THE SPORT AMERICANA®

Baseball Card

ALPHABETICAL CHECKLIST

NUMBER 5

By

DR. JAMES BECKETT

 Manufactured in the United States of America. Published by Edgewater Book Co. Inc., Box 40238, Cleveland, OH 44140.

ISBN 0-937424-59-5

Acknowledgments

A great deal of hard work went into this volume, and it could not have been done without a considerable amount of help from many people. Our thanks are extended to each and every one of you.

Those who have worked closely with us on this and many other books, have again proven themselves invaluable — Mike Aronstein, Frank and Vivian Barning (*Baseball Hobby News*), Chris Benjamin, Sy Berger (Topps), Cartophilium (Andrew Pywowarczuk), Mike Cramer (Pacific Trading Cards), Bill and Diane Dodge, Doubleheaders (Wayne Varner, Mike Wheat, and Bill Zimpleman), Fleer (Paul Mullan, Ted Taylor, and Jeff Massien), Gervise Ford, Steve Freedman, Craig W. Friedemann, Larry and Jeff Fritsch, Tony Galovich, Georgia Music and Sports (Dick DeCourcy), Dick Goddard, Bill Goodwin (St. Louis Baseball Cards), Mike and Howard Gordon, George Grauer, Wayne Grove, Bill Haber, Don Harrison (Tenth Inning), Alan Kaye (*Sports Card News*), Neil Lewis (Leaf), Lew Lipset, Mark Macrae, Major League Marketing (Dan Shedrick, Tom Day, and Julie Haddon), Don McPherson, Mid-Atlantic Sports Cards (Bill Bossert), Brian Morris, B.A. Murry, Oldies and Goodies (Nigel Spill), Optigraphics (Ed Fick), Jack Pollard, Jeff Prillaman, Gavin Riley, Alan Rosen (Mr. Mint), John Rumierz, San Diego Sport Collectibles (Bill Goepner and Nacho Arredondo), Kevin Savage (Sports Gallery), Mike Schechter, Barry Sloate, John E. Spalding, Phil Spector (Scoreboard, Inc.), Sports Collectors Store (Pat Quinn and Don Steinbach), Frank Steele, Murvin Sterling, Lee Temanson, Ed Twombly (New England Bullpen), Bill Wesslund (Portland Sports Card Co.), and Kit Young. Finally, we give a special acknowledgment to Dennis W. Eckes, "Mr. Sport Americana," whose untimely passing last year was a real loss to the hobby and to me personally. The success of the Beckett Price Guides has always been the result of a team effort.

I believe this edition of the *The Sport Americana Alphabetical Baseball Card Checklist* is our best yet. For that, you can thank all of the contributors nationwide (listed above and below) as well as our staff here in Dallas. Our company now boasts a substantial Technical Services team which has made (and is continuing to make) direct and important contributions to this work. Technical Services capably handled numerous technical details and provided able assistance in the preparation of this edition. That effort was directed by Technical Services manager Pepper Hastings. He was ably assisted by Technical Services coordinator Mary Gregory, Price Guide analysts Theo Chen, Mike Hersh, Dan Hitt, Mary Huston (special thanks for expertise on minor leaguers), Rich Klein, Tom Layberger, Allan Muir, Grant Sandground and Dave Sliepka. Also contributing to our Technical Services functions were Jana Threatt, Wendy Jewell, Peter Tepp and Scott Layton. I want to especially thank Scott Layton and Rich Klein for their dedication and hard work. Scott Layton in fact did most of the hard work and completely immersed himself in making this edition more complete, correct, and consistent. Rich Klein (incredibly) did most of the intensive proofing all by himself.

Many other people have provided checklist verifications, errata, and/or background information. We would like to individually thank Ab D Cards (Dale Wesolewski), Jerry Adamic, Dennis Anderson, Chuck Baldree, Karen Bell, D. Bruce Brown, Ira Cetron, Mike Christianson, Brian DeCaussin, Ben Defibaugh, Donald Dietrich, Robert Duke, Doak Ewing, Russell Ferris, Shirley Fortin, M.M. Gibson, Rob Grierson, John Grist, Hall's Nostalgia, Bill Henderson, William S. Herbert, Jim Hutchinson, Jack W. Kary, Frank J. Katen, Irv Lerner, Bill Ludlum, Mike McDonald (Sports Page), Andrew Menown, Joe Michalowicz, Tom Mohelnitzky, Mike O'Brien, Tom Pfirrmann, Tom Reid, Michael Riordan, Scott Rosen, David Rothlauf, Jack Rudley, Sandra Rufty, Garry Rust, Joe Sak, Gary Sawatzki, Randall L. Sheaffer, Vincent Tobin, Richard E. Walden, Richard West, and Robert Zanze.

We have appreciated all of the help we have received over the years from collectors across the country and, indeed, throughout the world. Every year we make active solicitations to individuals and groups for input for a specific edition and we are particularly appreciative of the help (large and small) provided for this volume. While we receive many inquiries, comments and questions — and, in fact, each and every one is read and digested — time constraints prevent us from personally replying to all but a few such letters. We hope that the letters will continue, and that even though no reply is received, you will feel that you are making significant contributions to the hobby through your interest and comments.

In the years since this guide debuted, Beckett Publications has grown beyond any rational expectation. A great many talented and hard working individuals have been instrumental in this growth and success. Our whole team is to be congratulated for what we together have accomplished. Our Beckett Publications team is led by Associate Publisher Claire Backus, Vice Presidents Joe Galindo and Fred Reed, and Director of Marketing Jeff Amano. They are ably assisted by Fernando Albieri, Theresa Anderson, Gena Andrews, Jeff Anthony, Patricia Bales, Airey Baringer II (special thanks to Airey for his late-night typesetting excellence), Barbara Barry, Nancy Bassi, Therese Bellar, Louise Bird, Wendy Bird, Cathryn Black, Terry Bloom, Lisa

The Sport Americana Baseball Card Alphabetical Checklist No. 5

Table of Contents

Player Listings

Index to Advertisers

Borden, Amy Brougher, Chris Calandro, Mary Campana, Renata Campos, Sammy Cantrell, Susan Catka, Deana Chapman, Theo Chen, Lynne Chinn, Catherine Colbert, Tommy Collins, Belinda Cross, Billy Culbert, Randy Cummings, Patrick Cunningham, Gail Docekal, Andrew Drago, Louise Ebaugh, Mila Egusquiza, Susan Elliott, Daniel Evans, Bruce Felps, Jorge Field, Sara Field, Jean Paul Figari, Jeany Finch, Robson Fonseca, Kim Ford, Eric Ford, Gayle Gasperin, Anita Gonzalez, Mary Gonzalez-Davis, Jeff Greer, Mary Gregory, Julie Grove, Marcio Guimaraes, Karen Hall, Carmen Hand, Lori Harmeyer, Beth Harwell, Jenny Harwell, Mark Harwell, Pepper Hastings, Joanna Hayden, Mike Hersh, Barbara Hinkle, Tracy Hinton, Dan Hitt, Charlie Hodges, Heather Holland, E.J. Hradek, Rex Hudson, Rhonda Hughes, Mary Huston, Don James, Marion Jarrell, Sara Jenks, Julia Jernigan, Wendy Jewell, Jay Johnson, Michael Johnson Jr., Matt Keifer, Fran Keng, Monte King, Debbie Kingsbury, Amy Kirk, Rudy Klancnik, Rich Klein, Frances Knight, Jane Layton, Scott Layton, Tom Liggitt, Lori Lindsey, Mark Manning, Louis Marroquin, Kaki Matheson, Teri McGahey, Kirk McKinney, Omar Mediano, Edras Mendez, Stephen Moore, Glen Morante, Elizabeth Morris, Daniel Moscoso, Daniel Moscoso Jr., Mike Moss, Randy Mosty, Allan Muir, Hugh Murphy, Wendy Neumann, Allen Neumann, LaQuita Norton, Robert Norton, Lisa O'Neill, Rich Olivieri, Abraham Pacheco, Guillermo Pacheco, Mike Payne, Suzee Payton, Ronda Pearson, Karen Penhollow, Julie Polomis, Reed Poole, Karen Quinn, Linda Rainwater, Roberto Ramirez, Nikki Renshaw, Patrick Richard, Jamile Romero, Grant Sandground, Gary Santaniello, Gabriel Santos, Maggie Seward, Carol Slawson, Steve Slawson, Dave Sliepka, Judi Smalling, Lisa Spaight, Mark Stokes, Cindy Struble, Peter Tepp, Jim Tereschuk, Christiann Thomas, Kimberly Thompson, Jana Threatt, Brett Tulloss, Valerie Voigt, Kim Whitesell, Mark Whitesell, Steve Wilson, Carol Ann Wurster, Robert Yearby. The whole Beckett Publications team has my thanks for jobs well done. Thank you, everyone.

I also thank my family, especially my wife, Patti, and daughters, Christina, Rebecca, and Melissa, for putting up with me again.

Introduction

One of the many problems collectors of baseball cards face is the identification of the many, many thousands of different baseball cards that exist. The best method devised thus far is the checklist. This technique involves breaking down all cards into levels with identifiable characteristics. The most common system begins at the most general level and proceeds to more specific levels. These levels are:

MAKER (Topps, Bowman, Goudey, etc.);

YEAR OF ISSUE;

NUMBER ON CARD (beginning with #1 or the lowest card number and continuing in numerical order until the last or highest card number is reached);

PLAYER ON CARD (corresponding to the particular number on the card); listed alphabetically if the particular year's issue is unnumbered, in which case the NUMBER ON CARD level may not be listed.

The Sport Americana Baseball Card Price Guide, the parent book of this one, adds two additional categories to each card's description:

CONDITION (Mint, Very Good-Excellent, Fair-Good);

PRICE (Value of the card in a given condition grade).

The common checklist format is effective for many (possibly most) situations; however, it is not an all-purpose answer to the collector's needs. There are times when neither the common checklist nor the Price Guide provide the right tools for the collector. This alphabetical checklist is intended to fill the void when the common checklist will not suffice.

The theory behind the alphabetical checklist is quite simple: The four levels of the common checklist are reordered. Their hierarchy in the alphabetical checklist is as follows:

PLAYER ON CARD (players are listed alphabetically);

YEAR OF ISSUE;

MAKER (producer or manufacturer);

NUMBER ON CARD (not applicable to unnumbered cards).

Simple in design, this restructuring provides the collector with an easy-to-use cross-reference to his card collection.

Today's baseball card collecting hobby is no longer dominated by the complete-set collector. While obtaining all cards of all sets still remains the ultimate accomplishment, the sheer numbers, costs and time involved to obtain them has given rise to large numbers of card collecting specialists. Such specialists collect only cards of particular players or teams (see *The Sport Americana Baseball Card Team Checklist*). The players

may be stars, superstars, players from a particular team, players born in a particular place, players with surnames of a particular nationality, or even such ephemeral common denominators as players who are lefthanded switch-hitters born east of the Mississippi below the Mason-Dixon line after 1933. As you can see, the possibilities are endless.

The Sport Americana Alphabetical Baseball Card Checklist presents at a glance all the cards issued for a particular player from virtually all the principal baseball card sets. No longer must a collector scan the entire 1957 Topps checklist to determine that the Brooks Robinson card of that year is #328. Nor must one go through four years of Bowman checklists to determine that the Bowman Rookie Card of Willie Mays is #305 in the 1951 series. The alphabetical checklist will show you without the necessity of having the actual card before you.

The concept of an alphabetical baseball card checklist is not new; however, we have attempted to make the current edition of *The Sport Americana Alphabetical Baseball Card Checklist* more complete, easier to use, and more attractive than any previous checklist of this kind. All of the cards of a particular player are listed consecutively below that player's name. There is no need to go to a second or third spot in the book to find that player's cards from another manufacturer or another time period.

Virtually all of the cards contained in any of the editions of *The Sport Americana Baseball Card Price Guide* and *The Sport Americana Baseball Collectibles Price Guide* are listed in this book. Many special cards are cross-referenced, as are checklist cards and team cards.

Errata

While a great deal of effort has been made to avoid errors of any type, it seems inevitable that some errors, misspellings, and inconsistencies may occur. Please inform the author of any you find, and corrections will be incorporated in the next edition. Send to: Dr. James Beckett, 4887 Alpha Road, Suite 200, Dallas, Texas 75244.

How to Collect

Card collecting is a hobby, a leisure pastime. There are no set rules for collecting baseball cards. The amount of time and funds available, and personal tastes, determine the path of a collector's interests. What is presented here is information and ideas that may help you enjoy this hobby.

Obtaining Cards

Several avenues are open to you to obtain cards. You can purchase current cards in the traditional way at local dandy, grocery, or drug stores, with bubblegum or other products included. You also can purchase complete recent sets from the many mail-order advertisers found in sports publications, such as *The Sporting News, Baseball Digest, Street & Smith's Baseball Yearbook, Baseball America*, and others. Occasionally, a few older cards and sets are advertised in these same publications. However, most serious card collectors obtain older cards from other collectors or dealers through hobby publications, at sports collectibles shows, or at sports card and memorabilia shops.

Nomenclature

Each hobby has its own language to describe its area of interest. The nomenclature traditionally used for trading cards is derived from the American Card Catalog, published in 1960 by Nostalgia Press. That catalog, written by Jefferson Burdick (who is called the "Father of Card Collecting" for his pioneering work), uses letter and number designations for each separate set of cards.

The letter used in the ACC designation refers to the generic type of card. While both sport and non-sport issues are classified in the ACC, we shall confine ourselves to the sport issues. The following list defines the letters and their meanings as used by the American Card Catalog.

(none) or N - 19th Century U.S. Tobacco
B - Blankets
D - Bakery Inserts Including Bread
E - Early Candy and Gum
F - Food Inserts
H - Advertising
M - Periodicals
PC - Postcards
R - Candy and Gum Cards, 1930 to Present
T - 20th Century U.S. Tobacco
UO - Gas and Oil Inserts
V - Canadian Candy
W - Exhibits, Strip Cards, Team Issues

Following the letter prefix and an optional hyphen are one-, two-, or three-digit numbers, 1-999. These typically represent the company or entity issuing the cards. In several cases, the ACC number is extended by an additional hyphen and another one- or two-digit numerical suffix. For example, the 1957 Topps regular series baseball card issue carries an ACC designation of R414-11. The "R" indicates a Candy or Gum Card produced since 1930. The "414" is the ACC designation for Topps Chewing Gum baseball card issues, and the "11" is the ACC designation for the 1957 regular issue (Topps' 11th baseball set).

Like other traditional methods of identification, this system provides order to the process of cataloging cards; however, most serious collectors learn the ACC designation of the popular sets by repetition and familiarity, rather than by attempting to "figure out" what they might or should be.

Since 1948, collectors and dealers more commonly have been referring to all sets by their year, maker, type of issue, and any other distinguishing characteristic. Such a characteristic could be an unusual issue or one of several regular issues put out by a specific maker in a single year. For example, in 1964, Topps issued three distinctly different baseball card sets. The regular issue is referred to as 1964 Topps; the postcard-sized issue is referred to as 1964 Topps Giants; and the die-cut issue is referred to as 1964 Topps Stand-Ups. Regional issues usually are referred to by year, maker, and sometimes by title or theme of the set.

Additional Reading

With the increase in popularity of the hobby in recent years, the amount of literature available on the subject also has increased. Below is a list of the books and periodicals which receive our highest recommendation and which we hope will further advance your knowledge and enjoyment of our great hobby.

The Sport Americana Baseball Card Price Guide by Dr. James Beckett (Fourteenth Edition, $15.95, released 1992, published by Edgewater Book Company) — the authoritative annual Price Guide to all the most popular baseball cards produced during the past century, 944 pages, illustrated, and priced in three condition grades, with an extensive introduction on the history of baseball cards and collecting.

The Official 1993 Price Guide to Baseball Cards by Dr. James Beckett (Twelfth Edition, $5.99, released 1992, published by The House of Collectibles) — an abridgment of The Sport Americana Price Guide in a convenient and economical pocket-size format providing Dr. Beckett's pricing of the major baseball sets since 1948.

The Sport Americana Price Guide to Baseball Collectibles by Dr. James Beckett (Second Edition, $12.95, released 1988, published by Edgewater Book Company) — the complete guide/checklist with values for box cards, coins, labels, Canadian cards, stamps, stickers, pins, etc.

The Sport Americana Football Card Price Guide by Dr. James Beckett (Eighth Edition, $14.95, released 1991, published by Edgewater Book Company) — the most comprehensive Price Guide and checklist ever issued on football cards. No serious football card hobbyist should be without it.

The Official Price Guide to Football Cards by Dr. James Beckett (Eleventh Edition, $5.99, released 1991, published by The House of Collectibles) — an abridgment of The Sport Americana Price Guide listed above in a convenient and economical pocket-size format providing Dr. Beckett's pricing of the major football sets since 1948.

The Sport Americana Hockey Card Price Guide by Dr. James Beckett (First Edition, $12.95, released 1991, published by Edgewater Book Company) — the most comprehensive Price Guide and checklist ever issued on hockey cards.

The Official Price Guide to Hockey Cards by Dr. James Beckett (First Edition, $5.99, released 1991, published by The House of Collectibles) — an abridgment of *The Sport Americana Price Guide* listed above in a convenient and economical pocket-size format providing Dr. Beckett's pricing of the major hockey sets since 1951.

The Sport Americana Basketball Card Price Guide and Alphabetical Checklist by Dr. James Beckett (First Edition, $12.95, released 1991, published by Edgewater Book Company) — the most comprehensive combination Price Guide and alphabetical checklist ever issued on basketball cards.

The Official Price Guide to Basketball Cards by Dr. James Beckett (First Edition, $5.99, released 1991, published by The House of Collectibles) — an abridgment of *The Sport Americana Price Guide* listed above in a convenient and economical pocket-size format providing Dr. Beckett's pricing of the major basketball sets since 1948.

The Sport Americana Alphabetical Baseball Card Checklist by Dr. James Beckett (Fifth Edition, $14.95, released 1992, published by Edgewater Book Company) — an alphabetical listing, by the last name of the player portrayed on the card, of virtually all baseball cards (Major League and Minor League) produced through the 1992 major sets.

The Sport Americana Price Guide to the Non-Sports Cards by Christopher Benjamin and Dennis W. Eckes (Third Edition [Part Two], $12.95, released 1988, published by Edgewater Book Company) — the definitive guide to all popular non-sports American tobacco and bubblegum cards. In addition to cards, illustrations and prices for wrappers also are included. Part Two covers non-sports cards from 1961 through 1987.

The Sport Americana Price Guide to the Non-Sports Cards 1930-1960 by Christopher Benjamin and Dennis W. Eckes ($14.95, released 1991, published by Edgewater Book Company) — the definitive guide to virtually all popular non-sports American tobacco and bubble gum cards issued between 1930 and 1960. In addition to cards, illustrations and prices for wrappers are also included.

The Sport Americana Baseball Address List by Jack Smalling and Dennis W. Eckes (Sixth Edition, $12.95, released 1990, published by Edgewater Book Company) — the definitive guide for autograph hunters, giving addresses and deceased information for virtually all major league baseball players past and present.

The Sport Americana Baseball Card Team Checklist by Jeff Fritsch and Dennis W. Eckes (Fifth Edition, $12.95, released 1990, published by Edgewater Book Company) — includes all Topps, Bowman, Donruss, Fleer, Score, Play Ball, Goudey and Upper Deck cards, with the players portrayed on the cards listed with the teams for which they played. The book is invaluable to the collector who specializes in an individual team because it is the most complete baseball card team checklist available.

The Encyclopedia of Baseball Cards, Volume I: 19th Century Cards by Lew Lipset ($11.95, released 1983, published by the author) — everything you ever wanted to know about 19th century cards.

The Encyclopedia of Baseball Cards, Volume II: Early Gum and Candy Cards by Lew Lipset ($10.95, released 1984, published by the author) — everything you ever wanted to know about Early Candy and Gum cards.

The Encyclopedia of Baseball Cards, Volume III: 20th Century Tobacco Cards, 1909-1932 by Lew Lipset ($12.95, released 1986, published by the author) — everything you ever wanted to know about old tobacco cards.

Beckett Baseball Card Monthly authored and edited by Dr. James Beckett — contains the most extensive and accepted monthly Price Guide, feature articles, "who's hot and who's not" section, convention calendar, and numerous letters to and responses from the editor. Published 12 times annually, it is the hobby's largest paid circulation periodical. *Beckett Football Card Monthly, Beckett Basketball Monthly, Beckett Hockey Monthly* and *Beckett Focus on Future Stars* are all similar to *Beckett Baseball Card Monthly* in style and content.

How to Use the Alphabetical Checklist

We are sure you will find this book an invaluable tool in your pursuit of card collecting enjoyment. Because of the large number of different card sets contained in this volume, it is extremely important that you familiarize yourself with the nomenclature used here. PLEASE READ THE FOLLOWING SECTION BEFORE ATTEMPTING TO USE THE CHECKLISTS.

Code Meanings

The codes following the players' names give the card sets and numbers within the sets in which the players appeared. Each entry consists of a number/letter combination indicating the particular set (Year, Maker, other set characteristic) followed by a dash, followed by a number/letter combination of the specific card and the type of card (if applicable) within that set. In short, the code before the dash describes the set, while the code after the dash describes the particular card within that set. Cards from unnumbered sets are sometimes listed by set name only.

Tips for Using this Checklist:

Entries for each player are listed in chronological order by year of issue and alphabetically by company within each year. Cards identified by ACC letter designation (rather than year) are listed last.

Some of the people listed herein are NOT baseball players, but are people who appear in the checklisted sets. In addition there are a number of ex-Major League players for whom no cards were produced; many of these players are listed with the designation "No cards."

The majority of the minor league cards were produced primarily by TCMA through 1985 and by ProCards since 1986. Other producers' cards, such as Larry Fritsch (Midwest League) or Mike Cramer's Pacific Trading Cards (PCL) sets are typically so designated.

Codes Used in this Checklist

Code	Example
A&P	76A&P/KC, 76A&P/Milw (A&P)
ActPacT	Action Packed Test
AmTract	American Tract Society
Arena	1991 Arena Holograms
Armour	1955 Armour Coins
Ault	1986 Ault Foods Blue Jays
B	48B (1948 Bowman)

Code	Example
BB	58BB through 62BB (Bell Brand)
BBBest	91BBBest (1991 Baseball's Best)
BBWit	1990 Baseball Wit
BeeHive	1961 Bee Hive Starch
Berg	1988 Cubs David Berg
BF#	1916 BF2 Felt Pennants
Bimbo	1989 Bimbo Bread Discs
BK	80BK/PHR (Burger King)
BLChew	1986 Big League Chew
BleachFT	1991 Bleachers 23K Frank Thomas
Bohem	1987 Bohemian Padres
Bond	1947 Bond Bread Jackie Robinson
Borden	1984 Borden's Reds
BR	51BR, 52BR (Berk Ross)
Brewer	1990 Brewers Miller Brewing
Briggs	53Briggs (Briggs Hot Dogs)
BU	35BU (1935 Batter Up)
BurgChef	1977 Burger Chef Discs
Buster	1909 Buster Brown Pins
Bz	59Bz (1959 Bazooka)
Cadaco	1989 Cadaco Ellis Game
Cain's	1985 Cain's Tigers Discs
Callahn	1950-1956 Callahan HOF
Carling	Carling Black Label Indians
CEA	Chicago Evening American pins
Centen	1943 Centennial Flour
Champion	1987 Champion Phillies
ChefBoy	1988 Chef Boyardee
CIGNA	85CIGNA (Phillies)
CircK	85CircK (Circle K)
Citgo	1969 Citgo Metal Coins
CJ	14CJ, 15CJ (Cracker Jack)
Classic	87Classic
Clover	1961-62 Cloverleaf Dairy
Coke	52Coke, 68Coke (Coca-Cola)
CokeK	Coke/Kroger
Colla	The Colla Collection
CollAB	Collect-A-Books
Conlon	1988 Conlon American All-Stars
CounHrth	Country Hearth Mariners
Cram	1980 Cramer Legends
Crane	1976 Crane Discs
Crown	1991 Crown Orioles
Crunch	1989 Topps Cap'n Crunch
D#	D301 through D350 (bread issues)
D	81D (1981 Donruss)
DanDee	54DanDee (1954 Dan Dee)
DennyGS	1991 Denny's Grand Slam
Det	1964 Detroit Tiger lids
Detroit	1981 Detroit News
Dexter	1968 Dexter Press
DF	1959 Darigold Farms
DG	Decade Greats
DH	1933 Doubleheader Discs
Dix	37Dix, 52Dix (Dixie Lids)
DL	33DL (1933 Delong)
Domino	1910 Domino Discs
Domino	1988 Domino's Tigers
Dorman	1986 Dorman's Cheese
DP	41DP (1941 Double Play)
Drake	81Drake (1981 Drake)
DS	34DS (1934 Diamond Stars)
Dunkin	1970 Dunkin Donuts Cubs
E#	E90/1 to E300 (candy issues)
EH	66EH (1966 East Hills)
EliteSenL	1990 Elite Senior League
Esskay	54Esskay, 55Esskay (Esskay)
Eureka	49 Eureka stamps
Exh	47Exh (Exhibits)
F	59F (1959 Fleer)

Code	Example
FanSam	1988 Fantastic Sam's Discs
FB	51FB (Fischer Baking Labels)
FleischBrd	1916 Fleischmann Bread
Foil	Foil Best (Minor League cards)
FrBauer	1963 French Bauer Caps
French	1988 French Bray Orioles
FresnoSt	Fresno State
FroJoy	28FroJoy (1928 Fro Joy)
FrRow	1991 Front Row Draft Picks
Fud's	1969 Fud's Photography
FunFood	1984 Fun Foods Pins
G	33G through 41G (Goudey)
Gard	83Gard (Gardner's Brewers)
Gator	86Gator (Gatorade Cubs)
GenMills	1985 General Mills
Glen	53Glen (Glendale)
Gol	1955 Golden Braves stamps
GP	61GP (Golden Press)
Granny	82Granny (Granny Goose)
Greyhound	Greyhound Heroes of the Base Paths
Griffey	1991 Griffey Gazette
Hawth	1952 Hawthorne-Mellody pins
HB	82HB/LS (Hillerich/Bradsby)
Helmar	1911 Helmar stamps
HenryH	1960 Henry House Wieners
Hires	58Hires (Hires)
Ho	75Ho (1975 Hostess)
Homer	1990 Homers Cookies
HomogBond	1947 Homogenized Bond
HotPlay	1990 Hottest 50 Players Stickers
HotRook	1990 Hottest 50 Rookies Stickers
HRDerby	1959 Home Run Derby
Hughes	1940 Hughes Solons
Hunter	53Hunter (1953 Hunter's)
Hygrade	Hygrade Expos
Icee	76Icee
IDL	1963 IDL Pirates
J	62J, 63J (Jello)
Jay's	1986 Jay's Potato Chip Discs
JB	69JB (Jack in the Box)
JC	53JC (1953 Johnston Cookies)
JDeanSig	1991 Jimmy Dean Signature
Jiffy	1986 Jiffy Pop Discs
JP	73JP (Johnny Pro)
K	70K (Kelloggs)
Kahn	55Kahn (1955 Kahn's)
Kaline	1983 Kaline Story
KAS	1986 KAS Cardinals Discs
KayBee	86KayBee
KDKA	68KDKA
Keller	1986 Keller's Phillies
Kelly	1969 Kelly Pins
KingB	1988 King-B Discs
Kitty	1986 Kitty Clover Discs
KMart	82KMart (K-Mart)
Kraft	1987 Kraft
L	48L (Leaf)
L#	L1 Leathers
Lake	60Lake (Lake to Lake)
LaPizza	1971 La Pizza Royale
Laugh	1972 Laughlin Great Feats
Leaf	1985 Leaf Canadian
Lennox	1989 Lennox HSE Astros
LineD	Line Drive (Minor League cards)
LitSun	1990 Little Sun Writers
LSU	Louisiana State University
M#	M101/4, M116 (periodical issues)
MajorLg	Major League Collector Pins
Mara	1989 Marathon Tigers
Master	1988 Master Bread Discs

Code	Example
MB	84MB (Milton Bradley)
McDon	70McDon (McDonald's)
MD	71MD (Milk Duds)
Meadow	1986 Meadow Gold Blank Back
MilSau	1963 Milwaukee Sausage
MLBPA	1969 MLBPA Baseball Pins
MnM's	87MnM's
MooTown	1991 MooTown Snackers
Morrell	59Morrell (Morrell Meats)
Mother	52Mother (Mother's Cookies)
Motor	1976 Motorola Old Timers
MP	43MP (MP & Co.)
MSA	76MSA/Disc (Mike Schecter Assoc.)
N#	N28 through N690 (19th century)
Nalley	1983 Nalley's Mariners
NatPhoto	86NatPhoto (Royals)
NB	53NB (Northland Bread Labels)
Negro	Negro League
Nes	84Nestle/792
Nestle	84Nestle/DT
NTea	52NTea (National Tea Labels)
NTF	69NTF (Nabisco Team Flakes)
NuCard	1960 Nu-Card Hi-Lites
NumNum	50NumNum, 52NumNum
NYJour	54NYJour (NY Journal American)
OhHenry	1986 Oh Henry Indians
OldLond	1965 Old London Coins
ONG	1939 Our National Game pins
OPC	89OPC (1989 O-Pee-Chee)
Orbit	1932-34 Orbit Pins Unnumbered
P	60P (1960 Post)
Pac	1988 Pacific Eight Men Out
PacBell	1958 Packard Bell
PapaG	1978 Papa Ginos Discs
Panini	Panini stickers
Park	Parkhurst
PB	39PB through 41PB (Play Ball)
Pep	63Pep, 77Pep (Pepsi)
PermaGr	Perma-Graphic
Peters	61Peters (Peter's Meats)
Petro	1991 Petro-Canada Standups
PG&E	Pacific Gas and Electric Giants
PhilBull	1964 Philadelphia Bulletin
Phill	Phillies (Tastykake, Medford)
Piedmont	1914 Piedmont stamps
PM#	Pins (PM1, PM10)
Pol	79Pol/Giants (Police/Safety)
Polar	1985 Polaroid Indians
Post	Post Cereal
Provigo	1986 Provigo Expos
PublInt	1990 Publications International
Quaker	86Quaker Oats
R#	R300-R346 ('30s gum issues)
Ralston	84Ralston
Rang	84Rangers
Rangers	83Rangers
Rawl	Rawl (Rawling's)
RedLob	1982 Cubs Red Lobster
Remar	46Remar (Remar Bread)
RFG	55RFG (W605 Robert F. Gould)
RH	54RH (Red Heart)
Rice	Rice Stix
RM	52RM through 55RM (Red Man)
Rodeo	Rodeo Meats
Royal	Royal Desserts
RoyRog	1983 Roy Rogers Discs
S	91S (1991 Score)
S#	S74 Silks
Salada	1962 Salada Coins
Salem	55Salem (Salem Potato Chips)
SanDiegoSt	San Diego State
Schnucks	1986 Schnucks Cardinals
Scrapps	Scrapps
Seven	84SevenUp (Cubs)
Seven	1985 Seven-Eleven Twins
Sf	88Sf (1988 Sportflics)
SFCallB	San Francisco Call-Bulletin
SFExam	San Francisco Examiner
Shirriff	1962 Shirriff coins
SilverSt	1991 SilverStar Holograms
SK	33SK (1933 Sport Kings)
SM	53SM through 55SM (Stahl Meyer)
Smok	85Smok/Angels (Smokey Bear)
Socko	1989 Socko Orel Hershiser
SpicSpan	Spic and Span Braves
Sqt	82Sqt (Squirt)
SSPC	76SSPC (1976 SSPC Pure Card)
StarCal	1952 Star Cal decals
Starshot	1991 Starshots Pinback Badges
Stuart	1983 Stuart Expos
Sugar	62Sugar, 63Sugar (Sugardale)
Sunflower	Sunflower Seeds
Sweet	1912 Sweet Caporal pins
SweetCap	1912 Sweet Caporal pins
Swell	48Swell (Swell Sport Thrills)
Swift	57Swift (Swift Meats)
T	51T (1951 Topps)
Target	1990 Target Dodgers
Tast	Tastee Freeze discs
TCMA	78TCMA, 79TCMA (TCMA)
TexGold	1986 Texas Gold Reds
ThomMc	1985 Thom McAn Discs
Thorn	83Thorn (Apple Valley)
Ticket	1971 Ticketron (Dodgers, Giants)
TipTop	47TipTop (TipTop Bread)
T/M	T and M Sports Umpires
Tor	87Tor/Fire (Toronto)
ToysRUs	87ToysRUs
Trans	69Trans, 70Trans (Transogram)
TrueVal	83TrueVal (True Value)
T#	T3 through T227 (Tobacco cards)
UD	89UD (1989 Upper Deck)
Union	Union Oil
USPlayC	U.S. Playing Cards All-Stars
USPS	1989 USPS Legends Stamp Cards
V#	V100 through V355 (Canadian issues)
VFJuice	1989 Very Fine Juice Pirates
W#	W501 through W711 (issued in strips)
Ward's	1934 Ward's Sporties pins
Wendy	85Wendy (Tigers)
West	1984 Doug West Series I
Weston	1974 Weston Expos
WG#	WG1 Card Game 1888
Wheat	35Wheat (Wheaties)
WichSt	Wichita State Game Day
Wiffle	1978 Wiffle Ball discs
Wilson	54Wilson (Wilson Wieners)
Windwlk	1990 Windwalker Discs
WonderBrd	1990 Wonder Bread Stars
Wool	85Wool (Woolworth)
Woolwth	85Woolwth (Woolworth)
Yank	1944 Yankee stamps
YellBase	1956 Yellow Basepath pins
Yueng	28Yueng (Yuenglings)
Zeller	Zeller's Expos

Set Code Suffixes

Code	Example
/A	R303A (Type A)
/A	82OrlTw/A (Orlando after season)
/AAS	84D/AAS (Action All-Stars)
/Aces	Baseball's Best Aces of the Mound
/A's	84Moth/A's (Oakland A's)
/AFGA	MSA AFGA film
/AL	American League
/Alb	1969 Topps Stamp albums
/Am	1988 Conlon American All-Stars
/Ames	Topps Ames (All-Stars, 20/20 Club)
/Angels	85Smok/Angels
/Arc53	1991 Topps Archive 1953
/AS	86F/AS (All-Stars)
/ASFan	1991 Score All-Star Fanfest
/ASG	1974 Laughlin All-Star Games
/ASIns	Fleer All-Star Inserts
/Ast	84Mother/Ast (Astros)
/ATG	63Bz/ATG (All Time Greats)
/Atl	62Kahn/Atl (Atlanta)
/AwardWin	87F/AwardWin (Award Winners)
/B	R303B (Type B)
/B	82OrlTw/B (Orlando before season)
/B	80Penin/B (Peninsula b&w set)
/Back	1988 Topps Sticker Backs
/BB	51T/BB (Blue Backs)
/BB	1988 Fleer Baseball All-Stars
/BBMVP	Fleer Baseball MVP's
/BC	N172/BC (Brown's Champs)
/Best	Best (Minor League cards)
/Best	1988 Donruss Baseball's Best
/BHN	Baseball Hobby News
/Big	1988 Topps Big
/Bk	1988 Donruss Mets Team Book
/BK	Burger King
/Black	1974 Laughlin Old Time Black Stars
/Blank	1986 Meadow Gold Blank Back
/blue	T213/blue (blue caption)
/BlueJ	Topps Toronto Blue Jays Fan Club
/Board	87T/Board (Boardwalk & Baseball)
/Bob	Bob's Camera (Minor League cards)
/Bon	The Bon (Minor League cards)
/Bonus	1989 Donruss Bonus MVP's
/Book	1988 Donruss Mets Team Book
/Box	1983 Topps sticker boxes
/Box	Box Scores (Minor League cards)
/BPro	Best/Pro (Minor League cards)
/Braves	85Ho/Braves
/Brew	82Pol/Brew (Brewers)
/brown	T213/brown (brown caption)
/bucks	62T/bucks (baseball bucks)
/BW	53B/BW (Black and White)
/C	80Penin/C (Peninsula color set)
/Cal	Cal League (Minor League cards)
/Can	1953 Exhibits Canadian
/Can	(Post) Canada
/Candl	Candl Coin (Minor League cards)
/Card	1988 Smokey Cardinals
/CAS	51T/CAS (Current All Stars)
/CB	70T/cb (Comic story booklet)
/CBatL	K-Mart Career Batting Leaders
/CC	Perma-Graphics Credit Cards
/Cereal	84T/Cereal
/Champs	84D/Champs
/Chong	Chong (Minor League cards)
/CJMini	Topps Cracker Jack Minis
/CL	Carolina League
/Classic	Homers Cookies Classics

Code	Example
/ClBest	Classic Best (Minor League cards)
/ClemIns	1992 Fleer Clemens Inserts
/Cloth	1972 Topps Test Cloth
/Clown	1976 Laughlin Indianapolis Clowns
/CM	51T/CM (Connie Mack)
/CMC	Collectors Marketing Corp.
/Coins	1964 Topps coins
/Col	53B/Col (Color)
/Comics	1973 Topps Comics
/ComRyan	Score Commemorative Nolan Ryan
/Coop	1989 Kahn's Cooperstown
/Cooper	1991 Score Cooperstown
/Cram	Cramer (Minor League cards)
/Crown	Crown Oil
/Crunch	1989 Topps Cap'n Crunch
/CS	77T/CS (Cloth Stickers)
/DC	1955 Spic and Span Die-Cut
/DE	69T/DE (Deckle Edge)
/DealP	1987 Sportflics Dealer Panels
/Dec	86S/Dec (Decade Greats)
/decal	69T/decal (decals)
/DH	55T/DH (Double Headers)
/DHTest	Topps Doubleheaders Test
/Dice	1961 Topps Dice Game
/DiMag	1992 Score Joe DiMaggio
/DIMD	Diamond (Minor League cards)
/Disc	76MSA/Disc
/DK	(Super) Diamond Kings
/DKsuper	85D/DKsuper
/Dodg	80Pol/Dodg (Dodgers)
/DP	1991 Front Row Draft Picks
/DT	84Nestle/DT (Dream Team)
/Duques	Negro League Duquesne
/E	65T/E (Embossed)
/Excit	1987 Fleer Exciting Stars
/Ext	1989 Upper Deck Extended
/FamFeat	1972 Fleer Famous Feats
/FamFun	1978 Padres Family Fun
/Fan	1984 Topps Mets Fan Club
/FB	84Shrev/FB (First Base)
/FFeat	1972 Fleer Famous Feats
/FinalEd	Upper Deck Final Edition
/Fire	87Tor/Fire (Toronto Fire)
/Frit	Larry Fritsch
/FrSt	Panini French Stickers
/G	68T/G (Game Cards)
/GameWin	87F/GameWin (Game Winners)
/Giants	79Pol/Giants
/GF	1972 Laughlin Great Feats
/GlossRk	87T/Glossy Rookie Jumbo 22
/Gloss22	84T/Gloss22 (All-Stars)
/Gloss40	83T/Gloss40 (Send In Glossy)
/Gloss60	86T/Gloss60 (Send In Glossy)
/GM	71T/GM (Greatest Moments)
/Gov	Rochester Governor's Cup
/GPromo	1992 Topps Gold Promo Sheet
/Great	Swell Baseball Greats
/GRook	1991 Leaf Gold Rookies
/GS	Grand Slam (Feder)
/GSlam	Donruss Grand Slammers
/HardC	Hardee's/Coke
/Head	1988 Fleer Headliners
/Hills	1989 Topps Hills Team MVP's
/HillsHM	1990 Topps Hills Hit Men
/HitM	Baseball's Best Hit Men
/HL	86D/HL (Highlights)
/Hocus	1956 Topps Hocus Focus
/HOF	48Exh/HOF (Hall of Fame)
/HotRook	1989 Score Hottest 100 Rookies
/HotStar	1989 Score Hottest 100 Stars

Code	Example
/Hottest	87F/Hottest (Hottest Stars)
/HT	81T/HT (Home Team Supers)
/Ind	83Wheat/Ind (Indians)
/Indians	82BK/Indians
/Jackson	Upper Deck Reggie Jackson Heroes
/JITB	Jack in the Box
/JP	Jones Photo (Minor League cards)
/JR	1947 Bond Bread Jackie Robinson
/Jub	1976 Laughlin Diamond Jubilee
/JumboR	1988 Topps Jumbo Rookies
/KC	76A P/KC (Kansas City)
/Kit	1988 CMC Mattingly Kit
/Ko	1988 Kodak Peoria Chiefs
/Kodak	1988 Kodak Peoria Chiefs
/L	1952 Star Cal Large
/Lead	K-Mart Leaders
/Learning	1990 Donruss Learning Series
/Leg	1980 Cramer Legends
/Legoe	Legoe
/Lewis	1991 Negro League Ron Lewis
/LF	Larry Fritsch (Minor League cards)
/LgStand	1990 Fleer League Standouts
/Lids	1964 Detroit Tiger lids
/Lim	85F/Lim (Limited Edition)
/LineD	Line Drive (Minor League cards)
/LJN	Topps LJN Talking Cards
/LJS	1990 Starline Long John Silver
/LL	86F/LL (League Leaders)
/LS	82HB/LS (Louisville Slugger)
/M	75T/M (Mini)
/M	70Trans/M (NY Mets)
/Mag	Padres Magazine
/MagRal	Padres Magazine/Rally's Hamburgers
/MagUno	Padres Magazine Unocal
/MantleP	1991 Score Mickey Mantle Promo
/Mar	Mariners
/Mara	Cubs Marathon
/Mast	Score Scoremasters
/Matting	1991 Coke Don Mattingly
/McDon	1990 Score McDonald's
/MetYank	1985 Police Mets/Yankees
/Mets	1988 Donruss Mets Team Book
/Milk	1986 Meadow Gold Milk
/MillB	Brewers Miller Brewing
/Milw	76A P/Milw (Milwaukee)
/Mini	86F/Mini
/Minn	1985 Seven-Eleven Twins
/MVP	1989 Donruss Bonus MVP's
/MWilliam	Mother's Cookies Matt Williams
/Nat	1988 Conlon National All-Stars
/Neg	1988 Conlon Negro All-Stars
/NL	National League
/num	1932-34 Orbit Pins Numbered
/NWest	Score Nat West Yankees
/OD	87D/OD (Opening Day)
/Orio	Orioles
/P	79BK/P (Phillies)
/Padres	84Smok/Padres
/PCL	49B/PCL (Pacific Coast League)
/PHR	80BK/PHR (Pitch, Hit, and Run)
/PI	67T/PI (Paper Insert)
/Pin	1909 Buster Brown Pins
/Pion	1975 Fleer Pioneers
/Pirates	Pittsburgh Pirates
/Pol	Police/safety sets
/PopUp	86D/PopUp
/Post	72T/Post (Posters)
/PostC	1954 Spic and Span Postcards
/PP	1967 Topps Test Pirates
/Prem	1949 Leaf Premiums
/Prev	Preview (Leaf, Score)
/ProC	ProCards (Minor League cards)
/Promo	1992 Topps Promo Sheet
/Proto	1985-86 Sportflics Prototypes
/ProV(F)	1991 Fleer Pro-Visions (Factory)
/Pucko	Pucko (Minor League cards)
/PW	Pizza World (Minor League cards)
/R	78BK/R (Rangers)
/Rang	Mother's Cookies Rangers
/RB	51T/RB (Red Backs)
/Rec	1989 Fleer For The Record
/RecBr	Baseball's Best Record Breakers
/RecSet	87F/RecSet (Record Setters)
/Red	1988 Classic Red
/Reds	1988 Kahn's Reds
/RedSox	1988 Donruss Red Sox Team Book
/Revco	1988 Topps Revco
/Riley	Riley's (Minor League cards)
/RiteAid	1988 Topps Rite-Aid
/Ritz	Topps Ritz Mattingly
/RO	66T/RO (Rub Offs)
/Rock	Rock's Dugout Wichita
/Rook	86D/Rook (Rookies)
/RookSIns	Fleer Rookie Sensations Inserts
/Royals	81Pol/Royals
/RSox	Boston Red Sox
/RyanL&T	Score Nolan Ryan Life and Times
/Ryan7NH	Pacific Nolan Ryan 7th No-Hitter
/RyanSIns	Pacific Nolan Ryan Silver Inserts
/RyanTE	Pacific Nolan Ryan Texas Express
/S	69T/S (Supers or Giant Size)
/SC	street clothes
/SchCd	Padres Schedule Cards
/SDP	84Moth/SDP (S.D. Padres)
/Sea	84Moth/Sea (Seattle)
/SenLg	Senior League (Pacific, T/M, Topps)
/SFG	83Moth/SFG (S.F. Giants)
/SilSlug	1991 Upper Deck Silver Sluggers
/Slug	86F/Slug (Sluggers vs. Pitchers)
/Sm	PM10 Small
/Smok	Smokey Bear
/SO	63T/SO (Stick Ons, Scratch Offs)
/SoarSt	1990 Fleer Soaring Stars
/SoCal	Smokey Southern California
/Soda	1990 MSA Soda Superstars
/SP	Sport Pro (Minor League cards)
/SpecOlym	1987 Leaf Special Olympics
/Sport	Conlon Sporting News
/SS	1988 Fleer Superstars
/ST	N172/ST (Spotted Ties)
/St	82F/St (Stickers, Stamps)
/Star	Star (Minor League cards)
/Stat	1986 Meadow Gold Stat Back
/StClub	Topps Stadium Club
/Strawb	Colla Darryl Strawberry
/Stud	Leaf Studio
/StudPrev	Leaf Studio Preview
/SU	64T/SU (Stand Ups)
/Sum	1988 Cape Cod Summer League
/Super	85T/Super
/T	51T/T, 58Hires/T (Team Cards, Test)
/T	78BK/T (Tigers)
/Taco	Taco Time (Minor League cards)
/TastyK	Phillies Tastykake
/tatt	60T/tatt (tattoo)
/TCMA	The Card and Memorabilia Associates
/Team	Team-issued set
/Test	Score Test Samples, Sportflics Test
/Test	1971 Bazooka Numbered Test
/Tips	1982 Post Tips

Code	Example
/TL	1988 Fleer Team Leaders
/TmLIns	Fleer Team Leaders Inserts
/TmPrev	Sportflics Team Preview
/ToroBJ	1991 Score Toronto Blue Jays
/Tr	76T/Tr (Traded)
/trans	65T/trans (transfers)
/Trib	Tribune
/Tul	63Pep/Tul (Tulsa Oilers)
/TVAS	1990 Topps TV All-Stars
/TVCard	1990 Topps TV Cardinals
/TVYank	1990 Topps TV Yankees
/Twink	75Ho/Twink (Twinkies)
/UK	88 Topps UK Minis
/Ultra(G)	Fleer Ultra (Gold)
/un	1932-34 Orbit Pins Unnumbered
/Up	87Classic/Up (Update)
/WaxBox	1985 Donruss Wax Box Cards
/WBTV	Charlotte TV station
/Wild	1973 Fleer Wildest Plays
/WS	85Coke/WS (White Sox)
/WS	1987 Fleer World Series
/WSox	White Sox (Kodak)
/Y	77BK/Y (Yankees)
/YB	Yearbook
/YS	1988 Score Young Superstars
/1	1988 Conlon Series 1
/100Ris	1990 Score 100 Rising
/100RisSt	Score 100 Rising Stars
/100St	1990 Score 100 Stars
/100Stars	1990 Score 100 Stars
/200	Classic Game 200
/3/4/500	1980 Laughlin 300/400/500 Club
/3D	68T/3D (three dimensional)
/4	1929-30 Exhibits 4-in-1
/8Men	1988 Pacific Eight Men Out

Individual Card Suffix Codes

Code	Example
a	autograph
ADM	administrator
AGM	assistant general manager
ALCS	AL Championship Series
ANN	announcer
AR	all-rookie
AS	all-star
ATHR	author
bb	batboy
BC	bonus card
BOX	boxer
CA	clubhouse attendant
CAPT	captain
CD	clinic director
CL	checklist
CO	coach
CY	Cy Young
DC	draft choice
DIR	director
DK	Diamond King
DP	draft pick
DR	doctor
DS	diamond skills
DT	dream team
EP	elite performer
EQMG(R)	equipment manager
FDP	first draft pick
FRAN	franchise
FS	father and son
FS	future star
GC	ground crew
GM	general manager
HL	highlight
HOR	horizontal pose
IA	in action
INS(T)	instructor
KM	K-Man
KP	kid picture (boyhood photo)
LL	league leader
M	multiple or misc.
MB	master blaster
MG	manager
MLP	major league performance
MOY	man of the year
MV(P)	MVP card
NH	no-hitter
NLCS	NL Championship Series
OF	outfielder
OLY	Olympics
org	organist
ow(n)	owner
P/CO	player coach
PER	office personnel
PRES	president
PV	Pro-vision
Pz	puzzle
R	rookie
RB	record breaker
RIF	rifleman
ROY	Rookie of the Year
RP	rookie prospect
RR	Rated Rookie
RS	rising star, record setter
SA	super action
SLUG	slugger
SR	star rookie
STAT	statistician
SV	super veteran
T	traded
TBC	turn back clock
TC	team checklist
TL	team leader
TP	top prospect
TR	traded or trainer
tr	trainer
UMP	umpire
VP	vice president
WS	World Series

Minor League Abbreviations

Code	Example
AAA	AAA All-Stars
Alaska	Alaska Goldpanners (amateur)
Albany	Albany-Colonie A's
Albuq	Albuquerque Dukes
AlexD	Alexandria Dukes
Amari	Amarillo Gold Sox
Anchora	Anchorage Glacier Pilots (amateur)
Ander	Anderson Braves
AppFx	Appleton Foxes
ArkTr	Arkansas Travelers
Ashvl	Asheville Tourists
AubAs	Auburn Astros
Augusta	Augusta Pirates
Bakers	Bakersfield Dodgers
Batavia	Batavia Clippers/Trojans
Baton	Baton Rouge Cougars
BBAmer	Baseball America All-Stars

Code	Example
BBAmerAA	Baseball America AA Prospects
BBCity	Baseball City Royals
Beaum	Beaumont Golden Gators
Belling	Bellingham Mariners
Beloit	Beloit Brewers
Bend	Bend Bucks/Phillies
Billings	Billings Mustangs
BirmB	Birmingham Barons
Bluefld	Bluefield Orioles
Boise	Boise Hawks
Bristol	Bristol Red Sox
BuffB	Buffalo Bisons
BurlAs	Burlington Astros
BurlB	Burlington Bees/Braves
BurlEx	Burlington Expos
BurlInd	Burlington Indians
BurlR	Burlington Rangers
Butte	Butte Copper Kings
Calgary	Calgary Cannons
CalLgAS	California Lg. All-Stars
Canton	Canton(-Akron) Indians
CapeCod	Cape Cod Prospects
CaroMud	Carolina Mudcats
Cedar	Cedar Rapids Reds
Charl	Charleston Charlies
CharlK	Charlotte Knights
CharlR	Charlotte Rangers
CharlO	Charlotte O's
CharR	Charleston Royals
CharRain	Charleston Rainbows
CharWh	Charleston Wheelers
Chatt	Chattanooga Lookouts
CLAS	Carolina League All-Stars
Clearw	Clearwater Phillies
Clinton	Clinton Dodgers/Giants
Clmbia	Columbia Mets
Cocoa	Cocoa Beach Astros
ColAst	Columbus Astros
ColClip	Columbus Clippers
ColInd	Columbus Indians
ColMud	Columbus Mudcats
ColoSp	Colorado Springs Sky Sox
Colum	Columbus Clippers
ColumAst	Columbus Astros
Columbia	Columbia Mets
ColumMud	Columbus Mudcats
Cram/PCL	Cramer PCL set
Danvl	Danville Suns
DayBe	Daytona Beach Astros
Denver	Denver Zephyrs
Dubuq	Dubuque Packers
Dunedin	Dunedin Blue Jays
Durham	Durham Bulls
EastLAS	Eastern League All-Stars
EastLDD	Eastern League Diamond Diplomacy
Edmon	Edmonton Trappers
Elizab	Elizabethton Twins
ElPaso	El Paso Diablos
Elmira	Elmira Pioneer Red Sox
Erie	Erie Cardinals/Orioles/Sailors
Eugene	Eugene Emeralds
Evansvl	Evansville Triplets
Everett	Everett Giants
Fayette	Fayetteville Generals
Freder	Frederick Keys
Fresno	Fresno Giants
FSLAS	Florida State League All-Stars
FtLaud	Ft. Lauderdale Yankees
FtMyr	Fort Myers Royals
Gaston	Gastonia Rangers
Gate	Gate City Pioneers
Geneva	Geneva Cubs
GlenF	Glen Falls White Sox
GreatF	Great Falls Dodgers
Green	Greenwood Braves
Greens	Greensboro Hornets
Greenvl	Greenville Braves
Hagers	Hagerstown Suns
Hamil	Hamilton Redbirds
Harris	Harrisburg Senators
Hawaii	Hawaii Islanders
Helena	Helena Brewers
HighD	High Desert Mavericks
Holyo	Holyoke Millers
Hunting	Huntington Cubs
Huntsvl	Huntsville Stars
Idaho	Idaho Falls Athletics/Braves
Indianap	Indianapolis Indians
IntLgAS	International League All-Stars
Iowa	Iowa Cubs
Jacks	Jackson Generals/Mets
James	Jamestown Expos
Jamestn	Jamestown Expos
Jaxvl	Jacksonville Expos/Suns
Johnson	Johnson City Cardinals
Kane	Kane County Cougars
Kenosha	Kenosha Twins
Kingspt	Kingsport Mets
Kinston	Kinston Blue Jays/Eagles/Indians
Kissim	Kissimmee Dodgers
Knoxvl	Knoxville Blue Jays/Knox Sox
Lafay	Lafayette Drillers
Lakeland	Lakeland Tigers
LasVegas	Las Vegas Stars
LitFalls	Little Falls Mets
LodiD	Lodi Dodgers
London	London Tigers
Louisvl	Louisville Redbirds
Lynch	Lynchburg Mets
LynchRS	Lynchburg Red Sox
LynnP	Lynn Pirates
LynnS	Lynn Sailors
Macon	Macon Braves/Pirates
Madis	Madison Muskies
Martins	Martinsville Phillies
Maine	Maine Guides
Medford	Medford Athletics
MedHat	Medicine Hat Blue Jays
Memphis	Memphis Chicks
Miami	Miami Marlins/Miracle/Orioles
MidldA	Midland Angels
MidldC	Midland Cubs
MidwLAS	Midwest League All-Stars
Modesto	Modesto A's
Myrtle	Myrtle Beach Blue Jays/Hurricanes
Nashua	Nashua Angels
Nashvl	Nashville Sounds
Newar	Newark Co-Pilots
NewBrit	New Britain Red Sox
Niagara	Niagara Falls Rapids
NiagFls	Niagara Falls Rapids
Ogden	Ogden A's
OkCty	Oklahoma City 89ers
Omaha	Omaha Royals
Oneonta	Oneonta Yankees
OrlTw	Orlando Twins
Orlan	Orlando Twins
OrlanSR	Orlando Sun Rays
OrlanTw	Orlando Twins
Osceola	Osceola Astros

Code	Example
PalmSp	Palm Springs Angels
Pawtu	Pawtucket Red Sox
Penin	Peninsula Pilots
Peoria	Peoria Chiefs
PeoriaCol	Peoria Collectors
Phoenix	Phoenix Firebirds/Giants
Pittsfld	Pittsfield Cubs/Mets
Pocatel	Pocatello Giants/Pioneers
PortChar	Port Charlotte Rangers
Portl	Portland Beavers
Princet	Princeton Patrios/Pirates/Reds
PrWill	Prince William Cannons/Pirates
Pulaski	Pulaski Braves
QuadC	Quad-City Cubs/Angels
Reading	Reading Phillies
Redwd	Redwood Pioneers
Reno	Reno Silver Sox
Richm	Richmond Braves
Richm25Ann	Richmond Braves 25th Anniversary
River	Riverside Red Wave
Riversi	Riverside Red Wave
RochR	Rochester Red Wings
Rockford	Rockford Expos
Sacra	Sacramento Solons
SALAS	South Atlantic League All-Stars
Salem	Salem Buccaneers/Dodgers/Pirates
Salinas	Salinas Spurs
SanAn	San Antonio Brewers/Missions
SanBern	San Bernadino Spirit
SanJose	San Jose Bees/Giants/Missions
Saraso	Sarasota White Sox
Savan	Savannah Braves/Cardinals
ScrantWB	Scranton-Wilkes-Barre
ScrWB	Scranton-Wilkes-Barre
Shrev	Shreveport Captains
SLAS	Southern League All-Stars
SLCity	Salt Lake City Gulls/Trappers
SoBend	South Bend White Sox
SoOreg	Southern Oregon A's
Spartan	Spartanburg Phillies
Spokane	Spokane Indians
SpokAT	Spokane All-Time Greats
SpokaAT	Spokane All-Time Greats
Spring	Springfield Cardinals
StCath	St. Catharines Blue Jays
StLucie	St. Lucie Mets
Stockton	Stockton Ports
StPete	St. Petersburg Cardinals
Sumter	Sumter Braves
Syrac	Syracuse Chiefs
Tacoma	Tacoma Tigers/Tugs
Tampa	Tampa Tarpons/Yankees
TexLgAS	Texas League All-Stars
Tidew	Tidewater Tides
Tigres	Tigres de Mexico
Toledo	Toledo Mud Hens
TriCit	Tri-Cities Triplets
Tucson	Tucson Toros
Tulsa	Tulsa Drillers
Utica	Utica Blue Jays/Blue Sox
Vanco	Vancouver Canadians
Ventura	Ventura Gulls
Vermont	Vermont Reds
VeroB	Vero Beach Dodgers
Virgini	Virginia Generals
Visalia	Visalia Oaks
Water	Waterbury Reds
Watertn	Watertown Indians/Pirates
Watlo	Waterloo Diamonds/Indians
Wausau	Wausau Mets/Timbers
Welland	Welland Pirates
WHave	West Haven A's/Yankees
Wichita	Wichita Aeros/Pilots/Wranglers
WinHaven	Winter Haven Red Sox
WinSalem	Winston-Salem Spirits
Wisco	Wisconsin Rapids Twins
Wmsprt	Williamsport Bills/Tomahawks
WPalmB	West Palm Beach Expos
Wythe	Wytheville Cubs
Yakima	Yakima Bears

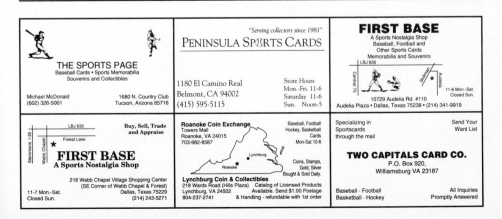

Aaron, Henry Louis
(Hank)
54JC-5
54SpicSpan/PostC-1
54T-128
55B-179
55Gol/Braves-1
55JC-44
55SpicSpan/DC-1
55T-47
55T/DH-105
56T-31
56T/Pin-16
56YellBase/Pin-1
57SpicSpan/4x5-1
57Swift-13
57T-20
58Hires-44
58T-30
58T-351M
58T-418M
58T-488AS
59Armour-1
59Bz
59HRDerby-1
59T-212M
59T-380
59T-467M
59T-561AS
60Armour-1A
60Armour-1B
60Bz-4
60Lake
60MacGregor-1
60NuCard-62
60SpicSpan-1
60T-300
60T-566AS
60T/tatt-1
61NuCard-462
61P-107
61T-415
61T-43LL
61T-484M
61T-577AS
61T/St-37
62Bz
62Exh
62J-149
62P-149
62P/Can-149
62Salada-180
62Shirriff-180
62T-320
62T-394AS
62T/bucks
62T/St-143
63Bz-9
63Exh
63J-152
63P-152
63Salada-24
63T-1LL
63T-242M
63T-390
63T-3LL
63T/SO
64Bz-9
64T-11LL
64T-300
64T-423M
64T-7LL
64T-9LL
64T/Coins-149AS
64T/Coins-83
64T/S-49
64T/St-84
64T/SU
64T/tatt
64Wheat/St-1
65Bz-9
65Kahn
65OldLond-1
65OPC-170
65OPC-2LL
65T-170
65T-2LL
65T/E-59
65T/trans-37
66Bz-30
66Kahn
66T-215LL
66T-500
66T/RO-117
67Bz-30
67Kahn
67OPC/PI-15
67T-242LL
67T-244LL
67T-250
67T/PI-15
67T/Test/SU-20
68Bz-5
68Coke
68Dexter-1
68Kahn
68OPC-110
68OPC-3LL
68OPC-5LL
68T-110
68T-370AS
68T-3LL
68T-5LL
68T/G-4
68T/Post-14
69Citgo-16
69Kahn
69MB-1
69MLB/St-109
69MLBPA/Pin-31
69NTF
69OPC-100
69T-100
69T/decal
69T/S-34
69T/St-1
69Trans-53
70MB-1
70MLB/St-1
70OPC-462AS
70OPC-500
70OPC-65LL
70T-462AS
70T-500
70T-65LL
70T/S-24
70T/SO
70Trans-4
71Bz
71Bz/Test-23
71MD
71MLB/St-1
71MLB/St-553
71OPC-400
71T-400
71T/Coins-137
71T/S-44
71T/tatt-9
72MB-1
72OPC-299
72OPC-300IA
72OPC-87LL
72OPC-89LL
72T-299
72T-300A
72T-87LL
72T-89LL
72T/Cloth-1
72T/Post-9
73OPC-100
73OPC-1M
73OPC-473LL
73T-100
73T-1LL
73T-473LL
73T/Comics-1
73T/Lids-1
73T/PinUps-1
74Laugh/ASG-72
74OPC-1
74OPC-2M
74OPC-3M
74OPC-4M
74OPC-5M
74OPC-6M
74OPC-7M
74OPC-8M
74OPC-9M
74T-1
74T-2M
74T-332M
74T-3M
74T-4M
74T-5M
74T-6M
74T/DE-57
74T/Puzzles-1
74T/St-1
75Ho-130
75Ho/Twink-130
75OPC-195MV
75OPC-1RB
75OPC-660
75T-195MV
75T-1RB
75T-660
75T/M-195MV
75T/M-1RB
75T/M-660
76A&P/Milw
76Crane-1
76Ho-94
76Laugh/Clown-34
76Laugh/Jub-8
76MSA/Disc
76OPC-1RB
76OPC-550
76SSPC-239
76T-1RB
76T-550
79T-412M
79T-413M
80Pac/Leg-7
80Laugh/3/4/5-16
81Detroit-54
81Pol/Atl-44C
82CJ-1
82KMart-43
83D/HOF-34
83MLBPA/Pin-19
83T/St-1F
84D/Champs-8
85CircK-1
85D/HOF-7
85Woolwth-1
86BLChew-1
86D-602Pz
86D/AS/WaxBox-PUZ
86D/WaxBox-PUZ
86Leaf-259PUZ
86Sf/Dec-40
87KMart-1
87Leaf/SpecOlym-H7
87Nestle/DT-29
88Pac/Leg-1
89HOF/St-44
89T-663TBC
89T/LJN-137
89T/LJN-161
90BBWit-6
90CollAB-22
90HOF/St-81
90MSA/AGFA-6
90Pac/Legend-1
90Swell/Great-2
91K/3D-2
91K/SU-1A
91K/SU-1B
91Swell/Great-102
91T/Archiv-317
91UD/Aaron-Set
91UD/Ext-HH1
Exh47
PM10/Sm-1
TCMA78-290
WG10-24
WG9-26

Aaron, Tommie Lee
63T-46
64T-454
65T-567
68T-394
69OPC-128
69T-128
70OPC-278
70T-278
71MLB/St-2
71OPC-717
71Richm/Team-1
71T-717
72MB-2
78Richm
82Pol/Atl-23C
90Richm25Ann/Team-1MG

Aaron, Wil
75SanAn
76Wmsprt

Aase, Donald William
(Don)
76OPC-597R
76T-597R
77T-472R
78OPC-233
78T-12
79T-368
80OPC-126
80T-239
81D-411
81F-286
81T-601
82D-267
82F-450
82F/St-212
82OPC-199
82T-199
83D-38
83F-76
83T-599
84Smok/Cal-1
85D-255
85F-293
85F/Up-U1
85T-86
85T/Tr-1T
86D-392
86D/HL-12
86F-268
86T-288
87Classic-99
87D-231
87D/AAS-47
87F-461
87F-627M
87F/Excit-1
87F/Mini-1
87F/St-1
87OPC-207
87Sf-165
87Sf-194M
87Seven-ME4
87T-766
87T/Mini-38
87T/St-228
88F-553
88French-41
88S-518
88T-467
89F/Up-100
89Kahn/Mets-49
89S-524
89T/Tr-1T
89UD-450
90F-196
90Mother/Dodg-27
90OPC-301
90S-377
90S/Tr-29T
90T-301
90UD-131
91Crown/Orio-1
91F-193
91S-289
91WIZMets-1

Abarbanel, Mickey
68T-287R

Abare, Bill
89StCath/ProC-2071
90Myrtle/ProC-2781
91Dunedin/ClBest-15
91Dunedin/ProC-212

Abbaticchio, Ed
12Sweet/Pin-65
D322-14
E254
E270/1
M116
T205
T206

Abbatiello, Pat
87Idaho-26

Abbey, Bert Wood
90Target-1

Abbey, Charles S.
(Charlie)
N300/SC

Abbot, Terry
78Green

Abbott, Frederick H.
(Fred)
E254
E270/1
T206

Abbott, Jim
88T/Tr-1T
89B-39
89Classic/Up/2-151
89D/Best-171
89D/Rook-16
89F/Up-11
89S/Tr-88
89T-573FDP
89T/Big-322
89T/HeadsUp-16
89T/Tr-2T
89UD/Ext-755
90B-288
90Bz-22
90Classic-40
90CollAB-27
90D-108
90D/Learning-44
90F-125
90F/SoarSt-10
90HotRook/St-1
90KingB/Discs-20
90Leaf/I-31
90MLBPA/Pins-95
90OPC-675
90Panini/St-34
90Post-13
90PublInt/St-362
90S-330
90S/100Ris-5
90S/YS/I-5
90Sf-99
90Smok/Angel-1
90T-675
90T/89Debut-1
90T/Big-329
90T/DH-1
90T/Gloss60-50
90T/HeadsUp-16
90T/JumboR-1
90T/St-172
90T/St-319FS
90ToysRUs-1
90UD-645
90WonderBrd-3
91B-200
91Classic/200-5
91Classic/III-T1
91D-78
91F-305
91F/Ultra-43
91Leaf/I-162
91Leaf/Stud-22
91MajorLg/Pins-23
91OPC-285
91Panini/FrSt-188
91Panini/St-140
91Post-20
91RedFoley/St-1
91S-105
91S/100SS-69
91Seven/3DCoin-1SC
91Smok/Angel-7
91T-285
91T/StClub/I-124
91UD-554
92Classic/I-T1
92D/I-130
92F-50
92S/100SS-19
92S/II-620
92T-406AS
92T-530
92UD-325
92UD-642DS
92UD-78
92UD-86

Abbott, John
85Elmira-1
86Greens-1
88WinHaven/Star-1

Abbott, Kurt
89Medford/Best-27
90Madison/Best-3
90Madison/ProC-2274
91Modesto/ClBest-1
91Modesto/ProC-3092

Abbott, Kyle
89QuadC/GS-13
90B-287
90OPC-444FDP
90S-673DC
90T-444
91B-187
91Edmon/LineD-151
91Edmon/ProC-1507
91UD-51

92Classic/I-T2
92D/I-3RR
92F-51
92S/II-849
92T-763
92T/91Debut-1
92UD-8SR

Abbott, Leander F.
(Dan)
No Cards.

Abbott, Ody Cleon
No Cards.

Abbott, Paul
86Kenosha-1
87Kenosha-24
88Visalia/Cal-165
88Visalia/ProC-92
89Orlan/Best-7
89Orlan/ProC-1348
89SLAS-14
90Portl/CMC-1
90Portl/ProC-168
91B-329
91D-639
91Portl/LineD-401
91Portl/ProC-1558
91S-363RP
91T/90Debut-1
91UD-487
92F-667
92S/II-697
92T-781

Abbott, Terry
89Augusta/ProC-515
90Cedar/Best-5CO
90Cedar/ProC-2338CO

Abbott, W. Glenn
(Glenn)
74OPC-602R
74T-602R
75OPC-591
75T-591
75T/M-591
76OPC-322
76SSPC-485
76T-322
77Ho-147
77OPC-219
77T-207
78Ho-17
78OPC-92
78T-31
79OPC-263
79T-497
80OPC-92
80T-166
81D-47
81F-615
81OPC-174
81Pol/Mariners-3
81T-699
82D-302
82F-502
82T-336TL
82T-571
84F-74
84Nes/792-356
84OPC-356
84T-356
86Jacks/TCMA-25
88Jacks/GS-5
89Tidew/CMC-26
90Huntsvl/Best-25CO
91Tacoma/LineD-550CO
91Tacoma/ProC-2322CO

Abe, Keiji
90Gate/ProC-3362CO

Abe, Osamu
83SanJose-8

Abel, Sid
51BR-C16

Aber, Albert Julius
(Al)
53T-233
54T-238
55B-24
56T-317
57T-141
91T/Archiv-233
D301

Abercrombie, John Jr.
91HighD/ClBest-14
91HighD/ProC-2397

Abernathie, William
(Bill)
No Cards.

Abernathy, Talmadge
No Cards.

Abernathy, Ted
57T-293
59T-169
60T-334
64T-64
65T-332
66OPC-2
66T-2
67T-597
68T-264
69MB-2
69T-483
69T/St-21
70T-562
71MLB/St-409
71OPC-187
71T-187
72MB-3
72OPC-519
72T-519
73OPC-22
73T-22
89Chatt/II/Team-1

Abernathy, Tom
V355-122

Abernathy, Virgil W.
(Woody)
No Cards.

Aberson, Clifford A.
(Cliff)
48L-136

Ables, Harry Terrell
No Cards.

Abner, Ben
86Macon-1
87Harris-26

Abner, Shawn
85Lynch-25
85T-282FDP
86Jacks/TCMA-19
87LasVegas-2
88D-33
88D/Best-21
88D/Rook-5
88F-576
88Leaf-33RR
88S-626
88Sf-223
88Smok/Padres-1
89D-323
89LasVegas/CMC-22
89LasVegas/ProC-21
89S-411
90Classic/III-20
90OPC-122
90S-352
90T-122
90UD-301
91D-561
91F-522
91F/Ultra-300
91Leaf/II-381
91OPC-697
91Padre/MagRal-8
91S-261
91T-697
91T/StClub/I-291
91UD/Ext-795
92D/II-736
92S/II-616
92T-338
92UD-502

Abone, Joseph
80Memphis-6
82Wichita-1

Abraham, Brian
77SanJose-23
79Ogden/TCMA-10
80Ogden-9
81WHave-18
82WHave-1

Abraham, Glenn
87Everett-10
87Pocatel/Bon-31

Abrams, Calvin Ross
(Cal)
51B-152
52B-86
52T-350
53B/Col-160
53NB
53T-98
54B-91
54Esskay
55B-55
55Esskay
89Rini/Dodg-34
90Target-2
91Crown/Orio-2
91T/Archiv-98

Abrams, George Allen
No Cards.

Abrego, Johnny
86D-32
86Iowa-1

Abrell, Thomas
86Sumter-1
87CharWh-26

Abreu, Armand
77Spartan

Abreu, Francisco
87DayBe-11

Abreu, Franklin
(Frank)
87Savan-20
88Spring/Best-21
89StPete/Star-1
91ArkTr/LineD-26

Abreu, Joseph L.
(Joe)
No Cards.

Abril, Ernest
(Odie)
85Greens-21
86FSLAS-1
86WinHaven-1
87WinHaven-15
88WinHaven/Star-2
89WinHaven/Star-1
90LynchRS/Team-14

Abstein, William H.
(Bill)
C46-86
E104
E254
T201
T206

Acker, James Austin
(Jim)
84D-146
84F-145
84Nes/792-359
84OPC-359
84T-359
84Tor/Fire-1
85F-96
85OPC-101
85T-101
85Tor/Fire-1
86Ault-31
86D-363
86F-50
86OPC-46
86T-569
86Tor/Fire-1
87D-659
87F-509
87Smok/Atl-10
87T-407
88F-531
88OPC-293
88S-576
88T-678
88T/St-43
89T-244
89UD-52
90D-558
90OPC-728
90T-728
90Tor/BlueJ-34
91D-368
91F-167
91OPC-71
91S-122
91S/ToroBJ-21
91T-71
91Tor/Fire-34
91UD-670
92F-322
92S/I-63
92T-178

Acker, Larry
85Cram/PCL-55
86Tucson-1
87BirmB/Best-8
88Memphis/Best-7

Acker, Thomas James
(Tom)
57Kahn
57T-219
58T-149
59Kahn
59T-201
60T-274

Ackerman, John
84Everett/Cram-27

Ackley, Florian F.
(Fritz)
64T-368R
65T-477R
66Pep/Tul
78TCMA-27

Ackley, John
80Elmira-12

Acosta, Bert
78Newar

Acosta, Carlos
86Tampa-1

Acosta, Clemente
90PalmSp/Cal-226
90PalmSp/ProC-2569
91London/LineD-426
91MidldA/ProC-426

Acosta, Cy
73OPC-379
73T-379
74OPC-22
74T-22
75OPC-634
75T-634
75T/M-634

Acosta, Ed
71OPC-343R
71T-343R
72OPC-123
72T-123
73OPC-244
73T-244

Acosta, Jose
87Watertn-17
88Augusta/ProC-371
89Augusta/ProC-492

Acosta, Oscar
89Gaston/ProC-1025
91Tulsa/LineD-600CO
91Tulsa/ProC-2789CO

Acta, Manuel
88Osceola/Star-1
89ColMud/Best-2
89ColMud/ProC-136
89ColMud/Star-1
90Osceola/Star-1
91BurlAs/ClBest-12
91BurlAs/ProC-2806

Adair, Kenneth Jerry
(Jerry)
60L-28
61T-71
62T-449
62T/St-2
63J-61
63P-61
63T-488
64T-22
65OPC-231
65T-231
66T-533
67T-484
68Coke
68Dexter-2
68T-346
69MB-3
69MLB/St-55
69OPC-159
69T-159
69T/St-181
70MLB/St-217
70OPC-525
70T-525
72MB-4
73OPC-179CO
73T-179C
91Crown/Orio-3

Adair, James Aubrey
(Jimmy)
No Cards.

Adair, Rick
81Wausau-14
82LynnS-1
83SLCity-8
84Chatt-23
87Watlo-29
89ColoSp/CMC-23
89ColoSp/ProC-247
90ColoSp/CMC-19CO
90ColoSp/ProC-56CO
91ColoSp/LineD-100CO
91ColoSp/ProC-2201CO

Adamczak, Jim
86Jacks/TCMA-1

Adames, Hernan
88Tampa/Star-1

Adames, Juan
88Wythe/ProC-1997
89Peoria/Ko-16

Adams, Ace Townsend
41DP-138
88Conlon/3-1

Adams, Art
91Bristol/ClBest-29
91Bristol/ProC-3594

Adams, Bob
77Evansvl/TCMA-1

Adams, Brian
90Spartan/Best-12
90Spartan/ProC-2493
90Spartan/Star-1

Adams, Bud
88BBCity/Star-1

Adams, Carl Ray
79Newar-15

Adams, Charles B.
(Babe)
16FleischBrd-1
21Exh-1
61F-90
80Laugh/FFeat-38
87Conlon/2-7
92Conlon/Sport-443
D322-9
D329-1
D350/2-1
E104
E120
E121/120
E126
E220
E254
E90/1
E96
M101/4-1
M101/5-1
M116
V100
V61-91
W501-84
W514-54
W515-6
W516-18
W573
W575

Adams, Charles Dwight
(Red)
47Signal
49B/PCL-24
53Mother-53
73OPC-569CO
73T-569C
74OPC-144CO
74T-144C

Adams, Craig
77Watlo
81Chatt-20
82Chatt-22

Adams, Daniel Leslie
(Dan)
No Cards.

Adams, Dan
75Lafay

Adams, Daryl
80Penin/C-2

Adams, Dave
91CharRain/ClBest-14
91CharRain/ProC-99
91QuadC/ClBest-1
91QuadC/ProC-2618

Adams, Derek
91Bluefld/ProC-4132
91Bluefld/ClBest-12
Adams, Earl John
(Sparky)
25Exh-17
26Exh-17
27Exh-9
29Exh/4-13
31Exh/4-15
33DH-1
33Exh/4-8
33G-213
34DS-24
35G-1H
35G-3F
35G-4F
35G-5F
Adams, Elvin Clark
(Buster)
No Cards.
Adams, Gary
90Gate/ProC-3352
91Sumter/ClBest-22
91Sumter/ProC-2347
Adams, George
No Cards.
Adams, Gerald
84Newar-20
85Newar-9
Adams, Glenn Charles
76OPC-389
76SSPC-108
76T-389
78T-497
79T-193
80T-604
81D-566
81F-562
82D-431
82F-545
82Syrac-19
82T-519
83OPC-374
83T-574
87Watlo-10MG
88CLAS/Star-21
Adams, Harold Douglas
(Doug)
No Cards.
Adams, Herbert Loren
(Herb)
No Cards.
Adams, James Irvin
(Willie)
No Cards.
Adams, James J.
(Jim)
No Cards.
Adams, Jason
90Kgsport/Star-30BB
Adams, John Bertram
(Bert)
11Helmar-153
14CJ-63
15CJ-63
T207
Adams, John
78BurlB
80Holyo-16
83ArkTr-10
84ArkTr-12
Adams, Joseph Edward
(Joe)
No Cards.
Adams, Karl Tutwiler
No Cards.
Adams, Ken
86Cram/PCL-46
88BBCity/Star-2
89BBCity/Star-1
Adams, Lionel
89Idaho/ProC-2012
89Sumter/ProC-1098
Adams, Mike
86Visalia-1
87Visalia-22
Adams, Moose
91Everett/ClBest-20
91Everett/ProC-3904
Adams, Morgan
90MedHat/Best-16
Adams, Pat
82AppFx-27
83AppFx/LF-8
85Cram/PCL-186
87Phoenix-21
88WPalmB/Star-1
Adams, Ralph
84LitFalls-6
86Lynch-1
Adams, Richard Leroy
(Dick)
No Cards.
Adams, Ricky Lee
78DaytB
80ElPaso-21
81Holyo-7
82Holyo-13
84Cram/PCL-104
84D-85
84Nes/792-487
84T-487
85Cram/PCL-188
86Phoenix-1
86T-153
Adams, Robert Andrew
(Bob)
No Cards.
Adams, Robert Burd.
(Bob)
No Cards.
Adams, Robert Henry
(Bobby)
48L-54
49Eureka-76
51B-288
52B-166
52T-249
53B/Col-108
53RM-NL2
53T-152
54B-108
54T-123
55B-118
55T-178
56T-287
58T-99
59T-249
91Crown/Orio-4
91T/Archiv-152
Adams, Robert Michael
(Mike)
74OPC-573
74T-573
Adams, Robert Melvin
(Bob)
No Cards.
Adams, Rollo
81Clinton-26
Adams, Spencer Dewey
(Spencer)
No Cards.
Adams, Steve
86Watertn-1
87Macon-13
88Salem/Star-1
89EastLDD/ProC-DD27
89Harris/ProC-295
89Harris/Star-1
90EastLAS/ProC-EL30
90Harris/ProC-1185
90Harris/Star-1
91CaroMud/LineD-101
91CaroMud/ProC-1078
Adams, Terry
76Cedar
Adams, Terry
91Hunting/ClBest-1
91Hunting/ProC-3324
Adams, Tommy
91Belling/ClBest-16
91Belling/ProC-3677
91Classic/DP-49
Adamson, Joel
90Princet/DIMD-1
Adamson, John Michael
(Mike)
69OPC-66R
69T-66R
71OPC-362R
71T-362R
91Crown/Orio-5
Adamson, Wade
80OrlTw-1
Adcock, Joseph Wilbur
(Joe)
51B-323
52B-69
52T-347
53B/Col-151
53JC-17
53SpicSpan/3x5-1
53SpicSpan/7x10-1
54B-96
54JC-9
54SpicSpan/PostC-2
55B-218
55Gol/Braves-2
55JC-9
55SpicSpan/DC-2
56T-320
56YellBase/Pin-2
57SpicSpan/4x5-2
57T-117
58T-325
58T-351M
59T-315
60Lake
60NuCard-33
60SpicSpan-2
60T-3
61NuCard-433
61P-104
61T-245
61T/St-38
62J-145
62P-145
62Salada-125
62Shirriff-125
62T-265
62T/bucks
62T/St-144
63F-46
63J-148
63P-148
63Sugar-4
63T-170
67T-563
72Laugh/GF-42
78TCMA-108
78TCMA-73
88Pac/Leg-31
89Swell-6
90HOF/St-50
90LSUGreat-12
91T/Archiv-285
Exh47
Adderly, Ken
87Miami-18
Addis, Robert Gorden
(Bob)
52T-259
53B/Col-94
53T-157
91T/Archiv-157
Adduci, James David
(Jim)
81Louisvl-19
82ArkTr-18
83Louisvl/Riley-19
84Louisvl-19
85Cram/PCL-206
86Vanco-1
87D-495
87Denver-16
88Pol/Brew-14
89F-176
89Phill/TastyK-37
89S-587
89T-338
90ScranWB/CMC-12
90ScranWB/ProC-604
Addy, Robert Edward
(Bob)
No Cards.
Aderholt, Morrie
90Target-888
Adkins, Adrian
89Princet/Star-1
Adkins, Grady Emmett
No Cards.
Adkins, John Dewey
(Dewey)
No Cards.
Adkins, Merle Theron
(Doc)
C46-18
E254
E270/2
T205
T206
Adkins, Richard Earl
(Dick)
No Cards.
Adkins, Steve
87FtLaud-22
87PrWill-20
88PrWill/Star-1
89BBAmerAA/BProC-AA3
89FtLaud/Star-1
90AlbanyDG/Best-28
90Classic/Up-T2
90ColClip/CMC-1
90ColClip/ProC-667
90T/TVYank-35
91ColClip/LineD-101
91ColClip/ProC-588
91S-716
91S/Rook40-16
91T/90Debut-2
Adkins, Terry
85PrWill-6
Adkinson, Henry Magee
(Henry)
No Cards.
Adler, Marcus
88Fayette/ProC-1085
89Lakeland/Star-1
Adlesh, David George
(Dave)
67OPC-51R
67T-51R
68T-576
69T-341
Adriana, Sharnol
91StCath/ClBest-5
91StCath/ProC-3400
Adriance, Dan
86Cram/PCL-190
87Beloit-23
88Beloit/GS-6
89Salinas/Cal-124
89Salinas/ProC-1818
Afenir, Troy
85Osceola/Team-13
86ColumAst-1
87ColAst/ProC-4
88ColAst/Best-23
89Huntsvl/Best-3
90Tacoma/CMC-22
90Tacoma/ProC-95
91F-1
91S-745
91Tacoma/LineD-526
91Tacoma/ProC-2308
92F-248
92S/I-407
Agado, David
89Batavia/ProC-1926
90Martins/ProC-3204
Agan, Tim
84Toledo-19
Agar, Jeff
86Lakeland-1
87GlenF-12
Agee, Tommie Lee
65OPC-166R
65T-166R
66OPC-164R
66T-164R
67Bz-2
67OPC/PI-4
67T-455
67T/PI-4
68Bz-15
68Bz-6
68Kahn
68T-465
69MB-4
69MLB/St-163
69T-364
69T/St-61
70K-11
70MLB/St-73
70OPC-307WS
70OPC-50
70T-307WS
70T-50
70T/PI-13
70T/S-42
70Trans/M-23
71Bz
71Bz/Test-16
71K-46
71MLB/St-145
71OPC-310
71T-310
71T/Coins-91
71T/tatt-9
72MB-5
72OPC-245
72T-245
72T/S-36
73OPC-420
73T-420
74OPC-630
74T-630
74T/Tr-630T
90Pac/Legend-2
90Swell/Great-19
91LineD-30
91Swell/Great-1
91WIZMets-2
Agganis, Harry
55T-152
Agler, Joseph Abram
(Joe)
E254
Agnew, Samuel Lester
(Sam)
D328-1
D329-2
D350/2-2
E135-1
M101/4-2
M101/5-2
Agostinelli, Sal
84Savan-22
86StPete-1
87ArkTr-15
88Louisvl-5
88Louisvl/CMC-21
88Louisvl/ProC-424
89Reading/Best-22
89Reading/ProC-654
89Reading/Star-1
90Reading/Best-13
90Reading/ProC-1222
90Reading/Star-1
90ScranWB/CMC-11
91ScranWB/LineD-476
91ScranWB/ProC-2540
Agosto, Juan Roberto
(Woody)
82Edmon-12
84D-208
84F-50
84Nes/792-409
84T-409
84TrueVal/WS-1
85Coke/WS-50
85D-526
85F-506
85T-351
86Coke/WS-50
86D-488
86F-197
86T-657
87T-277
87Tucson-1
88F-437
88Mother/Ast-24
88Pol/Ast-1
88S-558
88T/Tr-2T
89B-321
89D-354
89F-348
89Lennox/Ast-17
89Mother/Ast-23
89Panini/St-81
89S-283
89T-559
89UD-251
90D-477
90F-220
90Lennox-1
90Mother/Ast-26
90OPC-181
90PublInt/St-85
90S-284
90T-181
90UD-450
91B-402

91D-531
91F-497
91Leaf/II-404
91OPC-703
91Pol/Card-49
91S-591
91T-703
91T/StClub/II-570
91T/Tr-1T
91UD-569
91UD/Ext-788
92D/I-37
92F-574
92S/I-329
92T-421
92UD-693

Aguayo, Carmelo
82Tulsa-14

Aguayo, Luis
79OkCty
80OkCty
82D-622
82F-238
82T-449
83D-546
83Portl-1
83T-252
84Phill/TastyK-28
85D-503
85Phill/TastyK-11M
85Phill/TastyK-28
85T-663
86D-503
86F-433
86Phill/TastyK-16
86T-69
87F-169
87F-169
87OPC-18
87Phill/TastyK-16
87T-755
87T-755
88D-185
88F-297
88Phill/TastyK-1
88S-499
88T-356
88T/Big-226
89B-88
89D-551
89F-249
89S-436
89T-561
89UD-156
91Pawtu/LineD-351
91Pawtu/ProC-43

Aguilar, Jose
85Tigres-14

Aguilar, Mark
88Stockton/Cal-191
88Stockton/ProC-723
89Madis/Star-1

Aguilera, Rick
85Tidew-11
86D-441
86F-74
86KayBee-1
86Leaf-216
86T-599
87Classic-79
87D-620
87F-1
87F/Excit-2
87Leaf-89
87OPC-103
87T-103
88D-446
88D/Mets/Bk-446
88F-127
88Kahn/Mets-15
88Leaf-231
88S-521
88S/YS/II-21
88T-434
89D-526
89D/Best-265
89F-27
89Kahn/Mets-38
89S-327
89T-257
89UD-563
90B-405
90D-391
90D/BestAL-79
90F-365
90Leaf/I-38
90OPC-711
90PublInt/St-127
90S-519
90T-711
90T/Big-284
90UD-11
91B-334
91BBBest/Aces-1
91D-172
91F-602
91F/Ultra-185
91Leaf/II-471
91Leaf/Stud-81
91OPC-318
91Panini/FrSt-308
91Panini/St-243
91RedFoley/St-2
91S-170
91S/100SS-67
91T-318
91T/StClub/I-76
91UD-542
91USPlayC/AS-7H
91WIZMets-3
92D/I-95
92F-195
92S/100SS-4
92S/I-42
92T-44
92UD-130

Aguirre, Henry John
(Hank)
57T-96
58T-337
59T-36
60T-546
61T-324
61T/St-144
62T-407
63J-54
63P-54
63Salada-32
63T-257
63T-6LL
64Det/Lids-1
64T-39
64T/Coins-74
64T/St-38
64T/SU
64T/tatt
65T-522
66OPC-113
66T-113
67T-263
68T-553
69OPC-94
69T-94
70T-699
73OPC-81CO
73T-81C
74OPC-354CO
74T-354C
75Tucson-26
78TCMA-225
81Detroit-122
90Target-3

Ahearn, Charles
(Charlie)
No Cards.

Ahern, Brian
88CapeCod/Sum-30
89Eugene/Best-23
90AppFox/Box-2
90AppFox/ProC-2086

Ahern, Jeff
82Danvl-3
83Redwd-1

Ahr, Jeff
88Hagers/Star-1

Ahrens, Kelly
90Clinton/Best-3
90Clinton/ProC-2551

Aiello, Talbot
81Wisco-20

Aikens, Willie Mays
75QuadC
77SLCity
78Cr/PCL-20
80OPC-191
80T-368
81Coke
81D-220
81F-43
81OPC-23
81Pol/Royals-1
81T-524
81T/SO-27
81T/St-84
82D-412
82F-404
82F/St-206
82OPC-35
82T-35
82T/St-196
83D-212
83F-104
83OPC-136
83Pol/Royals-1
83T-136
84D-155
84F-341
84F/X-1
84Nes/792-685
84OPC-137
84T-685
84T/St-276
84T/Tr-1
84Tor/Fire-2
85F-97
85OPC-147
85T-436
85Tor/Fire-2
89Pac/SenLg-147
89T/SenLg-57
89TM/SenLg-2
90EliteSenLg-107
90ElPasoATG/Team-43

Ainge, Daniel Rae
(Danny)
78Syrac
80Syrac-20
81D-569
81F-418
81T/Tr-727
82D-638
82F-608
82OPC-125
82T-125

Ainsmith, Edward W.
(Eddie)
90Target-4
D329-3
D350/2-3
E120
E286
M101/4-3
M101/5-3
T207
W572
W573

Aitcheson, Kevin
83Knoxvl-15

Aitchison, Raleigh L.
90Target-889

Ake, John Leckie
(John)
No Cards.

Aker, Jack Delane
66T-287
67OPC-110
67T-110
68T-224
69MLB/St-91
69T-612
69T/St-221
70MLB/St-241
70OPC-43
70T-43
71MLB/St-481
71OPC-593
71T-593
72T-769
73OPC-262
73T-262
74OPC-562
74T-562
78TCMA-274
81Tidew-21MG
82Tidew-19MG
83BuffB-25MG
84BuffB-18MG
85Water-22MG
86OhHenry-CO
87Gator-CO
91WIZMets-4

Akerfelds, Darrel
84Madis/Pol-25
85Huntsvl/BK-32
86Tacoma-1
87Tacoma-2
88ColoSp/CMC-1
88ColoSp/ProC-1537
88S-632
88T-82
89OkCty/CMC-1
89OkCty/ProC-1532
89Smok/R-1
90F/Up-U41
90Leaf/II-526
90Phill/TastyK-1
90T/Tr-1T
91B-493
91D-110
91F-386
91OPC-524
91Phill/Medford-1
91S-223
91T-524
91T/StClub/II-581
91UD-619

Akers, Albert Earl
(Jerry)
No Cards.

Akers, Howard
86Kinston-1

Akers, Thomas Earnest
(Bill)
No Cards.

Akimoto, Ratoo
87SanJose-14

Akins, Sid
85BurlR-12
85T-390OLY
87Durham-5
88Richm-16
88Richm/CMC-7
88Richm/ProC-14
89Greenvl/ProC-1151

Akins, Tom
88Indianap/ProC-525M
89Indianap/ProC-1216

Ako, Gerry
80Holyo-23
81ElPaso-9
81Vanco-22

Alario, Dave
86Bakers-1

Alba, Gibson
85Syrac-1
86Syrac-1
87BuffB-14
88Louisvl-6
88Louisvl/CMC-6
88Louisvl/ProC-442
89Louisvl-7
89Louisvl/CMC-1
89Louisvl/ProC-1252
90Louisvl/CMC-2
90Louisvl/ProC-393
90T/TVCard-37
91Richm/ProC-2559

Albanese, Joseph P.
(Joe)
No Cards.

Alberro, Hector
87Beloit-20
90Johnson/Star-1

Albert, August P.
(Gus)
N172

Albert, Richard
(Rick)
83Ander-2
86Greenvl/Team-1CO
87Richm/Crown-26CO
87Richm/TCMA-26
88Sumter/ProC-416

Alberts, Francis Burt
(Butch)
77SLCity
78Syrac
80Syrac-10

Alberts, Frederick J.
(Cy)
No Cards.

Albertson, John
88Idaho/ProC-1839

Alborano, Pete
88CLAS/Star-22
88Virgini/Star-1
89BBCity/Star-2
89Star/Wax-62
90Memphis/Best-3
90Memphis/ProC-1020
90Memphis/Star-1
91London/LineD-401
91Memphis/ProC-665

Albosta, Edward John
(Ed)
47Signal
90Target-5

Albrecht, Andrew
88CapeCod/Sum-159
91Oneonta/ProC-4164

Albrecht, Edward A.
(Ed)
No Cards.

Albright, Dave
81CharR-9

Albright, Eric
89NiagFls/Pucko-2
90Lakeland/Star-1
91Lakeland/ClBest-14
91Single/ClBest-39

Albright, Gilbert
80Clinton-25

Albright, Harold John
(Jack)
No Cards.

Albury, Victor
(Vic)
72T-778R
74OPC-605R
74T-605R
75OPC-368
75T-368
75T/M-368
76OPC-336
76SSPC-205
76T-336
77T-536
82Watlo/B-27C
82Watlo/C-3C
83Charl-20
83Watlo/LF-27CO
84Maine-9

Alcala, Jesus
82Oneonta-12

Alcala, Julio
86FSLAS-2
86FtMyr-1
87Memphis-24
87Memphis/Best-5
89Memphis/Best-6
89Memphis/ProC-1183
89Memphis/Star-1

Alcala, Santo
76OPC-589R
76T-589R
77Pep-52
77T-636
78OPC-36
78T-321
81Portl-3

Alcantara, Francisco
90Niagara/Pucko-15

Alcazar, Jorge
86Penin-1
88Vanco/CMC-23
88Vanco/ProC-772

Alcaraz, Angel Luis
(Luis)
69T-437
90Target-6

Alcock, John Forbes
(Scotty)
No Cards.

Alder, Jimmy
90Bristol/ProC-3168
90Bristol/Star-1
91Fayette/ClBest-17
91Fayette/ProC-1176

Alderson, Dale L.
No Cards.

Aldred, Scott
87Fayette-11
88Lakeland/Star-1
89London/ProC-1368
90B-344

90Toledo/CMC-2
90Toledo/ProC-141
91B-147
91D-422RR
91OPC-658
91S-740RP
91S/Rook40-3
91T-658
91T/90Debut-3
91T/StClub/II-429
91Toledo/LineD-576
91Toledo/ProC-1922
91UD-7
92Classic/I-T3
92D/II-486
92F-127
92S/100RisSt-41
92S/II-729
92T-198

Aldrete, Mike
86F/Up-U1
86Phoenix-2
87D-450
87F-264
87Mother/SFG-24
87T-71
88D-362
88D/Best-191
88F-76
88Mother/Giants-5
88OPC-351
88Panini/St-426
88RedFoley/St-1
88S-556
88S/YS/I-35
88Sf-80
88T-602
88T/Big-119
88T/St-89
89B-368
89D-140
89D/Tr-25
89F-323
89F/Up-95
89OPC-9
89Panini/St-219
89S-82
89S/Tr-68
89T-158
89T/St-80
89UD-239
89UD/Ext-738
90OPC-589
90S-220
90T-589
90UD-415
91F-224
91OPC-483
91S-447
91T-483
92D/II-621
92F-102
92S/I-351
92T-256

Aldrete, Richard
87Everett-6
88CalLgAS-7
88SanJose/Cal-116
88SanJose/ProC-119
89Shreve/ProC-1847
90Shrev/ProC-1448
90Shrev/Star-1
91Phoenix/LineD-376
91Phoenix/ProC-78

Aldrich, Jay
83Beloit/LF-8
86ElPaso-1
87Denver-4
88D-460
88Denver/CMC-7
88Denver/ProC-1270
88F-155
88Pol/Brew-33
88S-578
88T-616
89Denver/CMC-1
89Denver/ProC-42
90RochR/CMC-6
90RochR/ProC-695
91Crown/Orio-6

Aldrich, Russell
80Water-20
81Water-18

Aldrich, Tom
88Bristol/ProC-1881
89London/ProC-1386
90London/ProC-1272

Aldridge, Vic
E120
V61-74
W573

Alegre, Paul
90Salinas/Cal-133
90Salinas/ProC-2729

Aleno, Charles
(Chuck)
45Centen-1

Aleshire, Troy
86AubAs-1

Alesio, Chris
90Hamil/Best-22
90Hamil/Star-1

Alexander, Charles
(Chuck)
88BurlInd/ProC-1785
89Watertn/Star-1

Alexander, Dave
89SLCity-22
90Miami/II/Star-1

Alexander, David Dale
(Dale)
29Exh/4-23
31Exh/4-23
32Orbit/num-27
32Orbit/un-1
33DH-2
33G-221
61F-91
81Detroit-69
88Conlon/4-1
92Conlon/Sport-616
R300
R305
R308-181
R316

Alexander, Don
90AubAs/Best-23CO
90AubAs/ProC-3418CO
91AubAS/ClBest-25CO
91AubAS/ProC-4290CO

Alexander, Doyle L.
72T-579
73JP
73OPC-109
73T-109
74OPC-282
74T-282
75OPC-491
75T-491
75T/M-491
76OPC-638
76SSPC-374
76T-638
77Ho-140
77T-254
78BK/R-4
78OPC-52
78T-146
79OPC-230
79T-442
80T-67
81D-448
81T-708
81T/Tr-728
82D-96
82F-383
82T-364
82T/Tr-1T
83D-451
83T-512
84D-439
84F-146
84Nes/792-677
84OPC-112
84T-677
84Tor/Fire-3
85D-561
85F-98
85Leaf-134
85OPC-218
85OPC/Post-21
85SpokAT/Cram-1
85T-218
85T/St-365
85Tor/Fire-3
86Ault-33
86D-390
86F-51
86F/LimEd-1
86Leaf-182
86OPC-196
86Sf-133M
86T-196
86T/Mini-34
86Tor/Fire-2
87D-657
87D/HL-52
87F-510
87OPC-249
87T-686
88D-584
88D/Best-13
88F-51
88F/Mini-21
88F/St-23
88OPC-316
88Pep/T-19
88Pol/T-1
88S-610
88T-492
88T/Big-34
89B-94
89D-178
89D/AS-12
89D/Best-125
89F-128
89F/BBAS-1
89Mara/Tigers-19
89OPC-77
89Pol/Tigers-19
89RedFoley/St-1
89S-129
89Sf-211
89T-77
89T/Big-182
89T/St-274
89UD-298
90D-62
90F-599
90KayBee-1
90OPC-748
90PubIInt/St-467
90S-237
90T-748
90Target-7
90UD-330
91Crown/Orio-8

Alexander, Eric
89Bluefld/Star-1
91Bluefld/ProC-4138
91Bluefld/ClBest-11

Alexander, Gary
88TexLgAS/GS-4
88Tulsa-12
89Pac/SenLg-141
89TexLAS/GS-31
89Tulsa/GS-5
89Tulsa/Team-1
90EastLAS/ProC-EL19
90Foil/Best-291
90Reading/Best-14
90Reading/ProC-1224
90Reading/Star-2
91ScranWB/LineD-477
91ScranWB/ProC-2542

Alexander, Gary Wayne
75Lafay
76Phoenix
77Phoenix
77T-476R
78OPC-72
78T-624
79Ho-57
79OPC-168
79T-332
80OPC-78
80T-141
81D-200
81F-398
81T-416
81T/Tr-729
82F-475
82T-11

Alexander, Gerald
90CharlR/Star-1
90OkCty/ProC-422
91Classic/III-11
91D-419RR
91F-278
91Mother/Rang-27
91OkCty/LineD-301
91OkCty/ProC-170
91S-733RP
91T/90Debut-4
91UD/FinalEd-72F
92D/II-578
92F-297
92S/100RisSt-99
92S/I-163

Alexander, Grover C.
14CJ-37
15CJ-37
16FleischBrd-2
21Exh-2
25Exh-18
27Exh-29
28Exh-29
29Exh/4-15
40PB-119
48Exh/HOF
48Swell-11
49Leaf/Prem-1
50Call
51T/CM
60Exh/HOF-1
60F-5
61F-2
61GP-2
63Bz/ATG-29
69Bz-2
69Bz/Sm
72F/FFeat-13
72Laugh/GF-41
76Motor-10
80Pac/Leg-124
80Laugh/3/4/5-8
80Laugh/FFeat-40
80SSPC/HOF
83D/HOF-23
85Woolwth-2
86Conlon/1-3
87Conlon/2-4
88Conlon/3-2
89HOF/St-72
90Swell/Great-30
91Conlon/Sport-32
91Swell/Great-128
92Conlon/Sport-534
92Conlon/Sport-630
BF2-81
D327
D328-2
D329-4
D350/2-4
E120
E121/120
E121/80
E122
E126-13
E135-2
E210-44
E220
L1-114
M101/4-4
M101/5-4
R332-19
R332-48
S81-89
T222
V100
V61-69
W501-59
W502-44
W512-2
W514-65
W515-49
W516-9
W572
W573
W575
WG5-1
WG6-1

Alexander, Hugh
No Cards.

Alexander, Jon
88BBCity/Star-3
89BBCity/Star-3

Alexander, Manny
89Bluefld/Star-2
90Foil/Best-241
90Wausau/Best-20
90Wausau/ProC-2135
91CLAS/ProC-CAR4
91Freder/ClBest-15
91Freder/ProC-2369
91Single/ClBest-97
92T-551M

Alexander, Matthew
(Matt)
76OPC-382
76SSPC-501
76T-382
77T-644
78T-102
81Portl-4
81T-68
82T-528

Alexander, Pat
78Cedar
81Shrev-23

Alexander, P.
N172

Alexander, Rob
88Madis-1
89Modesto/Cal-270
89Modesto/Chong-7

Alexander, Robert S.
(Bob)
52Park-63
53Exh/Can-34
55Esskay
91Crown/Orio-7

Alexander, Roberto
82VeroB-1
84Cram/PCL-166

Alexander, Roger
79Richm-12

Alexander, Tim
80Ander-6
83Durham-27
84Durham-10

Alexander, Tommy
87Wichita-3
88Jaxvl/Best-9
88Jaxvl/ProC-982

Alexander, Walter E.
(Walt)
16FleischBrd-3
D328-3
E135-3

Alexander, William H.
(Nin)
No Cards.

Alexis, Juan
91Martins/ClBest-28
91Martins/ProC-3442

Aleys, Maximo
89Everett/Star-1
90Clinton/Best-22
90Clinton/ProC-2548
91SanJose/ClBest-13
91SanJose/ProC-1
91Single/ClBest-87

Alfaro, Flavio
85Durham-18
85T-391OLY

Alfaro, Jesus
80Wichita-14
84CharlO-19
86ElPaso-3
87ElPaso-15
87TexLgAS-30
88MidldA/GS-19
89ElPaso/GS-20
90ElPasoATG/Team-4

Alfaro, Jose
74Cedar
75Dubuq

Alfonso, Carlos
75Iowa/TCMA-1
76Indianap-24
82AubAs-18
86Tucson-2MG

Alfonso, Edgar
86QuadC-1
87PalmSp-20
88PalmSp/Cal-96
88QuadC/GS-19
89PalmSp/Cal-44
89PalmSp/ProC-464
91PalmSp/ProC-2021

Alfonso, Ossie
84Visalia-6
85Orlan-14

Alfredson, Tom
86QuadC-2
87PalmSp-19

88MidldA/GS-15
89MidldA/GS-4
90BirmB/Best-5
90BirmB/ProC-1394

Alicano, Pedro
91Peoria/ClBest-2
91Peoria/ProC-1333

Alicea, Edwin
89Greenvl/ProC-1156
89Greenvl/Star-1
89Greenvl/Best-6
90Durham/Team-13
91Miami/ClBest-26
91Miami/ProC-419

Alicea, Luis
85Anchora-1
86Erie-1
87ArkTr-16
88D/Rook-52
88F/Up-U116
88Louisvl-7
88Louisvl/CMC-20
88Louisvl/ProC-436
88S/Tr-98T
88Smok/Card-24
88T/Tr-3T
89D-466
89F-443
89Louisvl-8
89Louisvl/CMC-14
89Louisvl/ProC-1263
89Panini/St-175
89RedFoley/St-2
89S-231
89T-261TL
89T-588
89T/St-37
89UD-281
91Louisvl/LineD-226
91Louisvl/ProC-2919
92D/II-560
92S/II-607

Alicea, Miguel
80Penin/B-4
80Penin/C-6
85Beloit-24
87CharlO/WBTV-16
88Edmon/CMC-11
88Edmon/ProC-582
89PalmSp/Cal-55

Allaire, Karl
85Osceola/Team-16
86ColumAst-2
87ColAst/ProC-14
88Tucson/CMC-17
88Tucson/ProC-167
88Tucson/JP-1
90Edmon/CMC-22
90Edmon/ProC-521
91Toledo/LineD-577
91Toledo/ProC-1937

Allanson, Andy
84BuffB-7
85Water-24
86D/Rook-43
86F/Up-U2
86OhHenry-6
86T/Tr-1T
87BuffB-3
87D-95
87F-241
87Gator-6
87Leaf-102
87T-436
87T/GlossRk-1
87T/St-311
87ToysRUs-1
88D-465
88D/Best-5
88F/Up-U21
88Gator-6
88S-586
88T-728
88T/Big-231
89B-83
89D-138
89F-396
89OPC-283
89Panini/St-323
89S-46
89T-283
89T/Big-311
89T/St-207
89UD-217
90F-483
90OPC-514
90PublInt/St-551
90S-452
90T-514
90UD-590
91CokeK/Tiger-10
91Leaf/II-455
92D/I-42
92F-128
92S/II-537
92T-167

Allard, Brian M.
77Ashvl
79Tucson-4
80Charl-5
80T-673R
81Spokane-10
82T-283
83SLCity-6
84Cram/PCL-171
85IntLgAS-43
85Maine-30
86Watlo-1CO
87Wmsprt-16CO
88EastLAS/ProC-50CO
88Wmsprt/ProC-1311CO
89Kenosha/ProC-1080CO
90AS/Cal-26
90Visalia/Cal-80CO
90Visalia/ProC-2171CO
91Visalia/ClBest-26CO
91Visalia/ProC-1758CO

Allcott, Charles
N172

Allen, Bernard Keith
(Bernie)
61Clover-1
62T-596R
63J-2
63P-2
63T-427
64T-455
65OPC-237
65T-237
66T-327
67OPC-118
67T-118
68T-548
69MB-5
69MLB/St-100
69OPC-27
69T-27
69T/St-231
70MLB/St-277
70T-577
71MLB/St-529
71OPC-427
71T-427
72MB-6
72T-644
73OPC-293
73T-293

Allen, Bob
88CapeCod/Sum-157

Allen, Chad
89Burllnd/Star-1
90Watertn/Star-1
91CLAS/ProC-CAR11
91Kinston/ClBest-1
91Kinston/ProC-313

Allen, Cyrus Alban
(Jack)
No Cards.

Allen, David
88Batavia/ProC-1684
90AubAs/Best-16
90AubAs/ProC-3414
91BurlAs/ClBest-1
91BurlAs/ProC-2792
91Single/ClBest-222

Allen, Edward
83Butte-23
83CharR-10

Allen, Ethan Nathan
(Ethan)
33G-46
34DS-92
35BU-76
35G-1E
35G-3C
35G-5C
35G-6C
R314
R316
V353-46

Allen, Fletcher M.
(Sled)
No Cards.

Allen, Frank Leon
16FleischBrd-4
90Target-9

Allen, Greg
78Wisco

Allen, Harold
88Ashvl/ProC-1060
89Osceola/Star-1
90ColMud/Best-11
90ColMud/ProC-1337
90ColMud/Star-1
90Foil/Best-161
91Tucson/LineD-601
91Tucson/ProC-2204

Allen, Harold Andrew
(Hank)
67T-569R
68T-426
69MB-6
69T-623
70OPC-14
70T-14
71MLB/St-3
72MB-7

Allen, Hezekiah
No Cards.

Allen, Horace Tanner
No Cards.

Allen, James
(Jim)
82QuadC-17
83QuadC-18

Allen, James Bradley
(Jamie)
80LynnS-18
81Spokane-31
82SLCity-2
84Cram/PCL-182
84D-267
84F-604
84Nes/792-744
84T-744
84T/St-350

Allen, Jesse Hall
(Pete)
No Cards.

Allen, Jim
89Johnson/Star-1

Allen, John Marshall
No Cards.

Allen, John Thomas
(Johnny)
32Orbit/num-103
34G-42
35G-8E
35G-9E
37OPC-122
39Wheat-2
90Target-10
92Conlon/Sport-384
R312
V300
V354-96
W753

Allen, Kim Bryant
(Kim)
75QuadC
78Cr/PCL-15
80Spokane-19
81F-612
81Spokane-27
89Pac/SenLg-99
89T/SenLg-53
91Pac/SenLg-99

Allen, Larry
86Penin-2
87CharWh-11

Allen, Lee
90LitSun-6

Allen, Lloyd Cecil
71OPC-152R
71T-152R
72OPC-102
72T-102
73OPC-267
73T-267
74OPC-539
74T-539
76SSPC-140

Allen, Matt
91James/ClBest-7
91James/ProC-3547

Allen, Mike
80Buffa-11
80Wichita-13

Allen, Myron Smith
N172

Allen, Neil
78Tidew
80T-94
81Coke
81D-276
81F-322
81F/St-84
81OPC-322
81T-322
81T/HT
81T/St-198
82D-506
82F-520
82K-20
82OPC-205
82T-205
82T/St-66
83D-98
83F-536
83K-34
83OPC-268
83T-575
83T/St-265
83T/Tr-1
84D-109
84F-318
84Jacks/Smok-1
84Nes/792-435
84OPC-183
84T-435
84T/St-147
85D-205
85F-219
85OPC-234
85T-731
85T/St-144
86Coke/WS-33
86D-610
86F-98
86F/Up-U3
86T-663
86T/Tr-2T
87Coke/WS-19
87D-507
87F-484
87OPC-113
87RedFoley/St-93
87T-113
87T/St-292
88D-597
88T-384
89ColoSp/CMC-6
89D-196
89F-250
89S-375
89T-61
89UD-567
90Nashvl/CMC-23
90Nashvl/ProC-223
91WIZMets-5

Allen, Newt
78Laugh/Black-3
86Negro/Frit-104
90Negro/Star-30

Allen, Paul
89Welland/Pucko-32

Allen, Richard A.
(Richie)
64PhilBull-1
64T-243R
65OldLond-2
65T-460
65T/E-36
65T/trans-38
66Bz-4
66OPC-80
66T-80
66T/RO-74
67Bz-4
67T-242LL
67T-244LL
67T-309
67T-450
67T/Test/SU-18
68Bz-14
68Coke
68Dexter-3
68T-225
68T/G-23
68T/Post-15
69Citgo-17
69MB-7
69MLB/St-172
69MLBPA/Pin-33
69NTF
69OPC-6LL
69OPC/DE-1
69T-350
69T-6LL
69T/DE-26
69T/decal
69T/S-53
69T/St-71
69Trans-57
70K-33
70MLB/St-133
70OPC-40
70T-40
70T/SO
71Bz/Test-44
71K-57
71MLB/St-97
71OPC-650
71T-650
71T/S-40
71T/tatt-7
71Ticket/Dodg-1
72MB-8
72OPC-240
72T-240
73K-26
73OPC-310
73OPC-62LL
73OPC-63LL
73T-310
73T-62LL
73T-63LL
73T/Comics-2
73T/Lids-2
73T/PinUps-2
74K-33
74OPC-332AS
74OPC-70
74T-332M
74T-70
74T/DE-39
74T/Puzzles-2
74T/St-151
75K-42
75OPC-210MV
75OPC-307LL
75OPC-400
75T-210MV
75T-307LL
75T-400
75T/M-210MV
75T/M-307LL
75T/M-400
76OPC-455
76SSPC-473
76T-455
82KMart-21
89Kodak/WSox-1M
90Target-8
PM10/L-1

Allen, Rick
88Alaska/Team-1
89Billings/ProC-2045
90Cedar/Best-8
90Cedar/ProC-2331
91Chatt/LineD-151
91Chatt/ProC-1964

Allen, Robert
(Bob)
No Cards.

Allen, Robert Earl
No Cards.

Allen, Robert Gilman
(Bob)
N172

Allen, Robert Gray
(Bob)
61T-452
62T-543
63Sugar-33
63T-266
64T-209

66T-538
67OPC-24
67T-24
68OPC-176
68T-176

Allen, Robert
(Robbie)
82VeroB-15
84Cram/PCL-156
86ElPaso-2
87MidldA-23

Allen, Roderick B.
(Rod)
79Knoxvl/TCMA-24
82SLCity-3
83SLCity-14
85RochR-10
87BuffB-24
88ColoSp/CMC-19
88ColoSp/ProC-1545
89F-397

Allen, Ron
91Batavia/ClBest-25
91Batavia/ProC-3474

Allen, Ronald F.
(Ron)
No Cards.

Allen, Ronnie
91FrRow/DP-13

Allen, Scott
88BurlInd/ProC-1784

Allen, Shane
81QuadC-7

Allen, Sterling
76Baton

Allen, Steve
88Butte-26
89Gaston/ProC-1022
89Gaston/Star-1
90Tulsa/ProC-1148
91SanAn/LineD-526
91SanAn/ProC-2965

Allen, Tracy
90WinHaven/Star-1
91WinHaven/ClBest-1
91WinHaven/ProC-481

Allenson, Gary M.
80T-376
81D-455
81T-128
82Coke/BOS
82D-386
82F-287
82OPC-273
82T-686
83D-30
83F-177
83T-472
84D-335
84F-388
84Nes/792-56
84OPC-56
84T-56
85F-148
85Syrac-3
85T-259
87Oneonta-24
88Oneonta/ProC-2064
89Lynch/Star-23
89Pac/SenLg-41
89TM/SenLg-3
90EliteSenLg-92
90LynchRS/Team-27
91NewBrit/LineD-474MG
91NewBrit/ProC-367
91Pac/SenLg-111

Allenson, Kelvin
88Oneonta/ProC-2064

Alley, Leonard Eugene
(Gene)
64T-509R
65OPC-121
65T-121
66EH-14
66T-336
67Kahn
67T-283
67T/Test/PP-1
68Kahn
68KDKA-22
68OPC-53
68T-368AS
68T-53
68T/G-25
69MB-8
69MLB/St-181
69T-436
69T/St-81
70MLB/St-97
70T-566
71MLB/St-193
71OPC-416
71T-416
72MB-9
72OPC-286
72T-286
73OPC-635
73T-635

Alleyne, Isaac
87SLCity/Taco-9
88James/ProC-1903
89Rockford/Team-1

Allie, Gair R.
54T-179
55T-59
55T/DH-71

Allietta, Robert G.
(Bob)
76OPC-623
76T-623
79Tacoma-15
80Tacoma-11

Allinger, Bob
83Miami-21

Allison, Arthur A.
(Art)
No Cards.

Allison, Bubba
86Cram/PCL-151

Allison, Dana
89Medford/Best-28
90Modesto/Cal-153
90Modesto/ProC-2203
91B-238
91S/RookTr-94T
91Tacoma/ProC-2295
91UD/Ext-771
92T/91Debut-2

Allison, Douglas L.
(Doug)
No Cards.

Allison, Jamie
88CalLgAS-21
88Reno/Cal-279
89Kinston/Star-1
90Kinston/Team-13

Allison, Jeff
87Idaho-5
88Miami/Star-1
88SLCity-9

Allison, Jim
83TriCit-12
85BurlR-27
85Utica-1
86DayBe-1

Allison, Mack P.
No Cards.

Allison, Milo Henry
No Cards.

Allison, Tommy
90Pittsfld/Pucko-32

Allison, William R.
(Bob)
59HRDerby-2
59T-116
60Armour-2
60NuCard-66
60T-320
60T/tatt-2
61NuCard-466
61P-91
61T-355
61T/St-176
62Bz
62J-83
62P-83
62P/Can-83
62Salada-22
62Shirriff-22
62T-180
62T/St-73
63J-7
63P-7
63T-75
64T-10LL
64T-290
64T/Coins-19
64Wheat/St-2
65OldLond-21
65OPC-180
65T-180
65T/E-38
65T/trans-1
66T-345
67OPC-194
67T-194
67T-334M
68Coke
68Dexter-4
68T-335
69MB-9
69MLB/St-64
69OPC-30
69T-30
69T/St-191
70MLB/St-229
70T-635
72MB-10
78TCMA-26
83MLBPA/Pin-1
89Chatt/II/Team-2
89Pac/Leg-165
89Swell-27

Allred, Beau
88CLAS/Star-23
88Kinston/Star-1
89BBAmerAA/BProC-AA7
89Canton/Best-4
89Canton/ProC-1302
89Canton/Star-1
90ColoSp/CMC-9
90ColoSp/ProC-48
90D-691
90F/Up-U88
90OPC-419
90S/Tr-70T
90T-419
90T/89Debut-2
91B-80
91F-358
91F/Ultra-104
91Leaf/II-316
91S-338RP
91S/100RisSt-56
91S/Rook40-22
91UD/Ext-784

Almada, Baldomero M.
(Mel)
35BU-147
39PB-43
40Hughes-1
40PB-71
90Target-11
91Conlon/Sport-234
92Conlon/Sport-550
R313
R314

Almante, Tom
86ArkTr-1

Almaraz, Johnny
88Billings/ProC-1825
89Greens/ProC-431

Almeida, Rafael D.
T207

Almon, William F.
(Bill)
74Hawaii
77Padre/SchCd-1
77Padre/SchCd-6
77T-490R
78Padre/FamFun-1
78T-392
79K-53
79T-616
80OPC-225
80T-436
81F-332
81T-163
81T/Tr-730
82D-637
82F-335
82F/St-185
82OPC-119
82T-521
82T/St-167
83D-356
83F-228
83OPC-362
83T-362
83T/Tr-2
84D-467
84F-436
84Mother/A's-11
84Nes/792-241
84OPC-241
84T-241
84T/St-334
85D-589
85F-414
85F/Up-U2
85T-273FDP
85T-607
85T/Tr-2T
86D-479
86F-602
86OPC-48
86T-48
86T/St-131
87D-326
87F-601
87OPC-159
87T-447
87T/Tr-1T
88D-487
88Phill/TastyK-2
88T-787
91WIZMets-6

Aloi, Dave
74Cedar
75Dubuq

Aloma, Luis
51B-231
52T-308
54B-134
54T-57

Alomar, Conde Santos
(Sandy)
65OPC-82R
65T-82R
66T-428
67T-561
68T-541
69JB
69T-283
69T/St-151
70MLB/St-169
70OPC-29
70T-29
71JB
71MLB/St-337
71OPC-745
71T-745
71T/Coins-28
72MB-11
72OPC-253
72T-253
73OPC-123
73T-123
74OPC-347
74T-347
74T/St-141
75OPC-266
75T-266
75T/M-266
76OPC-629
76SSPC-441
76T-629
77T-54
78BK/R-15
78T-533
79T-144
88Smok/Padres-3CO
89B-258M
89Padre/Mag-9CO
90Padre/MagUno-22CO
91WIZMets-7

Alomar, Rafael
61Union

Alomar, Roberto
87TexLgAS-8
87Wichita-4
88D-34RR
88D/Best-42
88D/Rook-35
88F/Up-U122
88LasVegas/CMC-20
88LasVegas/ProC-231
88Leaf-34RR
88S/Tr-105T
88Smok/Padres-2
88T/Tr-4T
89B-458
89Bimbo/Discs-12
89Classic-127
89Coke/Padre-1
89D-246
89D/Best-21
89F-299
89F-630M
89F/Superstar-1
89OPC-206
89Padre/Mag-14
89Padre/Mag-9
89Panini/St-191
89RedFoley/St-3
89S-232
89S/HotRook-72
89S/YS/I-28
89Sf-20
89T-206
89T-231TL
89T/Big-102
89T/Gloss60-19
89T/JumboR-1
89T/St-104
89ToysRUs-1
89UD-471
90 USPlayC/AS-4D
90B-221
90Classic-61
90Coke/Padre-1
90D-111
90D/BestNL-35
90F-149
90F/LL-1
90Leaf/I-75
90OPC-517
90Padre/MagUno-10
90Panini/St-349
90PublInt/St-43
90PublInt/St-607
90S-12
90Sf-93
90T-517
90T/Big-9
90T/Coins-37
90T/Gloss60-27
90T/Mini-77
90T/St-109
90T/TVAS-35
90UD-346
91B-9
91Classic/200-113
91Classic/I-94
91Classic/II-T81
91Colla/Alomar-Set
91D-12DK
91D-682
91D/SuperDK-12
91F-523
91F/Ultra-358
91F/Up-U63
91Leaf/II-267
91Leaf/Stud-131
91OPC-315
91OPC/Premier-1
91Panini/FrSt-92
91Panini/St-96
91RedFoley/St-3
91S-25
91S-887DT
91S/100SS-100
91S/RookTr-44T
91S/ToroBJ-13
91S/ToroBJ-39AS
91Sunflower-19
91T-315
91T/StClub/II-304
91T/Tr-2T
91Tor/Fire-12
91UD-335
91UD/Ext-763
91UD/FinalEd-83F
91USPlayC/AS-12H
92Classic/I-T4
92D/I-28AS
92D/I-58
92F-323
92F-698M
92S/100SS-82
92S/I-15
92T-225
92UD-355
92UD-81M

Alomar, Santos Jr.
(Sandy)
86Beaum-1
87TexLgAS-10

87Wichita-5
88AAA/ProC-20
88LasVegas/CMC-22
88LasVegas/ProC-236
89AAA/CMC-31
89AAA/ProC-6
89B-258M
89B-454
89Classic-79
89D-28RR
89D/Rook-21
89F-300
89F-630M
89LasVegas/CMC-11
89LasVegas/ProC-7
89Padre/Mag-2
89Padre/Mag-9
89Panini/St-192
89S-630M
89S/YS/II-1
89Sf-223M
89T-648FS
89UD-5
90B-337
90Classic/III-76
90Classic/Up-T3
90D-30
90D/BestAL-97
90D/Learning-40
90D/Rook-1
90F-150
90F/Up-U89
90HotRook/St-2
90Leaf/I-232
90OPC-353
90S-577
90S/McDon-2
90S/Tr-18T
90T-353
90T/Big-265
90T/Tr-2T
90UD-655
90UD/Ext-756
90USPlayC/AS-2S
90Windwlk/Discs-1
91B-57
91Bz-20
91Classic/200-194
91Classic/I-39
91Classic/II-T68
91D-13DK
91D-489
91D-51AS
91D-693ROY
91D/SuperDK-13DK
91F-359
91F/Ultra-105
91JDeanSig-8
91KingB/Discs-17
91Leaf/I-189
91Leaf/II-528CL
91Leaf/Prev-17
91Leaf/Stud-41
91MajorLg/Pins-18
91MooTown-10
91OPC-165
91OPC/Premier-2
91Panini/FrSt-166
91Panini/FrSt-215
91Panini/St-172
91Panini/Top15-109
91Petro/SU-9
91Post-6
91Post/Can-23
91RedFoley/St-113
91S-400AS
91S-694RF
91S-793
91S-851FRAN
91S-879ROY
91S/100RisSt-1
91S/HotRook-6
91Sunflower-21
91T-165
91T/CJMini/I-5
91T/StClub/I-61
91T/SU-2
91ToysRUs-1
91UD-144
91UD-46
91UD/FinalEd-81F
91USPlayC/AS-11D
91Woolwth/HL-6
92D/I-203
92D/I-29AS
92F-103
92F-698M
92S/100SS-49
92S/II-510
92T-420
92UD-156
92UD-81M

Alonso, Julio
77Evansvl/TCMA-2

Alonzo, Ray
83Madis/LF-6

Alou, Felipe Rojas
59T-102
60L-6
60T-287
61T-565
62AmTract-52A
62AmTract-52B
62AmTract-52C
62J-133
62P-133
62P/Can-133
62Salada-130
62Shirriff-130
62T-133
62T/St-193
63J-107
63P-107
63T-270
64T-65
64T/Coins-11
64T/St-62
65T-383
66Kahn
66OPC-96
66T-96
67Kahn
67OPC/PI-30
67T-240LL
67T-530
67T/PI-30
68Coke
68Dexter-5
68Kahn
68OPC-55
68T-55
69MB-10
69MLB/St-110
69MLBPA/Pin-32
69OPC-2LL
69T-2LL
69T-300
69T/DE-17
69T/decal
69T/S-35
69T/St-2
69Trans-51
70MLB/St-253
70OPC-434
70T-434
71K-7
71MLB/St-505
71OPC-495
71T-495
71T/Coins-8
72MB-12
72OPC-263
72T-263
73OPC-650
73Syrac/Team-1
73T-650
74OPC-485
74T-485
74T/Tr-485T
78Memphis/Team-1
82D-650
82Wichita-2
84Mother/Giants-19
84Stuart-6CO
84Stuart-38CO
85Indianap-2MG
86WPalmB-1MG
88FSLAS/Star-2CO
88Pac/Leg-58
90FSLAS/Star-23
90WPalmB/Star-29
91WPalmB/ClBest-1MG
91WPalmB/ProC-1244

Alou, Jesus M. R.
(Jesus)
64T-47R
65T-545
66T-242
66T/RO-3
67T-332
68Coke
68Dexter-6
68T-452
69MB-11
69MLB/St-136
69OPC-22
69T-22
69T/St-51
70MLB/St-37
70OPC-248
70T-248
71MLB/St-73
71OPC-337
71T-337
72MB-13
72T-716
73OPC-93
73T-93
74OPC-654
74T-654
75OPC-253
75T-253
75T/M-253
76OPC-468
76SSPC-538
76T-468
78BK/Ast-22
79T-107
80T-593
91WIZMets-8

Alou, Jose
87BurlEx-10
88WPalmB/Star-2
89WPalmB/Star-1

Alou, Marty
73Syrac/Team-2

Alou, Mateo Rojas
(Matty)
61T-327
62T-413
63Salada-25
63T-128
64T-204
65T-318
66EH-18
66OPC-94
66T-94
67Bz-47
67Kahn
67OPC-10
67OPC/PI-29
67T-10
67T-240LL
67T/PI-29
67T/Test/PP-2
67T/Test/PP-28
68Bz-2
68Kahn
68KDKA-18
68OPC-1LL
68T-1LL
68T-270
68T/G-1
69Kahn
69MB-12
69MLB/St-182
69OPC-2LL
69T-2LL
69T-490
69T/S-56
69T/St-82
69Trans-58
70K-28
70MLB/St-98
70OPC-30
70OPC-460AS
70T-30
70T-460AS
71K-53
71MLB/St-265
71OPC-720
71T-720
71T/Coins-47
72MB-14
72OPC-395
72T-395
73OPC-132
73T-132
74OPC-430
74T-430
78TCMA-75
88Pac/Leg-37
91Swell/Great-2

Alou, Moises
86Watertn-2
87Watertn-27
88Augusta/ProC-360
89Salem/Star-1
89Star/Wax-93
90A&AASingle/ProC-29
90B-178
90BuffB/Team-1
90F-650M
90Harris/ProC-1204
90Harris/Star-2
90S-592
91Classic/I-60
91D-38RR
91Leaf/Stud-191
91OPC-526A
91OPC-526B
91OPC/Premier-3
91S-813
91T-526A
91T-526B
91T/90Debut-5
91T/StClub/I-31
91UD-665
92S/100RisSt-9

Alperman, Charles A.
(Whitey)
90Target-890
C46-7
E270/2
T204
T206

Alpert, George
81Batavia-25
82Watlo/B-20
82Watlo/C-27

Alstead, Jason
91Freder/ClBest-21
91Freder/ProC-2375

Alston, Thomas E.
(Tom)
53Mother-24
54Hunter
55B-257
55Hunter

Alston, Walter E.
52Park-66MG
53Exh/Can-61MG
55Gol/Dodg-1MG
56T-8MG
58PacBell-1MG
58T-314M
60BB-18MG
60Morrell
60T-212MG
61BB-24MG
61T-136MG
62BB-24MG
62T-217MG
63T-154MG
64T-101MG
65OPC-217MG
65T-217MG
66OPC-116MG
66T-116MG
67T-294MG
68T-472MG
69OPC-24MG
69T-24MG
70OPC-242MG
70T-242MG
71OPC-567MG
71T-567MG
71Ticket/Dodg-2MG
72T-749MG
73OPC-569MG
73T-569MG
74OPC-144MG
74T-144MG
75OPC-361MG
75T-361MG
75T/M-361MG
76SSPC-90MG
76T-46MG
80Pac/Leg-14MG
87Smok/Dodg-1MG
88Smok/Dodg-1MG
89Smok/Dodg-1MG
90Target-12

Alston, Wendell
(Dell)
78Cr/PCL-68
78T-710R
79T-54
79Tacoma-19
80T-198
80Tacoma-24
81D-322

Altaffer, Todd
90SoBend/ClBest-12
91SoBend/ProC-2848

Altamirano, Porfirio
80OkCty
81OkCty/TCMA-1
83F-153
83Portl-15
83T-432
84Iowa-23
84Nes/792-101
84T-101

Alten, Ernest M.
(Ernie)
No Cards.

Altenberger, Peter
88CapeCod/Sum-48

Altenburg, Jesse H.
No Cards.

Altizer, David Tildon
(Dave)
E254

Altman, George Lee
59T-512
60T-259
61P-195
61T-551
61T/St-1
62J-187
62P-187
62P/Can-187
62Salada-128
62Shirriff-128
62T-240
62T/bucks
62T/St-103
63J-171
63P-171
63Salada-31
63T-357
64Bz-23
64T-95
64T/St-69
64T/SU
65T-528
66OPC-146
66T-146
67OPC-87
67T-87
91WIZMets-9

Altman, John
77Visalia

Altobelli, Joseph S.
75IntAS/TCMA-16
77T-211MG
78T-256MG
79Pol/Giants-6CO
79T-356MG
80Colum-8
83T/Tr-3
84D-88
84F-643IA
84F/St-125MG
84Nes/792-21MG
84T-21MG
85T-574MG
85T/Gloss22-12MG
88Berg/Cubs-CO
90Cub/Mara-28CO
90T/TVCub-2CO
91Cub/Mara-x

Alton, George Wilson
No Cards.

Altrock, Nicholas
(Nick)
61F-3
87Conlon/2-8
88Conlon/5-1
91Conlon/Sport-226
E210-40
E254
R312/M
WG2-1

Alusik, George J.
62T-261
63T-51
64T-431
Alva, John
86Sumter-2
87Durham-25
88Greenvl/Best-6
89Greenvl/ProC-1154
89Greenvl/Star-2
89Greenvl/Best-7
90Greenvl/Star-1
90Richm/CMC-23
90Richm/ProC-263
91Richm/LineD-426
91Richm/ProC-2574
Alvarado, Arnaldo
75Dubuq
Alvarado, Jose
85Tigres-15
Alvarado, Luis Cesar
70OPC-317R
70T-317R
71OPC-489
71T-489
72T-774
73OPC-627
73T-627
74OPC-462
74T-462
91WIZMets-10
Alvarez, Alex
88CapeCod/Sum-7
Alvarez, Carmelo
82VeroB-16
Alvarez, Chris
86FSLAS-3
86FtLaud-1
87Albany-15
88Colum/CMC-24
88Colum/Pol-13
88Colum/ProC-323
89Colum/ProC-739
90London/ProC-1273
Alvarez, Clemente
88Utica/Pucko-2
89SoBend/GS-30
90Saraso/Star-1
91Saraso/ClBest-12
91Saraso/ProC-1115
91Single/ClBest-142
Alvarez, David
89Elmira/Pucko-1
90Elmira/Pucko-2
Alvarez, Emenegilda
91MedHat/ProC-4112
Alvarez, Javier
89Eugene/Best-15
Alvarez, Jesus O.
(Orlando)
77SLCity
Alvarez, Jorge
89Salem/Team-5
90BBCity/Star-29CO
90VeroB/Star-1
90VeroB/Star-30CO
91SanAn/LineD-527
Alvarez, Jose
76Dubuq
Alvarez, Jose Lino
79Savan-12
81Richm-15
82Richm-1
83Richm-1
84Cram/PCL-51
86Greenvl/Team-2
88F/Up-U70
88Richm/CMC-8
88Richm/ProC-12
89D-405
89F-585
89Panini/St-31
89T-253
89UD/Ext-734
90D-389
90F-574
90OPC-782
90Publint/St-106
90S-148
90T-782
90UD-634
Alvarez, Mike
81Miami-11
82FtMyr-12
83Omaha-1
84Omaha-19
85FtMyr-27
86FtMyr-2
87AppFx-18
88Savan/ProC-353
91London/LineD-425CO
91Memphis/ProC-670CO
Alvarez, Orlando
74Albuq/Team-1
90Target-891
Alvarez, Oswaldo
85Tigres-4
Alvarez, Oswaldo G.
(Ossie)
59T-504
Alvarez, Robbie
81Chatt-3
82Miami-12
Alvarez, Rogelio H.
63T-158R
Alvarez, Tavo
91Single/ClBest-48
91Sumter/ClBest-1
91Sumter/ProC-2324
Alvarez, Wilson
88Gaston/ProC-1017
89CharlR/Star-1
89Tulsa/Team-2
90T/89Debut-3
90UD/Ext-765
90Vanco/CMC-1
90Vanco/ProC-481
91B-354
91BirmB/LineD-51
91BirmB/ProC-1446
91F/UltraUp-U13
91OPC-378
91Single/ClBest-285
91T-378
91UD/FinalEd-42F
92Classic/I-T5
92D/II-495HL
92D/II-630
92F-684RS
92F-74
92S/I-428NH
92S/II-760
92T-452
92UD-573
Alvis, Andy
80Batavia-20
Alvis, Dave
86Watlo-2
87Watlo-7
Alvis, Roy Maxwell
(Max)
63Sugar-14
63T-228R
64Kahn
64T-545
64T/Coins-48
64T/S-46
64T/St-7
64T/SU
64T/tatt
65Kahn
65OPC-185
65T-185
65T/E-3
65T/trans-2
66Kahn
66T-415
66T/RO-68
67Kahn
67T-520
67T/Test/SU-16
68Bz-9
68Kahn
68T-340
68T/Post-2
69Kahn
69MB-13
69MLB/St-37
69MLBPA/Pin-1
69OPC-145
69T-145
69T/St-161
70McDon-6
70MLB/St-193
70OPC-85
70T-85
72MB-15
78TCMA-83
Exh47
Alvord, William C.
(Billy)
N172
Alyea, Brant Jr.
88Gaston/ProC-1007
88SALAS/GS-16
89StLucie/Star-1
90Tulsa/ProC-1165
Alyea, Garrabrant R.
(Brant)
66OPC-11R
66T-11R
69OPC-48
69T-48
70OPC-303
70T-303
71MLB/St-457
71OPC-449
71T-449
72MB-16
72OPC-383
72T-383
Amador, Bruce
82Madis-30
Amalfitano, John J.
(Joey)
55B-269
55Gol/Giants-1
55T-144
60T-356
61T-87
62J-144
62P-144
62P/Can-144
62Salada-193
62Shirriff-193
62T-456
62T/St-123
63F-36
63T-199
64T-451
65T-402
73OPC-252CO
73T-252CO
74OPC-78CO
74T-78CO
76SSPC-629CO
77Padre/SchCd-2CO
78TCMA-96
81D-522CO
81T-676MG
85Coke/Dodg-1CO
86Coke/Dodg-1CO
89Smok/Ast-15
90Mother/Dodg-28M
90Pol/Dodg-x
91Mother/Dodg-28CO
91Pol/Dodg-x
Aman, Kevan
77Wausau
Amante, Tom
87StPete-10
90SpringDG/Best-4
Amaral, Rich
86Pittsfld-1
87Pittsfld-22
88Pittsfld/ProC-1362
89BirmB/Best-14
89BirmB/ProC-91
90Vanco/CMC-13
90Vanco/ProC-493
91Calgary/LineD-51
91Calgary/ProC-520
92T/91Debut-3
Amaras, Marcos
89Medford/Best-24
Amaro, Ruben
59T-178
61T-103
62J-194
62P-194
62P/Can-194
62Salada-163
62Shirriff-163
62T-284
62T/St-163
63F-50
63T-455
64PhilBull-2
64T-432
65T-419
66OPC-186
66T-186
67T-358
68OPC-138
68T-138
69T-598
76OkCty/Team-1
78TCMA-28
83Thorn-26C
90Bristol/ProC-3175CO
Amaro, Ruben Jr.
88CalLgAS-32
88PalmSp/Cal-97
88PalmSp/ProC-1434
89Bristol/Star-29
89QuadC/Best-30
89QuadC/GS-18
91AAAGame/ProC-AAA12
91B-208
91Classic/III-19
91Edmon/LineD-152
91Edmon/ProC-1526
92D/II-733
92F-52
92T-269
92T/91Debut-4
Amaya, Ben
86Chatt-1
Ambler, Wayne H.
39PB-117
41G-7
Ambos, Willie
88SLCity-13
89SanBern/Best-9
89SanBern/Cal-66
91SLCity/ProC-3202
Ambrose, Mark
87ElPaso-11
88ElPaso/Best-15
89Stockton/Best-10
89Stockton/Cal-159
89Stockton/ProC-377
Ambrosio, Ciro
90StCath/ProC-3467
91Myrtle/ClBest-15
91Myrtle/ProC-2949
Amelung, Edward
(Ed)
81VeroB-1
83Albuq-19
84Cram/PCL-163
85Cram/PCL-158
86Albuq-1
87Edmon-11
88SanDiegoSt-1
90Target-13
Amerson, Archie
78SanJose-21
79Toledo-4
Ames, Doug
86Madis-1
86Madis/Pol-1
Ames, Ken
80Ander-10
Ames, Leon Kessling
(Red)
10Domino-1
11Helmar-120
12Sweet/Pin-106
91Conlon/Sport-153
92Conlon/Sport-334
D328-4
D329-5
D350/2-5
E104
E135-4
E254
E270/1
E270/2
E93
E96
M101/4-5
M101/5-5
M116
S74-79
T202
T205
T206
T213/blue
T215/blue
T215/brown
T3-77
W555
WG3-1
Amole, Morris George
(Doc)
No Cards.
Amor, Vincente A.
No Cards.
Amoros, Edmundo I.
(Sandy)
53Exh/Can-43
55Gol/Dodg-2
55T-75
55T/DH-54
56T-42
56T/Pin-49
57T-201
58T-93
60T-531
89Rini/Dodg-2
90Target-14
PM10/Sm-2
Amos, Perry
91Hunting/ClBest-2
91Hunting/ProC-3325
Anaya, Mike
89Star/Wax-22
90Kgsport/Best-15
90Kgsport/Star-1
91Pittsfld/ClBest-22
91Pittsfld/ProC-3414
Ancker, Walter
No Cards.
Anders, Scott
86Peoria-1
Andersen, Larry E.
75OkCty
78T-703R
79Tacoma-4
80Port-23
80T-665R
82D-428
82T-52
83D-181
83F-470
83Portl-3
83T-234
84Phill/TastyK-14
85D-570
85F-244
85Phill/TastyK-13
85Phill/TastyK-9
85T-428
86D-355
86F-434
86Phill/TastyK-47
86T-183
87D-640
87F-49
87Mother/Ast-21
87Pol/Ast-1
87T-503
88D-332
88F-438
88Mother/Ast-21
88Pol/Ast-2
88S-133
88T-342
89B-325
89D-359
89F-349
89Lennox/Ast-18
89Mother/Ast-20
89S-523
89T-24
89UD-404
90B-67
90D-359
90F-221
90Leaf/II-386
90Lennox-2
90Mother/Ast-20
90Publint/St-86
90S-282
90UD-407
91B-660
91D-665
91F-83
91F/Up-U120
91Leaf/II-407
91Leaf/Stud-241
91OPC-761
91Padre/MagRal-17
91S-848

91S/RookTr-71T
91T-761
91T/StClub/II-390
91UD-41
91UD/Ext-793
92D/II-687
92F-597
92S/I-263
92T-616
92UD-587

Andersh, Kevin
86Macon-2
89Augusta/ProC-512

Anderson, Alfred W.
(Alf)
No Cards.

Anderson, Allan
83Wisco/LF-3
84Visalia-20
85Toledo-1
86D/Rook-3
86Toledo-1
87D-368
87F-533
87Portl-4
87T-336
88F/Up-U41
88Portl/ProC-654
88T-101
89B-149
89Classic/Up/2-178
89D-419
89D/Best-270
89F-102
89F/LL-1
89OPC-20
89Panini/St-381
89S-394
89S/YS/I-34
89Sf-220
89T-672
89T/Mini-60
89UD-85
90B-409
90D-64
90D/BestAL-52
90F-366
90Leaf/I-5
90OPC-71
90Panini/St-117
90PublInt/St-320
90PublInt/St-593
90RedFoley/St-1
90S-292
90Sf-59
90T-71
90T/St-296
90UD-219
91B-327
91D-527
91F-603
91Leaf/I-259
91OPC-223
91S-135
91T-223
91T/StClub/I-188
91UD-503
92F-196
92S/II-731
92T-417
92UD-506

Anderson, Andy
88ElPaso/Best-16
88Portl/CMC-1

Anderson, Andy Holm
52Park-17
86Negro/Frit-41

Anderson, Arnold R.
(Red)
No Cards.

Anderson, Bernie
86Lakeland-2
87Lakeland-10
88GlenF/ProC-928
89London/ProC-1364

Anderson, Brady
85Elmira-2
86FSLAS-4
86WinHaven-2
87NewBrit-7
88D/RedSox/Bk-NEW
88D/Rook-14
88S/Tr-70T
88T/Tr-5T
89B-18
89D-519
89F-606
89French-9
89OPC-161
89S-563
89S/YS/I-26
89T-757
89T/JumboR-2
89T/UK-1
89ToysRUs-2
89UD-408
90B-258
90D-638
90F-172
90MLBPA/Pins-119
90OPC-598
90PublInt/St-572
90S-33
90T-598
90UD-290
91B-100
91Crown/Orio-9
91D-668
91F-466
91OPC-97
91S-249
91T-97A
91T-97B
91T/StClub/II-410
91UD-349
92F-1
92S/I-365
92T-268
92UD-185

Anderson, Chad
90Martins/ProC-3205
91Martins/ClBest-27
91Martins/ProC-3443

Anderson, Dave
76Cedar
77Cedar

Anderson, David C.
(Dave)
82Albuq-14
84D-642
84Nes/792-376
84Pol/Dodg-10
84T-376
85Coke/Dodg-2
85D-275
85F-366
85T-654
86Coke/Dodg-2
86F-123
86OPC-29
86Pol/Dodg-10
86T-758
87F-436
87Mother/Dodg-17
87Pol/Dodg-4
87T-73
88D-475
88F-508
88Mother/Dodg-17
88OPC-203
88Panini/St-313
88Pol/Dodg-10
88S-166
88T-456
89D-434
89F-53
89Mother/Dodg-17
89OPC-117
89Pol/Dodg-7
89S-478
89T-117
89UD-89
90D-486
90F/Up-U59
90Mother/Giant-19
90OPC-248
90PublInt/St-1
90S-238
90T-248
90Target-15
90UD-510
91F-252
91F/Ultra-314
91Leaf/Stud-251
91Mother/Giant-19
91OPC-572
91PG&E-18
91S-641
91T-572
92D/II-759
92F-625
92S/I-167
92UD-290

Anderson, David S.
(Dave)
No Cards.

Anderson, Doug
91Belling/ClBest-19
91Belling/ProC-3654

Anderson, Dwain C.
72OPC-268R
72T-268R
73OPC-241
73T-241

Anderson, Ed
88SLCity-30M

Anderson, Edward
76Dubuq
77Cocoa

Anderson, Edward John
(Goat)
No Cards.

Anderson, Eric
82AubAs-6

Anderson, Ferrell J.
90Target-16

Anderson, Fred
16FleischBrd-5

Anderson, Garret
91QuadC/ClBest-22
91QuadC/ProC-2641
91Single/ClBest-258

Anderson, George A.J.
No Cards.

Anderson, George Lee
(Sparky)
59T-338
60L-125
60T-34
61BeeHive-1
70OPC-181MG
70T-181MG
71OPC-688MG
71T-688MG
72OPC-358MG
72T-358MG
73OPC-296MG
73T-296MG
74OPC-326MG
74T-326MG
75OPC-531MG
75T-531MG
75T/M-531MG
76SSPC-22
76T-104MG
77T-287MG
78T-401MG
79T-259MG
81D-370MG
81Detroit-18MG
81F-460MG
81T-666MG
82D-29MG
83D-533MG
83T-660MG
84Nes/792-259MG
84T-259MG
85F-628MG
85F/St-125MG
85Seven-2MG
85T-307MG
85Wendy-1MG
86D/AAS-58MG
86T-411MG
86T/Gloss22-1MG
87T-218MG
88Pac/Leg-46
88Pep/T-11MG
88Pol/T-2MG
88T-14MG
89Mara/Tigers-11MG
89Pol/Tigers-MG
89T-193MG
89T/LJN-132
90CokeK/Tiger-1MG
90OPC-609MG
90T-609MG
91CokeK/Tiger-11MG
91Leaf/Stud-261MG
91OPC-519MG
91T-519MG
92T-381MG

Anderson, Glen
86Cram/PCL-141

Anderson, Greg
76BurlB

Anderson, Harold
(Hal)
No Cards.

Anderson, Harry W.
57T-404
58T-171
59T-85
60T-285
61T-76
PM10/Sm-3

Anderson, James Lea
(Jim)
78Cr/PCL-93
79T-703R
80T-183
81D-165
81F-598
81Pol/Mariners-4
81T-613
82D-181
82F-503
82T-497
83Rangers-46
84Nes/792-353
84Rangers-14
84T-353
85OKCty-6
87Clinton-5
88Clinton/ProC-703
89Shreve/ProC-1835

Anderson, Jeff
86Penin-3

Anderson, Jesse
81AppFx-1
82AppFx-10
83Albany-1

Anderson, John
84Butte-2
88Martins/Star-1

Anderson, John C.
62T-266
90Target-17
91Crown/Orio-10

Anderson, John Fred
(Fred)
D328-5
E135-5

Anderson, John Joseph
E107
T204
T206

Anderson, Jon
91QuadC/ProC-2629

Anderson, Karl Adam
(Bud)
79Spokane-20
79T-712R
81Chatt-25
82Charl-1
83T-367
83Wheat/Ind-1
84D-590
84F-533
84Maine-8
84Nes/792-497
84T-497
91Pac/SenLg-4

Anderson, Kent
86PalmSp-1
88Edmon/CMC-17
88Edmon/ProC-574
89Edmon/CMC-17
89T/Tr-3T
90D-490
90HotRook/St-3
90OPC-16
90PublInt/St-363
90S-412
90S/100Ris-86
90T-16
90T/89Debut-4
90UD-691
91B-194
91D-525
91Edmon/LineD-153
91Edmon/ProC-1520
91F-306
91OPC-667
91S-224
91T-667
91T/StClub/I-241

Anderson, Lawrence D.
(Larry)
76OPC-593R
76SSPC-249
76T-593R
77T-487R

Anderson, Matthew
89Bluefld/Star-26
90Wausau/Best-6
90Wausau/ProC-2119
90Wausau/Star-1
91Kane/ClBest-3
91Kane/ProC-2650

Anderson, Michael A.
(Mike)
72OPC-14R
72T-14R
73OPC-147
73T-147
74JP
74OPC-619
74T-619
75OPC-118
75T-118
75T/M-118
76OPC-527
76SSPC-469
76T-527
77T-72
78T-714
79T-102
80BurlB-18
80OkCty
80T-317
81Portl-5
82Vanco-22
84Cram/PCL-46
85Louisvl-29
91Crown/Orio-11

Anderson, Mike
85LitFalls-1
86LitFalls-1
87Columbia-20
87PalmSp-24
88PalmSp/Cal-98
88PalmSp/ProC-1438
89Greens/ProC-428
89Reno/Cal-239
90Cedar/Best-20
90Cedar/ProC-2318
91Chatt/LineD-152
91Chatt/ProC-1950

Anderson, Norman C.
(Craig)
62T-593R
63T-59
91WIZMets-11

Anderson, Paul
91Spring/ClBest-1
91Spring/ProC-731

Anderson, Richard A.
(Rick)
79Jacks-16
81Tidew-26
82Tidew-12
84Tidew-19
85IntLgAS-19
85Tidew-6
86Tidew-1
87F-2
87Omaha-22
87T-594
88Omaha/CMC-1
88Omaha/ProC-1512
89S-441
90Kenosha/Best-28CO
90Kenosha/ProC-2311CO
90Kenosha/Star-26CO
91Kenosha/ClBest-20CO
91Kenosha/ProC-2092CO
91WIZMets-12

Anderson, Richard Lee
(Rick)
76Shrev
77WHave
79Colum-21
80Spokane-20
81Spokane-28
81T-282R

Anderson, Robert Carl
(Bob)
58T-209
59T-447
60T-412
61T-283
61T/St-2
62T-557
63T-379
Anderson, Roy
85Madis-4
85Madis/Pol-1
86Modesto-1
86Modesto-2
Anderson, Scott
82Madis-10
85Tulsa-33
88OkCty/CMC-1
89Indianap/CMC-6
89Indianap/ProC-1234
90Indianap/CMC-7
90Indianap/ProC-280
91F-225
91S-734RP
Anderson, Spike
90WichSt-2
Anderson, Steve
83Beloit/LF-12
91Oneonta/ProC-4159
Anderson, Steve
(Nub)
76Laugh/Clown-14
76Laugh/Clown-25
Anderson, Tim
87Bakers-22
Anderson, Todd
91Pocatel/ProC-3794
Anderson, Tom
78Watlo
91AubAS/ClBest-8
Anderson, Varney S.
N172
Anderson, Walter Carl
No Cards.
Anderson, William
(Bill)
No Cards.
Anderson, William E.
(Bill)
No Cards.
Anderson, Wingo C.
(Wingo)
No Cards.
Andrade, Herberto
88Peoria/Ko-1
89CharWh/Best-13
89CharWh/ProC-1759
Andre, John Edward
No Cards.
Andres, Ernest Henry
(Ernie)
No Cards.
Andrews, Elbert D.
No Cards.
Andrews, Fred Jr.
76OkCty/Team-2
78Tidew
Andrews, George E.
N162
N172
N284
N690
WG1-46
Andrews, Hubert Carl
(Hub)
No Cards.
Andrews, Ivy Paul
32Orbit/num-1
32Orbit/un-2
35BU-106
35BU-115M
36Exh/4-15
92Conlon/Sport-420
R300
R305
R313
Andrews, James Pratt
(Jim)
No Cards.
Andrews, Jay III
91BBCity/ClBest-23
91BBCity/ProC-1409

Andrews, Jeff
87PortChar-12
88Tulsa-9CO
89Tulsa/GS-3
89Tulsa/Team-3CO
90Tulsa/ProC-1174CO
91OkCty/LineD-303
91OkCty/ProC-194CO
Andrews, John
88SanDiegoSt-2
Andrews, John Richard
No Cards.
Andrews, Michael Jay
(Mike)
67T-314R
67T/Test/RedSox-7
68Coke
68Dexter-7
68T-502
69MB-14
69MLB/St-10
69OPC-52
69T-52
69T/St-131
70MLB/St-157
70OPC-406
70T-406
71OPC-191
71T-191
72MB-17
72OPC-361
72T-361
73OPC-42
73T-42
Andrews, Nathan H.
(Nate)
No Cards.
Andrews, Robert P.
(Rob)
75IntAS/TCMA-10
76OPC-568
76SSPC-54
76T-568
77T-209
78T-461
79Pol/Giants-21
79T-34
80T-279
Andrews, Shane
90Classic/DP-11
90Classic/III-88
91B-452
91OPC-74
91S-674FDP
91Sumter/ClBest-10
91Sumter/ProC-2339
91T-74
91T/CJMini/II-13
Andrews, Stanley J.
(Stan)
41G-24
90Target-18
Andrews, William W.
(Wally)
N172
Andrezejewski, Joe
89Helena/SP-1
90Beloit/Best-3
90Beloit/Star-1
90Foil/Best-52
91Erie/ClBest-15
91Erie/ProC-4059
Andrus, William M.
(Bill)
No Cards.
Andrus, Frederick H.
(Fred)
No Cards.
Andujar, Hector
91Watertn/ClBest-16
91Watertn/ProC-3371
Andujar, Joaquin
77T-67
78BK/Ast-7
78T-158
78T/Zest-1
79OPC-246
79T-471
80K-55
80OPC-324
80T-617
81D-381
81F/St-48

81OPC-329
81T-329
81T/Tr-731
82D-607
82F-110
82T-533
83D-316
83D/AAS-27
83F-1
83OPC-228
83T-228
83T-561TL
83T/St-179
84D-181
84F-319
85FunFood/Pin-90
84Nes/792-785
84OPC-371
84T-785
85D-13
85D-449
85D/DKsuper-13
85F-220
85F/St-85
85Leaf-13DK
85OPC-231
85Seven-6C
85T-655
85T/Gloss40-12
85T/St-136
85T/Super-38
86D-231
86F-26
86F/LimEd-2
86F/Up-U4
86KAS/Disc-11
86Mother/A's-4
86Mother/Ast-15
86OPC-150
86Sf-101
86Sf-133M
86Sf-185M
86T-150
86T/Mini-58
86T/St-44
86T/Tr-3T
87D-548
87F-385
87F/Hottest-1
87F/Mini-2
87Leaf-162
87OPC-284
87RedFoley/St-11
87Smok/A's-1
87T-775
87T/St-172
88Mother/Ast-26
88Pol/Ast-3
88S-193
88T-47
89S-472
89T/SenLg-93
89UD-79
Andujar, Juan
89Johnson/Star-2
90Foil/Best-13
90Spring/Best-1
91Single/ClBest-80
91Spring/ClBest-2
91Spring/ProC-746
Angelini, Norman S.
(Norm)
73OPC-616R
73T-616R
Angelo, Mark
83Erie-12
84Savan-11
Angero, Jose
87Omaha-2
Anglero, Jose
88BBCity/Star-4
89BBCity/Star-4
90BBCity/Star-1
91Lakeland/ClBest-18
91Lakeland/ProC-271
Angley, Thomas S.
(Tom)
No Cards.
Anglin, Russ
83Ander-25
Angotti, Donald
90Osceola/Star-2
91AubAS/ClBest-12

91AubAS/ProC-4276
Angulo, Ken
83Redwd-2
85MidldA-15
Anicich, Mike
82Jacks-14
82Tidew-25
83MidldC-20
Ankenman, Fred N.
(Pat)
90Target-892
Annee, Tim
89Medford/Best-23
Annis, William P.
(Bill)
N172
Ansley, Willie
89Ashvl/ProC-950
89B-332
89SALAS/GS-3
89T-607FDP
90A&AASingle/ProC-57
90ColMud/Best-1
90ColMud/ProC-1356
90ColMud/Star-2
90Foil/Best-3
91B-549
91Jacks/LineD-551
91Jacks/ProC-935
91Single/ClBest-135
Anson, Adrian C.
(Cap)
50Callahan
60Exh/HOF-2
60F-44
61F-4
63Bz/ATG-39
69Bz/Sm
75F/Pion-1
80SSPC/HOF
89HOF/St-5
90BBWit-66
90HOF/St-9
E223
N162
N172
N28
N284
N300/unif
WG1-10
Anthony, Andy
86VeroB-1
Anthony, Dane
82Chatt-8
83Watlo/LF-21
Anthony, Eric
89BBAmerAA/BProC-AA11
89ColMud/Best-1
89ColMud/ProC-134
89ColMud/Star-2
89SLAS-3
89Star/Wax-1
89Tucson/JP-1
90B-81
90Classic-70
90ColMud/Star-3
90D-34
90D/BestNL-28
90D/Rook-49
90F-222
90HotRook/St-4
90Leaf/I-82
90Leaf/Prev-7
90Lennox-3
90Mother/Ast-3
90OPC-608
90Panini/St-379
90S-584
90S/100Ris-45
90S/DTRook-B10
90S/YS/I-42
90Sf-179
90T-608
90T/89Debut-5
90T/Big-197
90ToysRUs-2
90UD-28
91B-540
91Classic/200-139
91Classic/II-T34
91D-333
91F-498
91F/Ultra-131

91Leaf/I-181
91Leaf/Stud-171
91MajorLg/Pins-44
91OPC-331
91S-146
91S/100RisSt-42
91T-331
91T/CJMini/II-3
91T/StClub/I-229
91Tucson/LineD-602
91Tucson/ProC-2223
91UD-533
92F-424
92S/100RisSt-8
92S/I-315
Anthony, Greg
91Classic/DP-27
91FrRow/DP-19
92T-336DP
Anthony, Lee
49B/PCL-1
Anthony, Mark
91Spokane/ClBest-12
91Spokane/ProC-3959
Anthony, Paul
77Salem
Antigua, Felix
89Augusta/ProC-497
89Princet/Star-2
90Augusta/ProC-2466
90SALAS/Star-26
Antolick, Joseph
(Joe)
No Cards.
Antonelli, John A.
(Johnny)
49Eureka-3
50B-74
51B-243
52T-140
53JC-2
53SpicSpan/3x5-2
53T-106
54B-208
54NYJour
54RM-NL21
54T-119
55Armour-1
55B-124
55Gol/Giants-2
55RM-NL13
56T-138
57T-105
58Hires-50
58Hires/T
58PacBell-2
58SFCallB-1
58T-152
59Armour-2
59T-377
60Bz-35
60T-572AS
60T-80
60T/tatt-3
61P-142
61T-115
61T/St-132
83Beloit/LF-6
84Mother/Giants-13
91T/Archiv-106
Exh47
PM10/Sm-4
PM10/Sm-5
Rawl
Antonelli, John L.
No Cards.
Antonello, William J.
(Bill)
53T-272
72T/Test-5
90Target-19
91T/Archiv-272
Antunez, Martin
82Beloit-23
Anyzeski, Fred
75AppFx
Aparicio, Luis E.
56T-292
56YellBase/Pin-3
57T-7
58T-483AS
58T-85
59T-310

59T-408M
59T-560AS
60Bz-22
60L-1
60T-240
60T-559AS
61Bz-35
61P-19
61T-440
61T-574AS
61T/St-120
62Bz
62Exh
62J-49
62P-49
62P/Can-49
62Salada-71
62Shirriff-71
62T-325
62T-469AS
62T/St-22
63Exh
63J-37
63P-37
63Salada-50
63T-205
63T/SO
64T-540
64T/Coins-127AS
64T/Coins-31
64T/S-39
64Wheat/St-3
65T-410
65T/trans-3
66OPC-90
66T-90
67OPC-60
67T-60
68T-310
69Kelly/Pin-1
69MB-15
69MLB/St-28
69MLBPA/Pin-2
69OPC-75
69OPC/DE-2
69T-75
69T/DE-6
69T/decal
69T/S-10
69T/St-152
69Trans-24
70K-22
70MLB/St-181
70OPC-315
70T-315
70T/S-3
70T/SO
71Bz
71Bz/Test-8
71K-19
71MD
71MLB/St-313
71MLB/St-554
71OPC-740
71T-740
71T/Coins-16
71T/GM-51
71T/S-23
71T/tatt-6
72MB-18
72OPC-313
72OPC-314IA
72T-313
72T-314A
72T/Cloth-2IA
73OPC-165
73T-165
74OPC-61
74T-61
74T/St-131
78TCMA-250
84TrueVal/WS-2
84West/1-2
86Sf/Dec-37M
87Nestle/DT-15
88Pac/Leg-91
89HOF/St-18
89Kodak/WSox-6M
90BBWit-23
90MSA/AGFA-9
91Crown/Orio-12
Exh47

Apodaca, Robert John
(Bob)
74OPC-608R
74T-608R
75OPC-659
75T-659
75T/M-659
76OPC-16
76SSPC-548
76T-16
77T-225
78T-592
79OPC-98
79T-197
80T-633
82Jacks-23
86Columbia-1CO
87Columbia-2CO
89Jacks/GS-21CO
91Tidew/LineD-575CO
91Tidew/ProC-2527CO
91WIZMets-13

Apolinario, Oswaldo
90BurlB/Best-6
90BurlB/ProC-2354
90BurlB/Star-1

Aponte, Edwin
80SanJose/JITB-2
81LynnS-15
83Watlo/LF-2
84BuffB-19

Aponte, Luis Eduardo
81Pawtu-8
83D-109
83F-178
83T-577
84D-371
84F-389
84F/X-2
84Nes/792-187
84T-187
84T/Tr-2
84Wheat/Ind-38
85F-437

Aponte, Newlan
89Wythe/Star-1

Aponte, Ricardo
78DaytB
87AubAs-19
90Ashvl/ClBest-27CO
90Ashvl/ProC-2765CO
91Ashvl/ProC-585CO

Appier, Kevin
88BBCity/Star-5
89F/Up-35
89Omaha/CMC-4
89Omaha/ProC-1720
90B-367
90D/Rook-21
90F-100
90OPC-167
90S-625
90S/100Ris-13
90T-167
90T/89Debut-6
90UD-102
91B-309
91Bz-21
91D-740
91F-549
91F/Ultra-143
91OPC-454
91Panini/Top15-72
91Panini/Top15-95
91Pol/Royal-1
91S-268
91S/100RisSt-73
91T-454
91T/StClub/II-501
91ToysRUs-2
91UD-566
92D/II-455
92F-150
92S/II-542
92T-281
92UD-159

Applegate, Fred
No Cards.

Applegate, Russ
85Madis-5
85Madis/Pol-2
86Modesto-3

Appleton, Edward Sam
(Ed)
90Target-893
D328-6
E135-6

Appleton, Peter W.
(Pete)
33G-83
39PB-137
40PB-128
91Conlon/Sport-76

Appling, Lucas B.
(Luke)
31Exh/4-19
34DS-95
34Exh/4-10
34G-27
35BU-124
35G-1I
35G-2F
35G-6F
35G-7F
36Exh/4-10
36Wheat-3
37Exh/4-10
37OPC-115
38Exh/4-10
39Exh
40Wheat-12
41DP-70
48L-59
49B-175
49Royal-16
50B-37
60F-27
60T-461C
80Pac/Leg-22
80SSPC/HOF
83D/HOF-8
84Pol/Atl-55C
88Conlon/AmAS-1
88Pac/Leg-4
89Kodak/WSox-6M
89Swell-30
90Pac/Legend-3
90Swell/Great-18
91Swell/Great-3
92Conlon/Sport-475
Exh47
PR1-1
R303/A
R303/B
R314
R326-7A
R326-7B
R342-7
R346-10
V300
V354-84
V355-113
WG8-1

Aquedo, Vasquez
87FtMyr-16

Aquino, Luis
86Syrac-2
87D-655
87OPC-301
87Syrac-10
87Syrac/TCMA-1
87T-301
88Omaha/CMC-2
88Omaha/ProC-1520
89D-534
89F-275
89T-266
90D-179
90F-101
90OPC-707
90PublInt/St-341
90S-432
90T-707
90UD-274
91D-718
91F-550
91OPC-169
91Pol/Royal-2
91T-169
91T/StClub/II-451
91UD-504
92D/II-544
92F-151
92S/I-369
92T-412
92UD-219

Aquino, Pedro
87Spokane-20
88Spokane/ProC-1929

Arace, Pasquale
91Augusta/ClBest-19
91Augusta/ProC-816

Aragon, Angel V. Sr.
No Cards.

Aragon, Angel V. Jr.
(Jack)
No Cards.

Aragon, Joey
86Visalia-2
87Visalia-19
88OrlanTw/Best-11

Aragon, Reno
76Dubuq
77Cocoa

Aragon, Steve
82Wisco-23
83Visalia/LF-3
84Visalia-24
85Orlan-1
86Orlan-1

Arangure, Maurillo
85Tigres-3

Aranzamendi, Jorge
77StPete
79ArkTr-12
80ArkTr-3
81ArkTr-8
82ArkTr-24
83ArkTr-24

Aranzullo, Mike
91SLCity/ProC-3215

Araujo, Andy
86NewBrit-1
87Pawtu-14
87Pawtu/TCMA-1
88Pawtu/CMC-5
88Pawtu/ProC-446
89Pawtu/CMC-8
89Pawtu/Dunkin-23
89Pawtu/ProC-679

Archdeacon, Maurice
No Cards.

Archer, Carl
91Pulaski/ClBest-4
91Pulaski/ProC-4010

Archer, James Peter
(Jimmy)
09Buster/Pin-1
10Domino-2
11Helmar-90
12Sweet/Pin-79A
12Sweet/Pin-79B
14CJ-64
15CJ-64
90Target-20
BF2-62
D328-7
D329-6
D350/2-6
E135-7
E224
E254
E90/3
E91
M101/4-6
M101/5-6
M116
PM1-1
T202
T204
T205
T222
WG4-1

Archer, James William
(Jim)
61T-552
62J-98
62P-98
62Salada-75
62Shirriff-75
62T-433
62T/bucks
62T/St-52

Archer, Kurt
91Single/ClBest-223
91Stockton/ClBest-8
91Stockton/ProC-3023

Archibald, Dan
88James/ProC-1920
89James/ProC-2142
90Rockford/ProC-2684

Archibald, Jaime
86Columbia-2
87Lynch-9

Archie, George Albert
No Cards.

Arcia, Jose R. Orta
68T-258R
69MB-16
69T-473
69T/St-91
70T-587
71MLB/St-217
71OPC-134
71T-134
72MB-19
73OPC-466
73T-466

Ard, Johnny
89AS/Cal-13
89B-153
89Visalia/Cal-96
89Visalia/ProC-1427
90A&AASingle/ProC-39
90B-406
90Foil/Best-60
90OrlanSR/Best-23
90OrlanSR/ProC-1075
90OrlanSR/Star-1
91B-634
91Phoenix/LineD-385
91Phoenix/ProC-58

Ardell, Daniel Miers
(Dan)
No Cards.

Ardizoia, Rinaldo J.
(Rugger)
46Remar-20

Ardner, Joseph
N172

Arellanes, Frank J.
E96
M116
T204
T206

Arena, Rich
89Oneonta/ProC-2120
90Greens/Best-29CO
90Greens/ProC-2681CO
90Greens/Star-26CO
90Tampa/DIMD-28CO

Arendas, Dan
87FtLaud-13
88FtLaud/Star-1

Arendas, David
88CapeCod/Sum-100

Arendt, Jim
91Princet/ClBest-29

Arft, Henry Irven
(Hank)
49B-139
51B-173
52B-229
52T-284
53Mother-26

Argo, Billy
88Bakers/Cal-244
89VeroB/Star-1

Arguelles, Fernando
89Salem/Star-2
90SanBern/Best-16
90SanBern/Cal-100
90SanBern/ProC-2636
91Jaxvl/LineD-326
91Jaxvl/ProC-152

Arias, Alex
88CharWh/Best-9
88SALAS/GS-13
89Peoria/Ko-17
90T/TVCub-36
91CharlK/LineD-126
91CharlK/ProC-1693
91Single/ClBest-10
92T-551M

Arias, Amador
91Cedar/ClBest-16
91Cedar/ProC-2724
91Erie/ClBest-1
91Erie/ProC-4074
91Single/ClBest-340

Arias, Francisco
87Pocatel/Bon-26
88Augusta//ProC-2078

Arias, German
90Martins/ProC-3207

Arias, Jose
90Hamil/Star-2
90Savan/ProC-2058
91Johnson/ClBest-27
Arias, Juan
78Salem
Arias, Pedro
88Burllnd/ProC-1787
Arias, Rodolfo M.
(Rudy)
59T-537
Arias, Tony
85Madis/Pol-3
86Madis-2
86Madis/Pol-2
88Modesto-19
Arigoni, Scott
82ArkTr-1
83Spring/LF-9
Ariola, Anthony
88SoOreg/ProC-1696
89Madis/Star-2
89Star/Wax-64
90Tacoma/CMC-4
90Tacoma/ProC-84
Arita, Shuzo
91Salinas/ClBest-27CO
91Salinas/ProC-2261CO
Arland, Mark
90CharWh/Best-20
90CharWh/ProC-2250
91CharWh/ClBest-21
91CharWh/ProC-2898
Arlas, Antonio
85Madis-6
Arlett, Russell Loris
(Buzz)
28Exh/PCL-1
31Exh/4-11
WG7-1
Arlich, Donald Louis
(Don)
No Cards.
Arlin, Stephen Ralph
(Steve)
72OPC-78
72T-78
73OPC-294
73T-294
74OPC-406
74T-406
75OPC-159
75T-159
75T/M-159
Arline, James
78Richm
79Richm-23
Armas, Antonio Rafael
(Tony)
77T-492R
78T-298
79T-507
80T-391
81D-239
81Drake-30
81F-575
81F/St-5
81OPC-151
81Sqt-24
81T-629
81T/SO-6
81T/St-116
82D-365
82Drake-1
82F-85
82F/St-128
82Granny
82K-35
82OPC-60
82PermaGr/CC-17
82T-162LL
82T-60
82T/St-224
82T/St-4LL
83D-71
83F-513
83OPC-353
83T-1RB
83T-435
83T/St-108
83T/St-191
83T/St-192
83T/Tr-4
84D-294
84F-390
84F/St-21
85FunFood/Pin-24
84Nes/792-105
84OPC-105
84T-105
84T/Gloss40-20
84T/St-218
85D-249
85Drake-1
85F-149
85F/St-12
85F/St-28
85Leaf-112
85OPC-394
85T-707AS
85T-785
85T/Gloss40-18
85T/St-194
85T/St-209
85T/St-95
85T/Super-10
86D-127
86D-5
86D/DKsuper-5
86F-339
86Leaf-5DK
86OPC-255
86Sf-140M
86Sf-61M
86T-255
86T/St-254
86Woolwth-1
87D-498
87F-26
87Mother/A's-21
87OPC-174
87T-535
87T/Board-15
88F-484
88S-487
88Smok/Angels-5
88T-761
89B-51
89D-580
89F-467
89Panini/St-295
89S-182
89T-332
89T/Big-99
89UD-212
90D-525
90F-126
90OPC-603
90PublInt/St-364
90S-378
90T-603
90UD-58
Armas, Marcos
90Madison/Best-4
91Huntsvl/ClBest-1
91Huntsvl/LineD-276
91HuntsvlProC-1807
91Modesto/ProC-3093
Armbrister, Edison R.
(Ed)
72OPC-524R
72T-524R
74OPC-601R
74T-601R
75OPC-622R
75T-622R
75T/M-622R
76OPC-652
76SSPC-42
76T-652
77T-203
78Indianap-8
78T-556
Armbrust, Orville M.
No Cards.
Armbruster, Charles
No Cards.
Armbruster, Herman
(Harry)
T206
Armer, Rick
77Wausau
Armstrong, George N.
No Cards.
Armstrong, Howard E.
No Cards.
Armstrong, Jack
88Kahn/Reds-40
88Nashvl/CMC-1
88Nashvl/ProC-484
88Nashvl/Team-1
88S/Tr-78T
88T/Tr-6T
89AAA/CMC-12
89Classic-97
89D-493
89Panini/St-63
89S-462
89S/HotRook-99
89T-317
89UD-257
90 USPlayC/AS-JK
90Classic/III-74
90D-544
90D/BestNL-142
90F-412
90Kahn/Reds-1
90Leaf/II-374
90OPC-642
90S/YS/II-11
90T-642
90T/Big-314
90UD-684
91B-679
91BBBest/Aces-2
91Classic/200-6
91D-439AS
91D-571
91F-55
91Kahn/Reds-40
91Leaf/II-459
91OPC-175
91Panini/FrSt-165
91Panini/St-126
91Pep/Reds-1
91RedFoley/St-114
91S-231
91S/100SS-83
91T-175
91T/StClub/II-510
91UD-373
92D/II-762
92F-398
92S/II-488
92T-77
92UD-296
Armstrong, Jimmy
91Idaho/ProC-4319
Armstrong, Kevin
85LitFalls-2
86Columbia-3
87Wichita-2
88River/Cal-206
89SanAn/Best-6
Armstrong, Michael D.
(Mike)
80Hawaii-16
81F-503
82Omaha-1
82T-731
83F-105
83T-219
84D-217
84F-342
84Nes/792-417
84T-417
84T/Tr-3
85D-602
85F-120
85T-612
86Colum-1
86Colum/Pol-1
87Colum-25
87Colum/Pol-1
Armstrong, William
83Evansvl-23tr
84Evansvl-20tr
Arndt, Harry J.
T206
Arndt, Larry
86Madis-3
86Madis/Pol-3
89Tacoma/CMC-22
89Tacoma/ProC-1557
90T/89Debut-7
90Tacoma/CMC-23
90Tacoma/ProC-97
Arner, Michael
90A&AASingle/ProC-80
90Foil/Best-200
90Gaston/Best-19
90Gaston/ProC-2511
90Gaston/Star-1
90SALAS/Star-1
91CharlR/ClBest-1
91CharlR/ProC-1305
Arnerich, Ken
82QuadC-18
Arnett, Curt
74Gaston
Arney, Jeff
82Wisco-25
83Visalia/LF-2
85Water-14
86Water-1
Arnold, Bryan
88Watertn/Pucko-14
Arnold, Chris
72OPC-232R
72T-232R
73OPC-584
73T-584
74OPC-432
74T-432
76SSPC-99
77Phoenix
77T-591
Arnold, Gary
88Geneva/ProC-1636
Arnold, Greg
89Pulaski/ProC-1912
Arnold, Jeff
84Newar-25
Arnold, Ken
91Hunting/ClBest-3
91Hunting/ProC-3339
Arnold, Ron
84Albany-2
84Cram/PCL-75
Arnold, Scott
86FSLAS-5
86StPete-2
87ArkTr-13
87TexLgAS-21
88Louisvl-8
88TexLgAS/GS-20
89Louisvl-9
89Louisvl/CMC-2
89Louisvl/ProC-1248
90Louisvl/CMC-1
90Louisvl/ProC-394
90SpringDG/Best-18
90T/TVCard-38
Arnold, Sheila
88Geneva/ProC-1660
Arnold, Tim
86FSLAS-6
86WPalmB-2
87Jaxvl-2
88Visalia/Cal-149
88Visalia/ProC-97
89Orlan/Best-8
89Orlan/ProC-1353
Arnold, Tony
84CharlO-26
85CharlO-8
86RochR-1
87French-57
88Albuq/CMC-5
88Albuq/ProC-261
89SanAn/Best-5
90Yakima/Team-19CO
91Crown/Orio-13
91Yakima/ProC-4265CO
Arnovich, Morris
(Morrie)
38Exh/4-6
39PB-46
40PB-97
40Wheat-4
41DP-139
41G-25
41G-25
41PB-57
92Conlon/Sport-500
W711/2
Arnsberg, Brad
84Greens-10
85Albany-1
86Colum-2
86Colum/Pol-2
87Colum-28
87Colum/Pol-2
87Colum/TCMA-1
88F-202
88T-159
89Mother/R-15
89Smok/R-2
90AlbanyDG/Best-27
90Leaf/II-495
90OkCty/CMC-7
90OkCty/ProC-423
90S/100Ris-72
90T/Tr-3T
91B-279
91D-633
91F-279
91F/Ultra-346
91Mother/Rang-25
91OPC-706A
91OPC-706B
91S-510
91T-706A
91T-706B
91T/StClub/II-540
91UD-608
92F-298
Arnsberg, Tim
86Ashvl-1
87Osceola-26
Arntzen, Orie Edgar
No Cards.
Arola, Bruce
88Madis-2
89Boise/ProC-1996
91Salinas/ClBest-22
91Salinas/ProC-2234
Arredondo, Joe
90Pittsfld/Pucko-6
91Pittsfld/ClBest-13
91Pittsfld/ProC-3427
Arredondo, Roberto
90CharRain/Best-9
90CharRain/ProC-2045
91MidwLAS/ProC-MWL29
91Waterlo/ClBest-14
91Waterlo/ProC-1261
Arrigo, Gerald W.
(Jerry)
64T-516R
65OPC-39
65T-39
66T-357
67T-488
68Kahn
68T-302
69Kahn
69OPC-213
69T-213
69T/St-22
70OPC-274
70T-274
72MB-20
78TCMA-64
78TCMA-86
91WIZMets-14
Arrington, Sam
82Amari-23
82Orlan-23
83Visalia/LF-4
Arrington, Tom
86BurlEx-1
Arrington, Warren
88Peoria/Ko-2
89Peoria/Ko-23
Arroyd, Freddie
86SanJose-1
Arroyo, Carlos R.
79OkCty
80OkCty
81OkCty/TCMA-2
86Clearw-1CO
87Clearw-15CO
88Reading/ProC-888CO
90Batavia/ProC-3084CO
91Batavia/ClBest-18CO
91Batavia/ProC-3501CO
Arroyo, Felipe
80Ander-11
Arroyo, Fernando
76OPC-614
76T-614
78T-607
81T-408
82D-177

82F-546
82T-18
82T-396TL
91Lakeland/ClBest-17CO
91Lakeland/ProC-283CO
Arroyo, Hector
81CharR-2
Arroyo, Luis Enrique
56T-64
56T/Pin-45
57T-394
61T-142
61T/St-188
62J-12
62P-12
62P/Can-12
62T-455
63T-569
78TCMA-258
PM10/L-2
Arroyo, Rudolph Jr.
(Rudy)
No Cards.
Arsenault, Ed
75SanAn
76Wmsprt
Arst, Matt
90WichSt-3
Artiaga, Sal
90AS/Cal-28COM
Arundel, Harry
No Cards.
Arundel, John Thomas
(Tug)
N172
N284
Arvesen, Scott
89Welland/Pucko-2
90Augusta/ProC-2455
91Augusta/ClBest-2
91Augusta/ProC-795
Arzola, Richard
86StPete-3
Asadoor, Randy
84Tulsa-18
85Cram/PCL-116
86LasVegas-1
87D-574
87F-650M
87LasVegas-7
87Sf-158M
Asai, Itsuki
90Gate/ProC-3345
Asbe, Daryl
86BurlEx-2
Asbell, Frank
40Hughes-2AS
Asbell, James Marion
(Jim)
No Cards.
Asbell, John
81Watlo-5
Asbjornson, Robert A.
(Asby)
No Cards.
Ascencio, Juan
86Cram/PCL-152
Asche, Scott
91Miami/ClBest-5
91Miami/ProC-399
Ash, Kenneth Lowther
(Ken)
92Conlon/Sport-601
Ashburn, Don Richard
(Richie)
49B-214
49Eureka-127
49Lummis
50B-84
51B-186
51BR-A9
51T/BB-3
52B-53
52BR
52Dix
52RM-NL2
52StarCal/L-77A
52T-216
53B/Col-10
53Dix
53NB
53RM-NL3
54B-15
54Dix
54RH
54RM-NL1
54T-45
55B-130
55RFG-22
55RM-NL1
56T-120
56YellBase/Pin-4
57Swift-17
57T-70
58Hires-10
58T-230
59Armour-3
59Bz
59T-300
59T-317M
60Bz-24
60MacGregor-2
60T-305
60T/tatt-4
60T/tatt-87
61P-192
61T-88
61T/St-3
62J-186
62P-186
62P/Can-186
62Salada-171
62Shirriff-171
62T-213
62T/bucks
63J-197
63P-197
63Salada-27
63T-135
63T/SO
80Pac/Leg-94
85West/2-38
88Pac/Leg-8
88Phill/TastyK-39ANN
89B/I-1
89Swell-85
90Pac/Legend-70
90Phill/TastyK-29
90Phill/TastyK-35BC
91Swell/Great-4
91T/Archiv-311
91WIZMets-15
Exh47
PM10/Sm-6
R423-1
Rawl
Ashby, Alan Dean
76OPC-209
76SSPC-514
76T-209
77Ho-124
77OPC-148
77T-564
77T/CS-1
78OPC-76
78T-319
79Ho-142
79OPC-14
79T-36
80OPC-105
80T-187
81Coke
81D-259
81F-64
81OPC-146
81T-696
82D-317
82F-212
82OPC-184
82T-433
82T/St-48
83D-144
83F-445
83OPC-84
83T-774
83T/St-241
84D-539
84F-220
84Mother/Ast-3
84Nes/792-217
84OPC-217
84T-217
84T/St-72
85D-283
85F-343
85Mother/Ast-13
85OPC-29
85T-564
86D-405
86F-292
86OPC-331
86Pol/Ast-8
86T-331
87D-332
87D/OD-17
87F-50
87Mother/Ast-11
87Pol/Ast-21
87T-112
88D-163
88D/Best-8
88F-439
88Mother/Ast-11
88OPC-48
88Panini/St-291
88Pol/Ast-4
88RedFoley/St-2
88S-73
88Sf-219
88T-48
88T/St-32
89B-327
89D-88
89F-350
89Mother/Ast-10
89OPC-359
89RedFoley/St-4
89S-366
89T-492
89T/DH-20
89UD-305
90EliteSenLg-63
90MLBPA/Pins-39
Ashby, Andrew
(Andy)
86Cram/PCL-139
87Spartan-13
90A&AASingle/ProC-22
90Foil/Best-46
90Reading/Best-7
90Reading/ProC-1211
90Reading/Star-3
91B-485
91F/Up-U105
91Phill/Medford-2
91ScranWB/LineD-478
91ScranWB/ProC-2530
91UD/FinalEd-64F
92Classic/I-T6
92D/I-11RR
92F-521
92S/I-396
92T-497
92T/91Debut-5
92UD-19SR
Ashford, Thomas S.
(Tucker)
78Padre/FamFun-2
78T-116
79T-247
80Charl-16
81Colum-2
82Colum-2
82Colum/Pol-12
83Tidew-26
84Nes/792-492
84T-492
88Jacks/GS-4
91WIZMets-16
Ashkinazy, Alan
85Greens-2
86Greens-2
Ashley, Billy
90Bakers/Cal-260
91Single/ClBest-210
91VeroB/ClBest-24
91VeroB/ProC-785
Ashley, Duane
91James/ClBest-16
91James/ProC-3534
Ashley, Shon
86Beloit-1
87Beloit-4
88CalLgAS-14
88Stockton/Cal-194
88Stockton/ProC-724
89ElPaso/GS-25
89TexLAS/GS-14
91ElPaso/LineD-176
91ElPaso/ProC-2758
Ashman, Mike
82Madis-23
83Albany-11
84Albany-21
85Cram/PCL-136
86Nashua-1
90AlbanyDG/Best-2
Ashmore, Mitch
82CharR-7
82Omaha-13
84Memphis-8
Ashworth, Mike
88BurlInd/ProC-1793
89SLCity-28
Asmussen, Thomas W.
(Tom)
No Cards.
Asp, Bryan
89Elizab/Star-1
Aspray, Mike
88Peoria/Ko-3
90Visalia/Cal-59
90Visalia/ProC-2151
Aspromonte, Ken
58T-405
59T-424
60T-114
61P-65
61T-176
61T/St-133
62J-19
62P-19
62P/Can-19
62Salada-7A
62Salada-7B
62Shirriff-7
62T-563
63T-464
64T-252
72T-784MG
73OPC-449MG
73T-449MG
74OPC-521MG
74T-521MG
Aspromonte, Robert T.
(Bob)
60T-547
61T-396
62Bz-9
62T-248
62T/St-124
63Exh
63F-37
63J-187
63P-187
63Pep
63T-45
63T/SO
64T-467
64T/Coins-163AS
64T/Coins-84
64T/St-16
64T/SU
65Bz-19
65OPC-175
65T-175
65T/E-61
65T/trans-39
66Bz-24
66T-273M
66T-352
66T/RO-12
67Bz-24
67T-274
68Coke
68Dexter-8
68OPC-95
68T-95
69MB-17
69MLB/St-111
69T-542
69T/St-31
70MLB/St-2
70OPC-529
70T-529
71MLB/St-146
71OPC-469
71T-469
72MB-21
72T-659
89Smok/Ast-16
90Target-21
91WIZMets-17
Exh47
Asselstine, Brian H.
77T-479R
78T-372
79T-529
81D-186
81F-256
81Pol/Atl-30
81T-64
82D-184
82F-428
82T-214
83Phoenix/BHN-4
Assenmacher, Paul
84Durham-20
85Durham-1
86D/Rook-28
86F/Up-U5
86Pol/Atl-30
86Sf/Rook-24
86T/Tr-4T
87D-290
87F-511
87Leaf-164
87Smok/Atl-8
87T-132
87T/St-37
87ToysRUs-2
88F-532
88T-266
89B-265
89D-357
89F-586
89Panini/St-33
89S-373
89T-454
89UD-566
90Cub/Mara-1
90D-459
90F-25
90Leaf/II-493
90OPC-644
90PublInt/St-107
90T-644
90T/TVCub-7
90UD-660
91B-431
91Cub/Mara-45
91D-144
91F-413
91Leaf/I-53
91OPC-12
91S-147
91T-12
91T/StClub/II-586
91UD-491
92D/I-159
92F-375
92S/I-360
92T-753
92UD-590
Astacio, Pedro
90VeroB/Star-2
90Yakima/Team-12
91SanAn/ProC-2966
91Single/ClBest-280
91VeroB/ClBest-1
91VeroB/ProC-762
Astacio, Rafael
91Erie/ClBest-2
91Erie/ProC-4075
Astroth, Joseph Henry
(Joe)
51B-298
52B-170
52T-290
53B/Col-82
53T-103
54B-131
55B-119
55Rodeo
56Rodeo
56T-106
91T/Archiv-103
Astroth, Jon
74Gaston
Atha, Jeff
88James/ProC-1901
Atherton, Charles
No Cards.
Atherton, Keith Rowe
80WHave-16
81WHave-2

82Tacoma-23
83Tacoma-1
84D-497
84F-437
84Mother/A's-26
84Nes/792-529
84T-529
85D-340
85F-415
85Mother/A's-17
85T-166
86F-410
86Mother/A's-17
86T-353
87D-272
87F-534
87T-52
88D-318
88D/Best-270
88F-1
88S-613
88T-451
89D-273
89F-103
89F/Up-24
89S-381
89T-698
89T/Tr-4T
89UD-599
90PubIInt/St-552

Atilano, Luis
75Clinton

Atkins, Francis M.
(Tommy)
E270/2
M116

Atkins, James Curtis
(Jim)
No Cards.

Atkinson, William C.
(Bill)
78OPC-144
78T-43
80OPC-133
80T-415
83AppFx/LF-19C

Atkinson, Hubert B.
(Lefty)
No Cards.

Atkisson, Albert W.
(Al)
No Cards.

Attardi, Jay
76AppFx

Attell, Abe
88Pac/8Men-28M
T3/Box-52

Attreau, Richard G.
(Dick)
No Cards.

Atwater, Buck
90Gate/ProC-3353
91Pocatel/ProC-3787

Atwell, Gary
75Lafay

Atwell, Maurice D.
(Toby)
52T-356
53B/Col-112
53T-23
54B-123
55B-164
56T-232
91T/Archiv-23
Exh47
V362-34

Atwood, Derek
91Pocatel/ProC-3773

Atwood, William F.
(Bill)
40PB-240

Atz, Jacob Henry
E270/2
T206

Aube, Richard
83CharR-14

Aubin, Kevin
91Princet/ClBest-1
91Princet/ProC-3516

Aubrey, Harvey H.
No Cards.

Auchard, Dan
89Kingspt/Star-1

Aucoin, Derek
90James/Pucko-13
91Sumter/ClBest-2
91Sumter/ProC-2325

Audain, Miguel
87Penin-13

Aude, Rich
90Augusta/ProC-2469
91Salem/ClBest-3
91Salem/ProC-957

Audley, Jim
90WichSt-4

Auerbach, Frederick
(Rick)
72OPC-153
72T-153
73OPC-427
73T-427
74OPC-289
74T-289
75OPC-588
75T-588
75T/M-588
76OPC-622
76SSPC-74
76T-622
78T-646
79T-174
80T-354
82T-72
90Target-22

Aufdermauer, Bud
85Anchora-44

August, Don
85T-392OLY
86Tucson-3
87Ashvl-20
87Denver-17
88D-602
88Denver/CMC-8
88Denver/ProC-1259
88F/Up-U37
88S/Tr-104T
88T/Tr-7T
89B-130
89Brewer/YB-38
89D-410
89F-177
89Gard-15
89Panini/St-365
89Pol/Brew-38
89S-419
89S/HotRook-83
89S/YS/II-28
89Sf-131
89T-696
89T/Big-33
89UD-325
90Classic-124
90D-617
90Denver/CMC-20
90Denver/ProC-616
90OPC-192
90Pol/Brew-38
90PubIInt/St-488
90S-144
90T-192
90UD-295
91Brewer/MillB-1
91Pol/Brew-1
92D/I-140
92S/II-533

August, Sam
88Osceola/Star-2
89ColMud/ProC-140
91Jacks/LineD-552
91Jacks/ProC-916
91Single/ClBest-298

Augustine, David R.
(Dave)
74OPC-598R
74T-598R
75OPC-616R
75T-616R
75T/M-616R
78Charl
79Charl-12
81Portl-6
82Portl-18

Augustine, Gerald Lee
(Jerry)
77BurgChef-82
77T-577
78T-133
79T-357
80T-243
81D-445
81F-514
81T-596
82D-332
82F-133
82Pol/Brew-46
82T-46
83F-26
83Pol/Brew-46
83T-424
84F-194
84Nes/792-658
84Pol/Brew-46
84T-658
85RochR-14

Auker, Eldon Leroy
35BU-120
39PB-4
40PB-139
41PB-45
81Detroit-91
88Conlon/3-3
R309/2
R313
W753

Aulds, Leycester D.
No Cards.

Aulenback, Jim
83AlexD-13
84PrWill-14

Ault, Douglas Reagan
(Doug)
77OPC-202
77T-477R
78OPC-202
78T-267
79OPC-205
79Syrac-15
79T-392
80Syrac-2
81F-424
82Syrac-24
83Knoxvl-20
85Syrac-21
86Syrac-3MG
87Syrac-7
87Syrac/TCMA-23
90StCath/ProC-3482MG
91StCath/ClBest-26MG
91StCath/ProC-3411MG

Ausanio, Joe
88Watertn/Pucko-2
89Salem/Star-3
90A&AASingle/ProC-12
90Harris/ProC-1186
91B-528
91Single/ClBest-186

Ausmus, Brad
89Oneonta/ProC-2110
90PrWill/Team-5
91PrWill/ClBest-13
91PrWill/ProC-1429
91Single/ClBest-17
92T-58M

Aust, Dennis Kay
63Pep/Tul
66OPC-179R
66Pep/Tul
66T-179R

Austin, Dero
76Laugh/Clown-13
76Laugh/Clown-2
76Laugh/Clown-28

Austin, Frank
52Mother-18
86Negro/Frit-74

Austin, James
(Bubba)
86Cram/PCL-178
87CharRain-7
88River/Cal-207
88Wichita-25
89ElPaso/GS-3
90ElPasoATG/Team-22
91Brewer/MillB-2
91Denver/LineD-127
91Denver/ProC-114
91James/ClBest-5
91James/ProC-3557
92S/II-747
92T/91Debut-6

Austin, James Phillip
(Jimmy or Pepper)
10Domino-3
11Helmar-60
12Sweet/Pin-51A
12Sweet/Pin-51B
14CJ-40
15CJ-40
91Conlon/Sport-236
D327
D328-8
D329-7
D350/2-7
E135-8
E220
E224
E254
E286
E94
E97
M101/4-7
M101/5-7
M116
T202
T205
T207
T222
V100
W555

Austin, Pat
87Lakeland-18
88GlenF/ProC-914
89Toledo/CMC-18
89Toledo/ProC-766
90Hagers/ProC-1418
90Hagers/Star-1
90Louisvl/CMC-23
90Louisvl/ProC-406
90S-626

Austin, Rick Gerald
71MLB/St-361
71OPC-41
71T-41
76OPC-269
76SSPC-248
76T-269

Austin, Rick
82Orlan-14
83Toledo-11

Austin, Terry
81QuadC-12

Auten, Jim
83Memphis-16
84MidldC-19

Auth, Bob
86QuadC-3

Autry, Albert Jr.
(Al)
No Cards.

Autry, Bucky
84LitFalls-18

Autry, Gene
61NuCard-414

Autry, Martin Gordon
29Exh/4-20

Autry, William Askew
(Chick)
No Cards.

Avent, Stephen
91Spartan/ClBest-13
91Spartan/ProC-898

Averill, Earl D. Jr.
59T-301
60L-110
60T-39
61T-358
62J-80
62P-80
62P/Can-80
62Salada-24A
62Salada-24B
62Shirriff-24
62T-452
63T-139

Averill, Howard Earl
(Earl)
28Exh/PCL-2
29Exh/4-22
31Exh/4-22
32Orbit/num-12
32Orbit/un-3
33DH-3
33Exh/4-11
33G-194
34DS-100
34DS-35
34Exh/4-11
35BU-113
35BU-24
35Exh/4-11
35G-1L
35G-2E
35G-6E
35G-7E
36Exh/4-11
36Wheat
37Exh/4-11
37OPC-103
38Exh/4-11
39Exh
39PB-143
40PB-46
55Salem
60F-71
61F-5
80Pac/Leg-4
86Sf/Dec-15M
88Conlon/AmAS-2
89Pac/Leg-203
91Conlon/Sport-31
92Conlon/Sport-597
PR1-2
R300
R303/A
R305
R306
R308-160
R310
R311/Gloss
R313
R314
R315-A1
R315-B1
V300
W517-51
WG8-2

Aversa, Joe
90Johnson/Star-2
91Spring/ClBest-3
91Spring/ProC-747

Avery, Larry
81BurlB-29
82BurlR-27GM

Avery, Steve
89B-268
89BBAmerAA/BProC-AA13
89Durham/Team-1
89Durham/Star-1
89Greenvl/Best-28
89Star/Wax-67
89T-784FDP
90B-9
90Classic/Up-T4
90D-39RR
90D/Rook-42
90F/Up-U1
90Leaf/II-481
90Richm/Bob-7
90Richm/CMC-1
90Richm/ProC-252
90Richm/Team-1
90S/Tr-109T
90T/Tr-4T
90UD-65
91B-566
91Classic/200-138
91Classic/II-T26
91D-187
91F-681
91F/Ultra-1
91Leaf/II-510
91Leaf/Stud-141
91OPC-227
91RedFoley/St-105
91S-80
91S/100RisSt-5
91T-227
91T/90Debut-6
91T/StClub/I-48
91ToysRUs-3
91UD-365
92Classic/I-T7
92Classic/I-xx
92D/I-81
92F-349

92S/100SS-34
92S/I-241
92S/II-797HL
92S/Prev-4
92T-574
92UD-41
92UD-475

Avila, Roberto G.
(Bobby)
50NumNum
51B-188
52B-167
52NumNum-14
52RM-AL2
52T-257
53B/Col-29
53RM-AL26
54B-68
54DanDee
54RM-AL1
55B-19
55Gol/Ind-1
55RM-AL15
55Salem
56T-132
57Sohio/Ind-1
57T-195
58Hires-33
58T-276
59T-363
60L-59
60T-90
91Crown/Orio-14

Aviles, Brian Keith
84Durham-25
87Greenvl/Best-15

Aviles, Ramon Antonio
79OkCty
80T-682R
81F-23
81T-644
82F-239
82OkCty-4
82T-152
83Portl-10
86Reading-1CO
87Spartan-11CO
88Maine/CMC-24CO
88Maine/ProC-302CO
89Reading/Best-25CO
89Reading/ProC-671CO
90Reading/Best-6CO
90Reading/ProC-1236CO
90Reading/Star-27CO
91Batavia/ClBest-27MG
91Batavia/ProC-3500MG

Avram, Brian
91Johnson/ClBest-23
91Johnson/ProC-3968

Avrea, James Epherium
(Jim)
No Cards.

Ayala, Adan
91CharRain/ClBest-12
91CharRain/ProC-97

Ayala, Benigno Felix
(Benny)
75OPC-619R
75T-619R
75T/M-619R
75Tidew/Team-1
80T-262
81D-236
81F-185
81T-101
82D-581
82F-157
82T-331
83D-331
83F-52
83T-59
84D-270
84Nes/792-443
84T-443
84T/St-22WS
85Polar/Ind-12
85T-624
85T/Tr-3T
85ThomMc/Discs-1
91Crown/Orio-15
91WIZMets-18

Ayala, Bobby
90Cedar/Best-15
90Cedar/ProC-2314
91Chatt/LineD-153
91Chatt/ProC-1951

Ayala, Eric
80Ander-20

Aydelott, Jacob S.
(Jake)
No Cards.

Ayer, Jack
82ArkTr-20
84Louisvl-21
85Louisvl-21
86Louisvl-4
87Louisvl-3

Ayers, Jim
75Cedar

Ayers, Kevin
86VeroB-2

Ayers, Lenny
91Everett/ClBest-22

Ayers, Scott
86WPalmB-3
87Jamestn-19

Ayers, William Oscar
(Bill)
47TipTop

Ayers, Yancy Wyatt
(Doc)
No Cards.

Aylmer, Bobby
90StCath/ProC-3465
91Myrtle/ClBest-1
91Myrtle/ProC-2935

Aylward, Jim
88QuadC/GS-22
88Reno/Cal-280
89QuadC/Best-8
89QuadC/GS-27

Aylward, Richard John
(Dick)
No Cards.

Ayoub, Sam
71Richm/Team-2
81Richm-25
82Richm-30
83Richm-7
84Richm-22
85Richm-24
86Richm-1TR
87Richm/Crown-x
87Richm/TCMA-29
88Richm-TR
88Richm/ProC-6
89Richm/CMC-14
89Richm/Ko-TR
89Richm/ProC-820
90Richm/CMC-18TR
90Richm/Team-2TR
90Richm25Ann/Team-2TR

Ayrault, Bob
89Reno/Cal-240
90A&AASingle/ProC-23
90EastLAS/ProC-EL31
90Foil/Best-303
90Reading/Best-2
90Reading/ProC-1212
90Reading/Star-4
91ScranWB/LineD-479
91ScranWB/ProC-2531

Ayrault, Joe
91Pulaski/ClBest-1
91Pulaski/ProC-4007

Ayres, Lenny
90Everett/Best-24
90Everett/ProC-3117
91Everett/ProC-3905

Azar, Todd
88Wausau/GS-15

Azcue, Jose Joaquin
(Joe)
62T-417
63T-501
64T-199
64T/Coins-110
65Kahn
65T-514
66T-452
67T-336
68Bz-4
68T-443
69JB
69MB-18
69MLB/St-38
69OPC-176
69T-176
69T/St-162
69Trans-1
70MLB/St-170
70OPC-294
70T-294
71MLB/St-338
71OPC-657
71T-657
72MB-22
78TCMA-36

Azocar, Oscar
88Albany/ProC-1347
89Albany/Best-19
89Albany/ProC-332
89Albany/Star-1
90ColClip/CMC-13
90ColClip/ProC-688
90F/Up-111
90S/Tr-71T
90T/TVYank-36
91B-652
91Classic/I-62
91D-331
91F-655
91LasVegas/ProC-247
91LasVegas/LineD-276
91OPC-659
91Panini/FrSt-329
91Panini/St-270
91S-72
91S/100RisSt-46
91T-659
91T/90Debut-7
91T/StClub/II-450
91UD-464
92F-598
92S/II-692
92T-112

Baar, Bryan
89GreatF-19
90Bakers/Cal-256
91SanAn/LineD-528
91SanAn/ProC-2978
91Single/ClBest-292

Babb, Charles Amos
(Charlie)
90Target-23
E254

Babbitt, Gene
47Sunbeam

Babbitt, Troy
91Eugene/ClBest-5
91Eugene/ProC-3730

Babcock, Bill
82AppFx-19

Babcock, Robert E.
(Bob)
77Tucson
78Cr/PCL-106
80Charl-17
81T-41R
82D-565
82T-567
83SLCity-3

Babe, Loren Rolland
No Cards.

Babich, John Charles
(Johnny)
34DS-82
35BU-167
40PB-191
41DP-127
41PB-40
43Centen-1
44Centen-1
48Signal
48Smith-22
90Target-24
R309/2

Babington, Charles P.
(Charlie)
No Cards.

Babitt, Mack Neal II
(Shooty)
80Ogden-21
80WHave-17
82D-556
82F-86
82T-578
82Tacoma-28
83Memphis-1
84Indianap-14

Babki, Blake
91James/ClBest-2
91James/ProC-3558

Baca, Mark A.
88PalmSp/Cal-99
88PalmSp/ProC-1456

Baccioccu, Jack
49Sommer-19

Bach, Jan
78Clinton

Bach, Rich
78Clinton
80BurlB-16

Bachman, Kent
86WPalmB-4

Backman, Lester John
(Les)
M116

Backman, Walter W.
(Wally)
79Jacks-2
80Tidew-4
81F-336
81Tidew-8
83D-618
83F-537
83T-444
83Tidew-3
84Jacks/Smok-2
85D-319
85F-72
85Leaf-79
85OPC-162
85T-677
85T/Mets/Fan-1
85T/St-106
86D-238
86F-75
86OPC-191
86T-191
86T/Mets/Fan-1
86T/St-97
87D-316
87F-3
87Leaf-59
87OPC-48
87Sf-124
87T-48
87T/St-100
88D-241
88D/Mets/Bk-241
88F-128
88Kahn/Mets-6
88Leaf-202
88OPC-333
88Panini/St-340
88S-303
88T-333
89B-159
89D-383
89D/Best-186
89D/Tr-10
89F-28
89F/Up-43
89OPC-72
89S-315
89S/Tr-34
89T-508
89T/Big-300
89T/Tr-5T
89UD-188
89UD/Ext-732
90B-177
90D-155
90D/BestNL-130
90F-367
90F/Up-U47
90Homer/Pirate-1
90Leaf/II-341
90OPC-218
90PublInt/St-321
90S-281
90S/Tr-37T
90T-218
90T/Big-233
90T/Tr-5T
90UD-158
91B-490
91D-177
91F-29
91F/UltraUp-U98
91F/Up-U106
91Leaf/II-482
91OPC-722
91Phill/Medford-3
91RedFoley/St-5
91S-16
91S/RookTr-8T
91T-722
91T/StClub/II-368
91T/Tr-3T
91UD-185
91UD/Ext-790
91WIZMets-19
92D/II-478
92S/I-177
92T-434
92UD-350

Backs, Jason
89Spartan/ProC-1038
89Spartan/Star-1
91Reading/LineD-501
91Reading/ProC-1362

Backus, Jerry
88Boise/ProC-1618

Bacon, Edgar Suter
(Eddie)
No Cards.

Bacosa, Al
88Idaho/ProC-1848

Bacsik, Michael James
(Mike)
74Gaston
77T-103
77Tucson
78Cr/PCL-43
80T-453

Baczewski, Fred
54B-60
55B-190

Badacour, Bob
90Martins/ProC-3189

Badcock, Tom
75Water

Bader, Arthur Herman
(Art)
No Cards.

Bader, Loren Verne
No Cards.

Badgro, Morris Hiram
(Red)
88Conlon/4-2

Badorek, Mike
91Hamil/ClBest-5
91Hamil/ProC-4026

Baecht, Edward Joseph
(Ed)
No Cards.

Baehr, Dave
82Idaho-1
83Wisco/LF-25

Baer, Max
33SK-44

Baerga, Carlos
86CharRain-1
87CharRain-2
88TexLgAS/GS-32
88Wichita-15
89LasVegas/CMC-18
89LasVegas/ProC-9
90B-339
90Classic/III-35
90D/Rook-19
90F/Up-U90
90Leaf/II-443
90S/Tr-74T
90S/YS/II-32
90T/Big-229
90T/Tr-6T
90UD/Ext-737
91B-69
91Classic/III-22
91D-274
91F-360
91F/Ultra-106
91Leaf/I-225
91OPC-147
91Panini/FrSt-218
91Panini/St-180
91S-74
91S/100RisSt-30
91T-147
91T/90Debut-8
91T/StClub/I-115
91ToysRUs-4
91UD-125

92D/I-120
92F-104
92S/I-128
92T-33
92UD-231

Baerwald, Rudolph
E254
E270

Baez, Angel
81Buffa-17

Baez, Francisco
90AppFox/Box-3
90AppFox/ProC-2087
91AppFx/ClBest-1
91AppFx/ProC-1707

Baez, Igor
89Greens/ProC-408

Baez, Jesse
79LodiD-9
81Wausau-13
83Wausau/LF-17

Baez, Jose Antonio
75Water
78T-311

Baez, Kevin
88LitFalls/Pucko-2
89Clmbia/Best-12
89Clmbia/GS-6
89SALAS/GS-19
91T/90Debut-9
91Tidew/LineD-551
91Tidew/ProC-2515
91WIZMets-20

Baez, Pedro
88Madis-3
89Modesto/Cal-267
89Modesto/Chong-8

Bafia, Bob
86WinSalem-2
87WinSalem-8
88Pittsfld/ProC-1363
89CharlK-22
90Iowa/CMC-11
90Iowa/ProC-323
90T/TVCub-37
91Huntsvl/ClBest-2
91Huntsvl/LineD-277
91HuntsvlProC-1800

Bagby, James C.J. Jr.
(Jim)
39PB-40
40PB-32
61F-92

Bagby, James C.J. Sr.
(Jim)
21Exh-3
92Conlon/Sport-487
D327
D328-9
E120
E121
E135-9
E220
V100
W501
W572
W575
WG7-2

Baggott, Dave
89SLCity-4GM

Bagiotti, Aldo
81Redwd-10

Bagley, Eugene T.
(Gene)
No Cards.

Bagnall, Jim
83Butte-16
83CharR-4

Bagshaw, Lance
87SLCity/Taco-7bb

Bagshaw, Ryan
87SLCity/Taco-7bb

Bagwell, Jeff
88CapeCod-4
88CapeCod/Sum-57
90A&AASingle/ProC-26
90EastLAS/ProC-EL40
90Foil/Best-132
90NewBrit/Best-7
90NewBrit/Star-1
91B-183
91Classic/200-90
91Classic/II-T84
91D/Rook-30
91F/UltraUp-U79
91F/Up-U87
91Leaf/GRook-BC14
91Leaf/Stud-172
91Mother/Ast-8
91S/RookTr-96T
91T/StClub/II-388
91T/Tr-4T
91UD/Ext-702
91UD/Ext-755
92Classic/I-T8
92D/DK-DK11
92D/I-358
92D/II-BC6ROY
92F-425
92F/RookSIns-4
92S/100RisSt-35
92S/II-576
92S/II-793ROY
92T-520
92T/91Debut-7
92UD-276

Bagwell, William M.
(Bill)
No Cards.

Baham, Leon
82Idaho-16
87SanBern-14
88Tampa/Star-2

Bahns, Ed
79AppFx-4

Bahnsen, Stanley R.
(Stan)
67OPC-93R
67T-93R
68T-214R
69Citgo-9
69T-380
69T/St-201
70T-568
71MD
71MLB/St-482
71OPC-184
71T-184
72T-662
73OPC-20
73T-20
74OPC-254
74T-254
74T/St-152
75OPC-161
75T-161
75T/M-161
76OPC-534
76SSPC-486
76T-534
77BurgChef-112
77T-384
78OPC-54
78T-97
79OPC-244
79T-468
80OPC-345
80T-653
81D-452
81F-156
81OPC-267
81T-267
82D-392
82F-183
82OPC-131
82T-131
83Portl-23
89Pac/SenLg-78
89Swell-39
89T/SenLg-62
89TM/SenLg-4

Bahr, Edson Garfield
(Ed)
No Cards.

Bahret, Frank J.
No Cards.

Baichley, Grover C.
No Cards.

Baier, Marty
82Clinton-15
83Clinton/LF-7

Bailes, Scott
83AlexD-10
85Nashua-1
86D/Rook-25
86F/Up-U6
86OhHenry-43
86Sf/Rook-9
86T/Tr-5T
87D-227
87F-242
87Gator-43
87OPC-134
87T-585
87ToysRUs-3
88D-104
88D/Best-285
88F-600
88Gator-43
88OPC-107
88Panini/St-68
88T-107
88T/St-206
89D-202
89F-398
89S-424
89T-339
89T/St-217
89UD-209
90D-468
90F-484
90Leaf/II-380
90OPC-784
90PublInt/St-553
90RedFoley/St-2
90S-218
90S/Tr-64T
90Smok/Angel-19
90T-784
91B-205
91S-535
91UD-190
92D/I-357
92F-53
92S/I-331
92T-95

Bailey, Abraham L.
(Sweetbreads)
No Cards.

Bailey, Ace
33SK-29

Bailey, Arthur Eugene
(Gene)
No Cards.

Bailey, Brandon
86Columbia-4
87Columbia-3

Bailey, Buddy
80Ander-17
82Durham-23
86Durham-1MG
87Sumter-10
88BBAmer-30
89Greenvl/ProC-1178
89Greenvl/Best-20
89SLAS-23
90Greenvl/ProC-1143MG
90Greenvl/Star-24MG
91CLAS/ProC-CAR21
91LynchRS/ClBest-25
91LynchRS/ProC-1215

Bailey, Cory
91Elmira/ClBest-16
91Elmira/ProC-3261

Bailey, Darryl
77BurlB
78BurlB
79Holyo-22

Bailey, Greg
83TriCit-21
86Tulsa-18

Bailey, Howard Lee
82Evansvl-1
82Evansvl-1
82T-261R
84D-212
84Evansvl-2
84F-75
84Nes/792-284
84T-284

Bailey, James Hopkins
(Jim)
No Cards.

Bailey, Jim
82Idaho-2

Bailey, John Mark
(Mark)
84F/X-3
85D-450
85F-344
85Mother/Ast-17
85OPC-64
85T-64
86D-354
86F-293
86Pol/Ast-14
86T-432
86T/St-30
87D-235
87D-429
87Mother/Ast-15
87Pol/Ast-2
87T-197
88Mother/Ast-15
88Pol/Ast-5
88T/Big-248
89Tidew/CMC-29
89Tidew/ProC-1949
90Phoenix/CMC-13
90Phoenix/ProC-13
91Phoenix/LineD-377
91Phoenix/ProC-69

Bailey, Lash
89Belling/Legoe-17
90Penin/Star-1

Bailey, Lemuel
(King)
No Cards.

Bailey, Lonas Edgar
(Ed)
53T-206
54T-184
55T-69
55T/DH-30
56Kahn
57Kahn
57Sohio/Reds-1
57Swift-5
57T-128
58Kahn
58T-330
58T-386M
58T-490AS
59Kahn
59T-210
60Kahn
60T-411
61Kahn
61T-418
61T/St-13
62J-137
62P-137
62P/Can-137
62Salada-113A
62Salada-113B
62Shirriff-113
62T-459
62T/St-194
63T-368
64T-437
64Wheat/St-4
65T-559
66T-246
78TCMA-173
78TCMA-37
79TCMA-11
84Mother/Giants-17
91T/Arc53-206
Exh47

Bailey, Mike
91Eugene/ClBest-25
91Eugene/ProC-3714

Bailey, Pat
86Cram/PCL-31
87AppFx-19

Bailey, Robert Jr.
89Welland/Pucko-3
90Salem/Star-1
91Salem/ClBest-4
91Salem/ProC-958

Bailey, Robert S.
(Bob)
63IDL-1
63Kahn
63T-228R
64Kahn
64T-91
64T/S-4
65Kahn
65T-412
66EH-7
66Kahn
66T-485
67OPC-32
67T-32
68T-580
69Fud's-1
69MLB/St-154
69T-399
69T/St-52
70Expos/Pins-2
70MLB/St-62
70OPC-293
70T-293
71LaPizza-1
71MLB/St-121
71OPC-157
71T-157
71T/Coins-59
72MB-23
72OPC-493KP
72T-493
72T-526
73OPC-505
73T-505
74OPC-97
74T-97
74T/St-51
74Weston-3
75Ho-55
75OPC-365
75T-365
75T/M-365
76OPC-338
76SSPC-333
76T-338
76T/Tr-338T
77T-221
78PapaG/Disc-20
78T-457
79OPC-282
79T-549
86Penin-4MG
87Hawaii-26MG
90Target-25

Bailey, Roy
90Hamil/Best-2
90Hamil/Star-3
91Savan/ClBest-1
91Savan/ProC-1642

Bailey, Steven John
(Steve)
No Cards.

Bailey, Troy
88Wythe/ProC-2003
89Wythe/Star-2

Bailey, Vince
79BurlB-18

Bailey, William F.
(Bill)
E254
E90/1
E92
M116
T205

Bailor, Robert M.
(Bob)
76SSPC-386
77OPC-48
77T-474R
78Ho-148
78K-39
78OPC-148
78T-196
78Tastee/Discs-26
79Ho-105
79OPC-259
79T-492
80K-16
80OPC-304
80T-581
81F-409
81OPC-297
81T-297
81T/Tr-732
82D-308
82F-521
82T-79
83D-506
83F-538
83T-343
83T/St-260
84D-595
84F-580
84F/X-4
84Nes/792-654

84Pol/Dodg-21
84T-654
84T/St-109
84T/Tr-4
85Coke/Dodg-3
85D-397
85F-367
85T-728
86F-124
86T-522
87Dunedin-6
88Syrac/CMC-24
88Syrac/ProC-817
89Syrac/CMC-25
89Syrac/ProC-796
89Syrac/Team-25MG
90AAAGame/ProC-AAA11MG
90Syrac/CMC-26MG
90Syrac/ProC-588MG
90Syrac/Team-1MG
90Target-26
91Crown/Orio-16
91Syrac/LineD-524MG
91Syrac/ProC-2496MG
91WIZMets-21

Bain, Herbert Loren
(Loren)
No Cards.

Bain, Paul
77Clinton
78LodiD
79LodiD-3

Baine, John T.
(Tom)
86Erie-2
87Spring/Best-8
88TexLgAS/GS-16
89Louisvl-10
89Louisvl/CMC-20
89Louisvl/ProC-1265
90SpringDG/Best-23

Baines, Harold D.
78Knoxvl
81F-346
81OPC-347
81T-347
82D-568
82F-336
82F/St-184
82OPC-56
82T-684
83D-143
83F-229
83K-16
83OPC-177
83T-177
83T/St-52
83TrueVal/WSox-3
84D-58
84D/AAS-11
84F-51
84F/St-4
85FunFood/Pin-110
84Nes/792-434
84OPC-197
84T-434
84T/St-242
84TrueVal/WS-3
85Coke/WS-3
85D-58
85D/AAS-58
85Drake-2
85F-507
85F/St-21
85Leaf-231
85OPC-249
85Seven-6G
85T-249
85T-275FDP
85T/Gloss40-34
85T/St-234
85T/Super-51
86Coke/WS-3
86D-13DK
86D-180
86D/AAS-49
86D/DKsuper-13
86Drake-24
86F-198
86F/LimEd-3
86F/Mini-42
86F/Slug-M1
86F/St-1
86Jay's-1
86Leaf-13DK
86OPC-65
86Sf-52M
86Sf-7
86T-755
86T/Mini-8
86T/St-288
86T/Super-9
87Classic-42
87Coke/WS-2
87D-429
87D/AAS-25
87D/OD-236
87Drake-22
87F-485
87F-643M
87F/GameWin-1
87F/Hottest-2
87F/BB-1
87F/Mini-3
87F/St-2
87Ho/St-21
87KayBee-1
87Kraft-13
87Leaf-52
87MnM's-8
87OPC-309
87RedFoley/St-119
87Sf-153M
87Sf-171
87Seven-C1
87Smok/AL-4
87T-772
87T/Board-16
87T/Coins-1
87T/Gloss60-14
87T/St-284
88Coke/WS-1
88D-211
88D/AS-12
88D/Best-11
88F-391
88F/Excit-1
88Kodak/WSox-5
88Leaf-157
88OPC-35
88Panini/St-62
88RedFoley/St-3
88S-590
88Sf-33
88T-35
88T/Big-224
88T/Coins-5
88T/RiteAid-16
88T/St-293
88T/UK-1
89B-72
89Cadaco-1
89Coke/WS-5
89D-148
89D/Best-81
89F-491
89F/Excit-1
89F/Superstar-2
89KMart/DT-22
89Kodak/WSox-4M
89OPC-152
89Panini/St-310
89S-128
89S/Tr-62
89Sf-157
89T-585
89T/Big-266
89T/Coins-33
89T/Hills-1
89T/LJN-23
89T/St-304
89T/UK-2
89UD-211
89UD-692TC
90B-501
90Classic-69
90D-402
90D-660AS
90D/BestAL-69
90F-290
90F/ASIns-1
90Leaf/I-126
90Mother/Rang-6
90OPC-345
90Panini/St-167
90Panini/St-200
90PublInt/St-275
90PublInt/St-383
90S-470
90Sf-125
90T-345
90T/Big-157
90T/HillsHM-30
90T/St-158AS
90T/St-245
90UD-353
91B-231
91Classic/200-13
91D-748
91F-2
91F/UltraUp-U45
91Leaf/I-196
91Leaf/StudPrev-8
91Mother/A's-14
91OPC-166
91RedFoley/St-6
91S-291
91SFExam/A's-1
91T-166
91T/StClub/II-303
91UD-562
91USPlayC/AS-9D
92D/DK-DK14
92D/I-68
92F-249
92F-707M
92S/I-137
92T-635
92UD-158

Bair, Charles Douglas
(Doug)
78OPC-229
78T-353
79Ho-3
79OPC-58
79T-126
80OPC-234
80T-449
81D-73
81F-213
81OPC-73
81T-73
82T-262
83D-372
83F-2
83T-627
83T/Tr-5
84D-369
84F-76
84Nes/792-536
84T-536
85Cain's-1
85D-369
85F-1
85T-744
85Wendy-2
87F-386
87Maine-2
87Phill/TastyK-58
88Syrac/CMC-9
88Syrac/ProC-816
89Syrac/CMC-1
89Syrac/ProC-807
89Syrac/Team-1
90Homer/Pirate-2
90S-517

Bair, Rich
84Newar-9

Baird, Albert Wells
(Al)
No Cards.

Baird, Allard
89AppFx/ProC-870

Baird, Chris
85Durham-19

Baird, Howard D.
(Doug)
90Target-894
D328-10
D329-8
E135-10
M101/4-8

Baird, Robert Allen
(Bob)
No Cards.

Bajus, Mark
80Batavia-3
81Batavia-1
81Watlo-6

Bakely, Edward Enoch
(Jersey)
No Cards.

Bakenhaster, David L.
(Dave)
64T-479R

Baker, Albert Jones
(Al)
75Clinton

Baker, Andy
89BurlInd/Star-2
91ColInd/ClBest-8
91ColInd/ProC-1475

Baker, Charles
(Bock)
No Cards.

Baker, Charles A.
(Charlie)
No Cards.

Baker, Charles Joseph
(Chuck)
78Padre/FamFun-3
79Hawaii-16
79T-456
80Hawaii-1
81F-500
82F-561
82T-253

Baker, Curt
78Wausau

Baker, Darnell
78Cedar

Baker, David Glen
(Dave)
79Syrac-11
80Syrac-17
81Syrac-11
82Syrac-14
83Toledo-13
84Toledo-20

Baker, Delmar David
(Del)
54T-133
60T-456C
81Detroit-58MG
88Conlon/5-2
V355-31

Baker, Derrell
86Indianap-13
87WPalmB-7
88Jaxvl/Best-14
88Jaxvl/ProC-968
89Rockford/Team-28CO

Baker, Douglas
(Doug)
83BirmB-8
84Evansvl-13
85T-269
86Nashvl-1
87Toledo-17
87Toledo/TCMA-20
88Portl/CMC-13
88Portl/ProC-647
89Portl/CMC-14
89Portl/ProC-230
90BirmDG/Best-4
90F-368
90Portl/CMC-18
90Portl/ProC-182
90PublInt/St-322
91Tucson/LineD-603
91Tucson/ProC-2217

Baker, Ernest Gould
(Ernie)
No Cards.

Baker, Ernie
89Johnson/Star-7
90Savan/ProC-2059
91StPete/ClBest-1
91StPete/ProC-2265

Baker, Eugene Walter
(Gene)
52Mother-45
55B-7
56T-142
56YellBase/Pin-5
57T-176
58Hires-65
58Kahn
58T-358
59T-238
60T-539
61T-339
79TCMA-48
Exh47

Baker, Floyd Wilson
47TipTop
48L-153
49B-119
50B-146
51B-87
52T-292
53B/BW-49

Baker, Frank Watts
71OPC-213
71T-213
72OPC-409
72T-409
73JP
74OPC-411
74T-411
91Crown/Orio-17

Baker, Frank
70T-704
71OPC-689
71T-689

Baker, George F.
No Cards.

Baker, Gerald
86QuadC-4

Baker, Greg
81Shrev-16

Baker, Howard Francis
No Cards.

Baker, Jack Edward
No Cards.

Baker, Jay
88Gaston/ProC-999

Baker, Jesse Eugene
No Cards.

Baker, Jesse Ormond
No Cards.

Baker, Jim
80Utica-4
83Syrac-4
84Syrac-29

Baker, John Franklin
(Home Run)
10Domino-4
11Helmar-52
12Sweet/Pin-40
14CJ-2
15CJ-2
21Exh-4
40PB-177
50Callahan
60Exh/HOF-3
60F-41
61F-1M
61F-6
61GP-21
75F/Pion-16
80Pac/Leg-41
80SSPC/HOF
89Pac/Leg-146
92Conlon/Sport-565
BF2-32
D327
D328-11
D329-9
D350/2-8
E120
E121/80
E122
E135-11
E220
E224
E254
E300
E90/1
E91
E96
L1-120
M101/4-9
M101/5-8
S74-26
S81-95
T201
T202
T205
T206
T208
T213/blue
T215/brown
T227
T3-78
V100
W514-75

W515-15
W573
W575
WG4-2
WG5-2
Baker, John
83Ander-7
Baker, Johnny B.
(Dusty)
71OPC-709R
71Richm
71Richm/Team-3
71T-709R
72T-764
73OPC-215
73T-215
73T/Lids-3
74OPC-320
74T-320
74T/St-2
75Ho-117
75OPC-33
75T-33
75T/M-33
76OPC-28
76SSPC-16
76T-28
76T/Tr-28T
77T-146
78Ho-50
78T-668
79OPC-290
79T-562
80OPC-135
80Pol/Dodg-12
80T-255
81D-179
81F-115
81F/St-62
81PermaGr/CC-27
81Pol/Dodg-12
81Sqt-17
81T-495
81T/HT
81T/SO-71
81T/St-182
82D-336
82F-1
82F/St-4
82K-50
82OPC-375
82Pol/Dodg-12
82T-311TL
82T-375
82T/St-52
83D-462
83F-201
83OPC-220
83Pol/Dodg-12
83Seven-6
83T-220
83T/Gloss40-22
83T/St-245
84D-226
84D/AAS-47
84F-96
84F/X-5
84Nes/792-40
84OPC-40
84Seven-18W
84T-40
84T/St-80
84T/Tr-5
85D-445
85F-602
85F/Up-U3
85Mother/A's-15
85OPC-165
85T-165
85T/Tr-4T
86D-467
86F-411
86Leaf-231
86Mother/A's-3
86OPC-31
86T-645
87F-387
87Smok/Dodg-2
87T-565
88Smok/Dodg-21M
88Smok/Dodg-22
89Smok/Dodg-93
90Mother/Giant-21M
90Pac/Legend-71
90Richm25Ann/Team-3
90Target-27
91Mother/Giant-27CO
Baker, Ken
89Smok/FresnoSt-1
90BirmDG/Best-6
Baker, Kenny
79WHave-12
82BirmB-10
83Evansvl-17
85Omaha-27
Baker, Kerry
84PrWill-32
85Nashua-2
86Nashua-2
Baker, Kirtley
No Cards.
Baker, Mark
83QuadC-6
85Osceola/Team-3
86ColumAst-3
87ColAst/ProC-13
Baker, Mike
86Elmira-1
87Greens-21
88WinHaven/Star-3
89Lynch/Star-1
Baker, Neal Vernon
No Cards.
Baker, Norman Leslie
(Norm)
No Cards.
Baker, Philip
(Phil)
No Cards.
Baker, Rick
(Ricky)
81Chatt-15
82Chatt-7
83MidldC-25
84MidldC-18
Baker, Sam
90BurlInd/ProC-3001
91CollInd/ClBest-9
91CollInd/ProC-1476
91Watertn/ClBest-1
91Watertn/ProC-3356
Baker, Scott
90Johnson/Star-3
91Savan/ProC-1643
Baker, Steven Byrne
(Steve)
80Evansvl/TCMA-12
81Syrac-1
83T/Tr-6
84Louisvl-25
85Indianap-6
Baker, Thomas Calvin
(Tom)
No Cards.
Baker, Thomas Henry
(Tom)
90Target-28
Baker, Tracy Lee
No Cards.
Baker, William
(Bill)
49Eureka-177
W711/2
Bakley, Edward
N172
Balabon, Anthony
86FtLaud-2
Balabon, Rick
87PrWill-9
89SanBern/Best-4
89SanBern/Cal-74
90CLAS/CL-45
90Penin/Star-2
91Calgary/LineD-52
91Calgary/ProC-508
Balas, Mitchell F.
(Mike)
No Cards.
Balaz, John Lawrence
76OPC-539
76T-539
Balboni, Stephen C.
(Steve)
80Nashvl
81Colum-11
82Colum-4
82Colum/Pol-35
82T-83R
83Colum-15
83D-73
83OPC-8
83T-8
84F/X-6
84Nes/792-782
84T-782
84T/Tr-6
85D-419
85F-196
85Leaf-95
85OPC-152
85T-486
85T/St-271
86D-222
86Drake-20
86F-1
86Kitty/Disc-17
86Leaf-98
86NatPhoto-45
86OPC-164
86Sf-186M
86T-164
86T/Gloss60-6
86T/Mini-17
86T/St-265
87D-102
87D/OD-199
87F-362
87Leaf-262
87OPC-240
87RedFoley/St-85
87T-240
87T/St-263
88D-424
88F-251
88S-273
88S/Tr-46T
88T-638
89D-143
89D/Best-188
89D/Tr-48
89F-538
89F/Up-45
89OPC-336
89S-353
89S/NWest-17
89S/Tr-27
89T-336
89T/St-222
89T/Tr-6T
89UD-111
90B-436
90D-315
90F-436
90Leaf/II-373
90MLBPA/Pins-66
90OPC-716
90PublInt/St-424
90S-327
90S/NWest-25
90T-716
90T/Big-160
90T/TVYank-22
90UD-497
91D-650
91F-656
91OPC-511
91S-159
91T-511
91T/StClub/I-134
Balcena, Robert R.
(Bobby)
52Park-20
Baldrick, Bob
83Wausau/LF-22
86Chatt-2
Baldschun, Jack
62T-46
62T/St-164
63T-341
64PhilBull-3
64T-520
64T/Coins-69
64T/St-90
64T/SU
65T-555
65T/E-34
66T-272
67OPC-114
67T-114
70OPC-284
70T-284
78TCMA-104
Baldwin, Brian
88Wausau/GS-21
89SanBern/Best-8
89SanBern/Cal-73
Baldwin, Charles
E223
N172
N403
Scrapp
Baldwin, Clarence G.
(Kid)
N172
Baldwin, Dave
68T-231
69OPC-132
69T-132
70T-613
71MLB/St-433
71OPC-48
71T-48
Baldwin, Frank DeWitt
No Cards.
Baldwin, Henry Clay
No Cards.
Baldwin, Jeff
86Ashvl-2
87Osceola-10
88Osceola/Star-3
89ColMud/Best-13
89ColMud/ProC-135
89ColMud/Star-3
90ColMud/Best-9
90ColMud/ProC-1357
90ColMud/Star-4
91Jacks/LineD-553
91Jacks/ProC-930
91T/90Debut-10
Baldwin, Johnny
83Greens-1
84Nashvl-1
Baldwin, Kirk
89Eugene/Best-3
90AppFox/Box-4
90AppFox/ProC-2088
Baldwin, Lady
90Target-895
Baldwin, Marcus E.
(Mark)
E223
N172
Baldwin, O.F.
No Cards.
Baldwin, Reginald C.
(Reggie)
79Charl-4
80T-678R
80Tidew-13
Baldwin, Rickey Alan
(Rick)
76OPC-372
76SSPC-552
76T-372
77T-587
78SanJose-11
91WIZMets-22
Baldwin, Robert H.
(Billy)
76SSPC-370
91WIZMets-23
Baldwin, Tony
88Sumter/ProC-391
89BurlB/ProC-1608
89BurlB/Star-1
90BurlB/Best-19
90BurlB/ProC-2361
90BurlB/Star-2
Balelo, Nesi
87Chatt/Best-19
88Vermont/ProC-949
Balenti, Michael R.
(Mike)
No Cards.
Balentine, Bryant
91Princet/ClBest-24
91Princet/ProC-3504
Bales, Tom
88LitFalls/Pucko-3
Bales, Wesley Owen
(Lee)
67OPC-51R
67T-51R
Balfanz, John
88StPete/Star-1
89AS/Cal-37
89Reno/Cal-261
Ball, Arthur
(Art)
No Cards.
Ball, Cornelius
(Neal)
10Domino-5
11Helmar-21
12Sweet/Pin-16
91Conlon/Sport-203
T202
T204
T205
T206
T207
T215/brown
Ball, Harrison
(Harry)
88CapeCod-19
88CapeCod/Sum-27
90Johnson/Star-4
Ball, James Chandler
(Jim)
T204
Ball, Jeff
90AubAs/Best-9
90AubAs/ProC-3408
90Boise/ProC-3310
91Osceola/ClBest-16
91Osceola/ProC-690
Ball, Jim
77QuadC
Ball, Robert
80Ashvl-10
81Tulsa-26
82Tulsa-21
Balla, Gary
77QuadC
Ballanfant, Lee
55B-295ump
Ballanger, Mike
77Jaxvl
Ballard, Dan
78Green
Ballard, Glenn
(Butch)
77Spartan
80OrlTw-14
Ballard, Jeff
86Hagers-1
87RochR-25
87RochR/TCMA-1
88D-520
88F-554
88French-34
88RochR/Team-1
88RochR/CMC-1
88RochR/ProC-199
88T-782
89B-7
89D-495
89D/Best-30
89F-607
89French-29
89Panini/St-253
89S-551
89T-69
89T/St-230
89UD-595
90B-244
90Classic-89
90D-51
90D/BestAL-29
90F-173
90F/AwardWin-1
90HagersDG/Best-1
90HotRook/St-5
90KMart/SS-27
90Leaf/I-118
90MLBPA/Pins-110
90OPC-296
90OPC-394AS
90Panini/St-13
90PublInt/St-573
90RedFoley/St-3
90S-349
90S/YS/I-25
90Sf-123
90T-296

90T-394AS
90T/Big-278
90T/DH-2
90T/Gloss60-17
90T/Mini-1
90T/St-232
90T/TVAS-27
90UD-259
91B-98
91Crown/Orio-18
91D-279
91F-467
91Leaf/II-522
91OPC-546
91S-243
91T-546
91T/StClub/I-283
91UD-260
92D/I-74
92S/I-129
92T-104

Ballard, Tim
82CharR-13

Ballenger, Pelham A.
No Cards.

Baller, Jay Scott
(Jay)
82Reading-1
83Charl-1
83Wheat/Ind-2
84BuffB-9
85Iowa-12
86Cub/Unocal-1
86D-613
86F/Up-U7
86Gator-48
87Iowa-5
88Calgary/CMC-5
88Calgary/ProC-792
88T-717
89Indianap/CMC-7
89Indianap/ProC-1231
90Omaha/CMC-1

Ballinger, Mark A.
No Cards.

Ballou, Bill
89Utica/Pucko-29CO
91Utica/ClBest-22CO
91Utica/ProC-3258CO

Ballou, Win
90Target-896

Balmer, Steve
83QuadC-7

Balsley, Darren
86Modesto-4
87Dunedin-9
88Knoxvl/Best-10
89Knoxvl/Best-3
89Knoxvl/ProC-1137
89Knoxvl/Star-5
90StCath/ProC-3484CO
91Myrtle/ClBest-28CO
91Myrtle/ProC-2962CO

Balthazar, Doyle
87CharWh-28
87Lakeland-8
88Lakeland/Star-2
89London/ProC-1384
90FSLAS/Star-25
90Lakeland/Star-2
91London/LineD-376
91London/ProC-1880

Baltz, Nick
76Baton

Bamberger, George I.
50Remar
53Mother-38
59T-529
73OPC-136CO
73T-136C
74OPC-306CO
74T-306C
79T-577MG
80T-659MG
83T-246MG
85Gard-1MG
85Pol/Brew-31MG
85T/Tr-5T
86Pol/Brew-31MG
86T-21MG
87T-468MG
90Pac/Legend-11
90Swell/Great-23
91Crown/Orio-19

Bamberger, Harold E.
(Hal)
No Cards.

Ban, Mark
86QuadC-5

Banach, Joe
81Clinton-1

Banasiak, Edward
87Elmira/Black-24
87Elmira/Red-24
88WinHaven/Star-4

Bancells, Richard
81RochR-20
83RochR-24

Bancroft, David James
(Dave)
16FleischBrd-6
21Exh-5
25Exh-1
26Exh-4
27Exh-1
28Exh-5
28Yueng-19
29Exh/4-4
61F-7
89HOF/St-20
89Smok/Dodg-2
90Target-29
91Conlon/Sport-17
92Conlon/Sport-598
BF2-82
D327
D328-12
D329-10
D350/2-9
E120
E121/120
E121/80
E126-52
E135-12
E210
E220
M101/4-10
M101/5-9
V100
V61-73
W501-64
W502-19
W512-1
W514-40
W515-4
W516-30
W572
W573
W575
WG7-3

Bancroft, Frank C.
T204

Bando, Christopher M.
(Chris)
81Charl-8
81T-451R
82D-551
82T-141R
82Wheat/Ind
83D-33
83F-400
83T-227
83Wheat/Ind-3
84D-224
84F-534
84Nes/792-431
84T-431
84Wheat/Ind-23
85D-520
85F-438
85Leaf-39
85OPC-14
85Polar/Ind-23
85T-14
86D-373
86F-579
86OhHenry-23
86OPC-211
86T-594
87D-501
87D/OD-105
87F-243
87Gator-23
87T-322
88Chatt/Team-1
88D-95
88F-601
88Gator-23
88OPC-51
88Panini/St-71
88S-172
88T-604
88T/St-209
90AS/Cal-29MG
90Stockton/Best-27MG
90Stockton/Cal-200
90Stockton/ProC-2200MG
91Stockton/ClBest-24MG
91Stockton/ProC-3047MG

Bando, Salvatore L.
(Sal)
67OPC-33R
67T-33R
68OPC-146
68T-146
69MLB/St-82
69T-371
69T-556M
69T/St-211
70K-51
70MLB/St-254
70OPC-120
70T-120
70T/S-2
70T/SO
71MLB/St-506
71OPC-285
71T-285
71T/Coins-132
71T/GM-5
71T/S-57
71T/tatt-1
72K-52
72MB-24
72OPC-348KP
72T-348KP
72T-650
73OPC-155
73T-155
73T/Lids-4
74K-51
74OPC-103
74T-103
74T/St-221
75Ho-4
75Ho/Twink-4
75OPC-380
75T-380
75T/M-380
76OPC-90
76SSPC-497
76T-90
77BurgChef-87
77Ho-126
77OPC-145
77T-498
78Ho-94
78OPC-174
78T-265
78Wiffle/Discs-1
79Ho-119
79OPC-283
79T-550
80OPC-363
80T-715
81D-84
81F-510
81OPC-276
81T-623
82D-592
82F-134
87Mother/A's-4
88Pac/Leg-99
89Swell-63
90Pac/Legend-4
90Swell/Great-7

Bandy, Ken
87QuadC-28

Bane, Edward Lee
(Ed)
74OPC-592
74T-592
76SSPC-212
77T-486

Banes, Alan
80Elmira-1

Banes, Dave
82Nashvl-1

Baney, Richard Lee
(Dick)
70OPC-88R
70T-88R
74OPC-608R
74T-608R

Bangert, Greg
81Clinton-10

Bangston, Pat
88Kenosha/ProC-1406
88MidwLAS/GS-34
89Orlan/Best-9
89Orlan/ProC-1338
90Portl/CMC-2
90Portl/ProC-169
91OrlanSR/LineD-476
91OrlanSR/ProC-1842

Banister, Jeff
86Watertn-3
87Macon-4
88Harris/ProC-855
89EastLDD/ProC-DD28
89Harris/ProC-306
89Harris/Star-2
90Harris/ProC-1195
90Harris/Star-3
91BuffB/LineD-26
91BuffB/ProC-544
92T/91Debut-8

Bankhead, Daniel R.
(Dan)
51B-225
52Park-64
79TCMA-159
86Negro/Frit-102
90Target-30

Bankhead, Sam
78Laugh/Black-31
86Negro/Frit-97

Bankhead, Scott
85T-393OLY
86D/Rook-36
86F/Up-U8
86Omaha-1
86Omaha/TCMA-25
86Sf/Rook-39
87F-363
87F/Up-U1
87Mother/Sea-13
87T-508
87T/Tr-2T
88D-70
88F-368
88Mother/Sea-13
88OPC-246
88Panini/St-180
88S-238
88S/YS/II-37
88T-738
89B-203
89D-463
89D/Best-219
89F-539
89Mother/Sea-13
89OPC-79
89Panini/St-429
89S-341
89S/YS/I-42
89T-79
89UD-316
90B-466
90D-261
90D/BestAL-40
90F-505
90Leaf/I-127
90Mother/Mar-24
90OPC-213
90Panini/St-147
90PublInt/St-426
90S-555
90Sf-41
90T-213
90T/St-222
90UD-561
91B-254
91CounHrth-11
91D-189
91F-442
91Leaf/II-345
91OPC-436
91S-817
91T-436
91T/StClub/II-597
91UD-294
92D/I-304
92S/II-594
92T-155

Bankowski, Chris
81Redwd-27
83Redwd-3

Banks, Darryl
82QuadC-1
83MidldC-12
84MidldC-8

Banks, Dave
86AubAs-2

Banks, Dean
91Pocatel/ProC-3788

Banks, Ernest
(Ernie)
54T-94
55B-242
55RFG-26
55T-28
55T/DH-32
56T-15
56T/Pin-5
56YellBase/Pin-6
57T-55
58T-310
58T-482AS
59Armour-4
59Bz
59HRDerby-3
59T-147M
59T-350
59T-469M
59T-559AS
60Armour-3
60Bz-1
60NuCard-20
60T-10
60T-560AS
60T-tatt
60T/tatt-5
61Bz-19
61NuCard-420
61P-191
61T-350
61T-43LL
61T-485MV
61T-575AS
61T/RO
61T/St-4
62Bz
62Exh
62J-188
62P-188
62P/Can-188
62Salada-177A
62Salada-177B
62Shirriff-177
62T-25
62T/bucks
62T/St-104
63Bz-3
63Exh
63J-169
63P-169
63Salada-17
63T-242M
63T-380
63T-3LL
63T/SO
64T-55
64T/Coins-42
64T/St-25
64T/SU
64T/tatt
65OldLond-3
65T-510
65T/E-58
66OPC-110
66T-110
66T/RO
67T-215
68T-355
69Kelly/Pin-2
69MB-19
69MLB/St-118
69MLBPA/Pin-34
69OPC-20
69OPC-6LL
69Sunoco/Pin-1
69T-20
69T-6LL
69T/St-11
69Trans-40
70Dunkin-1
70K-40

70MB-3
70MLB/St-13
70T-630
70T/CB
70Trans-3
71K-50
71MD
71MLB/St-25
71MLB/St-555
71OPC-525
71T-525
71T/GM-36
72MB-25
73OPC-81CO
73T-81C
75OPC-196MV
75OPC-197MV
75T-196MV
75T-197MV
75T/M-196MV
75T/M-197MV
76Laugh/Jub-2
78TCMA-255
79TCMA-5
80Pac/Leg-33
80Laugh/3/4/5-27
82CJ-14
85CircK-10
85Woolwth-3
86BLChew-9
86Sf/Dec-29
87Nestle/DT-26
88Pac/Leg-36
89HOF/St-6
89T/LJN-65
90BBWit-19
90CollAB-11
90Pac/Legend-5
90Swell/Great-95
91K/3D-4
91K/SU-2A
91K/SU-2B
91LineD-18
91Swell/Great-5
Exh47

Banks, George Edward
61Clover-2
63T-564
64T-223
65T-348
66T-488

Banks, Lance
90CharRain/Best-2
90CharRain/ProC-2032
91Waterlo/ClBest-1
91Waterlo/ProC-1248

Banks, William John
(Bill)
No Cards.

Banks, Willie
88Kenosha/ProC-1380
89AS/Cal-4
89Visalia/Cal-101
89Visalia/ProC-1426
90A&AASingle/ProC-40
90B-411
90Classic/III-31
90Foil/Best-11
90OrlanSR/Best-1
90OrlanSR/ProC-1076
90OrlanSR/Star-2
91B-341
91Classic/II-T57
91F/Ultra-373MLP
91Leaf/GRook-BC5
91Portl/LineD-402
91Portl/ProC-1559
91UD-74
92D/II-760
92F-657
92T-747
92T/91Debut-9
92UD-14SR

Bankston, Wilborn E.
(Bill)
No Cards.

Banning, Doug
86MidldA-1
87Edmon-7
87MidldA-6

Banning, James M.
(Jim)
N172

Bannister, Alan
77T-559
78K-38
78T-213
79T-134
80OPC-317
80T-608
81T-632
82D-159
82F-359
82T-287
82Wheat/Ind
83D-285
83F-401
83OPC-348
83T-348
83Wheat/Ind-4
84D-154
84F-535
84F/X-7
84Mother/Ast-21
84Nes/792-478
84Rangers-2
84T-478
84T/St-257
84T/Tr-7
85F-555
85Rangers-5
85T-76
86D-525
86F-556
86T-784
88Rockford-1
89Jaxvl/Best-2
89Jaxvl/ProC-151
89Pac/SenLg-14
89Rockford-1MG
89T/SenLg-30
89TM/SenLg-5
91Phoenix/LineD-400CO
91Phoenix/ProC-84CO

Bannister, Floyd F.
78BK/Ast-6
78T-39
79OPC-154
79T-306
80OPC-352
80T-699
81D-286
81F-599
81OPC-166
81Pol/Mariners-2
81T-166
81T/St-128
82D-100
82F-504
82T-468
82T/St-234
83D-21DK
83D-50
83F-471
83K-41
83OPC-203
83T-545
83T-706
83T/St-113
83T/St-18
83T/Tr-7
83TrueVal/WSox-24
84D-366
84F-52
84F/St-84
84Nes/792-280
84OPC-280
84T-280
84T/St-247
84TrueVal/WS-4
85Coke/WS-24
85D-379
85F-508
85OPC-354
85T-274FDP
85T-725
86Coke/WS-19
86D-244
86F-199
86Leaf-118
86OPC-64
86T-64
86T/Mini-9
87Coke/WS-12
87D-211
87F-486
87F/Lim-1
87F/St-3
87OPC-356
87T-737
87T/St-286
88AlaskaAS70/Team-18
88D-383
88D/Best-7
88F-392
88OPC-357
88Panini/St-52
88RedFoley/St-4
88S-622
88S/Tr-63T
88Smok/Royals-8
88T-357
88T/Big-174
88T/Tr-8T
89B-112
89D-262
89F-276
89OPC-194
89RedFoley/St-5
89S-249
89Sf-154
89T-638
89T/St-269
89UD-549
90OPC-116
90PublInt/St-342
90T-116
90UD-695
91B-190
91F/Up-U8
91Leaf/II-439

Bannister, Tim
77BurlB
78BurlB

Bannon, James Henry
(Jimmy)
N300/unif

Bannon, Thomas Edward
(Tom)
No Cards.

Banta, John Kay
(Jack)
49Eureka-28
50B-224
78TCMA-203
90Target-31

Banton, Scott
89Hamil/Star-1
90Savan/ProC-2079
91Spring/ClBest-4
91Spring/ProC-753

Baptist, Travis
91MedHat/ProC-4089

Baranoski, Jim
89Idaho/ProC-2025

Barba, Doug
84Cedar-4

Barba, Michael
82Holyo-1
83ArkTr-6

Barbara, Daniel
(Dan)
89SanBern/Best-7
89SanBern/Cal-76
90Penin/Star-3

Barbara, Don
91MidwLAS/ProC-MWL24
91QuadC/ClBest-15
91QuadC/ProC-2633

Barbare, Walter L.
21Exh-6
E120

Barbary, Donald O.
(Red)
No Cards.

Barbe, Jim
(Yogi)
78Ashvl
79Tulsa-17

Barbeau, William J.
(Jap)
E91
T206

Barbee, David Monroe
(Dave)
No Cards.

Barber, Brian
91Classic/DP-18
91FrRow/DP-21
91Johnson/ClBest-18
91Johnson/ProC-3969
92S/II-803
92T-594

Barber, Charles D.
(Charlie)
No Cards.

Barber, Red
89Rini/Dodg-28M
89Rini/Dodg-29

Barber, Stephen David
(Steve)
60T-514
61P-74
61T-125
61T/St-97
62Salada-11
62Shirriff-11
62T-355
62T-57LL
63Exh
63F-1
63J-64
63P-64
63T-12
64Bz-3
64T-450
64T/Coins-8
64T/St-54
64T/SU
64T/tatt
64Wheat/St-5
65OPC-113
65T-113
66T-477
67OPC-82
67T-82
68T-316
69MB-20
69MLB/St-92
69T-233
69T/St-222
70MLB/St-265
70OPC-224
70T-224
72MB-26
72OPC-333
72T-333
73OPC-36
73T-36
74OPC-631
74T-631
78TCMA-57
91Crown/Orio-20
Exh47

Barber, Steve Lee
(Steve)
No Cards.

Barber, Tyrus Turner
(Turner)
21Exh-7
E120
E121
E220
V100
W501-60
W573

Barberich, Frank F.
C46-16

Barberie, Bret
88T/Tr-9T
89Star/Wax-32
89T/Big-19
89WPalmB/Star-2
90Jaxvl/Best-3
90Jaxvl/ProC-1379
91F/UltraUp-U90
91Indianap/LineD-176
91Indianap/ProC-465
91UD/FinalEd-67F
92Classic/I-T9
92D/II-449
92F-472
92S/100RisSt-14
92S/I-419
92T-224
92T/91Debut-10
92UD-363

Barbieri, James P.
(Jim)
67OPC-76
67T-76
90Target-32

Barbosa, Rafael
84Durham-11

Barclay, Curtis C.
(Curt)
57T-361
58Hires-70
58SFCallB-2
58T-21
59T-307

Barclay, George O.
No Cards.

Barczi, Scott
87Watertn-7
88Augusta/ProC-368
89Salem/Star-4
90Harris/ProC-1196
90Harris/Star-4

Bard, Michael
91BendB/ClBest-26
91BendB/ProC-3699

Bard, Paul Z.
81VeroB-2
82VeroB-12
84CharlO-21

Barden, Steve
89Richm/ProC-819

Bardot, Gene
76Wausau

Bare, Raymond Douglas
(Ray)
76OPC-507
76SSPC-613
76T-507
77T-43
78RochR

Barefoot, Mike
89Miami/I/Star-1

Barfield, Jesse Lee
78Dunedin
82OPC-203R
82T-203R
82T/Tr-2T
83D-595
83F-424
83OPC-257
83T-257
83T/St-307
84D-193
84F-147
84Nes/792-488
84OPC-316
84T-488
84T/St-372
84Tor/Fire-4
85D-195
85F-99
85Leaf-209
85OPC-24
85OPC/Post-20
85T-24
85T/St-362
85Tor/Fire-4
86Ault-29
86D-193
86F-52
86F/Mini-12
86F/St-2
86Leaf-254
86OPC-234
86Sf-76
86T-593
86T/St-192
86Tor/Fire-3
87Classic-58
87D-121
87D/AAS-23
87D/OD-34
87F-219
87F-643M
87F/Excit-3
87F/BB-2
87F/LL-1
87F/Mini-4
87F/Slug-2
87F/St-4
87F/WaxBox-C2
87Ho/St-1
87KayBee-2
87Kraft-41
87Leaf-127
87OPC-24
87RedFoley/St-3
87Sf-14
87Sf-153M

87T-655
87T/Coins-2
87T/Gloss60-35
87T/HL-9
87T/Mini-73
87T/St-184
87Tor/Fire-1
87Woolwth-9
88D-442
88D/Best-216
88F-102
88F/RecSet-1
88F/St-70
88Ho/Disc-19
88Leaf-225
88OPC-140
88Panini/St-223
88S-8
88Sf-13
88T-140
88T/Big-92
88T/Gloss60-2
88T/St-192
88T/St/Backs-46
88Tor/Fire-29
89T/Ames-1
89B-257
89Classic-66
89D-425
89D/Best-132
89D/GrandSlam-11
89F-225
89F/Up-46
89OPC-325
89Panini/St-471
89RedFoley/St-6
89S-160
89S/NWest-5
89S/Tr-22
89Sf-9
89T-325
89T/Tr-7T
89Tor/Fire-29
89UD-149
89UD/Ext-702
90B-433
90Classic-99
90D-74
90D/BestAL-109
90F-437
90Leaf/I-201
90MLBPA/Pins-61
90OPC-740
90Pac/Legend-110
90Panini/St-120
90PublInt/St-530
90RedFoley/St-4
90S-222
90S/NWest-5
90Sf-10
90T-740
90T/Big-188
90T/HillsHM-24
90T/St-314
90T/TVYank-29
90UD-476
91B-169
91Classic/200-61
91D-498
91F-657
91F/Ultra-228
91Leaf/II-308
91Leaf/Stud-91
91OPC-85
91Panini/FrSt-330
91S-148
91S-414RIF
91T-85
91T/StClub/I-103
91UD-485
92D/I-316
92F-221
92S/II-565
92T-650
92UD-139
92UD-644DS

Barfield, John
87PortChar-5
88TexLgAS/GS-17
88Tulsa-14
89OkCty/CMC-2
89OkCty/ProC-1518
90OkCty/CMC-9
90OkCty/ProC-424
90T/89Debut-8
91D-688
91F/Up-U58
91Mother/Rang-13
91OPC-428
91S-573
91T-428
91UD-629
92D/I-168
92S/II-683
92UD-691

Barfoot, Clyde R.
No Cards.

Bargar, Gregory R.
(Greg)
80Memphis-5
83Memphis-20
84Indianap-13
84Nes/792-474
84OPC-292
84T-474
85Indianap-13
87Louisvl-4
88Louisvl-9

Bargas, Rob
91WPalmB/ClBest-18
91WPalmB/ProC-1234

Barger, Bob
76Wausau

Barger, Eros Bolivar
(Cy)
10Domino-6
11Helmar-82
12Sweet/Pin-69
14CJ-141
14Piedmont/St-1
15CJ-141
M116
S74-48
T202
T205
T206
T207
T213/blue

Barger, Vince
85Durham-2

Bargerhuff, Brian
83Clinton/LF-17
86Chatt-3

Bargfeldt, John
79QuadC-19

Bark, Brian
88CapeCod/Sum-114
90Pulaski/Best-1
90Pulaski/ProC-3101
91Durham/ClBest-2
91Durham/ProC-1535

Barker, Bob
87Albany-3

Barker, Jeff
78Holyo

Barker, Leonard H.
(Len)
74Gaston
77T-489R
77Tucson
78BK/R-9
78T-634
79OPC-40
79T-94
80T-227
81D-320
81F-408
81OPC-3
81T-432
81T-6LL
81T/St-5
81T/St-72
82D-137
82D-6DK
82F-360
82F-639M
82F/St-200
82K-37
82OPC-360
82T-166LL
82T-360
82T/St-113
82T/St-12
82T/St-178
82Wheat/Ind
83D-111
83F-402
83F-642
83K-33
83OPC-120
83T-120
83T/St-57
83Wheat/Ind-5
84D-443
84F-170
84Nes/792-614
84OPC-309
84Pol/Atl-39
84T-614
85D-165
85F-318
85Ho/Braves-2
85Pol/Atl-39
85T-557
86D-409
86F-507
86Indianap-20
86T-24
91Pac/SenLg-153

Barker, Raymond H.
(Ray)
61T-428
65T-546R
66T-323
67T-583
91Crown/Orio-21

Barker, Timothy
(Tim)
86Tampa-2
87Beloit-17
88Charl/ProC-1221
89GreatF-14
90AS/Cal-8
90Bakers/Cal-255
91SanAn/LineD-529
91SanAn/ProC-2980

Barkley, Jeff
83Watlo/LF-20
84Maine-15
85Maine-1
85Polar/Ind-49
86T-567

Barkley, Red
90Target-33

Barkley, Samuel E.
(Sam)
N172
N284
N284/StL

Barley, Ned
90MedHat/Best-12

Barlick, Al
55B-265ump
90TM/Umpire-71

Barling, Glenn
82Clinton-6

Barlow, Andy
90James/Pucko-31

Barlow, Clem
91Belling/ClBest-1
91Belling/ProC-3678

Barlow, Mike
76SSPC-298
77SLCity
78Cr/PCL-97
78T-429
80Syrac-13
80T-312
81OPC-77
81T-77
82Syrac-1

Barlow, Ricky
86GlenF-1
87Toledo-9
87Toledo/TCMA-19

Barmes, Bruce R.
No Cards.

Barna, Herbert Paul
(Babe)
No Cards.

Barnard, Jeff
81AppFx-2

Barnard, Steve
85PrWill-11

Barnard, Tom
88Watertn/Pucko-32

Barnes, Brian
88CapeCod/Sum-130
90A&AASingle/ProC-36
90Foil/Best-261
90Jaxvl/Best-14
90Jaxvl/ProC-1365
91B-438
91Classic/200-8
91D-415RR
91Leaf/Stud-192
91OPC-211
91OPC/Premier-4
91S-708RP
91S/Rook40-10
91T-211
91T/90Debut-11
91T/StClub/I-114
91UD-12
92D/I-117
92F-473
92S/100RisSt-78
92S/II-715
92T-73
92UD-361

Barnes, Charlie
48Sommer-30M

Barnes, Chris
88CapeCod/Sum-115

Barnes, Craig
75Lafay

Barnes, Donald L.
W753

Barnes, Emile Deering
(Red)
No Cards.

Barnes, Everett Duane
(Eppie)
No Cards.

Barnes, Frank
60T-538

Barnes, Jesse L.
25Exh-2
90Target-34
92Conlon/Sport-355
E120
V100
V117-1
W514-120
W516-12
W572
W573
W575

Barnes, John Francis
(Honey)
No Cards.

Barnes, John S.
N172

Barnes, Jon
91Classic/DP-47
91FrRow/DP-20

Barnes, Luther Owen
(Lute)
91WIZMets-24

Barnes, Mike
80Buffa-1

Barnes, Richard
78Knoxvl
79Knoxvl/TCMA-5
82Edmon-19
84D-608
84Maine-6

Barnes, Roscoe C.
(Ross)
No Cards.

Barnes, Samuel Thomas
(Sam)
No Cards.

Barnes, Virgil
28Exh-17

Barnes, William H.
(Bill)
No Cards.

Barnes, William Henry
(Skeeter)
79Nashvl
80Water-15
81Indianap-29
82Water-13
83Indianap-31
84Wichita/Rock-16
85D-530
86Indianap-16
88BuffB/CMC-23
88BuffB/ProC-1487
88Nashvl/Team-2
89AAA/CMC-6
89AAA/ProC-15
89Nashvl/CMC-13
89Nashvl/ProC-1289
89Nashvl/Team-1
90Nashvl/CMC-13
90Nashvl/ProC-244
91T/Tr-5T
91Toledo/LineD-578
91Toledo/ProC-1942
92D/II-749
92S/II-569
92T-221
92UD-470

Barnett, Larry
88TM/Umpire-7
89TM/Umpire-5
89TM/Umpire-60M
90TM/Umpire-5

Barnett, Mike
90SoBend/Best-26CO
91Saraso/ClBest-28CO
91Saraso/ProC-1130CO

Barney, Edmund J.
(Ed)
No Cards.

Barney, Rex
47HomogBond-1
48B-41
49B-61
49Eureka-29
50B-76
51B-153
90Target-35
D305

Barnhart, Clyde Lee
21Exh-8
E120
E126-2
V61-108

Barnhart, Edgar V.
(Ed)
No Cards.

Barnhart, Leslie Earl
(Les)
No Cards.

Barnhart, Rick
79Wausau-13

Barnhart, Victor Dee
(Vic)
No Cards.

Barnhill, Dave
86Negro/Frit-101

Barnhouse, Scott
83Wausau/LF-18

Barniak, Jim
90Phill/TastyK-36BC

Barnicle, George B.
No Cards.

Barnicle, Ted
76Cedar
79Knoxvl/TCMA-21
80GlenF/B-11
80GlenF/C-19

Barnie, William H.
(Billy)
90Target-36
N172

Barnowski, Edward A.
(Ed)
66T-442R
67T-507R
91Crown/Orio-22

Barns, Jeff
88PalmSp/Cal-100
88PalmSp/ProC-1451
89MidldA/GS-5
91London/LineD-427
91MidldA/ProC-438

Barnwell, Richard
(Rich)
89Oneonta/ProC-2117
90FtLaud/Star-1
91FtLaud/ClBest-24
91FtLaud/ProC-2438

Barnwell, Rob
87Watertn-21

Barojas, Salome
83D-67
83F-230
83TrueVal/WSox-30
84D-570
84F-53

84TrueVal/WS-5
85D-605
85F-482
85Mother/Mar-19

Baron, Sean
88BurlInd/ProC-1778

Barone, Richard A.
(Dick)
61Union

Barr, Bob
76Watlo

Barr, Hyder Edward
(Bob)
No Cards.

Barr, James Leland
(Jim)
72OPC-232R
72T-232R
73OPC-387
73T-387
74OPC-233
74T-233
75Ho-13
75Ho/Twink-13
75OPC-107
75T-107
75T/M-107
76OPC-308
76SSPC-92
76T-308
77BurgChef-103
77Ho-83
77OPC-119
77T-609
78OPC-19
78T-62
79T-461
80OPC-275
80T-529
81D-412
81F-287
81T-717
83D-398
83F-252
83T-133
84D-79
84F-365
84Nes/792-282
84T-282
88AlaskaAS60/Team-9

Barr, Robert A.
(Bob)
90Target-897

Barr, Robert M.
(Bob)
No Cards.

Barr, Steven Charles
(Steve)
76OPC-595R
76T-595R

Barr, Tim
78Green
80OrlTw-2

Barragan, Facundo A.
(Cuno)
59DF
62T-66
63T-557

Barragan, Gerry
87Madis-12
88Modesto/Cal-73

Barragan, Jaime
(Jimmy)
88Spartan/ProC-1036
88Spartan/Star-1
88Spartan/Star-17
89Clearw/Star-1
90Clearw/Star-1

Barranca, German
76Watlo
77Jaxvl
81Indianap-25
83Evansvl-25
84OKCty-24
85Water-17

Barranco, Vince
88BurlInd/ProC-1777

Barreiro, Efrain
90Ashvl/ClBest-1
90AubAs/Best-5
90AubAs/ProC-3413
91Ashvl/ProC-559

Barreiro, Fernando
91Spring/ClBest-5
91Spring/ProC-732

Barrera, Nelson
85BuffB-7

Barrett, Charles H.
(Red)
39Exh
47TipTop
49B-213
49Eureka-4
52Park-14

Barrett, Charles
77LodiD

Barrett, Dick
47Centen-1

Barrett, Francis J.
(Frank)
No Cards.

Barrett, James E.
(Jimmy)
E107
T201
WG2-2

Barrett, Jeff
87Indianap-17

Barrett, John Joseph
(Johnny)
No Cards.

Barrett, Kewpie
47Signal

Barrett, Martin F.
(Marty)
No Cards.

Barrett, Martin Glen
(Marty)
81Pawtu-14
83Pawtu-14
84F/X-8
84Nes/792-683
84T-683
85D-127
85F-150
85Leaf-229
85T-298
85T/St-219
86D-294
86F-340
86Leaf-169
86OPC-314
86T-734
86T/St-250
87Classic-61
87D-523
87D/OD-188
87F-27
87F/AwardWin-1
87F/Lim-2
87F/St-5
87F/WS-6
87Leaf-165
87OPC-39
87Sf-112M
87Sf-182
87Seven-ME2
87T-39
87T/HL-17
87T/St-18
87Woolwth-17
88D-276
88D/Best-9
88D/RedSox/Bk-276
88F-343
88Leaf-141
88OPC-338
88Panini/St-28
88S-155
88Sf-157
88T-525
88T/Big-54
88T/St-248
89B-28
89D-184
89D/Best-252
89F-78
89OPC-155
89Panini/St-276
89S-63
89Sf-198
89T-155
89T/Big-278
89T/St-257
89UD-173
90B-282
90D-240
90F-266
90OPC-355
90Panini/St-15
90Pep/RSox-1
90PublInt/St-446
90S-15
90T-355
90T/Big-44
90T/St-256
90T/TVRSox-21
90UD-133
91B-648
91F-84
91Leaf/II-474
91OPC-496
91Padre/MagRal-10
91S-228
91T-496
91UD-90

Barrett, Robert S.
(Bob)
90Target-37

Barrett, Tim
86Indianap-34
87Indianap-9
88Indianap/CMC-5
88Indianap/ProC-502
89Indianap/CMC-1
89Indianap/ProC-1229

Barrett, Tom
84Nashvl-2
85Colum-13
85Colum/Pol-1
86Albany/TCMA-5
87Reading-7
88Maine/CMC-16
88Maine/ProC-284
88Phill/TastyK-27
89ScrWB/CMC-11
89ScrWB/ProC-725
89T-653
89T/Big-177
90AlbanyDG/Best-15
90S-633
91Pawtu/LineD-352
91Pawtu/ProC-44

Barrett, Tracey S.
(Dick)
No Cards.

Barrett, William J.
(Bill)
No Cards.

Barretto, Saul M.
87Gaston-6
88Gaston/ProC-1022

Barrick, Andy
88Batavia/ProC-1687

Barrilleaux, John
89Oneonta/ProC-2099

Barringer, Reggie
85PrWill-20
86PrWill-1
87Salem-23

Barrios, Eugene
85Greens-24

Barrios, Francisco
77T-222
78T-552
79Ho-21
79T-386
80OPC-58
80T-107
81F-352

Barrios, Gregg
86WinHaven-3

Barrios, Jose Manuel
76Cedar
80Phoenix-17
81Phoenix-12
82Phoenix

Barron, Anthony
(Tony)
89Star/Wax-26
89VeroB/Star-2
90VeroB/Star-3
91SanAn/LineD-530
91SanAn/ProC-2986

Barron, David Irenus
(Red)
No Cards.

Barros, Ellie
82Danvl-17

Barrow, Ed
50Callahan
60F-23
80SSPC/HOF
81Detroit-77MG
89HOF/St-94

Barrow, Mel
76SanAn/Team-1
79Tucson-22
79Tulsa-21
80Tulsa-11
81Tulsa-6
90TulsaDG/Best-26

Barrows, Roland
(Cuke)
No Cards.

Barrs, Stan
88Savan/ProC-349

Barry, Jeff
90James/Pucko-7
91Single/ClBest-365
91WPalmB/ClBest-24
91WPalmB/ProC-1239

Barry, John C.
(Shad)
T206

Barry, John Joseph
(Jack)
10Domino-7
11Helmar-53
12Sweet/Pin-41
14CJ-28
14Piedmont/St-2
15CJ-28
16FleischBrd-7
88Conlon/3-4
91Conlon/Sport-139
BF2-1
D303
D304
D327
D328-13
D329-11
D350/2-10
E101
E104
E105
E106
E135-13
E254
E270/1
E300
E90/1
E91
M101/4-11
M101/5-10
M116
S74-27
T201
T202
T205
T206
T207
T208
T216
T222

Barry, John
86Clinton-1
88Fresno/Cal-10
88Fresno/ProC-1227

Barry, Richard D.
(Rich)
No Cards.

Bartell, Mike
75Clinton

Bartell, Richard
(Dick)
29Exh/4-13
31Exh/4-12
32Orbit/num-15
32Orbit/un-4
33DH-4
33Exh/4-6
33G-28
34DS-101
34Exh/4-6
35BU-4
35G-2A
35G-4A
35G-7A
38G-248
38G-272
41DP-56
55B-234
88Conlon/4-3
92Conlon/Sport-452
PM10/Sm-7
R300
R305
R308-158
R309/2
R310
R314
R337-424
V353-28
V355-37

Bartels, Bill
85Anchora-2
87VeroB-26
88Lynch/Star-1

Barthelson, Robert E.
(Bob)
47Sunbeam

Barthold, John F.
No Cards.

Bartholomew, Lester
No Cards.

Bartholow, Bud
83Reading-1

Bartirome, Anthony J.
(Tony)
52T-332
53T-71
91T/Arc53-71

Bartlett, Bob
75Tidew/Team-2

Bartley, Boyd Owen
90Target-898

Bartley, Greg
84Chatt-29
86Calgary-1
87Chatt/Best-3

Bartley, William J.
(Bill)
E254

Bartling, Irving H.
(Irv)
No Cards.

Bartolomucci, Tony
86AppFx-1

Barton, Harry Lamb
No Cards.

Barton, Jeff
89Spokane/SP-21
90CharRain/Best-3
90CharRain/ProC-2051

Barton, Ken
76Cedar
77Cedar
81Charl-10

Barton, Larry
40Hughes-3
47Signal

Barton, Paul
91StCath/ClBest-18
91StCath/ProC-3386

Barton, Robert Wilbur
(Bob)
66T-511R
67T-462
68T-351
69OPC-41
69T-41
70OPC-352
70T-352
71MLB/St-218
71OPC-589
71T-589
72MB-27
72OPC-39
72OPC-40IA
72T-39
72T-40A
73OPC-626
73T-626

Barton, Shawn
86Reading-2
86SanJose-2
87Maine-6
87Maine/TCMA-1
87Phill/TastyK-x
87SanJose-29
88Jacks/GS-19
89AS/Cal-42
89Reno/Cal-260

89Tidew/CMC-8
89Tidew/ProC-1969
90Reno/Cal-272
90T/TVMets-35
90Tidew/CMC-1
90Tidew/ProC-534
91Jaxvl/LineD-327
91Jaxvl/ProC-141

Barton, Vincent David
(Vince)
No Cards.

Bartosch, David R.
(Dave)
No Cards.

Bartson, Charles F.
(Charlie)
No Cards.

Barun, Barton
82Redwd-24

Basgall, Romanus
(Monty)
49Eureka-152
52T-12
73OPC-569CO
73T-569CO
74OPC-144CO
74T-144C
85Coke/Dodg-4CO
86Coke/Dodg-3CO

Bashang, Albert C.
(Al)
No Cards.

Bashore, Walter F.
(Walt)
No Cards.

Basinski, Edward F.
(Eddie)
47TipTop
52Mother-6
53Mother-32
90Target-899

Baskette, James B.
(Jim)
No Cards.

Bass, Barry
83BurlR-1
83BurlR/LF-9
84Tulsa-22
85Tulsa-26
87ElPaso-27
88ElPaso/Best-17

Bass, Bart
77Cedar

Bass, Ed
85FtMyr-1

Bass, Jerry
78Clinton
79LodiD-16
82BirmB-18

Bass, John E.
No Cards.

Bass, Kevin
77Newar
78BurlB
79Holyo-5
79T-708R
80Holyo-13
81Vanco-24
82Pol/Brew-26
82Vanco-4
84D-450
84F-221
84Nes/792-538
84T-538
85D-136
85F-345
85F/St-52
85Mother/Ast-22
85T-326
86D-548
86D/HL-21
86F-294
86OPC-52
86Pol/Ast-4
86T-458
86T/St-28
87Classic-17
87D-410
87D/AAS-40
87D/OD-14
87Drake-17
87F-51
87F/Hottest-3
87F/Mini-5
87F/Slug-1
87F/St-6
87Leaf-211
87Mother/Ast-9
87OPC-85
87Pol/Ast-22
87Sf-117M
87Sf-175
87T-85
87T/Gloss60-34
87T/Mini-7
87T/St-34
88D-286
88D/Best-38
88F-440
88F/Excit-2
88F/Mini-77
88F/St-85
88Leaf-137
88Mother/Ast-9
88OPC-175
88Panini/St-298
88Pol/Ast-6
88S-33
88Sf-55
88T-175
88T/Big-77
88T/St-29
89T/Ames-2
89D-325
89F-351
89Lennox/Ast-5
89Mother/Ast-8
89OPC-102
89Panini/St-91
89S-226
89Sf-11
89T-646
89T/Big-187
89T/LJN-63
89T/St-14
89UD-425
90B-240
90D-589
90D/BestNL-36
90D/GSlam-10
90F-223
90F/Up-U60
90Leaf/II-305
90MLBPA/Pins-45
90Mother/Giant-24
90OPC-281
90Panini/St-261
90PublInt/St-87
90S-279
90S/100St-100
90S/Tr-2T
90Sf-198
90T-281
90T/Big-236
90T/St-17
90T/Tr-7T
90UD-302
90UD/Ext-793
91B-625
91D-630
91F-253
91F/Ultra-315
91Leaf/II-365
91Mother/Giant-24
91OPC-752
91PG&E-10
91S-616
91SFExam/Giant-1
91T-752
91T/StClub/I-29
91UD-287
92D/I-373
92F-626
92S/I-139
92T-513
92UD-107

Bass, Norm
62T-122
63T-461

Bass, Randy William
79T-707R
82D-439
82F-566
82T-307
89T/SenLg-50
90EliteSenLg-49

Bass, Regan
86DayBe-2

Bass, William Capers
(Doc)
No Cards.

Bassett, Charles E.
(Charley)
N172
N284
WG1-28

Bassett, Matt
84Omaha-29
85Omaha-2

Bassett, Pepper
86Negro/Frit-103

Bassler, John Landis
(Johnny)
21Exh-9
25Exh-89
26Exh-89
27Exh-45
92Conlon/Sport-414
E120
E126-55
V100
V117-10
W572
W573
WG7-4

Basso, Michael A.
(Mike)
86Cram/PCL-167
87CharRain-20
88TexLgAS/GS-23
88Wichita-16
89AubAs/ProC-9
89Wichita/Rock-16
89Wichita/Rock/HL-12
90LasVegas/CMC-11
90LasVegas/ProC-126
91Wichita/LineD-601
91Wichita/ProC-2601

Bast, Steven
(Steve)
86Elmira-2
87NewBrit-11
89NewBrit/ProC-608
89Pawtu/Dunkin-30
90Pawtu/CMC-9
90Pawtu/ProC-452
90T/TVRSox-36

Bastable, John M.
76OkCty/Team-3

Bastian, Charles J.
(Charlie)
N172
N284
N690
WG1-47

Bastian, John K.
(Jack)
T206

Bastian, Jose
79RochR-17
81Toledo-3

Bastian, Robert
81Redwd-1
83Nashua-1
85Cram/PCL-21
86Edmon-1

Batch, Emil Henry
C46-48
T205
T206

Batchelder, Joseph E.
(Joe)
No Cards.

Batchelor, Rich
91FSLAS/ProC-FSL11
91FtLaud/ClBest-1
91FtLaud/ProC-2416
91Single/ClBest-54

Bateman, John Alvin
63Pep
63T-386R
64T-142
64T/Coins-107
65T-433
66OPC-86
66T-86
67T-231
68Coke
68Dexter-9
68T-592
69Expos/Pins-1
69Fud's-2
69MB-21
69MLB/St-155
69OPC-138
69T-138
69T/St-53
70Expos/Pins-3
70MLB/St-61
70OPC-417
70T-417
71MLB/St-122
71OPC-31
71OPC-628
71T-628
71T/Coins-19
72MB-28
72OPC-5
72T-5

Bates, Billy
86ElPaso-4
87Denver-7
88Denver/CMC-17
88Denver/ProC-1271
89AAA/ProC-41
89Denver/CMC-15
89Denver/ProC-38
90ElPasoATG/Team-1
90Idaho/ProC-3265
90Pol/Brew-34
90S-608
90S/100Ris-80
90T/89Debut-9
91Nashvl/LineD-251

Bates, Charles W.
No Cards.

Bates, Delbert O.
No Cards.

Bates, Eric
89Billings/ProC-2061

Bates, Hubert Edgar
(Buddy)
R314/Can
V355-126

Bates, John William
(Johnny)
10Domino-8
11Helmar-109
12Sweet/Pin-94
E104
E254
E94
M116
S74-97
T202
T204
T205
T206
W555

Bates, Kevin
84Shrev/FB-1

Bates, Raymond
(Ray)
No Cards.

Bates, Richard
(Dick)
No Cards.

Bates, Steve
88Clearw/Star-1

Bates, Tommy
91Watertn/ClBest-17
91Watertn/ProC-3372

Batesole, Michael
86Bakers-2
87VeroB-15
88VeroB/Star-1

Bathe, Bill
82WHave-10
83Tacoma-10
84Cram/PCL-80
85Cram/PCL-148
86D/Rook-41
86F/Up-U9
86Mother/A's-23
87D-281
88AAA/ProC-16
88Iowa/CMC-23
88Iowa/ProC-527
89Phoenix/CMC-11
89Phoenix/ProC-1495
90B-234
90D-680
90Mother/Giant-22
91OPC-679
91T-679

Bathe, Bob
84Albany-23
85Cram/PCL-143
86Iowa-2

Batista, Francisco
82Spring-24
83ArkTr-20
83StPete-20
90SpringDG/Best-5

Batista, Miguel
86CharRain-2A
86CharRain-2B

Batista, Rafael
No Cards.

Batiste, Chris
89Bluefld/Star-3

Batiste, Kevin
87Dunedin-19
88Knoxvl/Best-7
89Knoxvl/Best-2
89Knoxvl/ProC-1124
89Knoxvl/Star-7
90Greenvl/Best-18
90Greenvl/ProC-1140
90Greenvl/Star-2
90T/89Debut-10
90UD-115

Batiste, Kim
88Spartan/ProC-1035
88Spartan/Star-18
88Spartan/Star-2
89Clearw/Star-2
90EastLAS/ProC-EL20
90Foil/Best-227
90Reading/Best-15
90Reading/ProC-1225
90Reading/Star-5
91B-488
91ScranWB/LineD-480
91ScranWB/ProC-2543
92Classic/I-10
92D/II-402
92F-522
92S/II-833
92T-514
92T/91Debut-11
92UD-422

Batsch, William M.
(Bill)
No Cards.

Battam, Lawrence
(Larry)
No Cards.

Battell, Mark
88Hamil/ProC-1725
89Hamil/Star-2

Batten, George B.
No Cards.

Batten, Mark
80SanJose/JITB-3
81Wausau-8

Battey, Earl Jesse
57T-401
58T-364
59T-114
60L-66
60T-328
61Bz-28
61Clover-3
61P-97
61Peters-22
61T-315
61T-582AS
61T/Dice-1
61T/St-177
62Bz
62J-90
62P-90
62P/Can-90
62Salada-19
62Shirriff-19
62T-371
62T/bucks
62T/St-74
63Exh
63J-8
63P-8
63Salada-44
63T-306M
63T-410
64T-90

64T/Coins-101
64T/Coins-136AS
64T/St-71
64T/SU
64Wheat/St-6
65T-490
65T/E-70
66T-240
66T/RO-55
67OPC-15
67T-15
78TCMA-113
88Pac/Leg-35
Exh47

Battin, Joseph V.
(Joe)
No Cards.

Battle, Howard
90MedHat/Best-26
91Myrtle/ClBest-16
91Myrtle/ProC-2950
91SALAS/ProC-SAL36
91Single/ClBest-29

Battle, James Milton
(Jim)
No Cards.

Batton, Chris
76Tucson-10
77T-475R

Batts, Matthew Daniel
(Matt)
48L-108
51B-129
52B-216
52T-230
53B/BW-22
53Glen
54B-183
54T-88
55B-161
76Baton/MG
Exh47

Bauer, Alice
52Wheat

Bauer, Dave
89Penin/Star-1

Bauer, Eric
85Spokane/Cram-1
87Wichita-22
88Wichita-33

Bauer, Henry Albert
(Hank)
50B-219
51B-183
51BR-A4
51T/RB-24
52B-65
52BR
52Coke
52T-215
52TipTop
53B/Col-44M
53B/Col-84
53Briggs
53RM-AL2
53SM
54B-129
54DanDee
54NYJour
54RM-AL23
54SM
54T-130
55B-246
55RM-AL22
55SM
55T-166
56T-177
57T-240
58T-9
59T-240
60T-262
61P-90
61T-119M
61T-398
61T/St-156
62T-127M
62T-463
64T-178
65T-323
66T-229
67OPC-1M
67T-1M
67T-534
68T-513
69OPC-124MG
69T-124
79TCMA-22
89Pac/Leg-144
89Swell-82
91T/Arc53-290
Exh47
PM10/L-3

Bauer, Mark
85Huntsvl/BK-26

Bauer, Marlene
52Wheat

Bauer, Matt
91Bristol/ClBest-21
91Bristol/ProC-3595

Bauer, Peter
(Pete)
86LitFalls-2
87Lynch-14
88Clmbia/GS-2
89Jacks/GS-23
90Osceola/Star-3
91Jacks/LineD-554
91Jacks/ProC-917

Bauer, Phil
76Clinton
79AppFx-14

Bauers, Russell
40PB-219
52Park-4

Baum, Jeff
88AppFx/ProC-158

Bauman, Brad
81Shrev-10

Baumann, Charles John
(Paddy)
T207

Baumann, David
91VeroB/ClBest-2
91VeroB/ProC-763
91Yakima/ClBest-21

Baumann, Frank
58T-167
59T-161
60T-306
61P-34
61T-46LL
61T-550
62T-161
63T-381
64T-453
65OPC-161
65T-161

Baumer, James Sloan
(Jim)
61T-292

Baumgardner, George
14CJ-131
15CJ-131
T222

Baumgarten, Ross
79T-704R
80T-138
81D-41
81OPC-328
81T-398
82D-104
82F-337
82OPC-322
82T-563
82T/Tr-3T
83F-302
83T-97

Baumgartner, John E.
No Cards.

Baumholtz, Frank C.
49B-21
52B-195
52T-225
54B-221
54RH
54T-60
55B-227
55T-172
56T-274
Exh47
R423-3

Baur, Al
89Martins/Star-1
90Batavia/ProC-3056

Bauta, Ed
61Union
62T-344
63T-336
91WIZMets-25

Bautista, Antonio
77WHave

Bautista, Benny
85Newar-12
87Hagers-6

Bautista, Dan
90Bristol/ProC-3154
91Fayette/ClBest-23
91Fayette/ProC-1182

Bautista, German
86Miami-1

Bautista, Hector
90Wausau/Best-25
90Wausau/ProC-2139
90Wausau/Star-2

Bautista, Jose
85Lynch-9
88D/Rook-41
88F/Up-U1
88French-48
88T/Tr-10T
89B-3
89D-451
89F-608
89French-48
89S-573
89T-469
89T/St-229
89UD-574
90Publint/St-574
90RochR/CMC-20
90RochR/ProC-696
90UD-8
91Crown/Orio-23
92F-2

Bautista, Ramon
80Clinton-4
82Clinton-13
83Clinton/LF-8
88Watlo/ProC-676
89Kinston/Star-2
90Kinston/Team-16
91Canton/LineD-76
91Canton/ProC-983

Bavasi, Buzzie
77Padre/SchCd-4GM

Baxes, Jim
59T-547
60T-318
90Target-38

Baxes, Michael
(Mike)
58T-302
59T-381

Baxter, Bob
90James/Pucko-14
91Rockford/ClBest-1
91Rockford/ProC-2037

Baxter, Jim
88Watlo/ProC-671
89Lakeland/Star-2
91London/LineD-402
91Memphis/ProC-657

Baxter, John
No Cards.

Baxter, William
C46-80

Bay, Harry Elbert
E107
T206
T213/brown
WG2-3

Bayer, Chris
86Columbia-5

Bayer, Christopher A.
(Burley)
No Cards.

Bayless, Harry Owen
(Dick)
E254
E270/1

Baylor, Don Edward
71OPC-709R
71T-709R
72OPC-474R
72T-474R
73JP
73OPC-384
73T-384
74OPC-187
74T-187
74T/St-121
75OPC-382
75T-382
75T/M-382
76Ho-118
76OPC-125
76SSPC-394
76T-125
77Ho-129
77OPC-133
77T-462
78OPC-173
78T-48
79Ho-63
79OPC-335
79T-635
80BK/PHR-12
80K-56
80OPC-150
80T-285
80T-203LL
80T/S-9
81D-413
81F-271
81F/St-122
81K-15
81OPC-309
81T-580
81T/HT
81T/St-51
82D-493
82F-451
82F/St-220
82KMart-35
82OPC-234
82T-415
82T/St-158
83D-493
83Drake-1
83F-77
83K-29
83OPC-105
83T-105
83T/St-40
83T/Tr-8
84D-152
84Drake-1
84F-119
84F/St-45
85FunFood/Pin-39
84Nes/792-335
84Nes/792-486TL
84OPC-335
84T-335
84T/St-320
85D-173
85D/HL-35
85Drake-3
85F-121
85F/St-49
85Leaf-146
85OPC-70
85T-70
85T/St-311
86D-347
86F-631M
86F-99
86F/St-3
86F/Up-U10
86OPC-184
86Sf-57M
86T-765
86T/St-300
86T/Tr-6T
86Woolwth-2
87Classic-14
87D-339
87D/OD-186
87F-28
87F/GameWin-2
87F/Hottest-4
87F/Mini-6
87F/St-7
87KayBee-3
87Leaf-232
87OPC-230
87OPC-A
87Sf-163
87Seven-E2
87T-230
87T-A
87T/Board-17
87T/Gloss60-27
87T/St-252
88D/A's/Bk-NEW
88F-2
88F/St-S1
88F/WS-11
88Mother/A's-8
88OPC-A
88S-250
88S/Tr-55T
88T-545
88T/Big-162
88T/St-10
88T/Tr-11T
88T/WaxBox-A
88Woolwth-1
88Woolwth-29
89T/Ames-3
89F-1
89S-205
89Smok/Angels-13
89T-673
89UD-601
90BBWit-5
90Brewer/MillB-32CO
90Pac/Legend-6
90Pol/Brew-x
91Brewer/MillB-32CO
91Crown/Orio-24
91K/3D-14
91LineD-14
91Pol/Brew-x
91Swell/Great-6

Bayne, William
E120

Beach, Jackson S.
(Jack)
No Cards.

Beacom, Chris
89StCath/ProC-2085
90Dunedin/Star-1

Beahan, Scott
83Greens-2

Beal, Sally
78Newar-GM

Beal, Tony
86NewBrit-2

Beall, John Woolf
(Johnny)
No Cards.

Beall, Mike
89AppFx/ProC-864
90BBCity/Star-2

Beall, Robert Brooks
(Bob)
76SSPC-21
79T-222
80Richm-19
81Portl-7

Beals, Bryan
88GreatF-19
89Bakers/Cal-197
90Bakers/Cal-257

Beals, Greg
91Pittsfld/ClBest-2
91Pittsfld/ProC-3425

Beals, Thomas L.
(Tommy)
No Cards.

Beamesderfer, Kurt
87CharlO/WBTV-19

Beamon, Charles Alon.
(Charlie)
59T-192
60HenryH-30
91Crown/Orio-25

Beamon, Charles Alph.
77SanJose-9
78SanJose-12
79Spokane-6
80Spokane-24
80T-672R
81Syrac-12
82Syrac-15

Beamon, Nick
(Pepper)
79WHave-22M
80WHave-18

Beams, Mike
88Ashvl/ProC-1054
88AubAs/ProC-1962
89Ashvl/ProC-968
90Osceola/Star-4

91NewBrit/LineD-451
91NewBrit/ProC-362
Bean, Billy
87Portl-5
88T-267
88Toledo/CMC-12
88Toledo/ProC-595
89Classic-33
89S/HotRook-19
89Toledo/ProC-772
90Albuq/CMC-25
90Albuq/ProC-356
90Albuq/Trib-1
90Target-39
91Albuq/LineD-1
91Albuq/ProC-1152
Bean, Joseph William
(Joe)
No Cards.
Bean, Kenneth
88Martins/Star-2
89Martins/Star-2
Beanblossom, Brad
88CapeCod/Sum-147
91StPete/ClBest-17
91StPete/ProC-2280
Beane, William Lamar
(Billy)
82Jacks-19
84Jacks-17
85IntLgAS-7
85Tidew-14
86D-647
86F/Up-U11
87F-535
87T-114
87Toledo-26
91WIZMets-26
Beard, Cramer T.
(Ted)
51B-308
52T-150
Beard, Dave
80Ogden-15
81T-96R
81Tacoma-24
82F-87
83D-113
83F-514
83Granny-33
83T-102
84D-218
84F-438
84F/X-9
84Mother/Mar-11
84Nes/792-513
84OPC-149
84T-513
84T/St-336
84T/Tr-8
85F-483
85Maine-2
85T-232
86Richm-2
88Toledo/CMC-1
88Toledo/ProC-586
89Toledo/CMC-10
89Toledo/ProC-777
Beard, Garrett
89Salem/Team-6
90Yakima/Team-1
Beard, Mike
76OPC-53
76T-53
Beard, Oliver Perry
(Ollie)
N172
Beard, Ralph
55B-206
Bearden, Gene
46Remar-17
49B-57
50NumNum
51B-284
52B-173
52NTea
52T-229
53Exh/Can-3
55B-93
79TCMA-222
Exh47
Beardman, Larry
84Madis/Pol-24
Beardsley, Chris
89PalmSp/Cal-58
Beare, Gary Ray
78T-516
79OkCty
Bearnarth, Larry
63T-386R
64T-527
65OPC-258
65T-258
66T-464
78TCMA-61
80Memphis-8
86Provigo-14CO
91WIZMets-27
Bearse, Kevin
88CLAS/Star-24
88Kinston/Star-2
89Canton/Best-1
89Canton/ProC-1306
90B-330
90F/Up-U91
90UD/Ext-715
91F-361
91Indianap/LineD-177
91Indianap/ProC-453
91T/90Debut-12
Beasley, Andy
90Hamil/Star-4
91Spring/ClBest-6
91Spring/ProC-743
Beasley, Bud
46Sunbeam
47Signal
47Sunbeam
Beasley, Chris
86Water-2
87Wmsprt-22
89PalmSp/ProC-488
90Edmon/CMC-4
90Edmon/ProC-509
91Edmon/ProC-1508
92F-54
92T/91Debut-12
92UD-614
Beasley, Lewis Paige
(Lew)
77Tucson
Beasley, Tony
89Erie/Star-1
90Freder/Team-4
91CLAS/ProC-CAR5
91Freder/ClBest-16
91Freder/ProC-2370
Beatin, Ebenezer
N172
Beatle, David
(Dave)
No Cards.
Beattie, Burt
87Kenosha-8
Beattie, Jim
77WHave
79BK/Y-7
79Colum-8
79OPC-86
79T-179
80T-334
81D-166
81Spokane-29
81T-443
82D-478
82T-22
83D-176
83F-472
83OPC-191
83T-675
83T-711
84D-191
84F-605
84Mother/Mar-12
84Nes/792-288
84OPC-288
84T-288
84T/St-346
85D-313
85F-484
85Leaf-85
85Mother/Mar-15
85OPC-303
85T-505
85T/St-334
86D-196
86F-458
86Mother/Mar-27
86T-729
87T-117
Beatty, Aloysius D.
(Des)
No Cards.
Beatty, Blaine
87Hagers-12
88Jacks/GS-15
88TexLgAS/GS-18
89Tidew/CMC-9
89Tidew/ProC-1964
90B-130
90F-197
90HagersDG/Best-2
90S-632
90T/89Debut-11
90T/TVMets-7
90UD-23
91Tidew/LineD-552
91Tidew/ProC-2500
91WIZMets-28
92S/II-843
Beatty, Gary
91Batavia/ClBest-30TR
Beauchamp, James E.
(Jim)
62Kahn/Atl
63Pep/Tul
64T-492R
65T-409R
66OPC-84R
66T-84R
67T-307
69T-613
71MLB/St-266
71OPC-322
71T-322
72T-594
73OPC-137
73T-137
74OPC-424
74T-424
78Charl
79Charl-2
80Indianap-2MG
81Indianap-2MG
82Syrac-26MG
83Syrac-1MG
84Syrac-1MG
86Greenvl/Team-3MG
87Greenvl/Best-1MG
87SLAS-22
88Richm-9MG
88Richm/CMC-23MG
88Richm/ProC-15MG
89AAA/ProC-53MG
89Richm/Bob-1MG
89Richm/CMC-25MG
89Richm/Ko-9MG
89Richm/ProC-822MG
90Richm/CMC-7MG
90Richm/ProC-274MG
90Richm/Team-3MG
90Richm25Ann/Team-4
91WIZMets-29
Beauchamp, Kash
86Knoxvl-1
87Syrac/TCMA-29
88Knoxvl/Best-9
89Richm/Bob-2
89Richm/CMC-23
89Richm/Ko-7
89Richm/ProC-836
90Phoenix/CMC-17
90Phoenix/ProC-21
Beaulac, Joe
90Miami/II/Star-2
Beaumont, Clarence H.
(Ginger)
E107
E254
M116
T206
WG3-2
Beavers, Mark
85Anchora-3
86Cram/PCL-55
87Madis-20
88Modesto/Cal-61
89River/Best-2
89River/Cal-23
89River/ProC-1390
BeBop, Spec
76Laugh/Clown-20
Bechtel, George A.
No Cards.
Beck, Brian
90CharRain/Best-4
90CharRain/ProC-2050
91CharRain/ClBest-20
91CharRain/ProC-106
Beck, Clyde Eugene
29Exh/4-5
Beck, Dion
85Bend/Cram-1
87Reading-8
Beck, Ervin Thomas
(Erve)
90Target-900
E107
Beck, Frederick T.
(Fred)
M116
T205
T206
Beck, Rich
66T-234R
Beck, Rod
88Clinton/ProC-695
88MidwLAS/GS-5
89SanJose/Best-2
89SanJose/Cal-209
89SanJose/ProC-459
89SanJose/Star-1
89Star/Wax-82
90Shrev/ProC-1435
90Shrev/Star-2
91Phoenix/LineD-378
91Phoenix/ProC-59
92D/II-461
92F-627
92S/II-746
92T/91Debut-13
Beck, Walter
(Boom Boom)
34G-50
40PB-217
90Target-40
Beck, Wynn
90Madison/Best-28
90Madison/ProC-2271
Beck, Zinn Bertram
11Helmar-140
D329-12
M101/4-12
S74-42
Beckendorf, Henry W.
(Heinie)
09Buster/Pin-2
M116
Becker, Beals
10Domino-9
11Helmar-121
12Sweet/Pin-107
14CJ-96
14Piedmont/St-3
15CJ-96
16FleischBrd-8
E254
S74-80
T202
T205
T206
T207
T213/brown
Becker, Gregory
87StPete-23
88MidwLAS/GS-27
88Spring/Best-5
89Star/Wax-47
89StPete/Star-2
Becker, Heinz R.
No Cards.
Becker, Joseph Edward
(Joe)
52Park-1
55Gol/Dodg-3
60T-463CO
79TCMA-187
Becker, Martin Henry
(Marty)
No Cards.
Becker, Rich
90Elizab/Star-1
91Kenosha/ClBest-25
91Kenosha/ProC-2086
91Single/ClBest-345
Becker, Tim
87FtLaud-1
88Albany/ProC-1341
89Albany/Best-20
89Albany/ProC-315
89Albany/Star-2
Becker, Tom
88LitFalls/Pucko-4
Beckert, Glenn Alfred
65T-549R
66T-232
67T-296
68OPC-101
68T-101
69Kelly/Pin-3
69MB-22
69MLB/St-119
69OPC-171
69Sunoco/Pin-2
69T-171
69T/St-12
70Dunkin-2
70K-43
70MLB/St-14
70OPC-480
70T-480
71K-71
71MD
71MLB/St-26
71OPC-390
71T-390
71T/Coins-143
71T/S-50
72K-24
72MB-29
72OPC-45
72OPC-46IA
72OPC-85LL
72T-45
72T-46A
72T-85LL
73OPC-440
73T-440
74McDon
74OPC-241
74T-241
74T/St-11
75Ho-103
75Ho/Twink-103
75OPC-484
75T-484
75T/M-484
89Pac/Leg-142
89Swell-116
Beckett, Robbie
90Classic/DP-25
91B-655
91CharRain/ClBest-1
91CharRain/ProC-87
91S-673FDP
91Single/ClBest-162
Beckley, Jacob Peter
(Jake)
80SSPC/HOF
E107
N172
T206
WG3-3
Beckman, Bernie
74Albuq/Team-2
83Syrac-2
Beckman, Bill
92Conlon/Sport-623
Beckwith, Joe
78Cr/PCL-36
79Albuq-20
80Albuq-2
80Pol/Dodg-27
80T-679R
81Pol/Dodg-27
81T-231
82Albuq-1
83F-202
83Pol/Dodg-27
84D-337
84F-97
84F/X-10
84Nes/792-454
84T-454

84T/Tr-9
85D-541
85F-197
85T-77
86F-2
86Syrac-4
86T-562
90Target-41
Beckwith, John
74Laugh/Black-6
86Negro/Frit-67
90Negro/Star-22
Becquer, Julio V.
58T-458
59T-93
60L-43
60T-271
61T-329
Bedell, Howard W.
61T-353
62Salada-217
62Shirriff-217
62T-76
Bedell, Jeff
86FtMyr-3
Bedford, James Elred
(Jim)
No Cards.
Bedrosian, Dave
76Wausau
Bedrosian, Steve
79Savan-14
81Richm-12
82BK/Lids-2
82D-401
82Pol/Atl-32
82T-502R
82T/Tr-4T
83D-173
83F-129
83OPC-157
83Pol/Atl-32
83T-157
84D-565
84F-171
84Nes/792-365
84OPC-365
84Pol/Atl-32
84T-365
84T/St-38
85D-628
85F-319
85Ho/Braves-3
85Leaf-51
85OPC-25
85Pol/Atl-32
85Seven-6S
85T-25
85T/St-23
86CIGNA-11
86D-199
86F-508
86F/Up-U12
86OPC-181
86Phill/TastyK-40
86T-648
86T/St-40
86T/Tr-7T
87D-185
87D/HL-9
87F-170
87F/Lim-3
87F/Slug-M1
87F/St-8
87OPC-233
87Phill/TastyK-40
87RedFoley/St-98
87Sf-110
87Smok/NL-7
87T-736
87T/Mini-27
87T/St-124
88Classic/Blue-222
88D-62
88D/AS-61
88D/Best-16
88F-298
88F-627M
88F/AwardWin-1
88F/Mini-98
88F/SS-1
88F/St-107
88Leaf-82
88MSA/Disc-18
88Nestle-25
88OPC-344
88OPC-B
88Panini/St-351
88Panini/St-440
88Phill/TastyK-3
88S-161
88S-656
88Sf-70
88Sf-222M
88T-407
88T-440
88T/Big-23
88T/Coins-34
88T/Gloss60-28
88T/Mini-64
88T/Revco-11
88T/St-116
88T/St-6
88T/St/Backs-31
88T/UK-2
88T/WaxBox-B
88Woolwth-10
89B-395
89Classic-34
89D-24DK
89D-75
89D/Best-303
89D/DKsuper-24DK
89F-562
89F/BBMVP's-1
89Panini/St-145
89Phill/TastyK-1
89S-260
89S/HotStar-29
89S/Tr-49
89Sf-63
89T-20
89T/Big-137
89T/LJN-96
89T/St-112
89T/Tr-8T
89Tetley/Discs-15
89UD-511
90B-226
90Classic-62
90D-295
90D/BestNL-99
90F-50
90Leaf/I-3
90Mother/Giant-6
90OPC-310
90Panini/St-364
90Publint/St-232
90S-379
90S/100St-31
90Sf-104
90T-310
90T/Big-275
90T/St-86
90UD-618
91B-317
91D-207
91F-254
91Leaf/II-505
91Leaf/Stud-82
91OPC-125
91OPC/Premier-5
91RedFoley/St-7
91S-459
91S/RookTr-14T
91T-125
91T/StClub/II-531
91T/Tr-6T
91UD-422
91UD/Ext-738
92D/I-184
92F-197
92S/I-17
92T-267
92UD-622
Beebe, Fred
12Sweet/Pin-95
C46-54
E270/2
M116
T204
Beecher, Edward H.
(Ed)
N284
Beecroft, Mike
82BirmB-6
Beeler, Joseph Sam
(Jodie)
No Cards.
Beeler, Pete
87Tampa-27
88Cedar/ProC-1147
88MidwLAS/GS-8
89Cedar/Star-25
89Chatt/Best-11
89Chatt/GS-4
91Chatt/LineD-154
91Nashvl/ProC-2158
Beene, Andy
82ElPaso-14
84Cram/PCL-26
Beene, Fred
70OPC-121R
70T-121R
71MLB/St-219
73OPC-573
73T-573
74OPC-274
74T-274
75OPC-181
75T-181
75T/M-181
76SSPC-504
79OkCty
80Tidew-14
91Crown/Orio-26
Beene, Steve
76Watlo
77DaytB
Beer, Darrin
89Geneva/ProC-1863
Beerbower, Dan
76QuadC
Befort, Curt
87Clearw-3
Beggs, Joe
Exh47
W711/2
Begley, James L.
(Jim)
No Cards.
Begue, Roger
82Lynch-18
Behel, Steven A. D.
(Steve)
N172/ST
Behenna, Rick
81Durham-15
83Pol/Atl-49
84D-346
85Polar/Ind-32
Behney, Mel
72OPC-524R
72T-524R
73OPC-602R
73T-602R
Behnsch, Bobby
87Clearw-7
Behny, Mark
86Erie-3
87Savan-24
88Savan/ProC-339
Behrend, Mike
83Erie-11
84Savan-26
Behrens, Scott
91Idaho/ProC-4320
91Pulaski/ClBest-16
91Pulaski/ProC-3995
Behrman, Henry
(Hank)
49Eureka-101
50Remar
90Target-42
Beitey, Dan
75Cedar
Beja, Aaron
91Fayette/ClBest-25
Bejma, Aloysius Frank
(Ollie)
35BU-55
35BU-93
R312/M
Belan, Lance
86PrWill-2
Belanger, Lee
82Orlan-2
83Visalia/LF-1
Belanger, Mark Henry
67T-558R
68Coke
68Dexter-10
68OPC-118
68T-118
69T-299
69T/St-121
70MLB/St-145
70T-615
71MLB/St-289
71OPC-99
71T-99
72OPC-224WS
72OPC-456
72T-456
73JP
73OPC-253
73T-253
74OPC-329
74T-329
74T/St-122
75OPC-74
75T-74
75T/M-74
76OPC-505
76T-505
77BurgChef-38
77Ho-71
77OPC-154
77T-135
78OPC-125
78T-315
79OPC-27
79T-65
80OPC-217
80T-425
81D-472
81F-175
81F/St-39
81T-641
82F-158
82F/St-148
82OPC-42
82Pol/Dodg-8
82T-776
82T/Tr-5T
83D-514
83T-273
90Target-43
91Crown/Orio-27
Belardi, Carroll W.
(Wayne)
55B-36
79TCMA-110
90Target-44
Belbru, Juan
89Savan/ProC-356
90Hamil/Star-5
Belcher, Glenn
87Fayette-27
88Fayette/ProC-1080
89Fayette/ProC-1568
Belcher, Kevin
88Gaston/ProC-1010
89Gaston/ProC-1004
89Gaston/Star-2
89SALAS/GS-30
90A&AASingle/ProC-67
90Tulsa/ProC-1166
91D-46RR
91F-280
91Leaf/Stud-121
91OkCty/LineD-302
91OkCty/ProC-189
91S-714RP
91S/Rook40-15
91T/90Debut-13
91UD-26
Belcher, Tim
84Madis/Pol-9
85Huntsvl/BK-31
85T-281FDP
87Tacoma-21
88D-587
88D/Best-10
88D/Rook-28
88F-509
88Mother/Dodg-23
88Pol/Dodg-49M
88S/Tr-101T
88T/Tr-12T
89B-336
89Bz-1
89Classic-57
89D-203
89D/Best-234
89F-54
89F/Superstar-3
89F/WS-2
89KMart/DT-9
89Mother/Dodg-23
89OPC-177
89Panini/St-21
89Panini/St-95
89Pol/Dodg-25
89S-418
89S/HotRook-94
89S/YS/I-36
89Sf-121
89T-456
89T/Big-145
89T/Gloss60-30
89T/JumboR-3
89T/St-317
89ToysRUs-3
89UD-648
89Woolwth-19
89Woolwth-29
90B-85
90D-79
90D/BestNL-17
90F-389
90F/AwardWin-2
90F/LL-2
90F/WaxBox-C2
90Leaf/I-200
90Mother/Dodg-9
90OPC-173
90Panini/St-281
90Pol/Dodg-49
90Publint/St-2
90Publint/St-608
90S-126
90T-173
90T/Big-246
90T/Coins-38
90T/Mini-57
90Target-45
90UD-547
91B-605
91BBBest/Aces-3
91D-70
91F-194
91F/Ultra-159
91Leaf/II-508
91Mother/Dodg-9
91OPC-25
91Pol/Dodg-49
91S-187
91T-25
91T/StClub/I-152
91UD-576
92D/I-78
92F-447
92S/I-368
92T-688
92UD-668
Belcik, Keith
84LitFalls-2
Belden, Ira Allison
No Cards.
Belen, Lance
85PrWill-14
87Harris-11
88Harris/ProC-844
Belen, Mattie
89Bluefld/Star-4
Belford, John
89Welland/Pucko-35M
Belinda, Stan
87Macon-17
88CLAS/Star-3
88Salem/Star-2
89AAA/CMC-13
89Harris/ProC-305
89Harris/Star-3
90BuffB/CMC-1
90BuffB/ProC-365
90F/Up-U48
90Leaf/II-486
90OPC-354
90S-634
90T-354
90T/89Debut-12
90UD/Ext-759
91D-699
91F-30
91F/Ultra-273

91OPC-522
91S-296
91S/100RisSt-8
91T-522
91T/StClub/II-453
91UD-161
92D/II-501
92F-548
92S/I-325
92T-466
92UD-202

Belinskas, Dan
86Cedar/TCMA-1

Belinsky, Bo
62T-592R
63T-33
64T-315
65OPC-225
65T-225
66T-506
67T-447
69T-366
89Pac/Leg-130
89Swell-16

Belk, Chuck
79Wisco-20

Bell, Bobby
86PalmSp-2
86PalmSp/Smok-5
87PalmSp-25
88PalmSp/ProC-1459

Bell, Brent
91Martins/ClBest-14
91Martins/ProC-3457

Bell, Cliff
86Negro/Frit-100

Bell, David
90Spring/Best-3
91Collnd/ClBest-22
91Collnd/ProC-1489
91Single/ClBest-104

Bell, David Gus
(Buddy)
73OPC-31
73T-31
74K-10
74OPC-257
74T-257
74T/DE-37
74T/St-161
75Ho-30
75Ho/Twink-30
75OPC-38
75T-38
75T/M-38
76Ho-95
76OPC-358
76OPC-66FS
76SSPC-517
76T-358
76T-66FS
77BurgChef-57
77Ho-69
77OPC-86
77Pep-11
77T-590
77T/CS-2
78Ho-15
78OPC-234
78PapaG/Disc-34
78T-280
78Tastee/Discs-1
78Wiffle/Discs-2
79Ho-147
79K-14
79OPC-367
79T-690
80K-53
80OPC-107
80T-190
80T-47
81D-145
81F-625
81F/St-11
81K-64
81MSA/Disc-1
81OPC-66
81T-475
81T/HT
81T/Nat/Super-1
81T/SO-21
81T/St-130
82D-23DK
82D-368
82Drake-2
82F-313
82F/St-172
82F/St-239
82K-33
82OPC-50
82T-50
82T/St-238
83D-215
83D/AAS-40
83F-562
83F-632M
83K-12
83OPC-330
83Rangers-25
83T-330
83T-412
83T/Gloss40-9
83T/St-119
84D-56
84D/AAS-12
84F-413
85FunFood/Pin-76
84Nes/792-37TL
84Nes/792-665
84OPC-347
84Rangers-25
84Seven-11W
84T-665
84T/St-351
85D-56
85D/AAS-11
85F-556
85F/LimEd-1
85F/St-7
85GenMills-13
85Leaf-174
85OPC-176
85Rangers-25
85T-131FS
85T-745
85T/St-347
85T/Super-53
85ThomMc/Discs-2
86D-447
86F-172
86F/Mini-37
86OPC-285
86Sf-151
86T-285
86T/St-139
86TexGold-25
86TrueVal-20
87D-556
87D/OD-196
87F-193
87Kahn-25
87Leaf-169
87OPC-104
87RedFoley/St-38
87Sf-141
87T-545
87T/Board-21
87T/St-143
88D-206
88F-227
88Jiffy-1
88Leaf-192
88Nestle-30
88OPC-130
88Panini/St-279
88RedFoley/St-5
88S-99
88Sf-147
88T-130
88T/St-138
88T/Tr-13T
89B-229
89F-352
89Mother/R-9
89OPC-92
89S-610
89Smok/R-3
89T-461
89T/Big-270
89T/St-18
89UD-112
90ColoSp/ProC-55CO
90Pac/Legend-74
90PublInt/St-404
91Swell/Great-7

Bell, David Russell
(Gus)
51B-40
51T/RB-17
52T-170
53B/BW-1
53NB
53T-118
54B-124
54RH
54RM-NL19
55B-243
55Kahn
55RFG-16
55RM-NL23
56Kahn
56T-162
57Kahn
57Sohio/Reds-2
57T-180
58Kahn
58T-75
59Kahn
59T-365
60Kahn
60MacGregor-3
60T-235
60T-352
61Kahn
61P-186
61T-215
61T-25
61T/St-14
62J-120
62P-120
62P/Can-120
62Salada-158A
62Salada-158B
62Shirriff-158
62T-408
62T/St-153
63T-547
64T-534
76OPC-66FS
76T-66FS
79TCMA-89
85T-131FS
88Pac/Leg-65
91T/Arc53-118
91WIZMets-30
PM10/Sm-8

Bell, Derek
88Myrtle/ProC-1171
88OPC-311
88SALAS/GS-20
89Knoxvl/Best-1
89Knoxvl/ProC-1149
89Knoxvl/Star-1
90S/Tr-81T
90Syrac/CMC-14
90Syrac/ProC-582
90Syrac/Team-2
91AAAGame/ProC-AAA42
91Classic/III-28
91D-32RR
91F-168
91S/100RisSt-32
91S/ToroBJ-20
91Syrac/LineD-501
91Syrac/ProC-2491
91T/Tr-7T
91UD/FinalEd-26F
92Classic/I-11
92D/II-581
92F-324
92S/100RisSt-64
92S/I-402
92T-121
92T/91Debut-14
92UD-26SR

Bell, Eric
84Newar-2
87D-39RR
87D/Rook-2
87F/Up-U2
87French-45
87Leaf-39RR
87Sf/Rook-1
87T/Tr-3T
88Classic/Red-193
88D-125
88F-555
88OPC-383
88Panini/St-4
88RochR/Team-2
88RochR/CMC-2
88RochR/ProC-194
88S-101
88S/YS/II-38
88T-383
88T/St-224
90HagersDG/Best-3
90RochR/ProC-697
91Canton/LineD-77
91Canton/ProC-971
91Crown/Orio-28

Bell, Fern Lee
No Cards.

Bell, Frank Gustav
No Cards.

Bell, Gary
59Kahn
59T-327
60Kahn
60T-441
61Kahn
61P-58
61T-274
62Kahn
62Salada-213
62Shirriff-213
62Sugar-2
62T-273
62T/bucks
63Sugar-2
63T-129
64T-234
65T-424
66T-525
67T-479
68Coke
68Dexter-11
68OPC-43
68T-43
69MB-23
69MLB/St-93
69T-377
69T/St-223
89Pac/Leg-213

Bell, George G.
10Domino-10
11Helmar-83
12Sweet/Pin-70A
12Sweet/Pin-70B
D304
E254
E90/1
M116
S74-49
T20
T204
T205
T3-79

Bell, Greg
86WinSalem-1
87Pittsfld-2

Bell, Herman
(Hi)
34G-52
92Conlon/Sport-632

Bell, James
(Cool Papa)
74Laugh/Black-24
80SSPC/HOF
83D/HOF-25
86Negro/Frit-3
86Negro/Frit-90
87Leaf/SpecOlym-H12
88Conlon/HardC-1
88Conlon/NegAS-1
88Negro/Duques-14
89Kahn/Coop-1
90Negro/Star-28

Bell, Jay
85Visalia-8
86Water-4
87BuffB-4
88D-637
88D/Best-61
88F-602
88Gator-16
88T-637
89AAA/ProC-7
89BuffB/CMC-4
89BuffB/ProC-1679
89D-350
89S-352
89T-144
89UD-489
89VFJuice-3
90B-174
90D-488
90D/BestNL-136
90F-459
90Homer/Pirate-4
90Leaf/I-248
90OPC-523
90OPC-724
90Panini/St-321
90RochR/CMC-13
90RochR/ProC-707
90S-563
90S/YS/II-12
90T-523
90T/89Debut-13
90UD-517
91B-522
91B-96
91Crown/Orio-29
91D-289
91F-31
91F-468
91F/Ultra-274
91Leaf/I-130
91Leaf/I-262
91Leaf/Stud-221
91Leaf/StudPrev-1
91OPC-293
91OPC/Premier-7
91Panini/FrSt-118
91Panini/St-110
91S-323
91S/100RisSt-59
91T-293
91T/StClub/I-84
91UD-183
91UD/FinalEd-59F
92Classic/I-12
92D/DK-DK17
92D/I-100
92D/II-479
92F-3
92F-549
92S/I-180
92S/II-646
92T-52
92T-779
92UD-115

Bell, Jerry
72OPC-162R
72T-162R
73OPC-92
73T-92
74OPC-261
74T-261
74T/St-191
75SanAn

Bell, Jorge Antonio
(George)
82D-54
82F-609
82OPC-254
82Syrac-20
82T-254
83Syrac-21
84D-73
84F-148
85FunFood/Pin-113
84Nes/792-278
84OPC-278
84T-278
84Tor/Fire-5
85D-146
85F-100
85F/St-39
85Leaf-248
85OPC-59
85OPC/Post-18
85T-698
85T/St-360
85Tor/Fire-5
86Ault-11
86D-4
86D-71
86D/DKsuper-4
86F-53
86F/Mini-13
86Leaf-4DK
86OPC-338
86OPC-A
86Sf-102
86T-338
86T-718AS

86T/Gloss60-47
86T/St-187
86T/Super-10
86T/WaxBox-A
86Tor/Fire-4
87Classic-56
87D-271
87D/OD-39
87F-220
87F/AS-9
87F/AwardWin-2
87F/GameWin-3
87F/Lim-4
87F/Mini-7
87F/Slug-3
87F/St-9
87Ho/St-3
87Kraft-43
87Leaf-184
87OPC-12
87Sf-51
87Sf-80M
87T-612AS
87T-681
87T/Coins-3
87T/Gloss60-45
87T/Mini-74
87T/St-193
87Tor/Fire-2
88Bz-1
88ChefBoy-4
88Classic/Blue-242
88D-656
88D-BC19
88D/AS-6
88D/Best-31
88D/PopUp-6
88Drake-22
88F-103
88F-623M
88F/AS-5
88F/AwardWin-2
88F/BB/AS-1
88F/BB/MVP-1
88F/Excit-3
88F/Hottest-1
88F/LL-1
88F/Mini-59
88F/RecSet-2
88F/Slug-1
88F/SS-2
88F/St-71
88F/TL-1
88FanSam-7
88Ho/Disc-22
88KayBee-1
88KMart-1
88Leaf-213CG
88Leaf-214MVP
88Leaf-254
88Nestle-34
88OPC-173
88Panini/St-224
88Panini/St-230M
88RedFoley/St-6
88S-540
88S/WaxBox-6
88Sf-4
88T-390AS
88T-590
88T/Big-15
88T/Coins-1
88T/Gloss22-6
88T/Gloss60-31
88T/Mini-37
88T/Revco-18
88T/RiteAid-26
88T/St-158
88T/St-188
88T/St/Backs-47
88T/UK-3
88Tor/Fire-11
88Woolwth-9
89T/Ames-4
89B-256
89Classic-43
89D-149
89D/Best-272
89F-226
89F/BBAS-2
89F/BBMVP's-2
89F/Heroes-1
89KMart/DT-17
89OPC-50
89Panini/St-472
89RedFoley/St-7
89S-347
89S/HotStar-91
89Sf-25
89T-1RB
89T-50
89T/Big-318
89T/Gloss60-27
89T/LJN-46
89T/Mini-75
89T/St-1
89T/St-193
89T/UK-3
89Tor/Fire-11
89UD-255
89Woolwth-7
90B-515
90Classic-84
90D-206
90D/BestAL-139
90D/Bon/MVP-BC13
90D/Learning-25
90F-628
90F-76
90F/BBMVP-1
90F/LL-3
90Holsum/Discs-1
90HotPlay/St-1
90Leaf/I-185
90MLBPA/Pins-67
90OPC-170
90Panini/St-180
90PublInt/St-276
90PublInt/St-509
90S-286
90S/100St-27
90S/McDon-20
90Sf-17
90T-170
90T/Ames-22
90T/Big-153
90T/Coins-5
90T/DH-3
90T/Gloss60-24
90T/HillsHM-12
90T/Mini-41
90T/St-192
90T/TVAS-21
90Target-46
90Tetley/Discs-9
90Tor/BlueJ-11
90UD-127
90UD-95TC
90USPlayC/AS-12C
90Windwlk/Discs-6
91B-418
91BBBest/HitM-1
91Classic/200-104
91Classic/II-T30
91Cub/Mara-11
91D-642
91F-169
91F/Ultra-55
91F/Up-U77
91Leaf/II-389
91Leaf/Stud-151
91OPC-440
91OPC/Premier-6
91Panini/FrSt-340
91Panini/St-158
91S-195
91S/100SS-40
91S/RookTr-13T
91T-440
91T/StClub/II-504
91T/Tr-8T
91UD-532
91UD/Ext-725
91UD/Ext-742
91USPlayC/AS-6S
92D/DK-DK7
92D/I-127
92F-376
92S/100SS-88
92S/I-45
92T-320
92UD-236

Bell, Juan
87Bakers-7
88BBAmer-23
88SanAn/Best-24
89B-11
89Classic/Up/2-170
89RochR/CMC-21
89RochR/ProC-1658
89UD-20
89UD/Ext-747
90S-603
90T-724

Bell, Kevin Robert
75AppFx
77T-83
78T-463
79T-662
80OPC-197
80T-379
81D-39
81F-343
81Tacoma-25
82Tacoma-13

Bell, Lenny
88Peoria/Ko-4
89WinSalem/Star-1

Bell, Lester Rowland
(Les)
25Exh-57
26Exh-57
28Yueng-58
92Conlon/Sport-651
E210-58
R309/2
W502-58

Bell, Michael
87Sumter-16
88CLAS/Star-25
88Durham/Star-1
89Greenvl/ProC-1173
89Greenvl/Star-3
89Greenvl/Best-4
89Star/Wax-34
90A&AASingle/ProC-64
90Greenvl/ProC-1134
90Greenvl/Star-3
91F-682
91Richm/LineD-427
91Richm/ProC-2575
91S-375RP
91T/90Debut-14
91UD-644
92F-350
92S/I-249

Bell, Robert
86Cram/PCL-34

Bell, Ron
77SanJose-20

Bell, Roy Chester
(Beau)
30CEA/Pin-1
37OPC-105
38Exh/4-15
38Wheat-7
39PB-136
40PB-138
V300

Bell, Rudolph Fred
(Rudy)
No Cards.

Bell, Terry
86Chatt-4
87Memphis-17
87Memphis/Best-23
88Greenvl/Best-2
88Richm-14
89Greenvl/ProC-1162
89Greenvl/Star-4
89Greenvl/Best-19

Bell, Tom
88Fresno/Cal-27
88Fresno/ProC-1248

Bell, William
86Negro/Frit-99

Bella, John
(Zeke)
59T-254

Bellacetin, Juan
85Tigres-27

Bellaman, Mike
86Water-3
87Wmsprt-10

Belle, Joey
(Albert)
88Kinston/Star-3
89Canton/Star-25
89F/Up-25
89S/Tr-106
90B-333
90Classic-100
90D-390
90F-485
90HotRook/St-6
90Leaf/I-180
90OPC-283
90S-508
90S/100Ris-9
90S/YS/I-3
90Sf-159
90T-283
90T/89Debut-14
90T/JumboR-2
90T/St-212
90ToysRUs-3
90UD-446
91B-81
91Classic/III-37
91F/Ultra-107
91F/Up-U16
91Leaf/I-239
91OPC/Premier-8
91T/StClub/II-465
91UD/Ext-764
92Classic/I-13
92D/II-500
92F-105
92S/100SS-39
92S/I-31
92T-785
92UD-137

Belliard, Rafael
83LynnP-14
87D-538
87D/OD-165
87F-602
87T-541
88F-321
88S-453
88T-221
88T/Big-175
89F-201
89OPC-119
89S-379
89T-723
89T/Big-196
89T/St-133
89UD-90
89VFJuice-6
90D-252
90F-460
90Homer/Pirate-3
90OPC-143
90PublInt/St-148
90S-520
90T-143
90UD-208
91B-578
91F-32
91F/UltraUp-U65
91F/Up-U70
91Leaf/II-453
91OPC-487
91S/RookTr-76T
91T-487
91T/StClub/II-404
91T/Tr-9T
91UD/Ext-706
92D/I-107
92F-351
92S/I-116
92T-367
92UD-510

Bellinger, Clayton
89Everett/Star-2
90Clinton/Best-1
90Clinton/ProC-2558
90Foil/Best-33
91AS/Cal-41
91SanJose/ClBest-4
91SanJose/ProC-15

Bellino, Frank
85Newar-25
86Hagers-2
87Hagers-21
88Fresno/Cal-8
89EastLDD/ProC-DD39
89Reading/Best-18
89Reading/ProC-659
89Reading/Star-2
90Foil/Best-266
90Reading/Best-20
90Reading/ProC-1230
90Reading/Star-6

Bellman, John H.
No Cards.

Bello, Duben
88Fayette/ProC-1091

Belloir, Robert E.
(Bob)
77T-312
78T-681

Bellomo, Kevin
91Everett/ClBest-28
91Everett/ProC-3926

Bellver, Juan
86Miami-2

Belmonte, Nick
91SLCity/ProC-3227MG

Belru, Juan
90Hamil/Best-26

Beltran, Angel
89Welland/Pucko-4

Beltran, Julio
78DaytB
82Miami-13

Beltran, Rigo
91Hamil/ClBest-6
91Hamil/ProC-4027

Beltre, Esteban
85Utica-12
86WPalmB-5
87Jaxvl-11
88Jaxvl/Best-17
88Jaxvl/ProC-991
89Rockford/Team-2
90Indianap/CMC-24
90Indianap/ProC-281
91Denver/LineD-128
91Denver/ProC-127
92F-75
92S/II-766
92T/91Debut-15

Beltre, Sergio
79Jacks-9
81Tidew-10

Belyeu, Randy
91Hunting/ClBest-4
91Hunting/ProC-3336

Bemis, Harry Parker
E101
E105
E107
E254
E90/1
E92
M116
T216

Ben, Elijah
83BurlR-12
83BurlR/LF-8

Benavides, Alfredo
89Chatt/Best-12
89Chatt/GS-5

Benavides, Freddie
88Cedar/ProC-1142
89Nashvl/Team-2
91B-672
91F/Up-U84
91Kahn/Reds-57
91Nashvl/LineD-252
91Nashvl/ProC-2161
91S/RookTr-98T
91UD/FinalEd-32F
92D/II-573
92F-399
92S/100RisSt-53
92T/91Debut-16

Benbow, Lou Jr.
91StCath/ClBest-3
91StCath/ProC-3401

Bench, Johnny Lee
68Kahn
68T-247R
69MB-24
69MLB/St-127
69MLBPA/Pin-35
69OPC-95
69T-430AS
69T-95
69T/St-23
70K-58
70MLB/St-25
70OPC-464AS
70T-464AS
70T-660

70T/Pl-11
70T/S-8
71Bz
71Bz/Test-29
71MD
71MLB/St-49
71MLB/St-556
71OPC-250
71OPC-64LL
71OPC-66LL
71T-250
71T-64LL
71T-66LL
71T/Coins-149
71T/GM-13
71T/S-32
71T/tatt-11
71T/tatt-11a
72MB-30
72OPC-433
72OPC-434IA
72T-433
72T-434A
73OPC-380
73OPC-62LL
73OPC-63LL
73T-380
73T-62LL
73T-63LL
73T/Comics-3
73T/Lids-5
73T/PinUps-3
74K-28
74OPC-10
74OPC-331AS
74T-10
74T-331M
74T/DE-71
74T/Puzzles-3
74T/St-21
75Ho-83
75K-7
75OPC-208MV
75OPC-210MV
75OPC-260
75OPC-308LL
75T-208MV
75T-210MV
75T-260
75T-308LL
75T/M-208MV
75T/M-210MV
75T/M-260
75T/M-308LL
76Crane-2
76Ho-22
76Ho/Twink-22
76Icee
76K-36
76MSA/Disc
76OPC-195LL
76OPC-300
76SSPC-31
76T-195LL
76T-300
77BurgChef-205
77Ho-6
77OPC-100
77Pep-44
77T-2LL
77T-3LL
77T-70
78Ho-44
78OPC-50
78T-700
78Wiffle/Discs-3
79Ho-128
79OPC-101
79T-200
79T/Comics-21
80K-52
80OPC-55
80T-100
80T/S-3
81Coke
81D-182
81D-62
81F-196
81F/St-37
81K-65
81MSA/Disc-2
81OPC-286
81PermaGr/CC-1
81Sqt-20
81T-201RB
81T-600
81T/HT
81T/Nat/Super-2
81T/SO-64
81T/St-160
82Coke/Reds
82D-400
82D-628M
82Drake-3
82F-57
82F/St-17
82K-30
82KMart-18
82KMart-22
82OPC-18
82OPC-304IA
82PermaGr/CC-1
82T-400
82T-401A
82T/St-35
83D-22DK
83D-500
83D/AAS-14
83F-584
83OPC-60
83OPC-61SV
83T-60
83T-61SV
83T/St-229
84D-660LLB
84D/Champs-51
84F-462
84F-640IA
84F/St-96
84Nes/792-6HL
84T-6HL
84T/Gloss22-22
85CircK-22
87KMart-12
87Nestle/DT-30
88Pac/Leg-110
89Kahn/Coop-2
89T/LJN-53
90BBWit-54
90OPC-664TBC
90T-664TBC

Bencomo, Omar
85Kingst-2
87Knoxvl-14
88Knoxvl/Best-17

Bender, Charles A.
(Chief)
10Domino-11
11Helmar-54
12Sweet/Pin-42A
12Sweet/Pin-42B
14CJ-19
15CJ-19
40PB-172
50Callahan
60F-7
61F-8
61GP-18
63Bz/ATG-11
69Bz/Sm
80Pac/Leg-93
80SSPC/HOF
86Conlon/1-39
91Conlon/Sport-20
92Conlon/Sport-335
BF2-83
D303
D304
D329-13
E101
E102
E103
E104
E105
E106
E107
E224
E286
E90/1
E91
E92
E93
E95
E98
L1-119
M101/4-13
M116
S74-28
S81-94
T201
T202
T204
T205
T206
T207
T208
T213/brown
T215/blue
T227
T3-80
W555
WG2-4
WG5-3
WG6-2

Bendorf, Jerry
82VeroB-17

Bene, Bill
88GreatF-1
89B-340
89Bakers/Cal-184
89Salem/Team-7
89T-84FDP
90VeroB/Star-4
91VeroB/ClBest-3
91VeroB/ProC-764

Benedetti, Don
75Cedar

Benedict, Arthur M.
(Art)
No Cards.

Benedict, Bruce Edwin
78Richm
79T-715R
80T-675
81D-208
81F-248
81Pol/Atl-20
81T-108
82BK/Lids-1
82D-375
82F-429
82OPC-168
82Pol/Atl-20
82T-424
82T/St-21
83D-299
83F-130
83OPC-204
83Pol/Atl-20
83T-521
83T/St-151
83T/St-152
83T/St-217
84D-409
84F-172
84Nes/792-255
84OPC-255
84Pol/Atl-20
84T-255
84T/St-34
85D-263
85F-320
85Ho/Braves-4
85Leaf-196
85OPC-335
85Pol/Atl-20
85T-335
85T/St-31
86D-554
86F-509
86OPC-78
86Pol/Atl-20
86T-78
87D-448
87F-512
87Smok/Atl-11
87T-186
88S-423
88T-652
89B-271
89D-475
89F-587
89OPC-353
89S-502
89T-778
89T/Big-83
89UD-121
90OPC-583
90Publint/St-108
90T-583

Benedict, Tom
91Pac/SenLg-94

Benes, Andy
88T/Tr-14T
89AAA/CMC-43
89AubAs/ProC-8
89B-448
89BBAmerAA/BPro-AA24
89T-437FDP
89T/Big-114
89TexLAS/GS-10
89Wichita/Rock-30
89Wichita/Rock/HL-3
89Wichita/Rock/Up-19
89Wichita/Rock/Up-5
90B-207
90Classic-120
90Coke/Padre-2
90D-41
90D/BestNL-47
90F-151
90HotRook/St-7
90Leaf/I-56
90OPC-193
90Padre/MagUno-9
90Panini/St-382
90S-578
90S/100Ris-69
90S/YS/II-13
90Sf-90
90T-193
90T/89Debut-15
90T/Big-260
90T/JumboR-3
90ToysRUs-4
90UD-55
91B-665
91Classic/200-85
91Classic/III-T7
91D-627
91F-524
91F/Ultra-301
91Leaf/II-275
91Leaf/Stud-242
91OPC-307
91Padre/MagRal-18
91Panini/FrSt-99
91Panini/St-92
91S-538
91T-307
91T/StClub/I-51
91UD-275
92Classic/I-14
92D/II-524
92F-599
92S/I-133
92T-682
92UD-323

Benes, Joseph Anthony
(Joe)
82Wausau-7

Benge, Brett
91Bluefld/ProC-4119
91Bluefld/ClBest-22

Benge, Ray
29Exh/4-12
31Exh/4-11
33Exh/4-6
33G-141
34G-24
35BU-11
35BU-99
35G-8A
35G-9A
90Target-47
V354-49
V355-13

Bengough, Bernard O.
(Benny)
29Exh/4-25
33G-1
49Eureka-128
91Conlon/Sport-103
R315-A2
R315-B2
V353-1

Benhardt, Chris
91Spokane/ClBest-24
91Spokane/ProC-3937

Beniquez, Juan Jose
74OPC-647
74T-647
75OPC-601
75T-601
75T/M-601
76OPC-496
76SSPC-406
76T-496
77BurgChef-27
77T-81
78T-238
79BK/Y-22
79T-478
80T-114
81D-518
81F-596
81T-306
81T/Tr-733
82D-587
82F-452
82T-572
83D-640
83F-78
83T-678
84D-207
84F-508
84Nes/792-53
84Smok/Cal-2
84T-53
85D-573
85F-294
85Smok/Cal-14
85T-226
85ThomMc/Discs-3
86D-352
86F-148
86F/St-4
86F/Up-U13
86Leaf-156
86OPC-325
86T-325
86T/St-185
86T/Tr-8T
87D-371
87F-462
87F/Up-U3
87OPC-173
87T-688
87T/Tr-4T
88F-104
88OPC-77
88OPC-C
88T-541
88T/St-12
88T/WaxBox-C
88Tor/Fire-21
89Bimbo/Discs-8
89Pac/SenLg-119
89T/SenLg-131
89TM/SenLg-6
90EliteSenLg-108
91Crown/Orio-30

Benitez, Christian
89Bluefld/Star-5
90Wausau/Best-22
90Wausau/ProC-2136
90Wausau/Star-3

Benitez, Luis
89CharWh/Best-12
89CharWh/ProC-1749
89Geneva/ProC-1870
90Geneva/ProC-3050
90Geneva/Star-1

Benitez, Manuel
86Bakers-3
87VeroB-12

Benjamin, Alfred S.
(Stan)
No Cards.

Benjamin, Bobby
91Beloit/ClBest-17
91Beloit/ProC-2114

Benjamin, Jerry
86Negro/Frit-82

Benjamin, Mike
88Shreve/ProC-1283
88TexLgAS/GS-11
89Phoenix/CMC-16
89Phoenix/ProC-1500
90F-51
90Phoenix/CMC-22
90Phoenix/ProC-15
90T/89Debut-16
90UD/Ext-750
91Classic/I-6
91D-432RR
91Leaf/Stud-252

91OPC-791
91PG&E-20
91S-345RP
91S/Rook40-25
91SFExam/Giant-2
91T-791
91T/StClub/I-143
91UD-651
92S/100RisSt-7
92S/II-649
92UD-268

Benners, Isaac
(Ike)
No Cards.

Bennes, L.D.
91Kingspt/ClBest-25TR

Bennett, Albert
88Martins/Star-3
89Batavia/ProC-1920
91Spartan/ClBest-21
91Spartan/ProC-906

Bennett, Bob
89Smok/FresnoSt-3
89Smok/FresnoSt-4

Bennett, Brad
82Spring-23

Bennett, Brian
89Ashvl/ProC-954

Bennett, Charles W.
(Charlie)
81Detroit-2
N172
N28
N284
N526
Scrapp
WG1-19

Bennett, Chris
89WPalmB/Star-3
90Foil/Best-213
90Jaxvl/Best-15
90Jaxvl/ProC-1366
91Indianap/ProC-454

Bennett, Dave
64T-561R
65T-521R

Bennett, Dennis
63T-56
64PhilBull-4
64T-396
65OPC-147
65T-147
66T-491
67T-206
67T/Test/RedSox-1
78TCMA-93
91WIZMets-31

Bennett, Doug
91Yakima/ClBest-22
91Yakima/ProC-4237

Bennett, Eric
88CapeCod/Sum-153

Bennett, Erik
89BendB/Legoe-1

Bennett, Gary
90Martins/ProC-3190
91Martins/ClBest-16
91Martins/ProC-3454

Bennett, Herschel E.
No Cards.

Bennett, James Fred
(Red)
No Cards.

Bennett, Jim
82WHave-20
83Tacoma-14
84Albany-1
87Memphis-25
87Memphis/Best-7
89Wausau/GS-17
90SanBern/Best-4
90SanBern/Cal-91
90SanBern/ProC-2625

Bennett, Jose
86Cram/PCL-104
87Wausau-11

Bennett, Joseph R.
(Joe)
No Cards.

Bennett, Justin Titus
(Pug)
No Cards.

Bennett, Keith
86Watlo-3
87Erie-13
87Wmsprt-2
88ColoSp/ProC-1535
88Watlo/ProC-684

Bennington, Jeff
91BurlAs/ClBest-23
91BurlAs/ProC-2803

Benoit, Dickens
87Everett-28
89Salinas/Cal-137
89Salinas/ProC-1827

Bensching, Bruce
91Waterlo/ClBest-2
91Waterlo/ProC-1249

Benson, Coach
80WHave-23bb

Benson, Gene
91Negro/Lewis-27

Benson, Nate
90Kgsport/Best-18
90Kgsport/Star-2

Benson, Randy
76Baton
80Syrac-18

Benson, Steve
80OrlTw-11
83ColumAst-8

Benson, Tom
89Elizab/Star-2
90Elizab/Star-2

Benson, Vernon A.
(Vern)
53T-205
61Union
73OPC-497CO
73T-497C
74OPC-236CO
74T-236C
78Syrac
79Syrac-2
80Pol/Giants-8C
91T/Arc53-205

Bentley, Blake
91Princet/ClBest-20
91Princet/ProC-3525

Bentley, John N.
(Jack)
26Exh-41
27Exh-17
W515-12
WG7-5

Benton, Alfred Lee
(Butch)
76Wausau
79Tidew-8
80Tidew-8
82Iowa-1
89Pac/SenLg-24
89T/SenLg-66
91Pac/SenLg-145
91WIZMets-32

Benton, John Alton
50NumNum
52T-374
53Mother-27
81Detroit-57

Benton, John C.
(Rube)
L1-113
S81-88
T222
W513-69
WG7-6

Benton, Lawrence
25Exh-3
26Exh-1
29Exh/4-9
33G-45
35G-8L
35G-9L
91Conlon/Sport-182
R310
R315-A3
R315-B3
R316
V353-45

Benton, Stanley
(Stan)
No Cards.

Benz, Joseph Louis
15CJ-175
BF2-8
D328-14
D350/2-13
E135-14
E300
M101/5-13
T207

Benza, Brett
82Tulsa-26
83Spring/LF-10

Benzinger, Todd
86Pawtu-2
87D/Rook-30
87Pawtu-7
87Pawtu/TCMA-13
87Sf/Rook-44
88Classic/Blue-245
88D-297
88D/Best-289
88D/RedSox/Bk-297
88F-344
88F-630M
88Leaf-111
88OPC-96
88S-546
88S/YS/I-31
88T-96
88ToysRUs-1
89B-312
89D-358
89D/Best-174
89D/Tr-47
89F-79
89F/Up-83
89Kahn/Reds-25
89OPC-188
89Panini/St-275
89S-371
89S/Tr-15
89T-493
89T/Tr-9T
89UD-184
89UD/Ext-785
90B-55
90D-257
90D/BestNL-101
90D/GSlam-8
90F-413
90Kahn/Reds-2
90Leaf/I-15
90OPC-712
90Panini/St-250
90PublInt/St-22
90S-65
90Sf-56
90T-712
90T/Big-14
90T/St-138
90UD-186
91D-640
91F-56
91F/Ultra-87
91F/UltraUp-U25
91Kahn/Reds-25
91OPC-334
91Panini/FrSt-127
91Pep/Reds-2
91S-90
91T-334
91T/StClub/I-113
91UD-280
91UD/FinalEd-41F
92D/II-536
92F-152
92S/II-563
92T-506
92UD-518

Berardino, Dick
79Elmira-21
80Elmira-29
86Pawtu-1CO
87Greens-3
90T/TVRSox-2CO

Berardino, John
(Johnny)
47TipTop
51B-245
52T-253
W753

Berberet, Louis J.
(Lou)
56T-329
57T-315
58T-383
59T-96
60L-24
60MacGregor-4
60T-6
61P-43

Bere, Jason
90SoBend/ClBest-13
91SoBend/ProC-2849

Berenguer, Juan
78Tidew
79T-721R
79Tacoma-6
80Tidew-3
81T-259R
82D-580
82Evansvl-2
82OPC-107
82OPC/Post-12
82T-437
84D-125
84F-77
84Nes/792-174
84T-174
85Cain's-2
85D-272
85F-2
85T-672
85Wendy-3
86F-221
86Mother/Giants-27
86T-47
86T/Tr-9T
87D-616
87F-265
87F/Up-U4
87T-303
87T/Tr-5T
88D-395
88D/Best-298
88F-3
88Master/Disc-3
88T-526
88T/Big-222
89B-152
89D-81
89D/Best-46
89F-104
89OPC-294
89S-414
89T-294
89T/Big-117
89T/St-291
89UD-232
90B-410
90D-301
90F-369
90Leaf/I-169
90OPC-709
90PublInt/St-323
90S-223
90T-709
90UD-440
91B-572
91D-340
91F-604
91F/UltraUp-U66
91F/Up-U71
91Leaf/II-526
91OPC-449
91S-111
91S/RookTr-73T
91T-449
91T/StClub/II-460
91UD-411
91WIZMets-33
92D/I-205
92F-352
92S/I-216
92T-172
92UD-493

Berenyi, Bruce
79Indianap-14
80Indianap-9
81T-606R
82Coke/Reds
82F-58
82T-459
83D-103
83F-585
83OPC-139
83T-139
84D-487
84F-463
84Nes/792-297
84OPC-297
84T-297
84T/Tr-10
85D-625
85F-73
85Indianap-32
85OPC-27
85T-27
85T/Mets/Fan-2
86T-339
87T-582
91WIZMets-34

Berg, Morris
(Moe)
30CEA/Pin-11
33BU-149
33G-158
39PB-103
40PB-30
88Conlon/5-3
90Target-48
91Conlon/Sport-184
R313
R316
V353-84

Berg, Patty
52Wheat

Berg, Rich
88Modesto-4
89Madis/Star-3
90Huntsvl/Best-2
91Stockton/ClBest-7
91Stockton/ProC-3024

Berg, Rick
90Richm/Bob-22CO
90Richm/ProC-278CO
90Richm/Team-4
91Richm/ProC-2584CO

Bergamo, August S.
(Augie)
No Cards.

Berge, Jordan
84Cedar-10
86Vermont-1

Berge, Lou
86LitFalls-3

Bergen, Martin
(Marty)
No Cards.

Bergen, William A.
(Bill)
10Domino-12
12Sweet/Pin-71
90Target-49
E101
E105
E300
E92
M116
S74-50
T201
T202
T205
T206
T216
T3-2
WG3-4

Bergendahl, Wray
83Wausau/LF-28
85Lynch-7
86Jacks/TCMA-3

Berger, Carl
28Exh/PCL-3

Berger, Charles
(Heinie)
E254
E270/1
M116
T206

Berger, Clarence E.
No Cards.

Berger, John Henne
(Johnny)
No Cards.

Berger, John Henry
(Tun)
No Cards.

Berger, Joseph August
(Joe)
No Cards.

Berger, Ken
77Spartan

Berger, Louis William
(Boze)
35BU-84
Berger, Mike
84PrWill-7
85Nashua-3
86Nashua-3
87Jaxvl-6
88Indianap/CMC-20
88Indianap/ProC-519
89OkCty/CMC-11
89OkCty/ProC-1515
90OkCty/CMC-10
90OkCty/ProC-434
91OkCty/ProC-181
Berger, Walter Anton
(Wally)
31Exh/4-2
32Orbit/num-51
32Orbit/un-5
33DH-5
33Exh/4-1
33G-98
34DS-108
34DS-25
34Exh/4-1
35BU-1
35BU-172
35Exh/4-1
35Wheat
36Exh/4-1
36G-1
37Exh/4-1
38ONG/Pin-1
39PB-99
40PB-81
88Conlon/3-5
88Conlon/NatAS-1
91Conlon/Sport-229
R300
R305
R309/2
R310
R313
R326-13A
R326-13B
R328-19
R332-12
R342-13
V355-35
W711/1
Bergeron, Gilles
87Jamestn-22
Bergert, Ned
76QuadC
77QuadC
Bergh, John Baptist
No Cards.
Berghammer, Martin A.
(Marty)
No Cards.
Bergman, Alfred Henry
(Al)
No Cards.
Bergman, David Bruce
(Dave)
76SSPC-454
78BK/Ast-21
78T-705R
79Charl-8
79T-697
81D-139
81F-76
81T-253
81T/Tr-734
82D-146
82T-498
83D-550
83F-253
83Mother/Giants-18
83T-32
84D-624
84F-366
84F/X-11
84Nes/792-522
84T-522
84T/Tr-11
85Cain's-3
85D-537
85F-3
85OPC-368
85T-368
85Wendy-4
86Cain's-1
86D-471
86F-222
86T-101
87Cain's-4
87Coke/Tigers-9
87D-420
87F-144
87OPC-256
87T-700
88D-373
88F-52
88Pep/T-14
88Pol/T-3
88S-217
88T-289
89D-389
89F-129
89Mara/Tigers-14
89Pol/Tigers-14
89S-469
89T-631
89UD-266
90B-355
90CokeK/Tiger-2
90D-445
90F-600
90Leaf/I-244
90OPC-77
90Panini/St-67
90PublInt/St-468
90S-254
90T-77
90T/St-285
90UD-381
91CokeK/Tiger-14
91D-342
91F-331
91F/Ultra-120
91Leaf/I-92
91OPC-412
91Panini/St-241
91S-562
91T-412
91T/StClub/II-386
91UD-599
92S/II-543
92T-354
Bergman, Sean
91Niagara/ClBest-24
91Niagara/ProC-3624
Beringer, Carroll
73OPC-486CO
73T-486C
74OPC-119CO
74T-119C
Beringhele, Vince
85VeroB-17
Berkelbach, Francis
No Cards.
Berley, John
V355-118
Berlin, Randy
89Hamil/Star-12
90Spring/Best-4
91Freder/ClBest-17
91Freder/ProC-2371
Berman, Gary
86Cram/PCL-150
87Clearw-18
88Reading/ProC-873
Berman, Robert Leon
(Bob)
No Cards.
Bernabe, Sam
85Iowa-18
Bernal, Vic
77Padre/SchCd-3
79Hawaii-8
Bernard, Curtis Henry
(Curt)
No Cards.
Bernard, Dwight
75Tidew/Team-3
78Tidew
79T-721R
79Tidew-6
81Vanco-4
82Pol/Brew-47
83D-28
83F-27
83Gard-2
83T-244
84Cram/PCL-55
86Macon-4
87Kenosha-16
88Kenosha/ProC-1381
89Orlan/Best-4
89Orlan/ProC-1342
91WIZMets-35
Bernard, Erik
84Albany-16
85Albany-29
86Alban/TCM-12bb
Bernardo, Rick
87PortChar-18
88CharlR/Star-1
89CharlR/Star-2
89Miami/II/Star-1
Bernardo, Robert
86Wausau-1
Bernazard, Antonio
(Tony)
75WPalmB
80OPC-351R
80T-680R
81D-449
81F-168
81OPC-194
81T-413
81T/Tr-735
82D-143
82F-338
82T-206
82T/St-171
83D-482
83F-231
83OPC-369
83T-698
83T/St-49
83T/X-9
83TrueVal/WSox-14
84D-240
84F-606
84F/X-12
84Nes/792-41
84OPC-41
84T-41
84T/St-340
84T/Tr-12
84Wheat/Ind-4
85D-102
85F-439
85OPC-171
85Polar/Ind-4
85T-533
85T/St-252
85ThomMc/Discs-4
86D-520
86F-580
86Leaf-249
86OhHenry-4
86OPC-354
86T-354
86T/St-210
87D-377
87D/OD-110
87F-244
87F/GameWin-4
87F/Mini-8
87Gator-4
87OPC-394
87RedFoley/St-105
87Sf-112M
87Sf-60
87T-607AS
87T-758
87T/Gloss60-43
87T/St-207
88D-344
88F-275
88OPC-122
88S-604
88T-122
91B-143
Bernhard, William H.
E107
T206
T213/brown
Bernhardt, Bill
WG2-5
Bernhardt, Cesar
89SoBend/GS-24
90BirmB/Best-6
90BirmB/ProC-1114
90Foil/Best-80
91B-360
91Vanco/LineD-626
91Vanco/ProC-1599
92T-179M
Bernhardt, Juan Ramon
77T-494R
78SanJose-13
78T-698
79OPC-189
79Spokane-24
79T-366
Berni, Denny
91LynchRS/ClBest-11
91LynchRS/ProC-1201
Bernier, Carlos R.
53T-243
54B-171
91T/Arc53-243
Bernstine, Pookie
83Watlo/LF-16
84BuffB-23
86Iowa-3
87Iowa-16
88Peoria/Ko-5
89Geneva/ProC-1886
89Peoria/Ko-29
Bero, Albert
48Sommer-30M
Bero, John George
(Johnny)
No Cards.
Berra, Dale Anthony
78Colum
79T-723R
80T-292
81D-153
81F-369
81OPC-147
81T-147
82D-250
82F-476
82T-588
83D-185
83F-303
83OPC-271
83T-433
83T/St-279
84D-430
84F-245
84Nes/792-18
84OPC-18
84T-18
84T/St-136
85D-444
85F-461
85F/Up-U4
85OPC-305
85T-132FS
85T-305
85T/St-133
85T/Tr-6T
86D-295
86F-100
86OPC-366
86T-692
87Tucson-8
88RochR/Team-3
88RochR/CMC-12
88RochR/Gov-3
88RochR/ProC-193
Berra, Lawrence Peter
(Yogi)
47HomogBond-2
47TipTop
48B-6
49B-60
49MP-117
50B-46
50Drake-24
51B-2
51BR-B4
51T/CAS
51T/RB-1
52B-1
52BR
52NTea
52RM-AL3
52StarCal/L-70C
52T-191
52TipTop
52Wheat
53B/Col-121
53B/Col-44M
53RM-AL3
53T-104
54B-161
54NYJour
54RM-AL20
54T-50
55Armour-2
55B-168
55RM-AL16
55T-198
56T-110
56T/Pin-27
56YellBase/Pin-7
57T-2
57T-407M
58T-370
59T-180
60Bz-8
60NuCard-28
60T-480
60T/tatt-6
61NuCard-453
61P-1
61T-425
61T-472MV
61T/RO
61T/St-189
62Exh
62J-7
62P-7
62P/Can-7
62Salada-33
62Shirriff-33
62T-360
62T/bucks
62T/St-83
63Exh
63J-17
63P-17
63Salada-62
63T-340P/CO
64T-21MG
65T-470P/CO
73OPC-257MG
73T-257MG
74OPC-179MG
74T-179MG
75OPC-189M
75OPC-192M
75OPC-193M
75OPC-421MG
75T-189MV
75T-192MV
75T-193MV
75T-421MG
75T/M-189MV
75T/M-192MV
75T/M-193MV
75T/M-421MG
79TCMA-2
80Pac/Leg-67
81D-351CO
82D-387CO
83D/HOF-24
83MLBPA/Pin-2
84T/Tr-13MG
85CircK-33
85T-132FS
85T-155MG
85West/2-31
85Woolwth-4
86Sf/Dec-31
87Leaf/SpecOlym-H2
87Nestle/DT-19
88Pac/Leg-53
89B/I-2
90BBWit-24
90MSA/AGFA-22
90Pac/Legend-7
90Swell/Great-105
91CollAB-35
91K/3D-11
91K/SU-3A
91K/SU-3B
91LineD-7
91Swell/Great-8
91T/Arc53-104
91WIZMets-36
D305
Exh47
PM10/L-4
PM10/Sm-10
PM10/Sm-9A
PM10/Sm-9B

R423-5
WG9-1
Berran, Dennis Martin
(Joe)
No Cards.
Berres, Raymond F.
(Ray)
39PB-156
40PB-164
60T-458C
90Target-50
Berringer, John
87Peoria-10
88WinSalem/Star-1
Berrios, Hector
87Fayette-1
88GlenF/ProC-935
90Lakeland/Star-3
91PalmSp/ProC-2007
Berroa, Ed
79Elmira-22
Berroa, Geronimo
85Kingst-21
86Ventura-1
87Knoxvl-15
87SLAS-3
88AAA/ProC-36
88D-659
88Syrac/CMC-13
88Syrac/ProC-808
89B-279
89D/Rook-19
89F/Up-72
89S-632
89S/HotRook-30
89S/YS/II-17
89Sf-225M
89T/Big-297
89T/Tr-10T
90Classic-83
90D-104
90F-575
90OPC-617
90Richm/Bob-15
90Richm/CMC-16
90Richm/ProC-269
90Richm/Team-5
90S-151
90S/100Ris-36
90T-617
90T/89Debut-17
90UD-531
91ColoSp/ProC-2195
Berry, Allen Kent
(Ken)
65T-368R
66OPC-127
66T-127
67OPC-67
67T-67
68T-485
69MB-25
69MLB/St-29
69T-494
69T/St-153
70MLB/St-182
70OPC-239
70T-239
71JB
71MLB/St-339
71OPC-466
71T-466
72MB-31
72OPC-379
72T-379
73OPC-445
73T-445
74OPC-163
74T-163
75OPC-432
75T-432
75T/M-432
78TCMA-53
82Oneonta-4MG
87AppFx-24MG
89BirmB/Best-20MG
89BirmB/ProC-89MG
90BirmB/Best-28MG
90BirmB/ProC-1397MG
90BirmDG/Best-3MG
Berry, Charles F.
(Charlie)
31Exh/4-17
33CJ/Pin-1
33Exh/4-10
33Exh/4-9
33G-184
35G-2C
35G-4C
35G-7C
36Exh/4-14
40PB-190
55B-281ump
92Conlon/Sport-398
R313
Berry, Charles Joseph
(Charlie)
No Cards.
Berry, Claude Elzy
No Cards.
Berry, Cornelius John
(Neil)
49B-180
50B-241
51B-213
52B-219
91Crown/Orio-31
Berry, Joseph H. Jr.
(Joe)
W575
Berry, Joseph H.
(Joe)
No Cards.
Berry, Kevin
90Billings/ProC-3211
91Cedar/ClBest-1
91Cedar/ProC-2709
Berry, Kirk
85Cedar-14
86FSLAS-7
86Macon-3
86Tampa-3
87Vermont-24
Berry, Mark
87Nashvl-1
88Greens/ProC-1575
89Greens/ProC-405
90CharWh/Best-25CO
90CharWh/ProC-2256CO
91Cedar/ClBest-27CO
91Cedar/ProC-2736CO
Berry, Perry
91Osceola/ClBest-17
91Osceola/ProC-691
Berry, Sean
86Cram/PCL-38
87FtMyr-7
88BBCity/Star-6
89BBCity/Star-5
90A&AASingle/ProC-49
90Foil/Best-86
90Memphis/Best-6
90Memphis/ProC-1016
90Memphis/Star-2
91Omaha/LineD-326
91Omaha/ProC-1039
91S-764RP
91T/90Debut-15
91UD-10
92Classic/I-15
92D/II-651
92F-680
92S/II-678
Berry, Tony
89Gaston/ProC-1009
89Gaston/Star-3
Berryhill, Damon
86Pittsfld-2
87Iowa-15
88Berg/Cubs-9
88D-639
88D/Best-261
88D/Cubs/Bk-639
88D/Rook-31
88F-642R
88F/Up-U75
88Iowa/CMC-12
88Iowa/ProC-537
88S/Tr-82T
88T/Tr-15T
89B-288
89Bz-2
89D-275
89D/Best-116
89F-418
89KMart/DT-8
89Mara/Cubs-9
89OPC-6
89Panini/St-52
89S-336
89S/HotRook-77
89S/YS/I-24
89Sf-216
89T-543
89T/Big-60
89T/Gloss60-39
89T/JumboR-4
89T/St-318
89T/St-51
89ToysRUs-4
89UD-455
90B-33
90D-167
90F-26
90MLBPA/Pins-52
90OPC-362
90Panini/St-234
90PeoriaUp/Team-U3
90PublInt/St-190
90S-163
90Sf-164
90T-362
90T/St-49
90T/TVCub-19
90UD-322
91Cub/Mara-9
91D-631
91F-414
91F/Ultra-56
91Leaf/I-156
91OPC-188
91S-881
91T-188
91T/StClub/I-28
91UD-319
92D/II-771
92T-49
Bertaina, Frank
65T-396
66T-579R
68OPC-131
68T-131
69MB-26
69T-554
70T-638
71MLB/St-267
71OPC-422
71T-422
72MB-32
91Crown/Orio-32
Berte, Harry Thomas
No Cards.
Bertell, Richard G.
(Dick)
61T-441
62T/St-105
63J-176
63P-176
63T-287
64T-424
65OPC-27
65T-27
66T-587
Berthel, Dan
89Erie/Star-2
90CLAS/CL-6
90Freder/Team-19
91Freder/ClBest-22
91Freder/ProC-2376
Berti, Don
83DayBe-14
Bertman, Skip
90LSUGreat-1CO
90LSUPol-1CO
Bertoia, Reno Peter
54T-131
55T-94
57T-390
58T-232
59T-84
60T-297
61P-95
61Peter-20
61T-392
61T/St-178
Bertolani, Jerry
86Penin-5
87DayBe-22
88BirmB/Best-23
88SLAS-8
89BirmB/Best-12
89BirmB/ProC-100
Bertolotti, Fulvio
78StPete
79ArkTr-15
Bertoni, Jeff
80SLCity-9
81SLCity-16
82Spokane-13
83Evansvl-13
Bertotti, Mike
91Utica/ClBest-4
91Utica/ProC-3232
Bertucio, Charlie
83SanJose-3
Berube, George
(Luc)
87FtLaud-11
87Oneonta-31
88FtLaud/Star-2
Berumen, Andres
91BBCity/ClBest-1
91BBCity/ProC-1388
91Single/ClBest-65
Besana, Fred
91Crown/Orio-33
Bescher, Robert Henry
(Bob)
10Domino-13
11Helmar-110
12Sweet/Pin-96
14CJ-110
15CJ-110
D303
D329-15
D350/2-14
E101
E102
E105
E106
E224
E254
E270/2
E90/1
E92
E94
M101/4-15
M101/5-14
M116
S74-72
T202
T205
T206
T207
T216
T3-81
W555
WG5-4
WG6-3
Bessard, Lloyd
79Elmira-1
Besse, Herman
47Signal
49B/PCL-29
Bessent, Don
56T-184
57T-178
58T-401
59T-71
90Target-51
Best, Bill
81CharR-21
82FtMyr-18
84Memphis-5
Best, Jayson
89Elizab/Star-3
90Foil/Best-225M
90Kenosha/Best-17M
90Kenosha/ProC-2286M
90Kenosha/Star-1M
91Visalia/ClBest-1M
91Visalia/ProC-1735M
Best, Jim
83AppFx/LF-6TR
Best, Karl
80LynnS-11
81LynnS-1
82LynnS-2
83SLCity-5
84Cram/PCL-189
85Cram/PCL-76
85F/Up-U5
86D-511
86F-459
86Mother/Mar-19
86Sf-179M
86T-61
87Calgary-10
87D-198
87F-579
87T-439
88Portl/CMC-2
88Portl/ProC-646
Beswick, James W.
(Jim)
79Hawaii-10
79T-725R
80Hawaii-8
83Nashua-17
Betances, Marcos
88Bristol/ProC-1882
89Fayette/ProC-1574
89NiagFls/Pucko-3
90Hamil/Best-3
90Hamil/Star-6
90Savan/ProC-2060
Betcher, Frank Lyle
No Cards.
Betemit, Manuel
77Newar
78BurlB
Bethancourt, Jose
90Elizab/Star-3
Bethea, Scott
90LSUPol-10
91LynchRS/ClBest-14
91LynchRS/ProC-1204
Bethea, Steve
89Spokane/SP-25
90Riversi/Best-2
90Riversi/Cal-7
90Riversi/ProC-2612
91HighD/ClBest-18
91HighD/ProC-2401
91Single/ClBest-148
Bethea, William Lamar
(Bill)
60DF
Bethke, James
65T-533R
91WIZMets-37
Bettencourt, Lawrence
No Cards.
Bettendorf, Dave
88Hagers/Star-2
89Hagers/Best-9
89Hagers/ProC-273
89Hagers/Star-1
90Hagers/ProC-1419
90HagersDG/Best-4
Bettendorf, Jeff
83Lynch-4
84Jacks-9
84Mother/A's-25
85Tidew-4
86ColumAst-4
87BirmB/Best-9
87SLAS-21
Betts, Walter
(Huck)
34G-36
E120
V354-83
Betz, Robert
52Park-80
Betzel, Christian
(Bruno)
D328-15
D329-16
D350/2-15
E135-15
M101/4-16
M101/5-15
Beuder, John
87SLCity/Taco-4
88Bakers/Cal-246
Beuder, Mike
83VeroB-1
Beuerlein, Ed
90Ashvl/ProC-2751
91Osceola/ClBest-14
91Osceola/ProC-867
Beuerlein, John
86Stockton-1

87Denver-14
Beulac, Joe
89SLCity-24
Beumiller
E254
E270/1
Bevacqua, Kurt A.
72OPC-193
72T-193
74OPC-454
74T-454
74T/Tr-454T
76OPC-427
76OPC-564M
76SSPC-233
76T-427
76T-564M
77T-317
77Tucson
78BK/R-16
78T-725
79T-44
80T-584
81F-382
81T-118
82F-477
82T-267
82T/Tr-6T
83F-352
83T-674
84D-80
84F-294
84F/St-43
84Mother/Padres-6
84Nes/792-346
84Smok/Padres-1
84T-346
85D-647
85F-26
85Mother/Padres-14
85T-478
85T/St-16WS
86D-528
86F-315
86T-789
Bevan, Harold Joseph
(Hal)
53B/BW-43
55Rodeo
60HenryH-10
60Union-22
61T-456
Bevenour, Keith
89Watertn/Star-2
Bevens, Floyd
(Bill)
47TipTop
48B-22
60NuCard-3
Beville, Henry Monte
(Monte)
No Cards.
Bevington, Terry
78BurlB
79Holyo-2
80Vanco-6
81BurlB-30
82Beloit-24
84ElPaso-12
86Vanco-2MG
87Denver-13
88Vanco/ProC-778
90Coke/WSox-30CO
91Kodak/WSox-x
Beyeler, Arnie
87Fayette-19
88Lakeland/Star-3
89London/ProC-1371
90EastLAS/ProC-EL7
90London/ProC-1274
91Toledo/LineD-579
91Toledo/ProC-1938
Beyers, Tom
87VeroB-22
89Salem/Team-1MG
90Bakers/Cal-244
91AS/Cal-23
Bezdek, Hugo
92Conlon/Sport-396
W514-83
Bhagwat, Tom
80ElPaso-13

Biagini, Greg
87CharlO/WBTV-24
87SLAS-24
88CharlK/Pep-23
89RochR/CMC-25
89RochR/ProC-1660
90RochR/CMC-25MG
90RochR/ProC-720MG
91AAAGame/ProC-AAA39MG
91RochR/LineD-474MG
91RochR/ProC-1918MG
Bialas, Dave
82Spring-2
83Spring/LF-22
84ArkTr-14
86FSLAS-8MG
86StPete-4MG
87StPete-18
90SpringDG/Best-22MG
91StPete/ClBest-9MG
91StPete/ProC-2292MG
Biancalana, Roland A.
(Buddy)
82Omaha-14
83Omaha-13
85T-387
86D-605
86F-3
86Kitty/Disc-2
86NatPhoto-1
86Sf-200
86T-99
86T/St-21WS
87D-527
87D/OD-202
87F-364
87Smok/AL-7
87T-554
88Omaha/CMC-20
88Omaha/ProC-1502
88S-383
Biancamano, John
91Spokane/ClBest-22
91Spokane/ProC-3953
Bianchi, Ben
86Visalia-3
87Portl-16
89Orlan/Best-10
89Orlan/ProC-1329
Bianchi, Steve
77Ashvl
79Tucson-9
Bianco, Robert
75AppFx
Bianco, Ron
86Sumter-3
Bianco, Thomas A.
(Tommy)
76SSPC-250
77Evansvl/TCMA-3
78RochR
79RochR-11
Biasatti, Henry A.
(Hank)
V362-44
Biasucci, Joe
91WinSalem/ClBest-16
91WinSalem/ProC-2833
Bibb, Mitch
90Wausau/Star-29TR
91Freder/ClBest-30TR
Bibby, Jim
72OPC-316R
72T-316R
74OPC-11
74T-11
74T/St-231
75OPC-155
75T-155
75T/M-155
76OPC-324
76T-324
77T-501
78OPC-61
78T-636
79OPC-39
79T-92
80T-229
81Coke
81D-134
81F-370
81F/St-65
81OPC-93

81T-430
81T/SO-105
81T/St-216
81T/St-260
82D-171
82F-478
82F/St-106
82F/St-70
82OPC-170
82T-170
82T/St-86
83T-355
84F-246
84Nes/792-566
84T-566
85Lynch-2CO
86Lynch-2CO
87Lynch-20CO
89Lynch/Star-24CO
89Pac/SenLg-52
89T/SenLg-128
89TM/SenLg-7
90LynchRS/Team-26CO
91LynchRS/ClBest-26CO
91LynchRS/ProC-1216CO
Biberdorf, Cam
88GreatF-24
89Bakers/Cal-190
90FSLAS/Star-1
90VeroB/Star-5
91SanAn/LineD-531
Bible, Mike
89SLCity-21
Bichette, Dante
86PalmSp-3
88Edmon/CMC-23
88Edmon/ProC-576
89Classic/Up/2-199
89D-634
89D/Rook-29
89F-468
89Panini/St-283
89T-761
89UD-24
90Classic/III-11
90F-127
90Leaf/II-340
90OPC-43
90PublInt/St-365
90S/YS/II-10
90T-43
90UD-688
91B-31
91Brewer/MillB-3
91D-303
91F-307
91F/Up-U29
91Leaf/I-242
91OPC-564
91Panini/FrSt-186
91Panini/St-139
91Pol/Brew-2
91S-463
91S/RookTr-37T
91T-564
91T/StClub/I-211
91T/Tr-10T
91UD-317
91UD/Ext-712
92D/I-347
92F-173
92S/I-316
92T-371
92UD-378
Bickford, Vern
49B-1
50B-57
51B-42
51FB
52B-48
52T-252
53JC-3
53SpicSpan/3x5-3
53T-161
54B-176
79TCMA-114
91Crown/Orio-34
91T/Arc53-161
Bickhardt, Eric
89Butte/SP-5
90Gaston/Best-14
90Gaston/ProC-2512
90Gaston/Star-2
91CharlR/ClBest-2

91CharlR/ProC-1306
Bicknell, Charlie
49Eureka-129
Bicknell, Greg
89StCath/ProC-2090
90Myrtle/ProC-2767
91Myrtle/ClBest-2
91Myrtle/ProC-2936
Bieger, Philip
87Anchora-1
Biehl, Rod
91AubAS/ClBest-4
91AubAS/ProC-4267
Bieksha, Steve
88Wausau/GS-18
Bielanin, Ray
89GreatF-11
Bielaski, Oscar
No Cards.
Bielecki, Mike
82Buffa-16
83LynnP-1
84Cram/PCL-131
85D-28
85F-650M
86F-603
86T/Tr-10T
87D-415
87T-394
87Vanco-1
88AAA/ProC-18
88D-484
88D/Cubs/Bk-NEW
88S-611
88T-436
89D-512
89D/Best-194
89F-419
89Mara/Cubs-36
89T-668
90B-22
90Cub/Mara-2
90D-373
90D-9DK
90D/BestNL-3
90D/SuperDK-9DK
90F-27
90Leaf/I-45
90OPC-114
90Panini/St-242
90PublInt/St-191
90S-484
90T-114
90T/Big-129
90T/Mini-48
90T/St-54
90T/TVCub-8
90UD-359
91B-422
91Cub/Mara-36
91D-87
91F-415
91F/Ultra-57
91OPC-501
91S-453
91T-501
91T/StClub/I-109
91UD-597
92D/II-776
92T-26
Bielenberg, Bruce
85Iowa-33
90Miami/II/Star-30PER
Bienek, Vince
79AppFx-18
80GlenF/B-20
80GlenF/C-11
81GlenF-17
Bierbauer, Louis W.
(Lou)
N172
N690
Biercevicz, Greg
78SanJose-3
79Spokane-21
79T-712R
80Spokane-3
81Spokane-8
81T-282R
82Tidew-17
83Tidew-15
85RochR-30

Bierley, Brad
85Visalia-7
86Orlan-2
87Orlan-14
88Portl/CMC-16
88Portl/ProC-639
89Portl/CMC-18
89Portl/ProC-231
90Iowa/CMC-22
90Iowa/ProC-329
90T/TVCub-38
91Iowa/LineD-201
91Iowa/ProC-1073
Bierscheid, Gene
87Spartan-3
Bieser, Steve
89Batavia/ProC-1934
90Batavia/ProC-3078
91Spartan/ClBest-22
91Spartan/ProC-907
Bigbee, Carson Lee
21Exh-10
25Exh-49
26Exh-49
E120
E121/120
E121/80
V61-54
W501
W573
W575
Bigbee, Lyle Randolph
No Cards.
Bigelow, Elliott A.
No Cards.
Biggers, Allan
89Hamil/Star-3
89Savan/ProC-362
Biggers, Brian
91SLCity/ProC-3216
Biggerstaff, Kent
75Tidew/Team-4
78Holyo
79Vanco-22
80Vanco-12
81Portl-27
Biggio, Craig
88F/Up-U89
88S/Tr-103T
88Tucson/CMC-15
88Tucson/ProC-166
88Tucson/JP-2
89Classic-51
89D-561
89D/Best-176
89F-353
89Lennox/Ast-24
89Mother/Ast-14
89Panini/St-79
89S-237
89S/HotRook-98
89S/YS/II-33
89T-49
89UD-273
90B-78
90Classic-57
90D-306
90D/BestNL-89
90F-224
90KMart/SS-8
90Leaf/I-37
90Lennox-4
90Mother/Ast-5
90OPC-157
90OPC-404AS
90Panini/St-259
90PublInt/St-88
90S-275
90Sf-22
90T-157
90T-404AS
90T/Big-111
90T/Coins-39
90T/Gloss60-54
90T/HeadsUp-6
90T/St-23
90T/TVAS-41
90UD-104
91B-556
91Classic/200-7
91Classic/III-T2
91D-2DK
91D-595

91D/SuperDK-2
91DennyGS-24
91F-499
91F/Ultra-132
91JDeanSig-16
91KingB/Discs-13
91Leaf/I-12
91Leaf/Prev-4
91Leaf/Stud-173
91MooTown-22
91Mother/Ast-5
91OPC-565
91Panini/FrSt-6
91Panini/St-10
91RedFoley/St-8
91S-161
91S-872FRAN
91S/100SS-55
91Seven/3DCoin-1T
91T-565
91T/StClub/I-176
91UD-158
91USPlayC/AS-9C
92D/I-75
92F-426
92S/100SS-52
92S/II-460
92S/II-888DT
92T-393AS
92T-715
92UD-162
92UD-31TC

Biggs, Doug
88Bristol/ProC-1864

Biggus, Bengie
80BurlB-29

Bigham, Craig
88Spokane/ProC-1931

Bigham, David
89Elizab/Star-4
90Elizab/Star-4
91Kenosha/CIBest-12
91Kenosha/ProC-2066

Bigham, Scott
89River/Best-3
89River/Cal-1
89River/ProC-1396
90Riversi/Best-3
90Riversi/Cal-8
90Riversi/ProC-2613

Bignal, George W.
No Cards.

Bigusiak, Mike
76Clinton
86SanJose-3

Biittner, Larry David
72OPC-122
72T-122
73OPC-249
73T-249
75OPC-543
75T-543
75T/M-543
76OPC-238
76SSPC-336
76T-238
77T-64
78T-346
79OPC-224
79T-433
80OPC-334
80T-639
81D-515
81F-314
81T-718
81T/Tr-736
82Coke/Reds
82D-43
82F-59
82T-159
83D-440
83F-586
83Rangers-14
83T-527
83T/X-10
84D-342
84F-414
84Nes/792-283
84T-283

Biko, Tom
80OrlTw-3
82Amari-14

Bilak, Paul
86PalmSp-4TR
86PalmSp/Smok-4
87PalmSp-6

Bilardello, Dann J.
83T/X-11
84D-408
84F-464
84Nes/792-424
84T-424
84T/St-57
85D-243
85T-28
86Provigo-2
86T-253
87F-313
87OPC-217
87T-577
87Vanco-21
88Omaha/CMC-17
88Omaha/ProC-1518
89BuffB/CMC-13
89BuffB/ProC-1677
90BuffB/CMC-13
90BuffB/ProC-375
90BuffB/Team-2
90OPC-682
90T-682
91LasVegas/ProC-237
91LasVegas/LineD-277
91S-659
92S/II-719

Bilbert, Roy
91Hagers/LineD-230

Bilello, John
88Boise/ProC-1605
88Fresno/Cal-18
88Fresno/ProC-1224
89Boise/ProC-1997
89Reno/Cal-241

Bilko, Steven Thomas
(Steve)
51B-265
52T-287
53Hunter
54B-206
54Hunter
54T-116
55B-88
55T-93
55T/DH-117
58T-346
59DF
59T-43
60L-106
60T-396
61T-184
62J-74
62P-74
62P/Can-74
62Salada-17A
62Salada-17B
62Shirriff-17
62T-422
62T/St-63
63J-24
63P-24
79TCMA-177
88MinorLg/Leg-6
90Target-52
Exh47

Bill, Bob
79Newar-4
83TriCit-28
86Tulsa-26TR
88Watertn/Pucko-33

Billanueva, Gil
89Reno/Cal-247

Billeci, Craig
91Batavia/CIBest-6
91Batavia/ProC-3488

Billingham, Jack
68T-228R
69OPC-92
69T-92
70T-701
71MLB/St-74
71OPC-162
71T-162
72T-542
73OPC-89
73T-89
74OPC-158
74T-158
74T/St-22
75OPC-235
75T-235
75T/M-235
76OPC-155
76SSPC-23
76T-155
77Pep-53
77T-512
78BK/T-6
78T-47
79T-388
80T-603
85SpokaAT/Cram-2
87Osceola-18CO
89Swell-43
90Osceola/Star-28CO
90Target-53
91Osceola/ProC-700CO

Billings, John A.
(Josh)
No Cards.

Billings, Richard A.
(Dick)
71OPC-729
71T-729
72OPC-148
72T-148
73OPC-94
73T-94
74OPC-466
74T-466
76SSPC-288

Billingsley, Rod
89Spokane/SP-3
90Waterlo/Best-7
90Waterlo/ProC-2380

Billmeyer, Mickey
86Hagers-3
87Miami-11
87PortChar-16
88Miami/Star-2
89CharlR/Star-3
91AS/Cal-15
91PalmSp/ProC-2018

Billoni, Mike
87BuffB-27
89BuffB/CMC-1

Bingham, Mark
82Danvl-5

Binks, George Eugene
V362-21

Biras, Stephen A.
(Steve)
No Cards.

Birch, Brock
86Cram/PCL-23
87Clinton-20

Birchall, A. Judson
(Jud)
No Cards.

Bird, Bill
90Pittsfld/Pucko-29PER

Bird, David
88Alaska/Team-2
89Welland/Pucko-5
90A&AASingle/ProC-75
90Augusta/ProC-2456
91Salem/CIBest-14
91Salem/ProC-944

Bird, Doug
74OPC-17
74T-17
75OPC-364
75T-364
75T/M-364
76A&P/KC
76OPC-96
76SSPC-180
76T-96
77BurgChef-68
77OPC-191
77T-556
78T-183
79BK/P-12
79T-664
80T-421
81F-106
81T-516
81T/Tr-737
82D-504
82F-586
82RedLob
82T-273
83D-48
83F-490
83T-759
83T/X-12
84F-391
84Nes/792-82
84T-82
89Pac/SenLg-90
90EliteSenLg-65

Bird, Frank Zepherin
No Cards.

Bird, Steven
88Kinston/Star-4

Birkbeck, Mike
86Vanco-3
87D-33RR
87D/Rook-19
87F/Up-U5
87Leaf-33
87Pol/Brew-40
87T-229
88D-49
88Pol/Brew-40
88S-369
88T-692
89B-132
89Brewer/YB-40
89D-501
89F-178
89Pol/Brew-40
89S-596
89T-491
90Denver/CMC-21
90Denver/ProC-617
90Pol/Brew-40
90PublInt/St-489
91Canton/ProC-972

Birkofer, Ralph
35BU-90
90Target-901

Birmingham, Joseph L.
(Dode)
10Domino-14
11Helmar-22
12Sweet/Pin-17
14CJ-106
14Piedmont/St-4
15CJ-106
E254
E270/2
E97
M116
T202
T205
T206
T207
W555
WG5-5
WG6-4

Birrell, Bob
79Elmira-24
83Pawtu-1

Birrer, Werner
(Babe)
56T-84
90Target-54
91Crown/Orio-35

Birriel, Jose
86NewBrit-3
87NewBrit-24
88EastLAS/ProC-19
88NewBrit/ProC-902
89Lynch/Star-2

Birtsas, Tim
82Oneonta-8
85F/Up-U6
86D-462
86F-412
86F/St-5
86Leaf-227
86Mother/A's-25
87Tacoma-23
88F/Up-U82
88Kahn/Reds-48
88Nashvl/CMC-2
88Nashvl/ProC-477
88T-501
89F-152
89Kahn/Reds-48
89S-454
89T-103
89UD-638
90D-493
90F-414
90Kahn/Reds-3
90OPC-687
90S-408
90T-687
90UD-137
91OPC-289
91S-648
91T-289

Bisceglia, Dave
81Water-20

Bisceglia, James
86Cram/PCL-90
87QuadC-14
88PalmSp/ProC-1458
89PalmSp/Cal-52

Bischoff, John George
No Cards.

Bish, Brent
91CharRain/CIBest-15
91CharRain/ProC-100

Bishop, Charles
52Park-98
53T-186
55Rodeo
55T-96
55T/DH-110
91T/Arc53-186

Bishop, Craig
90Bakers/Cal-243
90Yakima/Team-27

Bishop, Frank H.
No Cards.

Bishop, James
83Kinston/Team-1
86Knoxvl-2
87Wmsprt-8
88Cedar/ProC-1165
89Miami/I/Star-2
91Salinas/CIBest-9
91Salinas/ProC-2249

Bishop, Max F.
25Exh-105
26Exh-105
29Exh/4-28
33G-61
34DS-6
35G-1G
35G-3E
35G-5E
35G-6E
88Conlon/4-4
91Conlon/Sport-183
R308-187
R315-A4
R315-B4
R316
V353-61

Bishop, Michael D.
(Mike)
77QuadC
80ElPaso-12
81SLCity-14
82Spokane-10
83Tidew-6
87Anchora-2
91WIZMets-38

Bishop, Tim
87Oneonta-28
88PrWill/Star-2

Bishop, William
N172

Bisland, Rivington M.
No Cards.

Bispo, Randy
86SanJose-4

Bissonette, Del
29Exh/4-4
31Exh/4-4
90Target-55
R314/Can
R316

Bitker, Joe
86Beaum-2
87LasVegas-1
88LasVegas/CMC-1
88LasVegas/ProC-230
89LasVegas/CMC-1
89LasVegas/ProC-4
90AAAGame/ProC-AAA47
90Tacoma/CMC-9
90Tacoma/ProC-85

91D-624
91F-281
91OkCty/ProC-171
91T/90Debut-16
91UD/Ext-797
92S/100RisSt-87
92S/II-743

Bittiger, Jeff
82Jacks-1
83Tidew-13
84Tidew-13
85IntLgAS-20
85Tidew-8
86Portl-1
87Portl-1
88S/Tr-66T
88Vanco/CMC-1
89B-60
89S-512
89T-209
89UD-509
89Vanco/CMC-1
90Albuq/CMC-2
90Albuq/ProC-335
90Albuq/Trib-2
91ColoSp/LineD-77
91ColoSp/ProC-2176

Bittmann, Henry
(Red)
No Cards.

Bivens, William E.
87Spring/Best-10
88Spring/Best-7
89StPete/Star-3
89TexLAS/GS-25

Bjorkman, George A.
80ArkTr-2
82Louisvl-1
83ColumAst-1
84Indianap-20
84Nes/792-116
84T-116
85Indianap-20
85RochR-31

Black, Allen
82QuadC-2

Black, Bob
89Richm/CMC-9

Black, Don
R346-28

Black, Harry
(Bud)
80SanJose
80SanJose/JITB-4
81LynnS-2
83D-322
83F-107
83F-644M
83Omaha-2
83T-238
84D-130
84F-343
84Nes/792-26
84T-26
84T/St-283
85D-100
85F-198
85Leaf-202
85OPC-47
85T-412
85T/St-275
86D-374
86F-4
86Kitty/Disc-7
86Leaf-170
86NatPhoto-40
86OPC-319
86T-697
86T/St-261
87D-404
87F-365
87OPC-315
87T-669
88D-301
88F-252
88OPC-301
88SanDiegoSt-3
88SanDiegoSt-4
88S-313
88S/Tr-11T
88Smok/Royals-9
88T-301
88T/Tr-16T
89B-82
89D-556
89OPC-5
89S-404
89T-509
89T/St-209
89UD-466
90D-556
90D/BestAL-118
90F-486
90Leaf/II-451
90OPC-144
90PublInt/St-554
90S-197
90T-144
90T/Big-223
90T/St-213
90UD-498
91B-639
91D-719
91F/UltraUp-U115
91F/Up-U128
91Leaf/II-312
91Leaf/Stud-260M
91Mother/Giant-7
91OPC-292
91OPC/Premier-9
91PG&E-19
91S/RookTr-46T
91SFExam/Giant-3
91T-292
91T/StClub/II-302
91T/Tr-11T
91UD/Ext-799
92D/I-93
92F-628
92S/I-358
92T-774
92UD-697

Black, Joe
52T-321
53RM-NL4
53T-81
54NYJour
54T-98
55Gol/Dodg-4
55T-156
56Kahn
56T-178
56T/Pin-54
79TCMA-160
89Pac/Leg-177
89Swell-69
90Target-56
91Swell/Great-9
91T/Arc53-81
PM10/Sm-11
PM10/Sm-12
PM10/Sm-13

Black, John Falconer
(Jack)
No Cards.

Black, John William
(Bill)
No Cards.

Black, Keith
91Hamil/ClBest-23
91Hamil/ProC-4043

Black, Robert B.
(Bob)
No Cards.

Blackaby, Ethan Allan
75Phoenix-25
76Phoenix
77Phoenix
78Cr/PCL-107
79Phoenix
80Phoenix-24
82Phoenix
83Phoenix/BHN-26GM

Blackburn, Earl S.
No Cards.

Blackburn, Jackie
85FtMyr-24

Blackburn, James Ray
49B-160
51B-287
79TCMA-259

Blackburn, Ron
58T-459
59T-401
60T-209

Blackburne, Russell
(Lena)
E90/3
M116
T205
T206
T207

Blackerby, George F.
(George)
No Cards.

Blackmon, Anthony
87SLCity/Taco-22

Blackmon, Tom
80Batavia-7
83Knoxvl-1

Blackmun, Ben
85Bend/Cram-2

Blackshear, Steve
87Reading-18

Blackwell, Barry
85Anchora-4
89Kinston/Star-3

Blackwell, Eric
90Yakima/Team-30
91VeroB/ProC-786
91Yakima/ClBest-8
91Yakima/ProC-4259

Blackwell, Ewell
47HomogBond-3
48B-2
48L-39
49Eureka-77
49Royal-9
50B-63
51B-24
52BR
52RM-NL3
52Royal
52T-344
53T-31
79TCMA-119
89Pac/Leg-188
91T/Arc53-31
D305
Exh47
R346-4

Blackwell, Fred
No Cards.

Blackwell, Juan
91FtLaud/ClBest-19
91FtLaud/ProC-2432

Blackwell, Larry
86Kenosha-2
87Orlan-26
88Visalia/Cal-159
88Visalia/ProC-83
89Orlan/Best-11
89Orlan/ProC-1340

Blackwell, Orlando
83Clinton/LF-11
84Shrev/FB-2

Blackwell, Teddy
89BurlInd/Star-29TR
90Watertn/Star-26TR
91CollInd/ClBest-30TR

Blackwell, Timothy P.
(Tim)
76SSPC-415
78OPC-223
78T-449
80T-153
81Coke
81D-559
81F-304
81OPC-43
81T-553
81T/HT
82D-99
82F-587
82Hygrade
82T-374
82T/St-28
82T/Tr-7T
83D-214
83OPC-57
83Stuart-26
83T-57
84Cram/PCL-241C
86Fres/Smok-1MG
88Phoenix/CMC-25M
89Pittsfld/Star-24MG
90FSLAS/Star-24
91SALAS/ProC-SAL12MG

Blackwell, Todd
90Reno/Cal-268

Blackwell, Tom
88Phoenix/ProC-53

Blades, Francis R.
(Ray)
21Exh-11
25Exh-58
26Exh-58
28Exh-30
54T-243CO
91Conlon/Sport-130
92Conlon/Sport-646

Bladt, Richard Alan
74OPC-601R
74Syrac/Team-2
74T-601R
76SSPC-444

Blaeholder, George
32Orbit/num-9
32Orbit/un-6
33G-16
34DS-13
34G-1F
35G-3D
35G-5D
35G-6D
R305
R314
V353-12
V353-169

Blaemire, Rae Bertram
No Cards.

Blaine, Tom
88ArkTr/GS-8

Blair, Clarence Vick
(Footsie)
No Cards.

Blair, Dennis
75OPC-521
75T-521
75T/M-521
76OPC-642
76SSPC-344
76T-642
77OPC-189
77T-593
78T-466
79Hawaii-22
80Hawaii-9

Blair, Dirk
91Pulaski/ClBest-17
91Pulaski/ProC-3996

Blair, Garnett
91Negro/Lewis-19

Blair, Lonnie
91Negro/Lewis-18

Blair, Louis Nathan
(Buddy)
No Cards.

Blair, Paul
65T-473R
66OPC-48
66T-48
67OPC-153WS
67T-153WS
67T-319
68Coke
68Dexter-12
68OPC-135
68T-135
69MB-27
69MLB/St-1
69T-506
70MLB/St-146
70OPC-285
70T-285
71K-35
71MLB/St-290
71OPC-53
71T-53
71T/tatt-6
72MB-33
72T-660
73JP
73OPC-528
73T-528
74OPC-92
74T-92
74T/St-123
75Ho-12
75Ho/Twink-12
75OPC-275
75T-275
75T/M-275
76OPC-473
76SSPC-395
76T-473
77BK/Y-21
77BurgChef-39
77T-313
78BK/Y-22
78T-114
79OPC-304
79T-582
80OPC-149
80T-281
84Everett/Cram-19
88CalLgAS-4
88SanJose/Cal-117
88SanJose/ProC-109
89Pac/SenLg-76
89Shreve/ProC-1834
89TM/SenLg-8
90EliteSenLg-77
90RochR/CMC-7CO
90RochR/ProC-722
90WinSalem/Team-4
91CharlK/LineD-127
91CharlK/ProC-1694
91Crown/Orio-36

Blair, Walter Allan
14CJ-126
14Piedmont/St-5
15CJ-126
T201
T202
T204

Blair, William E.
N172

Blair, Willie
87Dunedin-22
89Syrac/CMC-6
89Syrac/ProC-805
89Syrac/Team-2
90B-504
90Classic/III-52
90D/Rook-29
90F/Up-126
90Leaf/II-449
90S/Tr-88T
90T/Tr-8T
90Tor/BlueJ-27
91ColoSp/LineD-78
91ColoSp/ProC-2177
91D-267
91F-170
91OPC-191
91S-57
91S/100RisSt-19
91T-191
91T/90Debut-17
91UD-427
92F-106
92S/II-730

Blake, Bob
79Wisco-5

Blake, Ed
52T-144

Blake, Harry Cooper
No Cards.

Blake, John Frederick
(Sherriff)
26Exh-18
92Conlon/Sport-478

Blakely, Dave
85Everett/Cram-1
86Clinton-2
87Visalia-10

Blakely, Lincoln H.
(Link)
R314/Can

Blakeman, Todd
90Elizab/Star-5
91Kenosha/ClBest-3
91Kenosha/ProC-2080

Blakiston, Robert J.
(Bob)
No Cards.

Blanchard, John Edwin
(Johnny)
59T-117
60L-89
60T-283
61P-18
61T-104
61T/St-190

62J-11
62P-11
62P/Can-11
62T-93
63J-21
63P-21
63T-555
64T-118
65T-388
66T-268
89Swell-92
PM10/L-5
WG10-1
WG9-2

Blanche, Prosper A.
(Al)
35BU-83

Blanco, Damasco
No Cards.

Blanco, Gil
65T-566R
67T-303

Blanco, Henry
90Kissim/DIMD-1

Blanco, Oswaldo C.
(Ossie)
No Cards.

Blanco, Romauldo
73Cedar
75Dubuq

Bland, Lance
90SanBern/Cal-116TR

Blanding, Fred
(Fritz)
14CJ-109
15CJ-109
T207

Blank, Frank Ignatz
(Coonie)
No Cards.

Blanke, Scott
83Clinton/LF-26

Blankenship, Bob
89Billings/ProC-2060

Blankenship, Cliff
E90/1
T204

Blankenship, Kevin
85Durham-3
86Greenvl/Team-4
87Greenvl/Best-19
88Greenvl/Best-16
88SLAS-28
89AAA/ProC-44
89D-658
89Iowa/CMC-7
89Iowa/ProC-1699
89UD/Ext-762
90B-24
90F-28
90Iowa/CMC-3
90Iowa/ProC-311
90S-646
90UD-47
91BuffB/ProC-533

Blankenship, Lance
86Cram/PCL-69
87Modesto-10
88AAA/ProC-38
88Tacoma/CMC-11
88Tacoma/ProC-630
89D-621
89F-2
89S-641
89S/HotRook-20
89Tacoma/CMC-12
89Tacoma/ProC-1539
89UD-15
90F-1
90HotRook/St-8
90Mother/A's-21
90OPC-132
90S-536
90S/100Ris-82
90S/YS/II-36
90T-132
90T/Big-173
90UD-687
91D-701
91F-3
91Mother/A's-21
91OPC-411
91S-303
91T-411
91T/StClub/II-437
92D/II-768
92F-250
92S/I-279

Blankenship, Ted
26Exh-73
27Exh-37
92Conlon/Sport-457

Blanks, Daryl
88Idaho/ProC-1834
89BurlB/ProC-1621
89BurlB/Star-2
90BurlB/Best-23
90BurlB/ProC-2362
90BurlB/Star-3

Blanks, Larvell
73OPC-609R
73T-609R
75OPC-394
75T-394
75T/M-394
76OPC-127
76SSPC-8
76T-127
76T/TR-127T
77Pep-6
77T-441
78OPC-213
78T-61
79T-307
80T-656
89Pac/SenLg-206
89T/SenLg-92

Blanton, Darrell
(Cy)
34DS-57
35BU-88
35G-8K
35G-9K
37Exh/4-7
38Exh/4-7
91Conlon/Sport-134
R312
R313
R314
V355-3

Blanton, Garrett
91Hamil/ClBest-16
91Hamil/ProC-4049

Blaser, Mark
83Greens-16
85Albany-14
86WPalmB-6

Blasingame, Donald L.
(Don)
56T-309
57T-47
58T-199
59Armour-5
59T-491
60T-397
61P-148
61T-294
61T/St-73
62J-117
62P-117
62P/Can-117
62Salada-103
62Shirriff-103
62T-103
63FrBauer-1
63J-126
63Kahn
63P-126
63T-518
64T-327
65OPC-21
65T-21
78TCMA-84
Exh47

Blasingame, Wade
65OPC-44
65T-44
66Kahn
66T-355
67OPC-119
67T-119
68T-507
69MB-28
69T-308
71OPC-79
71T-79
72T-581

Blass, Steve
65OPC-232
65T-232
66EH-28
66T-344
67T-562
67T/Test/PP-4
68KDKA-28
68T-499
69Kahn
69OPC-104
69T-104
69T/S-57
69T/St-83
70OPC-396
70T-396
71MLB/St-194
71OPC-143
71T-143
72K-44
72MB-34
72OPC-229WS
72OPC-320
72T-229WS
72T-320
73K-11
73OPC-95
73T-95
74OPC-595
74T-595

Blasucci, Tony
85PrWill-18
86PrWill-3
87DayBe-5
88BirmB/Best-2
89BirmB/Best-10
89BirmB/ProC-94
90Calgary/CMC-2
90Calgary/ProC-644

Blateric, Steve
73OPC-616R
73T-616R

Blatnick, John Louis
(Johnny)
49B-123

Blattner, Robert G.
(Buddy)
40Hughes-4
47TipTop
49Eureka-130

Blauser, Jeff
86Durham-2
87Richm/Crown-2
87Richm/TCMA-11
87Sf/Rook-48
88D-513
88F-533
88Richm-2
88Richm/CMC-22
88Richm/ProC-18
88S-562
88S/YS/II-14
89D-592
89F-588
89Panini/St-41
89S-589
89T-83
89T/Big-317
89UD-132
90B-15
90Classic-123
90D-271
90D/BestNL-74
90F-576
90Leaf/I-191
90OPC-251
90Panini/St-217
90PublInt/St-109
90S-178
90T-251
90T/Big-180
90T/St-28
90UD-406
91D-229
91F-683
91F/Ultra-2
91Leaf/I-115
91OPC-623
91Panini/FrSt-22
91S-52
91T-623
91T/StClub/II-377
91UD-382
92D/I-228
92F-353
92S/I-362
92T-199
92UD-370

Blaylock, Gary
59T-539

Blaylock, Marvin E.
(Marv)
55B-292
57T-224

Blaylock, Robert
59T-211
62-Pep/Tul

Blazier, Ron
90Princet/DIMD-2
91Batavia/ClBest-26
91Batavia/ProC-3475

Blefary, Curtis LeRoy
(Curt)
65OPC-49R
65T-49R
66Bz-28
66T-460
66T/RO-87
67Bz-28
67OPC-180
67T-180
67T-521M
68Coke
68Dexter-13
68T-312
69MB-29
69MLB/St-137
69T-458
69T/S-44
69T/St-122
70MLB/St-242
70OPC-297
70T-297
71MLB/St-483
71OPC-131
71T-131
72MB-35
72T-691
72T-692A
91Crown/Orio-37

Blessitt, Isiah
(Ike)
77Holyo
89Pac/SenLg-190
89T/SenLg-20

Bleuberg, Jim
91Jaxvl/ProC-142

Blevins, Brad
83QuadC-8

Blevins, Greg
91Gaston/ClBest-13
91Gaston/ProC-2690

Bligh, Edwin Forrest
(Ned)
N172

Bliss, Bill
91FrRow/DP-45
91Geneva/ClBest-1
91Geneva/ProC-4207

Bliss, Elmer Ward
No Cards.

Bliss, Howard Frank
No Cards.

Bliss, John J.A.
11Helmar-166
E90/1
M116
T206

Blobaum, Jeff
84Cram/PCL-19

Block, James John
(Bruno)
11Helmar-6
E286
M116
T204
T207

Block, Richard
79Newar-19

Block, Seymour
(Cy)
V362-9

Blocker, Terry
82Jacks-20
84Tidew-20
85IntLgAS-16
85Tidew-19
86Tidew-2
87Tidew-5
87Tidew/TCMA-19
89F-589
89Richm/CMC-17
89Richm/Ko-19
89S-605
89T-76
89UD-399
91WIZMets-39

Blohm, Pete
89Augusta/ProC-516
89SALAS/GS-45
90Dunedin/Star-3
90Knoxvl/Best-3
90Knoxvl/ProC-1246
90Knoxvl/Star-1
91Knoxvl/LineD-351
91Syrac/ProC-2475

Blomberg, Ronald Mark
(Ron)
72OPC-203
72T-203
73OPC-462
73Syrac/Team-3
73T-462
74K-54
74OPC-117
74Syrac/Team-1
74T-117
74T/DE-60
74T/St-211
75OPC-68
75T-68
75T/M-68
76Ho-38
76Ho/Twink-38
76OPC-354
76SSPC-450
76T-354
77T-543
78Ho-147
78T-506
79OPC-17
79T-42
88T-663TBC

Blomberg, Steve
76Shrev

Blomdahl, Ben
91Niagara/ClBest-19
91Niagara/ProC-3625

Blong, Joseph Myles
(Joe)
No Cards.

Blong, Wesley C.
(Wes)
No Cards.

Blood, Ed
33SK-9

Bloodworth, James H.
(Jimmy)
40PB-189
49Eureka-78
51B-185

Bloomfield, Clyde S.
62Pep/Tul
63Pep/Tul
64T-532R

Blosser, Greg
89LittleSun-21
90B-278
90CLAS/CL-12
90LynchRS/Team-1
90S-681DC
90T/TVRSox-37
91B-115
91NewBrit/LineD-452
91NewBrit/ProC-363
91Single/ClBest-226
91UD-70

Blott, Jack Leonard
No Cards.

Blouin, Gary
86Cram/PCL-45
87FtMyr-3

Blount, Bill
85Spokane/Cram-2
86CharRain-3
87LasVegas-16
88River/Cal-230
88River/ProC-1421

Blowers, Michael
86Jamestn-1
87WPalmB-13
88Jaxvl/Best-16
88Jaxvl/ProC-975
89Indianap/CMC-14
89Indianap/ProC-1221
90B-441
90Classic/Up-T5
90D-656
90D/Rook-26
90F-438
90Leaf/I-109
90S-624
90S/YS/II-34
90T/89Debut-18
90T/Tr-9T
90T/TVYank-23
90UD/Ext-767
91D-63
91OPC-691
91S-838
91S/100RisSt-17
91T-691
91UD/Ext-730

Blue, Bird Wayne
(Bert)
No Cards.

Blue, Luzerne Atwell
(Lu)
26Exh-90
28Exh-57
29Exh/4-30
31Exh/4-20
33Exh/4-10
81Detroit-115
90Target-57
E120
E126-54
R316
V61-5
W517-50
W572
W573

Blue, Vida
70OPC-21R
70T-21R
71MLB/St-507
71OPC-544
71T-544
72K-9
72OPC-169
72OPC-170IA
72OPC-92LL
72OPC-94LL
72OPC-96LL
72T-169
72T-170IA
72T-92LL
72T-94LL
72T-96LL
72T/Post-8
73OPC-430
73T-430
74OPC-290
74T-290
74T/St-222
75OPC-209MV
75OPC-510
75T-209MV
75T-510
75T/M-209MV
75T/M-510
76Crane-3
76Ho-20
76Ho/Twink-20
76K-47
76MSA/Disc
76OPC-140
76OPC-200LL
76SSPC-481
76T-140
76T-200LL
77BurgChef-114
77Ho-52
77OPC-75
77T-230
77T/CS-4
78OPC-177
78T-680
78Wiffle/Discs-4
79Ho-74
79K-23
79OPC-49
79Pol/Giants-14
79T-110
79T/Comics-33
80BK/PHR-1
80K-42
80OPC-14
80Pol/Giants-14
80T-30
80T/S-59
81D-433
81F-432
81F/St-63
81K-23
81OPC-310
81T-310
81T/SO-108
81T/St-239
82D-222
82D-4DK
82F-384
82F/St-61
82K-63
82KMart-19
82OPC-267
82OPC-82IA
82T-430
82T-431A
82T-576TL
82T/St-111
82T/Tr-8T
83D-34
83D-648M
83F-106
83F-643M
83OPC-178
83T-471TL
83T-570
84Mother/Giants-25
85F/Up-U7
85Mother/Giants-10
86D-509
86F-533
86Leaf-247
86Mother/Giants-10
86Sf-132M
86Sf-142M
86Sf/Dec-63M
86T-770
87D-362
87F-266
87Mother/A's-7
87OPC-260
87RedFoley/St-128
87T-260
89Pac/Leg-198
89Pac/SenLg-215
89T/SenLg-48
89TM/SenLg-9
90EliteSenLg-121
90EliteSenLg-50
90Pac/Legend-8
90Swell/Great-89
91Pac/SenLg-81
91Swell/Great-10

Blueberg, James
86Cram/PCL-120
87Wausau-2
88CalLgAS-30
88SanBern/Best-15
88SanBern/Cal-47
89SanBern/Best-6
90Wmsprt/Best-2
90Wmsprt/ProC-1049
90Wmsprt/Star-1
91Jaxvl/LineD-328

Bluege, Oswald Louis
(Ossie)
25Exh-121
26Exh-121
29Exh/4-31
31Exh/4-32
33G-113
33G-159
34DS-71
35BU-105
36Exh/4-16
61F-93
91Conlon/Sport-295
R313
V353-83
V355-87

Bluege, Otto Adam
No Cards.

Bluestone, Brad
86Erie-4tr
87Sprn/Best-27tr
88Spring/Best-27
90Louisvl/CMC-29TR

Bluhm, Bill
87Everett-25
88Watlo/ProC-668
89Reno/Cal-262

Bluhm, Brandon
91Burllnd/ProC-3290

Bluhm, Harvey Fred
(Red)
No Cards.

Blum, Brent
86Albany/TCMA-30
87Albany-22
88PrWill/Star-3

Bluma, Jeff
90WichSt-5

Blumberg, Rob Jr.
89StCath/ProC-2088
90A&AASingle/ProC-89
90Myrtle/ProC-2768
90SALAS/Star-27
91Kane/ClBest-4
91Kane/ProC-2651

Blume, David
81Wausau-11

Blundin, Barry
88Burllnd/ProC-1791

Bluthardt, Jay
88Watertn/Pucko-15

Blyleven, Bert
71MLB/St-458
71OPC-26
71T-26
72OPC-515
72T-515
73K-35
73OPC-199
73T-199
74K-46
74OPC-98
74T-98
74T/DE-47
74T/St-201
75Ho-74
75OPC-30
75T-30
75T/M-30
76Ho-116
76K-11
76OPC-204LL
76OPC-235
76SSPC-219
76T-204LL
76T-235
77BurgChef-22
77OPC-101
77T-630
77T/CS-5
78Ho-74
78K-53
78OPC-113
78T-131
78Wiffle/Discs-5
79Ho-133
79OPC-155
79T-308
80K-5
80OPC-238
80T-457
81D-135
81F-383
81OPC-294
81T-554
81T/Tr-738
82D-111
82F-361
82F/St-199
82OPC-164
82T-559TL
82T-685
82T/Tr-11T
82Wheat/Ind
83D-589
83OPC-280
83T-280
83Wheat/Ind-6
84D-129
84D/AAS-45
84D/Champs-42
84F-536
85FunFood/Pin-106
84Nes/792-716LL
84Nes/792-789
84OPC-126
84T-716ATL
84T-789
84T/St-261
84Wheat/Ind-28
85D-224
85D-4DK
85D/DKsuper-4
85F-440
85F/LimEd-2
85F/St-112
85F/St-81
85F/St-92
85Leaf-4DK
85OPC-355
85Polar/Ind-28
85Seven-7G
85T-355
85T/Gloss40-17
85T/St-247
85T/Super-35
86D-649
86D/AAS-52
86D/HL-31
86F-386
86F/Mini-82
86F/Slug-1
86F/St-6
86Leaf-88
86OPC-272
86Quaker-21
86Sf-103
86Sf-142M
86Sf-64M
86T-445
86T/3D-1
86T/Mini-23
86T/St-279
86T/Super-11
87D-71
87D/OD-226
87F-536
87F/AwardWin-3
87F/Mini-9
87F/St-10
87F/St-S3
87Leaf-100
87OPC-25
87RedFoley/St-101
87Sf-81
87T-25
87T/Mini-61
87T/St-278
88D-71
88D/Best-18
88F-4
88F/St-41
88Leaf-52
88Master/Disc-1
88OPC-295
88Panini/St-132
88S-90
88Sf-92
88Smok/Minn-6
88T-295
88T/Big-180
88T/St-20
88T/St-276
88Woolwth-21
89B-41
89D-119
89D/Best-3
89D/Tr-35
89F-105
89F/Up-12
89OPC-204
89S-215
89S/Tr-17
89T-555
89T/LJN-55
89T/St-285
89T/Tr-11T
89UD-225
89UD/Ext-712
90B-285
90Classic-142
90D-331
90D/BestAL-4
90F-128
90F/AwardWin-3
90F/BBMVP-2
90KayBee-2
90Leaf/I-63
90MLBPA/Pins-96
90OPC-130
90Panini/St-28
90PublInt/St-366
90RedFoley/St-5
90S-180
90S/100St-12
90Sf-193
90Smok/Angel-2
90T-130
90T/Big-114
90T/Mini-7
90T/St-165
90UD-527
90Woolwth/HL-7
91BBBest/RecBr-1
91D-453
91F-308
91Leaf/Stud-23
91OPC-615
91S-235
91T-615
91T/StClub/I-175
91T/WaxBox-A
91UD-571
91Woolwth/HL-7
92T-375
92UD-632

Blyth, Robert
(Bert)
82Iowa-14

Blyzka, Michael
(Mike)
54Esskay
54T-152
91Crown/Orio-38

Boag, Jack
78StPete

Boak, Chester Robert
(Chet)
No Cards.

Boatright, Dennis
83Butte-1

Bobb, Mark Randall
(Randy)
70OPC-429R
70T-429R
71OPC-83R
71T-83R

Bobo, Elgin
91Boise/ClBest-10
91Boise/ProC-3882

Boccabella, John D.
64T-192R
66T-482R
67T-578
68T-542
69MB-30
69T-466
70OPC-19
70T-19
71LaPizza-2
71MLB/St-123
71OPC-452
71T-452
72OPC-159
72T-159
73OPC-592
73T-592
74OPC-253
74T-253
74T/St-52
74Weston-12
75OPC-553
75T-553
75T/M-553
78TCMA-291

Bocek, Milton Frank
(Milt)
No Cards.

Bochesa, Greg
86WinHaven-4
87NewBrit-13
88NewBrit/ProC-900

Bochte, Bruce Anton
74SLCity
75OPC-392
75T-392
75T/M-392
76OPC-637
76SSPC-200

76T-637
77T-68
78Ho-81
78PapaG/Disc-29
78T-537
78Tastee/Discs-25
79Ho-123
79OPC-231
79T-443
80K-59
80OPC-80
80T-143
80T/S-55
81D-403
81Drake-25
81F-600
81F/St-8
81K-62
81MSA/Disc-3
81OPC-18
81Sqt-31
81T-723
81T/SO-30
81T/St-123
82D-505
82F-505
82F/St-222
82OPC-224
82T-224
82T/St-232
83D-127
83F-473
83OPC-28
83T-28
83T-711
83T/St-111
84F/X-13
84Mother/A's-6
85D-253
85F-416
85Mother/A's-10
85OPC-391
85T-632
85T/St-331
86D-400
86F-413
86F/Mini-86
86F/St-7
86Leaf-189
86Mother/A's-10
86OPC-378
86T-378
86T/St-170
87F-388
87T-496
87T/St-169

Bochtler, Doug
90Rockford/ProC-2694
91WPalmB/ClBest-2
91WPalmB/ProC-1218

Bochy, Bruce Douglas
76Dubuq
77Cocoa
79T-718R
80T-289
81D-20
81F-69
81Tidew-2
82Tidew-6
84Cram/PCL-225
84Nes/792-571
84T-571
85D-505
85Mother/Padres-12
85T-324
86D-551
86T-608
87D-311
87F-411
87T-428
88LasVegas/CMC-21
88LasVegas/ProC-241
88S-469
88T-31
89Pac/SenLg-194
89River/Best-25CO
89River/Cal-29CO
89River/ProC-1405CO
89Spokane/SP-4
90EliteSenLg-51
90Riversi/Best-22MG
90Riversi/Cal-24MG
91HighD/ClBest-29MG
91HighD/ProC-2412MG
91WIZMets-40

Bock, Doug
88AppFx/ProC-157

Bock, Paul
75AppFx
77Clinton

Bockewitz, Stan
76Wmsprt

Bockhorn, Glen
81Durham-11
86BuffB-1

Bockman, Joseph E.
(Eddie)
49B-195
49Eureka-153

Bockus, Randy
84Shrev/FB-3
86Phoenix-3
87F/Up-U6
87Phoenix-3
88F/Up-U127
88Phoenix/CMC-1
88Phoenix/ProC-55
89B-96
89T-733
89Toledo/CMC-1
89Toledo/ProC-769
91Edmon/LineD-155

Boddicker, Mike
80RochR-6
81RochR-1
81T-399R
82RochR-1
84D-123
84F-1
84F-645IA
84F/St-110
85FunFood/Pin-121
84Nes/792-191
84Nes/792-426TL
84Seven-9E
84T-191
84T/St-13
84T/St-375
85D-291
85Drake-34
85F-170
85F/St-80
85F/St-90
85Leaf-109
85OPC-225
85Seven-6E
85T-225
85T-709AS
85T/3D-26
85T/Gloss40-4
85T/St-202
85T/Super-16
85ThomMc/Discs-5
86D-47
86D-8DK
86D/DKsuper-8
86F-269
86F/Mini-57
86Leaf-8DK
86OPC-367
86Sf-104
86T-575
86T/St-233
87D-125
87D/OD-140
87F-463
87F/LL-2
87F/St-11
87French-52
87Leaf-76
87OPC-149
87RedFoley/St-40
87Sf-56
87Seven-ME8
87T-455
87T/St-227
88AlaskaAS70/Team-23
88D-89
88D/Best-317
88F-556
88F/St-1
88F/Up-U5
88French-52
88OPC-281
88Panini/St-5
88S-67
88Sf-146
88T-725
88T/St-231
89B-21
89Classic-139
89D-612
89D/Best-297
89F-80
89OPC-71
89S-549
89Sf-122
89T-71
89T/Big-296
89T/St-261
89UD-542
90B-267
90D-280
90D/BestAL-3
90F-267
90Leaf/I-19
90OPC-652
90Panini/St-20
90Pep/RSox-2
90Publlnt/St-447
90S-31
90T-652
90T/Big-258
90T/St-258
90T/TVRSox-7
90UD-652
91B-296
91Crown/Orio-39
91D-680
91F-85
91Leaf/II-330
91Leaf/Stud-61
91OPC-303
91OPC/Premier-10
91Panini/Top15-108
91Pol/Royal-3
91S-232
91S/RookTr-45T
91T-303
91T/StClub/II-400
91T/Tr-12T
91UD-438
91UD/Ext-719
92D/I-176
92F-153
92S/I-102
92T-106
92UD-213

Boddie, Eric
89Bakers/Cal-193
90VeroB/Star-6

Boddie, Rodney
(Rod)
88James/ProC-1905
89Rockford/Team-3
90WPalmB/Star-1

Bodenhamer, Don
74Gaston

Bodie, Frank Stephan
(Ping)
11Helmar-7
14CJ-79
15CJ-79
28Exh/PCL-4
D327
D328-16
E121/80
E122
E135-16
E224
T207
W514-66
W516-3
W575

Bodie, Keith
76Wausau
79Jacks-11
86AubAs-3MG
87Ashvl-4
88FSLAS/Star-3
89Clinton/ProC-898
90SanBern/Best-26MG
90SanBern/Cal-114
90SanBern/ProC-2649
91Calgary/LineD-74
91Calgary/ProC-530

Boeckel, Norman Doxie
(Tony)
E120
V100
V61-80
W572
W573

Boehler, George
90Target-58

Boehling, John Joseph
14CJ-72
15CJ-72
D328-17
E135-17

Boehmer, Leonard J.
(Len)
69T-519R

Boelter, Tarry
79Wisco-14

Boemier, Bill
53Mother-63

Boever, Dan
85Cedar-21
88Nashvl/CMC-15
88Nashvl/ProC-476
88Nashvl/Team-3
89Calgary/CMC-12
89Calgary/ProC-535
89Canton/Best-7
89Canton/ProC-1325
89Canton/Star-3
90CedarDG/Best-33

Boever, Joe
83StPete-1
86Louisvl-6
87Louisvl-5
88AAA/ProC-34
88F-534
88Richm-36
88Richm/CMC-9
88Richm/ProC-22
88S-542
88T-627
89D-168
89T-586
90D-357
90F-577
90Leaf/II-349
90OPC-410
90Panini/St-220
90Publlnt/St-110
90S-81
90SpringDG/Best-14
90T-410
90T/St-34
90UD-408
91B-502
91D-578
91F-387
91Leaf/I-68
91OPC-159
91Phill/Medford-4
91T-159
91T/StClub/II-462
91UD-430
92D/II-493
92F-523
92S/II-647
92T-696
92UD-402

Boffek, Scott
91VeroB/ClBest-19

Bogar, Tim
89Jacks/GS-3
90T/TVMets-36
90Tidew/CMC-14
90Tidew/ProC-549
91Wmsprt/LineD-626
91Wmsprt/ProC-298

Bogart
N172

Bogatyrev, Ilya
89EastLDD/ProC-DD17

Bogener, Terrence W.
(Terry)
79Tulsa-15
83D-520
83OKCty-3
84Wichita/Rock-13

Boggess, Dusty
55B-297ump

Boggetto, Brad
91Yakima/ClBest-20
91Yakima/ProC-4238

Boggs, Tommy
77T-328
78T-518
79Richm-22
79T-384
81D-597
81F-267
81Pol/Atl-40
81T-132
82BK/Lids-3
82D-249
82F-430
82T-61
83D-349
83F-131
83T-649
85OKCty-7

Boggs, Wade Anthony
81Pawtu-15
83D-586
83F-179
83T-498
83T/St-308
84D-151
84D-26DK
84D/AAS-22
84D/Champs-16
84Drake-2
84F-392
84F-630IA
84F/St-11
84F/St-28
84F/St-52
85FunFood/Pin-43
84MiltBrad-1
84Nes/792-131LL
84Nes/792-30
84Nes/792-786TL
84OPC-30
84Ralston-11
84Seven-10E
84T-131LL
84T-30
84T-786TL
84T/Cereal-11
84T/Gloss40-8
84T/St-100
84T/St-216
84T/St/Box-7
84T/Super-7
85D-172
85D/AAS-38
85D/HL-49
85F-151
85F/LimEd-3
85F/St-6
85Leaf-179
85OPC-350
85Seven-7E
85Seven-8C
85T-350
85T/St-210
86BK/AP-9
86D-371
86D/AAS-47
86D/AS/WaxBox-PC7
86D/HL-11
86D/HL-13
86Dorman-18
86Drake-27
86F-341
86F-634M
86F-639M
86F/LimEd-4
86F/LL-1
86F/Mini-72
86F/Slug-2
86F/St-8
86F/St-S2
86Jiffy-2
86Leaf-168
86Meadow/Blank-1
86Meadow/Milk-1
86Meadow/Stat-9
86OPC-262
86OPC-B
86Quaker-22
86Sf-180M
86Sf-183M
86Sf-184M
86Sf-3
86Sf-75M
86Sf/Dec-68
86T-510
86T/3D-3
86T/Gloss60-26
86T/Mini-3
86T/St-164

86T/St-247
86T/Super-12
86T/WaxBox-B
86TrueVal-30
86Woolwth-3
87BK-1
87Classic/Up-105
87Classic-60
87D-252
87D/AAS-7
87D/HL-14
87D/HL-44
87D/OD-181
87D/PopUp-7
87Drake-16
87F-29
87F-637M
87F/Excit-4
87F/GameWin-5
87F/HL-1
87F/BB-3
87F/LL-3
87F/Mini-10
87F/Slug-4
87F/St-12
87F/St-S2
87F/WS-2M
87Ho/St-19
87Jiffy-20
87KayBee-4
87KMart-23
87Kraft-7
87Leaf-193
87MnM's-5
87MSA/Discs-13
87OPC-150
87Ralston-3
87RedFoley/St-96
87Sf-114M
87Sf-197M
87Sf-2
87Seven-E5
87Seven-ME6
87Sportflic/DealP-2
87T-150
87T-608AS
87T/Board-31
87T/Coins-4
87T/Gloss22-15
87T/Gloss60-18
87T/HL-10
87T/Mini-41
87T/St-148
87T/St-253
87Woolwth-10
88ActPacT-1
88Bz-2
88ChefBoy-22
88Classic/Blue-214
88Classic/Red-155
88D-153
88D-BC7
88D/AS-31
88D/AS-7
88D/Best-65
88D/PopUp-7
88D/RedSox/Bk-153
88Drake-4
88F-345
88F/AS-8
88F/AwardWin-3
88F/BB/AS-2
88F/BB/MVP-2
88F/Excit-4
88F/Hottest-2
88F/LL-2
88F/Mini-4
88F/RecSet-3
88F/Slug-2
88F/SS-3
88F/St-5
88F/TL-2
88FanSam-8
88Jiffy-2
88KayBee-2
88KMart-2
88Leaf-65
88MSA/Disc-1
88Nestle-32
88OPC-200
88Panini/St-228M
88Panini/St-29
88S-2
88S/WaxBox-4
88Sf-50
88Sf/Gamewin-3
88T-21TL
88T-200
88T-388
88T/Big-32
88T/Coins-4
88T/Gloss22-4
88T/Gloss60-51
88T/Mini-1
88T/Revco-16
88T/RiteAid-14
88T/St-157
88T/St-244
88T/St/Backs-40
88T/UK-4
88Woolwth-13
89B-32
89Bz-3
89Cadaco-2
89Classic-102
89Classic-2
89D-68
89D/AS-7
89D/Best-140
89D/PopUp-7
89F-633M
89F-81
89F/BBAS-3
89F/BBMVP's-3
89F/Excit-2
89F/Heroes-2
89F/LL-2
89F/Rec-1
89F/Superstar-4
89F/WaxBox-C2
89Holsum/Discs-2
89KayBee-1
89KingB/Discs-3
89KMart/DT-14
89KMart/Lead-1
89Master/Discs-5
89Nissen-2
89OPC-184
89Panini/St-242AS
89Panini/St-245AS
89Panini/St-277
89Panini/St-7
89RedFoley/St-8
89S-175
89S-654HL
89S/HotStar-100
89S/Mast-17
89Sf-100
89Sf-221M
89T-2RB
89T-399AS
89T-600
89T/Big-241
89T/Coins-32
89T/DH-3
89T/Gloss22-4
89T/Gloss60-5
89T/HeadsUp-11
89T/Hills-2
89T/LJN-62
89T/Mini-45
89T/St-147
89T/St-260
89T/St-9
89T/St/Backs-7
89T/UK-4
89Tetley/Discs-7
89UD-389
89UD-687TC
89Woolwth-8
90B-281
90Classic-26
90CollAB-26
90D-68
90D-712AS
90D/BestAL-86
90D/Learning-21
90D/Preview-11
90F-268
90F-632M
90F/AwardWin-4
90F/BB-1
90F/BBMVP-3
90F/LgStand-5
90F/LL-4
90HotPlay/St-2
90KayBee-3
90KingB/Discs-9
90KMart/CBatL-1
90KMart/SS-19
90Leaf/I-51
90MLBPA/Pins-68
90MSA/Soda-3
90OPC-387AS
90OPC-760
90Panini/St-19
90Panini/St-199M
90Pep/RSox-3
90Post-17
90PublInt/St-277
90PublInt/St-448
90RedFoley/St-6
90S-245
90S-683DT
90S-704
90S/100St-80
90Sf-2
90Starline/LJS-17
90Starline/LJS-22
90Starline/LJS-6
90T-387AS
90T-760
90T/Ames-16
90T/Big-77
90T/Coins-6
90T/DH-4
90T/Gloss22-15
90T/Gloss60-22
90T/HillsHM-19
90T/Mini-3
90T/St-156AS
90T/St-253
90T/St-8HL
90T/TVAS-20
90T/TVRSox-22
90T/WaxBox-A
90Tetley/Discs-7
90UD-555
90USPlayC/AS-11C
90Windwlk/Discs-2
90Woolwth/HL-8
91B-129
91BBBest/HitM-2
91Classic/200-192
91Classic/I-19
91Classic/III-T3
91CollAB-16
91D-178
91D-55AS
91F-86
91F/Ultra-27
91KingB/Discs-11
91Leaf/II-273
91Leaf/Prev-14
91Leaf/Stud-11
91MajorLg/Pins-9
91MooTown-11
91OPC-450
91OPC/Premier-11
91Panini/FrSt-169
91Panini/FrSt-266
91Panini/St-214
91Panini/Top15-30
91RedFoley/St-115
91RedFoley/St-9
91S-12
91S-393AS
91S-889DT
91S/100SS-3
91S/Cooper-B1
91Seven/3DCoin-1NE
91Sunflower-2
91T-450
91T/CJMini/I-29
91T/StClub/I-170
91T/SU-3
91UD-546
91UD/FinalEd-84F
91USPlayC/AS-WC
92D/DK-DK9
92D/Elite-E9
92D/I-210
92D/I-23AS
92D/Preview-1
92F-32
92F-707M
92F/TmLIns-13
92S/100SS-30
92S/I-434AS
92S/II-660
92S/II-885
92T-10
92T-399AS
92UD-443
92UD-646DS

Bogues, Muggsy
91Gaston/ClBest-29

Bohanon, Brian
88CharlR/Star-2
90B-489
90D/Rook-13
90F/Up-122
90Mother/Rang-13
90UD/Ext-731
91S/100RisSt-53
91T/90Debut-18
92S/II-672
92T-149

Bohlke, Scott
88Durham/Star-2

Bohn, Charles
(Charlie)
No Cards.

Bohn, Matt
88CalLgAS-23

Bohne, Sammy Arthur
21Exh-12
90Target-59
E120
V117-20
V61-67

Bohnenkamp, Dave
89Clinton/ProC-880

Bohnet, Bob
79Wisco-13
82Holyo-14

Bohnet, John
81Chatt-13
82Charl-2
84BuffB-14

Bohrofen, Brent
91Hamil/ClBest-22
91Hamil/ProC-4050

Boisclair, Bruce A.
75Tidew/Team-5
77T-399
78T-277
79OPC-68
79T-148
80T-654
91WIZMets-41

Boitano, Danny
76OkCty/Team-4
79Vanco-9
80T-668R
80Vanco-14
81Tidew-27
91WIZMets-42

Bojcun, Pat
91Batavia/ClBest-21
91Batavia/ProC-3476

Bokelman, Dick
53T-204
79TCMA-249
91T/Arc53-204

Boken, Robert A.
(Bob)
34G-74

Boker, Mike
91BendB/ClBest-11
91BendB/ProC-3685

Boland, Edward John
(Ed)
No Cards.

Bolar, Wendell
86Cram/PCL-106
87Wausau-9
88Boise/ProC-1607

Bold, Charles Dickens
(Charlie)
No Cards.

Bolek, Ken
76Clinton
78Watlo
83ColumAst-23
86Ashvl-3MG
87Osceola-6
88Watlo/ProC-687
89Kinston/Star-25
90Canton/Best-4MG
90Canton/ProC-1309MG
90Canton/Star-20MG
91Canton/LineD-99
91Canton/ProC-995

Boles, Carl Theodore
63T-428

Boles, John
83AppFx/LF-25MG
85BuffB-1
86Omah/TCM-23MG
86Omaha-2MG

Boley, John Peter
(Joe)
31Exh/4-27

Bolger, James Cyril
(Jim)
55T-179
57T-289
58T-201
59T-29
61Union

Bolick, Frank
76SanAn/Team-2

Bolick, Frank C.
88Beloit/GS-4
89Beloit/I/Star-1
89Beloit/II/Star-1
90A&AASingle/ProC-152
90AS/Cal-11
90Stockton/Best-7
90Stockton/Cal-193
90Stockton/ProC-2192
91B-534
91Jaxvl/LineD-329
91Jaxvl/ProC-154
91Single/ClBest-381
92T-473M

Bolin, Bobby
61T-449
62T-329
63T-106
64T-374
65T-341
66OPC-61
66T-61
67T-252
68Coke
68Dexter-14
68OPC-169
68T-169
69OPC-8LL
69T-505
69T-8LL
69T/St-101
70McDon-1
70MLB/St-266
70T-574
71MLB/St-314
71OPC-446
71T-446
72MB-36
72OPC-266
72T-266
73OPC-541
73T-541
74OPC-427
74T-427
78TCMA-109

Boling, John
86AppFx-2
87BirmB/Best-12
88BirmB/Best-18
90Target-60

Bolling, Frank Elmore
55B-204
57T-325
58T-95
59T-280
60T-482
61P-41
61T-335
61T/St-145
62J-146
62P-146
62P/Can-146
62Salada-140
62Shirriff-140
62T-130
62T-211M
62T/St-145
63F-44
63J-149
63P-149
63Salada-18
63T-570
64T-115
65Kahn

65OPC-269
65T-269
66Kahn
78TCMA-9
81Detroit-103

Bolling, John Edward
No Cards.

Bolling, Milton J.
(Milt)
53T-280
54B-130
54T-82
55B-48
55T-91
55T/DH-92
56T-315
57T-131
58T-188
91T/Arc53-280

Bollo, Greg
65T-541R
66T-301
78TCMA-30

Bollweg, Donald R.
(Don)
52T-128
54B-115
55B-54
55Rodeo
PM10/Sm-14

Bolster, Bob
80GlenF/B-29bb
80GlenF/C-23bb

Bolt, James
86SanJose-5

Bolton, Cecil G.
No Cards.

Bolton, Rod
90Utica/Pucko-14
91FSLAS/ProC-FSL27
91Saraso/ClBest-1
91Saraso/ProC-1104
91Single/ClBest-56

Bolton, Tom
80Elmira-2
87Pawtu-12
87Pawtu/TCMA-27
88F-346
88Pawtu/CMC-9
88Pawtu/ProC-452
88T-442
89AAA/ProC-17
89D-539
89Pawtu/CMC-1
89Pawtu/Dunkin-15
89Pawtu/ProC-680
89S-531
89T-269
89UD-545
90Pawtu/ProC-453
90T/TVRSox-38
90UD-351
91B-114
91D-609
91F-87
91F/Ultra-28
91Leaf/I-47
91OPC-37
91Pep/RSox-1
91S-781
91T-37
91T/StClub/II-588
91UD-86
92F-33
92S/I-99
92T-708
92UD-110

Bolton, William C.
(Cliff)
34DS-47
34G-65
92Conlon/Sport-505
R313
R314
V355-133

Boltz, Brian
90Foil/Best-87
90Greenvl/Best-7
90Greenvl/ProC-1122
90Greenvl/Star-4

Bomback, Mark
77Holyo
79Vanco-7
81F-323
81OPC-264
81T-567
81T/Tr-739
82D-559
82F-610
82OPC-307
82T-707
83Syrac-5
84Syrac-23
89Pac/SenLg-39
91WIZMets-43

Bombard, Marc
86FSLAS-9CO
87Tampa-8
88Cedar/ProC-1144
88MidwLAS/GS-15
89ElPaso/GS-1
90CedarDG/Best-28MG
90EastLAS/ProC-EL29
90Harris/ProC-1208
90Harris/Star-23
91CaroMud/LineD-124
91CaroMud/ProC-1101

Bombard, Rich
82AubAs-13
83DayBe-3
86ColumAst-5
87Cedar-26
88Chatt/Best-5
89Chatt/Best-8
89Chatt/GS-2
91Fayette/ClBest-12

Bomgardner, Rich
89Clmbia/Best-25
89Clmbia/GS-3

Bonacquista, Jeff
87Anchora-3

Bonaparte, Elijah
77Spartan
80OkCty
81OkCty/TCMA-3
82Toledo-19
83RochR-19

Bonarigo, Nick
43Centen-2

Bonchek, Jeff
88Burllnd/ProC-1779
89Miami/I/Star-3

Boncore, Steve
82VeroB-13
83VeroB-14

Bond, Daven
86AubAs-4
87Ashvl-6
88Osceola/Star-4
89Osceola/Star-2
90ColMud/Best-14
90ColMud/ProC-1338
90ColMud/Star-5
91ColClip/LineD-102
91ColClip/ProC-589

Bond, David
87Spokane-16
88Charl/ProC-1196
89CharRain/ProC-993

Bond, Doug
88Billings/ProC-1809

Bond, Michael
91Belling/ClBest-11
91Belling/ProC-3670

Bond, Thomas Henry
(Tommy)
No Cards.

Bond, Walter F.
(Walt)
60T-552
61T-334
62Salada-208
62Shirriff-208
63T-493
64T-339
65OPC-109
65T-109
65T/E-50
65T/trans-4
66T-431
67T-224

Bonds, Barry
86D/Rook-11
86F/Up-U14
86Sf/Rook-13
86T/Tr-11T
87Classic/Up-113
87D-361
87D/OD-163
87F-604
87F/Hottest-5
87Leaf-219
87OPC-320
87T-320
87T/Gloss60-30
87T/St-131
87ToysRUs-4
88D-326
88D/Best-17
88F-322
88F/SS-4
88KingB/Disc-11
88Leaf-113
88OPC-267
88Panini/St-376
88RedFoley/St-7
88S-265
88S/YS/II-12
88Sf-119
88T-450
88T/Big-89
88T/St-135
88T/UK-5
89T/Ames-5
89B-426
89Classic-117
89D-92
89D/Best-73
89F-202
89F/Heroes-3
89OPC-263
89Panini/St-172
89RedFoley/St-9
89S-127
89S/HotStar-31
89Sf-146
89T-620
89T/Big-5
89T/LJN-95
89T/St-127
89T/St/Backs-46
89T/UK-5
89UD-440
89VFJuice-24
90B-181
90Classic-82
90Classic/III-68
90D-126
90D/BestNL-45
90F-461
90Homer/Pirate-5
90Leaf/I-91
90MLBPA/Pins-37
90OPC-220
90Panini/St-322
90PublInt/St-149
90RedFoley/St-7
90S-4
90S/100St-53
90S/McDon-11
90Sf-143
90Sunflower-9
90T-220
90T/Big-128
90T/Coins-40
90T/DH-5
90T/Mini-70
90T/St-123
90T/St-9HL
90UD-227
90USPlayC/AS-13D
91B-380SLUG
91B-513
91Bz-1
91Classic/200-195
91Classic/I-81
91Classic/II-T78
91Colla/Bonds-Set
91CollAB-26
91D-495
91D-4DK
91D-762MVP
91D/Elite-E1
91D/GSlam-5
91D/Preview-10
91D/SuperDK-4DK
91F-33
91F-710M
91F/ASIns-5
91F/ProVF-1F
91F/Ultra-275
91F/Ultra-391EP
91F/UltraG-1
91JDeanSig-4
91KingB/Discs-21
91Leaf/I-261
91Leaf/II-364CL
91Leaf/Prev-9
91Leaf/Stud-222
91MajorLg/Pins-57
91MooTown-3
91OPC-401AS
91OPC-570
91OPC/Premier-12
91Panini/FrSt-119
91Panini/St-114
91Panini/Top15-105
91Panini/Top15-12
91Panini/Top15-20
91Panini/Top15-33
91Panini/Top15-43
91Pep/SS-7
91Petro/SU-16
91Post-21
91Post/Can-5
91S-330
91S-668AS
91S-868FRAN
91S-876MVP
91S/100SS-26
91Seven/3DCoin-1F
91Seven/3DCoin-2NE
91Seven/3DCoin-2T
91T-401AS
91T-570
91T/CJMini/I-19
91T/StClub/I-220
91T/SU-4
91UD-154
91UD-94
91UD/SilSlug-SS5
91Woolwth/HL-1
92Classic/I-16
92Classic/I-xx
92D/I-243
92D/Preview-2
92F-550
92F/ASIns-3
92S/100SS-26
92S/II-555
92S/II-777AS
92T-380
92T-390AS
92UD-134

Bonds, Bobby Lee
69MB-31
69T-630
70MLB/St-121
70OPC-425
70T-425
71MLB/St-241
71OPC-295
71T-295
71T/Coins-13
71Ticket/Giant-1
72MB-37
72T-711
72T-712A
73K-8
73OPC-145
73T-145
73T/Lids-6
74K-39
74Laugh/ASG-73
74OPC-30
74T-30
74T/Puzzles-4
74T/St-101
75Ho-145
75OPC-55
75T-55
75T/M-55
76Ho-18
76Ho/Twink-18
76OPC-2RB
76OPC-380
76SSPC-436
76T-2RB
76T-380
76T/Tr-380T
77BurgChef-124
77OPC-173
77T-570
78Ho-42
78OPC-206
78T-150
78Wiffle/Discs-6
79OPC-142
79T-285
80BK/PHR-23
80OPC-215
80T-410
81D-71
81F-548
81OPC-223
81T-635
81T/Tr-740
82F-588
82OPC-27
82T-580
84Mother/Giants-12
85Polar/Ind
86OhHenry-CO
87Gator-CO
89Pac/SenLg-128
89T/SenLg-40
89TM/SenLg-10
89TM/SenLg-119M
90EliteSenLg-109
90EliteSenLg-122
91Swell/Great-11

Bone, George D.
No Cards.

Bone, Pat
82Oneonta-10

Bones, Ricardo
(Ricky)
86Cram/PCL-163
87CharRain-21
88CalLgAS-41
88River/Cal-208
88River/ProC-1426
89AubAs/ProC-16
89Wichita/Rock-10
89Wichita/Rock/HL-2
90Wichita/Rock-2
91B-643
91LasVegas/ProC-226
91LasVegas/LineD-278
92D/II-545
92F-600
92S/II-758
92T-711
92T/91Debut-17
92UD-623

Bongiovanni, Anthony
(Nino)
W711/1

Bonham, Bill
72OPC-29
72T-29
73OPC-328
73T-328
74OPC-528
74T-528
75OPC-85
75T-85
75T/M-85
76OPC-151
76SSPC-303
76T-151
77BurgChef-192
77OPC-95
77T-446
78T-276
79K-31
79OPC-182
79T-354
80OPC-26
80T-47
81F-215
81Indianap-13
81T-712
86AubAs-5CO

Bonham, Ernie
(Tiny)
43MP-1
44Yank/St-1
47TipTop
49B-77
49Eureka-154

Boni, Joel
82Madis-2

Bonine, Eddie
90Gate/ProC-3363CO

Bonikowski, Joe
61Clover-4

62T-592R
Bonilla, Bobby
83AlexD-16
86Coke/WS-26
86D/Rook-30
86F/Up-U15
86Sf/Rook-26
86T/Tr-12T
87D-558
87D/OD-167
87F-605
87T-184
88Classic/Blue-236
88D-238
88D/Best-33
88F-323
88F/BB/AS-3
88F/Hottest-3
88F/Mini-103
88F/Slug-3
88F/St-114
88Leaf-188
88OPC-189
88Panini/St-372
88S-116
88S/YS/II-9
88Sf-131
88T-681
88T/Big-25
88T/Coins-37
88T/St-129
89B-422
89Cadaco-3
89D-151
89D-2DK
89D/AS-39
89D/Best-33
89D/DKsuper-2DK
89D/PopUp-39
89F-203
89F-637M
89F/AS-1
89F/BBAS-4
89Nissen-15
89OPC-142
89Panini/St-171
89Panini/St-234AS
89RedFoley/St-10
89S-195
89S/HotStar-42
89Sf-182
89T-388AS
89T-440
89T/Big-159
89T/Coins-5
89T/DH-15
89T/Gloss22-15
89T/Gloss60-24
89T/LJN-127
89T/Mini-30
89T/St-131
89T/St-158
89T/St/Backs-40
89T/UK-6
89UD-578
89VFJuice-25
90B-169
90Classic-143
90Classic/III-73
90D-290
90D/BestNL-70
90D/Bon/MVP-BC16
90F-462
90F/BB-2
90F/BBMVP-4
90Homer/Pirate-6
90HotPlay/St-3
90KingB/Discs-8
90Leaf/I-196
90Leaf/Prev-10
90MLBPA/Pins-38
90OPC-273
90Panini/St-325
90PublInt/St-150
90PublInt/St-253
90S-170
90S/100St-37
90Sf-195
90Starline/LJS-31
90Starline/LJS-5
90T-273
90T/Big-208
90T/Coins-41
90T/DH-6
90T/Mini-71
90T/St-129
90T/TVAS-59
90Tetley/Discs-11
90UD-16TC
90UD-366
90USPlayC/AS-11H
91B-381SLUG
91B-525
91Classic/200-144
91Classic/II-T92
91Classic/III-T4
91Classic/III-xx
91D-325
91D/GSlam-2
91DennyGS-17
91F-34
91F-711M
91F/Ultra-276
91Leaf/II-357
91Leaf/Stud-223
91OPC-403AS
91OPC-750
91Panini/FrSt-120
91Panini/St-111
91Panini/Top15-18
91Panini/Top15-50
91Pep/SS-15
91Post-14
91RedFoley/St-10
91S-315
91S-402MB
91S-670AS
91S/100SS-42
91Sunflower-3
91T-403AS
91T-750
91T/CJMini/II-15
91T/StClub/I-139
91T/SU-5
91UD-152
91UD/FinalEd-99F
91UD/SilSlug-SS15
91USPlayC/AS-JK
92D/II-427AS
92D/II-610
92F-551
92F-699M
92F/ASIns-4
92F/TmLIns-9
92S/100SS-80
92S/I-225
92T-160
92T-392AS
92UD-225
Bonilla, George
85Everett/Cram-2A
85Everett/Cram-2B
86Clinton-3
88Shreve/ProC-1289
89Shreve/ProC-1855
90Phoenix/CMC-4
90Phoenix/ProC-2
Bonilla, Juan G.
78Watlo
80Tacoma-19
82D-220
82F-567
82T-464
83D-346
83F-353
83T-563
84D-234
84F-295
84Nes/792-168
84OPC-168
84T-168
84T/St-152
85Colum-26
85IntLgAS-26
86T/Tr-13T
87F-464
87OPC-131
87T-668
88Chatt/Team-2
91Crown/Orio-40
Bonin, Ernest Luther
(Luther)
No Cards
Bonin, Greg
88TM/Umpire-56
89TM/Umpire-54
90TM/Umpire-52
Bonine, Eddie
83Tucson-1
84Cram/PCL-64
85Cram/PCL-70
Bonitto, Arturo
77QuadC
Bonk, Thomas
85Greens-5
Bonneau, Rob
88Wythe/ProC-1976
Bonnell, Robert Barry
(Barry)
78Ho-142
78T-242
79T-496
80OPC-331
80T-632
81D-272
81F-413
81OPC-82
81OPC/Post-19
81T-558
82D-432
82F-611
82OPC-99
82T-99
82T/St-251
83D-430
83F-425
83OPC-281
83T-766
83T/St-133
84D-559
84F-149
84F/X-14
84Mother/Mar-2
84Nes/792-302
84OPC-302
84T-302
84T/St-370
84T/Tr-14
85D-191
85F-485
85Leaf-195
85Mother/Mar-10
85OPC-107
85T-423
85T/St-342
86F-460
86Mother/Mar-10
86OPC-119
86T-119
91Pac/SenLg-123
Bonner, Frank J.
No Cards.
Bonner, Jeffry
(Jeff)
89Clinton/ProC-892
90Clinton/Best-5
90Clinton/ProC-2560
91SanJose/ClBest-9
91SanJose/ProC-22
91Single/ClBest-76
Bonner, Mark
82Danvl-25
83Redwd-4
85MidldA-5
Bonner, Robert A.
(Bob)
80RochR-1
81RochR-2
82D-610
82T-21R
83F-53
83RochR-14
84RochR-13
91Crown/Orio-41
Bonura, Henry John
(Zeke)
34DS-65
35BU-141
35BU-65
35Exh/4-10
35G-8B
35G-9B
36Exh/4-10
36G
37Exh/4-10
37OPC-116
37Wheat
38G-252
38G-276
38Wheat
39PB-144
40PB-131
88Conlon/5-4
91Conlon/Sport-237
R312/M
R313
R314
V300
V355-112
WG8-3
Bonura, Tony
86Cram/PCL-93
Booe, Everitt Little
No Cards.
Booker, Eric
90A&AASingle/ProC-168
90SoOreg/Best-10
90SoOreg/ProC-3429
91Modesto/ClBest-16
91Modesto/ProC-3101
91Single/ClBest-286
Booker, Greg
84Cram/PCL-218
85F-27
85Mother/Padres-22
85T-262
86LasVegas-2
86T-429
87T/Tr-6T
88Coke/Padres-51
88D-311
88F-577
88S-447
88Smok/Padres-4
88T-727
89S-417
89T-319
89T/Big-194
89UD-641
90Phoenix/CMC-9
90Phoenix/ProC-3
90PublInt/St-44
Booker, Richard Lee
(Buddy)
No Cards.
Booker, Rod
82OrlTw/A-1
82Toledo-12
83ArkTr-19
84Louisvl-12
86ArkTr-2
86Louisvl-7
87F/Up-U7
87Louisvl-6
88Louisvl-10
88T-483
89Louisvl-11
89Louisvl/CMC-8
89Louisvl/ProC-1264
89T/Big-256
89UD-644
90Phill/TastyK-2
91F-388
91OPC-186
91Phill/Medford-5
91T-186
Bool, Albert
(Al)
No Cards.
Boone, Antonio
91Hamil/ClBest-13
91Hamil/ProC-4028
Boone, Bret
88Alaska/Team-3
91B-261
91Jaxvl/LineD-330
91Jaxvl/ProC-155
Boone, Danny
79SLCity-23
82D-187
82F-568
82T-407
83Tucson-2
84Cram/PCL-36
85Anchora-5
90ElPasoATG/Team-38
90RochR/CMC-27
90RochR/ProC-698
91Crown/Orio-42
91Pac/SenLg-44
91S-715RP
Boone, Isaac Morgan
(Ike)
87Conlon/2-24
88MinorLg/Leg-3
90Target-61
R314/Can
Boone, Lute Joseph
(Luke)
D350/2-12
M101/5-12
Boone, Raymond Otis
(Ray)
50NumNum
51B-54
51T/RB-23
52B-214
52NumNum-13
52T-55
53B/Col-79
53T-25
54T-77
55RFG-11
55RM-AL1
55T-65
55T/DH-113
56T-6
56T/Hocus-A7
56T/Hocus-B9
56T/Pin-36
57T-102
58T-185
59T-252
60Lake
60T-281
76OPC-67FS
76T-67FS
79TCMA-179
81Detroit-84
83Kaline-15M
85T-133FS
91T/Arc53-25
Boone, Robert Raymond
(Bob)
73OPC-613R
73T-613R
74JP
74OPC-131
74T-131
74T/St-71
75OPC-351
75T-351
75T/M-351
76OPC-318
76OPC-67FS
76SSPC-471
76T-318
76T-67M
77BurgChef-164
77OPC-68
77T-545
78Ho-29
78OPC-141
78T-161
79BK/P-2
79Ho-113
79OPC-38
79T-90
80BK/P-2
80OPC-246
80T-470
81Coke
81D-262
81F-4
81F/St-79
81OPC-290
81T-290
81T/HT
81T/St-203
82D-471
82F-240
82OPC-23
82OPC-392IA
82T-615
82T-616A
82T/St-77
82T/Tr-9T
83D-192
83F-79
83OPC-366
83T-765
83T/St-45
84D-158
84F-509
84F-637
84Nes/792-520
84OPC-174
84Smok/Cal-3

84T-520
84T/St-234
85D-230
85F-295
85OPC-348
85Smok/Cal-3
85T-133FS
85T-348
85T/St-228
86D-17
86D-230
86D/DKsuper-17
86F-149
86Leaf-17DK
86OPC-62
86Smok/Cal-3
86T-62
86T/St-179
87D-233
87D/HL-41
87F-73
87F/AwardWin-4
87Leaf-202
87OPC-166
87T-166
87T/St-180
88AlaskaAS60/Team-10
88D-305
88D/Best-3
88F-485
88Leaf-151
88OPC-158
88OPC-D
88Panini/St-39
88S-63
88Sf-212
88Smok/Angels-9
88T-498
88T/Big-30
88T/St-182
88T/St-5
88T/UK-6
88T/WaxBox-D
89B-119
89Classic/Up/2-187
89D-170
89D/Best-263
89D/Tr-5
89F-469
89F/Up-36
89OPC-243
89Panini/St-287
89S-233
89S/HotStar-81
89S/Tr-74
89Sf-40
89Smok/Angels-17
89T-243
89T-404AS
89T/Big-269
89T/LJN-48
89T/St-175
89T/St/Backs-22
89T/Tr-12T
89UD-119
89UD/Ext-767
90B-373
90D-326
90D/BestAL-50
90F-102
90F/AwardWin-5
90Leaf/I-46
90MLBPA/Pins-107
90OPC-671
90PublInt/St-278
90PublInt/St-343
90S-60
90Sf-40
90T-671
90T/Big-268
90UD-271
91D-356
91F-551
91UD-502

Boone, Ron
75Iowa/TCMA-2

Bootay, Kevin
86Salem-1
86Tulsa-16
88TexLgAS/GS-9
88Tulsa-13
89ScrWB/CMC-24
89ScrWB/ProC-713

Booth, Amos Smith
No Cards.

Booth, David
88Pocatel/ProC-2098
89SanJose/Best-10
89SanJose/Cal-228
89SanJose/ProC-440
89SanJose/Star-2

Booth, Edward H.
(Eddie)
No Cards.

Boothby, John
90Wausau/Star-4

Boozer, John
63T-29R
64PhilBull-5
64T-16
65OPC-184
65T-184
66T-324
68OPC-173
68T-173
69T-599
89Chatt/II/Team-3

Boras, Scott
77StPete

Borbon, Ernie
82VeroB-2
83Albuq-21
84Cram/PCL-159

Borbon, Pedro
70OPC-358
70T-358
71OPC-613
71T-613
73OPC-492
73T-492
74OPC-410
74T-410
74T/St-23
75OPC-157
75T-157
75T/M-157
76OPC-77
76SSPC-24
76T-77
77Pep-54
77T-581
78OPC-199
78T-220
79OPC-164
79T-326
80T-627
89Pac/SenLg-49
89T/SenLg-77
89TM/SenLg-11
90EliteSenLg-93

Borbon, Pedro Jr.
90A&AASingle/ProC-124
90BurlB/Best-1
90BurlB/ProC-2340
90BurlB/Star-4
90Foil/Best-31
91Durham/ClBest-10
91Durham/ProC-1536

Borcherding, Mark
89Billings/ProC-2066
90Cedar/Best-24
90CharWh/ProC-2232
91Cedar/ClBest-2
91Cedar/ProC-2710
91MidwLAS/ProC-MWL21
91Single/ClBest-372

Borchers, Rick
79Tacoma-3
80Tacoma-21
81Chatt-18
82Chatt-20

Borchert, Shane
89Clinton/ProC-889
90Madison/Best-27TR
91Madison/ClBest-21

Bordagaray, Stanley
(Frenchy)
36Exh/4-2
36G-3
39PB-75
90Target-62
R312/M
R314
W711/1

Border, Bob
80ElPaso-10

Border, Mark
82Idaho-3

Borders, Pat
85Kingst-15
86Knoxvl-3
87Knoxvl-20
88D/Rook-12
88F/Up-U65
88S/Tr-99T
88T/Tr-17T
88Tor/Fire-10
89D-560
89F-227
89OPC-343
89Panini/St-464
89S-198
89S/HotRook-91
89S/YS/I-11
89T-693
89T/St-191
89Tor/Fire-10
89UD-593
90B-521
90Classic/III-39
90D-560
90F-77
90Leaf/II-343
90OPC-191
90Panini/St-175
90PublInt/St-510
90S-288
90Sf-45
90T-191
90T/Big-60
90Tor/BlueJ-10
90UD-112
91B-14
91D-317
91F-171
91F/Ultra-359
91Leaf/I-23
91OPC-49A
91OPC-49B
91Panini/FrSt-335
91Panini/St-156
91S-425
91S/ToroBJ-11
91T-49A
91T-49B
91T/StClub/I-266
91Tor/Fire-10
91UD-147
92D/I-379
92F-325
92S/I-288
92T-563
92UD-140

Bordi, Rich
81Tacoma-10
82SLCity-4
82T-531R
83Iowa-1
84SevenUp-42
85D-289
85F-49
85F/Up-U8
85Leaf-166
85T-357
85T/Tr-7T
86D-518
86F-101
86F/Up-U16
86T-94
86T/Tr-14T
87Colum-22
87Colum/Pol-3
87Colum/TCMA-2
87D-213
87F-465
87T-638
88Tacoma/CMC-1
88Tacoma/ProC-627
89Tacoma/CMC-1
89Tacoma/ProC-1544
90Phoenix/ProC-4
91Crown/Orio-43

Bordick, Michael
(Mike)
87Modesto-6
88Huntsvl/BK-1
88SLAS-4
89Tacoma/CMC-23
89Tacoma/ProC-1565
90Tacoma/ProC-98
91Classic/II-T58
91S-339RP
91T/90Debut-19
91Tacoma/LineD-527
92D/II-505
92F-251
92S/II-681
92T-317

Bordley, Bill
79Phoenix
80Phoenix-10

Borelli, Dean
88SoOreg/ProC-1705
89Madis/Star-4
90Modesto/Cal-164

Borg, Gary
86Visalia-4
87Orlan-16
88OrlanTw/Best-12
89AS/Cal-34
89Stockton/Best-18
89Stockton/Cal-164
89Stockton/ProC-396
89Stockton/Star-1

Borgatti, Mike
87Hagers-1
88Virgini/Star-2
89Watlo/ProC-1793
89Watlo/Star-1
90Hagers/Best-19
90Hagers/ProC-1402
90Hagers/Star-2

Borges, George
83MidldC-15
84PrWill-33

Borges, Jose
89Butte/SP-9

Borgese, Jeff
88CapeCod/Sum-20
90A&AASingle/ProC-194
90Martins/ProC-3201

Borgmann, Bennie
40Hughes-5

Borgmann, Glenn D.
73OPC-284
73T-284
74OPC-547
74T-547
75OPC-127
75T-127
75T/M-127
76OPC-498
76SSPC-213
76T-498
77T-87
78T-307
79T-431
80T-634
81D-159
81T-716

Borgogno, Mate
89Alaska/Team-17
90ClintUp/Team-U1
90Everett/Best-16
90Everett/ProC-3132
91Clinton/ClBest-11
91Clinton/ProC-839

Borhinger, Helms
90Yakima/Team-4

Boris, Paul
81Colum-7
83T-266
83Toledo-1
84Richm-4

Bork, Frank
65T-592
66OPC-123R
66T-123R

Borkowski, Robert V.
(Bob)
52T-328
53T-7
54T-138
55T-74
55T/DH-63
91T/Arc53-7

Borland, Scott
83AlexD-4
84PrWill-18
85PrWill-15

Borland, Toby
88Martins/Star-4
89Spartan/ProC-1037
89Spartan/Star-2
90Clearw/Star-2
91Reading/LineD-502
91Reading/ProC-1363
91Single/ClBest-336

Borland, Tom
60L-26
60T-117
61T-419
89Smok/Ast-6

Borman, Dave
89Utica/Pucko-9

Bormann, Mike
83Durham-16
85Durham-4

Bornw, Tony
89Tidew/CMC-27

Borom, Edward Jones
(Red)
No Cards.

Boros, Stephen
(Steve)
58T-81
59T-331
61T-348
61T/St-146
62J-16
62P-16
62P/Can-16
62Salada-50
62Shirriff-50
62T-62
62T-72M
62T/St-42
63J-47
63P-47
63T-532
65OPC-102
65T-102
65T-131
78TCMA-88
83Granny-14MG
83T/X-13MG
84Mother/A's-1MG
84Nes/792-531MG
84T-531
86T/Tr-15T
87T-143MG

Boroski, Stan
83Beloit/LF-28
86FtMyr-4
87FtMyr-2

Borowicz, Ray
88BurlInd/ProC-1801

Borowski, Rich
83Idaho-20
84Madis/Pol-23

Borowsky, Erez
83Visalia/LF-15
84Visalia-3
85Orlan-2

Borowski, Joe
91Kane/ClBest-2
91Kane/ProC-2652

Borowy, Henry
(Hank)
39Exh
44Yank/St-2
49B-134
49Eureka-131
49Lummis
50B-177
51B-250

Borrelli, Dean
90Modesto/ProC-2214
91Huntsvl/ClBest-3
91Huntsvl/LineD-278
91HuntsvlProC-1798

Borriello, Sebby
82Wisco-13

Borruel, Jeff
78Cedar

Borski, Jeff
91Belling/ClBest-23
91Belling/ProC-3655

Borton, William Baker
(Babe)
No Cards.

Borucki, Ray
80Penin/B-19
80Penin/C-25

Borzello, Aaire
91Johnson/ClBest-3

Bosarge, Scott
91Belling/ClBest-15
91Belling/ProC-3667
Bosch, Donald John
(Don)
68T-572
69Fud's-3
69T-578
70OPC-527
70T-527
72MB-38
91WIZMets-44
Bosco, Joseph
90Peoria/Team-37ATHR
Bosco, Mike
89Reno/Cal-253
Bosetti, Richard Alan
(Rick)
76OkCty/Team-5
78T-710R
79OPC-279
79T-542
80OPC-146
80T-277
80T/S-51
81D-152
81OPC-46
81OPC/Post-18
81T-46
81T/Tr-741
82D-626
82F-88
82T-392
82Tacoma-33
Bosio, Chris
83Beloit/LF-27
86Vanco-4
87D-478
87D/Rook-20
87F-338
87Pol/Brew-29
87Sf/Rook-2
87T-448
88D-117
88D/Best-295
88F-156
88OPC-137
88Pol/Brew-29
88S-38
88S/YS/I-4
88T-137
89B-134
89Brewer/YB-29
89D-412
89D/Best-109
89F-179
89Pol/Brew-29
89RedFoley/St-11
89S-243
89T-311
89UD-292
90B-389
90Brewer/MillB-1
90Classic/III-42
90D-20DK
90D-57
90D/BestAL-9
90D/SuperDK-20DK
90ElPasoATG/Team-2
90F-316
90Leaf/I-26
90OPC-597
90Panini/St-99
90Pol/Brew-29
90PublInt/St-490
90RedFoley/St-8
90S-283
90Sf-25
90T-597
90T/Big-139
90T/Mini-19
90T/St-205
90UD-293
91B-43
91Brewer/MillB-4
91D-160
91F-576
91Leaf/II-518
91OPC-217
91Pol/Brew-3
91S-43
91T-217
91T/StClub/I-164
91UD-529
92D/II-471
92S/I-37
92T-638
92UD-615
Boskie, Shawn
87Peoria-8
89CharlK-17
90Classic/III-43
90Cub/Mara-3
90D/Learning-31
90D/Rook-18
90F/Up-U7
90Iowa/CMC-1
90Iowa/ProC-312
90Leaf/II-519
90Peoria/Team-20M
90S/Tr-94T
90T/Tr-10T
90T/TVCub-39
90UD/Ext-722
91Cub/Mara-47
91D-241
91F-416
91Leaf/I-221
91Leaf/Stud-152
91OPC-254
91S-59
91S/100RisSt-4
91T-254
91T/90Debut-20
91T/StClub/II-521
91UD-471
92F-377
92S/II-713
92T-229
Bosley, Rich
86Beloit-2
Bosley, Thaddis
(Thad)
75QuadC
77SLCity
78T-619
79T-127
80T-412
81D-162
81F-353
82T-350
83Thorn-20
84Iowa-7
84Nes/792-657
84SevenUp-27
84T-657
85D-388
85SevenUp-27
85T-432
86Cub/Unocal-2
86D-483
86F-361
86Gator-27
86T-512
87D-191
87F-555
87F/Up-U8
87T-58
87T/Tr-7T
88D-348
88F-253
88T-247
89UD-591
90Mother/Rang-16
Bosman, Dick
67T-459R
68T-442
69T-607
70MLB/St-278
70OPC-175
70OPC-68LL
70T-175
70T-68LL
70T/S-22
70T/SO
71MLB/St-530
71OPC-60
71T-60
71T/Coins-70
71T/GM-49
71T/S-7
71T/tatt-1
72MB-39
72OPC-365
72T-365
73OPC-640
73T-640
73T/Lids-7
74OPC-465
74T-465
75Ho-114
75OPC-354
75OPC-7M
75T-354
75T-7M
75T/M-354
75T/M-7M
76OPC-298
76SSPC-483
76T-298
77T-101
86BuffB-2CO
89RochR/CMC-24CO
89RochR/ProC-1641CO
89Swell-124
90EliteSenLg-3
90RochR/CMC-26CO
90RochR/ProC-721CO
91RochR/LineD-475CO
91RochR/ProC-1919CO
Boss, David
89Hamil/Star-5
90Hamil/Best-8
90Hamil/Star-7
Boss, Elmer Harley
(Harley)
No Cards.
Bostick, Henry L.
No Cards.
Bostock, Lyman W.
76OPC-263
76T-263
77BurgChef-54
77Ho-102
77K-16
77OPC-239
77T-531
78Ho-145
78K-46
78T-655
Bostock, Lyman Sr.
91Negro/Lewis-4
Boston, D.J.
91MedHat/ProC-4105
Boston, Daryl L.
82AppFx-24
83GlenF-1
85Coke/WS-8
85D-33RR
85F/Up-U9
85T/Tr-8T
86BuffB-3
86Coke/WS-8
86D-86
86T-139
87Coke/WS-4
87D-137
87F-487
87T-482
88Coke/WS-2
88F-393
88S-582
88T-739
89B-70
89Coke/WS-6
89D-455
89F-492
89Panini/St-311
89S-443
89T-633
89UD-496
90B-317
90D/BestNL-135
90F/Up-U33
90Leaf/II-514
90OPC-524
90Panini/St-52
90PublInt/St-384
90S-213
90S/Tr-47T
90T-524
90T/Big-54
90T/Tr-11T
90UD-529
91B-476
91D-210
91F-140
91F/Ultra-211
91Kahn/Mets-8
91Leaf/I-202
91Leaf/Stud-201
91OPC-83
91Panini/FrSt-84
91S-618
91T-83
91T/StClub/I-125
91UD-159
91WIZMets-45
92D/II-612
92F-495
92S/I-276
92T-227
Boswell, Dave
67T-575
68Coke
68T-322
69T-459
70MLB/St-230
70OPC-325
70OPC-70LL
70T-325
70T-70LL
71MLB/St-459
71OPC-675
71T-675
72MB-40
91Crown/Orio-44
Boswell, Kenneth G.
(Ken)
68Dexter-15
69T-402
70OPC-214
70T-214
70Trans/M-22
71MLB/St-147
71OPC-492
71T-492
72MB-41
72OPC-305
72OPC-306IA
72T-305
72T-306A
73OPC-87
73T-87
74OPC-645
74T-645
75OPC-479
75T-479
75T/M-479
76OPC-379
76SSPC-55
76T-379
77T-429
91WIZMets-46
Boswell, Mike
88Peoria/Ko-6
Botelho, Derek
83Omaha-3
84Iowa-xx
85Iowa-13
87Omaha-10
88Louisvl-11
90Martins/ProC-3209CO
91CharWh/ClBest-27CO
91CharWh/ProC-2903CO
91Pac/SenLg-38
Botkin, Alan
88CapeCod/Sum-81
89Johnson/Star-3
90Hamil/Star-8
90Spring/Best-5
91Spring/ClBest-7
91Spring/ProC-733
Botkin, Mike
83DayBe-24
Bottarini, John C.
No Cards.
Bottenfield, Kent
87BurlEx-5
88WPalmB/Star-3
89Jaxvl/Best-9
89Jaxvl/ProC-163
90Jaxvl/Best-16
90Jaxvl/ProC-1367
91Indianap/LineD-178
91Indianap/ProC-455
Bottenfield, Keven
88Boise/ProC-1628
Botting, Ralph
75QuadC
76QuadC
80SLCity-1
80T-663R
81SLCity-2
81T-214R
82Omaha-2
Bottomley, James L.
(Jim)
21Exh-13
25Exh-59
26Exh-59
27Exh-30
29Exh/4-15
31Exh/4-15
33DH-6
33G-44
34DS-59
34Exh/4-4
35BU-115M
35BU-179
35BU-8
35Exh/4-4
35G-1H
35G-1K
35G-3B
35G-3F
35G-4F
35G-5B
35G-6B
40PB-236
60F-45
61F-9
69Bz-7
72F/FFeat-6
72Laugh/GF-13
80Pac/Leg-64
90BBWit-83
90HOF/St-26
91Conlon/Sport-22
91Conlon/Sport-302
92Conlon/Sport-440
92Conlon/Sport-645
R300
R308-205
R310
R311/Gloss
R315-A5
R315-B5
R316
V117-19
V353-44
V355-85
Botts, Jake
90Kissim/DIMD-2
Bouchee, Edward F.
(Ed)
57T-314
59T-39
60T-347
61T-196
61T/St-5
62J-182
62P-182
62P/Can-182
62Salada-116
62Shirriff-116
62T-497
91WIZMets-47
Boucher, Alexander F.
(Al)
No Cards.
Boucher, Denis
88Myrtle/ProC-1168
88SALAS/GS-23
89Dunedin/Star-1
90Dunedin/Star-2
91B-29
91D/Rook-45
91OPC/Premier-13
91Tor/Fire-35
91UD/Ext-761
92D/II-604
92S/II-848
92T/91Debut-18
Boucher, Medric C.
No Cards.
Boudreau, Jim
84MidldC-4
Boudreau, Louis
(Lou)
39Exh
41DP-132
43MP-2
47HomogBond-4
48L-106
49B-11
49MP-100

50B-94
50NumNum
51B-62
53B/Col-57MG
55B-89MG
55Rodeo
56Rodeo
60F-16
61F-94
79TCMA-287
80Pac/Leg-79
83D/HOF-12
86Sf/Dec-17
88Pac/Leg-106
89Pac/Leg-166
89Swell-80
90Pac/Legend-9
90Swell/Great-31
91Swell/Great-12
91T/Arc53-304MG
D305
PM10/Sm-15
PM10/Sm-16
R346-22

Boudreau, Tommy
91Belling/ClBest-3
91Belling/ProC-3679

Boudreaux, Eric
87Clearw-12
89Reading/Best-19
89Reading/ProC-668
90Reading/Best-3
90Reading/ProC-1214
90Reading/Star-7
90ScranWB/CMC-1

Bouldin, Carl
63T-496R
64T-518

Bourjos, Christopher
(Chris)
77Cedar
79Phoenix
80Phoenix-11
81RochR-21
81T-502R
83Portl-14

Bourne, Kendrick
86Elmira-3
87Elmira/Black-6
87Elmira/Red-6
88WinHaven/Star-5
89Clearw/Star-3

Bournigal, Rafael
89Star/Wax-27
89VeroB/Star-3
91VeroB/ClBest-17
91VeroB/ProC-778

Bourque, Patrick D.
(Pat)
73OPC-605R
73T-605R
74OPC-141
74T-141
75OPC-502
75T-502
75T/M-502

Bouton, Jim
62T-592R
63T-401
64T-219M
64T-470
64T-4LL
64T/Coins-138AS
64T/Coins-4
64T/St-45
64Wheat/St-7
65OPC-137WS
65OPC-30
65T-30
65T/E-25
65T-137WS
65T/trans-5
66T-276
67T-393
68T-562
78TCMA-77
88Pac/Leg-20
89Swell-66
90LitSun-22
91Swell/Great-123
WG10-2
WG9-3

Bouton, Tony
91Gaston/ClBest-1
91Gaston/ProC-2678

Bowa, Lawrence Robert
(Larry)
70OPC-539R
70T-539R
71MLB/St-169
71OPC-233
71T-233
71T/tatt-16
72OPC-520
72T-520
73OPC-119
73T-119
74JP
74OPC-255
74T-255
74T/DE-70
74T/St-72
75OPC-420
75T-420
75T/M-420
76Crane-4
76Ho-145
76MSA/Disc
76OPC-145
76SSPC-464
76T-145
77BurgChef-170
77Ho-62
77OPC-17
77T-310
78Ho-71
78K-26
78OPC-68
78T-90
79BK/P-15
79Ho-134
79K-44
79OPC-104
79T-210
80BK/P-7
80K-39
80OPC-330
80T-630
80T/S-34
81Coke
81D-142
81F-2
81F-645M
81F/St-20
81F/St-43M
81K-43
81OPC-120
81T-120
81T/HT
81T/St-201
82D-63
82F-241
82F/St-107M
82F/St-56
82OPC-194
82OPC-374IA
82RedLob
82T-515
82T-516A
82T/St-80
82T/Tr-10T
83D-435
83F-491
83OPC-305
83T-305
83Thorn-1
84D-239
84F-486
85FunFood/Pin-126
84Nes/792-705LL
84Nes/792-757
84OPC-346
84SevenUp-1
84T-705LL
84T-757
84T/St-46
85D-361
85D/HL-7
85F-50
85OPC-56
85SevenUp-1
85T-484
85T/St-45
86LasVegas-1
87Bohem-10MG
87T/Tr-8T
88Coke/Pad-10MG
88Phill/TastyK-31CO
88T-284MG
89Phill/TastyK-2CO
90Phill/TastyK-34CO
91Phill/Medford-6CO
91WIZMets-48

Bowcock, Benjamin J.
(Benny)
No Cards.

Bowden, David Timon
(Tim)
No Cards.

Bowden, James
84Butte-3

Bowden, Mark
81Cedar-22
86Reading-3
87Reading-17
88RochR/Team-4
88RochR/CMC-4
88RochR/Gov-2
88RochR/ProC-208
90Iowa/ProC-313

Bowden, Merritt
91Elizab/ProC-4310

Bowden, Steve
85Bend/Cram-3
87Hagers-15
88Fresno/Cal-16

Bowen, Emmons Joseph
(Chick)
No Cards.

Bowen, John
89Erie/Star-3

Bowen, Kenny
88Memphis/Best-5
89Memphis/Best-8
89Memphis/ProC-1207
89Memphis/Star-2

Bowen, Ryan
87Ashvl-5
88Osceola/Star-5
89ColMud/Best-18
89ColMud/ProC-126
89ColMud/Star-4
90Foil/Best-245
90Tucson/CMC-1
90Tucson/ProC-196
91B-539
91Tucson/LineD-604
91Tucson/ProC-2205
91UD/FinalEd-45F
92Classic/I-17
92D/II-671
92S/II-762
92T-254
92T/91Debut-19
92UD-354

Bowen, Samuel Thomas
(Sam)
78PapaG/Disc-6
81Pawtu-18

Bowens, Samuel Edward
(Sam)
64T-201R
65OPC-188
65T-188
66T-412
67T-491
68OPC-82
68T-82
69MB-32
91Crown/Orio-45

Bowens, Steve
83Idaho-1

Bowerman, Frank E.
T204
T206

Bowers, Brent
90MedHat/Best-10
91Myrtle/ClBest-23
91Myrtle/ProC-2957

Bowers, Grover Bill
(Billy)
52Park-6

Bowers, Mickey
80LynnS-15
81LynnS-25
82LynnS-18
83Chatt-12

Bowers, Tom
58SFCallB-3

Bowes, Frank M.
No Cards.

Bowie, Jim Jr.
86Cram/PCL-102
87Wausau-15
88CalLgAS-27
88SanBern/Best-16
88SanBern/Cal-30
89Calgary/CMC-17
89Calgary/ProC-525
90Foil/Best-258
90Wmsprt/Best-3
90Wmsprt/ProC-1067
90Wmsprt/Star-2
91Jaxvl/LineD-331
91Jaxvl/ProC-156

Bowlan, Mark
89Hamil/Star-4
91Spring/ClBest-8
91Spring/ProC-734

Bowlin, Allan
80Elmira-3

Bowlin, Lois Weldon
(Hoss)
No Cards.

Bowling, Stephen S.
(Steve)
79Indianap-20

Bowman, Billy
90Mother/Ast-27CO

Bowman, Don
(General Manager)
88Pulaski/ProC-1771

Bowman, Elmer W.
No Cards.

Bowman, Ernest F.
(Ernie)
62T-231
63T-61
66T-302

Bowman, Joseph Emil
(Joe)
39PB-128
40PB-162

Bowman, Michael
89Bristol/Star-1

Bowman, Robert LeRoy
(Bob)
57T-332
58T-415
59T-221

Bowman, Roger
55B-115

Bowman, William G.
(Bill)
No Cards.

Bowman, William
77StPete

Bowser, James H.
(Red)
No Cards.

Bowsfield, Edward
(Ted)
59T-236
60T-382
61T-216
62T-369
62T/St-64
63T-339
64T-447

Box, Newt
80Cedar-2

Boxberger, Rod
83Nashua-2

Boyan, Michael
88CapeCod/Sum-155

Boyce
N172

Boyce, Bob
82Miami-14

Boyce, Joe
90Erie/Star-1

Boyce, Randy
78Newar
79BurlB-19

Boyce, Tommy
88SLCity-10
89Kenosha/Star-1
89Miami/II/Star-2
90Miami/II/Star-3

Boyd, Bob
76QuadC
77QuadC

Boyd, Daryl
86Watertn-4
89WPalmB/Star-4

Boyd, Dennis
(Oil Can)
80Elmira-4
83Pawtu-2
84D-457
84F-393
85D-151
85F-152
85T-116
86D-50
86F-342
86F/St-9
86Leaf-35
86OPC-259
86Sf-152
86T-605
86T/Mini-4
86T/St-249
87Classic-85
87D-51
87F-30
87F/Excit-5
87F/BB-4
87Leaf-248
87OPC-285
87RedFoley/St-122
87Sf-47
87S/Test-121
87Smok/AL-2
87T-285
87T/St-249
88D-462
88D/RedSox/Bk-462
88F-347
88Leaf-252
88Panini/St-20
88S-121
88T-704
89D-476
89F-82
89OPC-326
89Panini/St-269
89S-238
89T-326
89UD-415
90B-102
90D-633
90F/Up-U26
90Leaf/I-159
90OPC-544
90PublInt/St-449
90S-137
90S/Tr-24T
90T-544
90T/Tr-12T
90UD-484
90UD/Ext-749
91B-456
91Classic/200-9
91D-194
91F-226
91F/Ultra-197
91Leaf/I-167
91Leaf/Stud-193
91OPC-48
91Panini/FrSt-147
91S-202
91T-48
91T/StClub/I-142
91UD-359
91UD/FinalEd-51F
92D/II-447
92S/II-531
92T-428
92UD-559

Boyd, Frank John
No Cards.

Boyd, Gary Lee
70OPC-7R
70T-7R

Boyd, Jacob Henry
(Jake)
N172

Boyd, Randy
77SanJose-16

Boyd, Robert Richard
(Bob)
53T-257
54B-118

54T-113
57T-26
58Hires-75
58T-279
59T-82
60L-13
60T-207
61T-199
61T/St-157
86Negro/Frit-49
91Crown/Orio-46
91T/Arc53-257

Boyer, Cletis Leroy
(Clete)
57T-121
59T-251
60L-46
60T-109
61P-11
61T-19
61T/St-191
62Exh
62J-3
62P-3
62P/Can-3
62Salada-80
62Shirriff-80
62T-163M
62T-490
62T/St-84
63Exh
63J-14
63Kahn
63P-14
63T-361
64T-69
65T-475
66OPC-9
66T-9
67T-328
68Bz-1
68Coke
68Dexter-16
68Kahn
68T-550
69T-489
69T/St-3
70OPC-206
70T-206
71MLB/St-4
71OPC-374
71T-374
72MB-42
78Green
87Colum-3
88Pac/Leg-13
89Pac/SenLg-149
89Swell-94
89T/SenLg-4
89TM/SenLg-12
90ColClip/CMC-24CO
90ColClip/ProC-693CO
90EliteSenLg-34
90Pac/Legend-10
90Swell/Great-102
91ColClip/LineD-125CO
91Pac/SenLg-43MG
91Pac/SenLg-54M
91Swell/Great-109
Exh47
PM10/L-6
WG10-3
WG9-4

Boyer, Cloyd
51B-228
52T-280
53B/Col-115
53Hunters
53T-60
55B-149
55Rodeo
85Syrac-30
88Pulaski/ProC-1770
90Pulaski/Best-28CO
90Pulaski/ProC-3113CO
91Pulaski/ClBest-20CO
91Pulaski/ProC-4023CO
91T/Arc53-60

Boyer, Kenton Lloyd
(Ken)
55Hunter
55T-125
56T-14
56T/Pin-46
57Swift-8
57T-122
58T-350
59Bz
59HRDerby-4
59T-325
59T-557AS
60Armour-4
60Bz-9
60L-12
60T-160M
60T-485
61Bz-14
61P-171
61T-375
61T-43LL
61T-573AS
61T/St-85
62Bz
62J-159
62P-159
62P/Can-159
62Salada-167
62Shirriff-167
62T-370
62T-392AS
62T-52LL
62T/bucks
62T/St-183
63F-60
63J-160
63P-160
63Salada-15
63T-375
63T/SO
64Bz-35
64T-11LL
64T-160
64T/Coins-145AS
64T/Coins-25
64T/S-57
64T/St-61
64T/SU
64T/tatt
64Wheat/St-8
65Bz-35
65OldLond-4
65OPC-100
65OPC-135WS
65OPC-6LL
65T-100
65T-6LL
65T/E-47
65T/trans-40
66T-385
66T/RO-41
67Bz-33
67Kahn
67OPC-105
67T-105
68T-259
69MB-33
69T-379
74Laugh/ASG-56
75OPC-202MV
75T-202MV
75T/M-202MV
78TCMA-67
79T-192MG
82KMart-6
88Pac/Leg-12
90Target-63
91WIZMets-49

Boykin, Tyrone
91Boise/ClBest-5
91Boise/ProC-3893

Boylan, Brad
84Cram/PCL-193TR
86Toledo-2TR
87Portl-24
88Portl/ProC-648

Boyland, Dorian Scott
78Colum
79Portl-7
80Port-2
80T-683R
81Portl-8
82Phoenix

Boyle, Edward J.
(Eddie)
No Cards.

Boyle, Gary
76QuadC

Boyle, Henry J.
N172
N284
WG1-29

Boyle, John Anthony
(Jack)
No Cards.

Boyle, John Bellew
(Jack)
No Cards.

Boyle, Ralph Francis
(Buzz)
90Target-64
R310

Boyles, John
85Cedar-1
86Vermont-2
89Wausau/GS-6

Boyne, Bryan
76Cedar

Braase, John
88GreatF-14
90Bakers/Cal-241

Brabender, Gene
66T-579R
67OPC-22
67T-22
68OPC-163
68T-163
69T-393
70McDon-3
70OPC-289
70T-289
71MLB/St-340
71OPC-666
71T-666
91Crown/Orio-47

Brabinski, Marek
90Idaho/ProC-3268

Bracho, Jose
52Park-24

Brack, Gilbert Herman
(Gib)
39PB-127

Bradbury, Miah
88Alaska/Team-4
90Miami/I/Star-1
91Miami/ClBest-16
91Miami/ProC-410
91Single/ClBest-110

Braddy, Leonard
84Visalia-9

Brader, Tim
88Bristol/ProC-1865
89Fayette/ProC-1583

Bradford, Charles W.
(Buddy)
68OPC-142R
68T-142R
69MB-34
69OPC-97
69T-97
70MLB/St-183
70OPC-299
70T-299
71MLB/St-362
71OPC-552
71T-552
72MB-43
74OPC-357
74T-357
75OPC-504
75T-504
75T/M-504
76OPC-451
76SSPC-281
76T-451

Bradford, Henry V.
(Vic)
No Cards.

Bradford, Larry
78Richm
79Richm-17
80T-675R
81D-584
81F-265
81Pol/Atl-34
81T-542
82D-553
82F-431
82T-271
83Portl-24

Bradford, Mark
88Batavia/ProC-1672

Bradford, Troy
88CapeCod/Sum-103
90Geneva/ProC-3030
90Geneva/Star-2
91CLAS/ProC-CAR39
91WinSalem/ClBest-1
91WinSalem/ProC-2820

Bradford, Vincent
90Bristol/ProC-3169
90Bristol/Star-2
91Bristol/ClBest-15
91Bristol/ProC-3617

Bradish, Mike
90Utica/Pucko-29

Bradley, Bert
80WHave-10
81WHave-3
82WHave-2
83Tacoma-2
84Cram/PCL-92
85Colum-2
85Colum/Pol-2
87Madis-1
88Madis-4
90Madison/Best-26CO
90Madison/ProC-2284CO
91Huntsvl/ClBest-17CO
91Huntsvl/LineD-300CO
91HuntsvlProC-1812CO

Bradley, David
91Welland/ClBest-23

Bradley, Eric
90Myrtle/ProC-2769

Bradley, George W.
90HOF/St-1
N172

Bradley, Hugh F.
M116
T207

Bradley, J. Nichols
(Nick)
No Cards.

Bradley, John Thomas
(Jack)
No Cards.

Bradley, Len
80GlenF/C-2
81GlenF-23
82Edmon-17

Bradley, M.
N172

Bradley, Mark
77LodiD
82Albuq-19
83Pol/Dodg-22
84F-581
84Nes/792-316
84T-316
90Target-65
91WIZMets-50

Bradley, Mike
91CharRain/ClBest-2
91CharRain/ProC-88

Bradley, Philip Poole
(Phil)
83SLCity-11
84F/X-15
84Mother/Mar-24
84T/Tr-15
85D-631
85F-486
85Leaf-50
85Mother/Mar-21
85OPC-69
85T-449
86D-191
86D-22DK
86D/AAS-41
86D/DKsuper-22
86F-461
86F/LimEd-5
86F/Mini-96
86F/St-10
86Leaf-22DK
86Mother/Mar-8
86OPC-305
86Sf-77
86T-305
86T/Gloss60-54
86T/St-217
86T/Super-13
87D-270
87D/OD-122
87F-580
87F/LL-4
87F/Mini-11
87F/St-13
87Ho/St-29
87Leaf-200
87Mother/Sea-6
87OPC-170
87Sf-89
87T-525
87T/Mini-70
87T/St-221
88D-243
88D/Best-47
88F-369
88F/Up-U107
88OPC-55
88Panini/St-191
88Phill/TastyK-4
88S-66
88S/Tr-34T
88Sf-93
88T-55
88T/Mini-33
88T/St-218
88T/Tr-18T
89T/Ames-6
89B-17
89D-369
89D/Best-198
89D/Tr-41
89F-563
89F/Up-1
89French-16
89OPC-308
89Panini/St-154
89S-79
89S/Tr-44
89T-608
89T/St-113
89T/Tr-13T
89UD-229
89UD/Ext-749
90B-261
90D-259
90F-174
90KMart/CBatL-20
90Leaf/I-138
90OPC-163
90Panini/St-4
90PublInt/St-575
90S-24
90S/100St-36
90S/Tr-44T
90Sf-95
90T-163
90T/Big-202
90T/Mini-2
90T/St-241
90UD-194
91Crown/Orio-48
91D-646
91F-114
91OPC-717
91S-560
91T-717
91UD-641

Bradley, Rick
77Phoenix
78Cr/PCL-75
79Phoenix

Bradley, Scott W.
83Nashvl-1
84Colum-11
84Colum/Pol-2
85D-37RR
86BuffB-4
86D-396
86T-481
87D-440
87F-581
87F/BB-5
87Mother/Sea-14
87T-376
87T/St-217
88D-147
88D/Best-24
88F-370
88Leaf-75
88Mother/Sea-14
88OPC-199
88Panini/St-183
88RedFoley/St-8
88S-151

88T-762
88T/St-222
89B-209
89D-261
89F-540
89Mother/Sea-14
89OPC-279
89Panini/St-432
89S-324
89T-279
89T/St-225
89UD-226
90B-483
90D-581
90F-506
90Leaf/II-404
90Mother/Mar-25
90OPC-593
90PublInt/St-427
90S-228
90T-593
90T/Big-181
90T/St-229
90UD-383
91B-239
91CounHrth-5
91D-287
91F-443
91F/Ultra-332
91Leaf/I-99
91OPC-38
91S-113
91T-38
91T/StClub/I-252
91UD-130
92D/II-713
92F-273
92S/I-304
92T-608
92UD-390

Bradley, Tom
71OPC-588
71T-588
72OPC-248
72T-248
73OPC-336
73T-336
74OPC-455
74T-455
74T/St-102
75OPC-179
75Phoenix-9
75T-179
75T/M-179
76OPC-644
76T-644
76Tucson-35

Bradley, Wayne
75Cedar

Bradley, William J.
(Bill)
E107
E90/1
E97
T206
T213/blue
W555
WG2-6

Bradshaw, Dallas C.
No Cards.

Bradshaw, George T.
No Cards.

Bradshaw, Joe
90Target-903

Bradshaw, Kevin
87Lakeland-7
88GlenF/ProC-934
89Toledo/CMC-19
89Toledo/ProC-783
91Bristol/ClBest-30CO

Bradshaw, Terry
90Hamil/Best-23
91SALAS/ProC-SAL41
91Savan/ClBest-23
91Savan/ProC-1664
91Single/ClBest-269

Brady, Brian
86MidldA-2
87MidldA-5
88Edmon/CMC-16
88Edmon/ProC-572
90Phoenix/CMC-12
90Phoenix/ProC-16
90T/89Debut-19

Brady, Clifford F.
(Cliff)
No Cards.

Brady, Dave
83Redwd-6

Brady, Doug
91Utica/ClBest-2
91Utica/ProC-3244

Brady, James J.
56T-126

Brady, Jim
77Salem

Brady, Lawrence
86Watertn-5

Brady, Mike
89Myrtle/ProC-1476
91StLucie/ProC-702
91VeroB/ClBest-4
91VeroB/ProC-765

Brady, Pat
89Salinas/Cal-138
89Salinas/ProC-1815
90SanJose/Best-4
90SanJose/Cal-31
90SanJose/ProC-2023
90SanJose/Star-1
90SanJose/Star-26M
91Clearw/ClBest-15
91Clearw/ProC-1626
91FSLAS/ProC-FSL6

Brady, Robert Jay
(Bob)
No Cards.

Brady, Stephen A.
(Steve)
E223
N172/ST

Bragan, Jimmy
89Chatt/II/Team-4MG

Bragan, Peter
89Jaxvl/Best-23

Bragan, Robert R.
(Bobby)
47TipTop
53Mother-4
59DF
60T-463CO
63T-73MG
64T-506MG
65T-346MG
66T-476MG
90Target-66

Braggs, Glenn
86Sf/Rook-21
86Vanco-5
87D-337
87D/OD-52
87F-339
87Pol/Brew-26
87T-622
88D-240
88D/Best-15
88F-157
88OPC-263
88Panini/St-127
88Pol/Brew-26
88S-59
88S/YS/II-2
88T-263
88T-639TL
88T/St-197
89B-145
89Brewer/YB-26
89Classic/Up/2-169
89D-103
89D/Best-277
89F-180
89Gard-12
89OPC-271
89Panini/St-375
89Pol/Brew-26
89S-147
89Sf-29
89T-718
89T/Big-204
89T/St-196
89UD-504
90B-403
90D-264
90ElPasoATG/Team-3
90F-317
90F/Up-U11
90Kahn/Reds-4
90Leaf/II-466
90OPC-88
90Panini/St-97
90Pol/Brew-26
90PublInt/St-491
90S-105
90S/Tr-56T
90T-88
90T/Big-10
90T/St-206
90T/Tr-13T
90UD-456
90UD/Ext-714
91B-669
91D-253
91F-57
91F/Ultra-88
91Kahn/Reds-15
91Leaf/II-362
91OPC-444
91Pep/Reds-3
91S-18
91T-444
91T/StClub/I-187
91UD-631
92D/I-363
92F-400
92S/I-393
92T-197
92UD-341

Brahms, Russ
82QuadC-3

Brain, David Leonard
(Dave)
T206

Brainerd, Frederick
(Fred)
No Cards.

Brake, Greg
85Madis/Pol-4

Brakebill, Mark
89Belling/Legoe-21
90Penin/Star-4
91Penin/ClBest-18
91Penin/ProC-383

Brakeley, Bill
89Helena/SP-9
91Beloit/ClBest-1
91Beloit/ProC-2094

Braley, Jeffrey
(Jeff)
89Bristol/Star-2
90A&AASingle/ProC-85
90Fayette/ProC-2397
90SALAS/Star-2
91FSLAS/ProC-FSL19
91Lakeland/ClBest-1
91Lakeland/ProC-257

Brame, Ervin Beckham
(Erv)
No Cards.

Bramhall, Arthur W.
(Art)
No Cards.

Branca, Ralph
47HomogBond-5
47TipTop
49B-194
49Eureka-30
50B-59
51B-56
51FB
51T/BB-20
52B-96
52T-274
52TipTop
53B/BW-52
53Exh/Can-8
79TCMA-32
89Rini/Dodg-7
89Smok/Dodg-51
90Pac/Legend-13
90Swell/Great-133
90Target-67
91B-410M
91Swell/Great-14
91T/Arc53-293
D305
Exh47
R423-4

Brancato, Albert
(Al)
41DP-48
41PB-43

Branch, Roy
80Spokane-7
89Pac/SenLg-210
91Pac/SenLg-57

Branconier, Paul
89Salem/Team-8
90Ashvl/ClBest-2
90Yakima/Team-31
91Ashvl/ProC-560

Brand, Ronald George
(Ron)
64T-326
65OPC-212
65T-212
66T-394
68Coke
68Dexter-17
68T-317
69Expos/Pins-2
69T-549
70MLB/St-63
70OPC-221
70T-221
71MLB/St-124
71OPC-304
71T-304
72MB-44
72T-773
78TCMA-41

Brandon, Darrell
66T-456R
67OPC-117
67T-117
67T/Test/RedSox-2
68Coke
68Dexter-18
68OPC-26
68T-26
69MB-35
69T-301
72OPC-283
72T-283
73OPC-326
73T-326
89Pac/SenLg-44

Brandt, Ed
(Dutch/Lefty)
33DH-7
33G-50
34Exh/4-1
34T-5
35BU-107
35BU-2
35Exh/4-1
35G-1J
35G-2E
35G-3A
35G-4A
35G-4E
35G-5A
35G-7E
36Exh/4-2
90Target-68
91Conlon/Sport-298
R306
R328-28
V353-50
V354-62

Brandt, John George
(Jackie)
59T-297
60T-53
61P-76
61T-515
61T/RO-27
61T/St-98
62J-31
62P-31
62P/Can-31
62Salada-53A
62Salada-53B
62Shirriff-53
62T-165
62T/bucks
62T/St-3
63J-58
63P-58
63T-65
64T-399
65OPC-33
65T-33
66T-383
67OPC-142
67T-142
78TCMA-33
91Crown/Orio-49
Exh47

Brandt, Randy
77Salem

Brannan, Otis Owen
No Cards.

Brannon, Cliff
89Hamil/Star-6
90Savan/ProC-2080
91ArkTr/LineD-27
91ArkTr/ProC-1298

Branom, Edgar Dudley
(Dudley)
No Cards.

Bransfield, William
(Kitty)
12Sweet/Pin-124
E104
E254
E270/1
E90/1
E97
M116
T204
T205
T206
T3-82
W555

Branson, Jeff
88T/Tr-19T
89Cedar/Best-1
89Cedar/ProC-928
89Cedar/Star-1
89T/Big-69
90B-52
90CedarDG/Best-20
91Chatt/LineD-155
91Chatt/ProC-1965

Brant, Marshall Lee
78Tidew
79Tidew-13
80Colum-20
81Colum-13
82Colum-6
82Colum/Pol-33
83Colum-16

Brantley, Cliff
88Clearw/Star-2
89Reading/Best-11
89Reading/ProC-662
90Clearw/Star-3
90Reading/Star-8
91Reading/LineD-503
91Reading/ProC-1364
92D/II-722
92F-662
92S/II-854
92T-544
92T/91Debut-20

Brantley, Jeff
86Shrev-1
87Phoenix-28
87Shrev-13
88Phoenix/CMC-5
88Phoenix/ProC-78
89D/Rook-41
89F/Up-127
89Mother/Giants-17
89S/Tr-101
89T/Tr-14T
90D-466
90F-52
90HotRook/St-9
90Leaf/II-357
90Mother/Giant-25
90OPC-703
90S-371
90S/100Ris-22
90S/YS/I-24
90T-703
90UD-358
90USPlayC/AS 3H
91B-620
91Classic/200-143
91Classic/II-T47
91D-319
91F-255
91F/Ultra-316
91Leaf/I-136
91Mother/Giant-25

91OPC-17
91Panini/FrSt-75
91Panini/St-70
91PG&E-7
91S-160
91SFExam/Giant-4
91T-17
91T/StClub/II-567
91UD-424
92D/I-295
92F-629
92S/I-157
92T-491
92UD-581

Brantley, Mickey
84Chatt-26
85Cram/PCL-88
86Calgary-2
86F-651R
86Sf/Rook-45
87D-656
87D/Rook-27
87F-582
87Mother/Sea-15
87T-347
88D-610
88D/Best-80
88F-371
88F/Excit-5
88F/Mini-51
88Leaf-258
88Mother/Sea-15
88Panini/St-192
88S-213
88S/YS/II-15
88T-687
89Chatt/II/Team-5
89D-212
89F-541
89Mother/Sea-7
89OPC-369
89Panini/St-439
89S-89
89Sf-6
89T-568
89T/Big-38
89T/St-219
89UD-550
90Calgary/CMC-15
90PublInt/St-428
91Denver/LineD-129
91Denver/ProC-133

Brashear, Robert N.
(Kitty)
No Cards.

Brashear, Roy Parks
T206

Brassil, Tom
85Beaum-14
86Beaum-3
87Wichita-19
88LasVegas/CMC-23
88LasVegas/ProC-238
89Spokane/SP-13

Bratcher, Joseph W.
(Joe)
No Cards.

Bratchi, Frederick O.
(Fred)
No Cards.

Bratlien, Erik
88Batavia/ProC-1673
89Batavia/ProC-1941
89Reading/Star-3

Braun, Bart
81Redwd-29

Braun, John Paul
65OPC-82R
65T-82R

Braun, Randy
83DayBe-17
86Calgary-3
87Calgary-15
88Jaxvl/Best-21
88Jaxvl/ProC-976
88SLAS-20
89Indianap/CMC-16
89Indianap/ProC-1213
90Indianap/CMC-19
90Indianap/ProC-283

Braun, Stephen R.
(Steve)
72OPC-244
72T-244
73OPC-16
73T-16
74OPC-321
74T-321
74T/St-202
75K-41
75OPC-273
75T-273
75T/M-273
76Ho-96
76OPC-183
76SSPC-221
76T-183
77Ho-134
77OPC-123
77T-606
77T/CS-6
78T-422
79T-502
80T-9
81F-427
82D-418
82F-111
82T-316
83F-3
83T-734
84F-320
84F/St-42
84Nes/792-227
84T-227
85F-221
85F/St-51
85T-152
86D-534
86F-27
86KAS/Disc-4
86Louisvl-5
86T-631
88Louisvl-4
90T/TVCard-2CO

Braunecker, Darek
91James/ClBest-24
91James/ProC-3535

Brauning, Jeff
90SanJose/Best-5
90SanJose/Cal-34
90SanJose/ProC-2015
90SanJose/Star-2

Bravo, Angel Alfonso
(Angel)
70OPC-283
70T-283
71MLB/St-50
71OPC-538
71T-538

Bravo, Luis
79Wisco-17
83Albany-17

Braxton, Garland
91Conlon/Sport-248

Braxton, Glenn
86AppFx-3
87Penin-16
89Utica/Pucko-2

Bray, Clarence W.
(Buster)
No Cards.

Bray, Scott
89SLCity-23

Brazell, Don
78Wausau

Brazill, Frank Leo
(Frank)
V100

Brazle, Alpha
47TipTop
49B-126
49Eureka-178
50B-126
51B-157
52B-134
52T-228
53B/Col-140
53Hunter
54B-142
54Hunter
55B-230

Breadon, Sam
W754

Bream, Scott
90CharRain/ProC-2049
91CharRain/ClBest-16
91CharRain/ProC-101
91Single/ClBest-184
91Spokane/ClBest-23
91Spokane/ProC-3954

Bream, Sidney Eugene
(Sid)
82VeroB-18
83Albuq-15
84Cram/PCL-149
85D-470
85T-253
86D-566
86F-604
86T-589
87D-79
87D/OD-168
87F-606
87F/Excit-6
87F/Mini-12
87F/Slug-5
87F/St-14
87Leaf-239
87OPC-35
87T-35
87T/St-126
88D-188
88D/Best-45
88F-324
88F/Excit-6
88F/St-113
88OPC-304
88Panini/St-370
88S-260
88Sf-98
88T-478
88T/Big-205
88T/St-130
89B-419
89D-252
89D/Best-89
89F-204
89OPC-126
89S-48
89T-126
89T/Big-106
89T/Mini-31
89T/St-125
89UD-556
89VFJuice-5
90B-175
90D-329
90D/BestNL-33
90F-463
90Homer/Pirate-7
90OPC-622
90PublInt/St-151
90S-423
90T-622
90Target-69
90UD-250
91B-585
91D-644
91F-35
91F/Up-U72
91Leaf/II-379
91Leaf/Stud-142
91OPC-354
91Panini/FrSt-115
91Panini/St-119
91S-304
91S/RookTr-12T
91T-354
91T/StClub/II-427
91T/Tr-13T
91UD-109
91UD/Ext-710
92D/I-202
92F-354
92S/I-131
92T-770
92UD-495

Breaux, Greg
88Martins/Star-5

Breazeale, James Leo
(Jim)
71Richm/Team-4
73OPC-33
73T-33
79AppFx-17
83Miami-25

Brecheen, Harry
47HomogBond-6
48L-158
49B-158
49Eureka-179
50B-90
51B-86
51FB
51T/BB-28
52B-176
52T-263
53Exh/Can-14
54Esskay
54T-203CO
55Esskay
55T-113CO
55T/DH-74CO
56T-229CO
60L-132CO
60T-455C
79TCMA-166
D305
Exh47
R423-8

Brecht, Mike
83Phoenix/BHN-17

Breckinridge
N172/PCL

Brede, Brent
90Elizab/Star-6
91Elizab/ProC-4311
91Kenosha/ClBest-7
91Kenosha/ProC-2087

Bree, Charlie
89Pac/SenLg-217M

Breeden, Daniel R.
(Danny)
69T-536R
70OPC-36R
70T-36R
71MLB/St-27

Breeden, Harold Noel
(Hal)
72T-684
73OPC-173
73T-173
74OPC-297
74T-297
75OPC-341
75T-341
75T/M-341
76SSPC-329

Breeden, Joe
89Memphis/Best-25
89Memphis/ProC-1193
90AppFox/Box-5
90AppFox/ProC-2111MG
91AppFx/ClBest-26
91AppFx/ProC-1731

Breeden, Scott
82Iowa-26
83Iowa-27
85Cedar-32
86TexGold-CO
88Kahn/Reds-CO

Breeding, Marvin E.
(Marv)
60T-525
61P-77
61T-321
61T/St-99
62J-28
62P-28
62P/Can-28
62Salada-65A
62Salada-65B
62Shirriff-65
62T-6
63T-149
90Target-70
91Crown/Orio-50

Breedlove, Larry R.
87Spring/Best-21

Breen, Dick
C46-88

Breining, Fred
78Colum
80Phoenix-9
82D-186
82F-385
82T-144
83D-503
83F-254
83Mother/Giants-7
83T-747
84D-387
84F-367
84F/X-16
84Nes/792-428
84Stuart-35
84T-428
84T/Tr-16
85F-392
85Indianap-10
85OPC-36
85T-36
86Nashvl-2

Breitenbucher, Karl
87Pocatel/Bon-21
89Clinton/ProC-888

Breitenstein, Ted
T206
T213/brown

Bremer, Bernard
85Albany-28

Bremer, Herbert F.
(Herb)
No Cards.

Bremigan, Nick
88TM/Umpire-19
89TM/Umpire-15
90TM/Umpire-63

Brenegan, Olaf Selmer
(Sam)
No Cards.

Brenly, Robert Earl
(Bob)
77Cedar
81Phoenix-4
82D-574
82T-171R
83D-377
83F-255
83Mother/Giants-6
83T-494
84D-616
84F-368
84Nes/792-378
84T-378
84T/St-174
85D-187
85D-26
85D/DKsuper-26
85F-603
85Leaf-26DK
85Mother/Giants-7
85OPC-215
85T-215
85T/Gloss40-3
85T/St-158
86D-323
86F-534
86Leaf-194
86Mother/Giants-5
86OPC-307
86T-625
86T/St-92
87D-485
87D/OD-95
87F-267
87Mother/SFG-4
87OPC-125
87T-125
87T/St-87
88D-189
88F-77
88Mother/Giants-4
88OPC-69
88Panini/St-419
88S-134
88T-703
88T/Big-143
88T/St-92
89B-249
89D-453
89OPC-52
89S-395
89T-52
89Tor/Fire-9
89UD-479

Brennan, Addison
14CJ-115
15CJ-115

Brennan, James A.
(Jim)
N172

Brennan, James D.
32Orbit/num-92
35BU-178

Brennan, Thomas M.

(Tom)
75OkCty
77Watlo
79Tacoma-5
80Tacoma-12
81Charl-1
81T-451R
82T-141R
82Wheat/Ind
83F-403
83T-524
84D-102
84F-537
84Nes/792-662
84T-662
84TrueVal/WS-6
85Coke/Dodg-5
90Target-71

Brennan, Tom
80Wausau-1
81Wausau-5
83GlenF-12

Brennan, William
85VeroB-15
87Albuq/Pol-5
88Albuq/CMC-6
88Albuq/ProC-250
89Albuq/CMC-1
89Albuq/ProC-65
89D-589
89S-622
89S/HotRook-9
89UD-16
90Target-72
90Tucson/CMC-8
90Tucson/ProC-197

Brennen, James
87DayBe-9

Brenzel, William R.
(Bill)
No Cards.

Bresnahan, Dave
86Watlo-4
87Wmsprt-14

Bresnahan, Roger P.
10Domino-15
11Helmar-167
12Sweet/Pin-145A
12Sweet/Pin-145B
14CJ-17
15CJ-17
48Exh/HOF
50Callahan
60Exh/HOF-4
60F-8
61F-10
75F/Pion-7
80Pac/Leg-102
80SSPC/HOF
89HOF/St-55
92Conlon/Sport-459
D303
D350/2-16
E103
E106
E254
E270/2
E90/1
E91
E98
L1-129
M101/5-16
M116
S74-117
S81-104
T201
T202
T204
T205
T206
T207
T213/blue
T215/blue
T216
T222
T3-4
WG3-5
WG5-6
WG6-5

Bressler, Raymond B.
(Rube)
25Exh-25
26Exh-25
27Exh-13
90Target-73
91Conlon/Sport-173
W514-28

Bressoud, Edward F.
(Ed)
58SFCallB-4
58T-263
59T-19
60T-253
61P-152
61T-203
61T/St-74
62Salada-182A
62Salada-182B
62Shirriff-182
62T-504
63J-78
63P-78
63T-188
64T-352
65T-525
66T-516
67OPC-121
67T-121
78TCMA-164
78TCMA-39
91WIZMets-51
PM10/Sm-17

Breton, John F.
(Jim)
No Cards.

Brett, George Howard
75OPC-228
75T-228
75T/M-228
76A&P/KC
76Ho-114
76OPC-19
76SSPC-167
76T-19
77BurgChef-71
77Ho-36
77K-6
77OPC-170
77OPC-1LL
77OPC-261RB
77Pep-32
77T-1LL
77T-231M
77T-580RB
77T-631M
77T/CS-7
78Ho-27
78OPC-215
78PapaG/Disc-36
78T-100
78Tastee/Discs-9
78Wiffle/Discs-7
79Ho-68
79K-50
79OPC-167
79T-330
79T/Comics-9
80BK/PHR-13
80K-9
80OPC-235
80T-450
80T/S-14
81Coke
81D-100
81D-491MVP
81Drake-5
81F-28
81F-655
81F/St-116
81K-8
81MSA/Disc-4
81OPC-113
81PermaGr/AS-10
81PermaGr/CC-3
81Pol/Royals-2
81Sqt-1
81T-1LL
81T-700
81T/Nat/Super-3
81T/SO-1
81T/St-243
81T/St-82
81T/St-9
82D-15DK
82D-34
82Drake-4
82F-405
82F/St-202
82K-3
82KMart-38
82OPC-200
82OPC-201IA
82OPC-261AS
82PermaGr/AS-9
82PermaGr/CC-19
82Sqt-3
82T-200
82T-201A
82T-549AS
82T-96TL
82T/St-133
82T/St-190
83D-338
83D/AAS-42
83F-108
83K-4
83OPC-3
83OPC-388AS
83PermaGr/AS-1
83PermaGr/CC-19
83Pol/Royals-2
83T-388AS
83T-600
83T/Gloss40-31
84D-53
84D/AAS-55
84D/Champs-15
84Drake-3
84F-344
84F-638IA
84F/St-36
85FunFood/Pin-6
84MiltBrad-2
84Nes/792-399AS
84Nes/792-500
84Nes/792-710LL
84Nestle/DT-3
84OPC-212
84OPC-223AS
84Ralston-13
84Seven-5C
84Seven-5E
84Seven-5W
84T-399AS
84T-500
84T-710LL
84T/Cereal-13
84T/Gloss22-4
84T/Gloss40-12
84T/St-198
84T/St-275
84T/Super-13
85D-53
85D/AAS-26
85D/HL-11
85D/HL-25
85Drake-4
85F-199
85F/LimEd-4
85GenMills-14
85Leaf-176
85OPC-100
85Seven-2C
85Seven-2E
85Seven-2G
85T-100
85T-703AS
85T/3D-4
85T/Gloss22-15
85T/St-188
85T/St-268
85T/Super-46
86BK/AP-20
86D-53
86D/AAS-12
86D/HL-3
86D/PopUp-12
86Dorman-1
86Drake-14
86F-5
86F-634M
86F/AS-3
86F/LimEd-6
86F/LL-2
86F/Mini-1
86F/Slug-3
86F/St-11
86F/WaxBox-C2
86Jiffy-4
86Kitty/Disc-20
86Leaf-42
86Meadow/Blank-2
86Meadow/Milk-2
86Meadow/Stat-1
86NatPhoto-5
86OPC-300
86OPC-C
86Quaker-23
86Sf-1
86Sf-180M
86Sf-186M
86Sf-52M
86Sf-63M
86Sf/Dec-64
86T-300
86T-714AS
86T/3D-5
86T/Gloss22-4
86T/Gloss60-18
86T/Mini-18
86T/St-157
86T/St-16ALCS
86T/St-23
86T/St-256
86T/St-3
86T/Super-14
86T/WaxBox-C
86TrueVal-17
86Woolwth-4
87Classic-47
87D-15DK
87D-54
87D/AAS-27
87D/DKsuper-15
87D/OD-206
87Drake-14
87F-366
87F/GameWin-6
87F/Hottest-6
87F/LL-5
87F/Lim-5
87F/Mini-13
87F/RecSet-1
87F/Slug-6
87F/St-15
87F/WaxBox-C3
87Ho/St-24
87Jiffy-5
87KayBee-5
87KMart-24
87Kraft-21
87Leaf-15DK
87Leaf-96
87MnM's-14
87OPC-126
87RedFoley/St-111
87Sf-114M
87Sf-197M
87Sf-5
87Sportflic/DealP-4
87T-400
87T/Board-13
87T/Coins-5
87T/Gloss60-31
87T/Mini-57
87T/St-254
88Classic/Blue-248
88D-102
88D/Best-39
88F-254
88F/BB/AS-4
88F/Hottest-4
88F/St-30
88FanSam-2
88KingB/Disc-7
88KMart-3
88Leaf-93
88OPC-312
88Panini/St-104
88S-11
88Sf-150
88Smok/Royals-20
88T-700
88T/Big-157
88T/Gloss60-53
88T/St-259
88T/St/Backs-41
88T/UK-7
89B-121
89Cadaco-4
89Classic-47
89T/Crunch-9
89D-204
89D/AS-11
89D/Best-7
89D/MVP-BC7
89F-277
89F/BBMVP's-4
89F/Superstar-5
89F/WaxBox-C3
89KayBee-2
89KMart/Lead-5
89Master/Discs-9
89OPC-200
89Panini/St-355
89MSA/SS-9
89RedFoley/St-12
89S-75
89S/HotStar-4
89S/Mast-11
89Sf-64
89T-200
89T/Big-46
89T/Coins-34
89T/Gloss60-14
89T/Hills-3
89T/LJN-42
89T/Mini-54
89T/St-270
89T/St/Backs-1
89T/UK-7
89T/WaxBox-A
89Tastee/Discs-1
89UD-215
89UD-689TC
90B-382
90Classic/Up-T6
90CollAB-21
90D-144
90D/BestAL-35
90D/Learning-1DK
90F-103
90F-621MVP
90F/BBMVP-5
90HOF/St-93
90KayBee-4
90KMart/CBatL-5
90Leaf/I-178
90MLBPA/Pins-101
90MSA/Soda-1
90OPC-60
90Panini/St-91
90Post-4
90PublInt/St-344
90RedFoley/St-9
90S-140
90S/100St-76
90S/McDon-19
90Sf-214
90T-60
90T/Ames-2
90T/HillsHM-10
90T/St-265
90T/WaxBox-B
90UD-124
90Woolwth/HL-9
91B-300
91BBBest/HitM-3
91Bz-10
91Classic/200-137
91Classic/I-46
91Classic/II-T70
91CollAB-28
91D-201
91D-396MVP
91D-BC19
91D/Elite-E2
91F-552
91F/Ultra-144
91JDeanSig-12
91Leaf/I-264CL
91Leaf/II-335
91Leaf/Stud-62
91MajorLg/Pins-21
91MooTown-19
91OPC-2RB
91OPC-540
91OPC/Premier-14
91Panini/FrSt-276
91Panini/St-224
91Panini/Top15-5
91Petro/SU-13
91Pol/Royal-4
91Post-26
91Post/Can-29
91RedFoley/St-11
91S-120
91S-769HL
91S-853FRAN

91S/100SS-85
91S/Cooper-B5
91Seven/3DCoin-1MW
91Seven/3DCoin-1NW
91Seven/3DCoin-2F
91Sunflower-4
91T-2RB
91T-540
91T/CJMini/I-15
91T/StClub/I-159
91T/SU-6
91T/WaxBox-B
91UD-525
91Woolwth/HL-8
92D/I-143
92F-154
92S/100SS-21
92S/II-650
92T-620
92UD-444

Brett, Kenneth Alvin
(Ken)
69T-476R
71MLB/St-315
71OPC-89
71T-89
72MB-45
72OPC-517
72T-517
73OPC-444
73T-444
74OPC-237
74T-237
75K-52
75OPC-250
75T-250
75T/M-250
76OPC-401
76SSPC-569
76T-401
76T/Tr-401T
77Ho-65
77OPC-21
77T-157
77T-631M
78T-682
79T-557
80Pol/Dodg-34
80T-521
81T-47
82D-364
82F-406
82T-397
85Utica-24
90Swell/Great-52
90Target-74

Breuer, Marvin
44Yank/St-3

Brevell, Ron
(Bubba)
86Kinston-2
88Miami/Star-3

Brewer, Anthony Bruce
(Tony)
83Albuq-20
84Cram/PCL-161
85Cram/PCL-152
85D-31RR
90Target-76

Brewer, Billy
90James/Pucko-15

Brewer, Chet
78Laugh/Black-23

Brewer, Jim
61T-317
61T/St-6
62T-191
63T-309
64T-553
65T-416
66OPC-158
66T-158
67OPC-31
67T-31
68T-298
69MB-36
69T-241
70T-571
71MLB/St-98
71OPC-549
71T-549
71Ticket/Dodg-3
72MB-46
72OPC-151
72T-151
73OPC-126
73T-126
74K-14
74OPC-189
74T-189
75OPC-163
75T-163
75T/M-163
76OPC-459
76T-459
78TCMA-243
87Smok/Dodg-3
88Smok/Dodg-14
89Smok/Dodg-79
90Target-75

Brewer, John H.
48Sommer-2
49B/PCL-8
49Sommer-2

Brewer, Mark
91SLCity/ProC-3228CO

Brewer, Marvin
40PB-183

Brewer, Matt
91Everett/ClBest-21
91Everett/ProC-3927

Brewer, Mike
84Omaha-9
85Maine-26
86Omaha-3
86Omaha/TCMA-13

Brewer, Omar
88CharlR/Star-3

Brewer, Rodney
88Spring/Best-19
89ArkTr/GS-3
90Louisvl/CMC-12
90Louisvl/ProC-407
90T/TVCard-39
91Classic/I-92
91Louisvl/LineD-227
91Louisvl/ProC-2925
91T/90Debut-21
92S/II-864

Brewer, Tom
55B-178
55T-83
55T/DH-128
56T-34
57T-112
58T-220
59T-346M
59T-55
60T-439
61P-50
61T-434
61T/St-108
62Salada-4
62Shirriff-4
Exh47

Brewington, Michael
(Mike)
89Welland/Pucko-6
90Augusta/ProC-2476
91Salem/ClBest-10
91Salem/ProC-964

Brewster, Charles L.
(Charlie)
No Cards.

Brewster, Rich
76QuadC
77QuadC
80ElPaso-20

Brian, Braden
87Jamestn-17

Brickell, Fritz D.
(Fritzie)
61BeeHive-2
61T-333

Brickell, George F.
(Fred)
33G-38
35G-1E
35G-3C
35G-5C
35G-6C
V353-38

Brickey, Josh
90Kgsport/Star-30BB

Brickhouse, Jack
89Pac/Leg-209

Brickley, Geroge V.
No Cards.

Brideweser, James E.
(Jim)
53B/Col-136
55B-151
57T-382
91Crown/Orio-51

Bridge, Eric
89Smok/FresnoSt-5

Bridges, Everett L.
(Rocky)
52T-239
53B/BW-32
54B-156
55B-136
56T-324
57Sohio/Reds-3
57T-294
58T-274
59T-318
60L-31
60T-22
61T-508
62J-75
62P-75
62P/Can-75
75Phoenix-1
76Phoenix
77Phoenix
78Cr/PCL-50
79Phoenix
80Phoenix-22
81Phoenix-25
82Phoenix
84Everett/Cram-28MG
86PrWill-4MG
87Vanco-8
88BuffB/CMC-25
88BuffB/Polar-1
88BuffB/ProC-1478
89Salem/Star-25
90Target-77
90Welland/Pucko-33CO
V362-1

Bridges, Jason
88Oneonta/ProC-2045
89PrWill/Star-1
90PrWill/Team-6

Bridges, Jim
85BurlR-28

Bridges, Marshall
58Union
78TCMA-48
WG9-5

Bridges, Thomas
33G-199
34DS-5
34G-44
35BU-81
35BU-9
35G-1D
35G-2D
35G-6D
35G-7D
35Wheat
37OPC-133
37Wheat
38Exh/4-12
38Wheat
39PB-104
41PB-65
61F-95
81Detroit-56
88Conlon/AmAS-3
91Conlon/Sport-180
R308-177
R313
R314
V300
V354-87
V355-33

Bridges-Clements, Tony
88BBCity/Star-9
89Memphis/Best-7
89Memphis/ProC-1202
89Memphis/Star-3
91Memphis/ProC-659

Bridwell, Albert H.
(Al)
10Domino-16
11Helmar-77
12Sweet/Pin-108
14CJ-42
14Piedmont/St-6
15CJ-42
91Conlon/Sport-170
D303
E101
E104
E105
E106
E254
E90/1
E91
E92
E98
M116
S74-81
T201
T202
T204
T205
T206
T213/blue
T215/brown
T216
T3-83

Brief, Anthony V.
(Bunny)
No Cards.

Brier, Coe
83Wisco/LF-1

Briggs, Daniel Lee
(Dan)
77T-592
79T-77
80T-352
82OPC-102
82T-102
82T/Tr-11T
84Colum-5
84Colum/Pol-3
85Colum-14
85Colum/Pol-3
85IntLgAS-33

Briggs, David
88Spokane/ProC-1938
89CharRain/ProC-994

Briggs, Grant
No Cards.

Briggs, John Edward
64PhilBull-6
64T-482R
65OPC-163
65T-163
66T-359
67T-268
68T-284
69MB-37
69MLB/St-173
69OPC-73
69T-73
69T/St-72
70MLB/St-85
70T-564
71MLB/St-170
71OPC-297
71T-297
72MB-47
72OPC-197
72T-197
73OPC-71
73T-71
74OPC-218
74T-218
74T/St-192
75K-16
75OPC-123
75T-123
75T/M-123
76OPC-373
76T-373

Briggs, John T.
59T-177
60T-376

Briggs, Ken
91Salinas/ClBest-1
91Salinas/ProC-2246

Briggs, Kenny
83Wausau/LF-29

Briggs, Stoney
91MedHat/ProC-4113

Briggs, Walter O.
81Detroit-50WN

Bright, Brian
91Elmira/ClBest-1
91Elmira/ProC-3281

Bright, Don
74Gaston
76SanAn/Team-3
78Cr/PCL-86

Bright, Harry James
59T-523
60T-277
61T-447
62T-551
63J-95
63P-95
63T-304
64T-259
65T-584
76Tucson-23MG
78TCMA-214
85Durham-14
WG9-6

Bright, Tom
77AppFx

Briles, Nelson
(Nellie)
65T-431R
66T-243
67T-404
68OPC-153WS
68T-540
69MB-38
69MLB/St-208
69OPC-60
69T-60
69T/St-111
70MLB/St-134
70OPC-435
70T-435
71MLB/St-195
71OPC-257
71T-257
72MB-48
72OPC-227WS
72T-605
73OPC-303
73T-303
74OPC-123
74T-123
74T/St-81
74T/Tr-123T
75OPC-495
75T-495
75T/M-495
76OPC-569
76SSPC-159
76T-569
77T-174
78T-717
79T-262
89Swell-79
91Crown/Orio-52

Briley, Greg
86Cram/PCL-107
87Chatt/Best-17
88Calgary/CMC-13
88Calgary/ProC-799
88S/Tr-74T
89F/Up-57
89S/HotRook-54
89T-781
89T/Big-247
89UD/Ext-770
90B-482
90Bz-17
90Classic-54
90D-463
90F-507
90Leaf/II-391
90Mother/Mar-14
90OPC-288
90Panini/St-148
90S-303
90S/100Ris-60
90S/YS/I-12
90Sf-43
90T-288
90T/Big-35
90T/Gloss60-19
90T/JumboR-4
90T/St-226
90T/St-320FS
90ToysRUs-5
90UD-455
91B-256
91CounHrth-4

91D-352
91F-444
91Leaf/I-194
91OPC-133
91S-494
91T-133
91T/StClub/I-130
91UD-479
92D/II-487
92F-274
92S/I-387
92T-502
92UD-369

Brilinski, Tyler
86Modesto-5
88Tacoma/CMC-12
88Tacoma/ProC-617
89Tacoma/CMC-13
89Tacoma/ProC-1561

Brill, Clinton
83Ander-26

Brill, Tim
78Watlo
79Savan-6

Brill, Todd
88Oneonta/ProC-2042

Brimhall, Bradley
90Madison/ProC-2260
90SoOreg/Best-22
90SoOreg/ProC-3439
91Madison/ClBest-5
91Madison/ProC-2122

Bringhurst, Stewart
78Wausau

Brink, Brad
87Clearw-23
88Maine/CMC-5
88Maine/ProC-289
88Phill/TastyK-27
89ScrWB/ProC-721

Brink, Craig
88Oneonta/ProC-2051

Brinker, William H.
(Bill)
No Cards.

Brinkman, Charles E.
(Chuck)
71OPC-13R
71T-13R
72T-786
73OPC-404
73T-404
74OPC-641
74T-641

Brinkman, Edwin A.
(Ed)
63T-479
64T-46
64T/Coins-108
64T/S-27
65T-417
66T-251
67T-311
68OPC-49
68T-49
69MB-39
69MLB/St-101
69OPC-153
69T-153
69T/St-232
70MLB/St-279
70T-711
71MLB/St-385
71OPC-389
71T-389
71T/Coins-46
72MB-49
72T-535
73OPC-5
73T-5
74OPC-138
74T-138
74T/St-171
75OPC-439
75T-439
75T/M-439
76SSPC-447
81Detroit-70
82BirmB-24MG

Brinkman, Greg
84Butte-8
88Vermont/ProC-957
89Orlan/Best-30
89Visalia/ProC-1428

Brinkman, Joe
88TM/Umpire-15
89TM/Umpire-13
90TM/Umpire-13

Brinkopf, Leon C.
No Cards.

Brinson, Hugh
86Ventura-2
87Dunedin-5
88Knoxvl/Best-24

Briody, Charles F.
(Fatty)
No Cards.

Brisbin, Steve
75QuadC

Brisco, Jamie
83Erie-9
84Savan-13
86Stockton-2
87ElPaso-10
88ElPaso/Best-4

Briscoe, John
90Modesto/Cal-150
90Modesto/ProC-2204
91Huntsvl/LineD-279
91S/RookTr-108T
92T/91Debut-21

Briskey, Dick
45Centen-2

Brison, Sam
76Laugh/Clown-11
76Laugh/Clown-29
76Laugh/Clown-37
76Laugh/Clown-4

Brissie, Lou
48L-31
49B-41
49Royal-8
50B-48
50Drake-4
51B-155
51T/BB-31
52B-79
52NTea
52NumNum-1
52Royal
52T-270
52TipTop
Exh47

Bristol, Dave
67OPC-21MG
67T-21
68OPC-148MG
68T-148MG
69T-234MG
70McDon-5MG
70T-556MG
71OPC-637MG
71T-637MG
72T-602MG
73OPC-377CO
73T-377C
74OPC-531CO
74T-531C
76T-631MG
77T-442MG
79Pol/SFG-1MG
80Pol/SFG-1MG
80T-499MG
81D-436MG
81T-686MG
84Phill/TastyK-9CO
85Phill/TastyK-3CO
85Phill/TastyK-8CO
88Phill/TastyK-29CO

Bristow, George
No Cards.

Bristow, Richie
90Kgsport/Best-21
90Kgsport/Star-3

Brito, Bernardo
81Batavia-20
81Watlo-31
83Watlo/LF-17
86Water-5
87Wmsprt-23
88OrlanTw/Best-28
88SLAS-13
89Portl/CMC-21
89Portl/ProC-212
90Portl/CMC-23
90Portl/ProC-190
91Portl/LineD-403
91Portl/ProC-1575

Brito, Jorge
88Modesto-17
88Modesto/Cal-68
89Modesto/Cal-282
90Foil/Best-180
90Huntsvl/Best-13
91Tacoma/LineD-528
91Tacoma/ProC-2309

Brito, Jose Oscar
80Water-12
81Indianap-11
81Louisvl-14
82Louisvl-3
83Louisvl/Riley-14
85CharlO-26
85RochR-15

Brito, Luis
89Martins/Star-3
90Princet/DIMD-3
91Martins/ClBest-13
91Martins/ProC-3458

Brito, Mario
87Jamestn-20
88MidwLAS/GS-45
88Rockford-3
89Rockford-2
90Jaxvl/Best-17
90Jaxvl/ProC-1368
91Vanco/LineD-627
91Vanco/ProC-1586

Britt, Bob
88Spartan/ProC-1046

Britt, Doug
78Charl
81Buffa-3
82DayBe-10

Britt, Patrick
87Modesto-21

Brittain, August S.
(Gus)
No Cards.

Brittain, Grant
90A&AASingle/ProC-198
90Idaho/ProC-3251
91Macon/ClBest-17
91Macon/ProC-870

Britton, James Alan
64T-94R
68OPC-76R
68T-76R
69OPC-154
69T-154
70T-646
71OPC-699
71T-699
72MB-50

Britton, Jimmy W.
72OPC-351R
72T-351R

Britton, Stephen G.
(Gil)
No Cards.

Brizzolara, Tony
79Richm-25
80OPC-86
80Richm-7
80T-156
81Richm-2
82Richm-2
83Richm-2
84Richm-9
85IntLgAS-11
85Richm-1
86BuffB-5
90Richm25Ann/Team-5

Broaca, Johnny
35BU-192
92Conlon/Sport-517

Broadfoot, Scott
87Erie-15
88StPete/Star-2
89Spring/Best-6

Broas, Rick
77Newar

Broberg, Pete
72OPC-64
72T-64
73K-41
73OPC-162
73T-162
74OPC-425
74T-425
75OPC-542
75T-542
75T/M-542
76A&P/Milw
76Ho-74
76OPC-39
76SSPC-245
76T-39
77Ho-145
77OPC-55
77T-409
78T-722
79OPC-301
79T-578
89T/SenLg-87

Brocail, Doug
87CharRain-23
88Charl/ProC-1211
89AubAs/ProC-13
89Wichita/Rock-28
90Wichita/Rock-3
91Wichita/LineD-602
91Wichita/ProC-2590

Brock, Don
88Pocatel/ProC-2073
89SanJose/Best-6
89SanJose/Cal-210
89SanJose/ProC-442
89SanJose/Star-3
90SanJose/Best-18
90SanJose/Cal-50
90SanJose/ProC-2004
90SanJose/Star-3

Brock, Gregory Allen
(Greg)
82Albuq-15
83D-579
83F-203
83Pol/Dodg-17
83Seven-12
83T/X-14
84D-296
84F-98
84Nes/792-555
84OPC-242
84Pol/Dodg-9
84T-555
84T/St-376YS
85Coke/Dodg-6
85F-368
85OPC-242
85T-753
86Coke/Dodg-4
86D-296
86F-125
86OPC-368
86Pol/Dodg-9
86T-368
86T/St-67
87D/OD-50
87F-437
87F/Up-U9
87OPC-26
87Pol/Brew-9
87T-26
87T/St-68
87T/Tr-9T
88D-337
88D/Best-71
88F-158
88Leaf-148
88OPC-212
88Panini/St-121
88Pol/Brew-9
88S-234
88Sf-184
88T-212
88T/Big-217
89B-143
89Brewer/YB-9
89D-57
89D/Best-239
89F-181
89Gard-11
89OPC-163
89Panini/St-371
89Pol/Brew-9
89S-307
89T-517
89T/Big-100
89T/St-201
89UD-543
90B-395
90Brewer/MillB-2
90D-293
90D/BestAL-142
90F-318
90Leaf/II-454
90OPC-139
90Panini/St-104
90PublInt/St-492
90S-485
90T-139
90T/Big-47
90T/St-208
90Target-78
90UD-514
91B-41
91D-572
91F-577
91F/Ultra-172
91OPC-663
91Panini/FrSt-204
91Pol/Brew-4
91RedFoley/St-12
91S-522
91T-663
91T/StClub/I-269
91UD-289

Brock, John Roy
No Cards.

Brock, Louis Clark
(Lou)
62T-387
63T-472
64T-29
64T/Coins-97
65T-540
66OPC-125
66T-125
67OPC-63M
67T-285
67T-63M
68Bz-15
68OPC-151WS
68T-151WS
68T-372AS
68T-520
69Kelly/Pin-4
69MB-40
69MLB/St-209
69MLBPA/Pin-36
69NTF
69OPC-165WS
69OPC-85
69T-165WS
69T-428AS
69T-85
69T/St-112
69Trans-31
70K-44
70MB-2
70MLB/St-135
70OPC-330
70T-330
70T/PI-4
70T/S-11
71K-17
71MD
71MLB/St-268
71OPC-625
71T-625
71T/Coins-87
71T/GM-27
71T/S-25
72K-48
72MB-51
72OPC-200
72T-200
73K-40
73OPC-320
73OPC-64LL
73T-320
73T-64LL
73T/Lids-8
74Greyhound-2
74Greyhound-6M
74OPC-204LL
74OPC-60
74T-204LL
74T-60
74T/DE-20
74T/St-111
75Ho-23
75Ho/Twink-23
75K-39
75OPC-2RB

75OPC-309LL
75OPC-540
75T-2RB
75T-309LL
75T-540
75T/M-2M
75T/M-309LL
75T/M-540
76Crane-5
76Ho-7
76Ho/Twink-7
76K-40
76Laugh/Jub-14
76MSA/Disc
76OPC-10
76OPC-197LL
76SSPC-275
76T-10
76T-197LL
77BurgChef-15
77Ho-32
77OPC-51
77T-355
77T/CS-8
78K-7
78OPC-204
78OPC-236RB
78T-1RB
78Tastee/Discs-6
78Wiffle/Discs-8
79OPC-350
79T-415HL
79T-665
80T-1M
85West/2-28
85Woolwth-5
86Sf/Dec-59
87KMart-13
89Kahn/Coop-3
89T-662TBC
89T/LJN-101
90HOF/St-86
90Pac/Legend-12
90Swell/Great-71
91CollAB-11
91K/3D-10
91K/SU-4A
91K/SU-4B
91LineD-24
91Swell/Great-13
91UD-636A
91UD-636B

Brock, Norman
86FSLAS-10
86Osceola-1
87ColAst/ProC-24
88ColAst/Best-27
89Cedar/Best-18
89Cedar/ProC-938
89Cedar/Star-2

Brock, Russell
91SoOreg/ClBest-10
91SoOreg/ProC-3832

Brock, Tarrik
91Bristol/ClBest-6
91FrRow/DP-52

Brocker, John
(Gene)
49Sommer-26

Brockett, Lew
11Helmar-39
C46-55
E254
E270/1

Brocki, Mike
87SanBern-16
88SanBern/Best-26
88SanBern/Cal-40
89Wmsprt/ProC-629
91Pac/SenLg-92

Brockil, Dave
86Cram/PCL-162

Brocklander, Fred
88TM/Umpire-38
89TM/Umpire-36
90TM/Umpire-34

Brockway, Kevin
86Cram/PCL-188

Broderick, Matthew T.
(Matt)
No Cards.

Broderick, Stan
83QuadC-24

Brodie, Walter Scott
(Steve)
No Cards.

Brodowski, Dick
52T-404
53T-69
54T-221
55T-171
56T-157
59Kahn
59T-371
91T/Arc53-69

Broersma, Eric
82Orlan/B-3
82OrlTw/A-13
83Orlan-19
83Toledo-26
84Toledo-17
85Toledo-2
86Toledo-3
87Tacoma-11

Broglio, Ernie
59T-296
60L-41
60T-16
61Bz-16
61P-179
61T-420
61T-451M
61T-45LL
61T-47LL
61T-49LL
62J-164
62P-164
62P/Can-164
62Salada-132
62Shirriff-132
62T-507
63J-165
63P-165
63T-313
64T-59
64T/Coins-95
64T/St-77
64T/SU
65T-565
66T-423
78TCMA-18

Brogna, Dennis
81Watlo-3
83MidldC-6
84MidldC-13

Brogna, Rico
88Bristol/ProC-1885
89B-102
89Lakeland/Star-3
90A&AASingle/ProC-30
90B-351
90EastLAS/ProC-EL4
90London/ProC-1275
91B-134
91Classic/200-197
91Classic/II-T12
91Leaf/GRook-BC11
91S-741RP
91Toledo/LineD-580
91Toledo/ProC-1939
91UD-73
92T-126M
92UD-74TP

Brohamer, John A.
(Jack)
73OPC-181
73T-181
74OPC-586
74T-586
75OPC-552
75T-552
75T/M-552
76OPC-618
76SSPC-518
76T-618
76T/Tr-618T
77BurgChef-78
77T-293
78PapaG/Disc-3
78T-416
79OPC-25
79T-63
80T-349
81F-393
81T-462

Brohm, Jeff
90BurlInd/ProC-3019
91Watertn/ClBest-24
91Watertn/ProC-3379

Bromby, Scott
88Rockford-2
89Rockford-3
89Rockford/Team-4

Bronkey, Jeff
87Orlan-21
88Visalia/Cal-166
88Visalia/ProC-95
89Orlan/Best-12
89Orlan/ProC-1337
91OkCty/LineD-305
91OkCty/ProC-172

Bronkie, Herman C.
No Cards.

Brookens, Andy
91Eugene/ClBest-3
91Eugene/ProC-3731

Brookens, Thomas D.
(Tom)
77Evansvl/TCMA-4
80T-416
81D-6
81F-473
81T-251
82D-202
82F-263
82OPC-11
82T-753
83D-454
83F-327
83T-119
84D-578
84F-78
84Nes/792-14
84T-14
85Cain's-4
85D-593
85F-4
85T-512
85Wendy-5
86Cain's-2
86D-537
86F-223
86OPC-286
86T-643
87Cain's-1
87Coke/Tigers-17
87D-296
87F-145
87OPC-232
87T-713
88D-107
88F-53
88Panini/St-93
88Pep/T-16
88Pol/T-4
88S-233
88T-474
89D-508
89D/Tr-53
89F-130
89OPC-342
89Panini/St-340
89S-269
89S/NWest-21
89S/Tr-73
89T-342
89T/St-278
89UD-106
90F-439
90S-297
90UD-138
91D-658
91F-362
91OPC-268
91S-106
91T-268
91UD-102

Brooks, Billy
87Bakers-6
88Bakers/Cal-250

Brooks, Bob
89AS/Cal-54UMP
90AS/Cal-33UMP
91AS/Cal-28UMP

Brooks, Brian Todd
87CharRain-1
88River/Cal-216
88River/ProC-1410
89Wichita/Rock-25
89Wichita/Rock/Up-12

Brooks, Craig
81Bristol-1

Brooks, Damon
86AubAs-6
87AubAs-5

Brooks, Desi
86Lynch-3
87Lynch-6

Brooks, Eric
89Myrtle/ProC-1460
91Dunedin/ClBest-12
91Dunedin/ProC-208

Brooks, Hubert
(Hubie)
79Jacks-3
80Tidew-15
81T-259R
81T/Tr-742
82D-476
82F-522
82F/St-81
82K-10
82OPC-266
82T-246TL
82T-494
82T/St-68
83D-49
83F-539
83OPC-134
83T-134
83T/St-261
84D-607
84F-582
84Jacks/Smok-3
84Nes/792-368
84OPC-368
84T-368
84T/St-103
85D-197
85F-74
85F/Up-U10
85Leaf-214
85OPC-222
85OPC/Post-5
85T-222
85T/St-104
85T/Tr-9T
86D-55
86D/HL-15
86F-244
86F/LimEd-7
86F/Mini-52
86F/St-12
86Leaf-44
86OPC-308
86Provigo-1
86Sf-187
86T-555
86T/St-77
86T/Super-15
87D-17DK
87D-88
87D/AAS-48
87D/DKsuper-17
87D/OD-91
87F-314
87F/GameWin-7
87F/LL-6
87F/Mini-14
87F/St-16
87Ho/St-4
87KayBee-6
87Kraft-42
87Leaf-142
87Leaf-17DK
87OPC-3
87RedFoley/St-91
87Sf-18
87Sf-197M
87Sf-79M
87T-650
87T/Coins-27
87T/Gloss60-46
87T/St-76
88D-468
88D/AS-45
88D/Best-12
88F-179
88Ho/Disc-5
88Leaf-257
88OPC-50
88Panini/St-328
88S-305
88Sf-187
88T-50
88T/Big-81
88T/St-81
88T/St/Backs-10
88T/UK-8
89B-367
89D-220
89D/Best-292
89F-371
89F/BBMVP's-5
89OPC-221
89Panini/St-123
89RedFoley/St-13
89S-53
89Sf-96
89T-485
89T/Big-301
89T/LJN-40
89T/Mini-21
89T/St-72
89T/UK-8
89UD-122
90B-100
90Classic-129
90Classic/III-75
90D-130
90D/BestNL-115
90F-341
90F/Up-U19
90Leaf/I-16
90Mother/Dodg-10
90OPC-745
90Pol/Dodg-21
90PublInt/St-169
90S-299
90S/Tr-34T
90T-745
90T/Big-262
90T/St-77
90T/Tr-14T
90UD-197
90UD/Ext-791
91B-461
91BBBest/HitM-4
91Classic/200-77
91D-349
91F-195
91F/UltraUp-U94
91F/Up-U100
91Kahn/Mets-7
91Leaf/II-295
91OPC-115
91OPC/Premier-15
91Panini/FrSt-59
91Panini/St-56
91RedFoley/St-13
91S-196
91S/RookTr-5T
91T-115
91T/StClub/II-325
91T/Tr-14T
91UD-217
91UD/Ext-787
91WIZMets-52
92D/I-64
92F-496
92S/I-107
92T-457
92UD-114

Brooks, Jerry
88GreatF-11
89AS/Cal-18
89Bakers/Cal-203
91AAAGame/ProC-AAA1
91Albuq/LineD-2
91Albuq/ProC-1153

Brooks, John
25Exh-19

Brooks, Jonathan J.
(Mandy)
No Cards.

Brooks, Kevin
88Virgini/Star-3

Brooks, Michael
75OkCty
75SanAn
76Baton
82Redwd-1

Brooks, Monte
87Spokane-12
88Charl/ProC-1204
89River/Best-27
89River/Cal-10

89River/ProC-1417
90CharRain/ProC-2048
Brooks, Rayme
91Eugene/ClBest-7
91Eugene/ProC-3728
Brooks, Robert
(Bobby)
70OPC-381R
70T-381R
71OPC-633R
71T-633R
Brooks, Rodney
88Hamil/ProC-1740
Brooks, Trey
83MidldC-16
84Iowa-14
85Iowa-3
86Iowa-4
Broome, Kim
89Welland/Pucko-7
Brosious, Frank
82BurlR-14
Brosius, Scott
88Madis-5
88MidwLAS/GS-50
89Huntsvl/Best-12
90Foil/Best-74
90Huntsvl/Best-15
91Tacoma/LineD-529
91Tacoma/ProC-2310
92Classic/I-19
92D/II-591
92F-671
92S/II-846
92T/91Debut-22
92UD-312
Broskie, Sigmund T.
(Siggy)
No Cards.
Brosnan, Jason
89GreatF-10
90AS/Cal-17
90Bakers/Cal-234
91SanAn/LineD-532
Brosnan, Jim
55B-229
57T-155
58T-342
59T-194
60L-124
60T-449
61T-513
61T/RO-25
61T/St-15
62J-125
62Kahn
62P-125
62T-2
63T-116
90LitSun-10
Brosnan, Timothy
N172
Bross, Terry
88LitFalls/Pucko-15
89StLucie/Star-2
90B-129
90D-502
90T/TVMets-37
91D-34RR
91Tidew/ProC-2501
92F-653
92S/II-763
92T/91Debut-23
92UD-531
Brothers, John
91Princet/ClBest-25
91Princet/ProC-3505
Brottem, Anton C.
(Tony)
No Cards.
Broughton, Cecil C.
(Cal)
N172
Brouhard, Mark Steven
82D-154
82F-135
82Pol/Brew-29
82T-517
83D-532
83F-28
83Gard-3
83T-167
84D-211
84F-195
84Gard-2
84Nes/792-528
84Pol/Brew-29
84T-528
85D-149
85F-576
85Gard-2
85Pol/Brew-29
85T-653
86OPC-21
86T-473
Brouthers, Arthur H.
(Art)
No Cards.
Brouthers, Dennis J.
(Dan)
50Callahan
75F/Pion-6
80SSPC/HOF
81Detroit-80
89HOF/St-7
89Smok/Dodg-3
90BBWit-102
90Target-79
N162
N172
N284
N300/unif
Scrapp
WG1-20
Brovia, Joseph John
(Joe)
48Sommer-11
52Mother-51
53Mother-18
Brow, Dennis
88PrWill/Star-4
89PrWill/Star-2
Brow, Scott
90StCath/ProC-3458
91Dunedin/ClBest-1
91Dunedin/ProC-197
Brow, Steve
87FtLaud-28
Browder, Bubba
88Wythe/ProC-1987
Brower, Bob
83BurlR-13
83BurlR/LF-11
83Tulsa-13
85OKCty-21
86OKCty-1
87D-651
87D/Rook-49
87F/Up-U10
87Mother/Rang-18
87Sf/Rook-3
87Smok/R-26
87T/Tr-10T
88D-346
88F-461
88Mother/R-18
88OPC-252
88RedFoley/St-9
88S-236
88Smok/R-16
88T-252
88ToysRUs-2
89B-182
89D-411
89F-514
89S-344
89T-754
89UD-439
90Publint/St-531
90T/TVYank-37
Brower, Louis Lester
(Lou)
No Cards.
Brown, Adam
88Bakers/Cal-242
88CalLgAS-48
89SanAn/Best-10
90Albuq/CMC-14
90Albuq/ProC-347
90Albuq/Trib-3
91FSLAS/ProC-FSL36
91VeroB/ClBest-14
91VeroB/ProC-775
Brown, Alvin
91Elizab/ProC-4302
91Kenosha/ClBest-1
91Kenosha/ProC-2077
Brown, Anthony
90Welland/Pucko-10
91Augusta/ProC-817
91Single/ClBest-246
Brown, Charles E.
(Buster)
E90/1
M116
Brown, Clinton
35BU-189
35BU-82
91Conlon/Sport-132
Brown, Craig
83AlexD-19
84PrWill-26
85Nashua-4
86Nashua-4
87Harris-8
Brown, Curt S.
84Colum-15
84Colum/Pol-1
85Colum-3
85Colum/Pol-4
86Indianap-25
87Indianap-13
88CharlK/Pep-24
88RochR/Gov-4
Brown, Curtis Jr.
(Curt)
81Holyo-11
Brown, Dan
91Martins/ClBest-26
91Martins/ProC-3444
Brown, Dana
88CapeCod/Sum-95
89Batavia/ProC-1932
90Spartan/Best-19
90Spartan/ProC-2502
90Spartan/Star-2
91Reading/LineD-504
91Reading/ProC-1380
Brown, Daren
89StCath/ProC-2073
90Myrtle/ProC-2770
91Dunedin/ClBest-2
91Dunedin/ProC-198
Brown, Darrell Wayne
80Evansvl/TCMA-11
84F-556
84Nes/792-193
84T-193
84T/St-311
85D-558
85F-270
85RochR-11
85T-767
85T/St-306
Brown, Dave
78Laugh/Black-27
90Negro/Star-12
Brown, Dave
89Erie/Star-4
Brown, Delos Hight
No Cards.
Brown, Dickie
90Burllnd/ProC-3002
91Collnd/ClBest-10
91Collnd/ProC-1477
Brown, Don
87Cedar-22
88Greens/ProC-1572
89Cedar/Star-26
89Chatt/Best-22
89Chatt/GS-6
Brown, Drummond Nic.
No Cards.
Brown, Duane
90Ashvl/ClBest-3
91Ashvl/ProC-561
Brown, Edward P.
(Ed)
No Cards.
Brown, Edward William
(Eddie)
28Exh-1
90Target-80
E126-44
E126-50
W575
Brown, Edwin Randolph
(Randy)
No Cards.
Brown, Elmer
90Target-81
Brown, Eric
74Cedar
82Idaho-4
Brown, Fred Herbert
No Cards.
Brown, George
WG3-6
Brown, Greg
78Wausau
Brown, Greg
91Batavia/ClBest-24
91Batavia/ProC-3477
Brown, Hector Harold
53T-184
54T-172
55B-221
55T-148
57T-194
58Hires-18
58T-394
59T-487
60T-89
61T-218
61T-46LL
62T-488
63T-289
64T-56
91CharRain/ProC-89
91Crown/Orio-54
91T/Arc53-184
Brown, Isaac
(Ike)
70OPC-152
70T-152
71MLB/St-387
71OPC-669
71T-669
72OPC-284
72T-284
72T/Cloth-3
73OPC-633
73T-633
74OPC-409
74T-409
Brown, J.B.
83GlenF-2
Brown, Jackie G.
71MLB/St-531
71OPC-591
71T-591
74OPC-89
74T-89
75OPC-316
75T-316
75T/M-316
76OPC-301
76T-301
77OPC-36
77T-147
78Cr/PCL-23
78OPC-126
78T-699
86Hawaii-1CO
87Vanco-2CO
88BuffB/ProC-1479CO
89BuffB/CMC-25CO
89BuffB/ProC-1683CO
90BuffB/ProC-390CO
90BuffB/Team-3CO
91BuffB/LineD-50CO
91BuffB/ProC-557CO
Brown, James D.
(Don)
No Cards.
Brown, James Murray
(John)
67OPC-72R
67T-72R
Brown, James Roberson
(Jimmy)
39PB-132
40PB-112
41DP-146
41PB-12
W754
Brown, Jarvis
87Kenosha-14
88Kenosha/ProC-1390
88MidwLAS/GS-33
89Visalia/Cal-106
89Visalia/ProC-1437
90OrlanSR/Best-9
90OrlanSR/ProC-1095
90OrlanSR/Star-3
91Portl/LineD-404
91Portl/ProC-1576
92D/II-770
92F-669
92S/II-870
92T/91Debut-24
Brown, Jeff
85Anchora-6
85FtMyr-14
87SanAn-12
87VeroB-16
88Bakers/Cal-234
88CalLgAS-46
91CharRain/ClBest-3
Brown, Jerald Ray
(Jake)
75Lafay
Brown, Jim
76QuadC
76Wausau
Brown, Jimmy
90Kissim/DIMD-3
91Niagara/ClBest-2
91Niagara/ProC-3639
Brown, John C.
(Chris)
80Clinton-16
84Cram/PCL-23
85F/Up-U11
85Mother/Giants-18
85T/Tr-10T
86D-553
86F-535
86F/LimEd-8
86F/Mini-108
86F/St-13
86KayBee-2
86Leaf-215
86Mother/Giants-18
86OPC-383
86Sf-78
86T-383
86T/Gloss60-10
86T/St-311
86T/St-85
87Classic-65
87D-11DK
87D-80
87D/AAS-44
87D/DKsuper-11
87D/OD-100
87F-268
87F/LL-7
87F/Mini-15
87F/RecSet-2
87F/Up-U11
87Leaf-11DK
87Leaf-236
87Mother/SFG-5
87OPC-180
87Sf-115M
87Sf-13
87T-180
87T/St-86
88Coke/Padres-35
88D-483
88D/Best-77
88F-578
88Leaf-221
88OPC-112
88Panini/St-408
88S-363
88Smok/Padres-5
88T-568
88T/Big-130
88T/St-111
89B-106
89D-183
89D/Tr-9
89F-301
89S-369
89T-481
89T/St-103
89UD-193
89UD/Ext-784
90Publint/St-469
Brown, John Lindsay
(Lindsay)
90Target-82

Brown, Keith
87Cedar-10
88Chatt/Best-3
88Nashvl/Team-4
89Chatt/II/Team-6
89D-115
89F-154
89Nashvl/CMC-2
89Nashvl/ProC-1296
89Nashvl/Team-3
90CedarDG/Best-32
90Nashvl/CMC-9
90Nashvl/ProC-224
91F-58
91Nashvl/LineD-253
91Nashvl/ProC-2149
Brown, Ken
88PrWill/Star-5
Brown, Kevin
87D-627
87Sumter-7
87Wichita-21
88BBAmer-25
88Tulsa-15
88Wichita-32
89D-613
89D/Best-256
89D/Rook-44
89F-641M
89F/Up-63
89Mother/R-18
89S/Tr-89
89Smok/R-4
89T/Tr-15T
89UD/Ext-752
90B-488
90Classic/III-41
90D-343
90D/BestAL-13
90F-291
90Leaf/I-47
90Mother/Rang-21
90OPC-136
90Panini/St-168
90PublInt/St-405
90S-210
90S/100Ris-28
90S/YS/I-29
90Sf-73
90T-136
90T/Big-261
90T/JumboR-5
90T/St-248
90ToysRUs-6
90TulsaDG/Best-32
90UD-123
91B-274
91D-314
91F-282
91F/Ultra-347
91Leaf/I-250
91Mother/Rang-21
91OPC-584
91Panini/St-208
91S-846
91T-584
91T/90Debut-22
91T/StClub/I-56
91UD-472
92D/I-55
92F-299
92S/II-709
92T-297
92UD-578
Brown, Kevin D.
86Lynch-4
89Jacks/GS-26
89Tidew/ProC-1962
90B-127
90T/TVMets-38
90Tidew/CMC-2
90Tidew/ProC-535
91B-49
91Brewer/MillB-5
91D-674
91Leaf/II-475
91Pol/Brew-5
91WIZMets-53
92F-174
Brown, Knock-out
T3/Box-66
Brown, Kurt
86AppFx-4
87Penin-26
88Tampa/Star-3
89Saraso/Star-1
90BirmB/Best-2
90BirmB/ProC-1111
90Foil/Best-189
91Vanco/LineD-628
91Vanco/ProC-1596
Brown, Larry Lesley
64T-301
65T-468
66OPC-16
66T-16
67OPC-145
67T-145
68Kahn
68T-197
69MB-42
69MLB/St-39
69T-503
69T/St-163
70MLB/St-194
70OPC-391
70T-391
71MLB/St-363
71OPC-539
71T-539
72MB-53
72OPC-279
72T-279
73JP
84Cram/PCL-238
91Crown/Orio-55
Brown, Larry
78Laugh/Black-2
86Negro/Frit-26
Brown, Leon
75Phoenix-21
91WIZMets-54
Brown, Lewis J.
(Lew)
No Cards.
Brown, Lloyd
90Target-83
91Conlon/Sport-181
Brown, Mace
40PB-220
41DP-36
90Target-84
R303/A
R312
Brown, Mark
81Miami-4
83RochR-2
85Toledo-3
86T-451
86Toledo-4
89Erie/Star-28
91Crown/Orio-56
Brown, Marty
86Cedar/TCMA-14
87Vermont-5
88AAA/ProC-26
88Nashvl/CMC-18
88Nashvl/ProC-481
88Nashvl/Team-5
89F-645M
89Nashvl/CMC-14
89Nashvl/ProC-1292
89Nashvl/Team-4
89S/HotRook-70
90CedarDG/Best-29
90D/Rook-39
91ColoSp/LineD-79
91ColoSp/ProC-2188
91Crown/Orio-57
Brown, Matt
90Elizab/Star-7
91Single/ClBest-93
91Visalia/ClBest-12
91Visalia/ProC-1743
Brown, Michael
90Welland/Pucko-2
91Augusta/ClBest-24
91Augusta/ProC-809
91Single/ClBest-88
Brown, Michael C.
(Mike)
81Holyo-8
82Spokane-19
84Cram/PCL-117
84D-42
84F/X-17
84Nes/792-643
84T-643
85D-207
85F-296
85Smok/Cal-4
85T-258
86D-642
86F-605
86F/Mini-117
86Leaf-256
86T-114
87D-168
87F-607
87Richm/Crown-42
87Richm/TCMA-27
87T-341
89Edmon/CMC-18
89Edmon/ProC-558
Brown, Michael G.
(Mike)
83T/X-15
84D-517
84F-394
84Nes/792-472
84T-472
86Pawtu-3
87Calgary-7
87D-563
87F-583
87T-271
90PrWill/Team-1
91FtLaud/ClBest-29CO
91FtLaud/ProC-2444
Brown, Mike
86Osceola-2
87Osceola-3
88ColoSp/CMC-2
88ColoSp/ProC-1526
88Toledo/CMC-24
88Toledo/ProC-611
89Kinston/Star-26
90Reno/Cal-286MG
91Collnd/ProC-1504MG
Brown, Mordecai
10Domino-17
11Helmar-91
12Sweet/Pin-80A
12Sweet/Pin-80B
14CJ-32
14Piedmont/St-7
15CJ-32
50Callahan
60Exh/HOF-5
60F-9
61F-11
63Bz/ATG-13
69Bz/Sm
75F/Pion-23
76Motor-5
80Pac/Leg-71
80SSPC/HOF
89HOF/St-60
90BBWit-89
92Conlon/Sport-555
BF2-63
D329-17
D350/2-23
E103
E270/2
E300
E90/1
E90/3
E91
E93
E96
E98
M101/4-17
M101/5-23
M116
S74-58
T201
T202
T204
T205
T206
T213/blue
T215/blue
T222
T3-1
W555
WG1-1
WG3-7
Brown, Ollie Lee
66T-524R
67OPC-83
67T-83
68T-223
69MLB/St-190
69OPC-149
69T-149
69T/S-63
69T/St-92
70K-55
70MLB/St-109
70OPC-130
70T-130
70T/PI-18
70T/S-36
71MLB/St-220
71OPC-505
71T-505
71T/Coins-133
72MB-54
72T-551
72T-552A
73OPC-526
73T-526
74OPC-625
74T-625
75OPC-596
75T-596
75T/M-596
76OPC-223
76SSPC-466
76T-223
77T-84
Brown, Oscar Lee
71MLB/St-5
71OPC-52R
71T-52R
72OPC-516
72T-516
73OPC-312
73T-312
Brown, Paul D.
62T-181
63T-478
64T-319
Brown, Paul
87Elmira/Black-34
88Lynch/Star-2
90LynchRS/Team-15
91WinHaven/ClBest-2
91WinHaven/ProC-482
Brown, Randy
76Wausau
Brown, Randy
90Elmira/Pucko-3
91Single/ClBest-131
91WinHaven/ClBest-15
91WinHaven/ProC-495
Brown, Reggie
89Helena/SP-3
Brown, Renard
87Stockton-9
Brown, Richard Ernest
(Dick)
58T-456
59T-61
60T-256
61T-192
62J-21
62P-21
62P/Can-21
62Salada-37
62Shirriff-37
62T-438
63J-52
63P-52
63T-112
78TCMA-95
91Crown/Orio-53
Brown, Rick
86LitFalls-4
87Columbia-12
Brown, Rob
90CharlR/Star-2
91Tulsa/LineD-576
91Tulsa/ProC-2765
Brown, Robert M.
34G-81
Brown, Robert W.
(Bobby)
47TipTop
49B-19
50B-101
51B-110
51BR-B6
52B-105
52BR
91Swell/Great-15
R346-9
Brown, Rogers Lee
(Bobby)
79Colum-27
80T-670R
81D-469
81F-95
81OPC-107
81T-418
82D-552
82F-30
82T-791
82T/Tr-12T
83T-287
84D-478
84F-296
84Mother/Padres-14
84Nes/792-261
84Smok/Padres-2
84T-261
84T/St-157
85D-383
85F-28
85Mother/Padres-23
85OPC-92
85T-583
85Utica-17
86T-182
Brown, Ronnie
89Wythe/Star-3
Brown, Samuel W.
(Sam)
No Cards.
Brown, Scott
80Indianap-17
81Indianap-19
82F-60
82T-351R
83Omaha-4
Brown, Sid
89Panini/St-169
Brown, Stacy
89Burllnd/Star-3
Brown, Steven E.
80ElPaso-16
81SLCity-3
82Spokane-1
85Indianap-24
Brown, Tab
89Pulaski/ProC-1899
90Foil/Best-62
90Sumter/Best-2
90Sumter/ProC-2425
Brown, Terry
87Beloit-15
89Kenosha/ProC-1068
89Kenosha/Star-2
Brown, Thomas D.
76Baton
78SanJose-16
79Tacoma-2
80Syrac-8
81Syrac-2
Brown, Thomas Michael
(Tom)
49B-178
49Eureka-31
52B-236
52T-281
53B/Col-42
90Target-85
Brown, Thomas T.
(Tom)
N172
N284
N526
Brown, Thomas William
(Tom)
64T-311
Brown, Timothy
88StCath/ProC-2007
89Myrtle/ProC-1464
90Dunedin/Star-4
91Dunedin/ClBest-3
91Dunedin/ProC-199
Brown, Todd
86Reading-4
86Stockton-3
87ElPaso-17
88Denver/CMC-19

88Denver/ProC-1278
Brown, Tom
89Hagers/Best-11
89Hagers/ProC-283
89Pac/SenLg-139
90Hagers/Best-5CO
90Hagers/ProC-1432CO
90Hagers/Star-27CO
Brown, Tony
87Reading-2
88EastLAS/ProC-31
88Reading/ProC-867
89Tidew/ProC-1974
90Foil/Best-298
90Huntsvl/Best-20
91Augusta/ClBest-23
Brown, Walter G.
(Jumbo)
33G-192
39PB-124
40PB-154
92Conlon/Sport-454
Brown, Willard
90Negro/Star-7
Brown, Willard Jessie
E223
N172
N338/2
Brown, William James
(Gates)
64T-471
65OPC-19
65T-19
66T-362
67OPC-134
67T-134
68T-583
69MB-41
69T-256
70OPC-98
70T-98
71MLB/St-386
71OPC-503
71T-503
72MB-52
72OPC-187
72T-187
73OPC-508
73T-508
74OPC-389
74T-389
75OPC-371
75T-371
75T/M-371
76SSPC-371
81Detroit-106
88Domino-1
89Pac/SenLg-199
89TM/SenLg-13
Brown, William Verna
(Bill)
No Cards.
Brown, Winston
61T-391
Brown, Winston
89Spring/Best-8
Browne, Byron Ellis
66OPC-139R
66T-139R
67T-439
68T-296
70OPC-388
70T-388
71MLB/St-171
71OPC-659
71T-659
Browne, Earl James
No Cards.
Browne, George Edward
E90/3
E91
T206
T3-84
Browne, Jerry
86Tulsa-9A
87Classic/Up-146
87D-41RR
87D/OD-170
87D/Rook-29
87F-647M
87F/Up-U12
87Leaf-41RR
87Mother/Rang-22
87Sf/Rook-4
87Smok/R-31
87T/Tr-11T
88D-408
88F-462
88Leaf-236
88Mother/R-22
88OPC-139
88Panini/St-201
88S-278
88S/YS/II-13
88Smok/R-15
88T-139
88T/Big-163
88T/JumboR-21
88ToysRUs-3
89B-85
89D-529
89D/Best-280
89D/Tr-44
89F/Up-26
89T-532
89T/Big-236
89T/Tr-16T
89UD-314
90B-332
90Classic-53
90D-138
90F-487
90Leaf/I-48
90OPC-442
90Panini/St-54
90Publlnt/St-555
90S-52
90Sf-111
90T-442
90T/Big-256
90T/Coins-7
90T/St-210
90TulsaDG/Best-27
90UD-426
91B-71
91D-162
91F-363
91F/Ultra-108
91Leaf/I-43
91OPC-76
91Panini/FrSt-217
91S-481
91T-76
91T/StClub/I-25
91UD-116
92F-107
92S/II-496
92T-219
92UD-340
Browne, Prentice A.
(Pidge)
89Smok/Ast-20
Browning, Jim
33SK-41
Browning, Louis R.
(Pete)
90Target-86
N172
Browning, Mike
82Nashvl-2
83Nashvl-2
84Cram/PCL-114
86Miami-3
87Miami-15
88Miami/Star-4
89ColMud/Best-17
89ColMud/ProC-122
89ColMud/Star-5
90ColMud/Best-20
90ColMud/ProC-1339
90ColMud/Star-6
Browning, Tom
83Tampa-5
84Wichita/Rock-5
85D-634
85D/HL-43
85F/Up-U12
85T/Tr-11T
86D-384
86Drake-37
86F-173
86F/Mini-38
86F/Slug-4
86F/St-14
86F/WaxBox-C6
86KayBee-3
86Leaf-179
86Sf-185M
86Sf-79
86T-652
86T/Gloss60-49
86T/Mini-40
86T/St-141
86T/St-313
86T/Super-16
86TexGold-32
87Classic-78
87D-63
87D/OD-194
87F-194
87Kahn-32
87Leaf-138
87OPC-65
87T-65
87T/St-137
88D-63
88D/Best-335
88F-228
88Kahn/Reds-32
88S-132
88T-577
88T/Big-96
89B-306
89Classic-126
89D-71
89D/Best-62
89F-153
89F-629M
89Kahn/Reds-32
89OPC-234
89Panini/St-4
89Panini/St-65
89S-554
89S-658HL
89S/HotStar-61
89Sf-180
89Sf-222M
89T-234
89T/Big-14
89T/Gloss60-46
89T/Mini-6
89T/St-141
89T/St-7
89T/St/Backs-61
89UD-617
89Woolwth-9
90B-43
90Classic/Up-T7
90D-308
90D/BestNL-27
90D/Learning-54
90F-415
90Kahn/Reds-5
90Leaf/I-110
90MLBPA/Pins-20
90OPC-418
90Panini/St-247
90Publlnt/St-23
90S-165
90S/100St-33
90Sf-91
90T-418
90T/Big-48
90T/St-135
90UD-189
91B-684
91Classic/200-10
91D-528
91F-59
91F/Ultra-89
91Kahn/Reds-32
91Leaf/I-88
91Leaf/Stud-161
91OPC-151
91Pep/Reds-4
91S-229
91S/100SS-32
91T-151
91T/StClub/I-235
91UD-633
91USPlayC/AS-5S
92D/I-136
92F-401
92S/II-642
92T-339
92UD-461
Broyles, Jason
90Kissim/DIMD-4
91Yakima/ClBest-19
91Yakima/ProC-4239
Brubaker, Bruce
65T-493R
67T-276
90Target-904
Brubaker, John
89Oneonta/ProC-2128
90FtLaud/Star-2
Brubaker, Wilbur L.
(Bill)
34G-4
36G
39PB-130
40PB-166
R314
Brucato, Bob
89CharRain/ProC-973
Bruce, Andy
91Johnson/ClBest-5
91Johnson/ProC-3981
Bruce, Bob
60T-118
61T-83
62T-419
63Pep
63T-24
64T-282
65OPC-240
65T-240
66OPC-64
66T-64
66T/RO-8
67T-417
89Smok/Ast-1
Bruce, Louis
(Lou)
No Cards.
Bruck, Tom
90BurlB/Best-5
90BurlB/ProC-2341
90BurlB/Star-5
Brucker, Earle F. Jr.
No Cards.
Brueggemann, Jeff
80Toledo-18
83Visalia/LF-14GM
Brueggemann, Steve
85LitFalls-3
Bruehl, Darin
89AubAs/ProC-2179
Bruett, Joseph T.
88CapeCod/Sum-168
89Kenosha/ProC-1074
89Kenosha/Star-3
90A&AASingle/ProC-154
90AS/Cal-13
90Portl/CMC-24
90Visalia/Cal-74
90Visalia/ProC-2165
91Portl/LineD-405
91Portl/ProC-1577
Bruggy, Frank Leo
No Cards.
Brugo, Dale
91LynchRS/ClBest-1
Bruhert, Mike
78Tidew
79T-172
79Tucson-3
82Colum-7
82Colum/Pol-25
91WIZMets-55
Brumfield, Harvey
87Clearw-9
88Reading/ProC-881
89Reading/Best-20
89Reading/ProC-667
89Reading/Star-4
Brumfield, Jacob
87FtMyr-33
88Memphis/Best-6
89Memphis/Best-3
89Memphis/ProC-1188
89Memphis/Star-4
90BBCity/Star-3
90FSLAS/Star-26
91Omaha/LineD-327
91Omaha/ProC-1045
92T-591M
Brumley, Duff
90Johnson/Star-5
91Hamil/ClBest-10
91Hamil/ProC-4029
Brumley, Mike
86Iowa-5
87Iowa-13
88AAA/ProC-21
88D-609
88LasVegas/CMC-19
88LasVegas/ProC-235
89D-302
89D/Rook-39
89F-302
89F/Up-30
89Mara/Tigers-12
89T/Big-324
90D-533
90Mother/Mar-26
90OPC-471
90S/100Ris-88
90T-471
90UD-312
91F-445
91Pawtu/LineD-353
91Pawtu/ProC-45
91S-624
92S/I-363
Brumley, Tony Mike
(Mike)
60DF
64T-167R
65T-523
66OPC-29
66T-29
Brummer, Glenn Edward
82Louisvl-2
82T-561R
83D-418
83F-4
83T-311
84D-138
84F-321
84Nes/792-152
84T-152
85D-290
85Rangers-7
86F-557
86Hawaii-2
86T-616
Brummer, Jeff
90Yakima/Team-7
Brummett, Greg
88Alaska/Team-5
89Everett/Star-26
90Clinton/Best-7
90Clinton/ProC-2546
91Clinton/ClBest-23
Brunansky, Thomas A.
(Tom)
80ElPaso-17
81SLCity-21
82Spokane-20
82T-653R
82T/Tr-13T
83D-555
83F-607
83OPC-232
83T-232
83T/St-309
83T/St-90
84D-242
84F-557
85FunFood/Pin-130
84Nes/792-447
84OPC-98
84T-447
84T/St-304
85D-364
85F-271
85GenMills-15
85Leaf-36
85OPC-122
85Seven/Minn-7
85T-122
85T/Gloss40-39
85T/St-299
85T/Super-57
86D-192
86D-24DK
86D/AAS-44
86D/DKsuper-24
86F-387
86F/LimEd-9
86F/Mini-83
86F/St-15
86KayBee-4
86Leaf-24DK
86OPC-392

86Sf-80
86T-565
86T/St-276
87D-194
87D/OD-222
87F-537
87F/Hottest-7
87F/St-17
87Leaf-244
87OPC-261
87RedFoley/St-75
87Sf-134
87T-776
87T/St-280
88D-245
88D/Best-19
88F-5
88F/Slug-4
88F/St-42
88F/Up-U117
88Master/Disc-12
88OPC-375
88Panini/St-142
88S-194
88S/Tr-5T
88Sf-194
88Smok/Card-25
88T-375
88T/Big-211
88T/St-15
88T/St-275
88T/Tr-20T
89B-444
89Classic/Up/2-186
89D-112
89D/Best-187
89F-444
89F/Heroes-4
89OPC-60
89Panini/St-187
89RedFoley/St-14
89S-184
89Sf-161
89Smok/Cards-1
89T-261TL
89T-60
89T/Big-54
89T/Hills-4
89T/LJN-116
89T/St-41
89T/UK-9
89UD-272
90B-202
90Classic-119
90D-399
90D/BestAL-130
90ElPasoATG/Team-34
90F-242
90F/Up-U70
90Leaf/II-447
90MLBPA/Pins-31
90OPC-409
90Panini/St-344
90PublInt/St-211
90S-72
90S/Tr-49T
90T-409
90T/Big-94
90T/St-45
90T/Tr-15T
90T/TVCard-31
90UD-257
90UD/Ext-708
91B-125
91Classic/200-11
91D-513
91F-88
91F/Ultra-29
91Leaf/I-164
91OPC-675
91Panini/FrSt-270
91Pep/RSox-2
91RedFoley/St-14
91S-245
91T-675
91T/StClub/I-297
91UD-163
92D/II-490
92F-34
92S/I-46
92T-296
92UD-543

Brundage, Dave
87Clearw-20
88Vermont/ProC-951
89Wmsprt/ProC-642
89Wmsprt/Star-1
90Wmsprt/Star-3
91Calgary/LineD-53
91Calgary/ProC-525

Brune, Jim
88Billings/ProC-1804
88Cedar/ProC-1154

Brunelle, Rodney
85Bend/Cram-4
87CharWh-7
88Clearw/Star-3

Brunenkant, Barry
84OKCty-15
85Tulsa-14
86Maine-1
87BuffB-5

Brunet, George
58T-139
63T-538
64T-322
65OPC-242
65T-242
66T-393
67OPC-122
67T-122
68T-347
69MB-43
69MLB/St-19
69MLBPA/Pin-3
69T-645
69T/St-141
70MLB/St-267
70OPC-328
70T-328
71MLB/St-269
71OPC-73
71T-73
72MB-55
91Crown/Orio-58

Brunner, Tom
79Elmira-26

Bruno, Joe
80Penin/B-15
80Penin/C-21
87Cedar-12
88Chatt/Best-17
88SLAS-37
89Chatt/Best-21
89Chatt/GS-7
89SLAS-18

Bruno, Julio
90CharRain/Best-5
90CharRain/ProC-2046
91Single/ClBest-367
91Waterlo/ClBest-15
91Waterlo/ProC-1262

Bruno, Paul
91Kenosha/ClBest-23
91Kenosha/ProC-2078
91Single/ClBest-343

Bruno, Thomas
77OPC-32
79T-724R

Brunsberg, Arlo A.
No Cards.

Brunson, Eddie
78Newar
80Holyo-7

Brunswick, Mark
85LitFalls-13
86Columbia-6
87Lynch-25

Brunswick, Tom
77Spartan

Brush, Robert
(Bob)
No Cards.

Bruske, James
87Kinston-17
88Wmsprt/ProC-1323
89Kinston/Star-4
90Canton/Best-18
90Canton/ProC-1285
90Canton/Star-1
91Canton/LineD-78
91Canton/ProC-973

Brusky, Brad
86Cedar/TCMA-2
87Vermont-1
88Cedar/ProC-1156
89Wmsprt/ProC-644
89Wmsprt/Star-2

Brusstar, Warren
78T-297
79BK/P-9
79T-653
80T-52
81OkCty/TCMA-4
81T-426
82F-242
82T-647
83Thorn-41
84D-442
84F-487
84Nes/792-304
84SevenUp-41
84T-304
85D-533
85F-51
85SevenUp-41
85T-189
86D-555
86F-362
86T-564
87SanJose-21

Brust, Dave
90Durham/Team-20
91Durham/ClBest-8
91Durham/ProC-1550

Brust, Jerry
76QuadC

Brutcher, Lenny
90Foil/Best-28
90SoBend/Best-1
91Saraso/ClBest-2
91Saraso/ProC-1105
91UD-75

Bruton, William Haron
(Bill)
53JC-22
53SpicSpan/3x5-4
53SpicSpan/7x10-2
53T-214
54B-224
54JC-38
54SpicSpan/PostC-3
54T-109
55B-11
55Gol/Braves-3
55JC-38
55RFG-15
55SpicSpan/DC-3
56T-185
56YellBase/Pin-8
57SpicSpan/4x5-3
57T-48
58T-355
59T-165
60Lake
60SpicSpan-3
60T-37
61P-109
61T-251
61T/St-39
62J-18
62P-18
62P/Can-18
62Salada-92
62Shirriff-92
62T-335
62T/St-43
63J-49
63P-49
63T-437
64Det/Lids-2
64T-98
81Detroit-101
91T/Arc53-214
Exh47
PM10/Sm-18

Bruyette, Edward T.
(Ed)
No Cards.

Bryan, Frank
87SanJose-9
88Fresno/Cal-17
88Fresno/ProC-1222
89PalmSp/Cal-47
89PalmSp/ProC-487

Bryan, William Ronald
(Billy)
63T-236
65OPC-51
65T-51
66T-332
67T-601
68T-498
78TCMA-47

Bryand, Renay
88Spokane/ProC-1941
89CharRain/ProC-996
90Riversi/Best-4
90Riversi/Cal-13
90Riversi/ProC-2597
91HighD/ClBest-1
91HighD/ProC-2384
91Wichita/ProC-2591

Bryans, Jason
91Eugene/ClBest-27
91Eugene/ProC-3715

Bryant, Bobby
79Jacks-19
79Tidew-21

Bryant, Chris
87Idaho-12

Bryant, Clay
74OPC-521CO
74T-521CO

Bryant, Derek Roszell
77SanJose-4
80Ogden-4
80T-671R
81Tacoma-9

Bryant, Donald Ray
(Don)
69T-499R
70OPC-473
70T-473
74OPC-403CO
74T-403C
77T-597C

Bryant, Erick
89Wausau/GS-25

Bryant, Erwin
81Bristol-16

Bryant, Franklin S.
81VeroB-3

Bryant, George
No Cards.

Bryant, James
86Chatt-5
87Chatt/Best-7

Bryant, John
82CharR-5
83CharR-15
86Cedar/TCMA-23
87Vermont-15

Bryant, Keith
89Belling/Legoe-3

Bryant, Mike
80Elmira-25

Bryant, Neil
82Amari-15
83MidldC-5

Bryant, Patrick
91Collnd/ClBest-29
91Collnd/ProC-1496
91Single/ClBest-57

Bryant, Phil
87Gaston-7
88CharlR/Star-4
89Tulsa/GS-6
89Tulsa/Team-4
90Tulsa/ProC-1149

Bryant, Ralph
82VeroB-21
83VeroB-22
85Cram/PCL-161
86Albuq-2
87Albuq/Pol-25
87D-587
87F-649M
87F/Up-U13
87Pol/Dodg-24
87T/Tr-12T
88F-510
90Target-87

Bryant, Ron
70OPC-433
70T-433
71MLB/St-242
71OPC-621
71T-621
72OPC-185
72OPC-186IA
72T-185
72T-186IA
73OPC-298
73T-298
74OPC-104
74OPC-205LL
74T-104
74T-205LL
74T/DE-21
74T/St-103
75OPC-265
75T-265
75T/M-265

Bryant, Scott
90A&AASingle/ProC-129
90B-59
90Cedar/Best-1
90Cedar/ProC-2336
90CedarDG/Best-30
90Foil/Best-64
90S-667DC
91Chatt/LineD-156
91Chatt/ProC-1970
91Single/ClBest-69
91UD/FinalEd-5F

Bryant, Shawn
90Burllnd/ProC-3003
91Kinston/ClBest-2
91Kinston/ProC-314

Bryden, Thomas R.
(T.R.)
82Danvl-4
83Redwd-7
85MidldA-11
87Edmon-21
87T-387
88Portl/CMC-3
88Portl/ProC-663

Brye, Stephen Robert
(Steve)
71OPC-391R
71T-391R
72OPC-28R
72T-28
73OPC-353
73T-353
74OPC-232
74T-232
75OPC-151
75T-151
75T/M-151
76OPC-519
76SSPC-215
76T-519
77T-424
78T-673
79Hawaii-12
79T-28

Bryeans, Chris
82CharR-10
83CharR-5

Brynan, Charles
N172

Brzezinski, George
88Geneva/ProC-1657

Bubalo, Mike
91Everett/ProC-3934

Bubrewicz, Tim
91Elmira/ProC-3262

Bubser, Harold Fred
(Hal)
No Cards.

Buccheri, James
88SoOreg/ProC-1692
89Madis/Star-5
89Star/Wax-65
90Modesto/Cal-162
90Modesto/ProC-2217
91Huntsvl/ClBest-5
91Huntsvl/LineD-280
91HuntsvlProC-1801

Bucci, Mike
76SanAn/Team-4
78Cr/PCL-115
79Tucson-5
80Tacoma-13
81Charl-11
82Wausau-12
83Chatt-9
85BurlR-10
86Salem-2MG
87BuffB-26MG
88Burllnd/ProC-1786

Buccola, Vic

47Signal
48Smith-16
Bucha, John George
(Johnny)
52T-19
53Glen
54B-215
Buchanan, Bob
81Cedar-23
82Water-7
83Indianap-28
87Tidew-26
87Tidew/TCMA-27
88Omaha/CMC-3
88Omaha/ProC-1514
89Omaha/CMC-1
89Omaha/ProC-1724
91Omaha/LineD-328
91Omaha/ProC-1027
Buchanan, Reggie
81Buffa-25
Buchanan, Rob
88Eugene/Best-13
89AppFx/ProC-868
89Eugene/Best-21
Buchanan, Shawn
91Utica/ClBest-5
91Utica/ProC-3252
Buchek, Gerald Peter
(Jerry)
61Union
62Kahn/Atl
62T-439
64T-314
65T-397
66T-454
67T-574
68T-277
69MB-44
91WIZMets-56
Bucher, James Quinter
(Jim)
90Target-88
R313
Buchheister, Don
(Bucky)
73Cedar
74Cedar
75Cedar
76Cedar
77Cedar
78Cedar
80Cedar-21
81Cedar-20
82Cedar-27
83Cedar-26
84Cedar-19
85Cedar-28
86Cedar/TCMA-27
88Cedar/ProC-1136
89Cedar/Best-24
89Cedar/ProC-931
90CedarDG/Best-34GM
Buckels, Gary
88MidwLAS/GS-25
88QuadC/GS-28
89MidldA/GS-6
90Edmon/CMC-3
90Edmon/ProC-510
91Edmon/LineD-156
91Edmon/ProC-1509
Buckenberger, Albert
N172
Buckholz, Steven
88Watertn/Pucko-3
90Salem/Star-2
91Salem/ProC-945
Buckle, Larry
80Cedar-5
82Water-2
Buckley, Brian
81Redwd-2
82Holyo-2
84PrWill-10
Buckley, Joe
89Spokane/SP-7
Buckley, John
83BurlR-2
83BurlR/LF-20
83Tulsa-16
84Tulsa-27
90TulsaDG/Best-14
Buckley, Kevin John
82BurlR-15
84OKCty-16
85Maine-15
86Maine-2
87LasVegas-8
Buckley, Mike
81QuadC-6
Buckley, Richard D.
(Dick)
N172
Buckley, Travis
90A&AASingle/ProC-78
90Gaston/Best-4
90Gaston/ProC-2513
90Gaston/Star-3
91CharlR/ClBest-3
91CharlR/ProC-1307
Buckley, Troy
88CapeCod/Sum-170
90AS/Cal-15
90Visalia/Cal-75
90Visalia/ProC-2157
91Single/ClBest-203
91Visalia/ClBest-13
91Visalia/ProC-1744
Buckmier, Jim
83AlexD-29
84PrWill-2
Buckner, Jim
79Tidew-10
79Toledo-14
80Buffa-5
81Omaha-20
Buckner, William J.
(Bill)
70OPC-286R
70T-286R
71MLB/St-99
71OPC-529R
71T-529R
72OPC-114
72T-114
73OPC-368
73T-368
74OPC-505
74T-505
74T/St-41
75Ho-97
75K-32
75OPC-244
75T-244
75T/M-244
76OPC-253
76SSPC-91
76T-253
77BurgChef-195
77Ho-54
77T-27
78Ho-46
78OPC-127
78T-473
78Wiffle/Discs-10
79Ho-27
79OPC-177
79T-346
80OPC-75
80T-135
81Coke
81D-482
81Drake-13
81F-292
81F/St-29
81MSA/Disc-5
81OPC-202
81Sqt-6
81T-1LL
81T-625
81T/HT
81T/SO-55
81T/St-153
81T/St-17
82D-403
82Drake-5
82F-589
82F/St-96
82K-2
82OPC-124
82RedLob
82T-456TL
82T-760
82T/St-29
83D-14DK
83D-99
83D/AAS-7
83Drake-2
83F-492
83K-59
83OPC-250
83PermaGr/CC-1
83T-250
83T/Gloss40-24
83T/St-223
83Thorn-22
84D-117
84D/AAS-28
84D/Champs-18
84Drake-4
84F-488
84F/X-18
85FunFood/Pin-100
84Nes/792-545
84OPC-96
84T-545
84T/St-42
84T/Super-14
84T/Tr-17
85D-416
85F-153
85Leaf-254
85OPC-65
85SpokaAT/Cram-3
85T-65
85T/St-214
85ThomMc/Discs-6
86D-151
86Drake-17
86F-343
86F/St-16
86Leaf-77
86OPC-239
86Sf-135M
86Sf-81
86T-443
86T/St-252
86T/Super-17
86Woolwth-5
87D-462
87D/OD-183
87F-31
87F/LimWaxBox-C2
87Leaf-241
87OPC-306
87Sf-70
87T-764
87T/Board-14
87T/St-250
88D-456
88F-486
88OPC-147
88S-591
88S/Tr-36T
88T-147
89F-278
89S-214
89T/WaxBox-B
89UD-639
90D-474
90Pep/RSox-4
90PublInt/St-345
90S-396
90T/TVRSox-23
90Target-89
90UD-252
Bucz, Bruce
88Visalia/Cal-171
90Visalia/Cal-81GM
Bucz, Joseph
90Visalia/Cal-83PER
Budaska, Mark David
79Ogden/TCMA-18
80Ogden-7
81Tacoma-13
82T-531R
Buddin, Donald Thomas
(Don)
58T-297
59T-32
60T-520
61P-53
61T-99
62J-59
62P-59
62P/Can-59
62Salada-68A
62Salada-68B
62Shirriff-68
62T-332
89Smok/Ast-19
Budke, Todd
85Visalia-17
86Orlan-3
Budner, Scott
90SoOreg/Best-30CO
90SoOreg/ProC-3450CO
91Madison/ClBest-13CO
91Madison/ProC-2147CO
Budnick, Michael
47TipTop
Budrewicz, Timothy
91Elmira/ClBest-17
Buechele, Steve
82Tulsa-27
83Tulsa-22
84OKCty-13
85OKCty-17
86D-544
86F-558
86Rangers-22
86T-397
87D-180
87D/OD-179
87F-121
87Mother/Rang-7
87OPC-176
87Smok/R-11
87T-176
87T/St-242
88D-224
88D/Best-312
88F-463
88Mother/R-7
88OPC-2
88Panini/St-204
88S-306
88Smok/R-12
88T-537
88T/Big-104
88T/St-235
89B-232
89D-174
89D/Best-223
89F-515
89Mother/R-8
89OPC-83
89Panini/St-453
89S-368
89Smok/R-5
89T-729TL
89T-732
89T/Big-156
89T/St-250
89UD-418
90B-493
90D-107
90F-292
90Leaf/I-179
90Mother/Rang-14
90OPC-279
90Panini/St-169
90PublInt/St-406
90S-221
90T-279
90T/Big-63
90T/St-251
90TulsaDG/Best-15
90UD-685
91B-268
91D-357
91F-283
91Mother/Rang-5
91OPC-464
91Panini/FrSt-254
91Panini/St-209
91S-257
91S/RookTr-77T
91T-464
91T/StClub/II-337
91UD-650
92D/II-699
92F-552
92S/II-695
92T-622
92UD-488
Buelow, Frederick W.
(Fritz)
E107
Bues, Arthur F.
(Art)
No Cards.
Buettemeyer, Kim
80Wichita-3
Buffamoyer, John
75BurlB
77Holyo
Buffinton, Charles G.
(Charlie)
E223
N172
N690
Buffolino, Rocco
87Pocatel/Bon-24
88Fresno/Cal-24
88Fresno/ProC-1231
Buford, Bobby
76Clinton
Buford, Damon
91Freder/ClBest-23
91Freder/ProC-2377
91Single/ClBest-198
Buford, Don Jr.
88Hagers/Star-3
89EastLDD/ProC-DD38
89Hagers/Best-15
89Hagers/ProC-277
89Hagers/Star-2
90Hagers/ProC-1420
90Hagers/Star-3
91Freder/ProC-2382DIR
Buford, Donald Alvin
(Don)
64T-368R
65OPC-81
65T-81
66T-465
67OPC-143M
67T-143M
67T-232
68Coke
68Dexter-19
68OPC-194
68T-194
69MB-45
69MLB/St-2
69T-478
69T/St-123
70MLB/St-147
70OPC-305WS
70OPC-428
70T-428
71MLB/St-291
71OPC-29
71OPC-328WS
71T-29
71T-328WS
72MB-56
72OPC-370
72T-370
73OPC-183
73T-183
74Greyhound-5M
86Indianap-29
88French-2CO
90Smok/SoCal-1
91Crown/Orio-59
Buggs, Michael J.
82AppFx-26
Buggs, Ron
(Doc)
77Newar
78Newar
79BurlB-9
Buhe, Tim
89Kingspt/Star-2
90Pittsfld/Pucko-9
Buheller, Tim
86Elmira-4
87WinHaven-1
88Lynch/Star-3
89Lynch/Star-3
Buhl, Bob
53JC-4
53SpicSpan/3x5-5
53SpicSpan/7x10-3
54JC-10
54SpicSpan/PostC-4
54T-210
55B-43
55Gol/Braves-4
55JC-10
55SpicSpan/DC-4
56T-244
57SpicSpan/4x5-4
57T-127

58T-176
59T-347
60Lake
60SpicSpan-4
60T-230M
60T-374
61P-103
61T-145
61T/St-40
62J-154
62P-154
62P/Can-154
62Salada-117
62Shirriff-117
62T-458
63T-175
64T-96
65OPC-264
65T-264
66OPC-185
66T-185
67OPC-68
67T-68
89Swell-21

Buhner, Jay
87Colum-19
87Colum/Pol-4
87Colum/TCMA-19
88Classic/Blue-244
88Colum/CMC-23
88Colum/Pol-18
88Colum/ProC-329
88D-545
88D/Rook-11
88D/Y/Bk-545
88S/Tr-95T
88Sf-223
88T/Tr-21T
89B-219
89Bz-4
89Calgary/CMC-13
89Calgary/ProC-544
89D-581
89D/Best-136
89F-542
89KMart/DT-5
89OPC-223
89Panini/St-440
89S-530
89S/YS/I-6
89Sf-89
89T-223
89T/Big-20
89T/Coins-35
89T/Gloss60-9
89T/JumboR-5
89T/St-319
89T/UK-10
89ToysRUs-5
89UD-220
90B-477
90D-448
90F-508
90Leaf/I-114
90Mother/Mar-7
90OPC-554
90S-521
90T-554
90UD-534
91B-247
91CounHrth-13
91D-509
91D/GSlam-6
91F-446
91F/UltraUp-U49
91Leaf/I-62
91OPC-154
91Panini/FrSt-234
91Panini/St-190
91S-125
91T-154
91T/StClub/I-153
91UD-128
92Classic/I-20
92D/I-61
92F-275
92S/I-64
92T-327
92UD-441

Buice, DeWayne
78Cedar
81WHave-4
82Tacoma-1
83Tacoma-3
86MidldA-3
87D/Rook-6
87F/Up-U14
87Sf/Rook-26
87T/Tr-13T
88D-58
88F-487
88OPC-396
88S-376
88Smok/Angels-7
88T-649
88T/JumboR-4
88T/Mini-4
88T/St-180
88ToysRUs-4
88UD/Sample-1
89S-153
89Syrac/CMC-8
89Syrac/ProC-811
89Syrac/Team-3
89T-147
89UD-147

Buitimea, Martin
85Tigres-5

Buker, Henry L.
(Harry)
No Cards.

Buksa, Ken
88Watertn/Pucko-16

Bulkeley, Morgan
50Callahan
80SSPC/HOF

Bullard, George D.
No Cards.

Bullard, Jason
91Welland/ClBest-28
91Welland/ProC-3563

Bullard, Larry
(Rocky)
78Dunedin

Bullas, Simeon E.
(Sam)
No Cards.

Bullett, Scott
90Welland/Pucko-11
91Augusta/ClBest-25
91Augusta/ProC-818
91SALAS/ProC-SAL3
91Single/ClBest-245
92T/91Debut-25

Bulling, Terry C.
(Bud)
78OrlTw
78T-432
79Spokane-23
80Spokane-10
82D-612
82T-98
83D-226
83F-630
83SLCity-15
83T-519

Bullinger, Jim
86Geneva-1
87WinSalem-10
88Pittsfld/ProC-1367
89CharlK-6
90WinSalem/Team-17
91CharlK/LineD-128
91CharlK/ProC-1681
91Single/ClBest-176

Bullinger, Matt
81Chatt-6
82Jacks-2

Bullock, Craig
91CharRain/ClBest-17
91CharRain/ProC-102

Bullock, Eric
82DayBe-12
83ColumAst-9
85Cram/PCL-52
87Tucson-19
88Portl/CMC-17
88Portl/ProC-640
89F-106
89Phill/TastyK-38
90Indianap/CMC-17
90Indianap/ProC-285
91B-457
91Leaf/II-470
92D/II-683
92F-474
92S/II-661

Bulls, Dave
86Portl-2

Bumbry, Alonza B.
(Al)
73JP
73OPC-614R
73T-614R
74OPC-137
74T-137
75OPC-358
75T-358
75T/M-358
76OPC-307
76SSPC-396
76T-307
77BurgChef-37
77Ho-90
77OPC-192
77T-626
78T-188
79T-517
80OPC-36
80T-65
81D-355
81F-172
81F/St-30
81OPC-34
81T-425
81T/SO-29
81T/St-35
82D-153
82F-159
82F/St-147
82OPC-265
82T-265
83D-383
83F-54
83OPC-272
83T-655
84D-210
84F-2
84Nes/792-319
84T-319
85D-350
85F-171
85F/Up-U13
85Mother/Padres-25
85T-726
85T/St-205
85T/Tr-12T
86F-316
86T-583
87Elmira/Black-29
87Elmira/Red-29
89Pac/SenLg-47
89T/SenLg-27
89TM/SenLg-14
90EliteSenLg-94
90Swell/Great-29
90T/TVRSox-3CO
91Crown/Orio-60

Bumgarner, Jeff
86Kenosha-3
87ColAst/ProC-25
87Orlan-1
88Portl/CMC-4
88Portl/ProC-659
89Jacks/GS-10
90Freder/Team-27
91Hagers/LineD-226
91Hagers/ProC-2447

Bumstead, Mark
78StPete

Bunce, Joshua
(Josh)
No Cards.

Bundy, Lorenzo
83AlexD-31
84Cram/PCL-127
89Indianap/CMC-17
89Indianap/ProC-1223
90Jaxvl/Best-27CO
90Jaxvl/ProC-1389CO
91Sumter/ClBest-26MG
91Sumter/ProC-2351

Bunker, Wally
64T-201R
65OPC-9LL
65T-290
65T-9LL
66T-499
67T-585
68T-489
69MLB/St-56
69OPC-137
69T-137
69T/St-182
70K-70
70MLB/St-218
70OPC-266
70T-266
70T/CB
71MLB/St-410
71OPC-528
71T-528
72MB-57
91Crown/Orio-61

Bunning, Jim
57T-338
58T-115
59T-149
60L-144
60T-502
61P-39
61T-46LL
61T-490
61T-50LL
61T/St-147
62J-26
62P-26
62P/Can-26
62Salada-13
62Shirriff-13
62T-460
62T-57LL
62T-59LL
62T/bucks
62T/St-44
63J-53
63P-53
63Salada-33
63T-10LL
63T-218M
63T-365
63T-8LL
63T/SO
64PhilBull-7
64T-265
64T-6LL
64T/Coins-93
64T/S-10
64Wheat/St-9
65Bz-21
65OldLond-5
65OPC-20
65T-20
65T/E-17
65T/trans-6
66Bz-31
66T-435
66T/RO-78
67Bz-31
67T-238LL
67T-560
68Bz-7
68KDKA-14
68OPC-11LL
68OPC-7LL
68OPC-9LL
68T-11LL
68T-215
68T-7LL
68T-9LL
69Citgo-20
69MB-46
69MLB/St-183
69OPC-175
69T-175
69T/St-84
70MLB/St-86
70OPC-403
70T-403
71MLB/St-172
71OPC-574
71T-574
71T/Coins-3
71T/GM-43
72MB-58
74Laugh/ASG-61
76Laugh/Jub-10
76OkCty/Team-6
81Detroit-97
83Kaline-15M
83Kaline-24M
88Pac/Leg-92
89Swell-7
90Pac/Legend-76
90Target-90
PM10/L-7

Buonantony, Rich
82QuadC-4
86Louisvl-8
87Louisvl-7
88Louisvl-12
88Louisvl/CMC-7
88Louisvl/ProC-445
90Reading/Star-9

Burba, David
(Dave)
88SanBern/Best-17
88SanBern/Cal-49
89Wmsprt/ProC-630
90Calgary/CMC-6
90Calgary/ProC-645
91B-263
91Calgary/LineD-54
91Calgary/ProC-509
91D/Rook-12
91F-447
91S-742RP
91T/90Debut-23
92Classic/I-21
92D/II-566
92S/II-611
92T-728

Burbach, Bill
69T-658R
70OPC-167
70T-167
71MLB/St-484
71OPC-683
71T-683

Burbank, Dennis
88CapeCod-6
88CapeCod/Sum-151
91Oneonta/ProC-4145

Burbrink, Nelson E.
(Nels)
56T-27

Burch, Albert William
(Al)
E254
E270/2
M116
T206

Burch, Ernest W.
N172
N28

Burcham, Timothy
(Tim)
86QuadC-6
87PalmSp-21
88MidldA/GS-6
89Edmon/CMC-5
89Edmon/ProC-553
89MidldA/GS-7
90Edmon/CMC-4
90Edmon/ProC-511
91Edmon/LineD-157
91Edmon/ProC-1510

Burchart, Larry
69T-597R
70OPC-412
70T-412

Burchell, Fred
C46-14
T204
T206

Burchett, Kerry D.
81ArkTr-10

Burda, Edward Robert
(Bob)
61Union
62Kahn/Atl
69T-392
70OPC-357
70T-357
71OPC-541
71T-541
72T-734

Burden, John
80Wausau-2
81Chatt-2
83Chatt-20
86Chatt-6CO

Burdette, Freddie
64T-408R

Burdette, Lew
52B-244
53B/BW-51

53JC-5
53SpicSpan/3x5-6
53SpicSpan/7x10-4
54B-192
54JC-33
54RM-NL24
54SpicSpan/PostC-5
55B-70
55Gol/Braves-5
55JC-33
55SpicSpan/DC-5
56T-219
57SpicSpan/4x5-5
57T-208
58T-10
58T-289M
59T-440
60Lake
60NuCard-35
60SpicSpan-5
60T-230M
60T-70
60T/tatt-7
61NuCard-408
61NuCard-435
61P-102
61T-320
61T-47LL
62Exh
62J-153
62P-153
62P/Can-153
62Salada-166
62Shirriff-166
62T-380
62T/bucks
62T/St-146
63Exh
63J-155
63P-155
63T-429
64T-523
65OPC-64
65T-64
66T-299
67T-265
73OPC-237CO
73T-237CO
78TCMA-276
88Pac/Leg-68
91LineD-15
91Swell/Great-16
91T/Arc53-310
Exh47

Burdette, Ricky
77Spartan
80Ashvl-24

Burdick, Kevin
87Watertn-11
88Salem/Star-3
89EastLDD/ProC-DD22
89Harris/ProC-297
89Harris/Star-4
89Star/Wax-19
90BuffB/CMC-16
90BuffB/ProC-378
90BuffB/Team-4
91ColoSp/LineD-80
91ColoSp/ProC-2189

Burdick, Stacey
87Miami-3
89Freder/Star-1
90EastLAS/ProC-EL43
90Foil/Best-255
90Hagers/Best-17
90Hagers/ProC-1403
90Hagers/Star-4
91Hagers/LineD-227
91Hagers/ProC-2448

Burdick, William B.
N172

Burdock, John Joseph
(Jack)
90Target-91
N172
N284

Burdy, B.J.
(Mascot)
91Tor/Fire-x

Burg, Joseph Peter
(Pete)
No Cards.

Burgess, Bob
89Welland/Pucko-34GM
90Welland/Pucko-34GM

Burgess, Forrest H.
(Smokey)
49Eureka-52
51B-317
52B-112
52T-357
53B/Col-28
53T-10
54B-31
55B-209
55RFG-12
56Kahn
56T-192
57Kahn
57Sohio/Reds-4
57T-228
58Kahn
58T-49
59Kahn
59T-432
60Kahn
60T-393
61Kahn
61P-138
61T-461
61T/St-61
62J-176
62Kahn
62P-176
62P/Can-176
62Salada-114
62Shirriff-114
62T-389
62T/St-173
63F-55
63IDL-2
63J-144
63Kahn
63P-144
63T-18M
63T-425
64T-37
65OPC-198
65T-198
66T-354
67T-506
72Laugh/GF-28
78Green
78TCMA-1
88Pulaski/ProC-1750
89Pac/Leg-201
89Swell-32
90Pac/Legend-77
91T/Arc53-10

Burgess, Gus
80Elmira-26
83Pawtu-20
84Pawtu-9
85Pawtu-1

Burgess, Thomas R.
54Hunter
79Richm-15MG
80Charl-1MG
81Tulsa-20MG
82Tulsa-22MG
83OKCty-2MG
84OKCty-3MG
86Lakeland-3MG
87GlenF-3MG
90TulsaDG/Best-28MG

Burguillos, Carlos
91Niagara/ClBest-17
91Niagara/ProC-3644

Burgmeier, Tom
69T-558
70OPC-108
70T-108
71MLB/St-411
71OPC-431
71T-431
72OPC-246
72T-246
73OPC-306
73T-306
75OPC-478
75T-478
75T/M-478
76OPC-87
76SSPC-206
76T-87
77T-398
78PapaG/Disc-16
78T-678
79OPC-272
79T-524
80T-128
81Coke
81D-97
81F-228
81OPC-320
81T-228
81T/HT
82Coke/BOS
82D-361
82F-288
82T-455
83D-235
83F-180
83Granny-39
83OPC-213
83T-213
83T/X-16
84D-522
84F-439
84Mother/A's-18
84Nes/792-33
84OPC-33
84T-33
85D-400
85F-417

Burgo, Dale
88WinHaven/Star-6
89Lynch/Star-4
91LynchRS/ProC-1190

Burgo, William Ross
(Bill)
No Cards.

Burgos, Enrique
87Knoxvl-17
88Syrac/ProC-815
89Dunedin/Star-2

Burgos, John
87Gaston-27
89Savan/ProC-351
91Reading/LineD-505
91Reading/ProC-1365

Burgos, Paco
87SanJose-17
88CharlR/Star-5
89CharlR/Star-4
90Tulsa/ProC-1160
91OkCty/LineD-306
91OkCty/ProC-183

Burich, William Max
(Bill)
No Cards.

Burk, Mack Edwin
57T-91
58T-278

Burkam, Robert
(Bob)
No Cards.

Burke, Curtis
83DayBe-25
85Osceola/Team-22

Burke, Daniel L.
(Dan)
No Cards.

Burke, Don
86Jamestn-2
87WPalmB-12
87WPalmB-24

Burke, Edward D.
(Eddie)
33SK-33

Burke, Edward
N566-177

Burke, Frank A.
No Cards.

Burke, Glenn L.
75Water
78T-562
79OPC-78
79T-163
90Target-92

Burke, James Timothy
(Jimmy)
T206
W514-89

Burke, John Patrick
No Cards.

Burke, Kevin
85Newar-24
87Hagers-20

Burke, Leo Patrick
63T-249
64T-557
65OPC-202
65T-202
91Crown/Orio-62

Burke, Leslie K.
(Les)
No Cards.

Burke, Michael E.
(Mike)
86Bakers-4
87VeroB-25

Burke, Patrick Edward
(Pat)
No Cards.

Burke, Robert J.
33G-71
35G-2C
35G-4C
35G-7C
92Conlon/Sport-362
V354-25

Burke, Steve
77Jaxvl
78T-709R
79Spokane-22

Burke, Tim
82Buffa-15
83Colum-7
83Nashvl-3
84Indianap-23
85F/Up-U14
86D-421
86F-245
86Leaf-198
86OPC-258
86Provigo-17
86T-258
87D-222
87F-315
87Leaf-205
87OPC-132
87T-624
87T/St-78
88D-98
88D/Best-34
88F-180
88F/Mini-87
88F/St-95
88Ho/Disc-2
88Leaf-84
88OPC-14
88S-187
88T-529
89B-360
89D-274
89D/Best-180
89F-372
89OPC-48
89Panini/St-113
89RedFoley/St-15
89S-228
89Sf-73
89T-48
89T/St-69
89UD-456
90B-103
90D-334
90D/BestNL-42
90F-342
90F/BB-3
90Leaf/I-28
90OPC-195
90Panini/St-294
90PublInt/St-170
90RedFoley/St-10
90S-127
90S/100St-34
90Sf-199
90T-195
90T/Big-187
90T/Mini-61
90T/St-72
90T/TVAS-60
90UD-515
91D-125
91F-227
91F/Ultra-198
91F/UltraUp-U95
91Leaf/I-124
91OPC-715
91Panini/FrSt-148
91RedFoley/St-15
91S-181
91T-715
91T/StClub/II-514
91UD-215
91UD/FinalEd-70F
92D/I-366
92F-497
92S/II-651
92T-322
92UD-433

Burke, Todd
87Visalia-18

Burke, Tom
77Charl

Burke, William I.
E254
T206

Burkett, Jesse Cail
50Callahan
80SSPC/HOF
89HOF/St-33
E254
E286
T204
W575

Burkett, John
86Shrev-2
87Shrev-14
87TexLgAS-33
88F-651
88Phoenix/CMC-2
88Phoenix/ProC-76
89Phoenix/CMC-1
89Phoenix/ProC-1483
90Classic/III-T6
90D/BestNL-12
90D/Rook-51
90F/Up-U61
90Leaf/II-384
90Mother/Giant-26
90Phoenix/ProC-5
90S/Tr-73T
90T/Tr-16T
90UD/Ext-735
91B-637
91Classic/200-86
91D-638
91F-256
91F/Ultra-317
91Leaf/I-56
91Leaf/Stud-253
91Mother/Giant-26
91OPC-447
91Panini/FrSt-74
91Panini/St-78
91PG&E-3
91S-70
91S/100RisSt-7
91Seven/3DCoin-1NC
91SFExam/Giant-5
91T-447
91T/StClub/I-119
91UD-577
92D/I-257
92F-630
92S/II-522
92T-762
92UD-148

Burkhart, Ken
47TipTop

Burks, Ellis
86NewBrit-4
87D/Rook-5
87F/Up-U15
87Pawtu-23
87Pawtu/TCMA-22
87Sf/Rook-5
87T/Tr-14T
88Classic/Blue-229
88D-174
88D/Best-121
88D/RedSox/Bk-174
88F-348
88F-630M
88F/Slug-5
88F/St-6
88Leaf-174
88MSA/Disc-2
88OPC-269
88Panini/St-31
88RedFoley/St-10
88S-472

88S/YS/I-37
88Sf-144
88T-269
88T/Big-80
88T/Gloss60-50
88T/JumboR-2
88T/St-250
88T/St-310
88ToysRUs-5
89T/Ames-7
89Classic/Up/2-152
89Classic/Up/2-175M
89D-303
89D/Best-9
89D/GrandSlam-12
89F-83
89Nissen-3
89OPC-311
89Panini/St-278
89S-9
89S/HotStar-43
89S/Mast-25
89Sf-191
89T-785
89T/Big-259
89T/HeadsUp-12
89T/St-254
89UD-434
90B-280
90Classic/Up-T8
90D-228
90D-23DK
90D/BestAL-30
90D/SuperDK-23DK
90F-269
90Leaf/I-261
90OPC-155
90Panini/St-21
90Pep/RSox-5
90PublInt/St-450
90PublInt/St-594
90RedFoley/St-11
90S-340
90S/100St-16
90Sf-80
90T-155
90T/Big-107
90T/Coins-8
90T/DH-7
90T/St-259
90T/TVRSox-28
90UD-343
90USPlayC/AS-7C
91B-109
91B-373SLUG
91Classic/200-12
91D-235
91DennyGS-1
91F-89
91F/Ultra-30
91Leaf/I-121
91Leaf/Stud-12
91MajorLg/Pins-11
91OPC-70
91Panini/FrSt-269
91Panini/St-212
91Panini/Top15-114
91Pep/RSox-3
91S-8
91S/100SS-48
91T-70
91T/CJMini/II-8
91T/StClub/I-108
91UD-436
91UD/SilSlug-SS10
92D/I-234
92F-35
92S/100SS-83
92S/I-270
92T-416
92UD-525
92UD-94TC

Burks, Robert E.
N172

Burleson, Richard P.
(Rick)
75OPC-302
75T-302
75T/M-302
76Ho-44
76Ho/Twink-44
76OPC-29
76SSPC-410
76T-29
77BurgChef-28
77Ho-68
77OPC-237
77T-585
78OPC-37
78PapaG/Disc-7
78T-245
79OPC-57
79T-125
80OPC-339
80T-645
81D-454
81F-225
81F/St-33
81K-49
81OPC-172
81Sqt-13
81T-455
81T/HT
81T/SO-37
81T/St-52
81T/Tr-743
82D-342
82F-453
82F/St-219
82K-44
82OPC-55
82T-55
82T/St-134
82T/St-157
83D-318
83F-80
83OPC-315
83T-315
84F-510
84Nes/792-735
84OPC-376
84Smok/Cal-4
84T-735
84T/St-238
86Smok/Cal-15
86T/Tr-16T
87D/OD-134
87F-74
87OPC-152
87T-579
91Crown/Orio-63
91Mother/A's-28CO

Burley, Tony
82Cedar-16
83Tampa-1

Burley, Travis
90MedHat/Best-4

Burlingame, Ben
91Geneva/ClBest-2
91Geneva/ProC-4208

Burlingame, Dennis
88SALAS/GS-28
88Sumter/ProC-393
89Durham/Team-2
89Durham/Star-2
91Durham/ClBest-7
91Durham/ProC-1537

Burlingame, Greg
89SanBern/Best-5
89SanBern/Cal-70

Burn
T222

Burnau, Ben
89Wausau/GS-10

Burnett, Hercules H.
No Cards.

Burnett, John H.
(Johnny)
91Conlon/Sport-82
92Conlon/Sport-543
R314/Can

Burnett, John P.
No Cards.

Burnett, Lance
88Pocatel/ProC-2083

Burnett, Ora
46Remar-9
47Remar-5
47Signal
47Smith-17
49B/PCL-36

Burnett, Roger
91Oneonta/ProC-4160

Burnette, Wallace
57T-13
58T-69

Burney, Wayne
74Albuq/Team-3

Burnham, George W.
N172

Burnitz, Jeromy
88CapeCod/Sum-145
90Classic/DP-17
90Pittsfld/Pucko-31
91B-474
91Classic/I-4
91S-380FDP
91Single/ClBest-68
91Wmsprt/LineD-627
91Wmsprt/ProC-304
92T-591M
92UD-65TP

Burnos, Jim
83Wisco/LF-20

Burns, Bill
(Sleepy)
88Pac/8Men-17M
88Pac/8Men-18

Burns, Britt
79Knoxvl/TCMA-6
81Coke
81D-279
81F-342
81OPC-218
81T-412
81T/HT
81T/St-63
82D-230
82F-339
82F/St-189
82T-44
83D-193
83D-23DK
83F-232
83K-43
83T-541
83T/St-48
83TrueVal/WSox-40
84D-424
84F-54
84Nes/792-125
84OPC-125
84T-125
84TrueVal/WS-7
85Coke/WS-40
85D-257
85F-509
85OPC-338
85T-338
86D-58
86F-200
86F/St-17
86OPC-174
86Sf-105
86T-679
86T/Mini-10
86T/St-292
90T/TVYank-38

Burns, Dan
83ElPaso-1

Burns, Daren
88Wythe/ProC-1985

Burns, Edward James
(Ed)
11Helmar-111
16FleischBrd-9
D327
D328-18
D329-18
D350/2-17
E135-18
E270/2
M101/4-18
M101/5-17

Burns, George Henry
21Exh-14
26Exh-81
27Exh-41
D327
D328-19
D329-19
E120
E121/80
E135-19
E210-9
E220
M101/4-19
V100
W502-9
W514-24
W516-10
W572
W573
W575

Burns, George Joseph
16FleischBrd-10
21Exh-15
28Yueng-9
32Orbit/num-64
32Orbit/un-7
91Conlon/Sport-158
91Conlon/Sport-201
91Conlon/Sport-309
D327
D328-20
D329-20
D350/2-18
E120
E121/80
E122
E135-20
E220
M101/4-20
M101/5-18
V100
W515-54
W572
W573
W575

Burns, George
21Exh-16
21Exh-17
80Laugh/FFeat-35
BF2-73
V61-1
V61-70
WG7-7

Burns, Gregory
85Madis-7

Burns, James M.
(Jim)
N172

Burns, James
83StPete-16

Burns, John Irving
(Jack)
33G-198
34DS-75
34Exh/4-15
35BU-18
35BU-191
35Exh/4-15
35G-8C
35G-9C
91Conlon/Sport-131
R305
R326-1A
R326-1B
R342-1

Burns, John Joseph
No Cards.

Burns, Joseph Francis
(Joe)
No Cards.

Burns, Joseph James
(Joe)
No Cards.

Burns, Kerry
83TriCit-4

Burns, Michael
91BurlAs/ClBest-24
91BurlAs/ProC-2804

Burns, Patrick
(Pat)
No Cards.

Burns, Richard Simon
(Dick)
No Cards.

Burns, Thomas E.
(Tom)
80Batavia-8
81Batavia-2
81Watlo-7
83Wausau/LF-4
85Lynch-11
86Tidew-3

Burns, Thomas P.
(Oyster)
90Target-905
E223
N172
N284
WG1-11

Burns, Todd
85Madis-8
85Madis/Pol-5
86SLAS-18
88F/Up-U52
88S/Tr-106T
88Tacoma/CMC-2
88Tacoma/ProC-632
89Classic/Up/2-171
89D-564
89F-3
89Mother/A's-24
89Panini/St-411
89S-465
89S/HotRook-100
89S/YS/II-4
89Sf-87
89T-174
89T/Big-10
89UD/Ext-718
90D-446
90F-2
90Leaf/II-458
90Mother/A's-20
90OPC-369
90PublInt/St-299
90S-64
90T-369
90UD-689
91B-221
91D-479
91F-4
91F/Ultra-243
91Mother/A's-20
91OPC-608
91S-41
91T-608
91T/StClub/I-207
91UD-405
92S/I-341

Burns, William T.
T206
T3-85

Burnside, Pete
58T-211
59T-354
60T-261
61P-46
61T-507
62T-207
63T-19
91Crown/Orio-64

Burnside, Sheldon
80Indianap-3
81F-220

Burr, Alexander T.
(Alex)
No Cards.

Burrell, Frank Andrew
(Buster)
90Target-93

Burrell, Kevin
85Lynch-14
86Shrev-3
87Phoenix-8
88Memphis/Best-11
88SLAS-2
89Omaha/CMC-10
89Omaha/ProC-1733
90Omaha/ProC-68
91Omaha/LineD-329
91Omaha/ProC-1037

Burress, Davey
76Clinton

Burright, Larry
62T-348
63T-174
90Target-94
91WIZMets-57

Burris, Paul Robert
54JC-29

Burris, Pierre
91Billings/ProC-3765

Burris, Ray
74OPC-161
74T-161
75OPC-566
75T-566
75T/M-566
76Ho-60
76Ho/Twink-60
76OPC-51
76T-51

77BurgChef-194
77Ho-67
77OPC-197
77T-190
78T-371
78Wiffle/Discs-9
79OPC-43
79T-98
80T-364
81D-524
81F-328
81OPC-323
81T-654
81T/Tr-744
82D-414
82F-184
82Hygrade
82OPC-227
82T-227
82Zeller-20
83D-36
83F-277
83OPC-12
83Stuart-16
83T-474
84D-331
84F-270
84F/X-19
84Mother/A's-22
84Nes/792-552
84OPC-319
84T-552
84T/Tr-18
85D-218
85F-418
85F/Up-U15
85Leaf-116
85OPC-238
85Pol/Brew-48
85T-758
85T/St-328
85T/Tr-13T
86D-107
86F-482
86T-106
89Helena/SP-26
89T/SenLg-108
90Brewer/MillB-32CO
90EliteSenLg-18
90Pol/Brew-x
91Brewer/MillB-32CO
91Pol/Brew-x
91WIZMets-58

Burroughs, Darren
82OkCty-23
83Reading-2
84Cram/PCL-235
86BuffB-6
88Calgary/CMC-1
88Calgary/ProC-780

Burroughs, Eric
90Billings/ProC-3233

Burroughs, Jeffrey A.
(Jeff)
72OPC-191
72T-191
73OPC-489
73T-489
74K-16
74OPC-223
74T-223
74T/DE-48
74T/St-232
75Ho-94
75K-8
75OPC-212MV
75OPC-308LL
75OPC-470
75T-212MV
75T-308LL
75T-470
75T/M-212MV
75T/M-308LL
75T/M-470
76Crane-6
76Ho-111
76MSA/Disc
76OPC-360
76SSPC-269
76T-360
77BurgChef-214
77OPC-209
77Pep-58
77T-55
78Ho-61
78K-15
78OPC-134
78T-130
78Tastee/Discs-4
78Wiffle/Discs-11
79Ho-20
79K-12
79OPC-124
79T-245
80OPC-283
80T-545
81D-66
81F-245
81Pol/Mariners-1
81T-20
81T/Tr-745
82D-379
82F-506
82F/St-220
82KMart-25
82OPC-309
82T-440
82T/St-231
82T/Tr-14T
83D-323
83F-515
84D-156
84D/Champs-7
84F-440
84Mother/A's-17
84Nes/792-354
84OPC-354
84T-354
84T/St-329
85D-542
85F/Up-U16
85OPC-91
85T-272FDP
85T-91
85T/Tr-14T
85Tor/Fire-6
86F-54
86OPC-168
86T-168

Burroughs, Kenny
89Utica/Pucko-3
90Yakima/Team-8

Burrows, Terry
91Gaston/ClBest-2
91Gaston/ProC-2679
91Single/ClBest-265

Burrus, Maurice L.
(Dick)
25Exh-4
26Exh-3

Burt, Frank J.
No Cards.

Burton, Bob
89Wausau/GS-4
90SALAS/Star-48TR

Burton, Chris
89Idaho/ProC-2022
90Idaho/ProC-3259
91Miami/ClBest-27
91Miami/ProC-420
91Single/ClBest-163

Burton, Darren
91AppFx/ClBest-22
91AppFx/ProC-1727
91MidwLAS/ProC-MWL1

Burton, Ellis N.
59T-231
60T-446
61BeeHive-3
63T-262
64T-269

Burton, Jim
76OPC-471
76SSPC-418
76T-471

Burton, Ken
76Cedar

Burton, Michael
89Smok/FresnoSt-6
90A&AASingle/ProC-99
90Foil/Best-268
90Gaston/ProC-2526
90Gaston/Star-4
90SALAS/Star-3
91Tulsa/LineD-577
91Tulsa/ProC-2777

Burtschy, Ed
55B-120
55Rodeo

Burtt, Dennis
81Bristol-21
83Pawtu-3
84Pawtu-5
85IntLgAS-39
85Toledo-4
87Albuq/Pol-6
88Albuq/CMC-7
88Albuq/ProC-276
89Albuq/CMC-2
89Albuq/ProC-68
90Toledo/CMC-3
90Toledo/ProC-142
91Kissim/ProC-4205CO

Burwell, Bill
60T-467C

Burwell, Phil
83Erie-17

Busby, James F.
(Jim)
51B-302
52B-68
52BR
52StarCal/L-73F
52T-309
53B/Col-15
53Briggs
53NB
54B-8
54RM-AL2
55B-166
55RFG-8
55RM-AL2
55Salem
56T-330
57Sohio/Ind-2
57T-309
58Hires-68
58Hires/T
58T-28
59T-185
60L-11
60T-232
62Salada-30
62Shirriff-30
73OPC-237CO
73T-237CO
74OPC-634CO
74T-634CO
77T-597CO
79TCMA-66
91Crown/Orio-65

Busby, Paul Miller
No Cards.

Busby, Steve
73OPC-608R
73T-608R
74OPC-365
74T-365
74T/St-181
75Ho-124
75K-24
75OPC-120
75OPC-7M
75T-120
75T-7M
75T/M-120
75T/M-7M
76A&P/KC
76Ho-71
76K-33
76Laugh/Jub-15
76OPC-260
76SSPC-183
76T-260
78T-336
80T-474
81F-33
90Smok/SoCal-2

Busby, Wayne
89SoBend/GS-23
90Saraso/Star-2
91BirmB/LineD-52
91BirmB/ProC-1458

Busch, Edgar John
(Ed)
No Cards.

Buschorn, Don
65T-577R

Bush, Guy T.
30CEA/Pin-12
32Orbit/num-16
32Orbit/un-8
33G-67
35BU-158
35Exh/4-7
35G-1E
35G-3C
35G-4C
35G-5C
36Exh/4-7
88Conlon/NatAS-2
91Conlon/Sport-196
R305
R306
R308-189
R316
V353-67

Bush, Kalani
89Geneva/ProC-1872

Bush, Leslie Ambrose
(Joe)
15CJ-166
21Exh-18
92Conlon/Sport-345
D328-21
D329-21
D350/2-19
E120
E121/120
E121/80
E126-3
E135-21
E220
M101/4-21
M101/5-19
V61-4
W501-34
W515-27
W572
W575
WG7-8

Bush, Owen Joseph
(Donie)
09Buster/Pin-3
11Helmar-27
14CJ-122
15CJ-122
21Exh-19
81Detroit-38MG
86Indianap-2
BF2-24
D303
D327
D328-22
D329-22
D350/2-20
E106
E135-22
E224
E254
E270/2
E286
E90/1
F61-96
M101/4-22
M101/5-20
M116
T206
T216
T222
W514-30
W575

Bush, Robert Randall
(Randy)
80Toledo-8
82OrlTw/A-2
82Toledo-20
83T/X-17
84D-513
84F-558
84Nes/792-429
84OPC-84
84T-429
84T/St-314
85D-633
85F-272
85T-692
86F-388
86OPC-214
86T-214
87D-441
87F-538
87T-364
88D-272
88F-6
88F/WS-2
88Master/Disc-7
88Panini/St-450IA
88S-292
88Smok/Minn-9
88T-73
89B-164
89D-537
89D/Best-214
89F-107
89OPC-288
89Panini/St-391
89S-212
89T-577
89T/Big-282
89UD-158
90B-416
90D-199
90F-370
90Leaf/I-83
90OPC-747
90Panini/St-109
90PublInt/St-324
90S-278
90T-747
90T/Big-92
90T/St-294
90UD-493
91D-382
91F-605
91F/UltraUp-U34
91Leaf/I-26
91OPC-124
91S-574
91T-124
92D/II-728
92F-198
92S/I-377
92T-476

Bushelman, John
(Jack)
T207

Bushing, Chris
89Penin/Star-2
90A&AASingle/ProC-111
90Rockford/ProC-2695
91WPalmB/ClBest-3
91WPalmB/ProC-1219

Bushong, Albert John
(Doc)
90Target-95
N172
N172/BC
N284
N370
Scrapps

Busick, Warren
86DayBe-3

Buskey, Joseph Henry
(Joe)
No Cards.

Buskey, Michael T.
(Tom)
74Syrac/Team-3
75OPC-403
75T-403
75T/M-403
76OkCty/Team-7
76OPC-178
76SSPC-505
76T-178
77T-236
80OPC-265
80T-506
81D-270

Buss, Scott
86Chatt-7
87Kinston-5

Busse, Raymond Edward
(Ray)
72OPC-101R
72T-101R
73OPC-607R
73T-607R
75Iowa/TCMA-3

Bustabad, Juan
83Pawtu-15
84Pawtu-25
85Pawtu-2
87SanAn-9
88SanAn/Best-12
89Albuq/CMC-20

89Albuq/ProC-78
90Yakima/Team-5
Bustamante, Eddie
89Smok/FresnoSt-7
Bustamante, Rafael
90CharWh/Best-14
90CharWh/ProC-2245
90Foil/Best-201
91CharWh/ClBest-15
91CharWh/ProC-2892
Bustillos, Albert
89Star/Wax-28
89VeroB/Star-4
Buszka, John
77Watlo
78Watlo
Butcher, A. Maxwell
40PB-222
Butcher, Arthur
89Beloit/II/Star-2
90Beloit/Best-20
90Beloit/Star-2
Butcher, Henry Joseph
(Hank)
T207
Butcher, John
78Ashvl
79Tulsa-16
80Charl-13
81F-635
81T-41R
82T-418
83D-37
83F-563
83Rangers-29
83T-534
84D-220
84F-415
84F/X-20
84Nes/792-299
84T-299
84T/Tr-19
85D-314
85F-273
85Leaf-71
85OPC-356
85Seven/Minn-5
85T-741
85T/St-305
86D-120
86F-389
86T-638
87F-245
87T-107
Butcher, Matthew
84Visalia-17
Butcher, Max
90Target-96
Butcher, Mike
86Cram/PCL-40
87AppFx-10
88BBCity/Star-7
89MidldA/GS-8
91London/LineD-428
91MidldA/ProC-427
Butera, Brian
80Elmira-35
Butera, Salvatore P.
(Sal)
79Toledo-8
81D-530
81F-570
81T-243
82D-532
82F-548
82T-676
83T-67
84Indianap-5
85Indianap-15
86OPC-261
86T-407
86TexGold-22
87F-195
87T-358
88S-361
88Syrac/CMC-16
88Syrac/ProC-826
88T-772
89Pac/SenLg-209
89Syrac/CMC-11
89Syrac/ProC-802
89Syrac/Team-4
89T/SenLg-42
89TM/SenLg-15
89Tor/Fire-26
90Osceola/Star-27MG
91Osceola/ClBest-26
91Osceola/ProC-700
Butka, Edward Luke
(Ed)
No Cards.
Butler, Arthur Edward
(Art)
D329-23
D350/2-21
E90/1
M101/4-23
M101/5-21
T201
Butler, Brett Morgan
80Ander-26
81Richm-8
82BK/Lids-4
82D-275
82Pol/Atl-22
82T-502R
83D-636
83F-132
83Pol/Atl-22
83T-364
84D-141
84F-173
84F/X-21
84Nes/792-77
84T-77
84T/Tr-20
84Wheat/Ind-2
85D-216
85D/AAS-23
85F-441
85F/St-56
85Leaf-186
85OPC-241
85Polar/Ind-2
85T-637
85T/St-246
86D-102
86D-12DK
86D/DKsuper-12
86F-581
86F/Mini-114
86F/St-18
86Leaf-12DK
86OhHenry-2
86OPC-149
86Sf-26
86T-149
86T/Gloss60-52
86T/Mini-12
86T/St-206
86T/Super-18
87Classic-36
87D-219
87D/OD-113
87F-246
87F/Hottest-8
87Gator-2
87Leaf-183
87OPC-197
87RedFoley/St-79
87Sf-69
87T-723
88D-279
88D/Best-23
88F-603
88F/Up-U128
88Mother/Giants-14
88OPC-202
88Panini/St-78
88S-122
88S/Tr-3T
88Sf-153
88T-479
88T/Big-166
88T/St-212
88T/Tr-22T
89B-480
89Classic-38
89D-217
89D/Best-274
89F-324
89Mother/Giants-5
89OPC-241
89Panini/St-220
89S-216
89Sf-31
89T-241
89T/Big-62
89T/Coins-6
89T/LJN-128
89T/Mini-39
89T/St-85
89T/UK-11
89UD-218
90B-237
90D-249
90D/BestNL-139
90F-53
90Leaf/I-251
90MLBPA/Pins-27
90Mother/Giant-7
90OPC-571
90Panini/St-365
90PublInt/St-64
90RedFoley/St-12
90Richm25Ann/Team-6
90S-236
90S/100St-47
90Sf-136
90T-571
90T/Big-259
90T/Mini-83
90T/St-87
90UD-119
91B-597
91Classic/200-4
91D-143
91F-257
91F/UltraUp-U85
91F/Up-U91
91Leaf/II-411
91Leaf/Stud-181
91Mother/Dodg-6
91OPC-325
91OPC/Premier-16
91Panini/FrSt-72
91Panini/St-75
91Panini/Top15-25
91Panini/Top15-44
91Panini/Top15-51
91Pol/Dodg-22
91S-455
91S/RookTr-23T
91T-325
91T/StClub/II-389
91T/Tr-15T
91T/WaxBox-C
91UD-270
91UD/Ext-732
91USPlayC/AS-8S
92D/DK-DK18
92D/I-369
92F-448
92F-702M
92S/II-465
92S/II-778AS
92T-655
92T/GPromo-655
92T/Promo-325
92UD-307
Butler, Cecil
62T-239
63T-201
Butler, Chris
89Kingspt/Star-3
Butler, Frank Dean
No Cards.
Butler, Frank E.
No Cards.
Butler, Jason
91Pulaski/ClBest-21
91Pulaski/ProC-3997
Butler, John Albert
90Target-906
Butler, John S.
(Johnny)
C46-46
T206
Butler, John
90Peoria/Team-3GM
Butler, John Stephen
(Johnny)
26Exh-9
27Exh-5
90Target-97
Butler, Mark
83SanJose-11
Butler, Mick
86PalmSp-5
86PalmSp/Smok-17
Butler, Richard H.
(Dick)
No Cards.
Butler, Robert
91StCath/ClBest-8
91StCath/ProC-3406
Butler, Todd
88BurlInd/ProC-1782
Butler, W. J.
(Bill)
69T-619R
70MLB/St-219
70OPC-377
70T-377
71MLB/St-412
71OPC-681
71T-681
72MB-59
75OPC-549
75T-549
75T/M-549
76OPC-619
76SSPC-207
76T-619
78Cr/PCL-1
Butler, Willis E.
(Kid)
No Cards.
Butterfield, Brian
82Nashvl-3
87Oneonta-14
89Oneonta/ProC-2098
90Greens/Best-27MG
90Greens/ProC-2679
90Greens/Star-26
Butterfield, Chris
89Pittsfld/Star-1
91StLucie/ClBest-10
91StLucie/ProC-715
Butters, Dave
85PrWill-28
Butters, Tom
63T-299R
64T-74R
65OPC-246
65T-246
Button, Dick
51BR-B17
Butts, David
87Sumter-29
88Durham/Star-3
89Durham/Team-3
89Durham/Star-3
Butts, Randy
86Erie-5
87StPete-24
88Hamil/ProC-1735
Butts, Tom
82Iowa-29
Butts, Tommy
78Laugh/Black-11
Buxton, Ralph
(Buck)
46Remar-21
47Remar-6
47Signal
47Smith-11
48Signal
48Smith-11
49Remar
Buzard, Brian
90WichSt-6
91Watertn/ClBest-2
91Watertn/ProC-3357
Buzas, Joseph John
(Joe)
47Centen-2
Buzhardt, John
59T-118
60T-549
61T-3
61T/St-49
62J-200
62P-200
62P/Can-200
62Salada-129A
62Salada-129B
62Shirriff-129
62T-555
63T-35
64T-323
65T-458
66T-245
67OPC-178
67T-178
68T-403
91Crown/Orio-66
Buzzard, Buddy
87Kenosha-7
Buzzard, Dale
89James/ProC-2130
Byam, George
V362-47
Byerly, Eldred
(Bud)
52T-161
58T-72
60T-371
Byerly, Rodney
(Rod)
89Augusta/ProC-518
89Welland/Pucko-8
90BurlB/Best-26
90BurlB/ProC-2342
90BurlB/Star-6
Byers, James W.
(Bill)
No Cards.
Byers, John William
C46-74
E254
Byers, Randell
86Beaum-4
87LasVegas-14
88D-605
88F-653R
88LasVegas/CMC-13
88LasVegas/ProC-224
89LasVegas/CMC-12
89LasVegas/ProC-6
89Louisvl-12
89Louisvl/CMC-23
89Louisvl/ProC-1245
Byington, John
88CapeCod/Sum-21
89Beloit/II/Star-3
90Beloit/Best-15
90Beloit/Star-3
90Foil/Best-254
91ElPaso/LineD-177
91ElPaso/ProC-2752
91Single/ClBest-356
Byrd, Bill
86Negro/Frit-52
Byrd, Felan
76Clinton
Byrd, Harry
53B/Col-38
53T-131
54B-49
54NYJour
55B-159
55Esskay
58T-154
79TCMA-172
91Crown/Orio-67
91T/Arc53-131
Byrd, Jeff
76SanAn/Team-5
78OPC-211
78Syrac
78T-667
Byrd, Jim
89Star/Wax-10
89WinHaven/Star-2
90CLAS/CL-13
90LynchRS/Team-5
91LynchRS/ClBest-15
91LynchRS/ProC-1205
Byrd, Leland
77Visalia
Byrd, Paul
90LSUPol-4
Byrd, Samuel D.
(Sammy)
32Orbit/num-96
33G-157
35BU-56
35G-2F
35G-4F
35G-7F
91Conlon/Sport-281
R313
R314
V353-86
Byrne, Robert M.

(Bobby)
10Domino-18
11Helmar-154
12Sweet/Pin-133
16FleischBrd-11
D322
D328-23
D329-24
D350/2-22
E135-23
E224
E270/2
E300
E94
M101/4-24
M101/5-22
M116
S74-106
T201
T202
T205
T206
T207
T213/blue
T213/brown
T215/blue
T215/brown
T222

Byrne, T.J.
81Holyo-4

Byrne, Thomas Joseph
(Tommy)
44Yank/St-4
51B-73
51BR-D4
51T/BB-35
52B-61
52T-241
53T-123
55B-300
56T-215
57T-108
79TCMA-198
91T/Arc53-123

Byrnes, Chris
87Oneonta-20

Byrnes, James Joseph
(Jim)
No Cards.

Byrnes, Milton John
(Milt)
No Cards.

Byron, Bill
73F/Wild-20

Byron, Tim
82Oneonta-11
85Albany-2

Bystrom, Marty
77Spartan
79OkCty
80OkCty
81T-526R
82D-93
82T-416R
83D-93
83F-154
83T-199
84D-259
84F-24
84Nes/792-511
84Phill/TastyK-15
84T-511
85F-122
85T-284
86D-591
86F-102
86T-723
87FtLaud-2
88Maine/CMC-1
88Maine/ProC-292

Ca, Adam
87SLCity/Taco-19

Caballero, Ed
88Peoria/Ko-7
89WinSalem/Star-2
90WinSalem/Team-18
91WinSalem/ClBest-2
91WinSalem/ProC-2821

Caballero, Jose
82Miami-8

Caballero, Ralph J.
(Putsy)
49Eureka-132

Cabassa, Carlos
80Penin/B-3
80Penin/C-3

Cabell, Billy
83Clinton/LF-4

Cabell, Enos Milton
73OPC-605R
73T-605R
75OPC-247
75T-247
75T/M-247
76OPC-404
76SSPC-61
76T-404
77BurgChef-2
77Ho-94
77T-567
78BK/Ast-14
78Ho-9
78OPC-44
78T-132
79Ho-70
79OPC-269
79T-515
80BK/PHR-24
80OPC-201
80T-385
81D-138
81F-58
81F/St-36
81OPC-45
81T-45
81T/Tr-746
82D-272
82F-386
82F/St-64
82OPC-311
82T-627
82T/St-105
82T/Tr-15T
83D-202
83F-328
83OPC-225
83T-225
84D-456
84F-79
84F/X-22
84Mother/Ast-11
84Nes/792-482
84T-482
84T/St-273
84T/Tr-21
85D-110
85F-346
85Leaf-161
85Mother/Ast-10
85T-786
85T/St-61
86Coke/Dodg-5
86D-418
86F-126
86Pol/Dodg-23
86T-197
87F-438
87T-509
90Target-98
91Crown/Orio-68

Cabella, Jim
89BurlInd/Star-27

Cabello, Bobby
86Cram/PCL-83

Cabral, Irene
91Erie/ClBest-3
91Erie/ProC-4080

Cabral, Joaquin
91Hunting/ClBest-5
91Hunting/ProC-3340

Cabrera, Alfredo A.
(Al)
No Cards.

Cabrera, Antonio
(Tony)
86Madis-4
86Madis/Pol-4

Cabrera, Basilio
87Fayette-5
88Lakeland/Star-4
89Lakeland/Star-4
90London/ProC-1278
91London/LineD-377
91London/ProC-1888

Cabrera, Carlos
80Utica-3

Cabrera, Francisco
86Ventura-3
87Myrtle-28
88BBAmer-20
88Dunedin/Star-1
88SLAS-22
89AAA/CMC-16
89AAA/ProC-16
89F/Up-68
89Syrac/CMC-20
89Syrac/ProC-791
89Syrac/Team-5
90D-646
90F/Up-U2
90OPC-254
90Richm/CMC-13
90Richm/ProC-264
90Richm/Team-6
90S/Tr-67T
90T-254
90T/89Debut-20
90UD-64
91D-341
91F-684
91F/Ultra-3
91OPC-693
91S-63
91S/100RisSt-33
91T-693
91UD-439
92D/II-482
92F-355
92S/II-581

Cabrera, Fremio
86Wausau-2

Cabrera, Jolbert
91Sumter/ProC-2340

Cabrera, Juan
91Beloit/ClBest-13
91Beloit/ProC-2107
91SoOreg/ProC-3852

Cabrera, Miguel
91AubAS/ProC-4284

Cabrera, Nasusel
88Madis-6

Cabrera, Victor
86CharRain-4

Cacciatore, Frank
88AubAs/ProC-1967
89Tucson/ProC-202
89Tucson/JP-2
90Ashvl/ClBest-26MG
90Ashvl/ProC-2764
91Ashvl/ProC-584

Cacciatore, Paul
76Wausau
77Wausau
79Jacks-10

Cacek, Craig Thomas
78Charl
79Portl-18
80Port-3
81Portl-9
82Spokane-14

Caceres, Edgar
86WPalmB-7
87Jaxvl-9
89Saraso/Star-2
90BirmB/Best-7
90BirmB/ProC-1395
90Foil/Best-206

Caci, Bob
86Beloit-3

Cacini, Ron
91AubAS/ProC-4279

Cadahia, Aurelio
(Chino)
80OrlTw-13
81Toledo-11
82Orlan/B-15
82OrlTw/A-3
83Orlan-10
86DayBe-4MG
87Gaston-3

Cadahia, Ben
81CharR-15
82FtMyr-4
86Tulsa-12

Cadaret, Greg
85Huntsvl/BK-34
88D-528
88D/A's/Bk-528
88Modesto-35
88Mother/A's-26
88T-328
89D-479
89F-4
89Mother/A's-20
89S-340
89S/Tr-69
89T-552
90D-545
90F-440
90OPC-659
90PublInt/St-300
90S/NWest-19
90T-659
90T/TVYank-7
90UD-549
91B-157
91D-236
91F-658
91F/Ultra-229
91Leaf/II-415
91OPC-187
91S-188
91T-187
91T/StClub/II-536
91UD-343
92D/II-628
92F-222
92S/II-454
92T-18
92UD-412

Cadian, Larry
89Portl/CMC-7

Cadore, Leon
21Exh-20
61T-403M
72F/FFeat-19M
72Laugh/GF-37M
90HOF/St-22
90Target-99
E120
E220
V100
V61-97
W572

Cady, Charles B.
(Charlie)
No Cards.

Cady, Forrest LeRoy
(Hick)
BF2-2
D328-24
D329-25
E135-24
M101/4-25
T205

Cafego, Thomas
(Tom)
No Cards.

Caffie, Joseph C.
(Joe)
58T-182

Caffrey, Bob
85T-394OLY
87WPalmB-10
88Jaxvl/Best-25
88Jaxvl/ProC-979
88SLAS-19

Caffyn, Benjamin T.
(Ben)
No Cards.

Cage, Wayne Levell
76Wmsprt
78T-706R
79OPC-70
79T-150
79Tacoma-26
80T-208
80Tacoma-4

Cahill, John F.P.
(Patsy)
N172
N284

Cahill, Mark
80Wausau-3
81LynnS-3
83Chatt-21

Cahill, Thomas H.
(Tom)
No Cards.

Cain, Aaron
81Hawaii-9
82Hawaii-9

Cain, Bob
50B-236
51B-197
52B-19
52T-349
53B/Col-56
53T-266
54B-195
54T-61
91T/Arc53-266

Cain, Cal
86Cedar/TCMA-19
87Cedar-18

Cain, Jerald
83VeroB-23

Cain, John
88Rockford-4
89Rockford-4TR

Cain, Les
69T-324R
71K-29
71MLB/St-388
71OPC-101
71T-101
72T-783

Cain, Tim
91BendB/ClBest-2
91BendB/ProC-3686

Caines, Arturo
(Art)
89Bristol/Star-3
90Fayette/ProC-2419

Cairncross, Cameron
91CharRain/ClBest-4
91CharRain/ProC-90

Cairo, Sergio
89Bluefld/Star-6
90Wausau/Best-14
90Wausau/ProC-2142
90Wausau/Star-5
91CLAS/ProC-CAR6
91Freder/ClBest-24
91Freder/ProC-2378

Caithamer, George T.
No Cards.

Cajide, Al
78DaytB

Cakora, Matthew
(Matt)
88CharWh/Best-17
89CharlK-20
89CharWh/Best-22
89CharWh/ProC-1770
90Miami/I/Star-2

Cala, Craig A.
88CapeCod/Sum-92
90SanJose/Best-6
90SanJose/Cal-35
90SanJose/ProC-2022
90SanJose/Star-4

Calcagno, Dan
91Everett/ProC-3916

Calderon, Ivan
81Wausau-26
82Wausau-10
83Chatt-27
84Cram/PCL-173
85F/Up-U17
85Mother/Mar-26
86D-435
86F-462
86Leaf-204
86Mother/Mar-15
86OPC-382
86T-382
87Coke/WS-14
87D/OD-230
87F-488
87F/Slug-7
87T/Tr-15T
88Coke/WS-3
88D-182
88D-25DK
88D-BC5
88D/Best-25
88D/DKsuper-25DK
88F-394
88F/BB/MVP-4
88F/LL-3
88F/Mini-14
88F/St-14
88Kodak/WSox-4
88Leaf-175

88Leaf-25DK
88OPC-184
88Panini/St-63
88S-607
88S/YS/II-22
88Sf-166
88T-184
88T/Big-63
88T/Coins-6
88T/Mini-7
88T/St-285
88T/UK-9
89B-68
89Coke/WS-7
89D-371
89D/Best-193
89F-493
89OPC-101
89RedFoley/St-16
89S-331
89T-656
89T/Big-289
89T/St-297
89UD-650
90B-316
90Coke/WSox-1
90D-294
90D/BestAL-141
90F-529
90Leaf/I-89
90OPC-569
90Panini/St-47
90Publint/St-385
90RedFoley/St-13
90S-94
90Sf-167
90T-569
90T/Big-80
90T/Coins-9
90T/Mini-11
90T/St-299
90UD-503
91B-440
91Classic/III-T5
91D-203
91F-115
91F/Ultra-199
91F/Up-U97
91Leaf/II-338
91Leaf/Stud-194
91OPC-93
91OPC/Premier-17
91Panini/FrSt-318
91Panini/St-258
91S-254
91S/RookTr-6T
91T-93
91T/StClub/II-383
91T/Tr-16T
91UD-285
91UD/Ext-786
91UD/FinalEd-96F
91USPlayC/AS-13C
92D/I-48
92D/II-431
92F-475
92S/100SS-61
92S/I-83
92T-775
92UD-226

Calderon, Jose
81Buffa-16
84Cram/PCL-207
85Maine-3
87ArkTr-4
87Louisvl-8

Calderone, Jeff
90BurlB/Best-10
90BurlB/ProC-2343
90BurlB/Star-7

Calderone, Samuel F.
(Sammy)
53T-260
54JC-42
54T-68
79TCMA-236
91T/Arc53-260

Caldwell, Bruce
90Target-100

Caldwell, Earl W.
47TipTop

Caldwell, Ralph M.
(Mike)
73OPC-182
73T-182
74OPC-344
74T-344
75OPC-347
75T-347
75T/M-347
76OPC-157
76SSPC-93
76T-157
77T-452
78T-212
79Ho-14
79OPC-356
79T-651
80OPC-269
80T-515
81D-86
81F-512
81OPC-85
81T-85
81T/St-97
82D-330
82F-136
82OPC-378
82Pol/Brew-48
82T-378
83D-154
83F-29
83Gard-4
83OPC-142
83Pol/Brew-48
83T-142
83T/St-184
83T/St-185
84D-237
84F-196
84Gard-3
84Nes/792-605
84OPC-326
84Pol/Brew-48
84T-605
85D-490
85F-577
85T-419
85T/St-289

Caldwell, Raymond B.
(Ray)
14CJ-129
15CJ-129
16FleischBrd-12
D329-27
D350/2-25
M101/4-27
M101/5-25

Caldwell, Rich
84Newar-17
85CharlO-19

Calhoun, Brad
77AppFx

Calhoun, Gary
91Niagara/ClBest-29MG
91Niagara/ProC-3650MG

Calhoun, Jeff
83ColumAst-13
85F/Up-U18
85Mother/Ast-24
86D-426
86F-295
86Pol/Ast-19
86T-534
87D-578
87F-52
87Maine-14
87Maine/TCMA-2
87T-282
87T/Tr-16T
88D-509
88F-299
88Phill/TastyK-5
88T-38
89UD-33

Calhoun, John Charles
No Cards.

Calhoun, Ray
89GreatF-30
90VeroB/Star-7
91FSLAS/ProC-FSL37
91VeroB/ClBest-5
91VeroB/ProC-766

Calhoun, William D.
(Bill)
No Cards.

Calini, Ron
91AubAS/ClBest-11

Calise, Michael S.
(Mike)
80ArkTr-6
81Louisvl-21
82Louisvl-4
83Louisvl/Riley-21
84RochR-5
85Cram/PCL-63

Call, Keith
82Madis-26
83Madis/LF-14
84Nashvl-3

Callaghan, Martin F.
(Marty)
E120
V61-66
W573

Callahan, Ben
82Nashvl-4
83Colum-14
83Nashvl-4

Callahan, Edward J.
(Ed)
No Cards.

Callahan, James J.
(Nixey)
10Domino-19
11Helmar-8
12Sweet/Pin-8
14CJ-111
16FleischBrd-13
D329-26
D350/2-24
E107
E224
E270/2
E300
M101/4-26
M101/5-24
T207
WG5-7
WG6-6

Callahan, Leo
90Target-107A

Callahan, Mike
83DayBe-4

Callahan, Patrick B.
79WHave-6
81Colum-4
82Nashvl-5

Callahan, Patrick H.
(Pat)
No Cards.

Callahan, Steve
89Everett/Star-3
90Clinton/Best-2
90Clinton/ProC-2545
91SanJose/ClBest-14
91SanJose/ProC-2

Callahan, Wesley L.
(Wes)
No Cards.

Callari, Ray
91Rockford/ClBest-17
91Rockford/ProC-2052
91Single/ClBest-316

Callas, Pete
87CharWh-6
88Clearw/Star-4

Callaway, Frank B.
E120

Calley, Robert
85Visalia-10
86Visalia-5

Callis, Al
75Clinton

Callison, John W.
(Johnny)
59T-119
60L-118
60T-17
61T-468
61T/St-50
62Bz
62P/Can-118
62Salada-204
62Shirriff-204
62T-17
62T/St-165
63Bz-15
63Exh
63F-51
63J-179
63P-179
63Salada-26
63T/SO
64Bz-15
64PhilBull-8
64T-135
64T/Coins-50
64T/S-36
64T/St-80
64T/SU
64T/tatt
65Bz-15
65OPC-4LL
65T-310
65T-4LL
65T/E-32
65T/trans-41
66Bz-12
66OPC-52M
66T-230
66T-52M
66T/RO
67Bz-12
67OPC-85
67OPC/PI-14
67T-309M
67T-85
67T/PI-14
68T-415
69MB-47
69MLB/St-174
69MLBPA/Pin-37
69OPC-133
69T-133
69T/St-73
70MLB/St-15
70OPC-375
70T-375
71MLB/St-28
71OPC-12
71T-12
72MB-60
72OPC-364
72T-364
72T/Cloth-4
73OPC-535
73Syrac/Team-4
73T-535
74Laugh/ASG-64
78TCMA-29
Exh47
PM10/L-8

Callistro, Robby
91Pocatel/ProC-3774

Calmus, Dick
64T-231
68T-427
90Target-101

Calufetti, Larry
76Wausau

Calvert, Art
87PrWill-8
88FtLaud/Star-3
89Star/Wax-48
89StPete/Star-4

Calvert, Chris
85Visalia-12
87Visalia-13
88Clearw/Star-5
88Reading/ProC-886
89EastLDD/ProC-DD34
89Reading/Best-21
89Reading/ProC-664
89Reading/Star-5

Calvert, Mark
81Phoenix-9
83Phoenix/BHN-2
84Cram/PCL-2
85Maine-4

Calvey, Jack
46Sunbeam

Calvo, Jacinto
(Jack)
No Cards.

Calzado, Francis
84Everett/Cram-23

Calzado, Johnny
89Johnson/Star-4
90Savan/ProC-2081
91Single/ClBest-79
91Spring/ClBest-9
91Spring/ProC-754

Calzado, Lorenzo
89Savan/ProC-360

Camacho, Adulfo
85Tigres-18

Camacho, Ernie
81T-96R
84Wheat/Ind-13
85D-129
85F-442
85Polar/Ind-13
85T-739
85T/St-253
86F-582
86OhHenry-13
86T-509
87D-350
87F-247
87Gator-13
87OPC-353
87T-353
87T/St-209
88Mother/Ast-16
88Tucson/ProC-189
89Phoenix/CMC-6
89Phoenix/ProC-1494
90B-229
90Mother/Giant-27
90T/TVCard-51
91Pac/SenLg-132

Camarena, Miguel
90Hunting/ProC-3272
91Hunting/ClBest-6
91Hunting/ProC-3326

Cambria, Fred
71OPC-27R
71T-27R
72OPC-392R
72T-392R

Camelli, Henry R.
(Hank)
47TipTop

Camelo, Pete
86Jaxvl/TCMA-6
87Jaxvl-4

Cameron, John S.
No Cards.

Cameron, Paul
84CharlO-5
85CharlO-30
87CharlO/WBTV-xx

Cameron, Stanton
89Pittsfld/Star-2
91StLucie/ClBest-4
91StLucie/ProC-722

Camilli, Adolf Louis
(Dolph)
34G-91
35BU-150
36Exh/4-6
36G-5
37Exh/4-6
38Exh/4-2
38Wheat-16
39Exh
39PB-86
40PB-68
40Wheat-11
41DP-20
41PB-51
61F-97
89Smok/Dodg-42
90Target-102
PM10/Sm-19
R302
R312
R313
R314
WG8-4

Camilli, Douglass J.
(Doug)
61Union
62T-594R
63T-196
64T-249
65OPC-77
65T-77
66T-593
67T-551
73OPC-131CO
73T-131C
85Greens-1MG

86Greens-3MG
87WinHaven-24
90Target-103
90WinHaven/Star-27CO

Camilli, Kevin
86Greens-4
88Fayette/ProC-1099

Camilli, Louis Steven
(Lou)
71MLB/St-364
71OPC-612R
71T-612R

Caminiti, Ken
85Osceola/Team-17
86ColumAst-6
87Sf/Rook-37
87SLAS-10
88Classic/Blue-228
88D-308
88F-441
88OPC-64
88S-164
88S/YS/I-29
88Sf-124
88T-64
88T/St-33
88ToysRUs-6
88Tucson/CMC-11
88Tucson/ProC-182
88Tucson/JP-3
89D-542
89D/Best-262
89Lennox/Ast-21
89Mother/Ast-25
89T-369
89T/Big-210
89UD-141
90B-73
90D-424
90D/BestNL-126
90F-225
90Leaf/I-253
90Lennox-5
90MLBPA/Pins-42
90Mother/Ast-6
90OPC-531
90Panini/St-260
90PublInt/St-89
90S-76
90Sf-209
90T-531
90T/Big-170
90T/St-20
90T/TVAS-37
90UD-122
91B-543
91D-221
91F-500
91F/Ultra-133
91Leaf/II-502
91Leaf/Stud-174
91Mother/Ast-6
91OPC-174
91Panini/FrSt-9
91Panini/St-17
91S-186
91S-415RIF
91T-174
91T/StClub/II-520
91UD-180
92D/I-66
92F-427
92S/I-69
92T-740
92UD-279

Camnitz, Samuel H.
(Howard)
10Domino-20
11Helmar-155
12Sweet/Pin-134A
12Sweet/Pin-134B
14CJ-16
14Piedmont/St-8
15CJ-16
D322
E224
E254
E270/1
E90/1
E97
L1-124
M116
S74-107
S81-99
T202
T205
T206
T207
T213/blue
T215/blue
T215/brown
T3-7

Camp, Howard Lee
(Howie)
No Cards.

Camp, Llewellan R.
No Cards.

Camp, Rick
77T-475R
78T-349
79Richm-21
79T-105
81D-197
81F-246
81OPC-87
81Pol/Atl-37
81T-87
81T/St-150
82BK/Lids-5
82D-223
82F-432
82OPC-138
82Pol/Atl-37
82T-637
83D-149
83F-133
83Pol/Atl-37
83T-207
84D-165
84F-174
84Nes/792-597
84OPC-136
84Pol/Atl-37
84T-597
85D-409
85F-321
85Ho/Braves-5
85Leaf-130
85OPC-167
85Pol/Atl-37
85T-491
86D-385
86F-510
86T-319

Camp, Scott
86Osceola-3

Campa, Eric
90Madison/Best-5

Campagno, Steve
82Oneonta-9

Campanella, Roy
49B-84
49Eureka-32
50B-75
50Drake-6
51B-31
52B-44
52BR
52StarCal/L-79C
52T-314
52TipTop
52Wheat
53B/Col-46
53Exh/Can-20
53RM-NL5
53SM
53T-27
54B-90
54NYJour
54RM-NL13
54Wilson
55B-22
55Gol/Dodg-5
56T-101
57T-210
57T-400M
58BB
59T-550
60NuCard-29
61NuCard-429
61T-480MV
75OPC-189MV
75OPC-191MV
75OPC-193MV
75T-189MV
75T-191MV
75T-193MV
75T/M-189MV
75T/M-191MV
75T/M-193MV
79TCMA-43
79TCMA-8
80Pac/Leg-90
80SSPC/HOF
83D/HOF-39
83MLBPA/Pin-20
84West/1-22
86Sf/Dec-33
87Leaf/SpecOlym-H3
88Pac/Leg-47
89HOF/St-54
89Rini/Dodg-9
89Smok/Dodg-4
90BBWit-30
90Target-104
91T/Arc53-27
Exh47
PM10/Sm-20A
PM10/Sm-20B
PM10/Sm-21
R423-12

Campaneris, Blanco D.
(Bert)
65OPC-266
65T-266
66Bz-44
66OPC-175
66T-175
66T/RO-108
67Bz-44
67OPC/PI-2
67T-515
67T/PI-2
68OPC-109
68T-109
69MB-48
69MLB/St-83
69T-423AS
69T-495
69T-556M
69T/S-29
69T/St-212
70K-39
70MLB/St-255
70OPC-205
70T-205
70T/PI-23
71Bz
71Bz/Test-31
71MLB/St-508
71OPC-440
71T-440
71T/Coins-64
71T/GM-6
71T/S-31
71T/tatt-7
72MB-61
72OPC-75
72T-75
73OPC-209WS
73OPC-295
73OPC-64LL
73T-209WS
73T-295
73T-64LL
74Greyhound-5M
74K-4
74OPC-155
74OPC-335AS
74OPC-474WS
74OPC-478WS
74T-155
74T-335AS
74T-474WS
74T-478WS
74T/DE-46
74T/St-223
75Ho-28
75Ho/Twink-28
75OPC-170
75T-170
75T/M-170
76Ho-61
76OPC-580
76SSPC-492
76T-580
77BurgChef-19
77Ho-149
77K-2
77OPC-74
77T-373
78BK/R-14
78T-260
78T/Zest-2
78Wiffle/Discs-12
79OPC-326
79T-620
80OPC-264
80T-505
81D-50
81F-280
81T-410
82D-593
82F-454
82T-772
83Colum-17
83T/Tr-18
84F-120
84Nes/792-139
84Nes/792-711LL
84Nes/792-714LL
84T-139
84T-711LL
84T-714LL
87Mother/A's-1
89Pac/Leg-157
89Pac/SenLg-63
89T/SenLg-32
89TM/SenLg-16
90EliteSenLg-78
90HOF/St-67
90Pac/Legend-15
90Swell/Great-121
91Swell/Great-110

Campanis, Alexander
(Al)
90Target-105

Campanis, James A.
(Jim)
67OPC-12R
67T-12R
68T-281
69T-396
70T-671
71MLB/St-196
74OPC-513
74T-513
90Target-106

Campanis, Jim Jr.
88T/Tr-23T
89SanBern/Best-1
89SanBern/Cal-85
90Penin/Star-5
91Jaxvl/LineD-332
91Jaxvl/ProC-153
92D/II-647
92T-58M

Campas, Mike
89Hamil/Star-7
90Spring/Best-6
91StPete/ClBest-18
91StPete/ProC-2281

Campau, Charles C.
(Count)
N172

Campbell, Arthur V.
(Vin)
15CJ-168
D322
M116

Campbell, Bill
74OPC-26
74T-26
75OPC-226
75T-226
75T/M-226
76OPC-288
76SSPC-208
76T-288
77OPC-12
77OPC-8LL
77T-166
77T-8LL
78Ho-107
78OPC-87
78OPC-8LL
78PapaG/Disc-22
78T-208LL
78T-545
79OPC-195
79T-375
80T-15
81F-240
81OPC-256
81T-396
82D-487
82F-289
82RedLob
82T-619
82T/Tr-16T
83D-504
83F-493
83T-436
83Thorn-39
84D-555
84F-489
84F/X-23
84Nes/792-787
84Phill/TastyK-16
84T-787
84T/Tr-22
85D-163
85F-245
85F/Up-U19
85OPC-209
85Phill/TastyK-9
85T-209
85T/Tr-15T
86D-571
86F-28
86F/Up-U17
86T-112
86T/Tr-17T
87F-146
87OPC-362
87T-674
89Pac/Leg-191
89Pac/SenLg-34
89T/SenLg-106
89TM/SenLg-17
90EliteSenLg-95
91Pac/SenLg-125

Campbell, Bruce D.
35BU-152
41PB-37
92Conlon/Sport-539
R305
R313

Campbell, Clarence
(Soup)
40PB-200
41DP-131

Campbell, D.C
90Durham/Team-8

Campbell, Darrin
89Saraso/Star-3
90Saraso/Star-3
91BirmB/LineD-53
91BirmB/ProC-1456

Campbell, David Alan
(Dave)
78T-402
79T-9

Campbell, David W.
(Dave)
69T-324R
70MLB/St-110
70T-639
71MLB/St-221
71OPC-46
71T-46
72OPC-384
72T-384
73OPC-488
73T-488
74OPC-556
74T-556
78Padre/FamFun-4ANN
84Smok/Padres-3ANN

Campbell, Donovan
88Idaho/ProC-1845
89BurlB/ProC-1620
89BurlB/Star-3

Campbell, Greg
83BurlR-28
83BurlR/LF-25TR
84Tulsa-TR
85OKCty-14
86OKCty-2TR

Campbell, James A.
81Detroit-130GM
83Kaline-22GM
83Kaline-44GM
83Kaline-54GM

Campbell, James R.
(Jim)
63Pep

63T-373
64T-303
Campbell, Jim
88Memphis/Best-10
89F-646M
89Memphis/Best-17
89Memphis/ProC-1194
89Memphis/Star-5
89Smok/Ast-13
90A&AASingle/ProC-15
90Foil/Best-311
90Memphis/Best-22
90Memphis/ProC-1002
90Memphis/Star-3
91Spokane/ClBest-3
91Spokane/ProC-3938
91T/90Debut-24
Campbell, Joseph Earl
(Joe)
No Cards.
Campbell, Keiver
91StCath/ClBest-2
91StCath/ProC-3407
Campbell, Kevin
87VeroB-17
88VeroB/Star-2
89Bakers/Cal-182
91AAAGame/ProC-AAA45
91Tacoma/LineD-530
91Tacoma/ProC-2296
92S/II-855
92T/91Debut-26
Campbell, Marc T.
(Hutch)
No Cards.
Campbell, Mark
82DayBe-17
Campbell, Mike
86Cedar/TCMA-4
87Calgary-14
87Tampa-21
88D-30
88D/Best-163
88D/Rook-2
88F-372
88Leaf-30RR
88Mother/Sea-18
88T-246
89D-497
89F-543
89Mother/Sea-18
89S-568
89S/HotRook-86
89S/YS/II-30
89T-143
89UD-337
90Vanco/CMC-7
90Vanco/ProC-482
Campbell, Paul M.
No Cards.
Campbell, Ronald T.
(Ron)
67T-497
Campbell, Samuel
(Sam)
No Cards.
Campbell, Scott
91James/ClBest-8
91James/ProC-3550
Campbell, Steve
82Idaho-23
Campbell, William G.
(Gilly)
32Orbit/num-34
32Orbit/un-9
35BU-164
35G-8D
35G-9D
90Target-107B
Campbell, William J.
E270/1
T206
T213/blue
T213/brown
Camper, Cardell
78T-711R
91Pac/SenLg-96
Campisi, Sal
70T-716R
71OPC-568
71T-568
Campos, Francisco J.
(Frank)
52T-307
53T-51
91T/Arc53-51
Campos, Frank
88CharWh/Best-24
89CharWh/Best-23
89CharWh/ProC-1767
90SoBend/ClBest-14
90Utica/Pucko-15
91SoBend/ProC-2850
Campusano, Genaro
90Welland/Pucko-3
91Augusta/ClBest-29
91Augusta/ProC-810
91Single/ClBest-161
Campusano, Silvestre
(Sil)
86Knoxvl-4
87Syrac-1
87Syrac/TCMA-18
88D/Rook-42
88F/Up-U66
88S/Tr-93T
88T/Tr-24T
88Tor/Fire-6
89Classic-137
89D-584
89OPC-191
89S-473
89Syrac/CMC-21
89Syrac/ProC-808
89Syrac/Team-6
89T-191
89Tor/Fire-6
89UD-45
90Classic/III-66
90Phill/TastyK-3
91F-389
91OPC-618
91Phill/Medford-7
91S-847
91ScranWB/ProC-2549
91T-618
91T/StClub/II-484
91UD-469
Campusano, Teo
89AubAs/ProC-2162
Canady, Chuckie
82BurlR-16
83Tulsa-14
84OKCty-17
85OKCty-29
90TulsaDG/Best-2
Canale, George
87Stockton-18
88ElPaso/Best-5
89Denver/CMC-19
89Denver/ProC-35
90B-392
90D-699
90Denver/CMC-17
90Denver/ProC-630
90ElPasoATG/Team-28
90F-641R
90OPC-344
90S-656
90T-344
90T/89Debut-21
90UD-59
91CharlK/LineD-129
91CharlK/ProC-1695
91Denver/LineD-130
91Denver/ProC-128
91F-578
91S/100RisSt-27
Canan, Dick
86Peoria-2
87Peoria-5
89WinSalem/Star-3
Canate, William
90Watertn/Star-2
91Kinston/ClBest-23
91Kinston/ProC-335
Canavan, James Edward
(Jimmy)
90Target-108
N172
Cancel, Danny
91Peoria/ProC-1353
Cancel, Victor
88Wythe/ProC-1980
89Wythe/Star-4
90Geneva/ProC-3034
90Geneva/Star-3
90Peoria/Team-15
91Peoria/ClBest-18
Candaele, Casey
85Indianap-25
86Indianap-33
87Classic/Up-128
87D-549
87D/Rook-33
87F/Up-U16
87Sf-158M
87Sf/Rook-6
87T/Tr-17T
88D-179
88D/Best-68
88F-181
88Ho/Disc-12
88Leaf-199
88OPC-87
88Panini/St-329
88RedFoley/St-11
88S-97
88S/YS/I-34
88Sf-140
88T-431
88T/Gloss60-60
88T/JumboR-11
88T/St-305
88T/St-77
88ToysRUs-7
89Tucson/CMC-16
89Tucson/ProC-197
89Tucson/JP-3
89UD-58
90Lennox-6
90Mother/Ast-25
90T/Tr-17T
91B-559
91D-324
91F-501
91F/Ultra-134
91Leaf/I-114
91Mother/Ast-25
91OPC-602
91Panini/FrSt-8
91S-577
91T-602
91T/StClub/II-434
91UD-511
92D/I-150
92F-428
92S/I-147
92T-161
92UD-387
Candelari, Rick
89Wausau/GS-21
Candelaria, Al
83Ander-9
Candelaria, John
76Crane-7
76Ho-92
76MSA/Disc
76OPC-317
76SSPC-563
76T-317
77BurgChef-188
77Ho-80
77K-7
77OPC-59
77Pep-63
77T-510
78Ho-104
78K-18
78OPC-221
78OPC-7LL
78T-190
78T-207LL
79Ho-86
79K-34
79OPC-29
79T-70
80OPC-332
80T-635
81Coke
81D-374
81F-375
81OPC-265
81T-265
82D-297
82F-479
82OPC-3
82T-425
83D-549
83F-304
83OPC-127
83T-291TL
83T-755
83T/St-282
84D-357
84F-247
84F/St-57
85FunFood/Pin-50
84Nes/792-330
84OPC-330
84T-330
84T/St-127
85D-430
85F-462
85F/St-98
85Leaf-157
85OPC-50
85T-50
85T/St-123
86D-499
86F-150
86OPC-140
86Sf-129M
86Smok/Cal-16
86T-140
87D-551
87F-75
87F/AwardWin-5
87F/LimWaxBox-C3
87Leaf-242
87OPC-313
87Sf-148
87Smok/AL-3
87Smok/Cal-1
87T-630
88D-608
88D/Best-20
88D/Y/Bk-NEW
88F/Up-U46
88S-293
88S/Tr-40T
88T-546
88T/Tr-25T
89B-171
89D-192
89F-251
89OPC-285
89Panini/St-397
89S-246
89S/NWest-8
89Sf-202
89T-285
89T/St-306
89UD-248
90KayBee-5
90Leaf/II-492
90OPC-485
90PublInt/St-532
90S/Tr-54T
90T-485
90T/Tr-18T
90UD/Ext-720
91F/Up-U92
91Leaf/II-324
91Mother/Dodg-22
91OPC-777
91Pol/Dodg-54
91S-791
91S/RookTr-32T
91T-777
91T/StClub/II-538
91T/Tr-17T
91UD/FinalEd-40F
91WIZMets-59
92D/I-125
92F-449
92S/I-350
92T-363
92UD-482
Candelaria, Jorge
88Oneonta/ProC-2055
89Boise/ProC-1998
89Reno/Cal-242
Candini, Mario
49Remar
51B-255
Candiotti, Tom
81ElPaso-22
84Cram/PCL-32
84D-393
84F-197
84Nes/792-262
84T-262
86F/Up-U18
86OhHenry-49
86T/Tr-18T
87D-342
87D/OD-104
87F-248
87F/Mini-16
87F/St-18
87Gator-49
87Leaf-81
87OPC-296
87T-463
87T/Mini-50
87T/St-211
88D-377
88D/Best-112
88F-604
88Gator-49
88OPC-123
88Panini/St-69
88S-595
88Sf-37
88T-123
88T/Big-93
89B-80
89D-256
89D/Best-117
89F-399
89Panini/St-317
89RedFoley/St-17
89S-239
89T-599
89T/Big-267
89T/St-211
89UD-470
90B-324
90D-256
90D/BestAL-89
90ElPasoATG/Team-32
90F-488
90Leaf/I-55
90OPC-743
90Panini/St-57
90PublInt/St-556
90S-269
90Sf-126
90T-743
90T/Coins-10
90T/St-216
90UD-388
91B-62
91Classic/200-54
91D-115
91F-364
91F/Ultra-109
91F/UltraUp-U59
91F/Up-U64
91Leaf/I-79
91Leaf/Stud-132
91OPC-624
91Panini/FrSt-223
91Panini/St-174
91RedFoley/St-16
91S-488
91S/100SS-36
91S/RookTr-31T
91S/ToroBJ-28
91T-624
91T/StClub/II-405
91T/Tr-18T
91UD-218
91UD/FinalEd-49F
92D/II-459
92F-326
92S/II-575
92T-38
92UD-447
Caneira, John
75QuadC
77SLCity
78Cr/PCL-55
Canestro, Art
88Oneonta/ProC-2060
89Oneonta/ProC-2104
90PrWill/Team-7
91FtLaud/ClBest-2
91FtLaud/ProC-2417
Cangelosi, John
83AppFx/LF-13
86Coke/WS-44
86D/HL-51
86D/Rook-51
86F/Up-U19
86Sf/Rook-31
86T/Tr-19T

87D-162
87F-489
87Leaf-251
87OPC-201
87Sf-157M
87Seven-C3
87T-201
87T/GlossRk-2
87T/Mini-49
87T/St-293
87T/Tr-18T
88D-435
88F-325
88OPC-328
88Panini/St-377
88S-418
88T-506
89S-601
89T-592
89UD-67
89VFJuice-44
90D-565
90Homer/Pirate-8
90OPC-29
90S-367
90T-29
90UD-370
91Vanco/LineD-629
91Vanco/ProC-1605

Cangemi, Jamie
87Beloit-7
89Beloit/II/Star-4
89Stockton/Best-6
89Stockton/Cal-150
89Stockton/ProC-389
89Stockton/Star-13
90Stockton/Best-21
90Stockton/Cal-182
90Stockton/ProC-2182
91Stockton/ClBest-1
91Stockton/ProC-3025

Canino, Carlos
88Geneva/ProC-1655

Cannell, Virgin Wirt
(Rip)
No Cards.

Cannizzaro, Chris Jr.
86Pawtu-4
87Pawtu-27
87Pawtu/TCMA-2
88Pawtu/CMC-15
88Pawtu/ProC-451
89Pawtu/CMC-11
89Pawtu/Dunkin-7
89Pawtu/ProC-686

Cannizzaro, Chris
61T-118
62T-26
65OPC-61
65T-61
66T-497
69OPC-131
69T-131
70OPC-329
70T-329
71MLB/St-222
71OPC-426
71T-426
71T/Coins-109
71T/tatt-6
72T-759
75OPC-355
75T-355
75T/M-355
81Redwd-28MG
82Redwd-25MG
90Target-109
91WIZMets-60

Cannon, Joseph Jerome
(J.J.)
75Dubuq
78Charl
79Syrac-7
80OPC-118
80T-221
81Syrac-17
82Knoxvl-18
83Kinston/Team-2
86Knoxvl-5
87Knoxvl-26
89Knoxvl/Best-25
89Knoxvl/ProC-1129
89Knoxvl/Star-24
90Knoxvl/Best-10CO
90Knoxvl/ProC-1260CO
90Knoxvl/Star-25CO
91MedHat/ProC-4117MG

Cannon, Robby
91Boise/ProC-3894

Cannon, Scott
86Kinston-3

Cannon, Stan
79Wisco-16

Cannon, Tim
83Miami-22

Cano, Jose
83Ander-8
84Durham-22
87Osceola-27
88Tucson/CMC-7
88Tucson/ProC-171
88Tucson/JP-4
89ColMud/Best-25
90B-68
90ColMud/Best-25
90ColMud/ProC-1340
90Lennox-7
90T/89Debut-22
90UD-43

Canseco, Jose
83Madis/LF-13
85Huntsvl/BK-44
86D-39RR
86D/HL-55
86D/Rook-22
86F-649R
86F/LL-3
86F/Mini-87
86F/Slug-5
86F/St-19
86F/Up-U20
86Mother/A's-9
86Sf-178R
86Sf/Rook-11
86SLAS-14
86T/Tr-20T
87Classic-46
87Classic/Up-125
87D-6DK
87D-97
87D-PC12
87D/AAS-21
87D/DKsuper-6
87D/HL-40M
87D/OD-24
87D/WaxBox-PC12
87Drake-4
87F-389
87F-625M
87F-628M
87F-633M
87F/AwardWin-6
87F/Excit-7
87F/GameWin-8
87F/HL-2
87F/Hottest-9
87F/BB-6
87F/LL-8
87F/Lim-6
87F/Mini-17
87F/RecSet-3
87F/Slug-8
87F/St-131M
87F/St-19
87Ho/St-28
87KayBee-7
87Kraft-35
87Leaf-151
87Leaf-6DK
87MnM's-10
87Mother/A's-26
87Mother/A's-27M
87MSA/Discs-17
87OPC-247
87RedFoley/St-63
87Sf-80M
87Sf-90
87Smok/A's-2
87Smok/AL-1
87T-620
87T/Coins-6
87T/Gloss60-59
87T/GlossRk-3
87T/HL-12
87T/Mini-68
87T/St-164
87T/St-304
87ToysRUs-5
87Woolwth-12
88Bz-3
88Classic/Red-165
88Classic/Red-197M
88D-302
88D/A's/Bk-302
88D/Best-22
88F-276
88F-624M
88F/AwardWin-4
88F/BB/AS-5
88F/BB/MVP-3
88F/Excit-7
88F/Hottest-5
88F/LL-4
88F/Mini-45
88F/RecSet-4
88F/Slug-6
88F/SS-5
88F/St-54
88F/TL-3
88KayBee-3
88KMart-4
88Leaf-138
88Mother/A's-7
88Nestle-37
88OPC-370
88Panini/St-173
88S-45
88S/YS/I-30
88Sf-201
88T-370
88T/Big-13
88T/Coins-7
88T/Gloss60-55
88T/Mini-30
88T/St-173
88T/St/Backs-48
88T/UK-10
89T/Ames-8
89B-201
89Bz-5
89Cadaco-5
89Classic-103
89Classic-3
89CMC/Canseco-Set
89T/Crunch-1
89D-643HL
89D-91
89D/AS-2
89D/AS-30
89D/Best-57
89D/GrandSlam-1
89D/MVP-BC5
89D/PopUp-2
89F-5
89F-628M
89F-634M
89F/AS-2
89F/BBAS-5
89F/BBMVP's-6
89F/Excit-3
89F/Heroes-5
89F/LL-3
89F/Superstar-6
89F/WaxBox-C4
89F/WS-3
89Holsum/Discs-5
89KayBee-3
89KingB/Discs-17
89KMart/DT-18
89Master/Discs-10
89Modesto/Chong-34
89Mother/A's-7
89Mother/Canseco-1
89Mother/Canseco-2
89Mother/Canseco-3
89Mother/Canseco-4
89Mother/ROY's-1
89Mother/ROY's-4M
89Nissen-5
89OPC-389
89Panini/St-238AS
89Panini/St-246
89Panini/St-422
89Panini/St-477
89Panini/St-480
89Panini/St-8
89MSA/SS-12
89RedFoley/St-18
89S-1
89S-582M
89S-655HL
89S/HotStar-1
89S/Mast-40
89Sf-1
89Sf-221M
89T-401AS
89T-500
89T/Big-190
89T/Coins-29
89T/DH-5
89T/Gloss22-6
89T/Gloss60-12
89T/HeadsUp-18
89T/Hills-5
89T/LJN-74
89T/Mini-68
89T/St-11
89T/St-148
89T/St-171
89T/St/Backs-13
89T/UK-12
89Tacoma/ProC-1536
89Tetley/Discs-18
89UD-371
89UD-659MVP
89UD-664M
89UD-670TC
89Woolwth-1
89Woolwth-23
90B-460
90BBWit-11
90Classic-22
90Classic/III-32
90Colla/Canseco-Set
90CollAB-25
90D-125
90D/BestAL-81
90D/Learning-6
90F-3
90F-629MVP
90F/AwardWin-6
90F/BB-4
90F/BBMVP-6
90F/LgStand-4
90F/LL-5
90F/WS-10M
90F/WS-5
90HOF/St-95
90HotPlay/St-4
90KMart/SS-21
90Leaf/I-108
90MLBPA/Pins-78
90Mother/A's-6
90Mother/Canseco-1
90Mother/Canseco-2
90Mother/Canseco-3
90Mother/Canseco-4
90MSA/Soda-15
90OPC-250
90Panini/St-142
90Pep/Canseco-Set
90Post-16
90PublInt/St-279
90PublInt/St-301
90RedFoley/St-14
90S-375
90S/100St-5
90Sf-23
90T-250
90T/Ames-29
90T/Big-270
90T/DH-8
90T/Gloss60-31
90T/HeadsUp-18
90T/HillsHM-7
90T/St-177
90T/TVAS-11
90Tetley/Discs-4
90UD-66
90USPlayC/AS-WC
90Windwlk/Discs-8
90WonderBrd-14
91B-227
91B-372SLUG
91BBBest/RecBr-2
91Classic/200-135
91Classic/II-T19
91Classic/III-T6
91CollAB-13
91D-50AS
91D-536
91D/Elite-E3
91D/GSlam-4
91D/Preview-11
91F-5
91F/ASIns-8
91F/ProV-6
91F/Ultra-244
91F/WS-3
91JDeanSig-19
91Leaf/I-182
91Leaf/Stud-101
91MajorLg/Pins-38
91MooTown-1
91Mother/A's-6
91OPC-390AS
91OPC-700
91OPC/Premier-18
91Panini/FrSt-173
91Panini/FrSt-198
91Panini/St-149
91Panini/Top15-15
91Panini/Top15-24
91Panini/Top15-39
91Pep/SS-17
91Post-4
91RedFoley/St-116
91RedFoley/St-17
91S-1
91S-398AS
91S-441DT
91S-690MB
91S/100SS-1
91Seven/3DCoin-2NC
91Seven/3DCoin-2NW
91Seven/3DCoin-2SC
91Seven/3DCoin-3T
91Seven/3DCoin-6A
91SFExam/A's-2
91T-390AS
91T-700
91T/CJMini/I-10
91T/StClub/I-155
91T/SU-7
91UD-155
91UD/SilSlug-SS4
92Classic/I-22
92D/II-548
92F-252
92F-688LL
92F/ASIns-24
92F/TmLIns-19
92S/100SS-67
92S/II-500
92T-100
92T-401AS
92UD-333
92UD-640CL
92UD-649DS

Canseco, Ozzie
83Greens-3
87Madis-6
88Madis-7
88MidwLAS/GS-51
89Huntsvl/Best-28
89UD/Ext-756
90F/Up-117
90Foil/Best-162
90Huntsvl/Best-21
90Leaf/II-516
91MajorLg/Pins-41
91OPC-162
91S-346RP
91T-162
91T/90Debut-25
91UD-146

Cantrell, Dave
89Salinas/Cal-129
89Salinas/ProC-1826

Cantrell, Guy
90Target-110

Cantres, Jorge
90Yakima/Team-35

Cantu, Mike
91Hamil/ClBest-19
91Hamil/ProC-4044

Cantwell, Ben
33G-139
35BU-96
35G-8L
35G-9L
90Target-111
91Conlon/Sport-211
R308-168
R332-25
V354-14
WG8-5

Cantwell, Rob
88Spokane/ProC-1924

89Watlo/ProC-1780
89Watlo/Star-2
Cantz, Bartholomew L.
(Bart)
N172
Capel, Mike
84MidldC-10
86Pittsfld-3
87Iowa-4
88D/Rook-46
88Iowa/CMC-1
88Iowa/ProC-547
89F-643R
89Iowa/CMC-1
89Iowa/ProC-1706
89T-767
90Denver/CMC-5
90Denver/ProC-618
91Tucson/LineD-605
91Tucson/ProC-2206
92F-429
92S/II-687
Capellan, Carlos
88Kenosha/ProC-1396
89AS/Cal-6
89Visalia/Cal-112
89Visalia/ProC-1441
90AS/Cal-9
90Visalia/Cal-71
90Visalia/ProC-2159
91OrlanSR/LineD-477
91OrlanSR/ProC-1854
Capello, Pete
87AppFx-4
88Virgini/Star-4
89AppFx/ProC-865
Capilla, Doug
78OPC-11
78T-477
80T-628
81D-587
81F-309
81T-136
82T-537
82Wichita-3
89Pac/SenLg-172
Capowski, Jim
78Ashvl
79Tulsa-4
Cappadona, Pete
86NewBrit-5
Cappuzzello, George
77Evansvl/TCMA-5
78Indianap-15
79Indianap-16
81Evansvl-2
82F-264
82T-137
82Tucson-20
83T-422
84Colum-7
84Colum/Pol-4
Capra, Lee
(Buzz)
72OPC-141R
72T-141R
75OPC-105
75OPC-311LL
75T-105
75T-311LL
75T/M-105
75T/M-311LL
76Ho-85
76OPC-153
76SSPC-1
76T-153
77T-432
78T-578
83Ander-6
86AppFx-5CO
87BurlEx-21
88Spartan/ProC-1047
88Spartan/Star-23
88Spartan/Star-7
90Spartan/Best-26CO
90Spartan/ProC-2508CO
90Spartan/Star-27CO
91Spartan/ClBest-29CO
91Spartan/ProC-914CO
91WIZMets-61
Capra, Nick Lee
79Tulsa-20
80Tulsa-8
83OKCty-4
84OKCty-11
85OKCty-25
86BuffB-7
87OKCty-23
88Omaha/CMC-12
88Omaha/ProC-1499
89F-279
89Omaha/CMC-19
89Omaha/ProC-1742
90OkCty/CMC-16
90OkCty/ProC-443
91OkCty/LineD-307
91OkCty/ProC-190
Capri, Patrick N.
(Pat)
No Cards.
Capriati, Jeff
91Pac/SenLg-76
Caprillo, Matias
85Tigres-25
Capron, Ralph Earl
No Cards.
Caraballo, Felix
88Madis-8
88Modesto-5
90Reno/Cal-281
Caraballo, Gary
90AppFox/Box-6
90AppFox/ProC-2100
91AppFx/ClBest-15
91AppFx/ProC-1721
91MidwLAS/ProC-MWL2
91Single/ClBest-211
Caraballo, Ramon
85Phill/TastyK-41
86Phill/TastyK-x
87Clearw-11
88Clearw/Star-6
90A&AASingle/ProC-131
90BurlB/Best-4
90BurlB/ProC-2360
90BurlB/Star-8
90Foil/Best-260
91B-584
91Durham/ClBest-24
91Durham/ProC-1551
91Single/ClBest-376
Caraballo, Wilmer
85Lynch-21
86Lynch-5
87BirmB/Best-6
Carabello, Nelson
89Welland/Pucko-9
Caray, Harry
88Peoria/Ko-8
Carballo, Lee
88SLCity-28
88Virgini/Star-5
Carbine, John C.
No Cards.
Carbo, Bernardo
(Bernie)
70OPC-36R
70T-36R
71MLB/St-51
71OPC-478
71T-478
72OPC-463
72T-463
73OPC-171
73T-171
74OPC-621
74T-621
75OPC-379
75T-379
75T/M-379
76OPC-278
76SSPC-411
76T-278
77T-159
78T-524
79T-38
80T-266
89Pac/SenLg-45
89T/SenLg-13
89TM/SenLg-18
90EliteSenLg-96
Carcione, Thomas
(Tom)
88SoOreg/ProC-1699
89Madis/Star-6
89Modesto/Chong-19
90Modesto/Cal-167
90Modesto/ProC-2215
91Huntsvl/ClBest-6
91Huntsvl/LineD-281
91HuntsvlProC-1799
Cardenal, Jose
65T-374R
66T-505
66T/RO-80
67OPC-193
67T-193
68OPC-102
68T-102
69MB-49
69MLB/St-40
69T-325
69T/S-15
69T/St-164
69Trans-5
70MLB/St-136
70T-675
71K-26
71MLB/St-270
71OPC-435
71T-435
72MB-62
72OPC-12
72T-12
72T-757TR
73OPC-393
73T-393
74Greyhound-6M
74OPC-185
74T-185
74T/DE-55
74T/St-12
75Ho-65
75Ho/Twink-65
75K-29
75OPC-15
75T-15
75T/M-15
76Crane-8
76Ho-37
76Ho/Twink-37
76MSA/Disc
76OPC-430
76T-430
77BurgChef-197
77Ho-85
77OPC-127
77T-610
77T/CS-9
78T-210
79BK/P-18
79T-317
80T-512
81T-473
89Pac/Leg-149
89Swell-61
91WIZMets-62
Cardenas, Daniel
90Yakima/Team-10
Cardenas, Leonardo L.
(Leo)
60T-119
61T-244
61T/St-16
62Kahn
62T-381
63FrBauer-2
63J-127
63Kahn
63P-127
63T-203
64Kahn
64T-72
65Kahn
65T-437
66Kahn
66T-370
67Kahn
67OPC/PI-10
67T-325
67T/PI-10
68Kahn
68OPC-23
68T-23
68T-480M
69MB-50
69T-265
70MLB/St-231
70OPC-245
70T-245
71MLB/St-460
71OPC-405
71T-405
71T/Coins-148
71T/tatt-8
72K-30
72MB-63
72T-561
72T-562A
73OPC-522
73T-522
75OPC-518
75T-518
75T/M-518
76OPC-587
76SSPC-261
76T-587
78TCMA-69
83Wisco/LF-15
Cardieri, Ron
82Miami-9
Cardinal, Conrad
(Randy)
63T-562R
Cardona, Isbel
91MedHat/ProC-4090
Cardona, James
91Welland/ClBest-6
91Welland/ProC-3585
Cardona, Jose
91Gaston/ClBest-3
91Gaston/ProC-2680
Cardoz, Don
78RochR
Cardwell, Buddy
77Wausau
Cardwell, Don
57T-374
58T-372
59T-314
60T-384
61NuCard-410
61P-194
61T-393M
61T-564
62T-495
62T/bucks
62T/St-106
63IDL-3
63Sugar-A
63T-575
64T-417
65T-502
66EH-43
66T-235
67T-555
68T-437
69MB-51
69OPC-193
69T-193
70OPC-83
70T-83
72MB-64
78TCMA-89
90Swell/Great-72
91WIZMets-63
Cardwood, Alfredo
85Orlan-15
86Visalia-6
87WPalmB-4
Carew, Rodney Cline
(Rod)
67T-569R
68Bz-13
68Coke
68Dexter-20
68OPC-80
68T-363AS
68T-80
68T/G-29
69MB-52
69MLB/St-65
69MLBPA/Pin-4
69OPC/DE-3
69T-419AS
69T-510
69T/DE-12
69T/St-192
70K-47
70MB-4
70MLB/St-232
70OPC-290
70OPC-453AS
70OPC-62LL
70T-290
70T-453AS
70T-62LL
70T/PI-16
71MLB/St-461
71OPC-210
71T-210
71T/Coins-24
71T/tatt-15
72MB-65
72T-695
72T-696IA
73K-51
73OPC-330
73OPC-61LL
73T-330
73T-61LL
73T/Lids-9
74Greyhound-3
74Greyhound-5M
74K-30
74OPC-201LL
74OPC-333AS
74OPC-50
74T-201LL
74T-333AS
74T-50
74T/DE-32
74T/DE-36
74T/St-203
75Ho-56
75K-33
75OPC-306LL
75OPC-600
75T-306LL
75T-600
75T/M-306LL
75T/M-600
76Crane-9
76Ho-33
76Ho/Twink-33
76K-48
76MSA/Disc
76OPC-192LL
76OPC-400
76SSPC-214
76T-192LL
76T-400
77BurgChef-51
77Ho-9
77K-53
77OPC-143
77Pep-2
77T-120
77T/CS-10
78Ho-140
78K-29
78OPC-1LL
78OPC-230
78PapaG/Disc-35
78T-201LL
78T-580
78Tastee/Discs-8
78Wiffle/Discs-13
79Ho-38
79K-13
79OPC-151
79T-1LL
79T-300
79T/Comics-11
80BK/PHR-14
80K-60
80OPC-353
80T-700
80T/S-12
81D-169
81D-49
81Drake-2
81F-268
81F/St-40
81K-26
81MSA/Disc-6
81OPC-100
81PermaGr/AS-11
81PermaGr/CC-22
81Sqt-9
81T-100
81T/HT
81T/Nat/Super-4
81T/SO-18
81T/St-49
82D-216
82Drake-6

82F-455
82F/St-217
82K-51
82KMart-31
82OPC-187
82OPC-363IA
82OPC-36AS
82PermaGr/CC-21
82T-276TL
82T-500
82T-501IA
82T-547AS
82T/St-131
82T/St-160
83D-8DK
83D-90
83D/AAS-38
83Drake-3
83F-81
83K-1
83OPC-200
83OPC-201SV
83OPC-386AS
83PermaGr/AS-2
83PermaGr/CC-20
83Seven-1
83T-200
83T-201SV
83T-386AS
83T-651TL
83T/Gloss40-29
83T/St-39
84D-352
84D/Champs-21
84Drake-5
84F-511
84F/St-103
84F/St-12
84F/St-54
85FunFood/Pin-35
84MiltBrad-3
84Nes/792-276TL
84Nes/792-600
84Nes/792-710LL
84Nes/792-711LL
84OPC-26
84Ralston-17
84Seven-8W
84Smok/Cal-5
84T-276LL
84T-600
84T-710LL
84T-711LL
84T/Cereal-17
84T/Gloss22-2
84T/Gloss40-26
84T/St-227
84T/St/Box-11
85D-85
85D/HL-31
85F-297
85F/LimEd-5
85Leaf-132
85OPC-300
85Seven-6W
85Smok/Cal-5
85T-300
85T/Gloss22-13
85T/St-184
85T/St-223
85ThomMc/Discs-7
86D-280
86F-151
86F-629M
86F/HOF-4
86F/LL-4
86F/St-20
86OPC-371
86Sf-106
86Sf-146M
86Sf-180M
86Sf-182M
86Sf-69M
86Sf-74M
86T-400
86T/Gloss60-16
86T/St-176
86T/St-4
86Woolwth-6
87KMart-14
87Nestle/DT-12
89Smok/Angels-10
89T/LJN-97
90MSA/AGFA-7
90Pac/Legend-17
90Swell/Great-4
91B-1
91B-2
91B-3
91B-4
91B-5
91Swell/Great-103
91T/Ruth-8

Carey, Andrew Arthur
(Andy)
53T-188
54NYJour
54T-105
55T-20
55T/DH-36
56T-12
57T-290
58T-333
59T-45
60T-196
61T-518
61T/St-158
62J-52
62P-52
62P/Can-52
62Salada-86A
62Salada-86B
62Shirriff-86
62T-418
79TCMA-243
90Target-112
91T/Arc53-188
PM10/L-9

Carey, Brooks M.
81RochR-3
82Indianap-9

Carey, Frank
90Clinton/Best-4
90Clinton/ProC-2555
90Foil/Best-67
91Shrev/LineD-301
91Shrev/ProC-1826

Carey, George C.
(Scoops)
E107
T206

Carey, Jeff
82WHave-3

Carey, Max George
11Helmar-156
14CJ-73
15CJ-73
21Exh-21
25Exh-50
26Exh-50
28Exh-6
28Yueng-32
40PB-178
61F-12
72Laugh/GF-9
80Laugh/FFeat-12
80SSPC/HOF
89HOF/St-38
89Smok/Dodg-5
90BBWit-88
90Target-113
91Conlon/Sport-24
BF2-90
D327
D329-28
D350/2-26
E120
E121/120
E121/80
E122
E126-32
E126-32
E210-32
E220
M101/4-28
M101/5-26
T206
T207
T213/brown
V100
V61-71
W501-86
W502-32
W514-22
W573
W575

Carey, P.J.
89Belling/Legoe-30MG
91Billings/ProC-3770MG

Carey, Paul
90Miami/I/Star-3
91Hagers/LineD-228
91Hagers/ProC-2466
91Single/ClBest-190

Carey, Pete
86FtMyr-5
87Tampa-2

Carey, Roger J.
No Cards.

Carey, Thomas Francis
(Tom)
35BU-89
39PB-62
40PB-39

Cargo, Robert J.
(Chick)
No Cards.

Caridad, Rolando
90SoBend/ClBest-15
90Utica/Pucko-16
91SoBend/ProC-2851

Caridad, Ron
91Elizab/ProC-4293

Cariel, Rafael
76Shrev

Carisch, Frederick B.
(Fred)
No Cards.

Carisen, Robert
91Madison/ClBest-25

Carista, Mike
85Elmira-3
86WinHaven-5
87Greens-5
88EastLAS/ProC-20
88NewBrit/ProC-909
89NewBrit/ProC-605
90NewBrit/Best-12
90NewBrit/Star-2

Carl, Frederick E.
(Fred)
No Cards.

Carl, Jeff
83Memphis-5

Carleton, James
(Tex)
34G-48
35G-1A
35G-2A
35G-6A
35G-7A
90Target-114
92Conlon/Sport-378
R310
V354-90

Carley, Dave
87Beloit-19

Carlin, James Arthur
(Jim)
No Cards.

Carlin, Mike
89Spartan/ProC-1035
89Spartan/Star-3

Carlisle, Matthew
86Negro/Frit-85

Carlisle, Walter G.
No Cards.

Carlo
C46-85

Carlos, Cisco
68T-287R
69OPC-54
69T-54
70OPC-487
70T-487
72MB-66

Carlos, Gil
84Iowa-20

Carlsen, Robert
91Madison/ProC-2137

Carlson, Bill
87Clinton-11
87Pocatel/Bon-13
88Clinton/ProC-700
89SanJose/Best-9
89SanJose/Cal-229
89SanJose/ProC-439
89SanJose/Star-4
90Salinas/Cal-131
90Salinas/ProC-2730
91Salinas/ClBest-30
91Salinas/ProC-2250

Carlson, Bob
91Elizab/ProC-4294

Carlson, Dan
90Everett/Best-3
90Everett/ProC-3119
91Clinton/ClBest-1
91Clinton/ProC-826

Carlson, Hal
R316
V100
W513-75

Carlson, Lynn
90Welland/Pucko-19
91Augusta/ClBest-3
91Augusta/ProC-796

Carlson, Tom
76Clinton

Carlstrom, Albin O.
(Swede)
No Cards.

Carlton, Andy
90StCath/ProC-3476
91Myrtle/ClBest-17
91Myrtle/ProC-2951

Carlton, Scott
91Spartan/ClBest-1
91Spartan/ProC-886

Carlton, Steve
65T-477R
67OPC-146
67T-146
68T-408
69T-255
70MLB/St-137
70OPC-220
70OPC-67LL
70T-220
70T-67LL
71MLB/St-271
71OPC-55
71T-55
71T/Coins-115
72MB-67
72OPC-420
72OPC-93LL
72T-420
72T-751TR
72T-93LL
73K-7
73OPC-300
73OPC-65LL
73OPC-66LL
73OPC-67LL
73T-300
73T-65LL
73T-66LL
73T-67LL
73T/Comics-4
73T/Lids-10
73T/PinUps-4
74JP
74OPC-95
74T-95
74T/DE-5
74T/St-73
75Ho-63
75OPC-185
75OPC-312LL
75T-185
75T-312LL
75T/M-185
75T/M-312LL
76Crane-10
76MSA/Disc
76OPC-355
76SSPC-459
76T-355
77BurgChef-171
77Ho-117
77K-57
77OPC-93
77T-110
77T/CS-11
78Ho-49
78K-1
78OPC-170
78OPC-5LL
78T-205LL
78T-540
78Wiffle/Discs-14
79BK/P-4
79Ho-71
79K-18
79OPC-9
79T-25
80BK/P-15
80BK/PHR-2
80K-14
80OPC-113
80T-210
81Coke
81D-481CY
81D-73
81Drake-23
81F-6
81F-660M
81F/St-85
81K-50
81MSA/Disc-7
81OPC-203
81PermaGr/CC-16
81T-202HL
81T-5LL
81T-630
81T-6LL
81T/HT
81T/SO-104
81T/St-206
81T/St-25
81T/St-261
81T/St-28
81T/St-29
82D-42
82Drake-7
82F-243
82F-641M
82F/St-240M
82F/St-241M
82F/St-54
82K-27
82OPC-122IA
82OPC-68
82PermaGr/CC-10
82T-1M
82T-480
82T-481IA
82T-636TL
82T/St-129
82T/St-75
83D-16DK
83D-219
83D/AAS-24
83F-155
83K-45
83OPC-384AS
83OPC-70
83OPC-71SV
83PermaGr/CC-2
83T-229TL
83T-406AS
83T-70
83T-705LL
83T-706LL
83T-71SV
83T/Gloss40-36
83T/St-203
83T/St-204
83T/St-267
84D-111
84D/AAS-24
84D/Champs-38
84F-25
84F-642IA
84F/St-101
84F/St-78
85FunFood/Pin-30
84MiltBrad-4
84Nes/792-136LL
84Nes/792-1HL
84Nes/792-395AS
84Nes/792-4HL
84Nes/792-706LL
84Nes/792-707LL
84Nes/792-708LL
84Nes/792-780
84Nestle/DT-21
84OPC-214
84OPC-395AS
84Phill/TastyK-17
84Phill/TastyK-5HOF
84Ralston-16
84Seven-12E
84T-1HL
84T-136LL

84T-395AS
84T-4HL
84T-706LL
84T-707LL
84T-708LL
84T-780
84T/Cereal-16
84T/Gloss40-27
84T/St-1
84T/St-119
84T/St-15
84T/St-184
84T/St-2
84T/Super-16
85CIGNA-12
85D-305
85D/AAS-55
85Drake-35
85F-246
85F/LimEd-6
85Leaf-113
85OPC-360
85Phill/TastyK-14
85Phill/TastyK-9M
85Seven-2S
85Seven-3E
85T-360
85T/3D-25
85T/St-112
85T/Super-24
85ThomMc/Discs-25
85Woolwth-6
86BK/AP-6
86D-183
86D/HL-35
86F-435
86F/HOF-2
86F/Mini-91
86F/Slug-M2
86F/St-21
86Keller-1
86Leaf-117
86Meadow/Milk-3
86OPC-120
86Phill/TastyK-32
86Sf-27
86Sf-70M
86Sf/Dec-54
86T-120
86T-246M
86T/St-116
87D-617
87F-490
87F-635M
87F/Excit-8
87F/Up-U17
87KMart-15
87OPC-271
87OPC-B
87Sf-200
87T-718
87T-B
87T/HL-1
87T/Tr-19T
87Woolwth-1
88F-7
89Swell-95
89T/LJN-145
90BBWit-43
90HOF/St-78
90MSA/AGFA-15
90Pac/Legend-16
90Phill/TastyK-30
90Swell/Great-110
91K/3D-8
91K/SU-5A
91K/SU-5B
91LineD-9
91Swell/Great-17

Carlucci, Dave
86Bakers-5

Carlucci, Rich
81Water-1
82Indianap-19
83Indianap-16
84RochR-2
86Syrac-6

Carlucci, Tony
83TriCit-14

Carlyle, Hiram Cleo
(Cleo)
No Cards.

Carlyle, Roy Edward
No Cards.

Carman, Don
80Penin/B-11
80Penin/C-5
82OkCty-24
83Reading-3
84Cram/PCL-204
84Phill/TastyK-41
85F/Up-U20
85Phill/TastyK-15
85Phill/TastyK-9M
85T/Tr-16T
86CIGNA-2
86D-427
86F-436
86F/St-22
86Leaf-200
86Phill/TastyK-42
86T-532
87D-432
87F-171
87Leaf-174
87OPC-355
87Phill/TastyK-42
87Sf-108
87T-355
87T/St-122
88D-385
88D/Best-72
88F-300
88Phill/TastyK-6
88S-401
88T-415
89B-392
89D-396
89F-564
89OPC-154
89Panini/St-146
89Phill/TastyK-3
89S-222
89T-154
89T/St-121
89UD-409
90D-604
90F-552
90OPC-731
90Phill/TastyK-4
90PublInt/St-233
90T-731
90UD-420
91D-377
91F-390
91Kahn/Reds-36
91OPC-282
91S-237
91T-282
91UD-288

Carman, George W.
No Cards.

Carmel, Leon James
(Duke)
60T-120
61Union
63T-544R
64T-44
64T/Coins-81
65OPC-261
65T-261
91WIZMets-64
WG10-4

Carmichael, Al
85Lynch-15
86Lynch-6

Carmody, Kevin
89Beloit/I/Star-2
89Beloit/II/Star-5
90Stockton/Best-20
90Stockton/Cal-181
90Stockton/ProC-2181

Carmona, Greg
89StPete/Star-5
90T/TVCard-40
91ArkTr/LineD-28
91ArkTr/ProC-1291
91B-392
91Louisvl/ProC-2920

Carmona, Williams
89Martins/Star-4
90Martins/ProC-3181
91Pocatel/ProC-3795

Carnera, Primo
33SK-43
47HomogBond-7BOX
D305

Carnes, Scott
77QuadC
80ElPaso-3
81SLCity-17
82Spokane-15

Carnett, Edwin E.
(Eddie)
43Centen-3

Carney, John Joseph
(Jack)
N172

Carney, Patrick J.
(Pat)
No Cards.

Carney, Ron
78Ashvl
79Tulsa-18
80Ashvl-14
81Tulsa-10

Carney, William John
(Bill)
No Cards.

Caro, Joe
91Boise/ProC-3900CO

Caro, Jorge
91Bristol/ClBest-2
91Bristol/ProC-3611

Carosielli, Marc
88Wythe/ProC-1999

Carpenter, Cris
88D/Rook-50
88Louisvl-13
88Louisvl/CMC-8
88Louisvl/ProC-428
89Classic/Up/2-185
89D-39RR
89D/Rook-40
89F/Up-117
89Louisvl-13
89S/Tr-81
89S/YS/II-37
89T-282
89T/Big-307
89UD-8
90D-634
90F-243
90HotRook/St-10
90Louisvl/CMC-3
90Louisvl/ProC-395
90OPC-443
90PublInt/St-212
90S/100Ris-74
90T-443
90T/TVCard-7
90UD-523
91F-628
91F/UltraUp-U105
91Leaf/II-507
91OPC-518
91T-518
91T/StClub/II-499
92D/I-79
92F-575
92S/I-160
92T-147
92UD-686

Carpenter, Doug
84Greens-9
85Albany-20
86FtLaud-3
87Miami-7
89Reno/Cal-254
90Lakeland/Star-27CO
91Lakeland/ClBest-10CO
91Lakeland/ProC-284CO

Carpenter, Glenn
83DayBe-18
86Tucson-4
87Tucson-2
88Tucson/CMC-12
88Tucson/ProC-173
88Tucson/JP-5

Carpenter, John
45Centen-3

Carpenter, Kevin
90Johnson/Star-6

Carpenter, Paul
44Centen-2
47Centen-3

Carpenter, Rob
90Kgsport/Best-10
90Kgsport/Star-4

Carpenter, Warren W.
(Hick)
N172

Carper, Mark
88CapeCod/Sum-172
91Freder/ClBest-1
91Freder/ProC-2355

Carpin, Frank
66OPC-71
66T-71

Carpine, Bill
91Clinton/ClBest-16TR

Carpio, Jorge
82QuadC-5
84MidldC-6

Carr, Charles Carbitt
(Charlie)
E107
E254
E270/1
E270/2
T206

Carr, Chuck
88MidwLAS/GS-56
88Wausau/GS-8
89Jacks/GS-2
89TexLAS/GS-28
90F/Up-U34
91F-141
91T/90Debut-26
91Tidew/ProC-2521
91UD-514
91WIZMets-65
92S/II-857

Carr, Ernie
88GreatF-4
89Bakers/Cal-200

Carr, Lewis Smith
(Lew)
No Cards.

Carr, Terence
86Cram/PCL-95
87QuadC-1
88QuadC/GS-9
89Reno/Cal-255
90PalmSp/Cal-203
90PalmSp/ProC-2589

Carrano, Rick
86Miami-4TR

Carranza, Javier
83StPete-2

Carrara, Giovanni
91StCath/ClBest-13
91StCath/ProC-3387

Carrasco, Carlos
88Bakers/Cal-251
89Reno/Cal-243
90Salinas/Cal-127
90Salinas/ProC-2718
91Salinas/ClBest-23
91Salinas/ProC-2235

Carrasco, Claudio
86Watlo-5
87Watlo-26
88Wmsprt/ProC-1320
89QuadC/Best-23
89QuadC/GS-29
89Reno/Cal-259

Carrasco, Ernie
83Erie-22
84Savan-15
86ArkTr-3

Carrasco, Hector
89Kgsport/Star-4
90Kgsport/Best-16
90Kgsport/Star-5
91Pittsfld/ClBest-21
91Pittsfld/ProC-3415

Carrasco, Norman
82Danvl-28
83Redwd-5
85Cram/PCL-22
86Edmon-2
87Edmon-19
88MidldA/GS-25
89Toledo/CMC-20
89Toledo/ProC-768

Carrasquel, Alfonso
(Chico)
51B-60
51FB
51T/BB-26
52B-41
52BR
52Dix-53
52StarCal/L-73D
52T-251
53B/Col-54
53Exh/Can-4
54B-54
54RM-AL19
55B-173
55RFG-4
55RM-AL23
55Salem
56T-230
57Sohio/Ind-3
57T-67
58Hires-11
58T-55
59T-264
79TCMA-74
91Crown/Orio-69
Exh47
PM10/Sm-22
R423-9

Carrasquel, Emilio
82BirmB-22

Carraway, Rod
82Watlo/B-14
82Watlo/C-9

Carreno, Amalio
87PrWill-19
88Albany/ProC-1329
89Reading/Star-6
90Foil/Best-140
90Reading/Best-5
90Reading/ProC-1213
90Reading/Star-11
91ScranWB/LineD-481
91ScranWB/ProC-2532
92S/II-867
92T/91Debut-27

Carreon, Camilo G.
(Cam)
60L-88
60T-121
61T-509
62T-178
62T/St-23
63T-308
64T-421
65T-578
66T-513
91Crown/Orio-70

Carreon, Mark
83Lynch-14
84Jacks-20
85Tidew-25
86Tidew-4
87Tidew-21
87Tidew/TCMA-20
88AAA/ProC-39
88F-129
88Tidew/CANDL-14
88Tidew/CMC-22
88Tidew/ProC-1588
89B-389
89Classic-84
89D/Rook-18
89F-29
89Kahn/Mets-32
89S/HotRook-16
89S/Tr-108
89Tidew/Candl-14
89Tidew/CMC-24
90Classic-112
90D-454
90F-198
90HotRook/St-11
90Kahn/Mets-45
90Leaf/II-488
90OPC-434
90S-363
90S/100Ris-67
90S/YS/I-17
90T-434
90T/JumboR-6
90T/TVMets-30
90ToysRUs-7
90UD-135
91D-731
91F-142
91Kahn/Mets-45
91OPC-764
91S-165

91T-764
91T/StClub/I-196
91WIZMets-66
92D/II-465
92F-498
92S/I-19
92T-111
92UD-398

Carrick, William
E107

Carrigan, William F.
(Bill)
10Domino-21
11Helmar-1
12Sweet/Pin-1A
12Sweet/Pin-1B
14CJ-27
14Piedmont/St-9
15CJ-27
16FleischBrd-14
E95
E97
M116
S74-1
T202
T204
T205
T206
T207
T3-86
WG6-7

Carriger, Rick
87Hagers-18
88Jaxvl/Best-1
88Jaxvl/ProC-988
89Jaxvl/Best-19
89Jaxvl/ProC-168

Carrillo, Matias
86Nashua-5
87Salem-10
88ElPaso/Best-12
89Denver/CMC-22
89Denver/ProC-49
91Denver/LineD-131
91Denver/ProC-134
92T/91Debut-28

Carrion, Jesus
86Osceola-4

Carrion, Leonel
80Memphis-12
83Memphis-15
84Indianap-3C
86Jaxvl/TCMA-9C

Carrithers, Don
71MLB/St-243
72OPC-76
72T-76
73OPC-651
73T-651
74OPC-361
74T-361
75OPC-438
75T-438
75T/M-438
76OPC-312
76SSPC-348
76T-312
77OPC-18
77T-579
78Cr/PCL-80
78T-113
79Phoenix

Carroll, Bob
77Visalia

Carroll, Carson
83Orlan-25
83Wisco/LF-7
84Visalia-15
86Albany/TCMA-3
87Albany-14

Carroll, Chris
86FtLaud-4
87FtLaud-5

Carroll, Clay
65T-461R
66T-307
67T-219
68Coke
68Dexter-21
68T-412
69Kahn
69OPC-26
69T-26
70OPC-133
70T-133
71MLB/St-52
71OPC-394
71T-394
72MB-68
72OPC-311
72OPC-312IA
72T-311
72T-312A
73OPC-195
73OPC-68LL
73T-195
73T-68LL
74OPC-111
74T-111
75OPC-345
75T-345
75T/M-345
76K-6
76OPC-211
76SSPC-25
76T-211
76T/Tr-211T
77T-497
78T-615
79Vanco-14

Carroll, Don
88GreatF-12
89Salem/Team-9
90Kissim/DIMD-5
91Yakima/ClBest-18
91Yakima/ProC-4240

Carroll, Dorsey Lee
(Dixie)
No Cards.

Carroll, Ed
78Holyo
79Holyo-4
80Holyo-19

Carroll, Edward
(Chick)
No Cards.

Carroll, Frederick H.
(Fred)
N172
N284

Carroll, James
86Cram/PCL-71
87Madis-21
88Madis-9
88Modesto-6
89Clearw/Star-4

Carroll, Joe
78Ashvl

Carroll, John E.
(Scrappy)
N172

Carroll, Kevin
91StLucie/ClBest-12
91StLucie/ProC-713

Carroll, Owen
33DH-8
33G-72
90Target-115
92Conlon/Sport-496
R310
R316
V354-46

Carroll, Patrick
(Pat)
No Cards.

Carroll, Ralph A.
(Doc)
No Cards.

Carroll, Samuel C.
(Cliff)
N172
N284
WG1-55

Carroll, Shadow
C46-39

Carroll, Steve
83Iowa-24
85Iowa-30

Carroll, Thomas E.
(Tommy)
55T-158
56T-139
57T-164
59T-513

Carroll, Thomas M.
75OPC-507
75T-507
75T/M-507
76Indianap-12
76OPC-561
76T-561

Carruth, Jim
76Baton

Carsey, Wilfred
(Kid)
90Target-908

Carsley, Jeff
78Dunedin

Carson, Henry
83StPete-3
86StPete-5

Carson, Paul
89Martins/Star-5

Carson, Ted
84Savan-23

Carson, Walter Lloyd
(Kit)
R313

Carstensen, Chris
77Newar
78BurlB

Carswell, Frank W.
53Glen

Cartaya, Joel
86Salem-3
87PortChar-21
88Tulsa-16
89CharlR/Star-5

Cartelli, John
(Doc)
86Modesto-6TR
87Modesto-22

Carter, Andy
88SALAS/GS-27
88Spartan/Star-19
88Spartan/Star-3
89Clearw/Star-5
90Clearw/Star-4
91Reading/LineD-506
91Reading/ProC-1366

Carter, Bruce
86Clearw-2
86Cram/PCL-189

Carter, Conrad P.
W514-45

Carter, David
90Gate/ProC-3361
91Erie/ClBest-14
91Erie/ProC-4060

Carter, Dell
85Elmira-4

Carter, Dennis
87ArkTr-1
88StPete/Star-3
89ArkTr/GS-4
90Louisvl/CMC-10
90Louisvl/ProC-414

Carter, Dick
60T-466C

Carter, Don
83Memphis-7
84BuffB-21

Carter, Dwight
75Clinton

Carter, Ed
90StPete/Star-1

Carter, Eddie
87Erie-7
88Savan/ProC-354
89Savan/ProC-358

Carter, Fred
87FtLaud-29
88Reno/Cal-290
89PalmSp/Cal-45
89PalmSp/ProC-479

Carter, Gary Edmund
75IntAS/TCMA-21
75OPC-620R
75T-620R
75T/M-620R
76Ho-62
76K-34
76OPC-441
76SSPC-334
76T-441
77BurgChef-154
77Ho-41
77OPC-45
77T-295
78Ho-146
78OPC-135
78T-120
79Ho-24
79OPC-270
79T-520
80OPC-37
80T-70
80T/S-52
81D-90
81F-142
81F/St-73
81OPC-6
81OPC/Post-8
81PermaGr/AS-1
81PermaGr/CC-32
81T-660
81T/SO-66
81T/St-184
81T/St-259
82D-114
82D-2DK
82F-185
82F/St-39
82Hygrade
82K-24
82OPC-244
82OPC-344AS
82OPC/Post-16
82PermaGr/AS-10
82PermaGr/CC-4
82Sqt-19
82T-344AS
82T-730
82T/St-128
82T/St-61
82Zeller-1
82Zeller-13
82Zeller-16
82Zeller-19
82Zeller-6
83D-340
83D/AAS-58
83Drake-4
83F-278
83F-637M
83F-638M
83K-55
83OPC-314AS
83OPC-370
83PermaGr/AS-10
83PermaGr/CC-3
83Stuart-8
83T-370
83T-404AS
83T/Gloss40-20
83T/St-178
83T/St-255
83T/St/Box-2
84D-55
84D/Champs-58
84Drake-6
84F-271
85FunFood/Pin-3
84MiltBrad-5
84Nes/792-393AS
84Nes/792-450
84OPC-366
84OPC-393AS
84Ralston-28
84Seven-15C
84Stuart-15
84Stuart-36AS
84T-393AS
84T-450
84T/Cereal-28
84T/Gloss22-20
84T/Gloss40-9
84T/St-183FOIL
84T/St-90
84T/Super-18
85D-55
85D/AAS-57
85D/HL-21M
85D/HL-47
85Drake-5
85F-393
85F-631IA
85F/St-16
85F/St-26
85F/St-35
85F/Up-U21
85GenMills-1DP
85Leaf-241
85OPC-230
85Pol/MetYank-M2
85Seven-9C
85T-230
85T-719AS
85T/3D-5
85T/Gloss22-9
85T/Gloss40-36
85T/Mets/Fan-3
85T/St-180
85T/St-192
85T/St-83
85T/Super-13
85T/Tr-17T
86D-68
86Dorman-3
86Drake-1
86F-76
86F/AS-4
86F/LimEd-10
86F/LL-5
86F/Mini-17
86F/Slug-M3
86F/St-23
86F/WaxBox-C7
86Jiffy-19
86Leaf-63
86OPC-170
86Quaker-4
86Sf-126M
86Sf-137M
86Sf-28
86Sf/Dec-72M
86T-170
86T-708AS
86T/3D-2
86T/Gloss60-23
86T/Mets/Fan-2
86T/Mini-50
86T/St-96
86T/Super-19
86TrueVal-16
86Woolwth-7
87BK-2
87Classic-5
87D-69
87D/AAS-19
87D/OD-130
87D/PopUp-19
87Drake-20
87F-4
87F-629M
87F-634M
87F/AS-2
87F/AwardWin-7
87F/Excit-9
87F/GameWin-9
87F/BB-7
87F/Mini-18
87F/St-20
87F/WS-4
87Ho/St-12
87KayBee-8
87KMart-25
87Leaf-109
87MnM's-12
87MSA/Discs-8
87OPC-20
87Ralston-9
87RedFoley/St-110
87Sf-151M
87Sf-50
87Seven-E1
87Seven-ME1
87T-20
87T-602AS
87T/Board-11
87T/Coins-28
87T/Gloss22-9
87T/Gloss60-11
87T/HL-25
87T/Mets/Fan-1
87T/Mini-20
87T/St-101
87T/St-14LCS
87T/St-158
87T/St-22WS
87Woolwth-25
88ChefBoy-10
88D-199
88D/AS-41
88D/Best-14
88D/Mets/Bk-199

88D/PopUp-19
88Drake-10
88F-130
88F-636M
88F/St-S2
88Jiffy-3
88Kahn/Mets-8
88Leaf-156
88Nestle-26
88OPC-157
88Panini/St-232M
88Panini/St-338
88S-325
88S/WxBx-10
88Sf-28
88Sf/Gamewin-14
88T-530
88T/Big-37
88T/Gloss22-20
88T/Gloss60-7
88T/Mets/Fan-8
88T/St-105
88T/St-152
88T/St/Backs-22
88T/UK-11
89B-379
89Cadaco-6
89Classic-64
89D-53
89D/AS-41
89D/Best-182
89D/PopUp-41
89F-30
89F/Superstar-7
89Kahn/Mets-8
89KayBee-4
89OPC-324
89Panini/St-136
89Panini/St-228AS
89RedFoley/St-19
89S-240
89Sf-155
89T-393AS
89T-3RB
89T-680
89T/Big-325
89T/DHTest-4
89T/Gloss22-20
89T/Gloss60-17
89T/LJN-138
89T/Mets/Fan-8
89T/St-160
89T/St-2
89T/St-94
89T/St/Backs-55
89UD-390
89Woolwth-10
90B-236
90BBWit-32
90D-147
90D/BestNL-48
90D/Learning-5
90F-199
90F/Up-U62
90KayBee-6
90Leaf/I-134
90MLBPA/Pins-17
90Mother/Giant-3
90OPC-790
90PublInt/St-128
90S-416
90S/Tr-35T
90T-790
90T/Tr-19T
90UD-168
90UD/Ext-774
91B-598
91BBBest/RecBr-3
91D-151
91D-BC8
91F-258
91F/UltraUp-U86
91F/Up-U93
91Leaf/II-457
91Leaf/Stud-182
91Mother/Dodg-16
91OPC-310
91OPC/Premier-19
91Pol/Dodg-12
91S-215
91S/RookTr-26T
91T-310
91T/StClub/II-424
91T/Tr-19T
91UD-176
91UD/Ext-758
91WIZMets-67
92D/I-36
92F-450
92S/II-489
92T-45
92UD-267

Carter, Glenn
89QuadC/Best-1
89QuadC/GS-8
91London/LineD-429
91MidldA/ProC-428
91Single/ClBest-305

Carter, Herbert
82Wisco-10

Carter, Jeff
85Everett/II/Cram-1
86Clinton-4
87Jamestn-27
88Rockford-5
88Shreve/ProC-1291
89Rockford-5
89Shreve/ProC-1846
89TexLAS/GS-29
89WPalmB/Star-5
90A&AASingle/ProC-38
90Foil/Best-316
90Jaxvl/Best-18
90Jaxvl/ProC-1369
90Phoenix/CMC-18
90Phoenix/ProC-17
91B-348
91Phoenix/LineD-379
91Phoenix/ProC-71
91Vanco/LineD-630
91Vanco/ProC-1587
92S/II-770
92T/91Debut-29

Carter, Joe
83Iowa-20
83Thorn-33
84D-41RR
84Iowa-25
84Wheat/Ind-30
85D-616
85F-443
85Polar/Ind-30
85T-694
86D-224
86D/HL-42
86F-583
86OhHenry-30
86OPC-377
86T-377
86T/St-213
87Classic/Up-127
87D-156
87D/OD-109
87F-249
87F/AwardWin-8
87F/BB-8
87F/LL-9
87F/Lim-7
87F/Mini-19
87F/St-21
87Gator-30
87KayBee-9
87Kraft-15
87Leaf-133
87MnM's-16
87OPC-220
87RedFoley/St-27
87Sf-176
87Smok/AL-5
87T-220
87T/Coins-7
87T/Gloss60-16
87T/Mini-51
87T/St-208
88D-254
88D-BC9
88D/Best-56
88F-605
88F/Mini-18
88F/Slug-7
88F/SS-6
88F/St-18
88Gator-30
88KayBee-4
88Leaf-184
88Nestle-36
88OPC-75
88OPC-I
88Panini/St-72
88S-80
88Sf-5
88T-75
88T/Big-71
88T/Coins-8
88T/Gloss60-44
88T/RiteAid-17
88T/St-213
88T/St/Backs-49
88T/UK-12
88T/WaxBox-I
89T/Ames-9
89B-91
89Cadaco-7
89Classic-11
89D-83
89D/Best-56
89D/MVP-BC3
89F-400
89F/Excit-4
89F/Heroes-6
89KingB/Discs-8
89OPC-164
89Panini/St-327
89RedFoley/St-20
89S-213
89S/HotStar-55
89S/Mast-34
89Sf-104
89T-420
89T/Big-155
89T/Coins-36
89T/Gloss60-3
89T/Hills-6
89T/LJN-87
89T/St-216
89T/St/Backs-14
89T/UK-13
89UD-190
90B-220
90Classic-138
90Classic/Up-T9
90Coke/Padre-3
90D-114
90D/BestNL-72
90F-489
90F/Up-U55
90HotPlay/St-5
90Leaf/II-379
90Leaf/Prev-2
90OPC-580
90Padre/MagUno-27
90Panini/St-65
90Post-30
90PublInt/St-280
90PublInt/St-557
90RedFoley/St-15
90S-319
90S/100St-59
90S/Tr-19T
90Sf-120
90T-580
90T/Ames-27
90T/Big-245
90T/Coins-42
90T/DH-9
90T/Gloss60-33
90T/HillsHM-28
90T/Mini-13
90T/St-209
90T/Tr-20T
90T/TVAS-43
90UD-375
90UD-53TC
90UD/Ext-754
90WichSt-7
91B-11
91Classic/200-91
91Classic/I-21
91Classic/II-T98
91Colla/Carter-Set
91D-298
91D-409MVP
91D/GSlam-1
91F-525
91F/Ultra-360
91F/Up-U65
91Leaf/II-353
91Leaf/Stud-133
91OPC-120
91OPC/Premier-20
91Panini/FrSt-95
91Panini/St-90
91Panini/Top15-19
91S-9
91S/100SS-81
91S/RookTr-11T
91S/ToroBJ-1
91S/ToroBJ-37AS
91T-120
91T/StClub/II-513
91T/Tr-20T
91Tor/Fire-29
91UD-226
91UD/Ext-765
91USPlayC/AS-4H
92D/DK-DK3
92D/Elite-E10
92D/II-677HL
92D/II-693
92F-327
92F-685RS
92F-703M
92F/ASIns-21
92F/TmLIns-14
92S/100SS-35
92S/I-435AS
92S/I-90
92T-402AS
92T-790
92UD-224

Carter, John Howard
(Howard)
No Cards.

Carter, Larry
89Beloit/II/Star-6
89Salinas/Cal-126
89Salinas/ProC-1816
90Beloit/Best-4
90Beloit/Star-4
91Beloit/ClBest-2
91Beloit/ProC-2095
91MidwLAS/ProC-MWL32
91Shrev/LineD-302
91Shrev/ProC-1814

Carter, Marlin
86Negro/Frit-50

Carter, Michael
91Beloit/ClBest-22
91Beloit/ProC-2108
91MidwLAS/ProC-MWL33
91Single/ClBest-214

Carter, Otis Leonard
(Jackie)
No Cards.

Carter, Richard
87Lakeland-13
88Lakeland/Star-6
89SanBern/Best-3
89SanBern/Cal-68

Carter, Richie
86PalmSp-6
86PalmSp/Smok-14

Carter, Ron
86Madis-5
86Madis/Pol-5
87SanBern-8

Carter, Steve
87Watertn-10
88Augusta/ProC-385
89BuffB/ProC-1665
89D/Rook-8
90AAAGame/ProC-AAA17
90B-179
90BuffB/CMC-22
90BuffB/ProC-385
90BuffB/Team-5
90OPC-482
90T-482
90T/89Debut-23
90UD-368
91D-418RR
91F/Ultra-374MLP
91Iowa/LineD-202
91Iowa/ProC-1074
91Lakeland/ClBest-8

Carter, Tim
91Beloit/ClBest-14
91Beloit/ProC-2109

Cartwright, Alan
84ElPaso-19
86ElPaso-5
87Denver-19
88ElPaso/Best-13

Cartwright, Alexander J.
50Call
80SSPC/HOF
89HOF/St-90
90BBWit-96

Cartwright, Edward C.
(Ed)
N172
N300/SC

Cartwright, Mark
83Visalia/LF-16

Carty, Jorge
77Charl

Carty, Ricardo A.
(Rico)
64T-476R
65Kahn
65OPC-2LL
65T-2LL
65T-305
65T/trans-7
66OPC-153
66T-153
67Kahn
67OPC-35
67T-240LL
67T-35
68Coke
68Dexter-22
68T-455
69MLB/St-112
69T-590
70MLB/St-3
70OPC-145
70T-145
71Bz
71Bz/Test-28
71MD
71MLB/St-557
71MLB/St-6
71OPC-270
71OPC-62LL
71T-270
71T-62LL
71T/Coins-113
71T/GM-3
71T/S-29
71T/tatt-11
72T-740
73OPC-435
73T-435
75OPC-655
75T-655
75T/M-655
76OPC-156
76SSPC-519
76T-156
77OPC-114
77Pep-9
77T-465
78T-305
79OPC-291
79T-565
80OPC-25
80T-46
91Swell/Great-18

Caruthers, Robert Lee
(Bob)
90Target-116
N162
N172
N172/BC
N28
N284
N370
Scrapps

Carvajal, Jovina
90Oneonta/ProC-3375
91FSLAS/ProC-FSL12
91FtLaud/ClBest-25
91FtLaud/ProC-2439

Carver, Billy Paul
87AubAs-6
88Ashvl/ProC-1049
88SALAS/GS-4
89ColMud/Best-23
89Osceola/Star-3

Cary, Chuck
82BirmB-9
83BirmB-14
86F/Up-U21
86Nashvl-3
87Richm/Crown-47
87D-461
87F-147

87Richm/TCMA-1
87T-171
89Colum/CMC-7
89Colum/Pol-1
89Colum/ProC-745
89S/NWest-27
89T/Tr-17T
89UD-396
90Classic-125
90D-429
90Leaf/I-50
90OPC-691
90Panini/St-123
90S-393
90S/NWest-15
90T-691
90T/St-315
90T/TVYank-8
90UD-528
91B-176
91D-179
91F-659
91Leaf/I-66
91OPC-359
91Panini/FrSt-331
91S-566
91T-359
91T/StClub/I-40
91UD-409

Cary, Jeff
80LynnS-12
81Wausau-15
82Madis-31

Casado, Cancio
89Martins/Star-6

Casagrande,Tom
55T-167

Casale, Jerry
59T-456
60MacGregor-5
60T-38
61T-195
61T/St-169

Casano, Andy
88Watlo/ProC-666
89Kinston/Star-5

Casanova, Ortiz P.
(Paul)
67OPC-115
67T-115
68Bz-1
68T-560
69MB-53
69MLB/St-102
69NTF
69T-486
69T/St-233
70MLB/St-280
70OPC-84
70T-84
71MLB/St-532
71OPC-139
71T-139
71T/Coins-146
72MB-69
72T-591
73OPC-452
73T-452
74OPC-272
74T-272
75OPC-633
75T-633
75T/M-633
76Laugh/Clown-24
89Pac/SenLg-58

Casarotti, Rich
88MidwLAS/GS-17
89Durham/Team-4
89Durham/Star-4
89Star/Wax-68
90Greenvl/Best-10
90Greenvl/ProC-1135
90Greenvl/Star-5
91Greenvl/ClBest-14
91Greenvl/LineD-201
91Greenvl/ProC-3008

Cascarella, Joe
35BU-162
W711/1

Case, George W.
39PB-138
40PB-15
41DP-76
41DP-88
41G-16
41PB-69
Exh47
R303/A
R303/B

Casey, Dan
N172
N284
N690
WG1-48

Casey, Dennis Patrick
No Cards.

Casey, Hugh
39PB-151
40PB-148
47TipTop
49B-179
49Eureka-155
80Laugh/FFeat-27
90Target-118
Exh47

Casey, James Peter
(Doc)
90Target-117
E107
T206

Casey, Jas.
WG3-8

Casey, Joie
87SLCity/Taco-x
88SLCity-30M

Casey, Joseph Felix
(Joe)
14CJ-87
15CJ-87
E101
E92

Casey, Keith
90Gate/ProC-3338

Casey, Kim
87SLCity/Taco-x

Casey, Orrin Robinson
(Bob)
No Cards.

Casey, Pat
83Beaum-16
84Beaum-16
85Cram/PCL-86
86Calgary-4
87Portl-7

Casey, Timothy
(Tim)
86Stockton-4
87ElPaso-13
89Huntsvl/Best-14
90Tacoma/CMC-12
90Tacoma/ProC-104

Cash, Bill
86Negro/Frit-57
91Negro/Lewis-2

Cash, David
(Dave)
70OPC-141R
70T-141R
71MLB/St-197
71OPC-582
71T-582
72OPC-125
72T-125
73OPC-397
73T-397
74JP
74OPC-198
74T-198
75Ho-93
75K-48
75OPC-22
75T-22
75T/M-22
76Crane-11
76Ho-40
76Ho/Twink-40
76K-16
76MSA/Disc
76OPC-295
76SSPC-465
76T-295
77BurgChef-162
77Ho-133
77OPC-180
77Pep-66
77T-649
77T/CS-12
78Ho-23
78OPC-18
78T-495
78Tastee/Discs-17
78Wiffle/Discs-15
79OPC-207
79T-395
80OPC-3
80T-14
81D-121
81F-492
81T-707
88Batavia/ProC-1663
89Pac/SenLg-192
89ScrWB/CMC-6
89T/SenLg-64
89TM/SenLg-19
90Batavia/ProC-3084MG
91Pac/SenLg-58
91Pac/SenLg-80

Cash, Earl
85Osceola/Team-4
86Osceola-5
87ColAst/ProC-19

Cash, Johnny
86Durham-3

Cash, Mike
75Cedar
78Cr/PCL-94

Cash, Norman Dalton
(Norm)
59T-509
60T-488
61P-40
61T-95
61T/St-148
62Bz
62Exh
62J-14
62P-14
62P/Can-14
62Salada-72
62Shirriff-72
62T-250
62T-466AS
62T-51LL
62T-90LL
62T/bucks
62T/St-45
63Exh
63J-46
63P-46
63T-445
63T-4LL
64Bz-20
64Det/Lids-3
64T-331M
64T-425
64T/Coins-79
64T/St-49
64T/SU
64T/tatt
65OPC-153
65T-153
66T-218LL
66T-315
67T-216M
67T-540
68T-256
69MB-54
69MLB/St-46
69OPC-80
69T-80
69T/St-171
70MLB/St-205
70T-611
71MLB/St-389
71OPC-599
71T-599
72MB-70
72OPC-150
72OPC-90LL
72T-150
72T-90LL
73OPC-485
73T-485
74OPC-367
74T-367
74T/St-172
78TCMA-49
81Detroit-73
83Kaline-19M
83Kaline-22M
83Kaline-24M
83MLBPA/Pin-3
85CircK-25
88Domino-2
Exh47

Cash, Ronald Forrest
(Ron)
74OPC-600R
74T-600R

Cash, Timothy
88VeroB/Star-3

Cash, Todd
86Clinton-5

Cashion, Jay Carl
14CJ-62
E270/1

Casian, Larry
88OrlanTw/Best-20
88SLAS-29
89Portl/ProC-223
90Portl/CMC-3
90Portl/ProC-170
91B-325
91Leaf/II-481
91OPC-374
91T-374
91T/90Debut-27
92F-199
92S/100RisSt-94

Casillas, Adam
88Greens/ProC-1562
89Cedar/Best-14
89Cedar/ProC-922
89Cedar/Star-3
90CedarDG/Best-18
91Nashvl/LineD-254
91Nashvl/ProC-2168

Caskin, Edward James
(Ed)
No Cards.

Casper, Tim
91Everett/ClBest-13
91Everett/ProC-3920

Cassady, Harry D.
No Cards.

Cassels, Chris
88Beloit/GS-23
89Stockton/Best-19
89Stockton/Cal-163
89Stockton/ProC-392
89Stockton/Star-14
90AS/Cal-41
90Stockton/Best-14
90Stockton/Cal-199
90Stockton/ProC-2199
91Harris/LineD-251
91Harris/ProC-640

Cassidy, David
(Dave)
89Hamil/Star-9
91StPete/ProC-2266

Cassidy, Howard
(Hop)
79Colum-25
90Tampa/DIMD-28CO

Cassidy, John P.
No Cards.

Cassidy, Joseph P.
(Joe)
No Cards.

Cassidy, Mike
91StPete/ClBest-2

Cassidy, Peter F.
(Pete)
90Target-909
T206

Cassini, Jack Dempsey
No Cards.

Castaigne, Arcilio
80Ander-2

Castain, Maurice
83Idaho-26
84Madis/Pol-22

Castaldo, Joe
91Hamil/ClBest-1
91Hamil/ProC-4030

Castaldo, Vince
91Single/ClBest-264
91Stockton/ClBest-19
91Stockton/ProC-3036

Castaneda, Nick
82AlexD-13
83AlexD-5
84PrWill-31
85Tigres-23
89Omaha/CMC-13
89Omaha/ProC-1722
91Louisvl/LineD-228
91Louisvl/ProC-2921

Castaneda, Robbie
91BendB/ProC-3687

Casteel, Brent
86WinSalem-3

Castellano, Miguel
91Gaston/ClBest-16
91Gaston/ProC-2693

Castellano, Pete
89Wythe/Star-5
90Peoria/Team-8
90Peoria/Team-9M
91CLAS/ProC-CAR40
91Single/ClBest-173
91WinSalem/ClBest-17
91WinSalem/ProC-2834

Castello, Brian
89Salinas/Cal-149TR

Caster, George
W753

Castiglione, Peter P.
(Pete)
49Eureka-156
50B-201
51B-17
52B-47
52T-260
54B-174

Castilla, Vinny
90Foil/Best-278
90SALAS/Star-28
90Sumter/Best-28
90Sumter/ProC-2439
91Greenvl/ClBest-15
91Greenvl/LineD-202
91Greenvl/ProC-3009
92F-666
92S/II-860
92T/91Debut-30

Castillo, Ace
75QuadC

Castillo, Alberto
89Kingspt/Star-5
90Pittsfld/Pucko-23

Castillo, Anthony
(Tony)
79Hawaii-24
80Hawaii-21
85Iowa-1
85Kingst-3
87Dunedin-12
88Dunedin/Star-2
89B-244
89D/Rook-12
90D-592
90OPC-620
90T-620
90UD-551
91F-685
91OPC-353
91Richm/LineD-428
91Richm/ProC-2560
91S-582
91T-353
91UD-458
92D/II-739
92F-499
92S/II-682

Castillo, Axel
88BurlInd/ProC-1781

Castillo, Ben
(Benny)
88Bristol/ProC-1892
89Fayette/ProC-1580
91SLCity/ProC-3222

Castillo, Bobby
79Albuq-22
79T-641
80Pol/Dodg-37
81D-298
81F-137
81Pol/Dodg-37
81T-146
82D-236
82F-2
82T-48
82T/Tr-17T

83F-608
83T-327
83T-771TL
84D-436
84F-559
84Nes/792-491
84OPC-329
84T-491
85Coke/Dodg-7
85F-274
85F/Up-U22
85T-588
85T/Tr-18T
86F-127
86T-252
90Target-119

Castillo, Braulio
89AS/Cal-9
89Bakers/Cal-202
91Classic/II-T85
91SanAn/LineD-533
91SanAn/ProC-2987
91Single/ClBest-307
92D/II-753
92S/II-824
92T-353
92T/91Debut-31
92UD-21SR

Castillo, Carlos
91Yakima/ClBest-23
91Yakima/ProC-4241

Castillo, Esteban M.
(Manny)
81Omaha-15
81T-66R
83D-253
83F-474
83T-258
84F-607
84Nes/792-562
84Syrac-24
84T-562

Castillo, Felipe
87Gaston-1
88Gaston/ProC-1008
89CharlR/Star-6
89Tulsa/GS-7
89Tulsa/Team-5
90Tulsa/ProC-1150

Castillo, Frank
89WinSalem/Star-4
91D/Rook-20
91Iowa/LineD-203
91UD/FinalEd-27F
92D/II-492
92F-378
92S/100RisSt-61
92S/I-399
92T-196
92T/91Debut-32
92UD-526

Castillo, Jeff
88GreatF-8

Castillo, Juan
80BurlB-22
80Utica-13
81BurlB-20
83ElPaso-10
84ElPaso-16
85Cram/PCL-205
86F/Up-U22
86Pol/Brew-3
87D-249
87F/Up-U18
87Pol/Brew-3
87T/Tr-20T
88D-363
88F-159
88OPC-362
88Pol/Brew-3
88S-429
88T-362
88T/Big-117
89D-530
89T-538
89T/Big-9
89UD-522
90ColoSp/ProC-41
90Pittsfld/Pucko-20
91Denver/LineD-132
91Denver/ProC-129
91SALAS/ProC-SAL13

Castillo, Luis T.
82Wausau-16
87Stockton-17
88ElPaso/Best-8

Castillo, M. Carmelo
(Carmen)
81Chatt-16
82Charl-19
83F-404
84Wheat/Ind-8
85D-590
85F-444
85OPC-184
85Polar/Ind-8
85T-184
85T/St-255
86D-460
86F-584
86OhHenry-8
86T/Tr-21T
87D-588
87F-250
87Gator-8
87T-513
88D-403
88F-606
88Gator-8
88S-581
88T-341
89D-374
89F-401
89S-497
89S/Tr-23
89T-637
89T/Big-91
89T/Tr-18T
89UD-487
90D-554
90F-371
90OPC-427
90S-123
90T-427
90UD-281
91F-606
91OPC-266
91S-608
91T-266

Castillo, Martin H.
(Marty)
80Evansvl-19
81Evans
82Evansvl-11
82F-265
82T-261R
83Evansvl-11
84D-247
84Nes/792-303
84T-303
85Cain's-5
85D-394
85F-5
85T-461
85Wendy-6
86T-788
89Pac/SenLg-88
89T/SenLg-10
90EliteSenLg-66
91Pac/SenLg-2

Castillo, Tomas
80Utica-12

Castino, John A.
77Orlan
78OrlTw
80OPC-76
80T-137
81D-488
81Drake-29
81F-554
81F/St-112
81OPC-304
81Sqt-29
81T-304
81T/SO-33
81T/St-99
82D-256
82F-549
82F/St-230
82K-29
82OPC-73
82T-396TL
82T-644
82T/St-209
83D-303
83F-609
83OPC-93
83T-93
83T/St-89
84D-120
84D-4
84D/AAS-7
84F-560
84Nes/792-237
84OPC-237
84T-237
84T/St-307
85OPC-298
85T-452

Castle, Donald Hardy
(Don)
77WHave

Castle, John Francis
No Cards.

Castleberry, Kevin
88CapeCod/Sum-111
90Durham/Team-6
91Miami/ClBest-18
91Miami/ProC-412

Castleman, Clydell
36G
R314
V355-36

Castleman, Foster E.
55Gol/Giants-3
56T-271
57T-237
58T-416
79TCMA-225
91Crown/Orio-71

Castner, Rodger
87Watertn-2
88Watertn/Pucko-4

Castro, Antionio
85Tigres-24

Castro, Bill
76OPC-293
76T-293
77T-528
78T-448
79T-133
80T-303
81D-578
81F-517
81T-271
82Tacoma-4
83F-109

Castro, Earnest
89Wausau/GS-3

Castro, Edgar
82Miami-15

Castro, Fidel
88MinorLg/Leg-11

Castro, Frank
85Beaum-15
86Beaum-5

Castro, Genaro
86LitFalls-5

Castro, Guillermo
82DayBe-1
83DayBe-5

Castro, Jose
81OkCty/TCMA-24
82Edmon-2
85BuffB-8
86Syrac-7
87Syrac-18
87Syrac/TCMA-12
88Omaha/CMC-24
88Omaha/ProC-1509
89Omaha/CMC-14
89Omaha/ProC-1731
90Indianap/CMC-23
90Indianap/ProC-287
90James/Pucko-29CO
91Rockford/ClBest-13CO
91Rockford/ProC-2063CO

Castro, Liliano
87Fayette-21
88Fayette/ProC-1101

Castro, Louis M.
No Cards.

Castro, Nelson
90Kissim/DIMD-6

Castro, Pablo
88StCath/ProC-2012

Castro, Tony
91Eugene/ClBest-1
91Eugene/ProC-3737

Cataline, Dan
81QuadC-16
83VeroB-24

Cater, Danny Anderson
64PhilBull-9
64T-482R
65OPC-253
65T-253
66T-398
67OPC-157
67T-157
68T-535
69MB-55
69MLB/St-84
69OPC-1LL
69OPC-44
69T-1LL
69T-44
69T-556M
69T/St-213
69Trans-12
70MLB/St-243
70OPC-437
70T-437
71K-30
71MD
71MLB/St-485
71OPC-358
71T-358
71T/Coins-14
72MB-71
72T-676
73OPC-317
73T-317
74OPC-543
74T-543
75OPC-645
75T-645
75T/M-645

Cates, Eli Eldo
No Cards.

Cates, Tim
83Memphis-11
85Indianap-8

Cathcart, Gary
86FtLaud-5
87Albany-9
88Albany/ProC-1335

Cather, Theodore P.
(Ted)
15CJ-145

Cato, Keefe
81Water-2
82Water-3
83Water-1
84Wichita/Rock-14
85Cram/PCL-118
85T-367
86Omaha-4

Cato, Wayne
76Cedar
80Clinton-26MG

Caton, James Howard
(Buster)
No Cards.

Catterson, Thomas H.
(Tom)
90Target-910

Caudill, Bill
76ArkTr
80T-103
81D-586
81F-306
81OPC-346
81T-574
81T/St-152
82D-426
82F-590
82T-303
82T/Tr-18T
83D-302
83F-475
83Nalley-5
83OPC-78
83T-78
83T/St-118
84D-118
84F-608
84F/St-76
84F/X-24
84Mother/A's-12
84Nes/792-769
84OPC-299
84T-769
84T/St-345
84T/Tr-23
85D-96
85F-419
85F/St-100
85F/Up-U23
85Leaf-154
85OPC-275
85OPC/Post-23
85T-685
85T/St-322
85T/Tr-19T
85Tor/Fire-7
86Ault-36
86D-317
86F-55
86OPC-207
86T-435
86Tor/Fire-5
87F-221
87Mother/A's-24
87OPC-156
87T-733

Caughey, Wayne
79Toledo-11
80Albuq-18
81Albuq/TCMA-14
82Portl-12

Cauley, Chris
88Tampa/Star-4
89Saraso/Star-4

Caulfield, John J.
No Cards.

Caulfield, Tom
83Erie-23

Causey, Cecil
(Red)
E120
E121/80
E122
W501-65

Causey, James Wayne
(Wayne)
62Salada-100
62Shirriff-100
62T-496
63T-539
64T-75
64T/Coins-102
64T/Coins-161AAS
64T/Coins-161BAS
64T/S-45
64T/St-87
64T/SU
64T/tatt
65T-425
65T/E-21
65T/trans-8
66T-366
67T-286
68T-522
69OPC-33
69T-33
78TCMA-8
91Crown/Orio-72

Cavalier, Kevin
87Jamestn-26
88WPalmB/Star-4

Cavallo, Pablo
77Newar
78Newar

Cavanaugh, John J.
No Cards.

Cavarretta, Phil
35BU-101
39Exh
41DP-104
47TipTop
48L-168
49B-6
49Eureka-53
50B-195
51B-138
52B-126
52StarCal/L-80F
52T-295
52TipTop
53B/Col-30MG
54T-55MG
55B-282MG
74Laugh/ASG-44
76SSPC-617CO

89Pac/Leg-131
91T/Arc53-295MG
PM10/Sm-23
PR1-3
R312/M
R314
R423-13
V355-54
WG8-6

Cavazzoni, Ken
91Princet/ClBest-5
91Princet/ProC-3519

Caveney, James C.
(Ike or Jimmy)
21Exh-22
E120
V61-116
W573

Cavers, Mike
89Freder/Star-2
90Hagers/Best-25
90Hagers/ProC-1404
90Hagers/Star-5

Cayson, Tony
89Belling/Legoe-25

Cebuhar, John
88Hamil/ProC-1721
89Hamil/Star-8

Ceccarelli, Art
55Rodeo
58T-191
59T-226
60T-156
91Crown/Orio-73

Cecchetti, George
81Chatt-14
82Chatt-14
83BuffB-22
84BuffB-2
85Water-20
86Maine-3

Cecchini, Jim
86Jaxvl/TCMA-3

Cecena, Jose
86Reading-5
88D/Rook-6
88F/Up-U62
88Mother/R-12
88T/Tr-26T
89F-516
89S/HotRook-35
89T-683
89UD-560

Cecil, Rex
47Centen-4
49Remar

Cecil, Timothy
90CharWh/Best-12
90CharWh/ProC-2233
91CharWh/ClBest-1
91CharWh/ProC-2878
91Single/ClBest-262

Cedeno, Andujar
89Ashvl/ProC-952
90A&AASingle/ProC-58
90B-77
90ColMud/Best-3
90ColMud/ProC-1351
90ColMud/Star-7
90Foil/Best-72
91B-563
91Classic/200-200
91Classic/I-43
91F-502
91F/Ultra-135
91Leaf/GRook-BC20
91Leaf/StudPrev-12
91MajorLg/Pins-45
91OPC-646
91S-753RP
91S/Rook40-40
91T-646
91T/90Debut-28
91T/StClub/II-476
91Tucson/LineD-606
91Tucson/ProC-2218
91UD-23SR
92Classic/I-23
92D/II-549
92F-430
92S/100RisSt-65
92S/II-599
92T-288
92UD-257

Cedeno, Blas
91Bristol/ClBest-19
91Bristol/ProC-3596

Cedeno, Cesar
71OPC-237
71T-237
71T/S-15
72OPC-65
72T-65
73K-13
73OPC-290
73T-290
74OPC-200
74OPC-337AS
74T-200
74T-337AS
74T/St-31
75Ho-17
75Ho/Twink-17
75OPC-590
75T-590
75T/M-590
76Crane-12
76Ho-47
76Ho/Twink-47
76MSA/Disc
76OPC-460
76SSPC-63
76T-460
77BurgChef-7
77Ho-58
77OPC-131
77T-90
77T/S-13
78BK/Ast-18
78Ho-50
78OPC-226
78T-650
78Wiffle/Discs-16
79Ho-91
79OPC-294
79T-570
80BK/PHR-25
80K-36
80OPC-193
80T-370
80T/S-56
81Coke
81D-263
81Drake-20
81F-59
81F/St-35
81K-14
81MSA/Disc-8
81OPC-190
81PermaGr/CC-25
81T-190
81T/HT
81T/SO-77
81T/St-167
81T/St-258
82Coke/Reds
82D-118
82F-213
82F/St-41
82OPC-48
82T-640
82T/St-47
82T/Tr-19T
83D-43
83F-587
83OPC-238
83T-351TL
83T-475
83T/St-231
84D-306
84F-465
85FunFood/Pin-42
84Nes/792-705LL
84Nes/792-725
84OPC-191
84T-705LL
84T-725
84T/St-54
85D-447
85F-531
85Leaf-87
85OPC-54
85T-54
85T/St-55
85ThomMc/Discs-26
86Coke/Dodg-6
86D-648
86F-29
86Mother/Ast-11
86OPC-224
86T-224
89Pac/SenLg-62
89T/SenLg-69
89TM/SenLg-118M
89TM/SenLg-20
90EliteSenLg-79
90Swell/Great-41
90Target-120
91LineD-36
91Pac/SenLg-40
91Pac/SenLg-53
91Swell/Great-104

Cedeno, Domingo
89Myrtle/ProC-1456
90Dunedin/Star-5
90Visalia/Cal-68
90Visalia/ProC-2166
91Knoxvl/LineD-352
91Knoxvl/ProC-1773

Cedeno, Ramon
88Ashvl/ProC-1053
89Osceola/Star-4

Cedeno, Vinicio
86MidldA-4
87MidldA-8
88MidldA/GS-4
89MidldA/GS-9

Centala, Scott
88CapeCod/Sum-123
89Eugene/Best-7
90Foil/Best-29
90Memphis/Best-14
90Memphis/ProC-1001
90Memphis/Star-4

Centeno, Jose
75Clinton

Cento, Tony
86AppFx-6
87Penin-28

Cepeda, Octavio
86Macon-5
87Salem-5

Cepeda, Orlando M.
58SFCallB-5
58T-343
59Bz
59T-390
59T-553AS
60Bz-10
60L-128
60T-450
60T/tatt-8
61P-144
61T-435
61T/St-75
62Bz
62Exh
62J-136
62P-136
62P/Can-136
62Salada-175
62Shirriff-175
62T-390AS
62T-40
62T-401M
62T-54LL
62T/bucks
62T/St-195
63Bz-22
63Exh
63F-64
63J-101
63P-101
63Salada-13
63T-3LL
63T-520
63T/SO
64T-306
64T-390
64T-9LL
64T/Coins-142AS
64T/Coins-63
64T/S-55
64T/St-50
64T/SU
64T/tatt
64Wheat/St-10
65OldLond-6
65OPC-4LL
65T-360
65T-4LL
65T/E-45
65T/trans-9
66OPC-132
66T-132
67OPC-20
67OPC/PI-9
67T-20
67T/PI-9
67T/Test/SU-13
68Bz-6
68OPC-3LL
68T-200
68T-362AS
68T-3LL
68T/G-32
68T/Post-12
69MB-56
69MLB/St-113
69MLBPA/Pin-38
69T-385
69T/St-113
70MLB/St-4
70T-555
70T/CB
71Bz
71Bz/Test-33
71MD
71MLB/St-7
71OPC-605
71T-605
71T/Coins-61
71T/GM-26
71T/tatt-3
72MB-72
72OPC-195
72T-195
73OPC-545
73T-545
74K-24
74OPC-83
74T-83
74T/St-132
75OPC-205MV
75T-205MV
75T/M-205MV
78TCMA-50
80GlenF/B-26CO
80GlenF/C-25CO
82KMart-12
83Kaline-51M
83MLBPA/Pin-21
84Mother/Giants-11
85CircK-24
86Sf/Dec-48M
88Pac/Leg-94
89Swell-8
90Pac/Legend-65
90Swell/Great-28
91Swell/Great-105
Exh47
PM10/Sm-24
PM10/Sm-25

Cepicky, Scott
90Foil/Best-173
90SoBend/Best-2
91FSLAS/ProC-FSL28
91Saraso/ClBest-15
91Saraso/ProC-1118
91Single/ClBest-86

Cerame, Mike
89Pulaski/ProC-1903
90Pulaski/Best-29
91Pulaski/ClBest-30TR

Cerdan, Marcel
47HomogBond-8BOX
D305

Cerefin, Mike
85Osceola/Team-5

Cermak, Edward Hugo
(Ed)
No Cards.

Cerny, Chris
88Bakers/Cal-252
89Boise/ProC-1999

Cerny, Mark
89Billings/ProC-2054
90Erie/Star-2

Cerny, Marty
87PortChar-7
88Gaston/ProC-1016
89Miami/I/Star-4
89Miami/II/Star-3

Cerny, Scott
86Cram/PCL-86
87QuadC-24
88CalLgAS-33
88PalmSp/Cal-101
88PalmSp/ProC-1440
89MidldA/GS-10

Cerone, Richard Aldo
(Rick)
76SSPC-516
77OPC-76
77T-476R
78OPC-129
78T-469
79OPC-72
79T-152
80OPC-311
80T-591
81D-346
81F-83
81F/St-88
81OPC-335
81T-335
81T/HT
81T/SO-28
81T/St-109
81T/St-248
82D-199
82F-31
82F/St-118
82F/St-238M
82OPC-45
82T-45
82T/St-218
83D-577
83F-376
83OPC-254
83RoyRog/Disc-1
83T-254
84D-492
84F-121
84Nes/792-617
84OPC-228
84T-617
85D-274
85F-123
85F/Up-U24
85Ho/Braves-6
85OPC-337
85Pol/Atl-5
85T-429
85T/Tr-20T
86D-310
86F-511
86F/Up-U23
86OPC-203
86Pol/Brew-11
86T-747
86T/Tr-22T
87F-340
87T-129
87T/Tr-21T
88D-351
88D/Best-332
88D/RedSox/Bk-NEW
88F-203
88F/Up-U6
88Panini/St-151
88S-486
88S/Tr-21T
88T-561
88T/Tr-27T
89D-398
89D/Best-308
89F-84
89OPC-96
89S-396
89T-96
89T/Big-119
89UD-152
90B-435
90D-305
90F-270
90OPC-303
90PublInt/St-451
90S-139
90S/NWest-28
90S/Tr-63T
90T-303
90T/St-1HL
90T/Tr-21T
90T/TVYank-20
90UD-405
91B-468

91F-660
91F/UltraUp-U96
91F/Up-U101
91Kahn/Mets-13
91Leaf/II-493
91OPC-237
91S-580
91S/RookTr-41T
91T-237
91T/StClub/II-511
91T/Tr-21T
92D/I-335
92T-643

Cerqueira, Jeff
88CapeCod/Sum-83

Cerrud, Roberto
80Utica-14

Cerutti, John
83Knoxvl-3
84Syrac-31
85Syrac-27
86D/Rook-20
86F/Up-U24
86Sf/Rook-36
86Syrac-8
86T/Tr-23T
87D-442
87F-222
87Leaf-210
87OPC-282
87T-557
87Tor/Fire-3
87ToysRUs-6
88D-321
88F-105
88Leaf-152
88OPC-191
88S-98
88T-191
88Tor/Fire-55
89B-247
89D-467
89F-228
89OPC-347
89S-304
89T-347
89Tor/Fire-55
89UD-129
90B-507
90D-645
90F-78
90Leaf/I-27
90OPC-211
90Panini/St-177
90PublInt/St-511
90S-429
90Sf-86
90T-211
90T/St-195
90Tor/BlueJ-55
90UD-485
91B-139
91CokeK/Tiger-55
91D-467
91F-172
91F/Up-U22
91Leaf/II-270
91OPC-687A
91OPC-687B
91S-786
91S/RookTr-40T
91T-687A
91T-687B
91T/StClub/II-445
91UD-585
92D/II-709
92F-129
92S/I-179
92T-487
92UD-487

Cerv, Robert Henry
(Bob)
53T-210
55B-306
56T-288
57T-269
58T-329
59Armour-6
59Bz
59HRDerby-5
59T-100
60Bz-15
60T-415
61P-13
61T-563
61T/St-170
62T-169
79TCMA-162
91T/Arc53-210
Exh47

Cesari, Jeff
89Geneva/ProC-1868

Cesarlo, Jim
83TriCit-23

Cespedes, Teodoro
89Everett/Star-4

Cey, Ronald Charles
(Ron)
72T-761R
73OPC-615R
73T-615R
74OPC-315
74T-315
74T/St-42
75Ho-61
75Ho/Twink-61
75OPC-390
75T-390
75T/M-390
76Crane-13
76Ho-63
76MSA/Disc
76OPC-370
76SSPC-75
76T-370
77BurgChef-153
77Ho-89
77K-18
77OPC-199
77T-50
77T/CS-14
78Ho-93
78K-24
78OPC-130
78T-630
78Wiffle/Discs-17
79Ho-28
79OPC-94
79T-190
80K-19
80OPC-267
80Pol/Dodg-10
80T-510
81D-296
81F-126
81F/St-3
81OPC-260
81Pol/Dodg-10
81T-260
81T/HT
81T/SO-73
81T/St-177
82D-210
82F-3
82F/St-3
82K-46
82OPC-216
82OPC-367IA
82Pol/Dodg-10
82T-410
82T-411IA
82T/St-51
83D-84
83D/AAS-21
83F-204
83OPC-15
83T-15
83T/St-244
83T/Tr-19
83Thorn-11
84D-361
84Drake-7
84F-490
85FunFood/Pin-89
84Nes/792-357
84OPC-357
84SevenUp-11
84T-357
84T/St-41
85D-320
85Drake-6
85F-52
85F/St-19
85Leaf-84
85OPC-366
85SevenUp-11
85T-768
85T/St-42
86Cub/Unocal-3
86D-198
86F-363
86Gator-11
86OPC-194
86Sf-150M
86T-669
87F-556
87OPC-322
87OPC-C
87Smok/Dodg-4
87T-767
87T-C
87T/Tr-22T
88Smok/Dodg-15M
88Smok/Dodg-21M
88Smok/Dodg-27
89Smok/Dodg-82
90Target-121

Chacon, Elio R.
60T-543
62T-256
66Pep/Tul
91WIZMets-68

Chacon, Troy
88CapeCod/Sum-183

Chadbourne, Chester
No Cards.

Chadwick, Henry
50Call
80SSPC/HOF
90LitSun-2

Chadwick, Ray
86Edmon-3
87D-505
88BirmB/Best-4
90Omaha/CMC-2
90Omaha/ProC-58

Chadwick, Robert
86NewBrit-6TR
87NewBrit-9TR
88NewBrit/ProC-893

Chafin, John
88Utica/Pucko-14
91Elmira/ClBest-23
91Elmira/ProC-3263

Chagnon, Leon
R314/Can

Chajin, David
91Johnson/ProC-3970

Chakales, Bob
52NumNum-9
52T-120
55B-148
57T-261
61BeeHive-4
91Crown/Orio-74

Chalk, David Lee
(Dave)
74OPC-597R
74T-597R
75Ho-46
75Ho/Twink-46
75OPC-64
75T-64
75T/M-64
76Ho-59
76Ho/Twink-59
76OPC-52
76SSPC-194
76T-52
77BurgChef-119
77T-315
78T-178
79OPC-362
79T-682
80OPC-137
80T-261
81D-101
81F-35
82D-590
82F-407
82T-462

Chalmers, George
D329-29
D350/2-27
M101/4-29
M101/5-27
T207
T222

Chamberlain, Bill
78Wausau

Chamberlain, Craig
80T-417
81Omaha-4
81T-274
82Phoenix
83Phoenix/BHN-23
88CharlK/Pep-12

Chamberlain, Elton
N172

Chamberlain, Joseph
No Cards.

Chamberlain, Tom
78StPete
79ArkTr-19

Chamberlain, Wesley
(Wes)
87Watertn-12
88Augusta/ProC-359
89BBAmerAA/BPro-AA1
89Harris/ProC-296
89Harris/Star-5
90BuffB/CMC-23
90BuffB/ProC-386
90BuffB/Team-6
91B-505
91Classic/200-92
91Classic/I-80
91Classic/III-T8
91D-423RR
91D/Rook-3
91F-391
91F/Ultra-258
91Leaf/I-178
91Leaf/Stud-211
91OPC-603
91Phill/Medford-8
91S-713RP
91S/Rook40-14
91ScranWB/ProC-2550
91T-603A
91T-603B
91T/90Debut-29
91T/StClub/II-317
91UD-626
92D/I-384
92F-524
92F/RookSlns-6
92S/100RisSt-25
92S/I-384
92T-14
92UD-347

Chamberlin, Buck
79Toledo-13
80Toledo-14
81Toledo-2
82Toledo-24

Chambers, Albert E.
(Al)
81LynnS-20
82SLCity-5
83D-649
83SLCity-21
84Cram/PCL-188
85Cram/PCL-80
85D-389
85T-277FDP
87ColAst/ProC-1

Chambers, Carl
87Watlo-17

Chambers, Cliff
47Signal
49Eureka-157
50B-202
51B-131
51FB
51T/RB-25
52B-14
52RM-NL4
52StarCal/L-81C
52T-68
53Hunter
54B-126

Chambers, Jeff
89Elizab/Star-31

Chambers, Mark
91Pulaski/ClBest-11
91Pulaski/ProC-4017

Chambers, Travis
86Clearw-3
87Maine-19
87Maine/TCMA-3
88Maine/CMC-2
88Maine/ProC-283
89Jaxvl/Best-10
89Jaxvl/ProC-162
90Indianap/CMC-4
90Indianap/ProC-282

Chambliss, Carroll C.
(Chris)
72OPC-142
72T-142
73OPC-11
73T-11
74OPC-384
74T-384
74T/DE-15
74T/St-162
75OPC-585
75T-585
75T/M-585
76Ho-58
76Ho/Twink-58
76OPC-65
76SSPC-434
76T-65
77BK/Y-12
77BurgChef-173
77Ho-98
77K-52
77OPC-49
77T-220
78BK/Y-12
78K-13
78OPC-145
78T-485
78Wiffle/Discs-18
79BK/Y-12
79K-37
79OPC-171
79T-335
80OPC-328
80T-625
81D-219
81F-252
81F/St-81
81OPC-155
81Pol/Atl-10
81T/St-147
82BK/Lids-6
82D-47
82F-433
82F/St-70
82K-52
82OPC-320
82OPC-321IA
82Pol/Atl-10
82T-320
82T-321IA
82T/St-17
83D-123
83F-134
83OPC-11
83Pol/Atl-10
83T-792
83T/St-212
84D-537
84D/AAS-29
84F-175
85FunFood/Pin-123
84Nes/792-50
84OPC-50
84Pol/Atl-10
84T-50
84T/St-28
85D-287
85F-322
85Ho/Braves-7
85Leaf-168
85OPC-187
85Pol/Atl-10
85T-518
85T/St-29
86D-618
86F-512
86Pol/Atl-10
86T-293
87F-513
87OPC-204
87T-777
89London/ProC-1378MG
91Greenvl/ClBest-25MG
91Greenvl/LineD-224MG
91Greenvl/ProC-3018MG

Champ, Jeff
89Penin/Star-3

Champagne, Boo
86Cram/PCL-44
87FtMyr-8

Champion, Billy
70OPC-149
70T-149
71MLB/St-173
71OPC-323
71T-323
72T-599
73OPC-74
73T-74
74OPC-391
74T-391
75Ho-118
75OPC-256
75T-256
75T/M-256
76OPC-501
76T-501
Champion, Brian
89Durham/Team-5
89Durham/Star-5
89Star/Wax-69
90CLAS/CL-31
90Durham/Team-3
90Greenvl/Best-3
91Greenvl/ClBest-16
91Greenvl/LineD-203
91Greenvl/ProC-3010
91Single/ClBest-177
Champion, Keith
88Savan/ProC-337
89Savan/ProC-344
90Spring/Best-26MG
Champion, Kirk
89SoBend/GS-5
90SoBend/Best-27CO
90SoBend/ClBest-26CO
91SoBend/ProC-2874CO
Champion, Randall
83StPete-14
87ArkTr-8
Champion, Robert M.
(Mike)
77Padre/SchCd-5
77Padre/SchCd-6
77T-494R
78Padre/FamFun-5
78T-683
79Tacoma-14
80Tacoma-16
Chance, Dean
62T-194
63Exh
63J-32
63P-32
63T-355
63T-6LL
64T-32
64T/Coins-67
64T/S-16
65Bz-5
65OldLond-22
65OPC-11LL
65OPC-140
65OPC-7LL
65OPC-9LL
65T-11LL
65T-140
65T-7LL
65T-9LL
65T/E-66
65T/trans-10
65T/trans-42
66Bz-25
66T-340
66T/RO-83
67Bz-25
67T-380
67T/Test/SU-12
68Bz-10
68Coke
68Dexter-23
68OPC-10LL
68OPC-12LL
68T-10LL
68T-12LL
68T-255
68T/G-16
68T/Post-1
69MB-57
69MLB/St-66
69MLBPA/Pin-5
69T-620
69T/S-21
69T/St-193
70K-67
70MLB/St-195
70T-625
71MLB/St-148
71OPC-36
71T-36
72MB-73
89Smok/Angels-2
89Swell-89
91WIZMets-69
Exh47
Chance, Frank Leroy
10Domino-22
11Helmar-92
12Sweet/Pin-81A
12Sweet/Pin-81BLL
14CJ-99
14Piedmont/St-10
40PB-234
48Exh/HOF
50Callahan
60Exh/HOF-6
60F-50
61F-98
63Bz/ATG-25
69Bz/Sm
73F/Wild-2
76Motor-11
80Pac/Leg-84
80SSPC/HOF
D304
D350/2-28
E101
E103
E105
E107
E224
E254
E270/1
E270/2
E286
E90/1
E90/3
E91
E92
E93
E94
E95
E98
M101/5-28
M116
PM1-2
S74-59
T201
T202
T204
T205
T206
T207
T213/blue
T213/brown
T215/blue
T215/brown
T216
T222
T3-47
W555
WG3-9
WG4-3
WG5-8
WG6-8
Chance, Robert
(Bob)
64T-146R
65Bz-18
65OPC-224
65T-224
66T-564
67T-349
69T-523
78TCMA-82
Chance, Tony
86Macon-6
86PrWill-5
87Salem-25
88Harris/ProC-854
89UD-3SR
90RochR/CMC-19
90RochR/ProC-713
91RochR/LineD-451
91RochR/ProC-1913
Chandler, A.B.
(Happy)
49Eureka-1
50Callahan
80SSPC/HOF
89HOF/St-97
Chandler, Bob
90Padre/MagUno-16ANN
Chandler, Ed
52Mother-63
90Target-122
Chandler, Ken
81Wisco-13
Chandler, Spud
40PB-181
44Yank/St-5
89Pac/Leg-136
Exh47
Chaney, Darrel Lee
69T-624R
70OPC-3
70T-3
71MLB/St-53
71OPC-632
71T-632
72OPC-136
72T-136
73OPC-507
73T-507
74OPC-559
74T-559
75OPC-581
75T-581
75T/M-581
76OPC-259
76SSPC-33
76T-259
76T/Tr-259T
77BurgChef-216
77Ho-57
77OPC-134
77T-384
78T-443
79OPC-91
79T-184
Chaney, Keith
91Pulaski/ClBest-5
91Pulaski/ProC-4011
Chaney, Norma
89Welland/Pucko-35M
Channell, Lester C.
(Les)
No Cards.
Chant, Charles J.
(Charlie)
75Tucson-7
Chanye, Bruce
83MidldC-10
Chapin, Darrin
88FtLaud/Star-4
89Albany/ProC-340
89Albany/Star-3
89Colum/CMC-30
90A&AASingle/ProC-19
90Albany/ProC-1029
90Albany/Star-1
90ColClip/CMC-20
90ColClip/ProC-668
91ColClip/LineD-103
91ColClip/ProC-590
92D/II-745
92T/91Debut-33
Chaplin, Bert Edgar
(Ed)
No Cards.
Chapman, Calvin Louis
No Cards.
Chapman, Dan
(AGM)
88Stockton/Cal-205
88Stockton/ProC-751
89Stockton/Best-28
89Stockton/Cal-174
89Stockton/ProC-398
89Stockton/Star-23
Chapman, Glenn J.
90Target-911
Chapman, Harry E.
No Cards.
Chapman, John Curtis
(Jack)
No Cards.
Chapman, Kelvin Keith
77Wausau
79Tidew-18
80Tidew-18
81Syrac-13
82Tidew-2
83Tidew-7
84Tidew-27
85D-626
85F-75
85T-751
86T-492
91WIZMets-70
Chapman, Mark
88Beloit/GS-10
88MidwLAS/GS-59
89ElPaso/GS-4
91ElPaso/LineD-178
91ElPaso/ProC-2739
Chapman, Nathan
79Colum-22
82Nashvl-6
Chapman, Raymond J.
(Ray)
BF2-21
D327
D328-26
D329-30
D350/2-29
E135-26
M101/4-30
M101/5-29
Chapman, Ron
85Albany-15
Chapman, Samuel Blake
(Sam)
40PB-194
41DP-125
41PB-44
48L-26
49B-112
50B-104
51B-9
51T/BB-52
52Mother-33
52NTea
Chapman, William B.
(Ben)
32Orbit/num-99
33G-191
34DS-38
34G-9
35BU-188
35BU-62
37OPC-130
41DP-74
52T-391MG
88Conlon/3-6
88Conlon/AmAS-4
90Target-123
R303/A
R303/B
R310
R313
R332-40
V300
V354-51
V355-90
Chappas, Harold Perry
(Harry)
80T-347
Chappell, Laverne A.
(Larry)
No Cards.
Chappelle, William
T206
T213/blue
Charboneau, Joseph
(Joe)
81D-82
81Drake-21
81F-397
81K-54
81OPC-13
81Sqt-32
81T-13
81T/SO-12
81T/St-66
82D-363
82F-362
82F/St-192
82OPC-211
82T-630
82Wheat/Ind
83BuffB-23
84PrWill-15
88Chatt/Team-3
Charbonnet, Mark
89BurlInd/Star-4
90Reno/Cal-269
90Watertn/Star-3
91ColInd/ClBest-7
91ColInd/ProC-1497
Charland, Colin
86Cram/PCL-76
87PalmSp-9
88CalLgAS-31
88PalmSp/Cal-85
88PalmSp/ProC-1447
89Edmon/CMC-6
89Edmon/ProC-565
90F-640M
Charles, Edwin
(Ed)
62T-595R
63J-89
63P-89
63T-67
64T-475
64T/Coins-117
64T/St-1
64T/SU
65OPC-35
65T-35
66T-422
66T/RO-106
67OPC-182
67T-182
68T-563
69MB-58
69MLB/St-164
69T-245
69T/St-62
78TCMA-25
90Swell/Great-123
91WIZMets-71
Charles, Ezzard
51BR-A13
Charles, Frank
91Everett/ClBest-11
91Everett/ProC-3917
Charles, Raymond
(Chappy)
M116
T206
T213/brown
Charleston, Oscar
74Laugh/Black-34
76Laugh/Clown-30
86Negro/Frit-24
86Negro/Frit-4
86Negro/Frit-8
88Conlon/NegAS-2
88Negro/Duques-7
90Negro/Star-36
Charlton, Norm
86Vermont-3
87Nashvl-2
88Nashvl/CMC-3
88Nashvl/ProC-488
88Nashvl/Team-6
89D-544
89F-155
89Kahn/Reds-37
89S-646
89S/YS/II-15
89T-737
89UD/Ext-783
90D-426
90F-416
90Kahn/Reds-6
90Leaf/II-334
90OPC-289
90PublInt/St-24
90S-248
90T-289
90UD-566
91B-690
91D-384
91F-60
91F/Ultra-90
91Kahn/Reds-37
91Leaf/II-414
91OPC-309
91Pep/Reds-5
91S-530
91T-309
91T/StClub/II-305
91UD-394

92D/I-102
92F-402
92S/I-267
92T-649
92UD-677

Charno, Joe
88Ashvl/ProC-1055
89Ashvl/ProC-962

Charpia, Reed
89Helena/SP-16

Charry, Stephen
83Madis/LF-2TD

Chartak, Michael G.
(Mike)
No Cards.

Charton, Frank
(Pete)
64T-459R
66T-329

Chase, Dave
80Ander-12

Chase, Harold Homer
(Hal)
10Domino-23
11Helmar-40
12Sweet/Pin-32A
12Sweet/Pin-32B
14Piedmont/St-11
75F/Pion-22
88Conlon/4-5
91Conlon/Sport-160
D303
D304
E101
E102
E103
E106
E254
E270/2
E300
E90/1
E92
E93
E98
M116
S74-20
T201
T202
T205
T206
T213/blue
T213/brown
T216
T3-6
W514-114
W555
WG5-9
WG6-9

Chase, Ken
39PB-59
40PB-19

Chase, Scott
89Oneonta/ProC-2107

Chasey, Mark
88Utica/Pucko-4
89SoBend/GS-21
90Saraso/Star-4
91BirmB/LineD-54
91BirmB/ProC-1459

Chasin, David
91Johnson/ClBest-22

Chasteen, Steve
83Idaho-2

Chatham, Charles L.
(Buster)
No Cards.

Chatterton, James M.
(Jim)
No Cards.

Chauncey, Keathel
76SanAn/Team-6
77Tucson
78Cr/PCL-58
79Tucson-19
80WHave-21
81Toledo-19

Chavarria, Oswaldo Q.
(Ossie)
67T-344

Chaves, Rafael
86CharRain-5

Chavez, Devin
91Hunting/ClBest-7
91Hunting/ProC-3341

Chavez, Harold P.
WG7-9

Chavez, Joe
86Beaum-6TR
88Wichita-TR
89Wichita/Rock-TR

Chavez, Pedro
83BirmB-21
86Nashvl-4
87GlenF-21
88Toledo/CMC-17
88Toledo/ProC-601

Chavez, Rafael
88CalLgAS-42
88River/Cal-209
88River/ProC-1429
89AubAs/ProC-25
89Wichita/Rock-14
90Wichita/Rock-4
91Wichita/LineD-603
91Wichita/ProC-2592

Chavez, Raul
91BurlAs/ClBest-13
91BurlAs/ProC-2807

Chavez, Samuel
(Sam)
88Cedar/ProC-1160
89SoBend/GS-9
90Huntsvl/Best-3

Chech, Charles
E90/1
T204

Checo, Pedro
89Bristol/Star-4

Cheek, Carey
86PrWill-6

Cheek, Harry G.
(Harry)
No Cards.

Cheek, Patrick
90Princet/DIMD-4
91Batavia/ClBest-7
91Batavia/ProC-3489

Cheetham, Sean
90A&AASingle/ProC-185
90Hunting/ProC-3273
91B-414
91Single/ClBest-231
91WinSalem/ClBest-3
91WinSalem/ProC-2822

Cheeves, Virgil
(Chief)
E120
E126-23
V61-84

Chelette, Mark
80SanJose/JITB-5
81Wausau-23

Chelini, Dan
83Butte-2

Chelini, Italo
35BU-114

Chenevey, Jim
88Madis-10
88MidwLAS/GS-53

Cheney, Larry
14CJ-89
15CJ-89
16FleischBrd-15
90Target-124
D328-27
D329-31
D350/2-30
E135-27
M101/4-31
M101/5-30
WG4-4

Cheney, Tom
57T-359
61T-494
63Exh
63F-27
63J-99
63P-99
78TCMA-85
Exh47
WG9-27

Cherry, Gus
85Omaha-6

Cherry, Joe
76Laugh/Clown-15
76Laugh/Clown-32

Cherry, Lamar
91Martins/ClBest-12
91Martins/ProC-3459

Cherry, Michael
85VeroB-23
86VeroB-3

Cherry, Paul
83Spring/LF-3
86ArkTr-4
87Louisvl-9
88Toledo/CMC-9
88Toledo/ProC-591

Chervinko, Paul
90Target-912

Chesbro, Jack
48Exh/HOF
50Callahan
61F-13
61T-407M
63Bz/ATG-3
69Bz/Sm
72F/FFeat-39
72Laugh/GF-12
79T-416M
80SSPC/HOF
85Woolwth-7
E107
T206
WG2-7

Cheshire, Donnie
78StPete

Chesnes, Bob
49B-13
50B-70

Cheso, Reno
49Sommer-11
53Mother-33

Chestnut, Troy
87Knoxvl-7

Chevalier, Bonel
89Belling/Legoe-23

Chevez, Tony
78RochR
79RochR-19
91Crown/Orio-75

Chevolek, Tom
80ElPaso-5

Chiamparino, Scott
88Huntsvl/BK-2
88Modesto-8
88Modesto/Cal-64
90AAAGame/ProC-AAA49
90S/Tr-108T
90Tacoma/CMC-3
90Tacoma/ProC-86
91B-282
91Classic/200-183
91Classic/I-84
91D-42RR
91D/Preview-3
91F/Ultra-375MLP
91Leaf/II-401
91Leaf/Stud-122
91MajorLg/Pins-37
91Mother/Rang-14
91OPC-676
91S-352A
91S-352B
91S/100RisSt-14
91S/Rook40-29
91T-676
91T/90Debut-30
91T/StClub/II-384
91UD-8SR
92S/II-688
92T-277

Chick, Bruce
91CLAS/ProC-CAR22
91LynchRS/ClBest-20
91LynchRS/ProC-1210
91Single/ClBest-13

Chicken, San Diego
82D-531
83D-645
84D-651
84Smok/Padres-4

Chiffer, Floyd
81Hawaii
83D-44
83F-354
83T-298
85Toledo-32
87Richm/Crown-28
87Richm/TCMA-2

Chikida, Honen
89Salinas/ProC-1812

Childers, Bob
88Alaska/Team-6

Childers, Jeffrey
85Beaum-1
88Modesto-7
88Wichita-30

Childress, Chip
83Durham-1
84Durham-13
85Durham-20
86Greenvl/Team-5

Childress, Rocky
85Cram/PCL-31
85Phill/TastyK-45
86Phill/TastyK-50
87Tucson-10
88D-554
88F-442
88T-643
88Tucson/CMC-8
88Tucson/ProC-181
88Tucson/JP-6
89Tucson/CMC-1
89Tucson/ProC-194
89Tucson/JP-4
90Tidew/CMC-3
90Tidew/ProC-536

Childress, Willie J.
87Greenvl/Best-11

Childs, Clarence A.
(Cupid)
N172

Childs, Peter Pierre
(Pete)
No Cards.

Chiles, Barry
90Pulaski/Best-2
90Pulaski/ProC-3100
91Macon/ClBest-1
91Macon/ProC-855

Chiles, Pearce Nuget
No Cards.

Chiles, Richard F.
(Rich)
72OPC-56
72T-56
73OPC-617
73T-617
78T-193
79T-498
79Tacoma-20
91WIZMets-72

Chimelis, Joel
88SoOreg/ProC-1703
89Modesto/Cal-279
89Modesto/Chong-22
90Reno/Cal-267
91Huntsvl/ClBest-7
91Huntsvl/LineD-282
91HuntsvlProC-1802

Ching, Maurice
(Mo)
83Greens-17
84Greens-22
86Albany/TCMA-18

Chiozza, Louis Peo
(Lou)
34DS-80
38ONG/Pin-2
39PB-58
40PB-157
41G-3
41G-3

Chipman, Robert
(Bob)
47TipTop
49B-184
49Eureka-54
50B-192
52B-228
52T-388
90Target-125

Chipple, Walter John
(Walt)
No Cards.

Chireno, Manny
87Beloit-24

Chism, Thomas R.
(Tom)
78RochR
79RochR-18
81RochR-4
82RochR-21
83RochR-23
91Crown/Orio-76

Chisum, Dave
91Burllnd/ProC-3306

Chiti, Dom
79Savan-1
85CharlO-13C
86RochR-2C
87RochR-15C
87RochR/TCMA-25C
88RochR/Team-5
88RochR/Gov-28
88RochR/ProC-212

Chiti, Harry Dominick
53B/Col-7
55B-304
56T-179
58T-119
59T-79
60T-339
61T-269
61T/St-149
62T-253
91WIZMets-73

Chitren, Stephen
(Steve)
87Anchora-4
89Medford/Best-20
90Foil/Best-279
90Huntsvl/Best-4
91B-214
91D-431RR
91F/Ultra-376MLP
91Leaf/II-486
91Mother/A's-27
91S-760RP
91T/90Debut-31
91UD/Ext-753
92D/I-385
92F-253
92F/RookSlns-17
92S/I-202
92T-379
92UD-471

Chittum, Nelson
60T-296

Chiyomaru, Akihiko
90Gate/ProC-3339

Chlupsa, Bob
71OPC-594R
71T-594R

Chmil, Steve
83Durham-2

Choate, Don
61Union

Choate, Mark
90MedHat/Best-6
91Myrtle/ClBest-18
91Myrtle/ProC-2952

Cholowsky, Dan
91Classic/DP-35
91FrRow/DP-5

Chouinard, Felix G.
No Cards.

Chozen, Harry Kenneth
No Cards.

Chris, Mike
80Evansvl-5
80T-666R
81Evansvl-3
82Phoenix
85Cram/PCL-149

Chrisley, Barbra O.
(Neil)
57T-320
58T-303
59T-189
60L-117
60T-273
62T-308

Chrisman, Jim
91AppFx/ClBest-2
91AppFx/ProC-1708

Christ, Michael
87Chatt/Best-11
88Calgary/CMC-6

Christenbury, Lloyd
V100

Christensen, Bruce R.
75Phoenix-15
76Phoenix
Christensen, Jim
82Toledo-13
Christensen, John L.
84Tidew-4
86D-360
86Pawtu-5
86Pawtu-6
86T-287
87Mother/Sea-27
87T/Tr-23T
88Calgary/CMC-17
88Calgary/ProC-794
88S-419
88T-413
89F-108
89Portl/CMC-19
89Portl/ProC-214
91WIZMets-74
Christensen, Walter
(Cuckoo)
No Cards.
Christenson, Gary
81Omaha-5
Christenson, Kim
83AppFx/LF-4
84PrWill-25
85Nashua-5
Christenson, Larry
74OPC-587
74T-587
75OPC-551
75T-551
75T/M-551
76OPC-634
76SSPC-460
76T-634
77OPC-194
77T-59
78OPC-17
78T-247
79BK/P-5
79OPC-260
79T-493
80BK/P-16
80OPC-89
80T-161
81F-8
81T-346
82D-219
82F-244
82T-544
83D-345
83F-156
83OPC-286
83T-668
84Nes/792-252
84T-252
Christian, Rick
86Erie-6
87Erie-1
88Hamil/ProC-1724
89StPete/Star-6
91ArkTr/LineD-29
91ArkTr/ProC-1299
Christian, Robert
69OPC-173R
69T-173R
70OPC-51
70T-51
Christiansen, Clay
82Nashvl-7
83Colum-9
84Colum-12
84Colum/Pol-5
85Colum-4
85Colum/Pol-5
85D-396
85T-211
86Albany/TCMA-28
86Colum-3
86Colum/Pol-3
88Tucson/ProC-179
Christiansen, Jim
83Tacoma-30A
Christianson, Alex
79Wausau-19
Christman, Mark J.
49B-121
Christmas, Stephen R.
(Steve)
80Water-3
81Water-12
82Indianap-22
83Tucson-12
85BuffB-4
86Gator-18
86Iowa-6
Christofferson, Bob
83Tacoma-25B
Christopher, Fred
86Cram/PCL-143
87Spartan-27
88Clearw/Star-7
89Clearw/Star-6
89Reading/Star-7
90Reading/ProC-1215
Christopher, Joe
61T-82
63T-217
64T-546
65Bz-20
65T-495
65T/E-52
65T/trans-43
66T-343
78TCMA-7
91WIZMets-75
WG10-25
Christopher, Lloyd
43Centen-4
44Centen-3
47Signal
47TipTop
48Signal
48Smith
49Remar
50Remar
Christopher, Mike
86FtLaud-6
87FtLaud-8
88Albany/ProC-1337
89Albany/Best-22
89Albany/ProC-321
89Albany/Star-4
90Albuq/CMC-1
90Albuq/ProC-336
90Albuq/Trib-4
91Albuq/LineD-3
91Albuq/ProC-1134
92F-654
92T/91Debut-34
Christopherson, Eric
90A&AASingle/ProC-170
90Classic/DP-19
90Classic/III-87
90Everett/Best-13
90Everett/ProC-3129
91B-635
91Clinton/ClBest-14
91Clinton/ProC-836
91MidwLAS/ProC-MWL3
91S-672FDP
91Single/ClBest-320
Christopherson, Gary
91BurlAs/ClBest-14
91BurlAs/ProC-2808
Christy, Al
83Peoria/LF-19
Christy, Claude
53Mother-47
Chue, Jose
80Clinton-3
81Clinton-7
Chumas, Steve
83Idaho-18
Church, Dan
80Ander-1
Church, Donald
86Cram/PCL-138
Church, Emory
(Bubba)
51B-149
52B-40
52T-323
53B/Col-138
53T-47
55B-273
91T/Arc53-47
Exh47
Church, Hiram Lincoln
(Hi)
No Cards.
Churchill, James
82AlexD-16
Churchill, Norman
77Watlo
79QuadC-27
Churchill, Tim
88Martins/Star-6
89Batavia/ProC-1919
89Spartan/ProC-1053
89Spartan/Star-4
90Spartan/Best-14
90Spartan/ProC-2496
90Spartan/Star-3
Churn, Chuck
59DF
60DF-13
90Target-126
Churry, John
No Cards.
Chylak, Nestar
55B-283ump
Ciaffone, Lawrence T.
(Larry)
No Cards.
Ciaglo, Paul
88CapeCod/Sum-6
89James/ProC-2135
90WPalmB/Star-2
Ciampa, Mike
80Elmira-27
Cianfrocco, Angelo
87Jamestn-2
Cianfrocco, Archie
88Rockford-6
89Jaxvl/Best-11
89Jaxvl/ProC-160
89Rockford-6
90Jaxvl/Best-4
90Jaxvl/ProC-1380
91Harris/LineD-252
91Harris/ProC-634
Ciardi, Mark
86Vanco-6
87Pol/Brew-34
88Denver/CMC-9
88Denver/ProC-1272
88T-417
Cias, Darryl
80WHave-14
81WHave-5
82Tacoma-11
83Tacoma-9
84Nes/792-159
84T-159
86SanJose-6
Ciccarella, Joe
89Alaska/Team-4
Cicero, Joseph F.
No Cards.
Cicione, Mike
84Everett/Cram-3
Cicotte, Al
57T-398
58T-382
59T-57
60T-473
61T-241
62T-126
89Smok/Ast-2
Cicotte, Eddie
10Domino-24
11Helmar-2
12Sweet/Pin-2
14CJ-94
15CJ-94
87Conlon/2-29
88Pac/8Men-104
88Pac/8Men-14
88Pac/8Men-19
88Pac/8Men-22M
88Pac/8Men-38
88Pac/8Men-58
88Pac/8Men-59
88Pac/8Men-6
D327
D328-28
D329-31
E135-28
E270/1
E286
E94
E95
M101/4-31
M116
S74-2
T201
T202
T204
T205
T206
T207
W514-81
W516-21
Cicotte, Greg
80BurlB-17
Ciczczon, Steve
89ColoSp/CMC-25
Cienscyk, Frank
90Mother/A's-28EQMG
Ciesla, Theodore
90James/Pucko-1
91Rockford/ClBest-18
91Rockford/ProC-2053
Cieslak, Mark
85Cedar-2
Cieslak, Thaddeus W.
(Ted)
No Cards.
Cifarelli, Gerard
89CharRain/ProC-980
Cihocki, Albert J.
(Al)
V362-4
Cihocki, Edward J.
(Ed)
No Cards.
Cijntje, Sherwin
85Newar-13
86Hagers-4
87CharlO/WBTV-2
88CharlK/Pep-25
88RochR/Team-6
88RochR/CMC-20
88RochR/ProC-198
89Hagers/Best-7
89Hagers/Star-3
89RochR/CMC-15
89RochR/ProC-1632
Cimino, Pete
66T-563R
67OPC-34
67T-34
68OPC-143
68T-143
Cimo, Matt
87CharlO/WBTV-15
88RochR/Team-7
88RochR/CMC-11
88RochR/Gov-5
88RochR/ProC-203
89ScrWB/CMC-14
89ScrWB/ProC-730
Cimoli, Gino Nicholas
52Park-70
57T-319
58BB
58Hires-63
58T-286
59T-418
60Kahn
60L-142
60T-58
61Kahn
61P-136
61T-165
62J-150
62P-150
62P/Can-150
62Salada-148
62Shirriff-148
62T-402
63J-88
63P-88
63T-321
64T-26
65T-569
89Smok/Dodg-62
90Target-127
91Crown/Orio-77
V362-22
Cimorelli, Frank
89Johnson/Star-5
90Spring/Best-23
91Spring/ClBest-10
91Spring/ProC-735
Cina, Randy
88Lynch/Star-4
Cinnella, Doug
87Hagers-29
88FSLAS/Star-4
88WPalmB/Star-5
89WPalmB/Star-6
91Tidew/LineD-553
91Tidew/ProC-2502
Ciocca, Eric
91Spokane/ClBest-1
91Spokane/ProC-3939
Cipolloni, Joe
86Phill/TastyK-x
86Portl-3
87Maine-18
87Maine/TCMA-8
87Phill/TastyK-23
Cipot, Ed
76Wausau
78Tidew
79Tidew-14
80Tidew-7
81Toledo-20
Cipres, Mark
83TriCit-6
Ciprian, Francis
88Modesto-18
88Modesto/Cal-78
Cipriani, Frank D.
62T-333
Cirbo, Dennis
78StPete
Cisar, George Joseph
90Target-913
Cisarik, Brian
88Spokane/ProC-1940
89AubAs/ProC-5
89Wichita/Rock-32
90Wichita/Rock-5
91Wichita/LineD-604
91Wichita/ProC-2609
Cisco, Galen
61Union
62T-301
63T-93
64T-202
64TS-47
65T-364
67T-596
69OPC-211
69T-211
73OPC-593CO
73T-593CO
74T-166CO
83Stuart-13CO
84Stuart-4CO
88Syrac/CMC-25CO
88Syrac/ProC-818CO
89Syrac/ProC-799CO
89Syrac/Team-25CO
90Tor/BlueJ-42CO
91Tor/Fire-42CO
91WIZMets-76
Cisco, Jeff
86CharRain-6
Cissell, Chalmer W.
(Bill)
28Exh-37
29Exh/4-19
30CEA/Pin-13
31Exh/4-19
32Orbit/num-23
32Orbit/un-10
33CJ/Pin-2
33G-26
34Exh/4-9
35BU-13
35G-1G
35G-3E
35G-5E
35G-6E
92Conlon/Sport-411
R305
R315-C1
R315-D1
R316
V353-26
W517-5
Ciszczon, Steve
80Tacoma-26
83Charl-21TR
85Maine-31
86Maine-4TR
88ColoSp/ProC-1539

89ColoSp/ProC-250
Ciszkowski, Jeff
84LitFalls-16
86Lynch-7
87Lynch-13
89Stockton/Best-11
89Stockton/Cal-154
89Stockton/ProC-399
89Stockton/Star-17
Citarella, Ralph A.
81ArkTr-18
81Louisvl-16
82Louisvl-5
83Louisvl/Riley-16
84Louisvl-16
85Cram/PCL-44
85D-504
85Phill/TastyK-46
86Louisvl-9
86Tacoma-2
87Hawaii-6
Citari, Joe
86Omaha-5
86Omaha/TCMA-14
87Omaha-9
88Omaha/CMC-21
88Omaha/ProC-1519
89Reading/Star-8
Citronnelli, Ed
87SLCity/Taco-13
Clabaugh, John W.
(Moose)
90Target-128
Clack, Marvin
82AlexD-12
83AlexD-7
Clack, Robert S.
(Bobby)
No Cards.
Claire, David M.
(Danny)
No Cards.
Clancey, William E.
(Bill)
E254
T206
Clancy, Albert H.
No Cards.
Clancy, Jim
76SanAn/Team-7
78OPC-103DP
78T-496
79OPC-61
79T-131
80OPC-132
80T-249
81F-412
81OPC-19
81OPC/Post-21
81T-19
81T/St-143
82D-227
82F-612
82OPC-28
82T-665
83D-101
83F-426
83OPC-345
83T-345
83T/St-132
84D-119
84D-19DK
84D/AAS-49
84F-150
84Nes/792-575
84OPC-337
84T-575
84T/St-367
84Tor/Fire-6
85D-439
85F-101
85OPC-188
85T-746
85Tor/Fire-8
86Ault-18
86D-268
86F-56
86Leaf-141
86OPC-213
86T-412
86T-96M
86Tor/Fire-6
87D-639
87D/HL-11
87F-223
87Leaf-90
87OPC-122
87Sf-189
87T-122
87T/St-189
87Tor/Fire-5
88D-74
88D/Best-48
88F-106
88Ho/Disc-13
88Leaf-73
88OPC-54
88S-530
88Sf-215
88T-54
88T/Big-258
88T/St-184
88Tor/Fire-18
89B-324
89D-267
89D/Best-206
89D/Tr-32
89F-229
89F/Up-88
89Lennox/Ast-7
89Mother/Ast-15
89OPC-219
89S-538
89S/Tr-42
89T-219
89T/Tr-19T
89UD-282
90D-69
90F-226
90Lennox-8
90Mother/Ast-23
90OPC-648
90PubIInt/St-90
90S-424
90T-648
90UD-203
91B-554
91Mother/Ast-23
91UD-682
92D/II-639
92S/II-627
92T-279
Clancy, John William
(Bud)
29Exh/4-19
33G-32
90Target-129
R315-D2
V353-32
Clanton, Ucal
(Uke)
No Cards.
Clapham, Mark
78OrlTw
Clapp, Aaron Bronson
No Cards.
Clapp, John Edgar
No Cards.
Clarey, Douglas W.
(Doug)
77Holyo
Clark, Al
88TM/Umpire-24
89TM/Umpire-22
90TM/Umpire-21
Clark, Alfred A.
(Allie)
49B-150
50B-233
50NumNum
51B-29
52B-130
52T-278
53B/Col-155
Clark, Alfred Robert
(Fred)
No Cards.
Clark, Bailey Earl
(Earl)
33G-57
40Wheat-4
V354-41
Clark, Bob
84Nes/792-626
86OPC-352
90Target-130
Clark, Bryan
77Salem
78Charl
80Spokane-8
82D-596
82F-507
82SLCity-6
82T-632
83D-603
83F-476
83T-789
84D-562
84F-609
84F/X-26
84Nes/792-22
84T-22
84T/Tr-25
84Tor/Fire-7
85Maine-5
85OPC-217
85Polar/Ind-43
85T-489
85T/Tr-21T
86BuffB-8
89AAA/CMC-41
89AAA/ProC-39
89Tacoma/CMC-7
89Tacoma/ProC-1563
Clark, Casey
77Salem
78Charl
Clark, Chris
81Holyo-9
82Holyo-19
84Cram/PCL-108
85Cram/PCL-18
Clark, Dan
84Butte-4
Clark, Daniel Curran
(Danny)
21Exh-23
Clark, Dave
85Water-15
86Maine-5
87BuffB-6
87D-623
87F-644M
87Gator-12
87Sf-118M
88D-473
88Gator-25
88Rockford-7
88S-633
88T-49
89D-585
89F-402
89Rockford-7
89T-574
89UD-517
90Cub/Mara-4
90D-492
90F-490
90OPC-339
90PubIInt/St-558
90S-141
90T-339
90T/TVCub-29
90UD-449
91D-616
91F-417
91OPC-241
91S-542
91T-241
91UD-314
92S/II-657
Clark, Dera
88BBCity/Star-8
89Memphis/Best-18
89Memphis/ProC-1199
89Memphis/Star-6
89Star/Wax-40
90Omaha/CMC-3
90Omaha/ProC-59
Clark, Garry
87Clearw-13
87Spartan-7
88Clearw/Star-8
90Reno/Cal-284
Clark, Geoff
89Salem/Team-4TR
91Yakima/ClBest-30TR
Clark, Glen Ester
No Cards.
Clark, Harry
(Pep)
No Cards.
Clark, Isaiah
86Beloit-4
87Stockton-11
88Modesto-20
89River/Best-29
89River/Cal-9
89River/ProC-1404
90Foil/Best-196
90SanBern/Best-7
90SanBern/Cal-103
90SanBern/ProC-2638
Clark, Jack Anthony
75Lafay
76Phoenix
77T-488R
78T-384
79Ho-116
79K-40
79OPC-268
79Pol/Giants-22
79T-512
79T/Comics-32
80K-57
80OPC-93
80Pol/Giants-22
80T-167
80T/S-54
81D-315
81Drake-15
81F-433
81F/St-52
81MSA/Disc-9
81OPC-30
81Sqt-18
81T-30
81T/SO-70
81T/St-234
82D-46
82Drake-8
82F-387
82F/St-65
82T-460
82T/St-106
83D-222
83D/AAS-29
83Drake-5
83F-256
83K-48
83Mother/Giants-2
83OPC-210
83T-210
83T/Gloss40-32
83T/St-162
83T/St-300
84D-65
84D-7DK
84D/AAS-31
84F-369
85FunFood/Pin-19
84Mother/Giants-7
84Nes/792-690
84OPC-381
84T-690
84T/St-167
85D-65
85D/AAS-30
85F-604
85F/Up-U25
85Leaf-207
85OPC-208
85T-740
85T/St-160
85T/Tr-22T
86D-168
86D/AAS-23
86F-30
86F/LL-6
86F/Mini-6
86F/St-24
86KAS/Disc-9
86Leaf-96
86OPC-350
86Quaker-5
86Sf-107
86Schnucks-1
86T-350
86T/Gloss60-4
86T/Mini-59
86T/St-50
87Classic/Up-148
87D-111
87D/OD-67
87F-289
87F/LimWaxBox-C4
87F/Slug-9
87OPC-331
87Sf-195M
87Smok/Cards-13
87T-520
87T/Board-25
87T/St-52
88Classic/Blue-205
88D-15DK
88D-183
88D/AS-33
88D/Best-49
88D/DKsuper-15DK
88D/PopUp-11
88D/Y/Bk-NEW
88F-26
88F/AS-11
88F/BB/AS-6
88F/Excit-8
88F/Mini-39
88F/RecSet-5
88F/SS-7
88F/Up-U47
88Jiffy-4
88KayBee-5
88KMart-5
88Leaf-15DK
88Leaf-181
88Nestle-17
88OPC-100
88Panini/St-232M
88Panini/St-388
88RedFoley/St-12
88S-650
88S-78
88S/Tr-1T
88S/WxBx-11
88Sf-18
88Sf/Gamewin-25
88T-100
88T-397
88T/Big-262
88T/Coins-9
88T/Gloss22-13
88T/Gloss60-41
88T/Mini-69
88T/Revco-4
88T/RiteAid-10
88T/St-150
88T/St-46
88T/St/Backs-1
88T/Tr-28T
88T/UK-13
89B-456
89Classic/Up/2-158
89Coke/Padre-2
89T/Crunch-14
89D-311
89D/Best-98
89D/Tr-2
89F-252
89F/Up-123
89KayBee-5
89OPC-3
89Padre/Mag-6
89RedFoley/St-21
89S-25
89S/HotStar-27
89S/Tr-3
89Sf-26
89T-410
89T/Big-240
89T/Coins-7
89T/Gloss60-56
89T/LJN-94
89T/Mini-65
89T/St-308
89T/Tr-20T
89T/UK-14
89UD-346
89UD/Ext-773
90B-214
90Coke/Padre-4
90D-128
90D/BestNL-109
90D/GSlam-11
90F-152
90F/AwardWin-8
90Leaf/II-287
90MLBPA/Pins-56
90OPC-90

90Padre/MagUno-18
90Panini/St-348
90Publint/St-45
90RedFoley/St-16
90S-20
90Sf-28
90T-90
90T/Ames-12
90T/Big-39
90T/HillsHM-18
90T/Mini-78
90T/St-104
90T/TVAS-44
90UD-342
91B-122
91Classic/200-154
91Classic/II-T99
91D-618
91F-526
91F/UltraUp-U5
91F/Up-U4
91Leaf/I-201
91Leaf/Stud-13
91OPC-650
91OPC/Premier-21
91Panini/FrSt-91
91Panini/St-98
91Pep/RSox-4
91RedFoley/St-18
91S-523
91S/RookTr-4T
91T-650
91T/StClub/II-500
91T/Tr-22T
91UD-331
91UD/Ext-735
92D/I-169
92F-36
92S/I-318
92T-207
92UD-521

Clark, James Edward
(Jim)
No Cards.

Clark, James Francis
(Jim)
E96

Clark, James
(Jim)
No Cards.

Clark, Jeff
89Pulaski/ProC-1910
90BurlB/Best-16
90BurlB/ProC-2363
90BurlB/Star-9
91Durham/ClBest-20
91Durham/ProC-1558

Clark, Jerald
85Spokane/Cram-3
87Wichita-24
88LasVegas/CMC-12
88LasVegas/ProC-229
89AAA/CMC-37
89AAA/ProC-49
89B-462
89D-599
89F-642M
89LasVegas/CMC-13
89LasVegas/ProC-10
89S-644
89Sf-179
89UD-30
90Classic/Up-10
90D-593
90D/Rook-48
90Leaf/II-510
90Publint/St-46
90S-660
90S/YS/II-41
90UD-624
91B-658
91D-74
91F/UltraUp-U110
91F/Up-U121
91Leaf/II-265
91OPC-513
91Padre/MagRal-15
91Padre/MagRal-7
91S-242
91T-513
91T/StClub/II-468
91UD-624
92D/I-144
92F-601
92S/I-257
92T-749
92UD-292

Clark, John Carroll
(Cap)
No Cards.

Clark, Joshua B.
(Pepper)
T206

Clark, Leroy
76Dubuq

Clark, Mark
87Sumter-11
88Hamil/ProC-1736
89Savan/ProC-370
90StPete/Star-2
90T/TVCard-41
92T/91Debut-35

Clark, Melvin Earl
(Mel)
53B/Col-67
54B-175
55B-41

Clark, Mike J.
53Hunter
53T-193
91T/Arc53-193

Clark, Owen F.
(Spider)
No Cards.

Clark, Phil
87Fayette-23
88FSLAS/Star-31
88Lakeland/Star-7
89London/ProC-1383
90Toledo/CMC-23
90Toledo/ProC-152
91F-332
91S-756RP
91S/Rook40-7
91Toledo/LineD-581
91Toledo/ProC-1934

Clark, Philip J.
58T-423
59T-454

Clark, Randy
79QuadC-14

Clark, Rickey
70T-586
71OPC-697
71T-697
72OPC-462
72T-462
73OPC-636
73T-636

Clark, Rob
83Tulsa-4
84OKCty-2
85Tulsa-27
86OKCty-3
90TulsaDG/Best-33

Clark, Robert Cale
(Bobby)
76QuadC
79SLCity-12
80SLCity-23
80T-663R
81D-572
81T-288
82D-318
82F-456
82T-74
83D-444
83F-82
83T-184
84D-524
84F-512
84F/X-25
84Gard-4
84Nes/792-626
84Pol/Brew-25
84T-626
84T/Tr-24
85Cram/PCL-204
85D-481
85F-578
85Gard-3
85T-553
86Edmon-4
86T-452
87Tacoma-4

Clark, Robert H.
(Bob)
N172

Clark, Rodney
85Utica-13

Clark, Ronald Bruce
(Ron)
67OPC-137R
67T-137R
68T-589R
69T-561
70OPC-531
70T-531
71MLB/St-509
75IntAS/TCMA-13
76OkCty/Team-8
82OkCty-6MG
83Kinston/Team-3MG
86Clearw-4MG
90Coke/WSox-30CO

Clark, Roy
79Tulsa-24M

Clark, Roy
80LynnS-20
81Spokane-6
82SLCity-7

Clark, Royal
No Cards.

Clark, Russell
76Wausau
79Jacks-20
79Tidew-22

Clark, Skip
81Miami-12

Clark, Terry
83ArkTr-3
84Louisvl-24
86MidldA-5
87Edmon-22
88Edmon/CMC-1
88Edmon/ProC-569
89AAA/ProC-27
89D-607
89F-470
89OPC-129
89S-566
89S/HotRook-89
89T-129
89UD-234
90Tucson/CMC-3
90Tucson/ProC-198
91Tucson/LineD-607
91Tucson/ProC-2207

Clark, Tim
90Beloit/Star-5
90LSUPol-14
91Stockton/ClBest-23
91Stockton/ProC-3042

Clark, Tom
90LitSun-18

Clark, Tony
86DayBe-5
90A&AASingle/ProC-189
90Bristol/ProC-3173
90Bristol/Star-3
91Niagara/ClBest-13
91Niagara/ProC-3645

Clark, Will
86D/HL-1
86D/Rook-32
86F/Slug-6
86F/Up-U25
86Mother/Giants-7
86Sf/Rook-6
86T/Tr-24T
87BK-3
87D-66
87D/OD-96
87F-269
87F/Excit-10
87F/Lim-8
87F/Slug-M2
87F/St-22
87Leaf-144
87Mother/SFG-2
87OPC-361
87RedFoley/St-50
87Sf-95
87T-420
87T/St-88
87ToysRUs-7
88Classic/Blue-225
88D-204
88D-21DK
88D-BC24
88D/Best-79
88D/DKsuper-21DK
88Drake-27
88F-78
88F/AwardWin-5
88F/BB/AS-7
88F/BB/MVP-5
88F/Excit-9
88F/Hottest-6
88F/LL-5
88F/Mini-116
88F/RecSet-6
88F/Slug-8
88F/SS-8
88F/St-126
88F/TL-4
88FanSam-12
88Jiffy-5
88KMart-6
88Leaf-170
88Leaf-21DK
88Mother/Giants-2
88Mother/WClark-1
88Mother/WClark-2
88Mother/WClark-3
88Mother/WClark-4
88MSA/Disc-10
88Nestle-14
88OPC-350
88Panini/St-420
88Panini/St-421TL
88S-78
88S/YS/I-25
88Sf-9
88Sf/Gamewin-4
88T-261TL
88T-350
88T/Big-9
88T/Coins-38
88T/RiteAid-12
88T/St-87
88T/UK-14
89B-476
89Cadaco-8
89Classic-150
89Classic-18
89Classic/Up/2-180
89T/Crunch-19
89D-249
89D/AS-33
89D/Best-23
89D/MVP-BC22
89D/PopUp-33
89F-325
89F-631M
89F-632M
89F/AS-3
89F/BBAS-6
89F/BBMVP's-7
89F/Excit-5
89F/Heroes-7
89F/LL-4
89F/Superstar-8
89F/WaxBox-C6
89KayBee-6
89KingB/Discs-22
89KMart/DT-23
89Mother/Giants-2
89Mother/WClark-1
89Mother/WClark-2
89Mother/WClark-3
89Mother/WClark-4
89OPC-321
89Panini/St-212
89Panini/St-232AS
89RedFoley/St-22
89S-195M
89S-450
89S/HotStar-85
89S/Mast-10
89Sf-170
89T-660
89T/Big-146
89T/Coins-8
89T/DH-13
89T/Gloss22-13
89T/Gloss60-11
89T/HeadsUp-2
89T/Hills-7
89T/LJN-22
89T/Mini-40
89T/St-159
89T/St-88
89T/St/Backs-34
89T/UK-15
89Tetley/Discs-4
89UD-155
89UD-678TC
90B-231
90B/Ins-1
90Classic-150
90Classic-6
90Classic-87
90Classic/III-T7
90Classic/Up-11
90Colla/Clark-Set
90CollAB-4
90D-230
90D-707AS
90D/BestNL-24
90D/GSlam-6
90D/Learning-23
90D/Preview-12
90F-54
90F-630MVP
90F-637M
90F/ASIns-2
90F/AwardWin-7
90F/BB-5
90F/BBMVP-7
90F/LL-6
90F/WS-10M
90F/WS-4
90Holsum/Discs-11
90HotPlay/St-6
90KMart/SS-1
90Leaf/I-172
90Leaf/II-444CL
90MLBPA/Pins-28
90Mother/Clark-1
90Mother/Clark-2
90Mother/Clark-3
90Mother/Clark-4
90Mother/Giant-2
90MSA/Soda-18
90OPC-100
90OPC-397AS
90Panini/St-207M
90Panini/St-363
90Post-7
90Publint/St-254
90Publint/St-65
90RedFoley/St-17
90S-300
90S-684DT
90S-699M
90S/100St-30
90S/McDon-1
90Sf-5
90Sunflower-17
90T-100
90T-397AS
90T/Ames-31
90T/Big-224
90T/Coins-43
90T/DH-10
90T/Gloss22-2
90T/Gloss60-52
90T/HeadsUp-2
90T/HillsHM-2
90T/Mini-84
90T/St-147AS
90T/St-85
90T/TVAS-34
90UD-50M
90UD-556
90USPlayC/AS-12D
90WonderBrd-19
90Woolwth/HL-24
91B-616
91BBBest/HitM-5
91Classic/200-48
91Classic/II-T94
91Classic/III-T9
91Classic/III-xx
91D-441AS
91D-86
91DennyGS-3
91F-259
91F/ProV-2
91F/Ultra-318
91F/UltraG-2
91JDeanSig-1
91KingB/Discs-15
91Leaf/I-238
91Leaf/Prev-12
91Leaf/Stud-254
91MajorLg/Pins-63

91Mother/Giant-2
91OPC-500
91OPC/Premier-22
91Panini/FrSt-158
91Panini/FrSt-67
91Panini/St-79
91Petro/SU-20
91PG&E-14
91Post-3
91Post/Can-9
91RedFoley/St-117
91RedFoley/St-19
91S-664AS
91S-7
91S-871FRAN
91S-886DT
91S/100SS-4
91S/Cooper-B6
91Seven/3DCoin-3NC
91SFExam/Giant-6
91T-500
91T/CJMini/I-35
91T/StClub/I-5
91T/SU-8
91UD-445
91UD/FinalEd-92F
91USPlayC/AS-WC
92Classic/I-24
92D/DK-DK2
92D/Elite-E11
92D/I-214
92D/II-428AS
92D/Preview-3
92F-631
92F-699M
92F/ASIns-13
92F/TmLIns-8
92S/100SS-24
92S/I-3
92S/II-773AS
92S/II-883DT
92T-330
92T-386AS
92UD-175

Clark, William Otis
(Willie)
No Cards.

Clark, William Watson
(Lefty)
32Orbit/num-8
32Orbit/un-11
33DH-9
33G-17
35G-1G
35G-3E
35G-4E
35G-5E
90Target-131
R305
R337-407
V353-17
V355-86

Clark, William Winf.
(Bill)
No Cards.

Clarke, Arthur F.
(Archie)
No Cards.

Clarke, Fred C.
10Domino-25
11Helmar-112
11Helmar-157
12Sweet/Pin-135A
12Sweet/Pin-135B
14CJ-70
14Piedmont/St-12
15CJ-70
48Exh/HOF
50Callahan
63Bz/ATG-26
73F/Wild-21
80SSPC/HOF
86Conlon/1-53
D322
E107
E254
E270/1
E270/2
E300
E90/1
E90/2
E91
E93
E96
E98
M116
S74-108
T201
T205
T206
T3-8
W555
WG3-10
WG5-10
WG6-10

Clarke, Harry Corson
No Cards.

Clarke, Horace M.
66T-547
67OPC-169
67T-169
68T-263
69MB-59
69MLB/St-73
69OPC-87
69T-87
69T/St-202
70MLB/St-244
70T-623
71MLB/St-486
71OPC-715
71T-715
72MB-74
72OPC-387
72T-387
73OPC-198
73Syrac/Team-5
73T-198
74OPC-529
74T-529

Clarke, Jay Austin
(Nig)
E254
E270/1
E270/2
M116
T202
T206

Clarke, Jeff
91AppFx/ClBest-16
91AppFx/ProC-1722

Clarke, Joshua B.
(Josh)
No Cards.

Clarke, Richard Grey
(Dick)
No Cards.

Clarke, Stan
83Knoxvl-2
84Syrac-19
84Tor/Fire-8
85Syrac-4
86Syrac-5
87Calgary-18
88T-556
88Toledo/CMC-2
88Toledo/ProC-607
89Omaha/CMC-2
89Omaha/ProC-1737
90Louisvl/CMC-4
90Louisvl/ProC-396
90T/TVCard-42
91Louisvl/LineD-229

Clarke, Sumpter Mills
No Cards.

Clarke, Thomas A.
(Tommy)
16FleischBrd-16
D328-29
D329-33
D350/2-32
E135-29
M101/4-33
M101/5-32
M116
T207

Clarke, Tim
82QuadC-6

Clarke, William H.
N172

Clarke, William Jones
(Boileryard)
E107
E270/2

Clarke, William S.
(Stu)
No Cards.

Clarkin, Mike
86WinHaven-6
87NewBrit-1
88NewBrit/ProC-891

Clarkson, Buster
86Negro/Frit-44

Clarkson, James B.
(Buzz)
No Cards.

Clarkson, John Gibson
75F/Pion-26
80SSPC/HOF
E223
N172
N28
N284
N300/unif
N403
WG1-2

Clary, Ellis
60T-470C
88Chatt/Team-5

Clary, Marty
85Richm-2
86D-36RR
87Richm/Crown-34
87Richm/TCMA-3
88F-535
88Richm-32
88Richm/CMC-10
88Richm/ProC-11
89Richm/CMC-1
89Richm/Ko-32
89Richm/ProC-826
90D-381
90F-578
90OPC-304
90T-304
90UD/Ext-779
91F-686
91Louisvl/LineD-230
91Louisvl/ProC-2906
91OPC-582
91T-582
91UD-478

Clatterbuck, Don
79Newar-9

Claus, Todd
91Boise/ClBest-1
91Boise/ProC-3885

Clawson, Chris
86Ashvl-4

Clawson, Ken
87PortChar-1

Clay, Billy
79Newar-17

Clay, Dain Elmer
No Cards.

Clay, Danny
83Wisco/LF-16
85Orlan-16
86Toledo-5
87Portl-11
88F/Up-U108
88Maine/ProC-297
89ScrWB/ProC-706
90Indianap/CMC-2
90Indianap/ProC-284
90T/TVCub-40

Clay, Dave
82Durham-14
83Durham-17
85Richm-3
86ElPaso-6
87Denver-1

Clay, Frederick C.
(Bill)
No Cards.

Clay, Jeff
81Cedar-21
82Cedar-26
86Salem-4TR

Clay, Ken
78T-89
79OPC-225
79T-434
80T-159
81F-633
81Pol/Mariners-8
81T-305
81T/Tr-747
82F-508
82T-649
89Pac/SenLg-72

Clayton, Craig
91Belling/ClBest-13
91Belling/ProC-3671

Clayton, Kenny
82Beloit-14
82Idaho-22

Clayton, Royal
88CLAS/Star-4
88PrWill/Star-6
89Albany/Best-6
89Albany/ProC-318
89Albany/Star-5
89Star/Wax-96
90Albany/Best-23
90Albany/ProC-1030
90Albany/Star-2
90AlbanyDG/Best-10
90EastLAS/ProC-EL13
90Foil/Best-287
91ColClip/LineD-104
91ColClip/ProC-591

Clayton, Royce
89B-472
89Clinton/ProC-895
90A&AASingle/ProC-156
90AS/Cal-49
90Foil/Best-114
90SanJose/Best-7
90SanJose/Cal-36
90SanJose/ProC-2018
90SanJose/Star-5
91B-641
91Classic/III-10
91Shrev/LineD-303
91Shrev/ProC-1827
91Single/ClBest-251
91UD-61TP
91UD/FinalEd-4F
92Classic/I-25
92D/II-397RR
92F-632
92S/II-841
92T-786
92T/91Debut-36
92UD-2SR

Clear, Mark
76QuadC
77QuadC
80T-638
81D-291
81T-12
81T/Tr-748
82Coke/BOS
82D-452
82F-290
82OPC-169
82T-421
82T/St-154
83D-361
83F-181
83F-629M
83OPC-162
83T-162
83T/St-36
84D-611
84F-395
84Nes/792-577
84OPC-148
84T-577
85D-538
85F-154
85Leaf-32
85T-207
86D-493
86F-344
86F/Up-U26
86Pol/Brew-25
86T-349
86T/Tr-25T
87D-355
87F-341
87F/BB-9
87F/St-23
87OPC-244
87Pol/Brew-25
87T-640
87T/St-195
88D-372
88F-160
88Pol/Brew-25
88S-446
88T-742
89D-528
89F-182
89S-430
89T-63
90ElPasoATG/Team-37

Cleary, Tony
79Elmira-16
86Pawtu-7TR
87Pawtu-15
88Pawtu/CMC-14
88Pawtu/ProC-467
89Pawtu/Dunkin-TR
89Pawtu/ProC-683

Clem, John
86Wausau-3

Clemans, Sherri
90Miami/II/Star-30

Clemens, Chester S.
(Chet)
No Cards.

Clemens, Clement L.
(Clem)
No Cards.

Clemens, Douglas H.
(Doug)
67T-489

Clemens, Roger
84F/X-27
84Pawtu-22
85D-273
85F-155
85F/St-123
85Leaf-99
85T-181
86D-172
86D/HL-17
86D/HL-18
86D/HL-26
86D/HL-5
86D/HL-6
86F-345
86F/Mini-73
86F/Slug-7
86OPC-98
86T-661
87BK-4
87Classic-84
87Classic/Up-114
87D-276
87D-2DK
87D/AAS-8
87D/AS/Wax-PC14
87D/DKsuper-2
87D/PopUp-8
87Drake-31
87F-32
87F-634M
87F-640M
87F/AS-11
87F/AwardWin-9
87F/Excit-11
87F/GameWin-10
87F/Hottest-10
87F/BB-10
87F/LL-10
87F/Lim-9
87F/Mini-20
87F/RecSet-4
87F/Slug-10
87F/St-24
87F/WS-3
87Jiffy-12
87KayBee-10
87Kraft-45
87Leaf-190
87Leaf-2DK
87MnM's-7
87MSA/Discs-2
87OPC-340
87Ralston-10
87RedFoley/St-70
87Sf-10
87Sf-111M
87Sf-159M
87Sf-196M
87Seven-E8
87Seven-ME10
87Sportflic/DealP-1
87T-1RB
87T-340
87T-614AS
87T/Coins-8
87T/Gloss22-21
87T/Gloss60-5

87T/HL-7
87T/Mini-42
87T/St-154
87T/St-2
87T/St-244
87T/St-3
87Woolwth-7
88Bz-4
88ChefBoy-23
88Classic/Blue-217
88Classic/Red-158
88D-51
88D/Best-57
88D/RedSox/Bk-51
88Drake-30
88F-349
88F/AS-4
88F/AwardWin-6
88F/BB/AS-8
88F/BB/MVP-6
88F/Excit-10
88F/Hottest-7
88F/LL-6
88F/Mini-5
88F/RecSet-7
88F/Slug-9
88F/SS-9
88F/St-7
88F/TL-5
88Jiffy-6
88KingB/Disc-20
88KMart-7
88Leaf-56
88MSA/Disc-9
88Nestle-1
88OPC-70
88Panini/St-21
88RedFoley/St-13
88S-110
88S/YS/II-23
88Sf-207
88Sf/Gamewin-20
88T-394
88T-70
88T/Big-118
88T/Coins-2
88T/Gloss60-13
88T/Mini-2
88T/Revco-28
88T/St-251
88T/St/Backs-58
88T/UK-15
88Woolwth-11
89B-26
89Cadaco-9
89Classic-119
89T/Crunch-18
89D-280
89D/AS-14
89D/Best-65
89F-85
89F/BBAS-7
89F/BBMVP's-8
89F/Excit-6
89F/Heroes-8
89F/LL-5
89F/Rec-2
89F/Superstar-9
89Holsum/Discs-16
89KayBee-7
89KMart/DT-20
89Nissen-16
89OPC-121
89Panini/St-249
89Panini/St-270
89MSA/SS-7
89RedFoley/St-23
89S-350
89S/HotStar-90
89S/Mast-20
89Sf-3
89T-405AS
89T-450
89T/Big-42
89T/Coins-37
89T/DH-9
89T/Gloss60-23
89T/Hills-8
89T/LJN-66
89T/Mini-46
89T/St-259
89T/St/Backs-25
89T/UK-16
89Tetley/Discs-8
89UD-195
90B-268
90Classic-51
90CollAB-19
90D-184
90D/BestAL-58
90F-271
90F-627MVP
90F/BBMVP-8
90F/WaxBox-C3
90HotPlay/St-7
90Leaf/I-12
90MLBPA/Pins-69
90MSA/Soda-8
90OPC-245
90Panini/St-24
90Pep/RSox-6
90Post-2
90PublInt/St-281
90PublInt/St-452
90RedFoley/St-18
90S-310
90S/100St-79
90S/McDon-18
90Sf-149
90Sunflower-18
90T-245
90T/Big-22
90T/DH-11
90T/Mini-4
90T/St-255
90T/TVAS-25
90T/TVRSox-8
90UD-323
90UD-57TC
90USPlayC/AS-1S
90Windwlk/Discs-3
90WonderBrd-2
91B-118
91BBBest/Aces-4
91Classic/200-149
91Classic/I-18
91Classic/II-T65
91Classic/II-T97
91CollAB-1
91D-395MVP
91D-81
91D-9DK
91D/SuperDK-9DK
91F-90
91F/ASIns-10
91F/ProV-9
91F/Ultra-31
91JDeanSig-18
91Leaf/I-174CL
91Leaf/II-488
91Leaf/Stud-14
91Leaf/StudPrev-2
91MajorLg/Pins-8
91OPC-530
91OPC/Premier-23
91Panini/FrSt-271
91Panini/St-215
91Panini/Top15-63
91Panini/Top15-69
91Panini/Top15-80
91Panini/Top15-94
91Pep/RSox-5
91Pep/SS-6
91Petro/SU-3
91Post-12
91Post/Can-18
91RedFoley/St-20
91S-399AS
91S-655
91S-684KM
91S-850FRAN
91S/100SS-50
91Seven/3DCoin-3F
91Seven/3DCoin-3NE
91Seven/3DCoin-4T
91T-530
91T/CJMini/I-22
91T/StClub/II-309
91T/SU-9
91UD-655
91USPlayC/AS-10H
92Classic/I-26
92Classic/I-xx
92D/I-244
92D/II-BC3CY
92F-37
92F/ClemIns-Set
92S/100SS-74
92S/I-21
92S/II-790CY
92T-150
92T-405AS
92UD-545
92UD-641DS

Clemens, Troy
90Spring/Best-7

Clement, Wallace Oaks
(Wally)
90Target-914
E90/1

Clemente, Roberto W.
55T-164
56T-33
57Kahn
57T-76
58Kahn
58T-52
59Kahn
59T-478
59T-543M
60Bz-7
60Kahn
60T-326
61Kahn
61P-132
61T-388
61T-41LL
62Bz-11
62Exh
62J-173
62Kahn
62P-173
62P/Can-173
62Salada-150
62Shirriff-150
62Sugar-B
62T-10
62T-52LL
62T/bucks
62T/St-174
63Bz-14
63Exh
63F-56
63IDL-4
63J-143
63Kahn
63P-143
63Salada-23
63T-18M
63T-540
63T/SO
64Bz-14
64Kahn
64T-440
64T-7LL
64T/Coins-150AS
64T/Coins-55
64T/S-11
64T/St-27
64T/SU
64Wheat/St-11
65Bz-14
65MacGregor-1
65OPC-160
65OPC-2LL
65T-160
65T-2LL
65T/E-19
65T/trans-44
66Bz-26
66EH-21
66Kahn
66T-215LL
66T-300
66T/RO-47
67Bz-26
67OPC/PI-11
67T-242LL
67T-400
67T/PI-11
67T/Test/PP-27
67T/Test/PP-6
67T/Test/SU-7
68Bz-12
68Coke
68Dexter-24
68KDKA-21
68OPC-150
68OPC-1LL
68OPC-3LL
68T-150
68T-1LL
68T-374AS
68T-3LL
68T-480M
68T/3D
68T/G-6
68T/Post-6
69MB-60
69MLB/St-184
69MLBPA/Pin-39
69OPC-50
69OPC/DE-4
69T-50
69T/DE-27
69T/decal
69T/S-58
69T/St-85
69Trans-56
70K-27
70MB-5
70MLB/St-99
70OPC-350
70OPC-61LL
70T-350
70T-61LL
70T/PI-21
70T/S-12
70Trans-5
71Bz
71Bz/Test-38
71K-5
71MLB/St-198
71MLB/St-558
71OPC-630
71T-630
71T/Coins-71
71T/S-37
72K-49
72MB-75
72OPC-226WS
72OPC-309
72OPC-310IA
72T-226WS
72T-309
72T-310A
72T/Cloth-6
73OPC-50
73T-50
74Laugh/ASG-62
75OPC-204MV
75T-204MV
75T/M-204MV
78TCMA-13
79TCMA-23
80Pac/Leg-50
80Laugh/FFeat-21
82KMart-10
83D/HOF-17
83MLBPA/Pin-22
84West/1-3
86CharRain-7
86Sf/Dec-43
87D-612PUZ
87D/AS/WaxBox-PUZ
87D/DKsuper-28
87D/WaxBox-PUZ
87KMart-2
87Leaf-163
87Nestle/DT-27
87T-313TBC
89HOF/St-46
89Pac/Leg-135
89Swell-125
89T/LJN-149
89USPS-1
90CollAB-35
90MSA/AGFA-8
90Swell/Great-20
91Homer/Classic-7
91LineD-39
91Swell/Great-132
Exh47
PM10/Sm-26

Clements, Dave
83Spring/LF-2
84ArkTr-2
85Louisvl-14
86ArkTr-5

Clements, Edward
(Ed)
89Pac/SenLg-54

Clements, John T.
(Jack)
N172
N284
N690
WG1-49

Clements, Pat
85F/Up-U26
85Smok/Cal-22
85T/Tr-23T
86D-600
86F-606
86OPC-283
86T-754
87D-390
87F-608
87T-16
88Colum/CMC-1
88Colum/Pol-1
88Colum/ProC-318
88D-52
88F-204
88S-389
88T-484
89B-452
89LasVegas/ProC-15
89T-159
90F-153
90OPC-548
90T-548
91LasVegas/ProC-227
92F-602
92S/II-714

Clements, Tony
91London/LineD-403

Clements, Wes
83Tucson-14
84Cram/PCL-53
85Beloit-14
87GlenF-5
89Pac/SenLg-176

Clemo, Scott
86Jamestn-3
87Indianap-28
88WPalmB/Star-6

Clemons, Lance
72OPC-372R
72T-372R

Clemons, Mark
85Kingst-1
86Orlan-4
87Orlan-10
88Jaxvl/Best-8
88Jaxvl/ProC-977

Clemons, Robert
E270/2

Clemons, Vern
V61-85

Clemons, Verne James
E120
V100
W573

Clendenon, Donn Alvin
62T-86
63IDL-5
63Kahn
63T-477
64Kahn
64T-163
64T/Coins-15
64T/St-76
64T/SU
65Kahn
65T-325
65T/E-9
66EH-17
66OPC-99M
66T-375
66T-99M
67T-266M
67T-535
67T/Test/PP-30
67T/Test/PP-7
68KDKA-17
68T-344
69MB-61
69OPC-208
69T-208
69T/decal
69T/St-54
70MLB/St-74
70OPC-280
70OPC-306WS
70T-280
70T-306WS
70Trans/M-24
71MLB/St-149

71OPC-115
71T-115
71T/Coins-151
71T/S-4
71T/tatt-6
72MB-76
72T-671
78TCMA-237
90Swell/Great-82
91WIZMets-77

Cleveland, Elmer E.
N172

Cleveland, Reggie
70T-716R
71OPC-216R
71T-216R
72OPC-375
72T-375
73OPC-104
73T-104
74OPC-175
74T-175
74T/St-112
74T/Tr-175T
75OPC-32
75T-32
75T/M-32
76OPC-419
76T-419
77OPC-111
77T-613
78BK/R-10
78T-105
79OPC-103
79T-209
80T-394
81D-206
81F-523
81T-576
82D-456
82F-137
82T-737
91Pac/SenLg-61
91Pac/SenLg-79

Clevenger, Tex
58T-31
59T-298
60T-392
61T-291
63T-457

Cleverly, Gary
75SanAn

Cliburn, Stanley Gene
(Stan)
75QuadC
76QuadC
78Cr/PCL-74
82Portl-10
83LynnP-11
84Cram/PCL-132
85Cram/PCL-242
86Edmon-5M
86Edmon-6
87Richm/Crown-29
87Richm/TCMA-28
88BuffB/CMC-24
88BuffB/ProC-1480
88Watertn/Pucko-31
89Augusta/ProC-514
89Pac/SenLg-150
89SALAS/GS-1
89T/SenLg-54
90Salem/Star-25MG
91Pac/SenLg-30
91Pac/SenLg-51M
91Salem/ClBest-25MG
91Salem/ProC-968MG

Cliburn, Stewart
77Salem
80Port-13
81Buffa-9
83Nashua-3
84Cram/PCL-113
85Cram/PCL-19
85F/Up-U27
86D-301
86Edmon-5M
86Edmon-7
86F-152
86Sf-177M
86T-179
87D-530
88Smok/Angels-19
89D-462
89Edmon/CMC-7
89Edmon/ProC-566
89F-471
89S-445
89T-649
89UD-483
91Pac/SenLg-29
91Pac/SenLg-51M
91PalmSp/ProC-2034CO

Clifford, Jeff
90SoOreg/Best-13
90SoOreg/ProC-3440

Clift, Harland Benton
36Exh/4-15
37Exh/4-15
37OPC-104
38Exh/4-15
38Wheat
41DP-148
41G-2
41PB-66
V300
W753

Clifton, Herman Earl
(Flea)
R314
V355-32

Cline, John
(Monk)
N172

Cline, Steve
75Cedar
81Clinton-3
82Clinton-3
84Shrev/FB-4CO
88Shreve/ProC-1286
89Shreve/ProC-1837
90Clinton/Best-10CO
91Clinton/ClBest-27CO
91Clinton/ProC-853CO

Cline, Tyrone A.
(Ty)
61T-421
62Kahn
62Sugar-8
62T-362
62T/St-32
63J-74
63P-74
63T-414
64T-171
65OPC-63
65T-63
66T-306
67T-591
68T-469
69MB-62
69MLB/St-156
69T-442
70MLB/St-64
70OPC-164
70T-164
71MLB/St-54
71OPC-199NLCS
71OPC-201NLCS
71OPC-319
71T-199NLCS
71T-201NLCS
71T-319
72MB-77
78TCMA-149
78TCMA-191

Clines, Eugene
(Gene)
71OPC-27R
71T-27R
72OPC-152
72T-152
73OPC-333
73T-333
74OPC-172
74T-172
75OPC-575
75T-575
75T/M-575
76OPC-417
76SSPC-543
76T-417
77T-237
78T-639
79T-171
89Pac/SenLg-146
89TM/SenLg-21
90Mother/Mar-27M
91WIZMets-78

Clingman, William F.
(Billy)
No Cards.

Clinton, James L.
(Jim)
No Cards.

Clinton, James
(Jim)
89Butte/SP-11
90Gaston/Best-24
90Gaston/ProC-2527
90Gaston/Star-5
91CharlR/ProC-1320

Clinton, Luciean L.
(Lu)
60T-533
61Union
62T-457
63F-6
63J-82
63P-82
63T-96
64T-526
65OPC-229
65T-229
67T-426

Cloherty, John
76Dubuq
78DaytB

Cloninger, Darin
85Albany-3

Cloninger, Greg
88Sumter/ProC-406
89BurlB/ProC-1601
89BurlB/Star-4

Cloninger, Todd
86Geneva-2
87WinSalem-3

Cloninger, Tom
87Oneonta-33

Cloninger, Tony
62T-63
63J-157
63P-157
63T-367
64T-575
65Kahn
65T-520
66Bz-27
66Kahn
66OPC-10
66T-10
66T-223LL
66T/RO-116
67Bz-27
67Kahn
67T-396M
67T-490
68Coke
68Dexter-25
68OPC-93
68T-93
69Kahn
69MLB/St-128
69T-492
70MLB/St-26
70T-705
71MLB/St-55
71OPC-218
71T-218
72T-779
78TCMA-20
88Albany/ProC-1353
90HOF/St-70
91Pac/SenLg-31

Close, Casey
88Colum/CMC-21
88Colum/Pol-19
88Colum/ProC-325
90Calgary/CMC-19
90Calgary/ProC-661

Clossen, Bill
86Durham-4
87PrWill-15

Closter, Alan
66T-549R
69OPC-114R
69T-114R
72OPC-124R
72T-124R
73OPC-634
73Syrac/Team-6
73T-634

Clough, Edgar George
(Ed)
No Cards.

Cluck, Bob
74Cedar
75Dubuq
76Dubuq
81Tucson-5
84Cram/PCL-239MG
85Cram/PCL-110MG
90Mother/Ast-27CO
91Mother/Ast-28CO

Cluff, Paul
89Boise/ProC-2006

Clutterbuck, Bryan
82Beloit-20
83ElPaso-15
84ElPaso-5
85Cram/PCL-222
86Vanco-7
87D-397
87Denver-23
87F-342
87T-562
89Pol/Brew-48
89T/Tr-21T
90OPC-264
90T-264
90UD-239

Clyde, David
74OPC-133
74T-133
74T/St-233
75OPC-12
75T-12
75T/M-12
76Laugh/Jub-19
77Tucson
79T-399
80T-697

Clymer, Otis Edgar
E254
E270/2
T204

Clymer, William J.
T206

Coachman, Pete
86PalmSp-7
86PalmSp/Smok-22
87Edmon-13
88Edmon/CMC-13
88Edmon/ProC-578
89Edmon/CMC-12
89Edmon/ProC-563
90Edmon/CMC-20
90Edmon/ProC-522
91S-344RP
91T/90Debut-32
91Tacoma/LineD-531
91Tacoma/ProC-2311

Coakley, Andrew
T204

Coan, Gilbert F.
(Gil)
49B-90
50B-54
51B-18
52B-51
52RM-AL4
52T-291
53B/Col-34
53T-133
54B-40
54Esskay
55B-78
55Esskay
88Chatt/Team-6
91Crown/Orio-78
91T/Arc53-133
R302-114

Coates, Jim
59T-525
60L-35
60T-51
61P-17
61T-531
62T-553
63T-237
67T-401
78TCMA-217
78TCMA-267

Coates, Thomas
91Idaho/ProC-4339

Coatney, Rick
81Durham-16
82Durham-15

Cobb, Joseph S.
No Cards.

Cobb, Mark
88Spartan/Star-20
88Spartan/Star-4
89Clearw/Star-7
89Star/Wax-11

Cobb, Marvin
89BendB/Legoe-2
90PalmSp/Cal-219
90PalmSp/ProC-2570
91London/LineD-430
91MidldA/ProC-429

Cobb, Tyrus Raymond
(Ty)
09Buster/Pin-4
10Domino-26
11Helmar-28
12Sweet/Pin-22A
12Sweet/Pin-22B
14CJ-30
14Piedmont/St-13
15CJ-30
16FleischBrd-17
21Exh-24
25Exh-90
26Exh-91
27Exh-53
28Yueng-27
33SK-1
48Exh/HOF-2
50Callahan
60Exh/HOF-7
60F-42
60NuCard-43
61F-14
61F-1M
61GP-25
61NuCard-443
63Bz/ATG-35
69Bz-1
69Bz-7
69Bz-8
72F/FFeat-15
72K/ATG-15
72Laugh/GF-35
73F/Wild-35M
73OPC-471LL
73OPC-475LL
73T-471LL
73T-475LL
75F/Pion-14
76Motor-3
76OPC-346AS
76T-346AS
79T-411M
79T-414M
80Pac/Leg-31
80Laugh/3/4/5-4
80Laugh/FFeat-28
80SSPC/HOF
81Detroit-17
83D/HOF-1
84D/Champs-26
84West/1-8
85Woolwth-8
86Conlon/1-2
86Conlon/1-24
86Conlon/1-41
86Conlon/1-6
87Conlon/2-5
87Nestle/DT-7
88Conlon/4-6
88Conlon/HardC-2
89HOF/St-37
89Pac/Leg-117
89Swell-2
89T/LJN-85
90BBWit-56
90HOF/St-19
90Swell/Great-15
91Conlon/Sport-250
91Homer/Classic-4
91LineD-48
91Swell/Great-127
92Conlon/Sport-425
92Conlon/Sport-525
92S/II-878
B18

BF2-25
D303
D304
D327
D328-30
D329-38
E101
E102
E103
E105
E106
E120
E121/120
E121/80
E126-17
E135-30
E210-27
E220
E224
E254
E270/1
E270/2
E300
E90/1
E92
E93
E94
E95
E98
L1-127
M101/4-38
M116
PM1-3
R328-14
R423-14
S74-13
S81-102
T201
T202
T205
T206
T213/blue
T213/brown
T215/blue
T215/brown
T216
T227
T3-9
V100
V117-22
V61-30
W501-8
W502-27
W512-3
W514-43
W515-10
W516-6
W555
W572
W573
WG4-5
WG5-11
WG6-11

Coble, David Lamar
(Dave)
No Cards.

Coble, Drew
88TM/Umpire-45
89TM/Umpire-43
90TM/Umpire-41

Cobleigh, Mike
89Modesto/Chong-5

Cocanower, Jaime
81Vanco-1
82Vanco-20
84F/X-28
84Pol/Brew-47
84T/Tr-26
85Cram/PCL-210
85D-455
85F-579
85Gard-4
85Pol/Brew-47
85T-576
85T/St-288
86D-393
86F-483
86Pol/Brew-47
86T-277
86T/Tr-24T
87Albuq/Pol-7
87T-423
87T/GlossRk-4

Coccia, Dan
88Martins/Star-7

Cochran, Arnold
81Batavia-12
81Watlo-20

Cochran, Dave
84Jacks-21

Cochran, George L.
No Cards.

Cochran, Greg
79Colum-17
80Colum-21
81Colum-12
82Colum-8
82Colum/Pol-27

Cochran, Jamie
91Johnson/ClBest-17
91Johnson/ProC-3971

Cochrane, Dave
87Hawaii-13
87Sf-158M
87Seven-C5
88Calgary/CMC-14
88Calgary/ProC-785
89Calgary/CMC-14
89Calgary/ProC-542
90Calgary/CMC-11
90OPC-491
90T-491
91Calgary/LineD-55
91Calgary/ProC-518
92D/II-539
92S/100RisSt-70
92S/II-461

Cochrane, Gordon S.
(Mickey)
28Exh-53
29Exh/4-27
31Exh/4-28
32Orbit/num-28
32Orbit/un-12
33DH-10
33DL-6
33Exh/4-14
33G-76
34DS-4
34Exh/4-12
34Exh/4-14
34G-2
35BU-25
35Exh/4-12
35G-1D
35G-1J
35G-2D
35G-3A
35G-5A
35G-6A
35G-6D
35G-7D
35Wheat
36Exh/4-12
36G
36Wheat
37Exh/4-12
40PB-180
48Exh/HOF
49Leaf/Prem-2
50Callahan
51T/CMAS
60F-24
60NuCard-19
61F-15
61GP-12
61NuCard-419
63Bz/ATG-34
69Bz/Sm
72K/ATG-4
76OPC-348AS
76T-348AS
80Pac/Leg-38
80SSPC/HOF
81Detroit-3
85West/2-29
86Conlon/1-7
86Sf/Dec-13
87Nestle/DT-8
88Conlon/3-7
88Conlon/AmAS-5
89HOF/St-56
89Pac/Leg-151
90Swell/Great-3
91Conlon/Sport-266
91Conlon/Sport-51
91LineD-49
91Swell/Great-142
92Conlon/Sport-432
92Conlon/Sport-551
R305
R306
R308-155
R308-186
R309/2
R310
R311/Gloss
R312
R314
R328-12
R332-32
V353-69
V354-59
V355-45
W517-37
W517-54

Cock, J.R.
91BendB/ClBest-1
91BendB/ProC-3688

Cockman, James
(Jim)
No Cards.

Cockrell, Alan
86Shrev-4
87Phoenix-15
88Phoenix/CMC-19
88Phoenix/ProC-68
89Portl/CMC-20
89Portl/ProC-224
90AAAGame/ProC-AAA50
90ColoSp/CMC-23
90ColoSp/ProC-49
91Calgary/LineD-56
91Calgary/ProC-526
92T-591M

Codinach, Antonio
84Visalia-19

Codiroli, Chris
82WHave-4
83T/Tr-20
84D-345
84F-441
84Mother/A's-10
84Nes/792-61
84OPC-61
84T-61
84T/St-330
85D-462
85F-420
85Mother/A's-9
85T-552
85T/St-327
86D-278
86F-414
86Leaf-151
86Mother/A's-15
86OPC-388
86T-433
86T/St-173
87D-226
87F-390
87T-217
89T-6

Cody
N172

Coentopp, Kevin
86Cram/PCL-175

Cofer, Brian
90Watertn/Star-4
91Collnd/ClBest-11
91Collnd/ProC-1478

Coffey, John Francis
(Jack)
No Cards.

Coffey, Mike
85Cedar-3
86Elmira-5
87WinHaven-11

Coffey, Stephen
90Geneva/ProC-3047
90Geneva/Star-4
91Peoria/ProC-1346

Coffman, George David
39PB-147
40PB-55
41G-32

Coffman, Jim
82Amari-12

Coffman, Kevin
85Durham-5
86Durham-5
87Greenvl/Best-20
87SLAS-19
88D/Rook-49
88F-536
88T/Tr-29T
89B-282
89OPC-44
89T-488
91Jacks/LineD-555
91Jacks/ProC-918

Coffman, Samuel R.
(Dick)
33G-101
35BU-92
35G-1F
35G-3D
35G-5D
35G-6D
39PB-24
40PB-140
91Conlon/Sport-321
V354-23

Coggins, Franklin
68OPC-96R
68T-96R

Coggins, Richard A.
(Rich)
73JP
73OPC-611R
73T-611R
74OPC-353
74T-353
75OPC-167
75T-167
76OPC-572
76SSPC-446
75T/M-167
76T-572
91Crown/Orio-79

Coghen, Al
77Wausau
78Wausau

Coghill, Dave
80Ander-7

Cogswell, Edward
(Ed)
No Cards.

Cohea, Dave
77Clinton
82Albuq-25
83Albuq-24

Cohen, Albert
(Alta)
90Target-132

Cohen, Andrew Howard
(Andy)
33G-52
60T-466C
V353-52

Cohen, John
91Single/ClBest-78
91Visalia/ClBest-20
91Visalia/ProC-1752

Cohen, Tony
87Macon-23
88Augusta/ProC-380

Cohick, Emmitt
91QuadC/ClBest-23
91QuadC/ProC-2642

Cohoon, Don
86Wausau-4
88CharWh/Best-18
89WinSalem/Star-5

Coin, Mike
85Beloit-5

Coker, Jimmie Goodwin
60T-438
61T-144
63T-456
64T-211
65OPC-192
65T-192
66T-292
67OPC-158
67T-158

Coker, Larry
88Fayette/ProC-1084

Colarusso, Sam
88CapeCod/Sum-105

Colavito, Rocco D.
(Rocky)
55Salem
57Sohio/Ind-4
57Swift
57T-212
58T-368
59Bz
59HRDerby-6
59Kahn
59T-166M
59T-420
59T-462HL
60Armour-5
60Bz-30
60NuCard-68
60T-260M
60T-400
60T/tatt-88
60T/tatt-9
61Bz-17
61NuCard-468
61P-36
61T-330
61T-44LL
62Exh
62P-19
62P/Can-19
62Salada-28
62Shirriff-28
62T-20
62T-314IA
62T-472AS
62T/bucks
62T/St-46
63Bz-33
63Exh
63J-50
63P-50
63Salada-58
63T-240
63T-4LL
63T/SO
64Bz-33
64T-320
64T/Coins-46
64T/S-9
64T/St-65
64T/SU
64T/tatt
65Bz-33
65OldLond-23
65T-380
65T/E-46
65T/trans-45
66Bz-15
66OPC-150
66T-150
66T-220LL
66T/RO-72
67Bz-15
67OPC-109M
67T-109M
67T-580
68OPC-99
68T-99
73OPC-449CO
73T-449CO
79TCMA-216
81Detroit-99
83Kaline-19M
85CircK-27
89Swell-126
90Pac/Legend-18
90Swell/Great-119
90Target-133
91Swell/Great-116
Exh47

Colavito, Steve
88Watlo/ProC-679

Colbern, Michael M.
(Mike)
79T-704R
80T-664R
81T-522
82Richm-22
88Indianap/ProC-499M

Colbert, Craig
88Clinton/ProC-707
89Shreve/ProC-1844
89TexLAS/GS-30
90Phoenix/CMC-16
90Phoenix/ProC-18
91Phoenix/LineD-380

91Phoenix/ProC-70
Colbert, Nathan
(Nate)
66T-596R
69MB-63
69T-408
70MLB/St-111
70OPC-11
70T-11
70T/SO
71K-72
71MLB/St-223
71OPC-235
71T-235
71T/Coins-77
71T/GM-28
71T/S-22
71T/tatt-1
72K-41
72MB-78
72T-571
72T-572IA
73K-33
73OPC-340
73T-340
73T/Comics-5
73T/Lids-11
73T/PinUps-5
74K-19
74McDon
74OPC-125
74T-125
74T/DE-34
74T/St-91
75Ho-76
75OPC-599
75T-599
75T/M-599
76Laugh/Jub-16
76OPC-495
76SSPC-330
76T-495
77T-433HL
87Wichita-6
88Wichita-17
89Padre/Mag-12
89River/Best-24
89River/Cal-27CO
89River/ProC-1391CO
90HOF/St-80
90Riversi/Best-19CO
90Riversi/Cal-26CO
90Riversi/ProC-2622CO
Colbert, Rick
81Bristol-10
85Cram/PCL-59
87Louisvl-10
88ArkTr/GS-1
89Spring/Best-27
90Savan/ProC-2084MG
91Hamil/ClBest-29
91Hamil/ProC-4056
Colbert, Vince
71MLB/St-365
71OPC-231R
71T-231R
72OPC-84
72T-84
Colborn, Jim
71MLB/St-29
71OPC-38
71T-38
72OPC-386
72T-386
73OPC-408
73T-408
74OPC-75
74T-75
74T/DE-49
74T/St-193
75OPC-305
75T-305
75T/M-305
76A&P/Milw
76OPC-521
76SSPC-226
76T-521
77T-331
78OPC-116
78T-129
79OPC-137
79T-276
85Iowa-29CO
86Iowa-7CO
Colbrunn, Greg
88MidwLAS/GS-42
88Rockford-8
89Rockford-8
89WPalmB/Star-7
90A&AASingle/ProC-53
90Foil/Best-5
90Jaxvl/Best-1
90Jaxvl/ProC-1377
91B-449
91D-425RR
91OPC-91
91T-91
91T/StClub/I-215
91UD-15SR
92D/II-557
Cole, Albert G.
E120
V100
W573
Cole, Alex
86FSLAS-11
86StPete-6
87ArkTr-20
88Louisvl-14
88Louisvl/CMC-11
88Louisvl/ProC-438
89AAA/CMC-14
89Louisvl-14
89Louisvl/CMC-21
89Louisvl/ProC-1266
89StPete/Star-7
90F-244
90LasVegas/CMC-16
90LasVegas/ProC-133
90UD/Ext-751
91B-64
91Classic/I-36
91D-383
91F-365
91F/Ultra-110
91Leaf/I-108
91OPC-421
91OPC/Premier-24
91Panini/FrSt-222
91Panini/Top15-48
91S-555
91S/100RisSt-13
91T-421
91T/90Debut-33
91T/StClub/II-392
91ToysRUs-5
91UD-654
92D/I-220
92F-108
92S/II-463
92T-170
92UD-197
Cole, Bert
V61-28
Cole, Butch
91AppFx/ClBest-23
91AppFx/ProC-1728
Cole, Chris
89BurlInd/Star-5
Cole, David
52B-132
53B/BW-38
53JC-6
Cole, Howard
90Reno/Cal-283
Cole, Joey
79QuadC-13
Cole, Leonard
(King)
11Helmar-93
E286
E300
E90/3
T201
T207
Cole, Mark
90Lakeland/Star-4
Cole, Marvin
88Wythe/ProC-1982
90PeoriaUp/Team-U5
91WinSalem/ClBest-18
91WinSalem/ProC-2835
Cole, Michael
81Wisco-15
Cole, Popeye
90CLAS/CL-30
90Durham/Team-12
91Greenvl/ClBest-20
91Greenvl/LineD-204
91Greenvl/ProC-3014
Cole, Richard Roy
(Dick)
52Mother-35
53SpicSpan/3x5-7
54B-27
54T-84
55B-28
57T-234
58Union
Cole, Robert
(Bob)
88Sumter/ProC-392
89BurlB/ProC-1627
89BurlB/Star-5
Cole, Rodger
85Cram/PCL-45
85Phill/TastyK-42
86Indianap-17
Cole, Stewart
(Stu)
89Memphis/Best-9
89Memphis/ProC-1184
89Memphis/Star-7
89Star/Wax-41
90Memphis/Best-4
90Memphis/ProC-1014
90Memphis/Star-5
91Omaha/LineD-330
91Omaha/ProC-1040
92T/91Debut-37
Cole, Tim
78Green
79Savan-20
82Richm-3
83Durham-18
Cole, Victor
89Memphis/Best-19
89Memphis/ProC-1185
89Memphis/Star-8
90Memphis/Best-20
90Memphis/ProC-1006
90Memphis/Star-6
91Omaha/LineD-331
91Omaha/ProC-1028
Cole, Willis Russell
No Cards.
Cole, Winston
76Baton
77Salem
Coleman, Billy
91Oneonta/ProC-4146
Coleman, Clarence
(Choo Choo)
61T-502
63Exh
63T-27
64T-251
66T-561
89Tidew/Candl-5
91WIZMets-79
Exh47
Coleman, Curtis H.
(Curt)
No Cards.
Coleman, Dale
91SanAn/ProC-2967
91VeroB/ClBest-6
91VeroB/ProC-767
Coleman, David Lee
(Dave)
79Toledo-17
80Colum-19
81Colum-18
Coleman, DeWayne
86Visalia-7
87WinSalem-25
88CharWh/Best-19
Coleman, Gerald F.
(Jerry)
49B-225
50B-47
50Drake-26
51B-49
51BR-A6
51T/RB-18
52B-73
52BR
52StarCal/L-70E
52T-237
54B-81
55B-99
55RFG-25
56T-316
57T-192
78Padre/FamFun-6
79TCMA-36
84Smok/Padres-5
90Padre/MagUno-8ANN
91Swell/Great-19
Exh47
PM10/L-10
PM10/Sm-27
R423-10
Coleman, Glenn
91Bluefld/ProC-4139
91Bluefld/ClBest-14
Coleman, Gordon C.
(Gordy)
60HenryH-5
60T-257
60Union-19
61Kahn
61T-194
62J-116
62Kahn
62P-116
62P/Can-116
62Salada-110
62Shirriff-110
62T-508
62T/St-113
63FrBauer-3
63J-125
63Kahn
63P-125
63T-90
64T-577
65Kahn
65T-289
66T-494
67OPC-61
67T-61
Exh47
Coleman, J. Dale
89VeroB/Star-5
Coleman, Joe H.
66T-333R
67OPC-167R
67T-167R
68T-573
69MB-64
69MLB/St-103
69T-246
69T/St-234
70MLB/St-281
70OPC-127
70T-127
71MLB/St-390
71OPC-403
71T-403
72K-18
72MB-79
72OPC-96LL
72T-640
72T-96LL
73K-48
73OPC-120
73T-120
74K-3
74OPC-240
74T-240
74T/DE-53
74T/St-173
75OPC-42
75T-42
75T/M-42
76OPC-456
76OPC-68FS
76SSPC-358
76T-456
76T-68FS
77T-219
78T-554
79OPC-166
79Portl-11
79T-329
80Spokane-5
80T-542
81Detroit-126
81Spokane-19
83Peor/LF-29MG
89Pac/SenLg-109
Coleman, Joe P.
50B-141
51B-120
53T-279
54Esskay
54NYJour
54T-156
55B-3
55Esskay
55RFG-20
55RM-AL17
55T-162
76T-68FS
91Crown/Orio-80
91T/Arc53-279
Coleman, John Francis
E223
N172
N284
WG1-56
Coleman, Ken
89Utica/Pucko-4
Coleman, Matthew
89Bristol/Star-5
Coleman, Parke Edward
(Ed)
34G-28
35G-8J
35G-9J
V354-76
Coleman, Paul
89Johnson/Star-6
89LittleSun-10
90B-199
90OPC-654FDP
90Savan/ProC-2082
90S-662DC
90T-654
90T/TVCard-43
91B-385
91Spring/ProC-755
Coleman, Raymond L.
(Ray)
50B-250
51B-136
52B-201
52Hawth/Pin-1
52T-211
Coleman, Rickey
85Beaum-2
Coleman, Rico
89Spokane/SP-24
90CharRain/Best-6
90CharRain/ProC-2053
Coleman, Ronnie
91BurlInd/ProC-3314
Coleman, Scott
91Martins/ClBest-25
91Martins/ProC-3445
Coleman, Solomon
(Hampton)
52Park-65
53Exh/Can-52
Coleman, Ty
80BurlB-14
Coleman, Vince
84Louisvl-20
85D/HL-29M
85D/HL-54
85F/Up-U28
85Louisvl-5
85T/Tr-24T
86D-181
86D-651M
86F-31
86F-636M
86F-637IA
86F/LimEd-11
86F/LL-7
86F/Mini-7
86F/Slug-M4
86F/St-25
86KAS/Disc-1
86KayBee-5
86Leaf-115
86Leaf-225M
86OPC-370
86OPC-D
86Quaker-3
86Sf-136M
86Sf-176M
86Sf-24
86Schnucks-2
86T-201RB
86T-370

86T-D
86T/Gloss60-21
86T/Mini-60
86T/St-306
86T/St-47
86T/St-5
86T/Super-8
86T/WaxBox-D
87Classic-30
87D-263
87D/HL-36
87D/OD-60
87F-290
87F/LL-11
87F/Lim-10
87F/Mini-21
87F/Slug-M3
87F/St-25
87KayBee-11
87Kraft-18
87Leaf-194
87OPC-119
87RedFoley/St-8
87Sf-152M
87Sf-199M
87Sf-65
87Smok/Cards-24
87T-590
87T/Coins-29
87T/Gloss60-38
87T/Mini-32
87T/St-50
88Bz-5
88Classic/Blue-223
88D-293
88D/Best-44
88F-27
88F-634M
88F/BB/MVP-7
88F/Excit-11
88F/LL-7
88F/Mini-106
88F/St-117
88F/WS-6
88Jiffy-7
88KMart-8
88Leaf-128
88MSA/Disc-11
88OPC-260
88Panini/St-394
88S-652HL
88S-68
88S/YS/II-24
88Sf-221
88Sf-67
88Smok/Card-19
88T-1RB
88T-260
88T/Big-5
88T/Mini-70
88T/Revco-3
88T/St-4
88T/St-47
88T/UK-16
88Woolw-2
89B-443
89Bz-6
89Cadaco-10
89D-181
89D-19DK
89D/AS-38
89D/Best-19
89D/DKsuper-19DK
89D/PopUp-38
89F-445
89F/BBAS-8
89F/Excit-7
89F/LL-6
89OPC-90
89Panini/St-188
89Panini/St-229AS
89S-155
89S/HotStar-86
89S/Mast-35
89Sf-113
89Smok/Cards-2
89T-90
89T/Big-124
89T/Gloss22-17
89T/LJN-72
89T/Mini-33
89T/St-154
89T/St-43
89UD-253
90B-198
90BBWit-45
90Bz-8
90Classic-105
90D-279
90D/BestNL-138
90F-245
90F/AwardWin-9
90HOF/St-100
90Holsum/Discs-15
90KayBee-7
90Leaf/I-90
90MLBPA/Pins-35
90OPC-660
90OPC-6RB
90Panini/St-216
90Panini/St-336
90Panini/St-383
90Publint/St-213
90Publint/St-609
90RedFoley/St-19
90S-260
90S/100St-73
90Sf-142
90Smok/Card-1
90SpringDG/Best-31
90T-660
90T-6RB
90T/Big-184
90T/DH-12
90T/Mini-73
90T/St-39
90T/St-4HL
90T/TVCard-32
90UD-223
90UD-68TC
90Woolwth/HL-10
91B-471
91BBBest/RecBr-4
91Bz-12
91Classic/200-93
91Classic/I-91
91D-487
91F-629
91F/Ultra-212
91F/Up-U102
91Kahn/Mets-1
91Leaf/II-427
91Leaf/Stud-202
91OPC-160
91OPC/Premier-25
91Panini/FrSt-35
91Panini/St-35
91Panini/Top15-41
91Post-5
91RedFoley/St-21
91S-450
91S/RookTr-57T
91T-160
91T/StClub/II-498
91T/Tr-23T
91UD-461
91UD/Ext-768
92D/I-218
92F-500
92S/100SS-79
92S/I-95
92T-500
92UD-131

Coleman, W. Rip
57T-354
59T-51
60T-179
61BeeHive-5
91Crown/Orio-81
D301

Coles, Cadwallader R.
(Cad)
T206

Coles, Charles Edward
(Chuck)
59T-120

Coles, Darnell
81Wausau-19
83Chatt-1
84Cram/PCL-190
84D-630
84Mother/Mar-26
85Cram/PCL-96
85D-118
85T-108
86D-557
86F/Up-U27
86T-337
86T/Tr-26T
87Cain's-2
87Coke/Tigers-14
87D-230
87D/OD-215
87F-148
87OPC-388
87Seven-DT1
87T-411
87T/St-271
88D-572
88D/Best-185
88OPC-46
88S-554
88T-46
88T/Big-255
89B-217
89D-566
89F-544
89Mother/Sea-23
89S-83
89T-738
89T/Big-133
89UD-339
90B-480
90D-212
90F-509
90Mother/Mar-22
90OPC-232
90Panini/St-145
90Publint/St-429
90S-62
90T-232
90T/St-227
90UD-311
91F-333
91OPC-506
91Phoenix/LineD-381
91Phoenix/ProC-79
91S-629
91T-506

Colescott, Rob
85LitFalls-15
86LitFalls-6
87Columbia-27
88SALAS/GS-24
88Savan/ProC-335
89Spring/Best-5

Coletta, Chris
75IntAS/TCMA-12
75IntAS/TCMA-27

Coletti, Mike
91Billings/ProC-3745

Colgan, William H.
(Bill)
No Cards.

Coliver, William J.
(Bill)
No Cards.

Colletti, Manny
82Omaha-15
82OrlTw/A-4

Colley, Jay
88RochR/ProC-220

Collier, Anthony
89GreatF-22
90VeroB/Star-8
91AS/Cal-17

Collins, Allen
86WPalmB-8
87WPalmB-15
88WPalmB/Star-7
90Canton/Best-25
90Canton/ProC-1286
90Canton/Star-2

Collins, Charles
(Chub)
No Cards.

Collins, Chris
86QuadC-7
87MidldA-4
88MidldA/GS-7

Collins, Cyril Wilson
No Cards.

Collins, Daniel T.
(Dan)
No Cards.

Collins, Dave
83Madis/LF-3DB

Collins, David S.
(Dave)
76OPC-363
76SSPC-191
76T-363
77OPC-248
77T-431
78T-254
79T-622
80T-73
81Coke
81D-185
81F-201
81OPC-175
81T-175
81T/HT
81T/SO-84
81T/St-162
82D-169
82F-61
82F/St-14
82OPC-349
82T-595
82T/St-33
82T/Tr-20T
83D-234
83F-377
83OPC-359
83T-359
83T/Tr-21
84D-650
84F-151
84Nes/792-733
84OPC-38
84T-733
84Tor/Fire-9
85D-241
85F-102
85F/St-55
85F/Up-U29
85Leaf-172
85Mother/A's-14
85OPC-164
85T-463
85T/St-363
85T/Tr-25T
86Cain's-3
86D-218
86F-415
86F/Up-U28
86OPC-271
86T-271
86T/St-172
86T/Tr-27T
87D-215
87F-149
87T-148
88Kahn/Reds-22
88S-371
89Kodak/WSox-2M
89S-267
89TM/SenLg-22
89UD-351
90Smok/Card-2
90T/TVCard-33

Collins, Don
80Tacoma-5
82Spring-18

Collins, Edw.T. Jr.
(Eddie)
No Cards.

Collins, Edw.T. Sr.
(Eddie)
10Domino-27
11Helmar-55
12Sweet/Pin-43A
12Sweet/Pin-43B
14CJ-7
14Piedmont/St-14
15CJ-7
21Exh-25
25Exh-73
26Exh-74
27Exh-54
33G-42
48Exh/HOF
50Callahan
51T/CM
60Exh/HOF-8
60F-20
61F-16
61GP-28
63Bz/ATG-41
69Bz/Sm
72F/FFeat-18
72K/ATG-10
72Laugh/GF-43
75F/Pion-20
80Pac/Leg-26
80Laugh/FFeat-32
80SSPC/HOF
87Conlon/2-27
88Conlon/5-5
88Pac/8Men-8
88Pac/8Men-99
90BBWit-76
91Conlon/Sport-21
91Conlon/Sport-312
92Conlon/Sport-582
BF2-9
D303
D304
D327
D328-31
D329-34
E101
E102
E103
E104
E105
E106
E120
E121/120
E121/80
E122
E126-16
E135-31
E210-47
E221
E254
E90/1
E92
E93
E98
L1-125
M101/4-34
M116
R328-1
S74-29
S81-100
T202
T204
T205
T206
T207
T208
T213/blue
T215/blue
T215/brown
T216
V117-4
V353-42
V61-29
W501-38
W514-25
W515-58
W517-52
W555
W572
W573
W575
WG4-6

Collins, Frankie
80GlenF/C-29M

Collins, George H.
(Hub)
N172

Collins, Harry W.
(Rip)
W575

Collins, Hugh
No Cards.

Collins, James Joseph
(Jimmy)
35Wheat
50Callahan
51T/CMAS
60Exh/HOF-9
60F-25
61F-99
63Bz/ATG-23
69Bz/Sm
80SSPC/HOF
89HOF/St-23
E104
E107
E220
E91
E95
R310
T204
T205

T206
T3-87
W555
WG2-8
Collins, James A.
(Rip)
35BU-146
35BU-78
35G-51
88Conlon/NatAS-3
92Conlon/Sport-656
R312
R312/M
R313
V355-18
WG8-7
Collins, John Edgar
(Zip)
No Cards.
Collins, John Francis
(Shano)
11Helmar-9
21Exh-26
88Pac/8Men-98
BF2-10
D327
D328-32
D329-35
D350/2-34
E120
E135-32
M101/4-35
M101/5-34
V100
W572
Collins, Joseph E.
(Joe)
52B-181
52BR
52T-202
53T-9
54NYJour
54T-83
55T-63
55T/DH-65
56T-21
56T/Pin-28
57T-295
79TCMA-21
91T/Arc53-9
PM10/L-11
Collins, Kevin M.
65T-581R
69OPC-127
69T-127
70T-707
71OPC-553
71T-553
91WIZMets-80
Collins, Orth Stein
No Cards.
Collins, Patrick T.
26Exh-97
28Exh-49
29Exh/4-1
91Conlon/Sport-118
E126-35
V61-35
Collins, Phil
32Orbit/num-22
32Orbit/un-13
33G-21
35Exh/4-6
R305
V353-21
Collins, Ray
15CJ-169
16FleischBrd-18
M116
Collins, Robert J.
(Bob)
No Cards.
Collins, Ron
88Eugene/Best-18
89Eugene/Best-20
Collins, Scott
81Batavia-19
Collins, Sean
89Eugene/Best-24
90BBCity/Star-4
Collins, Sherman
89VeroB/Star-6
Collins, Stacey
91Rockford/ClBest-3
91Rockford/ProC-2038
Collins, Terry
78Cr/PCL-41
80Albuq-19
82VeroB-26
84Cram/PCL-167
85Cram/PCL-156MG
86Albuq-3MG
87Albuq/Pol-1MG
88AAA/ProC-47
88Albuq/CMC-25
88Albuq/ProC-270
89BuffB/CMC-24
89BuffB/ProC-1668
90AAAGame/ProC-AAA36MG
90BuffB/CMC-3MG
90BuffB/ProC-389MG
90BuffB/Team-7MG
91BuffB/LineD-49MG
91BuffB/ProC-556MG
Collins, Tharon L.
(Pat)
E120
W573
Collins, Tim
85Bend/Cram-5
Collins, Tony
86Geneva-3
86Peoria-3
Collins, William J.
(Bill)
N172
Collins, William S.
(Bill)
90Target-915
C46-34
Collucio, Bob
74T/St-194
Collum, Jack
54B-204
55B-189
57T-268
90Target-134
V362-30
Colman, Frank Lloyd
52Park-9
Colombino, Carlo
86Ashvl-5
87Osceola-4
88ColAst/Best-19
88SLAS-10
89Tucson/CMC-21
89Tucson/ProC-206
89Tucson/JP-5
91Tucson/LineD-608
91Tucson/ProC-2219
Colombino, Chris
90Osceola/Star-5
Colon, Cristobal
87PortChar-22
88Gaston/ProC-1005
89Gaston/ProC-1014
89Gaston/Star-4
90CharlR/Star-3
90SALAS/Star-4
91CharlR/ClBest-17
91CharlR/ProC-1321
91Single/ClBest-183
Colon, David
88Sumter/ProC-411
90Waterlo/Best-2
90Waterlo/ProC-2389
91PalmSp/ProC-2027
Colon, Felix
90WinHaven/Star-2
91Elmira/ClBest-2
91Elmira/ProC-3275
Colon, Hector
91Johnson/ClBest-14
91Johnson/ProC-3988
Colon, Jose
91Burllnd/ProC-3291
Colon, Tony
89Geneva/ProC-1875
Colpaert, Dick
73OPC-608R
73T-608R
Colpitt, Mike
87Spartan-28
Colson, Bruce
88Cedar/ProC-1145
Colson, Loyd
71OPC-111R
71T-111R
Colston, Frank
87Miami-16
87SLCity/Taco-18
88Wausau/GS-24
Colton, Lawrence
68T-348R
69T-454R
Coluccio, Robert P.
(Bob)
74OPC-124
74T-124
75OPC-456
75T-456
75T/M-456
76OPC-333
76SSPC-150
76T-333
78Charl
Colvard, Benny
(Ben)
88Billings/ProC-1830
89Cedar/Best-19
89Cedar/ProC-916
89Cedar/Star-4
91Chatt/ProC-1971
Colzie, Rick
80Batavia-22
81Watlo-2
Combe, Geoff
79Indianap-19
80Indianap-7
81Indianap-3
81T-606R
82Edmon-23
82F-62
82T-351R
Combs, Bobby
75AppFx
77AppFx
Combs, Earle Bryan
26Exh-98
28Yueng-21
29Exh/4-25
31Exh/4-25
32Orbit/num-111
33G-103
40PB-124
44Yank/St-6
54T-183
61F-17
80Pac/Leg-105
80SSPC/HOF
91Conlon/Sport-105
91Conlon/Sport-262
92Conlon/Sport-466
92Conlon/Sport-583
R314
R316
R328-5
R332-28
V354-21
W502-21
W513-86
W517-1
Combs, Mark
87SanBern-9
88Fresno/Cal-2
Combs, Merrill R.
48Signal
48Smith-23
52T-18
Combs, Pat
88T/Tr-30T
89B-398
89BBAmerAA/BPro-AA10
89Clearw/Star-8
89Reading/ProC-676
89Reading/Star-9
89Star/Wax-12
89T/Big-227
90B-148
90Classic/Up-12
90D-44
90D/BestNL-49
90D/Rook-3
90F-553
90Leaf/I-78
90OPC-384
90Phill/TastyK-5
90S-623RP
90S/DTRook-B2
90S/YS/II-4
90T-384
90T/89Debut-24
90T/Big-136
90UD/Ext-763
91B-498
91Classic/200-94
91Classic/II-T41
91D-60
91F-392
91F/Ultra-259
91Leaf/I-32
91OPC-571
91Phill/Medford-9
91S-440
91S/100RisSt-72
91T-571
91T/StClub/I-36
91ToysRUs-6
91UD-537
92D/I-76
92F-525
92S/I-106
92T-456
92UD-442
Comeau, Drew
88CapeCod/Sum-124
Comer, H. Wayne
69T-346
70McDon-2
70MLB/St-268
70OPC-323
70T-323
88Domino-3
Comer, Steve
79T-463
80T-144
81T-592
82D-341
82F-314
82F/St-177
82T-16
82T/St-242
83D-163
83F-564
83T-353
84Wheat/Ind-31
85T-788
86Maine-6C
88OrlanTw/Best-7
Comforti, Dave
81Holyo-5M
Comiskey, Charles A.
(Charlie)
14CJ-23
15CJ-23
50Callahan
61F-18
80SSPC/HOF
87Conlon/2-26
88Pac/8Men-24
88Pac/8Men-80
BF2-11
D329-36
D350/2-35
M101/4-36
M101/5-35
N172
N172/BC
N28
N284
N370
Scrapps
Command, James Dalton
(Jim)
No Cards.
Como, George
82Holyo-25
83Nashua-26
85Nashua-28
Comoletti, Glenn
78StPete
Comorosky, Adam A.
31Exh/4-13
33G-77
34G-85
35BU-44
35G-1H
35G-1K
35G-3B
35G-3F
35G-4F
35G-5B
35G-5F
35G-6B
91Conlon/Sport-73
V353-70
Compos, Rafael
89Ashvl/ProC-949
Compres, Fidel
87Watlo-1
90CharlR/Star-4
91ArkTr/ProC-1276
91Louisvl/LineD-231
Compton, Anna S.
(Pete)
No Cards.
Compton, Kenny
86Fres/Smok-27bb
Compton, Michael Lynn
(Mike)
71MLB/St-174
71OPC-77
71T-77
77Spartan
80Water-10
Comstock, Brad
87Everett-27
88Fresno/Cal-25
88Fresno/ProC-1226
Comstock, Keith
77QuadC
80WHave-19
81WHave-6
82Tacoma-39
82WHave-5
83BirmB-22
84Toledo-16
88F-579
88LasVegas/CMC-2
88LasVegas/ProC-246
88S-438
88T-778
89LasVegas/CMC-2
89LasVegas/ProC-14
90B-467
90BirmDG/Best-5
90F-510
90Leaf/II-522
90Mother/Mar-23
91CounHrth-20
91D-246
91OPC-337
91S-502
91T-337A
91T-337B
91T/StClub/II-556
Conatser, Clinton A.
(Clint)
49Eureka-5
Concepcion, Carlos
84CharlO-6
Concepcion, David E.
(Dave)
71MLB/St-56
71OPC-14
71T-14
72OPC-267
72T-267
72T/Cloth-7
73OPC-554
73T-554
74OPC-435
74T-435
74T/St-24
75Ho-47
75OPC-17
75T-17
75T/M-17
76Ho-128
76Icee
76OPC-48
76SSPC-34
76T-48
77BurgChef-200
77Ho-95
77OPC-258
77Pepsi-47
77T-560
78Ho-108
78OPC-220
78T-180
78Wiffle/Discs-19
79Ho-85

79OPC-234
79T-450
80OPC-117
80T-220
81Coke
81D-181
81F-197
81F/St-15
81K-28
81OPC-83
81PermaGr/AS-2
81T-375
81T/HT
81T/SO-95
81T/St-161
82Coke/Reds
82D-421
82F-63
82F/St-109M
82K-22
82OPC-221IA
82OPC-340AS
82OPC-86
82PermaGr/AS-11
82Sqt-15
82T-340
82T-660
82T-661A
82T/St-124
82T/St-37
83D-148
83D/AAS-47
83F-588
83F-631M
83K-57
83OPC-102
83OPC-32AS
83T-400
83T-720
83T/Gloss40-34
83T/St-227
84D-121
84D-2
84F-466
85FunFood/Pin-23
84MiltBrad-6
84Nes/792-55
84OPC-55
84Ralston-20
84T-55
84T/Cereal-20
84T/St-56
85D-203
85D/HL-8
85F-532
85Leaf-131
85OPC-21
85T-515
85T/St-48
86D-243
86F-174
86OPC-195
86Sf-131M
86Sf-153
86T-366M
86T/St-137
86TexGold-13
87F-196
87Kahn-13
87OPC-193
87RedFoley/St-12
87T-731
88D-329
88F-229
88Kahn/Reds-13
88OPC-336
88Panini/St-275
88S-210
88Sf-218
88T-422
88T/Big-144
89F-156
89S-166
89UD-196

Concepcion, Onix
81Omaha-16
83D-516
83F-110
83T-52
84D-95
84F-345
84Nes/792-247
84T-247
85D-155
85F-200
85T-697
85ThomMc/Discs-8
86D-252
86F-6
86Kitty/Disc-5
86OPC-163
86T-596

Concepcion, Yamil
91Princet/ClBest-19
91Princet/ProC-3520

Conde, Ramon Luis
60DF-14
61Union

Cone, David
82CharR-19
84Memphis-25
85Omaha-25
86Omaha-6
86Omaha/TCMA-16
87D-502
87D/Rook-35
87Sf/Rook-39
87T/Tr-24T
88D-653
88D/Best-40
88D/Mets/Bk-653
88F-131
88Kahn/Mets-44
88S-49
88T-181
88ToysRUs-8
89B-375
89Cadaco-11
89Classic-100
89Classic-125
89D-388
89D-9DK
89D/AS-44
89D/Best-96
89D/DKsuper-9DK
89F-31
89F-636M
89F/BBAS-9
89F/Excit-8
89F/Heroes-9
89F/LL-7
89F/WaxBox-C7
89Holsum/Discs-19
89Kahn/Mets-44
89Nissen-19
89OPC-384
89Panini/St-129
89RedFoley/St-24
89S-221
89S/HotStar-2
89S/YS/I-9
89Sf-51
89T-710
89T/DHTest-6
89T/Gloss60-6
89T/Hills-9
89T/Mets/Fan-44
89T/Mini-24
89T/St-96
89T/St/Backs-58
89T/UK-17
89Tetley/Discs-2
89UD-584
90B-125
90D-265
90D/BestNL-43
90F-200
90F/LL-7
90Kahn/Mets-44
90Leaf/I-40
90Mets/Fan-44
90MLBPA/Pins-11
90OPC-30
90Panini/St-301
90Publint/St-129
90S-430
90Sf-201
90T-30
90T/Big-11
90T/Mini-65
90T/St-93
90T/TVMets-8
90UD-224
91B-460
91D-154
91F-143
91F/Ultra-213
91Kahn/Mets-17
91Leaf/I-253
91OPC-680
91Panini/St-80
91Panini/Top15-73
91S-409KM
91S-549
91T-680
91T/StClub/II-367
91UD-366
91WIZMets-81
92Classic/I-27
92D/I-97
92F-501
92F-687RS
92S/100SS-16
92S/II-680
92S/II-795HL
92T-195
92UD-364

Conely, Greg
91HighD/ClBest-15

Confreda, Gene
83Beaum-23
87Ashvl-3
88Ashvl/ProC-1076
90Osceola/Star-30TR

Congalton, William M.
(Bunk)
E254
E270/2
T206

Conigliaro, Anthony
(Tony)
64T-287R
65OPC-55
65T-55
65T/trans-11
66Bz-6
66T-218LL
66T-380
66T/RO-113
67Bz-6
67T-280
67T/Test/RSox-3
67T/Test/RSox-30
68Bz-4
68OPC-140
68T-140
69T-330
70OPC-340
70T-340
71Bz/Test-45
71JB
71MLB/St-342
71OPC-105
71OPC-63LL
71T-105
71T-63LL
71T/Coins-142
71T/tatt-10
78TCMA-206
PM10/Sm-28
PM10/Sm-29

Conigliaro, William
(Billy)
69T-628R
70OPC-317R
70T-317R
71MLB/St-316
71OPC-114
71T-114
72MB-80
72OPC-481
72T-481
74OPC-545
74T-545

Conine, Jeff
88BBCity/Star-10
89BBCity/Star-6
90A&AASingle/ProC-48
90Foil/Best-156
90Memphis/Best-8
90Memphis/ProC-1017
90Memphis/Star-7
91B-184
91Classic/200-96
91Classic/I-47
91D-427RR
91F-553
91F/Ultra-145
91Leaf/Stud-63
91Omaha/LineD-332
91Omaha/ProC-1041
91OPC/Premier-26
91S-722RP
91S/HotRook-5
91S/Rook40-19
91T/90Debut-34
91T/StClub/II-578
91UD-27RS
92S/100RisSt-21

Conklin, Chip
82Wausau-28
83Wausau/LF-11
85Huntsvl/BK-17

Conkright, Dan
88BirmB/Best-21

Conlan, John Bertrand
(Jocko)
55B-303ump
80Pac/Leg-59
80SSPC/HOF
88TM/Umpire-63
89HOF/St-98

Conley, Bob
78Watlo

Conley, D. Eugene
(Gene)
53T-215
54JC-22
54SpicSpan/PostC-6
54T-59
55Gol/Braves-6
55JC-22
55SpicSpan/DC-6
55T-81
55T/DH-34
56T-17
56T/Pin-17
57SpicSpan/4x5-6
57T-28
58T-431
59T-492
60Armour-6
60T-293
61P-124
61T-193
61T/St-119
62T-187
63T-216
64T-571
90Pac/Legend-79
91T/Arc53-215

Conley, Greg
88Spokane/ProC-1922
89CharRain/ProC-974
90Waterlo/Best-22
90Waterlo/ProC-2381
91HighD/ProC-2398

Conley, Matt
91Sumter/ClBest-3
91Sumter/ProC-2326

Conley, Robert Burns
(Bob)
59T-121

Conley, Virgil
83Tampa-2
84Cedar-8
85Cedar-4
86Penin-6
87Penin-27
88Jacks/GS-11

Conlon, Arthur Joseph
(Art)
No Cards.

Conlon, Charles M.
86Conlon/1-59
91Conlon/Sport-327

Conn, Albert Thomas
(Bert)
No Cards.

Conn, Gary
75BurlB
76BurlB
77Holyo

Connally, Fritzie Lee
81QuadC-5
83Iowa-13
84Cram/PCL-224
85F/Up-U30
91Crown/Orio-82

Connally, George
(Sarge)
33G-27
91Conlon/Sport-247
R337-406
V353-27

Connally, Mervin T.
(Bud)
No Cards.

Connatser, Broadus M.
(Bruce)
No Cards.

Connaughton, Frank H.
No Cards.

Connell, Eugene J.
(Gene)
No Cards.

Connell, Joseph B.
(Joe)
No Cards.

Connell, Peter J.
(Pete)
N172

Connelly, Bill
53T-126
91T/Arc53-126

Connelly, Daron
86Cram/PCL-196
87Clinton-24
88SanJose/Cal-130
88SanJose/ProC-135

Connelly, David
86Cram/PCL-197

Connelly, Thomas M.
(Tom)
No Cards.

Conner, Greg
88SanJose/Cal-118
88SanJose/ProC-129
89Shreve/ProC-1839

Conner, Jeff
81Holyo-12
82Holyo-3
83Nashua-4
84Evansvl-18
86Nashvl-5

Conner, John
90AppFox/Box-7
90AppFox/ProC-2089
91BBCity/ClBest-2
91BBCity/ProC-1389
91Single/ClBest-71

Connolly, Chris
91Eugene/ClBest-29
91Eugene/ProC-3716

Connolly, Craig
90SoOreg/Best-20
90SoOreg/ProC-3441
91Madison/ClBest-6
91Madison/ProC-2123

Connolly, Edward J.
(Ed)
65T-543

Connolly, John M.
(Red)
No Cards.

Connolly, Joseph A.
(Joe)
15CJ-155
D329-37
D350/2-36
M101/4-37
M101/5-36

Connolly, Joseph G.
(Joe)
No Cards.

Connolly, Matt
91Erie/ClBest-16
91Erie/ProC-4061

Connolly, Steve
87Pocatel/Bon-4
88Clinton/ProC-696
88MidwLAS/GS-6
89Shreve/ProC-1830
90Shrev/ProC-1437
90Shrev/Star-3

Connolly, Thomas F.
(Blackie)
No Cards.

Connolly, Thomas H.
50Callahan
80SSPC/HOF
89TM/Umpire-63

Connolly, Tommy
92Conlon/Sport-469

Connor, James Matthew
(Jim)

No Cards.
Connor, Joseph F.
(Joe)
No Cards.
Connor, Joseph
(Joe)
No Cards.
Connor, Mark
90T/TVYank-2CO
Connor, Roger
80SSPC/HOF
89HOF/St-9
E223
N167
N172
N284
N690
WG1-37
Connors, Billy
67T-272R
83Thorn-26CO
90T/TVYank-3CO
91Cub/Mara-x
91WIZMets-82CO
Connors, Jeremiah
(Jerry)
No Cards.
Connors, Joseph P.
(Joe)
No Cards.
Connors, Kevin Joseph
(Chuck)
52Mother-4
80Pac/Leg-28
88Pac/Leg-71
89Rini/Dodg-21
90Target-135
V362-2
Connors, Mervyn James
(Merv)
No Cards.
Conquest, Tom
82Idaho-5
83Madis/LF-12
Conroy, Bernard P.
(Ben)
No Cards.
Conroy, Brian
90CLAS/CL-9
90LynchRS/Team-16
91NewBrit/LineD-453
91NewBrit/ProC-344
Conroy, Mike
88Stockton/ProC-752
89Stockton/Best-31M
89Stockton/ProC-402M
89Stockton/Star-28M
Conroy, Tim
80WHave-22
81WHave-7
84D-340
84F-442
84Mother/A's-24
84Nes/792-156TL
84Nes/792-189
84T-156TL
84T-189
85D-156
85F-421
85Mother/A's-16
85T-503
86F/Up-U29
86Schnucks-3
86T/Tr-28T
87F-291
88Louisvl-15
88Louisvl/CMC-5
88S-384
88T-658
89Harris/ProC-288
89Harris/Star-6
Conroy, William E.
(Wid)
11Helmar-67
46Sunbeam
E254
E91
M116
T204
T206
T215/brown
Conroy, William F.
(Pep)
No Cards.
Conroy, William G.
(Bill)
No Cards.
Consolo, William A.
(Billy)
54T-195
55T-207
57T-399
58T-148
59T-112
60T-508
61P-100
61Peters-26
61T-504
88Pep/T-CO
89Mara/Tigers-CO
90CokeK/Tiger-28CO
91CokeK/Tiger-x
Constable, Jimmy
59T-451
63T-411
Constant, Andres
89Freder/Star-3
90Freder/Team-25
91Freder/ClBest-2
91Freder/ProC-2356
Consuegra, Sandy
51B-96
52B-143
53B/Col-89
54B-166
55B-116
55RM-AL25
56T-265
79TCMA-170
91Crown/Orio-83
Conte, Michael
(Mike)
89Medford/Best-1
90Madison/ProC-2276
91Huntsvl/ClBest-4
91HuntsvlProC-1808
Conti, Guy
86Watertn-6CO
88Bakers/Cal-263CO
89AS/Cal-24CO
89Bakers/Cal-207CO
Conti, Joe
88CapeCod/Sum-15
Contreras, Frank
82Miami-21
Contreras, Henry
81BurlB-15
Contreras, Joaquin
85LitFalls-22
86Columbia-7
87TexLgAS-16
88Jacks/GS-20
88Tidew/CANDL-15
88Tidew/CMC-17
89Tidew/CMC-16
89Tidew/ProC-1960
90RochR/ProC-719
91RochR/LineD-452
Contreras, Nardi
75Tidew/Team-6
82Edmon-14CO
85BuffB-2CO
87Richm/Crown-43CO
87Richm/TCMA-22CO
88Jaxvl/Best-23CO
88Jaxvl/ProC-969CO
88SLAS-40CO
89Jaxvl/Best-26CO
89Jaxvl/ProC-173CO
90Jaxvl/Best-26CO
90Jaxvl/ProC-1392CO
91Indianap/LineD-200CO
91Indianap/ProC-478CO
Converse, Jim
91Penin/ClBest-2
Converse, Mike
86Cedar/TCMA-3
87Tampa-3
Conway, Jack Clements
No Cards.
Conway, James P.
N172
Conway, John
52Park-96
Conway, Owen S.
No Cards.
Conway, Peter J.
(Pete)
N172
Scrapps
Conway, Richard D.
(Rip)
N172
Conway, William
(Bill)
No Cards.
Conwell, Edward J.
(Ed)
No Cards.
Conyers, Herbert L.
(Herb)
No Cards.
Coogan, Dale Roger
50B-244
52T-87
Coogan, Daniel George
(Dan)
No Cards.
Cook, Andy
88Oneonta/ProC-2041
89PrWill/Star-3
90Albany/Best-2
90Albany/ProC-1031
90Albany/Star-3
91Albany/ProC-999
Cook, Dennis
86Fresno/Smok-16
87Shrev-4
88Phoenix/CMC-3
88Phoenix/ProC-80
89D-646
89D/Best-327
89F-652R
89F/Up-104
89Panini/St-207
89Phill/TastyK-39
89Phoenix/CMC-3
89Phoenix/ProC-1482
89UD/Ext-779
90Classic-80
90D-193
90D/BestNL-93
90F-554
90HotRook/St-12
90Leaf/II-342
90OPC-633
90Panini/St-320
90Phill/TastyK-6
90S-545
90S/100Ris-75
90T-633
90UD-71
91Albuq/LineD-4
91D-657
91F-196
91Leaf/I-257
91OPC-467
91Pol/Dodg-25
91T-467
91T/StClub/II-411
91UD-612
92F-451
Cook, Doug
81CharR-12
83CharR-16
84Memphis-12
91Idaho/ProC-4321
Cook, Glen
82BurlR-17
83BurlR-3
83BurlR/LF-12
83Tulsa-2
84OKCty-22
85OKCty-8
86OKCty-4
86T-502
87OKCty-14
Cook, James Fitchie
(Jim)
No Cards.
Cook, James
86Kenosha-4
Cook, Jeff
86PrWill-7
87Harris-10
88EastLAS/ProC-13
88Harris/ProC-835
89Harris/ProC-304
89Harris/Star-7
90BuffB/CMC-24
90BuffB/ProC-387
Cook, Kerry
83SanJose-13
86WPalmB-9
Cook, Larry
86PalmSp-8
86PalmSp/Smok-11
Cook, Luther Almus
(Doc)
D350/2-37
M101/5-37
Cook, Mike
86MidldA-6
88Edmon/CMC-2
88Edmon/ProC-567
89F-472
90AAAGame/ProC-AAA21
90Portl/CMC-4
90Portl/ProC-171
91Calgary/LineD-57
Cook, Mitch
83QuadC-9
86ColumAst-7
87ColAst/ProC-9
Cook, Paul
N172
Cook, Raymond C.
(Cliff)
61T-399
62T-41
63T-566
91WIZMets-83
Cook, Ron
88Fayette/ProC-1096
89Lakeland/Star-5
90Lakeland/Star-5
91London/LineD-378
Cook, Ron W.
71MLB/St-75
71OPC-583
71T-583
72OPC-339
72T-339
72T/Cloth-8
Cook, Stan
89Boise/ProC-1982
90Erie/Star-3
Cook, Tim
79Holyo-12
81ElPaso-20
82Vanco-12
84Beaum-12
Cooke, Allan Lindsey
(Dusty)
35BU-148
92Conlon/Sport-418
W711/1
Cooke, Frederick B.
(Fred)
No Cards.
Cooke, Mitch
82QuadC-7
Cooke, Stephen
90Welland/Pucko-20
91Augusta/ClBest-4
91Augusta/ProC-797
Cookson, Brent
91SoOreg/ClBest-11
91SoOreg/ProC-3860
Coolbaugh, Mike
90MedHat/Best-1
91StCath/ClBest-7
91StCath/ProC-3402
Coolbaugh, Scott
88TexLgAS/GS-12
88Tulsa-18
89AAA/CMC-5
89AAA/ProC-26
89OkCty/CMC-21
89OkCty/ProC-1512
90B-494
90Classic/III-24
90D-43
90D/Rook-32
90F-293
90F/SoarSt-5
90HotRook/St-13
90Leaf/II-363
90S-612
90S/100Ris-79
90Sf-180
90T/89Debut-25
90T/Tr-22T
90TulsaDG/Best-1
90UD-42
91B-649
91F/Up-U122
91LasVegas/ProC-241
91Leaf/II-397
91LasVegas/LineD-280
91OPC-277
91S/100RisSt-36
91T-277
91T/StClub/II-493
91T/Tr-24T
91UD-451
91UD/FinalEd-37F
92S/I-205
Cooley, Dick Gordon
(Duff)
E107
Cooley, Fred
89Medford/Best-9
90A&AASingle/ProC-126
90Madison/Best-6
90Madison/ProC-2275
91Huntsvl/ClBest-8
91Huntsvl/LineD-283
91HuntsvlProC-1803
91Modesto/ProC-3094
91Single/ClBest-228
Cooley, Jack
91Pac/SenLg-90
Coombs, Cecil L.
(Cecil)
No Cards.
Coombs, Daniel
65T-553R
66T-414
67T-464
68T-547
69T-389
71OPC-126
71T-126
71T/Coins-49
Coombs, Glenn
91Welland/ClBest-25
91Welland/ProC-3564
Coombs, John W.
(Jack)
16FleischBrd-19
86Conlon/1-40
90Target-136
D350/2-38
E224
E270/2
E286
E98
M101/5-38
M116
T201
T204
Coomer, Ronald
(Ron)
88CalLgAS-9
88Modesto-21
88Modesto/Cal-72
90Huntsvl/Best-16
91BirmB/LineD-55
91BirmB/ProC-1460
Coonan, Bill
86Cram/PCL-58
Cooney, Ed
88CapeCod/Sum-14
Cooney, James E.
26Exh-19
Cooney, James Edward
(Jimmy)
N172
Cooney, John Walter
(Johnny)
39PB-85
40PB-60
41DP-41
41PB-50
54JC-28CO
55Gol/Braves-7CO
55JC-28CO
60T-458C
90Target-137
91Conlon/Sport-94
Cooney, Phillip
(Phil)
No Cards.

Cooney, Terry
88TM/Umpire-21
89TM/Umpire-19
90TM/Umpire-18
Cooney, William A.
(Bill)
No Cards.
Coons, Wilbur K.
(William)
No Cards.
Cooper, Arley Wilbur
16FleischBrd-20
E120
E121/120
E220
W501-80
W514-42
W516-19
W572
W573
Cooper, Bill
86Lakeland-4
87GlenF-8
88GlenF/ProC-933
Cooper, Cecil C.
72OPC-79R
72T-79R
74OPC-523
74T-523
75OPC-489
75T-489
75T/M-489
76OPC-78
76SSPC-404
76T-78
77OPC-102
77T-235
78Ho-119
78K-41
78OPC-71
78T-154
79Ho-36
79OPC-163
79T-325
80OPC-52
80T-95
80T/S-33
81D-83
81Drake-16
81F-639
81F/St-16
81K-32
81MSA/Disc-10
81OPC-356
81PermaGr/CC-15
81Sqt-30
81T-3LL
81T-555
81T/Nat/Super-5
81T/SO-2
81T/St-10
81T/St-13
81T/St-241
81T/St-93
82D-258
82Drake-9
82F-138
82F/St-140
82K-60
82OPC-167
82PermaGr/AS-2
82PermaGr/CC-18
82Pol/Brew-15
82Sqt-1
82T-675
82T-703TL
82T/St-199
83D-106
83D/AAS-19
83Drake-6
83F-30
83Gard-5
83K-28
83OPC-190
83PermaGr/CC-21
83Pol/Brew-15
83T-190
83T/Gloss40-15
83T/St-173
83T/St-181
83T/St-80
84D-351
84D/Champs-24
84Drake-8
84F-198
84F/St-31
85FunFood/Pin-48
84Gard-5
84MiltBrad-7
84Nes/792-133LL
84Nes/792-420
84Nes/792-710LL
84OPC-43
84Pol/Brew-15
84Ralston-27
84Seven-8C
84T-133LL
84T-420LL
84T-710LL
84T/Cereal-27
84T/Gloss40-34
84T/St-200A
84T/St-291
85D-170
85F-580
85Gard-5
85Leaf-246
85OPC-290
85Pol/Brew-15
85T-290
85T/St-287
85ThomMc/Discs-9
86D-170
86D-7DK
86D/AAS-54
86D/AS/WaxBox-PC9
86D/DKsuper-7
86F-484
86F/LimEd-12
86F/Mini-100
86F/St-26
86Jay's-2
86Leaf-7DK
86OPC-385
86Pol/Brew-15
86Sf-140M
86Sf-180M
86Sf-29
86T-385
86T/St-196
86T/Super-20
86Woolwth-8
87D-363
87F-343
87F/AwardWin-10
87F/Mini-22
87Leaf-230
87OPC-10
87OPC-D
87Pol/Brew-15
87RedFoley/St-48
87Sf-169
87T-10
87T-D
87T/Board-6
87T/HL-2
87T/St-198
87Woolwth-2
88F-161
88S-169
88T-769
89Pac/SenLg-42
89TM/SenLg-23
Cooper, Claude W.
No Cards.
Cooper, Craig
86Cram/PCL-168
88Wichita-24
89Wichita/Rock-34
89Wichita/Rock/Up-8
Cooper, Darren
90Martins/ProC-3200
Cooper, Dave
87Lakeland-23
88Toledo/CMC-8
88Toledo/ProC-608
89London/ProC-1362
Cooper, Don
79WHave-3
82F-550
82T-409
82Toledo-1
83Syrac-6
84Colum-17
84Colum/Pol-6
85Colum-5
85Colum/Pol-6
86Syrac-9
90Saraso/Star-27CO
91Pac/SenLg-22
91Saraso/ClBest-16CO
91Saraso/ProC-1131CO
Cooper, Gary N.
74Gaston
79Savan-2
81Durham-6
Cooper, Gary
86AubAs-7
87Osceola-21
88ColAst/Best-21
89Tucson/CMC-22
89Tucson/ProC-184
89Tucson/JP-6
90Hamil/Best-19
90Hamil/Star-9
90Tucson/CMC-10
90Tucson/ProC-213
91AAAGame/ProC-AAA51
91Tucson/LineD-609
91Tucson/ProC-2224
92D/II-774
92S/II-840
92T/91Debut-38
Cooper, Jamie
87Everett-9
88Clinton/ProC-715
88MidwLAS/GS-4
89SanJose/Best-3
89SanJose/Cal-230
89SanJose/ProC-458
89SanJose/Star-5
89Star/Wax-83
90Shrev/ProC-1457
90Shrev/Star-4
91Shrev/ProC-1833
Cooper, Jeff
91SLCity/ProC-3217
Cooper, Kent
84Everett/Cram-7
Cooper, Mark
85Kingst-12
Cooper, Morton
(Mort)
39PB-131
40PB-113
91Conlon/Sport-301
92Conlon/Sport-624
Exh47
PM10/Sm-30
R302
W754
Cooper, Neal
76Dubuq
Cooper, Orge
(Pat)
No Cards.
Cooper, Paul
78DaytB
Cooper, Scott
86Elmira-6
87Greens-10
88CLAS/Star-5
88Lynch/Star-5
89BBAmerAA/BPro-AA9
89NewBrit/ProC-609
89NewBrit/Star-3
90B-277
90Classic/Up-13
90Pawtu/CMC-14
90Pawtu/ProC-467
90S-651RPs
90T/TVRSox-39
91AAAGame/ProC-AAA29
91D-496
91F-91
91Pawtu/LineD-354
91Pawtu/ProC-46
91T/90Debut-35
91UD-22
92Classic/I-28
92D/II-570
92S/100RisSt-88
92S/II-876
92T-488
92UD-541
Cooper, Tim
90Tampa/DIMD-1
91Greens/ProC-3064
Cooper, Virgil
88Utica/Pucko-15
89SoBend/GS-10
Cooper, Wilbur
21Exh-27
V61-57
Cooper, William W.
(Walker)
48B-9
49B-117
49Eureka-79
50B-111
51B-135
52B-208
52T-294
53B/BW-30
53Exh/Can-58
53JC-14
53SpicSpan/3x5-8
54DanDee
56T-273
57T-380
60T-462C
79TCMA-69
92Conlon/Sport-633
Exh47
R302
R423-11
W754
Cope, Gary
91Kissim/ProC-4175
Copeland, Mark
90AubAs/Best-24TR
Coplon, Mitch
82DayBe-2
Copp, Bill
86Watertn-7
87Salem-19
88Harris/ProC-853
Coppell, Shannon
89Clinton/ProC-902
Coppenbarger, Frank
77QuadC
Coppeta, Greg
90Niagara/Pucko-16
91Fayette/ClBest-1
91Fayette/ProC-1161
Cora, Joey
85Spokane/Cram-4
86Beaum-7
87Bohem-4
87D/OD-147
88AAA/ProC-22
88F-580
88LasVegas/CMC-18
88LasVegas/ProC-234
88S-420
88T-91
89AAA/CMC-33
89LasVegas/CMC-14
89LasVegas/ProC-23
90B-211
90D-538
90F-154
90Leaf/II-366
90S/YS/II-14
90UD-601
91F-527
91F/Up-U11
91Kodak/WSox-21
91Leaf/II-375
91S-253
91UD-291
92D/I-108
92F-76
92S/I-326
92T-302
92UD-359
Corbell, Charlie
86Shrev-5
87Phoenix-6
88Tacoma/CMC-3
88Tacoma/ProC-636
Corbell, Eric
91Kingspt/ClBest-17
91Kingspt/ProC-3804
Corbett
N284
Corbett, Doug
79Indianap-12
81D-546
81F-555
81F/St-227
81OPC-162
81T-162
81T/St-106
82D-53
82F-551
82OPC-157
82T-560
82T/St-210
82T/Tr-21T
83F-83
83T-27
84Cram/PCL-111
85D-474
85F-298
85Smok/Cal-18
85T-682
86Smok/Cal-8
86T-234
87D-333
87F-76
87T-359
89Pac/SenLg-193
89T/SenLg-114
89TM/SenLg-24
90EliteSenLg-52
91Crown/Orio-84
Corbett, Eugene Louis
(Gene)
46Sunbeam
Corbett, Ray
81Cedar-8
82Water-11
83Indianap-15
85RochR-1
90CedarDG/Best-25
Corbett, Sherman
86MidldA-7
87Edmon-18
88F/Up-U11
89D-407
89Edmon/CMC-8
89Edmon/ProC-547
89F-473
89T-99
89ToysRUs-6
89UD-464
90Edmon/CMC-5
90Edmon/ProC-512
91London/LineD-431
91MidldA/ProC-430
Corbin, A. Ray
72OPC-66
72T-66
73OPC-411
73T-411
74OPC-296
74T-296
74T/St-204
75OPC-78
75T-78
75T/M-78
76OPC-474
76SSPC-209
76T-474
Corbin, Archie
89Clmbia/Best-5
89Clmbia/GS-7
91London/LineD-404
91Memphis/ProC-646
91Single/ClBest-293
92D/II-400RR
92T/91Debut-39
Corbitt, Claude E.
No Cards.
Corbitt, Cord
91Spokane/ClBest-19
91Spokane/ProC-3940
Corcino, Luis
86BurlEx-3
87FtMyr-22
88Virgini/Star-6
Corcoran, Arthur A.
(Art)
No Cards.
Corcoran, John A.
No Cards.
Corcoran, John H.
No Cards.
Corcoran, Lawrence J.
(Larry)
No Cards.
Corcoran, Lawrence
N172
Corcoran, Lori
83GlenF-23
Corcoran, Michael J.

(Mickey)
C46-49
Corcoran, Thomas W.
(Tommy)
90Target-138
E107
E270/2
N300/unif
WG3-11
Corcoran, Timothy M.
(Tim)
77Evansvl/TCMA-6
78BK/T-20
78T-515
79T-272
81D-367
81Evansvl-18
81F-479
81T-448
82OkCty-3
83Portl-11
84Phill/TastyK-34
85CIGNA-6
85D-381
85F-247
85Phill/TastyK-12M
85Phill/TastyK-34
85T-302
86D-381
86F-437
86T-664
86Tidew-5
87Maine/TCMA-24
88Reading/ProC-887
91WIZMets-84
Cordani, Richard
88CapeCod/Sum-8
90LSUPol-6
Cordero, Wil
(Wilfredo)
89WPalmB/Star-8
90Foil/Best-128
90Jaxvl/Best-5
90Jaxvl/ProC-1381
91B-436
91Classic/II-T2
91Indianap/LineD-179
91Indianap/ProC-466
91Leaf/GRook-BC3
91UD-60TP
92D/I-2RR
92T-551M
92UD-16SR
Cordner, Steve
83QuadC-19
Cordoba, Wilfrido
82AlexD-9
83LynnP-2
84PrWill-13
Cordoua, Marty
89Elizab/Star-5
Cordova, Antonio
82QuadC-21
84MidldC-2
Cordova, Rocky
78Clinton
79LodiD-7
Corey, Frederick H.
(Fred)
No Cards.
Corey, Mark M.
79RochR-15
79T-701R
80RochR-5
80T-661R
81F-193
81T-399R
82Evansvl-23
86Jaxvl/TCMA-20
87Indianap-30
89Pac/SenLg-195
91Crown/Orio-85
Corgan, Charles H.
(Chuck)
90Target-916
Corhan, Roy George
No Cards.
Corkhill, John S.
(Pop)
90Target-139
N172
Corkins, Mike
70T-573R
71MLB/St-224
71OPC-179
71T-179
72T-608
73OPC-461
73T-461
74OPC-546
74T-546
Cormack, Terry
83Durham-3
84Durham-6
85Durham-21
Corman, Dave
85Beaum-20
90HagersDG/Best-5
Cormier, Rheal
89StPete/Star-8
91B-396
91Louisvl/ProC-2907
92D/II-712
92S/II-851
92T-346
92T/91Debut-40
92UD-574
Cormier, Russ
89Medford/Best-21
91Huntsvl/ClBest-9
91Huntsvl/LineD-284
91HuntsvlProC-1788
Cornejo, Mardie
78Tidew
91WIZMets-85
Cornelius, Brian
89NiagFls/Pucko-4
90Fayette/ProC-2420
91FSLAS/ProC-FSL20
91Lakeland/ClBest-23
91Lakeland/ProC-277
91Single/ClBest-15
Cornelius, Reid
89Rockford/Team-5
90WPalmB/Star-3
91B-458
91FSLAS/ProC-FSL42
91Single/ClBest-52
91WPalmB/ClBest-4
91WPalmB/ProC-1220
Cornelius, Willie
78Laugh/Black-17
Cornell, Daren
90Beloit/Best-16
Cornell, Jeff
83Phoenix/BHN-7
84Cram/PCL-12
85Cram/PCL-200
85T-514
86Iowa-8
Cornutt, Terry
75Lafay
76Phoenix
78Cr/PCL-71
79Phoenix
80Phoenix-8
Corona, John
90Spring/Best-22
91StPete/ClBest-3
91StPete/ProC-2267
Corrado, Gary
77Wausau
Corrales, Patrick
(Pat)
65OPC-107R
65T-107R
66OPC-137
66T-137
67OPC-78
67T-78
69T-382
70OPC-507
70T-507
71MLB/St-57
71OPC-293
71T-293
72T-705
72T-706IA
73OPC-542
73T-542
74OPC-498
74T-498
79T-499MG
81F-623MG
83D-626MG
83T-637MG
84Nes/792-141MG
84T-141MG
84Wheat/Ind-18MG
85Polar/Ind-18MG
85T-119MG
86OhHenry-7MG
86T-699MG
87Gator-7MG
87Gator-MG
87T-268MG
88Chatt/Team-4
88Toledo/CMC-25
88Toledo/ProC-590
Correa, Amilcar
89Wythe/Star-6
90Geneva/ProC-3051
90Geneva/Star-5
91Peoria/ClBest-3
91Peoria/ProC-1334
Correa, Edwin
83AppFx/LF-17
86D/Rook-4
86F/Up-U30
86Rangers-18
86Sf/Rook-2
87Classic/Up-143
87D-57
87F-122
87Leaf-145
87Mother/Rang-19
87OPC-334
87Smok/R-22
87T-334
88D-57
88F-464
88Panini/St-196
88S-523
88Smok/R-18
88T-227
89RedFoley/St-25
89UD-598
90VeroB/Star-9
Correa, Ramser
89Helena/SP-15
90Beloit/Best-1
90Foil/Best-24
Correia, Rod
88SoOreg/ProC-1702
89Modesto/Cal-277
89Modesto/Chong-23
90Modesto/Cal-163
90Modesto/ProC-2218
91Tacoma/ProC-2312
Correll, Victor C.
(Vic)
75OPC-177
75T-177
75T/M-177
76OPC-608
76SSPC-14
76T-608
77T-364
78Indianap-19
78T-527
79T-281
80T-419
81T-628
Correnti, Chris
91BurlAs/ClBest-28TR
Corridan, Phillip
No Cards.
Corriden, John M. Jr.
90Target-140
R346-17
Corriden, John M. Sr.
(Red)
No Cards.
Corridon, Frank
C46-17
E90/1
M116
T205
Corrigan, Larry
75Water
Corsaro, Robby
89Batavia/ProC-1945
Corsi, James
(Jim)
83Greens-4
85Greens-16
86NewBrit-7
87Modesto-25
88Tacoma/CMC-7
88Tacoma/ProC-625
89F-649R
89S/HotRook-36
89T-292
89Tacoma/CMC-2
89Tacoma/ProC-1560
90D-422
90F-4
90OPC-623
90S-553
90T-623
90UD-521
91F/UltraUp-U80
91Mother/Ast-21
92D/II-467
92F-431
92S/II-524
Cort, Barry
75BurlB
79Holyo-26
80Holyo-4
Cortazzo, John F.
(Shine)
No Cards.
Cortes, Argenis
91BirmB/LineD-56
Cortes, Hernan
89Penin/Star-4
90FtLaud/Star-3
91Wmsprt/LineD-628
91Wmsprt/ProC-299
Cortez, Conde
87DayBe-12
91BirmB/ProC-1447
Cortez, Dave
87Wichita-18
Corwin, Elmer
(Al)
52B-121
53B/Col-126
53B/Col-149
54B-137
55B-122
55Gol/Giants-4
79TCMA-232
Cosby, Rob
84Everett/Cram-13A
Coscarart, Joseph M.
(Joe)
No Cards.
Coscarart, Peter J.
(Pete)
36G
39PB-141
40PB-63
49B/PCL-21
89Smok/Dodg-46
90Target-141
R314
Cosey, Donald Ray
(Ray)
79Ogden/TCMA-16
80Ogden-2
Cosgrove, Mike
75Iowa/TCMA-4
75OPC-96
75T-96
75T/M-96
76Ho-96
76OPC-122
76T-122
77T-589
Cosio, Raymundo
78Cedar
Cosman, James H.
66Pep/Tul
67T-384R
70OPC-429R
70T-429R
Cosman, Jim
89Martins/Star-7
Coss, Mike
91Bluefld/ProC-4133
91Bluefld/ClBest-10
Costas, Bob
89Chatt/II/Team-7ANN
Costell, Arnie
75Dubuq
Costello, Bob
83Wisco/LF-14
Costello, Brian
89Salinas/ProC-1828
90Clinton/Best-12
Costello, Daniel F.
(Dan)
D350/2-39
M101/5-39
Costello, Fred
88Ashvl/ProC-1063
89ColMud/Best-16
89ColMud/ProC-129
89ColMud/Star-6
90ColMud/Best-16
90ColMud/ProC-1341
90ColMud/Star-8
90Foil/Best-218
91Osceola/ClBest-1
91Osceola/ProC-673
Costello, John
83Erie-18
84Savan-4
85Spring-5
86StPete-7
87ArkTr-25
88F/Up-U118
88Louisvl-16
88Louisvl/CMC-1
88Louisvl/ProC-440
88S/Tr-107T
89Classic-142
89D-518
89F-446
89Panini/St-176
89S-534
89S/HotRook-75
89Smok/Cards-3
89T-184
89UD-625
90D-555
90F-246
90OPC-36
90Publint/St-214
90S-347
90SpringDG/Best-10
90T-36
90T/TVCard-8
90UD-486
91LasVegas/ProC-228
91LasVegas/LineD-281
92S/II-614
Costello, Mike
86Beaum-8
87Wichita-15
88Wichita-26
89Denver/CMC-5
89Denver/ProC-45
89ElPaso/GS-5
Costello, Tim
77Visalia
Costner, Kevin
89Durham/Star-29
Costo, Tim
90Classic/DP-8
91B-79
91Canton/LineD-79
91Canton/ProC-984
91Classic/200-58
91Classic/I-38
91Leaf/GRook-BC18
91OPC-103
91S-680FDP
91Single/ClBest-389
91T-103FDP
91UD-62TP
Cota, Chris
87DayBe-20
89BendB/Legoe-3
Cota, Francisco
83Miami-4
85Tigres-11
Cota, Tim
87Visalia-4
Cote, Brice
80Elmira-5
Cote, Henry Joseph
No Cards.
Cote, Warren Peter
(Pete)
No Cards.
Cotes, Eugenio
77Salem
79Portl-10
79T-723R
Cotner, Andrew
91Kingspt/ClBest-28

91Kingspt/ProC-3805
Cotter, Edward C.
(Ed)
No Cards.
Cotter, Harvey L.
No Cards.
Cotter, Richard R.
(Dick)
No Cards.
Cotter, Thomas B.
(Tom)
No Cards.
Cottier, Charles K.
(Chuck)
60L-138
60Lake
60SpicSpan-6
60T-417
61P-113
61T-13
62J-66
62P-66
62P/Can-66
62Salada-20
62Shirriff-20
62T-27
62T/bucks
62T/St-93
63F-28
63J-98
63P-98
63T-219
64T-397
69T-252
77QuadC
78TCMA-189
85Mother/Mar-1MG
85T-656MG
86T-141MG
88Berg/Cubs-CO
90Cub/Mara-28CO
90T/TVCub-3CO
91Cub/Mara-x
Cotto, Hector
88Miami/Star-5
Cotto, Henry
81QuadC-15
83Iowa-21
84SevenUp-28
85D-411
85F-53
85F/Up-U31
85T-267
87Colum/TCMA-20
87T-174
88D/Best-51
88F-205
88F/Up-U58
88Mother/Sea-6
88OPC-172
88S-368
88S/Tr-48T
88T-766
88T/Big-125
88T/Tr-31T
89D-109
89F-545
89Mother/Sea-6
89OPC-207
89Panini/St-441
89S-209
89T-468
89T/Big-160
89T/St-218
89UD-134
90B-476
90D-644
90F-511
90Mother/Mar-9
90OPC-31
90PublInt/St-430
90S-161
90T-31
90T/Big-156
90UD-207
91B-244
91CounHrth-18
91D-343
91F-448
91F/Ultra-333
91Leaf/I-113
91OPC-634
91Panini/FrSt-232
91S-282
91T-634
91T/StClub/II-525
91UD-110
92D/I-356
92F-276
92S/I-390
92T-311
92UD-616
Cotton, John
89BurlInd/Star-6
90Watertn/Star-5
91CollInd/ClBest-23
91CollInd/ProC-1490
Cottrell, Steve
84Everett/Cram-8
Couch, Richard
77Ashvl
Couchee, Mike
82Amari-16
85CharlO-31
85Cram/PCL-123
86Tulsa-4CO
88QuadC/GS-2
88SanDiegoSt-5
Coughlin
N172
Coughlin, Kevin
90SoBend/ClBest-9
90Utica/Pucko-1
91SoBend/ProC-2868
Coughlin, Red
85Syrac-24
86Syrac-10TR
87Syrac/TCMA-33
88Syrac/ProC-819
Coughlin, William P.
(Bill)
E107
Coughlon, Kevin
82Madis-7
84Madis/Pol-21
Coughtry, James M.
(Marlan)
61Union
62T-595R
Coulon, Johnny
T3/Box-54
Coulson, Robert
T207
Coulson, Steven
77WHave
Coulter, Chris
91BurlInd/ProC-3292
Coulter, Darrell
88Spartan/ProC-1029
88Spartan/Star-21
88Spartan/Star-5
89Spartan/ProC-1042
89Spartan/Star-5
Coulter, Roy
75AppFx
76AppFx
Coulter, Thomas Lee
(Tom)
No Cards.
Coumbe, Fred
(Fritz)
D328-33
E135-33
Counts, Rick
78Dunedin
Courtney, Clinton D.
(Clint)
53B/Col-70
53NB
53T-127
54B-69
54Dix
55B-34
56T-159
57T-51
58T-92
59T-483
60T-344
61T-342
79TCMA-169
91Crown/Orio-86
91T/Arc53-127
Courtney, Ernest E.
(Ernie)
E254
Courtney, Harry
E120
Courtright, John
91Billings/ProC-3746
Cousineau, Edward T.
(Dee)
No Cards.
Cousins, Derryl
88TM/Umpire-40
89TM/Umpire-38
90TM/Umpire-36
Cousy, Bob
51BR-A11
60P
Couture, Mike
91Stockton/ClBest-15
91Stockton/ProC-3043
Coveleski, Harry
81Detroit-39
BF2-26
D327
D328-34
D329-39
D350/2-40
E135-34
M101/4-39
M101/5-40
M116
T206
Coveleski, Stan
21Exh-28
25Exh-122
26Exh-122
28Yueng-57
61F-100
80SSPC/HOF
92Conlon/Sport-462
E120
E121/120
E210-57
E220
E254
E93
T3-88
V100
W501-21
W502-57
W555
W572
W575
Coveney, Jim
89Ashvl/ProC-961
Coveney, John P.
(John)
No Cards.
Coveney, Patrick
86Clearw-5
87DayBe-13
Covington, Clarence
(Sam)
No Cards.
Covington, John W.
(Wes)
57SpicSpan/4x5-7
57T-283
58T-140
59T-290
59T-565AS
60Lake
60T-158
61P-108
61T-296
61T/St-41
62Salada-105
62Shirriff-105
62T-157
63J-182
63P-182
63T-529
64PhilBull-10
64T-208
65T-583
66OPC-52M
66T-484
66T-52M
78TCMA-132
90Target-142
Covington, William
(Tex)
T207
Cowan, Billy Roland
64T-192R
65OPC-186
65T-186
69T-643
71MLB/St-341
71OPC-614
71T-614
72OPC-19
72T-19
78TCMA-282
91WIZMets-86
Cowan, Ed
77DaytB
Cowens, Alfred Edward
(Al)
75OPC-437
75T-437
75T/M-437
76A&P/KC
76Ho-28
76Ho/Twink-28
76OPC-648
76SSPC-175
76T-648
77T-262
78Ho-67
78K-5
78OPC-143
78T-46
79OPC-258
79T-490
80OPC-174
80T-330
81Coke
81D-369
81F-471
81OPC-123
81T-123
82D-207
82F-266
82OPC-103
82T-575
82T/St-182
82T/Tr-22T
83D-554
83F-477
83Nalley-2
83OPC-193
83T-763
83T/St-115
84D-511
84F-610
84Mother/Mar-19
84Nes/792-622
84T-622
84T/St-344
85D-196
85F-487
85Leaf-239
85Mother/Mar-6
85OPC-224
85T-224
85T/St-333
85ThomMc/Discs-10
86D-389
86F-463
86Leaf-184
86Mother/Mar-6
86OPC-92
86T-92
89Pac/SenLg-145
89TM/SenLg-25
Cowger, Tracy
80Tulsa-18
81Tulsa-2
82Tulsa-12
83OKCty-5
83Tulsa-17
Cowley, Joe
78Green
79Savan-15
82Pol/Atl-38
83Richm-3
83T-288
84Colum-13
84Colum/Pol-7
85D-613
85F-124
85Leaf-58
85T-769
85T/St-318
86BuffB-9
86Coke/WS-40
86D-608
86D/HL-44
86F-103
86F/Up-U31
86T-427
86T/Tr-29T
87D-552
87F-491
87F/LL-12
87Leaf-240
87Phill/TastyK-39A
87Sf-196M
87T-27
87T/St-290
Cox, Boyce
89Bristol/Star-31
90Bristol/Star-30PRES
Cox, Carl
47Signal
Cox, Carl
86VeroB-4
Cox, Dalene
81ArkTr-23M
Cox, Danny
82Spring-12
83StPete-4
84D-449
85D-571
85F-222
85T-499
86D-382
86F-32
86KAS/Disc-5
86Leaf-177
86OPC-294
86Sf-108
86Schnucks-4
86T-294
86T/Mini-61
86T/St-48
87D-553
87F-292
87F/Excit-12
87Leaf-160
87OPC-202
87Smok/Cards-6
87T-621
87T/Mini-33
88D-60
88D/Best-75
88F-28
88Leaf-72
88Louisvl-17
88OPC-59
88Panini/St-383
88S-415
88Sf-84
88Smok/Card-2
88T-59
88T/Big-111
88Woolwth-27
89D-348
89F-447
89OPC-158
89S-613
89T-562
89UD-535
90OPC-184
90PublInt/St-215
90Smok/Card-3
90SpringDG/Best-9
90T-184
90T/TVCard-9
91Leaf/II-350
91Phill/Medford-10
91T/Tr-25T
92D/II-614
92F-526
92S/II-568
92T-791
Cox, Darren
87Idaho-21
Cox, Darron
88CapeCod/Sum-97
89Billings/ProC-2067
90CharWh/Best-1
90CharWh/ProC-2243
90Foil/Best-20
90SALAS/Star-5
91Cedar/ClBest-13
91Cedar/ProC-2720
Cox, Doug
87Bakers-13
88VeroB/Star-4

Cox, Elmer Joseph
(Dick)
90Target-917
E120
E126-5
W573
Cox, Frank Bernhardt
No Cards.
Cox, J. Casey
66T-549R
67T-414
68OPC-66
68T-66
69T-383
70OPC-281
70T-281
71MLB/St-533
71OPC-82
71T-82
72MB-81
72OPC-231
72T-231
73OPC-419
73T-419
Cox, James Charles
(Jim)
74OPC-600R
74T-600R
76SSPC-325
Cox, Jeffrey Linden
(Jeff)
79Ogden/TCMA-12
80Ogden-19
81D-230
81T-133
81Tacoma-19
82Evansvl-14
83Omaha-14
86Vermont-4
87Vanco-3
87Watertn-30
88Augusta/ProC-382
88Chatt/Team-7
89Memphis/Best-24
89Memphis/ProC-1195
90Memphis/Best-26MG
90Memphis/ProC-1025MG
90Memphis/Star-26MG
91London/LineD-424
91Memphis/ProC-669MG
Cox, Jim
85Elmira-5
Cox, Larry Eugene
76SSPC-596
77T-379
78T-541
79T-489
80OPC-63
80T-116
81D-285
81F-604
81T-249
81T/Tr-749
83QuadC-2
85Iowa-28
86Iowa-9MG
87Iowa-22MG
88Berg/Cubs-CO
Cox, Robbie
76Baton
Cox, Robert Joe
(Bobby)
69MB-65
69T-237
78T-93MG
79T-302MG
81D-426MG
81F-247MG
81Pol/Atl-6MG
81T-675MG
83OPC-34MG
83T-606MG
84Nes/792-202MG
84OPC-202MG
84T-202MG
84Tor/Fire-10MG
85OPC-135MG
85T-411
85Tor/Fire-9MG
86OPC-359MG
86T-471MG
90T/Tr-23TMG
91OPC-759MG
91T-759MG
92T-489MG
Cox, Terry
71OPC-559R
71T-559R
Cox, William Richard
(Billy)
47TipTop
49B-73
49Eureka-33
50B-194
51B-224
51T/BB-48
52B-152
52Dix
52T-232
53B/BW-60
53NB
54B-26
54NYJour
54RH
54RM-NL2
55B-56
55Esskay
79TCMA-83
90Target-143
91Crown/Orio-87
PM10/Sm-31
PM10/Sm-32
Cox, William Ted
(Ted)
78T-706R
79T-79
80T-252
81D-283
81F-602
81Spokane-16
Coyle, Joseph
(Rocky)
87Knoxvl-6
87Syrac/TCMA-27
Coyne, Toots
No Cards.
Cozzolino, Paul
82VeroB-3
Crabbe, Bruce
86Pittsfld-4
87Iowa-12
88Iowa/CMC-13
88Iowa/ProC-550
89Iowa/CMC-14
89Iowa/ProC-1714
90Richm/Bob-5
90Richm/CMC-14
90Richm/ProC-265
90Richm/Team-7
91Richm/LineD-429
91Richm/ProC-2576
Crable, George
90Target-918
Crabtree, Chris
91Yakima/ClBest-24
91Yakima/ProC-4242
Crabtree, Estel C.
V355-134
W754
Craddock, Walt
59T-281
Craft, Harry Francis
39PB-65
40PB-79
55Rodeo
62T-12MG
63T-491MG
64T-298MG
78TCMA-244
89Smok/Ast-27
W711/1
W711/2
Craft, Mark
90SoOreg/Best-16
90SoOreg/ProC-3442
Craig, Dale
89Wythe/Star-7
90WinSalem/Team-8
91Geneva/ClBest-3
91Geneva/ProC-4220
Craig, Dean
78Clinton
79Wausau-18
82Nashvl-8
Craig, Morris
90Hunting/ProC-3287
91Geneva/ClBest-4
91Peoria/ProC-1347
Craig, Pete
65T-466R
66OPC-11R
66T-11R
67T-459R
Craig, Rodney Paul
79Spokane-5
80T-672R
81Charl-19
81D-288
81F-597
81T-282R
82Wheat/Ind
83Charl-15
83D-515
84Maine-19
Craig, Roger
56T-63
57T-173
58T-194
60BB-15
60L-8
60Morrell
60T-62
61BB-38
61T-543
62Salada-189
62Shirriff-189
62T-183
62T/bucks
62T/St-154
63Exh
63F-47
63J-200
63P-200
63T-197
64T-295
65T-411
66T-543
74OPC-31CO
74T-31CO
76SSPC-628CO
77Padre/SchCd-7CO
78Padre/FamFun-7MG
78TCMA-201
79T-479MG
86Mother/SFG-1MG
86T-111MG
87Mother/SFG-1MG
87T-193MG
88Mother/Giants-1MG
88T-654MG
89Mother/Giants-1MG
89Pac/Leg-145
89Rini/Dodg-15
89T-744MG
89T/LJN-79MG
90KMart/SS-33MG
90Mother/Giant-1MG
90OPC-351MG
90T-351MG
90T/TVAS-66MGM
90Target-144
91Mother/Giant-1MG
91OPC-579MG
91PG&E-6MG
91T-579MG
91WIZMets-87
92T-109MG
Exh47
Craig, Tom
82Syrac-25
83Syrac-3
84Syrac-3
Crain, Gregg
91Cedar/ClBest-29TR
Cram, Jerry
71OPC-247R
71T-247R
75Tidew/Team-7
76SSPC-559
81Omaha-2
82Omaha-26
83Omaha-25
84Omaha-13
91WIZMets-88
Cramer, Bill
90Rockford/ProC-2698
91WPalmB/ClBest-15
91WPalmB/ProC-1231
Cramer, George
35Exh/4-14
Cramer, Michael J.
(Mike)
75Phoenix-26
Cramer, Rob
86Visalia-8
Cramer, Roger Maxwell
(Doc)
34G-25
35BU-53
35G-8J
35G-9J
39PB-101
40PB-29
81Detroit-24
89Pac/Leg-181
92Conlon/Sport-451
R314
V354-74
Cramer, William B.
(Dick)
No Cards.
Crandall, Bob
80Elmira-33
Crandall, Delmar W.
(Del)
50B-56
51B-20
52T-162
53JC-15
53SpicSpan/3x5-9
53SpicSpan/7x10-5
53T-197
54B-32
54JC-1
54RM-NL3
54SpicSpan/PostC-7
54T-12
55Armour-3
55B-217
55Gol/Braves-8
55JC-1
55RM-NL2
55SpicSpan/DC-7
56T-175
57SpicSpan/4x5-7
57T-133
58T-351M
58T-390
59Armour-7
59Bz
59T-425
59T-567AS
60Armour-7
60Bz-36
60Lake
60MacGregor-6
60SpicSpan-7A
60SpicSpan-7B
60T-170
60T-568AS
61P-110
61T-390
61T-583AS
61T/Dice-2
61T/St-42
62T-351M
62T-443
62T/St-147
63J-153
63P-153
63Salada-11
63T-460
64T-169
65OPC-68
65T-68
66T-339
73OPC-646MG
73T-646MG
74T-99MG
75OPC-384MG
75T-384MG
75T/M-384MG
78Cr/PCL-30MG
78TCMA-144
79TCMA-68
80Albuq-23MG
81Albuq/TCMA-25MG
82Albuq-24MG
83Albuq-23MG
84D-632MG
84Mother/Mar-1MG
84Nes/792-721MG
84T-721MG
88Pac/Leg-98
89Swell-132
91T/Arc53-197
Exh47
PM10/L-12
WG9-28
Crandall, Ducky
75Lafay
Crandall, James Otis
(Doc)
10Domino-28
11Helmar-122
12Sweet/Pin-109
14CJ-67
15CJ-67
D304
E104
E254
M116
S74-82
T202
T204
T205
T206
T207
T213/blue
T215/blue
T215/brown
Crane, Edward N.
(Cannonball)
N172
Crane, Rich
89GreatF-3
89Smok/FresnoSt-8
90Bakers/Cal-235
Crane, Samuel Byren
(Sam)
E120
Crane, Samuel N.
(Sam)
90Target-919
N172
N284
Scrapps
Cranston, William
T206
Cravath, Clifford C.
(Gavvy)
14CJ-82
15CJ-82
91Conlon/Sport-277
BF2-84
D327
D328-35
D329-40
D350/2-41
E135-35
E254
E270/1
M101/4-40
M101/5-41
T206
W514-11
Craven, Britt
91QuadC/ClBest-2
91QuadC/ProC-2619
Craver, William H.
(Bill)
No Cards.
Crawford, Carlos
91BurlInd/ProC-3293
Crawford, Clifford R.
(Pat)
No Cards.
Crawford, Forrest
No Cards.
Crawford, George
No Cards.
Crawford, Glenn M.
47Remar-25
Crawford, Jack
82Danvl-8
83Peoria/LF-15
Crawford, Jerry
88TM/Umpire-28
89TM/Umpire-26
90TM/Umpire-25
Crawford, Jim
74OPC-279
74T-279
76OPC-428
76SSPC-47
76T-428

76T/Tr-428T
77T-69
89Gaston/ProC-1015
Crawford, Joe
91Kingspt/ClBest-16
91Kingspt/ProC-3806
Crawford, Kenneth D.
(Ken)
No Cards.
Crawford, Rufus
55B-121
Crawford, Samuel Earl
(Sam)
11Helmar-29
14CJ-14
15CJ-14
72F/FFeat-27
80Pac/Leg-55
80SSPC/HOF
81Detroit-121
87Conlon/2-30
89HOF/St-50
90BBWit-78
BF2-27
D303
D304
D327
D328-36
E101
E102
E103
E104
E106
E135-36
E90/1
E92
E94
E95
M116
T201
T206
T213/blue
T215/brown
T216
T3-5
W514-95
W555
WG2-9
WG5-12
WG6-12
Crawford, Shag
89Pac/Leg-199
Crawford, Steve
82Coke/BOS
82D-564
82F-291
82T-157
83Pawtu-4
83T-419
84Pawtu-14
85D-395
85F-156
85T-661
86D-416
86F-346
86Leaf-193
86T-91
87D-399
87F-33
87T-589
88F-350
88S-289
88T-299
90Leaf/II-494
91F-554
91OPC-718
91Pol/Royal-5
91S-287
91T-718
92S/I-349
Crawford, Willie M.
65T-453R
68T-417
69T-327
70K-26
70OPC-34
70T-34
71MLB/St-100
71OPC-519
71T-519
71Ticket/Dodg-4
72T-669
73OPC-639
73T-639
74OPC-480
74T-480
74T/St-43
75OPC-186
75T-186
75T/M-186
76OPC-76
76SSPC-84
76T-76
77BurgChef-107
77T-642
78T-507
78TCMA-157
85SpokAT/Cram-4
90Target-146
Creager, Mack
66Pep/Tul
Creamer, George W.
No Cards.
Creamer, Robert
90LitSun-14
Credeur, Todd
85Anchora-7
86Ashvl-6
87Osceola-28
88Osceola/Star-6
89ColMud/Best-26
89Osceola/Star-5
90ColMud/Best-17
90ColMud/ProC-1342
90ColMud/Star-9
Cree, William F.
(Birdie)
10Domino-29
11Helmar-41
12Sweet/Pin-33
E224
M116
T206
T213/blue
T213/brown
T215/blue
T215/brown
Creech, Ed
91James/ClBest-28MG
91James/ProC-3561MG
Creed, Bennett
90Miami/II/Star-30PER
Creeden, Patrick F.
(Pat)
No Cards.
Creedon, Cornelius C.
(Connie)
No Cards.
Creegan, Martin
(Marty)
No Cards.
Creek, Doug
91Hamil/ProC-4031
Creekmore, Niles
87SLCity/Taco-17
Creel, Keith
82Omaha-3
83D-574
83Omaha-5
84F-346
84Omaha-15
85Maine-6
86Maine-7
87OKCty-7
Creely, August L.
(Gus)
No Cards.
Cregan, Peter James
(Pete)
No Cards.
Creger, Bernard Odell
(Bernie)
47TipTop
Crenshaw, Ken
89Princet/Star-28
Crespi, Frank A.
(Creepy)
41DP-145
W754
Crespo, Felipe
91MedHat/ProC-4106
Crespo, Michael
91Gaston/ClBest-14
91Gaston/ProC-2691
Cresse, Mark
85Coke/Dodg-8CO
86Coke/Dodg-7CO
90Mother/Dodg-28M
90Pol/Dodg-x
91Mother/Dodg-28CO
91Pol/Dodg-x
Crew, Ken
87Memphis-20
87Memphis/Best-8
88ColAst/Best-6
Crews, Larry
82Clinton-19
84Shrev/FB-5
85Cram/PCL-178
Crews, Tim
81BurlB-10
83ElPaso-17
84ElPaso-10
86ElPaso-7
87Albuq/Pol-8
88Albuq/CMC-8
88Albuq/ProC-264
88D-464
88D/Rook-20
88F-511
88Pol/Dodg-52M
88S-641RB
88Sf-224
88T-57
89D-486
89Mother/Dodg-24
89Panini/St-96
89Pol/Dodg-27
89S-505
89T-22
89UD-611
90D-550
90ElPasoATG/Team-29
90F-390
90Mother/Dodg-26
90OPC-551
90Pol/Dodg-52
90S-164
90T-551
90Target-147
90UD-670
91D-294
91F-197
91F/UltraUp-U87
91Leaf/I-141
91Mother/Dodg-26
91OPC-737
91Pol/Dodg-52
91S-302
91T-737
91T/StClub/II-375
91UD-596
92D/II-437
92F-452
92S/I-238
92T-642
92UD-687
Cribb, Buddy
89Alaska/Team-19
Crider, Jerry
69T-491R
71OPC-113
71T-113
Criger, Louis
E107
E90/1
M116
T205
T206
T3-89
WG2-10
Crim, Chuck
83Beloit/LF-22
84ElPaso-6
85Cram/PCL-220
86Vanco-8
87D/Rook-18
87F/Up-U19
87Pol/Brew-32
87T/Tr-25T
88D-355
88F-162
88Pol/Brew-32
88S-402
88T-286
89B-136
89Brewer/YB-32
89D-617
89D/Best-127
89F-183
89OPC-99
89Pol/Brew-32
89S-272
89T-466
89UD-501
90Brewer/MillB-3
90D-221
90ElPasoATG/Team-7
90F-319
90Leaf/I-58
90OPC-768
90Panini/St-103
90Pol/Brew-32
90PublInt/St-493
90S-108
90T-768
90UD-511
91B-51
91Brewer/MillB-6
91D-684
91F-579
91F/Ultra-173
91Leaf/I-28
91OPC-644
91Pol/Brew-6
91S-99
91T-644
91T/StClub/I-112
91UD-391
92D/I-103
92F-175
92S/I-22
92T-169
92UD-496
Crimian, Jack
53Hunter
56T-319
57T-297
Cripe, David Gordon
(Dave)
83DayBe-1
85Osceola/Team-1
86ColumAst-8MG
Criscione, Dave G.
78RochR
91Crown/Orio-88
Criscola, Anthony P.
(Tony)
47Centen-5
Crisham, Patrick L.
(Pat)
No Cards.
Crisler, Joel
77QuadC
79SLCity-15
80ElPaso-11
Crisler, Thomas
81Redwd-3
Crisp, Joseph Shelby
(Joe)
No Cards.
Criss, Dode
E254
M116
T206
Criss, Matt
90WichSt-8
Crist, Chester Arthur
(Ches)
No Cards.
Crist, Clark
81LynnS-28
81Wausau-21
82LynnS-10
84Chatt-7
91AubAS/ClBest-24CO
91AubAS/ProC-4291CO
Crist, Jack
71Richm/Team-5
Cristelli, Pat
77SLCity
78Cr/PCL-5
Criswell, Brian
85Madis-9
85Madis/Pol-6
86Madis-6
86Madis/Pol-6
88Huntsvl/BK-3
Criswell, Tim
86Durham-6
87Durham-7
Critz, Hugh Melville
(Hughie)
25Exh-26
26Exh-26
28Exh-13
29Exh/4-7
31Exh/4-9
33Exh/4-5
33G-238
33G-3
34G-17
35Exh/4-5
35G-2A
35G-4A
35G-7A
61F-101
87Conlon/2-10
88Conlon/5-6
91Conlon/Sport-290
R316
R332-46
V353-3
V354-72
W517-25
WG7-10
Crnich, Jeff
89Belling/Legoe-36BB
Croak, David
90Martins/ProC-3188
Crockett, Claude
77StPete
Crockett, David S.
(Davey)
No Cards.
Crockett, Rusty
88Peoria/Ko-9
89WinSalem/Star-6
90T/TVCub-41
91CharlK/LineD-130
91CharlK/ProC-1696
Croft, Arthur F.
(Art)
No Cards.
Croft, Henry T.
No Cards.
Croft, Paul
78Wisco
90HagersDG/Best-6
Croghan, Andy
89Alaska/Team-10
91Oneonta/ProC-4147
Croghan, John
N172
Crolius, Fred J.
No Cards.
Cromartie, Warren L.
78OPC-117
78T-468
79OPC-32
79T-76
80OPC-102
80T-180
81D-332
81F-142
81F/St-92
81OPC-345
81OPC/Post-5
81T-345
81T/SO-78
81T/St-188
82D-340
82F-186
82F/St-33
82Hygrade
82OPC-61
82OPC-94TL
82OPC/Post-13
82T-526TL
82T-695
82T/St-60
82Zeller-18
82Zeller-7
83D-466
83F-279
83OPC-351
83Stuart-18
83T-495
84F-272
84Nes/792-287
84OPC-287
84T-287
91B-315
91F/Up-U25

91Leaf/II-458
91Leaf/Stud-64
92S/II-637
Cromer, Tripp
89Hamil/Star-10
90StPete/Star-3
91StPete/ClBest-19
91StPete/ProC-2282
Crompton, Edward
(Ned)
No Cards.
Crompton, Herbert B.
(Herb)
No Cards.
Cromwell, Nate
88Myrtle/ProC-1174
89Dunedin/Star-3
90Knoxvl/Best-27
90Knoxvl/ProC-1238
90Knoxvl/Star-2
91Knoxvl/LineD-353
91Knoxvl/ProC-1760
91Single/ClBest-91
Cron, Chris
86Durham-7
87QuadC-23
88CalLgAS-34
88PalmSp/Cal-102
88PalmSp/ProC-1441
89MidldA/GS-11
89TexLAS/GS-2
90Edmon/CMC-21
90Edmon/ProC-523
91Edmon/LineD-158
91Edmon/ProC-1521
92Classic/I-29
92D/II-698
92F-656
92S/II-847
92T/91Debut-41
Crone, Bill
81LynnS-16
82LynnS-11
83SLCity-18
84Cram/PCL-172
85Cram/PCL-93
86Calgary-5
87Tucson-4
Crone, Ray
85Newar-18
Crone, Raymond H.
54JC-20
54SpicSpan/PostC-8
54T-206
55Gol/Braves-9
55JC-12
55T-149
56T-76
57SpicSpan/4x5-8
57T-68
58SFCallB-6
58T-272
Cronin, Chuck
47Sunbeam
Cronin, Daniel
(Dan)
No Cards.
Cronin, James John
90Target-148
Cronin, Jeff
91Durham/ClBest-5
91Durham/ProC-1538
Cronin, Joseph Edward
(Joe)
31Exh/4-31
33DH-11
33G-109
33G-63
34Exh/4-16
35BU-183
35BU-32
35Exh/4-9
35G-1G
35G-3E
35G-5E
35G-6E
36Exh/4-9
37Exh/4-9
37OPC-124
38Exh/4-9
38ONG/Pin-3
40PB-134
40Wheat-7
41DP-59
41DP-82
41PB-15
61GP-14
80Pac/Leg-39
80SSPC/HOF
83D/HOF-20
86Conlon/1-9
86Sf/Dec-7
88Conlon/AmAS-6
89HOF/St-19
89Pac/Leg-167
91Conlon/Sport-314
91Conlon/Sport-50
92Conlon/Sport-600
R300
R302
R303/A
R303/B
R306
R308-176
R310
R311/Gloss
R312/M
R313
R314
R328-7
R332-37
V300
V353-63
V355-63
WG8-8
Cronin, William P.
(Bill)
No Cards.
Cronk, Doug
89Gaston/ProC-1013
89Gaston/Star-5
89SALAS/GS-29
90CharlR/Star-5
Cronkright, Dan
86Penin-7
Cronkright, Dave
87DayBe-24
Crooks, John Charles
N172
Crooks, Thomas A.
(Tom)
No Cards.
Crosby, Edward C.
(Ed)
71OPC-672
71T-672
73OPC-599
73T-599
76OPC-457
76SSPC-520
76T-457
78SanJose-5
79Spokane-1
Crosby, Ken
76OPC-593R
76SSPC-602
76T-593R
Crosby, Pat
86LitFalls-7
Crosby, Todd
87Spartan-15
88Clearw/Star-9
89Star/Wax-49
89StPete/Star-9
90Louisvl/CMC-24
90Louisvl/ProC-408
90T/TVCard-44
91Louisvl/LineD-232
91Louisvl/ProC-2922
Crosetti, Frank P.
(Frankie)
33G-217
34DS-86
35BU-182
36G-9
38ONG/Pin-4
41DP-113
44Yank/St-7
47TipTop
52B-252CO
52T-384CO
60T-465C
68Bz-13
88Conlon/3-8
90Pac/Legend-19
90Swell/Great-48
91Swell/Great-20
R303/A
R311/Leath
R313
R314
R346-24
R423-17
V355-91
WG8-9
Crosnoe, Cory
91Pulaski/ClBest-6
91Pulaski/ProC-4012
Cross, Amos C.
No Cards.
Cross, Bob
79Newar-16
Cross, Clarence
No Cards.
Cross, Frank Atwell
No Cards.
Cross, Jesse
89Myrtle/ProC-1473
90Dunedin/Star-6
90FSLAS/Star-27
91Knoxvl/LineD-354
91Knoxvl/ProC-1761
Cross, Joffre
(Jeff)
47TipTop
Cross, LaFayette N.
(Lave)
90Target-149
E107
N172
N300/unif
WG2-11
Cross, Leach
T3/Box-69
Cross, Montford M.
(Monte)
E107
T206
WG2-12
Crossin, Frank P.
No Cards.
Crossley, William
N172
Crotty, Joseph P.
(Joe)
N172
N172/ST
Crouch, Bill
41G-27
90Target-150
W754
Crouch, Jack Albert
No Cards.
Crouch, Matt
86BurlEx-4
88Memphis/Best-8
89Omaha/CMC-5
89Omaha/ProC-1717
Crouch, Zach
85Greens-9
87NewBrit-2
88Pawtu/CMC-6
88Pawtu/ProC-457
89NewBrit/ProC-612
89NewBrit/Star-4
90T/TVRSox-40
Croucher, Frank D.
No Cards.
Crough, Bill
41G-27
Crouse, Clyde E.
(Buck)
92Conlon/Sport-509
Crow, Donald Leroy
(Don)
80Albuq-27
81Albuq/TCMA-13
82Albuq-12
90Target-151
Crow, Roger
(Gabby)
79QuadC-4
81QuadC-32
82QuadC-12
83QuadC-1
Crowder, Alvin
33G-122
33G-95
34DS-93
34Exh/4-16
34G-15
35BU-161
35G-1H
35G-3F
35G-5F
35G-6F
61F-102
88Conlon/AmAS-7
91Conlon/Sport-257
R308-185
R310
R312/M
V353-71
V354-65
Crowe, George Daniel
52T-360
53JC-18
53SpicSpan/3x5-10
53T-3
55JC-39
56T-254
57Kahn
57T-73
58Kahn
58T-12
59T-337
60T-419
61T-52
91T/Arc53-3
Crowe, Ron
89Everett/Star-5
90Clinton/Best-21
90Clinton/ProC-2557
90Foil/Best-170
91SanJose/ClBest-5
91SanJose/ProC-16
Crowell, William
N172
Crowley, Brian
89Butte/SP-8
Crowley, Edgar Jewel
(Ed)
No Cards.
Crowley, Jim
91Elmira/ClBest-3
91Elmira/ProC-3276
Crowley, John A.
No Cards.
Crowley, Ray
78Memphis/Team-2
80Memphis-11
Crowley, Terrence M.
(Terry)
70OPC-121R
70T-121R
71MLB/St-292
71OPC-453
71T-453
72T-628
73JP
73OPC-302
73T-302
74OPC-648
74T-648
74T/Tr-648T
75OPC-447
75T-447
75T/M-447
76OPC-491
76SSPC-35
76T-491
79T-91
80T-188
81D-507
81F-190
81OPC-342
81T-543
82D-383
82F-160
82T-232
83D-457
83F-55
83T-372
83T/Tr-22
84Nes/792-732
84OPC-246
84T-732
87French-10CO
88French-10CO
91Crown/Orio-89
Crowley, Terry Jr.
88Salem/Star-4
89Salem/Star-5
90Harris/ProC-1198
90Harris/Star-5
91CaroMud/LineD-104
91CaroMud/ProC-1091
Crowley, William M.
N284
Cruise, Walton Edwin
(Walt)
21Exh-29
E120
E220
V100
Crum, George
83BurlR-14
83BurlR/LF-4
85Tulsa-4
86Water-6
Crumling, Eugene Leon
(Gene)
No Cards.
Crump, Arthur Elliott
(Buddy)
No Cards.
Crump, Jamie
90Pulaski/Best-15
90Pulaski/ProC-3095
Crutcher, Dave
79Tulsa-19
80Tulsa-2
81Tulsa-15
Crutchfield, Jim
(Jimmie)
78Laugh/Black-35
86Negro/Frit-29
91Negro/Lewis-8
Cruthers, Charles P.
(Press)
No Cards.
Cruz, Andres
90Memphis/Best-23
90Memphis/ProC-1003
90Memphis/Star-8
91London/LineD-405
91Memphis/ProC-647
Cruz, Arcadio
77Charl
Cruz, Cirilio Dilan
(Tommy)
78Cr/PCL-105
79Colum-13
Cruz, Daniel
90Bristol/ProC-3162
90Bristol/Star-4
Cruz, Fausto
91Modesto/ProC-3095
Cruz, Georgie
83Memphis-2
Cruz, Hector Dilan
(Heity)
76OPC-598R
76T-598R
77T-624
78T-257
79Pol/Giants-9
79T-436
80T-516
81F-206
81T-52
81T/Tr-750
82D-57
82F-214
82OPC-364
82T-663
91Pac/SenLg-60
Cruz, Henry Acosta
74Albuq/Team-4
76OPC-590R
76SSPC-85
76T-590R
78T-316
90Target-152
Cruz, Ismael
89Martins/Star-8
90Batavia/ProC-3071
Cruz, Ivan
90FSLAS/Star-28
90Lakeland/Star-6
91B-153
91London/LineD-379
91London/ProC-1882

91Single/ClBest-18
Cruz, J.J.
91Erie/ClBest-4
91Erie/ProC-4071
Cruz, Javier
85Tigres-26
Cruz, Jose Dilan
72OPC-107
72T-107
73OPC-292
73T-292
74OPC-464
74T-464
74T/St-113
75OPC-514
75T-514
75T/M-514
76OPC-321
76SSPC-62
76T-321
77BurgChef-9
77Ho-75
77K-50
77OPC-147
77T-42
78BK/Ast-17
78Ho-72
78K-16
78OPC-131
78T-625
79Ho-58
79OPC-143
79T-289
80OPC-367
80T-722
81Coke
81D-383
81F-60
81F/St-78
81OPC-105
81T/HT
81T/SO-83
81T/St-169
82D-244
82Drake-10
82F-214
82F/St-50
82OPC-325
82T-325
82T/St-44
83D-41
83F-446
83OPC-327
83T-585
83T/St-242
84D-182
84F-222
84F/St-24
84F/St-8
85FunFood/Pin-129
84Mother/Ast-8
84Nes/792-422
84Nes/792-66TL
84OPC-189
84Seven-19W
84T-66TL
84T-422
84T/St-65
84T/St/Box-13
85D-20DK
85D-304
85D/DKsuper-20
85Drake-7
85F-347
85Leaf-20DK
85Mother/Ast-4
85OPC-95
85Seven-10C
85T-95
85T/Gloss40-20
85T/St-59
85T/Super-34
85ThomMc/Discs-27
86D-60
86D/AAS-19
86F-296
86F/LimEd-13
86F/LL-8
86F/Mini-62
86F/St-27
86Leaf-49
86Mother/Ast-20
86OPC-96
86Pol/Ast-12
86Sf-30
86T-186M
86T-640
86T/St-26
87D-85
87D/OD-13
87F-53
87F/BB-11
87F/St-26
87F/St-S4
87Leaf-116
87Mother/Ast-3
87OPC-343
87Pol/Ast-3
87RedFoley/St-95
87Sf-152M
87Sf-42
87T-670
87T/St-29
88D/Y/Bk-NEW
88F-443
88Panini/St-299
88S-28
88T-278
89Pac/SenLg-188
89T/SenLg-78
89TM/SenLg-26
90EliteSenLg-53
90Kissim/DIMD-7
91Pac/SenLg-36
Cruz, Juan
83Madis/LF-21
85MidldA-23
Cruz, Julio Luis
75QuadC
78T-687
79Ho-111
79OPC-305
79T-583
80BK/PHR-26
80OPC-16
80T-32
81D-163
81F-601
81OPC-121
81Pol/Mariners-6
81T-397
81T/St-126
82D-250
82F-509
82F/St-225
82OPC-130
82T-130
82T/St-114
82T/St-235
83D-379
83F-478
83OPC-113
83T-414
83T/St-112
83T/Tr-23
84D-379
84F-55
84F/St-95
84Nes/792-257
84OPC-257
84T-257
84T/St-248
84TrueVal/WS-9
85Coke/WS-12
85D-452
85F-510
85OPC-71
85T-749
85T/St-239
86Coke/WS-12
86D-257
86F-201
86OPC-14
86T-14
87F-492
87OPC-53
87T-790
89Stockton/Cal-179CO
90Swell/Great-88
91LineD-32
91Swell/Great-21
Cruz, Luis
83Wisco/LF-19
86Pittsfld-5
87WinSalem-9
88CLAS/Star-26
88WinSalem/Star-2
89CharlK-8
89Iowa/CMC-15
89Iowa/ProC-1692
89NiagFls/Pucko-5A
Cruz, Nandi
90Saraso/Star-5
91Dunedin/ClBest-16
91Dunedin/ProC-213
Cruz, Pablo
77Salem
78Salem
Cruz, Rafael
86DayBe-6
87Gaston-13
Cruz, Ruben
91BurlAs/ClBest-19
91BurlAs/ProC-2813
Cruz, Todd Ruben
80T-492
81Coke
81F-341
81T-571
83D-505
83F-479
83Nalley-4
83OPC-132
83T-132
84D-148
84F-3
84Nes/792-773
84T-773
85F-172
85T-366
87SanBern-20
91Crown/Orio-90
91Pac/SenLg-147
91Salinas/ClBest-5
91Salinas/ProC-2251
Cruz, Victor
78Syrac
79T-714R
80OPC-54
80T-99
81D-321
81F-407
81OPC-252
81T-252
81T/Tr-751
82F-480
82T-263
83OKCty-6
84OKCty-20
88Pocatel/ProC-2089
Csefalvay, John
83ColumAst-3
84Nashvl-4
Cubanich, Creighton
91SoOreg/ClBest-23
Cubbage, Michael Lee
(Mike)
75OPC-617R
75T-617R
75T/M-617R
76OPC-615
76T-615
77BurgChef-50
77T-149
78T-219
79OPC-187
79T-362
80OPC-262
80T-503
81D-492
81F-566
81T-657
81T/Tr-752
82F-523
82T-43
82Tidew-26
85Lynch-1
86Jacks/TCMA-24
87Tidew-12
87Tidew/TCMA-23
88AAA/ProC-54
88Tidew/CANDL-3MG
88Tidew/CMC-24MG
88Tidew/ProC-1586MG
89Tidew/CMC-21MG
90Kahn/Mets-4CO
90T/TVMets-2CO
91Kahn/Mets-4CO
91WIZMets-89
Cuccinello, Alfred E.
(Al)
No Cards.
Cuccinello, Anthony
(Tony)
33G-99
34DS-55
35BU-79
35Exh/4-2
38Exh/4-1
39Exh
39PB-61
40PB-61
49Eureka-80
55Gol/Ind-3
55Salem
60T-458C
89Pac/Leg-170
89Smok/Dodg-37
90Target-153
R314
Cucjen, Romy
87Shrev-9
88Shreve/ProC-1293
89Louisvl-15
89Louisvl/CMC-15
89Louisvl/ProC-1257
90Indianap/CMC-22
90Indianap/ProC-289
Cudjo, Lavell
89Greens/ProC-406
89SALAS/GS-34
90Cedar/Best-9
90Cedar/ProC-2332
Cudworth, James A.
(Jim)
N172
Cuellar, Bobby
76SanAn/Team-8
77Tucson
78Cr/PCL-111
79Tacoma-7
80T-665R
80Tacoma-6
81Charl-2
84Cram/PCL-192
85Cram/PCL-84
86Wausau-5MG
87Wausau-1MG
88SanBern/Best-27
88SanBern/Cal-54
89Wmsprt/ProC-627
89Wmsprt/Star-3
90Wmsprt/Best-26CO
90Wmsprt/ProC-1073CO
90Wmsprt/Star-26CO
91Jaxvl/LineD-350CO
91Jaxvl/ProC-167CO
Cuellar, Mike
59T-518
60T-398
65T-337
66T-566
67OPC-97
67T-234LL
67T-97
68Coke
68Dexter-26
68T-274
69MB-66
69T-453
69T-532M
70MLB/St-148
70OPC-199ALCS
70OPC-68LL
70OPC-70LL
70T-199ALCS
70T-590
70T-68LL
70T-70LL
70T/CB
71K-49
71MLB/St-293
71OPC-170
71OPC-69LL
71T-170
71T-69LL
71T/Coins-150
71T/tatt-16
72K-27
72MB-82
72OPC-70
72T-70
73JP
73K-47
73OPC-470
73T-470
74OPC-560
74T-560
75Ho-42
75OPC-410
75T-410
75T/M-410
76Ho-121
76OPC-285
76SSPC-375
76T-285
77T-162
86Mother/Ast-5
89Pac/SenLg-46
89TM/SenLg-27
91Crown/Orio-91
Cuen, Eleno
73Cedar
75Dubuq
81Portl-26
82Buffa-14
Cuervo, Ed
78Wausau
83ColumAst-2
Cuesta, Jamie
89Durham/Team-6
89Durham/Star-6
Cueto, Manuel Melo
No Cards.
Cuevas, Angelo
86Lynch-8
88Jacks/GS-21
88TexLgAS/GS-10
89Jacks/GS-14
Cuevas, Johnny
86Sumter-4
87Durham-8
88Sumter/ProC-397
89BurlB/ProC-1597
89BurlB/Star-6
90Durham/Team-16
91Greenvl/ClBest-11
91Greenvl/LineD-205
91Greenvl/ProC-3005
Cuevas, Rafael
78Newar
Cuff, John J.
No Cards.
Culberson, Calvain
88Pulaski/ProC-1760
89Sumter/ProC-1101
Culberson, Charles
86Fresno/Smok-25
87FtMyr-15
88Memphis/Best-17
91Utica/ClBest-24CO
91Utica/ProC-3259CO
Culberson, Delbert Leon
47TipTop-1
Culkar, Steve
88Virgini/Star-7
89Hagers/Best-8
89Hagers/ProC-276
89Hagers/Star-4
90Hagers/Best-16
90Hagers/ProC-1405
90Hagers/Star-6
91Hagers/ProC-2449
Cullen, John
(Jack)
63T-54R
66OPC-31
66T-31
Cullen, Mike
85Kingst-4
Cullen, Tim
67OPC-167R
67T-167R
68T-209
69T-586
70K-30
70OPC-49
70T-49
71MLB/St-534
71OPC-566
71T-566
72OPC-461
72T-461
Cullenbine, Roy
81Detroit-43
90Target-154
W753
Culler, Richard

47TipTop
Cullers, Steve
85BurlR-5
Cullop, Henry Nick
29Exh/4-3
31Exh/4-7
87Conlon/2-11
88Conlon/4-7
90Target-156
W514-59
Culmer, Will
80Penin/B-8
80Penin/C-19
82OkCty-25
83Charl-16
83Wheat/Ind-7
84Maine-14
Culp, Ray
60L-75
63T-29R
64PhilBull-11
64T-412
64T/Coins-35
64T/St-96
64T/SU
64T/tatt
64Wheat/St-12
65T-505
66OPC-4
66T-4
67OPC-168
67T-168
68T-272
69MB-67
69MLB/St-11
69T-391
69T/S-6
69T/St-132
70K-35
70MLB/St-158
70OPC-144
70T-144
71MD
71MLB/St-317
71OPC-660
71T-660
71T/tatt-13
72MB-83
72OPC-2
72T-2
78TCMA-197
Culver, George
65OPC-166R
65T-166R
67T-499R
68T-319
69Kahn
69T-635
70OPC-92
70T-92
71MLB/St-76
71OPC-291
71T-291
72MB-84
72T-732
73OPC-242
73T-242
74OPC-632
74T-632
83Portl-12
84Cram/PCL-215
86Reading-6MG
87Reading-1MG
88Maine/CMC-23
88Maine/ProC-300
89ScrWB/ProC-724
90Reading/Best-25CO
90Reading/ProC-1235CO
90Reading/Star-28CO
90Target-155
Culver, Lanell C.
83Tampa-3
84Cedar-16
Cumberbatch, Abdiel
90Tampa/DIMD-2
Cumberland, John
69OPC-114R
69T-114R
71MLB/St-244
71OPC-108
71T-108
72OPC-403
72T-403
83Lynch-13
85Tidew-26CO
86Tidew-6CO
87Tidew-18CO
87Tidew/TCMA-24CO
88Tidew/CANDL-2PC
88Tidew/CMC-25CO
88Tidew/ProC-1579CO
90Tidew/CMC-28CO
90Tidew/ProC-561CO
91Wichita/LineD-625CO
91Wichita/ProC-2615CO
Cummings, Audelle
89GreatF-8
Cummings, Bob
80Clinton-24
84Shrev/FB-6
85Cram/PCL-197
Cummings, Brian
88Batavia/ProC-1689
89Batavia/ProC-1943
89BurlB/ProC-1618
89BurlB/Star-7
90Durham/Team-19
Cummings, Dick
84Iowa-21
85Iowa-25
Cummings, John
91SanBern/ClBest-1
91SanBern/ProC-1977
Cummings, Midre
91Kenosha/ClBest-24
91Kenosha/ProC-2088
91Single/ClBest-318
Cummings, Steve
87Dunedin-2
88Knoxvl/Best-20
88SLAS-27
89Syrac/CMC-7
89Syrac/ProC-803
89Syrac/Team-7
90D-698
90OPC-374
90S/Tr-78T
90Syrac/CMC-3
90Syrac/Team-3
90T-374
90T/89Debut-26
91ColoSp/LineD-81
91ColoSp/ProC-2178
Cummings, William
(Candy)
50Callahan
80SSPC/HOF
89HOF/St-64
90BBWit-60
Cunha, Steve
91SLCity/ProC-3223
Cunningham, Bill
86WPalmB-10
87Jaxvl-17
Cunningham, Bill
V61-112
Cunningham, Chip
85PrWill-5
Cunningham, Dave
88Ashvl/ProC-1075
89Watlo/ProC-1795
89Watlo/Star-3
Cunningham, Earl
89LittleSun-2
89Wythe/Star-8
90B-34
90OPC-134FDP
90Peoria/Team-1
90Peoria/Team-2
90Peoria/Team-9M
90PeoriaCol/Team-1
90PeoriaCol/Team-2
90PeoriaCol/Team-3
90PeoriaCol/Team-4
90S-670DC
90T-134FDP
90T/TVCub-42
91B-420
91Peoria/ClBest-8
91Peoria/ProC-1354
Cunningham, Ellsworth
N172
Cunningham, Everett
88Butte-27
89Gaston/ProC-1000
89Gaston/Star-6
89SALAS/GS-43
90CharlR/Star-6
90FSLAS/Star-29
91Tulsa/LineD-578
91Tulsa/ProC-2766
Cunningham, Glen
51BR-D16
Cunningham, Joseph R.
(Joe)
55T-37
55T/DH-38
57T-304
58T-168
59T-285
60Bz-27
60T-40
60T-562AS
60T/tatt-10
61P-172
61T-520
62J-195
62P-195
62P/Can-195
62Salada-173A
62Salada-173B
62Shirriff-173
62T-195
63Exh
63J-35
63P-35
63T-100
64T-340
65T-496
65T/E-63
66T-531
79TCMA-105
90Johnson/Star-29CO
91Johnson/ClBest-30CO
91Johnson/ProC-4172CO
Exh47
Cunningham, Joseph R. Jr.
87StPete-8
88StPete/Star-4
89Hamil/Star-28
Cunningham, Kenn
90Bristol/ProC-3174MG
90Bristol/Star-27MG
Cunningham, Sean
87BurlEx-25
88Rockford-9
89Jaxvl/Best-22
89Jaxvl/ProC-158
89Rockford-9TR
90WPalmB/Star-31
91WPalmB/ClBest-30TR
Cunningham, Troy
89Spokane/SP-17
90CharRain/Best-7
90CharRain/ProC-2034
Cunningham, Wm. A.
E120
W515-1
W573
W575
Cunningham, Wm. J.
E102
E220
T207
Cupples, Michael
85Madis-10
85Madis/Pol-7
86Madis-7
86Madis/Pol-7
87Madis-16
Curbelo, Jorge
82Miami-10
Curley, Tim
89Princet/Star-3
Curnal, Jim
78Cr/PCL-96
Curnow, Robert
88Spokane/ProC-1939
89Watlo/ProC-1777
89Watlo/Star-4
90CharRain/Best-8
90CharRain/ProC-2042
Curran, Bud
88Cedar/ProC-1161
Curran, Dave
80Holyo-22
Curran, Shawn
91Classic/DP-48
91FrRow/DP-27
Curren, Bud
85Cedar-30
Currence, Delaney
(Lafayette)
76SSPC-251
Current, Matt
88Martins/Star-8
89Martins/Star-9
90Spartan/Best-13
90Spartan/ProC-2494
90Spartan/Star-4
91Clearw/ClBest-13
91Clearw/ProC-1624
Currie, Brian
89Boise/ProC-2000
90Erie/Star-4
Currier, Lenny
86Albuq-4TR
87Albuq/Pol-4TR
88Albuq/ProC-272TR
Currin, Wes
88Sumter/ProC-395
89Durham/Team-7
89Durham/Star-7
89Star/Wax-70
Curry, Clinton
83TriCit-25
Curry, Dell
91Gaston/ClBest-27
Curry, G. Tony
60T-541
61P-120
61T-262
61T/St-51
Curry, Stephen T.
(Steve)
86NewBrit-8
87Pawtu-3
87Pawtu/TCMA-3
88AAA/ProC-31
88Pawtu/CMC-7
88Pawtu/ProC-468
88S/Tr-81T
89F-86
89Panini/St-267
89Pawtu/CMC-2
89Pawtu/Dunkin-35
89Pawtu/ProC-691
89S/HotRook-53
89T-471
90Pawtu/ProC-454
90T/TVRSox-41
Curry, Steve
81Richm-17
86Greenvl/Team-6
86Richm-3
89BurlB/ProC-1613
90Idaho/ProC-3262MG
91Idaho/ProC-4344MG
Curtis, Chad
91AAAGame/ProC-AAA13
91Edmon/LineD-159
91Edmon/ProC-1522
Curtis, Clinton
(Cliff)
90Target-920
M116
Curtis, Craig
90Ashvl/ProC-2753
91Osceola/ClBest-22
91Osceola/ProC-696
Curtis, Ed
C46-90
Curtis, Irvin
N172
Curtis, Jack P.
61T-533
62T-372
Curtis, John D.
72T-724R
73OPC-143
73T-143
74OPC-373
74T-373
74T/Tr-373T
75OPC-381
75T-381
75T/M-381
76OPC-239
76T-239
77T-324
78T-486
79Pol/Giants-40
79T-649
80T-12
81F-491
81OPC-158
81T-531
81T/St-231
82F-569
82T-219
83D-170
83F-84
83T-777
84F-513
84Nes/792-158
84Smok/Cal-6
84T-158
89Princet/Star-4
90Welland/Pucko-12
Curtis, Mike
86Geneva-4
87WinSalem-27
88Harris/ProC-843
90Canton/Best-26
90Canton/ProC-1287
90Canton/Star-3
90EastLAS/ProC-EL38
90Foil/Best-119
91Canton/LineD-80
91Canton/ProC-974
Curtis, Randy
91Pittsfld/ClBest-6
91Pittsfld/ProC-3434
Curtwright, Guy
Exh47
Cusack, Rocky
87Lakeland-12
88CharlK/Pep-13
Cusak, John
88Pac/8Men-12
Cushing, Steve
81Batavia-4
81Watlo-32
82Watlo/B-1
82Watlo/C-15
Cushman, Ed
N172
N172/ST
N284
N690
Cusick, Anthony
N172
Cusick, Jack
52B-192
Cutshall, Bill
86Jaxvl/TCMA-24
87Nashvl-3
88OrlanTw/Best-27
Cutshaw, George
16FleischBrd-21
21Exh-30
90Target-157
D327
D328-37
E100
E120
E135-37
E220
E99
V100
W573
Cutty, Fran
81CharR-11
82FtMyr-15
Cuyler, Hazen
(KiKi)
25Exh-51
26Exh-51
27Exh-25
29Exh/4-6
30CEA/Pin-2
31Exh/4-6
32Orbit/num-6
32Orbit/un-14
33CJ/Pin-3
33DL-8
33G-23
34DS-31
34G-90
35G-1F
35G-3D
35G-4D
35G-5D
36G

36G-10
38Wheat
60F-75
61F-19
73F/Wild-14
80Pac/Leg-92
80SSPC/HOF
89Smok/Dodg-6
90Target-158
91Conlon/Sport-12
92Conlon/Sport-587
R305
R308-152
R312
R312/M
R314
R332-29
R332-3
V353-23
V355-55
W517-19
WG8-10

Cuyler, Milt
87Fayette-8
88FSLAS/Star-32
88Lakeland/Star-8
89Toledo/CMC-21
89Toledo/ProC-787
90B-358
90S-583
90S/100Ris-84
90Toledo/CMC-21
90Toledo/ProC-160
91B-141
91Classic/200-191
91Classic/I-42
91CokeK/Tiger-22
91D-40RR
91D/Rook-6
91F-334
91F/UltraUp-U22
91Leaf/I-251
91Leaf/Stud-51
91OPC-684
91OPC/Premier-27
91T-684
91T/90Debut-36
91T/StClub/II-470
91UD-556
92D/I-232
92F-130
92F/RookSIns-11
92S/100RisSt-1
92S/I-26
92T-522
92UD-536

Cvejdlik, Kent
76Watlo

Cyburt, Phil
78Salem

Cypret, Greg
81Tucson-1
82Tucson-6
83Tucson-15
84Cram/PCL-54

Czajkowski, Jim
87Sumter-19
88Durham/Star-4
89Durham/Team-8
89Durham/Star-8
90Harris/ProC-1187
90Harris/Star-6
91ElPaso/LineD-179
91ElPaso/ProC-2740

Czarnik, Chris
89BurlB/ProC-1617
89BurlB/Star-8
90Durham/Team-9

D'Acquisto, John F.
(John)
74OPC-608R
74T-608R
75OPC-372
75T-372
75T/M-372
76OPC-628
76SSPC-94
76T-628
77Padre/SchCd-8
77T-19
78Padre/FamFun-8
79T-506
80T-339
81F-163
81OPC-204
81T-427
82Richm-4
82T-58
83F-516
89Pac/SenLg-121
89T/SenLg-31

D'Alesandro, Mark
90A&AASingle/ProC-166
90Boise/ProC-3324
91MidwLAS/ProC-MWL25
91QuadC/ClBest-16
91QuadC/ProC-2634
91Single/ClBest-259

D'Alessandro, Sal
85Durham-22
86Greenvl/Team-7
87Richm/Crown-10
88Greenvl/Best-3

D'Alexander, Greg
90Miami/I/Star-4
91Miami/ClBest-19
91Miami/ProC-413

D'Amore, Louis
81Clinton-14

D'Boever, William
86Jamestn-4

D'Onofrio, Gary
83DayBe-20

D'Vincenzo, Mark
86LitFalls-8

Dabney, Fred
88Utica/Pucko-16
89SoBend/GS-11
90Saraso/Star-6
91Saraso/ClBest-3
91Saraso/ProC-1106

Dabney, Ty
85Everett/Cram-3
86Fresno/Smok-19
87Shrev-3
87TexLgAS-32
88Phoenix/CMC-22
88Phoenix/ProC-72

Daboll, Dennis
65T-561R

Dacko, Mark
82Evansvl-3
83Evansvl-1
84Evansvl-6

Dacosta, Bill
87Oneonta-11
88PrWill/Star-7

Dacus, Barry
86PalmSp-9
86PalmSp/Smok-19
87MidldA-28
88Edmon/CMC-10
88Edmon/ProC-568

Dade, Lonnie Paul
(Paul)
78K-14
78OPC-86
78T-662
79OPC-3
79T-13
80OPC-134
80T-254
81T-496

Dafforn, Mike
88Martins/Star-9
89Martins/Star-10

Dagres, Angelo George
(Angie)
91Crown/Orio-92

Dahle, Dave
52Mother-15

Dahlen, William F.
(Bill)
10Domino-30
11Helmar-84
12Sweet/Pin-72
14Piedmont/St-15
90Target-159
E107
E254
E286
E98
M116
N300/SC
S74-51
T202
T205
T206
T3-11
WG3-12
WG5-13

Dahlgren, Ellsworth
(Babe)
39PB-81
40PB-3
41PB-49
90Target-160

Dahse, David
84Newar-4

Dailey, William G.
63T-391
64T-156

Daily, Cornelius F.
(Con)
90Target-922
N172
N284

Daily, Edward M.
(Ed)
E223
N172
N284
N690/2

Dakin, Brian
90Everett/Best-17
90Everett/ProC-3133

Dal Canton, John B.
(Bruce)
69T-468R
70OPC-52
70T-52
71MLB/St-413
71OPC-168
71T-168
72T-717
73T-487
73OPC-487
74OPC-308
74T-308
75OPC-472
75T-472
75T/M-472
76OPC-486
76T-486
77T-114
79Knoxvl/TCMA-18
82Durham-22
85IntLgAS-23
85Richm-23CO
86Richm-4CO
91Richm/LineD-450CO
91Richm/ProC-2585CO

Dale, Emmett Eugene
(Gene)
D329-42
D350/2-43
M101/4-42
M101/5-43

Dale, Phil
86Tampa-4
87Cedar-2
88Chatt/Best-18
89Greens/ProC-427
90CedarDG/Best-22
91Idaho/ProC-4345CO

Dalena, Pete
83Nashvl-5
84Colum-18
84Colum/Pol-8
84Nashvl-5
85Colum-15
85Colum/Pol-7
86Colum-4
86Colum/Pol-4
87Colum-11
87Colum/Pol-5
87Colum/TCMA-12
88Colum/CMC-16
88Colum/Pol-14
88Colum/ProC-321
89AAA/ProC-36
89ColoSp/CMC-12
89ColoSp/ProC-235
90T/89Debut-27
90Vanco/CMC-14
90Vanco/ProC-494
91Harris/ProC-617CO

Daley, Jud
90Target-923

Daley, Leavitt Leo
(Buddy)
55Salem
58T-222
59T-263
60Armour-8
60Bz-2
60T-8
60T/tatt-11
61Bz-4
61P-83
61T-422
61T-48LL
61T/St-159
61T/St-201
62Salada-203
62Shirriff-203
62T-376
63T-38
64T-164
65OPC-262
65T-262
78TCMA-257
Exh47

Daley, Peter Harvey
(Pete)
55T-206
57T-388
58T-73
59T-276
60T-108
61T-158
62T/St-94

Daley, William
(Bill)
N172

Dalkowski, Steve
63T-496R

Dallas, Gershon
90Ashvl/ProC-2759
91Osceola/ClBest-23
91Osceola/ProC-697

Dallessandro, Dom
41DP-101
49B/PCL-9

Dalrymple, Abner F.
(Abner)
N172
WG1-57

Dalrymple, Clayton E.
(Clay)
60L-143
60T-523
61T-299
61T/St-52
62J-197
62P-197
62P/Can-197
62Salada-141
62Shirriff-141
62T-434
62T/St-166
63F-52
63J-184
63P-184
63T-192
64PhilBull-12
64T-191
65T-372
66T-202
67OPC-53
67T-53
68T-567
69MB-68
69OPC-151
69T-151
69T/St-74
70OPC-319
70T-319
71MLB/St-294
71OPC-617
71T-617
78TCMA-203
91Crown/Orio-93
PM10/L-13

Dalson, Kevin
89Wythe/Star-9

Dalton, Harry
82Pol/Brew-GM

Dalton, Jack
90Target-161

Dalton, Mike
86Pawtu-8
87Pawtu-16
87Pawtu/TCMA-4
88NewBrit/ProC-896
89NewBrit/ProC-607
89Pawtu/Dunkin-27
90Pawtu/CMC-24
90Pawtu/ProC-455
90T/TVRSox-42
91Toledo/LineD-582
91Toledo/ProC-1923
92F-131
92S/100RisSt-95
92T/91Debut-42

Dalton, Rich
78OrlTw

Daly, James J.
(Sun)
N172

Daly, Mark
81Tidew-25

Daly, Thomas Peter
(Tom)
90Target-162
E107
N172
N300/SC

Damian, Leonard
(Len)
86Peoria-4
87Pittsfld-13
88Iowa/CMC-2
88Iowa/ProC-544
89Iowa/CMC-2
89Iowa/ProC-1705
90T/TVCub-43

Damon, John
83Memphis-4

Dana, Derek
91Everett/ClBest-12
91Everett/ProC-3918

Dancy, Bill
80Penin/B-27MG
80Penin/C-12MG
83Reading-23
85Cram/PCL-35MG
87Maine/TCMA-23
89ScrWB/CMC-25
89ScrWB/ProC-1208
90AAAGame/ProC-AAA27MG
90ScranWB/CMC-18MG
91ScranWB/LineD-499MG
91ScranWB/ProC-2555MG

Dando, Patrick
90A&AASingle/ProC-191
90Pulaski/Best-16
90Pulaski/ProC-3096
91Durham/ClBest-18
91Durham/ProC-1552

Dandos, Mike
85Everett/II/Cram-2

Dandridge, Ray
(Hooks)
74Laugh/Black-26
86Negro/Frit-7
87D/HL-18
88Negro/Duques-17
89HOF/St-26
90Negro/Star-14
91Negro/Lewis-5

Danek, Bill
86Peoria-5
87WinSalem-5

Danforth, David C.
(Dave)
21Exh-31
E120
E121/120
T207
V61-26
W501-101
W572
W573

Danforth, Perry
77Spoka

Daniel, Clay
85Cedar-5
86Vermont-5
88Harris/ProC-860
90Miami/I/Star-5

Daniel, Dian
81ArkTr-23M

Daniel, Jake
90Target-924

Daniel, Jim

86CharRain-8TR
87CharlO/WBTV-11
88CharlK/Pep-16
88River/Cal-231
88River/ProC-1412
89River/Best-28
89River/ProC-1407
90Riversi/Best-21TR
Daniel, Keith
90Kissim/DIMD-8
Daniel, Lee
90MedHat/Best-21
Daniel, Michael
91James/ProC-3548
Daniel, Scott
91James/ClBest-29PER
Daniel, Steve
85BurlR-25
Daniels, Bennie
58T-392
59T-122
60L-7
60T-91
61T-368
62Salada-42
62Shirriff-42
62T-378
62T/bucks
62T/St-95
63T-497
64T-587
65OPC-129
65T-129
78TCMA-145
Daniels, Bernard E.
(Bert)
E270/1
E286
T207
Daniels, Dave
79AppFx-11
82VeroB-4
Daniels, Gary
90Erie/Star-5
Daniels, Greg
87Miami-19
Daniels, Harold Jack
(Jack)
53B/Col-83
Daniels, Jerry
87Erie-23
88StPete/Star-5
Daniels, Jim
89River/Cal-28TR
Daniels, Kal
83Cedar-22
83Cedar/LF-17
86D-27RR
86F-646M
86Sf/Rook-43
86TexGold-28
87Classic/Up-130
87D-142
87D/OD-192
87F-197
87F/LL-13
87Kahn-28
87T-466
87ToysRUs-8
88Classic/Red-161
88D-14DK
88D-289
88D/Best-6
88D/DKsuper-14DK
88F-230
88F/AwardWin-7
88F/Mini-72
88F/St-82
88Kahn/Reds-28
88Leaf-14DK
88Leaf-150
88OPC-53
88Panini/St-281
88RedFoley/St-14
88S-86
88S/YS/I-39
88Sf-112
88T-622
88T/Big-48
88T/St-139
89T/Ames-10
89B-314
89Classic-74
89D-198
89D/Best-118
89D/MVP-BC18
89F-157
89F/LL-8
89F/Superstar-10
89Kahn/Reds-28
89OPC-45
89Panini/St-75
89RedFoley/St-26
89S-7
89S/Tr-48
89Sf-52
89T-45
89T/Big-323
89T/LJN-59
89T/Mini-7
89T/St-144
89UD-160
90B-99
90CedarDG/Best-2
90Classic/III-64
90D-432
90D/BestNL-127
90F/Up-U20
90Leaf/II-313
90Mother/Dodg-3
90OPC-585
90Panini/St-280
90Pol/Dodg-28
90Publlnt/St-25
90Publlnt/St-610
90S-490
90T-585
90T/Big-238
90Target-925
90UD-603
91B-600
91Classic/200-14
91D-336
91D/GSlam-3
91F-198
91F/Ultra-160
91Leaf/I-112
91MooTown-7
91Mother/Dodg-3
91OPC-245
91Panini/FrSt-60
91Panini/St-58
91Pol/Dodg-28
91RedFoley/St-22
91S-20
91S/100SS-53
91Sunflower-5
91T-245
91T/StClub/I-116
91UD-166
92D/I-343
92F-453
92S/I-110
92T-767
92UD-284
Daniels, Lance
89Bristol/Star-6
Daniels, Lawrence L.
(Law)
N172
Daniels, Lee
91MedHat/ProC-4114
Daniels, Steve
80Cedar-24
Dann, Tom
79Newar-1
Danner, Deon
91Welland/ClBest-18
91Welland/ProC-3565
Danning, Harry
(Harry)
39PB-18
40PB-93
41DP-25
41DP-91
41PB-7
41Wheat-20
R302
V355-22
Danrel, Mike
91James/ClBest-6
Danson, Roger
76BurlB
Dantonio, Fats
90Target-921
Dantzler, Shawn
86Clearw-6
87Clearw-10
88Clearw/Star-10
Dapper, Cliff
90Target-163
Darby, Mike
86Wausau-6
Darcy, Patrick L.
(Pat)
75OPC-615R
75T-615R
75T/M-615R
76OPC-538
76SSPC-26
76T-538
Dare, Brian
90Idaho/ProC-3241
Dark, Alvin Ralph
(Alvin)
48L-51
49B-67
49Eureka-6
49Royal-18
50B-64
50Drake-20
51B-14
52B-34
52BR
52Royal
52StarCal/L-78B
52T-351
53B/Col-19
53T-109
54B-41
54NYJour
54RH
55B-2
55Gol/Giants-5
56T-148
57T-98
58T-125
59T-502
60T-472
61T-220MG
62T-322MG
63T-258MG
64T-529MG
66T-433MG
67T-389MG
68T-237MG
69OPC-91MG
69T-91MG
70OPC-524MG
70T-524MG
71OPC-397MG
71T-397MG
75OPC-561MG
75T-561MG
75T/M-561MG
76SSPC-488MG
78T-467MG
79TCMA-25
80Pac/Leg-80
87Mother/A's-13
88Pac/Leg-28
89Swell-77
90Pac/Legend-69
91LineD-23
91Swell/Great-22
91T/Arc53-109
Exh47
PM10/Sm-33
R302-116
R423-20
Darkis, Willie
83Reading-18
84Cram/PCL-211
86GlenF-2
Darley, Ned
91MedHat/ProC-4091
Darling, Dell Conrad
(Dell)
N172
N184
Darling, Gary
89TM/Umpire-58
90TM/Umpire-56
Darling, Ronald M.
(Ron)
81Tulsa-18
82Tidew-13
83Tidew-1
84D-30RR
84F/X-29
84T/Mets/Fan-2
84T/Tr-27
85D-434
85F/St-117
85Leaf-256
85OPC-138
85T-415
85T/St-105
86D-563
86D/AAS-37
86F-77
86F/Mini-18
86F/St-28
86KayBee-6
86Leaf-221
86OPC-225
86Sf-109
86T-225
86T/Mets/Fan-3
86T/St-98
87BK-6
87D-192
87Drake-28
87F-5
87F/Hottest-11
87F/LimWaxBox-C1
87F/Mini-23
87F/St-27
87F/WS-5
87Kraft-28
87Leaf-85
87MSA/Discs-3
87OPC-75
87Sf-53
87T-75
87T/HL-26
87T/Mets/Fan-2
87T/Mini-21
87T/St-105
87Woolwth-26
88D-6DK
88D-76
88D/Best-41
88D/DKsuper-6DK
88D/Mets/Bk-76
88F-132
88F/Slug-C1
88F/St-100
88Kahn/Mets-12
88Leaf-6DK
88Leaf-78
88OPC-38
88Panini/St-335
88S-141
88Sf-73
88T-685
88T/Big-85
88T/St-98
89B-372
89D-171
89D/Best-41
89F-32
89Kahn/Mets-12
89OPC-105
89Panini/St-130
89S-180
89S/HotStar-71
89Sf-32
89T-105
89T/Big-166
89T/DHTest-7
89T/LJN-15
89T/St-100
89UD-159
90D-289
90D/Learning-29
90F-201
90Kahn/Mets-15
90Leaf/II-304
90MLBPA/Pins-14
90OPC-330
90Panini/St-295
90Publlnt/St-130
90S-446
90T-330
90T/Big-113
90T/St-98
90T/TVMets-9
90TulsaDG/Best-18
90UD-241
91B-483
91D-472
91F-144
91F/Ultra-214
91Kahn/Mets-15
91Leaf/II-378
91OPC-735
91S-456
91T-735
91T/StClub/I-60
91UD-198
91UD/FinalEd-69F
91WIZMets-90
92D/II-723
92F-254
92S/II-710
92T-259
92UD-669
Darnbrough, William
N172
Darnell, Robert Jack
(Bob)
55B-39
79TCMA-257
90Target-164
Darnell, Steve
76Wausau
Darr, Michael Edward
(Mike)
78Syrac
Darretta, Dave
85BurlR-9
Darrow, Darrell
79SLCity-17
Darrow, George Oliver
(George)
34G-87
Darwin, Arthur B.
(Bobby)
69T-641R
73OPC-228
73T-228
74OPC-527
74T-527
74T/St-205
75Ho-98
75OPC-346
75T-346
75T/M-346
76Ho-31
76Ho/Twink-31
76OPC-63
76SSPC-247
76T-63
77T-617
90Lennox-9
90Target-165
Darwin, Danny Wayne
78Cr/PCL-81
79T-713R
80T-498
81D-147
81F-632
81OPC-22
81T-22
81T/St-136
82D-231
82F-315
82T-298
82T/St-237
83D-289
83F-565
83Rangers-44
83T-609
83T/St-121
84D-544
84F-416
84Nes/792-377
84Rangers-44
84T-377
84T/St-359
85D-98
85F-557
85F/Up-U32
85OPC-227
85Pol/Brew-18
85T-227
85T/St-352
85T/Tr-26T
86D-149
86F-485
86Leaf-75
86OPC-206
86Pol/Brew-18
86T-519
86T/St-205

87D-508
87F-54
87Mother/Ast-14
87OPC-157
87Pol/Ast-4
87T-157
88D-358
88F-444
88Mother/Ast-14
88Pol/Ast-7
88S-184
88T-461
89D-390
89F-354
89Lennox/Ast-13
89Mother/Ast-13
89S-553
89T-719
89UD-97
90B-66
90D-561
90D/BestNL-53
90F-227
90Leaf/II-346
90Mother/Ast-15
90OPC-64
90Publlnt/St-91
90S-402
90Sf-83
90T-64
90T/St-14
90UD-305
91B-111
91Classic/200-170
91Classic/I-44
91D-165
91D-401MVP
91F-503
91F/Up-U5
91Leaf/II-405
91OPC-666
91OPC/Premier-28
91Panini/FrSt-15
91Panini/St-18
91Panini/Top15-65
91Pep/RSox-6
91S-51
91S/RookTr-24T
91T-666
91T/StClub/II-394
91T/Tr-26T
91UD-586
91UD/Ext-705
92D/I-87
92F-38
92S/I-138
92T-324
92UD-678

Darwin, Jeff
89Belling/Legoe-4
90Penin/Star-6
91SanBern/ClBest-2
91SanBern/ProC-1978
91Single/ClBest-51

Dascenzo, Doug
86WinSalem-4
87Pittsfld-23
88Iowa/CMC-19
88Iowa/ProC-528
89D-491
89F-420
89Iowa/CMC-20
89Iowa/ProC-1702
89Panini/St-47
89S-621
89S/HotRook-4
89Sf-42
89T-149
89UD-10SR
90Cub/Mara-5
90OPC-762
90S/YS/II-40
90T-762
90T/TVCub-30
90UD-211
91Cub/Mara-29
91D-749
91F-418
91Leaf/II-483
91OPC-437
91S-209
91T-437
92D/I-38
92S/I-319
92T-509
92UD-239

Dascoli, Frank
55B-291ump

Dasso, Francis J.
(Frank)
47Signal

Dattola, Kevin
90SoOreg/Best-4
91Modesto/ClBest-25
91Modesto/ProC-3102
91Single/ClBest-115

Datz, Jeff
82AubAs-11
83DayBe-15
86ColumAst-9
87ColAst/ProC-2
88Tucson/CMC-9
88Tucson/ProC-187
88Tucson/JP-7
89Toledo/CMC-11
89Toledo/ProC-761
90ColClip/CMC-19
90ColClip/ProC-678
90T/89Debut-28

Daub, Dan
90Target-926

Daubach, Brian
91Kingspt/ClBest-6
91Kingspt/ProC-3818

Daubert, Jacob E.
(Jake)
11Helmar-85
14CJ-143
14Piedmont/St-16
15CJ-143
16FleischBrd-22
21Exh-32
75F/Pion-24
87Conlon/2-12
88Pac/8Men-95
90Target-166
91Conlon/Sport-307
BF2-57
D327
D328-38
D329-43
D350/2-44
E120
E121/80
E122
E135-38
E220
E254
E270/1
M101/4-43
M101/5-44
S74-52
T201
T202
T205
T207
V100
V61-99
W501-52
W514-68
W572
W575
WG5-14
WG6-13
WG7-11

Dauer, Richard F.
(Rich)
77T-477R
78T-237
79T-666
80OPC-56
80T-102
81D-232
81F-182
81OPC-314
81T-314
81T/St-36
82D-256
82F-161
82OPC-8
82T-8
82T/St-147
83D-477
83F-57
83OPC-192
83T-579
83T/St-27
84D-350
84F-4
84Nes/792-723
84OPC-374
84T-723
84T/St-214
85D-106
85F-173
85OPC-58
85T-494
85T/St-203
86F-270
86OPC-251
86T-251
87SanBer-7
89ColoSp/CMC-24
89ColoSp/ProC-242
89SanBer/Best-28M
90Smok/SoCal-3
91Crown/Orio-94
91Pac/SenLg-105

Daugherty, Jack
86Jaxvl/TCMA-25
87Indianap-10
88Indianap/CMC-21
88Indianap/ProC-521
89OkCty/CMC-13
89OkCty/ProC-1525
90B-503
90D-461
90F-294
90Leaf/II-521
90Mother/Rang-11
90OPC-52
90S-564
90S/100Ris-61
90T-52
90UD-614
91B-277
91D-576
91F-284
91Leaf/I-17
91Mother/Rang-11
91OPC-622
91S-309
91T-622
91T/StClub/I-276
91UD-284
92D/II-569
92F-300
92S/II-622
92T-344

Daugherty, Jim
90Ashvl/ClBest-4
91Ashvl/ProC-562
91SALAS/ProC-SAL1

Daugherty, Pat
90James/Pucko-27MG

Daughterty, Mike
83SanJose-19

Daughtry, Dorian
89SanBern/Best-2
89SanBern/Cal-88

Daulton, Darren
83Reading-11
84Cram/PCL-198
85Cram/PCL-42
85F/Up-U33
85Phill/TastyK-10M
85Phill/TastyK-24
86CIGNA-7
86D-477
86F-438
86Phill/TastyK-10
86T-264
87D-262
87F-172
87Maine/TCMA-21
87OPC-57
87Phill/TastyK-10
87T-636
88D-309
88Phill/TastyK-7
88S-473
88T-468
89D-549
89D/Best-128
89Phill/TastyK-4
89S-413
89T-187
89UD-448
90B-158
90D-194
90D/BestNL-20
90F-555
90Leaf/II-369
90OPC-542
90Phill/TastyK-7
90Publlnt/St-234
90S-389
90T-542
90UD-418
91B-507
91Classic/200-81
91D-316
91F-393
91F/Ultra-260
91Leaf/I-192
91Leaf/Stud-212
91OPC-89
91Panini/FrSt-102
91Panini/St-109
91Phill/Medford-11
91S-246
91T-89
91T/StClub/I-4
91UD-408
92D/I-198
92F-527
92S/II-506
92T-244
92UD-429

Dauphin, Philip J.
90Geneva/ProC-3036
90Geneva/Star-6
91MidwLAS/ProC-MWL7
91Peoria/ClBest-25
91Peoria/ProC-1355

Dauss, George August
(Hooks)
21Exh-33
25Exh-91
26Exh-92
27Exh-46
81Detroit-74
88Conlon/5-7
D327
D328-39
E120
E121/120
E121/80
E122
E135-39
V100
V117-11
V61-18
W501-110
W573
W575

Davalillo, Victor J.
(Vic)
63Sugar-24
63T-324R
64Kahn
64T-435
64T/Coins-86
64T/St-100
64T/tatt
65Kahn
65OldLond-24
65OPC-128
65T-128
66Kahn
66T-216LL
66T-325
66T/RO-70
67OPC-69
67T-69
68T-397
69MB-70
69MLB/St-20
69T-275
69T/S-9
69T/St-142
70MLB/St-138
70OPC-256
70T-256
71MLB/St-199
71OPC-4
71T-4
72MB-86
72T-785
73OPC-163
73T-163
74OPC-444
74T-444
78T-539
79T-228
81F-132
90Target-167
WG10-26

DaVanon, Frank G.
(Jerry)
69T-637R
71OPC-32
71T-32
75Iowa/TCMA-5
76OPC-551
76T-551
77T-283
91Crown/Orio-95

Davenport, Adell
87Anchora-5
89Clinton/ProC-882
90AS/Cal-47
90Foil/Best-58
90SanJose/Best-8
90SanJose/Cal-39
90SanJose/ProC-2019
90SanJose/Star-6
91AS/Cal-29
91SanJose/ClBest-6
91SanJose/ProC-17

Davenport, Arthur D.
(Dave)
D327

Davenport, Gary
86Fresno/Smok-2CO

Davenport, James H.
(Jim)
58SFCallB-7
58T-413
59Bz
59T-198
60T-154
61P-149
61T-55
61T/Dice-3
61T/St-76
62J-134
62P-134
62P/Can-134
62Salada-169
62Shirriff-169
62T-9
62T/St-196
63F-65
63J-104
63P-104
63Salada-19
63T-388
64T-82
64T/St-63
65OPC-213
65T-213
66OPC-176
66T-176
67T-441
68Coke
68Dexter-27
68T-525
69MB-69
69OPC-102
69T-102
69T/St-102
70MLB/St-122
70OPC-378
70T-378
72MB-85
76SSPC-626
78TCMA-131
79Pol/SFG-12
79TCMA-288
80Pol/SFG-12
84Mother/SFG-6
85Mother/SFG-1MG
85T/Tr-27T
86Phill/TastyK-2CO
87Phill/TastyK-x
89Pac/Leg-118
91CokeK/Tiger-x
91Hamil/ClBest-24
91Hamil/ProC-4051
PM10/Sm-34

Davenport, Neal
86Cedar/TCMA-26
87Tampa-23TR

Davey, Michael Gerard
(Mike)
79Spokane-14
80Port-19

Daviault, Ray
91WIZMets-91
David, Andre
82Orlan/B-16
82OrlTw/A-5
83Toledo-19
84Toledo-11
85T-43
85Toledo-20
86Toledo-7
87D-519
87Tidew-24
87Tidew/TCMA-12
88Tidew/CANDL-7
88Tidew/CMC-18
88Tidew/ProC-1596
89ElPaso/GS-26
David, Brian
83Wausau/LF-6
86Chatt-8
87Chatt/Best-23
David, Gregory
87Dunedin-20
88Myrtle/ProC-1176
89Myrtle/ProC-1454
90Wichita/Rock-6
91Kingspt/ClBest-24MG
91Kingspt/ProC-3829MG
91Wichita/LineD-605
91Wichita/ProC-2603
Davidsmeier, Dan
82ElPaso-5
84Cram/PCL-29
85Cram/PCL-201
86Vanco-9
87Denver-22
Davidson, Bob
88TM/Umpire-44
89TM/Umpire-42
90TM/Umpire-40
Davidson, Bobby
86Albany/TCMA-31
87PrWill-3
88Albany/ProC-1334
89Albany/Best-3
89Albany/ProC-327
89Albany/Star-6
89Star/Wax-97
90ColClip/CMC-26
90ColClip/ProC-669
90T/89Debut-29
90T/TVYank-39
91Louisvl/LineD-233
91Louisvl/ProC-2908
Davidson, Grady
91Watertn/ClBest-3
91Watertn/ProC-3358
Davidson, Jackie
86Pittsfld-6
87Iowa-3
88Pittsfld/ProC-1375
89CharlK-19
Davidson, John
91Kissim/ProC-4176
Davidson, Mark
85Orlan-3
86Toledo-6
87D/OD-225
87D/Rook-22
87F/Up-U20
88D-519
88F-8
88S-570
88T-19
89F-109
89Portl/CMC-22
89Portl/ProC-227
89S-107
89T-451
89T/Big-320
89UD-577
90Lennox-10
90Mother/Ast-11
90OPC-267
90T-267
91D-540
91F-504
91F/Ultra-136
91Leaf/I-143
91Mother/Ast-11
91OPC-678
91T-678
91T/StClub/II-584
92F-432
92S/I-289
Davidson, Mike
88Bristol/ProC-1871
89Fayette/ProC-1593
Davidson, Randy
78Indianap-24
79Indianap-13
81Cedar-19
82Cedar-25
Davidson, Thomas E.
(Ted)
65OPC-243R
65T-243R
66OPC-89
66T-89
67T-519
68OPC-48
68T-48
Davidson, William J.
M116
T206
Davie, Gerald Lee
(Jerry)
59T-256
60T-301
Davies, Bob
52Wheat
Davila, J.D.
(Jose)
91Spokane/ProC-3941
91Spokane/ClBest-18
Davila, Vic
83Butte-17
Davin, D.
N172
Davino, Mike
89Utica/Pucko-5
90Saraso/Star-7
91BirmB/LineD-57
91BirmB/ProC-1448
Davins, Jim
86Macon-7
87Kenosha-1
88Portl/CMC-10
88Portl/ProC-660
89Portl/CMC-1
89Portl/ProC-211
90Indianap/CMC-11
90Indianap/ProC-286
91Denver/LineD-133
91Denver/ProC-115
Davis, Allen
(Bo)
89Bluefld/Star-7
90Wausau/Best-26
90Wausau/ProC-2140
90Wausau/Star-6
91Kane/ClBest-21
91Kane/ProC-2668
Davis, Alvin
83Chatt-8
84F/X-30
85FunFood/Pin-37
84Mother/Mar-23
84T/Tr-28
85D-18DKs86D-
85D-69
85D/AAS-16
85D/DKsuper-18
85Drake-8
85F-488
85F/LimEd-7
85F/St-15
85GenMills-16
85Leaf-18DK
85Mother/Mar-2
85OPC-145
85Seven-7W
85T-145
85T/Gloss40-8
85T/St-332
85T/St-368YS
85T/Super-6
86D-69
86F-464
86F/LL-9
86F/Mini-97
86F/Slug-8
86F/St-29
86KayBee-7
86Leaf-65
86Mother/Mar-2
86OPC-309
86Sf-31
86Sf-74M
86T-440
86T/St-218
86TrueVal-21
87D-75
87D/OD-115
87F-584
87F/Excit-13
87F/Mini-24
87F/RecSet-5
87F/St-28
87Kraft-37
87Leaf-118
87Mother/Sea-2
87OPC-235
87RedFoley/St-71
87Sf-21
87T-235
87T/Coins-9
87T/St-220
88D-193
88D-BC25
88D/Best-107
88F-373
88F/RecSet-8
88F/SS-10
88F/St-59
88KayBee-6
88KingB/Disc-17
88Leaf-196
88Mother/Sea-2
88OPC-349
88Panini/St-185
88S-83
88Sf-52
88T-785
88T/Big-64
88T/Coins-10
88T/RiteAid-24
88T/St-219
88T/UK-17
89B-215
89Chatt/II/Team-8
89Classic-81
89D-345
89D/Best-24
89D/MVP-BC25
89F-546
89Mother/Sea-2
89OPC-57
89Panini/St-435
89RedFoley/St-27
89S-51
89S/HotStar-78
89Sf-33
89T-687
89T/Big-218
89T/Coins-38
89T/LJN-70
89T/Mini-72
89T/St-227
89T/UK-18
89UD-105
89UD-680TC
90B-479
90Classic-136
90D-109
90D/BestAL-26
90D/Bon/MVP-BC9
90F-512
90HotPlay/St-8
90Leaf/I-35
90MLBPA/Pins-116
90Mother/Mar-2
90OPC-373
90Panini/St-149
90PublInt/St-431
90S-205
90S/100St-26
90Sf-112
90T-373
90T/Ames-26
90T/Big-315
90T/Coins-11
90T/DH-13
90T/HillsHM-26
90T/Mini-33
90T/St-220
90UD-364
91B-258
91CounHrth-14
91D-482
91DennyGS-19
91F-449
91F/Ultra-334
91Leaf/II-429
91Leaf/Stud-111
91OPC-515
91Panini/St-185
91S-482
91Seven/3DCoin-3NW
91T-515
91T/StClub/I-82
91UD-457
92D/I-124
92F-277
92S/I-76
92T-130
92UD-386
Davis, Anthony
91Pac/SenLg-95
Davis, Arthur W.
(Bill)
65T-546R
66OPC-44R
66T-44R
67T-253R
68T-432R
69T-304R
Davis, Bill
82Idaho-17
Davis, Brad
85FtMyr-3
Davis, Braz
88CharWh/Best-20
89Peoria/Ko-2P
Davis, Bret
85Anchora-8
86Wausau-7
88James/ProC-1897
89Rockford/Team-6
90WPalmB/Star-4
Davis, Brian
88Tampa/Star-5
89Utica/Pucko-6
90SALAS/Star-29
91StLucie/ProC-723
Davis, Bryshear B.
(Brock)
63T-553R
71OPC-576R
71T-576R
72OPC-161
72T-161
73OPC-366
73T-366
Davis, Charles T.
(Chili)
78Cedar
82T-171R
82T/Tr-23T
83D-348
83F-257
83Mother/Giants-3
83OPC-115
83T-115
83T/St-319
84D-114
84F-370
85FunFood/Pin-38
84Nes/792-494
84OPC-367
84T-494
84T/St-171
85D-480
85Drake-9
85F-605
85F/St-10
85Leaf-66
85Mother/Giants-2
85OPC-245
85T-245
85T/St-162
85T/Super-40
86D-6DK
86D-65
86D/DKsuper-6
86F-536
86F/Mini-109
86Leaf-6DK
86Mother/Giants-2
86Sf-82
87D-268
87D/AAS-38
87D/OD-97
87F-270
87F/BB-12
87F/Mini-25
87F/St-29
87Kraft-46
87Leaf-208
87Mother/SFG-3
87OPC-162
87RedFoley/St-76
87Sf-45
87T-672
87T/St-95
88D-313
88F-79
88F/Up-U12
88OPC-15
88S-605
88S/Tr-28T
88Sf-172
88Smok/Angels-10
88T-15
88T/Big-235
88T/Tr-32T
89B-50
89Classic-80
89D-449
89D/Best-115
89F-474
89F/LL-9
89OPC-103
89Panini/St-296
89RedFoley/St-28
89S-54
89Sf-129
89T-525
89T/Big-294
89T/LJN-44
89T/St-177
89UD-126
90B-301
90D-136
90D/Bon/MVP-BC20
90F-129
90Leaf/II-288
90OPC-765
90Panini/St-39
90PublInt/St-367
90S-326
90Sf-21
90Smok/Angel-3
90T-765
90T/Big-280
90T/Coins-12
90T/St-173
90UD-38
91B-331
91Classic/III-12
91D-580
91F-309
91F/UltraUp-U35
91F/Up-U36
91Leaf/II-374
91OPC-355
91Panini/St-134
91S-803
91S/RookTr-70T
91T-355
91T/StClub/II-329
91T/Tr-27T
91UD-339
91UD/Ext-722
92D/I-115
92F-200
92S/I-94
92T-118
92UD-126
Davis, Chris
78StPete
79ArkTr-17
Davis, Chris
90Elmira/Pucko-15
91Elmira/ClBest-18
91Elmira/ProC-3264
Davis, Chuck
86NewBrit-9
87Pawtu-24
87Pawtu/TCMA-5
Davis, Courtney
90ClintUp/Team-U2
90Everett/Best-22
90Everett/ProC-3138
91Clinton/ProC-845
Davis, Curtis Benton
(Curt)

35BU-97
36Exh/4-6
36Wheat
90Target-168
91Conlon/Sport-282
R314

Davis, Darwin
91Kingspt/ClBest-3
91Kingspt/ProC-3819

Davis, Douglas
(Doug)
82BurlR-18
85MidldA-14
86MidldA-8
87MidldA-10
88Edmon/CMC-18
88Edmon/ProC-559
89Belling/Legoe-18
89Edmon/CMC-15
89Edmon/ProC-551
90Edmon/CMC-18
90Edmon/ProC-519
91Edmon/LineD-160
91Edmon/ProC-1518

Davis, Eric Keith
(Eric)
82Cedar-20
83Water-15
84Borden-44
84Wichita/Rock-15
85D-325
85F-533
85T-627
86D-164
86D/HL-30
86F-175
86T-28
86TexGold-44
87Classic-21
87Classic/Up-102
87Classic/Up-150M
87D-22DK
87D-265
87D/DKsuper-22
87D/HL-3
87D/HL-8
87D/OD-197
87F-198
87F/AwardWin-11
87F/Excit-14
87F/GameWin-11
87F/Hottest-12
87F/Mini-26
87F/Slug-11
87F/St-132M
87F/St-30
87Ho/St-9
87Kahn-44
87Kraft-10
87Leaf-179
87Leaf-22DK
87MSA/Discs-7
87OPC-228
87Sf-155M
87Sf-199M
87Sf-22
87T-412
87T/Coins-30
87T/Gloss60-44
87T/Mini-4
87T/St-136
88Bz-6
88ChefBoy-2
88Classic/Blue-201M
88Classic/Blue-213
88Classic/Red-154
88D-369
88D-BC2
88D/AS-38
88D/Best-62
88D/PopUp-16
88Drake-24
88F-231
88F-637M
88F/AS-7
88F/AwardWin-8
88F/BB/AS-9
88F/BB/MVP-8
88F/Excit-12
88F/Hottest-8
88F/LL-8
88F/Mini-73
88F/RecSet-9
88F/Slug-10
88F/SS-11
88F/St-83
88F/St-S6M
88F/TL-6
88FanSam-14
88Kahn/Reds-44
88KayBee-7
88KingB/Disc-22
88Leaf-149
88MSA/Disc-12
88Nestle-3
88OPC-150
88OPC-J
88Panini/St-235M
88Panini/St-282
88RedFoley/St-15
88S-10
88S-649M
88S/WaxBox-15
88S/YS/II-1
88Sf-10
88Sf/Gamewin-5
88T-150
88T/Big-20
88T/Coins-39
88T/Gloss22-17
88T/Gloss60-16
88T/Mini-46
88T/RiteAid-3
88T/St-141
88T/St-146
88T/St/Backs-14
88T/UK-18
88T/WaxBox-J
89T/Ames-11
89B-316
89Cadaco-12
89Classic-109
89Classic-9
89T/Crunch-13
89D-80
89D/Best-6
89F-158
89F-639M
89F/BBMVP's-9
89F/Excit-9
89F/Heroes-10
89F/LL-10
89F/Superstar-11
89Holsum/Discs-7
89Kahn/Reds-44
89KayBee-8
89Nissen-7
89OPC-330
89Panini/St-76
89RedFoley/St-29
89S-109
89S/HotStar-58
89S/Mast-18
89Sf-69
89T-111TL
89T-330
89T/Big-273
89T/Coins-9
89T/Gloss60-2
89T/HeadsUp-21
89T/LJN-38
89T/Mini-8
89T/St-138
89T/St/Backs-47
89T/UK-19
89Tetley/Discs-11
89UD-410
89UD-688TC
90B-58
90CedarDG/Best-1
90Classic-11
90CollAB-28
90D-233
90D-695AS
90D/BestNL-1
90D/Bon/MVP-BC23
90F-417
90F/AwardWin-10
90F/BB-6
90F/BBMVP-9
90F/LL-8
90F/WaxBox-C4
90HotPlay/St-9
90Kahn/Reds-7
90Leaf/I-189
90MLBPA/Pins-22
90OPC-260
90OPC-402AS
90Panini/St-209
90Panini/St-246
90Post-24
90PublInt/St-255
90PublInt/St-26
90RedFoley/St-20
90S-185
90S/100St-95
90Sf-97
90Starline/LJS-3
90Starline/LJS-38
90Sunflower-21
90T-260
90T-402AS
90T/Ames-28
90T/Big-72
90T/Coins-44
90T/DH-14
90T/Gloss22-7
90T/Gloss60-25
90T/HillsHM-1
90T/Mini-53
90T/St-134
90T/St-149AS
90T/TVAS-38
90UD-116
91B-686
91Classic/200-136
91Classic/I-34
91Classic/III-13
91D-84
91DennyGS-4
91F-61
91F/ProV-10
91F/Ultra-91
91F/WS-1
91Kahn/Reds-44
91Leaf/I-37
91Leaf/Stud-162
91Leaf/StudPrev-11
91MajorLg/Pins-70
91OPC-550
91OPC/Premier-29
91Panini/FrSt-131
91Panini/St-124
91Pep/Reds-6
91Petro/SU-6
91S-137
91S-403MB
91S-669AS
91S-696RF
91S-863FRAN
91S/100SS-9
91Seven/3DCoin-6SC
91T-550
91T/CJMini/I-16
91T/StClub/I-37
91T/SU-10
91UD-355
91Woolwth/HL-25
92D/II-503
92F-403
92S/100SS-44
92S/I-44
92T-610
92UD-125

Davis, Frank
(Dixie)
E120
E121/120
V100
V61-36
W501-3
W514-48
W573
W575

Davis, Freddie Jr.
89Lynch/Star-5
90CLAS/CL-10
90LynchRS/Team-17
90WinHaven/Star-3
91NewBrit/LineD-454
91NewBrit/ProC-345
91Single/ClBest-123

Davis, Geff
86BurlEx-5
87WPalmB-27

Davis, George Stacey
(George)
11Helmar-23
E107
E254
E90/1
N142
T206
V355-17

Davis, George Allen
(George)
D350/2-45
M101/5-45

Davis, George Willis
(Kiddo)
33G-236
92Conlon/Sport-502
W711/1

Davis, George
(Storm)
83D-619
83F-56
83T-268
83T/St-310
84D-585
84F-5
85FunFood/Pin-120
84Nes/792-140
84OPC-140
84T-140
85D-454
85F-174
85Leaf-81
85OPC-73
85T-599
86D-169
86F-271
86Leaf-99
86OPC-179
86T-469
86T/St-231
87Bohem-34
87D-273
87F-466
87F/Up-U22
87OPC-349
87T-349
87T/St-230
87T/Tr-26T
88D-595
88D/A's/Bk-595
88D/Best-282
88F-278
88Mother/A's-19
88T-248
89B-192
89D-210
89F-6
89Mother/A's-18
89Panini/St-413
89S-248
89T-701
89T/Big-121
89UD-153
90B-368
90Classic/Up-15
90D-479
90F-5
90F/Up-102
90Leaf/II-362
90OPC-606
90PublInt/St-302
90S-266
90S/Tr-21T
90T-606
90T/Mini-26
90T/Tr-25T
90UD-292
90UD/Ext-712
91B-293
91Classic/200-16
91Crown/Orio-97
91D-185
91F-556
91F/UltraUp-U26
91Leaf/I-161
91Leaf/Stud-65
91OPC-22
91Pol/Royal-7
91S-511
91T-22
91T/StClub/I-67
91UD-639
92D/II-529
92F-155
92S/I-264
92T-556
92UD-499

Davis, George
76Clinton

Davis, Gerald Edward
(Gerry)
82Amari-5

Davis, Gerrod
90Kgsport/Best-3

Davis, Gerry
88TM/Umpire-52
89TM/Umpire-50
90TM/Umpire-48

Davis, Glenn
52Wheat

Davis, Glenn Earl
(Glenn)
82DayBe-20
83ColumAst-11
84Cram/PCL-62
85Cram/PCL-65
85F-652R
86D-380
86F-297
86F/Mini-63
86Leaf-175
86OPC-389
86Pol/Ast-22
86Sf-188
86T-389
86T/Gloss60-59
86T/St-29
86T/St-314
87Classic-28
87Classic/Up-107
87D-61
87D/AAS-42
87D/OD-16
87F-55
87F-636M
87F/GameWin-12
87F/LL-14
87F/Lim-11
87F/Mini-27
87F/St-31
87F/St-S5
87KayBee-12
87Kraft-36
87Leaf-115
87Mother/Ast-10
87OPC-56
87Pol/Ast-23
87RedFoley/St-43
87Sf-17
87Sf-195M
87T-560
87T/Coins-31
87T/Gloss60-4
87T/Mini-8
87T/St-26
88Classic/Red-182
88D-184
88D/Best-64
88F-445
88F/Mini-78
88F/Slug-11
88F/SS-12
88F/St-86
88Leaf-186
88Mother/Ast-10
88OPC-159
88Panini/St-292
88Pol/Ast-8
88S-460
88Sf-102
88T-430
88T/Big-192
88T/St-35
88T/UK-19
89B-331
89Cadaco-13
89Classic-17
89Classic/Up/2-168
89D-236
89D-25DK
89D/Best-8
89D/DKsuper-25DK
89F-355
89F/BBMVP's-10
89F/Excit-10
89F/Heroes-11
89F/LL-11
89Lennox/Ast-26
89Mother/Ast-9
89OPC-378
89Panini/St-88
89RedFoley/St-30
89S-164

89S/HotStar-46
89Sf-137
89T-579TL
89T-765
89T/Big-89
89T/Coins-10
89T/Gloss60-32
89T/Hills-10
89T/LJN-67
89T/St-21
89T/St/Backs-35
89T/UK-20
89UD-443
90B-80
90Classic-71
90D-118
90D/BestNL-65
90D/Bon/MVP-BC21
90D/Learning-22
90F-228
90F/BB-7
90F/BBMVP-10
90F/LL-9
90F/WaxBox-C5
90HotPlay/St-10
90KMart/SS-16
90Leaf/I-30
90Lennox-11
90MLBPA/Pins-41
90Mother/Ast-2
90OPC-50
90Panini/St-258
90PublInt/St-92
90RedFoley/St-21
90S-272
90S/100St-52
90Sf-19
90Starline/LJS-15
90Starline/LJS-30
90T-50
90T/Big-122
90T/Coins-45
90T/DH-15
90T/Gloss60-3
90T/HillsHM-22
90T/Mini-55
90T/St-13
90T/TVAS-45
90UD-245
91B-83
91Classic/200-169
91Classic/II-T6
91Crown/Orio-496
91D-474
91F-505
91F/Ultra-14
91F/Up-U1
91Leaf/II-398
91Leaf/Stud-1
91OPC-350
91OPC/Premier-30
91Panini/FrSt-7
91Panini/St-19
91Post/Can-14
91RedFoley/St-23
91S-405MB
91S-830
91S/RookTr-7T
91Seven/3DCoin-1A
91Seven/3DCoin-4F
91Seven/3DCoin-5T
91Sunflower-6
91T-350
91T/StClub/II-391
91T/Tr-28T
91UD-535
91UD-81TC
91UD/Ext-757
92D/II-597
92F-4
92S/II-615
92T-190
92UD-654

Davis, Greg
90Kissim/DIMD-9

Davis, Harry H.
(Harry)
91Conlon/Sport-269
E101
E103
E104
E105
E107
E254
E270/1
E286
E90/1
E91
E92
E94
E96
E97
E98
M116
T206
T207
T208
T213/blue
T215/blue
T215/brown
T216
T222
W555
WG2-13

Davis, Harry
84Everett/Cram-5
86Fresno/Smok-26
88Shreve/ProC-1299
89Wmsprt/ProC-641
89Wmsprt/Star-4

Davis, Herman Thomas
(Tommy)
59DF
60T-509
61BB-12
61Morrell
61P-165
61T-168
61T/St-25
62BB-12
62J-105
62P-105
62P/Can-105
62Salada-154A
62Salada-154B
62Shirriff-154
62T-358
63Bz-36
63F-40
63J-117
63P-117
63T-1LL
63T-310
63T/SO
64Bz-36
64T-180
64T-7LL
64T/Coins-153AS
64T/Coins-57
64T/S-43
64T/St-64
64T/SU
64Wheat/St-13
65Bz-36
65T-370
65T/E-49
65T/trans-46
66OPC-75
66T-75
67Bz-37
67Kahn
67T-370
68Bz-10
68T-265
68T/G-10
69MB-72
69MLB/St-94
69OPC-135
69T-135
69T/DE-15
69T/decal
69T/S-32
69T/St-224
70MB-6
70MLB/St-38
70T-559
71OPC-151
71T-151
71T/Coins-93
72MB-87
72OPC-41
72OPC-42IA
72T-41
72T-42IA
73JP
74K-43
74OPC-396
74T-396
74T/St-124
75OPC-564
75T-564
75T/M-564
76OPC-149
76SSPC-398
76T-149
77T-362
78TCMA-87
82D-648CO
87Smok/Dodg-5
88Bakers/Cal-265
88Pac/Leg-83
88Smok/Dodg-8
89Smok/Dodg-70
90Target-171
91Crown/Orio-98
91WIZMets-92

Davis, I.M.
25Exh-77

Davis, Jacke S.
(Jacke)
62T-521
63T-117

Davis, James Bennett
(Jim)
52Mother-2
53Mother-46
55T-68
55T/DH-28
56T-102
57T-273

Davis, James J.
(Jumbo)
N172

Davis, Jay
90Kgsport/Star-6
91SALAS/ProC-SAL14

Davis, Jerry
90Johnson/Star-7

Davis, Jerry
84Cram/PCL-222
85D-162
85F/Up-U34
85Mother/Padres-26
85T/Tr-28T
86D-429
86F-317
86T-323
87Toledo-30
87Toledo/TCMA-24

Davis, Jody Richard
(Jody)
79Jacks-7
82D-225
82F-592
82RedLob
82T-508
83D-183
83F-494
83T-542
83T/St-226
83Thorn-7
84D-433
84F-491
85FunFood/Pin-51
84Jacks/Smok-4
84Nes/792-73
84OPC-73
84SevenUp-7
84T-73
84T/St-43
85D-76
85D/AAS-54
85F-54
85Leaf-180
85OPC-384
85SevenUp-7
85T-384
85T/St-37
86Cub/Unocal-4
86D-289
86F-364
86F/St-30
86Gator-7
86Jay's-3
86OPC-176
86T-767
86T/St-58
87Berg/Cubs-7
87D-269
87D/AAS-50
87D/OD-72
87F-557
87F/BB-13
87F/LL-15
87Kraft-6
87Leaf-48
87OPC-270
87RedFoley/St-68
87Sf-170
87Seven-C2
87Seven-ME3
87Smok/NL-3
87T-270
87T/St-64
88Berg/Cubs-7
88D-119
88D/Cubs/Bk-119
88F-414
88Leaf-69
88OPC-376
88Panini/St-258
88S-551
88Sf-60
88T-615
88T/St-60
88T/St/Backs-23
89B-270
89D-650
89D/Best-58
89F-421
89OPC-115
89RedFoley/St-31
89S-173
89S/Tr-64
89Sf-187
89T-115
89T/Big-3
89T/Tr-22T
89UD-148
89UD/Ext-795
90F-579
90OPC-453
90PublInt/St-111
90S-328
90T-453
90T/Big-26
90UD-429

Davis, Joel
86Coke/WS-52
86D-623
86F-202
86T/Tr-30T
87Coke/WS-26
87D-124
87T-299
88T-511
88Vanco/CMC-2
88Vanco/ProC-763
89ColoSp/CMC-7
89ColoSp/ProC-237

Davis, John Humphrey
(John or Red)
52Mother-27
61Union

Davis, John
75OkCty
76Wmsprt

Davis, John Kirk
83CharR-17
87Omaha-19
88CapeCod/Sum-56
88Coke/WS-5
88D-594
88D/Rook-48
88F-255
88F/Up-U15
88S-636
88Sf-224
88T-672
89S-608
89T-162
89UD-548
89Vanco/CMC-9
89Vanco/ProC-582
91Richm/LineD-430

Davis, Johnny
86Negro/Frit-95

Davis, Kelvin
88Eugene/Best-17

Davis, Kenny
87Visalia-15
88Visalia/Cal-145
88Visalia/ProC-81

Davis, Kevin
83Peoria/LF-3
83Redwd-8
85MidldA-18
87Salem-30
88EastLAS/ProC-14
88Harris/ProC-837
89BirmB/Best-6
89BirmB/ProC-98
91London/LineD-432
91MidldA/ProC-439

Davis, Larry
81Tacoma-1
82Tacoma-20
83Tacoma-22
90Mother/A's-28TR

Davis, Lefty
90Target-1102

Davis, Mark
84LitFalls-22
86Kenosha-5
87Penin-1
87Savan-12
88BirmB/Best-14
88Sumter/ProC-396
89BurlB/ProC-1599
89BurlB/Star-9
89Vanco/CMC-22
89Vanco/ProC-585
91Edmon/LineD-161
91Edmon/ProC-1527

Davis, Mark William
(Mark)
81OkCty/TCMA-6
82OkCty-12
82T-231R
83Phoenix/BHN-20
84D-201
84F-371
84Nes/792-343
84T-343
85D-553
85F-606
85Mother/Giants-20
85T-541
86D-265
86F-537
86Mother/Giants-20
86T-138
86T/St-91
87D-313
87F-271
87F/Up-U21
87Mother/SFG-14
87T-21
88Coke/Padres-48
88D-64
88D/Best-98
88F-581
88S-391
88Smok/Padres-6
88T-482
89B-447
89Coke/Padre-3
89D-65
89D/AS-46
89D/Best-133
89F-303
89F-635M
89F/BBAS-10
89F/Up-18
89OPC-59
89Padre/Mag-13
89RedFoley/St-32
89S-490
89S/HotStar-62
89Sf-74
89T-59
89T/St-110
89T/St/Backs-64
89UD-268
90B-369
90B/Ins-2
90Bz-3
90Classic/Up-14
90Classic/Up-NNO
90D-302
90D/BestAL-8
90F-155
90F-631M
90F/ASIns-3
90F/Up-101
90Holsum/Discs-6
90HotPlay/St-11
90KMart/SS-14

90Leaf/II-468
90OPC-205
90OPC-407AS
90Panini/St-215
90Panini/St-352
90PublInt/St-47
90RedFoley/St-22
90S-259
90S/100St-51
90S/Tr-26T
90Sf-62
90T-205
90T-407AS
90T/Big-312
90T/Coins-34
90T/DH-16
90T/Gloss60-58
90T/Mini-79
90T/St-102
90T/Tr-24T
90T/TVAS-12
90UD-431
90UD/Ext-710
90Woolwth/HL-4CY
91B-306
91BBBest/RecBr-5
91Classic/200-15
91D-560
91F-555
91Leaf/I-16
91OPC-116
91Pol/Royal-6
91RedFoley/St-24
91S-136
91T-116
91T/StClub/I-136
91UD-589
92D/I-54
92S/II-718
92T-766
92T/91Debut-43
92UD-607

Davis, Matt
91Clinton/ClBest-12
91Clinton/ProC-840

Davis, Michael Dwayne
(Mike)
81D-470
81F-586
81T-364
81Tacoma-11
82T-671
82Tacoma-34
83Granny-16
83T/Tr-24
84D-298
84F-443
84Mother/A's-5
84Nes/792-558
84T-558
84T/St-338
85D-223
85D/HL-3
85F-422
85Mother/A's-7
85T-778
86D-14DK
86D-96
86D/DKsuper-14
86F-416
86F/LimEd-14
86F/Mini-88
86F/St-31
86Leaf-14DK
86Mother/A's-7
86OPC-165
86Sf-83
86T-165
86T/St-166
87D-133
87D/OD-21
87F-391
87F/Lim-12
87F/Mini-28
87F/St-32
87Smok/A's-3
87T-83
87T/St-168
88D-281
88D/Best-36
88F-277
88Mother/Dodg-12
88OPC-217
88Panini/St-174
88Pol/Dodg-37
88RedFoley/St-16
88S-211
88S/Tr-53T
88Sf-206
88T-448
88T/Big-154
88T/St-171
88T/Tr-33T
89T/Ames-12
89B-352
89D-316
89F-55
89Mother/Dodg-12
89OPC-277
89Panini/St-193
89Panini/St-24
89Pol/Dodg-11
89S-376
89T-277
89T/Big-225
89UD-146
89Woolwth-32
90D-552
90F-391
90OPC-697
90PublInt/St-3
90S-437
90T-697
90Target-169
90UD-258

Davis, Michael
82Tidew-3
83Pawtu-16
84Pawtu-26
84Pawtu-7
85Tidew-23
86Tidew-7
89BurlInd/Star-7
89Kingspt/Star-6
90Watertn/Star-6
91Indianap/LineD-180
91Indianap/ProC-472

Davis, Nicky
90Ashvl/ClBest-12
90Pittsfld/Pucko-11
91Ashvl/ProC-573
91Single/ClBest-49

Davis, Odie Ernest
(Odie)
79Tucson-18
80Charl-15
81Charl-16

Davis, Piper
53Mother-54
86Negro/Frit-12
86Negro/Frit-47

Davis, Ray
(Peaches)
39PB-123
W711/1

Davis, Richard Earl
(Dick)
77Spoka
79T-474
80T-553
81D-528
81F-527
81T-183
81T/Tr-753
82D-147
82F-245
82T-352
82T/Tr-24T
83D-647
83F-305
83Portl-16
83T-667

Davis, Rick
89Spokane/SP-11
90Foil/Best-78
90Riversi/Best-5
90Riversi/Cal-14
90Riversi/ProC-2598
91Wichita/LineD-606
91Wichita/ProC-2593

Davis, Robert Edward
(Bob)
61T-246

Davis, Robert John
76OPC-472
76T-472
77Padre/SchCd-9
77T-78
78Padre/FamFun-9
78T-713
80OPC-185
80T-351
81D-30
81F-428
81OPC-221
81SLCity-26
81T-221

Davis, Robert
86FtMyr-6
89Bristol/Star-7

Davis, Ronald Gene
(Ron)
79Colum-14
80OPC-101
80T-179
81D-467
81F-86
81OPC-16
81T-16
82D-451
82F-32
82F/St-117
82F/St-242M
82OPC-283
82T-2M
82T-635
82T/Tr-25T
83D-228
83F-610
83OPC-380
83T-380
83T/St-94
84D-269
84F-561
84F/St-75
85FunFood/Pin-112
84Nes/792-519
84OPC-101
84T-519
84T/St-309
85D-120
85F-275
85F/St-103
85OPC-78
85Seven/Minn-8
85T-430
85T/St-297
86D-364
86F-390
86OPC-265
86T-265
86T/St-281
87Berg/Cubs-39
87D-438
87F-558
87OPC-383
87T-383
89Phoenix/ProC-1505
90Target-170
91Pac/SenLg-115

Davis, Ronald E.
(Ron)
67T-298
68Coke
68Dexter-28
68OPC-21
68T-21
69MB-71
69MLB/St-185
69T-553
70MLB/St-100

Davis, Russell
89FtLaud/Star-2
89Oneonta/ProC-2109
90CLAS/CL-18
90PrWill/Team-8
90Saraso/Star-29TR
91Albany/ProC-1014
91Single/ClBest-182

Davis, Sammy
78Watlo

Davis, Stan
77Newar
78Newar
79BurlB-21
81ElPaso-6
82Vanco-9
83ElPaso-6
84ElPaso-14

Davis, Steven K.
86Ault-25
86Tor/Fire-7
87Syrac-21
87Syrac/TCMA-2
88Syrac/CMC-1
88Syrac/ProC-814
89ColoSp/CMC-1
89ColoSp/ProC-249
90Albuq/CMC-4
90Albuq/ProC-337
90Albuq/Trib-6
90OPC-428
90S-187
90T-428
91Geneva/ClBest-5
91Geneva/ProC-4209
91Wmsprt/LineD-629
91Wmsprt/ProC-305

Davis, Steven Michael
(Steve)
81Syrac-14
87Tampa-19
88Cedar/ProC-1150

Davis, Ted
78Ashvl
79Wausau-20
80Tulsa-4
81Tulsa-8
82Jacks-3
83BirmB-18

Davis, Thomas Oscar
(Tod)
47Signal

Davis, Tim
90Elmira/Pucko-4

Davis, Trench
82Portl-19
84Cram/PCL-139
85Cram/PCL-238
86Hawaii-3
87Richm/Crown-32
87Richm/TCMA-17

Davis, Virgil L.
(Spud)
33G-210
39PB-37
40PB-163
88Conlon/NatAS-4
R314
V355-12
W711/1
WG8-11

Davis, Wallace M.
(Butch)
84D-277
85Omaha-12
85T-49
87Vanco-17
88CharlK/Pep-3
89AAA/CMC-21
89RochR/CMC-22
89RochR/ProC-1652
90Albuq/CMC-22
90Albuq/ProC-357
90Albuq/Trib-5
91Albuq/LineD-5
91Albuq/ProC-1154
91Crown/Orio-96

Davis, Wayne
87Myrtle-20
88Dunedin/Star-3

Davis, Willie Henry
(Willie)
60DF-8
61BB-3
61T-506
62BB-3
62J-106
62P-106
62P/Can-106
62Salada-161
62Shirriff-161
62T-108
63J-119
63P-119
63Salada-21
63T-229
64T-68
65OldLond-7
65T-435
66T-535
66T/RO-17
67OPC-160
67T-160
68T-208
68T/3D
69MB-73
69MLB/St-145
69MLBPA/Pin-40
69OPC-65
69T-65
69T/S-45
69T/St-41
69Trans-45
70MLB/St-49
70OPC-390
70T-390
70T/PI-3
70T/S-39
70Trans-2
71K-16
71MD
71MLB/St-101
71OPC-585
71T-585
71Ticket/Dodg-5
72K-3
72MB-88
72OPC-390
72T-390
72T/Cloth-9
73K-43
73OPC-35
73T-35
73T/Comics-6
73T/Lids-12
73T/PinUps-6
74K-45
74OPC-165
74T-165
74T/DE-42
74T/St-44
74T/Tr-165T
75OPC-10
75T-10
75T/M-10
76OPC-265
76SSPC-279
76T-265
77T-603
78TCMA-24
87Smok/Dodg-6
88Smok/Dodg-12
89Smok/Dodg-77
90Target-172

Davison, Julio
(Coco)
91StCath/ClBest-25CO
91StCath/ProC-3412CO

Davison, Michael Lynn
(Mike)
71MLB/St-245
71OPC-276R
71T-276R

Davison, Scott
89James/ProC-2145
90Rockford/ProC-2699
91WPalmB/ClBest-19
91WPalmB/ProC-1235

Davisson, Jay
83Reading-4
84Cram/PCL-213
85Cram/PCL-41

Dawley, Bill
79Nashvl
80Indianap-25
81Indianap-28
82Indianap-7
84D-328
84F-223
84F/St-108
84Mother/Ast-22
84Nes/792-248
84OPC-248
84T-248
84T/St-71
85D-354
85F-348
85Mother/Ast-16
85OPC-363
85T-634
86F-298
86F/Up-U32
86Mother/Ast-25
86T-376
87D-628
87F-493

87F/Up-U23
87Smok/Cards-9
87T-54
88D-331
88F-29
88S-328
88T-509
89Tacoma/CMC-5
89Tacoma/ProC-1555

Dawson, Andre Nolan
(Andre)
77T-473R
78OPC-180
78T-72
79OPC-179
79T-348
80OPC-124
80T-235
81D-212
81F-145
81F/St-123
81OPC-125
81OPC/Post-6
81PermaGr/AS-3
81T-125
81T/SO-90
81T/St-187
82D-88
82F-187
82F/St-35
82Hygrade
82OPC-341AS
82OPC-379
82OPC/Post-18
82PermaGr/AS-12
82Sqt-17
82T-341AS
82T-540
82T/St-125
82T/St-57
82Zeller-10
82Zeller-14
82Zeller-4
83D-518
83D/AAS-9
83F-280
83OPC-173AS
83OPC-303
83PermaGr/AS-11
83PermaGr/CC-4
83Stuart-4
83T-402
83T-680
83T/St-164
83T/St-252
84D-97
84D/AAS-18
84Drake-9
84F-273
84F/St-18
84F/St-25
84F/St-33
85FunFood/Pin-22
84MiltBrad-8
84Nes/792-200
84Nes/792-392AS
84Nestle/DT-16
84OPC-200
84OPC-392AS
84Ralston-6
84Seven-1C
84Seven-1E
84Seven-1W
84Stuart-11
84Stuart-36AS
84Stuart-37M
84T-200
84T-392AS
84T/Cereal-6
84T/Gloss22-18
84T/Gloss40-35
84T/St-181
84T/St-92
84T/Super-20
85D-421
85D/HL-41
85F-394
85F/LimEd-8
85GenMills-2
85Leaf-133
85OPC-133
85OPC/Post-9
85Seven-7S
85T-420
85T/St-86
86D-25DK
86D-87
86D/DKsuper-25
86F-246
86F/Mini-53
86F/St-32
86Leaf-25DK
86OPC-256
86Provigo-9
86Sf-110
86Sf-66M
86T-576TL
86T-760
86T/St-74
86TrueVal-29
87Berg/Cubs-8
87Classic/Up-124
87D-458
87D/HL-28
87D/HL-31
87D/OD-70
87F-316
87F/Hottest-13
87F/Slug-12
87F/St-33
87F/Up-U24
87Leaf-212
87OPC-345
87RedFoley/St-13
87Sf-139
87T-345
87T/Board-10
87T/St-77
87T/Tr-27T
88ActPacT-2
88Berg/Cubs-8
88ChefBoy-18
88Classic/Blue-216
88Classic/Red-157
88D-269
88D-9DK
88D-BC10
88D/AS-36
88D/Best-225
88D/Cubs/Bk-269
88D/DKsuper-9DK
88D/PopUp-14
88Drake-16
88F-415
88F/AS-6
88F/AwardWin-9
88F/BB/AS-10
88F/BB/MVP-9
88F/Excit-13
88F/Hottest-9
88F/LL-9
88F/Mini-67
88F/RecSet-10
88F/Slug-12
88F/SS-13
88F/St-79
88F/TL-7
88FanSam-15
88Jiffy-8
88KayBee-8
88KingB/Disc-14
88KMart-9
88Leaf-126
88Leaf-9DK
88Nestle-9
88OPC-247
88Panini/St-236M
88Panini/St-265
88RedFoley/St-17
88S-4
88S/WaxBox-16
88Sf-3
88T-401AS
88T-500
88T/Big-153
88T/Coins-33
88T/Gloss22-18
88T/Gloss60-1
88T/Mini-43
88T/Revco-2
88T/RiteAid-2
88T/St-148
88T/St-56
88T/St/Backs-13
88T/UK-20
88Woolwth-8
89T/Ames-13
89B-298
89Cadaco-14
89Classic-37
89T/Crunch-10
89D-167
89D/AS-36
89D/Best-4
89D/MVP-BC8
89D/PopUp-36
89F-422
89F/BBAS-11
89F/BBMVP's-11
89F/Excit-11
89F/Heroes-12
89F/LL-12
89F/Superstar-12
89KayBee-9
89Mara/Cubs-8
89OPC-10
89Panini/St-230AS
89Panini/St-59
89MSA/SS-2
89RedFoley/St-33
89S-2
89S/HotStar-80
89S/Mast-28
89Sf-95
89T-10
89T-391AS
89T-4RB
89T/Big-120
89T/Coins-11
89T/DH-17
89T/Gloss22-18
89T/Hills-11
89T/LJN-148
89T/Mini-3
89T/St-156
89T/St-5
89T/St-54
89T/St/Backs-48
89T/UK-21
89Tetley/Discs-14
89UD-205
89Woolwth-11
90B-39
90Classic-85
90Cub/Mara-6
90D-223
90D/BestNL-97
90D/Learning-52
90F-29
90HOF/St-96
90KayBee-8
90Leaf/I-177
90MLBPA/Pins-54
90MSA/Soda-24
90OPC-140
90Panini/St-240
90Publint/St-192
90Publint/St-256
90RedFoley/St-23
90S-265
90S/100St-74
90S/McDon-10
90Sf-108
90T-140
90T/Ames-9
90T/Big-91
90T/DH-17
90T/Gloss60-41
90T/HillsHM-15
90T/St-47
90T/TVCub-31
90T/WaxBox-C
90UD-357
90UD-73TC
90USPlayC/AS-9H
90Woolwth/HL-11
91B-429
91Classic/200-26
91Classic/III-14
91Cub/Mara-8
91D-129
91D-435AS
91D/Elite-E4
91DennyGS-14
91F-419A
91F-419B
91F-713M
91F/Ultra-58
91Leaf/II-400
91Leaf/Stud-153
91MajorLg/Pins-67
91OPC-640
91OPC/Premier-31
91Panini/FrSt-49
91Panini/St-41
91Pep/SS-2
91Post/Can-7
91RedFoley/St-118
91RedFoley/St-25
91S-445
91S/100SS-87
91Seven/3DCoin-2MW
91Sunflower-14
91T-640
91T/CJMini/II-7
91T/StClub/II-310
91T/SU-11
91T/WaxBox-D
91UD-454
91UD/Ext-725
91UD/FinalEd-98FAS
91USPlayC/AS-11C
91Woolwth/HL-9
92D/I-119
92D/II-422AS
92D/Preview-4
92F-379
92F/TmLIns-20
92S/100SS-48
92S/I-75
92T-460
92UD-124

Dawson, David
89Bakers/Cal-180

Dawson, Gary
83Madis/LF-24

Dawson, Larry
88AppFx/ProC-164

Day, Charles F.
(Boots)
70Expos/Pins-4
70T-654R
71MLB/St-125
71OPC-42
71T-42
72OPC-254
72T-254
73OPC-307
73T-307
74OPC-589
74T-589
74Weston-8
77Evansvl/TCMA-7

Day, Clyde Henry
(Pea Ridge)
90Target-173

Day, Dexter
83Water-16
84Cedar-13

Day, George
91AppFx/ClBest-17
91AppFx/ProC-1723

Day, Kevin
89Ashvl/ProC-943

Day, Leon
78Laugh/Black-5
90Negro/Star-13
91Negro/Lewis-6

Day, Mike
86WPalmB-11

Day, Ned
52Wheat

Day, Paul
88Augusta/ProC-388

Day, Randy
86Phill/TastyK-x
86Portl-4
87Syrac/TCMA-31

Day, Steve
77Newar

Dayett, Brian Kelly
(Brian)
79WHave-4
82Nashvl-9
83Colum-26
84Colum-4
84Colum/Pol-9
84D-45RR
85D-152
85F-125
85F/Up-U35
85Iowa-8
85SevenUp-24
85T-534
85T/Tr-29T
86T-284
87Berg/Cubs-24
87D/OD-73
87F/Up-U25
87T-369
88D-416
88F-416
88OPC-136
88S-205
88T-136

Dayley, Kenneth Grant
(Ken)
81Richm-19
82BK/Lids-7
82D-501
82Richm-25
83D-375
83F-135
83Richm-4
83T-314
84D-199
84F-176
84Nes/792-104
84T-104
84T/Tr-29
86D-303
86F-33
86KAS/Disc-2
86OPC-202
86Schnucks-5
86T-607
87D-357
87F-293
87T-59
88D-357
88D/Best-299
88F-30
88S-517
88Smok/Card-3
88T-234
89B-428
89D-299
89D/Best-268
89F-448
89OPC-396
89Smok/Cards-4
89T-409
89UD-114
90B-191
90D-281
90D/BestNL-22
90F-247
90Leaf/II-275
90OPC-561
90Publint/St-216
90Richm25Ann/Team-7
90S-556
90Smok/Card-4
90T-561
90T/St-36
90T/TVCard-10
90UD-280
91B-27
91D-735
91F-630
91Leaf/Stud-134
91OPC-41
91OPC/Premier-32
91S-607
91S/ToroBJ-27
91T-41
91T/StClub/II-552
91Tor/Fire-46
91UD-628
91UD/Ext-781
92S/II-685
92T-717

Deabenderfer, Blaine
87Madis-22

Deak, Brian
87Sumter-26
88MidwLAS/GS-16
89Durham/Team-9
89Durham/Star-9
89Star/Wax-71
90Durham/Team-4
91Greenvl/ClBest-12
91Greenvl/LineD-206
91Greenvl/ProC-3006

Deak, Darrel
88Alaska/Team-7
89Alaska/Team-12
91Johnson/ClBest-6
91Johnson/ProC-3982

Deal, Charles Albert
(Charlie)
21Exh-34
D327
D328-40
D329-44
D350/2-46
E121/80
E122
E135-40
E220
M101/4-44
M101/5-46
V100
W514-18
W575
Deal, Ellis Fergason
(Cot)
54Hunter
54T-192
60T-459C
78Colum
79OkCty
81OkCty/TCMA-22
82OkCty-5
Deal, Lindsay
90Target-927
Dealey, Patrick E.
(Pat)
N172
Dean, Alfred Lovill
(Chubby)
40PB-193
Dean, Bob
73Cedar
75Dubuq
Dean, Jay Hanna
(Dizzy)
32Orbit/num-14
32Orbit/un-15
33CJ/Pin-4
33G-223
34G-6
34Ward's/Pin-1
35BU-64
35Exh/4-8
35G-1A
35G-2A
35G-6A
35G-7A
35Wheat
36Exh/4-8
37Exh/4-8
38Exh/4-3
38ONG/Pin-5
38Wheat-1
39Exh
50Callahan
60NuCard-14M
61GP-8
61NuCard-476M
74Laugh/ASG-36
80Pac/Leg-12
80Laugh/FFeat-5
80SSPC/HOF
83D/HOF-29
86Conlon/1-10
86Sf/Dec-14M
88Conlon/4-8
88Conlon/NatAS-5
90BBWit-71
90Swell/Great-6
91Conlon/Sport-3
91Homer/Classic-8
91LineD-50
91Swell/Great-138
91T/Arc53-326M
92Conlon/Sport-428
92Conlon/Sport-635
PM10/Sm-35
PR1-4
R300
R305
R308-202
R310
R311/Gloss
R332-31
R332-35
R423-21
RiceStix
V354-55
V355-19
Dean, Jeff
83Miami-11
Dean, John
77Salem
Dean, Kevin
87WPalmB-9
88Jaxvl/Best-13
88Jaxvl/ProC-984
89Indianap/CMC-21
89Indianap/ProC-1225
90Greenvl/Star-6
90Tucson/CMC-23
90Tucson/ProC-214
91Jacks/LineD-556
91Jacks/ProC-936
Dean, Paul Dee
(Daffy)
35BU-143
35Exh/4-8
35Wheat
36Exh/4-8
39PB-19
40PB-156
60NuCard-14M
61NuCard-476M
88Conlon/3-9
92Conlon/Sport-363
92Conlon/Sport-631
RiceStix
Dean, Roger
85Utica-9
Dean, Tommy Douglas
(Tommy)
69T-641R
70OPC-234
70T-234
71MLB/St-225
71OPC-364
71T-364
90Target-174
DeAngelis, Steve
86Reading-7
87Maine-13
88Phill/TastyK-27
88Reading/ProC-877
89QuadC/Best-29
89QuadC/GS-26
DeArmas, Rollie
87Clearw-19
88Martins/Star-10
90Martins/ProC-3209MG
91Martins/ClBest-29MG
Dearse, Ed
46Remar-14
Dease, Don'l
90Idaho/ProC-3247
Deasley, Thomas H.
(Pat)
E223
N172
N403
DeBattista, Dan
77Salem
Debee, Rich
90Omaha/CMC-23CO
DeBerry, Joe
91Billings/ProC-3759
91FrRow/DP-30
DeBerry, John Herman
(Hank)
25Exh-9
29Exh/4-4
90Target-175
E120
E126-30
R316
V61-101
W572
W573
DeBord, Bob
83CharR-18
DeBottis, Marc
88Syrac/ProC-828
DeBrand, Genaro
90Niagara/Pucko-12
Debus, Jon Eric
81VeroB-4
84Cram/PCL-164
86Albuq-5
87Albuq/Pol-15
88Albuq/CMC-15
88Albuq/ProC-269
89Albuq/CMC-12
89Albuq/ProC-76
91VeroB/ProC-792CO
DeBusschere, David A.
(Dave)
63T-54R
64T-247
65T-297
78TCMA-246
DeButch, Mike
86Beaum-9
87TexLgAS-1
87Wichita-1
88Wichita-10
89Jacks/GS-19
89Tidew/ProC-1959
90T/TVMets-39
90Tidew/CMC-15
90Tidew/ProC-550
Decatur, A.R.
(Art)
25Exh-10
27Exh-21
90Target-176
DeChavez, Oscar
83Idaho-3
Decillis, Dean
88Lakeland/Star-9
89London/ProC-1372
90Toledo/CMC-20
90Toledo/ProC-154
91London/LineD-380
91London/ProC-1883
DeCinces, Douglas V.
(Doug)
75OPC-617R
75T-617R
75T/M-617R
76OPC-438
76SSPC-387
76T-438
77BurgChef-44
77Ho-15
77OPC-228
77T-216
78Ho-10
78OPC-192
78T-9
79Ho-54
79OPC-217
79T-421
80OPC-322
80T-615
81D-352
81F-173
81F/St-90
81OPC-188
81T-188
82D-279
82F-162
82F/St-142
82OPC-174
82T-564
82T/St-142
82T/Tr-26T
83D-216
83F-85
83OPC-341
83PermaGr/CC-22
83Seven-7
83T-341
83T/St-155
83T/St-171
83T/St-46
84D-230
84D/AAS-6
84F-514
85FunFood/Pin-73
84Nes/792-790
84OPC-82
84Smok/Cal-7
84T-790
84T/St-229
85D-179
85D-2DK
85D/AAS-51
85D/DKsuper-2
85F-299
85Leaf-2DK
85OPC-111
85Smok/Cal-6
85T-111
85T/St-222
86D-57
86D/HL-39
86D/WaxBox-PC6
86F-153
86OPC-257
86Sf-173
86Smok/Cal-6
86T-257
86T/St-178
87D-356
87D/OD-1
87F-77
87F/Hottest-14
87F/Mini-29
87F/St-34
87OPC-22
87Sf-106
87Seven-W1
87Smok/Cal-17
87T-22
87T/Gloss60-52
87T/St-182
88F-31
88OPC-141
88S-239
88Sf-185
88T-446
89Smok/Angels-16
91Crown/Orio-99
91LineD-19
91Swell/Great-23
Decker, Dee Martin
(Marty)
82OkCty-22
83Portl-18
84Cram/PCL-226
85Cram/PCL-107
Decker, Edward
N172
Decker, George Henry
(Joe)
71MLB/St-30
71OPC-98
71T-98
72T-612
73OPC-311
73T-311
74OPC-469
74T-469
74T/St-206
75Ho-96
75OPC-102
75T-102
75T/M-102
76OPC-636
76SSPC-210
76T-636
78SanJose-6
79Spokane-12
82SLCity-25
83SLCity-10
89T/SenLg-112
90Niagara/Pucko-29CO
91Pac/SenLg-101
Decker, Steve
89SanJose/Best-11
89SanJose/Cal-227
89SanJose/ProC-446
89SanJose/Star-6
89Star/Wax-84
90A&AASingle/ProC-72
90Shrev/ProC-1445
90Shrev/Star-5
91B-622
91Classic/200-198
91Classic/I-7
91Classic/II-T100
91Classic/II-T64
91D-428RR
91F-260
91F/Ultra-319
91Leaf/II-441
91Leaf/Stud-260M
91Leaf/StudPrev-16
91Mother/Giant-3
91OPC/Premier-33
91PG&E-13
91S-710RP
91S/ASFan-2
91S/HotRook-8
91S/Rook40-12
91Seven/3DCoin-4NC
91SFExam/Giant-7
91T/90Debut-37
91T/StClub/II-569
91T/Tr-29T
91UD-25SR
92D/I-389
92F-633
92S/100RisSt-56
92S/I-317
92T-593
92UD-173
DeCordova, David
87StPete-14
DeCosta, Bob
83Visalia/LF-8
DeDario, Joe
90Niagara/Pucko-31HOST
Dede, Artie
90Target-928
Dedeaux, Raoul
(Rod)
85T-389OLY
90Smok/SoCal-4CO
90Target-177
Dedmon, Jeffrey L.
(Jeff)
81Durham-17
82Durham-16
84T/Tr-30
85D-554
85F-323
85Richm-4
85T-602
86D-443
86F-513
86Pol/Atl-49
86T-129
87D-314
87F-514
87Smok/Atl-7
87T-373
88D-325
88F-537
88Gator-50
88S-498
88T-469
89Indianap/ProC-1214
Dedos, Felix
87WinHaven-2
89WinHaven/Star-3
Dedrick, James
91Kane/ClBest-5
91Kane/ProC-2653
Deer, Robert George
(Rob)
80Clinton-20
84Cram/PCL-4
85F-648R
85Mother/Giants-25
86F-538
86F/Up-U33
86Pol/Brew-45
86T-249
86T/Tr-31T
87Classic-43
87Classic/Up-141
87D-274
87D/OD-57
87F-344
87F/Excit-15
87F/BB-14
87F/Mini-30
87OPC-188
87Pol/Brew-45
87Sf-172
87T-547
87T/Coins-10
87T/Gloss60-22
87T/Mini-59
87T/St-194
88D-274
88D/Best-109
88F-163
88F/St-36
88OPC-33
88Panini/St-128
88Pol/Brew-45
88RedFoley/St-18
88S-95
88Sf-183
88T-33
88T/Big-151
88T/St-198
89B-146
89Brewer/YB-45
89Classic-39
89D-173
89D/Best-71

89F-184
89Gard-4
89OPC-364
89Panini/St-376
89Pol/Brew-45
89RedFoley/St-34
89S-72
89Sf-111
89T-364
89T-759TL
89T/Big-78
89T/St-202
89UD-442
90B-401
90Brewer/MillB-4
90D-55
90F-320
90Leaf/II-322
90MLBPA/Pins-80
90OPC-615
90Panini/St-102
90Pol/Brew-45
90PublInt/St-494
90RedFoley/St-24
90S-390
90Sf-137
90T-615
90T/Big-74
90T/St-204
90UD-176
91B-132
91CokeK/Tiger-44
91D-729
91F-580
91F/Up-U23
91Leaf/I-237
91Leaf/Stud-52
91OPC-192
91Panini/FrSt-209
91RedFoley/St-26
91S-248
91S/RookTr-47T
91T-192
91T/StClub/II-539
91T/Tr-30T
91UD-272
91UD/Ext-726
92D/II-532
92F-132
92S/I-56
92T-441
92UD-294

Dees, Charles Henry
(Charlie)
64T-159

DeFillippis, Art
76OPC-595R
76T-595R

DeFrancesco, Anthony
85Greens-25
86WinHaven-7
87NewBrit-15
88Chatt/Best-7
88Nashvl/Team-7
89Chatt/Best-3
89Chatt/GS-8
90Nashvl/ProC-235
91Nashvl/LineD-255
91Nashvl/ProC-2159

DeFreites, Arturo S.
(Art)
76Indianap-4
77Indianap-20
78Indianap-22
80T-677R
91Pac/SenLg-77

Degifico, Vincent
(Vince)
87Elmira/Black-16
87Elmira/Red-16
89WinHaven/Star-4
90NewBrit/Best-16
90NewBrit/Star-3

Degrasse, Tim
91Hamil/ClBest-2
91Hamil/ProC-4032

Deguero, Jerry
86Modesto-7

DeHart, Greg
78Newar
79BurlB-20
80BurlB-6
83SanJose-25

DeHart, Rick
87Birm/Best-28tr

Deiley, Lou
87Ashvl-23
88Osceola/Star-7

Deisel, Pat
90Target-929

Deitz, Tim
86Cedar/TCMA-5
88Chatt/Best-15
89Greenvl/ProC-1175
89Greenvl/Star-5
89Greenvl/Best-12

Dejak, Tom
78Dunedin

DeJardin, Bob
(Bobby)
88Oneonta/ProC-2044
89PrWill/Star-4
90Albany/Best-14
90Albany/ProC-1039
90Foil/Best-212
91Albany/ProC-1015
92T-179M

DeJardin, Brad
88Alaska/Team-8
91Kinston/ProC-336

DeJesus, Ivan
74Albuq/Team-5
76SSPC-76
78OPC-158
78T-152
79Ho-88
79OPC-209
79T-398
80OPC-349
80T-691
81Coke
81D-483
81F-297
81OPC-54
81T-54
81T/HT
81T/SO-94
81T/St-156
82D-14DK
82D-48
82F-593
82F/St-95
82OPC-313
82T-484
82T/St-32
82T/Tr-27T
83D-399
83F-157
83OPC-233
83T-587
83T/St-271
84D-427
84F-26
84Nes/792-279
84OPC-279
84Phill/TastyK-29
84T-279
84T/St-121
85D-204
85F-248
85Phill/TastyK-11
85T-791
85T/Tr-30T
85ThomMc/Discs-28
86D-449
86F-34
86T-178
89Toledo/ProC-774
89UD-355
90EliteSenLg-4
90Kissim/DIMD-29MG
90Target-178
91Kissim/ProC-4205MG

DeJesus, Jorge
78Newar
80BurlB-21

DeJesus, Jose
85FtMyr-12
85Tigres-19
86FtMyr-7
87Memphis-5
87Memphis/Best-9
88BBAmer-14
88Memphis/Best-18
89D-558
89F-280
89Omaha/CMC-6
89Omaha/ProC-1735
89UD/Ext-769
90F-104
90F/Up-U42
90Leaf/II-415
90OPC-596
90S-587RP
90S/100Ris-95
90ScranWB/ProC-592
90Sf-131
90T-596
90UD-255
91D-596
91F-394
91F/Ultra-261
91Leaf/I-200
91OPC-232
91Phill/Medford-12
91S-623
91S/100RisSt-16
91T-232
91T/StClub/I-104
91UD-486
92D/I-300
92F-528
92S/I-380
92T-471
92UD-631

DeJohn, Mark Stephen
(Mark)
75Tidew/Team-8
80Evansvl-2
81Evansvl-13
83Evansvl-24
87Savan-26
88Spring/Best-26
89Johnson/Star-24MG
90Johnson/Star-28MG
91Louisvl/LineD-249MG
91Louisvl/ProC-2932MG

Dejulio, Frank
80Cedar-15

DeKneef, Mike
91Single/ClBest-171
91WinHaven/ClBest-17
91WinHaven/ProC-496

DeKraai, Brad
81BurlB-21
82Beloit-22

DelaCruz, Anthony
89BurlInd/Star-8

DeLaCruz, Carlos
87DayBe-6
88Utica/Pucko-17
89SoBend/GS-12
90BirmB/Best-14
90BirmB/ProC-1102

DeLaCruz, Francisco
87Spokane-15

DeLaCruz, Gerry
77Clinton

DeLaCruz, Hector
87Dunedin-16
88Knoxvl/Best-8
89Syrac/CMC-18
89Syrac/ProC-816
89Syrac/Team-8
90Syrac/CMC-20
90Syrac/ProC-583
90Syrac/Team-4

Delahanty, Edward J.
(Ed)
50Callahan
72F/FFeat-38
72Laugh/GF-10
75F/Pion-10
80SSPC/HOF
89HOF/St-31
90BBWit-70
N142
N172
N300/SC

Delahanty, Frank G.
(Frank)
14CJ-81
15CJ-81
T206

Delahanty, James C.
(Jim)
10Domino-31
11Helmar-30
12Sweet/Pin-23
E104
E107
E254
E300
E91
E93
E96
M116
S74-14
T202
T205
T206
T207
W555

Delahanty, Joseph
C46-67

DeLaHoya, Javier
89LittleSun-13
90VeroB/Star-10
90Yakima/Team-2

DeLaHoz, Miguel A.
(Mike)
61T-191
62T-123
63Sugar-8
63T-561
64T-216
65OPC-182
65T-182
66T-346
67T-372

DeLaMata, Fred
87Miami-21

Delancer, Julio
86Kenosha-7

DeLancey, William P.
(Bill)
34DS-81
35Wheat
92Conlon/Sport-625
V355-15

DeLaNuez, Rex
89Elizab/Star-24
90Foil/Best-118
90Kenosha/Best-2
90Kenosha/ProC-2305
90Kenosha/Star-8
91Single/ClBest-147
91Visalia/ClBest-21
91Visalia/ProC-1753

Delany, Dennis
79ArkTr-16
81ArkTr-4

DeLao, Mike
85Durham-17
88Fayette/ProC-1105
89London/ProC-1367
90EastLAS/ProC-EL48TR
91Fayette/ClBest-30TR

DeLaRosa, Benny
77Charl
81Buffa-6

DeLaRosa, Cesar
87Spartan-24
88QuadC/GS-23
89PalmSp/Cal-43
89PalmSp/ProC-475

DeLaRosa, Domingo
87Pocatel/Bon-11
89Clinton/ProC-905

DelaRosa, Francisco
89Freder/Star-4
90A&AASingle/ProC-3
90Hagers/Best-23
90Hagers/ProC-1406
90Hagers/Star-7
91RochR/LineD-453
91RochR/ProC-1895
92T/91Debut-44

DeLaRosa, Jesus
75Iowa/TCMA-10
89Pac/SenLg-57

DeLaRosa, Juan
88Myrtle/ProC-1175
89Myrtle/ProC-1458
90Dunedin/Star-7
91Knoxvl/LineD-355
91Knoxvl/ProC-1779

DeLaRosa, Nelson
82AlexD-25
83AlexD-23
85Nashua-6

Delarwelle, Chris
90Foil/Best-229
91Visalia/ClBest-14
91Visalia/ProC-1746

Delas, Mickey
88Bristol/ProC-1883
89Fayette/ProC-1590

DeLeeuw, Karel
76Watlo

DeLeon, Felix
63Pep/Tul

DeLeon, Gerbacio
90Madison/Best-14

DeLeon, Huascar
90BBCity/Star-5
91BBCity/ClBest-13

DeLeon, Jesus
87FtMyr-11
88AppFx/ProC-155
88MidwLAS/GS-39
89RedFoley/St-35

DeLeon, John
81Miami-7

DeLeon, Jose
81Buffa-4
82Portl-1
84D-628
84F-248
84Nes/792-581
84T-581
85D-308
85F-463
85OPC-385
85T-385
86D-235
86F-607
86OPC-75
86T-75
87Coke/WS-16
87D-457
87F-494
87T-421
88D-59
88F-395
88F/St-15
88F/Up-U119
88OPC-23
88S-508
88S/Tr-7T
88Smok/Card-4
88T-634
88T/Big-194
88T/Tr-34T
89B-431
89D-437
89F-449
89OPC-107
89Panini/St-177
89S-115
89Smok/Cards-5
89T-107
89T/Mini-34
89UD-293
90B-186
90D-536
90D/BestNL-59
90F-248
90F/AwardWin-11
90Leaf/II-485
90OPC-257
90Panini/St-334
90PublInt/St-217
90RedFoley/St-25
90S-309
90Sf-76
90Smok/Card-6
90T-257
90T/Big-31
90T/Mini-74
90T/St-38
90T/TVCard-11
90UD-697
91B-400
91D-128
91F-631
91F/Ultra-288
91Leaf/I-190
91OPC-711
91Pol/Card-48
91S-221
91T-711
91T/StClub/II-455
91UD-220
92D/I-246

92F-576
92S/I-81
92T-85
92UD-458

DeLeon, Julio
87PortChar-20

DeLeon, Luis Antonio
(Luis)
80ArkTr-7
80Tacoma-27
81Chatt-4
82Charl-14
82D-588
82T-561R
83Charl-9
83D-296
83F-355
83OPC-323
83T-323
84D-162
84F-297
84Mother/Padres-17
84Nes/792-38
84Smok/Padres-6
84T-38
85D-406
85F-29
85Mother/Padres-11
85T-689
85ThomMc/Discs-29
86F-318
86T-286
87RochR-16
87RochR/TCMA-2
88Tucson/CMC-10
88Tucson/ProC-174
88Tucson/JP-8
89Calgary/CMC-1
91Crown/Orio-100

DeLeon, Paulo
73Cedar
74Cedar
75Dubuq

DeLeon, Pedro
86Ashvl-7
88Osceola/Star-8
89PrWill/Star-5
89Star/Wax-88

DeLeon, Pichy
84Maine-11

DeLeon, Rafael
86FtMyr-8

DeLeon, Roberto
89Sumter/ProC-1113
90BurlB/Best-11
90BurlB/ProC-2351
90BurlB/Star-10
90Foil/Best-166

Delgado, Alex
90WinHaven/Star-4
91LynchRS/ClBest-16
91LynchRS/ProC-1206

Delgado, Carlos
89StCath/ProC-2077
90A&AASingle/ProC-184
90StCath/ProC-3454
91Myrtle/ClBest-12
91Myrtle/ProC-2946
91SALAS/ProC-SAL37
91Single/ClBest-63

Delgado, Juan
83DayBe-19
86ColumAst-10
87Osceola-22

Delgado, Luis Felipe
(Luis)
78SanJose-14

Delgado, Pablo
89Geneva/ProC-1879
90Hunting/ProC-3296

Delgado, Richard
91Elmira/ClBest-19
91Elmira/ProC-3265
91WinHaven/ClBest-29

Delgado, Tim
90Geneva/ProC-3045
90Miami/II/Star-4
91Peoria/ClBest-4
91Peoria/ProC-1335

DelGreco, Robert G.
(Bobby)
52T-353
53T-48
57T-94
60T-486
61T-154
61T/St-53
62Salada-16
62Shirriff-16
62T-548
63J-91
63P-91
63T-282
78TCMA-259
91T/Arc53-48

DeLima, Rafael
86Kenosha-8
87Kenosha-6
88BBAmer-15
88OrlanTw/Best-22
88SLAS-11
89Portl/CMC-23
89Portl/ProC-222
90Portl/CMC-22
90Portl/ProC-191
91OrlanSR/LineD-478
91OrlanSR/ProC-1861

Delkus, Pete
88Kenosha/ProC-1398
88MidwLAS/GS-35
89Orlan/Best-13
89Orlan/ProC-1331
90Portl/CMC-5
90Portl/ProC-172
91OrlanSR/ProC-1843

Dell, Tim
88Batavia/ProC-1674
89Spartan/ProC-1052
89Spartan/Star-6
89Star/Wax-54
90Clearw/Star-5
91Stockton/ProC-3026

Dell, William George
(Wheezer)
16FleischBrd-23
D328-41
WG7-12

Deller, Bob
90Oneonta/ProC-3388
91Greens/ProC-3071

Deller, Tom
87Anchora-6
89Welland/Pucko-10
90Salem/Star-3

DelliCarri, Joseph
88CapeCod/Sum-16
89Pittsfld/Star-3
91Wmsprt/LineD-630
91Wmsprt/ProC-300

Delmas, Bert
90Target-930

Delmonte, John
82Lynch-4

DeLoach, Bobby
87Savan-1
89Savan/ProC-346
90FSLAS/Star-2
90StPete/Star-4
91Knoxvl/LineD-356
91Knoxvl/ProC-1780

DeLoach, Lee
89GreatF-16

Delock, Ivan Martin
(Ike)
52B-250
52T-329
55B-276
56T-284
57T-63
58T-328
59T-437
60T-336
61T-268
61T/St-110
62T-201
63T-136
91Crown/Orio-101

DelOrbe, Chico
75Lafay

DeLosSantos, Alberto
89Princet/Star-5
91Salem/ClBest-5
91Salem/ProC-959
91Single/ClBest-152

DeLosSantos, German
75Cedar
76Cedar

DeLosSantos, Luis
86SLAS-9
87Omaha-25
88AAA/ProC-30
88Omaha/CMC-22
88Omaha/ProC-1506
89AAA/CMC-2
89D-562
89D/Rook-33
89F-646M
89F/Up-37
89Omaha/ProC-1729
89Panini/St-347
89S-648
89S/HotRook-52
89UD-12
90Classic-9
90F-105
90HotRook/St-14
90Omaha/CMC-11
90Omaha/ProC-70
90OPC-452
90S-659
90S/100Ris-100
90S/DTRook-B4
90T-452
91B-152

DeLosSantos, Pedro
89Ashvl/ProC-951

DeLosSantos, Ramon
75Iowa/TCMA-11
84Cram/PCL-76

DeLosSantos, Reynoldo
91Martins/ClBest-5
91Martins/ProC-3466

Delpiano, Marc
89BurlInd/Star-9
90Watertn/Star-7

DelPozo, Roberto
90SanBern/Best-10
90SanBern/Cal-104
90SanBern/ProC-2643
91Penin/ClBest-23
91Penin/ProC-388

DelRosario, Manny
83Miami-18

DelRosario, Maximo
85Durham-6
86Durham-8
87Greenvl/Best-18
88Greenvl/Best-17
89Greenvl/ProC-1161
89Greenvl/Star-6
89Greenvl/Best-11
90Greenvl/ProC-1123
90Greenvl/Star-7

DelRosario, Sergio
83Miami-6

Delsing, James Henry
(Jim)
47Signal
51B-279
52B-157
52T-271
53B/BW-44
53Glen
53T-239
54B-55
54RM-AL24
54T-111
55B-274
55T-192
56T-338
59T-386
91T/Arc53-239

DeLuca, Kurt
85LitFalls-16
86Columbia-8

Delucchi, Ron
86PrWill-8

DeLucia, Richard
(Rich)
86Cram/PCL-121
88SanBern/Best-8
88SanBern/Cal-50
89Wmsprt/ProC-649
89Wmsprt/Star-5
90A&AASingle/ProC-134
90Foil/Best-228
90SanBern/Best-2
90SanBern/Cal-88
90SanBern/ProC-2626
90Wmsprt/Star-4
91B-242
91CounHrth-27
91D-426RR
91D/Rook-2
91F/UltraUp-U50
91F/Up-U52
91Leaf/I-222
91S-728RP
91S/Rook40-37
91T/90Debut-38
91T/Tr-31T
91UD/Ext-727
92D/I-118
92F-278
92F/RookSIns-15
92S/100RisSt-54
92S/I-135
92T-686
92UD-637

DelVecchio, Jim
77Clinton

Delyon, Gene
77Holyo

Delzer, Ed
85MidldA-22
86Kinston-4

DeMaestri, Joseph P.
(Joe)
52T-286
54B-147
55B-176
55Rodeo
56Rodeo
56T-161
57T-44
58T-62
59T-64
60L-139
60T-358
61T-116

Demaree, Albert W.
(Al)
14CJ-92
15CJ-92
37Wheat
D329-45
D350/2-47
M101/4-45
M101/5-47
PM1-4

Demaree, Joseph F.
(Frank)
33G-224
35BU-166
38G-244
38G-268
38ONG/Pin-6
39PB-34
40PB-90
41PB-58
91Conlon/Sport-212
WG8-12

DeMars, William L.
(Billy)
50B-252
51B-43
52Park-8
73OPC-486CO
73T-486CO
74OPC-119CO
74T-119CO
82Zeller-9
83Stuart-11CO
84Stuart-3CO
86TexGold-CO

Dembowski, Steve
79Newar-7

DeMeo, Bob M.
79OkCty
81OkCty/TCMA-21

DeMerit, John Stephen
(John)
61T-501
62Salada-192
62Shirriff-192
62T-4
78TCMA-129
91WIZMets-93

DeMerit, Thomas
88VeroB/Star-5

DeMerritt, Martin
75BurlB
76Dubuq
83Clinton/LF-25
86Shrev-6
87Shrev-24
88Phoenix/CMC-25M
88Phoenix/ProC-67
89Phoenix/CMC-7
89Phoenix/ProC-1486

Demerson, Tim
90Tampa/DIMD-3

Demery, Lawrence C.
(Larry)
75OPC-433
75T-433
75T/M-433
76OPC-563
76SSPC-564
76T-563
77T-607
78T-138

Demeter, Donald Lee
(Don)
58T-244
59T-324
60BB-14
60T-234
61BB-16
61T-23
62J-195
62P-195
62P/Can-195
62Salada-170
62Shirriff-170
62T-146
62T/bucks
62T/St-167
63F-53
63J-180
63P-180
63T-268
64Det/Lids-4
64T-58
64T/Coins-116
65T-429
66OPC-98
66T-98
67T-572
67T/Test/RSox-4
78TCMA-198
79TCMA-237
90Target-179

Demeter, Stephen
(Steve)
61BeeHive-6
77Salem
80Buffa-16
87Salem-29

Demeter, Todd
85Spring-6

Demetral, Chris
91Yakima/ClBest-7
91Yakima/ProC-4252

Demetre, Doug
90Oneonta/ProC-3383

Demmitt, Charles R.
(Ray)
C46-11
D303
E106
E254
E270/1
E90/1
M116
T206
T213/blue
T216
T222

DeMola, Donald John
(Don)
75OPC-391
75T-391
75T/M-391
76OPC-571
76T-571

DeMontreville, Eugene
90Target-180
E107

Demoran, Joe
43Centen-5
44Centen-4
45Centen-4

DeMoss, Bingo
74Laugh/Black-4

86Negro/Frit-66
90Negro/Star-6
Dempsay, Adam
87Lakeland-24
88GlenF/ProC-932
Dempsey, Cornelius F.
(Con)
48Sommer-3
49Sommer-4
52T-44
Dempsey, Jack
33SK-17
Dempsey, John
90Johnson/Star-8
91Johnson/ClBest-2
91Johnson/ProC-3979
91Spring/ClBest-12
91Spring/ProC-744
Dempsey, John Rikard
(Rick)
72T-778R
74OPC-569
74Syrac/Team-4
74T-569
75OPC-451
75T-451
75T/M-451
76OPC-272
76SSPC-438
76T-272
77T-189
78T-367
79Ho-73
79OPC-312
79T-593
80OPC-51
80T-91
81D-113
81F-177
81OPC-132
81T-615
81T/St-38
82D-77
82F-163
82F/St-146
82OPC-262
82T-489
83D-329
83F-58
83OPC-138
83T-138
83T/St-30
84D-413
84F-6
84F-644
84F/St-115
84Nes/792-272
84OPC-272
84Seven-21E
84T-272
84T/St-213
84T/St-23WS
85D-332
85F-175
85OPC-94
85T-521
85T/St-199
86D-106
86F-272
86OPC-358
86Sf-147M
86T-358
86T-726M
86T/St-232
87D-294
87F-467
87F/Up-U26
87Gator-24
87OPC-28
87RedFoley/St-92
87T-28
87T/St-225
87T/Tr-28T
88Mother/Dodg-15
88S-262
88S/Tr-32T
89B-343
89D-432
89Mother/Dodg-15
89Pol/Dodg-10
89S-556
89T-606
89T/Big-108
89UD/Ext-713
90D-557
90D/Learning-15
90F-392
90Mother/Dodg-16
90OPC-736
90Pol/Dodg-17
90Publint/St-4
90S-414
90T-736
90Target-181
91Brewer/MillB-7
91Crown/Orio-102
91Leaf/II-484
91OPC-427
91Pol/Brew-7
91S-816
91T-427
91T/StClub/II-553
Dempsey, Mark S.
(Mark)
81Shrev-11
82Phoenix
83Phoenix/BHN-21
Dempsey, Mike
76BurlB
77BurlB
78Holyo
Dempsey, Pat
77Modesto
79Ogden/TCMA-20
80Ogden-22
81T-96R
81Tacoma-7
82Tacoma-26
84Nashvl-6
85Maine-14
86Toledo-8
87Portl-2
Dempster, Kurt
88Billings/ProC-1828
89Billings/ProC-2053
89Greens/ProC-426
Demus, Joe
90Elmira/Pucko-13
91WinHaven/ClBest-11
91WinHaven/ProC-491
DeMuth, Dana
88TM/Umpire-53
89TM/Umpire-51
90TM/Umpire-49
DeMuth, Don
89Spartan/ProC-1056
Denbo, Gary
84Cedar-26
85Cedar-16
86Vermont-6
87Tampa-1
88Cedar/ProC-1143
89Greens/ProC-404
90CLAS/CL-19
90PrWill/Team-2
91ColClip/LineD-125CO
Denby, Darryl
83Lynch-6
84Jacks-19
86Greenvl/Team-8
Denehy, William F.
(Bill)
67T-581R
68T-526
91WIZMets-94
Denevi, Mike
77Jaxvl
Denkenberger, Ralph
88Watertn/Pucko-17
Denkinger, Don
88TM/Umpire-8
89TM/Umpire-6
90TM/Umpire-6
Denman, Brian John
(Brian)
81Bristol-7
83Pawtu-5
84Pawtu-24
86Nashvl-6
Dennis, Donald Ray
(Don)
63Pep/Tul
66OPC-142
66T-142
67T-259
Dennis, Ed
(Eddie)
78Dunedin
82Knoxvl-16
83Knoxvl-16
86Knoxvl-6
88StCath/ProC-2014
91Pac/SenLg-71
Dennison, Jim
90Elmira/Pucko-16
90WinHaven/Star-5
91LynchRS/ClBest-2
91LynchRS/ProC-1191
Dennison, Scott
91James/ClBest-10
91James/ProC-3551
Denny, Jeremiah D.
(Jerry)
N172
N284
WG1-30
Denny, John Allen
(John)
75OPC-621R
75T-621R
75T/M-621R
76OPC-339
76SSPC-295
76T-339
77BurgChef-14
77Ho-42
77OPC-109
77OPC-7LL
77T-541
77T-7LL
78Ho-129
78T-609
79Ho-1
79T-59
80OPC-242
80T-464
81T-122
82D-572
82F-363
82F/St-194
82T-773
82Wheat/Ind
83D-237
83F-158
83T-211
84D-407
84F-27
84F/St-56
85FunFood/Pin-49
84Nes/792-135LL
84Nes/792-17
84Nes/792-637TL
84Phill/TastyK-18
84Seven-19E
84T-135LL
84T-17
84T-637TL
84T/St-122
84T/St-177
84T/St-19WS
84T/Super-4
85CIGNA-13
85D-111
85F-249
85Leaf-228
85OPC-325
85Phill/TastyK-16
85Phill/TastyK-9M
85T-325
85T/St-119
86D-204
86F-439
86F/Up-U34
86OPC-268
86Sf-132M
86Sf-134M
86Sf-64M
86T-556
86T/Tr-32T
86TexGold-40
87D-329
87F-199
87OPC-139
87T-644
90Swell/Great-116
Denson, Andrew
(Drew)
86Durham-9
87Greenvl/Best-7
88Greenvl/Best-9
88SLAS-17
89Richm/Bob-4
89Richm/CMC-18
89Richm/Ko-39
89Richm/ProC-847
90Richm/CMC-11
90Richm/ProC-266
90Richm/Team-8
90T/89Debut-30
Dent, Eddie
90Target-182
Dent, Russell Earl
(Bucky)
74OPC-582
74T-582
75OPC-299
75T-299
75T/M-299
76Ho-119
76OPC-154
76SSPC-143
76T-154
77BK/Y-14
77BurgChef-81
77Ho-91
77OPC-122
77T-29
78BK/Y-15
78K-2
78OPC-164
78T-335
79BK/Y-14
79Ho-131
79OPC-254
79T-485
80OPC-33
80T-60
81D-465
81F-80
81F/St-110
81K-7
81MSA/Disc-11
81OPC-164
81PermaGr/AS-12
81T-650
81T/HT
81T/St-110
82D-209
82F-33
82OPC-240
82OPC-241IA
82OPC-298AS
82T-240
82T-241A
82T-550AS
83F-566
83OPC-279
83Rangers-7
83T-565
83T/St-122
84D-300
84F-417
84Nes/792-331
84OPC-331
84T-331
84T/St-362
87Colum-1MG
87Colum/Pol-6MG
87Colum/TCMA-23MG
88Colum/CMC-25MG
88Colum/Pol-24MG
88Colum/Pol-25MG
88Colum/ProC-306MG
89AAA/ProC-21MG
89Colum/CMC-25MG
89Colum/Pol-25MG
89Colum/ProC-757MG
89Swell-72
90OPC-519MG
90T-519MG
90T/TVYank-1MG
Dente, Samuel Joseph
(Sam)
50B-107
51B-133
52Hawth/Pin-2
52T-304
53B/Col-137
55Gol/Ind-4
55Salem
DePalo, Jim
79TCMA-82
DePastino, Rich
87Myrtle-22
88Dunedin/Star-5
89Myrtle/ProC-1628
90Dunedin/Star-8
DePew, Daren
88Boise/ProC-1627
DePrimo, John
85Greens-28
DeRicco, John
90Geneva/ProC-3043
90Geneva/Star-8
Deriso, Phil
81Batavia-8
Derksen, Rob
85Beloit-25
86Stockton-5CO
87Stockton-2
88CalLgAS-18
88Stockton/Cal-201
88Stockton/ProC-721
89Stockton/Best-30
89Stockton/Cal-177CO
89Stockton/ProC-385
89Stockton/Star-25
90Beloit/Best-26MG
90Beloit/Star-25MG
91Beloit/ClBest-27
91Beloit/ProC-2119
Dernier, Robert E.
(Bob)
80Reading
81OkCty/TCMA-5
82T-231R
82T/Tr-28T
83D-189
83F-159
83OPC-43
83T-43
83T/St-320
84D-541
84F-28
84F/X-31
85FunFood/Pin-127
84Nes/792-358
84OPC-358
84SevenUp-20
84T-358
84T/Tr-31
85D-510
85F-55
85Leaf-57
85OPC-334
85SevenUp-20
85T-589
85T/St-38
86Cub/Unocal-5
86D-266
86F-365
86Gator-20
86Jay's-4
86Leaf-139
86OPC-188
86T-188
86T/St-63
87Berg/Cubs-20
87D-146
87D/OD-68
87F-559
87OPC-138
87T-715
88D-392
88F-417
88OPC-183
88Phill/TastyK-8
88S-451
88S/Tr-45T
88T-642
89D-430
89F-565
89Panini/St-155
89Phill/TastyK-5
89S-357
89T-418
89T/Big-265
89UD-340
90OPC-204
90Publint/St-235
90T-204
DeRosa, Tom
77Newar
78BurlB
DeRosa, Tony
81Syrac-24tr
Derrick, Claud Lester
(Claud)

T207
Derringer, Paul
34G-84
35BU-190
35Exh/4-4
36Exh/4-4
36G
37Exh/4-4
38Exh/4-4
39Exh
39PB-15
40PB-74
41DP-7
41PB-4
60F-43
61F-20
80Pac/Leg-113
86Sf/Dec-14M
91Conlon/Sport-213
PR1-5
R303/A
R310
R311/Leath
R313
R314
R326-9A
R326-9B
R342-9
V355-66
W711/1
W711/2
WG8-13
Derrington, Charles
39PB-116
40PB-28
53Mother-60
Derrington, Chas. J.
(Jim)
58T-129
Derryberry, Tim
82RochR-9
Dersin, Eric
86Albany/TCMA-14
Dertli, Chuck
87WinSalem-21
DeSa, Joseph
(Joe)
79ArkTr-10
81Louisvl-7
82Louisvl-6
83Louisvl/Riley-7
85Coke/WS-20
86BuffB-10
86D-546
86T-313
DeSalvo, Steve
85FtMyr-22
DeSantis, Dominic
91Martins/ClBest-24
91Martins/ProC-3446
DeSanto, Tom
79Elmira-27
DeSapio, Jim
88AubAs/ProC-1968
89AubAs/ProC-2172
Desautels, Eugene A.
(Gene)
39PB-116
40PB-28
Desert, Harry
52Park-92
Deshaies, Jim
85Colum-23
85Colum/Pol-8
85IntLgAS-34
86D/HL-45
86D/Rook-34
86F/Up-U35
86Pol/Ast-24
86Sf/Rook-15
87Classic/Up-137
87D-184
87F-56
87F/Mini-31
87Leaf-255
87Mother/Ast-23
87Pol/Ast-19
87Sf-156M
87T-167
87T-2RB
87T/Gloss60-20
87T/St-1
87ToysRUs-9
88D-85
88D/Best-94
88F-446
88Leaf-96
88Mother/Ast-23
88OPC-24
88Panini/St-287
88Pol/Ast-9
88S-354
88Sf-190
88T-24
88T/St-27
89B-320
89D-241
89D/Best-120
89F-356
89Lennox/Ast-11
89Mother/Ast-22
89OPC-341
89S-546
89T-341
89T/Big-29
89UD-76
90B-70
90D-187
90D-7DK
90D/BestNL-4
90D/SuperDK-7
90F-229
90Leaf/I-168
90Lennox-12
90Mother/Ast-12
90OPC-225
90Panini/St-267
90PublInt/St-93
90RedFoley/St-26
90S-154
90Sf-32
90T-225
90T/Big-212
90T/St-21
90UD-221
91B-541
91D-652
91F-506
91F/Ultra-137
91Leaf/I-49
91Leaf/Stud-175
91Mother/Ast-9
91OPC-782
91Panini/St-11
91S-193
91T-782
91T/StClub/I-262
91UD-208
92D/II-515
92S/I-364
92T-415
92UD-297
DeShields, Delino
88MidwLAS/GS-44
88OPC-88DP
88Rockford-10
89BBAmerAA/BPro-AA15
89Jaxvl/Best-15
89Jaxvl/ProC-152
89Rockford-10
89SLAS-5
90B-119
90Classic-55
90Classic/III-95
90D-42RR
90D/BestNL-116
90D/Learning-47
90D/Rook-6
90F-653R
90F/Up-U27
90Leaf/I-193
90OPC-224
90S-645RP
90S/YS/II-3
90T-224
90T/Big-231
90UD/Ext-702M
90UD/Ext-746
91B-445
91Bz-14
91Classic/200-134
91Classic/I-61
91Classic/II-T71
91D-11DK
91D-555
91D-BC16
91D/SuperDK-11DK
91F-228
91F/Ultra-200
91Leaf/I-139
91Leaf/Stud-195
91MajorLg/Pins-78
91OPC-432
91OPC/Premier-34
91Panini/FrSt-140
91Panini/St-69
91Post/Can-1
91RedFoley/St-27
91S-545
91S/100RisSt-55
91T-432
91T/90Debut-39
91T/CJMini/II-35
91T/StClub/I-194
91ToysRUs-7
91UD-364
92D/I-277
92F-476
92S/I-16
92T-515
92UD-167
92UD-36TC
Deshong, James B.
(Jimmie)
34G-96
35G-8E
35G-9E
39PB-10
DeSilva, John
89NiagFls/Pucko-6
90FSLAS/Star-30
90Lakeland/Star-8
91B-148
91London/LineD-381
91London/ProC-1869
DeSimone, Jerry
81Hawaii-7
82Hawaii-7
84Cram/PCL-223
DesJardins, Brad
89Watertn/Star-29
Desjarlais, Keith
81AppFx-3
82Edmon-7
83GlenF-13
DeSonnaville, Erik
89AS/Cal-53UMP
Dessau, Frank Rolland
(Rube)
90Target-931
C46-61
M116
T206
Dest, Blanch
80WHave-18M
Dest, Vanna
80WHave-18M
Destrade, Orestes
82Oneonta-1
85Albany-16
86Colum-5
86Colum/Pol-5
87Colum-12
87Colum/Pol-7
87Colum/TCMA-13
88BuffB/CMC-20
88BuffB/ProC-1486
88S/Tr-110T
89BuffB/ProC-1687
89T-27
90AlbanyDG/Best-21
Detherage, Robert W.
(Bob)
75Water
81Omaha-21
Dettmer, John
91T/Tr-32T
Dettore, Thomas A.
(Tom)
75OPC-469
75T-469
75T/M-469
76OPC-126
76T-126
89Princet/Star-27
91Salem/ProC-969CO
Deutsch, John
89GreatF-17
90AS/Cal-3
90Bakers/Cal-249
91VeroB/ClBest-18
91VeroB/ProC-779
Deutsch, Mike
89Freder/Star-5
90Freder/Team-5
Devares, Cesar
89Bluefld/Star-8
90Foil/Best-133
90Wausau/Best-17
90Wausau/ProC-2130
90Wausau/Star-7
91CLAS/ProC-CAR7
91Freder/ClBest-12
91Freder/ProC-2366
Devereaux, Mike
87SanAn-10
87TexLgAS-28
88AAA/ProC-1
88Albuq/CMC-18
88Albuq/ProC-252
88D-546
88F-512
88Mother/Dodg-27
88S-637
89Classic/Up/2-181
89D-603
89D/Best-326
89D/Rook-51
89D/Tr-30
89F-56
89F/Up-2
89French-12
89S/HotRook-11
89S/YS/II-22
89T/Tr-23T
89UD-68
90B-260
90D-282
90F-175
90Leaf/I-223
90OPC-127
90Panini/St-12
90PublInt/St-576
90S-232
90S/100Ris-90
90Sf-114
90T-127
90T/Big-178
90T/JumboR-7
90Target-183
90ToysRUs-8
90UD-681
91B-93
91Crown/Orio-103
91D-444
91F-469A
91F-469B
91F/Ultra-15
91Leaf/I-138
91OPC-758
91Panini/FrSt-245
91Panini/St-196
91S-258
91T-758
91T/StClub/II-555
91UD-308
92D/I-354
92F-5
92S/I-36
92T-492
92UD-209
Devereaux, Todd
90FtLaud/Star-4
Devich, John
83Butte-24
Deville, Dan
89Spokane/SP-10
90Riversi/Best-6
90Riversi/Cal-15
90Riversi/ProC-2599
91HighD/ClBest-2
91HighD/ProC-2385
DeVincenzo, Rich
83AppFx/LF-7
Devine, Kevin
86VeroB-5
87VeroB-23
Devine, Paul Adrian
(Adrian)
74OPC-614
74T-614
77T-339
78T-92
79T-257
80T-528
81T-464
Devito, Fred
80WHave-13
Devlin, Arthur M.
(Art)
10Domino-32
11Helmar-123
12Sweet/Pin-110
E101
E103
E254
E91
E92
E94
E95
M116
S74-83
T202
T204
T205
T206
T207
T3-10
W555
Devlin, Bob
84Greens-21
86WPalmB-12
87Jaxvl-18
Devlin, James H.
(Tim)
N172
N690
Devlin, Paul
88Lynch/Star-6
89Lynch/Star-6
Devoe, Dan
91Kinston/ClBest-29TR
Devore, Joshua
(Josh)
10Domino-33
11Helmar-124
12Sweet/Pin-111
14CJ-47
15CJ-47
BF2-85
D329-46
E270/2
E300
E94
E97
M101/4-46
M116
S74-84
T202
T205
T206
T207
T213/blue
T215/blue
T215/brown
W555
Devore, Ted
91CharRain/ClBest-5
91CharRain/ProC-91
DeVormer, Albert E.
(Al)
E120
E121/120
W501-105
W513-80
W572
W573
W575
Dewechter, Pat
85Greens-14
Deweerdt, Dan
88Rockford-11
89Rockford-11
Dewey, Mark
87Everett-32
88Clinton/ProC-711
89AS/Cal-43
89SanJose/Best-7
89SanJose/Cal-211
89SanJose/ProC-448
89SanJose/Star-7
89Star/Wax-85
90A&AASingle/ProC-65
90Shrev/ProC-1436
90Shrev/Star-6
91Phoenix/LineD-382

91Phoenix/ProC-60
91S-371RP
91T/90Debut-40
91Tidew/ProC-2503

Dewey, Todd Alan
86Durham-10
87Greenvl/Best-10
88Richm/CMC-11
88Richm/ProC-4
89Durham/Team-10
89Durham/Star-10
90Durham/Team-25

DeWillis, Jeff
88S-583

DeWitt, William O.
63FrBauer-4
W753

DeWolf, Rob
85Beloit-7
86Stockton-6
87ElPaso-6
88ElPaso/Best-14
89Wichita/Rock-9
89Wichita/Rock/Up-15

DeWright, Wayne
78Dunedin

Dews, Robert
(Bobby)
66Pep/Tul
82Durham-25MG
85Pol/Atl-53C

DeYoung, Rob
87BurlEx-28
88WPalmB/Star-8
89WPalmB/Star-9

Dial, Bryan
85BurlR-20
86Salem-5

Dials, Lou
86Negro/Frit-14
86Negro/Frit-20

Diaz, Alberto
89Kingspt/Star-7
91StLucie/ClBest-9
91StLucie/ProC-716

Diaz, Alex
88Clmbia/GS-14
89StLucie/Star-3
90T/TVMets-40
90Tidew/CMC-23
90Tidew/ProC-555
91Indianap/LineD-181
91Indianap/ProC-473

Diaz, Andres
90Kissim/DIMD-10

Diaz, Angel
89Helena/SP-2

Diaz, Baudilio Jose
(Bo)
78T-708R
79T-61
80T-483
81D-517
81F-404
81T-362
82D-263
82F-364
82F/St-197
82OPC-258
82T-258
82T/St-176
82T/Tr-29T
83D-147
83F-160
83F-637M
83OPC-175
83T-175
83T-229TL
83T/St-273
84D-137
84F-29
84F/St-118
84Nes/792-535
84OPC-131
84Phill/TastyK-25
84T-535
84T/St-120
85F-250
85OPC-219
85Phill/TastyK-10
85Phill/TastyK-25
85T-737
86D-530
86F-176
86Leaf-258
86OPC-253
86T-639
86TexGold-6
87D-246
87D/HL-21
87D/OD-190
87F-200
87F/Mini-32
87Kahn-6
87OPC-41
87T-41
87T/St-142
88D-186
88D/AS-47
88D/Best-110
88F-232
88Kahn/Reds-6
88Leaf-191
88OPC-265
88Panini/St-273
88S-206
88Sf-117
88T-265
88T/St-143
89B-307
89D-242
89D/Best-293
89F-159
89Kahn/Reds-6
89OPC-201
89Panini/St-71
89RedFoley/St-36
89S-187
89T-422
89T/St-135
89UD-169
90D-139
90Publint/St-27
90S-434
90UD-664

Diaz, Carlos Antonio
(Carlos)
80Spokane-4
81Richm-13
82Richm-5
83D-562
83F-540
84D-600
84F-583
84F/X-32
84Nes/792-524
84Pol/Dodg-27
84T-524
84T/Tr-32
85Coke/Dodg-9
85F-369
85T-159
86Coke/Dodg-9
86D-348
86F-128
86Pol/Dodg-27
86T-343
87Dunedin-1
88Knoxvl/Best-12
89Knoxvl/Best-4
89Knoxvl/ProC-1125
89Knoxvl/Star-2
90Syrac/CMC-10
90Syrac/Team-5
90Target-184
91Bristol/ClBest-18
91Bristol/ProC-3612
91Denver/LineD-134
91Denver/ProC-124
91T/90Debut-41
91WIZMets-96

Diaz, Cesar
91Kingspt/ClBest-27
91Kingspt/ProC-3815

Diaz, Derek
85Beloit-23
86ElPaso-8
87ElPaso-16

Diaz, Eddie
83Watlo/LF-4

Diaz, Edgar
83Beloit/LF-23
86Vanco-10
87Pol/Brew-2
90Brewer/MillB-5
90ElPasoATG/Team-16
90F/Up-105
90Leaf/II-335
90Pol/Brew-2
90T/Tr-26T
91Belling/ClBest-5
91Belling/ProC-3672
91D-197
91F-581
91OPC-164
91S-576
91T-164
91UD-286

Diaz, Enrique
80Wausau-15
81Wausau-16

Diaz, German
90Geneva/ProC-3039
90Geneva/Star-9
91Peoria/ClBest-16
91Peoria/ProC-1348

Diaz, Johnny
87Elmira/Black-22
87Elmira/Red-22
88WinHaven/Star-7
89Elmira/Pucko-2

Diaz, Jorge
83Madis/LF-8

Diaz, Jose
87Myrtle-3
88Dunedin/Star-4
88FSLAS/Star-33
89Knoxvl/Best-5
89Knoxvl/Star-3

Diaz, Kiki
88Denver/CMC-18
88Denver/ProC-1256
89Denver/CMC-12
89Denver/ProC-47

Diaz, Mario
80Wausau-14
81LynnS-17
82LynnS-12
84Chatt-25
86Calgary-6
87Calgary-11
88Calgary/ProC-804
88F-649R
88F/Up-U59
88Mother/Sea-21
89F-547
89Mother/Sea-21
89Panini/St-427
89T-309
89UD-318
90Calgary/ProC-655
90OPC-781
90Publint/St-432
90T-781
91Leaf/II-363
91Mother/Rang-24
91WIZMets-97
92D/I-149
92F-301

Diaz, Mike
83Iowa-11
85Cram/PCL-50
85Phill/TastyK-41
86Sf/Rook-50
87D-267
87F-609
87T-469
88D-267
88F-326
88OPC-239
88Panini/St-378
88S-143
88T-567
89D-655
89F-494
89S-603
89T-142
89UD-606

Diaz, Ralph
90James/Pucko-16
91Rockford/ClBest-4
91Rockford/ProC-2039

Diaz, Remigio
90Stockton/Best-6
90Stockton/Cal-192
90Stockton/ProC-2191
91Stockton/ClBest-13
91Stockton/ProC-3036

Diaz, Rich
83Watlo/LF-25

Diaz, Roberto
78Newar
79BurlB-16

Diaz, Sandy
89Elizab/Star-6
90Elizab/Star-8
90Kenosha/Best-18
90Kenosha/ProC-2287
90Kenosha/Star-2
91Elizab/ProC-4295

Diaz, Steve
89Beloit/II/Star-7
90Stockton/Best-3
90Stockton/Cal-188
90Stockton/ProC-2187
91Beloit/ClBest-11
91Beloit/ProC-2105

Diaz, Tony
84Butte-9
88Miami/Star-6
89StLucie/Star-4

Diaz, Victor
87Myrtle-23
89BirmB/Best-4
89BirmB/ProC-101

Diaz, William
86Wausau-8
88SanBern/Best-9
88SanBern/Cal-37
89Wmsprt/ProC-640
89Wmsprt/Star-6

DiBartolomeo, Steve
90CLAS/CL-52
90WinSalem/Team-16
91CharlK/LineD-131
91CharlK/ProC-1682

Dibble, Rob
85Cedar-6
86Vermont-7
87Nashvl-4
88F/Up-U83
88Nashvl/CMC-4
88Nashvl/ProC-493
88Nashvl/Team-8
88S/Tr-86T
89B-305
89Classic-76
89D-426
89D/Best-334
89F-160
89Kahn/Reds-49
89S-618
89T-264
89UD-375
90B-42
90CedarDG/Best-16
90Classic-43
90D-189
90D/BestNL-76
90F-418
90Kahn/Reds-8
90Leaf/I-57
90OPC-46
90Panini/St-249
90Publint/St-28
90S-277
90S/YS/II-15
90T-46
90UD-586
90USPlayC/AS-WC
91B-667
91Classic/200-168
91Classic/I-23
91Classic/III-15
91D-321
91F-62
91F/Ultra-92
91Kahn/Reds-49
91Leaf/II-282
91Leaf/Stud-163
91OPC-662
91Panini/St-128
91Pep/Reds-7
91RedFoley/St-4
91S-17
91S-407KM
91T-662
91T/StClub/I-131
91UD-635
91USPlayC/AS-10S
91Woolwth/HL-23M
92D/I-139
92F-404
92S/100SS-41
92S/II-455
92S/II-891DT
92T-757
92T/GPromo-757
92T/Promo-131
92UD-142
92UD-30TC

DiCeglio, Tom
85Visalia-11
86Kenosha-6

Dick, Bill
76BurlB
77BurlB
77Holyo
78BurlB
78Holyo

Dick, Ed
79TCMA-81

Dick, Ralph
88SanBern/Best-14
88SanBern/Cal-53
89SanBern/Best-11
89SanBern/Cal-90MG

Dickerman, Leo
90Target-932

Dickerson, Bob
(Bobby)
87Oneonta-27
88FtLaud/Star-5
89Albany/Best-16
89Albany/ProC-319
89Albany/Star-7
90Albany/Best-15
90Albany/ProC-1040
90Albany/Star-4
91Hagers/LineD-229
91Hagers/ProC-2461

Dickerson, Jim
86Pittsfld-7

Dickey, George W.
47TipTop

Dickey, William M.
(Bill)
31Exh/4-25
33Exh/4-13
33G-19
34DS-103
34DS-11
34Exh/4-13
35BU-117
35BU-30
35Exh/4-13
35G-2D
35G-4D
35G-7D
37OPC-119
38Exh/4-13
39Exh
39PB-30
40PB-7
41DP-66
41PB-70
44Yank/St-8
48Swell-6
50Callahan
51B-290CO
52T-400CO
60NuCard-34
60T-465C
61GP-27
61NuCard-434
63Bz/ATG-40
80Pac/Leg-44
80SSPC/HOF
83D/HOF-26
86Sf/Dec-13
88Conlon/AmAS-8
92Conlon/Sport-474
PM10/Sm-36
PR1-6
R300
R302
R303/A
R303/B
R308-161
R310
R312
R314
R328-4
R332-11
R423-22
V300

V353-19
V355-34
WG8-14
Dickman, Dave
89Pulaski/ProC-1888
89Sumter/ProC-1100
Dickman, Geo. Emerson
39PB-17
40PB-37
41G-6
Dickman, Mark
85Kingst-5
86Ventura-4
Dickson, James Edward
(Jim)
64T-524R
65T-286R
66T-201
Dickson, Ken
87AubAs-21
88Ashvl/ProC-1050
Dickson, Lance
90A&AASingle/ProC-173
90Classic/DP-23
90Classic/III-85
90Geneva/ProC-3029
90Geneva/Star-10
90PeoriaUp/Team-U1
91B-411
91Classic/II-T55
91D-424RR
91Iowa/LineD-204
91Iowa/ProC-1053
91Leaf/Stud-154
91OPC-114
91OPC/Premier-35
91S-385FDP
91S/Rook40-24
91T-114
91T/90Debut-42
91T/StClub/I-44
91UD-9SR
91UD/FinalEd-3F
92D/II-421
92S/100RisSt-96
Dickson, Murry Monroe
(Murry)
49B-8
49Eureka-158
50B-34
51B-167
51T/BB-16
52B-59
52RM-NL5
52T-266
52TipTop
53RM-NL22
54B-111
55B-236
56T-211
57T-71
58T-349
59T-23
Exh47
R423-23
Dickson, Walter R.
(Walt)
T205
Didier, Robert Daniel
(Bob)
69T-611R
70MLB/St-5
70OPC-232
70T-232
71MLB/St-8
71OPC-432
71T-432
73OPC-574
73T-574
74OPC-482
74T-482
75Iowa/TCMA-6
80Vanco-11
81WHave-1
82WHave-26
83Tacoma-18
87Tucson-24
88Tucson/CMC-24
88Tucson/ProC-190
88Tucson/JP-9
90Mother/Mar-27M
Didrickson, Babe
33SK-45
Diehl, Charles
52Wheat
Diemido, Chet
87Penin-3
91Saraso/ProC-1132CO
Dierderger, George
78Wisco
79Wisco-4
Diering, Charles E.
(Chuck)
47TipTop
49Eureka-180
50B-179
51B-158
52B-198
52NTea
52T-265
54Esskay
55Esskay
55T-105
55T/DH-2
56T-19
56T/Pin-1
79TCMA-51
91Crown/Orio-104
Dierker, Lawrence E.
(Larry)
65T-409R
66T-228
67T-498
68T-565
69MLB/St-138
69T-411
69T/St-32
70MLB/St-39
70OPC-15
70T-15
70T/PI-15
70T/S-6
71Bz
71Bz/Test-24
71K-48
71MLB/St-77
71OPC-540
71T-540
71T/Coins-141
71T/GM-32
71T/S-30
71T/tatt-6
72MB-89
72OPC-155
72T-155
73K-53
73OPC-375
73T-375
73T/Lids-13
74OPC-660
74T-660
75OPC-49
75T-49
75T/M-49
76Ho-25
76Ho/Twink-25
76OPC-75
76T-75
77T-350
78T-195
86Mother/Ast-8
89Swell-78
Dietrich, William J.
(Bill)
41G-9
91Conlon/Sport-133
92Conlon/Sport-366
R313
Dietrick, Patrick J.
(Pat)
85Madis-12
85Madis/Pol-9
86Madis-8
86Madis/Pol-8
88Huntsvl/BK-4
89Tacoma/CMC-24
89Tacoma/ProC-1553
90Tacoma/CMC-13
90Tacoma/ProC-105
Dietz, Don
87Vermont-11
Dietz, Richard Allen
(Dick)
62Kahn/Atl
67T-341R
68OPC-104
68T-104
69T-293
69T/St-103
70MLB/St-123
70OPC-135
70T-135
71K-42
71MD
71MLB/St-246
71OPC-545
71T-545
71T/Coins-33
71T/tatt-4
71Ticket/Giant-2
72MB-90
72OPC-295
72OPC-296IA
72T-295
72T-296IA
73OPC-442
73T-442
84Mother/Giants-21
90SanJose/Best-28CO
90SanJose/ProC-2027
90SanJose/Star-28
90Target-185
91SanJose/ClBest-25
91SanJose/ProC-28
Diez, Scott
87Miami-14
88FSLAS/Star-5
88Miami/Star-7
DiFelice, Mike
91Hamil/ClBest-15
91Hamil/ProC-4041
Diggle, Ron
75Tidew/Team-9
77Spoka
79RochR-14
Diggs, Tony
89Helena/SP-8
91Beloit/ClBest-18
91Beloit/ProC-2115
DiGioia, John
85Spring-7
86PalmSp-10
86PalmSp/Smok-7
DiGiovanna, Charlie
55Gol/Dodg-6bb
Digirolama, Dave
83Butte-3
DiHigo, Martin
74Laugh/Black-29
86Negro/Frit-19
88Conlon/NegAS-3
88Negro/Duques-10
89HOF/St-63
90Negro/Star-23
DiLauro, Jack Edward
(Jack)
70OPC-382
70T-382
71MLB/St-78
71OPC-677
71T-677
91WIZMets-95
Dilks, Darren
84Indianap-27
Dillard, David Donald
(Don)
59T-123
60T-122
61T-172
63T-298
Dillard, Gordon
87Hagers-25
88CharlK/Pep-20
88RochR/Gov-6
89ScrWB/CMC-7
89ScrWB/ProC-714
90BuffB/CMC-2
90BuffB/ProC-366
91Crown/Orio-105
Dillard, Harrison
51BR-D18
Dillard, Jay
75Lafay
Dillard, Mike
87Elmira/Red-32
Dillard, Ron
81Miami-1
82Tulsa-18
83BurlR-15
83BurlR/LF-14
Dillard, Stephen B.
75IntAS/TCMA-22
77T-142
78BK/T-16
78T-597
79T-217
80T-452
81D-502
81F-298
81T-78
82D-174
82Edmon-4
82F-594
82T-324
89Pac/SenLg-140
90EliteSenLg-35
91AubAS/ClBest-26MG
91AubAS/ProC-4289
Dillhoefer, William
(Pickles)
W514-71
Dillinger, Robert B.
(Bob)
48L-144
49B-143
50B-105
51B-63
53Mother-61
Exh47
R346-14
Dillman, William H.
(Bill)
67T-558R
68T-466
69OPC-141
69T-141
70OPC-386
70T-386
91Crown/Orio-106
Dillmore, Phillip
87Kinston-6
Dillon, Frank Edward
(Pop)
90Target-186
E107
Dillon, James
(Jim)
90SoOreg/Best-11
90SoOreg/ProC-3443
91Madison/ClBest-7
91Madison/ProC-2124
91MidwLAS/ProC-MWL40
Dillon, Stephen E.
(Steve)
64T-556R
91WIZMets-98
Dilone, Miguel Angel
(Miguel)
78T-705R
79Ho-118
79OPC-256
79T-487
80T-541
81D-441
81F-391
81F/St-86
81OPC-141
81T-141
81T/St-67
82D-515
82F-365
82F/St-196
82OPC-77
82T-77
82Wheat/Ind
83D-85
83F-405
83T-303
83Wheat/Ind-8
84Stuart-25
85D-453
85F-395
85Leaf-135
85OPC-178
85T-178
DiMaggio, Dominic P.
(Dom)
41DP-108
41PB-63
47HomogBond-9
47TipTop
48L-75
49B-64
49Royal-4
50B-3
50Drake-33
51BR-A8
51T/RB-20
52BR
52NTea
52RM-AL5
52Royal
52StarCal/L-71F
52T-22
53Exh/Can-23
53RM-AL22
53T-149
91T/Arc53-149
D305
Exh47
PM10/Sm-37
PM10/Sm-38
R423-24
DiMaggio, Joseph Paul
(Joe)
37Exh/4-13
37OPC-118
37Wheat
38Exh/4-13
38G-250
38G-274
38ONG/Pin-7
38Wheat
39Exh
39PB-26
40PB-1
40Wheat
41DP-63
41PB-7
41Wheat
47HomogBond-10
48L-1
48Swell-15
50Callahan
51BR-B5
52BR
53Exh/Can-28
60NuCard-38
60NuCard-7
61GP-9
61NuCard-438
61NuCard-467
72Laugh/GF-1
73Syrac/Team-7
74Laugh/ASG-39
74Syrac/Team-5
76Laugh/Jub-25
79TCMA-1
80Pac/Leg-5
80SSPC/HOF
83MLBPA/Pin-4
84West/1-5
85Sportflic/Proto-1
86Sf/Dec-20
88Pac/Leg-100
89HOF/St-39
90BBWit-49
90HOF/St-39
92S/DiMag-1
92S/DiMag-2
92S/DiMag-3
92S/DiMag-4
92S/DiMag-5
92S/DiMag-x
D305
PM10/Sm-39
PM10/Sm-40
PM10/Sm-41A
PM10/Sm-41B
PM10/Sm-42
PM10/Sm-43
PR1-7
R302
R303/A
R303/B
R311/Leath
R312
R314
R314/M
R326-4A
R326-4B
R342-4
R346-16
R423-25
V300
V355-51

DiMaggio, Vincent P.
(Vince)
38Exh/4-1
41PB-61
47Signal
DiMarco, Steven
91Erie/ClBest-5
91Erie/ProC-4077
91Kane/ClBest-15
91Kane/ProC-2662
Dimas, Rodolfo
85Tigres-7
DiMascio, Dan
87GlenF-22
88EastLAS/ProC-6
88GlenF/ProC-931
89Toledo/CMC-17
89Toledo/ProC-788
Dimeda, Jose
91Macon/ClBest-21
DiMichele, Frank
86QuadC-8
87PalmSp-27
88Edmon/ProC-565
88MidldA/GS-8
89MidldA/GS-12
Dimmel, Michael Wayne
(Mike)
75Water
78RochR
80ArkTr-8
91Crown/Orio-107
Dimuro, Ray
91AS/Cal-53
Dineen, Kerry Michael
(Kerry)
76SSPC-452
79OkCty
Dinkelmeyer, John
75Clinton
Dinneen, William H.
(Bill)
92Conlon/Sport-374
E107
T204
T206
WG2-14
Diorio, Ronald M.
(Ron)
74OPC-599R
74T-599R
DiPietro, Fred
76Clinton
DiPino, Frank M.
78BurlB
80Holyo-12
81Vanco-17
82T-333R
82Vanco-16
83T/Tr-25
84D-502
84F-224
84F/St-72
84Mother/Ast-17
84Nes/792-172
84T-172
84T/St-74
85D-232
85F-349
85Mother/Ast-11
85OPC-376
85T-532
85T/St-66
86D-304
86F-299
86Pol/Ast-25
86T-26
87Berg/Cubs-33
87D-416
87F-560
87OPC-297
87T-662
88Berg/Cubs-33
88D-570
88D/Best-205
88D/Cubs/Bk-570
88F-418
88S-413
88T-211
89B-434
89D-393
89F-423
89F/Up-118
89S-146
89Smok/Cards-6
89T-439
89T/Tr-24T
89UD-61
90B-187
90D-518
90F-249
90Leaf/I-103
90OPC-788
90Publlnt/St-218
90S-462
90Smok/Card-5
90T-788
90T/TVCard-12
90UD-202
91D-360
91F-632
91OPC-112
91Pol/Card-35
91S-553
91T-112
91T/StClub/II-439
91UD-350
DiPino, Paul
90Idaho/ProC-3254
Dipoto, Jerry
89Watertn/Star-3
90CLAS/CL-36
90Kinston/Team-1
91Canton/LineD-81
91Canton/ProC-975
DiSalvo, Pio
77Evansvl/TCMA-8TR
DiSarcina, Gary
89BBAmerAA/BPro-AA30
89MidldA/GS-13
89TexLAS/GS-4
90B-290
90Edmon/CMC-19
90Edmon/ProC-524
90S/Tr-68T
90T/89Debut-31
90UD/Ext-761
91Edmon/LineD-162
91Edmon/ProC-1523
91S-768RP
91S/100RisSt-26
92D/II-497
92F-664
DiSarcina, Glenn
91Utica/ClBest-16
91Utica/ProC-3245
Disher, Dan
87Wausau-4
88SanBern/Best-10
88SanBern/Cal-31
Disher, David
86Cram/PCL-122
Dismuke, Jamie
91Cedar/ClBest-17
91Cedar/ProC-2725
91Single/ClBest-368
Distaso, Alec John
(Alec)
69T-602R
Distefano, Benny
83LynnP-19
84Cram/PCL-144
85Cram/PCL-231
85D-166
85T-162
86D-78
86Hawaii-4
87D-514
87T-651
88AAA/ProC-4
88BuffB/CMC-11
88BuffB/Polar-6
88BuffB/ProC-1489
89BuffB/CMC-11
89BuffB/ProC-1682
89F-205
89T/Tr-25T
89VFJuice-30
90F-464
90Publlnt/St-152
91RochR/LineD-454
91RochR/ProC-1907
Ditmar, Arthur J.
(Art)
55B-90
55Rodeo
56Rodeo
56T-258
57T-132
58T-354
59T-374
60L-78
60MacGregor-7
60T-430
61P-16
61T-46LL
61T-48LL
61T-510
61T/St-192
62J-100
62P-100
62P/Can-100
62Salada-202
62Shirriff-202
62T-246
79TCMA-220
Dittmar, Carl
28Exh/PCL-5
Dittmer, John D.
(Jack)
53JC-19
53SpicSpan/3x5-11
53SpicSpan/7x10-6
53T-212
54B-48
54JC-6
54SpicSpan/PostC-9
54T-53
55B-212
55Gol/Braves-10
55JC-6
55SpicSpan/DC-8
57T-282
91T/Arc53-212
Ditton, Julian
76Clinton
Divison, Julio
75Lafay
Dixon, Andrew
86Cram/PCL-11
88Shreve/ProC-1287
Dixon, Bryan
88StCath/ProC-2030
Dixon, Colin
90WinHaven/Star-6
91NewBrit/LineD-455
91NewBrit/ProC-356
Dixon, Dan
79Tulsa-7
Dixon, Dee
87Clinton-15
89Shreve/ProC-1836
Dixon, Dickie
91Kenosha/ClBest-13
91Kenosha/ProC-2067
Dixon, Eddie
86WPalmB-13
87WPalmB-21
88Jaxvl/Best-6
88Jaxvl/ProC-967
89Jaxvl/Best-5
89Jaxvl/ProC-159
90Indianap/CMC-10
90Indianap/ProC-288
91Indianap/LineD-182
91Indianap/ProC-456
Dixon, Hal
55B-309ump
Dixon, John Craig
(Sonny)
53Briggs
55B-211
55Rodeo
88Chatt/Team-8
Dixon, Ken
84CharlO-17
85D-270
85F/Up-U36
85T/Tr-31T
86D-148
86F-273
86T-198
87D-171
87F-468
87French-39
87T-528
88D-48
88F-557
88S-411
88T-676
91Crown/Orio-108
Dixon, Mason
90ColMud/Star-28
Dixon, Mike
81Watlo-8
Dixon, Rap
74Laugh/Black-2
86Negro/Frit-78
Dixon, Roger
90Elizab/Star-9
Dixon, Ronn
82Wausau-14
83Wausau/LF-7
Dixon, Steve
89Johnson/Star-8
90Savan/ProC-2061
91StPete/ClBest-4
91StPete/ProC-2268
Dixon, Thomas Earl
(Tom)
75Dubuq
79OPC-186
79T-361
80T-513
80Tidew-12
81Tidew-14
82Syrac-2
Dixon, Troy
83BirmB-23
Djakonow, Paul
75Shreve/TCMA-1
76Shrev
80Buffa-10
82Evansvl-15
Doak, William L.
(Bill)
21Exh-35
21Exh-36
90Target-187
D327
D328-42
D329-47
D350/2-48
E120
E121/120
E121/80
E122
E135-42
E220
M101/4-47
M101/5-48
V100
V61-65
W501-78
W514-51
W572
W573
W575
Dobbek, Daniel J.
(Dan)
59T-124
60T-123
61Peters-24
61T-108
62T-267
Dobbins, Joe
43Centen-6
44Centen-5
45Centen-5
Dobbs, Gary
78Wisco
79Wisco-15
Dobbs, John
90Target-188
Doberenz, Mark
82Idaho-32
83Idaho-33
Dobernic, Andrew J.
(Jess)
49B-200
49Eureka-81
Dobie, Reggie
85Lynch-5
86Jacks/TCMA-2
87Tidew-3
87Tidew/TCMA-1
88Tidew/ProC-1590
89Calgary/CMC-5
89Calgary/ProC-528
Dobson, Charles T.
(Chuck)
66T-588R
67T-438
68OPC-62
68T-62
69MB-74
69T-397
70MLB/St-256
70OPC-331
70T-331
71K-32
71MLB/St-510
71OPC-238
71T-238
72MB-91
72OPC-523
72T-523
75OPC-635
75T-635
75T/M-635
77SLCity
Dobson, Joseph Gordon
(Joe)
47TipTop-3
49B-7
50B-44
51B-36
52Hawth/Pin-3
52T-254
53B/Col-88
53RM-AL15
53T-5
91T/Arc53-5
Exh47
Dobson, Patrick E.
(Pat)
67T-526R
68OPC-22
68T-22
69T-231
70MLB/St-112
70OPC-421
70T-421
71MLB/St-295
71OPC-547
71T-547
72MB-92
72OPC-140
72T-140
73OPC-34
73T-34
74OPC-463
74Syrac/Team-6
74T-463
75OPC-44
75T-44
75T/M-44
76OPC-296
76SSPC-431
76T-296
76T/Tr-296T
77Pep-8
77T-618
78T-575
83Pol/Brew-45C
88Domino-4
88Smok/Padres-7CO
89Pac/SenLg-219M
89Pac/SenLg-87
89T/SenLg-96
89TM/SenLg-28
90EliteSenLg-64
90Padre/MagUno-22CO
91Crown/Orio-109
91Pac/SenLg-9
Doby, Lawrence Eugene
(Larry)
48L-138
49B-233
50B-39
50NumNum
51B-151
51T/CAS
52B-115
52BR
52NumNum-18
52RM-AL6
52StarCal/L-74A
52T-243
53B/Col-40
53Exh/Can-11
54B-84
54DanDee
54T-70
55Armour-4
55Gol/Ind-5

55RM-AL18
55Salem
56T-250
56YellBase/Pin-9
57T-85
58Hires-17
58T-424
59T-166
59T-455
73OPC-377CO
73T-377C
74OPC-531CO
74T-531C
79TCMA-27
82CJ-6
88Pac/Leg-102
89Swell-115
90Pac/Legend-20
90Swell/Great-43
91Swell/Great-24
91T/Arc53-333
Exh47
PM10/Sm-44
PM10/Sm-45
PM10/Sm-46
R302-124
R423-18

Dockins, George
90Target-189

Dodd, Bill
88Cedar/ProC-1138
88MidwLAS/GS-11
89Chatt/Best-14
89Chatt/GS-9
91Chatt/LineD-157
91Chatt/ProC-1952

Dodd, Daniel
88StCath/ProC-2018
89Myrtle/ProC-1471

Dodd, Lance
82AlexD-8

Dodd, Mike
75Cedar

Dodd, Robb
91Boise/ClBest-26
91Boise/ProC-3869

Dodd, Scott
91Billings/ProC-3747

Dodd, Tim
83Tampa-7
84Cedar-11

Dodd, Tom
86SLAS-12
87CharlO/WBTV-8
87SLAS-6
88Omaha/CMC-19
88Omaha/ProC-1505
89Omaha/CMC-11
89Omaha/ProC-1727
90Calgary/CMC-16
90Calgary/ProC-662
91Crown/Orio-110

Dodd, Tommie
82Nashvl-10

Dodge, Tom
91QuadC/ClBest-12
91QuadC/ProC-2630

Dodig, Jeff
87Idaho-25
88Durham/Star-5

Dodson, Bo
89Helena/SP-17
89LittleSun-11
90A&AASingle/ProC-150
90AS/Cal-38
90Stockton/Best-26
90Stockton/Cal-190
90Stockton/ProC-2189
91AS/Cal-55
91B-38
91Single/ClBest-358
91Stockton/ClBest-20
91Stockton/ProC-3038

Dodson, Pat
84Pawtu-19
85Pawtu-3
86Pawtu-9
87Classic-8
87D-44RR
87Leaf-44RR
87Pawt/TCMA-24
87Sf-118M
87Seven-E11
87T-449FS
88Pawtu/CMC-16
88Pawtu/ProC-466
88S-352
90OkCty/ProC-437
91Pol/Royal-25CO

Doerr, Robert P.
(Bobby)
38G-258
38G-282
39PB-7
40PB-38
41DP-106
41PB-64
47HomogBond-11
47TipTop-4
48L-83
49B-23
50B-43
50Drake-13
51T/BB-37
52BR
53Exh/Can-24
74Laugh/ASG-43
83MLBPA/Pin-5
86D/HL-32
88Pac/Leg-73
89HOF/St-11
89Pac/Leg-150
89Swell-110
89T/Gloss22-11
90Pac/Legend-21
90Swell/Great-96
91Swell/Great-25
92Conlon/Sport-467
D305
Exh47
R314
Rawl

Doerr, Tim
76Clinton

Does, Raymond
89Welland/Pucko-11

Doescher, Edward
C46-50

Doffek, Scott
90Yakima/Team-15
91VeroB/ProC-780

Doggett, George
85Lynch-26

Doggett, Jerry
71Ticket/Dodg-20ANN

Doherty, John Michael
(John)
75OPC-524
75T-524
75T/M-524
89NiagFls/Pucko-7
90Lakeland/Star-7
91London/LineD-382
91London/ProC-1870

Dohne, Heriberto
88Modesto/Cal-76

Doiron, Serge
91Geneva/ClBest-6
91Geneva/ProC-4221

Dolan, Cozy
90Target-190
V117-9

Dolan, John
88Elmira-7
89Lynch/Star-7

Dolan, Thomas J.
(Tom)
N172

Dolf, Mike
76Wmsprt

Doll, Chris
88Wausau/GS-4

Dolson, Andrew
91MedHat/ProC-4092

Dombrowski, Robert
89Billings/ProC-2055
90Cedar/ProC-2328

Domecq, Ray
90Martins/ProC-3192
91Spartan/ClBest-2
91Spartan/ProC-887

Dominguez, Frank
89Reno/Cal-256
90PalmSp/Cal-209
90PalmSp/ProC-2580
91PalmSp/ProC-2019

Dominguez, Jose
86Orlan-5
88Shreve/ProC-1281
88TexLgAS/GS-19
89Shreve/ProC-1854

Dominguez, Ken
90Oneonta/ProC-3390CO

Dominico, Ron
84LitFalls-26
85LitFalls-4

Dominquez, Jose
85Visalia-22

Donaghue, Ray
77StPete

Donahue, Chuck
86Tampa-5

Donahue, James A.
(Jim)
No Cards.

Donahue, Patrick W.
(Pat)
E107
E91
M116
T204
T205
T206

Donahue, Tim
90Reno/Cal-270
91Collnd/ClBest-24
91Collnd/ProC-1491

Donald, Richard Atley
(Atley)
40PB-121
41PB-38
44Yank/St-9

Donald, Tremayne
90Johnson/Star-9

Donaldson, John
78Laugh/Black-28
86Negro/Frit-77
90Negro/Star-8

Donaldson, John David
(John)
68T-244
69MB-75
69MLB/St-85
69OPC-217
69T-217
70MLB/St-269
70OPC-418
70T-418
72MB-93

Donatelli, Andy
85Utica-18

Donatelli, Augie
55B-313ump

Donlin, Michael J.
(Mike)
11Helmar-158
75F/Pion-25
92Conlon/Sport-450
E107
E90/1
E91
T204
T206
T207
T213/blue
T215/blue
T215/brown
WG3-13

Donnelly, Edward
(Ed)
T207

Donnelly, James B.
(Jim)
N172
N284
WG1-64

Donnelly, Rich
74Gaston
77Tucson
78Cr/PCL-8
79Tucson-8
89VFJuice-39CO
90Homer/Pirate-9CO

Donnelly, Sylvester
(Blix)
49B-145
49Eureka-133
50B-176
51B-208

Donnels, Chris
88Clmbia/GS-26
89StLucie/Star-5
90T/TVMets-41
91AAAGame/ProC-AAA47
91B-465
91Classic/III-16
91Leaf/II-447
91S/RookTr-104T
91Tidew/LineD-554
91Tidew/ProC-2516
91UD/FinalEd-61F
92D/II-619
92S/100RisSt-79
92S/I-212
92T-376
92T/91Debut-45
92UD-44

Donofrio, Larry
80Ashvl-22
81AppFx-13

Donohue, J.A.
E91

Donohue, Jack
N172
N172/ST

Donohue, James A.
(Jim)
N172
N284
N690

Donohue, James T.
(Jim)
60T-124
61T-151
62T-498

Donohue, John F.
(Jiggs)
No Cards.

Donohue, Peter J.
(Pete)
25Exh-27
26Exh-27
91Conlon/Sport-322
E120
R316
V61-77
W517-26
W572

Donohue, Steve
79WHave-19
82Colum-24M

Donohue, Thomas J.
(Tom)
77SLCity
78Cr/PCL-52
80T-454
81D-51
81F-281
81T-621

Donovan, Bret
88CapeCod/Sum-165

Donovan, Gary
77BurlB

Donovan, Jack
81Tucson-25

Donovan, Michael B.
(Mike)
80BurlB-3

Donovan, Patrick J.
(Patsy)
09Buster/Pin-5
11Helmar-31
12Sweet/Pin-24
90Target-191
E107
M116
WG2-15

Donovan, Richard E.
(Dick)
55T-146
56T-18
56T/Pin-32
57T-181
58T-290
59T-5
60L-72
60T-199
61Bz-10
61T-414
61T/St-202
62J-73
62Kahn
62P-73
62P/Can-73
62Sugar-3
62T-15
62T-55LL
62T/St-33
63Bz-10
63F-11
63J-75
63P-75
63Salada-34
63Sugar-3
63T-370
63T-8LL
63T/SO
64Kahn
79TCMA-34
Exh47

Donovan, William E.
(Wild Bill)
16FleischBrd-24
81Detroit-29
87Conlon/2-13
90Target-192
D303
D327
D328-43
D329-48
D350/2-49
E101
E102
E103
E104
E105
E106
E121/80
E122
E254
E300
E90/1
E92
E93
E96
M116
T201
T204
T206
T213/blue
T213/brown
T216
T3-12
V100
W555
W575

Dooin, Charles S.
(Red)
10Domino-34
11Helmar-141
12Sweet/Pin-125A
12Sweet/Pin-125B
14CJ-38
15CJ-38
BF2-74
D303
D329-49
D350/2-50
E101
E103
E104
E105
E106
E224
E270/2
E300
E90/1
E92
E93
E96
E98
L1-126
M101/4-49
M101/5-50
M116
S74-98
S81-101
T201
T202
T205
T206
T207
T215/blue
T215/brown

T216
T3-14
W555
WG3-14
WG5-15
WG6-14

Doolan, Michael J.
(Mickey)
10Domino-35
11Helmar-142
12Sweet/Pin-126A
12Sweet/Pin-126B
14CJ-120
15CJ-120
90Target-193
D303
D329-50
D350/2-51
E101
E104
E105
E106
E224
E254
E270/1
E92
E94
E97
M101/4-50
M101/5-51
M116
S74-99
T202
T205
T206
T213/blue
T213/brown
T215/blue
T215/brown
T216
T3-90
W555
WG3-15

Dooley
N172/PCL

Dooley, Marvin
89Princet/Star-6

Doolittle, James
33SK-28

Dooner, Glenn
82Toledo-2

Doornenweerd, Dave
91FrRow/DP-36

Dophied, Tracy
82AubAs-12

Dopson, John
86Indianap-12
88D/Rook-43
88F/Up-U99
88S/Tr-88T
89B-24
89Classic/Up/2-161
89D-392
89D/Best-177
89D/Tr-7
89F-373
89F/Up-8
89OPC-251
89S-466
89S/Tr-40
89T-251
89T/Tr-26T
89UD-57
90D-162
90F-272
90Leaf/I-130
90OPC-733
90Panini/St-18
90Pep/RSox-7
90S-331
90S/YS/I-26
90T-733
90T/St-260
90T/TVRSox-9
90UD-671
91D-193
91F-92
91OPC-94
91S-772
91T-94
91UD-88

Doran, Bill
82Tucson-7
83T/Tr-26
84D-580
84F-225
84Mother/Ast-4
84Nes/792-198
84OPC-198
84T-198
84T/St-377
85D-84
85F-350
85Mother/Ast-8
85OPC-299
85T-684
85T/St-68
86D-10DK
86D-110
86D/DKsuper-10
86F-300
86Leaf-10DK
86OPC-57
86Pol/Ast-5
86T-57
86T/St-25
87D-286
87D/OD-11
87F-57
87Leaf-197
87Mother/Ast-4
87OPC-243
87Pol/Ast-5
87RedFoley/St-69
87Sf-116M
87Sf-162
87T-472
87T/Mini-9
87T/St-31
88D-235
88D/Best-120
88F-447
88F/LL-10
88F/St-87
88Leaf-183
88Mother/Ast-4
88Nestle-19
88OPC-166
88Panini/St-295
88Pol/Ast-10
88S-52
88Sf-48
88T-745
88T/Big-51
88T/St-34
89B-329
89D-306
89D/Best-38
89F-357
89Lennox/Ast-8
89Mother/Ast-4
89OPC-226
89Panini/St-89
89RedFoley/St-37
89S-21
89Sf-57
89T-226
89T/Big-168
89T/St-16
89T/UK-22
89UD-101
90B-76
90D-236
90D/BestNL-102
90F-230
90Leaf/I-161
90Lennox-13
90MLBPA/Pins-44
90Mother/Ast-7
90OPC-368
90Panini/St-268
90PublInt/St-257
90PublInt/St-94
90S-182
90S/100St-8
90T-368
90T/Big-159
90T/St-15
90UD-198
91B-682
91D-756
91F-63
91F/Ultra-93
91Kahn/Reds-19
91Leaf/I-197
91OPC-577
91Pep/Reds-8
91S-775
91T-577
91T/StClub/I-148
91UD-398
92D/I-293
92F-405
92S/I-77
92T-136
92UD-280

Doran, John F.
(John)
N172

Doran, Mark
86PalmSp-11
87MidldA-21
88Edmon/CMC-24
88Edmon/ProC-570
89MidldA/GS-14

Dorante, Luis
87Elmira/Black-14
87Elmira/Red-14
88Elmira-12
89Elmira/Pucko-3
90LynchRS/Team-11
91WinHaven/ClBest-12
91WinHaven/ProC-492

Dorgan, Charles
77Clinton

Dorgan, Michael C.
(Mike)
N172
N284
N403
N690

Dorish, Harry
51B-266
52T-303
53T-145
54B-86
54T-110
55B-248
56T-167
80Port-14C
91Crown/Orio-111
91T/Arc53-145

Dorn, Chris
89Pittsfld/Star-4
91StLucie/ClBest-22
91StLucie/ProC-703

Dorner, Augustus
(Gus)
T204
T206

Dorsett, Brian
85Huntsvl/BK-22
85Madis-11
85Madis/Pol-8
86Tacoma-3
87Tacoma-22
88F-607
89Colum/CMC-14
89Colum/Pol-2
89Colum/ProC-759
90AAAGame/ProC-AAA14
90ColClip/ProC-679
90T/TVYank-40
91LasVegas/ProC-238
91LasVegas/LineD-279

Dorsey, James Edward
(Jim)
75QuadC
79SLCity-14
80SLCity-16
81Pawtu-9
81T-214R
83Pawtu-6
84Pawtu-6

Dorsey, Lee
90Utica/Pucko-30

Doscher, Jack
90Target-194

Doss, Dennis
77Watlo

Doss, Greg
88Savan/ProC-357

Doss, Jason
88Wythe/ProC-1998
89CharWh/Best-20
89CharWh/ProC-1765
90Peoria/Team-19
91Peoria/ClBest-5
91Peoria/ProC-1336

Doss, Larry
87Jamestn-9

Dostal, Bruce
88Bakers/Cal-247
89VeroB/Star-7
90FSLAS/Star-3
90VeroB/Star-11
91Reading/LineD-507
91Reading/ProC-1381

Doster, Zach
87Fayette-7
88Fayette/ProC-1090
89Miami/I/Star-5

Dotel, Mariano
91Myrtle/ClBest-19
91Myrtle/ProC-2953

Dotelson, Angel
91Kissim/ProC-4200

Dotson, J.
(Gene)
79ArkTr-8
81Louisvl-15
83Louisvl/Riley-15

Dotson, Larry
81Watlo-25

Dotson, Richard E.
(Rich)
78Knoxvl
79Knoxvl/TCMA-8
81Coke
81D-280
81F-356
81OPC-138
81T-138
81T/HT
81T/St-62
82D-356
82F-340
82F/St-186
82OPC-257
82T-457
82T/St-166
83D-319
83F-233
83OPC-46
83T-46
83TrueVal/WSox-34
84D-180
84F-56
84F/St-62
84Nes/792-216TL
84Nes/792-759
84OPC-24
84T-216TL
84T-759
84T/St-241
84TrueVal/WS-10
85Coke/WS-34
85D-3DK
85D-302
85D/DKsuper-3
85F-511
85Leaf-3DK
85OPC-364
85T-364
85T/St-233
86Coke/WS-34
86D-160
86F-203
86Jay's-5
86OPC-233
86Sf-133M
86T-156M
86T-612
87Coke/WS-20
87D-383
87D/OD-238
87F-495
87F/Mini-33
87OPC-211
87T-720
88D-124
88D/Best-52
88D/Y/Bk-NEW
88F-396
88F/Up-U48
88OPC-209
88Panini/St-53
88S-480
88S/Tr-60T
88T-209
88T/St-291
88T/Tr-35T
89D-277
89F-253
89OPC-357
89Panini/St-398
89S-278
89S/NWest-23
89S/Tr-80
89Sf-194
89T-511
89T/DHTest-22
89T/St-316
89UD-80
90OPC-169
90PublInt/St-533
90S-19
90T-169

Dotter, Gary Richard
(Gary)
65T-421R

Dotterer, Henry John
(Dutch)
58T-396
59T-288
60T-21
61T-332
61T/RO-24

Doty, Sean
89Billings/ProC-2052
90Billings/ProC-3212
91CharWh/ClBest-2
91CharWh/ProC-2879

Dotzler, Mike
86DayBe-7
87Salem-12
88OrlanTw/Best-21
89Visalia/Cal-105
89Visalia/ProC-1438

Doubleday, Abner
90BBWit-108

Doucet, Eric
89Boise/ProC-1983

Dougherty, Jim
88CapeCod/Sum-55

Dougherty, Mark
83Erie-7
86ArkTr-6
87Louisvl-11
88Louisvl-18
88Louisvl/CMC-23
88Louisvl/ProC-444

Dougherty, Pat
86BurlEx-6

Dougherty, Patrick H.
(Patsy)
10Domino-36
11Helmar-10
12Sweet/Pin-9
E101
E102
E105
E107
E254
E90/1
E90/3
E92
E94
M116
T201
T205
T206
T215/blue
T215/brown
T216
WG2-16

Doughty, Jamie
85Tulsa-9
86Tulsa-11

Douglas, Charles
(Whammy)
58T-306
59T-431

Douglas, Charles
88Boise/ProC-1624

Douglas, Dave
87Harris-16

Douglas, John
90Target-933

Douglas, Phillip B.
(Phil)
90Target-195
E120
E121/120
W501-74
W514-5

W575
Douglas, Preston
88Utica/Pucko-27
Douglas, Steve
82Orlan/B-17
82OrlTw/A-6
Douglas, William B.
(Klondike)
E107
Douma, Todd
90Pittsfld/Pucko-13
91FSLAS/ProC-FSL30
91StLucie/ClBest-24
91StLucie/ProC-704
Dour, Brian
88CapeCod/Sum-64
89Everett/Star-6
90Foil/Best-253
90SanJose/Best-21
90SanJose/Cal-42
90SanJose/ProC-2009
90SanJose/Star-7
91SanJose/ClBest-15
91SanJose/ProC-3
Douris, John D.
91Welland/ClBest-21
91Welland/ProC-3566
Douthit, Taylor Lee
(Taylor)
29Exh/4-16
31Exh/4-16
33Exh/4-4
33G-40
91Conlon/Sport-264
R316
V353-40
Dovalis, Alex
79Wisco-6
Dovey, Troy
89Ashvl/ProC-956
90Ashvl/ProC-2739
90Osceola/Star-6
91BurlAs/ClBest-2
91BurlAs/ProC-2793
Dowd, Snooks
90Target-196
Dowell, Ken
83Reading-13
84Cram/PCL-210
85Cram/PCL-46
86Portl-5
87F/Up-U27
87Maine-16
87Maine/TCMA-10
88Tidew/CANDL-8
88Tidew/CMC-14
88Tidew/ProC-1595
89Tidew/CMC-11
89Tidew/ProC-1963
90Richm/CMC-22
90Richm/ProC-267
90Richm/Team-9
Dowies, Butch
82Danvl-10
Dowless, Mike
81Water-3
82Indianap-16
83Indianap-23
84Cedar-24
Dowling, David B.
(Dave)
65OPC-116R
65T-116R
66T-482R
67T-272R
88AlaskaAS60/Team-12
Down, Rick
90Albany/ProC-1180MG
90Albany/Star-24
91ColClip/LineD-124
91ColClip/ProC-614
Downey, Alexander C.
(Red)
90Target-934
Downey, Thomas E.
(Tom)
10Domino-37
11Helmar-143
12Sweet/Pin-97A
12Sweet/Pin-97B
14CJ-107
15CJ-107
E254
M116
S74-73
T201
T205
T206
T207
T213/blue
T3-91
Downing, Alphonso E.
(Al)
62T-219
64T-219M
64T-86
64T/Coins-109
65MacGregor-2
65OPC-11LL
65T-11LL
65T-598
66T-384
67T-308
68Bz-12
68OPC-105
68T-105
69MB-76
69T-292
70T-584
71MLB/St-102
71OPC-182
71T-182
72MB-94
72OPC-460
72OPC-93LL
72T-460
72T-93LL
73OPC-324
73T-324
74OPC-620
74T-620
75OPC-498
75T-498
75T/M-498
76OPC-605
76SSPC-66
76T-605
90Target-197
WG10-5
WG9-7
Downing, Brian Jay
(Brian)
74OPC-601R
74T-601R
75OPC-422
75T-422
75T/M-422
76OPC-23
76SSPC-141
76T-23
77Ho-138
77OPC-246
77T-344
78T-519
79T-71
80OPC-315
80T-602
80T/S-49
81D-410
81F-282
81OPC-263
81T-263
81T/St-50
82D-115
82F-457
82F/St-215
82OPC-158
82T-158
83D-367
83F-86
83OPC-298
83T-442
84D-423
84F-515
84Nes/792-574
84OPC-135
84Smok/Cal-8
84T-574
84T/St-236
85D-158
85F-300
85Leaf-223
85OPC-374
85Smok/Cal-7
85T-374
85T/St-224
86D-108
86F-154
86Leaf-39
86OPC-205
86Sf-154
86Smok/Cal-7
86T-772
86T/St-183
87D-86
87D/HL-5
87D/OD-9
87F-78
87F/Excit-16
87F/BB-15
87F/Mini-34
87F/St-35
87OPC-88
87Sf-161
87Smok/Cal-19
87T-782
87T/St-178
88D-258
88D/Best-27
88F-488
88F/Mini-10
88F/St-11
88Leaf-203
88OPC-331
88Panini/St-46
88RedFoley/St-19
88S-44
88Sf-181
88Smok/Angels-18
88T-331
88T/Big-78
88T/Mini-5
88T/Revco-23
88T/St-181
89B-53
89D-254
89D/Best-321
89F-475
89OPC-17
89Panini/St-288
89S-76
89Sf-117
89Smok/Angels-12
89T-17
89T/St-178
89UD-485
90B-294
90D-10DK
90D-352
90D/SuperDK-10DK
90F-130
90OPC-635
90Panini/St-27
90PublInt/St-368
90S-26
90S/100St-46
90Sf-77
90Smok/Angel-4
90T-635
90T/St-169
90UD-146
91F-310
91F/UltraUp-U54
91Leaf/II-269
91Mother/Rang-17
91OPC-255
91S-104
91S/RookTr-30T
91T-255
91T/StClub/II-348
91T/Tr-33T
91UD-231A
91UD-231B
91UD/Ext-770
92D/I-167
92F-302
92S/II-579
92T-173
92UD-483
Downs, Dorley
84PrWill-12
85Nashua-7
86Macon-8
Downs, Jerome Willis
(Red)
90Target-198
T201
T206
Downs, John
91Eugene/ClBest-22
91Eugene/ProC-3717
Downs, Kelly
82OkCty-21
83Portl-9
84Cram/PCL-201
85Cram/PCL-189
86Phoenix-4
87D-573
87F-272
87Mother/SFG-17
87T-438
88Classic/Red-194
88D-145
88D/Best-106
88F-80
88Mother/Giants-17
88OPC-187
88Panini/St-415
88S-27
88S/YS/I-19
88Sf-203
88T-629
88T/JumboR-19
88ToysRUs-9
89B-465
89D-367
89D/Best-247
89F-326
89Mother/Giants-4
89OPC-361
89Panini/St-209
89S-124
89Sf-39
89T-361
89T/Big-112
89T/St-81
89UD-476
90D-177
90F-55
90Mother/Giant-4
90OPC-17
90PublInt/St-66
90S-534
90T-17
90UD-699
91B-633
91D-738
91F-261
91F/UltraUp-U116
91Mother/Giant-4
91OPC-733
91PG&E-4
91S-654
91T-733
91T/StClub/I-193
91UD-441
92D/I-303
92F-634
92S/I-191
92T-573
92UD-583
Downs, Kirk
80BurlB-24
Downs, Ron
88Augusta/ProC-378
88SALAS/GS-5
89Salem/Star-6
Doyel, Dan
89Savan/ProC-347
91StPete/ClBest-30TR
Doyle
N172/PCL
Doyle, Blake
78RochR
79RochR-4
80Indianap-20
Doyle, Brian Reed
(Brian)
78Cr/PCL-14
79T-710R
80Colum-13
80T-582
81F-104
81T-159
81T/Tr-754
82Syrac-16
Doyle, Carl
90Target-935
Doyle, Ian
91BurlInd/ProC-3294
Doyle, James
M116
Doyle, Jeffrey D.
(Jeff)
81ArkTr-7
81Louisvl-11
82Louisvl-7
83Louisvl/Riley-11
Doyle, John Joseph
(Jack)
90Target-199
E107
N566-178
Doyle, Judd Bruce
(Slow Joe)
T206
Doyle, Lawrence J.
(Larry)
10Domino-38
11Helmar-125
12Sweet/Pin-112A
12Sweet/Pin-112B
14CJ-4
14Piedmont/St-19
15CJ-4
16FleischBrd-25
91Conlon/Sport-317
BF2-75
D303
D328-44
D329-51
D350/2-52
E101
E102
E103
E104
E105
E106
E135-44
E224
E254
E270/2
E286
E91
E92
E95
M101/4-51
M101/5-52
M116
S74-85
T201
T202
T205
T206
T207
T213/blue
T215/blue
T215/brown
T216
T3-13
W514-81
W516-13
WG4-7
Doyle, Paul S.
(Paul)
70OPC-277
70T-277
72T-629
Doyle, Rich
82Watlo/B-2
82Watlo/C-23
83BuffB-3
84BuffB-11
85Water-6
86Beaum-10
88SanBern/Best-24
88SanBern/Cal-52
89Calgary/CMC-7
89Calgary/ProC-541
89EastLDD/ProC-DD32
Doyle, Robert Dennis
(Denny)
70OPC-539R
70T-539R
71MLB/St-175
71OPC-352
71T-352
72T-768
73OPC-424
73T-424
74OPC-552
74T-552
75OPC-187
75T-187
75T/M-187
76Ho-107
76OPC-381
76SSPC-407

76T-381
77Ashvl
77T-336
78OPC-111
78T-642

Doyle, Tim
91SoOreg/ClBest-4
91SoOreg/ProC-3833

Doyle, Tom
86Columbia-9TR
87Columbia-23
88Jacks/GS-7
88Martins/Star-11
90Waterlo/Best-26
90Waterlo/ProC-2383
91CharRain/ClBest-18
91CharRain/ProC-103

Doyle, William Carl
R313

Dozier, D.J.
90FSLAS/Star-4
90S/Tr-97T
91B-478
91Classic/200-89
91Classic/II-T4
91Single/ClBest-387
91UD-3SR
91Wmsprt/LineD-631
91Wmsprt/ProC-306
92D/I-20RR
92T-591M

Dozier, Tom
82Spring-15
83StPete-5
84Albany-11
85Cram/PCL-145
85Huntsvl/BK-15
86Tacoma-4
87Tacoma-1
88Greenvl/Best-18
90SpringDG/Best-8

Drabek, Doug
85Albany-4
86Colum-6
86Colum/Pol-6
86D/Rook-31
86F/Up-U36
87D-251
87D/HL-32
87F-96
87T-283
87T/Tr-29T
88D-79
88D/Best-73
88F-327
88Leaf-88
88OPC-143
88RedFoley/St-20
88S-51
88T-591
88T/Big-124
88T/St-134
89B-416
89D-211
89D/Best-17
89F-206
89OPC-37
89Panini/St-161
89S-117
89S/HotStar-87
89S/YS/I-21
89Sf-27
89T-478
89UD-597
89VFJuice-15
90AlbanyDG/Best-22
90B-164
90D-92
90D/BestNL-9
90F-465
90Homer/Pirate-10
90Leaf/II-296
90OPC-197
90Panini/St-332
90PublInt/St-153
90RedFoley/St-27
90S-505
90T-197
90T/Big-185
90T/St-130
90UD-422
91B-515
91BBBest/Aces-5
91Bz-4
91Classic/200-167
91Classic/I-82
91Classic/II-T79
91CollAB-29
91D-269
91D-411MVP
91D-750CY
91D/Elite-E5
91D/Preview-2
91F-36
91F/Ultra-277
91F/UltraG-3
91Leaf/II-516
91Leaf/Stud-224
91Leaf/StudPrev-15
91MajorLg/Pins-59
91OPC-405AS
91OPC-685
91Panini/FrSt-122
91Panini/St-116
91Panini/Top15-57
91Panini/Top15-92
91RedFoley/St-28
91S-472
91S-661AS
91S-878CY
91S/100SS-6
91T-405
91T-685
91T/CJMini/I-12
91T/StClub/I-202
91UD-278
91Woolwth/HL-3
92D/I-209
92F-553
92S/100SS-53
92S/I-115
92T-440
92UD-221
92UD-39TC

Drabinski, Marek
91Macon/ClBest-14
91Macon/ProC-867

Drabowsky, Myron W.
(Moe)
57T-84
58T-135
59T-407
60L-68
60T-349
61T-364
62T-331
64T-42
64T/St-82
64T/tatt-36
65T-439
66T-291
67OPC-125
67OPC-151WS
67T-125
67T-151WS
68Coke
68Dexter-29
68T-242
69MB-77
69MLB/St-57
69T-508
69T/St-183
70MLB/St-220
70T-653
71MLB/St-272
71OPC-685
71T-685
72MB-95
72T-627
78TCMA-121
87Birm/Best-3CO
88BirmB/Best-7CO
89Pac/Leg-215
89Swell-103
89Vanco/CMC-25CO
89Vanco/ProC-581CO
90Vanco/CMC-26CO
90Vanco/ProC-506CO
91Crown/Orio-112
91Vanco/LineD-650CO
91Vanco/ProC-1610CO

Drago, Richard A.
(Dick)
69T-662R
70OPC-37
70T-37
71MLB/St-414
71OPC-752
71T-752
72K-40
72OPC-205
72T-205
73OPC-392
73T-392
74OPC-113
74T-113
75OPC-333
75T-333
75T/M-333
76OPC-142
76SSPC-422
76T-142
77T-426
78PapaG/Disc-11
78T-567
79OPC-2
79T-12
80T-271
81D-336
81F-239
81OPC-332
81T-647
81T/Tr-755
82F-510
82T-742
89T/SenLg-17
89TM/SenLg-29
91Crown/Orio-113

Drahman, Brian
87Beloit-10
88Stockton/Cal-186
88Stockton/ProC-734
89ElPaso/GS-6
90BirmB/Best-15
90BirmB/ProC-1103
91B-363
91Kodak/WSox-50
91S/RookTr-81T
92F-77
92S/100RisSt-55
92S/II-734
92T-231
92T/91Debut-46

Drake, Bill
78Laugh/Black-8
86Negro/Frit-69

Drake, Delos Daniel
(Delos)
T207

Drake, H.P.
78LodiD

Drake, Kevin
74Cedar
75Dubuq

Drake, Sam
88CapeCod/Sum-131
89Helena/SP-22
90Beloit/Best-6
90Beloit/Star-6
91Stockton/ClBest-9
91Stockton/ProC-3027

Drake, Samuel H.
(Sammy)
62T-162
91WIZMets-99

Drake, Solomon L.
(Solly)
57T-159
59T-406
90Target-200

Drake, Tex
85Kingst-26
86Kinston-5bb
89Richm/ProC-819

Drake, Tom
90Target-201

Dramer, Tommy
90Kinston/Team-2

Draper, Mike
88Oneonta/ProC-2059
89PrWill/Star-6
90FtLaud/Star-5
91Albany/ProC-1000

Dravecky, David F.
(Dave)
79BuffB
80Buffa-4
81Hawaii-20
82Hawaii-20
83F-356
83T-384
84D-551
84D-8DK
84F-298
84Mother/Padres-11
84Nes/792-290
84Nes/792-366TL
84OPC-290
84Smok/Padres-7
84T-290
84T-366TL
84T/St-155
85D-112
85F-30
85Mother/Padres-8
85OPC-32
85T-530
85T/St-154
86D-162
86F-319
86Leaf-92
86OPC-276
86T-735
87Bohem-43
87D-187
87F-412
87F/Up-U28
87OPC-62
87T-470
87T/St-107
88D-485
88D/Best-135
88F-81
88F/BB/MVP-10
88F/St-127
88Mother/Giants-9
88S-564
88T-68
89F-327
89Mother/Giants-9
89T-601
89UD-39
90OPC-124
90Pac/Legend-80
90Panini/St-360
90Panini/St-386
90S-550
90T-124
90UD-679

Drawdy, Duke
77WHave

Drees, Tom
86Penin-8
87DayBe-4
88BirmB/Best-3
88SLAS-34
89AAA/ProC-29
89Vanco/CMC-10
89Vanco/ProC-588
90AAAGame/ProC-AAA38
90BirmDG/Best-7
90F-644R
90UD-3SR
90Vanco/CMC-3
90Vanco/ProC-483
91Vanco/LineD-631
91Vanco/ProC-1588
92T/91Debut-47

Dreifort, Darren
91T/Tr-34TUSA

Dreifort, Todd
90WichSt-9

Dreisbach, Bill
91Princet/ClBest-12
91Princet/ProC-3517

Drell, Tom
88CapeCod-1
88CapeCod/Sum-18
90Niagara/Pucko-17
91Lakeland/ClBest-2
91Lakeland/ProC-258

Dressen, Charles W.
(Chuck)
25Exh-28
26Exh-28
40PB-72
49Remar
50Remar
51B-259MG
52B-188MG
52T-377MG
53B/Col-124MG
53RM-NL1MG
53T-50MG
60Lake
60SpicSpan-8MG
60T-213MG
61T-137MG
64Det/Lids-5MG
64T-443MG
65T-538MG
66OPC-187MG
66T-187MG
79TCMA-56MG
83Kaline-29M
87Conlon/2-31
88Conlon/4-9
89Smok/Dodg-59
90Target-202
91T/Arc53-50MG
92Conlon/Sport-400
R312
R316
R346-8

Dressendorfer, Kirk
88CapeCod/Sum-134
90A&AASingle/ProC-163
90SoOreg/Best-3
90SoOreg/ProC-3425
91B-235
91Classic/200-159
91Classic/I-77
91Classic/II-T20
91D/Rook-24
91F/Up-U50
91Leaf/GRook-BC13
91Mother/A's-19
91OPC/Premier-36
91S/RookTr-97T
91T/Tr-35T
91UD/Ext-756
92D/II-594
92S/100RisSt-37
92S/II-728
92T-716
92T/91Debut-48

Dressler, Robert Alan
(Rob)
75Lafay
75Phoenix-11
76OPC-599R
76Phoenix
76T-599R
77Phoenix
77T-11
78Cram/PCL-57
79Spokane-19
80T-366
81D-405
81OPC-163
81T-508

Drew, Bob
75Lafay
82Madis-24M

Drew, Cameron
86Ashvl-8
87ColAst/ProC-7
87SLAS-7
88Tucson/CMC-14
88Tucson/ProC-188
88Tucson/JP-10
89B-334
89Classic-135
89D-30RR
89F-640R
89S-643RP
89S/HotRook-3
89Sf-225R

Drews, Karl August
(Karl)
49B-188
52T-352
53B/Col-113
53T-59
54B-191
91T/Arc53-59

Dreyer, Steve
91Gaston/ClBest-4
91Gaston/ProC-2681
91SALAS/ProC-SAL22

Dreyfuss, Barney
D322

Drezek, Karl
88AppFx/ProC-148
88Eugene/Best-21

Driessen, Daniel
(Dan)

74OPC-341
74T-341
74T/St-25
75OPC-133
75T-133
75T/M-133
76OPC-514
76SSPC-36
76T-514
77BurgChef-199
77OPC-31
77Pep-45
77T-23
78Ho-64
78OPC-84
78T-246
79K-26
79OPC-247
79T-475
80OPC-173
80T-325
81Coke
81D-301
81F-205
81F/St-22
81OPC-14
81T-655
81T/HT
81T/St-164
82Coke/Reds
82D-248
82F-64
82OPC-373
82T-785
83D-274
83F-589
83OPC-165
83T-165
83T/St-228
84D-243
84F-467
84Nes/792-585
84OPC-44
84T-585
84T/St-55
85D-619
85F-396
85Leaf-255
85OPC-285
85OPC/Post-2
85T-285
85T/St-92
86D-641
86F-539
86Leaf-255
86Mother/Giants-14
86T-65
86T/St-89
87Louisvl-12
88F/WS-7M
89Pac/SenLg-102
89Pac/SenLg-105IA
89T/SenLg-46
89TM/SenLg-30
90EliteSenLg-67
91Pac/SenLg-1

Driggers, Lee
90Augusta/ProC-2480MG
91Welland/ProC-3591MG

Drill, Lewis L.
(Lew)
E107

Drilling, Robert
49Sommer-20

Driscoll, James B.
(Jim)
71OPC-317R
71T-317R
85Water-19
86Water-7C

Driscoll, Jim
T3/Box-51

Driver, Ron
77Newar
78Holyo
79Holyo-11

Drizmala, Tom
83CharR-19

Drohan, Bill
88Eugene/Best-5
89AppFx/ProC-854
90BBCity/Star-6

Dromerhauser, Rob
85Newar-17

Dropo, Walter
(Walt)
50B-246
51T/CAS
52B-169
52T-235
53B/Col-45
53Glen
53RM-AL4
53T-121
54B-7
54T-18
55B-285
56T-238
57T-257
58T-338
59T-158
60T-79
61T-489
80Laugh/FFeat-36
89Swell-108
90Pac/Legend-22
90Swell/Great-57
91Crown/Orio-114
91Swell/Great-111
91T/Arc53-121
Exh47
R423-19

Droschak, Dave
83Spring/LF-5

Drott, Richard Fred
(Dick)
58T-80
59T-15
60L-76
60T-27
61T-231
79TCMA-64

Drucke, Louis
10Domino-39
11Helmar-126
12Sweet/Pin-113

Drummond, Tim
86PrWill-9
87Vanco-13
88Tidew/CANDL-18
88Tidew/CMC-4
88Tidew/ProC-1593
89Tidew/CMC-1
89Tidew/ProC-1952
90D-510
90D/Rook-50
90F/Up-107
90OPC-713
90S/Tr-103T
90T-713
91D-694
91F-607
91OPC-46
91Portl/LineD-406
91Portl/ProC-1560
91S-76
91S/100RisSt-95
91T-46
91UD-698

Drummonds, Lamar
63Pep/Tul

Drumright, Keith A.
78Charl
79Charl-1
81Tacoma-17
82D-616
82F-89
82T-673
82Tacoma-29

Drury, Scott
88Batavia/ProC-1668

Drysdale, Donald S.
(Don)
57T-18
58BB
58Hires-55
58T-25
59Bz
59Morrell
59T-262M
59T-387
60Armour-9
60Morrell
60P
60T-475
60T-570AS
60T/tatt-12
61Bz-26
61Morrell
61P-160
61T-260
61T-45LL
61T-49LL
61T/Dice-4
61T/St-26
62BB-53
62J-110
62P-110
62P/Can-110
62T-340
62T-398AS
62T-60LL
62T/bucks
62T/St-133
63Bz-17
63Exh
63F-41
63J-123
63P-123
63Salada-1
63T-360
63T-412M
63T-5LL
63T-7LL
63T-9LL
63T/SO
64T-120
64T-5LL
64T/Coins-34
64T/St-79
64T/SU
65OPC-12LL
65OPC-260
65OPC-8LL
65T-12LL
65T-260
65T-8LL
65T/E-15
65T/trans-47
66Bz-42
66T-223LL
66T-430
66T/RO-16
67Bz-42
67OPC-55
67OPC/PI-16
67T-55
67T/PI-16
67T/Test/SU-11
68Bz-15
68Bz-6
68OPC-145
68T-145
68T/Post-7
69MLBPA/Pin-41
69T-400
69T/decal
69T/S-46
69T/St-42
72Laugh/GF-38
78TCMA-3
82KMart-42
83MLBPA/Pin-23
84West/1-9
87Smok/Dodg-7
88Smok/Dodg-11
89AS/Cal-28
89Rini/Dodg-8
89Smok/Dodg-7
89T/LJN-153
90HOF/St-73
90Pac/Legend-29
90Swell/Great-62
90T/Gloss22-11CAPT
90Target-203
91CollAB-10
91LineD-1
91Swell/Great-26
Exh47

Drzayich, Emil
80Cedar-4
81Cedar-10

Duant, Rich
86LitFalls-9

Duarte, Luis
80Batavia-16
81Watlo

Dube, Greg
85Osceola/Team-6
87Wmsprt-19

DuBeau, Jack
78Watlo

Dubee, Rich
76Watlo
77DaytB
84Memphis-2
85Omaha-11
87Memphis-11
87Memphis/Best-3C
88Omaha/CMC-23
88Omaha/ProC-1494
89Omaha/ProC-1739
90Omaha/ProC-82CO
91Rockford/ClBest-16CO
91Rockford/ProC-2064CO

Dubiel, Walter John
(Monk)
47Centen-6
49Eureka-55
51B-283
52T-164

DuBois, Brian
86Hagers-5
87Hagers-4
88CLAS/Star-6
88Virgini/Star-8
89Hagers/Best-13
89Hagers/ProC-274
89Hagers/Star-5
90B-349
90Classic/Up-17
90CokeK/Tiger-3
90D-38RR
90D/Rook-4
90F-601
90HagersDG/Best-7
90Leaf/II-266
90OPC-413
90S-657RP
90T-413
90T/89Debut-32
90T/Big-272
90UD-78
91S/100RisSt-85

DuBose, Brian
90Bristol/ProC-3163
90Bristol/Star-5
91Niagara/ClBest-10
91Niagara/ProC-3640

Dubuc, Jean J.
(Jean)
15CJ-156
BF2-28
D329-52
D350/2-53
M101/4-52
M101/5-52
T206
T213/blue
T213/brown
T215/blue

Ducey, Rob
86Ventura-5
87D/HL-39
87Syrac-16
87Syrac/TCMA-19
87Tor/Fire-6
88F-107
88OPC-106
88S-629
88Syrac/CMC-14
88Syrac/ProC-825
88T-438
88Tor/Fire-40
89OPC-203
89Panini/St-459
89S/HotRook-7
89T-203
89T/Big-280
89Tor/Fire-40
89UD/Ext-721
90OPC-619
90PublInt/St-512
90S/YS/I-34
90Syrac/CMC-21
90Syrac/ProC-584
90Syrac/Team-6
90T-619
90UD-464
91AAAGame/ProC-AAA43
91D-705
91OPC-101
91S-821
91S/ToroBJ-22
91Syrac/LineD-502
91Syrac/ProC-2492
91T-101
91T/StClub/II-374
91Tor/Fire-20
92D/II-466
92F-328
92S/II-609
92T-739

Duchin, David
90LynchRS/Team-25TR
91LynchRS/ClBest-27TR

Duckett, Mahlon
86Negro/Frit-40
91Negro/Lewis-11

Duckworth, James R.
(Jim)
78TCMA-151
78TCMA-23

Dudek, Steve
91Johnson/ClBest-9
91Johnson/ProC-3983

Dudley, Clise
90Target-204

Duenas, Vernon
88CharWh/Best-11

Duensing, Larry
80Hawaii-3
81Hawaii-25
82Hawaii-25
84Cram/PCL-244tr

Dues, Hal Joseph
(Hal)
79OPC-373
79T-699
81OPC-71
81T-71

Duey, Kody
86Jamestn-5

Duey, Kyle
90MedHat/Best-5
91Myrtle/ClBest-3
91Myrtle/ProC-2937

Duezabou, Mel
47Remar-20
47Signal
47Smith-23
48Signal
48Smith-14
49Remar
50Remar

Duff, Dave
82Jacks-12

Duff, Scott
90Billings/ProC-3213
91CharWh/ClBest-3
91CharWh/ProC-2880

Duffalo, Jim
62T-578
63T-567
64T-573
65OPC-159
65T-159
78TCMA-204
78TCMA-249
80Phoenix-23
81Shrev-13

Duffee, Charles E.
(Charlie)
N172

Duffie, John
90Target-936

Duffy, Allen
86GlenF-3

Duffy, Darrin
86Cram/PCL-72
88Modesto-22
89WinSalem/Star-7
90T/TVCub-44

Duffy, Frank Thomas
(Frank)
71OPC-164R
71T-164R
72T-607
73OPC-376
73T-376
74OPC-81
74T-81
74T/St-163
75OPC-448
75T-448

75T/M-448
76Ho-115
76OPC-232
76SSPC-521
76T-232
77BurgChef-63
77OPC-253
77Pep-18
77T-542
78PapaG/Disc-17
78T-511
79OPC-47
79T-106

Duffy, Hugh
12Sweet/Pin-10A
12Sweet/Pin-10B
48Exh/HOF
50Callahan
63Bz/ATG-33
69Bz-4
80SSPC/HOF
87Conlon/2-33
90BBWit-67
90HOF/St-8
92Conlon/Sport-532
E90/1
M116
N172
N300/unif
S74-5
T205
T206
V100
WG3-16

Duffy, John
87GlenF-23
88Toledo/CMC-10
88Toledo/ProC-596
89Memphis/Best-2
89Memphis/ProC-1181
89Memphis/Star-9

Duffy, Tom
83VeroB-2

Dugan, Joseph Anthony
(Joe)
21Exh-37
21Exh-38
21Exh-39
28Yueng-3
29Exh/4-1
61F-103
88Conlon/5-8
91Conlon/Sport-112
E120
E210-3
E220
V100
W502-3
W513-66
W515-30
W573
WG7-13

Dugas, Augustin J.
(Gus)
R314/Can

Dugas, Shanie
81Watlo-21
82Chatt-13
83BuffB-15
84Maine-23
85Maine-17
87Albuq/Pol-18
88Albuq/CMC-22
88Albuq/ProC-266
89Albuq/CMC-13
89Albuq/ProC-85

Dugdale, Daniel E.
(Dan)
N172

Dugey, Oscar Joseph
(Oscar)
15CJ-60
D329-53
D350/2-54
M101/4-53
M101/5-54

Duggan, Tom
83Wausau/LF-21
86Salem-6

Dugger, Keith
91Spokane/ClBest-30

Dugger, Lonnie
81Holyo-13
82Holyo-4

Dugrahm
N172

Duke, Andy
89Billings/ProC-2056

Duke, Doug
87BurlEx-7
88Jaxvl/Best-22
89Jaxvl/Best-6
89Jaxvl/ProC-167

Duke, Ed
86ColumAst-11tr

Duke, Jerome
86Jamestn-6

Duke, Kyle
90Penin/Star-7
91BendB/ClBest-4
91BendB/ProC-3689

Duke, Martin F.
N172

Duke, Marvin
V355-116

Duke, Richard
87Idaho-6

Dukes, Jan Noble
(Jan)
70OPC-154R
70T-154R

Dukes, Kevin
82LynnS-3
83Chatt-19

Dukes, Thomas Earl
(Tom)
68OPC-128R
68T-128R
69T-223
71OPC-106
71T-106
91Crown/Orio-115

Dukes, Willie Jr.
90Elmira/Pucko-9
90WinHaven/Star-7
91WinHaven/ClBest-13
91WinHaven/ProC-493

Duliba, Robert John
(Bob)
60L-77
60T-401
62Kahn/Atl
62T-149
63T-97
64T-441
66OPC-53
66T-53
67T-599

Dulin, Tim
86Miami-5
87Hagers-10
88CharlK/Pep-5
88SLAS-9
89RochR/CMC-20
89RochR/ProC-1646
90RochR/CMC-16
90RochR/ProC-708

Dull, Darrell
83Idaho-19

Dull, Mike
87BurlEx-9
88WPalmB/Star-9
89Jaxvl/Best-7
89Jaxvl/ProC-164

Dulom, Kirk
90FtLaud/Star-6

Dumas, Don
87Savan-21

Dumouchelle, Pat
81Miami-8
84CharlO-13
90HagersDG/Best-8

Dumoulin, Dan
77Indianap-13
78Indianap-7
79Indianap-26

Dunbar, Matt
88CapeCod/Sum-65
90Oneonta/ProC-3382
91Greens/ProC-3050

Dunbar, Thomas Jerome
(Tommy)
82Tulsa-10
83OKCty-7
84D-28RR
84OKCty-18
84Rangers-13
85D-159
85F/Up-U37
85Rangers-13
85T-102
86D-221
86OKCty-5
86T-559
87Vanco-6
88Greenvl/Best-21
89Greenvl/ProC-1179
89Greenvl/Star-7
89Greenvl/Best-26
90Memphis/Best-11
90Memphis/ProC-1023
90Memphis/Star-9
90TulsaDG/Best-24
91Omaha/LineD-333
91Omaha/ProC-1046

Duncan, Andres
91Clinton/ClBest-13
91Clinton/ProC-841
91Single/ClBest-322

Duncan, C.
(Duke)
78Newar
79Holyo-27

Duncan, Chip
87Watertn-6
88Salem/Star-5
89Salem/Star-7
90Salem/Star-4
91CaroMud/LineD-105
91CaroMud/ProC-1079

Duncan, David Edwin
(Dave)
64T-528R
68T-261
69OPC-68
69T-68
69T/St-214
70T-678
71MLB/St-511
71OPC-178
71T-178
72OPC-17
72T-17
73OPC-337
73T-337
74OPC-284
74T-284
74T/St-164
75OPC-238
75OPC-626
75T-238
75T/M-238
76OPC-49
76SSPC-383
76T-49
77T-338
87Mother/A's-8CO
90Mother/A's-27M
91Crown/Orio-116
91Mother/A's-28CO

Duncan, Doug
76SanAn/Team-9
77Visalia

Duncan, Frank
86Negro/Frit-118

Duncan, John
83Wausau/LF-26

Duncan, Lindy
81Tulsa-25

Duncan, Louis Baird
(Pat)
21Exh-40
88Pac/8Men-94
E120
V100
V61-109
W572
WG7-14

Duncan, Mariano
83VeroB-16
85Coke/Dodg-10
85F/Up-U38
85T/Tr-32T
86Coke/Dodg-8
86D-128
86F-129
86F/LL-10
86F/Mini-27
86F/St-33
86KayBee-8
86Leaf-50
86OPC-296
86Pol/Dodg-25
86T-602
87D-253
87D/OD-84
87F-439
87Mother/Dodg-7
87OPC-199
87Pol/Dodg-12
87Seven-W2
87T-199
87T/Mini-13
87T/St-74
88Albuq/CMC-23
88Albuq/ProC-255
88D-155
88F-513
88OPC-181
88Pol/Dodg-25
88S-321
88T-481
89Mother/Dodg-26
89Pol/Dodg-15
90D-684
90D/BestNL-113
90F/Up-U12
90Kahn/Reds-9
90Leaf/I-202
90OPC-234
90S-506
90T-234
90T/Big-243
90Target-205
90UD-430
91B-675
91D-309
91F-64
91F/Ultra-94
91Kahn/Reds-7
91Leaf/II-494
91Leaf/Stud-164
91OPC-13
91Panini/FrSt-128
91Panini/St-123
91Pep/Reds-9
91S-479
91T-13
91T/StClub/I-251
91UD-112
92D/II-540
92F-406
92S/I-352
92T-589
92UD-659

Duncan, Michael
86Modesto-8
87Modesto-4

Duncan, Rick
78OrlTw

Duncan, Taylor M.
79T-658
89Pac/SenLg-70

Duncan, Tim
80Elmira-20

Duncun, John
86Chatt-9

Dundik, Alexander
89EastLDD/ProC-DD10

Dunegan, James W. Jr.
(Jim)
71OPC-121R
71T-121R

Dunlap, Frederick C.
(Fred)
N162
N172
N284
Scrapps
WG1-58

Dunlap, Joe
86Cedar/TCMA-15
87Vermont-10
89Calgary/CMC-18
89Calgary/ProC-529
89EastLDD/ProC-DD30

Dunlap, Paul
V355-125

Dunlap, Travis
90Pulaski/Best-3
90Pulaski/ProC-3099

Dunleavy, John E.
WG3-17

Dunlop, Harry
73OPC-593CO
73T-593CO
74T-166CO
84Smok/SDP-8CO

Dunn
N172

Dunn, Brian
90Pittsfld/Pucko-12

Dunn, Bubba
91BBCity/ClBest-3
91BBCity/ProC-1390

Dunn, Greg
82Spring-13
83Spring/LF-14
85Spring-8
86Louisvl-10

Dunn, James William
(Jim)
81Shrev-3

Dunn, John Joseph
(Jack)
90Target-206
C46-19
E107
E254
T205
T206

Dunn, Joseph Edward
(Joe)
T205
T206
T213/brown

Dunn, Mike
82Clinton-14

Dunn, Ronald Ray
(Ron)
76SSPC-322

Dunn, Steve
88QuadC/GS-10

Dunn, Steve R.
89Elizab/Star-7
89Kenosha/ProC-1073
89Kenosha/Star-4
90Foil/Best-12
90Kenosha/Best-1
90Kenosha/ProC-2299
90Kenosha/Star-3
90PalmSp/Cal-220
90PalmSp/ProC-2571
91Single/ClBest-241
91Visalia/ClBest-15
91Visalia/ProC-1747

Dunne, Mike
85T-395OLY
86Louisvl-11
87D/Rook-38
87F/Up-U29
87Sf/Rook-40
87T/Tr-30T
87Vanco-15
88Classic/Blue-237
88D-390
88D/Best-89
88F-328
88F/AwardWin-10
88F/BB/MVP-11
88F/Mini-104
88F/RecSet-11
88F/St-115
88Leaf-235
88OPC-224
88Panini/St-367
88S-432
88S/YS/I-26
88Sf-171
88T-619
88T/Big-236
88T/Coins-40
88T/Gloss60-19
88T/JumboR-16
88T/Mini-68
88T/RiteAid-9
88T/St-132
88T/St-307
88T/UK-21
88ToysRUs-10
89B-412
89D-269
89F-207
89OPC-165

89Panini/St-162
89S-285
89T-165
89T/St-130
89UD-518
89VFJuice-41
90Leaf/II-418
90OPC-522
90Padre/MagUno-19
90T-522
91OPC-238
91T-238
Dunnegan, Steve
82DayBe-11
Dunning, Stephen John
(Steve)
71OPC-294
71T-294
72T-658
73OPC-53
73T-53
78T-647
Dunnum, Rick
88AubAs/ProC-1969
89Ashvl/ProC-964
90Osceola/Star-7
91Reading/LineD-508
91Reading/ProC-1367
Dunster, Don
86Osceola-6
87Osceola-19
88ColAst/Best-2
Dunston, Shawon
83QuadC-20
84MidldC-22
85D-39RR
85F-649R
85T-280FDP
86Cub/Unocal-6
86D-311
86F-366
86F/Mini-77
86F/St-34
86Gator-12
86Jay's-6
86KayBee-9
86Leaf-181
86Sf-155
86T-72
87Berg/Cubs-12
87D-119
87D/OD-76
87F-561
87F/GameWin-13
87F/Mini-35
87F/RecSet-6
87F/St-36
87Leaf-128
87OPC-346
87RedFoley/St-94
87Sf-79M
87Sf-98
87Seven-C4
87T-346
87T/St-59
88Berg/Cubs-12
88D-146
88D/Best-37
88D/Cubs/Bk-146
88F-419
88Leaf-70
88OPC-277
88Panini/St-264
88S-529
88S/YS/II-18
88Sf-163
88T-695
88T/Big-225
88T/St-65
88T/St/Backs-11
89B-294
89Cadaco-15
89D-137
89D/AS-43
89D/Best-93
89F-424
89KMart/DT-26
89Mara/Cubs-12
89OPC-140
89Panini/St-58
89RedFoley/St-38
89S-235
89Sf-190
89T-140
89T/Big-233
89T/St-49
89T/St/Backs-43
89UD-107
90B-38
90Cub/Mara-7
90D-49
90D/BestNL-112
90F-30
90Leaf/I-229
90MLBPA/Pins-46
90OPC-415
90Panini/St-236
90PublInt/St-193
90S-169
90T-415
90T/Big-62
90T/DH-18
90T/Gloss60-45
90T/St-53
90T/TVCub-22
90UD-231
90USPlayC/AS-10D
91B-424
91Classic/200-27
91Cub/Mara-12
91D-686
91F-420
91F/Ultra-59
91Leaf/I-25
91Leaf/Stud-155
91OPC-765
91OPC/Premier-37
91Panini/FrSt-46
91Panini/St-47
91RedFoley/St-29
91S-201
91S-413RIF
91S/100SS-45
91T-765
91T/CJMini/II-23
91T/StClub/I-3
91UD-111
92D/II-613
92F-380
92S/II-634
92T-370
92T/GPromo-370
92T/Promo-3
92UD-122
92UD-35TC
Dunton, Kevin
86WPalmB-14
Dupont, Margaret
51BR-D13
Dupree, Michael D.
(Mike)
77T-491R
79Hawaii-19
Duquette, Bryan
83ElPaso-5
84ElPaso-11
85Cram/PCL-212
86Vanco-11
Duquette, Chuck
88Fayette/ProC-1089
Duran, Daniel James
(Dan)
74Gaston
76SanAn/Team-10
80Charl-12
Duran, Dave
(Pitcher)
81Holyo-14
82Holyo-5
Duran, Felipe
91BurlInd/ProC-3307
Duran, Ignacio
90Savan/ProC-2072
91Single/ClBest-283
91Spring/ClBest-13
91Spring/ProC-748
Duran, Rick
79Holyo-14
Durant, Mike
91Classic/DP-42
91FrRow/DP-17
Durant, Richard
87Columbia-25
88Clmbia/GS-3
89Stockton/Best-7
89Stockton/Cal-155
89Stockton/ProC-388
89Stockton/Star-19
Duren, Rinold George
(Ryne)
58T-296
59T-485
60L-22
60T-204
60T/tatt-13
61P-14
61T-356
62J-81
62P-81
62P/Can-81
62Salada-46A
62Salada-46B
62Shirriff-46
62T-388
63T-17
64T-173
65T-339
79TCMA-135
89Pac/Leg-141
91Crown/Orio-117
Durham, Donald Gary
(Don)
73OPC-548
73T-548
Durham, Edward Fant
(Bull)
34G-79
90Target-207
Durham, Joseph Vann
(Joe)
58T-96
90Hagers/Best-6CO
90Hagers/ProC-1433CO
90Hagers/Star-28CO
91Crown/Orio-118
91Hagers/LineD-250CO
91Hagers/ProC-2472CO
Durham, Leon
81Coke
81D-427
81F-540
81OPC-321
81T-321
81T/HT
81T/Tr-756
82D-151
82F-595
82F/St-94
82OPC-206
82RedLob
82T-607
82T/St-25
83D-477
83D/AAS-55
83F-495
83K-27
83OPC-125
83T-125
83T-51TL
83T/St-219
83Thorn-10
84D-5DK
84D-67
84F-492
85FunFood/Pin-107
84Nes/792-565
84OPC-209
84SevenUp-10
84T-565
84T/St-40
85D-189
85D/AAS-46
85F-56
85Leaf-238
85OPC-330
85Seven-8G
85SevenUp-10
85T-330
85T/Gloss40-11
85T/St-36
86Cub/Unocal-7
86D-320
86F-367
86F/LL-11
86F/Mini-78
86F/St-35
86Gator-10
86Leaf-190
86OPC-58
86Sf-111
86T-460
86T/St-60
87Berg/Cubs-10
87D-242
87D/OD-74
87F-562
87F/Hottest-15
87Leaf-125
87OPC-290
87RedFoley/St-120
87Sf-185
87Seven-C6
87T-290
87T/Board-26
87T/St-57
88D-191
88D/Cubs/Bk-191
88F-420
88Kahn/Reds-10
88OPC-65
88Panini/St-259
88S-378
88T-65
88T/Big-42
88T/St-63
89Louisvl-16
89Louisvl/CMC-16
89Louisvl/ProC-1260
89UD-354
Durham, Louis
E97
T206
W555
Durham, Ray
91Utica/ClBest-6
91Utica/ProC-3246
Durham, Shane
87Anchora-7
Durkin, Chris
91AubAS/ClBest-19
91AubAS/ProC-4285
91FrRow/DP-8
Durkin, Martin
(Marty)
88CapeCod/Sum-128
89Watertn/Star-4
90Miami/I/Star-6
90Miami/II/Star-5
91WPalmB/ClBest-25
91WPalmB/ProC-1240
Durnan, Bill
51BR-A17
Durney, Bill
88PalmSp/Cal-115
88PalmSp/ProC-1462
89BendB/Legoe-29TR
Durning, Dick
90Target-937
Durocher, Francois
86Osceola-7
Durocher, Leo Ernest
(Leo)
29Exh/4-26
31Exh/4-7
33G-147
34G-7
35BU-156
38Exh/4-2
39PB-6
41DP-142
49Eureka-102
50B-220MG
51B-233MG
52B-146MG
52RM-NL1
52T-315MG
53B/Col-55MG
55Gol/Giants-6
67T-481MG
68T-321MG
69OPC-147MG
69T-147
70OPC-291MG
70T-291MG
71OPC-609MG
71T-609MG
72T-576MG
73OPC-624MG
73T-624MG
79TCMA-201MG
80Pac/Leg-40
86Conlon/1-11
88Conlon/3-10
88Pac/Leg-27
89Rini/Dodg-28M
89Rini/Dodg-30
89Smok/Dodg-39
90Target-208
91T/Arc53-309MG
R310
R346-2
V353-74
V354-69
V355-25
Durrett, Red
90Target-938
Durrman, Jim
81WHave-8
83Albany-9
Durst, Cedric
91Conlon/Sport-108
DuRussel, Scott
91Niagara/ProC-3626
Duryea, James Whitney
(Jesse)
N172
Dusak, Ervin Frank
(Erv)
47TipTop
51B-310
52T-183
79TCMA-122
Dusan, Gene
75OkCty
77Watlo
79Tacoma-24
80Tacoma-23
82Jacks-22
84Wichita/Rock-22
86Cedr/TCM-25MG
Dustal, Robert Andrew
(Bob)
63T-299R
Duval, Michael
(Mickey)
79Indianap-27
82Madis-24M
DuVall, Brad
88Hamil/ProC-1722
89B-430
89Spring/Best-4
90StPete/Star-5
90T/TVCard-45
Dwyer, James Edward
(Jim)
75OPC-429
75T-429
75T/M-429
76OPC-94
76SSPC-341
76T-94
78T-644
79T-236
80T-577
81D-577
81F-235
81OPC-184
81T-184
81T/Tr-757
82D-64
82F-164
82T-359
83D-583
83F-59
83T-718
84D-454
84F-7
84F/St-117
84Nes/792-473
84T-473
85F-176
85T-56
86D-413
86F-274
86OPC-339
86T-653
87D-418
87F-469
87French-9
87T-246
88D-459
88F-558
88French-9
88S-229
88T-521
89D/Best-311
90D-484

90PublInt/St-325
91Crown/Orio-119
91Pac/SenLg-118
91Portl/LineD-425CO
91Portl/ProC-1582CO
91WIZMets-100

Dwyer, John Francis
(Frank)
N172

Dybzinski, Jerome M.
(Jerry)
78Watlo
79Tacoma-13
81D-438
81F-399
81OPC-198
81T-198
82D-647
82F-366
82T-512
82Wheat/Ind
83D-576
83F-406
83T-289
83T/Tr-27
84D-160
84F-57
84Nes/792-619
84T-619
84TrueVal/WS-11
85Cram/PCL-250
85F-512
85T-52
86Calgary-7

Dyce, George
89Nashvl/Team-27VP

Dyck, James Robert
(Jim)
53B/C-111
53NB
53T-177
54B-85
56T-303
91Crown/Orio-120
91T/Arc53-177

Dye, Mark
82Idaho-18

Dye, Scott
80Water-8
81Tidew-15
82Jacks-4
83Tidew-14

Dye, Steve
89Modesto/Cal-269
89Modesto/Chong-9

Dyer, Don Robert
(Duffy)
69T-624R
70T-692
71MLB/St-150
71OPC-136
71T-136
72OPC-127
72T-127
73OPC-493
73T-493
74OPC-536
74T-536
75OPC-538
75T-538
75T/M-538
76OPC-88
76SSPC-581
76T-88
77BurgChef-185
77T-318
78T-637
79T-286
80OPC-232
80T-446
81D-7
81T-196
83Thorn-26CO
86ElPaso-9MG
87ElPaso-14MG
88Denver/CMC-25
88Denver/ProC-1264
90Brewer/MillB-32CO
90ElPasoATG/Team-20
90Pol/Brew-x
91Brewer/MillB-32
91Pol/Brew-x
91WIZMets-101

Dyer, Eddie
49Eureka-181
92Conlon/Sport-618

Dyer, Hal
87CharWh-14

Dyer, John
78Green

Dyer, Linton
88AppFx/ProC-143
89AppFx/ProC-867
90BBCity/Star-7

Dyer, Mike
87Kenosha-11
88OrlanTw/Best-9
89Portl/CMC-8
89Portl/ProC-228
90D-642
90F-372
90OPC-576
90Portl/CMC-6
90Portl/ProC-173
90S-571
90T-576
90T/89Debut-33
90UD-374

Dyes, Andy
78Syrac
79Hawaii-5
80Hawaii-24

Dygert, James Henry
(Jimmy)
12Sweet/Pin-44
C46-45
E104
E90/1
E97
M116
S74-30
T201
T205
T206
T208
T3-92
W555

Dyke, Bill
89Knoxvl/ProC-1120

Dykes, James Joseph
(Jimmy)
21Exh-41
25Exh-106
26Exh-107
29Exh/4-28
31Exh/4-27
32Orbit/num-11
32Orbit/un-16
33DH-12
33DL-18
33G-6
34DS-42
34Ward's/Pin-2
35BU-159
35BU-29
35Exh/4-10
35G-1I
35G-2F
35G-6F
35G-7F
36Exh/4-10
36G
37Exh/4-10
40PB-187
47Signal
51B-226MG
52B-98MG
53B/Col-31MG
54Esskay
60T-214MG
61Kahn
61T-222MG
78TCMA-224
87Conlon/2-37
88Conlon/4-10
91Conlon/Sport-92
91T/Arc53-281MG
E120
E210-51
E220
R300
R305
R308-167
R311/Gloss
R314
R316
R337-410
V100
V353-6
V355-1
W517-22
W572

Dykstra, Kevin
90AS/Cal-32UMP

Dykstra, Len
83Lynch-15
84Jacks-18
85Tidew-20
86D-482
86F-78
86OPC-53
86T-53
87Classic-2
87D-611
87F-6
87F/Lim-13
87Leaf-88
87OPC-295
87Sf-58
87Seven-E4
87Seven-ME5
87T-295
87T/HL-23
87T/Mets/Fan-3
87T/St-13
87T/St-21WS
87T/St-98
87Woolwth-23
88D-364
88D/Best-264
88D/Mets/Bk-364
88F-133
88Kahn/Mets-4
88Leaf-135
88OPC-299
88Panini/St-345
88S-370
88S/YS/II-19
88Sf-106
88T-655
88T/Big-203
88T/Mini-59
89Classic-36
89D-353
89D/Best-159
89F-33
89F/Up-105
89OPC-349
89Panini/St-138
89Phill/TastyK-40
89S-84
89S/Tr-28
89Sf-123
89T-435
89T/Big-41
89T/DHTest-12
89T/St-90
89T/Tr-27T
89UD-369
90B-152
90Classic/Up-18
90D-313
90D/BestNL-118
90F-556
90Leaf/I-262
90MLBPA/Pins-5
90OPC-515
90Panini/St-313
90Phill/TastyK-8
90PublInt/St-131
90RedFoley/St-28
90S-427
90S/McDon-14
90Sf-156
90T-515
90T/Big-300
90T/St-118
90UD-472
90USPlayC/AS-9D
91B-501
91BBBest/HitM-6
91Classic/200-133
91Classic/I-78
91CollAB-8
91D-410MVP
91D-434AS
91D-523
91D-744M
91D-7DK
91D/SuperDK-7DK
91F-395
91F/Ultra-262
91Leaf/I-163
91Leaf/Prev-8
91Leaf/Stud-213
91MajorLg/Pins-60
91MooTown-18
91OPC-345
91Panini/FrSt-108
91Panini/FrSt-163
91Panini/St-103
91Panini/Top15-26
91Panini/Top15-4
91Pep/SS-16
91Phill/Medford-13
91Post-8
91Post/Can-6
91RedFoley/St-119
91RedFoley/St-30
91S-250
91S-867FRAN
91S/100SS-11
91Seven/3DCoin-4NE
91Sunflower-9
91T-345
91T/CJMini/I-21
91T/StClub/I-150
91T/SU-12
91UD-267
91UD-97TC
91WIZMets-102
92Classic/I-30
92D/I-57
92F-529
92F/TmLIns-10
92S/100SS-86
92S/II-560
92T-200
92UD-246

Dyson, Ted
88PalmSp/Cal-103

Dyson, Tim
88PalmSp/ProC-1453

Dzafic, Bernie
88Elmira-5
89WinHaven/Star-5

Dziadkowiec, Andy
87Myrtle-27
89Dunedin/Star-4
90Knoxvl/Best-17
90Knoxvl/Star-3
90Syrac/CMC-25
90Syrac/ProC-573
91Miami/ClBest-17
91Miami/ProC-411

Eagar, Brad
87Anchora-8
89Medford/Best-7

Eagar, Steve
86Lakeland-5

Eagelston, Chris
86Hagers-6

Eagen, Charles
E254
M116

Eakes, Steven
82Redwd-2
83Redwd-9

Ealy, Thomas
(Tom)
85Everett/Cram-4
86Clinton-6
86Cram/PCL-200
87Clinton-12
88Clinton/ProC-718
89SanJose/Best-14
89SanJose/Cal-231
89SanJose/ProC-434
89SanJose/Star-8
90Shrev/ProC-1454
90Shrev/Star-7
91Shrev/LineD-304
91Shrev/ProC-1834

Ealy, Tracey
90Johnson/Star-10
91Savan/ClBest-24
91Savan/ProC-1665

Eaman, Bob
89London/ProC-1359

Earl, Scottie
83BirmB-17
84Evansvl-14
85D-491
86Nashvl-7
87Toledo-1
87Toledo/TCMA-10
88Nashvl/CMC-19
88Nashvl/ProC-471
88Nashvl/Team-9
90BirmDG/Best-8

Earle, William
(Billy)
90Target-209
N172

Earley, Arnold Carl
(Arnie)
67T-388
78TCMA-209

Earley, Bill
83Iowa-2
84Iowa-2
85OKCty-30
86Louisvl-12
87Louisvl-13
88Wythe/ProC-1989
89CharWh/Best-24
89CharWh/ProC-1754
90WinSalem/Team-28
91WinSalem/ClBest-21
91WinSalem/ProC-2846CO

Earls, Peter
82Tucson-28M

Early, Jacob Willard
(Jake)
48L-61
49B-106

Earnshaw, George L.
(George)
32Orbit/num-38
32Orbit/un-17
33DH-13
34Exh/4-10
34G-41
35G-1I
35G-2F
35G-6F
35G-7F
40PB-233
90Target-210
91Conlon/Sport-88
R305
R306
R308-169
R310
R312/M
R328-29
R332-13
V354-93
W517-8

Easler, Michael A.
(Mike)
75Iowa/TCMA-7
76Tulsa
78Colum
78T-710R
80T-194
81Coke
81D-256
81F-372
81F/St-74
81OPC-92
81T-92
81T/SO-81
81T/St-212
82D-221
82F-481
82K-49
82OPC-235
82T-235
82T/St-84
83D-221
83F-306
83OPC-385
83T-385
84D-444
84F-249
84F/X-33
84Nes/792-589
84OPC-353
84T-589
84T/St-137
84T/Tr-33
85D-213
85F-157
85F/St-46
85Leaf-206

85OPC-349
85T-686
85T/St-213
86D-395
86F-347
86F/Up-U37
86T-477
86T/St-255
86T/Tr-33T
87D-277
87D/OD-155
87F-97
87F/AS-7
87Leaf-192
87OPC-135
87Phill/TastyK-34
87Sf-92
87T-135
87T/St-295
88F-206
88OPC-9
88S-220
88T-741
89T/SenLg-80
90EliteSenLg-19
90Miami/I/Star-28MG
90Miami/II/Star-26MG

Easley, Damion
89BendB/Legoe-16
91London/LineD-433
91MidldA/ProC-440
91Single/ClBest-121

Easley, Logan
83Greens-5
85Albany-5
86Albany/TCMA-17
88BuffB/CMC-1
88BuffB/ProC-1490
90AlbanyDG/Best-5
90Denver/ProC-619

Easley, Mike
90Reno/Cal-266
91CLAS/ProC-CAR12
91Kinston/ClBest-15
91Kinston/ProC-327

Eason, Greg
80Ashvl-26

Eason, Mal
90Target-939
92Conlon/Sport-375

Eason, Tommy
91Batavia/ClBest-3
91Batavia/ProC-3485

Easter, Dick
84Iowa-4

Easter, Luscious Luke
(Luke)
50NumNum
51B-258
51T/RB-26
52B-95
52NumNum-12
52T-24
53B/Col-104
53Exh/Can-2
53T-2
54B-116
54DanDee
54T-23
79TCMA-80
86Negro/Frit-83
88MinorLg/Leg-5
91T/Arc53-2
D301
Exh47
PM10/Sm-47

Easterly, James M.
(Jamie)
75OPC-618R
75T-618R
75T/M-618R
76OPC-511
76T-511
78T-264
79Richm-11
79T-684
82D-623
82F-139
82Pol/Brew-28
82T-122
83D-280
83F-31
83Pol/Brew-28
83T-528
83T/Tr-28
84F-538
84Nes/792-367
84T-367
84T/St-258
85F-445
85Polar/Ind-36
85T-764
86D-582
86F-585
86OhHenry-36
86T-31
87Gator-11
89Pac/SenLg-189
89TM/SenLg-31
90EliteSenLg-54

Easterly, Theodore H.
(Ted)
14CJ-117
15CJ-117
T206
T207

Eastman, Doug
88Cedar/ProC-1153
89Cedar/Best-20
89Cedar/ProC-923
89Cedar/Star-5

Eastwick, Rawlins J.
(Rawley)
75OPC-621R
75T-621R
75T/M-621R
76Icee
76OPC-469
76T-469
77OPC-140
77OPC-8LL
77Pep-55
77T-45
77T-8LL
78BK/Y-11
78T-405
79T-271
80T-692
82F-596
82T-117

Eatinger, Michael
90Foil/Best-222
90SoBend/Best-18

Eaton, Craig
76Watlo
77DaytB
80SLCity-3
81SLCity-4
82Spokane-2
83Evansvl-2
84Indianap-8

Eaton, Dann
91Spring/ClBest-14
91Spring/ProC-736

Eaton, Tom R.
81RochR-5

Eave, Gary
87Durham-19
88Richm-31
88Richm/CMC-5
88Richm/ProC-26
89Richm/Bob-5
89Richm/CMC-2
89Richm/Ko-31
89Richm/ProC-828
90B-471
90D-713
90S-621
91Jaxvl/LineD-333
91Jaxvl/ProC-143

Ebbetts, Charlie
90Target-940

Ebel, Brian
89Hagers/Best-16
89Hagers/ProC-284

Ebel, Dino
89VeroB/Star-8
90VeroB/Star-12
91SanAn/ProC-2981

Eberle, Mike
88CLAS/Star-7
88Hagers/Star-4
89Hagers/Best-12
89Hagers/ProC-270
89Hagers/Star-6
90Foil/Best-199
90Hagers/Best-4
90Hagers/ProC-1415
90Hagers/Star-8
91RochR/LineD-455
91RochR/ProC-1905

Eberle, Greg
89Peoria/Ko-27MG

Eberly, Ryan
90Tampa/DIMD-4

Ebersberger, Randy
82Clinton-24

Ebert, Scott
88Pocatel/ProC-2080
89Everett/Star-7
90ClintUp/Team-U3
90Everett/ProC-3118

Ebright, Chris
88CapeCod/Sum-33
89Geneva/ProC-1876
90Peoria/Team-16
91CLAS/ProC-CAR41
91WinSalem/ClBest-23
91WinSalem/ProC-3840

Ebright, Hiram C.
(Hi)
N172

Eccles, John
85Anchora-9
87Orlan-4
88CalLgAS-38
88Visalia/Cal-150
88Visalia/ProC-84
89Orlan/ProC-1351
90OrlanSR/Best-2
90OrlanSR/ProC-1086
90OrlanSR/Star-4

Eccleston, Tom
86Wausau-9

Echemendia, Idaiberto
(Bert)
88James/ProC-1906
89Star/Wax-33
89WPalmB/Star-10

Echevarria, Francisco
84Everett/Cram-17

Echevarria, Robert
87Elmira/Black-7
87Elmira/Red-7

Echols, Tony
76Wausau

Eckard, Paul
91Everett/ClBest-29TR

Eckersley, Dennis Lee
(Dennis)
76Ho-137
76K-19
76OPC-202LL
76OPC-98
76SSPC-506
76T-202LL
76T-98
77BurgChef-58
77Ho-106
77OPC-15
77Pep-13
77T-525
78Ho-78
78OPC-138
78PapaG/Disc-5
78T-122
78Wiffle/Discs-20
79Ho-145
79K-9
79OPC-16
79T-40
80OPC-169
80T-320
81Coke
81D-96
81F-226
81F/St-34
81OPC-109
81T-620
81T/HT
81T/St-48
82Coke/BOS
82D-30
82F-292
82F/St-165
82OPC-287
82PermaGr/AS-1
82T-490
83D-487
83F-182
83F-629M
83OPC-270
83T-270
83T/St-34
84D-639
84F-396
84F/X-34
84Nes/792-745
84OPC-218
84SevenUp-43
84T-745
84T/St-224
84T/Tr-34
85D-442
85F-57
85OPC-163
85SevenUp-43
85T-163
86Cub/Unocal-8
86D-239
86F-368
86Gator-43
86Leaf-113
86OPC-199
86Sf-129M
86T-538
86T/St-62
87D-365
87F-563
87F/Up-U30
87OPC-381
87Seven-C8
87T-459
87T/St-63
87T/Tr-31T
88D-349
88D/A's/Bk-349
88D/Best-43
88F-279
88F/Slug-13
88Mother/A's-10
88OPC-72
88S-104
88T-72
88T/St-170
89B-190
89Cadaco-16
89Classic-90
89D-67
89D/AS-16
89D/Best-134
89F-7
89F/AS-4
89F/BBAS-12
89F/Heroes-13
89Mother/A's-10
89OPC-370
89Panini/St-12
89Panini/St-414
89RedFoley/St-39
89S-276
89S/HotStar-16
89Sf-101
89Sf-222M
89T-370
89T/DH-11
89T/Gloss60-16
89T/Hills-12
89T/LJN-20
89T/Mini-69
89T/St-167
89T/St/Backs-31
89T/UK-23
89UD-289
89Woolwth-20
90B-451
90D-210
90D/BestAL-12
90F-6
90F/LL-11
90KayBee-9
90KMart/SS-29
90Leaf/I-29
90Leaf/Prev-3
90MLBPA/Pins-75
90Mother/A's-7
90OPC-670
90Panini/St-137
90PublInt/St-282
90PublInt/St-303
90RedFoley/St-29
90S-315
90Sf-170
90T-670
90T/Big-50
90T/DH-19
90T/Gloss60-53
90T/HeadsUp-4
90T/Mini-27
90T/St-182
90T/TVAS-13
90UD-513
90USPlayC/AS-8C
91B-237
91BBBest/Aces-6
91Classic/200-126
91Classic/II-T18
91D-270
91F-6
91F/Ultra-245
91Leaf/II-285
91Leaf/Stud-102
91Mother/A's-7
91OPC-250
91OPC/Premier-38
91Panini/FrSt-200
91Panini/St-148
91Panini/Top15-86
91RedFoley/St-31
91S-485
91S/100SS-73
91Seven/3DCoin-5NC
91SFExam/A's-3
91T-250
91T/StClub/II-332
91UD-172
91USPlayC/AS-10D
92D/I-147
92D/Preview-5
92F-255
92S/100SS-56
92S/I-190
92T-738
92UD-331

Eckhardt, Ox
90Target-211

Eckhardt, Tom
89Idaho/ProC-2030

Economy, Scott
88Billings/ProC-1814
89Cedar/Best-9
89Cedar/ProC-921
89Cedar/Star-6
90Cedar/ProC-2317

Eddings, Jay
88CharWh/Best-12
89CharWh/Best-21
89CharWh/ProC-1766
89Peoria/Ko-6
90Peoria/Team-21

Eddins, Glenn Jr.
79Elmira-6
81Bristol-18

Eddy, Donald Eugene
(Don)
72OPC-413R
72T-413R

Eddy, Jim
90Rockford/ProC-2691
91WPalmB/ClBest-5
91WPalmB/ProC-1221

Eddy, Martin
88BurlInd/ProC-1775

Eddy, Steven Allen
(Steve)
76QuadC
80SLCity-17

Edelen, Benny Joe
(Joe)
77StPete
80ArkTr-1
82F-65
83Indianap-8

Eden, Edward Michael
(Mike)
75Phoenix-16
76Phoenix
79RochR-9
80RochR-12

Edenfield, Ken
90Boise/ProC-3308
91QuadC/ClBest-3
91QuadC/ProC-2620
91Single/ClBest-260

Edens, Tom
83Butte-4

86Jacks/TCMA-4
87Tidew-9
87Tidew/TCMA-2
88Tidew/CANDL-19
88Tidew/CMC-5
88Tidew/ProC-1581
89Tidew/CMC-2
89Tidew/ProC-1956
90Brewer/MillB-6
90Denver/CMC-4
90Denver/ProC-620
91AAAGame/ProC-AAA35
91D-590
91F-582
91OPC-118
91Portl/LineD-407
91Portl/ProC-1561
91S-78
91S/100RisSt-2
91T-118
91UD-616
91WIZMets-103
92S/II-720

Edge, Alvin
76BurlB
78BurlB

Edge, Claude Lee Jr.
(Butch)
76BurlB
78Syrac
79Syrac-9
80OPC-329R
80Richm-3
80T-674R
81Richm-11
82Portl-2

Edge, Greg
86Clearw-7
87Reading-4
88EastLAS/ProC-32
88Reading/ProC-880
89ElPaso/GS-21
89Reading/Best-16
89Reading/ProC-666
91CaroMud/LineD-106
91CaroMud/ProC-1092

Edge, Tim
90Welland/Pucko-16
91Salem/ClBest-1
91Salem/ProC-955

Edgerton, Bill
No Cards.

Ediger, Lance
78Newar

Edler, David Delmar
(Dave)
80Spokane-15
81F-610
81Pol/Mariners-7
82Omaha-16
82T-711
83T-622

Edmonds, Bobby Joe
89Reading/Best-17
89Reading/ProC-673
89Reading/Star-10

Edmonds, Jim
89QuadC/Best-27
89QuadC/GS-6
90AS/Cal-6
91PalmSp/ProC-2028

Edmonds, Stan
82Wausau-4

Edmondson, Brian
91Bristol/ClBest-26
91Bristol/ProC-3597

Edmondson, Paul M.
(Paul)
70OPC-414
70T-414

Eduardo, Hector
77StPete
78StPete
79ArkTr-19

Edwards, Allen
82Madis-17
83Albany-2

Edwards, Bobby
88SLCity-11

Edwards, Charles B.
(Bruce)
47HomogBond-12
47TipTop
48B-43
49B-206
49Eureka-34
50B-165
51B-116
51T/BB-42
52B-88
52NTea
52T-224
89Smok/Dodg-52
90Target-212
D305
Exh47
R346-26

Edwards, Chuck
89Johnson/Star-9

Edwards, David L.
(Dave)
80T-657
81D-595
81F-568
81T-386
81T/Tr-758
82D-247
82T-151
83D-565
83F-357
83T-94
87Pocatel/Bon-17
88Pocatel/ProC-2084
90Everett/Best-28

Edwards, Glenn
85Water-5

Edwards, Henry Albert
(Hank)
48L-72
49B-136
49Eureka-56
50B-169
52B-141
52T-176
53T-90
90Target-213
91T/Arc53-90

Edwards, Howard R.
(Doc)
62T-594R
63T-296
64T-174
65OPC-239
65T-239
79RochR-10
80RochR-13
81RochR-22
82Charl-23
83Charl-22
84Maine-10
85IntLgAS-24
85Maine-29
86OhHenry-CO
87Gator-CO
88Gator-32MG
88T-374MG
89T-534MG
90Kahn/Mets-32CO
90T/TVMets-3CO
91Kahn/Mets-32CO

Edwards, Jeff
86Ashvl-9
86AubAs-8
87Albuq/Pol-9
87Ashvl-25
87SanBern-3
88ColAst/Best-16
89Canton/ProC-1316
89Canton/Star-4
89EastLDD/ProC-DD41
90ColoSp/CMC-6

Edwards, Jerome
90Princet/DIMD-5
91Batavia/ClBest-12
91Batavia/ProC-3495

Edwards, John Alban
(Johnny)
62Kahn
62Salada-191
62Shirriff-191
62T-302
62T/St-114
63FrBauer-5
63J-132
63P-132
63T-178
64Kahn
64T-507
64Wheat/St-14
65Kahn
65MacGregor-3
65T-418
66Kahn
66T-507
67Kahn
67T-202
68T-558
69MLB/St-139
69OPC-186
69T-186
69T/St-33
70MLB/St-40
70OPC-339
70T-339
71MLB/St-79
71OPC-44
71T-44
72MB-96
72OPC-416
72T-416
73OPC-519
73T-519
74OPC-635
74T-635

Edwards, Jovon
86Bakers-6

Edwards, Larry
77BurlB
78BurlB
79BurlB-1
80Ander-5
81GlenF-24

Edwards, Marshall L.
78Holyo
79Vanco-4
80Vanco-19
82F-140
82T-333R
83D-406
83F-32
83Gard-6
83Pol/Brew-16
83T-582
84Cram/PCL-47
84D-490
84Nes/792-167
84T-167

Edwards, Mel
91Spokane/ProC-3955

Edwards, Michael L.
(Mike)
75Shreve/TCMA-2
76Shrev
79T-201M
79T-613
80OPC-158
80T-301
81D-497

Edwards, Otis
91Watertn/ClBest-25
91Watertn/ProC-3380

Edwards, Ryan
90Billings/ProC-3223
91Cedar/ClBest-3
91Cedar/ProC-2711

Edwards, Samuel
90Princet/DIMD-6
91Martins/ClBest-23
91Martins/ProC-3447

Edwards, Todd
86Miami-6
91Beloit/ClBest-19
91Beloit/ProC-2116
91SLCity/ProC-3224

Edwards, Wayne
86Penin-9
87DayBe-15
88BirmB/Best-1
89BBAmerAA/BPro-AA22
89BirmB/Best-21
89BirmB/ProC-110
89SLAS-16
90B-309
90BirmDG/Best-9
90Coke/WSox-2
90Coke/WSox-28
90D/Rook-17
90F-652M
90F/Up-U83
90Leaf/II-352
90S/Tr-85T
90T/89Debut-34
90T/Tr-27T
90UD/Ext-762
91B-364
91D-327
91F-116
91Kodak/WSox-45
91Leaf/II-454
91OPC-751
91S-66
91S/100RisSt-10
91T-751
91T/StClub/I-129
91UD-697

Eenhoorn, Robert
90A&AASingle/ProC-182
90Oneonta/ProC-3384
91B-172
91PrWill/ClBest-16
91PrWill/ProC-1432
91UD/FinalEd-16F

Effrig, Mark
83ElPaso-7
84ElPaso-1

Egan, Richard Joseph
(Joe)
14Piedmont/St-20
16FleischBrd-26
T202
T205
T206

Egan, Richard Wallis
(Dick)
63T-169R
64T-572R
66T-536
67T-539
89Smok/R-6CO
90OkCty/CMC-22CO
90OkCty/ProC-449CO
90Target-214

Egan, Thomas Patrick
(Tom)
65T-486R
66T-263
67OPC-147
67T-147
69T-407
70MLB/St-171
70OPC-4
70T-4
71OPC-537
71T-537
72MB-97
72OPC-207
72T-207
73OPC-648
73T-648
75OPC-88
75T-88
75T/M-88
77Wausau-MG

Eggertsen, Todd
86PalmSp-12
86PalmSp/Smok-16
87PalmSp-29
88MidldA/GS-9

Eggleston, Darren
88CharWh/Best-10

Eggleston, Scott
91Spokane/ClBest-17
91Spokane/ProC-3942

Eggleston, Skip
88Geneva/ProC-1639

Egins, Paul C. III
89BurlB/ProC-1625

Egloff, Bruce
87Watlo-15
89Watertn/Star-5
90A&AASingle/ProC-11
90Canton/Best-20
90Canton/ProC-1288
90Foil/Best-251
91B-78
92S/II-751
92T/91Debut-49

Ehardt, Rube
90Target-941

Ehmig, Greg
88SLCity-14

Ehmke, Howard J.
(Howard)
21Exh-42
21Exh-43
25Exh-65
28Exh-54
61F-21
88Conlon/5-9
92Conlon/Sport-357
E120
R316
V100
W573
WG7-15

Ehret, Philip S.
(Red)
N172

Ehrhard, Jim
88FtLaud/Star-6

Ehrhard, Rod
87Oneonta-23
88Oneonta/ProC-2072
89PrWill/Star-7
90FtLaud/Star-7

Eichelberger, Juan T.
79Hawaii-21
80Hawaii-4
81T-478
81T/St-97
82D-442
82F-570
82T-366TL
82T-614
83D-422
83F-358
83OPC-168
83T-168
83T/Tr-29
84D-398
84F-539
84Nes/792-226
84T-226
86Richm-5
87Richm/Crown-15
87Richm/TCMA-4
88Richm/CMC-6
88Richm/ProC-10
89Pac/SenLg-175
89T/SenLg-123
89TM/SenLg-32
90EliteSenLg-20
91Pac/SenLg-119

Eichhorn, Dave
86Albuq-6
87SanAn-20
88SanAn/Best-13
89Albuq/CMC-6
89Albuq/ProC-61

Eichhorn, Mark A.
82Syrac-3
83Syrac-7
84Syrac-18
86D/Rook-13
86F/Up-U38
86Sf/Rook-38
86T/Tr-34T
86Tor/Fire-8
87D-321
87F-224
87F/GameWin-14
87F/Hottest-16
87F/Mini-36
87F/St-37
87Leaf-173CG
87Leaf-229
87OPC-371
87Sf-194M
87T-371
87T/Gloss60-49
87T/GlossRk-5
87T/St-187
87Tor/Fire-7
87ToysRUs-10
88D-121
88F-108
88F/Mini-60
88Ho/Disc-18
88Leaf-74
88OPC-116
88Panini/St-212
88S-198
88Sf-210
88T-749
88T/Big-208
88T/Revco-30

88Tor/Fire-38
89AAA/CMC-26
89F-230
89OPC-274
89Richm/ProC-825
89S-152
89T-274
89T/Big-188
90F-580
90F/Up-U77
90Leaf/II-472
90OPC-513
90T-513
90T/Tr-28T
91D-318
91F-311
91OPC-129
91S-504
91Smok/Angel-16
91T-129
91UD-519
92D/I-181
92F-55
92S/I-221
92T-435
92UD-287

Eierman, John
91Elmira/ClBest-4
91Elmira/ProC-3282

Eiland, Dave
87Oneonta-17
88Albany/ProC-1336
88EastLAS/ProC-1
89Colum/CMC-8
89Colum/Pol-3
89Colum/ProC-750
89D-481
89T-8
90AlbanyDG/Best-26
90ColClip/CMC-2
90ColClip/ProC-670
90S-652
90T/TVYank-41
91D-354
91F-661
91Leaf/I-184
91OPC-611
91S-826
91T-611
91T/StClub/II-477
92F-223
92S/II-679

Eilers, David Louis
(Dave)
66T-534R
78TCMA-245
91WIZMets-104

Einstein, Charles
90LitSun-11

Eischen, Joe
(Joey)
89Butte/SP-13
90Gaston/Best-6
90Gaston/ProC-2514
90Gaston/Star-6
91CharlR/ClBest-4
91CharlR/ProC-1308

Eisenreich, Charlie
87AppFx-15

Eisenreich, James M.
(Jim)
81Wisco-21
83T-197
87Memphis-27
87Memphis/Best-21
88D-343
88OPC-348
88S-456
88Smok/Royals-26
88T-348
89D/Best-306
89F/Up-38
89S-594
89T/Tr-28T
89UD-44
90B-374
90D-238
90D/BestAL-120
90F-106
90Leaf/II-278
90OPC-246
90Panini/St-80
90Publint/St-346
90S-179
90Sf-166
90T-246
90T/Big-234
90T/St-271
90UD-294
91B-304
91D-448
91F-557
91F/Ultra-146
91OPC-707
91Panini/FrSt-280
91Panini/St-229
91Pol/Royal-8
91S-154
91T-707
91T/StClub/II-373
91UD-658
92D/I-297
92F-156
92S/I-158
92T-469
92UD-539

Eisenstat, Harry
40PB-204
90Target-215

Eiterman, Tom
90AS/Cal-39
90Reno/Cal-263
91CLAS/ProC-CAR13
91Kinston/ClBest-25
91Kinston/ProC-337

Eklund, Troy
89Butte/SP-16
90Gaston/Best-12
90Gaston/ProC-2532
90Gaston/Star-7

Ekman, Rich
91Pocatel/ProC-3775

Elam, Scott
82Knoxvl-2
83Kinston/Team-4

Elam, Todd
88Batavia/ProC-1682
89Spartan/ProC-1028
89Spartan/Star-7
90Clearw/Star-6

Elberfeld, Norman A.
(Kid)
12Sweet/Pin-57A
12Sweet/Pin-57B
89Chatt/II/Team-9
90Target-216
92Conlon/Sport-557
E107
E254
M116
S74-38
T201
T202
T204
T205
T206
T213/blue
T215/blue
T215/brown
T3-15
WG2-17

Elder, Isaac
89James/ProC-2147
90Rockford/ProC-2706

Elders, Mike
76Clinton

Eldred, Calvin
(Cal)
89Beloit/II/Star-8
90A&AASingle/ProC-138
90B-387
90Foil/Best-61
90S-669DC
90Stockton/Best-1
90Stockton/Cal-174
90Stockton/ProC-2178
91B-56
91Denver/LineD-135
91Denver/ProC-116
92Classic/I-31
92D/II-718
92F-679
92S/II-834
92T-433
92T/91Debut-50
92UD-477

Eldredge, Ted
88SanBern/Best-11
88SanBern/Cal-41
89Wausau/GS-9

Eldridge, Rodney
90Hamil/Best-20
90Hamil/Star-10
91Savan/ClBest-16
91Savan/ProC-1657
91Single/ClBest-180

Elenes, Larry
74Cedar

Elguezabal, Jose
78SanJose-7

Elia, Lee Constantine
(Lee)
66T-529R
67T-406
68T-561
69T-312
75IntAS/TCMA-26
75IntAS/TCMA-8
79OkCty
82RedLob
83D-614MG
83T-456MG
83Thorn-26MG
84Cram/PCL-200MG
85Phill/TastyK-4CO
85Phill/TastyK-8CO
86Phill/TastyK-4CO
87Phill/TastyK-x
87T/Tr-32T
88Chatt/Team-9
88Phill/TastyK-32CO
88Phill/TastyK-9A
88Phill/TastyK-9B
88T-254MG
90Clearw/Star-26MG
91Clearw/ClBest-18MG
91Clearw/ProC-1638MG

Elick, Jason
90Visalia/Cal-84BB

Elkin, Rick
80Batavia-15
81Batavia-11

Ellam, Roy
T206
T213/brown

Eller, Horace Owen
(Hod)
88Pac/8Men-93
92Conlon/Sport-352
W514-38

Ellerbe, Francis R.
(Frank)
E120
V100
V61-51
W573

Elli, Rocky
88Clmbia/GS-4
91ScranWB/LineD-482
91ScranWB/ProC-2533

Ellingsen, H. Bruce
75OkCty
75OPC-288
75T-288
75T/M-288

Elliot, Corey
84Visalia-7

Elliot, Lawrence L.
(Larry)
63T-407R
64T-536R
67OPC-23
67T-23
91WIZMets-105

Elliot, Rowdy
90Target-942

Elliot, Terry
88StPete/Star-6
89StPete/Star-10

Elliott, Clay
79Savan-11

Elliott, Donnie
88Martins/Star-12
89Batavia/ProC-1925
90Spartan/Best-16
90Spartan/ProC-2482
90Spartan/Star-5
91Spartan/ClBest-3
91Spartan/ProC-888

Elliott, Glenn
43Centen-7
44Centen-6
45Centen-6
49Eureka-8

Elliott, Harry Lewis
(Harry)
55Hunters
55T-137

Elliott, James Thomas
(Jumbo)
33G-132
90Target-217
V354-6
W513-64

Elliott, John
86Ashvl-10
87Osceola-17
88ColAst/Best-13

Elliott, Mark
78Clinton

Elliott, Randy Lee
(Randy)
78T-719R

Elliott, Robert I.
(Bob)
39Exh
47HomogBond-13
48B-1
48L-65
49B-58
49Eureka-7
50B-20
50Drake-35
51B-66
51T/BB-32
52BR
52T-14
53Exh/Can-26
60T-215
D305
R346-38
R423-28

Ellis, Bull
91Utica/ProC-3233

Ellis, Dock Phillip
(Dock)
69T-286
70T-551
71MLB/St-200
71OPC-2
71T-2
71T/Coins-99
72OPC-179
72OPC-180IA
72T-179
72T-180IA
73OPC-575
73T-575
74OPC-145
74T-145
74T/St-82
75OPC-385
75T-385
75T/M-385
76OPC-528
76T-528
76T/Tr-528T
77K-4
77OPC-146
77T-71
78BK/R-6
78T-209
79T-691
80OPC-64
80T-117
89Pac/SenLg-15
89T/SenLg-116
89TM/SenLg-33
90EliteSenLg-5
91WIZMets-106

Ellis, Doug
87Macon-15

Ellis, George W.
(Rube)
E254
E270/1
E286
E90/1
M116
T207

Ellis, John Charles
(John)
70OPC-516R
70T-516R
71MLB/St-487
71OPC-263
71T-263
72OPC-47
72OPC-48IA
72T-47
72T-48IA
73OPC-656
74OPC-128
74T-128
74T/St-165
75Ho-54
75OPC-605
75T-605
75T/M-605
76Ho-27
76Ho/Twink-27
76OPC-383
76SSPC-515
76T-383
76T/Tr-383T
77T-36
78BK/R-3
78T-438
79T-539
80T-283
81D-26
82D-642
82F-316
82T-177
T73-656

Ellis, Paul
90Hamil/Best-13
90Hamil/Star-11
91FSLAS/ProC-FSL34
91Single/ClBest-81
91StPete/ClBest-15
91StPete/ProC-2278

Ellis, Robert Walter
(Rob)
76SSPC-240
77Spoka
79Tacoma-23
80Port-5
91Everett/ProC-3933MG
91Utica/ClBest-7

Ellis, Rufus
86FSLAS-12
86FtMyr-9
87FtMyr-18
88CharlR/Star-6

Ellis, Samuel Joseph
(Sammy)
63T-29R
64T-33R
65Kahn
65T-507
66Kahn
66T-250
66T/RO
67Kahn
67OPC-176
67T-176
68T-453
69OPC-32
69T-32
78TCMA-293
80Colum-14
81Colum-26
82Colum-24M
90Coke/WSox-30CO
91Kodak/WSox-x

Ellis, Tim
88Geneva/ProC-1643
90Kinston/Team-26
90Watertn/Star-8

Ellison, Darold
80Batavia-18

Ellison, Jeff
76Dubuq
77Cocoa

Ellison, Paul
88Spartan/Star-22
88Spartan/Star-6
89Spartan/ProC-1041
89Spartan/Star-8

Ellsworth, Ben
90Johnson/Star-11
91Hamil/ClBest-25
91Hamil/ProC-4045

Ellsworth, Richard C.

(Dick)
60T-125
61T-427
61T/St-7
62T-264
62T/St-107
63T-399
64Bz-28
64T-1LL
64T-220
64T/Coins-56
64T/S-17
64T/St-5
64T/SU
64T/tatt
65OPC-165
65T-165
65T/E-67
66T-447
67T-359
68Coke
68Dexter-30
68T-406
69MB-78
69MLB/St-12
69T-605
70MLB/St-196
70OPC-59
70T-59
71MLB/St-435
71OPC-309
71T-309
72MB-98

Ellsworth, Steve
86NewBrit-10
87Pawtu-17
87Pawtu/TCMA-6
88D/RedSox/Bk-NEW
88D/Rook-54
88S/Tr-83T
89Pawtu/CMC-7
89Pawtu/Dunkin-28
89Pawtu/ProC-704
89T-299

Elpin, Ralph
81Watlo-33
82Watlo/B-3
82Watlo/C-12

Elsea, Dottie
89Kingspt/Star-30
90Kgsport/Star-29GM

Elster, Kevin
84LitFalls-19
85Lynch-19
86Jacks/TCMA-13
87D-635
87F-7
87Tidew-32
87Tidew/TCMA-13
88Classic/Red-190
88D-37RR
88D/Best-70
88D/Mets/Bk-37
88D/Rook-34
88F/Up-U104
88Kahn/Mets-21
88Leaf-37RR
88S-624
88S/YS/II-40
88Sf/Gamewin-24
88T-8FS
88T/Mets/Fan-21
89B-383
89Classic-75
89D-289
89D/Best-97
89F-34
89Kahn/Mets-21
89Panini/St-127
89S-130
89Sf-71
89T-356
89T/Big-16
89T/JumboR-6
89Tidew/Candl-15
89ToysRUs-7
89UD-269
90B-137
90D-152
90D/BestNL-31
90F-202
90Kahn/Mets-21
90Leaf/I-8
90Mets/Fan-21
90MLBPA/Pins-12
90OPC-734
90Panini/St-296
90PublInt/St-132
90S-443
90Sf-118
90T-734
90T/Big-143
90T/St-2HL
90T/St-97
90T/TVMets-23
90UD-187
91B-469
91D-304
91F-145
91F/Ultra-215
91Kahn/Mets-21
91Leaf/II-305
91OPC-134
91Panini/FrSt-82
91RedFoley/St-32
91S-633
91T-134
91T/StClub/I-149
91UD-101
91WIZMets-107
92D/I-307
92F-502
92S/I-103
92T-251
92UD-385

Elston, Carey
89BurlInd/Star-10

Elston, Curt
C46-23

Elston, Donald Ray
(Don)
57T-376
58T-363
59T-520
60T-233
61P-200
61T-169
61T/St-8
62J-190
62P-190
62P/Can-190
62Salada-101
62Shirriff-101
62T-446
63T-515
64T-111
65T-436
78TCMA-143
90Target-218

Elston, Guy
82Nashvl-11
83Colum-13
84Maine-13

Elvira, Narciso
88Stockton/Cal-183
88Stockton/ProC-748
89Stockton/Star-6
91B-47
91Denver/LineD-136
91Denver/ProC-117
91T/90Debut-43
91UD-13

Elway, John
82Oneonta-13

Elwert
E270/2

Ely, Bones
90Target-943

Embree, Alan
90BurlInd/ProC-3004
91ColInd/ClBest-12
91ColInd/ProC-1479

Embree, Charles W.
(Red)
52Mother-22

Embry, Todd
90Waterlo/Best-4
90Waterlo/ProC-2370

Embser, Rich
85Spring-2
86ArkTr-7

Emery, Calvin Wayne
(Cal)
81Charl-24
89Vanco/CMC-21
89Vanco/ProC-572

Emerick, Chris
90Gate/ProC-3357

Emmerke, R.
N172

Emoto, Kouichi
90Salinas/Cal-121
90Salinas/ProC-2715

Empting, Mike
83Clinton/LF-15

Encarcion, Miguel
76BurlB

Encarnacion, Angie
91Welland/ClBest-10
91Welland/ProC-3574

Encarnacion, Juan
90Ashvl/ProC-2760

Encarnacion, Luis
86Water-8
87Wmsprt-5
88Memphis/Best-12
89Memphis/Best-20
89Memphis/ProC-1187
89Memphis/Star-10
89SLAS-22
90Omaha/CMC-4
90Omaha/ProC-60
91Omaha/LineD-334
91Omaha/ProC-1029
91T/90Debut-44

Endebrock, Kurt
91SoOreg/ClBest-25
91SoOreg/ProC-3853

Ender, Scott
81Cedar-24

Engel, Bob
88TM/Umpire-5
89TM/Umpire-3
90TM/Umpire-3

Engel, Joe
88Chatt/Team-10

Engel, Steve
86D-510
86Iowa-10
88ArkTr/GS-3

Engelkin, Gary
88Jaxvl/Best-28
88Jaxvl/ProC-990
89James/ProC-2149

Engelmeyer, Bob
77DaytB

Engeln, William
55B-301ump

England, Dave
82ArkTr-23
83ArkTr-25

Engle, Arthur Clyde
(Hack)
10Domino-40
11Helmar-3
12Sweet/Pin-3A
12Sweet/Pin-3B
14Piedmont/St-21
D303
E106
E254
E90/1
M116
T205
T206
T207
T213/brown
T216

Engle, Eleanor
91T/Arc53-332

Engle, Ralph David
(Dave)
79Toledo-7
80Toledo-15
81T-328R
82D-102
82F-552
82T-738
83D-646
83T-294
84D-598
84F-562
84Nes/792-463
84T-463
84T/St-313
85D-72
85F-276
85Leaf-173
85OPC-199
85T-667
85T/St-298
86D-438
86F-391
86F/Up-U39
86T-43
88OPC-196
88S-617
88T-196
89Pol/Brew-25
90OkCty/ProC-435
91Tucson/LineD-625CO
91Tucson/ProC-2229CO

Engle, Tom
89Kingspt/Star-8
89LittleSun-3
90Kgsport/Best-22
90Kgsport/Star-7

Englehart, Bill
84Greens-26

English, Elwood G.
(Woody)
28Exh-9
29Exh/4-6
30CEA/Pin-3
31Exh/4-6
32Orbit/num-32A
32Orbit/num-32B
32Orbit/un-18
33Exh/4-3
33G-135
34Exh/4-3
34G-4
35G-1F
35G-3D
35G-4D
35G-5D
37Exh/4-2
90Target-944
R305
R308-156
R308-193
R316
R332-18
V354-11
V354-50
WG8-15

English, Gil
90Target-219

Englishby, Steve
73Cedar
78DaytB

Englund, Tim
86Knoxvl-7
87Knoxvl-8

Engram, Duane
86Penin-10

Engram, Graylyn
87DayBe-21

Ennis, Alan
84Newar-8

Ennis, Delmar
(Del)
47HomogBond-14
48L-49
49Eureka-134
49Lummis
50B-31
50Drake-21
51B-4
51BR-A10
51T/BB-4
52B-76
52BR
52NTea
52T-223
53B/Col-103
53Exh/Can-60
53RM-N17
54B-127
54Wilson
55B-17
56T-220
57T-260
58T-60
59T-255
79TCMA-18
89Pac/Leg-121
89Swell-19
D305
Exh47
PM10/Sm-48
R302

Enno, Clayton
89Salem/Team-10

Enos, Dave
82Reading-13

Enos, Eric
88Batavia/ProC-1671

Enright, George A.
(George)
82QuadC-26
84MidldC-15

Enriquez, Graciano
91Beloit/ClBest-20
91Beloit/ProC-2117

Enriquez, Martin
82Wausau-15
83Wausau/LF-5

Ens, Jewel
92Conlon/Sport-499

Enyart, Terry Gene
(Terry)
79Ogden/TCMA-1
80Ogden-8

Enzmann, Johnny
90Target-220

Epley, Daren
89Kinston/Star-6
90Canton/Best-5
90Canton/ProC-1296
90Canton/Star-4
91Canton/LineD-82
91Canton/ProC-985

Eppard, Jim
84Albany-24
86Tacoma-5
87Edmon-1
88Edmon/CMC-21
88Edmon/ProC-558
88F-645
88F/Up-U13
89Edmon/CMC-14
89Edmon/ProC-548
89F-476
89S-607
89T-42
89UD-614
90Syrac/CMC-13
90Syrac/ProC-576
90Syrac/Team-7

Epperly, Al
90Target-221

Epple, Tom
82Spring-8
83StPete-6

Epps, Riley
86Salem-7

Epstein, Michael P.
(Mike)
67T-204R
68T-358
69MB-79
69MLB/St-104
69T-461
69T-539M
69T/St-235
69Trans-25
70K-24
70MLB/St-282
70OPC-235
70T-235
70T/CB
71K-34
71MLB/St-535
71OPC-655
71T-655
71T/Coins-126
72MB-99
72T-715
73OPC-38
73T-38
73T/Lids-14
74OPC-650
74T-650
74T/St-142
78TCMA-261
91Crown/Orio-121

Erardi, Joseph G.
(Joe)
77Holyo

Erautt, Edward L.S.
(Eddie)
49Eureka-82
52Mother-43
52T-171

53T-226
91T/Arc53-226

Erautt, Joseph M.
(Joe)
No Cards.

Erb, Gerry
77Newar

Erb, Mike
88PalmSp/Cal-86
88PalmSp/ProC-1443
89QuadC/Best-10
89QuadC/GS-14
90Edmon/CMC-6
90Edmon/ProC-513
91Edmon/LineD-154
91Edmon/ProC-1511

Erdahl, Jay Michael
82Wausau-21

Erdman, Brad
90Geneva/ProC-3033
90Geneva/Star-11
90Peoria/Team-4
91MidwLAS/ProC-MWL8
91Peoria/ClBest-10
91Peoria/ProC-1344

Erhard, Barney
91Belling/ClBest-9
91Belling/ProC-3673

Erhardt, Herb
88Oneonta/ProC-2046
89FtLaud/Star-3
90PrWill/Team-9
91CharWh/ClBest-16
91CharWh/ProC-2893

Ericks, John
89B-433
89SALAS/GS-36
89Savan/ProC-371
90B-190
90StPete/Star-6
90T/TVCard-46
91ArkTr/LineD-30
91ArkTr/ProC-1277
91B-393
91Single/ClBest-287
91UD-57TP

Erickson, Don
89Beloit/I/Star-3

Erickson, Eric G.
82Clinton-22
86Fresn/Smok-14
87Lynch-7

Erickson, Harold J.
(Hal)
53Glen

Erickson, Henry Nels
(Hank)
R314/Can

Erickson, Roger F.
79Ho-94
79OPC-34
79T-81
80T-256
81D-549
81F-561
81OPC-80
81T-434
81T/St-105
82D-303
82F-553
82T-153
82T/St-211
82T/Tr-30T
83F-378
83T-539
87SanJose-23
89Louisvl-17
89Louisvl/CMC-3
89Louisvl/ProC-1242
90Spring/Best-27CO
91Pac/SenLg-98
91Spring/ClBest-29CO
91Spring/ProC-760CO

Erickson, Scott
90A&AASingle/ProC-41
90Foil/Best-106
90OrlanSR/Best-16
90OrlanSR/ProC-1077
90OrlanSR/Star-5
90T/Tr-29T
91B-335
91Classic/200-160
91Classic/II-T16
91Classic/III-17
91Classic/III-xx
91D-767
91F-608
91F/UltraUp-U36
91Gaston/ClBest-5
91Gaston/ProC-2682
91Leaf/II-527
91Leaf/Stud-83
91OPC-234
91S-812
91T-234
91T/90Debut-45
91T/StClub/II-560
91UD-522
92D/DK-DK21
92D/II-463
92F-201
92F-693LL
92F/ASIns-10
92S/100SS-2
92S/I-438AS
92S/I-60
92S/II-889DT
92T-605
92UD-146
92UD-89TC

Erickson, Steve
87Oneonta-8
88FtLaud/Star-7
89FtLaud/Star-4

Erickson, Tim
87Wausau-28

Ericson, E.G.
V100

Ericson, Mark
88Kenosha/ProC-1394

Ericson, Mike
90Miami/I/Star-7
91Miami/ClBest-6
91Miami/ProC-400

Ermer, Calvin C.
(Cal)
68T-206MG
70McDon-2
79Toledo-3
80Toledo-3
81Toledo-1
82Toledo-23
83Toledo-23
84Toledo-6
85Toledo-26
88Chatt/Team-12

Ermis, Chris
91MedHat/ProC-4093

Erskine, Carl Daniel
(Carl)
51B-260
52B-70
52T-250
53B/Col-12
53Briggs
54B-10
54NYJour
54RH
54RM-NL4
54SM
54Wilson
55B-170
55Gol/Dodg-8
55RM-NL14
55SM
56T-233
57T-252
58T-258
59T-217
60NuCard-69
61NuCard-469
79TCMA-146
88Pac/Leg-75
89Rini/Dodg-23
89Rini/Dodg-25
89Smok/Dodg-60
89Swell-44
90Pac/Legend-14
90Swell/Great-36
90Target-222
91Swell/Great-27
91T/Arc53-308
PM10/Sm-49

Ervin, Chris
91Beloit/ClBest-21

Erwin, Ross Emil
(Tex)
10Domino-41
11Helmar-86
12Sweet/Pin-73
90Target-223
M116
T207

Erwin, Scott
88CapeCod/Sum-78
89Medford/Best-5
90Modesto/Cal-149
90Modesto/ProC-2205
91Modesto/ProC-3079

Erwin, Terry
75BurlB

Esasky, Nicholas A.
(Nick)
80Water-21
81Indianap-15
82Indianap-4
83Indianap-5
84D-602
84F-468
84Nes/792-192
84OPC-192
84T-192
84T/St-378YS
85D-121
85F-534
85Indianap-35
85OPC-253
85T-779
85T/St-51
86D-286
86F-177
86Leaf-162
86OPC-201
86T-677
86TexGold-12
87D-166
87F-201
87Kahn-12
87OPC-13
87T-13
88D-413
88D/Best-118
88F-233
88Kahn/Reds-12
88Leaf-240
88OPC-364
88Panini/St-274
88S-163
88T-364
88T/Big-167
88T/St-137
89B-31
89D-189
89D/Best-284
89D/Tr-18
89F-161
89F/Up-9
89OPC-262
89Panini/St-72
89S-64
89S/Tr-37
89T-554
89T/Big-316
89T/St-134
89T/Tr-29T
89UD-299
89UD/Ext-757
90B-20
90D-303
90D/BestNL-13
90F-273
90F/LL-10
90F/Up-U3
90Leaf/I-164
90OPC-206
90Panini/St-26
90Publlnt/St-453
90S-91
90S/Tr-3T
90Sf-72
90T-206
90T/Big-251
90T/Mini-5
90T/St-263
90T/Tr-30T
90UD-463
90UD/Ext-758
91F-687
91Leaf/Stud-143
91OPC-418
91T-418

Escalera, Carlos
86Beloit-5
86Cram/PCL-30
87AppFx-6
88BBCity/Star-11
88FSLAS/Star-34
89Memphis/Best-10
89Memphis/ProC-1182
89Memphis/Star-11

Escalera, Ruben
87Stockton-14
88CalLgAS-17
88Stockton/Cal-200
88Stockton/ProC-735
89ElPaso/GS-27
90Denver/CMC-24
90Denver/ProC-637
91ElPaso/LineD-180
91ElPaso/ProC-2759

Escarrega, Chico E.
(Ernesto)
83D-291
83F-234

Eschen, Jim
77Evansvl/TCMA-9
89Kingspt/Star-26
90Pittsfld/Pucko-25MG
91Wmsprt/LineD-650CO
91Wmsprt/ProC-310CO

Escobar, Angel
86Shrev-7
87Phoenix-7
88Phoenix/CMC-14
88Phoenix/ProC-63
89Huntsvl/Best-25

Escobar, John
88Martins/Star-13
89Batavia/ProC-1940
90Spartan/Best-15
90Spartan/ProC-2497
90Spartan/Star-6
91Clearw/ClBest-16
91Clearw/ProC-1627

Escobar, Jose
80Utica-15
83Kinston/Team-5
87Syrac-17
87Syrac/TCMA-13
88Knoxvl/Best-13
89Syrac/Team-9
90Syrac/CMC-15
90Syrac/ProC-577
90Syrac/Team-8
91B-74
92T/91Debut-51

Escobar, Oscar
86Ventura-6
87Myrtle-2
88Salem/Star-6

Escobar, Rodney
90WichSt-10

Escribano, Eddie
83Madis/LF-17

Eshelman, Vaughn
91Bluefld/ProC-4120
91Bluefld/ClBest-7

Eskew, Dan
88SoOreg/ProC-1711
89Modesto/Chong-10
90Foil/Best-51
90Huntsvl/Best-5
91Tacoma/LineD-532
91Tacoma/ProC-2297

Eskins, Mark
88Idaho/ProC-1856

Esmond, James J.
(Jimmy)
E270/2

Espinal, Bill
(Willie)
89Johnson/Star-11
90A&AASingle/ProC-76
90Savan/ProC-2062
91Spring/ClBest-15
91Spring/ProC-737

Espinal, Josue
88SoOreg/ProC-1700

Espinal, Mendy
87Cedar-9

Espinal, Sergio
86Geneva-5
87Peoria-4
88Peoria/Ko-10

Espino, Francisco
88Geneva/ProC-1648
89Geneva/ProC-1860
89Peoria/Ko-3

Espino, Juan
79WHave-24
80Colum-28
81Colum-15
82Colum-23
82Colum/Pol-29
83Colum-3
84D-92
84Maine-17
85Colum-11
85Colum/Pol-9
85IntLgAS-32
86Colum-7
86Colum/Pol-7
87Colum-8
87Colum/Pol-8
87Colum/TCMA-10
87T-239
88Richm-29
88Richm/CMC-20
88Richm/ProC-7

Espinosa, Anulfo A.
(Nino)
75Tidew/Team-10
77T-376
78T-197
79BK/P-11
79OPC-292
79T-566
80BK/P-17
80OPC-233
80T-447
81F-20
81T-405
89Tidew/Candl-7
91WIZMets-108

Espinosa, Philip
87Anchora-9

Espinosa, Santiago
86Cram/PCL-98
86QuadC-9
87QuadC-4

Espinoza, Alvaro
82Wisco-7
83Visalia/LF-23
84Toledo-3
85Toledo-15
86Toledo-9
87Portl-14
87T-529
88Colum/CMC-15
88Colum/Pol-15
88Colum/ProC-320
89D/Best-161
89F/Up-47
89S/NWest-3
89T/Tr-30T
90B-431
90D-245
90D/BestAL-123
90F-441
90Leaf/I-240
90OPC-791
90Panini/St-121
90S-101
90S/NWest-4
90T-791
90T/Big-8
90T/St-311
90T/TVYank-24
90UD-163
91B-163
91D-226
91F-662
91F/Ultra-230
91Leaf/I-198
91OPC-28
91Panini/FrSt-327
91Panini/St-269
91S-127
91T-28
91T/StClub/I-242
91UD-204
92D/II-474
92F-224
92S/I-41
92T-243
92UD-119

Espinoza, Andres
85LitFalls-17
86QuadC-10
87PalmSp-31
Espinoza, Carlos
90Gate/ProC-3343
Esposito, Nick
83TriCit-9
Esposito, Samuel
(Sammy)
57T-301
58T-425
59T-438
60T-31
61T-323
62T-586
63T-181
Espy, Cecil Edward
(Cecil)
81AppFx-14
82VeroB-22
86Hawaii-5
87OKCty-16
88D/Rook-9
88F-465
88Mother/R-13
88S/Tr-73T
88T/Tr-36T
89B-236
89Bz-7
89Classic-143
89D-292
89D/Best-335
89F-517
89KMart/DT-6
89Mother/R-12
89Panini/St-443
89S-401
89S/YS/II-10
89Smok/R-7
89T-221
89T/Big-36
89T/Gloss60-59
89T/JumboR-7
89T/St-240
89T/St-320
89ToysRUs-8
89UD-92
90B-502
90D-260
90F-295
90Mother/Rang-25
90OPC-496
90PublInt/St-407
90S-69
90T-496
90T/Big-37
90T/Mini-36
90T/St-249
90Target-224
90UD-371
91BuffB/LineD-27
91BuffB/ProC-551
92D/II-678
92S/II-673
Espy, Duane
77Spoka
79BurlB-17
80BurlB-10
84Shrev/FB-7MG
86Phoenix-5CO
87Phoenix-22
88SanJose/Cal-141
88SanJose/ProC-125
89AS/Cal-49MG
89SanJose/Best-28
89SanJose/Cal-235
89SanJose/ProC-453
90Phoenix/CMC-24
90Phoenix/ProC-27
91Phoenix/LineD-399
91Phoenix/ProC-83
Esquer, David
(Dave)
89QuadC/Best-7
89QuadC/GS-25
90PalmSp/Cal-204
90PalmSp/ProC-2583
Esquer, Mercedes
83Knoxvl-4
Essegian, Charles A.
(Chuck)
58T-460
59T-278
60BB-11
60T-166
61T-384
62J-45
62P-45
62P/Can-45
62T-379
63J-71
63P-71
63T-103
90Target-225
91Crown/Orio-122
Esser, Mark Gerald
(Mark)
80GlenF/B-14
80GlenF/C-5
Essian, James Sarkis
(Jim)
76SSPC-142
77T-529
78T-98
79OPC-239
79T-458
80OPC-179
80T-341
81Coke
81D-503
81F-593
81T-178
81T/Tr-759
82D-369
82F-341
82T-269
82T/Tr-31T
83D-478
83T-646
83T/St-117
83T/Tr-30
83Wheat/Ind-10
84D-629
84F-540
84F/X-35
84Mother/A's-19
84Nes/792-737
84T-737
84T/Tr-35
85F-423
85T-472
86WinSalem-7MG
87Pittsfld-4MG
88EastLAS/ProC-47MG
88Pittsfld/ProC-1360MG
89CharlK-3MG
90Iowa/CMC-24MG
90Iowa/ProC-333MG
91Cub/Mara-41MG
91Iowa/LineD-224MG
91Iowa/ProC-1076MG
91T/Tr-36T
Estalella, Roberto M.
(Bobby)
W753
Esteban, Felipe
87VeroB-21
88VeroB/Star-6
Estelle, Richard H.
(Dick)
65OPC-282R
65T-282R
66T-373R
Estep, Chris
87Anchora-10
88Watertn/Pucko-18
89Augusta/ProC-499
90CLAS/CL-25
90Salem/Star-5
91CaroMud/LineD-107
91CaroMud/ProC-1097
Estepa, Ramon
80SanJose/JITB-6
81LynnS-21
82LynnS-14
83Chatt-5
84Chatt-3
Estepan, Rafael
80Clinton-18
Esterbrook, Thomas J.
(Dude)
90Target-226
E223
N167
N172
N284
N690
WG1-31
Esterday, Henry
N172
Estes, Frank
(Doc)
78OrlTw
80OrlTw-9
81Toledo-21
85IntLgAS-8
85Richm-18
86Richm-6
87Syrac-22
87Syrac/TCMA-22
Estes, Joel
86AubAs-9
87Osceola-20
89ColMud/ProC-128
89ColMud/Star-7
90Foil/Best-97
90SanJose/Best-17
90SanJose/Cal-45
90SanJose/ProC-2007
90SanJose/Star-8
Estes, Marc
86Miami-7
Estes, Shawn
91Belling/ClBest-29
91Belling/ProC-3656
91Classic/DP-8
92T-624DP
Estevez, Juan
88Bristol/ProC-1866
Estrada, Charles L.
(Chuck)
60T-126
61Bz-13
61P-73
61T-395
61T-48LL
61T/St-100
62J-36
62P-36
62P/Can-36
62Salada-212
62Shirriff-212
62T-560
62T/bucks
62T/St-4
63T-465
64T-263
65T-378
67T-537
73OPC-549CO
73T-549C
78Padre/FamFun-10CO
82Charl-24
85Cram/PCL-129
86Tacoma-6CO
87Tacoma-12CO
88Tacoma/ProC-623CO
89Tacoma/CMC-9CO
89Tacoma/ProC-1564CO
90Tacoma/ProC-111CO
91Crown/Orio-123
91WIZMets-109
Estrada, Eduardo
86NewBrit-11
87NewBrit-25
88EastLAS/ProC-21
88NewBrit/ProC-903
89NewBrit/Star-1
89Pawtu/CMC-23
89Pawtu/ProC-698
Estrada, Francisco
91WIZMets-110
Estrada, Jay
87Spokane-5
88Charl/ProC-1213
89River/Best-4
89River/Cal-21
89River/ProC-1409
90Riversi/Best-7
90Riversi/Cal-16
90Riversi/ProC-2600
91HighD/ClBest-3
91HighD/ProC-2386
Estrada, Luis
79AppFx-16
81GlenF-1
Estrada, Manuel
(Manny)
78SanJose-22
79Spokane-25
80LynnS-13
81Spokane-29
82SLCity-23
83SLCity-25
84Butte-1
Estrada, Peter
(Pete)
88Elmira-8
89WinHaven/Star-6
90LynchRS/Team-18
91NewBrit/LineD-456
91NewBrit/ProC-346
Etchandy, Curt
76AppFx
Etchebarren, Andy
66OPC-27R
66T-27R
67T-457
68Coke
68Dexter-31
68T-204
69MB-80
69MLB/St-3
69T-634
70MLB/St-159
70OPC-213
70T-213
71MLB/St-296
71OPC-501
71T-501
72MB-100
72OPC-26
72T-26
73JP
73OPC-618
73T-618
74OPC-488
74T-488
75OPC-583
75T-583
75T/M-583
76OPC-129
76T-129
77T-454
78T-313
86Pol/Brew-8C
90Brewer/MillB-32CO
90Pol/Brew-x
91Brewer/MillB-32
91Crown/Orio-124
91Pol/Brew-x
Etchebarren, Ray
84Beaum-24
Etheredge, Jeff
89Batavia/ProC-1917
Etheridge, Bobby L.
(Bobby)
68OPC-126
68T-126
69T-604
70OPC-107
70T-107
Etten, Nicholas R.
(Nick)
41DP-123
44Yank/St-10
48Signal
48Smith-4
Ettles, Mark
89NiagFls/Pucko-8
90Lakeland/Star-9
91Lakeland/ClBest-3
91Lakeland/ProC-259
Etzweiler, Dan
88Myrtle/ProC-1177
Eubanks, Craig
91CharRain/ClBest-6
91CharRain/ProC-92
Eubanks, Larry
77Cocoa
Eufemia, Frank
83Visalia/LF-11
85Toledo-6
86D-513
86F-392
86T-236
86Toledo-10
Eusebio, Tony
88Osceola/Star-9
89ColMud/Best-15
89ColMud/ProC-125
89ColMud/Star-8
90ColMud/Best-5
90ColMud/ProC-1350
90ColMud/Star-10
90Foil/Best-112
91Jacks/LineD-557
91Jacks/ProC-928
92S/II-858
92T/91Debut-52
Evans, Alfred Hubert
(Al)
48L-22
49B-132
50B-144
51B-38
52T-152
Evans, Barry Steven
(Barry)
81F-499
81OPC-72
81T-72
82D-271
82F-571
82T-541
83Colum-19
85Maine-18
86Maine-8
Evans, Brian
89CharlR/Star-7
90A&AASingle/ProC-81
90Gaston/Best-13
90Gaston/ProC-2515
90Gaston/Star-8
Evans, Darrell
70T-621R
72OPC-171
72OPC-172IA
72T-171
72T-172IA
73OPC-374
73T-374
74OPC-140
74T-140
74T/DE-2
74T/St-3
75Ho-3
75Ho/Twink-3
75OPC-475
75T-475
75T/M-475
76Ho-24
76Ho/Twink-24
76OPC-81
76SSPC-9
76T-81
77T-571
78T-215
79Ho-64
79OPC-215
79Pol/Giants-41
79T-410
80OPC-81
80Pol/Giants-41
80T-145
81D-192
81F-436
81OPC-69
81T-648
81T/St-235
82D-398
82F-388
82OPC-17
82T-17
82T/St-112
83D-251
83F-258
83Mother/Giants-9
83OPC-329
83T-448
83T/St-305
84D-431
84F-372
84F/St-3
84F/X-36
85FunFood/Pin-117
84Mother/Giants-27
84Nes/792-325
84OPC-325
84T-325
84T/Gloss40-11
84T/St-163
84T/Tr-36
85Cain's-6
85D-227

85D/HL-51
85F-6
85Leaf-215
85OPC-319
85Seven-3D
85T-792
85Wendy-7
86Cain's-4
86D-369
86F-224
86F/St-36
86OPC-103
86Quaker-24
86Sf-183M
86Sf-189
86T-515
86T/3D-7
86T/Gloss60-60
86T/Mini-13
86T/St-165
86T/St-269
86T/Super-21
86Woolwth-9
87Cain's-6
87Coke/Tigers-13
87D-398
87D/OD-210
87F-150
87F/LL-16
87OPC-265
87Sf-132
87Seven-DT2
87T-265
87T/St-264
88D-250
88D/Best-35
88F-54
88KayBee-9
88KingB/Disc-12
88Leaf-173
88OPC-390
88OPC/WaxBox-E
88Panini/St-441
88Panini/St-89
88Pep/T-41
88Pol/T-5
88S-75
88Sf-188
88T-630
88T/Big-82
88T/Mini-10
88T/St-265
88T/St-8
88T/WaxBox-E
88Woolwth-3
89B-275
89D-533
89S-171
89S/Tr-65
89T/Tr-31T
89T/WaxBox-C
89UD-394
90F-581
90KayBee-10
90OPC-55
90PublInt/St-112
90Richm25Ann/Team-8
90S-302
90T-55
90T/St-31
90T/WaxBox-D
90UD-143
Evans, Dave
90SanBern/Best-5
90SanBern/Cal-97
90SanBern/ProC-2627
91Jaxvl/LineD-334
91Jaxvl/ProC-144
Evans, Duane
82Lynch-13
Evans, Dwight Michael
(Dwight)
73OPC-614R
73T-614R
74OPC-351
74T-351
75Ho-18
75Ho/Twink-18
75K-38
75OPC-255
75T-255
75T/M-255
76Ho-87
76OPC-575
76SSPC-408
76T-575
77BurgChef-30
77Ho-21
77OPC-259
77T-25
78Ho-54
78PapaG/Disc-24
78T-695
79Ho-33
79K-41
79OPC-73
79T-155
80OPC-210
80T-405
81Coke
81F-232
81OPC-275
81T-275
81T/HT
82Coke/BOS
82D-109
82Drake-11
82Drake-45
82F-293
82F/St-167
82OPC-355
82T-162LL
82T-355
82T/St-135
82T/St-153
82T/St-4LL
83D-452
83D-7DK
83D/AAS-2
83Drake-7
83F-183
83OPC-135
83T-135
84D-395
84F-397
85FunFood/Pin-62
84Nes/792-720
84OPC-244
84T-720
84T/St-219
85D-294
85D/AAS-15
85Drake-10
85F-158
85F/St-40
85Leaf-150
85OPC-271
85Seven-8E
85T-580
85T/St-212
85T/Super-33
86D-249
86Drake-2
86F-348
86F/Mini-74
86Leaf-127
86OPC-60
86Sf-32
86T-396M
86T-60
86T/Mini-5
86T/St-251
86T/Super-22
86Woolwth-10
87D-129
87D/HL-33
87D/OD-184
87F-34
87F/LL-17
87F/Mini-37
87F/St-38
87F/WS-9M
87Leaf-57
87OPC-368
87Sf-128
87T-3RB
87T-645
87T/Board-7
87T/HL-21
87T/St-20WS
87T/St-251
87T/St-4
87Woolwth-21
88D-16DK
88D-216
88D/AS-23
88D/Best-84
88D/DKsuper-16DK
88D/RedSox/Bk-216
88Drake-9
88F-351
88F/AwardWin-11
88F/BB/MVP-12
88F/LL-11
88F/Mini-6
88F/St-8
88F/WaxBox-C2
88KayBee-10
88Leaf-16DK
88Leaf-171
88OPC-221
88Panini/St-25
88RedFoley/St-21
88S-65
88Sf-137
88T-470
88T/Big-6
88T/Coins-11
88T/Coins-42
88T/Gloss60-21
88T/Mini-3
88T/Revco-24
88T/St-245
88T/St/Backs-50
88T/UK-22
89B-35
89Classic-44
89D-240
89D/Best-121
89F-87
89F/Excit-12
89KayBee-10
89OPC-205
89Panini/St-279
89RedFoley/St-40
89S-193
89S/HotStar-8
89Sf-204
89T-205
89T/Big-193
89T/Gloss60-36
89T/LJN-107
89T/Mini-47
89T/St-252
89T/St/Backs-15
89T/UK-24
89UD-366
90B-279
90Classic-77
90D-122
90D/BestAL-102
90D/GSlam-5
90F-274
90KayBee-11
90Leaf/I-235
90OPC-375
90Panini/St-17
90Pep/RSox-8
90PublInt/St-454
90S-3
90S/100St-54
90Sf-217
90T-375
90T/Ames-4
90T/Big-1
90T/HillsHM-23
90T/St-257
90T/TVAS-28
90T/TVRSox-29
90UD-113
90Woolwth/HL-12
91B-103
91Crown/Orio-497
91D-122
91F-93
91F/UltraUp-U1
91F/Up-U2
91Leaf/II-266
91Leaf/Stud-2
91OPC-155A
91OPC-155B
91OPC/Premier-39
91Panini/St-213
91S-225
91S/100SS-99
91S/RookTr-62T
91Seven/3DCoin-2A
91T-155A
91T-155B
91T/StClub/II-351
91T/Tr-37T
91T/WaxBox-E
91UD-549
91UD/Ext-776
91Woolwth/HL-10
92D/II-502
92F-6
92S/I-150
92T-705
92UD-248
Evans, Frank
91Negro/Lewis-23
Evans, Frank
85Louisvl-3
Evans, Freeman
76Clinton
Evans, Gary
82Beloit-17
Evans, Godfrey
78Memphis/Team-3
Evans, Jamie
91AubAS/ClBest-7
91AubAS/ProC-4268
Evans, Jim
77Clinton
Evans, Jim
88TM/Umpire-13
89TM/Umpire-11
90TM/Umpire-11
Evans, John
79BurlB-15
80BurlB-25
81ElPaso-21
82Tacoma-16
Evans, Louis Richard
10Domino-42
11Helmar-168
12Sweet/Pin-146
14CJ-128
15CJ-128
E254
M116
S74-118
T202
T205
T206
T207
T213/blue
Evans, Michael
91SoOreg/ClBest-18
91SoOreg/ProC-3834
Evans, Mike
90Spring/Best-28TR
91Spring/ClBest-30TR
Evans, Mike
82Wausau-22
84Chatt-1
87Erie-17
88Hamil/ProC-1734
89Hamil/Star-29
Evans, Phil
89SLCity-25
Evans, Randy
80GlenF/B-4
80GlenF/C-15
81GlenF-2
Evans, Richard (Dr.)
82Iowa-32
Evans, Rick
(Bubba)
76AppFx
77Charl
78Salem
80Buffa-8
Evans, Rob
87Tidew-29
Evans, Roy
90Target-945
Evans, Russell Edison
(Red)
39PB-159
90Target-227
Evans, Scott
87Miami-4
88Hagers/Star-5
Evans, Tony
83Tampa-4
Evans, Tory
89SanBern/Cal-65
Evans, Van
85PrWill-25
86Kinston-6
Evans, William L.
(Billy)
21Exh-44UMP
61F-22
80SSPC/HOF
89HOF/St-100
92Conlon/Sport-472
Evaschuk, Brad
88StCath/ProC-2010
Eveline, William
(Billy)
86AppFx-7
87DayBe-18
88Tampa/Star-6
89QuadC/Best-26
89QuadC/GS-30
Everett, Carl
90Classic/DP-10
90Tampa/DIMD-5
91B-156
91Greens/ProC-3072
91OPC-113DP
91SALAS/ProC-SAL25
91S-386DP
91T-113DP
Everett, Smokey
81Wisco-3
82Orlan-4
Evers, Bill
83Greens-28
86Clinton-7CO
87Clinton-17
88Clinton/ProC-712
89Shreve/ProC-1838
90Shrev/ProC-1458MG
90Shrev/Star-25MG
91Shrev/LineD-324MG
91Shrev/ProC-1838MG
Evers, John Joseph
(Johnny)
10Domino-43
11Helmar-94
12Sweet/Pin-82
14CJ-118
15CJ-118
16FleischBrd-27
40PB-174
48Exh/HOF
50Callahan
60Exh/HOF-10
60F-57
61F-23
63Bz/ATG-21
69Bz/Sm
72F/FFeat-7
75F/Pion-17
80SSPC/HOF
91Conlon/Sport-15
BF2-50
D303
D304
D327
D328-45
D329-54
D350/2-55
E101
E102
E105
E106
E121/80
E122
E135-45
E254
E270/1
E90/3
E91
E92
E93
E94
E95
E98
L1-134
M101/4-54
M101/5-55
M116
PM1-5
S74-60
S81-109
T201
T202
T204
T205
T206
T213/blue
T213/brown
T215/blue

T216
V100
W555
W575
WG5-16
WG6-15

Evers, Troy
87FtLaud-4
88Albany/ProC-1340
90Wmsprt/Best-4
90Wmsprt/ProC-1050
90Wmsprt/Star-5

Evers, Walter Arthur
(Hoot)
47TipTop
48L-78
49B-42
50B-41
51B-23
51FB
51T/CAS
52B-111
52StarCal/L-71H
52StarCal/L-72C
52T-222
53B/Col-25
54B-18
55Esskay
79TCMA-264
81Detroit-44
91Crown/Orio-125
91T/Arc53-291
Exh47
R302-123

Eversgerd, Bryan
89Johnson/Star-10
91Savan/ClBest-3
91Savan/ProC-1644

Everson, Gregory
(Greg)
88FSLAS/Star-35
88Lakeland/Star-10
89London/ProC-1380
90Memphis/Best-15
90Memphis/ProC-1005
90Memphis/Star-10
91Omaha/LineD-335
91Omaha/ProC-1030

Ewart, Ron
86WinSalem-8

Ewell, Doc
90Mother/Ast-28TR

Ewing, William
(Buck)
50Callahan
75F/Pion-3
80SSPC/HOF
89HOF/St-57
90BBWit-68
E223
N172
N284
N29
N300/unif
N338/2
N403
N43
WG1-38

Ewing, Bill
76QuadC
79SLCity-13

Ewing, George L.
(Long Bob)
E103
M116
S74-100
T204
T205
T206
WG3-18

Ewing, Jim
84Everett/Cram-10B

Ewing, John
(Long John)
N172

Ewing, Samuel James
(Sam)
77OPC-221
78OPC-112
78Syrac
78T-344
79OPC-271
79T-521
81AppFx-28

Ezell, Glenn
86Ventura-7MG
87Knoxvl-23
91Pol/Royal-26CO
88Omaha/CMC-25
88Omaha/ProC-1503

Faatz, Jay
N172

Fabbro, Arthur
52Park-55
53Exh/Can-45

Faber, Dick
52Mother-28

Faber, Urban
(Red)
21Exh-45
28Yueng-4
30CEA/Pin-14
33G-79
40PB-230
61F-24
80SSPC/HOF
88Pac/8Men-96
89HOF/St-61
91Conlon/Sport-41
92Conlon/Sport-483
BF2-12
D327
D328-46
D329-55
D350/2-56
E120
E121/120
E121/80
E126-6
E135-46
E210-4
E220
M101/4-55
M101/5-56
R316
V100
V353-54
V61-14
W501-48
W502-4
W514-69
W515-60
W572
W573
W575

Fabregas, Jorge
91Classic/DP-30

Fabri, Isidro
86Negro/Frit-73

Fabrique, Bunny
90Target-228

Faccio, John
89Beloit/I/Star-4
89Star/Wax-4

Faccio, Luis
85Bend/Cram-6
88PrWill/Star-8
89Spring/Best-7
90Savan/ProC-2063
91StPete/ClBest-6
91StPete/ProC-2269

Face, Elroy
53T-246
54T-87
56T-13
57Kahn
57T-166
58Hires-59
58Kahn
58T-74
59Kahn
59T-339
59T-425M
60Kahn
60L-16
60T-115M
60T-20
60T/tatt-14
60T/tatt-89
61Kahn
61P-133
61T-250M
61T-370
61T/St-62
62J-177
62P-177
62P/Can-177
62Salada-174
62Shirriff-174
62T-210
62T-423M
62T/St-175
63F-57
63IDL-6
63J-147
63P-147
63T-409
64T-539
65T-347
66EH-26
66T-461
67OPC-49
67T-49
67T/Test/PP-8
68KDKA-26
68T-198
69OPC-207
69T-207
72Laugh/GF-26
78TCMA-5
89Pac/Leg-178
89Swell-51
90HOF/St-58
91Swell/Great-28
91T/Arc53-246

Faedo, Len
80OrlTw-10
81Charl-12
82T-766R
83F-611
83T-671
84Evansvl-10
84F-563
84Nes/792-84
84T-84
84T/St-310

Fagan, Pete
87StPete-26
91Savan/ClBest-4TR

Fagan, William
N172

Fagnano, Phil
88Spartan/ProC-1032

Fagnant, Ray
90WinHaven/Star-8
91NewBrit/LineD-457
91NewBrit/ProC-354

Faherty, Sean
83AlexD-18
84PrWill-3

Fahey, Bill
72OPC-334R
72T-334R
73OPC-186
73T-186
74OPC-558
74T-558
75OPC-644
75T-644
75T/M-644
76OPC-436
76SSPC-259
76T-436
77T-511
78Cr/PCL-67
78T-388
80OPC-23
80T-44
81D-361
81F-490
81T-653
81T/Tr-760
82T-286
83D-281
83T-196
85Tulsa-28CO
89T-351TL
90Mother/Giant-21M
91Mother/Giant-27CO

Fahr, Gerald
52Park-23

Fahrow, Bryant
75QuadC

Fain, Ferris
48B-21
49B-9
49Royal-24
50B-13
51T/RB-3
52B-154
52BR
52Dix-53
52NTea
52RM-AL7
52Royal
52StarCal/L-76B
52T-21
52TipTop
53T-24
54B-214
54RH
54RM-AL22
54T-27
54Wilson
55T-11
55T/DH-116
91T/Arc53-24
Exh47

Fairchild, Glenn
86Watlo-6
87Watlo-25
88Kinston/Star-5

Fairey, Jim
68T-228R
69MLB/St-157
69OPC-117
69T-117
71MLB/St-126
71OPC-474
71T-474
72T-653
73OPC-429
73T-429
85SpokAT/Cram-5
90Target-229

Fairly, Ron
59T-125
60DF-21
60T-321
61T-492
62BB-6
62T-375
62T/St-134
63T-105
64T-490
64T/Coins-54
65OldLond-8
65OPC-196
65T-196
65T/E-2
66Bz-20
66T-330
66T/RO-18
67Bz-20
67OPC-94
67T-94
68T-510
68T/3D
69Expos/Pins-3
69MB-81
69MLB/St-146
69MLBPA/Pin-42
69OPC-122
69T-122
69T/St-43
70Expos/Pins-5
70MLB/St-65
70T-690
70T/PI-10
71LaPizza-3
71MLB/St-127
71OPC-315
71T-315
71T/Coins-83
72MB-101
72OPC-405
72T-405
73OPC-125
73T-125
74K-27
74OPC-146
74T-146
74T/St-53
75OPC-270
75T-270
75T/M-270
76OPC-375
76SSPC-276
76T-375
77T-127
78OPC-40
78T-85
79T-580
90Smok/SoCal-5
90Target-230

Fajardo, Hector
91Augusta/ClBest-5
91Augusta/ProC-798
91SALAS/ProC-SAL4
92Classic/I-32
92D/II-419RR
92S/II-842
92T/91Debut-53

Falco, Chris
91James/ClBest-9
91James/ProC-3552

Falcone, Dave
84CharlO-16
85RochR-4
87CharlO/WBTV-36
87SLAS-1
90HagersDG/Best-9

Falcone, Pete
76OPC-524
76T-524
76T/Tr-524T
77BurgChef-12
77Ho-24
77OPC-177
77T-205
78T-669
79OPC-36
79T-87
80T-401
81D-395
81F-327
81OPC-117
81T-117
82D-380
82F-524
82T-326
83D-182
83F-541
83Pol/Atl-33
83T-764
83T/Tr-31
84D-385
84F-177
84Nes/792-521
84OPC-51
84Pol/Atl-33
84T-521
85T-618
89Pac/SenLg-208
89T/SenLg-56
90EliteSenLg-55
91Pac/SenLg-110
91WIZMets-111

Falk, Bibb A.
21Exh-46
25Exh-74
26Exh-75
28Exh-38
29Exh/4-22
31Exh/4-22
39Yueng
61F-104
92Conlon/Sport-518
E120
E121/120
E210-39
V100
V61-15
W501-41
W502-39
W572
W573
W575

Falkenburg, Frederick
(Cy)
14CJ-20
15CJ-20
M116
T201

Falkner, Richard
88BurlInd/ProC-1773
89Kinston/Star-7
89Star/Wax-75
90Kinston/Team-18

Fallon, George
90Target-231

Fallon, Robert
81GlenF-3
85BuffB-17
85F/Up-U39

Falls, Bobby

86ColumAst-12
Falzone, Jim
87Miami-2
Faneyte, Rikkert
91Clinton/ClBest-22
Fannin, Cliff
47TipTop
48L-123
49B-120
50B-106
51B-244
51T/BB-36
52T-285
53T-203
91T/Arc53-203
Fanning, Jim
82D-492MG
82Hygrade
85OPC-267MG
85T-759MG
Fanning, Steve
88Hamil/ProC-1739
89Savan/ProC-363
91ArkTr/LineD-31
91ArkTr/ProC-1292
Fanok, Harry
62Kahn/Atl
63T-54R
64T-262R
Fanovich, Frank
49Eureka-83
52Park-84
54Esskay
Fansler, Stan
85Nashua-8
86Hawaii-7
87Vanco-7
88BuffB/CMC-2
88BuffB/ProC-1469
91CaroMud/LineD-102
91CaroMud/ProC-1080
Fanzone, Carmen
73OPC-139
73T-139
74OPC-484
74T-484
75OPC-363
75T-363
75T/M-363
Faria, Joe
47Smith-25
Faries, Paul
87Spokane-17
88CalLgAS-43
88River/Cal-217
88River/ProC-1422
89AubAs/ProC-18
89TexLAS/GS-7
89Wichita/Rock-22
89Wichita/Rock/HL-17
89Wichita/Rock/Up-3
90AAAGame/ProC-AAA8
90LasVegas/CMC-14
90LasVegas/ProC-128
91B-664
91D/Rook-16
91F-528
91F/Ultra-302
91Leaf/Stud-243
91MajorLg/Pins-55
91Padre/MagRal-20
91S-711RP
91T/90Debut-46
91T/StClub/II-557
91UD/Ext-751
92F-603
92S/100RisSt-22
92S/II-509
92T-162
92UD-310
Fariss, Monty
88Butte-22
88Tulsa-3
89B-233
89T-177FDP
89Tulsa/GS-8
89Tulsa/Team-6
90B-500
90Tulsa/ProC-1161
91AAAGame/ProC-AAA25
91B-285
91Classic/III-18
91D-455
91OkCty/LineD-308
91OkCty/ProC-184
92F-668
92S/II-772
92T-138
92T/91Debut-54
92UD-462
Farkas, Ron
82Indianap-24
Farley, Bob
61Union
62T-426
Farley, Brian
83Erie-10
87Spring/Best-20
Farlow, Kevin
91Waterlo/ClBest-16
91Waterlo/ProC-1263
Farmar, Damon
83QuadC-25
87MidldA-14
Farmer, Al
86Salem-8
Farmer, Billy
70OPC-444R
70T-444R
Farmer, Bryan Pierce
87Greenvl/Best-16
88Greenvl/Best-13
89Richm/Bob-6
89Richm/CMC-8
89Richm/Ko-12
89Richm/ProC-834
Farmer, Ed
72OPC-116
72T-116
73OPC-272
73T-272
74OPC-506
74T-506
80T-702
81Coke
81D-40
81F-339
81F/St-114
81OPC-36
81T-36
81T/HT
81T/SO-54
81T/St-64
82D-482
82F-342
82OPC-328
82T-328
82T/Tr-32T
83D-471
83F-161
83T-459
84Cram/PCL-247
86Hawaii-8
91Crown/Orio-126
Farmer, Gordon
88AubAs/ProC-1970
89Ashvl/ProC-953
91Osceola/ClBest-2
91Osceola/ProC-674
Farmer, Howard
87Jamestn-24
88MidwLAS/GS-46
88Rockford-12
89BBAmerAA/BPro-AA20
89Jaxvl/Best-12
89Jaxvl/ProC-155
89Rockford-12
90B-107
90Indianap/CMC-3
90Indianap/ProC-290
90S/Tr-91T
90UD/Ext-753
91D-734
91MajorLg/Pins-79
91OPC/Premier-40
91S-718RP
91S/100RisSt-20
91T/90Debut-47
91UD-362
92D/II-779
Farmer, Ken
86LitFalls-10
Farmer, Kevin
87Spokane-14
88River/Cal-218
88River/ProC-1408
89River/Best-5
89River/Cal-7
89River/ProC-1412
Farmer, Michael
90Martins/ProC-3182
91SALAS/ProC-SAL43
91Spartan/ClBest-23
91Spartan/ProC-908
Farmer, Randy
91Kingspt/ClBest-13
91Kingspt/ProC-3820
Farmer, Reggie
87Spokane-11
88Charl/ProC-1216
89Watlo/ProC-1796
89Watlo/Star-5
90Riversi/Best-8
90Riversi/Cal-9
90Riversi/ProC-2618
91HighD/ClBest-24
91HighD/ProC-2407
Farmer, William
N172
Farnsworth, Mark
82CharR-23
83CharR-26
85FtMyr-21
86FtMyr-10TR
87FtMyr-31
90BBCity/Star-31TR
Farnsworth, Ross
90Kissim/DIMD-11
Faron, Robert J.
87Spring/Best-11
88ArkTr/GS-9
90SpringDG/Best-21
Farr, Jim
80Tulsa-7
83OKCty-22
84Cram/PCL-9
Farr, Michael
86Watlo-7
87Kinston-15
88Wmsprt/ProC-1307
Farr, Steve
78Charl
80Buffa-7
81Buffa-18
82Buffa-13
84Maine-4
84Wheat/Ind-27
85D-653
85F-446
85T-664
86D-588
86NatPhoto-26
86T/Tr-35T
87D-301
87F-367
87OPC-216
87T-473
87T/St-255
88D-378
88F-256
88S-466
88Smok/Royals-10
88T-222
89B-114
89D-356
89D/Best-151
89F-281
89OPC-356
89Panini/St-349
89S-183
89T-507
89T/St-272
89Tastee/Discs-12
89UD-308
90B-366
90D-356
90F-107
90OPC-149
90Publint/St-347
90RedFoley/St-30
90S-356
90T-149
90T/St-270
90UD-680
91B-168
91D-365
91F-558
91Leaf/II-348
91Leaf/Stud-92
91OPC-301
91S-172
91S/RookTr-21T
91T-301
91T/StClub/II-419
91T/Tr-38T
91UD-660
91UD/Ext-717
92D/II-735
92F-225
92S/I-47
92T-46
92UD-48
Farrar, Sid
N172
N284
N690
WG1-50
Farrar, Terry
91Bluefld/ProC-4121
91Bluefld/ClBest-4
Farrell, Charles A.
(Duke)
90Target-233
E107
N172
Farrell, Dick
(Turk)
58Hires-43
58T-76
59T-175
60T-103
61P-115
61T-522
61T/St-54
62Salada-184
62Shirriff-184
62T-304
62T/bucks
62T/St-125
63Bz-8
63Exh
63F-38
63J-192
63P-192
63Pep
63Salada-2
63T-277
63T-9LL
63T/SO
64Bz-8
64T-560
64T/Coins-91
64T/S-22
64T/St-98
64T/SU
65OldLond-9
65OPC-80
65T-80
66T-377
67OPC-190
67T-190
68T-217
69MB-82
69T-531
78TCMA-202
78TCMA-256
86Mother/Ast-1
89Smok/Ast-8
90Target-232
Exh47
Farrell, Edward S.
(Doc)
26Exh-33
29Exh/4-1
33G-148
91Conlon/Sport-324
V353-73
Farrell, John A.
N172
N284
Farrell, John
85Water-21
86Water-9
87BuffB-15
88CapeCod/Sum-76
88Classic/Blue-239
88D-42RR
88D/Best-117
88F-608
88Gator-52
88Leaf-42RR
88S-620
88S/YS/I-33
88Sf-132
88T-533
88T/Big-213
89B-74
89D-320
89D/Best-285
89F-403
89OPC-227
89Panini/St-318
89S-266
89Sf-37
89T-227
89T/Big-135
89T/St-214
89UD-468
90D-232
90D/BestAL-19
90F-491
90Leaf/I-22
90OPC-32
90Panini/St-53
90Publint/St-559
90S-103
90T-32
90T/Big-237
90T/St-217
90UD-570
91B-82
91Classic/DP-20
91D-106
91F-366
91F/Ultra-111
91Leaf/Stud-42
91OPC-664
91S-50
91T-664
91T/StClub/I-185
91UD-692
Farrell, Jon
91FrRow/DP-12
91Welland/ClBest-1
91Welland/ProC-3575
92S/II-804FDP
92T-9DP
92UD-69TP
Farrell, Mike
76AppFx
Farrish, Keoki
91Yakima/ClBest-9
91Yakima/ProC-4260
Farrow, Doug
82Idaho-6
Farsaci, Dave
91Eugene/ClBest-17
91Eugene/ProC-3718
Farson, George
78Holyo
79Holyo-8
80Penin/C-11C
Farwell, Fred
87Bakers-20
Fascher, Stan
86Ashvl-11
87Osceola-11
Fassero, Jeff
85Spring-9
86FSLAS-13
86StPete-8
87ArkTr-6
88ArkTr/GS-5
89Louisvl-18
89Louisvl/CMC-4
89Louisvl/ProC-1246
90Canton/Best-19
90Canton/ProC-1289
90Canton/Star-5
91D/Rook-28
91Indianap/LineD-183
91Indianap/ProC-457
91T/Tr-39T
92D/II-717
92F-477
92F/RookSlns-5
92S/II-738
92T-423
92T/91Debut-55
92UD-685
Fast, Darcy
72OPC-457R
72T-457R
Faszholz, John
55Hunter

Fator, Laverne
33SK-13
Faul, Bill
63T-558R
64T-236
66T-322
Faulk, James
(Jim)
88Rockford-13
89Rockford-13
90FSLAS/Star-5
90WPalmB/Star-5
Faulk, Kelly
80Penin/B-6
80Penin/C-13
82Reading-2
85Colum-6
85Colum/Pol-10
86Colum-8
86Colum/Pol-8
87Indianap-24
Faulkner, Craig
88Hagers/Star-6
89Hagers/Best-14
89Hagers/ProC-266
89Hagers/Star-7
90Hagers/Best-10
90Hagers/ProC-1421
90Hagers/Star-9
90LSUGreat-6
91ElPaso/LineD-181
91ElPaso/ProC-2750
Faulkner, Jim
90Target-234
Faurot, Scott
90Yakima/Team-21TR
Faust, Nancy
84TrueVal/WS-12org
85Coke/WS-org
86Coke/WS-org
87Coke/WS-28org
88Coke/WS-6org
89Coke/WS-29org
Fava, Andres
85Anchora-10
Faw, Bryan
90Tampa/DIMD-6
91Greens/ProC-3051
Fayne, Jeff
89Johnson/Star-13
90Hamil/Star-12
91Spring/ClBest-16
91Spring/ProC-756
Fazekas, Robert
88CapeCod/Sum-160
90Niagara/Pucko-18
91Fayette/ClBest-9
91Fayette/ProC-1162
Fazio, Ernie
63Pep
78TCMA-215
Fazzini, Frank
86Beloit-6
Fears, Tom
52Wheat
Feder, Mike
76Wausau
Federici, Rick
78Charl
80Buffa-3
Federico, Gustavo
89Helena/SP-14
Federico, Joe
87Anchora-11
88Hamil/ProC-1738
89StPete/Star-11
90Foil/Best-93
90Spring/Best-8
91StPete/ClBest-20
91StPete/ProC-2283
Federoff, Al
53Mother-62
Fedor, Chris
84Greens-11
Fedor, Fritz
82Beloit-9
83Beloit/LF-24
86BurlEx-7
87Kinston-10
Feeley, James
82Madis-20
Feeley, Peter
91Niagara/ClBest-16
91Niagara/ProC-3646
Feinburg, Ken
77Cedar
78Cedar
Feist, Ken
91Everett/ClBest-9
91Everett/ProC-3928
Felda, Brian
75Cedar
Felden, Keith
88Utica/Pucko-18
89Miami/I/Star-6
Felder, Mike
83ElPaso-9
84ElPaso-23
85Cram/PCL-211
86D-634
86Pol/Brew-16
87D-295
87Pol/Brew-16
87T-352
88D-397
88F-164
88Pol/Brew-16
88S-388
88T-718
89Pol/Brew-16
89T-263
89UD-252
90Brewer/MillB-7
90D-609
90ElPasoATG/Team-12
90F-321
90Leaf/II-480
90OPC-159
90Pol/Brew-16
90PublInt/St-495
90S-268
90T-159
90UD-178
91D-535
91F-583
91F/UltraUp-U117
91F/Up-U129
91Leaf/II-445
91Mother/Giant-15
91OPC-44
91PG&E-28
91S-97
91T-44
91T/StClub/II-307
91UD-395
92D/I-182
92F-635
92S/I-251
92T-697
92UD-288
Felice, Jason
83Tampa-8
86Jacks/TCMA-20
87Tidew-7
Feliciano, Felix
80Utica-5
Felitz, Bill
89Johnson/Star-12
Felix, Antonio
89Augusta/ProC-510
90Salem/Star-6
Felix, Gus
90Target-946
Felix, Junior
87Myrtle-21
88SLAS-24
89D/Best-199
89D/Rook-55
89F/Up-69
89S/Tr-83
89Syrac/CMC-19
89Syrac/ProC-810
89Syrac/Team-10
89T/Tr-32T
89UD/Ext-743
90B-522
90Classic-50
90D-70
90D/BestAL-70
90F-79
90F/SoarSt-9
90HotRook/St-15
90Leaf/II-422
90OPC-347
90Panini/St-377
90S-258
90S/100Ris-18
90S/YS/I-9
90Sf-186
90T-347
90T/89Debut-35
90T/Big-210
90T/JumboR-8
90T/St-188
90Tor/BlueJ-47
90ToysRUs-9
90UD-106
91B-201
91Classic/200-190
91Classic/II-T48
91D-323
91F-173
91Leaf/II-435
91OPC-543
91OPC/Premier-41
91Panini/FrSt-342
91S-203
91S/RookTr-20T
91Smok/Angel-2
91T-543
91T/StClub/II-457
91T/Tr-40T
91UD-563
91UD/Ext-711
92D/I-217
92S/II-519
92T-189
92UD-303
Felix, Nathanael
90Tampa/DIMD-7
Felix, Nick
89Wausau/GS-16
90SanBern/Cal-92
91CharlR/ClBest-5
91CharlR/ProC-1309
Felix, Paul
83Wisco/LF-6
85Orlan-4
86GlenF-4
87GlenF-19
88Toledo/CMC-20
88Toledo/ProC-600
Felix, Sanchez
88Knoxvl/Best-2
Feliz, Adolfo
81Water-13
82Cedar-15
83Tampa-9
83Water-11
Feliz, Janiero
90Welland/Pucko-5
Feller, Bob
37Exh/4-11
37OPC-120
38Dix
38Exh/4-11
38G-264
38G-288
38ONG/Pin-8
38Wheat
39Exh
40Wheat
41DP-78
47HomogBond-15
48B-5
48L-93
48Swell-19
49B-27
50B-6
50NumNum
51B-30
51T/RB-22
51Wheat
52B-43
52BR
52NumNum-5
52RM-AL8
52StarCal/L-74E
52T-88
52Wheat
53B/Col-114
53Exh/Can-17
53T-54
54B-132
54DanDee
54Wilson
55B-134
55Gol/Ind-6
55Salem
56Carling-1
56T-200
60F-26
60NuCard-60
61F-25
61NuCard-460
72Laugh/GF-44
79TCMA-28
80Pac/Leg-53
80SSPC/HOF
81Watlo-34
82CJ-10
83D/HOF-36
83MLBPA/Pin-6
84West/1-10
86Sf/Dec-16
87Nestle/DT-20
88Pac/Leg-101
89HOF/St-62
89Pac/Leg-156
89Swell-75
90BBWit-13
90CollAB-36
90Pac/Legend-85
90Swell/Great-60
91Conlon/Sport-35
91Homer/Classic-6
91LineD-43
91Swell/Great-145
91T/Arc53-54
92Conlon/Sport-370
D305
PM10/Sm-50
PM10/Sm-51
PR1-8
R302-103
R303/A
R303/B
R326-8A
R326-8B
R342-8
R346-43
R423-31
V300
Fellows, Mark
82Madis-14
83Albany-3
Felsch, Oscar
(Happy)
88Pac/8Men-10
88Pac/8Men-109
88Pac/8Men-41
88Pac/8Men-55M
88Pac/8Men-76
D327
D328-47
D329-56
D350/2-57
E135-47
M101/4-56
M101/5-57
W514-3
Felske, John
73OPC-332
73OPC-45
73T-332
77Spoka
79Vanco-20
82Reading-22
83Portl-13
84Phill/TastyK-10CO
85Phill/TastyK-2MG
85Phill/TastyK-8MG
85T/Tr-33T
86Phill/TastyK-7MG
86T-621MG
87Phill/TastyK-7MG
87T-443MG
Felt, Jim
82AlexD-24
83AlexD-22
84PrWill-5
Felt, Rich
82VeroB-5
83VeroB-3
Felton, Fred
88Batavia/ProC-1686
Felton, Terry
79Toledo-9
80Toledo-7
81Toledo-4
83D-354
83F-612
83T-181
83Toledo-2
Felton, Todd
88Spartan/ProC-1043
Fendrick, Dave
74Gaston
Fennell, Mike
82Oneonta-14
83Greens-18
85Albany-26
Fennelly, Francis
N172
Fenwick, Bob
72T-679R
73OPC-567
73T-567
Feola, Lawrence
(Larry)
75Clinton
87SanJose-22
Ferguson, Alex
90Target-235
E126-40
Ferguson, Bruce
78Wausau
Ferguson, Charles
N172
N284
N690
Ferguson, Fergy
83Tampa-10
Ferguson, George
10Domino-44
12Sweet/Pin-66
E254
E270/1
E286
M116
T204
T205
T206
Ferguson, Greg
88SoOreg/ProC-1708
Ferguson, James
(Jim)
82Oneonta-15
87SLCity/Taco-6
88Savan/ProC-348
89Savan/ProC-354
90Savan/ProC-2075
91James/ClBest-23
91James/ProC-3536
Ferguson, Joe
72T-616
73OPC-621
73T-621
74OPC-86
74T-86
74T/DE-67
74T/St-45
75OPC-115
75T-115
75T/M-115
76OPC-329
76SSPC-81
76T-329
77BurgChef-8
77OPC-107
77T-573
78BK/Ast-2
78Ho-109
78T-226
79T-671
80OPC-29
80Pol/Dodg-13
80T-51
81D-177
81F-124
81Pol/Dodg-13
81T-711
82T-514
83D-604
83F-87
83T-416
87Smok/R-24CO
90Mother/Dodg-28M
90Pol/Dodg-x
90Target-236
91Mother/Dodg-28CO
91Pol/Dodg-x
Ferguson, Mark
83Albany-4

84Greens-19
85Albany-6
Ferguson, Mike
82Cedar-8
Ferlenda, Greg
86Salem-9
86Tulsa-15
88Kinston/Star-6
89Canton/Best-14
89Canton/Star-5
89Kinston/Star-8
90CLAS/CL-35
90Kinston/Team-19
Ferm, Ed
88Bristol/ProC-1886
90Lakeland/Star-10
91Lakeland/ClBest-4
91Lakeland/ProC-260
91Single/ClBest-289
Fermaint, Mike
91Penin/ClBest-19
91Penin/ProC-384
Fermin, Carlos
90Bristol/ProC-3149
90Bristol/Star-6
91Fayette/ClBest-18
91Fayette/ProC-1177
91Single/ClBest-374
Fermin, Felix
84PrWill-16
85Nashua-9
86Hawaii-9
87Harris-6
88BuffB/CMC-21
88BuffB/ProC-1465
88D-144
88F-643R
88T-547
89D-565
89D/Best-229
89D/Tr-33
89F-208
89F/Up-27
89S-620
89S/Tr-78
89T-303
89T/Tr-33T
89UD-88
90B-334
90D-191
90F-492
90OPC-722
90Panini/St-60
90Publlnt/St-560
90S-256
90S/YS/I-6
90T-722
90UD-409
91D-537
91F-367
91F/Ultra-112
91Leaf/I-137
91OPC-193
91Panini/FrSt-219
91S-139
91T-193
91T/StClub/I-238
91UD-104
92D/I-242
92F-109
92S/I-148
92T-632
92UD-160
Fermin, Pompilio
76Clinton
Fernandes, Eddie
47Sunbeam
Fernandez, Alex
90Classic/DP-4
90Classic/III-99
90F/Up-U84
90Foil/Best-250
90Foil/Best-321
91B-351
91Bz-5
91Classic/200-184
91Classic/II-T7
91D-59
91F-117
91F/UltraUp-U14
91Kodak/WSox-32
91Kodak/WSox-x
91Leaf/II-296
91Leaf/Stud-31
91OPC-278
91OPC/Premier-42
91S-382FDP
91S/100RisSt-66
91Seven/3DCoin-5F
91Seven/3DCoin-9MW
91T-278
91T/90Debut-48
91T/CJMini/II-36
91T/StClub/I-147
91UD-645
91Woolwth/HL-11
92D/I-191
92F-78
92S/I-82
92T-755
92UD-551
Fernandez, Chris
87Tampa-22
Fernandez, Dan
89SanJose/Best-8
89SanJose/Cal-232
89SanJose/ProC-441
89SanJose/Star-9
90SanJose/Best-12
90SanJose/Cal-40
90SanJose/ProC-2012
90SanJose/Star-9
91SanJose/ClBest-1
91SanJose/ProC-12
Fernandez, Frank
66T-584R
68T-214R
69T-557
70OPC-82
70T-82
71MLB/St-512
71OPC-468
71T-468
72MB-102
Fernandez, Froilan
(Nanny)
47TipTop
49Royal-23
Fernandez, Humberto
(Chico)
55B-270
57T-305
58Hires-16
58Hires/T
58T-348
59T-452
60T-314
61T-112
61T/St-150
62J-17
62P-17
62P/Can-17
62Salada-3
62Shirriff-3
62T-173
63T-278
79TCMA-274
88Cedar/ProC-1141
90Target-237
91Crown/Orio-127
91WIZMets-113
Fernandez, James
88StPete/Star-7
Fernandez, Joey
89StPete/Star-12
91ArkTr/LineD-32
91ArkTr/ProC-1293
91Louisvl/ProC-2926
Fernandez, Jose
86Negro/Frit-72
89Hamil/Star-11
90StPete/Star-7
91ArkTr/LineD-33
91ArkTr/ProC-1288
91Hunting/ClBest-8
91Hunting/ProC-3346
Fernandez, Julio
89Clinton/ProC-900
91Belling/ClBest-17
91Belling/ProC-3680
Fernandez, Mike
91Elizab/ProC-4305
Fernandez, Reynaldo
88Oneonta/ProC-2053
88PrWill/Star-9
Fernandez, Rolando
90Hunting/ProC-3297
91Peoria/ClBest-19
91Peoria/ProC-1356
Fernandez, Sid
82VeroB-6
84D-44RR
84Tidew-2
85D-563
85F-77
85OPC-390
85T-649
85Tidew-3
86D-625
86F-79
86KayBee-10
86Leaf-242
86T-104
86T/Mini-51
87Classic-74
87D-323
87D/AAS-26
87D/HL-4
87F-629M
87F-8
87F/BB-16
87F/Slug-13
87Leaf-93
87OPC-337
87Sf-63
87T-570
87T/Mini-22
87T/St-97
88D-118
88D/AS-58
88D/Mets/Bk-118
88F-134
88F/BB/MVP-13
88F/St-101
88Kahn/Mets-50
88Leaf-63
88OPC-30
88Panini/St-336
88RedFoley/St-22
88S-615
88Sf-177
88T-30
88T/Mets/Fan-50
88T/St-103
88T/St/Backs-28
89B-377
89D-471
89F-35
89Kahn/Mets-50
89OPC-34
89S-268
89T-790
89T/Big-276
89T/Mini-25
89UD-168
90B-131
90D-572
90D/BestNL-105
90F-203
90Kahn/Mets-50
90KMart/SS-11
90Leaf/I-66
90Mets/Fan-50
90OPC-480
90Panini/St-299
90Publlnt/St-133
90S-18
90Sf-113
90T-480
90T/Big-155
90T/Coins-46
90T/DH-20
90T/Mini-66
90T/St-92
90T/TVAS-61
90T/TVMets-10
90Target-238
90UD-261
91B-462
91D-97
91F-146
91F/Ultra-216
91Kahn/Mets-50
91OPC-230
91S-180
91T-230
91T/StClub/I-225
91UD-242
91WIZMets-112
92D/II-719
92F-503
92S/II-675
92T-382
92UD-671
Fernandez, Tony
82Syrac-17
83Syrac-16
84D-32
84F-152
84Syrac-9
84Tor/Fire-11
85D-390
85F-103
85Leaf-91
85OPC-48
85OPC/Post-16
85T-48
85Tor/Fire-10
86Ault-1
86D-119
86F-57
86F/Mini-14
86F/St-37
86KayBee-11
86Leaf-45
86OPC-241
86Sf-112
86T-241
86T/St-194
86Tor/Fire-9
87Classic-57
87D-72
87D/AAS-35
87D/OD-35
87F-225
87F/AS-3
87F/AwardWin-12
87F/Mini-38
87F/RecSet-7
87F/St-39
87Leaf-106
87OPC-329
87RedFoley/St-29
87Sf-113M
87Sf-187
87T-485
87T/Mini-75
87T/St-191
87Tor/Fire-8
88Bz-7
88D-12DK
88D-319
88D/AS-25
88D/Best-87
88D/DKsuper-12DK
88F-109
88F-635M
88F/BB/MVP-14
88F/Hottest-10
88F/Mini-61
88F/SS-C3
88F/St-72
88Ho/Disc-21
88Leaf-12DK
88Leaf-133
88OPC-290
88Panini/St-222
88S-20
88S-651M
88S/YS/II-6
88Sf-26
88T-290
88T/Big-187
88T/Coins-12
88T/Gloss60-15
88T/St-193
88T/St/Backs-43
88T/UK-23
88Tor/Fire-1
89B-254
89Classic-115
89D-206
89D/Best-48
89F-231
89F/Superstar-13
89OPC-170
89Panini/St-470
89RedFoley/St-41
89S-57
89S/HotStar-53
89Sf-93
89T-170
89T/Big-157
89T/Coins-39
89T/Gloss60-52
89T/LJN-92
89T/Mini-76
89T/St-189
89T/St/Backs-10
89T/UK-25
89Tor/Fire-1
89UD-139
90B-524
90D-149
90D/BestAL-113
90F-634M
90F-80
90F/AwardWin-12
90F/BB-9
90F/BBMVP-11
90KMart/CBatL-16
90Leaf/I-53
90OPC-685
90Panini/St-176
90Publlnt/St-283
90Publlnt/St-513
90RedFoley/St-31
90S-89
90Sf-6
90T-685
90T/Big-165
90T/DH-21
90T/Mini-42
90T/St-11HL
90T/St-194
90Tor/BlueJ-1
90UD-130
91B-642
91Classic/200-161
91Classic/II-T45
91D-524
91F-174
91F/UltraUp-U111
91F/Up-U123
91Leaf/II-315
91Leaf/Stud-244
91OPC-320
91OPC/Premier-43
91Panini/FrSt-339
91Panini/St-152
91RedFoley/St-33
91S-432
91S/RookTr-66T
91T-320
91T/StClub/II-515
91T/Tr-41T
91UD-126
91UD/Ext-754
92D/I-362
92F-604
92S/II-645
92T-60
92UD-272
Ferran, Alex
89Watertn/Star-6
90Reno/Cal-265
Ferran, George
86Shrev-8
87Phoenix-4
Ferrante, Joe
82DayBe-3
Ferrara, Al
64T-337R
65T-331R
66T-487
67T-557
68OPC-34
68T-34
69MLB/St-191
69NTF
69T-452
69T/DE-30
69T/St-93
70MLB/St-113
70OPC-345
70T-345
70T/CB
71MLB/St-226
71OPC-214
71T-214
71T/Coins-25
72MB-103
90Target-239
Ferrarese, Don
55T-185
56T-266
57T-146
58T-469

59T-247
60T-477
61T-558
62T-547
91Crown/Orio-128

Ferraro, Carl
86CharRain-9

Ferraro, Mike
68T-539R
69OPC-83
69T-83
72T-613
77WHave
78Cr/PCL-119MG
83T/Tr-32MG
83Wheat/Ind-11MG
90T/TVYank-4CO

Ferraro, Vincent
84Visalia-5

Ferrebee, Anthony
87Idaho-2

Ferreira, Arturo J.
(Jose)
85Madis-13
85Madis/Pol-10

Ferreira, Tony
82FtMyr-11
84Omaha-3
85Omaha-10
86Tidew-8
87Calgary-20
88Albany/ProC-1339
90Omaha/CMC-8
90Omaha/ProC-61

Ferreiras, Sal
86PrWill-10

Ferrell, Frank
75Cedar

Ferrell, Rick
31Exh/4-30
33Exh/4-15
33G-197
34DS-48
34Exh/4-9
35BU-10
35BU-126
35Exh/4-9
35G-8G
35G-9G
36Exh/4-9
36G
37Exh/4-9
37OPC-132
38Exh/4-16
39PB-39
40PB-21
61F-105
90Pac/Legend-23
90Swell/Great-86
91Swell/Great-29
92Conlon/Sport-471
R310
R312/M
R314
V300
W753
WG8-17

Ferrell, Wes
31Exh/4-21
33CJ/Pin-5
33DH-14
33Exh/4-11
33G-218
34DS-94
34Exh/4-11
35BU-12
35BU-174
35G-8G
35G-9G
37OPC-138
38Exh/4-16
61F-26
88Conlon/3-11
90HOF/St-30
90Target-240
91Conlon/Sport-198
92Conlon/Sport-361
92Conlon/Sport-446
R300
R306
R308-162
R311/Leath
R314
R332-21
V300
V355-40

Ferrer, Sergio
76OkCty/Team-9
78Tidew
79T-397
80T-619
80Tidew-5
81Indianap-31
89Pac/SenLg-2
90EliteSenLg-110
91WIZMets-114

Ferretti, Sam
88Watlo/ProC-680
89Canton/ProC-1307
89Kinston/Star-9
90Canton/Best-7
90Canton/ProC-1297
90Canton/Star-6
90Foil/Best-309
91Canton/LineD-83
91Canton/ProC-986

Ferreyra, Raul
77Indianap-19
78Indianap-21

Ferrick, Tom
39Exh
51B-182
60T-461C

Ferris, Albert
(Hobe)
E107
E254
E270/1
E270/2
T204
T206
WG2-18

Ferris, Bob
76QuadC
78Cr/PCL-60
79SLCity-10
80SLCity-24
81SLCity-5

Ferris, David
(Boo)
47TipTop
49B-211

Ferro, Bob
83Wisco/LF-11

Ferroni, Frank
81Miami-14

Ferry, John
11Helmar-159
T207

Ferry, Mike
90A&AASingle/ProC-195
90Billings/ProC-3214
91Cedar/ClBest-4
91Cedar/ProC-2712

Ferson, Alexander
N172

Ferst, Larry
78Clinton

Fessenden, Wallace
N172

Fette, Lou
38Wheat
90Target-241
PR1-9

Fetters, Michael
86Cram/PCL-97
87PalmSp-26
88MidldA/GS-10
89Edmon/CMC-9
90B-286
90D-35
90Edmon/CMC-7
90Edmon/ProC-514
90F-131
90OPC-14
90T-14
90T/89Debut-36
90UD/Ext-742
91D-565
91Edmon/LineD-163
91Edmon/ProC-1512
91F-312
91OPC-477
91S-497
91S/100RisSt-74
91T-477
91T/StClub/I-228
91UD-696
92D/II-491
92F-56
92S/100RisSt-38
92S/II-606
92T-602

Fetzer, John E.
81Detroit-81OWN
83Kaline-39OWN
83Kaline-44OWN

Fewster, Wilson
(Chick)
25Exh-81
26Exh-12
27Exh-6
90Target-242
E121/120
E220
W501-120
W575

Fiacco, Charlie
90Geneva/ProC-3035
90Geneva/Star-12

Fiala, Mike
86Bakers-7

Fiala, Neil
78StPete
79ArkTr-13
82Indianap-29

Fiala, Walter
52Park-67
53Exh/Can-48

Fichman, Mal
79Newar-6
88Boise/ProC-1632
90Erie/Star-29MG

Fick, Barry
85Cedar-7

Fick, Chuck
82WHave-11
90EliteSenLg-111
91Pac/SenLg-93

Ficklin, Winston
81Watlo-29
82Watlo/B-15
82Watlo/C-19
83Watlo/LF-18
85Water-4
86Water-10
87Wmsprt-3
88Portl/CMC-18
88Portl/ProC-652
89Iowa/CMC-21
89Iowa/ProC-1711

Fidler, Andy
89Kingspt/Star-9
90Pittsfld/Pucko-19

Fidrych, Mark
77BurgChef-92
77Ho-46
77K-26
77OPC-115
77OPC-7LL
77Pep-30
77T-265
77T-7LL
77T/CS-15
78BK/T-4
78OPC-235
78PapaG/Disc-32
78T-45
78Tastee/Discs-22
78Wiffle/Discs-21
79Ho-77
79OPC-329
79T-625
80Evansvl-6
80OPC-231
80T-445
81D-8
81Detroit-6
81Evansvl-4
81F-462
81OPC-150
81T-150
83Pawtu-7
88Pac/Leg-62
90Swell/Great-122

Fiedler, Mark
86LitFalls-11

Fiegel, Todd
91Kingspt/ClBest-15
91Kingspt/ProC-3807

Field, Greg
79Portl-3
83Richm-5
84Toledo-18

Field, James
E254

Fielder, Cecil
86Ault-23
86D-512
86F-653R
86OPC-386
86T-386
86Tor/Fire-10
87F/Up-U31
87OPC-178
87T-178
87Tor/Fire-9
88D-565
88F-110
88OPC-21
88S-399
88T-618
88Tor/Fire-23
89D-442
89F-232
89OPC-224
89S-120
89T-541
89UD-364
90B-357
90Classic/III-94
90CokeK/Tiger-4
90D/BestAL-133
90D/Learning-26
90F/Up-U95
90Leaf/I-165
90S/McDon-16
90S/Tr-9T
90T/Big-313
90T/Tr-31T
90UD/Ext-786
90USPlayC/AS-13S
90Windwlk/Discs-4
91B-136
91B-367SLUG
91Bz-8
91Classic/200-127
91Classic/I-41
91Classic/II-T69
91CokeK/Tiger-45
91CollAB-14
91D-397MVP
91D-3DK
91D-451
91D-BC5
91D/Elite-E6
91D/GSlam-7
91D/SuperDK-3
91DennyGS-2
91F-335
91F-709M
91F/ASIns-4
91F/Ultra-121
91F/Ultra-392EP
91JDeanSig-21
91KingB/Discs-14
91Leaf/I-106
91Leaf/Prev-18
91Leaf/Stud-53
91MajorLg/Pins-32
91MooTown-24
91OPC-386AS
91OPC-720
91OPC/Premier-44
91Panini/FrSt-288
91Panini/St-232
91Panini/Top15-13
91Panini/Top15-21
91Panini/Top15-37
91Panini/Top15-54
91Pep/SS-10
91Petro/SU-11
91Post-23
91Post/Can-19
91RedFoley/St-34
91S-168
91S-395AS
91S-693MB
91S-770HL
91S/100SS-88
91Seven/3DCoin-3MW
91Seven/3DCoin-6F
91Sunflower-8
91T-386AS
91T-720
91T/CJMini/I-31
91T/StClub/I-186
91T/SU-13
91UD-244
91UD-83TC
91UD/FinalEd-82F
91UD/SilSlug-SS12
91USPlayC/AS-12D
92Classic/I-33
92D/I-206
92D/I-27AS
92F-133
92F-692LL
92F-705M
92F/TmLIns-6
92S/100SS-66
92S/I-431AS
92S/I-50
92T-397AS
92T-425
92UD-255
92UD-647DS
92UD-96TC

Fields, Bruce
82BirmB-11
83SanJose-14
86Nashvl-8
87D-47RR
87Leaf-47RR
87Toledo-14
87Toledo/TCMA-9
88Mother/Sea-16
89AAA/CMC-36
89Calgary/CMC-19
89Calgary/ProC-534
89S/HotRook-43
89T-556
89UD-238
90BirmDG/Best-10
90Tacoma/CMC-14
90Tacoma/ProC-106
91Richm/ProC-2580

Fields, John James
N172

Fields, Wilmer
52Park-21
91Negro/Lewis-17

Fiene, Lou
T206

Fiener, Huck
91Myrtle/ClBest-4

Fiepke, Scott
86Nashua-6

Fier, Mike
90Gate/ProC-3350

Fierro, John
80Penin/B-24tr
80Penin/C-10tr
86Peoria-6

Fife, Dan
74OPC-421
74T-421

Figga, Michael
90Tampa/DIMD-8
91PrWill/ClBest-14
91PrWill/ProC-1430

Figueroa, Alexis
89Watlo/ProC-1774
89Watlo/Star-6

Figueroa, Bienvenido
86Erie-7
87Spring/Best-22
88ArkTr/GS-6
89Louisvl-19
89Louisvl/CMC-17
89Louisvl/ProC-1262
90Louisvl/CMC-17
90Louisvl/ProC-409
90T/TVCard-47
91Louisvl/LineD-234
91Louisvl/ProC-2923

Figueroa, Ed
75OPC-476
75T-476
75T/M-476
76OPC-27
76SSPC-190
76T-27
76T/Tr-27T
77BK/Y-5
77K-42

77OPC-164
77T-195
78BK/Y-5
78T-365
78T/Zest-3
79BK/Y-11
79OPC-13
79T-35
80OPC-288
80T-555
81F-624
81T-245
81Tacoma-32
82Tacoma-10
89Pac/SenLg-75
89T/SenLg-43
89TM/SenLg-34
90EliteSenLg-80

Figueroa, Fernando
87PrWill-22
88FtLaud/Star-8
89Miami/II/Star-4
90Wmsprt/Best-5
90Wmsprt/ProC-1051
90Wmsprt/Star-6
91Jaxvl/LineD-335
91Jaxvl/ProC-145

Figueroa, Jesus
77WHave
80Wichita-9
81D-556
81T-533
87Pocatel/Bon-25

Figueroa, Matt
91James/ClBest-22
91James/ProC-3537

Figueroa, Ray
88Geneva/ProC-1637

Figueroa, Rich
80Clinton-23
81Clinton-28

Figueroa, Vic
86Modesto-9

Filer, Thomas
79WHave-11
81Colum-24
82Iowa-15
83Iowa-3
83T-508
84Iowa-28
85Syrac-6
86D-439
86F-58
86Leaf-211
86OPC-312
86T-312
86Tor/Fire-11
88Denver/CMC-10
88Denver/ProC-1257
88T/Tr-37T
89F-185
89T-419
90B-385
90Brewer/MillB-8
90D-687
90F-322
90Pol/Brew-28

Filippi, James
86AppFx-8
87SanBern-10

Filkey, Bernard
89ArkTr/GS-6

Filkins, Les
81Evansvl-19
82Evansvl-19

Fillingim, Dana
21Exh-47
E120

Fillmore, Joe
86Negro/Frit-59

Filotei, Bobby
90Billings/ProC-3227
91Cedar/ProC-2726

Filson, Pete
82Colum-9
82Colum/Pol-30
82Toledo-26
84D-194
84F-564
84Nes/792-568
84T-568
85D-607
85F-277
85T-97
86BuffB-11
86D-436
86F-393
86T-122
87Colum-29
87Colum/Pol-9
87Colum/TCMA-3
90AAAGame/ProC-AAA23
90Omaha/CMC-9
90Omaha/ProC-62
91BBCity/ClBest-30CO
91BBCity/ProC-1414CO

Filter, Rusty
90StCath/ProC-3468

Fimple, Jack
81Watlo-18
82VeroB-14
83Albuq-11
84Cram/PCL-146
84D-372
84F-99
84Nes/792-263
84Pol/Dodg-31
84T-263
85Cram/PCL-163
86Albuq-7
87Edmon-23
90Target-243

Finch, Joel
79T-702R
80T-662R
81Pawtu-1

Finch, Steve
77Ashvl
79Tulsa-6
81Spokane-11
82SLCity-8
84Cram/PCL-106
85MidldA-13
86Edmon-8

Findlay, Bill
88Gaston/ProC-997

Fine, Tom
89Penin/Star-5
90Visalia/Cal-61
90Visalia/ProC-2147

Fine, Tommy
48Sommer-4

Fingers, Bob
87Modesto-18

Fingers, Rollie
69T-597R
70OPC-502
70T-502
71MLB/St-513
71OPC-384
71T-384
72OPC-241
72T-241
73OPC-84
73T-84
74OPC-212
74T-212
75Ho-52
75Ho/Twink-52
75K-55
75OPC-21
75OPC-463WS
75T-21
75T/M-21
75T-463WS
75T/M-463WS
76Ho-104
76OPC-405
76SSPC-480
76T-405
77BurgChef-133
77Ho-137
77K-51
77OPC-52
77Padre/SchCd-10
77T-523
78Ho-144
78OPC-201
78OPC-8LL
78Padre/FamFun-11
78T-140
78T-208LL
78Wiffle/Discs-22
79OPC-203
79T-390
79T-8LL
80BK/PHR-3
80OPC-343
80T-651
81D-2
81F-485
81F/St-47
81OPC-229
81T-229
81T-8LL
81T/St-31M
81T/Tr-761
82D-28
82F-141
82F-644M
82F/St-132
82K-7
82KMart-40
82OPC-176
82OPC-44
82PermaGr/CC-16
82Pol/Brew-34
82Sqt-11
82T-168LL
82T-585
82T-586IA
82T/St-16
82T/St-198
83D-2DK
83D-78
83D/AAS-33
83F-33
83Gard-7
83K-2
83OPC-35
83OPC-36SV
83PermaGr/CC-23
83Pol/Brew-34
83T-35
83T-36SV
83T/St-79
83T/St/Box-6
84D-LLA
84D/Champs-45
84F-199
85FunFood/Pin-10
84Gard-6
84Nes/792-495
84Nes/792-717LL
84Nes/792-718LL
84OPC-283
84Pol/Brew-34
84T-495
84T-717
84T-718
85D-292
85D/AAS-36
85D/HL-2
85F-581
85Gard-6
85Leaf-190
85OPC-182
85Pol/Brew-34
85T-750
85T/St-285
85Woolwth-10
86D-229
86F-486
86OPC-185
86Sf-130M
86Sf-146M
86Sf-150M
86Sf-65M
86T-185
86T/St-198
87Mother/A's-10
88Pac/Leg-103
89Pac/SenLg-161
89Padre/Mag-8
89T/SenLg-65
89TM/SenLg-35
90BBWit-51
90EliteSenLg-123
90EliteSenLg-21
90MSA/AGFA-18
91K/3D-7
91Pac/SenLg-126
91Swell/Great-30

Finigan, Jim
55Armour-5
55RFG-17
55Rodeo
55T-14
55T/DH-50
56Rodeo
56T-22
56T/Pin-12
57T-248
58T-136
59T-47
79TCMA-128
91Crown/Orio-129

Finigan, Kevin
87BurlEx-13
88James/ProC-1915

Fink, Eric
84PrWill-11

Finken, Steve
88GreatF-15
89AS/Cal-22
89Bakers/Cal-205
91SanAn/LineD-534
91SanAn/ProC-2982

Finley, Bob
45Centen-7

Finley, Brian
83Beloit/LF-18
86ElPaso-10
88Chatt/Best-13

Finley, Chuck
86QuadC-11
87D-407
87F-79
87Smok/Cal-6
87T-446
88D-530
88D/Best-283
88F-489
88Smok/Angels-15
88T-99
88T/Big-254
89B-36
89D-226
89D/Best-333
89F-477
89S-503
89T-708
89T/Big-76
89UD-632
90B-289
90D-344
90D/BestAL-103
90F-132
90KMart/SS-28
90Leaf/I-162
90OPC-147
90Panini/St-32
90PublInt/St-369
90S-380
90S/100St-24
90Sf-172
90Smok/Angel-5
90T-147
90T/Big-319
90T/Coins-13
90T/DH-22
90T/Mini-8
90T/St-171
90T/TVAS-14
90UD-667
90USPlayC/AS-9S
90Windwlk/Discs-5
91B-196
91BBBest/Aces-7
91Classic/I-95
91Classic/III-20
91D-26DK
91D-692
91D/SuperDK-26
91F-313
91F/Ultra-44
91Leaf/I-45
91Leaf/Prev-15
91Leaf/Stud-24
91OPC-395AS
91OPC-505
91Panini/FrSt-187
91Panini/St-135
91Panini/Top15-70
91RedFoley/St-35
91S-100
91S/100SS-90
91Smok/Angel-9
91Sunflower-7
91T-395AS
91T-505
91T/CJMini/II-12
91T/StClub/I-81
91UD-31
91UD-437
92D/I-255
92F-57
92S/100SS-6
92S/II-585
92T-247
92UD-244

Finley, David
88Modesto-23
88Modesto/Cal-70

Finley, Steve
88AAA/ProC-29
88Hagers/Star-7
88RochR/Gov-7
89B-15
89D/Rook-47
89F/Up-3
89French-10
89RochR/ProC-1639
89S/Tr-95
89UD/Ext-742
90D-215
90F-176
90HagersDG/Best-10
90Leaf/II-329
90OPC-349
90S-339
90S/100Ris-58
90S/YS/I-11
90T-349
90T/89Debut-37
90UD-602
91B-561
91Crown/Orio-130
91D-355
91F-470
91F/UltraUp-U81
91F/Up-U88
91Leaf/I-231
91Leaf/Stud-176
91Mother/Ast-2
91OPC-212
91Panini/FrSt-244
91S-266
91T-212
91T/StClub/II-376
91T/Tr-42T
91UD-330
91UD/Ext-794
92D/I-197
92F-433
92S/I-176
92T-86
92UD-368

Finn, John
89Beloit/II/Star-9
90Stockton/Best-11
90Stockton/Cal-196
90Stockton/ProC-2196
91AS/Cal-30
91Stockton/ClBest-18
91Stockton/ProC-3044

Finn, Neal (Mickey)
28Exh/PCL-7
33DH-15
90Target-244

Finney, Lou
40PB-197
41PB-30
92Conlon/Sport-512
R314
V355-64

Finney, Mark
91BendB/ClBest-5
91BendB/ProC-3690

Finnvold, Gar
90Elmira/Pucko-17
91LynchRS/ClBest-3
91LynchRS/ProC-1192
91Single/ClBest-192

Finzer, Kory
91AubAS/ClBest-27DIR

Fiore, Mike Jr.
88T/Tr-38T
89Spring/Best-1
89T/Big-8
90StPete/Star-8
91ArkTr/LineD-34
91ArkTr/ProC-1294

Fiore, Mike
69T-376R
70T-709
71MLB/St-318

71OPC-287
71T-287
72MB-104
72OPC-199
72T-199
78Colum
91Crown/Orio-131

Fiore, Tom
86Kenosha-9tr

Fiorillo, Nicholas
80Water-1
82Water-10
83Tampa-27

Fireovid, Steve
81Hawaii-13
82Hawaii-13
84Cram/PCL-214
85BuffB-18
86Calgary-8
87F-653M
87Syrac-6
87Syrac/TCMA-30
87T-357
88Omaha/CMC-4
88Omaha/ProC-1513
89Omaha/CMC-3
89Omaha/ProC-1718
90Indianap/CMC-1
90Indianap/ProC-292
91BuffB/LineD-28
91BuffB/ProC-534

Firova, Dan
80Spokane-22
86Calgary-9
89UD-32

Firsich, Steve
91Bluefld/ProC-4122
91Bluefld/ClBest-20

Fischback, Bruce
86Kinston-7tr

Fischer
N172

Fischer, Brad
82Madis-19MG
83Madis/LF-31MG
84Madis/Pol-1MG
85Huntsv/BK-25MG
88Tacoma/ProC-622MG
89Tacoma/CMC-25MG
89Tacoma/ProC-1551MG
90Tacoma/ProC-110MG

Fischer, Carl
43Centen-8
44Centen-7
45Centen-8
92Conlon/Sport-409

Fischer, Dan
81Omaha-7
82Omaha-4

Fischer, Hank
63T-554
64T-218
65T-585
66T-381
67T-342
67T/Test/RSox-5

Fischer, Jeff
86FSLAS-14
86WPalmB-15
87Indianap-15
88Indianap/CMC-6
88Indianap/ProC-503
89Albuq/CMC-3
89Albuq/ProC-86
90Albuq/CMC-3
90Albuq/ProC-338
90Albuq/Trib-7
90S-654
90Target-948

Fischer, Todd
82Idaho-7
83Madis/LF-4
84Albany-12
86Edmon-9

Fischer, Tom
89B-20
89Lynch/Star-8
90NewBrit/Star-4
91NewBrit/LineD-458

Fischer, William C.
58T-56
59T-230
60T-76
61T-553
63T-301
64T-409
72Laugh/GF-47
90T/TVRSox-4CO

Fischer, William C.
90HOF/St-64
90Target-947
D328-48
D329-57
D350/2-58
E135-48
M101/4-57
M101/5-58
W514-27

Fischetti, Art
75Water

Fischlin, Mike
78Charl
79Charl-6
79T-718R
80Tucson-17
81Charl-13
82Wheat/Ind
83D-489
83F-407
83T-182
83Wheat/Ind-12
84F-541
84Nes/792-689
84T-689
84Wheat/Ind-22
85D-495
85F-447
85Polar/Ind-22
85T-41
86F/Up-U40
86T-283
87Richm/Crown-18
87F-98
87Richm/TCMA-12
87T-434
88Greenvl/Best-23
88Richm-4
89Myrtle/ProC-1465
90Myrtle/ProC-2792MG
90SALAS/Star-47CO

Fishel, John
86FSLAS-15
86Osceola-8
87ColAst/ProC-12
88F/Up-U88
88Tucson/CMC-19
88Tucson/ProC-178
88Tucson/JP-11
89Colum/CMC-18
89Colum/Pol-4
89Colum/ProC-735
89D-443
89F-358
89Panini/St-80
89S/HotRook-42
90ColClip/CMC-14
90ColClip/ProC-689
90T/TVYank-42

Fisher, Brian
77Newar

Fisher, Brian K.
82Durham-17
84Richm-20
85Colum-7
85Colum/Pol-11
85F/Up-U40
86D-492
86F-104
86KayBee-12
86Sf-177M
86T-584
86T/Gloss60-30
86T/St-312
87D-340
87F-99
87F/Up-U32
87OPC-316
87T-316
87T/Tr-33T
88D-415
88D/Best-101
88F-329
88Leaf-244
88OPC-193
88Panini/St-368
88S-130
88T-193
88T/Big-159
89B-415
89D-126
89F-209
89OPC-303
89RedFoley/St-42
89S-24
89T-423
89UD-69
89VFJuice-54
90OPC-666
90PublInt/St-154
90S-547
90T-666
90Tucson/CMC-24
90Tucson/ProC-199
90UD-97
91Denver/LineD-137
91Denver/ProC-118

Fisher, Chauncey
90Target-949

Fisher, Eddie
60T-23
61T-366
63T-223
63T-6LL
64T-66
65T-328
66Bz-47
66OPC-85
66T-222LL
66T-85
66T/RO-22
67T-434
68T-418
69T-315
69T/St-143
70OPC-156
70T-156
71MLB/St-343
71OPC-631
71T-631
72T-689
73OPC-439
73T-439
91Crown/Orio-132

Fisher, Frederick
(Fritz)
64T-312R
66T-209R

Fisher, Glen
81Shrev-6
82Redwd-20

Fisher, Jack H.
60T-399M
60T-46
61T-463
62T-203
63T-474
64T-422
65OPC-93
65T-93
66T-316
66T/RO-6
67Kahn
67T-533
68T-444
69T-318
70T-684
89Clmbia/Best-23
89Clmbia/GS-2
91Crown/Orio-133
91WIZMets-115

Fisher, Kyle
89Augusta/ProC-521

Fisher, Ray
11Helmar-42
14CJ-102
15CJ-102
16FleischBrd-28
88Pac/8Men-92
D328-49
D329-58
D350/2-59
E135-49
M101/4-58
M101/5-59
T205
T207

Fisher, Tom
90NewBrit/Best-2
91Crown/Orio-134
91NewBrit/ProC-347
91Single/ClBest-306

Fisher, Robert
90Target-245
C46-43

Fisk, Carlton
72OPC-79R
72T-79R
73K-27
73OPC-193
73T-193
73T/Lids-15
74K-5
74OPC-105
74OPC-331AS
74T-105
74T-331AS
74T/DE-64
74T/St-133
75Ho-143
75OPC-80
75T-80
75T/M-80
76Crane-14
76Ho-64
76MSA/Disc
76OPC-365
76SSPC-403
76T-365
77BurgChef-33
77Ho-104
77OPC-137
77Pep-22
77T-640
78OPC-210
78PapaG/Disc-25
78T-270
78Wiffle/Discs-23
79Ho-106
79OPC-360
79T-680
80K-41
80OPC-20
80T-40
81D-335
81Drake-32
81F-224
81F/St-58
81MSA/Disc-12
81OPC-116
81PermaGr/AS-13
81T-480
81T/HT
81T/St-46
81T/Tr-762
82D-20DK
82D-495
82Drake-12
82F-343
82F/St-183
82K-25
82OPC-110
82OPC-111IA
82OPC-58AS
82PermaGr/AS-3
82Sqt-8
82T-110
82T-111IA
82T-554AS
82T/St-138
82T/St-170
83D-104
83D/AAS-43
83F-235
83F-638M
83K-56
83OPC-20
83OPC-393AS
83T-20
83T-393
83T/Gloss40-17
83T/St-177
83T/St-54
83TrueVal/WSox-72
84D-302
84D/Champs-52
84F-58
84F/St-39
85FunFood/Pin-72
84MiltBrad-9
84Nes/792-216TL
84Nes/792-560
84OPC-127
84Ralston-33
84Seven-12C
84T-216TL
84T-560
84T/Cereal-33
84T/Gloss40-40
84T/St-243
84T/Super-15
84TrueVal/WS-13
85Coke/WS-72
85D-208
85F-513
85GenMills-17
85Leaf-155
85OPC-49
85T-1RB
85T-770
85T/St-243
86Coke/WS-72
86D-366
86D/AAS-17
86D/PopUp-17
86F-204
86F-643M
86F/LimEd-15
86F/LL-12
86F/Mini-43
86F/St-38
86F/WaxBox-C8
86Jay's-7
86Leaf-163
86Meadow/Blank-3
86Meadow/Stat-13
86OPC-290
86OPC-E
86Sf-125
86Sf-67M
86Sf/Dec-62M
86T-290
86T-719AS
86T/Gloss22-9
86T/Gloss60-28
86T/Mini-11
86T/St-162
86T/St-286
86T/Super-23
86T/WaxBox-E
87Classic-41
87Coke/WS-27
87D-247
87D/OD-232
87F-496
87F/RecSet-8
87Leaf-199
87OPC-164
87RedFoley/St-41
87Sf-140
87Seven-C7
87T-756
87T/St-288
88Coke/WS-8
88D-260
88D/Best-67
88F-397
88F/AwardWin-12
88KingB/Disc-18
88Kodak/WSox-2
88Leaf-208
88Nestle-38
88OPC-385
88Panini/St-55
88RedFoley/St-23
88S-592
88Sf-43
88T-385
88T/Big-197
88T/Mini-8
88T/St-290
89B-62
89Cadaco-17
89Coke/WS-8
89D-101
89D-7DK
89D/Best-11
89D/DKsuper-7DK
89F-495
89KayBee-11
89Kodak/WSox-3M
89OPC-46
89Panini/St-304
89RedFoley/St-43
89S-449
89S/HotStar-39
89S/Mast-9
89Sf-219
89T-695

89T/Big-24
89T/Coins-40
89T/DH-8
89T/LJN-134
89T/St-299
89T/St/Backs-23
89T/UK-26
89UD-609
90B-314
90Classic-116
90Coke/WSox-29
90Coke/WSox-3
90D-58
90D/BestAL-5
90D/Bon/MVP-BC19
90D/Learning-49
90F-530
90F/AwardWin-13
90HotPlay/St-12
90KayBee-12
90Kodak/WSox-1
90Leaf/I-10
90Leaf/I-174CL
90MSA/Soda-21
90OPC-392AS
90OPC-420
90Panini/St-44
90PublInt/St-284
90PublInt/St-386
90RedFoley/St-32
90S-290
90S/100St-70
90S/McDon-4
90Sf-204
90T-392AS
90T-420
90T/Big-176
90T/DH-23
90T/Gloss60-46
90T/HillsHM-29
90T/St-303
90T/TVAS-8
90UD-367
90Woolwth/HL-13
91B-345
91BBBest/RecBr-6
91Classic/200-51
91Classic/III-21
91D-108
91D-BC6
91F-118
91F/Ultra-72
91KingB/Discs-22
91Kodak/WSox-72
91Kodak/WSox-x
91Leaf/II-384
91Leaf/Prev-16
91Leaf/Stud-32
91MajorLg/Pins-14
91OPC-170
91OPC-393AS
91OPC-3RB
91OPC/Premier-45
91Panini/FrSt-311
91Panini/St-255
91Petro/SU-7
91RedFoley/St-36
91S-265
91S-421HL
91S/100SS-41
91Seven/3DCoin-4MW
91T-170
91T-393AS
91T-3RB
91T/CJMini/II-2
91T/StClub/I-180
91T/SU-14
91T/WaxBox-F
91UD-29TC
91UD-643
91UD-677M
91USPlayC/AS-2D
91Woolwth/HL-12
92D/II-543
92F-79
92F/TmLIns-4
92S/100SS-72
92S/I-72
92T-630
92UD-571

Fister, Corby
90Idaho/ProC-3256

Fitzer, Doug
91SanBern/CIBest-3
91SanBern/ProC-1979
91Single/CIBest-362

Fitzgerald, Dave
89Beloit/I/Star-5
89Beloit/II/Star-10
90AS/Cal-54
90Stockton/Best-17
90Stockton/Cal-178
90Stockton/ProC-2177
91Stockton/CIBest-11

Fitzgerald, Ed
47Signal
47Sunbeam
49B-109
49Eureka-159
50B-178
52B-180
52T-236
53Briggs
54B-168
55B-208
56T-198
57T-367
58T-236
59T-33
60T-423

Fitzgerald, Kevin
86Cram/PCL-1

Fitzgerald, Matthew
E254
E270/1

Fitzgerald, Mike P.
85Spring-11
87ArkTr-21
87TexLgAS-26
88Louisvl-19
88Louisvl/CMC-18
88Louisvl/ProC-427
89Louisvl-20
89Louisvl/CMC-18
89Louisvl/ProC-1259
90SpringDG/Best-34

Fitzgerald, Mike R.
82Tidew-4
83Tidew-2
84D-482
84F/X-37
84T/Tr-37
85D-238
85F-78
85F/Up-U41
85OPC-104
85OPC/Post-1
85T-104
85T/St-108
85T/St-372YS
85T/Tr-34T
86D-97
86F-247
86Leaf-32
86OPC-313
86Provigo-26
86T-503
87D-345
87F-317
87Leaf-222
87OPC-212
87Smok/NL-14
87T-212
88D-159
88F-182
88Ho/Disc-6
88Leaf-81
88OPC-386
88Panini/St-322
88S-318
88T-674
88T/St-78
89D-456
89F-374
89OPC-23
89S-511
89T-23
89UD-133
90D-392
90F-343
90OPC-484
90PublInt/St-171
90S-361
90T-484
90T/Big-84
90UD-558
91B-453
91D-82
91F-229
91F/Ultra-201
91Leaf/Stud-196
91OPC-317
91Panini/FrSt-138
91S-198
91T-317
91T/StClub/I-128
91UD-516
91WIZMets-116
92F-478
92S/II-667
92T-761
92UD-210

Fitzmaurice, Shaun
71Richm/Team-6
91WIZMets-117

Fitzmorris, Al
70OPC-241R
70T-241R
71OPC-564
71T-564
72OPC-349
72T-349
72T/Cloth-10
73OPC-643
73T-643
74OPC-191
74T-191
75OPC-24
75T-24
75T/M-24
76A&P/KC
76Ho-8
76Ho/Twink-8
76OPC-144
76SSPC-160
76T-144
77T-449
78T-227
79Hawaii-17
79T-638

Fitzpatrick, Dan
84Newar-7
86Beloit-7
87Stockton-6
88CalLgAS-11
88Stockton/Cal-187
88Stockton/ProC-745
89Stockton/Best-12
89Stockton/Cal-151
89Stockton/ProC-395

Fitzpatrick, Dave
91Kissim/ProC-4177

Fitzpatrick, Edward
C46-70
T201

Fitzpatrick, Gary
83LynnP-27

Fitzpatrick, John
54T-213

Fitzpatrick, Mike
89EastLDD/ProC-DD48UMP

Fitzpatrick, Robert
90James/Pucko-2
91Rockford/CIBest-14
91Rockford/ProC-2049
91Single/CIBest-254

Fitzsimmons, Fred
31Exh/4-10
33Exh/4-5
33G-130
33G-235
35BU-72
35G-8A
35G-9A
39PB-110
40PB-65
41DP-143
52B-234
60T-462C
90Target-246
91Conlon/Sport-260
R315-A6
R315-B6
R316
V354-20
V355-14
WG8-16

Fitzsimmons, Tom
90Target-950

Fix, Greg
86Cram/PCL-91
87QuadC-17

Flack, Max
25Exh-60
D329-59
D350/2-60
E120
E121/120
M101/4-59
M101/5-60
V100
W501-117
W573

Flagstead, Ira
21Exh-48
25Exh-66
26Exh-65
27Exh-33
28Exh-33
87Conlon/2-34
91Conlon/Sport-291
E120
E121/120
E210-21
W501-7
W514-1
W573

Flaherty, John
55B-272ump

Flaherty, John
88Elmira-13
89WinHaven/Star-7
90Pawtu/CMC-11
90Pawtu/ProC-464
90T/TVRSox-43
91NewBrit/LineD-459
91NewBrit/ProC-355

Flaherty, Patrick
E254

Flammang, Chris
80SanJose/JITB-7
81Spokane-1

Flanagan, Dan
90ClintUp/Team-U4
90Everett/Best-4
90Everett/ProC-3120
91Clinton/CIBest-2
91Clinton/ProC-827

Flanagan, James
T206

Flanagan, Mike
76OPC-589R
76T-589R
77T-106
78Ho-134
78OPC-231
78T-341
79K-48
79OPC-76
79T-160
80K-3
80OPC-335
80T-640
81D-234
81F-171
81F/St-56
81K-60
81OPC-10
81T-10
82D-329
82F-165
82F/St-145
82OPC-153
82T-520
82T/St-148
83D-105
83F-60
83OPC-172
83T-445
83T/St-25
84D-169
84F-8
84F/St-63
84Nes/792-295
84OPC-295
84T-295
84T/St-12LCS
84T/St-210
85D-88
85F-177
85Leaf-175
85OPC-46
85T-780
85T/St-207
86D-576
86F-275
86Sf-57M
86T-365
87D-459
87F-470
87French-46
87OPC-112
87T-748
88D-636
88D/Best-272
88F/Up-U67
88OPC-164
88S-427
88T-623
88Tor/Fire-46
89B-241
89D-324
89D/Best-316
89F-233
89OPC-139
89RedFoley/St-44
89S-475
89T-139
89T/Big-243
89T/LJN-103
89T/St-190
89Tor/Fire-46
89UD-385
90D-324
90F-81
90OPC-78
90PublInt/St-514
90S-67
90T-78
90UD-483
91Crown/Orio-135
91Leaf/II-479
91S/RookTr-2T
92D/I-196
92F-7
92S/I-333
92S/I-427NH
92T-218
92UD-380

Flanigan, Thomas
N172

Flannelly, Tim
91Oneonta/ProC-4161

Flannery, John
76QuadC
79Knoxvl/TCMA-10
82BirmB-15

Flannery, Kevin
81AppFx-4
82AppFx-21
83Toledo-3

Flannery, Tim
80Hawaii-19
80T-685R
81F-493
81T-579
82D-61
82F-572
82T-249
83D-472
83F-359
83T-38
84D-202
84F-299
84Mother/Padres-12
84Nes/792-674
84Smok/Padres-9
84T-674
85D-551
85F-31
85Mother/Padres-20
85T-182
86D-383
86F-320
86OPC-387
86T-413
86T/St-112
87Bohem-11
87D-287
87F-413
87OPC-52
87T-763
87T/St-114
88Coke/Padres-11
88D-328
88F-582
88OPC-262

88Panini/St-404
88S-483
88Smok/Padres-8
88T-513
88T/St-108
89B-457
89Coke/Padre-4
89D-364
89Padre/Mag-15
89S-513
89T-379
89T/Big-174
89UD-603
90PublInt/St-48

Flater, John
E254

Flath, Daniel
90Saraso/Star-30BB

Fleet, Joe
91Watertn/ClBest-4
91Watertn/ProC-3359

Fleita, Oneri
89Freder/Star-6
90Wausau/ProC-2145CO
90Wausau/Star-28CO
91Kane/ClBest-28CO
91Kane/ProC-2675CO

Fleming, Bill
91Pac/SenLg-84

Fleming, Dave
90Foil/Best-57
91B-249
91Jaxvl/LineD-336
91Jaxvl/ProC-146
91Single/ClBest-284
92Classic/I-34
92D/II-404RR
92T-192
92T/91Debut-56
92UD-4SR

Fleming, Jack
77DaytB
80Tucson-7

Fleming, Jim
91James/ClBest-28CO
91James/ProC-3561CO

Fleming, Keith
87Stockton-20
88Stockton/Cal-185
88Stockton/ProC-725
89ElPaso/GS-7
90Beloit/Best-25
90Beloit/Star-7

Fleming, Les
49Eureka-160

Fleming, Paul
82Wisco-8

Flener, Huck
90StCath/ProC-3470
91Myrtle/ProC-2938

Fleshman, Richard
77WHave

Fletcher, Arthur
11Helmar-127
21Exh-49
40PB-125
44Yank/St-11CO
61F-106
87Conlon/2-32
88Conlon/4-11
91Conlon/Sport-117
92Conlon/Sport-490
D304
D327
D328-50
D329-60
D350/2-61
E120
E135-50
E220
M101/4-60
M101/5-61
M116
S74-86
T202
T205
T206
T207
T213/brown
T222
V61-107
W514-14
W516-14
W573
WG4-8

Fletcher, Bob
89GreatF-27
89Saraso/Star-5
90VeroB/Star-13

Fletcher, Darrin
88SanAn/Best-15
89Albuq/CMC-18
89Albuq/ProC-58
90AAAGame/ProC-AAA44
90Albuq/CMC-15
90Albuq/ProC-348
90Albuq/Trib-8
90S-622RP
90T/89Debut-38
90Target-951
91B-496
91Classic/II-T5
91D-47RR
91F/Ultra-377MLP
91F/Up-U107
91OPC-9
91Phill/Medford-14
91ScranWB/LineD-483
91ScranWB/ProC-2541
91T-9
91UD-428
92D/I-319
92F-530
92S/I-193
92T-159
92UD-108

Fletcher, David
90MedHat/Best-17

Fletcher, Dennis
90A&AASingle/ProC-77
90Savan/ProC-2064
91Spring/ClBest-17
91Spring/ProC-738

Fletcher, Don
76Clinton
91Pac/SenLg-103

Fletcher, Elburt
39PB-69
40PB-103
41DP-150
41G-26
41PB-62
47TipTop
49Eureka-9
R314

Fletcher, Mitch
80Tulsa-26

Fletcher, Paul
88Martins/Star-14
89Batavia/ProC-1921
90Spartan/Best-2
90Spartan/ProC-2483
90Spartan/Star-7
91Clearw/ClBest-2
91Clearw/ProC-1613
91Single/ClBest-111

Fletcher, Rob
90WPalmB/Star-6
91Modesto/ClBest-4
91Modesto/ProC-3096

Fletcher, Scott
82D-554
82Iowa-2
83TrueVal/WSox-1
84D-452
84F-59
84Nes/792-364
84T-364
84T/St-250
84TrueVal/WS-14
85Coke/WS-1
85D-330
85F-514
85T-78
85T/St-240
86D-282
86D/HL-28
86F-205
86F/Up-U41
86OPC-187
86Rangers-1
86T-187
86T/Tr-36T
87Classic/Up-118
87D-304
87D/OD-171
87F-123
87F/AwardWin-13
87Leaf-226
87Mother/Rang-6
87Sf-113M
87Sf-136
87Smok/R-13
87T-462
87T/St-237
88D-11DK
88D-180
88D/Best-32
88D/DKsuper-11DK
88F-466
88F/Mini-54
88F/St-63
88Leaf-11DK
88Leaf-155
88Mother/R-6
88OPC-345
88Panini/St-206
88RedFoley/St-24
88S-251
88Sf-77
88Smok/R-10
88T-345
88T/Big-19
88T/St-241
89B-230
89Cadaco-18
89D-142
89D/Best-167
89F-518
89F/Superstar-14
89Mother/R-13
89OPC-295
89Panini/St-454
89S-78
89S/Tr-47
89Sf-185
89Smok/R-8
89T-295
89T/Big-205
89T/St-246
89UD-420
90B-319
90Coke/WSox-4
90D-455
90D/BestAL-88
90F-531
90Kodak/WSox-5
90Leaf/I-141
90OPC-565
90Panini/St-43
90PublInt/St-408
90S-58
90Sf-220
90T-565
90T/Big-207
90T/St-307
90UD-310
91B-359
91D-276
91F-119
91F/Ultra-73
91Kodak/WSox-7
91Leaf/II-306
91Leaf/Stud-33
91OPC-785
91Panini/FrSt-313
91S-36
91T-785
91T/StClub/I-30
91UD-321
92F-80
92S/I-203
92T-648
92UD-186

Fletcher, Van
(Guy)
46Sunbeam
47Signal
47Sunbeam

Flick, Elmer
80SSPC/HOF
89HOF/St-53
E107
E254
E270/1
M116
T206
WG2-19

Flinn, Geoff
89Butte/SP-15

Flinn, John
79T-701R
81T-659R
81Vanco-21
82RochR-2
83RochR-3
85CharlO-24
87CharlO/WBTV-25
91Crown/Orio-136

Flinn, Mike
82Madis-4

Flint, Frank S.
E223
N172
N284
WG1-12

Floethe, Chris
72OPC-268R
72T-268R

Flood, Curt
58T-464
59T-353
60L-141
60T-275
61P-178
61T-438
61T/St-86
62J-166
62P-166
62P/Can-166
62Salada-139
62Shirriff-139
62T-590
63J-162
63P-162
63T-162M
63T-505
64T-103
64T/Coins-65
64T/St-28
64T/tatt
65T-415
66OPC-60
66T-60
67OPC-63M
67T-245
67T-63M
68Bz-11
68OPC-180
68T-180
68T/3D
69Kelly/Pin-5
69MB-83
69MLB/St-210
69MLBPA/Pin-43
69OPC/DE-5
69T-426AS
69T-540
69T/DE-28
69T/S-59
69T/St-114
70K-48
70MLB/St-87
70OPC-360
70T-360
71MLB/St-536
71OPC-535
71T-535
71T/S-41
72MB-105
78TCMA-240
89Pac/SenLg-220COM
89TM/SenLg-1COM
90EliteSenLg-1COM

Flood, Thomas J.
N172

Flood, Tim
90Target-247

Flora, Kevin
88QuadC/GS-5
89QuadC/Best-6
89QuadC/GS-11
91London/LineD-434
91MidldA/ProC-441
91Single/ClBest-19
92T/91Debut-57

Florence, Donald
88WinHaven/Star-8
89WinHaven/Star-8
90NewBrit/Best-10
90NewBrit/Star-5
91NewBrit/LineD-460
91NewBrit/ProC-348

Florence, Paul
V355-177

Flores, Adalberto
76BurlB
77BurlB
77Newar

Flores, Alex
87Greens-18

Flores, Gil
77SLCity
78Cr/PCL-40
78T-268
80T-478
80Tidew-6
81Tidew-11
82Tidew-7
83Tidew-22
84Tidew-7
91WIZMets-118

Flores, Jose
85Greens-23
86Greens-5
90Ashvl/ClBest-13
90AubAs/Best-6
90AubAs/ProC-3411
91Ashvl/ProC-574

Flores, Juan
91Stockton/ClBest-22
91Stockton/ProC-3034

Flores, Miguel
90BurlInd/ProC-3013
91CLAS/ProC-CAR14
91Kinston/ClBest-16
91Kinston/ProC-328

Flores, Norberto
(Bert)
85VeroB-12
86Bakers-8

Flores, Willi
82Wisco-21

Florez, Tim
91Everett/ClBest-10
91Everett/ProC-3921

Florie, Bryce
89CharRain/ProC-983
90Foil/Best-130
90Waterlo/Best-3
90Waterlo/ProC-2371
91Waterlo/ClBest-3
91Waterlo/ProC-1250

Flower, George
86WPalmB-16

Flowers, Bennett
55B-254

Flowers, D'Arcy
(Jake)
29Exh/4-3
31Exh/4-3
33G-151
90Target-248
V353-81

Flowers, Doug
91Kane/ClBest-29

Flowers, Kim
85Everett/Cram-5A
85Everett/Cram-5B
87Clinton-16
88Fresno/Cal-11
88Fresno/ProC-1223

Flowers, Perry
86Clinton-8

Flowers, Wes
90Target-952

Flowers, Willie
78Newar

Floyd, Chris
88Myrtle/ProC-1173

Floyd, Cliff
91Classic/DP-11
91FrRow/DP-49
92S/II-801
92T-186

Floyd, D.J.
90Erie/Star-6

Floyd, Robert
(Bobby)
69T-597R
70OPC-101
70T-101
71MLB/St-415
71OPC-646
71T-646

72OPC-273
72T-273
72T/Cloth-11
74OPC-41
74T-41
80LynnS-4MG
81LynnS-24MG
82SLCity-24MG
83SLCity-24MG
84Cram/PCL-191
85Cram/PCL-78MG
86Lynch-9MG
91Crown/Orio-137

Floyd, Stan
77Charl

Floyd, Tony
88SoOreg/ProC-1707

Flynn, Bob
75AppFx
76AppFx

Flynn, David
88CapeCod/Sum-13

Flynn, Errol
88Pulaski/ProC-1758

Flynn, John A.
(Jocko)
N172

Flynn, John Anthony
12Sweet/Pin-136
D322
M116
S74-109
T205

Flynn, R. Doug
76OPC-518
76SSPC-37
76T-518
77T-186
78T-453
79Ho-81
79OPC-116
79T-229
80OPC-32
80T-58
81Coke
81D-394
81F-330
81OPC-311
81T-634
81T/HT
81T/SO-93
81T/St-192
82D-427
82F-525
82F/St-87
82OPC-302
82T-302
82T/St-70
82T/Tr-33T
83D-240
83F-282
83OPC-169
83Stuart-7
83T-169
84D-254
84F-274
84Nes/792-749
84OPC-262
84Stuart-29
84T-749
84T/St-97
85D-463
85F-397
85Leaf-257
85OPC-112
85T-554
85T/St-93
86Cain's-5
86T-436
91WIZMets-119

Fobbs, Larry
78LodiD
81Albuq/TCMA-15
82Albuq-16

Fodge, Gene
58T-449

Fogarty, James
N172
N284
N29
N43
N690
WG1-51

Fogg, Kevin
76Baton

Foggie, Cornell
89Watertn/Star-7

Fogler, Seth
90Miami/II/Star-29TR
90Miami/II/Star-30PER

Fohl, Lee
V100
V117-5

Foiles, Hank
52Park-85
53T-252
55Gol/Ind-7
57T-104
58Hires-71
58Kahn
58T-4
59T-294
60T-77
61T-277
62T-112
63T-326
64T-554
91Crown/Orio-138
91T/Arc53-252

Foit, Jim
83Tulsa-20

Foldman, Harry
(Hal)
49Sommer-29

Foley, Bill
77Newar
78BurlB
79Holyo-3
82ElPaso-6

Foley, Jack
83Tampa-11

Foley, Jim
88Modesto-9
89Madis/Star-8
90Clinton/ProC-2549

Foley, Joe
87Anchora-12

Foley, Keith
86WPalmB-17
88Vermont/ProC-948

Foley, Mark
87Penin-4

Foley, Martin
87Spartan-17
88Spartan/ProC-1038
88Spartan/Star-23
88Spartan/Star-7
89Reading/Best-15
89Reading/ProC-672
89Reading/Star-11
90Reading/Best-16
90Reading/ProC-1226
90Reading/Star-12

Foley, Marvis
77AppFx
78Knoxvl
81D-399
81T-646
83D-652
83T-409
84Rangers-30
85D-500
85T-621
89Vanco/CMC-23
89Vanco/ProC-573
90AAAGame/ProC-AAA39
90Vanco/CMC-5MG
90Vanco/ProC-505MG
91Pac/SenLg-23
91Vanco/LineD-649MG
91Vanco/ProC-1609MG

Foley, Rick
79SLCity-18
80SLCity-15
81Holyo-15
82Spokane-3

Foley, Thomas
80Water-19
81Indianap-7
82Indianap-20
84D-81
84Nes/792-632
84T-632
85D-569
85F-535
85T-107
86D-549
86F-440
86Phill/TastyK-11
86T-466
87D-504
87F-318
87OPC-78
87T-78
88D-303
88F-183
88Ho/Disc-3
88Leaf-143
88OPC-251
88S-159
88T-251
89D-342
89D/Best-314
89F-375
89OPC-159
89Panini/St-121
89S-405
89T-529
89T/Big-261
89UD-441
90B-120
90D-274
90F-344
90Leaf/II-292
90OPC-341
90Panini/St-292
90Publint/St-172
90S-32
90T-341
90T/Big-58
90UD-489
91D-180
91F-230
91Leaf/StudPrev-13
91OPC-773
91S-526
91T-773
91UD-381
92D/II-538
92S/II-486
92T-666
92UD-492

Folga, Mike
85PrWill-12
87Peoria-26

Foli, Tim
71OPC-83R
71T-83R
72T-707
72T-708IA
73OPC-19
73T-19
73T/Lids-16
74OPC-217
74T-217
74T/DE-19
74T/St-54
74Weston-19
75Ho-9
75Ho/Twink-9
75OPC-149
75T-149
75T/M-149
76OPC-397
76SSPC-328
76T-397
77BurgChef-156
77OPC-162
77T-76
78OPC-169
78T-167
79OPC-213
79T-403
80OPC-131
81Coke
81D-13
81F-379
81OPC-38
82D-376
82F-482
82F/St-75
82OPC-97
82T-618
82T/St-88
82T/Tr-34T
83D-342
83F-88
83OPC-319
83T-738
84D-474
84F-516
84F/X-38
84Nes/792-342
84OPC-342
84T-342
84T/Tr-38
85F-126
85T-271FDP
85T-456
87Smok/R-29CO
91WIZMets-120

Folkers, Rich
71OPC-648R
71T-648R
73OPC-649
73T-649
74OPC-417
74T-417
75OPC-98
75T-98
75T/M-98
76OPC-611
76SSPC-114
76T-611
77Spoka
77T-372
91WIZMets-121

Followell, Vern
81Evansvl-14
82Evansvl-18
85Cram/PCL-57

Fondy, Dee
52B-231
52T-359
53B/BW-5
54B-173
54RH
55B-224
56T-112
57T-42
58Kahn
58T-157
79TCMA-47

Fong, Steve
87SLCity/Taco-21TR

Fonseca, Dave
80Clinton-13

Fonseca, Lew
29Exh/4-21
31Exh/4-22
32Orbit/num-20
32Orbit/un-19
33DH-16
33G-43
34DS-7
61F-27
91Conlon/Sport-283
R305
R308-184
R310
R316
V353-43
W517-48
WG7-16

Fonsecca, Angel
82Wausau-25

Fontenot, Ray
82Nashvl-12
84D-370
84F-122
84Nes/792-19
84T-19
85D-248
85F-127
85F/Up-U42
85SevenUp-31
85T-507
85T/Tr-35T
86Cub/Unocal-9
86D-361
86F-369
86Gator-31
86T-308
87T-124
87Tucson-12

Fontenot, Silton
83Colum-5

Fontes, Brad
88Butte-24
89Kenosha/ProC-1062
89Kenosha/Star-5

Fonville, Charlie
84Butte-10

Foor, Jim
72OPC-257R
72T-257R

Foote, Barry
74OPC-603R
74T-603R
75Ho-39
75OPC-229
75T-229
75T/M-229
76OPC-42
76T-42
77BurgChef-157
77OPC-207
77T-612
78T-513
79T-161
80OPC-208
80T-398
81D-558
81F-313
81OPC-305
81T-492
81T/St-154
81T/Tr-763
82D-43
82F-34
82T-706
83T-697
85Albany-23
86Colum-9MG
87Myrtle-7
89Knoxvl/Best-28
89Knoxvl/ProC-1128
89SLAS-24
90Coke/WSox-30CO
91Kodak/WSox-x

Forbes, Andre
78Green

Forbes, P.J.
90Boise/ProC-3320
90WichSt-11
91PalmSp/ProC-2022

Forbes, Willie
88Charl/ProC-1193

Ford, Allen
91MedHat/ProC-4094

Ford, Calvin
89Wythe/Star-15
90Hunting/ProC-3298

Ford, Curt
83Spring/LF-6
84ArkTr-16
85Louisvl-13
86F-648R
86Louisvl-13
87D-454
87F-294
87Smok/Cards-21
87T-399
88D-417
88F-32
88Panini/St-395
88S-288
88Smok/Card-20
88T-612
88T/St-23
88Woolwth-28
89B-408
89F-450
89Phill/TastyK-6
89T-132
89UD-309
90D-694
90F-557
90OPC-39
90Phill/TastyK-9
90S-183
90SpringDG/Best-30
90T-39
90UD-490
91Toledo/LineD-583
91Toledo/ProC-1943

Ford, Dale
88TM/Umpire-23
89TM/Umpire-21
89TM/Umpire-60M
90TM/Umpire-20

Ford, Darnell
(Dan)
76OPC-313
76SSPC-216
76T-313

77BurgChef-48
77Ho-121
77OPC-104
77T-555
77T/CS-16
78Ho-18
78OPC-34
78T-275
79OPC-201
79T-385
80OPC-7
80T-20
81D-54
81F-273
81OPC-303
81T-422
82D-468
82F-458
82F/St-216
82OPC-134
82T-134
82T/St-163
82T/Tr-35T
83D-509
83F-61
83OPC-357
83T-683
84D-367
84F-9
84Nes/792-530
84OPC-349
84T-530
84T/St-212
85D-489
85F-178
85T-252
86T-753
91Crown/Orio-139

Ford, Dave
79RochR-20
80T-661R
81D-552
81F-192
81T-706
82D-597
82F-166
82T-174
83RochR-4
84Cram/PCL-94
91Crown/Orio-140

Ford, Doug
47Centen-7

Ford, Edward C.
(Whitey)
51B-1
51BR-D5
53B/Col-153
53T-207
54B-177
54NYJour
54RM-AL16
54T-37
55Armour-6
55B-59
55RM-AL3
56T-240
57T-25
58T-320
59Armour-8
59T-430
60Armour-10
60T-35
60T/tatt-15
61P-6
61T-160
61T-586AS
61T/St-193
62Bz
62Exh
62J-9
62P-9
62P/Can-9
62Salada-8
62Shirriff-8
62T-310
62T-315IA
62T-475AS
62T-57LL
62T-59LL
62T/bucks
62T/St-85
63Exh
63J-19
63P-19
63T-446
63T-6LL
64T-380
64T-4LL
64T/Coins-139AS
64T/S-7
64Wheat/St-15
65T-330
66OPC-160
66T-160
66T/RO-60
67OPC-5
67T-5
74Syrac/Team-30
78TCMA-21
80SSPC/HOF
82CJ-11
83Kaline-16M
83MLBPA/Pin-7
85Woolwth-11
86Sf/Dec-44
87Nestle/DT-21
89B/I-3
89HOF/St-70
89Kahn/Coop-4
89Pac/Leg-210
89Swell-50
89T/LJN-121
90MSA/AGFA-16
90Swell/Great-8
91T/Arc53-207
Exh47
PM10/L-14
PM10/Sm-52
WG10-6
WG9-8

Ford, Horace E.
(Hod)
29Exh/4-8
31Exh/4-8
33G-24
90Target-249
E120
E126-57
R316
V353-24
V61-111
W573

Ford, Ken
82AlexD-23
83LynnP-20
85Nashua-10
86Nashua-7

Ford, Ondra
86Cram/PCL-33
89AppFx/ProC-859

Ford, Randy
82Knoxvl-3

Ford, Rick
76BurlB
77BurlB
77Holyo
78Clinton

Ford, Russ
10Domino-45
11Helmar-43
12Sweet/Pin-34A
12Sweet/Pin-34B
14CJ-83
14Piedmont/St-22
15CJ-83
E270/2
E286
E98
L1-115
M116
S74-21
S81-90
T201
T202
T205
T206
T213/blue
T215/blue
T215/brown

Ford, Rusty
86Beaum-11
87LasVegas-9
88Wichita-41

Ford, Steve
90Yakima/Team-20VP/GM

Ford, Stewart
90Pulaski/Best-4
90Pulaski/ProC-3098
91Pulaski/ClBest-18
91Pulaski/ProC-3998

Ford, Ted
71OPC-612R
71T-612R
72OPC-24
72T-24
73OPC-299
73T-299
74OPC-617
74T-617

Fordyce, Brook
89Kingspt/Star-10
90SALAS/Star-30
91FSLAS/ProC-FSL31
91Single/ClBest-220
91StLucie/ClBest-11
91StLucie/ProC-714
91UD-64

Fore, Chuck L.
78Syrac
79Syrac-14
81Syrac-3
83Richm-6

Foreman, Dave
87Anchora-40STAT

Foreman, Francis
N172

Foreman, Toby
91Belling/ClBest-21
91Belling/ProC-3657

Forer, Daniel Lynn
81VeroB-5

Forgeur, Freddy
79QuadC-21

Forgione, Chris
85Visalia-9
86Visalia-9
87Kenosha-22
88OrlanTw/Best-16

Forney, Jeff
87Tampa-25
88Cedar/ProC-1151
88MidwLAS/GS-10

Fornieles, Mike
54T-154
55B-266
57T-116
58T-361
59T-473
60T-54
61T-113
62T-512
62T/St-12
63T-28
79TCMA-132
91Crown/Orio-141

Forrest, Chris
87StPete-15
89Boise/ProC-2001

Forrest, Joel
87Macon-3
88Augusta/ProC-381
88Watertn/Pucko-5

Forrester, Gary
89Salem/Team-11
90Bakers/Cal-251
91QuadC/ProC-2635

Forrester, Tom
87Hawaii-7
88BirmB/Best-12
89Vanco/CMC-20
89Vanco/ProC-597
90BirmDG/Best-11
90SoBend/Best-19

Forry, Dewey
75Water

Forsch, Ken
71OPC-102R
71T-102R
72OPC-394
72T-394
73OPC-589
73T-589
74OPC-91
74T-91
75OPC-357
75T-357
75T/M-357
76OPC-357
76SSPC-48
76T-357
77BurgChef-4
77OPC-78
77T-21
77T-632M
78BK/Ast-8
78Ho-3
78K-50
78T-181
79Ho-51
79OPC-276
79T-534
80OPC-337
80T-642
81D-141
81F-52
81OPC-269
81T-269
81T/Tr-764
82D-393
82F-459
82F/St-221
82OPC-385
82T-276TL
82T-385
82T/St-159
83D-164
83F-89
83OPC-346
83T-625
84D-280
84F-517
84Nes/792-765
84OPC-193
84Smok/Cal-9
84T-765
84T/St-237
85F-301
85OPC-141
85Smok/Cal-8
85T-442
86F-155
86Mother/Ast-14
90Swell/Great-37

Forsch, Robert
75OPC-51
75T-51
75T/M-51
76OPC-426
76SSPC-294
76T-426
77T-381
77T-632M
78OPC-83
78T-58
79K-38
79OPC-117
79T-230
80OPC-279
80T-535
81Coke
81D-69
81F-537
81OPC-140
81T-140
82D-91
82F-112
82F/St-22
82OPC-34
82T-186TL
82T-775
82T/St-90
83D-64
83F-5
83OPC-197
83T-415
83T/St-289
84D-168
84F-322
84F-639M
84Nes/792-5HL
84Nes/792-75
84OPC-75
84T-5HL
84T-75
84T/St-288A
85F-223
85OPC-137
85T-631
86D-353
86F-35
86KAS/Disc-6
86Sf-129M
86Schnucks-6
86T-322
86T-66M
87D-540
87F-295
87F/AwardWin-14
87F/St-40
87Leaf-161
87OPC-257
87Sf-191
87Smok/Cards-7
87T-257
87T/St-47
88D-111
88F-33
88Panini/St-384
88S-264
88Sf-199
88Smok/Card-5
88T-586
89D-118
89Lennox/Ast-23
89Mother/Ast-11
89S-525
89T-163
90F-231
90Publint/St-95
90S-219

Forster, Guillermo
73Cedar
74Cedar

Forster, Terry
72T-539
73OPC-129
73T-129
74OPC-310
74T-310
74T/St-153
75Ho-14
75OPC-137
75OPC-313LL
75T-137
75T-313LL
75T/M-137
75T/M-313LL
76Ho-14
76Ho/Twink-14
76OPC-437
76SSPC-157
76T-437
77T-271
78T-347
79OPC-7
79T-23
80T-605
81Pol/Dodg-51
81T-104
82D-362
82F-4
82Pol/Dodg-51
82T-444
83D-453
83F-205
83Pol/Atl-51
83T-583
83T/Tr-33
84F-178
84Nes/792-791
84OPC-109
84Pol/Atl-51
84T-791
85F-324
85Ho/Braves-8
85OPC-248
85Pol/Atl-51
85T-248
86D-432
86F-514
86F/Up-U42
86Leaf-202
86Smok/Cal-23
86T-363
86T/Tr-37T
87F-80
87T-652
90Target-250

Forster, Tom
N172
N284

Fortaleza, Ray
84Greens-2

Fortenberry, Jim
86Clearw-8
86FSLAS-16
87Reading-21

Fortinberry, Bill

80Port-12
Fortugno, Tim
86Cram/PCL-115
88Reading/ProC-876
89Reno/Cal-244
89Stockton/Star-7
90Beloit/Best-7
90Beloit/Star-8
91ElPaso/LineD-182
91ElPaso/ProC-2741
Fortuna, Mike
89Salem/Star-8
89Welland/Pucko-12
Fortune, Steve
79Elmira-9
Fosnow, Gerald
65T-529
Foss, Larry
91WIZMets-122
Fossa, Dick
88CalLgAS-24
Fossas, Tony
80Ashvl-7
81Tulsa-16
83Tulsa-3
84OKCty-12
85OKCty-10
86Edmon-10
87Edmon-20
88OkCty/CMC-9
88OkCty/ProC-34
89Denver/CMC-3
89Denver/ProC-55
90D-457
90F-323
90OPC-34
90Pol/Brew-36
90S-567
90T-34
91Leaf/II-276
91OPC-747
91S-634
91T-747
92D/II-645
92S/I-389
92T-249
92UD-503
Fosse, Ray
69T-244R
70OPC-184
70T-184
71K-39
71MD
71MLB/St-366
71OPC-125
71T-125
71T/Coins-42
71T/S-51
71T/tatt-16
72OPC-470
72T-470
72T/Post-4
73K-18
73OPC-226
73T-226
73T/Lids-17
74OPC-420
74T-420
75OPC-486
75T-486
75T/M-486
76OPC-554
76SSPC-500
76T-554
76T/Tr-554T
77BurgChef-62
77Ho-122
77OPC-39
77Pep-17
77T-267
78Ho-57
78T-415
79T-51
80T-327
Foster, Alan
69T-266R
70OPC-369
70T-369
71MLB/St-367
71OPC-207
71T-207
72OPC-521
72T-521
73OPC-543
73T-543
74OPC-442
74T-442
75OPC-296
75T-296
75T/M-296
76OPC-266
76SSPC-115
76T-266
77T-108
85SpokAT/Cram-6
90Target-251
Foster, Andrew
(Rube)
74Laugh/Black-35
86Negro/Frit-18
88Conlon/NegAS-4
88Negro/Duques-1
90Negro/Star-16
91Conlon/Sport-138
Foster, Bob
79LodiD-17
Foster, Bryan
88Beloit/GS-12
89Stockton/Best-21
89Stockton/Cal-171
89Stockton/ProC-393
89Stockton/Star-20
Foster, Bud
46Remar-15
47Remar-9
47Signal
48Signal
49Remar
Foster, Doug
78Clinton
Foster, Edward C.
BF2-44
D327
D328-51
D329-61
D350/2-62
E121/120
E121/80
E122
E135-51
E270/2
M101/4-61
M101/5-62
M116
T201
W575
Foster, Edward Lee
M116
T206
Foster, Elmer
N172/ST
N338/2
N690
WG1-39
Foster, George
71OPC-276R
71T-276R
72OPC-256
72T-256
73OPC-202
73OPC-399
73T-399
74OPC-646
74T-646
75OPC-87
75T-87
75T/M-87
76Ho-106
76Icee
76OPC-179
76SSPC-44
76T-179
77BurgChef-201
77Ho-40
77K-1
77OPC-120
77OPC-3LL
77Pepsi-48
77T-347
77T-3LL
78Ho-2
78K-10
78OPC-2LL
78OPC-3LL
78OPC-70
78T-202LL
78T-203LL
78T-500
78Wiffle/Discs-24
79Ho-107
79K-32
79OPC-316
79T-2LL
79T-3LL
79T-600
80BK/PHR-15
80K-50
80OPC-209
80T-400
80T/S-24
81Coke
81D-65
81Drake-18
81F-202
81F-216
81F/St-41
81K-1
81OPC-200
81PermaGr/AS-4
81PermaGr/CC-9
81Sqt-2
81T-200
81T/HT
81T/SO-65
81T/St-159
82D-274
82Drake-13
82F-66
82F/St-12
82K-56
82KMart-32
82OPC-177IA
82OPC-336
82OPC-342AS
82Sqt-18
82T-342AS
82T-700
82T-701IA
82T/St-126
82T/St-40
82T/Tr-36T
83D-427
83D-6DK
83Drake-8
83F-542
83K-22
83OPC-80
83T-80
83T/St-263
84D-312
84D/Champs-2
84F-584
85FunFood/Pin-46
84Nes/792-350
84OPC-350
84T-350
84T/Mets/Fan-3
84T/St-105
85D-603
85F-79
85Leaf-42
85OPC-170
85Pol/MetYank-M1
85T-170
85T/Mets/Fan-4
85T/St-99
86D-116
86F-80
86OPC-69
86Sf-126M
86Sf-131M
86Sf-139M
86Sf-68M
86T-680
86T/St-100
86Woolwth-11
89Pac/Leg-173
89Pac/SenLg-114
89T/SenLg-1
89TM/SenLg-119
89TM/SenLg-36
90EliteSenLg-112
90EliteSenLg-124
90Pac/Legend-72
90Swell/Great-97
91LineD-37
91Swell/Great-112
91WIZMets-123
Foster, John
82Wisco-19
Foster, Ken
81Wisco-16
82Orlan/B-18
83Orlan-11
86SanJose-7
Foster, Kevin
89Rockford/Team-7
90WPalmB/Star-7
91Sumter/ClBest-4
91Sumter/ProC-2327
Foster, Lamar
75Tidew/Team-11
89Martins/Star-11
90Martins/ProC-3179
91Batavia/ClBest-8
91Batavia/ProC-3490
91WIZMets-124
Foster, Leo
74OPC-607R
74T-607R
75OPC-418
75T-418
75T/M-418
77T-458
78T-229
Foster, Lindsay
87Myrtle-15
88Dunedin/Star-6
89Canton/Best-15
89Canton/ProC-1304
89Canton/Star-6
90Kinston/Team-14
91BirmB/LineD-58
91BirmB/ProC-1461
Foster, Paul
87Fayette-16
88Lakeland/Star-11
Foster, Randy
87Oneonta-21
88PrWill/Star-10
Foster, Roy
71MLB/St-368
71OPC-107
71T-107
72OPC-329
72T-329
72T/Cloth-12
89Tidew/Candl-2
Foster, Russ
91Pac/SenLg-75
Foster, Stephen
(Steve)
88Billings/ProC-1818
89Cedar/Best-2
89Cedar/ProC-936
89Cedar/Star-7
91Chatt/LineD-158
91Chatt/ProC-1953
92Classic/I-35
92D/II-420RR
92T-528
92T/91Debut-58
Foster, Willie
74Laugh/Black-5
90Negro/Star-24
Fothergill, Robert
(Bob)
28Exh-45
81Detroit-85
91Conlon/Sport-72
Foucault, Steve
74OPC-294
74T-294
75OPC-283
75T-283
75T/M-283
76OPC-303
76SSPC-252
76T-303
77T-459
78BK/T-10
78T-68
Foulk, Leon
52Park-15
Fournier, Bruce
80Ogden-16
80WHave-5
81WHave-10
Fournier, Jacques F.
21Exh-50
21Exh-51
25Exh-11
26Exh-10
90Target-252
92Conlon/Sport-541
D327
D328-52
D329-62
D350/2-63
E120
E135-52
M101/4-62
M101/5-63
T207
V100
W573
Foussianes, George
83BirmB-11
85Tulsa-6
90BirmDG/Best-12
Foutz, Dave
90Target-253
N172/BC
N284
N300/unif
N370
N566-181
Scrapps
Fowler, Dick
49B-171
50B-214
52B-190
52T-210
Exh47
Fowler, Don
81Tacoma-14
82Tacoma-2
84Colum-6
84Colum/Pol-10
84Nashvl-7
89Watlo/ProC-1792
89Watlo/Star-7
Fowler, Dwayne
91Pulaski/ClBest-19
91Pulaski/ProC-3999
Fowler, Eddie
89Wythe/Star-10
Fowler, J. Art
55T-3
55T/DH-80
56Kahn
56T-47
56T/Pin-55
57T-233
59T-508
62T-128
63T-454
64T-349
73OPC-323CO
73T-323C
74OPC-379CO
74T-379C
90Target-254
Fowler, John
89Bluefld/Star-9
90Wausau/Best-21
90Wausau/ProC-2134
90Wausau/Star-8
Fowler, Mike
88Durham/Star-6
89Durham/Team-11
89Durham/Star-11
Fowler, Yale
89GreatF-13
90Yakima/Team-32
Fowlkes, Alan Kim
81Shrev-7
83D-46
83F-259
83T-543
84Cram/PCL-16
86Edmon-11
88Reno/Cal-268
Fowlkes, David
77Watlo
Fox, Andy
89LittleSun-8
90Foil/Best-263
90Greens/Best-16
90Greens/ProC-2668
90Greens/Star-1
90SALAS/Star-6
90T/TVYank-43
91CLAS/ProC-CAR30
91PrWill/ClBest-17
91PrWill/ProC-1433

91Single/ClBest-132
Fox, Blane
87Lakeland-22
88FSLAS/Star-36
88Lakeland/Star-12
89ColMud/Best-14
89ColMud/ProC-143
89ColMud/Star-9
91NewBrit/LineD-461
91NewBrit/ProC-364
Fox, Charlie
71OPC-517MG
71T-517MG
71Ticket/Giant-3MG
72OPC-129MG
72T-129MG
73OPC-252MG
73T-252MG
74OPC-78MG
74T-78MG
Fox, Dan
89Kenosha/ProC-1085
90Kenosha/Best-29TR
90Kenosha/Star-27TR
91Kenosha/ClBest-21TR
Fox, Eric
85Anchora-11
87Chatt/Best-16
88Vermont/ProC-945
89Huntsvl/Best-9
90Tacoma/CMC-15
90Tacoma/ProC-107
91Tacoma/LineD-533
91Tacoma/ProC-2317
Fox, Ervin
(Pete)
34G-70
35BU-195
35G-8F
35G-9F
38G-242
38G-266
39PB-80
40PB-43
81Detroit-110
91Conlon/Sport-197
R309/2
R312/M
R313
R314
V355-30
WG8-18
Fox, Howard
(Howie)
49Eureka-84
50B-80
51B-180
52B-125
52T-209
53B/Col-158
53T-22
54Esskay
54T-246
91Crown/Orio-142
91T/Arc53-22
Fox, Jacob Nelson
(Nellie)
51B-232
52B-21
52BR
52Dix-53
52Hawth/Pin-4
52RM-AL9
52StarCal/L-73G
53B/Col-18
53NB
53RM-AL5
54B-6
54RH
54RM-AL3
54Wilson
55B-33
55RM-AL4
56T-118
56YellBase/Pin-11
57Swift-7
57T-38
58T-400
58T-479AS
59Armour-9
59Bz
59T-30
59T-408M
59T-556AS
60Armour-11
60Bz-25
60NuCard-72
60T-100
60T-429M
60T-555AS
60T/tatt-16
61NuCard-472
61P-20
61T-30
61T-477MV
61T-570AS
62Exh
62J-47
62P-47
62P/Can-47
62Salada-12
62Shirriff-12
62T-73
62T/bucks
62T/St-24
63Exh
63J-36
63P-36
63T-525
64T-205
64T-81M
64T/S-13
64Wheat/St-16
65T-485P/CO
74Laugh/ASG-58
75OPC-197MV
75T-197MV
75T/M-197MV
76Laugh/Jub-24
79TCMA-15
80Pac/Leg-68
80Laugh/FFeat-7
83Kaline-20
83MLBPA/Pin-8
86Sf/Dec-37M
87Nestle/DT-13
88Pac/Leg-57
89Kodak/WSox-2M
91T/Arc53-331
Exh47
PM10/Sm-53
Fox, Kenneth
86Jamestn-7
Fox, Mike
87StPete-11
89ArkTr/GS-5
Fox, Terry
61T-459
62T-196
63T-44
64T-387
65T-576
66T-472
67OPC-181
67T-181
Foxen, Bill
M116
S74-61
T202
T205
Foxx, James Emory
(Jimmie)
29Exh/4-27
31Exh/4-28
32Orbit/num-18
32Orbit/un-20
33DH-17
33DL-21
33Exh/4-14
33G-154
33G-29
34DS-64
34Exh/4-14
34G-1
34Ward's/Pin-3
35BU-144
35BU-28
35Exh/4-14
35G-1B
35G-2B
35G-6B
35G-7B
35Wheat
36Exh/4-9
36Wheat
37Exh/4-9
37OPC-106
38Dix
38Exh/4-9
38G-249
38G-273
38ONG/Pin-9
38Wheat
39Exh
39Wheat-5
40PB-133
40Wheat-3
41DP-60
41PB-13
41Wheat-14
50Callahan
60F-53
61F-28
61GP-22
72F/FFeat-16
72Laugh/GF-19
73F/Wild-41
74Laugh/ASG-35
80Pac/Leg-16
80Laugh/3/4/5-21
80Laugh/FFeat-23
80SSPC/HOF
83D/HOF-13
85CircK-7
86BLChew-7
86Conlon/1-12
86Sf/Dec-2
87Nestle/DT-11
88Conlon/5-10
88Conlon/AmAS-9
90BBWit-61
90Swell/Great-101
91Conlon/Sport-2
91Conlon/Sport-303
91LineD-44
91Swell/Great-143
92Conlon/Sport-526
92Conlon/Sport-560
PR1-10
R300
R302-153
R303/A
R303/B
R305
R306
R308-153
R310
R311/
R311/Gloss
R312/M
R314
R315-A7
R315-B7
R316
R326-12A
R326-12B
R328-23
R337
R342-12
V300
V353-29
V353-85
V354-58
V355-47
W517-21
WG8-19
Foy, Joe
66T-456R
67T-331
67T/Test/RSox-6
68Coke
68Dexter-32
68T-387
69MB-84
69MLB/St-58
69OPC-93
69T-93
69T/DE-22
69T/decal
69T/S-22
69T/St-184
70MLB/St-75
70OPC-138
70T-138
71MLB/St-537
71OPC-706
71T-706
72MB-106
91WIZMets-125
Foytack, Paul
53Glen
57T-77
58T-282
59T-233
60T-364
61P-62
61T-171
62T-349
63T-327
64T-149
Frailing, Ken
74OPC-605R
74T-605R
75OPC-436
75T-436
75T/M-436
76SSPC-305
78Knoxvl
Fralick, Bob
90Miami/I/Star-28CO
90Miami/II/Star-27CO
91Miami/ClBest-30CO
91Miami/ProC-424
Frame, Michael
(Mike)
89GreatF-2
90Bakers/Cal-236
France, Todd
86Stockton-7TR
87Stockton-5
Franchi, Kevin
86Macon-9
87Salem-1
Franchuk, Orv
90Boise/ProC-3332CO
91Boise/ProC-3901CO
Francis, Earl
61T-54
62T-252
63IDL-7
63T-303
64T-117
78TCMA-226
Francis, Harry
81Redwd-13
82Holyo-20
83Nashua-12
Francis, Scott
91Pulaski/ClBest-22
91Pulaski/ProC-4000
Francis, Todd
83Wausau/LF-14
Francis, Tommy
83Miami-23
Francisco, Rene
89Geneva/ProC-1862
90Peoria/Team-17
Francisco, Vicente
91SoOreg/ClBest-22
91SoOreg/ProC-3854
Franco, John
82Albuq-2
84F/X-39
84Wichita/Rock-19
85D-164
85F-536
85F/St-120
85T-417
86D-487
86F-178
86F/St-39
86KayBee-13
86Leaf-240
86OPC-54
86Sf-156
86T-54
86T/St-142
86TexGold-31
87Classic-100
87D-289
87D/AAS-22
87F-202
87F-631M
87F/BB-17
87F/LL-18
87F/Lim-14
87F/Slug-14
87F/St-41
87Kahn-31
87Leaf-178
87OPC-305
87RedFoley/St-116
87Sf-192
87T-305
87T/Mini-5
87T/St-138
88D-123
88D/AS-53
88D/Best-54
88F-234
88F-627M
88F/Mini-74
88F/RecSet-12
88F/St-84
88Kahn/Reds-31
88Leaf-79
88Nestle-8
88OPC-341
88Panini/St-271
88S-535
88Sf-195
88T-730
88T/Big-232
88T/Coins-41
88T/Mini-47
88T/St-142
88T/St/Backs-32
88T/UK-24
89B-301
89Cadaco-19
89D-233
89D/Best-166
89F-162
89F/Heroes-14
89F/LL-13
89Kahn/Reds-31
89OPC-290
89Panini/St-66
89RedFoley/St-45
89S-575
89S/HotStar-97
89Sf-176
89T-290
89T/Coins-12
89T/DH-23
89T/LJN-28
89T/Mini-9
89T/St-136
89T/St-4
89T/St/Backs-65
89T/UK-27
89UD-407
89Woolwth-12
90B-128
90Classic-86
90Classic/Up-19
90D-124
90D-14DK
90D/BestNL-92
90D/SuperDK-14DK
90F-419
90F/Up-U35
90F/WaxBox-C7
90HotPlay/St-13
90Kahn/Mets-31
90Leaf/II-356
90OPC-120
90Panini/St-244
90Publint/St-258
90Publint/St-29
90RedFoley/St-33
90S-273
90S/100St-49
90S/McDon-7
90S/Tr-15T
90Sf-138
90T-120
90T/Big-264
90T/HeadsUp-11
90T/Mini-54
90T/St-144
90T/Tr-32T
90T/TVMets-11
90UD-139
90UD/Ext-709
90USPlayC/AS-7H
91B-475
91Classic/200-125
91Classic/I-65
91D-322
91F-147
91F-712M
91F/Ultra-217
91Kahn/Mets-31
91Leaf/II-437
91Leaf/Stud-203
91OPC-407AS
91OPC-510

91Panini/St-87
91Panini/Top15-81
91S-14
91S/100SS-29
91T-407AS
91T-510
91T/StClub/I-22
91UD-290
91WIZMets-126
92D/I-186
92F-504
92S/100SS-57
92S/II-605
92T-690
92UD-514

Franco, Julio
80Penin/B-21
80Penin/C-17
82OkCty-11
83D-525
83T/Tr-34
83Wheat/Ind-13
84D-216
84F-542
84F/St-111
84Nes/792-48
84OPC-48
84T-48
84T/St-379
84Wheat/Ind-14
85D-94
85F-448
85Leaf-213
85OPC-237
85Polar/Ind-14
85T-237
85T/St-245
86D-216
86F-586
86F/LimEd-16
86F/LL-13
86F/Mini-115
86F/Slug-9
86F/St-40
86KayBee-14
86Leaf-93
86OhHenry-14
86OPC-391
86Sf-33
86T-391
86T/St-211
87D-131
87D/OD-111
87F-251
87F/LL-19
87F/Lim-15
87F/Mini-39
87F/St-42
87Gator-14
87Leaf-131
87OPC-160
87RedFoley/St-1
87Sf-84
87T-160
87T/St-210
88Classic/Red-187
88D-10DK
88D-156
88D/Best-168
88D/DKsuper-10DK
88F-609
88F/AwardWin-13
88F/BB/AS-11
88F/BB/MVP-15
88F/Excit-14
88F/Hottest-11
88F/LL-12
88F/Mini-19
88F/RecSet-13
88F/St-19
88F/TL-8
88FanSam-10
88Gator-14
88Leaf-10DK
88Leaf-71
88OPC-49
88Panini/St-77
88RedFoley/St-25
88S-60
88S/YS/II-7
88Sf-58
88T-683
88T/Big-135
88T/St-207
89B-228
89Cadaco-20
89D-310
89D/Best-32
89D/Tr-31
89F-404
89F/AS-5
89F/Up-64
89KMart/Lead-14
89Master/Discs-11
89Mother/R-3
89OPC-55
89Panini/St-325
89S-11
89S/HotStar-36
89S/Mast-29
89S/Tr-35
89Sf-149
89Smok/R-9
89T-398AS
89T-55
89T/Big-288
89T/DH-2
89T/St-208
89T/St/Backs-4
89T/Tr-34T
89UD-186
89UD/Ext-793
90B-497
90Classic-67
90D-142
90D-701AS
90D/BestAL-112
90D/Bon/MVP-BC14
90D/Learning-17
90F-296
90F/BB-8
90KMart/CBatL-11
90KMart/SS-18
90Leaf/I-205
90Mother/Rang-10
90OPC-386AS
90OPC-550
90Panini/St-163
90Panini/St-201
90PublInt/St-285
90PublInt/St-409
90RedFoley/St-34
90S-160
90S/100St-84
90S/McDon-3
90Sf-158
90T-386AS
90T-550
90T/Ames-21
90T/Big-205
90T/DH-24
90T/Gloss22-14
90T/Gloss60-35
90T/Mini-37
90T/St-159AS
90T/St-243
90T/TVAS-2
90UD-103
90UD-82TC
90USPlayC/AS-JK
90Windwlk/Discs-6
91B-265
91B-368SLUG
91D-192
91F-285
91F/Ultra-348
91Leaf/I-228
91Leaf/Stud-123
91Mother/Rang-10
91OPC-387AS
91OPC-775
91Panini/FrSt-253
91Panini/St-210
91S-392AS
91S-493
91S/100SS-84
91Seven/3DCoin-6T
91T-387AS
91T-775
91T/StClub/I-173
91UD-227
91UD/SilSlug-SS1
91USPlayC/AS-6H
92Classic/I-36
92D/DK-DK4
92D/II-741
92F-303
92F-690LL
92F/ASIns-18
92S/100SS-38
92S/I-108
92S/I-432AS
92T-398AS
92T-490
92UD-241

Franco, Matthew
(Matt)
89CharWh/Best-11
89CharWh/ProC-1748
89SALAS/GS-14
90Peoria/Team-11
91Single/ClBest-134
91WinSalem/ClBest-19
91WinSalem/ProC-2836

Francois, Manny
85VeroB-5
87VeroB-11
88SanAn/Best-14
89SanAn/Best-2
90Canton/Best-8
90Canton/ProC-1298

Francona, John
(Tito)
57T-184
58T-316
59T-268
60Kahn
60T-260M
60T-30
60T/tatt-17
61Kahn
61P-64
61T-503
61T/St-134
62Exh
62J-40
62Kahn
62P-40
62P/Can-40
62Salada-15
62Shirriff-15
62Sugar-9
62T-97
62T/St-34
63Exh
63F-12
63J-67
63P-67
63Sugar-9
63T-248
63T-392M
64T-583
65OPC-256
65T-256
66OPC-163
66T-163
67T-443
68T-527
69MB-85
69T-398
69T/St-4
70MLB/St-257
70T-663
72MB-107
78TCMA-205
78TCMA-231
85T-134FS
89Pac/Leg-133
89Swell-76
91Crown/Orio-143
Exh47
WG9-29

Francona, Terry
80Memphis-13
82D-627
82F-188
82Hygrade
82OPC-118R
82OPC/Post-19
82T-118R
82Zeller-11
82Zeller-5
83D-592
83F-281
83OPC-267
83Stuart-14
83T-267
83T/St-321
84D-463
84F-275
84Nes/792-496
84OPC-89
84Stuart-18
84T-496
85D-132
85F-398
85Leaf-245
85OPC-258
85T-134FS
85T-578
85T/St-88
86D-401
86F-248
86F/Up-U43
86Gator-16
86Iowa-11
86Leaf-191
86OPC-374
86T-374
86T/St-80
86T/Tr-38T
87D/OD-193
87F-564
87Kahn-10
87OPC-294
87T-785
87T/Tr-34T
88ColoSp/CMC-20
88ColoSp/ProC-1541
88S-297
88T-686
89Pol/Brew-30
89S-597
89T-31
89T/Tr-35T
89UD-536
90OPC-214
90Pol/Brew-30
90S-216
90T-214
90T/TVCard-48
90UD-180

Franek, Ken
88CalLgAS-49

Franjul, Miguel
78Clinton
79LodiD-15

Frankhouse, Fred
33G-131
34DS-62
35BU-75
35G-2E
35G-4E
35G-7E
39PB-70
90Target-255
92Conlon/Sport-498
V354-19

Franklin, Elliott
76BurlB

Franklin, Glen
80Memphis-10
82Water-17
83Indianap-24

Franklin, Jay
89Butte/SP-17
90Gaston/Best-11
90Gaston/ProC-2516
90Gaston/Star-9

Franklin, Jeff
78Wausau

Franklin, Micah
90Kgsport/Best-7
90Kgsport/Star-8
91Pittsfld/ClBest-12
91Pittsfld/ProC-3428

Franklin, Tony
76Indianap-23
79RochR-7
90Saraso/Star-26MG
91BirmB/LineD-74MG
91BirmB/ProC-1469MG

Franko, Phil
82Wisco-18
83Visalia/LF-5

Franks, Herman
52T-385
65OPC-32MG
65T-32MG
66T-537MG
67OPC-116MG
67T-116MG
68T-267MG
77T-518MG
78T-234MG
79T-551MG
90Target-256
Rawl

Frascatore, John
91Hamil/ClBest-3
91Hamil/ProC-4033

Fraser, Chick
WG3-19

Fraser, Gretchen
52Wheat

Fraser, Will
(Willie)
86PalmSp-13
86PalmSp/Smok-9
87D-40RR
87D/Rook-9
87F-646R
87F/Up-U33
87Leaf-40RR
87Sf/Rook-27
87Smok/Cal-7
87T/Tr-35T
88D-135
88F-490
88OPC-363
88S-394
88Smok/Angels-14
88T-363
88T/Big-183
89D-567
89F-478
89S-157
89T-679
89T/Big-272
89UD-613
90D-587
90F-133
90OPC-477
90PublInt/St-370
90S-358
90Smok/Angel-6
90T-477
90UD-85
91B-6
91D-379
91F-314
91OPC-784
91OPC/Premier-46
91S-96
91T-784
91T/StClub/II-496
91UD-699
92D/II-755
92S/II-721

Frash, Roger
82Lynch-12

Frassa, Bob
88Bristol/ProC-1867

Fraticelli, Carl
90Visalia/Cal-66
90Visalia/ProC-2160

Frazier, Fred
74Syrac/Team-7
75IntAS/TCMA-15
75IntAS/TCMA-20
77SLCity
78Knoxvl

Frazier, George
76BurlB
77Holyo
79T-724R
80T-684R
81D-310
82D-584
82F-35
82T-349
83D-535
83F-379
83T-123
84D-591
84F-123
84F/X-40
84Nes/792-539
84OPC-139
84SevenUp-39
84T-539
84T/Tr-39
85D-167
85F-58
85OPC-19
85SevenUp-39
85T-19
86Cub/Unocal-10

86D-411
86F-370
86Gator-39
86T-431
87D-564
87F-539
87T-207
88D-443
88F-9
88S-332
88T-709
Frazier, Joseph F.
(Joe)
55Hunter
55T-89
55T/DH-83
56T-141
60DF-22
75Tidew/Team-12
76SSPC-610MG
76T-531MG
77T-259MG
82Louisvl-8
91Crown/Orio-144
Frazier, Keith
45Centen-9
Frazier, Ken
81Clinton-18
Frazier, Lou
87Ashvl-7
88Osceola/Star-10
89ColMud/Best-12
89ColMud/ProC-145
89ColMud/Star-10
90London/ProC-1276
91London/LineD-383
91London/ProC-1889
Frazier, Ron
88CapeCod/Sum-90
90Oneonta/ProC-3376
91Greens/ProC-3052
Frazier, Shawn
86Sumter-5
Frazier, Terance
89Smok/FresnoSt-9
Freck
E254
Frederick, Charlie
84CharlO-3
85CharlO-29
87CharlO/WBTV-xx
Frederick, John
34G-47
85Woolwth-12
88Conlon/NatAS-6
90HOF/St-34
90Target-257
R315-A8
R315-B8
V354-85
Frederiksen, Kelly
90Gate/ProC-3359
Fredlund, Jay
79Elmira-2
81Bristol-15
Fredrickson, Scott
91Waterlo/ClBest-4
91Waterlo/ProC-1251
Fredymond, Juan
85Durham-23
86Durham-11
87Durham-21
88Sumter/ProC-409
Freeburg, Larry
82Cedar-11
Freed, Daniel
(Dan)
88James/ProC-1899
89Rockford/Team-8
90FSLAS/Star-6
90WPalmB/Star-8
91Harris/LineD-253
91Harris/ProC-619
Freed, Roger
70OPC-477R
70T-477R
71MLB/St-176
71OPC-362R
71T-362R
72OPC-69
72T-69
78T-504
79T-111
80T-418
91Crown/Orio-145
Freehan, Bill
63T-466R
64Det/Lids-6
64T-407
64T/Coins-87
64T/S-30
64T/St-68
64T/tatt
65T-390
65T/E-41
65T/trans-12
66OPC-145
66T-145
66T/RO-63
67OPC-48
67T-48
68Bz-2
68Coke
68Dexter-33
68Kahn
68T-375AS
68T-470
68T/G-11
69Kahn
69MB-86
69MLB/St-47
69MLBPA/Pin-6
69NTF
69OPC/DE-6
69T-390
69T-431AS
69T/DE-10
69T/S-18
69T/St-172
70K-57
70MB-7
70MLB/St-206
70OPC-335
70OPC-465AS
70T-335
70T-465AS
70T/CB
70T/S-7
71Bz
71Bz/Test-37
71K-31
71MD
71MLB/St-391
71OPC-575
71T-575
71T/Coins-38
71T/GM-22
71T/S-12
71T/tatt-12
72MB-108
72OPC-120
72T-120
73OPC-460
73T-460
73T/Comics-7
73T/Lids-18
73T/PinUps-7
74OPC-162
74T-162
74T/St-174
75Ho-120
75OPC-397
75T-397
75T/M-397
76Ho-6
76Ho/Twink-6
76OPC-540
76T-540
77BurgChef-94
77T-22
78TCMA-285
81Detroit-72
83Kaline-33M
86Sf/Dec-49M
88Domino-5
88Pac/Leg-93
89Swell-106
WG10-27
Freeland, Dean
85Beloit-15
86Clinton-9
87Shrev-5
88Shreve/ProC-1285
89Shreve/ProC-1852
91Jacks/LineD-558
91Tucson/ProC-2208
Freeman, Clem Jr.
82Water-6
83Tampa-12
Freeman, Herschel
(Hersh)
55B-290
56Kahn
56T-242
57Kahn
57Sohio/Reds-5
57T-32
58T-27
79TCMA-120
Freeman, James J.
(Buck)
T204
T206
WG2-20
Freeman, Jimmy
73OPC-610R
73T-610R
Freeman, John
N172
Freeman, Julius
N172
Freeman, LaVell
86ElPaso-11
87ElPaso-1
87TexLgAS-25
88AAA/ProC-12
88Denver/CMC-20
88Denver/ProC-1277
89Denver/CMC-14
89Denver/ProC-48
89UD/Ext-788
90ElPasoATG/Team-31
90T/89Debut-39
90Toledo/CMC-17
90Toledo/ProC-161
Freeman, Mark
59T-532
79TCMA-265
Freeman, Marty
86GlenF-5
Freeman, Marvin
86Reading-8
87D-576
87F-651R
87Maine-12
87Maine/TCMA-4
87Phill/TastyK-48
87Sf/Rook-4
88Maine/CMC-4
88Maine/ProC-279
89D-631
89F-566
89S/HotRook-34
89ScrWB/CMC-1
89T-634
90OPC-103
90Publint/St-236
90ScranWB/CMC-2
90ScranWB/ProC-593
90T-103
91D-619
91F/Up-U73
92D/II-603
92F-356
92S/I-307
92T-68
92UD-491
Freeman, Pete
87Watertn-9
88Augusta/ProC-367
90Martins/ProC-3193
Freeman, Rick
89Elizab/Star-8
Freeman, Scott
90Yakima/Team-28
91Single/ClBest-357
91VeroB/ClBest-7
91VeroB/ProC-768
Freer, Mike
91Osceola/ClBest-27TR
Freese, Gene
55T-205
56T-46
58T-293
59T-472
60L-140
60MacGregor-8
60T-435
60T/tatt-18
61Kahn
61P-30
61T-175
61T/St-17
62J-118
62Kahn
62P-118
62P/Can-118
62Salada-137
62Shirriff-137
62T-205
62T/St-115
63F-33
63Kahn
63T-133
64T-266
65T-492
66T-319
Freese, George
55B-84
Fregin, Doug
82Toledo-27
Fregosi, Jim Jr.
85Spring-3
86StPete-9
87ArkTr-11
91BendB/ClBest-12CO
91BendB/ProC-3711CO
Fregosi, Jim
62T-209
63T-167
64Bz-22
64T-97
64T/Coins-128AS
64T/Coins-98
64T/S-18
64T/St-60
64T/SU
64T/tatt
65Bz-22
65OldLond-25
65OPC-210
65T-210
65T/E-39
65T/trans-13
66Bz-19
66OPC-5
66T-5
66T/RO-84
67Bz-19
67T-385
67T/Test/SU-9
68Coke
68Dexter-34
68OPC-170
68T-170
68T-367AS
68T/G-33
68T/Post-4
69Bz-28
69Citgo-7
69JB
69MB-87
69MLB/St-21
69MLBPA/Pin-7
69NTF
69T-365
69T/DE-5
69T/decal
69T/S-7
69T/St-144
69Trans-14
70K-36
70MB-8
70MLB/St-172
70T-570
70T/S-30
70Trans-14
71Bz
71Bz/Test-25
71JB
71K-64
71MD
71MLB/St-344
71OPC-360
71T-360
71T/Coins-136
71T/GM-16
71T/tatt-3
71T/tatt-3a
72MB-109
72OPC-115
72OPC-346KP
72T-115
72T-346KP
72T-755TR
72T/Cloth-13KP
73OPC-525
73T-525
74T-196
74T/St-234
75OPC-339
75T-339
75T/M-339
76OPC-635
76SSPC-262
76T-635
78T-323
78TCMA-170
79T-424MG
81F-274MG
81Louisvl-1MG
81T-663MG
83Louisvl/Riley-1MG
84Louisvl-1MG
85Louisvl-1MG
86Louisvl-1MG
86T/Tr-39T
87Coke/WS-10MG
87T-318MG
88ArkTr/GS-16MG
88Coke/WS-7MG
88T-714MG
89Smok/Angels-3
89T-414MG
89WPalmB/Star-11
91T/Tr-43TMG
91WIZMets-127
92T-669MG
Freigau, Howard
21Exh-52
25Exh-20
26Exh-20
90Target-953
Freiling, Howard
88VeroB/Star-7
89Jacks/GS-18
Freisleben, Dave
74OPC-599R
74T-599R
75OPC-37
75T-37
75T/M-37
76OPC-217
76SSPC-116
76T-217
77Padre/SchCd-11
77T-407
78Padre/FamFun-12
78T-594
79T-168
80OPC-199
80T-382
89Butte/SP-30
Freitas, Antonio
40Hughes-6
46Sunbeam
47Signal
47Sunbeam
49B/PCL-11
R314
Freitas, Mike
90Pittsfld/Pucko-24
French, Charlie
C46-25
French, Jim
69OPC-199
71MLB/St-538
71OPC-399
71Richm/Team-7
French, Larry
34G-29
35BU-132
41DP-1
88Conlon/NatAS-7
90Target-258
92Conlon/Sport-416
V354-79
WG8-20
French, Ray
28Exh/PCL-31
WG7-17
French, Richard J.
66T-333R
69T-199
70T-617
71T-399
French, Ron

90Johnson/Star-12
91Hamil/ClBest-27
91Hamil/ProC-4052
French, Steve
84Butte-11
French, Walt
92Conlon/Sport-397
Frew, Mike
85Beloit-16
86Stockton-8
87Stockton-15
Frey, Eric
77Newar
Frey, Benjamin R.
92Conlon/Sport-381
Frey, Jim
73OPC-136CO
73T-136CO
74OPC-306CO
74T-306CO
81D-464MG
81T-667MG
84Nes/792-51MG
84SevenUp-MG
84T-51MG
85SevenUp-MG
85T-241MG
86T-231MG
Frey, Linus R.
(Lonny)
34G-89
35G-1G
35G-3E
35G-4E
35G-5E
39PB-161
40PB-76
41DP-5
90Target-259
R310
R312
R314
W711/1
W711/2
Frey, Steve
85Albany-7
87Albany-23
87FtLaud-3
88Tidew/CANDL-20
88Tidew/CMC-6
88Tidew/ProC-1602
89Indianap/CMC-3
89Indianap/ProC-1218
90F-649R
90F/Up-U28
90OPC-91
90T-91
90T/89Debut-40
91B-451
91D-292
91F-231
91F/Ultra-202
91Leaf/I-153
91OPC-462
91Panini/FrSt-154
91S-436
91T-462
91UD-397
92D/II-660
92F-479
92T-174
Frias, Israel
89Bluefld/Star-10
Frias, Jesus M.
(Pepe)
73OPC-607R
73T-607R
74OPC-468
74T-468
75OPC-496
75T-496
75T/M-496
76OPC-544
76SSPC-231
76T-544
77OPC-225
77T-199
78OPC-171
78T-654
79OPC-146
79T-294
80OPC-48
80T-87
81F-134
81Pol/Dodg-36
89Pac/SenLg-106
90Target-260
91Clinton/ClBest-18
Frias, Joe
91Spokane/ClBest-27
91Spokane/ProC-3956
Friberg, A. Bernhardt
(Barney)
26Exh-42
29Exh/4-11
31Exh/4-12
33G-105
91Conlon/Sport-297
V354-10
Fricano, Marion
53T-199
54B-3
54T-124
55B-316
55Rodeo
91T/Arc53-199
Frick, Ford
49Eureka-2
59T-1COM
60F-74
61F-29
80SSPC/HOF
Frick, James
T205
Frick, Tod
91SoOreg/ProC-3848
Fricke, Dave
90Kgsport/Best-28
90Kgsport/Star-28TR
Fridley, Jim
52T-399
53T-187
54Esskay
72T/Test-6
91Crown/Orio-146
91T/Arc53-187
Fridman, Jason
91Elmira/ClBest-5
Friedel, Chuck
84LitFalls-5
Friederich, Mike
85Osceola/Team-7
86ColumAst-13
Friedland, Michael
90James/Pucko-12
91Rockford/ClBest-19
91Rockford/ProC-2054
Friedman, Jason
90Elmira/Pucko-5
90WinHaven/Star-9
91Elmira/ProC-3277
Friel, Bill
E107
E270/2
Friend, Bob
52B-191
52T-233
53B/Col-16
54B-43
54DanDee
55B-57
56T-221
56YellBase/Pin-10
57Kahn
57T-150
58Hires-24
58Hires/T
58Kahn
58T-315
58T-334
58T-492AS
59Kahn
59T-428M
59T-460
59T-569AS
60Kahn
60L-53
60T-437
61Kahn
61P-125
61T-270
61T-45LL
61T-585AS
61T/St-63
62J-178
62Kahn
62P-178
62P/Can-178
62Salada-157
62Shirriff-157
62T-520
62T/bucks
62T/St-176
63IDL-8
63J-145
63Kahn
63P-145
63T-450
64Bz-6
64Kahn
64T-1LL
64T-20
64T/Coins-77
64T/S-28
64T/St-66
64T/SU
64T/tatt
64Wheat/St-17
65Kahn
65OldLond-10
65T-392
66T-519
78TCMA-160
88Pac/Leg-78
89Swell-86
91T/Arc53-298
91WIZMets-128
Exh47
Friend, Owen
50B-189
51B-101
52T-160
53Glen
54B-212
55B-256
Frierson, John
83Miami-19
Frierson, Mike
80Wausau-19
Friesen, Rob
87Fayette-26
Frill, John E.
E270/2
M116
T206
Frink, Keith
88Wausau/GS-7
Frisch, Frank
(Frankie)
21Exh-53
25Exh-33
26Exh-34
28Exh-31
28Yueng-50
29Exh/4-15
31Exh/4-15
33CJ/Pin-6
33DH-18
33Exh/4-8
33G-49
34DS-17
34Exh/4-8
34G-13
34Ward's/Pin-4
35BU-173
35BU-33
35Exh/4-8
35G-1A
35G-2A
35G-6A
35G-7A
35Wheat
36Exh/4-8
40PB-167
48Exh/HOF
50B-229MG
50Callahan
51B-282MG
61F-30
61GP-19
76Motor-7
80Pac/Leg-46
80SSPC/HOF
85Woolwth-13
86Conlon/1-14M
88Conlon/5-11
88Conlon/NatAS-8
89HOF/St-13
89Pac/Leg-113
91Conlon/Sport-11
91Conlon/Sport-305
92Conlon/Sport-634
E120
E121/120
E121/80
E210-50
E220
R300
R306
R310
R311/Gloss
R313
R314
R315-A9
R315-B9
R316
R328-30
R332-4
R337-419
R423-32
V100
V353-49
V354-64
V355-107
V61-62
W501-104
W501-62
W502-50
W512-8
W515-14
W517-16
W572
W573
W575
WG8-21
Frisella, Dan
(Danny)
68OPC-191
68T-191
69T-343
71MLB/St-151
71OPC-104
71T-104
72OPC-293
72OPC-294IA
72T-293
72T-294A
72T/Cloth-14IA
73OPC-432
73T-432
74OPC-71
74T-71
75OPC-343
75T-343
75T/M-343
76OPC-32
76SSPC-117
76T-32
77T-278
89Tidew/Candl-1
91WIZMets-129
Fritz, Charles
T206
T213 brown
Fritz, Greg
91Utica/ClBest-19
91Utica/ProC-3234
Fritz, John
88PalmSp/Cal-87
88PalmSp/ProC-1445
90PalmSp/Cal-221
90PalmSp/ProC-2572
91Miami/ClBest-7
91Miami/ProC-401
Frobel, Doug
78Charl
81Buffa-22
82Portl-20
84D-38
84Nes/792-264
84T-264
85F-464
85T-587
85T/St-128
86Tidew-9
87BuffB-7
89BirmB/Best-7
89BirmB/ProC-105
Frock, Sam
C46-13
M116
Froemming, Bruce
88TM/Umpire-11
89TM/Umpire-9
90TM/Umpire-9
Frohwirth, Todd
86Clearw-9
87Phill/TastyK-52
87Reading-19
88D/Rook-3
88F-301
88Maine/CMC-10
88Maine/ProC-296
88Phill/TastyK-10
88T-378
89D-587
89F-567
89Phill/TastyK-7
89S-647
89S/HotRook-14
89T-542
90D-631
90OPC-69
90ScranWB/CMC-24
90ScranWB/ProC-594
90T-69
90UD-443
91RochR/LineD-456
91RochR/ProC-1896
92D/I-317
92S/II-534
92T-158
92T/Promo-18
92UD-318
Fromme, Art
10Domino-46
11Helmar-113
12Sweet/Pin-98
14Piedmont/St-23
D303
E106
E254
E270/2
E90/1
M116
S74-74
T202
T204
T205
T206
T207
T213/blue
T215/blue
T215/brown
T216
T3-93
Fronio, Jason
91Watertn/ClBest-5
91Watertn/ProC-3360
Frost, C. David
78Cr/PCL-83
79T-703R
80T-423
81D-52
81F-275
81SLCity-6
81T-286
82D-290
82F-460
82T-24
82T/Tr-37T
83F-111
83T-656
Frost, Jerald
87Sumter-1
89Durham/Team-12
89Durham/Star-12
Fruge, Chris
90Utica/Pucko-17
Fruge, Jeff
82QuadC-8
83QuadC-10
Fry, Brian
89Billings/ProC-2051
90Billings/ProC-3215
Fry, Jerry
79T-720R
Fry, W.J.
N172
Frye, Jeff
88Butte-14
89Gaston/ProC-1023
89Gaston/Star-7
89SALAS/GS-27
90CharlR/Star-7

91Tulsa/LineD-579
91Tulsa/ProC-2778

Frye, Paul
86Jamestn-8
87WPalmB-3
88Rockford-14
89Rockford-14

Fryer, Paul
82Reading-14

Fryhoff, John
83TriCit-10

Fryman, Travis
88Fayette/ProC-1094
89BBAmerAA/BPro-AA2
89London/ProC-1366
90AAAGame/ProC-AAA30
90B-360
90F/Up-U96
90T/Tr-33T
90Toledo/CMC-18
90Toledo/ProC-155
91B-145
91Classic/200-124
91Classic/I-40
91CokeK/Tiger-24
91D-768
91F-336
91F/Ultra-122
91Leaf/I-149
91Leaf/Stud-54
91MajorLg/Pins-34
91OPC-128
91RedFoley/St-106
91S-570
91S/100RisSt-68
91Seven/3DCoin-5MW
91T-128
91T/90Debut-49
91T/StClub/II-355
91ToysRUs-8
91UD-225
92D/I-349
92F-134
92S/I-65
92T-750
92UD-466
92UD-643DS

Fryman, Troy
91Utica/ClBest-27
91Utica/ProC-3247

Fryman, Woodie
66EH-22
66T-498R
67T-221
67T/Test/PP-9
68OPC-112
68T-112
69MB-88
69MLB/St-175
69OPC-51
69T-51
69T/St-75
70MLB/St-88
70T-677
71MLB/St-177
71OPC-414
71T-414
72MB-110
72OPC-357
72T-357
72T/Cloth-15
73OPC-146
73T-146
74OPC-555
74T-555
75OPC-166
75T-166
75T/M-166
76OPC-467
76SSPC-345
76T-467
77OPC-126
77T-28
78T-585
79OPC-135
79T-269
80OPC-316
80T-607
81D-331
81F-159
81OPC-170
81OPC/Post-10
81T-394
82D-68
82F-189
82Hygrade
82OPC-181
82T-788
82Zeller-12
83D-162
83F-283
83OPC-137
83Stuart-2
83T-137

Fucci, Dom
80GlenF/B-19
80GlenF/C-14
80GlenF/C-20M
81GlenF-11
82Edmon-18

Fuchs, Charlie
90Target-261

Fuentes, Miguel
70OPC-88R
70T-88R

Fuentes, Mike
84D-40RR
84Indianap-12
84Stuart-32
85Indianap-7
87Memphis-1
87Memphis/Best-25

Fuentes, Roberto
85Elmira-6
86WinHaven-8

Fuentes, Tito
66T-511R
67OPC-177
67T-177
70OPC-42
70T-42
71MLB/St-247
71OPC-378
71T-378
71Ticket/Giant-4
72OPC-427
72OPC-428IA
72T-427
72T-428IA
73OPC-236
73T-236
74OPC-305
74T-305
74T/St-104
75Ho-108
75OPC-425
75T-425
75T/M-425
76Crane-15
76MSA/Disc
76OPC-8
76SSPC-124
76T-8
77T-63
78T-385

Fuhrman, Alfred
(Ollie)
E120
W573

Fujimoto, Kenji
89Visalia/Cal-116
89Visalia/ProC-1432

Fulgencio, Elvin
85Cedar-22

Fulgham, John
77StPete
80T-152
81D-70
81Louisvl-20
81T-523
82Louisvl-9
83Louisvl/Riley-20

Fuller, Charles F.
(Nig)
90Target-954

Fuller, Harry
88AubAs/ProC-1956
89Ashvl/ProC-957

Fuller, James H.
(Jim)
74OPC-606R
74T-606R
75OPC-594
75T-594
75T/M-594
78Colum
91Crown/Orio-147

Fuller, Jon
90CharWh/ProC-2244
91Cedar/ClBest-14
91Cedar/ProC-2721

Fuller, Paul
88Utica/Pucko-5
89Saraso/Star-6
89Star/Wax-58

Fuller, Scott
88Utica/Pucko-19

Fuller, Tom
80Ander-4

Fuller, Vern
68OPC-71
68T-71
69T-291
70MLB/St-197
70T-558
72MB-111

Fuller, Wayne
88Batavia/ProC-1669

Fuller, William B.
N172
N566-179

Fullerton, Hugh
88Pac/8Men-29
88Pac/8Men-35M
88Pac/8Men-42M
88Pac/8Men-64

Fullis, Charles
(Chick)
33DH-19
35BU-74
88Conlon/NatAS-9
92Conlon/Sport-514
R308-166

Fully, Edward
90Kgsport/Best-11
90Kgsport/Star-9
91SALAS/ProC-SAL15

Fulmer, Chris
N172
N284

Fulmer, Mike
84Madis/Pol-20
86Stockton-9

Fulton, Bill
84Greens-12
86Albany/TCMA-26
87Colum-31
87Colum/Pol-10
87Colum/TCMA-4
88Colum/CMC-4
88Colum/Pol-2
88Colum/ProC-312
89Colum/CMC-1
89Colum/Pol-5
89Colum/ProC-746

Fulton, Ed
88Spring/Best-24
89StPete/Star-13
90T/TVCard-49
91Louisvl/LineD-235
91Louisvl/ProC-2916

Fulton, Greg
87Chatt/Best-18
88Vermont/ProC-942
89Calgary/ProC-524
89Wmsprt/ProC-648
90Calgary/CMC-9
90Calgary/ProC-656
91Harris/LineD-254
91Harris/ProC-631

Fults, Nathan
90Idaho/ProC-3260

Fultz, Bill
82Lynch-20
83Lynch-5
84Jacks-7

Fultz, David
E107

Funderburk, Mark
78Wisco
80OrlTw-19
82Orlan-7
83Omaha-15
85Orlan-5
86D-630
86F-652M
86Sf-178M
86Toledo-11
87Orlan-25
88OrlanTw/Best-5
89Orlan/Best-3
89Orlan/ProC-1344
90OrlanSR/Best-29CO
90OrlanSR/ProC-1099CO
90OrlanSR/Star-25CO
91OrlanSR/LineD-500CO
91OrlanSR/ProC-1866CO

Funk, Art
R314/Can

Funk, Brian
83Water-2
84Cedar-6

Funk, E.
31Exh/4-24

Funk, Frank
61T-362
62Sugar-4
62T-587
63T-476
64T-289
80Penin/B-26C
86Omaha-7CO
86Omaha/TCMA-24
87Omaha-1
91Cedar/ClBest-26MG
91Cedar/ProC-2735MG

Funk, Tom
86ColumAst-14
87Tucson-25
88ColAst/Best-18

Fuqua, David
75Lafay

Furcal, Lorenzo
89Madis/Star-9
89Medford/Best-17

Furcal, Manuel
90SanBern/Best-11
90SanBern/Cal-98
90SanBern/ProC-2628
91Penin/ClBest-4
91Penin/ProC-370

Furch, John
89Utica/Pucko-7

Furillo, Carl
47HomogBond-16
48Swell-20
49B-70
49Eureka-35
50B-58
50Drake-18
51B-81
52B-24
52Coke
52TipTop
53B/Col-78
54B-122
54NYJour
55B-169
55Gol/Dodg-9
56T-190
57T-400M
57T-45
58T-417
59Morrell
59T-206
60BB-8
60Morrell
60NuCard-32
60T-408
61NuCard-432
72T/Test-5
79TCMA-43
89Rini/Dodg-14
89Smok/Dodg-58
90Target-262
91T/Arc53-305
D305
Exh47
PM10/Sm-54
PM10/Sm-55
PM10/Sm-56
PM10/Sm-57

Furman, Jon
83BirmB-20

Furmanik, Dan
89Clmbia/Best-6
89Clmbia/GS-8
91SLCity/ProC-3203

Fusco, Thomas
90Hamil/Best-5
90Hamil/Star-13
91Savan/ProC-1645

Fuson, Grady
82Idaho-31
83Idaho-31
89Medford/Best-18
90SoOreg/Best-30MG
90SoOreg/ProC-3449MG
91SoOreg/ProC-3866MG

Fuson, Robin
78Watlo
82Chatt-18
83BuffB-1
84BuffB-24
85Pawtu-13

Fusselman, Les
52T-378
53Hunter
53T-218
91T/Arc53-218

Futrell, Mark
90Welland/Pucko-21
91Augusta/ClBest-6
91Augusta/ProC-799

Fye, Chris
89Clinton/ProC-885
90Foil/Best-159
90SanJose/Best-16
90SanJose/Cal-43
90SanJose/ProC-2002
90SanJose/ProC-2172M
90SanJose/Star-10

Fynan, Kevin
88Clearw/Star-11
89Clearw/Star-9
90Clearw/Star-7

Fyock, Wade
91AppFx/ClBest-3
91AppFx/ProC-1709
91Single/ClBest-249

Fzelykovskyi, Andrei
89EastLDD/ProC-DD13

Gabbani, Mike
90Hunting/ProC-3284
91WinSalem/ClBest-13
91WinSalem/ProC-2831

Gabella, Jim
90Watertn/Star-24MG
91ColoSp/LineD-100CO
91ColoSp/ProC-2202CO

Gabler, Frank
35BU-91
92Conlon/Sport-606

Gabler, John
60L-62

Gables, Kenneth
48Sommers-5
49Sommers-3

Gabriele, Dan
85Elmira-7
86Greens-6
87WinHaven-10
88NewBrit/ProC-898
89NewBrit/ProC-604
89NewBrit/Star-6

Gabriele, Mike
90Sumter/Best-3
90Sumter/ProC-2426

Gabrielson, Len
63T-253R
64T-198
65OPC-14
65T-14
66T-395
67T-469
68T-357
69MB-89
69MLB/St-147
69T-615
69T/St-44
70MLB/St-50
70OPC-204
70T-204
90Target-263
PM10/Sm-58

Gabrielson, Leonard
43Centen-9

Gaddie, Mike
90Johnson/Star-30TR

Gaddy, Robert
89Batavia/ProC-1928
90A&AASingle/ProC-95
90SALAS/Star-7
90Spartan/Best-3

90Spartan/ProC-2484
90Spartan/Star-8
91Clearw/ClBest-3
91Clearw/ProC-1614

Gaeckle, Chris
86Greens-7
87Greens-25

Gaedel, Eddie
60NuCard-26
61NuCard-426
73F/Wild-4

Gaeta, Chris
85Newar-19

Gaetti, Gary
80Wisco
82OrlTw/A-7
83D-53
83F-613
83T-431
83T/St-87
84D-314
84F-565
85FunFood/Pin-131
84Nes/792-157
84OPC-157
84T-157
84T/St-306
85D-242
85F-278
85Leaf-145
85OPC-304
85Seven/Minn-9
85T-304
85T/St-302
86D-314
86F-394
86OPC-97
86T-97
86T/St-283
87Classic-54
87D-122
87D/OD-219
87F-540
87F/GameWin-15
87F/Mini-40
87F/RecSet-9
87F/St-43
87Leaf-245
87OPC-179
87Sf-114M
87Sf-64
87T-710
87T/Gloss60-3
87T/Mini-62
87T/St-279
88Classic/Blue-233
88D-194
88D-19DK
88D/Best-46
88D/DKsuper-19DK
88F-10
88F/Hottest-12
88F/LL-13
88F/Mini-34
88F/St-43
88KayBee-11
88Leaf-19DK
88Leaf-200
88Master/Disc-9
88Nestle-4
88OPC-257
88Panini/St-140
88Panini/St-445
88RedFoley/St-26
88S-62
88Sf-154
88Smok/Minn-2
88T-578
88T/Big-127
88T/Coins-13
88T/RiteAid-31
88T/St-17
88T/St-277
88T/UK-25
88Woolwth-18
88Woolwth-22
89B-158
89Cadaco-21
89Classic-41
89D-64
89D/AS-13
89D/Best-102
89F-110
89F/Heroes-15
89Master/Discs-3
89OPC-220
89Panini/St-389
89RedFoley/St-46
89S-8
89S/HotStar-21
89S/Mast-16
89Sf-48
89T-220
89T/Big-264
89T/Gloss60-33
89T/LJN-35
89T/Mini-61
89T/St-289
89T/St/Backs-8
89UD-203
90B-417
90D-151
90D/BestAL-10
90F-373
90F/BB-10
90HotPlay/St-14
90Leaf/I-97
90Leaf/Prev-11
90MLBPA/Pins-100
90OPC-630
90Panini/St-106
90PublInt/St-286
90PublInt/St-326
90S-145
90S/100St-22
90Sf-51
90T-630
90T/Big-254
90T/Coins-14
90T/DH-25
90T/Gloss60-28
90T/St-288
90UD-454
91B-207
91Classic/200-49
91D-547
91F-609
91F/UltraUp-U8
91F/Up-U9
91Leaf/II-303
91Leaf/Stud-25
91OPC-430
91OPC/Premier-47
91Panini/FrSt-302
91Panini/St-250
91S-325
91S/RookTr-39T
91Smok/Angel-13
91T-430
91T/StClub/II-353
91T/Tr-44T
91UD-233
91UD-34TC
91UD/Ext-731
92D/I-96
92F-58
92S/I-39
92T-70
92UD-321

Gaff, Brent
78Wausau
79Wausau-1
81Tidew-17
82Tidew-20
83D-553
83Tidew-16
84Tidew-8
85F-80
85T-546
86T-18
91WIZMets-130

Gaffney, Bill
80SanJose/JITB-8

Gaffney, John H.
90Target-955
N172

Gagliano, Phil
61Union
62Kahn/Atl
64T-568R
65T-503
66T-418
67T-304
68T-479
69T-609
70OPC-143
70T-143
71OPC-302
71T-302
72MB-112
72OPC-472
72T-472
73OPC-69
73T-69
74OPC-622
74T-622

Gagliano, Ralph
65T-501R

Gagliardi, Joe
88CalLgAS-25
89AS/Cal-56PRES
90AS/Cal-27PRES
91AS/Cal-26

Gagne, Greg
82Orlan-8
83Toledo-14
84D-39RR
85F/Up-U43
85T/Tr-36T
86D-558
86F-395
86T-162
87D-395
87D/OD-223
87F-541
87T-558
87T/St-283
88D-441
88D/Best-74
88F-11
88Master/Disc-11
88OPC-343
88Panini/St-141
88S-214
88Smok/Minn-8
88T-343
88T/Big-58
88Woolwth-32WS7
89B-161
89D-318
89D/Best-158
89F-111
89OPC-19
89Panini/St-390
89S-159
89T-19
89T-429TL
89T/Big-186
89T/St-288
89UD-166
90B-414
90D-237
90D/BestAL-135
90F-374
90Leaf/II-302
90MLBPA/Pins-99
90OPC-448
90Panini/St-115
90PublInt/St-327
90S-102
90T-448
90T/Big-78
90T/St-295
90UD-217
91B-338
91D-284
91F-610
91F/Ultra-186
91Leaf/II-426
91Leaf/Stud-84
91OPC-216
91Panini/FrSt-303
91Panini/St-245
91RedFoley/St-37
91S-211
91T-216
91T/StClub/I-277
91UD-415
92D/I-204
92F-202
92S/I-182
92T-663
92UD-168

Gahbrielson, Rick
86Bakers-9CO

Gainer, Delos C.
BF2-3
D328-53
D329-63
D350/2-64
E135-53
M101/4-63
M101/5-64
T207

Gainer, Jay
91AS/Cal-7
91HighD/ClBest-19
91HighD/ProC-2402
91Single/ClBest-230

Gainer, Keith
79Newar-18

Gaines, A. Joe
62T-414
63T-319
64T-364
65T-595
66OPC-122
66T-122
91Crown/Orio-148

Gaines, Jerry
77Ashvl

Gainey, Ty
82DayBe-13
83ColumAst-10
85Cram/PCL-69
86D-31RR
86Tucson-5
87D-533
87Sf-118M
87Tucson-23
88D-578
88F-448
89ColoSp/CMC-22
89ColoSp/ProC-258
90ColoSp/CMC-11
90ColoSp/ProC-50

Gainous, Trey
88AppFx/ProC-151

Gaither, Horace
90Saraso/Star-8
90SoBend/ClBest-2
91SoBend/ProC-2862

Gajkowski, Steve
90BurlInd/ProC-3005
91ColInd/ClBest-13
91ColInd/ProC-1480
91Watertn/ClBest-6
91Watertn/ProC-3361

Gakeler, Dan
85Greens-20
86Greens-8
87NewBrit-19
88NewBrit/ProC-904
89Jaxvl/Best-24
89Jaxvl/ProC-157
90Indianap/CMC-6
90Indianap/ProC-294
90WPalmB/Star-9
91B-144
91Toledo/LineD-584
91Toledo/ProC-1924
92F-135
92S/II-831
92T-621
92T/91Debut-59

Galan, Augie
35BU-135
36Exh/4-3
37Exh/4-3
38Exh/4-3
41DP-102
48B-39
49B-230
49Eureka-103
50Remar
53Mother-7
54T-233
89Smok/Dodg-48
90Target-264
Exh47
R312/M
R314
V355-106
WG8-22

Galante, Matt
75BurlB
76BurlB
77Holyo
83Tucson-23
84Cram/PCL-50
90Mother/Ast-27CO
91Mother/Ast-28CO

Galarraga, Andres
85Indianap-3
86D-33
86D/Rook-7
86F-647R
86F/Up-U44
86Leaf-27RR
86Provigo-10
86Sf/Rook-27
86T/Tr-40T
87Classic-71
87D-303
87D/OD-90
87F-319
87F/BB-18
87F/Mini-41
87Leaf-221
87OPC-272
87T-272
87T/St-84
88D-282
88D/Best-90
88F-184
88F/LL-14
88F/Mini-88
88F/Slug-14
88F/St-96
88F/TL-9
88F/WaxBox-C3
88Ho/Disc-8
88Leaf-121
88OPC-25
88Panini/St-323
88S-19
88S/YS/II-8
88Sf-182
88T-25
88T/Big-55
88T/Gloss60-58
88T/Mini-56
88T/St-79
88T/St/Backs-2
89B-365
89Cadaco-22
89Classic-46
89D-130
89D-14DK
89D/AS-45
89D/Best-12
89D/DKsuper-14DK
89D/MVP-BC16
89F-376
89F-638M
89F/BBAS-13
89F/BBMVP's-12
89F/Excit-13
89F/Heroes-16
89F/LL-14
89F/Rec-3
89F/Superstar-15
89F/WaxBox-C8
89KayBee-12
89OPC-93
89Panini/St-119
89Panini/St-224
89RedFoley/St-47
89S-144
89S/HotStar-74
89S/Mast-33
89Sf-139
89T-386AS
89T-590
89T/Big-173
89T/Coins-13
89T/Gloss60-44
89T/Hills-13
89T/LJN-159
89T/Mini-22
89T/St-76
89T/St/Backs-36
89T/UK-28
89UD-115
89UD-677TC
90B-113
90Classic-115
90D-97
90D/BestNL-67
90F-345
90Holsum/Discs-4
90HotPlay/St-15
90Leaf/II-450
90OPC-720
90Panini/St-284
90PublInt/St-173
90PublInt/St-611
90RedFoley/St-35
90S-25

90S/100St-14
90Sf-148
90T-720
90T/Big-108
90T/HillsHM-31
90T/St-75
90T/TVAS-62
90UD-356
91B-446
91Classic/200-75
91D-68
91D/GSlam-9
91F-232
91F/Ultra-203
91Leaf/I-110
91Leaf/Stud-197
91OPC-610
91OPC/Premier-48
91Panini/FrSt-139
91Panini/Top15-100
91Post/Can-3
91S-443
91T-610
91T/StClub/I-69
91UD-456
92D/I-355
92F-480
92S/I-35
92T-240
92UD-474

Galasso, Bob
80T-711R
80Vanco-20
81Spokane-9
82T-598
84Richm-16
89Pac/SenLg-200
89T/SenLg-100
90EliteSenLg-56
91Pac/SenLg-114

Galatzer, Milt
R313

Galbato, Chan
86Jamestn-9

Gale, Bill
91StPete/ProC-2287

Gale, Rich
76Watlo
77Jaxvl
79OPC-149
79T-298
80T-433
81D-462
81F-40
81OPC-363
81Pol/Royals-3
81T-544
82D-138
82F-408
82OPC-67
82T-67
82T/Tr-38T
83D-172
83F-260
83OPC-243
83T-719
83T/Tr-35
84D-140
84F-469
84F/X-41
84Nes/792-142
84Pawtu-23
84T-142
84T/Tr-40
85T-606
89EastLDD/ProC-DD43CO
89NewBrit/ProC-602
89NewBrit/Star-24
89Pac/SenLg-95
90NewBrit/Best-26CO
90NewBrit/Star-26CO
91Pac/SenLg-19
91Pawtu/LineD-375CO
91Pawtu/ProC-55CO

Galehouse, Dennis
40PB-198
47TipTop
61F-107
W753

Galindez, Luis
89Watlo/ProC-1789
89Watlo/Star-8
90Foil/Best-171
90Waterlo/Best-5
90Waterlo/ProC-2372
91HighD/ClBest-4
91HighD/ProC-2387
91Single/ClBest-179

Galindez, Vilato
90Foil/Best-172

Galindo, Luis
88Lakeland/Star-5
89Lakeland/Star-6
90London/ProC-1277
91London/LineD-384
91London/ProC-1884

Gallagher
N690

Gallagher, Alan
71OPC-224
71T-224
72T-693
72T-694IA
78Green
81Durham-14
82Chatt-23
83BuffB-24

Gallagher, Bob
74OPC-21
74T-21
75OPC-406
75T-406
75T/M-406
76Phoenix
76SSPC-608
91WIZMets-131

Gallagher, Dave
80Batavia-25
81Watlo-26
82Chatt-17
82Watlo/C-11
83BuffB-19
84Maine-7
85IntLgAS-35
85Maine-27
86Maine-9CO
87Calgary-22
88D/Rook-7
88F/Up-U16
88S/Tr-89T
88Vanco/CMC-24
88Vanco/ProC-771
89B-71
89Bz-8
89Chatt/II/Team-10
89Coke/WS-9
89D-384
89D/Best-67
89F-496
89KMart/DT-7
89Panini/St-299
89S-455
89S/HotRook-96
89S/YS/I-4
89Sf-88
89T-156
89T/Big-310
89T/Gloss60-49
89T/JumboR-8
89T/St-295
89T/St-321
89ToysRUs-9
89UD-164
90Classic-49
90Coke/WSox-5
90D-219
90F-532
90OPC-612
90Panini/St-46
90Publint/St-387
90S-115
90S/100St-56
90Sf-105
90T-612
90T/St-305
90UD-328
91Crown/Orio-498
91F-471
91F/UltraUp-U9
91OPC-349
91T-349
91T/StClub/II-563
91UD-508
92D/I-377
92F-59
92S/I-239
92T-552
92UD-289

Gallagher, Joe
90Target-265

Gallardo, Luis
87QuadC-31
90Oneonta/ProC-3366
91Greens/ProC-3065

Galle, Mike
89GreatF-28
90Yakima/Team-26

Gallego, Mike
82Tacoma-30
82WHave-12
84Cram/PCL-81
85Mother/A's-24
86D-156
86T-304
86Tacoma-7
88D-379
88D/A's/Bk-379
88Modesto-33
88Mother/A's-22
88S-428
88T-702
88T/Big-103
89D-422
89F-8
89Mother/A's-23
89S-537
89T-102
89UD-583
90B-459
90D-361
90F-7
90Leaf/I-121
90Mother/A's-25
90OPC-293
90Publint/St-304
90S-323
90T-293
90T/Big-73
90UD-230
91B-219
91D-158
91F-7
91F/Ultra-246
91Leaf/I-78
91Mother/A's-25
91OPC-686
91S-476
91SFExam/A's-4
91T-686
91T/StClub/I-151
91UD-151
92D/I-314
92F-256
92S/I-43
92T-76
92UD-193

Gallegos, Matt
83Nashvl-6

Gallia, Melvin
(Bert)
D328-54
E135-54
W514-76

Gallivan, Phil
90Target-266

Gallo, Ben
81Clinton-6
90Reno/Cal-287CO

Gallo, Raymond
81BurlB-6
83ElPaso-14

Galloway, Clarence E.
(Chick)
21Exh-54
61F-108
E120
E126-15
E210-58
V100
W572
W573

Galloway, Gill
89Billings/ProC-2065

Galloway, Ike
88Batavia/ProC-1680

Galloway, Joseph
26Exh-106

Galloway, Troy
85Visalia-24
86Orlan-6
87Visalia-9

Galvan, Mike
88Utica/Pucko-20
89Utica/Pucko-8
90Saraso/Star-9
91Saraso/ClBest-4
91Saraso/ProC-1107

Galvez, Balvino
86Albuq-8
89Colum/CMC-10
89Colum/Pol-6
89Colum/ProC-748
90Indianap/ProC-296
90Target-267

Galvez, Roberto
78Dunedin

Galvin, James
(Pud)
75F/Pion-11
76Motor-8
80SSPC/HOF
89HOF/St-80
N172
WG1-59

Gamba, Tom J.
87Watlo-8
88Watlo/ProC-673

Gambee, Brad
86Cram/PCL-4
87Everett-29

Gambeski, Mike
83Spring/LF-23

Gamble, Billy
88Wythe/ProC-2000

Gamble, Fredie
89Bristol/Star-8

Gamble, John
74OPC-597R
74T-597R

Gamble, Lee
40PB-208
W711/1

Gamble, Oscar
70T-654R
71MLB/St-178
71OPC-23
71T-23
72OPC-423
72T-423
73OPC-372
73T-372
74OPC-152
74T-152
74T/St-166
75Ho-147
75OPC-213
75T-213
75T/M-213
76OPC-74
76SSPC-526
76T-74
76T/Tr-74T
77T-505
78Ho-100
78Padre/FamFun-13
78T-390
79OPC-132
79T-263
80T-698
81D-229
81F-98
81OPC-139
81T-139
82D-360
82F-36
82OPC-229
82T-472
83D-461
83F-380
83OPC-19
83T-19
84F-124
84Nes/792-512
84OPC-13
84T-512
85Coke/WS-0
85F/Up-U44
85OPC-93
85T-724
85T/Tr-37T
89Pac/SenLg-116
89TM/SenLg-37

Gamble, Robert
N172

Gamboa, Tom
90Toledo/CMC-22MG
90Toledo/ProC-164MG

Gamby, Steve
75Clinton

Gammage, Mark
82BurlR-19

Ganch, Tim
78Charl

Gandil, Charles
(Chick)
14CJ-39
15CJ-39
88Pac/8Men-106
88Pac/8Men-22M
88Pac/8Men-25
88Pac/8Men-46
88Pac/8Men-48M
88Pac/8Men-9
BF2-22
C46-65
D328-55
D329-64
E135-55
E90/3
M101/4-64
T206
T213/blue
W514-31

Gamez, Bobby
90Boise/ProC-3317
91QuadC/ClBest-4
91QuadC/ProC-2621

Gamez, Fabio
91Collnd/ClBest-27

Gamez, Francisco
91Beloit/ClBest-3
91Beloit/ProC-2096

Ganley, Robert
E91
T204
T206

Ganote, Joe
90StCath/ProC-3461
91Myrtle/ClBest-5
91Myrtle/ProC-2939
91SALAS/ProC-SAL38

Gant, Ronald Edwin
(Ronnie)
86Durham-12
87Greenvl/Best-13
87SLAS-13
88D-654
88D/Best-2
88D/Rook-47
88F-538
88Richm/CMC-12
88Richm/ProC-3
88S-647
88T/Big-249
88T/Tr-39T
89B-274
89Bz-9
89Classic-35
89D-50
89F-590
89KMart/DT-2
89OPC-196
89Panini/St-42
89S-372
89S/HotRook-87
89S/YS/I-16
89Sf-28
89T-296
89T/Big-43
89T/Gloss60-10
89T/JumboR-9
89T/St-322
89T/St-34
89T/UK-29
89ToysRUs-10
89UD-378
90D-475
90D/BestNL-111
90F-582
90Leaf/II-376
90OPC-567
90Publint/St-113
90Publint/St-612
90T-567
90T/Big-66
90UD-232

91B-583
91Classic/200-123
91Classic/I-5
91Classic/III-23
91Classic/III-24
91D-10DK
91D-507
91D/SuperDK-10
91F-688
91F/Ultra-4
91Leaf/I-129
91Leaf/Stud-144
91MajorLg/Pins-47
91OPC-725
91OPC/Premier-49
91Panini/FrSt-23
91Panini/St-27
91Panini/Top15-36
91Panini/Top15-52
91RedFoley/St-38
91S-448
91S/100SS-14
91T-725
91T/CJMini/II-19
91T/StClub/II-454
91UD-361
91UD-82TC
92D/I-284
92F-357
92S/100SS-76
92S/I-25
92T-25
92T-391AS
92UD-345

Gantner, Jim
77Spoka
77T-494R
79T-154
80T-374
81D-204
81F-522
81F/St-133
81OPC-122
81T-482
82D-406
82F-142
82OPC-207
82Pol/Brew-17
82T-613
83D-232
83F-34
83Gard-8
83OPC-88
83Pol/Brew-17
83T-88
84D-115
84F-200
84Gard-7
84Nes/792-298
84OPC-298
84Pol/Brew-17
84T-298
84T/St-298
85D-229
85D/AAS-2
85F-582
85Gard-7
85Leaf-217
85OPC-216
85Pol/Brew-17
85T-781
85T/St-295
86D-115
86F-487
86Jay's-8
86Leaf-43
86OPC-51
86Pol/Brew-17
86T-582
86T/St-202
87D-172
87D/OD-53
87F-345
87OPC-108
87Pol/Brew-17
87Smok/AL-15
87T-108
87T/St-197
88D-214
88D/Best-53
88F-165
88Leaf-161
88OPC-337
88Panini/St-124
88Pol/Brew-17
88S-197
88Sf-130
88T-337
88T/St-195
89B-141
89Brewer/YB-17
89D-264
89D/Best-295
89F-186
89Gard-3
89OPC-134
89Panini/St-372
89Pol/Brew-17
89S-313
89T-671
89T/Big-184
89T/St-203
89UD-274
90B-400
90Brewer/MillB-9
90D-291
90F-324
90MLBPA/Pins-81
90OPC-417
90Panini/St-94
90Pol/Brew-17
90PublInt/St-496
90S-382
90T-417
90T/Big-124
90T/St-207
90UD-218
91B-48
91Brewer/MillB-8
91D-703
91F-584
91F/Ultra-174
91Leaf/I-145
91OPC-23
91Pol/Brew-8
91S-532
91T-23
91T/StClub/I-183
91UD-618
92D/II-574
92F-176
92S/I-246
92T-248
92UD-360

Ganzel, Charles
N172
N300/unif
N526
Scrapp

Ganzel, John Henry
C46-26
T206

Garagiola, Joe
47TipTop
49Eureka-182
51B-122
52B-27
52T-227
53B/Col-21
54B-141
79TCMA-262
80Pac/Leg-76
90Pac/Legend-24
90Swell/Great-14
91Swell/Great-31
91T/Arc53-314

Garagozzo, Keith
91Oneonta/ProC-4148

Garber, Gene
74OPC-431
74T-431
75OPC-444
75T-444
75T/M-444
76OPC-14
76SSPC-458
76T-14
77T-286
78T-177
79OPC-331
79T-629
80OPC-263
80T-504
81D-77
81F-249
81OPC-307
81Pol/Atl-26
81T-307
81T/SO-42
81T/St-137
82BK/Lids-8
82D-123
82F-434
82F/St-234
82Pol/Atl-26
82T-32
82T/St-245
83D-223
83F-136
83OPC-255
83OPC-256SV
83Pol/Atl-26
83T-255
83T-256IA
83T/St-213
84D-287
84F-179
84Nes/792-466
84Nes/792-709LL
84OPC-167
84Pol/Atl-26
84T-466
84T-709LL
84T/St-35
85F-325
85Ho/Braves-9
85Pol/Atl-26
85T-129
86F-515
86Pol/Atl-26
86T-776
87D-414
87F-515
87F/Excit-17
87F/RecSet-10
87F/St-44
87Leaf-172
87Smok/Atl-9
87T-351
87T/St-40
88D-618
88D/Best-63
88F-257
88OPC-289
88S-565
88Sf-88
88Smok/Royals-11
88T-597

Garber, Jeff
88Eugene/Best-16
89AppFx/ProC-863
90BBCity/Star-8
91London/LineD-406
91Memphis/ProC-660

Garbey, Barbaro
81BirmB
82BirmB-2
83Evansvl-18
84F/X-42
84T/Tr-41
85Cain's-7
85D-456
85F-7
85F/St-121
85Leaf-121
85OPC-243
85T-243
85T/St-263
85Wendy-8
86D-349
86F-225
86OPC-88
86T-609
88OkCty/CMC-16
88OkCty/ProC-45
90BirmDG/Best-13

Garbould, Bob
44Centen-8

Garces, Jesus
90Princet/DIMD-7
91Batavia/ClBest-9
91Batavia/ProC-3491

Garces, Maduro
89Hagers/Best-6

Garces, Richard
(Rich)
89Kenosha/ProC-1076
89Kenosha/Star-6
89Star/Wax-51
90A&AASingle/ProC-140
90AS/Cal-18
90Visalia/Cal-62
90Visalia/ProC-2148
91B-324
91Classic/I-59
91D-420RR
91F/Ultra-378MLP
91OPC-594
91Portl/LineD-408
91Portl/ProC-1562
91T-594
91T/90Debut-50
91T/StClub/II-370
91UD/Ext-741
92D/II-516

Garces, Robinson
87Lakeland-21
88Fayette/ProC-1087
89Hagers/ProC-281
89Hagers/Star-8

Garcia, Alfonso
(Kiko)
77T-474R
78T-287
79T-543
80T-37
81D-514
81F-191
81OPC-192
81T-688
81T/Tr-765
82D-476
82F-215
82T-377
83D-569
83F-447
83Portl-25
83T-198
83T/Tr-36
84D-545
84F-30
84Nes/792-458
84T-458
85T-763

Garcia, Amadeo
89Elizab/Star-26

Garcia, Anastacio
90MedHat/Best-13
91Dunedin/ClBest-13
91Dunedin/ProC-209

Garcia, Anthony
89Salem/Team-3TR
90Bakers/Cal-245TR

Garcia, Apolinar
89Madis/Star-10
90Modesto/ProC-2206
91Tacoma/LineD-534
91Tacoma/ProC-2298

Garcia, Carlos
88Augusta/ProC-365
89Salem/Star-9
90A&AASingle/ProC-28
90EastLAS/ProC-EL25
90Harris/ProC-1199
90Harris/Star-7
91B-531
91BuffB/LineD-29
91BuffB/ProC-546
91F-37
91F/Ultra-278
91T/90Debut-51
92Classic/I-37
92D/I-14RR
92S/II-821
92UD-665

Garcia, Cheo
89Kenosha/ProC-1083
89Kenosha/Star-7
91OrlanSR/LineD-480
91OrlanSR/ProC-1855

Garcia, Chidez
89BirmB/Best-9

Garcia, Cornelio
86AppFx-9
88FSLAS/Star-37
88Tampa/Star-7
89BirmB/ProC-102
90BirmB/Best-9
90BirmB/ProC-1117

Garcia, Damaso
76FtLaud
77WHave
78Cr/PCL-49
79Colum-4
81D-269
81F-415
81OPC-233
81OPC/Post-14
81T-488
82D-479
82F-613
82OPC-293
82OPC/Post-2
82T-596
83D-54
83D/AAS-17
83F-427
83OPC-202TL
83OPC-222
83PermaGr/CC-24
83T-202TL
83T-222
83T/St-134
84D-241
84F-153
84Nes/792-124
84OPC-124
84T-124
84T/St-364
84Tor/Fire-12
85D-315
85D/AAS-6
85F-104
85Leaf-65
85OPC-353
85OPC/Post-15
85T-645
85T-702AS
85T/St-357
85Tor/Fire-11
86Ault-7
86D-241
86D/AAS-40
86F-59
86F/LimEd-17
86F/Mini-15
86F/St-41
86Leaf-116
86OPC-45
86Sf-34
86T-45
86T-713
86T/St-190
86Tor/Fire-12
87D-614
87F-226
87Leaf-92
87OPC-395
87Sf-183
87Smok/Atl-22
87T-395
87T/St-188
88D-414
88T-241
89T/Big-275
90F-346
90OPC-432
90T-432
90UD-649

Garcia, Danny
76Watlo
91Spokane/ClBest-28CO
91Spokane/ProC-3966CO

Garcia, Dave
73OPC-12CO
73T-12C
78T-656MG
81D-442MG
81T-665MG
82BK/Indians-1MG
82BK/Indians-2MG
82D-337MG
82Wheat/Ind
83Pol/Brew-C
83T-546MG

Garcia, Edward M.
(Mike)
50B-147
50NumNum
51B-150
51T/RB-40
52B-7
52NumNum-7
52T-272
53B/Col-43
53T-75
54B-100
54DanDee
55B-128

55Gol/Ind-8
55Salem
56Carling-2
56T-210
57Sohio/Ind-5
57T-300
58T-196
59T-516
60T-532
91T/Arc53-75

Garcia, Fermin
91Princet/ClBest-27
91Princet/ProC-3506

Garcia, Francisco
90AppFox/Box-8
90AppFox/ProC-2107

Garcia, Frank
80Ashvl-23
80Tulsa-12
83StPete-17

Garcia, Guillermo
91Kingspt/ClBest-14
91Kingspt/ProC-3821

Garcia, Joe
75SanAn

Garcia, Jose
90AS/Cal-4
90Visalia/Cal-78
90Visalia/ProC-2161

Garcia, Julio
89Princet/Star-26
91Augusta/ClBest-1CO
91Augusta/ProC-823CO

Garcia, Kiko
84Phill/TastyK-30
85Phill/TastyK-29
91Crown/Orio-150

Garcia, Leo
81AppFx-15
82AppFx-3
83Water-17
84Wichita/Rock-4
87Nashvl-5
89Toledo/CMC-16
89Toledo/ProC-767
90Nashvl/CMC-15
90Nashvl/ProC-245
91Nashvl/LineD-256
91Nashvl/ProC-2169

Garcia, Leonard
77SLCity
78Cr/PCL-88
79SLCity-23
80SLCity-19
81SLCity-1
86Edmon-12TR

Garcia, Librado
89Beloit/I/Star-6
89Beloit/II/Star-11
90Miami/I/Star-8

Garcia, Longo
89Miami/I/Star-7
89Miami/II/Star-5

Garcia, Luis
90LSUPol-13

Garcia, Manny
89Butte/SP-19
91Kane/ClBest-16
91Kane/ProC-2663

Garcia, Marcos
90Penin/Star-8
91AS/Cal-22
91SanBern/ClBest-4
91SanBern/ProC-1980

Garcia, Mario
90Princet/DIMD-8
91Hunting/ClBest-9
91Hunting/ProC-3327

Garcia, Michael
90A&AASingle/ProC-84
90Fayette/ProC-2398
90SALAS/Star-8
91Lakeland/ClBest-5
91Lakeland/ProC-261

Garcia, Miguel
75BurlB
76Clinton
80Ander-22
81Durham-2
82Durham-1
86PalmSp-14
86PalmSp/Smok-8
87MidldA-1
89BuffB/CMC-7
89BuffB/ProC-1686
89D-622
89F-647R
90Harris/ProC-1188
90Harris/Star-8
90UD-538

Garcia, Mike
89Bristol/Star-9

Garcia, Nelson Jose
75OkCty
80ArkTr-17

Garcia, Omar
90Kgsport/Best-13
90Kgsport/Star-10

Garcia, Oscar
89StCath/ProC-2075

Garcia, Pedro
73OPC-609R
73T-609R
74OPC-142
74T-142
74T/St-195
75OPC-147
75T-147
75T/M-147
76OPC-187
76SSPC-234
76T-187
77OPC-166
77T-453
77Watlo

Garcia, Ralph
73OPC-602R
73T-602R

Garcia, Ramon
90Saraso/Star-10
91BirmB/LineD-59
91BirmB/ProC-1449
91D/Rook-13
92D/II-658
92S/II-745
92T-176
92T/91Debut-60

Garcia, Raphael
90MedHat/Best-25
91Myrtle/ClBest-6
91Myrtle/ProC-2940

Garcia, Ray
85Utica-19

Garcia, Reggie
88Martins/Star-15
89Spartan/ProC-1039
89Spartan/Star-9

Garcia, Rene
86Bakers-10
87VeroB-27

Garcia, Rich
88TM/Umpire-22
89TM/Umpire-20
90TM/Umpire-19

Garcia, Santiago
88Vanco/CMC-13
88Vanco/ProC-764

Garcia, Steve
83Beaum-12
84Beaum-18
85Cram/PCL-115
86LasVegas-3
87LasVegas-20
88Albuq/CMC-24
88Albuq/ProC-249

Garcia, Victor
(Butch)
87Columbia-16
87Peoria-2
87Peoria/PW-1
88CLAS/Star-27
88PrWill/Star-11
88WinSalem/Star-3
89CharlK-7
89FtLaud/Star-5
89Greens/ProC-407
89Iowa/CMC-11
89Iowa/ProC-1693
90A&AASingle/ProC-122
90Cedar/Best-16
90Cedar/ProC-2315
90FtLaud/Star-8
91Albany/ProC-1001
91Chatt/LineD-159
91Chatt/ProC-1954

Garcia, Vinicio U.
(Chico)
54Esskay
91Crown/Orio-149

Garczyk, Ed
(Eddie)
89SLCity-9
90Miami/II/Star-6

Gardella, Mike
88CapeCod/Sum-69
89Oneonta/ProC-2103
90CLAS/CL-15
90PrWill/Team-10
91Albany/ProC-1002
91Single/ClBest-46

Gardenhire, Ron
81Tidew-5
82D-649
82T-623R
82T/Tr-39T
83D-175
83F-543
83T-469
83Tidew-20
85D-360
85F-81
85T-144
86T-274
86Tidew-10
87Portl-25
88Kenosha/ProC-1402
88MidwLAS/GS-36
89Orlan/Best-5
89Orlan/ProC-1355
90OrlanSR/Best-28MG
90OrlanSR/ProC-1098MG
90OrlanSR/Star-24MG
91WIZMets-132

Gardey, Rudy
88Idaho/ProC-1855
90Salinas/Cal-123

Gardiner, Mike
88Wausau/GS-25
89Wausau/GS-28
90A&AASingle/ProC-16
90EastLAS/ProC-EL17
90Wmsprt/Best-6
90Wmsprt/ProC-1052
90Wmsprt/Star-7
91Classic/III-25
91D-417RR
91D/Rook-46
91Pawtu/LineD-355
91Pawtu/ProC-31
91S-721RP
91T/90Debut-52
91UD-14RP
92D/I-290
92S/II-694
92T-694
92UD-588

Gardner, Art
73Cedar
75Iowa/TCMA-8
78Cr/PCL-2
86Tulsa-5CO
87Gaston-24

Gardner, Bill
88Eugene/Best-19

Gardner, Billy F.
52Park-88
55B-249
55Gol/Giants-7
55T-27
55T/DH-61
57T-17
58Hires-37
58T-105
59T-89
60T-106
61Clover-5
61P-96
61Peters-14
61T-123
61T/St-179
62Salada-211
62Shirriff-211
62T-163M
62T-338
63T-408
82D-591MG
83T-11MG
84Nes/792-771MG
84T-771MG
85T-213MG
87T/Tr-36T
91Crown/Orio-151
91Pittsfld/ClBest-27CO
91Pittsfld/ProC-3439CO

Gardner, Billy Jr.
90Pittsfld/Pucko-27CO

Gardner, Chris
90Ashvl/ProC-2741
91Jacks/ProC-919
92D/II-413RR
92T/91Debut-61

Gardner, Chuck
77Clinton

Gardner, Earl M.
11Helmar-44
M116
T201
T205
T207

Gardner, Floyd
(Jelly)
74Laugh/Black-7

Gardner, Franklin W.
N172

Gardner, Glen
88Pulaski/ProC-1756
89SALAS/GS-42
89Sumter/ProC-1097
90BurlB/Best-3
90BurlB/ProC-2355
90BurlB/Star-11
90Foil/Best-217

Gardner, Harry R.
16FleischBrd-29

Gardner, Jeff
86Lynch-10
87TexLgAS-7
88Jacks/GS-10
89Tidew/CMC-20
89Tidew/ProC-1966
90T/TVMets-42
90Tidew/CMC-16
90Tidew/ProC-551
91AAAGame/ProC-AAA48
91Tidew/LineD-555
91Tidew/ProC-2517
92F-675
92S/II-869
92T/91Debut-62

Gardner, Jim
(Jimmie)
86Peoria-7
87CharWh-20

Gardner, Jimmie C.
86Geneva-6

Gardner, Jimmie
T3/Box-62

Gardner, John
88CharWh/Best-15
89CharWh/Best-19
89CharWh/ProC-1769
90WinSalem/Team-6
91CharlK/LineD-132
91CharlK/ProC-1683

Gardner, Mark
86Jaxvl/TCMA-15
87Indianap-19
88Jaxvl/Best-7
88Jaxvl/ProC-987
89AAA/CMC-10
89AAA/ProC-10
89Indianap/CMC-8
89Indianap/ProC-1224
90B-106
90Classic/III-T4
90D-40RR
90D/Rook-20
90F-646R
90F/Up-U29
90Foil/Best-262
90HotRook/St-16
90Leaf/II-371
90OPC-284
90S-639
90S/100Ris-66
90T-284
90T/89Debut-41
90ToysRUs-10
90UD/Ext-743
91D-443
91F-233
91OPC-757
91Panini/St-67
91Panini/Top15-91
91S-518
91S/100RisSt-71
91T-757
91T/StClub/II-592
91UD-663
92D/I-238
92F-481
92S/II-586
92S/II-785HL
92T-119
92UD-557

Gardner, Myron
86Watlo-8
88SLCity-20

Gardner, Rob
66T-534R
67T-217
68T-219
71OPC-734
71T-734
72OPC-22
72T-22
73OPC-222
73T-222
91WIZMets-133

Gardner, Scott
82DayBe-4
83Miami-3
90Hunting/ProC-3274
91Hunting/ClBest-10
91Hunting/ProC-3328

Gardner, Vassie
81Charl-20
82Knoxvl-19

Gardner, Wes
83Lynch-23
84Tidew-3
85IntLgAS-21
85Tidew-9
88D-634
88D/RedSox/Bk-634
88F-352
88T-189
89B-23
89D-541
89F-88
89S-412
89T-526
90B-266
90D-541
90F-275
90Leaf/II-407
90OPC-38
90Pep/RSox-9
90Publlnt/St-455
90S-348
90T-38
90T/TVRSox-10
91B-653
91F-94
91OPC-629
91S-592
91T-629
91UD-214
91WIZMets-134

Gardner, William L.
(Larry)
21Exh-55
91Conlon/Sport-147
D327
D328-56
D329-65
D350/2-65
E120
E121/120
E121/80
E135-56
E220
E254
M101/4-65
M101/5-65
M116
V100
W501-24
W575

Gardner, Willie
90Hunting/ProC-3299
91Geneva/ClBest-7
91Geneva/ProC-4229
91Peoria/ClBest-20
91Peoria/ProC-1357

Garham, John
91AubAS/ClBest-29GM
Garibaldi, Art
40Hughes-7
Garibaldi, Bob
70T-681
71OPC-701
71T-701
Garibaldo, Chris
89AppFx/ProC-862
90BBCity/Star-9
Gariglio, Robert
81Chatt-1
Garland, Chaon
90SoOreg/Best-14
90SoOreg/ProC-3428
91Modesto/ClBest-5
91Modesto/ProC-3080
Garland, Tim
(Nookie)
90Greens/Best-21
90Greens/ProC-2673
90Greens/Star-2
91FtLaud/ClBest-26
91FtLaud/ProC-2440
Garland, Wayne
74OPC-596R
74T-596R
76OPC-414
76SSPC-376
76T-414
77BurgChef-59
77Ho-144
77K-21
77OPC-138
77Pep-14
77T-33
77T/CS-17
78Ho-137
78OPC-15
78T-174
78Wiffle/Discs-25
79T-636
80T-361
81D-440
81F-394
81OPC-272
81T-511
82D-489
82F-367
82T-446
87Nashvl-6CO
88Nashvl/CMC-24CO
88Nashvl/ProC-494CO
88Nashvl/Team-25CO
89Pac/SenLg-100
89TM/SenLg-38
90EliteSenLg-68
91Crown/Orio-152
Garman, Mike
71OPC-512R
71T-512R
72OPC-79R
72T-79R
73OPC-616R
73T-616R
75OPC-584
75T-584
75T/M-584
76OPC-34
76SSPC-293
76T-34
77T-302
78T-417
79OPC-88
79Portl-15
79T-181
90Target-268
Garman, Pat
88Gaston/ProC-1014
89CharlR/Star-8
90OkCty/CMC-12
90OkCty/ProC-438
91Tulsa/LineD-580
91Tulsa/ProC-2779
Garms, Debs
39PB-72
40PB-161
41DP-149
41G-29
41PB-11
91Conlon/Sport-296
Garner, Darrin
86DayBe-8
87Gaston-22
88CharlR/Star-7
88FSLAS/Star-38
89Tulsa/GS-9
89Tulsa/Team-7
90Tulsa/ProC-1162
91OkCty/LineD-309
91OkCty/ProC-185
Garner, Kevin
88River/Cal-220
88River/ProC-1431
89AubAs/ProC-17
89Wichita/Rock-33OF
91BirmB/LineD-60
91BirmB/ProC-1462
Garner, Mike
87VeroB-13
88Reno/Cal-277
Garner, Phil
75OPC-623R
75T-623R
75T/M-623R
76OPC-57
76SSPC-495
76T-57
77BurgChef-109
77Ho-11
77OPC-34
77T-261
78Ho-52
78OPC-203
78T-53
79Ho-75
79OPC-200
79T-383
80OPC-65
80T-118
81Coke
81D-372
81F-364
81F/St-71
81K-44
81OPC-99
81T-573
81T/SO-102
81T/St-209
81T/St-253
82D-544
82F-216
82Sqt-13
82T-683
83D-270
83F-448
83OPC-128
83T-478
83T/St-170
83T/St-237
84D-354
84F-226
84Mother/Ast-5
84Nes/792-752
84OPC-119
84T-752
84T/St-63
85D-161
85F-351
85Mother/Ast-3
85OPC-206
85T-206
85T/St-64
86D-527
86F-301
86F/Mini-64
86OPC-83
86Pol/Ast-9
86T-83
86T/St-32
87D-358
87D/OD-12
87F-58
87Mother/A's-16
87Mother/Ast-6
87OPC-304
87Pol/Ast-24
87T-304
87T/St-30
88Mother/Giants-25
88S-431
88T-174
90Mother/Ast-27CO
90Target-269
91Mother/Ast-28CO
91Swell/Great-113
92T-291MG
Garnett, Brad
82AlexD-11
Garr, Ralph
70OPC-172R
70T-172R
71MLB/St-9
71OPC-494R
71T-494R
72K-21
72OPC-260
72OPC-85LL
72T-260
72T-85LL
73K-37
73OPC-15
73T-15
74OPC-570
74T-570
74T/St-4
75Ho-87
75K-35
75OPC-306LL
75OPC-550
75T-306LL
75T-550
75T/M-306LL
75T/M-550
76OPC-410
76SSPC-17
76T-410
76T/Tr-410T
77BurgChef-80
77Ho-108
77K-13
77OPC-77
77Pep-26
77T-133
78K-37
78OPC-195
78PapaG/Disc-37
78T-628
78Tastee/Discs-21
78Wiffle/Discs-26
79OPC-156
79T-309
80OPC-142
80T-272
90Pac/Legend-25
90Richm25Ann/Team-9
90Swell/Great-46
Garrelts, Scott
80Clinton-10
81Shrev-20
83Phoenix/BHN-3
84Cram/PCL-5
84D-646
85Mother/Giants-23
85T/Tr-38T
86D-309
86D/AAS-35
86F-540
86F/LL-14
86F/Mini-110
86F/St-42
86Leaf-180
86Mother/Giants-19
86OPC-395
86Sf-157
86T-395
86T/St-86
87D-116
87F-273
87F/Hottest-17
87F/Mini-42
87F/St-45
87Leaf-75
87Mother/SFG-11
87OPC-37
87RedFoley/St-24
87Sf-68
87T-475
87T/St-89
88D-80
88D/Best-162
88F-82
88Mother/Giants-11
88OPC-97
88Panini/St-416
88S-533
88Sf-44
88T-97
88T/Big-240
88T/St-90
89B-467
89D-295
89D/Best-218
89F-328
89Mother/Giants-11
89OPC-214
89RedFoley/St-48
89S-258
89T-703
89UD-50
90B-228
90D-217
90D/BestNL-110
90F-56
90F/AwardWin-14
90F/BB-11
90Leaf/I-41
90Mother/Giant-16
90OPC-602
90Panini/St-367
90Publnt/St-67
90S-246
90Sf-39
90T-602
90T/Big-51
90T/Mini-85
90T/St-82
90UD-478
91B-626
91D-311
91F-262
91F/Ultra-320
91Leaf/I-5
91Leaf/Stud-255
91Mother/Giant-16
91OPC-361
91PG&E-29
91S-541
91SFExam/Giant-8
91T-361
91T/StClub/I-182
91UD-443
92F-636
92S/I-117
92T-558
Garrett, Bobby
81WHave-9
Garrett, Clifton
90Boise/ProC-3330
91MidwLAS/ProC-MWL26
91QuadC/ClBest-24
91QuadC/ProC-2643
91Single/ClBest-248
Garrett, Eric
83Idaho-15
84Madis/Pol-19
Garrett, Greg
70T-642R
71MLB/St-58
71OPC-377
71T-377
Garrett, H. Adrian
(Pat)
66T-553R
71OPC-576R
71T-576R
74OPC-656
74T-656
76OPC-562
76T-562
82AppFx-31
83GlenF-22
87Omaha-16
91Pol/Royal-25CO
Garrett, Lee
80Water-9
81Water-23
82Indianap-31tr
83Indianap-32tr
Garrett, Lynn
81WHave-11
82WHave-21
83Tacoma-15
Garrett, R. Wayne
70T-628
71MLB/St-152
71OPC-228
71T-228
72OPC-518
72T-518
73OPC-562
73T-562
74OPC-510
74T-510
74T/St-61
75OPC-111
75T-111
75T/M-111
76OPC-222
76SSPC-539
76T-222
77OPC-117
77T-417
78OPC-198
78T-679
79T-319
89Pac/SenLg-156
89TM/SenLg-39
91WIZMets-135
Garrett, Steve
80Elmira-6
Garrick, Darren
86SanJose-8
Garrido, Gil
61Union
64T-452R
69T-331R
70OPC-48
70T-48
71MLB/St-10
71OPC-173
71T-173
72T-758
89Sumter/ProC-1094
90BurlB/ProC-2366CO
90BurlB/Star-28CO
91Durham/ProC-1677CO
Garriott, Cece
47Signal
Garrison, Jim
87Watertn-18
88Augusta/ProC-369
Garrison, Marv
77LodiD
78LodiD
Garrison, Venoy
75Clinton
Garrison, Webster
85Kingst-16
87Dunedin-15
88SLAS-23
89Knoxvl/Best-6
89Knoxvl/ProC-1131
89Knoxvl/Star-4
90Syrac/CMC-16
90Syrac/ProC-578
90Syrac/Team-9
91Tacoma/LineD-535
91Tacoma/ProC-2313
Garrity, Pat
90LSUPol-3
Garside, Russ
90CharRain/Best-1
90CharRain/ProC-2038
90Foil/Best-35
Garver, Ned
49B-15
50B-51
51B-172
51FB
51T/BB-18
52B-29
52BR
52StarCal/L-75A
52T-212
52TipTop
53B/Col-47
53Glen
53T-112
54B-39
54T-44
55B-188
56T-189
57T-285
58T-292
59T-245
60T-471
61T-331
61T/St-171
89Pac/Leg-183
91T/Arc53-112
PM10/Sm-59
Garvey, Brian
75AppFx
Garvey, Don
91Welland/ClBest-4

91Welland/ProC-3577
Garvey, Steve
71MLB/St-103
71OPC-341
71T-341
71Ticket/Dodg-6
72T-686
73OPC-213
73T-213
74OPC-575
74T-575
75Ho-49
75Ho/Twink-49
75K-17
75OPC-140
75OPC-212M
75OPC-460NLCS
75T-140
75T-212MV
75T-460NLCS
75T/M-140
75T/M-212MV
75T/M-460NLCS
76Crane-16
76Ho-19
76Ho/Twink-19
76K-54
76MSA/Disc
76OPC-150
76SSPC-77
76T-150
77BurgChef-150
77Ho-35
77K-14
77OPC-255
77Pep-61
77T-400
77T/CS-19
78OPC-190
78T-350
78Tastee/Discs-3
78Wiffle/Discs-27
79Ho-8
79OPC-21
79T-50
79T/Comics-24
80K-31
80OPC-152
80Pol/Dodg-6
80T-290
80T/S-13
81D-176
81D-56
81Drake-11
81F-110
81F-606HL
81F/St-1
81K-10
81MSA/Disc-13
81OPC-251
81PermaGr/CC-12
81Pol/Dodg-6
81Sqt-4
81T-530
81T/HT
81T/Nat/Super-6
81T/SO-56
81T/St-176
81T/St-252
82D-3DK
82D-84
82Drake-14
82F-5
82F/St-9
82HB/LS
82K-47
82KMart-26
82OPC-179
82OPC-180IA
82P/Tips-1
82P/Tips-12
82PermaGr/CC-11
82Pol/Dodg-6
82T-179
82T-180IA
82T/St-54
83D-488
83F-206
83OPC-198
83T-610
83T/St-243
83T/Tr-37
84D-63
84D/AAS-38
84D/Champs-56
84Drake-10
84F-300
84F-628IA
85FunFood/Pin-9
84MiltBrad-10
84Mother/Padres-7
84Nes/792-380
84Nestle/DT-12
84OPC-380
84Ralston-18
84Seven-7W
84Smok/Padres-10
84T-380
84T/Cereal-18
84T/St-156
84T/Super-22
85D-307
85Drake-11
85F-32
85F-631IA
85F/LimEd-9
85GenMills-3
85Leaf-94
85Mother/Padres-6
85OPC-177
85Seven-8W
85SpokAT/Cram-7
85T-2RB
85T-450
85T/Gloss22-2
85T/St-1
85T/St-13
85T/St-14
85T/St-149
85T/St-176
85T/St-2
85T/Super-26
86BK/AP-18
86D-63
86D/AAS-3
86D/PopUp-3
86F-321
86F-640M
86F/LL-15
86F/Mini-67
86F/St-43
86F/St-S3
86Jiffy-18
86Leaf-56
86Meadow/Blank-4
86Meadow/Stat-15
86OPC-4
86Quaker-6
86Sf-137M
86Sf-35
86Sf-51M
86Sf/Dec-61
86T-660
86T/Gloss22-13
86T/Gloss60-38
86T/St-104
86T/St-148
86T/Super-24
86TrueVal-2
87BK-5
87Bohem-6
87Classic-27
87D-81
87D/OD-143
87F-414
87F/Excit-18
87F/GameWin-16
87F/Lim-16
87F/Mini-43
87F/St-46
87Kraft-20
87Leaf-114
87MnM's-20
87OPC-100
87Ralston-2
87RedFoley/St-61
87Sf-40
87Smok/Dodg-8
87Smok/NL-10
87T-100
87T/Board-18
87T/Coins-32
87T/St-115
88S-225
88Smok/Dodg-15M
88Smok/Dodg-17
88Smok/Dodg-21M
89Padre/Mag-20
89Smok/Dodg-83
90BBWit-26
90Pac/Legend-27
90Swell/Great-103
90Target-270
91LineD-8
91Swell/Great-32
Garvin, Ned
90Target-271
Garvin, Theodore
(Jerry)
78OPC-49
78T-419
79OPC-145
79T-293
80OPC-320
80T-611
81D-150
81F-429
81OPC-124
81T-124
82D-430
82F-614
82OPC-264
82T-768
83D-227
83F-428
83T-358
Garvin, Virgil
E107
Garza, Lonnie
83Redwd-10
Garza, Willie
88Watlo/ProC-670
Gash, Darius
91Waterlo/ClBest-20
91Waterlo/ProC-1267
Gaspar, Harry
10Domino-47
11Helmar-114
12Sweet/Pin-99
E254
M116
T201
T202
T205
T206
Gaspar, Rod
70OPC-371
70T-371
71MLB/St-227
71OPC-383
71T-383
91WIZMets-136
Gass, Jeff
83Erie-16
Gassaway, Charles
46Remar-7
47Remar-4
47Signal
47Smith-8
48Signal
48Smith-10
49B/PCL-10
49Remar
50Remar
Gasser, Steve
86Kenosha-10
87Orlan-11
87SLAS-18
88OrlanTw/Best-23
89Pittsfld/Star-5
Gast, Joe
89Penin/Star-6
Gast, John
91Princet/ClBest-4
91Princet/ProC-3521
Gastall, Tommy
91Crown/Orio-153
Gastelum, Macario
87Bakers-3
89Bakers/Cal-185
Gastfield, Ed
N172
Gaston, Alex
E121/120
W501-11
W575
Gaston, Clarence
(Cito)
69MB-90
69T-304R
70T-604
71Bz
71Bz/Test-12
71K-41
71MLB/St-228
71OPC-25
71T-25
71T/Coins-1
71T/tatt-4
72MB-113
72OPC-431
72OPC-432IA
72T-431
72T-432IA
73OPC-159
73T-159
74OPC-364SD
74T-364
75OPC-427
75T-427
75T/M-427
76OPC-558
76SSPC-18
76T-558
77T-192
78T-716
79T-208
84Tor/Fire-13CO
85Tor/Fire-12CO
86Tor/Fire-13CO
87Tor/Fire-10CO
88Tor/Fire-43CO
89T/Tr-36T
89Tor/Fire-43MG
90OPC-201MG
90T-201MG
90T/TVAS-33MG
90Tor/BlueJ-43MG
91OPC-81MG
91S/ToroBJ-36MG
91T-81MG
91Tor/Fire-43MG
92T-699MG
Gaston, John
83Greens-6
Gaston, Milt
33G-65
V353-65
Gaston, Russell
90Savan/ProC-2065
91Johnson/ClBest-19
91Savan/ClBest-5
91Savan/ProC-1646
Gaston, Welcome
90Target-956
Gastreich, Henry
N172
Gastright, Hank
90Target-272
Gate, Bill
91StPete/ClBest-24
Gateman, Wareham
88CapeCod-25
Gates, Brent
91Classic/DP-22
91FrRow/DP-22
91SoOreg/ClBest-24
91SoOreg/ProC-3855
92S/II-805DP
92T-216DP
Gates, Bryan
87Anchora-34BB
Gates, Eddie
81Evansvl-20
82Evansvl-20
Gates, Joe
77Jaxvl
78Knoxvl
Gates, Michael
80Memphis-9
82Wichita-4
83D-114
83OPC-195
83T-657
84Indianap-29
Gatewood, Aubrey
64T-127R
65T-422
66OPC-42
66T-42
Gatewood, Henry
85VeroB-11
86Visalia-10
87Orlan-5
88WinSalem/Star-4
Gatins, Frank
90Target-957
Gatlin, Mike
82Oneonta-16
Gaton, Frank
75BurlB
76BurlB
Gattis, Jim
89Miami/II/Star-6
Gaudet, Jim
77Jaxvl
79T-707R
80Evansvl-3
81Omaha-13
82Syrac-11
Gaughan, Hank
82Chatt-25
Gault, Raymond
77Watlo
Gaunt
C46-69
Gausepohl, Dan
81Hawaii-8
82Hawaii-8
Gautreau, Doc
92Conlon/Sport-545
Gautreaux, Sid
90Target-273
Gavan, John
E120
W573
Gavin, Dave
88Madis-11
89Modesto/Chong-28
89Watlo/ProC-1776
89Watlo/Star-9
Gavin, Tom
90Elizab/Star-10
91Visalia/ClBest-22
91Visalia/ProC-1754
Gay, Jeff
86Cram/PCL-78
87QuadC-26
89PalmSp/Cal-34
89PalmSp/ProC-466
91BirmB/LineD-61
91BirmB/ProC-1457
Gay, Scott
87FtLaud-17
88FtLaud/Star-9
89Salinas/ProC-1823
Gay, Steve
86Lynch-11
Gaylor, Bobby
86Jamestn-10
87BurlEx-18
88WPalmB/Star-10
Gaynor, Richard Kent
83Reading-5
84Cram/PCL-212
87BirmB/Best-11
88BirmB/Best-17
Gazella, Mike
91Conlon/Sport-121
Gazzilli, Dan
85Utica-26
Gbur, Paul
79AppFx-25
Gebhard, Bob
72OPC-28R
72T-28R
75IntAS/TCMA-29
Geddes, Jim
73OPC-561
73T-561
Gedeon, Elmer Joe
16FleischBrd-30
D327
D328-57
D329-66
D350/2-66
E135-57
M101/4-66
M101/5-66
W514-39
Gedman, Rich
81Pawtu-24
82Coke/BOS
82D-512
82F-294
82T-59

83D-156
83F-184
83T-602
84D-579
84F-398
84Nes/792-498
84OPC-296
84T-498
84T/St-222
85D-457
85F-159
85OPC-18
85T-529
85T/St-217
86D-273
86D/AAS-56
86F-349
86F-643M
86F/LimEd-18
86F/Mini-75
86F/St-44
86Leaf-145
86OPC-375
86Sf-84
86T-375
86T/St-248
87Classic-49
87D-153
87D/AAS-39
87F-35
87F/RecSet-11
87F/WS-9M
87Leaf-254
87OPC-137
87Sf-149
87Sf-154M
87T-740
87T/St-247
88D-129
88D/Best-140
88D/RedSox/Bk-129
88F-353
88OPC-245
88Panini/St-24
88S-241
88T-245
88T/Big-152
88T/St-252
89B-27
89D-162
89F-89
89OPC-178
89S-345
89T-652
89T/Big-72
89T/St-253
89UD-368
90D-346
90F-276
90Leaf/II-478
90MLBPA/Pins-72
90OPC-123
90Pep/RSox-10
90PublInt/St-456
90S-173
90T-123
90T/TVRSox-18
90UD-402
91Leaf/II-418
91Pol/Card-29
91UD-588
92D/II-553
92F-577
92S/II-689

Gee, Steve
82Tucson-28M

Gegan, Fred
87VeroB-9

Gehrig, Henry Louis
(Lou)
25Exh-97
26Exh-99
27Exh-49
28Exh-50
28Yueng-26
29Exh/4-26
31Exh/4-26
33CJ/Pin-7
33DL-7
33G-160
33G-92
34Exh/4-13
34G-37
34G-61
35Exh/4-13
35Wheat
36Exh/4-13
36Wheat
37Exh/4-13
38Exh/4-13
38ONG/Pin-11
39Exh
48Exh/HOF
48Swell-14
49Leaf/Prem-3
50Callahan
51T/CM
60Exh/HOF-11
60F-28
60NuCard-24
61F-31
61GP-16
61NuCard-424
61T-405M
63Bz/ATG-15
69Bz-5
69Bz/Sm
72F/FFeat-5
72K/ATG-13
72Laugh/GF-8
73OPC-472LL
73Syrac/Team-8
73T-472LL
74Syrac/Team-8
76Laugh/Jub-28
76OPC-341AS
76T-341M
80Pac/Leg-13
80Laugh/3/4/5-29
80Laugh/FFeat-10
80SSPC/HOF
81Detroit-50
85CircK-14
85D-635PUZ
85D/HOF-3
85D/WaxBox-PUZ
85Leaf-635PUZ
85West/2-25
85Woolwth-14
86Conlon/1-1
86Conlon/1-17
86Conlon/1-52
86Conlon/1-57
86Sf/Dec-10
87Conlon/2-1
87Nestle/DT-1
88Conlon/5-12
88Conlon/AmAS-10
88Conlon/HardC-3
89HOF/St-1
89Pac/Leg-174
89Swell-25
89T/LJN-81
89USPS-2
90BBWit-73
90CollAB-34
90HOF/St-38
90Swell/Great-25
91Conlon/Sport-111
91Conlon/Sport-310
91Homer/Classic-9
91Swell/Great-125
92Conlon/Sport-529
92S/II-881
PM10/Sm-60
PR1-11
R310
R315-A10
R315-B10
R316
R328-26
R332-20
R346-29
R423-35
V353-55
V354-92
V355-96
W502-26
W517-35

Gehringer, Charles
(Charlie)
26Exh-95
27Exh-47
29Exh/4-23
31Exh/4-23
33DH-20
33DL-5
33Exh/4-12
33G-222
34DS-77
34Exh/4-12
34G-23
34Ward's/Pin-5
35BU-130
35BU-42
35Exh/4-12
35G-1D
35G-2D
35G-6D
35G-7D
36Exh/4-12
36Wheat
37Dix
37Exh/4-12
37OPC-112
37Wheat-4
38Exh/4-12
38G-241
38G-265
38ONG/Pin-10
38Wheat
39Exh
39PB-50
40PB-41
41DP-54
41PB-19
50Callahan
60F-58
61F-32
61GP-10
80SSPC/HOF
81Detroit-14
83D/HOF-28
83Kaline-33M
83Kaline-39M
84West/1-16
86Conlon/1-43
86Sf/Dec-12
88Conlon/5-13
88Conlon/AmAS-11
90Pac/Legend-81
92Conlon/Sport-461
92Conlon/Sport-553
R300
R303/A
R308-183
R310
R311/Leath
R313
R314
R316
V300
V354-57
V355-42
WG8-23

Geiger, Burt
82Albuq-3
83Albuq-2

Geiger, Gary Jr.
87Everett-24
88Fresno/Cal-23
88Fresno/ProC-1229

Geiger, Gary Merle
58T-462
59T-521
60T-184
61T-33
61T/St-111
62J-60
62P-60
62P/Can-60
62Salada-38A
62Salada-38B
62Shirriff-38
62T-117
62T/St-13
63J-81
63P-81
63T-513
64T-93
65T-452
66T-286
67T-566
69T-278
77Evans/TCMA-10CO

Geisel, J. Dave
79T-716R
80T-676R
82D-633
82Syrac-4
84Cram/PCL-175
84D-645
84F-154
84Nes/792-256
84OPC-256
84T-256
85Mother/Mar-22
86OKCty-6

Geishert, Vern
70T-683R

Geiske, Mark
90Riversi/Cal-10

Geisler, Phillip
91Martins/ClBest-11
91Martins/ProC-3460

Geiss, Emil
N172

Geist, Pete
86FSLAS-17
86VeroB-6
87VeroB-6
88Dunedin/Star-7

Geivett, Billy
86PalmSp-15
86PalmSp/Smok-23
87MidldA-3

Gelatt, Dave
85LitFalls-18
86Columbia-10
87Lynch-18

Gelb, Jac
89Wythe/Star-11
90Peoria/Team-22

Gelbert, Charles M.
(Charlie)
29Exh/4-16
31Exh/4-16
33Exh/4-8
39PB-93
40PB-18
91Conlon/Sport-70
R306
R313
R314
V355-49

Gelfarb, Steve
81WHave-12
82WHave-13

Gelinas, Marc
78Salem

Gellinger, Mike
87DayBe-25
89Utica/Pucko-30CO
90BirmB/Best-24CO
90BirmB/ProC-1400CO
91Utica/ClBest-23MG
91Utica/ProC-3257MG

Gelnar, John
65OPC-143R
65T-143R
67T-472R
70McDon-4
70OPC-393
70T-393
71MLB/St-436
71OPC-604
71T-604

Gendron, Bob
84Shrev/FB-8

Genewich, Joseph
(Joe)
21Exh-56
25Exh-5
26Exh-5
27Exh-2
92Conlon/Sport-573

Genins, C. Frank
N172

Gentile, Gene
78Charl
81Bristol-4
83Pawtu-21
84Albany-3
86Kinston-8
87Harris-21
88Harris/ProC-856

Gentile, Jim
60T-448
61NuCard-401
61P-68
61T-559
61T/St-101
62Bz
62Exh
62J-27
62P-27
62P/Can-27
62Salada-1
62Shirriff-1
62T-290
62T-53LL
62T/bucks
62T/St-5
63Bz-11
63Exh
63J-57
63P-57
63T-260
63T-4LL
63T/SO
64Bz-11
64T-196
64T/S-15
64T/St-75
64T/SU
65T-365
66OPC-45
66T-45
78TCMA-4
85Woolwth-15
90Target-274
91Crown/Orio-154
Exh47
WG10-28

Gentile, Randy
89Elizab/Star-9
90Kenosha/Best-3
90Kenosha/ProC-2300
90Kenosha/Star-4

Gentle, Mike
83VeroB-4

Gentleman, J.P.
88Hamil/ProC-1743

Gentleman, Jean
88Savan/ProC-356

Gentry, Gary
69OPC-31R
69T-31R
70OPC-153
70T-153
70Trans/M-23
71MLB/St-153
71OPC-725
71T-725
72OPC-105
72T-105
73OPC-288
73T-288
74OPC-415
74T-415
75OPC-393
75T-393
75T/M-393
91WIZMets-137

Genzale, Henry
90Mother/Mar-28EQMG

George, Andre
88Pocatel/ProC-2075

George, Chris
89AS/Cal-38
89Stockton/Best-2
89Stockton/Cal-153
89Stockton/ProC-391
89Stockton/Star-8
90ElPasoATG/Team-21
91B-35
91Classic/II-T50
91Denver/LineD-138
91Denver/ProC-119
91Pittsfld/ClBest-23
91Pittsfld/ProC-3416
92D/II-746
92S/II-835
92T/91Debut-63
92UD-9SR

George, Don
33SK-40

George, Frankie
77SLCity

George, Greek
90Target-275

George, Leo
82QuadC-14

George, Nattie
84Greens-7

George, Phil
83Butte-5
85FtMyr-11

86FtMyr-11
87Memphis-2
87Memphis/Best-11
George, Steve
83Greens-7
84Greens-18
86Albany/TCMA-29
George, Thomas
(Lefty)
T207
George, Will
82Miami-1
83Miami-1
87Hagers-3
89Kinston/Star-27
90Canton/Best-2CO
90Canton/ProC-1363CO
91Canton/ProC-996CO
George, William
N172
N338/2
Georger, Joe
80LynnS-17
81LynnS-4
82LynnS-4
86Wausau-10CO
89QuadC/Best-3CO
89QuadC/GS-3CO
91QuadC/ClBest-28CO
91QuadC/ProC-2646CO
Gerace, Joanne
88Utica/Pucko-29
89Utica/Pucko-32GM
Geraghty, Ben
90Target-276
Gerald, Edward
(Ed)
89LittleSun-19
91AppFx/ClBest-24
91AppFx/ProC-1729
Gerber, Craig
82Redwd-3
83Nashua-13
84Cram/PCL-109
86D-545
86Edmon-13
86F-156
86T-222
88Edmon/ProC-583
88MidldA/GS-24
Gerber, Walter
(Wally)
21Exh-57
25Exh-113
26Exh-117
92Conlon/Sport-501
E120
E220
V61-49
W573
Geren, Bob
83Spring/LF-13
84ArkTr-11
87Albany-5
88AAA/ProC-9
88Colum/CMC-11
88Colum/Pol-12
88Colum/ProC-303
89Colum/CMC-11
89Colum/Pol-7
89Colum/ProC-758
89D/Rook-11
89F/Up-48
89S/HotRook-66
89S/NWest-25
89S/Tr-93
89T/Tr-37T
90AlbanyDG/Best-4
90B-438
90Bz-20
90Classic-25
90D-395
90F-442
90Leaf/I-182
90OPC-536
90Panini/St-128
90S-464
90S/100Ris-50
90S/NWest-9
90Sf-205
90SpringDG/Best-28
90T-536
90T/Big-209
90T/Gloss60-40
90T/JumboR-9
90T/St-316
90T/St-321FS
90T/TVYank-21
90ToysRUs-11
90UD-608
91D-114
91F-663
91F/Ultra-231
91OPC-716
91Panini/FrSt-323
91Panini/St-265
91S-435
91T-716
91T/StClub/I-171
91UD-202
92F-226
92S/I-170
92T-341
Gergen, Bob
83BurlR-16
83BurlR/LF-13
84Tulsa-26
85Tulsa-25
86Tulsa-14
Gerhardt, Allen
83Beaum-22
87Gaston-10
Gerhardt, Bill
83Miami-7
Gerhardt, John
N172
N284
N338/2
Gerhardt, Rusty
84OKCty-5
85OKCty-24
86OKCty-7CO
89CharlR/Star-27CO
Gerhart, Ken
84CharlO-22
85CharlO-1
86RochR-3
87D-30RR
87D/OD-141
87D/Rook-24
87F/Up-U34
87French-38
87Leaf-30
87Sf/Rook-7
87T/Tr-37T
88D-213
88F-559
88French-38
88OPC-271
88Panini/St-14
88RedFoley/St-27
88S-58
88T-271
88ToysRUs-11
89F-609
89OPC-192
89Phoenix/CMC-20
89Phoenix/ProC-1499
89S-506
89T-598
89UD-426
90HagersDG/Best-11
91Crown/Orio-155
Gering, Scott
79Elmira-13
Gerlach, Jim
81QuadC-27
83MidldC-21
German, Rene
83QuadC-11
Germann, Mark
86Cedar/TCMA-16
87Vermont-20
88Chatt/Best-10
89Nashvl/CMC-15
89Nashvl/ProC-1275
Germer, Glen
81Durham-18
Gernert, Dick
52StarCal/L-71G
52T-343
53B/BW-11
54B-146
57T-202
58T-38
59T-13
59T-519M
60T-86
61T-284
61T/St-151
62T-536
62T/bucks
89Smok/Ast-18
Geronimo, Cesar
71OPC-447
71T-447
72T-719
73OPC-156
73T-156
74OPC-181
74T-181
74T/St-26
75Ho-121
75K-50
75OPC-41
75T-41
75T/M-41
76Ho-150
76Icee
76OPC-24
76SSPC-45
76T-24
77BurgChef-202
77Ho-76
77K-40
77OPC-160
77Pep-49
77T-535
78OPC-32
78T-354
79OPC-111
79T-220
80OPC-247
80T-475
81D-305
81T-390
81T/Tr-766
82D-322
82F-409
82T-693
83D-448
83F-112
83T-194
84D-252
84Nes/792-544
84T-544
Gershberg, Howie
89BendB/Legoe-27CO
90Boise/ProC-3333CO
91Boise/ProC-3902CO
Gerstein, Ron
91Sumter/ClBest-5
91Sumter/ProC-2328
Gertz, Mike
82Watlo/B-16
82Watlo/C-14
83Watlo/LF-22
Gessler, Harry
(Doc)
14CJ-59
15CJ-59
M116
Gettel, Allen
50Remar
51B-304
52Mother-3
Getter, Kerry
76Clinton
Gettler, Chris
88Bakers/Cal-253
Gettman, Jake
C46-40
Getz, Gustave
(Gus)
90Target-277
D328-58
D329-67
D350/2-67
E135-58
E254
E270/2
M101/4-67
M101/5-67
Getzein, Charles
N172
N284
N29
N43
Scrapps
WG1-21
Gewecke, Steve
90Spring/Best-21
Geyer, Jacob
(Rube)
T213/blue
Gharriey, Joe
W514-109
Gharrity, Edward P.
(Patsy)
E120
E121/120
V100
V61-50
W501-12
W572
W573
W575
WG7-18
Ghelfi, Andrew
86Watlo-9
87Kinston-16
88Wmsprt/ProC-1308
Ghelfi, Tony
84Phill/TastyK-19
85Cram/PCL-40
85Phill/TastyK-17
88Wmsprt/ProC-1314
89LasVegas/CMC-5
89LasVegas/ProC-1
Giallombardo, Bob
59DF
59T-321
60DF-9
61Union
90Target-278
Giamatti, A.Bartlett
89Wichita/Rc/HL-16
90D-716
90OPC-396
90S/DTRook-B1
90T-396
90TM/Umpire-65
Giamdi, Jason
91T/Tr-45T
Giannelli, Ray
89Myrtle/ProC-1469
89SALAS/GS-35
90Dunedin/Star-9
91Knoxvl/LineD-357
91Knoxvl/ProC-1774
91S/ToroBJ-33
91Single/ClBest-26
92T/91Debut-64
Giannotta, Go
80Evansvl-13
Giansanti, Ralph
83Ander-21
Gianukakis, John
86Cram/PCL-146
Giard, Joe
91Conlon/Sport-119
Giaudrone, Charlie
90WichSt-12
Gibbon, Joe
60T-512
61T-523
62Kahn
62T-448
63IDL-9
63Kahn
63T-101
64T-307
65OPC-54
65T-54
66T-457
67T-541
68OPC-32
68T-32
69OPC-158
69T-158
70OPC-517
70T-517
72OPC-382
72T-382
78TCMA-219
Gibbons, Bill
89Clinton/ProC-907
Gibbons, John
82Beloit-8
85D-116
85IntLgAS-15
85Tidew-15
86ElPaso-12
86Tidew-11
87Chatt/Best-22
87D-626
87Tidew-6
87Tidew/TCMA-10
88Albuq/CMC-20
88Albuq/ProC-260
88Vermont/ProC-950
89OkCty/CMC-12
89OkCty/ProC-1531
90ScranWB/CMC-10
90ScranWB/ProC-602
91WIZMets-138
Gibbons, Michael
88SLCity-15
89Rockford/Team-9
Gibbs, Jake
62T-281
64T-281R
65OPC-226R
65T-226R
66OPC-117
66T-117
67T-375
68OPC-89
68T-89
69MB-91
69MLB/St-74
69T-401
69T/St-203
70MLB/St-245
70T-594
71MLB/St-488
71OPC-382
71T-382
72MB-114
WG10-7
WG9-9
Gibbs, James
88Spring/Best-9
89Medford/Best-4
Gibbs, Jim
90Madison/Best-15
Gibert, Pat
89Huntsvl/Best-21
Gibralter, Steve
91CharWh/ClBest-22
91CharWh/ProC-2899
91SALAS/ProC-SAL7
Gibree, Bob
86Wausau-11
Gibson, Frank
25Exh-6
Gibson, George
10Domino-48
11Helmar-160
12Sweet/Pin-137
92Conlon/Sport-516
D303
D322
D329-68
D350/2-68
E101
E103
E105
E106
E121/120
E254
E270/1
E270/2
E90/1
E90/2
E91
E92
E93
E96
M101/4-68
M101/5-68
M116
S74-110
T201
T202
T205
T206
T216
T3-94
V100
W501-88
W514-63
W555
Gibson, Hoot
81Durham-19

Gibson, J. Russ
67T-547R
68T-297
69MB-92
69OPC-89
69T-89
69T/St-133
70OPC-237
70T-237
71MLB/St-248
71OPC-738
71T-738
72MB-115
72T-643
Gibson, Joel
65T-368R
78TCMA-208
Gibson, Josh Jr.
74Laugh/Black-8
80SSPC/HOF
83D/HOF-4
86Negro/Frit-23
86Negro/Frit-30
86Negro/Frit-31
86Negro/Frit-4
86Negro/Frit-9
88Conlon/NegAS-5
88Negro/Duques-12
90Negro/Star-2
91Negro/Lewis-24
Gibson, Kirk
81Coke
81Detroit-20
81F-481
81OPC-315
81T-315
81T/St-78
82D-407
82Drake-15
82F-267
82F/St-161
82K-40
82OPC-105
82PermaGr/CC-24
82Sqt-6
82T-105
82T/St-184
83D-459
83F-329
83OPC-321
83T-430
83T/St-67
84D-593
84F-80
85FunFood/Pin-21
84Nes/792-65
84OPC-65
84T-65
84T/St-272
85Cain's-8
85D-471
85Drake-12
85F-8
85F/St-22
85Leaf-103
85OPC-372
85Seven-13D
85Seven-8S
85T-565
85T/St-11ALCS
85T/St-19WS
85T/St-267
85T/Super-27
85Wendy-9
86BK/AP-13
86Cain's-6
86D-1DK
86D-125
86D/DKsuper-1
86D/WaxBox-PC4
86Drake-28
86F-226
86F/LimEd-19
86F/Mini-47
86F/Slug-10
86F/St-45
86Leaf-1DK
86OPC-295
86Sf-21
86T-295
86T/Gloss60-29
86T/St-266
86T/Super-25
86TrueVal-8
87Cain's-9
87Classic-9
87Coke/Tigers-1
87D-50
87F-151
87F/GameWin-17
87F/Lim-17
87F/Mini-44
87F/St-47
87Kraft-19
87Leaf-104
87OPC-386
87RedFoley/St-10
87Sf-48
87Seven-DT3
87T-765
87T/Board-29
87T/Coins-11
87T/Mini-53
87T/St-273
87Toledo-28
88D-275
88D/Best-66
88F-55
88F/Mini-82
88F/St-24
88F/Up-U93
88Leaf-136
88Mother/Dodg-8
88OPC-201
88Panini/St-95
88Pol/Dodg-23
88S-525
88S/Tr-10T
88Sf-111
88T-605
88T/Big-191
88T/St-267
88T/Tr-40T
88T/UK-26
89T/Ames-14
89B-351
89Bz-10
89Cadaco-23
89Classic-120
89T/Crunch-2
89D-132
89D-15DK
89D/Best-10
89D/DKsuper-15DK
89F-57
89F/BBAS-14
89F/BBMVP's-13
89F/Excit-14
89F/Heroes-17
89F/LL-15
89F/Rec-4
89F/Superstar-16
89F/WaxBox-C10
89F/WS-5
89Holsum/Discs-20
89KayBee-13
89KingB/Discs-1
89Mother/Dodg-8
89OPC-340
89OPC-382
89Panini/St-107
89Panini/St-16
89Panini/St-17
89Panini/St-479
89Pol/Dodg-14
89RedFoley/St-49
89S-210
89S-582M
89S/HotStar-30
89Sf-65
89T-340
89T-396AS
89T/Big-299
89T/Coins-1
89T/DH-24
89T/Gloss60-55
89T/Hills-14
89T/LJN-102
89T/Mini-17
89T/St-66
89T/St/Backs-49
89T/UK-30
89UD-633
89UD-662MVP
89UD-676TC
89Woolwth-2
89Woolwth-24
90B-97
90Classic/Up-20
90D-368
90D/BestNL-41
90F-393
90KingB/Discs-5
90Leaf/I-173
90MLBPA/Pins-6
90Mother/Dodg-13
90OPC-150
90Panini/St-271
90Pol/Dodg-23
90PublInt/St-259
90PublInt/St-5
90S-487
90T-150
90T/Ames-20
90T/Big-326
90T/HillsHM-25
90T/St-60
90Target-279
90UD-264
91B-302
91Classic/200-57
91D-445
91F-199
91F/UltraUp-U27
91F/Up-U26
91Leaf/I-249
91Leaf/Stud-66
91OPC-490
91OPC/Premier-50
91Pol/Royal-9
91S-800
91S/RookTr-18T
91T-490
91T/StClub/II-344
91T/Tr-46T
91UD-634
91UD/Ext-737
92D/I-39
92F-157
92S/II-520
92T-720
92UD-180
Gibson, Leighton
N172
N690
Gibson, Monty
91Pocatel/ProC-3776
Gibson, Paul
80Cedar-18
82BirmB-23
83Orlan-20
86GlenF-6
86Nashvl-9
87Toledo-10
87Toledo/TCMA-17
88D/Rook-19
88F/Up-U26
88Pep/T-48
89B-99
89Bz-11
89Classic-140
89D-445
89F-131
89KMart/DT-10
89Mara/Tigers-48
89Panini/St-331
89S-595
89T-583
89T/Big-230
89T/Gloss60-20
89T/JumboR-10
89T/St-323
89ToysRUs-11
89UD-47
90BirmDG/Best-14
90CokeK/Tiger-5
90D-657
90F-602
90Leaf/II-298
90OPC-11
90PublInt/St-470
90S-261
90T-11
90UD-496
91CokeK/Tiger-48
91D-353
91F-337
91F/UltraUp-U23
91Leaf/I-55
91OPC-431
91S-152
91T-431
91UD-579
92D/I-375
92F-136
92S/I-261
92T-143
92UD-489
Gibson, Robert L.
(Bob L.)
79BurlB-14
82ElPaso-21
83Pol/Brew-40
84Cram/PCL-40
84D-246
84F-201
84Nes/792-349
84T-349
85D-393
85Pol/Brew-40
85T/Tr-39T
86D-271
86F-488
86T-499
86Vanco-12
87Tidew-33
87Tidew/TCMA-3
88RochR/Team-8
88RochR/CMC-5
88RochR/ProC-196
91WIZMets-139
Gibson, Robert
(Bob)
59T-514
60T-73
61T-211
62T-530
63F-61
63J-166
63P-166
63Salada-3
63T-415
63T-5LL
63T-9LL
64T-460
64T/Coins-59
64T/S-41
65Bz-23
65OPC-12LL
65OPC-138WS
65T-12LL
65T-138WS
65T-320
65T/E-69
65T/trans-14
66Bz-21
66T-225LL
66T-320
66T/RO-39
67Bz-21
67T-210
67T-236LL
68Bz-9
68OPC-100
68OPC-154WS
68T-100
68T-154WS
68T-378AS
69Kelly/Pin-6
69MLB/St-211
69MLBPA/Pin-44
69NTF
69OPC-107CL
69OPC-10LL
69OPC-12LL
69OPC-162WS
69OPC-168WS
69OPC-200
69OPC-8LL
69OPC/DE-7
69T-10LL
69T-12LL
69T-162WS
69T-168WS
69T-200
69T-432AS
69T-8LL
69T/DE-29
69T/decal
69T/S-60
69T/St-115
69Trans-33
70K-71
70MLB/St-139
70OPC-530
70OPC-67LL
70OPC-71LL
70T-530
70T-67LL
70T-71LL
70T/CB
70T/S-33
70Trans-5
71Bz
71Bz/Test-41
71K-51
71MD
71MLB/St-273
71MLB/St-559
71OPC-450
71OPC-70LL
71OPC-72LL
71T-450
71T-70LL
71T-72LL
71T/Coins-63
71T/GM-24
71T/S-48
71T/tatt-15
71T/tatt-15a
72K-26
72OPC-130
72T-130
73K-14
73OPC-190
73T-190
73T/Lids-19
74K-1
74OPC-350
74T-350
74T/DE-3
74T/Puzzles-5
74T/St-114
75Ho-119
75OPC-150
75OPC-206M
75OPC-3RB
75T-150
75T-206MV
75T-3RB
75T/M-150
75T/M-206MV
75T/M-3RB
78TCMA-60
82KMart-14
82Pol/Atl-45CO
83Pol/Atl-45CO
84Pol/Atl-45CO
86Sf/Dec-42
87KMart-3
87Nestle/DT-31
88T-664TBC
89Kahn/Coop-5
89T/LJN-89
90BBWit-31
90HOF/St-74
90Pac/Legend-28
90Swell/Great-120
91CollAB-23
91K/3D-5
91K/SU-6A
91K/SU-6B
91LineD-3
91Swell/Great-33
Gibson, Scott
82AppFx-22
84Visalia-22
Gibson, Steve
78Newar
79BurlB-13
80BurlB-1
81BurlB-11
Gibson, Thomas
91Niagara/ClBest-4
Giddens, Ron
84Cedar-20
86Macon-10
Giddings, Wayne
83Idaho-4
84Madis/Pol-18
85Huntsvl/BK-42
Gideon
BF2-33
Gideon, Brett
86PrWill-11
87Harris-18
88BuffB/CMC-3
88BuffB/ProC-1492
88F-330

89Indianap/CMC-5
89Indianap/ProC-1230
90B-105
Gideon, Jim
77T-478R
82Tulsa-9
89Pac/SenLg-81
89T/SenLg-26
Gideon, Ron
86Lynch-12
87Lynch-8
88Jacks/GS-1
89StLucie/Star-7
91StLucie/ClBest-27CO
91StLucie/ProC-728CO
Giebell, Floyd
81Detroit-88
Giegling, Matt
91Cedar/ClBest-15
91Cedar/ProC-2722
Giel, Paul
55B-125
55Gol/Giants-9
58SFCallB-8
58T-308
59T-9
60T-526
61Clover-6
61Peters-19
61T-374
Gierhan, Sam
78Newar
79BurlB-5
Gies, Chris
91Gaston/ClBest-6
91Gaston/ProC-2683
91Single/ClBest-191
Giesdal, Brent
82Oneonta-3
Gieseke, Mark
89Watlo/Star-30
90Riversi/ProC-2614
91AS/Cal-20
91HighD/ClBest-20
91HighD/ProC-2403
Giesecke, Rob
(Doc)
82VeroB-27
83VeroB-27
85VeroB-24
86VeroB-7TR
87VeroB-18
Giesen, Dan
87Reading-6
88Reading/ProC-874
Gifford, Frank
60P
Giggie, Bob
60Lake
Gigon, Norm
67T-576R
Gil, Benji
91Classic/DP-15
91FrRow/DP-50B
92S/II-808
92T-534DP
Gil, Carlos
83MidldC-7
Gil, Danny
90Boise/ProC-3336
91PalmSp/ProC-2020
Gil, Jose
82Wisco-15
Gil, T. Gus
67T-253R
69T-651
82Danvl-2MG
Gilbert, Andrew
(Andy)
73OPC-252CO
73T-252CO
74OPC-78CO
74T-78CO
Gilbert, Angelo
80Batavia-1
82Idaho-8
Gilbert, Brent
90Tampa/DIMD-9
91PrWill/ClBest-1
91PrWill/ProC-1417
Gilbert, Charles M.
(Charlie)
90Target-280
Gilbert, Dennis
80ElPaso-2
81Holyo-10
82Holyo-21
83Redwd-11
Gilbert, Drew E.
(Buddy)
60HenryH-16
60T-359
60Union-6
Gilbert, Greg
84Everett/Cram-6A
86Fresno/Smok-7
87Anchora-13
87Idaho-15
88Sumter/ProC-405
Gilbert, Harold
(Tookie)
50B-235
52Mother-31
52T-61
Gilbert, Jeff
83SanJose-21
84CharlO-18
85CharlO-20
Gilbert, Lawrence W.
(Larry)
16FleischBrd-31
Gilbert, Mark
79QuadC-12
80Water-14
81Water-19
82Water-18
83Indianap-22
84Wichita/Rock-12
85BuffB-13
Gilbert, Pat
86Cram/PCL-59
87Madis-7
88Modesto-26
88Modesto/Cal-79
Gilbert, Pete
90Target-958
Gilbert, Robbie
86Cram/PCL-62
Gilbert, Roy
89Freder/Star-7
90Freder/Team-14
91Freder/ProC-2379
Gilbert, Shawn
88MidwLAS/GS-32
88Visalia/Cal-151
88Visalia/ProC-91
89Visalia/Cal-104
89Visalia/ProC-1439
90Foil/Best-88
90OrlanSR/Best-4
90OrlanSR/ProC-1089
90OrlanSR/Star-6
91OrlanSR/LineD-481
91OrlanSR/ProC-1856
Gilbert, Walter John
(Wally)
90Target-959
92Conlon/Sport-404
Gilbert, William O.
(Billy)
E107
T206
Gilbreath, Rod
74OPC-93
74T-93
75OPC-431
75T-431
75T/M-431
76OPC-306
76SSPC-10
76T-306
77T-126
78T-217
79OPC-296
79T-572
80Port-22
87Idaho-9
Gilchrist, John
88Eugene/Best-24
89Eugene/Best-22
90AppFox/Box-9
90AppFox/ProC-2108
91BBCity/ClBest-24
91BBCity/ProC-1410
Gilcrease, Doug
84Memphis-19
85FtMyr-17
Gile, Don
61T-236
62T-244
Gile, Mark
83TriCit-16
85Tulsa-10
Giles, Brian
81Tidew-4
82Tidew-8
83F-544
83T-548
83T/St-322
84D-563
84F-585
84Jacks/Smok-5
84Nes/792-676
84OPC-324
84T-676
84T/St-111
84Tidew-24
85Pol/Brew-26
87Hawaii-8
88Calgary/CMC-15
88Calgary/ProC-784
89ColoSp/CMC-13
89ColoSp/ProC-253
90Watertn/Star-9
91CLAS/ProC-CAR15
91Kinston/ClBest-26
91Kinston/ProC-338
91Single/ClBest-16
91WIZMets-140
Giles, George
86Negro/Frit-51
91Negro/Lewis-1
Giles, Troy
87QuadC-2
88QuadC/GS-15
89PalmSp/Cal-32
89PalmSp/ProC-473
Giles, Warren
56T-2PRES
57T-100M
58T-300M
59T-200PRES
60F-73
61F-33
80SSPC/HOF
89HOF/St-92
Gilhooley, Frank
16FleischBrd-32
D328-59
E135-59
Gilkey, Otis Bernard
(Bernard)
87Spring/Best-25
88Spring/Best-13
89ArkTr/GS-6
90AAAGame/ProC-AAA19
90Leaf/II-353
90Louisvl/CMC-9
90Louisvl/ProC-415
90S/Tr-106T
90T/TVCard-50
91B-408
91Classic/200-165
91Classic/I-93
91D-30RR
91F-633
91Leaf/II-286
91Leaf/Stud-231
91OPC-126
91OPC/Premier-51
91Pol/Card-23
91S-709RP
91S/Rook40-11
91T-126
91T/90Debut-53
91T/StClub/II-402
91UD-16
92D/I-376
92F-578
92S/100RisSt-24
92S/II-544
92T-746
92UD-552
Gilks, Robert
N172
Gill, Chris
89Billings/ProC-2046
90CharWh/Best-15
90CharWh/ProC-2246
90Foil/Best-141
91CharWh/ClBest-17
91CharWh/ProC-2894
Gill, John
45Centen-10
WG8-24
Gill, Shawn
82Idaho-14
83Madis/LF-11
84Madis/Pol-17
Gill, Steve
91Waterlo/ClBest-21
91Waterlo/ProC-1268
Gill, Turner
87Wmsprt-25
88Wmsprt/ProC-1312
Gillaspie, Mark
83Beaum-15
84Beaum-5
85IowaC-22
88Memphis/Best-13
Gillen, Kevin
76Watlo
77Jaxvl
Gillenwater, Carden
90Target-960
V362-32
Gilles, Bob
83VeroB-15
Gilles, Mark
87Kinston-3
88Kinston/Star-7
89Canton/Best-13
89Canton/ProC-1323
89Canton/Star-7
Gilles, Tom
87AppFx-16
88Kenosha/ProC-1387
89Knoxvl/Best-7
89Knoxvl/ProC-1143
90Syrac/CMC-4
90Syrac/ProC-564
90Syrac/Team-10
91T/90Debut-54
Gillespie, Don
89Wythe/Star-12
Gillespie, John
E120
Gillespie, Patrick
N172
N284
N690
Gillespie, Paul
47Smith-20
Gillespie, Robert
52Mother-21
Gillette, Mike
90Fayette/ProC-2409
91Lakeland/ClBest-15
91Lakeland/ProC-269
Gilliam, Darryl
86Bakers-11
86Cram/PCL-199
Gilliam, Ed
78BurlB
Gilliam, James
(Junior)
52Park-68
53T-258
54B-74
54NYJour
54RH
54RM-NL14
54T-35
55Armour-7
55B-98
55Gol/Dodg-10
55T-5
55T/DH-129
56T-280
57Swift-10
57T-115
58BB
58PacBell-3
58T-215
59Morrell
59T-306
60BB-4
60L-18
60MacGregor-9
60T-255
60T/tatt-19
61BB-19
61P-158
61T-238
62BB-19
62J-112
62P-112
62P/Can-112
62Salada-201
62Shirriff-201
62T-486
63J-114
63P-114
63T-80
64T-310
64Wheat/St-18
73OPC-569CO
73T-569CO
74OPC-144CO
74T-144CO
78TCMA-45
79TCMA-290
86Negro/Frit-76
88Pac/Leg-44
90Target-281
91T/Arc53-258
PM10/L-15
PM10/Sm-61
PM10/Sm-62
Gilliam, Keith
83Kinston/Team-6
85Syrac-7
86Knoxvl-8
87Knoxvl-13
Gilliam, Melvin
80Ashvl-4
Gilliam, Sean
90Greens/Best-22
90Greens/ProC-2674
90Greens/Star-3
91Greens/ProC-3073
Gilliford, Paul
91Crown/Orio-156
Gilligan, Andrew
N172
N284
Gilligan, John
90MedHat/Best-19
91SLCity/ProC-3204
Gilligan, Larry
91Johnson/ClBest-7
91Johnson/ProC-3984
Gilligan, Jim
87SLCity/Taco-11MG
Gillis, Jack
91Oneonta/ProC-4168MG
Gillis, Tim
90BurlB/Best-13
90BurlB/ProC-2356
90BurlB/Star-12
90Foil/Best-134
91CLAS/ProC-CAR1
91Durham/ClBest-17
91Durham/ProC-1553
Gills, Amy
85Anchora-35TR
87Anchora-14TR
Gills, Jack
87Oneonta-32
Gillum, K.C.
89Billings/ProC-2042
90A&AASingle/ProC-196
90Billings/ProC-3237
90CharWh/ProC-2251
91Cedar/ClBest-25
91Cedar/ProC-2731
91Single/ClBest-369
Gilmartin, Dan
78Newar
79BurlB-10
82Beloit-18
Gilmore, Bill
87AppFx-2
Gilmore, Bob
79Richm-9M
Gilmore, Frank T.
N172
Gilmore, Joel
91Martins/ProC-3448
Gilmore, Lenny
88BurlInd/ProC-1774
Gilmore, Matt

90BurlInd/ProC-3014
Gilmore, Terry
87Spokane-19
88TexLgAS/GS-29
88Wichita-20
89LasVegas/CMC-4
89LasVegas/ProC-16
90AAAGame/ProC-AAA18
90LasVegas/CMC-4
90LasVegas/ProC-113
91LasVegas/ProC-229
91LasVegas/LineD-282
Gilmore, Tony
80Utica-16
Gilmore, Tony R.
90AubAs/ProC-3397
91BurlAs/ClBest-25
91BurlAs/ProC-2805
91MidwLAS/ProC-MWL15
91Single/ClBest-325
Gilson, Bob
89London/ProC-1358
Gilson, Hal
66Pep/Tul
68OPC-162R
68T-162R
69OPC-156R
69T-156R
Gimenez, Issac
75Clinton
Gimenez, Ray
75Clinton
Ging, Adam
85Spokane/Cram-5
87Columbia-8
Gingrich, Gary
76BurlB
77BurlB
Ginsberg, Myron
(Joe)
52T-192
53B/Col-6
53Glen
54B-52
57T-236
58T-67
59T-66
60T-304
61T-79
79TCMA-52
91Crown/Orio-157
91WIZMets-141
Gioia, Joe
86Cram/PCL-194
Gionfriddo, Al
48Swell-9
90Target-282
V362-24
Giordano, Marc
89Princet/Star-7
90Miami/I/Star-9
90Miami/II/Star-7
91Miami/ClBest-20
91Miami/ProC-414
Giordano, Mike
83Orlan-21
Giovanola, Ed
90Idaho/ProC-3269
91Durham/ClBest-14
91Durham/ProC-1554
Girardi, Joe
87WinSalem-17
88BBAmer-8
88EastLAS/ProC-25
88Pittsfld/ProC-1359
89D/Rook-23
89F-644R
89Mara/Cubs-7
89S/Tr-84
89UD/Ext-776
90Cub/Mara-8
90D-404
90D/BestNL-87
90F-31
90Leaf/II-289
90OPC-12
90S-535
90S/100Ris-33
90S/YS/II-29
90T-12
90T/89Debut-42
90T/TVCub-20
90UD-304
91B-415
91Cub/Mara-7
91D-184
91F-421
91F/Ultra-60
91Leaf/I-258
91Leaf/Stud-156
91OPC-214
91Panini/FrSt-42
91Panini/St-49
91S-585
91T-214
91T/StClub/I-247
91UD-113
92D/I-175
92S/II-701
92T-529
92UD-351
Giron, Ysidro
86FtLaud-7
87PrWill-17
Gisselman, Bob
82Wausau-31
Githens, John
86Watlo-10
87Watlo-13
88Kinston/Star-8
89Hagers/Best-2
89Hagers/ProC-262
89Hagers/Star-9
Giuliani, Tony
90Target-283
Giusti, Dave
62T-509
63T-189
64T-354
65T-524
66T-258
67T-318
68Coke
68Dexter-36
68OPC-182
68T-182
69MB-93
69OPC-98
69T-98
69T/St-95
70OPC-372
70T-372
71MLB/St-202
71OPC-562
71T-562
72MB-116
72OPC-190
72T-190
73OPC-465
73T-465
74OPC-82
74T-82
74T/St-83
75OPC-53
75T-53
75T/M-53
76OPC-352
76SSPC-565
76T-352
77T-154
89Smok/Ast-3
89Swell-58
Giustino, Gerard
89SLCity-26
Givens, Brian
85LitFalls-5
86Columbia-11A
86Columbia-11B
87Lynch-28
88Jacks/GS-14
89Jacks/GS-27
90Tidew/CMC-4
90Tidew/ProC-537
Givens, James
91Bristol/ClBest-1
91Bristol/ProC-3613
Givler, Doug
87Chatt/Best-9
88ColAst/Best-7
89ColMud/Best-11
89ColMud/ProC-124
89ColMud/Star-11
Gjesdal, Brent
86Beaum-12
Glabman, Barry
76Dubuq
Gladd, Jim
52Mother-53
53Mother-29
Gladden, Dan
(Danny)
81Shrev-9
82Phoenix
83Phoenix/BHN-8
84Cram/PCL-17
85D-567
85F-607
85F/St-118
85Leaf-30
85Mother/Giants-3
85T-386
85T/St-166
85T/St-374YS
86D-187
86F-541
86Mother/Giants-3
86OPC-336
86T-678
86T/St-90
87D-189
87D/OD-224
87F-274
87F/Up-U36
87OPC-46
87T-46
87T/St-93
87T/Tr-38T
88D-491
88D/Best-130
88F-12
88F/WS-1
88OPC-206
88Panini/St-143
88S-324
88Smok/Minn-10
88T-502
88T/St-19
88T/St-281
88Woolwth-20
89B-163
89D-391
89D/Best-298
89F-112
89OPC-387
89Panini/St-392
89RedFoley/St-50
89S-62
89T-426
89T/St-286
89UD-400
90B-420
90Classic-148
90D-182
90D-22DK
90D/BestAL-108
90D/SuperDK-22DK
90F-375
90Leaf/I-254
90OPC-298
90Panini/St-111
90PublInt/St-328
90S-61
90Sf-190
90T-298
90T/Big-147
90T/St-292
90UD-238
91B-318
91D-228
91F-611
91F/Ultra-187
91Leaf/I-76
91Leaf/Stud-85
91OPC-778
91Panini/FrSt-304
91S-163
91T-778
91T/StClub/I-54
91UD-659
92D/II-585
92F-203
92S/I-28
92T-177
92UD-332
Gladden, Jeff
81CharR-17
82FtMyr-13
83Clinton/LF-28
Gladding, Fred
64T-312R
65OPC-37
65T-37
66T-337
67OPC-192
67T-192
68T-423
69OPC-58
69T-58
70MLB/St-41
70OPC-208
70T-208
71MLB/St-80
71OPC-381
71T-381
72MB-117
72OPC-507
72T-507
73OPC-17
73T-17
78TCMA-158
79Tacoma-25
86Ashvl-12CO
87ColAst/ProC-3
88ColAst/Best-20
89ColMud/Best-10
89ColMud/ProC-139
90Kinston/Team-27CO
91Kinston/ClBest-17CO
91Kinston/ProC-341CO
Glade, Fred
WG2-21
Gladu, Mike
88Wythe/ProC-1993
Glanville, Doug
91Classic/DP-9
91Geneva/ClBest-24
91Geneva/ProC-4230
Glanz, Scott
83Peoria/LF-4
Glaser, Gordy
81Charl-3
82Charl-3
83BuffB-4
Glaser, Kris
91Eugene/ClBest-28
91Eugene/ProC-3719
Glasker, Stephen
86Salem-10
87PortChar-15
89CharlR/Star-9
Glass, Bobby
77Jaxvl
Glass, Steve
87Idaho-22
89BurlB/ProC-1607
89BurlB/Star-10
90Sumter/Best-29CO
90Sumter/ProC-2452CO
Glass, Tim
78Watlo
81Chatt-11
82Chatt-6
83BuffB-11
84BuffB-3
85Water-18
Glasscock, John
(Jack)
75F/Pion-21
86Indianap-5
N162
N172
N284
N300
WG1-32
Glasscock, Larry
83Memphis-18
Glaviano, Thomas
(Tommy)
49Eureka-183
51B-301
51T/RB-47
52T-56
53T-140
91T/Arc53-140
Glavine, Tom
86Greenvl/Team-9
86SLAS-23
87Richm/Crown-14
87Richm/TCMA-5
88D-644
88F-539
88S-638
88T-779
88T/St-44
89B-267
89Classic/Up/2-159
89D-381
89D/Best-2
89F-591
89Panini/St-34
89S-442
89S/YS/II-23
89T-157
89UD-360
90B-2
90Classic-36
90D-145
90D/BestNL-2
90D/Learning-53
90F-583
90Leaf/I-13
90OPC-506
90Panini/St-219
90RedFoley/St-36
90S-481
90Sf-34
90T-506
90T/Big-99
90T/St-26
90UD-571
91B-576
91Classic/200-17
91Classic/III-26
91D-132
91F-689
91F/Ultra-5
91Leaf/I-172
91Leaf/Stud-145
91OPC-82
91RedFoley/St-39
91S-206
91T-82
91T/StClub/II-558
91UD-480
91UD/FinalEd-90FAS
91USPlayC/AS-1S
92Classic/I-38
92D/II-426AS
92D/II-629
92D/II-BC4CY
92F-358
92F-694LL
92F/ASIns-6
92F/TmLIns-11
92S/100SS-15
92S/II-450
92S/II-791CY
92S/II-890DT
92T-305
92T-395AS
92UD-342
Glazner, Charles
(Whitey)
E120
E121/120
E220
W501-87
W572
W573
W575
Gleason, Harry
E107
Gleason, Roy
90Target-961
Gleason, William G.
N172
N172/BC
N284
N370
Scrapps
Gleason, William J.
(Kid)
88Conlon/5-14
88Pac/8Men-102
88Pac/8Men-23
88Pac/8Men-73
E107
E223
N172
Gleason, William P.
D327
D328-60
E121/120
E121/80
E122
E135-60
V100

W501-39
W514-112
W575
Gleaton, Jerry Don
80T-673R
80Tulsa-1
81T-41R
82T-371
83SLCity-2
84Cram/PCL-186
85BuffB-19
85T-216
86BuffB-12
86T-447
88D-547
88F-258
88Omaha/CMC-5
88Omaha/ProC-1497
88S-343
88Smok/Royals-7
88T-116
89D-444
89F-282
89S-423
89T-724
90CokeK/Tiger-6
90TulsaDG/Best-17
91CokeK/Tiger-19
91D-661
91F-338
91Leaf/I-135
91OPC-597
91S-316
91T-597
91T/StClub/II-574
92D/II-607
92S/I-375
92T-272
92UD-601
Gleckel, Scott
82OrlTw/A-14
Gledhill, Chance
91Boise/ClBest-4
91Boise/ProC-3870
Gleissner, James
82FtMyr-17
Glenn, Edward C.
N172
Glenn, Joe
35BU-87
92Conlon/Sport-510
Glenn, John
62Kahn/Atl
Glenn, Leon Jr.
90Beloit/Best-17
90Beloit/Star-9
90Foil/Best-271
91Beloit/ClBest-24
91Beloit/ProC-2110
91BendB/ClBest-25
91BendB/ProC-3700
91Single/ClBest-215
Glenn, Simon
80Elmira-28
Glick, Tom
90James/Pucko-31
Glinatsis, Mike
76Cedar
82Miami-2
Gline, Steve
90Clinton/ProC-2566CO
Glinton, James
91CharlR/ClBest-16
Glisson, Robert
86Erie-8
87Spring/Best-18
88Spring/Best-1
Globig, Dave
76BurlB
Glossop, Alban
(Al)
47Signal
49B/PCL-17
90Target-284
Glover, Jeff
86Cram/PCL-68
87Madis-17
88Modesto-10
88Modesto/Cal-60
Glover, Reggie
88Reno/Cal-271
Glover, Terence
88SLCity-23
Glynn, Dennis
86Jacks/TCMA-14
Glynn, Ed
77Evansvl/TCMA-11
77T-487R
79T-343
80T-509
81Charl-4
81T-93
82Charl-4
83Charl-19
83D-537
83F-408
83T-614
83Wheat/Ind-14
84Maine-22
86Tidew-12
87Tidew-15
87Tidew/TCMA-4
89Pac/SenLg-129
91Pac/SenLg-82
91WIZMets-142
Glynn, Gene
84Indianap-22
85Utica-25
86WPalmB-18CO
87Jamestn-16
88Rockford-15
89Jaxvl/Best-27
89Jaxvl/ProC-174
89Rockford-15CO
90Waterlo/Best-23CO
90Waterlo/ProC-2395CO
91Spokane/ClBest-29MG
91Spokane/ProC-3965MG
Glynn, William V.
(Bill)
52Mother-56
53T-171
54T-178
55T-39
55T/DH-59
91T/Arc53-171
V362-42
Gnacinski, Paul
84Pawtu-8
86Greenvl/Team-10
Gobel, Donnie
91Augusta/ClBest-7
91Augusta/ProC-800
Gobbo, Michael
85Beloit-8
86Stockton-10
87ElPaso-26
Gochnaur, John
90Target-285
E107
Godfrey, Tyson
90Hunting/ProC-3275
91Peoria/ClBest-12
91Peoria/ProC-1337
Godin, Steven
91Kane/ClBest-22
91Kane/ProC-2669
Godwin, Glenn
83Madis/LF-25
Goedde, Mike
85Cedar-8
89Billings/ProC-2049
Goedhart, Darrell
89Martins/Star-12
90Spartan/Best-4
90Spartan/ProC-2485
90Spartan/Star-9
91Clearw/ClBest-4
91Clearw/ProC-1615
Goergen, Todd
89Batavia/ProC-1927
90Spartan/Best-5
90Spartan/ProC-2486
90Spartan/Star-10
91Spartan/ClBest-4
91Spartan/ProC-889
Goetz, Barry
91CharlR/ClBest-6
91CharlR/ProC-1310
Goetz, Jack
75Dubuq
Goetz, Lawrence
55B-311ump
Goff, Jerry L.
86Cram/PCL-110
87Wausau-17
88SanBern/Best-12
88SanBern/Cal-33
89Wmsprt/ProC-631
89Wmsprt/Star-7
90B-112
90Indianap/CMC-13
90Indianap/ProC-291
90Leaf/II-476
91D-499
91Indianap/LineD-184
91Indianap/ProC-467
91Panini/FrSt-153
91S-834
91T/90Debut-55
Goff, Mike
86Greens-9
88MidwLAS/GS-57
88Wausau/GS-27
89AS/Cal-14
89SanBern/Best-24
89SanBern/Cal-72
90Wmsprt/Best-7
90Wmsprt/ProC-1053
90Wmsprt/Star-8
Goff, Tim
86Cram/PCL-32
87FtMyr-17
Goff, Wally
79Wausau-8
80Penin/B-7
80Penin/C-14
Goggin, Chuck
74OPC-457
74T-457
Gogolewski, Bill
71MLB/St-539
71OPC-559R
71T-559R
72OPC-424
72T-424
73OPC-27
73T-27
74OPC-242
74T-242
Gogolewski, Doug
(Gogo)
87Oneonta-10
88FtLaud/Star-10
89FtLaud/Star-6
90Albany/ProC-1032
90Albany/Star-5
Gohl, Lefty
52Park-78
Gohmann, Ken
86Lakeland-6
87Lakeland-26
88GlenF/ProC-930
89Saraso/Star-7
Gohr, Greg
90B-347
90Lakeland/Star-11
90S-679DC
91B-142
91London/LineD-385
91London/ProC-1871
91Toledo/ProC-1925
Goins, Scott
87Everett-3
89SanJose/Best-27
89SanJose/Cal-233
89SanJose/ProC-438
89SanJose/Star-10
Gokey, Steve
87Modesto-8
88Modesto-30
89Modesto/Cal-289CO
89Modesto/Chong-6
Gold, Bret
81Miami-20
Gold, Mark
87Wausau-23
Goldberg, Marc
91StLucie/ClBest-29DIR
Golden, Brian
89Hamil/Star-16
90Erie/Star-7
Golden, Ike
81AppFx-16
Golden, Jim
61T-298
62T-568
63T-297
89Smok/Ast-4
90Target-286
Goldetsky, Larry
78Memphis/Team-4
80Memphis-7
83Memphis-6
Goldman, J.
31Exh/4-21
Goldsberry, Gordon
52T-46
53T-200
91T/Arc53-200
Goldsby, Walt
N172
Goldstein, David R.
80WHave-20
Goldstein, Ike
87Visalia-12
Goldthorn, Burk
82AlexD-15
83LynnP-12
85PrWill-30
86Hawaii-10
Goldy, Purnal
63T-516
Golenbock, Peter
90LitSun-21
Goliat, Mike
50B-205
51B-77
51BR-B10
61Union
Gollehon, Chris
88Bristol/ProC-1875
89Spokane/SP-20
Golmont, Van
90Erie/Star-8
Goltz, Dave
73OPC-148
73T-148
74OPC-636
74T-636
75OPC-419
75T-419
75T/M-419
76OPC-136
76SSPC-218
76T-136
77BurgChef-47
77Ho-48
77OPC-73
77T-321
78Ho-96
78K-35
78OPC-142
78OPC-5LL
78T-205LL
78T-249
79Ho-16
79OPC-10
79T-27
80OPC-108
80Pol/Dodg-38
80T-193
81F-127
81OPC-289
81Pol/Dodg-38
81T-548
82D-604
82F-6
82Pol/Dodg-38
82T-674
83F-90
83T-468
90Target-287
Gomez, Art
81Clinton-8
Gomez, Dana
87WinHaven-30
Gomez, Fabio
88BurlInd/ProC-1788
89Watertn/Star-8
90Kinston/Team-7
91Kinston/ProC-329
Gomez, Henry
88CharWh/Best-14
90Peoria/Team-23
91CharlK/LineD-133
91CharlK/ProC-1684
Gomez, Jorge
80Ashvl-3
82BurlR-20
83Tulsa-1
84Tulsa-4
Gomez, Jose L.R.
(Chile)
R313
Gomez, Jose Luis
(Luis)
77T-13
78OPC-121
78T-573
79OPC-128
79T-254
80OPC-95
80T-169
81D-88
81F-253
81Pol/Atl-9
81T-477
82T-372
89Pac/SenLg-17
89T/SenLg-16
91Pac/SenLg-143
Gomez, Jose
83Miami-14
Gomez, Juan A.
75Tucson-9
76Tucson-33
Gomez, Leo
87Hagers-5
89Hagers/Best-1
89Hagers/ProC-280
89Hagers/Star-10
90AAAGame/ProC-AAA10
90B-262
90HagersDG/Best-12
90RochR/CMC-10
90RochR/ProC-709
91B-88
91Classic/200-164
91Classic/I-12
91Classic/III-31
91Crown/Orio-158
91D-35RR
91F-472
91F/Ultra-16
91Leaf/I-35
91Leaf/Prev-13
91Leaf/Stud-3
91OPC/Premier-52
91S-725RP
91S/Rook40-20
91Seven/3DCoin-3A
91T/90Debut-56
91T/Tr-47T
91UD-6
92D/I-199
92F-8
92S/100RisSt-66
92S/I-240
92T-84
92UD-161
Gomez, Marcos
82Beloit-10
Gomez, Miguel
78Dunedin
Gomez, Orlando
82Tulsa-23
83BurlR-26
83BurlR/LF-27MG
84Tulsa-23MG
85Tulsa-23MG
86Water-11MG
87BuffB-25
88Gaston/ProC-1009MG
89Gaston/ProC-1017MG
89SALAS/GS-2
90Gaston/Best-25MG
90Gaston/ProC-2536MG
90Gaston/Star-26MG
90SALAS/Star-24CO
91Mother/Rang-28CO
Gomez, Pat
87Peoria-13
87Peoria/PW-2
88CharWh/Best-13
89WinSalem/Star-8
90Foil/Best-49
90Greenvl/Best-4
91Greenvl/ClBest-1
91Greenvl/LineD-207
91Greenvl/ProC-2995
91Huntsvl/ClBest-26
Gomez, Pedro
(Preston)

60DF-10
61Union
69OPC-74MG
69T-74MG
70OPC-513MG
70T-513MG
71OPC-737MG
71T-737MG
72T-637MG
73OPC-624CO
73T-624CO
74OPC-31MG
74T-31MG
75OPC-487MG
75T-487MG
75T/M-487MG

Gomez, Pierre
90Miami/II/Star-8

Gomez, Randy
84Cram/PCL-20
85Cram/PCL-179
86Phoenix-6
87Hawaii-24

Gomez, Ruben
54NYJour
54T-220
55Gol/Giants-10
55T-71
55T/DH-89
56T-9
56T/Pin-39P
57T-58
58SFCallB-9
58T-335
59T-535
60T-82
61T-377
67T-427
79TCMA-80
PM10/L-16
PM10/Sm-64

Gomez, Rudy
91Geneva/ClBest-8
91Geneva/ProC-4223

Gomez, Steve
86Orlan-7
87Orlan-13

Gomez, Vernon
(Lefty)
32Orbit/num-120
33CJ/Pin-8
33DL-14
33G-216
34Exh/4-13
35BU-23
35BU-86
35Exh/4-13
36Exh/4-13
36G
36Wheat-1
37Exh/4-13
38Exh/4-13
38ONG/Pin-12
39Exh
39PB-48
39Wheat-3
40PB-6
41DP-61
41PB-72
60F-54
61F-34
72Laugh/GF-18
80Pac/Leg-117
80SSPC/HOF
86Conlon/1-45
86Sf/Dec-9
87Conlon/2-2
88Conlon/5-15
88Conlon/AmAS-12
89HOF/St-76
90Swell/Great-84
91Conlon/Sport-67
91Homer/Classic-3
91Swell/Great-129
92Conlon/Sport-536
PM10/Sm-63
PR1-12
R303/A
R303/B
R308-151
R309/2
R310
R312/M
R313
R314
R328-31
V355-56

Gonder, Jesse
63FrBauer-6
63T-29R
64T-457
64T/Coins-43
64T/St-30
64T/SU
65T-423
66EH-20
66T-528
67T-301
67T/Test/PP-10
69T-617
78TCMA-122
78TCMA-238
91WIZMets-143

Goninger, Gerry
89Cedar/ProC-930

Gonring, Doug
87Ashvl-8

Gonsalves, Dennis
83Madis/LF-7
84Madis/Pol-16

Gonzales, Arturo
73Cedar
74Cedar

Gonzales, Benjamin
(Ben)
89AubAs/ProC-2171
90Ashvl/ProC-2740
91BurlAs/ClBest-3
91BurlAs/ProC-2794

Gonzales, Dan
77Evansvl/TCMA-12
80Evansvl-20

Gonzales, Eddie
87SanJose-25

Gonzales, Frank
90Fayette/ProC-2399
91Lakeland/ClBest-6
91Lakeland/ProC-262

Gonzales, John
90Ashvl/ClBest-21
91Ashvl/ProC-579

Gonzales, Larry
89QuadC/Best-21
89QuadC/GS-28
91London/LineD-435
91MidldA/ProC-436

Gonzales, Rene C.
83Memphis-3
84Indianap-25
85Indianap-11
86Indianap-10
88D-582
88F-560
88French-88
88T-98
88T/Big-209
89D-377
89French-88
89OPC-213
89S-585
89T-213
89T/Big-87
89T/St-234
90D-401
90OPC-787
90S-118
90T-787
91B-25
91Crown/Orio-159
91F-473
91Leaf/II-490
91OPC-377
91OPC/Premier-53
91S-638
91S/ToroBJ-14
91T-377
91T/StClub/II-406
91Tor/Fire-88
92D/I-274
92S/II-582
92T-681

Gonzales, Todd
87Watlo-11
88Kinston/Star-9
89Canton/Best-16
89Canton/ProC-1320
89Canton/Star-8

Gonzalez, Angel
86WinHaven-9
87NewBrit-4
88NewBrit/ProC-910
88Pawtu/CMC-17
88Pawtu/ProC-462
89Pawtu/CMC-22
89Pawtu/Dunkin-12
89Pawtu/ProC-684
90Pawtu/CMC-15
90Pawtu/ProC-468
90T/TVRSox-44
91Nashvl/LineD-257
91Nashvl/ProC-2162

Gonzalez, Arturo
85Cram/PCL-33
86Phill/TastyK-x
86Portl-6

Gonzalez, Carlos
86FtMyr-12
87AppFx-14
88BBCity/Star-12
89BBCity/Star-7

Gonzalez, Cecilio
90Johnson/Star-13
91Johnson/ClBest-26
91Johnson/ProC-3972

Gonzalez, Cliff
85LitFalls-23
86LitFalls-12
87Columbia-4
89Saraso/Star-8
90Saraso/Star-11
91AS/Cal-46

Gonzalez, David
91London/LineD-407
91Memphis/ProC-661

Gonzalez, Denio
(Denny)
82Portl-13
84Cram/PCL-130
85Cram/PCL-229
85D-600
86D-410
86F-608
86T-746
88BuffB/CMC-15
88BuffB/ProC-1473
89ColoSp/CMC-14
89ColoSp/ProC-248
90T/TVMets-43
90Tidew/CMC-17
90Tidew/ProC-552
91Nashvl/LineD-258
91Nashvl/ProC-2163

Gonzalez, Eddie
90WPalmB/Star-10

Gonzalez, Felipe
86Fresno/Smok-5
87Clinton-7

Gonzalez, Ferdi
83Greens-14
84Greens-6
86Albany/TCMA-6
86FtLaud-8
87Albany-20
90Miami/I/Star-28CO
90Miami/II/Star-28CO
91Miami/ClBest-1MG
91Miami/ProC-423MG

Gonzalez, Fred
(Freddy)
90VeroB/Star-14
91SanAn/LineD-535

Gonzalez, German
87Kenosha-26
88BBAmer-18
88OrlanTw/Best-17
88SLAS-30
89D-590
89D/Rook-24
89F-113
89Panini/St-379
89S/HotRook-49
89T-746
90F-376
90HotRook/St-17
90OPC-266
90S-133
90S/100Ris-81
90T-266
90UD-352
91Kissim/ProC-4193

Gonzalez, Gilberto
80Elmira-32

Gonzalez, Henry
84Newar-18
85Newar-10

Gonzalez, Javier
88Clmbia/GS-12
91Wmsprt/LineD-632
91Wmsprt/ProC-296

Gonzalez, Jesus
91Burllnd/ProC-3295

Gonzalez, Jimmy
91Classic/DP-36
91FrRow/DP-32
92T-564DP

Gonzalez, Jose
82ArkTr-13
83Louisvl/Riley-13

Gonzalez, Jose Fern.
(Fernando)
74OPC-649
74T-649
74T/Tr-649T
78Colum
78Padre/FamFun-14
78T-433
79T-531
80SLCity-25
80T-171
81SLCity-18
82AlexD-7
83LynnP-3

Gonzalez, Jose Rafael
86Albuq-9
87Albuq/Pol-26
87D-525
87F-649M
87Pol/Dodg-25
88Albuq/CMC-19
88Albuq/ProC-258
88D-341
88S-364
89Albuq/CMC-17
89Albuq/ProC-80
89D/Best-260
89S/HotRook-29
89UD-626
90Classic-96
90D-314
90F-394
90Mother/Dodg-11
90OPC-98
90Pol/Dodg-38
90S-368
90S/YS/I-16
90T-98
90Target-288
90UD-666
91D-543
91Mother/Dodg-11
91OPC-279
91Pol/Dodg-38
91S-614
91T-279A
91T-279B
91T/StClub/I-208
92S/II-733

Gonzalez, Juan
76Clinton

Gonzalez, Juan A.
87Gaston-4
88CharlR/Star-8
89BBAmerAA/BPro-AA26
89TexLAS/GS-34
89Tulsa/GS-10
89Tulsa/Team-8
90AAAGame/ProC-AAA12
90B-492
90Classic/Up-21
90D-33
90F-297
90OkCty/CMC-17
90OkCty/ProC-444
90OPC-331
90S-637
90T-331
90T/89Debut-43
90TulsaDG/Best-25
90UD-72
91B-180
91Classic/200-122
91Classic/I-70
91Classic/II-T74
91D-371
91F-286
91F/UltraUp-U55
91Leaf/I-119
91Leaf/Stud-124
91MajorLg/Pins-36
91Mother/Rang-4
91OPC-224
91OPC/Premier-54
91RedFoley/St-107
91S-805
91S/100RisSt-41
91S/HotRook-9
91Seven/3DCoin-7T
91T-224
91T/StClub/I-237
91UD-646
92D/I-393
92F-304
92S/100SS-69
92S/I-11
92T-27
92UD-243

Gonzalez, Julian
83Peoria/LF-23
85MidldA-25
87SanJose-24

Gonzalez, Julio C.
78BK/Ast-13
78T-389
79T-268
80T-696
81F-73
82D-645
82T-503
83Evansvl-14
83T-74

Gonzalez, Larry
89Salem/Team-12

Gonzalez, Luis
78Ashvl
80Tulsa-14

Gonzalez, Luis E.
88AubAs/ProC-1973
89Osceola/Star-6
89Star/Wax-15
90A&AASingle/ProC-59
90ColMud/Best-4
90ColMud/ProC-1352
90ColMud/Star-11
90Foil/Best-95
91B-550
91Classic/II-T91
91D-690
91D/Rook-17
91F-507
91F/UltraUp-U82
91Leaf/GRook-BC2
91Mother/Ast-13
91S/RookTr-99T
91T/90Debut-57
91T/StClub/II-576
91T/Tr-48T
91UD-567
91UD/Ext-702
92D/I-270
92F-434
92S/100RisSt-6
92S/I-210
92T-12
92UD-372

Gonzalez, Marcos
82Miami-3
87Fayette-20

Gonzalez, Melvin
91Elmira/ClBest-21
91Elmira/ProC-3266

Gonzalez, Miguel
21Exh-58
28Yueng-34
40PB-115
86Conlon/1-14M
92Conlon/Sport-655
D328-61
E121/80
E135-61
E210-34
W502-34
W575
W754

Gonzalez, Mike
(Pitcher)
75Shreve/TCMA-3

76Shrev
Gonzalez, Mike
89BurlInd/Star-11
90Watertn/Star-10
Gonzalez, Orlando
75OkCty
77T-477R
79OkCty
80BurlB-7
80OkCty
81F-585
83Tampa-13
87Nashvl-7
88Miami/Star-8
89Pac/SenLg-82
89T/SenLg-83
91Pac/SenLg-35
Gonzalez, Otto
82BurlR-21
83BurlR/LF-17
85Tulsa-35
86DayBe-9
86FSLAS-18
88OkCty/CMC-12
88OkCty/ProC-47
89MidldA/GS-15
Gonzalez, Paul
91HighD/ClBest-21
91HighD/ProC-2404
91Single/ClBest-82
Gonzalez, Pedro
63T-537R
64T-581R
65OPC-97
65T-97
66Kahn
66T-266
67T-424
WG10-8
WG9-10
Gonzalez, Pedro
(Pete)
90VeroB/Star-15
91VeroB/ClBest-15
91VeroB/ProC-776
Gonzalez, Rich
91StPete/ClBest-25
91StPete/ProC-2288
Gonzalez, Ruben
88Wausau/GS-6
89AS/Cal-12
89SanBern/Best-23
89SanBern/Cal-82
90Foil/Best-198
90Wmsprt/Best-8
90Wmsprt/ProC-1062
91Jaxvl/LineD-337
91Jaxvl/ProC-157
91Single/ClBest-28
Gonzalez, Tommy
75Phoenix-5
76Phoenix
79Phoenix
80Phoenix-25
81Phoenix-26
82Phoenix
83Phoenix/BHN-28
Gonzalez, Tony
60T-518
61T-93
61T/St-55
62T-534
62T/St-168
63Exh
63J-181
63P-181
63T-32
64PhilBull-13
64T-379
64T/Coins-58
64T/S-14
64T/St-58S6
64T/SU
65OPC-72
65T-72
66T-478
67T-548
68Bz-8
68OPC-1LL
68T-1LL
68T-245
68T/G-20
69MB-94
69MLB/St-192
69T-501
69T/decal
69T/St-94
70MLB/St-6
70OPC-105
70T-105
71MLB/St-345
71OPC-256
71T-256
72MB-118
77Spartan/C
82Danvl-13C
Exh47
Gonzalez, Wallace
90Pulaski/Best-13
90Pulaski/ProC-3093
91Macon/ClBest-15
91Macon/ProC-868
Gooch, John B.
(Johnny)
31Exh/4-8
90Target-289
91Conlon/Sport-244
E120
E126-1
Gooch, Ron
79Tucson-7
79Tulsa-11
80Tulsa-17
81Tulsa-28
Good, Wilbur
D329-69
D350/2-69
M101/4-69
M101/5-69
T205
T206
Goodale, Jeff
89NiagFls/Pucko-9
90Lakeland/Star-12
91Lakeland/ClBest-24
91Lakeland/ProC-278
Goodchild, Chris
80Clinton-6
Goode, William
14Piedmont/St-24
Gooden, Dwight
83Lynch-10
84F/X-43
85FunFood/Pin-27
84T/Tr-42
85D-190
85D/AAS-47
85D/HL-32
85D/HL-33
85D/HL-48
85D/WaxBox-PC1
85Drake-36
85F-634IA
85F-82
85F/St-113
85F/St-87
85F/St-95
85Leaf-234
85OPC-41
85Pol/MetYank-M3
85Seven-9E
85T-3RB
85T-620
85T/3D-19
85T/Gloss40-38
85T/Mets/Fan-5
85T/St-107
85T/St-280
85T/St-3
85T/St-371M
85T/St-4
85T/Super-7
85Woolwth-16
86BK/AP-17
86D-26DK
86D-75
86D/AAS-28
86D/DKsuper-26
86D/HL-8
86Dorman-5
86Drake-35
86F-626M
86F-638M
86F-641M
86F-81
86F/AS-10
86F/LimEd-20
86F/LL-16
86F/Mini-19A
86F/Mini-19B
86F/Slug-11
86F/St-132CL
86F/St-46
86Jiffy-20
86KayBee-16
86Leaf-26DK
86Meadow/Blank-5
86Meadow/Milk-4
86Meadow/Stat-3
86OPC-250
86OPC-F
86Quaker-2
86Sf-100
86Sf-136M
86Sf-143M
86Sf-176M
86Sf-184M
86Sf-185M
86Sf/Dec-75
86Sf/Rook-47M
86T-202RB
86T-250
86T-709AS
86T/3D-4
86T/Gloss60-41
86T/Mets/Fan-4
86T/Mini-52
86T/St-6
86T/St-94
86T/Super-4
86T/WaxBox-F
87Classic-72
87D-199
87D/AAS-18
87D/PopUp-18
87Drake-26
87F-629M
87F-9
87F/AwardWin-15
87F/Excit-19
87F/GameWin-18
87F/HL-3
87F/Hottest-18
87F/BB-19
87F/LL-20
87F/Lim-18
87F/Mini-45
87F/RecSet-12
87F/Slug-15
87F/St-48
87F/WaxBox-C4
87F/WS-7
87Jiffy-9
87KayBee-13
87KMart-26
87Leaf-84
87OPC-130
87RedFoley/St-6
87Sf-100
87Sf-120M
87Sf-159M
87Seven-E7
87Seven-ME9
87Sportflic/DealP-4
87T-130
87T-603AS
87T/Coins-33
87T/Gloss22-10
87T/Gloss60-51
87T/Mini-23
87T/St-163
87T/St-5
87T/St-6
87T/St-96
87Tidew-31
87Tidew/TCMA-30
88ActPacT-3
88Bz-8
88Classic/Red-171
88D-69
88D/Best-96
88D/Mets/Bk-69
88Drake-28
88F-135
88F/AwardWin-14
88F/BB/AS-12
88F/BB/MVP-16
88F/Excit-15
88F/Head-5
88F/Hottest-13
88F/LL-15
88F/Mini-92
88F/RecSet-14
88F/Slug-15
88F/SS-14
88F/St-102
88F/TL-10
88Kahn/Mets-16
88KMart-10
88Leaf-48
88MSA/Disc-19
88Nestle-21
88OPC-287
88Panini/St-337
88S-350
88S/YS/II-3
88Sf-200
88Sf/Gamewin-9
88T-405ASs
88T-480
88T/Big-11
88T/Gloss60-54
88T/Mets/Fan-16
88T/Mini-60
88T/St-101
88T/St/Backs-25
88T/UK-27
89B-376
89Classic-107
89Classic-7
89Classic/Up/2-189
89T/Crunch-17
89D-270
89D/AS-40
89D/Best-14
89D/PopUp-40
89F-36
89F-635M
89F/BBAS-15
89F/BBMVP's-14
89F/Excit-15
89F/Heroes-18
89F/LL-16
89F/Superstar-17
89Kahn/Mets-16
89KayBee-14
89KMart/DT-31
89OPC-30
89Panini/St-131
89Panini/St-227AS
89RedFoley/St-51
89S-200
89S/HotStar-15
89S/Mast-26
89Sf-140
89T-30
89T-661TBC84
89T/Big-304
89T/Coins-14
89T/DHTest-5
89T/Gloss22-21
89T/Gloss60-37
89T/HeadsUp-3
89T/LJN-86
89T/Mets/Fan-16
89T/Mini-26
89T/St-162
89T/St-99
89T/St/Backs-59
89T/UK-31
89Tetley/Discs-6
89UD-565
90B-126
90B/Ins-3
90BBWit-35
90Classic-58
90CollAB-2
90D-171
90D/BestNL-7
90D/Learning-10
90F-204
90F/BBMVP-12
90HOF/St-98
90HotPlay/St-16
90Kahn/Mets-16
90KMart/SS-10
90Leaf/I-139
90Mets/Fan-16
90MLBPA/Pins-9
90MSA/Soda-6
90OPC-510
90Panini/St-297
90Post-29
90PublInt/St-134
90PublInt/St-260
90RedFoley/St-37
90S-313
90S/100St-99
90Sf-145
90T-510
90T/Big-174
90T/DH-26
90T/Gloss60-23
90T/HeadsUp-3
90T/St-96
90T/TVAS-58
90T/TVMets-12
90T/WaxBox-E
90Tetley/Discs-10
90UD-114
90UD-62TC
91B-472
91BBBest/Aces-8
91Classic/200-121
91Classic/I-99
91Classic/II-T39
91Colla/Gooden-Set
91CollAB-17
91D-266
91D/Preview-8
91F-148
91F/ProV-7
91F/Ultra-218
91JDeanSig-25
91Kahn/Mets-16
91KingB/Discs-8
91Leaf/I-165
91Leaf/Prev-7
91Leaf/Stud-204
91Leaf/StudPrev-14
91MajorLg/Pins-74
91OPC-330
91OPC/Premier-55
91Panini/FrSt-86
91Panini/St-89
91Panini/Top15-60
91Panini/Top15-74
91Pep/SS-1
91Petro/SU-12
91RedFoley/St-40
91S-540
91S-685KM
91S-866FRAN
91S/100SS-65
91Seven/3DCoin-5NE
91Seven/3DCoin-8F
91Sunflower-10
91T-330
91T/CJMini/I-28
91T/StClub/I-100
91T/SU-15
91UD-224
91WIZMets-144
92D/DK-DK15
92D/Elite-E12
92D/II-446
92F-505
92S/100SS-25
92S/I-10
92T-725
92UD-135
92UD-84M
Gooden, Maury
85LitFalls-24
Goodenough, Randy
86Cram/PCL-39
87FtMyr-23
Goodfellow, Michael
N172
Goodin, Craig
83CharR-6
Goodin, Rich
83CharR-20
Goodlow, Sebastian
89Salem/Team-13
Goodman, Billy
48L-30
49B-39
50B-99
51B-237
51BR-C2
51FB
51T/RB-46
52B-81
52StarCal/L-71E
52T-23
53B/Col-148

53Exh/Can-63
54B-82
55B-126
56T-245
57T-303
58T-225
59T-103
60T-69
61T-247
79TCMA-96
91Crown/Orio-160
91T/Arc53-334
Exh47
PM10/Sm-65

Goodman, Billy
80Ashvl-1

Goodman, Ival
35BU-127
35G-8D
35G-9D
38Exh/4-4
41DP-115
R303/A
R303/B
W711/1
W711/2

Goodson, J. Ed
73OPC-197
73T-197
74K-18
74OPC-494
74T-494
74T/St-105
75OPC-322
75T-322
75T/M-322
76OPC-386
76SSPC-588
76T-386
77T-584
78T-586
90Target-290

Goodson, Kirk
91Hunting/ClBest-11
91Hunting/ProC-3329

Goodwin, Danny
77SLCity
79Ogden/TCMA-15
79T-322
80T-362
81D-474
81T-527
82D-305
82F-554
82T-123
82Tacoma-14
83Tacoma-25A
84Cram/PCL-91
85Cram/PCL-134

Goodwin, David
88Geneva/ProC-1641
89CharWh/Best-18
89CharWh/ProC-1768

Goodwin, Mike
86PrWill-12

Goodwin, Tom
89GreatF-1
89Smok/FresnoSt-10
89Smok/FresnoSt-11
90B-96
90Bakers/Cal-261
90S-668DC
91Albuq/LineD-6
91Albuq/ProC-1155
91B-608
91Classic/III-32
91UD/FinalEd-9F
92Classic/I-39
92F-652
92S/II-830
92T/91Debut-65
92UD-20SR

Goossen, Greg
67T-287R
68T-386
70McDon-5
70OPC-271
70T-271
91WIZMets-145

Gorbould, Bob
45Centen-11

Gorbous, Glen
56T-174

Gordon, Anthony
89Belling/Legoe-5
90Penin/Star-9

Gordon, Don
83BirmB-2
85Syrac-13
86Ault-39
86Tor/Fire-14
87RochR/TCMA-29
87Syrac-5
87Syrac/TCMA-26
87Syrac/TCMA-4
88ColoSp/CMC-3
88ColoSp/ProC-1538
88S/Tr-92T
88T-144
89ColoSp/CMC-2
89ColoSp/ProC-260
89F-405
89S-547
90Denver/CMC-18
90Denver/ProC-621
91ElPaso/LineD-183
91ElPaso/ProC-2742

Gordon, Joe
39Exh
41DP-67
41DP-83
41Wheat-21
44Yank/St-12
47HomogBond-17
48L-117
49B-210
49Royal-13
50B-129
50NumNum
52Mother-19
59Kahn
60T-216MG
61T-224MG
61T/RO-30
69T-484MG
86Sf/Dec-24M
D305
R303/A
R303/B
R423-36

Gordon, Keith
90Billings/ProC-3228
91CharWh/ClBest-23

Gordon, Kevin
85PrWill-21
86Nashua-8

Gordon, Sid
47HomogBond-18
47TipTop
48B-27
48L-131
49B-101
49Eureka-104
50B-109
50Drake-16
51B-19
51T/RB-2
52B-60
52Dix
52NTea
52RM-NL6
52T-267
52TipTop
53B/Col-5
53Dix
53JC-23
53NB
53SpicSpan/3x5-12
53T-117
54B-11
54DanDee
54Dix
55B-163
55RFG-24
79TCMA-67
91T/Arc53-117
D305

Gordon, Tom
(Tommy)
87FtMyr-25
88AppFx/ProC-149
88MidwLAS/GS-40
89B-115
89Classic/Up/2-182
89D-45RR
89D/Best-287
89D/Rook-4
89F-284
89S-634RP
89S/HotRook-68
89S/Mast-7
89S/YS/II-2
89T/Tr-38T
89UD/Ext-736
90B-365
90Bz-21
90Classic-4
90D-297
90F-108
90F/AwardWin-15
90F/SoarSt-7
90HotRook/St-18
90Leaf/I-14
90OPC-752
90Panini/St-89
90PublInt/St-348
90S-472
90S/100Ris-1
90Sf-30
90T-752
90T/Big-252
90T/Coins-15
90T/Gloss60-30
90T/HeadsUp-21
90T/JumboR-10
90T/Mini-15
90T/St-268
90T/St-322FS
90ToysRUs-12
90UD-365
91B-311
91D-242
91F-559
91F/Ultra-147
91Leaf/I-132
91OPC-248
91Panini/FrSt-284
91Panini/St-231
91Pol/Royal-10
91S-197
91T-248
91T/StClub/I-254
91UD-431
92D/I-250
92F-158
92S/I-130
92T-431
92UD-476

Gore, Arthur
55B-289ump

Gore, Bryan
90CharlR/Star-8
91Tulsa/LineD-581
91Tulsa/ProC-2767

Gore, George
90HOF/St-6
N172
N284
N338/2
WG1-40

Gore, Kevin
89Geneva/ProC-1865

Gore, Ricky
89Idaho/ProC-2017

Gorin, Charles
54JC-15
55Gol/Braves-11
55JC-15

Gorinski, Bob
78T-386
79Tidew-24

Gorman, Bill
82Omaha-24
83Omaha-23
84Omaha-14
85Omaha-1

Gorman, Dave
89Utica/Pucko-9
90Utica/Pucko-18

Gorman, Dirk
90Kissim/DIMD-12

Gorman, Mike
86GlenF-7

Gorman, Thomas A.
(Tom)
53B/BW-61
54B-17
55Rodeo
56T-246
57T-87
58T-235
59T-449

Gorman, Thomas P.
(Tom)
80Memphis-4
82Wichita-5
83Tidew-11
84Nes/792-774
84T-774
84Tidew-14
85F-83
85T-53
86F-82
86Portl-7
86T-414
91WIZMets-146

Gorman, Tom
55B-293ump

Gorsica, John
47TipTop

Gorski, Gary
86Cram/PCL-82
88Modesto-11
88Modesto/Cal-62
89Modesto/Chong-12

Gorton, Chris
89Hamil/Star-15
90Foil/Best-181
90Spring/Best-20
91StPete/ClBest-7
91StPete/ProC-2270

Goryl, John
58T-384
59T-77
61Clover-7
62T-558
63T-314
64T-194
78OrlTw
81D-527MG
81T-669MG
82BK/Indians-3CO
82BK/Indians-4CO
82Wheat/Ind
83Wheat/Ind-15CO
85Polar/Ind-xx
86OhHenry-CO
87Gator-CO
88Gator-45CO

Goselin, Scott
88Pulaski/ProC-1751
89Sumter/ProC-1107

Gosger, Jim
63T-553R
66OPC-114
66T-114
67OPC-17
67T-17
68T-343
69MB-95
69T-482
70Expos/Pins-6
70T-651
71LaPizza-4
71MLB/St-128
71OPC-284
71T-284
72MB-119
91WIZMets-147

Goshay, Henry Lee
88VeroB/Star-8
89Dunedin/Star-5

Goshgarian, Dee Marge
91Salinas/ClBest-28

Goslin, Leon
(Goose)
25Exh-123
26Exh-123
27Exh-61
28Exh-61
29Exh/4-31
31Exh/4-29
33CJ/Pin-9
33DH-21
33Exh/4-15
33G-110
33G-168
34Exh/4-12
35BU-85
35Exh/4-12
35G-1H
35G-3F
35G-5F
35G-6F
36Exh/4-12
37Exh/4-12
37OPC-111
40PB-232
48Swell-13
61F-35
80Pac/Leg-104
80SSPC/HOF
81Detroit-124
87Conlon/2-38
91Conlon/Sport-62
92Conlon/Sport-437
E120
E210-49
R300
R308-173
R309/2
R312/M
R313
R314
R315-A11
R315-B11
R316
R332-27
V300
V355-43
V61-8
W502-49
W517-47
W573

Goss, Howie
62T-598R
63T-364

Gossage, Rich
(Goose)
73OPC-174
73T-174
74OPC-542
74T-542
75OPC-554
75T-554
75T/M-554
76Ho-77
76OPC-180
76OPC-205LL
76SSPC-156
76T-180
76T-205LL
77Ho-128
77T-319
78BK/Y-10
78K-8
78T-70
79BK/Y-10
79Ho-48
79OPC-114
79T-225
79T-8LL
80OPC-77
80T-140
81D-347
81F-89
81F/St-118
81K-41
81MSA/Disc-14
81OPC-48
81T-460
81T/HT
81T/Nat/Super-7
81T/St-113
81T/St-251
81T/St-8
82D-283
82F-37
82F/St-116
82K-32
82OPC-117IA
82OPC-286AS
82OPC-396
82T-557AS
82T-770
82T-771IA
82T/St-140
82T/St-217
83D-157
83F-381
83K-10
83OPC-240
83OPC-241SV
83RoyRog/Disc-2
83T-240
83T-241SV

83T/Gloss40-11
83T/St-100
84D-396
84F-125
84F/X-44
85FunFood/Pin-85
84Mother/Padres-2
84Nes/792-670
84Nes/792-718LL
84OPC-121
84Seven-22E
84T-670
84T-718LL
84T/St-316
84T/Tr-43
85D-185
85D/AAS-14
85F-33
85F/LimEd-10
85F/St-108
85Leaf-204
85Mother/Padres-5
85OPC-90
85Seven-9W
85T-90
85T/3D-27
85T/Gloss40-19
85T/St-147
85T/Super-49
85ThomMc/Discs-30
86D-185
86D-2DK
86D/AAS-31
86D/DKsuper-2
86F-322
86F/Mini-68
86F/Slug-12
86Leaf-2DK
86Meadow/Stat-20
86OPC-104
86Sf-190
86Sf-55M
86T-530
86T/3D-6
86T/Gloss60-56
86T/St-107
86T/Super-26
87Bohem-54
87Classic-96
87D-483
87F-415
87F/LL-21
87OPC-380
87RedFoley/St-9
87T-380
87T/St-109
88Berg/Cubs-54
88D-434
88D/Best-26
88D/Cubs/Bk-NEW
88F-583
88F/Up-U76
88OPC-170
88S-331
88S/Tr-14T
88T-170
88T/Tr-41T
89D-158
89F-425
89Mother/Giants-27
89OPC-162
89S-223
89T-415
89T/LJN-75
89T/WaxBox-D
89UD-452
90D-678
90PublInt/St-68
91B-271
91Classic/III-98
91F/Up-U59
91Leaf/I-236
91Leaf/Stud-125
91Mother/Rang-16
92D/II-555
92F-305
92S/II-538
92T-215

Gosse, John
80WHave-19

Gotay, Julio
62T-489
63IDL-10
63J-161
63P-161
63T-122
65T-552
68Coke
68Dexter-35
68OPC-41
68T-41
69MB-96

Gotay, Ruben
83ArkTr-2

Gott, James
(Jim)
81ArkTr-17
83D-353
83OPC-62
83T-506
84D-268
84F-155
84Nes/792-9
84OPC-9
84T-9
84Tor/Fire-14
85D-632
85F-105
85F/Up-U45
85Leaf-136
85Mother/Giants-21
85OPC-311
85T-311
85T/Tr-40T
86D-358
86F-542
86Mother/Giants-21
86OPC-106
86T-463
87F/Up-U35
87Mother/SFG-19
87T/Tr-39T
88D-606
88D/Best-213
88F/Up-U112
88Leaf-253
88S-320
88T-127
89B-411
89D-362
89F-210
89F/Excit-16
89F/Superstar-18
89OPC-172
89Panini/St-163
89S-257
89S/HotStar-98
89Sf-83
89T-752
89T/Mini-41
89UD-539
89VFJuice-35
90D-605
90F-466
90Mother/Dodg-24
90OPC-292
90Pol/Dodg-35
90PublInt/St-155
90S-515
90T-292
90UD-89
90UD/Ext-701
91D-601
91F-200
91Leaf/I-229
91Mother/Dodg-24
91OPC-606
91Pol/Dodg-35
91S-621
91T-606
91UD-690
92D/II-601
92F-454
92S/I-172
92T-517

Goucher, Steve
91BendB/ClBest-6
91BendB/ProC-3691

Goughan, Bob
88RochR/Gov-32

Gould, Bob
85Madis-14
85Madis/Pol-11
86Madis-9
86Madis/Pol-9
87Modesto-11

Gould, Frank
90Everett/Best-5
90Everett/ProC-3121

Goulding, Rich
77Clinton
78LodiD

Gouldrup, Gary
85Elmira-8

Governor, Tony
28Exh/PCL-8

Gowdy, Hank
11Helmar-78
14CJ-138
15CJ-138
16FleischBrd-33
21Exh-59
21Exh-60
40PB-82
72F/FFeat-33
87Conlon/2-39
88Conlon/3-12
91Conlon/Sport-209
BF2-51
D327
D328-62
D329-70
D350/2-70
E120
E121/120
E121/80
E122
E135-62
E220
M101/4-70
M101/5-70
R313
T207
V100
W501-90
W514-67
W516-23
W572
W573
W575
W711/1
W711/2

Gowell, Larry
73Syrac/Team-9

Gozzo, Mauro
(Goose)
84LitFalls-21
86Lynch-13
87Memphis-3
87Memphis/Best-20
88Memphis/Best-16
89Knoxvl/Best-8
89Knoxvl/ProC-1145
89Knoxvl/Star-6
90D-655
90F-82
90OPC-274
90S-610
90S/100Ris-48
90Sf-168
90Syrac/CMC-2
90Syrac/ProC-565
90Syrac/Team-11
90T-274
90T/89Debut-44
91ColoSp/LineD-82
91ColoSp/ProC-2179
91MajorLg/Pins-19
91S-843

Grabarkewitz, Bill
70OPC-446
70T-446
71K-56
71MD
71MLB/St-104
71OPC-85
71T-85
71T/Coins-21
71T/tatt-5
71Ticket/Dodg-7
72T-578
73OPC-301
73T-301
74OPC-214
74T-214
74T/St-74
75OPC-233
75T-233
75T/M-233
75Tucson-8
87Smok/Dodg-9
89Smok/Dodg-76
90Target-291

Graber, Red
61Union

Grable, Rob
91Niagara/ClBest-14
91Niagara/ProC-3641

Grabowski, Al F.
No Cards.

Grabowski, Joe
R310

Grabowski, Johnny
91Conlon/Sport-124

Grabowski, Reggie J.
No Cards.

Grace, Joe
52Mother-5
V355-103
W753

Grace, Mark
86Peoria-8
87Pittsfld-10
88Berg/Cubs-17
88D-40RR
88D/Best-4
88D/Cubs/Bk-40
88D/Rook-1
88F-641R
88F/Mini-68
88F/Up-U77
88IowaC/CMC-14
88IowaC/ProC-539
88Leaf-40RR
88Peoria/Ko-11
88Peoria/Ko-34M
88S/Tr-80T
88T/Tr-42T
89B-291
89Bz-12
89Classic-13
89Classic/Up/2-155
89D-17DK
89D-255
89D/DKsuper-17DK
89F-426
89F/BBMVP's-15
89F/Excit-17
89F/LL-17
89F/Superstar-19
89Holsum/Discs-12
89KMart/DT-1
89Mara/Cubs-17
89Nissen-12
89OPC-297
89Panini/St-55
89S-362
89S/HotRook-78
89S/Mast-22
89S/YS/I-3
89Sf-15
89T-465
89T/Big-189
89T/Coins-15
89T/Gloss60-29
89T/HeadsUp-15
89T/JumboR-11
89T/St-324
89T/St-50
89ToysRUs-12
89UD-140
90B-29
90Classic-8
90CollAB-31
90Cub/Mara-9
90D-577
90D/BestNL-51
90F-32
90F/BB-12
90F/LgStand-6
90F/LL-12
90HotPlay/St-17
90Leaf/I-137
90MLBPA/Pins-51
90OPC-240
90Panini/St-241
90Post-19
90PublInt/St-194
90PublInt/St-613
90RedFoley/St-38
90S-150
90S/100St-60
90Sf-15
90Starline/LJS-16
90Starline/LJS-2
90Starline/LJS-40
90T-240
90T/Big-19
90T/DH-27
90T/Gloss60-12
90T/Mini-49
90T/St-56
90T/TVAS-63
90T/TVCub-23
90UD-128
91B-433
91Classic/200-105
91Classic/I-27
91CollAB-20
91Cub/Mara-17
91D-199
91F-422
91F/Ultra-61
91Leaf/I-170
91Leaf/Stud-157
91MajorLg/Pins-66
91OPC-520
91Panini/FrSt-43
91Panini/St-48
91Post-22
91S-175
91S/100SS-91
91Seven/3DCoin-6MW
91T-520
91T/CJMini/I-24
91T/StClub/I-290
91T/SU-16
91UD-134
91UD-99TC
92D/I-281
92F-381
92S/100SS-20
92S/II-445
92T-140
92UD-143

Grace, Michael
87Anchora-15
89SLCity-14
90Rockford/ProC-2702
91Batavia/ClBest-22
91Batavia/ProC-3478
91WinSalem/ClBest-20
91WinSalem/ProC-2837

Grace, Mike
77Indianap-12
78Indianap-16
79Indianap-18
80Indianap-4
83ColumAst-4

Grace, Robert Earl
34DS-69
34G-58
35BU-69
R314

Grachen, Tim
83QuadC-12

Grady, Pat
80Batavia-26

Graff, Milt
57T-369
58T-192
59T-182

Graff, Stephen
86Erie-9

Graffagnino, Anthony
91Idaho/ProC-4335

Graham, Bert
M116

Graham, Bill
91WIZMets-148

Graham, Brian
83Madis/LF-28
84Albany-6
85Huntsvl/BK-14
87Kinston-11
88EastLAS/ProC-51
88Wmsprt/ProC-1313
89Watertn/Star-11
90CLAS/CL-32MG
90Kinston/Team-28MG
91CLAS/ProC-CAR16MG
91Kinston/ClBest-28MG
91Kinston/ProC-340MG

Graham, Bruce
85Everett/II/Cram-3TR
87Everett-33TR
89Phoenix/ProC-1488TR

Graham, Dan
79Toledo-6
80T-669R
81D-233
81F-189
81OPC-161
81T-161
82D-455
82F-167
82RochR-10
82T-37
91Crown/Orio-161
Graham, Derick
91Billings/ProC-3766
Graham, Everett
82Clinton-10
86Phoenix-7
87Shrev-1
88Phoenix/CMC-20
88Phoenix/ProC-60
89MidldA/GS-16
Graham, George
(Peaches)
11Helmar-95
C46-63
E270/2
E90/1
M116
S74-43
S74-62
T201
T202
T204
T205
T206
T207
T3-95
Graham, Gordie
91Bluefld/ProC-4134
91Bluefld/ClBest-2
Graham, Greg
91WinHaven/ClBest-18
91WinHaven/ProC-497
Graham, Jack
50B-145
90Target-292
Graham, Jeffrey L.
87Spring/Best-9
Graham, John
(Johnny)
88AubAs/ProC-1971
89AubAs/ProC-2177
90AubAs/Best-20MG
Graham, Lee
81Pawtu-19
83Pawtu-22
84Pawtu-2
85Richm-19
86Richm-7
Graham, Lew
84LitFalls-23
Graham, Lindsey
74Gaston
Graham, Otto
52Wheat
Graham, Randy
83Greens-8
84Nashvl-8
85Albany-8
86Colum-10
86Colum/Pol-9
87Colum-23
87Colum/Pol-11
87Colum/TCMA-5
Graham, Steve
88Hamil/ProC-1745
89Hamil/Star-13
90StPete/Star-9
Graham, Tim
90Elmira/Pucko-1
91Elmira/ClBest-6
91Elmira/ProC-3283
Graham, Wayne
91WIZMets-149
Graham, William
T206
Grahe, Joe
91Classic/200-50
91Classic/III-27
91D-737
91Edmon/LineD-164
91Edmon/ProC-1513
91OPC-426
91S-367RP
91T-426
91T/90Debut-58
91UD-657
92D/II-445
92S/100RisSt-97
92S/II-674
92T-496
92UD-542
Grahek, Larry
81CharR-22
Grahovac, Mike
89Everett/Star-8
90ClintUp/Team-U5
91Clinton/ProC-837
Gralewski, Bob
88CapeCod-5
88CapeCod/Sum-154
Grammas, Alex
54Hunter
54T-151
55B-186
55Hunter
55T-21
55T/DH-107
56T-37
57Sohio/Reds-6
57T-222
58T-254
59T-6
60T-168
61P-177
61T-64
61T/St-87
62J-168
62P-168
62P/Can-168
62Salada-197
62Shirriff-197
62T-223
63T-416
73OPC-296CO
73T-296CO
74OPC-326CO
74T-326CO
76SSPC-620
76T-606MG
77T-51MG
88Pep/T-CO
89Mara/Tigers-CO
90CokeK/Tiger-28CO
91CokeK/Tiger-xCO
Granco, Julio
86Cram/PCL-79
Grandas, Bob
79Ogden/TCMA-25
80Ogden-11
81Tacoma-27
82Tacoma-35
83Evansvl-19
Grandquist, Ken
82IowaC-27
83IowaC-29
84IowaC-5
85IowaC-26
Graney, Jack
92Conlon/Sport-481
D327
D328-63
D329-71
D350/2-71
E120
E121/120
E121/80
E135-63
E220
M101/4-71
M101/5-71
T207
W501-112
W573
W575
Grange, Red
33SK-4
Granger, George
R314/Can
Granger, Jeff
91T/Tr-49T
Granger, Lee
82Miami-19
83SanJose-4
84RochR-7
85CharlO-2
Granger, Wayne
69T-551
70MLB/St-27
70OPC-73
70T-73
71MLB/St-59
71OPC-379
71T-379
72T-545
73OPC-523
73T-523
74OPC-644
74T-644
76OPC-516
76T-516
89Pac/SenLg-202
Grant, Bob
77Wausau
Grant, Charles
52Park-10
Grant, Charlie
74Laugh/Black-23
86Negro/Frit-70
Grant, Ed
10Domino-49
11Helmar-115
12Sweet/Pin-100
E104
E270/2
E90/1
E94
M116
S74-75
T201
T202
T205
Grant, Frank
74Laugh/Black-17
Grant, Jim
(Mudcat)
58T-394
59Kahn
59T-186
60Kahn
60L-25
60T-14
61Kahn
61P-60
61T-18
61T/St-135
62Kahn
62Salada-26
62Shirriff-26
62T-307
63Sugar-23
63T-227
64Kahn
64T-133
64T/Coins-99
64T/St-37S4
64Wheat/St-19
65T-432
66Bz-37
66OPC-40
66T-224LL
66T-40
66T/RO-3
67T-545
68T-398
69Fud's-4
69MLB/St-158
69T-306
69T/St-55
71MLB/St-201
71OPC-509
71T-509
72MB-120
72OPC-111
72T-111
78TCMA-200
85Durham-15C
89Pac/Leg-186
89Swell-84
90Target-293
91Swell/Great-34
Grant, Ken
86QuadC-12
87PalmSp-7
88QuadC/GS-21
88Visalia/Cal-152
88Visalia/ProC-86
Grant, Larry
90Elmira/Pucko-6
91WinHaven/ClBest-19
91WinHaven/ProC-498
Grant, Mark
82Clinton-23
84Cram/PCL-3
85Cram/PCL-199
85D-601
86Phoenix-8
87D-644
87Mother/SFG-26
88Coke/Padres-55PAN
88D-511
88D/Best-133
88F-584
88Smok/Padres-9
88T-752
89Coke/Padre-5
89F-304
89S-349
89S/YS/I-12
89T-178
89T/Big-154
89UD-622
90Coke/Padre-5
90D-441
90F-156
90OPC-537
90Padre/MagUno-20
90Publint/St-49
90S-466
90T-537
90UD-412
91D-361
91F-690
91OPC-287
91S-824
91T-287
91UD-301
Grant, Tom
82IowaC-3
83IowaC-22
84IowaC-30
85IowaC-9
Grantham, George
25Exh-52
26Exh-52
31Exh/4-14
33CJ/Pin-10
33Exh/4-4
33G-66
91Conlon/Sport-292
R316
V353-66
W513-76
Grapenthin, Dick
84Indianap-16
86LasVegas-4
87Louisvl-14
88AAA/ProC-24
88Louisvl-20
88Louisvl/CMC-2
88Louisvl/ProC-426
89Colum/CMC-23
89Colum/Pol-9
89Colum/ProC-747
Graser, Rick
80SanJose/JITB-9
80Wausau-18
Grasso, Newton M.
(Mickey)
49B/PCL-6
51B-205
52B-174
52T-90
53B/Col-77
53Briggs
53T-148
54B-184
91T/Arc53-148
Grate, Don
88Chatt/Team-13
Grater, Mark
87Savan-11
88Spring/Best-2
89StPete/Star-14
90Louisvl/CMC-21
90Louisvl/ProC-397
91Louisvl/LineD-236
91Louisvl/ProC-2909
92T/91Debut-66
Graupmann, Tim
83Wisco/LF-9
84Visalia-16
Graven, Tim
79Savan-7
Graves, Chris
87QuadC-22
88QuadC/GS-27
89PalmSp/Cal-40
89PalmSp/ProC-483
Graves, Frank M.
N172
Graves, Joe
83Lynch-20
84Jacks-8
86Jaxvl/TCMA-11
Graves, John
89Butte/SP-21
90A&AASingle/ProC-82
90Gaston/Best-23
90Gaston/ProC-2517
90Gaston/Star-10
90SALAS/Star-9
Graves, Kenley
85Bend/Cram-7
Graves, Kenny
90T/TVMets-44
Graves, Randy
90Kissim/DIMD-13
Gray, Dan
91Yakima/ClBest-10
91Yakima/ProC-4250
Gray, Dave
64T-572R
Gray, David
88Lynch/Star-7
89Lynch/Star-9
Gray, Dennis Jr.
89Alaska/Team-16
91StCath/ClBest-16
91StCath/ProC-3388
Gray, Dick
58T-146
59T-244
60T-24
90Target-294
Gray, Elliott
89Martins/Star-13
90Batavia/ProC-3057
91Clearw/ClBest-1
91Clearw/ProC-1616
91Single/ClBest-141
Gray, Gary
76SanAn/Team-11
77Tucson
78Cr/PCL-38
79Tucson-1
80Tacoma-17
81F-402
81T/Tr-767
82F-511
82OPC-78
82SLCity-9
82T-523
82T/St-233
83D-637
83F-480
83T-313
Gray, Jeff
86Vermont-8
87Nashvl-8
88Nashvl/CMC-5
88Nashvl/ProC-478
88Nashvl/Team-10
89Nashvl/CMC-3
89Nashvl/ProC-1288
89Nashvl/Team-5
90Pawtu/CMC-25
90Pawtu/ProC-456
91D-721
91F-95
91Leaf/II-356
91OPC-731
91Pep/RSox-7
91S-586
91T-731
91T/StClub/I-271
91UD-685
92D/I-122
92S/I-187
Gray, John L.
55Rodeo
55T-101
55T/DH-48
Gray, Lorenzo

77AppFx
80GlenF/B-22
80GlenF/C-20M
80GlenF/C-26
82Edmon-10
84Maine-12
84Nes/792-163
84T-163
86SanJose-9

Gray, Pete
88MinorLg/Leg-2

Gray, Samuel
25Exh-107
29Exh/4-29
31Exh/4-30
33Exh/4-15
91Conlon/Sport-75

Gray, Scott
86AubAs-10

Gray, Stanley
43Centen-10
44Centen-9

Gray, Steve
89Clinton/ProC-899
89Salinas/ProC-1802

Gray, Ted
49B-10
50B-210
51B-178
52B-199
52T-86
53B/Col-72
53T-52
54B-71
55B-86
81Detroit-131
91Crown/Orio-162
91T/Arc53-52

Gray, Terry
77StPete

Gray, William
(Dolly)
11Helmar-68
12Sweet/Pin-58
E90/1
T202
T205
T206

Graybill, Dave
87Jaxvl-15
89PalmSp/Cal-59

Grayner, Paul
82Nashvl-13
83Nashvl-7TR

Grayson, Mike
89Beloit/I/Star-7

Grayston, Joe
85BurlR-1

Grayum, Richie
89Geneva/ProC-1871
91WinSalem/ClBest-24
91WinSalem/ProC-2841

Grba, Eli
60T-183
61T-121
62T-96
63T-231
64T-464
65T-203
82Vanco-23
88Vanco/ProC-769
89Reno/Cal-265MG
90Princet/DIMD-28MG
91Martins/ProC-3471CO

Grebe, Brett
90Pulaski/Best-5
90Pulaski/ProC-3103

Grebeck, Brian
90Boise/ProC-3321
91QuadC/ClBest-17
91QuadC/ProC-2636

Grebeck, Craig
87Penin-10
88BirmB/Best-24
89BirmB/Best-17
89BirmB/ProC-111
90B-318
90BirmDG/Best-15
90Coke/WSox-28
90Coke/WSox-6
90D/Rook-9
90F/Up-U85
90S/Tr-105T
90UD/Ext-721
91D-378
91F-120
91F/UltraUp-U15
91Kodak/WSox-14
91OPC-446
91S-69
91S/100RisSt-35
91T-446
91T/90Debut-59
91T/StClub/II-559
92D/II-546
92F-81
92S/II-561
92T-273
92UD-603

Greco, George
80Elmira-7

Green, Bob
86FtLaud-9
87FtLaud-6
88Albany/ProC-1331
89Albany/Best-10
89Colum/CMC-20
89Colum/Pol-8
89Colum/ProC-734

Green, Charlie
87Watertn-29

Green, Christopher
82AlexD-6
85Cram/PCL-240
86Edmon-14
87RochR/TCMA-22

Green, Daryl
86Cram/PCL-88
87QuadC-10
88QuadC/GS-13
89Modesto/Cal-271
89Modesto/Chong-11
90Huntsvl/Best-6
91StPete/ClBest-8
91StPete/ProC-2271

Green, David A.
80Holyo-14
82Louisvl-10
83D-166
83F-6
83T-578
83T/St-323
84D-425
84D-625
84F-323
84Nes/792-362
84OPC-362
84T-362
84T/St-149
85D-303
85F-224
85F/Up-U46
85Leaf-191
85Mother/Giants-17
85OPC-87
85T-87
85T/St-145
85T/Tr-41T
86D-114
86F-543
86OPC-122
86T-727
87Louisvl-15
88F-34
88Louisvl-21
88Louisvl/CMC-14
88Louisvl/ProC-421
91Tulsa/LineD-582
91Tulsa/ProC-2784

Green, Donald
(Don)
89Hamil/Star-18
90Savan/ProC-2066

Green, Edward
(Danny)
E107

Green, Elijah
(Pumpsie)
60T-317
61T-454
62Salada-187
62Shirriff-187
62T-153
63T-292
64T-442
91WIZMets-151

Green, Fred
60T-272
61T-181

Green, G. Dallas
60L-52
60T-366
61T-359
62Salada-219
62Shirriff-219
62T-111
63T-91
64T-464
65OPC-203
65T-203
78TCMA-187
80BK/P-1MG
81D-415MG
81T-682MG
89S/NWest-31MG
89T-104MG
91WIZMets-150

Green, Gary
85Beaum-18
85T-396OLY
86LasVegas-5
87LasVegas-22
88LasVegas/CMC-17
88LasVegas/ProC-232
89UD/Ext-722
90OkCty/CMC-13
90OkCty/ProC-439
91OPC-184
91T-184
91T/StClub/II-323

Green, Gene
58T-366
59T-37
60L-82
60T-269
61T-206
62J-72
62P-72
62P/Can-72
62Salada-70
62Shirriff-70
62T-78
63Sugar-10
63T-506
91Crown/Orio-163

Green, Harvey
90Target-962

Green, Jeff
83BuffB-8

Green, John
86Geneva-7
86Peoria-9
87Peoria-3
87Peoria/PW-3
89FtLaud/Star-7

Green, Larry
76Dubuq

Green, Lenny
58T-471
59T-209
60T-99
61Clover-8H
61Peters-15
61T-4
62J-87
62P-87
62P/Can-87
62Salada-69A
62Salada-69B
62Shirriff-69
62T-84
62T/bucks
62T/St-75
63J-6
63P-6
63T-198
64T-386
65T-588
66T-502
91Crown/Orio-164

Green, Nat
85Bend/Cram-8

Green, Otis
86Syrac-11
87Syrac-15
87Syrac/TCMA-14
88Syrac/CMC-19
88Syrac/ProC-831
89Syrac/CMC-12
89Syrac/ProC-793
89Syrac/Team-11
90Indianap/CMC-18
90Indianap/ProC-293
91Stockton/ClBest-2
91Stockton/ProC-3028

Green, Randy
80Ogden-5

Green, Richard
64T-466R
65OPC-168
65T-168
66T-545
67OPC-54
67T-54
68T-303
69MB-97
69T-515
69T/St-215
70MLB/St-258
70OPC-311
70T-311
71MLB/St-514
71OPC-258
71T-258
72MB-121
72T-780
73OPC-456
73T-456
74OPC-392
74T-392
75OPC-91
75T-91
75T/M-91

Green, Rick
77Visalia

Green, Shawn
92T-276
92UD-55TP

Green, Stephen W.
88Bakers/Cal-248
89VeroB/Star-9
90London/ProC-1279

Green, Steve
78Holyo
80OrlTw/B-4
82OrlTw/A-15

Green, Terry
86Osceola-9
87Osceola-25
88ColAst/Best-22

Green, Tom
(Tom)
90Welland/Pucko-13
91Augusta/ClBest-20
91Augusta/ProC-819

Green, Tyler
90WichSt-13
91Batavia/ClBest-20
91Batavia/ProC-3479
91Classic/DP-7
91FrRow/DP-34
92S/II-810DP
92T-764DP
92UD-68TP

Greenberg, Hank
34DS-54
34G-62
35BU-57
35G-8F
35G-9F
36G
36Wheat
37OPC-107
38Exh/4-12
38G-253
38G-277
38ONG/Pin-13
38Wheat
39Exh
39PB-56
39Wheat-7
40PB-40
41DP-52
41DP-85
41PB-18
41Wheat-16
55Gol/Ind-9
60NuCard-42
61GP-4
61NuCard-442
63Bz-19
80Pac/Leg-30
80SSPC/HOF
81Detroit-133
83D/HOF-16
83Kaline-39M
85T/Gloss22-22
85West/2-33
86Sf/Dec-4
89Pac/Leg-195
91Conlon/Sport-14
92Conlon/Sport-430
92Conlon/Sport-590
PR1-13
R302
R303-B
R303/A
R309/2
R311/Gloss
R312
R313
R314
R346-35
R423-38
V300
V355-41

Greenberg, Steve
76Dubuq

Greene, Altar
(Al)
80Evansvl-8
80T-666R

Greene, Ed
86Beloit-8

Greene, Grant
76Laugh/Clown-8

Greene, Henry
77DaytB

Greene, Ira Thomas
(Tommy)
86Sumter-7
87Greenvl/Best-23
88Richm-33
88Richm/CMC-1
88Richm/ProC-2
89AAA/ProC-54
89Richm/Bob-7
89Richm/CMC-3
89Richm/Ko-33
89Richm/ProC-831
90B-1
90Classic/Up-22
90D-576
90F-584
90Richm/Bob-9
90Richm/CMC-20
90Richm/ProC-253
90Richm/Team-10
90S-640
90S/YS/II-24
90Sf-224
90T/89Debut-45
90UD-49
91Classic/200-66
91D-635
91F/UltraUp-U99
91F/Up-U108
91Leaf/II-524
91OPC-486
91Phill/Medford-15
91S-808
91T-486
91T/StClub/II-549
91UD/FinalEd-62F
92D/I-109
92D/I-94HL
92F-531
92S/I-336
92S/I-426NH
92T-83
92UD-567

Greene, James
(Joe)
78Laugh/Black-13

Greene, Jeff
86Sumter-6
87Durham-22
87Penin-20
88Tampa/Star-8

Greene, Keith
86Cram/PCL-137
87Spartan-8

Greene, Nelson
90Target-963

Greene, Steve

77BurlB
Greene, Todd
91T/Tr-50T
Greene, Willie
90A&AASingle/ProC-96
90Augusta/ProC-2470
90B-173
90S-682DC
91B-448
91Single/ClBest-350
91WPalmB/ClBest-20
91WPalmB/ProC-1236
Greenfield, Kent
90Target-295
92Conlon/Sport-617
Greengrass, Jim
53T-209
54B-28
54T-22
55B-49
56T-275
56YellBase/Pin-12
58Union
91T/Arc53-209
Exh47
Greenhalgh, Ted
46Sunbeam
Greenlee, Gus
88Negro/Duques-5OWN
Greenlee, Robert
87SanBern-19
Greenwell, Mike
85IntLgAS-44
85Pawtu-4
86Pawtu-10
86Sf-178R
87D-585
87D/Rook-4
87F/Up-U37
87Sf/Rook-8
87T-259
88Classic/Blue-227
88D-339
88D/Best-177
88D/RedSox/Bk-339
88F-354
88F-630M
88F/Excit-16
88F/Hottest-14
88F/Mini-7
88F/St-9
88Leaf-153
88OPC-274
88Panini/St-32
88S-175
88S/YS/I-24
88Sf-118
88T-493
88T/Big-233
88T/Coins-14
88T/Gloss60-20
88T/JumboR-3
88T/St-249
88T/St-312
88ToysRUs-12
89B-34
89Cadaco-24
89Classic-149
89D-186
89D-1DK
89D/AS-15
89D/Best-28
89D/DKsuper-1DK
89D/GrandSlam-5
89D/MVP-BC13
89F-90
89F/AS-6
89F/BBAS-16
89F/BBMVP's-16
89F/Excit-18
89F/Heroes-19
89F/LL-18
89F/Superstar-20
89F/WaxBox-C11
89KayBee-15
89Nissen-6
89OPC-374
89Panini/St-280
89S-659HL
89S-66
89S/HotStar-70
89S/Mast-36
89Sf-143
89Sf-221M
89T-402AS
89T-630
89T/Big-211
89T/Coins-41
89T/DH-6
89T/Gloss60-31
89T/HeadsUp-22
89T/Hills-15
89T/LJN-147
89T/Mini-48
89T/St-255
89T/St/Backs-16
89T/UK-32
89UD-432
90B-274
90Classic-47
90D-66
90D/BestAL-115
90D/Bon/MVP-BC17
90D/Learning-32
90F-277
90F-632M
90F/BB-13
90F/BBMVP-13
90F/LL-13
90F/WaxBox-C8
90Leaf/I-143
90MLBPA/Pins-71
90OPC-70
90Panini/St-16
90Pep/RSox-11
90PublInt/St-287
90PublInt/St-457
90RedFoley/St-39
90S-345
90S/100St-67
90Sf-50
90T-70
90T/Big-61
90T/DH-28
90T/St-254
90T/TVAS-22
90T/TVRSox-30
90Tetley/Discs-18
90UD-354
91B-116
91Classic/200-18
91Classic/III-29
91D-553
91D/GSlam-14
91F-96
91F/ProV-8
91F/Ultra-32
91Leaf/I-19
91Leaf/Stud-15
91OPC-792
91Panini/FrSt-268
91Panini/Top15-32
91Pep/RSox-8
91S-130
91S/100SS-82
91T-792
91T/CJMini/II-34
91T/StClub/I-253
91UD-165
91UD-43TC
92D/II-523
92F-39
92S/100SS-10
92S/II-545
92T-113
92UD-275
Greenwell, Richard
89LittleSun-12
Greenwood, Bob
55B-42
Greenwood, John
88Pulaski/ProC-1753
Greenwood, Mike
87Pocatel/Bon-9
Greenwood, William
N172
Greer, Brian K.
80T-685R
82Amari-2
Greer, Edward C.
N172
N403
Greer, Ken
88Oneonta/ProC-2047
89PrWill/Star-8
90FtLaud/Star-9
91FtLaud/ClBest-4
91FtLaud/ProC-2418
Greer, Randy
80Penin/B-14
80Penin/C-20
Greer, Rusty
91CharlR/ClBest-21
91CharlR/ProC-1325
91FSLAS/ProC-FSL4
91Single/ClBest-172
Gregg, Eric
88TM/Umpire-34
89TM/Umpire-32
90TM/Umpire-31
Gregg, Hal
47TipTop
49Eureka-161
52T-318
90Target-296
Gregg, Tommy
86Nashua-9
87Harris-19
88BuffB/CMC-12
88BuffB/ProC-1474
88D-203
88F/Up-U113
88S/Tr-69T
89Classic/Up/2-192
89D-121
89D/Best-170
89F-592
89Panini/St-32
89T/Tr-39T
89UD/Ext-751
90D-239
90F-585
90Leaf/I-86
90OPC-223
90Panini/St-224
90PublInt/St-114
90S-78
90S/YS/I-39
90T-223
90UD-121
91D-244
91F-691
91F/Ultra-6
91Leaf/I-144
91OPC-742
91Panini/FrSt-19
91S-606
91T-742
91T/StClub/II-571
92D/II-485
92S/II-623
92T-53
Gregg, Sylvanus
16FleischBrd-34
Gregg, Vean
14CJ-29
15CJ-29
T207
W514-33
WG5-17
WG6-16
Gregory, Brad
90Miami/I/Star-10
Gregory, Grover
(Lee)
62Kahn/Atl
Gregory, John
83VeroB-17
Gregory, Paul
47Signal
Gregory, Scott
78Dunedin
Gregson, Glenn
83MidldC-3
84MidldC-14
87WinSalem-12
Gregson, Goose
88GreatF-27
89GreatF-33
90Bakers/Cal-246
91AS/Cal-24
Greif, Bill
72OPC-101R
72T-101R
73T-583
74McDon
74OPC-102
74T-102
75OPC-168
75T-168
75T/M-168
76OPC-184
76T-184
77OPC-243
77T-112
Greiner, Dan
W514-80
Grejtak, Bryan
91Bluefld/ProC-4130
91Bluefld/ClBest-13
Greminger, Edward
T206
T213/brown
Grennan, Steve
91Pocatel/ProC-3777
Gresham, Kris
91Bluefld/ProC-4131
91Bluefld/ClBest-1
Gress, Loren
90Idaho/ProC-3270
91Idaho/ProC-4336
91Macon/ProC-871
Grewal, Ranbir
90James/Pucko-17
91MidwLAS/ProC-MWL45
91Rockford/ClBest-5
91Rockford/ProC-2040
Grich, Bob
71OPC-193
71T-193
72OPC-338
72T-338
73JP
73K-39
73OPC-418
73T-418
74OPC-109
74T-109
74T/DE-8
74T/St-125
75Ho-72
75K-4
75OPC-225
75T-225
75T/M-225
76Ho-13
76Ho/Twink-13
76OPC-335
76SSPC-388
76T-335
77BurgChef-126
77Ho-131
77K-39
77OPC-28
77Pepsi-25
77T-521
78Ho-62
78OPC-133
78T-18
79Ho-112
79OPC-248
79T-447
80OPC-326
80T-621
81D-289
81F-269
81F/St-50
81OPC-182
81T-182
81T/HT
81T/St-53
82D-90
82F-461
82F/St-218
82K-38
82OPC-284
82PermaGr/AS-5
82T-162LL
82T-284
82T/St-162
82T/St-4LL
83D-468
83F-91
83K-60
83OPC-381
83OPC-387AS
83Seven-11
83T-387
83T-790
83T/St-43
84D-179
84F-518
84Nes/792-315
84OPC-315
84Smok/Cal-10
84T-315
84T/St-228
85D-280
85F-302
85Leaf-88
85OPC-155
85Smok/Cal-12
85T-465
85T/St-230
86D-207
86F-157
86OPC-155
86Smok/Cal-12
86T-155
86T-486M
86T/St-181
86Woolwth-12
87D-456
87F-81
87OPC-4
87RedFoley/St-30
87Sf-184
87T-677
89Smok/Angels-11
90Pac/Legend-31
90Swell/Great-58
91Crown/Orio-165
Grief
E270/2
Grief, Bill
73OPC-583
74T/St-92
Grier, Antron
87Erie-12
88Hamil/ProC-1723
88Savan/ProC-355
89Spring/Best-3
90StPete/Star-10
Grier, Dave
80BurlB-5
82ElPaso-17
Grier, Mark
79Newar-14
Griesser, Grant
90AppFox/Box-10
90AppFox/ProC-2097
Grieve, Tom
71MLB/St-540
71OPC-167
71T-167
72T-609
73OPC-579
73T-579
74OPC-268
74T-268
75Ho-38
75OPC-234
75T-234
75T/M-234
76Ho-130
76OPC-106
76SSPC-270
76T-106
77BurgChef-25
77Ho-93
77T-403
78T-337
79OPC-138
79T-277
79Tucson-14
91WIZMets-152
Grieve, William
55B-275ump
Griffen, Leonard
91Cedar/ClBest-5
91Cedar/ProC-2713
Griffey, Craig
92UD-51CL
92UD-85M
Griffey, G. Ken
74OPC-598R
74T-598R
75OPC-284
75T-284
75T/M-284
76Crane-17
76Icee
76K-44
76MSA/Disc
76OPC-128

76SSPC-40
76T-128
77BurgChef-206
77Ho-59
77K-49
77OPC-11
77Pep-50
77T-320
78K-4
78OPC-140
78T-80
79Ho-45
79K-39
79OPC-216
79T-420
80OPC-285
80T-550
81Coke
81D-184
81F-199
81F/St-60
81OPC-280
81T-280
81T/HT
81T/SO-91
81T/St-163
82D-634
82F-67
82F/St-16
82OPC-171IA
82OPC-330
82T-620
82T-621SA
82T-756TL
82T/St-38
82T/St-38
82T/Tr-40T
83D-486
83F-382
83OPC-110
83RoyRog/Disc-3
83T-110
83T/St-98
84D-613
84D/AAS-21
84D/Champs-25
84F-126
84Nes/792-770
84OPC-306
84T-770
84T/St-317
85D-347
85F-128
85Leaf-193
85OPC-380
85T-380
86D-126
86F-105
86Leaf-48
86OPC-40
86T-40
86T/Tr-41T
87D-513
87D/OD-42
87F-516
87F/Mini-46
87F/St-49
87OPC-114
87Smok/Atl-19
87T-711
88D-202
88D/Best-141
88F-540
88Leaf-165
88OPC-255
88Panini/St-248
88RedFoley/St-28
88S-390
88Sf-178
88T-443
88T/Big-110
88T/St-38
89B-259FS
89F/Up-84
89Kahn/Reds-30
89S-609
89T/Tr-40T
90B-60
90D-469
90F-420
90Kahn/Reds-10
90KayBee-13
90OPC-581
90PublInt/St-30
90S-338
90T-581
90T/Big-100
90UD-682
91B-255
91Classic/200-141
91Classic/II-T21
91CounHrth-19
91CounHrth-28M
91D-452
91F/Ultra-335
91Griffey-4M
91Leaf/II-503
91Leaf/Stud-113
91MajorLg/Pins-5
91Mother/Griffey-2
91Mother/Griffey-3M
91Mother/Griffey-4M
91OPC-465
91S-835
91S-841M
91Seven/3DCoin-4NW
91T-465
91T/StClub/II-342
91UD-572
92T-250
92UD-335
92UD-85M

Griffey, Ken Jr.
88CalLgAS-26
88SanBern/Best-1
88SanBern/Cal-34
89B-220
89B-259FS
89Classic-131
89Classic/Up/2-193
89D-33RR
89D/Best-192
89D/Rook-3
89F-548
89Mother/Griffey-1
89Mother/Griffey-2
89Mother/Griffey-3
89Mother/Griffey-4
89Mother/Sea-3
89S/Mast-30
89S/Tr-100
89S/YS/II-18
89T/HeadsUp-5
89T/Tr-41T
89UD-1
90B-481
90Bz-18
90Classic-20
90Classic/III-T1
90CollAB-3
90D-365
90D-4DK
90D/BestAL-1
90D/Learning-8
90D/SuperDK-4DK
90F-513
90F/AwardWin-16
90F/BB-14
90F/BBMVP-14
90F/LL-14
90F/SoarSt-6
90F/WaxBox-C10
90HotRook/St-19
90KingB/Discs-16
90Leaf/I-245
90Leaf/Prev-4
90MLBPA/Pins-117
90Mother/Mar-3
90MSA/Soda-17
90OPC-336
90Panini/St-155
90Post-23
90PublInt/St-433
90PublInt/St-595
90RedFoley/St-40
90S-560
90S/100Ris-3
90Sf-7
90Sunflower-2
90T-336
90T/89Debut-46
90T/Big-250
90T/Coins-16
90T/DH-29
90T/Gloss60-20
90T/HeadsUp-5
90T/JumboR-11
90T/St-225
90T/St-323FS
90Tetley/Discs-8
90ToysRUs-13
90UD-156
90UD-24TC
90USPlayC/AS-11S
90Windwlk/Discs-7
90WonderBrd-18
91Arena-2
91B-246
91BBBest/HitM-7
91Classic/200-120
91Classic/I-3
91Classic/II-T1
91Classic/III-30
91Colla/Griffey-Set
91CollAB-4
91CounHrth-15
91CounHrth-28M
91D-392MVP
91D-49AS
91D-77
91D/Preview-4
91F-450A
91F-450B
91F-710M
91F/ASIns-7
91F/Ultra-336
91F/UltraG-4
91Griffey-1
91Griffey-2
91Griffey-3
91Griffey-4M
91JDeanSig-2
91KingB/Discs-6
91Leaf/II-372
91Leaf/Stud-112
91MajorLg/Pins-4
91MooTown-4
91Mother/Griffey-1
91Mother/Griffey-3M
91Mother/Griffey-4M
91OPC-392AS
91OPC-790
91OPC/Premier-56
91Panini/FrSt-172
91Panini/FrSt-233
91Panini/St-189
91Panini/Top15-116
91Pep/Griffey-Set
91Petro/SU-23
91Post-11
91Post/Can-26
91RedFoley/St-120
91RedFoley/St-41
91S-2
91S-396AS
91S-697RF
91S-841M
91S-858FRAN
91S-892DT
91S/100SS-5
91S/Cooper-B3
91Seven/3DCoin-3SC
91Seven/3DCoin-4A
91Seven/3DCoin-4NW
91Seven/3DCoin-5NW
91Seven/3DCoin-6NC
91Seven/3DCoin-6NE
91Seven/3DCoin-7F
91Seven/3DCoin-7MW
91Seven/3DCoin-8T
91Sunflower-11
91T-392AS
91T-790
91T/CJMini/I-36
91T/StClub/I-270
91T/SU-17
91UD-555
91UD/FinalEd-79FCL
91UD/FinalEd-87FAS
91USPlayC/AS-1D
92Classic/I-40
92D/Elite-E13
92D/I-165
92D/I-24AS
92D/Preview-7
92F-279
92F-709PV
92F/ASIns-23
92F/TmLIns-15
92S/100SS-1
92S/I-1
92S/I-436AS
92S/Prev-1
92T-50
92UD-424
92UD-650DS
92UD-85M

Griffin, Alan
75Tucson-21
76Tucson-34
78SanJose-9

Griffin, Alfredo
79T-705R
80OPC-290
80T-558
81D-149
81F-430
81OPC-277
81OPC/Post-15
81T-277
81T/St-140
82D-101
82F-615
82F/St-236
82OPC-148
82T-677
82T/St-252
83D-180
83F-429
83OPC-294
83T-488
83T/St-129
84D-605
84F-156
84Nes/792-76
84OPC-76
84T-76
84T/St-369
84Tor/Fire-15
85D-73
85F-106
85F/Up-U47
85Leaf-230
85Mother/A's-5
85OPC-361
85T-361
85T/St-366
85T/Tr-42T
86D-101
86F-417
86Leaf-34
86Mother/A's-5
86OPC-121
86Sf-136M
86T-566
86T/St-168
87D-256
87D/OD-28
87F-392
87Leaf-198
87OPC-111
87Sf-164
87Smok/A's-4
87T-111
87T/St-166
88D-226
88D/Best-92
88F-280
88F/Up-U94
88Mother/Dodg-7
88OPC-42
88Panini/St-172
88Pol/Dodg-7
88S-88
88S/Tr-37T
88Sf-156
88T-726
88T/Big-247
88T/St-169
88T/Tr-43T
89B-345
89D-79
89D/Best-178
89F-58
89Mother/Dodg-7
89OPC-62
89Pol/Dodg-5
89S-167
89T-62
89T/St-59
89UD-631
90B-95
90D-195
90D/BestNL-103
90F-395
90Leaf/I-95
90Mother/Dodg-8
90OPC-643
90Panini/St-270
90Pol/Dodg-7
90PublInt/St-6
90S-156
90T-643
90T/Big-18
90T/St-58
90Target-297
90UD-338
91B-592
91D-488
91F-201
91F/Ultra-161
91Leaf/II-344
91Mother/Dodg-8
91OPC-226
91Panini/FrSt-58
91Pol/Dodg-7
91S-442
91T-226
91T/StClub/II-524
91T/WaxBox-G
91UD-119
92D/II-692
92F-455
92S/I-254
92T-418
92UD-282

Griffin, Barry
88Boise/ProC-1614

Griffin, Dave
83Ander-20
84Durham-8
85Durham-24
86Greenvl/Team-11
87Richm/Crown-24
87Richm/TCMA-13
88Richm-34
88Richm/CMC-19
88Richm/ProC-20
89Colum/CMC-27
89Toledo/CMC-12
89Toledo/ProC-785

Griffin, Doug
71OPC-176R
71T-176R
72T-703
72T-704IA
73OPC-96
73T-96
74OPC-219
74T-219
75OPC-454
75T-454
75T/M-454
76OPC-654
76SSPC-412
76T-654
77T-191
89Pac/SenLg-53

Griffin, Frankie
83Reading-6

Griffin, Greg
83Knoxvl-17

Griffin, Ivy M.
V100

Griffin, Mark
89Star/Wax-29
89VeroB/Star-10
90VeroB/Star-16
91FSLAS/ProC-FSL38
91Single/ClBest-236
91VeroB/ClBest-27
91VeroB/ProC-787

Griffin, Michael
N172
N300/unif

Griffin, Mike
77Ashvl
79WHave-17
81Colum-10
81F-107
81T-483
82D-553
82T-146
83OKCty-8
84OKCty-7
85Omaha-13
86Omaha-8
86Omaha/TCMA-15
87French-42

87RochR-9
87RochR/TCMA-3
88D-494
88F-561
88RochR/Team-9
88RochR/CMC-7
88RochR/Gov-8
88RochR/ProC-210
89Nashvl/CMC-4
89Nashvl/ProC-1274
89Nashvl/Team-6
90CharWh/Best-27CO
90CharWh/ProC-2258CO
90Target-298
91Chatt/LineD-175CO
91Chatt/ProC-1975CO

Griffin, Nuje
91Crown/Orio-166

Griffin, Rick
90Mother/Mar-28TR

Griffin, Terry
88LitFalls/Pucko-16
89StLucie/Star-8

Griffin, Tim
91VeroB/ClBest-20
91VeroB/ProC-781
91Yakima/ClBest-11
91Yakima/ProC-4253

Griffin, Tom
69T-614R
70T-578
71MLB/St-81
71OPC-471
71T-471
72MB-122
73OPC-468
73T-468
74OPC-256
74T-256
75OPC-188
75T-188
75T/M-188
76OPC-454
76T-454
77Padre/SchCd-12
77T-39
78T-318
79Pol/Giants-43
79T-291
80Pol/Giants-43
80T-649
81D-75
81F-456
81T-538
82D-474
82F-389
82T-777

Griffin, Ty
88T/Tr-44T
89B-289
89CharlK-14
89Peoria/Ko-1
89T-713FDP
89T/Big-170
90B-37
90T/TVCub-45
91CharlK/LineD-134
91CharlK/ProC-1700

Griffith, Clark C.
10Domino-50
11Helmar-69
12Sweet/Pin-101A
12Sweet/Pin-101B
14Piedmont/St-25
48Exh/HOF
50Callahan
60Exh/HOF-12
60F-15
61F-36
63Bz/ATG-37
80Pac/Leg-37
80SSPC/HOF
92Conlon/Sport-464
D329-72
E220
E93
M101/4-72
M116
N172
S74-76
T202
T204
T205
T206
T213/blue
T215/blue
T215/brown
T3-77
W514-41
W555
WG2-22
WG5-18
WG6-17

Griffith, Jeff
87Watertn-22
88Augusta/ProC-363

Griffith, Kerry
86Erie-10

Griffith, Robert D.
(Derrell)
65OPC-112
65T-112
66T-573
67T-502
90Target-299

Griffith, Thomas H.
(Tommy)
15CJ-167
16FleischBrd-35
90Target-300
91Salinas/ClBest-6
91Salinas/ProC-2255
D327
D328-64
D329-73
D350/2-72
E120
E121/120
E121/80
E122
E135-64
M101/4-73
M101/5-72
V100
V61-58
W501-106
W515-35
W572
W575

Griffith, Tommy
89Boise/ProC-1984

Griffiths, Brian
89Ashvl/ProC-955
90Osceola/Star-8
91Osceola/ClBest-3
91Osceola/ProC-675

Grifol, Pedro
91Elizab/ProC-4303

Griggs, Hal
58T-455
59T-434
60L-34
60T-244

Grijak, Kevin
91Idaho/ProC-4337

Grilione, Dave
86Cram/PCL-94
87QuadC-29

Grilk, Jim
40Hughes-8

Grilli, Guido
66T-558R

Grilli, Steve
76OPC-591R
76T-591R
77T-506
78Syrac
79Syrac-17
81Syrac-4

Grim, Bob
55B-167
55RM-AL5
55T-80
55T/DH-58
56T-52
57T-36
58T-224
59T-423
60L-10
60T-78
62T-564

Grim, John
90Target-964

Grimes, Bob
88CharWh/Best-27
89Peoria/Ko-32TR

Grimes, Burleigh A.
21Exh-61
25Exh-12
26Exh-11
27Exh-7
28Yueng-1
32Orbit/num-26
32Orbit/un-21
33G-64
35G-1F
35G-3D
35G-4D
35G-5D
60F-59
61F-37
80Pac/Leg-51
80SSPC/HOF
83D/HOF-21
89Smok/Dodg-8
90Target-301
91Conlon/Sport-25
92Conlon/Sport-433
E120
E210-1
R305
R308-191
R315-A12
R315-B12
R316
V100
V353-64
V61-89
W502-1
W513-72
W515-16
W572

Grimes, David
(Dave)
89Spring/Best-2
90StPete/Star-11
91ArkTr/LineD-35
91ArkTr/ProC-1278

Grimes, John
84Everett/Cram-25
86Shrev-9
87Shrev-22

Grimes, Lee
87WinSalem-14
88CharWh/Best-6

Grimes, Michael
(Mike)
88CapeCod/Sum-122
89Medford/Best-6
91Madison/ClBest-4

Grimes, Oscar Ray
21Exh-62
44Yank/St-13
E120
V61-105
W572
W573

Grimes, Steve
76Cedar
78Holyo

Grimm, Charlie
21Exh-63
25Exh-21
26Exh-21
27Exh-10
29Exh/4-6
30CEA/Pin-4
31Exh/4-6
32Orbit/num-37
32Orbit/un-22
33CJ/Pin-11
33Exh/4-3
33G-51
34Exh/4-3
34G-3
34Ward's/Pin-6
35Exh/4-3
40PB-228
53B/Col-69MG
53JC-1MG
54JC-40MG
55B-298MG
55Gol/Braves-12MG
55JC-40MG
60T-217
80Pac/Leg-75
87Conlon/2-40
88Conlon/4-12
91Conlon/Sport-95
91T/Arc53-321MG
E120
E121/120
E126-19
E220
R300
R305
R332-15
R337-423
V100
V353-51
V354-61
V355-89
W501-82
W575
WG8-25

Grimshaw, Myron
(Moose)
E254
T206

Grimsley, Jason
85Bend/Cram-9
88Clearw/Star-12
89BBAmerAA/BPro-AA4
89Reading/Best-10
89Reading/ProC-670
89Reading/Star-12
90B-151
90F-653R
90OPC-493
90Phill/TastyK-10
90S-649RP
90ScranWB/CMC-3
90ScranWB/ProC-595
90T-493
90T/89Debut-47
90UD-27SR
91D-653
91F-396
91Leaf/II-288
91OPC-173
91Phill/Medford-16
91S-818
91T-173
91T/StClub/I-294
92D/II-599
92F-532
92S/II-711
92UD-406

Grimsley, Ross
72OPC-99
72T-99
73OPC-357
73T-357
74OPC-59
74T-59
74T/Tr-59T
75K-2
75OPC-458
75T-458
75T/M-458
76OPC-257
76SSPC-377
76T-257
77BurgChef-40
77OPC-47
77T-572
78T-691
79Ho-5
79K-3
79OPC-4
79T-15
79T/Comics-26
80K-1
80OPC-195
80T-375
81F-406
81T-170
84Chatt-8
86Calgary-10C
87Calgary-5CO
89BurlB/ProC-1614
89Pac/SenLg-117
89TM/SenLg-40
90EliteSenLg-81
90Penin/Star-26CO
91Calgary/LineD-75CO
91Calgary/ProC-531CO
91Crown/Orio-167

Griner, Dan
90Target-965

Grisham, Wes
90LSUPol-2
90Welland/Pucko-15

Grissom, Antonio
90Martins/ProC-3195
91Batavia/ClBest-13
91Batavia/ProC-3496
91Spartan/ClBest-24
91Spartan/ProC-909

Grissom, Lee
38Wheat
39PB-2
90Target-302
W711/1

Grissom, Marquis
88James/ProC-1910
89BBAmerAA/BPro-AA14
89Jaxvl/Best-1
89Jaxvl/ProC-175
90B-115
90Classic-65
90D-36RR
90D/BestNL-128
90D/Rook-45
90F-347
90HotRook/St-20
90Leaf/I-107
90OPC-714
90S-591RP
90S/100Ris-99
90S/DTRook-B9
90S/YS/II-6
90Sf-134
90T-714
90T/89Debut-48
90T/Big-138
90UD-9SR
90UD/Ext-702M
91B-435
91Classic/200-119
91Classic/II-T38
91D-307
91F-234
91F/Ultra-204
91Leaf/I-22
91Leaf/Stud-198
91OPC-283
91Panini/FrSt-151
91S-234
91S/100RisSt-38
91T-283
91T/StClub/I-8
91ToysRUs-9
91UD-477
92D/I-137
92F-482
92S/I-66
92T-647
92UD-455

Grissom, Marv
54NYJour
55B-123
55Gol/Giants-11
55RM-NL25
56T-301
57T-216
58Hires-64
58SFCallB-10
58T-399
59T-243

Groat, Dick
52T-369
53T-154
54T-43
55T-26
55T/DH-100
56T-24
56T/Hocus-A1
56T/Hocus-B3
56T/Pin-42SS
57Kahn
57T-12
58Hires-21
58Kahn
58T-45
59Kahn
59T-160
60Kahn
60T tattoo
60T-258
60T/tatt-20
61Bz-8
61Kahn
61NuCard-413
61P-129
61T-1
61T-41LL

61T-486MV
61T/Dice-5
61T/St-64
62Exh
62J-172
62Kahn
62P-172
62P/Can-172
62Salada-138
62Shirriff-138
62Sugar-A
62T-270
62T/bucks
62T/St-177
63Exh
63J-139
63Kahn
63P-139
63Salada-16
63T-130
64Bz-2
64T-40
64T-7LL
64T/Coins-147AS
64T/Coins-5
64T/S-19
64T/St-81S9
64T/SU
64T/tatt
64Wheat/St-20
65OldLond-11
65OPC-275
65T-275
65T/trans-15
66OPC-103
66T-103
67T-205
75OPC-198MV
75T-198MV
75T/M-198MV
78TCMA-150
85West/2-40
88Pac/Leg-108
89Swell-91
90Pac/Legend-26
90Swell/Great-49
91Swell/Great-35
91T/Arc53-154
Exh47
WG10-29
WG9-30

Grob, Connie
59DF

Groch, Dick
89EastLDD/ProC-DD47CO

Groennert, John
87SLCity/Taco-8
88Billings/ProC-1815

Groh, Don
83Peoria/LF-5
85Cram/PCL-4

Groh, Heinie
15CJ-159
16FleischBrd-36
21Exh-64
21Exh-65
25Exh-34
88Pac/8Men-81
91Conlon/Sport-163
D327
D328-65
D329-74
D350/2-73
E120
E121/120
E121/80
E135-65
E220
M101/4-74
M101/5-73
V61-88
W501-67
W514-46
W515-52
W516-2
W572
W573
W575
WG7-19

Grohs, Mike
91Spokane/ClBest-4
91Spokane/ProC-3943

Gromek, Steve
49B-198
50B-131
50NumNum
51B-115
52B-203
52NumNum-8
52T-258
53B/BW-63
54B-199
55B-203
56T-310
56YellBase/Pin-13
57T-258
79TCMA-133
Exh47

Groninger, Gerry
88Billings/ProC-1803
89Cedar/Best-23
89Cedar/Star-23
90Billings/ProC-3238MG
91Fayette/ClBest-14MG
91Fayette/ProC-1186MG

Groom, Bob
10Domino-51
11Helmar-70
12Sweet/Pin-59
14CJ-46
14Piedmont/St-26
15CJ-46
92Conlon/Sport-350
D328-66
E135-66
E270/2
E90/1
E91
T202
T205
T206
T213/blue
T215
T3-96

Groom, Buddy
88Tampa/Star-9
89BirmB/Best-24
89BirmB/ProC-109
89SLAS-17
90BirmB/Best-16
90BirmB/ProC-1104
91London/LineD-386
91London/ProC-1872

Groppuso, Mike
91Classic/DP-39
91FrRow/DP-39

Gross, Bob
87Gaston-5

Gross, Deryk
89Kenosha/ProC-1064
89Kenosha/Star-8
90Kenosha/Best-4
90Kenosha/ProC-2306
90Kenosha/Star-5

Gross, Don
57Kahn
57Sohio/Reds-7
57T-341
58T-172
59T-228
60T-284

Gross, George
78DaytB
80Tucson-10
81Tucson-22

Gross, Greg
75Ho-101
75K-5
75OPC-334
75T-334
75T/M-334
76Ho-90
76K-56
76OPC-171
76SSPC-64
76T-171
77T-614
78T-397
79BK/P-22
79OPC-302
79T-579
80BK/P-12
80OPC-364
80T-718
81D-598
81F-18
81T-459
82D-371
82F-246
82T-53
83D-441
83F-162
83T-279
84D-285
84F-31
84Nes/792-613
84Phill/TastyK-35
84T-613
85CIGNA-5
85D-407
85F-251
85F/St-53
85OPC-117
85Phill/TastyK-12M
85Phill/TastyK-35
85T-117
86CIGNA-5
86D-163
86F-441
86OPC-302
86Phill/TastyK-21
86T-302
87D-385
87F-173
87OPC-338
87Phill/TastyK-21
87RedFoley/St-20
87T-702
88D-412
88F-302
88Phill/TastyK-11
88S-386
88T-518
89F-568
89Lennox/Ast-2
89Mother/Ast-12
89S-125
89T-438
89T/WaxBox-E
89UD-534
91Padre/MagRal-12CO

Gross, John
90AppFox/Box-11
91BBCity/ClBest-4
91BBCity/ProC-1391
91Single/ClBest-35

Gross, Kevin
83Portl-5
84D-381
84F-32
84Nes/792-332
84Phill/TastyK-20
84T-332
85CIGNA-14
85D-477
85F-252
85Phill/TastyK-18
85Phill/TastyK-9M
85T-584
86CIGNA-8
86D-529
86F-442
86Phill/TastyK-46
86T-764
86T/St-119
87D-236
87F-174
87OPC-163
87Phill/TastyK-46
87T-163
88D-113
88D/Best-103
88F-303
88OPC-20
88Phill/TastyK-12
88S-468
88T-20
88T/St-118
89B-355
89D-194
89D/AS-48
89D/Best-202
89D/MVP-BC12
89D/Tr-3
89F-569
89F/Up-96
89OPC-215
89Panini/St-147
89S-227
89S/Tr-39
89Sf-213
89T-215
89T/St-116
89T/Tr-42T
89UD-31
89UD/Ext-719
90B-109
90D-248
90D/BestNL-18
90F-348
90Leaf/I-61
90OPC-465
90PublInt/St-174
90S-251
90T-465
90T/Big-3
90T/St-76
90UD-468
91B-611
91D-569
91F-235
91F/Up-U94
91Leaf/II-279
91Mother/Dodg-17
91OPC-674A
91OPC-674B
91Pol/Dodg-45
91S-22
91S/RookTr-51T
91T-674A
91T-674B
91UD-380
91UD/Ext-713
92D/I-279
92F-456
92S/I-34
92T-334
92UD-515

Gross, Kip
87Lynch-5
88FSLAS/Star-6
89Jacks/GS-22
91Nashvl/LineD-259
91Nashvl/ProC-2150
91T/90Debut-60
92F-407
92S/100RisSt-92
92S/II-740
92T-372

Gross, Wayne
76Tucson-25
77T-479R
78Ho-141
78OPC-106
78T-139
79T-528
80OPC-189
80T-363
81D-237
81F-587
81OPC-86
81T-86
81T/St-118
82D-139
82F-90
82F/St-124
82Granny-2
82OPC-303
82T-692
83D-591
83F-517
83Granny-10
83T-233
84D-375
84F-444
84F/X-45
84Nes/792-741
84OPC-263
84T-741
84T/St-333
84T/Tr-44
85D-228
85F-179
85OPC-233
85T-416
86D-535
86F-276
86OPC-173
86T-173
87Mother/A's-17
91Crown/Orio-168

Grossman, Bob
75OkCty
75SanAn
76Wmsprt

Grossman, Dave
82Edmon-24
86IowaC-12tr
88IowaC/ProC-531
89IowaC/ProC-1703

Grossman, Jim
87Kinston-8

Grote, Bob
79Jacks-8

Grote, Gerald
(Jerry)
64T-226R
65T-504
66T-328
67T-413
68T-582
69MB-98
69MLB/St-165
69OPC-55
69T-55
69T/St-63
70MLB/St-76
70OPC-183
70T-183
70Trans-22
71MLB/St-154
71OPC-278
71T-278
71T/GM-54
72MB-123
72T-655
73OPC-113
73T-113
74OPC-311
74T-311
74T/St-62
75OPC-158
75T-158
75T/M-158
76Ho-78
76OPC-143
76T-143
78T-464
79T-279
89Pac/SenLg-120IA
89Pac/SenLg-125
89T/SenLg-34
89TM/SenLg-41
90Target-303
91LineD-17
91Swell/Great-36
91WIZMets-153

Grotewald, Jeff
87Spartan-21
88Clearw/Star-13
89Clearw/Star-10
90Reading/Best-17
90Reading/ProC-1227
90Reading/Star-10
91ScranWB/LineD-484
91ScranWB/ProC-2544

Groth, Bill
52StarCal/L-72F

Groth, Ernest
50Remar

Groth, John
(Johnny)
50B-243
51B-249
51T/BB-11
52B-67
52NTea
52RM-AL10
52T-25
52TipTop
53T-36
54B-165
54Wilson
55B-117
56T-279
56YellBase/Pin-14
57T-360
58T-262
59T-164
60L-133
60T-171
79TCMA-38
81Detroit-33
91T/Arc53-36
Exh47

Grott, Matthew
90A&AASingle/ProC-115

90Madison/ProC-2261
91Huntsvl/ClBest-11
91Huntsvl/LineD-285
91HuntsvlProC-1789
Grout, Ron
79Wisco-7
Grove, George M.
WG7-20
Grove, LeRoy Orval
48L-66
Exh47
Grove, Robert M.
(Lefty)
29Exh/4-27
31Exh/4-28
32Orbit/un-23
33CJ/Pin-12
33DL-23
33Exh/4-14
33G-220
34DS-1
34Exh/4-14
34Exh/4-9
34G-19
35BU-153
35BU-31
35Exh/4-9
35Wheat
36Exh/4-9
36Wheat
37Exh/4-9
37OPC-137
37Wheat-9
38Exh/4-9
38Wheat
39Exh
41DP-105
48Exh/HOF
50Callahan
60F-60
61F-38
61GP-17
72K/ATG-7
72Laugh/GF-16
76OPC-350AS
76T-350AS
80Pac/Leg-27
80Laugh/3/4/5-19
80Laugh/FFeat-8
80SSPC/HOF
86Conlon/1-47
86Sf/Dec-3
88Conlon/4-13
88Conlon/AmAS-13
89HOF/St-74
89Pac/Leg-185
89Swell-15
90BBWit-94
90HOF/St-31
90Swell/Great-70
91Conlon/Sport-23
91Conlon/Sport-255
91Swell/Great-139
92Conlon/Sport-431
92Conlon/Sport-533
PR1-14
R300
R305
R306
R308-182
R310
R312/M
R313
R315-A13
R315-B13
R316
R328-27
R332-49
R337-408
R423-39
V300
V354-54
V355-88
W517-39
Grove, Scott
88Pulaski/ProC-1752
89Sumter/ProC-1114
90BurlB/Best-18
90BurlB/ProC-2344
90BurlB/Star-13
Groves, Jeff
86Greenvl/Team-12
Groves, Larry
86Indianap-27
Grovom, Carl
86AubAs-11
87CharWh-15
88Osceola/Star-11
91Jacks/ProC-920
Grow, Lorin
76Indianap-14
Grubb, Cary
88Reno/Cal-281
Grubb, John
(Johnny)
74McDon
74OPC-32SD
74T-32
74T/St-93
75Ho-109
75K-43
75OPC-298
75T-298
75T/M-298
76OPC-422
76SSPC-130
76T-422
77OPC-165
77Pep-10
77T-286
78T-608
79OPC-99
79T-198
80OPC-165
80T-313
81D-148
81F-631
81T-545
82D-467
82F-317
82OPC-193
82T-496
83D-341
83F-567
83T-724
83T/St-123
83T/Tr-38
84D-90
84F-81
84Nes/792-42
84T-42
85Cain's-9
85D-578
85F-9
85T-643
85Wendy-10
86Cain's-7
86D-615
86F-227
86T-243
87Cain's-12
87Coke/Tigers-18
87D-476
87F-152
87T-384
87T/St-265
88Richm-27
88S-199
88T-128
89Pac/SenLg-191
89Richm/Bob-8CO
89Richm/CMC-24CO
89Richm/Ko-CO
89Richm/ProC-821CO
89TM/SenLg-42
90EliteSenLg-57
90Richm/CMC-2CO
90Richm/ProC-275CO
90Richm/Team-11CO
91Richm/ProC-2586CO
Grubb, Sean
89Hamil/Star-17
Grube, Frank
32Orbit/num-5
32Orbit/un-24
34G-64
35G-8C
35G-9C
92Conlon/Sport-399
R305
W753
Gruber, Henry
N172
Gruber, Kelly
80Batavia-21
81Watlo-22
82Chatt-16
83BuffB-16
84Syrac-27
84Tor/Fire-16
85F-645R
85IntLgAS-37
85Syrac-22
85Tor/Fire-13
86Ault-17
86D/Rook-16
86Tor/Fire-15
87D-444
87F-227
87OPC-191
87T-458
87Tor/Fire-11
88D-244
88D/Best-255
88F-111
88OPC-113
88Panini/St-221
88S-422
88T-113
88T/Big-134
88Tor/Fire-17
89B-251
89D-113
89D/Best-31
89F-234
89OPC-29
89Panini/St-469
89S-194
89S/YS/II-12
89Sf-163
89T-201TL
89T-29
89T/Big-95
89T/St-187
89Tor/Fire-17
89UD-575
90B-519
90Classic/III-70
90D-113
90D-12DK
90D/BestAL-84
90D/Learning-30
90D/SuperDK-12DK
90F-83
90Leaf/I-106
90OPC-505
90Panini/St-171
90PublInt/St-515
90RedFoley/St-41
90S-425
90S/McDon-9
90Sf-57
90T-505
90T/Big-17
90T/St-193
90Tor/BlueJ-17
90UD-111
90USPlayC/AS-5S
90Windwlk/Discs-5
91B-18
91B-369SLUG
91Classic/200-19
91D-149
91DennyGS-6
91F-175
91F/Ultra-361
91Leaf/I-9
91Leaf/Stud-135
91OPC-370
91OPC-388AS
91OPC/Premier-57
91Panini/FrSt-338
91Panini/St-161
91Panini/Top15-112
91Panini/Top15-22
91Petro/SU-26
91Post/Can-15
91RedFoley/St-42
91S-595
91S/100SS-64
91S/ToroBJ-15
91Sunflower-12
91T-370
91T-388AS
91T/CJMini/II-4
91T/StClub/II-331
91Tor/Fire-17
91UD-374
91UD-44TC
91UD/SilSlug-SS7
92D/I-65
92D/Preview-8
92F-329
92S/100SS-64
92S/II-495
92T-298
92UD-324
Grudzielanek, Mark
91James/ClBest-4
91James/ProC-3553
Grudzinski, Gary
85PrWill-19
Grunard, Dan
86QuadC-13
87PalmSp-8
Grundler, Frank
75Shreve/TCMA-4
76Shrev
Grunhard, Dan
(Danny)
85Anchora-12
88MidldA/GS-16
89MidldA/GS-17
90Edmon/CMC-16
90Edmon/ProC-528
91Edmon/LineD-165
91Edmon/ProC-1528
Grunsky, Gary
76Baton
Grundt, Ken
91Everett/ClBest-18
91Everett/ProC-3906
Grunwald, Al
60T-427
Grygiel, Joe
91Spokane/ClBest-16
91Spokane/ProC-3944
Gryskevich, Larry
89Hamil/Star-14
90Savan/ProC-2073
Grzenda, Joe
69OPC-121
69T-121
70T-691
71MLB/St-541
71OPC-518
71T-518
72OPC-13
72T-13
91WIZMets-154
Grzybeck, Ben
77DaytB
Gsellman, Bob
87CharWh-8
Guanchez, Harry
91AppFx/ClBest-18
91AppFx/ProC-1724
Guante, Cecilio
81Portl-10
82Portl-3
83D-423
84D-78
84F-250
84Nes/792-122
84T-122
85D-357
85F-465
85T-457
86D-142
86F-609
86T-668
87D-238
87F-610
87F/Up-U38
87OPC-219
87T-219
87T/St-127
87T/Tr-40T
88D/Best-276
88D/Y/Bk-NEW
88T-84
89D-260
89F-519
89Mother/R-23
89S-439
89Smok/R-10
89T-766
89UD-576
90D-403
90F-298
90Leaf/II-365
90OPC-532
90PublInt/St-410
90S-438
90T-532
Guarache, Jose
88StCath/ProC-2011
Guardado, Eddie
91Elizab/ProC-4296
Gubanich, Creighton
91SoOreg/ProC-3850
Gubicza, Mark
84F/X-46
84T/Tr-45
85D-344
85F-201
85OPC-127
85T-127
86D-583
86F-8
86Kitty/Disc-19
86Leaf-226
86NatPhoto-23
86T-644
87D-466
87F-368
87F/Excit-20
87F/Mini-47
87Leaf-238
87OPC-326
87T-326
88D-54
88D/Best-95
88F-259
88F/RecSet-15
88OPC-378
88S-516
88Smok/Royals-12
88T-507
88T/Big-199
88T/St-262
89B-117
89Cadaco-25
89Classic-138
89D-179
89D/AS-18
89D/Best-119
89F-283
89F/BBAS-17
89F/Excit-19
89OPC-379
89Panini/St-350
89S-291
89S/HotStar-69
89S/YS/II-14
89Sf-102
89T-430
89T/Big-26
89T/Mini-55
89T/St-271
89T/St/Backs-26
89T/UK-33
89Tastee/Discs-9
89UD-202
90B-363
90D-204
90D/BestAL-77
90F-109
90F-633M
90F/BB-15
90F/LL-15
90Leaf/I-145
90MLBPA/Pins-105
90OPC-20
90Panini/St-82
90PublInt/St-349
90S-121
90T-20
90T/Big-201
90T/St-272
90UD-676
91Classic/200-20
91D-145
91F-560
91F/Ultra-148
91Leaf/Stud-67
91OPC-265
91Panini/St-228
91Pol/Royal-11
91S-212
91T-265
91T/StClub/I-240
91UD-541
92D/I-282
92F-159
92S/II-459
92T-741

92UD-459
Guenther, Bob
87Myrtle-26
Guercio, Maurice
86FSLAS-19
86FtLaud-10
87Albany-6
Guerra, Fermin
(Mike)
49B-155
50B-157
51B-202
Guerra, Pete
91BurlInd/ProC-3303
Guerra, Rich
75SanAn
76Wmsprt
Guerrero, Alex
75QuadC
Guerrero, Inocencio
(Ino)
83Durham-4
86Greenvl/Team-13
87Greenvl/Best-17
88Greenvl/Best-4
89Durham/Team-26CO
89Durham/Star-28
Guerrero, Juan
87Pocatel/Bon-27
88Clinton/ProC-701
89SanJose/Best-21
89SanJose/Cal-219
89SanJose/ProC-451
89SanJose/Star-11
89Star/Wax-86
90Shrev/ProC-1450
90Shrev/Star-8
91Shrev/LineD-305
91Shrev/ProC-1828
Guerrero, Mario
73OPC-607R
73T-607R
74OPC-192
74T-192
75OPC-152
75T-152
75T/M-152
76OPC-499
76SSPC-285
76T-499
77T-628
78T-339
79Ho-78
79K-43
79OPC-131
79T-261
80T-49
81F-591
81T-547
89Pac/SenLg-36
89TM/SenLg-43
Guerrero, Mike
88Beloit/GS-15
89Beloit/I/Star-8
90Stockton/Best-8
90Stockton/ProC-2193
91ElPaso/ProC-2754
Guerrero, Patrick
88StCath/ProC-2038
Guerrero, Pedro
78Cr/PCL-11
79Albuq-16
79T-719R
80Pol/Dodg-28
81Pol/Dodg-28
81T-651
82D-136
82F-7
82F/St-6
82OPC-247
82Pol/Dodg-28
82T-247
82T/St-55
82T/St-260
83D-110
83Drake-9
83F-207
83K-20
83OPC-116
83PermaGr/CC-5
83Pol/Dodg-28
83Seven-4
83T-425
83T-681
83T/St-248
84D-174
84D-24DK
84D/AAS-17
84Drake-11
84F-100
84F/St-19
84F/St-34
85FunFood/Pin-26
84MiltBrad-11
84Nes/792-306TL
84Nes/792-90
84OPC-90
84Pol/Dodg-28
84Ralston-30
84Seven-14W
84T-90
84T-306TL
84T/Cereal-30
84T/Gloss40-25
84T/St-75
84T/Super-24
85Coke/Dodg-11
85D-174
85D/AAS-34
85D/HL-19
85Drake-13
85F-370
85Leaf-211
85OPC-34
85Seven-10W
85T-575
85T/St-70
85T/Super-44
85ThomMc/Discs-31
86Coke/Dodg-10
86D-174
86Drake-6
86F-130
86F/AS-8
86F/LimEd-21
86F/Mini-28
86F/Slug-13
86F/St-47
86Leaf-105
86Meadow/Blank-6
86Meadow/Stat-18
86OPC-145
86OPC/WaxBox-G
86Pol/Dodg-28
86Sf-14
86Sf-148M
86Sf-181M
86Sf/Dec-74M
86T-145
86T-706AS
86T/3D-8
86T/Gloss60-25
86T/Mini-44
86T/St-65
86T/Super-27
86T/WaxBox-G
86TrueVal-1
87BK-7
87Classic-39
87D-53
87F-440
87F/Slug-16
87Jiffy-10
87KayBee-14
87Leaf-237
87Mother/Dodg-2
87OPC-360
87Pol/Dodg-14
87RedFoley/St-83
87Sf-27
87Seven-W4
87Smok/Dodg-10
87T-360
87T/Board-27
87T/St-69
88D-278
88D-BC16
88D/AS-48
88D/Best-122
88Drake-26
88F-514
88F-623M
88F/AwardWin-15
88F/Mini-83
88F/Slug-16
88F/St-91
88FanSam-20
88KayBee-12
88KMart-11
88Leaf-101
88Mother/Dodg-2
88Nestle-24
88OPC-111
88Panini/St-314
88Pol/Dodg-28
88RedFoley/St-29
88S-9
88Sf-97
88Smok/Dodg-28
88T-409TL
88T-550
88T/Big-171
88T/Coins-43
88T/Gloss60-24
88T/Mini-52
88T/RiteAid-5
88T/St-75
88T/St/Backs-15
88T/UK-28
89T/Ames-15
89B-440
89Cadaco-26
89Classic-60
89D-418
89D/Best-75
89F-451
89KayBee-16
89KingB/Discs-20
89KMart/DT-33
89KMart/Lead-6
89OPC-68
89Panini/St-183
89RedFoley/St-52
89S-564
89S/HotStar-44
89Smok/Cards-7
89Smok/Dodg-94
89T-780
89T/Big-285
89T/Coins-16
89T/LJN-130
89T/St-40
89T/UK-34
89UD-306
90B-201
90Classic-146
90D-63
90D-674AS
90D/BestNL-95
90D/Bon/MVP-BC6
90F-250
90F/BB-16
90F/BBMVP-15
90F/LL-16
90F/WaxBox-C11
90HOF/St-85
90HotPlay/St-18
90KMart/CBatL-6
90KMart/SS-15
90Leaf/I-44
90MLBPA/Pins-32
90OPC-610
90Panini/St-211
90Panini/St-335
90Post-22
90PublInt/St-219
90RedFoley/St-42
90S-13
90S/100St-61
90Sf-66
90Smok/Card-7
90Sunflower-10
90T-610
90T/Big-13
90T/Coins-47
90T/DH-30
90T/Gloss60-32
90T/HillsHM-6
90T/Mini-75
90T/St-151AS
90T/St-35
90T/TVAS-50
90T/TVCard-25
90Target-304
90UD-244
91B-403
91BBBest/HitM-8
91Classic/200-21
91D-25DK
91D-558
91D/SuperDK-25DK
91DennyGS-22
91F-634
91F/Ultra-289
91Leaf/I-204
91Leaf/Stud-232
91OPC-20
91OPC/Premier-58
91Panini/FrSt-31
91Panini/St-37
91Pol/Card-28
91RedFoley/St-43
91S-140
91T-20
91T/CJMini/I-8
91T/StClub/II-314
91UD-327
91UD-98TC
92D/I-158
92F-579
92S/I-376
92T-470
92UD-357
Guerrero, Ramces
88Idaho/ProC-1844
89Idaho/ProC-2010
Guerrero, Sandy
(Epy)
86Ventura-8
87Stockton-4
88CalLgAS-15
88Stockton/Cal-196
88Stockton/ProC-727
89ElPaso/GS-22
91Denver/LineD-139
91Denver/ProC-130
Guerrero, Tony
81Wisco-4
83Orlan-22
85Visalia-21
Guetterman, Lee
84Chatt-16
86F/Up-U45
87D-322
87F-585
87T-307
88D-270
88D/Y/Bk-NEW
88F-374
88OPC-382
88S-323
88Sf-45
88T-656
89D/Best-108
89S/NWest-24
89T/Tr-43T
90D-127
90F-443
90Leaf/II-333
90OPC-286
90Panini/St-118
90PublInt/St-534
90S-294
90S/NWest-17
90T-286
90T/TVYank-9
90UD-318
91D-124
91F-664
91F/Ultra-232
91Leaf/I-52
91OPC-62
91S-34
91T-62
91T/StClub/II-361
91UD-481
92D/II-507
92F-227
92S/I-244
92T-578
92UD-610
Guggiana, Todd
91B-697
91CharlR/ClBest-18
91CharlR/ProC-1322
91Single/ClBest-204
Guidi, Jim
91SLCity/ProC-3205
Guidry, Ron
76OPC-599R
76T-599R
77BK/Y-11
77T-656
78BK/Y-4
78Ho-25
78PapaG/Disc-28
78T-135
79BK/Y-4
79Ho-89
79K-11
79OPC-264
79T-202RB
79T-500
79T-5LL
79T-7LL
79T/Comics-13
80BK/PHR-4
80K-4
80OPC-157
80T-300
80T/S-7
81D-227
81F-88
81F/St-76
81K-45
81OPC-250
81T-250
81T/St-112
82D-548
82D-558M
82F-38
82F/St-120
82K-26
82OPC-10IA
82OPC-9
82Sqt-9
82T-10IA
82T-9
83D-17DK
83D-31
83D/AAS-15
83F-383
83OPC-104
83RoyRog/Disc-4
83T-440
83T/St-102
84D-173
84D/AAS-51
84F-127
85FunFood/Pin-96
84MiltBrad-12
84Nes/792-110
84Nes/792-406AS
84Nes/792-486TL
84Nes/792-717LL
84Nestle/DT-10
84OPC-110
84OPC-204AS
84Ralston-31
84Seven-16E
84T-110
84T-406AS
84T-486TL
84T-717LL
84T/Cereal-31
84T/Gloss40-14
84T/St-194
84T/St-318
84T/Super-17
85D-214
85F-129
85Leaf-237
85OPC-388
85Pol/MetYank-Y3
85T-790
85T/St-313
85ThomMc/Discs-11
86D-103
86Drake-32
86F-106
86F/Mini-22
86F/Slug-14
86F/St-48
86Leaf-36
86OPC-109
86OPC/WaxBox-H
86Sf-149M
86Sf-18
86Sf-185M
86Sf-57M
86Sf/Dec-71
86T-610
86T-721
86T/3D-9
86T/Gloss60-12
86T/Mini-26
86T/St-302
86T/Super-28

86T/WaxBox-H
87Classic-68
87D-93
87F-100
87F/AwardWin-16
87Leaf-101
87OPC-375
87RedFoley/St-54
87Sf-83
87T-375
87T/St-301
88D-175
88D/Y/Bk-175
88F-207
88F/St-S3
88Leaf-180
88OPC-127
88S-310
88T-535
88T/Big-50
88T/St-296
88T/St/Backs-61
89S-342
89S/NWest-28
89T-255
89T/LJN-111
89UD-307
90HOF/St-97

Guifoyle, Mike
90Bristol/ProC-3166
90Bristol/Star-7
91Fayette/ClBest-2
91Fayette/ProC-1163

Guiheen
T206

Guillen, Ozzie
83Beaum-2
84Cram/PCL-236
85Coke/WS-13
85D/HL-55
85F/Up-U48
85T/Tr-43T
86Coke/WS-13
86D-208
86F-206
86F/LL-17
86F/Mini-44
86F/St-49
86F/WaxBox-C3
86Jay's-9
86KayBee-16
86Leaf-140
86OPC-254
86Quaker-20
86Sf-176M
86Sf-22
86T-254
86T/Gloss60-58
86T/St-294
86T/St-309
86T/Super-7
87Coke/WS-7
87D-87
87D/OD-235
87F-497
87F/AwardWin-17
87F/Mini-48
87F/RecSet-13
87F/St-50
87Kraft-11
87Leaf-117
87OPC-89
87RedFoley/St-67
87Sf-186
87Seven-C9
87T-89
87T/St-287
88Coke/WS-9
88D-137
88D/Best-81
88F-398
88F/Mini-15
88F/RecSet-16
88F/St-16
88Kodak/WSox-1
88Leaf-59
88Nestle-7
88OPC-296
88Panini/St-61
88S-603
88S/YS/I-21
88Sf-14
88T-585
88T/Big-27
88T/St-284
89B-64
89Classic/Up/2-175M
89Coke/WS-10
89D-176
89D/Best-137
89D/MVP-BC23
89F-497
89F/BBAS-18
89KingB/Discs-6
89Kodak/WSox-6M
89OPC-195
89Panini/St-309
89RedFoley/St-53
89S-433
89S/HotStar-51
89Sf-85
89T-195
89T/Big-148
89T/LJN-104
89T/St-303
89T/UK-35
89UD-175
90B-315
90Classic-92
90Coke/WSox-29
90Coke/WSox-7
90D-135
90D-15DK
90D/BestAL-74
90D/Learning-13
90D/SuperDK-15DK
90F-533
90Kodak/WSox-3
90Leaf/I-128
90OPC-365
90Panini/St-41
90PublInt/St-388
90S-6
90S/McDon-21
90Sf-48
90T-365
90T/Big-215
90T/St-298
90T/TVAS-3
90UD-267
90UD-79TC
90USPlayC/AS-6C
90Windwlk/Discs-9
91B-356
91BBBest/HitM-9
91Classic/200-53
91D-577
91F-121
91F/Ultra-74
91Kodak/WSox-13
91Kodak/WSox-xM
91Leaf/II-331
91MooTown-12
91OPC-620
91Panini/FrSt-315
91Panini/St-261
91Panini/Top15-113
91RedFoley/St-44
91S-11
91S-394AS
91S/100SS-15
91Seven/3DCoin-8MW
91T-620
91T/StClub/I-70
91UD-325
91USPlayC/AS-2H
92D/I-229
92F-706M
92F-82
92S/100SS-13
92S/I-92
92T-210
92UD-436

Guin, Greg
82ArkTr-14
83ArkTr-17
84ArkTr-10

Guindon, Bob
65T-509R

Guinn, Brian
86SLAS-8
87Pittsfld-11
88IowaC/CMC-15
88IowaC/ProC-526
89IowaC/CMC-16
89IowaC/ProC-1709
90Iowa/CMC-12
90Iowa/ProC-324
90T/TVCub-46
91Iowa/LineD-206
91Iowa/ProC-1066

Guinn, Drannon E.
(Skip)
69T-614R
70OPC-316
70T-316
71MLB/St-82
71OPC-741
71T-741

Guinn, Wayne
80Cedar-26

Guintini, Ben
48Sommer-14

Guise, Witt
W711/2

Guisto, Lou
D328-67
E135-67

Gulbit, German
89EastLDD/ProC-DD3

Gulden, Brad
77LodiD
78Cr/PCL-46
79Colum-1
80Colum-6
80T-670R
81Spokane-30
83Colum-4
85D-365
85F-537
85OPC-251
85T-251
86Mother/Giants-25
90Target-305

Gull, Sterling
80SLCity-20

Gulledge, Hugh
90Madison/Best-16
91Madison/ProC-2125

Gulledge, William
91Madison/ClBest-8

Gullett, Don
71MLB/St-60
71OPC-124
71T-124
72OPC-157
72T-157
73OPC-595
73T-595
74OPC-385
74T-385
74T/St-27
75Ho-107
75OPC-65
75T-65
75T/M-65
76Crane-18
76Ho-45
76Ho/Twink-45
76Icee
76K-3
76MSA/Disc
76OPC-390
76SSPC-27
76T-390
77BK/Y-6
77BurgChef-172
77Ho-143
77OPC-250
77Pepsi-35
77T-15
78BK/Y-8
78OPC-30
78T-225
78Wiffle/Discs-28
79OPC-64
79T-140
80T-435
91Nashvl/LineD-275CO
91Nashvl/ProC-2173CO

Gullickson, Bill
81D-91
81F-150
81OPC-41
81T-203RB
81T-578
82D-162
82F-190
82Hygrade
82OPC-172
82OPC-94TC
82OPC/Post-21
82T-172
82T-526TL
82Zeller-15
83D-288
83F-284
83OPC-31
83Stuart-15
83T-31
84D-401
84F-276
84Nes/792-318
84OPC-318
84Stuart-16
84T-318
84T/St-96
85D-97
85F-399
85Leaf-236
85OPC-143
85T-687
85T/St-91
86D-331
86D/HL-40
86F-249
86F/Up-U46
86OPC-229
86T-229
86T/St-78
86T/Tr-42T
86TexGold-34
87D-369
87F-203
87F/AwardWin-18
87F/Mini-49
87F/RecSet-14
87F/St-51
87Kahn-34
87Smok/NL-4
87T-489
87T/St-140
88D-586
88F-208
88OPC-329
88S-585
88T-711
90B-65
90Lennox-14
90Mother/Ast-13
90T/Tr-34T
90UD/Ext-799
91B-133
91CokeK/Tiger-36
91F-508
91Leaf/II-402
91Leaf/Stud-55
91S-177
91S/RookTr-56T
91UD-590
92D/I-131
92F-137
92S/I-242
92T-508
92UD-317

Gulliver, Glenn
77Evansvl/TCMA-13
80Evansvl-21
81Evansvl-15
82RochR-12
83D-131
83F-62
83RochR-15
83T-293
84RochR-11
85Richm-13
86Hagers-7
86RochR-4
87Hagers-11
91Crown/Orio-169
91Pac/SenLg-155

Gully, Scott
91Oneonta/ProC-4149

Gumbert, Addison
90Target-306
N172

Gumbert, Harry
39PB-54
40PB-86
41DP-27
41DP-92
41PB-26
49B-192
50B-171
W754

Gumbert, Rich
83Greens-9

Gumbs, Lincoln Jr.
90AubAs/Best-17
90AubAs/ProC-3409

Gumpert, Dave
82BirmB-5
83Evansvl-3
84Evansvl-8
84Nes/792-371
84T-371
85IowaC-14
86IowaC-13
87F-565
87T-487
90BirmDG/Best-16

Gumpert, Randy
49B-87
50B-184
51B-59
52B-106
52T-247

Gumpf, John
90Elizab/Star-11
91Kenosha/ClBest-9
91Kenosha/ProC-2089

Gundelfinger, Matt
81Redwd-14
83Spring/LF-18

Gunderson, Eric
87Everett-13
88CalLgAS-5
88SanJose/Cal-131
88SanJose/ProC-114
89Shreve/ProC-1833
90B-225
90Phoenix/CMC-7
90S/Tr-99T
90UD/Ext-752
91B-628
91D-416RR
91S-744RP
91S/100RisSt-57
91T/90Debut-61
91UD-315
92F-637

Gunderson, Greg
89Batavia/ProC-1938
90Spartan/Best-6
90Spartan/ProC-2487
90Spartan/Star-11

Gunn, Clay
86Cram/PCL-126
87Wausau-10
88SanBern/Best-18
88SanBern/Cal-32

Gunn, Jeffrey
90Princet/DIMD-9

Gunnarson, Bob
86Chatt-10
87Chatt/Best-13

Gunning, Thomas
N172
N690

Gunson, Joseph
N172

Gunter, Chet
76Shrev

Gunter, Reid
87Pocatel/Bon-8

Gura, Larry
71OPC-203
71T-203
73OPC-501
73T-501
74OPC-616
74T-616
74T/Tr-616T
75OPC-557
75T-557
75T/M-557
76OPC-319
76T-319
77T-193
78T-441
79T-19
80OPC-154
80T-295
81Coke
81D-461
81F-38
81F/St-102
81K-59

81OPC-130
81T-130
81T/SO-51
81T/St-88
82D-338
82F-410
82F/St-205
82OPC-147
82T-790
82T-96TL
82T/St-195
83D-160
83F-113
83K-42
83OPC-340
83OPC-395AS
83T-340
83T-395AS
83T/St-77
84D-100
84F-347
84Nes/792-625
84Nes/792-96TL
84OPC-264
84T-625
84T-96TL
84T/St-285
85D-217
85F-202
85T-595
85T/St-278

Gurchiek, Chris
88AppFx/ProC-156
88Boise/ProC-1609

Gurtcheff, Jeff
86Watertn-8

Gust, Chris
88Madis-12

Gustafson, Edward
(Ed)
89Everett/Star-9
90A&AASingle/ProC-118
90Clinton/Best-6
90Clinton/ProC-2550
90Foil/Best-85
91Visalia/ClBest-2
91Visalia/ProC-1736

Gustave, Michael
78Wisco

Gustavson, Duane
82FtMyr-10
83CharR-25
85FtMyr-26
86FtMyr-13MG
87Memphis-21
87Memphis/Best-2C
88OrlanTw/Best-3

Gustine, Frank
47TipTop
48L-88
49B-99
49Eureka-57
Exh47

Guthrie, Mark
88Visalia/Cal-167
89Orlan/Best-14
89Orlan/ProC-1335
89SLAS-19
90D-622
90LSUGreat-9
90OPC-317
90Portl/ProC-174
90T-317
90T/89Debut-49
90UD-436
91D-64
91F-612
91Leaf/I-171
91OPC-698
91S-778
91T-698
91T/StClub/I-219
91UD-505
92D/II-691
92S/I-164
92T-548
92UD-604

Gutierrez, Anthony
90Ashvl/ProC-2742
91BurlAs/ClBest-4
91BurlAs/ProC-2795

Gutierrez, Cesar
69OPC-16R
69T-16R
70OPC-269
70T-269
71MLB/St-392
71OPC-154
71T-154
72T-743

Gutierrez, Dimas
85PrWill-8
86Nashua-10
87Harris-22
88EastLAS/ProC-15
88Harris/ProC-841
89Miami/I/Star-8

Gutierrez, Felipe
85VeroB-7

Gutierrez, Israel
78Ashvl
79Wausau-7

Gutierrez, Jackie
84F/X-47
84T/Tr-46
85D-335
85F-160
85T-89
85T/St-216
85T/St-373YS
86D-335
86F-350
86F/Up-U47
86OPC-73
86T-633
87D-601
87F-471
87T-276
88Phill/TastyK-33
89Pawtu/CMC-19
89Pawtu/Dunkin-21
89Pawtu/ProC-694
89UD-430
90Miami/I/Star-11
90Miami/II/Star-9
91Crown/Orio-170

Gutierrez, Jim
89Belling/Legoe-6
90Penin/Star-10
91SanBern/ClBest-5
91SanBern/ProC-1981

Gutierrez, Joaquin
79Elmira-7

Gutierrez, Julian
78StPete
80ArkTr-16
82ArkTr-15

Gutierrez, Ricky
89Freder/Star-8
90CLAS/CL-4
90Freder/Team-18
91Hagers/LineD-231
91Hagers/ProC-2462
91Single/ClBest-55

Gutierrez, Robert
(Bob)
84Newar-21
85Newar-15

Gutrirrez, Willie
79Knoxvl/TCMA-13

Gutteridge, Don
60T-458C
70OPC-123MG
70T-123MG
92Conlon/Sport-636

Guzik, Rob
(Robbi)
89Kingspt/Star-11
90Pittsfld/Pucko-5

Guzman, Correa
88Knoxvl/Best-18

Guzman, Doinini
89Medford/Best-10

Guzman, Hector
83VeroB-18

Guzman, Johnny
90A&AASingle/ProC-144
90Modesto/ProC-2207
91Tacoma/LineD-536
91Tacoma/ProC-2299
92T/91Debut-67

Guzman, Jose
83BurlR-4
83BurlR/LF-7
84Tulsa-29
85OKCty-11
86D-30RR
86D/Rook-24
86F-559
86Rangers-23
86T/Tr-43T
87D-101
87F-124
87Leaf-50
87Mother/Rang-23
87Smok/R-3
87T-363
88D-136
88D/Best-88
88F-467
88Leaf-55
88Mother/R-23
88OPC-98
88S-322
88Smok/R-20
88T-563
89Bimbo/Discs-11
89Bristol/Star-10
89D-284
89F-520
89Mother/R-25
89OPC-209
89Panini/St-445
89S-143
89S/YS/II-11
89Smok/R-11
89T-462
89T/St-241
89UD-73
90Fayette/ProC-2400
90OPC-308
90PublInt/St-411
90T-308
90UD-617
91F/Up-U60
92D/I-271
92F-306
92S/II-502
92T-188
92UD-204

Guzman, Juan
86VeroB-8
87Bakers-5
89Syrac/CMC-9
89Syrac/ProC-797
89Syrac/Team-12
90Foil/Best-79
90Knoxvl/Best-8
90Knoxvl/ProC-1242
91F/UltraUp-U60
91S/ToroBJ-25
91Syrac/LineD-504
91Syrac/ProC-2476
92D/II-534
92F-330
92F/RookSlns-16
92S/100RisSt-27
92S/I-424
92T-662
92T/91Debut-68
92UD-625

Guzman, Luis
79Knoxvl/TCMA-3
80Utica-17

Guzman, Pedro
(Pete)
90CharRain/Best-10
90CharRain/ProC-2037

Guzman, Ruben
83Water-18
86GlenF-8
87GlenF-1

Guzman, Santiago
70T-716R
72OPC-316R
72T-316R

Gwinn, Tony
87PrWill-27

Gwosdz, Doug
81Hawaii
82T-731R
84D-383
84Mother/Padres-16
84Nes/792-753
84Smok/Padres-11
84T-753
85Mother/Giants-22
86Jacks/TCMA-11
87Calgary-23
88Nashvl/CMC-16
88Nashvl/ProC-480
88Nashvl/Team-11
89Nashvl/CMC-11
89Nashvl/ProC-1277
89Nashvl/Team-7

Gwynn, Anthony
(Tony)
81Hawaii-10
82Hawaii-10
83D-598
83F-360
83OPC-143
83T-482
84D-324
84F-301
85FunFood/Pin-28
84Mother/Padres-9
84Nes/792-251
84Smok/Padres-12
84T-251
84T/St-160
85D-25DK
85D-63
85D/AAS-19
85D/DKsuper-25
85Drake-14
85F-34
85F/LimEd-11
85F/St-8
85Leaf-25DK
85Mother/Padres-2
85OPC-383
85Seven-11W
85T-660
85T-717AS
85T/3D-13
85T/Gloss22-6
85T/Gloss40-29
85T/St-146
85T/St-170
85T/St-174
85T/Super-5
85ThomMc/Discs-32
86D-112
86D/AAS-1
86D/PopUp-1
86F-323
86F/LimEd-22
86F/Mini-69
86F/Slug-15
86F/St-50
86KayBee-17
86Leaf-41
86OPC-10
86Quaker-7
86Sf-13
86Sf-135M
86Sf-181M
86T-10
86T/Gloss22-17
86T/Gloss60-57
86T/Mini-65
86T/St-105
86T/St-146
86T/Super-29
86Woolwth-13
87Bohem-19
87Classic-26
87D-64
87D/AAS-16
87D/HL-12
87D/OD-146
87D/PopUp-16
87Drake-11
87F-416
87F/AwardWin-19
87F/BB-19
87F/Lim-19
87F/Mini-50
87F/Slug-17
87F/St-52
87Ho/St-16
87KayBee-15
87Kraft-44
87Leaf-235
87MnM's-23
87MSA/Discs-16
87OPC-198
87RedFoley/St-113
87Sf-117M
87Sf-197M
87Sf-31
87Sportflic/DealP-3
87T-530
87T-599AS
87T/Coins-34
87T/Gloss22-6
87T/Gloss60-2
87T/HL-16
87T/Mini-35
87T/St-106
87T/St-155
87Woolwth-16
88Bz-9
88ChefBoy-6
88Classic/Blue-220
88Coke/Padres-19
88D-164
88D/AS-51
88D/Best-154
88D/MVP-BC6
88Drake-14
88F-585
88F-631M
88F-634M
88F/AwardWin-16
88F/BB/AS-13
88F/BB/MVP-17
88F/Excit-17
88F/Hottest-15
88F/LL-16
88F/Mini-112
88F/RecSet-17
88F/Slug-17
88F/St-123
88F/TL-11
88FanSam-18
88KayBee-13
88KingB/Disc-5
88KMart-12
88Leaf-90
88Nestle-40
88OPC/WaxBox-360
88OPC-F
88Panini/St-410
88Panini/St-437
88SanDiegoSt-7M
88SanDiegoSt-8
88S-385
88Sf-16
88Smok/Padres-10
88T-360
88T-402AS
88T-699M
88T/Big-161
88T/Coins-36
88T/Gloss60-38
88T/Mini-74
88T/Revco-1
88T/RiteAid-11
88T/St-115
88T/St/Backs-16
88T/UK-29
88T/WaxBox-F
88Woolwth-12
89B-461
89Bz-13
89Cadaco-27
89Classic-30
89Coke/Padre-6
89T/Crunch-5
89D-128
89D-6DK
89D/Best-42
89D/DKsuper-6DK
89D/MVP-BC20
89F-305
89F/BBAS-19
89F/BBMVP's-17
89F/Excit-20
89F/Heroes-20
89F/LL-19
89F/Superstar-21
89F/WaxBox-C12
89Holsum/Discs-6
89KayBee-17
89KingB/Discs-21
89KMart/DT-29
89KMart/Lead-2
89OPC-51
89Padre/Mag-3
89Panini/St-203
89Panini/St-222
89RedFoley/St-54
89S-90
89S/HotStar-40
89S/Mast-37

89Sf-160
89T-570
89T-699M
89T/Big-58
89T/Coins-4
89T/Gloss60-58
89T/HeadsUp-1
89T/Hills-16
89T/LJN-82
89T/Mini-38
89T/St-109
89T/St/Backs-50
89T/UK-36
89UD-384
89UD-683TC
90B-217
90BBWit-2
90Bz-6
90Classic-17
90Classic-87
90Coke/Padre-6
90CollAB-17
90D-705AS
90D-86
90D/BestNL-11
90D/Bon/MVP-BC4
90D/Learning-48
90D/Preview-6
90F-157
90F/BBMVP-16
90F/LL-17
90F/WaxBox-C12
90Holsum/Discs-18
90HotPlay/St-19
90KayBee-14
90KingB/Discs-3
90KMart/CBatL-2
90KMart/SS-5
90Leaf/I-154
90MLBPA/Pins-55
90MSA/Soda-14
90OPC-403AS
90OPC-730
90Padre/MagUno-1
90Padre/MagUno-15
90Panini/St-207M
90Panini/St-351
90Post-5
90PublInt/St-261
90PublInt/St-50
90RedFoley/St-43
90S-255
90S-685DT
90S/100St-3
90Sf-98
90Starline/LJS-29
90Starline/LJS-4
90Sunflower-11
90T-403AS
90T-730
90T/Big-93
90T/Coins-36
90T/DH-31
90T/Gloss22-8
90T/Gloss60-56
90T/HeadsUp-1
90T/Mini-80
90T/St-101
90T/St-146AS
90T/TVAS-39
90UD-344
90USPlayC/AS-11D
90WonderBrd-12
91B-647
91BBBest/HitM-10
91Classic/200-156
91Classic/II-T93
91Classic/III-33
91CollAB-19
91D-243
91F-529
91F/Ultra-303
91Leaf/II-290
91Leaf/Prev-11
91Leaf/Stud-245
91MajorLg/Pins-54
91MooTown-6
91OPC-180
91OPC/Premier-59
91Padre/MagRal-22
91Panini/FrSt-97
91Panini/St-99
91Panini/Top15-104
91Petro/SU-24
91Post-10
91S-500
91S/100SS-94
91Seven/3DCoin-4SC
91T-180
91T/CJMini/I-26
91T/StClub/II-308
91T/SU-18
91UD-255
91UD/FinalEd-97FAS
91USPlayC/AS-1C
92D/Elite-E14
92D/II-425AS
92D/II-441
92F-605
92F/ASIns-2
92F/TmLIns-7
92S/100SS-81
92S/II-625
92S/II-779AS
92S/II-886DT
92T-270
92UD-274
92UD-83TC

Gwynn, Chris
87Albuq/Pol-27
88AAA/ProC-2
88Albuq/CMC-12
88Albuq/ProC-259
88F-647R
88SanDiegoSt-6
88SanDiegoSt-7M
88S-640RP
89Albuq/CMC-15
89Albuq/ProC-64
89F-59
89S/HotRook-21
89UD-607
90Classic-111
90Leaf/II-411
90Mother/Dodg-14
90OPC-456
90Pol/Dodg-15
90S/YS/II-39
90T-456
90Target-307
90UD-526
91D-598
91F-202
91Mother/Dodg-14
91OPC-99
91Pol/Dodg-15
91S-178
91T-99
91T/StClub/II-480
91UD-560
92D/II-648
92F-457
92S/II-449
92T-604
92UD-689

Gyarmati, Jeff
83Beloit/LF-4
89Boise/ProC-1985

Gyselman, Dick
43Centen-11
44Centen-10

Haas, Berthold
(Bert)
49Eureka-105
90Target-308
Exh47

Haas, Bill
63T-544R
64T-398R

Haas, Bryan
(Moose)
75BurlB
78T-649
79T-448
80T-181
81D-85
81F-516
81OPC-327
81T-327
81T/St-98
82D-206
82F-143
82F/St-139
82OPC-12
82Pol/Brew-30
82T-12
83D-204
83F-35
83Gard-9
83OPC-317
83Pol/Brew-30
83T-503
84D-368
84F-202
84F/St-61
84Gard-8
84Nes/792-271
84Nes/792-726TL
84OPC-271
84Pol/Brew-30
84T-271
84T-726TL
84T/St-292
85D-473
85F-583
85Gard-8
85OPC-151
85Pol/Brew-30
85T-151
85T/St-293
86D-237
86F-489
86F/Up-U48
86Mother/A's-16
86OPC-9
86T-759
86T/St-201
86T/Tr-44T
87D-528
87F-393
87Leaf-54
87OPC-369
87Smok/A's-5
87T-413
88S-177
88T-606

Haas, Dave
87Anchora-16
89Lakeland/Star-7
90London/ProC-1263
91B-151
91Toledo/LineD-585
91Toledo/ProC-1926
92S/II-825
92T-665
92T/91Debut-69

Haas, G. Edwin
(Eddie)
59T-126
79Savan-16
81Richm-21
82Richm-27
83Richm-23
84Richm-27
85Ho/Braves-1MG
85Pol/Atl-22MG
85T/Tr-44T

Haas, George W.
(Mule)
29Exh/4-27
31Exh/4-28
32Orbit/num-19
32Orbit/un-25
33G-219
35BU-170
35G-8B
35G-9B
40PB-184
61F-109
91Conlon/Sport-323
PR1-15
R305
R310
R312/M
R314
R315-A14
R315-B14
V355-68
W517-32
WG8-26

Haas, Randy
75Clinton

Haase, Dean
91Utica/CIBest-11
91Utica/ProC-3242

Haberle, Dave
83Cedar-18
83Cedar/LF-11
84Cedar-28
91Eugene/CIBest-2
91Eugene/ProC-3732

Habyan, John
85CharlO-21
86D-45RR
86RochR-5
87Classic-95
87D-494
87French-54
87RochR-24
87RochR/TCMA-4
88D-354
88F-562
88RochR/Team-10
88RochR/CMC-6
88RochR/Gov-9
88RochR/ProC-215
88S-353
88T-153
90ColClip/CMC-3
90ColClip/ProC-671
90T/TVYank-44
91B-167
91Crown/Orio-171
91F/UltraUp-U40
91F/Up-U42
91Leaf/II-480
91T/StClub/II-590
92D/I-32
92F-228
92S/II-451
92T-698

Hack, Stan
34DS-107
34DS-34
35BU-137
40Wheat-12
41DP-2
41DP-97
41Wheat-21
47TipTop
52Mother-60
53Mother-49
54Wilson
55T-6MG
55T/DH-24MG
61F-110
80Pac/Leg-83
91Conlon/Sport-126
R302
R312/M
R313
V355-105
WG8-27

Hacker, Rich
90T/TVCard-3CO
91Tor/Fire-7

Hacker, Warren
51B-318
52Dix
52StarCal/L-80G
52T-324
53B/Col-144
53Dix
53NB
53RM-NL23
54B-125
55B-8
56T-282
57Kahn
57Sohio/Reds-8
57T-370
58T-251

Hackett, John
86Erie-11

Haden, Paris
90Hagers/Best-11

Haddix, Harvey
53Hunter
53T-273
54Hunter
54T-9
55Armour-8
55Hunter
55T-43
55T/DH-42
56T-77
56T/Hocus-A6
56T/Hocus-B8
56T/Pin-47P
57T-265
58Kahn
58T-118
59T-184
60Kahn
60NuCard-9
60T-340
61Kahn
61NuCard-478
61P-134
61T-100
61T-410HL
61T/RO-33
62J-180
62Kahn
62P-180
62P/Can-180
62T-67
63IDL-11
63Kahn
63T-239
64T-439
65OPC-67
65T-67
76Laugh/Jub-31
76SSPC-623CO
79TCMA-39
82D-651CO
88Pac/Leg-11
89Swell-13
90HOF/St-57
90Swell/Great-73
91Crown/Orio-172
91T/Arc53-273

Haddock, Darren
91BendB/CIBest-7
91BendB/ProC-3692

Haddock, George
N172
N300/unif

Hadley, Irving
(Bump)
32Orbit/num-24
32Orbit/un-26
33G-140
34Exh/4-15
35G-1C
35G-275
35G-2C
35G-6C
35G-7C
38G-251
38ONG/Pin-14
61F-111
92Conlon/Sport-508
R305
R316
V354-15

Hadley, Kent
59T-127
60L-135
60T-102
61Union

Haeberle, Kevin
89Idaho/ProC-2037
90Sumter/Best-27
90Sumter/ProC-2427

Haefner, Mickey
49B-144
50B-183

Haeger, Greg
90Bristol/ProC-3159
90Bristol/Star-8
91Fayette/CIBest-3
91Fayette/ProC-1164

Hafey, Charles J.
(Chick)
29Exh/4-16
31Exh/4-16
32Orbit/un-27
33DL-19
33Exh/4-4
34DS-18
34Exh/4-4
34G-34
35BU-16
35Exh/4-4
61F-39
80Pac/Leg-116
80SSPC/HOF
87Conlon/2-14
88Conlon/NatAS-10
89HOF/St-34
91Conlon/Sport-33
92Conlon/Sport-657
R300
R305
R308-207

R310
R316
R328-8
R332-5
V354-78
V355-94
W517-29
Hafey, Daniel A.
(Bud)
35BU-163
Hafey, Tom
46Remar-12
47Remar-11
47Signal
47Smith-18
48Smith-12
Hafey, Will
47Remar-16
47Smith-19
48Signal
48Smith-3
Haffley, Jay
90WichSt-15
Hagan, Kevin
81Louisvl-6
83Louisvl/Riley-6
84Louisvl-11
84Nes/792-337
85Louisvl-7
88Tucson/CMC-5
88Tucson/ProC-180
88Tucson/JP-12
Hageman, Kurt
T207
Hagemann, Tim
80Clinton-9
Hagen, Kevin
81ArkTr-16
82ArkTr-2
84T-337
86Maine-10
87Portl-13
87Tucson-17
Hagen, Walter
33SK-8
Hagermann, Ken
79Elmira-3
Haggerty, Roger
86Elmira-7
87WinHaven-26
88WinHaven/Star-9
Hagman, Keith
81Durham-9
82Durham-2
Hague, Joe
69T-559R
70OPC-362
70T-362
71MLB/St-274
71OPC-96
71T-96
71T/Coins-139
72T-546
73OPC-447
73T-447
Hagy, Gary
91Boise/ClBest-19
91Boise/ProC-3886
Hahn, Brent
90Salinas/Cal-134
90Salinas/ProC-2725
Hahn, Don
71MLB/St-129
71OPC-94
71T-94
72OPC-269
72T-269
74OPC-291
74T-291
75OPC-182
75T-182
75T/M-182
77Phoenix
91WIZMets-155
Hahn, Ed
E254
E90/3
M116
T206
Hahn, Eric
87Savan-5
Hahn, Frank
E107
Hahn, Willie
N172
Hailey, Fred
(Freddie)
87Oneonta-15
88FtLaud/Star-11
89FtLaud/Star-8
90Albany/Best-20
90Albany/ProC-1044
90Albany/Star-6
Hailey, Roger
88Pulaski/ProC-1766
89Pulaski/ProC-1907
90A&AASingle/ProC-93
90Foil/Best-160
90SALAS/Star-31
90Sumter/Best-4
90Sumter/ProC-2428
91Durham/ProC-1539
Hain, Bill
60HenryH-6
60Union-7
Haines, Allan
(Abner)
80GlenF/B-27tr
80GlenF/C-22tr
Haines, Dennis
77SanJose-11
79Ogden/TCMA-8
Haines, Jesse
21Exh-66
32Orbit/un-28
33G-73
40PB-227
61F-40
80SSPC/HOF
89Pac/Leg-208
91Conlon/Sport-43
92Conlon/Sport-358
92Conlon/Sport-647
E120
E121/120
E210-30
R305
R316
V100
V354-44
V355-93
V61-103
W501-76
W513
W573
W575
Haines, Michael
86Jamestn-11
Hainline, Jeff
88Butte-25
Hairston, Jerry
74OPC-96
74T-96
75OPC-327
75T-327
75T/M-327
76OPC-391
76SSPC-153
76T-391
83D-616
83F-236
83T-487
83TrueVal/WSox-17
84D-86
84F-60
84Nes/792-177
84T-177
84TrueVal/WS-15
85Coke/WS-17
85D-135
85F-515
85T-596
86Coke/WS-17
86D-424
86F-207
86T-778
87Coke/WS-11
87D-285
87F-498
87OPC-299
87T-685
88D-285
88T-281
Hairston, John
90SoBend/Best-3
90SoBend/ClBest-8
91SoBend/ProC-2863
Hairston, Rodd
91Burllnd/ProC-3308
Hairston, Sam Sr.
87BirmB/Best-2CO
89BirmB/Best-29
89BirmB/ProC-112CO
90BirmB/Best-26CO
90BirmB/ProC-1398CO
91BirmB/LineD-75CO
91BirmB/ProC-1470CO
Hajeck, David
90A&AASingle/ProC-102
90Ashvl/ProC-2754
90SALAS/Star-10
91Osceola/ClBest-18
91Osceola/ProC-692
Halama, Scott
87Erie-22
88Hamil/ProC-1720
89Johnson/Star-14
Halberg, Eric
83Clinton/LF-2
Hale, A. Odell
36Wheat-8
37OPC-128
38Exh/4-11
92Conlon/Sport-415
R313
R314
V300
Hale, Bob
56T-231
57T-406
59T-507
60T-309
61T-532
79TCMA-129
91Crown/Orio-173
Hale, Chip
88OrlanTw/Best-18
89Portl/CMC-24
89Portl/ProC-208
90D-690
90OPC-704
90Portl/CMC-19
90Portl/ProC-183
90S-588RP
90S/100Ris-98
90Sf-223
90T-704
90T/89Debut-50
90UD-475
91Portl/LineD-409
91Portl/ProC-1570
91S/100RisSt-39
Hale, Dan
86Greens-10
87Greens-20
Hale, DeMarlo
86NewBrit-12
88Huntsvl/BK-5
88Madis-13
Hale, Diane
81ArkTr-23M
Hale, John
76OPC-228
76T-228
77T-523
78T-584
79OPC-23
79T-56
80Indianap-6
81RochR-6
90Target-309
Hale, Samuel
(Sammy)
25Exh-108
29Exh/4-28
91Conlon/Sport-293
W517-44
Hale, Shane
91Freder/ClBest-3
91Freder/ProC-2357
Haley, Bart
86Elmira-8
87WinHaven-6
88Lynch/Star-8
89Lynch/Star-10
Haley, Bill
78Green
Haley, Mark
85Anchora-13CO
90SoBend/ClBest-23CO
91SoBend/ProC-2875CO
Haley, Ryan
91Niagara/ClBest-5
91Niagara/ProC-3635
Haley, Sam
83Wausau/LF-23
86WPalmB-19
Halicki, Ed
75OPC-467
75T-467
75T/M-467
76OPC-423
76T-423
77T-343
78Ho-12
78T-107
79OPC-354
79Pol/Giants-28
79T-672
80OPC-115
80Pol/Giants-28
80T-217
81D-53
81T-69
89Pac/SenLg-74
Halicki, Kevin
82Redwd-4
Hall, Albert
82Richm-19
83Richm-18
85F-326
85Ho/Braves-10
85Pol/Atl-2
85T-676
86Richm-8
87F/Up-U39
87Smok/Atl-25
87T/Tr-41T
88D-290
88D/Best-253
88F-541
88OPC-213
88Panini/St-249
88S-148
88T-213
88T/St-39
89F-593
89OPC-153
89S-74
89T-433
89T/Big-104
89T/St-30
89UD-93
Hall, Andy
86Cram/PCL-198
86Macon-11
88CLAS/Star-8
88Salem/Star-7
89BuffB/CMC-10
89BuffB/ProC-1672
89Harris/Star-8
Hall, Billy
90WichSt-16
Hall, Bob
49Eureka-10
90Target-1103
Hall, Carl
90WichSt-17
Hall, Charles Louis
E90/1
M116
T207
Hall, Chris
89Bristol/Star-11
90Bristol/ProC-3155
90Bristol/Star-9
Hall, Darren
87Myrtle-4
88Dunedin/Star-8
89Dunedin/Star-6
90Knoxvl/Best-21
90Knoxvl/ProC-1244
90Knoxvl/Star-4
91Knoxvl/LineD-358
91Knoxvl/ProC-1762
Hall, Dave
63MilSau-1
Hall, Dave
81Cedar-26
82Cedar-19
83Tampa-14
Hall, Dean
78Newar
Hall, Drew
86Pittsfld-8
87D-594
87Iowa-2
88D/Cubs/Bk-NEW
88T-262
89B-221
89D-522
89F-643R
89OkCty/ProC-1517
89Smok/R-12
89T-593
89UD-324
90F-299
90Leaf/II-423
90OPC-463
90S-516
90T-463
90UD-631
91F-236
91OPC-77
91S-581
91T-77
Hall, Gardner C.
87BirmB/Best-14
Hall, Grady
88Vanco/CMC-8
88Vanco/ProC-761
89BirmB/Best-11
89BirmB/ProC-108
89F-650R
90Vanco/CMC-6
90Vanco/ProC-484
91Vanco/LineD-632
91Vanco/ProC-1589
Hall, Greg
85Spokane/Cram-6
87CharRain-5
88River/Cal-219
88River/ProC-1415
89River/Best-26
89River/Cal-6
89River/ProC-1397
89Spokane/SP-8
Hall, Jeff
80Elmira-11
Hall, Jimmie
64T-73
64T/Coins-16
64T/St-3
65T-580
66OPC-190
66T-190
66T/RO-51
67T-432
68OPC-121
68T-121
69MB-99
69OPC-61
69T-61
70T-649
Hall, Joe
88Hamil/ProC-1747
89StPete/Star-15
91Vanco/LineD-633
91Vanco/ProC-1600
Hall, Johnny
90Target-968
Hall, Kevin
88Pocatel/ProC-2093
89Everett/Star-10
Hall, Lamar
88Idaho/ProC-1840
89Sumter/ProC-1106
Hall, Marty
86Madis-10
86Madis/Pol-10
87Ashvl-10
Hall, Matthew
86Chatt-11
87Chatt/Best-21
Hall, Mel
82Iowa-4
83D-126
83T/Tr-39
83Thorn-27
84D-411
84F-493
84F/St-106
84Nes/792-508
84OPC-4

84T-508
84T/St-380YS
84T/Tr-47
84Wheat/Ind-34
85D-338
85F-449
85OPC-263
85Polar/Ind-27
85T-263
85T/St-254
86D-276
86F-587
86OhHenry-27
86OPC-138
86T-647
87D-473
87F-252
87F/Excit-21
87F/St-53
87Gator-27
87OPC-51
87Sf-180
87T-51
87T/St-206
88D-342
88D/Best-173
88F-610
88Gator-27
88Leaf-109
88OPC-318
88Panini/St-79
88S-441
88Sf-189
88T-318
88T/Big-114
88T/St-205
89D-73
89D/Tr-36
89F-406
89F/Up-49
89OPC-173
89Panini/St-328
89RedFoley/St-55
89S-17
89S/NWest-20
89S/Tr-54
89Sf-144
89T-173
89T/Big-13
89T/Tr-44T
89UD-538
89UD/Ext-729
90B-437
90D-598
90D/BestAL-66
90F-444
90Leaf/I-227
90MLBPA/Pins-92
90OPC-436
90Panini/St-122
90PublInt/St-535
90S-383
90S/NWest-7
90T-436
90T/Big-123
90T/St-313
90T/TVYank-30
90UD-458
91B-179
91Classic/III-34
91D-442
91F-665
91F/Ultra-233
91Leaf/II-283
91OPC-738
91S-166
91T-738
91T/StClub/II-333
91UD-392
92D/I-248
92F-229
92S/I-154
92T-223
92UD-291

Hall, Richard W.
55T-126
55T/DH-57
56T-331
57T-308
60T-308
61T-197
61T/St-160
62T-189
63T-526
67T-508
68OPC-17
68T-17
70OPC-182
70T-182
71MLB/St-297
71OPC-417
71T-417
91Crown/Orio-174

Hall, Robert L.
55B-113

Hall, Robert P.
T206

Hall, Rocky
78Newar
79BurlB-6
79Holyo-24

Hall, Roy
85Greens-15

Hall, Tim
91Spokane/ClBest-26
91Spokane/ProC-3950

Hall, Todd
87Penin-24
88Tampa/Star-10
89Saraso/Star-9
90BirmB/Best-17
90BirmB/ProC-1105

Hall, Tom E.
69T-658R
70OPC-169
70T-169
71MLB/St-462
71OPC-313
71T-313
72MB-124
72OPC-417
72T-417
73OPC-8
73T-8
74OPC-248
74T-248
75OPC-108
75T-108
75T/M-108
76OPC-621
76SSPC-556
76T-621
91WIZMets-156

Hall, William
(Bill)
59T-49

Hall, William B.
(Bill)
90Target-967

Halla, John
E254
E270/1

Hallahan, Bill
31Exh/4-16
32Orbit/num-72
32Orbit/un-29
33Exh/4-8
33G-200
34DS-23
34Exh/4-8
34G-82
35BU-121
35BU-40
87Conlon/2-15
91Conlon/Sport-214
92Conlon/Sport-639
R305
R313
R314
V355-70
WG8-28

Halland, Jon
91Belling/ClBest-4
91Belling/ProC-3674
91Penin/ProC-385

Hallandsworth, Todd
91FrRow/DP-46

Hallas, Bob
83Madis/LF-16
84Albany-13

Hallberg, Lance
78Wisco
80OrlTw-8
82OrlTw/A-11

Halle, Andrew
88BurlInd/ProC-1797

Haller, Jim
90A&AASingle/ProC-87
90Greens/Best-7
90Greens/ProC-2653
90Greens/Star-4
91PrWill/ClBest-29
91PrWill/ProC-1418
91Single/ClBest-144

Haller, Tom
62T-356
63J-108
63P-108
63T-85
64T-485
65T-465
65T/trans-16
66T-308
67OPC-65
67T-65
68OPC-185
68T-185
69MB-100
69MLB/St-148
69OPC/DE-10
69T-310
69T/DE-23
69T/decal
69T/S-47
69T/St-45
70K-25
70MB-9
70MLB/St-51
70T-685
71MLB/St-105
71OPC-639
71T-639
72MB-125
72OPC-175
72OPC-176IA
72T-175
72T-176IA
73OPC-454
73T-454
79Pol/Giants-5
84Mother/Giants-5
87Smok/Dodg-11
89Smok/Dodg-74
90Target-310

Hallgren, Robert
76Dubuq
77Cocoa
78Ashvl

Hallgren, Tim
80SanJose/JITB-11
86Salem-11C

Halliday, Doc
90Idaho/ProC-3264

Hallinan, Ed
T207

Hallion, Tom
88TM/Umpire-57
89TM/Umpire-55
90TM/Umpire-53

Hallman, William W.
(Bill)
90Target-311
E107
N172
N300/SC
T206

Halls, Gary
77BurlB

Hallstrom, Charles
N172

Hally
E254

Halter, Shane
91Eugene/ClBest-4
91Eugene/ProC-3733

Ham, Michael
(Mike)
87Everett-17
88Clinton/ProC-709
89Phoenix/ProC-1478
89SanJose/Best-26
89SanJose/Cal-220
89SanJose/ProC-461
89SanJose/Star-12
90Shrev/ProC-1447
90Shrev/Star-9

Hambright, Roger
72OPC-124R
72T-124R
74Syrac/Team-9

Hamelin, Bob
88Eugene/Best-1
89BBAmerAA/BPro-AA17
89Memphis/Best-1
89Memphis/ProC-1201
89Memphis/Star-12
89SLAS-9
89Star/Wax-42
90B-379
90Omaha/CMC-24
90Omaha/ProC-71
90UD-45
91B-310
91Omaha/LineD-336
91Omaha/ProC-1042
92F-672

Hamilton, Billy
61F-112
80SSPC/HOF
89HOF/St-43
BF2-40
N172
N300/SC

Hamilton, Bob
85VeroB-1
87SanAn-18

Hamilton, Carl
86Pittsfld-9
87Iowa-1
88Peoria/Ko-13
91CaroMud/LineD-108
91CaroMud/ProC-1081

Hamilton, Charlie
91Kissim/ProC-4205TR

Hamilton, Darryl
85Anchora-14
87Stockton-8
88Denver/CMC-24
88Denver/ProC-1274
88F/Up-U38
88S/Tr-72T
89Denver/CMC-13
89Denver/ProC-39
89F-187
89S/HotRook-44
89T-88
89UD-301
90B-397
90Brewer/MillB-10
90F-325
90Pol/Brew-24
90T/Tr-35T
91Brewer/MillB-9
91D-517
91F-585
91F/UltraUp-U30
91OPC-781
91Pol/Brew-9
91S-107
91T-781
91T/StClub/I-234
91UD-42
92D/II-593
92F-177
92S/II-497
92T-278
92UD-460

Hamilton, Dave
73OPC-214
73T-214
74OPC-633
74T-633
75OPC-428
75T-428
75T/M-428
76OPC-237
76T-237
77OPC-224
77T-367
78T-288
79T-147
80T-86
81Tacoma-8

Hamilton, Earl
15CJ-171
92Conlon/Sport-339
D328-68
D329-75
D350/2-74
E120
E135-68
M101/4-75
M101/5-74
T207
T222
V61-68
W573

Hamilton, Jack
62T-593R
63T-132
65T-288
66T-262
67OPC-2
67T-2
68OPC-193
68T-193
69T-629
91WIZMets-157

Hamilton, Jamie
80ElPaso-23

Hamilton, Jeff
86Albuq-10
87Albuq/Pol-19
87D-464
87Pol/Dodg-16
87T-266
88D-525
88F-515
88Mother/Dodg-19
88Panini/St-312
88Pol/Dodg-33
88T-62
89D-550
89D/Best-290
89F-60
89Mother/Dodg-19
89Pol/Dodg-3
89S-570
89T-736
89UD-615
90B-94
90D-321
90F-396
90Leaf/II-306
90Mother/Dodg-23
90OPC-426
90Pol/Dodg-3
90PublInt/St-7
90S-132
90S/YS/II-17
90T-426
90T/Big-98
90T/St-67
90Target-312
90UD-296
91Leaf/II-509
91Mother/Dodg-23
91OPC-552
91Pol/Dodg-3
91T-552
91T/StClub/II-550
91UD/Ext-779
92S/II-684
92T-151

Hamilton, Joey
92UD-67TP

Hamilton, Kenny
91Yakima/ClBest-17
91Yakima/ProC-4243

Hamilton, Mike
88Butte-1

Hamilton, Robert
80Water-13

Hamilton, Scott W.
86Erie-12
87Spring/Best-17
88StPete/Star-8
90Stockton/Best-19
90Stockton/Cal-180
90Stockton/ProC-2180

Hamilton, Steve
63T-171
64T-206
65T-309
66T-503
67T-567
68T-496
69MB-101
69MLB/St-75
69OPC-69
69T-69
70MLB/St-246
70OPC-349
70T-349
71OPC-627
71T-627

72MB-126
72T-766
WG10-9
WG9-11
Hamilton, Z.B.
89Princet/Star-8
Hamlin, Jonas
91StPete/ClBest-21
91StPete/ProC-2284
Hamlin, Ken
60T-542
61P-89
61T-263
62Salada-34A
62Salada-34B
62Shirriff-34
62T-296
66OPC-69
66T-69
Hamlin, Luke
39PB-13
40PB-70
41PB-53
90Target-313
Hamm, Pete
71OPC-74R
71T-74R
72OPC-501
72T-501
Hamm, Stacy
91Pocatel/ProC-3796
Hamm, Tim
81Hawaii-18
82Hawaii-18
Hammagren, Tucker
88CapeCod/Sum-166
Hammaker, Atlee
81Omaha-6
82T-471R
83D-298
83F-261
83Mother/Giants-13
83T-342
83T/St-324
84D-236
84F-373
84F/St-65
84Mother/Giants-9
84Nes/792-137LL
84Nes/792-576TL
84Nes/792-85
84OPC-85
84Seven-15W
84T-137TL
84T-576TL
84T-85
84T/Gloss40-7
84T/St-165
84T/St-175
85D-509
85F-608
85Mother/Giants-6
85OPC-351
85T-674
85T/St-165
86D-445
86F-544
86Leaf-220
86Mother/Giants-6
86T-223
87F/Up-U40
87OPC-358
87Phoenix-24
87T-781
88D-450
88F-83
88Mother/Giants-19
88S-528
88T-157
88T/Big-259
89D-414
89F-329
89Mother/Giants-19
89OPC-2
89S-422
89T-572
89T/Big-21
89UD-544
90D-532
90F-57
90Mother/Giant-13
90OPC-447
90Publint/St-69
90S-231
90T-447
90UD-620
91D-707
91F-530
91Leaf/Stud-246
91OPC-34
91T-34
91T/StClub/II-347
92S/I-233
Hamman, Ed
76Laugh/Clown-1
76Laugh/Clown-12
76Laugh/Clown-23
76Laugh/Clown-32
76Laugh/Clown-40
Hammargren, Roy
90Billings/ProC-3225
91CharWh/ClBest-12
91CharWh/ProC-2889
Hammer, James
(Pete)
77Wausau
79Jacks-12
Hammett, Ann
81ArkTr-23M
Hammon, Randy
78Cr/PCL-85
79Phoenix
Hammond, Arthur S.
81VeroB-6
Hammond, Chris
87Tampa-15
88BBAmer-17
88Chatt/Best-2
88SLAS-36
89Nashvl/ProC-1279
89Nashvl/Team-8
90AAAGame/ProC-AAA51
90F-421
90Nashvl/CMC-5
90Nashvl/ProC-225
90S-629RP
90UD-52
91B-680
91D-759
91D/Rook-19
91F-65
91F/UltraUp-U76
91Kahn/Reds-45
91Leaf/II-373
91Leaf/Stud-165
91OPC-258
91OPC/Premier-60
91T-258
91T/90Debut-62
91T/StClub/II-575
91UD/Ext-748
92D/I-172
92F-408
92S/100RisSt-89
92S/II-513
92T-744
92UD-105
Hammond, David
90Princet/DIMD-10
Hammond, Greg
91CharWh/ClBest-13
91CharWh/ProC-2890
Hammond, Steve
78Green
80Richm-6
81Richm-16
83F-114
83Omaha-18
84Omaha-10
86Iowa-14
Hammonds, Jeffrey
91T/Tr-51T
Hammonds, Reggie
86Nashua-11
Hamner, Granny
49Eureka-135
49Lummis
50B-204
51B-148
51BR-B7
51T/BB-29
52B-35
52NTea
52RM-NL7
52T-221
52TipTop
53B/Col-60
53RM-NL18
53T-146
54B-47
54T-24
55B-112
55RFG-18
55RM-NL15
56T-197
57T-335
58Hires-20
58T-268
59T-436
79TCMA-309
91T/Arc53-146
PM10/Sm-66
Rawl
Hamner, Ralph
49B-212
Hampton, Anthony
86Osceola-10
Hampton, Isaac
(Ike)
76SSPC-601
78T-503
91WIZMets-158
Hampton, Mark
90AubAs/Best-14
90AubAs/ProC-3401
Hampton, Mike
91SanBern/ClBest-6
91SanBern/ProC-1982
Hampton, Ray
82Evansvl-21
Hampton, Tony
85Osceola/Team-23
Hamric, Odbert
(Bert)
55T-199
58T-336
91Crown/Orio-175
Hamric, Rusty
80Penin/B-18
80Penin/C-24
82OkCty-10
84Cram/PCL-216
Hamrick, Ray
47Remar-17
47Smith-6
48Signal
48Smith-7
49Remar
50Remar
Hamrick, Stephen
78SanJose-15
Hamza, Tony
86Geneva-8
86Peoria-10
Hance, Bill
83TriCit-13
84Tulsa-28
Hancock, Andy
80Ashvl-5
Hancock, Chris
89Clinton/ProC-890
89Everett/Star-11
90A&AASingle/ProC-119
90Clinton/Best-8
90Clinton/ProC-2543
90Foil/Best-113
Hancock, Garry
79T-702R
81F-229
82Coke/BOS
82D-608
82F-295
82T-322
84F-445
84Mother/A's-16
84Nes/792-197
84T-197
Hancock, Jeff
89Watertn/Star-9
Hancock, Lee
89SanBern/Best-16
89SanBern/Cal-71
90Foil/Best-32
90Wmsprt/Best-1
90Wmsprt/ProC-1054
90Wmsprt/Star-9
91CaroMud/LineD-109
91CaroMud/ProC-1082
Hand, James
82Tucson-23
Hand, Rich
71MLB/St-369
71OPC-24
71T-24
71T/tatt-8
72OPC-317
72T-317
73OPC-398
73T-398
74OPC-571
74T-571
Handford, Charles
C46-21
Handler, Marve
80Elmira-34
Handley, Gene
40Hughes-9
49B/PCL-34
52Mother-7
53Mother-21
Handley, Jim
76AppFx
Handley, Lee E.
40PB-221
41DP-33
49B/PCL-28
Hands, William Alfred
(Bill)
66T-392R
67OPC-16
67T-16
68T-279
69MLB/St-120
69OPC-115
69T-115
69T/St-13
70MLB/St-16
70OPC-405
70T-405
71MLB/St-31
71OPC-670
71T-670
72MB-127
72OPC-335
72T-335
73OPC-555
73T-555
74OPC-271
74T-271
75OPC-412
75T-412
75T/M-412
76OPC-509
76SSPC-253
76T-509
Hanebrink, Harry
58T-454
59T-322
Hanel, Marcus
90Welland/Pucko-17
91Augusta/ClBest-13
91Augusta/ProC-807
Haney, Chris
90James/Pucko-18
91B-443
91D/Rook-44
91Harris/LineD-255
91Harris/ProC-620
91Single/ClBest-23
91UD/FinalEd-23F
92Classic/I-41
92D/I-291
92F-483
92S/100RisSt-15
92S/II-873
92T-626
92T/91Debut-70
92UD-662
Haney, Fred G.
26Exh-66
27Exh-34
29Exh/4-16
47Signal
52Mother-13
54T-75MG
57SpicSpan/4x5-9MG
58T-475AS
59T-551AS
87Conlon/2-16
91T/Arc53-316MG
Haney, Joe
86Beloit-9
Haney, Todd
88Wausau/GS-14
89SanBern/Best-25
89SanBern/Cal-81
89Wmsprt/Star-8
90AAAGame/ProC-AAA43
90Calgary/CMC-18
90Calgary/ProC-657
91Indianap/LineD-185
91Indianap/ProC-468
Haney, Wallace Larry
(Larry)
67T-507R
68OPC-42
68T-42
69OPC-209
69T-209
70T-648
73OPC-563
73T-563
75OPC-626
75T-626
75T/M-626
76OPC-446
76SSPC-502
76T-446
77T-12
78T-391
78TCMA-228
83Pol/Brew-12CO
86Pol/Brew-12CO
90Brewer/MillB-32CO
90Pol/Brew-x
91Brewer/MillB-32CO
91Crown/Orio-176
91Pol/Brew-x
Hanford, Charles
E254
E270/2
T205
Hanggie, Dan
84Chatt-4
85Orlan-6
Hanifin, Pat
90Target-970
Hanisch, Ron
89Beloit/II/Star-12
90Ashvl/ClBest-29TR
90Stockton/Best-23
90Stockton/Cal-202
Hanker, Fred
88Madis-14
Hankins, Mike
90Oneonta/ProC-3385
91CLAS/ProC-CAR31
91PrWill/ClBest-5
91PrWill/ProC-1434
91Single/ClBest-143
Hankinson, Frank
E223
N172
N172/ST
N284
N690/2
Hanks, Chris
89Elmira/Pucko-4
89WinHaven/Star-9
90LynchRS/Team-12
Hanley, John
79Knoxvl/TCMA-15
81AppFx-17
Hanlin, Rich
89Belling/Legoe-26
Hanlon, Edward J.
(Ned)
75F/Pion-9
90Target-314
E107
N172
N284
Scrapps
WG1-22
WG3-20
Hanna, Dave
83Idaho-5
Hanna, Preston
79T-296
80T-489
81D-523
81F-264
81Pol/Atl-49
81T-594

82BK/Lids-9
82F-435
82Pol/Atl-49
83T-127
Hannah, Joe
61BeeHive-7
Hannah, Mike
75OkCty
75SanAn
76Wmsprt
Hannah, Truck
28Exh/PCL-9
Hannahs, Gerald
(Gerry)
79Albuq-9
80Albuq-25
81Toledo-5
90Target-315
Hannahs, Mitch
88CapeCod/Sum-45
89Beloit/II/Star-13
91ElPaso/LineD-184
91ElPaso/ProC-2755
Hannan, Jim
63T-121
64T-261
65T-394
66T-479
67T-291
69OPC-106
69T-106
69T/St-236
70T-697
71OPC-229
71T-229
72MB-128
Hannifan, John J.
T206
Hannon, John
76BurlB
77Holyo
Hannon, Phil
87WinSalem-6
88Peoria/Ko-12
89WinSalem/Star-9
90T/TVCub-47
91Geneva/ClBest-29CO
91Geneva/ProC-4235CO
Hanrahan, William
N172
Hansel, Damon
87Macon-18
Hansell, Greg
90WinHaven/Star-10
91AS/Cal-14
Hanselman, Carl
88Pocatel/ProC-2099
89Clinton/ProC-903
89Everett/Star-12
90Clinton/Best-14
90Clinton/ProC-2540
91AS/Cal-45
91SanJose/ClBest-16
91SanJose/ProC-4
Hansen, Andy
49Eureka-106
52T-74
53B/BW-64
Hansen, Bob
75OPC-508
75T-508
75T/M-508
Hansen, Darel
83Idaho-6
84Madis/Pol-15
85Madis-15
85Madis/Pol-12
86Modesto-10
Hansen, Dave
87Bakers-21
88FSLAS/Star-7
88VeroB/Star-9
89SanAn/Best-17
90AAAGame/ProC-AAA45
90Albuq/CMC-17
90Albuq/ProC-350
90Albuq/Trib-9
90B-93
90F-642R
90F/Up-U21
91Albuq/LineD-7
91Albuq/ProC-1145
91Classic/200-155
91Classic/II-T35
91D-45RR
91F-203
91T/90Debut-63
91UD-4
92D/II-506
92S/II-754
Hansen, Guy
83Butte-31
89Memphis/Best-26CO
89Memphis/ProC-1192CO
90Memphis/Best-25CO
90Memphis/ProC-1026CO
90Memphis/Star-26CO
91Omaha/LineD-350CO
91Omaha/ProC-1050CO
Hansen, Jon
82ElPaso-11
Hansen, Mike
87Lakeland-16
88FSLAS/Star-39
88Lakeland/Star-13
89London/ProC-1376
Hansen, Ray
86Greens-11
87Greens-17
Hansen, Roger
81CharR-6
82CharR-2
84Memphis-18
86Omaha-9
86Omaha/TCMA-5
87Chatt/Best-14
88Calgary/CMC-21
88Calgary/ProC-790
89Calgary/CMC-15
89Calgary/ProC-530
Hansen, Ron Jr.
83TriCit-17
Hansen, Ron
59T-444
60T-127
61P-72
61T-240
61T/St-102
62J-30
62P-30
62P/Can-30
62Salada-89
62Shirriff-89
62T-245
62T/St-6
63F-2
63J-60
63P-60
63T-88
64T-384
64T/Coins-41
65MacGregor-4
65OPC-146
65T-146
66T-261
67OPC-9
67T-9
68T-411
69MB-102
69T-566
70MLB/St-184
70OPC-217
70T-217
71MLB/St-489
71OPC-419
71T-419
72MB-129
72T-763
78TCMA-142
83Pol/Brew-18C
86Provigo-28CO
91Crown/Orio-177
Hansen, Terrel
87Jamestn-10
89Rockford/Team-10
90A&AASingle/ProC-54
90Foil/Best-169
90Jaxvl/Best-9
90Jaxvl/ProC-1384
91Tidew/LineD-556
91Tidew/ProC-2522
Hansen, Todd
86Macon-12
88Charl/ProC-1206
89River/Best-6
89River/Cal-22
89River/ProC-1413
90Wichita/Rock-7
Hanson, Craig
91Spokane/ClBest-15
91Spokane/ProC-3945
Hanson, Erik
87Chatt/Best-10
88Calgary/ProC-786
89B-206
89Chatt/II/Team-11
89Classic-145
89D-32RR
89D/Best-320
89D/Rook-49
89F-549
89Mother/Sea-16
89T/Tr-45T
89UD/Ext-766
90B-469
90Classic/III-78
90D-345
90D/BestAL-68
90F-514
90Leaf/II-430
90Mother/Mar-8
90OPC-118
90PubIInt/St-434
90S-530
90S/100Ris-85
90S/YS/II-18
90T-118
90T/Big-289
90UD-235
91B-260
91Classic/200-147
91Classic/II-T22
91CounHrth-24
91D-550
91F-451
91F/Ultra-337
91Leaf/I-142
91Leaf/Stud-114
91OPC-655
91Panini/FrSt-235
91Panini/St-186
91Panini/Top15-79
91S-486
91S-688KM
91Seven/3DCoin-6NW
91T-655
91T/StClub/I-9
91UD-551
92D/I-138
92F-280
92S/I-8
92T-71
92UD-572
Hanyuda, Tad
88SanJose/Cal-119
88SanJose/ProC-128
Haraguchi, Ted
87SanJose-10
Hard, Shelby
90Everett/Best-23
Hardamon, Derrick
86Geneva-9
Harden, Curry
88CapeCod/Sum-67
Harden, Ty
85BurlR-21
86DayBe-10
Harder, Mel
32Orbit/num-29
32Orbit/un-30
34G-66
35BU-134
35Exh/4-11
35G-8I
35G-9I
36Exh/4-11
41DP-134
55Gol/Ind-10CO
55Salem
60T-460C
62Sugar-15
63Sugar-15
88Conlon/AmAS-14
89Pac/Leg-205
89Swell-41
R305
R311/Gloss
R311/Leath
R312
R313
R314
WG8-29
Hardgrave, Eric
86Beaum-13
87ElPaso-7
88GlenF/ProC-915
Hardgrove, Tom
88CapeCod/Sum-132
89Martins/Star-14
90Foil/Best-38
90Spartan/Best-1
90Spartan/ProC-2498
90Spartan/Star-12
Hardin, Jim
68T-222
69MB-103
69T-532M
69T-610
69T/St-124
70T-656
71MLB/St-298
71OPC-491
71T-491
72MB-130
72OPC-287
72T-287
73OPC-124
73T-124
91Crown/Orio-178
Harding, Greg
88StCath/ProC-2029
89Myrtle/ProC-1468
Hardtke, Jason
91Collnd/ClBest-25
91Collnd/ProC-1492
91Single/ClBest-7
Hardwick, Anthony
86Bakers-12
Hardwick, Willie
82Amari-19
83Beaum-18
84ArkTr-15
Hardy, Alex
C46-78
Hardy, Carlton
91Martins/ClBest-10
91Martins/ProC-3461
Hardy, Carroll
58T-446
59T-168
60T-341
61T-257
62Salada-220
62Shirriff-220
62T-101
63Pep
63T-468
Hardy, Howard L.
(Larry)
75OPC-112
75T-112
75T/M-112
76SSPC-120
78Charl
79Charl-15
80Utica-1
82Knoxvl-21
84Syrac-2
86Knoxvl-9MG
87Phoenix-11
90Phoenix/CMC-26CO
90Phoenix/ProC-29CO
91Phoenix/LineD-400CO
91Phoenix/ProC-85CO
Hardy, Jack
87Hawaii-3
88Vanco/CMC-10
88Vanco/ProC-755
89Vanco/CMC-5
89Vanco/ProC-586
90OkCty/CMC-1
90OkCty/ProC-425
90T/89Debut-51
Hardy, John Graydon
87BirmB/Best-18
Hardy, Mark
86Jamestn-12
Hare, Shawn
89Lakeland/Star-8
90Toledo/CMC-14
90Toledo/ProC-162
91Toledo/LineD-586
91Toledo/ProC-1944
92S/II-828RP
92T/91Debut-71
Harer, Wayne
80Colum-4
81Colum-19
82Colum-3
82Colum/Pol-22
Harford, Bill
90Peoria/Team-34VP
Hargan, Steve
66T-508
67Kahn
67T-233LL
67T-440
68Kahn
68OPC-35
68T-35
68T/G-15
69T-348
70OPC-136
70T-136
71MLB/St-370
71OPC-375
71T-375
71T/Coins-110
72MB-131
72T-615
75OPC-362
75T-362
75T/M-362
76K-1
76OPC-463
76SSPC-254
76T-463
77OPC-247
77T-37
Hargesheimer, Al
81F-457
81Phoenix-13
81T-502R
82Phoenix
83Iowa-4
84Omaha-4
85Omaha-26
86Omaha/TCMA-21
87Omaha-13
88Omaha/CMC-6
88Omaha/ProC-1517
Hargis, Dan
89Rockford/Team-11
90James/Pucko-34
91Rockford/ProC-2050
Hargis, Gary
76Shrev
78Colum
79Portl-13
80Port-15
81Buffa-15
Hargis, Steve
91Rockford/ClBest-29
Hargrave, Eugene F.
(Bubbles)
28Exh-14
28Yueng-33
E120
V61-60
W501-33
W572
W573
WG7-21
Hargrave, William M.
(Pinky)
26Exh-113
27Exh-57
33G-172
91Conlon/Sport-245
Hargraves, Charles R.
28Exh-7
29Exh/4-14
90Target-316
Hargrove, Dudley M.
(Mike)
75Ho-106
75OPC-106
75T-106
75T/M-106
76Ho-88
76K-51
76OPC-485
76SSPC-263
76T-485
77BurgChef-24

77Ho-18
77K-30
77OPC-35
77Pep-5
77T-275
77T/CS-20
78BK/R-11
78Ho-41
78K-56
78OPC-176
78T-172
79Ho-148
79OPC-311
79T-591
80OPC-162
80T-308
81D-78
81F-387
81K-66
81MSA/Disc-15
81OPC-74
81T-74
81T/SO-32
81T/St-68
82D-389
82Drake-16
82F-368
82F/St-198
82OPC-310
82T-310
82T-559TL
82T/St-180
82Wheat/Ind
83D-450
83F-409
83OPC-37
83T-660
83T/St-56
83Wheat/Ind-16
84D-495
84F-543
85FunFood/Pin-101
84Nes/792-546TL
84Nes/792-764
84OPC-79
84Seven-10C
84T-546TL
84T-764
84T/St-260
84Wheat/Ind-21
85D-398
85F-450
85GenMills-18
85OPC-252
85Polar/Ind-21
85T-425
85T/St-248
85ThomMc/Discs-12
86D-590
86F-588
86Leaf-228
86T-136
88EastLAS/ProC-52
88Wmsprt/ProC-1306
89ColoSp/CMC-10
89ColoSp/ProC-246
91T/Tr-52TMG
92T-609MG

Harigen, Charlie
81Tacoma-29M

Harkey, Mike
88BBAmer-2
88EastLAS/ProC-26
88Peoria/Ko-35M
88Pittsfld/ProC-1377
89B-286
89D-43RR
89F-427
89Iowa/CMC-5
89Iowa/ProC-1704
89Panini/St-48
89S-624RP
89S/HotRook-48
89S/YS/II-31
89Sf-132
89T-742FS
89UD-14SR
90B-28
90Classic/III-47
90Cub/Mara-10
90D-522
90D/Rook-22
90F-33
90Leaf/II-309
90Peoria/Team-20M
90T/Tr-36T
90T/TVCub-9
90UD-107
91B-417
91Classic/200-22
91Cub/Mara-22
91D-447
91F-423
91F/Ultra-62
91Leaf/I-90
91OPC-376
91Panini/FrSt-51
91Panini/St-46
91S-322
91S/100RisSt-63
91T-376
91T/StClub/I-197
91ToysRUs-10
91UD-475
92D/I-241
92F-382
92S/I-67
92T-98
92UD-218

Harkins, John
N172

Harkness, Don
77Cocoa
78DaytB

Harkness, Thomas W.
(Tim)
61Union
62T-404
63T-436
64T-57
90Target-317
91WIZMets-159

Harlan, Dan
88BBCity/Star-13

Harley, Al
90Ashvl/ClBest-14
91Ashvl/ProC-575
91Single/ClBest-101

Harley, Richard
E107

Harlow, Larry
76SSPC-397
78T-543
79T-314
80T-68
81F-289
81T-121
82F-462
82T-257
89T/SenLg-103
91Crown/Orio-179
91Pac/SenLg-20

Harmes, Kris
90MedHat/Best-20
91Dunedin/ClBest-29
91Dunedin/ProC-210
91StCath/ClBest-4
91StCath/ProC-3397

Harmon, Charles
(Chuck)
54T-182
55T-82
55T/DH-55
56T-308
57T-299
58T-48

Harmon, Kevin
86Sumter-8TR
87Sumter-12

Harmon, Mark
89SanBern/Best-28M

Harmon, Robert
10Domino-52
11Helmar-169
12Sweet/Pin-147
16FleischBrd-37
D329-76
E286
E300
M101/4-76
M116
T202
T205
T207

Harmon, Terry
69T-624R
70OPC-486
70T-486
71MLB/St-179
71OPC-682
71T-682
72OPC-377
72T-377
72T/Cloth-16
73OPC-166
73T-166
74OPC-642
74T-642
75OPC-399
75T-399
75T/M-399
76OPC-247
76T-247
77T-388
78T-118

Harmon, Tommy
83MidldC-2

Harmon, Wayne
83Cedar-28
83Cedar/LF-6TR

Harms, Tom
88Hagers/Star-8
89Freder/Star-9

Harnisch, Pete
88BBAmer-11
88CharlK/Pep-18
88RochR/Gov-10
88SLAS-32
89B-4
89D-44RR
89French-42
89RochR/ProC-1649
89S/Tr-110
89UD/Ext-744
90B-247
90Classic-44
90D-596
90D/BestAL-101
90F-177
90Leaf/I-39
90OPC-324
90S-355
90S/100Ris-76
90S/YS/II-19
90T-324
90T/JumboR-12
90ToysRUs-14
90UD-623
91B-555
91Crown/Orio-180
91D-181
91F-474
91F/UltraUp-U83
91F/Up-U89
91Leaf/I-245
91Leaf/Stud-177
91Mother/Ast-3
91OPC-179
91RedFoley/St-45
91S-492
91S/RookTr-36T
91T-179
91T/StClub/II-343
91T/Tr-53T
91UD-302
91UD/Ext-772
91USPlayC/AS-3S
92D/I-235
92F-435
92S/100SS-12
92S/I-224
92T-765
92UD-635

Haro, Sam
84PrWill-22
85Nashua-11
86Hawaii-11
87Vanco-10

Harper, Brian
80ElPaso-9
81SLCity-15
84D-142
84Nes/792-144
84T-144
85D-566
85F-466
85T-332
86D-547
86F-36
86KAS/Disc-8
86Nashvl-10
86T-656
88F/Up-U42
88Martins/Star-16
88Portl/CMC-11
88Portl/ProC-651
89B-155
89D-641
89F-114
89S-408
89T-472
89UD-379
90D-355
90D/BestAL-37
90ElPasoATG/Team-35
90F-377
90Leaf/II-479
90OPC-47
90Panini/St-116
90PublInt/St-329
90S-189
90Sf-121
90T-47
90T/St-290
90UD-391
91B-333
91Classic/III-35
91D-22DK
91D-398MVP
91D-582
91D/SuperDK-22DK
91F-613
91F/Ultra-188
91Leaf/I-54
91Leaf/Stud-86
91OPC-554
91Panini/FrSt-299
91Panini/St-242
91S-312
91S/100SS-46
91T-554
91T/StClub/II-589
91UD-212
92D/I-83
92F-204
92S/I-215
92T-217
92UD-527

Harper, Charles W.
E107

Harper, David
77Tucson
78Cr/PCL-28

Harper, Devallon
83Kinston/Team-7

Harper, George W.
21Exh-68
25Exh-41
26Exh-43
27Exh-18
29Exh/4-2
91Conlon/Sport-246
E121/120
W501-107
W513-85

Harper, Greg
88Idaho/ProC-1847
88Sumter/ProC-401
89Sumter/ProC-1117
90BurlB/Best-22
90BurlB/Star-14

Harper, Harry C.
90Target-318
D327
D328-69
E135-69
W575

Harper, Jon
77Cedar

Harper, Marshal
76AppFx
77AppFx

Harper, Milt
86Water-12
87Kinston-22
88Wmsprt/ProC-1327
90Reno/Cal-275

Harper, Terry Joe
(Terry)
79Richm-14
80Richm-17
81Pol/Atl-19
81T-192R
82BK/Lids-10
82Richm-24
82T-507
83D-607
83F-137
83Pol/Atl-19
83T-339
84F-180
84Nes/792-624
84Pol/Atl-19
84T-624
85F-327
85Pol/Atl-19
85T/Tr-45T
86D-627
86F-516
86Leaf-246
86OPC-247
86Pol/Atl-19
86T-247
86T/St-41
87D/OD-217
87F-517
87F/Excit-22
87T-49
87T/Tr-42T
88F-331
90Greenvl/ProC-1145CO
90Greenvl/Star-24CO
91Greenvl/ClBest-27CO
91Greenvl/LineD-225CO
91Greenvl/ProC-3019CO

Harper, Terry
82Redwd-22
83Redwd-12

Harper, Tommy
63FrBauer-7
63T-158R
64Kahn
64T-330
64T/Coins-40
64T/St-43
65Kahn
65OPC-47
65T-47
66Kahn
66T-214
67Kahn
67T-392
68T-590
69MB-104
69MLB/St-95
69OPC-42
69Sunoco/Pin-10
69T-42
69T/St-225
70K-74
70McDon-5
70MLB/St-270
70OPC-370
70T-370
70T/CB
70T/S-9
71Bz
71Bz/Test-30
71K-47
71MD
71MLB/St-437
71OPC-260
71T-260
71T/Coins-140
71T/GM-42
71T/S-63
71T/tatt-2
72MB-132
72OPC-455
72T-455
73OPC-620
73T-620
74Greyhound-5M
74OPC-204LL
74OPC-325
74T-204LL
74T-325
74T/St-134
75OPC-537
75T-537
75T/M-537
76OPC-274
76T-274
77T-414
91Crown/Orio-181

Harrah, Toby
72OPC-104
72T-104

73OPC-216
73T-216
74OPC-511
74T-511
74T/St-235
75Ho-14
75Ho/Twink-14
75OPC-131
75T-131
75T/M-131
76Ho-48
76Ho/Twink-48
76OPC-412
76SSPC-264
76T-412
77BurgChef-26
77Ho-37
77OPC-208
77T-301
78BK/R-13
78Ho-123
78OPC-74
78T-44
79Ho-150
79OPC-119
79T-234
80OPC-333
80T-636
81D-318
81F-389
81OPC-67
81T-721
81T/SO-46
81T/St-65
82D-72
82F-369
82F/St-193
82OPC-16
82T-532
82T/St-177
82Wheat/Ind
83D-13DK
83D-337
83D/AAS-39
83F-410
83F-635M
83K-44
83OPC-356
83PermaGr/CC-25
83T-141TL
83T-480
83T/Gloss40-13
83T/St-58
83Wheat/Ind-17
84D-251
84F-544
84F/X-48
84Nes/792-348
84OPC-348
84T-348
84T/St-251
84T/Tr-48
85F-130
85F/Up-U49
85Rang-11
85T-94
85T/Tr-46T
86D-159
86F-560
86Leaf-86
86OPC-72
86Rang-11
86T-535
86T/Mini-32
86T/St-238
87D-408
87F-125
87OKCty-12
87T-152
88AAA/ProC-51
88OkCty/CMC-25
88OkCty/ProC-46
89Pac/SenLg-162
89Smok/R-13
89T/SenLg-58
89TM/SenLg-44
90EliteSenLg-22
90Mother/Rang-27M
91LineD-10
91Mother/Rang-28CO
91Swell/Great-37

Harrel, Donny
91AppFx/ClBest-12
91AppFx/ProC-1718

Harrell, Bill
58T-443
59T-433
61T-354
63MilSau-2

Harrell, Greg
87PortChar-13
88Tulsa-27TR
89Tulsa/GS-4
89Tulsa/Team-9TR

Harrell, John
70OPC-401R
70T-401R

Harrelson, Bill
69T-224R

Harrelson, Derrel M.
(Bud)
67T-306
68OPC-132
68T-132
69MB-105
69MLB/St-166
69MLBPA/Pin-45
69T-456
69T/St-64
70K-68
70MLB/St-77
70T-634
70Trans/M-25
71K-66
71MD
71MLB/St-155
71OPC-355
71T-355
71T/Coins-67
71T/GM-55
71T/tatt-13
72MB-133
72OPC-496KP
72OPC-53
72OPC-54IA
72T-496KP
72T-53
72T-54IA
72T/Post-22
73OPC-223
73T-223
73T/Lids-20
74OPC-380
74T-380
74T/St-63
75Ho-45
75OPC-395
75T-395
75T/M-395
76Ho-52
76Ho/Twink-52
76OPC-337
76SSPC-545
76T-337
77BurgChef-144
77OPC-172
77T-44
78T-403
79T-118
80OPC-294
80T-566
81T-694
84LitFalls-13
88Kahn/Mets-3CO
89Kahn/Mets-3CO
90Kahn/Mets-3CO
90Swell/Great-111
90T/Tr-37TMG
90T/TVMets-4MG
91Kahn/Mets-3MG
91OPC-261MG
91Swell/Great-38
91T-261MG
91WIZMets-160

Harrelson, Ken
64T-419
65T-479
66OPC-55
66T-55
66T/RO-107
67OPC-188
67T-188
68T-566
69MB-106
69MLB/St-13
69MLBPA/Pin-8
69OPC-3LL
69OPC-5LL
69OPC/DE-8
69T-240
69T-3LL
69T-417AS
69T-5LL
69T/DE-3
69T/S-4
69T/St-134
70K-68
70MLB/St-198
70OPC-545
70T-545
70T/PI-6
71Bz/Test-15
71MLB/St-371
71OPC-510
71T-510
71T/Coins-134
72MB-134
78TCMA-247
86Coke/WS-xx
88Pac/Leg-14

Harridge, Will
56T-1PRES
57T-100M
58T-300M
80SSPC/HOF

Harriger, Dennis
89Pittsfld/Star-6
91StLucie/ClBest-21

Harring, Ken Jr.
89Idaho/ProC-2014
90Durham/Team-5

Harrington, Jody
89Elizab/Star-10
90Kenosha/Best-19
90Kenosha/ProC-2288
90Kenosha/Star-6

Harrington, John
86Miami-8
87Miami-20

Harris, Adoldo
90Tampa/DIMD-10

Harris, Alonzo
(Candy)
67T-564R
68OPC-128R
68T-128R

Harris, Anthony S.
(Spence)
E120
E220

Harris, B. Gail
56T-91
57T-281
58T-309
59T-378
60T-152
79TCMA-275

Harris, Carry
83Knoxvl-10

Harris, Craig
80WHave-11

Harris, Dannie
90Foil/Best-126
90Huntsvl/Best-7

Harris, David Stanley
25Exh-7
33G-9
R337-412
V353-9

Harris, Donald
89Butte/SP-4
90B-499
90OPC-314FDP
90S-661DC
90T-314FDP
90Tulsa/ProC-1167
91B-269
91Single/ClBest-12
91Tulsa/LineD-583
91Tulsa/ProC-2785
92D/II-652
92F-660
92T-554
92T/91Debut-72
92UD-11SR

Harris, Doug
91AppFx/ClBest-4
91AppFx/ProC-1710

Harris, Doyle
81Louisvl-29
83Louisvl/Riley-29
84Louisvl-7

Harris, Frank
77Evansvl/TCMA-14
80Ogden-12
82Madis-18
89Clmbia/Best-26

Harris, Franklyn
89Medford/Best-3

Harris, Gene
86Jamestn-13
87WPalmB-26
88Jaxvl/Best-5
88Jaxvl/ProC-980
89D/Best-325
89F/Up-58
89T/Tr-46T
90D-247
90F-515
90Leaf/II-378
90Mother/Mar-15
90OPC-738
90S-548
90S/100Ris-54
90T-738
90T/89Debut-52
90UD-565
91D-651
91F-452
91OPC-203
91S-627
91T-203

Harris, Glenn
84Savan-18

Harris, Greg
(Lefty)
87Wichita-11
88Wichita-19
89Wichita/Rock-19

Harris, Greg A.
79Jacks-21
80Tidew-11
81Tidew-23
82Coke/Reds
82Indianap-13
82T-783
82T/Tr-41T
83D-295
83F-590
83Indianap-6
83T-296
84Stuart-22
85F-35
85Rang-27
85T-242
85T/Tr-47T
86D-465
86F-561
86OPC-128
86Rang-27
86T-586
86T/St-245
87D-382
87F-126
87F/St-54
87Leaf-82
87Mother/Rang-11
87OPC-44
87Sf-126
87Smok/R-2
87T-44
87T/St-238
88AlaskaAS70/Team-15
88D-427
88F-468
88Phill/TastyK-34
88S-179
88T-369
89D-548
89F-570
89Phill/TastyK-8
89S-476
89T-627
90D-582
90F/Up-U71
90Leaf/II-499
90OPC-529
90PublInt/St-237
90T-529
90T/TVRSox-11
91D-306
91F-97
91Leaf/I-83
91OPC-123
91Pep/RSox-9
91S-109
91T-123
91T/StClub/II-324
91UD-509
91WIZMets-161
92D/I-113
92S/I-156
92T-468
92UD-658

Harris, Greg W.
85Spokane/Cram-7
86Cram/PCL-161
87TexLgAS-23
88AAA/ProC-23
88F/Up-U109
88LasVegas/CMC-3
88LasVegas/ProC-227
89D-34
89D/Rook-46
89F-306
89Padre/Mag-18
89S/Tr-87
89T-194
89UD/Ext-724
90Classic/III-13
90Coke/Padre-7
90D-65
90F-158
90Leaf/II-452
90OPC-572
90Padre/MagUno-24
90Panini/St-353
90S-257
90S/100Ris-24
90S/YS/I-18
90T-572
90T/JumboR-13
90UD-622
91B-657
91D-131
91F-531
91F/Ultra-304
91F/Ultra-33
91Leaf/II-422
91OPC-749
91Padre/MagRal-13
91S-251
91T-749
91T/StClub/I-205
91UD-489
92D/I-49
92F-606
92S/I-378
92T-636
92UD-306

Harris, Gregg S.
86CharRain-10
87CharRain-3

Harris, James William
(Billy)
69T-569
70OPC-512
70T-512

Harris, James
89Kingspt/Star-12
90SALAS/Star-32
91StLucie/ClBest-8
91StLucie/ProC-717

Harris, Joe
28Yueng-51
90Target-319
E120
W502-51
W513-81
W572

Harris, John
77QuadC
79SLCity-16
80SLCity-12
81T-214R
82D-444
82F-463
82Spokane-16
82T-313
83Indianap-29
84Evansvl-15

Harris, Keith
89Utica/Pucko-10

Harris, Larry
81Wisco-5

Harris, Lenny
84Cedar-25
86Vermont-9
87Nashvl-9

88Nashvl/CMC-12
88Nashvl/ProC-489
88Nashvl/Team-12
89F-645R
89Kahn/Reds-7
89UD/Ext-781
90CedarDG/Best-3
90D-434
90F-397
90Leaf/II-437
90Mother/Dodg-18
90OPC-277
90Pol/Dodg-29
90PublInt/St-31
90S-23
90S/100Ris-83
90S/YS/I-37
90T-277
90Target-320
90UD-423
91B-607
91D-224
91F-204
91F/Ultra-162
91Mother/Dodg-18
91OPC-453
91Panini/FrSt-57
91Panini/St-51
91Pol/Dodg-29
91S-144
91T-453
91T/StClub/I-65
91UD-239
92D/I-226
92F-458
92S/I-291
92T-92
92UD-191

Harris, Luman
60T-455CO
65OPC-274MG
65T-274MG
66OPC-147MG
66T-147MG
68T-439MG
69OPC-196MG
69T-196MG
70OPC-86MG
70T-86MG
71OPC-346MG
71T-346MG
72OPC-484MG
72T-484MG

Harris, Mark
(Infielder)
79WHave-26

Harris, Mark
90LitSun-19

Harris, Maurice
(Mickey)
47TipTop
48L-27
49B-151
50B-160
51B-311
52B-135
52T-207

Harris, Mike
82Spring-19
83ArkTr-13
84ArkTr-26

Harris, Pep
91BurlInd/ProC-3296

Harris, Rafael
80Utica-6

Harris, Ray
88SoOreg/ProC-1713

Harris, Reggie
87Elmira/Red-30
88Lynch/Star-9
89WinHaven/Star-10
90B-446
91Classic/I-71
91D-704
91OPC-177
91S-643RP
91S/100RisSt-49
91T-177
91T/90Debut-64
91Tacoma/ProC-2300
91UD-672
92D/II-781
92S/100RisSt-48

Harris, Robert A.
W753

Harris, Robert
87Watertn-3
88Augusta/ProC-386
90Harris/ProC-1205
90Harris/Star-9

Harris, Rusty
87AubAs-2
88Osceola/Star-12
89Osceola/Star-7
90ColMud/Best-7
90ColMud/ProC-1353
90ColMud/Star-12
91Jacks/LineD-559
91Jacks/ProC-931

Harris, Sam
21Exh-69

Harris, Stanley
(Bucky)
25Exh-124
26Exh-124
28Exh-62
28Yueng-41
34DS-91
36G
40PB-129
51B-275MG
52B-158MG
53B/BW-46
80SSPC/HOF
81Detroit-105MG
86Conlon/1-25
91Conlon/Sport-61
91T/Arc53-313MG
92Conlon/Sport-593
E120
E210-41
E220
R310
R312/M
R313
R314
V100
V117-21
V355-130
W502-14
W517-9
W572

Harris, Steve
85Bend/Cram-10

Harris, Tracy
80SanJose/JITB-10
81LynnS-5
82SLCity-10
83Chatt-17

Harris, Twayne
83Idaho-21
86Modesto-11

Harris, Vic
73OPC-594
73T-594
74OPC-157
74T-157
74T/St-13
75OPC-658
75T-658
75T/M-658
76SSPC-321
77Phoenix
78T-436
79T-338
79Vanco-2
80Vanco-21
84Louisvl-18

Harris, Vince
88Utica/Pucko-6
89CharRain/ProC-976
90AS/Cal-5
90Foil/Best-315
90Riversi/Best-9
90Riversi/Cal-12
90Riversi/ProC-2619
91Wichita/LineD-607
91Wichita/ProC-2610

Harris, Walt
88Hagers/Star-9
89RochR/CMC-19
89RochR/ProC-1651
90Hagers/Star-10

Harris, Walter
(Buddy)
71OPC-404R
71T-404R

Harris, William
(Bill)
60DF-18
60T-128
90Target-971

Harris, William
V100

Harrison, Brett
87StPete-7
88ArkTr/GS-13
88TexLgAS/GS-13

Harrison, Brian Lee
86Cram/PCL-164
87CharRain-8
88River/Cal-210
88River/ProC-1428
89River/Best-7
89River/Cal-17
89River/ProC-1410
90A&AASingle/ProC-133
90Foil/Best-27
90Riversi/Best-10
90Riversi/Cal-17
90Riversi/ProC-2601

Harrison, Charles
(Chuck)
66T-244R
67OPC-8
67T-8
69OPC-116
69T-116

Harrison, Doug
78Clinton
80Albuq-9

Harrison, Keith
86Cram/PCL-173
86Elmira-9
87CharRain-22
88Charl/ProC-1207

Harrison, Mack
79Ogden/TCMA-7

Harrison, Mathew
(Matt)
86FSLAS-20
86FtLaud-11
87Albany-13
88Colum/CMC-5
88Colum/Pol-3
88Colum/ProC-317
90AlbanyDG/Best-8

Harrison, Mike
91Billings/ProC-3756

Harrison, Pat
89Alaska/Team-7

Harrison, Phil
86Geneva-10
87Peoria-23
88CLAS/Star-28
88WinSalem/Star-5
89CharlK-21
90T/TVCub-48

Harrison, R.J.
80LynnS-19
81LynnS-6
82Wausau-17
83Wausau/LF-30MG
86Chatt-12MG

Harrison, Robert Lee
(Bob)
79TCMA-76
91Crown/Orio-182

Harrison, Robert
77StPete

Harrison, Robert
89Johnson/Star-26TR
90Hamil/Star-28TR

Harrison, Ron
82Madis-21
83Albany-18
87Beloit-16
87Denver-8

Harrison, Roric E.
72OPC-474R
72T-474R
73OPC-229
73T-229
74OPC-298
74T-298
74T/St-5
75OPC-287
75T-287
75T/M-287
76OPC-547
76SSPC-507
76T-547
77Evansvl/TCMA-15
78T-536
91Crown/Orio-183

Harrison, Wayne
85Durham-25
86Durham-13

Harriss, Bryan
(Slim)
28Exh-34
E126-46
V61-38

Harriss, William
(Slim)
21Exh-70
E120
W573

Harrist, Earl
50Remar
52T-402
53T-65
91T/Arc53-65

Harry, Whitney
82BurlR-22
83BurlR-18
83BurlR/LF-15
84Tulsa-20

Harryman, Jeff
77Newar
78BurlB

Harsh, Nick
82FtMyr-7

Harshman, Jack
54T-173
55RM-AL6
55T-104
55T/DH-66
56T-29
56T/Pin-33
57T-152
58T-217
59T-475
60T-112
79TCMA-33
91Crown/Orio-184

Hart, Brian
89BurlInd/Star-12

Hart, Chris
90SoOreg/Best-18
90SoOreg/ProC-3431
91Modesto/ProC-3103
91SoOreg/ProC-3861

Hart, Darrin
89Watlo/Star-10
89Watlo/Star-29

Hart, James Henry
T206
T213/brown

Hart, James M.
81RochR-7
83Colum-24

Hart, Jeff
89CharRain/ProC-987
89Watlo/ProC-1781
90Waterlo/Best-6
90Waterlo/ProC-2373

Hart, Jim Ray
64T-452R
65OPC-4LL
65T-395
65T-4LL
65T/E-4
66T-295
66T/RO-28
67T-220
68Coke
68Dexter-37
68OPC-73
68T-73
69MB-107
69MLB/St-199
69MLBPA/Pin-46
69T-555
69T/St-104
70MLB/St-124
70OPC-176
70T-176
71MLB/St-249
71OPC-461
71T-461
72MB-135
72T-733
73OPC-538
73T-538
74OPC-159
74T-159
78TCMA-269
84Mother/Giants-20
PM10/Sm-67

Hart, John
85CharlO-14
86RochR-6MG
87RochR-3
87RochR/TCMA-24
88French-47CO
90OPC-141MG
90T-141MG

Hart, Kim
82Iowa-31
83Iowa-28

Hart, Mike
79Tucson-17
80Charl-10
80LynnS-7
81Spokane-7
82SLCity-11
83Toledo-20
85IntLgAS-30
85Toledo-21
86RochR-7
87RochR-10
87RochR/TCMA-18
88CLAS/Star-2
88T-69
89Reading/ProC-658
90FtLaud/Star-23MG
91CLAS/ProC-CAR32MG
91Crown/Orio-185
91PrWill/ClBest-24
91PrWill/ProC-1442MG

Hart, Shelby
90Everett/ProC-3139
91Clinton/ClBest-17
91Clinton/ProC-846

Hart, William F.
90Target-321
N172
N284
N526
T206
T213/brown

Hart, William W.
46Remar-6
47Smith-15
90Target-972

Hartenstein, Chuck
68OPC-13
68T-13
69T-596
70OPC-216
70T-216
77OPC-157
77T-416
80Hawaii-11
81Hawaii-24
82Hawaii-24
84Cram/PCL-134CO
86Penin-11CO

Harter, Andy
88Ashvl/ProC-1052

Hartgraves, Dean
87AubAs-24
88Ashvl/ProC-1072
89Ashvl/ProC-960
90ColMud/Best-6
90ColMud/ProC-1343
90ColMud/Star-13
91Jacks/LineD-560
91Jacks/ProC-921

Hartje, Chris
90Target-973

Hartley, Grover
11Helmar-128
92Conlon/Sport-520
D328-70
E135-70
T207
W753

Hartley, Michael
(Mike)
83StPete-7
85Spring-13
87Bakers-1
88Albuq/CMC-9

88Albuq/ProC-263
89Albuq/CMC-4
89Albuq/ProC-67
90B-87
90Classic/III-63
90D/Rook-34
90F-651R
90F/Up-U22
90Pol/Dodg-46
90S-641
90SpringDG/Best-15
90T/89Debut-53
90Target-974
91D-545
91F-205
91Mother/Dodg-19
91OPC-199
91Pol/Dodg-46
91S-252
91S/100RisSt-67
91T-199
91UD-686
92D/II-726
92S/II-670
92T-484
92UD-613

Hartley, Todd
86Cram/PCL-63

Hartley, Tom
86AppFx-10

Hartman, Albert
82BurlR-23

Hartman, Ed
87Watertn-16
88Augusta/ProC-366
89Salem/Star-10
89Star/Wax-94

Hartman, Harry
W711/1ANN
W711/2ANN

Hartman, J.C.
61T/St-161
63Pep
63T-442

Hartman, Jeff
86VeroB-9
88VeroB/Star-10

Hartman, Ralph
(Doc)
81Redwd-26
82Redwd-27

Hartman, Robert
59T-128
60T-129

Hartmann, Reid
89Kingspt/Star-13

Hartnett, Charles
(Gabby)
21Exh-67
25Exh-22
26Exh-22
27Exh-11
28Exh-10
28Yueng-5
29Exh/4-5
30CEA/Pin-5
31Exh/4-5
32Orbit/un-31
33CJ/Pin-13
33G-202
35BU-136
35Exh/4-3
36Exh/4-3
36Wheat
37Dix
37Exh/4-3
38Dix
38Exh/4-3
38ONG/Pin-15
39Exh
50Callahan
60F-29
61F-41
61GP-11
80Pac/Leg-72
80SSPC/HOF
86Sf/Dec-13
87Conlon/2-17
91Conlon/Sport-313
91Conlon/Sport-59
92Conlon/Sport-586
E120
E210-5
PM10/Sm-68
PR1-16
R305
R306
R308-200
R311/Leath
R312/M
R314
R332-38
V355-57
W502-5
WG8-30

Hartnett, Dave
86Cram/PCL-101
87Wausau-22

Harts, Greg
91WIZMets-162

Hartsel, Tully
(Topsy)
10Domino-53
12Sweet/Pin-45
E101
E106
E107
E254
E90/1
E92
E97
S74-31
T205
T206
T208
T213/brown
T215/blue
T215/brown
T216
W555

Hartsfield, Bob
75Cedar
76Clinton
82AubAs-2MG

Hartsfield, Roy
51B-277
52B-28
52T-264
73OPC-237CO
73T-237CO
77OPC-238MG
77T-113MG
78OPC-218MG
78T-444MG
79OPC-262MG
79T-282MG
79TCMA-123
83Indianap-3MG

Hartshorn, Kyle
85Lynch-12
86Jacks/TCMA-5
88Jacks/GS-6

Hartsock, Brian
82Danvl-24
83Peoria/LF-24
86MidldA-9
87SanBern-13
89Reno/Cal-249

Hartsock, Jeff
88GreatF-21
89AS/Cal-15
89Bakers/Cal-183
91Albuq/LineD-8
91Albuq/ProC-1135

Hartung, Andrew
90A&AASingle/ProC-180
90Geneva/ProC-3044
90Geneva/Star-13
91Peoria/ClBest-28
91Peoria/ProC-1349

Hartung, Clinton
47TipTop
48B-37
49B-154
49Eureka-107
50B-118
50Drake-2
51B-234
52BR
52T-141
R346-47

Hartwig, Dan
77Cedar

Hartwig, Rob
90Batavia/ProC-3079
91Spartan/ClBest-25
91Spartan/ProC-910

Hartzell, Paul
75QuadC
77BurgChef-118
77T-179
78T-529
79OPC-212
79T-402
80OPC-366
80T-721
84ElPaso-20

Hartzell, Pete
91Crown/Orio-186

Hartzell, Roy A.
16FleischBrd-38
92Conlon/Sport-544
D303
D329-77
D350/2-76
E126
E254
E270/1
E90/1
E91
M101/4-77
M101/5-76
M116
T201
T204
T216

Hartzog, Cullen
90PrWill/Team-11
90T/TVYank-45
91Albany/ProC-1003

Harvell, Rod
89GreatF-26

Harvey, Bob
91Negro/Lewis-3

Harvey, Bryan
86PalmSp-16
86PalmSp/Smok-12
87MidldA-25
88D/Rook-53
88Edmon/CMC-5
88F/Up-U14
88S/Tr-87T
88Smok/Angels-21
88T/Tr-45T
89B-40
89D-525
89D/Best-317
89F-479
89F/BBMVP's-18
89F/Heroes-21
89OPC-287
89Panini/St-284
89S-185
89S/HotRook-92
89S/YS/I-30
89Sf-130
89T-632
89T/St-180
89ToysRUs-13
89UD-594
90D-372
90F-134
90Leaf/I-116
90OPC-272
90RedFoley/St-44
90S-8
90Sf-31
90Smok/Angel-7
90T-272
90T/St-175
90UD-686
91B-211
91D-206
91F-315
91F/Ultra-45
91Leaf/I-213
91OPC-153
91S-108
91Smok/Angel-17
91T-153
91T/StClub/I-98
91UD-592
91USPlayC/AS-7D
92Classic/I-42
92D/I-211
92F-61
92F-696LL
92S/I-322
92T-407AS
92T-568
92UD-434

Harvey, Craig
77Watlo

Harvey, Don
88Pac/8Men-16

Harvey, Greg
88Eugene/Best-3
89AppFx/ProC-853
90BBCity/Star-10
90FSLAS/Star-31
91BBCity/ClBest-5
91BBCity/ProC-1392

Harvey, Harold
(Doug)
84Smok/SDP-13ump
88TM/Umpire-1
89TM/Umpire-1
90TM/Umpire-1

Harvey, Ken
87SanAn-23

Harvey, Randy
82BirmB-12
86QuadC-14

Harvey, Raymond
91Collnd/ClBest-1
91Collnd/ProC-1498

Harvey, Robert
90SanBern/Cal-BB

Harvey, Steve
82Reading-20

Harvick, Brad
87Erie-19
88Savan/ProC-345
89Savan/ProC-365

Harwell, David
88Kinston/Star-10

Harwell, Ernie
81Detroit-62ANN
83Kaline-26ANN
88Domino-6ANN
89Pac/Leg-172ANN

Harwell, Jim
61Union

Haryd, Mark
87BurlEx-20

Haselman, Bill
88CharlR/Star-9
89TexLAS/GS-33
89Tulsa/GS-11
89Tulsa/Team-10
90A&AASingle/ProC-68
90Tulsa/ProC-1158
91D-679
91F-287
91OkCty/LineD-310
91OkCty/ProC-182
91S-377RP
91T/90Debut-65

Hasler, Curt
89Saraso/Star-10
91Vanco/LineD-634
91Vanco/ProC-1590

Haslerig, Bill
78Green
79Savan-4

Hasley, Mike
75Dubuq
76Dubuq

Haslin, Mickey
35BU-104

Haslock, Chris
88Spokane/ProC-1945
89CharRain/ProC-981
90Riversi/Best-11
90Riversi/Cal-18
90Riversi/ProC-2602
91HighD/ClBest-5
91HighD/ProC-2388

Hassamaer, William L.
N172

Hassett, John
(Buddy)
39Exh
39PB-57
40PB-62
41DP-121
90Target-322
R303/A

Hassey, Ron
79Tacoma-1
80T-222
81D-80
81F-405
81OPC-187
81T-564
81T/St-71
82D-463
82F-370
82OPC-54
82T-54
82Wheat/Ind
83D-159
83F-411
83F-642M
83T-689
83T/St-62
83Wheat/Ind-18
84D-460
84F-545
84F/X-49
84Nes/792-308
84OPC-308
84SevenUp-15
84T-308
84T/St-262
84T/Tr-49
85F/Up-U50
85T-742
85T/Tr-48T
86D-370
86F-107
86OPC-157
86T-157
87Coke/WS-15
87D-532
87F-499
87OPC-61
87T-667
87T/St-285
88D-580
88D/A's/Bk-NEW
88D/Best-302
88F-399
88Mother/A's-16
88S/Tr-33T
88T-458
88T/Tr-46T
89B-194
89D-361
89F-9
89Mother/A's-15
89OPC-272
89S-334
89T-272
89T/Big-171
89T/St-173
89UD-564
90B-464
90D-450
90F-8
90Leaf/II-326
90Mother/A's-12
90OPC-527
90Publint/St-305
90S-168
90T-527
90T/Big-4
90UD-195
91D-476
91F-8
91F/Up-U98
91Leaf/II-359
91OPC-327
91OPC/Premier-61
91S-806
91S/RookTr-43T
91T-327
91T/StClub/II-490
91UD-401
92S/I-273

Hassinger, Brad
90Princet/DIMD-11
91Single/ClBest-140
91Spartan/ClBest-5
91Spartan/ProC-890

Hassler, Andy
75OPC-261
75T-261
75T/M-261
76OPC-207
76SSPC-186
76T-207
77T-602
78T-73
79T-696

80T-353
81D-581
81F-290
81T-454
81T/St-55
82D-519
82F-464
82T-94
83D-290
83F-92
83T-573
84ArkTr-25
84D-255
84F-519
84Nes/792-719
84T-719
85Louisvl-6
91WIZMets-163

Hasty, Robert
E120
V100

Hatcher, Billy
83MidldC-13
84Iowa-24
85D-41RR
85F-649R
85Iowa-10
85SevenUp-22
86D-433
86F-371
86F/Up-U49
86Pol/Ast-23
86T-46
86T/Tr-45T
87D-481
87D/OD-18
87F-59
87F/RecSet-15
87Mother/Ast-26
87Pol/Ast-6
87T-578
88D-23DK
88D-261
88D/Best-150
88D/DKsuper-23DK
88F-449
88Leaf-110
88Leaf-23DK
88Mother/Ast-6
88OPC-306
88Panini/St-300
88Pol/Ast-11
88RedFoley/St-30
88S-505
88Sf-63
88T-306
88T/Big-3
88T/Mini-49
88T/St-28
88T/UK-30
89D-187
89D/Best-150
89F-359
89Lennox/Ast-1
89Mother/Ast-5
89OPC-252
89Panini/St-92
89S-61
89Sf-174
89T-252
89T/Big-118
89T/St-19
89UD-344
90D-616
90D/BestNL-125
90F-467
90F/Up-U13
90Homer/Pirate-11
90Kahn/Reds-11
90Leaf/I-241
90OPC-119
90PublInt/St-96
90S-562
90S/Tr-42T
90T-119
90T/Big-222
90T/Tr-38T
90UD-598
90UD/Ext-778
91B-670
91D-196
91D-763WS
91F-66
91F/Ultra-95
91F/WS-2
91Kahn/Reds-22
91Leaf/I-205
91Leaf/Stud-166
91OPC-604
91Panini/FrSt-132
91Pep/Reds-10
91RedFoley/St-46
91S-469
91T-604
91T/StClub/II-371
91UD-114
91Woolwth/HL-27
92D/II-537
92F-409
92S/II-447
92T-432
92UD-699

Hatcher, Christopher
90AubAs/ProC-3395
91BurlAs/ClBest-20
91BurlAs/ProC-2814
91MidwLAS/ProC-MWL16
91Single/ClBest-312

Hatcher, Hal
81CharR-5
82FtMyr-2
84Memphis-20

Hatcher, Johnny
83Durham-5
84Durham-5
85Durham-26
87Greenvl/Best-25

Hatcher, Mickey
79Albuq-11
80Pol/Dodg-44
80T-679R
81D-526
81F-135
81Pol/Dodg-44A
81T-289
81T/Tr-768
82D-480
82F-467
82OPC-291
82T-467
82T/St-212
83D-615
83F-614
83T-121
84D-147
84F-566
84Nes/792-746
84T-746
85D-194
85F-279
85Leaf-224
85Seven/Minn-3
85T-18
85T/St-304
86D-269
86F-396
86Leaf-143
86OPC-356
86T-356
86T-786M
87D-491
87F-542
87F/Up-U41
87Mother/Dodg-25
87OPC-341
87T-504
87T/St-276
87T/Tr-43T
88D-299
88F-516
88Leaf-122
88Mother/Dodg-25
88OPC-339
88Pol/Dodg-9
88S-298
88T-607
88T/St-71
89B-347
89D-346
89F/WS-1
89Mother/Dodg-25
89OPC-254
89OPC-390
89Panini/St-105
89Panini/St-23
89Pol/Dodg-6
89S-332
89T-483
89T/Big-63
89UD/Ext-709
89Woolwth-31
90D-439
90F-398
90Leaf/II-332
90Mother/Dodg-6
90OPC-226
90Pol/Dodg-8
90PublInt/St-8
90S-359
90T-226
90Target-323
90UD-283
91F-206
91OPC-152
91S-153
91T-152
91UD-666

Hatcher, Rick
82Durham-18

Hatfield, Fred
52B-153
52T-354
53B/Col-125
53Glen
53T-163
54B-119
55B-187
56T-318
57T-278
58T-339
59DF
80Richm-5MG
86Miami-9MG
91T/Arc53-163

Hatfield, Gilbert
(Gil)
90Target-975
N172
N338/2

Hatfield, Rob
86Macon-13
87Salem-4

Hathaway, Hilly
90A&AASingle/ProC-157
90Boise/ProC-3311

Hathaway, Shawn
88Spring/Best-6
89Star/Wax-50
89StPete/Star-16

Hattabaugh, Matt
91Utica/ClBest-10
91Utica/ProC-3243

Hattaway, Wayne
85Orlan-23
88OrlanTw/Best-26
89Orlan/Best-27
89Orlan/ProC-1336
90OrlanSR/Best-26
90OrlanSR/Star-28MG

Hatteberg, Scott
91Classic/DP-38
91FrRow/DP-15
92T-734

Hatten, Joe
47HomogBond-19
47TipTop
49B-116
49Eureka-36
50B-166
51B-190
52B-144
52T-194
90Target-324
D305

Hatton, Grady
49B-62
49Eureka-85
50B-26
51B-47
51T/RB-34
52T-6
53T-45
54T-208
55T-131
55T/DH-72
56T-26
56T/Pin-23
66T-504MG
67T-347MG
68T-392MG
73OPC-624CO
73T-624C
74OPC-31CO
74T-31C
91Crown/Orio-187
91T/Arc53-45
Exh47
PM10/Sm-69

Haugen, Troy
89Helena/SP-7
90Beloit/Best-24
90Beloit/Star-10
91Stockton/ClBest-12
91Stockton/ProC-3039

Haughey, Chris
90Target-976

Haugstad, Phil
52T-198
90Target-325

Haurado, Yanko
87PrWill-2

Hauser, Arnold
10Domino-54
11Helmar-170
12Sweet/Pin-148
14Piedmont/St-27
S74-119
T201
T202
T205

Hauser, Jeff
88Rockford-16
89Rockford-16

Hauser, Joe
26Exh-108
28Exh-55
61F-113
88MinorLg/Leg-10
92Conlon/Sport-548
E120
V61-53
W572

Hausladen, Bob
83BurlR-19
83BurlR/LF-1

Hausman, George
49Eureka-109

Hausman, Thomas
(Tom)
74Sacra
76OPC-452
76T-452
77Spoka
77T-99
78Tidew
79OPC-339
79T-643
80T-151
81D-396
81F-333
81T-359
82D-301
82F-526
82T-524
83T-417
91WIZMets-164

Hausmann, Clem
V362-13

Hausterman, David
86DayBe-11TR

Havens, Brad
82D-382
82OrlTw/A-16
82T-92
83D-480
83F-615
83T-751
84Nes/792-509
84T-509
84Toledo-8
85IntLgAS-40
85RochR-16
86D-599
87F-472
87RochR-17
87RochR/TCMA-5
87T-398
87T/Tr-44T
88F-517
88Mother/Dodg-22
88Pol/Dodg-41
88T-698
89F-407
89T-204
90Target-326
91Crown/Orio-188

Hawarny, Dave
82BirmB-16
83BirmB-6

Hawblitzel, Ryan
90Hunting/ProC-3276
91CLAS/ProC-CAR42
91WinSalem/ClBest-4
91WinSalem/ProC-2823
92UD-59TP

Hawes, Roy Lee
55B-268
88Chatt/Team-14

Hawkins, Andy
81Hawaii-14
82Hawaii-14
84F-302
84Mother/Padres-18
84Nes/792-778
84T-778
85D-528
85D/HL-14
85D/HL-15
85F-36
85Mother/Padres-13
85T-299
86D-284
86F-324
86F/Mini-70
86F/St-51
86Leaf-158
86OPC-5
86Sf-191
86T-478
86T/St-108
87Bohem-40
87D-264
87F-417
87T-183
88F-586
88S-347
88Smok/Padres-11
88T-9
88T/Big-257
89B-166
89D-583
89D/Best-52
89D/Tr-52
89F-307
89F/Up-50
89Panini/St-194
89S-118
89S/NWest-19
89S/Tr-14
89Sf-84
89T-533
89T/St-111
89T/Tr-47T
89UD-495
89UD/Ext-708
90Classic-135
90D-159
90F-445
90Leaf/II-281
90OPC-335
90Panini/St-130
90PublInt/St-536
90S/NWest-18
90T-335
90T/Big-36
90T/St-317
90T/TVYank-10
90UD-339
91D-611
91D-BC12A
91D-BC12B
91F-666
91F/Ultra-234
91F/WaxBox-6
91OPC-635
91Panini/FrSt-357
91Panini/St-6
91S-47
91S-704NH
91T-635
91T/StClub/II-487
91UD-333

Hawkins, Cedric
86LitFalls-13

Hawkins, Chris
87AubAs-11

Hawkins, Craig

91Elizab/ProC-4306
Hawkins, Hersey
88Peoria/Ko-14
Hawkins, Joe
90Pittsfld/Pucko-28TR
91StLucie/ClBest-30TR
Hawkins, John
84Nashvl-9
85Albany-32
86FSLAS-21
86FtLaud-12
90SoBend/ClBest-28
Hawkins, Todd
87Everett-18
88Fresno/Cal-9
88Fresno/ProC-1242
Hawkins, Ty
91SoBend/ProC-2869
Hawkins, Walter
87Idaho-11
Hawkins, Wynn
60T-536
61T-34
63T-334
Hawks, Larry
91BendB/ClBest-24
91BendB/ProC-3696
91Waterlo/ClBest-28
91Waterlo/ProC-1258
Hawks, Nelson
25Exh-42
W575
Hawley, Billy
83Cedar/LF-10
86Vermont-10
87Tampa-26
Haydel, Hal
71OPC-692R
71T-692R
72OPC-28R
72T-28R
Hayden, Alan
86Columbia-12
87Lynch-11
88Jacks/GS-25
89Chatt/Best-25
89Chatt/GS-23
89Jacks/GS-30
89Nashvl/Team-9
Hayden, David
91Batavia/ClBest-10
91Batavia/ProC-3492
Hayden, John F.
T206
Hayden, Paris
89Freder/Star-10
90Freder/Team-13
90Hagers/ProC-1427
90Hagers/Star-11
91FSLAS/ProC-FSL22
91Miami/ClBest-28
91Miami/ProC-421
Hayden, Richard
84Butte-12
Hayes, Ben
82Indianap-21
83F-591
84F-470
84Nes/792-448
84T-448
85Louisvl-25
Hayes, Bill
80Wichita-5
82Iowa-5
83Iowa-12
84Iowa-15
85Iowa-2
86Omaha-10
86Omaha/TCMA-1
87Iowa-14
88Geneva/ProC-1654
90Geneva/ProC-3053MG
90Geneva/Star-26MG
91Peoria/ClBest-22MG
91Peoria/ProC-1359MG
Hayes, Brian
78LodiD
79LodiD-19
Hayes, Charlie
86Shrev-11
87Shrev-17
87TexLgAS-27
88Phoenix/CMC-15
88Phoenix/ProC-57
89F-330
89F/Up-106
89Phill/TastyK-41
89Phoenix/CMC-13
89Phoenix/ProC-1487
89S-628
89S/HotRook-39
89UD/Ext-707
90Classic-98
90D-548
90D/BestNL-106
90F-558
90HotRook/St-21
90Leaf/I-131
90OPC-577
90Phill/TastyK-11
90S-507
90S/100Ris-12
90S/YS/I-38
90Sf-36
90T-577
90T/Big-69
90UD-437
91B-508
91D-278
91F-397
91F/Ultra-263
91Leaf/I-214
91Leaf/Stud-214
91OPC-312
91Panini/FrSt-105
91Panini/St-102
91Phill/Medford-17
91S-238
91S/100SS-19
91T-312
91T/StClub/I-163
91UD-269
92D/II-547
92F-533
92S/I-301
92T-754
92UD-208
Hayes, Chris
87Modesto-13
Hayes, Damon
47Remar-21
47Smith-21
48Smith-13
Hayes, Dan
84Newar-13
Hayes, Frank
(Blimp)
39PB-108
40PB-24
41DP-47
41G-13
41PB-41
47TipTop
92Conlon/Sport-380
Hayes, Jim
(Jimmy)
88Bristol/ProC-1874
90Tampa/DIMD-11
Hayes, Minter
(Jackie)
29Exh/4-32
34G-63
35BU-111M
35G-8B
35G-9B
37OPC-102
91Conlon/Sport-71
V300
Hayes, Terry
82Wausau-29
Hayes, Todd
87SanBern-22
88SanBern/Best-25
88SanBern/Cal-51
Hayes, Tom
81Durham-7
84Richm-6
Hayes, Von
80Watlo
81Charl-15
82D-237
82F-371
82T-141R
82T/Tr-42T
82Wheat/Ind
83D-324
83F-412
83OPC-325
83T-325
83T/St-311
83T/Tr-40
84D-477
84F-33
84Nes/792-587
84OPC-259
84Phill/TastyK-36
84T-587
84T/St-124
85CIGNA-2
85D-326
85D/HL-16
85F-253
85Leaf-93
85OPC-68
85Phill/TastyK-12M
85Phill/TastyK-36
85T-68
85T/St-115
86CIGNA-3
86D-305
86F-443
86F/Mini-92
86F/St-52
86Keller-2
86Leaf-176
86OPC-146
86Phill/TastyK-9
86T-420
86T/St-120
87BK-8
87Champion-1
87Classic-63
87D-113
87D-12DK
87D/DKsuper-12
87D/OD-152
87Drake-3
87F-175
87F/Excit-23
87F/GameWin-19
87F/Mini-51
87F/St-55
87Kraft-24
87Leaf-12DK
87Leaf-130
87OPC-389
87Phill/TastyK-9
87RedFoley/St-72
87Sf-193
87T-666
87T/Coins-35
87T/Mini-28
87T/St-121
88D-207
88D/Best-128
88Drake-17
88F-304
88F/Excit-18
88F/Mini-99
88F/St-108
88Leaf-197
88OPC-215
88Panini/St-356
88Phill/TastyK-13
88S-515
88Sf-62
88T-215
88T/Big-139
88T/St-117
89B-406
89D-160
89D/Best-47
89F-571
89KingB/Discs-18
89OPC-385
89Panini/St-151
89Phill/TastyK-9
89RedFoley/St-56
89S-38
89Sf-181
89T-385
89T/Big-302
89T/St-115
89UD-246
90B-160
90Classic-113
90D-278
90D/BestNL-140
90D/Bon/MVP-BC25
90D/Learning-18
90F-559
90F/AwardWin-17
90F/BB-17
90KingB/sDiscs-7
90Leaf/I-52
90MLBPA/Pins-2
90OPC-710
90Panini/St-319
90Phill/TastyK-12
90Post-27
90PubInt/St-238
90RedFoley/St-45
90S-36
90S/100St-62
90Sf-147
90Sunflower-12
90T-710
90T/Coins-48
90T/DH-32
90T/Mini-69
90T/St-114
90T/TVAS-54
90UD-453
90UD-7TC
91B-487
91Classic/200-25
91D-222
91F-398
91F/Ultra-264
91F/Ultra-398CL
91Leaf/II-280
91OPC-15
91Panini/FrSt-107
91Panini/St-105
91Phill/Medford-18
91RedFoley/St-47
91S-426
91T-15
91T/CJMini/II-5
91T/StClub/I-127
91UD-368
92D/II-580
92F-534
92S/I-207
92T-135
92UD-427
Hayford, Don
79Elmira-10
Haynes, Heath
91James/ClBest-25
91James/ProC-3538
Haynes, Joe
49B-191
51B-240
52B-103
52T-145
54T-223
Haynes, Marvin
87Vermont-26
Haynes, Rick
75Dubuq
Hays, Darrin
89Butte/SP-23
90CharlR/Star-9
Hays, David
89EastLDD/ProC-DD50EQMG
Hays, Rob
91Waterlo/ClBest-5
91Waterlo/ProC-1252
Hayward, Jeff
86Tampa-6
Hayward, Ray
83Beaum-19
84Cram/PCL-219
85Cram/PCL-104
86LasVegas-6
87D-632
87LasVegas-12
88F/Up-U63
88Mother/R-16
88OkCty/CMC-7
88OkCty/ProC-49
88S/Tr-67T
88T/Tr-47T
89D-521
89F-521
89S-514
90OkCty/ProC-426
Haywood, Albert
78Laugh/Black-20
Haywood, Buster
86Negro/Frit-42
Hayworth, Ray
34DS-90
35BU-165
39PB-140
40PB-155
90Target-327
R300
R314
V355-50
WG8-31
Hazelette, Moe
83Kinston/Team-8
Hazewood, Drungo L.
81RochR-8
83RochR-20
91Crown/Orio-189
Hazle, Robert S.
(Hurricane)
58T-83
Hazlett, Steve
91Elizab/ProC-4307
Head, Ed
90Target-328
Headley, Kent
88Virgini/Star-9
Heakins, Craig
86Watertn-9
87Macon-19
Healey, John
N172
N284
Healy, Bob
77QuadC
Healy, Fran
72T-663
73OPC-361
73T-361
74OPC-238
74T-238
74T/St-182
75OPC-120
75OPC-251
75T-251
75T/M-251
76OPC-394
76SSPC-184
76T-394
77BK/Y-3
77T-148
78T-582
Heard, Jehosie
54Esskay
54T-226
91Crown/Orio-190
91Negro/Lewis-15
Hearn, Ed
83Lynch-22
84Jacks-xx
85IntLgAS-10
85Tidew-21
86D/Rook-54
86Tidew-13
87D-446
87D/OD-201
87F-10
87T-433
87ToysRUs-11
88S-569
88T-56
89AAA/ProC-4
89D-297
89Omaha/CMC-12
89Omaha/ProC-1732
89T-348
89UD-42
91WIZMets-165
Hearn, Jim
49B-190
49Eureka-184
50B-208
51B-61
52B-49
52BR
52RM-NL8
52T-337
52TipTop
53B/Col-76
53NB
53T-38
54NYJour
55B-220
55Gol/Giants-12
56T-202

57T-348
58T-298
59T-63
91T/Arc53-38
R423-44
Hearn, Tommy
86Miami-10
Hearne, Hugh
90Target-977
Hearron, Jeff
86Tor/Fire-16
87D-490
87Knoxvl-21
87OPC-274
87Syrac/TCMA-3
87T-274
87Tor/Fire-13
89LasVegas/CMC-17
89LasVegas/ProC-11
90Iowa/CMC-23
90Iowa/ProC-320
90T/TVCub-49
Heath, Al
82AppFx-28
83AppFx/LF-29
84Madis/Pol-8
86Kinston-9
87PalmSp-2
Heath, Dave
83Peoria/LF-6
85MidldA-6
86MidldA-10
87Edmon-3
Heath, John Jeffrey
(Jeff)
39Exh
47TipTop
49B-169
49Eureka-11
79TCMA-97
R303/A
R303/B
Heath, Kelly
81Omaha-17
83Omaha-16
84Colum-2
84Colum/Pol-11
85Colum-16
85Colum/Pol-12
85IntLgAS-31
86Richm-9
87Richm/Crown-1
87Richm/TCMA-18
88Syrac/CMC-20
88Syrac/ProC-811
89Syrac/CMC-17
89Syrac/ProC-800
89Syrac/Team-13
90ScranWB/CMC-13
90ScranWB/ProC-605
Heath, Lee
89Pulaski/ProC-1911
90Sumter/Best-5
90Sumter/ProC-2445
91Macon/CIBest-23
91Macon/ProC-876
Heath, Mickey
28Exh/PCL-10
Heath, Mike
76FtLaud
77WHave
79T-710R
80T-687
81D-120
81F-583
81T-437
82D-413
82F-91
82Granny-3
82OPC-318
82T-318
83D-517
83F-518
83Granny-2
83T-23
83T/St-104
84D-223
84F-446
84Mother/A's-9
84Nes/792-567
84T-567
84T/St-337
85D-298
85F-422
85F-424
85Mother/A's-4
85OPC-396
85T-662
85T/St-326
86D-253
86F-418
86F/Up-U50
86OPC-148
86Schnucks-7
86T-148
86T/St-174
86T/Tr-46T
87Cain's-3
87Coke/Tigers-8
87D-496
87D/OD-214
87F/Up-U42
87T-492
88D-338
88D/Best-69
88F-56
88Pep/T-8
88RedFoley/St-31
88S-156
88T-237
89D-271
89D/Best-147
89F-132
89Mara/Tigers-8
89S-131
89T-609TL
89T-743
89UD-654
90B-352
90Classic/III-40
90CokeK/Tiger-7
90D-209
90D/BestAL-90
90F-603
90Leaf/I-60
90MLBPA/Pins-91
90OPC-366
90Panini/St-66
90PublInt/St-471
90S-172
90T-366
90T/Big-166
90T/St-280
90UD-306
91B-589
91D-230
91F-339
91Leaf/II-320
91OPC-16
91Panini/FrSt-287
91Panini/St-237
91S-112
91S/RookTr-69T
91T-16
91T/StClub/II-393
91UD-318
91UD/Ext-701
92S/I-344
92T-512
92T/GPromo-512
92T/Promo-16
92UD-304
Heath, Thomas
52Mother-46
53Mother-43
R314/Can
Heath, William
66T-539R
67OPC-172
67T-172
70OPC-541
70T-541
Heathcock, Jeff
83ColumAst-14
84Cram/PCL-65
86D-182
86F-302
86Tucson-6
87Tucson-18
88F-450
88Mother/Ast-18
88Pol/Ast-12
89Tucson/CMC-7
89Tucson/ProC-196
89Tucson/JP-7
90Edmon/CMC-9
90Edmon/ProC-515
Heathcote, Clifton E.
21Exh-71
26Exh-23
27Exh-12
33G-115
E120
E210-35
V354-9
Heathcott, Mike
91Utica/CIBest-8
91Utica/ProC-3235
Heaton, Neal
82Charl-5
83Wheat/Ind-19
84D-373
84F-546
84F/St-113
84Wheat/Ind-44
85D-373
85F-451
85Polar/Ind-44
86D-338
86F-589
86Leaf-203
86OhHenry-44
87D-615
87F-543
87F/Up-U43
87T/Tr-45T
88D-134
88D/Best-124
88F-185
88F/Mini-89
88Ho/Disc-10
88OPC-354
88Panini/St-319
88RedFoley/St-32
88S-430
88Sf-81
88T-765
88T/Big-33
88T/St-80
88T/St/Backs-29
89D-224
89F-377
89F/Up-113
89OPC-197
89S-253
89T-197
89UD-99
89VFJuice-26
90D-658
90F-468
90Homer/Pirate-12
90Leaf/II-460
90OPC-539
90PublInt/St-156
90T-539
90T/Big-255
90UD-86
90USPlayC/AS-7D
91BBBest/Aces-9
91D-475
91F-38
91F/Ultra-279
91OPC-451
91Panini/FrSt-123
91Panini/St-115
91S-233
91T-451
91T/StClub/I-53
91UD-36
92D/II-522
92F-554
92S/II-723
92T-89
92UD-417
Heaverlo, Dave
76OPC-213
76SSPC-95
76T-213
77Phoenix
77T-97
78T-338
79T-432
80T-177
81D-407
81F-594
81Tacoma-26
82Tacoma-3
83Tacoma-21
Hebb, Michael
91Kane/CIBest-6
91Kane/ProC-2654
Heble, Kurt
91StCath/CIBest-11
91StCath/ProC-3403
Hebner, Rich
69OPC-82R
69T-82R
70MLB/St-101
70OPC-264
70T-264
71MLB/St-203
71OPC-212
71T-212
72MB-136
72T-630
73OPC-2
73T-2
74/DE-35
74OPC-450
74T-450
74T/St-84
75Ho-57
75K-57
75OPC-492
75T-492
75T/M-492
76OPC-376
76SSPC-579
76T-376
77OPC-168
77T-167
78OPC-194
78T-26
79OPC-293
79T-567
80OPC-175
80T-331
81Coke
81D-125
81F-474
81OPC-217
81T-217
82D-328
82F-268
82OPC-96
82T-603
83F-307
83T-778
84F-251
84F/X-50
84Nes/792-433
84SevenUp-18
84T-433
84T/Tr-50
85D-564
85F-59
85SevenUp-18
85T-124
86T-19
88Myrtle/ProC-1188
88SALAS/GS-1MG
90T/TVRSox-5CO
91WIZMets-166
Hebrard, Mike
82Amari-24
Hechinger, Mike
90Target-978
Hecht, Steve
89AS/Cal-35
89SanJose/Best-24
89SanJose/Cal-221
89SanJose/ProC-457
89SanJose/Star-13
90Shrev/ProC-1451
90Shrev/Star-10
91Indianap/LineD-186
91Indianap/ProC-474
Heckel, Wally
90StCath/ProC-3477
Hecker, Guy
90HOF/St-3
N172
Heckman, Tom
82Madis-8
Hedfelt, Pancho
85Utica-10
Hedge, Pat
89Erie/Star-5
91Freder/CIBest-25
91Freder/ProC-2380
Hedgearner, Pat
90Freder/Team-28
Hedley, Darren
90Martins/ProC-3183
Hedlund, Mike
65T-546R
69T-591
70OPC-187
70T-187
71OPC-662
71T-662
72MB-137
72OPC-81
72T-81
73OPC-591
73T-591
Hedrick, Craig
78Cedar
Heep, Danny
80Tucson-1
81F-72
81T-82R
82F-217
82T-441
83D-443
83F-449
83T-538
83T/Tr-41
84D-434
84F-586
84Nes/792-29
84T-29
85D-556
85F-84
85OPC-339
85T-339
86D-556
86F-83
86T-619
87D-649
87F-11
87T-241
88Mother/Dodg-20
88Pol/Dodg-12
88S-417
88T-753
89D-368
89F-61
89S-343
89S/Tr-57
89T-198
90B-276
90D-358
90F-278
90OPC-573
90S-113
90T-573
90T/Big-90
90T/TVRSox-24
90Target-329
91S-827
91Vanco/LineD-635
91Vanco/ProC-1601
91WIZMets-167
Heffernan, Bert
89Beloit/I/Star-9
89Beloit/II/Star-14
91Albuq/LineD-9
91Albuq/ProC-1143
Heffner, Don
39PB-44
40PB-51
41DP-147
41G-11
60T-462C
66T-269MG
92Conlon/Sport-521
W753
Heffner, Robert
64T-79
65OPC-199
65T-199
66T-432
Hegan, J. Mike
67T-553R
68T-402
69Sunoco/Pin-11
69T-577
70McDon-3
70MLB/St-271
70OPC-111
70T-111
70T/SO
71MLB/St-438
71OPC-415
71T-415

71T/Coins-116
72T-632
73OPC-382
73T-382
74OPC-517
74Syrac/Team-10
74T-517
75OPC-99
75T-99
75T/M-99
76A&P/Milw
76Laugh/Jub-21
76OPC-377
76OPC-69FS
76SSPC-235
76T-377
76T-69FS
77T-507

Hegan, Jim
48L-28
50B-7
50NumNum
51B-79
51T/RB-12
52B-187
52NumNum-2
52RM-AL11
52StarCal/L-74D
52T-17
53B/Col-102
53T-80
54DanDee
54RH
54T-29
55Gol/Ind-11
55RFG-5
55RM-AL7
55Salem
55T-7
55T/DH-67
56Carling-3
56T-48
56T/Pin-8C
57Sohio/Ind-6
57T-136
58T-345
59T-372
73OPC-116CO
73T-116CO
76OPC-69FS
76T-69FS
79TCMA-139
83Kaline-15M
91T/Arc53-80
Exh47
PM10/Sm-70

Hegman, Bob
81CharR-10
84Memphis-13
85Omaha-30
86Omaha-11
86Omaha/TCMA-8

Hehl, Jake
90Target-979

Heidemann, Jack
71MLB/St-372
71OPC-87
71T-87
72OPC-374
72T-374
73OPC-644
73T-644
75OPC-649
75T-649
75T/M-649
76SSPC-544
77T-553
79Spokane-15
91WIZMets-168

Heiden, Shawn
89Bluefld/Star-11
90Foil/Best-110
90Wausau/Best-13
90Wausau/ProC-2126
90Wausau/Star-9

Heidenreich, Curt
82Cedar-3
83Water-3
84Wichita/Rock-9

Heiderscheit, Pat
89James/ProC-2143

Heidrick, John
E107

Heifferon, Mike
86Albany/TCMA-11
87PrWill-14
88Albany/ProC-1354
89AAA/ProC-3
89Colum/Pol-24M
90ColClip/CMC-24CO
90ColClip/ProC-693CO

Height, Ron
88LitFalls/Pucko-5

Heilgeist, Jim
90Gate/ProC-3346

Heilmann, Harry E.
21Exh-72
25Exh-92
26Exh-93
27Exh-48
29Exh/4-24
31Exh/4-7
50Callahan
60F-65
61F-42
63Bz/ATG-2
80Laugh/3/4/5-28
80SSPC/HOF
81Detroit-40
86Conlon/1-42
91Conlon/Sport-52
D327
D328-71
E120
E121/120
E122
E135-71
E210-22
E220
R423-46
V100
V61-27
W501-6
W502-22
W515-18
W517-14
W573
W575

Heimach, Fred
90Target-330
92Conlon/Sport-480

Heimer, Todd
79Tacoma-8
80Tacoma-18
81Chatt-10

Heimueller, Gorman
81WHave-20
82Tacoma-5
83Tacoma-4
84Cram/PCL-95
84D-131
85Orlan-25
86Toledo-12
87Visalia-24
88Visalia/Cal-174
88Visalia/ProC-105
89Visalia/Cal-119CO
89Visalia/ProC-1420
90OrlanSR/Best-24CO
90OrlanSR/ProC-1100CO
90OrlanSR/Star-26CO
91Portl/LineD-425CO
91Portl/ProC-1583CO

Heinen, Joe
75Cedar

Heinkel, Don
83BirmB-9
84Evansvl-19
86Nashvl-11
87Toledo-7
87Toledo/TCMA-2
88F/Up-U27
88S/Tr-79T
89B-427
89F-133
89Louisvl-21
89S-168
89T-499
90BirmDG/Best-17
90WichSt-14

Heinle, Dana
87Kenosha-15
88Visalia/Cal-168
88Visalia/ProC-82
89VeroB/Star-11

Heins, Jim
89NiagFls/Pucko-10

Heintzelman, Ken
49B-108
49Eureka-136
50B-85
51B-147
51BR-C10
52B-148
52T-362
53T-136
79TCMA-78
91T/Arc53-136
R423-42

Heintzelman, Tom
74OPC-607R
74T-607R
75Phoenix-17
76Phoenix
79Phoenix

Heise, Benjamin
75OkCty

Heise, Larry Wayne
84Newar-19
87Greenvl/Best-22

Heise, Robert
70OPC-478
70T-478
71MLB/St-250
71OPC-691
71T-691
72OPC-402
72T-402
73OPC-547
73T-547
74T/Tr-51T
74OPC-51
74T-51
75OPC-441
75T-441
75T/M-441
91WIZMets-169

Heist, Al
58Union
61T-302
62Salada-195
62Shirriff-195
62T-373
62T/St-126
89Smok/Ast-24

Heitmuller, William
(Heinie)
E90/1
M116

Held, Matt
83Idaho-16

Held, Mel
91Crown/Orio-191

Held, Woodie
58T-202
59Kahn
59T-226
60Kahn
60L-2
60T-178
61Bz-33
61Kahn
61NuCard-405
61T-60
61T/St-136
62Bz
62J-44
62Kahn
62P-44
62P/Can-44
62Salada-5
62Shirriff-5
62Sugar-12
62T-215
62T/bucks
62T/St-35
63J-69
63P-69
63Sugar-12
63T-435
64Kahn
64T-105
64T/Coins-29
64T/St-29S3
64T/SU
64T/tatt
65T-336
66OPC-136
66T-136
67T-251
68T-289
69MB-108
69T-636
78TCMA-284
79TCMA-174
91Crown/Orio-192

Heller, John
83Lynch-17

Heller, Mark
86Albuq-11

Helfand, Eric
89Alaska/Team-3
90A&AASingle/ProC-167
90SoOreg/Best-2
90SoOreg/ProC-3426
91Modesto/ClBest-21
91Single/ClBest-128

Helling, Rick
91T/Tr-54T

Hellman, Anthony
N172

Hellman, Jeff
87FtLaud-25

Helm, J. Ross
T206

Helm, Wayne
89BendB/Legoe-4
90Boise/ProC-3315

Helmick, Tony
89GreatF-6
90Bakers/Cal-238

Helmquist, Doug
84BuffB-25

Helms, Mike
90Everett/Best-18
90Everett/ProC-3134

Helms, Tommy
65OPC-243R
65T-243R
66T-311R
67Kahn
67T-505
68T-405
69MB-109
69MLB/St-129
69MLBPA/Pin-47
69OPC-70
69OPC/DE-9
69T-418AS
69T-70
69T/DE-20
69T/decal
69T/S-40
69T/St-24
70MLB/St-28
70OPC-159
70T-159
71MLB/St-61
71OPC-272
71T-272
72MB-138
72OPC-204
72T-204
73OPC-495
73T-495
74OPC-67
74T-67
74T/St-32
75OPC-119
75T-119
75T/M-119
76OPC-583
76SSPC-56
76T-583
76T/Tr-583T
77T-402
78T-618
86TexGold-CO
88Kahn/Reds-CO
90OPC-110MG
90T-110MG
91Utica/ClBest-17
91Utica/ProC-3248

Helsom, Bob
83StPete-21
84ArkTr-7

Helton, Keith
88CalLgAS-29
88SanBern/Best-19
88SanBern/Cal-44
89Wmsprt/ProC-645
89Wmsprt/Star-9
90Calgary/CMC-21
90Calgary/ProC-646
91Calgary/LineD-58
91Calgary/ProC-510

Heman, Russell
59T-283

Hemm, Warren
78Memphis/Team-5

Hemmerich, Mike
89Pittsfld/Star-7

Hemmerly, John
89Erie/Star-6

Hemond, Scott
87Madis-3
88Huntsvl/BK-6
89Huntsvl/Best-1
90B-453
90F-646R
90S-598RP
90T/89Debut-54
90Tacoma/CMC-16
90Tacoma/ProC-99
90UD/Ext-727
91B-232
91S/100RisSt-22
91Tacoma/ProC-2314
92D/II-637
92S/II-617

Hempen, Hal
88Savan/ProC-342

Hempfield, Keith
83CharR-7

Hemphill, Charles
12Sweet/Pin-35
E107
E97
S74-22
T204
T205
T206
W555

Hemsley, Ralston
(Rollie)
34Exh/4-15
35BU-71
35Exh/4-15
35G-8C
35G-9C
36Exh/4-15
36G
36Wheat
37Exh/4-15
40PB-205
41DP-133
41PB-34
44Yank/St-14
47Centen-8
54T-143CO
91Conlon/Sport-299
PR1-17
R312/M
R314
WG8-32

Hemus, Solly
52B-212
52T-196
53B/Col-85
53Hunter
53T-231
54B-94
54Hunter
54T-117
55B-107
55Hunter
57T-231
58T-207
59T-527
60T-218MG
61T-139MG
79TCMA-93
91T/Arc53-231

Hence, Sam
90BurlInd/ProC-3020
91BurlInd/ProC-3315

Henderson, Bill
88Fayette/ProC-1102
89Lakeland/Star-9

Henderson, Brad
86FSLAS-22TR
86StPete-10TR
87ArkTr-24TR
88ArkTr/GS-2TR

Henderson, Craig

82Wisco-26
83Visalia/LF-20
85Orlan-26
Henderson, Dave
80Spokane-16
82T-711R
83F-481
83T-732
84D-557
84F-611
84Mother/Mar-3
84Nes/792-154
84OPC-154
84T-154
84T/St-343
85F-489
85Mother/Mar-4
85OPC-344
85T-344
85T/St-338
86D-318
86F-465
86Leaf-187
86Mother/Mar-4
86OPC-221
86T-221
86T-546M
86T/St-222
87D-622
87D/OD-189
87F-36
87F/Hottest-19
87F/WS-10M
87Leaf-103
87T-452
87T/HL-22
87T/St-23WS
87Woolwth-22
88D/A's/Bk-NEW
88F-84
88F/Up-U53
88Mother/A's-14
88S-228
88S/Tr-49T
88T-628
88T/Big-131
88T/Tr-48T
89AubAs/ProC-2185
89B-200
89D-20DK
89D-450
89D/Best-190
89D/DKsuper-20DK
89F-10
89Mother/A's-13
89OPC-327
89Panini/St-423
89S-533
89Sf-127
89T-527
89T/Big-326
89T/St-164
89T/St/Backs-17
89UD-174
90B-458
90D-243
90D/BestAL-39
90F-9
90Mother/A's-18
90OPC-68
90Osceola/Star-9
90Panini/St-133
90PublInt/St-306
90S-325
90T-68
90T/Big-309
90T/St-184
90UD-206
90Woolwth/HL-29
91B-226
91BurlAs/ClBest-15
91BurlAs/ProC-2809
91Classic/III-36
91D-326
91F-9
91F/Ultra-247
91Leaf/I-232
91Leaf/Stud-103
91Mother/A's-18
91OPC-144
91Panini/FrSt-197
91Panini/St-150
91S-644
91SFExam/A's-5
91T-144
91T/StClub/I-284
91UD-108
91UD/FinalEd-88FAS
91USPlayC/AS-13H
92D/I-21AS
92D/I-311
92F-257
92S/100SS-92
92S/I-5
92T-335
92UD-172
Henderson, Derek
89Pittsfld/Star-8
91StLucie/ClBest-7
91StLucie/ProC-718
Henderson, Frank
88AppFx/ProC-154
88Eugene/Best-23
89AppFx/ProC-857
Henderson, Harry IV
89Billings/ProC-2059
Henderson, James H.
(Hardie)
N172
N184
Henderson, Jeff
91Kingspt/ClBest-1
91Kingspt/ProC-3808
Henderson, Joe
76Indianap-5
77Indianap-3
77T-487R
81Clinton-22
82Beloit-2
83ElPaso-3
84MidldC-1
Henderson, John
77QuadC
Henderson, Kenneth J.
91Everett/ClBest-19
91Everett/ProC-3929
Henderson, Kenneth Joseph
65T-497R
66OPC-39
66T-39
67T-383
68T-309
70OPC-298
70T-298
71MLB/St-251
71OPC-155
71T-155
71T/Coins-97
71T/tatt-2
71Ticket/Giant-5
72OPC-443
72OPC-444IA
72T-443
72T-444IA
73OPC-101
73T-101
74OPC-394
74T-394
74T/St-154
75Ho-136
75Ho/Twink-136
75OPC-59
75T-59
75T/M-59
76OPC-464
76SSPC-147
76T-464
76T/Tr-464T
77T-242
78Ho-126
78T-212
79T-73
80T-523
91WIZMets-170
Henderson, Lee
90CharRain/Best-11
90CharRain/ProC-2041
91Waterlo/ClBest-12
91Waterlo/ProC-1259
Henderson, Matt
79Wisco-8
Henderson, Mike
78Holyo
79Holyo-17
80Vanco-17
Henderson, Pedro
90BurlInd/ProC-3021
91CollInd/ProC-1499
91Watertn/ClBest-26
91Watertn/ProC-3381
Henderson, Ramon
86Reading-9
87Reading-15
88Maine/CMC-19
88Maine/ProC-295
89Reading/Best-13
89Reading/ProC-653
89Reading/Star-13
90Princet/DIMD-29CO
91Clearw/ClBest-5CO
91Clearw/ProC-1639CO
Henderson, Rats
86Negro/Frit-34
Henderson, Rickey
77Modesto
79Ogden/TCMA-9
80T-482
81D-119
81F-351HL
81F-574
81F/St-54
81K-33
81OPC-261
81PermaGr/CC-19
81Sqt-28
81T-261
81T-4LL
81T/SO-39
81T/St-115
81T/St-15
82D-113
82F-643HL
82F-92
82F/St-123
82Granny-4
82K-4
82OPC-268
82PermaGr/AS-6
82PermaGr/CC-23
82T-156TL
82T-164LL
82T-610
82T/St-221
82T/St-8
83D-11DK
83D-35
83D/AAS-22
83F-519
83F-639HL
83F-646IA
83Granny-35
83K-8
83OPC-180
83OPC-391AS
83PermaGr/CC-26
83T-180
83T-2M
83T-391AS
83T-531TL
83T-704LL
83T/Gloss40-33
83T/St-103
83T/St-159
83T/St-197
83T/St-198
83T/St-199
83T/St-200
83T/St-201
83T/St-202
83T/St-21
83T/St/Box-8
84D-54
84D/AAS-9
84F-447
84F/St-53
84F/St-92
85FunFood/Pin-17
84MiltBrad-13
84Mother/A's-2
84Nes/792-134LL
84Nes/792-156TL
84Nes/792-230
84Nes/792-2HL
84OPC-230
84Ralston-15
84Seven-21W
84T-134LL
84T-156TL
84T-2LL
84T-230
84T/Cereal-15
84T/Gloss40-6
84T/St-202
84T/St-3
84T/St-327
84T/St-4
84T/Super-19
85D-176
85D/HL-17
85D/HL-42
85F-425
85F-629IA
85F/St-54
85F/Up-U51
85Leaf-208
85OPC-115
85Seven-12W
85T-115
85T-706AS
85T/3D-10
85T/St-283
85T/St-321
85T/Super-14
85T/Tr-49T
85Woolwth-17
86D-51
86D/AAS-10
86D/PopUp-10
86Dorman-7
86Drake-5
86F-108
86F/AS-7
86F/LimEd-23
86F/Mini-23
86F/St-53
86Leaf-37
86OPC-243
86Quaker-25
86Sf-184M
86Sf-6
86Sf/Dec-69
86T-500
86T-716AS
86T/3D-11
86T/Gloss22-7
86T/Gloss60-5
86T/Mini-27
86T/St-155
86T/St-297
86T/Super-30
87BK-9
87Classic-12
87D-228
87D/AAS-6
87D/OD-248
87D/PopUp-6
87Drake-12
87F-101
87F/Excit-24
87F/HL-4
87F/Hottest-20
87F/Mini-52
87F/Slug-18
87F/St-56
87Jiffy-14
87KayBee-16
87KMart-27
87Kraft-31
87Leaf-191
87Mother/A's-20
87MSA/Discs-18
87OPC-7
87OPC/WaxBox-E
87RedFoley/St-80
87Sf-157M
87Sf-159M
87Sf-198M
87Sf-4
87Seven-E3
87Sportflic/DealP-4
87T-311TBC
87T-735
87T/WaxBox-E
87T/Board-8
87T/Coins-12
87T/Gloss22-18
87T/Gloss60-21
87T/HL-3
87T/Mini-64
87T/St-147
87T/St-296
87Woolwth-3
88ChefBoy-20
88Classic/Blue-234
88D-277
88D/AS-4
88D/Best-76
88D/PopUp-4
88D/Y/Bk-277
88Drake-7
88F-209
88F/Hottest-16
88F/Mini-40
88F/Slug-C2
88F/SS-C2
88F/St-S4
88KMart-13
88Leaf-145
88OPC-60
88OPC/WaxBox-M
88Panini/St-158
88Panini/St-231M
88Panini/St-434
88S-13
88S/WaxBox-7
88Sf-11
88Sf/Gamewin-8
88T-60
88T/Big-165
88T/Gloss22-7
88T/Gloss60-25
88T/Mini-26
88T/St-155
88T/St-297
88T/St/Backs-51
88T/UK-31
88T/WaxBox-M
89T/Ames-16
89B-181
89Bz-14
89Cadaco-28
89Classic-50
89D-245
89D/AS-4
89D/Best-78
89D/PopUp-4
89F-254
89F/BBAS-20
89F/Excit-21
89F/Superstar-22
89F/Up-54
89KayBee-18
89KMart/Lead-15
89Modesto/Chong-33
89OPC-282
89Panini/St-239AS
89Panini/St-408
89S-657HL
89S-70
89S/HotStar-45
89S/Tr-50
89Sf-145
89T-380
89T/Big-271
89T/DHTest-16
89T/Gloss22-7
89T/Gloss60-35
89T/LJN-54
89T/Mini-66
89T/St-145
89T/St-312
89T/St/Backs-18
89T/Tr-48T
89T/UK-37
89T/WaxBox-F
89UD-210
90B-457
90BBWit-37
90Bz-9
90Classic-37
90Classic/III-27
90CollAB-8
90D-304
90D/BestAL-124
90D/Learning-7
90F-10
90F/AwardWin-18
90F/BBMVP-17
90F/LL-18
90F/WS-11
90HOF/St-87
90Holsum/Discs-8
90HotPlay/St-20
90KayBee-15
90KingB/Discs-19
90KMart/CBatL-21
90KMart/SS-23
90Leaf/I-160
90Leaf/I-84CL

90Mother/A's-4
90MSA/Soda-5
90OPC-450
90OPC-7RB
90Panini/St-138
90Post-25
90PublInt/St-288
90PublInt/St-537
90S-360
90S-686DT
90S-698M
90S/100St-90
90S/McDon-5
90Sf-208
90Sunflower-13
90T-450
90T-7RB
90T/Ames-13
90T/Big-292
90T/Coins-17
90T/DH-33
90T/Gloss60-37
90T/Mini-28
90T/St-181
90T/St-7HL
90T/TVAS-10
90T/WaxBox-F
90UD-334
90USPlayC/AS-13C
90Windwlk/Discs-8
90Woolwth/HL-14
90Woolwth/HL-23
90Woolwth/HL-31
91B-213
91B-371SLUG
91B-692
91BBBest/RecBr-7
91Bz-2
91Classic/200-189
91Classic/I-72
91Classic/II-T75
91CollAB-25
91D-387MVP
91D-53AS
91D-648
91D-761MVP
91D/Elite-E7
91F-10
91F/ASIns-6
91F/ProVF-2F
91F/Ultra-248
91F/Ultra-393EP
91F/UltraG-5
91F/WS-4
91JDeanSig-17
91KingB/Discs-5
91Leaf/GRook-BC26
91Leaf/I-101
91Leaf/Prev-23
91Leaf/Stud-104
91MajorLg/Pins-40
91Mother/A's-4
91OPC-391AS
91OPC-670
91OPC/Premier-62
91Panini/FrSt-171
91Panini/FrSt-196
91Panini/St-146
91Panini/Top15-38
91Panini/Top15-45
91Panini/Top15-53
91Panini/Top15-6
91Pep/Henderson-Set
91Pepsi/Discs-1
91Pepsi/Discs-2
91Pepsi/Discs-3
91Pepsi/Discs-4
91Petro/SU-21
91Post-27
91Post/Can-24
91RedFoley/St-121
91RedFoley/St-48
91S-10
91S-397AS
91S-857FRAN
91S-875MVP
91S-890DT
91S/100SS-10
91S/Cooper-B4
91Seven/3DCoin-5A
91Seven/3DCoin-7NC
91Seven/3DCoin-7NE
91Seven/3DCoin-7NW
91SFExam/A's-6
91SilverSt-1
91T-391AS
91T-670
91T/CJMini/I-18
91T/StClub/I-120
91T/SU-19
91T/WaxBox-H
91UD-444
91UD-636
91UD/Ext-SP2M
91UD/FinalEd-86FAS
91UD/SilSlug-SS3
91USPlayC/AS-11H
91Woolwth/HL-2
91Woolwth/HL-26
92Classic/I-43
92D/Elite-L1
92D/I-193
92D/I-215HL
92D/I-30AS
92F-258
92F-681RS
92S/100SS-100
92S/I-430HL
92S/I-441DT
92S/II-480
92T-2RB
92T-560
92UD-155
92UD-640CL
92UD-648DS
92UD-90TC

Henderson, Steve
77Indianap-14
78OPC-53
78T-134
79OPC-232
79T-445
80OPC-156
80T-299
81Coke
81D-157
81F-321
81K-25
81OPC-44
81T-619
81T/SO-79
81T/St-193
81T/Tr-769
82D-183
82F-597
82F/St-98
82OPC-89
82RedLob
82T-89
82T/St-30
83D-252
83F-496
83T-335
83T/Tr-42
84D-389
84F-612
84Mother/Mar-21
84Nes/792-501
84OPC-274
84T-501
84T/St-341
85D-145
85F-490
85F/Up-U52
85Mother/A's-26
85OPC-38
85T-640
85T/Tr-50T
86D-375
86F-419
86Mother/A's-20
86T-748
87Tacoma-13
88Mother/Ast-12
88Pol/Ast-13
88S-547
88T-527
89AAA/CMC-9
89AAA/ProC-22
89BuffB/CMC-14
89BuffB/ProC-1676
89Pac/SenLg-5
89T/SenLg-9
89TM/SenLg-45
90BuffB/ProC-391CO
90BuffB/Team-8CO
90EliteSenLg-17
91Pac/SenLg-144
91WIZMets-171

Henderson, Ted
81Tacoma-29M

Henderson, Valentine
89Welland/Pucko-13

Henderson, Wendell
82QuadC-15

Hendley, Brett
91Madison/ClBest-15
91Madison/ProC-2134
91MidwLAS/ProC-MWL41

Hendley, C. Bob
61T-372
62T-361
63T-62
64T-189
64T/Coins-94
65T-444
66OPC-82
66T-82
67T-256
68T-345
69OPC-144
69T-144
91WIZMets-172

Hendrick, George
72OPC-406
72T-406
73OPC-13
73OPC-201ALCS
73T-13
73T-201ALCS
74OPC-303
74T-303
74T/St-167
75Ho-140
75K-46
75OPC-109
75T-109
75T/M-109
76OPC-570
76SSPC-527
76T-570
77BurgChef-129
77Ho-123
77OPC-218
77Padre/SchCd-13
77Pep-40
77T-330
78Ho-82
78OPC-178
78T-30
79Ho-66
79OPC-82
79T-175
80OPC-184
80T-350
81Coke
81D-430
81Drake-22
81F-542
81K-35
81OPC-230
81T-230
81T/SO-85
81T/St-22
81T/St-220
81T/St-256
82D-40
82D-9DK
82Drake-17
82F-113
82F/St-25
82OPC-295
82Sqt-16
82T-420
82T/St-91
83D-404
83Drake-10
83F-7
83K-25
83OPC-148
83PermaGr/CC-6
83T-650
83T/St-153
83T/St-154
83T/St-285
84D-475
84D/AAS-32
84Drake-12
84F-324
84F/St-9
85FunFood/Pin-52
84Nes/792-386AS
84Nes/792-540
84OPC-163
84OPC-386AS
84T-386AS
84T-540
84T/Gloss40-23
84T/St-139
84T/St-185
84T/St/Box-11
85D-181
85F-225
85F/St-27
85F/Up-U53
85Leaf-259
85OPC-60
85T-60
85T/St-134
85T/Tr-51T
86F-158
86OPC-190
86Smok/Cal-14
86T-190
87D/OD-3
87F-82
87OPC-248
87Smok/Cal-22
87T-725
88D-479
88S-308
88Smok/Angels-24
88T-304
89Pac/SenLg-61
89T/SenLg-12
89TM/SenLg-46
90EliteSenLg-82

Hendrick, Harvey
29Exh/4-3
34DS-41
90Target-331
92Conlon/Sport-522
R315-C2
R316
W513-63

Hendrick, Pete
86ElPaso-14

Hendricks, Elrod
(Ellie)
69MB-110
69T-277
70OPC-528
70T-528
71MLB/St-299
71OPC-219
71T-219
72MB-139
72OPC-508
72T-508
75OPC-609
75T-609
75T/M-609
76OPC-371
76SSPC-384
76T-371
87French-44CO
88French-44CO
89French-44CO
89Swell-64
91Crown/Orio-193

Hendricks, Steve
87Spokane-22
88River/Cal-221
88River/ProC-1409
89AubAs/ProC-7
89Watlo/ProC-1772
89Watlo/Star-11
90AS/Cal-7
90Riversi/Best-12
90Riversi/Cal-11
90Riversi/ProC-2615
91NewBrit/LineD-462
91NewBrit/ProC-357

Hendrickson, Craig
77QuadC

Hendrickson, Dan
89Everett/Star-13

Hendriksen, Claude
16FleischBrd-39

Hendrix, Claude
14CJ-76
15CJ-76
92Conlon/Sport-343
BF2-64
D328-72
D329-78
D350/2-77
E135-72
E220
M101/4-78
M101/5-77
W514-9
WG4-9

Hendrix, James
87CharWh-2
88Virgini/Star-10

Hendry, Ted
88TM/Umpire-35
89TM/Umpire-33
90TM/Umpire-32

Henerson, Rob
78Cedar

Hengel, Dave
86Calgary-11
87Calgary-9
88Calgary/CMC-18
88Calgary/ProC-1550
88D-629
88F-375
89Chatt/II/Team-12
89ColoSp/CMC-18
89ColoSp/ProC-243
89T-531

Hengle, Emory
N172

Henika, Ron
84Cedar-27
86Vermont-11
87Nashvl-10
90CedarDG/Best-17

Henion, Scott
87Columbia-17
88Salem/Star-8
89WPalmB/Star-12

Henke, Rick
83Watlo/LF-26TR
86Water-13TR
87Wmsprt-15

Henke, Tom
82Tulsa-1
83OKCty-9
84D-134
84OKCty-10
85D-403
85IntLgAS-41
85Syrac-8
85Tor/Fire-14
86Ault-50
86D-437
86F-60
86F/St-54
86Leaf-206
86OPC-333
86T-333
86T/St-189
86Tor/Fire-17
87D-197
87F-228
87F/Excit-25
87F/Slug-19
87F/St-57
87Leaf-73
87OPC-277
87Smok/AL-14
87T-510
87T/Mini-76
87T/St-185
87Tor/Fire-12
88D-490
88D/AS-28
88D/Best-104
88F-112
88F/AS-2
88F/AwardWin-18
88F/Excit-19
88F/LL-17
88F/Mini-62
88F/St-73
88F/TL-12
88Ho/Disc-23
88OPC-220
88Panini/St-213
88RedFoley/St-33
88S-57
88Sf-65
88T-220

88T-396
88T/Big-41
88T/Gloss60-35
88T/Mini-38
88T/Revco-31
88T/St-186
88T/St/Backs-64
88T/UK-32
88Tor/Fire-50
89B-246
89D-385
89D/Best-301
89F-235
89F/Excit-22
89OPC-75
89Panini/St-461
89S-318
89S/HotStar-63
89Sf-126
89T-75
89T/LJN-143
89T/St-195
89Tor/Fire-50
89UD-264
90B-506
90D-349
90D/BestAL-14
90F-84
90Holsum/Discs-3
90Leaf/I-158
90OPC-695
90PublInt/St-516
90S-157
90Sf-42
90T-695
90T/Big-101
90T/St-196
90Tor/BlueJ-50
90TulsaDG/Best-19
90UD-282
91B-16
91D-205
91F-176
91F/Ultra-362
91Leaf/II-517
91OPC-110
91OPC/Premier-63
91Panini/FrSt-345
91S-579
91S/ToroBJ-2
91T-110
91T/StClub/I-24
91Tor/Fire-50
91UD-149
92D/I-141
92F-331
92S/100SS-31
92S/I-385
92S/I-439AS
92T-451
92UD-395

Henkel, Rob
91Elmira/ClBest-20
91Elmira/ProC-3267

Henkemeyer, Dick
82Wisco-17

Henley, Dan
85Anchora-15
88Bakers/Cal-235
89SanAn/Best-12
90Albuq/CMC-18
90Albuq/ProC-351
90Albuq/Trib-10
91Vanco/LineD-636
91Vanco/ProC-1602

Henley, Mike
83AppFx/LF-11

Henley, Weldon
90Target-332
E107
E254

Henline, Noah
C46-64

Henline, Walter
(Butch)
25Exh-43
26Exh-44
27Exh-8
87Conlon/2-18
90Target-333
92Conlon/Sport-581
E120
E126-31
E220
V100
V61-59
W572

Henneman, Mike
86Nashvl-12
87D/Rook-32
87F/Up-U44
87Sf/Rook-29
87T/Tr-46T
87Toledo-16
87Toledo/TCMA-13
88Classic/Blue-241
88D-420
88D/Best-91
88F-57
88F/St-25
88OPC-3
88Pep/T-39
88S-520
88S/YS/I-15
88Sf-129
88T-582
88T/Big-256
88T/Gloss60-10
88T/JumboR-7
88ToysRUs-13
89B-98
89Classic-94
89D-327
89D/Best-237
89F-134
89F/Excit-23
89Mara/Tigers-39
89OPC-365
89Panini/St-333
89Pol/Tigers-39
89S-293
89S/HotStar-59
89Sf-56
89T-365
89T/Big-252
89T/St-273
89UD-373
90B-345
90BirmDG/Best-18
90CokeK/Tiger-8
90D-296
90D/BestAL-105
90F-604
90Leaf/I-2
90OPC-177
90Panini/St-69
90PublInt/St-472
90S-184
90Sf-144
90T-177
90T/Big-41
90T/St-282
90UD-537
91CokeK/Tiger-39
91D-76
91F-340
91F/Ultra-123
91Leaf/I-18
91OPC-641
91Panini/St-236
91RedFoley/St-49
91S-142
91S/100SS-51
91T-641
91T/StClub/I-287
91UD-386
92D/I-253
92F-138
92S/I-217
92T-293
92UD-339

Hennessey, Scott
91BBCity/ClBest-25
91BBCity/ProC-1411

Hennessy, Brendan
83BurlR-20
83BurlR/LF-18
83TriCit-24

Hennessy, Mike
82Cedar-9
86Sumter-9

Hennigan, Phil
71MLB/St-373
71OPC-211
71T-211
72T-748
73OPC-107
73T-107
91WIZMets-173

Henning, Rich
90Bristol/ProC-3176CO
90Bristol/Star-28CO

Henninger, Rai
88Idaho/ProC-1852

Henninger, Rich
74OPC-602R
74T-602R
75OkCty

Hennis, Randall
(Randy)
87AubAs-10
88FSLAS/Star-8
88Osceola/Star-13
89ColMud/Best-9
89ColMud/ProC-137
89ColMud/Star-12
90Tucson/CMC-6
90Tucson/ProC-200
91Classic/I-45
91S-752RP
91T/90Debut-66
91Tucson/LineD-611
91Tucson/ProC-2209

Henrich, Bobby
58T-131

Henrich, Tom
39PB-52
40PB-4
41DP-111
41PB-39
47TipTop
48B-19
48L-55
49B-69
49Royal-12
50B-10
50Drake-23
51B-291
51BR-B3
53Exh/Can-27
79TCMA-35
Exh47
PM10/Sm-71
PM10/Sm-72
R302
R303/A
R346-42
R423-47

Henrichs, Shawn
91Everett/ClBest-16
91Everett/ProC-3907

Henriksen, Olaf
16FleischBrd-40
D328-73
D329-79
D350/2-78
E135-73
M101/4-79
M101/5-78
T207

Henrikson, Dan
91Clinton/ClBest-3
91Clinton/ProC-828

Henry, Bill F.
68T-384R

Henry, Bill R.
55B-264
59T-46
60Kahn
60T-524
61T-66
62Kahn
62T-562
63FrBauer-8
63T-378
64T-49
65T-456
66OPC-115
66T-115
67T-579
68T-239

Henry, Butch
88Cedar/ProC-1159
88MidwLAS/GS-12
89Chatt/Best-9
89Chatt/GS-11
90CedarDG/Best-23
91Tucson/LineD-612
91Tucson/ProC-2210

Henry, Carlos
88Ashvl/ProC-1074
89Ashvl/ProC-965

Henry, Chris
80Wausau-17

Henry, Dan
77Clinton
77LodiD

Henry, Doug
86Beloit-10
87Beloit-12
88Stockton/Cal-177
88Stockton/ProC-747
89ElPaso/GS-8
90Stockton/Cal-184
91AAAGame/ProC-AAA9
91Denver/LineD-140
91Denver/ProC-120
92D/II-663
92S/I-421
92T-776
92T/91Debut-73
92UD-43

Henry, Dutch
90Target-334

Henry, Dwayne
82BurlR-24
83Tulsa-11
84Tulsa-36
85Tulsa-29
86D-603
86F-562
86Sf-179R
87D-637
87OKCty-18
88OkCty/CMC-2
88OkCty/ProC-33
88T-178
89Richm/Bob-9
89Richm/CMC-4
89Richm/Ko-38
89Richm/ProC-844
89T-496
89UD-51
91F-692
91Leaf/II-329
91Mother/Ast-24
91OPC-567
91T-567
92D/I-114
92F-436
92S/I-204
92T-668
92UD-430

Henry, Harold
91Utica/ClBest-18
91Utica/ProC-3253

Henry, Jimmy
90Bristol/ProC-3171
90Bristol/Star-10
91Niagara/ClBest-25
91Niagara/ProC-3627

Henry, John M.
N172

Henry, John Park
D327
D328-74
D329-80
D350/2-79
E135-74
M101/4-80
M101/5-79
T222

Henry, Jon
90Elizab/Star-12
91Visalia/ClBest-3
91Visalia/ProC-1737

Henry, Kevin
88Idaho/ProC-1846

Henry, Mark
86Penin-12
87DayBe-10

Henry, Michael
87Savan-10
88Spring/Best-4

Henry, Scott
90Madison/Best-7
90SoOreg/Best-29
91Madison/ClBest-17
91Madison/ProC-2135

Henry, Tim
82BurlR-1
82Tulsa-6
83Tulsa-10

Henshaw, Roy
90Target-335

Hensich, Phil
R314/Can
V355-123

Hensley, Chuck
82WHave-6
83Tacoma-5
84Cram/PCL-86
86Phoenix-9
87Richm/Crown-37
87Richm/TCMA-6
88Albuq/CMC-10
88Albuq/ProC-273
89Calgary/CMC-2
89Calgary/ProC-531
90Wmsprt/Best-9
90Wmsprt/ProC-1055
90Wmsprt/Star-10

Hensley, Mike
89Savan/ProC-364
90Foil/Best-235
90Spring/Best-19
91StPete/ProC-2272

Henson, Mickey
91Gaston/ClBest-7
91Gaston/ProC-2684
91Single/ClBest-22

Hentgen, Pat
87Myrtle-10
88Dunedin/Star-9
89Dunedin/Star-7
90A&AASingle/ProC-45
90Foil/Best-295
90Knoxvl/Best-4
90Knoxvl/ProC-1240
90Knoxvl/Star-5
91B-23
91Syrac/LineD-505
91Syrac/ProC-2477
92D/II-704
92T/91Debut-74

Hepler, William
66T-574R
67OPC-144
67T-144
91WIZMets-174

Herbel, Ron
61Union
63T-208R
64T-47R
65OPC-84
65T-84
66T-331
67OPC-156
67T-156
68T-333
69T-251
70OPC-526
70T-526
71MLB/St-11
71OPC-387
71T-387
72MB-140
72OPC-469
72T-469
91WIZMets-175

Herberholz, Craig
81BurlB-7

Herbert, Ray
53Glen
54T-190
55Rodeo
55T-138
55T/DH-106
58T-379
59T-154
60T-252
60T/tatt-21
61P-87
61T-498
61T/St-162
62Salada-6
62Shirriff-6
62T-8
62T/St-25
63Bz-29
63Exh
63F-9
63J-45
63P-45
63Salada-42
63T-560

63T-8LL
63T/SO
64T-215
65T-399
66OPC-121
66T-121
Exh47

Heredia, Geysi
86Osceola-11

Heredia, Gilbert
(Gil)
87Everett-2
88CalLgAS-2
88SanJose/Cal-132
88SanJose/ProC-130
90Phoenix/CMC-3
90Phoenix/ProC-6
91Phoenix/LineD-383
91Phoenix/ProC-61
92D/II-737
92F-665
92S/II-771
92T/91Debut-75

Heredia, Hector
87Albuq/Pol-10
88Albuq/CMC-11
88Albuq/ProC-274
89Albuq/CMC-5
89Albuq/ProC-66

Heredia, Julian
91Boise/ClBest-29
91Boise/ProC-3871

Heredia, Ubaldo
77LodiD
78LodiD
87Indianap-11

Herman, Billy
28Yueng-22
32Orbit/num-67
32Orbit/un-33
33G-227
35BU-138
36Exh/4-3
36Wheat
37Exh/4-3
37Wheat-10
38Exh/4-3
38Wheat
40Wheat-10
41DP-3
50Remar
52T-394CO
54T-86CO
55Gol/Dodg-11CO
55T-19CO
55T/DH-53CO
60T-456CO
65OPC-251MG
65T-251MG
66OPC-37MG
66T-37
78Padre/FamFun-15CO
80Pac/Leg-23
80SSPC/HOF
89Kahn/Coop-6
89Smok/Dodg-9
90Pac/Legend-30
90Swell/Great-59
90Target-337
91Swell/Great-39
92Conlon/Sport-421
92Conlon/Sport-473
R303/A
R303/B
R305
R312/M
V355-16
WG8-33

Herman, Floyd C.
(Babe)
29Exh/4-4
31Exh/4-4
32Orbit/un-32
33G-5
35G-8K
35G-9K
36Exh/4-4
61F-114
88Conlon/5-16
90Target-336
91Conlon/Sport-169
R305
R306
R308-195
R312/M
R314
R315-A15
R315-B15
R316
R337-418
V353-5
W513-84

Herman, Greg
77AppFx

Herman, Ty
80Elmira-8

Hermann, Jeff
86GlenF-9
87GlenF-18
88Wichita-27

Hermann, LeRoy
R314/Can

Hermanski, Gene
47TipTop
48L-102
49B-20
49Eureka-37
50B-113
51B-55
51T/RB-11
52B-136
52T-16
52TipTop
53T-179
54T-228
79TCMA-165
89Rini/Dodg-36
90Target-338
91T/Arc53-179
Exh47

Hermoso, Angel
70OPC-147
70T-147

Hernaiz, Jesus R.
76OkCty/Team-10
83Colum-12
88SoOreg/ProC-1718
91Kingspt/ClBest-26CO
91Kingspt/ProC-3830CO

Hernandez, Arned
90AppFox/Box-12
90AppFox/ProC-2110

Hernandez, Carlos
85BurlR-19
87Bakers-25
88Bakers/Cal-243
89SanAn/Best-13
89TexLAS/GS-17
90Albuq/CMC-16
90Albuq/ProC-349
90Albuq/Trib-11
90D/Rook-37
91AAAGame/ProC-AAA2
91Albuq/LineD-10
91Albuq/ProC-1144
91D-711
91F-207
91Madison/ClBest-24
91Madison/ProC-2138
91T/90Debut-67
92Classic/I-44
92D/II-778

Hernandez, Cesar
86BurlEx-8
87WPalmB-14
88Rockford-17
89Rockford-17
90Jaxvl/Best-10
90Jaxvl/ProC-1385
91Harris/LineD-256
91Harris/ProC-641
92T-618R

Hernandez, Chuck
86PalmS-17C
86PalmS/Smk-3C
87MidldA-18
88Edmon/ProC-563
89Edmon/CMC-24
89Edmon/ProC-562
90Edmon/CMC-8CO
90Edmon/ProC-532CO

Hernandez, Enrique
89Oneonta/ProC-2100
90PrWill/Team-12

Hernandez, Enzo
71MLB/St-229
71OPC-529R
71T-529R
72OPC-7
72T-7
73OPC-438
73T-438
74McDon
74OPC-572
74T-572
75OPC-84
75T-84
75T/M-84
76OPC-289
76SSPC-125
76T-289
77BurgChef-135
77Padre/SchCd-14
77T-522
78Cr/PCL-84
90Target-339

Hernandez, Fernando
91BurlInd/ProC-3297

Hernandez, Henry
90StPete/Star-12

Hernandez, Jackie
68T-352
69T-258
69T/St-185
70MLB/St-221
70T-686
71MLB/St-204
71OPC-144
71T-144
72MB-141
72OPC-502
72T-502
73OPC-363
73T-363
74OPC-566
74T-566

Hernandez, Javier
90Ashvl/ClBest-5
91Ashvl/ProC-563

Hernandez, Jeremy
87Erie-26
88Spring/Best-3
89StPete/Star-17
90Wichita/Rock-8
91LasVegas/ProC-230
91LasVegas/LineD-283
92D/II-756
92T-211
92T/91Debut-76
92UD-42

Hernandez, Jose
89Gaston/ProC-1018
89Gaston/Star-8
90CharlR/Star-10
91Single/ClBest-94
91Tulsa/LineD-584
91Tulsa/ProC-2780
92D/II-530
92F-307
92S/II-866
92T-237
92T/91Debut-77

Hernandez, Keith
75OPC-623R
75T-623R
75T/M-623R
76OPC-542
76T-542
77BurgChef-11
77Ho-115
77OPC-150
77T-95
78Ho-22
78OPC-109
78T-143
79Ho-108
79OPC-371
79T-695
80BK/PHR-16
80K-43
80OPC-170
80T-201LL
80T-321
80T/S-26
81Coke
81D-67
81F-545
81K-31
81MSA/Disc-16
81OPC-195
81PermaGr/CC-8
81T-420
81T/SO-67
81T/St-18
81T/St-219
82D-278
82F-114
82F/St-23
82K-23
82KMart-36
82OPC-210
82PermaGr/CC-8
82T-186TL
82T-210
82T/St-92
83D-152
83D-20DK
83D/AAS-20
83F-8
83K-49
83OPC-262
83PermaGr/CC-7
83T-700
83T/Gloss40-4
83T/St-188
83T/St-290
83T/Tr-43
84D-238
84D/AAS-23
84D/Champs-46
84Drake-13
84F-587
84F/St-49
85FunFood/Pin-104
84Nes/792-120
84OPC-120
84Ralston-32
84Seven-24E
84T-120
84T/Cereal-32
84T/Mets/Fan-4
84T/St-107
84T/St/Box-6
84T/Super-26
85D-68
85D/AAS-41
85D/HL-21M
85D/HL-27
85Drake-15
85F-85
85F/LimEd-12
85F/St-25
85Leaf-62
85OPC-80
85Pol/MetYank-M5
85Seven-10E
85T-712AS
85T-80
85T/3D-11
85T/Gloss40-13
85T/Mets/Fan-6
85T/St-98
85T/Super-36
85ThomMc/Discs-33
86D-190
86Dorman-9
86Drake-10
86F-84
86F/Mini-20
86F/St-55
86Leaf-124
86OPC-252
86Sf-127M
86Sf-15
86Sf-181M
86Sf-62M
86T-203HL
86T-520
86T-701AS
86T/3D-10
86T/Gloss60-7
86T/Mets/Fan-5
86T/Mini-53
86T/St-99
86T/Super-31
86Woolwth-14
87BK-10
87Classic-4
87D-76
87D/AAS-11
87D/OD-124
87D/PopUp-11
87Drake-10
87F-12
87F-629M
87F-637M
87F/HL-5
87F/Hottest-21
87F/Lim-20
87F/Mini-53
87F/St-58
87F/WaxBox-C6
87F/WS-2M
87Jiffy-4
87KayBee-17
87Leaf-233
87MSA/Discs-4
87OPC-350
87RedFoley/St-32
87Sf-133
87Sf-195M
87Seven-E10
87Seven-ME13
87Sportflic/DealP-3
87T-350
87T-595AS
87T/Board-12
87T/Coins-36
87T/Gloss22-2
87T/Gloss60-26
87T/HL-31
87T/Mini-24
87T/St-102
87T/St-157
87Woolwth-31
88ChefBoy-12
88D-316
88D/AS-49
88D/Best-152
88D/Mets/Bk-316
88Drake-5
88F-136
88F-639M
88F/Hottest-17
88F/LL-18
88F/Mini-93
88F/St-103
88Jiffy-9
88Kahn/Mets-17
88KMart-14
88Leaf-117
88Nestle-42
88OPC-68
88Panini/St-339
88S-400
88Sf-31
88Sf/Gamewin-11
88T-610
88T/Big-59
88T/Gloss60-32
88T/Mets/Fan-17
88T/St-97
88T/St/Backs-3
88T/UK-33
89B-385
89Classic-59
89D-117
89D/Best-208
89D/GrandSlam-8
89F-37
89Kahn/Mets-17
89KMart/Lead-8
89OPC-63
89Panini/St-137
89RedFoley/St-57
89S-41
89S/HotStar-23
89Sf-60
89T-291TL
89T-480
89T/Big-185
89T/DHTest-8
89T/LJN-26
89T/St-93
89T/WaxBox-G
89UD-612
90B-342
90BBWit-20
90Classic/III-36
90D-388
90D/BestAL-33
90F-205
90KayBee-16
90KMart/CBatL-10
90Leaf/II-470
90MLBPA/Pins-10
90OPC-230

90PublInt/St-135
90PublInt/St-262
90S-193
90S/100St-29
90S/Tr-57T
90Sf-106
90T-230
90T/Ames-8
90T/Big-301
90T/Tr-39T
90UD-222
90UD/Ext-777
91F-368
91S-89
91WIZMets-177

Hernandez, Kiki
91Greens/ProC-3062
91SALAS/ProC-SAL26

Hernandez, Krandall
91Hunting/ClBest-12
91Hunting/ProC-3337

Hernandez, Leo
83T/Tr-44
84Nes/792-71
84RochR-15
84T-71
85RochR-5
86Colum-11
86Colum/Pol-10
91Crown/Orio-194

Hernandez, Leonardo
78Clinton

Hernandez, Luis
90Bristol/ProC-3153
90Bristol/Star-11
91Bristol/ClBest-5
91Bristol/ProC-3614

Hernandez, Manny
82DayBe-5
83DayBe-6
84Cram/PCL-59
85Cram/PCL-56
86Tucson-7
87Tucson-7
88D-481
88Tucson/CMC-1
88Tucson/ProC-169
88Tucson/JP-13
89Portl/CMC-2
89Portl/ProC-221
90T/TVMets-45
90Tidew/CMC-5
90Tidew/ProC-538
91Tidew/LineD-557
91Tidew/ProC-2504
91WIZMets-176

Hernandez, Marino
88Pocatel/ProC-2085
89Clinton/ProC-884
90Clinton/Best-16

Hernandez, Martin
86Nashua-12
87Salem-11

Hernandez, Nick
78Newar
79BurlB-8

Hernandez, Pedro J.
81Syrac-15
82Syrac-21
85Cram/PCL-71

Hernandez, Pete
78DaytB

Hernandez, Rafael
91Kingspt/ClBest-11
91Kingspt/ProC-3822

Hernandez, Ramon
67T-576R
68T-382
73OPC-117
73T-117
74OPC-222
74T-222
75OPC-224
75T-224
75T/M-224
76OPC-647
76SSPC-567
76T-647
77T-468
91Billings/ProC-3760

Hernandez, Robert
(Bobby)
86LitFalls-14
87Columbia-15

Hernandez, Robert
86Cram/PCL-100
87Kenosha-2

Hernandez, Roberto
87QuadC-8
88QuadC/GS-20
89MidldA/GS-18
90BirmB/Best-18
90BirmB/ProC-1106
90Foil/Best-216
91B-343
91Vanco/LineD-637
91Vanco/ProC-1591
92Classic/I-45
92D/I-19RR
92F-677
92S/II-874
92T-667
92T/91Debut-78
92UD-7SR

Hernandez, Rudy A.
61T-229

Hernandez, Rudy J.
89StLucie/Star-9
91Wmsprt/LineD-633
91Wmsprt/ProC-301

Hernandez, Toby
80Utica-18
83Syrac-14
84Syrac-15
85Toledo-13

Hernandez, Tom
91Gaston/ClBest-15
91Gaston/ProC-2692

Hernandez, Willie
(Guillermo)
76OkCty/Team-11
78T-99
79T-614
80T-472
81D-589
81F-310
81T-238
82RedLob
82T-23
83D-174
83F-497
83T-568
83T/Tr-45
84D-163
84F-34
84F/X-51
85FunFood/Pin-79
84Nes/792-199
84OPC-199
84T-199
84T/Tr-51
85Cain's-10
85D-212
85Drake-37
85F-10
85F/St-101
85Leaf-235
85OPC-333
85Seven-10D
85Seven-1G
85Seven-7C
85T-333
85T/St-257
85T/Super-2
85Wendy-11
86Cain's-8
86D-227
86D/AAS-43
86D/WaxBox-PC5
86F-228
86F/LL-18
86F/St-56
86Leaf-102
86OPC-341
86Sf-65M
86Sf-85
86T-670
86T/St-275
87Cain's-13
87Coke/Tigers-15
87D-522
87D/AAS-43
87F-153
87F/Excit-26
87F/GameWin-20
87F/Mini-54
87F/St-59
87OPC-339
87Sf-105
87Seven-DT4
87T-515
87T/Mini-54
87T/St-272
87Toledo-27
88D-398
88D/Best-125
88F-58
88Panini/St-84
88Pep/T-21
88S-507
88T-713
88T/Big-206
89Bimbo/Discs-9
89D-62
89F-135
89Mara/Tigers-21
89OPC-43
89Pol/Tigers-21
89S-275
89T-43
89UD-279
90D-610
90F-605
90PublInt/St-473
90RedFoley/St-46
90S-267
90UD-518

Hernandez, Xavier
88Myrtle/ProC-1178
88SALAS/GS-21
89Knoxvl/Best-9
89Knoxvl/ProC-1144
89Syrac/Team-14
90D-682
90D/Rook-33
90Leaf/II-517
90Lennox-15
90T/89Debut-55
90UD-26
91B-545
91D-708
91F-509
91Leaf/II-462
91Mother/Ast-26
91OPC-194
91S-564
91T-194
91T/StClub/I-74
92D/II-782
92F-437
92T-640

Herndon, Larry
75Phoenix-20
76Phoenix
77BurgChef-104
77Ho-47
77OPC-169
77T-397
78T-512
79OPC-328
79Pol/Giants-31
79T-624
80Pol/Giants-31
80T-257
81D-196
81F-451
81OPC-108
81T-409
81T/St-236
82D-172
82F-390
82OPC-182
82T-182
82T/St-109
82T/Tr-43T
83D-585
83D/AAS-5
83F-330
83OPC-13
83T-13
83T-261TL
83T/St-68
84D-349
84F-82
84Nes/792-333
84OPC-333
84T-334
84T/St-264
85Cain's-11
85D-150
85F-11
85Leaf-249
85OPC-9
85Seven-4D
85T-591
85T/St-266
85Wendy-12
86Cain's-9
86D-593
86F-229
86Leaf-230
86OPC-61
86T-688
86T/St-271
87Cain's-11
87Coke/Tigers-2
87D/OD-211
87F-154
87Seven-DT5
87T-298
88D-353
88F-59
88OPC-146
88Pep/T-31
88Pol/T-6
88RedFoley/St-34
88S-138
88T-743
88T/Big-56
89S-279
89UD-49

Herr, Edward
N172

Herr, Thomas
(Tommy)
77StPete
80T-684R
81Coke
81D-68
81F-550
81T-266
82D-530
82F-115
82F/St-30
82T-27
83D-217
83F-9
83OPC-97
83T-489
83T/St-286
84D-596
84F-325
84Nes/792-649
84OPC-117
84T-649
84T/St-142
85D-425
85D/AAS-43
85F-226
85OPC-113
85T-113
85T/St-142
86D-83
86D/AAS-2
86D/PopUp-2
86Drake-21
86F-37
86F/AS-2
86F/Mini-8
86F/St-57
86KAS/Disc-15
86Leaf-79
86OPC-94
86Sf-113
86Schnucks-8
86T-550
86T-702AS
86T/Gloss22-14
86T/Gloss60-32
86T/Mini-62
86T/St-147
86T/St-49
86T/Super-32
87D-140
87D/OD-61
87F-296
87F/LL-22
87Leaf-121
87OPC-181
87RedFoley/St-60
87Smok/Cards-20
87T-721
87T/St-49
88D-208
88D/Best-326
88F-35
88F/Hottest-18
88F/Up-U43
88F/WS-10
88F/WS-7M
88Leaf-201
88OPC-310
88Panini/St-391
88S-84
88S/Tr-8T
88Sf-141
88T-310
88T/Big-31
88T/St-50
88T/St/Backs-4
88T/Tr-49T
89B-403
89Classic/Up/2-166
89D-301
89D/Best-72
89D/Tr-4
89F-115
89F/Up-107
89Phill/TastyK-10
89S-191
89S/Tr-9T
89T-709
89T/Big-283
89T/Tr-49T
89UD-558
89UD/Ext-720
90B-159
90D-21DK
90D-75
90D/BestNL-32
90D/Learning-16
90D/SuperDK-21DK
90F-560
90F/BBMVP-18
90Leaf/I-184
90MLBPA/Pins-1
90OPC-297
90Panini/St-309
90Phill/TastyK-13
90PublInt/St-239
90RedFoley/St-47
90S-171
90S/100St-77
90Sf-63
90T-297
90T/Big-206
90T/Coins-49
90T/St-122
90UD-488
91B-480
91D-610
91F-149
91F/Ultra-219
91Kahn/Mets-28
91Leaf/I-48
91Leaf/Stud-205
91OPC-64
91S-820
91T-64
91T/StClub/II-532
91UD-416
91WIZMets-178

Herrera, Ezequiel
90Foil/Best-41
90Spring/Best-9
91StPete/ClBest-26
91StPete/ProC-2289

Herrera, Hector
87AubAs-20

Herrera, Jose
91MedHat/ProC-4115

Herrera, Jose C.
69T-378

Herrera, Juan
(Poncho)
58T-433
59T-129
60L-5
60T-130
61Bz-27
61P-121
61T-569AS
61T/RO-36
61T/St-56
62J-192
62P-192
62Salada-122
62Shirriff-122

Herrera, Ramon
26Exh-67
86Negro/Frit-84
Herrholtz, John
91Utica/ClBest-3
91Utica/ProC-3236
Herrick, Neal
81Miami-16
Herring, Art
90Target-340
Herring, Paul
80Water-5
81Indianap-27
82Water-16
Herring, Vince
90SanJose/Best-20
90SanJose/Cal-48
90SanJose/ProC-2010
90SanJose/Star-11
91SanJose/ClBest-17
91SanJose/ProC-5
Herrmann, Ed
69T-439R
70OPC-368
70T-368
71OPC-169
71T-169
72OPC-452
72T-452
73OPC-73
73T-73
74OPC-438
74T-438
74T/St-155
75Ho-86
75OPC-219
75T-219
75T/M-219
76OPC-406
76SSPC-440
76T-406
77T-143
78BK/Ast-3
78T-677
79OPC-194
79T-374
Herrmann, Tim
89NiagFls/Pucko-11
90Fayette/ProC-2401
Herrnstein, John
63T-553R
64PhilBull-14
64T-243R
65T-534
66T-304
78TCMA-124
Herron, Tony
84Pawtu-11A
84Pawtu-11B
85Pawtu-16
Herrscher, Rick
91WIZMets-179
Hersh, Dave
77BurlB
Hersh, Earl
61BeeHive-8
Hershberger, N. Mike
62T-341
63T-254
64T-465
65OPC-89
65T-89
66T-236
67T-323
68OPC-18
68T-18
69MB-111
69MLB/St-86
69T-655
70McDon-3
70MLB/St-272
70T-596
71OPC-149
71T-149
72MB-142
78TCMA-287
Hershberger, Willard
39PB-119
40PB-77
W711/1
W711/2
Hershiser, Gordon
88VeroB/Star-11
89SanAn/Best-7
Hershiser, Orel
82Albuq-4
83Albuq-3
85FunFood/Pin-83
84Pol/Dodg-55
85Coke/Dodg-12
85D-581
85F-371
85F/St-96
85Leaf-38
85OPC-273
85T-493
85T/St-74
86Coke/Dodg-11
86D-18
86D-226
86D/DKsuper-18
86Drake-31
86F-131
86F/LimEd-24
86F/Slug-16
86F/St-58
86Leaf-18DK
86OPC-159
86Pol/Dodg-55
86Sf-9
86T-159
86T/3D-12
86T/Gloss60-24
86T/Mini-45
86T/St-73
86T/Super-33
87Classic-92
87D-106
87D/HL-13
87D/OD-79
87F-441
87F/RecSet-16
87Leaf-246
87Mother/Dodg-6
87OPC-385
87Pol/Dodg-28
87RedFoley/St-5
87Sf-43
87Seven-W6
87Smok/Dodg-12
87T-385
87T/Mini-14
88D-94
88D/AS-56
88D/Best-148
88F-518
88F-632M
88F/AwardWin-17
88F/BB/AS-14
88F/Excit-20
88F/Hottest-19
88F/LL-19
88F/Mini-84
88F/RecSet-18
88F/Slug-18
88F/SS-15
88F/St-92
88F/TL-13
88Leaf-62
88Mother/Dodg-6
88OPC-40
88Panini/St-303
88Pol/Dodg-55
88S-470
88Sf-160
88T-40
88T/Big-91
88T/Mini-53
88T/Revco-12
88T/St-68
88T/UK-34
89B-341
89Bz-15
89Cadaco-29
89Classic-1
89Classic-105
89Classic/Up/2-173
89T/Crunch-3
89D-197
89D-648HL
89D/AS-50
89D/Best-225
89D/MVP-BC4
89F-62
89F/AS-7
89F/BBAS-21
89F/BBMVP's-19
89F/Excit-24
89F/Heroes-22
89F/LL-20
89F/Superstar-23
89F/WaxBox-C14
89F/WS-11
89F/WS-6
89Holsum/Discs-18
89KayBee-19
89KingB/Discs-12
89Mother/Dodg-6
89Nissen-18
89OPC-380
89OPC-41
89Panini/St-13LCS
89Panini/St-18
89Panini/St-19
89Panini/St-225
89Panini/St-25
89Panini/St-474
89Panini/St-9
89Panini/St-97
89Pol/Dodg-29
89MSA/SS-5
89RedFoley/St-58
89S-370
89S-582M
89S-653HL
89S/HotStar-35
89S/Mast-21
89Sf-222M
89Sf-36
89Smok/Dodg-100
89Socko-Set
89T-394AS
89T-550
89T-5RB
89T-669TL
89T/Big-1
89T/Coins-2
89T/DH-21
89T/Gloss60-48
89T/Hills-17
89T/LJN-162
89T/Mini-18
89T/St-12
89T/St-65
89T/St/Backs-60
89T/UK-38
89Tetley/Discs-10
89UD-130
89UD-661CY
89UD-665M
89UD-667M
89Woolwth-21
89Woolwth-25
89Woolwth-33
89Woolwth-4
90B-84
90BBWit-1
90Classic-81
90CollAB-6
90D-197
90D/BestNL-54
90D/Bon/MVP-BC5
90F-399
90F/BB-18
90F/BBMVP-19
90F/WaxBox-C14
90HOF/St-99
90Holsum/Discs-12
90HotPlay/St-21
90Leaf/II-280
90MLBPA/Pins-8
90Mother/Dodg-12
90MSA/Soda-9
90OPC-780
90Panini/St-275
90Pol/Dodg-55
90Post-8
90PublInt/St-263
90PublInt/St-9
90RedFoley/St-48
90S-50
90S/100St-94
90Sf-197
90T-780
90T/Big-82
90T/DH-34
90T/Mini-58
90T/St-63
90T/TVAS-46
90Target-341
90UD-10TC
90UD-256
90WonderBrd-4
91B-595
91Classic/200-23
91Classic/III-38
91D-280
91F-208
91F/UltraUp-U88
91Leaf/I-243
91Leaf/Stud-183
91Mother/Dodg-12
91OPC-690
91OPC/Premier-64
91Petro/SU-22
91Pol/Dodg-55
91SanAn/ProC-2968
91S-550
91Seven/3DCoin-5SC
91T-690
91T/CJMini/II-17
91T/StClub/I-244
91UD-524
92D/I-247
92F-459
92S/II-653
92T-175
92UD-261
Hershmann, William
87StPete-21
88Savan/ProC-340
89Savan/ProC-366
Hertel, Rick
78Dunedin
Hertz, Steve
64T-544R
Hertzler, Paul
85Indianap-18
86Jacks/TCMA-15
Herz, Steve
80Toledo-13
81Toledo-12
82Spokane-11
82Vanco-11
84Cram/PCL-142
85Cram/PCL-244
Herzig, Lynn
(Spike)
77Holyo
78Holyo
Herzog, Charles
(Buck)
11Helmar-129
12Sweet/Pin-114
12Sweet/Pin-67
14CJ-85
15CJ-85
16FleischBrd-41
40PB-229
75F/Pion-27
92Conlon/Sport-489
BF2-71
D304
D327
D328-75
D329-81
D350/2-80
E135-75
E96
M101/4-81
M101/5-80
M116
S74-44
T201
T205
T206
T207
T213/blue
T215/blue
T3-45
W514-104
Herzog, Hans
84Savan-8
86StPete-11
87StPete-16
Herzog, Whitey
57T-29
58T-438
59T-392
60L-71
60T-92
61P-88
61T-106
61T/St-163
62T-513
63T-302
73OPC-549MG
73T-549MG
76SSPC-185
76T-236MG
77T-371MG
78T-299MG
79T-451MG
81T-684MG
82D-190MG
83D-530MG
83T-186MG
84Nes/792-561MG
84T-561MG
84T/Gloss22-12MG
85T-683MG
86T-441MG
87D/AAS-20MG
87D/PopUp-20MG
87Smok/Cards-25MG
87T-243MG
87T/Gloss22-1MG
88Smok/Card-1MG
88T-744MG
89D/AS-42MG
89D/PopUp-42MG
89Smok/Cards-8MG
89T-654MG
89T/Gloss22-12MG
90OPC-261MG
90Smok/Card-8MG
90T-261MG
90T/TVCard-1MG
91Crown/Orio-195
Exh47
Hesketh, Joe
83Memphis-19
84Indianap-6
85D-157
85F-652R
85T/Tr-52T
86D-341
86F-250
86Leaf-150
86OPC-42
86Provigo-21
86Sf-177M
86T-472
86T/Gloss60-19
87D-134
87F-320
87Leaf-62
87OPC-189
87T-189
88D-504
88Indianap/ProC-512
88OPC-371
88T-371
89D-460
89F-378
89OPC-74
89S-498
89T-614
89UD-60
90D-511
90F-349
90Leaf/II-507
90OPC-24
90PublInt/St-175
90S-483
90T-24
90T/Tr-40T
90UD-512
91OPC-269
91T-269
92D/II-611
92F-40
92S/I-359
92T-521
92UD-570
Heslet, Harry
V362-27
Hester, Steve
88Greens/ProC-1570
89Cedar/Best-29
89Cedar/ProC-919
89Cedar/Star-27
89Cedar/Star-8
90Cedar/Best-26
90Cedar/ProC-2323
Hetki, John
53T-235
54T-161

55T/DH-62
91T/Arc53-235
Hetrick, Kent
87SLCity/Taco-3
88Beloit/GS-13
89Stockton/Best-9
89Stockton/Cal-161
89Stockton/ProC-376
89Stockton/Star-10
Hetzel, Eric
85Greens-18
87WinHaven-22
88Pawtu/CMC-8
88Pawtu/ProC-449
89D-660
89Pawtu/CMC-3
89Pawtu/Dunkin-31
89Pawtu/ProC-703
90D-539
90F-279
90LSUGreat-5
90OPC-629
90S-543
90S/100Ris-23
90T-629
90T/89Debut-56
90T/TVRSox-45
90UD-673
91Pawtu/LineD-356
91Pawtu/ProC-32
Heuer, Mark
87SanAn-24
Heving, Joseph W.
(Joe)
29Exh/4-17
35BU-43
39PB-20
40PB-35
41DP-136
Heving, John A.
(Johnnie)
92Conlon/Sport-455
Hewatt, B.
88Pocatel/ProC-2090
Hewes, Pat
87Savan-9
88StPete/Star-9
89Penin/Star-7
Heydeman, Greg
74Albuq/Team-6
Hiatt, Jack
65T-497R
66T-373R
67T-368
68Coke
68Dexter-38
68T-419
69MB-112
69OPC-204
69T-204
70OPC-13
70T-13
71MLB/St-83
71OPC-371
71T-371
72MB-143
72T-633
73OPC-402
73T-402
80Wichita-8
82Holyo-23
83ColumAst-22
88Pocatel/ProC-2101
Hiatt, Phil
91BBCity/ClBest-17
91BBCity/ProC-1403
91FSLAS/ProC-FSL1
91Single/ClBest-151
Hibbard, Greg
86Cram/PCL-43
87AppFx-27
87FtMyr-6
88Vanco/CMC-11
88Vanco/ProC-770
89Vanco/CMC-3
89Vanco/ProC-584
90B-303
90Coke/WSox-8
90D-384
90F-534
90Leaf/II-523
90OPC-769
90S-369
90S/100Ris-77
90S/YS/II-20
90T-769
90T/89Debut-57
90T/JumboR-14
90UD-543
91D-159
91F-122
91F/Ultra-75
91Kodak/WSox-27
91Leaf/II-438
91Leaf/Stud-34
91OPC-256
91Panini/FrSt-319
91Panini/St-254
91S-128
91T-256
91UD-679
92D/I-178
92F-83
92S/I-266
92T-477
92UD-420
Hibbett, Wendell
78Charl
Hibbs, Al
85Utica-11
86Cram/PCL-132
Hibbs, Loren
84Everett/Cram-15
90WichSt-40
Hibner, Dave
78Ashvl
80Ashvl-8
Hice, Bob
84CharlO-1
85CharlO-27
87CharlO/WBTV-xx
Hickerson, Bryan
87Clinton-28
89SanJose/Best-15
89SanJose/Cal-212
89SanJose/ProC-443
89SanJose/Star-14
90Shrev/ProC-1438
90Shrev/Star-11
91Shrev/LineD-306
91Shrev/ProC-1815
92D/II-783
92F-638
92S/II-750
92T-8
92T/91Debut-79
92UD-667
Hickey, Bob
75SanAn
Hickey, James Joseph
85BuffB-20
87BirmB/Best-16
89ColMud/Best-19
91BurlAs/ClBest-26CO
91BurlAs/ProC-2818CO
Hickey, Kevin
79AppFx-6
80GlenF/B-10
80GlenF/C-7
82D-631
82F-344
82OPC-362
82T-778
83D-445
83F-237
83T-278
83TrueVal/WSox-45
84D-135
84F-61
84Nes/792-459
84T-459
86Portl-8
87Hawaii-18
88RochR/Gov-11
89F/Up-4
89French-23
90D-583
90F-178
90OPC-546
90PublInt/St-577
90S-214
90T-546
90UD-299
91Crown/Orio-196
91F-475
91Hagers/LineD-237
91Hagers/ProC-2450
Hickman, Charles
E107
T201
T213/brown
WG2-23
Hickman, Dave J.
90Target-342
Hickman, Gordon J.
T206
Hickman, Jim
61Union
62T-598R
63T-107
64T-514
64T/Coins-92
65OPC-114
65T-114
66T-402
67T-346
69MB-113
69OPC-63
69Sunoco/Pin-3
69T-63
70T-612
71K-11
71MD
71MLB/St-32
71OPC-175
71T-175
71T/Coins-27
72T-534
73OPC-565
73T-565
90Target-343
91WIZMets-180
Hickox, Tom
88CapeCod/Sum-86
Hicks, Aman
89Erie/Star-7
90Wausau/Best-24
90Wausau/ProC-2138
90Wausau/Star-10
91Kane/ClBest-23
91Kane/ProC-2670
Hicks, Clay
77AppFx
Hicks, Ed
76Wausau
89Pac/SenLg-130
Hicks, Jim
67T-532
69T-559R
70OPC-173
70T-173
Hicks, Mike
77Ashvl
Hicks, Rob
86Portl-9
87Reading-26
88ElPaso/Best-27
Hicks, Robert
82Spring-7
Hicks, William J.
(Joe)
60L-74
61T-386
62T-428
79QuadC-11CO
83Iowa-14CO
84Iowa-9CO
86Iowa-15CO
87PrWill-26CO
89Pac/SenLg-69
89T/SenLg-105
91WIZMets-181
Hierholzer, David
91AppFx/ClBest-5
91AppFx/ProC-1711
Higbe, Kirby
39Exh
41DP-24
41PB-52
47TipTop
48L-129
49B-215
49Eureka-108
50B-200
89Smok/Dodg-50
90Target-344
Exh47
Higginbotham, Robin
91Niagara/ClBest-15
91Niagara/ProC-3647
Higgins, Bill
90Martins/ProC-3184
Higgins, Bob
90Target-980
T207
Higgins, Dennis
66T-529R
67OPC-52
67T-52
68T-509
69T-441
69T/St-237
70OPC-257
70T-257
71MLB/St-374
71OPC-479
71T-479
72MB-144
72OPC-278
72T-278
Higgins, Frank
36Exh/4-14
WG8-34
Higgins, Kevin
89Spokane/SP-19
90Foil/Best-102
90Riversi/Best-13
90Riversi/Cal-6
90Riversi/ProC-2610
91LasVegas/ProC-239
91LasVegas/LineD-284
Higgins, Mark
80BurlB-23
81BurlB-23
86Watlo-11
87Wmsprt-9
88ColoSp/CMC-13
88ColoSp/ProC-1544
89ColoSp/CMC-15
89ColoSp/ProC-255
90Denver/CMC-16
90Denver/ProC-631
90T/89Debut-58
Higgins, Mike
(Pinky)
34G-78
35BU-171
35G-1B
35G-2B
35G-6B
35G-7B
36B
40PB-199
41DP-55
41PB-35
55T-150MG
61T-221MG
62T-559MG
72F/FFeat-30
72Laugh/GF-11
81Detroit-89
88Conlon/AmAS-15
90HOF/St-37
PM10/Sm-73
R303/A
R303/B
R313
R314
W501-26
Higgins, Ted
86FSLAS-23
86FtLaud-13
87Albany-8
Higgs, Darrel
87Orlan-24
High, Andrew
(Andy)
21Exh-73
26Exh-2
27Exh-3
33G-182
88Conlon/3-13
90Target-345
92Conlon/Sport-648
R316
High, Hugh
16FleischBrd-42
D328-76
D329-82
D350/2-81
E135-76
M101/4-82
M101/5-81
Hightower, Barry
86Columbia-13
87Columbia-1
88Spokane/ProC-1942
Higson, Chuck
86Cram/PCL-185
88Fresno/Cal-22
88Fresno/ProC-1225
Higuera, Ted
(Teddy)
84ElPaso-15
85F/Up-U54
85Pol/Brew-49
85T/Tr-53T
86D-351
86F-490
86F/St-59
86Jay's-10
86Leaf-157
86Pol/Brew-49
86Sf-114
86T-347
87Classic/Up-147
87D-16DK
87D-49
87D/AAS-57
87D/DKsuper-16
87D/OD-56
87F-346
87F/Excit-27
87F/GameWin-21
87F/Hottest-22
87F/LL-23
87F/Lim-21
87F/Mini-55
87F/Slug-20
87F/St-60
87Leaf-16DK
87Leaf-95
87OPC-250
87Pol/Brew-49
87RedFoley/St-74
87Sf-11
87Sf-111M
87T-250
87T-615AS
87T/Gloss22-22
87T/Mini-60
87T/St-199
88D-90
88D/Best-127
88F-166
88F/AS-3
88F/AwardWin-19
88F/BB/AS-15
88F/BB/MVP-18
88F/Excit-21
88F/Hottest-20
88F/LL-20
88F/Mini-30
88F/RecSet-19
88F/Slug-19
88F/SS-16
88F/St-37
88F/TL-15
88Leaf-53
88OPC-110
88Panini/St-116
88Pol/Brew-49
88S-280
88Sf-20
88T-110
88T/Big-87
88T/Mini-18
88T/St-196
88T/UK-35
89B-129
89Brewer/YB-49
89Classic-136
89D-175
89D/Best-183
89ElPaso/GS-16
89F-188
89F/BBMVP's-20
89F/Heroes-23
89F/Superstar-24
89Gard-7
89OPC-292
89Panini/St-366
89Pol/Brew-49
89RedFoley/St-59
89S-132
89S/HotStar-49

89Sf-47
89T-595
89T/Mini-57
89T/St-198
89T/St/Backs-28
89T/UK-39
89UD-424
90B-384
90Brewer/MillB-11
90Classic/III-T9
90D-339
90D/BestAL-92
90ElPasoATG/Team-6
90F-326
90Leaf/II-506
90MLBPA/Pins-83
90OPC-15
90Panini/St-96
90Pol/Brew-49
90PublInt/St-289
90PublInt/St-497
90S-305
90Sf-44
90T-15
90T/Big-322
90T/St-201
90UD-627
91B-54
91BBBest/Aces-10
91Brewer/MillB-10
91Classic/200-24
91D-629
91F-586
91F/Ultra-175
91Leaf/StudPrev-6
91OPC-475
91Pol/Brew-10
91S-260
91T-475
91T/StClub/I-46
91UD-341
92D/I-294
92F-178
92S/I-126
92T-265
92UD-138

Hilbert, Adam
88Pocatel/ProC-2081

Hildebrand, George
90Target-346

Hildebrand, Oral
34G-38
35BU-123
35G-1L
35G-2E
35G-6E
35G-7E
36G
37Exh/4-15
40PB-123
91Conlon/Sport-278
R308-163
R313
R314

Hildebrand, Tom
86Penin-13

Hildebrand, Umpire
21Exh-74

Hildreth, Brad
89Erie/Star-8
90Freder/Team-30
90Wausau/Star-11

Hilgenberg, Scot
86Cedar/TCMA-17
87Tampa-24

Hilgendorf, Tom
63Pep/Tul
70OPC-482
70T-482
74OPC-13
74T-13
75OPC-377
75T-377
75T/M-377
76OPC-168
76T-168

Hill, A.J.
77AppFx
80GlenF/B-21
80GlenF/C-20M
80GlenF/C-30
81AppFx-18
83MidldC-26
84Chatt-20

Hill, Brad
85BurlR-4
86Salem-12

Hill, Chris
88LitFalls/Pucko-17
89Clmbia/Best-13
89Clmbia/GS-9
89SALAS/GS-15
91Wmsprt/LineD-634
91Wmsprt/ProC-286

Hill, Clay
85Cram/PCL-100
86Calgary-12
88Miami/Star-9

Hill, Darryl
78Dunedin

Hill, Don
(Clay)
83Chatt-15
84Chatt-27

Hill, Donnie
82WHave-14
83Tacoma-11
84D-96
84F-448
84Mother/A's-13
84Nes/792-265
84T-265
85D-375
85F-426
85Mother/A's-12
85T/Tr-54T
86D-340
86F-420
86Leaf-148
86Mother/A's-12
86OPC-310
86T-484
87Coke/WS-9
87D-405
87D/OD-237
87F-394
87T-339
87T/Tr-47T
88Coke/WS-10
88D-87
88F-400
88OPC-132
88S-572
88T-132
88T/Big-137
88T/St-286
89S-583
89T-512
89Tacoma/CMC-18
89Tacoma/ProC-1562
89UD-527
91D-376
91F-316
91F/Ultra-46
91Leaf/I-177
91OPC-36
91Smok/Angel-12
91T-36
91UD-211
92F-60
92S/I-183
92T-731
92UD-413

Hill, Elmore
(Moe)
78Wisco

Hill, Eric
90Batavia/ProC-3058
91Spartan/ClBest-6
91Spartan/ProC-891

Hill, Fred
89Wythe/Star-13

Hill, Garry
70OPC-172R
70T-172R

Hill, Glenallen
85Kingst-19
86Knoxvl-10
86SLAS-16
87D-561
87Syrac-23
87Syrac/TCMA-20
88Syrac/CMC-15
88Syrac/ProC-812
89AAA/CMC-22
89AAA/ProC-31
89Syrac/CMC-15
89Syrac/ProC-804
89Syrac/Team-15
90B-514
90Classic-88
90D-627
90D/Rook-24
90F/Up-127
90Leaf/II-317
90OPC-194
90S-601RP
90S/YS/II-33
90T-194
90T/89Debut-59
90Tor/BlueJ-24
90UD/Ext-776
91B-24
91D-380
91F-177
91F/Ultra-363
91F/UltraUp-U19
91F/Up-U17
91Leaf/II-311
91Leaf/Stud-43
91OPC-509
91Panini/FrSt-347
91S-514
91S/100RisSt-60
91T-509
91T/StClub/II-425
91T/Tr-55T
91Tor/Fire-24
91ToysRUs-11
91UD-276
91UD/FinalEd-52F
92D/II-643
92F-110
92S/II-448
92T-364
92UD-558

Hill, H.A.
79Knoxvl/TCMA-22

Hill, Herman
70OPC-267R
70T-267R

Hill, Jim
47Centen-9

Hill, Ken
87ArkTr-19
89D-536
89D/Best-304
89D/Rook-31
89F-652R
89F/Up-119
89Louisvl-22
89Louisvl/ProC-1268
89S/Tr-98
89Smok/Cards-9
89T/Tr-50T
90AAAGame/ProC-AAA53
90D-397
90F-251
90OPC-233
90S-233
90S/100Ris-34
90S/YS/I-32
90T-233
90T/JumboR-15
90T/TVCard-13
90ToysRUs-15
90UD-336
91B-390
91D-670
91F-635
91F/UltraUp-U106
91Leaf/II-376
91OPC-591
91Pol/Card-43
91S-567
91T-591
91T/StClub/II-435
91UD-647
92D/I-31
92F-580
92S/I-104
92T-664
92UD-628

Hill, Lew
87Oneonta-1
89Oneonta/ProC-2111
90Greens/Best-23
90Greens/ProC-2675
91Greens/ProC-3074

Hill, Marc
75OPC-620R
75T-620R
75T/M-620R
76OPC-577
76SSPC-100
76T-577
77T-57
78T-359
79Pol/Giants-2
79T-11
80OPC-125
80Pol/Giants-2
80T-236
81T-486
81T/Tr-770
82T-748
83D-230
83T-124
83TrueVal/WSox-7
84D-330
84F-62
84Nes/792-698
84T-698
84TrueVal/WS-16
85Coke/WS-7
85D-160
85F-516
85T-312
86Coke/WS-7
86T-552

Hill, Milton
88Cedar/ProC-1163
89Chatt/Best-6
89Chatt/GS-10
90Nashvl/CMC-1
90Nashvl/ProC-226
91Nashvl/LineD-261
91Nashvl/ProC-2151
92D/II-659
92S/II-820
92T/91Debut-80

Hill, Nate
85Spokane/Cram-8

Hill, Orsino
83Cedar-23
83Cedar/LF-23
88Jaxvl/Best-12
88Jaxvl/ProC-965
89CharlK-24
90AAAGame/ProC-AAA41
90Vanco/CMC-17
90Vanco/ProC-499
91Vanco/LineD-638
91Vanco/ProC-1606

Hill, Perry W.
86DayBe-12C
90Gaston/Star-28INST
91Gaston/ProC-2705INST

Hill, Pete
74Laugh/Black-10

Hill, Quency
76OkCty/Team-12
78Knoxvl
82QuadC-27

Hill, Roger
88Watlo/ProC-685

Hill, Ron
80Elmira-9

Hill, Sandy
78Salem

Hill, Stephen F.
(Steve)
85Anchora-16
86StPete-12
87Peoria-7
87Peoria/PW-4
87Spring/Best-12
88StPete/Star-10
88WinSalem/Star-6
89ArkTr/GS-7
89SanBern/Best-15
89SanBern/Cal-84

Hill, Tony
86Elmira-10
87Greens-14

Hill, Tyrone
91Classic/DP-12
92S/II-807DP
92T-444DP

Hill, William C.
(Still Bill)
90Target-981

Hillegas, Shawn
87Albuq/Pol-11
87Sf/Rook-30
88Albuq/CMC-1
88Albuq/ProC-265
88D-35RR
88F-519
88Leaf-35RR
88Pol/Dodg-57M
88S-612
88T-455
89B-58
89Coke/WS-11
89D-503
89F-498
89Panini/St-301
89S-488
89S/YS/II-29
89T-247
89UD-478
90D-619
90F-535
90OPC-93
90PublInt/St-389
90S-329
90T-93
90Target-982
90UD-541
90Vanco/CMC-8
90Vanco/ProC-485
91D-589
91F/Up-U18
91Leaf/II-513
91S/RookTr-65T
92D/I-72
92F-111
92S/I-93
92T-523

Hillemann, Charles
(Charlie)
87Spokane-9
88Charl/ProC-1197
89AubAs/ProC-4
89TexLAS/GS-9
89Wichita/Rock-18
89Wichita/Rock/Up-6
90LasVegas/CMC-18
90LasVegas/ProC-134
90Wichita/Rock-9
91Single/ClBest-50
91Wichita/LineD-608
91Wichita/ProC-2611

Hiller, Chuck
61T-538
62Salada-106
62Shirriff-106
62T-188
63J-102
63P-102
63T-185
64T-313
65T-531
66OPC-154
66T-154
67T-198
68T-461
73OPC-549CO
73T-549CO
91WIZMets-182

Hiller, Frank
52B-114
52T-156
R346-37

Hiller, John
66T-209R
68T-307
69MB-114
69T-642
70OPC-12
70T-12
71MLB/St-393
71OPC-629
71T-629
72MB-146
73OPC-448
73T-448
74/DE-17
74OPC-208LL
74OPC-24
74T-208LL
74T-24
74T/St-175
75K-19
75OPC-415
75T-415

75T/M-415
76OPC-37
76SSPC-353
76T-37
77BurgChef-95
77Ho-28
77OPC-257
77T-595
78BK/T-9
78T-258
79OPC-71
79T-151
80OPC-229
80T-614
81Detroit-12
83Kaline-52M
86GlenF-10CO
87Toledo-25
88Domino-7

Hillman, Dave
57T-351
58T-41
59T-319
60T-68
61T-326
62T-282
91WIZMets-183

Hillman, Eric
88Clmbia/GS-5
89Clmbia/Best-11
89Clmbia/GS-10
91Tidew/LineD-558
91Tidew/ProC-2505

Hillman, Joe
88SoOreg/ProC-1716
89Modesto/Cal-275
89Modesto/Chong-29

Hillman, Stewart
90Clinton/Best-18
90Clinton/ProC-2542

Hillman, Trey
86Watlo-12
87Kinston-19
90ColClip/CMC-24CO
90ColClip/ProC-693CO
90Oneonta/ProC-3389MG
91Greens/ProC-3075MG
91SALAS/ProC-SAL27MG

Hilpert, Adam
89Clinton/ProC-883

Hilton, Dave
73T-615R
74OPC-148
74T-148
75OPC-509
75T-509
75T/M-509
77OPC-139
77T-163
81Portl-11
89Pac/SenLg-216
89SnJos/Cal-238C
90EliteSenLg-113
91Pac/SenLg-124
91Pac/SenLg-133

Hilton, Howard
86StPete-13
87Spring/Best-13
88ArkTr/GS-12
89Louisvl-23
89Louisvl/CMC-6
89Louisvl/ProC-1251
90B-189
90Louisvl/CMC-6
90Louisvl/ProC-398
90T/TVCard-14
91T/90Debut-68

Hilton, John
84Visalia-10

Hilton, Stan
88Wmsprt/ProC-1316
89Burllnd/Star-28CO
89ColoSp/ProC-244
90Burllnd/ProC-3027
91Burllnd/ProC-3321CO

Hina, Fred
88Clmbia/GS-18

Hinchman, Harry
E254
E270/1
T201
T206

Hinchman, William
(Bill)
91Conlon/Sport-155
E97
T206
W555

Hinde, Michael
88CapeCod/Sum-62
89Elizab/Star-11

Hindman, Randy
86Cedar/TCMA-18

Hinds, Kevin
81Cedar-11

Hinds, Sam
77Spoka
78T-303
79Holyo-29
79Vanco-19

Hines, Ben
86Coke/Dodg-12CO
87Albuq/Pol-2CO
90Mother/Dodg-28M
90Pol/Dodg-x
91Mother/Dodg-28CO
91Pol/Dodg-x

Hines, Henry
(Hunkey)
90Target-347
N172

Hines, Keith
90MedHat/Best-14
91StCath/ClBest-12
91StCath/ProC-3408

Hines, Maurice
90Martins/ProC-3187

Hines, Paul
N172
N284
WG1-33

Hines, Richard
90Tampa/DIMD-12
91Greens/ProC-3053
91SALAS/ProC-SAL28

Hines, Tim
89Pittsfld/Star-9
89StLucie/Star-10
90Salem/Star-7
91CaroMud/LineD-110
91CaroMud/ProC-1089

Hinkel, John
78Wausau

Hinkle, Mike
87Erie-28
88Savan/ProC-331
89ArkTr/GS-8
90Louisvl/CMC-5
90Louisvl/ProC-399
90T/TVCard-52

Hinnrichs, Dave
84Everett/Cram-16
86Fresn/Smok-13

Hinrichs, Phil
81Phoenix-17
83Phoenix/BHN-11

Hinshaw, George
82Amari-1
84Cram/PCL-234
85Cram/PCL-113
87Albuq/Pol-28
88Albuq/CMC-13
88Albuq/ProC-268
90Phoenix/CMC-15
90Phoenix/ProC-22

Hinsley, Jerry
64T-576R
65T-449R
91WIZMets-184

Hinson, Bo
82AubAs-10

Hinson, Dean
91Welland/ClBest-9II
91Welland/ProC-3576

Hinson, Gary
82BirmB-14

Hinton, Chuck
62T-347
62T/St-96
63Bz-25
63Exh
63J-93
63P-93
63T-2LL
63T-330
63T/SO
64Bz-25
64T-52
64T/Coins-162AS
64T/Coins-38
64T/S-20
64T/St-47
64T/SU
65Bz-3
65Kahn
65OldLond-26
65OPC-235
65T-235
65T/E-60
65T/trans-48
66T-391
67OPC-189
67T-189
68T-531
69MB-115
69MLB/St-22
69T-644
70MLB/St-199
70OPC-27
70T-27
71MLB/St-375
71OPC-429
71T-429
72MB-147
78TCMA-252
78TCMA-265
89Swell-93
Exh47

Hinton, Rich
72T-724R
73OPC-321
73T-321
76Indianap-20
76OPC-607
76SSPC-158
76T-607

Hinton, Steve
91Eugene/ClBest-9
91Eugene/ProC-3734

Hinzo, Thomas
87Kinston-21
88ColoSp/CMC-14
88ColoSp/ProC-1527
88D-526
88F-611
88OPC-294
88Panini/St-73
88S-567
88T-576
89ColoSp/CMC-16
89ColoSp/ProC-256
89UD-34

Hippauf, Herb A.
66T-518R
87Idaho-18CO
88Idaho/ProC-1860CO

Hirose, Sam
87SanJose-1
88SanJose/Cal-142
88SanJose/ProC-123

Hirsch, Chris
91Sumter/ClBest-13
91Sumter/ProC-2336

Hirsch, Jeff
86Peoria-11
87WinSalem-23
88Iowa/CMC-6
88Iowa/ProC-532
89CharlK-18
90Peoria/Team-20M

Hirschbeck, John
88TM/Umpire-50
89TM/Umpire-48
90TM/Umpire-46

Hirschbeck, Mark
89TM/Umpire-59
89Umpires-59
90TM/Umpire-57

Hirtensteiner, Rick
88CapeCod/Sum-25
89BendB/Legoe-20
91SLCity/ProC-3225

Hiser, Gene
72OPC-61R
72T-61R
74OPC-452
74T-452
76SSPC-314

Hisey, Jason
88Alaska/Team-9
91Hamil/ClBest-11
91Hamil/ProC-4034

Hisey, Steve
88SanBern/Best-20
88SanBern/Cal-39

Hisle, Larry
68T-579R
69OPC-206R
69T-206R
70K-45
70MLB/St-89
70OPC-288
70T-288
71MLB/St-180
71OPC-616
71T-616
72MB-148
72OPC-398
72T-398
73OPC-622
73T-622
74OPC-366
74T-366
75Ho-128
75OPC-526
75T-526
75T/M-526
76Ho-73
76OPC-59
76SSPC-220
76T-59
77BurgChef-49
77OPC-33
77T-375
78Ho-13
78OPC-3LL
78PapaG/Disc-38
78T-203LL
78T-520
78Tastee/Discs-24
78Wiffle/Discs-29
79Ho-95
79OPC-87
79T-180
79T/Comics-10
80K-22
80OPC-222
80T-430
81D-87
81F-509
81F/St-94
81OPC-215
81T-215
82D-358
82F-144
82Pol/Brew-9
82T-93
83T-773

Hiss, William
75SanAn
77Watlo

Hitchcock, Billy
51B-191
52B-89
52T-182
53Glen
53T-17
60T-461C
62T-121MG
63T-213MG
67T-199MG
91T/Arc53-17

Hitchcock, Sterling
90A&AASingle/ProC-88
90Greens/Best-2
90Greens/ProC-2654
90Greens/Star-5
90T/TVYank-46
91PrWill/ClBest-2
91PrWill/ProC-1419
91Single/ClBest-385

Hithe, Victor
87Ashvl-19
88Osceola/Star-14
89Hagers/Best-5
89Hagers/ProC-272
89Hagers/Star-11
90Foil/Best-135
90Hagers/Best-14
90Hagers/ProC-1426
90RochR/CMC-22
90RochR/ProC-714

Hitt, Daniel
(Danny)
89Savan/ProC-369
90StPete/Star-13

Hitta, Chief Powa
78Richm

Hitting, Scott
90Batavia/ProC-3084CO

Hittle, Floyd
(Red)
48Smith-21
53Mother-42

Hivizda, Jim
88Butte-2

Hixon, Alan
86Miami-11

Hiyama, Yasuhiro
87SLCity/Taco-20

Hoag, Myril
34G-95
39PB-109
40PB-52
91Conlon/Sport-233
R312/M
R313
R314

Hoak, Don
52Park-57
53Exh/Can-33
53T-176
54T-211
55B-21
55Gol/Dodg-13
55T-40
55T/DH-26
56T-335
57Kahn
57Sohio/Reds-9
57T-274
58Kahn
58T-160
59Kahn
59T-25
60Kahn
60T-373
61Kahn
61P-130
61T-230
61T/St-65
62Exh
62J-171
62Kahn
62P-171
62P/Can-171
62Salada-107
62Shirriff-107
62Sugar-C
62T-95
62T/bucks
62T/St-178
63Exh
63J-140
63P-140
63T-305
64T-254
79TCMA-273
90Target-348
91T/Arc53-176
Exh47

Hoban, John
81Watlo-9
82Beloit-7

Hobaugh, Brian
83Wisco/LF-17
84Visalia-12

Hobaugh, Ed
60T-131
61T-129
62T-79
63T-423

Hobbie, Glen
58T-467
59T-334
60Bz-32
60L-20
60T-182
60T/tatt-22
61P-197
61T-264
61T-393M
62Salada-145
62Shirriff-145

62T-585
62T/St-108
63F-31
63T-212
64T-578

Hobbs, Jack
82Orlan/B-5
82OrlTw/A-17
83Orlan-16

Hobbs, Jon
88Fresno/Cal-4
88Fresno/ProC-1237

Hobbs, Rodney
80LynnS-3
81LynnS-22
82WHave-22
84Albany-4
86Nashvl-13

Hoblitzell, Richard C.
(Doc)
10Domino-55
11Helmar-116
12Sweet/Pin-102
14CJ-55
15CJ-55
16FleischBrd-43
91Conlon/Sport-148
D328-77
D329-83
D350/2-82
E135-77
E270/2
M101/4-83
M101/5-82
M116
PM1-6
S74-77
T202
T204
T206
T213/blue
T215/blue
T215/brown
T3-97
WG5-19
WG6-18

Hobson, Butch
77T-89
78Ho-1
78OPC-187
78PapaG/Disc-4
78T-155
79Ho-129
79OPC-136
79T-270
80OPC-216
80T-420
81D-542
81F-227
81OPC-7
81T-595
81T/HT
81T/St-54
81T/Tr-771
82D-577
82F-465
82F/St-213
82OPC-357
82T-357
82T/St-164
83Colum-21
83T-652
84Colum-16
84Colum/Pol-12
85Colum-17
85Colum/Pol-13
87Columbia-10
88Clmbia/GS-1
89NewBrit/ProC-617
89NewBrit/Star-23
89Pac/SenLg-32
89T/SenLg-49
89TM/SenLg-47
90EastLAS/ProC-EL11MG
90NewBrit/Best-23MG
90NewBrit/Star-25MG
91Pawtu/LineD-374MG
91Pawtu/ProC-54MG

Hobson, Todd
91AubAS/ClBest-18
91AubAS/ProC-4286

Hockenbury, Bill
52Park-81

Hockett, Oris
90Target-349

Hocking, David
89Everett/Star-14

Hocking, Denny
91Kenosha/ClBest-4
91Kenosha/ProC-2081
91MidwLAS/ProC-MWL37

Hocutt, Mike
86Indianap-22
88Louisvl-22

Hodapp, Urban J.
(Johnny)
33DH-22
88Conlon/AmAS-16
92Conlon/Sport-538
R316

Hodde, Rodney
82BurlR-2

Hoderlein, Mel
53Briggs
54B-120

Hodge, Clarence
E120
E121/120
W501-42
W573

Hodge, Eddie
80OrlTw-5
82Orlan-24
83Toledo-4
84F/X-52
85F-280
85T-639
85Toledo-8

Hodge, Gomer
81Watlo-1
82Watlo/B-26MG
82Watlo/C-2MG
83Watlo/LF-28MG
86Beloit-11MG
87Beloit-18MG
88Beloit/GS-1MG
89Jaxvl/Best-20
90Indianap/ProC-308CO
91Indianap/LineD-200CO
91Indianap/ProC-479CO

Hodge, Kevin
88BuffB/ProC-1482

Hodge, Pat
83Durham-6
84Durham-4

Hodge, Tim
88StCath/ProC-2016
89Myrtle/ProC-1457
90Dunedin/Star-10
91Dunedin/ClBest-20
91Dunedin/ProC-218

Hodges, Darren
90A&AASingle/ProC-177
90Oneonta/ProC-3377
91CLAS/ProC-CAR33
91PrWill/ClBest-3
91PrWill/ProC-1420

Hodges, Gil
47HomogBond-20
49B-100
49Eureka-38
50B-112
50Drake-11
51B-7
51FB
51T/RB-31
52B-80
52BR
52Coke
52StarCal/L-79A
52T-36
52TipTop
53B/Col-92
53Briggs
53Exh/Can-13
53SM
54B-138
54DanDee
54NYJour
54RM-NL22
54SM
54T-102
54Wilson
55B-158
55Gol/Dodg-12
55RM-NL3
55SM
55T-187
56T-145
56T/Pin-50
56YellBase/Pin-15
57T-400M
57T-80
58BB
58PacBell-4
58T-162
59HRDerby-7
59Morrell
59T-270
60Bz-23
60Morrell
60NuCard-41
60T-295
61BB-14
61NuCard-441
61P-168
61T-460
62Bz
62J-101
62P-101
62P/Can-101
62Salada-146A
62Salada-146B
62Shirriff-146
62T-85
62T/bucks
62T/St-155
63J-193
63P-193
63T-245
63T-68M
64T-547MG
65OPC-99MG
65T-99MG
66T-386MG
67T-228MG
68OPC-27MG
68T-27MG
69T-564MG
70OPC-394MG
70T-394MG
71OPC-183MG
71T-183MG
72OPC-465MG
72T-465MG
79TCMA-43
79TCMA-71
80Pac/Leg-63
85CircK-29
85West/2-30
86Sf/Dec-38M
88Pac/Leg-87
89B/I-4
89Rini/Dodg-31
89Smok/Dodg-54
89Swell-33
89T-664TBC
90Swell/Great-132
90Target-350
91Swell/Great-131
91T/Arc53-296
91WIZMets-185
D305
Exh47
PM10/Sm-74A
PM10/Sm-74B
PM10/Sm-75
PM10/Sm-76

Hodges, Ronald W.
(Ron)
74OPC-448
74T-448
75Cedar
75OPC-134
75T-134
75T/M-134
75Tidew/Team-13
76Cedar
77T-329
78T-653
79T-46
80T-172
81T-537
82F-527
82T-234
83D-476
83F-445
83T-713
84D-603
84F-588
84Nes/792-418
84T-418
85T-363
91WIZMets-186

Hodges, Steve
90Idaho/ProC-3242

Hodgin, Elmer Ralph
47TipTop
49B/PCL-3

Hodgson, Gordon
79QuadC-18

Hodgson, Paul
82Knoxvl-13
83Knoxvl-18

Hodo, Doug
86Cram/PCL-134

Hoeft, Billy
52T-370
53B/BW-18
53Glen
53T-165
54B-167
54Dix
56T-152
57T-60
58T-13
59T-343
60L-90
60T-369
61T-256
62T-134
63T-346
64T-551
65T-471
66T-409
79TCMA-37
81Detroit-32
91Crown/Orio-197
91T/Arc53-165

Hoeksema, Dave
83Memphis-9
85Indianap-23

Hoeme, Steve
88Eugene/Best-2
89AppFx/ProC-852
90BBCity/Star-11

Hoenstine, Dave
80Cedar-3
81Cedar-12

Hoerner, Joe
64T-544R
66T-544R
67OPC-41
67T-41
68T-227
69T-522
70MLB/St-90
70OPC-511
70T-511
71MLB/St-181
71OPC-166
71T-166
72OPC-482
72T-482
73OPC-653
73T-653
74OPC-493
74T-493
75OPC-629
75T-629
75T/M-629
77T-256

Hoerner, Troy
90Kenosha/Best-5
90Kenosha/ProC-2307
90Kenosha/Star-7

Hofer, John
89AppFx/ProC-878

Hoff, Chester
(Red)
T207

Hoff, Jim
83Tampa-28
88Billings/ProC-1827

Hoff, Michael
86VeroB-11

Hoffinger, Glenn
86Cram/PCL-61

Hoffman, Danny
14CJ-9
15CJ-9
E300
E90/3
E91
E95
M116
T205
T206
T213/brown
W575

Hoffman, Dennis
88Martins/Star-17

Hoffman, Frank J.
N172

Hoffman, Fred
28Exh-35
92Conlon/Sport-575
W753

Hoffman, Glenn
81D-95
81F-237
81OPC-349
81T-349
81T/HT
82Coke/BOS
82D-460
82F-296
82F/St-168
82T-189
83D-282
83F-185
83OPC-108
83T-108
84D-606
84F-399
84Nes/792-523
84OPC-141
84T-523
84T/St-223
85T-633
86D-457
86F-351
86OPC-38
86T-38
87Pawtu-13
87T-374
88Pawtu/CMC-13
88Pawtu/ProC-465
88T-202
90Albuq/CMC-26CO
90Albuq/ProC-352
90Albuq/Trib-12
90D-407
90Target-351

Hoffman, Guy
80T-664R
82Edmon-6
86F/Up-U51
86Gator-50
86Iowa-16
87F-566
87F/Up-U45
87Kahn-30
87T/Tr-48T
88D-452
88F-235
88S-609
88T-496

Hoffman, Harry C.
T206

Hoffman, Hunter
89Wausau/GS-18
90Fayette/ProC-2410

Hoffman, Jeff
88Oneonta/ProC-2057
90Foil/Best-230
90Greens/Best-3
90Greens/ProC-2655
90Greens/Star-6
90SALAS/Star-11
91PrWill/ClBest-4
91PrWill/ProC-1421

Hoffman, John
88Wausau/GS-9
89SanBern/Cal-77

Hoffman, Rich
89StPete/Star-18

Hoffman, Rob
90Kissim/DIMD-14

Hoffman, Trevor
89Billings/ProC-2068
90CharWh/Best-16
90CharWh/ProC-2247
91Cedar/ClBest-6
91Cedar/ProC-2714

Hoffmann, Greg

85Iowa-24
Hoffner, Jamie
89Pittsfld/Star-27
91StLucie/ClBest-6
91StLucie/ProC-719
Hoffner, William
N172
Hofman, Arthur
(Solly)
10Domino-56
11Helmar-96
12Sweet/Pin-52
E254
M116
T201
T206
T213/blue
T215/blue
T215/brown
T3-98
Hofman, Robert G.
(Bobby)
49B-223
50Remar
52T-371
53T-182
54NYJour
54T-99
55Gol/Giants-13
55T-17
55T/DH-96
56T-28
56T/Pin-40
78TCMA-59
91T/Arc53-182
Hogan, Ben
51BR-A16
52Wheat
Hogan, J. Francis
(Shanty)
28Exh-18
29Exh/4-10
31Exh/4-9
33DH-23
33G-30
34DS-20
34Exh/4-1
34G-20
35Exh/4-1
35G-2E
35G-4E
35G-7E
87Conlon/2-42
91Conlon/Sport-294
R310
R316
V353-30
V354-66
Hogan, Mike
82AubAs-8
83DayBe-8
86Modesto-12
88Phoenix/CMC-6
88Phoenix/ProC-73
Hogan, Robert
N172
Hogan, William
(Happy)
E270/2
T207
Hogg, David
82Edmon-16
Hogue, Bobby
49Eureka-12
52T-9
Hogue, Cal
53T-238
54T-134
91T/Arc53-238
Hohn, Bill
90TM/Umpire-60
Hohn, Eric
86Erie-13
Hoiles, Chris
87GlenF-2
88Toledo/CMC-19
88Toledo/ProC-597
89RochR/ProC-1640
90B-259
90F/Up-U65
90Leaf/II-513
90S/Tr-96T
90T/89Debut-60
91B-99
91Classic/I-13
91Crown/Orio-198
91D-358
91F-476
91F/Ultra-17
91Leaf/I-131
91Leaf/Stud-4
91OPC-42
91OPC/Premier-65
91S-334RP
91S/100RisSt-34
91T-42
91T/StClub/II-489
91UD-306
92D/I-156
92F-9
92S/II-641
92T-125
92UD-183
Hokanson, Mark
91Kingspt/ClBest-21
91Kingspt/ProC-3809
Hoke, Leon
81Miami-17
83SanJose-23
Hokuf, Ken
91Modesto/ClBest-6
91Modesto/ProC-3081
Holbert, Aaron
90Classic/DP-18
90Johnson/Star-14
91B-399
91S-676FDP
Holbert, Ray
89Watlo/ProC-1791
89Watlo/Star-12
90Foil/Best-9
90Waterlo/Best-1
90Waterlo/ProC-2384
91HighD/ClBest-22
91HighD/ProC-2405
Holbert, William
N172
N172/ST
Holcomb, Scott
87Modesto-24
88Huntsvl/BK-7
89Huntsvl/Best-16
Holcomb, Ted
86Bakers-13
87Bakers-18
88Durham/Star-7
Holcombe, Ken
49B/PCL-19
51B-267
52T-95
Holden, Gary
81Batavia-21
Holder, Brooks
46Remar
47Remar-3
47Signal
47Smith-4
48Signal
48Smith-2
49Sommer
Holdridge, Dave
88QuadC/GS-11
89Clearw/Star-11
90Foil/Best-17
90Reading/Best-1
90Reading/ProC-1216
90Reading/Star-13
91Reading/LineD-510
91Reading/ProC-1368
91Single/ClBest-155
Holdsworth, Fred
74OPC-596R
74T-596R
75OPC-323
75T-323
75T/M-323
77T-466
80Vanco-18
81Tacoma-21
91Crown/Orio-199
Holifield, Rick
(Rickey)
91Myrtle/ClBest-24
91Myrtle/ProC-2958
Holke, Walter
21Exh-75
21Exh-76
25Exh-44
91Conlon/Sport-207
92Conlon/Sport-491
D327
D328-78
E120
E121/120
E121/80
E122
E135-78
V100
W501-91
W575
Hollacher, Charlie
V61-110
Holland, Al
77Shrev
78Colum
79Portl-1
80Pol/Giants-19
81F-445
81T-213
82D-377
82F-391
82T-406
83D-146
83F-262
83T-58
83T/St-306
83T/Tr-46
84D-204
84F-35
84F/St-68
85FunFood/Pin-87
84Nes/792-138LL
84Nes/792-564
84Nestle/DT-22
84OPC-206
84Phill/TastyK-21
84T-138LL
84T-564
84T/St-125
84T/St-289
84T/Super-10
85D-427
85F-254
85F-637IA
85F/St-107
85F/Up-U55
85Leaf-151
85OPC-185
85Phill/TastyK-19
85Phill/TastyK-9M
85T-185
85T/St-113
85T/Tr-55T
86Colum-12
86Colum/Pol-11
86D-573
86F-159
86OPC-369
86T-369
87Colum-26
87Colum/Pol-12
87Colum/TCMA-6
89Pac/SenLg-113
89Pac/SenLg-26
90EliteSenLg-114
91Pac/SenLg-139
Holland, Bill
78Laugh/Black-21
Holland, Donny
82Wausau-20
Holland, John
81Buffa-2
82Buffa-12
Holland, Michael
90Erie/Star-9
Holland, Mike
74Cedar
Holland, Monty
80Batavia-9
Holland, Randy
86Knoxvl-11TR
87Knoxvl-22
88AAA/ProC-53
88Syrac/CMC-2
89Syrac/CMC-13
89Syrac/ProC-795
89Syrac/Team-25TR
90Syrac/Team-12
Holland, Sid
91Gaston/ClBest-23
91Gaston/ProC-2700
Holland, Tim
89Watlo/ProC-1779
89Watlo/Star-13
90CLAS/CL-5
90Freder/Team-15
91Hagers/LineD-232
91Hagers/ProC-2463
Holle, Gary
77Holyo
78Holyo
Hollenback, Dave
88Modesto-3tr
88Modesto/Cal-83TR
89Modesto/Cal-290TR
89Modesto/Chong-3TR
90Modesto/Cal-173TR
91Modesto/ClBest-19TR
Holley, Bobby
88Eugene/Best-22
90BBCity/Star-12
91CLAS/ProC-CAR28
91Penin/ClBest-21
91Penin/ProC-386
Holley, Ed
34G-55
R310
Holley, Kenny
88Wythe/ProC-1994
Holliday, James
N172
Hollifield, David
76QuadC
77QuadC
Hollingsworth, Al
90Target-352
W711/1
Hollins, Dave
87Spokane-8
88CalLgAS-44
88River/Cal-222
88River/ProC-1418
89AubAs/ProC-12
89Wichita/Rock-7
89Wichita/Rock/HL-11
90B-161
90Classic/III-14
90D/Rook-47
90F/Up-U43
90Phill/TastyK-14
90S/Tr-75T
90S/YS/II-35
90T/Tr-41T
90UD/Ext-785
91F-399
91OPC-264
91Phill/Medford-19
91S-61
91S/100RisSt-96
91ScranWB/ProC-2545
91T-264
91T/90Debut-69
91UD-518
92D/II-685
92F-535
92S/II-553
92T-383
92UD-586
Hollins, Jesse
89Wythe/Star-16
90A&AASingle/ProC-175
90Geneva/ProC-3041
90Geneva/Star-14
91B-423
91Single/ClBest-36
91WinSalem/ClBest-5
91WinSalem/ProC-2824
Hollins, Paul
86Chatt-13
Hollins, Steve
90Princet/DIMD-12
Hollinshed, Joe
86Erie-14
Hollis, Jack
52Mother-62
Hollis, Jack
90CharWh/Best-21
90CharWh/ProC-2252
Hollmig, Stan
49Eureka-137
Hollocher, Charles J.
21Exh-77
E120
E121/120
E121/80
E122
E220
V100
W501-57
W514-53
W515-59
W572
W573
W575
Holloman, Bobo
90BBWit-69
90HOF/St-47
91T/Arc53-306
Holloway, Crush
78Laugh/Black-24
86Negro/Frit-22
Holloway, K.
29Exh/4-22
Holloway, Rick
81WHave-13
Hollowell, Chuck
80Batavia-12
Holly, Jeff
78OrlTw
79T-371
Holm, Dave
75Clinton
Holm, Mike
85Newar-8
Holm, Roscoe
33G-173
Holman, Brad
91Penin/ClBest-5
91Penin/ProC-371
Holman, Brian
86Jaxvl/TCMA-23
86SLAS-21
87Jaxvl-24
88F/Up-U100
88Indianap/CMC-9
88Indianap/ProC-504
89B-357
89D-511
89F-379
89T/Tr-51T
89UD-356
90Classic-66
90D-143
90F-516
90Leaf/II-273
90Mother/Mar-20
90OPC-616
90Panini/St-146
90PublInt/St-176
90S-387
90S/YS/I-7
90T-616
90T/Big-282
90UD-362
91B-240
91CounHrth-21
91D-539
91F-453
91F/Ultra-338
91Leaf/I-11
91Leaf/Stud-115
91OPC-458
91S-285
91T-458
91T/StClub/I-106
91UD-252
92D/I-43
92F-281
92S/I-228
92T-239
92UD-595
Holman, Craig
91Batavia/ClBest-28
91Batavia/ProC-3480
Holman, Dale
82Albuq-20

86Syrac-12
87Richm/Crown-25
87Richm/TCMA-23

Holman, Ed
76SanAn/Team-12

Holman, Gary
69T-361

Holman, Nat
33SK-3

Holman, R. Scott
77Wausau
79Tidew-17
82Tidew-18
83D-224
84F-589
84Nes/792-13
84T-13
84Tidew-1
85Iowa-15
91WIZMets-187

Holman, Shawn
84PrWill-4
85PrWill-16
86Nashua-13
87Harris-1
88EastLAS/ProC-7
88GlenF/ProC-929
89Toledo/CMC-5
89Toledo/ProC-781
90F-606
90S-620RP
90T/89Debut-61
90Toledo/CMC-4
90Toledo/ProC-143

Holman, Steve
78Cedar

Holmberg, Dennis
75BurlB
76BurlB
77Newar
78Dunedin
85Syrac-28
87Dunedin-7C
90Dunedin/Star-26MG
90FSLAS/Star-48
91Dunedin/ClBest-25MG
91Dunedin/ProC-223MG

Holmes, Bill
89Princet/Star-9
90Augusta/ProC-2471

Holmes, Bob
C46-79

Holmes, Carl
86Cram/PCL-158

Holmes, Chris
88Reno/Cal-282

Holmes, Darren
86VeroB-10
87VeroB-5
89SanAn/Best-4
90Albuq/CMC-6
90Albuq/ProC-339
90Albuq/Trib-13
91Brewer/MillB-11
91D-669
91Denver/LineD-141
91Leaf/II-387
91T/90Debut-70
92D/II-504
92F-179
92S/100RisSt-39
92S/II-753
92T-454

Holmes, Ducky
C46-60

Holmes, Stan
83Visalia/LF-10
85Toledo-22
86Orlan-8
87MidldA-17
88Edmon/CMC-14
88Edmon/ProC-571
89Edmon/CMC-11
89Edmon/ProC-555

Holmes, Tim
88Watertn/Pucko-6

Holmes, Tommy
39Exh
47HomogBond-21
48L-133
49B-72
49Eureka-13
50B-110
51T/RB-52
52T-289
53Exh/Can-18
90Target-353
D305

Holmes, William
WG2-24

Holmquist, Doug
83Nashvl-8MG
85Colum-25

Holsman, Richard
(Rich)
87Spokane-6
88River/Cal-211
88River/ProC-1427
89AubAs/ProC-20
89TexLAS/GS-12
89Wichita/Rock-17
89Wichita/Rock/Up-20
90Wichita/Rock-10
91Harris/LineD-257
91Harris/ProC-621

Holt, Darren
90Visalia/Cal-86PER

Holt, Dave
79Elmira-14
86FSLAS-24MG
86WinHaven-10
87NewBrit-18
90WinHaven/Star-26MG
91Elmira/ClBest-27MG
91Elmira/ProC-3287MG

Holt, Gene
44Centen-11

Holt, Goldie
49Eureka-162

Holt, Jim
71MLB/St-463
71OPC-7
71T-7
72T-588
73OPC-259
73T-259
74OPC-122
74T-122
74T/St-207
75OPC-607
75T-607
75T/M-607
76OPC-603
76SSPC-498
76T-603
76Tucson-37
77T-349

Holt, Mike
78Clinton

Holt, Roger
79Colum-18
80Colum-7

Holton, Brian
81Albuq/TCMA-10
82Albuq-5
83Albuq-4
84Cram/PCL-168
85Cram/PCL-164
86Albuq-12
87D-598
87D/Rook-54
87Mother/Dodg-26
87Pol/Dodg-27
87T/Tr-49T
88D-402
88Mother/Dodg-26
88Pol/Dodg-51
88RedFoley/St-35
88S-208
88T-338
89B-2
89D-439
89D/Tr-20
89F-63
89F/Up-5
89French-37
89S-507
89S/Tr-59
89T-368
89T/Tr-52T
89UD-72
90D-635
90F-179
90Leaf/II-487
90OPC-179
90Publnt/St-578
90S-177
90T-179
90Target-354
90UD-175
91Crown/Orio-200

Holton, Mark
80Utica-19

Holtz, Ed
76AppFx-GM
84Chatt-6GM
88Sumter/ProC-420GM
89Sumter/ProC-1088GM

Holtz, Fred
75AppFx
76AppFx

Holtz, Gerald
87CharlO/WBTV-17
88CharlK/Pep-19
88RochR/Gov-12
89Reading/Star-14

Holtzclaw, Shawn
90A&AASingle/ProC-100
90Myrtle/ProC-2788
90SALAS/Star-33
91Dunedin/ClBest-21
91Dunedin/ProC-219

Holtzman, Ken
67OPC-185
67T-185
68Bz-4
68OPC-60
68T-380AS
68T-60
69MB-116
69T-288
70MLB/St-18
70OPC-505
70T-505
71MD
71MLB/St-33
71OPC-410
71T-410
72MB-149
72T-670
73OPC-60
73T-60
74K-31
74OPC-180
74T-180
74T/St-224
75Ho-16
75Ho/Twink-16
75OPC-145
75T-145
75T/M-145
76OPC-115
76SSPC-482
76T-115
77BK/Y-8
77T-625
78T-387
79T-522
80T-298
87Mother/A's-11
89Pac/Leg-138
89Swell-129
91Crown/Orio-201
91LineD-21
91Swell/Great-40

Holub, Edward
88Boise/ProC-1612

Holum, Brett
90Ashvl/ProC-2755

Holway, John
90LitSun-20

Holyfield, Vince
85Bend/Cram-11
87Spartan-20
88Reading/ProC-883
89Reading/Best-14
89Reading/ProC-661
89Reading/Star-15
90EastLAS/ProC-EL23
90Reading/Best-21
90Reading/ProC-1231
90Reading/Star-14

Holzemer, Mark
89QuadC/Best-9
89QuadC/GS-21

Homstedt, Vic
78Watlo

Honeycutt, Rick
79T-612
80T-307
81D-46
81OPC-33
81T-33
81T/Tr-772
82D-494
82F-318
82T-751
83D-415
83F-568
83Rang-40
83T-557
84D-494
84F-101
84F/St-66
84Nes/792-137LL
84Nes/792-222
84Nes/792-37TL
84OPC-222
84Pol/Dodg-40
84T-137LL
84T-222
84T-37TL
84T/St-176
84T/St-84
85Coke/Dodg-13
85D-215
85F-372
85Leaf-156
85OPC-174
85T-174
85T/St-78
86Coke/Dodg-13
86D-372
86F-132
86Pol/Dodg-40
86T-439
87Classic-93
87D-402
87F-442
87F/Excit-28
87Mother/Dodg-16
87OPC-167
87Pol/Dodg-20
87T-753
87T/St-71
88D-590
88D/A's/Bk-590
88D/Best-211
88F-281
88Mother/A's-23
88S-87
88T-641
89B-187
89D-328
89D/Best-313
89F-11
89Mother/A's-25
89S-416
89T-328
89UD-278
89Woolwth-28
90B-450
90D-386
90F-11
90Leaf/II-372
90Mother/A's-13
90OPC-582
90Publnt/St-307
90S-317
90T-582
90T/Big-42
90Target-355
90UD-151
91D-373
91F-11
91F/Ultra-249
91Leaf/I-210
91Leaf/Stud-105
91Mother/A's-13
91OPC-67
91S-539
91SFExam/A's-7
91T-67
91T/StClub/II-415
91UD-379
92D/I-269
92F-259
92S/II-456
92T-202
92UD-684

Honeywell, Brent
90Augusta/ProC-2457

Honochick, Jim
55B-267ump

Hood, Dennis
86Sumter-10
87Durham-27
88Greenvl/Best-5
89Greenvl/ProC-1169
89Greenvl/Star-8
89Greenvl/Best-1
90Richm/Bob-18
90Richm/CMC-15
90Richm/ProC-270
90Richm/Team-12
91Calgary/LineD-59
91Calgary/ProC-527

Hood, Don
74OPC-436
74T-436
75OPC-516
75T-516
75T/M-516
76OPC-132
76SSPC-508
76T-132
77T-296
78T-398
79T-667
80T-89
81Omaha-8
82Omaha-5
83D-390
83F-115
83T-443
84F-348
84Nes/792-743
84T-743
89Pac/SenLg-108
91Crown/Orio-202

Hood, Mike
80Wausau-16

Hood, Randy
91Stockton/ClBest-16
91Stockton/ProC-3045

Hood, Scott
82Durham-3
83Durham-7
84Durham-17

Hood, Wally
28Exh/PCL-11
90Target-983

Hoog, James
88CapeCod/Sum-178

Hoog, Michael
90Idaho/ProC-3244

Hook, Chris
90CharWh/Best-2
90CharWh/ProC-2234
91CharWh/ClBest-4
91CharWh/ProC-2881

Hook, Ed
90HagersDG/Best-13

Hook, Jay
60Kahn
60T-187
61Kahn
61T-162
62T-94
62T/St-156
63T-469
64T-361
91WIZMets-188

Hook, Mike
88Ashvl/ProC-1073
89FtLaud/Star-9
91Freder/ClBest-4
91Freder/ProC-2358

Hooker, W.E.
(Buck)
T206

Hooks, Alex
R314

Hooper, Ed
W516-27

Hooper, Harry
12Sweet/Pin-4
14CJ-35
15CJ-35
25Exh-75
40PB-226
80SSPC/HOF
87Conlon/2-35
89HOF/St-52
91Conlon/Sport-135
92Conlon/Sport-470

BF2-4
D327
D328-79
D329-84
D350/2-83
E120
E121/120
E121/80
E135-79
E220
E224
E254
E270/1
E91
M101/4-84
M101/5-83
M116
T207
V100
V61-13
W501-47
W514-64
W572
W573
W575

Hooper, Jeff
88Wausau/GS-16
89Wmsprt/ProC-639
89Wmsprt/Star-10
90Wmsprt/Best-10
90Wmsprt/ProC-1060
90Wmsprt/Star-11

Hooper, Mike
91Beloit/ClBest-25
91Beloit/ProC-2097

Hooper, Robert
(Bob)
51B-33
52B-10
52T-340
53T-84
54B-4
55B-271
55Salem
91T/Arc53-84

Hooten, Leon
75Tucson-10
76Tucson-16
77OPC-67
77T-478R

Hooton, Burt
72OPC-61R
72T-61R
73OPC-367
73T-367
74OPC-378
74T-378
74T/St-14
75Ho-11
75Ho/Twink-11
75OPC-176
75T-176
75T/M-176
76OPC-280
76SSPC-67
76T-280
77T-284
78K-42
78T-41
79Ho-49
79OPC-370
79T-694
80OPC-96
80Pol/Dodg-46
80T-170
81D-541
81F-113
81F/St-61
81OPC-53
81Pol/Dodg-46
81T-565
81T/HT
81T/St-180
82D-32
82F-8
82F/St-5
82K-15
82OPC-315
82Pol/Dodg-46
82T-311TL
82T-315
82T/St-53
83D-32
83F-208
83OPC-82
83Pol/Dodg-46
83T-775
84D-459
84F-102
84Nes/792-15
84OPC-15
84Pol/Dodg-46
84T-15
85D-104
85F-373
85F/Up-U56
85OPC-201
85Rang-46
85T-201
85T/Tr-56T
86D-300
86F-563
86OPC-36
86T-454
86T/St-242
87Smok/Dodg-13
88Smok/Dodg-19
89Pac/Leg-219
89Salem/Team-2CO
89Smok/Dodg-95
90Target-356
91SanAn/ProC-2992CO

Hoover, Charles
N172

Hoover, John
85CharlO-22
85T-397OLY
87CharlO/WBTV-20
88Jaxvl/Best-4
88Jaxvl/ProC-989
89Tulsa/Team-11
90OkCty/CMC-3
90OkCty/ProC-427
91T/90Debut-71

Hoover, William
N172

Hope, John
89LittleSun-18
91Welland/ClBest-26
91Welland/ProC-3567

Hopke, Fred
60L-91

Hopkins, Dave
83BurlR-5
83BurlR/LF-23

Hopkins, Don
76Tucson-11
77SanJose-13

Hopkins, Gail
70OPC-483
70T-483
71MLB/St-416
71OPC-269
71T-269
72T-728
73OPC-441
73T-441
74OPC-652
74T-652
90Target-357

Hopkins, Randy
75Shreve/TCMA-5
76Shrev
78Colum

Hopkins, Rick
86WinSalem-9
87Pittsfld-20

Hopp, Dean
91Martins/ClBest-17
91Martins/ProC-3455

Hopp, John
(Johnny)
48L-139
49B-207
49Eureka-163
50B-122
51B-146
52T-214
54T-193
89Pac/Leg-139
90Target-358
Exh47
W754

Hoppe, Denny
91Kenosha/ClBest-10
91Kenosha/ProC-2068
91Single/ClBest-341

Hoppe, Willie
33SK-36

Hopper, Brad
88Eugene/Best-9
90BBCity/Star-13
91BBCity/ClBest-6
91BBCity/ProC-1393

Hopper, Clay
52Mother-55MG
53Mother-51MG

Hopper, Jim
47Centen-10

Hopper, Lefty
90Target-984

Hoppert, Dave
88Stockton/ProC-740

Horan, Dave
89Salinas/Cal-128
89Salinas/ProC-1800

Horlen, Joel
62T-479
63T-332
64T-584
65OPC-7LL
65T-7LL
65T-480
66T-560
66T/RO-5
67OPC-107
67T-107
67T-233LL
68Bz-11
68Kahn
68OPC-125
68OPC-8LL
68T-125
68T-377AS
68T-8LL
69Kahn
69Kelly/Pin-7
69MB-117
69MLB/St-30
69MLBPA/Pin-9
69T-328
69T/S-12
69T/St-154
70K-23
70MLB/St-185
70OPC-35
70T-35
70T/PI-1
70T/S-20
71OPC-345
71T-345
71T/Coins-120
72MB-150
72T-685
88Clmbia/GS-28CO
89Pac/Leg-217
91Wmsprt/LineD-638CO
91Wmsprt/ProC-311CO

Horn, Sam
86NewBrit-13
87Pawtu-2
87Pawtu/TCMA-14
87Sf/Rook-38
88Classic/Blue-204
88D-498
88D/RedSox/Bk-498
88F-355
88F/Mini-8
88Leaf-237
88OPC-377
88S-201
88S/YS/I-3
88Sf-114
88T-377
88T/Big-252
88T/St-246
88ToysRUs-14
90Classic/III-28
90PublInt/St-458
90T/Big-307
90T/Tr-42T
90UD/Ext-796
91Crown/Orio-203
91D-733
91F-477
91Leaf/II-332
91Leaf/Stud-5
91OPC-598
91S-605
91T-598
91T/StClub/II-316
91UD-530
92D/I-278
92F-10
92S/I-290
92T-422
92UD-338

Horn, Terry
91Classic/DP-46
91FrRow/DP-24

Horn, Walt
82WHave-29TR
86Tacoma-8TR
89Tacoma/ProC-1543TR

Hornacek, Jay
86Bakers-14
87VeroB-20
88Bakers/Cal-245
89SoBend/GS-29
90Saraso/Star-12

Horne, Jeffrey
82AlexD-5
84Greens-5

Horne, Tyrone
90Gate/ProC-3348
91Sumter/ClBest-23
91Sumter/ProC-2348

Horner, Bob
79Ho-98
79T-586
79T/Comics-18
80OPC-59
80T-108
80T/S-27
81D-99
81Drake-17
81F-244
81F/St-99
81K-61
81MSA/Disc-17
81OPC-355
81PermaGr/CC-6
81Pol/Atl-5
81T-355
81T/SO-61
81T/St-145
81T/St-20
82BK/Lids-11
82D-173
82Drake-18
82F-436
82F/St-69
82K-13
82OPC-145
82Pol/Atl-5
82T-145
82T/St-18
83D-58
83D/AAS-46
83Drake-11
83F-138
83K-54
83OPC-50
83Pol/Atl-5
83T-50
83T/Gloss40-12
83T/St-214
84D-14DK
84D-535
84D/AAS-10
84Drake-14
84F-181
85FunFood/Pin-122
84Nes/792-760
84OPC-239
84Pol/Atl-5
84Seven-10W
84T-760
84T/Gloss40-13
84T/St-30
85D-77
85F-328
85Ho/Braves-11
85Leaf-240
85OPC-262
85Pol/Atl-11
85T-276FDP
85T-410
85T/St-24
85ThomMc/Discs-34
86D-188
86D/HL-22
86F-517
86F-635M
86F/LL-19
86F/Mini-104
86F/St-60
86Leaf-121
86OPC-220
86Pol/Atl-11
86Sf-115
86Sf-66M
86T-220
86T/Gloss60-44
86T/St-34
87Classic-38
87D-389
87F-518
87F-632M
87F/Hottest-23
87F/LL-24
87F/St-61
87F/St-S7
87Leaf-136
87OPC-116
87RedFoley/St-21
87Sf-196M
87Sf-73
87T-660
87T/Board-23
87T/Mini-1
87T/St-41
88F/Mini-107
88F/Up-U120
88Smok/Card-14
88T/Big-245
88T/Tr-50T
89F-452
89OPC-255
89S-68
89T-510
89T/St-35
89UD-125
90HOF/St-89
90Pac/Legend-54

Horner, William F.
N172

Hornsby, Dave
84Everett/Cram-11
85Everett/II/Cram-4
86Clinton-10

Hornsby, Rogers
21Exh-78
25Exh-61
26Exh-60
27Exh-19
28Exh-2
28Yueng-13
29Exh/4-5
30CEA/Pin-6
31Exh/4-5
32Orbit/un-34
33G-119
33G-188
34DS-44
35BU-35
37OPC-140
48Exh/HOF
50Callahan
61F-43
61GP-7
61T-404HL
63Bz/ATG-32
69Bz/Sm
72F/FFeat-2
72K/ATG-2
72Laugh/GF-15
76OPC-342AS
76T-342M
79T-414M
80Pac/Leg-20
80Laugh/3/4/5-17
80Laugh/FFeat-39
80SSPC/HOF
84D/Champs-20
85Woolwth-18
86Conlon/1-44
87Nestle/DT-2
88Conlon/3-14
89Pac/Leg-148
89Swell-20
90BBWit-97
90HOF/St-27
90Swell/Great-51
91Conlon/Sport-1
91Conlon/Sport-251
91Swell/Great-137
91T/Arc53-289MG

92Conlon/Sport-527
92Conlon/Sport-622
D327
D328-80
E120
E121/120
E121/80
E122
E135-80
E210-13
E220
R305
R310
R311/Leath
R312
R312/M
R313
R315-A16
R315-B16
R316
R328-11
R332-7
R423-48
V100
V300
V354-1
V61-81
W501-114
W512-9
W514-56
W515-55
W516-7
W517-38
W572
W573
W575

Hornung, Michael
N172
N284
WG1-3

Horowitz, Ed
88CapeCod/Sum-140
89Erie/Star-9
90Freder/Team-21
91CLAS/ProC-CAR8
91Freder/ClBest-13
91Freder/ProC-2367

Horsley, Clinton
88Savan/ProC-343

Horsman, Vince
87Myrtle-6
88Dunedin/Star-10
89Dunedin/Star-8
90Dunedin/Star-11
91Knoxvl/ProC-1763
92T/91Debut-81

Horta, Nedar
86Ashvl-13
87Ashvl-15
88Ashvl/ProC-1057
88AubAs/ProC-1965

Horton, David
86Erie-15
87StPete-12

Horton, Ricky
81Louisvl-23
82ArkTr-3
82Louisvl-11
83Louisvl/Riley-23
84F/X-53
84T/Tr-52
85D-83
85F-227
85Leaf-253
85OPC-321
85T-321
86D-138
86F-38
86Schnucks-9
86T-783
87D-234
87F-297
87OPC-238
87Smok/Cards-5
87T-542
88Coke/WS-11
88D-430
88F-36
88F/Up-U17
88Kodak/WSox-3
88OPC-34
88S-412
88S/Tr-24T
88T-34
88T/St-48
88T/Tr-51T
89B-338
89D-582
89Mother/Dodg-20
89Pol/Dodg-18
89S-145
89T-232
89UD-629
90D-666
90OPC-133
90Publint/St-10
90Smok/Card-9
90T-133
90T/TVCard-15
90Target-985
91ColoSp/LineD-83

Horton, Tony
68Kahn
69Kahn
69MB-118
69MLB/St-41
69MLBPA/Pin-10
69NTF
70MLB/St-200
71K-69
71MLB/St-376
72MB-151
78TCMA-128

Horton, Willie
64T-512R
65OPC-206
65T-206
66Bz-2
66OPC-20
66T-20
66T-218LL
66T-220LL
66T/RO-62
67T-465
68Bz-8
68Kahn
68T-360
69Citgo-6
69MB-119
69MLB/St-48
69MLBPA/Pin-11
69OPC-180
69OPC-5LL
69OPC/DE-11
69T-180
69T-429AS
69T-5LL
69T/DE-9
69T/decal
69T/S-16
69T/St-173
69Trans-2
70MLB/St-207
70OPC-520
70T-520
71MLB/St-394
71MLB/St-560
71OPC-120
71T-120
71T/Coins-130
72MB-152
72OPC-494KP
72T-494KP
72T-750
73OPC-433
73T-433
74K-23
74OPC-115
74T-115
74T/DE-72
74T/St-176
75Ho-36
75Ho/Twink-36
75OPC-66
75T-66
75T/M-66
76Crane-19
76Ho-26
76Ho/Twink-26
76MSA/Disc
76OPC-320
76SSPC-360
76T-320
77BurgChef-97
77Pepsi-31
77T-660
78T-290
79OPC-252
79T-239
80OPC-277
80T-532
81Detroit-78
81Portl-12
82Portl-14
88Domino-8
90Pac/Legend-83
91LineD-29
91Swell/Great-41

Hoscheidt, John
77DaytB

Hoscheit, Vern
73OPC-179CO
73T-179CO

Hosey, Dwayne
89Madis/Star-11
90AS/Cal-42
90Modesto/Cal-169
90Modesto/ProC-2225
91Huntsvl/ClBest-12
91Huntsvl/LineD-286
91HuntsvlProC-1809

Hosey, Steve
89Everett/Star-15
89Smok/FresnoSt-12
90B-242
90Foil/Best-15
90SanJose/Best-1
90SanJose/Cal-28
90SanJose/ProC-2025
90SanJose/Star-12
90SanJose/Star-26M
90S-666DC
91B-629
91Shrev/LineD-307
91Shrev/ProC-1835
91Single/ClBest-233
92T-618M
92UD-62TP

Hoskins, Dave
54T-81
55Salem
55T-133
55T/DH-7
86Negro/Frit-81

Hoskinson, Keith
86Lakeland-7

Hosley, Tim
72OPC-257R
72T-257R
76OPC-482
76SSPC-313
76T-482
77SanJose-10
78T-261
79Ogden/TCMA-2
80Ogden-1
82Tacoma-12
89Pac/SenLg-93

Hostetler, Dave
79Memphis
83D-89
83F-569
83OPC-339
83Rang-12
83T-584
83T/St-312
84D-159
84F-418
84Nes/792-62
84OPC-62
84T-62
85Indianap-17
85Iowa-23

Hostetler, Jeff
91FrRow/DP-37
91James/ClBest-20
91James/ProC-3539

Hostetler, Tom
87Everett-16
88Clinton/ProC-697
88MidwLAS/GS-7
89SanJose/Best-19
89SanJose/Cal-213
89SanJose/ProC-444
89SanJose/Star-15
90A&AASingle/ProC-66
90Shrev/ProC-1439
90Shrev/Star-12
91Shrev/LineD-308
91Shrev/ProC-1816

Hotaling, Pete
E223
N172

Hotchkiss, John
83Tacoma-12
84Cram/PCL-93
86MidldA-11
87MidldA-11

Hotchkiss, Thomas
90MedHat/Best-23

Hotz, Todd
90Utica/Pucko-19

Houck, Byron Simon
T222

Hough, Charlie
72OPC-198R
72T-198R
73OPC-610R
73T-610R
74OPC-408
74T-408
75OPC-71
75T-71
75T/M-71
76OPC-174
76SSPC-68
76T-174
77K-47
77T-298
78T-22
79OPC-266
79T-508
80Pol/Dodg-49
80T-644
81T-371
82D-447
82F-319
82T-718
83D-69
83F-570
83OPC-343
83Rang-49
83T-412TL
83T-479
83T/St-125
83T/St-312
84D-638
84F-419
85FunFood/Pin-114
84Nes/792-118
84OPC-118
84Rang-49
84T-118
84T/St-356
85D-422
85F-558
85Leaf-108
85OPC-276
85Rang-49
85SpokAT/Cram-8
85T-571
85T/St-345
86D-342
86F-564
86F/St-61
86Leaf-152
86OPC-275
86Rang-49
86T-275
86T-666M
86T/Mini-33
86T/St-241
87D-470
87D-7DK
87D/AAS-49
87D/DKsuper-7
87D/OD-178
87F-127
87F-641M
87F/BB-21
87F/Mini-56
87F/St-62
87Leaf-7DK
87Mother/Rang-3
87OPC-70
87RedFoley/St-26
87Smok/AL-12
87Smok/R-1
87T-70
87T/St-240
88D-99
88D/Best-256
88F-469
88F/AwardWin-20
88F/BB/AS-16
88F/BB/MVP-19
88F/Mini-55
88F/St-64
88Leaf-89
88Mother/R-3
88OPC-121
88Panini/St-197
88S-140
88Sf-87
88Smok/R-13
88T-680
88T/Big-47
88T/Coins-15
88T/Mini-36
88T/Revco-32
88T/St-236
88T/UK-36
89B-224
89D-165
89F-522
89Mother/R-4
89OPC-345
89Panini/St-446
89RedFoley/St-60
89S-295
89Sf-92
89Smok/R-14
89T-345
89T/LJN-146
89T/St-245
89T/UK-40
89UD-437
90D-411
90F-300
90KayBee-17
90Leaf/II-390
90Mother/Rang-5
90OPC-735
90Publint/St-412
90S-202
90T-735
90T/Big-242
90Target-359
90UD-314
91B-355
91D-146
91F-288
91F/Up-U12
91Kodak/WSox-49
91Leaf/II-472
91Leaf/Stud-35
91OPC-495
91S-141
91T-495
91T/StClub/II-579
91T/Tr-56T
91UD-313
91UD/Ext-792
92D/I-69
92F-84
92S/I-302
92T-191
92UD-418

Hough, Stan
79Jacks-22
79Tidew-16
83DayBe-2
85Cram/PCL-62
86Osceola-12C
88Tulsa-11CO
89OkCty/CMC-24CO
89OkCty/ProC-1521CO
90OkCty/CMC-23CO
90OkCty/ProC-450CO
91OkCty/LineD-325CO
91OkCty/ProC-195CO

Houk, Ralph
52T-200
60T-465C
61T-133MG
62T-88MG
63T-382MG
67T-468MG
68OPC-47MG
68T-47MG
69T-447MG
70OPC-273MG
70T-273MG
71OPC-146MG
71T-146MG
72T-533MG
73OPC-116MG
73Syrac/Team-10MG

73T-116MG
74OPC-578MG
74T-578MG
75OPC-18MG
75T-18MG
75T/M-18MG
76SSPC-352MG
76T-361MG
77T-621MG
78BK/T-1MG
78T-684MG
81T-662MG
82D-282MG
83T-786MG
84Nes/792-381MG
84T-381MG
85T-11MG
89Swell-42
90Swell/Great-131
91LineD-25
91Swell/Great-42
91T/Arc53-282

Houk, Tom
91Kenosha/ClBest-26
91Kenosha/ProC-2082
91Single/ClBest-351

Houp, Scott
85Osceola/Team-24

House, Brian
86WinSalem-10
87Pittsfld-7
88EastLAS/ProC-27
88Pittsfld/ProC-1361
89Iowa/CMC-17
89Iowa/ProC-1700
90OkCty/CMC-14
90OkCty/ProC-440

House, Gary
77Newar

House, H. Frank
52T-146
54T-163
55T-87
55T/DH-14
56T-32
56T/Pin-37
57T-223
58T-318
59T-313
60T-372
79TCMA-214

House, Mike
89Elizab/Star-12
90Visalia/Cal-73
90Visalia/ProC-2167

House, Mitch
91Welland/ClBest-7
91Welland/ProC-3578

House, Thomas R.
69T-331R
72OPC-351R
72T-351R
74OPC-164
74T-164
75OPC-525
75T-525
75T/M-525
76OPC-231
76SSPC-2
76T-231
76T/Tr-231T
77T-358
78T-643
79T-31
82Amari-25C
84Cram/PCL-232C
87Smok/R-20CO
88AlaskaAS60/Team-8
89Smok/R-15CO
90Mother/Rang-27M
90Richm25Ann/Team-10
91Mother/Rang-28CO

Householder, Brian
87CharlO/WBTV-21
88CharlK/Pep-1
88SLAS-33

Householder, Ed
90Target-986

Householder, Paul
79Nashvl
80Indianap-15
81D-303
81F-217
81Indianap-4
81T-606R
82Coke/Reds
82D-314
82F-68
82T-351R
83D-566
83F-592
83T-34
84F-471
84Nes/792-214
84T-214
84T/St-61
85Pol/Brew-7
86D-414
86F-491
86Pol/Brew-7
86T-554

Houser, Ben
T207

Houser, Brett
78StPete

Houser, Chris
87Erie-24
88Hamil/ProC-1719

Housey, Joe
81QuadC-20
84MidldC-7
86Geneva-12
87Peoria-11
89WinSalem/Star-20
90Geneva/ProC-3054CO
91Geneva/ClBest-28CO

Housie, Wayne
87Lakeland-1
88GlenF/ProC-913
89London/ProC-1382
90Salinas/ProC-2731
91NewBrit/LineD-463
91NewBrit/ProC-365
92S/II-836
92T-639
92T/91Debut-82
92UD-664

Houston, Barry
82Wisco-16

Houston, K.R.
(Ken)
81Evansvl-21TR
82Evansvl-24TR
83Wausau/LF-1TR
86Osceola-13TR
87Osceola-24TR

Houston, Kevin
78DaytB
82Buffa-10

Houston, Maceo
91Hunting/ClBest-13
91Hunting/ProC-3347

Houston, Mel
86WPalmB-20
87WPalmB-19
88Indianap/CMC-23
88Indianap/ProC-507
89Jaxvl/Best-3
89Jaxvl/ProC-170
90Indianap/CMC-20
90Indianap/ProC-295
91Indianap/LineD-196
91Indianap/ProC-469

Houston, Pete
88Reno/Cal-289

Houston, Tyler
89Idaho/ProC-2021
89LittleSun-5
90A&AASingle/ProC-104
90B-14
90Foil/Best-16
90Foil/Best-324
90OPC-564FDP
90S-677DC
90Sumter/Best-1
90Sumter/ProC-2436
90T-564FDP
91B-581
91Macon/ClBest-16
91Macon/ProC-869
91SALAS/ProC-SAL32
91Single/ClBest-267

Houtteman, Art
50B-42
51B-45
52T-238
53B/Col-4
53Glen
54B-20
54DanDee
55B-144
55Gol/Ind-12
55Salem
56Carling-4
56T-281
57T-385
79TCMA-242
81Detroit-46
91Crown/Orio-204

Hovley, Steve
70McDon-2
70MLB/St-273
70OPC-514
70T-514
71MLB/St-515
71OPC-109
71T-109
72T-683
73OPC-282
73T-282

Howard, Brent
89AS/Cal-52UMP
90AS/Cal-35UMP

Howard, Bruce
64T-107R
65OPC-41R
65T-41R
66T-281
67OPC-159
67T-159
68T-293
69T-226
91Crown/Orio-205

Howard, Chris
87PrWill-11
88CLAS/Star-9
88PrWill/Star-12
89FtLaud/Star-10
89Star/Wax-78
89Wausau/GS-27
90Albany/ProC-1033
90Foil/Best-239
90Wmsprt/Best-11
90Wmsprt/ProC-1061
90Wmsprt/Star-12
91BirmB/LineD-62
91BirmB/ProC-1450
91Calgary/LineD-60
91Calgary/ProC-519
92T/91Debut-83

Howard, David
(Dave)
87FtMyr-32
88AppFx/ProC-145
89BBCity/Star-9
89Princet/Star-10
90Memphis/Best-5
90Memphis/ProC-1015
90Memphis/Star-11
91B-295
91F/Up-U27
91Leaf/II-325
91S/RookTr-83T
92D/II-567
92F-160
92S/100RisSt-2
92S/II-704
92T-641
92T/91Debut-84
92UD-216

Howard, Dennis
80Utica-20
82Knoxvl-4
83Syrac-8
84Syrac-4
85Syrac-9
86Syrac-13

Howard, Doug
77OPC-112
88SLCity-19

Howard, Elston
55B-68
56T-208
57T-82
58T-275
59T-395
60T-65
61P-2
61T-495
61T/St-194
62J-8
62P-8
62P/Can-8
62Salada-95
62Shirriff-95
62T-400
62T-473AS
62T-51LL
62T/bucks
62T/St-86
63J-18
63Kahn
63P-18
63Salada-45
63T-306M
63T-60
64Bz-29
64T-100
64T/Coins-135AS
64T/Coins-23
64T/S-21
64T/St-72
64T/SU
64Wheat/St-21
65Bz-29
65OPC-1LL
65T-1LL
65T-450
65T/trans
66T-405
67OPC-25
67T-25
68OPC-167
68T-167
73OPC-116CO
73T-116CO
74Syrac/Team-11
75OPC-201MV
75T-201MV
75T/M-201MV
76SSPC-619CO
78TCMA-236
79TCMA-271
82KMart-3
86Sf/Dec-49M
88Pac/Leg-19
Exh47
PM10/L-17
PM10/Sm-77
WG10-10
WG9-12

Howard, Ernest E.
T206

Howard, Frank
60DF-17
60T-132
61Morrell
61T-280
61T/RO-34
61T/St-27
62BB-25
62Bz
62T-175
62T/bucks
62T/St-135
63Exh
63T-123
64T-371
64T/Coins-61
64T/S-24
64T/St-83
64T/SU
64T/tatt
65OPC-40
65T-40
65T/trans-49
66Bz-3
66T-515
66T/RO-33
67Bz-3
67OPC/PI-7
67T-255
67T/PI-7
67T/Test/SU-15
68Bz-7
68OPC-6LL
68T-320
68T-6LL
68T/G-21
68T/Post-3
69Citgo-10
69MB-120
69MLB/St-105
69MLBPA/Pin-12
69OPC-170
69OPC-3LL
69OPC-5LL
69OPC/DE-12
69T-170
69T-3LL
69T-5LL
69T/DE-16
69T/decal
69T/S-30
69T/St-238
69Trans-29
70K-6
70MB-10
70MLB/St-283
70OPC-66LL
70T-550
70T-66LL
70T/PI-22
70T/S-16
70Trans-12
71Bz
71Bz/Test-20
71K-14
71MD
71MLB/St-542
71MLB/St-561
71OPC-620
71OPC-63LL
71OPC-65LL
71T-620
71T-63LL
71T-65LL
71T/Coins-22
71T/GM-48
71T/S-17
71T/tatt-8
71T/tatt-8a
72MB-153
72OPC-350
72T-350
72T/Cloth-17
73OPC-560
73T-560
78TCMA-220
81T-685MG
83MLBPA/Pin-9
83T/Tr-47MG
84Nes/792-621MG
84T-621MG
85CircK-23
85Woolwth-19
86Pol/Brew-33C
87Mother/Mar-28CO
88Mother/Mar-27CO
88Pac/Leg-17
88Smok/Dodg-3
90HOF/St-75
90Target-360
Exh47

Howard, Fred
77AppFx
78Knoxvl
80T-72

Howard, George Elmer
(Del)
E254
T204
T206
T215/brown
WG3-21

Howard, Ivan Chester
D328-81
D329-85
D350/2-84
E135-81
M101/4-85
M101/5-84

Howard, Jim
86Knoxvl-12
87Albany-12

Howard, Larry
71OPC-102R
71T-102R

Howard, Mathew
(Matt)
88CapeCod/Sum-120
89GreatF-23
90AS/Cal-14
90Bakers/Cal-253
91FSLAS/ProC-FSL39
91VeroB/ClBest-21
91VeroB/ProC-782

Howard, Mike
75QuadC
79Jacks-14
81Pawtu-2
81Tidew-12
82Tidew-5
83Tidew-18
84Cram/PCL-135
91WIZMets-189

Howard, Ron
88Bristol/ProC-1870
89Fayette/ProC-1592
90Fayette/ProC-2413
91Lakeland/ClBest-19
91Lakeland/ProC-272

Howard, Steve
83Idaho-27
86Modesto-13
88Huntsvl/BK-8
88SLAS-3
89Tacoma/CMC-21
89Tacoma/ProC-1552
90T/Tr-43T
90Tacoma/CMC-17
90Tacoma/ProC-108
91S-364RP
91T/90Debut-72
91UD-277

Howard, Thomas
86Cram/PCL-171
87TexLgAS-18
87Wichita-13
88LasVegas/CMC-11
88LasVegas/ProC-239
89LasVegas/CMC-15
89LasVegas/ProC-8
89UD/Ext-726
90B-212
90F/Up-U56
90LasVegas/ProC-135
91B-644
91D-746
91F-532
91F/Ultra-305
91LasVegas/ProC-248
91Padre/MagRal-3
91S-335RP
91S/100RisSt-9
91T/90Debut-73
91T/StClub/II-403
91UD/FinalEd-39F
92D/I-266
92F-607
92S/I-293
92T-539
92UD-416

Howard, Tim
89Pittsfld/Star-10
90SALAS/Star-34
91B-538
91Single/ClBest-232
91StLucie/ClBest-23
91StLucie/ProC-720

Howard, Wilbur
74OPC-606R
74T-606R
75OPC-563
75T-563
75T/M-563
76OPC-97
76SSPC-65
76T-97
77T-248
78BK/Ast-20
78T-534
79Charl-17
79T-642

Howarth, Jim
73OPC-459
73T-459
74OPC-404
74T-404

Howe, Art
76SSPC-585
78BK/Ast-16
78T-13
79OPC-165
79T-327
80OPC-287
80T-554
81Coke
81D-258
81F-51
81OPC-129
81T-129
81T/HT
81T/SO-99
81T/St-170
82D-92
82F-218
82K-34
82OPC-248
82T-453
82T-66TL
82T/St-43
82T/Tr-48T
83D-396
83F-450
83OPC-372
83T-639
83T/St-236
84F-227
84F/X-54
84Nes/792-679
84T-679
84T/Tr-53
85F-228
85T-204
87Smok/R-25CO
89Lennox/Ast-25CO
89Mother/Ast-1MG
89T/Tr-53MG
90Lennox-16MG
90Mother/Ast-1MG
90OPC-579MG
90T-579MG
91Mother/Ast-1MG
91OPC-51MG
91T-51MG
92T-729

Howe, Gordie
83Kaline-13M

Howe, Greg
83Visalia/LF-21
85Toledo-23

Howe, Steve
81D-511
81F-136
81OPC-159
81Pol/Dodg-57
81T-693
81T/HT
82D-158
82F-9
82OPC-14
82Pol/Dodg-57
82T-14
83D-630
83F-209
83OPC-170
83Pol/Dodg-57
83T-170
84F-103
84Nes/792-425
84OPC-196
84T-425
85Coke/Dodg-14
86SanJose-10
87Smok/Dodg-14
88D-593
88S-543
89London/ProC-1357
89Smok/Dodg-98
90Salinas/Cal-117
90Target-361
91ColClip/LineD-105
91ColClip/ProC-592
91F/Up-U43
91Leaf/II-440
91Leaf/Stud-93
91T/StClub/II-401
91UD/FinalEd-31F
92D/I-106
92F-230
92S/I-275
92T-318
92UD-630

Howell, David
(Dave)
89Oneonta/ProC-2113
90PrWill/Team-13
91FtLaud/ClBest-20
91FtLaud/ProC-2433

Howell, Harry
90Target-363
E107
E90
E92
M116
T204
T206
T213/brown
WG2-25

Howell, Homer
(Dixie)
48Sommer-19
49Eureka-86
51B-252
52B-222
52T-135
53T-255
90Target-362
91T/Arc53-255

Howell, Jack
85Cram/PCL-24
86D-524
86Edmon-15
86OPC-127
86T-127
87D-305
87F-83
87OPC-2
87Smok/Cal-16
87T-422
88D-333
88D/Best-59
88F-491
88OPC-114
88Panini/St-44
88S-124
88Smok/Angels-3
88T-631
88T/Big-121
88T/St-175
89B-48
89D-288
89D/Best-307
89F-480
89OPC-216
89Panini/St-293
89RedFoley/St-61
89S-261
89T-216
89T/Big-228
89T/St-181
89UD-138
90B-296
90D-254
90D/BestAL-45
90F-135
90Leaf/II-327
90OPC-547
90PublInt/St-371
90S-206
90Smok/Angel-8
90T-547
90T/Big-34
90UD-19
91D-247
91F/Ultra-47
91OPC-57
91Panini/FrSt-182
91S-842
91Smok/Angel-11
91T-57
91T/StClub/I-198
91UD-213
92D/II-646
92S/II-706
92T-769
92UD-419

Howell, Jay
79Indianap-24
80Indianap-11
82Iowa-16
82T-51R
83D-587
84F-128
84Nes/792-239
84T-239
85D-103
85D/HL-18
85F-131
85F/Up-U57
85Leaf-244
85Mother/A's-18
85T-559
85T/Tr-57T
86D-223
86D/AAS-57
86F-421
86F/Mini-89
86F/St-62
86Leaf-100
86Mother/A's-18
86OPC-115
86Sf-192
86T-115
86T/St-175
86T/Super-34
87D-503
87F-395
87F/St-63
87Mother/A's-25
87OPC-391
87RedFoley/St-89
87Smok/A's-6
87T-391
88D-55
88D/AS-11
88F-282
88F/Up-U95
88Mother/Dodg-16
88OPC-91
88Pol/Dodg-50
88S-522
88S/Tr-35T
88Sf-86
88T-690
88T/St-166
88T/Tr-52T
89B-335
89D-610
89D/Best-36
89F-64
89Mother/Dodg-16
89OPC-212
89Panini/St-22
89Panini/St-98
89Pol/Dodg-26
89S-378
89Smok/Dodg-89
89T-425
89T/Big-79
89T/St-61
89UD-610
89Woolwth-30
90B-83
90D-203
90D/BestNL-66
90F-400
90KMart/SS-13
90Leaf/I-42
90Mother/Dodg-15
90OPC-40
90Panini/St-274
90Pol/Dodg-50
90PublInt/St-11
90RedFoley/St-49
90S-227
90Sf-78
90T-40
90T/Mini-59
90T/St-65
90T/TVAS-47
90Target-364
90UD-508
91B-603
91D-486
91F-209
91F/Ultra-163
91Leaf/I-98
91Mother/Dodg-15
91OPC-770
91Pol/Dodg-50
91S-29
91T-770
91T/StClub/I-278
91UD-558
92D/I-395
92F-460
92S/I-119
92T-205
92UD-511

Howell, Ken
84Cram/PCL-165
85Coke/Dodg-15
85D-592
85F-374
85T/Tr-58T
86Coke/Dodg-14
86D-275
86F-133
86OPC-349
86Pol/Dodg-43
86T-654
86T/St-69
87D-229
87F-443
87Mother/Dodg-19
87OPC-187
87Phill/TastyK-37
87Pol/Dodg-22
87T-477
88D-130
88F-520
88Mother/Dodg-24
88OPC-149
88Pol/Dodg-43
88S-406
88T-149
89B-394
89D/Best-184
89F/Up-108
89Phill/TastyK-11
89T-93
89T/Tr-54T
90B-147
90D-430
90D/BestNL-44
90F-561
90Leaf/II-316
90OPC-756
90Panini/St-314
90Phill/TastyK-15
90PublInt/St-240
90T-756
90T/Big-269
90T/St-116
90Target-365
90UD-559
91D-204
91F-400
91F/Ultra-265
91OPC-209
91Panini/FrSt-110
91Panini/St-108
91Phill/Medford-20
91S-458
91T-209
91T/StClub/I-71
91UD-488

Howell, Millard
(Dixie)
56T-149
57T-221
58T-421

Howell, Pat
89Pittsfld/Star-11
90SALAS/Star-35
91FSLAS/ProC-FSL32
91Single/ClBest-217
91StLucie/ClBest-25
91StLucie/ProC-724

Howell, Roy Lee
74Spoka
76OPC-279
76SSPC-265
76T-279
77T-608
78Ho-84
78OPC-31
78T-394
79Ho-137
79K-54
79OPC-45
79T-101
80OPC-254
80T-488
81D-392
81F-417
81OPC-40
81T-581
81T/Tr-773
82D-204
82F-145
82Pol/Brew-13
82T-68
83D-358
83F-36
83Pol/Brew-13
83T-218
84F-203
84Gard-9
84Nes/792-687
84Pol/Brew-13
84T-687
85D-577
85T-372

89Pac/SenLg-12
89T/SenLg-88
89TM/SenLg-48
90EliteSenLg-6

Howerton, Bill
50B-239
51B-229
52B-119
52T-167
53Mother-16

Howerton, Rick
77Watlo

Howerton, Troy
84Newar-3

Howes, Jeff
84LitFalls-12

Howes, John
87BurlEx-22
88WPalmB/Star-11

Howes, William
N172

Howey, Todd
87Clearw-26
88Clearw/Star-14

Howie, Mark
85Madis-16
85Madis/Pol-13
86Madis-11
86Madis/Pol-11
88EastLAS/ProC-39
88Wmsprt/ProC-1322
89MidldA/GS-19
90LSUGreat-2
91London/LineD-436
91MidldA/ProC-442

Howitt, Dann
86Cram/PCL-67
87Modesto-20
88Modesto-27
88Modesto/Cal-67
89Huntsvl/Best-7
90F-644R
90T/89Debut-62
90Tacoma/CMC-20
90Tacoma/ProC-100
90UD/Ext-747
91B-229
91Tacoma/LineD-538
91Tacoma/ProC-2315
91UD-442
92D/II-751
92S/100RisSt-68
92S/II-861

Howley, Dan
33G-175

Howser, Dick
61T-416
62Bz-10
62J-94
62P-94
62P/Can-94
62Salada-31
62Shirriff-31
62T-13
62T/bucks
62T/St-53
63F-15
63T-124
64T-478
65Kahn
65OPC-92
65T-92
66T-567
67T-411
68T-467
69MB-121
73OPC-116CO
73T-116C
78TCMA-233
81F-84MG
83D-590MG
83T-96MG
84Nes/792-471MG
84T-471MG
85T-334MG
86NatPhoto-10MG
86T-199MG
87D/AAS-10MG
87D/PopUp-10MG
87T-18MG
87T/Gloss22-12MG
90OPC-661TBC
90T-661TBC

Howze, Ben
89Rockford/Team-12
91Rockford/ClBest-6
91Rockford/ProC-2041

Hoy, Pete
89Elmira/Pucko-5
90WinHaven/Star-11
91NewBrit/LineD-464
91NewBrit/ProC-349

Hoy, William
(Dummy)
73F/Wild-8
N172
WG1-65

Hoyer, Brad
88Spokane/ProC-1937
89Watlo/ProC-1794
89Watlo/Star-14
90Waterlo/Best-8
90Waterlo/ProC-2374
91LynchRS/ClBest-4
91LynchRS/ProC-1193

Hoyt, Dave
82Wisco-5
83Spring/LF-16

Hoyt, LaMarr
78AppFx
81D-160
81T-164
82D-117
82F-345
82F/St-190
82T-428
83D-632
83F-238
83OPC-226
83T-591TL
83T-618
83T-705LL
83T/St-16
83T/St-53
83TrueVal/WSox-31
84D-488
84F-63
85FunFood/Pin-91
84Nes/792-135LL
84Nes/792-405AS
84Nes/792-97
84Nestle/DT-9
84OPC-177AS
84OPC-97
84Seven-23C
84T-135LL
84T-405AS
84T-97
84T/Gloss40-32
84T/St-11LCS
84T/St-178
84T/St-192
84T/St-240
84T/Super-3
84TrueVal/WS-17
85D-86
85D/HL-23
85F-517
85F/Up-U58
85Leaf-37
85Mother/Padres-17
85OPC-312
85T-520
85T/Tr-59T
86D-139
86D/AAS-9
86D/PopUp-9
86F-325
86F/LimEd-25
86F/St-63
86Leaf-61
86OPC-380
86Sf-193
86Sf-57M
86T-380
86T/Gloss22-21
86T/St-113
86T/St-154
87D-434
87F-418
87T-275

Hoyt, Waite
28Yueng-30
29Exh/4-25
31Exh/4-24
33G-60
35G-1E
35G-3C
35G-4C
35G-5C
40PB-118
60F-69
61F-44
80SSPC/HOF
86Conlon/1-26
89HOF/St-71
89Smok/Dodg-10
90Target-366
91Conlon/Sport-115
92Conlon/Sport-468
E120
E220
R310
R313
R314
R316
V100
V117-7
V353-60
V355-39
V61-44
W501-32
W502-30
W513-62
W515-8
W572
W573
W575

Hrabar, Shaun
91Kane/ClBest-1
91Kane/ProC-2671

Hrabcsak, Edward
52Park-87

Hrabosky, Al
71OPC-594R
71T-594R
73OPC-153
73T-153
74OPC-108
74T-108
75OPC-122
75T-122
75T/M-122
76Crane-20
76Ho-50
76Ho/Twink-50
76K-23
76MSA/Disc
76OPC-205LL
76OPC-315
76SSPC-291
76T-205LL
76T-315
77BurgChef-10
77Pep-37
77T-495
78T-230
78Wiffle/Discs-30
79Ho-25
79OPC-19
79T-45
80OPC-306
80T-585
81D-550
81F-262
81OPC-354
81Pol/Atl-39
81T-636
82BK/Lids-12
82D-97
82F-438
82OPC-393
82Pol/Atl-39
82T-393
83D-475
89Pac/Leg-115
89Pac/SenLg-179
89T/SenLg-15
89TM/SenLg-49
91Swell/Great-43

Hrbek, Kent
80Wisco
82D-557
82T-766R
82T/Tr-44T
83D-179
83D-19DK
83D/AAS-49
83F-616
83F-633M
83K-53
83OPC-251
83T-690
83T-771TL
83T/Gloss40-35
83T/St-313
83T/St-88
84D-70
84D/AAS-37
84F-567
85FunFood/Pin-111
84Nes/792-11TL
84Nes/792-345
84OPC-345
84Seven-11C
84T-11TL
84T-345
84T/St-305
85D-70
85D/AAS-40
85Drake-16
85F-281
85F/LimEd-13
85Leaf-200
85OPC-308
85Seven-11C
85Seven/Minn-4
85T-510
85T/St-296
85T/Super-41
85ThomMc/Discs-13
86D-70
86D/HL-19
86Dorman-6
86F-397
86F/LL-20
86F/Mini-84
86F/Slug-17
86F/St-64
86Leaf-67
86OPC-63
86Sf-36
86T-430
86T/St-277
86TrueVal-24
87Classic-53
87D-73
87D/OD-228
87F-544
87F/Excit-29
87F/Lim-22
87F/Mini-57
87F/St-64
87Kraft-25
87Leaf-99
87OPC-161
87RedFoley/St-49
87Sf-15
87T-679
87T/Board-28
87T/Coins-13
87T/Gloss60-25
87T/St-281
88Classic/Red-192
88D-320
88D/Best-102
88F-13
88F/BB/AS-17
88F/LL-21
88F/Mini-35
88F/SS-17
88F/St-44
88F/TL-14
88F/WS-9
88Jiffy-10
88Leaf-139
88Master/Disc-10
88OPC-45
88Panini/St-136
88S-43
88Sf-95
88Smok/Minn-3
88T-45
88T/Big-84
88T/Gloss60-8
88T/Mini-22
88T/St-24
88T/St-274
88T/UK-37
88Woolwth-30WS6
89B-157
89Cadaco-30
89Classic-55
89D-199
89D/Best-18
89F-116
89KMart/Lead-16
89OPC-265
89Panini/St-387
89RedFoley/St-62
89S-382
89S/HotStar-14
89Sf-188
89T-265
89T/Big-209
89T/Coins-42
89T/Gloss60-7
89T/LJN-112
89T/St-287
89T/UK-41
89UD-213
90B-418
90Classic/Up-23
90D-81
90D/BestAL-65
90D/Learning-36
90F-378
90F/BBMVP-20
90KMart/CBatL-22
90Leaf/I-228
90MLBPA/Pins-97
90MSA/Soda-20
90OPC-125
90Panini/St-112
90PublInt/St-290
90PublInt/St-330
90RedFoley/St-50
90S-381
90Sf-203
90T-125
90T/Ames-19
90T/Big-27
90T/Coins-18
90T/HillsHM-11
90T/St-287
90UD-452
91B-321
91Classic/200-118
91Classic/II-T15
91D-95
91DennyGS-7
91F-614
91F/Ultra-189
91Leaf/II-313
91Leaf/Stud-87
91OPC-710
91Panini/FrSt-300
91Panini/St-251
91RedFoley/St-50
91S-292
91S/100SS-78
91Sunflower-13
91T-710
91T/CJMini/II-24
91T/StClub/I-248
91UD-167
92D/I-326
92F-205
92S/100SS-98
92S/II-530
92T-347
92UD-334

Hriniak, Walt
69T-611R
70OPC-392
70T-392
90Coke/WSox-30CO
91Kodak/WSox-x

Hrovat, Dale
76Watlo
77Holyo

Hrusovsky, John
91Princet/ClBest-8
91Princet/ProC-3507

Hrynko, Larry
81Watlo-4
82Charl-6
83Charl-3

Hubbard, Cal
55B-315ump
80SSPC/HOF
89HOF/St-99
90BBWit-75

Hubbard, Don
78Watlo

Hubbard, Glenn
78Richm

79T-715R
80Richm-15
81D-459
81F-260
81OPC-247
81Pol/Atl-17
81T-247
81T/St-149
82BK/Lids-13
82D-436
82F-437
82Pol/Atl-17
82T-482
82T/St-23
83D-184
83F-139
83OPC-322
83Pol/Atl-17
83T-624
83T/St-215
84D-432
84F-182
84Nes/792-25
84OPC-25
84Pol/Atl-17
84T-25
84T/St-29
85D-199
85F-329
85Ho/Braves-12
85Leaf-242
85OPC-195
85Pol/Atl-17
85T-195
85T/St-33
86D-141
86F-518
86Leaf-71
86OPC-112
86Pol/Atl-17
86T-539
86T/St-36
87D-634
87D/OD-48
87F-519
87OPC-68
87Smok/Atl-21
87T-745
88D-22DK
88D-314
88D/A's/Bk-NEW
88D/DKsuper-22DK
88F-542
88Leaf-22DK
88Mother/A's-18
88OPC-325
88Panini/St-243
88RedFoley/St-36
88S-111
88S/Tr-58T
88T-325
88T/Big-200
88T/Tr-53T
89B-199
89D-568
89F-12
89Mother/A's-19
89S-34
89T-237
89T/Big-232
89UD-395
90Richm25Ann/Team-11
91Macon/ClBest-10CO
91Macon/ProC-882CO

Hubbard, Jeff
89CharlR/Star-28CO
90CharlR/Star-30CO
91Tulsa/LineD-600CO
91Tulsa/ProC-2790CO

Hubbard, Joe
90Elizab/Star-26TR

Hubbard, Mark
91Oneonta/ProC-4165

Hubbard, Trent
86AubAs-12
87Ashvl-2
88Osceola/Star-15
89ColMud/ProC-132
89ColMud/Star-13
91Jacks/LineD-561
91Jacks/ProC-932

Hubbard, Ty III
83Tampa-15

Hubbell, Carl
33G-230
33G-234
33SK-42
33SK-42
34DS-39
34Exh/4-5
34G-12
35BU-5
35Exh/4-5
35Wheat
36Exh/4-5
36Wheat
37Dix
37Exh/4-5
37Wheat-6
38Dix
38Exh/4-5
38ONG/Pin-16
38Wheat
39Exh
39PB-53
40PB-87
41DP-140
41G-20
41G-20
41PB-6
48Exh/HOF
48Swell-8
50Callahan
60F-4
60NuCard-11
61F-45
61GP-6
61NuCard-479
72Laugh/GF-36
74Laugh/ASG-34
80Pac/Leg-89
80SSPC/HOF
83D/HOF-33
84D/Champs-55
85West/2-32
86Conlon/1-15
86Sf/Dec-6
87Nestle/DT-10
88Conlon/3-15
88Conlon/NatAS-11
89HOF/St-75
90BBWit-95
90HOF/St-32
91Conlon/Sport-10
91Conlon/Sport-253
92Conlon/Sport-360
92Conlon/Sport-552
PM10/Sm-78A
PM10/Sm-78B
R302
R314
R315-A17
R315-B17
R332-22
V354-71
WG8-35

Hubbell, Wilbert
21Exh-79
25Exh-45
90Target-987
E120
E220
V61-96
W572

Hubbs, Ken
62T-461
63Bz-27
63Exh
63J-174
63P-174
63T-15
63T/SO
64T-550
Exh47

Huber, Clarence
26Exh-45

Huber, Jeff
91CharRain/ClBest-7
91CharRain/ProC-93

Hudek, John
89Saraso/Star-11
89Star/Wax-59
90BirmB/Best-19
90BirmB/ProC-1107
90Foil/Best-296
91BirmB/LineD-63
91BirmB/ProC-1451

Hudgens, Dave
83Tacoma-16
84Cram/PCL-74

Hudik, Matt
90StCath/ProC-3452

Hudler, Rex
82Nashvl-14
84Colum-8
84Colum/Pol-13
85Colum-18
85Colum/Pol-14
85D-469
86RochR-8
87RochR/TCMA-28
88F/Up-U101
88Indianap/CMC-10
88Indianap/ProC-513
89B-364
89D-452
89F-380
89OPC-346
89S-470
89T-346
89T/Big-248
89UD-405
90D-366
90Leaf/II-439
90OPC-647
90Publint/St-177
90S-287
90Smok/Card-10
90T-647
90UD-411
91B-409
91Crown/Orio-206
91D-599
91F/Up-U116
91Leaf/I-212
91Leaf/Stud-233
91OPC-228
91Panini/FrSt-37
91Pol/Card-10
91S-589
91T-228
91T/StClub/I-280
91UD-482
92D/II-438
92F-581
92S/I-184
92T-47
92UD-670

Hudlin, Willis
33G-96
34DS-79
35BU-103
35BU-48
35G-1K
35G-3B
35G-5B
35G-6B
R313
R316
V353-72

Hudson, Charles
83Portl-19
84D-448
84F-36
84Nes/792-432
84Phill/TastyK-22
84T-432
84T/St-17
85CIGNA-16
85D-355
85F-255
85OPC-379
85Phill/TastyK-20
85Phill/TastyK-9M
85T-379
85T/St-120
86CIGNA-13
86D-622
86F-444
86Leaf-239
86Phill/TastyK-49
86T-792
87D-630
87F-176
87F/Up-U46
87T-191
87T/Tr-50T
88D-374
88D/Y/Bk-374
88F-210
88T-636
88T/Big-212
89D-514
89D/Tr-50
89Mara/Tigers-27
89OPC-236
89S-415
89T-236
89T/Big-88
89UD-586
90Publint/St-474
90UD-520

Hudson, David
(Hap)
86Louisvl-3tr
87Louisvl-29
88Louisvl-51
88Louisvl/ProC-434
89AAA/ProC-12
89Louisvl-38
89Louisvl/CMC-5
89Louisvl/ProC-1253

Hudson, Deryk
90Rockford/ProC-2701

Hudson, Jack
76Watlo

Hudson, Jesse James
70OPC-348R
70T-348R
91WIZMets-190

Hudson, Jim
89BBCity/Star-10

Hudson, John
39PB-154
40PB-147
90Target-367

Hudson, Kevin
89Billings/ProC-2039

Hudson, Lance
86Miami-12
88Lakeland/Star-14
90Miami/II/Star-10

Hudson, Nathaniel
N172
N172/BC
N370
Scrapps

Hudson, Rex
74Albuq/Team-7

Hudson, Robert
81Wausau-3
83Chatt-14

Hudson, Sid
41PB-46
48L-84
50B-17
51B-169
51T/RB-44
52B-123
52T-60
53B/BW-29
53T-251
54B-194
54T-93
55B-318
91T/Arc53-251

Hudson, Teressa
81ArkTr-23M

Hudson, Tony
80Tulsa-3
81Tulsa-21
82BurlR-3
85Tulsa-20
86Knoxvl-13
87Syrac-12

Huebner, John
88GreatF-18
89Bakers/Cal-196

Huey, John
83Madis/LF-26
84MidldC-5

Huff, Brad
88Wythe/ProC-1979
89Wythe/Star-14
90Geneva/ProC-3032
90Geneva/Star-15
91WinSalem/ClBest-14

Huff, Matt
87SLCity/Taco-23
88Miami/Star-10

Huff, Mike
87SanAn-16
88SanAn/Best-19
88TexLgAS/GS-33
89AAA/CMC-38
89AAA/ProC-48
89Albuq/CMC-24
89Albuq/ProC-79
90AAAGame/ProC-AAA46
90Albuq/CMC-24
90Albuq/ProC-358
90Albuq/Trib-14
90Classic/Up-24
90F-649
90S-597
90T/89Debut-63
91B-73
91F-210
91Leaf/GRook-BC22
91S/RookTr-52T
92D/II-579
92F-85
92S/II-664
92T-532

Huffman, Kris
88Savan/ProC-351
89Spring/Best-9

Hüffman, Phil
80OPC-79
80Syrac-9
80T-142
81OPC-2
81Syrac-5
81T-506
82Omaha-6
85RochR-17
86RochR-9
87RochR-1
87RochR/TCMA-6
91Crown/Orio-207

Huffman, Rod
91Clinton/ClBest-5
91Clinton/ProC-829
91MidwLAS/ProC-MWL4

Hufford, Scott
87Spartan-26
88Lakeland/Star-15

Huffstickler, Danny
79Elmira-4

Hufft, Fuzzy
28Exh/PCL-12

Huggins, Miller
10Domino-57
11Helmar-171
12Sweet/Pin-149A
12Sweet/Pin-149B
14CJ-75
14Piedmont/St-28
15CJ-75
61F-46
80SSPC/HOF
86Conlon/1-16
91Conlon/Sport-101
91Conlon/Sport-271
92Conlon/Sport-649
BF2-93
D329-86
D350/2-85
E121/120
E121/80
E270/2
E300
M101/4-86
M101/5-85
M116
S74-120
T201
T202
T204
T205
T206
T207
T213/blue
T213/brown
T215/blue
T215/brown
T222
V100
W514-34
W515-36
W575
WG3-22
WG5-20
WG6-19

Hughes, Butch
82Reading-3
83Phoenix/BHN-18

86Modesto-14
87Modesto-9
Hughes, Gregory
80Water-22
81Tulsa-23
Hughes, Jim R.
52Park-56
53T-216
54NYJour
54T-169
55B-156
55Gol/Dodg-14
55T-51
55T/DH-20
79TCMA-268
90Target-369
91T/Arc53-216
Hughes, Jim
76Ho/Twink-53
76OPC-11
76SSPC-211
76T-11
77T-304
78Cr/PCL-62
78T-395
90Target-368
Hughes, Jim
N172
Hughes, John
83Clinton/LF-16
Hughes, Keith
85Albany-35
86Albany/TCMA-7
87Colum-21
87Colum/Pol-13
87Colum/TCMA-21
88D-643
88F-305
88RochR/Team-11
88RochR/CMC-15
88RochR/Gov-13
88RochR/ProC-213
88S-635
88T-781
89AAA/ProC-23
89RochR/CMC-13
89RochR/ProC-1659
90AAAGame/ProC-AAA6
90AlbanyDG/Best-32
90T/TVMets-46
90Tidew/CMC-24
90Tidew/ProC-556
91ColClip/LineD-106
91ColClip/ProC-601
91Crown/Orio-208
91WIZMets-191
Hughes, Leo
(Doc)
48Sommer-29
49Sommer-23
Hughes, Michael
(Mickey)
90Target-370
Hughes, Richard
(Dick)
62Kahn/Atl
62Pep/Tul
67T-384R
68T-253
69OPC-39
69T-39
Hughes, Roy
92Conlon/Sport-566
Hughes, Sammy T.
78Laugh/Black-15
86Negro/Frit-111
90Negro/Star-35
Hughes, Steve
80Cedar-8
Hughes, Terry W.
73OPC-603R
73T-603R
74OPC-604R
74T-604R
75OPC-612
75T-612
75T/M-612
Hughes, Thomas
(Tom)
11Helmar-71
91Conlon/Sport-161
C46-66
E254
E91
M116
Hughes, Tim
75Cedar
Hughes, Troy
90Pulaski/Best-20
90Pulaski/ProC-3088
91Macon/ClBest-24
91Macon/ProC-877
Hughs, Eric
89Alaska/Team-18
Hughson, Cecil
(Tex)
47TipTop
49B-199
Exh47
Huismann, Mark
81CharR-18
82FtMyr-16
84D-339
85D-583
85F-203
85Omaha-15
85T-644
86NatPhoto-38
87F-586
87Mother/Sea-16
87T-187
88AAA/ProC-42
88Toledo/CMC-11
88Toledo/ProC-588
89RochR/CMC-10
89RochR/ProC-1650
90BuffB/CMC-4
90BuffB/ProC-367
90BuffB/Team-9
91BuffB/LineD-30
91BuffB/ProC-535
91Crown/Orio-209
Huisman, Rick
90ClintUp/Team-U6
91AS/Cal-31
91SanJose/ClBest-27
91SanJose/ProC-6
91Single/ClBest-32
Hulett, Tim
81GlenF-12
84TrueVal/WS-18
85Coke/WS-32
85D-645
85F/Up-U59
85T/Tr-60T
86Coke/WS-32
86D-404
86F-208
86OPC-87
86T-724
86T/St-295
87Coke/WS-18
87D-260
87D/OD-231
87F-500
87OPC-286
87T-566
87T/St-289
88Indianap/CMC-17
88Indianap/ProC-522
88T-158
89RochR/CMC-16
89RochR/ProC-1653
90F/Up-U66
91Crown/Orio-210
91D-706
91F-478
91OPC-468
91S-632
91T-468
91T/StClub/II-517
92F-11
92S/I-391
Hull, Jeff
85FtMyr-8
86FtMyr-14
88EastLAS/ProC-35
88Vermont/ProC-961
89Calgary/CMC-8
89Calgary/ProC-526
90OrlanSR/Best-8
90OrlanSR/ProC-1085
Hulme, Pat
90Utica/Pucko-20
Hulse, David
91CharlR/ClBest-22
91CharlR/ProC-1326
91Single/ClBest-197
Hulse, Jeff
88Eugene/Best-14
89AppFx/ProC-866
90Clearw/Star-8
Hulstrom, Bruce
87Penin-14
Hulswitt, Rudy
E254
E270/1
E270/2
M116
T206
Humber, Frank
89GreatF-21
90Bakers/Cal-239
Hume, Thomas
(Tom)
76Indianap-9
77Indianap-5
78T-701R
79T-301
80T-149
81F-211
81OPC-292
81T-419
81T-8LL
81T/HT
81T/St-166
81T/St-31M
82Coke/Reds
82D-229
82F-69
82OPC-79
82T-763
83D-229
83F-593
83OPC-86
83T-86
84D-550
84F-472
84Nes/792-607
84OPC-186
84T-607
84T/St-59
85D-408
85F-538
85OPC-223
85T-223
86D-365
86F-179
86F/Up-U52
86Phill/TastyK-41
86T-573
86T/Tr-47T
87F-177
87OPC-251
87Phill/TastyK-41
87T-719
88F-236
88S-494
Hummel, Dean
86Shrev-10
Hummel, John E.
10Domino-58
11Helmar-87
12Sweet/Pin-74
14CJ-50
14Piedmont/St-29
15CJ-50
90Target-371
E254
E270/2
E300
M116
S74-53
T202
T204
T205
T206
T213/blue
T215/blue
T215/brown
Humphrey, Al
90Target-988
Humphrey, Daryl
83Greens-10
Humphrey, Sly
83Idaho-28
Humphrey, Terry
72OPC-489R
72T-489R
73OPC-106
73T-106
76OPC-552
76SSPC-373
76T-552
77T-369
78T-71
79T-503
Humphreys, Mike
87SLCity/Taco-16
88Spokane/ProC-1926
89AS/Cal-10
89River/Best-8
89River/Cal-5
89River/ProC-1400
90Wichita/Rock-11
91B-162
91ColClip/LineD-107
91ColClip/ProC-608
91UD/FinalEd-35F
92D/II-769
92F-231
92S/II-815
92T/91Debut-85
92UD-432
Humphreys, Robert W.
(Bob)
65OPC-154
65T-154
66T-342
67T-478
68T-268
69OPC-84
69T-84
70OPC-538
70T-538
71MLB/St-439
71OPC-236
71T-236
72MB-154
81Syrac-23MG
83Syrac-26MG
Humphries, Joe
87Myrtle-25
88SanAn/Best-20
Humphry, Brandt
80ElPaso-1
81Holyo-22
Hund, John
75QuadC
Hundhammer, Paul
84Pawtu-10A
84Pawtu-10B
85Pawtu-5
Hundley, Randy
66T-392R
67OPC-106
67T-106
68OPC-136
68T-136
69MB-122
69MLB/St-121
69Sunoco/Pin-4
69T-347
69T/St-14
70Dunkin-3
70K-31
70MLB/St-17
70OPC-265
70T-265
71Bz
71Bz/Test-46
71MD
71MLB/St-34
71OPC-592
71T-592
71T/Coins-51
71T/tatt-3
72MB-155
72OPC-258
72T-258
73OPC-21
73T-21
74OPC-319
74T-319
74T/St-15
74T/Tr-319T
76OPC-351
76SSPC-121
76T-351
77T-502
89Pac/Leg-207
Hundley, Todd
88LitFalls/Pucko-6
89Clmbia/Best-1
89Clmbia/GS-11
89SALAS/GS-17
90B-142
90Classic/III-100
90F/Up-U36
90S/Tr-76T
90T/Tr-44T
90T/TVMets-47
90UD/Ext-726
91AAAGame/ProC-AAA49
91B-467
91D-641
91F-150
91F/Ultra-220
91MajorLg/Pins-75
91OPC-457
91OPC/Premier-66
91RedFoley/St-108
91S-340RP
91S/100RisSt-79
91S/Rook40-23
91T-457
91T/90Debut-74
91T/StClub/II-349
91Tidew/LineD-559
91Tidew/ProC-2513
91UD-440
91WIZMets-192
92D/II-568
92F-506
92S/100RisSt-80
92S/II-602
92T-673
92UD-260
Hunger, Chris
81Wausau-9
83Chatt-3
Hungler
N172
Hungling, Bernard
(Bernie)
90Target-989
E120
Hunington, Neal
91James/ClBest-29PER
Hunnefield, William
26Exh-76
27Exh-38
30CEA/Pin-15
31Exh/4-21
Hunsacker, Frank
77StPete
80ArkTr-15
Hunsinger, Alan
82Spring-17
83ArkTr-18
90SpringDG/Best-7
Hunt, Ben
75Clinton
Hunt, Ken L.
60L-33
60T-522
61T-156
61T/St-172
62J-79
62P-79
62P/Can-79
62Salada-76A
62Salada-76B
62Shirriff-76
62T-68
62T/bucks
62T/St-65
63T-207
64Bz-26
64T-294
64T/Coins-89
65Bz-26
Hunt, Ken R.
61T-556
62J-129
62Kahn
62P-129
62P/Can-129
62T-364
Hunt, Randy
82Spring-20
83ArkTr-11
85Louisvl-11
86Indianap-6
86T-218

87D-625
88Memphis/Best-15
90SpringDG/Best-33

Hunt, Ronald K.
(Ron)
63T-558R
64T-235
64T/Coins-164AS
64T/S-6
64T/St-93
64T/SU
65OldLond-12
65T-285
65T/E-35
65T/trans-50
66T-360
67OPC/PI-31
67T-525
67T/PI-31
68Coke
68Dexter-39
68OPC-15
68T-15
69MB-123
69MLB/St-200
69T-664
69T/St-105
70Expos/Pins-7
70MLB/St-125
70OPC-276
70T-276
71MLB/St-130
71OPC-161
71T-578
72MB-156
72OPC-110
72T-110
73OPC-149
73T-149
74K-25
74OPC-275
74T-275
74T/St-55
74Weston-33
75OPC-610
75T-610
75T/M-610
78TCMA-212
90Pac/Legend-84
90Target-372
91WIZMets-193

Hunt, Ronald
81Redwd-15
82Holyo-15
82Redwd-21

Hunt, Tom
80LynnS-16
81Wausau-28
82Wausau-30
83Chatt-23
84Chatt-10
86Chatt-14tr
87Chatt/Best-26tr

Hunter, Bert
86Ashvl-14
86AubAs-13
87Ashvl-16
88Osceola/Star-16
89ColMud/ProC-148
89ColMud/Star-14
90ColMud/Best-8
90ColMud/ProC-1358
90ColMud/Star-14
91Jacks/LineD-562
91Jacks/ProC-937

Hunter, Bob
(Bobby)
88Oneonta/ProC-2056
91Augusta/ClBest-8

Hunter, Brian
88MidwLAS/GS-18
89Greenvl/ProC-1158
89Greenvl/Star-9
89Greenvl/Best-2
89Star/Wax-35
90Ashvl/ProC-2761
90Richm/CMC-19
90Richm/ProC-271
90Richm/Team-13
91Classic/III-39
91D/Rook-9
91F/UltraUp-U67
91Osceola/ClBest-24
91Osceola/ProC-698
91Richm/LineD-431
91Richm/ProC-2581
91UD/FinalEd-54F
92D/I-163
92F-359
92S/100RisSt-3
92S/I-417
92T-611
92T/91Debut-86
92UD-366

Hunter, George
90Target-990
E254
M116
T206
T213/brown

Hunter, Gordon
(Billy)
53T-166
54B-5
54T-48
55B-69
57T-207
58T-98
59T-11
73OPC-136CO
73T-136CO
74OPC-306CO
74T-306CO
78BK/R-1MG
78T-548CO
79TCMA-118
91Crown/Orio-211
91T/Arc53-166

Hunter, Greg
91SanBern/ClBest-15
91SanBern/ProC-1992
91Single/ClBest-178

Hunter, Herb H.
16FleischBrd-44

Hunter, James
88ElPaso/Best-28

Hunter, Jeff
80Elmira-21

Hunter, Jim
(Catfish)
65T-526R
66OPC-36
66T-36
67T-369
67T/Test/SU-23
68Bz-2
68T-385
68T/Post-5
69MB-124
69MLB/St-87
69T-235
69T/St-216
70MLB/St-259
70T-565
71Bz
71Bz/Test-48
71MD
71MLB/St-516
71OPC-45
71T-45
71T/Coins-80
71T/tatt-9
72K-22
72MB-157
72OPC-330
72T-330
73K-20
73OPC-235
73OPC-344KP
73T-235
73T-344KP
73T/Lids-21
74K-44
74OPC-196
74OPC-339AS
74T-339AS
74T-7
74T/DE-6
74T/St-225
75Ho-148
75K-44
75OPC-230
75OPC-310LL
75OPC-311LL
75T-230
75T-310LL
75T-311LL
75T/M-230
75T/M-310LL
75T/M-311LL
76Crane-21
76Ho-141
76K-5
76Laugh/Jub-7
76MSA/Disc
76OPC-100
76OPC-200LL
76OPC-202LL
76SSPC-425
76T-100
76T-200LL
76T-202LL
77BK/Y-4
77BurgChef-178
77Ho-79
77OPC-10
77T-280
77T/CS-21
78BK/Y-7
78OPC-69
78T-460
78Wiffle/Discs-31
79BK/Y-6
79OPC-352
79T-670
83MLBPA/Pin-10
86Sf/Dec-63M
87D/HL-19
87Mother/A's-6
88Pac/Leg-16
88T/Gloss22-11
89HOF/St-82
89Pac/Leg-193
89Swell-10

Hunter, Jim
86BurlEx-9
87Stockton-19
89ElPaso/GS-9
90Pac/Legend-68
91Brewer/MillB-12
92S/II-741
92T/91Debut-87

Hunter, Marion
81Redwd-16

Hunter, Willard
90Target-373
91WIZMets-194

Huntz, Steve
69OPC-136R
69T-136R
70OPC-282
70T-282
71MLB/St-252
71OPC-486
71T-486
72OPC-73
72T-73
76SSPC-126

Hunziker, Kent
76Clinton
77AppFx

Huppert, David B.
81RochR-9
83RochR-11
84Cram/PCL-37
86ElPaso-13
88CalLgAS-19
88Stockton/Cal-202MG
89Stockton/Best-29MG
89Stockton/Cal-176MG
89Stockton/ProC-386MG
89Stockton/Star-22MG
91Crown/Orio-212MG
91ElPaso/LineD-199MG
91ElPaso/ProC-2762MG

Hurd, Thomas
55T-116
55T/DH-120
56T-256

Hurdle, Clinton
76Watlo
78T-705R
79T-547
80OPC-273
80T-525
81D-224
81F-45
81OPC-98
81Pol/Royals-4
81T-98
81T/St-85
82Coke/Reds
82D-516
82F-411
82T-297
83Tidew-4
84Tidew-28
86D-434
86Schnucks-10
86T-438
87F-298
87OPC-317
87T-317
87Tidew-1
87Tidew/TCMA-22
89Pac/SenLg-111
89StLucie/Star-6
89T/SenLg-98
89Tidew/Candl-12
89TM/SenLg-50
90EliteSenLg-115
91WIZMets-195
91Wmsprt/LineD-649MG
91Wmsprt/ProC-309MG

Hurdle, Mike
80Utica-29

Hurlbert, Gordon
90EastLAS/ProC-EL47TR
90NewBrit/Best-15TR
90NewBrit/Star-27TR

Hurlbutt, Robert
90Ashvl/ClBest-18
90AubAs/Best-7
90AubAs/ProC-3416
91Ashvl/ProC-570

Hurley, Battling
T3/Box-71

Hurley, Edwin
55B-260ump

Hurley, Pat
90Target-991

Hurni, Rick
88SLCity-12

Hursey, Darren
87Fayette-13
88Lakeland/Star-16
89London/ProC-1370
90Lakeland/Star-13
91London/LineD-387
91London/ProC-1873

Hurst, Bill
91Johnson/ProC-3973

Hurst, Bruce
81Pawtu-3
81T-689R
82F-297
82T-381R
83D-134
83F-186
83T-82
84D-213
84F-400
84Nes/792-213
84OPC-213
84T-213
84T/St-226
85D-493
85F-161
85Leaf-73
85OPC-134
85T-451
85T/St-211
86D-517
86D/HL-47
86F-352
86OPC-193
86T-581
86T/Mini-6
87Classic-83
87D-174
87F-37
87F/BB-22
87F/St-65
87F/WS-1
87Leaf-253
87OPC-31
87Sf-38
87T-705
87T/HL-19
87T/HL-28
87T/Mini-43
87T/St-19WS
87Woolwth-19
87Woolwth-28
88D-252
88D/AS-14
88D/Best-233
88D/RedSox/Bk-252
88F-356
88F/BB/AS-18
88F/St-10
88Leaf-179
88OPC-125
88Panini/St-22
88RedFoley/St-37
88S-380
88Sf-197
88T-125
88T/St-253
88T/St/Backs-62
89B-451
89Classic/Up/2-194
89Coke/Padre-7
89D-423
89D/Best-77
89D/Tr-45
89F-91
89F/Up-124
89Padre/Mag-21
89Panini/St-271
89S-325
89S/HotStar-79
89S/Tr-19
89Sf-175
89T-675
89T/Gloss60-28
89T/LJN-115
89T/Mini-49
89T/St/Backs-29
89T/Tr-55T
89T/UK-42
89UD-387
89UD/Ext-792
90B-208
90Classic-102
90Coke/Padre-8
90D-183
90D/BestNL-84
90F-159
90F/BB-19
90Leaf/I-23
90MLBPA/Pins-57
90OPC-315
90Padre/MagUno-23
90Panini/St-357
90PublInt/St-51
90S-270
90S/100St-18
90Sf-47
90T-315
90T/Big-324
90T/Mini-81
90T/St-108
90T/TVAS-48
90UD-433
91B-661
91Classic/200-84
91D-83
91F-533
91F/Ultra-306
91Leaf/II-469
91MajorLg/Pins-56
91OPC-65
91Padre/MagRal-19
91Padre/MagRal-5
91Panini/Top15-90
91S-145
91T-65
91T/StClub/II-475
91UD-602
92D/I-123
92F-608
92S/I-111
92T-595
92UD-437

Hurst, Charles
(Charlie)
89Martins/Star-15
90Batavia/ProC-3059
91Spartan/ClBest-7
91Spartan/ProC-892

Hurst, Frank O.
(Don)
29Exh/4-11
31Exh/4-12
33Exh/4-6
34Exh/4-6

34G-33
92Conlon/Sport-519
R316
V354-80
Hurst, Jody
88CapeCod/Sum-110
89NiagFls/Pucko-12
90Lakeland/Star-14
Hurst, Jonathan
88CharlR/Star-10
89CharlR/Star-10
90Foil/Best-105
90Gaston/Best-9
90Gaston/ProC-2518
90Gaston/Star-11
90SALAS/Star-12
91FSLAS/ProC-FSL23
91Miami/ClBest-8
91Miami/ProC-402
91Single/ClBest-199
Hurt, Mike
89Reading/Best-26
Hurta, Robert
(Bob)
88Spartan/ProC-1026
88Spartan/Star-24
88Spartan/Star-8
90AubAs/Best-2
90AubAs/ProC-3399
91BurlAs/ClBest-5
91BurlAs/ProC-2796
Hurtado, Jose
85Bend/Cram-12
Husband, Perry
85Visalia-3
Huseby, Ken
87Tampa-4
88Greens/ProC-1564
89Augusta/ProC-503
Huskey, Butch
90Kgsport/Star-11
91SALAS/ProC-SAL16
Huslig, James
90ClintUp/Team-U7
90Everett/Best-6
90Everett/ProC-3122
Huson, Jeff
86BurlEx-10
87WPalmB-23
88Jaxvl/Best-18
88Jaxvl/ProC-966
88SLAS-18
89AAA/CMC-4
89AAA/ProC-11
89Indianap/CMC-18
89Indianap/ProC-1233
89S/HotRook-69
90D-693
90D/BestAL-83
90D/Rook-11
90F-350
90F/Up-123
90Leaf/II-285
90Mother/Rang-23
90OPC-72
90S-615
90S/100Ris-14
90S/DTRook-B7
90S/Tr-41T
90S/YS/I-41
90Sf-176
90T-72
90T/Tr-45T
90UD-434
90UD/Ext-788
91B-273
91Bz-16
91D-305
91F-289
91F/Ultra-349
91Leaf/I-134
91Mother/Rang-23
91OPC-756
91Panini/FrSt-255
91Panini/St-206
91S-263
91S/100RisSt-18
91T-756
91T/StClub/I-160
91ToysRUs-12
91UD-195
92D/II-456
92F-308
92S/II-466
92T-314
92UD-196
Hust, Gary
91SoOreg/ClBest-16
91SoOreg/ProC-3862
Huston, Pat
91Geneva/ClBest-9
91Geneva/ProC-4224
Hutcheson, Joe
90Target-992
Hutcheson, Todd
83Miami-28TR
84Beaum-23TR
85Beaum-23TR
86LasVegas-7TR
87LasVegas-13TR
88LasVegas/ProC-226TR
89LasVegas/ProC-28TR
90LasVegas/CMC-25TR
Hutchings, John R.
W711/2
Hutchingson, Chris
86Osceola-14
Hutchins, Lance
88SanJose/Cal-144
88SanJose/ProC-124
Hutchinson, Don
88CapeCod/Sum-68
Hutchinson, Fred
47TipTop
48L-163
49B-196
50B-151
51B-141
52B-3
52StarCal/L-72E
52T-126
53B/Col-132
53NB
53T-72
60T-219MG
61T-135MG
62T-172MG
63FrBauer-9MG
63T-422MG
64T-207MG
79TCMA-138
80Pac/Leg-25
81Detroit-48MG
91T/Arc53-72
Exh47
R303/A
Hutchinson, Ira
39PB-142
90Target-374
W754
Hutchinson, Ray
(Harpo)
76Dubuq
Hutchinson, Sean
89Pulaski/ProC-1909
Hutchinson, William
N172
Huth, Ken
84Savan-7
Hutson, Jason
90Myrtle/ProC-2771
Hutson, Roy
90Target-993
Hutson, Scott
89StCath/ProC-2074
Hutto, Jim
75IntAS/TCMA-11
75IntAS/TCMA-17
76SSPC-385
84Newar-23
84RochR-4
91Crown/Orio-213
Hutto, Paul
90Gate/ProC-3351
Hutton, Mark
89Oneonta/ProC-2118
90Greens/Best-4
90Greens/ProC-2656
90Greens/Star-7
91FSLAS/ProC-FSL13
91FtLaud/ClBest-5
91FtLaud/ProC-2419
Hutton, Tom
67T-428R
69T-266R
72T-741R
73OPC-271
73T-271
74OPC-443
74T-443
75OPC-477
75T-477
75T/M-477
76OPC-91
76SSPC-472
76T-91
77T-264
78Ho-103
78T-568
79OPC-355
79T-673
80OPC-219
80T-427
81D-93
81F-164
81OPC-374
81T-374
85SpokAT/Cram-9
90Swell/Great-87
90Target-375
Huyke, Woody
78Charl
Huyler, Mike
88Watertn/Pucko-19
89Augusta/ProC-509
90CLAS/CL-22
90Salem/Star-8
91CaroMud/LineD-111
91CaroMud/ProC-1093
91Single/ClBest-300
Hvizda, James
(Jim)
89Gaston/ProC-1019
89Gaston/Star-9
89SALAS/GS-25
90CharlR/Star-11
91Beloit/ClBest-28
91Beloit/ProC-2098
Hyatt, Robert Ham
D322
E104
E286
E90/2
M116
T207
Hyde, Bubba
91Negro/Lewis-29
Hyde, Dick
57T-403
58T-156
59T-498
60T-193
91Crown/Orio-214
Hyde, Matt
91QuadC/ClBest-5CO
91QuadC/ProC-2647CO
Hyde, Mickey
89Batavia/ProC-1931
91Clearw/ClBest-21
91Clearw/ProC-1632
Hyde, Rich
91Everett/ProC-3908
Hyers, Tim
90MedHat/Best-3
91Myrtle/ClBest-20
91Myrtle/ProC-2954
Hyman, Don
81QuadC-2
83MidldC-17
84MidldC-3
Hyman, Pat
89Clmbia/Best-24
Hymel, Gary
90LSUPol-7
Hypes, Kyle
75Lafay
76Phoenix
77Phoenix
78Cr/PCL-22
79Phoenix
Hyson, Cole
89AubAs/ProC-2170
90Osceola/Star-10
91Osceola/ClBest-4
91Osceola/ProC-676
Hyzdu, Adam
90A&AASingle/ProC-169
90Classic/DP-15
90Classic/III-90
90Everett/Best-1
90Everett/ProC-3140
91B-617
91Clinton/ClBest-20
91Clinton/ProC-847
91S-388FDP
91Single/ClBest-321
Iacona, Andy
87SLCity/Taco-7BB
Iadarola, George
80WHave-18
Iannini, Steve
87Modesto-15
Iasparro, Donnie
86Visalia-11
Iaverone, Greg
87Peoria-9
90Tulsa/ProC-1159
91Tulsa/LineD-585
91Tulsa/ProC-2775
Ibarguen, Ricky
89Bristol/Star-12
Ibarguen, Steve
82Jacks-5
Ibarra, Carlos
82Edmon-1
Ibarra, Luis
85Tigres-28
Ickes, Mike
87WinHaven-25
Iglesias, Luis
87Spartan-18
88Clearw/Star-15
Iglesias, Michael
91Kissim/ProC-4178
Ignasiak, Mike
89AS/Cal-39
89Stockton/Best-3
89Stockton/Cal-157
89Stockton/ProC-400
89Stockton/Star-5
90Stockton/Best-16
90Stockton/Cal-177
90Stockton/ProC-2176
91Denver/LineD-142
91Denver/ProC-121
92S/II-837RP
92T/91Debut-88
Ikesue, Kazutaka
91Salinas/ClBest-21
91Salinas/ProC-2236
Ikeue, Kouichi
87SLCity/Taco-15
Ilsley, Blaise
86Ashvl-15
87ColAst/ProC-8
88ColAst/Best-17
89Osceola/Star-8
91Tucson/LineD-613
91Tucson/ProC-2211
Imes, Rodney
(Rod)
87Oneonta-25
88FtLaud/Star-12
89Albany/Best-21
89Albany/ProC-314
89Albany/Star-8
89BBAmerAA/BPro-AA8
90AlbanyDG/Best-16
90Nashvl/CMC-7
90Nashvl/ProC-227
91Nashvl/LineD-262
91Nashvl/ProC-2152
Impagliazzo, Joe
86Albany/TCMA-27
Inagaki, Shuji
87Miami-13
88Miami/Star-12
Incaviglia, Pete
86D/Rook-23
86F/Up-U53
86Rang-29
86Sf/Rook-3
86T/Tr-48T
87Classic-16
87Classic/Up-131
87D-224
87D/OD-175
87F-128
87F-625M
87F/Hottest-24
87F/LL-25
87F/Mini-58
87F/Slug-21
87F/St-66
87Kraft-39
87Leaf-185
87Mother/Rang-2
87OPC-384
87RedFoley/St-130
87Sf-37
87Smok/R-15
87T-550
87T/Coins-14
87T/Gloss60-29
87T/GlossRk-6
87T/St-236
87T/St-308
87ToysRUs-12
88Classic/Red-177
88D-304
88D/Best-55
88F-470
88F/Mini-56
88F/Slug-20
88F/SS-C1
88F/St-65
88Leaf-147
88Mother/R-2
88Nestle-20
88OPC-280
88Panini/St-207
88S-485
88S/YS/I-32
88Sf-169
88Smok/R-4
88T-280
88T/Big-73
88T/St-239
89B-238
89D-3DK
89D-56
89D/Best-144
89D/DKsuper-3DK
89F-523
89F/LL-21
89KingB/Discs-24
89Mother/R-10
89OPC-42
89Panini/St-455
89RedFoley/St-63
89S-201
89Sf-112
89Smok/R-16
89T-706
89T/Big-127
89T/LJN-16
89T/St-249
89UD-484
90B-491
90D-48
90F-301
90Leaf/I-231
90Mother/Rang-4
90OPC-430
90Panini/St-157
90PublInt/St-413
90S-93
90T-430
90T/Big-81
90T/St-247
90UD-333
91B-131
91CokeK/Tiger-29
91D-464
91F-290
91Leaf/II-366
91OPC-172
91OPC/Premier-67
91Panini/FrSt-258
91RedFoley/St-51
91S-278
91S/RookTr-3T
91T-172
91T/StClub/I-78
91T/Tr-57T
91UD-453
91UD/Ext-747
92F-139
92S/I-306
92T-679
92UD-271
Incavigua, Tony
81Buffa-20
Infante, Alexis

85Syrac-14
86Syrac-14
87Syrac-8
87Syrac/TCMA-15
88Syrac/CMC-21
88Syrac/ProC-813
89D/Rook-30
90B-17
90PublInt/St-517

Infante, Kennedy
(Ken)
86StPete-14
87ArkTr-5
88ArkTr/GS-11
89Cedar/Best-15
89Cedar/Star-28
90Clearw/Star-9

Infante, Tom
89Hamil/Star-19
90Spring/Best-17

Ingalls, Rick
89BendB/Legoe-28CO

Ingle, Mike
86Kinston-10

Ingle, Randy
83Ander-4
84Durham-29
86Greenvl/Team-14
87Greenvl/Best-4
89Greenvl/ProC-1177
89Greenvl/Best-21
90Greenvl/ProC-1146CO
90Greenvl/Star-24CO
90Pulaski/Best-26MG
90Pulaski/ProC-3114MG
91Greenvl/ClBest-28CO
91Pulaski/ClBest-14MG
91Pulaski/ProC-4022MG

Ingram, Gerald
(Garey)
88Eugene/Best-26
91AS/Cal-12

Ingram, Jeff
89Utica/Pucko-11
90SoBend/Best-5

Ingram, John
90Batavia/ProC-3061
91Martins/ClBest-22
91Martins/ProC-3449

Ingram, Linty
89Fayette/ProC-1572
90Fayette/ProC-2402

Ingram, Riccardo
89Lakeland/Star-10
90London/ProC-1280
91London/LineD-388
91London/ProC-1890

Ingram, Todd
91SoOreg/ClBest-9
91SoOreg/ProC-3835

Inks, Bert
90Target-994

Inman, Bert
91Oneonta/ProC-4150

Innis, Brian
83VeroB-5

Innis, Jeff
84Jacks-6
85Lynch-4
86Jacks/TCMA-6
87Tidew-8
87Tidew/TCMA-5
88D/Mets/Bk-NEW
88F/Up-U105
88T/Tr-54T
88Tidew/CANDL-21
88Tidew/CMC-3
88Tidew/ProC-1582
89Tidew/CMC-3
89Tidew/ProC-1950
90D-408
90F-206
90Kahn/Mets-40
90OPC-557
90T-557
90T/TVMets-13
90Tidew/CMC-6
90Tidew/ProC-539
90UD-562
91F/UltraUp-U97
91F/Up-U103
91Kahn/Mets-40
91OPC-443
91T-443
91T/StClub/II-547
91WIZMets-196
92D/II-587
92F-507
92S/I-327
92T-139
92UD-298

Intorcia, Trent
87Wausau-21
88Miami/Star-13

Iorg, Dane
76OkCty/Team-13
80T-139
81D-311
81F-543
81T-334
82D-166
82F-116
82T-86
83D-469
83F-10
83T-788
83T/St-189
83T/St-190
84D-571
84F-326
84F/X-55
84Nes/792-416
84T-416
84T/Tr-54
85D-252
85F-204
85T-671
86F-9
86F/Up-U54
86Kitty/Disc-9
86Sf-186M
86T-269
86T/St-18WS
86T/Tr-49T
87OPC-151
87T-690

Iorg, Garth
75FtLaud
78T-704R
79Syrac-12
80Syrac-1
81F-423
81OPC-78
81OPC/Post-16
81T-444
82D-353
82F-616
82OPC-83
82T-518
83D-306
83F-430
83OPC-326
83T-326
84D-561
84F-157
84Nes/792-39
84OPC-39
84T-39
84Tor/Fire-17
85D-363
85F-107
85OPC-168
85T-168
85Tor/Fire-15
86Ault-16
86D-640
86F-61
86Leaf-252
86OPC-277
86T-694
86Tor/Fire-18
87D-394
87F-229
87OPC-59
87T-751
87Tor/Fire-14
88D-444
88F-113
88OPC-273
88Panini/St-220
88S-204
88T-273
89Pac/SenLg-152
89T/SenLg-86
89TM/SenLg-51
90EliteSenLg-36
91Myrtle/ClBest-27MG
91Myrtle/ProC-2961MG
91Pac/SenLg-41

Ireland, Billy
83Miami-13

Ireland, Tim
77Jaxvl
81Omaha-18
81T-66R
89Pac/SenLg-104
89Salinas/Cal-146MG
89Salinas/ProC-1822MG
89T/SenLg-67
89TM/SenLg-52
90EliteSenLg-69
90Phoenix/CMC-25CO
90Phoenix/ProC-28CO

Irish, Jeffrey
90Dunedin/Star-12
90StCath/ProC-3475

Irvin, Kyle
88Eugene/Best-7

Irvin, Monte
51B-198
51T/RB-50
52B-162
52BR
52Dix
52RM-NL9
52StarCal/L-78F
52T-26
53B/Col-51
53Briggs
53Dix
53Exh/Can-6
53NB
53SM
53T-62
54DanDee
54Dix
54NYJour
54RM-NL5
54SM
54T-3
55Gol/Giants-14
55SM
55T-100
55T/DH-3
56T-194
79TCMA-168
80SSPC/HOF
83D/HOF-15
86Negro/Frit-6
86Negro/Frit-89
88Negro/Duques-20
88Pac/Leg-79
89HOF/St-32
90Negro/Star-9
90Pac/Legend-32
90Swell/Great-85
91LineD-42
91Negro/Lewis-20
91Swell/Great-44
91T/Arc53-62
Exh47
PM10/Sm-79
PM10/Sm-80
PM10/Sm-81

Irvine, Daryl
85Greens-17
86WinHaven-11
87NewBrit-14
88NewBrit/ProC-890
89NewBrit/ProC-611
89NewBrit/Star-7
90Pawtu/CMC-5
90Pawtu/ProC-457
90T/TVRSox-46
91AAAGame/ProC-AAA30
91F-98
91F/Ultra-34
91OPC-189
91Pawtu/ProC-33
91S-333RP
91T-189
91T/90Debut-75
91T/StClub/I-122
92F-41
92S/II-726

Irvine, Ed
81ElPaso-1
82Vanco-8
84Cram/PCL-44

Irwin, Arthur
N172
N284
N690
WG1-52
WG1-66

Irwin, Charles
90Target-376
E90/1

Irwin, Dennis
78Cr/PCL-9

Irwin, John
N172

Irwin, Michael
90AubAs/Best-13
90AubAs/ProC-3412

Isa, Kelsey
87Penin-21

Isaac, Joe Keith
78Wisco

Isaac, Luis
76Wmsprt
81Batavia-28
88Gator-7CO

Isaacson, Christopher
88Kinston/Star-11

Isales, Orlando
79OkCty
80OkCty
81OkCty/TCMA-8
82Indianap-10
83Indianap-18

Isbell, Frank
WG2-26

Isbell, William
E107
E90/1
T206

Ishmael, Michael
(Mike)
87BurlEx-19
87Jamestn-3

Issac, Richard
86AppFx-11

Ithier, Pete
76Wmsprt
78SanJose-10

Iverson, Tom
89Greens/ProC-430
90CharWh/Best-28TR
91Princet/ClBest-30TR

Ivie, Lonnie
81Miami-15

Ivie, Mike
72OPC-457R
72T-457R
73OPC-613R
73T-613R
76Ho-103
76OPC-134
76SSPC-127
76T-134
77BurgChef-134
77OPC-241
77Padre/SchCd-15
77T-325
78T-445
79Pol/Giants-15
79T-538
80OPC-34
80Pol/Giants-15
80T-62
81D-312
81F-435
81OPC-236
81T-236
81T/Tr-744
82D-396
82T-734
82T/Tr-45T
83D-485
83F-331
83OPC-117
83T-613

Ivie, Tom
91CharRain/ClBest-27

Jabalera, Francisco
83ColumAst-12

Jablonowski, Pete
33G-83
V354-34

Jablonski, Ray
53Hunter
53T-189
54Hunter
54T-26
54Wilson
55RM-NL21
55T-56
55T/DH-51
56Kahn
56T-86
57Kahn
57T-218
58Hires-35
58SFCallB-11
58T-362
59T-342
61Union-H1
91T/Arc53-189

Jacas, Andre
86Madis-12
86Madis/Pol-12

Jacas, David
(Dave)
87Kenosha-12
88Kenosha/ProC-1389
89AS/Cal-8
89Visalia/Cal-109
89Visalia/ProC-1447
90Portl/CMC-20
90Portl/ProC-192
91ElPaso/LineD-186
91ElPaso/ProC-2760

Jaccar, Mike
77Ashvl

Jacklitsch, Fred
90Target-377
C46-62
D303
E101
E104
E105
E106
E107
E92
M116
T205
T206
T216

Jackman, Bill
86Negro/Frit-68

Jackowski, Bill
55B-284ump

Jackson, Alvin
62T-464
63Bz-19
63F-48
63T-111
63T/SO
64T-494
64T/Coins-17
64T/St-85
64T/SU
64T/tatt
65T-381
65T/trans-17
66T-206
67OPC-195
67T-195
68T-503
69MB-125
69T-649
70OPC-443
70T-443
83Tidew-24CO
84Tidew-22CO
88LitFalls/Pucko-27
89French-31
91WIZMets-197

Jackson, Bo
86D/HL-43
86D/Rook-38
86Sf/Rook-40
86SLAS-13
86T/Tr-50T
87Classic-15
87Classic/Up-109
87D-35RR
87D/OD-205
87D/Rook-14
87F-369
87F/Slug-M4
87F/St-132M
87Leaf-35RR
87Sf-190

87T-170
87ToysRUs-13
88Classic/Blue-208
88D-220
88D/Best-119
88F-260
88Leaf-187
88OPC-8
88Panini/St-110
88RedFoley/St-38
88S-180
88Sf-148
88Smok/Royals-5
88T-750
88T/Big-49
88T/St-258
89T/Ames-17
89B-126
89Classic-122
89Classic/Up/2-157
89D-208
89D/Best-169
89F-285
89KingB/Discs-11
89OPC-84
89Panini/St-358
89RedFoley/St-64
89S-330
89S/Mast-1
89S/YS/I-5
89Sf-70
89T-540
89T-789TL
89T/Big-238
89T/HeadsUp-8
89T/St-265
89T/UK-43
89Tastee/Discs-6
89UD-221
90B-378
90B/Ins-4
90Classic-2
90Classic-59
90Classic/Up-25
90CollAB-1
90D-1DK
90D-61
90D-650AS
90D/BestAL-63
90D/Bon/MVP-BC1
90D/GSlam-12
90D/Learning-38
90D/Preview-1
90D/SuperDK-1DK
90F-110
90F-635M
90F/AwardWin-19
90F/BB-20
90F/BBMVP-21
90F/LL-19
90F/WaxBox-C15
90HotPlay/St-22
90KingB/Discs-17
90Leaf/I-125
90MLBPA/Pins-104
90MSA/Soda-7
90OPC-300
90Panini/St-198M
90Panini/St-384
90Panini/St-84
90Post-14
90PublInt/St-350
90PublInt/St-596
90RedFoley/St-51
90S-280
90S-566AS
90S-687DT
90S-697M
90S/100St-40
90S/YS/I-1
90Sf-200
90Sunflower-4
90T-300
90T/Big-6
90T/Coins-19
90T/DH-35
90T/Gloss22-17
90T/Gloss60-44
90T/HeadsUp-8
90T/Mini-16
90T/St-155AS
90T/St-264
90T/TVAS-5
90Tetley/Discs-5
90UD-105
90UD-32TC
90UD-75HL
90WonderBrd-1
91Classic/200-186
91Classic/I-48
91D-632
91D-BC10
91F-561
91F/ProV-5
91F/Ultra-149
91F/UltraG-6
91Kodak/WSox-8
91Leaf/Prev-19
91MajorLg/Pins-20
91OPC-600
91Panini/FrSt-281
91Panini/St-226
91Pol/Royal-12
91S-412RIF
91S-420HL
91S-5
91S-692MB
91S-773HL
91S/100SS-2
91S/RookTr-1T
91T-600
91T/CJMini/I-25
91T/StClub/I-224
91T/SU-20
91T/Tr-58T
91UD-545
91UD/Ext-744
92D/II-470
92F-701M
92F-86
92S/I-361
92T-290
92UD-555

Jackson, Bubba
88Tulsa-17

Jackson, Chuck
85Cram/PCL-67
86Tucson-8
87D/Rook-55
87F/Up-U47
88Mother/Ast-25
88Pol/Ast-14
88S-222
88T-94
89S-584
89Tucson/CMC-20
89Tucson/ProC-205
89Tucson/JP-8
89UD-323
91Calgary/LineD-61
91Calgary/ProC-521

Jackson, Danny
82CharR-6
83Omaha-6
84D-461
85D-374
85F-205
86D-95
86F-10
86Kitty/Disc-16
86Leaf-30
86NatPhoto-25
86Sf-186M
87D-157
87D/OD-203
87F-370
87T/Tr-51T
88D-132
88D/Best-166
88F-261
88F/Slug-21
88F/Up-U84
88Kahn/Reds-20
88OPC-324
88S-398
88S/Tr-2T
88T-324
88T/Tr-55T
89B-304
89Cadaco-31
89Classic-123
89D-124
89D/AS-52
89D/Best-54
89F-163
89F-636M
89F/BBAS-22
89F/BBMVP's-21
89F/Excit-25
89F/Heroes-24
89F/LL-22
89F/WaxBox-C15
89Kahn/Reds-20
89KingB/Discs-23
89OPC-319
89Panini/St-225
89Panini/St-67
89Richm/Ko-CO
89S-555
89S/HotStar-75
89S/YS/II-41
89Sf-80
89T-395AS
89T-730
89T/DH-22
89T/Gloss60-57
89T/Hills-18
89T/LJN-99
89T/Mini-10
89T/St-143
89T/St/Backs-62
89UD-640
90B-44
90D-80
90F-422
90Kahn/Reds-13
90Leaf/II-279
90OPC-445
90Panini/St-255
90PublInt/St-264
90PublInt/St-32
90S-289
90Sf-89
90T-445
90T/St-142
90UD-120
91B-412
91Classic/200-69
91Cub/Mara-32
91D-678
91D-96
91F-67
91F/UltraUp-U70
91F/Up-U78
91Leaf/II-268
91OPC-92
91OPC/Premier-68
91S-601
91S/RookTr-17T
91T-92
91T/StClub/II-433
91T/Tr-59T
91UD-414
91UD/Ext-723
92D/I-91
92F-383
92S/I-120
92T-619
92UD-104

Jackson, Darrell
78OrlTw
79T-246
79Toledo-18
80T-386
81D-547
81F-567
81OPC-89
81T-89
82D-179
82F-555
82T-193

Jackson, Darrin
82QuadC-22
84MidldC-16
86Pittsfld-10
87Iowa-25
88Berg/Cubs-30
88D/Cubs/Bk-NEW
88D/Rook-45
88F-641R
88F/Up-U78
88S/Tr-109T
88T/Tr-56T
89F-428
89S-360
89T-286
89T/JumboR-12
89ToysRUs-14
89UD-214
90D-641
90F-160
90OPC-624
90Padre/MagUno-6
90PublInt/St-195
90S-541
90T-624
90UD-414
91F/UltraUp-U112
91F/Up-U124
91Leaf/II-346
91OPC-373
91Padre/MagRal-6
91S-169
91T-373
92D/I-292
92F-609
92S/II-521
92T-88
92UD-328

Jackson, Doug
78DaytB

Jackson, Gayron
86AubAs-14

Jackson, Grant
66T-591R
67T-402R
68T-512
69OPC-174
69T-174
70MLB/St-91
70OPC-6
70T-6
71Bz
71MLB/St-300
71OPC-392
71T-392
72MB-158
72OPC-212
72T-212
73JP
73OPC-396
73T-396
74OPC-68
74T-68
74T/St-126
75OPC-303
75T-303
75T/M-303
76OPC-233
76SSPC-378
76T-233
77T-49
78T-661
79T-117
80OPC-218
80T-426
81D-15
81F-378
81OPC-232
81T-519
82D-518
82F-191
82OPC-104
82T-779
82T/Tr-46T
88EastLAS/ProC-48
89CharlK-2
89Chatt/II/Team-13
89Pac/SenLg-66
89TM/SenLg-53
91Crown/Orio-215
91Iowa/LineD-225CO
91Iowa/ProC-1077CO

Jackson, Greg
86Cram/PCL-85
87QuadC-30

Jackson, James B.
T206

Jackson, Jason
88NewBrit/ProC-912
90Canton/Star-7

Jackson, Jeff
89Martins/Star-16
90B-157
90Batavia/ProC-3080
90OPC-74FDP
90S-678DC
90T-74DP
91B-491
91Single/ClBest-125
91Spartan/ClBest-26
91Spartan/ProC-911

Jackson, Jelly
86Negro/Frit-96

Jackson, Joe
(Shoeless)
14CJ-103
15CJ-103
40PB-225
80Pac/Leg-107
80Laugh/3/4/5-13
80Laugh/FFeat-24
88Pac/8Men-110
88Pac/8Men-13
88Pac/8Men-31
88Pac/8Men-32
88Pac/8Men-36
88Pac/8Men-37
88Pac/8Men-55M
88Pac/8Men-62
88Pac/8Men-69
88Pac/8Men-77
89Pac/Leg-220
92Conlon/Sport-444
D327
D328-82
D329-87
D350/2-86
E135-82
E224
E90/1
M101/4-87
M101/5-86
W514-15

Jackson, Joe
76Clinton

Jackson, John
90Everett/Best-25
90Everett/ProC-3141
91SanJose/ClBest-26
91SanJose/ProC-23
91SanJose/ProC-26M
91Single/ClBest-255

Jackson, Ken
86Reading-10
87Maine-7
87Maine/TCMA-11
88Maine/ProC-287
89ScrWB/CMC-17
89ScrWB/ProC-729

Jackson, Kenny
85Phill/TastyK-44
86Cram/PCL-37
87AppFx-28
87Phill/TastyK-51
88BBCity/Star-14
88Maine/CMC-17
89Beloit/II/Star-15
90Stockton/Best-12
90Stockton/Cal-197
90Stockton/ProC-2197
91ElPaso/LineD-187
91ElPaso/ProC-2761

Jackson, Larry
81Cedar-1

Jackson, LaVerne
85Greens-26
86WinHaven-12
87WinHaven-8
89EastLDD/ProC-DD31
89NewBrit/ProC-615
89NewBrit/Star-2
90Canton/ProC-1303

Jackson, Lawrence C.
(Larry)
55Hunters-1
56T-119
57T-196
58T-97
59T-399
60L-15
60T-492
61P-174
61T-535
61T-75M
61T/St-88
62J-165
62P-165
62P/Can-165
62T-306M
62T-83
62T/bucks
62T/St-184
63T-95
64T-444
64T/Coins-114
64T/St-13
64T/tatt

64Wheat/St-22
65Bz-2
65OPC-10LL
65T-10LL
65T-420
66T-595
67T-229
68OPC-81
68T-81
69MB-126
78TCMA-222
78TCMA-286

Jackson, Lee
90Canton/Best-13

Jackson, Lloyd
85Everett/II/Cram-5
86Clinton-11

Jackson, Lonnie
91Kissim/ProC-4201

Jackson, Lou
59T-130
61BeeHive-9
64T-511
78TCMA-115
91Crown/Orio-216

Jackson, Mark
86Cedar/TCMA-20
87Tampa-18

Jackson, Miccal
91Savan/ClBest-17
91Savan/ProC-1658

Jackson, Michael
86Reading-11
87D/Rook-36
87F/Up-U48
87Phill/TastyK-33
87Sf/Rook-33
88D-139
88F-306
88F/Up-U60
88Mother/Sea-19
88RedFoley/St-39
88S-144
88S/Tr-62T
88T-651
89B-207
89D-652
89F-550
89F/BBMVP's-22
89Mother/Sea-19
89OPC-169
89S-398
89S/YS/I-14
89T-169
89UD-142
90F-517
90Leaf/II-351
90Mother/Mar-19
90OPC-761
90PublInt/St-435
90S-546
90T-761
90UD-494
91CounHrth-23
91D-676
91F-454
91F/UltraUp-U51
91Leaf/II-452
91OPC-534
91S-91
91T-534
91UD-496
92D/II-584
92F-282
92S/I-194
92T-411
92UD-593

Jackson, Mikki
83Madis/LF-20

Jackson, Randy
52B-175
52StarCal/L-80C
52T-322
53B/BW-12
54B-189
55B-87
56T-223
57T-190
58T-301
59T-394
90Target-378

Jackson, Ray
91Everett/ClBest-7
91Everett/ProC-3930

Jackson, Reginald M.
(Reggie)
69MB-127
69T-260
69T/decal
69T/S-28
70K-32
70MB-11
70MLB/St-260
70OPC-140
70OPC-459AS
70OPC-64LL
70OPC-66LL
70T-140
70T-459AS
70T-64LL
70T-66LL
70T/CB
70T/S-28
70Trans-11
71Bz/Test-18
71MLB/St-517
71MLB/St-562
71OPC-20
71T-20
71T/Coins-108
71T/GM-47
71T/S-38
71T/tatt-3
72K-20
72MB-159
72OPC-435
72OPC-436IA
72OPC-90LL
72T-435
72T-436IA
72T-90LL
73K-22
73OPC-255
73T-255
73T/Comics-8
73T/Lids-22
73T/PinUps-8
74K-20
74Laugh/ASG-71
74OPC-130
74OPC-202LL
74OPC-203LL
74OPC-338AS
74OPC-470ALCS
74OPC-477WS
74T-130
74T-202LL
74T-203LL
74T-338AS
74T-470ALCS
74T-477WS
74T/DE-61
74T/Puzzles-6
74T/St-226
75Ho-88
75K-54
75OPC-211M
75OPC-300
75OPC-461WS
75T-211MV
75T-300
75T-461WS
75T/M-211MV
75T/M-300
75T/M-461WS
76Crane-22
76Ho-146
76K-8
76MSA/Disc
76OPC-194LL
76OPC-500
76SSPC-494
76T-194LL
76T-500
77BK/Y-17
77BurgChef-176
77Ho-3
77OPC-200
77Pep-34
77T-10
77T/CS-22
78BK/Y-21
78Ho-47
78OPC-110
78OPC-242RB
78PapaG/Disc-26
78T-200
78T-413WS
78T-7RB
78Wiffle/Discs-32
79BK/Y-21
79K-46
79OPC-374
79T-700
79T/Comics-12
80BK/PHR-17
80K-26
80OPC-314
80T-600
80T/S-6
81D-228
81D-348
81D-468
81Detroit-120
81Drake-10
81F-650HL
81F-79
81F/St-115
81F/St-CLI
81K-3
81MSA/Disc-18
81OPC-370
81PermaGr/AS-14
81PermaGr/CC-7
81Sqt-5
81T-2LL
81T-400
81T/HT
81T/Nat/Super-8
81T/SO-3
81T/St-107
81T/St-11M
81T/St-245
82D-535
82D-575M
82Drake-19
82F-39
82F-646M
82F/St-110M
82F/St-112
82K-14
82KMart-23
82OPC-300
82OPC-301IA
82OPC-377AS
82PermaGr/AS-7
82PermaGr/CC-20
82Sqt-5
82T-300
82T-301IA
82T-551AS
82T/St-216
82T/Tr-47T
83D-115
83D-3DK
83D/AAS-3
83Drake-12
83F-640M
83F-645M
83F-93
83K-3
83OPC-219SV
83OPC-390AS
83OPC-56
83PermaGr/CC-27
83Seven-5
83T-390
83T-500
83T-501SV
83T-702AS
83T/Gloss40-39
83T/St-163
83T/St-17M
83T/St-41
83T/St-5
83T/St/Box-4
84D-57
84D/AAS-36
84D/Champs-9
84Drake-15
84F-520
85FunFood/Pin-16
84MiltBrad-14
84Nes/792-100
84Nes/792-711LL
84Nes/792-712LL
84Nes/792-713LL
84OPC-100
84Ralston-19
84Seven-12W
84Smok/Cal-11
84T-100
84T-711
84T-712
84T-713
84T/Cereal-19
84T/St-102B
84T/St-231
84T/Super-21
85CircK-13
85D-57
85D/AAS-39
85Drake-17
85F-303
85F-639IA
85F/LimEd-14
85GenMills-19
85Leaf-170
85OPC-200
85Seven-12C
85Seven-13W
85Smok/Cal-2
85T-200
85T/3D-14
85T/Gloss22-19
85T/Gloss40-15
85T/St-187
85T/St-220
85T/Super-29
86BK/AP-12
86D-377
86D/HL-10
86Dorman-11
86Drake-3
86F-160
86F/HOF-6
86F/LimEd-26
86F/Mini-32
86F/Slug-18
86F/St-65
86Jiffy-8
86Leaf-173
86Meadow/Blank-7
86Meadow/Stat-6
86OPC-394
86OPC/WaxBox-I
86Quaker-26
86Sf-145M
86Sf-147M
86Sf-37
86Sf-59M
86Sf-61M
86Sf-71M
86Sf/Dec-53
86Smok/Cal-2
86T-700
86T/3D-13
86T/Gloss60-2
86T/St-177
86T/Super-35
86T/WaxBox-I
86TrueVal-13
86Woolwth-15
87Classic-24
87D-210
87D/OD-22
87F-84
87F/Up-U49
87KMart-16
87Leaf-201
87Mother/A's-27M
87Mother/A's-5
87OPC-300
87RedFoley/St-108
87Sf-44
87Smok/A's-7
87T-300
87T-312TBC
87T/Coins-15
87T/Gloss60-54
87T/HL-4
87T/Tr-52T
87Woolwth-4
88F-283
88Panini/St-175
88S-500
88S-504
88Sf-120
89Pac/Leg-111
89Smok/Angels-15
89T/LJN-33
90BBWit-42
90HOF/St-88
90UD/Jackson-Set
91BBBest/RecBr-8
91Crown/Orio-217
91Mother/A's-28CO

Jackson, Reggie
83Lynch-1
84Jacks-5

Jackson, Robert
85Everett/II/Cram-6

Jackson, Roland
(Sonny)
65OPC-16R
65T-16R
66T-244R
67T-415
68Coke
68Dexter-40
68OPC-187
68T-187
69MB-128
69OPC-53
69T-53
69T/St-5
70OPC-413
70T-413
71MLB/St-12
71OPC-587
71T-587
72MB-160
72OPC-318
72T-318
73OPC-403
73T-403
74Greyhound-6M
74OPC-591
74T-591
79Savan-8CO
80Ander-8CO
83Pol/Atl-36
84Durham-30CO
85Richm-25CO
87Greenvl/Best-3CO
89Richm/Bob-10CO
89Richm/CMC-24CO
89Richm/ProC-832
90Richm/CMC-2CO
90Richm/ProC-277CO
90Richm/Team-14CO
91Richm/LineD-450CO
91Richm/ProC-2587CO

Jackson, Ron H.
55Armour-9
55T-66
55T/DH-49
56T-186
58T-26
59T-73
60L-29
60T-426

Jackson, Ron
85Louisvl-30
86Bakers-15
87Gaston-20
88Vanco/ProC-768
89BirmB/Best-26
89BirmB/ProC-113

Jackson, Ronnie D.
75SLCity
77BurgChef-120
77T-153
78T-718
79K-59
79OPC-173
79T-339
80OPC-5
80T-18
81D-489
81F-557
81OPC-271
81T-631
81T/St-103
82D-602
82F-269
82OPC-359
82Spokane-21
82T-488
82T/Tr-48T
83D-639
83F-94
83T-262
84D-133
84F-521
84Nes/792-548
84Smok/Cal-12
84T-548
89Pac/SenLg-92

89T/SenLg-117
89TM/SenLg-54
90EliteSenLg-70
90Saraso/Star-28CO
91Crown/Orio-218
91Pac/SenLg-5

Jackson, Roy Lee
78Tidew
79Tidew-1
80Tidew-19
81D-36
81T-223
81T/Tr-775
82D-541
82OPC-71
82OPC/Post-7
82T-71
83D-479
83F-431
83OPC-194
83T-427
84D-195
84F-158
84Nes/792-339
84OPC-339
84T-339
84Tor/Fire-18
85D-606
85F-108
85Leaf-106
85OPC-37
85T-516
85T/St-364
86F-326
86T-634
87F-545
87T-138
91WIZMets-198

Jackson, Travis C.
(Stonewall)
25Exh-35
29Exh/4-10
31Exh/4-9
33CJ/Pin-14
33G-102
34DS-63
35BU-180
35G-1K
35G-3B
35G-4B
35G-5B
35Wheat
40PB-158
61F-115
80Pac/Leg-87
91Conlon/Sport-42
R315-A18
R315-B18
V354-24
W517-12
WG4-10
WG5-21
WG6-20

Jackson, Vince
91Kissim/ProC-4202

Jacob, Mark
83SanJose-12

Jacobo, Ed
85VeroB-10
86VeroB-12

Jacobs, Anthony R.
55T-183

Jacobs, Elmer
WG7-22

Jacobs, Forrest
(Spook)
52Park-54
53Exh/Can-46
54T-129
55Rodeo
55T-61
55T/DH-47
56T-151
56T/Hocus-A17
88Chatt/Team-15
PM10/Sm-82

Jacobs, Frank
91Pittsfld/ClBest-4
91Pittsfld/ProC-3429

Jacobs, Jake
89Eugene/Best-4
90AppFox/Box-13
90AppFox/ProC-2090
91BBCity/ClBest-7
91BBCity/ProC-1394

Jacobs, Ron
77Holyo
78Holyo
79Vanco-3

Jacobsen, Nels
87BurlEx-3
88FSLAS/Star-9
88WPalmB/Star-12

Jacobsen, Robert
85VeroB-16
86VeroB-13

Jacobson, Albert
WG2-27

Jacobson, Jeff
82AubAs-3
85CharlO-3

Jacobson, Kevin
82Redwd-23

Jacobson, Merwin
90Target-379

Jacobson, William
(Baby Doll)
21Exh-80
25Exh-114
26Exh-114
87Conlon/2-43
88Conlon/4-14
D327
E120
E121/120
E121/80
E122
E126-45
E220
V100
V117-18
W514-61
W572
W573
W575

Jacobucci, Steve
89Pittsfld/Star-26TR
91Elmira/ClBest-30

Jacoby, Brook
80Ander-27
82Richm-13
83Richm-13
84D-542
84F/X-56
84T/Tr-55
84Wheat/Ind-26
85D-154
85F-452
85OPC-327
85Polar/Ind-26
85T-327
85T/St-251
85T/St-370YS
86D-154
86F-590
86F/Mini-116
86Leaf-82
86OhHenry-26
86OPC-116
86T-116
86T/St-207
87Classic-40
87D-104
87D-8DK
87D/AAS-37
87D/DKsuper-8
87D/OD-112
87F-253
87Gator-26
87Ho/St-22
87Leaf-134
87Leaf-8DK
87OPC-98
87RedFoley/St-53
87Sf-109
87T-405
87T/St-212
88D-131
88D/Best-229
88F-612
88F/Excit-22
88F/St-20
88Gator-26
88Leaf-51
88OPC-248
88Panini/St-76
88S-39
88Sf-72
88T-555
88T/Big-17
88T/St-211
88T/UK-38
89B-86
89D-114
89D/Best-61
89F-408
89OPC-1
89Panini/St-326
89RedFoley/St-65
89S-19
89Sf-192
89T-141TL
89T-739
89T/Big-195
89T/St-212
89UD-198
90B-341
90D-83
90D/BestAL-75
90F-493
90Leaf/I-74
90OPC-208
90Panini/St-58
90PublInt/St-561
90Richm25Ann/Team-12
90S-56
90Sf-155
90T-208
90T/Big-276
90T/St-219
90UD-459
90USPlayC/AS-5C
91B-59
91D-176
91DennyGS-9
91F-369
91F/Ultra-113
91F/UltraUp-U46
91Leaf/II-421
91Leaf/Stud-44
91OPC-47
91Panini/FrSt-216
91Panini/St-178
91S-162
91S/100SS-92
91T-47
91T/StClub/I-286
91UD-137
91UD/FinalEd-78F
92Classic/I-46
92D/II-670
92F-260
92S/II-577
92T-606
92UD-528

Jacoby, Don
91BurlInd/ProC-3322CO

Jacome, Jason
91Kingspt/ClBest-23
91Kingspt/ProC-3810

Jacques, Eric
89Wythe/Star-17
90Peoria/Team-24
91WinSalem/ClBest-6
91WinSalem/ProC-2825

Jaeckel, Paul
65T-386R

Jaffee, Irving
33SK-34

Jagnow, Jim
85BurlR-17

Jaha, John
86Cram/PCL-195
87Beloit-3
88Stockton/Cal-193
88Stockton/ProC-743
89AS/Cal-45
89Stockton/Best-16
89Stockton/Cal-165
89Stockton/ProC-380
89Stockton/Star-3
91ElPaso/LineD-188
91ElPaso/ProC-2756
91Single/ClBest-291
92D/II-398RR
92T-126M

Jaime, Ismael
85Tigres-16

Jaime, Juan
90Myrtle/ProC-2780
91Myrtle/ClBest-13
91Myrtle/ProC-2947

Jaime, Jorge
89LittleSun-17

Jakubowski, John
81Batavia-30

Jakubowski, Stan
77Ashvl
79Tucson-6

Jakucki, Sigmund
(Jack)
47Centen-11
47Signal

James, Art
79RochR-6

James, Artie
77Evansvl/TCMA-16

James, Bob
82Hygrade
84D-87
84F-277
84Nes/792-579
84OPC-336
84Stuart-10
84T-579
85Coke/WS-43
85D-279
85F-400
85F/Up-U60
85OPC-114
85T-114
85T/Tr-61T
86Coke/WS-43
86D-379
86F-209
86F/St-66
86OPC-284
86Sf-158
86T-467
86T/St-290
86T/Super-36
87Coke/WS-24
87D-493
87F-501
87F/St-67
87OPC-342
87RedFoley/St-15
87T-342
88D-507
88F-401
88OPC-232
88Panini/St-54
88T-232
88T/St-289

James, Calvin
86Osceola-15
87Osceola-7
88ColAst/Best-26

James, Charles
(Charlie)
60T-517
61T-561
62T-412
63J-163
63P-163
63T-83
64T-357
65OPC-141
65T-141
78TCMA-292

James, Chris
85Cram/PCL-29
85Phill/TastyK-43
86F/Up-U55
86Phill/TastyK-26
86Portl-10
87D-42RR
87F/Up-U50
87Leaf-42RR
87Phill/TastyK-18
87T/Tr-53T
88D-453
88D/Best-159
88F-307
88OPC-1
88Panini/St-362
88Phill/TastyK-14
88S-409
88S/YS/I-14
88T-572
88T/St-122
89B-404
89Coke/Padre-8
89D-312
89D/Best-266
89F-572
89OPC-298
89Padre/Mag-23
89Panini/St-156
89Phill/TastyK-12
89RedFoley/St-66
89S-202
89S/Tr-46
89T-298
89T/St-119
89T/Tr-56T
89UD-513
90B-340
90D-323
90D/GSlam-3
90F-161
90F/Up-U92
90Leaf/II-319
90OPC-178
90Panini/St-350
90PublInt/St-241
90S-498
90S/Tr-60T
90T-178
90T/St-105
90T/Tr-46T
90UD-435
90UD/Ext-798
91B-67
91D-227
91F-370
91F/Ultra-114
91Leaf/I-175
91Leaf/Stud-45
91OPC-494
91Panini/St-181
91S-491
91T-494
91T/StClub/II-422
91UD-140
92D/I-82
92F-112
92S/I-262
92T-709
92UD-560

James, Cleo
72OPC-117
72T-117
90Target-380

James, Darin
84Everett/Cram-6B
85Everett/II/Cram-7

James, Dewey
82Beloit-11
83Beloit/LF-3

James, Dion
82ElPaso-2
84D-31RR
84F/X-57
84Pol/Brew-14
85D-211
85F-584
85Gard-9
85Leaf-162
85Pol/Brew-14
85T-228
86D-89
86T-76
86Vanco-13
87Classic/Up-144
87D/OD-44
87F/Up-U51
87Smok/Atl-24
87T/Tr-54T
88D-190
88D/Best-29
88F-543
88F/Mini-64
88F/St-76
88OPC-82
88Panini/St-250
88S-395
88S/YS/I-7
88Sf-36
88T-408
88T/Big-220
88T/Coins-44
88T/Mini-40
88T/St-42
88T/UK-39
89B-277

89D-340
89D/Best-253
89F-594
89Panini/St-44
89S-163
89S/Tr-51T
89T-678
89T/Big-223
89T/St-24
89UD-587
90B-331
90D-428
90ElPasoATG/Team-14
90F-494
90OPC-319
90Panini/St-64
90PublInt/St-115
90S-514
90T-319
90T/Big-132
90UD-591
91D-348
91F-371
91OPC-117
91S-131
91T-117
91UD-399

James, Duane
85Tulsa-29
86Salem-13

James, Howard
90Cedar/Best-27GM

James, Jeff
69T-477
70OPC-302
70T-302

James, Joey
89Watertn/Star-10
90A&AASingle/ProC-127
90Clinton/Best-20
90Clinton/ProC-2554
90Foil/Best-127
91AS/Cal-33
91SanJose/ClBest-29
91SanJose/ProC-18
91Single/ClBest-378

James, John
60T-499
61T-457

James, Keith
87Pocatel/Bon-22

James, Mike
88GreatF-23
89Bakers/Cal-186
91SanAn/LineD-536
91SanAn/ProC-2969

James, Paul
86DayBe-13

James, Richard
83StPete-22

James, Robert Byrne
33G-208

James, Skip
75Phoenix-14
76Phoenix
77Phoenix
79Vanco-1

James, Sonny
84Savan-1

James, Todd
89PalmSp/Cal-56
91London/LineD-437
91MidldA/ProC-431

James, Troy
86Columbia-14
87Lynch-23
88Visalia/Cal-164
88Visalia/ProC-88

James, William
15CJ-153
88Conlon/5-17
BF2-52
D328-84
D329-88
D350/2-87
E135-84
M101/4-88
M101/5-87

Jamieson, Charles
21Exh-81
25Exh-82
28Exh-41
33G-171
D328-85
E120
E126-21
E135-85
R316
V100
W572

Jamison, Bob
87Nashvl-25M
89Nashvl/Team-26ANN

Janeski, Gerry
71MLB/St-543
71OPC-673
71T-673

Janikowski, Randy
88Boise/ProC-1619

Janney, Barry
77Spartan

Janowicz, Vic
53T-222
54B-203
54T-16
55B-114
72T/Test-8
91T/Arc53-222

Jansen, Larry
47HomogBond-22
48B-23
48L-56
49B-202
49Eureka-110
50B-66
51B-162
51FB
51T/RB-21
52B-90
52BR
52RM-NL10
52StarCal/L-78D
52T-5
52TipTop
53B/BW-40
54B-169
54NYJour
54T-200
73OPC-81CO
73T-81C
79TCMA-255
D305
R346-6

Jantzen, A.C.
N172

Janus, Ed
82Madis-33
83Madis/LF-1GM

Janvrin, Harold
15CJ-149
16FleischBrd-45
90Target-381
91Conlon/Sport-144
D327
D328-83
D329-89
D350/2-88
E135-83
M101/4-89
M101/5-88

Jaramillo, Rudy
76SanAn/Team-13
90Mother/Ast-27CO
91Mother/Ast-28CO

Jarlett, Al
46Sunbeam

Jarquin, Gersan
(Skeeter)
78RochR
79Holyo-13

Jarrell, Joe
87CharlO/WBTV-13
88CharlK/Pep-9

Jarrett, Mark
82Madis-12

Jarvis, John
90Greens/Best-14
90Greens/ProC-2666
90Greens/Star-8
91PrWill/ClBest-15
91PrWill/ProC-1431

Jarvis, Kevin
91Princet/ClBest-23
91Princet/ProC-3508

Jarvis, LeRoy
47TipTop
49Sommer-9
90Target-382

Jarvis, Ray
70OPC-361
70T-361
71OPC-526
71T-526

Jarvis, Robert Pat
(Pat)
67OPC-57
67T-57
68Coke
68Dexter-41
68OPC-134
68T-134
69MB-129
69MLB/St-114
69T-282
69T/St-6
70MLB/St-7
70OPC-438
70T-438
71MLB/St-13
71OPC-623
71T-623
71T/Coins-85
72MB-161
72T-675
73OPC-192
73T-192
78TCMA-264

Jaster, Larry
66Pep/Tul
67T-356
68OPC-117
68T-117
69T-496
69T/St-56
70OPC-124
70T-124
71MLB/St-14
71Richm/Team-8
72MB-162
86Durham-14CO
87Sumter-21
88Sumter/ProC-415
89Durham/Star-27
90Durham/Team-28CO
91Durham/ClBest-16CO
91Durham/ProC-1678CO

Jaster, Scott
86Columbia-15
87Lynch-21
88Clmbia/GS-25
89StLucie/Star-11
90Salinas/ProC-2732
91BirmB/LineD-64
91BirmB/ProC-1465

Jata, Paul
72OPC-257R
72T-257R

Jauss, Dave
90WPalmB/Star-30
91WPalmB/ClBest-27
91WPalmB/ProC-1245CO

Javier, Alfredo
73Cedar
75Iowa/TCMA-9

Javier, Ignacio
80Wichita-10

Javier, M. Julian
60T-133
61T-148
61T/St-89
62T-118
62T/St-185
63J-159
63P-159
63T-226
64T-446
64Wheat/St-23
65T-447
66T-436
67T-226
68Bz-5
68OPC-25
68T-25
69MB-130
69MLB/St-212
69T-497
69T/St-116
70MLB/St-140
70OPC-415
70T-415
71MLB/St-275
71OPC-185
71T-185
71T/Coins-39
72MB-163
72T-745
78TCMA-288

Javier, Stan
83Greens-24
84Nashvl-10
85Huntsvl/BK-20
86D-584
86F/Up-U56
86Tacoma-9
87D-590
87F/Up-U52
87T-263
88D/A's/Bk-NEW
88D/Best-155
88Mother/A's-15
88S-367
89D-185
89F-13
89Mother/A's-21
89OPC-248
89S-322
89T-622
89T/Big-277
89UD-581
90D-568
90F-12
90F/Up-U23
90Leaf/II-445
90Mother/A's-23
90OPC-102
90PublInt/St-308
90S-394
90S/Tr-52T
90S/YS/II-21
90T-102
90T/Tr-47T
90UD-209
91B-599
91D-239
91F-211
91Leaf/I-155
91Mother/Dodg-27
91OPC-61
91Panini/FrSt-61
91Pol/Dodg-5
91S-281
91T-61
91T/StClub/I-39
91UD-688
92D/I-322
92F-461
92S/II-583
92T-581

Javier, Vicente
88Billings/ProC-1824
89Greens/ProC-422
90Cedar/Best-4
90Cedar/ProC-2327
91Cedar/ClBest-18
91Cedar/ProC-2727

Jay, Joe
54JC-47
54T-141
55Gol/Braves-13
55JC-47
55T-134
58T-472
59T-273
60L-23
60Lake
60SpicSpan-9
60T-266
61Kahn
61T-233
61T/St-43
62Bz-13
62J-124
62Kahn
62P-124
62P/Can-124
62Salada-126
62Shirriff-126
62T-263M
62T-440
62T-58LL
62T/bucks
62T/St-116
63Exh
63FrBauer-10
63J-133
63Kahn
63P-133
63T-225
63T-7LL
64Kahn
64T-346
65Kahn
65OPC-174
65T-174
66T-406
78TCMA-216
90BBWit-81
Exh47

Jean, Domingo
90SoBend/ClBest-16
91MidwLAS/ProC-MWL10
91SoBend/ProC-2852

Jeannette, Joe
T3/Box-68

Jeansonne, Kevin
77Watlo

Jeffcoat, George
90Target-383

Jeffcoat, Hal
49Eureka-58
51B-211
52B-104
52T-341
53B/BW-37
53T-29
54B-205
55B-223
56T-289
57Kahn
57Sohio/Reds-10
57T-93
58Kahn
58T-294
59T-81
91T/Arc53-29

Jeffcoat, Mike
81Watlo-10
82Watlo-4
83Charl-2
84D-43RR
84F/X-58
84T/Tr-56
84Wheat/Ind-46
85D-251
85F-453
85T-303
86F-545
86Phoenix-10
86T-571
87OKCty-10
89F-524
89OkCty/CMC-4
89OkCty/ProC-1520
90D-521
90F-302
90Leaf/II-416
90Mother/Rang-19
90OPC-778
90S-158
90T-778
91B-278
91F-291
91Leaf/II-386
91Mother/Rang-19
91OPC-244
91S-174
91T-244
91T/StClub/I-216
92D/I-351
92F-309
92S/I-174
92T-464
92UD-597

Jefferies, Gregg
86Columbia-16
87TexLgAS-11
88AAA/ProC-40
88Classic/Blue-243
88D-657
88D/Mets/Bk-657
88F-137
88F/Mini-94
88Leaf-259
88S-645
88Tidew/CANDL-9
88Tidew/CMC-15

88Tidew/ProC-1600
89B-381
89Bz-16
89Classic-6
89Classic/Up/2-154
89D-35RR
89D/Best-152
89D/Rook-2
89F-38
89F/Excit-26
89F/LL-23
89F/Superstar-25
89Holsum/Discs-11
89Kahn/Mets-9
89KMart/DT-11
89Nissen-11
89OPC-233FS
89Panini/St-128
89S-600
89S/HotRook-1
89S/Mast-39
89S/YS/I-1
89Sf-223R
89Sf-90
89T-233FS
89T/Big-253
89T/DHTest-2
89T/HeadsUp-10
89T/JumboR-13
89T/LJN-19
89T/Mets/Fan-9
89T/UK-44
89ToysRUs-15
89UD-9RS
89Woolwth-22
90B-140
90Bz-14
90Classic/Up-T1
90D-270
90D/BestNL-117
90F-207
90HotRook/St-22
90Kahn/Mets-9
90Leaf/I-171
90Mets/Fan-9
90MLBPA/Pins-18
90OPC-457
90Panini/St-298
90PubIInt/St-136
90PubIInt/St-614
90S-468
90S/100Ris-10
90Sf-14
90Starline/LJS-12
90Starline/LJS-32
90T-457
90T/Big-57
90T/DH-36
90T/Gloss60-60
90T/JumboR-16
90T/St-324FS
90T/TVMets-24
90ToysRUs-16
90UD-166
91B-481
91BBBest/HitM-11
91Classic/200-117
91Classic/II-T40
91D-79
91F-151
91F/Ultra-221
91F/Ultra-397CL
91Kahn/Mets-9
91Leaf/II-465
91Leaf/Stud-206
91MajorLg/Pins-77
91OPC-30
91Panini/FrSt-80
91Panini/St-83
91Post-9
91S-660
91S/100SS-80
91Seven/3DCoin-8NE
91T-30
91T/StClub/I-257
91UD-156
91UD-95TC
91WIZMets-199
92D/I-372
92F-508
92S/I-192
92T-707
92UD-133

Jeffers, Steve
87Erie-6
88Spring/Best-20

Jefferson, George
86Negro/Frit-105

Jefferson, Jesse
73OPC-604R
73T-604R
74OPC-509
74T-509
75OPC-539
75T-539
75T/M-539
76OPC-47
76T-47
77OPC-184
77T-326
78BK/R-8
78OPC-22
78T-144
79OPC-112
79T-221
80OPC-244
80T-467
81F-419
82F-466
82F/St-173
82RedLob
82T-682
82T/Tr-49T
91Crown/Orio-219

Jefferson, Jim
86FSLAS-25
86Tampa-7
87Vermont-2
88Chatt/Best-19
88Nashvl/Team-13

Jefferson, Reggie
87Cedar-14
88Cedar/ProC-1146
89Chatt/Best-1
89Chatt/GS-12
90B-51
90CedarDG/Best-9
90Nashvl/CMC-22
90Nashvl/ProC-238
91B-678
91Classic/I-35
91D/Rook-55
91F/Ultra-379MLP
91Leaf/II-514
91Nashvl/LineD-263
91Nashvl/ProC-2164
91T/Tr-60T
91UD/Ext-746
91UD/FinalEd-73F
92D/I-12RR
92F-113
92S/I-409
92T-93
92T/91Debut-89
92UD-656

Jefferson, Stan
86Tidew-14
87Bohem-22
87D-642
87D/Rook-43
87F/Up-U53
87Sf/Rook-9
87T/Tr-55T
88Coke/Padres-22
88D-187
88F-587
88OPC-223
88Panini/St-411
88S-114
88S/YS/I-11
88Smok/Padres-12
88T-223
88T/Big-86
88T/St-109
89B-180
89Colum/CMC-28
89S-519
89T-689
89T/Big-165
91ColoSp/LineD-84
91Crown/Orio-220
91WIZMets-200

Jeffery, Scott
88Greens/ProC-1553
89Cedar/Best-3
89Cedar/ProC-913
89Cedar/Star-9
90Cedar/Best-25
91Chatt/ProC-1955

Jeffries, James
T3/Box-55

Jeffries, James
82BurlR-4

Jefts, Chris
86Penin-14
87DayBe-16

Jelic, Chris
86FtMyr-15
87Lynch-4
88Jacks/GS-8
89Jacks/GS-5
90T/TVMets-48
90Tidew/CMC-18
90Tidew/ProC-553
91Classic/I-66
91LasVegas/ProC-249
91LasVegas/LineD-285
91T/90Debut-76
91WIZMets-201

Jelinek, Joey
91Martins/ClBest-9
91Martins/ProC-3462

Jelks, Greg
86Portl-11
87Maine-9
87Maine/TCMA-12
87Phill/TastyK-45
88F-648
88Maine/CMC-18
88Maine/ProC-298
89Louisvl-24
89Louisvl/CMC-19
89Louisvl/ProC-1258

Jelks, Pat
85Greens-22
86NewBrit-14
88River/Cal-228
88River/ProC-1411
88Wichita-28

Jeltz, Steve
82Reading-15
83Portl-6
84Cram/PCL-205
85CIGNA-10
85D-44RR
85F-653R
85Phill/TastyK-11M
85Phill/TastyK-30
85T/Tr-62T
86CIGNA-9
86Phill/TastyK-30
86T-453
87Champion-2
87D-359
87D/OD-157
87F-178
87Phill/TastyK-30
87T-294
88D-576
88F-308
88OPC-126
88Panini/St-361
88Phill/TastyK-15
88S-435
88T-126
89D-431
89D/Best-271
89F-573
89Phill/TastyK-13
89S-355
89T-707
89T/Big-52
89T/St-114
89UD-219
90D-133
90F-562
90OPC-607
90PubIInt/St-242
90RedFoley/St-52
90S-421
90S/Tr-59T
90T-607
90T/St-113
90UD-495
91OPC-507
91RochR/LineD-457
91RochR/ProC-1908
91S-272
91T-507

Jemenez, Miguel
91SoOreg/ClBest-14

Jemison, Greg
77Ashvl
79WHave-15
83BurlR-27CO
83BurlR/LF-26CO
84Tulsa-14CO

Jendra, Rick
80Cedar-11

Jenkins, Anthony
91Savan/ClBest-25
91Savan/ProC-1666

Jenkins, Bernie
88AubAs/ProC-1959
89Osceola/Star-9
90ColMud/Best-10
90ColMud/ProC-1359
90ColMud/Star-15
90Foil/Best-66
91Jacks/LineD-563
91Jacks/ProC-938

Jenkins, Buddy Jr.
91James/ClBest-21
91James/ProC-3540

Jenkins, Dee
91Princet/ClBest-14
91Princet/ProC-3522

Jenkins, Fats
74Laugh/Black-28
86Negro/Frit-113

Jenkins, Fergie
66T-254R
67T-333
68Bz-10
68Kahn
68OPC-11LL
68OPC-9LL
68T-11LL
68T-410
68T-9LL
69MB-131
69MLB/St-122
69OPC-10LL
69OPC-12LL
69Sunoco/Pin-5
69T-10LL
69T-12LL
69T-640
69T/decal
69T/S-37
69T/St-15
70MLB/St-19
70OPC-240
70OPC-69LL
70OPC-71LL
70T-240
70T-69LL
70T-71LL
71Bz/Test-13
71MD
71MLB/St-35
71MLB/St-563
71OPC-280
71OPC-70LL
71OPC-72LL
71T-280
71T-70LL
71T-72LL
71T/Coins-7
71T/S-42
71T/tatt-10
71T/tatt-10a
72K-8
72MB-164
72OPC-410
72OPC-93LL
72OPC-95LL
72T-410
72T-93LL
72T-95LL
72T/Post-10
73K-28
73OPC-180
73T-180
73T/Lids-23
74Laugh/ASG-67
74OPC-87
74T-87
74T/DE-59
74T/St-236
75Ho-116
75K-22
75OPC-310LL
75OPC-60
75T-310LL
75T-60
75T/M-310LL
75T/M-60
76Ho-138
76OPC-250
76SSPC-255
76T-250
76T/Tr-250T
77BurgChef-31
77K-3
77OPC-187
77T-430
78BK/R-8
78T-420
79T-544
80K-47
80OPC-203
80T-390
81D-146
81F-622
81F/St-84
81T-158
82D-643
82F-320
82OPC-137
82T-624
83D-300
83F-498
83OPC-230
83OPC-231SV
83T-230
83T-231SV
83T-51TL
83T/St-224
83Thorn-31
84D-189
84D/Champs-33
84F-494
84Nes/792-456TL
84Nes/792-483
84Nes/792-706LL
84OPC-343
84Seven-20C
84T-456TL
84T-483
84T-706LL
84T/St-48
85West/2-46
88OkCty/CMC-6
88OkCty/ProC-50
88Pac/Leg-43
89Chatt/II/Team-14
89OkCty/CMC-25
89OkCty/ProC-1513
89Pac/SenLg-29
89T/SenLg-119
89TM/SenLg-55
90EliteSenLg-125
90EliteSenLg-97
91Pac/SenLg-108
91Swell/Great-45
91UD/HOF-H3
91UD/HOF-x

Jenkins, Garrett
89Elmira/Pucko-6
90FSLAS/Star-32
90WinHaven/Star-12
91Single/ClBest-72
91WinHaven/ClBest-22
91WinHaven/ProC-501

Jenkins, Jack
70OPC-286R
70T-286R
90Target-384

Jenkins, Jerry
77Newar
78BurlB
82ElPaso-13

Jenkins, Jon
90SoBend/ClBest-17
91Single/ClBest-219
91SoBend/ProC-2853

Jenkins, Jonathan
90Utica/Pucko-21

Jenkins, Mack
88Greens/ProC-1566
90Billings/ProC-3239CO
91Billings/ProC-3771CO
91Cedar/ClBest-28CO
91Cedar/ProC-2737CO

Jenkins, Norm
90Peoria/Team-3DIR

Jennings, Doug
86PalmSp-18
86PalmSp/Smok-26
87MidldA-16
87TexLgAS-4
88D/A's/Bk-NEW
88D/Rook-13
88F/Slug-22
88F/Up-U54
88Mother/A's-24
89D-505
89F-14
89S-459
89T-166
89Tacoma/CMC-19
89Tacoma/ProC-1541
89UD-585
90Tacoma/CMC-18
90Tacoma/ProC-101
91F-12
91S-819
91Tacoma/LineD-539

Jennings, Hugh
09Buster/Pin-6
10Domino-59
11Helmar-32
12Sweet/Pin-25A
12Sweet/Pin-25B
14CJ-77
15CJ-77
16FleischBrd-46
40PB-223
48Exh/HOF
50Callahan
60F-67
61F-47
72Laugh/GF-23
80SSPC/HOF
81Detroit-34MG
89HOF/St-16
89Smok/Dodg-11
90Target-385
91Conlon/Sport-16
92Conlon/Sport-556
D303
D327
D328-86
D329-90
D350/2-89
E101
E103
E104
E105
E106
E121/80
E135-86
E254
E270/2
E90/1
E92
E93
E94
E96
E98
L1-128
M101/4-90
M101/5-89
M116
S81-103
T201
T202
T205
T206
T213/blue
T215/blue
T215/brown
T216
T222
T3-18
W514-206
W515-34
W555
W575
WG4-11
WG5-22
WG6-21

Jennings, Lance
91AppFx/ClBest-13
91AppFx/ProC-1719

Jennings, William
52Park-5

Jenny, Shane
88Kenosha/ProC-1401

Jensen, Dave
85Lynch-8

Jensen, Forrest
(Woody)
R313
R314

Jensen, Jackie
49Remar
51B-254
52B-161
52Dix-53
52T-122
53B/Col-24
53Briggs
53Dix
53NB
53RM-AL6
53T-265
54B-2
54Dix
54T-80
55Armour-10
55RM-AL19
55T-200
56T-115
56T/Pin-24OF
57Swift-15
57T-220
58Hires-56
58T-130
58T-489AS
59Armour-10
59Bz
59HRDerby-8
59T-400
60Bz-21
60T/tatt-23
60T/tatt-90
61T-173M
61T-476MV
61T-540
61T/St-112
62J-62
62P-62
62P/Can-62
62Salada-73
62Shirriff-73
75OPC-196MV
75T-196MV
75T/M-196MV
79TCMA-229
91T/Arc53-265
Exh47
PM10/Sm-83
PM10/Sm-84
PM10/Sm-85

Jensen, John
(Swede)
49B/PCL-13

Jensen, John
89WinSalem/Star-10
90WinSalem/Team-15
91CLAS/ProC-CAR43
91WinSalem/ClBest-25
91WinSalem/ProC-2842

Jensen, Marcus
90A&AASingle/ProC-171
90Everett/Best-14
90Everett/ProC-3130

Jenson, Jeff
91SoOreg/ProC-3836

Jernigan, Pete
63MilSau-3
63T-253R

Jesperson, Bob
91Billings/ProC-3767

Jessup, Steve
88Utica/Pucko-28

Jestadt, Garry
70OPC-109R
70T-109R
71OPC-576R
71T-576R
72OPC-143
72T-143
77Phoenix

Jester, Billy
86Clearw-10

Jeter, John
70OPC-141R
70T-141R
71MLB/St-205
71OPC-47
71T-47
72OPC-288
72T-288
73OPC-423
73T-423
74OPC-615
74T-615

Jeter, Shawn
87Dunedin-21
88Dunedin/Star-12
89Knoxvl/Best-10
89Knoxvl/ProC-1130
89Knoxvl/Star-8
90Knoxvl/Best-6
90Knoxvl/ProC-1257
90Knoxvl/Star-6
91Syrac/LineD-506
91Syrac/ProC-2493

Jethroe, Sam
50B-248
51B-242
51BR-D10
51T/BB-12
52B-84
52T-27
53B/Col-3
53Exh/Can-10
79TCMA-44
86Negro/Frit-38
89Pac/Leg-206
89Swell-62

Jevne, Frederick
N172

Jewell, Jim
43Centen-12

Jewell, Mike
91Watertn/ClBest-7
91Watertn/ProC-3362

Jewett, Earl
89Pulaski/ProC-1897
90Sumter/Best-7
90Sumter/ProC-2429
91Macon/ClBest-2
91Macon/ProC-856

Jewett, Trent
89Salem/Star-11
90Harris/ProC-1197
90Harris/Star-10
91CaroMud/LineD-125CO

Jewtraw, C.
33SK-11

Jimaki, Jim
88CapeCod/Sum-84

Jimenez, Alex
88Clmbia/GS-15
89Clmbia/Best-29
89Clmbia/GS-12
91Tidew/LineD-560
91Tidew/ProC-2518

Jimenez, Cesar
86Durham-15
87Durham-1
88Durham/Star-8
88F/Up-U72

Jimenez, Felix
(Elvio)
65OPC-226R
65T-226R
69T-567R

Jimenez, German
88F/Up-U72
89Greenvl/ProC-1153
89Greenvl/Star-10
89Greenvl/Best-23
89T-569
89UD-113

Jimenez, Houston
83Toledo-15
84Nes/792-411
84T-411
85D-269
85F-282
85T-562
85Toledo-16
87Vanco-12

Jimenez, Juan
86BurlEx-11C

Jimenez, Manuel
62T-598R
63J-87
63P-87
63T-195
64T-574
66T-458
67T-586
68T-538
69MB-132

Jimenez, Manuel
75QuadC

Jimenez, Manuel
91Pulaski/ClBest-7
91Pulaski/ProC-4013

Jimenez, Miguel
91SoOreg/ProC-3837

Jimenez, Ramon
90Foil/Best-40
90Greens/Best-17
90Greens/ProC-2669
90Greens/Star-9
90SALAS/Star-13
91PrWill/ClBest-18
91PrWill/ProC-1435

Jimenez, Ray
83Peoria/LF-1

Jimenez, Roberto
90Burllnd/ProC-3011

Jiminez, Alex
86LitFalls-15
87Columbia-28

Jiminez, Luis
78Charl

Jiminez, Vincent
90Pulaski/Best-14
90Pulaski/ProC-3092

Jirschele, Mike
78Ashvl
79Wausau-21
80Ashvl-28
80Tulsa-15
81Tulsa-29
82Tulsa-19
83OKCty-10
84OKCty-9
85OKCty-4
89Omaha/CMC-17
90AppFox/Box-14CO
90AppFox/ProC-2112CO
90TulsaDG/Best-20
91AppFx/ClBest-27CO
91AppFx/ProC-1732CO

Job, Ryan
85Osceola/Team-18
86ColumAst-15

Jockish, Mike
88StCath/ProC-2031
89StCath/ProC-2078
90Erie/Star-10

Jodo, Daijiro
88SanJose/Cal-120

Johdo, Joe
88SanJose/ProC-136

John, Oliver
E270/2

John, Tommy
64T-146R
65OPC-208
65T-208
66T-486
67T-609
68OPC-72
68T-72
69MB-133
69MLB/St-31
69NTF
69T-465
69T/St-155
69Trans-22
70MLB/St-186
70OPC-180
70T-180
71K-74
71MD
71OPC-520
71T-520
71T/Coins-56
72MB-165
72OPC-264
72T-264
73OPC-258
73T-258
74OPC-451
74T-451
75OPC-47
75T-47
75T/M-47
76OPC-416
76SSPC-69
76T-416
77T-128
78Ho-7
78K-36
78T-375
79BK/Y-9
79OPC-129
79T-255
80OPC-348
80T-690
81D-107
81F-81
81F/St-121
81K-52
81OPC-96
81T-550
81T/HT
81T/SO-52
81T/St-114
81T/St-250
81T/St-2M
82D-409
82D-558M
82F-40
82F/St-115
82OPC-75
82T-486TL
82T-75
82T/St-214
83D-570
83F-95
83OPC-144SV
83OPC-196
83Seven-9
83T-735
83T-736A
84D-301
84D/Champs-36
84F-522
85FunFood/Pin-92
84Nes/792-415
84Nes/792-715LL
84OPC-284
84Smok/Cal-13
84T-415
84T-715LL
84T/St-232
85D-423
85F-304
85OPC-179
85Smok/Cal-23
85T-179
85T/St-229
86F-422
86F/Up-U57
86T-240
87F-102
87OPC-236
87Smok/Dodg-15
87T-236
88D-17DK
88D-401
88D/Best-220
88D/DKsuper-17DK
88D/Y/Bk-401
88F-211
88Leaf-17DK
88Leaf-230
88Panini/St-148
88S-240
88Sf-122
88T-611
89Classic-40
89F-255
89S-477
89Smok/Dodg-91
89T-359
89T/LJN-64
89T/St-310
89UD-230
90Target-386

Johnigan, Steve
87Watlo-4

Johns, Douglas
90SoOreg/Best-5
91Madison/ClBest-9
91Madison/ProC-2126

Johns, Ronald M.
86FSLAS-26
86StPete-15
87Spring/Best-6
88Harris/ProC-849

Johnson, Abner
78Wisco

81CharR-19
Johnson, Alex
64PhilBull-15
65T-352
66OPC-104
66Pep/Tul
66T-104
67OPC-108
67T-108
68T-441
69Kahn
69T-280
69T/St-25
70MLB/St-173
70OPC-115
70T-115
71JB
71K-54
71MD
71MLB/St-346
71MLB/St-564
71OPC-590
71OPC-61LL
71T-590
71T-61LL
71T/Coins-84
71T/GM-17
71T/S-8
71T/tatt-15
72MB-166
72OPC-215
72T-215
73OPC-425
73T-425
74OPC-107
74T-107
74T/St-237
75OPC-534
75T-534
75T/M-534
77T-637
Johnson, Andre
91Pulaski/CIBest-12
91Pulaski/ProC-4018
Johnson, Anthony
80Memphis-3
83D-629
83Syrac-22
84Syrac-7
90Pulaski/Best-21
90Pulaski/ProC-3086
Johnson, Arthur
91Niagara/CIBest-3
Johnson, Avery
89Burllnd/Star-13
Johnson, Ban
50Callahan
61F-48
63Bz/ATG-16
69Bz-Sm
80SSPC/HOF
88Pac/8Men-78
89HOF/St-96
WG1-4
WG2-28
Johnson, Ben
60T-528
Johnson, Ben
88Alaska/Team-10
90Welland/Pucko-6
Johnson, Bert
82CharR-9
Johnson, Bill
83Reading-7
84Iowa-29
85Iowa-16
Johnson, Billy
87Louisvl-30
89Spokane/SP-12
90CharRain/Best-12
90CharRain/ProC-2040
91CharRain/CIBest-8
91CharRain/ProC-94
Johnson, Bob
79Wausau-12
Johnson, Bobby E.
78Ashvl
80Tulsa-21
82T-418R
83D-494
83Rang-8
83T/Tr-48
84D-500
84F-420
84Nes/792-608
84T-608
Johnson, Brian
88Burllnd/ProC-1798
89Kinston/Star-10
90CLAS/CL-40
90Foil/Best-214
90Greens/Best-13
90Greens/ProC-2665
90Greens/Star-10
90Kinston/Team-6
90SALAS/Star-14
90T/TVYank-47
91ColoSp/LineD-85
91ColoSp/ProC-2186
91FSLAS/ProC-FSL14
91FtLaud/CIBest-16
91FtLaud/ProC-2429
91Single/CIBest-9
Johnson, C. Barth
(Bart)
70T-669R
71OPC-156
71T-156
72OPC-126
72T-126
73OPC-506
73T-506
74OPC-147
74T-147
75OPC-446
75T-446
75T/M-446
76OPC-513
76T-513
77BurgChef-77
77T-177
Johnson, Carl
88VeroB/Star-12
89Kenosha/ProC-1065
89Kenosha/Star-9
90Burllnd/ProC-3006
91Kinston/CIBest-3
91Kinston/ProC-315
Johnson, Charles
81GlenF-4
Johnson, Charles
91T/Tr-61T
Johnson, Charles
(Chuck)
87Savan-2
88Spring/Best-12
89StPete/Star-19
Johnson, Chet
45Centen-12
Johnson, Chris
88Beloit/GS-25
89Beloit/I/Star-10
89Beloit/II/Star-16
90A&AASingle/ProC-137
90AS/Cal-56
90Stockton/Best-15
90Stockton/Cal-176
90Stockton/ProC-2174
91B-45
91ElPaso/LineD-189
91ElPaso/ProC-2743
91Single/CIBest-282
91UD-56
Johnson, Cliff
75OPC-143
75T-143
75T/M-143
76OPC-249
76SSPC-51
76T-249
77T-514
78BK/Y-3
78T-309
79BK/Y-3
79OPC-50
79T-114
80OPC-321
80T-612
81D-484
81F-303
81OPC-17
81T-17
81T/Tr-776
82F-93
82Granny-5
82OPC-333
82T-422
82T/St-226
83D-601
83F-520
83T-762
83T/Tr-49
84D-512
84F-159
84Nes/792-221
84OPC-221
84T-221
84T/St-366
84Tor/Fire-19
85D-512
85F-109
85F/Up-U61
85Leaf-115
85OPC-7
85Rang-44
85T-4RB
85T-568
85T/St-367
85T/Tr-63T
85Woolwth-20
86Ault-44
86D-639
86F-62
86Leaf-250
86OPC-348
86T-348
86Tor/Fire-19
87D-645
87F-230
87OPC-118
87T-663
90EliteSenLg-83
Johnson, Clifford
(Connie)
56T-326
57T-43
58T-266
59T-21
91Crown/Orio-222
Johnson, Clinton
81Bristol-20
Johnson, Curtis
88StCath/ProC-2022
89Myrtle/ProC-1470
Johnson, Dana
87Dunedin-8
Johnson, Dante
88Billings/ProC-1812
89Greens/ProC-417
Johnson, Daron
89Welland/Pucko-14
Johnson, Darrell
54Esskay
57T-306
58T-61
59T-533
60T-263
62T-16
74OPC-403MG
74T-403MG
75OPC-172MG
75T-172MG
75T/M-172MG
76SSPC-417MG
76T-118MG
77T-597MG
78T-79MG
79T-659MG
83T-37MG
91Crown/Orio-223
Johnson, David Allen
(Davey)
65T-473R
66T-579R
67T-363
68Coke
68Dexter-42
68T-273
69MB-135
69MLB/St-4
69OPC-203
69T-203
69T/St-125
70MLB/St-150
70OPC-45
70T-45
71MD
71MLB/St-301
71OPC-595
71T-595
71T/Coins-2
71T/tatt-4
72K-43
72MB-168
72OPC-224WS
72T-224WS
72T-680
73OPC-550
73T-550
74K-50
74OPC-45
74T-45
74T/St-6
75OPC-57
75T-57
75T/M-57
78T-317
83Tidew-23
84Jacks/Smk-6MG
84T/Mets/Fan-1MG
84T/Tr-57MG
85Pol/MetYank-M2MG
85T-492MG
86T-501MG
87T-543MG
88D/AS-42MG
88D/PopUp-20MG
88Kahn/Mets-5MG
88T-164MG
88T/Gloss22-12MG
89Kahn/Mets-5MG
89T-684MG
90Kahn/Mets-5MG
90OPC-291MG
90Pac/Legend-33
90Swell/Great-61
90T-291MG
90T/TVMets-1MG
91Crown/Orio-224
91LineD-34
91Swell/Great-46
Johnson, David C.
77T-478R
78T-627
91Crown/Orio-225
Johnson, David M.
77SanJose-24
78StPete
79ArkTr-21
80ArkTr-14
Johnson, David Wayne
(Dave)
84PrWill-30
85Nashua-12
86Hawaii-12
86QuadC-15
87Vanco-9
88BuffB/CMC-4
88BuffB/Polar-2
88BuffB/ProC-1476
89RochR/CMC-11
89RochR/ProC-1656
90D-702
90F/Up-U67
90Leaf/II-434
90OPC-416
90S-528
90S/100Ris-43
90T-416
90UD-425
91Crown/Orio-226
91D-126
91F-479
91F/Ultra-18
91Leaf/I-248
91OPC-163
91Panini/St-199
91T-163
91T/StClub/I-117
91UD-299
92F-12
92S/II-604
92T-657
Johnson, David
83AlexD-20
87PalmSp-3
Johnson, Dean
85LitFalls-25
Johnson, Deron Jr.
86Cram/PCL-105
87Wausau-18
88Albany/ProC-1351
88Watertn/Pucko-20
Johnson, Deron
59T-131
60T-134
61T-68
62T-82
64T-449
65Kahn
65MacGregor-5
65OPC-75
65T-75
66Kahn
66T-219LL
66T-440
67Kahn
67OPC-135
67T-135
68Kahn
68T-323
69MB-136
69T-297
70OPC-125
70T-125
70T/CB
71MLB/St-182
71OPC-490
71T-490
71T/Coins-79
71T/S-58
72MB-169
72OPC-167
72OPC-168IA
72T-167
72T-168A
73OPC-590
73T-590
74OPC-312
74T-312
74T/St-227
76OPC-529
76T-529
78Cr/PCL-10
78TCMA-213
84Phill/TastyK-11CO
85Mother/Mar-27CO
86Mother/Mar-28CO
90Augusta/ProC-2472
90Swell/Great-34
Johnson, Dodd
86Sumter-11
87Durham-28
88Durham/Star-9
89Penin/Star-8
Johnson, Dominick
87Pocatel/Bon-15
89Clinton/ProC-904
90SanJose/Best-25
90SanJose/Cal-47
90SanJose/ProC-2011
90SanJose/Star-13
Johnson, Don
47TipTop
52T-190
53B/BW-55
54T-146
55B-101
55Esskay
55T-165
91Crown/Orio-227
Johnson, Earl
47TipTop
49B-231
50B-188
51B-321
52Mother-14
Johnson, Earnie
91Saraso/CIBest-5
91Saraso/ProC-1108
Johnson, Erik
87Pocatel/Bon-29
88Clinton/ProC-708
88MidwLAS/GS-3
89Shreve/ProC-1845
90Phoenix/ProC-19
90Shrev/Star-13
91Shrev/LineD-309
91Shrev/ProC-1829
Johnson, Ernest R.
21Exh-82
E120
E220
V100
W573
Johnson, Ernest T.

53JC-7
53SpicSpan/3x5-13
54B-144
54JC-32
54SpicSpan/PostC-10
55B-157
55Gol/Braves-14
55JC-32
55SpicSpan/DC-9
56T-294
57SpicSpan/4x5-10
57T-333
58T-78
59T-279
60T-228
91Crown/Orio-228

Johnson, Frank
69T-227
71MLB/St-253
71OPC-128
71T-128
75Phoenix-23

Johnson, George
78Laugh/Black-25

Johnson, Greg
77QuadC
79Savan-10

Johnson, Greg
87AubAs-18
88Ashvl/ProC-1051
89Ashvl/ProC-959
90A&AASingle/ProC-42
90OrlanSR/Best-15
90OrlanSR/ProC-1078
90OrlanSR/Star-7
91OrlanSR/LineD-482
91OrlanSR/ProC-1844
91Single/ClBest-105

Johnson, Hank
33G-14
92Conlon/Sport-382
R314/Can
R337-409
V353-14

Johnson, Home Run
74Laugh/Black-22
86Negro/Frit-109

Johnson, Howard
81BirmB
83D-328
83F-332
85D-247
85F-12
85F/Up-U62
85OPC-192
85T-192
85T/St-262
85T/Tr-64T
86D-312
86F-85
86OPC-304
86T-751
86T/Mets/Fan-6
86T/St-101
87D-646
87D/HL-43
87D/OD-132
87F-13
87OPC-267
87T-267
88D-569
88D/Best-97
88D/Mets/Bk-569
88F-138
88F/Mini-95
88F/RecSet-20
88F/St-104
88Kahn/Mets-20
88KayBee-14
88Leaf-238
88OPC-85
88OPC/Waxbox-K
88Panini/St-343
88Panini/St-439
88RedFoley/St-40
88S-69
88Sf-138
88Sf/Gamewin-17
88T-85
88T/Big-129
88T/Gloss60-52
88T/Mets/Fan-20
88T/Mini-61
88T/St-99
88T/WaxBox-K
89T/Ames-18
89D-235
89D/Best-126
89F-39
89Kahn/Mets-20
89OPC-383
89S-136
89T-383
89T/Big-208
89T/DHTest-10
89T/Gloss60-22
89T/St-91
89T/St/Backs-41
89UD-582
90B-133
90BirmDG/Best-2
90Classic-144
90D-18DK
90D-654AS
90D-99
90D/BestNL-19
90D/Bon/MVP-BC2
90D/Preview-8
90D/SuperDK-18DK
90F-208
90F-639M
90F/ASIns-4
90F/AwardWin-20
90F/BB-21
90F/BBMVP-22
90F/WaxBox-C16
90Holsum/Discs-10
90Kahn/Mets-20
90KMart/SS-3
90Leaf/II-272
90Mets/Fan-20
90MLBPA/Pins-16
90OPC-399AS
90OPC-680
90Panini/St-210
90Panini/St-306
90Panini/St-385
90PublInt/St-137
90PublInt/St-265
90S-124
90S/100St-83
90Sf-109
90Sunflower-3
90T-399AS
90T-680
90T/Big-216
90T/Coins-50
90T/DH-37
90T/Gloss22-4
90T/Gloss60-43
90T/HillsHM-33
90T/Mini-67
90T/St-150AS
90T/St-90
90T/TVAS-53
90T/TVMets-25
90Tetley/Discs-2
90UD-263
90WonderBrd-17
91B-464
91BBBest/RecBr-9
91Classic/200-76
91Classic/III-40
91D-454
91DennyGS-11
91F-152
91F/Ultra-222
91Kahn/Mets-20
91Leaf/I-34
91Leaf/Stud-207
91OPC-470
91Panini/FrSt-81
91Panini/St-86
91RedFoley/St-52
91S-185
91S/100SS-86
91T-470
91T/CJMini/II-33
91T/StClub/I-86
91UD-124
91USPlayC/AS-4C
91WIZMets-203
92Classic/I-47
92D/Elite-E15
92D/I-341
92F-509
92F-689LL
92F/TmLIns-2
92S/100SS-68
92S/II-550
92S/II-776AS
92T-388AS
92T-590
92UD-256
92UD-37TC

Johnson, J.J.
91Classic/DP-33
91FrRow/DP-48
91Yakima/ClBest-6

Johnson, Jack
T3/Box-76

Johnson, James H.
21Exh-83

Johnson, James
81Clinton-19

Johnson, Jay
87Sumter-30

Johnson, Jeff
88Oneonta/ProC-2069
89PrWill/Star-9
90FtLaud/Star-10
91B-159
91ColClip/LineD-108
91ColClip/ProC-593
91D/Rook-47
91F/Up-U44
91S/RookTr-110T
91T/Tr-62T
92D/I-275
92S/100RisSt-40
92S/II-523
92T-449
92T/91Debut-90
92UD-626

Johnson, Jerry
69T-253
70OPC-162
70T-162
71MLB/St-254
71OPC-412
71T-412
72OPC-35
72OPC-36IA
72T-35
72T-36A
73OPC-248
73T-248
75OPC-218
75T-218
75T/M-218
76OPC-658
76T-658
78OPC-184
78T-169
84Louisvl-26

Johnson, Jerry
81ArkTr-11
81Hawaii-5
82Hawaii-5
83ArkTr-9
84Beaum-19
85RochR-18

Johnson, Jim
(Jimmy)
80Tucson-9
81Tucson-12
82Tucson-24MG
85Cram/PCL-53MG

Johnson, Jim
88GreatF-26

Johnson, Joe
84Richm-21
85IntLgAS-17
86D-624
86F-519
86Pol/Atl-38
86Syrac-15
87D-650
87F-231
87Leaf-91
87T/Tr-56T
87Tor/Fire-15
88Edmon/CMC-7
88Edmon/ProC-560
88OPC-347
88T-347
90Pawtu/CMC-7
90Pawtu/ProC-458
90T/TVRSox-47

Johnson, Joel
91Eugene/ClBest-26
91Eugene/ProC-3720

Johnson, John Henry
75Cedar
76Cedar
79Ho-39
79K-6
79OPC-361
79T-681
80OPC-97
80T-173
81T-216
82D-550
82F-321
82T-527
84D-91
84F-401
84Nes/792-419
84T-419
85Cram/PCL-246
85F-162
85T-734
86Vanco-14
87F-347
87Pol/Brew-38
87T-377

Johnson, John Ralph
N172

Johnson, John
87FtLaud-23

Johnson, Josh
86Negro/Frit-13
86Negro/Frit-63
91Negro/Lewis-26

Johnson, Judd
89Sumter/ProC-1102
90Foil/Best-193
90Greenvl/Best-13
90Greenvl/Star-8
91Greenvl/ClBest-2
91Greenvl/LineD-208
91Greenvl/ProC-2996

Johnson, Karl
89Elizab/Star-13

Johnson, Ken T.
60T-135
61BeeHive-10
61T-24
62T-278
63Pepsi
63T-352
64T-158
64T/S-2
64T/St-70
64T/SU
64T/tatt
65OldLond-13
65T-359
66T-466
66T/RO-96
67Kahn
67OPC-101
67T-101
68Coke
68Dexter-43
68T-342
69T-238
78TCMA-232
89Smok/Ast-5

Johnson, Ken
49Eureka-185
51B-293
D301

Johnson, Kevin
80Clinton-12

Johnson, Kevin
91Spokane/ClBest-20
91Spokane/ProC-3951

Johnson, Lamar
76OPC-596R
76T-596R
77BurgChef-76
77T-443
78Ho-59
78T-693
79Ho-43
79OPC-192
79T-372
80T-242
81Coke
81D-38
81F-350
81OPC-366
81T-589
81T/HT
81T/SO-26
81T/St-58
82D-269
82F-346
82T-13
82T/Tr-50T
83D-142
83F-571
83T-453
90EliteSenLg-7
91Denver/LineD-150CO
91Denver/ProC-138CO

Johnson, Lance
86ArkTr-8
87Louisvl-16
88Coke/WS-12
88D-31RR
88F-37
88Leaf-31RR
88T/Big-251
89AAA/ProC-30
89D-606
89F-499
89Panini/St-312
89RedFoley/St-67
89S/HotRook-33
89T-122
89Vanco/CMC-18
89Vanco/ProC-576
90Coke/WSox-9
90D-573
90F-536
90Leaf/I-259
90OPC-587
90S-570
90S/YS/II-38
90T-587
90T/Big-274
90UD-90
91B-349
91D-259
91F-123
91F/Ultra-76
91Kodak/WSox-1
91Leaf/II-403
91OPC-243
91Panini/FrSt-317
91Panini/St-253
91S-157
91T-243
91T/StClub/I-199
91UD-248
92D/I-267
92F-87
92S/I-146
92T-736
92UD-188

Johnson, Larry D.
80RochR-20
81Evansvl-12

Johnson, Lee
90Greenvl/ProC-1124
90Greenvl/Star-9
91Osceola/ClBest-5
91Osceola/ProC-677

Johnson, Lindsey
86Kinston-11
89Miami/II/Star-7
89Miami/I/Star-9

Johnson, Lloyd
34G-86

Johnson, Lou
60T-476
61BeeHive-11
63T-238
66OPC-13
66T-13
67T-410
68OPC-184
68T-184
69JB
69MB-137
69T-367
90Target-387

Johnson, Luther
88Martins/Star-18
89AubAs/ProC-2176
90Ashvl/ProC-2762
91Osceola/ClBest-25
91Osceola/ProC-699

Johnson, Marcel

90Kgsport/Best-23
90Kgsport/Star-12
Johnson, Mark
88CapeCod-2
88CapeCod/Sum-1
91Augusta/ClBest-15
91Augusta/ProC-811
91Eugene/ClBest-11
91Eugene/ProC-3738
Johnson, Mark
88TM/Umpire-51
89TM/Umpire-49
90TM/Umpire-47
Johnson, Mike
79AppFx-10
82Wausau-18
84Chatt-14
Johnson, Mitch
80Elmira-18
85Pawtu-19
86Pawtu-11
87Pawtu-8
87Pawtu/TCMA-7
88Pawtu/CMC-3
88Pawtu/ProC-455
89Tucson/CMC-2
89Tucson/ProC-187
89Tucson/JP-9
Johnson, North
91Kinston/ClBest-30
Johnson, Otis
T201
Johnson, Owen
66T-356R
Johnson, Paul
89Pittsfld/Star-12
Johnson, Perry
83Idaho-7
Johnson, Randall G.
81Richm-22
82BK/Lids-14
82Pol/Atl-6
83Pol/Atl-6
83T-596
84D-321
84F-183
84Nes/792-289
84Pol/Atl-6
84T-289
85D-531
85F-330
85Richm-14
85T-458
86Phoenix-11
89Everett/Star-16
90Clinton/Best-15
90Clinton/ProC-2561
Johnson, Randall S.
(Randy)
80GlenF/B-18
80GlenF/C-4
81GlenF-18
82T/Tr-51T
83D-305
83F-617
83T-354
83Toledo-21
85BuffB-14
Johnson, Randy
86WPalmB-21
87Jaxvl-23
87SLAS-16
88Indianap/CMC-1
88Indianap/ProC-510
89Classic-95
89D-42RR
89D/Best-80
89D/Rook-43
89F-381
89F/Up-59
89OPC-186
89Pac/SenLg-181
89Panini/St-111
89S-645RP
89S/HotRook-63
89S/Tr-77T
89S/YS/II-32
89Sf-224R
89T-647
89T/Big-287
89T/Tr-57T
89UD-25
89Woolwth-13
90B-468
90Classic/III-22
90D-379
90D/BestAL-111
90EliteSenLg-23
90F-518
90HotRook/St-23
90Leaf/II-483
90Mother/Mar-13
90OPC-431
90Panini/St-154
90S-415
90S/100Ris-52
90Sf-64
90T-431
90T/St-230
90UD-563
90USPlayC/AS-3S
91B-253
91Classic/200-35
91CounHrth-26
91D-134
91D-BC2
91F-455
91F/Ultra-339
91F/WaxBox-2
91Leaf/II-319
91Leaf/Stud-116
91MajorLg/Pins-6
91OPC-225
91Panini/FrSt-353
91Panini/St-188
91Panini/St-2
91RedFoley/St-53
91S-290
91S-700NH
91Seven/3DCoin-9NW
91T-225
91T/StClub/II-409
91UD-376
92D/DK-DK22
92D/I-207
92F-283
92S/II-584
92T-525
92UD-164
Johnson, Rich
86Ashvl-16
87ColAst/ProC-23
88ColAst/Best-14
Johnson, Robert Dale
70T-702R
71OPC-365
71OPC-71LL
71T-365
71T-71LL
72MB-167
72OPC-27
72T-27
73OPC-657
73T-657
74OPC-269
74T-269
74T/Tr-269T
91WIZMets-202
Johnson, Robert Lee
(Indian Bob)
34G-68
35BU-20
35Exh/4-14
35G-8J
35G-9J
36Exh/4-14
37Exh/4-14
37OPC-123
38Exh/4-14
38Wheat-6
39Exh
39PB-97
40PB-25
41DP-49
41PB-22
47Centen-12
47Signal
91Conlon/Sport-96
92Conlon/Sport-547
R314
V100
Johnson, Robert Wallace
62T-519
62T/St-97
63J-96
63P-96
63T-504
64T-304
65T-363
66OPC-148
66T-148
67OPC-38
67T-38
68T-338
69MB-134
69T-261
70T-693
78TCMA-79
91Crown/Orio-221
91WIZMets-204
Johnson, Roger
86Kinston-12
Johnson, Ron
90BBCity/Star-30CO
91BBCity/ClBest-29CO
91BBCity/ProC-1415CO
Johnson, Rondin
81Omaha-19
82Omaha-17
84Indianap-24
84Omaha-25
85Omaha-21
86Omaha-12
86Omaha/TCMA-2
87FtMyr-34
87Omaha-11
88Omaha/CMC-10
88Omaha/ProC-1515
Johnson, Roy
32Orbit/un-35
33G-8
34Exh/4-9
35BU-63
38Exh/4-1
44Centen-12
88Conlon/AmAS-17
91Conlon/Sport-199
R305
R316
R337
V353-8
Johnson, Roy
82Wichita-6
82Wichita-7M
83D-492
84Indianap-7
85Indianap-5
87Tacoma-15
88Tacoma/CMC-15
88Tacoma/ProC-621
Johnson, Scott
81Miami-21
87Watlo-9
88Kinston/Star-12
89SoBend/GS-6
90SoBend/Best-25TR
Johnson, Sean
88SLCity-30M
Johnson, Silas
33DH-24
35BU-54
47TipTop
R332-34
Johnson, Stan
61Union
Johnson, Steve
83Beaum-3
84Beaum-20
86Watlo-13
Johnson, Sylvester
39PB-28
40PB-99
43Centen-13
44Centen-13
45Centen-13
92Conlon/Sport-654
E120
V117-13
V61-24
W572
W573
Johnson, Terence
(T.J.)
84LitFalls-14
85LitFalls-19
Johnson, Terry
83BurlR-6
83BurlR/LF-10
83Tulsa-24
84Tulsa-34
85Tulsa-30
Johnson, Tim
74OPC-554
74T-554
75OPC-556
75T-556
75T/M-556
76A&P/Milw
76OPC-613
76T-613
77T-406
78T-542
79OPC-89
79T-182
80OPC-155
80T-297
89AS/Cal-23MG
89Bak/Cal-206MG
90Indianap/CMC-25MG
90Indianap/ProC-307MG
Johnson, Todd
91T/Tr-63T
Johnson, Tom
83MidldC-23
86BurlEx-12
87FtMyr-19
Johnson, Tom R.
75OPC-618R
75T-618R
75T/M-618R
76OPC-448
76T-448
77BurgChef-46
77T-202
78K-9
78T-54
79OPC-77
79T-162
80GlenF/B-3
80GlenF/C-28
81QuadC-13
88Virgini/Star-11
89BBCity/Star-11
Johnson, Tookie
90LSUPol-16
Johnson, Wallace
(Wally)
82F-192
82Wichita-8
83F-285
85Indianap-21
86Indianap-19
87F-321
87OPC-234
87T-588
88F-186
88OPC-228
88S-433
88T-228
89D-484
89F-382
89OPC-138
89Panini/St-120
89S-196
89T-138
89UD-124
90D-570
90F-351
90Leaf/II-344
90OPC-318
90PublInt/St-178
90S-479
90T-318
90T/Big-46
Johnson, Walter P.
10Domino-60
11Helmar-72
12Sweet/Pin-60A
12Sweet/Pin-60B
14CJ-57
15CJ-57
21Exh-84
25Exh-125
26Exh-125
27Exh-62
40PB-120
48Exh/HOF
48Swell-4
49Leaf/Prem-4
50Callahan
51T/CM
60Exh/HOF-13
60F-6
60NuCard-40
61F-49
61GP-29
61NuCard-440
61T-409HL
63Bz/ATG-12
69Bz-6
69Bz-Sm
72F/FFeat-8
72K/ATG-1
72Laugh/GF-2
73OPC-476LL
73OPC-478LL
73T-476LL
73T-478LL
76OPC-349AS
76T-349AS
79T-417LL
79T-418LL
80Pac/Leg-45
80Laugh/3/4/5-3
80Laugh/FFeat-25
80SSPC/HOF
83D/HOF-2
84D/Champs-37
85Woolwth-21
86Conlon/1-4
87Conlon/2-6
87Nestle/DT-9
89Pac/Leg-192
89Swell-3
90BBWit-62
90HOF/St-28
90Swell/Great-75
91Conlon/Sport-258
91Conlon/Sport-9
91LineD-45
91Swell/Great-130
92Conlon/Sport-353
92Conlon/Sport-564
BF2-45
D327
D328-87
D329-91
D350/2-90
E120
E121/120
E121/80
E122
E126-28
E135-87
E210-45
E224
E300
E91
L1-135
M101/4-91
M101/5-90
M116
PM1-7
PM10/Sm-86
R310
R423-54
S74-39
S81-110
T201
T202
T204
T205
T206
T207
T213/blue
T215/blue
T215/brown
T222
T3-99
V100
V117-30
V61-47
W501-17
W514-94
W515-38
W516-8
W573
W575
WG5-23
WG6-22
WG7-23
Johnson, Wayne
82Watlo/B-5
82Watlo/C-25
83BuffB-2
85Water-10
91Martins/ClBest-4

91Martins/ProC-3467
Johnson, William
44Yank/St-15
48B-33
48L-14
49B-129
50B-102
51B-74
51BR-A5
51T/BB-21
52B-122
52T-83
53Hunter
53T-21
79TCMA-230
91T/Arc53-21
Exh47
R346-1
Johnson, William
(Judy)
74Laugh/Black-36
78Laugh/Black-29
86Negro/Frit-4
86Negro/Frit-5
88Conlon/NegAS-6
88Negro/Duques-9
90Negro/Star-18
Johnson, Willy
88Sumter/ProC-417
89Sumter/ProC-1092
90Sumter/Best-26TR
Johnson, Ching
33SK-30
Johnston, Chris
83Knoxvl-11
Johnston, Craig
88Martins/Star-19
89Kingspt/Star-14
Johnston, Dan
88Geneva/ProC-1644
90Greens/Best-5
90Greens/ProC-2657
90Greens/Star-11
91PrWill/ClBest-6
91PrWill/ProC-1422
Johnston, Fred Ivy
90Target-388
Johnston, Greg
78Cr/PCL-47
79Phoenix
79T-726R
80T-686R
81T-328R
Johnston, James H.
25Exh-13
90Target-389
D327
D328-88
E120
E121/80
E122
E135-88
E220
V100
W515-41
W572
W575
Johnston, Jody
82Jacks-6
82Lynch-22
Johnston, Joel
88Eugene/Best-11
89BBCity/Star-12
90Memphis/Best-17
90Memphis/ProC-1010
91B-297
91Omaha/LineD-337
91Omaha/ProC-1031
92F-673
92S/II-764
92T-328
92T/91Debut-91
Johnston, John
16FleischBrd-47
Johnston, Mark
79WHave-1
82ElPaso-10
83Beloit/LF-10
Johnston, Richard
E223
N172
N284
N526

Johnston, Ryan
88Savan/ProC-352
Johnston, Stan
86Bakers-16TR
87Bakers-14TR
88Bakers/Cal-264
89Albuq/ProC-74
Johnston, Wheeler
(Doc)
15CJ-150
E120
W573
Johnstone, Jay
67T-213
68T-389
69JB
69MB-138
69OPC-59
69T-59
70MLB/St-174
70OPC-485
70T-485
70T/CB
71OPC-292
71T-292
72MB-170
72OPC-233
72T-233
75OPC-242
75T-242
75T/M-242
76OPC-114
76SSPC-463
76T-114
77BurgChef-166
77K-35
77OPC-226
77Pep-71
77T-415
78T-675
79BK/Y-5
79OPC-287
79T-558
80OPC-15
80Pol/Dodg-21
80T-31
81D-300
81F-128
81OPC-372
81Pol/Dodg-21
81T-372
82D-262
82F-10
82Pol/Dodg-21
82RedLob
82T-774
82T/Tr-52T
83D-561
83F-499
83OPC-152
83T-152
83T/St-220
83Thorn-21
84D-540
84F-495
84Nes/792-249
84SevenUp-21
84T-249
84T/St-50
85Coke/Dodg-16
86T-496
90Target-390
Johnstone, John
89Pittsfld/Star-13
90FSLAS/Star-7
91Single/ClBest-64
91Wmsprt/LineD-635
91Wmsprt/ProC-287
Joiner, Dave
88Clmbia/GS-16
89Clmbia/Best-8
89Clmbia/GS-13
Joiner, Roy
(Pop)
40PB-211
Jok, Stan
52Park-93
54T-196
55B-251
Jolley, Mike
91Savan/ClBest-6
91Savan/ProC-1647
Jolley, Smead
28Exh/PCL-13
30CEA/Pin-16
31Exh/4-20
32Orbit/num-25
32Orbit/un-36
87Conlon/2-23
88MinorLg/Leg-8
R305
R315-C3
R315-D3
V355-98
Jolly, Dave
53JC-8
53SpicSpan/3x5-14
54JC-17
54SpicSpan/PostC-11
54T-188
55B-71
55Gol/Braves-15
55JC-16
55SpicSpan/DC-10
55T-35
55T/DH-95
57T-389
58T-183
Jonas, John
90Salinas/Cal-144GM
Jonas, Pete
43Centen-14
47Centen-13
47Signal
Jones, Al
82AppFx-7
83AppFx/LF-20
85D-404
85T-437
86BuffB-13
86T-227
87Denver-26
Jones, Barry
85PrWill-3
86Hawaii-13
86Sumter-12
87D-602
87Durham-2
87F-611
87T-494
88F/Up-U114
88Greenvl/Best-8
88SLAS-14
88T-168
89Coke/WS-12
89D-647
89F-500
89Richm/Bob-11
89Richm/CMC-20
89Richm/Ko-18
89Richm/ProC-846
89S-333
89T-539
89T/SenLg-3
89UD-457
90Coke/WSox-10
90Leaf/II-431
90OPC-243
90Publint/St-390
90Richm/Bob-11
90Richm/CMC-12
90Richm/ProC-272
90Richm/Team-15
90S-152
90T-243
91B-439
91ColoSp/LineD-86
91ColoSp/ProC-2196
91D-534
91F-124
91F/UltraUp-U91
91Leaf/II-406
91OPC-33
91OPC/Premier-69
91Panini/St-259
91S-115
91S/RookTr-75T
91T-33
91T/StClub/II-551
91T/Tr-64T
91UD-39
91UD/Ext-789
92D/I-155
92F-484
92S/I-297
92T-361
92UD-681

Jones, Bill
86StPete-16
Jones, Bobby
(Ducky)
28Exh/PCL-14
Jones, Bobby
89BendB/Legoe-21
91MidldA/ProC-445
Jones, Bobby
91Classic/DP-32
91FrRow/DP-11
91London/LineD-438
Jones, Bobby
(Golfer)
33SK-38
Jones, Brian
85PrWill-31
86PrWill-13
87Harris-17
Jones, Bryan
76Watlo
Jones, Calvin
87Chatt/Best-6
88Vermont/ProC-962
89SanBern/Cal-64
89Wmsprt/Star-11
90SanBern/Best-3
90SanBern/Cal-96
90SanBern/ProC-2629
91Calgary/LineD-62
91Calgary/ProC-511
92D/II-690
92S/II-868
92T/91Debut-92
Jones, Carl
87Sumter-14
Jones, Charles
E107
T204
Jones, Charlie
83VeroB-6
Jones, Chipper
90Classic/DP-1
90Classic/DP-NNO
90Classic/III-92
90Classic/III-NO
91B-569
91Macon/ClBest-19
91Macon/ProC-872
91OPC-333FDP
91SALAS/ProC-SAL33
91S-671FDP
91Single/ClBest-268
91T-333FDP
91UD-55TP
92T-551M
Jones, Chris
78Wausau
82Tucson-2
83Tucson-19
84Cram/PCL-52
85Cram/PCL-51
Jones, Chris C.
86Cedar/TCMA-21
86Phoenix-12
87Dunedin-17
87Phoenix-1
87Vermont-22
88Chatt/Best-6
88Idaho/ProC-1843
88Knoxvl/Best-16
88SanDiegoSt-9
89Knoxvl/Best-11
89Knoxvl/ProC-1134
89Knoxvl/Star-9
89Nashvl/CMC-20
89Nashvl/ProC-1290
90Knoxvl/Best-20
90Knoxvl/ProC-1243
90Knoxvl/Star-7
90Nashvl/CMC-16
90Nashvl/ProC-246
91Albuq/LineD-11
91Albuq/ProC-1136
91B-676
91D/Rook-50
91S/RookTr-92T
91T/Tr-65T
92D/II-464
92F-410
92S/100RisSt-69
92S/II-811
92T-332

92T/91Debut-93
Jones, Chris L.
88CapeCod/Sum-164
Jones, Clarence W.
68T-506
86Sumter-13
87Sumter-6
88Richm/CMC-25
88Richm/ProC-17
Jones, Cleon Joseph
65T-308R
66OPC-67R
66T-67R
67Kahn
67OPC-165
67OPC/PI-13
67T-165
67T/PI-13
68T-254
69MB-139
69MLB/St-167
69T-512
69T/S-50
69T/St-65
70K-3
70MLB/St-78
70OPC-61LL
70T-575
70T-61LL
70T/CB
70Trans-1
70Trans/M-24
71MLB/St-156
71OPC-527
71T-527
71T/Coins-103
71T/tatt-1
72MB-171
72OPC-31
72OPC-32IA
72T-31
72T-32IA
73OPC-540
73T-540
74OPC-245
74OPC-476WS
74T-245
74T-476WS
74T/St-64
75Ho-123
75K-21
75OPC-43
75T-43
75T/M-43
91WIZMets-207
Jones, Craig
84Richm-13
Jones, D.J.
87Durham-23
Jones, Dan
83Miami-15
Jones, Dan
91Welland/ClBest-29
91Welland/ProC-3568
Jones, Darryl
78Cr/PCL-24
79Colum-28
80T-670R
Jones, David
11Helmar-33
81Detroit-19
E103
E104
E107
E254
E270/1
E93
M116
S74-15
T202
T205
T3-100
W555
Jones, David
85Durham-7
86Sumter-14
Jones, Dax
91Everett/ClBest-8
91Everett/ProC-3931
Jones, Dennis
87Myrtle-13
88BBAmer-19
88Knoxvl/Best-19

89Knoxvl/Best-12
89Knoxvl/ProC-1136
89Knoxvl/Star-10
90Knoxvl/Best-24
90Knoxvl/Star-8

Jones, DeWayne
88SoOreg/ProC-1698

Jones, Donny
77QuadC
80ElPaso-18

Jones, Doug
78Newar
79BurlB-12
81ElPaso-11
82Pol/Brew-45
82Vanco-13
84Cram/PCL-39
84ElPaso-7
85Water-12
86Maine-11
87Gator-46
88D-588
88D/Best-325
88F-613
88Gator-11
88S-594
88T-293
89B-78
89Classic-89
89D-438
89D/AS-20
89D/Best-173
89F-409
89F/BBAS-23
89F/BBMVP's-23
89OPC-312
89Panini/St-319
89Panini/St-5
89S-387
89S-656HL
89S/HotStar-41
89Sf-38
89T-690
89T-6RB
89T/LJN-152
89T/Mini-51
89T/St-215
89T/St-3
89T/St/Backs-32
89UD-540
89Woolwth-14
90B-328
90Classic-114
90D-320
90D/BestAL-61
90ElPasoATG/Team-15
90F-495
90F/BB-22
90F/LL-20
90Leaf/I-153
90OPC-75
90Panini/St-63
90PublInt/St-562
90S-130
90Sf-96
90T-75
90T/Big-316
90T/St-215
90UD-632
90USPlayC/AS-7S
91B-77
91Classic/200-55
91D-232
91F-372
91F/Ultra-115
91Leaf/I-57
91Leaf/Stud-46
91OPC-745
91Panini/FrSt-224
91Panini/St-173
91Panini/Top15-87
91RedFoley/St-54
91S-45
91S-884DT
91S/100SS-54
91T-745
91T/StClub/I-145
91UD-216
92D/II-674
92F-114
92S/I-53
92T-461

Jones, Earl
(Lefty)
48Signal
49Remar

Jones, Elijah
C46-52

Jones, Eric
81Batavia-22

Jones, Eugene
89Greens/ProC-416
90CharWh/Best-22
90CharWh/ProC-2253
90Foil/Best-207
91Cedar/ClBest-22
91Cedar/ProC-2732

Jones, Fielder
87Conlon/2-44
90HOF/St-20
90Target-391
BF2-41
D328-89
D329-92
D350/2-91
E135-89
M101/4-92
M101/5-91
T206
W514-50
WG2-29

Jones, Gary
71OPC-559R
71T-559R

Jones, Gary
91Madison/ClBest-22MG
91Madison/ProC-2146MG

Jones, Gary
83QuadC-21
86Fresno/Smok-4
87Tacoma-5
88SanJose/Cal-121
88SanJose/ProC-112
88Tacoma/CMC-23
88Tacoma/ProC-612
89Huntsvl/Best-17

Jones, Geary
86Columbia-17
87Lynch-17
88Jacks/GS-3

Jones, George
85Everett/Cram-6A
85Everett/Cram-6B

Jones, Glenn
82Clinton-21

Jones, Gordon
55Hunter
55T-78
55T/DH-6
59T-458
60L-73
60T-98
61T-442
91Crown/Orio-229

Jones, Gordon
82Redwd-5

Jones, Grover
(Deacon)
63T-253R

Jones, Gus
86Cram/PCL-47
87FtMyr-14

Jones, Hank
77LodiD
78LodiD
79LodiD-20

Jones, Harold
62T-49

Jones, J. Dalton
64T-459R
65OPC-178
65T-178
66T-317
67OPC-139
67T-139
67T/Test/RSox-8
68Coke
68Dexter-44
68OPC-106
68T-106
69MB-140
69T-457
70T-682
71MLB/St-395
71OPC-367
71T-367
72MB-172
72OPC-83
72T-83
73OPC-512
73T-512
89Pac/SenLg-55

Jones, James
88CapeCod-3
88CapeCod/Sum-70
89BendB/Legoe-5

Jones, Jeffrey A.
79Ogden/TCMA-23
81T-687
82D-213
82F-94
82F/St-130
82T-139
82Tacoma-24
83D-651
83T-259
83Tacoma-28
84Cram/PCL-82
84Nes/792-464
84T-464
85T-319

Jones, Jeffrey R.
80Cedar-19
81Cedar-16
82Cedar-24
84D-262
84MidldC-20
87GlenF-4
88GlenF/ProC-936
89Fayette/ProC-1570
90CedarDG/Best-19
90Toledo/CMC-26CO
90Toledo/ProC-165CO
91London/LineD-400CO
91London/ProC-1893CO
91Pac/SenLg-32

Jones, Jim
84Madis/Pol-14
86Modesto-15
87SLAS-12
88Tacoma/ProC-618
89Denver/ProC-40
89SanJose/Best-23
89SanJose/Cal-222
89SanJose/ProC-460
89SanJose/Star-16
90SanJose/Best-11
90SanJose/Cal-38
90SanJose/ProC-2016
90SanJose/Star-14

Jones, Jimmy
84Beaum-1
85Beaum-8
86Cram/PCL-25
86LasVegas-8
87D-557
87F-650R
87F/Up-U54
87LasVegas-17
87Pocatel/Bon-7
87Sf/Rook-35
88Coke/Padres-45PAN
88D-141
88D/Best-189
88F-588
88Huntsvl/BK-9
88S-246
88Smok/Padres-13
88T-63
88Tacoma/CMC-21
89AS/Cal-30
89B-169
89Colum/CMC-9
89Colum/Pol-10
89Colum/ProC-752
89D-247
89D/Best-217
89Denver/CMC-17
89F-308
89S-294
89S/NWest-26
89T-748
89T/Tr-58T
89UD-286
90ColClip/CMC-23
90ColClip/ProC-672
90OPC-359
90S/NWest-21
90T-359
90T/TVYank-48
91B-553
91F-667
91Leaf/II-371
91Mother/Ast-12
91S-583
92D/I-272
92F-438
92S/I-33
92T-184
92UD-392

Jones, Joe
77Spartan

Jones, Keith
(Kiki)
89GreatF-18
90AS/Cal-20
90B-86
90Bakers/Cal-230
90S-676DC
91Johnson/ClBest-16
91Johnson/ProC-3989
91Single/ClBest-212
91UD-59TP
91VeroB/ClBest-8
91VeroB/ProC-769

Jones, Keith
82BurlR-5
84Tulsa-6

Jones, Ken
78Wausau
81Water-4
82Water-4
83Water-4
87Madis-14

Jones, Kevin
85Osceola/Team-28BB
89Everett/Star-17
90Billings/ProC-3229
90CharWh/Best-17

Jones, Kirk
80Batavia-6

Jones, Kirk
85Osceola/Team-29BB

Jones, Lance
88CapeCod/Sum-133

Jones, Larry K.
80RochR-7
81RochR-19
82Iowa-17
82WHave-17
83Iowa-5

Jones, Lee
83Redwd-13

Jones, Lynn
78Indianap-20
80T-123
81T-337
82D-542
82F-270
82T-64
83F-333
83T-483
84Nes/792-731
84T-731
84T/Tr-58
85T-513
86D-466
86F-11
86NatPhoto-35
86T-671
91Pol/Royal-26CO

Jones, Mack
62T-186
63T-137
65OPC-241
65T-241
66Kahn
66T-446
67T-435
68Kahn
68T-353
69Fud's-5
69MLB/St-159
69T-625
69T/St-57
70Expos/Pins-8
70MLB/St-66
70OPC-38
70T-38
70T/SO
71MLB/St-131
71OPC-142
71T-142
71T/Coins-135
72MB-173
76Laugh/Jub-20

Jones, Mark
88Visalia/Cal-173

Jones, Marty
90AubAs/Best-15
90AubAs/ProC-3403

Jones, Michael C.
(Mike)
81Omaha-9
81T-66R
82Clinton-7
82F-412
82T-471R
84Omaha-20
84Shrev/FB-9
85D-640
85T-244
86D-419
86F-12
86Richm-10
86Shrev-12
86T-514
86Ventura-9
87Dunedin-4

Jones, Mike
74Cedar

Jones, Mike
88Bristol/ProC-1889
88Knoxvl/Best-4
88Nashvl/CMC-6
88Nashvl/ProC-485
88Nashvl/Team-14
89Lakeland/Star-11
89RochR/CMC-1
89RochR/ProC-1657
89Star/Wax-31
90RochR/CMC-4
90WichSt-18
91Billings/ProC-3761

Jones, Norm
89Denver/ProC-56

Jones, Odell
78Colum
78T-407
80Port-17
80T-342
81Portl-13
82Portl-4
83Rang-21
83T/Tr-50
84D-256
84F-421
84Nes/792-734
84OPC-382
84Rang-21
84T-734
85D-525
85F-560
85RochR-19
85T-29
86RochR-10
87D-582
87Syrac/TCMA-5
88Pol/Brew-28
89F-189
89Pac/SenLg-171
89S-579
89TM/SenLg-56
89UD-608
91Crown/Orio-231
91Pac/SenLg-27

Jones, Oscar
90Target-392

Jones, Percy
92Conlon/Sport-456
E120
E126-18
R316

Jones, Randy
74McDon
74OPC-173SD
74T-173
74T/St-94
75OPC-248
75T-248
75T/M-248
76Crane-23
76Ho-143
76K-4
76MSA/Disc
76OPC-199LL
76OPC-201LL

76OPC-310
76SSPC-118
76T-199LL
76T-201LL
76T-310
77BurgChef-132
77Ho-26
77K-17
77OPC-113
77OPC-5LL
77Padre/SchCd-16
77Padre/SchCd-17
77T-550
77T-5LL
78Ho-121
78OPC-101
78Padre/FamFun-16
78T-56
78Wiffle/Discs-33
79Ho-99
79OPC-95
79T-194
80OPC-160
80T-305
81Coke
81D-122
81F-487
81OPC-148
81T-458
81T/Tr-777
82F-528
82OPC-274
82T-626
83F-546
83OPC-29
83T-29
89Padre/Mag-16
91WIZMets-205

Jones, Rex
83ColumAst-24
84Cram/PCL-56
85Cram/PCL-74TR
86Tucson-9TR
88Tucson/ProC-192

Jones, Rick
88Portl/CMC-14
88Portl/ProC-656
89Spartan/ProC-1032
90Spartan/Best-27CO
90Spartan/ProC-2509CO
90Spartan/Star-27CO
91Crown/Orio-230

Jones, Ricky
83RochR-16
85CharlO-23
85RochR-6
86RochR-11
87CharlO/WBTV-7

Jones, Robert O.
(Bobby)
77T-16
78Cr/PCL-79
83OKCty-11
83Rang-6
84Nes/792-451
84Rang-6
84T-451
85D-134
85F-559
85Rang-6
85T-648
86OKCty-8
86T-142]
87Beloit-8
89CharlR/Star-26MG
89Pac/SenLg-98
90CharlR/Star-29MG
90EliteSenLg-71
91Pac/SenLg-59
91Tulsa/LineD-599MG
91Tulsa/ProC-2788MG

Jones, Robert Walter
E120
V100

Jones, Robert
(Bobby)
88CalLgAS-13
88Stockton/Cal-190
88Stockton/ProC-732
89Stockton/Best-24
89Stockton/Cal-166
89Stockton/ProC-383
89Stockton/Star-15
89AS/Cal-32
90FSLAS/Star-50

Jones, Ron
85Bend/Cram-13
86Clearw-11
86FSLAS-27
87Maine-23
87Maine/TCMA-17
88Maine/CMC-14
88Maine/ProC-280
88Phill/TastyK-27
89B-407
89Classic-96
89D-40RR
89D/Rook-42
89F-574
89Panini/St-143
89Phill/TastyK-14
89S-639RP
89S/HotRook-25
89S/YS/II-3
89Sf-178
89Sf-225M
89T-349
89ToysRUs-16
89UD-11
90D-487
90F-563
90OPC-129
90Phill/TastyK-16
90PublInt/St-243
90S-364
90S/100Ris-31
90ScranWB/CMC-19
90ScranWB/ProC-610
90T-129
90UD-94
91S-653
92D/II-738
92S/I-342

Jones, Ronnie
81BurlB-25

Jones, Ross
82Albuq-17
83Albuq-16
84Tidew-18
85BurlR-26
85Tidew-22
85Utica-2
86Chatt-15
86DayBe-14
87Gaston-17
88F-262
88S-598
88T-169
88WPalmB/Star-13
89WPalmB/Star-13
91WIZMets-208

Jones, Ruppert
77T-488R
78OPC-20
78T-141
79OPC-218
79T-422
80OPC-43
80T-78
81D-349
81F-101
81OPC-225
81T-225
81T/HT
81T/Tr-778
82D-346
82F-573
82F/St-102
82OPC-217
82T-511
82T/St-99
83D-373
83F-361
83OPC-287
83T-695
83T/Gloss40-38
83T/St-295
84D-261
84F-303
84F/X-U59
84Nes/792-327
84OPC-327
84T-327
84T/St-158
84T/Tr-59
85D-612
85F-13
85F/Up-U63
85Smok/Cal-19
85T-126
85T/Tr-65T
86D-423
86F-161
86OPC-186
86Smok/Cal-19
86T-464
86T/St-184
87D-428
87F-85
87Smok/Cal-21
87T-53
88F-492
88Panini/St-47
88S-333

Jones, Sam P.
21Exh-85
28Exh-63
28Yueng
29Exh/4-32
33G-81
91Conlon/Sport-140
91Conlon/Sport-174
92Conlon/Sport-356
E120
R316
V100
V354-31
V61-43
W502-38
W514-8
W515-43
W573

Jones, Sam
75BurlB
76BurlB
77DaytB

Jones, Samuel
(Sad Sam)
52NumNum-19
52T-382
53T-6
56T-259
57T-287
58T-287
59T-75
60L-14
60T-410
60T/tatt-24
61P-143
61T-49LL
61T-555
61T/RO-31
62J-138
62P-138
62P/Can-138
62Salada-162
62Shirriff-162
62T-92
62T/St-127
84Mother/Giants-15
86Negro/Frit-80
91Crown/Orio-232
91T/Arc53-6

Jones, Scott
83Cedar-2
83Cedar/LF-18

Jones, Shannon
89Geneva/ProC-1881
90CLAS/CL-46
90WinSalem/Team-12
91CharlK/LineD-135
91CharlK/ProC-1685

Jones, Sheldon
(Available)
47HomogBond-23
48B-34
49B-68
49Eureka-111
50B-83
50Drake-7
51B-199
52B-215
52BR
52NTea
52T-130
D305

Jones, Sherman
61T-161
91WIZMets-206

Jones, Slim
86Negro/Frit-79

Jones, Stacy
89Freder/Star-11
90Freder/Team-12
91Hagers/LineD-233
91Hagers/ProC-2451
92F-701M
92S/II-832RP
92T/91Debut-94

Jones, Steve
91Johnson/ClBest-25
91Johnson/ProC-3974

Jones, Steve H.
69OPC-49R
69T-49R

Jones, Terry R.
76OkCty/Team-14

Jones, Terry
87FtMyr-21

Jones, Thomas F.
(Rick)
77T-118
79Portl-23
82RochR-13

Jones, Thomas
09Buster/Pin-7
12Sweet/Pin-26
E254
E270/1
M116
T205
T206

Jones, Tim
75Shreve/TCMA-6
77Clinton
78Clinton
78T-703R

Jones, Todd
90Osceola/Star-12
91Osceola/ClBest-6
91Osceola/ProC-678
91Single/ClBest-333

Jones, Tommy
80Clinton-27
81Phoenix-16
83Butte-30
87Albany-19
88Albany/ProC-1352
89Wausau/GS-2
90Batavia/ProC-3060
90Calgary/CMC-23MG
90Calgary/ProC-664MG
91SanBern/ClBest-27MG
91SanBern/ProC-2003MG

Jones, Tracy
83Tampa-26
86D/Rook-2
86F/Up-U58
86TexGold-29
87D-413
87F-651M
87F/Up-U55
87Kahn-29
87T-146
88Classic/Red-185
88D-310
88D/Best-174
88F-237
88Kahn/Reds-29
88Leaf-107
88OPC-101
88Panini/St-283
88S-326
88S/YS/I-38
88Sf-38
88T-553
89B-479
89D-574
89F-383
89F/Up-31
89Mother/Giants-14
89OPC-373
89Panini/St-124
89S-510
89S/Tr-43
89T-373
89UD-96
89UD/Ext-798
90CokeK/Tiger-9
90D-636
90F-607
90OPC-767
90PublInt/St-70
90S-291
90T-767
90UD-309
91CounHrth-16
91D-594
91F/Up-U53
91OPC-87
91S-87
91T-87
91T/StClub/II-446
92D/II-519
92F-284
92S/I-206
92T-271

Jones, Vernal
(Nippy)
49Eureka-186
50B-238
52T-213
58Union
R302-111
R423-51

Jones, Victor
91Collnd/ClBest-2
91Collnd/ProC-1500

Jones, William Timothy
(Tim)
87ArkTr-14
87Louisvl-17
88Louisvl-23
88Louisvl/CMC-13
88Louisvl/ProC-433
89B-439
89D-555
89D/Rook-28
89F-453
89S-649
89S/HotRook-28
89Smok/Cards-10
89UD-348
90D-686
90OPC-533
90S-579
90S/100Ris-62
90Smok/Card-11
90T-533
90T/TVCard-26
90UD-501
91D-66
91F/Up-U117
91OPC-262
91T-262
91T/StClub/I-121

Jones, Willie
49B-92
49Eureka-138
49Lummis
50B-67
51B-112
51BR-B8
51FB
51T/BB-43
52B-20
52RM-NL11
52T-47
52TipTop
53B/Col-133
53T-88
54B-143
54T-41
55B-172
56T-127
57T-174
58Hires-60
58T-181
59T-208
60L-98
60T-289
61T-497
79TCMA-29
91T/Arc53-88
PM10/Sm-87

Jongewaard, Steve
87Erie-8

Jonnard, Clarence
35G-1E
35G-3C
35G-5C
35G-6C

Jonson, Greg
81CharR-1
82FtMyr-6

Joost, Edwin
(Eddie)

39PB-67
40PB-151
41DP-117
47HomogBond-24
48B-15
48L-62
49B-55
50B-103
51B-119
51FB
51T/BB-15
52B-26
52RM-AL12
52T-45
52TipTop
53B/Col-105
53RM-AL7
54B-35
55B-263
61F-116
D305
R302-115
R423-50
W711/1
W711/2

Jordan
N172

Jordan, Adolph
(Dutch)
90Target-995
E254
E270/1
T206
T213/brown

Jordan, Adrian
90Bristol/ProC-3152
90Bristol/Star-12

Jordan, Baxter
(Buck)
34DS-49
34G-31
38Wheat
R314
V354-75

Jordan, Brian
91Louisvl/LineD-238
91Louisvl/ProC-2927
92UD-3SR

Jordan, Harry K.
75Phoenix-24
76Phoenix
77Phoenix
78Cr/PCL-117
79Phoenix
80Phoenix-26
81Phoenix-2
82Phoenix

Jordan, Jim
78BurlB

Jordan, Jim
R310

Jordan, Joe
85Everett/II/Cram-8

Jordan, Kevin
90A&AASingle/ProC-181
90Oneonta/ProC-3386
91FSLAS/ProC-FSL15
91FtLaud/ClBest-21
91FtLaud/ProC-2434
91Single/ClBest-96

Jordan, Michael
91UD-SP1

Jordan, Milton
53Glen

Jordan, Ricardo
91Myrtle/ClBest-7
91Myrtle/ProC-2941

Jordan, Ricky
86Phill/TastyK-x
86Reading-12
87Reading-16
88F/Up-U110
88Maine/CMC-11
88Maine/ProC-286
88Phill/TastyK-35
88S/Tr-68T
89B-401
89Bz-17
89Classic-129
89D-624
89D/Best-103
89F-575
89F/BBAS-24
89F/Excit-27
89F/Heroes-25
89Panini/St-144
89Phill/TastyK-15
89S-548
89S/HotRook-88
89S/YS/I-15
89Sf-44
89T-358
89T/Big-246
89T/Coins-17
89T/HeadsUp-4
89T/JumboR-14
89T/UK-45
89ToysRUs-17
89UD-35
90B-156
90Classic-32
90D-76
90D/BestNL-8
90F-564
90F/LL-21
90F/SoarSt-11
90HotPlay/St-23
90Leaf/I-236
90MLBPA/Pins-3
90OPC-216
90Panini/St-315
90Phill/TastyK-17
90PublInt/St-244
90PublInt/St-615
90S-16
90Sf-153
90T-216
90T/Big-172
90T/DH-38
90T/St-112
90UD-576
91B-494
91D-466
91DennyGS-13
91F-401
91F/UltraUp-U100
91Leaf/Stud-215
91OPC-712
91Panini/FrSt-103
91Phill/Medford-21
91RedFoley/St-55
91S-15
91T-712
91T/StClub/I-192
91UD-160
92D/II-458
92F-536
92S/II-476
92T-103
92UD-106

Jordan, Scott
86Watlo-14
87Kinston-12
88EastLAS/ProC-40
88Wmsprt/ProC-1326
89D-609

Jordan, Steve
81BurlB-16

Jordan, Tim
77Newar
78Newar

Jordan, Tim
C46-87
E103
E254
E90/1
M116
T206
T213/blue
T3-20

Jordan, Tim
90Johnson/Star-15
90Target-393
91Savan/ClBest-26
91Savan/ProC-1667

Jordan, Tony
80Wausau-4

Jorgens, Arndt
34G-72
39PB-42
40PB-2
91Conlon/Sport-78

Jorgensen, Mike
70OPC-348R
70T-348R
71OPC-596
71T-596
72OPC-16
72T-16
73OPC-281
73T-281
74OPC-549
74T-549
74T/St-56
74Weston-16
75Ho-105
75OPC-286
75T-286
75T/M-286
76Ho-144
76OPC-117
76SSPC-327
76T-117
77OPC-9
77T-368
78T-406
79T-22
80T-213
81D-274
81F-324
81T-698
82D-224
82F-529
82T-566
83F-547
83T-107
83T/Tr-51
84Nes/792-313
84Pol/Atl-11
84T-313
84T/Tr-60
85F-229
85T-783
86T-422
87Louisvl-1MG
88Louisvl-1MG
88Louisvl/CMC-25
88Louisvl/ProC-441MG
89Louisvl-6MG
89Louisvl/CMC-25MG
89Louisvl/ProC-1256MGs
91WIZMets-209

Jorgenson, John
(Spider)
47TipTop
49Eureka-39
53Mother-55
90Target-394

Jorgenson, Terry
88OrlanTw/Best-15
89Orlan/Best-15
89Orlan/ProC-1352
89SLAS-12
90Portl/CMC-17
90Portl/ProC-184
90S-655
90T/89Debut-64
91Portl/LineD-410
91Portl/ProC-1571

Jorn, David A.
78StPete
80ArkTr-25
81ArkTr-12
90Greens/Best-30CO
90Greens/ProC-2680CO
90Greens/Star-26CO
91Albany/ProC-1024CO

Jose, Elio
88CharWh/Best-23

Jose, Domingo Felix
85Madis-17
85Madis/Pol-14
86Modesto-16
88Tacoma/CMC-24
88Tacoma/ProC-614
89D-38RR
89F-15
89Mother/A's-22
89S-629RP
89S/HotRook-22
89Tacoma/CMC-14
89Tacoma/ProC-1542
89UD-22SR
90B-455
90Classic/III-33
90D-564
90D/Rook-5
90F-13
90HotRook/St-24
90Leaf/II-385
90Mother/A's-17
90OPC-238
90S-321
90S/YS/I-19
90T-238
90UD-228
91B-401
91Bz-17
91Classic/200-64
91Classic/III-41
91D-656
91F-636
91F/UltraUp-U107
91Leaf/II-392
91OPC-368
91Pol/Card-34
91S-784
91S/100RisSt-90
91T-368
91T/StClub/II-366
91ToysRUs-13
91UD-387
91USPlayC/AS-9S
92D/DK-DK13
92D/I-233
92F-582
92F/ASIns-1
92S/100SS-99
92S/I-40
92T-105
92UD-264

Jose, Manny
85Greens-4
86WinHaven-13
87WinHaven-17
88NewBrit/ProC-897
89London/ProC-1385
91Nashvl/LineD-265
91Nashvl/ProC-2170

Joseph, Ricardo
68T-434
69T-329
70OPC-186
70T-186
72MB-174

Joseph, Sam
86QuadC-16tr

Josephson, Duane
67T-373R
68T-329
69MB-141
69MLB/St-32
69T-222
69T/St-156
70MLB/St-187
70OPC-263
70T-263
71OPC-56
71T-56
71T/Coins-92
72MB-175
72T-543

Josephson, Paul
83Albany-5
84Durham-21

Joshua, Von
71OPC-57
71T-57
73OPC-544
73T-544
74OPC-551
74T-551
75OPC-547
75T-547
75T/M-547
76A&P/Milw
76K-39
76OPC-82
76SSPC-109
76T-82
77BurgChef-85
77T-651
78T-108
80T-209
85SpokAT/Cram-10
88Albuq/ProC-254
89Albuq/ProC-73
90Albuq/CMC-28CO
90Albuq/ProC-362CO
90Albuq/Trib-15CO
90Target-395
91Albuq/LineD-25CO
91Albuq/ProC-1158CO

Joslin, Chris
83BurlR-7
83BurlR/LF-16

Joslyn, John
88Virgini/Star-12

Joss, Adrian
(Addie)
61F-117
80Pac/Leg-114
80SSPC/HOF
91Conlon/Sport-272
E107
E254
E90/1
E93
M116
T205
T206
T3-19
W555
WG2-30

Joyce, James
91Pocatel/ProC-3784

Joyce, Jim
90TM/Umpire-59

Joyce, Kevin
78Clinton

Joyce, Michael
63T-66
64T-477

Joyce, Robert Emmett
48Sommer-6

Joyce, Tom
76AppFx

Joyce, William
(Bill)
90Target-396
N300/unif

Joyner, Wally
85Cram/PCL-2
86D/HL-23
86D/Rook-1
86F/Slug-19
86F/Up-U59
86Sf/Rook-7
86Smok/Cal-22
86T/Tr-51T
87BK-11
87Classic-6
87Classic/Up-108
87D-135
87D-1DK
87D/AAS-1
87D/DKsuper-1
87D/HL-35
87D/OD-7
87D/PopUp-1
87Drake-2
87F-628M
87F-86
87F/Excit-30
87F/GameWin-22
87F/Hottest-25
87F/BB-23
87F/LL-26
87F/Lim-23
87F/Mini-59
87F/RecSet-17
87F/Slug-22
87F/St-68
87F/WaxBox-C7
87Ho/St-20
87KayBee-18
87Kraft-9
87Leaf-1DK
87Leaf-252
87MnM's-1
87MSA/Discs-10
87OPC-80
87RedFoley/St-82
87Sf-26
87Sf-75M
87Seven-W3
87Smok/Cal-12
87Sportflic/DealP-2
87T-80
87T/Coins-16
87T/Gloss22-13
87T/Gloss60-39
87T/GlossRk-7
87T/Mini-45
87T/St-150
87T/St-174

87T/St-313
87ToysRUs-14
88Bz-10
88Classic/Blue-206
88D-110
88D-BC13
88D/Best-115
88F-493
88F-622M
88F/AwardWin-21
88F/BB/AS-19
88F/BB/MVP-20
88F/Excit-23
88F/Hottest-21
88F/LL-22
88F/Mini-11
88F/RecSet-21
88F/SS-18
88F/St-12
88F/TL-16
88F/WaxBox-C4
88FanSam-4
88Jiffy-11
88KayBee-15
88KingB/Disc-9
88Leaf-50
88Nestle-44
88OPC-168
88Panini/St-40
88RedFoley/St-41
88S-7
88S/YS/I-27
88Sf-75
88Smok/Angels-17
88T-420
88T/Big-52
88T/Coins-16
88T/Gloss60-48
88T/Mini-6
88T/RiteAid-15
88T/St-179
88T/St/Backs-34
88T/UK-40
88UD/Sample-700
89B-47
89Classic-29
89D-52
89D/Best-139
89D/MVP-BC21
89F-481
89F/Excit-28
89F/Superstar-26
89F/WaxBox-C16
89Holsum/Discs-1
89Master/Discs-7
89Nissen-1
89OPC-270
89Panini/St-291
89RedFoley/St-68
89S-65
89S/HotStar-73
89Sf-2
89Smok/Angels-18
89T-270
89T/Big-201
89T/LJN-30
89T/St-183
89T/UK-46
89UD-573
89UD-668TC
90B-299
90Classic/Up-42
90D-94
90D/BestAL-31
90F-136
90HotPlay/St-24
90Leaf/I-24
90MLBPA/Pins-93
90OPC-525
90Panini/St-31
90PublInt/St-372
90S-120
90S/100St-81
90Sf-49
90Smok/Angel-9
90Sunflower-19
90T-525
90T/Ames-30
90T/Big-168
90T/St-166
90UD-693
91B-195
91Classic/III-42
91D-677
91DennyGS-23
91F-317
91F/Ultra-48
91Leaf/I-31
91Leaf/Stud-26
91OPC-195
91Panini/FrSt-180
91Panini/St-141
91RedFoley/St-56
91S-470
91S-873FRAN
91S/100SS-57
91Seven/3DCoin-7SC
91Smok/Angel-6
91T-195
91T/StClub/I-2
91UD-575
92D/I-333
92F-62
92S/100SS-29
92S/II-535
92T-629
92UD-343

Juarbe, Ken
90Oneonta/ProC-2114
90Greens/Best-6
90Greens/ProC-2658
90Greens/Star-12

Juday, Richard
91Erie/ClBest-6
91Erie/ProC-4076

Judd, Oscar
40Hughes-10

Juden, Jeff
90B-64
90Foil/Best-243
90FSLAS/Star-8
90OPC-164FDP
90Osceola/Star-11
90T-164FDP
91B-547
91Classic/III-43
91Jacks/LineD-564
91Jacks/ProC-922
91Single/ClBest-302
91UD-52TP
92D/II-405RR
92T-34
92T/91Debut-95
92UD-6SR

Judge, Joe
21Exh-86
25Exh-126
26Exh-126
28Yueng-35
29Exh/4-31
31Exh/4-32
33DH-25
33Exh/4-16
33G-155
61F-118
88Conlon/3-16
90Target-397
91Conlon/Sport-68
BF2-46
D327
D328-90
D329-93
E120
E121/80
E122
E126-26
E135-90
E220
M101/4-93
R316
V100
V353-88
W501-13
W502-35
W517-53
W572
W575

Judnich, Walt
41PB-67
47TipTop
49Sommer-28
52Mother-8
Exh47
W753

Judson, Erik
90Batavia/ProC-3072
91Spartan/ClBest-16
91Spartan/ProC-900

Judson, Howard
(Howie)
50B-185
51B-123
52B-149
52NTea
52T-169
53B/BW-42
53T-12
55B-193
91T/Arc53-12

Juelsgaard, Jarod
91Everett/ClBest-14
91Everett/ProC-3909

Juenke, Dan
86FSLAS-28
86Miami-13

Jundy, Lorin
85LitFalls-6
86LitFalls-16
89BBCity/Star-13

Junker, Lance
81Clinton-27
83Redwd-14

Jurado, Pat
91Rockford/ClBest-7
91Rockford/ProC-2042

Jurak, Ed
81Bristol-12
84D-127
84F-402
84Nes/792-628
84T-628
85D-579
85T-233
86T-749
87TexLgAS-9
88AAA/ProC-6
88D/A's/Bk-NEW
88Tacoma/CMC-13
88Tacoma/ProC-615
89Mother/Giants-20
90Calgary/CMC-10
90Calgary/ProC-658
90TulsaDG/Best-21

Jurgens, Scott
89Boise/ProC-1980

Jurges, Bill
32Orbit/num-33A
32Orbit/num-33B
32Orbit/un-37
33G-225
35BU-139
39PB-35
40PB-89
41PB-59
60T-220MG
R305
R312/M
V355-97
WG8-36

Jury, Frank
88Boise/ProC-1630

Justice, Dave
86Sumter-15
87Greenvl/Best-9
88Richm-18
88Richm/CMC-17
88Richm/ProC-24
89Richm/CMC-15
89Richm/Ko-20
89Richm/ProC-838
89S/HotRook-26
90Classic/III-97
90D-704
90D/Rook-14
90F-586
90Leaf/II-297
90Richm/CMC-9
90Richm/ProC-273
90Richm/Team-16
90S-650RP
90T/89Debut-65
90T/Tr-48T
90UD/Ext-711
91B-574
91Bz-18
91Classic/200-193
91Classic/I-11
91Classic/I-NO
91Classic/II-T63
91Classic/III-24
91Colla/Justice-Set
91CollAB-33
91D-402MVP
91D-548
91D-683ROY
91D/Preview-1
91DennyGS-25
91F-693
91F/Ultra-394EP
91F/Ultra-7
91JDeanSig-14
91KingB/Discs-18
91Leaf/I-77
91Leaf/I-84CL
91Leaf/Prev-1
91Leaf/Stud-146
91Leaf/StudPrev-10
91MajorLg/Pins-46
91MooTown-9
91OPC-329
91OPC/Premier-70
91Panini/FrSt-25
91Panini/St-29
91Pep/SS-9
91Post-1
91Post/Can-12
91S-55
91S-861FRAN
91S-880ROY
91S/100RisSt-45
91S/HotRook-1
91Seven/3DCoin-10NW
91Seven/3DCoin-7A
91Seven/3DCoin-9F
91SilverSt-3
91Sunflower-15
91T-329
91T/CJMini/I-14
91T/StClub/I-26
91T/SU-21
91ToysRUs-14
91UD-363
91Woolwth/HL-5
92D/DK-DK6
92D/I-327
92F-360
92F-713PV
92S/100SS-42
92S/I-4
92S/Prev-2
92T-80
92UD-29
92UD-546

Justis, Walter
C46-42

Jutze, Alfred Henry
(Skip)
73OPC-613R
73T-613R
74OPC-328
74T-328
76OPC-489
76SSPC-52
76T-489
78T-532

Kaage, George
77Clinton
78LodiD

Kaaihue, Kala
87Hawaii-20

Kaat, Jim
60T-136
61Clover-9
61Peters-7
61T-63
61T/St-180
62T-21
63F-22
63J-10
63P-10
63Salada-40
63T-10LL
63T-165
64T-567
65OPC-62
65T-62
66T-224LL
66T-445
67Bz-18
67T-235LL
67T-237LL
67T-300
68Coke
68Dexter-45
68OPC-67CL
68T-450
68T-67CL
69MB-142
69MLB/St-67
69T-290
69T/St-194
70MLB/St-233
70OPC-75
70T-75
71MLB/St-464
71OPC-245
71T-245
71T/GM-7
72MB-176
72T-709
72T-710IA
73OPC-530
73T-530
74OPC-440
74T-440
75Ho/Twink-110
75OPC-243
75T-243
75T/M-243
76Crane-24
76Ho-110
76K-25
76MSA/Disc
76OPC-80
76SSPC-136
76T-80
76T/Tr-80T
77BurgChef-169
77T-638
78T-715
79T-136
80T-250
81D-536
81F-536
81T-563
82D-217
82F-117
82F/St-240M
82T-367
83D-343
83F-11
83OPC-211
83OPC-383SV
83T-672
83T-673SV
83T/St-135
83T/St-136
88Chatt/Team-16
88Pac/Leg-88
89Swell-88

Kable, David
81ArkTr-9
81Louisvl-28
82Louisvl-12
83Louisvl/Riley-28
84Louisvl-29
85Louisvl-9
86ArkTr-9

Kaczmarski, Randy
82Amari-21
83Beaum-4

Kaelin, Kris
91Pocatel/ProC-3789

Kahanamoku, Duke
33SK-20

Kahmann, Jim
86WPalmB-22TR
87Jaxvl-28
88Jaxvl/ProC-974
89Orlan/Best-6
89Orlan/ProC-1349

Kahn, Roger
90LitSun-13

Kahoe, Michael
E107
T204

Kain, Marty
82Amari-20
84Cram/PCL-100
85Cram/PCL-11

Kainer, Don W.
(Don)
79Tucson-11

Kainer, Ronald
76Watlo

Kairis, Bob
88BurlInd/ProC-1794

Kaiser, Bart
86Clearw-12
87Clearw-25
Kaiser, C. Don
56T-124
57T-134
Kaiser, Jeff
85Mother/A's-25
86Tacoma-10
87BuffB-16
88ColoSp/CMC-4
88ColoSp/ProC-1531
88Gator-47
89ColoSp/CMC-3
89F-410
89Salinas/Cal-142
89Salinas/ProC-1805
90ColoSp/CMC-10
90T/Tr-49T
91Denver/LineD-143
91Denver/ProC-122
91OPC-576
91T-576
Kaiser, Keith
88Greens/ProC-1573
89Chatt/Best-2
89Chatt/GS-13
91Jacks/LineD-565
91Jacks/ProC-923
Kaiser, Ken
88TM/Umpire-31
89TM/Umpire-29
90TM/Umpire-28
Kaiser, Nick
91Eugene/ClBest-6
91Eugene/ProC-3735
Kaiserling, George
15CJ-157
Kajima, Ken
89Salinas/Cal-148CO
Kalas, Harry
88Phill/TastyK-39ANN
90Phill/TastyK-35BC
Kaler
T207
Kalin, Frank
53Mother-44
Kaline, Al
54T-201
55B-23
55T-4
55T/DH-45
56T-20
56T/Pin-38OF
56YellBase/Pin-16
57T-125
58T-304M
58T-70
59HRDerby-9
59T-360
59T-463HL
59T-562AS
60Armour-12
60Bz-18
60NuCard-65
60P
60T-50
60T-561AS
60T/tatt-25
61Bz-20
61NuCard-465
61P-35
61T-429
61T-580AS
61T/Dice-6
61T/St-152A
61T/St-152B
62Bz-12
62Exh
62J-20
62P-20
62P/Can-20
62Salada-67
62Shirriff-67
62T-150
62T-470AS
62T-51LL
62T/bucks
62T/St-47
63Bz-34
63Exh
63J-51
63P-51
63Salada-63
63T-25
63T/SO
64Bz-34
64Det/Lids-7
64T-12LL
64T-250
64T-331M
64T-8LL
64T/Coins-100
64T/Coins-129AS
64T/S-12
64T/St-95
64T/SU
64T/tatt
64Wheat/St-24
65Bz-34
65OldLond-27
65OPC-130
65T-130
65T/E-13
65T/trans-51
66Bz-46
66T-410
66T/RO-66
67Bz-46
67OPC-30
67OPC/PI-21
67T-216M
67T-239LL
67T-30
67T/PI-21
67T/Test/SU-10
68Bz-1
68OPC-2LL
68T-240
68T-2LL
68T/G-13
68T/Post-9
69Kelly/Pin-8
69MB-143
69MLB/St-49
69MLBPA/Pin-13
69NTF
69OPC-166WS
69T-166WS
69T-410
69T/St-174
69Trans-6
70K-52
70MLB/St-208
70T-640
70T/SO
70Trans-14
71Bz/Test-14
71K-44
71MLB/St-396
71MLB/St-565
71OPC-180
71T-180
71T/Coins-62
71T/GM-19
71T/S-54
71T/tatt-5
71T/tatt-5a
72MB-177
72T-600
73K-52
73OPC-280
73T-280
73T/Lids-24
74Laugh/ASG-57
74OPC-215
74T-215
74T/St-177
75OPC-4RB
75T-4HL
75T/M-4HL
78TCMA-40
79TCMA-184
80Pac/Leg-65
80SSPC/HOF
81Detroit-100
81Detroit-132
82CJ-12
83D/HOF-18
83Kaline-Set
83MLBPA/Pin-11
84West/1-12
85CircK-21
86Sf/Dec-51M
87Leaf/SpecOlym-H10
88Domino-9
88Pac/Leg-104
89Swell-40
89T/LJN-93
90HOF/St-52
90MSA/AGFA-5
91Swell/Great-53
Exh47
Rawl
WG10-30
WG9-31
Kaline, Louise
83Kaline-32M
83Kaline-7M
Kaline, Mark
83Kaline-28M
83Kaline-32M
Kaline, Michael
83Kaline-28M
83Kaline-32M
Kaline, Naomi
83Kaline-65M
Kaline, Nicholas
83Kaline-65M
Kallevig, Dane
90Watertn/Star-11
Kallevig, Greg
86Peoria-12
87WinSalem-2
88MidwLAS/GS-28
88Peoria/Ko-18
89CharlK-16
90Iowa/CMC-4
90Iowa/ProC-314
90T/TVCub-50
Kallio, Rudy
28Exh/PCL-15
Kamanaka, Masaaki
89VeroB/Star-12
Kamei, Kat
87SanJose-8
Kamerschen, Robbie
90Martins/ProC-3199
Kamieniecki, Scott
87PrWill-6
88FtLaud/Star-13
89Albany/Best-25
89Albany/ProC-316
90Albany/Best-5
90Albany/ProC-1034
90Albany/Star-7
90Foil/Best-63
90T/TVYank-49
91ColClip/LineD-109
91ColClip/ProC-594
91D/Rook-51
91F/Up-U45
91T/StClub/II-568
91T/Tr-66T
91UD/FinalEd-33F
92D/I-195
92F-232
92S/100RisSt-23
92S/I-415
92T-102
92T/91Debut-96
92UD-46
Kamm, Willie
21Exh-87
25Exh-76
26Exh-77
27Exh-39
28Yueng-40
29Exh/4-19
30CEA/Pin-17
31Exh/4-19
32Orbit/num-10
32Orbit/un-38
33G-75
34Exh/4-11
34G-14
35BU-39
35Exh/4-11
35G-1J
35G-1L
35G-2E
35G-3A
35G-5A
35G-6A
35G-6E
35G-7E
91Conlon/Sport-166
R305
R308-164
R316
V353-68
V354-60
W502-40
W515-42
W517-13
Kammeyer, Bob
78Cr/PCL-34
79Colum-23
80Colum-10
Kammeyer, Tim
82Redwd-6
83Redwd-15
Kampouris, Alex
35G-8D
35G-9D
36Exh/4-4
41DP-13
90Target-398
R314
W711/1
Kampsen, Doug
85Cedar-9
Kane, Frank
90Target-997
Kane, Joey
88Alaska/Team-11
89Alaska/Team-13
Kane, John
M116
Kane, Kevin
81Bristol-3
85Pawtu-18
Kane, Thomas
91NewBrit/LineD-465
91NewBrit/ProC-350
Kane, Tom
86Greens-12
87Greens-1
Kanehl, Rod
62T-597R
63F-49
63J-199
63P-19
63T-371
64T-582
90Swell/Great-44
91WIZMets-210
Kaney, Joe
47Centen-14
Kannenberg, Scott
86QuadC-17
87QuadC-9
88PalmSp/Cal-88
88PalmSp/ProC-1444
Kanter, John
85Madis-18
85Madis/Pol-15
86Modesto-17
Kantlehner, Erving
16FleischBrd-48
Kantor, Brad
91Watertn/ClBest-18
91Watertn/ProC-3373
Kanwisher, Gary
85Beloit-20
86Stockton-11
87Stockton-25
Kapano, Corey
89BendB/Legoe-17
91AS/Cal-16
91PalmSp/ProC-2023
Kappell, Henry
N172
Kappesser, Bob
89Helena/SP-19
90AS/Cal-48
90Stockton/Best-4
90Stockton/Cal-189
90Stockton/ProC-2188
91Visalia/ClBest-25
91Visalia/ProC-1745
Karasinski, Dave
89BurlB/ProC-1611
89BurlB/Star-11
90Durham/Team-26
91Salinas/ClBest-20
91Salinas/ProC-2237
Karcher, Kevin
86Cram/PCL-41
Karcher, Rick
90Idaho/ProC-3255
91Macon/ClBest-20
91Macon/ProC-873
Karchner, Matt
89Eugene/Best-6
90AppFox/Box-15
90AppFox/ProC-2091
91BBCity/ClBest-8
91BBCity/ProC-1395
Karczewski, Ray
88SLCity-7
89SLCity-7SS
Karger, Edwin
10Domino-61
12Sweet/Pin-5
E90/1
E91
E96
M116
T204
T205
T206
Karkovice, Ron
83AppFx/LF-22
86SLAS-5
87Coke/WS-3
87D-334
87D/OD-234
87F-645R
87Seven-C11
87T-491
88S-374
88T-86
88Vanco/CMC-15
88Vanco/ProC-773
89Coke/WS-13
89T-308
89UD-183
90BirmDG/Best-19
90Coke/WSox-11
90D-413
90Leaf/II-307
90OPC-717
90PublInt/St-391
90S-22
90T-717
90UD-69
91D-220
91D/GSlam-12
91F-125
91F/UltraUp-U16
91Kodak/WSox-20
91Leaf/II-515
91OPC-568
91S-833
91T-568
91T/StClub/I-102
91UD-209
92D/I-374
92F-88
92S/II-532
92T-153
92UD-169
Karli, Todd
90Reno/Cal-291ANN
Karmeris, Joe
85VeroB-14
Karpuk, Greg
86Watlo-15
87Wmsprt-26
Karr, Benjamin
E120
E126-20
W573
Karr, Jeff
84LitFalls-7
Karros, Eric
88GreatF-2
89AS/Cal-2
89Bakers/Cal-201
91Albuq/LineD-12
91Albuq/ProC-1164
91B-604
91Classic/200-171
91Classic/II-T36
91F/Ultra-380MLP
91UD-24
92D/I-16RR
92F-462
92S/II-827
92T-194
92T/91Debut-97
92UD-534
Karsay, Steve
90A&AASingle/ProC-179

90StCath/ProC-3472
91B-12
91Classic/200-88
91Classic/II-T60
91Myrtle/ClBest-8
91Myrtle/ProC-2942
91S-675FDP
91S/ToroBJ-31
91Single/ClBest-119
91UD-54TP

Kaseda, Yuki
89Salinas/Cal-130
89Salinas/ProC-1808

Kasko, Eddie
57T-363
58T-8
59T-232
60Kahn
60L-9
60T-61
61Kahn
61P-185
61T-534
61T/St-18
62J-119
62Kahn
62P-119
62P/Can-119
62Salada-147
62Shirriff-147
62T-193
62T/St-117
63FrBauer-11
63J-128
63Kahn
63P-128
63T-498
70OPC-489MG
70T-489MG
71OPC-578MG
71T-31MG
72OPC-218MG
72T-218MG
73OPC-131MG
73T-131MG
78TCMA-249

Kasper, Kevin
89Everett/Star-18
90Clinton/Best-17
90Clinton/ProC-2556
91SanJose/ClBest-7
91SanJose/ProC-19

Kaspryzak, Dennis
77Jaxvl

Kastelic, Bruce
82Lynch-5

Kasunick, Joe
83Butte-29

Katalinas, Ed
81Detroit-127

Kating, Jim
87Bakers-11
88SanAn/Best-9
89Huntsvl/Best-6
90Huntsvl/Best-17

Kats, Bill
43Centen-15
45Centen-14

Katt, Ray
54B-121
54NYJour
55B-183
55Gol/Giants-15
57T-331
58Hires-57
58T-284
60T-468C
61Union
62Sugar-17
79TCMA-235

Katzaroff, Robert
(Robbie)
88CapeCod/Sum-163
90James/Pucko-8
91Harris/LineD-258
91Harris/ProC-642
91Single/ClBest-20

Kaub, Keith
88James/ProC-1911
89Miami/I/Star-21
89Rockford/Team-13
90Rockford/ProC-2704

Kauff, Benjamin
(Bennie)
15CJ-160
16FleischBrd-49
92Conlon/Sport-484
BF2-76
D327
D328-92
D329-94
D350/2-92
E135-92
M101/4-94
M101/5-92
PM1-9
W514-100
W516-16

Kaufman, Al
T3/Box-73

Kaufman, Curt
82Colum-5
82Colum/Pol-24
83Colum-11
84Smok/Cal-14
85Cram/PCL-20
85D-524
85F-305
85T-61

Kaufman, Ron
82QuadC-9

Kaufman, Tony
21Exh-88

Kaufmann, Anthony
47TipTop

Kaull, Kurt
83Erie-25
84Savan-5

Kausnicka, Jay
90Visalia/Cal-72

Kautz, Scott
88Harris/ProC-862

Kautzer, Bill
75AppFx
76AppFx

Kavanagh, Mike
75Shrev/TCMA-7

Kavanaugh, Tim
83Erie-19

Kawabata, Yasuhiro
89VeroB/Star-13

Kawano, Rye
91Salinas/ClBest-11
91Salinas/ProC-2256

Kay, Belinda
90ColMud/Star-29

Kaye, Jeff
86Clearw-13
87Clearw-8
87Phill/TastyK-x
88Reading/ProC-872

Kayser, Tom
77Holyo
79Holyo-30
80Holyo-10
81Holyo-3

Kazak, Edward
(Eddie)
49Eureka-187
50B-36
51B-85
52T-165
53T-194
79TCMA-16
91T/Arc53-194

Kazanski, Ted
54T-78
55T-46
55T/DH-5
57T-27
58T-36
59T-99

Kazmierczak, William
87Peoria-28
88WinSalem/Star-7

Kealey, Steve
69T-224R
71OPC-43
71T-43
72OPC-146
72T-146
73OPC-581
73T-581

Keane, Johnny
60T-468C
62T-198MG
63T-166MG
64T-413MG
65OPC-131MG
65T-131MG
66T-296MG

Kearney, Robert
(Bob)
78Cedar
80Phoenix-15
81Tacoma-5
82Tacoma-27
83D-539
83T/Tr-52T
84D-462
84F-449
84F/X-U60
84Mother/Mar-4
84Nes/792-326
84T-326
84T/St-381YS
84T/Tr-61T
85D-362
85F-491
85Mother/Mar-13
85OPC-386
85T-679
85T/St-335
86D-74
86F-466
86Mother/Mar-23
86OPC-13
86T-13
87D-445
87F-587
87Mother/Sea-12
87OPC-73
87T-498

Kearns, John
83Wisco/LF-10

Kearse, Edward
47Remar-7
47Smith-14

Keas
N172

Keathley, Don
91Modesto/ProC-3090

Keathley, Robin
83TriCit-8
85BurlR-22

Keating, Dave
89NiagFls/Pucko-5B
90Bristol/Star-13

Keating, Dennis
79AppFx-2

Keating, Mike
90Savan/ProC-2074

Keating, Ray H.
14CJ-95
15CJ-95
16FleischBrd-50
28Exh/PCL-32
T222

Keatley, Greg
81Omaha-14
82Omaha-11

Keckler, Mike
85FtMyr-23

Keedy, Pat
81Holyo-16
82Holyo-16
84Cram/PCL-118
85Cram/PCL-1
86Edmon-16
87Hawaii-27
88T-486
88Tucson/CMC-22
88Tucson/ProC-175
88Tucson/JP-14

Keefe, George
N172

Keefe, Kevin
78Cr/PCL-104
79Albuq-8
80Albuq-17
81Albuq/TCMA-11

Keefe, Timothy
(Tim)
80SSPC/HOF
90HOF/St-4
E223
N162
N172
N28
N284
N403
WG1-41

Keefer, Paul
89Welland/Pucko-15

Keegan, Ed
61T-248
62T-249

Keegan, Robert
(Bob)
53T-196
54T-100
55T-10
55T/DH-52
56T-54
57T-99
58T-200
59T-86
60T-291
77T-436M
91T/Arc53-196

Keehn, Mike
83TriCit-18

Keeler, Jay
(Devo)
83Watlo/LF-9

Keeler, Willie
40PB-237
48Exh/HOF
50Callahan
63Bz/ATG-31
69Bz/Sm
72F/FFeat-40
72Laugh/GF-31
80Pac/Leg-99
80SSPC/HOF
89HOF/St-51
89Smok/Dodg-12
90BBWit-74
90Target-399
E107
E254
E270/2
E90/1
E97
T204
T206
T3-101
W555
WG2-31

Keeley, Robert
54JC-35
54T-176
55JC-35

Keeline, Jason
91Pulaski/ClBest-8
91Pulaski/ProC-4014

Keenan, James
N172
V100

Keenan, Kerry
77Ashvl
79Wausau-4
80Ashvl-15

Keenan, Kevin
80Elmira-10

Keener, Jeff
81Louisvl-10
82ArkTr-4
83Louisvl/Riley-10
84Louisvl-22
85Louisvl-8

Keenum, Larry
76Baton

Keeter, Lonnie
90Wichita/Rock-26CO
91HighD/ProC-2413CO

Keeton, Garry
83AppFx/LF-26

Keeton, Rickey
(Buster)
79Vanco-10
82D-618
82F-146
82T-268
82Tucson-13
83Tucson-3
84Omaha-6
85Omaha-28
91Augusta/ClBest-27CO
91Augusta/ProC-824CO

Kehn, Chet
90Target-998

Keighley, Steve
91Rockford/ClBest-15
91Rockford/ProC-2051

Keim, Chris
89Billings/ProC-2062
90Billings/ProC-3216

Keitges, Jeff
89Wausau/GS-24
90SanBern/Best-6
90SanBern/Cal-110
90SanBern/ProC-2639
91SanBern/ClBest-16
91SanBern/ProC-1993

Kekich, Mike
65T-561R
69T-262
70OPC-536
70T-536
71MLB/St-490
71OPC-703
71T-703
72OPC-138
72T-138
73OPC-371
73Syrac/Team-11
73T-371
74OPC-199
74T-199
76OPC-582
76T-582
78SanJose-24
89Pac/SenLg-73
89TM/SenLg-57
90EliteSenLg-84
90Target-400

Kelbe, Frank
89Watertn/Star-27

Keliher, Paul
91Pulaski/ClBest-2

Keliipuleole, Carl
88Kinston/Star-13
89Canton/Best-18
89Canton/ProC-1300
89Canton/Star-9
90Canton/Best-21
90Canton/ProC-1290
90Canton/Star-8
90Foil/Best-137
91Harris/ProC-622

Keling, Korey
91Boise/ClBest-25
91Boise/ProC-3872

Kell, Everett
(Skeeter)
52B-242

Kell, George
47TipTop
48L-120
49B-26
49Royal-3
50B-8
51B-46
51FB
51T/CAS
52B-75
52BR
52RM-AL13
52Royal
52StarCal/L-72A
52T-246
52TipTop
53B/Col-61
53RM-AL8
53T-138
54B-50
54RH
54RM-AL4
55B-213
56T-195
57T-230
58T-40
79TCMA-86
80Pac/Leg-118
81Detroit-10
83Kaline-26ANN
83Kaline-30M
83Kaline-39M
83Kaline-57M
83Kaline-58M
86Sf/Dec-24M
88Pac/Leg-69
89HOF/St-24

90Pac/Legend-86
91Crown/Orio-233
91Swell/Great-47
91T/Arc53-138
Exh47
R423-57

Kelleher, Frank
47Signal
49B/PCL-27
53Mother-37

Kelleher, John
90Target-401
E120
V61-87

Kelleher, Mick
76SSPC-605
77T-657
78T-564
79T-53
80T-323
81D-513
81T-429
81T/Tr-779
82D-601
82T-184
82T/Tr-53T
83T-79

Kellelmark, Joe
87VeroB-19

Keller, Carlton
(Buzz)
77ArkTr

Keller, Charlie
39Exh
39PB-88
40PB-9
41DP-64
41DP-84
41PB-21
44Yank/St-16
47HomogBond-25
47TipTop
49B-209
50B-211
51B-177
89Pac/Leg-194
90Swell/Great-22
91Swell/Great-48
D305
Exh47
R346-48

Keller, Clyde
90Foil/Best-82
90Spring/Best-18
91MidwLAS/ProC-MWL14
91Spring/ClBest-18
91Spring/ProC-739

Keller, David
(Dave)
86Tampa-8C
88Billings/ProC-1802
89Billings/ProC-2048
90BurlInd/ProC-3026
91BurlInd/ProC-3320MG
91Canton/LineD-100CO
91Canton/ProC-997CO

Keller, Jerry
79Richm-19
80Richm-12
81Richm-3
82Richm-10
83Portl-7
84Syrac-10
85Syrac-18
90Richm25Ann/Team-13

Keller, Phil
74Albuq/Team-8

Keller, Steve
89Spartan/ProC-1055
89Spartan/Star-10

Kellert, Frank
55Gol/Dodg-15
56T-291
90Target-402
91Crown/Orio-234

Kelley, Anthony
86ColumAst-16
87Tucson-21
88Tucson/CMC-2
88Tucson/ProC-186
88Tucson/JP-15
89Tucson/CMC-3
89Tucson/JP-10
90FSLAS/Star-9
90Miami/I/Star-13
90Miami/II/Star-11

Kelley, Dean Alan
87Oneonta-29
88CLAS/Star-10
90Wichita/Rock-12
91LasVegas/ProC-242
91LasVegas/LineD-286

Kelley, Harry
37Exh/4-14
37OPC-121
38Exh/4-14
V300

Kelley, Jack
C46-15

Kelley, Joe
80SSPC/HOF
89HOF/St-35
89Smok/Dodg-13
90Target-403
C46-27
E107
T206
WG3-23

Kelley, M.
W516-26

Kelley, Rich
91Niagara/ClBest-18
91Niagara/ProC-3628

Kelley, Richard
64T-476R
66OPC-84R
66T-84R
67OPC-138
67T-138
68T-203
69MLB/St-193
69T-359
70MLB/St-114
70OPC-474
70T-474
72MB-178
72OPC-412
72T-412

Kelley, Steve
75QuadC

Kelley, Thomas
64T-552R
66OPC-44R
66T-44R
67T-214
71OPC-463
71T-463
72OPC-97
72T-97

Kelliher, Paul
91Idaho/ProC-4332
91Pulaski/ProC-4008

Kellman, Howard
88Indianap/ProC-525M
89Indianap/ProC-1216

Kellner, Alex
49B-222
50B-14
51B-57
51FB
52B-226
52T-201
53B/Col-107
53Exh/Can-64
54B-51
55B-53
55Rodeo
56T-176
57T-280
58T-3
59T-101
79TCMA-55
Exh47

Kellner, Frank
90Osceola/Star-13
91Osceola/ClBest-19
91Osceola/ProC-693

Kellogg, Geoffrey
91Beloit/ClBest-4
91Beloit/ProC-2099

Kellogg, Jeff
89EastLDD/ProC-DD48UMP

Kelly, Anthony
86SLAS-22
89Tucson/ProC-186

Kelly, Bill
47Signal

Kelly, Bill
80Indianap-23
81Indianap-22
82Omaha-7

Kelly, Brian
75Clinton

Kelly, Bryan
83Evansvl-4
86Nashvl-14
87Toledo-29

Kelly, Charles H.
N172

Kelly, Dale Patrick
(Pat)
75QuadC
78Syrac
79T-714R
80OPC-329R
80Syrac-15
80T-674R
82F-372
83GlenF-11
86CharRain-11MG
88Wichita-40MG
89Pac/SenLg-134
89TexLAS/GS-1MG
89Wichita/Rock-6MG
89Wichita/Rock/Up-2MG
90LasVegas/CMC-22MG
90LasVegas/ProC-136MG
90Sumter/Best-8MG
90Sumter/ProC-2440MG
91Durham/ProC-1555MG
91Pac/SenLg-56
91Rockford/ClBest-27MG
91Rockford/ProC-2062MG

Kelly, Dean
88PrWill/Star-13
89FtLaud/Star-11

Kelly, Eliqio
78Newar

Kelly, George L.
21Exh-89
28Yueng-20
29Exh/4-7
40PB-141
49Remar
50Remar
80Pac/Leg-62
80SSPC/HOF
87Conlon/2-45
89HOF/St-8
89Smok/Dodg-14
90Target-404
91Conlon/Sport-60
92Conlon/Sport-561
E120
E121/120
E121/80
E122
E126-60
E210-20
E220
V100
V61-119
W501-72
W502-20
W515-32
W517-11
W572
W575

Kelly, Harold Patrick
(Pat)
69T-619R
70MLB/St-222
70OPC-57
70T-57
71OPC-413
71T-413
72MB-179
72OPC-326
72T-326
73OPC-261
73T-261
74K-47
74OPC-46
74T-46
74T/St-156
75OPC-82
75T-82
75T/M-82
76OPC-212
76SSPC-152
76T-212
77T-469
78T-616
79T-188
80T-543
81D-600
82T-417
91Crown/Orio-235

Kelly, Hal
79Tulsa-22

Kelly, Jimy
88Knoxvl/Best-5
89Dunedin/Star-9

Kelly, John O.
N172

Kelly, Joseph
(Joe)
88CapeCod/Sum-173
90Yakima/Team-17

Kelly, John
90Johnson/Star-16
91SALAS/ProC-SAL42
91Savan/ClBest-7
91Savan/ProC-1648
91Single/ClBest-166

Kelly, Kevin
89BurlB/ProC-1623
89BurlB/Star-12
90BurlB/Best-21
90BurlB/ProC-2345
90BurlB/Star-15

Kelly, Leonard
87BurlEx-1

Kelly, Michael
88CapeCod/Sum-10
88WinHaven/Star-10
89Alaska/Team-6
90EastLAS/ProC-EL39
90Foil/Best-191
90NewBrit/Best-11
90NewBrit/Star-6
91Classic/DP-2
91Durham/ClBest-6
91DurhamUp/ProC-1

Kelly, Michael
(King)
50Callahan
75F/Pion-8
80SSPC/HOF
E223
N162
N172
N172
N28
N284
N403
N526
N690/2
WG1-5

Kelly, Mike
87Elmira/Black-15
87Elmira/Red-15
89Lynch/Star-11

Kelly, Pat F.
88Oneonta/ProC-2043
89PrWill/Star-10
89Star/Wax-89
90A&AASingle/ProC-32
90Albany/Best-16
90Albany/ProC-1041
90Albany/Star-8
90EastLAS/ProC-EL21
91B-155
91Classic/III-44
91ColClip/LineD-110
91ColClip/ProC-602
91D/Rook-1
91F/Ultra-381MLP
91F/UltraUp-U41
91F/Up-U46
91Leaf/GRook-BC17
91S/RookTr-107T
91T/StClub/II-381
91T/Tr-67T
91UD-76
92Classic/I-48
92D/I-370
92F-233
92S/100RisSt-5
92S/I-185
92T-612
92T/91Debut-98
92UD-435

Kelly, Rafael
75QuadC
76QuadC

Kelly, Robert Edward
52T-348

Kelly, Roberto
83Greens-19
84Greens-4
86Albany/TCMA-2
87Colum-18
87Colum/Pol-14
87Colum/TCMA-22
88D-635
88D/Rook-16
88D/Y/Bk-635
88F-212
88S-634RP
88T/Tr-57T
89B-183
89Classic/Up/2-167
89D-433
89D/Best-273
89F-256
89Panini/St-395
89S-487
89S/HotRook-90
89S/NWest-18
89S/YS/II-25
89T-691
89T/Big-152
89ToysRUs-18
89UD-590
90AlbanyDG/Best-3
90B-444
90Classic/Up-27
90D-192
90D/BestAL-94
90F-446
90Leaf/I-17
90OPC-109
90Panini/St-119
90PublInt/St-538
90PublInt/St-597
90S-100
90S/100St-57
90S/NWest-6
90Sf-184
90T-109
90T/Big-247
90T/St-312
90T/TVYank-31
90UD-193
91B-166
91Classic/200-28
91D-400MVP
91D-538
91F-668
91F/Ultra-235
91Leaf/I-38
91Leaf/Stud-94
91OPC-11
91Panini/FrSt-328
91Panini/St-268
91Panini/Top15-31
91Panini/Top15-47
91RedFoley/St-57
91S-119
91S/100SS-96
91Seven/3DCoin-9NE
91T-11
91T/CJMini/II-16
91T/StClub/II-319
91UD-372
92D/I-73
92F-234
92S/100SS-96
92S/I-324
92T-266
92UD-577

Kelly, Tim
86Bakers-17CO
87PalmSp-18
88MidldA/GS-3

Kelly, Tom
82Orlan/B-13MG
82OrlTw/A-12MG
87T-618MG
88T-194MG
89D/AS-10MG
89D/PopUp-10MG
89T-14MG
89T/Gloss22-1MG

90OPC-429MG
90T-429MG
91OPC-201MG
91T-201MG
92T-459MG

Kelly, Van
71Richm/Team-9

Kelly, William J.
D304
E254
E270/2
E97
T207
T213/blue
T215/blue

Kelso, Bill
65OPC-194R
65T-194R
67T-367R
68T-511

Kelso, Jeff
89BendB/Legoe-22
90PalmSp/Cal-214
90PalmSp/ProC-2590

Keltner, Ken
39Exh
41DP-79
47HomogBond-26
48L-45
49B-125
50B-186
89Pac/Leg-143
89Swell-87
D305
Exh47
R303/A
R303/B
R311/Gloss

Kemmerer, Russ
55B-222
55T-18
55T/DH-4
58T-137
59T-191
60T-362
61T-56
61T/St-121
62T-576
63T-338

Kemmler, Rudolph
N172
N172/BC
N370
Scrapps

Kemnitz, Brent
85Anchora-17CO
87Anchora-17CO
90WichSt-41

Kemp, Hugh
84Cedar-7
87Nashvl-11
88AAA/ProC-27
88Nashvl/CMC-7
88Nashvl/ProC-479
88Nashvl/Team-15
89Nashvl/CMC-5
89Nashvl/ProC-1294
89Nashvl/Team-10
90BuffB/CMC-5
90BuffB/ProC-368
90BuffB/Team-10

Kemp, Joe
88SanBern/Best-21
88SanBern/Cal-35
89Modesto/Cal-280

Kemp, Rod
79LodiD-1

Kemp, Steve
77T-492R
78BK/T-18
78Ho-55
78OPC-167
78T-21
79Ho-15
79OPC-97
79T-196
80K-33
80OPC-166
80T-315
80T/S-29
81Coke
81D-249
81Detroit-86
81Drake-27
81F-459
81F/St-7
81MSA/Disc-19
81OPC-152
81Sqt-27SP
81T-593
81T/SO-11
81T/St-74
82D-594
82F-271
82F/St-160
82K-39
82OPC-296
82T-666TL
82T-670
82T/St-185
82T/Tr-54T
83D-269
83Drake-13
83F-239
83OPC-260
83RoyRog/Disc-5
83T-260
83T/St-50
83T/Tr-53
84D-469
84Drake-16
84F-129
85FunFoodPin-58
84Nes/792-440
84OPC-301
84T-440
85D-225
85F-132
85F/Up-U64
85Leaf-100
85OPC-120
85T-120
85T/Tr-66T
86D-200
86F-610
86LasVegas-9
86T-387
87OKCty-11
88AlaskaAS70/Team-19
88Mother/R-8
89Pac/SenLg-10
89T/SenLg-52
89TM/SenLg-58
90EliteSenLg-8
90Smok/SoCal-6

Kemper, Robbie
89Clinton/ProC-896
90Erie/Star-11

Kenaga, Jeff
82Evansvl-22
83Evansvl-20
84CharlO-8

Kendall, Fred
72T-532
73OPC-221
73T-221
74McDon
74OPC-53SD
74T-53
74T/St-95
75OPC-332
75T-332
75T/M-332
76OPC-639
76SSPC-122
76T-639
77OPC-213
77T-576
78PapaG/Disc-13
78T-426
79T-83
80T-598

Kendall, Phil
91Billings/ProC-3748

Kendrick, Pete
83Madis/LF-23
84Albany-14
87ElPaso-4
88Denver/ProC-1269

Kenins, John N.
N172

Kennedy, Bo
87Penin-23
89Saraso/Star-12
90BirmB/Best-20
90BirmB/ProC-1108
91BirmB/LineD-65
91BirmB/ProC-1452

Kennedy, Dan
89WinSalem/Star-11
89Wythe/Star-18

Kennedy, Dave
89Elmira/Pucko-23

Kennedy, John E.
64T-203
65OPC-119
65T-119
66T-407
67OPC-111
67T-111
69T-631
70McDon-2
70OPC-53
70T-53
71MLB/St-319
71OPC-498
71T-498
72T-674
73OPC-437
73T-437
86Alban/TCM-24C
90Target-407

Kennedy, Junior
76Indianap-13
77Phoenix
79T-501
80T-377
81D-424
81F-203
81T-447
82D-188
82F-70
82RedLob
82T-723
82T/Tr-55T
83D-529
83F-500
83T-204

Kennedy, Kevin
78RochR
79RochR-3
80RochR-11
81RochR-10
87Bakers-15
88SanAn/Best-23
88TexLgAS/GS-22
89Albuq/ProC-72
90AAAGame/ProC-AAA32MG
90Albuq/CMC-27MG
90Albuq/ProC-361MG
90Albuq/Trib-16MG
91Albuq/LineD-24MG
91Albuq/ProC-1157MG

Kennedy, Lloyd Vernon
37Exh/4-10
37OPC-135
38G-256
38G-280
92Conlon/Sport-365
V300
WG8-37

Kennedy, Mike
91SoOreg/ClBest-21
91SoOreg/ProC-3849

Kennedy, Monte
47TipTop
49B-237
49Eureka-112
50B-175
51B-163
52B-213
52BR
52T-124

Kennedy, Robert D.
47TipTop
51B-296
51T/RB-29
52NumNum-16
52T-77
53T-33
54Esskay
54T-155
55Esskay
55T-48
55T/DH-87
56T-38
56T/Pin-34
57T-149
64T-486CO
65T-457CO
68OPC-183MG
68T-183
85T-135FS
90Target-405
91Crown/Orio-236
91T/Arc53-33

Kennedy, Terry
78ArkTr
79T-724R
80T-569
81D-428
81F-541
81OPC-353
81T-353
81T/Tr-780
82D-121
82Drake-20
82F-574
82F/St-105
82OPC-65
82T-65
82T/St-100
83D-220
83D-26DK
83D/AAS-11
83F-362
83OPC-274
83T-274
83T-742TL
83T/Gloss40-6
83T/St-293
84D-112
84D/AAS-8
84F-304
85FunFoodPin-47
84Mother/Pad-5
84Nes/792-366TL
84Nes/792-455
84OPC-166
84Seven-17W
84Smok/Pad-14
84T-366TL
84T-455
84T/St-154
85D-429
85F-37
85Leaf-33
85Mother/Pad-10
85OPC-194
85T-135FS
85T-635
85T/St-148
86D-356
86D/AAS-7
86D/PopUp-7
86F-327
86OPC-230
86T-230
86T-306M
86T/Gloss22-20
86T/St-111
86T/St-152
87D-205
87D/OD-142
87F-419
87F/Up-U56
87French-15
87OPC-303
87T-540
87T/St-108
87T/Tr-57T
88D-150
88D/AS-9
88D/Best-30
88D/PopUp-9
88F-563
88French-15
88Leaf-99
88OPC-180
88Panini/St-227M
88Panini/St-7
88S-123
88S/WaxBox-1
88Sf-94
88T-180
88T/Gloss22-9
88T/St-161
88T/St-225
88T/St/Backs-55
89B-470
89D-141
89F-610
89F/Up-128
89Mother/Giants-8
89OPC-309
89Panini/St-256
89S-123
89S/Tr-30T
89T-705
89T/Big-180
89T/St-235
89T/Tr-59T
89UD-469
90B-241
90D-602
90D/BestNL-132
90F-58
90Leaf/I-67
90Mother/Giant-12
90OPC-372
90PublInt/St-71
90S-7
90T-372
90T/Big-16
90UD-397
91B-631
91Crown/Orio-237
91D-94
91F-263
91F/Ultra-321
91F/Ultra-399CL
91Leaf/I-216
91Mother/Giant-12
91OPC-66
91Panini/FrSt-66
91PG&E-5
91S-548
91T-66
91T/StClub/I-91
91UD-404
92S/II-503
92T-253
92UD-192

Kennedy, Theodore A.
N172

Kennedy, William G.
(Bill)
49B-105
52T-102
53T-94
60HenryH-25
91T/Arc53-94

Kennedy, William V.
(Brickyard)
90Target-406

Kennedy, William
N284
N300/unif

Kennelley, Steve
87Columbia-11

Kennemur, Paul
76Baton

Kenner, Jeff
86ArkTr-10

Kenney, Jerry
69T-519R
70OPC-219
70T-219
71MLB/St-491
71OPC-572
71T-572
72MB-180
72OPC-158
72T-158
73OPC-514
73T-514

Kenny, Brian
91Geneva/ClBest-10
91Geneva/ProC-4210

Kenny, Terry
75Cedar

Kent, Bernard
85Beloit-12

Kent, Dave
89Oneonta/ProC-2119

Kent, Jeff
88CapeCod/Sum-169
89StCath/ProC-2091
90Dunedin/Star-13
90FSLAS/Star-33
91Knoxvl/LineD-360
91Knoxvl/ProC-1775
91Single/ClBest-108

Kent, John
(Bo)

86Cram/PCL-73
87Modesto-1
88Huntsvl/BK-10
Kent, Lewis
87Kinston-7
88Kinston/Star-14
Kent, Matt
86Stockton-12
Kent, Maury
90Target-999
Kent, Troy
88Martins/Star-20
89Spartan/ProC-1033
89Spartan/Star-11
91SanBern/ClBest-7
91SanBern/ProC-1983
Kent, Wes
81AppFx-26
82AppFx-13
83GlenF-3
Kenworthy, Dick
68OPC-63
68T-63
Kenworthy, William
(Duke)
WG7-24
Kenyon, J.J.
N172
Kenyon, Robert
81VeroB-7
82VeroB-7
Keon, Kevin
90Niagara/Pucko-19
Keough, Joseph
69T-603
70T-589
71MLB/St-417
71OPC-451
71T-451
72OPC-133
72T-133
Keough, Matt
78T-709R
79Ho-59
79OPC-284
79T-554
80OPC-74
80T-134
81D-358
81F-588
81OPC-301
81T-301
82D-71
82F-95
82F/St-129
82Granny-6
82OPC-87
82T-87
82T/St-225
83D-239
83F-521
83Granny-27
83T-413
83T/St-109
83T/Tr-54
84D-627
84F-130
84Nes/792-203
84OPC-203
84T-203
85Louisvl-16
87Mother/A's-18
88Chatt/Team-17
90Swell/Great-127
Keough, R. Marty
58T-371
59T-303
60T-71
61T-146
62J-69
62P-69
62P/Can-69
62Salada-79
62Shirriff-79
62T-258
63FrBauer-12
63J-135
63P-135
63T-21
64T-166
65OPC-263
65T-263
66T-334
Kepshire, Kurt
81Cedar-2
82Cedar-5
83ArkTr-4
84Louisvl-17
85D-382
85F-230
85T-474
86D-504
86F-39
86KAS/Disc-13
86Louisvl-14
86Schnucks-11
86T-256
88Indianap/CMC-2
88Indianap/ProC-506
89Portl/CMC-3
89Portl/ProC-215
Kerdoon, Randy
87SLCity/Taco-21ANN
Kerfeld, Charlie
85Cram/PCL-73
86D/Rook-6
86F-303
86Pol/Ast-10
86Sf/Rook-23
86T/Tr-52T
87D-209
87F-60
87F/Excit-31
87Leaf-195
87Mother/Ast-12
87OPC-145
87Sf-146
87T-145
87T/St-28
87ToysRUs-15
88ColAst/Best-1
88OPC-392
88S-479
88T-608
89Tucson/CMC-8
89Tucson/ProC-188
89Tucson/JP-11
Kerfut, George
90FSLAS/Star-10
90Miami/I/Star-14
90Miami/II/Star-12
91Miami/ClBest-15
91Miami/ProC-403
Keriazakos, Const.
(Gus)
55B-14
Kerkes, Kevin
89Wausau/GS-22
Kern, Jim
75OkCty
75OPC-621R
75T-621R
75T/M-621R
76SSPC-509
77Pep-7
77T-41
78OPC-165
78T-253
79OPC-297
79T-573
80OPC-192
80T-369
81D-27
81F-618
81F/St-18
81OPC-197
81T-197
82Coke/Reds
82D-89
82F-322
82OPC-59
82T-463
82T/Tr-56T
83D-355
83F-240
83T-772
83TrueVal/WSox-67
86OhHenry-46
Kern, Lloyd D.
77WHave
79WHave-28
79WHave-29M
80LynnS-22
81LynnS-26
Kernek, George B.
66Pep/Tul
66T-544R
Kerns, Russ
V362-38
Kerr, Jason
91Yakima/ClBest-16
91Yakima/ProC-4244
Kerr, John Francis
33G-214
49Remar
Kerr, John J.
(Buddy)
47HomogBond-27
48B-20
49B-186
49Eureka-113
50B-55
50Drake-15
51B-171
79TCMA-113
D305
R302-102
Kerr, John L.
28Exh/PCL-16
29Exh/4-19
Kerr, Richard
(Dickie)
21Exh-90
88Pac/8Men-47
88Pac/8Men-56
88Pac/8Men-97
E121/120
E121/80
E122
E220
W501-37
W514-23
W575
Kerr, Zackary
(Zach)
89Erie/Star-10
90CLAS/CL-1
90Freder/Team-10
91Freder/ClBest-5
Kerrigan, Joe
77OPC-171
77T-341
78OPC-108
78T-549
79RochR-2
79T-37
81Indianap-24
82OkCty-13
84Stuart-33
86Provigo-14CO
87Jaxvl-26
88Indianap/ProC-499M
90Indianap/ProC-309CO
91Crown/Orio-238
91Harris/LineD-275CO
91Harris/ProC-618CO
Kerrigan, Rob
87Jamestn-21
88James/ProC-1898
88Rockford-18
89Rockford-18
89Rockford/Team-14
90WPalmB/Star-11
Kershaw, Scott
86AppFx-12
Keshock, Christopher
87CharWh-22
Kesler, Mike
87QuadC-13
Kesselmark, Joe
88SanAn/Best-11
89SanAn/Best-9
90Canton/Best-10
90Canton/ProC-1304
Kesses, Steve
76Wausau
Kessinger, Don
66OPC-24
66T-24
67T-419
68OPC-159
68T-159
69Kelly/Pin-9
69MB-144
69MLB/St-123
69MLBPA/Pin-48
69Sunoco/Pin-6
69T-225
69T-422AS
69T/S-18
69T/St-16
70Dunkin-4
70MLB/St-20
70OPC-456AS
70OPC-80
70T-456AS
70T-80
71K-9
71MD
71MLB/St-36
71OPC-455
71T-455
71T/Coins-119
71T/tatt-15
72MB-181
72OPC-145
72T-145
73OPC-285
73T-285
74OPC-38
74T-38
74T/DE-52
74T/St-16
75Ho-77
75Ho/Twink-77
75OPC-315
75T-315
75T/M-315
76Crane-25
76Ho-134
76MSA/Disc
76OPC-574
76SSPC-315
76T-574
77T-229
78T-672
79T-404MG
79T-467
89Swell-112
90Pac/Legend-34
90Swell/Great-69
91Swell/Great-115
Kessinger, Keith
89Bluefld/Star-12
90Wausau/Best-18
90Wausau/ProC-2131
Kessinger, Robert
90Wausau/Star-12
91Freder/ClBest-29
Kessler, Greg
89Wythe/Star-19
90Geneva/ProC-3037
90Geneva/Star-16
Kester, Rick
70T-621R
71OPC-494R
71Richm/Team-10
71T-494
72OPC-351R
72T-351
Ketchel, Stanley
T3/Box-67
Ketchen, Douglas
90Ashvl/ClBest-6
90AubAs/Best-8
91Ashvl/ProC-564
Ketchen, J.B.
90AubAs/ProC-3415
Ketleers, Cotuit
88CapeCod-24
Keuter, Greg
89Wythe/Star-30TR
Key, Denny
91Burllnd/ProC-3298
Key, Greg
83Redwd-16
85MidldA-3
Key, Jimmy
84F/X-U61
84T/Tr-62T
84Tor/Fire-20
85D-559
85F-110
85OPC-193
85T-193
85Tor/Fire-16
86Ault-22
86D-561
86D/AAS-53
86F-63
86F-642M
86KayBee-18
86Leaf-219
86OPC-291
86T-545
86T/Mini-35
86T/St-191
86Tor/Fire-20
87D-244
87D/OD-37
87F-232
87Leaf-187
87OPC-29
87T-29
87T/St-192
87Tor/Fire-16
88Classic/Blue-249
88D-72
88D/Best-143
88F-114
88F/AwardWin-22
88F/Excit-24
88F/Hottest-22
88F/LL-23
88F/Mini-63
88F/RecSet-22
88F/SS-19
88F/St-74
88F/TL-17
88Ho/Disc-24
88Leaf-67
88OPC-47
88Panini/St-214
88RedFoley/St-42
88S-216
88Sf-116
88T-395AS
88T-682
88T/Coins-17
88T/Mini-39
88T/Revco-27
88T/St-190
88Tor/Fire-22
89B-243
89D-188
89D/Best-87
89F-236
89OPC-229
89Panini/St-462
89S-480
89Sf-167
89T-229
89T/LJN-24
89T/St-186
89Tor/Fire-22
89UD-291
90B-509
90D-231
90D/BestAL-42
90F-85
90Leaf/I-211
90OPC-371
90Panini/St-181
90PublInt/St-518
90RedFoley/St-53
90S-407
90T-371
90T/St-191
90Tor/BlueJ-22
90UD-462
91B-19
91Classic/200-63
91Classic/III-45
91D-98
91F-178
91F/Ultra-364
91Leaf/I-103
91OPC-741
91OPC/Premier-71
91Panini/FrSt-351
91S-422
91S/ToroBJ-3
91S/ToroBJ-38AS
91T-741
91T/StClub/I-221
91Tor/Fire-22
91UD-667
91USPlayC/AS-8D
92D/I-219
92F-332
92S/I-96
92T-482
92UD-302
Keyes, Stewart
88CapeCod/Sum-148
Keyser, Brian

89Utica/Pucko-12
90Saraso/Star-13
91Saraso/ClBest-6
91Saraso/ProC-1109

Khalifa, Sammy
83AlexD-2
85Cram/PCL-227
86D-308
86F-611
86Leaf-178
86T-316
86T/St-127
87T-164
87Vanco-11
89BuffB/CMC-15
89BuffB/ProC-1667

Khoury, Mike
86Watertn-10

Khoury, Scott
86Hagers-8
87Hagers-26
88Watlo/ProC-672
89Canton/Best-19
89Canton/ProC-1310
89Canton/Star-10

Kibbe, Jay
81Redwd-4
84Cram/PCL-119

Kibler, John
88TM/Umpire-4
89TM/Umpire-2
90TM/Umpire-2

Kibler, Russell
85Madis-19
85Madis/Pol-16
86Madis-13
86Madis/Pol-13

Kida, Masao
88Miami/Star-14

Kidd, Dennis
90Miami/I/Star-12
90Miami/II/Star-13
91Miami/ClBest-29
91Miami/ProC-422

Kiecker, Dana
86NewBrit-15
87NewBrit-17
88Pawtu/CMC-10
88Pawtu/ProC-461
89Pawtu/CMC-4
89Pawtu/Dunkin-19
89Pawtu/ProC-701
90D/Rook-28
90F/Up-U72
90Leaf/II-525
90S/Tr-102T
90T/Tr-50T
90T/TVRSox-12
91B-108
91D-347
91F-99
91F/UltraUp-U6
91Leaf/II-341
91OPC-763
91Pep/RSox-10
91S-77
91S/100RisSt-92
91T-763
91T/90Debut-77
91T/StClub/I-140
91ToysRUs-15
91UD-507
92S/II-732
92T-163

Kiefer, Mark
89Beloit/I/Star-11
89Beloit/II/Star-17
91ElPaso/LineD-190
91ElPaso/ProC-2744

Kiefer, Steve
82Madis-3
83Albany-12
84Cram/PCL-78
85Cram/PCL-139
85D-35
85F-647
85Leaf-27
86D-420
86Vanco-15
87Denver-18
88D-542
88F-167
88Pol/Brew-30
88S-630
88T-187
89Colum/CMC-15
89Colum/Pol-11
89Colum/ProC-740
90BuffB/CMC-17
90BuffB/ProC-379
90BuffB/Team-11

Kiely, John
89Lakeland/Star-12
90A&AASingle/ProC-18
90London/ProC-1264
91Toledo/LineD-587
91Toledo/ProC-1927
92T/91Debut-99

Kiely, Leo
52T-54
54T-171
55T-36
55T/DH-43
58T-204
59T-199
60T-94

Kiernan, J.F.
T206

Kierst, Kevin
87Knoxvl-24

Kies, Norman
V355-120

Kiess, Paul
80Penin/B-17
80Penin/C-23

Kilduff, Pete
D327
E121/120
E121/80
E122
E220
V100
W501-93
W575

Kile, Darryl
89BBAmerAA/BProC-AA12
89ColMud/Best-4
89ColMud/ProC-133
89ColMud/Star-15
89Tucson/JP-12
90B-61
90Tucson/CMC-4
90Tucson/ProC-201
91B-548
91D/Rook-5
91F/UltraUp-U84
91F/Up-U90
91Leaf/Stud-178
91Mother/Ast-27
91S/RookTr-86T
91T/Tr-68T
91UD/Ext-774
92Classic/I-49
92D/I-309
92F-439
92S/100RisSt-4
92S/II-494
92T-134
92T/91Debut-100
92UD-374

Kiley, Craig
84LitFalls-15

Kilgo, Rusty
89James/ProC-2156
90A&AASingle/ProC-110
90Rockford/ProC-2685
91FSLAS/ProC-FSL43
91WPalmB/ClBest-6
91WPalmB/ProC-1222

Kilgus, Paul
86Tulsa-20
87OKCty-1
88D-469
88D/Best-111
88F-471
88Mother/R-19
88S-536
88T-427
89B-285
89D-283
89D/Best-149
89D/Tr-42
89F-525
89F/Up-76
89Mara/Cubs-39
89OPC-276
89S-271
89T-276
89T/Tr-60T
89UD-335
89UD/Ext-797
90B-508
90D-276
90F-34
90OPC-86
90PublInt/St-196
90S-196
90Syrac/CMC-9
90Syrac/ProC-566
90Syrac/Team-13
90T-86
90Tor/BlueJ-39
90UD-155
91Crown/Orio-499
92S/I-268

Kilkenny, Mike
69T-544
70MLB/St-209
70OPC-424
70T-424
71MLB/St-397
71OPC-86
71T-86
72OPC-337
72T-337
73OPC-551
73T-551

Killebrew, Cameron
79Wausau-22

Killebrew, Harmon
55T-124
55T/DH-111
56T-164
58T-288
59HRDerby-10
59T-515
60Bz-20
60NuCard-49
60P
60T-210
60T/tatt-26
60T/tatt-91
61Clover-10
61NuCard-449
61P-92
61Peters-18
61T-80
61T/St-181
62Bz
62Exh
62J-85
62P-85
62P/Can-85
62Salada-36
62Shirriff-36
62T-316IA
62T-53LL
62T-70
62T/bucks
62T/St-76
63Bz-7
63Exh
63J-5
63P-5
63T-4LL
63T-500
63T/SO
64Bz-7
64T-10LL
64T-12LL
64T-177
64T-81M
64T/Coins-112
64T/Coins-133AS
64T/S-38
64T/St-34
64T/SU
64T/tatt
64Wheat/St-25
65Bz-7
65OldLond-28
65OPC-3LL
65OPC-5LL
65T-3LL
65T-400
65T-5LL
65T/E-56
65T/trans-52
66Bz-11
66OPC-120
66T-120
66T/RO-50
67Bz-11
67OPC/PI-23
67T-241LL
67T-243LL
67T-334M
67T-460
67T/PI-23
67T/Test/SU-6
68Bz-8
68Coke
68Dexter-46
68OPC-4LL
68OPC-6LL
68T-220
68T-361AS
68T-490M
68T-4LL
68T-6LL
68T/G-5
68T/Post-10
69Citgo-4
69MB-145
69MLB/St-68
69MLBPA/Pin-14
69T-375
69T/decal
69T/S-19
69T/St-195
69Trans-11
70K-61
70MB-12
70MLB/St-234
70OPC-150
70OPC-64LL
70OPC-66LL
70T-150
70T-64LL
70T-66LL
70T/S-4
70T/SO
70Trans-15
71Bz
71Bz/Test-17
71K-55
71MD
71MLB/St-465
71MLB/St-566
71OPC-550
71OPC-65LL
71T-550
71T-65LL
71T/Coins-100
71T/GM-8
71T/S-60
71T/tatt-6
71T/tatt-6a
72MB-182
72OPC-51
72OPC-52IA
72OPC-88LL
72T-51
72T-52IA
72T-88LL
72T/Post-20
73OPC-170
73T-170
73T/Comics-9
73T/Lids-25
73T/PinUps-9
74OPC-400
74T-400
74T/St-208
75OPC-207MV
75OPC-640
75T-207MV
75T-640
75T/M-207MV
75T/M-640
76Laugh/Jub-13
76SSPC-168
78TCMA-90
80Pac/Leg-69
80Laugh/3/4/5-14
82CJ-15
82KMart-15
84West/1-23
85CircK-5
86BLChew-5
86Sf/Dec-48M
87KMart-4
87Nestle/DT-22
88Chatt/Team-18
88Pac/Leg-86
89Kahn/Coop-7
89Pac/Leg-163
89Swell-70
89T/LJN-49
90MSA/AGFA-3
90Pac/Legend-35
91CollAB-34
91K/3D-6
91LineD-41
91Swell/Great-49
91UD/HOF-H1
91UD/HOF-x
Exh47
PM10/Sm-88
Rawl

Killian, Ed
12Sweet/Pin-27
81Detroit-87
E254
T201
T205
T206
T213/brown

Killefer, Wade H.
(Red)
16FleischBrd-51

Killifer, William
09Buster/Pin-8
14CJ-135
14Piedmont/St-30
15CJ-135
21Exh-91
BF2-86
D327
D328-93
D329-95
D350/2-93
E121/120
E121/80
E122
E135-93
E254
E286
M101/4-95
M101/5-93
M116
V100
W501-56
W514-87

Killingsworth, Kirk
83Tulsa-12
85Tulsa-32
86Tulsa-3
87OKCty-9

Killingsworth, Sam
75BurlB

Kilner, John Steven
86Durham-16
87Greenvl/Best-14
88Greenvl/Best-20
89Greenvl/Star-11
89Richm/Ko-30
90Foil/Best-289
90Greenvl/Best-21
90Greenvl/ProC-1125
90Greenvl/Star-10

Kilroy, Mathew
N172
N284

Kim, Wendell
75Lafay
77Phoenix
78Cr/PCL-98
81Clinton-2
82Clinton-2
86Shrev-13
86Shrev-14
87Phoenix-23
88Phoenix/CMC-24
88Phoenix/ProC-65
90Mother/Giant-21M
91Mother/Giant-27CO

Kimball, Newt
90Target-409

Kimball, Ricky
88CapeCod/Sum-142
91SoOreg/ClBest-6
91SoOreg/ProC-3838

Kimball, Scott
90Beloit/Best-8
90Beloit/Star-11
90Foil/Best-124

Kimberlin, Keith
89NiagFls/Pucko-13
90FSLAS/Star-34
90Lakeland/Star-15
91London/LineD-389
91London/ProC-1885
91Single/ClBest-170
Kimbler, Doug
90Niagara/Pucko-2
91Fayette/ClBest-19
91Fayette/ProC-1178
Kimbrough, Larry
86Negro/Frit-37
86Negro/Frit-61
Kimm, Bruce
77T-554
81F-355
81T-272
83Cedar-1
83Cedar/LF-22
86TexGold-CO
88Kahn/Reds-CO
89VFJuice-36CO
90CedarDG/Best-27MG
Kimsey, Chad
92Conlon/Sport-511
Kimsey, Keith
91Bristol/ClBest-12
91Bristol/ProC-3618
Kin, Clinton
82Clinton-32
Kindall, Jerry
58T-221
59T-274
60T-444
61P-199
61T-27
62AmTract-51A
62AmTract-51B
62J-191
62P-191
62P/Can-191
62Sugar-13
62T-292
63F-13
63J-68
63P-68
63Sugar-13
63T-36
78TCMA-218
78TCMA-271
Kinder, Ellis
50B-152
51B-128
52T-78
53T-44
54B-98
54T-47
55T-115
55T/DH-130
56T-336
57T-352
79TCMA-115
91T/Arc53-44
Exh47
R423-55
Kindred, Curt
83Visalia/LF-22
84Visalia-2
86Cedar/TCMA-6
87Cedar-4
Kindred, Vincent L.
87Spring/Best-23
89Savan/ProC-355
90Foil/Best-302
90Spring/Best-10
Kiner, Ralph
47HomogBond-28
47TipTop
48B-3
48L-91
49B-29
49Eureka-164
50B-33
51BR-C1
51T/CAS
51T/RB-15
52B-11
52BR
52Dix-53
52RM-NL12
52StarCal/L-77B
52Wheat
53B/Col-80
53Exh/Can-22
53RM-NL15
53T-191
54B-45
54Dix
54RH
55B-197
55Gol/Ind-13
55Salem
60F-79
61F-50
74Laugh/ASG-51
77T-437HL
79TCMA-13
80Pac/Leg-81
80SSPC/HOF
82CJ-16
83D/HOF-38
85CircK-30
85West/2-36
86Sf/Dec-35
88Pac/Leg-9
89T/LJN-141
90Pac/Legend-36
90Swell/Great-80
91CollAB-12
91K/3D-15
91Swell/Great-50
91T/Arc53-191
D305
Exh47
PM10/Sm-89
R302-110
R346-7
R423-58
King, Bryan
88SanBern/Best-22
88SanBern/Cal-28
89SanBern/Best-20
89SanBern/Cal-80
90Wmsprt/Best-12
90Wmsprt/ProC-1063
90Wmsprt/Star-13
91SanBern/ClBest-17
91SanBern/ProC-1994
King, Charles F.
(Silver)
N172
King, Charles G.
(Chick)
55B-133
59T-538
King, Clyde
51B-299
52B-56
52T-205
69T-274MG
70T-624MG
71Richm/Team-11
75OPC-589MG
75T-589MG
75T/M-589MG
83T-486MG
89Rini/Dodg-12
90Swell/Great-117
90Target-410
91Swell/Great-51
V362-26
King, David
90AppFox/Box-16
90AppFox/ProC-2101
91BBCity/ClBest-18
91BBCity/ProC-1404
King, Douglas
90Cedar/Best-21
90CharWh/ProC-2235
91CharWh/ClBest-5
91CharWh/ProC-2882
King, Edward Lee
E120
W572
King, Eric
86D/Rook-27
86Sf/Rook-42
86T/Tr-53T
87Cain's-19
87D-250
87F-155
87T-36
87T/GlossRk-8
87ToysRUs-16
88D-50
88F-60
88OPC-108
88Pep/T-25
88S-471
88T-499
88T/St-271
88Toledo/CMC-5
88Toledo/ProC-592
89Coke/WS-14
89D-535
89D/Best-235
89D/Tr-37
89F-136
89F/Up-19
89S-471
89S/Tr-26
89S/YS/II-7
89T-238
89T/Tr-61T
89UD-493
90B-304
90Coke/WSox-12
90D-337
90D/BestAL-46
90F-537
90Leaf/I-43
90OPC-786
90Publlnt/St-392
90S-28
90T-786
90UD-651
91B-63
91Classic/200-56
91D-271
91F-126
91Leaf/II-382
91Leaf/Stud-47
91OPC-121
91S-124
91S/RookTr-60T
91T-121
91T/StClub/II-328
91UD-281
91UD/Ext-782
92F-115
92S/I-144
92T-326
92UD-679
King, Frank J.
T206
King, Hal
76Laugh/Clown-32
R314/Can
V355-121
King, Hank
85Phill/TastyK-8CO
King, Harold
(Hal)
69MB-146
70OPC-327
70T-327
71MLB/St-15
71OPC-88
71T-88
72T-598
74OPC-362
74T-362
King, James H.
56T-74
57T-186
58T-332
61T-351
62T-42
63T-176
64T-217
65OPC-38
65T-38
65T/E-54
65T/trans-53
66T-369
67T-509
78TCMA-207
King, Jason
90Pittsfld/Pucko-8
King, Jeff
87Salem-24
88EastLAS/ProC-16
88F-653R
88Harris/ProC-859
89BuffB/CMC-16
89BuffB/ProC-1671
89F/Up-114
90D-480
90F-469
90Homer/Pirate-13
90HotRook/St-25
90Leaf/I-163
90OPC-454
90S-549
90S/100Ris-71
90S/YS/II-16
90T-454
90T/89Debut-66
90T/Big-117
90T/JumboR-17
90UD-557
91B-520
91D-233
91F-39
91F/Ultra-280
91Leaf/I-71
91OPC-272
91Panini/FrSt-117
91S-244
91T-272
91T/StClub/II-528
91UD-687
92D/II-468
92F-555
92S/II-511
92T-693
92UD-111
King, Jerome
83Tacoma-6
King, Jerry
81Bristol-13
King, Joe
82Danvl-22
83Peoria/LF-2
King, Kenny
87Miami-1
88Bakers/Cal-254
King, Kevin
80Wausau-20
81Wausau-27
83Chatt-18
84Chatt-2
86MidldA-12
87Edmon-8
88CapeCod/Sum-99
88Edmon/CMC-25
88Edmon/ProC-573
91Penin/ClBest-6
91Penin/ProC-372
King, Lee
V100
V61-92
King, Lynn
40Hughes-11
43Centen-16
King, Michael J.
87CharRain-4
88Charl/ProC-1202
89Watlo/ProC-1787
89Watlo/Star-15
King, Mike
81QuadC-17
84Nashvl-11
King, Nelson
55T-112
57T-349
79TCMA-247
King, Randy
85Newar-2
King, Richard
76Laugh/Clown-31
76Laugh/Clown-5
King, Ron
86Salem-14
King, Steve
86Jamestn-14
89Boise/ProC-2002
91London/LineD-439
91MidldA/ProC-432
King, Tom
75AppFx
76Clinton
Kingery, Mike
82CharR-12
84Memphis-7
85Omaha-23
86Omaha-13
86Omaha/TCMA-4
86Sf/Rook-37
87D-424
87D/OD-119
87F-371
87F/Up-U57
87Mother/Sea-17
87T-203
87T/Tr-58T
88D-322
88F-376
88Leaf-104
88Mother/Sea-17
88OPC-119
88Panini/St-193
88S-178
88T-532
88T/Big-160
89Calgary/CMC-20
89Calgary/ProC-545
89T-413
90D-601
90Phoenix/CMC-11
90Phoenix/ProC-23
91D-573
91Leaf/I-224
91Mother/Giant-21
91OPC-657
91PG&E-16
91S-547
91T-657
Kingman, Brian
77SanJose-19
79Ogden/TCMA-13
80T-671R
81D-360
81F-529
81T-284
82D-87
82F-96
82OPC-231
82T-476
82Tacoma-25
83F-522
83T-312
84Cram/PCL-15
Kingman, Dave
72OPC-147
72T-147
73K-44
73OPC-23
73T-23
74OPC-610
74T-610
74T/St-106
75Ho-85
75OPC-156
75T-156
75T/M-156
76Crane-26
76Ho-15
76Ho/Twink-15
76MSA/Disc
76OPC-193LL
76OPC-40
76SSPC-542
76T-193LL
76T-40
77BurgChef-141
77Ho-60
77K-35
77OPC-98
77Pep-69
77T-500
77T/CS-24
78Ho-26
78T-570
78Tastee/Discs-19
78Wiffle/Discs-34
79Ho-146
79OPC-191
79T-370
79T/Comics-20
80K-6
80OPC-127
80T-240
80T/S-16
81Coke
81D-553
81Drake-19
81F-291
81F/St-111
81OPC-361
81PermaGr/CC-18
81Sqt-14
81T-450
81T/HT
81T/St-151

81T/St-69
81T/Tr-781
82D-17DK
82D-182
82Drake-21
82F-530
82F/St-85
82K-19
82OPC-276
82T-690
82T/St-72
83D-301
83Drake-14
83F-548
83OPC-160
83OPC-161SV
83T-160
83T-161SV
83T-702LL
83T/St-11
83T/St-207
83T/St-259
84D-360
84D/Champs-3
84F-590
84F/X-U62
85FunFoodPin-36
84Mother/A's-15
84Nes/792-573
84Nes/792-703LL
84OPC-172
84T-573LL
84T-703LL
84T/Tr-63T
85CircK-26
85D-54
85D/AAS-32
85F-427
85F/LimEd-15
85F/St-14
85F/St-29
85F/St-48
85Leaf-182
85Mother/A's-2
85OPC-123
85T-730
85T/3D-12
85T/Gloss40-5
85T/St-320
85T/Super-59
86D-54
86F-423
86F/St-67
86Mother/A's-2
86OPC-322
86Sf-116
86Sf-145M
86Sf-68M
86T-410
86T/St-167
86Woolwth-16
87D-425
87F-396
87F/LL-27
87OPC-266
87RedFoley/St-115
87Sf-178
87T-709
87T/Mini-69
87T/St-173
88AlaskaAS60/Team-7
89Pac/Leg-175
89Pac/SenLg-164
89Pac/SenLg-186
89T/SenLg-101
89TM/SenLg-59
90EliteSenLg-126
90EliteSenLg-24
90Pac/Legend-87
90Smok/SoCal-7
91Swell/Great-52
91WIZMets-211

Kingman, Eamon
88CapeCod/Sum-17

Kingsolver, Kurt
80BurlB-19
82ElPaso-4

Kingwood, Tyrone
88WPalmB/Star-14
90SanBern/Cal-102
90SanBern/ProC-2644
91Hagers/LineD-234
91Hagers/ProC-2467
91Single/ClBest-304

Kinnard, Kenneth Joe
(Ken)
83Kinston/Team-9
86Ventura-10
87Greenvl/Best-27

Kinney, Brad
84Butte-13

Kinney, Dennis
75SanAn
79Hawaii-18
81D-363
81Evansvl-22
81F-505
81T-599
82Tacoma-6

Kinney, Tom
91Savan/ClBest-8
91Savan/ProC-1649
91Single/ClBest-139

Kinnunen, Mike
81Toledo-6
83Memphis-24
85Omaha-18
86RochR-12
88AAA/ProC-10
88Colum/CMC-9
88Colum/Pol-4
88Colum/ProC-316
89Denver/CMC-4
89Denver/ProC-33
91Crown/Orio-239

Kinsel, David
83AppFx/LF-23

Kinsella, W.P.
90LitSun-15

Kinslow, Thomas
90Target-1000
N300/unif

Kinyoun, Tavis
89Bristol/Star-13
91BBCity/ClBest-14
91BBCity/ProC-1400

Kinzer, Matt
85Spring-14
86StPete-17
88ArkTr/GS-14
88Louisvl-24
89Louisvl-25
89Louisvl/CMC-7
89Louisvl/ProC-1255
90F-652R
90S-628RP
90SpringDG/Best-13
90T/89Debut-67
90Toledo/CMC-5
90Toledo/ProC-144

Kipfer, Greg
82Wisco-2

Kipila, Jeff
89BendB/Legoe-18
90PalmSp/Cal-205
90PalmSp/ProC-2584
91QuadC/ClBest-18
91QuadC/ProC-2637

Kipp, Fred
59T-258
60T-202
90Target-1001

Kipper, Bob
83Peoria/LF-25
83TriCit-3
86D-44RR
86D/Rook-46
86F-648R
86T/Tr-54T
87D-572
87F-612
87T-289
88D-115
88F-332
88T-723
88T/Big-141
89B-414
89D-409
89F-211
89S-354
89T-114
89UD-520
89VFJuice-16
90D-362
90F-470
90Homer/Pirate-14
90OPC-441
90T-441
90UD-560
91D-720
91F-40
91OPC-551
91S-646
91T-551
91T/StClub/II-334
91UD-407
92D/II-622
92F-556
92S/I-340
92T-64

Kipper, Thornton
54T-108
55T-62
55T/DH-10

Kirby, Butch
81BurlB-18
82Beloit-15
83Beloit/LF-1

Kirby, Chris
78Wausau

Kirby, Clay
69T-637R
70MLB/St-115
70OPC-79
70T-79
71MLB/St-230
71OPC-333
71T-333
72OPC-173
72OPC-174IA
72T-173
72T-174A
73OPC-655
73T-655
73T/Lids-26
74OPC-287
74T-287
74T/St-96
75OPC-423
75T-423
75T/M-423
76OPC-579
76SSPC-28
76T-579
76T/Tr-579T

Kirby, Wayne
76Tucson-15
85VeroB-8
86VeroB-14
87Bakers-23
88Bakers/Cal-249
88SanAn/Best-8
89SanAn/Best-8
90Albuq/CMC-23
90Albuq/ProC-359
90Albuq/Trib-17
91ColoSp/LineD-87
91ColoSp/ProC-2197
92F-670
92T/91Debut-101

Kirchenwitz, Arno
78StPete
79ArkTr-1

Kirk, Chuck
90Hunting/ProC-3277
91Peoria/ClBest-6
91Peoria/ProC-1338

Kirk, Thomas
52Park-79

Kirk, Tim
86Watertn-11
87Salem-8
88CLAS/Star-11
88Salem/Star-9
89Penin/Star-9

Kirke, Judson
T207

Kirkland, Willie
58SFCallB-12
58T-128
59T-484
60T-172
61Kahn
61P-146
61T-15
62J-41
62Kahn
62P-41
62P/Can-41
62Salada-61
62Shirriff-61
62Sugar-11
62T-447
63J-72
63P-72
63Sugar-11
63T-187
64T-17
65OPC-148
65T-148
66T-434
91Crown/Orio-240

Kirkpatrick, Bill
75IntAS/TCMA-14

Kirkpatrick, Ed
63T-386R
64T-296
65T-393
66OPC-102
66T-102
67T-293
68T-552
69MB-147
69MLB/St-59
69T-529
70MLB/St-223
70OPC-165
70T-165
70T/PI-19
71MLB/St-418
71OPC-299
71T-299
72MB-183
72T-569
72T-570IA
73OPC-233
73T-233
74OPC-262
74T-262
74T/St-183
74T/Tr-262T
75OPC-171
75T-171
75T/M-171
76OPC-294
76SSPC-580
76T-294
77T-582
78T-77

Kirkpatrick, Enos
90Target-411

Kirkpatrick, Stephen
88Clearw/Star-16
88Spartan/Star-9
88Spartan/Star-9
89Clearw/Star-12
90Reading/Best-22
90Reading/ProC-1232
90Reading/Star-15

Kirkwood, Don
76OPC-108
76T-108
77T-519
78T-251
79OPC-334
79T-632

Kirsch, Paul
82Cedar-14
84Cedar-5
85Cedar-26
86Cedar/TCMA-24
87Cedar-24
91Portl/LineD-425CO
91Portl/ProC-1584CO

Kirt, Tim
90Niagara/Pucko-3

Kiser, Bob
88CapeCod-10
88CapeCod/Sum-74

Kiser, Dan
89Modesto/Chong-4

Kiser, Garland
86Cram/PCL-154
89Watertn/Star-12
90CLAS/CL-37
90Kinston/Team-12
91Canton/LineD-84
91Canton/ProC-976
91CLAS/ProC-CAR17
92T/91Debut-102

Kiser, Larry G.
76OkCty/Team-15

Kish, Bobby
82Spring-14
83StPete-8
84Savan-12

Kisinger, Charles S.
(Rube)
T206

Kison, Bruce
72OPC-72
72T-72
73OPC-141
73T-141
75OPC-598
75T-598
75T/M-598
76OPC-161
76SSPC-568
76T-161
77T-563
78T-223
79T-661
80T-28
81F-284
81T-340
82D-66
82F-467
82T-442
83D-267
83F-96
83T-712
84D-499
84F-523
84Nes/792-201
84OPC-201
84Smok/Cal-15
84T-201
84T/St-235
85D-377
85F-306
85F/Up-U65
85T-544
85T/Tr-67T
86D-616
86F-353
86T-117
89Pac/SenLg-136
89T/SenLg-11
89TM/SenLg-60
90EliteSenLg-37

Kissell, George
73OPC-497CO
73T-497CO
74OPC-236CO
74T-236CO
90Johnson/Star-28CO

Kissinger, John
C46-72

Kistaitis, Dale
90MedHat/Best-18

Kisten, Dale
88Hamil/ProC-1728
89Spring/Best-20
90SpringDG/Best-19
91ArkTr/LineD-36
91ArkTr/ProC-1279

Kite, Dan
88Elmira-6
90LSUGreat-3
90WinHaven/Star-13
91WinHaven/ClBest-3
91WinHaven/ProC-483

Kitson, Frank R.
90Target-412
E107

Kittle, Hub
73OPC-624CO
73T-624C
74OPC-31CO
74T-31C
77StPete

Kittle, Ron
77Clinton
79Knoxvl/TCMA-12
81GlenF-19
82Edmon-13
83F-241
83T/Tr-55T
83TrueVal/WSox-42
84D-18DK
84D-244
84Drake-17
84F-64
84F/St-109
84F/St-22

84MiltBrad-15
84Nes/792-480
84OPC-373
84Seven-17C
84T-480
84T/St-382YS
84T/Super-11
84TrueVal/WS-19
85Coke/WS-40
85D-180
85D/AAS-13
85D/WaxBox-PC3
85F-518
85F/LimEd-16
85FunFoodPin-53
85Leaf-210
85OPC-105
85T-105
85T/St-232
86Coke/WS-42
86D-526
86F-210
86F/Mini-45
86F/St-68
86Jay's-11
86Leaf-257
86OPC-288
86Sf-67M
86Sf-86
86T-574
86T/St-289
87D-351
87F-103
87T-584
88D-422
88F-213
88Gator-33
88Leaf-251
88S-449
88S/Tr-44T
88T-259
88T/Tr-58T
89B-69
89Coke/WS-15
89D-428
89D/Best-249
89D/Tr-51
89F/Up-20
89OPC-268
89S-96
89T-771
89T/Tr-62T
89UD-228
89UD/Ext-711
90Coke/WSox-13
90D-148
90F-538
90Kodak/WSox-4
90Leaf/II-405
90OPC-79
90Panini/St-51
90PublInt/St-393
90RedFoley/St-54
90S-529
90T-79
90T/St-302
90UD/Ext-790
91Crown/Orio-241
91D-613
91F-480
91OPC-324A
91OPC-324B
91T-324A
91T-324B

Kittredge, Malachi
E107

Kizer, Craig
82AubAs-14

Kizer, Hal
(Bubba)
79QuadC-15

Kizziah, Daren
89StCath/ProC-2076
90Myrtle/ProC-2772
91Dunedin/ClBest-4
91Dunedin/ProC-200

Klages, Fred
67T-373R
68T-229
69MB-148

Klancnik, Joe
88James/ProC-1919
89James/ProC-2155
91QuadC/ProC-2622

Klaus, Robert
61T/St-203
64T-524R
65OPC-227
65T-227
66OPC-108
66T-108
69T-387
91WIZMets-212

Klaus, William
(Billy)
55B-150
56T-217
57T-292
58T-89
59T-299
60T-406
61P-79
61T-187
62J-67
62P-67
62P/Can-67
62Salada-10
62Shirriff-10
62T-571
63T-551
78TCMA-19
79TCMA-251
91Crown/Orio-242
Exh47

Klavitter, Clay
91Belling/ClBest-2
91Belling/ProC-3668
91SanBern/ClBest-13
91SanBern/ProC-1989

Klawitter, Tom
84Toledo-14

Klebba, Rob
80WHave-6

Kleean, Tom
86Beloit-12

Klein, Bob
75AppFx

Klein, Bruce
89Augusta/ProC-513

Klein, Chuck
31Exh/4-11
33DH-26
33DL-22
33Exh/4-6
33G-128
34Exh/4-3
34G-10
35BU-185
35Exh/4-3
35G-1F
35G-3D
35G-4D
35G-5D
35Wheat
36G
38Exh/4-6
39PB-82
40PB-102
41PB-60
49Exh
60F-30
61F-51
72F/FFeat-36
80Pac/Leg-112
80Laugh/FFeat-6
80SSPC/HOF
88Conlon/NatAS-12
89HOF/St-48
91Conlon/Sport-30
91Conlon/Sport-300
92Conlon/Sport-438
92Conlon/Sport-531
PR1-18
R300
R306
R308-157
R314
R315-A19
R315-B19
R316
R328-21
R332-17
V354-56
V355-13
W517-10
WG8-38

Klein, Gary
83Butte-6

Klein, Larry
85BurlR-3
86Tulsa-24
88OkCty/CMC-17
88OkCty/ProC-32

Klein, Lou
49Eureka-188
60T-457C

Kleinke, Norbert
40Hughes-12

Kleinow, John
(Red)
E101
E102
E105
E92
E94
E97
T204
T205
T206
T216
T3-21
W555

Klem, Bill
21Exh-92
50Callahan
72F/FFeat-31
80SSPC/HOF
86Conlon/1-5
88Conlon/4-15
89TM/Umpire-63
92Conlon/Sport-460
R332-6

Klenoshek, Bill Jr.
88CapeCod/Sum-50

Klesko, Ryan
89LittleSun-20
90A&AASingle/ProC-106
90Foil/Best-236
90Sumter/Best-9
90Sumter/ProC-2441
91B-590
91Classic/II-T53
91Greenvl/ClBest-17
91Greenvl/LineD-209
91Greenvl/ProC-3011
91Leaf/GRook-BC21
91Single/ClBest-388
91UD/FinalEd-1FCL
91UD/FinalEd-8F
92D/I-13RR
92D/Preview-9
92T-126M
92UD-1CL
92UD-24SR

Kleven, Jay
75Tidew/Team-14
91WIZMets-213

Kleven, Mark
88Charl/ProC-1205

Klimas, Phil
77Cocoa
80Tulsa-13
81Tulsa-3
90TulsaDG/Best-22

Klimchock, Lou
60L-116
60T-137
61T-462
62T-259
63T-542
65T-542
66T-589
70OPC-247
70T-247
91WIZMets-214

Klimkowski, Ron
70T-702R
71MLB/St-492
71OPC-28
71T-28
72OPC-363
72T-363
72T/Cloth-18
73Syrac/Team-12

Kline, Bob
84Newar-24

Kline, Doug
88Visalia/Cal-169
88Visalia/ProC-107
89WPalmB/Star-14
91Wmsprt/LineD-636
91Wmsprt/ProC-288

Kline, Greg
75Clinton
76Clinton

Kline, John Robert
55T-173

Kline, Kris
83Peoria/LF-7

Kline, Ron
53T-175
56T-94
57Kahn
57T-256
58Hires-31
58Kahn
58T-82
59Kahn
59T-265
59T-428M
60Kahn
60L-105
60T-197
61T-127
61T/St-90
62T-216
63T-84
64T-358
65OPC-56
65T-56
65T/trans-54
66T-453
67OPC-133
67T-133
68KDKA-27
68T-446
69MB-149
69T-243
69T/St-86
78TCMA-251
91T/Arc53-175

Kline, Steve
71MLB/St-493
71OPC-51
71T-51
72OPC-467
72T-467
73K-50
73OPC-172
73Syrac/Team-13
73T-172
74OPC-324
74Syrac/Team-12
74T-324
75OPC-639
75T-639
75T/M-639
76SSPC-532

Klinefelter, David
88AubAs/ProC-1972

Kling, John
11Helmar-79
61F-52
E254
E300
E91
E96
E98
M116
S74-63
T201
T202
T205
T206
T207
T3-102
WG3-24

Klingbell, Scott
85Visalia-23

Klinger, Robert
39PB-90
40PB-165
41DP-35
41DP-98
48Smith-25

Klink, Joe
85Lynch-13
86Orlan-9
89Huntsvl/Best-27
90Classic/III-26
90Leaf/II-503
90Mother/A's-26
90T/Tr-51T
91D-591
91F-13
91Leaf/II-461
91Mother/A's-26
91OPC-553
91S-588
91T-553
91UD-468
92D/I-183
92S/I-151
92T-678
92UD-530

Klippstein, John
51B-248
52T-148
53T-46
54B-29
54T-31
55B-152
56Kahn
56T-249
57Kahn
57Sohio/Reds-11
57T-296
58T-242
59T-152
60BB-12
60T-191
61T-539
61T/St-204
62T-151
63T-571
64T-533
65T-384
66T-493
67T-588
79TCMA-62
90Target-413
91T/Arc53-46

Klipstein, Dave
84ElPaso-18
86Vanco-16
87Denver-12
88Nashvl/CMC-20
88Nashvl/ProC-474

Kloff, August
N172

Klonoski, Jason
88CapeCod/Sum-127
91Kenosha/ClBest-27
91Kenosha/ProC-2069
91Single/ClBest-370

Klopp, Frank
85PrWill-26

Klopper, Rod
88Alaska/Team-12

Klugman, Joe
90Target-1002

Klump, Ken
83Wisco/LF-21
85Orlan-17

Klumpp, Elmer
90Target-414

Klusener, Matt
90WichSt-19

Klusman, William F.
N172

Kluss, Dennis
90Watertn/Star-12

Kluszewski, Ted
48L-38
49Eureka-87
50B-62
51B-143
51FB
51T/RB-39
52Dix-53
52T-29
53B/Col-62
53NB
53RM-NL6
53T-162
54Dix
54RH
54RM-NL6
54T-7
55Armour-11
55Kahn
55RFG-10
55RM-NL16
55T-120
55T/DH-121
56Kahn

56T-25
56T/Hocus-A12
56T/Hocus-B14
56T/Pin-56
56YellBase/Pin-17
57Kahn
57Sohio/Reds-12
57T-165
58Hires-67
58Kahn
58T-178
58T-321M
59Kahn
59T-17M
59T-35
60Kahn
60MacGregor-10
60NuCard-57
60T-505
61Bz-18
61NuCard-457
61P-31
61T-65
61T/St-173
62P-82
73OPC-296CO
73T-296C
74OPC-326CO
74T-326C
76SSPC-618CO
79TCMA-12
85West/2-48
86Sf/Dec-38M
88Pac/Leg-72
89Kodak/WSox-1M
91T/Arc53-162
Exh47
PM10/Sm-90

Klutts, Gene
(Mickey)
77T-490R
78T-707R
80T-717
81D-110
81F-584
81T-232
82F-97
82T-148
83D-465
83T-571
83T/Tr-56T

Kluttz, Clyde
52T-132
V362-41

Kmak, Joe
85Everett/Cram-7
86Fresno/Smok-6
88Shrev/ProC-1280
89AS/Cal-46
89Reno/Cal-252
91Denver/LineD-144
91Denver/ProC-125

Knabe, Franz Otto
(Otto)
11Helmar-144
14CJ-1
15CJ-1
D303
E101
E102
E104
E105
E106
E254
E270/2
E92
M116
T206
T207
T213/blue
T213/brown
T216

Knabenshue, Chris
85Spokane/Cram-9
86CharRain-12
87Wichita-7
88TexLgAS/GS-34
88Wichita-14
89LasVegas/CMC-23
89LasVegas/ProC-19
90ScranWB/CMC-20
90ScranWB/ProC-611
91ScranWB/LineD-485
91ScranWB/ProC-2551

Knackert, Brent
88FSLAS/Star-40
88Tampa/Star-11
89Saraso/Star-13
90D/Rook-52
90Mother/Mar-18
90T/Tr-52T
91CounHrth-17
91D-662
91OPC-563
91S-774
91T-563
91T/90Debut-78
91UD-378
92D/II-608

Knapland, Greg
91Watertn/ClBest-8
91Watertn/ProC-3363

Knapp, John
87CharWh-12
88Bakers/Cal-236
89VeroB/Star-14
90VeroB/Star-17

Knapp, Michael
86Cram/PCL-87
87QuadC-27
88MidldA/GS-13
88TexLgAS/GS-36
89MidldA/GS-20
91CharlK/LineD-136
91CharlK/ProC-1691

Knapp, Rick
86Tulsa-9B
88Gaston/ProC-1000

Knapp, Robert C.
(Chris)
77T-247
78T-361
79T-453
80T-658
81D-173
81SLCity-7
81T-557
82Iowa-18
83Kinston/Team-10

Knecht, Bobby
88AppFx/ProC-161
88MidwLAS/GS-41

Knell, Phillip
N172

Knepper, Bob
75Phoenix-10
76Phoenix
77Phoenix
78T-589
79Ho-52
79K-35
79OPC-255
79Pol/Giants-39
79T-486
80OPC-61
80Pol/Giants-39
80T-111
81D-194
81F-447
81OPC-279
81T-279
81T/Tr-782
82D-41
82F-219
82F/St-49
82K-31
82OPC-389
82T-672
82T/St-45
83D-92
83F-451
83T-382
84D-572
84Mother/Ast-16
84Nes/792-93
84OPC-93
84T-93
85D-476
85F-352
85Leaf-61
85Mother/Ast-20
85OPC-289
85T-455
85T-721AS
85T/St-62
86D-161
86F-304
86Leaf-90
86Mother/Ast-22
86OPC-231
86Pol/Ast-15
86T-590
87D-112
87F-61
87F/AwardWin-20
87F/GameWin-23
87F/Mini-60
87Leaf-249
87Mother/Ast-5
87OPC-129
87Pol/Ast-20
87RedFoley/St-17
87Sf-29
87T-722
87T/Gloss60-13
87T/Mini-10
87T/St-32
88D-138
88D/Best-176
88F-451
88Mother/Ast-5
88Pol/Ast-15
88S-344
88T-151
89D-123
89D/AS-54
89F-360
89F/BBAS-25
89Lennox/Ast-10
89Mother/Ast-7
89OPC-280
89Panini/St-82
89S-273
89S/HotStar-38
89T-280
89T/St-22
89T/St/Backs-63
89UD-422
90D-485
90OPC-104
90Phoenix/ProC-7
90PublInt/St-97
90T-104
90UD-599

Knetzer, Elmer
14CJ-84
15CJ-84
16FleischBrd-52
90Target-1003
T207

Kneuer, Frank
83Nashvl-9

Knicely, Alan
75Dubuq
76Dubuq
80T-678R
80Tucson-14
81T-82R
81Tucson-4
83D-620
83F-452
83T-117
83T/Tr-57
84F-473
84Nes/792-323
84T-323
84Wichita/Rock-18
85T/Tr-68T
86Louisvl-15
86OPC-316
86T-418
87OKCty-22

Knickerbocker, Wm.
(Bill)
35BU-58
35G-8I
35G-9I
40PB-182
91Conlon/Sport-79
R313
R314

Kniffen, Chuck
88Wausau/GS-2
89SanBern/Best-10
89SanBern/Cal-89CO
90SanBern/Best-8CO
90SanBern/Cal-115CO
90SanBern/ProC-2650CO
91SanBern/ClBest-26CO
91SanBern/ProC-2004CO

Knight, Brock
85Elmira-9

Knight, C. Ray
(Ray)
76Indianap-3
78T-674
79OPC-211
79T-401
80OPC-98
80T-174
81Coke
81D-61
81F-198
81OPC-325
81T-325
81T/HT
82D-374
82F-71
82F/St-18
82OPC-319
82T-525
82T/St-39
82T/Tr-57T
83D-522
83F-453
83OPC-275
83T-275
83T-441
83T/Gloss40-18
83T/St-238
84D-12DK
84D-232
84F-229
84F/St-10
84Mother/Ast-6
84Nes/792-660
84OPC-321
84T-660
84T/St-68
84T/St/Box-9
85D-617
85F-86
85Indianap-28
85OPC-274
85T-590
86D-597
86F-86
86Mother/Ast-24
86OPC-27
86T-27
87D-586
87D/OD-137
87F-14
87F/AwardWin-21
87F/RecSet-18
87F/Up-U58
87F/WS-11M
87F/WS-12
87French-25
87Leaf-166
87OPC-275
87Sf-88
87T-488
87T/HL-30
87T/HL-33
87T/St-24WS
87T/Tr-59T
87Woolwth-30
87Woolwth-33
88D-108
88F-564
88F/Up-U28
88OPC-124
88Panini/St-12
88Pep/T-22
88RedFoley/St-43
88S-96
88S/Tr-17T
88Sf-115
88T-124
88T/St-229
88T/Tr-59T
89S-135
89UD-259
91Crown/Orio-243
91WIZMets-215

Knight, Dennis
83TriCit-5

Knight, John
10Domino-62A
10Domino-62B
11Helmar-73
12Sweet/Pin-36A
12Sweet/Pin-36B
14Piedmont/St-31
E101
E105
E254
E90/1
E92
M116
S74-23
T202
T204
T205
T206
T216

Knight, Steve
80SanJose/JITB-12

Knight, Tim
82Nashvl-15
83Nashvl-10
84Nashvl-12
85Albany-33
85Colum-20
85Colum/Pol-15
86Portl-12

Knoblauch, Chuck
88CapeCod-15
88CapeCod/Sum-94
90A&AASingle/ProC-56
90B-415
90Foil/Best-146
90Foil/Best-322
90OrlanSR/Best-3
90OrlanSR/ProC-1090
90OrlanSR/Star-8
90S-672DC
91B-330
91Classic/III-46
91D-421RR
91D/Rook-39
91F/Ultra-382MLP
91F/UltraUp-U37
91F/Up-U37
91Leaf/II-396
91S/ASFan-10
91S/RookTr-93T
91T/StClub/II-548
91T/Tr-69T
91UD-40
92Classic/I-50
92D/I-390
92D/II-BC5ROY
92F-206
92F/RookSIns-19
92S/100RisSt-11
92S/II-572
92S/II-792ROY
92T-23
92T/91Debut-103
92UD-446

Knoblaugh, Jay
88Oneonta/ProC-2067
89Penin/Star-10
90FSLAS/Star-35
90FtLaud/Star-11
91Albany/ProC-1019

Knoop, Bobby
64T-502R
65OPC-26
65T-26
65T/trans-18
66T-280
66T/RO-81
67OPC-175
67OPC/PI-17
67T-175
67T/PI-17
68Bz-3
68T-271
69MB-150
69MLB/St-23
69T-445
69T/St-145
69Trans-17
70MLB/St-188
70T-695
71OPC-506
71T-506
72MB-184
72T-664
75QuadC
78TCMA-234
89Smok/Angels-4
90ElPasoATG/Team-44MG

Knorr, Randy
87Myrtle-12
88Myrtle/ProC-1182

89Dunedin/Star-10
90Foil/Best-273
90Knoxvl/Best-26
90Knoxvl/ProC-1248
90Knoxvl/Star-9
91Knoxvl/LineD-361
91Knoxvl/ProC-1770
91Single/ClBest-21
92T/91Debut-104

Knott, Jack
39PB-91
40PB-13
41PB-68
91Conlon/Sport-178

Knout, Edward
(Fred)
N172

Knowles, Darold
64T-418R
65T-577R
66OPC-27R
66T-27R
67T-362
68T-483
70OPC-106
70T-106
71MLB/St-544
71OPC-261
71T-261
72T-583
73OPC-274
73T-274
74OPC-472WS
74OPC-57
74T-472WS
74T-57
75OPC-352
75T-352
75T/M-352
76OPC-617
76SSPC-307
76T-617
77T-169
78T-414
79OPC-303
79T-581
80T-286
88Louisvl-3
89Phill/TastyK-16CO
90Phill/TastyK-34CO
91Clearw/ClBest-10CO
91Clearw/ProC-1640CO
91Crown/Orio-244

Knox, Jeff
86Clearw-14
87Albany-17

Knox, John
74OPC-604R
74T-604R
75OPC-546
75T-546
75T/M-546
76Indianap-21
76OPC-218
76SSPC-361
76T-218

Knox, Kerry
89Spokane/SP-14
90Foil/Best-221
90Riversi/Best-14
90Riversi/ProC-2603
91Wichita/LineD-609
91Wichita/ProC-2594

Knox, Mike
83Cedar-4
83Cedar/LF-9
83Durham-8
84Durham-15

Knox, Scott
85PrWill-29

Knudsen, Kurt
89Lakeland/Star-13
90Lakeland/Star-16
91London/ProC-1874

Knudson, Mark
83DayBe-7
85Cram/PCL-60
86Tucson-10
87Denver-20
88D-495
88Denver/CMC-1
88Denver/ProC-1275
88T-61
89Pol/Brew-41
90Brewer/MillB-12
90D-575
90F-327
90Leaf/II-348
90OPC-566
90Pol/Brew-41
90S-539
90T-566
91Brewer/MillB-13
91D-328
91F-587
91F/Ultra-176
91Leaf/I-159
91OPC-267
91Panini/FrSt-211
91Panini/St-165
91Pol/Brew-12
91S-239
91T-267
91UD-393
92S/I-373

Knudtson, Jim
87Cedar-27

Kobel, Kevin
74OPC-605R
74T-605R
75OPC-337
75T-337
75T/M-337
76OPC-588
76T-588
77Spoka
79OPC-6
79T-21
80OPC-106
80T-189
91WIZMets-216

Kobernus, Jeff
82Madis-25

Kobetitsch, Kevin
91Eugene/ClBest-16
91Eugene/ProC-3721

Kobza, Greg
89Utica/Pucko-13
90SoBend/Best-15
91Saraso/ClBest-14
91Saraso/ProC-1116
91Single/ClBest-73

Koch, Barney
90Target-1004

Koch, Donn
82AppFx-18

Koch, Ken
87Orlan-8

Kochanski, Mark
82Idaho-9

Kocher, Bradley W.
16FleischBrd-53
C46-82

Koegel, Pete
71OPC-633R
71T-633R
72OPC-14R
72T-14R
77Jaxvl

Koehnke, Odie
75AppFx
76AppFx

Koelling, Brian
91Billings/ProC-3762

Koenecke, Leonard
(Len)
34Exh/4-2
90Target-415

Koenig, Fred
83Thorn-26CO
88Pulaski/ProC-1749
89Pulaski/ProC-1900
91Pulaski/ClBest-23CO
91Pulaski/ProC-4024CO

Koenig, Gary
90BBCity/Star-14

Koenig, Mark
29Exh/4-26
31Exh/4-24
32Orbit/num-30
32Orbit/un-39
33G-39
34G-56
35E-8A
35G-9A
87Conlon/2-41
88Conlon/4-16
91Conlon/Sport-125
R305
R315-A20
R315-B20
R316
V353-39
W513-83

Koenigsfeld, Ron
82ElPaso-3
84Cram/PCL-25

Koga, Hide
90Salinas/Cal-142MG
90Salinas/ProC-2735MG
91Salinas/ClBest-24MG
91Salinas/ProC-2260MG

Koh, Joe
87Idaho-20

Kohlogi, Acey
(Asst.)
89Visalia/Cal-121

Kohno, Takayuki
90Salinas/Cal-143CO
90Salinas/ProC-2736CO
91Salinas/ClBest-26CO
91Salinas/ProC-2262CO

Koklys, Wayne
91Idaho/ProC-4322

Kokos, Dick
49B-31
50B-50
51B-68
51T/RB-19
53T-232
54B-37
54Esskay
54T-106
91Crown/Orio-245
91T/Arc53-232

Kolarek, Frank
79Ogden/TCMA-19

Kolb, Gary
62Pep/Tul
63Pep/Tul
64T-119
65T-287
68KDKA-10
68T-407
69MB-151
69T-307
78TCMA-268
78TCMA-283
91WIZMets-217

Kolb, Pete
86ElPaso-15TR
87ElPaso-9
88Denver/ProC-1252
89Denver/ProC-50

Kolbe, Brian
82Jacks-7

Koller, Jerry
91Idaho/ProC-4323

Koller, Mark
87Watertn-25
88Watertn/Pucko-7

Koller, Mike
88Bristol/ProC-1880
89Fayette/ProC-1576
90Fayette/ProC-2403

Koller, Rodney
91Burlind/ProC-3299

Kolloway, Don
49B-28
50B-133
51B-105
52B-91
52T-104
53T-97
91T/Arc53-97
Exh47

Kolodny, Mike
80Batavia-5

Kolotka, Chuck
82Madis-6
83Miami-8
84Beaum-22

Kolp, Ray
33G-150
V100
V353-82

Kolstad, Harold
(Hal)
62T-276
63T-574

Komadina, Tony
75AppFx

Komazaki, Yukiichi
83SanJose-9

Komminsk, Brad
80Ander-28
81Durham-10
83Richm-19
84D-36RR
84F/X-U63
84Richm-10M
84Richm-11
85D-321
85F-331
85Ho/Braves-13
85Pol/Atl-36
85T-292
86F-520
86OPC-210
86Richm-11
86T-698
87Denver-6
88D-583
88Denver/CMC-21
88Denver/ProC-1263
89F/Up-28
90D-350
90F-496
90Leaf/II-303
90OPC-476
90Richm25Ann/Team-14
90S-496
90S/Tr-53T
90T-476
90T/Tr-53T
90UD-428
91Crown/Orio-246
91S-259
91Tacoma/LineD-540
92S/II-735

Konderla, Mike
83Cedar-7
83Cedar/LF-14
84Cedar-9
87Nashvl-12
88Denver/CMC-2
88Denver/ProC-1276

Konetchy, Ed
10Domino-63
11Helmar-172
12Sweet/Pin-150
14CJ-118
15CJ-118
16FleischBrd-54
21Exh-93
90Target-416
91Conlon/Sport-263
92Conlon/Sport-638
D328-94
D329-96
D350/2-94
E135-94
E254
E270/2
E96
M101/4-96
M101/5-94
M116
PM1-8
S74-121
T202
T204
T205
T206
T207
T213/blue
T215/blue
T3-103
W514-93
WG5-24
WG6-23

Konieczki, Dom
91Erie/ClBest-17
91Erie/ProC-4062

Konieczny, Doug
75OPC-624R
75T-624R
75T/M-624R
76OPC-602
76SSPC-49
76T-602

Konopa, Bob
82Orlan/B-6
82OrlTw-18/A
84CharlO-15
90HagersDG/Best-14

Konopki, Mark
91Elmira/ClBest-22
91Elmira/ProC-3268

Konstanty, Jim
49Eureka-139
50B-226
51B-27
51BR-D6
51FB
51T/CAS
52T-108
53B/BW-58
55B-231
56T-321
61T-479MV
79TCMA-53
90HOF/St-44
Exh47
PM10/Sm-91
R423-56
Rawl

Koob, Ernie
92Conlon/Sport-349

Kooiman, Bill
90Idaho/ProC-3267

Kooman, Chris
87Everett-14

Koonce, Cal
63T-31
65OPC-34
65T-34
66T-278
67OPC-171
67T-171
68T-486
69T-303
70OPC-521
70T-521
71MLB/St-320
71OPC-254
71T-254
72MB-185
91WIZMets-218

Koontz, Jim
81ElPaso-10
82ElPaso-20
84Cram/PCL-45

Koopman, Bob
86PrWill-14
87Salem-20

Koosman, Jerry
68OPC-177R
68T-177R
69Citgo-12
69MLB/St-168
69MLBPA/Pin-49
69OPC-90
69T-434AS
69T-90
69T/DE-25
69T/decal
69T/S-51
69T/St-66
69Trans-46
70MLB/St-79
70OPC-309WS
70OPC-468AS
70T-309WS
70T-468AS
70T-610
70Trans-5
70Trans/M-22
71MLB/St-157
71OPC-335
71T-335
71T/Coins-23
71T/tatt-3
72MB-186
72T-697
72T-698IA
73OPC-184
73T-184
74OPC-356
74T-356
74T/St-65
75OPC-19
75T-19
75T/M-19

76Crane-27
76Laugh/Jub-22
76MSA/Disc
76OPC-64
76SSPC-609
76T-64
77BurgChef-143
77Ho-77
77K-29
77OPC-26
77T-300
78Ho-80
78T-565
78Tastee/Discs-12
78Wiffle/Discs-35
79Ho-149
79OPC-345
79T-655
80BK/PHR-5
80OPC-144
80T-275
80T/S-38
81D-531
81F-552
81F/St-19
81OPC-298
81T-476
81T/St-104
82D-603
82F-347
82OPC-63
82T-714
83D-39
83F-242
83OPC-153
83T-153
83TrueVal/WSox-36
84D-501
84F-65
84F/X-64
84Nes/792-311
84Nes/792-716LL
84OPC-311
84Phill/TastyK-23
84T-311
84T-716LL
84T/Tr-64
85CIGNA-7
85D-233
85F-256
85Leaf-178
85OPC-15
85Phill/TastyK-21
85Phill/TastyK-9
85T-15
85T/St-117
86D-23DK
86D/DKsuper-23
86Leaf-23DK
86OPC-343
86Sf-64M
86T-505
88Pac/Leg-66
89Swell-109
90Pac/Legend-88
91Pittsfld/ClBest-26CO
91Pittsfld/ProC-3440CO
91WIZMets-219

Kopacz, George
71OPC-204R
71T-204R

Koperda, Mike
80Ander-21

Kopetsky, Brian
86Bakers-18

Kopf, Dave
86Pittsfld-11
87Iowa-10
88Pittsfld/ProC-1373

Kopf, William
88Pac/8Men-91
E120
E220
W514-118
W572

Koplitz, Howard
62T-114
63T-406
64T-372
66OPC-46
66T-46
78TCMA-221

Koppe, Joe
59T-517
60T-319
61T-179
62Salada-209
62Shirriff-209
62T-39
63J-26
63P-26
63T-396
64T-279

Kopyta, Jeff
86Cram/PCL-66
87Madis-18
88Modesto-12
88Modesto/Cal-63
89Modesto/Cal-272

Korcheck, Steve
58T-403
59T-284
60L-79
60T-56

Korczyk, Steve
82Toledo-3
83Toledo-5

Kordish, Steve
83TriCit-2
84Tulsa-30
86Salem-15

Korince, George
67OPC-72R
67T-526R
67T-72R
68T-447R

Korn, Ray
91Erie/ClBest-27CO
91Erie/ProC-4085CO

Korneev, Leonid
89EastLDD/ProC-DD15

Kornfeld, Craig
79QuadC-16

Korolev, Sergey
89EastLDD/ProC-DD4

Kortright, Jim
88Idaho/ProC-1858
89Idaho/ProC-2031

Korwan, Jim
90Target-1005

Kosc, Greg
88TM/Umpire-25
89TM/Umpire-23
90TM/Umpire-22

Kosco, Andrew
(Dru)
87Wausau-14
88Wausau/GS-26
89Wmsprt/ProC-626
90Wmsprt/Best-13
90Wmsprt/ProC-1068
90Wmsprt/Star-14

Kosco, Andy
66T-264R
67T-366
68T-524
69MB-152
69OPC-139
69T-139
69T/St-204
70OPC-535
70T-535
71MLB/St-440
71OPC-746
71T-746
72MB-187
72OPC-376
72T-376
74OPC-34
74T-34
90Target-417

Kosco, Bryn
88James/ProC-1896
89Rockford/Team-15
90Jaxvl/Best-6
90Jaxvl/ProC-1382
91Harris/LineD-259
91Harris/ProC-635

Kosenski, John
88CapeCod/Sum-108
91Fayette/ClBest-4
91Fayette/ProC-1165

Koshevoy, Alexei
89EastLDD/ProC-DD7

Koshorek, Clem
52T-380
53B/Col-147
53T-8
91T/Arc53-8

Koslo, George B.
(Dave)
47TipTop
48B-48
49B-34
49Eureka-114
50B-65
51B-90
52B-182
52BR
52T-336
54Esskay
55Gol/Braves-16
55JC-20
79TCMA-231
91Crown/Orio-247

Koslofski, Kevin
86FtMyr-16
87FtMyr-24
88BBCity/Star-15
89BBCity/Star-14
90Memphis/Best-10
90Memphis/ProC-1021
90Memphis/Star-12
91London/LineD-408
91Memphis/ProC-666

Kostich, Billy
89LittleSun-15
91Penin/ClBest-7
91Penin/ProC-373

Kostickhka, Steve
87Beloit-6

Kostro, Frank
63T-407R
65T-459
68OPC-44
68T-44
69T-242

Kotch, Darrin
90James/Pucko-19
91Sumter/ClBest-6
91Sumter/ProC-2329

Kotchman, Randy
89Miami/II/Star-8
90Boise/ProC-3325

Kotchman, Tom
86PalmSp-19MG
86PalmSp/Smok-2
87Edmon-12
88Edmon/CMC-22
88Edmon/ProC-580
89AAA/ProC-28
89Edmon/CMC-25
89Edmon/ProC-549
90Boise/ProC-3331MG
91Boise/ProC-3899MG

Kotes, Chris
91StCath/ClBest-17
91StCath/ProC-3389

Kouba, Curtis
82Wausau-5

Koufax, Sandy
55Gol/Dodg-16
55T-123
56T-79
57T-302
58BB
58T-187
59Morrell
59T-163
60BB-9
60Morrell
60T-343
61BB-32
61Morrell
61T-207M
61T-344
61T-49LL
62BB-32
62Bz
62Exh
62J-109
62P-109
62P/Can-109
62Salada-109
62Shirriff-109
62T-5
62T-60LL
62T/bucks
62T/St-136
63Exh
63F-42
63J-121
63P-121
63Salada-4
63T-210
63T-412M
63T-5LL
63T-9LL
63T/SO
64Bz-32
64T-1LL
64T-200
64T-3LL
64T-5LL
64T/Coins-106
64T/Coins-159AS
64T/S-3
64T/St-91
64T/SU
64T/tatt
65Bz-32
65OPC-8LL
65T-300
65T-8LL
65T/E-8
65T/trans-55
66Bz-1
66OPC-100
66T-100
66T-221LL
66T-223LL
66T-225LL
66T/RO-14
67T-234LL
67T-236LL
67T-238LL
72Laugh/GF-4
75OPC-201MV
75T-201MV
75T/M-201MV
76Laugh/Jub-4
78TCMA-130
79TCMA-49
80Pac/Leg-10
80SSPC/HOF
81Albuq/TCMA-23B
82KMart-4
83MLBPA/Pin-24
87Smok/Dodg-16
88Smok/Dodg-4
88Smok/Dodg-6M
89HOF/St-79
89Smok/Dodg-15
90HOF/St-69
90OPC-665TBC
90T-665TBC
90Target-418
Exh47

Koukalik, Joe
90Target-1006

Kounas, Tony
88CapeCod/Sum-144
91Penin/ClBest-14
91Penin/ProC-380

Koupal, Lou
90Target-1007

Kovach, Ty
89Watertn/Star-13
90CLAS/CL-34
90Kinston/Team-4
91Canton/LineD-85
91Canton/ProC-977
91Single/ClBest-309

Kowar, Frank
90StCath/ProC-3462

Kowitz, Brian
90A&AASingle/ProC-192
90Pulaski/Best-22
90Pulaski/ProC-3087
91Durham/ClBest-25
91Durham/ProC-1559
91Single/ClBest-66

Koy, Ernest
41DP-118
90Target-419

Koza, Dave
81Pawtu-16
83Pawtu-17

Kozar, Al
49B-16
50B-15
R302

Kozyrez, Alexander
89EastLDD/ProC-DD18

Kracl, Darin
89Medford/Best-13
90A&AASingle/ProC-114
90Madison/ProC-2262

Kraeger, Don
79AppFx-23

Kraemer, Joe
86Peoria-13
87Iowa-9
88Iowa/CMC-7
88Iowa/ProC-549
89Iowa/CMC-3
89Iowa/ProC-1715
90D/Rook-10
90F/Up-U8
90T/89Debut-68
90T/TVCub-10
90UD/Ext-740
91Iowa/LineD-207
91Iowa/ProC-1054
91S-755RP

Kraft, Ken
86Clearw-15

Kraft, Mike
89Johnson/Star-15
90Spring/Best-11

Krafve, Keith
86Cram/PCL-24

Krahenbuhl, Ken
90Hunting/ProC-3278
91Peoria/ClBest-26

Krajewski, Chris
80SanJose/JITB-13

Krakauskas, Joe
40PB-188
41DP-77
47Signal
91Conlon/Sport-228

Kralick, Jack
61Clover-11
61Peters-6
61T-36
62T-346
62T/St-77
63J-11
63P-11
63Sugar-28
63T-448
64Kahn
64T-338
65Kahn
65T-535
65T/E-72
66OPC-129
66T-129
67T-316
78TCMA-134

Kraly, Steve
54NYJour
55T-139

Kramer, Jack
52Wheat

Kramer, Joe
85Madis-20
85Madis/Pol-17
86Modesto-18

Kramer, John
(Jack)
41G-14
47TipTop
49B-53
50B-199
51B-200
79TCMA-107
W753

Kramer, Mark
85BurlR-18
86DayBe-15
87PortChar-19
88CharlR/Star-11
89Miami/II/Star-9

Kramer, Randy
83BurlR-8
83BurlR/LF-5
86Kinston-13
86Tulsa-23
87Vanco-16
88BuffB/CMC-5
88BuffB/ProC-1464
89D-480
89D/Best-213

89D/Rook-48
89F-647R
89F/Up-U115
89Panini/St-159
89S/HotRook-57
89T-522
90BuffB/Team-12
90D-409
90F-471
90Homer/Pirate-15
90HotRook/St-26
90OPC-126
90Panini/St-327
90S/100Ris-41
90T-126
90UD-519
91Richm/LineD-432
91Richm/ProC-2561

Kramer, Tommy
88MidwLAS/GS-22
88Watlo/ProC-689
89Kinston/Star-11
89Star/Wax-76
90CLAS/CL-38
91Canton/LineD-86
91Canton/ProC-978
92T/91Debut-105

Kranepool, Ed
63T-228R
64T-393M
64T-566
65OPC-144
65T-144
65T/E-6
65T/trans-56
66Bz-9
66T-212
66T/RO-20
67Kahn
67OPC-186M
67T-186M
67T-452
68OPC-92
68T-92
69MB-153
69MLB/St-169
69T-381
69T/St-67
70K-1
70MLB/St-80
70T-557
70Trans/M-21
71MLB/St-158
71OPC-573
71T-573
72MB-188
72OPC-181
72OPC-182IA
72T-181
72T-182IA
73OPC-329
73T-329
74OPC-561
74T-561
75OPC-324
75T-324
75T/M-324
76OPC-314
76SSPC-533
76T-314
77BurgChef-136
77OPC-60
77T-201
78OPC-205
78T-49
78Wiffle/Discs-36
79OPC-265
79T-505
80OPC-336
80T-641
89Pac/Leg-114
89Swell-28
91WIZMets-220
Exh47
PM10/Sm-92

Kranitz, Rick
80Holyo-1
81ElPaso-17
82Vanco-19
86WinSalem-11C
88Peoria/Ko-19
89Peoria/Ko-31
91CharlK/LineD-150CO
91CharlK/ProC-1705CO

Krattli, Tom
77DaytB

Kraus, Jeff
77Spartan

Kraus, Ralph
87PrWill-5
88FtLaud/Star-14
89FtLaud/Star-12

Krause, Andrew
85Madis-21
85Madis/Pol-18

Krause, Harry
10Domino-64
11Helmar-56
12Sweet/Pin-46
28Exh/PCL-17
E104
E90/1
E91
E95
M116
S74-32
T202
T205
T206
T207
T208
T213/blue
T215/blue
T215/brown
T3-22
WG7-25

Krauss, Ron
82CharR-15
90Rockford/ProC-2700
91WPalmB/ClBest-21

Krauss, Timothy
81Redwd-17
82Holyo-17
84Cram/PCL-98
85Cram/PCL-17
86BuffB-14
87Hawaii-23

Krausse, Lew
63T-104
64T-334
65T-462
66T-256
67T-565
68T-458
69MB-154
69OPC-23
69Sunoco/Pin-12
69T-23
69T/St-217
70McDon-4
70OPC-233
70T-233
71MLB/St-441
71OPC-372
71T-372
71T/Coins-20
72T-592
73OPC-566
73T-566
75OPC-603
75T-603
75T/M-603
75Tucson-20

Krauza, Ron
89BuffB/CMC-19

Kravec, Ken
77T-389
78T-439
79OPC-141
79T-283
80OPC-299
80T-575
81T-67
81T/Tr-783
82D-378
82Iowa-19
82RedLob
82T-639
87FtMyr-28
88Memphis/Best-14
89Pac/SenLg-151
91Pac/SenLg-10

Kravitz, Dan
57T-267
58T-444
59T-536
60T-238
61T-166

Krawczyk, Ray
82AlexD-4
84Cram/PCL-129
85Cram/PCL-245
86Hawaii-14
87Hawaii-17
89Denver/CMC-7
89Denver/ProC-32

Krebs, Dave
87Savan-3
88Savan/ProC-338

Kreevich, Mike
38Exh/4-10
39Exh
R303/A
R303/B
R312/M
WG8-39

Krehmeyer, Charles
N172/PCL

Kremblas, Frank
90Cedar/ProC-2324
91Chatt/LineD-160
91Chatt/ProC-1966

Kremer, Ken
89Beloit/I/Star-12
89Beloit/II/Star-18

Kremer, Remy
(Ray)
25Exh-53
26Exh-53
27Exh-26
28Exh-25
29Exh/4-14
31Exh/4-14
33G-54
91Conlon/Sport-279
R306
V354-38
WG7-26

Kremers, Jimmy
89Greenvl/ProC-1163
89Greenvl/Star-12
89Greenvl/Best-24
89SLAS-8
90F/Up-U4
90Richm/Bob-12
90Richm/CMC-10
90Richm/ProC-261
90Richm/Team-17
91D-739
91F-694
91Indianap/LineD-187
91Indianap/ProC-464
91S-736RP
91T/90Debut-79
91UD-262

Krenchicki, Wayne
78RochR
80RochR-16
80T-661R
82Coke/Reds
82F-168
82T-107
82T/Tr-58T
83D-314
83F-594
83T-374
84D-334
84F-83
84F/X-65
84Nes/792-223
84T-223
84T/Tr-65T
84Wichita/Rock-7
85D-140
85F-539
85T-468
86D-140
86F-180
86F/Up-U60
86OPC-81
86Provigo-20
86T-777
86T/Tr-55T
87D-406
87F-322
87OPC-81
87T-774
87Tacoma-6
88Louisvl-25
88Tacoma/CMC-14
88Tacoma/ProC-635
89Pac/SenLg-157
89T/SenLg-75
90EliteSenLg-38
91Crown/Orio-248
91Pac/SenLg-42

Kress, Charlie
(Chuck)
54T-219
90Target-420

Kress, Ralph
(Red)
29Exh/4-29
31Exh/4-30
33G-33
35BU-169
35G-2C
35G-4C
35G-7C
39PB-115
40PB-45
54T-160CO
55Gol/Ind-14
55Salem
55T-151
60T-460C
92Conlon/Sport-383
PR1-19
R316
V353-33

Kretlow, Lou
52B-221
52T-42
53B/Col-50
54B-197
54Esskay
55B-108
55Esskay
57T-139
91Crown/Orio-249

Kreuter, Chad
86Salem-16
87PortChar-25
88TexLgAS/GS-3
88Tulsa-19
89Classic-27
89D-579
89F-526
89Panini/St-444
89S-638
89S/HotRook-51
89S/YS/II-40
89Sf-43
89Smok/R-17
89T-432
89UD-312
90D-520
90F-303
90OPC-562
90PublInt/St-414
90S-406
90S/100Ris-51
90T-562
90TulsaDG/Best-23
90UD-609

Kreutzer, Frank
64T-107R
65T-371
66T-211
78TCMA-116

Krevokuch, James
(Krev)
91Welland/ClBest-8
91Welland/ProC-3579

Krichell, Paul
E270/2

Krieg, William
N172
N284

Kries, John
89Salem/Team-14

Kripner, Mike
80Cedar-23
82Water-12

Krippner, Curt
88Beloit/GS-16
89Beloit/II/Star-19
90Stockton/Cal-185
90Stockton/ProC-2184
91Erie/ProC-4063

Krist, Howie
W754

Kristan, Kevin
85Cram/PCL-124
87WPalmB-22

Krivda, Ricky
91Bluefld/ProC-4123
91Bluefld/ClBest-18

Krizmanich, Mike
75IntAS/TCMA-23
75IntAS/TCMA-3

Kroc, Ray
78Padre/FamFun-17OWN

Krock, August
E223
N172
N403

Kroener, Chris
86Visalia-12

Kroh, Floyd
(Rube)
12Sweet/Pin-83
E254
E97
M116
T205
T206

Krol, David
88CapeCod/Sum-180

Krol, Jack
84Smok/SDP-15CO
87LasVegas-3MG
88Charl/ProC-1219MG
89CharRain/ProC-991MG
90CharRain/Best-26MG
90CharRain/ProC-2054MG

Kroll, Gary
65T-449R
66T-548
66T/RO-2
78TCMA-27
91WIZMets-221

Kroll, Todd
87Bakers-8
88Bakers/Cal-255

Kromy, Ted
79Wisco-19
82Orlan/B-19
82OrlTw/A-19
83Orlan-17

Krsnich, Mike
62T-289

Krsnich, Rocco
(Rocky)
53T-229
91T/Arc53-229

Krueger, Arthur T.
E286
M116
T206

Krueger, Bill
82WHave-7
84Cram/PCL-84
84F-450
84Nes/792-178
84OPC-178
84T-178
85D-467
85F-428
85Mother/A's-21
85T-528
86D-298
86F-424
86Mother/A's-21
86T-58
87T-238
88Albuq/CMC-3
88Albuq/ProC-271
90Brewer/MillB-13
90F-328
90Leaf/II-421
90OPC-518
90Pol/Brew-47
90S-366
90T-518
90Target-421
91B-248
91D-647
91F-588
91F/UltraUp-U52
91F/Up-U54
91OPC-417
91S-598
91T-417
91T/Tr-70T
91UD/FinalEd-60F

92D/II-672
92F-285
92S/I-253
92T-368
92UD-403

Krueger, Ernie
90Target-422

Krueger, Kirby
81Wisco-6
83Orlan-18

Krueger, Steve
81LynnS-7
82LynnS-5

Krug, Everett B.
(Chris)
62Pep/Tul
63Pep/Tul
66OPC-166
66T-166

Krug, Martin
E120

Kruk, John
83Beaum-11
84Cram/PCL-228
84Cram/PCL-250
85Cram/PCL-103
86D/Rook-42
86F/Up-U61
86Sf/Rook-1
86T/Tr-56T
87Bohem-8
87D-328
87F-420
87Leaf-217
87Sf-61
87T-123
87T/St-113
87ToysRUs-17
88Classic/Blue-203
88Classic/Red-162
88Coke/Padres-8
88D-205
88D/Best-245
88F-589
88F/Mini-113
88F/SS-20
88F/St-124
88Leaf-176
88OPC-32
88OPC/WaxBox-G
88Panini/St-403
88RedFoley/St-44
88S-36
88S/YS/I-17
88Sf-64
88Smok/Padres-14
88T-596
88T/Big-60
88T/Coins-45
88T/Mini-75
88T/St-110
88T/UK-41
88T/WaxBox-G
89B-460
89D-86
89D/Best-240
89F-309
89F/Up-109
89OPC-235
89Padre/Mag-5
89Panini/St-200
89Phill/TastyK-42
89RedFoley/St-69
89S-148
89S/Tr-70T
89Sf-184
89T-235
89T/Big-216
89T/LJN-88
89T/St-102
89T/Tr-63T
89UD-280
90B-154
90Classic/III-T3
90D-160
90D/BestNL-69
90F-565
90Leaf/II-284
90OPC-469
90Panini/St-310
90Phill/TastyK-18
90Publint/St-52
90S-467
90Sf-124
90T-469
90T/Big-214
90T/St-117
90UD-668
91B-503
91Classic/III-47
91D-260
91F-402
91F/Ultra-266
91Leaf/II-278
91OPC-689
91Panini/St-107
91Phill/Medford-22
91S-94
91T-689
91T/StClub/I-227
91UD-199
91USPlayC/AS-4S
92D/DK-DK12
92D/I-230
92F-537
92S/I-235
92T-30
92UD-326
92UD-38TC

Krukow, Mike
77T-493R
78T-17
79T-592
80OPC-223
80T-431
81Coke
81F-312
81OPC-176
81T-176
81T/HT
82D-351
82F-598
82F/St-92
82OPC-215
82T-215
82T/St-31
82T/Tr-59T
83D-119
83F-163
83Mother/Giants-12
83OPC-331
83T-331
83T/Tr-58T
84D-509
84F-374
84Nes/792-633
84OPC-37
84T-633
85D-630
85F-609
85Mother/Giants-11
85OPC-74
85T-74
85T/St-163
86D-143
86D/HL-49
86F-546
86Mother/Giants-11
86OPC-126
86T-752
86T/St-93
87BK-12
87Classic-67
87D-609
87D/AAS-58
87D/AS/Wax-PC15
87D/OD-98
87F-275
87F-630M
87F/GameWin-24
87F/Lim-24
87F/Mini-61
87F/St-69
87Ho/St-17
87Leaf-86
87Mother/SFG-6
87OPC-241
87Sf-62
87Smok/NL-12
87T-580
87T/Mini-36
87T/St-92
88D-116
88D/Best-50
88F-85
88Mother/Giants-6
88OPC-393
88Panini/St-417
88RedFoley/St-45
88S-185
88T-445
89Classic-114
89D-258
89D/Best-135
89F-331
89Mother/Giants-6
89OPC-125
89S-190
89T-125
89T/St-83
89UD-46
90OPC-241
90Publint/St-72
90S-215
90T-241
90UD-639

Krum, Sandy
89Chatt/Best-24
89Chatt/GS-3
90Salem/Star-27TR
91Salem/ClBest-24

Krumback, Mark
88Boise/ProC-1625
89Greens/ProC-425
90Cedar/Best-12
90Cedar/ProC-2335
91AS/Cal-34

Krume, Sandy
88Cedar/ProC-1140

Krumm, Todd
90Lakeland/Star-17
91London/LineD-390
91London/ProC-1875

Krupenchemkov, Alexander
89EastLDD/ProC-DD14

Krusinski, Clar
89Peoria/Ko-33ow

Kryhoski, Dick
49B-218
49Remar
50B-242
52B-133
52T-149
53B/Col-127
54B-117
54Esskay
54T-150
79TCMA-241
91Crown/Orio-250

Kryka, Mark
77Clinton
78Clinton

Kryzanowski, Rusty
86AubAs-15
87Kenosha-9
88Kenosha/ProC-1383
89Kenosha/ProC-1077
89Kenosha/Star-10

Kuahn, Bill
89Welland/Pucko-33

Kubala, Brian
86SanJose-11

Kubek, Tony
57T-312
58T-393
59T-505
60T-83
61P-9
61T-265
61T/Dice-7
61T/St-195
62J-4
62P-4
62P/Can-4
62Salada-18
62Shirriff-18
62T-311IA
62T-430
62T/St-87
63Kahn
63T-20
64T-415
65OPC-65
65T-65
65T/E-71
79TCMA-244
88Pac/Leg-29
89Swell-68
Exh47
WG10-11
WG9-13

Kubiak, Ted
68OPC-79
68T-79
69Sunoco/Pin-13
69T-281
70McDon-1
70T-688
71MLB/St-442
71OPC-516
71T-516
72MB-189
72OPC-23
72T-23
73OPC-652
73T-652
74OPC-228
74T-228
75OPC-329
75T-329
75T/M-329
76OPC-578
76SSPC-129
76T-578
77T-158
89Modesto/Chong-1MG
90Modesto/Cal-171MG
90Modesto/ProC-2229MG
91Modesto/ClBest-17MG
91Modesto/ProC-3106MG

Kubicki, Marc
91Utica/ClBest-1
91Utica/ProC-3237

Kubit, Joe
83Visalia/LF-17

Kuboto, Masahiro
90Salinas/Cal-148TR

Kubski, Gil
78Cr/PCL-35
79SLCity-16
80SLCity-21
81Syrac-18
81Vanco-9
82Indianap-28
91Hunting/ProC-3354CO

Kucab, John
52T-358

Kucek, Jack
75OPC-614R
75T-614R
75T/M-614R
76OPC-597R
76T-597R
77T-623
79OkCty
80Syrac-11
81Syrac-6

Kucharski, Joe
84RochR-18
85RochR-20
87CharlO/WBTV-37
87RochR/TCMA-27

Kucks, John
56T-88
57T-185
58T-87
59T-289
60L-96
60T-177
61T-94
62Kahn/Atl
62T-241

Kuder, Jeff
89Augusta/ProC-491
89Welland/Pucko-16

Kuecker, Mark
77Cedar
79Phoenix

Kuehl, John
88Spokane/ProC-1934
89CharRain/ProC-986
89SALAS/GS-12
91MidwLAS/ProC-MWL30
91Single/ClBest-354
91Waterlo/ClBest-17
91Waterlo/ProC-1264

Kuehl, Karl
75IntAS/TCMA-25MG
76SSPC-611MG
76T-216MG

Kuehne, William
N172
WG1-60

Kuenn, Harvey
53Glen
54B-23
54RH
54T-25
54Wilson
55Armour-12A
55Armour-12B
55B-132
56T-155
57T-88
58T-304M
58T-434
59Armour-11
59Bz
59T-70
60Bz-34
60Kahn
60NuCard-59
60T-330
60T-429M
60T/tatt-27
61Bz-15
61NuCard-459
61P-57
61T-500
61T/St-77
62J-135
62P-135
62P/Can-135
62Salada-121
62Shirriff-121
62T-480
62T/bucks
62T/St-197
63Exh
63J-105
63P-105
63T-30
64T-242
65OPC-103
65T-103
66T-372
73OPC-646CO
73T-646CO
74T-99CO
78Newar
79TCMA-104
80Pac/Leg-66
81Detroit-96
82D-578MG
83D-608MG
83Gard-1MG
83Kaline-15M
83Kaline-16M
83Pol/Brew-32MG
83T-726MG
84Nes/792-321MG
84T-321MG
84T/Gloss22-1MG
88Pac/Leg-56
89Swell-9
91Swell/Great-114
91T/Arc53-301
Exh47

Kuhaulua, Fred
77SLCity
79Hawaii-20
80Hawaii-25
81Hawaii-17
82Hawaii-17
82T-731R

Kuhel, Joe
33G-108
34DS-78
34Exh/4-16
34G-16
35BU-128
35BU-80
35G-8H
35G-9H
37Exh/4-16
37OPC-127
38G-243
38G-267
40PB-185
41PB-31
47TipTop
49Exh
61F-119
88Conlon/5-18
88Conlon/AmAS-18
91Conlon/Sport-188
R310

R313
R314
V300
V354-52
V355-63

Kuhlman, Eric
88Idaho/ProC-1851
89Idaho/ProC-2028

Kuhlmann, Hank
62Pep/Tul

Kuhn, Bowie
83Kaline-64COM

Kuhn, Chad
88Spokane/ProC-1935
89Watlo/ProC-1797
89Watlo/Star-16
90Madison/Best-17
90Madison/ProC-2263
91Huntsvl/ClBest-13
91Huntsvl/LineD-287
91HuntsvlProC-1790

Kuhn, Ken
55Salem
57T-266

Kuhn, Walter
(Red)
T207

Kuilan, Jorge
88WinHaven/Star-11

Kuiper, Duane
76OPC-508
76SSPC-522
76T-508
77BurgChef-55
77OPC-233
77Pep-19
77T-85
78Ho-34
78OPC-39
78T-332
79Ho-13
79OPC-67
79T-146
80OPC-221
80T-429
81D-319
81OPC-226
81T-612
82D-198
82F-373
82OPC-233
82T-233
82T/Tr-60T
83F-263
83Mother/Giants-11
83T-767
84D-553
84F-375
84Nes/792-542
84OPC-338
84T-542
84T/St-169
85F-610
85T-22

Kuiper, Glen
85Spokane/Cram-10
86Erie-16

Kulakov, Vadim
89EastLDD/ProC-DD5

Kuld, Pete
88Watlo/ProC-682
89Miami/I/Star-22
90Huntsvl/Best-14
91Wichita/LineD-610
91Wichita/ProC-2602

Kume, Mike
52Park-100

Kunkel, Jeff
84Rang-20
85D-587
85F-561
85OKCty-3
85OPC-288
85T-136FS
85T-288
85T/St-350
86OKCty-9
87Mother/Rang-24
88OkCty/CMC-18
88OkCty/ProC-30
88S-407
89B-231
89D-496
89F-527
89Mother/R-19
89S-484
89Smok/R-18
89T-92
89UD-463
90D-496
90F-304
90Mother/Rang-18
90OPC-174
90PublInt/St-415
90S-431
90T-174
90T/St-246
90UD-394
91F-292
91Leaf/Stud-126
91OPC-562
91S-783
91T-562
91T/StClub/II-580

Kunkel, Kevin
86Cram/PCL-70
87Madis-19

Kunkel, William
(Bill)
61T-322
62T-147
63T-523
85T-136FS

Kuntz, Lee
86Watlo-16tr
88Wmsprt/ProC-1303
90Canton/Best-3
90Canton/Star-21TR

Kuntz, Rusty
78Knoxvl
81D-282
81T-112R
82Edmon-20
82F-348
82T-237
84F-568
84F/X-U66
84Nes/792-598
84T-598
84T/Tr-66T
85D-516
85F-14
85T-73
85Wendy-13
90Mother/Mar-27M

Kuoda, Masa
89Salinas/Cal-134
89Salinas/ProC-1804

Kupsey, John
89Pulaski/ProC-1913
90Sumter/Best-10
90Sumter/ProC-2442

Kurczewski, Tommy
88Watlo/ProC-665
89BurlB/ProC-1603

Kurosaki, Ryan
77ArkTr
80ArkTr-13

Kurowski, George
(Whitey)
47TipTop
48L-81
62Pep/Tul
Exh47

Kurpiel, Ed
78Tidew

Kush, Emil
47TipTop
49Eureka-59

Kusick, Craig
75OPC-297
75T-297
75T/M-297
77T-38
78T-137
79T-472
80Hawaii-7
80OPC-374
80T-693
81Evansvl-16

Kusnyer, Art
72OPC-213R
72T-213R
77Spoka
89Mother/A's-27CO
90Mother/A's-27M
91Mother/A's-28CO

Kustus, Joe
90Target-1008

Kutcher, Randy
80Clinton-14
83Phoenix/BHN-15
84Cram/PCL-18
85Cram/PCL-177
86Phoenix-13
87D-547
87F-276
87Phoenix-12
88Pawtu/CMC-11
88Pawtu/ProC-464
89T/Tr-64T
90OPC-676
90PublInt/St-459
90S-551
90T-676
90T/TVRSox-31
91F-100
91S-837

Kutina, Joe
T207

Kutner, Mike
82Miami-20

Kutsukos, Pete
84Beaum-2
85Beaum-7

Kutyna, Marty
60T-516
61T-546
62T-566

Kutzler, Jerry
88Tampa/Star-12
89BirmB/Best-15
89BirmB/ProC-117
89SLAS-15
90Coke/WSox-14
90Coke/WSox-28
90D-503
90D/Rook-25
90S/Tr-80T
91S-749RP
91T/90Debut-80
91Vanco/LineD-639
91Vanco/ProC-1592

Kuykendall, Kevin
87Watlo-12

Kuzava, Robert
(Bob)
50B-5
51B-97
51T/BB-22
52B-233
52BR
52T-85
53B/BW-33
54Esskay
54NYJour
54T-230
55B-215
55Esskay
91Crown/Orio-251

Kuzma, Greg
88Butte-3

Kuzniar, Paul
(Kooz)
87Watlo-19
88Wmsprt/ProC-1321
89Canton/Best-20
89Canton/ProC-1305
89Canton/Star-11
90NewBrit/Star-7

Kvansnicka, Jay
89Kenosha/ProC-1063
89Kenosha/Star-11
90Visalia/ProC-2168
91OrlanSR/LineD-483
91OrlanSR/ProC-1862

Kwolek, Joe
86Osceola-16

Kyles, Stan
81QuadC-19
83MidldC-19
84Albany-15
85Cram/PCL-138
87Tacoma-3
88Albuq/CMC-2
88Albuq/ProC-275
91BendB/ClBest-3CO
91BendB/ProC-3712CO

Laabs, Chester
40PB-206
V362-31
W753

Laake, Pete
91Gaston/ProC-2694

LaBare, Jay
80Elmira-39

Labay, Steve
86Reading-13

Labine, Clem
52T-342
53T-14
54B-106
54NYJour
54T-121
55Gol/Dodg-17
55T-180
56T-295
57T-53
58Hires-34
58T-305
59Morrell
59T-262M
59T-403
60BB-6
60L-60
60T-29
61T-22
79TCMA-31
89Rini/Dodg-19
89Smok/Dodg-61
90Pac/Legend-89
90Target-423
91Swell/Great-54
91T/Arc53-14
91WIZMets-222

Labossiere, Dave
80Tucson-12
81Tucson-14
82Tucson-27
83Tucson-25
90Mother/Ast-28TR

Laboy, Carlos
87AubAs-14
88Ashvl/ProC-1056
89Osceola/Star-10
91PalmSp/ProC-2029

Laboy, Jose A.
(Coco)
66Pep/Tul
69Expos/Pins-4
69Fud's-6
69T-524R
70Expos/Pins-9
70K-66
70MLB/St-67
70OPC-238
70T-238
71LaPizza-5
71MLB/St-132
71OPC-132
71T-132
72MB-190
72T-727
73OPC-642
73T-642
87FtLaud-20
88PrWill/Star-14

Labozzetta, Al
86GlenF-11

LaCasse, Michael
79Newar-10

Lacer, Mike
86Pittsfld-12tr

LaCerra, Tony
88Reno/Cal-270

Lacey, Robert
76Tucson-19
77SanJose-14
78T-29
79T-647
80OPC-167
80T-316
81D-240
81F-578
81T-481
81T/Tr-784
82T-103
85Cram/PCL-191
85F-611

LaChance, George
(Candy)
90Target-424
E107

Lachemann, Bill
83Clinton/LF-29
86QuadC-18MG
87PalmSp-17
88CalLgAS-35
88PalmSp/Cal-112
88PalmSp/ProC-1436
89PalmSp/Cal-63MG
89PalmSp/ProC-489

Lachemann, Bret
91QuadC/ClBest-6
91QuadC/ProC-2623

Lachemann, Marcel
71MLB/St-518
71OPC-84
71T-84
82Danvl-14

Lachemann, Rene
65T-526R
66OPC-157
66T-157
67T-471
68T-422
77SanJose-2MG
78SanJose-2MG
79Spokane-16MG
80Spokane-18MG
81Spokane-13MG
82D-600MG
83T-336MG
84F-655M
84Gard-1MG
84Pol/Brew-9MG
84T/Tr-67T
85T-628MG
88Chatt/Team-19
88Mother/A's-27CO
89Mother/A's-27CO
90Mother/A's-27M
91Mother/A's-28CO

Lachmann, Tom
89BurlInd/Star-14

Lachowetz, Anthony J.
81VeroB-8
82VeroB-23

Lachowicz, Al
82Tulsa-7
84OKCty-1
85Tulsa-36

Lackey, John
83LynnP-4

Lacko, Rich
87Lakeland-14
88GlenF/ProC-920

Lacks, Charles K.
55Gol/Braves-17

LaCock, R. Pete
75OPC-494
75T-494
75T/M-494
76OPC-101
76SSPC-317
76T-101
77T-561
78T-157
79T-248
80OPC-202
80T-389
81D-344
81F-47
81T-9
89Pac/SenLg-33
89T/SenLg-99
90EliteSenLg-98
91Pac/SenLg-120
91Pac/SenLg-53

LaCorte, Frank
76OPC-597R
76SSPC-612
76T-597R
78Richm
80T-411
81D-143
81F-55
81OPC-348
81T-513
82D-270
82F-220
82T-248
83D-218
83F-454
83T-14

84D-283
84F-230
84F/X-67
84Nes/792-301
84Smok/Cal-16
84T-301
84T/Tr-68T
85OPC-153
85T-153

LaCoss, Mike
77Indianap-11
78Indianap-4
79T-717R
80OPC-111
80T-199
81D-183
81OPC-134
81T-474
82D-440
82F-72
82T-294
82T/Tr-61T
83D-344
83F-455
83T-97
84D-206
84F-231
84Mother/Ast-24
84Nes/792-507
84T-507
85D-405
85F-353
85F/Up-U66
85T-666
85T/Tr-69T
86F/Up-U62
86Mother/Giants-17
86T-359
86T/Tr-57T
87D-636
87F-277
87Mother/SFG-21
87T-151
88D-436
88F-86
88Mother/Giants-21
88Panini/St-418
88S-465
88T-754
89D-602
89F/Up-129
89Mother/Giants-21
89RedFoley/St-70
89S-500
89T-417
89UD-48
90D-652
90F-59
90Leaf/II-463
90Mother/Giant-11
90OPC-53
90Publint/St-73
90S-253
90T-53
90UD-140
91F-264
91Leaf/II-309
91Mother/Giant-11
91OPC-242
91PG&E-17
91S-652
91SFExam/Giant-9
91T-242
91T/StClub/II-479
91UD-691

Lacy, Lee
73OPC-391
73T-391
74OPC-658
74T-658
75OPC-631
75T-631
75T/M-631
76OPC-99
76SSPC-78
76T-99
76T/Tr-99T
77T-272
78T-104
79OPC-229
79T-441
80T-536
81D-376
81F-374
81T-332
82D-276
82F-483
82F/St-80
82T-752
83D-276
83F-308
83OPC-69
83T-69
84D-479
84F-252
84Nes/792-462
84OPC-229
84T-462
84T/St-138
85D-508
85F-467
85F/St-9
85F/Up-U67
85Leaf-40
85T-669
85T/St-126
85T/Tr-70T
86D-228
86F-277
86Leaf-104
86OPC-226
86Sf-87
86T-226
86T/St-229
87D-336
87F-473
87French-27
87OPC-182
87Sf-86
87T-182
87T/St-231
88F-565
88S-173
88T-598
89Pac/SenLg-184
89T/SenLg-72
89TM/SenLg-61
90EliteSenLg-25
90Swell/Great-94
90Target-425
91Crown/Orio-252

Lacy, Steve
76Watlo
77DaytB

Ladd, Pete
80T-678R
81Tucson-19
82Vanco-17
83F-37
83Pol/Brew-27
84D-124
84F-204
84F/St-77
84Gard-10
84Nes/792-243
84Pol/Brew-27
84T-243
85D-271
85F-585
85Gard-10
85Pol/Brew-27
85T-471
86F-492
86F/Up-U63
86Mother/Mar-17
86T-163
86T/Tr-58T
87Albuq/Pol-12
87D-660
87F-588
87T-572

Lade, Doyle
49B-168
49Eureka-60
50B-196
51B-139

Ladnier, Deric
86FtMyr-17
87AppFx-8
89Memphis/Best-11
89Memphis/ProC-1189
89Memphis/Star-13
89Star/Wax-43
91London/LineD-409
91Memphis/ProC-662

Lafata, Joe
49Eureka-115

LaFever, Greg
86Watlo-17
87Wmsprt-17
88SanAn/Best-4

Lafitte, Edward
(Doc)
E254
E270/2

Lafitte, James A.
T206

LaFountain, James
77Visalia

LaFrancois, Roger
81Pawtu-23
83D-534
83Pawtu-12
83T-344
84Richm-14
85Durham-27
88James/ProC-1894
89SoBend/GS-4
90Vanco/CMC-27CO
90Vanco/ProC-507CO
91Vanco/LineD-650CO
91Vanco/ProC-1611

Laga, Mike
82Evansvl-16
83Evansvl-15
84D-491
84Evansvl-16
86D-578
86T/Tr-59T
87D-293
87Louisvl-23
87Smok/Cards-15
87T-321
88Louisvl-26
89Phoenix/CMC-17
89Phoenix/ProC-1493
89S-536
90BirmDG/Best-20
90Phoenix/CMC-21

LaGrow, Lerrin
71OPC-39R
71T-39R
73OPC-369
73T-369
74OPC-433
74T-433
75OPC-116
75T-116
75T/M-116
76OPC-138
76SSPC-356
76T-138
78OPC-152
78T-14
79T-527
80T-624
90Target-426

LaHonta, Ken
76Dubuq

Lahoud, Joe
69OPC-189R
69T-189R
70OPC-78
70T-78
71MLB/St-321
71OPC-622
71T-622
72MB-191
72OPC-321
72T-321
72T/Cloth-19
73OPC-212
73T-212
74OPC-512
74T-512
75Ho-10
75Ho/Twink-10
75OPC-317
75T-317
75T/M-317
76OPC-612
76SSPC-20
76T-612
78T-382

Lahrman, Tom
86Penin-15
87Penin-22
88Tampa/Star-13

Lahti, Jeffrey Allen
80Water-2
81Indianap-16
82Louisvl-13
83F-12
83T-284
84D-327
84F-327
84Nes/792-593
84T-593
85F-231
85T-447
86D-475
86F-40
86KAS/Disc-18
86Leaf-233
86Schnucks-12
86T-33
87D-577
87F-299
87T-367

Lain, Marty
83Beaum-9

Laird, Tony
85Nashua-13
86Nashua-14

Lairsey, Eric
91Pulaski/ClBest-24
91Pulaski/ProC-4001

Lajeskie, Dick
48Sommer-22
49B/PCL-16
49Sommer-12

Lajoie, Napoleon
(Nap)
10Domino-65
11Helmar-24
12Sweet/Pin-18
14CJ-66
15CJ-66
33G-106
40PB-173
48Exh/HDF
50Callahan
60F-1
61F-120
61GP-31
63Bz/ATG-8
69Bz/Sm
72F/FFeat-28
73F/Wild-35M
75F/Pion-18
76Motor-2
80Pac/Leg-74
80Laugh/3/4/5-9
80SSPC/HOF
89HOF/St-10
92Conlon/Sport-528
BF2-35
D303
D304
D329-97
E101
E102
E103
E105
E106
E107
E254
E270/2
E300
E90/1
E92
E93
E94
E96
E98
L1-121
M101/4-97
M116
PM1-10
S81-96
T201
T206
T213/blue
T215/blue
T215/brown
T216
T3-23
W514-62
W555
WG2-32
WG4-12
WG5-25
WG6-24

Lajszky, Werner
80Wausau-21

Lak, Carlos
91Clinton/ProC-842

Lake, Dan
85Anchora-18

Lake, Edward
47TipTop
49B-107
50B-240
51B-140
Exh47

Lake, Fred
M116

Lake, Joe
11Helmar-61
E94
M116
T201
T206
T215/blue
W555

Lake, Ken
89James/ProC-2148
89Miami/I/Star-10
90WPalmB/Star-12
91Harris/LineD-260
91Harris/ProC-643

Lake, Mike
77LodiD
78LodiD

Lake, Steve
80Holyo-17
81Vanco-25
82Tucson-5
83Thorn-16
84D-198
84Nes/792-691
84T-691
85SevenUp-16
85T-98
86Gator-29
86T-588
87D-604
87F-300
87Smok/Cards-10
87T-84
88D-510
88F-38
88S-596
88Smok/Card-11
88T-208
89B-399
89F-454
89Phill/TastyK-17
89S-363
89S/Tr-12
89T-463
89T/Tr-65T
90D-431
90F-566
90Leaf/II-395
90OPC-183
90Phill/TastyK-19
90Publint/St-245
90S-435
90T-183
90T/Big-191
90UD-491
91D-334
91F-403
91Leaf/II-385
91Leaf/Stud-216
91OPC-661
91Phill/Medford-23
91S-572
91T-661
91T/StClub/II-395
92S/II-467
92T-331

Lakeman, Al
49Eureka-14

Laker, Tim
88James/ProC-1904
89James/ProC-2137
90Rockford/ProC-2696
91Single/ClBest-205
91WPalmB/ClBest-16
91WPalmB/ProC-1232

Lamabe, Jack
62T-593R
63T-251
64T-305
65OPC-88
65T-88

66T-577
67T-208
68T-311
85Beaum-24C
91WIZMets-223
Lamanno, Ray
49B-113
Lamanske, Frank
90Target-1009
Lamar, Bill
90Target-427
LaMar, Danny
82Cedar-12
83Tampa-16
84Cedar-18
LaMarche, Michel
87Spartan-10
LaMaster, Wayne
90Target-428
Lamb, Randy
77Cocoa
78Wausau
Lamb, Ray
70OPC-131R
70T-131R
71MLB/St-377
71OPC-727
71T-727
72OPC-422
72T-422
73OPC-496
73T-496
85SpokAT/Cram-11
90Target-429
Lamb, Todd
84Durham-19
86Durham-17
Lambert, Gene
82Clinton-17
83Clinton/LF-10
Lambert, Ken
87VeroB-10
Lambert, Layne
90AubAs/ProC-3396
91BurlAs/ClBest-16
91BurlAs/ProC-2810
Lambert, Reese
87Madis-23
88Tacoma/CMC-4
88Tacoma/ProC-631
89Tacoma/CMC-3
89Tacoma/ProC-1548
90Tacoma/CMC-8
90Tacoma/ProC-87
Lambert, Reggie
86PalmSp-20
86PalmSp/Smok-27
87PalmSp-5
88PalmSp/Cal-113
88PalmSp/ProC-1461
Lambert, Rob
87PrWill-25
88Colum/CMC-14
88Colum/ProC-319
Lambert, Tim
82Idaho-10
84Albany-17
85Cram/PCL-140
86Tacoma-11
87Memphis-13
87Memphis/Best-16
90AlbanyDG/Best-24
Lamle, Adam
88CharlR/Star-12
88FSLAS/Star-41
89Miami/II/Star-10
89Tulsa/GS-12
Lammon, John
90Elmira/Pucko-14
91Elmira/ClBest-7
91Elmira/ProC-3272
Lamonde, Larry
82AlexD-3
84Cram/PCL-124
85Nashua-14
Lamont, Gene
71OPC-39R
71T-39R
75OPC-593
75T-593
75T/M-593
84Omaha-2
85Omaha-22MG
89VFJuice-36CO
90Homer/Pirate-16CO
LaMotta, Jake
47HomogBond-29BOX
D305
Lamp, Dennis
78T-711R
79T-153
80OPC-129
80T-54
81D-573
81F-305
81T-331
81T/Tr-785
82D-619
82F-349
82T-216TL
82T-622
83D-165
83F-243
83OPC-26
83T-434
83TrueVal/WSox-53
84D-526
84F-66
84F/X-U68
84Nes/792-541
84T-541
84T/St-239
84T/Tr-69T
84Tor/Fire-21
85D-119
85F-111
85OPC-83
85T-774
85Tor/Fire-17
86Ault-53
86D-626
86F-64
86Leaf-244
86OPC-219
86T-219
86T/St-193
86Tor/Fire-21
87F-233
87OPC-336
87T-768
88D/RedSox/Bk-NEW
88F-284
88S-616
88S/Tr-6T
89D-633
89F-92
89S-508
89T-188
89T/Big-169
89UD-503
90D-423
90F-280
90Leaf/II-315
90OPC-338
90Pep/RSox-12
90PublInt/St-460
90S-471
90T-338
90T/TVRSox-13
91D-138
91F-101
91OPC-14
91Pep/RSox-11
91S-612
91T-14
92F-42
92S/I-335
92T-653
Lampard, C. Keith
(Keith)
70OPC-492R
70T-492R
71OPC-728R
71T-728R
72OPC-489R
72T-489R
Lampe, Ed
88Hamil/ProC-1742
Lampert, Ken
86VeroB-15
Lamphere, Lawrence
(Larry)
88AubAs/ProC-1947
89Ashvl/ProC-967
89SALAS/GS-4
90Osceola/Star-14
Lampkin, Tom
87Watlo-23
88BBAmer-7
88EastLAS/ProC-41
88Wmsprt/ProC-1304
89AAA/ProC-35
89ColoSp/ProC-254
89D-639
90ColoSp/CMC-12
90ColoSp/ProC-39
90OPC-172
90T-172
91Leaf/II-512
91Padre/MagRal-4
91S-720RP
91S/100RisSt-70
91T/StClub/II-530
92F-610
92S/I-338
Lamson, Chuck
78Ashvl
80Tulsa-20
Lancaster, Lester
(Les)
86WinSalem-12
87D/Rook-10
88Berg/Cubs-50
88D-561
88D/Best-172
88D/Cubs/Bk-561
88F-421
88S-602
88T-112
89D-341
89F-429
89Iowa/CMC-8
89Iowa/ProC-1689
89Mara/Cubs-50
89S-60
89T-694
89UD-84
90Cub/Mara-11
90D-628
90D/BestNL-38
90F-35
90Leaf/II-361
90OPC-437
90S-413
90T-437
90T/TVCub-11
90UD-584
91Cub/Mara-50
91D-256
91F-424
91F/Ultra-63
91OPC-86
91S-293A
91S-293B
91T-86
92D/I-296
92F-384
92S/I-348
92T-213
92UD-481
Lance, Gary
79Spokane-11
83Idaho-32
84Madis/Pol-2
85Huntsvl/BK-24
87CharRain-9
88Charl/ProC-1212
89AubAs/ProC-28
89Wichita/Rock-38CO
90LasVegas/CMC-23CO
90LasVegas/ProC-138CO
90Martins/ProC-3191CO
91Pac/SenLg-62
91Sumter/ClBest-27CO
91Sumter/ProC-2352CO
Lance, Mark
83Durham-19
84Durham-2
Lancellotti, Rick
78Salem
80Port-20
81Hawaii-11
82Hawaii-11
84Cram/PCL-230
85Tidew-1
86Phoenix-14
89Pawtu/Dunkin-29
90Pawtu/CMC-19
90Pawtu/ProC-472
90T/TVRSox-48
91Pac/SenLg-122
91Pawtu/LineD-358
91Pawtu/ProC-47
Landers, Hank
83Beloit/LF-7
Landestoy, Rafael
75Water
78Cr/PCL-6
79T-14
80T-268
81Coke
81D-19
81F-70
81OPC-326
81T-597
81T/St-168
81T/Tr-786
82Coke/Reds
82F-73
82T-361
83F-595
83T-684
83T/Tr-59
84Nes/792-477
84Pol/Dodg-17
84T-477
85Albany-17
85Cram/PCL-61
87Pocatel/Bon-2MG
89Pac/SenLg-60
89T/SenLg-5
89TM/SenLg-62
90EliteSenLg-85
90Target-430
91Pac/SenLg-24
Landinez, Carlos
90Spring/Best-12
91Savan/ClBest-18
91Savan/ProC-1659
Landis, Craig
78Cedar
80Phoenix-14
81Richm-5
Landis, Jim
57T-375
58T-108
59T-493
60MacGregor-11
60T-550
61P-27
61T-271
61T/St-122
62Bz
62Exh
62P-50
62P/Can-50
62Salada-49
62Shirriff-49
62T-50
62T-540
62T/bucks
62T/St-26
63Exh
63F-10
63J-40
63P-40
63Salada-60
63T-485
64T-264
65T-376
66OPC-128
66T-128
67T-483
89Kodak/WSox-4M
Exh47
Landis, Kenesaw M.
(Judge)
50Callahan
60F-64
61F-53
63Bz-30
80SSPC/HOF
88Pac/8Men-66
88Pac/8Men-67
88Pac/8Men-79
89HOF/St-95
Landis, William
68OPC-189
68T-189
69T-264
72MB-192
Landmark, Neil
85Visalia-20
Landphere, Ed
90Salinas/Cal-130
90Salinas/ProC-2728
Landreaux, Ken
79T-619
80OPC-49
80T-88
81D-565
81F-553
81F/St-46
81K-30
81OPC-219
81Pol/Dodg-44B
81T-219
81T/SO-41
81T/St-101
81T/Tr-787
82D-388
82F-11
82OPC-114
82Pol/Dodg-44
82T-114
82T/St-49
83D-236
83F-210
83Pol/Dodg-44
83T-376
83T/St-246
84D-470
84F-104
84F/St-2
84Nes/792-533
84OPC-216
84Pol/Dodg-44
84Smok/Dodg-1
84T-533
84T/St-76
85Coke/Dodg-17
85D-494
85F-375
85T-418
85T/St-75
86Coke/Dodg-15
86D-470
86F-134
86OPC-2
86Pol/Dodg-44
86T-782
87D-352
87D/OD-81
87F-444
87Mother/Dodg-24
87OPC-123
87Pol/Dodg-23
87T-699
88RochR/Gov-14
88S-247
88T-23
89T/SenLg-109
89TM/SenLg-63
90EliteSenLg-9
90ElPasoATG/Team-41
90Target-431
91Pac/SenLg-134
Landress, Roger
91Eugene/ClBest-24
91Eugene/ProC-3722
Landreth, Harry
83Chatt-25
84Chatt-15
Landreth, Larry
78T-701R
Landrith, Dave
83Butte-13
Landrith, Hobie
54B-220
55B-50
56T-314
57T-182
58T-24
59T-422
60T-42
61P-150
61T-114
61T/St-78
62Salada-181
62Shirriff-181
62T-279
62T/St-157
63T-209
91Crown/Orio-253
91WIZMets-224
Landrum

46Sunbeam
Landrum, Bill
82Water-1
83Water-5
84Wichita/Rock-17
87Kahn-43
88F-238
88Iowa/CMC-8
88Iowa/ProC-541
88T-42
89BuffB/CMC-2
89BuffB/ProC-1674
89F/Up-U116
89VFJuice-43
90B-166
90D-668
90D/BestNL-58
90F-472
90Homer/Pirate-17
90Leaf/I-222
90OPC-425
90Panini/St-326
90PublInt/St-157
90S-456
90T-425
90T/Big-164
90T/St-128
90UD-442
91B-523
91D-350
91F-41
91F/Ultra-281
91Leaf/Stud-225
91OPC-595
91S-98
91T-595
91T/StClub/II-431
91UD-614
92D/I-221
92F-557
92S/I-196
92T-661
92UD-636
Landrum, Cedric
86Geneva-13
87WinSalem-4
88Pittsfld/ProC-1370
89CharlK-4
90Iowa/CMC-19
90Iowa/ProC-330
90T/TVCub-51
91Classic/III-49
91D/Rook-11
91Iowa/LineD-208
91Iowa/ProC-1075
92D/II-662
92F-385
92S/100RisSt-30
92S/I-418
92T-81
92T/91Debut-106
92UD-50
Landrum, Darryl
86Ventura-11
87Dunedin-11
88Wmsprt/ProC-1319
Landrum, Don
58T-291
61P-175
61T-338
62T-323
63T-113
64T-286
65T-596
66OPC-43
66T-43
66T/RO-99
Landrum, Terry
(Tito)
76ArkTr
77ArkTr
78StPete
79ArkTr-4
81F-539
81Louisvl-12
81T-244R
82D-292
82F-118
82T-658
83D-498
83F-13
83Louisvl/Riley-12
83T-357
84F/X-69
84T/St-14LCS
85D-168
85F-232
85OPC-33
85T-33
86D-425
86F-41
86KAS/Disc-3
86OPC-171
86Schnucks-13
86T-498
86T/St-19WS
87D-386
87D/OD-66
87F-301
87OPC-288
87Smok/Cards-23
87T-288
88Pol/Dodg-21M
88RochR/CMC-22
88T-581
89Nashvl/Team-11
89Pac/SenLg-168
89T/SenLg-94
89TM/SenLg-64
90EliteSenLg-26
90Miami/I/Star-15
90Target-432
91Crown/Orio-254
91Pac/SenLg-149
Landry, Greg
89Beloit/I/Star-13
89Helena/SP-10
90Beloit/Best-9
Landry, Howard
89WinHaven/Star-11
90LynchRS/Team-19
Landuyt, Doug
78Cedar
81Shrev-14TR
83Phoenix/BHN-25tr
Landy, Brian
88Billings/ProC-1820
89Greens/ProC-412
Lane, Brian
88Greens/ProC-1555
88SALAS/GS-7
89BBAmerAA/BProC-AA16
89Chatt/Best-4
89Chatt/GS-14
90B-48
90Nashvl/CMC-20
90Nashvl/ProC-239
Lane, Gene
82Durham-24
90BurlB/Best-29TR
90BurlB/Star-31TR
Lane, Heath
89Beloit/I/Star-14
90Riversi/Best-26
90Riversi/Cal-19
90Riversi/ProC-2604
Lane, Ira
82DayBe-14
Lane, Jerald H.
(Jerry)
54T-97
Lane, Jerry
81ElPaso-7
Lane, Kevin
91BurlAs/ClBest-6
91BurlAs/ProC-2797
Lane, Marvin
77Evansvl/TCMA-17
Lane, Nolan
88CapeCod/Sum-46
89BurlInd/Star-15
90CLAS/CL-42
90Kinston/Team-10
91Canton/LineD-87
91Canton/ProC-990
Lane, Scott
88Rockford-19AGM
89Rockford-19AGM
Lane, William C.
52Park-50
Lanfair, Dave
75Water
Lanfranco, Luis
90SoOreg/Best-6
90SoOreg/ProC-3432
91Madison/ClBest-23
91Madison/ProC-2139
Lanfranco, Raphael
90Ashvl/ClBest-19
91Ashvl/ProC-571
Lang, Perry
88Pac/8Men-15
Lang, Robert
(Chip)
77OPC-216
77T-132
Langbehn, Gregg
89Pittsfld/Star-14
91StLucie/ClBest-20
91StLucie/ProC-705
Langdon, Ted
83Tampa-17
84Cedar-2
86Tampa-9
87Vermont-3
Langdon, Tim
91Kinston/ClBest-4
91Kinston/ProC-316
Lange, Clark
85Osceola/Team-19
87Visalia-26
Lange, Frank H.
E254
T205
T207
Lange, Fred
N172
Lange, Richard
74OPC-429
74T-429
75OPC-114
75T-114
75T/M-114
76OPC-176
76T-176
77SLCity
Langfield, Paul
80Utica-28
Langford, Rick
75Shrev/TCMA-8
78Ho-120
78OPC-33
78T-327
79T-29
80OPC-284
80T-546
81D-238
81F-572
81F/St-27
81K-55
81OPC-154
81T-154
81T/St-121
82D-161
82F-98
82F/St-126
82Granny-7
82OPC-43
82T-454
83D-365
83F-523
83Granny-22
83T-286
83T-531TL
83T/St-106
84F-451
84Nes/792-629
84OPC-304
84T-629
85T-347
85ThomMc/Discs-14
86F-425
86Mother/A's-14
86T-766
88Colum/CMC-10
88Colum/Pol-5
88Colum/ProC-308
91Billings/ProC-3749
91Cedar/ClBest-7
91Cedar/ProC-2715
91Single/ClBest-347
Langford, Sam
T3/Box-65
Langiotti, Fred
89Spring/Best-24
90Spring/Best-13
91StPete/ClBest-16
91StPete/ProC-2279
Langley, Lee
87VeroB-28
88Bakers/Cal-256
89Clearw/Star-13
90Clearw/Star-10
91Miami/ClBest-14
91Miami/ProC-404
Langowski, Ted
91MedHat/ProC-4107
Langston, Keith
88CapeCod/Sum-109
89NiagFls/Pucko-14
Langston, Mark
83Chatt-11
84F/X-U70
85FunFoodPin-18
84Mother/Mar-13
84T/Tr-70T
85D-557
85Drake-38
85F-492
85F/LimEd-17
85F/St-109
85Leaf-56
85Mother/Mar-3
85OPC-259
85T-625
85T/3D-22
85T/St-281
85T/St-337
85T/St-371M
85T/Super-20
86D-118
86F-467
86Mother/Mar-3
86OPC-198
86T-495
86T/St-225
87Classic-89
87D-568
87D/HL-34
87D/OD-116
87F-589
87F/AwardWin-22
87F/Hottest-26
87F/Mini-62
87F/St-70
87Leaf-55
87Mother/Sea-5
87OPC-215
87RedFoley/St-45
87Sf-102
87S/Test-30
87T-215
87T/Mini-71
87T/St-219
88Classic/Blue-250
88D-20DK
88D-317
88D/AS-26
88D/Best-136
88D/DKsuper-20DK
88F-377
88F/BB/AS-20
88F/BB/MVP-21
88F/Hottest-23
88F/LL-24
88F/Mini-52
88F/Slug-23
88F/St-60
88F/TL-18
88Leaf-123
88Leaf-20DK
88Mother/Sea-5
88OPC-80
88Panini/St-181
88RedFoley/St-46
88S-30
88Sf-46
88T-80
88T/Big-176
88T/Coins-18
88T/Mini-34
88T/Revco-33
88T/St-214
88T/St/Backs-63
88T/UK-42
89B-205
89D-227
89D/Best-68
89F-551
89F/Excit-29
89F/Superstar-27
89F/Up-97
89KMart/DT-21
89Mother/Sea-5
89OPC-355
89Panini/St-430
89RedFoley/St-71
89S-161
89S/HotStar-67
89S/Mast-13
89S/Tr-25
89Sf-159
89T-355
89T/Hills-19
89T/LJN-11
89T/Mini-73
89T/St-221
89T/Tr-66T
89T/UK-47
89UD-526
90B-284
90Classic-72
90Classic/Up-28
90D-338
90D/BestAL-17
90F-352
90F/Up-U78
90Leaf/I-155
90Leaf/Prev-6
90OPC-530
90Panini/St-287
90PublInt/St-179
90RedFoley/St-55
90S-401
90S-688DT
90S/100St-96
90S/Tr-11T
90Sf-110
90Smok/Angel-10
90T-530
90T/Big-232
90T/Mini-62
90T/St-70
90T/Tr-54T
90UD-647
90UD/Ext-783
91B-202
91D-190
91D-BC1M
91F-318
91F/Ultra-49
91F/WaxBox-1M
91Leaf/I-67
91Leaf/Stud-27
91MajorLg/Pins-25
91OPC-755
91Panini/FrSt-352
91Panini/St-1
91S-21
91S-411KM
91S-699
91Smok/Angel-8
91T-755
91T/CJMini/I-17
91T/StClub/I-27
91UD-234
91USPlayC/AS-5H
92D/DK-DK20
92D/II-531
92F-63
92S/100SS-32
92S/I-12
92T-165
92UD-305
Laniauskas, Vitas
89Ashvl/ProC-941
Lanier, H. Max
50B-207
51B-230
52B-110
52T-101
92Conlon/Sport-620
W754
Lanier, Hal
65OPC-118
65T-118
66OPC-156M
66T-156M
66T-271
67OPC-4
67T-4
68T-436
69MB-155
69MLB/St-201
69T-316
69T/St-106
70MLB/St-126
70T-583

71MLB/St-255
71OPC-181
71T-181
72MB-193
72T-589
73OPC-479
73T-479
74OPC-588
74T-588
78StPete
86Pol/Ast-6MG
86T/Tr-60T
87Mother/Ast-1
87Pol/Ast-7MG
87T-343MG
88Mother/Ast-1MG
88Pol/Ast-25MG
88T-684MG
89T-164MG
90Phill/TastyK-34CO
91Phill/Medford-24CO
PM10/Sm-93

Lankard, Steve
86Salem-17
87PortChar-3
88Tulsa-20
89TexLAS/GS-35
89Tulsa/GS-13
90OkCty/CMC-2
90OkCty/ProC-428

Lankford, Ray
88MidwLAS/GS-26
88Spring/Best-14
89ArkTr/GS-9
89BBAmerAA/BProC-AA23
89TexLAS/GS-22
90B-192
90Classic/Up-29
90Leaf/II-308
90Louisvl/CMC-14
90Louisvl/ProC-416
90S/Tr-84T
90SpringDG/Best-24
90T/TVCard-53
90UD/Ext-755
91B-388
91Classic/200-83
91Classic/III-48
91D-43RR
91D/Rook-8
91F-637
91F/Ultra-290
91Leaf/II-523
91Leaf/Prev-10
91Leaf/Stud-234
91MajorLg/Pins-50
91OPC-682
91OPC/Premier-72
91Pol/Card-16
91S-731RP
91S/ASFan-1
91S/HotRook-7
91S/Rook40-2
91Seven/3DCoin-10MW
91T-682
91T/90Debut-81
91T/StClub/II-537
91UD-346
92Classic/I-51
92D/I-350
92F-583
92F/RookSIns-8
92S/100RisSt-43
92S/I-223
92T-292
92UD-262

Lanning, David P.
81VeroB-9

Lanok, Dale
85BurlR-7

Lanoux, Marty
86Kenosha-11
87Visalia-23
88CalLgAS-39
88Visalia/Cal-153
88Visalia/ProC-104
89Orlan/Best-26
89Orlan/ProC-1328
90Portl/ProC-186

Lansford, Carney
76QuadC
79T-212
80OPC-177
80T-337
81Coke
81D-409
81F-270
81F/St-12
81OPC-245
81T-639
81T/HT
81T/SO-25
81T/St-43
81T/Tr-788
82Coke/BOS
82D-82
82F-298
82F/St-164
82K-41
82OPC-91
82PermaGr/CC-15
82T-161LL
82T-786TL
82T-91
82T/St-156
82T/St-2
83D-408
83F-187
83Granny-4
83OPC-318
83T-523
83T/St-32
83T/Tr-60T
84D-176
84D/AAS-39
84F-452
85FunFoodPin-55
84Mother/A's-7
84Nes/792-767
84OPC-59
84T-767
84T/St-328
85D-345
85D-8DK
85D/DKsuper-8
85F-429
85Leaf-8DK
85Mother/A's-8
85OPC-347
85T-422
85T/St-330
86D-131
86F-426
86Leaf-55
86Mother/A's-8
86OPC-134
86Sf-75M
86T-134
86T/St-169
86Woolwth-17
87D-158
87D/OD-20
87F-397
87F/BB-24
87F/Mini-63
87F/St-71
87OPC-69
87RedFoley/St-37
87Sf-138
87Smok/A's-8
87T-678
87T/St-171
88ActPacT-4
88D-178
88D/A's/Bk-178
88D/Best-246
88F-285
88F/Slug-C3
88F/St-55
88Leaf-195
88Mother/A's-6
88OPC-292
88Panini/St-169
88S-253
88Sf-202
88T-292
88T/Big-221
88T/St-167
89B-198
89D-243
89D/AS-17
89D/Best-22
89F-16
89F-633M
89KMart/Lead-20
89Mother/A's-5
89OPC-47
89Panini/St-421
89RedFoley/St-72
89S-179
89S/HotStar-12
89Sf-53
89T-47
89T/Big-57
89T/LJN-83
89T/St-170
89UD-562
90B-452
90Classic-12
90D-95
90D/BestAL-117
90ElPasoATG/Team-40
90F-14
90KMart/CBatL-12
90Leaf/I-213
90MLBPA/Pins-73
90Mother/A's-8
90OPC-316
90Panini/St-134
90Panini/St-184
90PublInt/St-309
90RedFoley/St-56
90S-296
90S/100St-20
90Sf-84
90T-316
90T/Big-83
90T/DH-39
90T/Gloss60-6
90T/Mini-29
90T/St-183
90T/TVAS-4
90UD-253
91BBBest/HitM-12
91D-273
91F-14
91F/Ultra-250
91Mother/A's-8
91OPC-502
91Panini/FrSt-194
91S-630
91T-502
91T/StClub/I-231
91UD-194
92D/II-775
92F-261
92S/II-648
92T-495
92UD-682

Lansford, Joe
81Hawaii-6
82Hawaii-6
84Cram/PCL-220
85Cram/PCL-146
87LasVegas-4

Lansing, Mike
90Miami/I/Star-16
90WichSt-20
91FSLAS/ProC-FSL24
91Miami/ClBest-21
91Miami/ProC-415
91Single/ClBest-45

Lantigua, Manny
75SanAn
79Portl-16

Lantrip, Rich
90Oneonta/ProC-3387
91Greens/ProC-3066

Lantz, Tom
75Clinton

LaPalme, Paul
52T-166
53B/BW-19
53T-201
54B-107
54DanDee
54T-107
55B-61
55Hunter
57T-344
91T/Arc53-201

Lapchick, Joe
33SK-32

Lapenta, Jerry
86Geneva-14
87Peoria-6
88Peoria/Ko-20
88Pittsfld/ProC-1366

LaPoint, Dave
77Newar
78BurlB
80Vanco-7
83D-544
83F-14
83T-438
84D-290
84F-328
84Nes/792-627
84T-627
84T/St-146
85D-138
85F-233
85F/Up-U68
85Mother/Giants-16
85OPC-229
85T-229
85T/St-143
85T/Tr-71T
86Cain's-10
86D-387
86F-547
86F/Up-U64
86OPC-162
86T-551
86T/Tr-61T
87D-607
87F-421
87OPC-319
87T-754
88Coke/WS-13
88D-552
88D/Best-123
88F-402
88F/BB/AS-21
88F/Slug-24
88S-589
88T-334
89B-165
89D-488
89D/Best-244
89D/Tr-27
89F-212
89OPC-89
89S-384
89S/NWest-15
89S/Tr-4
89T-89
89T/Tr-67T
89UD-600
89UD/Ext-706
90D-72
90OPC-186
90PublInt/St-539
90S-357
90S/NWest-12
90T-186
90T/TVYank-11
90UD-507
91D-481
91F-669
91OPC-484
91S-218
91T-484
91UD-483

LaPoint, J. Anthony
(Tony)
86Geneva-15
87CharWh-19

LaPorte, Frank
10Domino-66
11Helmar-62
12Sweet/Pin-53A
12Sweet/Pin-53B
14CJ-98
14Piedmont/St-48
15CJ-98
E254
M116
T201
T202
T205
T206
T213/brown

Lapp, John
BF2-13
D329-98
D350/2-96
E104
E300
M101/4-98
M101/5-96
M116
T201
T207
T208
T222

Lapple, Bob
80Cedar-10

Lara, Carlos
91Pulaski/ClBest-3
91Pulaski/ProC-4009

Lara, Crucito
87StPete-20
88StPete/Star-11
89StLucie/Star-12

Larcom, Mark
82Wisco-22
83Wisco/LF-12

Lardizabal, Ruben
91Modesto/ClBest-7
91Modesto/ProC-3082

Lardner, Ring
88Pac/8Men-30
88Pac/8Men-35M
88Pac/8Men-42M

Laribee, Russ
81Pawtu-20

Larios, John
86Cram/PCL-35
87AppFx-3

Lariviere, Chris 42
88Rockford-20
89Rockford-20

Larker, Norm
53Exh/Can-37
59Morrell
59T-107
60BB-1
60T-394
61BB-5
61Bz-34
61Morrell
61P-156
61T-130
61T-41LL
61T/St-28
62Bz
62J-113
62P-113
62P/Can-118
62Salada-194
62Shirriff-194
62T-23
62T/bucks
63J-188
63P-188
63T-536
89Smok/Ast-14
89Smok/Dodg-67
90Target-433

Larkin, Barry
86Sf/Rook-34
87Classic-18
87Classic/Up-133
87D-492
87D/OD-191
87F-204
87Kahn-15
87S/Test-72
87T-648
87ToysRUs-18
88D-492
88D/Best-222
88F-239
88Kahn/Reds-11
88Leaf-226
88OPC-102
88Panini/St-280
88S-72
88S/YS/II-34
88T-102
88T/Big-74
88T/St-140
89B-311
89Cadaco-32
89Classic-70
89Classic/Up/2-165
89D-257
89D/AS-47
89D/Best-110
89F-164
89F/BBAS-26
89Kahn/Reds-11
89OPC-363
89Panini/St-74
89RedFoley/St-73
89S-31
89S/HotStar-52

89S/Mast-24
89Sf-136
89T-515
89T/Big-199
89T/LJN-31
89T/Mini-11
89T/St-137
89T/St/Backs-44
89UD-270
90B-50
90Classic-48
90D-71
90D/BestNL-52
90D/Learning-51
90F-423
90F/BB-23
90F/LgStand-1
90F/LL-22
90Kahn/Reds-12
90Leaf/I-18
90Leaf/Prev-5
90MLBPA/Pins-21
90OPC-10
90Panini/St-253
90PublInt/St-266
90PublInt/St-33
90RedFoley/St-57
90S-155
90S-689DT
90Sf-160
90T-10
90T/Big-189
90T/Coins-51
90T/DH-40
90T/Gloss60-5
90T/St-136
90T/TVAS-36
90UD-167
90UD-99TC
90USPlayC/AS-6D
91B-379SLUG
91B-673
91BBBest/HitM-13
91Classic/200-142
91Classic/II-T33
91CollAB-31
91D-471
91D-5DK
91D/SuperDK-5DK
91F-68
91F-711M
91F/ASIns-2
91F/Ultra-96
91JDeanSig-10
91Kahn/Reds-11
91Leaf/I-168
91Leaf/Prev-3
91Leaf/Stud-167
91OPC-400AS
91OPC-730
91Panini/FrSt-130
91Panini/St-129
91Panini/Top15-28
91Pep/Reds-11
91Post-18
91RedFoley/St-58
91S-505
91S-666AS
91S-795WS
91S-888DT
91S/100SS-20
91S/Cooper-B2
91Seven/3DCoin-10F
91Sunflower-16
91T-400AS
91T-730
91T/CJMini/II-11
91T/StClub/I-92
91UD-353
91UD/SilSlug-SS18
91USPlayC/AS-6C
91Woolwth/HL-30
92D/I-185
92F-411
92F-704M
92F/ASIns-16
92S/100SS-77
92S/I-100
92S/II-775AS
92T-389AS
92T-465
92UD-144

Larkin, Gene
85Visalia-14
86Orlan-10
87D/Rook-23
87F/Up-U59
87Portl-19
87Sf/Rook-34
87T/Tr-60T
88D-564
88D/Best-158
88F-14
88OPC-384
88Panini/St-145
88RedFoley/St-47
88S-276
88Sf-107
88Smok/Minn-5
88T-746
88T/Big-264
88T/St-279
89B-160
89D-355
89F-117
89Panini/St-388
89S-280
89S/YS/II-6
89T-318
89T/Big-226
89T/St-294
89UD-580
90Classic/III-53
90D-436
90F-379
90Leaf/I-215
90OPC-556
90PublInt/St-331
90S-276
90T-556
90T/Big-302
90T/St-291
90UD-471
91D-152
91F-615
91F/Ultra-190
91Leaf/I-157
91OPC-102
91Panini/FrSt-306
91Panini/St-246
91S-471
91T-102
91T/StClub/I-132
91UD-501
92D/II-496
92F-207
92S/I-272
92T-284
92UD-187

Larkin, Henry
(Ted)
N172
N690

Larkin, Pat
84Evansvl-5

Larkin, Steve
34G-92

LaRoche, Dave
71OPC-174
71T-174
72OPC-352
72T-352
73OPC-426
73T-426
74OPC-502
74T-502
75OPC-258
75T-258
75T/M-258
76OPC-21
76SSPC-510
76T-21
77BurgChef-60
77OPC-61
77Pep-15
77T-385
78T-454
79OPC-317
79T-601
80T-263
81F-285
81T-529
81T/Tr-789
82D-569
82T-142
83F-384
83OPC-333
83OPC-334SV
83T-333
83T-334SV
85Albany-24
86Colum-13CO
87Syrac-19
87Syrac/TCMA-24
89Pac/SenLg-97
89T/SenLg-89
89TM/SenLg-65
90Coke/WSox-30CO
90Swell/Great-108
91Kodak/WSox-x

LaRocque, Gary
76BurlB
77Holyo
88Bakers/Cal-262CO

LaRosa, Bill
78Ashvl

Larosa, John
88Spartan/ProC-1031
88Spartan/Star-10
88Spartan/Star-10
89Pac/SenLg-43
89Spartan/ProC-1054
89Spartan/Star-12

LaRosa, Mark
88CapeCod/Sum-77
91James/ProC-3541

Larose, Steve
88Clmbia/GS-6
89StLucie/Star-13
91Jacks/LineD-566
91Jacks/ProC-924

LaRose, Vic
69T-404

Larregui, Ed
90Hunting/ProC-3300
91Geneva/ClBest-11
91Geneva/ProC-4231

Larsen, Bill
88Rockford-21
89Rockford-21AGM

Larsen, Dan
81OkCty/TCMA-7
86Kinston-14

Larsen, Don
54B-101
54Esskay
55B-67
56T-332
57T-175
58T-161
59T-205
59T-383M
60NuCard-18
60T-353
61NuCard-418
61T-177
61T-402HL
62T-33
63T-163
64T-513
65T-389
72Laugh/GF-45
76Laugh/Jub-17
78TCMA-211
78TCMA-266
79TCMA-272
88Pac/Leg-42
90BBWit-7
90HOF/St-54
91Crown/Orio-255
Exh47

Larsen, Jim
86Cram/PCL-36

Larson, Dan
77T-641
79OkCty
83Iowa-6
84Butte-14
84OKCty-6
86Wausau-12
87BurlEx-26
91Martins/ClBest-3
91Martins/ProC-3468

Larson, Duane
82Syrac-27

Larson, Jamie
85Anchora-36bb

Larson, Michael
(Mike)
88Boise/ProC-1620
89Boise/ProC-2003
90Erie/Star-12

LaRussa, Tony
64T-244
68T-571
72OPC-451
72T-451
78Knoxvl
78TCMA-229
81D-402MG
81F-344MG
82D-319MG
83D-571MG
83T-216MG
83TrueVal/WSox-10MG
84F/St-126MG
84Nes/792-591MG
84T-591MG
84TruVl/WS-20MG
85Coke/WS-10MG
85T-466MG
86Coke/WS-MG
86T-531MG
87T-68MG
88Mother/A's-1MG
88T-344
89Mother/A's-1MG
89Pac/Leg-140
89T-224MG
89T/LJN-36
90KMart/SS-33MG
90Mother/A's-1MG
90OPC-639MG
90Pac/Legend-90
90T-639MG
90T/Gloss22-12MG
90T/TVAS-33MG M
91Leaf/Stud-263MG
91Mother/A's-1MG
91OPC-171MG
91T-171MG
92T-429MG

Lary, Frank
55B-154
56T-191
57T-168
58T-245
59T-393
60L-3
60T-85
60T/tatt-28
61P-38
61T-243
61T-48LL
61T-50LL
61T/St-153
62J-22
62P-22
62P/Can-22
62Salada-58
62Shirriff-58
62T-474AS
62T-57LL
62T/bucks
62T/St-48
63F-14
63J-55
63P-55
63T-140
63T-218M
64Det/Lids-8
64T-197
65OPC-127
65T-127
78TCMA-253
79TCMA-183
81Detroit-125
91WIZMets-225

Lary, Lynford H.
(Lyn)
28Exh/PCL-18
31Exh/4-26
33G-193
35G-1C
35G-2C
35G-6C
35G-7C
90Target-434
91Conlon/Sport-318
R314

Lasek, Jim
77Spartan

Laseke, Eric
85Elmira-10
86WinHaven-14
87WinHaven-7
89WinHaven/Star-12

Laseter, Tom
76Watlo

Lasher, Fred
68T-447R
69T-373
70OPC-356
70T-356
71MLB/St-347
71OPC-707
71T-707
72MB-194
88Domino-10

Lashley, Mickey
77Clinton
78LodiD

Laskey, Bill
81Omaha-10
83D-424
83F-264
83Mother/Giants-15
83OPC-218
83T-171TL
83T-518
83T/St-325
84D-358
84F-376
84Nes/792-129
84OPC-129
84T-129
84T/St-172
85D-387
85F-612
85Mother/Giants-9
85OPC-331
85T-331
86D-585
86F-251
86Mother/Giants-24
86OPC-281
86T-603
87Toledo-21
87Toledo/TCMA-4
88Gator-17
90Richm/Bob-3
90Richm/CMC-24
90Richm/ProC-254
90Richm/Team-18

Lasky, Larry
85Osceola/Team-27TR
86Ashvl-17TR
87ColAst/ProC-21TR
88ColAst/Best-15TR
89Tucson/ProC-182TR

Lasorda, Tom
52Park-58
53Exh/Can-50
54T-132
55Gol/Dodg-18
73OPC-569CO
73T-569CO
74OPC-144CO
74T-144CO
77T-504MG
78T-189MG
79T-526MG
81D-420MG
81F-116MG
81Pol/Dodg-2MG
81T-679MG
82D-110MG
82F/St-111M
82Pol/Dodg-2MG
83D-136
83Pol/Dodg-2MG
83T-306MG
84F/St-124MG
84Nes/792-681MG
84Pol/Dodg-2
84T-681MG
85Coke/Dodg-18MG
85SpokAT/Cram-12
85T-601MG
86Coke/Dodg-16MG
86Pol/Dodg-2
86T-291MG
87Mother/Dodg-1MG
87Pol/Dodg-1MG
87Smok/Dodg-17MG
87T-493MG
88Mother/Dodg-1MG
88Pol/Dodg-2MG
88Pol/Dodg-MG

88Smok/Dodg-23MG
88T-74MG
89Mother/Dodg-1MG
89Pol/Dodg-2MG
89Rini/Dodg-13MG
89T-254MG
89T/LJN-50
89T/WaxBox-H
90Mother/Dodg-1MG
90OPC-669MG
90Pol/Dodg-1MG
90Pol/Dodg-x
90T-669MG
90T/Gloss22-1MG
90T/WaxBox-G
90Target-435
91Leaf/Stud-262MG
91Mother/Dodg-1MG
91OPC-789MG
91Pol/Dodg-x
91T-789MG
92T-261MG
92T/GPromo-261MG
92T/Promo-261MG
V362-45

Lassard, Paul
87FtLaud-14

Lata, Tim
88CapeCod/Sum-129
89Hamil/Star-20
90Foil/Best-267
90Spring/Best-16
91StPete/ClBest-29
91StPete/ProC-2273

Latham, Bill
83Lynch-3
84Tidew-6
85Tidew-10
87Portl-18
87Tidew-22
87Tidew/TCMA-28
91WIZMets-226

Latham, Chris
91Kissim/ProC-4194

Latham, John
89Welland/Pucko-17
90Salem/Star-9
91Augusta/ClBest-9
91Augusta/ProC-801

Latham, W. Arlie
12Sweet/Pin-115
N172
N172/BC
N284
N300/unif
N338/2
N370
Scrapps
T202
T205
T206
T207
T215/brown

Lathers, Charles
M116

Latimer, Tacks
90Target-1010

Latman, Barry
59T-477
60T-41
61T-560
61T/St-137
62Kahn
62Sugar-1
62T-145
62T-37M
62T/St-36
63Sugar-1
63T-426
64T-227
65T-307
66T-451
67OPC-28
67T-28

Latmore, Bob
86Miami-14
87Miami-10
88Hagers/Star-10
89Hagers/Best-4
89Hagers/ProC-271
89Hagers/Star-12
90EastLAS/ProC-EL34
90Hagers/Best-7
90Hagers/ProC-1422
90Hagers/Star-12

Latta, Greg
85BuffB-3
86BuffB-15TR
87Hawaii-25
89Vanco/ProC-574

Latter, Dave
89Medford/Best-12
90Madison/Best-18
90Madison/ProC-2264
91Huntsvl/ClBest-14
91Huntsvl/LineD-288
91HuntsvlProC-1791

Lattimore, William
T206

Lau, Charley
58T-448
60T-312
61T-261
62T-533
63T-41
64T-229
65OPC-94
65T-94
66T-368
67T-329
73OPC-593CO
73T-593CO
74T-166CO
91Crown/Orio-256

Lau, David
88Clmbia/GS-13
89StLucie/Star-14

Lauck, Jeff
84Savan-2

Laudner, Tim
80OrlTw-12
82D-549
82OrlTw/A-8
82T-766R
83D-177
83F-618
83T-529
83T/St-314
83T/St-93
84F-569
84Nes/792-363
84T-363
85D-652
85F-283
85Seven/Minn-12
85T-71
86D-391
86F-398
86T-184
87D-320
87F-546
87OPC-392
87T-478
88D-631
88F-15
88Master/Disc-5
88OPC-78
88Panini/St-135
88S-153
88Smok/Minn-7
88T-671
88T/Big-243
88T/St-278
89B-154
89D-615
89D/AS-19
89F-118
89OPC-239
89Panini/St-384
89S-134
89Sf-152
89T-239
89T/St-290
89UD-62
90D-419
90F-380
90OPC-777
90PublInt/St-332
90S-318
90T-777
90T/Big-218
90UD-419

Lauer, John Charles
N172

Laureano, Francisco
(Frank)
86BurlEx-13
87AppFx-7
88Virgini/Star-13
89BBCity/Star-15
90Memphis/Best-7
90Memphis/ProC-1018
90Memphis/Star-13
91Omaha/LineD-338
91Omaha/ProC-1043

Lauzerique, George
69T-358R
70McDon-6
70OPC-41
70T-41
75Dubuq
76Dubuq

Lav, David
87Columbia-5

Lavagetto, Harry
(Cookie)
35BU-51
39PB-74
40PB-69
41DP-17
47TipTop
48Signal
49Remar
50Remar
52T-365CO
59T-74M
60T-221MG
61Peters-10
61T-226MG
89Rini/Dodg-10
89Rini/Dodg-35
89Smok/Dodg-40
90HOF/St-43
90Target-436
R313
R314

LaValliere, Mike
83Reading-12
85Louisvl-22
86D/Rook-35
86F/Up-U65
86Schnucks-14
87D-331
87F-302
87F/Up-U60
87T-162
87T/Tr-61T
87ToysRUs-19
88D-312
88D/Best-129
88F-333
88F/Slug-25
88Leaf-112
88OPC-57
88Panini/St-369
88S-421
88Sf-193
88T-539
88T/Big-61
88T/St-131
89B-417
89D-244
89D/Best-201
89F-213
89OPC-218
89Panini/St-168
89RedFoley/St-74
89S-33
89Sf-98
89T-218
89T/Big-306
89T/LJN-12MG M
89T/St-128
89T/St/Backs-56
89UD-417
89VFJuice-12
90B-172
90Classic-42
90D-211
90D/BestNL-107
90D/Learning-43
90F-473
90Homer/Pirate-18
90Leaf/I-32
90OPC-478
90Panini/St-333
90PublInt/St-158
90S-116
90Sf-157
90T-478
90T/Big-104
90T/St-133
90T/TVAS-57
90UD-578
91B-514
91D-121
91F-42
91F/Ultra-282
91Leaf/I-15
91Leaf/Stud-226
91OPC-665
91Panini/FrSt-114
91S-222
91T-665
91T/StClub/I-279
91UD-129
92D/I-121
92F-558
92F/ASIns-5
92S/I-38
92T-312
92UD-113

Lavan, John
(Doc)
21Exh-94
BF2-42
D327
D328-95
D329-99
D350/2-97
E120
E121/120
E121/80
E122
E135-95
M101/4-99
M101/5-97
V100
V61-102
W501-108
W514-4
W575

Lavelle, Gary
75OPC-624R
75T-624R
75T/M-624R
76OPC-105
76SSPC-96
76T-105
77T-423
78Ho-32
78T-671
79Pol/Giants-46
79T-311
80Pol/Giants-46
80T-84
81D-314
81F-448
81OPC-62
81T-588
82D-60
82F-392
82OPC-209
82T-209
83D-60
83F-265
83Mother/Giants-14
83OPC-376
83T-791
84D-573
84D/AAS-1
84F-377
84Mother/Giants-10
84Nes/792-145
84OPC-145
84T-145
84T/St-164
85D-265
85F-613
85F/Up-U69
85Leaf-114
85OPC-2
85OPC/Post-24
85T-462
85T/St-159
85T/Tr-72T
85Tor/Fire-18
86Ault-46
86D-621
86F-65
86OPC-22
86T-622
86Tor/Fire-22
87Tor/Fire-17

Lavenda, John
91AS/Cal-27ADM

Lavender, James
(Jimmy)
14CJ-105
15CJ-105
92Conlon/Sport-344
BF2-65
D328-96
D329-100
D350/2-98
E135-96
M101/4-100
M101/5-98
T206
WG4-13

Lavender, Robert
88Gaston/ProC-996
89CharlR/Star-11

Laviano, Frank
90Tampa/DIMD-13
91Oneonta/ProC-4151

Lavigne, Martin
91Kissim/ProC-4179

LaVigne, Randy
82Iowa-6
83MidldC-24

Lavrusky, Chuck
87Idaho-7
88Boise/ProC-1621

Law, Joe
83Idaho-14
85Huntsvl/BK-40
87Modesto-19
89Tacoma/CMC-6
89Tacoma/ProC-1550
90Tacoma/CMC-10
90Tacoma/ProC-88

Law, Rudy
77LodiD
78Cr/PCL-56
79Albuq-19
79T-719R
81Albuq/TCMA-20
81D-180
81F-139
81Pol/Dodg-3
81T-127
82D-582
83D-521
83F-244
83T-514
83TrueVal/WSox-11
84D-257
84F-67
84F/St-93
84Nes/792-47
84OPC-47
84T-47
84T/St-245
84TrueVal/WS-21
85Coke/WS-23
85D-244
85F-519
85Leaf-117
85OPC-286
85T-286
85T/St-241
86D-632
86F-211
86F/Up-U66
86OPC-6
86T-637
86T/St-291
86T/Tr-62T
87D-343
87F-372
87T-382
90Target-437

Law, Travis
88Butte-23
89CharlR/Star-12

Law, Vance
79Portl-5
80Port-9
81Portl-14
81T-551R
82D-582
82F-484
82T-291
83D-117
83F-245
83OPC-98

83T-98
83TrueVal/WSox-5
84D-546
84F-68
84Nes/792-667
84T-667
84T/St-249
84TrueVal/WS-22
85D-122
85F-520
85F/Up-U70
85Leaf-183
85OPC-81
85T-137FS
85T-413
85T/St-242
85T/Tr-73T
86D-132
86F-252
86Leaf-57
86OPC-99
86Provigo-23
86T-787
86T/St-81
87D-212
87D/OD-94
87F-323
87OPC-127
87T-127
88Berg/Cubs-2
88D-212
88D/Best-60
88D/Cubs/Bk-NEW
88F-187
88F/Up-U79
88OPC-346
88Panini/St-324
88S-85
88S/Tr-16T
88Sf-41
88T-346
88T/Tr-60T
89B-293
89D-276
89D/AS-49
89F-430
89F/BBAS-27
89Mara/Cubs-2
89OPC-338
89Panini/St-57
89S-102
89Sf-162
89T-501
89T/Big-143
89T/St-46
89T/St/Backs-42
89UD-473
90D-629
90F-36
90OPC-287
90Publint/St-197
90S-73
90T-287
90UD-380
91B-222
91Leaf/II-355
91Mother/A's-12
91UD/Ext-760

Law, Vern
51B-203
52B-71
52T-81
54B-187
54T-235
55B-199
56T-252
57T-199
58Hires/T
58Kahn
58T-132
59Kahn
59T-12
59T-428M
60Kahn
60T-453
60T/tatt-29
61Kahn
61NuCard-406
61P-126
61T-250M
61T-400
61T-47LL
61T/St-66
62J-179
62P-179
62P/Can-179
62T-295
63F-58
63T-184
64T-472
65T-515
66Bz-18
66EH-32
66OPC-15
66T-15
66T-221LL
66T/RO-48
67T-351
67T/Test/PP-11
78TCMA-239
79TCMA-42
85T-137FS
90Pac/Legend-37
91Swell/Great-55
91T/Arc53-324

Lawless, Thomas
80Water-18
81Water-14
82Indianap-15
83D-400
83Indianap-12
83T-423
86Schnucks-15
86T-228
87Smok/Cards-19
87T-647
88Smok/Card-15
88T-183
88T/St-22
88Woolwth-25WS4
89B-255
89T-312
89Tor/Fire-18
90D-681
90OPC-49
90Publint/St-519
90T-49
90Tor/BlueJ-18

Lawless
N172

Lawrence, Andy
85Lynch-22
86Jacks/TCMA-16
87Jaxvl-7
88Jaxvl/Best-19
88Jaxvl/ProC-972

Lawrence, Bill
43Centen-17

Lawrence, Brooks
55B-75
55Hunter
55RM-NL4
56Kahn
56T-305
57Kahn
57Sohio/Reds-13
57T-66
58Kahn
58T-374
59T-67
60Kahn
60L-36
60T-434
79TCMA-217

Lawrence, Scott
86Erie-17
87Savan-25
88StPete/Star-12
89Spring/Best-13
90Tidew/CMC-30TR

Lawrenson, Scott
87Lynch-27

Lawson, Alfred V.
(Roxie)
38Wheat
92Conlon/Sport-513

Lawson, Cale
91Burllnd/ProC-3304

Lawson, James
(Jim)
88SoOreg/ProC-1712
89Madis/Star-12
90Madison/Best-19
90Modesto/Cal-152
90Modesto/ProC-2209

Lawson, Rex
V355-104

Lawson, Steve
73OPC-612R
73T-612R

Lawton, Marcus
86Lynch-14
87TexLgAS-24
88Tidew/ProC-1591
89Tidew/CMC-23
89Tidew/ProC-1967
90OPC-302
90T-302
90T/89Debut-69
90Vanco/CMC-16
90Vanco/ProC-500
91London/LineD-440
91MidldA/ProC-446

Laxamana, Brian
90AS/Cal-34UMP
91AS/Cal-50

Laxton, William
75Tidew/Team-15
76SSPC-615
77T-394

Laya, Jesus
87Pocatel/Bon-28
88Pocatel/ProC-2096
89Everett/Star-19

Layana, Tim
87Albany-11
88Albany/ProC-1333
89Albany/Best-5
89Albany/ProC-329
89Albany/Star-9
90AlbanyDG/Best-11
90B-41
90Classic/III-46
90D/Rook-23
90F/Up-U14
90Kahn/Reds-14
90Leaf/II-410
90S/Tr-107T
90T/Tr-55T
90UD/Ext-717
91B-689
91D-516
91F-69
91OPC-627
91S-64
91S/100RisSt-54
91T-627
91T/90Debut-82
91T/StClub/II-396
91UD-396
92S/II-628

Layne, Hillis
47Centen-15
47Signal
88Chatt/Team-21

Layne, Jerry
90TM/Umpire-58

Layton, Tom
83Kinston/Team-11
87Iowa-8

Lazar, John Dan
69T-439R
70T-669R
72MB-195

Lazor, Joe
87Cedar-5
88Chatt/Best-4
88SLAS-35
89Chatt/Best-5
89Chatt/GS-15

Lazor, John Paul
49B/PCL-30

Lazorko, Jack
80Tulsa-6
81Tulsa-19
83ElPaso-23
84Cram/PCL-48
85Cram/PCL-176
85T-317
86D-628
86Nashvl-15
87Edmon-2
87F/Up-U61
87T/Tr-62T
88D-160
88Edmon/CMC-3
88Edmon/ProC-556
88F-494
88S-437
88T-601
89Edmon/CMC-1
89F-482
89T-362
90TulsaDG/Best-13
91Pac/SenLg-113

Lazzeri, Anthony
(Tony)
26Exh-100
27Exh-50
28Yueng-29
29Exh/4-25
31Exh/4-25
32Orbit/num-107
33CJ/Pin-15
33Exh/4-13
33G-31
34DS-74
35BU-45
35Exh/4-13
35G-2D
35G-4D
35G-7D
36Exh/4-13
37Exh/4-13
37OPC-117
40PB-238
60Exh/HOF-14
60F-31
61F-54
69Bz-3
80Laugh/FFeat-26
88Conlon/3-17
88Conlon/AmAS-19
90Target-438
91Conlon/Sport-113
PR1-20
R311/Leath
R315-A21
R315-B21
R328-18
V300
V353-31
W502-29
W513-79
W517-27

Lea, Charles
79Memphis
80Memphis-2
81F-165
81OPC-293
81T-293
82D-320
82F-193
82Hygrade
82OPC-38
82T-38
83D-414
83F-286
83OPC-253
83Stuart-23
83T-629
84D-376
84F-278
84Nes/792-421
84Nes/792-516TL
84OPC-142
84OPC-332TL
84Stuart-8
84T-421
84T-516TL
84T/St-98
85D-177
85D-21DK
85D/DKsuper-21
85F-401
85Leaf-21DK
85OPC-345
85OPC/Post-10
85T-345
85T/Gloss22-10
85T/Gloss40-30
85T/St-182
85T/St-84
86D-376
86F-253
86Leaf-172
86OPC-376
86T-526
87WPalmB-17
88F/Up-U44
89D-473
89F-119
89S-501
89UD-81

Leach, Chris
89WinHaven/Star-13
90LynchRS/Team-2
91LynchRS/ClBest-21
91LynchRS/ProC-1211

Leach, Don
80Elmira-19

Leach, Fred
28Exh-21
33G-179
R315-A22
R315-B22
R316

Leach, Jalal
(Jay)
90A&AASingle/ProC-183
90Oneonta/ProC-3420
91FtLaud/ClBest-27
91FtLaud/ProC-2441
91Single/ClBest-270

Leach, Martin
82Tulsa-3
85Water-13

Leach, Rick
80Evansvl-24
82D-583
82F-272
82T-266
83D-81
83F-334
83T-147
84F-84
84F/X-U71
84Nes/792-427
84Syrac-6
84T-427
84T/Tr-71T
84Tor/Fire-22
85F-112
85IntLgAS-29
85OPC-52
85Syrac-11
85T-593
86T/Tr-63T
86Tor/Fire-23
87D-567
87F-234
87F/Up-U63
87OPC-5
87T-716
87Tor/Fire-18
88D-518
88F-115
88Leaf-247
88OPC-323
88S-258
88T-323
88Tor/Fire-9
89B-234
89D-638
89F-237
89Mother/R-16
89OPC-284
89S-540
89Smok/R-19
89T-682
89T/Tr-68T
89UD-554
90D-613
90F-305
90Leaf/II-436
90Mother/Giant-14
90OPC-27
90Publint/St-416
90S-426
90T-27
90T/Tr-56T
90UD-640

Leach, Terry
76Baton
79Savan-19
81Tidew-29
82T-623R
82Tidew-14
83D-634
83T-187
83Tidew-5
84Richm-19
84Tidew-26
85Tidew-2
86F-87
86T-774
86Tidew-15

87F/Up-U62
87T/Tr-63T
88D-603
88D/Mets/Bk-603
88F-139
88Kahn/Mets-26
88OPC-391
88S-203
88Sf-139
88T-457
89D-502
89F-40
89S-431
89S/Tr-24
89T-207
89T/Big-96
89T/Tr-69T
89UD-288
90D-534
90F-111
90Leaf/II-360
90OPC-508
90S-502
90S/Tr-43T
90T-508
90T/Tr-57T
90UD-642
91B-340
91D-715
91F-616
91S-556
91T/StClub/II-397
91WIZMets-227
92D/II-484
92F-208
92S/I-296
92T-644
92UD-311

Leach, Thomas
10Domino-67
11Helmar-161
12Sweet/Pin-138
12Sweet/Pin-138
14CJ-41
15CJ-41
91Macon/ClBest-3
91Macon/ProC-857
D322
E103
E107
E254
E286
E90
E90/2
E91
E93
E94
E95
M116
S74-111
T201
T202
T205
T206
T207
T213/blue
T215
T222
T3-3
W555
WG3-25

Leader, Ramon
77Cocoa
78DaytB

Leake, Jon
87SLCity/Taco-24

Leaks, Charles
54JC
55JC

Leal, Carlos
80Utica-27

Leal, Luis
81OPC-238R
81T-577R
82D-255
82F-617
82OPC-368
82OPC/Post-9
82T-412
83D-129
83F-432
83OPC-109
83T-109
84D-485
84F-160
84Nes/792-783
84OPC-207
84T-783
84T/St-371
84Tor/Fire-23
85D-317
85F-113
85Leaf-29
85OPC-31
85T-622
85T/St-361
85Tor/Fire-19
86D-315
86OPC-365
86Syrac-16
86T-459
88Syrac/ProC-806

Leard, Bill
90Target-1011

Leary, Rob
87WPalmB-1
88Rockford-22
89Rockford-22
89WPalmB/Star-15
90LSUGreat-8
90Rockford/ProC-2697CO

Leary, Timothy
82T-623R
83Tidew-9
84Jacks/Smok-7
85Cram/PCL-203
86D-577
86Pol/Brew-39
86T/Tr-64T
87D-232
87F-348
87Mother/Dodg-21
87Pol/Dodg-11
87T-32
87T/Tr-64T
88AlaskaAS70/Team-20
88F-521
88Mother/Dodg-21
88Pol/Dodg-54
88S-224
88T-367
89B-339
89D-552
89D/Best-309
89F-65
89F/Excit-30
89Mother/Dodg-21
89OPC-249
89Panini/St-99
89Pol/Dodg-28
89S-429
89S/HotStar-9
89S/Tr-52
89Sf-81
89T-249
89T/Big-17
89T/St-62
89UD-94
90B-429
90D-670
90D/BestAL-53
90F-424
90Leaf/I-148
90OPC-516
90PublInt/St-12
90S-504
90S/NWest-13
90S/Tr-27T
90T-516
90T/Tr-58T
90T/TVYank-12
90Target-439
90UD-662
90UD/Ext-705
91D-67
91F-670
91F/Ultra-236
91Leaf/I-206
91Leaf/Stud-95
91OPC-161
91S-631
91T-161
91T/StClub/II-423
91UD-693
91WIZMets-228
92D/II-433
92F-235
92S/I-286
92T-778

Leatherman, Jeff
91Welland/ClBest-17
91Welland/ProC-3580

Leatherwood, Del
78DaytB
81Tucson-2

Leavell, Gregg
91Welland/ClBest-12
91Welland/ProC-3586

Lebak, David
91Spokane/ClBest-7
91Spokane/ProC-3960

LeBlanc, Michael
88CapeCod/Sum-61
89Belling/Legoe-7

LeBlanc, Richie Jr.
88BBCity/Star-16
88FSLAS/Star-42
90Memphis/Best-16
90Memphis/ProC-1024
90Memphis/Star-14

Lebo, Mike
78Dunedin

LeBoeuf, Alan
85Cram/PCL-32
86Portl-13
87Maine-22
87Maine/TCMA-13
88Reading/ProC-864
90Clearw/Star-27CO
91Reading/LineD-525CO
91Reading/ProC-1386CO

Lebron, David
78Newar

LeBron, Jose
89Watlo/ProC-1775
89Watlo/Star-17
90Foil/Best-37
90Waterlo/Best-27
90Waterlo/ProC-2375
91HighD/ClBest-6
91HighD/ProC-2389

Leclair, Keith
88Idaho/ProC-1850

LeClair, Morgan
90WichSt-22

LeClaire, George
(Frenchy)
C46-3

Ledbetter, Gary
77Cedar

Ledbetter, Jeff
86ArkTr-11

Ledduke, Dan
79WHave-9

Ledee, Ricardo
90Tampa/DIMD-14

Ledesma, Aaron
90Kgsport/Best-1
90Kgsport/Star-13

Ledezma, Carlos
81Buffa-8
82Portl-26
84Cram/PCL-143
86Hawaii-15TR
87Vanco-4
88AAA/ProC-48
88BuffB/ProC-1481
89BuffB/CMC-3
89BuffB/ProC-1678
90BuffB/Team-13

Ledinsky, Ray
91Miami/ClBest-22
91Miami/ProC-416

Leduc, Jean
78Charl

Ledwik, Shannon
91Idaho/ProC-4324

Lee, Ben
87AppFx-13

Lee, Bob
85Visalia-15
86Kenosha-12
87Visalia-6
88Kenosha/ProC-1403
89Kenosha/ProC-1058

Lee, Chris
88Ashvl/ProC-1059

Lee, Derek
88Utica/Pucko-7
89SoBend/GS-27
90BirmB/Best-10
90BirmB/ProC-1118
90Foil/Best-144
91BirmB/LineD-66
91BirmB/ProC-1466
91Single/ClBest-272

Lee, Don
57T-379
59T-132
60T-503
61Clover-12
61Peters-9
61T-153
62T-166
63F-18
63T-372
64T-493
65T-595

Lee, Dudley
21Exh-95
28Exh/PCL-19

Lee, Eddie
79Elmira-11

Lee, Greg
88Pocatel/ProC-2086
89Salinas/Cal-141
89Salinas/ProC-1806

Lee, Hal
90Target-441
R310

Lee, Harvey
86FtLaud-14
87SanJose-5

Lee, John
76Dubuq

Lee, Leron
70OPC-96R
70T-96R
71MLB/St-276
71OPC-521
71T-521
72OPC-238
72T-238
73OPC-83
73T-83
74OPC-651
74T-651
75OPC-506
75T-506
75T/M-506
76OPC-487
76T-487
90Target-442

Lee, Manny
85F/Up-U71
85Tor/Fire-20
86Knoxvl-14
86OPC-23
86Syrac-17
86T-23
87D-518
87OPC-289
87Syrac-14
87Syrac/TCMA-16
87T-574
88D-650
88F-116
88OPC-303
88S-561
88T-722
88Tor/Fire-4
89D-504
89F-238
89OPC-371
89Panini/St-468
89S-326
89T-371
89T/Big-70
89Tor/Fire-4
89UD-271
90B-512
90D-620
90F-86
90Leaf/II-370
90OPC-113
90PublInt/St-520
90S-482
90T-113
90T/Big-219
90Tor/BlueJ-4
90UD-285
91B-21
91D-211
91F-179
91F/Ultra-365
91Leaf/II-399
91OPC-297
91Panini/FrSt-337
91S-534
91S/ToroBJ-16
91T-297
91T/StClub/I-168
91Tor/Fire-4
91UD-142
92D/II-499
92F-333
92S/II-518
92T-634
92UD-118

Lee, Mark
86Lakeland-8
87GlenF-15
87Lakeland-17
88Lakeland/Star-17
89Memphis/Best-4
89Memphis/ProC-1190
89Memphis/Star-14
91Brewer/MillB-14
91F/Up-U30
91Leaf/II-343
91OPC-721
91Pol/Brew-11
91S-372RP
91T-721
92D/I-313
92F-180
92S/I-277
92T-384
92UD-507

Lee, Mark L.
78Padre/FamFun-18
79T-138
80Hawaii-17
80T-557
81Portl-15
82Evansvl-4

Lee, Michael
60T-521

Lee, Robert D.
64T-502R
65OPC-46
65T-46
66T-481
67T-313
68Kahn
68T-543
90Target-440

Lee, Ronnie
53Exh/Can-51
V362-25

Lee, Terry
75Cedar
80Holyo-21
81Vanco-14

Lee, Terry James
83Cedar-19
83Cedar/LF-13
89Chatt/Best-10
89Chatt/GS-16
91AAAGame/ProC-AAA23
91B-683
91D-752
91F-70
91Nashvl/LineD-266
91Nashvl/ProC-2165
91T/90Debut-83
91UD-37
92T-262

Lee, Thomas
91Eugene/ClBest-23
91Eugene/ProC-3723

Lee, Thornton
35BU-109
47TipTop
89Pac/Leg-158
R313

Lee, Wiley
88MidwLAS/GS-24
88QuadC/GS-4
89AS/Cal-11
89PalmSp/Cal-39
89PalmSp/ProC-485

Lee, William C.
35BU-140
37Exh/4-3
39Exh

39Wheat-4
41DP-103
47TipTop
PM10/Sm-94
V355-109
WG8-40

Lee, William F.
70OPC-279
70T-279
71MLB/St-322
71OPC-58
71T-58
72T-636
73OPC-224
73T-224
74OPC-118
74T-118
74T/St-135
75Ho-66
75OPC-128
75T-128
75T/M-128
76K-29
76OPC-396
76SSPC-421
76T-396
77BurgChef-32
77T-503
78PapaG/Disc-9
78T-295
79OPC-237
79T-455
80OPC-53
80T-97
81D-211
81F-157
81OPC-371
81T-633
82D-194
82F-194
82OPC-323
82T-323
88AlaskaAS60/Team-6
89Chatt/II/Team-15GM
89Pac/SenLg-28
89T/SenLg-33
89TM/SenLg-66
90EliteSenLg-99
90Smok/SoCal-8
91Conlon/Sport-128
91Pac/SenLg-146

Lee, Wyatt
(Watty)
C46-71
E107
E270/2
T205

Leech, Skip
77Charl

Leek, Eugene
61T-527
62Salada-82A
62Salada-82B
62Shirriff-82

Leeper, Dave
83Omaha-22
84Omaha-22
85Omaha-24
86D-461
86Hawaii-16
87Vanco-14

Leever, Sam
10Domino-68
12Sweet/Pin-139
D322
E104
E107
E90/1
E90/2
E91
M116
T205

Lefebvre, Jim
65T-561R
66OPC-57
66T-57
67T-260
68Bz-2
68T-457
69MB-156
69MLB/St-149
69OPC-140
69T-140
69T/St-46
69Trans-47
70MLB/St-52
70T-553
71MLB/St-106
71OPC-459
71T-459
71Ticket/Dodg-8
72MB-196
72OPC-369
72T-369
72T/Cloth-20
78TCMA-263
80Pol/Giants-5
85Cram/PCL-187
86Phoenix-15MG
87Smok/Dodg-18
89Mother/Sea-1
89Smok/Dodg-71
89T/Tr-70TMG
90Mother/Mar-1MG
90OPC-459MG
90T-459MG
90Target-443
91CounHrth-1MG
91OPC-699MG
91T-699MG

Lefebvre, Joe
77FtLaud
79WHave-25
80Colum-26
81D-571
81F-103
81OPC-88
81T-88R
81T/Tr-790
82D-373
82F-575
82T-434
83D-523
83F-363
83T-644
83T/Tr-61T
84D-82
84F-37
84Nes/792-148
84Phill/TastyK-37
84T-148
85D-285
85F-257
85Phill/TastyK-12M
85Phill/TastyK-37M
85T-531
86Phill/TastyK-23
87Reading-3
88Maine/CMC-25
88Maine/ProC-301
89ScrWB/CMC-18CO
89ScrWB/ProC-722CO
90Albany/Best-25CO
90Albany/ProC-1181CO
90Albany/Star-25CO

Lefebvre, Tip
84Cram/PCL-14

Lefferts, Craig
82Iowa-20
83Thorn-32
84D-388
84F-496
84F/X-U72
84Mother/Padres-19
84Nes/792-99
84T-99
84T/Tr-72T
85D-261
85F-38
85Mother/Padres-15
85OPC-76
85T-608
86D-307
86F-328
86OPC-244
86T-244
87Bohem-37
87D-387
87F-422
87F/RecSet-19
87F/Up-U64
87OPC-287
87T-501
88D-515
88D/Best-330
88F-87
88Mother/Giants-24
88S-553
88T-734
89B-464
89D-59
89F-332
89Mother/Giants-24
89S-178
89T-372
89UD-541
90B-206
90Classic-109
90Coke/Padre-9
90D-376
90D/BestNL-23
90F-60
90F/Up-U57
90Leaf/II-339
90OPC-158
90Padre/MagUno-11
90Panini/St-362
90PublInt/St-74
90S-209
90S/Tr-22T
90Sf-130
90T-158
90T/St-80
90T/Tr-59T
90UD-399
90UD/Ext-792
91B-650
91D-515
91F-534
91F/Ultra-307
91Leaf/II-390
91OPC-448
91Padre/MagRal-21
91Panini/Top15-84
91RedFoley/St-59
91S-184
91T-448
91T/StClub/II-533
91UD-228
92D/I-162
92F-611
92S/I-175
92T-41
92UD-589

LeFlore, Ron
75OPC-628
75T-628
75T/M-628
76Greyhound-3
76Ho-69
76K-17
76OPC-61
76SSPC-363
76T-61
77BurgChef-98
77Ho-50
77K-25
77OPC-167
77Pep-28
77T-240
78BK/T-19
78Ho-95
78OPC-88
78T-480
78Wiffle/Discs-37
79Ho-34
79OPC-348
79T-4LL
79T-660
79T/Comics-8
80BK/PHR-27
80OPC-45
80T-80
81Coke
81D-576
81F-154
81F/St-2
81MSA/Disc-20
81OPC-104
81Sqt-26
81T-204M
81T-4LL
81T-710
81T/HT
81T/St-23
81T/Tr-791
82D-165
82F-350
82F/St-182
82OPC-140
82T-140
82T/St-172
83D-543
83F-246
83OPC-297
83T-560
89Pac/SenLg-4
89T/SenLg-111
89TM/SenLg-67
90EliteSenLg-39
91Pac/SenLg-63

Leftwich, Phil
90A&AASingle/ProC-158
90Boise/ProC-3306
91MidwLAS/ProC-MWL27
91QuadC/ClBest-7
91QuadC/ProC-2624
91Single/ClBest-247

Legendre, Rob
91Yakima/ClBest-25
91Yakima/ProC-4245

Leger, Frank
83LynnP-24

Legg, Greg
83Reading-14
85Cram/PCL-48
87Maine-4
87Maine/TCMA-14
87Phill/TastyK-11
88Reading/ProC-882
89ScrWB/CMC-19
89ScrWB/ProC-708
90ScranWB/ProC-609
91ScranWB/LineD-486
91ScranWB/ProC-2546

Leggatt, Rich
82Buffa-1
83Durham-20
84Durham-18
86Toledo-13

Legumina, Gary
83SanJose-15
85VeroB-9

Lehew, Jim
91Crown/Orio-257

Lehman, Bill
76AppFx

Lehman, Ken
55B-310
57T-366
58Hires-52
58T-141
59T-31
79TCMA-258
90Target-444
91Crown/Orio-258

Lehman, Mike
89Freder/Star-12
90Freder/Team-16
91Hagers/LineD-235
91Hagers/ProC-2459

Lehner, Paul
47TipTop
49B-131
50B-158
51B-8

Lehnerz, Daniel
88Idaho/ProC-1857

Lehnerz, Mike
89Kingspt/Star-15
91Pittsfld/ClBest-20
91Pittsfld/ProC-3417

Leiber, Hank
38Exh/4-5

Leibert, Allen
90Canton/Star-10
90Foil/Best-188

Leibold, Harry
(Nemo)
88Pac/8Men-101
D327
D328-97
D329-101
D350/2-99
E120
E121/80
E135-97
E220
M101/4-101
M101/5-99
T222
V100
W575

Leibrandt, Charles
79Indianap-7
81D-421
81F-208
81Indianap-5
81OPC-126
81T-126
82Coke/Reds
82F-74
82T-169
83D-421
83F-596
83Indianap-4
83T-607
84Omaha-1
85D-399
85D/HL-4
85D/HL-46
85F-206
85Indianap-33
85T-459
86D-297
86F-13
86F/LL-21
86F/Slug-20
86F/St-69
86Kitty/Disc-10
86Leaf-171
86NatPhoto-37
86OPC-77
86Sf-159
86Sf-186M
86T-77
86T/Mini-19
86T/St-262
86T/Super-37
87D-220
87F-373
87OPC-223
87T-223
87T/St-258
88D-157
88D/Best-151
88F-263
88F/St-31
88Leaf-76
88OPC-218
88Panini/St-100
88S-61
88Sf-21
88Smok/Royals-13
88T-569
88T/St-260
89B-116
89Classic-82
89D-89
89D/Best-231
89F-286
89OPC-301
89Panini/St-351
89S-133
89T-301
89Tastee/Discs-10
89UD-637
90B-8
90D-208
90F-112
90Leaf/II-428
90MLBPA/Pins-103
90OPC-776
90PublInt/St-351
90S-82
90T-776
90T/Tr-60T
90UD-658
91B-573
91D-562
91F-695
91Leaf/I-209
91OPC-456
91Panini/FrSt-27
91Panini/St-23
91S-536
91T-456
91T/StClub/II-527
91UD-460
92D/I-84
92F-361
92S/I-105
92T-152
92UD-170

Leiby, Brent
90Princet/DIMD-30TR
91Spartan/ClBest-30TR

Leifield, Albert

(Lefty)
10Domino-69
11Helmar-162
12Sweet/Pin-140
D322
M116
S74-112
T201
T202
T205
T206
T207
T215/blue
T215/brown

Leighton, John
N172

Leimeister, Eric
90Niagara/Pucko-20
91Lakeland/ClBest-7
91Lakeland/ProC-263

Lein, Chris
82Nashvl-16
83AlexD-14
85PrWill-13
87Salem-28
89Harris/ProC-301
90Salem/Star-26CO
91Bluefld/ProC-4142CO
91Bluefld/ClBest-25CO

Leinen, Michael
90Wausau/Star-13

Leinen, Pat
88CapeCod/Sum-102
89Erie/Star-11
90Foil/Best-96
90Wausau/Best-3
90Wausau/ProC-2116
91Freder/ProC-2359
91Hagers/ProC-2452

Leinhard, Steve
90Shrev/Star-14

Leiper, Dave
82Idaho-11
83Madis/LF-27
86Tacoma-12
87D-472
87F-398
87T-441
88D-557
88F/Up-U123
88S-348
88Smok/Padres-15
89D-465
89F-310
89S-515
89T-82
89UD-363
90OPC-773
90Publint/St-53
90S-212
90T-773
91Edmon/LineD-166
91Edmon/ProC-1514

Leiper, Tim
86FSLAS-29
86Lakeland-9
87GlenF-9
88GlenF/ProC-938
88Toledo/CMC-21
88Toledo/ProC-603
89London/ProC-1373
90EastLAS/ProC-EL5
90London/ProC-1281
91Tidew/LineD-561
91Tidew/ProC-2523

Leister, John
86Pawtu-12
87Pawtu-5
87Pawtu/TCMA-26
88Pawtu/CMC-4
88Pawtu/ProC-470
89Pawtu/CMC-5
89Pawtu/Dunkin-22
89Pawtu/ProC-681
90Pawtu/CMC-6
90Pawtu/ProC-459
90T/TVRSox-49

Leiter, Al
87Colum-30
87Colum/Pol-15
88Classic/Blue-238
88D-43RR
88D/Best-132
88D/Rook-27
88D/Y/Bk-43
88F/Up-U49
88Leaf-43RR
88S/Tr-97T
88T-18
89B-170
89Classic-112
89D-315
89F-257
89F/Up-70
89Panini/St-396
89S-580
89S/HotRook-80
89S/YS/I-17
89T-659
89T/Big-125
89T/JumboR-15
89T/Tr-71T
89ToysRUs-19
89UD-588
89UD/Ext-705
90D-543
90OPC-138
90Publint/St-521
90T-138
90Tor/BlueJ-28
91D-697
91OPC-233
91S/ToroBJ-4
91T-233
91Tor/Fire-28
92F-334

Leiter, Kurt
83SanJose-24
84CharlO-23
86Miami-15

Leiter, Mark
89Colum/CMC-29
89FtLaud/Star-13
90ColClip/CMC-4
90ColClip/ProC-673
90T/TVYank-51
91B-138
91CokeK/Tiger-23
91D/Rook-29
91S-727RP
91T/90Debut-84
91Toledo/LineD-588
92Classic/I-52
92D/II-633
92F-140
92S/II-626
92T-537
92UD-319

Leitner, Ted
90Padre/MagUno-16ANN

Leius, Scott
87Kenosha-21
88Visalia/Cal-154
88Visalia/ProC-102
89BBAmerAA/BProC-AA18
89Orlan/Best-16
89Orlan/ProC-1332
89SLAS-6
90B-423
90F-647R
90Portl/CMC-16
90Portl/ProC-185
91B-337
91D/Rook-4
91F/UltraUp-U38
91F/Up-U38
91Leaf/GRook-BC1
91S-370RP
91T/90Debut-85
91T/StClub/II-338
91T/Tr-71T
91UD-35
92D/I-359
92F-209
92F/RookSlns-14
92S/I-320
92T-74
92UD-313

Leiva, Jose
86Reading-14
87Reading-22
88Reading/ProC-884
89Canton/Best-22
89Canton/ProC-1312
89Canton/Star-24

Leix, Tom
81Wisco-2

Leja, Frank
54NYJour
54T-175
55T-99
60L-121

LeJohn, Don
(Ducky)
66OPC-41
66T-41
75Water
77Clinton
78Clinton
86Bakers-19MG
90Target-445

LeJeune, Larry
90Target-1105

Lekang, Anton
33SK-10

Leland, Stan
78DaytB
81Tucson-15

Lelivelt, William
E254
E270/1
T222

Lemanczyk, Dave
75OPC-571
75T-571
75T/M-571
76OPC-409
76SSPC-355
76T-409
77OPC-229
77T-611
78OPC-85
78T-33
79OPC-102
79T-207
80OPC-68
80T-124
81D-292
81T-391

LeMaster, Denny
63T-74
64T-152
65Kahn
65T-441
66Kahn
66T-252
67T-288
68Coke
68Dexter-47
68T-491
69MB-157
69OPC-96
69T-96
69T/St-34
70MLB/St-42
70OPC-178
70T-178
71MLB/St-84
71OPC-636
71T-636
72MB-197
72OPC-371
72T-371
78TCMA-17

LeMaster, Johnnie
75Phoenix-12
76OPC-596R
76Phoenix
76T-596R
77T-151
78T-538
79Pol/Giants-10
79T-284
80OPC-224
80Pol/Giants-10
80T-434
81D-432
81F-450
81OPC-84
81T-84
82D-524
82F-393
82T-304
82T/St-108
83D-125
83F-266
83Mother/Giants-4
83OPC-154
83T-154
83T/St-304
84D-649
84F-378
84Nes/792-663
84OPC-107
84T-663
84T/St-168
85D-114
85F-614
85Mother/Giants-14
85OPC-302
85T-772
85T/St-164
85T/Tr-74T
86OPC-289
86T-289
90Swell/Great-68

LeMasters, Jim
87Sumter-20
88MidwLAS/GS-20
89Greenvl/ProC-1176
89Greenvl/Star-13
89Greenvl/Best-10
89Star/Wax-36
90Omaha/CMC-5
90Omaha/ProC-63
91Omaha/LineD-339
91Omaha/ProC-1032

Lemay, Bob
91Niagara/ClBest-27
91Niagara/ProC-3629

Lemay, Richard
62T-71
63T-459
66Pep/Tul

Lembo, Steve
53Exh/Can-36
90Target-446
V362-7

Lemke, Mark
86Sumter-16
87Durham-26
88BBAmer-16
88Greenvl/Best-10
88SLAS-15
89AAA/CMC-18
89AAA/ProC-55
89Classic-52
89D-523
89Richm/Bob-13
89Richm/CMC-19
89Richm/Ko-16
89Richm/ProC-830
89T-327
89UD-19
90B-11
90D-624
90D/Rook-43
90F-587
90OPC-451
90S-593
90S/DTRook-B5
90S/YS/II-22
90T-451
90T/Big-120
90UD-665
91D-604
91F-696
91OPC-251
91S-779
91S/100RisSt-89
91T-251
91T/StClub/I-203
91UD-419
92D/II-606
92F-362
92S/I-386
92T-689
92UD-47

Lemle, Rob
88Clmbia/GS-21
89Clmbia/Best-4
89Clmbia/GS-14

Lemon, Chet
75Tucson-3
76OPC-590R
76T-590R
77BurgChef-73
77OPC-195
77T-58
78Ho-124
78OPC-224
78T-127
79Ho-40
79OPC-169
79T-333
79T/Comics-5
80K-46
80OPC-309
80T-589
80T/S-57
81Coke
81D-281
81F-354
81K-19
81OPC-242
81Sqt-33
81T-242
81T/HT
81T/SO-34
81T/St-57
82D-291
82F-351
82F/St-191
82K-54
82OPC-13
82T-216TL
82T-493
82T/St-168
82T/Tr-62T
83D-511
83F-335
83OPC-53
83T-727
84D-171
84F-85
85FunFoodPin-97
84Nes/792-611
84OPC-86
84T-611
84T/St-271
85Cain's-12
85D-90
85F-15
85Leaf-77
85OPC-20
85Seven-11D
85Seven-9G
85T-20
85T/Gloss22-18
85T/St-190
85T/St-21WS
85T/St-260
85Wendy-14
86Cain's-11
86D-90
86F-230
86Leaf-85
86OPC-160
86T-160
86T/St-274
87Cain's-10
87Coke/Tigers-10
87D-353
87D/OD-213
87F-156
87Leaf-227
87OPC-206
87Seven-DT6
87T-739
87T/St-268
88D-215
88D/Best-147
88F-61
88Leaf-166
88OPC-366
88Panini/St-96
88Pep/T-34
88Pol/T-7
88S-119
88T-366
88T/Big-147
89D-209
89D/Best-69
89F-137
89Mara/Tigers-34
89OPC-328
89Panini/St-344
89Pol/Tigers-34
89S-44
89Sf-171
89T-514
89T/Big-202
89T/St-283
89UD-128
90B-354
90CokeK/Tiger-10
90D-60

90D/BestAL-76
90F-608
90Leaf/I-133
90MLBPA/Pins-87
90OPC-271
90Panini/St-77
90PublInt/St-475
90S-106
90T-271
90T/Big-86
90T/St-278
90UD-348
91D-301
91F-341
91OPC-469
91Panini/FrSt-292
91S-557
91T-469
91T/StClub/I-23
91UD-389

Lemon, Don
89Idaho/ProC-2033

Lemon, Jim
54T-103
55B-262
57T-57
58T-15
59HRDerby-11
59T-215
59T-74M
60T-440
61Bz-12
61Clover-13
61P-93
61Peters-17
61T-44LL
61T-450
61T/St-182
62J-89
62P-89
62P/Can-89
62Salada-9A
62Salada-9B
62Shirriff-9
62T-510
63T-369
68T-341MG
69T-294MG
79TCMA-180
90Elizab/Star-25
91Elizab/ProC-4316CO
PM10/Sm-97

Lemon, Leo
81Redwd-19

Lemon, Robert
49B-238
50B-40
50NumNum
51B-53
51BR-A2
51FB
51T/CAS
52B-23
52BR
52Dix
52NumNum-4
52StarCal/L-74C
52T-268
52Wheat
53B/BW-27
53Dix
53Exh/Can-31
53NB
53RM-AL17
54B-196
54DanDee
54RH
54RM-AL21
55B-191
55Gol/Ind-15
55RM-AL8
55Salem
56Carling-5
56T-255
57Sohio/Ind-7
57T-120
58T-2
60T-460C
71OPC-91MG
71T-91MG
72OPC-449MG
72T-449MG
77T-418MG
78BK/Y-1
78T-574MG
79T-626MG
79TCMA-19
80Pac/Leg-120
80SSPC/HOF
82D-635MG
83D/HOF-30
85West/2-45
86Sf/Dec-39M
88Pac/Leg-32
89HOF/St-68
91T/Arc53-284
Exh47
PM10/Sm-95
PM10/Sm-96
R302-119
R423-59

Lemonds, Dave
71OPC-458R
71T-458R
72OPC-413R
72T-413R
73OPC-534
73T-534

Lemongello, Mark
77T-478R
78BK/Ast-9
78T-358
79T-187
80Wichita-22

Lemons, Tim
86BurlEx-14
87Spring/Best-7

Lemp, Chris
91Bluefld/ProC-4124
91Bluefld/ClBest-21

Lemperle, John
86Alban/TCM-19bb

Lemuth, Steve
89Medford/Best-19

Lenderman, Dave
86Pittsfld-13

Lenhardt, Don
51T/BB-33
52T-4
53B/Col-20
54B-53
54Esskay
54T-157
73OPC-131CO
73T-131C
91Crown/Orio-259

Lennon, Patrick
86Cram/PCL-128
87Wausau-7
88Vermont/ProC-947
89Wmsprt/ProC-632
89Wmsprt/Star-12
90Foil/Best-153
90SanBern/Best-9
90SanBern/Cal-101
90SanBern/ProC-2645
91B-250
91Calgary/LineD-63
91Calgary/ProC-528
91UD/FinalEd-43F
92D/I-17RR
92T/91Debut-107
92UD-13SR

Lennon, Robert
55T-119
56T-104
57T-371

Lennox, James E.
(Ed)
11Helmar-97
90Target-447
M116
T202
T205
T206
T207
T213/blue
T213/brown
T3-104

Lenti, Mike
81Clinton-23

Lentine, James
81Charl-17
81D-250
81F-476

Lentz, Harry
(Sentz, sic)
T206
T213/brown

Leon, Danilo
87Jamestn-23
88James/ProC-1913
88WPalmB/Star-15
89Jaxvl/Best-21
89Jaxvl/ProC-169

Leon, Eduardo
70OPC-292
70T-292
71MLB/St-378
71OPC-252
71T-252
72T-721
73OPC-287
73T-287
74OPC-501
74T-501
75OPC-528
75T-528
75T/M-528

Leon, Johnny
90Tampa/DIMD-15

Leon, Jose
89Elizab/Star-14

Leon, Maximino
75OPC-442
75T-442
75T/M-442
76OPC-576
76SSPC-3
76T-576
77T-213

Leon, Mike
87AppFx-22TR
88AppFx/ProC-163TR
89Memphis/Best-27TR
89Memphis/ProC-1191TR
90Memphis/Best-27TR
90Memphis/Star-27TR

Leon, Ron
85Spring-15
87Erie-5

Leonard, Andy
86BurlEx-15

Leonard, Bernardo
78Holyo

Leonard, Dennis
75OPC-615R
75T-615R
75T/M-615R
76A&P/KC
76OPC-334
76SSPC-164
76T-334
77BurgChef-70
77Ho-72
77OPC-91
77T-75
78Ho-88
78OPC-41
78OPC-5LL
78T-205LL
78T-665
79Ho-109
79OPC-109
79T-218
80OPC-293
80T-565
81Coke
81D-102
81F-42
81OPC-185
81Pol/Royals-5
81T-185
81T/St-87
82D-264
82F-413
82F/St-208
82OPC-369
82Sqt-10
82T-495
82T/St-191
83D-412
83F-116
83OPC-87
83Pol/Royals-3
83T-785
84F-349
84Nes/792-375
84OPC-375
84T-375
86F/Up-U67
86NatPhoto-22
86T/Tr-65T
87F-374
87OPC-38
87RedFoley/St-33
87T-38
89Pac/SenLg-84
89T/SenLg-125
89TM/SenLg-68
90EliteSenLg-72
90Pac/Legend-91

Leonard, Emil
(Dutch)
39PB-21
40PB-23
41PB-24
48B-24
48L-113
49B-115
49Eureka-61
50B-170
51B-102
52B-159
52StarCal/L-80B
52T-110
52TipTop
53B/BW-50
53T-155
55B-247
90Target-448
91T/Arc53-155

Leonard, Hubert
(Dutch)
16FleischBrd-56
61F-121
72F/FFeat-17
72Laugh/GF-34
79T-418M
85Woolwth-22
91Conlon/Sport-142
91Conlon/Sport-276
92Conlon/Sport-346
BF2-5
D327
D328-98
D329-102
D350/2-100
E135-98
E220
M101/4-102
M101/5-100

Leonard, Jeffery
80T-106
81D-264
81F-67
81T-469
82D-438
82T-47
83D-474
83Mother/Giants-8
83T-309
84D-567
84F-379
84Nes/792-576TL
84Nes/792-748
84T-576TL
84T-748
84T/St-166
85D-358
85F-615
85F/LimEd-18
85GenMills-4
85Leaf-92
85Mother/Giants-4
85OPC-132
85Seven-14W
85T-619
85T-718AS
85T/St-161
85ThomMc/Discs-35
86D-79
86F-548
86Leaf-74
86Mother/Giants-4
86OPC-381
86T-490
86T/St-84
87Classic-64
87D-391
87D/OD-103
87F-278
87F/GameWin-25
87F/Slug-23
87Mother/SFG-8
87OPC-280
87RedFoley/St-102
87T-280
87T/St-90
88Classic/Red-175
88D-327
88D/AS-54
88F-88
88F/Mini-117
88F/RecSet-23
88F/SS-21
88F/St-128
88F/Up-U39
88Leaf-118
88Mother/Giants-8
88OPC-152
88Panini/St-427
88Panini/St-446
88RedFoley/St-48
88S-580
88Sf-82
88T-570
88T/Coins-46
88T/RiteAid-32
88T/St-16
88T/St-86
88T/St/Backs-17
88T/Tr-61T
88T/UK-43
88Woolwth-17
89T/Ames-19
89B-218
89D-457
89D/Best-107
89D/Tr-1
89F-190
89F/Up-60
89Mother/Sea-8
89OPC-160
89S-557
89S/Tr-7
89T-160
89T/St-199
89T/Tr-72T
89UD-263
89UD/Ext-789
90B-472
90Classic-93
90D-93
90D/BestAL-125
90D/GSlam-2
90F-519
90Leaf/I-219
90Mother/Mar-4
90OPC-455
90Panini/St-150
90PublInt/St-436
90RedFoley/St-58
90S-98
90S/100St-91
90Sf-20
90T-455
90T/Big-303
90T/St-223
90Target-449
90UD-331
91F-456
91OPC-55
91S-44
91T-55
91UD-107

Leonard, Kathy
81Redwd-24

Leonard, Mark
86Cram/PCL-182
87Clinton-14
88CalLgAS-3
88SanJose/Cal-122
88SanJose/ProC-134
89Phoenix/CMC-5
89Phoenix/ProC-1498
90AAAGame/ProC-AAA52
90Phoenix/CMC-19
90Phoenix/ProC-24
91B-624
91D-526
91F-265
91F/Ultra-322
91Leaf/II-369
91Mother/Giant-13
91PG&E-22
91S-719RP
91S/Rook40-18

91T/90Debut-86
91UD-557
92D/II-761
92S/100RisSt-62
92S/II-499

Leonard, Mathew
88Geneva/ProC-1645
88Wythe/ProC-1996
89CharWh/Best-9
89CharWh/ProC-1758

Leonard, Tom
81Redwd-23

Leonard, Walter
(Buck)
74Laugh/Black-11
86Negro/Frit-1
88Conlon/NegAS-7
88Negro/Duques-16
90Negro/Star-26
91Negro/Lewis-22

Leonard, Wilfred
48Sommer-20

Leonardo, Juan
75AppFx

Leonette, Mark
83Idaho-8
85Madis-22
85Madis/Pol-19
87Pittsfld-16
88Pittsfld/ProC-1371

Leonhard, Dave
68OPC-56R
68T-56R
69MB-158
69T-228
70T-674
71MLB/St-302
71OPC-716
71T-716
72MB-198
72T-527
91Crown/Orio-260

Leopold, Jim
83Beaum-6
84Beaum-14
85Cram/PCL-119
86Nashua-15
88Louisvl-27
88Louisvl/CMC-10
88Louisvl/ProC-437

Lepcio, Ted
52T-335
53T-18
54B-162
54T-66
55T-128
55T/DH-126
57T-288
58T-29
59T-348
60T-97
61T-234
91T/Arc53-18

Lepel, Joel
91Kenosha/ClBest-19MG
91Kenosha/ProC-2091MG

Lepley, John
88Hamil/ProC-1737
89ArkTr/GS-10
91ArkTr/LineD-37
91ArkTr/ProC-1280

Leppert, Don
62T-36
63T-243
64T-463
64Wheat/St-26
73OPC-517CO
73T-517C
74OPC-489CO
74T-489CO
77T-113CO
78TCMA-101
78TCMA-110
86Kenosha-13MG
87Kenosha-27MG
88Kenosha/ProC-1399
89Kenosha/ProC-1070
91Crown/Orio-261

Lepson, Mark
79BurlB-11
80BurlB-4
81BurlB-9

Lerch, Randy
76OkCty/Team-16
76OPC-595R
76T-595R
77T-489R
78T-271
79BK/P-8
79T-52
80BK/P-18
80OPC-181
80T-344
81D-574
81F-25
81T-584
81T/Tr-792
82D-595
82F-147
82Pol/Brew-35
82T-466
83F-287
83OPC-22
83Stuart-28
83T-686
84F-380
85D-309
85F-616
85T-103
86Phill/TastyK-35
86Portl-14
89Pac/SenLg-23
89T/SenLg-23
90EliteSenLg-10

Lersch, Barry
69OPC-206R
69T-206R
71MLB/St-183
71OPC-739
71T-739
72OPC-453
72T-453
73OPC-559
73T-559
74OPC-313
74T-313
74T/Tr-313T
75OkCty

Leshnock, Don
75Shrev/TCMA-9

Leshnock, Donnie
91T/Tr-72T

Leskanic, Curtis
90Kinston/Team-5
91Kinston/ClBest-5
91Kinston/ProC-317
91Single/ClBest-297

Lesley, Brad
81Cedar-3
82Indianap-5
83D-547
83Indianap-26
85Cram/PCL-202
85T-597
90CedarDG/Best-21

Leslie, Reggie
91CharWh/ClBest-6
91CharWh/ProC-2883

Leslie, Roy Reid
E120

Leslie, Sam
34DS-68
34Exh/4-2
34G-49
35BU-46
35G-1G
35G-3E
35G-4E
35G-5E
37Exh/4-5
92Conlon/Sport-504
R314
V355-4

Lesslie, Bob
75Water

Lester, Jimmy
88Wichita-22
89CharRain/ProC-989CO
90CharRain/Best-27CO
90CharRain/ProC-2056CO
91Waterlo/ClBest-11
91Waterlo/ProC-1273CO

Letchas, Charlie
89Chatt/II/Team-16

Letendre, Mark
79Colum-11
80Colum-18
81Colum-25
91Mother/Giant-28TR

Letourneau, Jeff
91Erie/ClBest-18
91Erie/ProC-4064

Lett, Jim
80Cedar-22
82Water-23
83Water-19
84Cedar-12
86TexGold-CO
88Kahn/Reds-CO
90CharWh/Best-26MG
90CharWh/ProC-2257MG
91Nashvl/LineD-275CO
91Nashvl/ProC-2174CO

Letterio, Shane
88Greens/ProC-1556
89Miami/I/Star-11
89Miami/II/Star-11
90Wmsprt/Best-14
90Wmsprt/ProC-1064
90Wmsprt/Star-15
91Calgary/LineD-64
91Calgary/ProC-522

Levan, Jesse
88Chatt/Team-20

Levangie, Dana
91Elmira/ClBest-8
91Elmira/ProC-3273

LeVasseur, Tom
86Cram/PCL-169
88River/Cal-223
88River/ProC-1417
89AubAs/ProC-26
89Wichita/Rock-21SS
89Wichita/Rock/HL-13
90LasVegas/CMC-17
90LasVegas/ProC-129

Levenda, John
90AS/Cal-31ADM

Leverette, Gorham
(Dixie)
E120
W573

Levey, James
32Orbit/num-52
32Orbit/un-40
92Conlon/Sport-395
R305

Levi, Stan
80BurlB-27
83ElPaso-11

Levine, Al
91Utica/ClBest-21
91Utica/ProC-3238

Levinson, Davis
81Redwd-25

Levinson, Steve
81Redwd-30

Levis, Jesse
88CapeCod-13
88CapeCod/Sum-116
89BurlInd/Star-16
90CLAS/CL-39
90Kinston/Team-8
91Canton/LineD-88
91Canton/ProC-981

Lewallyn, Dennis
78Cr/PCL-110
79Albuq-7
80Albuq-8
82T-356
82Wheat/Ind
83VeroB-29
85VeroB-25
90Target-451
90VeroB/Star-30CO
91VeroB/ProC-793CO

Lewis, Alan
88Bakers/Cal-237
89VeroB/Star-15
90VeroB/Star-18

Lewis, Anthony
90Savan/ProC-2083
91Single/ClBest-137
91StPete/ClBest-27
91StPete/ProC-2290

Lewis, Brett
87Pocatel/Bon-3

Lewis, Craig
88Watertn/Pucko-8

Lewis, Curt
78OrlTw

Lewis, Dan
87AubAs-8
88Ashvl/ProC-1061
89Osceola/Star-11
90AS/Cal-40
91Shrev/LineD-310
91Shrev/ProC-1830

Lewis, Darren
89AS/Cal-33
89Modesto/Cal-278
89Modesto/Chong-30
90B-463
90Foil/Best-22
90Huntsvl/Best-1
91AAAGame/ProC-AAA33
91Classic/II-T54
91D/Rook-35
91F-15
91F/Ultra-323
91OPC-239
91OPC/Premier-73
91Phoenix/LineD-384
91Phoenix/ProC-80
91S-350RP
91S/Rook40-28
91T-239
91T/90Debut-87
91T/StClub/II-362
91UD-564
91UD/FinalEd-38F
92Classic/I-53
92D/II-615
92F-639
92F/RookSIns-10
92S/100RisSt-10
92S/II-562
92T-743
92UD-565

Lewis, George
(Duffy)
16FleischBrd-57
55JC
87Conlon/2-36
88Conlon/4-17
91Conlon/Sport-146
BF2-6
D327
D328-99
D329-103
D350/2-101
E121/80
E122
E135-99
E254
E270/2
M101/4-103
M101/5-101
T207
W575

Lewis, Harry
T3/Box-63

Lewis, Herman
80Utica-26

Lewis, Irving
T207

Lewis, James
89AubAs/ProC-14
91AubAS/ClBest-3
91AubAS/ProC-4269

Lewis, Jay
83Peoria/LF-18

Lewis, Jerry
78Newar

Lewis, Jim M.
79Spokane-13
80Colum-16
81Colum-6
82Colum-22
82Colum/Pol-21
83Toledo-6
84Cram/PCL-180
85Cram/PCL-77
86CharRain-13

Lewis, Jim S.
88River/Cal-212
88River/ProC-1423
89Wichita/Rock-20RHP
90LasVegas/CMC-6
90LasVegas/ProC-114
91Wichita/LineD-611
92F-612
92T/91Debut-108

Lewis, Jimmy
91Classic/DP-44
91FrRow/DP-28
92S/II-852

Lewis, Joe
89Gaston/ProC-1007
89Gaston/Star-10
90Gaston/Best-20
90Gaston/ProC-2523
90Gaston/Star-12

Lewis, John K.
(Buddy)
37OPC-101
37Wheat-7
38ONG/Pin-17
39PB-47
40PB-20
41PB-47
89Pac/Leg-119
Exh47
V300

Lewis, John
86Peoria-14
87WinSalem-16
88WinSalem/Star-8

Lewis, Johnny
62Kahn/Atl
62Pep/Tul
64T-479R
65OPC-277
65T-277
66T-282
66T/RO-24
67OPC-91
67T-91
74OPC-236CO
74T-236C
91WIZMets-229

Lewis, Ken
89Bristol/Star-14

Lewis, Mark
88BurlInd/ProC-1800
89B-87
89Kinston/Star-12
89T-222FDP
90A&AASingle/ProC-27
90B-338
90Canton/Best-1
90Canton/ProC-1299
90Canton/Star-9
90EastLAS/ProC-EL36
90Foil/Best-320
90Foil/Best-4
91B-70
91Classic/200-185
91Classic/I-37
91Classic/II-T11
91ColoSp/LineD-88
91ColoSp/ProC-2190
91D-29RR
91D/Rook-42
91F/Up-U19
91Leaf/II-289
91Leaf/Stud-48
91S/RookTr-106T
91T/StClub/II-492
91T/Tr-73T
91UD-17SR
92D/I-273
92F-116
92S/100RisSt-50
92S/II-528
92T-446
92T/91Debut-109
92UD-235

Lewis, Mica
88AubAs/ProC-1974
89Ashvl/ProC-966
89AubAs/ProC-2186
90Osceola/Star-15
91Visalia/ClBest-16
91Visalia/ProC-1748

Lewis, Phil
90Target-1012

Lewis, Richie
88Jaxvl/Best-10
88Jaxvl/ProC-992
90Jaxvl/Best-20
90WPalmB/Star-13
91Harris/ProC-623

Lewis, Rufus

91Negro/Lewis-30
Lewis, Scott
89MidldA/GS-21
89TexLAS/GS-5
90Edmon/CMC-10
90Edmon/ProC-516
91B-192
91S-759RP
91S/Rook40-9
91Smok/Angel-19
91T/90Debut-88
91UD-594
92S/I-165
Lewis, Steve
83AlexD-25
84PrWill-19
85PrWill-9
Lewis, T.R.
89Bluefld/Star-13
90Foil/Best-10
90Wausau/Best-1
90Wausau/ProC-2133
90Wausau/Star-14
91Freder/ClBest-18
91Freder/ProC-2372
91Single/ClBest-238
Lewis, Timothy
77WHave
79WHave-18
Lewis, Tony
87Spokane-3
88Charl/ProC-1214
89River/Best-9
89River/Cal-24
89River/ProC-1395
90Waterlo/Best-9
90Waterlo/ProC-2376
Lewis, Willie
T3/Box-74
Lexa, Michael
87Kenosha-10
88Kenosha/ProC-1395
Ley, Terry
72OPC-506R
72T-506R
Leyland, Jim
75Clinton
80Evansvl-17
81Evansvl-1
86T/Tr-66T
87T-93MG
88T-624MG
89T-284MG
89VFJuice-10MG
90Homer/Pirate-19MG
90OPC-699MG
90T-699MG
91OPC-381MG
91T-381MG
92T-141MG
Leyritz, Jim
87FtLaud-24
88Albany/ProC-1344
89Albany/Best-2
89Albany/ProC-325
89Albany/Star-10
90AlbanyDG/Best-6
90Classic/III-60
90ColClip/CMC-11
90ColClip/ProC-681
90F/Up-U112
90Leaf/II-465
90S/NWest-10
90S/Tr-83T
90T/Tr-61T
90T/TVYank-50
90UD/Ext-723
91B-171
91D-219
91F-671
91F/Ultra-237
91OPC-202
91Panini/FrSt-326
91S-65
91S/100RisSt-29
91T-202
91T/90Debut-89
91UD-243
92D/II-649
92UD-117
Leyva, Nick
77ArkTr
83ArkTr-23
89Phill/TastyK-18MG
89T-74MG
90OPC-489MG
90Phill/TastyK-20MG
90T-489MG
91OPC-141MG
91T-141MG
Lezcano, Carlos
81D-521
81F-307
81T-381R
82F-51
83Iowa-23
84Cram/PCL-79
91Penin/ProC-395CO
Lezcano, Sixto
74Sacra
76A&P/Milw
76OPC-353
76SSPC-241
76T-353
77BurgChef-89
77Ho-12
77K-27
77OPC-71
77T-185
78Ho-35
78OPC-102
78T-595
78Wiffle/Discs-38
79Ho-136
79OPC-364
79T-685
80OPC-114
80T-215
80T/S-31
81Coke
81D-207
81F-513
81OPC-25
81T-25
81T/SO-45
81T/St-218
81T/Tr-793
82D-64
82F-119
82OPC-271
82T-727
82T/St-95
82T/Tr-63T
83D-499
83F-364
83OPC-244
83T-455
83T/St-298
84F-38
84Nes/792-185
84OPC-185
84Phill/TastyK-38
84T-185
85D-529
85F-258
85F/Up-U72
85OPC-89
85T-556
85T/Tr-75T
86T-278
Libke, Al
44Centen-14
47Signal
Liborio, Dennis
90Mother/Ast-28EQMG
Liburdi, John
84Albany-10
85Albany-34
86Albany/TCMA-13
Lich, Rod
84Cedar-23
85Cedar-29
86Tampa-10TR
87Vermont-27
Lickert, John
83Pawtu-13
85Richm-11
Liddell, Dave
86Peoria-15
87Columbia-13
88Reno/Cal-287
89Jacks/GS-25
89Tidew/CMC-18
90T/TVMets-49
90Tidew/CMC-20
90Tidew/ProC-547
91T/90Debut-90
91WIZMets-230
Liddle, Don
53JC-9
53SpicSpan/3x5-15
54NYJour
54T-225
55B-146
55Gol/Giants-16
56T-325
Liddle, Steve
82Redwd-7
83Nashua-10
84Cram/PCL-105
85Cram/PCL-13
86Edmon-17
87Portl-10
88Portl/CMC-12
88Portl/ProC-655
89Kenosha/ProC-1084
89Kenosha/Star-25
90Kenosha/Best-27MG
90Kenosha/ProC-2310MG
90Kenosha/Star-25MG
91Visalia/ClBest-24MG
91Visalia/ProC-1757MG
Liebert, Allen
86Lakeland-10
87Fayette-15
88CLAS/Star-29
88Kinston/Star-15
89Canton/Best-21
89Canton/ProC-1314
89Canton/Star-12
90Canton/Best-6
90Canton/ProC-1294
90EastLAS/ProC-EL35
Lieberthal, Mike
90A&AASingle/ProC-193
90Classic/DP-3
90Classic/III-62
90Martins/ProC-3197
91B-506
91OPC-471
91SALAS/ProC-SAL44
91S-683FDP
91Single/ClBest-290
91Spartan/ClBest-14
91Spartan/ProC-899
91T-471
91UD-67TP
Liebhardt, Glenn
T206
Liebold, Harry
21Exh-96
21Exh-97
Lien, Al
48Sommer-7
49Sommer-5
52Mother-47
Lienhard, Steve
87Pocatel/Bon-5
88Clinton/ProC-694
89AS/Cal-47
89SanJose/Best-20
89SanJose/Cal-214
89SanJose/ProC-456
89SanJose/Star-17
90Shrev/ProC-1440
91ElPaso/LineD-185
91ElPaso/ProC-2745
Lieppman, Keith
76Tucson-6
79Ogden/TCMA-26
82Idaho-30
82WHave-27
84Albany-7
85Cram/PCL-126MG
86Tacoma-13MG
87Tacoma-14MG
Lifgren, Kelly
88Spokane/ProC-1925
89River/Best-10
89River/Cal-16
89River/ProC-1392
90Foil/Best-190
90Riversi/Best-15
90Riversi/Cal-22
90Riversi/ProC-2605
91HighD/ClBest-7
91HighD/ProC-2390
91Single/ClBest-120
Lightner, Ed
91BendB/ClBest-23
91BendB/ProC-3701
Lillard, Robert E.
37Wheat
46Sunbeam
47Remar-22
47Signal
47Smith-6
48Signal
48Smith-8
Lilliquist, Derek
88Richm-24
88Richm/CMC-2
88Richm/ProC-21
89B-264
89Classic/Up/2-172
89D-653
89D/Best-226
89D/Rook-54
89F/Up-73
89S-631
89S/HotRook-23
89T/Tr-73T
89UD/Ext-753
90B-7
90D-286
90F-588
90HotRook/St-27
90OPC-282
90Panini/St-223
90PublInt/St-116
90S-243
90S/100Ris-19
90S/YS/I-30
90Sf-24
90T-282
90T/89Debut-70
90T/Big-192
90T/JumboR-18
90ToysRUs-17
90UD-234
91D-570
91F-535
91LasVegas/ProC-231
91LasVegas/LineD-287
91OPC-683
91S-571
91T-683
91T/StClub/I-268
91UD-251
Lillis, Bob
59DF
59T-133
60T-3
61BB-11
61T-38
62Salada-108A
62Salada-108B
62Shirriff-108
62T-74
63J-191
63P-191
63Pep
63T-119
64T-321
74OPC-31CO
74T-31C
78TCMA-42
83T-66MG
84D-84MG
84Mother/Ast-15MG
84Nes/792-441MG
84T-441MG
85Mother/Ast-1MG
85T-186MG
86T-561MG
89Smok/Ast-17
90Mother/Giant-21M
90Target-452
91Mother/Giant-27CO
Lim, Ron
90LSUPol-12
Lima, Jose
90Bristol/ProC-3156
90Bristol/Star-14
Limbach, Chris
86Cram/PCL-147
88Clearw/Star-17
88FSLAS/Star-10
90SALAS/Star-15
90Spartan/Best-7
90Spartan/ProC-2488
90Spartan/Star-13
91Clearw/ClBest-6
91Clearw/ProC-1617
Limmer, Lou
52Park-86
54T-232
55B-80
55T-54
55T/DH-16
Limoncelli, Bill
79Elmira-23
80Elmira-34
87Elmira/Black-2
87Elmira/Red-2
88Elmira-27MG
Limoncelli, Jeff
90Elmira/Pucko-7
Linares, Antonio
88Martins/Star-22
89Spartan/ProC-1046
89Spartan/Star-13
89Star/Wax-55
90Spartan/Best-20
90Spartan/ProC-2503
90Spartan/Star-14
Linares, Mario
91AubAS/ClBest-15
91AubAS/ProC-4277
Linares, Rufino
79Savan
81Pol/Atl-25
82BK/Lids-15
82D-310
82F-439
82Pol/Atl-25
82T-244
83D-275
83F-140
83T-467
84Richm-2
85T-167
86Edmon-18
Linarez, Jose
87Pocatel/Bon-32
Lincoln, Lance
86Beloit-13
87Beloit-14
Lind, Carl
29Exh/4-21
Lind, Jack
83Redwd-30
87Nashvl-13MG
88Nashvl/CMC-23
88Nashvl/ProC-486
Lind, Jose
85PrWill-17
86Nashua-16
87Vanco-19
88Classic/Red-195
88D-38RR
88D/Best-145
88F-334
88Leaf-38RR
88Panini/St-371
88S-597
88S/YS/II-4
88T-767
88T/Big-106
88T/St-127
89B-421
89Bimbo/Discs-7
89Classic-20
89D-290
89D/Best-101
89F-214
89OPC-273
89Panini/St-170
89RedFoley/St-75
89S-87
89Sf-62
89T-273
89T/Big-25
89T/St-126
89UD-334
89VFJuice-13
90B-170
90D-172
90D/BestNL-82
90F-474
90Homer/Pirate-20
90Leaf/I-77
90OPC-168
90Panini/St-328
90PublInt/St-159
90PublInt/St-616

90S-83
90Sf-58
90T-168
90T/Big-196
90T/St-131
90UD-424
91B-530
91D-58
91F-43
91F/Ultra-283
91Leaf/I-146
91Leaf/Stud-227
91OPC-537
91Panini/FrSt-116
91Panini/St-117
91S-461
91S/100SS-33
91T-537
91T/StClub/I-233
91UD-258
92D/I-189
92F-559
92S/I-265
92T-43
92UD-205
Lind, Orlando
85PrWill-1
86Nashua-17
87Harris-14
88Harris/ProC-847
89Harris/ProC-300
89Harris/Star-9
90OrlanSR/Star-9
90Portl/ProC-175
91OrlanSR/LineD-484
91OrlanSR/ProC-1845
Lind, Randy
87Everett-11
Lindaman, Vivian
T206
Lindblad, Paul
66T-568R
67T-227
68OPC-127
68T-127
69T-449
70OPC-408
70T-408
71MLB/St-519
71OPC-658
71T-658
72OPC-396
72T-396
73OPC-406
73T-406
74OPC-369
74T-369
75OPC-278
75T-278
75T/M-278
76K-52
76OPC-9
76SSPC-479
76T-9
77BurgChef-117
77T-583
78T-314
79T-634
87ElPaso-20CO
88ElPaso/Best-10CO
89ElPaso/GS-2CO
91ElPaso/LineD-200CO
91ElPaso/ProC-2763CO
Lindell, John
44Yank/St-17
47HomogBond-30
47TipTop
48B-11
48L-82
48Swell-17
49B-197
50B-209
52Mother-1
53T-230
54B-159
54T-51
91T/Arc53-230
D305
Exh47
R346-5
Lindell, Rick
91Pac/SenLg-72
Lindeman, Ernest
E254
T204
Lindeman, Jim
86Louisvl-16
87Classic/Up-111
87D-37RR
87D/OD-59
87D/Rook-41
87F/Mini-64
87F/Up-U65
87Leaf-37RR
87Sf/Rook-43
87Smok/Cards-14
87T/Tr-65T
88D-540
88F-39
88Louisvl-28
88OPC-16
88S-302
88T-562
89Louisvl-26
89Smok/Cards-11
89T-791
90SpringDG/Best-29
90Toledo/CMC-15
90Toledo/ProC-156
91ScranWB/LineD-487
92D/II-701
92F-538
92S/I-321
92T-258
Lindemuth, John
90BBWit-87M
Linden, Mark
89Geneva/ProC-1878
Lindquist, Dan
83TriCit-11
84Visalia-25
Lindros, Eric
90S/Tr-100T
Lindsay, Chuck
80LynnS-5
Lindsay, Darian
90Kgsport/Best-2
90Kgsport/Star-14
91Pittsfld/ClBest-19
91Pittsfld/ProC-3418
Lindsay, Tim
91StCath/ClBest-21
91StCath/ProC-3390
Lindsey, Darrell
88Martins/Star-21
89Spartan/ProC-1040
89Spartan/Star-14
90Clearw/Star-11
91Reading/LineD-511
91Reading/ProC-1369
Lindsey, Don
89Eugene/Best-5
Lindsey, Douglas
(Doug)
82Danvl-12
88Spartan/ProC-1042
88Spartan/Star-11
88Spartan/Star-11
90Reading/Best-12
90Reading/ProC-1223
90Reading/Star-16
91Reading/LineD-512
91Reading/ProC-1372
91Single/ClBest-100
92T/91Debut-110
Lindsey, Elmer
(Bee)
62Pep/Tul
63Pep/Tul
Lindsey, Jim
90Target-453
Lindsey, Jon
82Reading-16
Lindsey, William D.
(Bill)
85Albany-12
86Albany/TCMA-22
87BirmB/Best-26
88F-403
88Vanco/CMC-16
88Vanco/ProC-758
Lindstrom, Fred
26Exh-36
27Exh-20
28Exh-19
29Exh/4-10
31Exh/4-9
33DL-11
33Exh/4-5
33G-133
35BU-122
36Exh/4-2
80Pac/Leg-100
80SSPC/HOF
88Conlon/NatAS-13
89Smok/Dodg-103
90Target-454
91Conlon/Sport-58
92Conlon/Sport-596
R306
R312/M
R314
R315-A23
R315-B23
R316
V354-17
V355-65
W517-24
Lines, Richard
61Union
67T-273
68T-291
Lingerman, Nemo
78Wisco
Link, Dave
83StPete-30
Link, Robert
86Water-14
87Wmsprt-7
88GlenF/ProC-937
89Toledo/CMC-6
89Toledo/ProC-778
Linke, Fred
M116
Linnert, Tom
75SanAn
76Wmsprt
Lino, Rivera Ortiz
87Gaston-9
Linskey, Mike
89Freder/Star-13
90A&AASingle/ProC-1
90Foil/Best-21
90Hagers/Best-20
90Hagers/ProC-1407
90HagersDG/Best-15
90RochR/ProC-718
91B-105
91RochR/LineD-468
91RochR/ProC-1897
92F-663
Lint, Royce
54Hunter
55B-62
Linton, Dave
85Utica-3
86DayBe-16
Linton, Doug
87Myrtle-5
88Knoxvl/Best-15
90Syrac/CMC-5
90Syrac/ProC-567
90Syrac/Team-14
91Syrac/LineD-507
91Syrac/ProC-2478
Lintz, Larry
74OPC-121
74T-121
75OPC-416
75T-416
75T/M-416
76OPC-109
76SSPC-286
76T-109
77T-323
Lintz, Ricky
81Watlo-11
82Watlo/B-6
82Watlo/C-5
Linz, Phil
62T-596R
63T-264
64T-344
65T-369
66T-522
67OPC-14
67T-14
68T-594
78TCMA-97
91WIZMets-231
Exh47
WG10-12
WG9-14
Linzy, Frank
65T-589R
66OPC-78
66T-78
67T-279
68Coke
68Dexter-48
68OPC-147
68T-147
69MLB/St-202
69T-345
70MLB/St-127
70OPC-77
70T-77
71MLB/St-277
71OPC-551
71T-551
72MB-199
72OPC-243
72T-243
73OPC-286
73T-286
Lipe, Perry H.
T206
Lipon, John
51B-285
52B-163
52T-89
53B/Col-123
53T-40
54T-19
61BeeHive-12
76Shrev
78Colum
79Portl-9
81Buffa-1
81Detroit-26
82AlexD-21
83AlexD-11
84PrWill-29
85Nashua-27
87Fayette-17
88FSLAS/Star-28
90FSLAS/Star-49
90Lakeland/Star-26MG
91Lakeland/ClBest-29MG
91Lakeland/ProC-282MG
91T/Arc53-40
Lipscomb, Bruce
89CharlR/Star-13
Lipski, Robert
63T-558R
Lipson, Marc
90A&AASingle/ProC-113
90Foil/Best-101
90Kenosha/Best-20
90Kenosha/ProC-2289
90Kenosha/Star-9
91Single/ClBest-229
91Visalia/ClBest-4
91Visalia/ProC-1738
Lipson, Stefan
83Butte-7
Lira, Felipe
90Bristol/ProC-3165
90Bristol/Star-15
Liranzo, Rafael
78RochR
Liriano, Felix
88Fayette/ProC-1093
Liriano, Julio
88Watlo/ProC-675
Liriano, Nelson
85Kingst-13
86Knoxvl-15
87Syrac-2
87Syrac/TCMA-17
88D-32RR
88F-117
88Leaf-32RR
88OPC-205
88S-621
88S/YS/I-13
88T-205
88T/Big-155
88Tor/Fire-2
89Classic/Up/2-196
89D-627
89D/Best-160
89F-239
89OPC-76
89S-577
89T-776
89T/Big-207
89Tor/Fire-2
89UD-109
90B-518
90D-267
90F-87
90OPC-543
90Panini/St-182
90PublInt/St-522
90S-77
90T-543
90T/Big-142
90T/St-197
90Tor/BlueJ-2
90UD-134
91D-603
91F-617
91OPC-18
91S-288
91T-18
91UD-360
Lis, Joe
70OPC-56R
70T-56R
71OPC-138R
71T-138R
74OPC-659
74T-659
75OkCty
75OPC-86
75T-86
75T/M-86
76SSPC-523
77Ho-125
77T-269
Lis, Joe Jr.
91StCath/ClBest-9
91StCath/ProC-3404
Liscio, Joe
59DF
Lisenbee, Horace
(Hod)
33G-68
92Conlon/Sport-540
V354-45
Lisi, Rick
79Tulsa-14
80Charl-9
82RochR-14
83RochR-21
84Richm-7
Lisiecki, David
91Belling/ClBest-22
91Belling/ProC-3658
Liska, Ad
R316
Liss, Tom
89Belling/Legoe-8
List, Paul
91Augusta/ClBest-21
91Augusta/ProC-820
Listach, Pat
89Stockton/Best-22
89Stockton/Cal-173
89Stockton/ProC-379
89Stockton/Star-4
90AS/Cal-36
90Stockton/Best-5
90Stockton/Cal-191
90Stockton/ProC-2190
91ElPaso/LineD-191
91ElPaso/ProC-2753
Littell, Mark
74OPC-596R
74T-596R
76OPC-593R
76SSPC-181
76T-593R
77T-141
78T-331
79T-466
80T-631
81D-580
81F-544
81T-255
82D-442
82F-120
82T-56
89Watlo/ProC-1784CO

89Watlo/Star-27CO
90CharRain/Best-25CO
90CharRain/ProC-2055CO
90Swell/Great-112
91HighD/ClBest-30CO
91HighD/ProC-2414CO
Littimer, Dave
91AS/Cal-54
Little, Bryan
83Stuart-24
83T/Tr-62T
84D-157
84F-279
84Nes/792-188
84OPC-188
84Stuart-30
84T-188
85BuffB-9
85F-402
85OPC-257
85T-257
86D-452
86F-212
86T-346
87Colum-14
87Colum/Pol-16
87Colum/TCMA-14
88BuffB/CMC-16
88BuffB/Polar-3
88BuffB/ProC-1491
89AubAs/ProC-27
89Wichita/Rock-4CO
90Waterlo/Best-19MG
90Waterlo/ProC-2393MG
91Waterlo/ClBest-25MG
91Waterlo/ProC-1272MG
Little, Doug
87DayBe-8
88BirmB/Best-26
89BirmB/Best-22
89BirmB/ProC-93
Little, Grady
84CharlO-10
85Kingst-24
89Durham/Team-28MG
89Durham/Star-26MG
90Durham/Team-29MG
90HagersDG/Best-16MG
91Durham/ClBest-15MG
91Durham/ProC-1676MG
Little, Jeff
75Lafay
78Cr/PCL-37
79Phoenix
82Toledo-4
83F-619
83T-499
83Toledo-7
Little, Martin
80Wausau-5
Little, Mike
89Wythe/Star-20
90Hunting/ProC-3301
91Peoria/ClBest-21
91Peoria/ProC-1358
Little, Randy
86Cram/PCL-119
Little, Richard
(Dick)
82Wichita-9
91Salinas/ClBest-25CO
91Salinas/ProC-2263CO
Little, Ronald
82Water-21
83Indianap-20
Little, Scott
84LitFalls-4
85Lynch-27
86Jacks/TCMA-21
88Harris/ProC-838
89BuffB/CMC-20
89BuffB/ProC-1681
90BuffB/CMC-25
90BuffB/ProC-388
90BuffB/Team-14
90T/89Debut-71
91BuffB/LineD-31
91BuffB/ProC-552
Little, Thomas
86Cram/PCL-109
Littlefield, John
77StPete
79ArkTr-6
81D-309
81F-535
81T-489
81T/Tr-794
82D-145
82F-576
82Syrac-5
82T-278
Littlefield, Richard
(Dick)
52B-209
54B-213
54Esskay
55B-200
57T-346
58T-241
79TCMA-14
91Crown/Orio-262
Littlejohn, Dennis
78Cr/PCL-61
79Phoenix
80Phoenix-16
80T-686R
81D-313
81F-455
81Phoenix-18
81T-561
Littleton, Larry
79Portl-19
80Tacoma-3
82Charl-20
Litton, Greg
84Everett/Cram-1
86Shrev-15
87Shrev-8
89F/Up-130
89S/Tr-86T
90D-453
90F-61
90HotRook/St-28
90Leaf/II-331
90Mother/Giant-18
90OPC-66
90Phoenix/ProC-20
90S-497
90S/100Ris-91
90S/YS/I-33
90T-66
90T/89Debut-72
90T/Big-308
90UD-677
91B-621
91D-198
91F-266
91F/Ultra-324
91Mother/Giant-18
91OPC-628
91PG&E-8
91S-533
91T-628
91T/StClub/I-45
92F-640
92S/II-603
92T-238
Littrell, Jack Jr.
78Clinton
79Wausau-15
Littrell, Jack Sr.
55Rodeo
Litwhiler, Dan
41DP-100
41DP-45
47TipTop
49B-97
49Eureka-88
50B-198
51B-179
Litzinger, Jeff
88CapeCod-8
88CapeCod/Sum-185
Livchak, Robert
87StPete-27
88StPete/Star-13
Lively, Everett
49Eureka-89
Lively, Henry
T207
Livengood, Wes
W711/1
Livernois, Derek
85Elmira-11
86Greens-13
87WinHaven-23
89Lynch/Star-12
90Foil/Best-307
90NewBrit/Best-24
90NewBrit/Star-8
90T/TVRSox-50
91B-123
91Pawtu/LineD-359
91Pawtu/ProC-34
Livesay, Jeff
87Anchora-19
88Oneonta/ProC-2052
89PrWill/Star-11
90FtLaud/Star-12
91Albany/ProC-1011
Livesey, Steve
91Oneonta/ProC-4162
Livin, Jeff
86Osceola-17
87ColAst/ProC-20
Livingston, Dennis
86Albuq-13
87Albuq/Pol-13
Livingston, Paddy
10Domino-70
11Helmar-25
12Sweet/Pin-47
E104
M116
T205
T206
T207
T208
Livingston, T.
(Mickey)
47TipTop
90Target-1013
Livingstone, Scott
89London/ProC-1381
90Toledo/CMC-16
90Toledo/ProC-157
91AAAGame/ProC-AAA46
91Classic/III-50
91Toledo/LineD-589
91Toledo/ProC-1940
91UD/FinalEd-53F
92Classic/I-54
92D/II-675
92F-141
92S/100RisSt-57
92S/I-414
92T-685
92T/91Debut-111
92UD-538
Livsey, Shawn
91Classic/DP-25
91FrRow/DP-38
92T-124
Llanes, Pedro
86Miami-16
87Savan-13
Llano, Jorge
82Miami-11
Llanos, Aurelio
88Martins/Star-23
89Martins/Star-17
90Princet/DIMD-13
Llenas, Winston
71OPC-152R
71T-152R
74OPC-467
74T-467
75OPC-597
75T-597
75T/M-597
76SSPC-195
83Nashua-20
85Cram/PCL-14MG
86Edmon-19MG
88Tor/Fire-57CO
Llewellyn, Paul
83Ander-28
Llodrat, Fernando
76Watlo
Lloyd, Graeme
88Myrtle/ProC-1167
91Dunedin/ClBest-5
91Dunedin/ProC-201
Lloyd, John Henry
(Pop)
74Laugh/Black-33
86Negro/Frit-16
88Conlon/NegAS-8
88Negro/Duques-6
90Negro/Star-5
Lloyd, Mike
89Elizab/Star-15
90Kenosha/Best-6
90Kenosha/ProC-2301
90Kenosha/Star-10
Lobb, Dave
71Richm/Team-12
Lobe, Bill
55Gol/Ind-16
55Salem
Lobert, John
(Hans)
10Domino-71
11Helmar-145
12Sweet/Pin-127
14Piedmont/St-32
15CJ-70
40PB-160
91Conlon/Sport-172
92Conlon/Sport-392
BF2-77
D303
D329-104
D350/2-102
E101
E102
E105
E106
E90/1
E92
E94
M101/4-104
M101/5-102
M116
S74-101
T201
T202
T204
T205
T206
T216
T222
T3-105
Lobozzetta, Al
87Cedar-1
Lochner, Dave
83Cedar-3
83Cedar/LF-8
Lock, Don
63T-47
64T-114
64T/Coins-53
64T/St-24
64T/SU
64T/tatt
65OldLond-29
65T-445
66OPC-165
66T-165
66T/RO-34
67T-376
68OPC-59
68T-59
69MB-159
69T-229
69T/St-76
78TCMA-34
Exh47
WG10-31
Locke, Bobby
60T-44
61T-537
62T-359
65T-324
68OPC-24
68T-24
Locke, Charlie
91Crown/Orio-263
Locke, Roger Dale
88Ashvl/ProC-1064
Locke, Ron
64T-556R
65T-511
91WIZMets-232
Locke, William H.
D322
Lockenmeyer, Mark
84Jacks-3
Locker, John
89Elmira/Pucko-29
90Elmira/Pucko-18
Locker, Robert
65T-541R
66T-374
67T-338
68OPC-51
68T-51
69T-548
70McDon-5
70MLB/St-274
70OPC-249
70T-249
71MLB/St-520
71OPC-356
71T-356
72T-537
73OPC-645
73T-645
74OPC-62
74T-62
74T/Tr-62T
75OPC-434
75T-434
75T/M-434
Lockett, Lester
91Negro/Lewis-28
Lockett, Ron
90Princet/DIMD-14
91Clearw/ClBest-17
91Clearw/ProC-1628
91FSLAS/ProC-FSL7
91Single/ClBest-348
Lockhart, Bruce
85Greens-6
86WinHaven-15
87WinHaven-13
Lockhart, Keith
87Cedar-13
88Chatt/Best-9
88SLAS-5
89Nashvl/CMC-16
89Nashvl/ProC-1278
89Nashvl/Team-12
90CedarDG/Best-12
90Nashvl/CMC-19
90Nashvl/ProC-247
91Nashvl/LineD-264
91Nashvl/ProC-2166
Lockhart, Tim
89Smok/FresnoSt-13
Lockie, Randy
83QuadC-13
Locklear, Dean
90SoBend/ClBest-18
91Single/ClBest-206
91SoBend/ProC-2854
Locklear, Gene
75OPC-13
75T-13
75T/M-13
76OPC-447
76T-447
Lockley, Blain
86Watertn-12
87Macon-12
Lockman, Carroll
(Whitey)
47HomogBond-31
47TipTop
48B-30
49B-2
49Eureka-116
50B-82
50Drake-8
51B-37
51T/RB-41
52B-38
52BR
52RM-NL13
52StarCal/L-78G
52TipTop
53B/Col-128
53Briggs
53RM-NL7
53SM
54B-153
54NYJour
54SM
55B-219
55Gol/Giants-17
55SM
56T-205
57T-232
58Hires-62
58SFCallB-13

58T-195
59T-411
60T-535
73OPC-81MG
73T-81MG
74OPC-354MG
74T-354MG
79TCMA-26
91Crown/Orio-264
91T/Arc53-292
D305
Exh47
PM10/Sm-98
R423-60

Lockwood, Claude
(Skip)
65T-526R
70OPC-499
70T-499
71MLB/St-443
71OPC-433
71T-433
72OPC-118
72T-118
73OPC-308
73T-308
74OPC-532
74T-532
75OPC-417
75T-417
75T/M-417
75Tucson-23
76OPC-166
76SSPC-549
76T-166
77BurgChef-139
77T-65
78T-379
79OPC-250
79T-481
80OPC-295
80T-567
81D-217
81T-233
91WIZMets-233

Lockwood, Rick
85CharlO-4
86Jacks/TCMA-18
88Louisvl-29

Lodbell, Dick
87Anchora-38

Lodding, Richard
89Belling/Legoe-9
91Penin/ClBest-8
91Penin/ProC-374

Lodgek, Scott
89Belling/Legoe-10
90Penin/Star-11

Lodigiani, Dario
41G-15
47Remar-19
47Signal
48Signal
48Smith-15
49Remar

Loe, Darin
89Belling/Legoe-11
90Penin/Star-12
91SanBern/ClBest-8
91SanBern/ProC-1984

Loeb, Marc
90MedHat/Best-24
91Myrtle/ClBest-14
91Myrtle/ProC-2948

Loehr, Ted
75AppFx

Loera, Javier
89GreatF-7

Loes, Billy
52B-240
52T-20
53B/Col-14
53T-174
54B-42
54NYJour
55B-240
55Gol/Dodg-19
56T-270
57T-244
58Hires-48
58T-359
59T-336
60T-181
61T-237
79TCMA-50
90Target-455
91Crown/Orio-265
PM10/L-18

Lofthus, Kevin
90Modesto/Cal-170
90Modesto/ProC-2219

Loftin, Bo
91Billings/ProC-3757

Lofton, Kenneth
88AubAs/ProC-1953
89AubAs/ProC-2166
90FSLAS/Star-11
90Osceola/Star-16
91AAAGame/ProC-AAA52
91B-565
91Tucson/LineD-614
91Tucson/ProC-2225
91UD/FinalEd-24F
92D/I-5RR
92F-655
92S/II-845
92T-69
92T/91Debut-112
92UD-25SR

Lofton, Rodney
89Freder/Star-14
90Hagers/Best-9
90Hagers/ProC-1423
90Hagers/Star-13
91Hagers/LineD-236
91Hagers/ProC-2464

Loftus, Dick
90Target-1014

Loftus, Thomas
N172

Logan, H. Dan
80RochR-4
81RochR-11
82RochR-15
83RochR-17

Logan, Joe Jr.
88CapeCod/Sum-19
89James/ProC-2158
90Rockford/ProC-2689
91FSLAS/ProC-FSL44
91WPalmB/ClBest-7
91WPalmB/ProC-1223

Logan, Johnny
53JC-20
53SpicSpan/3x5-16
53SpicSpan/7x10-7
53T-158
54B-80
54JC-23
54RM-NL20
54SpicSpan/PostC-12
54T-122
55B-180
55Gol/Braves-18
55JC-23
55RM-NL5
55SpicSpan/DC-11
56T-136
56YellBase/Pin-18
57SpicSpan/4x5-11
57Swift-12
57T-4
58T-110
59T-225
60Lake
60SpicSpan-10
60T-205
61P-105
61T-524
62T-573
63T-259
79TCMA-158
91T/Arc53-158
Exh47

Logan, Robert Dean
(Lefty Bob)
86Indianap-18
90Target-456

Logan, Todd
90Visalia/Cal-76
90Visalia/ProC-2157

Loggins, Mike
86FtMyr-18
87Memphis-4
87Memphis/Best-18
88Omaha/CMC-13
88Omaha/ProC-1504
89Omaha/CMC-20
89Omaha/ProC-1738
90Omaha/CMC-12
90Omaha/ProC-76
91Richm/LineD-433

LoGrande, Angelo
78Watlo
81Charl-14
82Charl-15
83Charl-10

Logsdon, Kevin
91Watertn/ClBest-9
91Watertn/ProC-3364

Logue, Matt
89NiagFls/Pucko-15

Lohbeck
N172

Lohrke, Jack
47TipTop
48B-16
49B-59
49Eureka-117
51B-235
52B-251
53B/BW-47

Lohrman, Bill
40PB-210
90Target-457

Lohry, Adin
90Oneonta/ProC-3367

Lohuis, Mark
81Shrev-21

Lois, Alberto
76Shrev
78Colum
79Portl-14
80T-683R

Lolich, Mickey
64T-128
65T-335
65T/E-55
66T-226LL
66T-455
66T/RO-65
67OPC-88
67T-88
68T-414
69Kelly/Pin-10
69MB-160
69MLB/St-50
69MLBPA/Pin-15
69OPC-168WS
69T-168WS
69T-270
69T/St-175
70K-65
70MB-13
70MLB/St-210
70OPC-72LL
70T-715
70T-72LL
71MLB/St-398
71OPC-133
71OPC-71LL
71T-133
71T-71LL
71T/Coins-106
71T/GM-23
71T/tatt-13
72K-38
72MB-200
72OPC-450
72OPC-94LL
72OPC-96LL
72T-450
72T-94LL
72T-96LL
72T/Post-5
73K-3
73OPC-390
73T-390
73T/Comics-10
73T/Lids-27
73T/PinUps-10
74OPC-166
74T-9
74T/St-178
75Ho-6
75Ho/Twink-6
75OPC-245
75T-245
75T/M-245
76Crane-28
76Laugh/Jub-3
76MSA/Disc
76OPC-385
76OPC-3RB
76SSPC-354
76T-385
76T-3RB
76T/Tr-385T
77T-565
78Padre/FamFun-19
79T-164
80T-459
81Detroit-55
83Kaline-62M
88Domino-11
88Pac/Leg-39
89Swell-97
90Swell/Great-81
91Swell/Great-56
91WIZMets-234

Lolich, Ron
71OPC-458R
71T-458R

Lollar, Sherm
50B-142
51B-100
51T/BB-24
52B-237
52Hawth/Pin-5
52NTea
52T-117
53B/Col-157
53T-53
54B-182
54RH
54RM-AL5
54T-39
55B-174
55T-201
56T-243
57T-23
58T-267
58T-491AS
59T-385
60T-495
60T-567AS
61P-28
61T-285
61T/St-123
62J-53
62P-53
62P/Can-53
62Salada-55
62Shirriff-55
62T-514
63J-42
63P-42
63T-118
79TCMA-73
89Kodak/WSox-3M
91T/Arc53-53

Lollar, Tim
79WHave-20
80Colum-1
81F-108
81T-424R
82T-587
83D-61
83D/AAS-37
83F-365
83OPC-185
83T-185
83T-742TL
83T/St-296
84D-284
84F-305
84Mother/Padres-3
84Nes/792-644
84OPC-267
84Smok/Padres-16
84T-644
85Coke/WS-46
85D-324
85F-39
85F/Up-U73
85Leaf-111
85OPC-13
85T-13
85T/St-153
85T/Tr-76T
86D-620
86F-354
86T-297
87F-38
87T-396

Loman, Doug
78BurlB
80Holyo-15
81ElPaso-8
82Vanco-10
84Cram/PCL-28
85D-46RR
85Pol/Brew-5

Lomastro, Jerry
83Orlan-12
85Toledo-24
86Toledo-14
87Hagers-7
87RochR/TCMA-26

Lombardi, Al
89Penin/Star-11

Lombardi, Ernie
32Orbit/num-58
32Orbit/un-41
34DS-105
34DS-36
34Exh/4-4
34G-35
35BU-129
35Exh/4-4
36Exh/4-4
37Exh/4-4
37Wheat
38Exh/4-4
38G-246
38G-270
38Wheat
39Exh
39Wheat-1
41DP-12
47TipTop
48Signal
60F-17
61F-55
80Pac/Leg-11
86D/HL-33
86Sf/Dec-23
89HOF/St-58
89Smok/Dodg-102
91Conlon/Sport-27
92Conlon/Sport-427
R303/A
R303/B
R305
R312
R314
V354-82
W711/1
W711/2

Lombardi, John
91MedHat/ProC-4102

Lombardi, Phil
83Greens-15
85Albany-13
86Colum-14
86Colum/Pol-12
87Colum-16
87Colum/Pol-17
87Colum/TCMA-15
87D-401
87F-648R
87Sf-118M
88T-283
88Tidew/CANDL-10
88Tidew/CMC-12
88Tidew/ProC-1578
89Tidew/CMC-12
89Tidew/ProC-1975
91WIZMets-235

Lombardi, Vic
47TipTop
49Eureka-165
51B-204
52Park-7
90Target-459

Lombardo, Chris
78StPete

Lombardozzi, Chris
87PrWill-13
89Cedar/Best-28
89Cedar/ProC-935
89Chatt/Best-17
89Chatt/GS-25
90Nashvl/ProC-240

Lombardozzi, Steve
83Orlan-6

84Toledo-1
85Toledo-17
86D-598
86D/Rook-18
86F/Up-U68
86Sf-178M
86Sf/Rook-17
87D-318
87D/OD-227
87F-547
87T/Tr-66T
88D-196
88F-16
88Master/Disc-6
88Panini/St-137
88S-174
88T-697
89D-554
89F-120
89OPC-376
89S-421
89T-376
89Tucson/CMC-23
89Tucson/ProC-181
89Tucson/JP-13
89UD-179
90D-688

Lombarski, Tom
82OkCty-14
83MidldC-14
84Iowa-17
85Iowa-4
86Peoria-16
87Tidew-17
87Tidew/TCMA-14

Lomeli, Michael
87Idaho-14
88Boise/ProC-1622
89Boise/ProC-2004
90Erie/Star-13

Lonborg, Jim
65T-573R
66OPC-93
66T-93
67T-371
67T/Test/RSox-9
67T/Test/SU-4
68Bz-11
68Coke
68Dexter-49
68OPC-10LL
68OPC-12LL
68OPC-155WS
68T-10LL
68T-12LL
68T-155WS
68T-460
68T/3D
68T/G-14
68T/Post-11
69Citgo-3
69MB-161
69MLB/St-14
69MLBPA/Pin-16
69NTF
69OPC-109
69T-109
69T/St-135
70K-49
70MLB/St-159
70T-665
71MLB/St-323
71OPC-577
71T-577
72MB-201
72OPC-255
72T-255
73OPC-3
73T-3
74JP
74OPC-342
74T-342
74T/St-75
75OPC-94
75T-94
75T/M-94
76OPC-271
76SSPC-462
76T-271
77K-41
77T-569
78T-52
79OPC-233
79T-446
88Pac/Leg-80
89Swell-48
90Swell/Great-124
91LineD-16
91Swell/Great-57

Lond, Joel
86FSLAS-30

London, Darren
90PrWill/Team-3

Londos, Jim
33SK-14

Long, Bruce
86Reading-15
87Reading-10

Long, Dale
55T-127
55T/DH-115
56T-56
56T/Pin-43
56YellBase/Pin-19
57Kahn
57Swift-3
57T-3
58T-7
59T-147M
59T-414
60T-375
61T-117
61T/St-205
62J-65
62P-65
62P/Can-65
62Salada-35
62Shirriff-35
62T-228
63T-484
72Laugh/GF-48
78TCMA-223
79TCMA-41
90HOF/St-53
90Pac/Legend-92
Exh47

Long, Danny
N172/PCL

Long, Dennis
81Tulsa-14
82Tulsa-4
83Tulsa-8

Long, Don
87QuadC-19
89BendB/Legoe-26MG
89PalmSp/Cal-60CO
89PalmSp/ProC-476
91London/LineD-449MG
91MidldA/ProC-449MG

Long, Herman
(Germany)
E107
N172
N300/unif

Long, James V.
88PalmSp/Cal-89
88PalmSp/ProC-1460

Long, Jeoff
62Pep/Tul
64T-497

Long, Joey
91Spokane/CIBest-2
91Spokane/ProC-3946

Long, Kevin
88CapeCod/Sum-98
89Eugene/Best-14
90BBCity/Star-15

Long, Richard
(Rich)
89Utica/Pucko-14
90SoBend/Best-10

Long, Robert E.
(Bob)
78Salem
80Port-21
81Portl-16
82Portl-5
82T-291R
84Cram/PCL-179
85Cram/PCL-95
86F-468
86Richm-12
87CharlO/WBTV-14
89Chatt/II/Team-17

Long, Ryan
91Classic/DP-40
91FrRow/DP-18

Long, Steve
90James/Pucko-20
91Sumter/CIBest-7
91Sumter/ProC-2330

Long, Thomas
D328-100
D329-105
D350/2-103
E135-100
M101/4-105
M101/5-103

Long, Tony
86Lakeland-11
91BBCity/CIBest-9
91BBCity/ProC-1396
91FSLAS/ProC-FSL2

Long, William
(Bill)
82Amari-18
84Beaum-11
85BuffB-21
86BuffB-16
87D/Rook-48
87F/Up-U66
87Hawaii-16
87T/Tr-67T
88Coke/WS-14
88D-306
88F-404
88OPC-309
88RedFoley/St-49
88S-539
88T-309
89B-56
89Coke/WS-16
89D-573
89F-501
89OPC-133
89S-351
89T-133
89UD-499
90Cub/Mara-12
90OPC-499
90PublInt/St-394
90S-526
90S/Tr-62T
90T-499
90T/TVCub-52
91F-425
91OPC-668
91S-559
91T-668
91UD-495

Longaker, Scott
91Hamil/CIBest-9
91Hamil/ProC-4035

Longenecker, Jere
83Butte-18
87Memphis-9
87Memphis/Best-19

Longmire, Tony
87Macon-8
88Salem/Star-10
91B-489
91Reading/LineD-513
91Reading/ProC-1382
91Single/CIBest-98

Longuil, Rich
87Sumter-15
88Durham/Star-10
89BurlB/ProC-1624
89BurlB/Star-14
90Durham/Team-21

Lonigro, Greg
87Cedar-15
88Cedar/ProC-1152
88MidwLAS/GS-9
89Chatt/Best-16
89Chatt/GS-17
91Chatt/LineD-161
91Chatt/ProC-1967

Lonnett, Joe
57T-241
58T-64
73OPC-356CO
73T-356C
74OPC-221CO
74T-221C

Lono, Joel
86Tampa-11
87Cedar-6

Look, Bruce
69T-317

Looney, Brian
91James/CIBest-17
91James/ProC-3542

Looney, Steve
91Fayette/CIBest-24
91Fayette/ProC-1183

Looper, Eddie
87Savan-18
88Savan/ProC-350
89Spring/Best-23

Lopat, Ed
47TipTop
49B-229
50B-215
51B-218
51BR-C6
51T/BB-39
52B-17
52BR
52Coke
52StarCal/L-70B
52T-57
52TipTop
53Exh/Can-15
53T-87
54NYJour
54T-5
55T-109
55T/DH-41
56T/Hocus-A2
60T-465C
61Peters-2
63T-23MG
64T-348MG
79TCMA-91
90Pac/Legend-38
90Swell/Great-24
91Crown/Orio-266
91Swell/Great-58
91T/Arc53-87
Exh47
PM10/L-19
R346-40
R423-61

Lopata, Stan
49B-177
49Eureka-140
50B-206
51B-76
51BR-B9
54B-207
55B-18
56T-183
57T-119
58Hires-29
58Hires/T
58T-353
59T-412
60T-515
79TCMA-151
PM10/Sm-99

Lopes, Dave
73OPC-609R
73T-609R
74Greyhound-4
74Greyhound-6M
74OPC-112
74T-112
74T/St-46
75Greyhound-2
75Greyhound-6
75Ho-67
75Ho/Twink-67
75OPC-93
75T-93
75T/M-93
76Greyhound-2
76Greyhound-6
76Ho-105
76OPC-197LL
76OPC-4RB
76OPC-660
76SSPC-79
76T-197LL
76T-4RB
76T-660
77BurgChef-145
77Ho-14
77OPC-4LL
77OPC-96
77T-180
77T-4LL
78Ho-112
78OPC-222
78T-440
78Wiffle/Discs-39
79Ho-114
79K-52
79OPC-144
79T-290
80BK/PHR-28
80K-29
80OPC-291
80Pol/Dodg-15
80T-560
80T/S-60
81D-416
81F-114
81F/St-67
81K-29
81OPC-50
81PermaGr/AS-5
81Pol/Dodg-15
81T-50
81T/HT
81T/SO-92
81T/St-175
82D-327
82F-12
82F/St-10
82Granny-8
82OPC-218
82OPC-338AS
82OPC-85IA
82T-338AS
82T-740
82T-741A
82T/Tr-64T
83D-339
83F-524
83Granny-15
83OPC-365
83T-365
83T/St-105
84D-400
84F-453
84Mother/A's-21
84Nes/792-669
84Nes/792-714LL
84OPC-17
84T-669
84T-714LL
84T/St-331
85D-604
85F-60
85OPC-12
85SevenUp-15
85SpokAT/Cram-13
85T-12
86Cub/Unocal-11
86D-388
86D-9DK
86D/DKsuper-9
86F-372
86Gator-15
86Leaf-9DK
86OPC-125
86Sf-144M
86Sf-194
86T-125
87D-455
87F-62
87Mother/Ast-16
87OPC-311
87Pol/Ast-8
87Smok/Dodg-19
87T-445
87T-4RB
87T/St-7
88S-489
88Smok/Dodg-15M
88Smok/Dodg-18
88T-226
89Smok/Dodg-96
89Smok/R-20
90Mother/Rang-27M
90Target-460
91Mother/Rang-28CO
91Single/CIBest-62

Lopez, Al
33DH-27
33Exh/4-2
34DS-28
34DS-97
34Exh/4-2
35BU-3
35Exh/4-2
37Exh/4-1

38G-257
38G-281
51B-295MG
52NumNum-20
53B/Col-143MG
54DanDee
55B-308MG
55Gol/Ind-17MG
55Salem
60MacGregor-12
60T-222MG
61T-132MG
61T-337M
62T-286MG
63T-458MG
64T-232MG
65T-414MG
69T-527MG
80Pac/Leg-98
80SSPC/HOF
86Indianap-21MG
89Pac/Leg-197
89Smok/Dodg-38
89Swell-90
90Target-461
91T/Arc53-329MG
R312/M
R314
V355-131

Lopez, Albie
91BurlInd/ProC-3300

Lopez, Antonio
79Wisco-1

Lopez, Art
65T-566R

Lopez, Aurelio
78Sprin
79T-444
80T-101
81Coke
81Detroit-75
81F-483
81OPC-291
81T-291
82D-359
82F-273
82T-278
83T/Tr-63T
84D-516
84F-86
85FunFood/Pin-98
84Nes/792-95
84OPC-95
84T-95
84T/St-268
85Cain's-13
85D-349
85F-16
85Leaf-160
85Seven-9D
85T-539
85T/St-265
85Wendy-15
86D-293
86F-231
86F/Up-U69
86T-367
87D-629
87F-63
87Mother/Ast-18
87Pol/Ast-13
87T-659

Lopez, Carlos
77T-492R
78OPC-219
78T-166
79RochR-8
79T-568
91Crown/Orio-267

Lopez, Fred
89Idaho/ProC-2016
90Sumter/Best-19
90Sumter/ProC-2437
91Greenvl/ClBest-13
91Greenvl/ProC-3007
91MedHat/ProC-4095

Lopez, Hector
55Rodeo
56Rodeo
56T-16
56T/Pin-13
57T-6
58T-155
59T-402
60T-163
61P-12
61T-28
62T-502
63T-92
64T-325
65T-532
66OPC-177
66T-177
78TCMA-272
79TCMA-195
PM10/L-20
WG9-15

Lopez, Javier
78Cedar

Lopez, Javier
89Pulaski/ProC-1892
90A&AASingle/ProC-132
90BurlB/Best-20
90BurlB/ProC-2352
90BurlB/Star-16
90Foil/Best-107
91B-587
91CLAS/ProC-CAR2
91Durham/ClBest-19
91Durham/ProC-1547

Lopez, Jose
90Johnson/Star-17
91Savan/ClBest-9
91Savan/ProC-1650

Lopez, Juan
77Spoka
79Vanco-12
80Evansvl-23
81Evansvl-17
82Evansvl-17
83Evansvl-16
83Watlo/LF-6
84Evansvl-1
87Fayette-18
87Osceola-2
88ColAst/Best-10
89NiagFls/Pucko-26
90Everett/ProC-3147CO
90Niagara/Pucko-28MG
91Bristol/ClBest-20MG
91Bristol/ProC-3622MG

Lopez, Luis
85VeroB-21
86FSLAS-31
86VeroB-16
87Bakers-10
88SanAn/Best-26
88Spokane/ProC-1930
88TexLgAS/GS-37
89CharRain/ProC-984
89SanAn/Best-15
90Albuq/CMC-21
90Albuq/ProC-360
90Albuq/Trib-18
90Riversi/Cal-5
90Riversi/ProC-2616
91ColoSp/LineD-90
91ColoSp/ProC-2191
91S/RookTr-109T
91T/90Debut-91
91Wichita/LineD-612
91Wichita/ProC-2604
92S/100RisSt-84
92S/II-716

Lopez, Marcelino
63T-549R
65T-537R
66OPC-155
66T-155
67T-513
70OPC-344
70T-344
71MLB/St-303
71OPC-137
71T-137
72T-652
91Crown/Orio-268

Lopez, Marcos
89Peoria/Ko-4

Lopez, Marcus
88CharWh/Best-16

Lopez, Pancho
73Cedar

Lopez, Pedro
89Watlo/ProC-1790
89Watlo/Star-18
90CharRain/Best-13
90CharRain/ProC-2043

Lopez, Rob
86FSLAS-32
86Tampa-12
87Vermont-9
88Nashvl/CMC-8
88Nashvl/ProC-487
89Nashvl/CMC-6
89Nashvl/ProC-1295
89Nashvl/Team-13
90Nashvl/CMC-8
90Nashvl/ProC-228
91Nashvl/LineD-267

Lopez, Steve
88Idaho/ProC-1859
89Sumter/ProC-1096

Lora, Jose
90Elmira/Pucko-10
91Elmira/ClBest-9
91Elmira/ProC-3284
91WinHaven/ClBest-28

Lora, Ramon Antonio
80OkCty
81Syrac-10
82Syrac-12

Lord, Bristol
10Domino-72
11Helmar-11
12Sweet/Pin-11A
12Sweet/Pin-11B
14Piedmont/St-33
E104
E224
E254
E270/1
M116
T205
T207
T208

Lord, Harry
14CJ-48
E103
E254
E270/1
E270/2
E91
E94
E95
M116
T201
T202
T204
T205
T206
T207
T215
T3-106

Lorenz, Joe
82Durham-4

Lorenzo, Gary
79AppFx-9

Lorms, John
90Watertn/Star-13
91Collnd/ClBest-20
91Collnd/ProC-1487

LoRosa, Mark
91James/ClBest-15

Losa, Bill
88Butte-13
88Gaston/ProC-1013
89CharlR/Star-14
90CharlR/Star-23
91Kinston/ClBest-14
91Kinston/ProC-325

Losauro, Carmelo
86DayBe-17
88Virgini/Star-14

Loscalzo, Bob
82Idaho-24
83Madis/LF-15
84Madis/Pol-13

Loseke, Scott
84Cedar-22

Lott, Bill
(Billy)
89LittleSun-4
90Bakers/Cal-259
90Yakima/Team-18

Lotzar, Greg
85Elmira-12
86FSLAS-33
86WinHaven-16
87NewBrit-6

Loubier, Stephen
88River/Cal-213
88River/ProC-1432
89AubAs/ProC-24
89River/Best-11
89River/Cal-20
89River/ProC-1389
90Wichita/Rock-13
91PalmSp/ProC-2008

Loubler, Steve
89Wichita/Rock/Up-14

Loucks, Scott
78DaytB
81Tucson-11
83Tucson-22
85Cram/PCL-228

Louden, William
D328-101
E135-101

Loudenslager, Charlie
90Target-1015

Loughlin, Mark
91AubAS/ClBest-1
91AubAS/ProC-4270

Louis, Joe
47HomogBond-32BOX
D305

Loun, Don
65OPC-181R
65T-181R

Lovdal, Stewart
89Martins/Star-18
90Batavia/ProC-3062

Love, Edward H.
(Slim)
16FleischBrd-58

Love, John
87Macon-6
88Salem/Star-11

Love, Sylvester
90Stockton/Best-9
90Stockton/Cal-194
90Stockton/ProC-2194

Love, William
(Will)
89Madis/Star-13
89Star/Wax-66
90Modesto/Cal-157
90Modesto/ProC-2210
91Modesto/ProC-3083

Lovelace, Vance
82QuadC-10
83VeroB-7
86MidldA-13
87MidldA-24
88Edmon/CMC-4
88Edmon/ProC-557
89Edmon/ProC-559
89F-651M
90Calgary/CMC-7
90Calgary/ProC-647
91Calgary/LineD-65
91Calgary/ProC-512

Lovell, Don
86Water-15
87BuffB-1
88ColoSp/CMC-15
88ColoSp/ProC-1523

Lovell, Jim
88Greenvl/Best-11
89Greenvl/ProC-1167
89Greenvl/Best-22
91Greenvl/ClBest-29TR

Lovett, Thomas
(Tom)
90Target-1016
N172
N300/unif

Loviglio, John
(Jay)
80OkCty
81T-526R
82Edmon-8
82T-599R
83Iowa-15
86Geneva-16MG
87WinSalem-13
89WinSalem/Star-19
91CharlK/LineD-149MG
91CharlK/ProC-1704MG

Lovinger, Allan
90Penin/Star-27TR

Lovins, Steve
(Sarge)
80Memphis-1

Lovitto, Joe
73OPC-276
73T-276
74OPC-639
74T-639
75OPC-36
75T-36
75T/M-36
76OPC-604
76SSPC-271
76T-604

Lovrich, Pete
63T-549R
64T-212

Lovullo, Torey
88EastLAS/ProC-8
88GlenF/ProC-923
89D/Rook-17
89F-648R
89Mara/Tigers-23
89Panini/St-332
89S/HotRook-17
89UD/Ext-782
90Toledo/CMC-24
90Toledo/ProC-158
90UD-332
91B-175
91ColClip/ProC-603

Lowdermilk, Grover
T207

Lowe, Chris
88Martins/Star-24
89Martins/Star-19
90Hamil/Star-14

Lowe, Donald
79Wausau-17

Lowe, Jamie
89Orlan/Best-29

Lowe, Q.V.
82Oneonta-6
83Greens-29
86Jaxvl/TCMA-10
87Jamestn-29CO
88James/ProC-2039CO
89James/ProC-2152CO
90James/Pucko-28CO
91James/ClBest-28CO
91James/ProC-3561CO

Lowe, Robert
N172
N300/unif

Lowe, Steve
(Doc)
76Wausau
78Wausau

Lowenstein, John
71OPC-231R
71T-231R
72OPC-486
72T-486
73OPC-327
73T-327
74OPC-176
74T-176
75OPC-424
75T-424
75T/M-424
76OPC-646
76SSPC-528
76T-646
77OPC-175
77T-393
78BK/R-21
78T-87
79T-173
80T-287
81D-235
81F-186
81OPC-199
81T-591
82D-599
82F-169
82T-747
82T/St-102
83D-153
83F-63
83OPC-337
83T-473
83T/St-24

84D-228
84D/AAS-26
84F-10
84F/St-116
84Nes/792-604
84T-604
84T/St-209
84T/St-20WS
85D-245
85F-180
85OPC-316
85T-316
85T/St-206
91Crown/Orio-269
Lowery, David
91Gaston/ClBest-18
91Gaston/ProC-2695
91SALAS/ProC-SAL23
Lowery, Josh
89Batavia/ProC-1942
Lowman, Mel
77DaytB
Lown, Omar
(Turk)
52B-16
52T-330
53B/Col-154
53T-130
54B-157
57T-247
58T-261
59T-277
60T-313
60T-57M
61P-32
61T-424
61T/RO-35
62T-528
91T/Arc53-130
V362-14
Lowrey, Harry
(Peanuts)
47TipTop
48L-33
49B-22
49Eureka-62
50B-172
51B-194
52B-102
52T-111
53Exh/Can-29
53Hunter
53T-16
54Hunter
54T-158
72T/Test-2
91T/Arc53-16
Exh47
Lowrey, Steve
82Cedar-4
Lowry, Dwight
83BirmB-4
87Cain's-5
87Coke/Tigers-11
87D-338
87F-157
87Seven-DT7
87T-483
87Toledo/TCMA-25
89Pac/SenLg-21
89T/SenLg-2
90Indianap/CMC-14
90Indianap/ProC-297
91Fayette/ClBest-11CO
91Fayette/ProC-1188CO
Lowry, Mike
78Wausau
Loy, Darren
86Reading-16
87Maine-21
87Maine/TCMA-9
87Phill/TastyK-x
88CharlR/Star-13
89OkCty/CMC-20
89OkCty/ProC-1526
89Tulsa/Team-12
Loynd, Mike
86Rang-46
86Tulsa-8
87D-506
87F/Up-U67
87Mother/Rang-21
87Smok/R-27
87T-126
88D-550
88F-472
88S-491
88T-319
88Tucson/CMC-3
88Tucson/ProC-185
89ColMud/ProC-147
89ColMud/Star-16
90Syrac/CMC-6
90Syrac/ProC-568
90Syrac/Team-15
Loyola, Juan
91Princet/ClBest-2
91Princet/ProC-3526
Lozado, Willie
79BurlB-7
81ElPaso-2
82Vanco-5
83Indianap-10
85D-595
85F-644R
85Louisvl-19
86OKCty-10
Lozano, Steve
89Smok/FresnoSt-14
Lozinski, Tony
89Batavia/ProC-1916
90Clearw/Star-12
Lubert, Dennis
83Durham-21
Lubratich, Steve
80SLCity-14
81SLCity-19
82Spokane-17
84Cram/PCL-112
84Cram/PCL-249
84D-377
84F-524
84Nes/792-266
84T-266
85Cram/PCL-106
86Beaum-14CO
86LasVegas-10
87Spokane-10
88LasVegas/ProC-243
88Spokane/ProC-1928
89River/Best-22MG
89River/Cal-25MG
89River/ProC-1411MG
90Wichita/Rock-25MG
91Wichita/LineD-624MG
91Wichita/ProC-2614MG
Luby, Hugh
48Sommer-23
Lucadello, John
W753
Lucarelli, Vito
79AppFx-3
Lucas, Arbrey
85Osceola/Team-8
Lucas, Brian
78Charl
Lucas, Charles Fred.
(Red)
29Exh/4-8
31Exh/4-8
32Orbit/num-40
32Orbit/un-42
33DH-28
33DH-29
33Exh/4-4
33G-137
34DS-106
34DS-46
35G-2B
35G-7B
91Conlon/Sport-190
R305
R313
R316
R332-43
V354-7
Lucas, Charles S.
R314/Can
Lucas, Gary
79Hawaii-9
81D-243
81F-502
81OPC-259
81T-436
82D-296
82F-577
82OPC-120
82T-120
83D-187
83F-366
83OPC-364
83T-761
84D-307
84F-306
84F/X-U73
84Nes/792-7
84OPC-7
84Stuart-12
84T-7
84T/St-161
84T/Tr-73T
85D-498
85F-403
85OPC-297
85T-297
86D-453
86F-254
86OPC-351
86T-601
87D-618
87F-87
87OPC-382
87Smok/Cal-4
87T-696
88D-579
88F-495
88T-524
91AS/Cal-48CO
91SanJose/ClBest-24CO
91SanJose/ProC-29CO
Lucas, Ray
90Target-462
Lucchesi, Frank
70T-662MG
71OPC-119MG
71T-119MG
72OPC-188MG
72T-188MG
74OPC-379CO
74T-379C
76SSPC-272
76T-172MG
77T-428MG
88Chatt/Team-22
88Nashvl/Team-25MG
88T-564
89Nashvl/CMC-25MG
89Nashvl/ProC-1284MG
89Nashvl/Team-30MG
Lucero, Kevin
91Hamil/ClBest-4
91Hamil/ProC-4036
Lucero, Robert
88Clinton/ProC-714
Lucia, Danny
78Green
81Durham-20
Luciani, Randy
88Fayette/ProC-1098
Luciano, Medina
89Pittsfld/Star-15
Luciano, Suliban
91Kingspt/ClBest-5
91Kingspt/ProC-3825
Luckham, Ken
89Salem/Team-15
90Osceola/Star-17
91Osceola/ClBest-7
91Osceola/ProC-679
Luderus, Fred
11Helmar-146
14CJ-45
15CJ-45
16FleischBrd-55
BF2-87
D328-102
D329-106
D350/2-104
E135-102
M101/4-106
M101/5-104
Ludwick, Bob
53Exh/Can-38
Ludwig, Jeff
89Geneva/ProC-1869
Ludwig, William
E254
Ludy, John
85Beloit-19
86Stockton-13
87Stockton-16
Luebber, Steve
72T-678
77T-457
79Syrac-20
80RochR-15
81RochR-12
83Evansvl-5
86Beaum-15CO
87Wichita-23
88Wichita-42
89LasVegas/ProC-26
89Pac/SenLg-94
90Riversi/Best-20CO
90Riversi/Cal-25CO
90Riversi/ProC-2623CO
91Crown/Orio-270
91Hagers/LineD-240CO
91Hagers/ProC-2473CO
91Pac/SenLg-7
Luebbers, Larry
90Billings/ProC-3217
91Cedar/ClBest-8
91Cedar/ProC-2716
91MidwLAS/ProC-MWL22
91Single/ClBest-373
Luebke, Dick
91Crown/Orio-271
Luecken, Rick
84Chatt-19
85Cram/PCL-98
86Chatt-16
87Memphis-18
87Memphis/Best-22
88Memphis/Best-20
89AAA/ProC-38
89Omaha/CMC-7
89Omaha/ProC-1734
90B-5
90D-562
90F-113
90OPC-87
90Richm/CMC-26
90Richm/Team-19
90T-87
90T/89Debut-73
90UD-621
Lugo, Angel
89Elizab/Star-16
90Miami/II/Star-14
91StCath/ClBest-23
91StCath/ProC-3391
Lugo, Rafael
82Danvl-26
83Peoria/LF-20
85Cram/PCL-9
Lugo, Urbano
85F/Up-U74
86D-329
86F-162
86T-373
87Smok/Cal-9
87T-92
88AAA/ProC-15
88Edmon/CMC-6
88Edmon/ProC-581
89Indianap/ProC-1232
90CokeK/Tiger-11
Luis, Joe
91LynchRS/ClBest-12
91LynchRS/ProC-1202
Lujack, Johnny
51Wheat
52Wheat
Lukachyk, Rob
88Utica/Pucko-1
89SoBend/GS-22
90Saraso/Star-14
91FSLAS/ProC-FSL29
91Saraso/ClBest-23
91Saraso/ProC-1124
Luketich, Stan
91Niagara/ClBest-30CO
91Niagara/ProC-3651CO
Lukevics, Mitch
76AppFx
78Knoxvl
79Knoxvl/TCMA-11
Lukish, Tom
80Utica-25
82Knoxvl-5
83Syrac-9
84Syrac-20
Lum, Mike
68T-579R
69MB-162
69T-514
70OPC-367
70T-367
71MLB/St-16
71OPC-194
71T-194
72T-641
73OPC-266
73T-266
74OPC-227
74T-227
74T/St-7
75Ho-33
75Ho/Twink-33
75OPC-154
75T-154
75T/M-154
76OPC-208
76SSPC-11
76T-208
76T/Tr-208T
77T-601
78T-326
79OPC-286
79T-556
80T-7
81F-258
81T-457
81T/Tr-795
82D-300
82F-599
82T-732
Luman, Charley
83Butte-8
Lumenti, Ralph
58T-369
59T-316
60L-130
61T-469
Lumley, Harry G.
90Target-464
E90/1
T204
T206
WG3-26
Lumley, Mike
89Lakeland/Star-14
90London/ProC-1265
91Lakeland/ClBest-9
91Lakeland/ProC-264
Lumpe, Jerry
58T-193
59T-272
60L-47
60T-290
61P-81
61T-119M
61T-365
61T/St-164
62J-93
62P-93
62P/Can-93
62Salada-25
62Shirriff-25
62T-127M
62T-305
62T/bucks
62T/St-54
63F-16
63J-86
63P-86
63T-256
63T/SO
64Det/Lids-9
64T-165
64T/Coins-124AS
64T/Coins-28
64T/St-86S9
64T/SU
65T-353
66OPC-161
66T-161
67T-247
78TCMA-55
Luna, Guillermo
(Memo)
52Mother-26
54B-222
54Hunter

Lunar, Luis
76Wausau
77Wausau
79Jacks-13
Lund, Don
53Glen
53T-277
54B-87
54T-167
90Target-465
91T/Arc53-277
Lund, Gordon
70T-642R
75AppFx
79Knoxvl/TCMA-4
Lund, Greg
89Everett/Star-27
Lundahl, Rich
86LitFalls-17
87Columbia-7
Lundblade, Rick
87Phill/TastyK-x
87Reading-13
88Maine/CMC-15
88Maine/ProC-291
89Tidew/CMC-19
89Tidew/ProC-1968
90Hagers/ProC-1424
Lundeen, Larry
88Boise/ProC-1615
Lundgren, Carl
T206
WG3-27
Lundgren, Jason
89BendB/Legoe-25BB
Lundgren, Kurt
86Jacks/TCMA-7
Lundstedt, Thomas
74OPC-603R
74T-603R
Lundy, Dick
78Laugh/Black-6
86Negro/Frit-75
90Negro/Star-25
Lundy, Gordy
82Edmon-22
Lung, Rod
88QuadC/GS-16
Lupien, Ulysses
(Tony)
47Signal
49B-141
Luplow, Al
62T-598R
63J-73
63P-73
63Sugar-19
63T-351
64T-184
66OPC-188
66T-188
67T-433
91WIZMets-236
Luque, Adolpho
(Dolph)
21Exh-98
28Exh-15
28Yueng-18
33G-209
40PB-231
61F-56
87Conlon/2-46
88Conlon/5-19
88Pac/8Men-90
90Target-466
92Conlon/Sport-413
E120
E210-18
V61-72
W502-18
W513-71
W514-17
Lusader, Scott
86GlenF-12
87Toledo-3
87Toledo/TCMA-8
88D-615
88F-62
88Toledo/CMC-13
88Toledo/ProC-594
89S/HotRook-15
89T-487
90D-696
90OPC-632
90S-575
90S/100Ris-42
90T-632
90Toledo/CMC-19
90Toledo/ProC-163
91B-174
91UD-241
Lush, John Charles
C46-33
E270/2
M116
T201
T204
T205
Lush, William L.
E107
Lusted, Chuck
84Shrev/FB-10
Luther, Brad
83StPete-18
85Spring-16
Luther, Tim
91Everett/ClBest-15
91Everett/ProC-3910
Lutticken, Bob
86Cram/PCL-156
87Spokane-18
88Charl/ProC-1217
89River/Best-1
89River/Cal-11
89River/ProC-1403
90Wichita/Rock-14
91HighD/ClBest-16
91HighD/ProC-2399
Luttrell, Lyle
57T-386
Luttrull, Bruce
85Bend/Cram-14
Lutz, Brent
91MedHat/ProC-4103
Lutz, Chris
88Geneva/ProC-1653
89CharWh/ProC-1760
90Peoria/Team-25
91WinSalem/ClBest-9
Lutz, Rollin Joseph
52Park-74
73OPC-449CO
73T-449CO
Lutzke, Walter
25Exh-83
26Exh-82
27Exh-42
Luzinski, Greg
71OPC-439R
71T-439R
72OPC-112
72T-112
73OPC-189
73T-189
73T/Lids-28
74JP
74K-9
74OPC-360
74T-360
74T/DE-24
74T/St-76
75Ho-27
75Ho/Twink-27
75OPC-630
75T-630
75T/M-630
76Crane-29
76Ho-125
76K-18
76MSA/Disc
76OPC-193LL
76OPC-195LL
76OPC-610
76SSPC-467
76T-193LL
76T-195LL
76T-610
77BurgChef-163
77Ho-25
77K-12
77OPC-118
77Pep-72
77T-30
78Ho-8
78K-33
78OPC-42
78T-420
78Tastee/Discs-5
78Wiffle/Discs-40
79BK/P-19
79Ho-30
79OPC-278
79T-540
80BK/P-11
80OPC-66
80T-120
81Coke
81D-175
81F-10
81F/St-75
81OPC-270
81T-270
81T/HT
81T/SO-74
81T/Tr-796
82D-193
82Drake-22
82F-352
82F/St-187
82OPC-152
82OPC-69IA
82T-720
82T-721IA
82T/St-165
83D-395
83D/AAS-4
83F-247
83K-50
83OPC-310
83T-310
83T-591TL
83T/St-51
83TrueVal/WSox-19
84D-122
84D/AAS-41
84D/Champs-13
84Drake-18
84F-69
84F/St-47
85FunFoodPin-34
84Nes/792-20
84Nes/792-712LL
84OPC-20
84Ralston-5
84T-20
84T-712LL
84T/Cereal-5
84T/St-244
84T/St-7
84T/St-8
84TrueVal/WS-23
85D-546
85F-521
85Leaf-75
85OPC-328
85T-650
85T/St-238
89Swell-24
Luzon, Bob
82Durham-5
83Durham-9
Lychak, Perry
83Kinston/Team-12
85Kingst-6
86Kinston-15
Lyden, Mitch
87Colum-9
87Colum/Pol-18
87Colum/TCMA-11
89Albany/Best-14
89Albany/ProC-320
89Albany/Star-11
89Star/Wax-98
90A&AASingle/ProC-33
90Albany/Best-11
90Albany/ProC-1037
90Albany/Star-9
90AlbanyDG/Best-34
90EastLAS/ProC-EL15
90Foil/Best-179
91Toledo/LineD-590
91Toledo/ProC-1935
Lydy, Scott
89Medford/Best-8
91Madison/ClBest-20
91Madison/ProC-2142
Lyle, Don
79Indianap-15
80Indianap-24
Lyle, Jeff
90Welland/Pucko-22
91Augusta/ProC-802
Lyle, Sparky
69MB-163
69T-311
70MLB/St-160
70OPC-116
70T-116
71MLB/St-324
71OPC-649
71T-649
72MB-202
72OPC-259
72T-259
73K-15
73OPC-394
73OPC-68LL
73Syrac/Team-14
73T-394
73T-68LL
74K-41
74OPC-66
74Syrac/Team-13
74T-66
74T/St-212
75Ho-134
75K-47
75OPC-485
75T-485
75T/M-485
76OPC-545
76SSPC-429
76T-545
77BK/Y-10
77OPC-89
77T-598
78BK/Y-9
78Ho-68
78K-43
78OPC-214
78OPC-237RB
78T-2RB
78T-35
79Ho-143
79OPC-188
79T-365
80OPC-62
80T-115
81D-284
81F-17
81F/St-91
81OPC-337
81T-719
82D-189
82F-247
82OPC-285
82T-285
83OPC-208
83OPC-92SV
83T-693
83T-694SV
90Pac/Legend-93
Lyman, Billy
44Centen-15
45Centen-15
Lynch, Charlie
80Elmira-40
Lynch, David
89Tulsa/GS-14
90OkCty/CMC-4
90OkCty/ProC-429
90TulsaDG/Best-16
91Albuq/LineD-13
91Albuq/ProC-1137
Lynch, Ed
78Ashvl
78Charl
79Tucson-20
80Tidew-21
81Tidew-16
82D-641
82F-531
82T-121
83D-308
83F-549
83T-601
84D-75
84F-591
84Nes/792-293
84T-293
85D-623
85F-87
85T-467
86D-631
86F-88
86OPC-68
86T-68
87Berg/Cubs-37
87D-516
87F-567
87OPC-16
87T-697
88D-77
88F-422
88S-506
88T-336
91WIZMets-237
Lynch, Jerry
54T-234
55T-142
55T/DH-73
56T-97
57T-358
58T-103
59Kahn
59T-97
60Kahn
60L-45
60T-198
60T-352M
61Kahn
61P-187
61T-97
61T/St-19
62J-127
62Kahn
62P-127
62P/Can-127
62Salada-198
62Shirriff-198
62T-487
63J-129
63Kahn
63P-129
63T-37
64Kahn
64T-193
65Kahn
65T-291
66EH-24
66OPC-182
66T-182
72Laugh/GF-22
Lynch, Joe
85Spokane/Cram-11
87TexLgAS-3
87Wichita-10
88LasVegas/CMC-9
88LasVegas/ProC-223
89LasVegas/CMC-3
89LasVegas/ProC-22
90LasVegas/CMC-10
90LasVegas/ProC-115
Lynch, John H.
N172
N172/SP
N690
Lynch, Mike
91Erie/ClBest-19
91Erie/ProC-4065
Lynch, Rich
80WHave-21
81WHave-22
Lynes, Mike
83Albany-6
Lynn, Chuck
86Lynch-15
Lynn, Fred
75OPC-622R
75T-622R
75T/M-622R
76Crane-30
76Ho-1
76Ho/Twink-1
76K-31
76MSA/Disc
76OPC-192LL
76OPC-196LL
76OPC-50
76SSPC-402
76T-192LL
76T-196LL
76T-50
77BurgChef-35
77Ho-51
77OPC-163
77Pep-21

77T-210
78OPC-62
78PapaG/Disc-19
78T-320
78Wiffle/Discs-41
79K-30
79OPC-249
79T-480
80BK/PHR-18
80K-40
80OPC-60
80T-110
80T/S-10
81D-218
81Drake-9
81F-223
81F/St-98
81K-40
81MSA/Disc-21
81OPC-313
81PermaGr/CC-20
81Sqt-25
81T-720
81T/HT
81T/SO-5
81T/St-42
81T/Tr-797
82D-367
82F-468
82F/St-214
82KMart-27
82OPC-251
82OPC-252IA
82PermaGr/AS-8
82T-251
82T-252IA
82T/St-161
83D-241
83D/AAS-59
83F-97
83K-51
83OPC-182
83OPC-392AS
83PermaGr/AS-3
83Seven-3
83T-392AS
83T-520
83T/St-158
83T/St-44
84D-108
84D-17DK
84D/AAS-27
84D/Champs-59
84Drake-19
84F-525
84F-626M
85FunFoodPin-54
84Nes/792-680
84OPC-247
84Ralston-29
84Seven-16W
84Smok/Cal-18
84T-680
84T/Cereal-29
84T/Gloss22-7
84T/St-230
84T/St-5
84T/St-6
84T/Super-23
85D-133
85F-307
85F/Up-U75
85Leaf-198
85OPC-220
85Seven-9S
85T-220
85T/St-225
85T/Tr-77T
86D-245
86F-278
86F/St-70
86Leaf-120
86OPC-55
86Sf-137M
86Sf-145M
86Sf-38
86Sf-63M
86Sf-71M
86Sf-73M
86Sf/Rook-46M
86T-55
86T/St-228
86Woolwth-18
87Classic-23
87D-108
87D-9DK
87D/DKsuper-9
87D/OD-135
87F-474
87F/Excit-32
87F/BB-25
87F/St-72
87French-19
87Leaf-83
87Leaf-9DK
87OPC-370
87Sf-198M
87Sf-49
87T-370
87T/St-226
88D-248
88D/Best-297
88F-566
88French-19
88Leaf-163
88Panini/St-15
88RedFoley/St-50
88S-42
88Sf-23
88T-707
88T/Big-169
89D-563
89F-138
89Mara/Tigers-9
89OPC-27
89Pol/Tigers-9
89RedFoley/St-76
89S-126
89Sf-68
89Smok/Angels-14
89T-416
89T/LJN-160
89UD/Ext-761
90B-216
90BBWit-28
90Classic/III-59
90Coke/Padre-10
90F-609
90HOF/St-83
90Leaf/I-188
90MLBPA/Pins-90
90OPC-107
90OPC-663TBC
90Padre/MagUno-17
90Panini/St-73
90PublInt/St-476
90S-131
90S/Tr-20T
90Smok/SoCal-9
90T-107
90T-663TBC
90T/Ames-10
90T/Big-277
90T/HillsHM-14
90T/St-279
90T/Tr-62T
90T/WaxBox-H
90UD-247
90UD/Ext-771
91Crown/Orio-272
91D-673
91F-536
91OPC-586
91S-554
91T-586
91UD-273

Lynn, Greg
83Clinton/LF-6tr
91Mother/Giant-28TR

Lynn, Japhet
(Red)
47Signal
53Mother-58

Lynn, Ken
83Ander-11

Lynn, Thomas
83LynnP-26

Lyons, Albert
52Mother-42

Lyons, Barry
86Tidew-16
87T/Tr-68T
88D-619
88D/Mets/Bk-619
88F-140
88Kahn/Mets-33
88S-387
88T-633
89D-572
89F/Up-101
89Kahn/Mets-33
89S-456
89T-412
89UD-176
90B-139
90D-526
90F-209
90Kahn/Mets-33
90Leaf/I-119
90OPC-258
90S-29
90T-258
90T/Big-97
90T/TVMets-20
90UD-473
91Mother/Dodg-25
91Pol/Dodg-40
91WIZMets-238

Lyons, Bobby
83AlexD-1

Lyons, Dennis
N172
N690

Lyons, Harry P.
N172

Lyons, Jimmie
74Laugh/Black-14
86Negro/Frit-114

Lyons, Steve
84Pawtu-18
85D-29RR
85F/Up-U76
86D-579
86F-355
86T-233
86T/Tr-67T
87Coke/WS-6
87D-409
87F-502
87T-511
88Coke/WS-15
88D-532
88D/Best-291
88F-405
88Panini/St-60
88T-108
89B-63
89Coke/WS-17
89D-253
89F-502
89Kodak/WSox-2M
89OPC-334
89Panini/St-308
89S-388
89T-334
89T/Big-105
89T/St-298
89UD-224
90B-321
90Coke/WSox-15
90D-651
90F-539
90OPC-751
90Panini/St-40
90PublInt/St-395
90S-88
90T-751
90T/Big-32
90T/St-301
90UD-390
91F-127
91F/Ultra-77
91F/UltraUp-U7
91F/Up-U6
91OPC-612
91S-269
91T-612
91UD-601
92D/II-758
92S/I-294
92T-349

Lyons, Ted
28Exh-39
31Exh/4-19
32Orbit/un-43
33CJ/Pin-16
33DH-30
33Exh/4-10
33G-7
34DS-43
35BU-111M
35BU-119
35BU-36
35Exh/4-10
35G-8B
35G-9B
36Exh/4-10
38Exh/4-10
50Callahan
61F-122
63Bz-38
80Pac/Leg-77
80SSPC/HOF
91Conlon/Sport-19
92Conlon/Sport-359
PR1-21
R305
R306
R308-172
R332-33
V353-7
W517-45

Lyons, William Allen
(Bill)
81Louisvl-27
82Louisvl-14
82Spring-4
83Louisvl/Riley-27
84Louisvl-14
85Louisvl-17
86Louisvl-17
87Louisvl-24
88Louisvl-30
88Louisvl/CMC-12
88Louisvl/ProC-432
90SpringDG/Best-32

Lysander, Richard
(Rick)
76Tucson-28
79Ogden/TCMA-11
80Ogden-6
81Tacoma-23
82Tucson-16
84D-560
84F-570
84Nes/792-639
84T-639
84Toledo-23
85D-560
85F-284
85T-383
86F-399
86T-482
89Pac/SenLg-143
89T/SenLg-68
90Syrac/CMC-12
90Syrac/ProC-569
90Syrac/Team-16
91Pac/SenLg-39
91Pac/SenLg-52

Lysgaard, Jim
77WHave
78Cr/PCL-59

Lytle, Wade
89Princet/Star-11

Lyttle, Jim
70OPC-516R
70T-516R
71OPC-234
71T-234
72T-648
74OPC-437
74T-437
76SSPC-337
90Target-467

Maack, Mike
83Wisco/LF-18

Maas, Duane
(Duke)
56T-57
57T-405
58T-228
59T-167
60T-421
61T-387
61T/RO-28
79TCMA-117

Maas, Jason
86FtLaud-15
87PrWill-24
88Albany/ProC-1346
89Albany/Best-24
89Albany/ProC-334
89Albany/Star-12
90ColClip/CMC-15
90ColClip/ProC-690
90T/TVYank-52
91ColClip/LineD-111
91ColClip/ProC-609

Maas, Kevin
87FtLaud-19
88EastLAS/ProC-2
88PrWill/Star-15
89AAA/CMC-24
89AAA/ProC-18
89Colum/CMC-17
89Colum/Pol-12
89Colum/ProC-737
90AlbanyDG/Best-12
90B-440
90Classic/Up-30
90ColClip/CMC-17
90ColClip/ProC-691
90Colla/Maas-Set
90F-641R
90F/Up-113
90Leaf/II-446
90S-606RP
90S/100Ris-27
90T/Tr-63T
90T/TVYank-53
90UD-70
91B-158
91Classic/200-130
91Classic/I-63
91Classic/I-NO
91Classic/III-51
91CollAB-21
91D-554
91F-672
91F/Ultra-238
91JDeanSig-23
91KingB/Discs-3
91Leaf/II-393
91Leaf/Stud-96
91MajorLg/Pins-2
91OPC-435
91OPC-4RB
91OPC/Premier-74
91Panini/St-264
91Post-30
91Post/Can-20
91S-600
91S/100RisSt-40
91S/HotRook-2
91Seven/3DCoin-10NE
91T-435
91T-4RB
91T/90Debut-92
91T/CJMini/I-20
91T/StClub/I-282
91T/SU-22
91ToysRUs-16
91UD-375
91Woolwth/HL-13
92D/I-153
92F-236
92S/100SS-46
92S/II-613
92T-710
92UD-377
92UD-98

Maasberg, Gary
88Spartan/ProC-1041

Mabe, Robert
(Bobby)
59T-356
60T-288
91Crown/Orio-273

Mabe, Todd
85FtMyr-2

Mabee, Vic
77Ashvl
79Wausau-6

Mabry, John
91Hamil/ClBest-17
91Hamil/ProC-4053

Macaluso, Nick
88Martins/Star-25

MacArthur, Mark
90Hamil/Best-21
90Hamil/Star-15
91Savan/ClBest-19
91Savan/ProC-1660

Macauley, Drew
80Buffa-6
81Buffa-7

Macavage, Joe

87Watertn-26
88Augusta/ProC-372
MacCormack, Franc
78SanJose-4
MacDonald, Bill
51B-239
52T-138
MacDonald, Jim
81Tucson-23
82Tucson-12
MacDonald, Kevin
79Newar-11
MacDonald, Robert
88Myrtle/ProC-1191
89Knoxvl/Best-13
89Knoxvl/ProC-1139
89Knoxvl/Star-11
90A&AASingle/ProC-44
90Knoxvl/ProC-1247
90Knoxvl/Star-10
91D-636
91F/UltraUp-U61
91S/ToroBJ-32
91Syrac/LineD-508
91T/90Debut-93
91T/StClub/II-585
92D/II-588
92F-335
92S/100RisSt-46
92S/I-405
92T-87
MacDonald, Ronald
79Jacks-23
80Tidew-9
81Tidew-3
82Tidew-10
Mace, Jeff
83BurlR-21
83BurlR/LF-24
85Tulsa-24
88Boise/ProC-1616
89Boise/ProC-1977
Macfarlane, Mike
87Omaha-24
88D/Rook-55
88F/Up-U31
88S/Tr-76T
88Smok/Royals-17
88T/Tr-62T
89B-118
89D-416
89F-287
89S-319
89S/HotRook-97
89S/YS/I-13
89T-479
89T/Big-86
89UD-546
90D-498
90F-114
90Leaf/II-389
90OPC-202
90Publlnt/St-352
90T-202
90UD-307
91B-301
91D-313
91F-562
91F/Ultra-151
91Leaf/I-30
91OPC-638
91Panini/FrSt-275
91Pol/Royal-13
91S-839
91T-638
91T/StClub/I-15
91UD-570
92D/I-161
92F-161
92S/I-27
92T-42
92UD-497
MacFayden, Dan
31Exh/4-18
33Exh/4-9
33G-156
35G-2F
35G-4F
35G-7F
36Exh/4-1
37Exh/4-1
38Exh/4-1
91Conlon/Sport-215
R314
V353-87
Macha, Ken
78Colum
78T-483
81D-540
81F-167
82F-618
82OPC-282
82T-282
86Provigo-28CO
Macha, Mike
78Richm
Machado, Julian
89Penin/Star-12
Machado, Julio
87Clearw-21
89AAA/CMC-28
89Jacks/GS-11
90Classic/Up-31
90D-47
90D/Rook-41
90F/Up-U37
90Kahn/Mets-48
90OPC-684
90S/Tr-92T
90T-684
90T/89Debut-74
90T/TVMets-14
90UD-93
91B-50
91Brewer/MillB-15
91D-764
91F/Up-U31
91Leaf/I-247
91OPC-434
91Pol/Brew-13
91S/100RisSt-87
91T-434
91UD/Ext-716
91WIZMets-240
92D/I-262
92F-181
92S/I-353
92T-208
92UD-479
Machalec, Mark
84Butte-15
Machemer, Dave
77SLCity
78Cr/PCL-25
80Evansvl-16
81Toledo-13
82Toledo-14
85Beloit-26
86Stockton-14MG
87Stockton-3
88ElPaso/Best-6
89Denver/CMC-25
89Denver/ProC-37
90AAAGame/ProC-AAA26MG
90Denver/CMC-25MG
90Denver/ProC-641MG
Machuca, Freddy
82Danvl-19
Macias, Angel
91Eugene/ClBest-19
91Eugene/ProC-3724
Macias, Bob
82Amari-6
Macias, Henry
77Cedar
78Cedar
Mack, Connie
14CJ-12
15CJ-12
32Orbit/un-44
40PB-132
48Exh/HOF
50Callahan
51T/CM
60F-14
61F-123
63Bz/ATG-18
69Bz/Sm
80Laugh/FFeat-37
80SSPC/HOF
85West/2-39
86Conlon/1-18
88Conlon/HardC-4
89HOF/St-85
90BBWit-99
90HOF/St-45
91Conlon/Sport-45
91Conlon/Sport-46
91Conlon/Sport-47
92Conlon/Sport-439
92Conlon/Sport-599
BF2-36
D329-107
D350/2-105
E104
E223
E96
E98
M101/4-107
M101/5-105
M116
N172
R305
R308-188
R311/Leath
R312/M
R423-67
T208
V100
V355-110
WG1-67
WG2-33
WG5-26
WG6-25
Mack, Earle
92Conlon/Sport-453
Mack, Henry
77Spartan
Mack, Jerry
86Kenosha-14
Mack, Joseph
N172
Mack, Quinn
88WPalmB/Star-16
89Jaxvl/Best-14
89Jaxvl/ProC-153
90Indianap/CMC-16
90Indianap/ProC-299
91Indianap/LineD-188
91Indianap/ProC-475
Mack, Raymond
89Wythe/Star-21
90Pulaski/ProC-3090
91Macon/ClBest-4
91Macon/ProC-858
Mack, Shane
85Beaum-4
85T-398OLY
86Beaum-16
87D/Rook-42
87LasVegas-18
87Sf/Rook-31
87T/Tr-69T
88D-411
88F-590
88LasVegas/CMC-10
88LasVegas/ProC-233
88OPC-283
88S-414
88S/YS/II-36
88Smok/Padres-16
88T-548
89D-538
89S-270
89UD-182
90Classic/III-17
90D/BestAL-122
90Leaf/I-136
90T/Tr-64T
91B-326
91D-320
91F-618
91F/Ultra-191
91Leaf/I-40
91Leaf/Stud-88
91OPC-672
91S-284
91T-672
91T/StClub/I-259
91UD-188
92Classic/I-55
92D/I-345
92F-210
92S/I-284
92S/Prev-6
92T-164
92UD-428
Mack, Tony Lynn
(Toby)
83Redwd-17
85Cram/PCL-6
86Edmon-20
87MidldA-19
88SanAn/Best-5
89Miami/II/Star-12
MacKanin, Pete
74OPC-597R
74T-597R
76OPC-287
76SSPC-324
76T-287
77OPC-260
77T-156
78T-399
79BK/P-17
81F-565
81T-509
82D-354
82F-556
82T-438
83OKCty-12
84Iowa-12
86Peoria-17MG
88Iowa/CMC-24
88Iowa/ProC-543
88Peoria/Ko-35M
89AAA/ProC-43
89Iowa/CMC-25
89Iowa/ProC-1707
90Nashvl/CMC-24MG
90Nashvl/ProC-249MG
91AAAGame/ProC-AAA24MG
91Nashvl/LineD-274MG
91Nashvl/ProC-2172MG
91Pac/SenLg-66
MacKay, Bill
83Ander-1
MacKay, Joey
83Greens-25
84Greens-8
MacKenzie, Gordon
77Jaxvl
83Evansvl-22
84Evansvl-4
89Phoenix/CMC-25
89Phoenix/ProC-1504
MacKenzie, Kenneth P.
60T-534
61T-496
62T-421
63T-393
64T-297
91WIZMets-239
MacKenzie, Shaun
86Cram/PCL-20
87Everett-20
Mackey, Biz
74Laugh/Black-27
86Negro/Frit-91
90Negro/Star-4
Mackie, Bart
81Batavia-9
82Wausau-6
Mackie, Scott
89Miami/I/Star-12
MacKiewicz, Felix
48Sommer-16
MacKinnon, Tim
88Boise/ProC-1629
Macko, Joe
90Mother/Rang-28EQMG
Macko, Steve
80T-676R
80Wichita-18
81D-535
81T-381R
MacLeod, Kevin
88SoOreg/ProC-1709
89Modesto/Cal-273
90Huntsvl/Best-8
Maclin, Lonnie
88StPete/Star-14
89Spring/Best-25
90StPete/Star-14
91Louisvl/LineD-239
91Louisvl/ProC-2928
MacMillan, Darrell
89Boise/ProC-1986
90Erie/Star-14
MacNeil, Tim
88Butte-4
89Gaston/ProC-1024
89Gaston/Star-11
90Miami/II/Star-15
Macon, Max
90Target-468
MacPhail, Larry
89Rini/Dodg-20
MacPherson, Bruce
78OrlTw
80Toledo-4
81Toledo-7
82RochR-3
Macrina, Eric
91SLCity/ProC-3218
Macu, Andres
90Kissim/DIMD-15
Macullar, James
N172
MacWhorter, Keith
81Pawtu-4
81T-689R
83Pawtu-8
84Maine-21
Macy, Frank
82Iowa-30
Madden, Bob
76AppFx
77AppFx
79QuadC-17
Madden, Michael
(Kid)
N172
N526
Madden, Mike
81ElPaso-14
82Vanco-14
83T/Tr-64T
84D-161
84F-232
84Mother/Ast-25
84Nes/792-127
84T-127
85T-479
86Pol/Ast-18
86T-691
Madden, Morris
83VeroB-8
86GlenF-13
87Toledo-18
87Toledo/TCMA-15
88BuffB/CMC-6
88BuffB/Polar-8
88BuffB/ProC-1466
89AAA/CMC-11
89S/HotRook-32
90Albuq/CMC-5
90Albuq/ProC-340
90Albuq/Trib-19
Madden, Scott
86Clearw-16
88Reno/Cal-273
Madden, Thomas
E254
E270/2
M116
Maddern, Clarence
49B-152
52Mother-44
53Mother-34
Maddon, Joe
76QuadC
85MidldA-10
86MidldA-14MG
Maddox, Elliott
71MLB/St-545
71OPC-11
71T-11
72OPC-277
72T-277
72T/Cloth-21
73OPC-658
73T-658
74OPC-401
74T-401
75Ho-90
75K-9
75OPC-113
75T-113
75T/M-113
76OPC-503
76SSPC-451
76T-503

77T-332
78Ho-133
78T-442
79OPC-28
79T-69
80OPC-357
80T-707
81D-397
81F-326
81OPC-299
81T-299
90Swell/Great-109
91Crown/Orio-274
91WIZMets-241

Maddox, Garry
73OPC-322
73T-322
74OPC-178
74T-178
74T/St-107
75Ho-43
75Ho/Twink-43
75K-37
75OPC-240
75T-240
75T/M-240
76OPC-38
76T-38
77BurgChef-167
77K-37
77OPC-42
77T-520
78Ho-40
78K-28
78OPC-93
78T-610
78Wiffle/Discs-42
79BK/P-20
79K-16
79OPC-245
79T-470
80BK/P-10
80OPC-198
80T-380
81Coke
81D-55
81F-19
81F/St-70
81OPC-160
81T-160
81T/HT
81T/St-204
82D-315
82F-248
82F/St-57
82OPC-20
82T-20
82T/St-73
83D-63
83F-164
83OPC-41
83T-615
84D-305
84F-39
84F/St-122
84Nes/792-755
84OPC-187
84Phill/TastyK-39
84T-755
84T/St-123
85CIGNA-11
85D-137
85F-259
85OPC-235
85Phill/TastyK-38
85T-235
85T/St-121
86D-407
86F-445
86OPC-362
86Phill/TastyK-31
86T-585
86T/St-117
88Phill/TastyK-39ANN
90Phill/TastyK-36BC

Maddox, Jerry
78Richm
79Richm-6

Maddox, Leland
87Madis-13

Maddox, Nicholas
10Domino-73
12Sweet/Pin-141
D322
E104
E254
E270/2
E90/1
E95
M116
T205
T206

Maddux, Greg
86Pittsfld-14
87Berg/Cubs-31
87D-36RR
87D/Rook-52
87F/Up-U68
87Leaf-36RR
87T/Tr-70T
88Berg/Cubs-31
88D-539
88D/Best-82
88D/Cubs/Bk-539
88F-423
88OPC-361
88Peoria/Ko-21
88Peoria/Ko-34M
88T-361
88T/St-59
89B-284
89Cadaco-33
89Classic-121
89D-373
89D/AS-56
89D/Best-37
89F-431
89F/BBMVP's-24
89F/Rec-5
89F/Superstar-28
89Mara/Cubs-31
89OPC-240
89Panini/St-49
89RedFoley/St-77
89S-119
89S/HotStar-48
89S/YS/I-39
89Sf-108
89T-240
89T/Mini-4
89T/St-48
89UD-241
90B-27
90Classic/Up-32
90Cub/Mara-13
90D-158
90D/BestNL-14
90F-37
90Leaf/I-25
90MLBPA/Pins-49
90OPC-715
90Panini/St-237
90Peoria/Team-20M
90Publlnt/St-198
90S-403
90Sf-211
90T-715
90T/Big-204
90T/DH-41
90T/Mini-50
90T/St-51
90T/TVCub-12
90UD-213
91B-426
91Classic/200-68
91Classic/III-52
91Cub/Mara-31
91D-374
91F-426
91F/Ultra-64
91Leaf/I-127
91OPC-35
91Panini/FrSt-50
91Panini/St-43
91Panini/Top15-98
91S-317
91T-35
91T/StClub/I-126
91UD-115
92D/II-520
92F-386
92S/I-269
92T-580
92UD-353

Maddux, Mike
85Cram/PCL-38
85Phill/TastyK-42
86Phill/TastyK-x
86Portl-15
87D-535
87F-179
87Maine/TCMA-5
87Phill/TastyK-44
87T-553
88F-309
88Phill/TastyK-16
88T-756
89B-391
89D-487
89F-576
89OPC-39
89Phill/TastyK-19
89S-393
89T-39
89T/Big-74
89UD-338
90Albuq/CMC-8
90Albuq/ProC-341
90Albuq/Trib-20
90D-312
90OPC-154
90Publlnt/St-246
90T-154
91F/UltraUp-U113
91Leaf/II-300
92D/II-450
92F-613
92S/I-313
92T-438
92UD-330

Mader, Perry
83Kinston/Team-13

Madison, Dave
52T-366
53Glen
53T-99
91T/Arc53-99

Madison, Helene
33SK-37

Madison, Scott
83Albuq-12
86Nashvl-16
87Omaha-17
88Smok/Royals-18
88T/Tr-63T
89AAA/ProC-2
89Nashvl/CMC-21
89Nashvl/ProC-1271
89Nashvl/Team-14

Madlock, Bill
74OPC-600R
74T-600R
75Ho-125
75Ho/Twink-125
75OPC-104
75T-104
75T/M-104
76Crane-31
76Ho-100
76K-20
76MSA/Disc
76OPC-191LL
76OPC-640
76SSPC-309
76T-191LL
76T-640
77BurgChef-198
77Ho-118
77K-43
77OPC-1LL
77OPC-56
77T-1LL
77T-250
77T/CS-25
78Ho-117
78OPC-89
78T-410
78Tastee/Discs-15
79Ho-138
79OPC-96
79Pol/Giants-18
79T-195
80OPC-30
80T-55
81Coke
81D-252
81F-381
81OPC-137
81T-715
81T/St-213
82D-653
82Drake-23
82F-485
82F/St-77
82K-55
82OPC-365
82PermaGr/CC-7
82T-161LL
82T-365
82T-696TL
82T/St-1
82T/St-83
83D-311
83D/AAS-30
83Drake-15
83F-309
83K-18
83OPC-335
83PermaGr/CC-8
83T-291TL
83T-645
83T/Gloss40-26
83T/St-275
84D-113
84D-20DK
84D/AAS-33
84D/Champs-22
84Drake-20
84F-253
84F/St-6
85FunFoodPin-31
84MiltBrad-16
84Nes/792-131LL
84Nes/792-250
84Nes/792-696TL
84Nes/792-701LL
84OPC-250
84Ralston-26
84Seven-11E
84T-131LL
84T-250
84T-696TL
84T-701LL
84T/Cereal-26
84T/Gloss40-19
84T/St-131
84T/St-99
84T/St/Box-12
84T/Super-8
85D-200
85F-468
85F/LimEd-19
85Leaf-185
85OPC-157
85Seven-11E
85T-560
85T/St-122
86Coke/Dodg-17
86D-617
86F-135
86F/Mini-29
86Leaf-238
86OPC-47
86Pol/Dodg-12
86Sf-131M
86Sf-181M
86Sf-58M
86Sf-88
86T-470
86T/St-12NLCS
86T/St-70
86TrueVal-23
86Woolwth-19
87D-155
87D/OD-78
87F-445
87F/Mini-65
87F/St-73
87F/Up-U69
87Leaf-120
87Mother/Dodg-8
87OPC-276
87Pol/Dodg-5
87RedFoley/St-109
87Sf-130
87T-734
87T/St-67
87T/Tr-71T
88D-496
88F-63
88Leaf-232
88OPC-145
88S-445
88Sf-123
88T-145
88T/St-266
89Pac/SenLg-214
89T/SenLg-71
89TM/SenLg-69
90EliteSenLg-116
90Target-469

Madrid, Alex
85Beloit-18
87Denver-10
88Denver/CMC-3
88Denver/ProC-1251
89D-604
89Phill/TastyK-20
89S/HotRook-58
89ScrWB/CMC-5
89ScrWB/ProC-720

Madrigal, Victor
91Gaston/ClBest-8
91Gaston/ProC-2685
91Single/ClBest-266

Madril, Bill
91Elmira/ClBest-10
91Elmira/ProC-3274
91WinHaven/ProC-494

Madril, Mike
83Redwd-18
85Cram/PCL-3
86MidldA-15

Madsen, Erik
89GreatF-24
90Yakima/Team-9

Madsen, Lance
89AubAs/ProC-2164
90Osceola/Star-18
91Jacks/LineD-567
91Jacks/ProC-933

Maebe, Art
80Clinton-11

Maeda, Koji
88SanJose/Cal-133
88SanJose/ProC-108

Maema, Takashi
90Gate/ProC-3358

Maffett, Chris
91Burllnd/ProC-3301

Mag, Rick
88Bristol/ProC-1862

Magadan, Dave
86Tidew-17
87Classic-19
87D-575
87D/Rook-34
87F-648R
87F/Up-U70
87Sf/Rook-10
87Sf/Rook-3
87T-512FS
87T/GlossRk-9
88Classic/Blue-230
88D-323
88D/Mets/Bk-323
88F-141
88Kahn/Mets-29
88Leaf-108
88MSA/Disc-13
88OPC-58
88RedFoley/St-51
88S-41
88S/YS/I-23
88Sf-83
88T-58
88T/St-104
89B-384
89D-408
89D/Best-264
89F-41
89Kahn/Mets-29
89OPC-81
89S-312
89T-655
89T/Big-71
89UD-388
90D-383
90D/BestNL-56
90F-210
90Kahn/Mets-10
90Leaf/II-330
90OPC-135
90Panini/St-300
90Publlnt/St-138
90S-46
90Sf-173
90T-135
90T/Big-24

90T/St-99
90T/TVMets-26
90UD-243
91B-484
91Classic/200-100
91Classic/I-67
91Classic/II-T72
91D-17DK
91D-362
91D/SuperDK-17DK
91F-153
91F/Ultra-223
91Kahn/Mets-10
91Leaf/I-20
91Leaf/Stud-208
91MajorLg/Pins-76
91MooTown-13
91OPC-480
91Panini/FrSt-79
91Panini/St-81
91Panini/Top15-3
91Post/Can-4
91S-190
91S/100SS-34
91T-480
91T/StClub/I-210
91UD-177
91WIZMets-242
92D/I-45
92F-510
92S/I-201
92T-745
92UD-112

Magallanes, Everado
88Kinston/Star-16
89Canton/Best-23
89Canton/ProC-1309
89Canton/Star-13
90ColoSp/CMC-13
90ColoSp/ProC-42
91B-61
91ColoSp/LineD-91
91ColoSp/ProC-2192
92T/91Debut-113

Magallanes, William
(Bobby)
86AppFx-13
90SanBern/Best-12
90SanBern/Cal-107
90SanBern/ProC-2640
91SanBern/ClBest-18
91SanBern/ProC-1995
91Single/ClBest-263

Magallanes, Willie
88BirmB/Best-25
90BirmB/Best-11
90BirmB/ProC-1396
90Foil/Best-125

Magee, Lee
15CJ-147
90Target-470
D328-103
D329-108
D350/2-106
E135-103
M101/4-108
M101/5-106

Magee, Sherry
11Helmar-147
12Sweet/Pin-128
14CJ-108
14Piedmont/St-34
15CJ-108
92Conlon/Sport-449
BF2-53
D328-104
D329-109
E101
E102
E135-104
E300
E92
E94
L1-123
M101/4-109
M116
S81-98
T202
T205
T206
T213/blue
T215/brown
T216
T222
T3-31

Magee, Warren
87Clearw-14
88EastLAS/ProC-33
88Reading/ProC-871
89Reading/Best-2
89Reading/ProC-674
89Reading/Star-16
90Reading/Best-9
90Reading/ProC-1218
90Reading/Star-17

Maggio, Aggie
79WHave-29M
80WHave-22

Magistri, Greg
85Elmira-13

Maglie, Sal
51B-127
52B-66
52BR
52RM-NL14
52StarCal/L-78C
52TipTop
53B/Col-96
53RM-NL8
54B-105
54NYJour
55B-95
55Gol/Giants-18
55RM-NL6
57T-5
58T-43
59T-309
60NuCard-70
60T-456C
61NuCard-470
67T/Test/RSox-17CO
79TCMA-256
88Pac/Leg-85
89NiagFls/Pucko-29
89Rini/Dodg-11
89Swell-99
90Swell/Great-38
90Target-471
91Swell/Great-59
91T/Arc53-303
Exh47
PM10/Sm-100

Magnante, Michael
(Mike)
89Memphis/Best-21
89Memphis/ProC-1198
89Memphis/Star-15
90Omaha/CMC-6
90Omaha/ProC-64
91Omaha/LineD-340
91Omaha/ProC-1033
92D/II-706
92S/II-739
92T-597
92T/91Debut-114

Magnante, Rick
89NiagFls/Pucko-25

Magner, Rich
75Water
79Albuq-17

Magnuson, Jim
72T-597

Magnusson, Brett
88GreatF-3
89Star/Wax-30
89VeroB/Star-16
90AS/Cal-2
90Bakers/Cal-254
91SanAn/LineD-537
91SanAn/ProC-2988

Magoon, George
90Target-472

Magrane, Joe
86ArkTr-12
87Classic/Up-117
87D/Rook-40
87F/Slug-24
87F/Up-U71
87Louisvl-25
87Sf/Rook-11
87T/Tr-72T
88Classic/Blue-240
88D-140
88D/Best-100
88F-40
88Louisvl-31
88OPC-380
88Panini/St-385
88RedFoley/St-52
88S-94
88S/YS/I-9
88Sf-128
88Smok/Card-6
88T-380
88T/Gloss60-40
88T/JumboR-20
88T/St-51
88ToysRUs-15
89B-432
89Classic-148
89D-201
89D/Best-131
89F-455
89F/LL-24
89OPC-264
89Panini/St-178
89S-460
89Smok/Cards-12
89T-657
89T/Big-203
89T/LJN-47
89T/Mini-35
89UD-103
90B-183
90Classic-145
90D-13DK
90D-163
90D/BestNL-46
90D/Learning-34
90D/SuperDK-13DK
90F-252
90F/ASIns-5
90KMart/SS-12
90Leaf/I-11
90OPC-406AS
90OPC-578
90Panini/St-346
90PublInt/St-220
90PublInt/St-267
90S-17
90Sf-151
90Smok/Card-12
90T-406AS
90T-578
90T/Big-271
90T/Coins-52
90T/DH-42
90T/Gloss60-36
90T/Mini-76
90T/St-41
90T/TVAS-64
90T/TVCard-16
90UD-242
91Classic/200-29
91D-295
91F-638
91F/Ultra-291
91Leaf/Stud-235
91OPC-185
91Panini/FrSt-38
91Panini/St-31
91S-575
91T-185
91T/StClub/I-85
91UD-465
92D/II-767
92T-783

Magrann, Tom
86Hagers-8
87Miami-24
89Canton/Best-10
89Canton/ProC-1313
89Canton/Star-14
90ColoSp/CMC-14
90ColoSp/ProC-40
90D-374
90T/89Debut-75
91BuffB/LineD-32
91BuffB/ProC-545

Magria, Javier
89Welland/Pucko-18
90Miami/II/Star-16

Magrini, Paul
91Bristol/ClBest-27
91Bristol/ProC-3598

Magrini, Pete
66T-558R

Maguire, Fred
29Exh/4-2
31Exh/4-2
33Exh/4-1
R316

Maguire, Mike
91Welland/ClBest-22
91Welland/ProC-3569

Mahaffey, Art
60T-138
61Bz-1
61T-433
61T/St-57
62Bz
62Exh
62J-199
62P-199
62P/Can-199
62Salada-112
62Shirriff-112
62T-550
62T/bucks
62T/St-171
63Bz-35
63Exh
63F-54
63J-183
63P-183
63Salada-10
63T-385
63T-7LL
63T/SO
64PhilBull-16
64T-104
65T-446
66T-570
Exh47
WG10-32
WG9-32

Mahaffey, Leroy
33G-196
34DS-10
35BU-15
35Exh/4-14
35G-1B
35G-2B
35G-6B
35G-7B
92Conlon/Sport-603
R308-175

Mahambitov, Igor
89EastLDD/ProC-DD20

Mahan, George
76Wmsprt

Mahaney, Dan
N172

Mahar, Eddie
87Syrac/TCMA-32

Mahlberg, Greg
77Tucson
78Cr/PCL-3
79Tucson-15
80Charl-6
80T-673R
81Indianap-12
88CharWh/Best-3
89CharWh/Best-25
89CharWh/ProC-1755
90Peoria/Team-31MG
91Geneva/ClBest-19MG
91Geneva/ProC-4234MG

Mahler, Mickey
78T-703R
79T-331
80Port-10
81SLCity-8
82Spokane-4
84Louisvl-28
85F/Up-U77
85Indianap-16
86F/Up-U70
86T/Tr-68T
87Louisvl-18
89T/SenLg-82
89TM/SenLg-70
91Pac/SenLg-37

Mahler, Rick
78Richm
80Richm-11
81Pol/Atl-42
82BK/Lids-16
82D-349
82F-440
82Pol/Atl-42
82T-126TL
82T-579
83D-527
83F-141
83OPC-76
83T-76
84Pol/Atl-42
85D-385
85F-332
85Ho/Braves-14
85OPC-79
85Pol/Atl-42
85T-79
85T/St-26
86D-21DK
86D-77
86D/DKsuper-21
86F-521
86Leaf-21DK
86OPC-39
86Pol/Atl-42
86T-437
86T/St-43
87D-190
87D/OD-41
87F-520
87OPC-242
87Smok/Atl-5
87T-242
87T/St-43
88D-389
88D/Best-114
88OPC-171
88Panini/St-239
88S-319
88T-706
89B-302
89D-222
89D/Best-286
89D/Tr-24
89F-595
89F/Up-85
89Kahn/Reds-42
89OPC-393
89Panini/St-35
89S-229
89S/Tr-79
89T-621
89T/St-29
89T/Tr-74T
89UD-74
89UD/Ext-760
90D-375
90F-425
90Kahn/Reds-15
90OPC-151
90PublInt/St-34
90Richm25Ann/Team-15
90S-87
90T-151
90T/St-139
90UD-220
91F-71
91Leaf/II-284
91OPC-363
91S-464
91T-363
91UD-613

Mahomes, Pat
89Kenosha/ProC-1067
89Kenosha/Star-12
90A&AASingle/ProC-141
90Visalia/Cal-60
90Visalia/ProC-2149
91OrlanSR/LineD-485
91OrlanSR/ProC-1846
92D/II-403RR
92T-676R

Mahoney, Jim
73OPC-356CO
73T-356CO
74OPC-221CO
74T-221CO
77Charl/MG
78Salem
80Port-6MG
81GlenF-22
88Portl/CMC-24
88Portl/ProC-650

Mahoney, Robert
52T-58

Mahony, Dan
91Erie/ClBest-7
91Erie/ProC-4072

Maietta, Bub
89LittleSun-7

Maietta, Ron

89Bristol/Star-15
90Bristol/ProC-3158
90Bristol/Star-16
Mails, John
E120
E121/120
E220
V100
W501-23
Mails, Walter
(Duster)
21Exh-99
28Exh/PCL-20
90Target-473
WG7-27
Main, Forrest
52T-397
53T-198
91T/Arc53-198
Main, Kevin
87CharWh-16
Mains, Willard
N172
Maisel, George
15CJ-158
21Exh-100
T222
WG4-14
Maitland, Mike
79AppFx-20
81GlenF-5
83GlenF-14
Majer, Steffen
90StPete/Star-15
91ArkTr/ProC-1281
Majeski, Carl
91Idaho/ProC-4325
Majeski, Hank
(Henry)
41DP-120
48L-149
49B-127
50B-92
51B-12
51T/BB-2
52B-58
52T-112
55B-127
55Gol/Ind-18
55Salem
91Crown/Orio-275
Exh47
R346-23
Majia, Alfredo
79LodiD-4
Majtyka, Roy
63Pep/Tul
77Indianap-2
78Indianap-2
79Indianap-2
82Evansvl-25MG
83BirmB-25
85IntLgAS-22
85Richm-26MG
86Richm-13MG
87/Richm/Crown-6MG
87Richm/TCMA-21
90BirmDG/Best-21MG
91Macon/ClBest-28MG
91Macon/ProC-881MG
91SALAS/ProC-SAL34MG
Makarewicz, Scott
89AubAs/ProC-2163
90FSLAS/Star-12
90Osceola/Star-19
91Jacks/LineD-568
91Jacks/ProC-929
Makemson, Jay
87Oneonta-18
88Oneonta/ProC-2063
89Penin/Star-13
Maki, Timothy
82BurlR-6
83BurlR-9
83BurlR/LF-19
Maksudian, Michael
(Mike)
88MidwLAS/GS-48
89Miami/II/Star-15
90Foil/Best-111
90Knoxvl/Best-11
90Knoxvl/ProC-1258
90Knoxvl/Star-11
91Syrac/LineD-509
91Syrac/ProC-2494
Malarcher, Dave
74Laugh/Black-20
86Negro/Frit-108
88Conlon/NegAS-9
Malarkey, William
C46-73
T206
Malave, Benito
86Wausau-13
87StPete-22
88ArkTr/GS-17
Malave, Jose
90Elmira/Pucko-11
Malave, Omar
85Kingst-17
86Ventura-12
87Knoxvl-4
88Myrtle/ProC-1181
89Knoxvl/Best-14
89Knoxvl/ProC-1127
89Knoxvl/Star-13
Malay, Charlie
90Target-1017
Malchesky, Tom
88Hamil/ProC-1741
89Spring/Best-19
Malden, Chris
79LodiD-18
Maldonado, Al
90Kissim/DIMD-16
Maldonado, Candy
79Clinton
81Albuq/TCMA-21
82Albuq-21
83Albuq-14
83D-262
83F-212
83Pol/Dodg-20
84D-93
84Nes/792-244
84Pol/Dodg-20
84T-244
85Coke/Dodg-19
85D-250
85F-376
85T-523
85T/St-81
86F-136
86F/Up-U71
86Mother/Giants-9
86T-87
86T/Tr-69T
87D-327
87D/OD-102
87F-279
87F/AwardWin-23
87Leaf-216
87Mother/SFG-7
87OPC-335
87Sf-78
87T-335
87T/Mini-37
87T/St-94
88D-391
88D/Best-247
88F-89
88F/BB/AS-22
88F/Mini-118
88F/St-129
88KingB/Disc-16
88Leaf-239
88Mother/Giants-7
88OPC-190
88Panini/St-428
88S-54
88Sf-126
88T-190
88T/Big-35
88T/St-95
88T/UK-44
89B-478
89Bimbo/Discs-2
89D-177
89F-333
89Mother/Giants-7
89OPC-269
89Panini/St-221
89RedFoley/St-78
89S-47
89T-495
89T/Big-197
89T/LJN-56
89T/St-89
89UD-502
90B-335
90Classic/III-34
90D-611
90D/BestAL-132
90D/Learning-42
90F-62
90F/Up-U93
90Leaf/II-338
90OPC-628
90PublInt/St-75
90S-138
90S/Tr-8T
90T-628
90T/Big-248
90T/Tr-65T
90Target-474
90UD-136
90UD/Ext-780
91Brewer/MillB-16
91D-391MVP
91D-480
91F-373
91Leaf/II-434
91Leaf/Stud-72
91OPC-723
91Panini/FrSt-220
91Panini/St-179
91Pol/Brew-14
91RedFoley/St-60
91S-93
91S/100SS-76
91S/RookTr-28T
91S/ToroBJ-29
91T-723
91T/StClub/II-350
91T/Tr-74T
91UD-138
91UD/Ext-739
91UD/FinalEd-28F
92D/II-664
92F-336
92S/II-591
92T-507
92UD-393
Maldonado, Carlos
88Bristol/ProC-1863
90A&AASingle/ProC-35
90Foil/Best-117
90Memphis/Best-21
90Memphis/ProC-1007
90Memphis/Star-15
91Fayette/ClBest-20
91Fayette/ProC-1179
91Omaha/LineD-341
91Omaha/ProC-1034
91T/90Debut-94
Maldonado, Felix
87Elmira/Black-30
Maldonado, Jerry
89Reno/Cal-264AGM
90Reno/Cal-290AGM
Maldonado, Johnny
89Sumter/ProC-1105
Maldonado, Pete
87Spartan-2
88Clearw/Star-18
Maldonado, Phil
87Idaho-3
88Durham/Star-11
89Durham/Team-13
89Durham/Star-13
90Durham/Team-22
Maler, James
(Jim)
80Spokane-14
81Spokane-22
83SLCity-17
83T-54
84Nes/792-461
84T-461
85OKCty-20
86OKCty-11
Malespin, Gus
79Elmira-19
82Spring-10
83Spring/LF-25
Maley, Dennis
83Miami-27
Malinak, Michael
(Mike)
87SLCity/Taco-2
88Cedar/ProC-1164
89Cedar/ProC-911
89Cedar/Star-29
Malinoski, Chris
91Rockford/ClBest-20
91Rockford/ProC-2055
Malinosky, Tony
90Target-475
Malkin, John
81Watlo-19
82Watlo/B-12
82Watlo/C-20
83BuffB-10
84Cram/PCL-145
85Cram/PCL-247
Malkmus, Robert
58T-356
59T-151
60T-251
61T-530
Mallea, Luis
88AppFx/ProC-138
Mallee, Johnny
91Martins/ClBest-8
91Martins/ProC-3463
Mallette, Malcolm
(Mal)
52Park-60
90Target-1018
Malley, Mike
89Greens/ProC-424
90CharWh/Best-3
90CharWh/ProC-2236
91Kinston/ClBest-6
91Kinston/ProC-318
91Watertn/ClBest-10
91Watertn/ProC-3365
Mallicoat, Rob
85Osceola/Team-9
86ColumAst-17
86Tucson-11
87ColAst/ProC-22
87SLAS-15
88F-452
88S/YS/II-10
89ColMud/ProC-131
89ColMud/Star-17
91Jacks/LineD-569
91Jacks/ProC-925
92D/II-673
92F-440
92S/II-819
92T-501
Mallinak, Mel
87Hagers-24
Mallon, Jim
90Welland/Pucko-32MG
Mallory, Sheldon
78Syrac
79Tacom-21
Mallory, Trevor
91Classic/DP-50
91FrRow/DP-53
Malloy, Bob
87Gaston-11
88Tulsa-22
89TexLAS/GS-37
89Tulsa/GS-15
89Tulsa/Team-13
90Foil/Best-43
90Jaxvl/Best-19
90Jaxvl/ProC-1370
Malmberg, Harry
60HenryH-2
61Union
Malone, Charles
(Chuck)
86Cram/PCL-136
87Clearw-4
88BBAmer-6
88EastLAS/ProC-34
88Reading/ProC-869
89Reading/Best-3
89Reading/ProC-656
89Reading/Star-17
90B-144
90ScranWB/CMC-4
90ScranWB/ProC-596
91B-497
91F-404
91S-724RP
91S/Rook40-21
91ScranWB/LineD-488
91ScranWB/ProC-2534
91T/90Debut-95
91UD-649
Malone, Earl
88Boise/ProC-1617
Malone, Ed
47Signal
49B/PCL-31
50Remar
53Mother-20
Malone, Eddie
82Idaho-25
Malone, Jack
89Boise/ProC-1990
Malone, Kevin
80Batavia-19
88James/ProC-1893
Malone, Lew
90Target-476
Malone, Perce
(Pat)
32Orbit/num-13
32Orbit/un-45
33G-55
35G-2D
35G-4D
35G-7D
91Conlon/Sport-219
R305
R308-192
R316
V354-30
Malone, Rubio
79Wisco-18
Malone, Todd
89Oneonta/ProC-2122
90Foil/Best-18
90Greens/Best-1
90Greens/ProC-2659
90Greens/Star-13
90Oneonta/ProC-3368
91Greens/ProC-3054
Maloney, Chris
85Lynch-17
88Spring/Best-25
89ArkTr/GS-2CO
90Hamil/Best-4CO
90Hamil/Star-27CO
91Johnson/ClBest-29
91Johnson/ProC-3994MG
Maloney, Jim
61Kahn
61T-436
62Kahn
63FrBauer-13
63Kahn
63T-444
64Bz-19
64Kahn
64T-3LL
64T-420
64T-5LL
64T/Coins-158AS
64T/Coins-60
64T/S-34
64T/St-32
64T/SU
65Kahn
65T-530
65T/E-68
65T/trans-19
66Bz-45
66Kahn
66OPC-140
66T-140
66T/RO-93
67Bz-45
67Kahn
67OPC-80
67T-80
68Kahn
68T-425
68T/3D
69Kahn
69MB-164
69MLB/St-130
69MLBPA/Pin-50
69T-362
69T/St-26
70K-10
70MLB/St-29
70OPC-320
70T-320

71MLB/St-348
71OPC-645
71T-645
72MB-203
72T-645
78TCMA-10
Maloney, Kevin
89Clmbia/Best-28
89Clmbia/GS-5
Maloney, Mark
88Kinston/Star-17
Maloney, Rich
87Sumter-18
88Durham/Star-12
89Durham/Team-14
89Durham/Star-14
90Greenvl/Best-14
90Greenvl/ProC-1139
90Greenvl/Star-11
91Greenvl/ClBest-18
91Greenvl/LineD-210
91Greenvl/ProC-3012
Maloney, William A.
T206
WG3-28
Maloof, Jack
77Indianap-24
83Beaum-21
85Spok/Cram-12MG
91Wichita/LineD-625CO
91Wichita/ProC-2616CO
Malpeso, Dave
84Pawtu-17
85Pawtu-7
Malpica, Omar
91Princet/ClBest-3
91Princet/ProC-3527
Malseed, James
(Jim)
87Pocatel/Bon-10
88Fresno/Cal-12
88Fresno/ProC-1232
89SanJose/Best-22
89SanJose/Cal-223
89SanJose/ProC-437
89SanJose/Star-18
Maltzberger, Gordon
49B/PCL-12
Malzone, Frank
55B-302
56T-304
57T-355
58T-260
58T-481AS
59Armour-12
59T-220
59T-519M
59T-558AS
60Armour-13A
60Armour-13B
60Bz-12
60T-310
60T-557AS
60T/tatt-30
61Bz-9
61P-48
61T-173M
61T-445
61T/St-113
62Exh
62J-58
62P-58
62P/Can-58
62Salada-14
62Shirriff-14
62T-225
62T/bucks
62T/St-14
63Exh
63J-79
63P-79
63T-232
64T-60
64T/Coins-126AS
64T/Coins-7
64T/St-6
64T/SU
64T/tatt
64Wheat/St-27
65T-315
65T/E-37
66OPC-152
66T-152
78TCMA-177
80Elmira-37C
87Elmira/Black-31
Exh47
PM10/Sm-101
PM10/Sm-102
WG10-33
WG9-33
Malzone, John
91WinHaven/ClBest-20
91WinHaven/ProC-499
Mamaux, Albert L.
(Al)
16FleischBrd-59
90Target-477
BF2-91
D327
D328-105
D329-110
D350/2-107
E120
E121/80
E122
E135-105
M101/4-110
M101/5-107
W514-19
W515-2
W575
Mammola, Mark
91Boise/ClBest-13
91Boise/ProC-3873
Manabe, Bullet
88Fresno/Cal-21
88Fresno/ProC-1235
Manahan, Anthony
90Foil/Best-83
91Jaxvl/ProC-158
Manahan, Austin
89B-420
90A&AASingle/ProC-97
90Augusta/ProC-2473
90SALAS/Star-36
91B-527
91Salem/ClBest-6
91Salem/ProC-960
91Single/ClBest-218
Mancini, Joe
88Boise/ProC-1626
88Fresno/Cal-3
88Fresno/ProC-1247
89Boise/ProC-1991
Mancini, Pete
85Newar-21
Mancuso, August
(Gus)
33G-237
33G-41
35BU-67
35G-1K
35G-2A
35G-3B
35G-4A
35G-4B
35G-5B
35G-7A
35Wheat
36Exh/4-5
37Exh/4-5
38ONG/Pin-18
40PB-207
41DP-38
90Target-478
91Conlon/Sport-129
R303/A
R303/B
R310
R332-24
V353-41
V355-9
W754
Mancuso, Frank
84Omaha-28
85Omaha-4
Mancuso, Paul
83Wisco/LF-22
84Visalia-18
85Orlan-18
86Beaum-17
Manderbach, Gary
75Tidew/Team-16
Manderfield, Steve
77Newar
78Newar
79BurlB-25
80BurlB-8
82ElPaso-15
Mandeville, Bob
86Peoria-18
Mandia, Sam
90StCath/ProC-3459
91Myrtle/ClBest-9
91Myrtle/ProC-2943
Mandl, Steve
89James/ProC-2151
Manering, Mark
87FtLaud-27
Manfre, Mike
83Cedar-20
83Cedar/LF-20
84Cedar-21
86Vermont-12
87Nashvl-14
Manfred, Jim
91Pittsfld/ClBest-18
91Pittsfld/ProC-3419
Mangham, Eric
87Bakers-19
88VeroB/Star-13
89SanAn/Best-3
91Toledo/LineD-591
91Toledo/ProC-1945
Mangham, Mark
85Osceola/Team-10
Mangiardi, Paul
83Erie-1
Mangrum, Lloyd
52Wheat
Mangual, Angel
70T-654R
71OPC-317R
71T-317R
72OPC-62
72T-62
73OPC-625
73T-625
75OPC-452
75T-452
75T/M-452
76SSPC-503
76Tucson-8
Mangual, Jose
(Pepe)
75OPC-616R
75T-616R
75T/M-616R
76OPC-164
76SSPC-335
76T-164
77T-552
78Tidew
79SLCity-22
80SLCity-22
81SLCity-22
82Spokane-22
91WIZMets-243
Mangum, Leo
33G-162
V353-92
Mangum, Wade
83Idaho-9
Manicchia, Bryan
90Princet/DIMD-15
91Batavia/ClBest-16
91Batavia/ProC-3481
91Spartan/ClBest-8
91Spartan/ProC-893
Manion, Clyde
33G-80
V354-35
Manion, George A.
T206
Mankowski, Phil
77T-477R
78BK/T-17
78T-559
79T-93
80T-216
81Tidew-6
82Tidew-9
91WIZMets-244
Mann, Bill
88Jaxvl/Best-15
Mann, Dave
61Union
Mann, Fred
N172
N690
Mann, Garth
(Red)
46Sunbeam
47Signal
47Sunbeam
Mann, Kelly
86Geneva-17
87Peoria-25
88CLAS/Star-30
88WinSalem/Star-9
89CharlK-9
89SLAS-4
90A&AASingle/ProC-63
90D-46RR
90F-642R
90Foil/Best-157
90Greenvl/Best-9
90Greenvl/ProC-1132
90Greenvl/Star-12
90HotRook/St-29
90OPC-744
90Richm/Bob-21
90S-627RP
90S/100Ris-56
90T-744
90T/89Debut-76
90UD-33
91D-736
91Leaf/Stud-147
91Richm/LineD-434
91Richm/ProC-2571
Mann, Les
D328-106
D329-111
D350/2-108
E135-106
M101/4-111
M101/5-108
W514-49
Mann, Scott
86WPalmB-23
87Jaxvl-8
88Jaxvl/ProC-964
Mann, Skip
79LodiD-5
81VeroB-10
Mann, Tom
90Hunting/ProC-3279
91Peoria/ClBest-7
91Peoria/ProC-1339
Manning, Dick
83GlenF-24
Manning, Henry
88CapeCod/Sum-150
Manning, James
N172
N284
Manning, Max
86Negro/Frit-54
91Negro/Lewis-13
Manning, Melvin
(Al)
77BurlB
78BurlB
81ElPaso-3
Manning, Rick
76Ho-12
76Ho/Twink-12
76OPC-275
76SSPC-529
76T-275
77BurgChef-56
77Ho-53
77K-15
77OPC-190
77Pep-12
77T-115
78Ho-91
78OPC-151
78T-11
79Ho-76
79OPC-220
79T-425
80OPC-292
80T-564
80T/S-44
81D-202
81F-403
81OPC-308
81T-308
81T/SO-19
81T/St-69
82D-85
82F-374
82F/St-195
82OPC-202
82T-202
82T/St-179
82Wheat/Ind
83D-198
83F-413
83OPC-147
83T-757
83T/St-60
83T/Tr-65
83Wheat/Ind-20
84D-170
84F-205
84Gard-11
84Nes/792-128
84OPC-128
84Pol/Brew-28
84T-128
84T/St-299
85D-237
85F-586
85Gard-11
85OPC-389
85Pol/Brew-28
85T-603
85T/St-291
86D-368
86F-493
86OPC-49
86Pol/Brew-28
86T-49
87D-521
87F-349
87OPC-196
87Pol/Brew-28
87T-706
88D-486
88F-168
88S-593
88T-441
89Pac/SenLg-86
89T/SenLg-39
89TM/SenLg-71
90EliteSenLg-73
Manning, Rube
T204
T206
T3-107
Manning, Tony
75SanAn
Manning, Vida
81ArkTr-23M
Mannion, Greg
90Salinas/Cal-132
Manon, Ramon
87PrWill-23
89FtLaud/Star-14
90Albany/Best-3
90Albany/ProC-1175
90Albany/Star-10
90Cedar/Best-17
90Cedar/ProC-2316
90F/Up-124
91Cedar/ClBest-9
91FtLaud/ClBest-6
91FtLaud/ProC-2420
91T/90Debut-96
Manos, Pete Charles
79OkCty
Manrique, Fred
82Syrac-18
83Syrac-17
84Syrac-12
85Indianap-12
86Louisvl-18
87Coke/WS-5
87F/Up-U72
88Coke/WS-17
88D-493
88F-406
88Panini/St-57
88S-139
88T-437
88T/JumboR-6
88ToysRUs-16
89B-66
89D-489
89F-503

89OPC-108
89S-457
89T-108
89T/Big-84
89T/St-300
89UD-628
90D-165
90F-306
90Leaf/II-518
90OPC-242
90Panini/St-158
90PublInt/St-396
90S-166
90T-242
90T/Tr-66T
90UD-392

Mansalino, Doug
85Crm/PCL-192C

Manser
C46-59
E254

Manship, Ray
78Newar

Mansolino, Doug
89Vanco/ProC-575

Manti, Sam
89Penin/Star-14

Mantick, Dennis
78OrlTw
79Toledo-21

Mantilla, Felix
57SpicSpan/4x5-12
57T-188
58T-17
59T-157
60Lake
60SpicSpan-11
60T-19
61T-164
61T/St-44
62Salada-183
62Shirriff-183
62T-436
62T/bucks
62T/St-158
63J-198
63P-198
63T-447
64T-228
65OPC-29
65T-29
66T-557
66T/RO-112
67T-524
91WIZMets-245

Mantle, Mickey
51B-253
52B-101
52BR
52StarCal/L-70G
52T-311
52TipTop
53B/Col-44M
53B/Col-59
53Briggs
53SM
53T-82
54B-65
54DanDee
54NYJour
54RH
54SM
55Armour-13A
55Armour-13B
55B-202
55SM
56T-135
56YellBase/Pin-20
57T-407M
57T-95
58T-150
58T-418M
58T-487AS
59Bz
59HRDerby-12
59T-10
59T-461HL
59T-564AS
60Armour-14
60Bz-31
60NuCard-22
60NuCard-50
60P
60T-160M
60T-350
60T-563AS
60T/tatt-31
60T/tatt-92
61Bz-2
61NuCard-422
61NuCard-450
61P-4
61T-300
61T-406HL
61T-44LL
61T-475MV
61T-578AS
61T/Dice-8
61T/St-196
62Bz
62Exh
62J-5
62P-5
62P/Can-5
62Salada-41
62Shirriff-41
62T-18M
62T-200
62T-318IA
62T-471AS
62T-53LL
62T/bucks
62T/St-88
63Bz-1
63Exh
63J-15
63P-15
63Salada-56
63T-173M
63T-200
63T-2LL
63T/SO
64Bz-1
64T-331M
64T-50
64T/Coins-120
64T/Coins-131AS
64T/S-25
64T/St-53
64T/SU
64T/tatt
65Bz-1
65OldLond-30
65OPC-134WS
65OPC-3LL
65OPC-5LL
65T-134WS
65T-350
65T-3LL
65T-5LL
65T/E-11
65T/trans-57
66Bz-7
66OPC-50
66T-50
66T/RO-57
67Bz-7
67OPC-103CL
67OPC-150
67OPC/PI-6
67T-103CL
67T-150
67T/PI-6
67T/Test/SU-8
68Bz-11
68T-280
68T-490M
68T/G-2
68T/Post-18
69T-412LL
69T-500
69T/decal
69T/S-24
69T/St-205
69Trans-30
72Laugh/GF-33
73Syrac/Team-15
74Syrac/Team-14
75OPC-194MV
75OPC-195MV
75OPC-200MV
75T-194MV
75T-195MV
75T-200MV
75T/M-194MV
75T/M-195MV
75T/M-200MV
78TCMA-262
79TCMA-7
80Pac/Leg-6
80Laugh/3/4/5-18
80SSPC/HOF
82CJ-5
82KMart-1
83D/HOF-43pz
83D/HOF-7
83Kaline-14M
83Kaline-16M
83Kaline-35M
83MLBPA/Pin-12
84D/Champs-50
84West/1-4
85CircK-6
85D/HOF-6
85Woolwth-23
86BLChew-6
86Sf/Dec-26
87KMart-5
87Leaf/SpecOlym-H1
87Nestle/DT-17
88Pac/Leg-7
89B/I-5
89B/I-6
89CMC/Mantle-Set
89HOF/St-40
90BBWit-3
90HOF/St-49
91S/MantleP-Set
91T/Arc53-82
Exh47
PM10/L-21
PM10/Sm-103
PM10/Sm-104
PM10/Sm-105
PM10/Sm-106
PM10/Sm-107
PM10/Sm-108
PM10/Sm-109
WG10-13
WG9-16

Manto, Jeff
86QuadC-19
87PalmSp-4
88BBAmer-29
88MidldA/GS-21
88TexLgAS/GS-39
89Edmon/CMC-20
89Edmon/ProC-570
89F/Up-13
90ColoSp/CMC-15
90ColoSp/ProC-43
90F-137
90F/Up-U94
91B-75
91D-602
91OPC-488
91S-337RP
91T-488
91T/90Debut-97
91T/StClub/II-582
91UD-238
92S/II-666

Mantrana, Manny
87Fayette-12
88Clmbia/GS-19

Manuare, Jose
91MedHat/ProC-4096

Manuel, Barry
88CharlR/Star-14
89Tulsa/GS-16
90CharlR/Star-12
90FSLAS/Star-36
90LSUGreat-16
91Tulsa/LineD-586
91Tulsa/ProC-2768
92D/II-401RR
92T/91Debut-115

Manuel, Charles
(Charlie)
70OPC-194
70T-194
71MLB/St-466
71OPC-744
71T-744
74Albuq/Team-9
76SSPC-86
83Wisco/LF-27
85Orlan-22
86Toledo-15MG
87Portl-22
88Gator-9CO
90Target-479
91ColoSp/LineD-99MG
91ColoSp/ProC-2200MG

Manuel, Jerry
76OPC-596R
76T-596R
77Evansvl/TCMA-18
82F-195
83Iowa-17
87Indianap-5
89T/SenLg-90
90Jaxvl/Best-25MG
90Jaxvl/ProC-1391MG
91Indianap/LineD-199
91Indianap/ProC-477

Manuel, Jose
88SanAn/Best-18

Manush, Heinie
29Exh/4-29
31Exh/4-31
33Exh/4-16
33G-107
33G-187
33G-47
34DS-30
34Exh/4-16
34G-18
35BU-77
35Exh/4-16
35G-1C
35G-2C
35G-6C
35G-7C
37Wheat-8
39PB-94
40PB-176
54T-187CO
60F-18
61F-57
80Pac/Leg-2
80SSPC/HOF
81Detroit-82
86Conlon/1-19
88Conlon/AmAS-20
89HOF/St-36
89Smok/Dodg-16
90Target-480
91Conlon/Sport-270
91Conlon/Sport-63
R308-178
R310
R314
R316
R337-416
V353-47
V354-68
V355-73
W517-28

Manwaring, Kirt
87Shrev-10
87TexLgAS-22
88D-39RR
88F-651R
88F/Mini-119
88Leaf-39RR
88Phoenix/CMC-12
88Phoenix/ProC-61
88S-627RP
88T/Tr-64T
89B-469
89D-494
89D/Best-330
89F-334
89Mother/Giants-23
89Panini/St-208
89S-619RP
89S/HotRook-46
89S/YS/I-22
89T-506
89UD-500
90D-59
90F-63
90OPC-678
90Phoenix/CMC-10
90Phoenix/ProC-14
90PublInt/St-76
90S-146
90T-678
90UD-457
91Mother/Giant-23
91OPC-472
91PG&E-25
91S-101
91T-472
92D/II-494
92F-641
92S/II-636
92T-726

Manzanillo, Josias
85Elmira-14
87NewBrit-21
89NewBrit/ProC-606
89NewBrit/Star-8
90Foil/Best-70
90NewBrit/Best-4
90NewBrit/Star-9
90T/TVRSox-51
91Pawtu/ProC-35
92S/II-838
92T/91Debut-116

Manzanillo, Ravelo
83AlexD-27
85Nashua-15
88FSLAS/Star-43
88Tampa/Star-14
89BirmB/Best-13
90Vanco/CMC-4
90Vanco/ProC-486
91Syrac/LineD-510

Manzon, Howard
86Kenosha-15

Mapel, Steve
79Wisco-9
80OrlTw-6
80Toledo-1
82OrlTw/B-20

Mapes, Cliff
50B-218
51B-289
51BR-D1
52B-13
52T-103
R346-33
R423-64

Maples, Tim
81Miami-18

Marabell, Scott
89Bakers/Cal-195
90VeroB/Star-19
91SanAn/ProC-2989

Marabella, Tony
90Gate/ProC-3347
91Sumter/ClBest-16
91Sumter/ProC-2341

Marak, Paul
87Sumter-9
88Durham/Star-13
89Greenvl/ProC-1174
89Greenvl/Star-14
89Greenvl/Best-17
90Richm/Bob-10
90Richm/CMC-8
90Richm/ProC-255
90Richm/Team-20
91Classic/II-T52
91D-413RR
91Leaf/I-260
91OPC-753
91Richm/ProC-2562
91S-712RP
91S/Rook40-13
91T-753
91T/90Debut-98

Maranda, Georges
60T-479
61Clover-15
61Union

Maranville, Walter
(Rabbit)
14CJ-136
15CJ-136
16FleischBrd-60
21Exh-101
25Exh-23
26Exh-15
31Exh/4-1
33CJ/Pin-17
33DL-13
33G-117
34DS-3
35BU-37
35G-1J
35G-3A
35G-4A
35G-5A
50Callahan
60Exh/HOF-15

60F-21
61F-124
63Bz-14
69Bz/Sm
80Pac/Leg-3
80SSPC/HOF
87Conlon/2-47
89HOF/St-17
89Smok/Dodg-18
90Target-481
91Conlon/Sport-4
BF2-54
D327
D328-107
D329-112
D350/2-109
E120
E121/120
E121/80
E122
E135-107
E220
M101/4-112
M101/5-109
R300
R316
R328-10
V100
V354-4
V355-129
V61-90
W501-83
W515-50
W572
W573
W575
WG4-15
WG7-28

Marberry, Fred
(Firpo)
31Exh/4-31
33DH-31
33Exh/4-16
33G-104
34Exh/4-12
35BU-66
35G-1H
35G-3F
35G-5F
35G-6F
61F-125
91Conlon/Sport-326
R310
R315-A24
R315-B24
R332-47
V354-8
V355-10

Marcell, Ziggy
86Negro/Frit-56

Marcelle, Oliver
74Laugh/Black-3
90Negro/Star-17

Marcero, Doug
89NiagFls/Pucko-16
90Niagara/Pucko-21
91Lakeland/ProC-265

Marchese, John
89QuadC/Best-18
89QuadC/GS-10

Marchese, Joseph
(Joe)
86Elmira-11
87Greens-11
88CLAS/Star-12
88Lynch/Star-10
89NewBrit/ProC-616
89NewBrit/Star-9
91WinHaven/ClBest-26CO
91WinHaven/ProC-506CO

Marcheskie, Lee
82AlexD-2
83LynnP-5
85Nashua-16

Marchildon, Phil
49B-187

Marchio, Frank
53Exh/Can-53

Marchok, Chris
87Jamestn-28
88Rockford-23
89Jaxvl/Best-4
89Jaxvl/ProC-166
89Rockford-23
90Indianap/CMC-5
90Indianap/ProC-300
91Harris/LineD-262
91Harris/ProC-624

Marcon, Dave
90StCath/ProC-3463
91SLCity/ProC-3206

Marcuci
46Sunbeam

Marcum, John
34G-69
35G-8J
35G-9J
92Conlon/Sport-574
R314
V355-58

Mardsen, Steve
84BuffB-17

Marett, John
89Bluefld/Star-14
90Wausau/ProC-2127
90Wausau/Star-15

Margheim, Greg
90Billings/ProC-3218
91Cedar/ClBest-10
91Cedar/ProC-2717

Margoneri, Joe
57T-191

Marguardt, Chuck
88Gaston/ProC-1023

Maria, Esteban
75BurlB

Mariano, Bob
84CharlO-12
85CharlO-18
89Albany/Best-28
89Albany/ProC-324
91Albany/ProC-1025CO

Marichal, Juan
61T-417
61T/St-79
62J-140
62P-140
62P/Can-140
62T-505
62T/St-198
63J-109
63P-109
63Salada-5
63T-440
64T-280
64T-3LL
64T/Coins-157AS
64T/Coins-36
64T/S-37
64T/St-39S4
64T/SU
64Wheat/St-28
65Bz-24
65OPC-10LL
65OPC-50
65T-10LL
65T-50
65T/trans-20
66Bz-10
66T-221LL
66T-420
66T/RO-29
67Bz-10
67OPC/PI-28
67T-234LL
67T-236LL
67T-500
67T/PI-28
68Bz-5
68Coke
68Dexter-50
68OPC-107CL
68T-107CL
68T-205
69Kelly/Pin-11
69MB-165
69MLB/St-203
69MLBPA/Pin-51
69NTF
69OPC-10LL
69OPC/DE-15
69T-10LL
69T-370
69T-572M
69T/DE-32
69T/S-64
69T/St-107
69Trans-32
70K-13
70MB-14
70MLB/St-128
70OPC-210
70OPC-466AS
70OPC-67LL
70OPC-69LL
70T-210
70T-466AS
70T-67LL
70T-69LL
70T/SO
70Trans-3
71Bz/Test-19
71MLB/St-256
71OPC-325
71T-325
71T/Coins-125
71T/tatt-1
71Ticket/Giant-6
72K-47
72MB-204
72T-567
72T-568IA
73OPC-480
73T-480
74OPC-330
74T-330
74T/Tr-330T
78TCMA-2
83MLBPA/Pin-25
84Mother/Giants-3
86Sf/Dec-46
87KMart-6
88Pac/Leg-54
89Smok/Dodg-17
90Target-482
PM10/Sm-110
WG10-34
WG9-34

Marichal, Victor
75BurlB

Marie, Larry
90Richm25Ann/Team-16

Marietta, Lou
78Cedar
82WHave-8

Marigny, Ron
87GlenF-11
87Lakeland-9
89Lakeland/Star-15
90Lakeland/Star-18
91Lakeland/ClBest-20
91Lakeland/ProC-273

Marin, Jose
91Elmira/ClBest-11
91Elmira/ProC-3278

Marina, Juan
87Columbia-18
88Clmbia/GS-7
89StLucie/Star-15

Marinaro, Bob
90PrWill/Team-4

Marino, Mark
86QuadC-20
87PalmSp-30
88Stockton/ProC-752
89Stockton/Best-31M
89Stockton/ProC-402M
89Stockton/Star-28M

Marion, Marty
39Exh
47TipTop
48B-40
48L-97
49B-54
49Eureka-189
50B-88
51B-34
52B-85
53B/Col-52
60F-19
61F-58
61NuCard-473
79TCMA-99
90BBWit-47
91T/Arc53-302
92Conlon/Sport-626
Exh47
PM10/Sm-111
R346-3
W754

Maris, Roger
57Sohio/Ind-8
58T-47
59T-202
60T-377
60T-565AS
60T/tatt-32
61Bz-5
61NuCard-416
61Post-7
61T-2
61T-44LL
61T-478MV
61T-576AS
61T/St-197
62Bz-14
62Exh
62J-6
62P-6
62P/Can-6
62Salada-23
62Shirriff-23
62T-1
62T-313IA
62T-401M
62T-53LL
62T/bucks
62T/St-89
63Exh
63J-16
63P-16
63Salada-57
63T-120
63T-4LL
64T-225
64T-331M
65OldLond-31
65OPC-155
65T-155
66T-365
67OPC-45
67T-45
68T-330
72Laugh/GF-50
75OPC-198MV
75OPC-199MV
75T-198MV
75T-199MV
75T/M-198MV
75T/M-199MV
76Laugh/Jub-30
78TCMA-11
79T-413LL
79TCMA-161
80Pac/Leg-101
85Woolwth-24
86T-405TBC
87KMart-7
88Pac/Leg-89
90HOF/St-63
90MSA/AGFA-10
Exh47
PM10/L-22
PM10/L-23
PM10/Sm-112
PM10/Sm-113
PM10/Sm-114
WG10-14
WG9-17

Markell, Duke
52Park-19

Markert, Jim
86Penin-16
88BirmB/Best-5

Markham, Bobby
80WHave-12

Markiewicz, Brandon
91Boise/ClBest-18
91Boise/ProC-3887

Markland, Gene
V362-37

Markle, Cliff
E120

Markley, Scot
86Ashvl-18
87Osceola-23

Marks, John
82Clinton-28
83Wisco/LF-26GM

Marks, Lansing
91Pulaski/ClBest-9
91Pulaski/ProC-4015

Markulike, Joe
90Idaho/ProC-3253

Marlowe, Richard
53Glen
55B-91

Marone, Lou
70T-703
71MLB/St-206

Maropis, Pete
76AppFx

Marquard, Richard
(Rube)
10Domino-75
11Helmar-130
12Sweet/Pin-116
16FleischBrd-61
72Laugh/GF-14
80SSPC/HOF
86Conlon/1-27
89HOF/St-66
89Smok/Dodg-19
90BBWit-91
90Target-483
91Conlon/Sport-252
92Conlon/Sport-342
BF2-58
D303
D304
D328-108
D329-113
D350/2-110
E106
E120
E135-108
E224
E254
E90/1
E96
L1-111
M101/4-113
M101/5-110
S74-87
S81-86
T202
T205
T206
T207
T213/blue
T213/brown
T215/blue
T215/brown
T215/brown
T216
T222
T227
V100
W572
WG4-16
WG5-27
WG6-26

Marquardt, Chuck
89Gaston/ProC-1010

Marquardt, John
84Madis/Pol-12
85Huntsvl/BK-18
86Orlan-11

Marquess, Mark
88T/Tr-65T

Marquez, Edgar
88Myrtle/ProC-1170
88StCath/ProC-2025
90StCath/ProC-3455

Marquez, Edwin
86QuadC-21
87MidldA-12
88Edmon/CMC-19
88Edmon/ProC-575
89Edmon/CMC-13
89Edmon/ProC-552
90Foil/Best-109
90Indianap/CMC-12
90Indianap/ProC-301
90Jaxvl/Best-29

Marquez, Gonzalo
73OPC-605R
73T-605R
74OPC-422
74T-422

Marquez, Isidrio
89SanAn/Best-16
91SanAn/ProC-2970

Marquis, Roger
91Crown/Orio-276

Marr, Alan
83Clinton/LF-18
85Everett/Cram-8CO
Marr, Charles
N172
Marrero, Conrado
51B-206
52T-317
53Briggs
53T-13
54B-200
91T/Arc53-13
Marrero, Kenny
91Erie/ClBest-8
91Erie/ProC-4073
Marrero, Oreste
89Beloit/I/Star-15
89Star/Wax-5
90Beloit/Best-18
90Beloit/Star-12
90Foil/Best-292
91Single/ClBest-194
91Stockton/ClBest-6
91Stockton/ProC-3040
Marrero, Roger
89AubAs/ProC-2181
Marrero, Vilato
89Beloit/I/Star-16
89Beloit/II/Star-20
90Beloit/Best-12
90Beloit/Star-13
91Stockton/ClBest-21
91Stockton/ProC-3041
Marrett, Scott
86PalmSp-21
86PalmSp/Smok-13
87SanBern-15
Marriott, Bill
90Target-484
Marris, Mark
(Moose)
87Oneonta-26
88PrWill/Star-16
89PrWill/Star-12
91FtLaud/ClBest-7
91FtLaud/ProC-2421
Marrow, Buck
90Target-485
Marrs, Terry
87Elmira/Black-10
87Elmira/Red-10
88Elmira-22
89WinHaven/Star-14
Marsans, Armando
14CJ-134
15CJ-134
D328-109
D350/2-111
E135-109
E224
M101/5-111
T207
Marsh, Fred
(Freddie)
52T-8
53T-240
54T-218
55Esskay
55T-13
55T/DH-39
56T-23
91Crown/Orio-277
91T/Arc53-240
Marsh, Quinn
88Greens/ProC-1552
89Cedar/Best-4
89Cedar/ProC-929
89Cedar/Star-10
90Salinas/Cal-124
90Salinas/ProC-2721
Marsh, Randy
88TM/Umpire-43
89TM/Umpire-41
89TM/Umpire-60M
90TM/Umpire-39
Marsh, Tom
88Batavia/ProC-1676
89Spartan/ProC-1047
89Spartan/Star-15
90Reading/Best-23
90Reading/ProC-1233
90Reading/Star-18
90Spartan/Best-28
90Spartan/ProC-2495
90Spartan/Star-15
91Reading/LineD-514
91Reading/ProC-1383
Marsh, Trent
89Stockton/Star-26M
Marshall, Bret
89SoBend/GS-13
Marshall, Charlie
V362-35
Marshall, Clarence
43Centen-18
52NTea
52T-174
Marshall, Dave
69T-464
70OPC-58
70T-58
71MLB/St-159
71OPC-259
71T-259
72MB-205
72T-673
73OPC-513
73T-513
91WIZMets-247
Marshall, John
88Martins/Star-26
89Spartan/ProC-1045
89Spartan/Star-16
89Star/Wax-56
Marshall, Keith
76Indianap-19
Marshall, Max
40Hughes-13
47Smith-22
Marshall, Mike A.
79LodiD-6
81Albuq/TCMA-16
82Albuq-22
82D-562
82F-13
82T-681R
83D-362
83F-211
83OPC-324
83Pol/Dodg-5
83T-324
84D-348
84F-105
84Nes/792-634
84OPC-52
84Pol/Dodg-5
84T-634
84T/St-85
85Coke/Dodg-20
85D-12DK
85D-296
85D/AAS-22
85D/DKsuper-12
85F-377
85FunFood/Pin-64
85Leaf-12DK
85OPC-85
85T-85
85T/St-72
86Coke/Dodg-18
86D-52
86Drake-8
86F-137
86F/Mini-30
86F/St-71
86Leaf-40
86OPC-26
86Pol/Dodg-5
86Sf-89
86T-728
86T/St-71
87D-176
87D/OD-77
87F-446
87F/Lim-25
87Mother/Dodg-5
87OPC-186
87Pol/Dodg-3
87RedFoley/St-31
87Sf-82
87Seven-W8
87Smok/Dodg-20
87Smok/Dodg-21
87T-664
87T/St-66
88D-229
88D/Best-178
88F-522
88Mother/Dodg-5
88OPC-249
88Panini/St-315
88Pol/Dodg-5
88S-135
88Sf-220
88Smok/Dodg-16
88Smok/Dodg-29
88T-249
88T/Big-133
88T/St-69
89B-350
89D-110
89D/Best-204
89D/GrandSlam-2
89F-66
89F/BBMVP's-25
89F/WS-7
89Mother/Dodg-5
89OPC-323
89Panini/St-108
89Pol/Dodg-4
89S-186
89Sf-54
89Smok/Dodg-101
89Smok/Dodg-84
89T-582
89T/Big-48
89T/Coins-18
89T/LJN-60
89T/St-67
89T/UK-48
89UD-70
89Woolwth-26
90B-132
90Classic/III-57
90D-84
90F-401
90HOF/St-79
90Kahn/Mets-6
90Leaf/I-224
90OPC-198
90Panini/St-272
90PublInt/St-13
90S-384
90T-198
90T/St-62
90T/Tr-67T
90T/TVMets-27
90Target-486
90UD-262
90UD/Ext-781
91D-625
91F-102
91F/Ultra-35
91OPC-356
91S-617
91T-356
91T/StClub/I-226
91UD-681
91WIZMets-246
91WIZMets-249
Marshall, Mike G.
68T-201
69OPC-17
69T-17
71MLB/St-133
71OPC-713
71T-713
72OPC-505
72T-505
73OPC-355
73T-355
73T/Lids-30
74OPC-208LL
74OPC-73
74T-208LL
74T-73
74T/St-57
74T/Tr-73T
75K-36
75OPC-313LL
75OPC-330
75OPC-6RB
75T-313LL
75T-330
75T-6M
75T/M-313LL
75T/M-330
75T/M-6M
76OPC-465
76T-465
77T-263
82F-532
90Target-487
Marshall, R. James
(Jim)
52Mother-9
58T-441
59T-153
60T-267
61T-188
62T-337
74OPC-354CO
74T-354C
75OPC-638MG
75T-638MG
75T/M-638MG
76SSPC-308
76T-277MG
84Nashvl-13MG
86BuffB-17MG
91Crown/Orio-278
91Pac/SenLg-127
91Pac/SenLg-133
91Pac/SenLg-54M
91WIZMets-248
Marshall, Randy
89Butte/SP-20
89Fayette/ProC-1581
90A&AASingle/ProC-83
90Fayette/ProC-2404
90Gaston/Best-18
90Gaston/ProC-2528
90Gaston/Star-13
91Gaston/ClBest-19
91Gaston/ProC-2696
91London/LineD-391
91London/ProC-1876
Marshall, Willard
47HomogBond-33
47TipTop
48B-13
49B-48
49Eureka-118
49Royal-17
50B-73
50Drake-17
51B-98
52B-97
52T-96
53B/Col-58
53T-95
54B-70
55B-131
79TCMA-124
91T/Arc53-95
D305
Exh47
R423-65
Marshall, William R.
(Doc)
T206
T213/brown
Marte, Alexis
83Kinston/Team-14
84Visalia-4
85Orlan-7
86Toledo-16
87Portl-17
89Tulsa/Team-14
Marte, Roberto
86Erie-18
87Erie-10
88Savan/ProC-341
89Spring/Best-21
91Erie/ClBest-26CO
91Erie/ProC-4086CO
Marte, Vic
78Charl
Martel, Ed
87Oneonta-30
88Oneonta/ProC-2040
89FtLaud/Star-15
90PrWill/Team-14
91Albany/ProC-1004
Martel, Jay
87Savan-7
Marten, Tom
88Kenosha/ProC-1405
Marteniz, Ivan
88Wythe/ProC-1995
Martes, Sixto
84Everett/Cram-14
Martig, Rich
86Modesto-19
Martin, Al
86Sumter-17
87Sumter-24
88MidwLAS/GS-19
89Durham/Team-15
89Durham/Star-15
90Foil/Best-220
90Greenvl/Best-17
90Greenvl/ProC-1141
91Greenvl/ClBest-23
91Greenvl/LineD-211
91Greenvl/ProC-3015
Martin, Alfred
(Billy)
48Signal
48Smith-17
49Remar
52BR
52T-175
53B/Col-118
53B/Col-93M
53T-86
54B-145
54RH
54T-13
56T-181
57T-62
58T-271
59Kahn
59T-295
60Kahn
60T-173
61T-89
61T/RO-26
61T/St-20
62J-84
62P-84
62P/Can-84
62Salada-43
62Shirriff-43
62T-208
69T-547MG
71OPC-208MG
71T-208MG
72OPC-33MG
72OPC-34IA
72T-33MG
72T-34IA
73OPC-323MG
73T-323MG
74OPC-379MG
74T-379MG
75OPC-511MG
75T-511MG
75T/M-511MG
76SSPC-453
76T-17MG
77T-387MG
78BK/Y-1
78T-721
79TCMA-143
81D-479
81Detroit-107
81Detroit-67MG
81F-581MG
81T-671MG
82D-491MG
82Granny-9MG
82T/St-115MG
83D-575MG
83Kaline-15M
83Kaline-16M
83Kaline-43M
83T-156MG
83T/Tr-66T
84Nes/792-81MG
84T-81
85Pol/MetYank-Y6
85T/Tr-78T
86T-651MG
87Mother/A's-23
90S/NWest-30
91T/Arc53-86
PM10/L-24
Martin, Boris
(Babe)
49B-167
Martin, Chris
88Kenosha/ProC-1397
91Harris/LineD-263
91Harris/ProC-636
Martin, Darryl
87Fayette-10

89Fayette/ProC-1585
89SALAS/GS-39
90Lakeland/Star-19

Martin, Derrell
61Union

Martin, Doug
91Niagara/ClBest-23
91Niagara/ProC-3630

Martin, Elwood
(Speed)
E121/120
W501-55

Martin, Fred
79TCMA-121

Martin, Gene
90Greenvl/Star-13
90Sumter/Best-11
90Sumter/ProC-2446

Martin, Gregg
89StCath/ProC-2070
90A&AASingle/ProC-91
90Myrtle/ProC-2773
91Dunedin/ClBest-6
91Dunedin/ProC-202
91Single/ClBest-193

Martin, Herschel
39PB-12
40PB-100
46Remar
47Remar-12
47Signal

Martin, Jake
56T-129

Martin, Jared
80Wichita-16
82Iowa-7

Martin, Jerry
76SSPC-475
77T-596
78T-222
79T-382
80OPC-256
80T-493
81D-555
81F-295
81OPC-103
81T-103
81T/SO-98
81T/Tr-798
82D-298
82F-394
82T-722
82T/Tr-65T
83D-138
83F-117
83OPC-309
83T-626
84F/X-74
84Nes/792-74
84T-74
84T/Tr-74
85T-517

Martin, Jim
91SLCity/ProC-3226

Martin, Joey
75Lafay
77Phoenix

Martin, John
77AppFx
80Evansvl-14
82D-343
82F-121
82Louisvl-15
82T-236
83D-617
83StPete-9
83T-721
84ArkTr-17
84Nes/792-24
84T-24
86ArkTr-13
87Louisvl-19
88Louisvl-32
88Louisvl/CMC-3
88Louisvl/ProC-423
89ScrWB/CMC-3
89ScrWB/ProC-719
90Clearw/Star-27CO
91Reading/LineD-509CO
91Reading/ProC-1387CO

Martin, John
(Pepper)
32Orbit/num-21
32Orbit/un-46
33DL-17
33G-62
34DS-26
34Exh/4-8
35BU-125
35BU-7
35Exh/4-8
35G-2F
35G-4F
35G-7F
35Wheat
36G
36Wheat
37Wheat
38Wheat
62Pep/Tul
63Pep/Tul
80Pac/Leg-106
86Conlon/1-22
88Conlon/3-18
88Conlon/NatAS-14
91Conlon/Sport-274
92Conlon/Sport-637
R305
R306
R308-159
R310
R311/Gloss
R312
R313
R314
R332-36
V353-62

Martin, Jon
90Welland/Pucko-4

Martin, Joseph C.
(J.C.)
60L-92
60T-346
61T-124
61T/St-124
62T-91
62T/St-27
63T-499
64T-148
65T-382
66OPC-47
66T-47
67T-538
68T-211
69MB-166
69OPC-112
69T-112
70OPC-308WS
70OPC-488
70T-308WS
70T-488
71MLB/St-37
71OPC-704
71T-704
72MB-206
72T-639
73OPC-552
73T-552
74OPC-354CO
74T-354C
89Pac/SenLg-197
89Pac/SenLg-6
89T/SenLg-14
91Pac/SenLg-14
91WIZMets-250
91WIZMets-251

Martin, Justin
89QuadC/Best-11
91QuadC/ClBest-8
91QuadC/ProC-2625

Martin, Lefty
49Eureka-40

Martin, Mark
87Idaho-4
88Oneonta/ProC-2068

Martin, Matt
91Billings/ProC-3763

Martin, Mike
82Amari-9
83Beaum-1
84Cram/PCL-227
85Cram/PCL-217
86Pittsfld-15

Martin, Morris
(Morrie)
52T-131
53B/BW-53
53T-227
54B-179
54T-168
58T-53
59T-38
90Target-488
91Crown/Orio-279
91T/Arc53-227

Martin, Norberto
87CharWh-25
88Tampa/Star-15
90Vanco/CMC-21
90Vanco/ProC-495
91B-346
91Vanco/LineD-640
91Vanco/ProC-1603

Martin, R. Hollis
81VeroB-11

Martin, Renie
80T-667R
81D-103
81F-39
81OPC-266
81T-452
82D-238
82F-414
82T-594
82T/Tr-66T
83D-272
83F-267
83T-263
84D-445
84F-381
84Nes/792-603
84T-603
85Omaha-14
86Omaha-14
91Pac/SenLg-65

Martin, Russ
87Jamestn-1

Martin, Sam
81Batavia-17
82Watlo/B-17
82Watlo/C-21
83Spring/LF-4

Martin, Steve
82VeroB-8
85Cram/PCL-172

Martin, Steve W.
89Spokane/SP-18
90Foil/Best-209
90Waterlo/Best-10
90Waterlo/ProC-2385
91B-662
91HighD/ClBest-25
91HighD/ProC-2408
91Single/ClBest-85

Martin, Stuart
37Exh/4-8
38Exh/4-8

Martin, T. Eugene
70T-599R

Martin, Thomas
(Tom)
89Bluefld/Star-15
90Foil/Best-178
90Wausau/Best-4
90Wausau/ProC-2117
90Wausau/Star-16
91Kane/ClBest-7
91Kane/ProC-2655

Martin, Todd
90Utica/Pucko-2

Martin, Tony
77LodiD

Martin, Vic
83Chatt-7
86Calgary-13

Martina, Mario
89PalmSp/Cal-37

Martindale, Denzel
77StPete

Martindale, Ryan
91Watertn/ClBest-13
91Watertn/ProC-3368

Martineau, Paul Peter
86Jamestn-15

Martinez, Alfredo
(Fred)
79Jacks-24
81D-172
81F-288
81SLCity-9
81T-227
82Spokane-5
82T-659

Martinez, Angel
88Modesto-24
88VeroB/Star-14
89Madis/Star-14
91MedHat/ProC-4104

Martinez, Art
84Memphis-4

Martinez, Bert
83TriCit-20

Martinez, Carlos
86Albany/TCMA-9
87Hawaii-21
88BirmB/Best-16
89D/Rook-14
89S/Tr-103
89Vanco/CMC-17
89Vanco/ProC-579
90B-322
90BirmDG/Best-22
90Bz-13
90Coke/WSox-16
90D-531
90F-540
90Leaf/II-438
90OPC-461
90Panini/St-374
90S-314
90S/100Ris-70
90S/YS/I-35
90Sf-213
90T-461
90T/Big-116
90T/Coins-20
90T/Gloss60-9
90T/JumboR-19
90T/St-300
90T/St-325FS
90ToysRUs-18
90UD-347
91Canton/LineD-89
91Canton/ProC-987
91D-465
91F-128
91OPC-156
91Panini/FrSt-312
91S-274
91T-156
91UD-625
92D/II-521
92F-117
92S/100RisSt-71
92S/II-593
92T-280
92UD-598

Martinez, Carmelo
83Iowa-16
84D-623
84F-497
84F/X-U75
84Mother/Padres-20
84Nes/792-267
84T-267
84T/St-383
84T/Tr-75T
85D-478
85F-40
85Mother/Padres-24
85OPC-365
85T-558
85T/St-157
85T/St-375
86D-324
86F-329
86OPC-67
86T-67
86T/St-109
87Bohem-14
87D/OD-151
87F-423
87OPC-348
87T-348
88Coke/Padres-14
88D-287
88F-591
88Leaf-142
88OPC-148
88Panini/St-412
88S-181
88Smok/Padres-17
88T-148
88T/Big-238
88T/Coins-47
88T/St-106
89B-459
89Bimbo/Discs-1
89Coke/Padre-9
89D-601
89F-311
89OPC-332
89Padre/Mag-10
89Panini/St-204
89S-517
89T-449
89T/Big-11
89UD-365
90B-162
90Classic-56
90D-482
90F-162
90F/Up-U44
90Leaf/II-448
90OPC-686
90Phill/TastyK-21
90Publint/St-54
90S-114
90S/Tr-10T
90T-686
90T/Big-287
90T/Tr-68T
90UD-592
91F-44
91Leaf/I-160
91Leaf/II-467
91OPC-779
91S-792
91T-779
91UD-92
92S/II-686
92UD-696

Martinez, Chito
85FtMyr-16
87Omaha-7
88Memphis/Best-21
89Memphis/Best-12
89Memphis/ProC-1200
89Memphis/Star-16
90Omaha/CMC-13
90Omaha/ProC-77
91AAAGame/ProC-AAA40
91D/Rook-54
91F/UltraUp-U2
91RochR/LineD-458
91RochR/ProC-1914
91UD/FinalEd-30F
92Classic/I-56
92D/II-558
92F-13
92F/RookSIns-7
92S/100RisSt-76
92S/I-400
92T-479
92T/91Debut-117
92UD-672

Martinez, Christian
83StPete-10

Martinez, Constantino
90Calgary/ProC-659

Martinez, Dave
83QuadC-26
86Iowa-17
87Berg/Cubs-1
87D-488
87T/Tr-73T
88D-438
88D/Best-149
88D/Cubs/Bk-438
88F-424
88Panini/St-266
88S-223
88T-439
89B-370
89D-102
89F-384
89OPC-395
89S-77
89T-763
89UD-444
90B-121
90D-452
90D/BestNL-79
90F-353
90Leaf/II-318
90OPC-228
90PalmSp/Cal-217

90PalmSp/ProC-2573
90Panini/St-293
90PublInt/St-180
90S-27
90T-228
90T/St-71
90UD-470
91B-455
91D-237
91F-237
91F/Ultra-205
91Leaf/I-8
91OPC-24
91Panini/FrSt-144
91Panini/St-66
91RochR/LineD-459
91RochR/ProC-1898
91S-82
91T-24
91T/StClub/II-346
91UD-186
92D/II-732
92F-485
92S/II-501
92T-309
92UD-382

Martinez, David
86PalmSp-22
87MidldA-2
88MidldA/GS-20
89MidldA/GS-22

Martinez, Domingo
86Ventura-13
87Dunedin-23
88Knoxvl/Best-6
88SLAS-25
89Knoxvl/Best-15
89Knoxvl/ProC-1148
89Knoxvl/Star-12
90Knoxvl/Best-15
90Knoxvl/ProC-1254
90Knoxvl/Star-12
91Syrac/LineD-511
91Syrac/ProC-2485

Martinez, Edgar
86Chatt-17
87Calgary-1
88Calgary/CMC-16
88Calgary/ProC-782
88D/Rook-36UER
88F-378
89B-216
89D-645
89D/Rook-15
89F-552
89Mother/Sea-11
89Panini/St-428
89S-637
89S/HotRook-40
89UD/Ext-768
90Calgary/CMC-12
90Classic/III-23
90D/Learning-45
90F-520
90Leaf/II-299
90Mother/Mar-10
90OPC-148
90PublInt/St-437
90S-324
90T-148
90UD-532
91B-243
91Classic/III-54
91CounHrth-7
91D-16DK
91D-606
91D/SuperDK-16DK
91F-457
91F/Ultra-340
91Leaf/II-477
91Leaf/Stud-117
91OPC-607
91Panini/FrSt-230
91Panini/St-187
91S-264
91S/100SS-17
91Seven/3DCoin-11NW
91T-607
91T/StClub/I-47
91UD-574
92D/I-286
92F-286
92S/100SS-17
92S/II-485
92T-553
92UD-367
92UD-91TC

Martinez, Eric
91AubAS/ClBest-13
91AubAS/ProC-4280
91Boise/ClBest-24
91Boise/ProC-3874

Martinez, Felix
(Tippy)
76OPC-41
76T-41
77OPC-254
77T-238
78T-393
79T-491
80T-706
81D-354
81F-179
81OPC-119
81T-119
82D-205
82F-171
82T-583
83D-357
83F-65
83OPC-263
83T-621
84D-472
84F-12
84F-635IA
84Nes/792-215
84OPC-215
84T-215
84T/St-208
85D-210
85F-182
85OPC-247
85T-445
85T/St-200
86D-514
86F-279
86OPC-82
86T-82
87OPC-269
87RedFoley/St-14
87T-728
89Pac/SenLg-144
89TM/SenLg-72
90EliteSenLg-40
91Crown/Orio-281
91Pac/SenLg-28

Martinez, Fili
89BendB/Legoe-7

Martinez, Fred
85Louisvl-20
86Louisvl-19

Martinez, Gabriel
(Tony)
63T-466R
64T-404
66T-581

Martinez, Gil
87Greens-15
88Lynch/Star-11
89Lynch/Star-13

Martinez, J. Dennis
77T-491R
78T-119
79OPC-105
79T-211
80OPC-2
80T-10
81D-533
81F-180
81OPC-367
81T-367
82D-79
82F-170
82OPC-135
82T-165LL
82T-712
82T/St-10LL
83D-231
83F-64
83OPC-167
83T-553
84D-633
84F-11
84Nes/792-631
84T-631
85D-514
85F-181
85T-199
86D-454
86F-280
86T-416
87F-324
87Indianap-31
87OPC-252
87T-252
88D-549
88D/Best-146
88F-188
88Leaf-262
88OPC-76
88S-601
88T-76
88T/St-84
89B-359
89Classic-45
89D-106
89D/Best-90
89F-385
89OPC-313
89Panini/St-114
89S-114
89S/HotStar-13
89Sf-106
89T-313
89T/St-74
89UD-377
90B-111
90D-156
90D/BestNL-30
90F-354
90Leaf/I-54
90OPC-763
90Panini/St-288
90PublInt/St-181
90S-47
90Sf-53
90T-763
90T/Big-133
90T/St-68
90UD-413
90USPlayC/AS-3D
91B-434
91BBBest/Aces-11
91Classic/200-30
91Classic/III-53
91Crown/Orio-280
91D-139
91F-238
91F/Ultra-206
91Leaf/II-274
91OPC-528
91OPC/Premier-75
91Panini/FrSt-150
91Panini/St-68
91S-454
91T-528
91T/StClub/I-273
91UD-385
91UD/FinalEd-50F
91USPlayC/AS-7S
92Classic/I-57
92D/DK-DK24
92D/I-276HL
92D/II-686
92F-486
92F-683RS
92F-695LL
92S/100SS-97
92S/II-470
92S/II-783HL
92S/II-784
92T-15
92T-394AS
92T/GPromo-15
92T/Promo-273
92UD-365

Martinez, John
(Buck)
70T-609
71OPC-163
71T-163
72OPC-332
72T-332
75OPC-314
75T-314
75T/M-314
76A&P/KC
76OPC-616
76SSPC-165
76T-616
77T-46
78T-571
79Ho-32
79T-243
80T-477
81D-444
81F-526
81T-56
81T/Tr-799
82D-561
82OPC-314
82T-314
83D-178
83F-433
83OPC-308
83T-733
84D-612
84F-161
84Nes/792-179
84OPC-179
84T-179
84Tor/Fire-24
85F-114
85OPC-119
85OPC/Post-13
85T-673
85Tor/Fire-21
86Ault-13
86F-66
86OPC-363
86T-518
86Tor/Fire-24
87F-235

Martinez, John
90BurlInd/ProC-3012
91Pocatel/ProC-3785

Martinez, Jose
70OPC-8
70T-8
71MLB/St-207
71OPC-712
71T-712
77DaytB/MG
79OkCty
80OkCty
88Berg/Cubs-CO
88StCath/ProC-2024
90Cub/Mara-28CO
90Cub/Mara-28CO
90T/TVCub-4CO
91Cub/Mara-x
91Cub/Mara-x
91SALAS/ProC-SAL17

Martinez, Julian
87Savan-19
88StPete/Star-15
89ArkTr/GS-11
89TexLAS/GS-20
90Louisvl/CMC-11
90Louisvl/ProC-410
90T/TVCard-54
91Louisvl/LineD-240
91Louisvl/ProC-2929

Martinez, Louis
(Louie)
89SanAn/Best-14
91AubAS/ClBest-6
91AubAS/ProC-4271

Martinez, Luis
86Cram/PCL-57
87Madis-8
88FSLAS/Star-11
88Modesto/Cal-74
89Savan/ProC-350
90Foil/Best-56
90Spring/Best-14
91Albuq/LineD-14
91Albuq/ProC-1147
91ArkTr/LineD-38
91ArkTr/ProC-1300

Martinez, Manuel
(Manny)
90SoOreg/Best-12
90SoOreg/ProC-3433
91AS/Cal-44
91Modesto/ClBest-24
91Modesto/ProC-3104
91Single/ClBest-145

Martinez, Martin
90Rockford/ProC-2693
91Rockford/ClBest-8
91Rockford/ProC-2043
91Single/ClBest-252

Martinez, Nicio
88Batavia/ProC-1667
90Savan/ProC-2076

Martinez, Orlando
(Marty)
67T-504
68T-578
69MB-167
69T-337
70OPC-126
70T-126
71MLB/St-85
71OPC-602
71T-602
72MB-207
72OPC-336
72T-336
72T/Cloth-22
76SanAn/Team-14
80Wausau-23
81Spokane-32MG

Martinez, Orlando
61Clover-16

Martinez, Pablo
90CharRain/Best-14
90CharRain/ProC-2044
91CharRain/ClBest-19
91CharRain/ProC-104

Martinez, Pedro
89CharRain/ProC-992
89SALAS/GS-11
90Wichita/Rock-15
91AS/Cal-2
91Classic/III-55
91SanAn/ProC-2971
91Single/ClBest-355
91UD/FinalEd-2F
91Wichita/LineD-613
91Wichita/ProC-2595
92UD-18SR
92UD-79M

Martinez, Porfi
86Lakeland-12

Martinez, Rafael
88StCath/ProC-2026
89Myrtle/ProC-1467

Martinez, Ramon
89Princet/Star-12
90Augusta/ProC-2458
91Augusta/ClBest-16
91Augusta/ProC-812
91PalmSp/ProC-2024

Martinez, Ramon J.
86Bakers-20
87VeroB-7
88BBAmer-21
88SanAn/Best-1
88TexLgAS/GS-28
89AAA/CMC-40
89AAA/ProC-47
89Albuq/CMC-7
89Albuq/ProC-69
89Classic-130
89D-464
89D/Rook-45
89F-67
89Pol/Dodg-24
89S-635
89S/HotRook-55
89S/YS/I-40
89Sf-224R
89T-225
89UD-18
90B-88
90Classic-76
90D-685
90D/BestNL-141
90F-402
90HotRook/St-30
90Leaf/I-147
90Mother/Dodg-17
90OPC-62
90Panini/St-380
90S-461
90S/100Ris-59
90S/McDon-13
90Sf-68
90T-62
90T/JumboR-20
90T/St-61
90Target-489
90ToysRUs-19
90UD-675
90USPlayC/AS-1H

91B-610
91BBBest/RecBr-10
91Classic/200-99
91Classic/I-52
91CollAB-18
91D-15DK
91D-557
91D/SuperDK-15DK
91F-212
91F/Ultra-164
91F/UltraG-7
91KingB/Discs-12
91Leaf/I-61
91Leaf/Prev-5
91Leaf/Stud-184
91MajorLg/Pins-52
91Mother/Dodg-10
91OPC-340
91Panini/FrSt-62
91Panini/St-50
91Panini/Top15-58
91Panini/Top15-75
91Pol/Dodg-48
91S-300
91S-408KM
91S-419HL
91S/100SS-16
91Seven/3DCoin-11F
91Seven/3DCoin-8SC
91T-340
91T/CJMini/II-25
91T/StClub/II-516
91T/SU-23
91UD-136
91UD-78TC
92D/II-656
92F-463
92F-706M
92F/ASIns-7
92S/100SS-75
92S/II-610
92S/II-780AS
92T-730
92UD-346
92UD-79M

Martinez, Randy
83Spring/LF-19

Martinez, Ray
81Batavia-13
83Watlo/LF-19

Martinez, Ray
90Kgsport/Best-8
90Kgsport/Star-15
90Madison/ProC-2265

Martinez, Rey
85Lynch-23

Martinez, Roman
89PalmSp/Cal-38
89PalmSp/ProC-467

Martinez, Sandy
91Kissim/ProC-4195

Martinez, Silvio
76Shrev
79T-609
80OPC-258
80T-496
81D-429
81F-546
81T-586
82Charl-7
82D-469
82F-122
82T-181

Martinez, Ted
71OPC-648R
71T-648R
72T-544
73OPC-161
73T-161
74OPC-487
74T-487
75OPC-637
75T-637
75T/M-637
76OPC-356
76SSPC-499
76T-356
78T-546
79OPC-59
79T-128
80Albuq-14
80Pol/Dodg-23
80T-191

90Target-490
91WIZMets-252

Martinez, Thomas
83AlexD-17

Martinez, Tino
88T/Tr-66T
89B-211
89BBAmerAA/BProC-AA6
89T/Big-93
89Wmsprt/ProC-635
89Wmsprt/Star-13
90B-484
90F/Up-119
90S-596
90UD-37
91AAAGame/ProC-AAA5
91B-257
91Calgary/LineD-66
91Calgary/ProC-523
91Classic/200-150
91Classic/I-2
91CounHrth-10
91D-28RR
91D/Preview-6
91F-458
91F/Ultra-341
91Leaf/Prev-24
91Leaf/Stud-118
91MajorLg/Pins-7
91OPC-482
91OPC/Premier-76
91S-798
91S/Rook40-38
91Seven/3DCoin-12NW
91T-482
91T/90Debut-99
91T/StClub/I-179
91UD-553
92D/II-410RR
92F-287
92S/100RisSt-51
92S/II-596
92T-481
92UD-554

Martinez, Wilfredo
83Erie-5

Martinez, William
90Gate/ProC-3344
91SALAS/ProC-SAL46
91Sumter/ClBest-8
91Sumter/ProC-2331

Marting, Tim
71OPC-423R
71T-423R

Martinson, Evon
78Clinton
79LodiD-21

Martinson, Mike
75QuadC
76QuadC

Marto, Johnny
T3/Box-61

Martorana, Dave
(Mutta)
91Utica/ClBest-12
91Utica/ProC-3249

Marty, Joe
40PB-216
41PB-28
46Sunbeam
47Signal
47Sunbeam
49B/PCL-26
52Mother-20

Martyn, Bob
58T-39
59T-41
79TCMA-254

Martz, Randy
80Wichita-7
81F-300
81T-381R
82D-126
82F-600
82RedLob
82T-188
82T-456TL
83D-151
83F-501
83T-22
84Richm-18
85Cram/PCL-66

Marx, Bill

86CharRain-14
88River/Cal-214
88River/ProC-1424
89River/Cal-14
89River/ProC-1416
90Riversi/Cal-20
90Riversi/ProC-2606

Marx, Jerry
62Pep/Tul
63Pep/Tul

Marx, William
90CharRain/Best-16

Marzan, Jose
88Visalia/Cal-155
88Visalia/ProC-89
89Visalia/Cal-111
89Visalia/ProC-1443
90OrlanSR/Best-6
90OrlanSR/ProC-1091
90OrlanSR/Star-10
91OrlanSR/LineD-486
91OrlanSR/ProC-1857

Marzano, John
85T-399OLY
86NewBrit-16
87Pawtu-1
87Pawtu/TCMA-11
87Sf/Rook-49
88Classic/Red-189
88D-421
88D/RedSox/Bk-421
88F-357
88Leaf-245
88S-584
88T-757
88ToysRUs-17
89Pawtu/CMC-17
89Pawtu/Dunkin-20
89Pawtu/ProC-687
90Pawtu/CMC-12
90Pawtu/ProC-465
90T/Tr-69T
90T/TVRSox-19
91B-119
91D-346
91F-103
91Leaf/I-179
91OPC-574
91Pep/RSox-12
91S-831
91T-574
91T/StClub/I-201
92D/II-448
92S/II-539
92T-677

Marze, Dickey
90BurlB/Best-15
90BurlB/ProC-2357
90BurlB/Star-17

Mashore, Clyde
71OPC-376R
71T-376R
73OPC-401
73T-401

Mashore, Damon
91SoOreg/ClBest-2
91SoOreg/ProC-3863

Mashore, Justin
91Bristol/ClBest-3
91Bristol/ProC-3619

Masi, Phil
49B-153
49Eureka-15
50B-128
51B-160
51T/RB-19
52T-283
R346-12

Maskery, Sam
N172

Maskovich, George
52Park-97

Mason, Don
66T-524R
69T-584
71MLB/St-231
71OPC-548
71T-548
72T-739

Mason, Henry
60L-80
60T-331

Mason, Jim

72OPC-334R
72T-334R
73OPC-458
73T-458
74OPC-618
74T-618
74T/Tr-618T
75OPC-136
75T-136
75T/M-136
76SSPC-448
77OPC-211
77T-212
78T-588
79T-67
80OPC-259
80T-497

Mason, Martin
(Marty)
82Spring-16
83Spring/LF-7
84ArkTr-19
86StPete-18CO
87StPete-19
88Savan/ProC-336
91ArkTr/LineD-50CO
91ArkTr/ProC-1303CO

Mason, Mike
82Tulsa-5
83OKCty-20
84F/X-U76
84Rang-16
84T/Tr-76T
85D-281
85F-562
85OPC-144
85Rang-16
85T-464
85T/St-354
86D-422
86F-565
86OPC-189
86Rang-16
86T-189
87D-284
87F-129
87F/Up-U73
87OPC-208
87Smok/R-4
87T-646
88T-87
91AppFx/ClBest-28INST
91AppFx/ProC-1733CO

Mason, Rob
88WPalmB/Star-17
89Rockford/Team-16
90WPalmB/Star-14

Mason, Roger
83BirmB-24
84Evansvl-21
85Cram/PCL-190
86D-633
86F/Up-U72
86Mother/Giants-23
86T/Tr-70T
87D-204
87F-280
87Mother/SFG-23
87T-526
88Phoenix/CMC-4
88Phoenix/ProC-62
89Tucson/CMC-4
89Tucson/ProC-195
89Tucson/JP-14
90BuffB/Team-15
91AAAGame/ProC-AAA3
91BuffB/LineD-33
91BuffB/ProC-536
92D/II-715
92S/II-727

Masone, Tony
80Cedar-9

Massarelli, John
87AubAs-1
88AubAs/ProC-1961
89Ashvl/ProC-945
90FSLAS/Star-13
90Osceola/Star-20
91Osceola/ClBest-15
91Osceola/ProC-688
91Single/ClBest-165

Masse, Bill
(Billy)

88T/Tr-67T
89PrWill/Star-13
89Star/Wax-90
89T/Big-179
90Albany/Best-21
90Albany/ProC-1045
90Albany/Star-11
91Albany/ProC-1020

Massey, Jim
86Cram/PCL-17
87Everett-21

Massicotte, Jeff
88Peoria/Ko-15
89Peoria/Ko-5
90WinSalem/Team-20

Massie, Bret
88Spartan/Star-24
88Spartan/Star-8

Masteller, Dan
90Visalia/Cal-67
90Visalia/ProC-2162
91OrlanSR/LineD-487
91OrlanSR/ProC-1858
91Single/ClBest-330

Masters, Burke
88CapeCod/Sum-101

Masters, David
(Dave)
86WinSalem-13
87Pittsfld-14
88Iowa/CMC-9
88Iowa/ProC-533
89Iowa/CMC-6
89Iowa/ProC-1698
90Iowa/CMC-2
90Iowa/ProC-315
91Indianap/LineD-189
91Indianap/ProC-458

Masters, Frank
86GlenF-14
88Madis-15
89Madis/Star-15

Masters, Wayne
90Augusta/ProC-2459

Masterson, Walt
49B-157
50B-153
51B-307
52B-205
52T-186
53B/BW-9
53Briggs

Mastropietro, Dave
90Niagara/Pucko-5

Masuyama, Daryl
86Shrev-16TR

Masuzawa, Hideki
90Gate/ProC-3342

Mata, Vic
83Nashvl-11
84Colum-10
84Colum/Pol-14
85Colum-1
85D-629
85F-644
86Colum-15
86Colum/Pol-13
88RochR/Team-12
88RochR/CMC-23
88RochR/Gov-15
88RochR/ProC-197

Matachun, Paul
91Gaston/ClBest-20
91Gaston/ProC-2697

Matas, Jim
86Geneva-18
87WinSalem-26
88WinSalem/Star-10

Matchett, Steve
89Bristol/Star-16

Matchick, J. Tom
67OPC-72R
67T-72R
68OPC-113R
68T-113R
69MB-168
69T-344
70T-647
71MLB/St-419
71OPC-321
71T-321
72MB-208
73OPC-631

73T-631
88Domino-12
91Crown/Orio-282

Mateo, Jose
90CharRain/Best-15
90CharRain/ProC-2047

Mateo, Luis
89Madis/Star-16

Matheson, Bill
43Centen-19
44Centen-16
45Centen-16

Mathews, Chuck
85Osceola/Team-11
86ColumAst-18

Mathews, Ed
86Sumter-18
87Durham-16
88Greenvl/Best-22
89Richm/Bob-14
89Richm/CMC-10
89Richm/Ko-26
89Richm/ProC-845
90Sumter/Best-12

Mathews, Edwin Lee
(Eddie)
52T-407
53B/Col-97
53JC-21
53SpicSpan/3x5-17
53SpicSpan/7x10-8
53T-37
54B-64
54JC-41
54RM-NL23
54SpicSpan/PostC-13
54T-30
55B-103
55Gol/Braves-19
55JC-41
55SpicSpan/DC-12
55T-155
56T-107
56T/Hocus-B21
56T/Pin-18
56YellBase/Pin-21
57SpicSpan/4x5-12
57T-250
58T-351M
58T-440
58T-480AS
59HRDerby-13
59T-212M
59T-450
60Armour-15
60P
60SpicSpan-12
60T-420
60T-558AS
60T/tatt-33
61Bz-11
61NuCard-412
61P-106
61T-120
61T-43LL
61T/St-45
62Bz
62Exh
62J-147
62P-147
62P/Can-147
62Salada-111
62Shirriff-111
62T-30
62T/bucks
62T/St-148
63Exh
63J-151
63P-151
63T-275
64T-35
64T/Coins-33
64T/St-97
64T/SU
64T/tatt
65Salada-28
65T-500
65T/E-26
66T-200
66T/RO-118
67OPC-166
67T-166
68OPC-58
68T-58
69MB-169
73OPC-237MG
73T-237MG
74OPC-634MG
74T-634MG
79TCMA-157
80Laugh/3/4/5-25
80SSPC/HOF
82CJ-2
83MLBPA/Pin-26
84West/1-17
85CircK-11
86BLChew-10
86Sf/Dec-34
87Nestle/DT-25
88Domino-13
89HOF/St-25
89Kahn/Coop-8
89Pac/Leg-116
89T/LJN-125
90Pac/Legend-66
90Swell/Great-65
91LineD-40
91Swell/Great-147
91T/Arc53-37
Exh47
WG10-35
WG9-35

Mathews, Greg
86D/Rook-26
86F/Up-U73
86Sf/Rook-41
87D-208
87F-303
87Smok/Cards-8
87T-567
87T/Gloss60-60
87ToysRUs-20
88D-84
88D/Best-324
88F-41
88Louisvl-33
88S-226
88S/YS/II-35
88Smok/Card-7
88T-133
88T/Big-177
89D-281
89F-456
89S-286
89T-97
89UD-531
90OPC-209
90PublInt/St-221
90S-537
90Smok/Card-13
90T-209
90T/TVCard-17
90UD-678

Mathews, Jeremy
89Belling/Legoe-22

Mathews, Jim
78Ashvl

Mathews, Nelson
63T-54R
64T-366
65OPC-87
65T-87

Mathews, Rick
81CharR-26
82FtMyr-22
84Memphis-1

Mathews, Robert
N172
N690

Mathews, Terry
88CharlR/Star-15
89Tulsa/GS-17
89Tulsa/Team-15
90Tulsa/ProC-1171
91OkCty/LineD-311
91OkCty/ProC-173
92D/II-694
92F-310
92S/II-737
92T/91Debut-118

Mathews, Tom
86Fresno/Smok-22

Mathewson, Christy
10Domino-76
11Helmar-131
12Sweet/Pin-117A
12Sweet/Pin-117B
14CJ-88
15CJ-88
16FleischBrd-62
40PB-175
48Exh/HOF
49Leaf/Prem-5
50Callahan
51T/CM
60Exh/HOF-16
60F-2
60NuCard-8
61F-59
61GP-24
61NuCard-477
61T-408HL
63Bz/ATG-4
69Bz/Sm
72F/FFeat-3
72Laugh/GF-25
73F/Wild-22
80Pac/Leg-34
80Laugh/3/4/5-5
80Laugh/FFeat-22
80SSPC/HOF
83D/HOF-3
85Woolwth-25
86Conlon/1-23
86Conlon/1-32
86Conlon/1-46
87Conlon/2-3
89HOF/St-65
90BBWit-104
90HOF/St-10
90Swell/Great-134
91Conlon/Sport-57
91Swell/Great-141
92Conlon/Sport-331
D303
D304
E101
E102
E103
E105
E106
E107
E224
E286
E90/1
E91
E93
E95
E98
L1-133
M116
PM1-11
R332-10
R423-68
S74-88
S81-108
T201
T202
T205
T206
T213/blue
T213/brown
T215/brown
T215blue
T216
T3-27
W514-72
W516-24
W555
WG4-17
WG5-28
WG6-27

Mathias, Carl
60T-139
61BeeHive-13

Mathile, Michael
90James/Pucko-21
91Rockford/ClBest-9
91Rockford/ProC-2044

Mathiot, Mike
89Kenosha/ProC-1059
89Kenosha/Star-13
90Kenosha/Best-7
90Kenosha/ProC-2302
90Kenosha/Star-11

Mathis, Ron
83Tucson-4
84Cram/PCL-72
85F/Up-U78
85Mother/Ast-26
85T/Tr-79T
86F-305
86T-476
86Tucson-12
87Tucson-14
88ColoSp/CMC-5
88ColoSp/ProC-1548

Mathis, Verdell
(Lefty)
86Negro/Frit-62
91Negro/Lewis-7

Mathis, Wayne
90Kgsport/Best-4
90Kgsport/Star-16

Mathison, Chuck
84Greens-15

Matias, John
70OPC-444R
70T-444R
71OPC-546
71T-546

Matilla, Pedro
88Elmira-14
89WinHaven/Star-15
90WinHaven/Star-14
91WinHaven/ClBest-14

Matlack, Jon
71OPC-648R
71T-648R
72OPC-141R
72T-141R
73K-12
73OPC-55
73T-55
74OPC-153
74OPC-471NLCS
74T-153
74T-471NLCS
74T/DE-44
74T/St-66
75K-10
75OPC-290
75T-290
75T/M-290
76Ho-97
76K-49
76OPC-190
76SSPC-554
76T-190
77BurgChef-137
77Ho-114
77OPC-132
77Pep-68
77T-440
78BK/R-5
78OPC-98
78T-25
78Wiffle/Discs-43
79Ho-122
79K-58
79OPC-159
79T-315
80OPC-312
80T-592
81D-266
81F-621
81F/St-51
81OPC-339
81T-656
81T/HT
81T/St-135
82D-215
82F-323
82F/St-176
82OPC-239
82T-239
83D-195
83F-572
83Rang-32
83T-749
84D-378
84F-422
84Nes/792-149
84T-149
89Pac/Leg-214
89Pac/SenLg-9
89River/Best-23
89River/Cal-26CO
89River/ProC-1408
89T/SenLg-102
89Tidew/Candl-3
89TM/SenLg-73
90EliteSenLg-11
90Wichita/Rock-27CO
91LasVegas/ProC-254CO
91LasVegas/LineD-300CO
91WIZMets-253

Matlock, Leroy
78Laugh/Black-32

Matos, Carlos
82Danvl-11

Matos, Domingo
90James/Pucko-3
91James/ClBest-14
91James/ProC-3554

Matos, Francisco
89Modesto/Cal-283
89Modesto/Chong-24
90Modesto/Cal-168
90Modesto/ProC-2220
91Huntsvl/ClBest-15
91Huntsvl/LineD-289
91HuntsvlProC-1804

Matos, Malvin
91Gaston/ClBest-24
91Gaston/ProC-2701

Matos, Rafael
84Butte-16

Matouzas, Jeff
90Tampa/DIMD-16

Matrisciano, Ron
80Clinton-7

Matsuo, Hideharu
87Miami-22

Mattaick, Denny
90Foil/Best-256

Mattern, Al
10Domino-77
11Helmar-80
12Sweet/Pin-68A
12Sweet/Pin-68B
E254
M116
S74-45
T201
T205
T206

Matthews
E254

Matthews, Gary
73OPC-606R
73T-606R
74OPC-386
74T-386
75Ho-31
75Ho/Twink-31
75OPC-79
75T-79
75T/M-79
76Ho-142
76OPC-133
76SSPC-110
76T-133
77BurgChef-210
77Ho-142
77T-194
78Ho-19
78OPC-209
78T-475
78Wiffle/Discs-44
79Ho-42
79OPC-35
79T-85
80K-48
80OPC-186
80T-355
81D-306
81F-251
81OPC-186
81T-228
81T/SO-76
81T/St-144
81T/Tr-800
82D-441
82F-249
82F/St-58
82OPC-151
82T-680
82T/St-79
83D-420
83Drake-16
83F-165
83OPC-64
83T-780
83T/St-269
84D-233
84Drake-21
84F-40

84F/St-121
84F/X-77T
85FunFoodPin-70
84Nes/792-637TL
84Nes/792-70
84OPC-70
84Seven-23E
84SevenUp-36
84T-70
84T/St-118
84T/St-18LCS
84T/Tr-77
85D-239
85Drake-18
85F-61
85F/St-24
85Leaf-220
85OPC-210
85Seven-10S
85SevenUp-36
85T-210
85T/St-44
85T/Super-19
86Cub/Unocal-12
86D-76
86F-373
86Gator-36
86OPC-292
86Sf-66M
86T-485
86T/St-59
87Berg/Cubs-36
87F-568
87OPC-390
87Seven-C10
87T-390
87T/St-62
88OPC-156
88S-599
88T-156
88T/St-223
89Swell-118

Matthews, Jeff
78Green

Matthews, Jeremy
89Wausau/GS-15

Matthews, Tom
90Kissim/DIMD-17

Matthews, W.C. (Wid)
21Exh-102

Mattick, Robert
80T-577MG
81D-570
81F-431
81T-674MG

Mattimore, Michael
N172

Mattingly, Don
81Nashvl
82Colum-21
82Colum/Pol-19
84D-248
84F-131
85FunFoodPin-77
84Nes/792-8
84OPC-8
84T-8
84T/St-325
85D-295
85D-651M
85D-7DK
85D/AAS-48
85D/DKsuper-7
85D/HL-36
85D/HL-44
85D/HL-45
85Drake-19
85F-133
85F/LimEd-20
85F/St-37
85F/St-4
85Leaf-140M
85Leaf-7DK
85OPC-324
85Seven-12E
85T-665
85T/3D-8
85T/Gloss40-27
85T/St-171
85T/St-310
85T/Super-4
86BK/AP-19
86D-173
86D/AAS-50
86D/HL-48
86D/HL-53
86Dorman-13
86Drake-7
86F-109
86F-627M
86F-639M
86F/AS-1
86F/LimEd-27
86F/LL-22
86F/Mini-24
86F/Slug-21
86F/St-72
86Jiffy-6
86KayBee-19
86Leaf-103
86Meadow/Blank-8
86Meadow/Milk-5
86Meadow/Stat-5
86OPC-180
86OPC/WaxBox-J
86Quaker-18
86Sf-176M
86Sf-179M
86Sf-180M
86Sf-183M
86Sf-184M
86Sf-2
86Sf-54M
86Sf-75M
86Sf/Dec-65
86T-180
86T-712AS
86T/3D-15
86T/Gloss60-31
86T/Mini-28
86T/St-296
86T/Super-1
86T/WaxBox-J
86TrueVal-5
86Woolwth-20
87BK-13
87Classic-10
87Classic/Up-104
87D-52
87D/AAS-33
87D/HL-17
87D/HL-23
87D/HL-48
87D/OD-241
87Drake-8
87F-104
87F-638M
87F/AS-1
87F/AwardWin-24
87F/Excit-33
87F/GameWin-26
87F/Hottest-27
87F/BB-26
87F/LL-28
87F/Lim-26
87F/Mini-66
87F/RecSet-20
87F/Slug-25
87F/St-131M
87F/St-74
87F/St-S8
87Ho/St-27
87Jiffy-6
87KayBee-19
87KMart-28
87Kraft-29
87Leaf-150
87MnM's-11
87MSA/Discs-6
87OPC-229
87Ralston-5
87RedFoley/St-106
87Sf-1
87Sf-159M
87Sf-75M
87Seven-E12
87Sportflic/DealP-1
87T-500
87T-606AS
87T/Board-32
87T/Coins-17
87T/Gloss60-1
87T/HL-15
87T/Mini-65
87T/St-294
87Woolwth-15
88ActPacT-5
88Bz-11
88ChefBoy-16
88Classic/Blue-211
88Classic/Blue-247M
88Classic/Red-151M
88Classic/Red-152
88CMC/Kit-1
88CMC/Kit-20
88D-217
88D-BC21
88D/AS-1
88D/Best-1
88D/PopUp-1
88D/Y/Bk-217
88Drake-1
88F-214
88F/AwardWin-23
88F/BB/AS-23
88F/BB/MVP-22
88F/Excit-25
88F/Head-1
88F/Hottest-24
88F/LL-25
88F/Mini-41
88F/RecSet-24
88F/Slug-26
88F/SS-22
88F/St-48
88F/TL-19
88FanSam-9
88KayBee-16
88KingB/Disc-15
88KMart-15
88Leaf-177
88MSA/Disc-3
88Nestle-15
88OPC-300
88Panini/St-152
88Panini/St-227M
88Panini/St-430
88RedFoley/St-53
88S-1
88S-650M
88S-658HL
88S/WaxBox-2
88Sf-1
88Sf-222M
88Sf/Gamewin-1
88T-2RB
88T-300
88T-386AS
88T/Big-229
88T/Coins-19
88T/Gloss22-2
88T/Gloss60-11
88T/Mini-27
88T/RiteAid-22
88T/St-156
88T/St-299
88T/St-3
88T/St/Backs-35
88T/UK-45
88Woolwth-4
89B-176
89Cadaco-34
89Classic-106
89Classic-5
89T/Crunch-8
89D-26DK
89D-74
89D/AS-21
89D/Best-1
89D/DKsuper-26DK
89F-258
89F/BBAS-28
89F/BBMVP's-26
89F/Excit-31
89F/Heroes-26
89F/LL-25
89F/Rec-6
89F/Superstar-29
89Holsum/Discs-15
89Holsum/Discs-4
89KayBee-20
89KMart/DT-12
89KMart/Lead-3
89Master/Discs-6
89Nissen-4
89OPC-26
89Panini/St-404
89MSA/SS-11
89RedFoley/St-79
89S-100
89S/HotStar-10
89S/Mast-6
89S/NWest-1
89Sf-50
89T-397AS
89T-700
89T/Big-50
89T/Coins-43
89T/DH-1
89T/DHTest-14
89T/Gloss60-51
89T/HeadsUp-19
89T/LJN-163
89T/St-314
89T/St/Backs-2
89T/UK-49
89Tetley/Discs-1
89Topps/Ritz-Set
89UD-200
89UD-693TC
90B-443
90B/Ins-5
90Classic-16
90Classic/III-12
90Classic/III-NO
90Colla/Matting-Set
90CollAB-13
90D-190
90D/BestAL-38
90D/Learning-12
90F-447
90F-626M
90F-638M
90F/AwardWin-21
90F/BB-24
90F/BBMVP-23
90F/LgStand-2
90F/LL-23
90F/WaxBox-C19
90HOF/St-90
90HotPlay/St-25
90KayBee-18
90KingB/Discs-14
90KMart/CBatL-4
90KMart/SS-17
90Leaf/I-69
90MLBPA/Pins-63
90MSA/Soda-11
90OPC-200
90Panini/St-125
90Post-1
90PublInt/St-291
90PublInt/St-540
90RedFoley/St-59
90S-1
90S/100St-10
90S/NWest-2
90Sf-150
90Starline/LJS-1
90Starline/LJS-28
90Starline/LJS-35
90Sunflower-8
90T-200
90T/Ames-18
90T/Big-85
90T/Coins-21
90T/DH-43
90T/Gloss60-11
90T/HeadsUp-19
90T/HillsHM-3
90T/Mini-24
90T/St-308
90T/TVAS-17
90T/TVYank-25
90Tetley/Discs-14
90UD-191
90WonderBrd-6
91B-178
91BBBest/HitM-14
91BBBest/RecBr-11
91Classic/200-98
91Classic/I-33
91Classic/III-56
91Coke/Matting-Set
91D-107
91DennyGS-8
91F-673
91F/ProV-11
91F/Ultra-239
91Leaf/II-425
91Leaf/Prev-22
91Leaf/Stud-97
91MajorLg/Pins-1
91MooTown-15
91OPC-100
91OPC/Premier-77
91Panini/FrSt-324
91Panini/St-267
91Pep/SS-11
91Petro/SU-19
91Post-29
91RedFoley/St-61
91S-23
91S-856FRAN
91S/100SS-23
91Seven/3DCoin-11NE
91T-100A
91T-100B
91T/CJMini/I-7
91T/StClub/I-21
91T/SU-24
91UD-354
92Classic/I-58
92D/II-596
92F-237
92F/TmLIns-1
92S/100SS-23
92S/I-23
92T-300
92UD-356

Mattingly, Earl
90Target-491

Mattingly, Steve
89Boise/ProC-1989

Mattocks, Rich
84Greens-24

Mattox, Frank
85Beloit-11
86Stockton-18
87ElPaso-8
88ElPaso/Best-29
88TexLgAS/GS-38
89ElPaso/GS-23
90Denver/CMC-14
90Denver/ProC-632

Mattson, Don
91Macon/ClBest-5

Mattson, Kurt
83Clinton/LF-22
84Shrev/FB-11

Mattson, Rob
91DurhamUp/ProC-3
91Macon/ProC-859

Mattson, Ronnie
77Spartan

Matula, Rick
80T-596
81D-317
81F-263
81T-611
82Evansvl-5

Matusyavichus, Edmuntas
89EastLDD/ProC-DD9

Matuszak, Mick
91AubAS/ClBest-23TR

Matuszek, Len
80OkCty
81OkCty/TCMA-10
82OkCty-8
83Portl-8
83T-357
84D-549
84F-41
84Nes/792-275
84OPC-275
84Phill/TastyK-31
84T-275
85D-259
85F-260
85F/Up-U79
85OPC-226
85T-688
85T/Tr-80T
85Tor/Fire-22
86Coke/Dodg-19
86D-494
86F-138
86Pol/Dodg-17
86T-109
87D-423
87F-447
87Mother/Dodg-20
87Pol/Dodg-8
87T-457
88Pol/Dodg-17M
88S-424
88T-92
90Target-492

Matzen, Mark
82Cedar-13
Matznick, Danny
90SoBend/Best-20
91Saraso/ClBest-7
91Saraso/ProC-1110
Mauch, Gene
49Eureka-63
51B-312
57T-342
61T-219MG
62T-374MG
63T-318MG
64PhilBull-17MG
64T-157MG
65T-489MG
66T-411MG
67T-248MG
68OPC-122MG
68T-122MG
69Expos/Pins-5MG
69T-606
70OPC-442MG
70T-442MG
71LaPizza-6
71OPC-59MG
71T-59MG
72OPC-276MG
72T-276MG
73OPC-377MG
73T-377MG
74OPC-531MG
74T-531MG
75OPC-101MG
75T-101MG
75T/M-101MG
76SSPC-597MG
76T-556MG
77T-228MG
78T-601MG
79T-41MG
82D-141MG
83T-276MG
85Smok/Cal-24MG
85T/Tr-81T
86Smok/Cal-24MG
86T-81MG
87T-518MG
88T-774MG
90Target-493
Mauch, Thomas
87StPete-17
88StPete/Star-16
Maul, Al
90Target-494
N172
N690
WG1-61
Mauldin, Eric
91Martins/ClBest-2
91Martins/ProC-3469
Mauldin, Weldon
(Hunky)
62Pep/Tul
63Pep/Tul
Mauney, Terry
84CharlO-2
85CharlO-28
87CharlO/WBTV-xx
Mauramatsu, Arihito
91Salinas/ProC-2257
Maurer, Rob
88Butte-15
89CharlR/Star-15
89Star/Wax-7
90A&AASingle/ProC-69
90Tulsa/ProC-1163
91AAAGame/ProC-AAA26
91AS/Cal-21
91OkCty/LineD-312
91OkCty/ProC-186
92D/II-703
92F-659RP
92S/II-767
92T/91Debut-119
92UD-10SR
Mauriello, Ralph
90Target-1019
Mauro, Carmen
52Park-71
53Exh/Can-47
79TCMA-109
90Target-495
Mauro, Mike
90Bristol/Star-17
Mauser, Timothy
(Tim)
88Spartan/Star-12
88Spartan/Star-12
89Clearw/Star-14
89Star/Wax-13
90Foil/Best-115
90Reading/Best-8
90Reading/ProC-1217
90Reading/Star-19
91Phill/Medford-25
91ScranWB/LineD-489
91ScranWB/ProC-2535
92S/II-744
92T/91Debut-120
Max, Bill
82Beloit-21
83ElPaso-13
84Jacks-12
89River/Best-12
Maxey, Kevin
88StPete/Star-17
Maxie, Larry
64T-94R
71Richm/Team-13
78TCMA-59
Maxson, Dan
78Newar
Maxvill, Dal
62Pep/Tul
63T-49
64T-563
65OPC-78
65T-78
66T-338
67T-421
68OPC-141
68T-141
69MB-174
69MLB/St-213
69T-320
69T/St-117
70MLB/St-141
70OPC-503
70T-503
71MLB/St-278
71OPC-476
71T-476
72MB-214
72OPC-206
72T-206
73OPC-483
73T-483
74OPC-358
74T-358
78TCMA-241
82Pol/Atl-53CO
83Pol/Atl-53CO
84Pol/Atl-53CO
Maxwell, Charlie
52T-180
55B-162
55Esskay
57T-205
58T-380
59T-34M
59T-481
60L-48
60T-443
61P-37
61T-37
61T/RO-22
61T/St-154
62J-25
62P-25
62P/Can-25
62T-506
63J-41
63P-41
63T-86
64T-401
81Detroit-76
91Crown/Orio-283
Maxwell, Jim
80Ashvl-16
Maxwell, John
90CharRain/Best-24
91CharRain/ClBest-28TR
Maxwell, Marty
78OrlTw
Maxwell, Pat
91Watertn/ClBest-20
91Watertn/ProC-3374
May, Carlos
69T-654R
70K-16
70OPC-18
70T-18
71K-45
71OPC-243
71T-243
71T/Coins-144
72MB-209
72OPC-525
72T-525
73K-45
73OPC-105
73T-105
74OPC-195
74T-195
74T/St-157
75Ho-44
75OPC-480
75T-480
75T/M-480
76Crane-32
76Ho-34
76Ho/Twink-34
76MSA/Disc
76OPC-110
76SSPC-148
76T-110
77BK/Y-22
77T-568
77T-633M
May, Dave
68OPC-56R
68T-56R
69OPC-113
69T-113
70OPC-81
70T-81
71MLB/St-444
71OPC-493
71T-493
72T-549
73OPC-152
73T-152
74K-13
74OPC-12
74T-12
74T/DE-58
74T/St-196
75OPC-650
75T-650
75T/M-650
76Ho-148
76OPC-281
76SSPC-19
76T-281
78T-362
83Ander-5C
91Crown/Orio-284
May, Davis
79Syrac-16
May, Derrick
87Peoria-12
88Peoria/Ko-35M
88WinSalem/Star-11
89CharlK-5
90F-645R
90Iowa/CMC-14
90Iowa/ProC-331
90T/TVCub-53
90UD/Ext-736
91Classic/200-153
91Classic/I-28
91D-36RR
91F-427
91F/Ultra-65
91Iowa/LineD-209
91MajorLg/Pins-69
91OPC-288
91S-379RP
91S/Rook40-36
91T-288
91T/90Debut-100
91T/StClub/I-73
91UD-334
92F-387
May, Frank
E122
May, Jakie
91Conlon/Sport-319
E126-56
May, Jerry
65OPC-143R
65T-143R
66EH-12
66OPC-123R
66T-123R
67T-379
67T/Test/PP-13
68KDKA-12
68T-598
69MB-170
69MLB/St-186
69T-263
69T/St-87
70MLB/St-102
70OPC-423
70T-423
71MLB/St-420
71OPC-719
71T-719
72MB-210
72OPC-109
72T-109
73OPC-558
73T-558
91WIZMets-254
May, Larry
82Orlan-20
May, Lee Jr.
88LitFalls/Pucko-1
89Clmbia/Best-10
89Clmbia/GS-15
89Pittsfld/Star-16
91Tidew/LineD-562
91Wmsprt/ProC-307
May, Lee Sr.
66T-424R
67Kahn
67T-222R
68Kahn
68T-487
69Kahn
69MB-171
69MLB/St-131
69T-405
69T/St-27
69Trans-52
70MLB/St-30
70OPC-225
70OPC-65LL
70T-225
70T-65LL
71MLB/St-62
71OPC-40
71T-40
71T/Coins-29
71T/tatt-5
72K-37
72MB-211
72OPC-480
72OPC-89LL
72T-480
72T-89LL
73OPC-135
73T-135
73T/Lids-31
74OPC-500
74T-500
74T/St-33
75Ho-142
75OPC-25
75T-25
75T/M-25
76Ho-98
76OPC-210
76SSPC-389
76T-210
77BurgChef-45
77Ho-55
77OPC-125
77OPC-3LL
77T-380
77T-3LL
77T-633M
78Ho-53
78OPC-47
78T-640
78Wiffle/Discs-45
79OPC-1
79T-10
80OPC-255
80T-490
81F-183
82D-570
82F-415
82T-132
83D-538
83F-118
83OPC-377
83OPC-378SV
83T-377
83T-378SV
83T/St-9
85CircK-34
86Mother/Ast-12
88Kahn/Reds-CO
90Pac/Legend-55
90Swell/Great-67
91Crown/Orio-285
May, Merrill
(Pinky)
39Exh
39PB-45
40PB-98
41DP-46
41PB-9
May, Milt
71OPC-343R
71T-343R
72OPC-247
72T-247
73OPC-529
73T-529
74OPC-293
74T-293
75Ho-35
75Ho/Twink-35
75OPC-279
75T-279
75T/M-279
76OPC-532
76SSPC-53
76T-532
76T/Tr-532T
77OPC-14
77T-98
78BK/T-2
78OPC-115
78T-176
79T-316
80OPC-340
80Pol/Giants-7
80T-647
81D-193
81OPC-273
81T-463
81T/St-237
82D-503
82F-395
82F/St-62
82OPC-242
82T-242
82T-576TL
82T/St-110
83D-312
83F-268
83T-84
83T/St-301
84D-386
84F-254
84Nes/792-788
84T-788
85D-410
85T-509
89VFJuice-39CO
90Homer/Pirate-21
May, Rudy
65T-537R
69JB
70MLB/St-175
70OPC-203
70T-203
71JB
71MLB/St-349
71OPC-318
71T-318
72T-656
73OPC-102
73T-102
74OPC-302
74T-302
75OPC-321
75T-321
75T/M-321
76OPC-481
76SSPC-427
76T-481
77T-56

78Ho-115
78T-262
79OPC-318
79T-603
80OPC-281
80T-539
81F-90
81OPC-179
81T-179
81T-7LL
81T/HT
81T/St-3
82D-325
82F-41
82OPC-128
82T-735
83D-135
83F-385
83T-408
84D-626
84Nes/792-652
84T-652
91Crown/Orio-286

May, Scott
86Albuq-14
87SanAn-11
88OkCty/CMC-3
88OkCty/ProC-27
89D-636
89OkCty/CMC-5
89OkCty/ProC-1523
91Iowa/LineD-210
91Iowa/ProC-1055

May, Ted
79QuadC-7

Mayberry, Greg
85VeroB-20
88VeroB/Star-15
89SanAn/Best-19
90Albuq/CMC-7
90Albuq/ProC-342
90Albuq/Trib-21

Mayberry, John
70OPC-227R
70T-227R
71MLB/St-86
71OPC-148
71T-148
72OPC-373
72T-373
73OPC-118
73T-118
73T/Lids-32
74K-29
74OPC-150
74T-150
74T/DE-51
74T/St-184
75Ho-92
75OPC-95
75T-95
75T/M-95
76A&P/KC
76Crane-33
76Ho-91
76K-46
76MSA/Disc
76OPC-194LL
76OPC-196LL
76OPC-440
76SSPC-169
76T-194LL
76T-196LL
76T-440
77BurgChef-69
77Ho-56
77OPC-16
77T-244
77T/CS-27
78OPC-168
78PapaG/Disc-40
78T-550
78Wiffle/Discs-46
79Ho-82
79OPC-199
79T-380
79T/Comics-17
80OPC-338
80T-643
81D-29
81Drake-31
81F-416
81OPC-169
81OPC/Post-13
81T-169
81T/SO-15
81T/St-139
82D-25DK
82D-306
82Drake-24
82F-619
82F/St-235
82OPC-382
82OPC-53TL
82OPC/Post-1
82T-470
82T-606TL
82T/St-248
82T/Tr-677
83F-386
83OPC-45
83T-45
85Syrac-20

Maye, A. Lee
(Lee)
60Lake
60SpicSpan-13
60T-246
61T-84
62J-156
62P-156
62P/Can-156
62Salada-216
62Shirriff-216
62T-518
63T-109
64T-416
65Kahn
65T-407
65T/E-62
65T/trans-21
66OPC-162
66T-162
67T-258
68OPC-94
68T-94
69MB-172
69T-595
69T/St-165
70OPC-439
70T-439
71OPC-733
71T-733
72MB-212
78TCMA-107
78TCMA-51

Maye, Stephen
(Steve)
86WinSalem-14
88Modesto-13
88Modesto/Cal-66
89Huntsvl/Best-10
90Salinas/Cal-128
91Salinas/ClBest-17
91Salinas/ProC-2238

Mayer, Ed
58T-461

Mayer, James Erskine
15CJ-172
D328-110
D329-114
D350/2-112
E135-110
M101/4-114
M101/5-112

Maynard, Ellerton
(Tow)
89Wausau/GS-7
90Foil/Best-84
90SanBern/Best-13
90SanBern/Cal-111
90SanBern/ProC-2646
91SanBern/ClBest-22
91SanBern/ProC-1999

Mayne, Brent
90A&AASingle/ProC-52
90B-372
90Foil/Best-8
90Memphis/Best-1
90Memphis/ProC-1012
90Memphis/Star-16
90S-664DC
91Classic/I-50
91D-617
91D/Rook-43
91F/Ultra-150
91F/Up-U28
91OPC-776
91S-765RP
91S/Rook40-8
91T-776
91T/90Debut-101
91T/StClub/II-418
91UD-72
92D/I-265
92F-162
92S/100RisSt-85
92S/I-84
92T-183

Mayo, Edward
47TipTop
49B-75
54T-247
Exh47

Mayo, John
(Jackie)
49B-228
49Eureka-141
V362-36

Mayo, Todd
88CapeCod/Sum-119
89James/ProC-2146
90WPalmB/Star-15
91WPalmB/ClBest-26
91WPalmB/ProC-1241

Mays, Al
N172/ST
N690
N690/2

Mays, Carl W.
21Exh-103
28Yueng-17
87Conlon/2-48
88Conlon/4-18
91Conlon/Sport-150
E120
E121/120
E121/80
E210-17
R332-8
V100
V61-7
W501-29
W502-17
W514-103
W515-20
W573
W575

Mays, Henry
77StPete

Mays, Jeff
86Salem-18
87PortChar-11
88CharlR/Star-16

Mays, Willie
51B-305
52B-218
52BR
52Coke
52RM-NL15
52StarCal/L-78E
52T-261
53Briggs
53T-244
54B-89
54NYJour
54RM-NL25
54SM
54T-90
55B-184
55Gol/Giants-20
55RFG-1
55RM-NL7
55T-194
56T-130
56T/Pin-41OF
57T-10
58Hires-25
58Hires/T
58PacBell-5
58SFCallB-14
58T-436M
58T-486AS
58T-5
59Bz
59HRDerby-14
59T-317M
59T-464HL
59T-50
59T-563AS
60Armour-16
60Bz-13
60MacGregor-13
60NuCard-27
60T-200
60T-564AS
60T-7M
60T/tatt-34
60T/tatt-93
61Bz-23
61NuCard-404
61NuCard-427
61P-145
61T-150
61T-41LL
61T-482MV
61T-579AS
61T/Dice-9
61T/St-80
62Bz
62Exh
62J-142
62P-142
62P/Can-142
62Salada-149
62Shirriff-149
62T-18M
62T-300
62T-395AS
62T-54LL
62T/bucks
62T/St-199
63Bz-12
63Exh
63F-5
63J-106
63P-106
63Salada-22
63T-300
63T-3LL
63T/SO
64Bz-12
64T-150
64T-306M
64T-423M
64T-9LL
64T/Coins-151AS
64T/Coins-80
64T/S-51
64T/St-20S2
64T/SU
64T/tatt
64Wheat/St-29
65Bz-12
65MacGregor-6
65OldLond-14
65OPC-250
65OPC-4LL
65OPC-6LL
65T-250
65T-4LL
65T-6LL
65T/E-27
65T/trans-58
66Bz-16
66OPC-1
66T-1
66T-215LL
66T-217LL
66T-219LL
66T/RO-27
67Bz-16
67OPC-191CL
67OPC/PI-12
67T-191CL
67T-200
67T-244LL
67T-423M
67T/PI-12
67T/Test/SU-19
68Bz-14
68Coke
68Dexter-51
68OPC-50
68T-490M
68T-50
68T/G-8
68T/Post-20
69Kelly/Pin-12
69MB-173
69MLB/St-204
69MLBPA/Pin-52
69NTF
69OPC-190
69OPC/DE-16
69T-190
69T/DE-33
69T/decal
69T/S-65
69T/St-108
69Trans-34
70K-12
70MB-15
70MLB/St-129
70T-600
70T/CB
70T/S-18
70Trans-1
71Bz
71Bz/Test-47
71K-10
71MD
71MLB/St-257
71MLB/St-567
71OPC-600
71T-600
71T/Coins-153
71T/GM-41
71T/S-56
71T/tatt-16
71T/tatt-16a
71Ticket/Giant-7
72K-54
72MB-213
72OPC-49
72OPC-50IA
72T-49
72T-50IA
72T/Post-17
73OPC-1M
73OPC-305
73T-1M
73T-305
73T/Lids-33
74Laugh/ASG-60
74OPC-473WS
74T-473WS
75OPC-192MV
75OPC-203MV
75T-192MV
75T-203MV
75T/M-192MV
75T/M-203MV
76Laugh/Jub-18
76SSPC-616
78TCMA-280
79TCMA-6
80Pac/Leg-48
80Laugh/3/4/5-10
80SSPC/HOF
82CJ-4
82KMart-8
83MLBPA/Pin-27
83T/St-3F
84Mother/Giants-1
84West/1-13
85CircK-3
85Woolwth-26
86BLChew-3
86Sf/Dec-50
86Sf/Rook-46M
86T-403TBC*
87KMart-8
87Nestle/DT-28
88Pac/Leg-24
89B/I-7
90BBWit-18
90HOF/St-65
90MSA/AGFA-1
91K/3D-3
91Negro/Lewis-21
91Swell/Great-106
91T/Arc53-244
91WIZMets-255
Exh47
PM10/L-25
PM10/L-26
PM10/Sm-115
PM10/Sm-116
PM10/Sm-117
PM10/Sm-118
PM10/Sm-119
PM10/Sm-120
PM10/Sm-121

Mayse, Gary
91Clinton/ClBest-15GM

Maysey, Matt
85Spokane/Cram-13
86CharRain-15

87CharRain-14
88Wichita-43
89LasVegas/CMC-6
89LasVegas/ProC-5
90LasVegas/CMC-3
90LasVegas/ProC-116
91Harris/LineD-264
91Harris/ProC-625

Mazeroski, Bill
57Kahn
57T-24
58Hires-36
58Kahn
58T-238
59Bz
59Kahn
59T-415
59T-555AS
60Kahn
60MacGregor-14
60T-55
61Bz-24
61Kahn
61NuCard-403
61P-128
61T-312WS
61T-430
61T-571AS
61T/Dice-10
61T/St-67
62J-170
62Kahn
62P-170
62P/Can-170
62Salada-131
62Shirriff-131
62T-353
62T-391AS
62T/St-179
63Bz-6
63Exh
63F-59
63IDL-12
63J-138
63Kahn
63P-138
63Salada-14
63T-323
63T/SO
64Kahn
64T-570
64T/Coins-143AS
64T/Coins-27
64T/St-40S4
64T/SU
64T/tatt
65Kahn
65OldLond-15
65OPC-95
65T-95
65T/E-23
65T/trans-59
66EH-9
66Kahn
66T-210
66T/RO-45
67Kahn
67T-510
67T/Test/PP-14
68Bz-7
68Coke
68Dexter-52
68Kahn
68KDKA-9
68T-390
69Kahn
69MB-175
69MLB/St-187
69T-335
69T/St-88
69Trans-60
70MLB/St-103
70OPC-440
70T-440
71Bz/Test-3
71MLB/St-208
71OPC-110
71T-110
71T/Coins-15
71T/tatt-11
72MB-215
72T-760
73OPC-517CO
73T-517CO
74OPC-489CO
74T-489CO
76Laugh/Jub-6
78TCMA-62
88Pac/Leg-60
89Swell-67
89T/LJN-73
90HOF/St-62
90Pac/Legend-39
90Swell/Great-93
91CollAB-24
91LineD-13
91Swell/Great-60
Exh47
WG10-36
WG9-36

Mazey, Randy
88BurlInd/ProC-1776
89Miami/I/Star-13

Mazur, Bob
77Salem

Mazzilli, Lee
77T-488R
78OPC-26
78T-147
79Ho-7
79K-42
79OPC-183
79T-355
80K-38
80OPC-11
80T-25
80T/S-8
81Coke
81D-34
81Drake-33
81F-316
81F/St-42
81K-46
81MSA/Disc-22
81OPC-167
81Sqt-21
81T-510
81T/HT
81T/SO-75
81T/St-191
82D-49
82F-533
82F/St-90
82OPC-243
82T-465
82T/St-67
82T/Tr-68T
83D-638
83F-387
83OPC-306
83T-685
83T/Tr-67
84D-166
84F-255
84Jacks/Smok-8
84Nes/792-225
84OPC-225
84T-225
85D-386
85F-469
85OPC-323
85T-748
86D-288
86F-612
86OPC-373
86T-578
87D-562
87F-15
87T-198
88D-614
88D/Best-209
88D/Mets/Bk-614
88Kahn/Mets-13
88Leaf-223
88OPC-308
88S-158
88T-308
89Kahn/Mets-13
89S-217
89T-58
89UD-657
90BBWit-8
90D-584
90F-88
90OPC-721
90PublInt/St-139
90S-459
90T-721
91WIZMets-256

Mazzone, Leo
75Tucson-18
79Savan-17
83Durham-29
84Durham-9
85Pol/Atl-52C
86Sumter-19CO
87Greenvl/Best-2C
87SLAS-25CO
88Richm/CMC-24CO
88Richm/ProC-16CO
89Richm/Bob-15CO
89Richm/CMC-24CO
89Richm/Ko-CO
89Richm/ProC-833CO
90Richm/CMC-2CO
90Richm/ProC-276CO
90Richm/Team-21CO

Mazzotti, Mauro
89Belling/Legoe-31CO

McAbee, Monte
82Madis-15
82WHave-15
83GlenF-4

McAfee, Brett
82Wausau-13

McAleer, James
M116
N172
T204
WG2-34

McAleese, John
T206

McAllister, Lewis
C46-57
E107
E270/2
T205

McAllister, Steve
83DayBe-21
85Nashua-17
86Nashua-18

McAlpin, Mike
88StCath/ProC-2015CO
89StCath/ProC-2093CO
90StCath/ProC-3483CO
91Knoxvl/LineD-375CO
91Knoxvl/ProC-1785CO

McAnally, Ernie
71OPC-376R
71T-376R
72OPC-58
72T-58
73OPC-484
73T-484
74OPC-322
74T-322
74Weston-21
75OPC-318
75T-318
75T/M-318

McAnany, Jim
88PalmSp/Cal-104
88PalmSp/ProC-1452

McAnarney, James
88Clmbia/GS-8

McAndrew, James
(Jim)
69T-321
70OPC-246
70T-246
71MLB/St-160
71OPC-428
71T-428
72T-781
73OPC-436
73T-436
91WIZMets-257

McAndrew, Jamie
89GreatF-5
90AS/Cal-22
90Bakers/Cal-237
91Albuq/LineD-15
91Albuq/ProC-1138
91B-601

McAuliffe, David
89Greens/ProC-411
89SALAS/GS-32
90A&AASingle/ProC-123
90Cedar/Best-22
90Cedar/ProC-2320
91Chatt/LineD-162
91Chatt/ProC-1956

McAuliffe, Dick
62T-527
63J-48
63P-48
63T-64
64Det/Lids-10
64T-363
65OPC-53
65T-53
66T-495
66T/RO-64
67OPC-170
67T-170
68Kahn
68T-285
69MB-176
69MLB/St-51
69T-305
69T/St-176
70MLB/St-211
70OPC-475
70T-475
71MLB/St-399
71OPC-3
71T-3
71T/Coins-10
71T/tatt-9
72MB-216
72T-725
73OPC-349
73T-349
74OPC-495
74T-495
78TCMA-94
81Detroit-134
88Domino-14
89Swell-14

McAvoy, Thomas
60L-108

McBean, Alvin
(Al)
62T-424
63IDL-13
63J-146
63P-146
63T-387
64Kahn
64T-525
64T/Coins-66
64T/St-17
65Kahn
65OPC-25
65T-25
65T/E-14
66EH-34
66T-353
67T-203
67T/Test/PP-12
68KDKA-34
68T-514
69MB-177
69OPC-14
69T-14
69T/St-96
70T-641
72MB-217
90Target-496

McBride, Bake
74OPC-601R
74T-601R
75Ho-41
75K-13
75OPC-174
75T-174
75T/M-174
76Crane-34
76Ho-93
76MSA/Disc
76OPC-135
76SSPC-277
76T-135
77BurgChef-17
77Ho-97
77K-34
77T-516
78OPC-156
78T-340
78Wiffle/Discs-47
79BK/P-21
79OPC-332
79T-630
80BK/P-9
80OPC-257
80T-495
81Coke
81D-404
81F-9
81F/St-31
81OPC-90
81T-90
81T/HT
81T/SO-58
81T/St-202
82D-497
82F-250
82OPC-92
82T-745
82T/Tr-69T
82Wheat/Ind
83F-414
83OPC-248
83T-248
83Wheat/Ind-21
84F-547
84Nes/792-569
84OPC-81
84T-569
84T/St-256
89Pac/SenLg-19
89Pac/SenLg-201
89TM/SenLg-74
90EliteSenLg-58

McBride, George
10Domino-78
11Helmar-74
12Sweet/Pin-61
14Piedmont/St-35
BF2-47
D327
D328-111
D329-115
D350/2-113
E135-111
E254
E270/1
E91
M101/4-115
M101/5-113
M116
T201
T202
T205
T206
T207
T213
T222
T3-110
V100

McBride, Ivan
88Watlo/ProC-677

McBride, Ken
60T-276
61P-33
61T-209
62Bz
62Salada-91A
62Salada-91B
62Shirriff-91
62T-268
62T/bucks
62T/St-66
63Exh
63Salada-41
63T-510
64Bz-4
64T-405
64T/Coins-52
64T/St-89
64T/SU
64T/tatt
64Wheat/St-30
65OPC-268
65T-268
65T/E-30
Exh47
WG10-37
WG9-37

McBride, Loy
89Visalia/Cal-107
89Visalia/ProC-1449
91Wmsprt/LineD-637
91Wmsprt/ProC-308

McBride, Thomas
49B-74

McCabe, Bill
90Target-1020

McCabe, James
T201
McCabe, Joseph
64T-564R
65OPC-181R
65T-181R
McCahan, Bill
48B-31
49B-80
McCain, Mike
82Orlan-10
83Orlan-7
83Toledo-27
McCall, John
(Windy)
55Gol/Giants-21
55T-42
55T/DH-88
56T-44
57T-291
79TCMA-200
McCall, Larry
78Cr/PCL-44
79Tucson-23
80Tacom-8
91Kane/ClBest-27CO
91Kane/ProC-2676CO
McCall, Robert
(Dutch)
47Signal
48L-57
McCall, Rod
91Collnd/ClBest-26
91Collnd/ProC-1493
91SALAS/ProC-SAL18
91Single/ClBest-175
McCall, Trey
85Bend/Cram-15
87Spartan-14
88Clearw/Star-19
89Clearw/Star-15
McCallum, Thomas
N172
McCament, Randy
85Everett/II/Cram-9
86Fresno/Smok-11
87Shrev-16
88Phoenix/CMC-9
88Phoenix/ProC-71
89Shrev/ProC-1853
90F-64
90OPC-361
90Phoenix/CMC-2
90Phoenix/ProC-8
90S-580
90T-361
90T/89Debut-77
90UD-657
McCann, Brian
82AlexD-19
83LynnP-25
86Wausau-14TR
87Pittsfld-6
88EastLAS/ProC-49
88Pittsfld/ProC-1364
89CharlK-23
90Iowa/CMC-25TR
McCann, Frank
77Jaxvl
82BirmB-19
McCann, Gene
90Target-1021
McCann, Joe
79Newar-12
89Pittsfld/Star-17
91StLucie/ClBest-19
91StLucie/ProC-706
McCarren, Bill
90Target-497
McCarter, Edward
86SanJose-12
McCarthy, Alex
E254
E270/2
T207
McCarthy, Danny
79WHave-22M
McCarthy, Dave
77Ashvl
McCarthy, Greg
88Spartan/ProC-1028
88Spartan/Star-13
88Spartan/Star-13
89Spartan/ProC-1034
89Spartan/Star-17
90Clearw/Star-13
McCarthy, Joe
30CEA/Pin-7
38ONG/Pin-19
44Yank/St-18MG
80Pac/Leg-58
80Laugh/FFeat-33
80SSPC/HOF
86Conlon/1-28
89HOF/St-87
91Conlon/Sport-28
92Conlon/Sport-589
R314/M
McCarthy, John A.
(Jack)
90Target-498
E107
N300/unif
McCarthy, John J.
40PB-215
49B-220
V355-53
McCarthy, Shawn
76BurlB
McCarthy, Steve
88Billings/ProC-1817
89Cedar/Best-10
89Cedar/ProC-914
89Cedar/Star-11
90Cedar/ProC-2319
90CharWh/Best-4
91Chatt/LineD-163
91Chatt/ProC-1957
McCarthy, Thomas F.
50Callahan
75F/Pion-13
80SSPC/HOF
89Smok/Dodg-20
90Target-499
N172
McCarthy, Tom
79Elmira-8
80Elmira-17
85Pawtu-17
86Tidew-19
87Tidew-13
87Tidew/TCMA-6
88Tidew/CANDL-22
88Tidew/CMC-7
88Tidew/ProC-1599
89T/Tr-75T
89Vanco/CMC-4
89Vanco/ProC-593
90F-541
90OPC-326
90S/100Ris-57
90T-326
91Richm/LineD-435
91Richm/ProC-2563
McCarty, David
91Classic/DP-3
92UD-75TP
McCarty, G. Lewis
90Target-500
D328-112
E135-112
W514-37
McCarty, John
N172
McCarty, Scott
91Madison/ClBest-10
91Madison/ProC-2127
McCarty, Tom
C46-89
T201
McCarver, Tim
62Kahn/Atl
62T-167
62T/St-186
63T-394
64T-429
64T/Coins-156AS
65T-294
65T/E-7
66T-275
66T/RO-40
67T-485
67T/Test/SU-14
68Bz-3
68T-275
68T-376AS
68T/G-18
68T/Post-19
69Kelly/Pin-13
69MB-178
69MLB/St-214
69MLBPA/Pin-53
69OPC-164WS
69T-164WS
69T-475
69T/decal
69T/S-61
69T/St-118
70K-34
70MLB/St-92
70OPC-90
70T-90
70T/S-61
70T/SO
71Bz/Test-1
71MLB/St-184
71OPC-465
71T-465
71T/Coins-107
71T/GM-25
71T/S-34
72MB-218
72OPC-139
72T-139
73OPC-269
73T-269
74OPC-520
74T-520
74T/St-115
75OPC-586
75T-586
75T/M-586
76OPC-502
76T-502
77T-357
78T-235
79BK/P-3
79T-675
80T-178
81F-27
WG10-38
McCaskill, Kirk
83Redwd-19
85Cram/PCL-7
86D-474
86F-163
86Smok/Cal-5
86T-628
87D-381
87F-88
87F/GameWin-27
87F/Hottest-29
87F/Mini-67
87F/St-75
87Leaf-223
87OPC-194
87Sf-127
87Seven-W5
87Smok/Cal-5
87T-194
87T/St-181
88D-381
88D/Best-83
88F-496
88Panini/St-36
88S-552
88Sf-78
88Smok/Angels-12
88T-16
88T/Big-168
89B-38
89D-136
89D/Best-83
89F-483
89OPC-348
89Panini/St-285
89S-181
89Sf-214
89T-421
89T/Big-149
89T/St-184
89UD-223
90B-283
90D-170
90F-138
90Leaf/I-247
90OPC-215
90Panini/St-37
90PublInt/St-373
90PublInt/St-598
90S-217
90S/100St-38
90Sf-169
90Smok/Angel-11
90T-215
90T/Mini-9
90T/St-167
90UD-506
91D-637
91F-319
91F/Ultra-50
91Leaf/I-199
91Leaf/Stud-28
91OPC-532
91S-590
91Smok/Angel-10
91T-532
91T/StClub/II-313
91UD-539
92D/I-340
92F-64
92S/I-79
92T-301
92UD-128
McCatty, Steve
78T-701R
80T-231
81D-478
81F-589
81OPC-59
81T-503
82D-35
82F-99
82F/St-131
82Granny-10
82OPC-113
82T-113
82T-156TL
82T-165LL
82T-167LL
82T/St-10LL
82T/St-14
82T/St-228
83D-491
83D/AAS-14
83F-525
83Granny-54
83T-493
84D-420
84F-454
84Mother/A's-8
84Nes/792-369
84OPC-369
84T-369
85D-497
85F-430
85Mother/A's-20
85T-63
85T/St-324
86BuffB-18
86F-427
86T-624
87SanJose-26
89Pac/SenLg-89
89T/SenLg-110
89TM/SenLg-75
91Pac/SenLg-16
McCauley
T206
McCauley, Drew
82Buffa-4
McCawley, Bill
52Mother-11
McCawley, James
N172
McCerod, George
86Pawtu-13
McClain, Charles
91Billings/ProC-3750
McClain, Joe Jr.
79QuadC-8
McClain, Joe Sr.
61T-488
62Salada-54
62Shirriff-54
62T-324
62T/St-98
63T-311
McClain, Michael
83Miami-2
85Beaum-12
86Beaum-18
McClain, Ron
76Indianap-25TR
77Indianap-26TR
78Indianap-26TR
79Indianap-30TR
McClear, Michael
86FtLaud-16
McClellan, Bobby
75AppFx
McClellan, Dan
74Laugh/Black-32
McClellan, Harvey
E120
V100
W573
McClellan, Paul
86Cram/PCL-2
87Clinton-21
88Shrev/ProC-1290
89Shrev/ProC-1850
90Phoenix/CMC-1
90Phoenix/ProC-9
91S-726RP
91Shrev/LineD-311
91Shrev/ProC-1817
91T/90Debut-102
92Classic/I-59
92D/II-700
92F-642
92S/II-703
92T-424
92UD-563
McClellan, William
N172
N284
McClelland, Tim
88TM/Umpire-46
89TM/Umpire-44
90TM/Umpire-42
McClendon, Lloyd
82Lynch-16
83Water-9
87F/Up-U74
87Kahn-23
88Kahn/Reds-30
88T-172
89B-287
89D-595
89D/Best-228
89F/Up-77
89Iowa/CMC-12
89Iowa/ProC-1695
89Mara/Cubs-10
89S-521
89T-644
89T/Tr-76T
89UD-446
90B-36
90Cub/Mara-14
90D-341
90D/BestNL-134
90F-38
90OPC-337
90S-176
90T-337
90T/Big-5
90T/TVCub-32
90UD-398
91F/Up-U111
91T/StClub/II-385
92D/I-338
92F-560
92S/II-566
92T-209
McClinton, Tim
89Kingspt/Star-16
90Pittsfld/Pucko-10
McClochlin, Mike
91Collnd/ProC-1481
McCloughan, Scott
90WichSt-23
McClure, Jack
44Centen-17
McClure, Jack
65T-553R
McClure, Rich
79QuadC-9
McClure, Robert
(Bob)
76OPC-599R
76SSPC-182
76T-599R
77T-472R

78T-243
79T-623
80T-357
81D-510
81F-520
81OPC-156
81T-156
82Pol/Brew-10
82T-487
83D-582
83F-38
83Gard-10
83Pol/Brew-10
83T-62
84D-359
84F-206
84Gard-12
84Nes/792-582
84Pol/Brew-10
84T-582
85D-536
85F-587
85Gard-12
85Pol/Brew-10
85T-203
86F-494
86Pol/Brew-10
86T-684
86T/Tr-71T
87F-325
87OPC-133
87T-707
88D-529
88F-189
88OPC-313
88S-381
88T-313
89B-43
89F-42
89F/Up-14
89S-572
89S/Tr-58T
89T-182
90D-470
90F-139
90OPC-458
90PublInt/St-374
90S-117
90Smok/Angel-20
90T-458
90UD-81
91OPC-84
91T-84
91WIZMets-258
92D/II-661
92S/II-717

McClure, Todd
87Ashvl-21
87AubAs-3
88FSLAS/Star-12
88Osceola/Star-17
89Kenosha/Star-14
89Star/Wax-52
89Visalia/ProC-1436

McCollom, Jim
87QuadC-21
88MidldA/GS-22
88TexLgAS/GS-27

McCollum, Greg
87Elmira/Black-23
87Elmira/Red-23
88Lynch/Star-12

McCollum, Lou
47Sunbeam

McConachie, Dale
89Albany/Best-26

McConathy, Doug
91Bluefld/ProC-4135
91Bluefld/ClBest-15

McConnell, Ambrose
11Helmar-12
E254
E91
E97
M116
S74-6
T202
T204
T205
T3-29
W555

McConnell, Walt
86FSLAS-34

86VeroB-17
87SanAn-14
88SanAn/Best-16
89Albuq/CMC-21
89Albuq/ProC-83
90Albuq/CMC-28CO
90Albuq/ProC-353
90Albuq/Trib-22
91Albuq/ProC-1148

McCool, Bill
64T-356R
65Kahn
65OPC-18
65T-18
66Kahn
66T-459
67Kahn
67T-353
68Kahn
68T-597
69MB-179
69MLB/St-194
69OPC-129
69T-129
70MLB/St-116
70OPC-314
70T-314
72MB-219

McCorkle, Dave
86Wausau-15
88Vermont/ProC-963

McCormack, Brian
88AppFx/ProC-152
89BBCity/Star-16
90Memphis/Best-19
90Memphis/ProC-1009
90Memphis/Star-17

McCormack, Don R.
79OkCty
80OkCty
81OkCty/TCMA-9
82Evansvl-12
88Batavia/ProC-1664
90Reading/Best-24MG
90Reading/ProC-1234MG
90Reading/Star-26MG
91Reading/LineD-524MG
91Reading/ProC-1385MG

McCormack, John
N172

McCormack, Mark
83Nashua-23

McCormack, Ron
83CharR-21

McCormack, Tim
86Jaxvl/TCM-26tr
87Indianap-32
88Indianap/ProC-498
89Indianap/CMC-9
89Indianap/ProC-1226

McCormick, Frank A.
(Buck)
39Exh
39PB-36
40PB-75
41DP-9
41PB-5
41Wheat-18
49B-239
91Conlon/Sport-306
W711/1
W711/2

McCormick, Glenn
90Madison/ProC-2277

McCormick, Harry
(Moose)
E254
T204
T206

McCormick, Jim
N172
N284

McCormick, John
89AppFx/ProC-873
90BBCity/Star-16
91BBCity/ClBest-10
91BBCity/ProC-1397

McCormick, Michael J.
(Kid or Dude)
90Target-501

McCormick, Mike F.
58SFCallB-15
58T-37
59T-148
60MacGregor-15
60T-530
61P-141
61T-305
61T-383M
61T-45LL
61T/St-81
62J-139
62P-139
62P/Can-139
62Salada-134
62Shirriff-134
62T-107
62T-319IA
62T-56LL
62T/bucks
62T/St-200
63T-563
64T-487
65T-343
66OPC-118
66T-118
67OPC-86
67T-86
68Bz-12
68Coke
68Dexter-53
68OPC-9LL
68T-400
68T-9LL
68T/G-17
69MB-180
69MLB/St-205
69T-517
70MLB/St-130
70OPC-337
70T-337
71MLB/St-494
71OPC-438
71T-438
72MB-220
72T-682
79TCMA-245
84Mother/Giants-16
88Pac/Leg-67
91Crown/Orio-287

McCormick, Mike
79ArkTr-14tr
80ArkTr-24tr

McCormick, Myron W.
(Mike)
41DP-116
49B-146
49Eureka-41
52Mother-57
90Target-1022
W711/2

McCormick, William J.
E107

McCosky, W. Barney
40PB-201
41DP-53
41PB-36
41Wheat-20
48B-25
48L-63
49B-203
51B-84
52T-300
81Detroit-114
Exh47

McCovey, Willie
60NuCard-67
60T-316
60T-554AS
61P-147
61T-517
61T/St-82
62J-131
62P-131
62P/Can-131
62Salada-142
62Shirriff-142
62T-544
63J-112
63P-112
63T-490
64Bz-21
64T-350
64T-41M
64T-9LL
64T/Coins-22
64T/St-94
64T/SU
64Wheat/St-31
65OPC-176
65T-176
66Bz-14
66T-217LL
66T-550
66T/RO-26
67Bz-14
67OPC/PI-32
67T-423M
67T-480
67T/PI-32
68Bz-13
68OPC-5LL
68T-290
68T-5LL
69Citgo-19
69MB-181
69MLB/St-206
69MLBPA/Pin-54
69OPC-4LL
69OPC-6LL
69OPC/DE-13
69T-416AS
69T-440
69T-4LL
69T-572M
69T-6LL
69T/DE-31
69T/decal
69T/S-66
69T/St-109
69Trans-36
70K-4
70MB-16
70MLB/St-131
70OPC-250
70OPC-450AS
70OPC-63LL
70OPC-65LL
70T-250
70T-450AS
70T-63LL
70T-65LL
70T/PI-7
70T/S-13
70Trans-2
71Bz
71Bz/Test-4
71K-33
71MD
71MLB/St-258
71OPC-50
71T-50
71T/Coins-57
71T/GM-52
71T/S-46
71T/tatt-13
71T/tatt-13a
71Ticket/Giant-8
72K-7
72MB-221
72OPC-280
72T-280
72T/Cloth-23
72T/Post-24
73OPC-410
73T-410
73T/Comics-11
73T/Lids-29
73T/PinUps-11
74Laugh/ASG-69
74McDon
74OPC-250
74T-250
74T/DE-28
74T/St-97
75Ho-19
75Ho/Twink-19
75OPC-207MV
75OPC-450
75T-207MV
75T-450
75T/M-207MV
75T/M-450
76Ho-124
76OPC-520
76T-520
77T-547
78Ho-73
78K-23
78OPC-185
78OPC-238RB
78T-34
78T-3MV
79K-17
79OPC-107
79Pol/Giants-44
79T-215
80Laugh/3/4/5-30
80OPC-176
80Pol/Giants-44
80T-335
81F-434
82KMart-16
83MLBPA/Pin-28
84Mother/Giants-2
85CircK-8
85T/Gloss22-11
86D/HL-34
86Sf/Dec-48M
87Leaf/SpecOlym-H11
89HOF/St-4
89Padre/Mag-4
89T/LJN-113
90MSA/AGFA-20
PM10/Sm-122
WG10-39
WG9-38

McCoy, Benjamin
41DP-130

McCoy, Brent
88Pulaski/ProC-1762
89Pulaski/ProC-1894
90A&AASingle/ProC-130
90BurlB/Best-27
90BurlB/ProC-2358
90BurlB/Star-18
90Foil/Best-59
91Durham/ClBest-23
91Durham/ProC-1556

McCoy, Kevin
80BurlB-2
81BurlB-3
83ElPaso-20

McCoy, Larry
88TM/Umpire-10
89TM/Umpire-8
90TM/Umpire-8

McCoy, Timothy
(Tim)
86Cram/PCL-13
88Shrev/ProC-1300
89PalmSp/Cal-57
89PalmSp/ProC-468
90Modesto/Cal-156
90Modesto/ProC-2208
91Tacoma/LineD-541

McCoy, Trey
88Butte-18
89Gaston/ProC-1012
89Gaston/Star-12
89SALAS/GS-28
90CharlR/Star-13
91Tulsa/LineD-587
91Tulsa/ProC-2781

McCrary, Arnold
77Ashvl
78Ashvl
79Wausau-23
80Wausau-22

McCrary, Sam
86Jacks/TCM-23tr
88Tidew/CANDL-1TR
88Tidew/ProC-1580
89Tidew/CMC-28

McCraw, Tom
64T-283
65T-586
66OPC-141
66T-141
67OPC-29
67T-29
68T-413
69MB-182
69MLB/St-33
69T-388
70MLB/St-189
70T-561
71OPC-373
71T-373
72MB-222
72T-767
73OPC-86
73T-86
74OPC-449

74T-449
75OPC-482
75T-482
75T/M-482
82BK/Indians-5CO
82BK/Indians-6CO
82BK/Indians-7CO
82Wheat/Ind
89French-40

McCray, Eric
89Gaston/ProC-1008
89Gaston/Star-13
90Tulsa/ProC-1151
91B-281

McCray, Justin
90Ashvl/ProC-2756
91Saraso/ClBest-17
91Saraso/ProC-1119

McCray, Rodney
(Rod)
86CharRain-16
89Saraso/Star-14
90BirmB/Best-12
90BirmB/ProC-1119
90Foil/Best-204
91OPC-523
91S-763RP
91T-523
91T/90Debut-103
91Vanco/LineD-641
91Vanco/ProC-1607
92S/II-517

McCray, Todd
90Boise/ProC-3307

McCreadie, Brant
89LittleSun-16
91Salinas/ClBest-8
91Salinas/ProC-2239

McCreary, Bob
88CapeCod/Sum-82
89Elizab/Star-17
90Visalia/Cal-69
90Visalia/ProC-2163
91OrlanSR/LineD-488
91OrlanSR/ProC-1859
91Single/ClBest-308

McCreedie, Judge
90Target-502

McCreery, Tom
90Target-503

McCue, Deron
86Shrev-17
87Shrev-19
88Phoenix/CMC-23
88Phoenix/ProC-58
90Everett/ProC-3145MG
91Clinton/ClBest-28CO
91Clinton/ProC-852CO

McCulla, Harry
82Spring-22
83Spring/LF-17
84Savan-16
85Spring-17
86ArkTr-14
90SpringDG/Best-3

McCullers, Lance
85Cram/PCL-109
86D-41RR
86F-330
86Sf/Rook-8
86T-44
87Bohem-41
87Classic-80
87D-237
87F-424
87F/Mini-68
87F/St-76
87OPC-71
87T-559
87T/St-111
88Coke/Padres-41
88D-451
88D/Best-210
88F-592
88F/Mini-114
88OPC-197
88Panini/St-399
88S-150
88Sf-85
88Smok/Padres-18
88T-197
88T/Big-38
88T/St-114
89B-168
89D-129
89D/Best-220
89D/Tr-13
89F-312
89OPC-307
89S-158
89S/NWest-14
89S/Tr-63
89S/YS/II-19
89Sf-76
89T-307
89T/St-108
89T/Tr-77T
89UD-382
89UD/Ext-710
90D-433
90F-448
90Leaf/II-456
90OPC-259
90PublInt/St-541
90S-186
90T-259
90T/TVYank-13
90UD-615
91D-133
91F-342
91S-313
91UD-203

McCullock, Alec
84BuffB-10

McCullough, Clyde
47TipTop
49B-163
49Eureka-166
50B-124
51B-94
52B-99
52T-218
55B-280
61Peters-21
72T/Test-8

McCune, Gary
83Knoxvl-22
88Knoxvl/Best-21
89Knoxvl/ProC-1121

McCurdy, Harry
28Exh-40
31Exh/4-12
33G-170

McCure, Gary
88Knoxvl/Best-21

McCutcheon, Greg
88StCath/ProC-2020
89StCath/ProC-2094
90Erie/Star-15

McCutcheon, James
87Gaston-21
88Gaston/ProC-1004
89Gaston/ProC-1011
89Gaston/Star-14

McDaniel, Jim
59T-134

McDaniel, Lindy
57T-79
58T-180
59T-479
60T-195
61P-175
61T-266
61T-75
61T/St-91
62J-163
62P-163
62P/Can-163
62Salada-144
62Shirriff-144
62T-306M
62T-522
62T/St-187
63J-167
63P-167
63T-329
64T-510
65OPC-244
65T-244
66T-496
67OPC-46
67T-46
68T-545
69MB-183
69OPC-191
69T-191
70OPC-493
70T-493
71MLB/St-495
71OPC-303
71T-303
72MB-223
72OPC-513
72T-513
73OPC-46
73Syrac/Team-16
73T-46
74OPC-182
74T-182
74T/Tr-182T
75OPC-652
75T-652
75T/M-652
79TCMA-280
Exh47

McDaniel, M. Von
58T-65
89Smok/Ast-21

McDaniel, Terry
88Clmbia/GS-22
89StLucie/Star-16
90T/TVMets-50
91Tidew/ProC-2524
92F-511
92S/II-765
92T/91Debut-121

McDavid, Ray
91CharRain/ClBest-21
91CharRain/ProC-107

McDermott, Maurice
(Mickey)
50B-97
50Drake-31
51B-16
51T/RB-43
52B-25
52T-119
53B/Col-35
53Briggs
53NB
53T-55
54B-56
55B-165
56T-340
57T-318
79TCMA-207
91T/Arc53-55

McDermott, Terry
74Albuq/Team-10
90Target-1023

McDevitt, Danny
58T-357
59T-364
60BB-3
60L-50
60T-333
61T-349
62T-493
90Target-504

McDevitt, Terry
86Cram/PCL-170
87CharRain-12
88River/Cal-224
88River/ProC-1430
89Watlo/Star-31
90Clearw/Star-14

McDonald, Ben
87Anchora-20
90A&AASingle/ProC-2
90B-243
90Bz-10
90Classic-130
90D-32RR
90D/BestAL-114
90D/Preview-2
90D/Rook-30
90F-180
90Foil/Best-7
90Hagers/Best-1
90Hagers/ProC-1408
90Leaf/I-249
90LSUGreat-7
90OPC-774
90Panini/St-373
90RochR/CMC-1
90RochR/ProC-699
90S-680DC
90S/100Ris-93
90S/YS/II-2
90T-774FDP
90T/89Debut-78
90T/Big-228
90T/Tr-70T
90UD-54
91B-86
91Classic/200-132
91Classic/I-14
91CollAB-9
91Crown/Orio-288
91D-485
91F-481
91F/Ultra-19
91KingB/Discs-4
91Leaf/I-117
91Leaf/Stud-6
91MajorLg/Pins-31
91OPC-497
91Panini/FrSt-247
91Panini/St-197
91RedFoley/St-109
91S-645
91S/100RisSt-50
91Seven/3DCoin-8A
91Sunflower-17
91T-497
91T/CJMini/II-6
91T/StClub/I-264
91T/SU-25
91ToysRUs-17
91UD-446
92D/II-436
92F-14
92S/100SS-94
92S/II-658
92T-540
92UD-163
92UD-93TC

McDonald, Chad
91WPalmB/ClBest-22
91WPalmB/ProC-1237

McDonald, Dave
91SanBern/ClBest-9
91SanBern/ProC-1985

McDonald, David B.
70OPC-189R
70T-189R

McDonald, Ed
T207

McDonald, George
45Centen-17

McDonald, James
86Jamestn-16

McDonald, Jason
91T/Tr-75T

McDonald, Jeff
84Chatt-28
86Chatt-18

McDonald, Jerry
77Salem
80Port-4

McDonald, Jim
55B-77
55Esskay
91Crown/Orio-289

McDonald, Jim
78DaytB
79WHave-10
80Colum-11
83ColumAst-15

McDonald, Kevin
91SLCity/ProC-3207

McDonald, Kirk
86Madis-14
86Madis/Pol-14
88Huntsvl/BK-11
89Modesto/Cal-274
89Modesto/Chong-13

McDonald, Manny
81OkCty/TCMA-12

McDonald, Mark
(Mac)
82Madis-29

McDonald, Michael
(Mike)
86Cram/PCL-103
87Wausau-20
88MidwLAS/GS-55
88Wausau/GS-11
89Everett/Star-20
89SanBern/Best-22
89SanBern/Cal-87
90Foil/Best-226
90Wmsprt/Best-15
90Wmsprt/ProC-1069
90Wmsprt/Star-16
91Jaxvl/LineD-338
91Jaxvl/ProC-162

McDonald, Rod
82Watlo/B-7
82Watlo/C-8
83BuffB-5

McDonald, Russ
83Tacom-7

McDonald, Rusty
78Clinton

McDonald, Shelby
88Spartan/ProC-1030
88Spartan/Star-14
89Clearw/Star-16
90Clearw/Star-15

McDonald, T.J.
84Everett/Cram-22B
86Fresno/Smok-24
87Shrev-18
88Shrev/ProC-1302
89SanJose/Best-25
89SanJose/Cal-224
89SanJose/ProC-436
89SanJose/Star-19

McDonald, Tony
82OkCty-15
82Reading-21

McDonald, Webster
78Laugh/Black-10

McDonough, Brian
82Miami-4
83SanJose-5

McDougal, John
90Target-1024

McDougal, Julius
86WinSalem-15
87Portl-12
88EastLAS/ProC-9
88GlenF/ProC-919
89Canton/Best-2
89Canton/ProC-1321
89Canton/Star-15
90NewBrit/Best-3
90NewBrit/Star-10
90Pawtu/CMC-16
90T/TVRSox-53
91Syrac/LineD-503
91Syrac/ProC-2486

McDougald, Gil
52B-33
52BR
52Coke
52RM-AL14
52T-372
52TipTop
53B/Col-63
53Briggs
53RM-AL23
53SM
53T-43
54B-97
54Dix
54NYJour
54RH
54RM-AL25
54SM
55B-9
55SM
56T-225
57Swift-9
57T-200
58T-20
59T-237M
59T-345
60MacGregor-16
60T-247
61P-10
79TCMA-155
90Pac/Legend-94
91T/Arc53-43
Exh47
PM10/L-27
PM10/Sm-123

McDowell, Jack
88Coke/WS-16
88D-47RR
88D/Rook-40
88F-407
88F/Hottest-25
88F/Mini-16

88Leaf-47RR
88S/Tr-85T
88T/Tr-68T
89B-61
89D-531
89F-504
89OPC-143
89Panini/St-302
89S-289
89T-486
89T/St-302
89ToysRUs-20
89UD-530
89Vanco/ProC-577
90B-305
90Coke/WSox-17
90T/Tr-71T
90UD-625
91B-352
91Classic/III-66
91D-57
91F-129
91F/Ultra-78
91Kodak/WSox-29
91Kodak/WSox-x
91Leaf/II-340
91Leaf/Stud-36
91OPC-219
91S-27
91T-219
91T/StClub/I-87
91UD-323
91USPlayC/AS-3H
92D/I-352
92F-89
92S/100SS-22
92S/I-62
92T-11
92UD-553

McDowell, Michael
(Mike)
89AubAs/ProC-2173
90Ashvl/ProC-2743
91BurlAs/ClBest-7
91BurlAs/ProC-2798

McDowell, Oddibe
85D/HL-24
85F/Up-U80
85OKCty-18
85Rang-0
85T-400OLY
85T/Tr-82T
86D-56
86F-566
86F/LimEd-28
86F/LL-23
86F/Mini-111
86F/St-73
86KayBee-20
86Leaf-46
86OPC-192
86OPC/WaxBox-K
86Rang-0
86Sf-160
86T-480
86T/Gloss60-1
86T/St-237
86T/St-307
86T/WaxBox-K
87Classic/Up-115
87D-161
87D/OD-177
87F-130
87F/Lim-27
87F/St-77
87Leaf-51
87Mother/Rang-4
87OPC-95
87RedFoley/St-78
87Sf-131
87Smok/R-16
87T-95
87T/St-243
88D-382
88F-473
88F/St-66
88Leaf-154
88Mother/R-4
88OPC-234
88Panini/St-208
88S-215
88S/YS/II-27
88Sf-175
88Smok/R-5
88T-617
88T/Big-198
88T/St-237
89B-90
89D-378
89D/Tr-49
89F-528
89OPC-183
89Panini/St-456
89S-59
89S/Tr-72T
89T-183
89T/Big-245
89T/LJN-123
89T/Tr-78T
89UD-333
89UD/Ext-796
90B-13
90D-340
90D/BestNL-100
90F-589
90Leaf/I-112
90OPC-329
90Panini/St-221
90PublInt/St-563
90S-476
90Sf-207
90T-329
90T/Big-148
90T/St-32
90UD-145
91D-450
91F-697
91F/Ultra-8
91OPC-533
91RedFoley/St-62
91RochR/ProC-1915
91S-121
91T-533
91UD-497

McDowell, Roger
85F/Up-U81
85T/Tr-83T
86D-629
86F-89
86KayBee-21
86Leaf-248
86OPC-139
86Sf-161
86T-547
86T/Gloss60-39
86T/Mets/Fan-7
86T/St-103
86T/St-312
87Classic-76
87D-241
87F-16
87F/AwardWin-25
87Leaf-49
87OPC-185
87Sf-160
87Smok/NL-6
87T-185
87T/Gloss60-8
87T/Mets/Fan-4
87T/St-104
88D-651
88D/Best-126
88D/Mets/Bk-651
88F-142
88F/BB/AS-24
88F/Mini-96
88F/St-105
88Kahn/Mets-42
88Leaf-243
88OPC-355
88S-188
88Sf-42
88T-355
88T/Big-101
88T/Mets/Fan-42
88T/Mini-62
88T/St-100
89D-265
89D/Best-16
89F-43
89F/Up-110
89OPC-296
89Panini/St-132
89Phill/TastyK-43
89S-281
89S/Tr-53
89Sf-79
89T-735
89T/LJN-43
89T/Mets/Fan-42
89T/St-92
89T/Tr-79T
89UD-296
90B-146
90Classic/III-69
90D-251
90D/BestNL-57
90F-567
90Leaf/I-20
90OPC-625
90Panini/St-308
90Phill/TastyK-22
90PublInt/St-140
90S-445
90Sf-75
90T-625
90T/Big-230
90T/St-121
90UD-416
91B-500
91Classic/200-80
91D-166
91F-405
91F/Ultra-267
91Leaf/II-410
91Leaf/Stud-217
91OPC-43
91Panini/FrSt-111
91Phill/Medford-26
91RedFoley/St-63
91S-537
91T-43
91T/StClub/II-506
91UD-406
91UD/FinalEd-57F
91WIZMets-259
92D/II-750
92F-464
92S/II-597
92T-713
92UD-484

McDowell, Sam
62T-591R
63Sugar-26
63T-317
64T-391
65Kahn
65OPC-76
65T-76
66Bz-17
66Kahn
66T-222LL
66T-226LL
66T-470
67Bz-17
67Kahn
67OPC/PI-8
67T-237LL
67T-295
67T-463M
67T/PI-8
68Kahn
68OPC-115
68OPC-12LL
68T-115
68T-12LL
69Kahn
69MB-184
69MLB/St-42
69MLBPA/Pin-17
69OPC-11LL
69OPC-7LL
69T-11LL
69T-220
69T-435AS
69T-7LL
69T/decal
69T/S-14
69T/St-166
70K-50
70MB-17
70MLB/St-201
70OPC-469AS
70OPC-72LL
70T-469AS
70T-650
70T-72LL
70T/S-10
70Trans-14
71Bz
71Bz/Test-11
71K-37
71MD
71MLB/St-379
71MLB/St-568
71OPC-150
71OPC-71LL
71T-150
71T-71LL
71T/Coins-86
71T/GM-50
71T/S-16
71T/tatt-4
71T/tatt-4a
72K-33
72MB-224
72T-720
73OPC-342KP
73OPC-511
73T-342KP
73T-511
74OPC-550
74Syrac/Team-15
74T-550
78TCMA-103
89Pac/Leg-155
89Swell-71

McDowell, Tim
90Salem/Star-10
91Salem/ClBest-16
91Salem/ProC-946

McElfish, Shawn
90BurlInd/ProC-3007

McElroy, Charles
(Chuck)
87Spartan-5
88Reading/ProC-875
89Reading/Best-1
89Reading/ProC-669
89Reading/Star-18
90B-150
90F-650R
90Phill/TastyK-23
90T/89Debut-79
90UD/Ext-706
91Cub/Mara-33
91D-709
91D/Rook-49
91F-406
91F/UltraUp-U71
91F/Up-U79
91S-374RP
91S/Rook40-34
91T/StClub/II-407
91UD/FinalEd-29F
92Classic/I-60
92D/II-650
92F-388
92S/100RisSt-63
92S/I-366
92T-727
92UD-220

McElroy, Glen
86Penin-17
87DayBe-26
89BirmB/ProC-116

McElveen, Pryor
90Target-1025
M116
T205
T206
T213brown

McEnaney, Will
75OPC-481
75T-481
75T/M-481
76Icee
76OPC-362
76T-362
77OPC-50
77T-160
78OPC-81
78T-603
80T-563
91Miami/ClBest-2CO
91Miami/ProC-424CO

McFadden, Leon
69OPC-156R
69T-156R
70T-672
72MB-225

McFarland, Charles A.
(Chappie)
90Target-505

McFarland, Dustin
85Anchora-19
87Anchora-21

McFarland, Ed
E107

McFarland, Herm
E107

McFarland, Kelly
85Anchora-43

McFarland, Packey
T3/Box-58

McFarland, Steve
85Anchora-20MG
87Anchora-22MG

McFarlane, Hemmy
85Newar-6

McFarlane, Orlando
62T-229
64T-509R
66T-569
67T-496
69MB-185

McFarlin, Jason
89Everett/Star-28
90Clinton/Best-13
90Clinton/ProC-2563
91AS/Cal-43
91SanJose/ClBest-10
91SanJose/ProC-24
91SanJose/ProC-26M
91Single/ClBest-70

McFarlin, Terry
91AS/Cal-9

McGaffigan, Andy
79WHave-14
80Nashvl
81Colum-8
82Phoenix
82T-83R
83Mother/Giants-20
83T/Tr-68T
84D-309
84F-382
84F/X-78
84Nes/792-31
84Stuart-34
84T-31
84T/Tr-78T
85D-646
85F-540
85T-323
86F-181
86F/Up-U74
86Provigo-4
86T-133
86T/Tr-72T
87D-380
87F-326
87Leaf-220
87OPC-351
87T-742
88D-380
88F-190
88OPC-56
88S-366
88T-488
89B-356
89D-338
89F-386
89OPC-278
89S-138
89T-278
89T/Big-315
89T/St-75
89UD-359
90D-574
90F-355
90Omaha/CMC-10
90OPC-559
90PublInt/St-182
90S-224
90T-559
90UD-597
91Omaha/LineD-342
91OPC-671
91Pol/Royal-14
91S-619
91T-671

McGaha, Mel
62Sugar-18
62T-242MG
65T-391MG

McGann, Dan
90Target-1026

McGann, Dennis
E254
T206
WG3-29
McGann, Don
83Greens-30
84Nashvl-14TR
86Nashvl-17TR
87Toledo-23
88Toledo/ProC-606
89Edmon/ProC-560
McGannon, Paul
81Omaha-3
82Omaha-27
83Omaha-26
McGarity, Jeremy
90Johnson/Star-18
91Savan/ClBest-10
91Savan/ProC-1651
McGarr, James
N172
McGeachy, John
(Jack)
N172
N284
McGee
10Domino-74
W555
McGee, Brian
91BendB/ClBest-22
91BendB/ProC-3697
McGee, Ron
80Spokane-6
McGee, Tim
86WinHaven-17
87Greens-16
88Lynch/Star-13
88NewBrit/ProC-901
McGee, Tony
89Spokane/SP-5
90Riversi/Best-16
90Riversi/Cal-4
90Riversi/ProC-2611
McGee, Willie D.
79WHave-13
82Louisvl-16
83D-190
83F-15
83OPC-49
83T-49
83T/St-147
83T/St-326
84D-353
84D-625M
84D/AAS-2
84F-329
85FunFoodPin-33
84Nes/792-310
84OPC-310
84Seven-9C
84T-310
84T/St-141
84T/St/Box-8
85D-475
85D/HL-29M
85D/HL-38
85D/HL-52
85F-234
85Leaf-125
85OPC-57
85T-757
85T/St-141
85ThomMc/Discs-36
86BK/AP-16
86D-109
86D-3DK
86D-651M
86D/AAS-36
86D/DKsuper-3
86Dorman-15
86Drake-23
86F-42
86F-636M
86F/LimEd-29
86F/LL-24
86F/Mini-9
86F/Slug-22
86F/St-74
86Jiffy-15
86KAS/Disc-20
86Leaf-225M
86Leaf-3DK
86Meadow/Blank-9
86Meadow/Milk-6
86Meadow/Stat-10
86OPC-117
86OPC/WaxBox-L
86Quaker-1
86Sf-176M
86Sf-183M
86Sf-184M
86Sf-19
86Schnucks-16
86T-580
86T-707AS
86T/3D-14
86T/Gloss60-9
86T/Mini-63
86T/St-144
86T/St-45
86T/Super-2
86T/WaxBox-L
86Woolwth-21
87Classic-31
87D-84
87Drake-9
87F-304
87F/Hottest-30
87F/BB-27
87F/LL-29
87Leaf-113
87OPC-357
87RedFoley/St-86
87Sf-74
87Smok/Cards-22
87T-440
87T/St-48
88Bz-12
88Classic/Red-173
88D-307
88D/AS-44
88D/Best-131
88F-42
88F/Mini-108
88F/St-118
88F/TL-20
88KayBee-17
88Leaf-103
88OPC-160
88Panini/St-396
88S-40
88Sf-91
88Smok/Card-21
88T-160
88T/Big-79
88T/Gloss60-36
88T/Mini-71
88T/St-55
88T/UK-46
88Woolwth-26WS
89B-442
89Classic-98
89D-161
89D/AS-51
89F-457
89KMart/Lead-12
89Louisvl-27
89OPC-225
89Panini/St-189
89S-88
89S/HotStar-93
89Sf-206
89Smok/Cards-13
89T-640
89T/Big-183
89T/LJN-7
89T/St-36
89UD-621
90B-194
90D-632
90D/BestNL-131
90F-253
90KMart/CBatL-14
90Leaf/II-367
90MLBPA/Pins-33
90OPC-285
90Panini/St-339
90Publint/St-222
90S-374
90Smok/Card-14
90T-285
90T/Big-158
90T/TVCard-34
90UD-505
91B-640
91Bz-11
91Classic/200-162
91Classic/I-74
91Classic/II-T76
91D-666
91D-BC22
91F-16
91F/Ultra-325
91F/UltraUp-U118
91F/Up-U130
91KingB/Discs-1
91Leaf/II-360
91Leaf/Stud-256
91Mother/Giant-6
91OPC-380
91OPC/Premier-78
91Panini/Top15-1
91PG&E-23
91RedFoley/St-64
91S-597
91S/100SS-37
91S/RookTr-19T
91SFExam/Giant-10
91T-380
91T/StClub/II-335
91T/Tr-76T
91T/WaxBox-I
91UD-584
91UD/Ext-721
92D/I-60
92F-643
92S/100SS-18
92S/I-112
92T-65
92UD-194
92UD-34
McGeehee, Connor
82Buffa-3
83LynnP-21
McGehee, Kevin
90Everett/ProC-3123
91AS/Cal-37
91SanJose/ClBest-18
91SanJose/ProC-7
McGhee, Warren E.
(Ed)
53T-195
54T-215
55T-32
55T/DH-78
91T/Arc53-195
McGilberry, Randy
77Jaxvl
79T-707R
80Tidew-25
McGinley, James
C46-2
E254
E270/1
T206
McGinn, Dan
69Fud's-7
69T-646R
70Expos/Pins-10
70OPC-364
70T-364
71MLB/St-134
71OPC-21
71T-21
72MB-226
72OPC-473
72T-473
73OPC-527
73T-527
McGinnis
N284
McGinnis, Russ
86Beloit-14
87Beloit-13
89Tacoma/CMC-16
89Tacoma/ProC-1556
90Tacoma/CMC-21
90Tacoma/ProC-96
91AAAGame/ProC-AAA18
91Iowa/LineD-211
91Iowa/ProC-1063
McGinnity, Joe
(Iron Man)
50Callahan
61F-126
72F/FFeat-1
72Laugh/GF-6
80SSPC/HOF
89Smok/Dodg-21
90HOF/St-11
90Target-506
C46-77
E107
E254
E270
E91
T201
T206
WG3-30
McGlone, Brian
91AubAS/ClBest-20
91AubAS/ProC-4281
McGlone, John
N172
McGlothen, Lynn
73OPC-114
73T-114
75K-20
75OPC-272
75T-272
75T/M-272
76OPC-478
76SSPC-297
77T-47
78T-478
78T-581
79T-323
80T-716
81D-562
81F-302
81T-609
82T-85
McGlothin, Ezra
(Pat)
52Park-53
90Target-1027
V362-10
McGlothlin, Jim
66T-417R
67OPC-19
67T-19
68Bz-8
68T-493
69JB
69MB-186
69MLB/St-24
69T-386
69T/St-146
70MLB/St-31
70OPC-132
70T-132
71MLB/St-63
71OPC-556
71T-556
71T/Coins-9
72K-36
72MB-227
72OPC-236
72T-236
73OPC-318
73T-318
74OPC-557
74T-557
McGlynn, Ulysses
T201
T206
McGonnigal, Brett
91Clinton/ClBest-4
91Everett/ClBest-5
91Everett/ProC-3932
McGorkle, Robbie
82DayBe-18
McGough, Greg
91Saraso/ClBest-13
91Saraso/ProC-1117
McGough, Keith
91Gaston/ClBest-9
91Gaston/ProC-2686
McGough, Tom
75OkCty
76Wmsprt
McGovern, Phil
T3/Box-70
McGovern, Steve
90Batavia/ProC-3063
McGowan, Donnie
85Elmira-15
86Greens-14
87WinHaven-5
88WinHaven/Star-12
McGrath
T222
McGrath, Charles
(Chuck)
83Erie-15
84Savan-6
85Spring-20
86StPete-19
87ArkTr-3
89ArkTr/GS-12
89Louisvl-28
90Denver/CMC-23
90Denver/ProC-622
McGraw, Bob
90Target-507
McGraw, Frank E.
(Tug)
65T-533R
66OPC-124
66T-124
67T-348
68T-236
69T-601
70OPC-26
70T-26
70Trans/M-24
71MLB/St-161
71OPC-618
71T-618
72MB-228
72OPC-163
72OPC-164IA
72T-163
72T-164A
73K-21
73OPC-30
73T-30
74OPC-265
74T-265
74T/St-67
75Ho-149
75OPC-67
75T-67
75T/M-67
76OPC-565
76SSPC-457
76T-565
77BurgChef-165
77OPC-142
77T-164
78T-446
78Wiffle/Discs-48
79BK/P-10
79OPC-176
79T-345
80BK/P-20
80OPC-346
80T-655
81Coke
81D-273
81F-657
81F-7
81F/St-83
81K-37
81T-40
81T/HT
81T/St-205
81T/St-262
82D-420
82F-251
82F/St-55
82OPC-250
82T-250
83D-371
83F-166
83OPC-166
83OPC-187SV
83T-510
83T-511SV
84D-547
84D/Champs-53
84F-42
84Nes/792-709LL
84Nes/792-728
84OPC-161
84Phill/TastyK-24
84T-709LL
84T-728
85F-261
85T-157
88Pac/Leg-96
89Swell-96
91WIZMets-260
McGraw, Gary
82Idaho-26
McGraw, Hank
71Richm/Team-14

McGraw, John J.
10Domino-79
11Helmar-132
12Sweet/Pin-118A
12Sweet/Pin-118B
14CJ-69
14Piedmont/St-36
15CJ-69
21Exh-104
28Yueng-42
40PB-235
48Exh/HOF
49Leaf/Prem-6
60Exh/HOF-17
60F-66
61F-60
61GP-23
63Bz/ATG-20
69Bz/Sm
72K/ATG-3
75F/Pion-15
80Pac/Leg-43
80SSPC/HOF
83D/HOF-35
86Conlon/1-29
88Conlon/5-20
89HOF/St-89
90BBWit-59
91Conlon/Sport-65
92Conlon/Sport-584
BF2-78
D303
D327
D328-113
D329-116
D350/2-114
E101
E104
E105
E106
E107
E121/120
E121/80
E122
E135-113
E210-42
E224
E286
E91
E92
E93
E94
E98
L1-116
M101/4-116
M101/5-114
M116
R332-41
S74-89
S81-91
T202
T205
T206
T207
T213/blue
T216
T3-26
V100
W501-103
W501-73
W502-42
W514-52
W515-45
W555
W575
WG3-31
WG4-18
WG5-29
WG6-28

McGraw, Tom
90Beloit/Star-14
91ElPaso/LineD-192
91ElPaso/ProC-2746

McGreachery
N172

McGregor, Scott
75OPC-618R
75T-618R
75T/M-618R
77T-475R
78T-491
79OPC-206
79T-393
80T-237
81D-114
81F-174
81F/St-10
81OPC-65
81T-65
81T/St-37
82D-331
82F-172
82F/St-149
82OPC-246AS
82OPC-316
82T-555AS
82T-617
82T/St-143
83D-483
83F-66
83OPC-216
83T-745
84D-594
84F-13
84F-646IA
84F/St-64
85FunFoodPin-102
84Nes/792-260
84OPC-260
84T-260
84T/St-207
85D-413
85F-183
85Leaf-72
85OPC-228
85T-550
85T/St-198
86D-291
86F-281
86F/St-75
86Leaf-165
86OPC-110
86T-110
86T/St-230
87D-520
87F-475
87French-16
87Leaf-243
87OPC-347
87T-708
88OPC-254
88S-315
88T-419
89Swell-56
91Crown/Orio-290

McGrew, Charley
86Beloit-15
87Stockton-12
88Beloit/GS-7
89Modesto/Cal-284

McGriff, Fred
85Syrac-2
85Syrac-25M
86D-28RR
86Leaf-28RR
86Syrac-18
87D-621
87D/HL-39
87D/OD-38
87D/Rook-31
87F/Up-U75
87Sf/Rook-12
87T/Tr-74T
87Tor/Fire-20
88D-195
88D/Best-160
88F-118
88Ho/Disc-15
88OPC-395
88RedFoley/St-54
88S-107
88S/YS/II-28
88Sf-168
88T-463
88Tor/Fire-19
88ToysRUs-18
89B-253
89Cadaco-35
89Classic-116
89D-16DK
89D-70
89D/Best-104
89D/DKsuper-16DK
89D/MVP-BC19
89F-240
89F/BBMVP's-27
89F/Heroes-27
89F/LL-26
89F/Superstar-30
89F/WaxBox-C19
89OPC-258
89Panini/St-467
89S-6
89S/HotStar-65
89Sf-14
89T-745
89T/Big-15
89T/Coins-44
89T/Hills-20
89T/Mini-77
89T/St-185
89T/UK-50
89Tor/Fire-19
89UD-572
89UD-671TC
90B-513
90Bz-5
90Classic-19
90D-188
90D/BestAL-56
90D/GSlam-9
90F-89
90F/AwardWin-22
90F/BBMVP-24
90F/LL-24
90Holsum/Discs-13
90HotPlay/St-26
90KingB/Discs-13
90KMart/SS-31
90Leaf/I-132
90OPC-295
90OPC-385AS
90Panini/St-170
90Publint/St-523
90Publint/St-599
90RedFoley/St-60
90S-271
90S/100St-45
90Sf-13
90T-295
90T-385AS
90T/Big-134
90T/Coins-22
90T/DH-44
90T/Gloss60-55
90T/Mini-43
90T/St-187
90T/TVAS-26
90Tor/BlueJ-19
90UD-108
91B-659
91Classic/200-163
91Classic/I-88
91Classic/II-T46
91D-261
91D-389MVP
91F-180
91F/Ultra-308
91F/Up-U125
91Leaf/II-342
91Leaf/Stud-247
91OPC-140
91OPC/Premier-79
91Padre/MagRal-24
91Panini/FrSt-336
91Panini/St-157
91Panini/Top15-16
91Panini/Top15-40
91RedFoley/St-65
91S-404MB
91S-480
91S/100SS-71
91S/RookTr-58T
91Seven/3DCoin-9SC
91T-140
91T/StClub/II-357
91T/Tr-77T
91UD-565
91UD/Ext-775
92Classic/I-61
92D/DK-DK26
92D/I-283
92F-614
92S/100SS-65
92S/I-7
92T-660
92UD-33TC
92UD-344

McGriff, Terrence
(Terry)
83Tampa-18
87D-512
88D-556
88F-240
88Kahn/Reds-8
88Nashvl/Team-16
88S-281
88T-644
89Nashvl/Team-15
89T-151
90Nashvl/CMC-4
90Nashvl/ProC-236
91Tucson/LineD-615
91Tucson/ProC-2215

McGuire, Bill
87Chatt/Best-15
88BBAmer-10
88Vermont/ProC-943
89Calgary/CMC-21
89Calgary/ProC-533
89F-553
90Calgary/CMC-14
90Calgary/ProC-653

McGuire, James
(Deacon)
90Target-508
E107
E286
M116
N172
N690
WG2-35

McGuire, Mike
88Wausau/GS-20
89Wausau/GS-1

McGuire, Steve
86QuadC-22
87MidldA-26
88MidldA/GS-12
89PalmSp/Cal-54
89QuadC/Best-14
89QuadC/GS-17

McGuire, Mickey
91Crown/Orio-291

McGunnigle, William
90Target-509
N172

McGwire, Mark
85T-401OLY
86SLAS-3
87Classic/Up-121
87Classic/Up-150M
87D-46RR
87D/HL-27
87D/HL-40M
87D/HL-46
87D/HL-54
87D/Rook-1
87F/Slug-26
87F/Up-U76
87Leaf-46RR
87Sf/Rook-13
87T-366
88Bz-13
88ChefBoy-1
88Classic/Blue-212
88Classic/Blue-247M
88Classic/Red-151M
88Classic/Red-153
88Classic/Red-197M
88D-1DK
88D-256
88D-BC23
88D/A's/Bk-256
88D/AS-19
88D/Best-169
88D/DKsuper-1DK
88Drake-6
88F-286
88F-624M
88F-629M
88F-633M
88F/AwardWin-24
88F/BB/AS-25
88F/BB/MVP-23
88F/Excit-26
88F/Head-2
88F/Hottest-26
88F/LL-26
88F/Mini-46
88F/RecSet-25
88F/Slug-27
88F/SS-23
88F/St-56
88F/St-S6M
88F/TL-21
88FanSam-3
88KayBee-18
88KingB/Disc-6
88KMart-16
88Leaf-194
88Leaf-1DK
88Mother/A's-2
88Mother/McGwire-1
88Mother/McGwire-2
88Mother/McGwire-3
88Mother/McGwire-4
88MSA/Disc-4
88Nestle-10
88OPC-394
88Panini/St-167
88Panini/St-438
88RedFoley/St-55
88S-5
88S-648M
88S-659HL
88S/YS/I-1
88Sf-100
88Sf-221
88Sf/Gamewin-2
88T-3RB
88T-580
88T/Big-179
88T/Coins-3
88T/Gloss60-39
88T/JumboR-13
88T/Mini-31
88T/Revco-17
88T/RiteAid-23
88T/St-1
88T/St-164
88T/St-309
88T/St/Backs-36
88T/UK-47
88ToysRUs-19
88Woolw-15
89B-197
89Cadaco-36
89Classic-104
89Classic-4
89Classic/Up/2-190
89T/Crunch-22
89D-95
89D/AS-1
89D/Best-43
89D/GrandSlam-7
89D/PopUp-1
89F-17
89F-634M
89F/BBAS-29
89F/BBMVP's-28
89F/Excit-32
89F/Heroes-28
89F/LL-27
89F/Superstar-31
89F/WS-8
89Holsum/Discs-14
89KayBee-21
89KingB/Discs-4
89Modesto/Chong-35
89Mother/A's-2
89Mother/McGwire-Set
89Mother/ROY's-2
89Mother/ROY's-4M
89Nissen-14
89OPC-174
89OPC-70
89Panini/St-20
89Panini/St-244AS
89Panini/St-420
89Pep/McGwire-Set
89RedFoley/St-80
89S-3
89S/HotStar-25
89S/Mast-32
89Sf-200
89T-70
89T/Big-34
89T/Coins-45
89T/DH-12
89T/Gloss22-2
89T/Gloss60-41
89T/HeadsUp-14
89T/LJN-90
89T/Mini-70
89T/St-151
89T/St-172
89T/St/Backs-3
89T/UK-51

89Tacoma/ProC-1537
89Tetley/Discs-3
89UD-300
89Woolwth-27
90B-454
90Classic-59
90Classic/Up-33
90D-185
90D-697AS
90D/BestAL-54
90D/GSlam-4
90F-15
90F-638M
90F/BB-25
90F/BBMVP-25
90F/LL-25
90F/WaxBox-C20
90HOF/St-91
90KMart/SS-32
90Leaf/I-62
90MLBPA/Pins-77
90Mother/A's-2
90Mother/McGwire-Set
90MSA/Soda-2
90OPC-690
90Panini/St-132
90Panini/St-204
90Post-12
90PublInt/St-310
90PublInt/St-600
90RedFoley/St-61
90S-385
90S/100St-25
90Sf-141
90Smok/SoCal-10
90Starline/LJS-11
90Starline/LJS-27
90Starline/LJS-9
90T-690
90T/Big-28
90T/DH-45
90T/Gloss22-13
90T/Gloss60-42
90T/HeadsUp-14
90T/Mini-30
90T/St-162AS
90T/St-176
90T/TVAS-1
90T/WaxBox-I
90Tetley/Discs-15
90UD-171
90UD-36TC
90USPlayC/AS-WCM
91B-234
91Classic/200-131
91Classic/I-73
91D-105
91D-56AS
91D-BC9
91D/GSlam-11
91DennyGS-10
91F-17
91F/ProV-4
91F/Ultra-251
91Leaf/II-487
91Leaf/Stud-106
91MajorLg/Pins-39
91Mother/A's-2
91OPC-270
91Panini/FrSt-167
91Panini/FrSt-192
91Panini/St-145
91Panini/Top15-110
91Panini/Top15-14
91Panini/Top15-23
91Post-2
91RedFoley/St-122
91S-324
91S/100SS-39
91Seven/3DCoin-9NC
91SFExam/A's-8
91Sunflower-18
91T-270A
91T-270B
91T/CJMini/I-27
91T/StClub/II-399
91T/SU-26
91UD-174
91UD-656HL
92D/I-348
92F-262
92S/100SS-63
92S/I-20
92T-450
92UD-153

McHenry, Austin
E120
V100

McHenry, Vance
80Spokane-9
81Spokane-20
82SLCity-12
85Syrac-23

McHugh, Chip
86Lakeland-13
87GlenF-25

McHugh, Mike
88GreatF-6

McHugh, Scott
87Jamestn-4

McHugh, Tom
82CharR-4

McIlwain, W. Stover
60L-114

McInerney, Steve
86GlenF-15TR
87GlenF-7
89Toledo/CMC-24
89Toledo/ProC-762
90Toledo/CMC-27TR

McInerny, Dan
83SanJose-7

McInnis, Bill
86NewBrit-17
87NewBrit-8
88Pawtu/CMC-12
88Pawtu/ProC-456

McInnis, John
(Stuffy)
14CJ-10
15CJ-10
21Exh-105
21Exh-106
25Exh-29
27Exh-22
28Yueng-60
80Laugh/FFeat-29
88Conlon/5-21
91Conlon/Sport-191
BF2-37
D328-114
D329-117
D350/2-115
E120
E121/120
E121/80
E122
E126-41
E135-114
E210-60
E90/1
M101/4-117
M101/5-115
M116
T222
V100
W501-18
W502-60
W514-20
W575
WG4-19
WG7-29

McIntire, Harry
11Helmar-98
12Sweet/Pin-84
90Target-510
S74-64
WG3-32

McIntire, John Reed
10Domino-81
M116
T202
T205
T206
T207
T3-28

McIntosh, Joe
76OPC-497
76T-497
76T/Tr-497T

McIntosh, Tim
87Beloit-26
88CalLgAS-12
88Stockton/Cal-189
88Stockton/ProC-733
89ElPaso/GS-18
89TexLAS/GS-13
90AAAGame/ProC-AAA24
90B-394
90Denver/CMC-15
90Denver/ProC-628
90ElPasoATG/Team-24
90F-329
91AAAGame/ProC-AAA10
91B-36
91Classic/I-55
91D-414RR
91Denver/LineD-145
91Denver/ProC-126
91F-589
91F/Ultra-177
91Leaf/Stud-71
91OPC-561
91S-347RP
91S/Rook40-35
91T-561
91T/90Debut-104
91T/StClub/II-321
91UD-547
92S/100RisSt-93
92S/II-469

McIntyre, James J.
80ArkTr-12

McIntyre, Matthew
09Buster/Pin-9
10Domino-82
11Helmar-13
12Sweet/Pin-12A
12Sweet/Pin-12B
E104
E254
E90/1
E95
E97
M116
T202
T204
T205
T206
T207
T213/brown
T3-25

McIver, Jeryl
76Wausau

McIver, Larry
82AubAs-9

McJames, Doc
90Target-1028

McKamie, Sean
91VeroB/ClBest-22
91VeroB/ProC-783

McKay, Alan
85Kingst-7
86Pittsfld-16

McKay, Dave
76OPC-592R
76T-592R
77Ho-130
77OPC-40
77T-377
79OPC-322
79T-608
81D-350
81F-592
81T-461
82D-391
82F-100
82T-534
83D-213
83F-526
83T-47
83Tacom-29B
90Mother/A's-27M
91Mother/A's-28CO

McKay, Karl
80BurlB-28
81BurlB-26

McKay, Troy
86Jaxvl/TCMA-16

McKean, Edward
N172

McKean, Jim
88TM/Umpire-20
89TM/Umpire-16
90TM/Umpire-15

McKechnie, William B.
(Bill)
16FleischBrd-63
40PB-153
80Pac/Leg-86
80SSPC/HOF
89HOF/St-88
91Conlon/Sport-34
92Conlon/Sport-592
T207
V117-25
V355-108
W711/1
W711/2

McKee, Matt
89Ashvl/ProC-940

McKee, Ron
80Ashvl-9GM
88Ashvl/ProC-1077
89Ashvl/ProC-942

McKelvey, Mitch
84PrWill-24
85Nashua-18
86FtMyr-19

McKelvie, Ron
83Visalia/LF-12tr

McKenna, Kit
90Target-1029

McKenzie, Don
81Wausau-10

McKenzie, Doug
83Peoria/LF-8
85MidldA-7

McKeon, Brian
90A&AASingle/ProC-109
90Foil/Best-264
90Waterlo/Best-11
90Waterlo/ProC-2377
91HighD/ClBest-8
91HighD/ProC-2391

McKeon, Jack
73OPC-593MG
73T-593MG
74T-166MG
75OPC-72MG
75T-72MG
75T/M-72MG
77T-74MG
78T-328MG
84Smok/Padres-17MG
88Coke/Pad-15MG
88T/Tr-69MG
89Coke/Padre-10MG
89Padre/Mag-1MG
89T-624MG
90Coke/Padre-11MG
90OPC-231MG
90Padre/MagUno-25MG
90T-231MG

McKeon, Joel
83AppFx/LF-5
85BuffB-22
86D/Rook-55
86F/Up-U75
87Coke/WS-25
87F-503
88LasVegas/CMC-4
88LasVegas/ProC-225
88T-409
89Indianap/ProC-1212
89Richm/Bob-16
90Hagers/Best-22
90Hagers/ProC-1409
90Hagers/Star-14
91Hagers/LineD-238
91Hagers/ProC-2453

McKeon, Kasey
89Bristol/Star-17
90Fayette/ProC-2411

McKeown, Dan
85Anchora-37bb

McKercher, Tim
88SLCity-24

McKinley, Pat
88Virgini/Star-15

McKinley, Tim
88Salem/Star-12
89Harris/ProC-312
89Harris/Star-11
90Miami/II/Star-17

McKinley, W.F.
55B-226ump

McKinney, C. Rich
(Rich)
71OPC-37
71T-37
72T-619
73OPC-587
73T-587
75Tucson-14
76SSPC-587
76Tucson-22

McKinney, Charlie
80Cedar-12

McKinney, Greg
81Cedar-25

McKinney, John
85Bend/Cram-16

McKinney, Lynn
79Hawaii-2

McKinnis, Tim
88QuadC/GS-26

McKinnon, Alex
N172

McKinnon, Tom
91Classic/DP-24
91FrRow/DP-41
91Johnson/ClBest-28
91Johnson/ProC-3975
92T-96DP

McKinzie, Phil
87AppFx-29

McKnight, Jack
83Knoxvl-5
86Phoenix-16
87Phoenix-14

McKnight, James
62Salada-199
62Shirriff-199
62T-597R

McKnight, Jeff
86Jacks/TCMA-17
87Tidew-4
87Tidew/TCMA-15
88Tidew/CANDL-16
88Tidew/CMC-19
88Tidew/ProC-1587
89Tidew/CMC-13
89Tidew/ProC-1953
90RochR/CMC-12
90RochR/ProC-710
90T/89Debut-80
90UD-162
91Crown/Orio-292
91OPC-319
91RochR/LineD-460
91RochR/ProC-1909
91S-369RP
91T-319
91WIZMets-261

McKnight, Jim
82DayBe-21

McKown, Steven
76Cedar

McKoy, Keith
91CharRain/ClBest-22
91CharRain/ProC-108

McKune, Jerry
81ArkTr-22
81Louisvl-3
82Louisvl-17
83Louisvl/Riley-3
84Louisvl-3
85Louisvl-4

McLain, Dennis
65OPC-236
65T-236
66T-226LL
66T-540
67Bz-24
67OPC/PI-20
67T-235LL
67T-420
67T/PI-20
68OPC-40
68T-40
69Citgo-1
69Kelly/Pin-14
69MB-187
69MLB/St-52
69MLBPA/Pin-18
69OPC-11LL
69OPC-150
69OPC-57CL
69OPC-9LL
69OPC/DE-14
69T-11LL
69T-150
69T-433AS
69T-57CL
69T-9LL

69T/DE-8
69T/decal
69T/S-17
69T/St-177
69Trans-4
70K-73
70MLB/St-212
70OPC-400
70OPC-467AS
70OPC-70LL
70T-400
70T-467AS
70T-70LL
70T/PI-24
70T/S-17
70Trans-11
71MLB/St-546
71MLB/St-569
71OPC-750
71T-750
71T/GM-20
72MB-229
72OPC-210
72T-210
72T-753TR
73OPC-630
73T-630
75OPC-206MV
75T-206MV
75T/M-206MV
78TCMA-210
81Detroit-15
81Detroit-79
81Detroit-94
82KMart-13
83Kaline-39M
85West/2-43
88Domino-15
90HOF/St-72

McLain, Tim
86Wausau-16
88SanBern/Cal-46

McLane, Larry
82BurlR-7
83Tulsa-6

McLaren, John
75Dubuq
83Knoxvl-19
86Tor/Fire-25CO
87Tor/Fire-21CO
88Maine/CMC-6
88Maine/ProC-281
88Tor/Fire-7CO
89Tor/Fire-7CO
90Tor/BlueJ-7CO

McLarnan, John
87Reading-23
90Reading/Best-4
90Reading/ProC-1219
90Reading/Star-20

McLauchlin, Dick
81Albuq/TCMA-26

McLaughlin, Burke
52Park-12

McLaughlin, Byron
78SanJose-17
79T-712R
80T-197
81D-287
81T-344
84Nes/792-442
84T-442

McLaughlin, Colin
82Knoxvl-6
83Syrac-10
85Syrac-15
86Knoxvl-16
87Syrac/TCMA-6
88Syrac/CMC-3
88Syrac/ProC-823
89Calgary/CMC-3
89Calgary/ProC-532

McLaughlin, Dave
83AppFx/LF-3

McLaughlin, Dick
(Mac)
77Clinton
78Clinton
82Albuq-26
83Albuq-25
84Cram/PCL-169CO
85Cram/PCL-160CO
86Albuq-15CO

McLaughlin, Joey
78Richm
79Richm-1
80T-384
81D-271
81F-420
81OPC-248
81T-248
82D-507
82F-620
82OPC-376
82OPC/Post-8
82T-739
83D-255
83F-434
83OPC-9
83T-9
84D-617
84F-162
84F/X-79
84Nes/792-556
84OPC-11
84Rang-53
84T-556
85T-678
86Tacom-14
87Hawaii-19

McLaughlin, Michael
(Bo)
77T-184
78Charl
78T-437
80Richm-23
80T-326
82T-217

McLaughlin, Steve
86AppFx-14tr

McLaughlin, Thomas
N172/ST

McLaughlin, Tom
81Clinton-24

McLaughlin, Wm.
40Hughes-14

McLaurine, Bill
77Spoka

McLean, John R.
(Larry)
10Domino-80
11Helmar-117
12Sweet/Pin-103A
12Sweet/Pin-103B
14Piedmont/St-37
E101
E103
E105
E254
E270/2
E300
E90/1
E92
E98
M116
T201
T202
T204
T205
T206
T207
T213/blue
T216
T222
WG5-30

McLean, Bobby
33SK-12

McLemore, Mark
83Peoria/LF-9
85MidldA-17
86D-35RR
86F-650R
86MidldA-16
87Classic/Up-119
87D-479
87D/OD-8
87D/Rook-7
87F/Up-U77
87Sf/Rook-14
87Smok/Cal-13
87T/Tr-75T
88D-181
88D/Best-251
88F-497
88Leaf-159
88OPC-162
88Panini/St-41
88S-152
88S/YS/II-29
88Smok/Angels-22
88T-162
89D-94
89F-484
89S-208
89T-51TL
89T-547
89T/Big-30
89UD-245
90Smok/Angel-12
90T/Big-310
91Leaf/I-86
91Mother/Ast-17

McLeod, Bill
63MilSau-4

McLeod, Brian
90Everett/Best-8
90Everett/ProC-3124
91Clinton/ProC-830

McLeod, Kevin
90Hamil/Best-6
90Hamil/Star-16

McLin, Joe Jr.
91Welland/ClBest-13
91Welland/ProC-3581

McLintock, Ron
87Pocatel/Bon-18

McLish, Cal
49Eureka-64
57T-364
58T-208
59T-445
60Kahn
60T-110
60T/tatt-35
61T-157
62T-453
63T-512
64T-365
69Fud's-8
73OPC-377CO
73T-377CO
74OPC-531CO
74T-531CO
79TCMA-221
90Target-511

McLish, Tom
78Newar

McLochlin, Mike
91Collnd/ClBest-14

McLoughlin, Tim
86Salem-19

McMahon, Don
58T-147
59T-3
60Lake
60SpicSpan-14
60T-189
61T-278
62T-483
63Pep
63T-395
64T-122
65Kahn
65T-317
66OPC-133
66T-133
67OPC-7
67T-7
67T/Test/RSox-10
68T-464
69T-616
70OPC-519
70T-519
71MLB/St-259
71OPC-354
71T-354
71Ticket/Giant-9
72OPC-509
72T-509
73OPC-252CO
73T-252C
74OPC-78CO
74T-78C
80Pol/SFG-47C
83Wheat/Ind-22
85Polar/Ind-xx
88Domino-16

McMahon, Jack
83Visalia/LF-9

McMahon, Sadie
90Target-1030

McManaman, Steve
80OrlTw-17

McManus, James M.
(Jim)
61Union

McManus, Jim
87Richm/TCMA-24

McManus, Martin
(Marty)
25Exh-115
26Exh-115
29Exh/4-23
31Exh/4-23
32Orbit/num-7
32Orbit/un-47
33DL-1
33G-48
34G-80
35G-1J
35G-3A
35G-4A
35G-5A
91Conlon/Sport-189
E120
E210-48
R305
V353-48
V61-41
W572
W573
WG7-30

McMath, Shelton
80Ashvl-27

McMichael, Chuck
81CharR-14

McMichael, Gregory
88Burllnd/ProC-1796
89Canton/Best-24
89Canton/ProC-1315
89Canton/Star-16
90Canton/Star-11
90ColoSp/CMC-7
90ColoSp/ProC-31
91DurhamUp/ProC-7

McMillan, Roy
52B-238
52T-137
53B/Col-26
53T-259
54B-12
54RH
54T-120
54Wilson
55Kahn
55T-181
56Kahn
56T-123
56T/Pin-57SS
57Kahn
57Sohio/Reds-14
57T-69
58Kahn
58T-360
59Bz
59Kahn
59T-405
60Bz-33
60Kahn
60T-45
61P-183
61T-465
61T/St-46
62J-148
62P-148
62P/Can-148
62Salada-159
62Shirriff-159
62T-211M
62T-393AS
62T/St-149
63J-150
63P-150
63T-156
64T-238
64T/Coins-148AS
64T/S-8
65OPC-45
65T-45
65T/E-44
66Bz-13
66T-421
70McDon-4CO
73OPC-257CO
73T-257CO
74OPC-179CO
74T-179C
77Visalia
79TCMA-154
80OrlTw-22MG
91T/Arc53-259
91WIZMets-262

McMillan, Stu
90Idaho/ProC-3261

McMillan, Thomas E.
75OkCty
77T-490R
78SanJose-18
89Pac/SenLg-40
90EliteSenLg-100
90Target-1032

McMillan, Thomas Law
M116

McMillan, Tim
86PrWill-15
87CharWh-17
88Salem/Star-13

McMillon, Billy
91T/Tr-78T

McMorris, Mark
86WinSalem-16
87WinSalem-1

McMullen, Dale
78Memphis/Team-6

McMullen, Ken
63T-537R
64T-214
65T-319
66T-401
66T/RO-35
67OPC-47
67T-47
68OPC-116
68T-116
69MB-188
69MLB/St-106
69T-319
69T/St-239
70MLB/St-284
70OPC-420
70T-420
71MLB/St-350
71OPC-485
71T-485
72MB-230
72T-756
73OPC-196
73T-196
74OPC-434
74T-434
75OPC-473
75T-473
75T/M-473
76OPC-566
76SSPC-80
76T-566
77T-181
90Target-512

McMullen, Kevin
91Greens/ProC-3063

McMullen, Rick
82Jacks-15

McMullin, Fred
88Pac/8Men-105
88Pac/8Men-15

McMurray, Brock
88GreatF-16
89Salem/Team-16
90Bakers/Cal-250
91VeroB/ClBest-28
91VeroB/ProC-788

McMurtrie, Dan
86LitFalls-18
87Columbia-24

McMurtry, Craig
82Richm-6
83Pol/Atl-29
83T/Tr-69T
84D-599
84F-184
84F/St-105
84Nes/792-126TL
84Nes/792-543
84OPC-219
84Pol/Atl-29

84T-126TL
84T-543
84T/St-384
85D-188
85F-333
85Ho/Braves-15
85Leaf-45
85OPC-362
85Pol/Atl-29
85T-362
85T/St-28
86Pol/Atl-29
86T-194
87T-461
87Tor/Fire-22
88OkCty/CMC-4
88OkCty/ProC-44
89D-520
89Mother/R-20
89Smok/R-21
89T-779
90OkCty/ProC-430
90OPC-294
90T-294
91S-602

McNabb, Buck
91Classic/DP-43
91FrRow/DP-42

McNabb, Glenn
89Augusta/ProC-508
89SALAS/GS-6
90Salem/Star-11

McNair, Bob
80Utica-24

McNair, Donald Eric
35BU-61
39PB-105
40PB-14
92Conlon/Sport-477
R303/A
R314

McNally, Bob
86Sumter-20
87Sumter-5

McNally, Dave
63T-562R
64T-161
65OPC-249
65T-249
66OPC-193
66T-193
67T-382
68Coke
68Dexter-54
68T-478
69Citgo-2
69MB-189
69MLB/St-5
69OPC-7LL
69OPC-9LL
69T-340
69T-532M
69T-7LL
69T-9LL
69T/decal
69T/S-1
69T/St-126
69Trans-15
70K-14
70MLB/St-151
70OPC-20
70OPC-70LL
70T-20
70T-70LL
71Bz
71Bz/Test-27
71K-59
71MD
71MLB/St-304
71OPC-196ALCS
71OPC-320
71OPC-69LL
71T-196ALCS
71T-320
71T-69LL
71T/Coins-26
71T/S
71T/tatt-12
72K-29
72MB-231
72OPC-223WS
72OPC-344KP
72OPC-490
72T-223WS
72T-344KP
72T-490
72T/Post-1
73OPC-600
73T-600
74OPC-235
74T-235
74T/St-127
75Ho-150
75OPC-26
75T-26
75T/M-26
78TCMA-270
88Pac/Leg-38
91Crown/Orio-293

McNally, Mike
E120
E121/120
E121/80
W501-33
W575

McNamara, Dennis
90Niagara/Pucko-4
91Lakeland/ClBest-25
91Lakeland/ProC-279

McNamara, James
86Cram/PCL-10
87Clinton-9
88SanJose/Cal-123
88SanJose/ProC-133
89Salinas/Cal-145
89Salinas/ProC-1811
91Shrev/LineD-312
91Shrev/ProC-1824

McNamara, John
70T-706MG
73OPC-252CO
73T-252C
74McDon
74OPC-78CO
74T-78CO
75OPC-146MG
75T-146MG
75T/M-146MG
76SSPC-123MG
76T-331MG
77Padre/SchCd-18MG
77T-134MG
81T-677MG
82D-526MG
83T/Tr-70T
84Nes/792-651MG
84Smok/Cal-19MG
84T-651MG
85T-732MG
85T/Tr-84T
86T-771MG
87T-368MG
88D/AS-10MG
88D/PopUp-10MG
88T-414MG
88T/Gloss22-1MG
90T/Tr-72T
91OPC-549MG
91T-549

McNamara, Mike
88CapeCod/Sum-85

McNamara, Reggie
33SK-15

McNamee, Bill
62Pep/Tul

McNaney, Scott
89Watlo/Star-32

McNary, Mike
88CapeCod/Sum-32

McNeal, Clyde
91Negro/Lewis-9

McNeal, Paul
86Hagers-10CO
87Hagers-2CO

McNealy, Derwin
83Nashvl-12
85Syrac-29
86Colum-16
86Colum/Pol-14

McNealy, Rusty
82WHave-23
83Tacom-17
86Chatt-19
87SanJose-27

McNeely, Earl
25Exh-127
26Exh-127
91Conlon/Sport-177

McNeely, Jeff
89Elmira/Pucko-30
90Elmira/Pucko-12
90WinHaven/Star-15
91B-113
91CLAS/ProC-CAR23
91Classic/III-67
91LynchRS/ClBest-22
91LynchRS/ProC-1212
91Single/ClBest-169
91UD/FinalEd-20F
92T-618R

McNees, Kevin
87Idaho-8
88Hagers/Star-11

McNeil, Johnny
86Columbia-18

McNertney, Gerald
(Jerry)
64T-564R
68OPC-14
68T-14
69MB-190
69T-534
69T/St-226
70McDon-4
70MLB/St-275
70OPC-158
70T-158
71MLB/St-279
71OPC-286
71T-286
71T/Coins-68
72MB-232
72T-584
79Colum-9
80Colum-22
81Colum-28
82Colum-24M
87Albany-10
87Colum-5

McNulty, Bill
73OPC-603R
73T-603R

McNutt, Larry
83Lynch-2

McPhail, Lee
83Kaline-54PRES

McPhail, Marlin
86Tidew-18
87BirmB/Best-5
88Vanco/CMC-25
88Vanco/ProC-777
89Vanco/CMC-15
89Vanco/ProC-596
90Vanco/CMC-18
90Vanco/ProC-501
91Indianap/LineD-190
91Indianap/ProC-470

McPhee, John
(Bid)
N172

McPheeters, Kourtney
87Anchora-35bb

McPherson, Barry
84Savan-3

McQuade, John H.
N172/ump

McQuaide, James H.
N172

McQueen, Mike
70T-621R
71OPC-8
71T-8
72OPC-214
72T-214

McQuillan, George
15CJ-152
D303
E103
E106
E120
E90/1
E96
M116
T206
T213/blue
T216

McQuillan, Hugh
26Exh-37
W515-33

McQuinn, George
39Exh
39PB-122
40PB-53
41G-5
41PB-23
49B-232
92Conlon/Sport-391

McRae, Brian
86Cram/PCL-28
87FtMyr-26
88BBCity/Star-17
89Memphis/Best-13
89Memphis/ProC-1205
89Memphis/Star-17
89Star/Wax-44
90A&AASingle/ProC-50
90Foil/Best-276
90Memphis/Best-13
90Memphis/ProC-1022
90Memphis/Star-18
91B-292
91Classic/200-157
91Classic/I-49
91Classic/III-68
91D-575
91D/Rook-31
91F-563
91F/Ultra-152
91Leaf/I-235
91Leaf/Stud-68
91OPC-222
91Pol/Royal-15
91S-331RP
91T-222
91T/90Debut-105
91T/StClub/II-478
91ToysRUs-18
91UD-543
92D/DK-DK16
92D/I-387
92F-163
92F/RookSIns-13
92S/II-478
92T-659
92UD-157

McRae, Hal
68T-384R
70T-683R
71MLB/St-64
71OPC-177
71T-177
72OPC-291
72OPC-292IA
72T-291
72T-292IA
72T/Cloth-24
73OPC-28
73T-28
74OPC-563
74T-563
75Ho-104
75K-53
75OPC-268
75T-268
75T/M-268
76A&P/KC
76Ho-135
76OPC-72
76SSPC-176
76T-72
77BurgChef-72
77Ho-17
77K-10
77OPC-215
77T-340
78Ho-6
78K-20
78T-465
78Wiffle/Discs-49
79Ho-90
79OPC-306
79T-585
80OPC-104
80T-185
81Coke
81D-463
81F-41
81F-653M
81OPC-295
81Pol/Royals-6
81T-295
81T/St-86
82D-196
82F-416
82F/St-210
82OPC-384
82T-625
83D-238
83D/AAS-16
83Drake-17
83F-110
83K-5
83OPC-25
83PermaGr/CC-28
83Pol/Royals-4
83T-25
83T-703LL
83T/St-19
83T/St-75
84D-11DK
84D-297
84D/AAS-25
84D/Champs-17
84F-350
84F/St-44
85FunFoodPin-63
84Nes/792-340
84Nes/792-96TL
84OPC-340
84T-96TL
84T-340
84T/St-278
84T/St/Box-3
85D-588
85F-207
85Leaf-34
85OPC-284
85T-773
85T/St-270
86D-521
86F-14
86Kitty/Disc-4
86Leaf-251
86NatPhoto-11
86OPC-278
86T-415
86T-606M
86Woolwth-22
87D-471
87F-375
87OPC-246
87RedFoley/St-59
87T-573
88Classic/Blue-235
89Pac/SenLg-133
89T/SenLg-122
89TM/SenLg-76
91T/Tr-79TMG
92T-519MG

McRae, Norm
70OPC-207R
70T-207R
71OPC-93R
71T-93R

McReynolds, Kevin
84D-34RR
84F-307
84Mother/SDP-13
84Smok/SDP-18
85D-139
85F-41
85Leaf-43
85Mother/SDP-3
86D-80
86F-331
86Leaf-76
87Classic/Up-126
87D-14DK
87D-451
87D/DKsuper-14
87D/OD-125
87F-425
87F/GameWin-28
87F/Up-U78
87Leaf-14DK
87Leaf-214
87RedFoley/St-35
87Sf-135
87Sf-155M
87T/Mets/Fan-5
87T/Tr-76T
88D-617
88D/Best-153
88D/Mets/Bk-617
88F-143
88F/SS-24
88Kahn/Mets-22
88Leaf-228

88OPC-37
88Panini/St-346
88RedFoley/St-56
88S-21
88Sf-56
88Sf/Gamewin-22
88T-735
88T/Big-158
88T/St-102
89T/Ames-20
89B-388
89Classic-24
89D-99
89D/Best-70
89D/GrandSlam-4
89F-44
89F/BBMVP's-29
89F/Heroes-29
89Kahn/Mets-22
89OPC-85
89Panini/St-139
89S-93
89S/HotStar-96
89Sf-97
89T-291TL
89T-7RB
89T-85
89T/Big-116
89T/DHTest-3
89T/Gloss60-26
89T/Mets/Fan-22
89T/Mini-27
89T/St-10
89T/St-95
89T/St/Backs-51
89T/UK-52
89UD-367
89Woolwth-15
90B-138
90Classic/III-56
90D-218
90D/BestNL-129
90F-211
90F/BB-26
90Kahn/Mets-22
90Leaf/I-198
90MLBPA/Pins-15
90OPC-545
90Panini/St-305
90Publlnt/St-141
90Publlnt/St-268
90RedFoley/St-62
90S-5
90Sf-127
90T-545
90T/Big-194
90T/DH-46
90T/St-94
90T/TVMets-31
90UD-265
91B-479
91Classic/200-31
91Classic/III-69
91D-191
91F-154
91F/Ultra-224
91Kahn/Mets-22
91Leaf/I-151
91Leaf/Stud-209
91OPC-105
91Panini/FrSt-83
91S-327
91T-105
91T/StClub/I-35
91UD-105
91WIZMets-263
92D/I-288
92F-512
92S/I-168
92T-625
92UD-362

McSherry, John
88TM/Umpire-12
89TM/Umpire-10
90TM/Umpire-10

McSparron, Greg
81Clinton-25

McTammy, James
N172

McVey, George
N172

McWane, Rick
88LitFalls/Pucko-28TR
89Visalia/Cal-122TR
89Visalia/ProC-1431TR
90OrlanSR/Best-25TR
90OrlanSR/Star-27TR

McWeeny, Douglas
26Exh-13
90Target-513
R316
V100

McWhirter, Kevin
78OrlTw
80OrlTw-20

McWilliam, Tim
89River/Best-13
89River/Cal-2
89River/ProC-1401
90Wichita/Rock-16
91Wichita/LineD-614
91Wichita/ProC-2612

McWilliams, Larry
79T-504
80T-309
81F-267
81Richm-14
81T-44
82BK/Lids-17
82D-527
82Pol/Atl-27
82T-733
83D-45
83F-310
83T-253
84D-566
84F-256
84F/St-58
84F/St-80
84Nes/792-668
84OPC-341
84T-668
84T/St-133
85D-78
85F-470
85Leaf-247
85OPC-183
85T-183
85T/St-132
86D-264
86F-613
86Leaf-136
86OPC-204
86T-425
87F-613
87OPC-14
87T-564
88S/Tr-23T
88Smok/Card-22
88T/Big-261
88T/Tr-70T
89B-397
89D-516
89F-458
89Phill/TastyK-21
89S-259
89T-259
89T/Tr-80T
89UD-143
90D-709
90Publlnt/St-247

Meacham, Bobby
83Colum-20
84D-336
84Nes/792-204
84T-204
85D-126
85F-134
85Leaf-147
85OPC-16
85T-16
85T/St-315
86D-638
86F-110
86OPC-379
86T-379
86T/St-304
87Colum-10
87Colum/Pol-19
87Colum/TCMA-16
87F-105
87T-62
88D-616
88D/Y/Bk-616
88F-215
88SanDiegoSt-10
88SanDiegoSt-11
88S-137
88T-659
89BuffB/CMC-17
89BuffB/ProC-1663
89S-509
89T-436
89UD-77
90Omaha/CMC-14
90Omaha/ProC-72

Meacham, Rusty
88Bristol/ProC-1868
89Fayette/ProC-1575
90A&AASingle/ProC-17
90EastLAS/ProC-EL6
90London/ProC-1266
91B-149
91D/Rook-53
91Toledo/LineD-592
91Toledo/ProC-1928
91UD/FinalEd-44F
92D/II-654
92S/100RisSt-67
92S/I-395
92T/91Debut-122
92UD-453

Mead, Timber
85Everett/II/Cram-10
86Clinton-12
87Tampa-16
88Chatt/Best-1
89Chatt/Best-13
89Chatt/GS-24
90Phoenix/CMC-23
90Phoenix/ProC-10
91AS/Cal-56

Meadows, Chuck
83AlexD-3

Meadows, Henry
D328-115
E120
E135-115
E220
W515-23
W572
W573

Meadows, Jeff
82AubAs-7

Meadows, Jim
86DayBe-18
86FSLAS-35

Meadows, Lee
21Exh-107
88Conlon/3-19
E126-4

Meadows, Louie
83DayBe-26
86Tucson-13
87Tucson-9
88F/Up-U92
88Tucson/CMC-20
88Tucson/ProC-177
89F-361
89T-643
89Tucson/CMC-14
89Tucson/ProC-191
89Tucson/JP-15
89UD-401
90OPC-534
90T-534
90Tucson/CMC-12
90Tucson/ProC-215
90UD-160
91ScranWB/LineD-490
91ScranWB/ProC-2552

Meadows, Scott
89Freder/Star-15
89Watlo/ProC-1773
89Watlo/Star-20
90A&AASingle/ProC-25
90EastLAS/ProC-EL9
90Foil/Best-294
90Hagers/Best-13
90Hagers/ProC-1428
90Hagers/Star-15
91Hagers/LineD-239
91Hagers/ProC-2468

Meads, Dave
86Ashvl-19
87D/Rook-46
87F/Up-U79
87Mother/Ast-17
87Pol/Ast-9
87T/Tr-77T
88D-455
88F-453
88RedFoley/St-57
88S-243
88T-199
88Tucson/CMC-4
88Tucson/ProC-183
88Tucson/JP-16
89D-424
89F-362
89Mother/Ast-26
89S-593
89T-589
89Tucson/CMC-5
89Tucson/ProC-180
89Tucson/JP-16

Meagher, Adrian
86Albuq-16
88ElPaso/Best-24

Meagher, Brad
77BurlB

Meagher, Tom
85Spokane/Cram-14
86CharRain-17
88SanJose/Cal-134
88SanJose/ProC-120

Mealy, Tony
87Macon-5
88Greens/ProC-1563
89Cedar/Best-21
89Cedar/ProC-926
89Cedar/Star-12

Meamber, Tim
87Erie-14
88Savan/ProC-344
89Spring/Best-22
90StPete/Star-16

Meares, Pat
89Alaska/Team-8
90WichSt-24
91Visalia/ClBest-17
91Visalia/ProC-1749

Mears, Ronnie
78Wisco

Mecerod, George
80Elmira-16

Meche, Carl
75QuadC

Meckes, Tim
83ColumAst-16
84Tulsa-24

Meddaugh, Dean
89Burllnd/Star-17

Mediavilla, Rick
91Hamil/ClBest-26
91Hamil/ProC-4054

Medich, George
(Doc)
73OPC-608R
73Syrac/Team-17
73T-608R
74OPC-445
74Syrac/Team-16
74T-445
74T/St-213
75Ho-78
75OPC-426
75T-426
75T/M-426
76Crane-35
76MSA/Disc
76OPC-146
76SSPC-430
76T-146
76T/Tr-146T
77OPC-222
77T-294
78BK/R-7
78Ho-86
78T-583
79OPC-347
79T-657
80T-336
81D-386
81F-627
81T-702
82D-142
82F-324
82T-36TL
82T-78
83F-39
89Swell-18
91WIZMets-264

Medina, Facanel
89Martins/Star-20
90Martins/ProC-3180
91Batavia/ClBest-14
91Batavia/ProC-3497

Medina, Luis
86Watlo-18
87Wmsprt-24
88AAA/ProC-8
88ColoSp/CMC-21
88ColoSp/ProC-1543
89Classic-67
89D-36RR
89D/Rook-20
89F-411
89Panini/St-315
89S-633RP
89S/HotRook-5
89S/YS/II-26
89T-528
89UD-2SR
90Classic-103
90ColoSp/CMC-16
90ColoSp/ProC-44
90HotRook/St-31
90Publlnt/St-564
91AAAGame/ProC-AAA6
91ColoSp/LineD-92
91ColoSp/ProC-2193

Medina, Patrico
90Martins/ProC-3186

Medina, Pedro
82Oneonta-17
83Greens-20
84Greens-23

Medina, Ricardo
89Wythe/Star-22
90Geneva/ProC-3031
90Geneva/Star-17
91Geneva/ClBest-12
91Geneva/ProC-4225

Medina, Val
82DayBe-22

Medina, Victor
89Bluefld/Star-16

Medlinger, Irving
52Park-11
V362-33

Medrick, John
91Eugene/ClBest-18
91Eugene/ProC-3725

Medvin, Scott
86Shrev-18
87Shrev-7
88BuffB/CMC-10
88BuffB/ProC-1484
89BuffB/CMC-6
89BuffB/ProC-1680
89D-597
89Panini/St-160
89S/HotRook-38
89T-756
90BuffB/CMC-6
90BuffB/ProC-369

Medwick, Joe
(Ducky)
34DS-66
35BU-145
35Wheat
36Exh/4-8
36Wheat
37Dix
37Exh/4-8
37Wheat
38Exh/4-8
38G-262
38G-286
38ONG/Pin-20
38Wheat
39Exh
39Wheat
40Wheat
41DP-22
60F-22
61F-61
74Laugh/ASG-37
80Laugh/FFeat-19
80SSPC/HOF
86Sf/Dec-15M
88Conlon/NatAS-15
89Pac/Leg-160
89Smok/Dodg-22
90Target-514
91Conlon/Sport-18

92Conlon/Sport-629
PR1-22
R302
R313
R314
R326-11A
R326-11B
R342-11
R423-69
V355-75
WG8-41
Mee, Jimmy
88Greens/ProC-1571
Mee, Tommy
78Green
Meek, Rich
89Erie/Star-12
Meeks, Tim
85Cram/PCL-169
86Albuq-17
87Albuq/Pol-14
88Tacoma/CMC-5
88Tacoma/ProC-633
90PalmSp/Cal-227
91BuffB/LineD-34
91BuffB/ProC-537
Mehl, Steve
87CharWh-9
88Utica/Pucko-8
89SoBend/GS-18
Mehrtens, Pat
88Tampa/Star-16
88Utica/Pucko-21
89Utica/Pucko-15
Meier, Brian
80Batavia-14
Meier, Dave
82Orlan-9
83Toledo-22
85D-147
85F-285
85T-356
86F-400
87OKCty-6
88Iowa/CMC-20
88Iowa/ProC-536
Meier, Jeff
89Sumter/ProC-1118
Meier, Kevin
87Pocatel/Bon-6
88SanJose/Cal-135
88SanJose/ProC-132
89AS/Cal-40
89SanJose/Best-18
89SanJose/Cal-215
89SanJose/ProC-447
89SanJose/Star-20
90Shrev/ProC-1441
90Shrev/Star-15
91Shrev/LineD-313
91Shrev/ProC-1818
Meier, Randy
82Wausau-8
83Wausau/LF-15
Meier, Scott
81AppFx-19
82AppFx-9
83GlenF-5
Meine, Heinie
33G-205
R332-50
Meissner, Scooter
90Beloit/Best-22TR
90Beloit/Star-27TR
Meister, Ralph
88Sumter/ProC-418
Meizosa, Gus
87Gaston-12
89Jacks/GS-9
Mejia, Cesar
88EastLAS/ProC-10
88GlenF/ProC-924
89RochR/CMC-4
89RochR/ProC-1635
90T/TVMets-51
90Tidew/CMC-7
90Tidew/ProC-540
Mejia, Delfino
91Modesto/ClBest-12
Mejia, Leandro
90Madison/Best-13
90Madison/ProC-2266
91Madison/ClBest-11
91Madison/ProC-2128
Mejia, Oscar
82Tulsa-16
84Tulsa-7
85Tulsa-7
86Water-16
87Wmsprt-4
Mejia, Secar
87Myrtle-14
Mejias, Fernando
91Martins/ClBest-21
91Martins/ProC-3450
Mejias, Marcos
75BurlB
Mejias, Roman
57T-362
58T-452
59T-218
60T-2
62T-354
63J-186
63P-186
63T-432
64T-186
Mejias, Sam
77T-479R
78OPC-99
78T-576
79OPC-42
79T-97
81F-219
81T-521
82D-295
82F-75
82T-228
91Princet/ClBest-28MG
91Princet/ProC-3531MG
Mejias, Simeon
87Peoria-21
Mejias, Teodulo
91Clinton/ClBest-19
91Clinton/ProC-838
Mele, Albert
(Dutch)
Exh47
V362-48
Mele, Sabath
(Sam)
49B-118
50B-52
51B-168
51T/BB-25
52B-15
52StarCal/L-73H
52T-94
54B-22
54Esskay
54RM-AL6
54T-240
55B-147
55Salem
60T-470C
61Peters-16
62T-482MG
63T-531MG
64T-54MG
65T-506MG
66OPC-3MG
66T-3MG
67T-418MG
80Elmira-36C
91Crown/Orio-294
Exh47
Melendez, Dan
91T/Tr-80T
Melendez, Diego
77Cocoa
78DaytB
Melendez, Francisco
83Reading-15
84Cram/PCL-199
85Cram/PCL-43
85Phill/TastyK-44
86Phill/TastyK-x
86Portl-16
87Phoenix-25
88Phoenix/ProC-64
89D-611
89French-43
89RochR/CMC-3
89RochR/ProC-1654
90Canton/Best-16
90Canton/ProC-1300
90Canton/Star-12
91Crown/Orio-295
Melendez, Jose
85PrWill-4
86PrWill-16
87Harris-5
88Harris/ProC-848
89Wmsprt/ProC-633
89Wmsprt/Star-14
90Calgary/CMC-22
90Calgary/ProC-648
91D/Rook-23
91LasVegas/ProC-232
91LasVegas/LineD-288
91T/90Debut-106
92D/II-572
92F-615
92S/100RisSt-19
92S/I-397
92T-518
92UD-566
Melendez, Luis A.
71OPC-216R
71T-216R
72T-606
73OPC-47
73T-47
74OPC-307
74T-307
75OPC-353
75T-353
75T/M-353
76OPC-399
76SSPC-282
76T-399
77Padre/SchCd-19
78Syrac
87Fayette-22
88Fayette/ProC-1083
88Hamil/ProC-1733
90Hamil/Best-27MG
90Hamil/Star-26MG
Melendez, Steve
86Geneva-19TR
88Peoria/Ko-16TR
89WinSalem/Star-21TR
90WinSalem/Team-27TR
91WinSalem/ClBest-28TR
Melendez, William
73Cedar
76Dubuq
Meleski, Mark
86NewBrit-18
87Pawtu/TCMA-28
88Pawtu/CMC-25
88Pawtu/ProC-454CO
89Pawtu/CMC-24CO
89Pawtu/Dunkin-5CO
89Pawtu/ProC-696CO
90Pawtu/CMC-8CO
90Pawtu/ProC-478CO
90T/TVRSox-35CO
91Pawtu/LineD-360
91Pawtu/ProC-56CO
Melillo, Oscar
(Ski)
26Exh-116
29Exh/4-30
31Exh/4-29
33DH-32
33DL-3
33Exh/4-15
34DS-53
34Exh/4-15
34G-45
35BU-151
35Exh/4-15
35G-1F
35G-3D
35G-5D
35G-6D
55Rodeo
61F-127
91Conlon/Sport-81
R300
R309/2
R310
R313
R316
R332-39
V354-94
Melito, Chuck
80Batavia-17
Mellix, Ralph
(Lefty)
88Negro/Duques-18
Mello, John
88MidwLAS/GS-43
88Rockford-24
89Rockford-24
89WPalmB/Star-16
90FSLAS/Star-14
90WPalmB/Star-16
Mellody, Honey
T3/Box-72
Meloan, Paul
M116
Melrose, Jeff
86DayBe-19
86Tulsa-21
88Gaston/ProC-1012
Melson, Gary
79Tacom-9
80Richm-8
Melton, Cliff
39PB-125
40PB-83
41DP-26
41DP-94
48Sommer-8
49Sommer-6
92Conlon/Sport-613
PM10/Sm-124
Melton, David
58T-391
Melton, Larry
86PrWill-17
87Salem-3
88EastLAS/ProC-17
88Harris/ProC-857
89BuffB/CMC-8
89BuffB/ProC-1673
Melton, Reuben
(Rube)
47TipTop
90Target-515
Melton, Sam
87Elmira/Black-11
87Elmira/Red-11
Melton, William
69T-481
70MLB/St-190
70OPC-518
70T-518
71Bz
71Bz/Test-21
71MD
71OPC-80
71T-80
71T/Coins-76
71T/GM-33
71T/S-47
71T/tatt-14
72K-12
72MB-233
72OPC-183
72OPC-184IA
72OPC-495KP
72OPC-90LL
72T-183
72T-184IA
72T-495KP
72T-90LL
72T/Post-3
73OPC-455
73T-455
74OPC-170
74T-170
74T/DE-68
74T/St-158
75Ho-8
75Ho/Twink-8
75OPC-11
75T-11
75T/M-11
76OPC-309
76SSPC-155
76T-309
76T/Tr-309T
77T-107
Melvin, Bob
82BirmB-7
83BirmB-12
84Evansvl-11
86D-456
86Mother/Giants-12
86T-479
87D-239
87F-281
87Mother/SFG-12
87T-549
88D-638
88F-90
88Mother/Giants-12
88OPC-41
88S-477
88T-41
89B-8
89F-335
89French-36
89OPC-329
89S-617
89S/Tr-61
89T-329
89T-351TL
89UD-227
90BirmDG/Best-23
90D-451
90F-181
90Leaf/II-382
90OPC-626
90PublInt/St-579
90S-453
90T-626
90UD-644
91B-89
91Crown/Orio-296
91D-335
91F-482
91F/UltraUp-U3
91Leaf/I-240
91OPC-249
91T-249
91T/StClub/II-312
91UD-310
92D/I-231
92F-15
92S/I-208
92T-733
92UD-692
Melvin, Doug
77WHav
Melvin, Ken
75Shrev/TCMA-10
Melvin, Scott
86Kinston-16
87Spring/Best-24
88StPete/Star-18
89StPete/Star-20
91ArkTr/LineD-50CO
91ArkTr/ProC-1295
Melvin, William
87CharWh-1
88Peoria/Ko-17
90WinSalem/Team-5
91WinSalem/ClBest-7
91WinSalem/ProC-2826
Mena, Andres
87SanAn-2
Menard, Dyrryl
86Osceola-18
Mendazona, Mike
89Gaston/ProC-1026
89Gaston/Star-15
Mendek, William
87Chatt/Best-24
88Vermont/ProC-958
Mendenhall, Kirk
90Niagara/Pucko-6
91FSLAS/ProC-FSL21
91Lakeland/ClBest-21
91Lakeland/ProC-274
Mendenhall, Shannon
88Lynch/Star-14
Mendez, Eddie
89Myrtle/ProC-1453
Mendez, Jesus
86StPete-20
87StPete-3
88ArkTr/GS-15
90Louisvl/CMC-18
90Louisvl/ProC-411
90T/TVCard-55
91Louisvl/ProC-2930
Mendez, Jose
74Laugh/Black-9
90Negro/Star-32
Mendez, Julio

89Savan/ProC-361
Mendez, Miguel
90Sumter/Best-13
90Sumter/ProC-2443
Mendez, Raul
86Cram/PCL-124
Mendez, Roberto
85Tigres-2
Mendon, Kevin
80Memphis-14
Mendonca, Robert
89Batavia/ProC-1918
Mendoza, Dave
76Cedar
Mendoza, Jesus
88Sumter/ProC-398
89BurlB/ProC-1605
89BurlB/Star-13
Mendoza, Mario
75OPC-457
75T-457
75T/M-457
76SSPC-606
78T-383
79T-509
80OPC-344
80T-652
81D-45
81F-613
81OPC-76
81T-76
81T/Tr-801
82D-394
82F-325
82OPC-212
82T-212
91PalmSp/ProC-2035CO
Mendoza, Mike
75Dubuq
76Dubuq
79Charl-19
80Tucson-21
81Tidew-19
Mendoza, Minnie
81Miami-6
88French-40CO
Menees, Gene
80Indianap-21
81Indianap-18
82Water-5
Menefee, John
E107
Menendez, Antonio G.
(Tony)
87BirmB/Best-10
88BirmB/Best-20
89BirmB/Best-3
89BirmB/ProC-103
90BirmDG/Best-24
Menendez, William
86WinSalem-17
Mengel, Brad
90Myrtle/ProC-2782
91Dunedin/ClBest-17
91Dunedin/ProC-214
Mengwasser, Brad
82Tulsa-2
Menhart, Paul
90StCath/ProC-3464
91Dunedin/ClBest-7
91Dunedin/ProC-203
91FSLAS/ProC-FSL9
Menke, Denis
62T-597R
63T-433
64T-53
64T/Coins-90
65Kahn
65T-327
66Kahn
66OPC-184
66T-184
66T/RO-119
67Kahn
67T-396M
67T-518
68Coke
68Dexter-55
68T-232
69MB-191
69MLB/St-140
69T-487
69T/St-35
70MB-18
70MLB/St-43
70OPC-155
70T-155
70T/CB
71K-8
71MLB/St-87
71OPC-130
71T-130
71T/Coins-89
72MB-234
72T-586
73OPC-52
73T-52
74OPC-134
74T-134
77BurlB
78Dunedin
78TCMA-58
82Tucson-26
86Mother/Ast-9
89Phill/TastyK-22CO
90Phill/TastyK-34CO
91Phill/Medford-27CO
Menosky, Mike
E120
V100
V61-46
W572
W573
Mentzer, Troy
89Everett/Star-21
90SanJose/Best-10
90SanJose/Cal-41
90SanJose/ProC-2013
90SanJose/Star-15
Meoli, Rudy
74OPC-188
74T-188
75OPC-533
75T-533
75T/M-533
76Indianap-10
76OPC-254
76SSPC-196
76T-254
77Indianap-18
78T-489
Mercado, Candy
75AppFx
76AppFx
77AppFx
77BurlB
Mercado, Manny
86Watlo-19
87Watlo-2
Mercado, Orlando
80LynnS-9
81Spokane-5
82SLCity-13
83T/Tr-71T
84D-318
84F-613
84Mother/Mar-14
84Nes/792-314
84T-314
85OKCty-1
85T-58
86OKCty-12
87Albuq/Pol-16
87D/OD-209
87T-514
88Tacoma/CMC-22
88Tacoma/ProC-624
89Portl/CMC-12
89Portl/ProC-209
89UD-624
90Kahn/Mets-35
90T/Tr-73T
90T/TVMets-21
90Target-517
90Tidew/CMC-21
90Tidew/ProC-548
91Tidew/LineD-563
91Tidew/ProC-2514
91WIZMets-265
Mercado, Rafael
90SoOreg/ProC-3434
91Madison/ClBest-27
91Madison/ProC-2140
91MidwLAS/ProC-MWL42
Merced, Orlando
86Macon-15
88Augusta/ProC-364
89AAA/CMC-15
89Harris/ProC-299
89Harris/Star-10
90BuffB/CMC-18
90BuffB/ProC-380
90BuffB/Team-16
91B-512
91BuffB/LineD-35
91Classic/III-57
91D/Rook-22
91F/Ultra-284
91F/Up-U112
91Leaf/II-489
91MajorLg/Pins-58
91S-747RP
91T/90Debut-107
91T/Tr-81T
91UD-84
92Classic/I-62
92D/I-310
92F-561
92F/RookSIns-3
92S/100RisSt-75
92S/I-153
92T-637
92UD-517
Mercedes, Guillermo
86Macon-14
Mercedes, Hector
89StCath/ProC-2080
90Myrtle/ProC-2783
Mercedes, Henry
89Modesto/Chong-20
90Madison/ProC-2272
91AS/Cal-38
91Modesto/ClBest-22
91Modesto/ProC-3091
91Single/ClBest-154
Mercedes, Juan
91Bluefld/ProC-4125
91Bluefld/ClBest-6
Mercedes, Luis
89Freder/Star-16
90A&AASingle/ProC-24
90EastLAS/ProC-EL44
90Foil/Best-313
90Hagers/Best-12
90Hagers/ProC-1429
90Hagers/Star-16
91B-94
91RochR/LineD-461
91RochR/ProC-1916
91UD/Ext-745
92Classic/I-63
92D/I-6RR
92F-16
92S/II-826
92T-603
92T/91Debut-123
92UD-652
Mercedes, Manuel
76QuadC
Mercer, Mark
78Ashvl
79Tulsa-10
80Charl-11
83OKCty-13
Mercerod, George
85Pawtu-21
Merchant, James A.
(Andy)
76OPC-594R
76T-594R
Merchant, John
81Batavia-18
Merchant, Mark
88Augusta/ProC-1576
89AS/Cal-3
89Augusta/ProC-496
89SanBern/Best-27
89SanBern/Cal-93
90Foil/Best-277
90Wmsprt/Best-16
90Wmsprt/ProC-1070
90Wmsprt/Star-17
91Penin/ClBest-24
91Penin/ProC-389
Mercker, Kent
87Durham-12
88CLAS/Star-31
88Durham/Star-14
89AAA/ProC-5
89Richm/Bob-17
89Richm/CMC-5
89Richm/Ko-24
89Richm/ProC-835
90B-6
90Classic-15
90D-31
90F-590
90Richm/Bob-8
90Richm/CMC-27
90Richm/Team-22
90S/Tr-72T
90T/89Debut-81
90UD-63
91B-568
91Classic/200-67
91D-299
91F/UltraUp-U68
91F/Up-U74
91Leaf/I-41
91OPC-772
91S-79
91S/100RisSt-58
91T-772
91T/StClub/II-341
91ToysRUs-19
91UD-642
92Classic/I-18
92D/I-116
92D/II-616M
92F-363
92F-700M
92S/I-178
92S/II-787M
92T-596
92UD-472
Mercurio, Tony
88Tidew/CANDL-30
Meredith, Steve
90Salinas/Cal-136
Merejo, Domingo
87Watertn-13
88Watertn/Pucko-21
89Salem/Star-12
90Salem/Star-12
Merejo, Jesus
88Utica/Pucko-9
89Utica/Pucko-16
Merejo, Luis
86Cram/PCL-92
87QuadC-11
88PalmSp/Cal-90
88PalmSp/ProC-1437
89MidldA/GS-23
89TexLAS/GS-6
Meridith, Ron
81Hawaii-16
81Tucson-16
82Hawaii-16
83Tucson-5
84Iowa-27
85Iowa-17
86D-533
86F-374
86Iowa-18
87Mother/Rang-16
87OKCty-13
88Louisvl-34
Merigliano, Frank
88Utica/Pucko-22
89SoBend/GS-8
90Saraso/Star-15
91BirmB/LineD-67
91BirmB/ProC-1453
Merkle, Cliff
E120
W573
Merkle, Fred
10Domino-83
11Helmar-133
12Sweet/Pin-119
14CJ-78
60NuCard-17
61NuCard-417
86Conlon/1-49
88Conlon/4-19
90Target-516
BF2-79
D304
D328-116
D329-118
D350/2-116
E135-116
E254
E270/2
E300
E95
M101/4-118
M101/5-116
M116
S74-90
T201
T202
T204
T205
T206
T213/blue
T215/brown
T3-108
W514-74
Merrifield, Bill
85MidldA-19
86MidldA-17
87Edmon-14
88OkCty/CMC-15
88OkCty/ProC-36
Merrifield, Doug
81Spokane-12
82SLCity-1
83SLCity-26
86Calgary-14TR
88Calgary/CMC-22
88Calgary/ProC-787
90Knoxvl/Best-7
Merrill, Carl
(Stump)
77WHave
79WHave-8
84Colum-23
84Colum/Pol-15MG
85Colum/Pol-16MG
89EastLDD/ProC-DD44CD
90ColClip/CMC-24CO
90ColClip/CMC-25MG
90ColClip/ProC-693MG
90S/NWest-1MG
90T/Tr-74TMG
91OPC-429MG
91T-429MG
Merrill, Durwood
88TM/Umpire-30
89TM/Umpire-28
90TM/Umpire-27
Merrill, Mike
86Durham-18TR
87Durham-17TR
Merriman, Brett
88BurlInd/ProC-1795
89Miami/I/Star-14
89Watertn/Star-14
90PalmSp/ProC-2574
91PalmSp/ProC-2009
Merriman, Lloyd
49Eureka-90
50B-173
51B-72
52B-78
55B-135
Merritt, George
E254
T205
T206
Merritt, Jim
66OPC-97
66T-97
67T-523
68OPC-64
68T-64
69MLB/St-132
69T-661
70MLB/St-32
70T-616
71Bz
71Bz/Test-7
71K-25
71MD
71MLB/St-65
71OPC-420
71T-420
71T/Coins-129
71T/tatt-15
72T-738
74OPC-318
74T-318
75OPC-83
75T-83

75T/M-83
Merritt, Lloyd
58T-231
84Savan-21MG
85Spring-10
Mersh, Neil
78Cr/PCL-19
79WHave-30
Merson, John
52T-375
Mertens, Warren
78OrlTw
Mertes, Sam
E107
Merullo, Matt
87DayBe-14
88BirmB/Best-22
88SLAS-7
89D/Rook-50
89F/Up-21
90BirmB/Best-3
90BirmB/ProC-1112
90BirmDG/Best-25
90F-542
90Foil/Best-167
90S-605
90T/89Debut-82
90UD-67
91F/Up-U13
91Kodak/WSox-5
91T/StClub/II-382
92D/I-264
92F-90
92S/I-367
92T-615
Mesa, Audy
91Pocatel/ProC-3790
Mesa, Baltazar
90Bakers/Cal-232
Mesa, Ivan
79AppFx-12
81GlenF-13
82Toledo-15
Mesa, Jose
85Kingst-8
86Ventura-14
87Knoxvl-1
88D-601
88RochR/Team-13
88RochR/CMC-3
88RochR/ProC-206
89Hagers/Best-3
89RochR/ProC-1636
90A&AASingle/ProC-4
90Hagers/Best-28
90Hagers/ProC-1410
90Hagers/Star-17
91B-91
91Crown/Orio-297
91D-765
91F/Up-U3
91Leaf/I-166
91OPC-512
91T-512
91T/StClub/II-380
91UD/Ext-703
92D/II-773
92F-17
92S/II-707
92T-310
Mesh, Mike
85Pawtu-8
86Pawtu-14
87Pawtu-18
87Pawtu/TCMA-15
88Pawtu/CMC-18
88Pawtu/ProC-463
89Omaha/CMC-16
89Omaha/ProC-1730
Mesner, Steve
46Sunbeam
47Signal
47Sunbeam
W754
Messaros, Mike
80Cedar-20
Messer, Doug
89Salinas/Cal-125
89Salinas/ProC-1817
Messerly, Michael
(Mike)
88SoOreg/ProC-1704
89Madis/Star-7
90Modesto/Cal-160
90Modesto/ProC-2221
91Modesto/ClBest-20
91Modesto/ProC-3097
91Single/ClBest-44
Messersmith, John
(Andy)
69JB
69T-296
70MLB/St-176
70OPC-430
70OPC-72LL
70T-430
70T-72LL
70T/PI-9
70T/S-25
71JB
71MD
71MLB/St-351
71OPC-15
71T-15
71T/Coins-112
72K-42
72MB-235
72OPC-160
72T-160
72T/Post-18
73OPC-515
73T-515
74OPC-267
74T-267
74T/St-47
75Ho-79
75Ho/Twink-79
75K-30
75OPC-310LL
75OPC-440
75T-310LL
75T-440
75T/M-310LL
75T/M-440
76Crane-36
76MSA/Disc
76OPC-199LL
76OPC-201LL
76OPC-203LL
76OPC-305
76SSPC-70
76T-199LL
76T-201LL
76T-203LL
76T-305
77BurgChef-213
77Ho-150
77K-54
77OPC-155
77T-80
77T/CS-28
78OPC-79
78T-156
78Wiffle/Discs-50
79OPC-139
79T-278
87Smok/Dodg-22
88AlaskaAS60/Team-5
89Smok/Dodg-85
90Target-518
Messier, Tom
84Everett/Cram-30A
86Fresno/Smok-10
Messitt, John
N172
Mestek, Barney
75Water
Metcalf, Thomas
64T-281R
WG10-15
WG9-18
Metheny, Bud
44Yank/St-19
Methven, Marlin
81Watlo-23
82Chatt-12
82Watlo/C-18
Metil, Bill
82Cedar-18
Metkovich, George
48Signal
49B/PCL-2
49Remar
50Remar
51B-274
52B-108
52T-310
53T-58
54JC-27
55Gol/Braves-20
91T/Arc53-58
Metkovich, John
52Park-89
Metoyer, Tony
86Ashvl-20
87Osceola-12
89Miami/II/Star-13
Metro, Charles
46Remar-11
66Pep/Tul
70OPC-16MG
70T-16
Mettler, Bradley
85Greens-27
Metts, Carey
89Erie/Star-13
Metzger, Clarence E.
(Butch)
75Hawaii
76OPC-593R
76T-593
77BurgChef-127
77Ho-99
77Padre/SchCd-20
77T-215
78T-431
80Richm-13
91WIZMets-266
Metzger, Curt
86ArkTr-15tr
Metzger, Roger
71OPC-404R
71T-404
72OPC-217
72T-217
73OPC-395
73T-395
74OPC-224
74T-224
74T/St-34
75Ho-115
75OPC-541
75T-541
75T/M-541
76Ho-67
76OPC-297
76SSPC-57
76T-297
77BurgChef-5
77Ho-20
77OPC-44
77T-481
78BK/Ast-15
78Ho-85
78T-697
79Pol/Giants-16
79T-167
80OPC-164
80Pol/Giants-16
80T-311
Metzler, Alex
29Exh/4-20
Meulens, Hensley
87PrWill-1
88Albany/ProC-1349
88BBAmer-1
88EastLAS/ProC-3
89Albany/Best-17
89Albany/ProC-337
89Albany/Star-13
89Classic-110
89D-547
89F/Up-U51
89S/HotRook-12
89Star/Wax-99
89UD/Ext-746
90AAAGame/ProC-AAA13
90AlbanyDG/Best-23
90Classic-133
90ColClip/CMC-9
90ColClip/ProC-682
90F-449
90OPC-83
90S-636RP
90S/100Ris-53
90T-83
90T/89Debut-83
90T/TVYank-54
90UD-546
91B-181
91Classic/200-179
91Classic/I-69
91D-31RR
91F/Ultra-240
91F/Up-U47
91Leaf/II-349
91Leaf/Stud-98
91MajorLg/Pins-3
91OPC-259
91OPC/Premier-80
91S-828RP
91S/100RisSt-84
91S/ASFan-4
91S/Rook40-39
91T-259
91T/StClub/II-503
91UD-675
92D/II-711
92F-238
92S/100RisSt-72
92S/I-89
92T-154
92UD-606
Meury, Bill
91Single/ClBest-339
91Waterlo/ClBest-18
91Waterlo/ProC-1265
Meusel, Robert W.
(Bob)
21Exh-114
25Exh-98
26Exh-101
27Exh-51
28Yueng-7
86Conlon/1-34
87Conlon/2-21
88Conlon/5-22
91Conlon/Sport-122
E126-39
E210-7
E220
V100
W501-35
W502-7
W515-21
W517-49
W572
W575
WG7-31
Meusel, Emil
(Irish)
25Exh-36
26Exh-38
87Conlon/2-22
90Target-519
E120
E121/120
E121/80
E126-34
E220
V100
V117-17
V61-55
W501-113
W501-36
W515-21
W572
W573
W575
Meyer, Alfred
77StPete
Meyer, Basil
88Kenosha/ProC-1404
89Visalia/Cal-94
89Visalia/ProC-1445
90OrlanSR/Best-17
90OrlanSR/ProC-1079
90OrlanSR/Star-11
Meyer, Benny
90Target-520
Meyer, Bob B.
64T-488R
65OPC-219
65T-219
70McDon-2
70T-667
71MLB/St-445
71OPC-456
71T-456
Meyer, Brad
88Gaston/ProC-1015
Meyer, Brian
86AubAs-16
87Osceola-13
88ColAst/Best-5
88SLAS-31
89B-319
89D-640
89Tucson/CMC-9
89Tucson/ProC-189
89Tucson/JP-17
90D-648
90F-232
90OPC-766
90T-766
90Tucson/CMC-2
90Tucson/ProC-202
90UD-22
91F-510
Meyer, Dan
75OPC-620R
75T-620R
75T/M-620R
76Ho-132
76OPC-242
76SSPC-365
76T-242
77Ho-135
77OPC-186
77T-527
78Ho-97
78K-12
78OPC-55
78T-57
79OPC-363
79T-683
80OPC-207
80T-396
81D-43
81F-603
81OPC-143
81Pol/Mariners-5
81T-143
81T/SO-40
81T/St-125
82D-176
82F-512
82T-413
82T/Tr-70T
83D-413
83F-527
83T-208
83T/St-110
84Cram/PCL-96
84F-455
84Nes/792-609
84T-609
85Mother/A's-23
89Pac/SenLg-155
89T/SenLg-97
89TM/SenLg-77
Meyer, Jack
56T-269
57T-162
58T-186
59T-269
60L-137
60T-64
61T-111
Meyer, Jay
91Hunting/ClBest-14
91Hunting/ProC-3330
Meyer, Joey
86Vanco-17
87D-460
87Denver-5
88D-36RR
88D/Best-239
88D/Rook-38
88F-645R
88F/Up-U40
88Leaf-36RR
88Pol/Brew-23
88S/Tr-75T
88T-312
89B-138
89Classic-10
89D-339
89F-191
89Gard-13
89OPC-136
89Panini/St-363
89Pol/Brew-23
89S-374
89S/HotRook-93
89S/YS/I-33

89Sf-135
89T-136
89T/Big-153
89UD-403
90OPC-673
90PubInt/St-498
90S-532
90T-673
91BuffB/LineD-36
91BuffB/ProC-547

Meyer, Lambert
(Dutch)
No Cards.

Meyer, Lee
E254

Meyer, Paul
91Kingspt/ClBest-9
91Kingspt/ProC-3823

Meyer, Randy
81CharR-20

Meyer, Rick
89Martins/Star-21
90Martins/ProC-3178

Meyer, Russ
49Lummis
51B-75
51BR-D7
52B-220
52T-339
53B/Col-129
54B-186
54NYJour
55B-196
55Gol/Dodg-20
56T-227
59T-482
79TCMA-194
88FSLAS/Star-29
89Albany/Best-27CO
89Albany/ProC-322CO
90Albany/Best-6CO
90Albany/ProC-1182CO
90Target-521
91ColClip/LineD-125CO

Meyer, Scott
80WHave-9
81WHave-21

Meyer, Stephen W.
86Erie-19
87Spring/Best-4
88Spring/Best-18

Meyer, William
49Eureka-167MG
51B-272MG
52B-155MG
52T-387MG
PM10/Sm-125

Meyers
WG1-34
WG1-68

Meyers, Benny
C46-28

Meyers, Brian
88AppFx/ProC-139

Meyers, Don
91Yakima/ClBest-12
91Yakima/ProC-4251

Meyers, Glenn
86QuadC-23

Meyers, Henry W.
V100

Meyers, Jim
90Foil/Best-223

Meyers, John
(Chief)
10Domino-84
11Helmar-134
12Sweet/Pin-120
14Piedmont/St-38
16FleischBrd-64
90Target-522
91Conlon/Sport-171
BF2-59
D304
D328-117
D329-119
D350/2-117
E135-117
E224
E254
E270/1
E286
E91
E96
E97
E98
M101/4-119
M101/5-117
S74-91
T201
T202
T205
T206
T213
T215/brown
T3-50
W501-94
W555
WG4-20
WG5-31
WG6-29

Meyers, Paul
87Shrev-2
88Shrev/ProC-1288
89Phoenix/CMC-22
89Phoenix/ProC-1490

Meyett, Don
89Beloit/I/Star-17
89Beloit/II/Star-21

Meza, Larry
91Hamil/ClBest-28
91Hamil/ProC-4046

Mezzanotte, Tom
91Bristol/ClBest-4
91Bristol/ProC-3607

Miceli, Danny
91Eugene/ClBest-21
91Eugene/ProC-3726

Micelotta, Bob
54T-212

Michael, Bill
75Clinton

Michael, Gene
66EH-45
67T-428R
68T-299
69T-626
70OPC-114
70T-114
71MLB/St-496
71OPC-483
71T-483
72T-713
72T-714IA
73OPC-265
73Syrac/Team-18
73T-265
74OPC-299
74Syrac/Team-17
74T-299
74T/St-214
75OPC-608
75T-608
75T/M-608
76SSPC-369
79Colum-7
81D-500MG
81T-670MG
86Gator-4MG
86T/Tr-73T
87Berg/Cubs-4
87T-43MG
90Target-523

Michael, Steve
82ElPaso-12
84ElPaso-4
87Elmira/Black-19
87Elmira/Red-19
88Elmira-3
89Elmira/Pucko-7
90WinHaven/Star-16

Michaels, Cass
47TipTop
48L-13
49B-12
50B-91
51B-132
51FB
52B-36
52T-178
53B/Col-130
54B-150
55B-85

Michalak, Tony
87Everett-15
88Clinton/ProC-710

Micheal, Matt
89Penin/Star-15

Michel, Domingo
86VeroB-18
87SanAn-7
88SanAn/Best-6
89Albuq/CMC-22
89Albuq/ProC-81
90Toledo/CMC-12
90Toledo/ProC-159
91London/LineD-392
91London/ProC-1886

Michel, John
82Idaho-19
83Madis/LF-19

Micheu, Buddy
89Butte/SP-25
90Gaston/Best-8
90Gaston/ProC-2524
90Gaston/Star-14

Michno, Tim
88WinSalem/Star-12

Michno, Tom
89CharlK-15
91FSLAS/ProC-FSL25
91Miami/ClBest-9
91Miami/ProC-405

Mickan, Dan
84Newar-5

Mickens, Glenn
90Target-1033

Middaugh, Scott
90Saraso/Star-16
91BirmB/LineD-68
91BirmB/ProC-1454

Middlekauff, Craig
89NiagFls/Pucko-17

Middleton, Damon
77Clinton

Mielke, Gary
88OkCty/CMC-5
88OkCty/ProC-35
89OkCty/CMC-6
89OkCty/ProC-1528
90D-679
90F/Up-125
90Mother/Rang-17
90OPC-221
90S-574
90T-221
90UD-612
91F-293
91OPC-54
91S-167
91T-54

Mielke, Greg
75AppFx
76AppFx

Mieses, Melanio
91Elizab/ProC-4297

Mieske, Matt
91AS/Cal-4
91B-694
91HighD/ClBest-26
91HighD/ProC-2409
91Single/ClBest-8

Mifune, Hideyuki
91AS/Cal-32
91Salinas/ClBest-4
91Salinas/ProC-2252

Miggins, Larry
53B/Col-142
53Hunter
79TCMA-285

Miggins, Mark
77Cocoa
79Charl-10
81Tucson-9
82Tucson-17
83Miami-26

Miglio, John
81QuadC-21
82Watlo/B-8
82Watlo/C-16
83Watlo/LF-11
85Water-8
87ElPaso-12
87TexLgAS-20
88Denver/CMC-4
88Denver/ProC-1260
89ElPaso/GS-10

Mijares, Willie
85Everett/Cram-9
87Clinton-6
88SanJose/Cal-124
88SanJose/ProC-110

Mikan, George
51Wheat
52Wheat

Mikesell, Larry James
82Wisco-12

Mikkelsen, Lincoln
90Erie/Star-16
91Stockton/ClBest-5
91Stockton/ProC-3029

Mikkelsen, Pete
64T-488R
65OPC-177
65T-177
66EH-19
66T-248
67T-425
67T/Test/PP-15
68T-516
71MLB/St-107
71Ticket/Dodg-9
90Target-524
WG10-16

Miksis, Eddie
47TipTop
49Eureka-42
51B-117
52B-32
52StarCal/L-80A
52T-172
53T-39
54B-61
55B-181
56T-285
57T-350
58T-121
59T-58
89Rini/Dodg-24
90Target-525
91Crown/Orio-298
91T/Arc53-39

Mikulik, Joe
86ColumAst-19
87ColAst/ProC-15
88Tucson/CMC-18
88Tucson/ProC-176
88Tucson/JP-17
90ColMud/Best-22
90ColMud/ProC-1360
90ColMud/Star-16
91Jacks/LineD-570
91Jacks/ProC-939

Milacki, Bob
86Hagers-11
87CharlO/WBTV-30
88AAA/ProC-35
88RochR/Gov-16
89Classic-92
89D-651
89D/Best-254
89D/Rook-22
89F-649R
89F/Up-U6
89French-18
89Panini/St-251
89S-651RP
89Sf-224R
89T-324
89UD/Ext-735
90D-333
90D/BestAL-2
90F-182
90Leaf/II-402
90OPC-73
90Panini/St-6
90PubInt/St-580
90PubInt/St-601
90S-239
90S/100Ris-68
90S/YS/I-20
90T-73
90T/JumboR-21
90T/St-240
90ToysRUs-20
90UD-635
91B-101
91Crown/Orio-299
91D-69
91F-483
91Hagers/ProC-2454
91OPC-788
91S-512
91T-788
91UD-328
92D/I-101
92F-18
92S/I-314
92S/I-427NH
92T-408
92UD-480

Milan, J. Clyde
10Domino-85
11Helmar-75
12Sweet/Pin-62
14CJ-56
15CJ-56
21Exh-108
40PB-130
BF2-48
D327
D328-118
D329-120
D350/2-118
E120
E121/120
E121/80
E122
E135-118
E220
E254
E91
M101/4-120
M101/5-118
M116
T202
T204
T205
T206
T207
V100
W501-15
W516-25
W573
W575
WG5-32
WG6-30

Milbourne, Larry
75OPC-512
75T-512
75T/M-512
76SSPC-58
78T-366
79OPC-100
79T-199
80T-422
81D-486
81F-611
81T-583
81T/Tr-802
82D-614
82F-42
82T-669
82T/Tr-71T
83D-411
83F-415
83T-91
83T/Tr-72T
84Mother/Mar-10
84Nes/792-281
84T-281
84T/Tr-79
85F-493
85T-754
89Pac/SenLg-112
89Pac/SenLg-203
90EliteSenLg-86
91Savan/ClBest-27MG
91Savan/ProC-1668MG

Milchin, Mike
89Hamil/Star-21
90SpringDG/Best-26
90StPete/Star-17
90T/TVCard-56
91ArkTr/LineD-39
91ArkTr/ProC-1282
91B-397
91Louisvl/ProC-2910
91Single/ClBest-107

Milene, Jeff
89Elizab/Star-18
90Kenosha/Best-8
90Kenosha/ProC-2296
90Kenosha/Star-12

Miles, Don

90Target-1034
Miles, Eddie
82AppFx-20
83GlenF-6
Miles, James
69T-658R
70OPC-154R
70T-154R
Miles, Wilson
(Dee)
40PB-195
Mileur, Jerome
83Nashua-25
85Nashua-29
Miley, Dave
81Cedar-9
83Water-10
84Wichita/Rock-2
87Vermont-17
89Cedar/Best-22MG
89Cedar/ProC-927MG
89Cedar/Star-22MG
90Cedar/Best-19MG
90Cedar/ProC-2337MG
91CharWh/ProC-2902MG
91SALAS/ProC-SAL8MG
Miley, Michael
(Mike)
76OPC-387
76T-387
77T-257
90LSUGreat-13
Milholland, Eric
86AppFx-15
87DayBe-3
88Tampa/Star-17
Militello, Sam Jr.
90A&AASingle/ProC-176
90Oneonta/ProC-3378
91B-693
91CLAS/ProC-CAR34
91PrWill/ClBest-7
91PrWill/ProC-1423
91Single/ClBest-150
92D/II-407RR
92T-676R
Miljus, John
90Target-526
V100
W513-65
Mill, Steve
91Pocatel/ProC-3778
Millan, Bernie
90Kgsport/Best-5
90Kgsport/Star-17
91Pittsfld/ClBest-11
91Pittsfld/ProC-3430
Millan, Felix
67OPC-89
67T-89
68T-241
69MB-192
69MLB/St-115
69OPC-210
69T-210
69T/St-7
70MLB/St-8
70OPC-452AS
70T-452AS
70T-710
71MD
71MLB/St-17
71OPC-81
71T-81
71T/Coins-5
71T/S-33
71T/tatt-12
72MB-236
72T-540
73OPC-407
73T-407
74K-53
74OPC-132
74T-132
74T/DE-26
74T/St-68
75Ho-111
75OPC-445
75T-445
75T/M-445
76Ho-120
76K-9
76OPC-245
76SSPC-536
76T-245
77BurgChef-138
77Ho-96
77OPC-249
77T-605
78T-505
78TCMA-31
89T/SenLg-85
89TM/SenLg-78
91WIZMets-267
Millares, Jose
91Kane/ClBest-17
91Kane/ProC-2664
Millay, Gar
87PortChar-23
88OkCty/CMC-13
88OkCty/ProC-40
88Tulsa-21
89Tulsa/GS-18
89Tulsa/Team-16
90OkCty/CMC-18
90OkCty/ProC-445
91OkCty/LineD-313
91OkCty/ProC-191
Miller, Barry
91Clinton/ClBest-21
91Clinton/ProC-843
Miller, Bill
89GreatF-31
89Idaho/ProC-2020
89Salem/Team-17
90Miami/I/Star-18
90Miami/II/Star-18
91Crown/Orio-300
91T/Arc53-100
Miller, Brent
91Kane/ClBest-18
91Kane/ProC-2665
Miller, C. Bruce
75OPC-606
75T-606
75T/M-606
76OPC-367
76Phoenix
76SSPC-102
76T-367
82Spring-3
Miller, Charles B.
(Molly)
T206
Miller, Damian
90Elizab/Star-13
Miller, Danny
75QuadC
Miller, Darrell
81Holyo-17
82Holyo-22
84Cram/PCL-107
85D-644
86Smok/Cal-18
86T-524
87Smok/Cal-11
87T-337
88D-551
88Edmon/CMC-12
88Edmon/ProC-579
88F-498
88S-463
88T-679
89Colum/CMC-19
89Colum/Pol-13
89Colum/ProC-733
89S-499
89T-68
89UD-462
90RochR/CMC-23
90RochR/ProC-705
Miller, Dave
87Durham-11
88Greenvl/Best-14
88Richm-20
89Freder/Star-17
89OkCty/CMC-7
89OkCty/ProC-1522
90Hagers/Best-24
90Hagers/ProC-1411
90Hagers/Star-18
90OkCty/CMC-6
90OkCty/ProC-431
Miller, Don
(Killer)
88Stockton/Cal-204GM
88Stockton/ProC-750GM
89Stockton/Best-27GM
89Stockton/Cal-175GM
89Stockton/ProC-397GM
89Stockton/Star-24GM
Miller, Dyar
75IntAS/TCMA-2
75OPC-614R
75T-614R
75T/M-614R
76OPC-555
76SSPC-379
76T-555
77T-77
78T-239
79T-313
80Tidew-10
81Louisvl-4
81T-472
82F-534
82Louisvl-18
82T-178
83Louisvl/Riley-4
84Louisvl-4
86Louisvl-2
89Pac/SenLg-211
89T/SenLg-129
90EliteSenLg-59
91Collnd/ProC-1505CO
91Crown/Orio-301
91Pac/SenLg-12
91WIZMets-270
Miller, Edmund
(Bing)
21Exh-109
25Exh-109
26Exh-109
31Exh/4-27
33G-59
40PB-137
60F-39
61F-62
91Conlon/Sport-192
E120
R315-A25
R315-B25
R316
V353-59
V61-23
W517-31
W573
Miller, Edward Lee
78Richm
79Richm-24
80Richm-22
80T-675R
81Pol/Atl-45
82D-425
82F-441
82T-451
83Portl-20
85Beaum-13
Miller, Edward R.
39PB-49
40PB-56
41PB-1
48L-68
Miller, Edward S.
R314/Can
Miller, Elmer
E120
E121/120
E121/80
V100
W573
W575
Miller, Gary
91StCath/ClBest-15
91StCath/ProC-3392
Miller, George
E223
N172
N284
N29
N403
N43
Miller, Gerry
81BurlB-24
82Beloit-3
Miller, Gregg
90WichSt-43
Miller, James
91Princet/ClBest-7
91Princet/ProC-3509
Miller, Jeff
89Wausau/GS-23
Miller, Jerry
86Miami-17C
Miller, Jim
77Charl
Miller, John Allen
69T-641R
Miller, John B.
(Dots)
14CJ-49
14Piedmont/St-39
15CJ-49
D303
D322
D329-121
E102
E104
E105
E106
E254
E270/2
E90/1
E90/2
E91
E92
M101/4-121
M116
T205
T206
T207
T213/blue
Miller, John E.
63T-208R
65OPC-49R
65T-49R
66T-427
67OPC-141
67T-141
90Target-1036
91Crown/Orio-302
Miller, Joseph
N172
Miller, Keith Alan
85Lynch-18
86Jacks/TCMA-27
87Sf/Rook-50
87Tidew-10
87Tidew/TCMA-16
88D-562
88D/Mets/Bk-562
88F-144
88S-639
88Sf-225
88T-382
88Tidew/CANDL-11
88Tidew/CMC-20
88Tidew/ProC-1604
89AAA/ProC-24
89B-380
89Classic-16
89D-623
89F-45
89S-464
89S/HotRook-62
89S/YS/I-23
89T-557
89T/Mets/Fan-25
89Tidew/CMC-14
89Tidew/ProC-1948
89UD/Ext-739
90B-136
90D-507
90Kahn/Mets-25
90Leaf/II-462
90Mets/Fan-25
90OPC-58
90S-559
90T-58
90T/TVMets-32
90UD-190
91D-248
91F-155
91F/Ultra-225
91Kahn/Mets-25
91OPC-719
91S-318
91T-719
91T/StClub/I-239
91UD-196
91WIZMets-272
92D/II-657
92F-513
92S/II-462
92T-157
92UD-383
Miller, Kenny
86Cram/PCL-142
87Spartan-9
Miller, Kevin
90Bristol/ProC-3151
90Bristol/Star-18
91Niagara/ClBest-11
91Niagara/ProC-3636
Miller, Kurt
90Classic/DP-5
90Welland/Pucko-1
91Augusta/ClBest-28
91Augusta/ProC-803
91B-521
91OPC-491FDP
91S-682FDP
91T-491FDP
91UD-68TP
92UD-70TP
Miller, Larry Don
65T-349
69T-323
91WIZMets-271
Miller, Larry
59DF
90Target-528
Miller, Lawrence H.
(Hack)
21Exh-110
90Target-1035
E120
V61-86
W573
WG7-32
Miller, Lemmie
83Albuq-22
84Cram/PCL-150
85Cram/PCL-165
90Target-1037
Miller, Lowell Otto
14CJ-53
15CJ-53
16FleischBrd-65
90Target-529
BF2-60
D121/80
D327
D328-119
D329-122
D350/2-119
E121/120
E122
E135-119
M101/4-122
M101/5-119
T207
V100
W501-95
W575
Miller, Mark
80Cedar-16
80ElPaso-8
80Indianap-18
Miller, Michael
83Butte-19
86Clearw-17
86Omaha-15
87Memphis/Best-15
87Pittsfld-9
87Reading-25
87WinSalem-20
88Clmbia/GS-9
88Memphis/Best-22
88SALAS/GS-14
89StLucie/Star-17
Miller, Mickey
76Baton
Miller, Mike
79Savan-25
Miller, Nancy
76Laugh/Clown-9UMP
Miller, Neal Keith
(Keith)
86Portl-17
86Reading-17
87Maine-8
87Maine/TCMA-15
88Maine/CMC-20
88Maine/ProC-290

88Phill/TastyK-27
88Phill/TastyK-36
89ScrWB/CMC-13
89ScrWB/ProC-716
89T-268
90AAAGame/ProC-AAA7
90ScranWB/CMC-21
90ScranWB/ProC-612
91BuffB/LineD-37
91BuffB/ProC-553

Miller, Norm
67T-412R
68OPC-161
68T-161
69OPC-76
69T-76
70T-619
71MLB/St-88
71OPC-18
71T-18
72MB-237
72OPC-466
72T-466
73OPC-637
73T-637
74OPC-439
74T-439

Miller, Orlando
89Oneonta/ProC-2124
90A&AASingle/ProC-101
90Ashvl/ProC-2757
90SALAS/Star-16
91Jacks/LineD-571
91Jacks/ProC-934
91Single/ClBest-377

Miller, Pat
91Beloit/ClBest-5
91Beloit/ProC-2100

Miller, Paul
89Salem/Star-13
90CLAS/CL-26
90Salem/Star-13
91CaroMud/LineD-112
91CaroMud/ProC-1083
92T/91Debut-124

Miller, Ralph
90Target-530

Miller, Ralph Jr.
77StPete
78StPete
83StPete-27GM

Miller, Randall
80OPC-351R
80T-680R
91Crown/Orio-303

Miller, Ray
86T-381MG
89VFJuice-31CO
90Homer/Pirate-22CO

Miller, Rhonda
90Miami/II/Star-30PER

Miller, Richard A.
(Rick)
72T-741R
74OPC-247
74T-247
74T/St-136
75OPC-103
75T-103
75T/M-103
76OPC-302
76SSPC-416
76T-302
77T-566
78T-482
79T-654
80OPC-27
80T-48
81D-294
81F-279
81OPC-239
81T-239
83OPC-188
84D-493
84F-403
84Nes/792-344
84T-344
85D-517
85F-163
85T-502
86T-424
91Modesto/ClBest-8

Miller, Richard
(Rich)
76Dubuq
78Tidew
79Jacks-18
86LitFalls-19MG
88Tidew/CANDL-4C
88Tidew/CMC-26
88Tidew/ProC-1585
89Tidew/CMC-25
90Tidew/CMC-29CO
90Tidew/ProC-562CO

Miller, Robert G.
(Bob)
54T-241
55T-9
56T-263
62T-572
91WIZMets-268

Miller, Robert J.
(Bob)
50B-227
51B-220
52T-187
55B-110
55T-157
55T/DH-60
56T-334
57T-46
58T-326
59T-379
79TCMA-289

Miller, Robert L.
(Bob)
60T-101
61T-314
62Salada-185
62Shirriff-185
62T-293
62T/St-159
63T-261
64T-394
65OPC-98
65T-98
66T-208
67T-461
68T-534
69T-403
70OPC-47
70T-47
71MLB/St-38
71OPC-542
71T-542
72OPC-414
72T-414
73OPC-277
73T-277
74OPC-624
74T-624
77T-113C
90Target-527
91WIZMets-269

Miller, Roger
77Spoka

Miller, Roger
88CapeCod/Sum-184
90Clinton/Best-19
90Clinton/ProC-2553
90Foil/Best-120
91SanJose/ClBest-2
91SanJose/ProC-13

Miller, Roscoe
E107

Miller, Roy
(Doc)
10Domino-86
11Helmar-163
12Sweet/Pin-142
D303
E286
S74-113
T201
T202
T207
T215/blue
T216

Miller, Scott
82QuadC-23
88CapeCod/Sum-87
90MedHat/Best-15
90Myrtle/ProC-2784
91Myrtle/ClBest-21
91Myrtle/ProC-2955

Miller, Steve
86Shrev-19
87Phoenix-26

Miller, Stu
53B/BW-16
53Hunter
53T-183
54B-158
54Hunter
54T-164
56T-293
58SFCallB-16
58T-111
59T-183
60T-378
61T-72
62J-143
62P-143
62P/Can-143
62Salada-205
62Shirriff-205
62T-155
62T/bucks
62T/St-201
63T-286
64T-565
65T-499
66T-265
67T-345
78TCMA-254
84Mother/Giants-18
91Crown/Orio-304
91T/Arc53-183

Miller, Ted
86Kenosha-16

Miller, Todd
85Everett/Cram-10
86Clinton-13
88Clinton/ProC-706
91Elmira/ClBest-24
91Elmira/ProC-3269

Miller, Tom
82Lynch-11

Miller, Tony
91AubAS/ClBest-2
91AubAS/ProC-4272

Miller, Trever
91Bristol/ClBest-14
91Bristol/ProC-3599
91Classic/DP-37
91FrRow/DP-7
92T-684DP

Miller, Walt
90Target-531

Miller, Ward
14CJ-5
15CJ-5
T207

Miller, Warren
M116

Miller, William Paul
(Bill)
52T-403
53B/BW-54
53T-100
54NYJour
55B-245
55Esskay
79TCMA-209
PM10/L-28

Miller-Jones, Gary
85Pawtu-9
86Pawtu-15
87Pawtu-19
87Pawtu/TCMA-16
88Pawtu/CMC-19
88Pawtu/ProC-459
89Pawtu/CMC-12
89Pawtu/Dunkin-11
89Pawtu/ProC-689

Millerick, Edwin
91Erie/ClBest-20
91Erie/ProC-4066

Milles, Rhadames G.
81ArkTr-6

Millette, Joe
89Batavia/ProC-1922
90Clearw/Star-16
90FSLAS/Star-15
91Clearw/ProC-1629
91Reading/ProC-1374

Millies, Walter
40PB-218
90Target-532

Milligan, John
N172
N690

Milligan, Randy
82Lynch-15
83Lynch-7
84Jacks-25
86Jacks/TCMA-26
86Tidew-20
87Tidew-28
87Tidew/TCMA-17
88D/Rook-32
88F/Up-U115
88S-623RP
89B-10
89F/Up-7
89French-15
89T/Tr-81T
89Tidew/Candl-13
89UD-559
89UD/Ext-740
90B-257
90D-519
90D/BestAL-85
90F-183
90Leaf/I-92
90OPC-153
90Panini/St-1
90S-252
90T-153
90T/Big-263
90T/St-233
90UD-663
91Crown/Orio-305
91D-542
91F-484
91F/Ultra-20
91Leaf/I-109
91Leaf/Stud-7
91OPC-416
91Panini/FrSt-240
91Panini/St-201
91S-86
91S/100SS-43
91Seven/3DCoin-9A
91T-416
91T/StClub/I-80
91UD-548
91WIZMets-273
92D/I-222
92F-19
92S/I-87
92T-17
92UD-181

Milligan, William J.
T206

Milliken, Bob
53Exh/Can-44
53T-221
54T-177
55T-111
55T/DH-118
62Kahn/Atl
79TCMA-234
90Johnson/Star-28CO
90Target-533
91T/Arc53-221

Millner, Tim
83MidldC-9

Mills, Alan
86Cram/PCL-81
87PrWill-7
88PrWill/Star-17
89FtLaud/Star-16
90B-428
90D/Rook-44
90F/Up-114
90Leaf/II-491
90S/NWest-29
90S/Tr-89T
90T/Tr-75T
90T/TVYank-14
91Classic/I-64
91ColClip/LineD-112
91ColClip/ProC-595
91D-338
91OPC-651
91S-73
91S/100RisSt-62
91T-651
91T/90Debut-108
91T/StClub/II-473
91UD-222

Mills, Art
47TipTop

Mills, Brad
80Memphis-15
82F-196
82Hygrade
82OPC-118R
82T-118R
83D-366
83F-288
83OPC-199
83Stuart-30
83T-744
84Indianap-9
85Cram/PCL-75
86Iowa-19
88CharWh/Best-2
89Peoria/Ko-30MG
90CLAS/CL-51CO
90WinSalem/Team-29CO
91CLAS/ProC-CAR44MG
91WinSalem/ClBest-12MG
91WinSalem/ProC-2845MG

Mills, Colonel
(Buster)
54T-227
90Target-534

Mills, Craig
86GlenF-16
87Lakeland-3

Mills, E.L.
N172

Mills, Gil
52Park-59
53Exh/Can-55

Mills, Gotay
82Louisvl-19
83ArkTr-21
84ArkTr-21

Mills, Jim
76Wausau

Mills, Ken
83Clinton/LF-19

Mills, Michael
85Beaum-17
86Beaum-19
88Wichita-31
89Dunedin/Star-11
89Knoxvl/Best-16
89Knoxvl/ProC-1141
89Knoxvl/Star-23

Mills, Richard Allen
71OPC-512R
71T-512R

Mills, Tony
90WichSt-25

Milnar, Al
40PB-202
41PB-33

Milne, William J.
(Pete)
49Eureka-119
53Mother-28

Milner, Brian
81OPC-238R
81T-577R
82Knoxvl-10
82OPC-203R
82T-203R
90Oneonta/ProC-3392CO
91Greens/ProC-3076

Milner, Eddie
79Indianap-10
80Indianap-10
81Indianap-9
82T/Tr-72T
83D-169
83F-597
83OPC-363
83T-449
84Borden-20
84D-365
84F-474
84Nes/792-34
84OPC-34
84T-34
84T/St-60
85D-428
85F-541
85OPC-198
85T-198
85T/St-53
86D-325

86F-182
86T-544
86TexGold-20
87D-433
87F-205
87Mother/SFG-15
87OPC-253
87T-253
87T/St-144
87T/Tr-78T
88F-91
88Kahn/Reds-9
88S-548
88T-677
91Pac/SenLg-25

Milner, John
72T-741R
73OPC-4
73T-4
74OPC-234
74T-234
74T/St-69
75Ho-15
75Ho/Twink-15
75OPC-264
75T-264
75T/M-264
76OPC-517
76SSPC-547
76T-517
77T-172
78T-304
79T-523
80OPC-38
80T-71
81D-377
81F-386
81T-618
82D-266
82F-197
82Hygrade
82OPC-331
82T-638
83F-311
91WIZMets-274

Milner, Ted
84Savan-9
86SanJose-13

Miloszewski, Frank
78Salem

Milstein, David
86Elmira-12
87WinHaven-14
88WinHaven/Star-13
89EastLDD/ProC-DD23
89NewBrit/ProC-621
89NewBrit/Star-10
90NewBrit/Best-5
90NewBrit/Star-11
91NewBrit/LineD-466
91NewBrit/ProC-358

Milton, Herb
90AppFox/Box-17
90AppFox/ProC-2092
91AppFx/ClBest-6
91AppFx/ProC-1712

Mimbs, Michael
91FSLAS/ProC-FSL40
91VeroB/ClBest-9
91VeroB/ProC-770

Mims, Fred
73Cedar
74Cedar

Mims, Larry
87Miami-23
88Hagers/Star-12
89AubAs/ProC-6
89Hagers/ProC-264
89Wichita/Rock/Up-13

Minarcin, John
78Wisco
79Wisco-10

Minarcin, Rudy
55T-174
56T-36

Minaya, Omar
81Wausau-22

Minaya, Robert
88Pulaski/ProC-1767
89Sumter/ProC-1111

Minch, John
87Modesto-7
88Huntsvl/BK-12

Mincher, Don
60T-548
61Clover-17
61Peters-5
61T-336
62T-386
63T-269
64T-542
65OPC-108
65T-108
66T-388
67T-312
68Bz-12
68OPC-75
68T-75
69MB-193
69MLB/St-96
69T-285
69T/decal
69T/S-33
69T/St-227
70K-75
70MB-19
70MLB/St-261
70OPC-185
70T-185
70T/PI-17
71K-27
71MLB/St-521
71OPC-680
71T-680
72MB-238
72OPC-242
72T-242
78TCMA-54
89Smok/Angels-5

Minchey, Nate
88OPC-6
88Rockford-25
89Rockford-25
89Rockford/Team-17
90Durham/Team-27
91DurhamUp/ProC-5
91Miami/ClBest-10
91Miami/ProC-406

Mincho, Tom
90Miami/I/Star-17

Minear, Clinton
91Kissim/ProC-4180

Miner, J.R.
86BurlEx-16MG
87BurlEx-24MG

Miner, James
82CharR-1
84Memphis-16
85Cram/PCL-72
86Tucson-14
87Tucson-13

Minetto, Craig
80Ogden-3
80T-494
81T-316
82RochR-4
83RochR-5
84Cram/PCL-69

Mingori, Steve
69T-339R
71OPC-612R
71T-612R
72OPC-261
72T-261
73OPC-532
73T-532
74OPC-537
74T-537
75OPC-544
75T-544
75T/M-544
76OPC-541
76SSPC-161
76T-541
77T-314
78T-696
79T-72
80T-219
86Syrac-19CO
87Dunedin-13CO
90Myrtle/ProC-2793CO
91Knoxvl/LineD-375CO
91Knoxvl/ProC-1786CO

Minick, Jeff
86Lakeland-14

Minier, Pablo
77Spartan

Minik, Tim
91BendB/ClBest-8
91BendB/ProC-3693

Minissale, Frank
88LitFalls/Pucko-29

Minium, Matt
80Batavia-24

Minker, Al
80WHave-1

Minnehan
N172

Minnema, Dave
86Lakeland-15

Minner, Paul
49Eureka-43
52B-211
52T-127
53B/Col-71
53T-92
54B-13
54T-28
56T-182
79TCMA-163
90Target-535
91T/Arc53-92

Minnick, Don
80LynnS-8

Minnifield, Wallace
89Kingspt/Star-17
90Pittsfld/Pucko-4

Minnis, Billy
91MidwLAS/ProC-MWL28
91QuadC/ClBest-19
91QuadC/ProC-2638

Minor, Blas
89Salem/Star-14
90Harris/ProC-1189
90Harris/Star-11
91BuffB/LineD-38
91BuffB/ProC-538

Minoso, Orestes
(Minnie)
52B-5
52BR
52RM-AL15
52StarCal/L-73E
52T-195
53B/Col-36
53NB
53T-66
54B-38
54Dix
54RH
54RM-AL7
55B-25
55RM-AL24
56T-125
56YellBase/Pin-22
57T-138
58T-295
59Kahn
59T-166M
59T-80
60T-365
61Bz-7
61P-25
61T-380
61T-42LL
61T/St-125
62J-51
62P-51
62P/Can-51
62Salada-39A
62Salada-39B
62Shirriff-39
62T-28
62T/bucks
62T/St-188
63T-190
64T-538
77OPC-262RB
77T-232RB
79TCMA-286
80Pac/Leg-96
84TrueVal/WS-24
86Coke/WS-CO
87Coke/WS-29
88Coke/WS-18
88Pac/Leg-51
89Coke/WS-30
89Kodak/WSox-4M
89Swell-59
91T/Arc53-66
Exh47
PM10/Sm-126

Minoso, Orestes Jr.
77AppFx

Minter, Larry
91Pocatel/ProC-3797

Minton, Greg
75Phoenix-8
77Phoenix
77T-489R
78Cr/PCL-102
78T-312
79T-84
80Pol/Giants-38
80T-588
81D-579
81F-449
81OPC-111
81T-111
81T/St-238
82D-348
82F-396
82OPC-144
82T-687
82T/St-107
83D-186
83D/AAS-10
83F-269
83K-46
83Mother/Giants-5
83OPC-107
83T-3RB
83T-470
83T/St-137
83T/St-138
83T/St-249
84D-187
84F-383
84F/St-69
84Mother/Giants-8
84Nes/792-205
84OPC-205
84T-205
85D-143
85F-617
85Mother/Giants-8
85OPC-45
85T-45
85T/St-167
86D-480
86F-549
86Mother/Giants-8
86T-310
86T-516M
87F-282
87F/Up-U80
87Mother/SFG-9
87OPC-333
87T-724
87T/Tr-79T
88D-505
88F-499
88OPC-129
88S-176
88Smok/Angels-11
88T-129
88T/St-176
89D-490
89D/Best-283
89F-485
89OPC-306
89S-543
89T-576
89UD-635
90D-116
90F-140
90OPC-421
90PublInt/St-375
90S-48
90T-421
90UD-83
91S-823

Minton, Jesse
87Sumter-17

Mintz, Alan
80Elmira-41

Mintz, Steve
90Yakima/Team-29

Minutelli, Gino
86Cedar/TCMA-7
87Tampa-20
88Chatt/Best-16
91B-677
91Nashvl/LineD-268
91Nashvl/ProC-2153
91T/90Debut-109
92S/I-408

Mirabella, Geno
91SLCity/ProC-3208

Mirabella, Paul
78Cr/PCL-48
79Colum-26
81D-151
81OPC-11
81T-382
82D-629
82OPC-163
82T-499
83D-541
83F-573
83T-12
84Mother/Mar-17
85Cram/PCL-89
85F-494
85T-766
86Mother/Mar-13
87Denver-9
88Denver/CMC-5
88Denver/ProC-1258
89D-654
89F-192
89Pac/SenLg-165
89Pol/Brew-27
89S-569
89T-192
89T/SenLg-51
89TM/SenLg-79
89UD-322
90Brewer/MillB-14
90EliteSenLg-27
90Pol/Brew-27
90PublInt/St-499
91Crown/Orio-306
91F-590
91S-558

Mirabelli, Doug
90WichSt-26

Mirabito, Tim
86Tampa-13
87Vermont-8

Miranda, Angel
88Stockton/Cal-180
88Stockton/ProC-749
89Beloit/II/Star-22
90A&AASingle/ProC-139
90AS/Cal-51
90Stockton/Best-25
90Stockton/Cal-175
90Stockton/ProC-2175
91B-53
91ElPaso/LineD-193
91ElPaso/ProC-2747

Miranda, Giovanni
90AppFox/Box-18
90AppFox/ProC-2102
91AppFx/ClBest-19
91AppFx/ProC-1725

Miranda, Willie
53T-278
54T-56
55B-79
55Esskay
55T-154
56T-103
56T/Pin-2SS
57T-151
58Hires-32
58T-179
59T-540
91Crown/Orio-307
91T/Arc53-278

Misa, Joe
91SoOreg/ClBest-28
91SoOreg/ProC-3839

Miscik, Bob
82Buffa-2
84Cram/PCL-136
85Cram/PCL-239
86Hawaii-17
87Edmon-4
88Edmon/CMC-15
88Edmon/ProC-577
90Freder/Team-3
91Kane/ClBest-26MG
91Kane/ProC-2674MG

Miscik, Dennis
77Cocoa
80Tucson-13
81OkCty/TCMA-11
Misuraca, Mike
89Elizab/Star-19
89Kenosha/ProC-1071
89Kenosha/Star-15
90Foil/Best-272
90Kenosha/Best-21
90Kenosha/ProC-2290
90Kenosha/Star-13
91Visalia/ClBest-5
91Visalia/ProC-1739
Mitchell, Albert
(Roy)
E270/2
Mitchell, Antonio
91Welland/ClBest-5
91Welland/ProC-3587
Mitchell, Charlie
84Pawtu-1
85D-40RR
85IntLgAS-18
85Pawtu-20
86Toledo-17
88Nashvl/Team-17
89Nashvl/CMC-1
89Nashvl/ProC-1273
89Nashvl/Team-16
90Nashvl/CMC-6
90Nashvl/ProC-229
91Nashvl/LineD-260
91Nashvl/ProC-2154
Mitchell, Clarence
10Domino-87
11Helmar-118
12Sweet/Pin-104
28Yueng-15
90Target-537
91Conlon/Sport-202
D328-120
E120
E135-120
E210-15
L1-118
S81-93
W502-15
W573
Mitchell, Craig
75Tucson-15
76OPC-591R
76T-591R
76Tucson-32
77SanJose-15
77T-491R
78T-711
79Ogden/TCMA-21
79Ogden/TCMA-5
Mitchell, Fred F.
90Target-539
C46-47
E107
E270/2
E90/1
M116
T206
V100
W514-96
Mitchell, Glenn
88Idaho/ProC-1837
88Sumter/ProC-408
89Sumter/ProC-1116
Mitchell, Howie
78Cr/PCL-116
Mitchell, J.W.
79QuadC-10
Mitchell, Jackie
88Chatt/Team-23
Mitchell, Joe
77Newar
Mitchell, Joe
90Denver/CMC-12
90Denver/ProC-633
Mitchell, John
83Beloit/LF-5
86Tidew-21
87D/Rook-37
87F/Up-U81
87Idaho-24
87T/Tr-80T
87Tidew-20
87Tidew/TCMA-7
88F-145
88S-249
88T-207
88Tidew/CANDL-23
88Tidew/CMC-8
88Tidew/ProC-1577
89Tidew/CMC-4
89Tidew/ProC-1970
90RochR/CMC-21
90RochR/ProC-700
90Target-540
91Calgary/LineD-67
91Calgary/ProC-513
91Crown/Orio-308
91D-710
91F-485
91OPC-708
91S-569
91T-708
91WIZMets-275
Mitchell, John
W575
Mitchell, Jorge
87Jamestn-11
88James/ProC-1916
Mitchell, Joseph
85Beloit-3
86Stockton-15
87ElPaso-2
88ElPaso/Best-25
89Denver/CMC-20
89Denver/ProC-43
Mitchell, Keith
88Sumter/ProC-390
89BurlB/ProC-1609
89BurlB/Star-15
90CLAS/CL-29
90Durham/Team-2
91B-575
91Classic/III-58
91Greenvl/ClBest-21
91Greenvl/LineD-212
91Greenvl/ProC-3016
91Single/ClBest-224
91UD/FinalEd-56F
92D/II-508
92F-364
92S/II-748
92T-542
92T/91Debut-125
92UD-454
92UD-80M
Mitchell, Kevin
82Lynch-6
84Tidew-23
85IntLgAS-4
85Tidew-18
86D/Rook-17
86F/Up-U76
86Sf/Rook-49
86T/Tr-74T
87Bohem-7
87D-599
87D/OD-145
87F-17
87F/RecSet-21
87F/Up-U82
87Leaf-170
87OPC-307
87Sf-144
87T-653
87T/Gloss60-50
87T/Tr-81T
87ToysRUs-21
88D-66
88F-92
88F/Hottest-27
88F/St-S5
88Leaf-87
88Mother/Giants-3
88OPC-387
88Panini/St-424
88Panini/St-448IA
88S-481
88T-497
88T/Big-57
88T/St-88
88T/UK-48
89B-474
89Classic-31
89Classic/Up/2-198
89D-485
89D/Best-281
89F-336
89Mother/Giants-3
89OPC-189
89Panini/St-216
89S-39
89S/Mast-12
89S/YS/II-38
89Sf-142
89T-189
89T/Big-129
89T/LJN-144
89T/St-84
89UD-163
90B-232
90B/Ins-6
90Bz-1
90Classic-150
90Classic-64
90CollAB-16
90D-11DK
90D-715AS
90D-98
90D/BestNL-85
90D/Bon/MVP-BC11
90D/Learning-2
90D/Preview-4
90D/SuperDK-11DK
90F-637M
90F-65
90F/ASIns-6
90F/AwardWin-23
90F/BB-27
90F/BBMVP-26
90F/LL-26
90F/WaxBox-C21
90F/WS-2
90Holsum/Discs-9
90HotPlay/St-27
90KingB/Discs-2
90KMart/SS-6
90Leaf/I-120
90MLBPA/Pins-24
90Mother/Giant-5
90OPC-401AS
90OPC-500
90Panini/St-208
90Panini/St-214
90Panini/St-361
90Post-15
90PublInt/St-617
90PublInt/St-77
90RedFoley/St-64
90S-343
90S/100St-50
90Sf-1
90Sunflower-1
90T-401AS
90T-500
90T/Big-137
90T/Coins-33
90T/DH-47
90T/Gloss22-6
90T/Gloss60-21
90T/HeadsUp-15
90T/HillsHM-5
90T/Mini-86
90T/St-148AS
90T/St-79
90T/TVAS-40
90Tetley/Discs-6
90UD-117
90UD-40TC
90USPlayC/AS-12H
90WonderBrd-7
90Woolwth/HL-2MVP
90Woolwth/HL-32
91B-636
91Classic/200-129
91Classic/I-10
91Classic/III-59
91CollAB-6
91D-255
91D-407MVP
91D-438AS
91F-267
91F/Ultra-326
91JDeanSig-13
91Leaf/I-85
91Leaf/Stud-257
91MajorLg/Pins-64
91MooTown-23
91Mother/Giant-5
91OPC-40
91OPC/Premier-81
91Panini/FrSt-162
91Panini/FrSt-71
91Panini/St-71
91Panini/Top15-11
91Panini/Top15-35
91PG&E-1
91Post-24
91RedFoley/St-123
91RedFoley/St-66
91S-406MB
91S-451
91S/100SS-98
91Seven/3DCoin-10NC
91SFExam/Giant-11
91T-40
91T/CJMini/I-30
91T/StClub/I-250
91T/SU-27
91UD-247
91WIZMets-276
92Classic/I-64
92D/II-583
92F-644
92S/100SS-93
92S/II-640
92T-180
92UD-266
92UD-80M
Mitchell, L. Dale
48L-165
49B-43
50B-130
50NumNum
51B-5
51T/RB-13
52B-239
52NumNum-15
52StarCal/L-74F
52T-92
52TipTop
53B/Col-119
53RM-AL9
53T-26
54B-148
54DanDee
55B-314
55Gol/Ind-19
55Salem
56T-268
79TCMA-140
90Target-538
91T/Arc53-26
Exh47
Mitchell, Mark
87Oneonta-22
88FtLaud/Star-15
Mitchell, Michael F.
14Piedmont/St-40
15CJ-62
E254
E270/2
E90/1
M116
S74-78
T202
T204
T205
T206
T207
T213/blue
T213/brown
T215/blue
T3-24
Mitchell, Paul
76OPC-393
76T-393
77SanJose-25
77T-53
78T-558
79OPC-118
79T-233
80T-131
81D-205
81T-449
91Crown/Orio-309
Mitchell, Robert
91Martins/ClBest-20
91Martins/ProC-3451
Mitchell, Robert V.
(Bobby Van)
79Albuq-18
80Albuq-20
81Albuq/TCMA-22
82F-14
82Toledo-28
83F-620
83T-647
83T/St-91
84Cram/PCL-202
84F-571
84Nes/792-307
84T-307
84Toledo-10
90Target-536
Mitchell, Robert V.
(Bobby Vance)
71OPC-111R
71T-111R
74OPC-497
74T-497
75OPC-468
75T-468
75T/M-468
76OPC-479
76SSPC-242
76T-479
79Hawaii-1
80Hawaii-10
81Portl-18
82Portl-15
Mitchell, Ron
75Shrev/TCMA-11
76Shrev
78Colum
79Portl-8
80Buffa-2
Mitchell, Scot
82Madis-11
Mitchell, Thomas
90Erie/Star-17
Mitchell, William
D329-123
D350/2-120
M101/4-123
M101/5-120
T207
Mitchelson, Mark
91Elmira/ClBest-25
91Elmira/ProC-3270
91Single/ClBest-168
91WinHaven/ClBest-4
91WinHaven/ProC-484
Mitchener, Mike
89SoBend/GS-14
90Foil/Best-131
90SoBend/Best-17
Mitta, Chris
88Pulaski/ProC-1763
Mitterwald, George
68T-301R
69T-491R
70OPC-118
70T-118
71MLB/St-467
71OPC-189
71T-189
72OPC-301
72OPC-302IA
72T-301
72T-302IA
74OPC-249
74T-249
74T/St-209
74T/Tr-249T
75OPC-411
75T-411
75T/M-411
76OPC-506
76SSPC-318
76T-506
77T-124
78SanJose-20
78T-688
86Orlan-12MG
87Orlan-9MG
Miyauchi, Hector
88Fresno/Cal-15
88Fresno/ProC-1233
Mize, John
38Exh/4-8
39Exh
40Wheat-6
41DP-39
41DP-99
47HomogBond-34
48B-4
48L-46
49B-85

49Eureka-120
50B-139
51B-50
51BR-A7
51FB
51T/BB-50
52B-145
52BR
52T-129
53B/BW-15
53NB
53RM-AL18
53T-77
60F-38
61F-63
72Laugh/GF-17
72T/Test-3
74Laugh/ASG-47
80Pac/Leg-49
83D/HOF-10
85CircK-32
85D/HOF-4
85West/2-44
86Sf/Dec-24M
88Pac/Leg-63
89HOF/St-3
89Pac/Leg-180
89Swell-55
90Swell/Great-90
91Conlon/Sport-53
91Swell/Great-62
91T/Arc53-77
92Conlon/Sport-435
92Conlon/Sport-628
D305
R302
R312
R346-30
R423-70
W754

Mize, Paul
80WHave-8
81Tacom-16
82Tacom-15
82WHave-16

Mizell, Wilmer
52T-334
53B/BW-23
53Hunters
53T-128
54T-249
56T-193
57T-113
58T-385
61Kahn
61P-140
91T/Arc53-128
91WIZMets-277

Mizerock, John
84D-380
85Cram/PCL-68
86D-502
86Tucson-15
87Richm/Crown-8
87D-653
87Richm/TCMA-10
87T-408
88Richm-25
88Richm/CMC-21
88Richm/ProC-19
89Richm/Bob-18
89Richm/CMC-12
89Richm/Ko-25
89Richm/ProC-827
90Richm/Bob-6
90Richm/CMC-21
90Richm/ProC-262
90Richm/Team-23

Mlicki, David
91Collnd/ClBest-6

Mmahat, Kevin
88FSLAS/Star-44
88FtLaud/Star-16
89Albany/Best-23
89Albany/ProC-341
89Albany/Star-14
90AAAGame/ProC-AAA15
90AlbanyDG/Best-25
90ColClip/CMC-5
90ColClip/ProC-674
90D-481
90S-643
90T/89Debut-84
90T/TVYank-55

Moates, Dave
76OPC-327
76T-327
77T-588
77Tucson

Moberg, Mike
91Rockford/ClBest-23
91Rockford/ProC-2058
91Single/ClBest-317

Mobley, Anton
89StCath/ProC-2084
90Myrtle/ProC-2789
90StCath/ProC-3479

Moccia, Mario
89NiagFls/Pucko-18
90Niagara/Pucko-7

Moeller, Daniel
C46-76
T206

Moeller, Dennis
86Cram/PCL-50
87AppFx-26
88AppFx/ProC-160
89BBCity/Star-17
90Memphis/Star-19

Moeller, Joe
63T-53
64T-549
65OPC-238
65T-238
66T-449
67OPC-149
67T-149
68T-359
69T-444
70OPC-97
70T-97
71MLB/St-108
71OPC-288
71T-288
71Ticket/Dodg-10
85SpokAT/Cram-14
90Target-541

Moeller, Ron
61T-466
63T-541
91Crown/Orio-310

Moen, Eric
90Yakima/Team-21TR
91BendB/ClBest-27TR

Moesche, Carl
84Butte-7

Moffet, Samuel
N172

Moffitt, G. Scott
76QuadC
77QuadC
80SLCity-4
81SLCity-23

Moffitt, Randy
73OPC-43
73T-43
74OPC-156
74T-156
75OPC-132
75T-132
75T/M-132
76OPC-553
76T-553
77BurgChef-101
77T-464
78T-284
78Wiffle/Discs-51
79Pol/Giants-17
79T-62
80Pol/Giants-17
80T-359
81D-195
81F-446
81T-622
83D-545
83F-456
83T-723
83T/Tr-73T
84D-390
84F-163
84Nes/792-108
84OPC-108
84T-108

Moford, Herb
59T-91
91WIZMets-278

Mogridge, George
92Conlon/Sport-376
E120
T207
V100
W572
W573

Mohart, George
90Target-1038

Moharter, Dave
77Tucson
78Cr/PCL-13
79Tucson-16
80Charl-7
87Macon-25
88Augusta/ProC-383

Mohler, Mike
90Madison/Best-20
90Madison/ProC-2267
91AS/Cal-42
91Modesto/ClBest-9
91Modesto/ProC-3084

Mohorcic, Dale
81Portl-17
83LynnP-6
85OKCty-26
86OKCty-13
86Rang-34
87D-531
87F-131
87Mother/Rang-15
87Smok/R-5
87T-497
88D-470
88D/Best-144
88F-474
88Mother/R-15
88OPC-163
88S-452
88Smok/R-6
88T-163
88T/St-242
89D-630
89F-259
89S-420
89S/NWest-16
89T-26
89UD/Ext-727
90F-450
90Indianap/CMC-8
90Indianap/ProC-298
90S-191
90UD-530
91F-239
91S-596

Mohr, Ed
79QuadC-2

Mohr, Tommy
83Butte-25
85FtMyr-19

Moisan, William
52Mother-64

Mokan, John
25Exh-46
26Exh-46
27Exh-23
E120

Moldes, Orestes
80Batavia-11

Molero, Juan
87Greens-13
88Lynch/Star-15
89Lynch/Star-14

Molesworth, Carlton
E270/2
T206
T213/brown

Molina, Albert
89Salem/Star-15

Molina, Islay
91Madison/ClBest-16
91Madison/ProC-2136
91MidwLAS/ProC-MWL43

Molina, Mario
88QuadC/GS-18
89PalmSp/ProC-477

Molinaro, Bob
77Evansvl/TCMA-19
79T-88
81Coke
81F-340
81T-466
81T/HT
81T/St-61
82D-417
82F-353
82RedLob
82T-363
83D-596
83F-167
83T-664
85RochR-12
86Hagers-12MG
87RochR-27
89Canton/Best-17
89Canton/ProC-1319
89Pac/SenLg-80
89T/SenLg-118
90ColoSp/CMC-24MG
90ColoSp/ProC-54MG
90EliteSenLg-87
90HagersDG/Best-17MG
91CharlR/ClBest-27MG
91CharlR/ProC-1330MG
91Crown/Orio-311
91Pac/SenLg-13

Moline, Stan
76Cedar

Molitor, Paul
78T-707R
79K-20
79OPC-8
79T-24
80OPC-211
80T-406
81D-203
81F-515
81F/St-82
81K-53
81OPC-300
81T-300
81T/SO-35
81T/St-91
82D-78
82F-148
82F/St-136
82OPC-195
82Pol/Brew-4
82T-195
82T/St-200
83D-484
83F-40
83Gard-11
83OPC-371
83Pol/Brew-4
83T-630
83T/St-139
83T/St-140
83T/St-156
83T/St-83
84D-107
84D/AAS-35
84D/Champs-54
84F-207
85FunFoodPin-105
84Gard-13
84Nes/792-60
84OPC-60
84Pol/Brew-4
84Seven-18C
84T-60
84T/St-294
85D-359
85F-588
85Gard-13
85OPC-395
85Pol/Brew-4
85T-522
86D-124
86D/AAS-39
86F-495
86F/LimEd-30
86F/Mini-101
86F/St-76
86Jay's-12
86Leaf-70
86OPC-267
86Pol/Brew-4
86Sf-128M
86Sf-39
86T-267
86T/St-203
87Classic-45
87D-117
87D/HL-29
87D/OD-54
87F-350
87F/St-78
87Leaf-71
87OPC-184
87Pol/Brew-4
87RedFoley/St-22
87Sf-54
87T-56
87T-741
87T/St-200
88Classic/Blue-232
88D-249
88D-7DK
88D-BC3
88D/Best-165
88D/DKsuper-7DK
88Drake-11
88F-169
88F/AS-12
88F/AwardWin-25
88F/LL-27
88F/Mini-31
88F/St-38
88F/TL-22
88FanSam-5
88Jiffy-12
88KayBee-19
88KingB/Disc-23
88KMart-17
88Leaf-168
88Leaf-7DK
88OPC-231
88Panini/St-125
88Panini/St-432
88Pol/Brew-4
88S-340
88S-660HL
88Sf-221
88Sf-79
88T-465
88T/Big-1
88T/Coins-20
88T/Gloss60-57
88T/Mini-19
88T/Revco-20
88T/RiteAid-20
88T/St-194
88T/St/Backs-42
88T/UK-49
89B-140
89Brewer/YB-4
89Cadaco-37
89Classic-12
89D-291
89D/AS-3
89D/Best-15
89D/MVP-BC9
89D/PopUp-3
89F-193
89F/AS-8
89F/BBAS-30
89Gard-1
89KMart/Lead-10
89Master/Discs-8
89OPC-110
89Panini/St-243AS
89Panini/St-373
89Pol/Brew-4
89RedFoley/St-81
89S-565
89S/HotStar-57
89Sf-209
89T-110
89T/Big-330
89T/Coins-46
89T/Gloss22-3
89T/Gloss60-43
89T/LJN-120
89T/Mini-58
89T/St-146
89T/St-204
89T/St/Backs-9
89T/UK-53
89UD-525
89UD-673TC
90B-399
90Brewer/MillB-15
90Classic/Up-34
90D-103
90D/BestAL-64
90D/Bon/MVP-BC15
90F-330
90F/BBMVP-27
90HotPlay/St-28
90KMart/CBatL-8
90Leaf/I-242

90MLBPA/Pins-79
90MSA/Soda-22
90OPC-360
90Panini/St-98
90Pol/Brew-4
90PublInt/St-500
90RedFoley/St-65
90S-460
90S/100St-98
90Sf-183
90T-360
90T/Ames-14
90T/Big-103
90T/Coins-23
90T/Mini-20
90T/St-199
90T/TVAS-29
90UD-254
91B-32
91Brewer/MillB-17
91Classic/200-79
91Classic/II-T14
91Classic/III-60
91D-85
91F-591
91F/Ultra-178
91Leaf/II-302
91Leaf/Prev-20
91Leaf/Stud-73
91MajorLg/Pins-42
91OPC-95
91OPC/Premier-82
91Panini/FrSt-205
91Panini/St-168
91Petro/SU-15
91Pol/Brew-15
91S-49
91S/100SS-13
91T-95
91T/CJMini/I-2
91T/StClub/I-245
91UD-324
91USPlayC/AS-8H
92D/DK-DK1
92D/I-51
92F-182
92F-702M
92S/100SS-8
92S/I-61
92T-600
92UD-423

Mollwitz, Fred
16FleischBrd-66
D329-124
D350/2-121
M101/4-124
M101/5-121

Moloney, Bill
81Bristol-2
83Pawtu-9

Moloney, Richard
71OPC-13R
71T-13R

Mompres, Danilo
91Pittsfld/ClBest-10
91Pittsfld/ProC-3431

Monasterio, Juan
76Wausau

Monastro, Frank
90BurlInd/ProC-3015

Monbouquette, Bill
59T-173
60T-544
61T-562
61T/St-114
62Salada-99
62Shirriff-99
62T-580
62T/St-15
63Bz-21
63F-7
63Salada-35
63T-480
63T/SO
64T-25
64T/Coins-47
64T/St-19
64T/tatt
65OPC-142
65T-142
66T-429
66T/RO-114
67T-482
68T-234
69OPC-64
69T-64
76Wausau
78TCMA-111
86Albany/TCMA-8
89Myrtle/ProC-1466
90Dunedin/Star-27CO
90Swell/Great-106
91Dunedin/ClBest-26CO
91Dunedin/ProC-224CO
PM10/Sm-127

Moncerratt, Pablo
84Butte-17
86Wausau-17

Monchak, Al
73OPC-356CO
73T-356CO
74OPC-221CO
74T-221CO
86Pol/Atl-52C

Moncrief, Homer
82BirmB-4
83GlenF-15

Moncrief, Tony
83Idaho-29

Monda, Greg
85Cedar-17
86Vermont-13
88Nashvl/CMC-13
88Nashvl/ProC-491

Monday, Rick
67T-542R
68Bz-10
68T-282
68T/G-26
69MB-194
69MLB/St-88
69MLBPA/Pin-19
69NTF
69OPC-105
69T-105
69T/DE-14
69T/decal
69T/S-27
69T/St-218
69Trans-10
70MLB/St-262
70T-547
71K-73
71MLB/St-522
71OPC-135
71T-135
71T/Coins-40
71T/tatt-15
72MB-239
72T-730
73OPC-44
73T-44
74K-2
74OPC-295
74T-295
74T/St-17
75Ho-113
75Ho/Twink-113
75OPC-129
75T-129
75T/M-129
76Crane-37
76Ho-80
76MSA/Disc
76OPC-251
76SSPC-311
76T-251
77BurgChef-146
77Ho-30
77OPC-230
77T-360
78T-145
79K-57
79OPC-320DP
79T-605
80OPC-243
80Pol/Dodg-16
80T-465
81F-122
81K-53
81OPC-177
81Pol/Dodg-16
81T-726
81T/HT
82D-514
82F-15
82F/St-2
82OPC-6
82Pol/Dodg-16
82T-577
83D-643
83F-213
83OPC-63
83Pol/Dodg-16
83Seven-10
83T-63
84F-106
84Nes/792-274
84Pol/Dodg-16
84T-274
84T/St-83
87Mother/A's-2
87Smok/Dodg-23
88AlaskaAS60/Team-1
89Smok/Dodg-90
90Pac/Legend-40
90Padre/MagUno-8ANN
90Target-542
91Swell/Great-65

Mondesi, Raul
91AS/Cal-3
91B-593
92UD-60TP

Mondile, Steve
89Freder/Star-18
90Freder/Team-7

Monegro, David
88Elmira-15

Monegro, Miguel
87Elmira/Black-4
87Elmira/Red-4
88WinHaven/Star-14
90LynchRS/Team-6

Monell, Johnny
85LitFalls-26
87Columbia-9
89Jacks/GS-16

Money, Don
69T-454R
70T-645
71MLB/St-185
71OPC-49
71T-49
71T/Coins-31
71T/tatt-7
72MB-240
72T-635
73OPC-386
73T-386
74OPC-413
74T-413
74T/St-197
75Ho-112
75Ho/Twink-112
75OPC-175
75T-175
75T/M-175
76A&P/Milw
76Ho-136
76OPC-402
76SSPC-236
76T-402
77T-79
78T-24
79OPC-133
79T-265
80OPC-313
80T-595
81D-443
81F-524
81OPC-106
81T-106
82D-384
82F-149
82OPC-294
82Pol/Brew-7
82T-709
83D-132
83F-41
83Gard-12
83OPC-259
83Pol/Brew-7
83T-608
84F-208
84Nes/792-374
84T-374

Money, Kyle
82Reading-4
83Portl-4
86Portl-18

Monge, Sid
75SLCity
76OPC-595R
76T-595R
77T-282
78T-101
79T-459
80OPC-39
80T-74
81D-81
81F-395
81OPC-333
81T-333
82D-620
82F-375
82T-601
82T/Tr-73T
83D-245
83F-168
83T-564
83T/St-274
83T/Tr-74T
84D-139
84F-308
84Mother/Padres-21
84Nes/792-224
84Smok/Padres-19
84T-224
84T/Tr-80T
85F-17
85T-408
89Pac/SenLg-180
90EliteSenLg-88
90Rockford/ProC-2711CO

Mongiello, Michael
90Foil/Best-282
90SoBend/Best-21
91Saraso/ClBest-8
91Saraso/ProC-1111

Monheimer, Len
88Augusta/ProC-389

Monico, Mario
86Stockton-16
87Stockton-7
88ElPaso/Best-26
88TexLgAS/GS-24
89ElPaso/GS-30
90Denver/CMC-13
90Denver/ProC-638

Monita, Greg
87Vermont-21

Monroe, Bill
74Laugh/Black-31
86Negro/Frit-110

Monroe, Gary
81QuadC-14

Monroe, Larry
75AppFx
78Knoxvl
79Knoxvl/TCMA-14

Monroe, Zack
59T-108
60T-329
79TCMA-219

Mons, Jeffrey
88VeroB/Star-17

Monson, Steve
(Mo)
87Beloit-5
88Stockton/Cal-175
88Stockton/ProC-722
89ElPaso/GS-11
89Stockton/Best-4
89Stockton/Cal-160
89Stockton/ProC-384
91Stockton/ClBest-3
91Stockton/ProC-3030

Montague, Ed
88TM/Umpire-27
89TM/Umpire-25
90TM/Umpire-24

Montague, John
75OPC-405
75T-405
75T/M-405
76OkCty/Team-17
78T-117
79OPC-172
79T-337
80T-253
81T-652

Montalvo, Rafael
83VeroB-9
85Cram/PCL-173
86Tucson-16
87Tucson-5
88Tucson/CMC-6
88Tucson/ProC-170
88Tucson/JP-18
90Edmon/CMC-11
90Edmon/ProC-517
91B-189
91Edmon/LineD-167
91Edmon/ProC-1515

Montalvo, Robert
88StCath/ProC-2021
90Myrtle/ProC-2875
90StCath/ProC-3466
91Dunedin/ClBest-28
91Dunedin/ProC-215

Montana, Joe
91Arena-1

Montanari, Dave
86PalmSp-23
86PalmSp/Smok-21

Montanez, Willie
71OPC-138R
71T-138R
72T-690
73OPC-97
73T-97
74JP
74OPC-515
74T-515
74T/St-77
75Ho-137
75K-31
75OPC-162
75T-162
75T/M-162
76OPC-181
76SSPC-103
76T-181
77BurgChef-211
77Ho-19
77K-31
77OPC-79
77T-410
77T/CS-29
78Ho-143
78OPC-43
78T-38
78T/Zest-4
79Ho-100
79OPC-153
79T-305
80OPC-119
80T-224
81F-506
81OPC-63
81OPC/Post-1
81T-559
82F-486
82T-458
91WIZMets-279

Montano, Francisco
85Tigres-8

Montano, Martin
85Beloit-22
86Stockton-17
87Stockton-13
88Fresno/ProC-1245

Monteagudo, Aurelio
64T-466R
65T-286R
66T-532
67T-453
71MLB/St-421
71OPC-129
71T-129
72OPC-458
72T-458
74OPC-139
74T-139
74T/Tr-139T
85MidldA-20CO
86MidldA-18CO
87Knoxvl-5CO

Monteau, Sam
75BurlB
76BurlB

Montefusco, John
76Crane-38
76Ho-41
76Ho/Twink-41
76MSA/Disc

76OPC-203LL
76OPC-30
76SSPC-97
76T-203LL
76T-30
77BurgChef-106
77Ho-31
77K-5
77OPC-232
77Pep-42
77T-370
77T/CS-30
78OPC-59
78T-142
79OPC-288
79Pol/Giants-26
79T-560
80OPC-109
80Pol/Giants-26
80T-195
81D-434
81F-439
81Pol/Atl-24
81T-438
81T/Tr-804
82F-442
82T-697
82T/Tr-74T
83D-313
83F-367
83OPC-223
83T-223
83T/St-297
84D-126
84F-132
84Mother/Giants-24
84Nes/792-761
84OPC-265
84T-761
85D-580
85F-135
85OPC-301
85T-301
85T/St-319

Monteiro, Dave
88Idaho/ProC-1841

Montejo, Steve
88Watertn/Pucko-22

Monteleone, Rich
86Calgary-15
87Calgary-24
87Mother/Sea-24
88Calgary/CMC-3
88Calgary/ProC-797
89Edmon/CMC-2
89Edmon/ProC-564
89S/Tr-92
90ColClip/CMC-8
90ColClip/ProC-675
90D-462
90F-648M
90OPC-99
90S-565
90T-99
90T/TVYank-56
91AAAGame/ProC-AAA7
91ColClip/LineD-113
91ColClip/ProC-596
92S/II-690

Montero, Alberto
90Ashvl/ClBest-15
91Ashvl/ProC-576

Montero, Cesar
90Hunting/ProC-3289

Montero, Sixto
89Martins/Star-22

Montes, Dan
89Everett/Star-22

Montgomery, Al
80Utica-23

Montgomery, Damin
91Billings/ProC-3768

Montgomery, Dan
87Bakers-2
88Bakers/Cal-238
89VeroB/Star-17

Montgomery, Don
91Everett/ClBest-6
91Everett/ProC-3919

Montgomery, Jeff
87Nashvl-15
88F-642R
88F/Up-U32
88Omaha/CMC-7
88Omaha/ProC-1501
88S-497
88S/Tr-71T
88T-447
89B-113
89D-440
89D/Best-319
89F-288
89S-367
89T-116
89UD-618
90B-370
90D-380
90F-115
90Leaf/II-520
90OPC-638
90Panini/St-85
90PublInt/St-353
90S-365
90T-638
90T/St-273
90UD-698
91B-308
91D-505
91F-564
91F/Ultra-153
91OPC-371
91Pol/Royal-16
91S-143
91T-371
91T/StClub/II-369
91UD-637
92D/II-666
92F-164
92S/I-14
92T-16
92UD-627

Montgomery, Larry
77BurlB
78BurlB
81ElPaso-12
85Cram/PCL-58

Montgomery, Mike
90Batavia/ProC-3064

Montgomery, Monty
72OPC-372R
72T-372R
73OPC-164
73T-164

Montgomery, Raymond
90AubAs/ProC-3394
91BurlAs/ClBest-21
91BurlAs/ProC-2815

Montgomery, Reggie
85MidldA-24
86Edmon-21
88RochR/ProC-207

Montgomery, Robert
71OPC-176R
71T-176R
72OPC-411
72T-411
73OPC-491
73T-491
74OPC-301
74T-301
75OPC-559
75T-559
75T/M-559
76OPC-523
76SSPC-414
76T-523
77T-288
78PapaG/Disc-10
78T-83
79OPC-219
79T-423
80T-618

Montoya, Albert
91MedHat/ProC-4097

Montoya, Norman
91QuadC/ClBest-9
91QuadC/ProC-2626

Montoyo, Charlie
88CalLgAS-16
88Stockton/Cal-199
88Stockton/ProC-737
89AS/Cal-29
89Stockton/Best-14
89Stockton/Cal-172
89Stockton/ProC-381
89Stockton/Star-12
91Denver/LineD-146
91Denver/ProC-131

Monzant, Ray
56T-264
58SFCallB-17
58T-447
59T-332
60T-338
79TCMA79-199

Monzon, Dan
90SoBend/ClBest-3
90Utica/Pucko-3

Monzon, Daniel F.
73OPC-469
73T-469
74OPC-613
74T-613
78Wausau
82Lynch-1

Monzon, Jose
89Myrtle/ProC-1459
91Knoxvl/LineD-362
91Knoxvl/ProC-1771

Moock, Joe
91WIZMets-280

Moody, James
89Oneonta/ProC-2105
90PrWill/Team-15

Moody, Kyle
91Spokane/ClBest-6
91Spokane/ProC-3957

Moody, Willis
88Negro/Duques-18

Moon, Glen
80Clinton-19

Moon, Wally
54T-137
55Hunter
55T-67
55T/DH-37
56T-55
56T/Pin-48OF
57T-65
58T-210
59T-530
60Bz-3
60Morrell
60T-5
60T/tatt-36
61BB-9
61P-159
61T-325
61T/St-29
62BB-9
62Exh
62Salada-124
62Shirriff-124
62T-190
62T-52LL
62T/bucks
62T/St-137
63Exh
63T-279
64T-353
65OPC-247
65T-247
79TCMA-137
88Pac/Leg-81
89Smok/Dodg-65
89Swell-81
90CLAS/CL-7MG
90Freder/Team-1MG
90Target-543
91Freder/ClBest-26MG
91Freder/ProC-2381MG
91Swell/Great-64
Exh47

Mooney, James
34G-83

Mooney, Troy
89Princet/Star-13
90Welland/Pucko-23
91Augusta/ClBest-10
91Augusta/ProC-804

Mooneyham, Bill
81Holyo-23
82Holyo-6
83Nashua-5
84Cram/PCL-110
85Huntsvl/BK-21
86D/Rook-50
86F/Up-U77
87D-302
87F-399
87T-548
87Tacom-18
88Denver/ProC-1254
88ElPaso/Best-9

Moore, Alvin
(Junior)
78Green
78T-421
79T-275
80T-186
81Durham-13

Moore, Archie
64T-581R

Moore, Balor
71OPC-747R
71T-747R
73OPC-211
73T-211
74OPC-453
74T-453
75OPC-592
75T-592
75T/M-592
78T-368
79OPC-122
79T-238
80OPC-6
80T-19
81Vanco-10

Moore, Bart
89Elmira/Pucko-9
90WinHaven/Star-17

Moore, Billy
86Indianap-35
87Indianap-18
88Indianap/CMC-13
88Indianap/ProC-497
89Indianap/CMC-13
89Indianap/ProC-1211
89RochR/ProC-1647
90Denver/CMC-11
90Denver/ProC-639

Moore, Bobby
88BBCity/Star-18
89BBCity/Star-18
90A&AASingle/ProC-51
90Foil/Best-231
90Memphis/Best-9
90Memphis/ProC-1019
90Memphis/Star-20
91Omaha/LineD-343
91Omaha/ProC-1047
92T/91Debut-126

Moore, Boo
90WinHaven/Star-18
91CLAS/ProC-CAR24
91LynchRS/ClBest-23
91LynchRS/ProC-1213
91Single/ClBest-43

Moore, Brad
86Cram/PCL-144
87Clearw-2
88Phill/TastyK-27
88Reading/ProC-866
89OPC-202
89ScrWB/CMC-8
89ScrWB/ProC-709
89T-202
90F/Up-U45
90ScranWB/ProC-597
91Tidew/LineD-564
91Tidew/ProC-2506

Moore, Calvin
75Cedar

Moore, Cary
89Erie/Star-14

Moore, Charlie
74OPC-603R
74T-603R
75OPC-636
75T-636
75T/M-636
76A&P/Milw
76OPC-116
76SSPC-231
76T-116
77BurgChef-84
77T-382
78T-51
79T-408
80OPC-302
80T-579
81D-324
81F-521
81OPC-237
81T-237
82D-280
82F-150
82OPC-308
82Pol/Brew-22
82T-308
83D-206
83F-42
83Gard-13
83Pol/Brew-22
83T-659
83T/St-157
84D-292
84F-209
84Gard-14
84Nes/792-751
84OPC-138
84Pol/Brew-22
84T-751
84T/St-301
85D-351
85F-589
85Gard-14
85Pol/Brew-22
85T-83
86D-246
86F-496
86F/St-77
86OPC-137
86Pol/Brew-22
86T-137
86T-426M
86T/St-204
87D-372
87F-351
87OPC-93
87SanJose-6
87T-676
87T/Tr-82T
88S-444

Moore, Daryl
90A&AASingle/ProC-107
90Foil/Best-121
90Wausau/Best-5
90Wausau/ProC-2118
91Freder/ProC-2360

Moore, Dave
78Indianap-11
79Indianap-4
81Albuq/TCMA-1
82Albuq-6

Moore, Dee
90Target-545

Moore, Don
81ArkTr-3
82ArkTr-17

Moore, Donnie
78T-523
79T-17
82Richm-7
84F-185
84Nes/792-207
84Pol/Atl-31
84T-207
85D-650
85F-334
85F/Up-U82
85OPC-61
85Smok/Cal-21
85T-699
85T/Tr-85T
86D-255
86D/AAS-46
86F-164
86Leaf-130
86OPC-345
86Smok/Cal-21
86T-345
86T/St-182
87D-110
87F-89
87F/LL-30
87OPC-115
87RedFoley/St-56
87Smok/Cal-8
87T-115
87T/Mini-46
87T/St-177
88D-621
88F-500
88OPC-204

88S-195
88Smok/Angels-20
88T-471
89S-535

Moore, Earl A.
11Helmar-148
14CJ-124
15CJ-124
92Conlon/Sport-373
E104
E107
E224
E94
E97
M116
T201
T207
W555
WG2-36

Moore, Ed
79QuadC-3

Moore, Eugene
(Gene)
39PB-160
40PB-143
41DP-122
41DP-37
41PB-25
90Target-547
91Conlon/Sport-77
R314

Moore, Graham E.
(Eddie)
33G-180
90Target-546

Moore, Gary D.
90Target-1039

Moore, Greg
86Knoxvl-17

Moore, J.B.
85PrWill-27

Moore, Jackie S.
65T-593R
70McDon-6
73OPC-549CO
73T-549CO
74OPC-379CO
74T-379CO
77T-113CO
84T/Tr-81T
85Mother/A's-1MG
85T-38MG
86Mother/A's-1
86T-591MG
90Kahn/Reds-27M
91Kahn/Reds-x

Moore, Jim
85FtMyr-25

Moore, Joe G.
(Jo-Jo)
33G-126
33G-231
37Wheat
38ONG/Pin-21
41DP-30
V355-8

Moore, John
90Wausau/Star-17

Moore, John F.
(Johnny)
30CEA/Pin-18
36Exh/4-6
37Exh/4-2
37Exh/4-6
38Wheat
R310

Moore, Kelvin
80Ogden-20
81Tacom-18
82D-534
82T-531R
82Tacom-31
83D-87
83Tacom-32
84Cram/PCL-31
84ElPaso-13
85BuffB-10

Moore, Kerwin
89Eugene/Best-17
90AppFox/Box-19
90AppFox/ProC-2109
91B-312
91BBCity/ClBest-26
91BBCity/ProC-1412
91Single/ClBest-38
91UD/FinalEd-19F

Moore, Lloyd
(Whitey)
39PB-162
40PB-150
W711/1
W711/2

Moore, Marcus
89BendB/Legoe-8
91Dunedin/ClBest-8
91Dunedin/ProC-204

Moore, Mark
80Cedar-1

Moore, Meredith
89WinHaven/Star-16

Moore, Michael
86Penin-18
88Boise/ProC-1608
91Watertn/ClBest-14
91Watertn/ProC-3369

Moore, Michael W.
(Mike)
83D-428
83F-482
83SLCity-7
83T-209
84D-634
84F-614
84Mother/Mar-5
84Nes/792-547
84T-547
85D-440
85F-495
85Mother/Mar-8
85T-279FDP
85T-373
86D-240
86F-469
86Leaf-114
86Mother/Mar-21
86Sf-162
86T-646
86T/Mini-30
86T/St-221
87D-70
87F-590
87Mother/Sea-3
87OPC-102
87Smok/AL-11
87T-727
87T/St-215
88D-75
88D/Best-192
88F-379
88Mother/Sea-3
88S-464
88T-432
88T/Big-241
89B-189
89D-448
89D/Best-246
89D/Tr-21
89F-554
89F/Up-55
89Mother/A's-12
89OPC-28
89Panini/St-431
89S-274
89S/Tr-5
89Sf-77
89T-28
89T/St-220
89T/Tr-82T
89UD-123
89UD/Ext-758
90B-445
90Classic-104
90D-214
90F-16
90F/WS-1
90Leaf/II-293
90Mother/A's-9
90OPC-175
90Panini/St-136
90PublInt/St-311
90S-190
90S/100St-42
90Sf-185
90T-175
90T/Big-200
90T/Mini-31
90T/St-178
90UD-275
90Woolwth/HL-27
91B-212
91D-161
91F-18
91F/Ultra-252
91Leaf/I-218
91Mother/A's-11
91OPC-294
91S-516
91SFExam/A's-9
91T-294
91T/StClub/II-464
91UD-423
92D/I-337
92F-263
92S/I-91
92T-359
92UD-661

Moore, Mike
80LynnS-1

Moore, Pat
87Erie-27

Moore, R. Barry
(Barry)
67OPC-11
67T-11
68T-462
69T-639
70OPC-366
70T-366
72MB-241

Moore, Randolph
31Exh/4-1
33G-69
35G-2E
35G-4E
35G-7E
90Target-548
R308-171
R314
V354-26

Moore, Randy
88Beloit/GS-21

Moore, Ray
55Esskay
55T-208
56T-43
57T-106
58T-249
59T-293
60T-447
61Clover-18
61Peters-13
61T-289
61T/RO-20
62T-437
63T-26
90Target-549
91Crown/Orio-312

Moore, Rick
86Chatt-20

Moore, Robert
(Bobby)
83GlenF-16
84Shrev/FB-12
86Phoenix-17
90Nashvl/CMC-2
90Nashvl/ProC-230

Moore, Ronald
86Cram/PCL-159

Moore, Roy Daniel
E120

Moore, Sam
86Fresno/Smok-8
87Clinton-23

Moore, Steve
82Tulsa-13

Moore, Terry
49B-174
92Conlon/Sport-641
R314
R423-71
W754

Moore, Tim
90Hunting/ProC-3290
90WinSalem/Team-19
91Elizab/ProC-4312
91Geneva/ClBest-13
91Geneva/ProC-4226
91Peoria/ClBest-17
91Peoria/ProC-1350

Moore, Tommy J.
89Pac/SenLg-148
91WIZMets-281

Moore, Tony
90Kgsport/Best-9
90Kgsport/Star-18

Moore, William Wilcey
(Cy)
90Target-544
91Conlon/Sport-109
W513-77

Moorhead, Bob
62T-593R
91WIZMets-282

Moose, Bob
68KDKA-38
68OPC-36R
68T-36R
69T-409
70MLB/St-104
70OPC-110
70T-110
70T/Cb
71MLB/St-209
71OPC-690
71T-690
71T/Coins-147
72MB-242
72T-647
73OPC-499
73T-499
74OPC-382
74T-382
75OPC-536
75T-536
75T/M-536
76OPC-476
76SSPC-570
76T-476

Mooty, J.T.
(Jake)
49B/PCL-23
R314/Can

Mora, Andres
77T-646
78T-517
79T-287
91Crown/Orio-313

Morales, Armando
91Princet/ClBest-11
91Princet/ProC-3510

Morales, Edwin
87PortChar-8

Morales, Joe Edwin
82Beloit-16
84ElPaso-21

Morales, Jorge
91Penin/ClBest-15
91Penin/ProC-381

Morales, Jose
76OPC-418
76SSPC-323
76T-418
77OPC-263RB
77OPC-90
77T-102
77T-233RB
78OPC-63
78T-374
79T-552
80OPC-116
80T-218
81D-495
81F-571
81T-43
81T/Tr-806
82D-203
82F-173
82T-648
82T/Tr-75T
83Pol/Dodg-43
83T/Tr-75T
84D-275
84F-107
84F-498
84Nes/792-143
84Pol/Dodg-43
84T-143
89Swell-38
90Target-550
91Crown/Orio-314

Morales, Julio
(Jerry)
70OPC-262R
70T-262R
71OPC-696
71T-696
73OPC-268
73T-268
74OPC-258
74T-258
74T/St-98
75OPC-282
75T-282
75T/M-282
76Crane-39
76Ho-140
76MSA/Disc
76OPC-79
76SSPC-312
76T-79
77BurgChef-196
77Ho-49
77T-639
78OPC-23
78T-175
79OPC-235
79T-452
80T-572
81F-338
81T-377
81T/Tr-805
82D-309
82F-601
82F/St-93
82RedLob
82T-33
83F-502
83T-729
83Thorn-24
91WIZMets-283

Morales, Manuel
85Tigres-20

Morales, Rich Jr.
91Pocatel/ProC-3800

Morales, Rich
69T-654R
70OPC-91
70T-91
71OPC-267
71T-267
72T-593
73OPC-494
73T-494
74OPC-387SD
74T-387
81QuadC-30
88Vermont/ProC-954
89Calgary/CMC-24
89Calgary/ProC-538
90SanBern/Cal-109
90Wmsprt/Best-25MG
90Wmsprt/ProC-1072MG
90Wmsprt/Star-25MG

Morales, William
87PrWill-29
88PrWill/Star-18

Moralez, Paul
86Kinston-17
87Bakers-24

Moran, Bill
(Bugs)
78Knoxvl

Moran, Dino
86Watertn-13

Moran, Frank
88Hamil/ProC-1746

Moran, Jim
53Mother-12

Moran, Joseph Herbert
16FleischBrd-67
90Target-1040
D350/2-122
M101/5-122
T206

Moran, Opie
87Erie-2
89ArkTr/GS-13

Moran, Owen
T3/Box-60

Moran, Pat J.
10Domino-88A
10Domino-88B
11Helmar-149
12Sweet/Pin-129
14Piedmont/St-41
15CJ-111

88Pac/8Men-89
BF2-88
D329-125
D350/2-123
E270/2
M101/4-125
M101/5-123
M116
S74-102
T202
T204
T205
T206
T207
T3-109
W514-12
WG7-33
Moran, Richard Alan
(Al)
63T-558R
64T-288
91WIZMets-284
Moran, Steve
86AppFx-16
Moran, William
(Billy)
58T-388
59T-196
61BeeHive-14
62T-539
63J-25
63P-25
63Salada-48
63T-57
64T-333
64T/St-67
65T-562
Morandini, Mickey
88T/Tr-71TOLY
89Spartan/ProC-1030
89Spartan/Star-18
89Star/Wax-57
89T/Big-162
90B-153
90ScranWB/CMC-14
90ScranWB/ProC-606
91B-492
91Classic/200-187
91Classic/I-79
91D-44RR
91F-407
91F/Ultra-268
91Leaf/II-383
91Leaf/Stud-218
91MajorLg/Pins-61
91OPC-342
91OPC/Premier-83
91Phill/Medford-28
91S-376RP
91S/Rook40-33
91ScranWB/LineD-491
91Seven/3DCoin-12NE
91T-342
91T/90Debut-110
91T/StClub/II-535
91UD-18
92D/II-669
92F-539
92S/I-143
92T-587
92UD-449
Morando, Dean
78Wisco
Moraw, Carl
86Beloit-16
87Stockton-21
88Stockton/Cal-184
88Stockton/ProC-746
89ElPaso/GS-12
89Stockton/Best-5
89Stockton/Cal-156
89Stockton/ProC-378
Mordecai, Mike
88CapeCod-17
88CapeCod/Sum-42
90CLAS/CL-28
90Durham/Team-7
91Durham/ClBest-13
91Durham/ProC-1557
Moreau, Guy
R314/Can
Morehart, Ray
91Conlon/Sport-102
Morehead, Dave
63T-299R
64T-376
65T-434
66OPC-135
66T-135
67T-297
67T/Test/RSox-11
68Coke
68Dexter-57
68T-212
69MLB/St-60
69OPC-29
69T-29
70MLB/St-224
70OPC-495
70T-495
71MLB/St-422
71OPC-221
71T-221
72MB-243
Morehead, Seth
59T-253
60L-87
60T-504
61T-107
Morehouse, Richard
86QuadC-24
87PalmSp-28
88PalmSp/Cal-91
88PalmSp/ProC-1449
89MidldA/GS-24
Morehouse, Scott
88CapeCod/Sum-162
Moreland, Keith
79OkCty
80BK/P-3
81D-382
81F-13
81T-131
82D-119
82F-252
82RedLob
82T-384
82T/Tr-76T
83D-309
83F-503
83OPC-58
83T-619
83T/St-222
83Thorn-6
84D-483
84F-499
84Nes/792-23
84Nes/792-456TL
84OPC-23
84SevenUp-6
84T-23
84T-456TL
84T/St-39
85D-117
85F-62
85Leaf-197
85OPC-197
85SevenUp-6
85T-538
85T/St-39
86Cub/Unocal-13
86D-167
86Drake-9
86F-375
86F/LL-25
86F/Mini-79
86F/St-78
86Gator-6
86Jay's-13
86Leaf-94
86OPC-266
86Sf-90
86T-266
86T/Mini-38
86T/St-54
87Berg/Cubs-6
87D-169
87D-24DK
87D/DKsuper-24
87D/OD-71
87Drake-7
87F-569
87F/LL-31
87F/Mini-69
87F/St-79
87Leaf-24DK
87Leaf-77
87OPC-177
87Sf-122
87S/Test-71
87Seven-C12
87Seven-ME7
87T-177
87T/St-65
88Coke/Padres-7
88D-201
88D/Best-266
88F-425
88F/Up-U124
88Leaf-160
88OPC-31
88Panini/St-263
88RedFoley/St-58
88S-71
88S/Tr-9T
88Sf-164
88Smok/Padres-19
88T-416
88T/Big-207
88T/St-58
88T/Tr-72T
89B-109
89D-111
89D/Best-203
89F-313
89Mara/Tigers-10
89OPC-293
89S-42
89S/Tr-29
89Sf-141
89T-773
89T/St-105
89T/Tr-83T
89UD-361
90PublInt/St-477
90S-444
90Sf-139
90UD-401
91Crown/Orio-315
Moreland, Owen III
84LitFalls-11
Morelli, Frank
89Elmira/Pucko-10
Morelock, Charlie
83Ander-12
86Durham-19
Moren, Lew
E104
M116
Morena, Jamie
87CharRain-18
Moreno, Angel
82F-469
84Cram/PCL-99
Moreno, Armando
86Jaxvl/TCMA-4
87Jaxvl-12
88Jaxvl/Best-27
88Jaxvl/ProC-983
88SLAS-21
89Indianap/CMC-19
89Indianap/ProC-1222
90BuffB/CMC-19
90BuffB/ProC-381
90BuffB/Team-17
91BuffB/LineD-39
91BuffB/ProC-548
92T-179R
Moreno, Carlos
82Miami-5
Moreno, Chris
89Stockton/Best-26M
Moreno, Douglas
86Macon-16
86Watertn-14
Moreno, Jaime
86CharRain-18
88Charl/ProC-1218
89Watlo/ProC-1785
89Watlo/Star-26
91CharRain/ClBest-26CO
91CharRain/ProC-111CO
Moreno, Jorge
73Cedar
74Cedar
75Dubuq
79Tidew-3
80Tidew-2
91WIZMets-285
Moreno, Jorge A.
91Bristol/ClBest-13
91Bristol/ProC-3615
Moreno, Jose D.
91Watertn/ClBest-15
91Watertn/ProC-3370
Moreno, Michael
83Wisco/LF-24
85Orlan-8
Moreno, Omar
77T-104
78T-283
79Ho-12
79OPC-321
79T-4LL
79T-607
80BK/PHR-29
80OPC-372
80T-165
81Coke
81D-17
81F-361
81F/St-100
81OPC-213
81T-535
81T/SO-100
81T/St-211
81T/St-24
82D-347
82F-487
82F/St-79
82OPC-395
82T-395
82T/St-81
83D-347
83F-312
83OPC-332
83T-485
83T/St-278
83T/Tr-76T
84D-637
84F-133
84Nes/792-16
84Nes/792-714LL
84OPC-16
84T-16
84T-714LL
84T/St-322
85D-591
85F-136
85T-738
86F-15
86F/Up-U78
86Pol/Atl-18
86T/Tr-75T
87F-521
87T-214
87T/St-44
89Pac/SenLg-138
89TM/SenLg-80
90EliteSenLg-41
91Pac/SenLg-46
Moreno, Ric
87Dunedin-14
Morenz, Howie
33SK-24
Moret, Rogelio
(Roger)
71OPC-692R
71T-692R
72OPC-113
72T-113
73OPC-291
73T-291
74OPC-590
74T-590
74T/St-137
75OPC-8
75T-8
75T/M-8
76OPC-632
76SSPC-420
76T-632
76T/Tr-632T
77T-292
78T-462
Moreta, Manuel
76Watlo
Morfin, Arvid
84Butte-18
86Cram/PCL-116
Morgan, Bill
79QuadC-5
Morgan, Bob M.
50B-222
52T-355
53B/Col-135
53T-85
55B-81
56T-337
58T-144
79TCMA-193
90Target-551
91T/Arc53-85
Morgan, Chris
86FSLAS-36
86Lakeland-16
87GlenF-17
Morgan, Curt
86Miami-18
Morgan, Eddie
31Exh/4-21
33Exh/4-11
33G-116
35BU-60
90Target-552
V354-2
Morgan, Gary
90Batavia/ProC-3081
Morgan, Gene
87Memphis-16
87Memphis/Best-17
Morgan, Harry
(Cy)
BF2-49
E104
E95
M116
T204
T207
T208
T222
Morgan, Jim
89Chatt/II/Team-18
Morgan, Joe L.
65OPC-16R
65T-16R
66OPC-195
66T-195
66T/RO-9
67OPC/PI-25
67T-337
67T/PI-25
68Coke
68Dexter-56
68OPC-144
68T-144
68T-364AS
69MB-195
69MLB/St-141
69OPC-35
69T-35
69T/St-36
70K-72
70MLB/St-44
70OPC-537
70T-537
71MLB/St-89
71OPC-264
71T-264
71T/Coins-117
71T/GM-34
72MB-244
72OPC-132
72T-132
72T-752TR
73K-34
73OPC-230
73T-230
74Greyhound-6M
74K-36
74OPC-333AS
74OPC-85
74T-333AS
74T-85
74T/St-28
75Greyhound-4
75Ho-5
75Ho/Twink-5
75K-27
75OPC-180
75T-180
75T/M-180
76Crane-40
76Greyhound-4
76Ho-2
76Ho/Twink-2

76Icee
76K-27
76MSA/Disc
76OPC-197LL
76OPC-420
76SSPC-38
76T-197LL
76T-420
77BurgChef-207
77Ho-2
77OPC-220
77Pep-46
77T-100
77T/CS-31
78Ho-87
78OPC-160
78T-300
78Wiffle/Discs-52
79Ho-61
79OPC-5
79T-20
80BK/PHR-30
80OPC-342
80T-650
81D-18
81F-78
81F/St-109
81K-22
81T-560
81T/Tr-807
82D-312
82F-397
82F/St-63
82KMart-28
82KMart-30
82OPC-146IA
82OPC-208
82T-754
82T-755IA
83D-24DK
83D-438
83D-648M
83F-270
83OPC-264SV
83OPC-81
83T-171TL
83T-603
83T-604SV
83T/St-303
83T/Tr-77T
84D-355
84D/Champs-44
84F-43
84F-636IA
84F/St-100
84F/St-120
84F/X-U80
85FunFoodPin-74
84Mother/A's-3
84Nes/792-210
84Nes/792-705LL
84OPC-210
84T-210
84T-705
84T/St-116
84T/Tr-82
85D-584
85F-431
85Leaf-28
85OPC-352
85T-352
85T-5RB
85T/St-325
85T/St-5
85T/St-6
86Mother/Ast-3
86Sf/Dec-56
89T/LJN-109
90MSA/AGFA-11

Morgan, Joe M.
60T-229
61T-511
62Kahn/Atl
81Pawtu-12MG
89T-714MG
90OPC-321MG
90T-321MG
90T/TVRSox-1MG
91OPC-21MG
91T-21MG

Morgan, Ken
87Visalia-3
88Visalia/Cal-146
88Visalia/ProC-90
89Orlan/Best-17
89Orlan/ProC-1341
90Foil/Best-30
90OrlanSR/Best-10
90OrlanSR/ProC-1096
90OrlanSR/Star-12
91Portl/LineD-411
91Portl/ProC-1578

Morgan, Kevin
91Niagara/ClBest-1
91Niagara/ProC-3642

Morgan, Michael
79Ogden/TCMA-3
80T-671R
83D-108
83F-388
83T-203
83T/Tr-78
84Nes/792-423
84OPC-6
84Syrac-22
84T-423
85Mother/Mar-25
86Mother/Mar-25
86T-152
87D-366
87F-591
87Mother/Sea-8
87T-546
88D-120
88D/Best-86
88F-380
88French-12
88S-295
88T-32
88T/Big-98
88T/Tr-73T
89D-164
89D/Best-122
89F/Up-91
89Mother/Dodg-13
89Pol/Dodg-23
89T-788
89T/Tr-84T
89UD-653
90D-132
90F-403
90Leaf/II-358
90Mother/Dodg-21
90OPC-367
90Pol/Dodg-36
90RedFoley/St-66
90S-342
90T-367
90Target-553
90UD-317
91Crown/Orio-316
91D-182
91F-213
91F/Ultra-165
91Leaf/I-193
91Mother/Dodg-21
91OPC-631
91Panini/FrSt-63
91Panini/St-52
91Panini/Top15-89
91Pol/Dodg-36
91RedFoley/St-67
91S-276
91T-631
91T/StClub/II-562
91UD-578
91USPlayC/AS-5C
92D/I-200
92F-465
92S/I-171
92T-289
92UD-513

Morgan, Ray
D327
D328-121
D329-126
D350/2-124
E135-121
M101/4-126
M101/5-124
T207

Morgan, Scott
91Kinston/ClBest-7
91Kinston/ProC-319

Morgan, Tom S.
52B-109
52BR
52T-331
53T-132
54NYJour
55B-100
57T-239
58T-365
59T-545
60L-97
60T-33
61T-272
62T-11
63T-421CO
73OPC-421CO
73T-421CO
74OPC-276CO
74T-276CO
91T/Arc53-132
PM10/L-29

Morgan, Vern
73OPC-49CO
73T-49C
74OPC-447CO
74T-447C

Morhardt, Greg
85Orlan-9
86Orlan-13
87Portl-20

Morhardt, Moe
62T-309

Mori, Dan
87SanJose-12

Moriarty, Edward
R314

Moriarty, George
09Buster/Pin-10
11Helmar-34
14CJ-114
15CJ-114
21Exh-111ump
D329-127
D350/2-125
E104
E254
E270/1
M101/4-127
M101/5-125
M116
S74-16
T202
T205
T206
T207

Moriarty, Todd
84Everett/Cram-26

Morillo, Ceasar
91BBCity/ClBest-19
91BBCity/ProC-1405
91Single/ClBest-60

Morillo, Santiago
91SoOreg/ClBest-17
91SoOreg/ProC-3840

Moritz, Chris
85Greens-7
86WinHaven-18
87NewBrit-23
88NewBrit/ProC-907
89NewBrit/ProC-603
89NewBrit/Star-11

Morlan, John
75OPC-651
75T-651
75T/M-651

Morland, Mike
91StCath/ClBest-1
91StCath/ProC-3398

Morlock, Allen
83Spring/LF-24
84ArkTr-8
86ArkTr-16
87Edmon-9

Morman, Russ
86BuffB-19
86Sf/Rook-33
87Coke/WS-8
87D-306
87F-645R
87Hawaii-22
87T-233
88Vanco/CMC-17
88Vanco/ProC-760
89Vanco/CMC-16
89Vanco/ProC-590
90Omaha/CMC-15
90Omaha/ProC-73
90WichSt-21
91Leaf/I-263

Morogiello, Dan
79Richm-18
80Richm-1
82Louisvl-20
83RochR-6
84Nes/792-682
84T-682
85Richm-5
91Crown/Orio-317

Morones, Gino
91Hunting/ClBest-15
91Hunting/ProC-3331

Moronko, Jeff
80Batavia-28
81Chatt-12
82Chatt-21
83BuffB-17
84BuffB-1
85Maine-19
85Tulsa-22
86OKCty-14
87Colum-15
87Colum/TCMA-17
88Colum/CMC-18
88Colum/Pol-20
88Colum/ProC-328
89Chatt/II/Team-19

Morphy, Pat
90Oneonta/ProC-3379
91Greens/ProC-3055

Morrill, John
E223
N172
N28
N284
N43
WG1-6

Morris, Aaron
91Watertn/ClBest-19
91Watertn/ProC-3375

Morris, Angel
81BurlB-14
82Beloit-26
85FtMyr-7
87FtMyr-30
88Virgini/Star-16
89Memphis/Best-14
89Memphis/ProC-1203
89Memphis/Star-18
90Miami/II/Star-19

Morris, Danny W.
69OPC-99R
69T-99R

Morris, Dave
81BurlB-1
83Ander-29
85Durham-8
85Everett/II/Cram-11
86Clinton-14

Morris, Don
80WHave-4
81WHave-16

Morris, Edward
N172

Morris, Fred
78DaytB

Morris, Hal
87Albany-21
88Colum/CMC-20
88Colum/Pol-21
88Colum/ProC-327
89AAA/CMC-17
89AAA/ProC-20
89Classic-28
89Colum/CMC-16
89Colum/Pol-14
89Colum/ProC-743
89D-545
89F-260
89S/HotRook-8
89S/NWest-29
90AlbanyDG/Best-18
90B-57
90Classic/Up-35
90D-514
90F/Up-U15
90HotRook/St-32
90Kahn/Reds-16
90Leaf/II-321
90OPC-236
90S-602RP
90S/100Ris-87
90S/YS/II-37
90T-236
90T/Tr-76T
90UD-31
91B-691
91Bz-13
91Classic/200-178
91Classic/I-98
91Classic/III-62
91D-141
91F-72
91F/Ultra-98
91Kahn/Reds-23
91Leaf/I-51
91Leaf/Stud-168
91MajorLg/Pins-71
91OPC-642
91Pep/Reds-12
91S-647
91S/100RisSt-98
91S/HotRook-3
91T-642
91T/StClub/II-339
91ToysRUs-20
91UD-351
92Classic/I-65
92D/DK-DK19
92D/I-258
92F-412
92S/100SS-14
92S/I-125
92T-773
92UD-121

Morris, Jack
77Evansvl/TCMA-20
78BK/T-8
78T-703R
79T-251
80T-371
81Coke
81D-127
81Detroit-128
81F-475
81OPC-284
81PermaGr/AS-15
81T-572
81T/St-80
82D-107
82F-274
82F/St-159
82K-5
82OPC-108
82OPC-47AS
82T-165LL
82T-450
82T-556AS
82T/St-10LL
82T/St-139
82T/St-183
83D-107
83D-5DK
83F-336
83K-35
83OPC-65
83T-65
83T/St-69
84D-415
84F-87
84F/St-83
85FunFoodPin-59
84Nes/792-136LL
84Nes/792-195
84Nes/792-666TL
84OPC-195
84T-136LL
84T-195
84T-666TL
84T/Gloss40-10
84T/St-263
85Cain's-14
85D-415
85F-18
85F/LimEd-21
85F/St-82
85Leaf-142
85OPC-382
85Seven-12D
85T-610
85T/3D-28
85T/Gloss40-26
85T/St-15WS
85T/St-256
85T/St-9ALCS

85T/Super-43
85ThomMc/Discs-15
85Wendy-16
86Cain's-12
86D-105
86D/AAS-18
86D/HL-27
86D/PopUp-18
86Dorman-2
86F-232
86F/Mini-48
86F/Slug-23
86F/St-79
86Leaf-38
86OPC-270
86Sf-117
86Sf-141M
86T-270
86T/3D-17
86T/Gloss22-10
86T/Mini-14
86T/St-163FOIL
86T/St-268
86T/Super-38
87Cain's-14
87Classic-90
87Coke/Tigers-7
87D-13DK
87D-173
87D/DKsuper-13
87D/OD-212
87Drake-27
87F-158
87F/BB-28
87F/Lim-28
87F/Mini-70
87F/Slug-27
87F/St-80
87Jiffy-3
87KayBee-20
87Leaf-135
87Leaf-13DK
87MnM's-6
87OPC-376
87RedFoley/St-114
87Sf-111M
87Sf-87
87Seven-DT8
87Smok/AL-6
87T-778
87T/Coins-18
87T/Gloss60-47
87T/Mini-55
87T/St-266
88ChefBoy-3
88Classic/Red-174
88Clinton/ProC-717
88D-127
88D/AS-24
88D/Best-181
88Drake-32
88F-626M
88F-64
88F/AwardWin-26
88F/BB/AS-26
88F/BB/MVP-24
88F/Excit-27
88F/Head-3
88F/Hottest-28
88F/LL-28
88F/Mini-22
88F/RecSet-26
88F/St-26
88F/TL-23
88Leaf-85
88OPC-340
88Panini/St-85
88Pep/T-47
88Pol/T-8
88S-545
88Sf-176
88T-340
88T/Big-170
88T/Coins-21
88T/Gloss60-17
88T/Mini-11
88T/RiteAid-27
88T/St-268
88T/St/Backs-59
88T/UK-50
89B-93
89Clinton/ProC-901
89D-234
89F-139
89F/BBMVP's-30
89Mara/Tigers-47
89OPC-266
89Panini/St-334
89Pol/Tigers-47
89RedFoley/St-82
89S-250
89S/Mast-8
89Sf-5
89T-645
89T/Big-61
89T/LJN-106
89T/St-277
89T/UK-54
89UD-352
90CokeK/Tiger-12
90D-639
90D/BestAL-34
90F-610
90F/LL-27
90KayBee-19
90Leaf/II-482
90OPC-555
90Panini/St-76
90PublInt/St-478
90S-203
90T-555
90T/St-276
90UD-573
91B-319
91Classic/II-T49
91Classic/III-61
91D-492
91F-343
91F/UltraUp-U39
91F/Up-U39
91Leaf/II-294
91Leaf/Stud-89
91OPC-75
91OPC/Premier-84
91Panini/FrSt-296
91S-114
91S/RookTr-74T
91T-75
91T/StClub/II-447
91T/Tr-82T
91UD-336
91UD-45TC
91UD/Ext-736
91UD/FinalEd-80FAS
91USPlayC/AS-1H
92Classic/I-66
92D/I-216
92D/I-25AS
92F-211
92S/II-652
92S/II-798HL
92T-235
92UD-315

Morris, Jeff
83Tucson-6
87Everett-26
90SanJose/Best-26CO
90SanJose/Cal-54CO
90SanJose/ProC-2028CO
90SanJose/Star-29CO

Morris, Jim
87Stockton-23
89Saraso/Star-15

Morris, Joe
90James/Pucko-23

Morris, John W.
69OPC-111
69T-111
70McDon-1
71MLB/St-446
71OPC-721
71T-721
75OPC-577
75T-577
75T/M-577

Morris, John
84Omaha-8
85D-32RR
85Louisvl-23
85Omaha-19
86Louisvl-20
87D-480
87F/Up-U83
87Louisvl-20
87Sf/Rook-42
87T-211
87T/GlossRk-10
88D-480
88F-43
88Louisvl-35
88S-346
88T-536
89Smok/Cards-14
89T-578
90D-516
90F-254
90OPC-383
90S-134
90Smok/Card-15
90T-383
90T/TVCard-35
91Crown/Orio-318
91F/Up-U109
91Leaf/II-496
91Phill/Medford-29
92D/I-92

Morris, Ken
88AubAs/ProC-1957

Morris, Marc
91Pocatel/ProC-3786

Morris, Rick
87Durham-20
88CLAS/Star-32
88Durham/Star-15
89Greenvl/ProC-1172
89Greenvl/Star-15
89Greenvl/Best-5
89Star/Wax-37
90Greenvl/Best-11
90Greenvl/ProC-1136
90Greenvl/Star-14
91Greenvl/ClBest-19
91Greenvl/LineD-213
91Greenvl/ProC-3013

Morris, Rod
88Butte-19
89CharlR/Star-16
89Star/Wax-8
90CharlR/Star-14
91Tulsa/LineD-588
91Tulsa/ProC-2786

Morris, Rossi
91Princet/ClBest-10
91Princet/ProC-3528

Morris, Steve
89Elizab/Star-20
89Kenosha/ProC-1060
89Kenosha/Star-16
89Star/Wax-53
90Foil/Best-185
90Kenosha/Best-9
90Kenosha/ProC-2308
90Kenosha/Star-14

Morrisette, James
89Clmbia/Best-15
89Clmbia/GS-16
89SALAS/GS-20
91Miami/ClBest-25
91StLucie/ClBest-3

Morrisey
N172
N284

Morrison, Anthony
87Oneonta-2

Morrison, Brian
87SanBern-17
88FSLAS/Star-13
88Miami/Star-15
89Knoxvl/Best-17
89Knoxvl/ProC-1146
90Salem/Star-14

Morrison, Bruce
83Lynch-9

Morrison, Dan
88TM/Umpire-47
89TM/Umpire-45
89TM/Umpire-60M
90TM/Umpire-43

Morrison, Jim
76OkCty/Team-18
79OkCty
79T-722R
80OPC-272
80T-522
81Coke
81D-158
81F-357
81T-323
81T/HT
81T/St-60
82D-395
82F-354
82OPC-154
82T-654
82T/Tr-77T
83D-150
83F-313
83T-173
84D-322
84F-257
84Nes/792-44
84T-44
85D-532
85F-471
85T-433
86D-386
86Elmira-13
86F-614
86OPC-56
86T-553
86T/St-133
87D-484
87D/OD-169
87F-614
87F/GameWin-29
87F/Mini-71
87F/St-81
87Greens-22
87Leaf-215
87OPC-237
87T-237
87T/St-133
88D-543
88F-65
88OPC-288
88S-272
88T-751
88T/Big-237
88T/St-272
89Elmira/Pucko-8
89Pac/SenLg-137
89T/SenLg-61
89TM/SenLg-81
89UD-568
90EliteSenLg-42
91WinHaven/ClBest-23
91WinHaven/ProC-502

Morrison, John
21Exh-112
90Target-554
E120
V100
V61-115
W572
W573

Morrison, Keith
90Pulaski/Best-6
90Pulaski/ProC-3104
91Macon/ClBest-6
91Macon/ProC-860

Morrison, Perry
80ElPaso-19
81Holyo-24
82Holyo-7

Morrison, Red
89FtLaud/Star-17

Morrison, Tony
88FSLAS/Star-45
88FtLaud/Star-17

Morrissey, Joe
33G-97
R310

Morrow, Ben
87Salem-9

Morrow, Brian
90WichSt-27

Morrow, Chris
88GreatF-5
89Bakers/Cal-204
89Salem/Team-18
90AS/Cal-12
90Bakers/Cal-247
91FSLAS/ProC-FSL41
91VeroB/ClBest-29
91VeroB/ProC-789

Morrow, David
86Jamestn-17
87BurlEx-17

Morrow, Red
88CalLgAS-50

Morrow, Steve
82FtMyr-23
84Memphis-22
87Memphis-26TR
87Memphis/Best-27
88Memphis/Best-4
89Omaha/CMC-24
89Omaha/ProC-1723

Morrow, Timmie
89Butte/SP-26
90Foil/Best-284
90Gaston/Best-17
90Gaston/ProC-2533
90Gaston/Star-15
91CharlR/ClBest-23
91CharlR/ProC-1327

Morse, Mike
81AppFx-20
83GlenF-7

Morse, Jacob C.
90LitSun-3

Morse, Matt
90Elizab/Star-14
91Kenosha/ClBest-5
91Kenosha/ProC-2083

Morse, Randy
84Shrev/FB-13

Morse, Scott
87PortChar-4
89CharlR/Star-17

Mortensen, Tony
89Smok/FresnoSt-15
91Waterlo/ClBest-6
91Waterlo/ProC-1253

Mortillaro, John
83Ander-13
84Durham-24

Mortimer, Bob
86Salem-20

Morton, Carl
69Fud's-9
69T-646R
70Expos/Pins-11
70OPC-109R
70T-109R
71K-23
71MLB/St-135
71OPC-515
71T-515
71T/Coins-35
71T/GM-4
71T/S-28
71T/tatt-16
72OPC-134
72T-134
73OPC-331
73T-331
74OPC-244
74T-244
74T/St-8
75OPC-237
75T-237
75T/M-237
76Ho-43
76Ho/Twink-43
76OPC-328
76SSPC-4
76T-328
77T-24

Morton, Guy
BF2-23
D327
D328-122
D329-128
D350/2-126
E121/80
E122
E135-122
M101/4-128
M101/5-126
W575
WG7-34

Morton, Kevin
88CapeCod-12
88CapeCod/Sum-139
89Elmira/Pucko-27
90A&AASingle/ProC-5
90EastLAS/ProC-EL32
90Foil/Best-211
90NewBrit/Best-14
90NewBrit/Star-12
90T/TVRSox-52
91B-130
91Classic/III-63
91D-37RR
91D/Rook-40
91Pawtu/LineD-361

91Pawtu/ProC-36
91UD/FinalEd-66F
92D/I-330
92S/100RisSt-36
92S/I-420
92T-724
92T/91Debut-127
92UD-676

Morton, Lew
52Park-13

Morton, Maurice
85Spokane/Cram-15

Morton, Ron
88Spokane/ProC-1946
89Watlo/ProC-1782
89Watlo/Star-21
90Waterlo/Best-12
90Waterlo/ProC-2378

Morton, Stan
80Clinton-22

Morton, Sydney
86Negro/Frit-36

Morton, Wycliffe
(Bubba)
62T-554
63T-164
67OPC-79
67T-79
68T-216
69MB-196
69T-342

Moryn, Walt
52Park-72
53Exh/Can-39
55B-261
57T-16
58T-122
59T-147
59T-488
60L-17
60T-74
60T/tatt-37
61T-91
61T/RO-32
79TCMA-141
90Target-555

Mosby, Linvel
78Ashvl
80Ashvl-20

Moscaret, Jeff
84MidldC-11

Moscat, Frank
85Lynch-20

Moschitto, Ross
65T-566R

Moscrey, Mike
88Cedar/ProC-1139
89Chatt/Best-19
89Chatt/GS-18

Moseby, Lloyd
80Syrac-16
81F-421
81OPC-52
81OPC/Post-24
81T-643
82D-129
82F-621
82OPC-223
82OPC/Post-4
82T-223
82T/St-246
83D-556
83F-435
83OPC-124
83T-452
83T/St-130
84D-363
84F-164
85FunFood/Pin-132
84Nes/792-403AS
84Nes/792-606TL
84Nes/792-92
84Nestle/DT-7
84OPC-289TL
84OPC-3AS
84OPC-92
84T-403AS
84T-606TL
84T-92
84T/St-191
84T/St-365
84T/St/Box-4
84Tor/Fire-25
85D-437
85D/AAS-5
85F-115
85F-636IA
85Leaf-143
85OPC-77
85OPC/Post-19
85T-545
85T/St-359
85T/Super-39
85Tor/Fire-23
86Ault-15
86D-73
86F-67
86F/LL-26
86Leaf-72
86OPC-360
86T-360
86T/St-195
86Tor/Fire-26
87D-21DK
87D-74
87D/AAS-59
87D/DKsuper-21
87D/OD-36
87F-236
87F/Lim-29
87F/Mini-72
87F/RecSet-22
87Leaf-105
87Leaf-21DK
87OPC-210
87RedFoley/St-55
87Sf-96
87T-210
87T/St-190
87Tor/Fire-23
88D-367
88D/Best-199
88F-119
88F/St-75
88Ho/Disc-20
88Leaf-140
88OPC-272
88Panini/St-225
88S-109
88Sf-74
88T-565
88T/Big-113
88T/St-189
88T/UK-51
88Tor/Fire-15
89D-231
89F-241
89OPC-113
89Panini/St-473
89RedFoley/St-83
89S-12
89T-113
89T/Big-262
89T/St-188
89Tor/Fire-15
89UD-381
90B-362
90CokeK/Tiger-13
90D-504
90D/BestAL-62
90F-90
90F/Up-U97
90Leaf/II-377
90OPC-779
90Publlnt/St-524
90S-404
90S/Tr-25T
90T-779
90T/Big-305
90T/Tr-77T
90UD-421
90UD/Ext-789
91B-135
91CokeK/Tiger-15
91D-188
91F-344
91F/Ultra-124
91Leaf/I-223
91Leaf/Stud-56
91OPC-632
91Panini/FrSt-293
91Panini/St-239
91S-133
91T-632
91T/StClub/II-364
91UD-559
92D/II-443
92F-142
92S/II-468
92UD-468

Moser, Larry
83Ander-30

Moser, Steve
86Watertn-15
87Salem-13

Moses, Gerald
(Gerry)
65T-573R
69T-476R
70OPC-104
70T-104
71MLB/St-352
71OPC-205
71T-205
71T/Coins-6
72OPC-356
72T-356
73OPC-431
73T-431
74OPC-19
74T-19
75OPC-271
75T-271
75T/M-271

Moses, John
81Wausau-25
83AppFx/LF-24
83SLCity-19
84Chatt-24
84D-74
84Nes/792-517
84T-517
85Cram/PCL-83
86Calgary-16
87D-393
87F-592
87Mother/Sea-18
87T-284
88D-440
88F-381
88F/Up-U45
88Portl/CMC-22
88Portl/ProC-643
88S-309
88T-712
89D-626
89F-121
89S-432
89T-72
89UD-242
90D-590
90F-381
90Leaf/II-433
90OPC-653
90Publlnt/St-333
90S-391
90T-653
90UD-240
91ColoSp/ProC-2198
91F-619
91OPC-341
91S-429
91T-341

Moses, Mark
80Ander-13

Moses, Steve
85Cram/PCL-30
86Reading-18
87Wmsprt-6

Moses, Wallace
(Wally)
35BU-98
37Dix
37Exh/4-14
37OPC-109
38Exh/4-14
38Wheat
39PB-64
40PB-26
41DP-126
41PB-42
51B-261
53B/Col-95
55B-294CO
60T-459C
91Conlon/Sport-90
R313
R314
R326-5A
R326-5B
R342-5
V300

Mosher, Peyton
82VeroB-9

Moskau, Paul
77Indianap-9
78Indianap-3
78OPC-181
78T-126
79OPC-197
79T-377
80T-258
81F-207
81OPC-358
81T-546
82D-355
82F-76
82T-97

Mosley, Reggie
83TriCit-15

Mosley, Tony
87Elmira/Black-17
87Elmira/Red-17
88WinHaven/Star-15
89Elmira/Pucko-11
90WinHaven/Star-19
91LynchRS/ClBest-5
91LynchRS/ProC-1194

Moss, Barry
77Indianap-23
87SLCity/Taco-x
88SLCity-18
89SLCity-15
91Erie/ClBest-28MG
91Erie/ProC-4084MG

Moss, Darren
87Anchora-36BB

Moss, J. Lester
47TipTop
50B-251
51B-210
52T-143
54B-181
54Esskay
55Esskay
57T-213
58T-153
59T-453
77Evansvl/TCMA-21
79T-66MG
91Crown/Orio-319

Moss, Ray
90Target-556

Mossi, Don
55B-259
55Gol/Ind-20
55Salem
55T-85
55T/DH-84
56T-39
56T/Pin-9P
57Sohio/Ind-9
57T-8
58T-35
59T-302
60T-418
60T/tatt-38
61P-42
61T-14
62J-23
62P-23
62P/Can-23
62T-105
62T-55LL
62T/St-49
63J-56
63P-56
63T-218M
63T-530
64T-335
66OPC-74
66T-74
79TCMA-215
81Detroit-49
90Pac/Legend-95

Mossor, Earl
90Target-1041

Mostil, Johnny A.
21Exh-113
28Yueng-24
61F-64
E120
E121/120
E210-24
V100
V61-45
W501-40
W502-24
W572
W573
WG7-35

Mota, Andres
(Andy)
87AubAs-7
88AubAs/ProC-1966
89Osceola/Star-12
89Star/Wax-16
90ColMud/Best-2
90ColMud/ProC-1354
90ColMud/Star-17
90Foil/Best-48
91Tucson/LineD-616
91Tucson/ProC-2220
91UD/FinalEd-22F
92D/II-598
92F-441
92S/II-872
92T-214
92T/91Debut-128
92UD-564

Mota, Carlos
88Burllnd/ProC-1783
89Watertn/Star-15
90Reno/Cal-271
91Kinston/ClBest-13
91Kinston/ProC-326
91Single/ClBest-118

Mota, Domingo
90Kissim/DIMD-18
91B-696

Mota, Jose
(Outfielder)
77Cocoa
78DaytB
80Cedar-13

Mota, Jose
(Infielder)
86Tulsa-27
89Huntsvl/Best-26
89Wichita/Rock/HL-15
89Wichita/Rock/Up-11
90LasVegas/CMC-13
90LasVegas/ProC-130
91F/Up-U126
91LasVegas/ProC-243
91LasVegas/LineD-289
92F-616
92S/100RisSt-47
92S/II-742
92T/91Debut-129

Mota, Manny
63T-141
64T-246
65T-463
66EH-15
66OPC-112
66T-112
67OPC-66
67T-66
67T/Test/PP-16
68KDKA-15
68T-325
69Fud's-10
69MB-197
69MLB/St-160
69T-236
69T/St-58
70MLB/St-53
70OPC-157
70T-157
71MLB/St-109
71OPC-112
71T-112
71Ticket/Dodg-11
72MB-245
72T-596
73OPC-412
73T-412
74K-49
74OPC-368
74T-368
75OPC-414
75T-414
75T/M-414
76OPC-548
76SSPC-87
76T-548

77T-386
78T-228
78T/Zest-5
79T-644
80T-3RS
81D-299
81F-141
85Coke/Dodg-21CO
86Coke/Dodg-20CO
87Smok/Dodg-24CO
88Smok/Dodg-5CO
89Smok/Dodg-80
90BBWit-25
90Mother/Dodg-28M
90Pac/Legend-41
90Pol/Dodg-x
90Swell/Great-26
90Target-557
91LineD-22
91Mother/Dodg-28CO
91Pol/Dodg-x
91Swell/Great-63

Mota, Manny Jr.
90AubAs/Best-1
90AubAs/ProC-3398

Mota, Miguel
87Bakers-4

Mota, Willie
89Elizab/Star-21
90Kenosha/Best-10
90Kenosha/ProC-2297
90Kenosha/Star-15
91Kenosha/ClBest-2

Motley, Darryl
81Omaha-22
82D-390
82F-417
82Omaha-19
82T-471R
83Evansvl-21
84D-344
84F/X-U81
85D-461
85F-208
85Leaf-69
85T-561
85T/St-276
86D-217
86F-16
86Kitty/Disc-14
86Leaf-95
86NatPhoto-24
86Sf-186M
86T-332
86T/St-22WS
87Richm/Crown-30
87OPC-99
87Richm/TCMA-19
87T-99
89Indianap/CMC-22
89Indianap/ProC-1238
90Nashvl/CMC-18
90Nashvl/ProC-248

Motton, Curt
68T-549R
69OPC-37
69T-37
70OPC-261
70T-261
71MLB/St-305
71OPC-684
71T-684
72MB-246
72OPC-393
72T-393
85Everett/II/Cram-12
86RochR-13C
87RochR-13
87RochR/TCMA-23
88RochR/Team-14
88RochR/CMC-25
88RochR/Gov-29
88RochR/ProC-218
91Crown/Orio-320

Motz, Willie
91Kenosha/ProC-2079

Moulder, Glen
49B-159
90Target-1042

Moulton, Brian
77Cedar

Mount, Chuck
86Cram/PCL-42
87AppFx-1
88BirmB/Best-27
89BirmB/Best-18
89BirmB/ProC-92
91Iowa/LineD-212
91Iowa/ProC-1056

Moure, Brian
88CapeCod/Sum-12

Moushon, Dan
89Spring/Best-28

Mouton, James
91AubAS/ClBest-17
91AubAS/ProC-4282

Mouton, Lyle
91Oneonta/ProC-4166

Mowrey, Harry
(Mike)
11Helmar-173
16FleischBrd-68
D328-123
D329-129
E135-123
E224
E300
E96
M101/4-129
M116
T213/blue
T213/brown
W555

Mowry, Joe
34G-59
R310

Moya, Felix
90James/Pucko-22
91WPalmB/ClBest-8
91WPalmB/ProC-1224

Moyer, Greg
81Shrev-22

Moyer, Jamie
86Gator-49
86Pittsfld-17
87Berg/Cubs-49
87D-315
87F-570
87T-227
88Berg/Cubs-49
88D-169
88D/Best-228
88D/Cubs/Bk-169
88F-426
88OPC-36
88Panini/St-255
88S-573
88T-36
88T/St-62
89B-223
89D-157
89D/Tr-39
89F-432
89F/Up-65
89Mother/R-17
89OPC-171
89S-263
89Smok/R-22
89T-549TL
89T-717
89T/St-53
89T/Tr-85T
89UD-63
89UD/Ext-791
90D-378
90F-307
90Mother/Rang-24
90OPC-412
90PublInt/St-417
90S-107
90T-412
90UD-619
91B-391
91F-294
91OPC-138
91S-437
91T-138
91T/StClub/II-481
91UD-610

Moyer, Jim
71MLB/St-260
72OPC-506R
72T-506R

Mraz, Don
76QuadC

Mrozinski, Ron
55B-287

Mueller, Clarence F.
25Exh-62
26Exh-61
V100

Mueller, Don
49Eureka-121
50B-221
51B-268
52B-18
52BR
52Coke
52Dix
52NTea
52T-52
52TipTop
53B/Col-74
53Brigg
53Dix
53SM
54B-73
54NYJour
54RM-NL7
54SM
54T-42
55Armour-14
55Gol/Giants-22
55RFG-9
55RM-NL8
55SM
56T-241
57T-148
58T-253
59T-368
79TCMA-149
Exh47
PM10/Sm-128

Mueller, Emmett
(Heinie)
39PB-63
40PB-96
91Conlon/Sport-179
92Conlon/Sport-643

Mueller, Pete
86Osceola-19

Mueller, Ray
49Eureka-122
51B-313
61F-128

Mueller, Willard
75BurlB
76BurlB
76Clinton
77BurlB
78Holyo
79Vanco-23
80T-668R
80Vanco-2
81Vanco-15
82Wichita-10

Muffett, Billy
58T-143
59T-241
61T-16
62T-336
76SSPC-614CO
88Pep/T-CO
89Mara/Tigers-CO
90CokeK/Tiger-28CO
91CokeK/Tiger-x

Muh, Steve
89Kenosha/ProC-1079
89Kenosha/Star-17
90OrlanSR/Best-20
90OrlanSR/ProC-1080
91OrlanSR/LineD-489
91OrlanSR/ProC-1847

Muhammad, Bob
89Beloit/I/Star-18

Muhlethaler, Mike
90SoOreg/Best-26
90SoOreg/ProC-3448

Muir, Joseph
52T-154

Mulcahy, Hugh
39PB-145
40PB-95
41G-1
49Exh

Mulden, Chris
78Clinton

Mulholland, Terry
84Everett/Cram-20
86Phoenix-18
87D-515
87Phoenix-5
87T-536
88Phoenix/CMC-10
88Phoenix/ProC-77
89F/Up-U111
89Phill/TastyK-44
89Phoenix/CMC-4
89Phoenix/ProC-1480
89S-474
89T-41
90Classic-127
90D-515
90F-568
90Leaf/II-474
90OPC-657
90Phill/TastyK-24
90S-542
90T-657
90UD-474
91B-504
91Classic/200-78
91D-541
91D-BC14
91F-408
91F/Ultra-269
91F/WaxBox-8
91Leaf/I-46
91Leaf/Stud-219
91OPC-413
91Panini/FrSt-359
91Panini/St-8
91Phill/Medford-30
91S-33
91S-706NH
91T-413
91T/StClub/I-58
91UD-426
92D/I-268
92F-540
92S/I-118
92T-719
92UD-129

Mull, Jack
75Phoenix-2
76Phoenix
77Cedar
78Cedar
81Shrev-1
83Phoenix/BHN-24
84Cram/PCL-24
86Clinton-15MG
87Shrev-25
87TexLgAS-6
88Shrev/ProC-1279MG
88TexLgAS/GS-1MG
89Phoenix/CMC-21
89Phoenix/ProC-1503
90Clinton/Best-9MG
90Clinton/ProC-2565MG
91Clinton/ClBest-26MG
91Clinton/ProC-851MG

Mullane, Anthony
(Count)
N172

Mullaney, Dominic
T206

Mulleavy, Greg
60T-463C

Mullen, Billy
90Target-1043

Mullen, Charles
14CJ-24
15CJ-24
E286

Mullen, Ford
43Centen-20

Mullen, Tom
81AppFx-5
81GlenF-6
83GlenF-17
85BuffB-23
86Omaha-16
86Omaha/TCMA-22
87Omaha-26
88Omaha/CMC-8
88Omaha/ProC-1507

Muller, Fred
37Wheat

Muller, Mike
87Memphis-22

Mulligan, Bill
86FtMyr-20
87FtMyr-1

Mulligan, Bob
82Orlan/A-21
83Toledo-8
84Toledo-9
85Orlan-19

Mulligan, Edward
E121/120
W501-45
W575

Mullin, George
09Buster/Pin-11
10Domino-89
11Helmar-35
12Sweet/Pin-28A
12Sweet/Pin-28B
81Detroit-119
92Conlon/Sport-338
E104
E254
E270/1
E90/1
E96
E97
E98
M116
S74-17
T202
T205
T206
T207
T213/blue
T215/blue
T215/brown
T3-30
W555
WG2-37

Mullin, Pat
47TipTop
49B-56
50B-135
51B-106
52B-183
52T-275
53B/BW-4
53Glen
54B-151
81Detroit-21
83Kaline-61M
83Kaline-8M

Mulliniks, S. Rance
(Rance)
75QuadC
77SLCity
78T-579
79SLCity-11
81D-504
81F-48
81T-433
82D-630
82F-418
82T-104
82T/Tr-78T
83D-432
83F-436
83OPC-277
83T-277
84D-584
84F-165
84Nes/792-762
84OPC-19
84T-762
84T/St-374
84Tor/Fire-26
85D-485
85F-116
85Leaf-153
85OPC-336
85OPC/Post-17
85T-336
85Tor/Fire-24
86Ault-5
86D-606
86F-68
86OPC-74
86T-74
86Tor/Fire-27
87D-319
87D/OD-32
87F-237
87OPC-91
87T-537
87Tor/Fire-24

88D-197
88D/Best-328
88F-120
88Ho/Disc-14
88Leaf-204
88OPC-167
88S-235
88T-167
88Tor/Fire-5
89B-250
89D-87
89F-242
89OPC-111
89S-385
89T-618
89T/St-192
89Tor/Fire-5
89UD-43
90D-607
90ElPasoATG/Team-42
90F-91
90OPC-466
90PublInt/St-525
90S-204RP
90T-466
90Tor/BlueJ-5
90UD-132
91D-663
91F-181
91F/Ultra-366
91OPC-229
91S-433
91S/ToroBJ-17
91T-229
91Tor/Fire-5
92D/II-542
92F-337
92S/I-132
92T-133

Mullino, Ray
87Peoria-1
88CharWh/Best-25
89WinSalem/Star-12
90Peoria/Team-26
90T/TVCub-54

Mullins, Fran
80GlenF/B-23
80GlenF/C-12
81T-112R
82Edmon-9
85Cram/PCL-180
85T-283
86OhHenry-22

Mullins, Ron
87Cedar-8
88Greens/ProC-1561
88SALAS/GS-9
89Miami/II/Star-14
90Penin/Star-13

Mulvaney, Michael
88Billings/ProC-1808
89Greens/ProC-410
89SALAS/GS-33
90Cedar/Best-7
90Cedar/ProC-2330

Mulvey, Joseph
(Joe)
90Target-558
N172
N28
N284
N690
WG1-53

Mulville, Duane
88Billings/ProC-1805
89Cedar/Best-11
89Cedar/ProC-924
89Cedar/Star-13

Mumaw, Steve
86Ventura-15
87Dunedin-10
88Dunedin/Star-11
89ArkTr/GS-14

Mumphrey, Jerry
76SSPC-289
77T-136
78T-452
79T-32
80OPC-196
80T-378
81D-124
81Drake-26
81F-494
81OPC-196
81Sqt-23
81T-556
81T/SO-97
81T/St-227
81T/Tr-808
82D-261
82F-43
82OPC-175
82T-175
82T-486TL
82T/St-220
83D-360
83F-389
83OPC-246
83RoyRog/Disc-6
83T-670
83T-81
83T/St-97
84D-426
84F-233
84Mother/Ast-9
84Nes/792-45
84OPC-45
84T-45
84T/St-70
85D-206
85F-354
85Leaf-124
85Mother/Ast-15
85OPC-186
85T-736
85T/St-60
86Cub/Unocal-14
86D-84
86F-306
86F/Up-U79
86Gator-22
86Mother/Ast-27
86OPC-282
86T-282
86T/Tr-76T
87Berg/Cubs-22
87D-324
87F-571
87F/Mini-73
87F/St-82
87T-372
87T/St-58
88Berg/Cubs-22
88D-447
88D/Cubs/Bk-447
88F-427
88F/Mini-69
88OPC-63
88Panini/St-267
88S-467
88T-466
88T/Big-70
89S-288

Muncrief, Bob
41G-8
47TipTop
49B-221
W753

Munda, Steve
91Oneonta/ProC-4152

Mundy, Rick
88Geneva/ProC-1640
89Geneva/ProC-1883
89Peoria/Ko-12C
90Peoria/Team-6
91Peoria/ClBest-11
91Peoria/ProC-1345

Munez, Jose
88Syrac/CMC-4

Munger, George
(Red)
47TipTop
49B-40
49Eureka-190
50B-89
51B-11
51T/BB-14
52B-243
52T-115

Mungin, Mike
88SoOreg/ProC-1710

Mungo, Van Lingle
34DS-102
34DS-19
35BU-131
35BU-26
35Exh/4-2
36Exh/4-2
36Wheat
37Exh/4-2
37Wheat
38Exh/4-2
38G-254
38G-278
38Wheat
39PB-111
40PB-64
89Smok/Dodg-45
90Target-559
PR1-23
R303/A
R311/Leath
R312
R313
R326-6A
R326-6B
R342-6
WG8-42

Munley, John
83TriCit-7

Munninghoff, Scott
80OkCty
81OkCty/TCMA-13
82Chatt-2

Munns, Les
90Target-560

Munoz, Bob
91FSLAS/ProC-FSL16
91FtLaud/ClBest-9
91FtLaud/ProC-2422

Munoz, J.J.
90A&AASingle/ProC-186
90Martins/ProC-3196
91Spartan/ClBest-9
91Spartan/ProC-894

Munoz, Jose
88Bakers/Cal-239
89VeroB/Star-18
90Bakers/Cal-258
91SanAn/LineD-538
91SanAn/ProC-2983

Munoz, Julio
90Ashvl/ProC-2744

Munoz, Lou
88Elmira-16
89Elmira/Pucko-12
90WinHaven/Star-20

Munoz, Luis
88WinHaven/Star-16

Munoz, Michael
87Bakers-27
88BBAmer-26
88SanAn/Best-7
88TexLgAS/GS-30
89Albuq/CMC-8
89Albuq/ProC-62
90D/Rook-8
90S-653
90T/89Debut-85
90Target-561
91S/100RisSt-93
91Toledo/LineD-593
91Toledo/ProC-1929

Munoz, Omer
87WPalmB-18
88WPalmB/Star-18
90Jaxvl/Best-7
90Jaxvl/ProC-1383
91Harris/LineD-265
91Harris/ProC-637

Munoz, Oscar
90Watertn/Star-14
91Kinston/ClBest-8
91Kinston/ProC-320
91Single/ClBest-149

Munoz, Pedro
87Dunedin-26
88Dunedin/Star-13
89Knoxvl/Best-18
89Knoxvl/ProC-1126
89Knoxvl/Star-14
90Syrac/ProC-585
90Syrac/Team-17
91B-336
91Classic/III-64
91D-758
91D/Rook-21
91F-620
91F/Ultra-192
91Leaf/I-186
91Portl/LineD-412
91Portl/ProC-1579
91S-332RP
91T/90Debut-111
91T/StClub/II-318
91UD-432
92D/I-305
92F-212
92S/100RisSt-74
92S/II-514
92T-613

Munoz, Roberto
90Foil/Best-192
90Greens/Best-8
90Greens/ProC-2660
90Greens/Star-14

Munson, Jay
83Cedar-25
83Cedar/LF-7

Munson, Joseph M.
26Exh-24

Munson, Thurman
70OPC-189R
70T-189R
71MD
71MLB/St-497
71OPC-5
71T-5
71T/Coins-118
71T/GM-1
71T/tatt-10
72OPC-441
72OPC-442IA
72T-441
72T-442IA
73OPC-142
73Syrac/Team-19
73T-142
73T/Lids-34
74OPC-340
74Syrac/Team-18
74T-340
74T/DE-7
74T/St-215
75Ho-138
75OPC-20
75T-20
75T/M-20
76Crane-41
76Ho-16
76Ho/Twink-16
76K-53
76MSA/Disc
76OPC-192LL
76OPC-650
76SSPC-433
76T-192LL
76T-650
77BK/Y-2
77BurgChef-177
77Ho-5
77K-23
77OPC-30
77Pep-36
77T-170
77T/CS-32
78BK/Y-2
78Ho-150
78K-30
78OPC-200
78PapaG/Disc-27
78T-60
78Tastee/Discs-7
78Wiffle/Discs-53
79BK/Y-2
79Ho-26
79OPC-157
79T-310
80Laugh/FFeat-13
82KMart-29
84West/1-15
86Sf/Dec-62M
88Pac/Leg-34
89S/NWest-32
91CollAB-22
91LineD-38
91Swell/Great-149

Mura, Steve
79T-725R
80T-491
81D-362
81F-496
81T-134
82D-523
82F-578
82T-641
82T/Tr-79T
83D-293
83F-16
83OPC-24
83T-24
84Cram/PCL-196
85Cram/PCL-147
86T-281

Murakami, Masanori
65OPC-282R
65T-282R
78TCMA-182

Murakami, Seiichi
90Salinas/Cal-119
90Salinas/ProC-2717

Muramatsu, Arihito
91Salinas/ClBest-10

Muratti, Rafael
86Macon-17
87Salem-17
88Miami/Star-16
91QuadC/ClBest-26
91QuadC/ProC-2644

Murcer, Bobby
66T-469R
67OPC-93R
67T-93R
69T-657
70K-60
70MLB/St-247
70OPC-333
70T-333
70T/CB
71Bz
71Bz/Test-9
71MLB/St-498
71OPC-635
71T-635
71T/Coins-54
71T/GM-46
72K-16
72MB-247
72OPC-86LL
72T-699
72T-700IA
72T-86LL
73K-19
73OPC-240
73OPC-343KP
73Syrac/Team-20
73T-240
73T-343KP
73T/Comics-12
73T/Lids-35
73T/PinUps-12
74K-22
74OPC-336AS
74OPC-90
74Syrac/Team-19
74T-336AS
74T-90
74T/DE-63
74T/Puzzles-7
74T/St-216
75Ho-141
75OPC-350
75T-350
75T/M-350
76Crane-42
76Ho-123
76K-38
76MSA/Disc
76OPC-470
76SSPC-111
76T-470
77BurgChef-105
77Ho-29
77OPC-83
77T-40
77T/CS-33
78Ho-90
78OPC-95
78T-590
79Ho-6
79OPC-63
79T-135
80OPC-190
80T-365
81D-111
81F-94
81OPC-253

81T-602
82D-486
82F-44
82T-208
83D-261
83F-390
83OPC-122
83OPC-304SV
83T-782
83T-783SV
84Mother/Giants-23
89Pac/Leg-196
91Swell/Great-117
PM10/Sm-129

Murch, Simeon
(Simmy)
90Target-562
E254

Murdock, Joe
89CharRain/ProC-982
90CharRain/Best-17
90CharRain/ProC-2036

Murdock, Kevin
88Tampa/Star-18

Murelli, Don
81Miami-5

Murff, John
(Red)
57T-321

Murillo, Javier
89Miami/I/Star5-15

Murillo, Ray
79Knoxvl/TCMA-19

Murnane, Tim
T204

Murphy, C.R.
N566-134

Murphy, Dale
77T-476R
78T-708R
79Ho-121
79OPC-15
79T-39
80OPC-143
80T-274
81D-437
81F-243
81F/St-119
81OPC-118
81Pol/Atl-3
81T-504
81T/SO-72
81T/St-146
82BK/Lids-18
82D-299
82F-443
82OPC-391
82PermaGr/AS-14
82Pol/Atl-3
82T-668
82T/St-19
83D-12DK
83D-47
83D/AAS-45
83Drake-18
83F-142
83K-52
83OPC-21AS
83OPC-23
83PermaGr/AS-12
83PermaGr/CC-9
83Pol/Atl-3
83T-401AS
83T-502TL
83T-703LL
83T-760
83T/Gloss40-16
83T/St-160
83T/St-206M
83T/St-211
84D-66
84D/AAS-40
84D/Champs-49
84Drake-22
84F-186
84F/St-17
84F/St-32
84F/St-50
85FunFoodPin-103
84MiltBrad-17
84Nes/792-126TL
84Nes/792-133LL
84Nes/792-150
84Nes/792-391AS
84Nestle/DT-18
84OPC-150
84OPC-391AS
84Pol/Atl-3
84Ralston-12
84Seven-3C
84Seven-3E
84Seven-3W
84T-126TL
84T-133LL
84T-150AS
84T-391AS
84T/Cereal-12
84T/Gloss22-19
84T/Gloss40-31
84T/St-180FOIL
84T/St-199
84T/St-27
84T/Super-2
85D-66
85D/AAS-25
85D/HL-5
85Drake-20
85F-335
85F/LimEd-22
85F/St-18
85F/St-33
85GenMills-5
85Ho/Braves-16
85Leaf-222
85OPC-320
85Pol/Atl-3
85Seven-1S
85Seven-3W
85Sportflic/Test-1
85T-320
85T-716AS
85T/3D-3
85T/Gloss22-7
85T/Gloss40-1
85T/St-177
85T/St-22
85T/St-96
85T/Super-11
86BK/AP-11
86D-66
86D/AAS-4
86D/HL-41
86D/PopUp-4
86Dorman-10
86Drake-12
86F-522
86F-635M
86F-640M
86F/LimEd-31
86F/LL-27
86F/Mini-105
86F/Slug-24
86F/St-132CL
86F/St-80
86F/WaxBox-C4
86Jiffy-16
86Leaf-60
86Meadow/Blank-10
86Meadow/Milk-7
86Meadow/Stat-4
86OPC/WaxBox-M
86Pol/Atl-3
86Quaker-8
86Sf-183M
86Sf-5
86Sf-62M
86Sf/Dec-67
86T-456M
86T-600
86T-705AS
86T/3D-16
86T/Gloss22-18
86T/Gloss60-37
86T/Mini-37
86T/St-145
86T/St-149
86T/St-35
86T/Super-39
86T/WaxBox-M
86TrueVal-10
86Woolwth-23
87Classic-37
87Classic/Up-106
87D-3DK
87D-78
87D-PC10
87D/AAS-14
87D/DKsuper-3
87D/OD-40
87D/PopUp-14
87D/WaxBox-PC10
87Drake-13
87F-522
87F/AwardWin-26
87F/GameWin-30
87F/Hottest-28
87F/BB-29
87F/Lim-30
87F/Mini-74
87F/RecSet-23
87F/Slug-28
87F/St-83
87F/WaxBox-C8
87Ho/St-7
87Jiffy-2
87KayBee-21
87KMart-29
87Kraft-2
87Leaf-141
87Leaf-3DK
87MnM's-9
87MSA/Discs-15
87OPC-359
87RedFoley/St-47
87Sf-155M
87Sf-159M
87Sf-3
87Smok/Atl-14
87Smok/NL-2
87Sportflic/DealP-3
87T-490
87T/Board-3
87T/Coins-37
87T/Gloss22-7
87T/Gloss60-6
87T/Mini-2
87T/St-161
87T/St-36
88ChefBoy-17
88Classic/Blue-201M
88Classic/Blue-215
88Classic/Red-156
88D-78
88D-BC14
88D/AS-46
88D/Best-113
88Drake-15
88F-544
88F-639M
88F/AwardWin-27
88F/BB/AS-27
88F/BB/MVP-25
88F/Excit-28
88F/Hottest-29
88F/LL-29
88F/Mini-65
88F/RecSet-27
88F/Slug-28
88F/SS-25
88F/St-77
88F/TL-24
88F/WaxBox-C6
88FanSam-13
88KayBee-20
88KingB/Disc-2
88KMart-18
88Leaf-83
88MSA/Disc-14
88Nestle-2
88OPC-90
88Panini/St-251
88RedFoley/St-59
88S-450
88Sf-170
88T-549TL
88T-90
88T/Big-14
88T/Coins-48
88T/Gloss60-26
88T/Mini-41
88T/RiteAid-1
88T/St-45
88T/St/Backs-18
88T/UK-52
89T/Ames-21
89B-276
89Classic-124
89T/Crunch-11
89D-104
89D/Best-29
89F-596
89F/Excit-33
89F/LL-28
89KayBee-22
89OPC-210
89Panini/St-45
89RedFoley/St-84
89S-30
89S/HotStar-66
89S/Mast-15
89Sf-110
89T-210
89T/Big-172
89T/Coins-19
89T/HeadsUp-23
89T/Hills-21
89T/LJN-98
89T/Mini-1
89T/St-32
89T/UK-55
89Tetley/Discs-20
89UD-357
89UD-672TC
90B-19
90BBWit-38
90Classic/Up-36
90D-168
90D/BestNL-62
90F-591
90F-623MVP
90F/BBMVP-28
90F/Up-U46
90HotPlay/St-29
90KayBee-20
90KingB/Discs-11
90Leaf/I-243
90OPC-750
90Panini/St-222
90Post-18
90PublInt/St-117
90RedFoley/St-67
90Richm25Ann/Team-17
90S-66
90S/100St-64
90S/Tr-31T
90Sf-189
90T-750
90T/Ames-11
90T/Big-40
90T/Coins-53
90T/HillsHM-16
90T/St-25
90UD-533
90Woolwth/HL-15
91B-486
91Classic/200-148
91Classic/I-96
91D-484
91D-744M
91F-409
91F/Ultra-270
91JDeanSig-3
91Leaf/II-412
91Leaf/Stud-220
91MajorLg/Pins-62
91OPC-545
91OPC/Premier-85
91Panini/FrSt-109
91Panini/St-104
91Petro/SU-14
91Phill/Medford-31
91S-650
91S/100SS-35
91Seven/3DCoin-13NE
91T-545
91T/StClub/I-243
91T/WaxBox-J
91UD-447
91Woolwth/HL-14
92D/I-146
92F-541
92S/100SS-40
92S/I-80
92T-680
92UD-127

Murphy, Daniel F.
(Danny)
10Domino-90
11Helmar-57
12Sweet/Pin-48
14CJ-140
14Piedmont/St-42
15CJ-140
16FleischBrd-69
BF2-14
D303
E101
E102
E105
E106
E107
E254
E270
E91
E92
M116
S74-33
T202
T205
T206
T208
T213/blue
T213/brown
T215/blue

Murphy, Daniel F.
61T-214
62T-119
63T-272
70OPC-146
70T-146

Murphy, Daniel Jr.
82Tulsa-17
83Tulsa-21
84OKCty-23
84Tulsa-16
85MidldA-9
86ElPaso-16
87ElPaso-22
89LasVegas/CMC-7
89LasVegas/ProC-2
90LasVegas/CMC-8
90LasVegas/ProC-117
90OPC-649
90T-649
90T/89Debut-86

Murphy, Dwayne
79T-711R
80T-461
81D-359
81F-590
81OPC-341
81T-341
81T/St-119
82D-239
82F-101
82F/St-122
82Granny-11
82K-57
82OPC-29
82T-29
82T/St-227
83D-161
83F-528
83Granny-21
83OPC-184
83T-598
83T/St-107
84D-101
84D-3DK
84F-456
85FunFoodPin-93
84Mother/A's-4
84Nes/792-103
84OPC-103
84T-103
84T/St-332
85D-420
85F-432
85F/St-30
85GenMills-20
85Leaf-74
85Mother/A's-6
85T-231
85T/St-323
86D-176
86F-428
86F/Mini-90
86Mother/A's-6
86OPC-8
86T-216M
86T-8
86T/St-171
86TrueVal-27
87D-379
87D/OD-27
87F-400
87OPC-121
87Smok/A's-9
87T-743

87T/St-170
88D-405
88F-287
88OPC-334
88Panini/St-176
88S-455
88T-424
89T/Ames-22
89Phill/TastyK-23
89S-545
89T-667
90F-569

Murphy, Eddie
48Smith-24

Murphy, Gary
86Ashvl-21
89QuadC/Best-16
89QuadC/GS-19

Murphy, James
88Geneva/ProC-1638
89CharWh/Best-10
89CharWh/ProC-1745
89Fayette/ProC-1586
90PeoriaUp/Team-U7
90WinSalem/Team-14

Murphy, Jeff
91Princet/ClBest-18
91Princet/ProC-3511

Murphy, John Edward
15CJ-165
D327
D329-130
D350/2-127
E121/80
E122
M101/4-130
M101/5-127
W575

Murphy, John J.
80ArkTr-21

Murphy, John Joseph
35BU-154
41DP-110
44Yank/St-20
88Conlon/3-20
91Conlon/Sport-84

Murphy, John V.
87Louisvl-21
87StPete-13
88Louisvl-36
88Louisvl/CMC-16
88Louisvl/ProC-429
88Spring/Best-22

Murphy, Kent
86Water-17
87BuffB-2
88Wmsprt/ProC-1305

Murphy, Micah
89Geneva/ProC-1880
90Hunting/ProC-3291

Murphy, Michael
86Water-18
87BuffB-17
90Martins/ProC-3198
91AubAS/ClBest-14
91AubAS/ProC-4278
91Martins/ClBest-1
91Martins/ProC-3470

Murphy, Miguel
87Kenosha-25
88Fayette/ProC-1100

Murphy, Mike
77ArkTr

Murphy, Morgan
N300/unif

Murphy, P.L.
N172

Murphy, Patrick J.
N172
N338/2

Murphy, Pete
87Macon-11
87Watertn-24
88Salem/Star-14
89Harris/ProC-308
89Harris/Star-12
90Harris/ProC-1190
90Harris/Star-12
91CaroMud/LineD-113
91CaroMud/ProC-1084

Murphy, Red
WG7-36

Murphy, Rob
82Cedar-2
83Cedar-13
83Cedar/LF-24
87Classic-70
87D-452
87F-206
87Kahn-46
87T-82
88D-82
88D/Best-230
88F-241
88Kahn/Reds-46
88S-559
88T-603
89B-22
89Classic/Up/2-183
89D-139
89D/Best-196
89D/Tr-15
89F-165
89F/Up-10
89OPC-182
89S-141
89S/Tr-8
89T-446
89T/Tr-86T
89UD-372
89UD/Ext-759
90B-269
90CedarDG/Best-13
90D-186
90F-281
90Leaf/I-183
90OPC-268
90Pep/RSox-13
90Publint/St-461
90S-181
90T-268
90T/Big-297
90T/St-261
90T/TVRSox-14
90UD-461
91D-250
91F-104
91OPC-542
91S-183
91S/RookTr-33T
91T-542
91UD-683
91UD/Ext-707
92D/I-329
92F-288
92S/II-492
92T-706
92UD-639

Murphy, Shaun
91MidwLAS/ProC-MWL46
91Rockford/ClBest-24
91Rockford/ProC-2059

Murphy, Tim
74Gaston

Murphy, Tom A.
69JB
69T-474
70OPC-351
70T-351
71OPC-401
71T-401
71T/tatt-5
72MB-248
72OPC-354
72T-354
73OPC-539
73T-539
74OPC-496
74T-496
74T/Tr-496T
75OPC-28
75T-28
75T/M-28
76OPC-219
76SSPC-227
76T-219
77T-396
78OPC-193
78T-103
79OPC-308
79T-588
89Pac/SenLg-122
89T/SenLg-28

Murphy, Tommy
T3/Box-59

Murphy, Wayne
87WinHaven-18

Murphy, William E.
66T-574R
91WIZMets-286

Murray, Bill
88SLCity-2
88SLCity-29
89SLCity-29OWN
90CLAS/CL-8M

Murray, Brian
88SLCity-2

Murray, Dale
75OPC-568
75T-568
75T/M-568
76OPC-18
76SSPC-350
76T-18
77T-252
78Ho-31
78T-149
79Ho-115
79OPC-198
79T-379
80OPC-274
80T-559
81Syrac-7
83D-381
83F-437
83OPC-42
83T-42
83T/Tr-79
84D-577
84F-134
84Nes/792-697
84OPC-281
84T-697
85F-137
85OKCty-27
85T-481
86OPC-197
91WIZMets-287

Murray, Dave
86Salem-21

Murray, Eddie
78K-25
78OPC-154
78T-36
79OPC-338
79T-640
79T/Comics-1
80K-24
80OPC-88
80T-160
80T/S-28
81D-112
81Drake-6
81F-184
81F/St-117
81K-18
81MSA/Disc-23
81OPC-39
81Sqt-15
81T-490
81T/SO-9
81T/St-34
82D-483
82Drake-25
82F-174
82F/St-151
82K-64
82OPC-390
82PermaGr/CC-22
82T-162LL
82T-163LL
82T-390
82T-426TL
82T/St-145
82T/St-4LL
82T/St-6
83D-405
83D/AAS-1
83Drake-19
83F-67
83K-11
83OPC-141
83PermaGr/CC-29
83T-21TL
83T-530
83T/Gloss40-37
83T/St-29
84D-22DK
84D-47
84D/AAS-50
84D/Champs-19
84Drake-23
84F-14
84F/St-23
84F/St-38
85FunFoodPin-119
84Nes/792-240
84Nes/792-397AS
84Nestle/DT-1
84OPC-240
84OPC-291AS
84Ralston-1
84Seven-6C
84Seven-6E
84Seven-6W
84T-240
84T-397AS
84T/Cereal-1
84T/Gloss40-4
84T/St-195FOIL
84T/St-203
84T/St-26WS
84T/St/Box-12
84T/Super-25
85D-47
85D/AAS-9
85D/HL-34
85Drake-21
85F-184
85F/LimEd-23
85F/St-20
85F/St-62SA
85F/St-63
85F/St-64
85F/St-65
85F/St-66
85F/St-67
85GenMills-21
85Leaf-203
85OPC-221
85Seven-1E
85Seven-4G
85Seven-4W
85T-700
85T-701AS
85T/3D-2
85T/Gloss40-28
85T/St-196
85T/Super-18
86BK/AP-14
86D-88
86D/AAS-13
86D/PopUp-13
86Dorman-12
86Drake-25
86F-282
86F/LimEd-32
86F/Mini-58
86F/Slug-25
86F/St-81
86Jiffy-10
86Leaf-83
86OPC-30
86Quaker-27
86Sf-140M
86Sf-4
86Sf-73M
86Sf/Dec-70
86Sf/Rook-48M
86T-30
86T/3D-19
86T/Gloss22-2
86T/Gloss60-33
86T/Mini-1
86T/St-158
86T/St-227
86T/Super-40
86TrueVal-3
86Woolwth-24
87Classic-51
87D-48
87D/AAS-31
87D/HL-37
87D/OD-136
87Drake-24
87F-476
87F-636M
87F/LL-32
87F/Lim-31
87F/Mini-75
87F/RecSet-24
87F/St-84
87French-33
87Ho/St-18
87KayBee-22
87KMart-30
87Kraft-1
87Leaf-110
87OPC-120
87Ralston-8
87RedFoley/St-66
87Sf-159M
87Sf-6
87Sf-75M
87Seven-ME12
87Sportflic/DealP-2
87T-120
87T/Board-2
87T/Coins-19
87T/Gloss60-12
87T/Mini-39
87T/St-224
88D-231
88D/Best-142
88Drake-21
88F-567
88F/BB/AS-28
88F/Mini-1
88F/St-2
88French-33
88Jiffy-13
88Leaf-172
88OPC-4
88Panini/St-442
88Panini/St-8
88S-18
88Sf-59
88T-495
88T-4RB
88T/Big-215
88T/Coins-22
88T/St-11
88T/St-233
88T/UK-53
88Woolwth-5
89B-346
89Classic/Up/2-160
89T/Crunch-15
89D-96
89D/Best-92
89D/Tr-12
89F-611
89F/Up-92
89KayBee-23
89KingB/Discs-2
89KMart/Lead-11
89Mother/Dodg-2
89OPC-148
89Panini/St-260
89Pol/Dodg-21
89RedFoley/St-85
89S-94
89S/HotStar-83
89S/Tr-31
89Sf-147
89T-625
89T/Big-319
89T/Coins-20
89T/Hills-22
89T/LJN-27
89T/Mini-44
89T/St-238
89T/Tr-87T
89T/UK-56
89UD-275
89UD/Ext-763
90B-101
90Classic/Up-37
90D-77
90D/BestNL-78
90F-404
90HotPlay/St-30
90KayBee-21
90KMart/CBatL-17
90Leaf/I-181
90Mother/Dodg-5
90OPC-305
90Panini/St-273
90Pol/Dodg-33
90Publint/St-14
90RedFoley/St-68
90S-80
90Sunflower-24
90T-305
90T/Ames-7
90T/Big-29
90T/HillsHM-13
90T/Mini-60

90T/St-57
90Target-563
90UD-277
90Woolwth/HL-16
91B-376SLUG
91B-614
91Classic/200-112
91Classic/I-51
91Classic/III-65
91Crown/Orio-321
91D-405MVP
91D-502
91D-BC18
91D/Preview-12
91DennyGS-15
91F-214
91F/Ultra-166
91Leaf/I-126
91Leaf/Stud-185
91MajorLg/Pins-53
91Mother/Dodg-5
91OPC-397AS
91OPC-590
91OPC/Premier-86
91Panini/FrSt-55
91Panini/St-53
91Panini/Top15-2
91Pol/Dodg-33
91Post/Can-11
91RedFoley/St-68
91S-310
91S/100SS-52
91Seven/3DCoin-10SC
91T-397AS
91T-590
91T/CJMini/II-1
91T/StClub/I-177
91T/WaxBox-K
91UD-237
91UD/SilSlug-SS6
91USPlayC/AS-2S
91Woolwth/HL-15
92D/I-392
92F-466
92S/100SS-78
92S/I-195
92T-780
92UD-265
92UD-32TC

Murray, George
R314/Can

Murray, Glenn
90James/Pucko-9
91MidwLAS/ProC-MWL47
91Rockford/ClBest-25
91Rockford/ProC-2060

Murray, Jack
14Piedmont/St-43

Murray, James
C46-5

Murray, Jed
80SanJose/JITB-14
81LynnS-8
82LynnS-6
83SLCity-9
84Cram/PCL-177
86Calgary-17
87Toledo-13
87Toledo/TCMA-18

Murray, Jeremiah
N172

Murray, Jim
75Clinton

Murray, John Joseph
10Domino-91
11Helmar-135
12Sweet/Pin-121
D350/2-128
E104
E254
E270/2
E91
E94
E96
E97
M101/5-128
M116
S74-92
T202
T205
T205
T206
T213/blue
T215/blue
T215/brown
T222
T3-48
W555
WG4-21

Murray, Joseph
52Park-99

Murray, Keith
91Gaston/ClBest-25
91Gaston/ProC-2702

Murray, Larry
76SSPC-449
80T-284

Murray, Matt
90BurlB/Best-2
90BurlB/ProC-2346
90BurlB/Star-19
90Foil/Best-285
91Durham/ClBest-4
91Durham/ProC-1540

Murray, Mike
87Myrtle-8
88Myrtle/ProC-1179
89Kingspt/Star-28

Murray, Pat
91Johnson/ClBest-4
91Johnson/ProC-3985

Murray, Ray
50NumNum
52B-118
52T-299
53B/BW-6
53T-234
54B-83
54Esskay
54T-49
91Crown/Orio-322
91T/Arc53-234

Murray, Rich
76Cedar
77Cedar
78Cr/PCL-32
79Phoenix
80Phoenix-19
81F-452
81Phoenix-24
81T-195
82Charl-16
83Phoenix/BHN-6
84Cram/PCL-6
85Omaha-8

Murray, Richard
82Wichita-11

Murray, Scott
86StPete-21
88SanJose/Cal-125
88SanJose/ProC-113

Murray, Steve
84Beaum-7
88SanBern/Cal-29
89Wausau/GS-20
90SanBern/Best-19CO
90SanBern/Cal-113CO
90SanBern/ProC-2651CO
91SanBern/ClBest-12CO
91SanBern/ProC-2005CO

Murray, Venice
78Cedar

Murrell, Ivan
68T-569R
69T-333
70OPC-179
70T-179
71MLB/St-232
71OPC-569
71T-569
72MB-249
72T-677
73OPC-409
73T-409
74OPC-628
74T-628
87Wmsprt-11
89Pac/SenLg-131
89T/SenLg-7

Murrell, Rodney
86LitFalls-20
87Columbia-22
88Clmbia/GS-17
89Penin/Star-16

Murtaugh, Danny
48L-142
49B-124
49Eureka-168
50B-203
51B-273
52NTea
59T-17MG
60T-223MG
61T-138MG
61T-567AS
62T-503MG
63IDL-14MG
63T-559MG
64T-141MG
64T-268MG
70OPC-532MG
70T-532MG
71OPC-437MG
71T-437MG
74OPC-489MG
74T-489MG
75OPC-304MG
75T-304MG
75T/M-304MG
76OPC-504MG
76SSPC-586MG
76T-504MG
PM10/Sm-130

Murtaugh, Tim
75Shrev/TCMA-12
76Shrev

Murtha, Brian
82Clinton-20

Muscat, Scott
89Helena/SP-24
90Beloit/Best-10
90Beloit/Star-15

Muser, Tony
73OPC-238
73T-238
74OPC-286
74T-286
75OPC-348
75T-348
75T/M-348
76OPC-537
76SSPC-390
76T-537
77T-251
78T-418
81ElPaso-23
82ElPaso-23
84Cram/PCL-27
86Pol/Brew-35C
90ElPasoATG/Team-17MG
91Crown/Orio-323
91Denver/LineD-149MG
91Denver/ProC-137MG

Musgraves, Dennis
91WIZMets-288

Musial, Stan
47HomogBond-35
48B-36
48L-4
49B-24
49Eureka-191
49Royal-1
51BR-B1
51Wheat
52B-196
52BR
52RM-NL16
52Royal
52StarCal/L-81E
52StarCal/L-81F
52Wheat
53B/Col-32
53Exh/Can-57
53Hunter
53RM-NL26
54Hunter
54RH
55Hunter
55Rawl-1
55Rawl-1A
55Rawl-2
55Rawl-2A
55Rawl-3
55Rawl-4
56YellBase/Pin-23
58T-476AS
59T-150
59T-470HL
60NuCard-21
60T-250
60T/tatt-39
60T/tatt-94
61NuCard-421
61T-290
61T/Dice-11
61T/St-92
62Exh
62T-317IA
62T-50
62T/bucks
62T/St-189
63Bz-23
63Exh
63T-1LL
63T-138M
63T-250
63T/SO
72Laugh/GF-24
74Laugh/ASG-55
79TCMA-9
80Pac/Leg-8
80SSPC/HOF
83D/HOF-32
83Kaline-67M
83MLBPA/Pin-29
85CircK-15
85D/HOF-5
85Woolwth-27
86Sf/Dec-30
87Leaf/SpecOlym-H4
87Nestle/DT-23
88D-641PUZ
88Leaf-263PUZ
88Pac/Leg-6
88T-665TBC
89HOF/St-30
89T/LJN-105
90BBWit-36
90HCF/St-51
D305
Exh47
PM10/Sm-131
PM10/Sm-132
PM10/Sm-133
R423-72

Musolino, Mike
88PalmSp/Cal-105
88QuadC/GS-30
89QuadC/Best-20
89QuadC/GS-15

Musselman, Jeff
86Ventura-16
87D-591
87D/Rook-53
87F/Up-U84
87Sf/Rook-15
87T/Tr-83T
87Tor/Fire-25
88D-630
88F-121
88Leaf-234
88OPC-229
88S-478
88S/YS/II-30
88T-229
88T/Big-69
88T/JumboR-22
88T/St-308
88Tor/Fire-13
88ToysRUs-20
89B-240
89D-656
89F-243
89OPC-362
89S-558
89T-591
89Tor/Fire-13
89UD-41
90D-623
90F-212
90Kahn/Mets-13
90OPC-382
90S-525
90T-382
90T/TVMets-15
90UD-585
91S-294
91Tacoma/LineD-542
91Tacoma/ProC-2301
91WIZMets-289

Musselman, Ron
80LynnS-23
81Spokane-17
82SLCity-14
83OKCty-14
85F/Up-U83
85Tor/Fire-25
86Syrac-20
87Portl-21

Musselwhite, Darren
90Kenosha/Best-16
90Kenosha/Star-28
91Visalia/ClBest-6
91Visalia/ProC-1740

Musser, Andy
88Phill/TastyK-39ANN
90Phill/TastyK-35ANN

Mussina, Mike
90Classic/DP-20
91B-97
91Classic/200-146
91Classic/I-17
91F/UltraUp-U4
91Leaf/GRook-BC12
91RochR/LineD-462
91RochR/ProC-1899
91S-383FDP
91UD-65TP
92Classic/I-67
92D/II-632
92F-20
92S/II-755
92T-242
92T/91Debut-130
92UD-675

Mustad, Eric
80Hawaii-5
81Tacom-4
82Tacom-7
84Indianap-11

Mustari, Frank
88VeroB/Star-16

Mute, Frank
89QuadC/Best-13

Muth, Bill
77Wausau

Mutis, Jeff
88BurlInd/ProC-1792
89Kinston/Star-13
90Canton/Best-22
90Canton/ProC-1291
90Canton/Star-13
90Foil/Best-290
91Canton/LineD-90
91Canton/ProC-979
91Single/ClBest-24
92D/II-411RR
92T/91Debut-131

Mutrie, James
E223
N172
N338/2

Mutz, Frank
88QuadC/GS-12
88Reno/Cal-276
89QuadC/GS-22

Mutz, Tommy
77Indianap-16
78Indianap-10
79Indianap-8

Myaer, Jeff
86Cram/PCL-153

Myatt, George
60Lake
60SpicSpan-15CO
60T-464C
V353-10
V355-26

Myatt, Glenn
25Exh-84
26Exh-83
27Exh-43
28Exh-42
33G-10
34DS-58
35G-1K
35G-3B
35G-5B
35G-6B
91Conlon/Sport-187
R314/Can
R337-417

Myer, Charles M.
(Buddy)
29Exh/4-32
31Exh/4-32
33G-153

Napoleon, Ed
78Cr/PCL-109
79WHave-2
82Nashvl-28CO
83Wheat/Ind-23CO
85Polar/Ind-xx
90Mother/Ast-27CO
Napp, Larry
55B-250ump
Naragon, Harold R.
(Hal)
55B-129
55Gol/Ind-21
55Salem
56T-311
57T-347
58T-22
59T-376
60T-231
61Clover-19
61Peters-8
61T-92
62T-164
Narcisse, Ron
85LitFalls-14
86LitFalls-21
Narleski, Bill
88Watlo/ProC-674
Narleski, Ray
55B-96
55Gol/Ind-22
55Salem
55T-160
56T-133
57Sohio/Ind-10
57T-144
58Hires-22
58T-439
59T-442
60T-161
Narleski, Steve
77Watlo
81Chatt-5
82Chatt-19
Narron, Jerry A.
(Jerry)
77WHave
78Cr/PCL-54
80T-16
81D-405
81OPC-249
81Pol/Sea-12
81T-637
82D-433
82F-513
82Spokane-12
82T-719
84Smok/Cal-20
85D-643
85Smok/Cal-10
85T-234
86D-451
86Smok/Cal-10
86T-543
87Calgary-21
87D-603
87T-474
88RochR/Team-15
88RochR/CMC-14
88RochR/Gov-17
88RochR/ProC-216
89Freder/Star-25
90Hagers/Best-29MG
90Hagers/ProC-1431MG
90Hagers/Star-26MG
91Hagers/LineD-249MG
91Hagers/ProC-2471MG
Narron, Johnny
75AppFx
Narron, Sam
49Eureka-44
60T-467CO
63IDL-15CO
Narum, L.F.
(Buster)
64T-418R
65OPC-86
65T-86
66T-274
78TCMA-44
91Crown/Orio-324
Nash, Charles F.
(Cotton)
71OPC-391R
71T-391R
Nash, Dave
86Cram/PCL-184
88Fresno/Cal-13
88Fresno/ProC-1228
Nash, Jim
67OPC-90
67T-90
68T-324
69MB-198
69MLB/St-89
69T-546
69T/St-219
70MLB/St-9
70OPC-171
70T-171
71MLB/St-18
71OPC-306
71T-306
72MB-250
72OPC-401
72T-401
73OPC-509
73T-509
Nash, Rob
91Batavia/ClBest-1
91Batavia/ProC-3498
Nash, William M.
(Billy)
N142
N172
N300/unif
N403
WG1-7
Nastu, Phil
77Cedar
78Cr/PCL-27
79Phoenix
80Phoenix-7
80T-686R
Natal, Bob
(Rob)
87Jamestn-18
88FSLAS/Star-14
88WPalmB/Star-19
89Jaxvl/Best-17
89Jaxvl/ProC-176
90Jaxvl/Best-2
90Jaxvl/ProC-1378
91Harris/LineD-266
91Harris/ProC-632
Na'te, Jeff
(Nikko)
90Beloit/Best-21CO
90Beloit/Star-26CO
Natera, Luis
85LitFalls-20
86LitFalls-22
87Columbia-14
Nattile, Sam
85Pawtu-10
86NewBrit-19
Nattress, William W.
(Natty)
C46-8
E254
T206
Natupsky, Hal
79Elmira-20
Naughton, Danny
87Columbia-19
88Clmbia/GS-23
89StLucie/Star-18
Naulty, Dan
89Alaska/Team-2
Naumann, Rick
81AppFx-6
Nava, Lipso
91SanBern/ClBest-19
91SanBern/ProC-1996
Navarro, Jaime
88Stockton/Cal-182
88Stockton/ProC-736
89ElPaso/GS-13
89F/Up-39
90B-388
90Brewer/MillB-16
90Classic/Up-38
90D-640
90ElPasoATG/Team-23
90F-331
90Leaf/I-85
90Pol/Brew-31
90S-569
90T/89Debut-87
90UD-646
91B-42
91Brewer/MillB-18
91D-216
91F-592
91F/UltraUp-U31
91Leaf/II-409
91OPC-548
91Pol/Brew-16
91S-102
91T-548
91T/StClub/II-436
91UD-476
92D/II-705
92F-183
92S/I-231
92T-222
92UD-633
Navarro, Julio
60T-140
63T-169R
64T-489
65T-563
66T-527
Navarro, Norberto
89Pittsfld/Star-18
Navarro, Tito
90SALAS/Star-37
91Wmsprt/LineD-639
91Wmsprt/ProC-302
Naveda, Edgar
86Kenosha-17
87Kenosha-5
88Visalia/Cal-156
88Visalia/ProC-103
89Orlan/Best-18
89Orlan/ProC-1347
90OrlanSR/Best-5
90Portl/CMC-15
90Portl/ProC-187
91Portl/LineD-413
91Portl/ProC-1580
Navilliat, James
86Cram/PCL-157
87CharRain-11
Naworski, Andy
86Bakers-21
86Cram/PCL-187
87FtMyr-9
Naylor, Earl
90Target-566
Naylor, Roleine C.
21Exh-116
E120
W573
Nazabal, Robert
85Bend/Cram-17
Neagle, Dennis
(Denny)
88CapeCod/Sum-53
89Elizab/Star-22
90A&AASingle/ProC-142
90AS/Cal-24
90OrlanSR/Star-13
90Visalia/ProC-2150
91AAAGame/ProC-AAA36
91B-323
91F/Ultra-383MLP
91Leaf/II-466
91Portl/LineD-414
91Portl/ProC-1563
91UD/FinalEd-34F
92Classic/I-68
92D/II-605
92F-213
92T-592
92T/91Debut-132
92UD-426
Neal, Bob
80Penin/B-25GM
80Penin/C-9GM
88AubAs/ProC-1964
89AubAs/ProC-2178
Neal, Bryan
82Durham-6
83Durham-10
Neal, Charles Lenard
(Charlie)
55B-278
56T-299
57T-242
58Hires-54
58T-16
59Morrell
59T-427
60Morrell
60T-155
60T-385AS
60T-386AS
60T-556AS
60T/tatt-40
61BB-43
61P-157
61T-423
61T/St-30
62J-102
62P-102
62P/Can-102
62Salada-102A
62Salada-102B
62Shirriff-102
62T-365
63Exh
63J-195
63P-195
63T-511
64T-436
89Smok/Dodg-66
90Target-567
91WIZMets-293
Exh47
Neal, Dave
89PalmSp/Cal-49
89PalmSp/ProC-474
Neal, Earl A.
21Exh-117
Neal, Scott
85PrWill-2
86Hawaii-18
87Harris-9
Neal, Willie
81CharR-25
82CharR-22
Neale, Alfred Earle
(Greasy)
88Conlon/4-20
88Pac/8Men-88
92Conlon/Sport-401
D327
D328-126
E120
E121/120
E135-126
E220
V100
W501-51
W514-6
W575
Nealeigh, Rod
83Memphis-13
Nebraska, David
89BurlInd/Star-18
Nedin, Tim
89Elizab/Star-23
90Foil/Best-306
90Kenosha/Best-22
90Kenosha/ProC-2291
90Kenosha/Star-16
91Single/ClBest-185
91Visalia/ClBest-7
Nee, John
T205
Needham, Thomas J.
(Tom)
10Domino-92
11Helmar-99
12Sweet/Pin-85
14Piedmont/St-44
E286
M116
S74-65
T202
T205
T206
T207
T213/blue
Neel, Troy
88MidwLAS/GS-21
88Watlo/ProC-681
89Canton/Best-25
89Canton/ProC-1324
89Canton/Star-17
89EastLDD/ProC-DD37
90ColoSp/CMC-17
90ColoSp/ProC-45
91Tacoma/LineD-543
91Tacoma/ProC-2318
Neely, Jeff
89Augusta/ProC-495
89SALAS/GS-7
91BuffB/LineD-40
91BuffB/ProC-539
Neeman, Calvin A.
(Cal)
57T-353
58T-33
59T-367
60T-337
79TCMA-142
Neff, Marty
91Welland/ClBest-16
91Welland/ProC-3588
Negray, Ron
56T-7
56T/Pin-20
57T-254
61BeeHive-15
90Target-568
Negron, Miguel
80LynnS-10
83Chatt-10
Nehf, Art N.
16FleischBrd-70
21Exh-118
25Exh-37
28Yueng-43
61F-65
75F/Pion-28
92Conlon/Sport-492
D327
D328-127
E120
E121/120
E121/80
E126-59
E135-127
E220
V61-93
W502-43
W515-22
W516-17
W572
W575
Neibauer, Gary
69T-611R
70OPC-384
70T-384
71OPC-668
71Richm/Team-15
71T-668
72OPC-149
72T-149
Neidinger, Joe
89Bristol/Star-18
91Fayette/ClBest-6
91Fayette/ProC-1166
Neidlinger, Jim
85PrWill-10
86Nashua-19
87Harris-20
88Harris/ProC-842
89Albuq/CMC-9
89Albuq/ProC-71
90Albuq/CMC-10
90Albuq/ProC-343
90Albuq/Trib-23
90Pol/Dodg-39
91Albuq/LineD-16
91Albuq/ProC-1139
91Classic/I-53
91D-713
91F-215
91OPC-39
91Pol/Dodg-31
91S-794
91T-39
91T/90Debut-115
91UD-632
Neiger, Al
61T-202
89Chatt/II/Team-20
Neill, Mike
91FrRow/DP-9
91SoOreg/ClBest-15
91SoOreg/ProC-3864
Neill, Scott

89Watertn/Star-16
90Kinston/Team-24
91CLAS/ProC-CAR18
91Kinston/ClBest-9
91Kinston/ProC-321

Neis, Bernard E.
(Bernie)
26Exh-6
27Exh-44
90Target-569
E220

Neitzer, R.A.
90Batavia/ProC-3073
91Clearw/ClBest-19
91Clearw/ProC-1630

Nelloms, Skip
88Oneonta/ProC-2048
89FtLaud/Star-18
90FtLaud/Star-13

Nelson, Albert
(Red)
E254
T207

Nelson, Battling
T3/Box-57

Nelson, Brian
90Niagara/Pucko-22
91Bristol/ClBest-22
91Bristol/ProC-3600

Nelson, Chester
77Newar

Nelson, Darren
87Erie-25
88StPete/Star-19

Nelson, David Earl
(Dave)
69MB-199
69T-579
70OPC-112
70T-112
71MLB/St-547
71OPC-241
71T-241
72T-529
73OPC-111
73T-111
74Greyhound-5M
74OPC-355
74T-355
74T/DE-4
74T/St-238
75OPC-435
75Shrev/TCMA-13
75T-435
75T/M-435
76OPC-535
76Shrev
76SSPC-273
76T-535

Nelson, Doug
75Shrev/TCMA-14
76Shrev

Nelson, Doug P.
88AppFx/ProC-141
89BBCity/Star-19
90Memphis/Best-24
90Memphis/ProC-1004
90Memphis/Star-21

Nelson, Eric
89Welland/Pucko-19

Nelson, Frank
47Sunbeam
49Remar
50Remar

Nelson, Gene
81T/Tr-809
82D-513
82F-45
82T-373
82T/Tr-80T
83D-55
83T-106
85Coke/WS-30
85D-615
85F-522
85T/Tr-86T
86Coke/WS-30
86D-501
86F-213
86Leaf-245
86T-493
87D-580
87F-504
87F/Up-U86
87T-273
87T/Tr-84T
88D-133
88D/A's/Bk-133
88F-288
88Mother/A's-25
88S-588
88T-621
89B-185
89D-540
89F-18
89Mother/A's-26
89OPC-318
89S-434
89T-581
89UD-643
89Woolwth-16
90D-540
90F-17
90Leaf/II-477
90Mother/A's-22
90OPC-726
90S-441
90T-726
90UD-80
91D-385
91F-19
91Leaf/II-328
91Mother/A's-22
91OPC-316
91S-478
91SFExam/A's-10
91T-316
91T/StClub/II-359
91UD-403
92D/II-696
92F-264
92S/I-383
92T-62
92UD-508

Nelson, Glenn Richard
(Rocky)
52Park-61
52T-390
53Exh/Can-49
54T-199
59T-446
60L-127
60T-157
61Kahn
61P-137
61T-304
61T/St-68
90Target-570

Nelson, Jackson
N172/SP
N284
N690

Nelson, James Lorin
(Jim)
71OPC-298
71T-298

Nelson, Jamie
83SLCity-16
84Cram/PCL-43
84Nes/792-166
84T-166
85Cram/PCL-221
87Memphis-8
87Memphis/Best-26
88Colum/CMC-12
88Colum/Pol-23
88Colum/ProC-305
89Edmon/CMC-19
89Edmon/ProC-569
90Portl/CMC-13
90Portl/ProC-180

Nelson, Jeff
86Bakers-22
88SanBern/Best-23
88SanBern/Cal-48
89Wmsprt/ProC-637
89Wmsprt/Star-15
90Wmsprt/Best-17
90Wmsprt/ProC-1056
90Wmsprt/Star-18
91Jaxvl/LineD-339
91Jaxvl/ProC-147
92D/II-408RR

Nelson, Jerome
86Modesto-20
87Modesto-5
88Huntsvl/BK-13
89Chatt/Best-23
89Chatt/GS-19

Nelson, Jim
81LynnS-13
82LynnS-9

Nelson, Kim
79Wisco-11

Nelson, Lynn B.
(Lynn)
34G-60
39PB-118
40PB-135

Nelson, Mel
60DF-11
61Union
63T-522R
64T-273
65T-564
66T-367
69OPC-181
69T-181

Nelson, Michael
90Peoria/Team-3GM

Nelson, Pat
78Ashvl

Nelson, Rick
84D-636
84F-615
84Nes/792-672
84T-672
84T/St-347
85Cram/PCL-91
85Everett/Cram-11A
85Everett/Cram-11B
85T-296
86Calgary-18
86Clinton-16
87Tidew-16
88Shrev/ProC-1294
90Shrev/ProC-1455
90Shrev/Star-16

Nelson, Rob
83Idaho-22
84Madis/Pol-11
85Huntsvl/BK-41
86Tacom-15
87D-595
87D/OD-25
87F-653R
88D-574
88LasVegas/CMC-16
88LasVegas/ProC-237
89LasVegas/CMC-16
89LasVegas/ProC-24
90B-213
90UD-51
91Vanco/LineD-642
91Vanco/ProC-1604

Nelson, Robert S.
(Bob)
56T-169
91Crown/Orio-325

Nelson, Roger
68T-549R
69MLB/St-61
69T-279
69T/S-23
69T/St-186
70MLB/St-225
70T-633
71OPC-581
71T-581
73OPC-251
73T-251
74OPC-491
74T-491
75OPC-572
75T-572
75T/M-572
75Tucson-25
78Colum
91Crown/Orio-326

Nelson, Ron
87Spartan-12

Nelson, Scott
88Clinton/ProC-698
89Salinas/Cal-127
89Salinas/ProC-1824

Nelson, Spike
49Eureka-192

Nelson, Thomas C.
(Tom)
47Sunbeam

Nemeth, Carey
86Erie-20
87Savan-16

Nemeth, Joe
79Wausau-9
80Ashvl-12
81Tulsa-11
82Reading-17
82Tulsa-24
83Tulsa-19

Nen, Richard LeRoy
(Dick)
64T-14R
65T-466R
66OPC-149
66T-149
67T-403
68T-591
69MB-200
90Target-571

Nen, Robb
88Butte-5
88Gaston/ProC-1003
89Gaston/ProC-1003
89Gaston/Star-16
90B-487
90CharlR/Star-15
91B-270
91Single/ClBest-240
91Tulsa/LineD-589
91Tulsa/ProC-2769

Nenad, David
82Clinton-9

Nerat, Dan
91SoOreg/ClBest-27
91SoOreg/ProC-3841

Nerone, Phil
75AppFx
76AppFx

Nettles, Graig
69OPC-99R
69T-99R
70OPC-491
70T-491
71MLB/St-380
71OPC-324
71T-324
72T-590
73OPC-498
73Syrac/Team-21
73T-498
74OPC-251
74Syrac/Team-20
74T-251
74T/St-217
75Ho-24
75Ho/Twink-24
75OPC-160
75T-160
75T/M-160
76Ho-81
76OPC-169
76SSPC-437
76T-169
77BK/Y-15
77BurgChef-174
77Ho-116
77OPC-217
77OPC-2LL
77T-20
77T-2LL
78BK/Y-14
78Ho-132
78OPC-10
78T-250
78Wiffle/Discs-54
79BK/Y-15
79Ho-110
79OPC-240
79T-460
80K-18
80OPC-359
80T-710
81D-105
81F-87
81F/St-72
81OPC-365
81T-365
81T/HT
82D-335
82Drake-26
82F-46
82F/St-119
82F/St-238M
82HB/LS
82OPC-21IA
82OPC-62
82T-505
82T-506IA
82T/St-215
83D-83
83F-391
83OPC-207SV
83OPC-293
83RoyRog/Disc-7
83T-635
83T-636SV
83T/St-13
84D-518
84D/Champs-12
84F-135
84F/X-U82
85FunFoodPin-66
84Mother/Padres-22
84Nes/792-175
84Nes/792-712LL
84Nes/792-713LL
84OPC-175
84T-175
84T-712LL
84T-713LL
84T/St-326
84T/Tr-83T
85D-234
85F-42
85Leaf-177
85Mother/Padres-4
85OPC-35
85T-35
85T/St-155
86D-478
86D/AAS-6
86D/PopUp-6
86F-332
86OPC-151
86Sf-91
86T-450
86T/Gloss22-15
86T/St-106
86T/St-151
87F-426
87OPC-205
87RedFoley/St-87
87Smok/Atl-15
87T-205
87T/Tr-85T
88AlaskaAS60/Team-4
88SanDiegoSt-12
88S-440
88S/Tr-25T
88T-574
89Pac/SenLg-115
89Pac/SenLg-132
89Pac/SenLg-158
89S-277
89T/SenLg-25
89TM/SenLg-82
90EliteSenLg-43
91LineD-26
91Swell/Great-67

Nettles, James W.
(Jim)
71OPC-74R
71T-74R
72OPC-131
72T-131
73OPC-358
73T-358
75OPC-497
75T-497
75T/M-497
80Colum-12
81Tacom-12
82Tacom-17
83Idaho-30
83Tacom-20
85Madis-23
85Madis/Pol-20
86Madis-15
86Madis/Pol-24
87Madis-4
88Madis-16
89Madis/Star-17
89Pac/SenLg-126A
89Pac/SenLg-126B
90EliteSenLg-44
90Penin/Star-25MG

91Jaxvl/LineD-349MG
91Jaxvl/ProC-166MG

Nettles, Morris Jr.
75OPC-632
75T-632
75T/M-632
76OPC-434
76SSPC-202
76T-434
76T/Tr-434T

Nettles, Robert
86Erie-21

Nettnin, Rodney
91Miami/ClBest-3

Neuendorff, Tony
83Durham-11
84Durham-16

Neuenschwander, Doug
80Water-4
81Water-5

Neufang, Gerry
82Tulsa-20
83Tulsa-23

Neuzil, Jeff
84Memphis-10

Neun, Johnny
91Conlon/Sport-204

Nevers, Ernie
92Conlon/Sport-394

Nevers, Tom
90Ashvl/ClBest-16
90Classic/DP-21
91Ashvl/ProC-577
91B-542
91SALAS/ProC-SAL2
91S-387FDP
91Single/ClBest-201
92UD-53TP

Nevill, Glenn
91Batavia/ClBest-19
91Batavia/ProC-3482

Neville, Dan
65T-398R

Neville, David
89BendB/Legoe-13

Nevin, Phil
91T/Tr-83T

Newberg, Tom
88Vermont/ProC-955TR
90Mother/Mar-28TR

Newby, Mike
90Hamil/Best-11
90Hamil/Star-17

Newcomb, Joe Dean
89Knoxvl/Best-19
89Knoxvl/ProC-1135
89Knoxvl/Star-15

Newcombe, Donald
(Don)
49Eureka-45
50B-23
51B-6
52B-128
52BR
52StarCal/L-79D
53Briggs
53Exh/Can-16
54B-154
54NYJour
54SM
55B-143
55Gol/Dodg-21
55RFG-21
55SM
56T-235
56YellBase/Pin-24
57T-130
58Hires-13
58T-340
59T-312
60Kahn
60L-19
60T-345
60T/tatt-41
61T-483MV
75OPC-194MV
75T-194MV
75T/M-194MV
79TCMA-182
86Sf/Dec-39M
88Pac/Leg-33
89Rini/Dodg-3
89Smok/Dodg-55
89Swell-122
90Pac/Legend-42
90Swell/Great-76
90Target-572
91Swell/Great-68
91T/Arc53-320
Exh47
PM10/L-30
PM10/Sm-134
PM10/Sm-135
PM10/Sm-136
R423-74
Rawl

Newell, Tom
86Clearw-18
87Maine-20
87Maine/TCMA-6
87Phill/TastyK-50
88D-604
88F-648R
88Maine/CMC-8
88Maine/ProC-293
90Albany/Best-4
90FtLaud/Star-14
91Albany/ProC-1005

Newfield, Marc
90Classic/DP-6
90Classic/III-89
91AS/Cal-1
91B-698
91Classic/200-62
91OPC-529FDP
91SanBern/ClBest-23
91SanBern/ProC-2000
91S-391FDP
91Single/ClBest-4
91T-529FDP
91UD/FinalEd-18F
92UD-64TP

Newhauser, Don
74OPC-33
74T-33

Newhouser, Hal
39Exh
48L-98
52StarCal/L-72B
53Exh/Can-12
53T-228
55Salem
55T-24
55T/DH-109
60F-68
61F-66
61NuCard-446
72T/Test-7
81Detroit-116
83Kaline-31M
83Kaline-39M
86Sf/Dec-19
90HOF/St-42
91T/Arc53-228
92Conlon/Sport-445
Exh47
R423-73

Newkirk, Craig
90Foil/Best-234
90Gaston/Best-22
90Gaston/ProC-2529
90Gaston/Star-16
91CharlR/ClBest-19
91CharlR/ProC-1323

Newlin, Jim
90AS/Cal-23
90Foil/Best-259
90SanBern/Best-23
90SanBern/Cal-89
90SanBern/ProC-2630
91Jaxvl/LineD-340
91Jaxvl/ProC-148

Newman, Al
84Beaum-4
85Indianap-14
86D/Rook-9
86F/Up-U80
86Provigo-18
87D-426
87F-327
87OPC-323
87T-323
87T/Tr-86T
88D-645
88F-17
88SanDiegoSt-13
88SanDiegoSt-14
88S-252
88Smok/Minn-11
88T-648
89B-156
89D-436
89F-122
89S-493
89T-503
89UD-197
90B-419
90D-506
90F-382
90Leaf/II-347
90OPC-19
90Panini/St-110
90PublInt/St-334
90S-128
90T-19
90T/Big-53
90T/St-293
90UD-199
91D-208
91F-621
91F/Ultra-193
91Leaf/II-446
91OPC-748
91Panini/FrSt-301
91S-424
91T-748
91T/StClub/I-146
91UD-413
91Visalia/ClBest-8
92D/I-339
92F-214
92S/I-357
92T-146
92UD-293

Newman, Alan
90A&AASingle/ProC-112
90Foil/Best-39
90Kenosha/Best-23
90Kenosha/ProC-2292
90Kenosha/Star-17
91AS/Cal-13

Newman, Danny
88Ashvl/ProC-1071

Newman, Fred
63T-496R
64T-569
65OPC-101
65T-101
66T-213
66T/RO-82
67T-451
69T-543

Newman, Jeff
76Tucson-12
77T-204
78T-458
79OPC-319
79T-604
80K-7
80OPC-18
80T-34
81D-477
81F-577
81T-587
81T/St-120
82D-517
82F-102
82Granny-12
82T-187
83D-635
83F-529
83T-784
83T/Tr-80T
84D-249
84F-404
84Nes/792-296
84T-296
85T-376
87Mother/A's-19
88Modesto-1MG
88Modesto/Cal-81MG
89Huntsvl/Best-20
89SLAS-25
90Huntsvl/Best-24MG
91Tacoma/LineD-549MG
91Tacoma/ProC-2321MG

Newman, Mark
82FtMyr-20

Newman, Randy
83Wausau/LF-25
86Calgary-19

Newman, Ray
72T-667
73OPC-568
73T-568

Newman, Todd
87AubAs-17

Newman, Tom
89Idaho/ProC-2036
90Idaho/ProC-3243
90Sumter/Best-14

Newsom, Gary
83VeroB-19
85VeroB-4
86Albuq-18
87Durham-9

Newsom, Norman
(Bobo)
35Exh/4-15
36Exh/4-16
36G
36Wheat
37Exh/4-16
37OPC-139
38Exh/4-15
39Exh
41DP-51
53T-15
54Esskay
55Esskay
60F-70
61F-67
81Detroit-64
88Chatt/Team-24
90Target-573
91Conlon/Sport-230
91T/Arc53-15
92Conlon/Sport-364
R313
R314
V300

Newsome, Lamar A.
(Skeeter)
39PB-84
R313

Newson, Warren
86Cram/PCL-174
88CalLgAS-45
88River/Cal-225
88River/ProC-1416
89AubAs/ProC-2
89TexLAS/GS-8
89Wichita/Rock-24
89Wichita/Rock/HL-10
89Wichita/Rock/Up-7
90LasVegas/CMC-15
90LasVegas/ProC-136
91D/Rook-15
91F/UltraUp-U17
91F/Up-U14
91Vanco/LineD-643
91Vanco/ProC-1608
92D/II-668
92F-91
92S/I-398
92T-355
92T/91Debut-133
92UD-621

Newton, Eustace
(Doc)
90Target-574
T204

Newton, Marty
86Cram/PCL-15

Newton, Steve
88LitFalls/Pucko-18
89Clmbia/Best-18
89Clmbia/GS-17
91CharRain/ClBest-9

Newton, Warren
(Newt)
87CharRain-16

Nezelek, Andy
88Greenvl/Best-19
89D-616
89Richm/Bob-19
89Richm/CMC-6
89Richm/Ko-34
89Richm/ProC-839
90B-3
90D-523
90Richm/Bob-13
90Richm/CMC-5
90Richm/ProC-256
90Richm/Team-24

Niarhos, Constantine
(Gus)
49B-181
50B-154
51B-124
52B-129
52T-121
53T-63
91T/Arc53-63
R346-25

Nicastro, Steve
79Newar-2

Nice, Bill
80Ander-14

Nicely, Roy M.
48Sommer-24
49Sommer-13

Nicely, Tony
78Charl

Nichioka, Tsuyoshi
91Salinas/ClBest-18

Nicholas, Franci
R314/Can

Nicholls, Simon B.
E104
E91
T204
T206
W555

Nichols, Brian
88Billings/ProC-1819
89Billings/ProC-2043
90Billings/ProC-3224
90Cedar/ProC-2326
90CharWh/Best-13

Nichols, Carl
83SanJose-20
85CharlO-9
87RochR-11
87RochR/TCMA-10
88D-477
88D/Rook-39
88RochR/Gov-18
89AAA/ProC-45
89F-612
89Tucson/CMC-15
89Tucson/ProC-185
89Tucson/JP-18
90Tucson/CMC-11
90Tucson/ProC-205
91Crown/Orio-327
91Leaf/I-217
91Mother/Ast-22
91OPC-119
91T-119
91T/StClub/II-440

Nichols, Charles A.
(Kid)
50Callahan
61F-129
80SSPC/HOF
E97
N172
N300/unif
WG3-33

Nichols, Chet
52B-120
52T-288
53SpicSpan/7x10-9
54JC-16
54SpicSpan/PostC-14
55B-72
55Gol/Braves-22
55JC-17
55SpicSpan/DC-13
56T-278
61T-301
62T-403
63T-307
90Wausau/ProC-2144CO
90Wausau/Star-28CO

Nichols, Dolan
59T-362

Nichols, Fred
74Gaston

Nichols, Gary
88Spring/Best-23
90Louisvl/CMC-25

Nichols, Howard Jr.
86Reading-19
87Reading-14

88Phill/TastyK-27
88Reading/ProC-879
89Iowa/CMC-18
89Iowa/ProC-1712
Nichols, Lance
82RochR-20
83RochR-1
Nichols, Rod
86Watlo-20
87Kinston-24
89D-649
89T-443
90D-546
90F-497
90OPC-108
90T-108
90UD-572
92D/I-194
92F-119
92S/II-559
92T-586
92UD-212
Nichols, Samuel
N172
Nichols, Scott
87Savan-6
89StPete/Star-21
90Louisvl/ProC-404
91Louisvl/ProC-2917
Nichols, Thomas Reid
(Reid)
81T-689R
82Coke/BOS
82D-632
82F-300
82T-124
83D-460
83F-189
83T-446
84D-614
84F-405
84Nes/792-238
84T-238
85D-636
85F-164
85T-37
86Coke/WS-20
86D-574
86F-214
86Leaf-224
86T-364
87D/OD-87
87F/Up-U89
87T-539
87T/Tr-87T
88F-191
88OPC-261
88T-748
Nichols, Ty
85Newar-3
86Hagers-13
88CharlK/Pep-22
89Hagers/Best-28
89Hagers/ProC-279
89Hagers/Star-13
90Hagers/Best-8
90Hagers/ProC-1425
90Hagers/Star-20
Nicholson, Carl
78Watlo
79Tacom-18
Nicholson, David L.
(Dave)
61T-182
62T-577
63T-234
64T-31
64T/Coins-32
64T/St-26
64T/tatt
65OPC-183
65T-183
66T-576
67OPC-113
67T-113
69T-298
78TCMA-99
91Crown/Orio-328
Nicholson, J.W.
N172
Nicholson, Keith
87Lakeland-2
88Fayette/ProC-1079
Nicholson, Larry
80Buffa-14
Nicholson, Rick
77Newar
78Holyo
Nicholson, Thomas
N172
Nicholson, William B.
(Bill)
49B-76
49Eureka-142
49Lummis
50B-228
51B-113
52T-185
53B/BW-14
R346-11
Nichting, Chris
88FSLAS/Star-15
88VeroB/Star-18
89SanAn/Best-22
Nickerson, Drew
74Gaston
77Cedar
Nickerson, Jim
77Spartan
Nicol, Hugh N.
(Hugh)
E223
N172
N172/BC
N284
N370
Scrapps
Nicolosi, Chris
59DF
60DF-1
Nicolosi, Sal
85Visalia-5
86Visalia-13
Nicometi, Tony
86Jaxvl/TCMA-1
Nicosia, Steven R.
(Steve)
75Shrev/TCMA-15
78Colum
80T-519
81D-373
81F-371
81OPC-212
81T-212
82D-45
82F-488
82T-652
83D-528
83F-314
83T-462
84Nes/792-98
84T-98
85F-618
85T-191
85T/Tr-87T
89Erie/Star-15
Nied, Dave
88Sumter/ProC-413
89Durham/Team-16
89Durham/Star-16
90Durham/Team-17
91Durham/ClBest-3
91Durham/ProC-1541
Niedenfuer, Tom
82Albuq-7
82F-16
82Pol/Dodg-49
83D-536
83F-214
83Pol/Dodg-49
83T-477
84D-128
84F-108
84Nes/792-112
84Pol/Dodg-49
84Smok/Dodg-2
84T-112
85Coke/Dodg-22
85D-153
85F-378
85OPC-281
85T-782
85T/St-80
86Coke/Dodg-21
86D-397
86F-139
86Leaf-186
86Pol/Dodg-49
86T-56
87D-218
87F-448
87French-49
87Leaf-204
87Mother/Dodg-14
87OPC-43
87Pol/Dodg-26
87T-538
87T/Tr-88T
88D-294
88D/Best-321
88F-568
88French-49
88OPC-242
88S-261
88T-242
88T/St-232
89B-204
89D-282
89D/Tr-54
89F-613
89Mother/Sea-12
89OPC-14
89Panini/St-254
89S-252
89T-651
89T/St-236
89UD-488
90OPC-306
90PublInt/St-438
90Smok/Card-16
90T-306
90Target-575
91Crown/Orio-329
91F-639
91S-217
Niehoff, John Albert
(Bert)
14CJ-125
15CJ-125
91Conlon/Sport-151
D328-128
D329-132
D350/2-130
E135-128
M101/4-132
M101/5-130
Niekro, Joe
67T-536R
68T-475
69OPC-43
69T-43
70OPC-508
70T-508
71MLB/St-400
71OPC-695
71T-695
72MB-251
72OPC-216
72T-216
73OPC-585
73T-585
74OPC-504
74T-504
75Iowa/TCMA-12
75OPC-595
75T-595
75T/M-595
76OPC-273
76SSPC-50
76T-273
78BK/Ast-5
77T-116
78T-306
80BK/PHR-6
80OPC-226
80T-436
81Coke
81D-380
81F-54
81OPC-102
81T-722
81T/St-174
81T/St-26
82D-167
82F-221
82F/St-45
82OPC-74
82T-611
83D-10DK
83D-470
83D-613M
83D/AAS-51
83F-457
83OPC-221
83T-221
83T-441TL
83T/St-240
84D-110
84F-234
85FunFoodPin-128
84Mother/Ast-2
84Nes/792-586
84OPC-384
84T-586
84T/St-69
85D-182
85F-355
85F/St-88
85Leaf-189
85Mother/Ast-6
85OPC-295
85T-295
85T/St-69
86D-601
86D-645M
86Leaf-243M
86Mother/Ast-17
86OPC-135
86T-135
87Classic/Up-120M
87D-217
87F-106
87F/Up-U87
87T-344
87T/Tr-89T
88F-18
88OPC-233
88S-237
88T-473
88T-5RB
Niekro, Phil
64T-541R
65T-461R
66OPC-28
66T-28
67T-456
68Coke
68Dexter-58
68OPC-7LL
68T-257
68T-7LL
69MB-201
69MLB/St-116
69T-355
70MB-20
70MLB/St-10
70OPC-160
70OPC-69LL
70T-160
70T-69LL
70T/PI-2
70T/S-15
71MLB/St-19
71OPC-30
71T-30
71T/Coins-37
72MB-252
72T-620
73K-29
73OPC-503
73T-503
74OPC-29
74T-29
74T/St-9
75Ho-99
75OPC-130
75OPC-310LL
75T-130
75T-310LL
75T/M-130
75T/M-310LL
76Ho-3
76Ho/Twink-3
76OPC-435
76SSPC-5
76T-435
77BurgChef-209
77Ho-111
77OPC-43
77T-615
78Ho-122
78OPC-155
78OPC-6LL
78T-10
78T-206LL
79Ho-62
79K-28
79OPC-313
79T-595
79T/Comics-19
80K-51
80OPC-130
80T-245
81D-328
81F-242
81F/St-23
81K-12
81OPC-201
81Pol/Atl-35
81T-387
81T/St-148
82BK/Lids-19
82D-10DK
82D-475
82F-444
82F/St-68
82K-36
82OPC-185
82Pol/Atl-35
82T-185
82T/St-20
83D-613M
83D-97
83D/AAS-12
83F-143
83OPC-316SV
83OPC-94
83Pol/Atl-35
83T-410
83T-411SV
83T-502TL
83T/St-218
84D-188
84D/Champs-34
84F-187
84F/X-U83
85FunFoodPin-115
84Nes/792-650
84OPC-29
84T-650
84T/St-31
84T/Tr-84T
85D-458
85D/AAS-49
85D/HL-50
85F-138
85F/St-93
85Leaf-138
85OPC-40
85Pol/MetYank-Y2
85Seven-11S
85T-40
85T/Gloss40-32
85T/St-309
86D-580
86D-645M
86F-112
86F-630M
86F/LL-28
86F/St-82
86F/Up-U81
86Leaf-243M
86OhHenry-35
86OPC-246
86Quaker-28
86Sf-130M
86Sf-163
86Sf-182M
86Sf-53M
86T-204RB
86T-790
86T/St-7
86T/Tr-77T
87D-465
87F-254
87F-626M
87F/RecSet-25
87Gator-35
87Leaf-181
87OPC-6
87Sf-147
87T-694
88Classic/Red-198
88Classic/Red-199
88Classic/Red-200
88S-555
88T-5RB
89Pac/Leg-212

89Swell-22
90Pac/Legend-96
91Richm/LineD-449MG
91Richm/ProC-2583MG

Nielsen, Dan
88Watertn/Pucko-9

Nielsen, Gerald
(Jerry)
88Oneonta/ProC-2062
89PrWill/Star-14
89Star/Wax-91
90PrWill/Team-16
91FtLaud/ClBest-10
91FtLaud/ProC-2423

Nielsen, Kevin
91Spring/ClBest-19
91Spring/ProC-740

Nielsen, Scott
84Nashvl-15
85Albany-9
87D-597
87Hawaii-15
87T-57
88AAA/ProC-11
88Colum/CMC-3
88Colum/Pol-6
88Colum/ProC-310
89Colum/CMC-2
89Colum/Pol-15
89Colum/ProC-754
89F-261
90AlbanyDG/Best-9
90T/TVMets-52
90Tidew/CMC-8
90Tidew/ProC-541

Nielsen, Steve
78Ashvl
79Tulsa-9
80Tulsa-19
81Tulsa-9
82BurlR-26C
83Tulsa-18
85BurlR-11

Nieman, Robert C.
(Bob)
53Glen
55B-145
56T-267
57T-14
58Hires-26
58T-165
59T-375
60T-149
61T-178
62Sugar-10
62T-182
79TCMA-211
91Crown/Orio-330

Niemann, Art
82AppFx-23

Niemann, Randy
80T-469
81F-77
81T-148
82D-473
82Portl-6
83T-329
85Tidew-7
86F/Up-U82
86T/Tr-78T
87F-18
87Portl-3
87T-147
88Tidew/CANDL-24
88Tidew/CMC-10
89Pac/SenLg-127
90Pittsfld/Pucko-26CO
91StLucie/ClBest-28CO
91StLucie/ProC-729CO
91WIZMets-294

Niemann, Tom
83Butte-14
85FtMyr-6

Nieporte, Jay
85Spokane/Cram-16

Niethammer, Darren
88CharlR/Star-17
90CharlR/Star-16
91CharlR/ClBest-13
91CharlR/ProC-1317
91FSLAS/ProC-FSL5

Nieto, Andy
87DayBe-23

Nieto, Thomas Andrew
(Tom)
81Louisvl-9
82ArkTr-12
83Louisvl/Riley-9
84Louisvl-8
85D-596
85F-235
85OPC-294
85T-294
86D-327
86F-43
86Indianap-30
86KAS/Disc-12
86T-88
87D/OD-220
87F/Up-U88
87OPC-124
87T-416
87T/Tr-90T
88D-612
88T-317
89Phill/TastyK-24
90ScranWB/ProC-603

Nieva, Wilfredo
88James/ProC-1895

Nieves, Adelberto
81Batavia-10
81Watlo-30

Nieves, Ernesto
90Billings/ProC-3219
90CharWh/Best-5
90CharWh/ProC-2237
91CharWh/ClBest-7
91CharWh/ProC-2884

Nieves, Fionel
90Ashvl/ClBest-7
91Ashvl/ProC-565

Nieves, Juan
86D-40RR
86D/Rook-12
86F/Up-U83
86Pol/Brew-20
86Sf/Rook-5
86T/Tr-79T
87Classic/Up-136
87D-90
87D/HL-1
87F-352
87OPC-79
87Pol/Brew-20
87T-79
87T/GlossRk-11
88D-126
88F-170
88OPC-104
88Panini/St-117
88Panini/St-431
88Pol/Brew-20
88RedFoley/St-60
88S-513
88S-655HL
88S/YS/II-33
88Sf-180
88Sf-211
88T-515
88T/Big-190
89B-131
89Bimbo/Discs-10
89Brewer/YB-20
89D-575
89Gard-10
89Pol/Brew-20
89S-410
89T-287
89UD-646
90OPC-467
90Pol/Brew-20
90Publlnt/St-501
90T-467
90UD-648

Nieves, Melvin
89Pulaski/ProC-1893
90A&AASingle/ProC-105
90Foil/Best-219
90Sumter/Best-15
90Sumter/ProC-2447
91Durham/ProC-1560

Nieves, Raul
76Dubuq

Niggling, John
W753

Niles, Harry Clyde
(Harry)
E91
M116
T204
T206
T3-111

Niles, Tommy
91WinHaven/ProC-485

Nilsson, Dave
88Beloit/GS-19
89Stockton/Best-1
89Stockton/Cal-162
89Stockton/ProC-374
89Stockton/Star-21
90A&AASingle/ProC-151
90Stockton/Best-2
90Stockton/Cal-187
90Stockton/ProC-2186
91ElPaso/LineD-194
91ElPaso/ProC-2751
91Single/ClBest-227
91UD/FinalEd-25F
92D/I-4RR
92T-58R
92UD-57TP

Nina, Robin
89Salem/Team-19
90VeroB/Star-20

Nipp, Mark
80Albuq-21

Nipper, Al
85D-614
85F-165
85T-424
86D-538
86F-356
86T-181
87D-297
87F-39
87OPC-64
87T-617
88Berg/Cubs-45
88D-523
88D/Best-250
88D/Cubs/Bk-NEW
88F-358
88S-527
88T-326
88T/Tr-75T
89D-394
89F-433
89S-532
89T-86
89UD-494
91Louisvl/LineD-241
91Louisvl/ProC-2911

Nipper, Mike
85Durham-28
86Durham-20

Nipper, Ronald
87Greenvl/Best-6

Nischwitz, Ron
62T-591R
63T-152
66OPC-38
66T-38

Nishimura, Hioetsugu
88VeroB/Star-19

Nishioka, Tsuyoshi
91Salinas/ProC-2241

Nitcholas, Otho
90Target-576

Nitschke, David
75Tucson-5

Nittoli, Mike
86SanJose-15

Nitz, Rick
74Albuq/Team-11

Nivens, Toby
87Orlan-12
88OrlanTw/Best-6
89Jacks/GS-6
91Wmsprt/LineD-640
91Wmsprt/ProC-289

Nix, Dave
81AppFx-21
82AppFx-15
83GlenF-8
86Madis-16
86Madis/Pol-15

Nix, John
75Cedar

Nixon, Al
90Target-577

Nixon, Donell
81Wausau-17
82Wausau-9
84Chatt-11
87Calgary-19
87D/OD-114
87Mother/Sea-19
88Calgary/CMC-11
88F-382
88F/Up-U129
88S-436
88T-146
89B-477
89F-337
89Mother/Giants-25
89S-481
89T-447
89T/Big-214
90D-571
90F-66
90MLBPA/Pins-25
90OPC-658
90Publlnt/St-78
90RochR/CMC-11
90RochR/ProC-715
90S-538
90T-658
91Crown/Orio-331

Nixon, Jason
90Augusta/ProC-2467

Nixon, Otis
83Colum-25
85Polar/Ind-20
86F-591
86OhHenry-20
86T/Tr-80T
87F-255
87Gator-20
87T-486
88Indianap/CMC-14
88Indianap/ProC-518
89B-366
89F-387
89OPC-54
89S-451
89T-674
89T/Big-234
89T/Mini-23
89UD-480
90D-456
90F-356
90OPC-252
90Publlnt/St-183
90S-241
90T-252
90T/Big-279
90UD-379
91B-571
91D-626
91F-241
91F/UltraUp-U69
91F/Up-U75
91Leaf/II-395
91OPC-558
91OPC/Premier-89
91Panini/FrSt-152
91S-431
91S/RookTr-29T
91T-558
91T/StClub/I-174
91T/Tr-84T
91UD-520
91UD/FinalEd-58F
92D/I-33HL
92D/I-41
92S/100SS-73
92S/I-429HL
92S/II-443
92T-340
92T/Promo-174
92UD-451

Nixon, Russell E.
(Russ)
57Sohio/Ind-11
58T-133
59Kahn
59T-344
60Kahn
60MacGregor-17
60T-36
61P-52
61T-53
61T/St-115
62T-523
62T/St-16
63T-168
64T-329
65OPC-162
65T-162
66T-227
67T-446
68Coke
68Dexter-59
68T-515
69T-363
83T-756
84Nes/792-351MG
84Stuart-5CO
84T-351MG
86Pol/Atl-2C
88T/Tr-76MG
89T-564MG
90OPC-171MG
90T-171MG
91Portl/LineD-424MG
91Portl/ProC-1581MG

Nixon, Willard
51B-270
52T-269
53B/BW-2
53T-30
54B-114
55B-177
56T-122
57T-189
58Hires-47
58T-395
59T-361
91T/Arc53-30

Noble, Rafael Miguel
(Ray)
50Remar
51B-269
52BR

Noble, Ray
85Utica-20
86Tucson-17

Nobles, Jim
79LodiD-10

Noboa, Milicades A.
(Junior)
81Batavia-15
82Watlo/B-18
82Watlo/C-28
83Watlo/LF-8
84BuffB-4
85Maine-20
86Maine-13
87BuffB-8
87Gator-17
88Edmon/ProC-564
88T-503
89AAA/CMC-3
89AAA/ProC-8
89Indianap/CMC-20
89Indianap/ProC-1235
90T/Tr-80T
91D-726
91F-242
91F/Ultra-207
91Leaf/I-255
91OPC-182
91S-423
91T-182
92D/II-765

Nocas, Luke
87AppFx-25
89AppFx/ProC-877

Nocciolo, Mark
80SLCity-5
81Holyo-18

Noce, Doug
90Gate/ProC-3356
91Sumter/ClBest-14
91Sumter/ProC-2337

Noce, Paul
83Miami-17
84MidldC-21
85Iowa-5
86Iowa-20
87D/Rook-51
87Iowa-11
88D-315
88D/Cubs/Bk-315
88F-428
88Iowa/CMC-16

88Iowa/ProC-538
88RedFoley/St-61
88S-329
88T-542
89Calgary/CMC-16
89Calgary/ProC-539
90Nashvl/CMC-14
90Nashvl/ProC-241
91Phoenix/ProC-72

Noch, Douglas
88VeroB/Star-20
89VeroB/Star-19

Nodell, Ray
83Miami-12

Noel, Mike
89Smok/FresnoSt-16

Noelke, Michael
88LitFalls/Pucko-7
89Clmbia/Best-9
89Clmbia/GS-18

Nokes, Matt
82Clinton-4
84Shrev/FB-14
86Nashvl-18
87Classic/Up-129
87D/Rook-12
87F/Up-U90
87Sf/Rook-16
87T/Tr-91T
88Classic/Blue-207
88Classic/Red-166
88D-152
88D/AS-16
88D/Best-237
88F-638M
88F-66
88F/AS-1
88F/BB/AS-29
88F/Excit-29
88F/Mini-23
88F/SS-26
88F/St-27
88Leaf-60
88MSA/Disc-5
88Nestle-41
88OPC-266
88Panini/St-88
88Pep/T-33
88Pol/T-9
88RedFoley/St-62
88S-15
88S-648M
88S/YS/I-5
88Sf-6
88Sf/Gamewin-18
88T-393AS
88T-645
88T/Big-185
88T/Gloss60-59
88T/JumboR-8
88T/St-269
88T/St-311
88T/St/Backs-56
88T/UK-54
88ToysRUs-22
89B-101
89Classic-113
89D-116
89D/Best-181
89F-140
89Holsum/Discs-13
89Mara/Tigers-33
89Nissen-13
89OPC-116
89Panini/St-339
89Pol/Tigers-33
89RedFoley/St-86
89S-23
89Sf-203
89T-445
89T/Big-303
89T/St-280
89UD-150
90Classic-141
90Classic/III-15
90CokeK/Tiger-14
90D-178
90D/BestAL-11
90F-611
90F/Up-115
90Leaf/I-192
90Leaf/II-314
90MLBPA/Pins-86
90OPC-131
90PublInt/St-479
90RedFoley/St-69
90S-55
90S/NWest-24
90S/Tr-38T
90T-131
90T/Tr-81T
90UD-226
90UD/Ext-744
91B-164
91Classic/200-32
91D-170
91F-674
91F/UltraUp-U42
91Leaf/I-89
91OPC-336
91S-551
91T-336
91T/StClub/I-64
91UD-673
92D/I-126
92F-239
92S/II-573
92T-404AS
92T-748
92UD-295

Nolan, Bob
75Phoenix-4
77SLCity

Nolan, Darin
91StCath/ClBest-22
91StCath/ProC-3393

Nolan, Gary
68OPC-196
68T-196
69MLB/St-133
69T-581
70K-53
70MLB/St-33
70OPC-484
70T-484
71K-36
71MLB/St-66
71OPC-75
71T-75
71T/tatt-4
72MB-253
72OPC-475
72T-475
73K-30
73OPC-260
73T-260
73T/Lids-36
74OPC-277
74T-277
75OPC-562
75T-562
75T/M-562
76Icee
76OPC-444
76SSPC-29
76T-444
77BurgChef-203
77Ho-113
77OPC-70
77Pep-51
77T-121

Nolan, Joseph W. Jr.
(Joe)
78T-617
79T-464
80T-64
81D-302
81F-212
81OPC-149
81T-149
81T/HT
82D-62
82F-77
82T-327
82T/Tr-81T
83D-79
83F-68
83T-242
84D-489
84F-15
84Nes/792-553
84T-553
85D-594
85F-185
85T-652
86T-781
91Crown/Orio-332
91WIZMets-295

Noland, J.D.
(James)
89Watlo/ProC-1778
89Watlo/Star-22
90Foil/Best-238
90Waterlo/Best-13
90Waterlo/ProC-2390
91AS/Cal-18
91HighD/ClBest-27
91HighD/ProC-2410

Nold, Dick
68OPC-96R
68T-96R

Noles, Dickie
79OkCty
80T-682R
81D-568
81F-12
81OkCty/TCMA-14
81T-406
82F-253
82RedLob
82T-530
82T/Tr-82T
83D-426
83F-504
83OPC-99
83T-99
83Thorn-48
84D-266
84F-500
84Nes/792-618
84Rang-36
84T-618
85OPC-149
85Rang-36
85T-149
86D-587
86F-567
86OhHenry-48
86T-388
87Berg/Cubs-47
87F-256
87F/Up-U91
87T-244
87T/Tr-92T
88RochR/Team-16
88RochR/CMC-8
88RochR/Gov-19
88RochR/ProC-219
88T-768
89Colum/CMC-3
89Colum/Pol-16
89Colum/ProC-749
90ScranWB/CMC-5
91Crown/Orio-333

Nolte, Eric
85Spokane/Cram-17
86CharRain-19
87Wichita-12
88D-534
88F-593
88S-568
88Smok/Padres-20
88T-694
89LasVegas/CMC-8
89LasVegas/ProC-12
90LasVegas/CMC-5
90LasVegas/ProC-118

Nonnenkamp, Leo W.
(Red)
40PB-196

Noonan, Dennis
90CLAS/CL-33TR
90Kinston/Team-29

Noonan, Jim
78Wausau

Noonan, Todd
87SLCity/Taco-10

Noore, Daryl
89Bluefld/Star-27

Nops, Jerry
90Target-578

Norbert, Ted
45Centen-18

Nordbrook, Timothy C.
(Tim)
76OPC-252
76SSPC-391
76T-252
78OPC-139
78T-369
79Vanco-6
80Vanco-10
83Beloit/LF-16
91Crown/Orio-334

Nordhagen, Wayne O.
76OkCty/Team-20
78T-231
79K-4
79T-351
80OPC-253
80T-487
81Coke
81D-401
81F-348
81T-186
81T/HT
81T/St-59
82D-67
82F-355
82OPC-139
82T-597
83F-438
83OPC-47
83T-714
89Pac/SenLg-154
89T/SenLg-47
90EliteSenLg-45

Nordstrom, Carl
88Billings/ProC-1831
88Cedar/ProC-1158
89Greens/ProC-429

Nored, Mike
76AppFx

Noren, Irving Arnold
(Irv)
50B-247
51B-241
51FB
51T/BB-38
52B-63
52T-40
53B/BW-45
53T-35
54NYJour
55B-63
55RM-AL9
56T-253
57T-298
58T-114
59T-59
60L-101
60T-433
73OPC-179CO
73T-179C
90Target-579
91T/Arc53-35
PM10/L-31

Noriega, Rey
90FtLaud/Star-15
91FSLAS/ProC-FSL17
91FtLaud/ClBest-22
91FtLaud/ProC-2435

Norko, Tom
80Utica-7

Norman, Bull
83Tampa-30

Norman, Daniel E.
(Dan)
77Indianap-10
78Tidew
79T-721R
79Tidew-11
80T-681R
81F-337
81Tidew-28
82Hygrade
83F-289
83OPC-237
83T-237
84MidldC-17
89Kingspt/Star-27CO
90Kgsport/Best-27CO
91Pac/SenLg-64
91WIZMets-296

Norman, Fred
64T-469R
65T-386R
70OPC-427
70T-427
71MLB/St-280
71OPC-348
71T-348
72OPC-194
72T-194
73OPC-32
73T-32
74OPC-581
74T-581
75OPC-396
75T-396
75T/M-396
76OPC-609
76SSPC-30
76T-609
77K-8
77OPC-181
77Pep-56
77T-139
78T-273
79OPC-20
79T-47
80OPC-362
80T-714
81D-92
81F-158
81OPC-183
81T-497
90Target-580

Norman, Greg
83BirmB-13

Norman, H. Willis
(Bill)
53T-245CO
91T/Arc53-245CO

Norman, Kenny
91Elizab/ProC-4313

Norman, Les
91Eugene/ClBest-13
91Eugene/ProC-3739

Norman, Nelson A.
78Cr/PCL-95
80Charl-4
80OPC-270
80T-518
81D-509
82Portl-16
83LynnP-15
84Cram/PCL-133
85RochR-7
86Jaxvl/TCMA-22
87Indianap-29
88Indianap/ProC-517

Norman, Ron
76SanAn/Team-16

Norman, Scott
83Clinton/LF-3
87Spring/Best-28

Norman, Terry
80Batavia-2

Normand, Guy
85Anchora-21
86AubAs-17
87Ashvl-13
88Osceola/Star-18
89Osceola/Star-13

Norrid, Tim
76Wmsprt
79T-705R
79Tacom-22
80Tacom-2
81Charl-9
82Charl-12
83Charl-14

Norris, Allen
59DF
60DF-23

Norris, Bill
91CLAS/ProC-CAR25
91LynchRS/ClBest-17
91LynchRS/ProC-1207

Norris, David
90Johnson/Star-19
91Spring/ClBest-20
91Spring/ProC-741

Norris, James Frances
(Jim)
75OkCty
78T-484
79T-611
80T-333
81D-388
81F-634
81T-264

Norris, Joe
91Sumter/ClBest-9
91Sumter/ProC-2332

Norris, Mike

76OPC-653
76SSPC-487
76T-653
77BurgChef-113
77T-284
78T-434
79T-191
80T-599
81D-118
81F-573
81F/St-6
81MSA/Disc-24
81OPC-55
81T-55
81T/SO-53
81T/St-122
81T/St-2M
81T/St-4
81T/St-6
82D-197
82D-19DK
82F-103
82F/St-125
82Granny-13
82K-59
82OPC-370
82T-370
82T/St-222
83D-139
83F-530
83Granny-17
83OPC-276
83T-620
84F-457
84Nes/792-493
84OPC-49
84T-493
85T-246
87Mother/A's-22
90Mother/A's-19
91Pac/SenLg-107

North, Jay
85Spring-21
86StPete-22
87StPete-25
88StPete/Star-20
89Savan/ProC-343
90StPete/Star-26CO
91StPete/ClBest-11CO
91StPete/ProC-2293CO

North, Mark
88Peoria/Ko-22
89Kenosha/ProC-1061
89Kenosha/Star-18

North, Roy
80Ander-18
81Durham-21

North, William Alex
(Billy)
73OPC-234
73T-234
74Greyhound-1
74Greyhound-5M
74OPC-345
74T-345
74T/St-228
75Greyhound-5
75K-23
75OPC-121
75OPC-309LL
75T-121
75T-309LL
75T/M-121
75T/M-309LL
76Greyhound-1
76Greyhound-5
76OPC-33
76SSPC-491
76T-33
77BurgChef-116
77Ho-33
77K-22
77OPC-106
77OPC-4LL
77T-4LL
77T-551
78Ho-76
78T-163
78Tastee/Discs-13
79OPC-351
79Pol/Giants-36
79T-668
80BK/PHR-31
80OPC-213
80Pol/Giants-36
80T-408
81D-76
81F-441
81OPC-47
81T-713
90Target-581

Northern, Hubbard
90Target-1144
T207

Northey, Ronald J.
(Ron)
49B-79
50B-81
51B-70
52T-204
57T-31
63IDL-16CO
Exh47

Northey, Scott R.
(Scott)
70OPC-241R
70T-241R
71OPC-633R
71T-633R

Northrup, George
E270/1

Northrup, James T.
(Jim)
65OPC-259R
65T-259R
66T-554
67T-408
68OPC-78
68T-78
69MB-202
69MLB/St-53
69OPC-167WS
69OPC-3LL
69T-167WS
69T-3LL
69T-580
69T/St-178
70MLB/St-213
70OPC-177
70T-177
71K-63
71MLB/St-401
71OPC-265
71T-265
71T/Coins-82
71T/GM-21
71T/S-55
72MB-254
72OPC-408
72T-408
73OPC-168
73T-168
74OPC-266
74T-266
75OPC-641
75T-641
75T/M-641
76SSPC-399
81Detroit-52
83Kaline-52M
88Domino-17
90Swell/Great-78
91Crown/Orio-335

Norton, Doug
83Beloit/LF-11
86Stockton-19

Norton, Rick
91SoOreg/ClBest-8
91SoOreg/ProC-3856

Norwood, Aaron
89Bluefld/Star-19

Norwood, Steve
78Newar
79BurlB-24
80BurlB-15
81BurlB-4

Norwood, Willie
78T-705R
79T-274
80T-432
80Toledo-10
81D-516

Nosek, Randy
88Lakeland/Star-18
89London/ProC-1377
90S-607RP
90T/89Debut-88
90Toledo/CMC-6
90Toledo/ProC-145
90UD-2SR
91Toledo/LineD-594
91Toledo/ProC-1930

Nossek, Joseph R.
(Joe)
64T-532R
65T-597R
66OPC-22
66T-22
67T-209
69OPC-143
69T-143
73OPC-646CO
73T-646C
74T-99C
90Coke/WSox-30CO
91Kodak/WSox-x

Nottebart, Don
60T-351
61T-29
62T-541
63T-204
64T-434
64T/Coins-119
65T-469
66OPC-21
66T-21
67T-269
68OPC-171
68T-171
69T-593
78TCMA-72

Nottle, Ed
74Gaston
77Tucson
80WHave-20
81Tacom-6
82Tacom-19
84Cram/PCL-90
86Pawtu-16MG
87Pawtu-22MG
87Pawtu/TCMA-21MG
88AAA/ProC-52MG
88Pawtu/CMC-24MG
88Pawtu/ProC-469
89Pac/SenLg-51
89Pawtu/CMC-25MG
89Pawtu/Dunk-17MG
89Pawtu/ProC-678MG
90Pawtu/CMC-10MG
90Pawtu/ProC-477MG
90T/TVRSox-34MG

Novak, Tom
87Tampa-11

Novick, Walter
52Park-77

Novikoff, Lou
43MP-18
47Centen-16
47Signal
88MinorLg/Leg-4

Novoa, Rafael
88CapeCod/Sum-36
90A&AASingle/ProC-116
90Clinton/Best-24
90Clinton/ProC-2541
90Foil/Best-89
91Classic/I-9
91Phoenix/LineD-386
91Phoenix/ProC-62
91S-366RP
91T/90Debut-116
91UD-674

Novotney, Rube
49Eureka-65

Nowak, Matt
88Hagers/Star-14

Nowak, Rick
90Myrtle/ProC-2774

Nowlan, Bill
81BurlB-28
82Beloit-25
83Beloit/LF-13

Nowlin, James
87Sumter-25

Noworyta, Steve
83AppFx/LF-9

Nozling, Paul
88Bristol/ProC-1890
89Fayette/ProC-1591

Nugent, Barney
86Reading-20TR
87Maine-10TR
88Maine/CMC-3TR
88Maine/ProC-299TR
89ScrWB/CMC-2TR
89ScrWB/ProC-712TR
90ScranWB/CMC-25TR

Nuismer, Jack
81Chatt-7
82Charl-8

Nunamaker, Leslie G.
(Les)
14CJ-132
15CJ-132
D350/2-131
E120
E121/120
M101/5-131
T207
W501-115
W514-7
W573

Nuneviller, Tom
90Batavia/ProC-3082
91Clearw/ClBest-22
91Clearw/ProC-1633

Nunez, Alex
90Kenosha/Best-11
90Kenosha/ProC-2303
90Kenosha/Star-18
91Visalia/ClBest-18
91Visalia/ProC-1750

Nunez, Bernardino
(Bernie)
88Myrtle/ProC-1169
89Dunedin/Star-12
90Knoxvl/Best-14
90Knoxvl/ProC-1256
90Knoxvl/Star-13
91Knoxvl/LineD-363
91Knoxvl/ProC-1781

Nunez, Dario
86PalmSp-24
86PalmSp/Smok-25
87PalmSp-22
88PalmSp/ProC-1448

Nunez, Edwin
80Wausau-6
81Wausau-4
83SLCity-1
84Cram/PCL-183
84D-435
85D-484
85F-496
85Mother/Mar-24
85T-34
86D-145
86F-470
86Leaf-66
86Mother/Mar-24
86OPC-364
86T-511
86T/St-223
87D-243
87F/Up-U92
87Mother/Sea-11
87T-427
88D-445
88D/Rook-36
88F-383
88Mother/Sea-11
88OPC-258
88Panini/St-182
88T-258
88T/St-216
89Toledo/ProC-773
90CokeK/Tiger-15
90D-563
90F/Up-U98
90Leaf/II-397
90OPC-586
90T-586
91B-40
91Brewer/MillB-19
91D-620
91F-345
91F/Up-U32
91Leaf/II-352
91OPC-106
91Pol/Brew-17
91T-106
91T/StClub/II-595
91WIZMets-297
92D/II-541
92F-184
92S/II-676
92T-352

Nunez, Jose
85FtMyr-13
87F/Up-U93
87Tor/Fire-26
88D-611
88F-122
88OPC-28
88S-312
88Syrac/ProC-820
88T-28
89Syrac/CMC-2
89Syrac/ProC-806
89Syrac/Team-16
89Tor/Fire-45
90D-467
90T/TVCub-13
90UD/Ext-716
91Iowa/ProC-1057

Nunez, Mauricio
86StPete-23
87StPete-6
88ArkTr/GS-10
89SALAS/GS-38
89Savan/ProC-357
90Louisvl/CMC-26
90Louisvl/ProC-417
90T/TVCard-57
91StPete/ClBest-28

Nunez, Rogelio
90SoBend/ClBest-22
90Utica/Pucko-4
91MidwLAS/ProC-MWL11
91Single/ClBest-277
91SoBend/ProC-2859

Nunley, Angelo
85Spring-22
86Tampa-14
87Vermont-13
88Chatt/Best-25

Nunn, Howard
59T-549
61T-346
62T-524

Nunn, Wally
77Spartan

Nurre, Peter
90Kissim/DIMD-19

Nuxhall, Joe
52T-406
53B/Col-90
53T-105
54B-76
55B-194
55Kahn
56Kahn
56T-218
57Kahn
57Sohio/Reds-15
57T-103
58Kahn
58T-63
59Kahn
59T-389
60Kahn
60T-282
61T-444
63FrBauer-14
63Kahn
63T-194
64Kahn
64T-106
65Kahn
65T-312
66T-485
67OPC-44
67T-44
78TCMA-65
89Pac/Leg-161
89Swell-53
90BBWit-105
91T/Arc53-105
Rawl

Nyce, Frederick
N172

Nye, Rich
67T-608R
68T-339
69MB-203
69OPC-88

69T-88
70OPC-139
70T-139
71LaPizza-7
72MB-255
78TCMA-281

Nyman, Christopher C.
(Chris)
78Knoxvl
82Edmon-5
84Nes/792-382
84T-382
86BuffB-20
86Nashvl-19

Nyman, Gerald
69OPC-173R
69T-173R
70T-644
71MLB/St-233
71OPC-656
71T-656
89Salinas/Cal-147CO
89Salinas/ProC-1820CO
90James/Pucko-10CO
90Welland/Pucko-33CO
91Welland/ProC-3592CO

Nyman, Nyls W.
(Nyls)
75OPC-619R
75T-619R
75T/M-619R
76OPC-258
76SSPC-149
76T-258

Nyquist, Mike
89SLCity-5

Nyssen, Dan
87AubAs-13
88Osceola/Star-19
89Osceola/Star-14
90Osceola/Star-21

O'Berry, Preston M.
(Mike)
80T-662R
82Coke/Reds
82D-538
82F-78
82T-562
84Colum-20
84Colum/Pol-16
84Nes/792-184
84T-184
84T/Tr-86
85Colum-12

O'Bradovich, James T.
(Jim)
78Charl

O'Brien, Charlie
83Albany-10
86Vanco-19
87Denver-24
88Denver/CMC-15
88Denver/ProC-1268
88Pol/Brew-11
88T-566
89F-194
89Pol/Brew-22
89S-606
89T-214
90Brewer/MillB-17
90D-410
90ElPasoATG/Team-30
90F-332
90Leaf/II-375
90OPC-106
90Pol/Brew-22
90PublInt/St-502
90T-106
90UD-650
90WichSt-28
91B-473
91D-623
91Kahn/Mets-5
91Leaf/I-122
91OPC-442
91S-829
91T-442
91T/StClub/I-157
91UD-420
91WIZMets-298
92D/II-777
92F-514
92S/II-621
92T-56
92UD-381

O'Brien, Dan
77StPete
80Richm-10
80T-684R
81Richm-18

O'Brien, Edward J.
(Eddie)
53T-249
54T-139M
56T-116
57T-259
91T/Arc53-249

O'Brien, John
91Hamil/ClBest-18
91Hamil/ProC-4047

O'Brien, John Joseph
(Jack)
T3/Box-75

O'Brien, John K.
(Jack)
N172
WG1-69

O'Brien, John Thomas
(Johnny)
53T-223
54T-139M
55T-135
56T-65
56T/Pin-44
58T-426
59T-499
60HenryH-4
90Target-584
91T/Arc53-223

O'Brien, Peter James
(Pete)
T206

O'Brien, Peter M.
(Pete)
80Ashvl-13
81Tulsa-16
83Rang-9
83T/Tr-81T
84D-281
84F-423
84Nes/792-534
84OPC-71
84Rang-9
84T-534
84T/St-357
85D-178
85F-563
85Leaf-201
85OPC-196
85Rang-9
85T-196
85T/St-344
86D-99
86F-568
86F/Mini-112
86OPC-328
86Rang-9
86T-328
86T/St-236
87Classic/Up-138
87D-259
87D/OD-174
87F-132
87F/GameWin-31
87F/Mini-76
87Ho/St-30
87Leaf-186
87Mother/Rang-9
87OPC-17
87Sf-52
87Smok/R-12
87T-17
87T/Mini-72
87T/St-239
88D-284
88D/Best-167
88F-475
88F/St-67
88Leaf-132
88Mother/R-9
88OPC-381
88Panini/St-200
88RedFoley/St-63
88S-29
88Sf-145
88Smok/R-2
88T-721
88T/Big-227
88T/St-240
89B-84
89Classic/Up/2-184
89D-107
89D/Best-5
89D/Tr-16
89F-529
89F/Up-29
89OPC-314
89Panini/St-452
89RedFoley/St-87
89S-22
89S/Tr-6
89Sf-8
89T-629
89T/Big-115
89T/St-248
89T/Tr-88T
89T/UK-57
89UD-54
89UD/Ext-800
90B-475
90Classic/III-38
90D-202
90D-24DK
90D/BestAL-98
90D/SuperDK-24DK
90F-498
90Leaf/I-9
90Mother/Mar-17
90OPC-265
90Panini/St-55
90PublInt/St-565
90S-175
90S/Tr-23T
90Sf-92
90T-265
90T/St-218
90T/Tr-82T
90TulsaDG/Best-4
90UD-110
90UD/Ext-719
91B-259
91CounHrth-8
91D-119
91F-459
91F/Ultra-342
91Leaf/I-244
91OPC-585
91Panini/FrSt-228
91S-509
91T-585
91T/StClub/I-285
91UD-459
92D/I-86
92F-289
92S/I-141
92T-455
92UD-388

O'Brien, Robert
72OPC-198R
72T-198R
90Target-583

O'Brien, Sydney L.
(Sid)
69T-628R
70OPC-163
70T-163
71MLB/St-353
71OPC-561
71T-561
72OPC-289
72T-289
72T/Cloth-25

O'Brien, Thomas
T207

O'Brien, William D.
(Darby)
90Target-1104
N172

O'Brien, William S.
(Billy)
R314/Can

O'Brien, William S.
N172
N284

O'Connell, Daniel F.
(Danny)
51B-93
53SpicSpan/3x5-18
53SpicSpan/7x10-10
53T-107
54B-160
54Dix
54JC-4
54SpicSpan/PostC-15
55B-44
55Gol/Braves-23
55JC-4
55SpicSpan/DC-14
56T-272
57SpicSpan/4x5-13
57T-271
58Hires-19
58SFCallB-18
58T-166
59T-87
60T-192
61T-318
62Salada-221
62Shirriff-221
62T-411
62T/St-99
91T/Arc53-107
PM10/Sm-137

O'Connell, James J.
(Jimmy)
W515-13
WG7-37

O'Connell, Mark
81Clinton-11

O'Connell, P.J.
N172

O'Connell, Shawn
91Bluefld/ProC-4126
91Bluefld/ClBest-23

O'Conner, Tim
86Kenosha-18
87Visalia-17

O'Conner, Tom
88OrlanTw/Best-2

O'Connor, Ben
90Yakima/Team-16
91Yakima/ClBest-15
91Yakima/ProC-4246

O'Connor, Bill
84Shrev/FB-15
85Visalia-4
86Visalia-14

O'Connor, Bob
82Clinton-25

O'Connor, Jack
82D-539
82F-557
82T-353
82Toledo-5
83D-51
83F-621
83T-33
83Toledo-29
84Nes/792-268
84T-268
84Toledo-15
85Indianap-22
86Calgary-20
87RochR-20
87RochR/TCMA-7
88S-434
88Syrac/CMC-10
88Syrac/ProC-805
89Syrac/CMC-3
89Syrac/ProC-812
89Syrac/Team-17
91Crown/Orio-336

O'Connor, James
91StCath/ClBest-14
91StCath/ProC-3394

O'Connor, John J.
(Jack)
E107
M116
N172

O'Connor, Kevin
90Idaho/ProC-3257
91Macon/ClBest-25
91Macon/ProC-878

O'Connor, Patrick F.
(Paddy)
D322
E90/1
M116

O'Day, Henry Francis
(Hank)
N172

O'Dea, James Kenneth
(Ken)
40PB-214
92Conlon/Sport-497
WG8-43

O'Dell, Bill
55T-57
55T/DH-8
57T-316
58T-84
59T-250
60T-303
61P-155
61T-383M
61T-96
61T/St-83
62T-429
63Exh
63F-66
63J-111
63P-111
63T-235
63T-7LL
63T-9LL
64T-18
64T/Coins-115
65T-476
66T-237
67OPC-162
67T-162
67T/Test/PP-17
91Crown/Orio-337
Exh47

O'Dell, James Wesley
(Jim)
85Osceola/Team-20
86ColumAst-20
87BirmB/Best-4
88CharlK/Pep-7

O'Donnell, Erik
91Belling/ClBest-10
91Belling/ProC-3659

O'Donnell, George
60DF-15

O'Donnell, Glen
86Elmira-14

O'Donnell, Stephen P.
88CapeCod-18
88CapeCod/Sum-41
89GreatF-25
90Bakers/Cal-248
91VeroB/ClBest-23
91VeroB/ProC-784

O'Donoghue, John Jr.
90LSUPol-15
91Freder/ClBest-6
91Freder/ProC-2361

O'Donoghue, John Sr.
64T-388R
65OPC-71
65T-71
66T-501
66T/RO-105
67OPC-127
67T-127
68T-456
70McDon-1
70OPC-441
70T-441
71LaPizza-8
71MLB/St-136
71OPC-743
71T-743
72MB-257
91Crown/Orio-338
91Freder/ClBest-27CO

O'Dougherty, Pat
44Yank/St-21

O'Doul, Francis J.
(Lefty)
29Exh/4-11
31Exh/4-3
32Orbit/num-31A
32Orbit/num-31B
32Orbit/un-48
33DH-33
33DL-10
33Exh/4-2
33G-232
33G-58
48Sommer-1
49Sommer-1
53Mother-9

60F-37
61F-130
72F/FFeat-34
80Pac/Leg-29
80Laugh/FFeat-31
88Conlon/5-23
90Target-585
91Conlon/Sport-165
92Conlon/Sport-447
R300
R305
R315-A26
R315-B26
R316
R328-24
R423-75
V353-58

O'Dowd,Tom
80Utica-22

O'Farrell, Robert A.
(Bob)
26Exh-62
27Exh-31
31Exh/4-10
33Exh/4-5
33G-34
35G-2F
35G-4F
35G-7F
61F-131
91Conlon/Sport-175
91Conlon/Sport-316
92Conlon/Sport-621
E120
E210-12
E220
R306
R310
R315-A27
R315-B27
V100
V353-34
V355-115
V61-76
W502-12
W572
W573

O'Halloran, Greg
89StCath/ProC-2079
90Dunedin/Star-14
90FSLAS/Star-38
91Dunedin/ClBest-14
91Dunedin/ProC-211
91Single/ClBest-30

O'Halloran, Mike
91MedHat/ProC-4098

O'Hara, Duane
88CapeCod/Sum-73

O'Hara, Pat
82Madis-27

O'Hara, William A.
C46-1
E101
E106
E92
M116
T204
T206
T216

O'Hearn, Bob
85BurlR-16
86Salem-22

O'Keeffe, Richard
76BurlB
80Water-11
81Water-6
82Syrac-27

O'Leary, Bill
84Butte-20

O'Leary, Charles T.
(Charley)
12Sweet/Pin-29
91Conlon/Sport-116
E104
E90/1
M116
T202
T202
T204
T205
T206
T215/blue
T215/brown
W575

O'Leary, Troy
89Beloit/I/Star-19
89Helena/SP-11
89Star/Wax-6
90Beloit/Best-5
90Beloit/Star-16
90Foil/Best-98
91AS/Cal-36
91Single/ClBest-160
91Stockton/ClBest-17
91Stockton/ProC-3046

O'Malley, Mike
81VeroB-12

O'Malley, Thomas P.
(Tom)
81Shrev-4
82Phoenix
83D-96
83F-271
83Mother/Giants-10
83T-663
84Cram/PCL-11
84D-601
84F-384
84Nes/792-469
84T-469
84T/St-170
86RochR-14
87F-477
87OKCty-20
87T-154
88AAA/ProC-28
88OkCty/CMC-19
88OkCty/ProC-48
88S-534
88Smok/R-1
88T-77
89AAA/CMC-20
89AAA/ProC-13
89Tidew/CMC-15
89Tidew/ProC-1965
90Kahn/Mets-27
90OPC-504
90T-504
90T/TVMets-28
91Crown/Orio-339
91F-157
91OPC-257
91S-439
91T-257
91WIZMets-299

O'Malley, Walter
89Rini/Dodg-22

O'Mara, Oliver E.
(Ollie)
16FleischBrd-72
D329-134
D350/2-133
M101/4-134
M101/5-133

O'Neal, Kelley
89Bristol/Star-19
90Niagara/Pucko-8
91Fayette/ClBest-21
91Fayette/ProC-1180
91SALAS/ProC-SAL20

O'Neal, Mark
90Savan/ProC-2084TR

O'Neal, Randy
82BirmB-8
83Evansvl-7
84Evansvl-17
85F-645R
86Cain's-13
86D-394
86F-233
86T-73
87D-584
87F-159
87Smok/Atl-3
87T-196
88Louisvl-37
88Louisvl/CMC-4
88Louisvl/ProC-430
89Phill/TastyK-25
89ScrWB/CMC-10
89ScrWB/ProC-726
90Mother/Giant-23
91F-268

O'Neil, Buck
86Negro/Frit-45

O'Neil, George M.
(Mickey)
21Exh-121
25Exh-8
26Exh-14
90Target-591
E120
V100
W573
WG3-34

O'Neil, Johnny
47Centen-17

O'Neil, William John
T206

O'Neill, Dan
87Fayette-3
88Lakeland/Star-19
89Lakeland/Star-16
90A&AASingle/ProC-6
91Pawtu/LineD-362
91Pawtu/ProC-37

O'Neill, Douglas
91James/ClBest-11
91James/ProC-3559

O'Neill, J.F.
21Exh-123

O'Neill, James E.
(Tip)
90HOF/St-7
E223
N172/BC
N184
N284
N370
Scrapps

O'Neill, John J.
(John)
47Signal

O'Neill, Paul
80Indianap-12
82Cedar-21
83Tampa-19
86D-37
86F-646R
87F/Up-U94
87Kahn-21
87Sf/Rook-17
88D-433
88F/Up-U85
88Kahn/Reds-21
88RedFoley/St-64
88S-304
88T-204
89B-313
89D-360
89D/Best-230
89F-166
89Kahn/Reds-21
89OPC-187
89Panini/St-77
89S-206
89S/YS/II-5
89T-604
89T/Big-39
89UD-428
90B-49
90CedarDG/Best-5
90Classic-117
90D-198
90D/BestNL-39
90F-427
90Kahn/Reds-20
90Leaf/I-70
90OPC-332
90Panini/St-245
90PublInt/St-36
90RedFoley/St-71
90S-295
90S/100St-17
90Sf-4
90T-332
90T/Big-30
90T/St-141
90UD-161
91B-685
91D-583
91F-76
91F/Ultra-100
91Kahn/Reds-21
91Leaf/I-219
91Leaf/Stud-169
91OPC-122
91Panini/FrSt-133
91Panini/St-120
91Pep/Reds-15
91S-227
91T-122
91T/StClub/I-218
91UD-133
91USPlayC/AS-2C
92D/I-63
92F-415
92S/100SS-58
92S/I-57
92T-61
92UD-464

O'Neill, Steve F.
15CJ-48
21Exh-122
35BU-160
51B-202MG
54T-127MG
81Detroit-11MG
88Conlon/3-21
91Conlon/Sport-186
91T/Arc53-307MG
D327
D328-129
D329-135
D350/2-134
E120
E121/120
E135-129
E220
M101/4-135
M101/5-134
R311/Leath
R312
R313
V100
V355-67
V61-22
W501-116
W514-26
W572
W573
W575
WG7-39

O'Neill, Ted
76Wausau

O'Quinn, Steven
87CharWh-21

O'Rear, John
78Cr/PCL-90
79Albuq-12
80Albuq-7

O'Regan, Dan
82Oneonta-5

O'Reilly, Jim
89CharWh/Best-26
89CharWh/ProC-1746
90Peoria/Team-33TR
91Peoria/ClBest-24

O'Reilly, Tom
90James/Pucko-31
91James/ClBest-29PER

O'Riley, Don
70T-552R
71OPC-679
71T-679

O'Rourke, Francis J.
(Frank)
25Exh-93
26Exh-94
29Exh/4-30
31Exh/4-29
33G-87
90Target-594
92Conlon/Sport-604
E254
V354-43

O'Rourke, James
50Callahan
73F/Wild-24
80SSPC/HOF
90BBWit-58
E223
N172
N284
N403
N690
WG1-42

O'Rourke, Thomas J.
(Tom)
N172

O'Toole, Dennis
73OPC-604R
73T-604R

O'Toole, Jack
85Anchora-24
87Anchora-23CO

O'Toole, Jim
59T-136
60Kahn
60T-32M
60T-325
61Kahn
61P-189
61T-328
61T/St-21
62J-126
62Kahn
62P-126
62P/Can-126
62T-450
62T-56L
62T-58L
62T-60L
62T/bucks
62T/St-118
63FrBauer-16
63J-136
63Kahn
63P-136
63T-70
64T-185
64T/Coins-85
64T/St-55
64T/SU
64Wheat/St-32
65Bz-6
65Kahn
65OPC-60
65T-60
65T/trans-22
66T-389
67T-467
78TCMA-92
89Pac/Leg-147
WG10-40
WG9-39

O'Toole, Martin J.
11Helmar-164
14CJ-54
15CJ-54
D304
E300
L1-112
S81-87
T207
WG5-33
WG6-31

Oakes, Ennis T.
(Rebel)
10Domino-93
11Helmar-174
12Sweet/Pin-151A
12Sweet/Pin-151B
14CJ-139
14Piedmont/St-45
15CJ-139
D303
E106
E254
E90/1
M116
S74-122
T202
T205
T206
T207
T213/blue
T213/brown
T215/blue
T216

Oakes, Todd
87Clinton-18
88SanJose/Cal-143
88SanJose/ProC-122
89AS/Cal-50CO
89SanJose/Best-29
89SanJose/Cal-236
89SanJose/ProC-455
90Shrev/ProC-1460
90Shrev/Star-26
91Shrev/LineD-325
91Shrev/ProC-1839

Oates, Johnny Lane
(Johnny)
72OPC-474R
72T-474R

73OPC-9
73T-9
74OPC-183
74T-183
74T/St-10
75OPC-319
75T-319
75T/M-319
76OPC-62
76SSPC-468
76T-62
77T-619
78T-508
79T-104
80Pol/Dodg-5
80T-228
81F-99
81T-303
82D-404
82F-47
82Nashvl-28MG
83Colum-1
88RochR/Team-17
88RochR/CMC-24
88RochR/Gov-30
88RochR/ProC-211
89French-46
90Target-582
91Crown/Orio-340
91T/Tr-85T
92T-579MG

Obal, Dave
76Baton

Obando, Sherman
89Oneonta/ProC-2102
90PrWill/Team-17
91PrWill/ClBest-28
91PrWill/ProC-1438
91Single/ClBest-116

Oberdank, Jeff
89QuadC/Best-5
89QuadC/GS-20
90PalmSp/Cal-206
90PalmSp/ProC-2585
91QuadC/ClBest-20
91QuadC/ProC-2639

Oberkfell, Kenneth R.
(Ken)
76ArkTr
80T-701R
81Coke
81D-583
81F-532
81OPC-32
81T-32
81T/St-222
82F-123
82F/St-21
82OPC-121
82T-474
82T/St-89
83D-246
83F-17
83OPC-206
83T-206
83T/St-287
84D-504
84F-330
84F/X-U84
84Nes/792-102
84OPC-102
84T-102
84T/St-148
84T/St/Box-2
84T/Tr-85T
85D-432
85F-336
85Ho/Braves-17
85Leaf-141
85OPC-307
85Pol/Atl-24
85T-569
85T/St-32
86D-531
86F-523
86OPC-334
86Pol/Atl-24
86T-334
86T/St-38
87D-437
87D/OD-46
87F-523
87Leaf-171
87OPC-1
87RedFoley/St-99
87Smok/Atl-16
87T-627
87T/St-38
88D-67
88D/Best-226
88F-545
88OPC-67
88Panini/St-244
88S-245
88Sf-165
88T-67
88T/St-37
89B-418
89D-506
89OPC-97
89S-139
89T-751
89UD-313
89VFJuice-14
90B-74
90D-494
90F-67
90Leaf/II-294
90Mother/Ast-16
90OPC-488
90S-422
90S/Tr-58T
90T-488
90UD-360
91D-109
91F-511
91Mother/Ast-16
91OPC-286
91S-214
91T-286
91T/StClub/II-414

Oberlander, Hartman
N172

Oberlin, Frank
T206

Obregon, Francisco
60HenryH-3
60Union-4

Ocasio, Javier
89Saraso/Star-16
90FSLAS/Star-37
90Saraso/Star-17
91BirmB/LineD-69
91BirmB/ProC-1463
91Single/ClBest-234

Oceak, Frank
60T-467C
63IDL-17CO

Ochoa, Alex
91FrRow/DP-29

Ochoa, Rafael
90Utica/Pucko-5
91Utica/ClBest-29
91Utica/ProC-3254

Ochs, Kevin
84Butte-19

Ochs, Tony
89Johnson/Star-16
90Savan/ProC-2070
91StPete/ClBest-22
91StPete/ProC-2285

Oddo, Ron
80Elmira-23

Odekirk, Rick
88OkCty/CMC-10
88OkCty/ProC-29

Odierno, Scott
88CapeCod/Sum-60

Odle, Page
86PrWill-18

Odom, Joe
84Madis/Pol-6

Odom, John
(Blue Moon)
65T-526R
67T-282
68T-501
69MB-204
69MLB/St-90
69OPC-195
69T-195
69T/St-220
69Trans-8
70K-38
70MLB/St-263
70OPC-55
70T-55
70Trans-15
71MLB/St-523
71OPC-523
71T-523
72MB-256
72T-557
72T-558IA
73OPC-207WS
73OPC-315
73T-207WS
73T-315
74OPC-461
74T-461
75OPC-69
75T-69
75T/M-69
76OPC-651
76T-651
77SanJose-3
78TCMA-68
87Mother/A's-3

Odom, Tim
87FtMyr-10
88AppFx/ProC-150
89Augusta/ProC-493

Odor, Rouglas
88Burllnd/ProC-1780
89Kinston/Star-15
89Watertn/Star-17
90CLAS/CL-41
90Kinston/Team-3
91Canton/LineD-91
91Canton/ProC-988

Odwell, Frederick W.
(Fred)
E254
T201

Oedewaldt, Larry
89Stockton/Best-15
89Stockton/Cal-167
89Stockton/ProC-375
89Stockton/Star-2

Oelkers, Bryan
83Toledo-28
84D-486
86Maine-14
87BuffB-18
87D-596
87F-257
87T-77
89Louisvl-29
89Louisvl/ProC-1244

Oertel, Chuck
91Crown/Orio-341

Oertli, Chuck
86Geneva-20

Oeschger, Joe
21Exh-119
61T-403M
72F/FFeat-19M
72Laugh/GF-37M
90HOF/St-22
90Target-586
E120
E121/120
E220
V100
V61-98
W501-92
W572
W575
WG7-38

Oester, Ronald John
(Ron)
77Indianap-6
78Indianap-6
79Indianap-3
79T-717R
81Coke
81D-423
81F-218
81OPC-21
81T-21
81T/HT
82Coke/Reds
82D-500
82F-79
82F/St-20
82T-427
82T/St-34
83D-526
83F-598
83OPC-269
83T-269
83T/St-230
84Borden-16
84D-62
84D/AAS-46
84F-475
84Nes/792-526
84Nes/792-756TL
84OPC-99
84T-526
84T-756TL
84T/St-53
85D-81
85F-542
85Indianap-30
85OPC-314
85T-314
85T/St-54
86D-81
86F-183
86Leaf-78
86OPC-264
86T-627
86T/St-138
86TexGold-16
87D-206
87D/OD-195
87F-207
87Kahn-16
87OPC-172
87T-172
87T/St-141
88D-246
88F-242
88OPC-17
88S-183
88T-17
88T/St-144
89B-310
89D-553
89Kahn/Reds-16
89S-615
89T-772
89T/Big-229
89UD-287
90D-317
90Kahn/Reds-18
90OPC-492
90Publint/St-35
90S-59
90T-492
90T/Big-55
90UD-118
91D-628
91F-74
91S-651
91UD-611

Oestreich, Mark
89Burllnd/Star-28CO

Offerman, Jose
88GreatF-22
89AS/Cal-1
89Bakers/Cal-194
89BBAmerAA/BProC-AA25
89SanAn/Best-27
90AAAGame/ProC-AAA31
90Albuq/CMC-19
90Albuq/ProC-354
90Albuq/Trib-24
90B-92
90Classic-45
90F/Up-U24
90Leaf/II-464
90UD-46
91Albuq/LineD-17
91Albuq/ProC-1149
91B-182
91Bz-6
91Classic/200-145
91Classic/II-T37
91D-33RR
91F-216
91F/Ultra-167
91Leaf/Stud-186
91MajorLg/Pins-51
91OPC-587
91OPC/Premier-90
91Pol/Dodg-30
91RedFoley/St-110
91S-343RP
91S/100RisSt-99
91S/HotRook-10
91S/Rook40-26
91Seven/3DCoin-11SC
91Seven/3DCoin-12F
91T-587
91T/90Debut-117
91T/StClub/II-340
91ToysRUs-23
91UD-356
92D/II-721
92F-467
92S/100RisSt-31
92S/II-699
92T-493
92UD-532

Office, Rowland J.
75OPC-262
75T-262
75T/M-262
76OPC-256
76SSPC-20
76T-256
77T-524
78T-632
79OPC-62
79T-132
80T-39
81D-213
81F-147
81OPC-319
81T-319
82F-198
82OkCty-2
82OPC-165
82T-479
83Colum-27

Officer, Jim
76QuadC

Ogawa, Kuni
79Vanco-15
80Holyo-8

Ogden, Charles
88CLAS/Star-33
88Kinston/Star-18
89Canton/Best-27

Ogden, John M.
33G-176

Ogden, Todd
89Canton/ProC-1322
89Canton/Star-18

Ogden, Warren
(Curly)
28Exh-58
33G-174

Ogea, Chad
90LSUPol-8

Ogier, Moe
68T-589R

Ogiwara, Mitsuru
88Miami/Star-17

Oglesbee, Mike
85Anchora-22
86Cram/PCL-29
87Ashvl-22

Oglesby, Ron
88River/Cal-232
88River/ProC-1407
89CharRain/ProC-978
90Waterlo/Best-20CO
90Waterlo/ProC-2394CO

Ogliaruso, Mike
89Myrtle/ProC-1463
90A&AASingle/ProC-90
90Myrtle/ProC-2775
90SALAS/Star-38
91Dunedin/ClBest-9
91Dunedin/ProC-205
91Single/ClBest-133

Oglivie, Benjamin A.
72T-761R
73OPC-388
73T-388
75OPC-344
75T-344
75T/M-344
76OPC-659
76SSPC-359
76T-659
77BurgChef-91
77OPC-236
77T-122
78T-286
79T-519
80T-53
81D-446
81F-508

81F/St-14
81K-20
81OPC-340
81PermaGr/CC-30
81Sqt-3
81T-2LL
81T-415
81T/SO-7
81T/St-11M
81T/St-14m
81T/St-92
82D-484
82F-151
82F/St-138
82OPC-280
82Pol/Brew-24
82T-280
82T/St-197
83D-384
83Drake-20
83F-43
83F-640M
83Gard-14
83OPC-91
83Pol/Brew-24
83T-750
83T/St-82
84D-229
84D/Champs-6
84F-210
85FunFoodPin-67
84Gard-15
84Nes/792-190
84OPC-190
84Pol/Brew-24
84T-190
84T/St-296
85D-333
85F-590
85Gard-15
85Leaf-123
85OPC-332
85Pol/Brew-24
85T-681
85T/St-292
86D-333
86F-497
86Leaf-199
86OPC-372
86Pol/Brew-24
86T-372
86T/St-200
86Woolwth-25
87D-419
87F-353
87F/RecSet-26
87F/St-85
87RedFoley/St-100
87T-586

Ogrodowski, Bruce
40Hughes-15
48Sommer-21

Ohlms, Mark
89PrWill/Star-15
89Star/Wax-92
90FtLaud/Star-16
91CLAS/ProC-CAR35
91PrWill/ClBest-8
91PrWill/ProC-1424

Ohman, Ed
89CharlR/Star-18
89Star/Wax-9

Ohnoutka, Brian
85Everett/II/Cram-13
86Shrev-20
87Shrev-12
88Phoenix/CMC-7
88Phoenix/ProC-79
90LasVegas/CMC-21
90LasVegas/ProC-119

Ohta, Katsumasa
91Salinas/ClBest-14
91Salinas/ProC-2242

Ohtsubo, Yukio
91Salinas/ClBest-16
91Salinas/ProC-2243

Ohtsuka, Kenichi
(Ken)
90Salinas/Cal-120
90Salinas/ProC-2716

Ohtsuka, Yoshiki
90Salinas/Cal-141
90Salinas/ProC-2722

Ojala, Kirt
90A&AASingle/ProC-178
90Oneonta/ProC-3380
91PrWill/ClBest-9
91PrWill/ProC-1425

Ojea, Alex
87Spring/Best-3
88Spring/Best-17

Ojeda, Bob
81Pawtu-5
82Coke/BOS
82D-540
82F-301
82T-274
83D-260
83F-190
83T-654
84D-538
84F-406
84Nes/792-162
84Nes/792-786TL
84OPC-162
84T-162
84T-786TL
85D-371
85F-166
85OPC-329
85T-477
86D-636
86F-357
86F/Up-U84
86OPC-11
86T-11
86T/Tr-81T
87Classic-73
87D-364
87D/OD-127
87F-19
87F/GameWin-32
87F/BB-30
87F/Mini-77
87F/St-86
87Leaf-94
87OPC-83
87Sf-36
87T-746
87T/Gloss60-36
87T/HL-24
87T/Mets/Fan-6
87T/Mini-25
87T/St-99
87Woolwth-24
88D-632
88D/Best-238
88D/Mets/Bk-632
88F-147
88Kahn/Mets-19
88S-563
88T-558
88T/Big-234
89B-371
89D-218
89D/Best-209
89F-47
89Kahn/Mets-19
89OPC-333
89S-116
89T-333
89UD-386
90D-117
90F-214
90Kahn/Mets-19
90OPC-207
90PublInt/St-143
90S-53
90T-207
90T/Big-131
90T/TVMets-16
90UD-204
91B-591
91D-584
91F-156
91F/UltraUp-U89
91F/Up-U95
91Leaf/II-476
91Leaf/Stud-187
91Mother/Dodg-13
91OPC-601
91OPC/Premier-91
91Pol/Dodg-17
91S-321
91S/RookTr-79T
91T-601
91T/StClub/II-449
91T/Tr-86T
91UD-179
91UD/Ext-715
91WIZMets-300
92D/I-157
92F-468
92S/II-527
92T-123
92UD-666

Ojeda, Luis
82ArkTr-16
83ArkTr-16
86Miami-19
87Miami-26

Ojeda, Ray
86Beloit-17
87Beloit-22

Oka, Yukitoshi
91Salinas/ClBest-15
91Salinas/ProC-2244

Okamoto, Yoshi
90Salinas/Cal-147OPMG

Okerlund, Ron
85Anchora-39GM

Okubo, Dave
86SanJose-16

Olah, Bob
89Clmbia/Best-7
89Clmbia/GS-19
89SALAS/GS-18

Olander, Jim
85Cram/PCL-36
86Reading-21
87Maine-1
87Maine/TCMA-18
87Phill/TastyK-38
88Maine/CMC-21
88Maine/ProC-277
89ScrWB/CMC-15
89ScrWB/ProC-723
90Tucson/CMC-17
90Tucson/ProC-216
91AAAGame/ProC-AAA11
91Denver/LineD-147
91Denver/ProC-135
92D/II-766
92S/II-839
92T-7
92T/91Debut-134

Olden, Paul
82Spokane-6

Oldham, J.C.
V100

Oldis, Robert Carl
(Bob)
53Briggs
53T-262
54T-91
55T-169
60T-361
61T-149
62T-269
63T-404
89Chatt/II/Team-22
91T/Arc53-262

Oldring, Reuben Henry
(Rube)
10Domino-94
11Helmar-58
12Sweet/Pin-49
14CJ-8
15CJ-8
16FleischBrd-71
BF2-38
D329-133
D350/2-132
E104
E286
E300
E91
M101/4-133
M101/5-132
M116
S74-34
T201
T202
T205
T206
T207
T208
T215/blue
T222

Oleksak, Mike
79Newar-8

Olerud, John
90B-510
90Classic-35
90Classic/III-96
90D-711
90D/BestAL-100
90D/Rook-2
90F/Up-U128
90Leaf/I-237
90S-589RP
90S/100Ris-39
90S/McDon-17
90S/YS/II-5
90T/89Debut-89
90T/Big-199
90T/Tr-83T
90Tor/BlueJ-9
90UD-56
91B-7
91Classic/200-116
91Classic/I-1
91Classic/II-T24
91D-530
91F-183
91F/Ultra-367
91KingB/Discs-7
91Leaf/I-125
91Leaf/Stud-136
91MajorLg/Pins-27
91OPC-168
91OPC/Premier-92
91Panini/FrSt-348
91Panini/St-159
91Post/Can-17
91S-625
91S-860FRAN
91S/100RisSt-100
91S/ToroBJ-18
91T-168
91T/StClub/II-482
91Tor/Fire-9
91ToysRUs-24
91UD-145
92D/I-98
92F-339
92S/100SS-71
92S/I-345
92T-777
92UD-375

Olin, Steve
88MidwLAS/GS-30
88Watlo/ProC-688
89AAA/CMC-42
89AAA/ProC-34
89ColoSp/ProC-252
90B-326
90D-438
90F-499
90OPC-433
90Panini/St-375
90S-590
90S/YS/II-23
90Sf-178
90T-433
90T/89Debut-90
90UD-553
91D-339
91F-374
91F/Ultra-116
91Leaf/I-94
91OPC-696
91S-496
91S/100RisSt-86
91T-696
91T/StClub/II-336
91UD-118
92D/I-151
92F-120
92S/II-644
92T-559
92UD-215

Oliva, Antonio Pedro
(Tony)
63T-228R
64T-116R
64T/S-44
65Bz-4
65MacGregor-7
65OPC-1LL
65T-1LL
65T-340
65T/trans-60
66Bz-41
66T-216LL
66T-220LL
66T-450
66T/RO-52
67Bz-41
67OPC-50
67OPC/PI-18
67T-239LL
67T-50
67T/PI-18
68Bz-9
68Coke
68Dexter-60
68OPC-165
68T-165
68T-371AS
68T-480M
69MB-205
69MLB/St-69
69MLBPA/Pin-20
69NTF
69OPC-1LL
69T-1LL
69T-427AS
69T-600
69T/decal
69T/S-20
69T/St-196
69Trans-7
70K-63
70MLB/St-235
70OPC-510
70OPC-62LL
70T-510
70T-62LL
70T/CB
70T/S-26
70Trans-13
71Bz/Test-36
71K-12
71MD
71MLB/St-468
71OPC-290
71OPC-61LL
71T-290
71T-61LL
71T/Coins-128
71T/GM-11
71T/S-11
71T/tatt-16
72K-25
72MB-258
72OPC-400
72OPC-86LL
72T-400
72T-86LL
72T/Post-7
73K-4
73OPC-80
73T-80
74OPC-190
74T-190
74T/DE-62
74T/St-210
75Ho-20
75Ho/Twink-20
75OPC-325
75T-325
75T/M-325
76Ho-10
76Ho/Twink-10
76OPC-35
76SSPC-217
76T-35
78TCMA-71
82CJ-7
83MLBPA/Pin-13
85West/2-41
86Sf/Dec-51M
88Pac/Leg-59
89Swell-12
89T-665TBC

Oliva, Jose
89Butte/SP-12
90Gaston/Best-21
90Gaston/ProC-2530
90Gaston/Star-17
91CharlR/ClBest-20
91CharlR/ProC-1324

Oliva, Steve
77QuadC

Olivares, Edward B.
(Ed)
62T-598R

Olivares, Jose
89Myrtle/ProC-1472
90Myrtle/ProC-2776

Olivares, Omar
87CharRain-13
88Charl/ProC-1210
88SALAS/GS-10
89AubAs/ProC-11
89TexLAS/GS-11
89Wichita/Rock-26
89Wichita/Rock/HL-4
89Wichita/Rock/Up-4
90Louisvl/CMC-20
90Louisvl/ProC-400
90T/TVCard-58
91D-503
91F/UltraUp-U108
91Louisvl/LineD-237
91Louisvl/ProC-2912
91OPC-271
91S-748RP
91S/Rook40-5
91T-271
91T/90Debut-118
91UD-463
92D/II-481
92F-584
92S/I-334
92T-193
92UD-478

Oliver, Albert
(Al)
69OPC-82R
69T-82R
70MLB/St-105
70OPC-166
70T-166
71MLB/St-210
71OPC-388
71T-388
72T-575
73OPC-225
73T-225
74OPC-52
74T-52
74T/St-85
75Ho-81
75K-15
75OPC-555
75T-555
75T/M-555
76Crane-43
76Ho-112
76MSA/Disc
76OPC-620
76SSPC-576
76T-620
77BurgChef-189
77Ho-45
77K-46
77OPC-203
77T-130
77T/CS-34
78BK/R-17
78OPC-97
78T-430
78Wiffle/Discs-55
79Ho-80
79OPC-204
79T-391
79T/Comics-16
80OPC-136
80T-260
81D-387
81Drake-24
81F-626
81F/St-64
81K-4
81OPC-70
81Sqt-22
81T-70
81T/HT
81T/SO-4
81T/St-131
81T/St-246
82D-116
82F-326
82F/St-178
82Hygrade
82K-61
82OPC-22IA
82OPC-326
82T-36TL
82T-590
82T-591IA
82T/St-239
82T/Tr-83T
83D-140
83D/AAS-6
83Drake-21
83F-290
83OPC-111TL
83OPC-311
83OPC-5SV
83PermaGr/AS-13
83PermaGr/CC-10
83Stuart-6
83T-111TL
83T-420
83T-421SV
83T-701LL
83T-703LL
83T/Gloss40-30
83T/St-174
83T/St-205
83T/St-206M
83T/St-251
84D-177
84D-9DK
84D/Champs-30
84Drake-24
84F-280
84F-632IA
84F/St-27
84F/X-85
84MiltBrad-18
84Nes/792-516TL
84Nes/792-620
84Nes/792-704LL
84OPC-307
84OPC-332TL
84T-516TL
84T-620
84T-704LL
84T/Gloss22-13
84T/Gloss40-21
84T/St-87
84T/St/Box-1
84T/Tr-87
85Coke/Dodg-23
85D-598
85F-262
85F/Up-U84
85Leaf-67
85OPC-130
85T-130
85T/St-118
85T/Tr-88T
86D-485
86F-69
86OPC-114
86Sf-126M
86Sf-135M
86Sf-164
86T-775
86T/St-14ALCS
86Woolwth-26
89Pac/SenLg-142
89T/SenLg-36
89TM/SenLg-83
90EliteSenLg-46
90Target-587

Oliver, Bruce
81Clinton-5

Oliver, Darren
89Gaston/ProC-1021
89Gaston/Star-17
89SALAS/GS-24
90CharlR/Star-17
91CharlR/ClBest-7
91CharlR/ProC-1311

Oliver, David Jacob
(Dave)
78T-704R
79T-705R
79Tacom-12
80Tacom-15
81Batavia-27
83TriCit-26
85OKCty-15
86OKCty-15MG
87Smok/R-30
89Smok/R-23
90Mother/Rang-27M
91Mother/Rang-28CO

Oliver, Eugene George
(Gene)
59T-135
60T-307
61T-487
62T-561
63F-62
63J-164
63P-164
63T-172
64T-316
65Kahn
65OPC-106
65T-106
66T-541
67OPC-18
67T-18
68T-449
69MB-206
69T-247
81QuadC-31C

Oliver, Harry
82Redwd-19

Oliver, Joe
84Cedar-14
87Vermont-19
88Nashvl/CMC-17
88Nashvl/ProC-483
89Nashvl/CMC-12
89Nashvl/ProC-1283
89Nashvl/Team-17
89S/Tr-104
90B-54
90CedarDG/Best-8
90Classic/III-98
90D-586
90D/BestNL-15
90F-426
90HotRook/St-33
90Kahn/Reds-19
90Leaf/II-453
90OPC-668
90Panini/St-378
90S-576
90S/100Ris-26
90S/YS/I-10
90Sf-71
90T-668
90T/89Debut-91
90T/Big-281
90UD-568
91B-671
91D-381
91F-75
91F/Ultra-99
91Kahn/Reds-9
91Leaf/I-73
91OPC-517
91Panini/FrSt-126
91Pep/Reds-14
91S-620
91T-517
91T/StClub/I-68
91UD-279
91Woolwth/HL-28
92D/I-261
92F-414
92S/I-370
92T-304
92UD-101

Oliver, Nathaniel
(Nate)
63T-466R
65OPC-59
65T-59
66T-364
68OPC-124
68T-124
69T-354
70OPC-223
70T-223
88Reno/Cal-291
89MidldA/GS-2
90PalmSp/Cal-228MG
90PalmSp/ProC-2594MG
90Target-588
91PalmSp/ProC-2033MG

Oliver, Rick
76Wmsprt
80SLCity-10

Oliver, Robert Lee
(Bob)
69T-662R
69T/St-187
70MLB/St-226
70T-567
71MLB/St-423
71OPC-470
71T-470
71T/Coins-48
71T/tatt-11
72MB-259
72OPC-57
72T-57
73OPC-289
73T-289
74OPC-243
74T-243
74T/St-143
75OPC-657
75T-657
75T/M-657
76OkCty/Team-21
79QuadC-26
91Crown/Orio-342

Oliver, Scott
82Danvl-16
83Redwd-20
85Cram/PCL-5

Oliver, Thomas
54Esskay
54T-207
R314/Can
V355-119

Oliver, Warren
82FtMyr-5

Oliveras, David
88Burllnd/ProC-1789
89Kinston/Star-16
90Kinston/Team-17

Oliveras, Francisco
81Miami-10
85CharlO-15
87CharlO/WBTV-12
88OrlanTw/Best-24
89D/Rook-9
89Portl/CMC-9
89Portl/ProC-229
90Leaf/II-515
90Portl/CMC-8
90Portl/ProC-176
90T/89Debut-92
91D-469
91OPC-52
91PG&E-24
91Phoenix/LineD-387
91Phoenix/ProC-63
91S-635
91T-52
92D/II-702
92F-645
92S/I-295
92UD-49

Oliveras, Herbie
84CharlO-27

Oliveras, Max
75Shrev/TCMA-16
86FSLAS-37CO
87MidldA-15
88MidldA/GS-1MG
89MidldA/GS-1
90Edmon/CMC-2MG
90Edmon/ProC-531MG
91AAAGame/ProC-AAA14
91Edmon/LineD-174
91Edmon/ProC-1531

Oliveras, Ossie
77Salem
78Colum
79Portl-2

Oliverio, Steve
85Cedar-10
86Vermont-14
87Vermont-14
88Nashvl/CMC-9
88Nashvl/ProC-482
88Nashvl/Team-18
89Calgary/CMC-4
89Calgary/ProC-543
89ColMud/Best-24

Olivo, Frederico
(Chi-Chi)
66T-578

Olivo, Mike
70OPC-381R
70T-381R

Olker, Joe
84Everett/Cram-4
86Fresno/Smok-12
88Shrev/ProC-1282
88TexLgAS/GS-8
89Phoenix/CMC-8
89Phoenix/ProC-1497

Ollar, Rick
78Clinton

Oller, Jeff
86Jamestn-18
87BurlEx-8
88WPalmB/Star-20
90CharlR/Star-18

Ollison, Scott
91BendB/ClBest-20
91BendB/ProC-3702

Ollom, James
67OPC-137R
67T-137R
68OPC-91
68T-91

Ollom, Mike
87Penin-9
88Tampa/Star-19
89BirmB/Best-2
89BirmB/ProC-95

Olmeda, Jose
89Idaho/ProC-2015
90Foil/Best-183
90Sumter/Best-16
90Sumter/ProC-2444
91Macon/ProC-874
91SALAS/ProC-SAL35

Olmo, Luis
90Target-589

Olmstead, Fred
T205

Olmstead, Reed
87Erie-4
87Savan-17
88Savan/ProC-346
89Spartan/ProC-1048
89Spartan/Star-19
90Foil/Best-257
90OrlanSR/Best-7
90OrlanSR/ProC-1092
90OrlanSR/Star-14
91OrlanSR/LineD-490
91OrlanSR/ProC-1860

Olmsted, Alan
80ArkTr-11
81T-244R
82Louisvl-21

Olsen, Al
86Ventura-18tr
87MidldA-9
88Edmon/ProC-584tr
89PalmSp/Cal-61tr
89PalmSp/ProC-480

Olsen, Lefty
52Mother-23

Olsen, Lew
77Jaxvl

Olsen, Rick
78Newar
79Holyo-9
80Vanco-22
81Vanco-13
82Vanco-15

Olson, Dan
89Boise/ProC-1995

Olson, Dean
77Visalia

Olson, Greg
83Lynch-8
84Jacks-xx
86Jacks/TCMA-12
87Tidew-19
87Tidew/TCMA-11
88Tidew/CANDL-6
88Tidew/CMC-13
88Tidew/ProC-1597
89Portl/CMC-13
89Portl/ProC-225
90Classic/III-19
90D/BestNL-25
90D/Rook-46
90F/Up-U5
90Leaf/II-323
90RedFoley/St-70
90S/Tr-69T
90T/Big-241
90T/Tr-84T
90USPlayC/AS-2D
91B-577
91D-285

91F-698
91F/Ultra-9
91Leaf/I-158
91OPC-673
91Panini/FrSt-18
91Panini/St-25
91Petro/SU-2
91S-56
91S/100RisSt-15
91T-673
91T/StClub/I-288
91UD-303
92D/I-386
92F-365
92S/II-474
92T-39
92UD-189

Olson, Gregg
89B-6
89Classic-132
89D-46RR
89D/Best-322
89D/Rook-35
89French-30
89S/Tr-96
89T-161FDP
89T/Tr-89T
89UD/Ext-723
90B-249
90B/Ins-7
90Bz-11
90Classic-3
90CollAB-32
90D-377
90D/BestAL-43
90D/Learning-27
90F-184
90F/AwardWin-24
90F/LL-28
90HagersDG/Best-19
90Holsum/Discs-20
90HotRook/St-34
90KingB/Discs-23
90Leaf/I-7
90MLBPA/Pins-114
90OPC-655
90Panini/St-2
90PublInt/St-581
90S-63
90S/100Ris-32
90S/YS/I-4
90Sf-215
90T-655
90T/89Debut-93
90T/Coins-3
90T/DH-48
90T/Gloss60-29
90T/HeadsUp-10
90T/JumboR-22
90T/St-10HL
90T/St-238
90T/TVAS-30
90ToysRUs-21
90UD-604
90USPlayC/AS-4C
90Woolwth/HL-5ROY
91B-92
91BBBest/Aces-13
91Classic/III-70
91Crown/Orio-343
91D-111
91D-23DK
91D-393MVP
91D/SuperDK-23
91F-486
91F/Ultra-21
91Leaf/II-519
91Leaf/Stud-8
91OPC-10
91OPC/Premier-93
91Panini/FrSt-248
91Panini/St-193
91Panini/Top15-88
91RedFoley/St-69
91S-490
91S/100SS-27
91Seven/3DCoin-10A
91T-10
91T/CJMini/II-22
91T/StClub/I-156
91UD-326
91UD-47
92D/I-110
92F-21
92F-701M
92S/100SS-91
92S/I-427NH
92S/I-71
92T-350
92UD-227

Olson, Ivan M.
(Ollie)
21Exh-120
90Target-590
E120
E220
T207
V100
W514-70

Olson, James Vincent
87BurlEx-2

Olson, Jimmy
86AubAs-18
87Ashvl-9

Olson, Karl Arthur
(Karl)
52T-72
54T-186
55T-72
55T/DH-35
56T-322
57T-153

Olson, Ken
91Salinas/ProC-2240

Olson, Kurt
88CapeCod/Sum-47
90Yakima/Team-6

Olson, Mike
81CharR-4

Olson, Warren
86Beloit-18
88WinHaven/Star-17

Olsson, Dan
86Tulsa-19

Olszta, Ed
75AppFx
77AppFx

Olwine, Ed
83Nashvl-13
84Tidew-11
85Tidew-12
86Richm-14
87D-560
87F-524
87Smok/Atl-6
87T-159
88S-379
88T-353
89Omaha/CMC-8
89Omaha/ProC-1725
89UD-435
90Richm/Bob-1
90Richm/CMC-6
90Richm/ProC-257
90Richm/Team-25

Omachi, George
88Fresno/ProC-1246

Omo, Bob
78Cedar

Ongarato, Mike
81Pawtu-21

Onichuk, Sergei
89EastLDD/ProC-DD11

Onis, Curly
90Target-1045

Ontiveros, Steve
(Steve)
83Albany-7
84Cram/PCL-83
86D-589
86F-429
86Mother/A's-22
86T-507
87D-221
87D/HL-15
87F-401
87T-161
88D-467
88D/A's/Bk-467
88F-289
88Mother/A's-13
88S-511
88T-272
89D-596
89D/Tr-11
89Phill/TastyK-26
89S-337
89T-692
89T/SenLg-79
89T/Tr-90T
90AlbanyDG/Best-7
90B-145
90EliteSenLg-117
91S-832

Ontiveros, Steven R.
(Steve)
74OPC-598R
74T-598R
75OPC-483
75T-483
75T/M-483
76OPC-284
76SSPC-104
76T-284
78K-44
78T-76
79OPC-150
79T-299
80OPC-268
80T-514

Opdyke, Paul
88Idaho/ProC-1854

Opie, James
83AlexD-6
85Cram/PCL-226
86Nashua-20
87Jaxvl-13

Oppenheimer, Jose
77BurlB

Oppenheimer, Juan
78Cedar

Opperman, Dan
88GreatF-10
89VeroB/Star-20
91Albuq/ProC-1140
91B-606
91Classic/II-T83
91F/Ultra-384MLP

Oquendo, Ismael
84RochR-8

Oquendo, Jorge
82Idaho-27

Oquendo, Jose Manuel
(Jose)
82Tidew-15
83Tidew-29
84D-643
84F-592
84Nes/792-208
84OPC-208
84T-208
84T/St-112
85F-88
85Louisvl-15
85T-598
86Schnucks-17
86T/Tr-82T
87D-510
87F-305
87Smok/Cards-18
87T-133
88D-234
88D/Best-313
88F-44
88S-248
88Smok/Card-16
88T-83
88T/St-18
89B-438
89Bimbo/Discs-5
89D-319
89D/Best-100
89F-459
89OPC-69
89Panini/St-184
89S-529
89S/YS/II-16
89Smok/Cards-15
89T-442
89T/Big-77
89T/St-45
89Tetley/Discs-19
89UD-514
90B-200
90D-161
90D/BestNL-108
90F-255
90Leaf/I-129
90MLBPA/Pins-59
90OPC-645
90Panini/St-341
90PublInt/St-223
90S-68
90Sf-85
90Smok/Card-17
90T-645
90T/Big-65
90T/St-44
90T/TVCard-27
90UD-319
91B-395
91D-281
91F-640
91F/Ultra-292
91Leaf/I-58
91Leaf/Stud-236
91OPC-343
91Panini/FrSt-32
91Panini/St-30
91Pol/Card-11
91S-622
91T-343
91T/StClub/I-190
91UD-193
91WIZMets-301
92D/I-280
92F-585
92S/I-305
92T-723
92UD-283

Oquist, Mike
89Erie/Star-16
90CLAS/CL-2
90Freder/Team-22
91Hagers/LineD-241
91Hagers/ProC-2455
91Single/ClBest-188

Oravetz, Ernest E.
(Ernie)
56T-51
57T-179
89Chatt/II/Team-23

Orengo, Joseph C.
(Joe)
41DP-29
47Sunbeam
90Target-592

Orensky, Herb
80Penin/B-23
80Penin/C-15
82OkCty-20

Orhan, Hugh
47Sunbeam

Orman, Richard
90MedHat/Best-7

Oropeza, Clemente
82Idaho-20

Oropeza, Dave
89Rockford/Team-19

Orosco, Jesse
79Tidew-23
80T-681R
81Tidew-20
82D-646
83D-434
83F-550
83T-369
84D-197
84F-593
84F/St-60
84Jacks/Smok-9
84Nes/792-396AS
84Nes/792-54
84OPC-396AS
84OPC-54
84T-396AS
84T-54
84T/Gloss40-33
84T/Mets/Fan-5
84T/St-104
85D-22DK
85D-75
85D/DKsuper-22
85F-89
85F/St-106
85Leaf-22DK
85OPC-250
85T-250
85T/Gloss40-2
85T/St-101
85T/Super-54
85ThomMc/Discs-37
86D-646
86F-90
86OPC-182
86T-465
87Classic-75
87D-439
87F-20
87F/Mini-78
87F/RecSet-27
87F/St-87
87Leaf-175
87OPC-148
87RedFoley/St-84
87Sf-76
87T-704
88D-192
88D/Best-234
88F-148
88F/Up-U96
88Mother/Dodg-13
88Pol/Dodg-47
88S-495
88S/Tr-64T
88Sf-89
88T-105
88T/Tr-77T
89B-81
89D-228
89D/Tr-26
89F-68
89S-356
89T-513
89T/Tr-91T
89UD-87
90D-154
90F-500
90Leaf/I-101
90OPC-636
90PublInt/St-566
90S-353
90T-636
90Target-593
90UD-588
91B-72
91D-171
91F-375
91OPC-346
91S-578
91T-346
91T/StClub/II-322
91UD-240
91WIZMets-302
92D/II-473
92F-121
92S/II-547
92T-79
92UD-580

Oroz, Felix Andres
81VeroB-13
84Cram/PCL-233

Orphal, John
47Centen-18

Orr, David L.
N172
N172/SP
N284
N338/2
N690

Orr, Geoff
90Idaho/ProC-3252
91Macon/ClBest-22
91Macon/ProC-875

Orr, William
T222

Orsag, Jim
86Greens-15
87WinHaven-28
88CLAS/Star-13
88Lynch/Star-16
89NewBrit/ProC-610
89NewBrit/Star-12
90Canton/Best-9
90Foil/Best-269

Orsatti, Ernesto R.
(Ernie)
33G-201
35G-1A
35G-2A
35G-6A
35G-7A
92Conlon/Sport-650

Orsino, John Joseph
(Johnny)
61Union

62T-377
63T-418
64T-63
64T/Coins-3
65T-303
65T/E-51
66OPC-77
66T-77
66T/RO-09
67T-207
91Crown/Orio-344

Orsulak, Joe
82AlexD-22
85F/Up-U85
85T/Tr-89T
86D-444
86F-615
86F/LL-29
86F/Mini-118
86F/St-83
86Leaf-218
86Sf-177M
86T-102
86T/St-132
87D-291
87F-615
87F/RecSet-28
87T-414
87T/St-132
88D/Best-310
88F/Up-U2
88French-6
88S/Tr-41T
88T/Tr-78T
89D-287
89D/Best-310
89F-614
89French-6
89Panini/St-263
89S-247
89T-727
89T/Big-181
89UD-429
90B-252
90Classic/III-50
90D-287
90D/BestAL-129
90F-185
90Leaf/II-355
90OPC-212
90Panini/St-5
90PublInt/St-582
90S-41
90Sf-38
90T-212
90T/Big-318
90T/St-234
90UD-270
91B-84
91Crown/Orio-345
91D-654
91F-487
91F/Ultra-22
91Leaf/I-152
91OPC-521
91Panini/FrSt-246
91Panini/St-200
91RedFoley/St-70
91S-508
91S/100SS-8
91T-521
91T/StClub/I-191
91UD-506
92D/II-475
92F-22
92S/II-551
92T-325
92UD-207

Orta, Jorge Nunez
(Jorge)
73OPC-194
73T-194
74OPC-376
74T-376
74T/St-159
75Ho-122
75Ho/Twink-122
75K-14
75OPC-184
75T-184
75T/M-184
76Ho-57
76Ho/Twink-57
76K-45
76OPC-560
76SSPC-144
76T-560
77BurgChef-74
77T-109
78Ho-105
78OPC-77
78T-42
78Wiffle/Discs-56
79Ho-126
79OPC-333
79T-631
80T-442
81D-439
81F-388
81OPC-222
81T-222
82D-211
82F-376
82OPC-26
82Pol/Dodg-31
82T-26
82T/St-175
82T/Tr-84T
83D-388
83F-215
83T-722
83T/Tr-82T
84D-317
84F-166
84F/X-U86
84Nes/792-312
84OPC-312
84T-312
84T/Tr-88T
85D-130
85F-209
85Leaf-226
85T-164
85T/St-273
86D-339
86F-17
86Kitty/Disc-6
86Leaf-205
86NatPhoto-3
86OPC-44
86T-541
87D-348
87F-376
87OPC-63
87T-738
90Target-595

Ortega, Dan
81AppFx-7

Ortega, Eduardo
89Batavia/ProC-1939
90Spartan/Best-17
90Spartan/ProC-2499
90Spartan/Star-16
91SLCity/ProC-3219

Ortega, Hector
90Gate/ProC-3341
91Sumter/ClBest-17
91Sumter/ProC-2342

Ortega, Kirk
81Clinton-16

Ortega, Phil
59DF
62T-69
63T-467
64T-291
65OPC-152
65T-152
66T-416
66T/RO-32
67T-493
68T-595
69MB-207
69T-406
90Target-596

Ortegon, Ronnie
89PalmSp/Cal-35
89PalmSp/ProC-478

Orteig, Ray
48Sommer-25
52Mother-50
53Mother-31

Orth, Albert Lewis
(Al)
E107
E254
T206

Ortiz, Adalberto Jr.
(Junior)
77Charl
78Charl
80Buffa
81Portl-19
82Portl-11
84D-319
84F-594
84Nes/792-161
84T-161
84T/St-114
85T-439
85ThomMc/Discs-38
86D-508
86T-682
87D-449
87D/OD-164
87F-616
87T-583
88D-168
88F-335
88S-404
88T-274
89AAA/ProC-46
89D-387
89D/Best-269
89F-215
89S-402
89T-769
89T/Big-66
89UD-86
89VFJuice-0
90F-475
90F/Up-108
90OPC-322
90PublInt/St-160
90S-143
90S/Tr-66T
90T-322
90T/Tr-85T
90UD-389
91B-328
91D-659
91F-622
91F/Ultra-194
91Leaf/II-498
91OPC-72
91S-438
91T-72
91T/StClub/I-13
91UD-170
91WIZMets-303
92D/II-684
92F-215
92S/II-473
92T-617
92UD-109

Ortiz, Alfredo
86Ventura-19CO
89Johnson/Star-25CO

Ortiz, Andy
83Watlo/LF-5
84BuffB-15

Ortiz, Angel
88Watlo/ProC-667
89Kinston/Star-17

Ortiz, Basilio
91Bluefld/ProC-4140
91Bluefld/ClBest-9

Ortiz, Darrell
80Tulsa-23

Ortiz, Hector Jr.
89Salem/Team-20
89VeroB/Star-21
90Yakima/Team-11
91VeroB/ClBest-16
91VeroB/ProC-777

Ortiz, Javier
84Tulsa-31
85Tulsa-31
86Tulsa-17
87OKCty-15
88SanAn/Best-22
89Albuq/CMC-25
89Albuq/ProC-84
90F/Up-U16
90Tucson/CMC-15
90Tucson/ProC-217
91B-562
91D-643
91T/90Debut-119
91Tucson/LineD-617
91Tucson/ProC-2226
92D/II-551
92S/I-403
92T-362
92UD-657

Ortiz, Joe
88Ashvl/ProC-1066
88CalLgAS-22
88Reno/Cal-285
89Beloit/I/Star-20
89Osceola/Star-15
90ColMud/Star-18
90Modesto/Cal-158
90Modesto/ProC-2216

Ortiz, Jorge
81Wisco-7

Ortiz, Lou
55T-114
55T/DH-91
D301

Ortiz, Miguel
80Utica-21

Ortiz, Ramon
89BurlInd/Star-19
90BurlInd/ProC-3022

Ortiz, Ray
90A&AASingle/ProC-153
90Visalia/Cal-70
90Visalia/ProC-2169
91OrlanSR/LineD-491
91OrlanSR/ProC-1863

Ortman, Doug
87Madis-9

Orton, John
85Anchora-23
88PalmSp/Cal-107
88PalmSp/ProC-1433
89MidldA/GS-25
90B-298
90Classic/III-61
90D/Rook-54
90F-647
90F/Up-U79
90Leaf/II-511
90S-582
90S/100Ris-64
90S/YS/II-30
90Sf-132
90T/89Debut-94
90UD-672
91D-714
91F-320
91Leaf/I-191
91OPC-176
91S-467
91Smok/Angel-20
91T-176
91T/StClub/II-591
92F-65
92S/II-712

Oruna, Roland
82CharR-17
83CharR-11

Osaka, Rocky
87SanJose-7

Osborn, Dan
76OPC-282
76SSPC-135
76T-282

Osborn, Don
47Signal
74OPC-489CO
74T-489CO

Osborn, Pat
No Cards.

Osborn, Wilfred
E254

Osborne, Donovan
90Classic/DP-13
90Hamil/Best-1
91ArkTr/LineD-40
91ArkTr/ProC-1283
91B-406
91S-677FDP
91Single/ClBest-27

Osborne, Jeff
89Augusta/ProC-494
89SALAS/GS-46
90Harris/ProC-1200
90Harris/Star-13

Osborne, Lawrence S.
(Bobo)
59T-524
60T-201
61T-208
62T-583
63T-514

Osborne, Tiny
90Target-1046

Osik, Keith
90LSUPol-5
91Salem/ClBest-2
91Salem/ProC-956

Osinski, Dan
63T-114
64T-537
65OPC-223
65T-223
66OPC-168
66T-168
67T-594
68T-331
69T-622

Osinski, Glenn
90Madison/Best-8
90SoOreg/Best-28
91Modesto/ClBest-10
91Modesto/ProC-3098

Osmon, Scott
89Idaho/ProC-2032

Osofsky, Alvin
75Dubuq

Osowski, Tom
83Butte-33
84Butte-6
85Everett/Cram-12
86PalmS/Smk-1GM

Osteen, Claude
59T-224
60T-206
62T-501
63J-100
63P-100
63T-374
64T-28
64T/Coins-13
64T/St-74
64T/SU
64T/tatt
65MacGregor-8
65T-570
66T-270
67T-330
68OPC-9LL
68T-440
68T-9LL
68T/G-12
69MB-208
69MLB/St-150
69T-528
69T/St-47
70MLB/St-54
70OPC-260
70T-260
70T/S-1
70T/SO
71Bz
71Bz/Test-39
71K-70
71MD
71MLB/St-110
71OPC-10
71T-10
71T/Coins-45
71T/S-27
71Ticket/Dodg-12
72K-34
72MB-260
72OPC-297
72OPC-298IA
72T-297
72T-298IA
73K-49
73OPC-490
73T-490
74OPC-42
74T-42
74T/DE-38
74T/St-48
74T/Tr-42T
75OPC-453
75T-453
75T/M-453
76OPC-488
76T-488
78TCMA-273
84Phill/TastyK-12CO

85Phill/TastyK-5CO
85Phill/TastyK-8CO
86Phill/TastyK-3CO
87Phill/TastyK-x
87Smok/Dodg-25
88Phill/TastyK-29
89Pac/Leg-132
89Smok/Dodg-73
89SanAn/Best-26
89Swell-17
90Albuq/CMC-28CO
90Albuq/ProC-363CO
90Albuq/Trib-25CO
90Target-597
91Albuq/LineD-25CO
91Albuq/ProC-1159CO

Osteen, Dave
87StPete-1
88ArkTr/GS-23
89ArkTr/GS-15
89TexLAS/GS-23
90Louisvl/CMC-7
90Louisvl/ProC-401
91Louisvl/LineD-242
91Louisvl/ProC-2913

Osteen, Gavin
89Medford/Best-29
90Madison/Best-21
90Madison/ProC-2268
91Huntsvl/ClBest-16
91Huntsvl/LineD-290
91HuntsvlProC-1792

Osteen, M. Darrell
66T-424R
67T-222R
68T-199R

Oster, Dave
88Geneva/ProC-1659

Oster, Paul
89Oneonta/ProC-2127
90PrWill/Team-18
91PrWill/ClBest-21
91PrWill/ProC-1439

Ostermeyer, Bill
91CharRain/ProC-105
91SALAS/ProC-SAL5
91Single/ClBest-196

Ostermueller, Fred
(Fritz)
34DS-73
34G-93
35G-8G
35G-9G
39PB-22
40PB-33
41G-12
47TipTop
49B-227
90Target-598
91Conlon/Sport-99
R314
W753

Ostopowicz, Rich
89Kingspt/Star-18

Ostrosser, Brian L.
(Brian)
75OkCty
91WIZMets-304

Ostrowski, Joe P.
49Royal-20
52BR
52Mother-2
52T-206

Ostrowski, John T.
(John)
47Signal

Osuna, Al
87AubAs-22
88Osceola/Star-20
89Osceola/Star-16
90A&AASingle/ProC-43
90ColMud/Best-19
90ColMud/ProC-1344
90ColMud/Star-19
90Foil/Best-312
91D/Rook-52
91Leaf/II-492
91Mother/Ast-20
91OPC-149
91S/RookTr-89T
91T-149
91T/90Debut-120
91UD/Ext-752
92D/I-318
92F-442
92S/100RisSt-83
92S/II-452
92T-614
92UD-259

Osuna, Antonio
91Kissim/ProC-4181

Otero, Regino J.
(Reggie)
47Signal
60T-459C
63FrBauer-15

Otero, Ricky
91Kingspt/ClBest-8
91Kingspt/ProC-3826

Otey, William
T206

Otis, Amos Joseph
(Amos)
69OPC-31R
69T-31R
70OPC-354
70T-354
71Bz
71Bz/Test-42
71K-38
71MLB/St-424
71OPC-610
71T-610
71T/Coins-96
71T/S-45
71T/tatt-4
72K-2
72OPC-10
72T-10
72T/Post-6
73K-1
73OPC-510
73T-510
73T/Lids-37
74Greyhound-5M
74K-17
74OPC-337AS
74OPC-65
74T-337AS
74T-65
74T/DE-1
74T/St-185
75Ho-50
75OPC-520
75T-520
75T/M-520
76A&P/KC
76Ho-51
76Ho/Twink-51
76OPC-198LL
76OPC-510
76SSPC-177
76T-198LL
76T-510
77BurgChef-65
77Ho-92
77OPC-141
77Pep-33
77T-290
78OPC-16
78T-490
79Ho-132
79OPC-185
79T-360
80OPC-72
80T-135
80T/S-50
81Coke
81D-104
81F-32
81F-483
81F/St-28
81OPC-288
81Pol/Royals-7
81T-585
82D-70
82F-419
82F/St-211
82OPC-162
82OPC-350IA
82T-725
82T-726IA
82T/St-194
83D-364
83F-120
83OPC-75
83Pol/Royals-5
83T-75
83T/St-72
84F-351
84F/X-U87
84Nes/792-655
84OPC-53
84T-655
84T/Tr-89T
88Smok/Padres-21
89Pac/SenLg-83
89T/SenLg-81
89Tidew/Candl-4
89TM/SenLg-84
90EliteSenLg-74
90Padre/MagUno-22CO
91Pac/SenLg-26
91WIZMets-305

Otis, David
86Madis-17

Ott, Melvin Thomas
(Mel)
29Exh/4-9
31Exh/4-10
33G-127
33G-207
34DS-50
34Exh/4-5
35BU-27
35Exh/4-5
35G-2A
35G-7A
35Wheat
36Exh/4-5
36Wheat
37Exh/4-5
38Exh/4-5
38ONG/Pin-22
39Exh
39PB-51
39Wheat
40PB-88
40Wheat
41DP-31
41DP-89
41G-33
41PB-8
43MP-19
50Callahan
52Mother-53
60Exh/HOF-18
60F-36
60NuCard-58
61F-68
61GP-1
61NuCard-458
63Bz-36
69Bz/Sm
72F/FFeat-25
73F/Wild-17
80Pac/Leg-35
80Laugh/3/4/5-12
80Laugh/FFeat-14
80SSPC/HOF
83D/HOF-40
85CircK-12
86BLChew-11
86Conlon/1-36
86Sf/Dec-8
88Conlon/4-21
89HOF/St-49
89Pac/Leg-189
90Swell/Great-55
91Conlon/Sport-225
91Conlon/Sport-7
91Swell/Great-144
R300
R302
R309/2
R310
R316
R326-3A
R326-3B
R342-3
R346-18
WG8-44

Ott, Nathan Edward
(Ed)
76OPC-594R
76T-594
77T-197
78OPC-161
78T-28
79Ho-31
79OPC-289
79T-561
80OPC-200
80T-383
81Coke
81D-133
81F-365
81OPC-246
81T-246
81T/St-214
81T/Tr-810
82D-192
82F-470
82OPC-225
82T-469
83F-98
83T-131
84Cram/PCL-120CO
85PrWill-23
86Watertn-16MG
91Mother/Ast-28CO

Ott, William
65T-354R

Otten, Brian
86Geneva-21
87Peoria-15
88WinSalem/Star-13

Otten, Jim
75OPC-624R
75T-624R
75T/M-624R
77T-493R

Otto, Dave
86Madis/Pol-16
88F-652R
89S/HotRook-60
89T-131
89Tacoma/CMC-10
89Tacoma/ProC-1547
89UD-4SR
90B-448
90S/Tr-101T
90Tacoma/CMC-7
90Tacoma/ProC-89
91ColoSp/LineD-93
91ColoSp/ProC-2180
91F-20
92D/II-730
92T-499
92UD-698

Otto, Steve
88Eugene/Best-4
89AppFx/ProC-876
90BBCity/Star-17

Ouellette, Phil
82Clinton-5
84Cram/PCL-1
85Cram/PCL-182
86Phoenix-19
88AAA/ProC-7
88Calgary/CMC-12
88Calgary/ProC-801
90Toledo/CMC-13
90Toledo/ProC-153

Outen, Chink
90Target-1049

Outlaw, James Paulus
(Jimmy)
39PB-155
47TipTop

Overall, Orval
12Sweet/Pin-86
E254
E90/1
E90/3
E91
M116
S74-66
T202
T205
T206
T3-32
WG3-35

Overeem, Steve
88James/ProC-1914

Overholser, Drew
91Spokane/ClBest-14
91Spokane/ProC-3947

Overmire, Frank
(Stubby)
47TipTop
48L-17
51B-280
52T-155

Overton, Jeff
82AppFx-2

Overton, Mike
79Newar-5

Overy, Mike
77SLCity
77T-489R
78Cr/PCL-108
79SLCity-9
80SLCity-26

Owchinko, Bob
77Padre/SchCd-21
78Padre/FamFun-20
78T-164
79OPC-257
79T-488
80OPC-44
80T-79
81D-563
81T-536
81T/Tr-811
82D-287
82F-104
82T-243
83D-265
83F-531
83T-338
84F/X-U88
85Cram/PCL-144
85D-506
85F-543
85T-752
86Indianap-9
91Pac/SenLg-83

Owen, Arnold Malcolm
(Mickey)
38G-263
38G-287
39PB-135
40PB-111
41DP-15
50B-78
51B-174
60NuCard-15
61NuCard-475
89Rini/Dodg-32
89Smok/Dodg-44
90Target-599

Owen, Billy
WG2-38

Owen, Dave
83Iowa-18
84Iowa-18
84SevenUp-19
85D-483
85Iowa-6
85T-642
86OKCty-16
87OKCty-3
88Omaha/CMC-16
88Omaha/ProC-1510
89Iowa/CMC-19
89Iowa/ProC-1694
89Lynch/Star-16
90A&AASingle/ProC-7
90NewBrit/Best-18
90NewBrit/Star-13
91B-110

Owen, Frank Malcomb
T206

Owen, Lawrence T.
(Larry)
79Richm-5
82Richm-11
82T-502R
83Pol/Atl-24
84Richm-8
85IntLgAS-9
85Richm-12
86Richm-15
88Omaha/CMC-18
88Omaha/ProC-1516
88S-230
89T-87
89UD-528
90Richm25Ann/Team-18

Owen, Marvin James
(Marv)
34DS-67
35BU-168
R314
V355-69

Owen, Spike D.

83SLCity-23
84D-313
84F-616
84Mother/Mar-6
84Nes/792-413
84T-413
84T/St-349
85D-435
85D/AAS-4
85F-497
85Leaf-167
85Mother/Mar-7
85T-84
85T/St-339
86D-362
86F-471
86Mother/Mar-20
86OPC-248
86T-248
86T/St-224
87D-633
87D/OD-185
87F-40
87Leaf-87
87T-591
88D-544
88D/RedSox/Bk-544
88F-359
88OPC-188
88Panini/St-30
88S-372
88T-21TL
88T-733
89B-363
89D-593
89D/Best-236
89D/Tr-14
89F-93
89F/Up-98
89S-218
89S/Tr-13
89T-123
89T/Big-221
89T/Tr-92T
89UD-161
89UD/Ext-717
90B-116
90D-102
90D/BestNL-6
90F-357
90Leaf/I-186
90OPC-674
90Panini/St-285
90PublInt/St-184
90S-247
90T-674
90T/Big-25
90T/St-73
90UD-291
91B-454
91D-251
91F-243
91F/Ultra-208
91Leaf/I-36
91OPC-372
91Panini/FrSt-142
91Panini/St-62
91S-452
91T-372
91T/StClub/I-236
91UD-189
92D/II-518
92F-488
92S/I-323
92T-443
92UD-206

Owen, Tim
85BurlR-14
86DayBe-20

Owen, Tommy
90Idaho/ProC-3248
91James/ClBest-13
91James/ProC-3549

Owens, Frank Walter
(Frank)
14CJ-74
15CJ-74
E254

Owens, Jay
90Foil/Best-224

Owens, Jim
55T-202
55T/DH-122
56T-114
59T-503
60L-39
60T-185
61P-116
61T-341
62T-212
63FrBauer-17
63T-483
64T-241
65T-451
66T-297
67T-582
73OPC-624CO
73T-624CO

Owens, Larry
88CapeCod/Sum-52
90Pulaski/Best-7
90Pulaski/ProC-3102

Owens, Markus
(Mark)
87Everett-30
88Clinton/ProC-704
88MidwLAS/GS-1
89Shrev/ProC-1849
90Shrev/ProC-1446
90Shrev/Star-17

Owens, Marty
88Geneva/ProC-1658

Owens, Michael
88Batavia/ProC-1675
89Batavia/ProC-1930
90Batavia/ProC-3074
91Spartan/ClBest-10
91Spartan/ProC-895

Owens, Paul
84F-643IA
84F/St-123MG
84Nes/792-229MG
84Phill/TastyK-8MG
84T-229MG
85T-92MG
85T/Gloss22-1MG

Owens, Steve
88CharWh/Best-8

Owens, Tom
79Wausau-25
81Watlo-12
82Chatt-9
83BuffB-6

Ownbey, Rick
82Tidew-1
83F-551
83T-739
84Louisvl-23
85Louisvl-26
86F/Up-U85
86Schnucks-18
91WIZMets-306

Oxner, Stan
83Butte-15

Oyler, Raymond F.
(Ray)
65OPC-259R
65T-259R
66OPC-81
66T-81
67T-352
68T-399
69MB-209
69MLB/St-97
69OPC-178
69T-178
69T/St-228
70MLB/St-264
70T-603
72MB-261
81Detroit-30
88Domino-18

Oyster, Jeff
87ArkTr-18
88ArkTr/GS-24
88Louisvl-38
89ArkTr/GS-16
90SpringDG/Best-11

Ozario, Claudio
91Sumter/ClBest-18
91Sumter/ProC-2343

Ozark, Danny
73OPC-486MG
73T-486MG
74OPC-119MG
74T-119MG
75OPC-46MG
75T-46MG
75T/M-46MG
76SSPC-476MG
76T-384MG
77T-467MG
78BK/P-1MG
78T-631MG
79T-112MG
85T-365MG

Ozawa, Kouichi
89Visalia/Cal-114
89Visalia/ProC-1422

Ozuna, Gabriel
89SALAS/GS-37
89Savan/ProC-345
91ArkTr/LineD-41
91ArkTr/ProC-1284

Ozuna, Mateo
89Savan/ProC-359
90Savan/ProC-2077
91Single/ClBest-244
91Spring/ClBest-21
91Spring/ProC-749

Pace, Jim
88Reno/Cal-288

Pace, Tubby
85Cedar-23

Pacella, John
78Tidew
79Tidew-2
81Colum-22
81T-414
82Colum-1
82Colum/Pol-17
83D-130
83F-622
83T-166
87Toledo-8
87Toledo/TCMA-14
91Crown/Orio-346
91WIZMets-307

Pacheco, Al
89Johnson/Star-17
90Savan/ProC-2067

Pacheco, Alex
90Welland/Pucko-24

Pacheco, Tony
74OPC-521CO
74T-521CO

Pacheo, Jose
91Hunting/ClBest-16
91Hunting/ProC-3332

Pacho, Juan
81Watlo-24
83Charl-11
89Greenvl/ProC-1155
89Greenvl/Star-16
89Greenvl/Best-8

Pacholec, Joe
87Watertn-23
88Augusta/ProC-373
89Salem/Star-16

Pacillo, Pat
85T-402OLY
87Kahn-35
87Nashvl-16
87T/Tr-93T
88D-536
88Nashvl/CMC-10
88Nashvl/ProC-472
88T-288
89Indianap/CMC-4
89Indianap/ProC-1236
90Calgary/CMC-1
90Calgary/ProC-649

Paciorek, Jim
83ElPaso-4
85Cram/PCL-213
86Vanco-20
87F/Up-U95
87Pol/Brew-14
90ElPasoATG/Team-11

Paciorek, Thomas M.
(Tom)
71OPC-709R
71T-709R
73OPC-606R
73T-606R
74OPC-127
74T-127
75OPC-523
75T-523
75T/M-523
76OPC-641
76SSPC-88
76T-641
77BurgChef-215
77T-48
78T-322
79OPC-65
79T-141
80T-481
81D-408
81F-614
81OPC-228
81Pol/Sea-11
81T-228
81T/SO-23
81T/St-124
82D-253
82F-514
82F/St-224
82OPC-371
82T-336TL
82T-678
82T/St-236
82T/Tr-85T
83D-243
83F-248
83OPC-72
83T-72
83T/St-47
83TrueVal/WSox-44
84D-282
84F-70
84Nes/792-777
84OPC-132
84T-777
84T/St-246
84TrueVal/WS-25
85Coke/WS-44
85D-488
85F-523
85OPC-381
85SpokAT/Cram-15
85T-572
86F-91
86F/Up-U86
86Rang-44
86T-362
86T/Tr-83T
87F-133
87Mother/Rang-8
87OPC-21
87Smok/R-14
87T-729
88S-531
89Pac/SenLg-204
89T/SenLg-107
89TM/SenLg-85
90EliteSenLg-60
90Pac/Legend-97
90Target-600
91WIZMets-308

Packard, Eugene
14CJ-142
15CJ-142

Packer, Bill
83Erie-6
84Savan-17

Pactwa, Joe
76OPC-589R
76T-589

Padden, Richard J.
(Dick)
E107

Padden, Thomas F.
(Tom)
35G-8K
35G-9K
92Conlon/Sport-607
R313
R314

Paddy, Marco
88Idaho/ProC-1835

Padget, Chris
86SLAS-7
87RochR-6
87RochR/TCMA-12
88RochR/Team-18
88RochR/CMC-13
88RochR/Gov-20
88RochR/ProC-204
89RochR/CMC-14
89RochR/ProC-1644
90RochR/CMC-17
90RochR/ProC-716

Padgett, Don W.
(Don)
39PB-157
40PB-109
49Remar
50Remar
90Target-601
W754

Padgett, Ernest
(Ernie)
21Exh-124
91Conlon/Sport-206

Padia, Steve
83Cedar-12
83Cedar/LF-25
86Orlan-14

Padilla, Freddy
88Bristol/ProC-1873
89Fayette/ProC-1595

Padilla, Livio
87WinHaven-3
88FSLAS/Star-46
88WinHaven/Star-18
89NewBrit/ProC-620
89NewBrit/Star-13

Padilla, Paul
79Albuq-23tr
80Albuq-24tr

Padula, Jim
78Newar
79BurlB-23

Paepke, Dennis Rae
(Dennis)
70T-552R

Pafko, Andrew
(Andy)
39Exh
47HomogBond-36
47TipTop
48L-125
49B-63
49Eureka-66
49MP-108
49Royal-6
50B-60
51B-103
51FB
51T/BB-27
52B-204
52Royal
52T-1
52TipTop
53B/BW-57
53JC-24
53SpicSpan/3x5-19
53SpicSpan/7x10-11
54B-112
54JC-48
54RM-NL8
54SpicSpan/PostC-16
54T-79
54Wilson
55B-12
55Gol/Braves-24
55JC-48
55SpicSpan/DC-15
56T-312
57SpicSpan/4x5-14
57T-143
58T-223
59T-27
60Lake
60SpicSpan-16CO
60T-464C
79TCMA-181
89Pac/Leg-123
89Rini/Dodg-16
89Swell-74
90Target-602
D305
Exh47
PM10/Sm-138
R423-82
RM53-NL9

Pagan, Dave
74Syrac/Team-21
75IntAS/TCMA-9
75OPC-648
75T-648
75T/M-648
76SSPC-432
77Ho-132

77OPC-151
77T-508
77T/CS-35
78Colum
91Crown/Orio-347
Pagan, Felix
83Idaho-23
Pagan, Jose Antonio
(Jose)
60T-67
61T-279
62J-132
62P-132
62P/Can-132
62Salada-200
62Shirriff-200
62T-565
63J-103
63P-103
63T-545
64T-123
65T-575
66EH-11
66OPC-54
66T-54
67T-322
67T/Test/PP-18
68KDKA-11
68T-482
69MB-210
69OPC-192
69T-192
70T-643
71MLB/St-211
71OPC-282
71T-282
72MB-262
72T-701
72T-702IA
73OPC-659
73T-659
78TCMA-102
79Ogden/TCMA-6
80Ogden-23
Page, Greg
90Salinas/Cal-126
90Salinas/ProC-2714
Page, Joe
47TipTop
48B-29
49B-82
50B-12
50Drake-27
51B-217
51BR-C5
51FB
51T/BB-10
52T-48
79TCMA-197
Exh47
PM10/Sm-139
Page, Kelvin
85LitFalls-7
Page, Marc J.
82Wisco-24
Page, Mike
85BurlR-2
Page, Mitchell Otis
(Mitchell)
75Shrev/TCMA-17
78Ho-38
78K-47
78OPC-75
78PapaG/Disc-39
78T-55
79Ho-17
79OPC-147
79T-295
79T/Comics-14
80OPC-307
80T-586
81D-480
81F-580
81T-35
82F-105
82OPC-178
82T-633
82Tacom-36
83T-737
84Nes/792-414
84T-414
85Cram/PCL-234
Page, Phil
49Eureka-91
Page, Sean
90Johnson/Star-20
91Savan/ClBest-20
91Savan/ProC-1661
Page, Ted
78Laugh/Black-16
86Negro/Frit-2
88Negro/Duques-15
Page, Thane
91Martins/ClBest-19
91Martins/ProC-3452
Page, Vance
41DP-2
Pagel, Dave
81QuadC-1
Pagel, Karl Douglas
(Karl)
79T-716R
80T-676R
80Wichita-1
81Charl-18
82Charl-21
83Charl-12
84Maine-16
Pagliari, Armando
88StCath/ProC-2005
89StCath/ProC-2092
91Myrtle/ClBest-30TR
Pagliaroni, James V.
(Jim)
60DF-2
61T-519
62J-63
62P-63
62P/Can-63
62Salada-81
62Shirriff-81
62T-81
63IDL-18
63Sugar-D
63T-159
64Kahn
64T-392
64T/Coins-62
65Kahn
65OPC-265
65T-265
66EH-10
66Kahn
66OPC-33
66T-33
67Kahn
67OPC-183
67T-183
67T/Test/PP-19
68T-586
69MB-211
69T-302
78TCMA-91
Pagliarulo, Mike
83Nashvl-14
84Colum-1
84Colum/Pol-17
85D-539
85F-139
85T-638
85T/St-317
86D-152
86F-113
86Leaf-80
86OPC-327
86T-327
87Classic-22
87D-298
87D/OD-239
87F-107
87F/LL-33
87Leaf-189
87OPC-195
87Sf-55
87Seven-E6
87Smok/AL-9
87T-195
87T/Gloss60-56
87T/St-300
88D-105
88D/Best-105
88D/Y/Bk-105
88F-216
88F/St-49
88OPC-109
88Panini/St-156
88S-170
88Sf-121
88Sf/Gamewin-23
88T-435
88T/Big-138
88T/St-295
89B-175
89D-127
89F-262
89OPC-211
89Panini/St-406
89S-189
89S/NWest-13
89S/Tr-11T
89Sf-153
89T-211
89T/Big-28
89T/DHTest-20
89T/St-311
89UD-569
90B-219
90Coke/Padre-12
90D-364
90D/BestNL-137
90F-163
90Leaf/II-320
90OPC-63
90Padre/MagUno-3
90PublInt/St-542
90S-494
90T-63
90T/Big-226
90T/St-106
90UD-329
91B-339
91D-140
91F-537
91F/Up-U40
91Leaf/II-339
91OPC-547
91Panini/FrSt-93
91S-199
91S/RookTr-42T
91T-547
91T/StClub/II-522
91T/Tr-87T
91UD-206
91UD/Ext-709
92D/I-62
92F-216
92S/I-173
92T-721
92UD-509
Paglino, Joseph
82AppFx-16
Pagnozzi, Tom
83Erie-20
86Louisvl-21
87Louisvl-22
87Smok/Cards-12
88D-577
88S-358
88Smok/Card-12
88T-689
89D-399
89S-483
89Smok/Cards-16
89T-208
89UD-602
90D-591
90Leaf/II-498
90OPC-509
90PublInt/St-224
90Smok/Card-18
90SpringDG/Best-35
90T-509
90T/TVCard-23
91B-389
91D-337
91F-641
91F/Ultra-293
91Leaf/I-72
91OPC-308
91Panini/FrSt-30
91Pol/Card-19
91S-797
91T-308
91T/StClub/I-223
91UD-91
92Classic/I-69
92D/I-254
92F-586
92S/I-136
92T-448
92UD-379
Paige, George L.
(Pat)
T206
Paige, LeRoy
(Satchel)
48L-8
49B-224
53T-220
72T/Test-1
74Laugh/Black-15
76Laugh/Clown-21
80Pac/Leg-60
80SSPC/HOF
83D/HOF-11
83MLBPA/Pin-14
85West/2-37
86Negro/Frit-10
86Negro/Frit-21
86Negro/Frit-4
88Conlon/NegAS-10
88Negro/Duques-11
89B/I-8
90BBWit-64
90Negro/Star-20
90Swell/Great-115
91Homer/Classic-2
91LineD-47
91Swell/Great-133
91T/Arc53-220
92S/II-882
Exh47
PM10/Sm-140
Rawl
Paine, Phil
54JC-11
55JC-11
58T-442
59DF
Painter, Gary
91FSLAS/ProC-FSL45
91Single/ClBest-129
91WinHaven/ClBest-6
91WinHaven/ProC-486
Painter, Lance
91Single/ClBest-352
91Waterlo/ClBest-7
91Waterlo/ProC-1254
Painton, Tim
80Clinton-15
89Smok/FresnoSt-17
Paixao, Paulino
85Utica-4
Pakele, Louis
90Boise/ProC-3309
91PalmSp/ProC-2010
Palacios, Rey
86GlenF-17
87Toledo-15
87Toledo/TCMA-1
88AAA/ProC-43
88Toledo/CMC-18
88Toledo/ProC-605
89F-648R
89UD-21SR
90B-381
91OPC-148
91T-148
Palacios, Vicente
87Vanco-22
88Classic/Red-191
88D-45RR
88F-336
88Leaf-45RR
88S-643RP
88Sf-224R
88T-322
89F-216
89S/HotRook-2
90BuffB/CMC-7
90BuffB/ProC-370
90BuffB/Team-18
91D-732
91F/Up-U113
91Leaf/II-442
91OPC-438
91T-438
91T/StClub/II-443
91UD/FinalEd-71F
92D/I-365
92S/I-109
92T-582
Palafox, Juan
85Tigres-12
Palermo, Pete
86Hagers-14
87Hagers-17
88Hagers/Star-16
Palermo, Steve
88TM/Umpire-29
89TM/Umpire-27
90TM/Umpire-26
Palica, Alex
45Centen-19
Palica, Ambrose
46Remar-22
47Remar-10
47Smith-12
Palica, Erv
51B-189
52T-273
54NYJour
55B-195
56T-206
60HenryH-21
61Union
79TCMA-233
90Target-603
91Crown/Orio-348
Palica, John
81Wisco-22
83Orlan-8
Pall, Donn Steven
86AppFx-17
87BirmB/Best-15
88AAA/ProC-45
88Vanco/CMC-9
88Vanco/ProC-759
89Coke/WS-18
89D/Rook-7
89F-505
89S/Tr-102
89T-458
90BirmDG/Best-26
90Coke/WSox-18
90D-606
90F-543
90Leaf/II-392
90OPC-219
90PublInt/St-397
90S-304
90S/100Ris-7
90T-219
90T/JumboR-23
90UD-386
91D-215
91F-130
91Kodak/WSox-22
91Leaf/II-468
91OPC-768
91S-132
91T-768
91UD-603
92D/I-56
92F-92
92S/II-484
92T-57
92UD-592
Pallas, Ted
82Beloit-27
Pallone, Dave
88TM/Umpire-37
89TM/Umpire-35
Palma, Brian
89Reno/Cal-258
91Salinas/ClBest-12
91Salinas/ProC-2258
Palma, Jay
83Ander-22
Palmeiro, Orlando
91Boise/ClBest-9
91Boise/ProC-3895
Palmeiro, Rafael
86Pittsfld-18
87D-43RR
87D/Rook-47
87Iowa-24
87Leaf-43RR
87Sf-158M
87Sf/Rook-32
87Sf/Rook-2
87T-634FS
87T/GlossRk-12
88Berg/Cubs-25
88D-324
88D/Best-93

88D/Cubs/Bk-324
88F-429
88F/Slug-C4
88OPC-186
88Panini/St-268
88Peoria/Ko-23
88Peoria/Ko-34M
88S-186
88T-186
89B-237
89Classic/Up/2-163
89D-49
89D/AS-53
89D/Best-88
89D/Tr-6
89F-434
89F-631M
89F/Up-66
89Mother/R-5
89OPC-310
89Panini/St-60
89RedFoley/St-88
89S-199
89S/HotStar-56
89S/Tr-1
89S/YS/I-35
89Sf-30
89Smok/R-24
89T-310
89T/Big-257
89T/Coins-47
89T/Mini-5
89T/St-47
89T/St/Backs-52
89T/Tr-93T
89T/UK-58
89UD-235
89UD/Ext-772
90B-496
90Classic-74
90D-225
90D/BestAL-41
90F-308
90Leaf/I-100
90Mother/Rang-9
90OPC-755
90Panini/St-164
90PublInt/St-418
90RedFoley/St-72
90S-405
90S/100St-58
90Sf-9
90T-755
90T/Big-127
90T/HeadsUp-12
90T/St-250
90UD-335
91B-286
91Classic/200-115
91Classic/I-85
91Classic/III-71
91D-19DK
91D-394MVP
91D-521
91D/SuperDK-19
91F-295
91F/Ultra-350
91Leaf/II-347
91Leaf/Stud-127
91Mother/Rang-9
91OPC-295
91Panini/FrSt-252
91Panini/St-211
91Panini/Top15-29
91Panini/Top15-7
91Pep/SS-14
91S-216
91S/100SS-56
91Seven/3DCoin-10T
91T-295
91T/StClub/II-502
91UD-30
91UD-474
91USPlayC/AS-6D
92D/I-46
92F-311
92F/ASIns-17
92F/TmLIns-12
92S/100SS-27
92S/I-55
92T-55
92UD-223

Palmer, Bob
75AppFx
82Holyo-11

Palmer, David
80OPC-21
80T-42
81D-451
81F-160
81OPC-243
81T-607
82F-199
82OPC-292
82T-292
83D-68
83F-291
83OPC-164
83T-164
84Stuart-23
85D-341
85F-404
85Leaf-105
85OPC-211
85OPC/Post-3
85T-526
86D-254
86F-255
86F/Up-U87
86OPC-143
86Pol/Atl-46
86T-421
86T/Tr-84T
87D-325
87F-525
87Smok/Atl-4
87T-324
87T/St-45
88D-266
88F-546
88F/Up-U111
88Phill/TastyK-17
88S-457
88T-732
88T/Tr-79T
89D-133
89F-577
89OPC-67
89S-544
89T-67
89Toledo/CMC-4
89Toledo/ProC-789
89UD-515

Palmer, Dean
87Gaston-8
88CharlR/Star-18
88FSLAS/Star-47
89BBAmerAA/BProC-AA27
89TexLAS/GS-32
89Tulsa/GS-19
89Tulsa/Team-17
90Classic/Up-39
90D-529
90HotRook/St-35
90OkCty/ProC-441
90S-594RP
90S/100Ris-38
90Sf-225R
90T/89Debut-95
90Tulsa/ProC-1170
90TulsaDG/Best-5
90UD-74SR
91B-288
91Classic/III-72
91D/Rook-48
91F/UltraUp-U56
91F/Up-U61
91OkCty/LineD-314
91OkCty/ProC-187
91S/100RisSt-28
91T/Tr-88T
91UD/FinalEd-74F
92D/I-177
92F-312
92S/100RisSt-60
92S/I-392
92T-567
92UD-465

Palmer, Denzil
76Clinton

Palmer, Donald
87BuffB-28

Palmer, Doug
85Visalia-2
86Orlan-15
87Orlan-17
88NewBrit/ProC-892

Palmer, Jim
66OPC-126
66T-126
67OPC-152WS
67T-152WS
67T-475
68T-575
69T-573
70OPC-449
70OPC-68LL
70T-449
70T-68LL
71K-60
71MD
71MLB/St-306
71OPC-197ALCS
71OPC-570
71OPC-67LL
71T-197ALCS
71T-570
71T-67LL
71T/Coins-90
71T/tatt-3
72K-13
72MB-263
72OPC-270
72OPC-92LL
72T-270
72T-92LL
73JP
73K-17
73OPC-160
73OPC-341KP
73T-160
73T-341KP
73T/Comics-13
73T/Lids-38
73T/PinUps-13
74K-6
74OPC-206LL
74OPC-40
74T-206LL
74T-40
74T/DE-45
74T/Puzzles-8
74T/St-128
75Ho-126
75OPC-335
75T-335
75T/M-335
76Crane-44
76Ho-56
76Ho/Twink-56
76K-37
76MSA/Disc
76OPC-200LL
76OPC-202LL
76OPC-450
76SSPC-380
76T-200LL
76T-202LL
76T-450
77BurgChef-42
77Ho-1
77OPC-5LL
77OPC-80
77Pep-20
77T-5LL
77T-600
77T/CS-36
78Ho-116
78OPC-179
78OPC-5LL
78PapaG/Disc-31
78T-160
78T-205LL
78Tastee/Discs-2
78Wiffle/Discs-57
79Ho-11
79K-5
79OPC-174
79T-340
80BK/PHR-7
80K-15
80OPC-310
80T-4M
80T-590
81D-353
81D-473
81F-169
81F/St-124
81K-2
81OPC-210
81PermaGr/CC-28
81T-210
81T/Nat/Super-9
81T/SO-50
81T/St-39
82D-231
82F-175
82F/St-143
82K-42
82OPC-80
82OPC-81IA
82T-80
82T-81IA
82T/St-146
83D-4DK
83D-77
83F-69
83K-39
83OPC-299
83OPC-328SV
83T-21TL
83T-490
83T-491SV
83T/Gloss40-19
83T/St-175
83T/St-23
83T/St/Box-5
84D-576
84D/Champs-35
84F-16
84F/St-102
84Nes/792-715LL
84Nes/792-717LL
84Nes/792-750
84OPC-194
84Ralston-23
84T-715LL
84T-717LL
84T-750
84T/Cereal-23
84T/St-21
84T/St-211
86Sf/Dec-58
87KMart-17
89Swell-105
90BBWit-33
90MSA/AGFA-17
91Crown/Orio-349

Palmer, Ken
76Baton

Palmer, Lowell
70OPC-252
70T-252
71OPC-554
71T-554
72T-746
89Pac/SenLg-174
89TM/SenLg-86

Palmer, Mickey
82FtMyr-8

Palmer, Mike
81QuadC-33tr

Palmieri, John
82Reading-5

Palmquist, Ed
60DF-7
90Target-604

Palyan, Vince
89Everett/Star-23
90Clinton/Best-26
90Clinton/ProC-2564

Palys, Stanley F.
(Stan)
58T-126

Pancoski, Tracey
88Fresno/Cal-7
88Fresno/ProC-1240

Panetta, Mario
83QuadC-4

Panick, Frank
77SLCity

Pankovits, James F.
(Jim)
77Cocoa
80Tucson-19
81Tucson-17
82Hawaii-4
83Tucson-16
84Cram/PCL-61
85D-502
85Mother/Ast-25
86D-450
86F-307
86Pol/Ast-1
86T-618
87D-605
87F-64
87Mother/Ast-22
87Pol/Ast-25
87T-249
88Mother/Ast-22
88Pol/Ast-16
88T-487
88T/Big-109
89BuffB/CMC-18
89BuffB/ProC-1664
89F-363
89S-192
89T-153
89UD-100
90Pawtu/CMC-18
90Pawtu/ProC-470
90T/TVRSox-55
91Pac/SenLg-89
91Pawtu/LineD-363
91Pawtu/ProC-48

Papa, John
91Crown/Orio-350

Papageorge, Greg
88Virgini/Star-17
89Penin/Star-17

Papai, Al
50B-245

Paparella, J.A.
55B-235ump

Pape, Kenneth Wayne
(Ken)
77Tucson
78Syrac
79Spokane-8
81Spokane-21

Pape, Lawrence
E270/1

Papi, Stanley Gerard
(Stan)
79OPC-344
79T-652
81D-246
81F-480
81T-273
82D-333
82F-280
82T-423

Papke, William
T3/Box-64

Pappageorgas, Bob
77Wausau

Pappas, Erik
86PalmSp-25
86PalmSp/Smok-6
87PalmSp-23
88MidldA/GS-14
89CharlK-12
90AAAGame/ProC-AAA34
90Iowa/CMC-17
90Iowa/ProC-321
90T/TVCub-55
91B-432
91S/RookTr-95T
92T/91Debut-135

Pappas, Milt
58T-457
59T-391
60Bz-5
60L-57
60T-12
60T-399M
60T/tatt-42
61P-71
61T-295
61T-48LL
61T/St-103
62Bz
62Exh
62J-34
62P-34
62P/Can-34
62Salada-98
62Shirriff-98
62T-55LL
62T-75
62T/St-7
63Exh
63F-3
63J-65
63P-65
63Salada-43
63T-358

64T-45
64T/Coins-70
64T/S-5
64T/St-4
64T/tatt
65OPC-270
65T-270
65T/E-20
65T/trans-61
66Bz-29
66Kahn
66OPC-105
66T-105
66T/RO-88
67T-254
68OPC-74
68T-74
69MB-212
69MLB/St-117
69OPC-79
69T-79
69T/St-8
70MLB/St-11
70T-576
71MD
71MLB/St-39
71OPC-441
71T-441
72MB-264
72OPC-208
72T-208
73OPC-70
73T-70
74OPC-640
74T-640
78TCMA-56
89Pac/Leg-204
89Swell-113
90Swell/Great-107
91Crown/Orio-351
91Swell/Great-69
Exh47
WG10-41
WG9-40

Paquette, Craig
89Medford/Best-22
90Modesto/ProC-2222
91B-236
92T-473M

Paquette, Darryl
78Wausau

Parachke, Greg
89Utica/Pucko-17

Parascand, Steve
87Fayette-4
88Fayette/ProC-1088

Pardo, Al
81Miami-2
83RochR-12
84CharlO-7
85RochR-2
86D-489
86RochR-15
86T-279
88Tidew/ProC-1594
89ScrWB/CMC-21
89ScrWB/ProC-711
90HagersDG/Best-20
91Crown/Orio-352

Pardo, Bed
89Eugene/Best-8

Pardo, Larry
86DayBe-21
87QuadC-6
88QuadC/GS-6
89QuadC/Best-12
89QuadC/GS-24
90PalmSp/ProC-2575

Paredes, German
91Kane/ClBest-24
91Kane/ProC-2672

Paredes, Jesus
87Jamestn-6
88Rockford-26
89Rockford-26
89Rockford/Team-20
90Indianap/CMC-21

Paredes, Johnny
86Jaxvl/TCMA-2
87Indianap-20
88D/Rook-29
88Indianap/CMC-11
88Indianap/ProC-516
89D-570
89F-388
89OPC-367
89S/HotRook-27
89T-367
89UD-477
90Indianap/ProC-303
91Toledo/LineD-595
91Toledo/ProC-1941

Parent, Eric
82Wausau-11
83Wausau/LF-10
84Greens-16

Parent, Frederick A.
(Freddy)
10Domino-95
11Helmar-14
12Sweet/Pin-13
14Piedmont/St-46
C46-44
E107
E254
M116
S74-7
T205
T206
WG2-39

Parent, Mark
82Amari-10
83Beaum-13
84Beaum-8
85Cram/PCL-105
86LasVegas-11
88Coke/Padres-27
88D/Rook-8
88F/Up-U125
88Smok/Padres-22
88T/Tr-80T
89Coke/Padre-11
89D-420
89F/Up-125
89S-576
89T-617
89UD-492
90Coke/Padre-13
90D-229
90F-164
90Leaf/II-497
90OPC-749
90Padre/MagUno-7
90PublInt/St-55
90S-119
90T-749
90UD-569
91D-506
91F-538
91OPC-358
91S-213
91T-358
91UD-470

Parese, Billy
89StCath/ProC-2082
90Myrtle/ProC-2786
91Dunedin/ClBest-18
91Dunedin/ProC-216

Parfrey, Brian
82Redwd-26

Parham, Bill
89Bakers/Cal-191

Paris, Juan
85Spokane/Cram-18
86CharRain-20
87Greens-12
88WinHaven/Star-19
89Lynch/Star-17
90NewBrit/Best-17
90NewBrit/Star-14
91NewBrit/LineD-467
91NewBrit/ProC-366

Paris, Kelly Jay
(Kelly)
77StPete
78StPete
80ArkTr-22
82Louisvl-22
84Cram/PCL-123
84D-384
84F-476
84Nes/792-113
84T-113
85IntLgAS-28
85RochR-8
86RochR-16
88Vanco/CMC-12
89F-506
89UD-192
89Vanco/CMC-11
89Vanco/ProC-594
91Crown/Orio-353

Paris, Zacarias
82Tucson-14
83ColumAst-17
86Ventura-20

Parish, Jack
76Clinton

Parisotto, Barry
89GreatF-20
90Bakers/Cal-242

Parke, Jim
77Charl

Parker, Bob
85Osceola/Team-21
86ColumAst-21

Parker, Carrol
86Erie-22
87Savan-14

Parker, Clay
86Wausau-18
88Colum/CMC-2
88Colum/Pol-7
88Colum/ProC-309
88F-649R
89Colum/CMC-4
89Colum/Pol-17
89Colum/ProC-751
89D/Best-164
89D/Rook-52
89S/NWest-30
89S/Tr-94
89T/Tr-94T
90D-363
90F-451
90LSUGreat-11
90OPC-511
90PublInt/St-543
90S-316
90S/100Ris-17
90S/YS/I-8
90T-511
90T/TVYank-15
91D-605
91F-346
91OPC-183
91T-183
91Tacoma/ProC-2302

Parker, Darrell
76Watlo
77Jaxvl

Parker, David Gene
(Dave)
74OPC-252
74T-252
74T/St-86
75OPC-29
75T-29
75T/M-29
76Crane-45
76Ho-133
76K-15
76MSA/Disc
76OPC-185
76SSPC-572
76T-185
77BurgChef-187
77K-19
77OPC-242
77T-270
78Ho-135
78K-52
78OPC-1LL
78OPC-60
78T-201LL
78T-560
78Wiffle/Discs-58
79Ho-53
79K-21
79OPC-223
79T-1LL
79T-430
79T/Comics-29
80BK/PHR-19
80K-23
80OPC-163
80T-310
80T/S-17
81Coke
81D-136
81Drake-4
81F-360
81F/St-26
81K-13
81MSA/Disc-25
81OPC-178
81PermaGr/AS-6
81PermaGr/CC-13
81Sqt-10
81T-640
81T/Nat/Super-10
81T/SO-59
81T/St-210
81T/St-257
82D-12DK
82D-95
82F-489
82F/St-241M
82F/St-71
82K-48
82KMart-34
82OPC-343AS
82OPC-40
82OPC-41IA
82T-343AS
82T-40
82T-41IA
82T/St-127
82T/St-87
83D-473
83F-315
83OPC-205
83PermaGr/CC-11
83T-205
83T/St-280
84Borden-39
84D-288
84D/Champs-57
84F-258
84F/X-U89
85FunFoodPin-80
84Nes/792-701LL
84Nes/792-775
84OPC-31
84T-701
84T-775
84T/St-130
84T/Tr-90T
85D-62
85D/AAS-35
85D/HL-13
85Drake-22
85F-544
85Leaf-169
85OPC-175
85T-175
85T/St-47
85T/Super-42
86D-203
86D/AAS-24
86Drake-4
86F-184
86F-640M
86F/AS-6
86F/LimEd-33
86F/LL-30
86F/Mini-39
86F/St-84
86Leaf-135
86OPC-287
86Quaker-9
86Sf-181M
86Sf-183M
86Sf-23
86Sf-58M
86T-595
86T/3D-18
86T/Gloss60-13
86T/Mini-41
86T/St-135
86T/Super-41
86TexGold-39
86Woolwth-27
87Classic-33
87D-388
87D/AAS-34
87D/OD-198
87Drake-18
87F-208
87F-639M
87F/AwardWin-27
87F/Mini-80
87F/Slug-29
87F/St-88
87F/WaxBox-C10
87Kahn-39
87KayBee-23
87Leaf-79
87OPC-352
87Ralston-7
87RedFoley/St-90
87Sf-117M
87Sf-35
87T-600AS
87T-691
87T/Board-20
87T/Coins-38
87T/Gloss60-17
87T/Mini-6
87T/St-145
88D-388
88D/A's/Bk-NEW
88D/Best-190
88F-243
88F/Mini-47
88F/Up-U55
88KayBee-21
88Mother/A's-5
88OPC-315
88Panini/St-284
88S-17
88S/Tr-50T
88Sf-101
88T-315
88T/Big-242
88T/Gloss60-34
88T/Mini-48
88T/St-136
88T/St/Backs-19
88T/Tr-81T
88T/UK-55
89T/Ames-23
89B-202
89D-150
89D/Best-336
89F-19
89KMart/Lead-13
89Mother/A's-4
89OPC-199
89Panini/St-424
89S-108
89Sf-49
89T-475
89T/Big-144
89T/LJN-135
89T/St-169
89UD-605
90B-398
90Brewer/MillB-18
90Classic-95
90Classic/III-10
90D-328
90D/BestAL-51
90D/Learning-33
90F-18
90F/Up-106
90F/WS-10M
90F/WS-9
90KayBee-22
90KMart/CBatL-13
90Leaf/I-190
90OPC-45
90Pol/Brew-39
90PublInt/St-312
90S-135
90S/Tr-12T
90T-45
90T/Ames-6
90T/Big-227
90T/HillsHM-21
90T/St-179
90T/Tr-86T
90T/WaxBox-J
90UD-192
90UD/Ext-766
90USPlayC/AS-12S
90Windwlk/Discs-1
91B-199
91B-375SLUG
91Classic/200-34
91D-142
91D-390MVP
91D-6DK
91D/SuperDK-6DK
91DennyGS-5
91F-593
91F/UltraUp-U10

91F/Up-U10
91Leaf/II-334
91Leaf/StudPrev-3
91OPC-235
91OPC/Premier-94
91Panini/FrSt-210
91Panini/St-171
91S-484
91S/100SS-44
91Smok/Angel-4
91T-235
91T/CJMini/I-11
91T/StClub/I-75
91T/Tr-89T
91T/WaxBox-L
91UD-274
91UD-48
91UD/Ext-733
91UD/SilSlug-SS14
91Woolwth/HL-16
92UD-522

Parker, Francis James
(Salty)
60T-469C
62Sugar-16
73OPC-421CO
73T-421C
74OPC-276CO
74T-276C
76Cedar

Parker, Harry
74OPC-106
74T-106
75OPC-214
75T-214
75T/M-214
91WIZMets-309

Parker, James
87Chatt/Best-4

Parker, Jarrod
89Pulaski/ProC-1906
90Pittsfld/Pucko-7

Parker, Joel
81BurlB-27

Parker, Mark
80Wichita-4
82Iowa-21

Parker, Maurice W.
(Wes)
64T-456R
65T-344
66OPC-134
66T-134
67T-218
68T-533
69MB-213
69MLB/St-151
69T-493
70MLB/St-55
70OPC-5
70T-5
71MLB/St-111
71OPC-430
71T-430
71T/Coins-121
71T/GM-30
71T/S-14
71T/tatt-8
71Ticket/Dodg-13
72K-17
72MB-265
72OPC-265
72T-265
73OPC-151
73T-151
88Smok/Dodg-10
90Target-605

Parker, Mike
89Idaho/ProC-2035

Parker, Olen
87Clearw-5

Parker, Richard
85Bend/Cram-18
87Clearw-1
88Reading/ProC-878
89BendB/Legoe-14
89Reading/Best-9
89Reading/ProC-660
89Reading/Star-19
90Classic/III-72
90F/Up-U63
90Leaf/II-398
90PalmSp/Cal-210
90PalmSp/ProC-2581
90Phoenix/ProC-26
90S/Tr-77T
90T/Tr-87T
90UD/Ext-732
91F-269
91OPC-218
91PG&E-26
91Phoenix/ProC-73
91S-58
91S/100RisSt-11
91T-218
91T/90Debut-121
92S/II-601

Parker, Rob
87ColAst/ProC-10

Parker, Stacy
89Butte/SP-1
91BendB/ClBest-21
91BendB/ProC-3706
91Clearw/ClBest-23
91Clearw/ProC-1634

Parker, Steve
87Peoria-24
88Pittsfld/ProC-1369
89WinSalem/Star-13
90Iowa/CMC-5
90Iowa/ProC-316
90T/TVCub-56

Parker, Tim
90A&AASingle/ProC-174
90Geneva/ProC-3049
90Geneva/Star-18
91CharlK/LineD-137
91CharlK/ProC-1686

Parker, William David
(Billy)
72OPC-213R
72T-213R
73OPC-354
73T-354

Parkins, Rob
86WinHaven-19

Parkinson, Eric
89Princet/Star-14
90Augusta/ProC-2460
91Salem/ClBest-17
91Salem/ProC-947

Parkinson, Frank J.
E120
V100

Parks, Art
90Target-1048

Parks, Danny
81Pawtu-6

Parks, Derek
87Kenosha-19
88BBAmer-12
88OrlanTw/Best-1
88SLAS-12
89Orlan/Best-19
89Orlan/ProC-1350
90B-422
90Classic/Up-40
90Portl/CMC-14
90Portl/ProC-181
91OrlanSR/LineD-492
91OrlanSR/ProC-1852
91Single/ClBest-159

Parks, Jack
55T-23
55T/DH-68

Parks, Jeff
85Spokane/Cram-19

Parmalee, LeRoy
33G-239
35BU-94
91Conlon/Sport-85
R312
V355-20

Parmenter, Gary
86Iowa-21
87Iowa-7
88Pittsfld/ProC-1378

Parnell, Mark
89AppFx/ProC-875
90BBCity/Star-18
91London/LineD-410
91Memphis/ProC-648
91Single/ClBest-301

Parnell, Mel
50B-1
51FB
51T/RB-10
52B-241
52BR
52Dix
52StarCal/L-71A
52T-30
53B/Col-66
53Dix
53NB
53RM-AL25
53T-19
54Dix
54RM-AL8
54T-40
55RFG-28
55T-140
55T/DH-119
56T/Hocus-A18
57T-313
63MilSau-5
79TCMA-58
90Pac/Legend-98
91Swell/Great-118
91T/Arc53-19
PM10/Sm-141
R423-77

Parra, Jose
90Kissim/DIMD-20

Parrett, Jeff
86F/Up-U88
86Provigo-25
88D-406
88F/Up-U102
88OPC-144
88T-588
89B-390
89D-334
89D/Best-296
89D/Tr-55
89F-389
89F/Up-112
89OPC-176
89Phill/TastyK-27
89S-377
89S/Tr-33
89S/YS/I-18
89T-176
89T/St-73
89T/Tr-95T
89UD-398
89UD/Ext-741
90B-149
90D-369
90F-570
90Leaf/I-210
90OPC-439
90Panini/St-312
90Phill/TastyK-25
90PublInt/St-248
90T-439
90T/St-119
90UD-92
91D-660
91F-699
91OPC-56
91S-565
91T-56
91T/StClub/II-544
91UD-417

Parrill, Marty
78RochR

Parris, Steve
88CapeCod/Sum-43
89Batavia/ProC-1923
90Batavia/ProC-3065
91Clearw/ClBest-7
91Clearw/ProC-1618

Parrish, Lance M.
77Evansvl/TCMA-22
78T-708R
79T-469
80K-54
80OPC-110
80T-196
81Coke
81D-366
81Detroit-90
81F-467
81OPC-8
81T-392
81T/SO-14
81T/St-73
82D-281
82F-276
82F/St-152
82OPC-214
82T-535
82T/St-188
83D-407
83D/AAS-50
83F-337
83K-40
83OPC-285
83PermaGr/CC-30
83T-285
83T-4RB
83T/Gloss40-27
83T/St-193
83T/St-194
83T/St-63
84D-15DK
84D-49
84D/AAS-34
84F-637IA
84F-88
85FunFoodPin-2
84Nes/792-640
84Nestle/DT-8
84OPC-158
84T-640
84T/Gloss40-2
84T/St-265
85Cain's-15
85D-49
85D/AAS-53
85Drake-23
85F-19
85F/St-31
85Leaf-41
85OPC-160
85Seven-13C
85Seven-14D
85T-160
85T-708AS
85T/Gloss22-20
85T/St-189
85T/St-259
85T/Super-55
85Wendy-17
86Cain's-14
86D-334
86F-234
86F/LL-31
86F/Mini-49
86F/St-85
86Jiffy-3
86Leaf-201
86OPC-147
86Sf-92
86Sf/Dec-72M
86T-36M
86T-740
86T/Gloss60-8
86T/Mini-15
86T/St-273
87D-91
87D/AAS-9
87D/OD-153
87D/PopUp-9
87F-160
87F/AwardWin-28
87F/Up-U96
87Jiffy-13
87Leaf-107
87MSA/Discs-19
87OPC-374
87Phill/TastyK-13
87RedFoley/St-36
87Sf-101
87Sf-154M
87T-613AS
87T-791
87T/Board-19
87T/Gloss22-20
87T/Gloss60-58
87T/St-149
87T/St-269
87T/Tr-94T
88D-359
88D/Best-184
88F-310
88KayBee-22
88Leaf-130
88OPC-95
88Panini/St-355
88Phill/TastyK-18
88RedFoley/St-65
88S-131
88Sf-143
88T-95
88T/Big-45
88T/St-123
89B-45
89D-278
89D/AS-55
89D/Best-59
89F-578
89F/Up-15
89OPC-114
89S-95
89S/Tr-36T
89Sf-59
89T-470
89T/Big-250
89T/Tr-96T
89UD-240
89UD/Ext-775
90B-295
90D-213
90D/BestAL-59
90D/Learning-41
90F-141
90Leaf/I-195
90MLBPA/Pins-94
90OPC-575
90Panini/St-38
90PublInt/St-376
90RedFoley/St-73
90S-35
90Smok/Angel-13
90T-575
90T/Big-323
90T/St-170
90UD-674
90USPlayC/AS-2C
91B-188
91B-374SLUG
91D-135
91D-388MVP
91F-321
91F/Ultra-51
91Leaf/II-368
91Leaf/Stud-29
91MooTown-20
91OPC-210
91Panini/FrSt-179
91Panini/St-133
91S-37
91Smok/Angel-5
91T-210
91T/StClub/I-166
91UD-552
91UD/SilSlug-SS11
92D/I-166
92F-66
92S/I-298
92T-360
92UD-431

Parrish, Larry A.
76Ho-126
76OPC-141
76SSPC-326
76T-141
77BurgChef-161
77OPC-72
77T-526
78OPC-153
78T-294
79OPC-357
79T-677
80OPC-182
80T-345
80T/S-53
81D-89
81F-146
81F/St-69
81OPC-15
81OPC/Post-4
81T-15
81T/SO-89
81T/St-183
82D-466
82F-200
82F/St-34
82OPC-353
82OPC/Post-15
82T-445
82T/St-64
82T/Tr-86T
83D-467
83F-574
83OPC-2

83Rang-15
83T-776
83T/St-120
84D-21DK
84D-422
84D/AAS-42
84F-424
84Nes/792-169
84OPC-169
84Rang-15
84T-169
84T/St-354
85D-300
85D/AAS-29
85F-564
85F/St-38
85Leaf-96
85OPC-203
85Rang-15
85T-548
85T/St-346
86D-178
86F-569
86F/St-86
86Leaf-110
86OPC-238
86Rang-15
86T-238
86T/St-240
87Classic-25
87Classic-50
87D-469
87D/HL-10
87D/OD-173
87F-134
87F/GameWin-33
87F/LL-34
87F/Mini-81
87F/RecSet-29
87F/St-89
87Leaf-209
87Mother/Rang-5
87RedFoley/St-104
87Sf-174
87Smok/R-18
87T-629
87T/St-234
88ChefBoy-9
88D-347
88D/AS-21
88D/Best-334
88F-476
88F/Mini-57
88F/RecSet-28
88F/St-68
88F/TL-25
88F/Up-U7
88KingB/Disc-21
88Leaf-119
88Mother/R-5
88OPC-226
88Panini/St-205
88RedFoley/St-66
88S-191
88S/Tr-65T
88Sf-49
88Smok/R-14
88T-490
88T/St-243
88T/UK-56
89F-94
89S-495
89T-354
89UD-36

Parrot, Steve
82ElPaso-19
83ElPaso-16

Parrott, Mike
79OPC-300
79T-576
80T-443
81Pol/Mar-10
81T-187
82D-226
82T-358
83Omaha-7
84Omaha-11
85OKCty-12
86OKCty-17
88Rockford-27CO
89Rockford-27CO
89Rockford/Team-29CO
91Crown/Orio-354
91WPalmB/ProC-1246

Parrotte, Brian
89Billings/ProC-2050

Parry, Bob
88Madis-17
89Modesto/Cal-286
89Modesto/Chong-31
90Modesto/ProC-2228

Parry, Dave
82Tucson-28M

Parsons, Bill
59DF

Parsons, Bill
72K-5
72OPC-281
72T-281
73OPC-231
73T-231
74OPC-574
74T-574
75OPC-613
75T-613
75T/M-613

Parsons, Bob
78Salem

Parsons, Casey R.
(Casey)
78Cr/PCL-42
79Phoenix
80Phoenix-13
81Spokane-26
82F-515
82SLCity-15
85Louisvl-27
86Louisvl-22
87BuffB-9
88Memphis/Best-9
90Madison/Best-25MG
90Madison/ProC-2283MG
91Huntsvl/ClBest-22MG
91Huntsvl/LineD-299MG
91HuntsvlProC-1811MG

Parsons, Charles
N172

Parsons, Scott
87LasVegas-5

Parsons, Thomas
62T-326
65T-308R
91WIZMets-310

Partee, Roy Robert
(Roy)
47TipTop
49B-149

Partin, Billy
89Sumter/ProC-1089

Partley, Calvin
74Cedar

Partrick, Dave
89QuadC/Best-24
90Boise/ProC-3327
90PalmSp/ProC-2591
91PalmSp/ProC-2030

Partridge, Glenn
77BurlB

Partridge, Jay
90Target-606

Pascarella, Andy
79Newar-24

Paschal, Ben
91Conlon/Sport-107

Paschall, Bill
77Jaxvl
80T-667R
81Omaha-11

Pascual, Camilo Jr.
83Idaho-10

Pascual, Camilo
55T-84
55T/DH-104
56T-98
57T-211
58T-219
59T-291
59T-413
60Bz-14
60L-4
60T-483
60T-569AS
60T/tatt-43
61Clover-20
61NuCard-411
61P-99
61Peters-23
61T-235
61T/Dice-12
61T/St-183
62J-91
62P-91
62P/Can-91
62Salada-78
62Shirriff-78
62T-230
62T-59LL
62T/bucks
62T/St-78
63Bz-13
63Exh
63J-9
63P-9
63Salada-36
63T-10LL
63T-220
63T-8LL
64Bz-13
64T-2LL
64T-4LL
64T-500
64T/Coins-137AS
64T/Coins-76
64T/S-32
64T/St-92
64T/SU
64T/tatt
65OPC-11LL
65OPC-255
65T-11LL
65T-255
65T/trans-23
66T-305
67OPC-71
67T-71
68T-395
69MB-214
69MLB/St-107
69T-513
69T/decal
69T/S-31
69T/St-240
69Trans-27
70OPC-254
70T-254
78TCMA-32
90Target-607
Exh47

Pascual, Jorge
89Salem/Team-21
90Martins/ProC-3203
90Miami/I/Star-19
90Miami/II/Star-20

Pashnick, Larry
81Evansvl-5
83D-233
83Evansvl-8
83F-338
84D-394

Pasillas, Andy
77AppFx
78Knoxvl
79Knoxvl/TCMA-20
80GlenF/B-15
80GlenF/C-6
81GlenF-10

Paskert, George H.
(Dode)
10Domino-96
11Helmar-150
12Sweet/Pin-130A
12Sweet/Pin-130B
14Piedmont/St-47
16FleischBrd-73
BF2-89
D327
D328-130
D329-136
D350/2-135
E135-130
E254
E270
M101/4-136
M101/5-135
M116
S74-103
T202
T204
T205
T206
T207
T213/blue
T213/brown
T215/blue
T215/brown
T3-112
V100
W514-55

Paskievitch, Tom
91Erie/ClBest-21
91Erie/ProC-4067

Pasley, Kevin P.
(Kevin)
74Albuq/Team-12
77T-476R
78T-702R
80Syrac-3
81Syrac-8
82BirmB-17
90Target-608

Pasqua, Dan
84Nashvl-16
85Colum-21
85Colum/Pol-17
85D-637
85F/Up-U86
86Colum-17
86Colum/Pol-15
86D-417
86F-114
86KayBee-22
86Leaf-195
86T-259
86T/Gloss60-20
87Classic-13
87D-474
87D/OD-244
87F-108
87F/Mini-79
87OPC-74
87Sf-143
87T-74
87T/St-297
88Coke/WS-19
88D-463
88D/Best-137
88F-217
88F/Up-U18
88OPC-207
88Panini/St-159
88S-196
88S/Tr-56T
88T-691
88T/Big-164
88T/Tr-82T
89B-67
89Coke/WS-19
89D-294
89D/Best-123
89F-507
89OPC-31
89Panini/St-313
89S-338
89T-558
89T/Big-44
89T/St-301
89UD-204
90B-313
90Coke/WSox-19
90D-176
90F-544
90Leaf/II-274
90OPC-446
90PublInt/St-398
90S-306
90T-446
90T/Big-144
90T/St-306
90T/St-309
90UD-286
91B-361
91D-103
91F-131
91F/Ultra-79
91Kodak/WSox-44
91Leaf/II-428
91OPC-364
91S-85
91T-364
91T/StClub/I-214
91UD-605
92D/I-142
92F-93
92S/I-237
92T-107
92UD-281

Pasquale, Jeff
91Hamil/ClBest-8
91Hamil/ProC-4037

Pasquali, Jeff
83Erie-13

Passalacqua, Ricky
76Watlo

Passeau, Claude W.
39Exh

Passero, Joe
45Centen-20

Passmore, Jay
76BurlB
77BurlB

Pastore, Frank
78Indianap-23
80T-677R
81F-204
81OPC-1
81T-499
82Coke/Reds
82D-122
82F-80
82F/St-13
82T-128
83D-62
83F-599
83OPC-119
83T-658
84D-164
84F-477
84Nes/792-87
84OPC-87
84T-87
85D-550
85F-545
85OPC-292
85T-727
86F-185
86T-314
86T/Tr-85T
87OKCty-4
87T-576

Pastorius, James
90Target-1047
E103
E90/1
E93
T206
W555

Pastornicky, Cliff
81CharR-16
82CharR-21
83Omaha-17
84Omaha-21
86Water-19

Pastors, Greg
82Buffa-5
83LynnP-16

Pastrovich, Steve
80GlenF/B-1
80GlenF/C-16
81AppFx-8
82AppFx-11
83GlenF-18

Patchett, Hal
45Centen-21

Patchin, Steve
75Water
80Evansvl-22

Pate, Robert Wayne
(Bobby)
81D-545
81OPC-136R
81T-479R
83Tucson-21
87BurlEx-23

Patek, Freddie Joe
69T-219
70OPC-94
70T-94
71MLB/St-425
71OPC-626
71T-626
72MB-266
72T-531
73OPC-334
73T-334
74Greyhound-5M
74OPC-88
74T-88

74T/St-186
75Ho-32
75Ho/Twink-32
75OPC-48
75T-48
75T/M-48
76A&P/KC
76OPC-167
76SSPC-170
76T-167
77BurgChef-67
77Ho-109
77K-36
77OPC-244
77T-422
78Ho-48
78OPC-4LL
78OPC-91
78T-204LL
78T-274
79Ho-46
79K-36
79OPC-273
79T-525
80OPC-356
80T-705
81D-170
81F-283
81T-311
82D-241
82F-471
82T-602

Paterson, Pat
78Laugh/Black-18
86Negro/Frit-106

Patrick, Bronswell
89Madis/Star-18
90Madison/Best-22
90Modesto/Cal-155
90Modesto/ProC-2211
91Modesto/ClBest-11
91Modesto/ProC-3085

Patrick, Dave
89QuadC/GS-9

Patrick, Davis
90PalmSp/Cal-212

Patrick, Hisel
59DF

Patrick, Ron
77Ashvl

Patrick, Tim
90VeroB/Star-21
90Yakima/Team-14
91VeroB/ClBest-10
91VeroB/ProC-771

Patrizi, Mike
91Kingspt/ClBest-4
91Kingspt/ProC-3816

Pattee, Harry Ernest
(Harry)
T206

Patten, Case
WG2-40

Patterson, Bob
83Beaum-7
84Cram/PCL-221
85Cram/PCL-117
86Hawaii-19
87D/OD-166
88BuffB/CMC-7
88BuffB/ProC-1467
88F-337
88T-522
89BuffB/ProC-1684
90B-168
90F/Up-U49
90T/Tr-88T
91D-345
91F-45
91OPC-479
91S-636
91T-479
91T/StClub/II-594
92D/II-590
92F-562
92S/II-548
92T-263

Patterson, Daryl
68OPC-113R
68T-113R
69OPC-101
69T-101
70T-592
71MLB/St-402
71OPC-481
71T-481
88Domino-19

Patterson, Dave
77LodiD
79Albuq-6
80Albuq-10
80T-679R
81Albuq/TCMA-2
82Tacom-8
86Cram/PCL-12
87Clinton-3
88CalLgAS-1
88SanJose/Cal-126
88SanJose/ProC-111
89Shrev/ProC-1843
90A&AASingle/ProC-73
90Shrev/ProC-1453
90Shrev/Star-18
90Target-609
91Shrev/LineD-315
91Shrev/ProC-1831
91Single/ClBest-253

Patterson, Gil
77T-472R

Patterson, Glenn
87Gaston-2
88Gaston/ProC-1021

Patterson, Greg
88WinSalem/Star-14
89Geneva/ProC-1882
90LSUGreat-14

Patterson, Jeff
89Martins/Star-23
90Clearw/Star-17
91Spartan/ClBest-11
91Spartan/ProC-896

Patterson, Jimmy
52Wheat

Patterson, Joe
62Pep/Tul
63Pep/Tul

Patterson, John
90A&AASingle/ProC-155
90Foil/Best-202
90SanJose/Best-9
90SanJose/Cal-33
90SanJose/ProC-2017
90SanJose/Star-17
91Shrev/LineD-316
91Shrev/ProC-1832
91Single/ClBest-314

Patterson, Ken
82CharR-16
86FtLaud-17
87FtLaud-30
88Vanco/CMC-6
88Vanco/ProC-757
89Coke/WS-20
89D/Rook-37
89F-508
89S/HotRook-61
89S/Tr-97
89T-434
90Coke/WSox-20
90D-371
90F-545
90OPC-156
90S-207
90S/100Ris-89
90S/YS/I-27
90T-156
91D-522
91F-132
91Kodak/WSox-34
91OPC-326
91T-326
91UD-283
92D/II-457
92F-94
92S/I-347
92T-784
92UD-440

Patterson, Larry
80LynnS-2
81Spokane-23
82Holyo-12
83Nashua-11

Patterson, Michael L.
79Ogden/TCMA-24
80WHave-15
82Colum-20
82Colum/Pol-14
83Colum-22

Patterson, Reggie
80GlenF/B-9
80GlenF/C-18
82Edmon-15
82T-599R
83Iowa-7
84Iowa-31
86F-376

Patterson, Rick
77Wausau

Patterson, Rick
88Utica/Pucko-26
89SoBend/GS-2
90SoBend/Best-24MG
91Saraso/ClBest-27
91Saraso/ProC-1129

Patterson, Roy
E107

Patterson, Scott
80Ander-9
81Durham-22
82Colum-19
82Colum/Pol-11
83Nashvl-15
84Colum-14
84Colum/Pol-18
85Albany-10
86Colum-18
86Colum/Pol-16

Patterson, Steve
91Pocatel/ProC-3779

Pattin, Jon
90Clinton/Best-28
90Clinton/ProC-2552
91SanJose/ClBest-3
91SanJose/ProC-14

Pattin, Marty
69Sunoco/Pin-14
69T-563
70McDon-6
70OPC-31
70T-31
71MLB/St-447
71OPC-579
71T-579
72OPC-144
72T-144
73OPC-415
73T-415
74OPC-583
74T-583
74T/St-187
75OPC-413
75T-413
75T/M-413
76OPC-492
76SSPC-162
76T-492
77T-658
78T-218
79T-129
80T-26
81D-343
81F-37
81T-389

Pattison, James
90Target-1050
R314/Can

Patton, Eric
89Helena/SP-20

Patton, Jack
88Bakers/Cal-266
89Reno/Cal-263GM
90Reno/Cal-292GM

Patton, Jeff
84PrWill-17

Patton, Owen
N172

Patton, Tom
91Crown/Orio-355

Paul, Corey
89Belling/Legoe-27
90Salinas/ProC-2733

Paul, Mike
69T-537
70T-582
71MLB/St-381
71OPC-454
71T-454
72MB-267
72T-577
73OPC-58
73T-58
74OPC-399
74T-399
85Cram/PCL-208
86Vanco-21CO
90Mother/Mar-27M

Paula, Carlos C.
(Carlos)
55T-97
56T-4
56T/Pin-58
58Union
79TCMA-205

Paulesic, David
66Pep/Tul

Paulino, Dario
91Idaho/ProC-4338

Paulino, Elvin
87Peoria-17
88Peoria/Ko-24
89Peoria/Ko-24
90CLAS/CL-48
90WinSalem/Team-24
91CharlK/LineD-138
91CharlK/ProC-1697

Paulino, Luis
87Hagers-14
88Hagers/Star-15
89Freder/Star-20

Paulino, Victor
84Savan-19

Paulis, George
89Watlo/Star-28

Paulsen, Troy
88Alaska/Team-13
91Clearw/ClBest-20
91Clearw/ProC-1631
91FSLAS/ProC-FSL8

Pautt, Juan
83Pawtu-23
84Pawtu-12

Paveloff, David
91Kane/ClBest-8
91Kane/ProC-2656

Pavlas, Dave
86WinSalem-18
87Pittsfld-15
88TexLgAS/GS-21
88Tulsa-23
89OkCty/CMC-8
89OkCty/ProC-1529
90Iowa/CMC-6
90Iowa/ProC-317
90T/TVCub-57
91Iowa/LineD-213
91Iowa/ProC-1058
91S-378RP
91T/90Debut-122

Pavletich, Donald S.
(Don)
59T-494
62T-594R
63FrBauer-18
65T-472
66OPC-196
66T-196
67Kahn
67T-292
68OPC-108
68T-108
69MB-215
69OPC-179
69T-179
70OPC-504
70T-504
71MLB/St-326
71OPC-409
71T-409
72OPC-359
72T-359

Pavlick, Greg
78Tidew
79Tidew-20
84Jacks-10
88Kahn/Mets-52CO
89Kahn/Mets-52CO
90Kahn/Mets-52CO
90T/TVMets-5CO
91Kahn/Mets-52CO

Pavlik, John
84PrWill-9

Pavlik, Roger
87Gaston-15
88Gaston/ProC-1020
89CharlR/Star-19
90CharlR/Star-19
91OkCty/LineD-315
91OkCty/ProC-174

Pawling, Eric
86Clinton-17
86Cram/PCL-193

Pawlowski, John
86Penin-19
87BirmB/Best-17
88Coke/WS-20
88D-457
89Vanco/CMC-7
89Vanco/ProC-595
90S-617
90Vanco/CMC-10
90Vanco/ProC-487

Paxton, Darrin
90WichSt-29

Paxton, Greg
90Reno/Cal-282

Paxton, Mike
78T-216
79OPC-54
79T-122
80T-388
80Tacom-27
81Charl-5
81F-401

Payne, Frederick T.
(Fred)
E90/3
M116
S74-8
T201
T202
T205
T206

Payne, Harley
90Target-610

Payne, Jeff
90Hamil/Best-25

Payne, Jim
79Wausau-24
81Wisco-17

Payne, Joe
V362-15

Payne, Larry
76Indianap-2
77Indianap-7
78Indianap-13

Payne, Mike
80Ander-15
81Durham-23
82Durham-19
85Richm-6
87Jaxvl-16

Paynter, Billy
88Wythe/ProC-1983
89Peoria/Ko-13
90Geneva/ProC-3040
90Geneva/Star-19
90Peoria/Team-5

Payton, Dave
87Erie-21
88Spring/Best-15
89Spring/Best-15

Payton, Ray
88MidwLAS/GS-49
89Saraso/Star-17
90Saraso/Star-18

Pazik, Mike
73Syrac/Team-22
76OPC-597R
76T-597R
77T-643
80GlenF/B-24MG
80GlenF/C-21MG
82AppFx-30
88CharlK/Pep-14
90Freder/Team-2

Peacock, John Gaston
(Johnny)
39PB-16
40PB-34
90Target-611

Pearce, Jeff
91CharRain/ClBest-23
91CharRain/ProC-109

Pearce, Jim

55T-170
Pearce, Steve
77Cedar
Pearn, Joe
87PortChar-27
88Gaston/ProC-1006
Pearse, Steve
88Rockford-30
89Rockford-28
Pearsey, Les
81Holyo-19
82Spokane-18
Pearson, Albert G.
(Albie)
58T-317
59T-4
60T-241
61T-288
62J-78
62P-78
62P/Can-78
62Salada-63A
62Salada-63B
62Shirriff-63
62T-343
62T/St-67
63F-19
63J-29
63P-29
63T-182
64T-110
64T/Coins-111
64T/Coins-132AS
64T/S-23
64T/St-42
64T/SU
64T/tatt
64Wheat/St-33
65T-358
66OPC-83
66T-83
78TCMA-16
91Crown/Orio-356
Exh47
Pearson, Darren
85Everett/Cram-13A
85Everett/Cram-13B
86Clinton-18
Pearson, Don
77Wausau
78Wausau
Pearson, Ike
47Centen-19
Pearson, Kevin
87Tampa-6
88Greens/ProC-1560
89Chatt/Best-18
89Chatt/GS-20
89Nashvl/Team-18
90Nashvl/CMC-17
90Nashvl/ProC-242
91Nashvl/LineD-269
91Nashvl/ProC-2167
Pearson, Monte
37OPC-131
39PB-71
40PB-5
92Conlon/Sport-369
R310
V300
V355-114
Pearson, Steve
87SLCity/Taco-14MG
88SLCity-16MG
Pechek, Wayne
76Cedar
81Phoenix-19
Peck, Hal
49B-182
90Target-612
Peck, Steve
90Madison/ProC-2269
91PalmSp/ProC-2011
Peckinpaugh, Roger
14CJ-91
15CJ-91
21Exh-125
21Exh-126
61F-132
86Conlon/1-37
91Conlon/Sport-308
D327
D328-131
D329-137
D350/2-136
E120
E121/120
E121/80
E122
E135-131
E210
E220
M101/4-137
M101/5-136
V100
V117-23
W502-56
W514-44
W516-20
W575
WG7-40
Pecota, Bill
82FtMyr-21
84Memphis-24
85Omaha-29
86Omaha-17
86Omaha/TCMA-12
87F/Up-U97
88D-466
88F-264
88S-377
88Smok/Royals-22
88T-433
89F-289
89Omaha/CMC-15
89S-339
89T-148
89T/Big-292
89UD-507
90B-377
90Omaha/CMC-16
91D-672
91F-565
91F/UltraUp-U28
91OPC-754
91Panini/FrSt-277
91Pol/Royal-17
91S-513
91T-754
92D/I-361
92F-165
92S/I-252
92T-236
92UD-240
Peden, Les
53T-256
91T/Arc53-256
Pedersen, Mark
81Wausau-6
Pedersen, Don
89NiagFls/Pucko-1
90Fayette/ProC-2414
Pederson, Stu
82VeroB-24
85Cram/PCL-167
86Albuq-19
87Albuq/Pol-29
89Syrac/CMC-16
89Syrac/ProC-798
89Syrac/Team-18
90Syrac/CMC-23
90Syrac/ProC-586
90Syrac/Team-18
90Target-613
91Syrac/LineD-512
91Syrac/ProC-2495
Pedraza, Nelson
83Watlo/LF-7
85Water-1
Pedraza, Rodney
91FrRow/DP-16
91James/ClBest-27
91James/ProC-3543
Pedre, Jorge
88AppFx/ProC-137
88MidwLAS/GS-37
89BBCity/Star-20
90Foil/Best-139
90Memphis/Best-2
90Memphis/ProC-1013
90Memphis/Star-22
91London/LineD-411
91Memphis/ProC-658
92S/II-844RP
92T/91Debut-136
Pedrique, Alfredo
(Al)
82Jacks-16
84Jacks-23
85IntLgAS-14
85Tidew-24
86Tidew-24
88D-361
88F-338
88Panini/St-375
88S-301
88T-294
88T/JumboR-17
88T/St-128
88T/St-304
88ToysRUs-23
89B-104
89Mara/Tigers-17
89S-614
89T-566
89T-699TL
90Tacoma/CMC-19
90Tacoma/ProC-102
91Tidew/LineD-565
91Tidew/ProC-2519
91WIZMets-311
Peek, Timothy
88Spartan/ProC-1027
88Spartan/Star-15
88Spartan/Star-15
90Madison/Best-23
91Huntsvl/ClBest-18
91Huntsvl/LineD-291
91HuntsvlProC-1793
Peel, Homer
34G-88
Peel, Jack
87CharWh-24
88Tampa/Star-20
89Saraso/Star-18
90CharlR/Star-20
Peguero, Jerry
87Modesto-17
88Huntsvl/BK-14
90Salinas/Cal-135
Peguero, Jose
89Beloit/I/Star-21
90Salinas/ProC-2726
Peguero, Julio
87Macon-16
88CLAS/Star-14
88Salem/Star-15
89Harris/ProC-294
89Harris/Star-13
90EastLAS/ProC-EL24
90Harris/ProC-1206
90Harris/Star-14
91ScranWB/LineD-492
91ScranWB/ProC-2553
Peguero, Pablo
77LodiD
78Cr/PCL-114
79Albuq-1
80Albuq-3
Pegues, Steve
88Fayette/ProC-1081
89Fayette/ProC-1594
90London/ProC-1282
91London/LineD-393
91London/ProC-1891
91Single/ClBest-126
Peitz, Henry
E107
E254
Pellagrini, Ed
49B-172
51B-292
52T-405
53T-28
91T/Arc53-28
Pellant, Gary
80LynnS-14
82Wausau-23
83Wausau/LF-3
Pellegrino, Tony
86Cram/PCL-172
88Charl/ProC-1194
89AubAs/ProC-3
89Wichita/Rock-12
Pells, Harry
76QuadC
77QuadC
Pelmmons, Scott
90CharWh/Best-6
Peltier, Dan
89Butte/SP-27
90A&AASingle/ProC-71
90Tulsa/ProC-1168
91B-266
91Classic/200-176
91Classic/II-T23
91OkCty/LineD-316
91OkCty/ProC-192
91UD-69TP
92T-618R
Pelty, Barney
10Domino-97
11Helmar-63
12Sweet/Pin-54
E286
M116
S74-35
T202
T204
T205
T206
T207
T215/blue
T215/brown
Peltz, Peter
81GlenF-14
Peltzer, Kurt
90Everett/Best-10
90Everett/ProC-3126
91Clinton/ClBest-7
91Clinton/ProC-832
Pemberton, Brock
75Tidew/Team-17
91WIZMets-312
Pemberton, Jose
87Elmira/Black-26
87Elmira/Red-26
Pemberton, Rudy
89Bristol/Star-20
90Fayette/ProC-2421
90SALAS/Star-17
91Lakeland/ClBest-26
91Lakeland/ProC-280
91Single/ClBest-181
92T-656M
Pena, Abelino
75BurlB
76BurlB
Pena, Adriano
81Wisco-8
Pena, Alejandro
79Clinton
81Albuq/TCMA-4
82Pol/Dodg-26
83Pol/Dodg-26
83T/Tr-83T
84D-250
84F-109
84Nes/792-324
84Pol/Dodg-26
84T-324
84T/St-82
85Coke/Dodg-24
85D-337
85F-379
85F/St-94
85Leaf-64
85OPC-110
85Seven-15W
85T-110
85T/Gloss40-33
85T/St-73
85T/Super-17
86Coke/Dodg-22
86F-140
86Pol/Dodg-26
86T-665
87F-449
87Mother/Dodg-18
87OPC-363
87Pol/Dodg-13
87T-787
88D-598
88F/Up-U97
88Mother/Dodg-18
88Pol/Dodg-26
88T-277
89D-557
89F-69
89Mother/Dodg-18
89Pol/Dodg-16
89S-389
89T-57
89UD-137
90B-124
90D-664
90F-405
90F/Up-U38
90Kahn/Mets-26
90Leaf/II-403
90OPC-483
90PubInt/St-15
90S-39
90S/Tr-32T
90T-483
90T/Tr-89T
90T/TVMets-17
90Target-614
90UD-279
90UD/Ext-703
91D-566
91F-158
91Kahn/Mets-26
91Leaf/I-70
91OPC-544
91S-204
91T-544
91T/StClub/II-583
91UD-388
91WIZMets-313
92Classic/I-18
92D/II-616HL
92D/II-772
92F-700M
92S/II-691
92S/II-787M
92T-337
92UD-694
Pena, Antonio
91SanBern/ClBest-10
91SanBern/ProC-1986
Pena, Bert
81Tucson-7
82Tucson-1
83Tucson-17
84Cram/PCL-67
86Tucson-18
87Mother/Ast-24
87Tucson-16
88Colum/CMC-13
88Colum/Pol-16
88Colum/ProC-322
Pena, Dan
87VeroB-4
88Bakers/Cal-257
Pena, George
73OPC-601R
73T-601R
75Iowa/TCMA-13
Pena, Geronimo
87Savan-4
88FSLAS/Star-16
88StPete/Star-21
90F/Up-U52
90Louisvl/CMC-19
90Louisvl/ProC-412
90T/TVCard-59
91D-712
91F/Up-U118
91OPC-636
91Pol/Card-7
91S-717RP
91S/Rook40-17
91T-636
91T/90Debut-123
91UD-20SR
92D/II-533
92F-587
92S/100RisSt-12
92S/II-516
92T-166
92UD-596
Pena, Hipolito
86Nashua-21
87Vanco-18
88Colum/CMC-7
88Colum/Pol-8
88Colum/ProC-315
89Colum/CMC-5
89Colum/Pol-18
89Colum/ProC-744
89D-598
89F-263
89T-109
90ColClip/CMC-6
91ColClip/LineD-114

91ColClip/ProC-597
Pena, Jaime
89Erie/Star-17
Pena, James
86Cram/PCL-14
87Clinton-19
89SanJose/Best-16
89SanJose/Cal-216
89SanJose/ProC-445
89SanJose/Star-21
90Shrev/ProC-1442
90Shrev/Star-19
91Shrev/LineD-317
91Shrev/ProC-1820
Pena, Jose
86Clinton-19
88Shrev/ProC-1292
88Utica/Pucko-23
89Shrev/ProC-1848
Pena, Jose G.
69T-339R
70OPC-523
70T-523
71MLB/St-112
71OPC-693
71T-693
72OPC-322
72T-322
90Target-615
Pena, Luis
86Macon-18
Pena, Manny
83Orlan-13
Pena, Orlando
59T-271
63T-214
64T-124
65T-311
66T-239
67T-449
68T-471
69T/St-97
73JP
74OPC-393
74T-393
75OPC-573
75T-573
75T/M-573
75Tucson-12
91Crown/Orio-357
Pena, Pedro
89Medford/Best-11
90Madison/ProC-2270
91SanJose/ClBest-19
91SanJose/ProC-8
Pena, Porfirio
90Batavia/ProC-3068
91Martins/ClBest-15
91Martins/ProC-3456
Pena, R. Roberto
65T-549R
66T-559
69OPC-184
69T-184
70OPC-44
70T-44
71MLB/St-448
71OPC-334
71T-334
Pena, Ramon
86GlenF-18
87GlenF-20
88Toledo/CMC-6
88Toledo/ProC-610
89Mara/Tigers-18
89Toledo/CMC-2
89Toledo/ProC-779
90T/89Debut-96
Pena, Tony
77Salem
80Port-24
81T-551R
82D-124
82F-490
82F/St-72
82T-138
83D-59
83D/AAS-35
83F-316
83OPC-133
83T-590
83T/St-281
84D-186
84D/AAS-3
84F-259
85FunFoodPin-88
84Nes/792-645
84Nestle/DT-19
84OPC-152
84Seven-18E
84T-645
84T/St-129
85D-24DK
85D-64
85D/AAS-10
85D/DKsuper-24
85F-472
85F/LimEd-24
85Leaf-24DK
85OPC-358
85T-358
85T/St-124
86BK/AP-1
86D-64
86D/AAS-22
86F-616
86F/LimEd-34
86F/Mini-119
86F/St-87
86Leaf-58
86OPC-260
86Sf-165
86Sf/Dec-72M
86T-260
86T/St-125
87BK-15
87Classic-34
87D-115
87D/AAS-46
87D/OD-64
87F-617
87F/BB-31
87F/LL-35
87F/Lim-32
87F/St-90
87F/Up-U98
87Ho/St-14
87Kraft-12
87Leaf-256
87MnM's-2
87MSA/Discs-5
87OPC-60
87RedFoley/St-25
87Sf-151M
87Sf-93
87S/Test-48
87Smok/Cards-11
87T-60
87T/Coins-39
87T/St-129
87T/Tr-95T
88D-170
88D/Best-156
88F-45
88F/WS-5M
88Leaf-95
88OPC-117
88Panini/St-387
88Panini/St-447IA
88Panini/St-449IA
88RedFoley/St-67
88S-48
88Sf-142
88Smok/Card-13
88T-410
88T/St-52
89B-435
89Cadaco-38
89D-163
89D/Best-299
89F-460
89KMart/DT-30
89OPC-94
89Panini/St-180
89S-36
89Smok/Cards-17
89T-715
89T/St-38
89UD-330
90B-271
90Classic/III-67
90D-181
90D/BestAL-44
90F-256
90F/Up-U74
90Leaf/I-104
90MLBPA/Pins-34
90OPC-115
90Pep/RSox-14
90Publint/St-225
90Publint/St-269
90S-122
90S/Tr-7T
90T-115
90T/Big-290
90T/Tr-90T
90T/TVRSox-20
90UD-276
90UD/Ext-748
91B-124
91D-456
91F-106
91F/Ultra-37
91Leaf/I-33
91Leaf/Stud-17
91OPC-375
91Panini/FrSt-263
91Panini/St-219
91Pep/RSox-14
91S-790
91T-375
91T/StClub/II-505
91UD-652
92D/I-208
92F-43
92S/II-446
92T-569
92UD-252
Penafeather, Pat
88AubAs/ProC-1952
Pendergast, Steve
W514-117
Pendleton, Jim
52Park-69
53JC-25
53SpicSpan/3x5-20
53T-185
54JC-3
54T-165
55Gol/Braves-25
55JC-2
55T-15
55T/DH-33
57T-327
58T-104
59T-174
62T-432
89Smok/Ast-25
91T/Arc53-185
Pendleton, Terry
83ArkTr-15
84Louisvl-15
85D-534
85F-236
85OPC-346
85T-346
86D-205
86F-44
86KAS/Disc-14
86KayBee-23
86Leaf-137
86OPC-321
86Schnucks-19
86T-528
86T/St-53
87D-183
87D/OD-62
87F-306
87Leaf-124
87OPC-8
87Smok/Cards-16
87T-8
87T/St-54
88D-454
88D/Best-187
88F-46
88F/AwardWin-28
88F/SS-27
88F/St-119
88Leaf-246
88OPC-105
88Panini/St-392
88RedFoley/St-68
88S-190
88Sf-159
88Smok/Card-17
88T-635
88T/Big-53
88T/St-49
88T/St/Backs-7
89B-437
89D-230
89D/Best-156
89F-461
89OPC-375
89Panini/St-185
89S-137
89Sf-99
89Smok/Cards-18
89T-375
89T/Big-151
89T/St-42
89UD-131
90B-197
90D-299
90D/BestNL-34
90F-257
90Leaf/I-260
90OPC-725
90Panini/St-337
90Publint/St-226
90S-208
90Sf-174
90Smok/Card-19
90T-725
90T/Big-135
90T/St-40
90T/TVCard-28
90UD-469
91B-570
91D-446
91F-642
91F/Ultra-10
91F/Up-U76
91Leaf/II-304
91Leaf/Stud-148
91OPC-485
91OPC/Premier-95
91S-230
91S/RookTr-50T
91T-485
91T/StClub/II-327
91T/Tr-90T
91UD-484
91UD/Ext-708
92Classic/I-70
92D/Elite-E16
92D/I-237
92D/II-BC2MVP
92F-366
92F-691LL
92F/ASIns-15
92S/100SS-45
92S/I-18
92S/II-789MVP
92T-115
92UD-229
Penigar, C.L.
86Clinton-20
88MidldA/GS-17
89BirmB/Best-23
89BirmB/ProC-115
90Vanco/CMC-9
90Vanco/ProC-502
Penland, Ken
88Butte-6
Penn, Shannon
91Gaston/ClBest-21
91Gaston/ProC-2698
Penn, Trevor
88Rockford-28
89Rockford-29
89WPalmB/Star-21
90Jaxvl/Best-11
90Jaxvl/ProC-1386
Penniall, David
77StPete
80ArkTr-10
Pennington, Art
86Negro/Frit-53
Pennington, Brad
89Bluefld/Star-18
90Foil/Best-65
90Wausau/Best-8
90Wausau/ProC-2121
90Wausau/Star-18
91Kane/ClBest-9
91Kane/ProC-2657
91Single/ClBest-390
Pennington, Ken
87Sumter-23
88Durham/Star-16
89Durham/Team-17
89Durham/Star-17
89Star/Wax-72
90EastLAS/ProC-EL16
90Foil/Best-177
90Wmsprt/Best-18
90Wmsprt/ProC-1065
90Wmsprt/Star-19
91Jaxvl/LineD-341
91Jaxvl/ProC-159
Pennock, Herb
28Yueng-8
31Exh/4-25
33Exh/4-13
33G-138
50Callahan
60Exh/HOF-19
60F-35
61F-133
63Bz/Sm
80Pac/Leg-111
80Laugh/FFeat-2
80SSPC/HOF
86Conlon/1-51
89HOF/St-67
91Conlon/Sport-120
91Conlon/Sport-143
92Conlon/Sport-465
92Conlon/Sport-594
E120
E210-8
E220
R315-A28
R315-B28
R316
R423-84
V100
V117-27
V354-16
W502-8
W513-68
Pennye, Darwin
88Watertn/Pucko-23
89Augusta/ProC-504
90CLAS/CL-24
90Salem/Star-15
91CaroMud/LineD-114
91CaroMud/ProC-1098
Pennyfeather, William
89Welland/Pucko-1
90Augusta/ProC-2477
90SALAS/Star-39
91B-517
91Salem/ClBest-11
91Salem/ProC-965
91Single/ClBest-158
Penrod, Jack
88Pocatel/ProC-2102
Penson, Paul
54T-236
Penton, Jack
28Exh/PCL-6
Pentz, Gene
77T-308
78BK/Ast-11
78T-64
79Portl-12
80Port-25
81Phoenix-20
Penvose, Randy
86Geneva-22
Peoples, James
N172
N284
Pepitone, Joe
62T-596R
63T-183
64T-360
64T/Coins-121AS
64T/St-22
64Wheat/St-34
65OPC-245
65T-245
66OPC-79
66T-79
67OPC/PI-22
67T-340
67T/PI-22
68Bz-5
68OPC-195
68T-195
69MB-216
69MLB/St-76
69MLBPA/Pin-21
69Sunoco/Pin-7

69T-589
69T/St-206
70K-59
70MLB/St-45
70T-598
70T-90
71MLB/St-40
71OPC-90
71T/GM-53
72MB-268
72OPC-303
72OPC-304IA
72T-303
72T-304IA
73OPC-580
73T-580
78TCMA-6
PM10/Sm-142
WG10-17
WG9-19
Pepper, Hugh
(Laurin)
55T-147
56T-108
Pepper, Stu
91Pac/SenLg-73
Pepper, Tony
75Phoenix-18
Peppers, Devin
90Elizab/Star-15
Pequignot, Jon
86VeroB-19
87SanAn-19
Peralta, Amado
85Tigres-21
Peralta, Martin
88SLCity-22
Peraza, Luis
86AppFx-18
Peraza, Oswald
86Knoxvl-18
87Knoxvl-18
88French-23
88S/Tr-77T
89B-1
89D-524
89F-615
89S-571
89T-297
89T/Big-219
89UD-651
90Hagers/Best-27
91Crown/Orio-358
91Hagers/LineD-242
91Hagers/ProC-2456
Percival, Troy
90Boise/ProC-3335
91Boise/ClBest-23
91Boise/ProC-3875
Perconte, Jack
77LodiD
79Albuq-13
80Albuq-16
81Albuq/TCMA-17
81T-302R
82T/Tr-87T
82Wheat/Ind
83Charl-13
83D-463
83F-417
83T-569
84F/X-U90
84Mother/Mar-15
85D-74
85F-498
85Leaf-221
85Mother/Mar-11
85T-172
85T/St-341
86F-472
86T-146
87Albuq/Pol-20
90Target-616
Perdomo, Felix
83Greens-21
86Columbia-19
87Lynch-12
88Jacks/GS-24
Perdue, Alphie
77Salem
Perdue, Doran
81Shrev-15
Perdue, Herbert R.
(Hub)
14CJ-121
15CJ-121
T206
T207
T213/brown
T222
Pereira, Ray
84LitFalls-8
Perez, Alex
88Kenosha/ProC-1385
Perez, Beban
89QuadC/Best-28
89QuadC/GS-23
90PalmSp/Cal-213
90PalmSp/ProC-2592
91PalmSp/ProC-2031
Perez, Benny
78Dunedin
Perez, Carlos
75QuadC
78Cr/PCL-99
79SLCity-18
80SLCity-13
81SLCity-10
Perez, Carlos
(Pitcher)
91Single/ClBest-92
91Sumter/ProC-2333
Perez, Cesar
90Greens/Best-9
90Greens/ProC-2661
90Greens/Star-15
90Oneonta/ProC-3369
91Greens/ProC-3056
Perez, Dario
91AppFx/ClBest-8
91AppFx/ProC-1714
Perez, David
89Butte/SP-2
90CharlR/Star-21
90FSLAS/Star-39
91Tulsa/LineD-590
91Tulsa/ProC-2770
Perez, Dick
85D/DKsuper-28
Perez, Eddie
89Sumter/ProC-1112
90Sumter/Best-17
90Sumter/ProC-2438
91Durham/ClBest-12
91Durham/ProC-1548
Perez, Eduardo
91Boise/ClBest-8
91Boise/ProC-3896
91Classic/DP-13
92UD-52TP
Perez, Eulogio
88Martins/Star-27
89Martins/Star-24
90Batavia/ProC-3075
90Spartan/ProC-2500
90Spartan/Star-17
91Spartan/ClBest-17
91Spartan/ProC-901
Perez, Francisco
86Erie-23
89Ashvl/ProC-963
89AubAs/ProC-2174
90Ashvl/ProC-2745
Perez, Fred
85Utica-21
Perez, Gorky
87Ashvl-26
87AubAs-15
88Ashvl/ProC-1062
89Osceola/Star-17
Perez, Hector
82Madis-32TR
83Madis/LF-29TR
84LitFalls-17
86Lynch-16
87Lynch-10
89Penin/Star-18
Perez, Joe
90Watertn/Star-15
91Collnd/ClBest-3
91Collnd/ProC-1501
Perez, Joel
77AppFx
79Knoxvl/TCMA-16
Perez, Jose
89Salem/Team-22
90Kissim/DIMD-21
90Yakima/Team-34
Perez, Julio
78Memphis/Team-7
80GlenF-16
83Reading-16
86Macon-19
87Macon-14
88Miami/Star-18
89Harris/ProC-307
89Harris/Star-14
90Harris/ProC-1201
90Harris/Star-15
Perez, Leo
88Beloit/GS-18
89Stockton/Best-13
89Stockton/Cal-158
89Stockton/ProC-373
89Wythe/Star-23
90Stockton/Best-24
90Stockton/Cal-186
90Stockton/ProC-2185
91Geneva/ClBest-14
91Geneva/ProC-4211
91WinSalem/ClBest-8
91WinSalem/ProC-2827
Perez, Manuel R.
48Sommer-17
49Sommer-8
Perez, Mario
85Bend/Cram-19
Perez, Marty
71OPC-529R
71T-529R
72OPC-119
72T-119
73OPC-144
73T-144
74OPC-374
74T-374
75OPC-499
75T-499
75T/M-499
76Dubuq
76Ho-65
76K-26
76OPC-177
76T-177
77BurgChef-100
77OPC-183
77T-438
78Ho-4
78T-613
78Tidew
Perez, Melido
86BurlEx-17
88Coke/WS-21
88D-589
88D/Best-179
88D/Rook-21
88F-265
88F/Up-U19
88S/Tr-108T
88T/Tr-83T
89B-59
89Classic-88
89Coke/WS-21
89D-58
89D/Best-179
89F-509
89OPC-88
89Panini/St-300
89RedFoley/St-89
89S-386
89S/HotRook-79
89S/YS/I-7
89Sf-118
89T-786
89T/Big-235
89T/JumboR-16
89T/St-296
89ToysRUs-21
89UD-243
90B-310
90Coke/WSox-21
90D-101
90D/BestAL-18
90F-546
90Kodak/WSox-2
90Leaf/I-36
90OPC-621
90Panini/St-42
90Publint/St-399
90Publint/St-602
90S-311
90T-621
90T/Big-195
90T/St-304
90UD-525
91B-344
91D-164
91D-BC13
91F-133
91F/Ultra-80
91F/WaxBox-7
91Kodak/WSox-33
91OPC-499
91Panini/FrSt-358
91Panini/St-7
91Panini/Top15-96
91S-179
91S-705NH
91T-499
91T/StClub/I-232
91UD-623
92D/II-509
92F-95
92S/I-29
92T-129
92UD-190
Perez, Michael I.
87Spring/Best-15
88ArkTr/GS-21
89ArkTr/GS-17
89TexLAS/GS-24
90AAAGame/ProC-AAA29
90Louisvl/CMC-8
90Louisvl/ProC-402
90SpringDG/Best-25
90T/TVCard-60
91D-615
91F-643
91OPC-205
91S-758RP
91T-205
91T/90Debut-124
91UD/Ext-728
92F-588
Perez, Ozzie
90Hamil/Best-18
90Hamil/Star-18
91Savan/ClBest-21
91Savan/ProC-1662
Perez, Paco
79Jacks-1
Perez, Pascual
77Charl
79Portl-20
80Port-7
81Portl-20
81T-551R
82F-491
82Portl-7
82T-383
83D-557
83F-144
83Pol/Atl-27
83T/Tr-84
84D-507
84F-188
84F/St-59
84Nes/792-675
84OPC-1
84Pol/Atl-27
84T-675
84T/St-36
85D-507
85D/AAS-18
85F-337
85Ho/Braves-18
85Leaf-55
85OPC-106
85Pol/Atl-27
85T-106
86F-524
86T-491
87D/HL-50
87Indianap-26
88D-591
88D/Best-236
88F-192
88Leaf-248
88OPC-237
88S-459
88T-647
88T/Big-196
89B-354
89Classic-85
89D-248
89D/Best-302
89F-390
89OPC-73
89Panini/St-115
89S-299
89T-73
89T/St-71
89UD-498
90B-430
90D-342
90D/BestAL-80
90F-358
90F/Up-116
90OPC-278
90Panini/St-282
90Publint/St-185
90S-486
90S/NWest-11
90S/Tr-5T
90T-278
90T/Big-291
90T/Tr-91T
90T/TVYank-16
90UD-487
90UD/Ext-769
91F-675
91Leaf/II-293
91OPC-701
91T-701
91T/StClub/II-485
91UD-671
92D/II-695
92F-240
92S/I-88
92T-503
Perez, Pedro
89Salem/Team-23
90VeroB/Star-22
90Yakima/Team-36
91Geneva/ClBest-15
91Geneva/ProC-4212
91Peoria/ProC-1340
Perez, Ramon
73Cedar
74Cedar
75Iowa/TCMA-14
78Charl
79Charl-9
Perez, Richard
91Hunting/ClBest-17
91Hunting/ProC-3342
Perez, Robert
90StCath/ProC-3456
91Dunedin/ClBest-22
91Dunedin/ProC-220
Perez, Segio
86Clearw-19
Perez, Tony
65T-581R
66OPC-72
66T-72
67Kahn
67T-476
68Bz-12
68Kahn
68OPC-130
68T-130
68T/3D
69Kahn
69MB-217
69MLB/St-134
69T-295
69T/St-28
70MLB/St-34
70OPC-380
70OPC-63LL
70T-380
70T-63LL
70T/SO
71K-58
71MD
71MLB/St-67
71OPC-580
71OPC-64LL
71OPC-66LL
71T-580
71T-64LL
71T-66LL
71T/Coins-105
71T/GM-14
71T/S-6
71T/tatt-9

72MB-269
72OPC-80
72T-80
73OPC-275
73T-275
74OPC-230
74T-230
74T/DE-54
74T/St-29
75Ho-127
75OPC-560
75T-560
75T/M-560
76Crane-46
76Ho-86
76Icee
76MSA/Disc
76OPC-195LL
76OPC-325
76SSPC-39
76T-195
76T-325
77BurgChef-160
77OPC-135
77T-655
77T/CS-37
78OPC-90
78T-15
78Wiffle/Discs-59
79OPC-261
79T-495
80OPC-69
80T-125
81Coke
81D-334
81F-241
81F/St-66
81K-17
81OPC-231
81T-575
81T/HT
81T/SO-8
81T/St-44
82Coke/BOS
82D-408
82F-302
82F/St-170
82OPC-255
82OPC-256IA
82T-255
82T-256IA
82T/St-152
83D-578
83F-191
83OPC-355
83OPC-74SV
83T-715
83T-716SV
83T/St-8
83T/Tr-85
84Borden-24
84D-503
84D/Champs-29
84F-44
84F-636IA
84F/X-U91
85FunFoodPin-99
84Nes/792-385
84Nes/792-702LL
84Nes/792-703LL
84Nes/792-704LL
84OPC-385
84T-385
84T-702LL
84T-703LL
84T-704LL
84T/St-126
84T/Tr-91
85CircK-28
85D/HL-9
85F-546
85OPC-212
85T-675
86D-15DK
86D-428
86D/DKsuper-15
86F-186
86Leaf-15DK
86OPC-85
86Sf-138M
86T-205RB
86T-85
86T/St-143
86T/St-8
86TexGold-24
87F-209
88Kahn/Reds-CO
90Kahn/Reds-27M
91Kahn/Reds-x

Perez, Victor
90Billings/ProC-3236

Perez, Vladimir
87Spartan-23
88LitFalls/Pucko-19
89Clmbia/Best-2
89Clmbia/GS-20

Perez, William
89Modesto/Chong-14

Perez, Yorkis
86Kenosha-19
87WPalmB-16
88Jaxvl/Best-11
88Jaxvl/ProC-973
89WPalmB/Star-17
90Jaxvl/Best-22
90Jaxvl/ProC-1372
91Richm/LineD-436
91Richm/ProC-2564
92D/II-754
92T/91Debut-137

Perezchica, Tony
84Everett/Cram-30B
86Fresn/Smok-20
87Shrev-6
88AAA/ProC-32
88Phoenix/CMC-16
88Phoenix/ProC-75
89F-338
89Phoenix/CMC-14
89Phoenix/ProC-1502
89S/HotRook-50
90B-235
90Phoenix/CMC-20
91D/Rook-10
91PG&E-30
91Phoenix/LineD-388
91Phoenix/ProC-74
91S-735RP
92S/II-702

Perigny, Don
90SoBend/CIBest-19
91SoBend/ProC-2855

Perkins, Bill
86Negro/Frit-94

Perkins, Broderick
78Padre/FamFun-21
79T-725R
80Hawaii-22
81D-525
81F-498
81T-393
81T/St-226
82D-397
82F-579
82F/St-103
82OPC-192
82T-192
82T/St-98
83D-121
83F-368
83T-593
83T/St-292
83T/Tr-86
83Wheat/Ind-24
84D-276
84F-548
84Nes/792-212
84T-212
84Wheat/Ind-15
85T-609

Perkins, Charlie
90Target-617

Perkins, Harold
82VeroB-19
83VeroB-20
89RochR/CMC-18
89RochR/ProC-1643

Perkins, Paul
91Penin/CIBest-9
91Penin/ProC-375

Perkins, Ralph
(Cy)
21Exh-127
25Exh-110
26Exh-110
91Conlon/Sport-185
E120
E210-29
E220
V100
V355-24
V61-11
W572
W573

Perkins, Ray
82AubAs-5
86FSLAS-38
86Miami-20

Perkins, Tom
75Clinton

Perkowski, Harry
52B-202
52T-142
53B/Col-87
53T-236
54B-44
54T-125
55T-184
91T/Arc53-236

Perlman, Jon
83Iowa-8
84Iowa-6
85Iowa-19
86Phoenix-20
87Phoenix-13
88ColoSp/CMC-6
88ColoSp/ProC-1542
88F-93
88F/Up-U22
89S-591
89T-476

Perlozzo, Sam
78T-704R
79Hawaii-11
79T-709R
81Tidew-22
83Lynch-11
84Jacks-16
86Tidew-23MG
88Kahn/Mets-34CO
89Kahn/Mets-34CO
90Kahn/Reds-27M
91Kahn/Reds-x

Perna, Robert
90Billings/ProC-3230
91CharWh/CIBest-18
91CharWh/ProC-2895
91SALAS/ProC-SAL9

Perno, Donn
87Everett-23

Pernoll, H. Hub
M116

Perodin, Ron
80Clinton-21

Perozo, Danny
88Billings/ProC-1813
89Billings/ProC-2058
89Greens/ProC-409
90CharWh/Best-23
90CharWh/ProC-2254
91Cedar/CIBest-23
91Cedar/ProC-2733

Perozo, Ed
90LynchRS/Team-3

Perozo, Ender
89Elmira/Pucko-13

Perpetuo, Nelson
91Bristol/CIBest-28
91Bristol/ProC-3601

Perranoski, Ron
61T-525
62BB-16
62T-297
63T-403
64T-30
64T/Coins-64
64T/St-46
64T/tatt
64Wheat/St-35
65T-484
66T-555
67T-197
68T-435
69OPC-77
69T-77
69T/St-197
70MLB/St-237
70OPC-226
70T-226
71MLB/St-469
71OPC-475
71T-475
71T/Coins-104
72OPC-367
72T-367
85Coke/Dodg-25CO
86Coke/Dodg-23CO
90Mother/Dodg-28M
90Pol/Dodg-xCO
90Target-618
91Mother/Dodg-28CO
91Pol/Dodg-x
WG10-42
WG9-41

Perrier, Hip
N172/PCL

Perring, George
14CJ-119
15CJ-119
M116
T206

Perritt, William D.
(Pol)
92Conlon/Sport-488
D327
D328-132
E135-132

Perry, Alonzo
49Remar

Perry, Bob
86Kenosha-20

Perry, David
89Boise/ProC-1981

Perry, Eric
88CharWh/Best-7
88Geneva/ProC-1633
89Peoria/Ko-19

Perry, Gaylord
61Union
62T-199
62T/bucks
63T-169R
64T-468
65OPC-193
65T-193
66T-598
67T-236LL
67T-320
68Coke
68Dexter-61
68OPC-11LL
68OPC-85
68T-11LL
68T-85
69MB-218
69MLB/St-207
69T-485
69T/St-110
70K-20
70MLB/St-132
70T-560
71K-6
71MD
71MLB/St-261
71OPC-140
71OPC-70LL
71T-140
71T-70LL
71T/Coins-73
71T/S-2
71Ticket/Giant-10
72MB-270
72OPC-285
72T-285
73K-38
73OPC-346KP
73OPC-400
73OPC-66LL
73T-346KP
73T-400
73T-66LL
73T/Comics-14
73T/Lids-39
73T/PinUps-14
74OPC-35
74T-35
74T/St-168
75Ho-84
75K-45
75OPC-530
75T-530
75T/M-530
76Ho-4
76Ho/Twink-4
76OPC-204LL
76OPC-55
76T-204LL
76T-55
77BurgChef-20
77Ho-73
77OPC-149
77T-152
78Ho-139
78Padre/FamFun-22
78T-686
78Wiffle/Discs-60
79Ho-83
79K-49
79OPC-161
79T-321
79T-5LL
80OPC-148
80T-280
81D-471
81F-91
81Pol/Atl-46
81T-582
81T/Tr-812
82D-543
82F-445
82F/St-67
82OPC-115
82T-115
82T/St-24
82T/Tr-88T
83D-307
83D/AAS-28
83F-483
83F-630M
83Nalley-1
83OPC-159SV
83OPC-96
83T-463
83T-464IA
83T/St-114
84D-LLA
84D/Champs-32
84F-352
84F-638IA
84F-641
84F/St-98
84Mother/Giants-4
84Nes/792-4HL
84Nes/792-6HL
84T-4HL
84T-6HL
89Pac/Leg-152
89Padre/Mag-24
89T/LJN-69
90BBWit-40
90Pac/Legend-43
90Swell/Great-66
91K/3D-1
91Swell/Great-70
91UD/HOF-H2
91UD/HOF-x
PM10/Sm-143

Perry, Gerald
82ArkTr-6
82Richm-14
83Richm-14
84D-263
84F/X-U92
84Pol/Atl-28
84T/Tr-92T
85D-443
85F-338
85Ho/Braves-19
85Pol/Atl-28
85T-219
86D-165
86F-525
86Richm-16
86T-557
87Smok/Atl-17
87T-639
88D-437
88D/Best-58
88F-547
88Leaf-216
88Panini/St-242
88S-136
88T-39
88T/Big-40
89B-273
89Cadaco-39
89Classic-118

89D-22DK
89D-239
89D/AS-57
89D/Best-291
89D/DKsuper-22DK
89D/MVP-BC24
89F-597
89F-638M
89F/BBAS-31
89F/BBMVP's-31
89F/Heroes-30
89OPC-130
89Panini/St-40
89RedFoley/St-90
89S-101
89S/HotStar-20
89Sf-164
89T-130
89T/Big-279
89T/Coins-21
89T/LJN-108
89T/Mini-2
89T/St-33
89T/UK-59
89UD-431
90B-383
90Classic/III-48
90D-153
90F-592
90F/Up-103
90Leaf/II-441
90OPC-792
90PublInt/St-118
90Richm25Ann/Team-19
90S-249
90S/Tr-28T
90T-792
90T/St-27
90T/Tr-92T
90UD-101
90UD/Ext-707
91B-405
91D-130
91F-566
91F/UltraUp-U109
91F/Up-U119
91Leaf/II-272
91OPC-384
91Panini/St-230
91Pol/Card-21
91S-286
91S/RookTr-63T
91T-384
91T/StClub/II-379
91UD-219
92D/II-634
92F-589
92S/II-491
92T-498
92UD-690

Perry, Herbert
91FrRow/DP-51
91Watertn/ClBest-21
91Watertn/ProC-3376

Perry, Herbert Scott
E220
E270/1

Perry, Jeff
84Savan-14
87Visalia-7

Perry, Jim
59Kahn
59T-542
60Kahn
60L-49
60T-324
61Bz-22
61Kahn
61P-59
61T-385
61T-48LL
61T-584AS
61T/St-138
62J-43
62Kahn
62P-43
62P/Can-43
62Salada-32
62Shirriff-32
62Sugar-5
62T-37M
62T-405
62T/St-37
63Sugar-5
63T-535
64T-34
65T-351
66T-283
67T-246
68T-393
69MB-219
69OPC-146
69T-146
70K-64
70MLB/St-236
70OPC-70LL
70T-620
70T-70LL
71K-3
71MD
71MLB/St-470
71OPC-500
71OPC-69LL
71T-500
71T-69LL
71T/Coins-12
71T/GM-10
71T/S-24
71T/tatt-14
72MB-271
72OPC-220
72OPC-497KP
72T-220
72T-497KP
73OPC-385
73T-385
74OPC-316
74T-316
75OPC-263
75T-263
75T/M-263
78TCMA-105
81Tacom-31
88Pac/Leg-18
89Swell-37
90BBWit-44

Perry, Melvin
(Bob)
64T-48

Perry, Parnell
86Geneva-23
87Peoria-22

Perry, Pat
83ColumAst-18
84ArkTr-18
85Louisvl-18
86D-596
86F/Up-U89
86Schnucks-20
87D-430
87F-307
87Smok/Cards-4
87T-417
88Berg/Cubs-37
88D-626
88F-244
88S-557
88T-282
89D-404
89F-435
89S-364
89T-186
89T/Big-329
89UD-345
90OPC-541
90PublInt/St-199
90S-436
90SpringDG/Best-17
90T-541
91S-527

Perry, Ron
80GlenF/B-17
80GlenF/C-1
81GlenF-15

Perry, Shawn
83Tacom-33

Perry, Steve
79LodiD-8
81VeroB-14
83Albuq-9
84Cram/PCL-154
90Oneonta/ProC-3370

Perschke, Greg
89Utica/Pucko-17
90Saraso/Star-19
91Vanco/LineD-644
91Vanco/ProC-1593

Persing, Tim
90Elizab/Star-16
91Kenosha/ClBest-8
91Kenosha/ProC-2070
91MidwLAS/ProC-MWL38
91Single/ClBest-371

Person, Carl
75QuadC

Person, Robert
90Kinston/Team-23
91BendB/ClBest-9
91BendB/ProC-3694
91Kinston/ClBest-10
91Kinston/ProC-322

Persons, Archie
T206
T213/brown

Pertica, William
E120

Perzanowski, Stan
76OPC-388
76T-388
77SLCity

Pesavento, Mike
85VeroB-22

Pesavento, Patrick
90Fayette/ProC-2415
90SALAS/Star-18

Pesky, Johnny
47HomogBond-37
47TipTop
48L-121
49B-86
50B-137
50Drake-32
51B-15
51T/BB-5
52B-45
52T-15
53B/Col-134
53Glen
54B-135
54T-63
55B-241
61Union
63T-343MG
64T-248MG
67T/Test/PP-20CO
76SSPC-625CO
91T/Arc53-315
D305
Exh47
PM10/Sm-144
R302

Pesut, Nick
47Sunbeam

Petagine, Roberto
91BurlAs/ClBest-17
91BurlAs/ProC-2811

Peterek, Jeff
86Stockton-20
87ElPaso-23
88ElPaso/Best-21
89Denver/CMC-8
89Denver/ProC-46
90D-530
90Denver/CMC-1
90Denver/ProC-623
90F-333
90T/89Debut-97

Peters, Dan
88Beloit/GS-20

Peters, Donald
90A&AASingle/ProC-161
90Classic/DP-26
90Classic/III-83
90SoOreg/Best-25
90SoOreg/ProC-3424
91B-224
91Classic/I-77
91Huntsvl/ClBest-19
91Huntsvl/LineD-292
91HuntsvlProC-1794
91S-381FDP
91Single/ClBest-288

Peters, Doug
91London/LineD-412
91Memphis/ProC-649

Peters, Frank
68T-409R

Peters, Gary
60T-407
61T-303
63T-522R
64Bz-27
64T-130
64T-2LL
64T/Coins-140AS
64T/Coins-71
64T/S-1
64T/St-56
64T/SU
64T/tatt
65Bz-27
65OldLond-32
65OPC-9LL
65T-430
65T-9LL
65T/E-18
65T/trans-62
66OPC-111
66T-111
67Bz-9
67T-233LL
67T-310
67T/Test/SU-2
68Bz-14
68Kahn
68OPC-8LL
68T-210
68T-379AS
68T-8LL
68T/G-13
68T/Post-13
69Kahn
69MB-220
69MLB/St-34
69OPC-34
69T-34
69T/St-157
70MLB/St-161
70OPC-540
70T-540
71MLB/St-327
71OPC-225
71T-225
71T/tatt-10
72MB-272
72OPC-503
72T-503
78TCMA-125
89Pac/Leg-159
Exh47

Peters, Jay
79SLCity-20
80SLCity-11

Peters, John
(Jack)
E120
V61-63

Peters, Oscar
T207

Peters, Ray
No Cards.

Peters, Reed
88PalmSp/Cal-108
88PalmSp/ProC-1439
89MidldA/GS-26
90Edmon/CMC-17
90Edmon/ProC-529
91Edmon/LineD-168
91Edmon/ProC-1529

Peters, Rex
89Salem/Team-24
90VeroB/Star-23
91AS/Cal-19

Peters, Richard D.
(Ricky)
81D-10
81F-470
81T-177
81T/St-77
82D-155
82F-277
82OPC-269
82T-504
83Tacom-29A
84F-458
84Nes/792-436
84T-436
85Cram/PCL-130
86Mother/A's-24
90AubAs/ProC-3417MG
91Pac/SenLg-117

Peters, Steve
87ArkTr-9
87TexLgAS-19
88D/Rook-22
88Louisvl-39
88Smok/Card-23
88T/Tr-84T
89F-462
89Louisvl-30
89Louisvl/CMC-9
89Louisvl/ProC-1247
89T-482
89UD/Ext-771
90LasVegas/CMC-2
90LasVegas/ProC-120
90SpringDG/Best-20
91OkCty/LineD-317
91OkCty/ProC-175

Peters, Tim
87SLCity/Taco-25
88MidwLAS/GS-47
89Jaxvl/Best-13
89Jaxvl/ProC-154
90Jaxvl/ProC-1373

Peterson, Adam C.
86Penin-20
87BirmB/Best-13
87SLAS-20
88F-646R
88Vanco/CMC-7
88Vanco/ProC-776
89AAA/CMC-45
89D-619
89Vanco/CMC-2
89Vanco/ProC-589
90B-307
90BirmDG/Best-27
90OPC-299
90T-299
90Vanco/CMC-2
90Vanco/ProC-488
91F-134
91LasVegas/ProC-233
91LasVegas/LineD-290
91OPC-559
91S-604
91S/100RisSt-94
91T-559
92UD-602

Peterson, Bart
91Kenosha/ClBest-14
91Kenosha/ProC-2071

Peterson, Brian
90Memphis/Best-28CO
90Memphis/ProC-1027CO
90Memphis/Star-26CO
91London/LineD-425CO
91London/LineD-425CO
91Memphis/ProC-671CO

Peterson, Carl
(Buddy)
52Mother-29
53Mother-8
91Crown/Orio-359

Peterson, Charles
(Cap)
64T-568R
65T-512
66T-349
67T-387
68OPC-188
68T-188
69T-571

Peterson, D. Scott
77Ashvl
78Ashvl

Peterson, Dave
85Greens-19
86NewBrit-20

Peterson, Eric
(Ricky)
77Charl
82Buffa-17C

Peterson, Erik
82Nashvl-17
83Nashvl-16
84Nashvl-17

Peterson, Fritz
66T-584R
67T-495
68T-246
69MLB/St-77
69OPC-46
69T-46
70MLB/St-248

70OPC-142
70T-142
71MD
71MLB/St-499
71OPC-460
71T-460
71T/Coins-138
71T/GM-44
71T/S-13
72T-573
72T-574IA
73OPC-82
73Syrac/Team-23
73T-82
74OPC-229
74Syrac/Team-22
74T-229
75OPC-62
75T-62
75T/M-62
76Ho-32
76Ho/Twink-32
76OPC-255
76SSPC-511
76T-255
90Swell/Great-79

Peterson, Geoff
86FtMyr-21

Peterson, Harding
58T-322

Peterson, Jerry
76Watlo

Peterson, Jim
77Clinton
90Target-619

Peterson, Kent
48L-42
49Eureka-92
51B-215

Peterson, Rick
88ColoSp/ProC-1530
89BirmB/Best-28
89BirmB/ProC-99CO
89Pac/SenLg-153
89T/SenLg-104
90BirmB/Best-25CO
91BirmB/LineD-75CO
91BirmB/ProC-1471CO
91Pac/SenLg-49

Peterson, Rob
89Welland/Pucko-20
90Welland/Pucko-18

Peterson, Robert A.
E254

Peterson, Tim
76Cedar

Petestio, Doug
84MidldC-12

Petit, Ricardo
91Idaho/ProC-4326
91Pulaski/ClBest-25
91Pulaski/ProC-4002

Petitt, Steven
86StPete-24

Petkovsek, Mark
88CharlR/Star-19
89TexLAS/GS-36
89Tulsa/GS-20
89Tulsa/Team-18
90OkCty/CMC-5
90OkCty/ProC-432
91OkCty/LineD-318
91OkCty/ProC-177
92T/91Debut-138

Petralli, Eugene J.
(Geno)
81Syrac-9
82Syrac-13
83D-623
83F-439
83Syrac-15
85Maine-16
85OKCty-5
86Rang-12
86T-296
87D-619
87F-135
87Mother/Rang-20
87Smok/R-8
87T-388
88D-506
88F-477
88Leaf-241
88Mother/R-20
88S-373
88Smok/R-3
88T-589
89D-343
89D/Best-312
89F-530
89Mother/R-11
89OPC-137
89Panini/St-451
89S-526
89Smok/R-25
89T-137
89T/Big-12
89T/St/Backs-24
89UD-482
90B-495
90D-56
90D/BestAL-27
90F-309
90Leaf/I-73
90Mother/Rang-7
90OPC-706
90Panini/St-161
90PublInt/St-419
90S-153
90T-706
90UD-633
91B-284
91D-137
91F-296
91F/Ultra-351
91Leaf/I-148
91Mother/Rang-7
91OPC-78
91Panini/FrSt-251
91S-191
91T-78
91T/StClub/I-10
91UD-492
92D/II-550
92F-313
92S/I-283
92T-409
92UD-599

Petrizzo, Tom
86DayBe-22CHM

Petrocelli, Rico
65OPC-74R
65T-74R
66T-298
67T-528
67T/Test/RSox-13
68Bz-5
68Coke
68Dexter-62
68OPC-156
68T-430
69Citgo-8
69MB-221
69MLB/St-15
69OPC-215
69T-215
69T/St-136
69Trans-21
70K-54
70MB-21
70MLB/St-162
70OPC-457AS
70T-457AS
70T-680
70T/CB
70T/S-14
70Trans-15
71Bz
71Bz/Test-10
71MD
71MLB/St-328
71OPC-340
71T-340
71T/Coins-30
71T/GM-39
71T/S-19
71T/tatt-11
72MB-273
72OPC-30
72T-30
73OPC-365
73T-365
74OPC-609
74T-609
75Ho-132
75OPC-356
75T-356
75T/M-356
76OPC-445
76SSPC-413
76T-445
77T-111
87BirmB/Best-1
87SLAS-23
88BirmB/Best-8
88SLAS-38
89Swell-123
90BirmDG/Best-28MG
90Pac/Legend-64
90Swell/Great-56
91LineD-31
91Swell/Great-71
PM10/Sm-145

Petry, Dan
80T-373
81D-128
81F-468
81T-59
82D-133
82F-278
82T-211
82T-666TL
83D-359
83F-339
83OPC-79
83T-261TL
83T-638
83T/St-70
84D-105
84F-89
85FunFoodPin-60
84Nes/792-147
84OPC-147
84T-147
84T/St-269
85Cain's-16
85D-334
85F-20
85F/St-83
85Leaf-188
85OPC-392
85Seven-7D
85T-435
85T/Gloss40-25
85T/St-264
85Wendy-18
86Cain's-15
86D-212
86D/AAS-42
86F-235
86Leaf-144
86OPC-216
86T-540
86T/St-270
87Cain's-15
87Coke/Tigers-12
87D-373
87F-161
87Leaf-228
87OPC-27
87Seven-DT9
87T-752
88D-476
88D/Best-139
88F-67
88S-461
88S/Tr-26T
88Smok/Angels-8
88T-78
88T/Tr-85T
89D-344
89F-486
89S-122
89T/Big-178
89UD-552
90CokeK/Tiger-16
90F-142
90Leaf/II-508
90OPC-363
90PublInt/St-377
90S-211
90S/Tr-39T
90T-363
90T/Tr-93T
90UD-690
91B-146
91CokeK/Tiger-46
91D-675
91F-347
91F/Ultra-125
91Panini/FrSt-295
91Panini/St-240
91RedFoley/St-71
91S-434
91UD-316
92S/II-705

Pettaway, Ike
78Green
83Durham-22

Pettee, Patrick E.
N172

Pettengill, Tim
89Savan/ProC-352

Pettibone, Jay
80Ashvl-17
82Orlan/B-22
83Orlan-14
84Toledo-24

Pettibone, Jim
82Cedar-10
83Water-6
84Cedar-3
85Cedar-11

Pettiford, Cecil
89BurlInd/Star-20
90AS/Cal-55
90Reno/Cal-279
91Kinston/ClBest-11
91Kinston/ProC-323

Pettini, Joe
78Memphis/Team-8
80Phoenix-20
81F-453
81Phoenix-21
81T-62
82F-398
82T-568
83T-143
84Cram/PCL-13
84Nes/792-449
84T-449
85Louisvl-12
86Louisvl-23
87Louisvl-2CO
88Louisvl-2CO
88Louisvl/CMC-24
88Louisvl/ProC-435
89Hamil/Star-27
90StPete/Star-26CO
91ArkTr/LineD-49MG
91ArkTr/ProC-1302MG

Pettis, Gary
81Holyo-20
82Spokane-23
84D-647
84F-526
84Smok/Cal-21
84T/Tr-93
85D-499
85F-308
85F/St-57
85OPC-39
85Smok/Cal-9
85T-497
85T/St-226
86D-158
86F-165
86F/Mini-33
86F/St-88
86Leaf-84
86OPC-323
86Smok/Cal-9
86T-604
86T/Mini-7
87Classic/Up-134
87D-160
87D/OD-10
87F-90
87F/AwardWin-29
87Leaf-152
87OPC-278
87Sf-157M
87Seven-W7
87Smok/Cal-20
87T-278
87T/Mini-47
87T/St-16
87T/St-175
88D-210
88D/Best-203
88F/Up-U29
88OPC-71
88Panini/St-48
88Pep/T-24
88S-255
88S/Tr-38T
88T-71
88T/St-178
88T/Tr-86T
89B-108
89D-60
89F-141
89Mara/Tigers-24
89OPC-146
89Panini/St-345
89S-26
89T-146
89T/Mini-53
89T/St-279
89UD-117
90B-498
90D-661
90D/BestAL-126
90F-612
90F/AwardWin-25
90Leaf/II-469
90Mother/Rang-12
90OPC-512
90Panini/St-78
90PublInt/St-480
90S-136
90S/Tr-6T
90Sf-202
90T-512
90T/Big-311
90T/Mini-14
90T/St-283
90T/Tr-94T
90UD-385
90UD/Ext-770
91B-276
91D-512
91F-297
91F/Ultra-352
91Leaf/StudPrev-9
91Mother/Rang-12
91OPC-314
91Panini/FrSt-256
91Panini/Top15-115
91S-182
91T-314
91T/StClub/I-141
91UD-229
92F-314
92S/I-308
92T-756
92UD-179

Pettis, Stacey
84PrWill-34
86PalmSp-26

Pettit
N172
WG1-13

Pettit, Bob
60P

Pettit, Paul
60HenryH-15

Petty, Brian
85Everett/Cram-14

Petty, Jesse
33G-90
90Target-620
V354-42

Petway, Bruce
78Laugh/Black-7
90Negro/Star-31

Pevey, Marty
86Louisvl-24
89Indianap/CMC-15
89Indianap/ProC-1217
90OPC-137
90T-137
90T/89Debut-98
90UD-628
91Syrac/LineD-513
91Syrac/ProC-2483

Peyton, Byron
82Cedar-17

Peyton, Eric
82ElPaso-1
83ElPaso-2
84Cram/PCL-41

Peyton, Mickey
88Augusta/ProC-362

Pezzoni, Ron
90Penin/Star-14
91CLAS/ProC-CAR29
91Penin/ClBest-20

91Penin/ProC-390
Pfaff, Bob
86Sumter-21
87Durham-4
89BurlB/ProC-1606
89BurlB/Star-16
Pfaff, Rich
89Beloit/I/Star-22
89Beloit/II/Star-23
Pfeffer, Edward
(Jeff)
90Target-621
D327
D328-133
D350/2-137
E121/80
E122
E135-133
E220
M101/5-137
V100
W575
Pfeffer, Francis
(Big Jeff)
M116
T206
W514-58
WG3-36
Pfeffer, Kurt
90Elizab/Star-17
91Kenosha/ClBest-11
91Kenosha/ProC-2090
Pfeffer, Nathaniel F.
E223
N172
N284
N300/Unif
WG1-14
Pfeil, Bobby
66Pep/Tul
70OPC-99
70T-99
72T-681
91WIZMets-314
Pfiester, John
12Sweet/Pin-87
E254
E96
M116
T204
T205
T206
T3-33
Pfister, Dan
62T-592R
63T-521
64T-302
Phanatic, Phillie
84Phill/TastyK-3
87TastyK-XX
88TastyK-30
90TastyK-33
Phelan, Art
C46-35
M116
T206
T222
Phelan, James D.
N172
Phelan, James F.
T205
T206
Phelan, John
89Spokane/SP-6
Phelps, Edward
10Domino-98
11Helmar-175
12Sweet/Pin-152
C46-36
E90/1
M116
T205
T206
Phelps, Ernest Gordon
(Babe)
37Exh/4-2
38Exh/4-2
39PB-96
40PB-66
89Smok/Dodg-41
90Target-622
R313
Phelps, Ken
76Watlo
77DaytB
77Jaxvl
82F-420
82Wichita-12
82Wichita-7M
85D-318
85F-499
85Leaf-129
85Mother/Mar-18
85OPC-322
85T-582
86Mother/Mar-18
86T-34
87D-317
87D/OD-118
87F-593
87F/GameWin-34
87F/Slug-30
87Mother/Sea-7
87T-333
87T/St-222
88D-489
88D/Best-248
88F-384
88F/Slug-29
88F/St-61
88Mother/Sea-7
88OPC-182
88RedFoley/St-69
88S-256
88T-182
88T/Big-189
89B-177
89D-363
89D/Best-276
89F-264
89S-242
89S/NWest-10
89T-741
89T/Big-293
89T/DHTest-24
89UD-167
90B-462
90D-675
90Mother/A's-14
90OPC-411
90Publint/St-544
90T-411
91Phoenix/ProC-75
Philley, Dave
48L-85
49B-44
50B-127
51B-297
52NTea
52T-226
53T-64
54B-163
54RM-AL9
54T-159
55Gol/Ind-23
55Salem
56T-222
57T-124
58Hires-12
58T-116
59T-92
60T-52
61T-369
62T-542
72Laugh/GF-46
79TCMA-192
90HOF/St-55
91Crown/Orio-360
91T/Arc53-64
Exh47
R423-80
Phillip, Jim
86WinSalem-19
Phillippe, Charles
(Deacon)
10Domino-99
12Sweet/Pin-143
72F/FFeat-37
D322
E104
E107
E254
E90/1
E91
E93
M116
S74-114
T202
T205
T206
W555
WG3-37
Phillips, Adolfo
66OPC-32
66T-32
67OPC-148
67T-148
68T-202
69MB-222
69T-372
69T/St-17
70T-666
71LaPizza-9
71MLB/St-137
71OPC-418
71T-418
Phillips, Bill
83CharR-8
86Peoria-19
Phillips, Charlie
77LodiD
80ElPaso-24
80SLCity-8
Phillips, Chris
83Knoxvl-6
Phillips, Dave
88TM/Umpire-9
89TM/Umpire-7
90TM/Umpire-7
Phillips, J.R.
89QuadC/Best-22
89QuadC/GS-7
90Boise/ProC-3319
90PalmSp/Cal-207
90PalmSp/ProC-2586
91PalmSp/ProC-2025
Phillips, Jack
52T-240
53Mother-57
57T-307
D301
Phillips, Jim
87Pittsfld-12
89Martins/Star-25
Phillips, John
(Bubba)
55B-228
57T-395
58T-212
59T-187
60T-243
61Kahn
61T-101
61T/St-140
62J-39
62Kahn
62P-39
62P/Can-39
62Salada-74
62Shirriff-74
62Sugar-14
62T-511
62T/St-38
63J-70
63P-70
63T-177
64Det/Lids-11
64T-143
65T-306
78TCMA-192
Phillips, Lanny
77Holyo
Phillips, Lefty
70OPC-376MG
70T-376MG
71JB
71OPC-279MG
71T-279MG
Phillips, Lonnie
87Everett-5
88Clinton/ProC-720
89SanJose/Best-5
89SanJose/Cal-217
89SanJose/ProC-452
Phillips, Mike
74OPC-533
74T-533
75OPC-642
75T-642
75T/M-642
76OPC-93
76SSPC-540
76T-93
77T-532
78T-88
79T-258
80T-439
81D-188
81F-538
81T-113
82F-201
82OPC-263
82T-762
91WIZMets-315
Phillips, Montie
88CalLgAS-8
89SanJose/Best-12
89SanJose/ProC-433
89SanJose/Star-22
91FSLAS/ProC-FSL26
91Osceola/ClBest-8
91Osceola/ProC-680
Phillips, Randy
90Pulaski/Best-27CO
90Pulaski/ProC-3113CO
Phillips, Richard E.
(Dick)
61Union
63T-544R
64T-559
78TCMA-179
79Hawaii-6
Phillips, Robbie
84Cedar-1
Phillips, Steve
85Lynch-16
86Lynch-17
Phillips, Steve
91Oneonta/ProC-4167
Phillips, Thomas G.
E120
W573
Phillips, Tony
80Memphis-16
81WHave-14
82Tacom-32
83T/Tr-87T
84D-278
84F-459
84Mother/A's-23
84Nes/792-309
84T-309
85D-101
85F-433
85T-444
85T/St-329
86D-542
86F-430
86Mother/A's-19
86T-29
87D-103
87D/OD-26
87F-402
87Smok/A's-10
87T-188
88D-221
88D/A's/Bk-221
88F-290
88Mother/A's-12
88OPC-12
88Panini/St-168
88S-294
88T-673
88T/St-165
89D/Best-211
89F/Up-56
89Mother/A's-11
89S-156
89T-248
89UD-267
90B-359
90Classic/III-79
90CokeK/Tiger-17
90D-91
90D/BestAL-20
90F-19
90F/Up-U99
90Leaf/II-324
90OPC-702
90S-84
90S/Tr-14T
90T-702
90T/Big-239
90T/Tr-95T
90UD-154
90UD/Ext-768
91B-137
91Classic/III-73
91CokeK/Tiger-4
91D-286
91F-348
91F/Ultra-126
91Leaf/I-4
91OPC-583
91Panini/FrSt-290
91S-38
91T-583
91T/StClub/I-41
91T/Tr-91T
91UD-131
92D/DK-DK25
92D/I-328
92F-143
92S/II-453
92T-319
92UD-184
Phillips, Vince
89PrWill/Star-16
90Albany/Best-22
90Albany/ProC-1046
90Albany/Star-12
90T/TVYank-57
91Albany/ProC-1021
Phillips, W. Taylor
57T-343
58T-159
59T-113
60T-211
Phillips, Wade
87Fayette-9
87Lakeland-15
88Lakeland/Star-20
Phillips, William
N172
N284
Philyaw, Dino
91Pocatel/ProC-3798
Philyaw, Thad
75Water
Phipps, Ron
83Peor/LF-26tr
Phoebus, Tom
67T-204R
68Coke
68Dexter-63
68OPC-97
68T-97
69MB-223
69MLB/St-6
69OPC-185
69T-185
69T-532M
69T/St-127
70MLB/St-152
70T-717
71MLB/St-234
71OPC-611
71T-611
72MB-274
72OPC-477
72T-477
91Crown/Orio-361
Phoenix, Steve
91Modesto/ProC-3086
Piatt, Bruce
83Butte-32
Piatt, Doug
88BurlInd/ProC-1790
89Kinston/Star-18
89Watertn/Star-18
90WPalmB/Star-17
91Indianap/LineD-191
91Indianap/ProC-459
91T/Tr-92T
92D/II-640
92S/I-422
92T-526
92T/91Debut-139
Piatt, Wiley
E107
Piazza, Anthony
87Everett-4
Piazza, Mike
89Salem/Team-25
90VeroB/Star-24
91AS/Cal-6
Picciolo, Dustin

87Spokane-25
Picciolo, Rob
76Tucson-9
78T-528
79T-378
80T-158
81D-357
81F-582
81T-604
81T/Tr-813
82D-465
82F-106
82Granny-14
82T-293
82T/Tr-89T
83D-456
83Pol/Brew-8
83T-476
84D-455
84Nes/792-88
84Smok/Cal-22
84T-88
84T/Tr-94
85Mother/A's-13
85T-756
85T/Tr-90T
86Cram/PCL-177
86D-497
86OPC-3
86T-672
87LasVegas-26
87Spokane-26
Pichardo, Francisco
90Elizab/Star-18
90Kenosha/Best-12
90Kenosha/ProC-2309
90Kenosha/Star-19
Pichardo, Hipolito
90BBCity/Star-19
91London/LineD-413
91Single/ClBest-296
Pichardo, Nelson
77WHave
Piche, Ron
61T-61
62T-582
63T-179
65T-464
66Pep/Tul
Picinich, Val J.
21Exh-128
21Exh-129
25Exh-67
29Exh/4-7
33G-118
90Target-623
92Conlon/Sport-479
E120
E220
V354-3
W573
Pickens, Kevin
89BBCity/Star-21
Pickering, Oliver
E107
E254
T206
Pickett, Antoine
88Modesto-28
Pickett, Danny
90CharRain/Best-18
90CharRain/ProC-2033
Pickett, John
N172
Pickett, Rich
83Lynch-21
84Tidew-12
Pickett, Tony
87AppFx-23
Picketts, William
90SoOreg/Best-7
90SoOreg/ProC-3435
91Madison/ClBest-26
91Madison/ProC-2141
Pico, Jeff
86WinSalem-20
87Pittsfld-19
88Berg/Cubs-41
88F/Up-U80
88Iowa/CMC-3
88Iowa/ProC-546
88Peoria/Ko-25
88S/Tr-94T
88T/Tr-87T
89D-513
89F-436
89Mara/Cubs-41
89Panini/St-50
89S-13
89T-262
89ToysRUs-22
89UD-491
90Cub/Mara-1541
90D-585
90F-39
90Iowa/CMC-7
90OPC-613
90Peoria/Team-20M
90PublInt/St-200
90S-428
90T-613
90T/TVCub-14
91F-428
91OPC-311
91S-326
91T-311
91Tacoma/LineD-537
91Tacoma/ProC-2303
Picota, Lenin
(Leny)
87Savan-23
88StPete/Star-22
89ArkTr/GS-18
91Louisvl/LineD-243
91Louisvl/ProC-2914
Piechowski, Tim
88James/ProC-1902
Piela, D.
88Pulaski/ProC-1765
Pieratt, Dan
91QuadC/ClBest-25TR
Pierce, Ben
89AppFx/ProC-874
90BBCity/Star-20
Pierce, Billy
51B-196
51T/BB-45
52B-54
52Hawth/Pin-6
52RM-AL16
52StarCal/L-73B
52T-98
53B/Col-73
53RM-AL16
53T-143
54B-102
54RH
54RM-AL10
55B-214
55RFG-27
56T-160
57Swift-4
57T-160
58T-334M
58T-50
59Bz
59T-156M
59T-410
59T-466HL
59T-572AS
60T-150
60T-571AS
60T/tatt-44
60T/tatt-95
61P-21
61T-205
61T/St-126
62J-54
62P-54
62P/Can-54
62Salada-2
62Shirriff-2
62T-260
63T-331M
63T-50
64T-222
79TCMA-16
88Coke/WS-22
89Pac/Leg-134
89Swell-57
90Pac/Legend-82
91T/Arc53-143
Exh47
Pierce, Chris
86PrWill-19
Pierce, Dominic
88Butte-16
89Gaston/ProC-1001
89Gaston/Star-18
89Star/Wax-38
Pierce, Don Diego
82Wausau-24
Pierce, Eddie
(Ed)
89Eugene/Best-9
91London/LineD-414
91Memphis/ProC-651
Pierce, G.
C46-68
D350/2-138
M101/5-138
Pierce, Jeff
91Utica/ClBest-13
91Utica/ProC-3255
Pierce, L. Jack
76OPC-162
76SSPC-386
76T-162
78SanJose-23
79Spokane-7
Pierce, Tony
67T-542R
68OPC-38
68T-38
Pierce, Walter
83ArkTr-5
84ArkTr-24
Piercy, Bill
21Exh-130
21Exh-131
Pieretti, Marino
(Chick)
49B-217
50B-181
50NumNum
52Mother-12
53Mother-35
Pierorazio, Wes
83Watlo/LF-23
85Visalia-19
86Visalia-15
87Orlan-22
Piersall, Jim
51B-306
52B-189
53B/BW-36
54B-210
54B-66B
54RM-AL11
55B-16
55RM-AL21
56T-143
57T-75
58T-280
59T-355
60T-159
61T-345
61T/St-139
62Bz
62Salada-88A
62Salada-88B
62Shirriff-88
62T-51LL
62T-90
62T/bucks
62T/St-100
63Exh
63F-29
63T-443
64T-586
65OPC-172
65T-172
66T-565
67T-584
79TCMA-188
89Pac/Leg-182
89Swell-83
90Pac/Legend-44
90Swell/Great-92
91LineD-20
91Swell/Great-72
91T/Arc53-286
91WIZMets-316
Exh47
PM10/Sm-146
Pierson, Larry
88StPete/Star-23
89StPete/Star-22
Piet, Tony
33G-228
34DS-72
34Exh/4-4
34G-8
35BU-142
35BU-70
35G-1H
35G-3F
35G-4F
35G-5F
88Conlon/NatAS-16
92Conlon/Sport-524
R314
V354-63
V355-95
Pietroburgo, Rob
79Spokane-18
80Tacoma
81Charl-23
82Charl-9
Pifer, Gary
87CharWh-10
88Lakeland/Star-21
Piggot, Rusty
81QuadC-4
Pignatano, Joe
58T-373
59T-16
60BB-10
60L-126
60T-292M
60T-442
61T-74
62J-97
62P-97
62P/Can-97
62Salada-45
62Shirriff-45
62T-247
73OPC-257CO
73T-257C
74OPC-179CO
74T-179C
79TCMA-204
82Pol/Atl-52C
83Pol/Atl-52C
84Pol/Atl-52C
90Target-624
91WIZMets-317
Pike, Mark
87Watlo-6
88Watlo/ProC-683
89Kinston/Star-19
Pilarcik, Al
57T-311
58Hires-76
58Hires/T
58T-259
59T-7
60T-498
61T-62
79TCMA-212
91Crown/Orio-362
Pilkington, Eric
86Clinton-21
88SanJose/Cal-136
88SanJose/ProC-127
Pilkinton, Lem
86Elmira-15
87Greens-23
89Penin/Star-19
90CLAS/CL-44
90Penin/Star-15
91Jaxvl/LineD-350CO
91Jaxvl/ProC-168CO
Pill, Mike
78Charl
Pilla, Tony
82Orlan-11
83Orlan-2
Pillette, Duane
51B-316
52T-82
53B/BW-59
53T-269
54B-133
54Esskay
54T-107
55B-244
55Esskay
55T-168
79TCMA-191
91Crown/Orio-363
91T/Arc53-269
Pillette, Herman
21Exh-132
46Sunbeam
E120
V61-19
W572
W573
Pimentel, Ed
90FtLaud/Star-17
Pimentel, Rafael D.
81ArkTr-13
82ArkTr-5
86MidldA-19
Pimentel, Wander
90Hamil/Best-16
90Hamil/Star-19
91Savan/ClBest-22
91Savan/ProC-1663
Pina, Horacio
71MLB/St-548
71OPC-497
71T-497
72T-654
73OPC-138
73T-138
74OPC-516
74T-516
74T/Tr-516T
75OPC-139
75T-139
75T/M-139
Pina, Mickey
87Elmira/Red-33
88Lynch/Star-17
89AAA/CMC-27
89NewBrit/ProC-619
89NewBrit/Star-14
90B-270
90Pawtu/CMC-20
90Pawtu/ProC-473
90S/Tr-104T
90T/TVRSox-56
90UD/Ext-764
91Pawtu/LineD-364
91Pawtu/ProC-50
Pina, Rafael
91Elizab/ProC-4298
Pinckes, Mike
90Burllnd/ProC-3016
91Collnd/ClBest-5
91Collnd/ProC-1494
Pinder, Chris
88Hagers/Star-17
89Hagers/Best-27
89Hagers/ProC-268
90Kinston/Team-20
Pineda, Gabriel
91AppFx/ClBest-9
91AppFx/ProC-1715
Pineda, Jose
91FtLaud/ClBest-17
91FtLaud/ProC-2430
Pineda, Rafael
87QuadC-15
Pinelli, Ralph
(Babe)
55B-307ump
87Conlon/2-20
88Conlon/4-22
92Conlon/Sport-476
E120
V61-78
W572
W573
WG7-41
Pinelli, Willie
87Bakers-29
Piniella, Lou
64T-167R
68OPC-16R
68T-16R
69T-394R
70MLB/St-227
70OPC-321
70T-321
70T/S-32
70T/SO
71MLB/St-426
71OPC-35
71T-35
71T/Coins-152
71T/GM-38
71T/S-62

71T/tatt-9
72MB-275
72OPC-491KP
72T-491KP
72T-580
73K-24
73OPC-140
73T-140
73T/Comics-15
73T/Lids-40
73T/PinUps-15
74OPC-390
74T-390
74T/St-188
74T/Tr-390T
75K-34
75OPC-217
75T-217
75T/M-217
76OPC-453
76SSPC-445
76T-453
77BK/Y-23
77K-48
77T-96
78BK/Y-18
78OPC-82
78T-159
79BK/Y-18
79Ho-69
79OPC-342
79T-648
80OPC-120
80T-225
81D-109
81F-85
81F/St-45
81OPC-306
81T-724
82D-135
82F-48
82F/St-114
82OPC-236
82T-538
83D-335
83F-392
83OPC-307
83RoyRog/Disc-8
83T-307
84D-274
84F-136
84Nes/792-408
84OPC-351
84T-408
86T/Tr-86T
87T-168MG
88T-44MG
90Kahn/Reds-21MG
90Pac/Legend-99
90T/Tr-96TMG
91Crown/Orio-364
91Kahn/Reds-41MG
91OPC-669MG
91Pep/Reds-16MG
91T-669MG
92T-321MG

Pinkerton, Wayne
76SanAn/Team-17
77Tucson
78Cr/PCL-33
79Tucson-12
80Charl-3

Pinkham, Bill
83Knoxvl-8

Pinkney, Alton
90Kissim/DIMD-22

Pinkney, George
90Target-625
N172

Pinkus, Jeff
77Salem

Pino, Rolando
83AppFx/LF-12
87BirmB/Best-19
89Kenosha/ProC-1082
89Kenosha/Star-19
90Greenvl/Best-20

Pinol, Juan
87Tampa-7

Pinson, Vada
58T-420
59Kahn
59T-448
60Armour-17
60Kahn
60T-176
60T-32M
61Kahn
61P-181
61T-110
61T-25M
61T/St-22
62Bz
62Exh
62J-121
62Kahn
62P-121
62P/Can-121
62Salada-118
62Shirriff-118
62T-52LL
62T-80
62T/bucks
62T/St-119
63Exh
63F-34
63FrBauer-19
63J-130
63Kahn
63P-130
63T-265
64Kahn
64T-162M
64T-80
64T/Coins-152AS
64T/Coins-45
64T/S-56
64T/St-2
64T/SU
65Kahn
65OldLond-16
65T-355
65T/E-42
65T/trans-24
66Kahn
66OPC-180
66T-180
67Kahn
67T-550
68Bz-9
68Kahn
68OPC-90
68T-90
69Kahn
69MB-224
69OPC-160
69T-160
69T/St-119
70MLB/St-202
70OPC-445
70T-445
70T/CB
70T/S-31
71MLB/St-382
71OPC-275
71T-275
71T/Coins-18
71T/GM-12
71T/tatt-5
72MB-276
72OPC-135
72T-135
73OPC-75
73T-75
74OPC-490
74T-490
74T/St-144
75OPC-295
75T-295
75T/M-295
76OPC-415
76SSPC-178
76T-415
77T-597C
78TCMA-146
82D-445CO
88Pep/T-CO
89Mara/Tigers-CO
90CokeK/Tiger-28CO
91CokeK/Tiger-xCO
Exh47

Pinto, Gustavo
89NiagFls/Pucko-19

Pipgras, Ed
90Target-626

Pipgras, George
33DH-34
33G-12
61F-134
91Conlon/Sport-123
R315-A29
R315-B29
R337-404

Piphus, Ben
83Watlo/LF-3

Pipik, Gary
89James/ProC-2138

Pipp, Wally
21Exh-133
25Exh-99
26Exh-29
27Exh-14
91Conlon/Sport-157
BF2-34
D328-134
D329-138
D350/2-139
E120
E121/120
E121/80
E122
E135-134
E220
M101/4-138
M101/5-139
V100
V61-48
W514-84
W515-39
W572
W573
W575
WG7-42

Pippen, Henry
(Cotton)
39PB-8
40PB-136
46Remar
47Remar
47Signal
47Smith-9

Pippin, Craig
83LynnP-7
86Maine-15
87Omaha-15

Pirkl, Greg
89Belling/Legoe-1
90Foil/Best-233
90SanBern/Best-14
90SanBern/Cal-105
90SanBern/ProC-2637
91Penin/ClBest-1
91SanBern/ClBest-14
91SanBern/ProC-1990

Pirruccello, Mark
83CharR-1
84Memphis-23

Pirtle, Jerry
79RochR-12
79T-720R
89Pac/SenLg-198

Pisacreta, Mike
89Pulaski/ProC-1890

Pisarkiewicz, Mike
77StPete
78StPete

Piscetta, Rob
89Bakers/Cal-187

Pisciotta, Marc
91Welland/ProC-3570

Pisel, Ron
78Cedar
83Phoenix/BHN-19

Pisker, Don
76Dubuq
78Charl
79Syrac-8
79T-718R
80Syrac-23
81SLCity-24

Piskol, Pete
84PrWill-8

Piskor, Steve
88LitFalls/Pucko-9
89Pittsfld/Star-19

Pisoni, Jim
57T-402
59T-259

Pitcher, Scott
89Wausau/GS-8
90SanBern/Best-17
90SanBern/Cal-95
90SanBern/ProC-2631
91SanBern/ClBest-11
91SanBern/ProC-1987

Pitler, Jake
49Eureka-46
52T-395CO
55Gol/Dodg-22CO
79TCMA-187

Pitlock, Lee
(Skip)
71OPC-19
71T-19
75OPC-579
75T-579
75T/M-579
76Tucson-44

Pittaro, Chris
85F/Up-U87
85T/Tr-91T
86D-150
86T-393
87Portl-6
88Portl/CMC-19
88Portl/ProC-653

Pittenger, Clark A.
29Exh/4-8
E120
V61-42
W573

Pittinger, Charley
WG3-38

Pittman, Doug
87Salem-27
88Kenosha/ProC-1388

Pittman, James
88OrlanTw/Best-8

Pittman, Joe
76Dubuq
80Tucson-3
81Tucson-3
82D-218
82F-222
82T-119
82T/Tr-90T
83D-247
83F-369
83T-346
89Pac/SenLg-38
89T/SenLg-19
90EliteSenLg-101
91Pac/SenLg-151

Pittman, Mike
82Spring-5
83Spring/LF-20

Pittman, Park
87Visalia-11
89Orlan/Best-20
89Orlan/ProC-1334
90B-408
90F/Up-109
90Portl/CMC-9
90Portl/ProC-177

Pitts, Gaylen
75Tucson-16
76Tucson-42
81ArkTr-21
81Louisvl-2
82ArkTr-22MG
82Louisvl-23
83Louisvl/Riley-2
84Louisvl-2
87Spring/Best-1
89ArkTr/GS-1MG
89TexLAS/GS-19MG
90Louisvl/CMC-27MG
90Louisvl/ProC-419MG
90SpringDG/Best-MG27
90T/TVCard-61MG

Pitz, Michael
87Bakers-28
88SanAn/Best-3
89SanAn/Best-23
91Jaxvl/LineD-342
91Jaxvl/ProC-149

Pivnick, Phil
85Albany-31

Pizarro, Juan
57T-383
59T-188
60L-51
60Lake
60SpicSpan-17
60T-59
61P-112
61T-227
62T-255
62T-59LL
62T/bucks
62T/St-28
63J-44
63P-44
63T-10LL
63T-160
64T-2LL
64T-430
64T/Coins-14
64T/S-53
64T/St-31
64T/SU
64Wheat/St-36
65OPC-125
65OPC-9LL
65T-125
65T-9LL
65T/trans-25
66T-335
67T-602
67T/Test/PP-5
68KDKA-29
68OPC-19
68T-19
69T-498
71MLB/St-41
71OPC-647
71T-647
72OPC-18
72T-18
78TCMA-79

Pizarro, Miguel
78Ashvl

Place, Michael
90Pulaski/Best-8
90Pulaski/ProC-3106

Placeres, Benigno
88StCath/ProC-2009

Pladson, Gordy
75Dubuq
76Dubuq
77Cocoa
79Charl-13
80Tucson-18
81T-491
81Tucson-18
82Tucson-21
83Tucson-7

Plainte, Brandon
80Elmira-15

Planco, Radhames
89Clmbia/GS-21

Plank, Ed
76Phoenix
77Phoenix
78Cr/PCL-66
79Phoenix
80Phoenix-6

Plank, Edward A.
14CJ-6
15CJ-6
48Exh/HOF
50Callahan
60F-46
61F-135
63Bz/ATG-9
69Bz/Sm
72F/FFeat-26
80Laugh/3/4/5-22
80SSPC/HOF
87Conlon/2-49
88Conlon/3-22
89HOF/St-78
92Conlon/Sport-463
D303
E104
E106
E107
E224
E90/1
E91
E93
E95
M116
T204
T206
T208

T216
W555
WG2-41
WG4-22

Plante, Bill
85Elmira-16
86Greens-16

Plantenberg, Erik
90Elmira/Pucko-19
91CLAS/ProC-CAR26
91LynchRS/ClBest-6
91LynchRS/ProC-1195

Plantier, Phil
87Elmira/Red-34
88WinHaven/Star-20
89Lynch/Star-18
90Pawtu/CMC-21
90Pawtu/ProC-474
90T/TVRSox-57
91AAAGame/ProC-AAA31
91B-117
91Classic/200-128
91Classic/I-22
91Classic/II-T66
91D-41RR
91F-107
91F/Ultra-38
91Leaf/Stud-18
91OPC-474
91Pawtu/LineD-365
91Pawtu/ProC-51
91Pep/RSox-15
91S-348RP
91T-474
91T/90Debut-125
91T/StClub/II-459
91UD-2SR
92Classic/I-71
92D/II-488
92F-44
92F/RookSIns-9
92S/100RisSt-86
92S/I-406
92T-782
92UD-425

Plants, Dan
84ElPaso-17

Plaskett, Elmo
63T-549R

Plaster, Allen
91Bluefld/ProC-4127
91Bluefld/ClBest-19

Platel, Mark
79AppFx-22
80GlenF/B-5
80GlenF/C-9
81AppFx-9

Platt, Mizell
48L-159
49B-89

Platts, Jim
87Spartan-1
88Spartan/ProC-1048

Plautz, Rick
82FtMyr-9

Plaza, Ron
62Kahn/Atl

Pleasac, Joe
86CharRain-21

Pledger, Kinnis
89SoBend/GS-19
90Saraso/Star-20
91BirmB/LineD-70
91BirmB/ProC-1467

Pleicones, Johnnie
86FtLaud-18

Pleis, Scott
83Erie-14

Pleis, William
62T-124
63T-293
64T-484
65OPC-122
65T-122
78TCMA-135

Plemel, Lee
88Hamil/ProC-1726
89Spring/Best-11
90StPete/Star-18
91ArkTr/LineD-42
91ArkTr/ProC-1285

Plemmons, Ron
89Utica/Pucko-18
90Foil/Best-36
90SoBend/Best-7
91Saraso/ClBest-24
91Saraso/ProC-1125

Plemmons, Scott
90CharWh/ProC-2238
90Foil/Best-299

Plesac, Dan
86D/Rook-14
86F/Up-U90
86Pol/Brew-37
86Sf/Rook-10
86T/Tr-87T
87D-214
87F-354
87Pol/Brew-37
87T-279
87T/St-201
87ToysRUs-22
88D-109
88D/AS-18
88D/Best-221
88F-171
88F-625M
88F/Mini-32
88F/St-39
88OPC-317
88Panini/St-118
88Pol/Brew-37
88RedFoley/St-70
88S-77
88S/YS/II-32
88Sf-191
88T-670
88T/Mini-20
88T/St-203
88T/St/Backs-65
89B-133
89Brewer/YB-37
89Cadaco-40
89D-382
89D/AS-22
89D/Best-165
89F-195
89F/LL-29
89F/Superstar-32
89Gard-8
89OPC-167
89Panini/St-367
89Pol/Brew-37
89S-320
89S/HotStar-32
89Sf-128
89T-740
89T/LJN-32
89T/St-197
89UD-630
90B-386
90Brewer/MillB-19
90D-175
90D/BestAL-36
90ElPasoATG/Team-5
90F-334
90F/BB-28
90F/LL-29
90KMart/SS-30
90Leaf/I-216
90MLBPA/Pins-85
90OPC-490
90Panini/St-95
90Pol/Brew-37
90Publint/St-503
90RedFoley/St-74
90S-86
90S/100St-86
90Sf-102
90T-490
90T/Big-33
90T/Mini-21
90T/St-200
90T/TVAS-31
90UD-477
91B-34
91Brewer/MillB-20
91Classic/200-33
91D-104
91F-594
91F/Ultra-179
91Leaf/II-287
91OPC-146
91Panini/FrSt-212
91Panini/St-163
91Pol/Brew-18
91RedFoley/St-72
91S-275
91T-146
91T/StClub/I-7
91UD-322
92D/II-682
92F-185
92S/II-567
92T-303
92UD-550

Pless, Rance
56T-339
79TCMA-176

Plews, Herb
57T-169
58T-109
59T-373
61BeeHive-16

Plitt, Norman
90Target-1051

Ploeger, Tim
91Spokane/ClBest-13
91Spokane/ProC-3948

Ploucher, George
77Cocoa

Plumb, Dave
87Sumter-13
88CLAS/Star-34
88Durham/Star-17
89Greenvl/ProC-1164
89Greenvl/Star-17
89Greenvl/Best-25
89Richm/Bob-20
90Greenvl/Best-2
90Greenvl/ProC-1133
90Greenvl/Star-15

Plummer, Bill
73OPC-177
73T-177
74OPC-524
74T-524
75OPC-656
75T-656
75T/M-656
76OPC-627
76SSPC-32
76T-627
77T-239
78SanJose-19
78T-106
79OPC-208
79Spokane-10
79T-396
80SanJose/JITB-1
81Wausau-29
84Chatt-9
86Calgary-21MG
87Calgary-4
88AAA/ProC-49
88Calgary/CMC-24
88Calgary/ProC-800
90Mother/Mar-27M
92T-171MG

Plummer, Dale
88LitFalls/Pucko-20
89Jacks/GS-28
89Star/Wax-23
89StLucie/Star-19
90T/TVMets-53
90Tidew/CMC-9
90Tidew/ProC-542
91Tidew/LineD-566
91Tidew/ProC-2507

Plunk, Eric
85Huntsvl/BK-33
86D/Rook-40
86F-649R
86Tacom-16
87D-178
87F-403
87T-587
88D-503
88D/A's/Bk-503
88D/Best-267
88F-291
88Mother/A's-20
88S-614
88T-173
89B-191
89D-125
89D/Best-49
89F-20
89Mother/A's-16
89OPC-141
89S-392
89T-448
89UD-353
90D-196
90F-452
90Leaf/II-504
90OPC-9
90Publnt/St-313
90S/NWest-20
90T-9
90T/TVYank-17
90UD-630
91D-593
91F-676
91F/Ultra-241
91OPC-786
91S-428
91T-786
91T/StClub/II-529
91UD-695
92D/II-554
92F-241
92S/I-379
92T-672
92UD-608

Plympton, Jeff
88Lynch/Star-18
89NewBrit/ProC-622
89NewBrit/Star-16
90A&AASingle/ProC-8
90EastLAS/ProC-EL33
90Foil/Best-242
90NewBrit/Best-20
90NewBrit/Star-15
91Pawtu/LineD-366
91Pawtu/ProC-38
92S/100RisSt-13
92S/II-823
92T/91Debut-140
92UD-71TP

Poat, Ray
48B-42

Pocekay, Walter
53Mother-10

Poche, Gerry
76Baton

Pocoroba, Biff
76OPC-103
76SSPC-15
76T-103
77T-594
78Ho-99
78T-296
79OPC-285
79T-555
80OPC-73
80T-132
81F-257
81Pol/Atl-4
81T-326
82BK/Lids-20
82F-446
82Pol/Atl-4
82T-88
83D-436
83F-145
83OPC-367
83Pol/Atl-4
83T-676
84D-77
84F-189
84Nes/792-438
84T-438

Podbielan, Clarence
(Bud)
52T-188
53B/BW-21
53T-237
54T-69
55T-153
56T-224
90Target-627
91T/Arc53-237
V362-12

Podres, Johnny
52Park-76
53T-263
54T-166
55B-97
55Gol/Dodg-23
55T-25
55T/DH-112
56T-173
57Swift-1
57T-277
58BB
58Hires-42
58T-120
59Armour-13
59Morrell
59T-262M
59T-495
60BB-19
60Morrell
60NuCard-2
60T-425
61BB-22
61NuCard-474
61P-169
61T-109
61T-207M
61T/St-31
62BB-22
62J-108
62P-108
62P/Can-108
62Salada-172
62Shirriff-172
62T-280
62T/bucks
62T/St-138
63Salada-9
63T-150
63T-412M
64T-580
65T-387
66T-468
67T-284
69T-659
73OPC-12CO
73T-12CO
78TCMA-156M
79TCMA-239M
79TCMA-267M
82D-566CO
87Smok/Dodg-26
88Pac/Leg-105
89Rini/Dodg-6
89Smok/Dodg-63
90Pac/Legend-45
90Swell/Great-104
90Target-628
91Phill/Medford-32CO
91Swell/Great-73
91T/Arc53-263
PM10/L-32
PM10/Sm-147
WG10-43
WG9-42

Poe, Charles
90SoBend/ClBest-10
91SoBend/ProC-2870

Poe, Rick
82Jacks-13

Poehl, Michael
86Watlo-21
87Kinston-9
88EastLAS/ProC-42
88Wmsprt/ProC-1325
91London/LineD-415
91Memphis/ProC-652

Poff, John William
79OkCty
80OkCty

Poffenberger, Boots
90Target-629

Pohle, Rich
88Idaho/ProC-1861

Pohle, Walt
85Beloit-2
86Stockton-21
87ElPaso-19

Poholsky, Tom
52T-242
54Hunter
54T-142
55B-76
55Hunter
56T-196
57T-235

Poindexter, Mike
81Batavia-5
83Watlo/LF-24

Pointer, Aaron
67T-564R

Poissant, Rod

86Lakeland-17
87GlenF-16
89SanBern/Cal-75
90Penin/Star-16

Polak, Rich
90PrWill/Team-19
91FtLaud/ClBest-11
91FtLaud/ProC-2424

Polanco, Carlos
91Boise/ClBest-21
91Boise/ProC-3888
91QuadC/ClBest-21
91QuadC/ProC-2640

Polanco, Giovanni
91Belling/ClBest-26
91Belling/ProC-3660

Polanco, Nicholas
89Kingspt/Star-19
90Kgsport/Best-12
90Kgsport/Star-19

Polanco, Radhames
88LitFalls/Pucko-10
89Clmbia/Best-21

Polanco, Roger
75Dubuq

Poland, Philip
T206

Polasek, John
90James/Pucko-24
91WPalmB/ClBest-9
91WPalmB/ProC-1225

Poldberg, Brian
82Nashvl-18
83Omaha-11
84Omaha-23
85Omaha-31
87AppFx-17
88AppFx/ProC-162
89AppFx/ProC-872
90BBCity/Star-28MG
91Omaha/LineD-350CO
91Omaha/ProC-1051

Pole, Dick
74OPC-596R
74T-596R
74T/Tr-596T
75OPC-513
75T-513
75T/M-513
76OPC-326
76T-326
77T-187
78T-233
80Port-11
83QuadC-3
86Pittsfld-19CO
87Iowa-21CO
88Berg/Cubs-CO
90Cub/Mara-28CO
90T/TVCub-5CO

Poles, Spot
74Laugh/Black-21

Polese, Joe
77Newar

Polewski, Steve
90Welland/Pucko-7
91Augusta/ClBest-17
91Augusta/ProC-813

Polhemus, Mark
N284

Poli, Crip
R314/Can
V355-84

Polidor, Gus
81Holyo-21
82Holyo-18
83Nashua-14
85Cram/PCL-12
86Edmon-22
86F-650R
87D-579
87Smok/Cal-18
88D-356
88F-501
88S-341
88Smok/Angels-6
88T-708
89Pol/Brew-14
90D-412
90OPC-313
90Pol/Brew-14
90T-313
90UD-480

Poling, Mark
88Clinton/ProC-699

Polinski, Bob
78Cr/PCL-82
79Colum-15

Polk, Riley
87Watlo-24

Polk, Ron
91T/Tr-93T

Polka, Fritz
86LitFalls-23
87Columbia-21
88FSLAS/Star-17

Pollack, Chris
87Jamestn-30
88Rockford-29
89Rockford-30
90WPalmB/Star-18
91Harris/LineD-267
91Harris/ProC-626

Pollack, Rick
88BirmB/Best-15

Pollard, Damon
91AppFx/ClBest-10
91AppFx/ProC-1716

Pollard, Jim
52Wheat

Pollet, Howard
(Howie)
39Exh
49B-95
49Eureka-193
50B-72
51B-263
51T/RB-7
52B-83
52T-63
53NB
53T-83
54T-89
55T-76
55T/DH-31
56T-262
60T-468CO
91T/Arc53-83
R423-83

Polley, Dale
88Greenvl/Best-12
89Greenvl/ProC-1160
89Greenvl/Star-18
89Greenvl/Best-15
90AAAGame/ProC-AAA4
90Richm/Bob-14
90Richm/CMC-3
90Richm/ProC-258
90Richm/Team-26
91Richm/LineD-437
91Richm/ProC-2565

Pollock, Syd
76Laugh/Clown-23
76Laugh/Clown-6

Polly, Nick
90Target-630

Poloni, John
76SanAn/Team-18
77Tucson
83Wausau/LF-2CO
87Myrtle-17
88Knoxvl/Best-23
89Knoxvl/Best-29
89Knoxvl/ProC-1147
89Knoxvl/Star-25
90Knoxvl/Best-19CO
90Knoxvl/ProC-1261CO
90Knoxvl/Star-26CO
91Syrac/LineD-522CO
91Syrac/ProC-2497CO

Polonia, Luis
84Madis/Pol-7
85Huntsvl/BK-11
86Tacom-17
87D/Rook-25
87F/Up-U99
87Sf/Rook-18
87T/Tr-96T
88D-425
88D/A's/Bk-425
88F-292
88Leaf-256
88OPC-238
88Panini/St-177
88RedFoley/St-71
88S-64
88S/YS/I-22
88Sf-71
88T-238
88T/Big-65
88T/JumboR-14
88T/St-172
88Tacoma/CMC-16
88Tacoma/ProC-638
88ToysRUs-24
89D-386
89F-21
89Mother/A's-17
89OPC-386
89Panini/St-425
89S-380
89S/NWest-4
89S/Tr-38
89Sf-133
89T-424
89UD-162
90D-547
90D/BestAL-116
90F/Up-U80
90Leaf/II-295
90OPC-634
90PublInt/St-314
90S-442
90S/Tr-46T
90T-634
90T/Tr-97T
90T/TVYank-32
90UD-316
91B-209
91D-93
91D/GSlam-10
91F-322
91F/UltraUp-U11
91KingB/Discs-10
91Leaf/I-81
91OPC-107
91S-587
91Smok/Angel-1
91T-107
91T/StClub/I-144
91UD-187
92D/I-252
92F-67
92S/I-68
92T-37
92UD-147

Polverini, Steve
87AubAs-9

Pomeranz, Mike
89Kenosha/ProC-1081
89Kenosha/Star-20
90CLAS/CL-20
90Salem/Star-16

Pomorski, John
V355-92

Ponce, Carlos
81BurlB-22
83ElPaso-19
84Cram/PCL-34
85Cram/PCL-224
86D-595
90ElPasoATG/Team-10
91Sumter/ClBest-28INST
91Sumter/ProC-2353CO

Ponder, Charles Elmer
V100
WG7-43

Ponder, Kevin
88Clmbia/GS-10
89Miami/I/Star-16
89Miami/II/Star-16
90Miami/II/Star-21

Pone, Vince
78Newar
79BurlB-22
80BurlB-11
81BurlB-2

Ponte, Edward
90Osceola/Star-22
91Osceola/ClBest-9
91Osceola/ProC-681

Pontiff, Wally
74Gaston

Pool, Harlin
R314/Can

Poole, Ed
E107

Poole, James
(Jimmy)
88T/Tr-88T
89T/Big-263
89VeroB/Star-22
91Classic/I-54
91D-655
91F-217
91OkCty/LineD-319
91OkCty/ProC-176
91S-357RP
91T/90Debut-126
92D/II-600
92F-23
92S/II-693
92T-683

Poole, Mark
83Kinston/Team-15
85Syrac-17
86Syrac-21
86Tulsa-1

Poole, Stine
82Evansvl-13
83Toledo-12

Poorman, Thomas
N172

Pope, Dave
55B-198
55Gol/Ind-24
55Salem
56T-154
57T-249
61BeeHive-17
91Crown/Orio-365

Pope, Greg
81Watlo-13

Pope, Mike
78StPete

Popham, Art
80Tacom-22
81Tacom-3
82Tacom-21
83Tacom-23

Popov, Andrey
89EastLDD/ProC-DD21

Popovich, Nick
77Spartan

Popovich, Paul
67T-536R
68T-266
69OPC-47
69T-47
69T/St-48
70OPC-258
70T-258
71MLB/St-42
71OPC-726
71T-726
72OPC-512
72T-512
73OPC-309
73T-309
74OPC-14
74T-14
75OPC-359
75T-359
75T/M-359
90Target-631

Popowski, Eddie
73OPC-131CO
73T-131C
74OPC-403CO
74T-403C
87Elmira/Black-32

Popplewell, Tom
87Oneonta-9
88PrWill/Star-19
89FtLaud/Star-19
90FSLAS/Star-40
90FtLaud/Star-18
91Albany/ProC-1006

Poquette, Tom
75OPC-622R
75T-622R
75T/M-622R
76A&P/KC
77BurgChef-66
77K-24
77OPC-66
77T-93
78OPC-197
78T-357
79T-476
80T-597
81T-153
82T-657
88Omaha/ProC-1495
89Omaha/ProC-1741
90Omaha/CMC-23CO
90Omaha/ProC-81CO

Porcelli, Joe
90Geneva/ProC-3038
90Geneva/Star-20
91WinSalem/ClBest-10
91WinSalem/ProC-2828

Porte, Carlos
80Cedar-6
83Water-12
85Cedar-18

Porter, Andy
86Negro/Frit-15

Porter, Bob
78Green
79Savan-22
81Richm-7
82Richm-21
83Richm-20
85Durham-16

Porter, Brad
84Everett/Cram-22A

Porter, Brian
89AubAs/ProC-2169
90AubAs/Best-21CO

Porter, Chuck
76QuadC
78Cr/PCL-65
79SLCity-19
81Vanco-2
82T-333R
82Vanco-21
84D-333
84F-211
84Nes/792-452
84Pol/Brew-43
84T-452
85D-115
85F-591
85Gard-16
85T-32
86T-292
86Vanco-22

Porter, Darrell
72OPC-162R
72T-162R
73OPC-582
73T-582
74OPC-194
74T-194
74T/St-198
75Ho-62
75OPC-52
75T-52
75T/M-52
76A&P/Milw
76Ho-117
76OPC-645
76SSPC-232
76T-645
77OPC-116
77T-214
78Ho-130
78OPC-66
78T-19
79Ho-4
79K-25
79OPC-295
79T-571
80K-12
80OPC-188
80T-360
80T/S-39
81Coke
81D-505
81F-36
81T-610
81T/St-224
81T/Tr-814
82D-498
82F-124
82F/St-29
82OPC-348IA
82OPC-98
82T-447
82T-448IA
82T/St-93
83D-278
83F-18
83OPC-103

83PermaGr/CC-12
83T-103
83T/St-148
83T/St-149
83T/St-182
83T/St-183
84D-303
84F-331
84MiltBrad-19
84Nes/792-285
84OPC-285
84T-285
84T/St-143
85D-353
85F-237
85Leaf-258
85OPC-246
85T-525
85T/St-140
86D-290
86F-45
86F/Up-U91
86KAS/Disc-16
86OPC-84
86Rang-17
86Sf-148M
86T-757
86T/Tr-88T
87D-593
87F-136
87Mother/Rang-10
87OPC-213
87RedFoley/St-52
87Smok/R-10
87T-689
88S-537

Porter, Dick
32Orbit/num-36
32Orbit/un-49
34G-43
R305
V354-88

Porter, Eric
82Wisco-20

Porter, Henry
E223
N172
N284

Porter, J.W.
53T-211
55T-49
55T/DH-9
58T-32
59T-246
91T/Arc53-211

Porter, Jeff
83Memphis-22
84Indianap-31TR

Porterfield, Erwin
(Bob)
49B-3
50B-216
52B-194
52RM-AL17
52T-301
52TipTop
53B/Col-22
53Briggs
53RM-AL19
53T-108
54B-24
54RM-AL10
54RM-AL18
55B-104
55RFG-7
56T-248
56YellBase/Pin-25
57T-118
58T-344
59T-181
79TCMA-284
91T/Arc53-108
Exh47
R423-81

Porterfield, Ron
88AubAs/ProC-1954
90ColMud/Star-26TR

Portocarrero, Arnold
(Arnie)
54T-214
55Rodeo
55T-77
55T/DH-12
56T-63
58T-465
59T-98
60T-254
79TCMA-196
91Crown/Orio-366

Portugal, Mark
82Wisco-14
83Visalia/LF-24
85Toledo-10
86D/Rook-44
87D-566
87F-548
87T-419
88Portl/CMC-5
88Portl/ProC-658
89B-318
89F-123
89S-482
89T-46
89Tucson/JP-19
89UD-358
90B-63
90Classic-121
90D-542
90Leaf/II-399
90Lennox-17
90Mother/Ast-10
90OPC-253
90S-552
90T-253
90UD-502
91B-552
91D-268
91F-512
91F/Ultra-138
91Leaf/I-63
91Mother/Ast-10
91OPC-647
91S-319
91T-647
91T/StClub/II-320
91UD-250
92D/I-188
92F-443
92S/I-243
92T-114
92UD-448

Posada, Jorge
91Oneonta/ProC-4156

Posada, Leo
61T-39
62J-96
62P-96
62P/Can-96
62Salada-62
62Shirriff-62
62T-168
62T/St-55
73Cedar
74Cedar
78DaytB/MG

Pose, Scott
89Billings/ProC-2063
90A&AASingle/ProC-103
90CharWh/Best-24
90CharWh/ProC-2255
90Foil/Best-91
90SALAS/Star-19
91Chatt/LineD-164
91Chatt/ProC-1972

Posedel, Bill
39PB-121
40PB-58
41G-19
41G-19
47Centen-20
49Eureka-169
52T-361CO
54Hunter
55Hunter
60T-469C
90Target-632

Posey, Bob
85Durham-29
86Durham-21

Posey, Cum
88Negro/Duques-3

Posey, John
87Hagers-13
88CharlK/Pep-11
89Hagers/Best-26
89Hagers/Star-14
89RochR/CMC-12

Posey, Marty
91Gaston/ClBest-26
91Gaston/ProC-2703
91SALAS/ProC-SAL24

Poss, David
87SLCity/Taco-27

Post, John
88Elmira-28TR

Post, Wally
52T-151
55B-32
55Kahn
56Kahn
56T-158
57Kahn
57Sohio/Reds-16
57T-157
58Hires-14
58Kahn
58T-387
59HRDerby-15
59T-398
60T-13
61Kahn
61T-378
61T/St-23
62J-128
62Kahn
62P-128
62P/Can-128
62T-148
63T-462
64T-253
79TCMA-90
91T/Arc53-294

Postema, Andy
90Erie/Star-18

Postier, Paul
87Gaston-16
88Tulsa-24
89Tulsa/GS-21
89Tulsa/Team-19
90Tulsa/ProC-1164
91OkCty/LineD-320
91OkCty/ProC-188

Postiff, J.P.
90Hunting/ProC-3292
91WinSalem/ProC-2838

Poston, Mark
85Beaum-16
86Beaum-20
87LasVegas-10

Potestio, Doug
86Iowa-22
87Iowa-6

Potestio, Frank
87DayBe-17
88Spring/Best-10
89ArkTr/GS-19
89Louisvl-31

Pott, Larry
85Tulsa-17

Potter, Mike
79Spokane-3

Potter, Nelson
41DP-129
47TipTop
49Eureka-16

Potter, Scott
89EastLDD/ProC-DD48UMP

Potthoff, Michael
89GreatF-4
90Bakers/Cal-240

Pottinger, Mark
86Clearw-20
87Lakeland-20

Potts, Dave
86AubAs-19
87Osceola-16
88Osceola/Star-21
89Osceola/Star-18

Pough, Clyde
89BurlInd/Star-21
90Reno/Cal-264
90Watertn/Star-16
91Kinston/ClBest-18
91Kinston/ProC-330

Poulin, Jim
88Beloit/GS-3
89Stockton/Best-25
89Stockton/Cal-178TR
89Stockton/ProC-387
89Stockton/Star-27

Poulis, George
90Waterlo/Best-21TR
91Waterlo/ClBest-27TR

Pounders, Brad
87TexLgAS-5
87Wichita-8
88LasVegas/CMC-15
88LasVegas/ProC-247
89F-642R

Powell, Alonzo
83Clinton/LF-14
86SLAS-15
86WPalmB-24
87D/OD-93
87Indianap-33
87Sf/Rook-8
88Indianap/CMC-15
88Indianap/ProC-520
89Indianap/ProC-1210
89WPalmB/Star-18
90Portl/ProC-193
91Calgary/LineD-69
91Calgary/ProC-529
91F/Up-U55
91Leaf/II-521
92D/I-213
92F-290
92S/I-413
92T-295

Powell, Alvin Jacob
(Jake)
38ONG/Pin-23
39PB-1
40PB-11
91Conlon/Sport-83

Powell, Charlie
78Charl

Powell, Colin
91B-533

Powell, Corey
91MidwLAS/ProC-MWL48
91Rockford/ClBest-10
91Rockford/ProC-2045

Powell, Dennis
85Cram/PCL-154
86Coke/Dodg-24
86D-250
86Pol/Dodg-48
87Calgary-6
87D-499
87F-450
87T-47
88Calgary/CMC-4
88Calgary/ProC-796
88T-453
89F/Up-61
89T/Tr-97T
90Brewer/MillB-20
90Denver/CMC-22
90Denver/ProC-624
90F-521
90S-308
90Target-634
90UD-229
91Calgary/LineD-68
91Calgary/ProC-514

Powell, Gordon Jr.
91Beloit/ClBest-15
91Beloit/ProC-2111

Powell, Grover
64T-113
91WIZMets-318

Powell, Hosken
79OPC-346
79T-656
80T-471
81D-567
81F-559
81T-137
82D-228
82F-558
82T-584
83D-644
83F-440
83OPC-77
83T-77
84Cram/PCL-38

Powell, James E.
N172

Powell, John J.
11Helmar-64
E107
M116
T204
T206

Powell, John
(Boog)
62T-99
63J-62
63P-62
63T-398
64T-89
64T/Coins-104
64T/St-36
64T/SU
64T/tatt
65Bz-11
65OldLond-33
65OPC-3LL
65T-3LL
65T-560
65T/E-29
65T/trans-63
66OPC-167
66T-167
67OPC/PI-1
67T-230
67T-241LL
67T-243LL
67T-521M
67T/PI-1
68Coke
68Dexter-64
68T-381
68T/3D
69MB-225
69MLB/St-7
69MLBPA/Pin-22
69OPC-15
69OPC/DE-17
69T-15
69T/DE-2
69T/St-128
70K-19
70MB-22
70MLB/St-153
70OPC-200ALCS
70OPC-410
70OPC-451AS
70OPC-64LL
70T-200ALCS
70T-410
70T-451AS
70T-64LL
70T/S-38
70T/SO
71K-20
71MD
71MLB/St-307
71MLB/St-570
71OPC-195ALCS
71OPC-327WS
71OPC-63LL
71OPC-700
71T-195ALCS
71T-327WS
71T-63LL
71T-700
71T/Coins-74
71T/S-5
71T/tatt-7
71T/tatt-7a
72MB-277
72OPC-250
72T-250
73JP
73OPC-325
73T-325
74OPC-460
74T-460
75OPC-208MV
75OPC-625
75T-208MV
75T-625
75T/M-208MV
75T/M-625
76Ho-75
76K-50
76OPC-45
76SSPC-524
76T-45
77T-206
78TCMA-80
82KMart-17

90BBWit-9
90Pac/Legend-46
90Swell/Great-16
90Target-633
91Crown/Orio-367
91K/3D-13
91Swell/Great-74
Exh47

Powell, Kenny
90Foil/Best-275
90Gaston/Best-5
90Gaston/ProC-2534
90Gaston/Star-18
91CharlR/ClBest-24
91CharlR/ProC-1328

Powell, Paul Ray
74Albuq/Team-13
76SSPC-82
90Target-635

Powell, Ray
21Exh-134
21Exh-135
E120
V100
V61-95
W572

Powell, Robert LeRoy
56T-144

Powell, Ross
89Cedar/Star-30
90CedarDG/Best-31
91Nashvl/LineD-270
91Nashvl/ProC-2155

Power, John
86Watlo-22

Power, Ted
80Albuq-22
81Albuq/TCMA-5
82F-17
84D-447
84F-478
84Nes/792-554
84T-554
85D-286
85F-547
85T-342
85T/St-50
86D-408
86F-187
86OPC-108
86Sf-166
86T-108
86T/St-140
86TexGold-48
87D-536
87F-210
87Kahn-48
87T-437
88D-142
88F-245
88F/Up-U33
88OPC-236
88Panini/St-272
88S-242
88Smok/Royals-14
88T-236
88T/Tr-89T
89D-153
89F-142
89Louisvl-32
89Louisvl/CMC-10
89Louisvl/ProC-1249
89OPC-331
89S-348
89T-777
90D-653
90F-258
90F/Up-U50
90Homer/Pirate-23
90Leaf/II-473
90OPC-59
90T-59
90Target-636
90UD-340
91B-688
91D-608
91F-46
91F/Up-U85
91Kahn/Reds-48
91OPC-621
91S-255
91T-621
91UD-450
92D/II-586
92F-416
92S/I-113
92UD-680

Power, Vic
54T-52
55Rodeo
55T-30
55T/DH-29
56T-67
56T/Pin-14
57T-167
58T-406
59Kahn
59T-229
60Bz-16
60Kahn
60L-65
60T-75
61Clover-21
61Kahn
61P-63
61T-255
61T/St-141
62J-37
62Kahn
62P-37
62P/Can-37
62Salada-44
62Shirriff-44
62T-445
62T/bucks
62T/St-39
63F-23
63J-1
63P-1
63T-40
64PhilBull-18
64T-355
65T-442
66OPC-192
66T-192
78TCMA-196
79TCMA-147
90HOF/St-56

Powers, John
58Kahn
58T-432
59T-489
60T-422
91Crown/Orio-368

Powers, Larry
79LodiD-11

Powers, Michael
E107
T206

Powers, Randy
90A&AASingle/ProC-159
90Boise/ProC-3305
91PalmSp/ProC-2012

Powers, Scott
87Elmira/Black-12
87Elmira/Red-12
88Lynch/Star-19
89Lynch/Star-19
90LynchRS/Team-7
91NewBrit/LineD-468
91NewBrit/ProC-359

Powers, Steve
75QuadC
77Salem

Powers, Steve
(Pitcher)
90Ashvl/ClBest-8
90AubAs/Best-11
90AubAs/ProC-3407
91Ashvl/ProC-566

Powers, Tad
89Penin/Star-20
90Reno/Cal-285
91SLCity/ProC-3209

Powers, Terry
91WinHaven/ClBest-7
91WinHaven/ProC-487

Powers, Thomas
N172/PCL

Powis, Carl
91Crown/Orio-369

Prager, Howard
88CapeCod/Sum-175
89AubAs/ProC-2175
90Osceola/Star-23
91Osceola/ProC-694

Pramesa, John
51B-324
52B-247
52T-105
PM10/Sm-148

Prather, Billy Ray
76Cedar

Prats, Mario
91Ashvl/ProC-567

Pratt, Crestwell
(Cressy)
82Water-22
83Tampa-20

Pratt, Derrill
(Del)
14CJ-93
15CJ-93
21Exh-136
21Exh-137
91Conlon/Sport-162
D327
D328-135
D329-139
D350/2-140
E120
E121
E135-135
E220
M101/4-139
M101/5-140
V100
W501-11

Pratt, Louis A.
79Savan-21
81ArkTr-20

Pratt, Steve
89Clinton/ProC-908

Pratt, Todd
85Elmira-17
86Greens-17
87WinHaven-29
88EastLAS/ProC-22
88NewBrit/ProC-906
89NewBrit/ProC-624
89NewBrit/Star-15
90NewBrit/Best-22
90NewBrit/Star-16
91Pawtu/LineD-367
91Pawtu/ProC-41

Pratte, Evan
91Niagara/ClBest-12
91Niagara/ProC-3643

Pratts, Alberto
(Tato)
88Elmira-2
89WinHaven/Star-17
90LynchRS/Team-20
91Elmira/ClBest-26
91Elmira/ProC-3271

Prendergast, Jim
V362-39

Prescott, George
61Union

Presko, Joe
52B-62
52T-220
53Hunter
54B-190
54Hunter
54T-135
79TCMA-178

Presley, Jim
80Wausau-13
81Wausau-20
82LynnS-13
84Cram/PCL-184
85D-240
85F-500
85Mother/Mar-20
85T/Tr-92T
86D-313
86F-473
86F/Mini-98
86F/St-89
86KayBee-24
86Leaf-183
86Mother/Mar-7
86OPC-228
86Sf-40
86T-598
86T/St-219
87Classic-48
87D-120
87D-23DK
87D/AAS-29
87D/DKsuper-23
87D/OD-123
87F-594
87F/Lim-33
87F/Mini-82
87F/St-91
87Leaf-154
87Leaf-23DK
87Mother/Sea-4
87OPC-45
87RedFoley/St-19
87Sf-179
87T-45
87T/St-214
88D-366
88D/Best-219
88F-385
88Mother/Sea-4
88OPC-285
88Panini/St-189
88S-46
88Sf-54
88T-285
88T/Big-90
88T/St-217
89B-214
89Chatt/II/Team-24
89D-379
89D/Best-331
89F-555
89Mother/Sea-4
89OPC-112
89Panini/St-437
89S-73
89Sf-7
89T-112
89T/Big-75
89T/St-223
89UD-642
90B-18
90Classic/III-21
90D-497
90D/BestNL-37
90F-522
90F/Up-U6
90Leaf/II-277
90OPC-346
90PublInt/St-439
90S-34
90S/Tr-36T
90T-346
90T/Big-304
90T/St-224
90T/Tr-98T
90UD-315
90UD/Ext-760
91B-646
91D-173
91F-700
91OPC-643
91Padre/MagRal-23
91Panini/FrSt-21
91Panini/St-24
91RedFoley/St-73
91S-771
91T-643
91UD-282
91UD/Ext-791

Pressnell, Forest
(Tot)
39PB-134
40PB-146
90Target-637

Preston, Dayton
88ColAst/Best-24

Preston, Steve
88Eugene/Best-20
89AppFx/ProC-861

Prevost, Eric
78Wisco

Prewitt, Larry
80Phoenix-5

Price, Al
81ElPaso-24
82ElPaso-24
83ElPaso-18
85Crm/PCL-225tr
87Denver-3

Price, Bill
81Wisco-18

Price, Bryan
85MidldA-2
86PalmSp-27
86PalmSp/Smk-15
88Vermont/ProC-940
89Calgary/CMC-9
89Calgary/ProC-540
89Wmsprt/Star-16
91Penin/ProC-396CO

Price, Harris
75AppFx
76AppFx

Price, Jimmie
67OPC-123R
67T-123R
68T-226
69T-472
70OPC-129
70T-129
71MLB/St-403
71OPC-444
71T-444
72MB-278
88Domino-20

Price, Joe
79Nashvl
80Indianap-5
81F-210
81T-258
82Coke/Reds
82D-481
82F-81
82T-492
83D-481
83F-600
83T-191
84D-506
84F-479
84Nes/792-686
84OPC-159
84T-686
84T/St-58
85D-627
85F-548
85OPC-82
85T-82
85T/St-56
86D-506
86F-188
86T-523
86TexGold-49
87F-211
87Phoenix-17
87T-332
88D-655
88Mother/Giants-26
88T-786
89D-376
89F-339
89Mother/Giants-26
89S-444
89T-217
89UD-505
90B-245
90F-282
90OPC-473
90T-473
91Crown/Orio-370
91F-488
91OPC-127
91RochR/LineD-464
91T-127

Price, John Thomas
46Remar-16

Price, Kevin
82Danvl-9
83Redwd-21
86Jaxvl/TCMA-14
86SLAS-25
87Jaxvl-20
87SLAS-17
88CharlK/Pep-4

Price, Phil
87Spartan-25
88Virgini/Star-18

Prichard, Brian
91Bristol/ClBest-8
91Bristol/ProC-3608

Priddy, Gerald
(Jerry)
41DP-109
48L-111
49B-4
50B-212

51B-71
51T/BB-46
52B-139
52Dix
52NTea
52T-28
53Dix
53Glen
53NB
53T-113
79TCMA-213
91T/Arc53-113
R423-79

Priddy, Robert
64T-74R
65T-482
66T-572
67OPC-26
67T-26
68T-391
69T-248
70T-687
71MLB/St-20
71OPC-147
71T-147

Pride, Curtis
89Pittsfld/Star-20
91FSLAS/ProC-FSL33
91StLucie/ClBest-2
91StLucie/ProC-725

Pries, Jeff
86Albany/TCMA-15
86Colum-19
86Colum/Pol-17
87Albany-18

Priessman, Kraig
83SanJose-17

Prieto, Arnie
88Miami/Star-19
89Miami/I/Star-23

Prieto, Pedro
(Pete)
76Dubuq
77Cocoa

Prim, Ray
47Signal

Prince, Ray
77DaytB

Prince, Tom
86PrWill-20
87Harris-3
88AAA/ProC-5
88BuffB/CMC-19
88BuffB/ProC-1488
88D-538
89D-527
89F-217
89S-626RP
89S/HotRook-45
89T-453
89UD-311
90B-176
90BuffB/CMC-14
90BuffB/ProC-376
90BuffB/Team-19
90Publint/St-161
92S/II-618

Prioleau, Laney
86Lakeland-18

Prior, Dan
82Reading-6

Pritchard, Harold
(Buddy)
58T-151

Pritchett, Anthony
91BendB/ClBest-18
91BendB/ProC-3707

Pritchett, Chris
91Boise/ClBest-2
91Boise/ProC-3889
91FrRow/DP-54

Pritikin, James
86Cram/PCL-113
88Wausau/GS-12
89SanBern/Best-14
89SanBern/Cal-86

Procopio, Jim
87Idaho-16
88Idaho/ProC-1853

Procter, Craig
88Spokane/ProC-1944

Proctor, Dave
88LitFalls/Pucko-21
89B-378
89StLucie/Star-20
91Single/ClBest-257
91StLucie/ProC-707

Proctor, Jim
60T-141

Proctor, Murph
91Yakima/ClBest-5
91Yakima/ProC-4254
92UD-51

Proffitt, Steve
89LittleSun-9

Prohaska, Tim
89NiagFls/Pucko-28

Proly, Michael
76Tulsa
79T-514
80T-399
81D-596
81F-358
81T-83
81T/Tr-815
82D-345
82F-254
82Iowa-22
82RedLob
82T-183
82T/Tr-92T
83D-225
83F-505
83T-597
83Thorn-36
84D-320
84F-501
84Nes/792-437
84Syrac-16
84T-437

Provence, Todd
86Ventura-21
87Knoxvl-11
88Myrtle/ProC-1192
89Myrtle/ProC-1455
90Myrtle/ProC-2790

Prts, Mario
90Ashvl/ClBest-9

Pruett, Hubert
(Hub)
87Conlon/2-50
88Conlon/5-24

Pruitt, Darrell Ray
86Penin-21
87BirmB/Best-21
88Chatt/Best-11
88SLAS-6
89Greenvl/ProC-1171
89Greenvl/Star-19
89Greenvl/Best-3

Pruitt, Donald
91Beloit/ClBest-6
91Beloit/ProC-2101
91MidwLAS/ProC-MWL34

Pruitt, Ed
86Jacks/TCMA-8

Pruitt, Jason
91Classic/DP-26
91FrRow/DP-26
92T-246DP

Pruitt, Ron
77T-654
78T-198
79T-226
80T-13
81T-442
82Phoenix
83Portl-21
89Pac/SenLg-103
89T/SenLg-74

Pruitt, Russell
79Elmira-12

Prusia, Greg
89AppFx/ProC-858

Prybylinski, Bruce
88Oneonta/ProC-2061
89PrWill/Star-17
90PrWill/Team-20
91FtLaud/ClBest-12
91FtLaud/ProC-2425

Prybylinski, Don
91ArkTr/LineD-43
91ArkTr/ProC-1289

Pryce, Ken
81QuadC-22
83MidldC-11
84Iowa-1
85Iowa-20
86Iowa-23

Pryor, Buddy
83Cedar-14
83Cedar/LF-2
86Vermont-15
87Nashvl-17
89Tacoma/CMC-15
89Tacoma/ProC-1558

Pryor, Greg
79T-559
80OPC-91
80T-164
81D-278
81F-359
81T-608
82D-521
82F-356
82T-76
82T/Tr-93T
83D-264
83F-121
83T-418
84D-374
84F-353
84Nes/792-317
84T-317
85D-277
85F-210
85T-188
86D-344
86NatPhoto-4
86T-773
87D-378
87OPC-268
87T-761

Pryor, Jim
76Cedar
77Cedar

Pryor, Randy
88CapeCod/Sum-107

Psaltis, Spiro
82CharR-20
85MidldA-16

Puccinelli, George
36Exh/4-14
38Exh/4-1
V355-127

Puchales, Javier
90Kissim/DIMD-23

Puchkov, Evgenyi
89EastLDD/ProC-DD6

Puckett, Kirby
83Visalia/LF-6
84F/X-U93
85D-438
85F-286
85F/St-122
85Leaf-107
85OPC-10
85Seven/Minn-1
85T-536
85T/St-307
85T/St-376YS
86D-72
86D/HL-7
86F-401
86F/LL-32
86F/Mini-85
86F/Slug-M5
86F/St-90
86KayBee-25
86Leaf-69
86OPC-329
86Sf-93
86T-329
86T/St-285
87Classic-55
87Classic/Up-112
87D-149
87D-19DK
87D/AAS-4
87D/DKsuper-19
87D/HL-30
87D/OD-221
87D/PopUp-4
87Drake-19
87F-549
87F-633M
87F/AS-5
87F/AwardWin-30
87F/BB-32
87F/LL-36
87F/Mini-83
87F/Slug-31
87F/St-92
87F/WaxBox-C11
87Ho/St-26
87KayBee-24
87Kraft-27
87Leaf-19DK
87Leaf-56
87MnM's-15
87OPC-82
87RedFoley/St-23
87Sf-198M
87Sf-7
87Smok/AL-8
87T-450
87T-611AS
87T/Coins-20
87T/Gloss22-19
87T/Gloss60-57
87T/Mini-63
87T/St-146
87T/St-274
88Bz-14
88ChefBoy-13
88Classic/Red-164
88D-368
88D-BC15
88D/AS-15
88D/Best-186
88Drake-19
88F-19
88F-638M
88F/AwardWin-29
88F/BB/AS-30
88F/BB/MVP-26
88F/Excit-30
88F/Hottest-30
88F/LL-30
88F/Mini-36
88F/RecSet-29
88F/Slug-30
88F/SS-28
88F/St-45
88F/TL-26
88F/WaxBox-C7
88F/WS-8
88FanSam-1
88KayBee-23
88KingB/Disc-3
88Leaf-144
88Master/Disc-8
88MSA/Disc-6
88Nestle-39
88OPC-120
88Panini/St-144
88Panini/St-444
88RedFoley/St-72
88S-24
88S-653HL
88Sf-180
88Sf-8
88Smok/Minn-12
88T-120
88T-391AS
88T/Big-36
88T/Coins-23
88T/Gloss60-27
88T/Mini-23
88T/Revco-21
88T/RiteAid-21
88T/St-283
88T/St/Backs-52
88T/UK-57
88Woolwth-31
89T/Ames-24
89B-162
89Cadaco-41
89Classic-15
89Classic/Up/2-176
89T/Crunch-20
89D-182
89D/AS-23
89D/Best-130
89D/MVP-BC1
89F-124
89F-639M
89F/BBAS-32
89F/BBMVP's-32
89F/Excit-34
89F/Heroes-31
89F/LL-30
89F/Superstar-33
89F/WaxBox-C20
89Holsum/Discs-8
89KayBee-24
89KMart/DT-16
89KMart/Lead-4
89Master/Discs-2
89Nissen-8
89OPC-132
89Panini/St-247
89Panini/St-393
89MSA/SS-8
89S-20
89S/HotStar-11
89S/Mast-19
89Sf-156
89T-403AS
89T-650
89T/Big-167
89T/Coins-48
89T/DH-7
89T/Gloss60-1
89T/HeadsUp-20
89T/Hills-23
89T/LJN-18
89T/Mini-62
89T/St-293
89T/St/Backs-19
89T/UK-60
89Tetley/Discs-12
89UD-376
90B-424
90Bz-7
90Classic-28
90CollAB-33
90D-269
90D-683AS
90D/BestAL-23
90D/Bon/MVP-BC8
90D/Learning-46
90D/Preview-10
90F-383
90F-635M
90F/ASIns-7
90F/AwardWin-26
90F/BB-29
90F/BBMVP-29
90F/LL-30
90F/WaxBox-C22
90Holsum/Discs-17
90HotPlay/St-31
90KayBee-23
90KingB/Discs-21
90KMart/CBatL-3
90KMart/SS-22
90Leaf/I-123
90MLBPA/Pins-98
90MSA/Soda-12
90OPC-391AS
90OPC-700
90Panini/St-105
90Panini/St-183
90Panini/St-199M
90Post-3
90Publint/St-292
90Publint/St-335
90RedFoley/St-75
90S-400
90S-690DT
90S/100St-1
90Sf-11
90Sunflower-5
90T-391AS
90T-700
90T/Ames-24
90T/Big-2
90T/Coins-4
90T/DH-49
90T/Gloss22-18
90T/Gloss60-48
90T/HeadsUp-20
90T/HillsHM-27
90T/Mini-23
90T/St-157AS
90T/St-286
90T/TVAS-6
90Tetley/Discs-13
90UD-236
90UD-48TC
90USPlayC/AS-8S
90Windwlk/Discs-2
90WonderBrd-9
91B-320
91BBBest/HitM-15
91Classic/200-111

91Classic/I-57
91Classic/III-74
91CollAB-7
91D-490
91F-623
91F/ProV-1
91F/Ultra-195
91F/UltraG-8
91JDeanSig-11
91KingB/Discs-23
91Leaf/I-208
91Leaf/Prev-21
91Leaf/Stud-90
91MajorLg/Pins-12
91MooTown-2
91OPC-300
91OPC/Premier-96
91Panini/FrSt-305
91Panini/St-248
91Pep/SS-13
91Petro/SU-17
91Post-28
91Post/Can-30
91RedFoley/St-74
91S-200
91S-855FRAN
91S-891DT
91S/100SS-7
91Seven/3DCoin-11A
91Seven/3DCoin-13F
91T-300
91T/CJMini/I-34
91T/StClub/I-110
91UD-544
91USPlayC/AS-4D
92Classic/I-72
92D/Elite-E17
92D/II-617
92F-217
92F-704M
92F/ASIns-22
92F/TmLIns-5
92S/100SS-7
92S/II-600
92S/II-796HL
92S/II-887DT
92T-575
92UD-254

Pudlo, Scott
91Erie/ClBest-22
91Erie/ProC-4068

Pueschner, Craig
90CharRain/Best-19
90CharRain/ProC-2052
90SALAS/Star-40
91Single/ClBest-366
91Waterlo/ClBest-22
91Waterlo/ProC-1269

Pugh, Scotty
91Spokane/ClBest-5
91Spokane/ProC-3958

Pugh, Tim
89Billings/ProC-2064
90A&AASingle/ProC-92
90CharWh/Best-7
90CharWh/ProC-2239
90Foil/Best-186
91Chatt/LineD-165
91Chatt/ProC-1958
91Single/ClBest-299

Puhl, Terry
75Dubuq
78BK/Ast-19
78T-553
79K-33
79T-617
80OPC-82
80T-147
81Coke
81D-24
81F-24
81K-42
81OPC-64
81T-411
81T/HT
81T/SO-88
81T/St-171
82D-370
82F-223
82F/St-44
82OPC-277
82T-277
82T/St-42
83D-167
83F-458
83OPC-39
83T-39
83T/S-239
84D-476
84F-235
84Mother/Ast-10
84Nes/792-383
84OPC-383
84T-383
84T/St-67
85D-426
85F-356
85GenMills-6
85Leaf-80
85Mother/Ast-7
85OPC-283
85Seven-14C
85T-613
85T/St-67
85ThomMc/Discs-39
86D-206
86F-308
86Leaf-138
86Mother/Ast-16
86OPC-161
86Pol/Ast-21
86T-763
87D-431
87F-65
87Mother/Ast-7
87OPC-227
87Pol/Ast-15
87T-693
88D-533
88F/Up-U90
88Mother/Ast-7
88Pol/Ast-17
88S-282
88T-587
89D-472
89D/Best-294
89F-364
89Lennox/Ast-22
89Mother/Ast-6
89S-567
89T-119
90D-354
90F-233
90Lennox-18
90MLBPA/Pins-60
90Mother/Ast-9
90OPC-494
90Panini/St-256
90PublInt/St-98
90S-473
90T-494
90UD-201

Puig, Ed
87Stockton-27
88ElPaso/Best-22
88TexLgAS/GS-31
89ElPaso/GS-14
90Denver/CMC-2
90Denver/ProC-625
91Denver/LineD-148
91Denver/ProC-123

Puig, Rich
91WIZMets-319

Puikunas, Ed
86Shrev-21
87Shrev-15
88Phoenix/CMC-11
88Phoenix/ProC-74
88Shrev/ProC-1301
89Phoenix/CMC-2
89Phoenix/ProC-1492

Pujols, Luis
73Cedar
74Cedar
75Dubuq
78Charl
79Charl-14
79T-139
81D-379
81F-68
81T-313
82D-576
82F-224
82T-582
83D-642
83F-459
83OPC-112
83T-752
83Tucson-13
84Cram/PCL-71
84F-236
84Nes/792-446
84T-446
85Rang-8
86OKCty-18
87Indianap-6
89Pac/SenLg-167
89T/SenLg-130

Pujols, Ruben
88Virgini/Star-19
89BBCity/Star-22

Pulchinski, Thomas
77Watlo
78Watlo

Puleo, Charles
80Knoxvl
81Tidew-13
82T/Tr-94T
83D-128
83F-552
83OPC-358
83T-549
83T/Tr-88T
84D-530
84F-480
84Nes/792-273
84T-273
84Wichita/Rock-1
86Richm-17
87Smok/Atl-2
88D-537
88F-548
88S-454
88T-179
89B-263
89D-286
89F-598
89Richm/Bob-21
89S-448
89T-728
89UD-589
90PublInt/St-119
91WIZMets-320

Pulford, Don
47Centen-21

Pulido, Alfonso
84Cram/PCL-121
85Colum-8
85Colum/Pol-18
85D-34RR
86Colum-20
86Colum/Pol-18
87Colum-24
87Colum/Pol-20
87Colum/TCMA-7
87T-642

Pulido, Carlos
90Kenosha/Best-24
90Kenosha/ProC-2293
90Kenosha/Star-20
91Visalia/ClBest-9

Pulido, Phil
77DaytB

Pulli, Frank
88TM/Umpire-14
89TM/Umpire-12
89TM/Umpire-60M
90TM/Umpire-12

Pulliam, Harry C.
WG3-39

Pulliam, Harvey Jr.
88BBCity/Star-19
89Memphis/Best-15
89Memphis/ProC-1204
89Memphis/Star-19
89SLAS-1
90Omaha/CMC-17
90Omaha/ProC-78
91B-303
91Omaha/LineD-344
91Omaha/ProC-1048
92F-166
92S/II-761
92T-687
92T/91Debut-141
92UD-457

Pullins, Jimmie
89Idaho/ProC-2011
90Pulaski/Best-23
90Pulaski/ProC-3110

Purcell, William
N172
N284

Purcey, Walter
R314/Can

Purdin, John
65T-331R
68T-336
69OPC-161
69T-161
71OPC-748
71T-748
85SpokAT/Cram-16
90Target-638

Purdy, Everett V.
(Pid)
29Exh/4-8
92Conlon/Sport-406

Purdy, Shawn
91Boise/ClBest-12
91Boise/ProC-3876

Purkey, Bob
54T-202
55T-118
55T/DH-114
57T-368
58Kahn
58T-311
59Kahn
59T-506
60Kahn
60L-67
60T-4
61Kahn
61P-184
61T-9
62J-123
62Kahn
62P-123
62P/Can-123
62Salada-153
62Shirriff-153
62T-120
62T-263M
62T/bucks
62T/St-120
63Bz-26
63F-35
63FrBauer-20
63J-134
63Kahn
63P-134
63Salada-6
63T-350
63T-5LL
63T-7LL
63T/SO
64Kahn
64T-480
65OPC-214
65T-214
66T-551
79TCMA-260
88Pac/Leg-77

Purnell, Byron
76Laugh/Clown-18

Purpura, Dan
82Amari-8
83Beaum-10

Purpura, Joe
78Clinton

Pursell, Joe
83Kinston/Team-16

Purtell, William
C46-30
E254
E90/3
M116
T206
T213/blue
T215/blue

Purvis, Glenn
77Visalia

Puryear, Nate
77Watlo
79Tacom-17
81Charl-22
82Chatt-1

Pust, John
87Visalia-21

Putman, Ed
80Evansvl-7
80T-59
81RochR-13

Putnam, Pat
77Tucson
78Cr/PCL-91
78T-706R
79T-713R
80OPC-8
80T-22
81D-265
81F-630
81OPC-302
81T-498
82D-520
82F-327
82F/St-180
82OPC-149
82T-149
82T/St-241
83T/Tr-89
84D-145
84F-617
84Mother/Mar-16
84Nes/792-336TL
84Nes/792-636
84OPC-226
84T-636
84T/St-339
85F-287
85Omaha-9
85T-535
89Pac/SenLg-85
89TM/SenLg-87
90EliteSenLg-75

Puttman, Ambrose
T206

Puzey, James W.
86StPete-25
87Spring/Best-5
88ArkTr/GS-22
88Louisvl-40
89Louisvl-33
89Louisvl/CMC-12
89Louisvl/ProC-1243

Pyburn, James
57T-276
91Crown/Orio-371

Pyburn, Jeff
81Hawaii-12
82Hawaii-12

Pye, Eddie
88GreatF-9
89AS/Cal-19
89Bakers/Cal-198
91Albuq/LineD-18
91Albuq/ProC-1150

Pyfrom, Joel
82Miami-6

Pyle, Scott
81WHave-23
82WHave-28
83Tacom-26

Pytlak, Frank A.
34Exh/4-11
37Exh/4-11
38G-245
38G-269
41DP-107
91Conlon/Sport-280
R308-180
R314

Pyznarski, Tim
83Albany-13
84Cram/PCL-87
85Cram/PCL-122
86LasVegas-12
87D-654
87Denver-2
87Sf-158M
87T-429FS
88AAA/ProC-13
88Denver/CMC-11
88Denver/ProC-1273
88RochR/Gov-21
89Omaha/ProC-1726

Quade, Mike
82AlexD-10
83AlexD-28
86Macon-20MG
87Jaxvl-27
89Rockford/Team-30MG
90Rockford/ProC-2710MG
91Harris/LineD-274MG
91Harris/ProC-644MG

Qualls, Jim

69T-602R
70OPC-192
70T-192
71OPC-731
71T-731
88Boise/ProC-1610

Qualters, Tom
54T-174
55T-33
55T/DH-108
58T-453
59T-341

Quantrill, Paul
89Elmira/Pucko-31
90WinHaven/Star-21
91NewBrit/LineD-469
91NewBrit/ProC-351

Quatrine, Mike
90Elmira/Pucko-26TR

Quealey, Steve
82BirmB-20

Queen, Mel D.
64T-33R
66T-556
67T-374
68T-283
69OPC-81
69T-81
71MLB/St-354
71OPC-736
71T-736
72OPC-196
72T-196
80Tacom-7
81Charl-21
82BK/Indians-8CO
82BK/Indians-9CO
82Wheat/Ind
87Syrac/TCMA-28

Queen, Mel J.
47TipTop
51B-309
52B-171

Querecuto, Juan
90StCath/ProC-3453

Quero, Juan
91CharlR/ClBest-8
91CharlR/ProC-1312

Quesada, Ed
89Everett/Star-24

Quezada, Rafael
80Ander-29

Quezada, Silvano
75Lafay
76Phoenix

Quick, Gene
76Clinton

Quick, Jim
88TM/Umpire-26
89TM/Umpire-24
90TM/Umpire-23

Quick, Ron
81Shrev-17

Quigley, Jerry
76QuadC

Quijada, Ed
90Ashvl/ProC-2758

Quiles, Henry
91Bristol/ProC-3602

Quilici, Frank
66T-207
68T-557
69MB-226
69T-356
70T-572
71MLB/St-471
71OPC-141MG
71T-141
72MB-279
73OPC-49MG
73T-49MG
74OPC-447MG
74T-447MG
75OPC-443MG
75T-443MG
75T/M-443MG

Quillin, Lee
T206

Quillin, Ty
91Kingspt/ClBest-7
91Kingspt/ProC-3827

Quinlan, Craig
91StCath/ClBest-10
91StCath/ProC-3399

Quinlan, Tom
87Myrtle-11
88Knoxvl/Best-25
89Knoxvl/Best-20
89Knoxvl/ProC-1123
89Knoxvl/Star-16
90A&AASingle/ProC-62
90Foil/Best-247
90Knoxvl/Best-22
90Knoxvl/ProC-1252
90Knoxvl/Star-14
91Syrac/LineD-514
91Syrac/ProC-2487
91T/90Debut-127

Quinn, Frank W.
51B-276

Quinn, James
77Newar

Quinn, John P.
(Jack)
10Domino-100
11Helmar-45
12Sweet/Pin-37
25Exh-68
26Exh-68
31Exh/4-4
33G-78
87Conlon/2-51
88Conlon/3-23
90Target-639
91Conlon/Sport-287
E120
E121/80
E126-14
S74-24
T202
T205
T206
T207
T213/blue
T215/brown
V353-53
W517-17
W572
W575

Quinn, Joseph J.
N172
N526

Quinn, Thomas G.
N172

Quinones, Elliot
90A&AASingle/ProC-197
90Billings/ProC-3234
91CharWh/ClBest-25
91CharWh/ProC-2900

Quinones, Hector
83Beloit/LF-26
86Fresno/Smok-18

Quinones, Luis
83Albany-14
84Maine-20
85Maine-21
86F/Up-U92
86Phoenix-21
87Iowa-20
87T-362
88D-365
88Nashvl/CMC-14
88Nashvl/ProC-490
88Nashvl/Team-19
88T-667
89Nashvl/CMC-17
89Nashvl/ProC-1272
90Classic-132
90D-595
90F-428
90Kahn/Reds-22
90OPC-176
90S-499
90T-176
90UD-593
91D-459
91F-77
91F/UltraUp-U77
91Kahn/Reds-10
91Leaf/I-233
91OPC-581
91S-822
91T-581
92F-417
92S/II-638
92T-356

Quinones, Rene
(Rey)
77BurlB
79Holyo-1
80Vanco-16
81Vanco-18
83BuffB-18
83ElPaso-8
84BuffB-5
86D/Rook-48
86F/Up-U93
86Pawtu-17
86T/Tr-89T
87D-638
87D/OD-121
87F-595
87Mother/Sea-20
87T-561
88D-198
88D/Best-275
88F-386
88Mother/Sea-20
88OPC-358
88Panini/St-190
88S-192
88T-358
88T/St-215
89B-213
89Bimbo/Discs-4
89D-330
89D/Best-185
89F-556
89OPC-246
89Panini/St-438
89S-361
89T-246
89T/St-224
89T/Tr-98T
89UD-508
89UD/Ext-750

Quintana, Al
86Watertn-17

Quintana, Carlos
85Elmira-18
86Greens-18
87NewBrit-12
88Pawtu/CMC-20
88Pawtu/ProC-453
89Classic-133
89D-37RR
89F-95
89Pawtu/CMC-13
89Pawtu/Dunkin-18
89Pawtu/ProC-688
89S-623RP
89S/HotRook-13
89T-704
89T/Big-142
89UD-26SR
90Classic/III-44
90D-517
90D/BestAL-140
90F-283
90HotRook/St-36
90Leaf/II-394
90OPC-18
90Pep/RSox-15
90S-658
90S/100Ris-49
90S/YS/II-42
90T-18
90T/Big-273
90T/TVRSox-32
90UD-465
91B-126
91Classic/III-75
91D-568
91F-108
91F/Ultra-39
91Leaf/II-473
91OPC-206
91Panini/FrSt-264
91Panini/St-221
91Pep/RSox-16
91S-149
91T-206
91T/StClub/I-12
91UD-232
92Classic/I-73
92D/II-609
92F-45
92S/I-189
92T-127
92UD-421

Quintana, Luis
77SLCity
82Wichita-13

Quintell, John
91Oneonta/ProC-4157

Quintero, Frank
77Visalia
78OrlTw

Quinzer, Paul
86Cram/PCL-165
88Wichita-23
89Wichita/Rock-27
89Wichita/Rock/Up-16
90LasVegas/ProC-121

Quirico, Rafael
90Foil/Best-147
90Greens/Best-10
90Greens/ProC-2662
90Greens/Star-16
90Oneonta/ProC-3371
91Greens/ProC-3057
91SALAS/ProC-SAL29

Quirk, Art
62T-591R
63T-522R
91Crown/Orio-372

Quirk, Jamie
76OPC-598R
76T-598R
77T-463
78T-95
79T-26
80T-248
81D-341
81F-50
81T-507
82D-212
82F-421
82T-173
83T-264
83T/Tr-90T
84F-332
84Nes/792-671
84T-671
85Omaha-16
87F-377
87T-354
88D-404
88F-266
88Panini/St-103
88S-577
88Smok/Royals-19
88T-477
89B-173
89F-290
89S-461
89T-702
89UD-620
90Mother/A's-15
91Crown/Orio-373
91D-588
91F-21
91Leaf/II-431
91Mother/A's-15
91OPC-132
91T-132
91T/StClub/II-573UER
92D/II-472
92F-265
92S/II-526
92T-19

Quiros, Gus
79Vanco-11
80Vanco-4
81Vanco-11

Quisenberry, Dan
75Watlo
76Watlo
77Jaxvl
80T-667R
81Coke
81D-222
81F-31
81F/St-24
81OPC-206
81T-493
81T-8LL
81T/St-7
82D-112
82F-422
82F/St-204
82T-264
83D-70
83F-122
83K-32
83OPC-155
83OPC-396AS
83Pol/Roy-6
83T-155
83T-396AS
83T-708LL
83T/St-165
83T/St-22
83T/St-74
84D-583
84D/AAS-56
84F-354
84F-635IA
84F/St-73
85FunFoodPin-25
84Nes/792-138LL
84Nes/792-3HL
84Nes/792-407AS
84Nes/792-570
84Nes/792-718LL
84Nestle/DT-11
84OPC-273
84OPC-69AS
84Ralston-25
84Seven-24C
84T-138LL
84T-3HL
84T-407AS
84T-570
84T-718LL
84T/Cereal-25
84T/Gloss40-38
84T/St-10
84T/St-279
84T/St-290
84T/St-9
84T/Super-9
85D-6DK
85D-95
85D/AAS-8
85D/DKsuper-6
85Drake-39
85F-211
85F/LimEd-25
85F/St-99
85Leaf-6DK
85OPC-270
85Seven-15C
85T-270
85T-711AS
85T/3D-24
85T/Gloss40-35
85T/St-173
85T/St-269
85T/Super-8
85ThomMc/Discs-16
85Woolwth-28
86D-541
86F-18
86F/AS-9
86F/Mini-2
86F/St-91
86Kitty/Disc-8
86Leaf-208
86NatPhoto-29
86OPC-50
86Quaker-29
86Sf-118
86Sf-186M
86Sf-55M
86T-50
86T-722AS
86T/3D-21
86T/Gloss60-35
86T/St-257
86T/Super-5
87D-177
87F-378
87F/BB-33
87F/Mini-84
87F/St-93
87OPC-15
87RedFoley/St-7
87Sf-167
87T-714
87T/St-257
88D-471
88F-267
88OPC-195
88Panini/St-101
88S-290

88S/Tr-18T
88Sf-76
88Smok/Royals-15
88T-195
88T/St-256
89F/Up-120
89OPC-13
89S-520
89Smok/Cards-19
89T-612
89UD-533
90D-437
90F-259
90OPC-312
90PublInt/St-227
90S-475
90T-312
90UD-659

Raabe, Brian
91AS/Cal-8
91Visalia/ClBest-19
91Visalia/ProC-1751

Raasch, Glen
91Penin/ProC-382

Rabb, John
81Shrev-2
82Phoenix
83Phoenix/BHN-1
84D-143
84Nes/792-228
84T-228
85Cram/PCL-183
85D-236
85IntLgAS-12
85Richm-22
85T-696
86Richm-18
87Richm/Crown-20
87Richm/TCMA-20

Rabe, Charles
58Kahn
58T-376

Rabouin, Andre
88AppFx/ProC-159
89AppFx/ProC-871
90AppFox/Box-20
90AppFox/ProC-2113CO

Rackley, Marv
47TipTop
90Target-640

Racobaldo, Mike
90Kissim/DIMD-24

Raczka, Mike
87CharlO/WBTV-10
88RochR/Gov-22
89RochR/CMC-5
89RochR/ProC-1648

Radachowsky, Gregg
90Niagara/Pucko-13
91Niagara/ProC-3637

Radatz, Dick
62T-591R
63T-363
64T-170
64T/Coins-30
64T/S-40
64T/St-41
64Wheat/St-37
65Bz-10
65OldLond-34
65T-295
65T/E-48
65T/trans-64
66T-475
66T/RO-111
67OPC-174
67T-174
69T-663
74Laugh/ASG-63
78TCMA-76
89Pac/Leg-122
89Swell-46
PM10/Sm-149
WG10-44
WG9-43

Radbourn, Charles
(Hoss)
50Callahan
75F/Pion-5
80SSPC/HOF
90BBWit-92
90HOF/St-2
N172
N284
N403

Radcliff, Ray
(Rip)
37OPC-125
37Wheat
38G-261
38G-285
91Conlon/Sport-98
PR1-24
R314
V300
WG8-45

Radcliffe, Ernest Jr.
87Erie-9
88Virgini/Star-20

Radcliffe, Ted
78Laugh/Black-36
86Negro/Frit-64
91Negro/Lewis-25

Rader, Dave
72OPC-232R
72T-232R
73OPC-121
73T-121
74OPC-213
74T-213
74T/St-108
75OPC-31
75T-31
75T/M-31
76Ho-21
76Ho/Twink-21
76OPC-54
76T-54
77T-427
78T-563
79OPC-369
79T-693
80T-296
81D-512
81OPC-359
81T-378

Rader, Doug
67T-412R
68T-332
69MB-227
69MLB/St-142
69OPC-119
69T-119
69T/St-37
70MLB/St-46
70OPC-355
70T-355
71MLB/St-90
71OPC-425
71T-425
71T/Coins-17
72K-14
72MB-280
72T-536
73OPC-76
73T-76
74OPC-395
74T-395
74T/DE-14
74T/St-35
75Ho-89
75OPC-165
75T-165
75T/M-165
76OPC-44
76SSPC-59
76T-44
76T/Tr-44T
77BurgChef-128
77Padre/SchCd-22
77T-9
78OPC-166
78T-651
80Hawaii-2
81Hawaii-23
82Hawaii-23
83Rang-11MG
83T/Tr-91
84Nes/792-412MG
84Rang-11
84T-412
85T-519MG
89T/Tr-99TMG
90OPC-51MG
90T-51MG
91OPC-231MG
91T-231MG

Rader, Keith
91SLCity/ProC-3220

Radford, Paul
N172

Radinsky, Scott
87Penin-12
89SoBend/GS-7
90B-308
90Classic/III-T5
90Coke/WSox-22
90Coke/WSox-28
90D/Rook-40
90F/Up-U86
90Leaf/II-484
90S/Tr-90T
90T/Tr-99T
90UD/Ext-725
91B-365
91Bz-22
91D-332
91F-135
91F/UltraUp-U18
91Kodak/WSox-31
91Leaf/II-463
91OPC-299
91S-62
91S/100RisSt-83
91T-299
91T/90Debut-128
91T/StClub/II-311
91ToysRUs-25
91UD-621
92D/I-299
92F-96
92S/II-444
92T-701
92UD-594

Radison, Dan
88Hamil/ProC-1732
89Spring/Best-29
91Albany/ProC-1023MG

Radloff, Scott
83Cedar-15
83Cedar/LF-21

Radovich, Robert
66Pep/Tul

Radtke, Jack
90Target-641

Radziewicz, Doug
91Johnson/ClBest-8
91Johnson/ProC-3986

Raeside, John
82Lynch-23

Raether, Richard
86Tulsa-22
87PortChar-9
88Tulsa-26
90TulsaDG/Best-10

Raffensberger, Ken
49B-176
49Eureka-93
51B-48
52B-55
52T-118
52TipTop
53B/Col-10
53T-276
54B-92
54T-46
91T/Arc53-276

Raffo, Greg
91Bristol/ClBest-16
91Bristol/ProC-3603

Raffo, Thomas
88CapeCod-9
88CapeCod/Sum-79
90Miami/I/Star-20
91CharWh/ClBest-19
91CharWh/ProC-2896
91SALAS/ProC-SAL10
91Single/ClBest-261

Ragan, Don C.P.
(Pat)
16FleischBrd-74
90Target-642
D329-140
M101/4-140
T207

Ragland, Tom
72OPC-334R
72T-334R
74OPC-441
74T-441

Ragland, Trace
91Welland/ClBest-14
91Welland/ProC-3589

Ragni, John
52Mother-34

Ragsdale, Jerry
83Ander-27

Raich, Eric
76OPC-484
76T-484
77T-62

Raimondi, Bill
46Remar
47Remar-1
47Signal
47Smith-2
48Signal
48Smith-1
49B/PCL-18
49Remar
53Mother-36

Raimondo, Pasquale
81VeroB-15

Rainbolt, Ray
74Gaston
76SanAn/Team-19
79Tulsa-8

Rainer, Rick
85Tidew-28
86Tidew-25TR
87Tidew-30
87Tidew/TCMA-25

Raines, Larry
58T-243

Raines, Mike
81Cedar-5

Raines, Tim
(Rock)
79Memphis
81D-538
81OPC-136R
81T-479R
81T/Tr-816
82D-214
82F-202
82F/St-31
82Hygrade
82K-53
82OPC-70
82OPC/Post-17
82PermaGr/AS-13
82PermaGr/CC-6
82T-164LL
82T-3RB
82T-70
82T/St-116
82T/St-62
82T/St-7
82Zeller-3
83D-540
83F-292
83OPC-227
83OPC-352AS
83PermaGr/AS-14
83Stuart-9
83T-403AS
83T-595
83T-704LL
83T/St-210
83T/St-253
84D-299
84F-281
84F-631IA
84F/St-51
84F/St-88
85FunFoodPin-41
84Nes/792-134LL
84Nes/792-370
84Nes/792-390AS
84Nestle/DT-17
84OPC-370
84OPC-390AS
84Seven-20E
84Stuart-20
84Stuart-36AS
84Stuart-37M
84T-134LL
84T-370
84T-390AS
84T/Gloss22-17
84T/Gloss40-37
84T/St-179
84T/St-201
84T/St-91
84T/St/Box-4
85D-299
85D/AAS-1
85Drake-24
85F-405
85F/LimEd-26
85F/St-42
85F/St-58
85Leaf-218
85Leaf-252CG
85OPC-277
85OPC/Post-7
85Seven-12S
85T-630
85T/3D-17
85T/St-282
85T/St-82
85T/Super-15
86D-177
86D/AAS-20
86Drake-15
86F-256
86F-632M
86F/LL-33
86F/Mini-54
86F/St-92
86Leaf-108
86OPC-280
86Provigo-7
86Quaker-10
86Sf-11
86Sf-127M
86Sf-144M
86Sf/Dec-74M
86T-280
86T/Gloss60-15
86T/Mini-49
86T/St-75
86T/Super-42
87Classic-29
87D-56
87D/AAS-36
87D/HL-16
87D/HL-7
87F-328
87F-642M
87F/AS-12
87F/Excit-34
87F/BB-34
87F/Mini-85
87F/RecSet-30
87F/Slug-32
87F/St-94
87KayBee-25
87Leaf-149
87OPC-30
87RedFoley/St-39
87Sf-152M
87Sf-197M
87Sf-199M
87Sf-34
87Sportflic/DealP-1
87T-30
87T/Board-24
87T/Gloss60-48
87T/HL-11
87T/Mini-17
87T/St-85
87Woolwth-11
88Bz-15
88Classic/Red-168
88D-2DK
88D-345
88D-BC18
88D/AS-57
88D/AS-62
88D/Best-180
88D/DKsuper-2DK
88Drake-2
88F-193
88F-631M
88F/AwardWin-30
88F/BB/AS-31
88F/BB/MVP-27
88F/Excit-31
88F/Head-6
88F/Hottest-31
88F/LL-31
88F/Mini-90
88F/RecSet-30
88F/SS-29
88F/St-97
88F/TL-27

88FanSam-16
88Ho/Disc-11
88Jiffy-14
88KayBee-24
88KMart-19
88Leaf-114
88Leaf-211MVP
88Leaf-2DK
88Nestle-31
88OPC-243
88Panini/St-330
88S-3
88S-649M
88Sf-2
88T-403AS
88T-720
88T/Big-116
88T/Coins-49
88T/Gloss60-12
88T/Mini-57
88T/Revco-5
88T/RiteAid-6
88T/St-76
88T/St/Backs-20
88T/UK-58
89B-369
89Classic-42
89D-97
89D/Best-258
89F-391
89KayBee-25
89KMart/DT-27
89KMart/Lead-7
89OPC-87
89Panini/St-125
89MSA/SS-6
89RedFoley/St-91
89S-40
89S/HotStar-95
89Sf-150
89T-560
89T-81TL
89T/Big-73
89T/Coins-22
89T/Gloss60-53
89T/LJN-154
89T/St-77
89T/UK-61
89UD-402
90B-118
90Classic-118
90D-216
90D/BestNL-104
90D/Bon/MVP-BC7
90F-359
90F/BBMVP-30
90Holsum/Discs-2
90HotPlay/St-32
90KayBee-24
90KingB/Discs-6
90KMart/CBatL-7
90Leaf/I-212
90OPC-180
90Panini/St-283
90PublInt/St-186
90S-409
90S/100St-75
90Sf-69
90Starline/LJS-23
90Starline/LJS-39
90Sunflower-14
90T-180
90T/Ames-17
90T/Big-154
90T/Coins-54
90T/DH-50
90T/Gloss60-38
90T/Mini-63
90T/St-69
90T/TVAS-55
90UD-177
90UD-29TC
91B-362
91BBBest/HitM-16
91Classic/200-174
91Classic/II-T9
91D-457
91DennyGS-26
91F-244
91F/Ultra-81
91F/Up-U15
91Kodak/WSox-30
91Leaf/II-413
91Leaf/Stud-37
91Leaf/StudPrev-4
91OPC-360
91OPC/Premier-97
91Panini/FrSt-143
91Panini/St-63
91RedFoley/St-75
91S-35
91S/100SS-89
91S/RookTr-10T
91T-360
91T/CJMini/I-3
91T/StClub/II-523
91T/Tr-94T
91UD-143
91UD/Ext-773
92D/I-312
92F-97
92S/II-635
92T-426
92UD-575

Rainey, Chuck
80T-662R
81T-199
82Coke/BOS
82F-303
82T-522
83D-334
83F-192
83T-56
83T/Tr-92
83Thorn-30
84D-76
84F-502
84Nes/792-334
84OPC-334
84T/St-47
85D-618

Rainey, Scott
83Clinton/LF-9
87Wichita-16

Rainout, Chief
87Peoria/PW-6

Raisanen, Keith
87Watertn-8
88Salem/Star-16
89Augusta/ProC-506
89SALAS/GS-9
90Salem/Star-17

Rajsich, Dave
78Cr/PCL-73
79T-710R
80T-548
81D-267
83OKCty-15
85RochR-21
86Louisvl-25
88Louisvl-41
88Louisvl/CMC-9
88Louisvl/ProC-443
89Pac/SenLg-3
91Beloit/ClBest-26CO
91Beloit/ProC-2120CO
91Pac/SenLg-154
91Pac/SenLg-160

Rajsich, Gary
77Cocoa
80Tucson-16
81Tidew-9
83D-599
83F-553
83T-317
83Tidew-8
84Louisvl-6
85Mother/Giants-24
89Pac/SenLg-7
89T/SenLg-124
90EliteSenLg-12
91Pac/SenLg-156
91Pac/SenLg-160
91WIZMets-321

Rakow, Ed
60T-551
61T-147
62T-342
63J-90
63P-90
63T-82
64Det/Lids-12
64T-491
65T-454
90Target-643

Raley, Dan
89Lakeland/Star-17
90Lakeland/Star-20
91London/LineD-400CO
91London/ProC-1894CO

Raley, Tim
88Beloit/GS-5
89Stockton/Best-20
89Stockton/Cal-169
89Stockton/ProC-401
89Stockton/Star-9
90Stockton/Best-13
90Stockton/Cal-198
90Stockton/ProC-2198
91Hagers/LineD-243
91Hagers/ProC-2469

Ralph, Curtis
90PrWill/Team-21
91PrWill/ClBest-10
91PrWill/ProC-1426

Ralston, Robert
(Bobby)
85Orlan-10
86Toledo-18
87Orlan-6
88Portl/CMC-21
88Portl/ProC-657
89Portl/CMC-15
89Portl/ProC-232
90Huntsvl/Best-18

Ramanouchi, Kenichi
91Salinas/ClBest-7
91Salinas/ProC-2254

Ramazzotti, Bob
49Eureka-67
51B-247
52T-184
53B/BW-41
90Target-644

Rambo, Dan
90A&AASingle/ProC-145
90AS/Cal-53
90Foil/Best-123
90SanJose/Best-23
90SanJose/Cal-44
90SanJose/ProC-2006
90SanJose/Star-18
91Shrev/LineD-318
91Shrev/ProC-1821

Rambo, Matt
88Spartan/ProC-1025
88Spartan/Star-16
88Spartan/Star-16
89Clearw/Star-17
91Osceola/ClBest-10
91Osceola/ProC-682
91Single/ClBest-53

Rameriez, Nick
88CharWh/Best-26

Rametta, Steve
75SanAn

Ramie, Vern
82Knoxvl-17
83Syrac-23

Ramirez, Alex
80OrlTw-18

Ramirez, D. Allan
(Allan)
82RochR-5
83RochR-7
84D-332
84Nes/792-347
84RochR-16
84T-347
85CharlO-25
91Crown/Orio-374

Ramirez, Daniel
91Kane/ClBest-19
91Kane/ProC-2666

Ramirez, Fausto
86Cram/PCL-125
88Wausau/GS-3

Ramirez, Francisco
91Elizab/ProC-4304

Ramirez, Frank
87Idaho-23

Ramirez, Hector
91Kingspt/ClBest-19
91Kingspt/ProC-3811

Ramirez, J.D.
89SLCity-11
90Rockford/ProC-2703
91WPalmB/ClBest-23
91WPalmB/ProC-1238

Ramirez, Jack
79Tulsa-12

Ramirez, Luis
78Newar

Ramirez, Manny
91BurlInd/ProC-3316
91Classic/DP-10
91FrRow/DP-47
92S/II-800Draft
92T-156DP
92UD-63TP

Ramirez, Mario
76Wausau
78Tidew
79Tidew-12
84F-309
84Mother/Padres-23
84Nes/792-94
84T-94
85Mother/Padres-16
85T-427
86D-568
86T-262
86Toledo-19
91WIZMets-322

Ramirez, Milt
71MLB/St-281
71OPC-702
71T-702
77SanJose-5
80Ogden-14

Ramirez, Nelson
90Hunting/ProC-3280

Ramirez, Nick
88Geneva/ProC-1634

Ramirez, Omar
91Watertn/ClBest-27
91Watertn/ProC-3382

Ramirez, Orlando
76SSPC-197
77T-131

Ramirez, Rafael
78Green
79Savan-23
80Richm-2
81F-266
81Pol/Atl-16
81T-192R
82BK/Lids-21
82D-546
82F-447
82Pol/Atl-16
82T-536
83D-310
83F-146
83Pol/Atl-16
83T-439
84D-589
84F-190
84F/St-26
84Nes/792-234
84OPC-234
84Pol/Atl-16
84T-234
84T/St-33
85D-141
85F-339
85Ho/Braves-20
85Leaf-86
85OPC-232
85Pol/Atl-16
85T-647
85T/St-27
86D-263
86F-526
86OPC-107
86Pol/Atl-16
86T-107
86T/St-42
87D-202
87F-526
87Smok/Atl-18
87T-76
87T/St-42
88D-448
88F/Up-U91
88Mother/Ast-17
88OPC-379
88Panini/St-247
88Pol/Ast-18
88S-426
88S/Tr-12T
88T-379
88T/Tr-90T
89B-330
89D-509
89D/Best-64
89F-365
89Lennox/Ast-16
89Mother/Ast-16
89OPC-261
89Panini/St-90
89S-113
89T-749
89T/Big-268
89T/St-17
89UD-341
90D-241
90D/BestNL-77
90F-234
90Leaf/I-135
90Lennox-19
90Mother/Ast-19
90OPC-558
90Panini/St-266
90PublInt/St-99
90S-42
90T-558
90T/Big-183
90T/St-18
90UD-144
91B-564
91D-586
91F-513
91F/Ultra-139
91Mother/Ast-19
91OPC-423
91Panini/FrSt-10
91S-305
91T-423
91T/StClub/I-107
91UD-210
92S/I-388
92UD-582

Ramirez, Randy
84Chatt-21

Ramirez, Ray
86Orlan-16TR
87OKCty-24
88OkCty/ProC-51
89OkCty/ProC-1533
90OkCty/CMC-24TR

Ramirez, Richard
87Gaston-23

Ramirez, Roberto
91Clinton/ProC-848
91Everett/ClBest-27
91Everett/ProC-3922
91Welland/ClBest-24
91Welland/ProC-3571

Ramirez, Russell
78Newar
79BurlB-2

Ramon, John
90Foil/Best-152

Ramon, Julio
87Oneonta-16

Ramon, Ray
86Reading-22

Ramos, Domingo
77WHave
78Cr/PCL-78
79Syrac-6
80Syrac-22
82SLCity-16
84D-440
84Nes/792-194
84T-194
85Mother/Mar-12
85T-349
86Mother/Mar-12
86T-462
87Mother/Sea-21
87T-641
88ColoSp/CMC-16
88ColoSp/ProC-1534
88D-622
88F/Up-U23
88S-362
88T-206
89Mara/Cubs-15
90Cub/Mara-16
90D-491
90Leaf/II-440
90OPC-37
90S-489

90T-37
90T/TVCub-24
90UD-150
91F-429
91OPC-541
91T-541
91UD-85

Ramos, Eddie
91Classic/DP-45
91FrRow/DP-33

Ramos, George
78Green

Ramos, Jairo
91MedHat/ProC-4116

Ramos, John
87PrWill-28
88CLAS/Star-15
88PrWill/Star-20
89Albany/Best-13
89Albany/ProC-336
89Albany/Star-15
89Star/Wax-100
90Albany/Best-12
90Albany/ProC-1177
90Albany/Star-13
90EastLAS/ProC-EL42
91ColClip/LineD-115
91ColClip/ProC-599
91F/Ultra-385MLP
92D/I-15RR
92F-242
92S/II-818
92T/91Debut-142

Ramos, Jorge
90SoBend/Best-8
90SoBend/ClBest-4
91SoBend/ProC-2864

Ramos, Jose
87Fayette-2
88Fayette/ProC-1086
89London/ProC-1387
90Toledo/CMC-7
90Toledo/ProC-146
90WichSt-30
91London/LineD-394
91London/ProC-1877

Ramos, Ken
90CLAS/CL-43
90Kinston/Team-9
91Canton/LineD-97
91Canton/ProC-991

Ramos, Pedro
56T-49
57T-326
58T-331
59T-291M
59T-78
60L-21
60T-175
61Clover-22
61P-98
61Peters-3
61T-50LL
61T-528
61T/St-184
62Sugar-19
62T-485
62T/bucks
62T/St-79
63Sugar-19
63T-14
64Kahn
64T-562
65OPC-13
65T-13
66T-439
67OPC-187
67T-187
89Pac/SenLg-217M
89Pac/SenLg-68
WG10-18

Ramos, Richard
82Wichita-14

Ramos, Roberto
(Bobby)
79SLCity
81F-162
81OPC-136R
81T-479R
82Colum-18
82Colum/Pol-31
82F-203
82OPC-354
82T-354
83Stuart-20
83T/Tr-93
84D-209
84F-282
84Nes/792-32
84OPC-32
84Stuart-9
84T-32
85Cram/PCL-15
85OPC-269
85T-407
86Iowa-24
87Omaha-21
88Phoenix/CMC-13
88Phoenix/ProC-69
89ColMud/Best-20
89ColMud/ProC-121
89Pac/SenLg-65
89T/SenLg-18
90Osceola/Star-29CO
91Osceola/ClBest-20CO
91Osceola/ProC-700CO

Ramos, Wolf
80Elmira-24

Ramppen, Frank
83Visalia/LF-7

Ramsdell, J. Willard
(Willie)
47Signal
47Sunbeam
51B-251
52B-22
52T-114
53Mother-3
79TCMA-279
90Target-645

Ramsey, Fernando
88CharWh/Best-22
89Peoria/Ko-25
90WinSalem/Team-11
91CharlK/LineD-139
91CharlK/ProC-1701

Ramsey, Jeff
90Rockford/ProC-2707

Ramsey, Michael James
(Mike)
87Albuq/Pol-30
87D/OD-80
87Mother/Dodg-11
88Albuq/CMC-14
88Albuq/ProC-267
88S-267
90Target-646

Ramsey, Michael Jeffery
(Mike)
76ArkTr
77ArkTr
81F-549
81T-366
82D-316
82F-125
82T-574
83D-568
83F-19
83T-128
84D-382
84F-333
84Nes/792-467
84T-467
85F-406
85OPC-62
85T-62
86Tampa-15
87Edmon-6
89Edmon/CMC-16
89Edmon/ProC-561
90Target-647
91Pac/SenLg-18
91Spring/ClBest-11MG
91Spring/ProC-759MG

Ramsey, Thomas
N172

Ramstack, Curt
76AppFx

Rand, Dick
54Hunter
58T-218

Rand, Kevin
85Albany-27
87Colum-2
89EastLDD/ProC-DD49TR

Randa, Joe
91Eugene/ClBest-14
91Eugene/ProC-3736

Randahl, Rick
81Tacom-2

Randall, Bob
74Albuq/Team-14
77BurgChef-52
77T-578
78T-363
79T-58
80OPC-90
80T-162
80Toledo-2

Randall, James
(Sap)
82Redwd-8
83Nashua-18
84Cram/PCL-101
85Cram/PCL-10
86MidldA-20
87Edmon-16
88AAA/ProC-46
88Vanco/CMC-20
88Vanco/ProC-765

Randall, Mark
89Martins/Star-26
90Clearw/Star-18
91Spartan/ClBest-12
91Spartan/ProC-897

Randall, Newton
T206

Randle, Carl
88Butte-7
89Gaston/ProC-1005
89Gaston/Star-19
90Gaston/Best-3
90Gaston/ProC-2519
90Gaston/Star-19
91CharlR/ClBest-9
91CharlR/ProC-1313

Randle, Len
72T-737
73OPC-378
73T-378
74OPC-446
74T-446
75OPC-259
75T-259
75T/M-259
76OPC-31
76SSPC-266
76T-31
77BurgChef-21
77T-196
78Ho-102
78K-22
78OPC-132
78T-544
79OPC-236
79T-454
81D-485
81F-301
81Pol/Mariners-9
81T-692
81T/TR-817
82D-307
82F-516
82OPC-312
82T-312
82T/ST-230
87Watlo-27
89Pac/SenLg-11
89T/SenLg-38
89TM/SenLg-88
90EliteSenLg-13
90Swell/Great-53
91Pac/SenLg-116
91WIZMets-323

Randle, Michael
87Kenosha-3
88CalLgAS-37
88Visalia/Cal-147
88Visalia/ProC-85
89Orlan/Best-21
89Orlan/ProC-1339
90OrlanSR/Best-11
90OrlanSR/ProC-1097
90OrlanSR/Star-15

Randle, Randy
86Osceola-20
87Osceola-5
88Modesto/Cal-77
89NewBrit/ProC-618
89NewBrit/Star-17
90NewBrit/Best-19
90NewBrit/Star-17
91NewBrit/LineD-470
91NewBrit/ProC-360

Randolph, Bob
81LynnS-26
83Chatt-13

Randolph, Willie
76OPC-592R
76SSPC-584
76T-592R
76T/Tr-592T
77BK/Y-13
77BurgChef-175
77OPC-110
77T-359
78BK/Y-13
78Ho-89
78OPC-228
78T-620
79BK/Y-13
79OPC-125
79T-250
80OPC-239
80T-460
81D-345
81F-109
81F/St-107
81OPC-60
81PermaGr/AS-16
81T-60
81T/HT
81T/So-36
81T/St-108
81T/St-242
82D-461
82F-49
82F/St-121
82OPC-159IA
82OPC-213AS
82OPC-37
82T-548AS
82T-569
82T-570IA
82T/St-219
83D-283
83F-393
83OPC-140
83RoyRog/Disc-9
83T-140
83T/St-95
84D-417
84F-137
85FunFoodPin-20
84Nes/792-360
84OPC-360
84T-360
84T/St-324
85D-92
85F-140
85Leaf-83
85OPC-8
85Pol/MetYank-Y1
85T-765
85T/St-312
86D-16DK
86D-92
86D/DKsuper-16
86F-115
86Leaf-16DK
86OPC-332
86T-276M
86T-455
86T/St-305
87D-154
87D/OD-246
87F-109
87F/BB-35
87Leaf-58
87OPC-377
87RedFoley/St-2
87T-701
87T/St-302
88D-228
88D/AS-3
88D/Best-108
88D/PopUp-3
88D/Y/Bk-228
88Drake-18
88F-218
88F/BB/AS-32
88F/BB/MVP-28
88F/Mini-42
88F/St-50
88Leaf-162
88Nestle-22
88OPC-210
88Panini/St-153
88Panini/St-228M
88S-266
88S/WaxBox-3
88Sf-47
88Sf/Gamewin-6
88T-210
88T-387
88T/Big-76
88T/Gloss22-3
88T/Gloss60-42
88T/Mini-28
88T/St-162
88T/St-294
88T/St/Backs-37
88T/UK-59
89B-344
89D-395
89D/Best-148
89D/Tr-8
89F-265
89F/Up-93
89Mother/Dodg-10
89OPC-244
89Panini/St-405
89Pol/Dodg-8
89RedFoley/St-92
89S-45
89S/Tr-41
89Smok/Dodg-57
89T-519TL
89T-635
89T/Big-244
89T/St-309
89T/Tr-100T
89UD-237
89UD/Ext-777
90B-90
90Classic-122
90Classic/III-71
90D-19DK
90D-250
90D/BestAL-110
90D/SuperDK-19DK
90F-406
90Leaf/II-345
90OPC-25
90Panini/St-279
90Pol/Dodg-12
90PublInt/St-16
90S-395
90S/100St-4
90S/Tr-51T
90Sf-175
90T-25
90T/Big-43
90T/Coins-55
90T/St-66
90T/Tr-100T
90Target-648
90UD-183
90UD/Ext-704
91B-46
91Brewer/MillB-21
91D-217
91D-766WS
91F-22
91F/UltraUp-U32
91F/Up-U33
91Leaf/II-419
91Leaf/Stud-74
91OPC-525
91Panini/FrSt-193
91Pol/Brew-19
91S-194
91S/RookTr-35T
91T-525
91T/StClub/II-545
91T/Tr-95T
91UD-421
91UD/Ext-720
92Classic/I-74
92D/II-625
92F-186
92S/I-30
92T-116
92UD-211

Randon, Gil
90Kgsport/Best-26CO

Ranew, Merritt

62T-156
64T-78
66OPC-62
66T-62
89Smok/Ast-11
Ranger, Rowdy
91Gaston/ClBest-30
Rannow, John
86Cram/PCL-19
87Clinton-10
Ransom, Gene
82Madis-9
83Madis/LF-18
Ransom, Jeff
81Phoenix-22
83Phoenix/BHN-5
87Toledo-24
87Toledo/TCMA-11
Rantz, Mike
83Idaho-24
Raper, Ron
88CapeCod/Sum-37
Rapp, Craig
91Idaho/ProC-4327
Rapp, Earl
49Remar
50Remar
53Mother-30
Rapp, Joe
(Goldie)
21Exh-138
E120
E220
V100
V61-104
W573
Rapp, Patrick
90A&AASingle/ProC-117
90Clinton/Best-23
90Clinton/ProC-2547
91AS/Cal-39
91SanJose/ClBest-20
91SanJose/ProC-9
91Single/ClBest-275
Rapp, Vern
77T-183MG
78T-324MG
83Stuart-3CO
84T/Tr-95MG
Rappoli, Paul
91Elmira/ClBest-12
91Elmira/ProC-3285
Rariden, William A.
(Bill)
14CJ-137
15CJ-137
16FleischBrd-75
88Pac/8Men-86
D327
D328-136
D329-141
D350/2-141
E135-136
E270
M101/4-141
M101/5-141
Raschi, Victor
(Vic)
49B-35
50B-100
51B-25
51BR-C4
52B-37
52BR
52StarCal/L-70D
53B/Col-27
53Exh/Can-5
54B-33
54Hunter
55B-185
55Hunter
55Rodeo
74Laugh/ASG-48
79TCMA-186
88Pac/Leg-70
90BBWit-53
Exh47
PM10/Sm-150
R346-32
Rashid, Ralph
90Peoria/Team-3PER
Rasmus, Tony
86Cram/PCL-191

Rasmussen
T207
Rasmussen, Dennis
81Holyo-25
83Colum-8
84Colum-25
84Colum/Pol-19
84D-446
85D-518
85F-141
85Leaf-48
85T-691
86D-336
86T-301
87Classic-87
87D-175
87D/OD-247
87F-110
87F/Excit-35
87F/GameWin-35
87F/Mini-86
87F/St-95
87Leaf-260
87OPC-364
87Sf-71
87T-555
87T/Mini-66
87T/St-303
88D-575
88F-246
88F/Up-U126
88S-560
88T-135
88T/St-145
88T/Tr-91T
89B-450
89Classic-86
89Coke/Padre-12
89D-559
89F-314
89OPC-32
89Padre/Mag-17
89Panini/St-195
89S-562
89Sf-212
89T-32
89UD-645
90B-205
90Coke/Padre-14
90D-420
90F-165
90Leaf/II-471
90OPC-449
90Padre/MagUno-4
90PublInt/St-56
90S-129
90T-449
90UD-594
91D-458
91F-539
91F/Ultra-309
91OPC-774
91Padre/MagRal-2
91S-457
91T-774
91T/StClub/I-169
91UD-230
92D/I-245
92F-617
92S/II-536
92T-252
92UD-439
Rasmussen, Harold
(Eric)
76OPC-182
76SSPC-296
76T-182
77T-404
78Padre/FamFun-23
78T-281
79T-57
80T-531
81D-123
81F-497
81T-342
83T-594
84Cram/PCL-49
84Nes/792-724
84OPC-377
84T-724
86Miami-21
86RochR-17
87RochR-8
87RochR/TCMA-8

88Watlo/ProC-686
89Canton/Best-11
89Canton/ProC-1308
89Pac/SenLg-107
90EliteSenLg-76
Rasmussen, Jim
81OkCty/TCMA-25
82OkCty-18
82Reading-7
84Nashvl-18
87Hawaii-11
Rasmussen, Neil
73Cedar
75BurlB
77Holyo
78Holyo
Rasp, Ronnie
88Wythe/ProC-2001
89CharWh/Best-17
89CharWh/ProC-1764
90Peoria/Team-27
90WinSalem/Team-13
Ratekin, Mark
91Boise/ClBest-28
91Boise/ProC-3877
Rath, Maurice
88Pac/8Men-85
E270
W514-57
Rather, Dody
86FSLAS-39
86Osceola-21
87ColAst/ProC-17
Rathjen, Dennis
80Clinton-2
Ratliff, Danny
86Stockton-22
Ratliff, Darryl
89Princet/Star-15
90Augusta/ProC-2478
91CLAS/ProC-CAR36
91Salem/ClBest-12
91Salem/ProC-966
Ratliff, Kelly Eugene
65T-553R
Ratliff, Paul
63T-549R
70OPC-267R
70T-267R
71OPC-607
71T-607
Ratzer, Steve
82Tidew-21
Rau, Doug
73OPC-602R
73T-602R
74OPC-64
74T-64
75OPC-269
75T-269
75T/M-269
76OPC-124
76SSPC-71
76T-124
77BurgChef-149
77K-11
77OPC-128
77T-421
78OPC-24
78T-641
79K-56
79OPC-178
79T-347
80Pol/Dodg-31
80T-527
81F-133
81Redwd-9
81T-174
81T/Tr-819
90Target-649
Raubolt, Art
86Lakeland-19
Rauch, Al
(Rocky)
78Watlo
Rauch, Bob
91WIZMets-324
Rauth, Chris
85LitFalls-8
86Columbia-20
87Lynch-15
89Jacks/GS-24
90Knoxvl/Best-16

Rautzhan, Clarence G.
(Lance)
75Water
78T-709R
79Holyo-25
79OPC-193
79T-373
80Vanco-9
90Target-650
Raven, Luis
91Boise/ClBest-3
91Boise/ProC-3897
Rawdon, Chris
86Elmira-16
Rawley, Billy
83Cedar-6
Rawley, Shane
75WPalmB
79OPC-30
79T-74
80OPC-368
80T-723
81D-167
81OPC-51
81Pol/Mar-16
81T-423
81T/St-129
82D-352
82F-517
82T-197
82T/Tr-95T
83D-513
83F-394
83T-592
84D-295
84F-138
84F/X-U94
84Nes/792-254
84OPC-254
84T-254
85CIGNA-15
85D-599
85D/HL-39
85F-263
85Leaf-31
85OPC-169
85Phill/TastyK-22
85Phill/TastyK-9M
85T-636
86CIGNA-6
86D-233
86F-446
86Leaf-109
86OPC-361
86Phill/TastyK-28
86T-361
86T/St-123
87D-83
87D/AAS-56
87D/OD-159
87F-180
87F/RecSet-31
87F/St-96
87Leaf-139
87OPC-239
87Phill/TastyK-28
87RedFoley/St-124
87Sf-181
87T-771
87T/St-120
88D-13DK
88D-83
88D/Best-240
88D/DKsuper-13DK
88F-311
88F/Hottest-32
88F/Mini-100
88F/SS-C4
88F/St-109
88F/WaxBox-C8
88Leaf-13DK
88Leaf-92
88OPC-66
88Panini/St-352
88Phill/TastyK-19
88S-375
88Sf-51
88T-406AS
88T-66
88T/Gloss60-45
88T/Mini-65
88T/St-121
89B-151
89D-251

89F-579
89F/Up-44
89OPC-24
89S-170
89T-494
89T/St-118
89T/Tr-101T
89UD-427
89UD/Ext-786
90D-537
90F-384
90OPC-101
90PublInt/St-336
90S-71
90T-101
90UD-438
Rawlings, John
E120
E121/120
E121/80
V100
W501-61
W573
W575
Ray
M116
Ray, Art
83AlexD-9
Ray, Bregg
84Butte-21
Ray, Glenn
81CharR-7
Ray, Jay
86Bakers-23
88VeroB/Star-21
Ray, Jim F.
68T-539R
69T-257
70OPC-113
70T-113
71MLB/St-91
71OPC-242
71T-242
72T-603
73OPC-313
73T-313
74OPC-458
74T-458
74T/Tr-458T
75Cedar
75OPC-89
75T-89
75T/M-89
Ray, Johnny
80Colum
81Tucson-10
82D-528
82F-492
82T-291R
82T/Tr-96T
83D-437
83F-317
83K-24
83OPC-149
83T-149
83T/St-327
84D-308
84F-260
85FunFoodPin-69
84Nes/792-387AS
84Nes/792-537
84Nestle/DT-13
84OPC-323
84OPC-387AS
84T-387AS
84T-537
84T/Gloss40-5
84T/St-134
84T/St-186
84T/St/Box-7
85D-186
85D/AAS-50
85F-473
85F/St-43
85GenMills-7
85Leaf-212
85OPC-96
85T-96
85T/St-130
85ThomMc/Discs-40
86D-186
86D-19DK
86D/DKsuper-19

86D/HL-9
86F-617
86F/St-93
86Leaf-19DK
86OPC-37
86T-615
86T/St-124
87D-144
87D/OD-162
87F-618
87F/AwardWin-31
87F/Excit-36
87F/Mini-87
87F/St-97
87Kraft-14
87Leaf-147
87OPC-291
87RedFoley/St-51
87Sf-116M
87Sf-121
87Smok/NL-8
87T-747
87T/Gloss60-55
87T/St-135
88D-428
88D/Best-171
88F-502
88F/Slug-31
88Leaf-260
88OPC-115
88S-254
88Sf-186
88Smok/Angels-2
88T-115
88T/Big-97
89B-49
89Cadaco-42
89D-12DK
89D-331
89D/AS-25
89D/Best-195
89D/DKsuper-12DK
89F-487
89F/BBAS-33
89F/Heroes-32
89KMart/Lead-18
89OPC-109
89Panini/St-292
89RedFoley/St-93
89S-14
89S/HotStar-99
89Sf-195
89Smok/Angels-20
89T-455
89T/Big-7
89T/Coins-49
89T/Hills-24
89T/Mini-50
89T/St-182
89T/UK-62
89UD-481
90B-302
90CharWh/Best-8
90CharWh/ProC-2240
90D-234
90D/BestAL-73
90F-143
90KMart/CBatL-18
90Leaf/I-208
90OPC-334
90Panini/St-33
90PublInt/St-378
90S-293
90Sf-82
90Smok/Angel-14
90T-334
90T/Big-95
90T/St-174
90UD-509
91CharWh/ClBest-8
91CharWh/ProC-2885
91D-622
91F-323
91OPC-273
91Panini/FrSt-181
91Panini/St-138
91S-31
91T-273
91UD-678

Ray, Larry
82Tucson-10
83Tucson-20
84Cram/PCL-70
86ColumAst-22
86SLAS-11
87Vanco-20

Ray, Rick
89Utica/Pucko-31TR
91Utica/ClBest-25TR

Ray, Steve
83Greens-11

Raybon, Shannon
86Visalia-16TR
87Visalia-27TR
88OrlanTw/Best-25TR

Raydon, Curt
59T-305
60T-49

Rayford, Floyd
79SLCity-20
80RochR-18
81RochR-14
81T-399R
83RochR-13
83T-192
84F-334
84F/X-U95
84Nes/792-514
84T-514
84T/Tr-96T
85D-576
85F-186
85T-341
86D-332
86F-283
86Leaf-197
86T-623
87French-6
87T-426
88S-359
88T-296
89ScrWB/CMC-22
89ScrWB/ProC-727
90ElPasoATG/Team-39
90ScranWB/CMC-22CO
91Crown/Orio-375
91ScranWB/LineD-500CO
91ScranWB/ProC-2556CO

Raymer, Greg
83Miami-9
86Jaxvl/TCMA-12

Raymond, Arthur
(Bugs)
E254
M116
S74-93
T202
T204
T205
T206
T3-113

Raymond, Claude
63T-519
64T-504
65OPC-48
65T-48
66T-586
67T-364
68OPC-166
68T-166
69T-446
70Expos/Pins-12
70MLB/St-68
70OPC-268
70T-268
71MLB/St-138
71OPC-202
71OPC-536
71T-536
78TCMA-46
86Mother/Ast-4

Raziano, Michael S.
87Spring/Best-19
88Spring/Best-16

Razook, Mark
87Anchora-24
89Wmsprt/Star-17
90Wmsprt/Best-19
90Wmsprt/ProC-1066
90Wmsprt/Star-20

Rea, Clarke
91Niagara/ClBest-8
91Niagara/ProC-3638

Rea, Shayne
91AppFx/ClBest-11
91AppFx/ProC-1717
91Single/ClBest-250

Read, James
88Pac/8Men-11

Reade, Bill
80Utica-30

Reade, Curtis
81VeroB-16

Ready, Randy
81BurlB-17
82ElPaso-7
84Pol/Brew-2
84T/Tr-97
85F-592
85Pol/Brew-2
86D-481
86F-498
86Pol/Brew-2
86T-209
87Bohem-5
87F/Up-U100
87T/Tr-97T
88Coke/Padres-5
88D-264
88F-594
88OPC-151
88Panini/St-407
88S-512
88Smok/Padres-23
88T-426
88T/Big-102
89Coke/Padre-13
89D-365
89D/Best-215
89F-315
89OPC-82
89Panini/St-201
89Phill/TastyK-45
89S-426
89S/Tr-60
89T-551
89T/St-106
89T/Tr-102T
89UD-474
90D-396
90ElPasoATG/Team-13
90F-571
90Leaf/II-500
90OPC-356
90Panini/St-311
90Phill/TastyK-26
90PublInt/St-57
90S-376
90T-356
90T/Big-150
90T/St-120
90UD-404
91B-495
91D-148
91F-410A
91F-410B
91F/Ultra-271
91Leaf/I-82
91OPC-137
91Panini/FrSt-104
91Phill/Medford-33
91S-615
91T-137
91T/StClub/I-265
91UD-540
92D/I-179
92F-542
92S/I-59
92T-63
92UD-408

Reagan, Edward
T206
T213/brown

Reagan, Kyle
89Billings/ProC-2047

Reagans, Javan
88James/ProC-1917

Reams, Ronald
90MedHat/Best-22
91Myrtle/ClBest-25
91Myrtle/ProC-2959

Reardon, Jeff
79Tidew-5
81D-156
81F-335
81OPC-79
81T-456
81T/Tr-819
82D-547
82F-204
82F/St-37
82Hygrade
82OPC-123
82OPC/Post-23
82T-667
83D-194
83F-293
83OPC-290
83Stuart-5
83T-290
83T/St-254
84D-279
84F-283
84F/St-71
84Jacks/Smok-10
84Nes/792-595
84OPC-116
84Stuart-13
84T-595
84T/St-89
85D-331
85F-407
85Leaf-126
85OPC-375
85OPC/Post-12
85T-375
85T/St-85
86D-209
86D/AAS-33
86D/HL-14
86F-257
86F/LimEd-35
86F/Slug-26
86F/St-94
86Leaf-214
86OPC-35
86Provigo-13
86Sf-119
86T-35
86T-711AS
86T/3D-20
86T/Gloss60-55
86T/St-76
86T/Super-6
87Classic-94
87D-98
87D-PC11
87D/AAS-52
87D/WaxBox-PC11
87F-329
87F/Lim-34
87F/Mini-88
87F/Slug-33
87F/St-98
87F/Up-U101
87Kraft-40
87Leaf-143
87OPC-165
87RedFoley/St-65
87Sf-77M
87T-165
87T/Gloss60-15
87T/Mini-18
87T/St-81
87T/Tr-98T
88D-122
88D/Best-242
88F-20
88F/AwardWin-31
88F/BB/AS-33
88F/Mini-37
88F/Slug-32
88F/St-46
88F/TL-28
88Master/Disc-4
88Nestle-27
88OPC-99
88Panini/St-133
88RedFoley/St-73
88S-91
88Sf-53
88Smok/Minn-4
88T-425
88T/Big-10
88T/Mini-24
88T/RiteAid-28
88T/St-14
88T/St-280
89B-148
89Cadaco-43
89D-155
89D/AS-24
89D/Best-242
89F-125
89F/Superstar-34
89OPC-86
89Panini/St-382
89RedFoley/St-94
89S-305
89S/HotStar-24
89Sf-168
89T-775
89T/Gloss60-54
89T/LJN-52
89T/Mini-63
89T/St-284
89T/St-8
89T/St/Backs-33
89UD-596
89Woolwth-17
90B-265
90Classic-101
90Classic/III-55
90D-119
90D/BestAL-72
90F-385
90F/Up-U75
90Leaf/II-276
90OPC-235
90Panini/St-108
90Pep/RSox-16
90PublInt/St-293
90PublInt/St-337
90RedFoley/St-76
90S-522
90S/Tr-17T
90Sf-37
90T-235
90T/Big-285
90T/St-289
90T/St-6HL
90T/Tr-101T
90T/TVRSox-15
90T/WaxBox-K
90UD-417
90UD/Ext-729
90Woolwth/HL-17
91B-107
91D-369
91F-109
91F/Ultra-40
91Leaf/I-252
91Leaf/Stud-19
91OPC-605
91OPC/Premier-98
91Panini/FrSt-272
91Panini/St-218
91Pep/RSox-17
91RedFoley/St-76
91S-164
91T-605
91T/StClub/II-354
91T/WaxBox-M
91UD-418
91USPlayC/AS-5D
91WIZMets-325
91Woolwth/HL-17
92D/I-89
92F-46
92S/100SS-5
92S/I-58
92T-182
92T-3RB
92UD-501

Reaves, Scott
88Clearw/Star-20
88Spartan/Star-1
88Spartan/Star-17
89Clearw/Star-18

Reberger, Frank
69T-637R
70MLB/St-117
70OPC-103
70T-103
71MLB/St-262
71OPC-251
71T-251
72T-548
83Nashua-21
84Cram/PCL-242
85Cram/PCL-23
86Edmon-23CO
87Edmon-17

Reboulet, James
83Erie-4
84Savan-10
86FSLAS-40
86StPete-26

87ArkTr-23
88BuffB/CMC-17
88BuffB/Polar-7
88BuffB/ProC-1470
Reboulet, Jeff
87Orlan-15
88OrlanTw/Best-19
89Orlan/ProC-1345
90LSUGreat-4
90OrlanSR/Best-27
90OrlanSR/ProC-1093
90OrlanSR/Star-16
91Portl/LineD-415
91Portl/ProC-1572
Rech, Ed
82Lynch-8
Redd, Rick R.
88Harris/ProC-840
Redding, Dick
(Cannonball)
74Laugh/Black-25
86Negro/Frit-112
90Negro/Star-3
Redding, Mike
86Kenosha-21
87Visalia-16
88Visalia/Cal-160
88Visalia/ProC-93
89Orlan/Best-22
89Orlan/ProC-1333
90OrlanSR/Best-19
90OrlanSR/ProC-1081
90OrlanSR/Star-17
Reddish, Mike
83Nashvl-17
85CharlO-10
86RochR-18
Redfern, Pete
77T-249
78T-81
79T-113
80T-403
81D-548
81F-560
81T-714
82D-51
82F-559
82T-309
83D-256
83F-623
83T-559
88AlaskaAS70/Team-14
Redfield, Joe
87MidldA-13
87TexLgAS-12
88Edmon/CMC-20
88Edmon/ProC-555
89ScrWB/CMC-20
89ScrWB/ProC-731
90AAAGame/ProC-AAA25
90Denver/CMC-9
90Denver/ProC-634
91BuffB/LineD-41
91BuffB/ProC-549
92F-563
92S/I-412
Redick, Kevin
86Cram/PCL-6
87Clinton-13
Redington, Thomas
88Sumter/ProC-412
89BurlB/ProC-1610
89BurlB/Star-17
90Foil/Best-75
90Greenvl/Best-5
90Greenvl/ProC-1137
90Greenvl/Star-16
91Single/ClBest-327
91Wichita/LineD-615
91Wichita/ProC-2605
92T-473R
Redman, Tim
87Erie-29
88Hamil/ProC-1729
89Hamil/Star-22
90StPete/Star-19
91ArkTr/ProC-1290
Redmon, Glen
75Phoenix-13
76Wmsprt
Redmond, Andre
89Princet/Star-16
90Welland/Pucko-25
91Augusta/ProC-805
Redmond, Dan
87Watlo-28
89Canton/Best-9
Redmond, H. Wayne
71OPC-728R
71T-728R
Redus, Gary
81Water-15
82Indianap-17
83T/Tr-94T
84Borden-2
84D-184
84D/AAS-16
84F-481
84Nes/792-475
84OPC-231
84T-475
84T/St-52
85D-306
85F-549
85Indianap-34
85Leaf-47
85OPC-146
85T-146
85T/St-49
86CIGNA-12
86D-306
86F-189
86F/Up-U94
86Keller-3
86OPC-342
86Phill/TastyK-22
86T-342
86T/Tr-90T
87Coke/WS-13
87D-288
87D/OD-229
87F-181
87F/Up-U102
87OPC-42
87T-42
87T/St-119
87T/Tr-99T
88Coke/WS-24
88D-370
88F-408
88OPC-332
88Panini/St-64
88S-443
88T-657
88T/Mini-9
89B-425
89D-605
89F-218
89OPC-281
89S-177
89T-281
89T/Big-131
89UD-419
89VFJuice-2
90B-180
90D-597
90F-476
90Homer/Pirate-24
90Leaf/I-209
90OPC-507
90Panini/St-331
90Publint/St-162
90S-14
90T-507
90T/Big-52
90T/St-127
90UD-248
91B-516
91D-587
91F-47
91F/Ultra-285
91Leaf/I-254
91OPC-771
91S-226
91T-771
91T/StClub/II-486
91UD-38
92D/I-67
92F-564
92S/I-303
92T-453
92UD-519
Reece, Jeff
86Stockton-23
87Wichita-14
Reece, Thad
83Madis/LF-9
84Albany-5
85Cram/PCL-135
86Tacom-18
87Tacom-10
88Memphis/Best-24
90AlbanyDG/Best-35
90Omaha/CMC-20
90Omaha/ProC-74
Reed, Billy
89LittleSun-23CO
89Watlo/ProC-1788
89Watlo/Star-23
90Foil/Best-314
90Waterlo/Best-14
90Waterlo/ProC-2379
91HighD/ClBest-9
91HighD/ProC-2392
Reed, Bob E.
70OPC-207R
70T-207R
71MLB/St-404
71OPC-732
71T-732
Reed, Bobby
91Tulsa/LineD-591
91Tulsa/ProC-2771
Reed, Chris
91Princet/ClBest-6
91Princet/ProC-3512
Reed, Curt
82AppFx-12
83GlenF-9
Reed, Darren
86Albany/TCMA-23
87Albany-16
88Tidew/CANDL-17
88Tidew/CMC-16
88Tidew/ProC-1603
89Tidew/CMC-17
89Tidew/ProC-1957
90AlbanyDG/Best-20
90F/Up-U39
90T/TVMets-54
90Tidew/CMC-25
90Tidew/ProC-557
91F-159
91S-368RP
91T/90Debut-129
91WIZMets-326
Reed, Dennis
87Anchora-25
90Ashvl/ClBest-10
91Ashvl/ProC-568
Reed, Howard
60L-84
61Union
65T-544
66T-387
70T-548
71LaPizza-10
71OPC-398
71T-398
90Target-651
Reed, Jamie
84CharlO-14
85RochR-28
87RochR-22
88RochR/Gov-31
88RochR/ProC-214
Reed, Jeff
81Wisco-14
83Orlan-5
84Toledo-2
85D-30RR
85IntLgAS-38
85Toledo-14
86F/Up-U95
87D/OD-92
87F-550
87T-247
87T/Tr-100T
88D-88
88F-194
88OPC-176
88S-408
88T-176
89D-469
89F-167
89Kahn/Reds-34
89S-99
89T-626
89T/Big-158
89UD-276
90D-351
90F-429
90Kahn/Reds-23
90Leaf/II-505
90OPC-772
90Publint/St-37
90S-147
90T-772
90UD-165
91D-741
91F-78
91F/Ultra-101
91Kahn/Reds-34
91Leaf/I-102
91OPC-419
91Pep/Reds-17
91T-419
91T/StClub/II-534
92D/II-451
92F-418
92S/I-311
92T-91
92UD-299
Reed, Jerry M.
80OkCty
82OkCty-9
83Charl-4
84Maine-2
85Maine-8
85Polar/Ind-35
86Calgary-22
86F-592
86T-172
87Mother/Sea-22
87T-619
88D-517
88F-387
88Mother/Sea-22
88S-488
88T-332
89D-657
89F-557
89Mother/Sea-22
89S-427
89T-441
89UD-529
90D-614
90F-523
90F/Up-U76
90Leaf/II-368
90OPC-247
90Publint/St-440
90S-492
90T-247
90T/TVRSox-58
90UD-210
91F-110
91Pac/SenLg-141
Reed, Jody
86NewBrit-21
87Pawtu-6
87Pawtu/TCMA-17
88D-41RR
88D/Best-196
88D/RedSox/Bk-41RR
88D/Rook-44
88F-360
88Leaf-41RR
88S-625RP
88Sf-225R
88T-152
88T/Big-202
89B-30
89D-305
89D/Best-289
89F-96
89OPC-232
89Panini/St-268
89RedFoley/St-95
89S-486
89S/HotRook-85
89S/YS/I-2
89Sf-210
89T-321TL
89T-734
89T/Big-97
89T/Gloss60-60
89ToysRUs-23
89UD-370
90B-272
90Classic/III-54
90D-398
90D/BestAL-16
90F-284
90Leaf/I-150
90OPC-96
90Panini/St-25
90Pep/RSox-17
90Publint/St-462
90S-11
90T-96
90T/Big-167
90T/Mini-6
90T/TVRSox-25
90UD-321
91B-120
91D-123
91F-111
91F/Ultra-41
91Leaf/I-69
91OPC-247
91Panini/FrSt-265
91Panini/St-220
91Pep/RSox-18
91S-173
91T-247
91T/StClub/I-33
91UD-184
92D/I-47
92F-47
92S/I-85
92T-598
92UD-404
Reed, Ken
87DayBe-7
Reed, Marty
86Kinston-18
87MidldA-27
87TexLgAS-15
88Edmon/CMC-9
88Edmon/ProC-562
Reed, Richard
(Rick)
87Macon-10
88Salem/Star-17
88TM/Umpire-48
89BuffB/CMC-9
89BuffB/ProC-1675
89TM/Umpire-46
90BuffB/CMC-8
90BuffB/ProC-371
90D-527
90F-477
90Leaf/II-427
90S-544
90S/100Ris-8
90TM/Umpire-44
91AAAGame/ProC-AAA4
91BuffB/LineD-42
91BuffB/ProC-540
91S-584
92S/100RisSt-73
Reed, Ron
68OPC-76R
68T-76R
69OPC-177
69T-177
69T/St-9
70MLB/St-12
70OPC-546
70T-546
71MLB/St-21
71OPC-359
71T-359
72MB-281
72T-787
73OPC-72
73T-72
74OPC-346
74T-346
75OPC-81
75T-81
75T/M-81
76OPC-58
76T-58
76T/Tr-58T
77T-243
78T-472
79BK/P-7
79OPC-84
79T-177
80BK/P-21
80OPC-318
80T-609
81D-44
81F-11
81T-376
82D-399

82F-255
82T-581
83D-567
83F-169
83T-728
84D-529
84F-45
84F/X-U96
84Nes/792-43
84T-43
84T/Tr-98T
84TrueVal/WS-26
85D-282
85F-524
85T-221
90Richm25Ann/Team-20

Reed, Sean
88Wythe/ProC-1981
89CharWh/Best-16
89CharWh/ProC-1762

Reed, Steve
78BurlB
80Holyo-18

Reed, Steve
88Pocatel/ProC-2082
89Clinton/ProC-906
90Shrev/ProC-1443
90Shrev/Star-20
91Shrev/LineD-319
91Shrev/ProC-1822

Reed, Tom
84Visalia-13

Reed, Toncie
89AubAs/ProC-2167
90Osceola/Star-24

Reeder, Bill E.
49Eureka-194
52Mother-48

Reeder, Mike
88CharWh/Best-5

Reedy, Jerry
78Cr/PCL-101

Reelhorn, John
81OkCty/TCMA-15
82OkCty-19

Rees, Rob
90Kgsport/Best-14
90Kgsport/Star-20

Rees, Sean
89Alaska/Team-11

Reese, Andrew
29Exh/4-9
R315-A30
R315-B30

Reese, Calvin
91Classic/DP-16
91FrRow/DP-23
91Princet/ClBest-15
91Princet/ProC-3523
92T-714

Reese, Chip
83Ander-10
89Boise/ProC-1979

Reese, Harold H.
(Pee Wee)
41DP-23
41PB-54
41Wheat-18
43MP-20
47HomogBond-38
48Swell-18
49B-36
49Eureka-47
49MP-106
49Royal-2
50B-21
50Drake-19
51B-80
52B-8
52BR
52Coke
52RM-NL17
52Royal
52StarCal/L-79B
52T-333
53B/Col-33
53Exh/Can-21
53RM-NL10
53T-76
54B-58
54NYJour
54RM-NL15
55Armour-15
55B-37
55Gol/Dodg-24
55RM-NL17
56T-260
56YellBase/Pin-26
57T-30
58BB
58Hires-23
58T-375
60NuCard-37
61NuCard-437
79TCMA-84
80Pac/Leg-52
85West/2-34
86Sf/Dec-21
87Leaf/SpecOlym-H8
88Pac/Leg-21
89Rini/Dodg-5
89Smok/Dodg-23
90Target-652
91T/Arc53-76
D305
Exh47
PM10/Sm-151
PM10/Sm-152
PM10/Sm-153
PM10/Sm-154
R302-106
R423-86

Reese, Jason
90MedHat/Best-2
91Pocatel/ProC-3780

Reese, Jimmie
28Exh/PCL-21
31Exh/4-26
73OPC-421CO
73T-421CO
74OPC-276CO
74T-276CO
76SSPC-630CO
91B-186CO
91Leaf/Stud-21CO

Reese, Kyle
86Erie-24
87FtMyr-27
88Virgini/Star-21
89Memphis/Best-16
89Memphis/ProC-1206
89Memphis/Star-20
90Memphis/Best-12
90Memphis/ProC-1011
90Memphis/Star-23

Reese, Rich
65T-597R
67T-486R
68OPC-111
68T-111
69MB-228
69OPC-56
69T-56
70MLB/St-238
70OPC-404
70T-404
71MLB/St-472
71OPC-349
71T-349
71T/Coins-72
72MB-282
72T-611
89Pac/Leg-112

Reeser, Jeffery
90Peoria/Team-3GM

Reeve, Bob
85Anchora-41

Reeves, Dave
91Billings/ProC-3751

Reeves, Jim
78StPete

Reeves, Matt
82VeroB-10

Reeves, Mel
47Smith-24

Reeves, Mickey
91Hunting/ClBest-18
91Hunting/ProC-3348

Reeves, Robert E.
29Exh/4-17
31Exh/4-17
31Exh/4-17

Regalado, Rudy
55B-142
60HenryH-14

Regalado, Uvaldo
82DayBe-6
83DayBe-9

Regan, Michael J.
E254

Regan, Phil
61T-439
62J-24
62P-24
62P/Can-24
62T-366
63T-494
64Det/Lids-13
64T-535
65OPC-191
65T-191
66T-347
67Bz-29
67OPC-130
67T-130
68OPC-88
68T-88
69MB-229
69MLB/St-124
69T-535
69T/St-18
70MLB/St-21
70OPC-334
70T-334
71MLB/St-43
71OPC-634
71T-634
72MB-283
72OPC-485
72T-485
87Smok/Dodg-27
88Smok/Dodg-9
89Smok/Dodg-72
90Target-653

Regan, William W.
29Exh/4-18
R316

Regira, Gary
89James/ProC-2154
90Rockford/ProC-2688
91WPalmB/ClBest-10
91WPalmB/ProC-1226

Rehbaum, Chris
80Batavia-27
81Batavia-23
82Watlo/B-22
82Watlo/C-17

Rehm, Vic
60L-61

Rehse
N172

Rehwinkel, Pat
89Helena/SP-4

Reiber, Frank
V355-111

Reich, Andy
89Clmbia/Best-19
89Clmbia/GS-22
89SALAS/GS-16
91StLucie/ClBest-18
91StLucie/ProC-708

Reich, Herman
49Eureka-68

Reichard, Clyde
(Bud)
78Wisco
85Tulsa-37
89Penin/Star-21CO
89Penin/Star-26CO

Reichardt, Rick
65OPC-194R
65T-194R
66T-321
67Bz-1
67OPC-40
67T-40
68T-570
69JB
69MB-230
69MLB/St-25
69MLBPA/Pin-23
69OPC-205
69T-205
69T/decal
69T/S-8
69T/St-147
69Trans-18
70K-18
70MLB/St-177
70T-720
70Trans-12
71OPC-643
71T-643
71T/Coins-102
72MB-284

Reichel, Tom
87Penin-19

Reichenbach, Eric
91Pittsfld/ClBest-24
91Pittsfld/ProC-3420

Reichle, Darrin
87Spokane-2
88Charl/ProC-1208
88SALAS/GS-11
89River/Best-14
89River/Cal-15
89River/ProC-1393
90Foil/Best-151
90Riversi/Best-24
90Riversi/Cal-23
90Riversi/ProC-2607
91Wichita/LineD-616
91Wichita/ProC-2596

Reichler, Joe
90LitSun-7

Reid, Derek
90A&AASingle/ProC-172
90Everett/Best-26
90Everett/ProC-3142
91SanJose/ClBest-28
91SanJose/ProC-25
91SanJose/ProC-26M
91Single/ClBest-273

Reid, Gregory
91Madison/ClBest-19
91Madison/ProC-2143

Reid, Jessie
84Shrev/FB-16
86Phoenix-22
87Phoenix-16
88F-643R
89Tacoma/CMC-17
89Tacoma/ProC-1549

Reid, John
91Niagara/ClBest-20

Reid, Scott D.
70OPC-56R
70T-56R
71OPC-439R
71T-439R

Reidy, Bill
90Target-654

Reilley, John
88Sumter/ProC-394
89Wausau/GS-5
90Salinas/Cal-129
90Salinas/ProC-2720

Reilly, Charles T.
N172

Reilly, Ed
83DayBe-10

Reilly, John G.
N172

Reilly, Mike
88TM/Umpire-33
89TM/Umpire-31
90TM/Umpire-30

Reilly, Neil
85BurlR-6

Reilly, Thomas H.
E254
T204

Reimer, Kevin
86Salem-23
87PortChar-26
88Tulsa-25
89F-641R
89OkCty/CMC-19
89OkCty/ProC-1527
89S/HotRook-59
90F-310
90OkCty/CMC-19
90OkCty/ProC-446
90TulsaDG/Best-30
91D-80
91F-298
91F/UltraUp-U57
91Mother/Rang-15
91OPC-304
91S-836
91T-304
91UD-494
92D/I-251
92F-315
92S/I-152
92T-737
92UD-201

Reimink, Robert
90Lakeland/Star-21
91London/LineD-395
91London/ProC-1887

Reimsnyder, Brian
90Erie/Star-19

Rein, Fred
77Charl

Reinbach, Mike
75IntAS/TCMA-5
91Crown/Orio-376

Reinebold, Jim
89SoBend/GS-3
90SoBend/Best-29
91SoBend/ProC-2876CO

Reincke, Corey
91Fayette/ClBest-7
91Fayette/ProC-1167
91Niagara/ClBest-28
91Niagara/ProC-3631

Reinhart, Art
91Conlon/Sport-242

Reinisch, Paul
90Bristol/ProC-3170
90Bristol/Star-19

Reinke, Jeff
75Clinton

Reis, Dave
88Pulaski/ProC-1757
89BurlB/ProC-1619
89BurlB/Star-18
90BurlB/Best-7
90BurlB/ProC-2347
90BurlB/Star-20
90Foil/Best-195

Reis, Paul
88Pulaski/ProC-1759
89Sumter/ProC-1090
90BurlB/Best-17
90BurlB/ProC-2359
90BurlB/Star-21

Reis, Robert
(Bobby)
90Target-655
R314

Reis, Tom
47Centen-22

Reiser, James
86Cram/PCL-52
87Madis-10
88Madis-18

Reiser, Pete
39Exh
41DP-18
43MP-21
48B-7
48L-146
48Swell-2
49B-185
49Eureka-17
50B-193
51B-238
52T-189
60T-463C
73OPC-81CO
73T-81CO
80Pac/Leg-88
89Smok/Dodg-47
90Target-656
PM10/Sm-155

Reish, Steve
83Kinston/Team-17
84Memphis-17

Reisling, Frank
(Doc)
90Target-1052
M116

Reiter, Gary
81Durham-24
82Durham-20
83Richm-8
84Richm-15
85Richm-7

Reitz, Ken
73OPC-603R
73T-603R
74OPC-372

74T-372
75OPC-27
75T-27
75T/M-27
76OPC-158
76SSPC-280
76T-158
76T/Tr-158T
77BurgChef-13
77K-38
77T-297
78Ho-106
78T-692
79Ho-23
79OPC-307
79T-587
80OPC-103
80T-182
81Coke
81D-307
81F-530
81OPC-316
81T-441
81T/HT
81T/So-101
81T/St-158
81T/Tr-820
82D-277
82F-602
82F/St-91
82OPC-245
82T-245
82T/St-26
85Tulsa-0
86SanJose-17
87SanJose-3
89Pac/SenLg-213
89T/SenLg-35
89TM/SenLg-89
90EliteSenLg-61
91Pac/SenLg-33
91Swell/Great-119

Reitzel, Mike
90Miami/II/Star-22

Relaford, Winnie
88Sumter/ProC-400
89Sumter/ProC-1103

Relmink, Bob
89NiagFls/Pucko-20

Rembielak, Rick
82Miami-16

Remlinger, Mike
87Everett-31
88Shrev/ProC-1296
89Shrev/ProC-1832
90B-227
90Shrev/ProC-1444
90Shrev/Star-21
91D/Rook-37
91PG&E-27
91Phoenix/LineD-390
91Phoenix/ProC-64
91UD/FinalEd-36F
92D/I-336
92F-646
92S/100RisSt-49
92S/I-410
92T/91Debut-143
92UD-585

Remmerswaal, Win
81D-98
81Pawtu-7
81T-38

Remo, Jeff
82QuadC-16

Remy, Jerry
76OPC-229
76SSPC-198
76T-229
77BurgChef-121
77K-44
77T-342
78Ho-66
78PapaG/Disc-2
79OPC-325
79T-618
80OPC-85
80T-155
81D-215
81F-238
81OPC-131
81T-549
82Coke/Bos
82D-156
82F-304
82F/St-171
82OPC-25
82Sqt-2
82T-25
82T/St-132
82T/St-149
83D-74
83F-193
83OPC-295
83T-295
83T/St-33
84D-172
84F-407
84Nes/792-445
84OPC-58
84T-445
84T/St-215
85F-167
85OPC-173
85T-761
85T/St-218

Rende, Sal
79Tacom-11
80Tacom-14
81Chatt-17
82Chatt-11
83BuffB-13
87Chatt/Best-1MG
88Chatt/Team-25
88Memphis/Best-26
89AAA/ProC-37
89Omaha/CMC-23
89Omaha/ProC-1740
90Fayette/ProC-2416
90Omaha/CMC-25MG
90Omaha/ProC-80MG
90SALAS/Star-20
91AAAGame/ProC-AAA27MG
91Lakeland/ClBest-22
91Lakeland/ProC-275
91Omaha/LineD-349MG
91Omaha/ProC-1049MG

Rendina, Mike
88Bristol/ProC-1877
89Bristol/Star-21
89Fayette/ProC-1584

Renfroe, Cohen
(Laddy)
86WinSalem-21
87Pittsfld-8
88Iowa/CMC-4
88Iowa/ProC-551
89CharlK-1
90Iowa/CMC-8
90Iowa/ProC-318
90T/TVCub-58
91AAAGame/ProC-AAA19
91Iowa/LineD-214
91Iowa/ProC-1059
92S/II-875
92T/91Debut-144

Renfroe, Marshall
60L-99

Renick, Rick
68T-301R
69MB-231
70OPC-93
70T-93
71MLB/St-473
71OPC-694
71T-694
72MB-285
72OPC-459
72T-459
83Memphis-23
86Provigo-28CO

Reniff, Hal
62T-139
62T-159
63T-546
64T-36
65T-413
66OPC-68
66T-68
67T-201
78TCMA-106
91WIZMets-327
WG10-19
WG9-20

Renko, Steve
69Expos/Pins-6
70OPC-87
70T-87
71MLB/St-139
71OPC-209
71T-209
72OPC-307
72OPC-308IA
72T-307
72T-308A
73OPC-623
73T-623
74OPC-49
74T-49
74T/St-58
74Weston-18
75Ho-69
75OPC-34
75T-34
75T/M-34
76OPC-264
76T-264
77T-586
78T-493
79T-352
80T-184
81D-337
81F-231
81T-63
81T/Tr-821
82D-38
82F-472
82T-702
83D-393
83F-99
83OPC-236
83T-236
83T/Tr-95
84F-355
84Nes/792-444
84T-444
91WPalmB/ClBest-11
91WPalmB/ProC-1227

Renna, Bill
54T-112
55Rodeo
55T-121
55T/DH-99
56T-82
58T-473
59T-72

Renneau, Charlie
77Visalia

Rennert, Dutch
88TM/Umpire-18
89TM/Umpire-18
90TM/Umpire-16

Rennicke, Dean
83Albuq-5
84Cram/PCL-160
85Cram/PCL-151

Renninger, Bob
74Cedar

Renteria, Edison
(Ed)
87AubAs-23
88Ashvl/ProC-1058
89Osceola/Star-19
90ColMud/Best-23
90ColMud/ProC-1355
90ColMud/Star-20
91Osceola/ClBest-21
91Osceola/ProC-695

Renteria, Rich
82AlexD-27
83LynnP-17
85Tigres-22
86Hawaii-20
87Mother/Sea-23
88Mother/Sea-23
89B-212
89Mother/Sea-20
89S-142
89T/Big-109
89UD-547

Rentschuler, Tom
83Peoria/LF-16
83Redwd-22

Renz, Kevin
86Penin-22
87Penin-2
88BirmB/Best-28

Replogle, Andy
77ArkTr
79T-427
79Vanco-8
81Vanco-16

Repoz, Craig
85LitFalls-21
86Columbia-21
87Lynch-1
89Jacks/GS-4
90Wichita/Rock-17

Repoz, Jeff
90Princet/DIMD-16

Repoz, Roger
66OPC-138
66T-138
67T-416
68T-587
69MB-232
69MLB/St-26
69OPC-103
69T-103
69T/St-148
70MLB/St-178
70OPC-397
70T-397
71MLB/St-355
71OPC-508
71T-508
72MB-286
72T-541

Repulski, Rip
53T-172
54B-46
54Hunter
54RM-NL17
54T-115
55B-205
55Hunter
55T-55
55T/DH-125
56T-201
57T-245
58Hires-15
58T-14
59T-195
60BB-5
60L-86
60T-265
61T-128
90Target-657
91T/Arc53-172

Rescigno, Xavier
47Signal
49B/PCL-5

Resendez, Oscar
91BurlInd/ProC-3302

Resetar, Gary
89Kenosha/ProC-1075
89Kenosha/Star-21
90Foil/Best-174
90OrlanSR/Best-12
90OrlanSR/ProC-1087
90OrlanSR/Star-18
91Canton/LineD-92
91Canton/ProC-982

Resinger, Grover
63Pep/Tul

Resnikoff, Bob
89Saraso/Star-19
90Saraso/Star-21
91Osceola/ProC-683

Restilli, Dino
48Sommer-12
49Sommer-17
50B-123

Restin, Eric
76BurlB
77BurlB

Retes, Lorenzo
85Tigres-10

Rettenmund, Merv
69OPC-66R
69T-66R
70T-629
71MLB/St-308
71OPC-393
71T-393
72K-11
72MB-287
72OPC-235
72OPC-86LL
72T-235
72T-86LL
73JP
73OPC-56
73T-56
74OPC-585
74T-585
74T/Tr-585T
75OPC-369
75T-369
75T/M-369
76OPC-283
76SSPC-46
76T-283
77Padre/SchCd-25
77T-659
78T-566
79T-48
80T-402
90Mother/A's-27M
91Crown/Orio-377

Retzer, Ed
83Madis/LF-10
83Tacom-31

Retzer, Ken
62T-594R
63J-94
63P-94
63T-471
64T-277
65OPC-278
65T-278

Reulbach, Ed
10Domino-101
11Helmar-100
12Sweet/Pin-88
14CJ-80
15CJ-80
69Bz-12
72F/FFeat-29
90HOF/St-12
90Target-658
92Conlon/Sport-549
E254
E286
E91
E95
M116
S74-67
T202
T204
T205
T206
T207
T213/blue
T215/blue
T215/brown
T222
WG3-40

Reuschel, Paul
77T-383
77T-634M
78T-663
79T-511

Reuschel, Rick
73OPC-482
73T-482
74OPC-136
74T-136
74T/St-18
75Ho-51
75OPC-153
75T-153
75T/M-153
76Ho-17
76Ho/Twink-17
76OPC-359
76SSPC-301
76T-359
77BurgChef-193
77Ho-103
77OPC-214
77T-530
77T-634M
78Ho-131
78K-45
78OPC-56
78T-50
79Ho-67
79K-47
79OPC-123
79T-240
80OPC-99
80T-175
81Coke
81D-561

81F-293
81F/St-93
81OPC-205
81T-645
81T/HT
81T/St-157
81T/Tr-822
82D-157
82F-50
82OPC-204
82T-405
84SevenUp-47
85Cram/PCL-230
85F-63
85F/Up-U88
85OPC-306
85T-306
85T/Tr-93T
86D-532
86F-618
86F/Slug-27
86F/St-95
86Leaf-207
86T-779
86T/Mini-57
86T/St-126
87D-188
87F-619
87OPC-154
87RedFoley/St-129
87T-521
87T/St-128
88D-613
88D/AS-52
88D/Best-218
88F-94
88F/LL-32
88F/St-130
88Leaf-219
88Mother/Giants-15
88OPC-278
88S-519
88Sf-136
88T-660
88T/Big-188
88T/Mini-76
88T/Revco-13
88T/RiteAid-30
89B-466
89D-11DK
89D-335
89D/Best-162
89D/DKsuper-11DK
89F-340
89Mother/Giants-15
89OPC-65
89Panini/St-210
89S-5
89S/HotStar-22
89Sf-72
89T-65
89T/LJN-3
89T/Mini-42
89T/St-79
89T/UK-63
89UD-194
90B-223
90D-112
90D-663AS
90F-68
90KayBee-25
90MLBPA/Pins-23
90Mother/Giant-8
90OPC-190
90Panini/St-206M
90Panini/St-370
90PublInt/St-79
90RedFoley/St-77
90S-465
90S/100St-7
90Sf-161
90T-190
90T/Big-328
90T/Gloss22-10
90T/Gloss60-18
90T/Mini-87
90T/St-154AS
90T/St-89
90T/WaxBox-L
90UD-696
90Woolwth/HL-18
91D-518
91F-270
91Mother/Giant-14
91OPC-422
91S-544
91T-422
91UD-249

Reuss, Jerry
70OPC-96R
70T-96R
71OPC-158
71T-158
72T-775
73OPC-446
73T-446
74OPC-116
74T-116
74T/St-38
75OPC-124
75T-124
75T/M-124
76Crane-47
76Ho-29
76Ho/Twink-29
76K-43
76MSA/Disc
76OPC-60
76SSPC-562
76T-60
77BurgChef-181
77Ho-119
77OPC-97
77Pep-65
77T-645
78T-255
79T-536
80Pol/Dodg-41
80T-318
81D-417
81F-118
81OPC-153
81Pol/Dodg-41
81T-440
81T/HT
81T/So-103
81T/St-181
82D-284
82F-18
82F/St-7
82OPC-278
82Pol/Dodg-41
82T-710
82T/St-259M
82T/St-56
83D-158
83F-216
83OPC-90
83Pol/Dodg-41
83T-90
83T/St-247
84D-418
84F-110
84Nes/792-170
84OPC-170
84Pol/Dodg-41
84T-170
84T/St-81
85Coke/Dodg-26
85D-226
85F-380
85OPC-66
85T-680
86Coke/Dodg-25
86D-104
86F-141
86OPC-236
86Pol/Dodg-41
86Sf-53M
86T-577
86T/St-66
87F-451
87OPC-373
87Pol/Dodg-21
87Smok/Dodg-28
87T-682
88Coke/WS-23
88S-270
88S/Tr-61T
88Smok/Dodg-6M
88T-216
89B-57
89Coke/WS-22
89D-413
89D/Best-305
89F-510
89S-489
89T-357
89UD-151
90D-528
90F-335
90KayBee-26
90OPC-424
90PublInt/St-400
90T-424
90Target-659
90UD-96

Reuteman, R.C.
(AGM)
88Tidew/CANDL-26

Reutter, Derrick
83Kinston/Team-18

Revak, Ray
86Greens-19

Revelle, R.H.
(Dutch)
T206

Revenig, Todd
90SoOreg/Best-8
90SoOreg/ProC-3445
91Madison/ProC-2130

Revering, Dave
76Indianap-7
77Indianap-4
78T-706R
79Ho-139
79OPC-113
79T-224
80OPC-227
80T-438
80T/S-58
81D-117
81F-576
81F/St-4
81OPC-57
81T-568
81T/So-22
81T/St-117
81T/Tr-823
82D-234
82F-51
82OPC-109
82T-109
82T/Tr-97T
83F-484
83OPC-291
83T-677
85Indianap-29

Rex, Mike
76Cedar
79Phoenix
80Phoenix-18
81Phoenix-11
82Phoenix

Rey, Everett
81Chatt-9
82Chatt-3
83BuffB-12

Reyan, Julio
89Belling/Legoe-2
91Belling/ProC-3661

Reyes, Carlos
86Ashvl-22

Reyes, Gilberto
85Cram/PCL-170
86Albuq-20
86D-581
87Albuq/Pol-17
87Pol/Dodg-7
88Albuq/CMC-21
88Albuq/ProC-257
89Indianap/CMC-11
89Indianap/ProC-1240
90Target-1053
91B-447
91F/UltraUp-U92
91F/Up-U99
91Leaf/II-451
92D/I-381
92F-489
92S/I-229
92T-286
92UD-230

Reyes, Giovanny
86Cram/PCL-77
86QuadC-26
87QuadC-5
88PalmSp/Cal-109

Reyes, Jesus
73Cedar
74Cedar

Reyes, Jose
77Clinton
80OrlTw-7
82OrlTw/A-22

Reyes, Joselito
84Memphis-21
85Kingst-18
86Omaha-18

Reyes, Juan
86Beloit-19
89BendB/Legoe-6
89Bristol/Star-22
91Clinton/ClBest-9
91Clinton/ProC-833

Reyes, Pablo
85Kingst-9
86Ventura-22

Reyes, Rafael
91Rockford/ClBest-11
91Rockford/ProC-2046

Reyes, Sergio
91Hunting/ClBest-19
91Hunting/ProC-3349

Reyes, Steve
88Billings/ProC-1810

Reyes, Wascar
78Charl

Reyna, Dion
88Madis-19

Reyna, Luis
86Ventura-23
87Knoxvl-9
88Syrac/CMC-12
88Syrac/ProC-810

Reynolds, Allie
47TipTop
48B-14
49B-114
50B-138
50Drake-28
51B-109
51BR-C3
51T/RB-6
52BR
52Dix
52StarCal/L-70A
52T-67
52TipTop
53B/Col-68
53Dix
53NB
53T-141
54B-113
54NYJour
55Armour-16
55B-201
61F-69
79TCMA-185
88Pac/Leg-41
89Swell-101
91Crown/Orio-378
91T/Arc53-141
PM10/L-33
R346-21
R423-89

Reynolds, Archie
71MLB/St-356
71OPC-664R
71T-664R
72T-672

Reynolds, Carl
29Exh/4-20
30CEA/Pin-19
31Exh/4-20
32Orbit/num-2
32Orbit/un-50
33CJ/Pin-18
33G-120
35BU-49
35BU-95
35G-1G
35G-3E
35G-5E
35G-6E
91Conlon/Sport-80
R300
R305
R310
R315-C4
V354-12

Reynolds, Charles
N172

Reynolds, Craig
76OPC-596R
76SSPC-582
76T-596R
77T-474R
78T-199
79K-51
79OPC-251
79T-482
80OPC-71
80T-129
81D-378
81F-74
81OPC-12
81T-617
81T/St-46
82D-344
82F-225
82OPC-57
82T-57
83D-317
83F-460
83T-328
84D-405
84F-237
84Mother/Ast-26
84Nes/792-776
84T-776
85D-328
85F-357
85Mother/Ast-14
85OPC-156
85T-156
85T/St-65
86D-232
86F-309
86Leaf-107
86Mother/Ast-18
86OPC-298
86Pol/Ast-13
86T-298
87D-384
87D/OD-19
87F-66
87Mother/Ast-19
87OPC-298
87Pol/Ast-10
87T-779
88D-209
88F-454
88Leaf-205
88Mother/Ast-19
88OPC-18
88Panini/St-297
88Pol/Ast-19
88S-207
88T-557
88T/Big-219
89B-328
89D-477
89F-366
89Lennox/Ast-15
89Mother/Ast-18
89S-468
89T-428
89T/Big-312
89UD-284
90OPC-637
90PublInt/St-100
90T-637

Reynolds, Dave
86AppFx-19
87Penin-11
88Tampa/Star-21
89Saraso/Star-20
90BirmB/Best-21
90BirmB/ProC-1109

Reynolds, Don
78Padre/FamFun-24
79Hawaii-13
79T-292
80Hawaii-23
88SanBern/Best-28
88SanBern/Cal-55
91Jacks/LineD-575CO
91Jacks/ProC-941CO

Reynolds, Doug
89Erie/Star-18
90Freder/Team-9
91Freder/ClBest-14
91Freder/ProC-2368

Reynolds, Harold
81Wausau-18
82LynnS-17
83SLCity-22

84Cram/PCL-185
85Mother/Mar-23
86Calgary-23
86D-484
86T-769
87D-489
87D/OD-117
87F-596
87Mother/Sea-10
87T-91
87T/St-216
88D-563
88D/AS-13
88D/Best-304
88F-388
88F/AwardWin-32
88F/Mini-53
88F/RecSet-31
88F/St-62
88Leaf-227
88Mother/Sea-10
88OPC-7
88Panini/St-188
88S-277
88Sf-127
88T-485
88T/Big-142
88T/Mini-35
88T/Revco-19
88T/St-221
88T/UK-60
89B-210
89Classic-147
89D-21DK
89D-93
89D/AS-27
89D/Best-51
89D/DKsuper-21DK
89F-558
89F/BBAS-34
89F/Heroes-33
89F/LL-31
89KMart/DT-13
89Mother/Sea-10
89OPC-208
89Panini/St-436
89RedFoley/St-96
89S-310
89S/HotStar-82
89Sf-165
89T-580
89T/Big-2
89T/LJN-80
89T/Mini-74
89T/St-226
89T/St/Backs-5
89UD-249
90B-478
90Classic-128
90D-227
90D/BestAL-138
90F-524
90F/AwardWin-27
90HotPlay/St-33
90Leaf/I-140
90MLBPA/Pins-118
90Mother/Mar-6
90OPC-161
90Panini/St-144
90PublInt/St-294
90PublInt/St-441
90S-167
90S/100St-43
90Sf-119
90T-161
90T/Big-321
90T/DH-51
90T/HeadsUp-17
90T/Mini-34
90T/St-221
90UD-179
91B-252
91Classic/200-47
91CounHrth-3
91D-175
91F-460
91F/Ultra-343
91Leaf/II-297
91Leaf/Stud-119
91OPC-260
91Panini/FrSt-229
91Panini/St-191
91Panini/Top15-111
91Panini/Top15-55
91S-48
91Seven/3DCoin-13NW
91T-260
91T/StClub/I-217
91UD-148
91UD-32TC
92D/I-239
92F-291
92S/I-250
92T-670
92UD-314

Reynolds, Jeff
83Syrac-19
86Jaxvl/TCMA-21
87Indianap-16
88Toledo/CMC-15
88Toledo/ProC-585
89Nashvl/Team-19

Reynolds, Ken
71OPC-664R
71T-664R
72OPC-252
72T-252
73OPC-638
73T-638
76SSPC-292
78Syrac
79Syrac-19
89Geneva/ProC-1885CO

Reynolds, Larry
80Tulsa-9
81Tulsa-7
82ArkTr-21
83ArkTr-22
84ArkTr-9

Reynolds, Mark
85Osceola/Team-14

Reynolds, Mike
79Richm-2
82Richm-18
84Richm-1
85Durham-30
86Durham-22

Reynolds, Neil
87SLCity/Taco-5

Reynolds, Robert J.
(R.J.)
81VeroB-17
84Cram/PCL-148
84F/X-U97
85Coke/Dodg-27
85D-128
85F-381
85T-369
86D-552
86F-619
86F/Mini-120
86Leaf-212
86OPC-306
86T-417
87D-65
87F-620
87OPC-109
87RedFoley/St-77
87T-109
87T/St-134
88D-65
88D/Best-201
88F-339
88OPC-27
88Panini/St-379
88S-34
88T-27
89D-134
89D/Best-257
89F-219
89S-91
89T-658
89UD-315
89VFJuice-23
90D-447
90F-478
90Homer/Pirate-25
90Leaf/II-381
90OPC-592
90PublInt/St-163
90S-469
90T-592
90T/St-126
90Target-660
90UD-540
91D-101
91F-48
91OPC-198
91S-273
91T-198
91UD-150

Reynolds, Robert
71OPC-664R
71T-664R
72OPC-162R
72T-162R
73JP
73OPC-612R
73T-612R
74OPC-259
74T-259
75OPC-142
75T-142
75T/M-142
82Iowa-28GM

Reynolds, Ronn
82Jacks-11
84Tidew-25
86F-92
86Phill/TastyK-29
86Portl-19
86T-649
87Phill/TastyK-29
87T-471
87Tucson-20
88Denver/CMC-16
88Denver/ProC-1262
90LasVegas/CMC-12
90LasVegas/ProC-127
91Pac/SenLg-109
91WIZMets-328

Reynolds, Shane
89AubAs/ProC-2161
90ColMud/Best-12
90ColMud/ProC-1345
91Jacks/LineD-572
91Jacks/ProC-926
91Single/ClBest-67

Reynolds, Thomas D.
(Tommie)
64T-528R
65T-333
67T-487
69T-467
70OPC-259
70T-259
71OPC-676
71T-676
77Spoka
86Modesto-21MG
87Modesto-23MG
88Huntsvl/BK-15
89Mother/A's-27M
90Mother/A's-27M
91Mother/A's-28CO
91WIZMets-329

Reynolds, Tim
83Cedar-9
83Cedar/LF-1

Reynolds, William
86Cram/PCL-56

Reynoso, Armando
91AAAGame/ProC-AAA38
91Richm/LineD-438
91Richm/ProC-2566
92F-367
92S/II-877
92T-631
92T/91Debut-145
92UD-674

Reynoso, Henry
90Beloit/Best-19
90Beloit/Star-17

Rhea, Allen
90StCath/ProC-3469

Rhem, Charles
(Flint)
33DH-35
33G-136
35G-8L
35G-9L
87Conlon/2-52
88Conlon/4-23
91Conlon/Sport-325
V354-5

Rhiel, William
90Target-661
R314
R314/Can
V355-81

Rhoades, James
88Augusta/ProC-387

Rhoads, Robert
T206
T213/brown
T3-114

Rhodas, Kevin
83Miami-10

Rhoden, Rick
74Albuq/Team-15
75OPC-618R
75T-618R
75T/M-618R
76OPC-439
76SSPC-72
76T-439
77BurgChef-148
77OPC-57
77T-245
78OPC-159
78T-605
79OPC-66
79T-145
80Port-27
80T-92
81F-377
81OPC-312
81T-312
82D-423
82F-493
82T-513
82T/St-82
83D-250
83F-318
83OPC-181
83T-781
84D-552
84F-261
84Nes/792-485
84Nes/792-696TL
84OPC-46
84T-485
84T-696TL
85D-552
85F-474
85F/St-97
85Leaf-63
85OPC-53
85T-695
85T/St-127
86D-166
86D/HL-20
86F-620
86OPC-232
86T-232
36T-756M
86T/St-130
87D-10DK
87D-435
87D/AAS-24
87D/DKsuper-10
87F-621
87F/Up-U103
87Leaf-10DK
87OPC-365
87RedFoley/St-103
87Sf-129
87Smok/Dodg-29
87T-365
87T/Mini-31
87T/St-130
87T/Tr-101T
88D-128
88D/Best-161
88D/Y/Bk-128
88F-219
88F/SS-30
88F/St-51
88Leaf-98
88OPC-185
88Panini/St-149
88RedFoley/St-74
88S-74
88Sf-104
88Sf/Gamewin-16
88T-185
88T/Big-108
88T/St-298
89B-323
89D-429
89D/Tr-40
89F-266
89F/Up-89
89Lennox/Ast-3
89Mother/Ast-24
89OPC-18
89Panini/St-399
89S-317
89Smok/Dodg-87
89T-18
89T/Big-237
89T/DHTest-23
89UD-56
90F-235
90OPC-588
90PublInt/St-101
90T-588
90Target-662
90UD-504

Rhodes, Arthur Lee
(Art)
89Erie/Star-19
90Freder/Team-29
91B-95
91Hagers/LineD-244
91Hagers/ProC-2457
91Leaf/GRook-BC6
91Single/ClBest-335
91UD/FinalEd-13F
92Classic/I-75
92D/II-727
92F-24
92S/II-736
92T-771
92T/91Debut-146
92UD-17SR

Rhodes, Charles
T206

Rhodes, Dusty
89Helena/SP-27

Rhodes, James L.
(Dusty)
28Exh/PCL-22
54NYJour
54T-170
55Gol/Giants-24
55RM-NL22
55SM
55T-1
55T/DH-27
56T-50
56T/Hocus-A4
56T/Hocus-B6
57T-61
61Union
79TCMA-190
91T/Arc53-299

Rhodes, Jeff
83Cedar-24
83Cedar/LF-15

Rhodes, Karl
87Ashvl-1
88FSLAS/Star-18
88Osceola/Star-22
89ColMud/Best-22
89ColMud/ProC-142
89ColMud/Star-19
90B-79
90Tucson/CMC-18
90Tucson/ProC-218
91B-544
91Classic/200-72
91D-698
91F-514
91Leaf/I-195
91Mother/Ast-14
91OPC-516
91S-365RP
91S/Rook40-32
91T-516
91T/90Debut-130
91T/StClub/I-52
91UD-466
91UD/Ext-702M

Rhodes, Mike
83ArkTr-1
86ArkTr-17
89FtLaud/Star-20
89Star/Wax-79
90Greens/Best-24
90Greens/ProC-2676
90Greens/Star-17

Rhodes, Ricky
89Oneonta/ProC-2123
90A&AASingle/ProC-86
90Foil/Best-249
90Greens/Best-11

90Greens/ProC-2663
90Greens/Star-18
91PrWill/ClBest-11
91PrWill/ProC-1427
91Single/ClBest-235

Rhodriguez, Rory
91Princet/ClBest-22
91Princet/ProC-3513

Rhomberg, Kevin
78Watlo
80Tacom-20
81Chatt-23
82Charl-17
83Charl-17
85Cram/PCL-193
88Chatt/Team-26

Rhown, Bobby
52Park-4

Rhyne, Hal
28Exh/PCL-23
29Exh/4-18
31Exh/4-18
33Exh/4-9
91Conlon/Sport-195

Ribant, Dennis
65OPC-73
65T-73
66T-241
67Kahn
67T-527
67T/Test/PP-3
68T-326
69T-463
91WIZMets-330

Ribbie
85Coke/WS
86Coke/WS
87Coke/WS-30M

Ricanelli, John
76QuadC
78Cr/PCL-69

Riccelli, Frank
74OPC-599R
74T-599R
75Lafay
76Phoenix
77Phoenix
80T-247
81Buffa-24
82Syrac-6
89Pac/SenLg-59
91Pac/SenLg-67

Ricci, Chuck
89Watlo/ProC-1783
89Watlo/Star-24
91Freder/ClBest-7
91Freder/ProC-2362

Ricci, Frank
82Nashvl-19
83Beaum-17

Ricciardi, J.P.
88SoOreg/ProC-1714

Riccitant, Chuck
90Freder/Team-26

Rice, David
89BendB/Legoe-9

Rice, Del
47TipTop
49Eureka-195
50B-125
51B-156
52B-107
52T-100
53B/Col-53
53Hunter
53T-68
54B-30
54Hunter
54RM-NL9
55B-106
55Hunter
57T-193
58T-51
59T-104
60T-248
61T-448
72T-718MG
91Crown/Orio-379
91T/Arc53-68
Exh47
R302-112
R423-87

Rice, Edgar
(Sam)
21Exh-140
29Exh/4-32
31Exh/4-32
33DH-36
33G-134
34DS-32
60F-34
61F-70
80SSPC/HOF
91Conlon/Sport-54
92Conlon/Sport-436
D327
D328-137
E120
E121/120
E121/80
E122
E126-29
E135-137
E210-3
E220
R316
V100
V354-18
W501-14
W502-36
W514-79
W572
W575
WG7-44

Rice, Grantland
90LitSun-5

Rice, Hal
51B-300
52T-398
53T-93
54B-219
54T-95
55B-52
91T/Arc53-93

Rice, Harry F.
29Exh/4-23
91Conlon/Sport-216
R316

Rice, Jim
75OPC-616R
75T-616R
75T/M-616R
76Ho-127
76K-10
76OPC-340
76SSPC-405
76T-340
77BurgChef-29
77OPC-62
77T-60
78Ho-45
78K-49
78OPC-163
78OPC-2LL
78PapaG/Disc-14
78T-202LL
78T-670
78Wiffle/Discs-61
79Ho-2
79K-15
79OPC-210
79T-2LL
79T-3LL
79T-400
79T/Comics-2
80BK/PHR-20
80K-46
80OPC-112
80T-200
80T/S-5
81Coke
81D-338
81Drake-8
81F-222
81F/St-53
81K-9
81OPC-68
81PermaGr/CC-23
81Sqt-7
81T-500
81T/HT
81T/Nat/Super-11
81T/So-13
81T/St-41
82Coke/Bos
82D-200
82Drake-27
82F-305
82F/St-163
82KMart
82OPC-366
82T-750
82T/St-150
83D-208
83Drake-22
83F-194
83K-13
83OPC-30
83PermaGr/AS-4
83PermaGr/CC-31
83T-30
83T-381TL
83T/St-37
84D-50
84D/AAS-52
84D/Champs-4
84Drake-25
84F-408
84F/St-20
84F/St-37
85FunFoodPin-5
84Nes/792-132LL
84Nes/792-133LL
84Nes/792-401AS
84Nes/792-550
84Nestle/DT-5
84OPC-184AS
84OPC-364
84Ralston-9
84Seven-15E
84T-132
84T-133
84T-401
84T-550
84T/Cereal-9
84T/Gloss22-6
84T/Gloss40-22
84T/St-102A
84T/St-189
84T/St-200B
84T/St-217
84T/Super-5
85D-15DK
85D-50
85D/AAS-27
85D/DKsuper-15
85Drake-25
85F-168
85F/LimEd-27
85F/St-13
85F/St-23
85GenMills-22
85Leaf-15
85OPC-150
85Seven-2W
85Seven-4E
85Sportflic/Test-1
85T-150
85T/3D-6
85T/Gloss40-6
85T/St-208
85T/Super-50
86BK/AP-8
86D-213
86D/AAS-16
86D/PopUp-16
86Dorman-20
86Drake-13
86F-358
86F/Mini-76
86F/St-96
86Jiffy-1
86Leaf-146
86Meadow/Stat-14
86OPC-320
86Quaker-30
86Sf-139M
86Sf-146M
86Sf-17
86Sf-52M
86Sf-61M
86Sf/Dec-57
86T-320
86T/3D-23
86T/Gloss22-6
86T/Gloss60-36
86T/St-161
86T/St-246
86T/Super-43
86TrueVal-7
86Woolwth-28
87BK-16
87Classic-59
87D-92
87D/AAS-45
87D/OD-182
87Drake-15
87F-41
87F-633M
87F/Excit-37
87F/HL-6
87F/Lim-35
87F/Mini-89
87F/St-99
87Jiffy-19
87KayBee-26
87KMart-18
87Kraft-5
87Leaf-247
87OPC-146
87OPC/WaxBox-F
87RedFoley/St-44
87Sf-80M
87Sf-97
87Seven-E14
87Seven-ME14
87Sportflic/DealP-3
87T-480
87T-610AS
87T/WaxBox-F
87T/Board-5
87T/Coins-21
87T/Gloss60-42
87T/HL-27
87T/HL-5
87T/Mini-44
87T/St-17
87T/St-248
87Woolwth-27
87Woolwth-5
88ChefBoy-21
88D-399
88D/Best-28
88D/RedSox/Bk-399
88F-361
88Leaf-215
88OPC-61
88Panini/St-33
88S-14
88Sf-158
88T-662TBC
88T-675
88T/Big-181
88T/St-247
89B-33
89D-122
89F-97
89KMart/Lead-9
89OPC-245
89Panini/St-281
89S-85
89Sf-173
89T-245
89T/Big-18
89T/LJN-119
89T/St-256
89T/WaxBox-I
89UD-413
90KayBee-27
90KMart/CBatL-9
90MLBPA/Pins-70
90OPC-785
90PublInt/St-463
90T-785
90T/Ames-3
90T/HillsHM-8
90T/WaxBox-M
90UD-373
91Pac/SenLg-148

Rice, Lance
88GreatF-7
89AS/Cal-5
89Bakers/Cal-192
90Calgary/CMC-4
90Calgary/ProC-650
91Calgary/LineD-70
91Calgary/ProC-515
91Classic/III-76
91SanAn/LineD-539
91SanAn/ProC-2979
92F-658
92S/I-423
92T/91Debut-147

Rice, Pat
87Wausau-24
88SanBern/Best-6
88SanBern/Cal-43
89Wmsprt/ProC-646
89Wmsprt/Star-18

Rice, Pete
83AlexD-8
85Nashua-19
86Nashua-22
87Salem-7
88Toledo/CMC-23
88Toledo/ProC-598

Rice, Tim
86WinSalem-22
87Pittsfld-24
88BBCity/Star-20

Rice, Woolsey
83Beloit/LF-2

Rich, Woody
R303/A

Richard, J.R.
72OPC-101R
72T-101R
74OPC-522
74T-522
74T/St-36
75OPC-73
75T-73
75T/M-73
76Ho-110
76OPC-625
76T-625
77BurgChef-1
77Ho-112
77OPC-227
77T-260
78BK/Ast-4
78Ho-92
78OPC-149
78T-470
79Ho-29
79K-10
79OPC-310
79T-203RB
79T-590
79T-6LL
79T/Comics-23
80BK/PHR-8
80K-57
80OPC-28
80T-50
80T-206LL
80T/S-25
81Coke
81D-140
81F-56
81F/St-44
81K-16
81MSA/Disc-26
81OPC-350
81T-350
82F-225
82OPC-190
82T-190
86Mother/Ast-21

Richard, Lee
(Bee Bee)
72OPC-476
72T-476
75OPC-653
75T-653
75T/M-653
76OPC-533
76SSPC-145
76T-533

Richard, Ron
91Yakima/ClBest-4
91Yakima/ProC-4255

Richardi, Rick
87Miami-8
88Miami/Star-20

Richardo, Hipolito
91Memphis/ProC-650

Richards, Dave
78LodiD
81Albuq/TCMA-8
81Hawaii-2
82Hawaii-2
88Fayette/ProC-1095
89Lakeland/Star-18
90London/ProC-1267
91Jaxvl/LineD-343
91Jaxvl/ProC-150

Richards, Eugene

(Gene)
76Hawaii
77Padre/SchCd-23
77T-473R
78Padre/FamFun-25
78T-292
79T-364
80OPC-323
80T-616
81D-4
81F-486
81F/St-17
81OPC-171
81T-171
81T/So-86
81T/St-225
82D-499
82F-580
82F/St-104
82OPC-253
82T-708
82T/St-103
83D-271
83F-370
83OPC-7
83T-7
83T/St-294
84D-429
84F-310
84F/X-U98
84Nes/792-594
84T-594
84T/Tr-99T
85F-619
85T-434
89Pac/SenLg-48
89T/SenLg-63
89TM/SenLg-90
90EliteSenLg-102
91London/LineD-450CO
91MidldA/ProC-450

Richards, Fred
(Fuzzy)
53Mother-50

Richards, Kevin
81Tulsa-22
82Tulsa-8

Richards, Nicky
83CharR-2

Richards, Paul
33G-142
51B-195MG
52B-93MG
52T-305MG
53B/Col-39MG
54Wilson
55B-225MG
60L-112MG
60T-224MG
61T-131MG
61T-566AS
81Detroit-40
88Conlon/5-25
90Target-663
91T/Arc53-322MG

Richards, Rusty
87Sumter-8
89Richm/Bob-22
89Richm/CMC-7
89Richm/Ko-40
89Richm/ProC-829
90Richm/Bob-17
90Richm/CMC-4
90Richm/ProC-259
90Richm/Team-27
90T/89Debut-99
91Richm/LineD-439

Richards, Todd
80Batavia-4
81Batavia-6

Richards, Vincent
33SK-23

Richardson, A.H.
(Hardy)
N172
N284
N526
Scrapps
WG1-23
WG1-43

Richardson, A.J.
88Visalia/Cal-157
88Visalia/ProC-87
89Orlan/Best-23
89Orlan/ProC-1346

Richardson, Bobby
57T-286
58T-101
59T-237M
59T-76
60T-405
61NuCard-415
61P-8
61T-180
61T/Dice-13
62AmTract-43A
62AmTract-43B
62AmTract-43C
62AmTract-43D
62J-2
62P-2
62P/Can-2
62Salada-64
62Shirriff-64
62T-65
62T/St-90
63F-25
63J-13
63Kahn
63P-13
63Salada-52
63T-173M
63T-420
63T/SO
64T-190
64T/Coins-123AS
64T/Coins-72
64T/St-12
64T/SU
64Wheat/St-38
65MacGregor-9
65OPC-115
65T-115
65T/E-65
65T/trans-26
66T-490
66T/RO-56
78TCMA-112
88Pac/Leg-74
89Swell-49
90HOF/St-61
90Pac/Legend-100
91LineD-4
91Swell/Great-75
Exh47
WG10-20
WG9-21

Richardson, C.N.
29Exh/4-24

Richardson, Daniel
(Danny)
90Target-664
E223
N172
N284
N338/2
N690

Richardson, David
89Spring/Best-16
90StPete/Star-20
91Louisvl/LineD-244
91Louisvl/ProC-2915

Richardson, Don
86WinSalem-23

Richardson, Gordon
62Pep/Tul
63Pep/Tul
66OPC-51
66T-51
91WIZMets-331

Richardson, James
88Kinston/Star-19
89Kinston/Star-20

Richardson, Jeff
85LitFalls-9
86Lynch-18
87Lynch-24
87Tampa-12
88Chatt/Best-22
88PalmSp/Cal-92
88PalmSp/ProC-1463
89Nashvl/CMC-18
89Nashvl/ProC-1291
89Nashvl/Team-20
89PalmSp/Cal-51
89PalmSp/ProC-469
90BuffB/CMC-12
90BuffB/ProC-382
90BuffB/Team-20
90T/89Debut-100
91B-198
91BuffB/LineD-43
91BuffB/ProC-550
91T/90Debut-131

Richardson, Jim
87Watlo-3
88Alaska/Team-14

Richardson, Jon
78Richm
79Richm-7

Richardson, Keith
88Watertn/Pucko-1
90Harris/ProC-1191
90Harris/Star-16

Richardson, Kenny
78Newar

Richardson, Kerry
87Kinston-23
88Wmsprt/ProC-1328

Richardson, Lenny
88CapeCod/Sum-5

Richardson, Mike
89Erie/Star-20
89Salem/Star-17
89Star/Wax-95
90Freder/Team-6

Richardson, Milt
88Eugene/Best-27
89Eugene/Best-18

Richardson, Ron
83MidldC-18

Richardson, Ronnie
87Elmira/Black-27
87Elmira/Red-27
88Lynch/Star-20

Richardson, Tim
86Hagers-15
87Hagers-19
90HagersDG/Best-21

Richardson, Tracey
90Watertn/Star-28

Richardt, Mike
80Charl-8
83D-368
83F-575
83Rang-2
83T-371
84Nes/792-641
84T-641

Richartz, Scott
75AppFx
76AppFx

Richbourg, Lance
29Exh/4-2
31Exh/4-2
33Exh/4-1
R316

Richert, Pete
62T-131
63T-383
64T-51
65OPC-252
65T-252
66Bz-43
66OPC-95
66T-95
66T/RO-36
67Bz-43
67T-590
68T-354
69MLBPA/Pin-24
69OPC-86
69T-86
70T-601
71MLB/St-311
71OPC-273
71T-273
72T-649
73OPC-239
73T-239
74OPC-348
74T-348
74T/Tr-348T
88Modesto-2CO
88Modesto/Cal-82CO
89Modesto/Cal-287CO
89Modesto/Chong-2CO
90Modesto/Cal-172CO
90Modesto/ProC-2230CO
90Target-665
91Crown/Orio-380
91Modesto/ClBest-18CO
91Modesto/ProC-3107CO

Richey, Rodney
88Idaho/ProC-1838
89Sumter/ProC-1104
90Durham/Team-24

Richie, Bennie
83Visalia/LF-19
84Visalia-1

Richie, Lewis
10Domino-102
11Helmar-101
12Sweet/Pin-89
E90/1
M116
T202
T204
T205

Richie, Rob
88BBAmer-3
88EastLAS/ProC-11
88GlenF/ProC-925
89AAA/CMC-29
89Toledo/ProC-765
90OPC-146
90T-146
90T/89Debut-101
90UD-76SR

Richmond, Bob
87Clinton-25

Richmond, Clarence
91Kissim/ProC-4203

Richmond, Don
51B-264
V362-43

Richmond, Ryan
89Pittsfld/Star-21

Richter
11Helmar-102

Richter, Francis C.
90LitSun-4

Rick, Dean
78Salem

Ricker, Drew
86Cram/PCL-9
87Clinton-22

Ricker, Troy
85Utica-22
86Jamestn-19
87Jamestn-13
88Rockford-31
89Rockford-31
89WPalmB/Star-19
90James/Pucko-25
90Rockford/ProC-2708
91WPalmB/ClBest-28
91WPalmB/ProC-1242

Rickert, Marv
47TipTop
52T-50

Rickert, Rick
49Eureka-18

Ricketts, Dave
65T-581R
66Pep/Tul
67T-589
68OPC-46
68T-46
69MB-233
69T-232
70T-626
72MB-288
73OPC-517CO
73T-517C
90T/TVCard-4CO

Ricketts, Dick
59T-137
60T-236

Rickey, W. Branch
14CJ-133
15CJ-133
60F-55
80SSPC/HOF
89HOF/St-91
90BBWit-101
V100
W754

Rickman, Andy
88Greens/ProC-1568
89Cedar/Best-13
89Cedar/ProC-932
89Cedar/Star-15

Ricks, Ed
89Madis/Star-19

Rico, Alfredo
70T-552R

Riconda, Harry
90Target-666

Riddle, David
89Erie/Star-21
90Foil/Best-317
90Wausau/Best-12
90Wausau/ProC-2125
90Wausau/Star-19
91Freder/ClBest-8
91Freder/ProC-2363

Riddle, Elmer
49Eureka-170
W711/2

Riddle, John L.
(Johnny)
53T-274
54Hunter
54T-147
55Hunter
55T-98
75Cedar
91T/Arc53-274

Riddleberger, Dennis
71OPC-93R
71T-93R
72T-642
73OPC-157
73T-157

Riddoch, Greg
88Smok/Padres-24
90Padre/MagUno-22CO
90T/Tr-102T
91OPC-109MG
91Padre/MagRal-1MG
91T-109MG
92T-351MG

Ridenour, Dana
87FtLaud-9
88Albany/ProC-1342
88EastLAS/ProC-4
89Wmsprt/ProC-647
90EastLAS/ProC-EL18
90Foil/Best-55
90Wmsprt/Best-20
90Wmsprt/ProC-1057
90Wmsprt/Star-21
91AAAGame/ProC-AAA16
91Indianap/LineD-192
91Indianap/ProC-460

Ridenour, Ryan
90Batavia/ProC-3069

Ridzik, Steve
53B/BW-48
54B-223
55B-111
57T-123
60T-489
61BeeHive-18
64T-92
65OPC-211
65T-211
66T-294

Riel, Franich
40Hughes-16

Riemer, Robin
86Cram/PCL-183

Riemer, Tim
89Watertn/Star-19

Riesgo, Nikco
88Spokane/ProC-1936
89CharRain/ProC-995
90FSLAS/Star-16
91B-536
91Reading/ProC-1375
92T/91Debut-148

Riewerts, Tom
82AubAs-15

Rigby, Kevin
81Durham-3

Riggar, Butch
79Holyo-18

Riggert, Joe
90Target-667

Riggins, Mark A.
81ArkTr-14
82ArkTr-7

83StPete-11
86ArkTr-18CO
87Spring/Best-2CO
89Louisvl/CMC-24CO
89Louisvl/ProC-1254
90Louisvl/CMC-28CO
90Louisvl/ProC-420CO
90T/TVCard-62CO
91Louisvl/LineD-250CO
91Louisvl/ProC-2933CO

Riggleman, James D.
75Water
77ArkTr
79ArkTr-5
80ArkTr-4
81ArkTr-19
83StPete-29
86ArkTr-19MG
87ArkTr-7MG
88ArkTr/GS-4MG
90T/TVCard-5CO
91LasVegas/ProC-253MG
91LasVegas/LineD-299MG

Riggs, Jim
82Oneonta-2
83Greens-22
85Albany-18
86Albany/TCMA-1

Riggs, Kevin
90Billings/ProC-3231
91Cedar/ClBest-19
91Cedar/ProC-2728

Riggs, Lew
34DS-96
37Exh/4-4
38Exh/4-4
39PB-77
40PB-78
41DP-141
90Target-668
92Conlon/Sport-567
R314
W711/1
W711/2

Righetti, Dave
79WHave-21
80Colum-17
81Colum-9
82D-73
82F-52
82T-439
83D-199
83F-395
83OPC-176
83T-176
83T-81
84D-10DK
84D-103
84D/AAS-59
84F-139
84F-639IA
84F/St-86
85FunFoodPin-116
84Nes/792-5HL
84Nes/792-635
84OPC-277
84T-5HL
84T-635
84T/Gloss40-28
84T/St-287B
84T/St-315
85D-336
85D/HL-37
85Drake-40
85F-142
85F/St-102
85Leaf-219
85OPC-260
85Pol/MetYank-Y5
85Seven-13E
85T-260
85T/St-314
85T/Super-58
86D-214
86D/HL-52
86F-116
86F/Mini-25
86F/St-97
86Leaf-89
86OPC-34
86Sf-141M
86Sf-41
86Sf-72M
86Sf/Rook-48M
86T-560
86T/St-303
86T/Super-44
87Classic-86
87D-128
87D/AAS-55
87F-111
87F-627M
87F/AwardWin-32
87F/Hottest-31
87F/Mini-90
87F/RecSet-32
87F/Slug-34
87F/St-100
87F/WaxBox-C12
87KayBee-27
87Leaf-53
87MSA/Discs-20
87OPC-40
87Sf-119M
87Sf-194M
87Sf-57
87Seven-E9
87T-40
87T-5RB
87T-616AS
87T/Coins-22
87T/Gloss60-24
87T/HL-14
87T/Mini-67
87T/St-299
87T/St-8
87T/St-9
87Woolwth-14
88Bz-16
88D-93
88D/AS-29
88D/Best-164
88D/Y/Bk-93
88F-220
88F-625M
88F/AwardWin-33
88F/Mini-43
88F/RecSet-32
88F/Slug-33
88F/St-52
88F/TL-29
88KMart-20
88Leaf-57
88Nestle-28
88OPC-155
88Panini/St-150
88RedFoley/St-75
88S-351
88Sf-135
88Sf/Gamewin-19
88T-790
88T/Mini-29
88T/St-300
88T/St/Backs-66
88Woolwth-16
89B-167
89D-78
89D/Best-76
89F-267
89OPC-335
89Panini/St-400
89RedFoley/St-97
89S-225
89S/HotStar-37
89S/NWest-6
89Sf-158
89T-335
89T/DHTest-18
89T/LJN-126
89T/St-307
89UD-59
90B-426
90Classic-41
90D-311
90D/BestAL-136
90D/Learning-14
90F-453
90OPC-160
90Panini/St-124
90PublInt/St-545
90RedFoley/St-79
90S-194
90S/100St-39
90S/NWest-16
90Sf-88
90T-160
90T/Big-102
90T/TVYank-18
90UD-479
91B-632
91BBBest/RecBr-12
91Classic/200-87
91D-21DK
91D-275
91D/SuperDK-21DK
91F-677
91F/Up-U131
91Leaf/II-301
91Leaf/Stud-258
91Mother/Giant-8
91OPC-410
91OPC/Premier-99
91Panini/FrSt-332
91Panini/St-266
91PG&E-15
91RedFoley/St-77
91S-24
91S/100SS-68
91S/RookTr-53T
91SFExam/Giant-12
91T-410
91T/StClub/II-356
91T/Tr-96T
91UD-448
91UD/Ext-778
92D/I-174
92F-647
92S/I-260
92T-35
92UD-171

Righetti, Steve
78Ashvl

Rightnowar, Ron
87Fayette-24
88Lakeland/Star-22
89London/ProC-1369
90London/ProC-1268
91Toledo/ProC-1931

Riginos, Tom
88CapeCod/Sum-58

Rigler, Umpire
21Exh-141

Rigney, Emory E.
21Exh-142
25Exh-94
26Exh-69
E120
E210-38
V61-17
W573

Rigney, John D.
41DP-72
47TipTop

Rigney, William J.
(Bill)
48B-32
49B-170
49Eureka-123
50B-117
51B-125
52BR
52NTea
52T-125
53B/BW-3
58PacBell-6MG
58SFCallB-19MG
60MacGregor-18
60T-225MG
60T-7M
61T-225MG
62T-549MG
63T-294MG
64T-383MG
65OPC-66MG
65T-66MG
66T-249MG
67T-494MG
68T-416MG
69OPC-182MG
69T-182MG
70OPC-426MG
70T-426MG
71OPC-532MG
71T-532MG
72OPC-389MG
72T-389MG
89Smok/Angels-1
91T/Arc53-328
PM10/Sm-156

Rigoli, Joe
79Newar-3
83Erie-2
85Louisvl-2
86Erie-25MG
87Erie-3

Rigos, John
83Erie-3
85Spring-1
86StPete-27
87Salem-14
88Harris/ProC-834

Rigsby, Rickey
88Pulaski/ProC-1761
89Idaho/ProC-2013

Rigsby, Tim
90Miami/I/Star-21
90Miami/I/Star-26
91Kinston/ClBest-19
91Kinston/ProC-331

Rijo, Jose
84F/X-U99
84T/Tr-100T
85Cram/PCL-133
85D-492
85F-143
85T-238
86D-522
86D/HL-2
86F-431
86Mother/A's-13
86T-536
87D-55
87F-404
87Leaf-119
87T-34
88D-548
88F/Up-U86
88Kahn/Reds-27
88S-392
88S/Tr-27T
88T-316
88T/Tr-92T
89B-300
89Classic-141
89D-375
89D/Best-278
89F-168
89Kahn/Reds-27
89OPC-135
89Panini/St-68
89S-552
89S/YS/I-31
89T-135
89T/Mini-12
89T/St-140
89UD-619
90B-45
90D-115
90F-430
90Kahn/Reds-24
90Leaf/II-282
90OPC-627
90Panini/St-243
90PublInt/St-38
90S-511
90T-627
90T/Big-257
90T/St-137
90UD-216
91B-681
91Classic/200-109
91Classic/I-97
91Classic/II-T31
91CollAB-27
91D-722
91D-742WS
91F-79
91F/Ultra-102
91F/WS-7
91Kahn/Reds-27
91KingB/Discs-24
91Leaf/II-326
91OPC-493
91Panini/FrSt-134
91Pep/Reds-18
91Pep/SS-5
91S-658
91T-493
91T/CJMini/I-9
91T/StClub/I-11
91UD-298
91Woolwth/HL-31
91Woolwth/HL-33
92D/I-223
92F-419
92S/100SS-43
92S/I-232
92T-220
92UD-258

Rijo, Rafael
89Salem/Team-26
90Yakima/Team-13
91VeroB/ClBest-25
91VeroB/ProC-790

Riker, Robert
90Bristol/ProC-3161
90Bristol/Star-20

Riles, Earnest
83ElPaso-21
84Cram/PCL-35
85Cram/PCL-207
85F/Up-U89
86D-359
86F-499
86F/LL-34
86F/Mini-102
86F/St-98
86Jay's-14
86KayBee-26
86Leaf-161
86Pol/Brew-1
86Sf-16
86T-398
86T/Gloss60-40
86T/St-310
87D-151
87F-355
87F/GameWin-36
87F/Mini-91
87Leaf-66
87OPC-318
87Pol/Brew-1
87T-523
87T/St-203
88D-478
88F-172
88F/Up-U130
88Pol/Brew-1
88S-349
88S/Tr-57T
88T-88
88T/Tr-93T
89B-475
89Classic-87
89D-625
89D/Best-50
89F-341
89Gard-14
89Mother/Giants-16
89S-458
89T-676
89UD-497
90B-239
90D-131
90ElPasoATG/Team-9
90F-69
90Mother/Giant-15
90OPC-732
90PublInt/St-80
90S-447
90T-732
90T/St-81
90UD-378
91B-217
91D-461
91F-271
91F/UltraUp-U47
91F/Up-U51
91Leaf/II-358
91Mother/A's-16
91OPC-408
91S-626
91S/RookTr-55T
91T-408
91T/StClub/II-432
91T/Tr-97T
91UD/Ext-780
92S/I-222
92T-187
92UD-494

Riley, Darren
85Cedar-24
86FSLAS-41
86Tampa-16
87Vermont-25
88Chatt/Best-24

Riley, Ed
89Elmira/Pucko-14
90WinHaven/Star-22

91LynchRS/ClBest-7
91LynchRS/ProC-1196

Riley, George
80Wichita-20
81D-588
81T-514
83Reading-8
84Cram/PCL-206

Riley, Mike
79Wisco-3
82Cedar-6

Riley, P.J.
89AubAs/ProC-2180

Riley, Randy
84Newar-1

Riley, Tim
77DaytB

Riley, Tom
83Cedar-16
83Cedar/LF-5
84Cedar-15
85Cedar-31

Rima, Tom
74Cedar
75Dubuq

Rincon, Andrew
(Andy)
80ArkTr-9
81Louisvl-17
81T-244R
82Louisvl-24
82T-135
83Louisvl/Riley-17
89ArkTr/GS-20
90Savan/ProC-2084CO

Rincones, Hector
81Water-16
83Water-13
84Wichita/Rock-3
85Cram/PCL-157

Rineer, Jeff
78RochR
79RochR-16
80RochR-8
91Crown/Orio-381

Rinehart, Robert Jr.
86Columbia-22

Ring, Dave
90Elmira/Pucko-20

Ring, James J.
21Exh-143
26Exh-39
28Exh-22
88Pac/8Men-87
92Conlon/Sport-614
E120
E126-24
E220
V100
V61-120
W516-11

Ringgold, Keith
90Everett/Best-27
90Everett/ProC-3143
91BendB/ClBest-19
91BendB/ProC-3708

Ringler, Tim
88Knoxvl/Best-22
89Knoxvl/Best-30
89Knoxvl/ProC-1122

Rings, Frank
N172

Rios, Carlos Rafael
77AppFx
78Charl
81Buffa-19
82Knoxvl-15
85IntLgAS-5
85Richm-15
86Greenvl/Team-15
87Greenvl/Best-5
88Richm-6
88Richm/CMC-18
88Richm/ProC-8
89Richm/Bob-23
89Richm/CMC-13
89Richm/Ko-6
89Richm/ProC-842

Rios, Enrique
87Kenosha-29
88CLAS/Star-16
88Lynch/Star-21

Rios, Jesus
85Tigres-1

Rios, Juan
69T-619R
70OPC-89
70T-89
72MB-289

Ripken, Bill
86SLAS-1
87D/Rook-16
87French-3
87RochR-12
87RochR/TCMA-13
87Sf/Rook-28
88Classic/Red-163
88D-336
88D-625M
88D/Best-254
88F-569
88F-640M
88French-7
88Leaf-134
88MSA/Disc-7
88OPC-352
88Panini/St-9
88S-200
88S/YS/I-20
88Sf-216
88T-352
88T/JumboR-1
88T/St-227
88ToysRUs-25
89B-12
89D-259
89D/Best-318
89F-616
89French-3
89OPC-22
89Panini/St-261
89RedFoley/St-98
89S-18
89T-571
89T/Big-27
89UD-283
90B-256
90D-164
90F-186
90HagersDG/Best-22
90Leaf/II-271
90MLBPA/Pins-113
90OPC-468
90Panini/St-3
90PublInt/St-583
90S-174
90T-468
90T/Big-244
90T/St-235
90UD-184
91B-87
91Crown/Orio-382
91D-167
91F-489
91F/Ultra-23
91Leaf/I-7
91OPC-677
91Panini/FrSt-241
91S-487
91Seven/3DCoin-12A
91T-677
91T/StClub/I-222
91UD-550
92D/II-734
92F-25
92S/I-97
92T-752
92UD-250
92UD-82M

Ripken, Cal Jr.
81RochR-15
82D-405
82F-176
82T-21R
82T/Tr-98T
83D-279
83D/AAS-52
83Drake-23
83F-70
83OPC-163
83T-163
83T/St-26
83T/St-315
84D-106
84D/AAS-20
84D/Champs-48
84Drake-26
84F-17
84F/St-15
84F/St-29
85FunFoodPin-118
84MiltBrad-20
84Nes/792-400AS
84Nes/792-426TL
84Nes/792-490
84Nestle/DT-4
84OPC-2AS
84OPC-363
84Seven-14E
84T-400AS
84T-426TL
84T-490
84T/St-197
84T/St-204
84T/St-24
84T/St/Box-13
84T/Super-1
85D-14DK
85D-169
85D/AAS-7
85D/DKsuper-14
85Drake-26
85F-187
85F-626IA
85F/LimEd-28
85F/St-41
85Leaf-14DK
85OPC-30
85Seven-14E
85T-30
85T-704AS
85T/3D-16
85T/Gloss22-16
85T/Gloss40-24
85T/St-185
85T/St-197
85T/Super-48
85ThomMc/Discs-17
86BK/AP-15
86D-210
86D/AAS-14
86D/PopUp-14
86Dorman-4
86Drake-11
86F-284
86F-633M
86F/AS-5
86F/LimEd-36
86F/LL-35
86F/Mini-59
86F/Slug-28
86F/St-99
86Jiffy-9
86Leaf-142
86Meadow/Blank-11
86Meadow/Milk-8
86Meadow/Stat-11
86OPC-340
86Quaker-31
86Sf-128M
86Sf-54M
86Sf-59M
86Sf-69M
86Sf-73M
86Sf-8
86Sf/Dec-73M
86Sf/Rook-48M
86T-340
86T-715AS
86T/Gloss22-5
86T/Gloss60-14
86T/Mini-2
86T/St-159
86T/St-226
86T/Super-45
86TrueVal-22
87Classic-52
87D-89
87D/AAS-5
87D/HL-38
87D/OD-133
87D/PopUp-5
87Drake-6
87F-478
87F/AwardWin-33
87F/GameWin-37
87F/BB-36
87F/Mini-92
87F/Slug-35
87F/St-101
87French-8
87Jiffy-8
87Kraft-3
87Leaf-98
87MnM's-13
87MSA/Discs-14
87OPC-312
87Ralston-12
87RedFoley/St-118
87Sf-113M
87Sf-9
87Seven-ME16
87Sportflic/DealP-49
87T-609AS
87T-784
87T/Board-22
87T/Coins-23
87T/Gloss22-16
87T/Gloss60-37
87T/Mini-40
87T/St-151
87T/St-233
88Bz-17
88ChefBoy-7
88Classic/Red-176
88D-171
88D-26DK
88D-625M
88D-BC1
88D/AS-5
88D/Best-198
88D/DKsuper-26DK
88D/PopUp-5
88Drake-25
88F-570
88F-635M
88F-640M
88F/RecSet-33
88F/Slug-34
88F/SS-31
88F/St-3
88F/TL-30
88French-8
88KayBee-25
88KingB/Disc-24
88KMart-21
88Leaf-100
88Leaf-26DK
88OPC-74
88Panini/St-13
88Panini/St-230M
88RedFoley/St-76
88S-550
88S-651M
88S/WaxBox-5
88Sf-152
88T-650
88T/Big-62
88T/Coins-24
88T/Gloss22-5
88T/Gloss60-6
88T/RiteAid-13
88T/St-160
88T/St-228
88T/St/Backs-44
88T/UK-61
89B-260FS
89B-9
89Cadaco-44
89Classic-56
89T/Crunch-6
89D-51
89D/AS-5
89D/Best-142
89D/MVP-BC15
89D/PopUp-5
89F-617
89F/BBAS-35
89F/Heroes-34
89F/LL-32
89French-8
89KMart/DT-15
89Master/Discs-12
89OPC-250
89Panini/St-241AS
89Panini/St-262
89RedFoley/St-99
89S-15
89S/HotStar-77
89S/Mast-3
89Sf-66
89T-250
89T/Big-286
89T/Coins-50
89T/Gloss22-5
89T/Gloss60-47
89T/LJN-142
89T/St-150
89T/St-237
89T/St/Backs-11
89T/UK-64
89T/WaxBox-J
89Tetley/Discs-16
89UD-467
89UD-682TC
90B-255
90Classic-24
90D-676AS
90D-96
90D/BestAL-57
90D/Bon/MVP-BC18
90D/Learning-19
90F-187
90F-624MVP
90F/ASIns-8
90F/BB-30
90F/BBMVP-31
90HotPlay/St-34
90KMart/SS-20
90Leaf/I-197
90MLBPA/Pins-112
90MSA/Soda-4
90OPC-388AS
90OPC-570
90OPC-8RB
90Panini/St-202
90Panini/St-388
90Panini/St-7
90Post-21
90PublInt/St-584
90RedFoley/St-78
90S-2
90S/100St-66
90Sf-100
90Sunflower-23
90T-388AS
90T-570
90T-8RB
90T/Ames-15
90T/Big-327
90T/Coins-24
90T/DH-52
90T/Gloss22-16
90T/Gloss60-51
90T/HillsHM-32
90T/St-160AS
90T/St-231
90T/St-5HL
90T/TVAS-19
90T/WaxBox-N
90UD-266
90USPlayC/AS-6S
90Windwlk/Discs-9
90Woolwth/HL-19
91B-104
91BBBest/RecBr-13
91Classic/200-110
91Classic/II-T3
91Classic/III-77
91Classic/III-xx
91CollAB-2
91Crown/Orio-383
91D-223
91D-52AS
91D-BC17
91DennyGS-20
91F-490
91F/Ultra-24
91JDeanSig-15
91Leaf/II-430
91Leaf/Stud-9
91MajorLg/Pins-29
91MooTown-14
91OPC-150
91OPC-5RB
91OPC/Premier-100
91Panini/FrSt-170
91Panini/FrSt-243
91Panini/St-192
91Pep/SS-8
91Petro/SU-1
91Post-19
91Post/Can-22
91RedFoley/St-124
91RedFoley/St-78
91S-849FRAN
91S-95
91S/100SS-21

91Seven/3DCoin-13A
91SilverSt-4
91T-150
91T-5RB
91T/CJMini/I-13
91T/StClub/II-430
91T/SU-28
91UD-347
91UD/FinalEd-85FAS
91USPlayC/AS-13D
91Woolwth/HL-18
92Classic/I-76
92D/DK-DK5
92D/Elite-S1
92D/I-22AS
92D/I-35
92D/II-BC1MVP
92D/Preview-10
92F-26
92F-703M
92F-711PV
92F/ASIns-20
92F/TmLIns-17
92S/100SS-89
92S/I-433AS
92S/II-540
92S/II-788MVP
92S/II-794MOY
92S/II-884DT
92T-40
92T-400AS
92T/GPromo-40
92UD-165
92UD-645DS
92UD-82M

Ripken, Cal Sr.
82D-579
87French-7MG
87T/Tr-102T
88D-625M
88F-635M
88T-444MG
89B-260FS
89French-7
90F-634M

Ripley, Allen
78PapaG/Disc-1
79T-702R
80T-413
81F-454
81T-144
82D-125
82F-399
82RedLob
82T-529
82T/Tr-99T
83D-57
83F-506
83T-73

Rippelmeyer, Brad
91Idaho/ProC-4333

Rippelmeyer, Ray
60HenryH-28
60Union-10
61T-276
62T-271
73OPC-486CO
73T-486C
74OPC-119CO
74T-119C
89Nashvl/CMC-24
89Nashvl/ProC-1280
89Nashvl/Team-29CO
90Nashvl/CMC-25CO
90Nashvl/ProC-250CO

Ripple, Charles
47Centen-23
47Signal

Ripple, Jimmy
38Exh/4-5
38ONG/Pin-24
39PB-66
41DP-11
41DP-95
44Centen-18
90Target-669
91Conlon/Sport-86
V355-28

Rippley, Steve
88TM/Umpire-49
89TM/Umpire-47
90TM/Umpire-45

Ripslager, Charles
N172/SP

Risberg, Charles
(Swede)
88Pac/8Men-103
88Pac/8Men-16
88Pac/8Men-26
88Pac/8Men-70
W514-105

Riscen, Fred
88SLCity-21

Risley, William
(Bill)
88Greens/ProC-1551
89Cedar/Best-6
89Cedar/ProC-912
89Cedar/Star-16
90A&AASingle/ProC-121
90Cedar/Best-14
90Cedar/ProC-2313
91Chatt/LineD-166
91Chatt/ProC-1959

Ritch, Harry
85VeroB-13

Ritchey, Claude
E107
E254
T206
WG3-41

Ritchey, Larry
86Cram/PCL-60

Ritchie, Dave
89Eugene/Best-11

Ritchie, Gregg
86Cram/PCL-5
87Clinton-4
88SanJose/Cal-127
88SanJose/ProC-131
89Shrev/ProC-1841
90Phoenix/CMC-14
90Phoenix/ProC-25
91Phoenix/LineD-391
91Phoenix/ProC-81

Ritchie, Jay
65T-494

Ritchie, Lewis
14Piedmont/St-49

Ritchie, Todd
90Classic/DP-12
90Elizab/Star-19
91B-332
91Classic/I-58
91Kenosha/ClBest-22
91Kenosha/ProC-2072
91MidwLAS/ProC-MWL39
91S-678FDP
91Single/ClBest-319

Ritchie, Wally
86Clearw-21
87F/Up-U104
87Maine-17
87T/Tr-103T
88D-555
88F-312
88OPC-322
88Phill/TastyK-20
88S-526
88T-494
89ScrWB/CMC-9
89ScrWB/ProC-715
90ScranWB/CMC-6
90ScranWB/ProC-598
91ScranWB/LineD-493
91ScranWB/ProC-2536
92D/II-631
92F-543
92S/II-619

Ritter, Chris
86PrWill-21
87Harris-25
88Harris/ProC-845

Ritter, Darren
89Pulaski/ProC-1905
90BurlB/Best-25
90BurlB/ProC-2348
90BurlB/Star-22
90Foil/Best-47
91DurhamUp/ProC-6
91Macon/ClBest-7
91Macon/ProC-861

Ritter, Ken
89Medford/Best-15

Ritter, Lawrence
90LitSun-12

Ritter, Louis
(Lou)
90Target-670
E254
T206

Ritter, Reggie
83Watlo/LF-15
85Water-11
86Maine-16
86OhHenry-53
87BuffB-19
88ColoSp/CMC-7
88ColoSp/ProC-1540

Ritter, William
D328-138
E135-138

Rittman, Alvin
89Belling/Legoe-24
90Spring/Best-2

Rittwage, James
65T-501R

Rittweger, Bill
82Jacks-18

Ritz, Kevin
87GlenF-6
88GlenF/ProC-926
89Toledo/CMC-7
89Toledo/ProC-786
90B-350
90Classic-131
90CokeK/Tiger-18
90D-415
90F-613
90HotRook/St-37
90OPC-237
90S-572
90S/100Ris-11
90Sf-29
90T-237
90T/89Debut-102
90Toledo/CMC-8
90Toledo/ProC-147
90UD-98
91CokeK/Tiger-31
91Toledo/LineD-596
91Toledo/ProC-1932

Rivard, John
89Miami/II/Star-17

Rivas, Javier
91Pulaski/ClBest-15
91Pulaski/ProC-4019

Rivas, Limbert
90Ashvl/ProC-2746

Rivas, Martin
77Charl

Rivas, Oscar
89Belling/Legoe-12
90Penin/Star-17
91SanBern/ProC-1988

Rivas, Rafael
80Utica-31

Rivas, Ralph
83Kinston/Team-19

Rivell, Robert
88CapeCod/Sum-72
91Waterlo/ClBest-19
91Waterlo/ProC-1266

Rivera, Angel
88James/ProC-1900

Rivera, Ben
88Sumter/ProC-410
89Durham/Team-18
89Durham/Star-18
90Greenvl/Best-6
90Greenvl/ProC-1126
90Greenvl/Star-17
91B-579
91Greenvl/ClBest-3
91Greenvl/LineD-214
91Greenvl/ProC-2997

Rivera, Carlos
87Fayette-14
88Elmira-11
88WinHaven/Star-21
89Elmira/Pucko-15

Rivera, Dave
77Ashvl
82Charl-22
91Kenosha/ClBest-6
91Kenosha/ProC-2084

Rivera, Elvin
86QuadC-27
87QuadC-16
88Reno/Cal-269

Rivera, German
78Clinton
83Albuq-17
84Pol/Dodg-25
85Cram/PCL-162
85D-638
85F-382
85T-626
86Nashvl-20
87Toledo-4
87Toledo/TCMA-3
88AAA/ProC-14
88Denver/CMC-12
88Denver/ProC-1253
90AAAGame/ProC-AAA9
90Indianap/ProC-305
90Target-671

Rivera, Hector
89WPalmB/Star-20
90Gate/ProC-3349
90Jaxvl/Best-23
90Jaxvl/ProC-1374
91B-444
91Harris/LineD-261
91Harris/ProC-627

Rivera, Jesus
(Bombo)
77OPC-54
77T-178
78T-657
79T-449
80OPC-22
80T-43
81D-593
81F-556
81Omaha-23
81T-256
82Omaha-20
83Omaha-19

Rivera, Jim
83Ander-14
84Durham-26

Rivera, Jose
83Greens-23
83QuadC-23
87Memphis-23
87Memphis/Best-4
88Memphis/Best-25

Rivera, Lino
88CharlR/Star-20
89Fayette/ProC-1573
89SALAS/GS-21
90Lakeland/Star-22
91Lakeland/ClBest-11
91Lakeland/ProC-266

Rivera, Luis
83VeroB-13
86Indianap-28
87F-330
87Indianap-27
88T/Big-223
88T/Tr-94T
89B-29
89D-578
89F-392
89OPC-257
89Pawtu/CMC-20
89Pawtu/Dunkin-14
89Pawtu/ProC-697
89S-169
89T-431
89T/St-68
89UD-423
90D-421
90F-285
90Leaf/II-283
90OPC-601
90Pep/RSox-18
90T-601
90T/TVRSox-26
90UD-482
91D-234
91F-112
91F/Ultra-42
91Leaf/II-408
91OPC-338
91Panini/FrSt-267
91Pep/RSox-19
91S-271
91T-338
91T/StClub/I-55
91UD-182
92D/I-332
92F-48
92S/I-159
92T-97
92UD-308

Rivera, Manuel J.
(Jim)
53T-156
54T-34
55T-58
55T/DH-90
56T-70
56T/Hocus-A11
56T/Hocus-B13
56T/Pin-35
57T-107
58T-11
59T-213
60L-55
60T-116
61P-33
61T-367
91T/Arc53-156

Rivera, Mariano
90Tampa/DIMD-17
91Greens/ProC-3058

Rivera, Pablo
89CharlK-25

Rivera, Rafael
91Salinas/ClBest-2
91Salinas/ProC-2247

Rivera, Ricardo
82AubAs-17
83DayBe-22

Rivera, Robert
89BurlInd/Star-22
90Watertn/Star-17
91ColInd/ClBest-15
91ColInd/ProC-1482

Rivero, Marty
88Peoria/Ko-26
89WinSalem/Star-14

Rivers, Ken
87Dunedin-27
88Knoxvl/Best-14
89Knoxvl/Best-21
89Knoxvl/ProC-1132
89Knoxvl/Star-17
90Myrtle/ProC-2779
91London/LineD-441
91MidldA/ProC-437

Rivers, Mickey Jr.
88Elmira-23
89WinHaven/Star-18
90LynchRS/Team-4
91Single/ClBest-90
91WinHaven/ClBest-24
91WinHaven/ProC-503

Rivers, Mickey Sr.
72OPC-272
72T-272
73OPC-597
73T-597
74OPC-76
74T-76
75Greyhound-1
75Ho-22
75Ho/Twink-22
75OPC-164
75T-164
75T/M-164
76Ho-102
76K-41
76OPC-198LL
76OPC-85
76SSPC-203
76T-198LL
76T-85
76T/Tr-85T
77BK/Y-18
77BurgChef-180
77K-51
77OPC-69
77T-305
78BK/Y-20
78Ho-110
78K-17
78OPC-182
78T-690
79BK/Y-20
79OPC-24
79T-60

80OPC-251
80T-485
81D-496
81F-617
81F/St-32
81OPC-145
81T-145
81T/HT
81T/So-31
81T/St-132
82D-242
82F-328
82F/St-174
82OPC-356
82OPC-51IA
82T-704
82T-705IA
82T/St-243
83D-394
83F-576
83OPC-224
83Rang-17
83T-224
84D-465
84F-425
84Nes/792-504
84OPC-269
84Rang-17
84T-504
84T/St-361
85D-465
85F-565
85Leaf-35
85OPC-371
85T-371
85T/St-355
89Pac/SenLg-163
89T/SenLg-115
89TM/SenLg-91
90EliteSenLg-28

Rixey, Eppa
21Exh-144
25Exh-30
26Exh-30
27Exh-15
28Yueng-16
33G-74
61F-71
80SSPC/HOF
89HOF/St-69
91Conlon/Sport-39
D327
D328-139
D329-142
D350/2-142
E120
E121/120
E121/80
E122
E135-139
E210
M101/4-142
M101/5-142
V100
V354-32
W501-54
W502-16
W572
W575

Rizza, Jerry
88SoOreg/ProC-1715
90Erie/Star-20

Rizzo, Johnny
39Exh
39PB-11
40PB-108
41DP-124
47Signal
47Sunbeam
90Target-672

Rizzo, Mike
83Peoria/LF-14

Rizzo, Rick
81CharR-23
82FtMyr-1
84Memphis-3

Rizzo, Tom
88Pulaski/ProC-1754
89Sumter/ProC-1087
90Idaho/ProC-3246

Rizzuto, Phil
41DP-62
47HomogBond-39
47TipTop
48B-8
48L-11
49B-98
49Royal-11
50B-11
50Drake-25
51B-26
51BR-A3
51T/CAS
51T/RB-5
52B-52
52BR
52Royal
52StarCal/L-70F
52T-11
52TipTop
52Wheat
53B/Col-9
53B/Col-93M
53Briggs
53Exh/Can-25
53RM-AL10
53SM
53T-114
54B-1
54DanDee
54NYJour
54RM-AL17
54SM
54T-17
55B-10
55SM
55T-189
56T-113
56T/Pin-29
60NuCard-45
61NuCard-445
61T-471MV
79TCMA-144
80Pac/Leg-82
83MLBPA/Pin-15
86Sf/Dec-22
88Pac/Leg-10
89Swell-111
90Pac/Legend-101
91T/Arc53-114
D305
Exh47
PM10/L-34
PM10/Sm-157

Roa, Hector
90Pulaski/Best-17
90Pulaski/ProC-3097
91Miami/ClBest-23
91Miami/ProC-417

Roa, Joe
90Pulaski/Best-9
90Pulaski/ProC-3107
91Macon/ClBest-8
91Macon/ProC-862

Roa, Pedro
89Belling/Legoe-19

Roach, Brett
88Bristol/ProC-1884
89Fayette/ProC-1589

Roach, John
N172

Roach, Mel
54T-181
55Gol/Braves-26
55T-117
59T-54
60Lake
60SpicSpan-18
60T-491
61P-163
61T-217
62T-581

Roadcap, Steve
83QuadC-16
86Pittsfld-20
88Wythe/ProC-1991
89Wythe/Star-29MG
90Hunting/ProC-3303MG
91Hunting/ClBest-30MG
91Hunting/ProC-3353MG

Roarke, Mike
61T-376
62T-87
63T-224
64T-292
83Pawtu-26
90T/TVCard-6CO

Roarke, Tom
82AubAs-1

Robarge, Dennis
88Elmira-29ASST
89Elmira/Pucko-26

Robbe, Fletcher
53Mother-5

Robbins, Bruce
80Evansvl-18
80T-666R
81D-129
81F-477
81T-79
82Evansvl-6
83BirmB-10

Robbins, Doug
88T/Tr-95T
89T/Big-49
90Foil/Best-53
90Hagers/Best-3
90Hagers/ProC-1416
90Hagers/Star-21
91Hagers/LineD-245
91Hagers/ProC-2460
92T-58R

Robbins, Leroy
80WHave-3

Roberge, Al
V362-46

Roberge, Bert
77Cocoa
80T-329
80Tucson-23
81Tucson-21
82Tucson-15
83D-496
83F-461
83T-611
83Tucson-8
85F-525
85T-388
85T/Tr-94T
86D-575
86F-258
86OPC-154
86Provigo-16
86T-154

Roberson, Kevin
88Wythe/ProC-1978
89CharWh/Best-7
89CharWh/ProC-1747
90WinSalem/Team-10
91CharlK/LineD-140
91CharlK/ProC-1702
91Single/ClBest-2

Roberts, Bill
76Dubuq

Roberts, Brent
88Burllnd/ProC-1772

Roberts, Chris
91T/Tr-98T

Roberts, Cliff
77DaytB

Roberts, Curt
54DanDee
54T-242
55T-107
55T/DH-11
56T-306
60DF-6
61Union

Roberts, Dave A.
69T-536R
70OPC-151
70T-151
71MLB/St-235
71OPC-448
71T-448
72K-15
72OPC-360
72OPC-91LL
72T-360
72T-91LL
73OPC-39
73T-39
74McDon
74OPC-177
74T-177
74T/St-37
74T/St-99
75OPC-301
75T-301
75T/M-301
76OPC-649
76T-649
76T/Tr-649T
77Ho-10
77OPC-193
77OPC-38
77Padre/SchCd-24
77T-363
78Padre/FamFun-26
78T-501
79Pol/Giants-25
79T-473
80T-212
81D-501
81F-636
81T-431
82Phoenix
91WIZMets-332

Roberts, Dave L.
63T-158R
66T-571

Roberts, Dave W.
73OPC-133
73T-133
74OPC-309
74T-309
75OPC-558
75T-558
75T/M-558
76OPC-107
76T-107
77T-537
78T-501
79T-342
80T-93
81D-490
81F-607
81T-57
81T/Tr-824
82D-625
82F-227
82T-218
83D-273
83T-148

Roberts, Drex
85Kingst-20

Roberts, Jay
83Ander-31

Roberts, Jeff
86Wausau-19

Roberts, Jim
90Target-673

Roberts, John
86Greens-20
87Greens-8
88EastLAS/ProC-23
88NewBrit/ProC-894
89Pawtu/CMC-21
89Pawtu/Dunkin-24
89Pawtu/ProC-693

Roberts, Keith
90Bristol/ProC-3150
90Bristol/Star-21

Roberts, Leon K.
(Leon)
75OPC-620R
75T-620R
75T/M-620R
76OPC-292
76SSPC-362
76T-292
76T/Tr-292T
77BurgChef-3
77T-456
79Ho-37
79OPC-81
79T-166
79T/Comics-15
80OPC-266
80T-507
81D-48
81F-608
81T-368
81T/Tr-825
82D-415
82F-329
82OPC-186
82T-688
83OPC-89
83T-89
83T/Tr-96
84D-399
84F-356
84Nes/792-784
84T-784
85T-217
86Nashvl-21MG
87Toledo-20
87Toledo/TCMA-21
88Fayette/ProC-1104
89Pac/SenLg-30
89T/SenLg-113
89TM/SenLg-92
90EliteSenLg-103
91Pac/SenLg-97

Roberts, Leon
(Bip)
84PrWill-1
85Nashua-20
86D/Rook-33
86F/Up-U96
86T/Tr-91T
87D-114
87F-427
87LasVegas-23
87T-637
88LasVegas/CMC-14
88LasVegas/ProC-245
89Coke/Padre-14
89F/Up-126
89T/Tr-103T
90B-222
90Coke/Padre-15
90D-347
90D/BestNL-60
90F-166
90Leaf/I-233
90OPC-307
90Padre/MagUno-26
90Panini/St-359
90S-51
90S/YS/I-23
90Sf-116
90T-307
90T/Big-149
90T/St-103
90UD-303
91B-654
91D-195
91F-540
91F/Ultra-310
91Leaf/II-478
91Leaf/Stud-248
91OPC-538
91Padre/MagRal-9
91Panini/FrSt-96
91Panini/St-97
91S-28
91T-538
91T/CJMini/II-31
91T/StClub/I-18
91UD-271
92D/I-371
92F-618
92S/I-123
92T-20
92T/GPromo-20
92T/Promo-20
92UD-141

Roberts, Lonell
90MedHat/Best-9
91Myrtle/ClBest-26
91Myrtle/ProC-2960
91Single/ClBest-99

Roberts, Mel
88SALAS/GS-2
88Spartan/ProC-1033
88Spartan/Star-22
88Spartan/Star-6
89Spartan/ProC-1050
90Spartan/Best-25MG
90Spartan/ProC-2508MG
90Spartan/Star-27MG
91Spartan/ClBest-28MG
91Spartan/ProC-913MG

Roberts, Mike
80Tulsa-5
81Tulsa-17

Roberts, Norman
86Hagers-16

Roberts, Pete
88LasVegas/CMC-5
88LasVegas/ProC-228
89LasVegas/CMC-9
89LasVegas/ProC-13
90LasVegas/CMC-7

90LasVegas/ProC-122
Roberts, Robin
49B-46
49Eureka-143
49Lummis
50B-32
51B-3
51BR-D8
51T/CAS
52B-4
52BR
52NTea
52RM-NL18
52T-59
52TipTop
53B/Col-65
53RM-NL11
54B-95
54RM-NL18
55B-171
56T-180
56YellBase/Pin-27
57T-15
58T-90
59T-156M
59T-352
60Bz-26
60MacGregor-19
60NuCard-44
60T-264
60T/tatt-45
61NuCard-444
61P-117
61T-20
61T/St-58
62J-198
62P-198
62P/Can-198
62T-243
63J-66
63P-66
63T-125
63T-6LL
64T-285
65OPC-15
65T-15
66T-530
79TCMA-4
80Pac/Leg-56
82CJ-9
83D/HOF-41
83MLBPA/Pin-30
86Phill/TastyK-36
86Sf/Dec-39M
88Pac/Leg-15
89T/LJN-157
90Pac/Legend-47
90Phill/TastyK-31
90Swell/Great-11
91Crown/Orio-384
91LineD-33
91Swell/Great-77
91T/Arc53-288
Exh47
PM10/Sm-158
PM10/Sm-159
Roberts, Scott
84Cram/PCL-42
85Cram/PCL-218
86Maine-17
87BuffB-20
Roberts, Tim
91Erie/ClBest-23
91Erie/ProC-4069
Robertson, Alfred J.
(Jim)
54B-211
54T-149
55B-5
55Rodeo
55T-177
Robertson, Andre
81Colum-3
82Colum-17
82Colum/Pol-2
82T-83r
83D-387
83F-396
83RoyRog/Disc-10
83T-281
83T/St-316
84Colum-9
84Colum/Pol-20
84D-347
84F-140
84Nes/792-592
84OPC-282
84T-592
84T/St-323
85F-144
85T-354
86Colum-21
86Colum/Pol-19
86D-469
86F-117
86T-738
87Chatt/Best-25
88Huntsvl/BK-16
88Tacoma/CMC-19
88Tacoma/ProC-634
89OkCty/CMC-14
89OkCty/ProC-1514
Robertson, Bill
90Beloit/Best-2
90Beloit/Star-18
Robertson, Bob E.
68OPC-36R
68T-36R
69T-468R
70T-664
71K-4
71MLB/St-212
71OPC-255
71T-255
72K-45
72OPC-429
72OPC-430IA
72T-429
72T-430IA
73OPC-422
73T-422
74OPC-540
74T-540
75OPC-409
75T-409
75T/M-409
76OPC-449
76SSPC-578
76T-449
77T-176
79OPC-158
79T-312
89Swell-107
90Ashvl/C1Best-28CO
90Ashvl/ClBest-28CO
90ColMud/Star-25CO
91Ashvl/ProC-586CO
91Ashvl/ProC-586CO
Robertson, Bryant
85LitFalls-27
Robertson, Charles
21Exh-145
92Conlon/Sport-354
E120
V61-10
W573
Robertson, Dale
81Pawtu-13
84Pawtu-4
Robertson, Daryl
62Pep/Tul
Robertson, David A.
16FleischBrd-76
D327
D328-140
D329-143
D350/2-143
E135-140
M101/4-143
M101/5-143
V100
Robertson, Doug
85Everett/II/Cram-14
86Clinton-22
87Clinton-1
88CalLgAS-6
88SanJose/Cal-137
88SanJose/ProC-115
89Shrev/ProC-1851
90ColoSp/CMC-5
90ColoSp/ProC-32
91London/LineD-442
91MidldA/ProC-433
Robertson, Eugene E.
(Gene)
92Conlon/Sport-386
Robertson, Jason
89LittleSun-14
90Foil/Best-288
90Greens/Best-25
90Greens/ProC-2677
90Greens/Star-19
91PrWill/ClBest-22
91PrWill/ProC-1440
Robertson, Jay
78Dunedin
80Syrac-6
Robertson, Jerry L.
69T-284R
70T-661
71OPC-651
71T-651
Robertson, Michael
86Jamestn-20
87StPete-5
88ArkTr/GS-20
89ArkTr/GS-21
Robertson, Richard P.
69OPC-16R
69T-16R
70OPC-229
70T-229
71MLB/St-263
71OPC-443
71T-443
72T-618
90Welland/Pucko-26
91Salem/ClBest-18
91Salem/ProC-948
Robertson, Roderick
(Rod)
86Cram/PCL-130
88Spartan/ProC-1034
88Spartan/Star-18
88Spartan/Star-2
89Clearw/Star-19
90Reading/Best-18
90Reading/ProC-1228
90Reading/Star-21
91Reading/LineD-515
91Reading/ProC-1376
Robertson, Shawn
91Spokane/ClBest-10
91Spokane/ProC-3961
Robertson, Sherry
50B-161
51B-95
52T-245
Robicheaux, Randy
86Watertn-18
Robidoux, Billy Jo
83Beloit/LF-21
86D-515
86F-652M
86F/Up-U97
86Pol/Brew-13
86Sf-178R
86Sf/Rook-28
86T/Tr-92T
87D-240
87D/OD-51
87F-356
87Pol/Brew-13
87T-401
87T/GlossRk-13
87T/St-202
88Denver/CMC-13
88Denver/ProC-1267
88S-334
89Coke/WS-23
90T/TVRSox-27
90UD/Ext-782
Robinette, Gary
81AppFx-22
Robinson, Aaron
47HomogBond-40
47TipTop
49B-133
50B-95
51B-142
53Mother-6
D305
Robinson, Bill H.
67T-442R
68T-337
68T/3D
69MB-234
69MLB/St-78
69T-313
69T/St-207
70MLB/St-249
70OPC-23
70T-23
72MB-290
73OPC-37
73T-37
74OPC-174
74T-174
74T/St-78
75OPC-501
75T-501
75T/M-501
76OPC-137
76SSPC-577
76T-137
77BurgChef-183
77T-335
78OPC-128
78T-455
79OPC-336
79T-637
80OPC-138
80T-264
81D-137
81F-373
81T-51
82D-402
82F-494
82T-543
82T/Tr-100T
83F-170
83T-754
85Pol/MetYank-M1CO
88Kahn/Mets-28CO
88QuadC/GS-8
89Kahn/Mets-28CO
90Swell/Great-114
Robinson, Bobby
86Negro/Frit-65
91Negro/Lewis-12
Robinson, Brad
88Greens/ProC-1557
Robinson, Brett
88Peoria/Ko-27
89Peoria/Ko-7P
Robinson, Brian
85Cedar-19
86Vermont-16
87Cedar-17
Robinson, Brooks
57T-328
58T-307
59T-439
60L-27
60T-28
61P-75
61T-10
61T-572AS
61T/Dice-14
61T/St-104
62J-29
62P-29
62P/Can-29
62Salada-40
62Shirriff-40
62T-45
62T-468AS
62T/bucks
62T/St-8
63Bz-30
63Exh
63F-4
63J-59
63P-59
63Salada-53
63T-345
63T/SO
64Bz-30
64T-230
64T/Coins-125AS
64T/Coins-18
64T/S-50
64T/St-21
64T/SU
64Wheat/St-39
65Bz-30
65OldLond-35
65OPC-150
65OPC-1LL
65OPC-5LL
65T-150
65T-1LL
65T-5LL
65T/trans-65
66Bz-34
66T-390
66T/RO-90
67Bz-34
67OPC-1M
67OPC/PI-3
67T-1M
67T-531CL
67T-600
67T/PI-3
68Bz-8
68Coke
68Dexter-65
68OPC-20
68T-20
68T-365AS
68T-530M
68T/G-9
69MB-235
69MLB/St-8
69MLBPA/Pin-25
69NTF
69OPC/DE-18
69T-421AS
69T-504CL
69T-550
69T/DE-1
69T/S-3
69T/St-129
69Trans-13
70K-21
70MLB/St-154
70OPC-230
70OPC-455AS
70T-230
70T-455AS
71Bz
71Bz/Test-22
71MD
71MLB/St-309
71MLB/St-571
71OPC-300
71OPC-331WS
71T-300
71T-331WS
71T/Coins-114
71T/GM-9
71T/S
71T/tatt-1
71T/tatt-1a
72MB-291
72OPC-222ALCS
72OPC-498KP
72T-222ALCS
72T-498KP
72T-550
73JP
73OPC-90
73T-90
73T/Comics-16
73T/Lids-41
73T/PinUps-16
74Laugh/ASG-66
74OPC-160
74OPC-334AS
74T-160
74T-334AS
74T/DE-25
74T/St-129
75Ho-144
75K-18
75OPC-202MV
75OPC-50
75T-202MV
75T-50
75T/M-202MV
75T/M-50
76Crane-48
76Ho-36
76Ho/Twink-36
76Laugh/Jub-11
76MSA/Disc
76OPC-95
76SSPC-392
76T-95
77BurgChef-43
77T-285
78OPC-239RB
78T-4RB
78TCMA-190
80Pac/Leg-54
82CJ-13
82KMart-5
83Kaline-69M

83MLBPA/Pin-16
84West/1-7
86Sf/Dec-45
87KMart-9
87Leaf/SpecOlym-H9
87Nestle/DT-14
88Pac/Leg-3
89Kahn/Coop-9
89Pac/Leg-129
89Swell-134
89T/LJN-37
90BBWit-17
90MSA/AGFA-13
90Pac/Legend-102
91Crown/Orio-385
91Swell/Great-146
Exh47

Robinson, Bruce
79Colum-16
79T-711R
80Colum-15
81T-424R
84Cram/PCL-73

Robinson, Chris
91Boise/ClBest-27
91Boise/ProC-3878

Robinson, Clyde
E254
W501-96

Robinson, Craig
74OPC-23
74T-23
74T/Tr-23T
75OPC-367
75T-367
75T/M-367
76SSPC-12
81Richm-23
82Richm-29
83Richm-24

Robinson, Darryl
88AppFx/ProC-144
88MidwLAS/GS-38
89AppFx/ProC-860
90BBCity/Star-21
91London/LineD-416
91Memphis/ProC-663

Robinson, David
(Admiral)
91Arena-5

Robinson, David T.
71OPC-262R
71T-262R
88SanDiegoSt-15

Robinson, Dewey
80T-664R
81T-487
82T-176
87Penin-7

Robinson, Don
79T-264
80T-719
81D-375
81F-366
81OPC-163
81T-168
82F-495
82OPC-332
82T-332
83D-171
83F-319
83OPC-44
83T-44
83T/St-277
84D-532
84F-262
84Nes/792-616
84OPC-22
84T-616
85D-264
85F-475
85OPC-129
85T-537
86D-357
86F-621
86Leaf-159
86T-731
87D-608
87F-622
87OPC-387
87T-712
88D-573
88F-95
88F/Mini-120
88F/St-131
88F/TL-31
88Mother/Giants-22
88S-619
88Sf-90
88T-52
88T/St-94
89B-463
89D-571
89D/Best-191
89F-342
89F/BBAS-36
89Mother/Giants-22
89Panini/St-211
89S-440
89T-473
89T/St-86
89UD-523
90D-258
90F-70
90Leaf/II-267
90Mother/Giant-20
90OPC-217
90PublInt/St-81
90S-112
90T-217
90T/Big-193
90T/St-84
90UD-616
91B-384SLUG
91B-619
91D-581
91F-272
91F/Ultra-327
91Leaf/I-188
91Mother/Giant-20
91OPC-104
91Panini/FrSt-73
91Panini/St-74
91PG&E-21
91Pulaski/ClBest-13
91Pulaski/ProC-4020
91S-639
91SFExam/Giant-13
91T-104
91T/StClub/I-167
91UD-402
91UD/SilSlug-SS16
92T-373

Robinson, Dwight
91Pittsfld/ClBest-3
91Pittsfld/ProC-3432

Robinson, Earl
60DF-20
61T-343
62T-272
78TCMA-81
90Target-674
91Crown/Orio-386

Robinson, Eli
91Princet/ClBest-17
91Princet/ProC-3524

Robinson, Emmett
86Kinston-19

Robinson, Floyd
62Salada-214
62Shirriff-214
62T-454
62T/bucks
62T/St-29
63Bz-24
63J-39
63P-39
63T-2LL
63T-405
63T/SO
64Bz-24
64T-195
64T/Coins-39
64T/St-18
64T/SU
65T-345
66OPC-8
66T-199M
66T-8
66T/RO-94
67OPC-120
67T-120
68T-404
71T/tatt-11
Exh47

Robinson, Frank
56Kahn
57Kahn
57Sohio/Reds-17
57Swift-16
57T-35
58Kahn
58T-285
58T-386M
58T-484AS
59Armour-14
59HRDerby-16
59Kahn
59T-435
60Bz-29
60Kahn
60MacGregor-20
60T-352M
60T-490
60T/tatt-46
61Bz-31
61Kahn
61P-182
61T-25M
61T-360
61T-581AS
61T/Dice-15
61T/St-24
62Bz
62J-122
62Kahn
62P-122
62P/Can-122
62Salada-165
62Shirriff-165
62T-350
62T-396AS
62T-54LL
62T/bucks
62T/St-121
63Bz-31
63Exh
63FrBauer-22
63J-131
63Kahn
63P-131
63Salada-29
63T-1LL
63T-3LL
63T-400
63T/SO
64Bz-31
64Kahn
64T-260
64T/Coins-154AS
64T/Coins-37
64T/S-29
64T/St-15
64T/SU
64T/tatt
65Bz-31
65Kahn
65OldLond-17
65OPC-120
65T-120
65T/E-22
65T/trans-66
66Bz-32
66T-219LL
66T-310
66T/RO-3
67Bz-32
67OPC-100
67OPC-1M
67OPC-62CL
67OPC/PI-19
67T-62CL
67T-100
67T-1M
67T-239LL
67T-241LL
67T-243LL
67T/PI-19
67T/Test/SU-3
68Bz-3
68Coke
68Dexter-66
68OPC-2LL
68OPC-4LL
68T-2LL
68T-373AS
68T-4LL
68T-500
68T-530M
68T/G-7
68T/Post-24
69MB-236
69MLB/St-9
69MLBPA/Pin-26
69NTF
69T-250
69T/decal
69T/S
69T/St-130
69Trans-16
70K-15
70MB-23
70MLB/St-155
70OPC-463AS
70T-463AS
70T-700
70T/PI-12
70T/S-37
70Trans-12
71Bz/Test-2
71K-15
71MD
71MLB/St-310
71MLB/St-572
71OPC-329WS
71OPC-63LL
71OPC-640
71T-329WS
71T-63LL
71T-640
71T/Coins-50WS
72MB-292
72OPC-100
72OPC-228WS
72OPC-88LL
72T-100
72T-228WS
72T-754TR
72T-88LL
73OPC-175
73T-175
73T/Lids-42
74Laugh/ASG-59
74OPC-55
74T-55
74T/DE-66
74T/St-145
75OPC-199MV
75OPC-204MV
75OPC-331MG
75OPC-580
75T-199MV
75T-204MV
75T-331MG
75T-580
75T/M-199MV
75T/M-204MV
75T/M-331MG
75T/M-580
76Crane-49
76Laugh/Jub-5
76MSA/Disc
76SSPC-525
76T-477MG
77T-18MG
78RochR
78TCMA-140
80Pac/Leg-123
80Laugh/3/4/5-23
82D-424MG
82KMart-9
83D-564MG
83D-648M
83D/HOF-19
83Mother/Giants-1
83T-576MG
83T/St-4
84D/Champs-43
84Nes/792-171MG
84T-171MG
85CircK-4
85D/HOF-8
85Woolwth-29
86BLChew-4
86Sf/Dec-41
86T-404TBC
87French-20CO
87KMart-10
87Nestle/DT-16
88French-20MG
88T/Tr-96MG
89French-20
89Smok/Angels-8
89Smok/Dodg-24
89T-774MG
90BBWit-48
90OPC-381MG
90T-381MG
90Target-675
91Crown/Orio-388
91OPC-639MG
91T-639MG
Exh47

Robinson, Henry
86FtMyr-22

Robinson, Humberto
55T-182
59T-366
60L-70
60T-416

Robinson, Jackie R.
47Bond/JR-1—13
47HomogBond-41
48L-79
48Swell-3
49B-50
49Eureka-48
50B-22
52BR
52StarCal/L-79G
52T-312
53Exh/Can-19
53T-1
54NYJour
54T-10
55Gol/Dodg-25
55T-50
55T/DH-25
56T-30
56T/Hocus-A14
56T/Pin-51
60NuCard-53
61NuCard-428
72T/Test-4
74Laugh/ASG-49
76Laugh/Jub-26
79TCMA-291
80Pac/Leg-15
80Laugh/FFeat-18
80SSPC/HOF
83D/HOF-6
83MLBPA/Pin-31
84West/1-1
86Negro/Frit-11
86Negro/Frit-25
86Sf/Dec-28
87Nestle/DT-24
88Pac/Leg-40
89B/I-9
89HOF/St-12
89Rini/Dodg-18
89Rini/Dodg-27
89Smok/Dodg-25
89USPS-3
90BBWit-52
90Target-676
91T/Arc53-1
D302-Set
D305
Exh47
PM10/Sm-160—166
R346-36
Rawl

Robinson, Jeffrey D.
(Jeff)
84F/X-U100
84T/Tr-101T
85D-201
85F-620
85OPC-5
85T-592
86Mother/Giants-15
86T/Tr-93T
87D-559
87F-283
87Mother/SFG-25
87T-389
88D-558
88D/Best-241
88OPC-244
88S-439
88T-244
88T/Big-123
88T/St-133
89B-410
89D-370
89D/Best-129
89F-220
89F/LL-33

89OPC-351
89Panini/St-164
89S-309
89T-681
89T/Big-45
89T/St-129
89UD-332
89VFJuice-49
90B-427
90D-134
90F-479
90Leaf/II-412
90OPC-723
90PubInt/St-164
90S/NWest-23
90T-723
90T/Tr-103T
90T/TVYank-19
90UD-403
91B-193
91D-291
91F-678
91Leaf/II-307
91OPC-19
91S-192
91Smok/Angel-18
91T-19
91T/StClub/II-542
91T/Tr-99T
92D/I-59
92S/I-274
92T-137

Robinson, Jeffrey M.
(Jeff)
85Cram/PCL-184
86Nashvl-22
87D/Rook-13
87F/Up-U105
87Sf/Rook-47
87T/Tr-104T
88D-296
88F-68
88Pep/T-44
88Pol/T-10
88S-549
88T-449
89B-97
89Classic-93
89D-18DK
89D-470
89D/DKsuper-18DK
89F-143
89Mara/Tigers-44
89OPC-267
89Panini/St-335
89Pol/Tigers-44
89S-284
89S/HotStar-34
89S/YS/II-8
89Sf-193
89T-267
89T/Big-274
89UD-472
90CokeK/Tiger-19
90D-417
90F-614
90Leaf/II-429
90OPC-42
90PubInt/St-481
90PubInt/St-603
90S-333
90T-42
90T/St-284
90UD-552
91B-90
91Crown/Orio-500
91D-245
91F-349
91Leaf/II-464
91OPC-766
91S-129
91T-766
91T/StClub/II-441
91T/Tr-100T
91UD-676
91UD/Ext-796
92D/I-77
92S/I-186
92UD-320

Robinson, Jerry
63T-466R

Robinson, Jim
78Newar
79BurlB-4

Robinson, Jim
90PeoriaUp/Team-U2
91Geneva/ClBest-16
91Geneva/ProC-4222

Robinson, Ken
91MedHat/ProC-4099

Robinson, Kevin
87Erie-20
88Hamil/ProC-1730

Robinson, Lee
74Albuq/Team-16

Robinson, M.C.
N172

Robinson, Marteese
88Madis-20
89Modesto/Cal-285
90Foil/Best-280

Robinson, Mike
83Erie-24
85Spring-25
86ArkTr-20
87ArkTr-2
88ArkTr/GS-19
88Louisvl-42

Robinson, Napoleon
89Salem/Team-27
90Bakers/Cal-233
91Greenvl/ClBest-4
91Greenvl/LineD-215
91Greenvl/ProC-2998

Robinson, Randall
87CharWh-27

Robinson, Randy
83Butte-9

Robinson, Raul
91Macon/ClBest-26
91Macon/ProC-879

Robinson, Ron
81Cedar-6
82Water-9
84Wichita/Rock-8
85D-649
85F-650
86D-121
86F-190
86T-442
86TexGold-33
87D-310
87F-212
87F/GameWin-38
87F/Mini-93
87Kahn-33
87T-119
88D-166
88D/Best-308
88F-247
88F/Mini-75
88Kahn/Reds-33
88OPC-342
88S-476
88T-517
89B-303
89D-308
89F-169
89Kahn/Reds-33
89OPC-16
89S-559
89T-16
89T/Big-132
89UD-187
90Brewer/MillB-21
90CedarDG/Best-14
90D-553
90F-431
90Leaf/II-467
90OPC-604
90S-495
90T-604
90T/Tr-104T
91B-39
91Brewer/MillB-22
91D-254
91F-595
91Leaf/I-14
91Leaf/Stud-75
91OPC-313
91Pol/Brew-20
91S-517
91T-313
91T/StClub/I-296
91UD-620
92F-187
92UD-198

Robinson, Scott
90Billings/ProC-3220
91Cedar/ClBest-11
91Cedar/ProC-2718

Robinson, Terry
91Pocatel/ProC-3799

Robinson, Wilbert
50Callahan
60F-33
63Bz-27
72F/FFeat-10
72Laugh/GF-30
80SSPC/HOF
89HOF/St-86
89Smok/Dodg-104
90Target-677A
D329-144
D350/2-144
E121/120
E210-43
M101/4-144
M101/5-144
N142
N172/BC
N300/SC
N690
W515-53
W575

Robinson, William E.
(Eddie)
49Royal-22
50B-18
51B-88
51T/RB-51
52B-77
52BR
52Hawth/Pin-7
52NTea
52RM-AL18
52Royal
52StarCal/L-73C
52T-32
53B/BW-20
53Mother-59
53RM-AL11
53T-73
54B-193
54NYJour
54T-62
55B-153
56T-302
57T-238
60T-455C
79TCMA-283
91Crown/Orio-387
91T/Arc53-73
Exh47

Robinson, William H.
N172
N284
N370
Scrapps

Robitaille, Martin
88James/ProC-1921

Robledo, Nilson
90SoBend/ClBest-24
91Single/ClBest-146
91SoBend/ProC-2860

Robles, Gabriel
(Gabby)
86Kinston-20
87WinSalem-18

Robles, Greg
82Idaho-21
83Madis/LF-22
84Albany-25

Robles, Javier
91BurlInd/ProC-3309

Robles, Jorge
89Wausau/GS-19
90Penin/Star-18

Robles, Josman
90Durham/Team-18

Robles, Rafael
69T-592R
70T-573R
71OPC-408
71T-408

Robles, Ruben
83Tucson-26
84Cram/PCL-66

Robles, Sergio
73OPC-601R
73T-601R
74OPC-603R
74T-603R
90Target-678B
91Crown/Orio-389

Robles, Scott
90Kenosha/Best-25
90Kenosha/ProC-2294
90Kenosha/Star-21

Robles, Silvano
75AppFx
76AppFx
76Clinton

Robson, Gary
88Beloit/GS-2
89Beloit/I/Star-26M

Robson, Tom
79Wausau-16
80Ashvl-2
87Smok/R-21CO
89Smok/R-26CO
90Mother/Rang-27M
91Mother/Rang-28CO

Roby, Ellis
86Sumter-22
87Durham-10
88Durham/Star-18
89Greenvl/ProC-1159
89Greenvl/Star-20
89Greenvl/Best-9

Roca, Gilbert
86Macon-21
87Salem-16
88Harris/ProC-851
89Jacks/GS-17
90T/TVMets-55

Rocco, Michael
(Mickey)
47Centen-24
48Sommer-26
49Sommer-14

Roche, Rod
86VeroB-20
87Bakers-17

Roche, Steve
80Wausau-7
81Chatt-8
82Chatt-15
82Watlo/C-10

Roche, Tim
77Clinton
78LodiD

Roche, Titi
88LitFalls/Pucko-11
89Star/Wax-24
89StLucie/Star-21

Rochelli, Lou
90Target-1055

Rochford, Mike
84Pawtu-21
86Pawtu-18
87Pawtu-9
87Pawtu/TCMA-9
88Pawtu/CMC-2
88Pawtu/ProC-447
89F-650M
89Pawtu/CMC-6
89Pawtu/Dunkin-26
89Pawtu/ProC-700
90B-264
90Pawtu/CMC-3
90Pawtu/ProC-460
90T/TVRSox-16
90UD-694
91S-739RP

Rock, Bob
77Charl
78Salem
80Buffa-12
81Buffa-10

Rock, Royal
C46-10
E254

Rockenfeld, Isaac B.
T206
T213/brown

Rockett, Pat
78T-502
79Richm-20
80Syrac-5

Rockey, Jim
86Durham-23

Rockman, Marv
88Gaston/ProC-995
89Tulsa/GS-22
89Tulsa/Team-20
90Tulsa/ProC-1152

Rockne, Knute
33SK-35

Rockweiler, Dean
86Jamestn-21

Rodas, Richard
(Rick)
82Albuq-9
83Albuq-6
84Cram/PCL-147
84Pol/Dodg-56
85Cram/PCL-174
90Target-678

Roddy, Phil
77Ashvl

Rode, Don
48Sommer-30M

Rodgers, Andre
57T-377
59T-216
60L-42
60T-431
61P-153
61T-183
62J-185
62P-185
62P/Can-185
62Salada-155A
62Salada-155B
62Shirriff-155
62T-477
63J-173
63P-173
63T-193
64T-336
65T-536
66EH-16
66T-592
67T-554
78TCMA-51

Rodgers, Charlie
91Miami/ClBest-11

Rodgers, Darrell
85Everett/II/Cram-15
86Fresno/Smok-15
88MidwLAS/GS-13
89Chatt/Best-15
89Chatt/GS-21

Rodgers, Doc
91Princet/ProC-3532CO

Rodgers, Dirk
79WHave-22M

Rodgers, Paul
87Myrtle-30
88Dunedin/Star-14
89Dunedin/Star-13
90Knoxvl/Best-12
90Knoxvl/ProC-1255
90Knoxvl/Star-15
91Knoxvl/LineD-364
91Knoxvl/ProC-1782
91Single/ClBest-3

Rodgers, Robert L.
(Buck)
62T-431
62T/St-68
63Bz-2
63F-20
63J-31
63P-31
63T-280
63T/SO
64T-426
64T-61M
65T-342
65T/trans-27
66T-462
67T-281
68T-433
69MB-237
69MLB/St-27
69OPC-157
69T-157
69T/St-149
73OPC-49CO
73T-49CO
74OPC-447CO
74T-447CO
78TCMA-63

81D-327MG
81T-668MG
82D-232MG
82Pol/Brew-37MG
84Indianap-2MG
85Indianap-36MG
85T/Tr-95T
86OPC-141MG
86Provigo-3MG
86T-171MG
87OPC-293MG
87T-293MG
88OPC-134MG
88T-504MG
89OPC-193MG
89T-474MG
90ElPasoATG/Team-19
90OPC-81MG
90T-81MG
91OPC-321MG
91T-321MG
92T-21MG
Exh47

Rodgers, Tim
83Kinston/Team-20
84Syrac-17
86Tulsa-7
87OKCty-17

Rodgers, William
16FleischBrd-77

Rodiles, Jose
85FtMyr-30
87ColumAst-18

Rodiles, Jose
87ColAst/ProC-18

Rodiles, Steve
85Iowa-36

Rodriguez, A.
86Ashvl-23

Rodriguez, Abimael
90James/Pucko-4
91Sumter/ClBest-19
91Sumter/ProC-2344

Rodriguez, Ahmed
89Johnson/Star-18
89Savan/ProC-353
90Hamil/Best-17
90Hamil/Star-20
91Spring/ClBest-22
91Spring/ProC-750

Rodriguez, Al
91Everett/ClBest-3
91Everett/ProC-3923

Rodriguez, Alex
75BurlB

Rodriguez, Andres
90PrWill/Team-22
91FtLaud/ClBest-23
91FtLaud/ProC-2436

Rodriguez, Andy
75SanAn

Rodriguez, Angel
85Beloit-10
87Stockton-10
88ElPaso/Best-23
88Stockton/Cal-198
88Stockton/ProC-742

Rodriguez, Anthony
91Kissim/ProC-4189

Rodriguez, Antonio H.
(Hector)
52Hawth/Pin-8
53B/Col-98

Rodriguez, Armando
90Pulaski/Best-24
90Pulaski/ProC-3109
91Idaho/ProC-4340

Rodriguez, Aurelio
69JB
69T-653
70MLB/St-179
70OPC-228
70T-228
71MLB/St-405
71OPC-464
71T-464
71T/Coins-124
72MB-293
72OPC-319
72T-319
72T/Cloth-27
73OPC-218
73T-218
74OPC-72
74T-72
74T/St-179
75OPC-221
75T-221
75T/M-221
76OPC-267
76SSPC-366
76T-267
77BurgChef-93
77Ho-120
77OPC-136
77T-574
78BK/T-14
78OPC-64
78T-342
79OPC-83
79T-176
80OPC-245
80T-468
81Detroit-47
81F-105
81T-34
82F-53
82OPC/Post-10
82T-334
82T/Tr-101T
83D-369
83F-249
83T-758
83T/Tr-97T
84Nes/792-269
84T-269
88ColoSp/CMC-25
88ColoSp/ProC-1536
90Toledo/CMC-25CO
90Toledo/ProC-166CO
91Crown/Orio-390

Rodriguez, Beto
90Johnson/Star-21
91Spring/ClBest-23
91Spring/ProC-751

Rodriguez, Buena
89James/ProC-2131
90Rockford/ProC-2705

Rodriguez, Carlos
88FtLaud/Star-18
89FtLaud/Star-21
90Albany/ProC-1178
90Albany/Star-14
90ColClip/ProC-683
90T/TVYank-58
91ColClip/LineD-116
91ColClip/ProC-604
91D/Rook-41
92S/I-411
92T/91Debut-149
92UD-77TP

Rodriguez, Chris
91Hunting/ClBest-20
91Hunting/ProC-3333

Rodriguez, Dave
83Tacom-30B

Rodriguez, Ed
84Cram/PCL-240
85Cram/PCL-108

Rodriguez, Eddie
83Peor/LF-28C
86QuadC-28
87QuadC-18
88QuadC/GS-1MG
89Bristol/Star-23
89QuadC/Best-2
89QuadC/GS-1

Rodriguez, Eddy
90Niagara/Pucko-23
91Fayette/ClBest-8
91Fayette/ProC-1168

Rodriguez, Edgar
87QuadC-3
88QuadC/GS-7
89PalmSp/Cal-41
89PalmSp/ProC-465
91PalmSp/ProC-2032

Rodriguez, Eduardo
74OPC-171
74T-171
75OPC-582
75T-582
75T/M-582
76OPC-92
76SSPC-228
76T-92
77BurgChef-86
77T-361
78T-623
79T-108
80T-273
81Holyo-1

Rodriguez, Edwin
83Colum-18
86LasVegas-13
87LasVegas-19

Rodriguez, Eligio
88Geneva/ProC-1646

Rodriguez, Eliseo
(Ellie)
69OPC-49R
69T-49R
70OPC-402
70T-402
71MLB/St-449
71OPC-344
71T-344
71T/Coins-124
72MB-294
72OPC-421
72T-421
73K-2
73OPC-45
73T-45
73T/Lids-43
74OPC-405
74T-405
74T/St-146
75Ho-34
75Ho/Twink-34
75OPC-285
75T-285
75T/M-285
76OPC-512
76SSPC-193
76T-512
77T-448
90Target-679

Rodriguez, Ernesto
91Myrtle/ClBest-22
91Myrtle/ProC-2956
91SALAS/ProC-SAL39
91Single/ClBest-40

Rodriguez, Ernie
85Bend/Cram-20
88Butte-28
89Butte/SP-28

Rodriguez, F. Boi
87Jamestn-7
88WPalmB/Star-21
89Jaxvl/Best-16
89Jaxvl/ProC-177
90Jaxvl/Best-8
91Greenvl/ClBest-24
91Greenvl/LineD-216

Rodriguez, Felix
91Kissim/ProC-4190

Rodriguez, Frankie
91Classic/DP-x
91Elmira/ClBest-14
91Elmira/ProC-3279
91FrRow/DP-1
91FrRow/DP-FR1
91FrRow/DP-FR2
91FrRow/DP-FR3
91FrRow/DP-FR4
91FrRow/DP-FR5
91UD/FinalEd-21F

Rodriguez, Gabriel
88FtLaud/Star-19
88Peoria/Ko-28
89FtLaud/Star-22
89Star/Wax-80
90Geneva/Star-21
90Osceola/Star-25

Rodriguez, Hector
91Augusta/ClBest-18
91Augusta/ProC-814

Rodriguez, Henry
89VeroB/Star-23
91Albuq/LineD-19
91Albuq/ProC-1156
91B-185
91Classic/II-T51
91F/Ultra-386MLP
91Leaf/GRook-BC8
91UD-21SR
92F-661
92T-656R

Rodriguez, Iggy
86WPalmB-25

Rodriguez, Ivan
78BurlB
80Holyo-6
81Vanco-8

Rodriguez, Ivan
(Pudge)
89Gaston/ProC-1006
89Gaston/Star-20
89SALAS/GS-26
90CharlR/Star-22
90FSLAS/Star-41
91B-272
91Classic/II-T82
91Classic/III-78
91D/Rook-33
91F/UltraUp-U58
91F/Up-U62
91S/RookTr-82T
91Single/ClBest-136
91T/Tr-101T
91Tulsa/LineD-592
91Tulsa/ProC-2776
91UD/FinalEd-55F
92Classic/I-77
92D/I-289
92F-316
92F/RookSIns-20
92S/100RisSt-77
92S/II-700
92T-78
92T/91Debut-150
92UD-245

Rodriguez, Jonis
84Greens-20

Rodriguez, Jose
79Wisco-21
81Buffa-13
82Jacks-8
82Portl-21
83LynnP-22
83StPete-23
86ArkTr-21
86BurlEx-18
87AppFx-20
89Bristol/Star-24
89Princet/Star-17

Rodriguez, Juan
77DaytB

Rodriguez, Luis E.
80OkCty
81OkCty/TCMA-16
82OkCty-16

Rodriguez, Manuel
90Johnson/Star-22
91Johnson/ClBest-24
91Johnson/ProC-3976

Rodriguez, Miguel
80Utica-32

Rodriguez, Mike
79Ogden/TCMA-4

Rodriguez, Ramon
85Spokane/Cram-20
86CharRain-22

Rodriguez, Richard
77Charl

Rodriguez, Ricardo
86Tacom-19
88ColoSp/CMC-8
88ColoSp/ProC-1549
89Vanco/CMC-8
89Vanco/ProC-580
91Phoenix/LineD-392
91Phoenix/ProC-65

Rodriguez, Richard
89AubAs/ProC-19
91Pocatel/ProC-3801CO

Rodriguez, Richard A.
(Rich)
84LitFalls-25
86Lynch-19
87Lynch-19
88F-293
88F/Up-U24
88Jacks/GS-13
88T-166
89Wichita/Rock-29LHP
90LasVegas/CMC-9
90LasVegas/ProC-123
91D-769
91F-541
91Leaf/II-448
91OPC-573
91Padre/MagRal-16
91S-593
91T-573
91T/90Debut-132
91T/StClub/II-565
91UD-640
92D/I-388
92F-619
92S/I-149
92T-462
92UD-568

Rodriguez, Rigo
85Beaum-10

Rodriguez, Roberto
68T-199R
69T-358R
71MLB/St-44
71OPC-424
71T-424

Rodriguez, Roman
89Princet/Star-18
90Augusta/ProC-2474
91Salem/ClBest-7
91Salem/ProC-961

Rodriguez, Rosario
88Greens/ProC-1567
90CedarDG/Best-24
90Nashvl/ProC-231
90T/89Debut-103
91BuffB/LineD-44
91BuffB/ProC-541
91OPC-688
91S-373RP
91T-688
92D/II-748
92F-565

Rodriguez, Ruben
83AlexD-26
85Nashua-21
86Nashua-23
87SLCity/Taco-7CO
87Vanco-23
89Boise/ProC-1992
89Denver/CMC-18
89Denver/ProC-34
90Erie/Star-21
91London/LineD-396
91London/ProC-1881

Rodriguez, Steve
91T/Tr-102T

Rodriguez, Tomas
88Billings/ProC-1816
89Billings/ProC-2044

Rodriguez, Tony
91Elmira/ClBest-13
91Elmira/ProC-3280

Rodriguez, Victor
82RochR-16
85Cram/PCL-101
85D-535
87Louisvl-26
88Portl/CMC-20
88Portl/ProC-649
89AAA/ProC-40
89Portl/CMC-17
89Portl/ProC-210
90Portl/CMC-12
90Portl/ProC-188
91Crown/Orio-391
91Portl/LineD-416
91Portl/ProC-1573

Roe, Preacher
47TipTop
49B-162
50B-167
50Drake-1
51B-118
51T/RB-16
52B-168
52BR
52Dix
52NTea
52StarCal/L-79F
52T-66
52Wheat
53B/BW-26
53Dix
53Exh/Can-1
53NB
53T-254
54B-218
54Dix

54NYJour
54T-14
55B-216
79TCMA-145
79TCMA-239
89Rini/Dodg-33
89Smok/Dodg-56
90Target-680
91T/Arc53-254
Exh47
PM10/Sm-167
Roe, Rocky
88TM/Umpire-42
89TM/Umpire-40
90TM/Umpire-38
Roebuck, Ed
52Park-75
53Exh/Can-41
55Gol/Dodg-26
55T-195
56T-58
58T-435
60BB-13
60T-519
61BB-37
61P-70
61T-6
61T/St-32
62BB-37
62T-535
63T-295
64PhilBull-19
64T-187
64T/Coins-20
64T/St-35
64T/SU
65OPC-52
65T-52
78TCMA-165
90Target-681
Roebuck, Joe
89Helena/SP-13
90Erie/Star-22
Roebuck, Ron
86Ashvl-24
86AubAs-20
Roebuck, Scott
83Wausau/LF-20
Roeder, Jack
82Wausau-3
Roeder, Steve
90Welland/Pucko-27
91Welland/ClBest-19
Roenicke, Gary
76SSPC-338
80T-568
81D-116
81F-187
81OPC-37
81T-37
82D-509
82F-177
82T-204
83D-27
83F-71
83OPC-382
83T-605
84D-392
84F-18
84Nes/792-372
84OPC-372
84T-372
84T/St-205
85D-123
85F-188
85OPC-109
85T-109
86D-472
86F-285
86F/Up-U98
86OPC-183
86T-494
86T/Tr-94T
87D/OD-47
87OPC-283
87Smok/Atl-23
87T-683
87T/Tr-105T
88Panini/St-252
88S-482
88T-523
91Crown/Orio-392
91Pac/SenLg-104
91Pac/SenLg-85
Roenicke, Ron
78LodiD
80Albuq-6
81Albuq/TCMA-9
82F-19
82Pol/Dodg-40
82T-681R
83D-327
83F-217
83Pol/Dodg-40
83T-113
84Cram/PCL-237
84D-484
84F-618
84Nes/792-647
84T-647
86F/Up-U99
86T-63
87D-412
87F-182
87Phill/TastyK-17
87T-136
87T-329
88Nashvl/CMC-21
88Nashvl/ProC-475
88Nashvl/Team-20
88S-566
88T-783
89OkCty/CMC-16
89OkCty/ProC-1519
90Target-682
91Pac/SenLg-106
91Pac/SenLg-85
91SanAn/ProC-2993CO
Roesch, John
77Newar
78Newar
Roesler, Mike
86Cedar/TCMA-8
87Tampa-5
88Nashvl/CMC-11
88Nashvl/ProC-492
89Nashvl/CMC-7
89Nashvl/ProC-1282
89Nashvl/Team-21
90BuffB/Team-21
90F-645
90OPC-203
90S-648
90T-203
90T/89Debut-104
91CaroMud/LineD-115
91CaroMud/ProC-1085
Roessler, Pat
90BirmB/Best-29CO
90BirmB/ProC-1399CO
91BirmB/LineD-75CO
91BirmB/ProC-1472CO
Roetter, Randy
82QuadC-28TR
88Wausau/GS-28TR
89Wmsprt/ProC-634TR
90Calgary/CMC-25TR
Roettger, Oscar F.L.
90Target-683
Roettger, Walter H.
(Wally)
31Exh/4-8
92Conlon/Sport-653
Rogaliner, Chris
90Niagara/Pucko-30TR
Rogalski, Wayne
86Ashvl-25
Rogan, Bullet
86Negro/Frit-32
90Negro/Star-29
Rogan, Pat
65T-486R
Rogascozv, Boris
89EastLDD/ProC-DD12
Rogell, William
33G-11
34DS-76
35BU-177
35G-1D
35G-2D
35G-6D
35G-7D
81Detroit-16
83Kaline-39MII
R313
R314
V353-11
V355-52
Rogers, Brad
88Batavia/ProC-1691
Rogers, Bryan
91Wmsprt/LineD-641
91Wmsprt/ProC-290
Rogers, Charlie
90Miami/I/Star-22
90Miami/I/Star-27
91Miami/ProC-407
91Single/ClBest-375
Rogers, Danny
87Sumter-22
90Niagara/Pucko-1
91Fayette/ClBest-22
91Fayette/ProC-1181
91Single/ClBest-379
Rogers, Darrell
88Cedar/ProC-1162
Rogers, Dennis
86Nashua-24MG
87Macon-24
Rogers, Doug
89Idaho/ProC-2027
Rogers, Dusty
86Tampa-17
87Cedar-11
Rogers, Jimmy
88Myrtle/ProC-1190
88SALAS/GS-22
89Knoxvl/Best-22
89Knoxvl/ProC-1133
89Knoxvl/Star-18
90Foil/Best-176
90Knoxvl/Best-2
90Knoxvl/ProC-1241
90Knoxvl/Star-16
91Knoxvl/LineD-365
91Knoxvl/ProC-1764
Rogers, Kenny
88Tulsa-28
89D/Best-315
89D/Rook-13
89Mother/R-21
89S/Tr-107
89Smok/R-27
89T/Tr-104T
90D-283
90F-311
90Leaf/II-311
90Mother/Rang-22
90OPC-683
90S-301
90S/100Ris-46
90S/YS/I-21
90Sf-216
90T-683
90T/89Debut-105
90T/JumboR-24
90ToysRUs-22
90UD-606
91B-290
91D-258
91F-299
91F/Ultra-353
91Leaf/I-105
91Mother/Rang-22
91OPC-332
91S-155
91T-332
91T/StClub/I-258
91UD-606
92D/I-368
92F-317
92S/I-101
92T-511
92UD-651
Rogers, Kevin
88Pocatel/ProC-2091
89Clinton/ProC-891
90AS/Cal-50
90Foil/Best-76
90SanJose/Best-24
90SanJose/Cal-51
90SanJose/ProC-2003
90SanJose/ProC-2172M
90SanJose/Star-19
91B-638
91Shrev/LineD-320
91Shrev/ProC-1823
91Single/ClBest-221
Rogers, Lee
90Target-684
Rogers, Mac
85Durham-9
86Durham-24
Rogers, Marte
85Elmira-19
Rogers, Packy
90Target-685
Rogers, Randy
78Tidew
83Ander-15
Rogers, Robbie
88Reno/Cal-283
Rogers, Steve
74OPC-169
74T-169
74T/DE-65
74T/St-59
75OPC-173
75T-173
75T/M-173
76Crane-50
76MSA/Disc
76OPC-71
76SSPC-349
76T-71
77BurgChef-159
77Ho-22
77OPC-153
77T-316
78OPC-9DP
78T-425
78Wiffle/Discs-62
79OPC-120
79T-235
80K-8
80OPC-271
80T-520
81D-330
81F-143
81F/St-57
81OPC-344
81OPC/Post-9
81T-725
81T/So-106
81T/St-190
82D-36
82F-205
82F/St-36
82Hygrade
82OPC-52
82OPC/Post-20
82PermaGr/AS-15
82T-605
82T/St-59
82Zeller-2
83D-18DK
83D-320
83F-294
83OPC-106AS
83OPC-111TL
83OPC-320
83Stuart-10
83T-111TL
83T-320
83T-405AS
83T-707LL
83T/St-208
83T/St-256
84D-219
84D/AAS-48
84F-284
84Nes/792-394AS
84Nes/792-708LL
84Nes/792-80
84OPC-394AS
84OPC-80
84Seven-20W
84Stuart-19
84Stuart-36AS
84T-394AS
84T-708LL
84T-80
84T/Gloss40-3
84T/St-182FOIL
84T/St-88
85D-219
85F-408
85Leaf-192
85OPC-205
85OPC/Post-11
85T-205
85T/St-89
Rogers, Stu
85BurlR-23
Rogers, Thomas
E121/120
W501-28
W575
Roggenburk, Garry
63T-386R
64T-258
66T-582
67T-429
68T-581
91Elmira/ClBest-28CO
91Elmira/ProC-3288
Rogodzinski, Mike
74OPC-492
74T-492
76SSPC-607
Rogon, Bullet
74Laugh/Black-19
Rogovin, Saul
52B-165
52RM-AL19
52T-159
52TipTop
53B/Col-75
54B-140
57T-129
91Crown/Orio-393
PM10/Sm-168
Rogozenski, Karl
83StPete-28
Rohan, Tony
85Newar-7
87Miami-9
88Miami/Star-22
Rohde, Brad
86Cram/PCL-112
86Wausau-20
Rohde, Dave
86AubAs-21
87Osceola-29
88ColAst/Best-11
89ColMud/Best-21
89ColMud/ProC-123
89ColMud/Star-20
89Star/Wax-2
89Tucson/JP-20
90B-75
90F/Up-U17
90Lennox-20
90Tucson/CMC-19
91B-558
91D-743
91Leaf/II-424
91Mother/Ast-18
91OPC-531
91S/100RisSt-69
91T-531
91T/90Debut-133
91T/StClub/I-137
91UD-662
Rohde, Dr. Richard
63FrBauer-21
Rohlfing, Wayne
79QuadC-6
Rohlof, Scott
86Visalia-17
Rohm, Dave
78Dunedin
Rohn, Andy
87Everett-7
Rohn, Dan
80Wichita-6
82Iowa-8
83Iowa-19
84Iowa-8
85IntLgAS-36
85Maine-22
86OhHenry-15
87Tacom-16
88OkCty/CMC-20
88OkCty/ProC-31
89OkCty/CMC-15
89OkCty/ProC-1530
91Pac/SenLg-21
Rohr, Les
68T-569R
91WIZMets-333
Rohr, William
67T-547R
68T-314R

Rohrmeier, Dan
88FSLAS/Star-48
88Tampa/Star-22
89Saraso/Star-21
90A&AASingle/ProC-70
90Tulsa/ProC-1169
91Tulsa/LineD-593
91Tulsa/ProC-2787
Rohrwild, Shawn
90Idaho/ProC-3266
91Macon/ClBest-9
91Macon/ProC-863
Roig, Tony
59DF
60DF-16
61Union
Rois, Luis
80GlenF/B-6
80GlenF/C-17
81GlenF-20
Rojas, Cookie
63T-221
64PhilBull-20
64T-448
65T-474
66OPC-170
66T-170
66T/RO-77
67T-595
68OPC-39
68T-39
69MB-238
69MLB/St-176
69T-507
69T/S-55
69T/St-77
69Trans-55
70MLB/St-142
70T-569
71MLB/St-427
71OPC-118
71T-118
72K-39
72MB-295
72OPC-415
72T-415
73OPC-188
73T-188
74K-42
74OPC-278
74T-278
74T/St-189
75Ho-2
75Ho/Twink-2
75OPC-169
75T-169
75T/M-169
76A&P/KC
76OPC-311
76SSPC-171
76T-311
77T-509
88Smok/Angels-1MG
88T/Tr-97MG
Rojas, Francisco
78Cedar
Rojas, Homar
85Tigres-17
87SanAn-21
88FSLAS/Star-19
88VeroB/Star-22
89SanAn/Best-21
Rojas, Jeff
85Visalia-18
Rojas, Luis
82WHave-24
Rojas, Melquiades
(Mel)
87BurlEx-27
89Jaxvl/Best-28
89Jaxvl/ProC-156
89SLAS-20
90B-108
90Indianap/ProC-302
90UD/Ext-772
91D-681
91F-245
91OPC-252
91OPC/Premier-101
91S-729RP
91S/Rook40-1
91T-252
91T/90Debut-134
91UD-357
92D/II-435
92F-490
92S/II-725
92T-583
92UD-683
Rojas, Mike
83Idaho-17
Rojas, Minnie
67OPC-104
67T-104
68T-305
69T-502
Rojas, Ricardo
89Wmsprt/Star-19
Rojas, Ricky
86FtMyr-23
87FtMyr-20
88EastLAS/ProC-36
88Vermont/ProC-959
90Foil/Best-73
90Wmsprt/Best-21
90Wmsprt/ProC-1058
90Wmsprt/Star-22
91Calgary/LineD-71
91Calgary/ProC-516
Rojas, Wilberto
90StCath/ProC-3478
Rojek, Stan
49B-135
49Eureka-171
49Royal-15
50B-86
51B-166
52B-137
52NTea
52T-163
90Target-686
PM10/Sm-169
Rokosz, Keith
77AppFx
Roland, James
63T-522R
64T-341
65OPC-171
65T-171
68T-276
69T-336
70T-719
71MLB/St-524
71OPC-642
71T-642
72OPC-464
72T-464
Roldan, Sal
88Miami/Star-21
88SLCity-27
Rolen, Steve
90Clinton/Best-25
90Clinton/ProC-2559
91SanJose/ClBest-11
91SanJose/ProC-20
91Single/ClBest-112
Rolfe, Robert
(Red)
34DS-104
34DS-29
34G-94
35BU-181
35BU-22
35G-8E
35G-9E
41DP-65MG
51B-319MG
52T-296MG
72F/FFeat-22
92Conlon/Sport-576
R314
V355-38
Rolland, Dave
86DayBe-23
87SanJose-15
Rollin, Rondal
82BirmB-13
84Evansvl-3
87BirmB/Best-7
87SLAS-2
90BirmDG/Best-29
Rollings, Bill
79Tulsa-23ow
Rollings, William R.
(Red)
33G-88
V354-40
Rollins, Patrick
(Pep)
91Utica/ClBest-28
91Utica/ProC-3250
Rollins, Rich
61Clover-23
62T-596R
63F-24
63J-4
63P-4
63Salada-49
63T-110
64Bz-10
64T-270
64T-8LL
64T/Coins-51
64T/St-52
64T/SU
65OPC-90
65T-90
66T-473
67OPC-98
67T-98
68Coke
68Dexter-67
68T-243
69MB-239
69MLB/St-98
69T-451
69T/St-229
70McDon-4
70MLB/St-276
70T-652
72MB-296
78TCMA-119
89Pac/Leg-169
Exh47
WG10-45
WG9-44
Rolls, David
88Eugene/Best-12
91SLCity/ProC-3213
Romagna, Randy
83Kinston/Team-21
85Kingst-14
86Kinston-21
Roman, Bob
77Spartan
Roman, Dan
87Oneonta-7
88FtLaud/Star-20
89FtLaud/Star-23
Roman, Jose
81Batavia-3
82Watlo/C-24
83Watlo/LF-12
84BuffB-8
85F-646
85Maine-13
86Maine-18
87BuffB-21
87Tidew-23
87Tidew/TCMA-29
88Tidew/CANDL-25
88Tidew/CMC-9
88Tidew/ProC-1601
Roman, Junior
77Watlo
78Wausau
Roman, Miguel
81Batavia-26
83Watlo/LF-13
86Water-20
87Wmsprt-13
88Jacks/GS-17
Roman, Ray
87Reading-11
88Reading/ProC-885
Roman, Vince
90Ashvl/ClBest-22
90AubAs/Best-10
90AubAs/ProC-3405
91Ashvl/ProC-580
Roman, William A.
65T-493R
Romanick, Ron
81Redwd-5
82Holyo-8
83Nashua-6
84F/X-101
84Smok/Cal-23
84T/Tr-102
85D-451
85F-309
85OPC-280
85Smok/Cal-11
85T-579
85T/St-231
86D-85
86F-166
86F/Mini-34
86F/St-100
86Leaf-81
86OPC-76
86Smok/Cal-11
86T-733
86T/St-180
87Colum-27
87Colum/Pol-21
87Colum/TCMA-8
87OPC-136
87T-136
88Stockton/Cal-176
88Stockton/ProC-731
Romano, James
52Park-73
90Target-1056
Romano, John
59T-138
60T-323
61Kahn
61T-5
61T/RO-19
61T/St-142
62Bz
62J-42
62Kahn
62P-42
62P/Can-42
62Salada-94
62Shirriff-94
62Sugar-7
62T-330
62T/bucks
62T/St-40
63Bz-18
63J-76
63P-76
63Salada-46
63Sugar-7
63T-392M
63T-72
63T/SO
64Kahn
64T-515
64T/Coins-9
64T/S-59
64T/St-48
64T/SU
64T/tatt
65OPC-17
65T-17
65T/E-10
66T-199M
66T-413
67OPC-196
67T-196
Romano, Scott
90Greens/Best-18
90Greens/ProC-2670
90Greens/Star-20
90Oneonta/ProC-3373
91Greens/ProC-3067
Romano, Thomas
82Madis-28
83Albany-19
84Cram/PCL-77
85Cram/PCL-131
86Indianap-7
87Indianap-14
88BuffB/CMC-13
88BuffB/Polar-4
88BuffB/ProC-1485
89BuffB/CMC-21
89BuffB/ProC-1670
Romanov, Vitalyi
89EastLDD/ProC-DD2
Romanovsky, Mike
86PalmSp-28
86PalmSp/Smok-10
87MidldA-22
Romay, Willie
89Belling/Legoe-28
91Penin/ClBest-17
91Penin/ProC-391
Rombard, Rich
91Fayette/ProC-1187CO
Romero, Al
83Nashua-19
85Cram/PCL-25
86Edmon-24
Romero, Brian
89Butte/SP-6
90A&AASingle/ProC-79
90Foil/Best-301
90Gaston/Best-7
90Gaston/ProC-2520
90Gaston/Star-20
90SALAS/Star-21
91Tulsa/LineD-594
91Tulsa/ProC-2772
Romero, Charlie
88QuadC/GS-24
89PalmSp/Cal-36
89PalmSp/ProC-470
Romero, Ed
76BurlB
77Holyo
79T-708R
79Vanco-17
80Vanco-13
81T-659R
82D-536
82Pol/Brew-11
82T-408
83D-584
83F-44
83Gard-15
83Pol/Brew-11
83T-271
84D-89
84F-212
84Gard-16
84Nes/792-146
84Pol/Brew-11
84T-146
85D-515
85F-593
85Gard-17
85Pol/Brew-11
85T-498
85ThomMc/Discs-18
86D-455
86F-500
86OPC-317
86T-317
86T/Tr-95T
87D-606
87F-42
87OPC-158
87T-675
88D-623
88D/RedSox/Bk-623
88F-362
88S-259
88T-37
89T/Tr-105T
89UD-40
90B-361
90CokeK/Tiger-20
91LasVegas/ProC-244
91LasVegas/LineD-291
Romero, Elbi
87Spartan-19
Romero, Elvis
86Cram/PCL-140
87Kenosha-23
Romero, Esmyel
82Redwd-9
Romero, Mandy
89Augusta/ProC-498
89SALAS/GS-10
90CLAS/CL-21
90Salem/Star-18
91CaroMud/LineD-103
91CaroMud/ProC-1090
Romero, Ramon
78Watlo
79Wausau-14
81AppFx-23
81Watlo-14
82AppFx-6
82Watlo-9
83BuffB-9
83GlenF-10
84BuffB-16
84Maine-1
85BuffB-11

85Polar/Ind-50
86D-495
86T-208
86Toledo-20
90HagersDG/Best-23
Romero, Ronaldo
89Gaston/ProC-1016
89Gaston/Star-21
90Gaston/Best-2
90Gaston/ProC-2521
90Gaston/Star-21
Romero, Scott
90Foil/Best-270
Romero, Tony
87Elmira/Black-21
87Elmira/Red-21
Romine, Kevin
84Pawtu-13
85Pawtu-11
86Pawtu-19
87Pawtu-4
87Pawtu/TCMA-18
87T-121
88D/RedSox/Bk-NEW
88F-363
88S-644
89F-98
89Pawtu/CMC-18
89Pawtu/Dunkin-16
89Pawtu/ProC-682
89S-541
89UD-524
90B-273
90D-476
90F-286
90Leaf/II-414
90Pep/RSox-19
90S-458
90T/Tr-105T
90T/TVRSox-33
90UD-441
91D-290
91F-113
91OPC-652
91S-116
91T-652
Rommel, Ed
21Exh-146
25Exh-111
26Exh-111
28Yueng-55
55B-239ump
87Conlon/2-19
E120
E210-55
R306
R316
V100
V61-9
W501-1
W501-102
W502-55
W515-5
W572
W573
W575
WG7-45
Rommell, Rick
80ElPaso-6
81Holyo-26
Romo, Enrique
78OPC-186
78T-278
79OPC-281
79T-548
80T-332
81D-255
81F-385
81OPC-28
81T-28
82D-59
82F-496
82T-106
83F-320
83T-226
Romo, Robert
87AubAs-16
Romo, Vicente
69T-267
70MLB/St-163
70OPC-191
70T-191
71MLB/St-329
71OPC-723
71T-723
72MB-297
72OPC-499
72T-499
73OPC-381
73T-381
74OPC-197SD
74T-197
75OPC-274
75T-274
75T/M-274
83F-218
83T-633
90Target-687
Romonosky, John
59T-267
60T-87
Ronan, Kernan
82Clinton-16
83Phoenix/BHN-10
84Shrev/FB-17
89PalmSp/Cal-62CO
89PalmSp/ProC-481
90PalmSp/Cal-229CO
90PalmSp/ProC-2595CO
91London/LineD-450CO
91MidldA/ProC-451CO
Ronan, Marc
88Alaska/Team-15
89Alaska/Team-15
90Hamil/Best-14
91Savan/ClBest-14
91Savan/ProC-1654
91Single/ClBest-5
Ronca, Joe
90Welland/Pucko-14
91Augusta/ClBest-22
91Augusta/ProC-821
Rondon, Alberto
76Dubuq
Rondon, Alfie
89Pac/SenLg-173
91Pac/SenLg-68
91Pac/SenLg-78
Rondon, Gilbert
89Pac/SenLg-196
90Kgsport/Star-27CO
91MedHat/ProC-4118CO
91Pac/SenLg-11
Rondon, Isidro
86Tampa-18
Ronk, Jeff
82Amari-7
83Beaum-14
84Beaum-25
Ronning, Al
52Park-49
53Exh/Can-56
Ronson, Tod
86Cram/PCL-21
87Clinton-8
88SanJose/Cal-128
88SanJose/ProC-126
89Salinas/Cal-143
89Salinas/ProC-1821
Roobarb
85Coke/WS
86Coke/WS
87Coke/WS-30M
Rood, Nelson
86Tucson-19
87Tucson-15
88Tucson/CMC-13
88Tucson/ProC-191
88Tucson/JP-19
90Edmon/CMC-14
90Edmon/ProC-525
Roof, Eugene L.
(Gene)
78StPete
79ArkTr-22
81Louisvl-5
82D-615
82Louisvl-25
82T-561R
83F-20
83Louisvl/Riley-5
84Louisvl-5
85Richm-20
86Nashvl-23
87Toledo-22
87Toledo/TCMA-22
88Toledo/ProC-599
89Fayette/ProC-1577
90Fayette/ProC-2423MG
90SALAS/Star-23MG
91London/LineD-399MG
91London/ProC-1892MG
Roof, Phil
63T-324R
64T-541R
65T-537R
66T-382
67OPC-129
67T-129
68T-484
69MB-240
69Sunoco/Pin-15
69T-334
70McDon-5
70OPC-359
70T-359
71MLB/St-450
71OPC-22
71T-22
72MB-298
72OPC-201
72T-201
73OPC-598
73T-598
74OPC-388
74T-388
75OPC-576
75T-576
75T/M-576
76OPC-424
76SSPC-224
76T-424
77OPC-121
77T-392
78Padre/FamFun-27CO
83Orlan-1
84Mother/Mar-27CO
85Mother/Mar-27CO
86Mother/Mar-28CO
87Mother/Mar-28CO
88Mother/Mar-27CO
90Cub/Mara-28CO
90Cub/Mara-28CO
90T/TVCub-6CO
91Cub/Mara-x
91Cub/Mara-x
Rooker, Dave
83Butte-26
86PrWill-22
87Harris-4
Rooker, Jim
69T-376R
70OPC-222
70T-222
71MLB/St-428
71OPC-730
71T-730
71T/Coins-32
72T-742
74OPC-402
74T-402
75OPC-148
75T-148
75T/M-148
76OPC-243
76SSPC-566
76T-243
77OPC-161
77T-82
78T-308
79T-584
80T-694
81F-368
Rooker, Michael
88Pac/8Men-9
Rooks, George
N172
N284
Roomes, Rolando
82QuadC-24
83QuadC-27
86WinSalem-24
87Pittsfld-25
89D-577
89F-644R
89F/Up-86
89Kahn/Reds-36
89Nashvl/CMC-22
89Nashvl/ProC-1286
89S/HotRook-37
89S/Tr-109T
89UD-6SR
90B-56
90Classic-38
90D-360
90F-432
90OPC-364
90Panini/St-254
90S-417
90S/100Ris-92
90S/YS/I-22
90T-364
90T/Big-87
90T/St-143
90UD-170
91Denver/ProC-136
Rooney, Jim
84Newar-16
Rooney, Pat
80Memphis-17
82Wichita-15
84Colum-3
84Colum/Pol-21
85Syrac-16
Root, Charley H.
28Exh-11
29Exh/4-6
30CEA/Pin-8
31Exh/4-6
32Orbit/un-51
33Exh/4-3
33G-226
60T-457C
88Conlon/3-24
91Conlon/Sport-93
R303/A
R305
R306
R308-190
R316
R332-44
Root, Mitchell
91Hunting/ClBest-21
91Hunting/ProC-3343
Roper, Brian
89Butte/SP-3
Roper, John
91CharWh/ClBest-9
91CharWh/ProC-2886
91SALAS/ProC-SAL11
91Single/ClBest-276
Roque, Jorge
72OPC-316R
72T-316R
73OPC-606R
73T-606R
Rosa, Julio
88Bristol/ProC-1869
89Fayette/ProC-1587
Rosado, Edwin
(Ed)
88Martins/Star-28
89Batavia/ProC-1944
89Spartan/ProC-1029
89Spartan/Star-20
90Clearw/Star-19
91Reading/LineD-516
91Reading/ProC-1373
Rosado, Luis
(Papo)
78Tidew
79Syrac-18
80Tidew-22
84RochR-12
85RochR-3
91WIZMets-334
Rosar, Warren
(Buddy)
41G-4
48B-10
48L-128
49B-138
50B-136
51B-236
R346-19
Rosario, Alfonso
78Cedar
Rosario, Angel
(Jimmy)
72OPC-366
72T-366
Rosario, David
87Peoria-16
88WinSalem/Star-15
89CharlK-13
91Iowa/LineD-215
91Iowa/ProC-1060
Rosario, Eliezel
90Ashvl/ProC-2747
Rosario, Francisco
88Savan/ProC-358
90Martins/ProC-3194
Rosario, Gabriel
91MedHat/ProC-4108
Rosario, Jose
78Dunedin
Rosario, Jossy
89CharWh/Best-8
89CharWh/ProC-1750
Rosario, Julio
86Elmira-17
87Elmira/Black-8
87Elmira/Red-8
88Elmira-18
88WinHaven/Star-22
89Elmira/Pucko-16
Rosario, Maximo
83Ander-16
Rosario, Mel
86Kinston-22
87FtLaud-26
88Albany/ProC-1343
89FtLaud/Star-24
Rosario, Sal
75BurlB
Rosario, Simon
76Dubuq
77Cocoa
78DaytB
81Tucson-8
84Durham-1
Rosario, Victor
85Elmira-20
86Greens-21
87Greens-19
88Martins/Star-29
89Reading/Star-20
89ScrWB/CMC-23
89ScrWB/ProC-710
90ScranWB/CMC-15
90ScranWB/ProC-607
91F-701
91Richm/LineD-440
91Richm/ProC-2577
91T/90Debut-135
Roscoe, Greg
88Watlo/ProC-691
89Kinston/Star-21
89Watertn/Star-20
90Canton/Best-23
90Canton/ProC-1308
90Canton/Star-15
91Canton/LineD-93
91Canton/ProC-980
Rose
53Exh/Can-42
Rose, Carl
86Watertn-19
Rose, Don
73OPC-178
73T-178
75Phoenix-7
91WIZMets-335
Rose, Guy
71Richm/Team-16
Rose, Kevin
79Newar-20
Rose, Mark
90Tampa/DIMD-28CO
Rose, Pete Jr.
82F-640M
89Erie/Star-22
89Freder/Star-27
90Classic-75
90Freder/Team-20
91Saraso/ClBest-18
91Saraso/ProC-1120
Rose, Pete
63FrBauer-23
63T-537R
64Kahn
64T-125
64T/Coins-82
65Kahn
65OPC-207

65T-207
66Bz-38
66Kahn
66OPC-30
66T-30
66T/RO-83
67Bz-38
67Kahn
67T-430
67T/Test/SU-1
68Bz-15
68Bz-6
68T-230
68T/G-30
68T/Post-23
69Citgo-14
69Kelly/Pin-15
69MB-241
69MLB/St-135
69MLBPA/Pin-55
69NTF
69OPC-120
69OPC-2LL
69T-120
69T-2LL
69T-424AS
69T/DE-21
69T/decal
69T/S-41
69T/St-29
69Trans-54
70K-2
70MB-24
70MLB/St-35
70OPC-458AS
70OPC-61LL
70T-458AS
70T-580
70T-61LL
70T/CB
70T/S-34
70Trans-1
71Bz
71Bz/Test-32
71K-65
71MD
71MLB/St-573
71MLB/St-68
71OPC-100
71T-100
71T/Coins-101
71T/GM-15
71T/S-20
71T/tatt-14
72K-6
72MB-299
72T-559
72T-560IA
72T/Post-11
73K-6
73OPC-130
73T-130
73T/Lids-44
74K-38
74OPC-201LL
74OPC-300
74OPC-336AS
74T-201LL
74T-300
74T-336AS
74T/DE-16
74T/St-30
75Ho-29
75Ho/Twink-29
75K-11
75OPC-211MV
75OPC-320
75T-211MV
75T-320
75T/M-211MV
75T/M-320
76Crane-51
76Ho-66
76Icee
76K-55
76MSA/Disc
76OPC-240
76SSPC-41
76T-240
77BurgChef-204
77Ho-8
77K-20
77OPC-240
77Pep-43
77T-450
77T/CS-38
78Ho-128
78OPC-100DP
78OPC-240RB
78T-20
78T-5RB
78Wiffle/Discs-63
79BK/P-13
79Ho-144
79K-22
79OPC-343
79T-204M
79T-650
79T/Comics-28
80BK/P-4
80BK/PHR-21
80K-35
80OPC-282
80T-4RB
80T-540
80T/S-19
81Coke
81D-131
81D-251
81D-371
81Drake-3
81F-1
81F-645M
81F/St-43M
81F/St-74
81K-63
81MSA/Disc-27
81OPC-180
81PermaGr/AS-7
81PermaGr/CC-5
81Sqt-11
81T-180
81T-205M
81T/HT
81T/Nat/Super-12
81T/So-62
81T/St-200
82D-168
82D-1DK
82D-585M
82Drake-28
82F-256
82F-640M
82F/St-107M
82F/St-109M
82F/St-51
82K-18
82KMart-24
82KMart-44
82OPC-24IA
82OPC-337AS
82OPC-361
82PermaGr/AS-16
82PermaGr/CC-9
82Sqt-12
82T-337AS
82T-4RB
82T-636TL
82T-780
82T-781IA
82T/St-117
82T/St-121
82T/St-78
83D-42
83D/AAS-31
83Drake-24
83F-171
83F-634M
83K-6
83OPC-100
83OPC-101SV
83OPC-373AS
83PermaGr/CC-13
83T-100
83T-101SV
83T-397AS
83T/Gloss40-14
83T/St-272
83T/St/Box-7
84D-61
84D/AAS-54
84D/Champs-27
84Drake-27
84F-46
84F-636IA
84F/St-119
84F/St-99
84F/X-U102
85FunFoodPin-4
84MiltBrad-21
84Nes/792-300
84Nes/792-701LL
84Nes/792-702LL
84OPC-300
84Ralston-4
84Seven-22C
84Stuart-17
84T-300
84T-701LL
84T-702LL
84T/Cereal-4
84T/Gloss40-1
84T/St-115
84T/Tr-103T
85D-254
85D-641
85D/HL-10
85D/HL-40
85F-550
85F-640IA
85F/LimEd-29
85F/St-1
85F/St-2
85F/St-3
85Leaf-144
85OPC-116
85Seven-10G
85Sportflic/Test-43
85T-547MG
85T-600
85T-6RB
85T/3D-5
85T/Gloss40-10
85T/St-57
85T/Super-32
85Woolwth-30
86BK/AP-4
86D-62
86D-644IA
86D-653M
86D/AAS-34
86D/DKsuper-27
86Drake-22
86F-191
86F-628IA
86F-638M
86F/HOF-1
86F/LimEd-37
86F/LL-36
86F/Mini-40
86F/Slug-29
86F/St-101
86Jiffy-11
86Leaf-209M
86Leaf-260M
86Leaf-53
86Meadow/Blank-12
86Meadow/Milk-9
86Meadow/Stat-8
86OPC-1
86OPC/WaxBox-N
86Quaker-11
86Sf-130M
86Sf-138M
86Sf-181M
86Sf-182M
86Sf-50
86Sf-51M
86Sf-56M
86Sf-58M
86Sf-69M
86Sf/Dec-60
86Sf/Rook-46M
86T-1
86T-206RB
86T-2M
86T-3M
86T-4M
86T-5M
86T-6M
86T-741MG
86T-7M
86T/3D-22
86T/Gloss60-51
86T/Rose-Set
86T/St-134
86T/St-1FOIL
86T/St-2
86T/Super-46
86T/WaxBox-N
86TexGold-14A
86TexGold-14B
86TexGold-14C
86TrueVal-4
86Woolwth-29
87Classic-1
87Classic/Up-103
87D-186
87F-213
87F/Excit-38
87F/Hottest-32
87F/BB-37
87F/LL-37
87F/Lim-36
87F/RecSet-33
87F/St-102
87KMart-19
87Kraft-34
87Leaf-129
87OPC-200
87RedFoley/St-64
87Sf-25
87T-200
87T-281TL
87T-393MG
87T/Gloss60-41
87T/St-139
88Classic/Blue-226
88Kahn/Reds-14
88KMart-22
88T-475MG
89Classic-71
89Kahn/Reds-14MG
89T-505MG
89T/LJN-133
90HOF/St-84
91T/Ruth-7

Rose, Robert

(Bobby)
86QuadC-29
88MidwLAS/GS-23
88QuadC/GS-14
89MidldA/GS-27
89TexLAS/GS-3
90B-293
90Classic/Up-41
90Edmon/CMC-15
90Edmon/ProC-526
90F-651R
90S-604
90T/89Debut-106
90UD-77
91B-206
91Edmon/LineD-169
91Edmon/ProC-1524
91F-324
92D/I-90
92F-68
92S/II-558
92T-652
92UD-611

Rose, Scott

91Modesto/ClBest-13
91Modesto/ProC-3087
91Oneonta/ProC-4169

Roseboro, Jaime

86LitFalls-24
87Columbia-6
88Clmbia/GS-24
89StLucie/Star-22
90B-134
90T/TVMets-56
91Tidew/ProC-2525

Roseboro, Johnny

58T-42
59Morrell
59T-441
60BB-7
60MacGregor-21
60Morrell
60T-292M
60T-88
61P-166
61T-363
61T/St-33
62BB-8
62J-107
62P-107
62P/Can-107
62Salada-133
62Shirriff-133
62T-32
62T-397AS
62T/St-139
63J-120
63Salada-12
63T-487
64T-88
65T-405
65T/trans-28
66OPC-189
66T-189
66T/RO-15
67T-365
68Bz-7
68Coke
68Dexter-68
68OPC-65
68T-65
69MB-242
69MLB/St-70
69OPC-218
69T-218
69T/St-198
70MLB/St-285
70T-655
72MB-300
73OPC-421CO
73T-421C
74OPC-276CO
74T-276C
78TCMA-185
87Smok/Dodg-30
88Smok/Dodg-2
89Smok/Dodg-64
90Target-688

Roselli, Bob

56T-131
61T-529
62T-363

Rosello, Dave

74OPC-607R
74T-607R
76OPC-546
76T-546
77T-92
78T-423
80T-122
81D-79
82Charl-18
82D-617
82F-377
82T-724

Roseman, James

E223
N172/ST
N284
N690
N690/2

Rosen, Al

50B-232
50NumNum
51B-187
51BR-A1
51T/RB-35
52B-151
52NTea
52NumNum-10
52StarCal/L-74B
52T-10
53B/Col-8
53NB
53RM-AL24
53T-135
54DanDee
54RH
54RM-AL12
54T-15
55Armour-17
55Gol/Ind-25
55RM-AL11
55Salem
55T-70
55T/DH-1
56Carling-6
56T-35
56T/Hocus-A8
56T/Pin-10
61T-474MV
72T/Test-6
74Laugh/ASG-54
75OPC-191M
75T-191MV
75T/M-191MV
79TCMA-175
90Pac/Legend-78
90Swell/Great-39
91Swell/Great-78
91T/Arc53-135
PM10/Sm-170

R423-85
Rosen, David
85Osceola/Team-30CO
Rosen, Goodwin
(Goody)
39PB-76
90Target-689
Rosenberg, Steve
87Albany-1
88Vanco/CMC-3
88Vanco/ProC-754
89Coke/WS-24
89D-219
89F/Up-22
89T-616
89UD/Ext-715
90AlbanyDG/Best-30
90D-253
90F-547
90OPC-379
90S-523
90T-379
90UD-522
90Vanco/CMC-11
90Vanco/ProC-489
91LasVegas/ProC-234
91LasVegas/LineD-292
Rosenfeld, Max
90Target-1057
Rosenfield, Dave
88Tidew/CANDL-5GM
Rosenthal, Wayne
87Gaston-18
88CharlR/Star-21
89CharlR/Star-20
89Tulsa/Team-21
90Tulsa/ProC-1153
91OkCty/LineD-321
91OkCty/ProC-178
92F-318
92S/II-749
92T-584
92T/91Debut-151
Rosfelder, Chris
89Elmira/Pucko-17
Rosinski, Brian
80Wichita-17
Roskom, Bryan
89Kenosha/ProC-1069
89Kenosha/Star-22
90Kenosha/Best-15
90Kenosha/Star-29
Roslund, John
75QuadC
Roso, James
(Jimmy)
89Bluefld/Star-17
90Wausau/Best-16
90Wausau/ProC-2129
90Wausau/Star-20
91Kane/ClBest-13
91Kane/ProC-2660
Ross, Chester
41G-31
Ross, Chuck
76BurlB
77BurlB
78Holyo
Ross, Dan
89London/ProC-1361
Ross, David
89Martins/Star-27
90Batavia/ProC-3066
91Peoria/ClBest-1
91Peoria/ProC-1341
Ross, Don
49B/PCL-20
90Target-690
Ross, Floyd
52T-298
54T-189
Ross, Gary Douglas
69T-404R
70T-694
71MLB/St-236
71OPC-153
71T-153
73OPC-112
73T-112
77T-544
78T-291
Ross, Gary Douglas
(Pitcher)
91Madison/ProC-2131
Ross, Joe
89Oneonta/ProC-2125
Ross, Mark
82Tucson-3
84Cram/PCL-68
85Cram/PCL-54
86Tucson-20
87Vanco-5
88Syrac/CMC-5
88Syrac/ProC-824
89Syrac/CMC-4
89Syrac/ProC-814
89Syrac/Team-19
90BuffB/CMC-9
90BuffB/ProC-372
90BuffB/Team-22
91Richm/LineD-441
91Richm/ProC-2567
Ross, Michael
88Hamil/ProC-1727
89Spring/Best-10
91Louisvl/LineD-245
91Louisvl/ProC-2931
Ross, Ron
89NiagFls/Pucko-27
Ross, Sean
87Sumter-27
89Durham/Team-19
89Durham/Star-19
91Greenvl/ClBest-22
91Greenvl/LineD-217
91Greenvl/ProC-3017
91Single/ClBest-156
Rosselli, Joe
90A&AASingle/ProC-165
90Everett/Best-11
90Everett/ProC-3127
91Clinton/ClBest-6
Rosser, Rex
75OkCty
Rossi, Joe
52T-379
53T-74
91T/Arc53-74
Rossi, Tom
83Erie-21
Rossiter, Mike
91Classic/DP-34
91FrRow/DP-14
92T-474DP
Rossler, Brett
(Ross)
91Kingspt/ClBest-12
91Kingspt/ProC-3817
Rossman, Claude
09Buster/Pin-12
E96
E97
T206
T213/brown
Rossum, Floyd
85Bend/Cram-21
Rossy, Elem
86Miami-22
Rossy, Rico
85Newar-14
87CharlO/WBTV-5
88BuffB/CMC-18
88BuffB/ProC-1471
89Harris/ProC-289
89Harris/Star-15
90Greenvl/ProC-1138
90Richm/Bob-19
91Richm/LineD-442
91Richm/ProC-2578
92F-676
92S/II-817
92T/91Debut-152
Rostel, Bud
87Anchora-26
Rotblatt, Marv
51B-303
Roth, Bob F.
D327
D328-141
D329-145
D350/2-145
E121/80
E135-141
M101/145
M101/5-145
W514-47
W575
Roth, Greg
89SoBend/GS-26
90BirmB/Best-8
90BirmB/ProC-1115
91BirmB/LineD-71
91BirmB/ProC-1464
Roth, Kris
86Peoria-20
87WinSalem-22
88Pittsfld/ProC-1376
Rothermal, Russ
75Iowa/TCMA-15
79Charl-3
Rothey, Mark
81Cedar-7
82Cedar-1
83Water-7
Rothford, Jim
81Shrev-19
Rothrock, John
29Exh/4-17
31Exh/4-17
34Exh/4-8
Rothschild, Larry
77Indianap-17
79Indianap-9
80Indianap-14
81Evansvl-6
82Evansvl-7
85Iowa-21
89Cedar/Best-26
89Cedar/ProC-933
90Kahn/Reds-27M
91Kahn/Reds-x
Rothstein, Arnold
88Pac/8Men-28M
Rountree, Brian
89Bristol/Star-25
90Fayette/ProC-2405
Rountree, Jerrold
91Spokane/ClBest-11
91Spokane/ProC-3962
Rountree, Mike
86Watlo-23
88Reno/Cal-284
Rouse, Chuck
77Charl
Rouse, Randy
76Dubuq
77Cocoa
78DaytB
Rousey, Steve
87WPalmB-25
Rousch, Ed
15CJ-161
16FleischBrd-78
25Exh-31
26Exh-31
28Exh-20
61F-72
80Pac/Leg-70
80SSPC/HOF
87Conlon/2-54
88Pac/8Men-84
89Pac/Leg-216
89Swell-35
90Swell/Great-35
91Conlon/Sport-55
91Swell/Great-134
D327
D328-142
D329-146
D350/2-146
E120
E121/120
E121/80
E135-142
E210-53
E220
M101/4-146
M101/5-146
R316
V100
V117-28
V61-79
W501-53
W502-53
W513-61
W514-85
W515-57
W517
W572
W575
W711/1
Rovasio, Dom
89Kenosha/ProC-1066
89Kenosha/Star-23
Rover, Vince
83Cedar-21
83Cedar/LF-19
Rowan, John Albert
10Domino-103
11Helmar-103
12Sweet/Pin-131
14Piedmont/St-50
E154
E286
M116
S74-104
T202
T205
Rowdon, Wade
82AppFx-5
83Water-14
84Wichita/Rock-21
85D-642
87Iowa-19
87T-569
88F-430
88RochR/Gov-23
91Crown/Orio-394
Rowe, Davis E.
N172
WG1-24
Rowe, Don
63T-562R
83Redwd-28CO
84Cram/PCL-243CO
87Hawaii-10CO
91Denver/LineD-150CO
91Denver/ProC-139CO
Rowe, Harold
(Butch)
78Wisco
Rowe, Jim
85Beloit-4
86Beloit-20TR
87Beloit-11
88ElPaso/Best-11
Rowe, John Charles
N172
Scrapps
Rowe, Ken
63T-562R
65T-518
82RochR-22CO
87Colum-4CO
89Colum/Pol-24CO
90ColClip/CMC-24CO
90ColClip/ProC-693CO
90Target-691
91Crown/Orio-395
91WIZMets-336
Rowe, Lynwood
(Schoolboy)
34DS-33
34DS-98
34Ward's/Pin-7
35BU-184
35Exh/4-12
35G-8F
35G-9F
36Exh/4-12
36Wheat
37Exh/4-12
37OPC-134
49B-216
49Eureka-144
49Lummis
54T-197CO
61F-73
80Laugh/FFeat-17
81Detroit-93P
90Target-692
91Conlon/Sport-256
PR1-25
R309/2
R311/Gloss
R312/M
R313
R314
V300
V355-44
Rowe, Matt
86Sumter-23
Rowe, Pete
78Dunedin
82AlexD-14
83LynnP-13
90Salinas/Cal-146CO
90Salinas/ProC-2737CO
91Dunedin/ClBest-27
Rowe, Ralph
73OPC-49CO
73T-49CO
74OPC-447CO
74T-447CO
76SSPC-603CO
89Sumter/ProC-1091CO
90Sumter/ProC-2453CO
Rowe, Tom A.
80RochR-9
81RochR-16
85IntLgAS-42
85Maine-9
86Maine-19
Rowell, Carvel
41DP-44
47TipTop
Rowen, Rob
87SanAn-6
88Fresno/Cal-19
88Fresno/ProC-1244
Rowland, Clarence
(Pants)
92Conlon/Sport-485
BF2-15
D328-143
D329-147
D350/2-147
E135-143
M101/4-147
M101/5-147
Rowland, Donnie
86FSLAS-42
86Lakeland-20
87Lakeland-6
88Toledo/CMC-22
88Toledo/ProC-589
89London/ProC-1363
Rowland, Mike
78Cr/PCL-17
79Phoenix
80Phoenix-4
81Phoenix-10
81T-502R
82Phoenix
Rowland, Rich
88Bristol/ProC-1872
89Fayette/ProC-1578
90London/ProC-1271
91Classic/II-T95
91T/90Debut-136
91Toledo/LineD-597
91Toledo/ProC-1936
92T-472
Rowley, Bill
87Indianap-36
Rowley, Steve
89Butte/SP-10
90CharlR/Star-24
91CharlR/ClBest-10
91CharlR/ProC-1314
Roy, Jean-Pierre
52Park-90
Roy, Kevin
83Wausau/LF-13
Roy, Luther
90Target-693
Roy, Norman
51B-278
Roy, Pat
76Cedar
Roy, Walt
90BurlB/Best-14
90BurlB/ProC-2349
90BurlB/Star-23
91Durham/ProC-1542
Royalty, Doug
87AubAs-26
88Ashvl/ProC-1065
Royer, Stan
88SoOreg/ProC-1701
89AS/Cal-31
89B-195
89Modesto/Cal-276

89Modesto/Chong-25
90Foil/Best-240
90Huntsvl/Best-19
91Louisvl/LineD-246
91Louisvl/ProC-2924
92D/II-602
92S/II-822
92T/91Debut-153

Royster, Jerry
74Albuq/Team-17
76OPC-592R
76T-592R
77BurgChef-212
77Ho-38
77OPC-251
77T-549
78T-187
79T-344
80OPC-241
80T-463
81D-339
81F-250
81Pol/Atl-1
81T-268
82BK/Lids-22
82D-555
82F-448
82Pol/Atl-1
82T-608
83D-425
83F-147
83Pol/Atl-1
83T-26
84D-531
84F-191
84Nes/792-572
84Pol/Atl-1
84T-572
84T/St-37
85F-340
85F/Up-U90
85Mother/Padres-18
85T-776
85T/Tr-96T
86D-446
86F-333
86OPC-118
86T-118
87Coke/WS-1
87D-534
87F-428
87OPC-324
87T-403
87T/Tr-106T
88D-660
88F-221
88T-257
89UD-433
90EliteSenLg-47
90Target-694
90Yakima/Team-23MG
91VeroB/ClBest-30MG
91VeroB/ProC-791MG

Royster, Willie
79RochR-5
82RochR-11
83Evansvl-12
91Crown/Orio-396

Rozek, Richard
52NumNum-11
52T-363

Rozema, Dave
75Clinton
78BK/T-5
78Ho-36
78K-21
78OPC-38
78T-124
79OPC-12
79T-33
80OPC-151
80T-288
81D-9
81F-464
81T-614
82D-259
82F-279
82F/St-153
82T-319
83D-133
83F-340
83T-562
84D-272
84F-90
84Nes/792-457
84OPC-133
84T-457
85D-125
85F-21
85F/Up-U91
85Rang-30
85Seven-5D
85T-47
85T/Tr-97T
86D-343
86F-570
86Leaf-154
86OPC-208
86T-739
91Pac/SenLg-135

Rozman, Richard
88SoOreg/ProC-1694

Roznovsky, Ron
75Iowa/TCMA-16

Roznovsky, Vic
65T-334
66T-467
67OPC-163
67T-163
68T-428
69T-368
91Crown/Orio-397

Rozook, Mark
89Wausau/GS-12

Rub, Jerry
88PrWill/Star-21
89Albany/Best-12
89Albany/ProC-328
89Albany/Star-16
90Albany/ProC-1035
90Albany/Star-15
91Albany/ProC-1007

Rub, Ron
87FtLaud-15

Rubel, John
83Butte-27

Rubel, Mike
82Tulsa-28
83Tulsa-15
84OKCty-14
85OKCty-22
87Phoenix-27
90TulsaDG/Best-12

Rubeling, Albert
52Park-82

Ruberto, John E.
(Sonny)
76Indianap-11
80ArkTr-5

Ruby, J. Gary
87QuadC-20
88CalLgAS-36
88PalmSp/Cal-114
88PalmSp/ProC-1435
89MidldA/GS-3
91Edmon/LineD-175CO
91Edmon/ProC-1532CO

Rucker, Dave
80Evansvl-9
82Evansvl-8
82T-261R
83D-641
83Evansvl-9
83F-341
83T-304
84D-260
84Nes/792-699
84T-699
85Cram/PCL-26
85D-260
85F-238
85F/Up-U92
85T-421
85T/Tr-98T
86D-448
86F-447
86Phill/TastyK-39
86T-39
87OKCty-27
88BuffB/CMC-8
88BuffB/ProC-1472
89BuffB/CMC-5
89BuffB/ProC-1662
89UD-436

Rucker, George
(Nap)
10Domino-104
11Helmar-88
12Sweet/Pin-75
12Sweet/Pin-75A
14CJ-51
15CJ-51
16FleischBrd-79
90Target-695
92Conlon/Sport-333
BF2-61
D304
D329-148
D350/2-148
E103
E254
E300
E96
L1-117
M101/4-148
M101/5-148
M116
S74-54
S81-92
T201
T202
T204
T205
T206
T207
T213/blue
T215/blue
T215/brown
T3-34
WG4-23
WG5-34
WG6-32

Rucker, Johnny
40PB-213
41DP-137
47Centen-25
49B/PCL-7

Ruckman, Scott
86Cram/PCL-133
88Spartan/ProC-1037
88Spartan/Star-19
88Spartan/Star-3

Rudi, Joe
69T-587
70OPC-102
70T-102
71MLB/St-525
71OPC-407
71T-407
72OPC-209
72T-209
73K-36
73OPC-360
73T-360
74OPC-264
74T-264
74T/St-229
75Ho-40
75Ho/Twink-40
75K-28
75OPC-45
75OPC-465WS
75T-45
75T-465WS
75T/M-45
75T/M-465WS
76K-7
76OPC-475
76SSPC-490
76T-475
77BurgChef-125
77Ho-146
77OPC-206
77T-155
77T/CS-39
78Ho-114
78OPC-28
78T-635
78Wiffle/Discs-64
79Ho-84
79OPC-134
79T-267
80OPC-289
80T-556
81D-174
81F-272
81F/St-113
81OPC-362
81T-701
81T/Tr-826
82D-586
82F-306
82OPC-388
82T-388
82T/Tr-102T
83D-287
83F-532
83T-87
87Mother/A's-9

Rudison, Karl
90Pulaski/Best-18
90Pulaski/ProC-3094

Rudolph, Blaine
88Bristol/ProC-1879
89Fayette/ProC-1579
90Dunedin/Star-15

Rudolph, F. Don
58T-347
59T-179
60HenryH-33
60Union-17
62T-224
63T-291
64T-427

Rudolph, Ken
70OPC-46
70T-46
71MLB/St-45
71OPC-472
71T-472
72OPC-271
72T-271
73OPC-414
73T-414
74OPC-584
74T-584
75OPC-289
75T-289
75T/M-289
76OPC-601
76SSPC-287
76T-601
91Crown/Orio-398

Rudolph, Mason
90Kgsport/Best-6
90Kgsport/Star-21

Rudolph, Richard
15CJ-154
16FleischBrd-80
BF2-55
C46-22
D328-144
D329-149
D350/2-149
E135-144
E254
M101/4-149
M101/5-149
T206
T213/blue
W514-13
W516-15

Rudstrom, Tom
89BendB/Legoe-15

Ruebel, Matt
91Welland/ClBest-20
91Welland/ProC-3572

Ruel, Harold
(Muddy)
21Exh-147
25Exh-128
26Exh-128
27Exh-63
28Exh-64
29Exh/4-31
33DH-37
33Exh/4-12
33G-18
35G-1J
35G-3A
35G-5A
35G-6A
40PB-127
91Conlon/Sport-284
E120
E121/120
E126-25
R306
R316
V100
V117-24
V353-18
W501-10
W573
W575

Ruether, Walter
(Dutch)
21Exh-139
28Yueng-2
88Pac/8Men-83
90Target-696
91Conlon/Sport-104
E120
E121/120
E210-2
V61-64
W501-98
W502-2
W514-108
W515-40
W573

Ruff, Dan
91Bristol/ClBest-24
91Bristol/ProC-3616

Ruffcorn, Scott
91Classic/DP-21
91FrRow/DP-4
92S/II-806DC
92T-36DP

Ruffin, Bruce
86Reading-23
86Sf/Rook-29
87D-555
87F-183
87F/Hottest-33
87Leaf-168
87Phill/TastyK-47
87T-499
87T/GlossRk-14
87T/St-123
87T/St-312
87ToysRUs-23
88D-165
88F-313
88OPC-268
88Panini/St-353
88Phill/TastyK-21
88S-492
88T-268
88T/St-119
89B-393
89D-515
89F-580
89OPC-222
89Panini/St-148
89Phill/TastyK-28
89S-328
89ScrWB/ProC-728
89T-518
89T/St-122
89UD-319
90F-572
90Leaf/I-151
90OPC-22
90Phill/TastyK-27
90T-22
90UD-580
91F-411
91OPC-637
91S-524
91ScranWB/LineD-494
91ScranWB/ProC-2537
91T-637
91T/StClub/I-89
91UD-410
92D/II-680
92F-544
92S/I-161
92T-307
92UD-309

Ruffin, Johnny
89Utica/Pucko-19
91B-347
91Saraso/ClBest-9
91Saraso/ProC-1112
91Single/ClBest-95

Ruffing, Charles H.
(Red)
25Exh-69
26Exh-70
29Exh/4-17
33CJ/Pin-19
33G-56
34DS-60
35G-2D
35G-4D
35G-7D
36Exh/4-13

37OPC-136
37Wheat
38ONG/Pin-25
39PB-3
40PB-10
40Wheat
41DP-68
41DP-86
43MP-22
60F-63
61F-74
80Pac/Leg-109
80SSPC/HOF
83D/HOF-31
86Sf/Dec-14M
89HOF/St-83
91Conlon/Sport-13
91Conlon/Sport-227
PM10/Sm-171
R300
R310
R311/Leath
R312
R316
R328-20
V300
V354-48
V355-102

Ruffner, Mark
89Reading/Best-24

Rugg, Rusty
89Helena/SP-6

Ruhle, Vern
75OPC-614R
75T-614R
75T/M-614R
76Ho-46
76Ho/Twink-46
76OPC-89
76T-89
77OPC-212
77T-311
78Charl
78T-456
79T-49
80T-234
81D-261
81F-53
81T-642
82D-293
82F-228
82T-539
83D-627
83F-462
83T-172
84D-564
84F-238
84Mother/Ast-23
84Nes/792-328
84T-328
85D-380
85F-358
85F/Up-U93
85Polar/Ind-48
85T-426
85T/Tr-99T
86F-593
86T-768
87F-91
87T-221
90Swell/Great-128
91Swell/Great-76

Ruiz, Augie
79LodiD-2
82Evansvl-9
83Richm-9

Ruiz, Benny
86GlenF-19
87GlenF-14
88Toledo/CMC-16
88Toledo/ProC-602

Ruiz, Hiraldo S.
(Chico)
63T-407R
64T-356R
65T-554
66OPC-159
66T-159
67T-339
68Kahn
68T-213
69MB-243
69T-469
70T-606
71MLB/St-357
71OPC-686
71T-686
72MB-301
78TCMA-35

Ruiz, Manuel
(Chico)
78Richm
79Richm-13
81Richm-9
82Richm-15
83Richm-15
90Richm25Ann/Team-21

Ruiz, Nelson
80Batavia-29

Ruiz, Stewart
91Bluefld/ProC-4136
91Bluefld/ClBest-3

Ruling, Steve
77Spoka

Rumer, Tim
90Tampa/DIMD-18
91FtLaud/ClBest-13
91FtLaud/ProC-2426

Rumfield, Toby
91FrRow/DP-35
91Princet/ClBest-13
91Princet/ProC-3518

Rumler, William G.
D328-145
E135-145

Rumsey, Dan
91Clinton/ProC-849

Rumsey, Derrell
91Visalia/ClBest-23
91Visalia/ProC-1755

Runge, Ed
55B-277ump
90TM/Umpire-64M

Runge, Paul
88TM/Umpire-17
89TM/Umpire-17
90TM/Umpire-17
90TM/Umpire-64M

Runge, Paul W.
81Richm-10
82Richm-16
83Richm-16
84Richm-24
85Pol/Atl-12
85T/Tr-100T
86Richm-19
86T-409
87Richm/Crown-12
87Richm/TCMA-14
88F/Up-U71
89LasVegas/CMC-21
89T-38
89T/Big-23
89UD-55
90Syrac/CMC-17
90Syrac/ProC-579
90Syrac/Team-19

Runge, Scott
86Watertn-20
87Watertn-5
88Augusta/ProC-376
89SanBern/Best-19
89Wmsprt/ProC-638

Runnells, Tom
81Phoenix-23
82Phoenix
83Phoenix/BHN-9
84Wichita/Rock-11
86D-569
87Vermont-16
88Chatt/Best-14
89Chatt/II/Team-25MG
89Indianap/CMC-25
89Indianap/ProC-1220
91T/Tr-103TMG
92T-51MG

Runnels, James E.
(Pete)
52T-2
53B/Col-139
53Briggs
53T-219
54T-6
55B-255
55RM-AL20
56T-234
57T-64
58Hires-38
58T-265
59T-370
59T-519M
60T-15
60T/tatt-47
61Bz-32
61NuCard-407
61P-47
61T-210
61T-42LL
61T/St-116
62J-57
62P-57
62Salada-47A
62Salada-47B
62Shirriff-47
62T-3
62T/bucks
62T/St-17
63Exh
63J-77
63P-77
63Pep
63Salada-61
63T-230
63T-2LL
64T-121
90Pac/Legend-103
91T/Arc53-219
Exh47

Ruocchio, James
91Boise/ClBest-6
91Boise/ProC-3890

Rupcich, Mike
89Smok/FresnoSt-18

Rupe, Brian
83Visalia/LF-25

Rupkey, Rich
90Hamil/Best-12
90Hamil/Star-21

Rupp, Mark
89Erie/Star-23

Rupp, Terry
89Spokane/SP-9
90Waterlo/Best-15
90Waterlo/ProC-2386

Rush, Andy
89Elmira/Pucko-18
90Target-1058
90WinHaven/Star-23
91LynchRS/ClBest-28
91LynchRS/ProC-1197

Rush, Bob
49Eureka-69
50B-61
51B-212
52NTea
52StarCal/L-80D
52T-153
53B/Col-110
54B-77
55B-182
55RFG-13
56T-214
57T-137
58T-313
59T-396
60Lake
60SpicSpan-19
60T-404
79TCMA-164

Rush, Edward
(Eddie)
88Cedar/ProC-1155
89Greens/ProC-418
90Cedar/Best-6
90Cedar/ProC-2329
91Cedar/ProC-2729
91MidwLAS/ProC-MWL23

Rush, Larry
79Holyo-20
80Vanco-1
81Vanco-12
82Vanco-7

Rush, Rod
84Everett/Cram-13B

Rusie, Amos
75F/Pion-12
80SSPC/HOF
86Indianap-8
87Conlon/2-53
92Conlon/Sport-535
N172
N300/unif
N566-175

Rusk, Troy
90Princet/DIMD-17
91Spartan/ClBest-15
91Spartan/ProC-902

Ruskin, Scott
87Macon-22
88Salem/Star-18
89Salem/Star-18
90B-167
90D/Rook-27
90Leaf/II-512
90T/Tr-106T
90UD/Ext-713
91D-612
91F-246
91F/Ultra-209
91OPC-589
91S-799
91T-589
91T/90Debut-137
91UD-383
92D/I-394
92F-491
92S/I-121
92T-692
92UD-384

Russ, Kevin
86Madis-18

Russell, Alan
91Boise/ClBest-30TR

Russell, Bill E.
70MLB/St-56
70OPC-304
70T-304
71MLB/St-113
71OPC-226
71T-226
71Ticket/Dodg-14
72T-736
73OPC-108
73T-108
74OPC-239
74T-239
74T/DE-40
74T/St-49
75Ho-91
75OPC-23
75T-23
75T/M-23
76OPC-22
76T-22
77T-322
78T-128
79T-546
80OPC-40
80Pol/Dodg-18
80T-75
81D-57
81F-117
81F/St-68
81OPC-20
81Pol/Dodg-18
81T-465
81T/HT
81T/St-179
82D-453
82F-20
82F/St-8
82Pol/Dodg-18
82T-279
83D-210
83F-219
83OPC-123
83Pol/Dodg-18
83T-661
83T/St-249
84D-587
84F-111
84Nes/792-792
84OPC-14
84Pol/Dodg-18
84T-792
84T/St-77
85Coke/Dodg-28
85D-93
85F-383
85Leaf-232
85OPC-343
85SpokAT/Cram-17
85T-343
85T/St-76
86Coke/Dodg-26
86D-153
86F-142
86Pol/Dodg-18
86T-506
86T-696M
87F-452
87Smok/Dodg-31
87T-116
88Smok/Dodg-13
88Smok/Dodg-15M
89Smok/Dodg-81
90Mother/Dodg-28M
90Pol/Dodg-x
90Target-697
91Mother/Dodg-28CO
91Pol/Dodg-x

Russell, Dan
88Modesto-25

Russell, Dave
80WHave-18

Russell, Ewell A.
(Reb)
14CJ-15
15CJ-15
92Conlon/Sport-482
BF2-16
D328-146
D329-150
D350/2-150
E135-146
M101/4-150
M101/5-150
V100
WG4-24

Russell, Fred
88Eugene/Best-15
89Eugene/Best-19
90AppFox/Box-21
90AppFox/ProC-2103
91BBCity/ClBest-20
91BBCity/ProC-1406
91Single/ClBest-122

Russell, Glen David
39Exh
47TipTop

Russell, Jack Erwin
33G-123
33G-167
R316

Russell, James W.
47TipTop
49B-235
49Eureka-20
50B-223
52Mother-52
52T-51
90Target-698

Russell, Jeff
82Water-8
83Indianap-14
84Borden-46
84D-569
84Nes/792-270
84T-270
85D-487
85F-551
85T-651
86OKCty-19
86Rang-40
87D-550
87F-137
87Mother/Rang-26
87Smok/R-32
87T-444
88D-531
88F-478
88Mother/R-26
88S-514
88Smok/R-17
88T-114
89B-226
89D-403
89D/AS-26
89D/Best-200
89F-531
89Mother/R-6
89OPC-166
89Panini/St-447
89S-438
89Smok/R-28
89T-565
89T/Big-309

89T/St-243
89UD-461
90B-485
90D-284
90D/BestAL-99
90F-312
90F-633M
90F/AwardWin-28
90Leaf/I-152
90Mother/Rang-8
90OPC-395AS
90OPC-80
90Panini/St-159
90PublInt/St-420
90RedFoley/St-80
90S-263
90S/100St-23
90Sf-192
90T-395AS
90T-80
90T/Big-15
90T/Mini-38
90T/St-252
90UD-638
91B-267
91D-202
91F-300
91F/Ultra-354
91Leaf/II-291
91Mother/Rang-8
91OPC-344
91S-277
91T-344
91T/StClub/II-421
91UD-648
92D/I-129
92F-319
92S/I-124
92T-257
92UD-695

Russell, Joe
79Tulsa-2
81Tulsa-27

Russell, John
83Portl-17
84Cram/PCL-208
84Phill/TastyK-42
85D-648
85F-653R
85Phill/TastyK-11N
85Phill/TastyK-31
86CIGNA-14
86D-82
86F-448
86Phill/TastyK-6
86T-392
87D-207
87F-184
87Phill/TastyK-6
87T-379
88Maine/CMC-12
88Maine/ProC-285
88Phill/TastyK-37
88T-188
89UD-532
90D-458
90Leaf/II-442
90Mother/Rang-26
90OkCty/CMC-11
90OkCty/ProC-436
90PublInt/St-120
90T/Tr-107T
90Target-699
91F-301
91Mother/Rang-26
91OPC-734
91S-802
91T-734
91T/StClub/II-474
91UD-191
92S/I-339

Russell, LaGrande
91Belling/ClBest-28

Russell, Larry
88CapeCod/Sum-28

Russell, Matt
89BendB/Legoe-25BB

Russell, Richard
91Belling/ProC-3662

Russell, Rob
85PrWill-7
86PrWill-23
87Harris-12
88Harris/ProC-858
89Harris/ProC-303
89Harris/Star-16

Russell, Ron
86DayBe-24

Russell, Todd
91Madison/ClBest-1

Russell, Tony
83Greens-26
85Albany-21
86Albany/TCMA-10
87Albany-2

Russo, Marius
41DP-112
44Yank/St-22

Russo, Pat
91Kenosha/ClBest-15
91Kenosha/ProC-2073

Russo, Paul
90Elizab/Star-20
91B-695
91Kenosha/ProC-2085
91Single/ClBest-344
92T-473M

Russo, Tony
87Erie-16
88Savan/ProC-333
89StPete/Star-23

Rusteck, Dick
91WIZMets-337

Ruth, George Herman
(Babe)
21Exh-148
21Exh-149
25Exh-100
26Exh-102
27Exh-52
28Exh-51
28FrJoy-Set
28Yueng-6
29Exh/4-26
31Exh/4-26
33Exh/4-13
33G-144
33G-149
33G-181
33G-53
33SK-2
34Exh/4-13
35Exh/4-1
35G-1J
35G-3A
35G-4A
35G-5A
48BRS-Set
48Exh/HOF
48L-3
48Swell-12
49Leaf/Prem-7
50Callahan
51T/CM
56T/Hocus-B1
60Exh/HOF-20
60F-3
60NuCard-1
60NuCard-16
60NuCard-47
61F-75
61GP-3
61NuCard-447
61NuCard-455
61T-401M
62T-135M
62T-136M
62T-137M
62T-138M
62T-139M
62T-140M
62T-141M
62T-142M
62T-143M
62T-144M
63Bz-17
69Bz-10
69Bz-11
69Bz-9
69Bz/Sm
72F/FFeat-20
72K/ATG-14
72K/ATG-6
72Laugh/GF-32
73F/Wild-34M
73OPC-1LL
73OPC-474LL
73Syrac/Team-24
73T-1LL
73T-474LL
74Laugh/ASG-33
74Syrac/Team-23
76Laugh/Jub-32
76Motor-9
76OPC-345ATG
76T-345ATG
80Pac/Leg-1
80Laugh/3/4/5-2
80Laugh/FFeat-16
80SSPC/HOF
81Detroit-54
83T/St-2F
84D/Champs-1
85CircK-2
85D/HOF-1
85West/2-47
85Woolwth-31
86BLChew-2
86Conlon/1-13
86Conlon/1-20
86Conlon/1-48
86Conlon/1-50
86Conlon/1-54
86Sf/Dec-1
87Nestle/DT-5
88Conlon/3-25
88Conlon/AmAS-21
89Cadaco-45
89CMC/Ruth-Set
89HOF/St-47
89Pac/Leg-176
89Smok/Dodg-26
89Swell-1
89T/LJN-77
89USPS-4
90BBWit-86
90CollAB-10
90HOF/St-25
90Swell/Great-10
91Conlon/Sport-110
91Conlon/Sport-145
91Homer/Classic-1
91Swell/Great-124
91T/Ruth-Set
92Conlon/Sport-426
92S/II-879
D327
D328-146
D329-151
D350/2-151
E120
E121/120
E121/80
E126-38
E135-146
E210-6
E220
M101/4-151
M101/5-151
PM10/Sm-172
R309/1
R310
R315-A31
R315-B31
R316
R328-32
R332-26
R332-42
R337-402
R423-92
Rawl
V100
V117-8
V353-80
V353-93
V354-28
V61-37
W501-49
W502-6
W512-6
W514-2
W515-3
W515-47
W516-1
W517-20
W517-4
W573
W575

Ruth, Pat
89Smok/FresnoSt-19
91Batavia/ClBest-4
91Batavia/ProC-3486

Rutherford, John
52T-320
53T-137
90Target-700
91T/Arc53-137

Ruthven, Dick
74OPC-47
74T-47
75OPC-267
75T-267
75T/M-267
76OPC-431
76SSPC-477
76T-431
77BurgChef-208
77Ho-74
77T-575
78T-75
79BK/P-6
79T-419
80BK/P-19
80T-136
81D-153
81F-16
81OPC-285
81T-691
81T/HT
82D-525
82F-257
82F/St-52
82OPC-317
82T-317
83D-497
83F-172
83OPC-313
83T-484
83T/Tr-98
83Thorn-44
84D-510
84F-503
84Nes/792-736
84OPC-156
84SevenUp-44
84T-736
84T/St-49
85F-64
85OPC-268
85SevenUp-44
85T-563
86D-564
86F-377
86T-98

Rutledge, Jeff
82QuadC-19
86Pittsfld-21

Ruyak, Craig
90Johnson/Star-23

Ruzek, Don
77LodiD
78LodiD
83AppFx/LF-27

Ryal, Mark
82Omaha-21
83Omaha-20
84Omaha-24
85BuffB-15
86Edmon-25
87D-583
87Smok/Cal-14
88F-503
88Louisvl-43
88T-243
90BuffB/CMC-20
90BuffB/ProC-383
90BuffB/Team-23

Ryan, Bobby
90Watertn/Star-18
91Rockford/ClBest-12
91Rockford/ProC-2047

Ryan, Colin
88CapeCod/Sum-71
89Eugene/Best-13
90AppFox/Box-22
90AppFox/ProC-2098
91BBCity/ClBest-15
91BBCity/ProC-1401
91Single/ClBest-130

Ryan, Connie
47TipTop
49Eureka-19
51B-216
52B-164
52T-107
53B/Col-131
53NB
53T-102
54T-136
74OPC-634CO
74T-634CO
91T/Arc53-102

Ryan, Craig
79Vanco-5
80Vanco-15

Ryan, Dan
89SLCity-8LHP

Ryan, Duffy
81Redwd-11

Ryan, Jack
90Target-1059

Ryan, James E.
E107
E223
N172
N28
N284
N300/SC
N403
N43
WG1-15

Ryan, Jody
86Cram/PCL-117
87Wausau-3
88SanBern/Best-7
88SanBern/Cal-42
89SanBern/Best-21
89SanBern/Cal-67

Ryan, John Budd
90Target-701
E254
E270/2
T207

Ryan, John C.
(Blondy)
34DS-40
34Exh/4-5
34G-32
35Exh/4-6
R310
V354-73

Ryan, Kenny Jr.
86Elmira-18
87Greens-6
88Lynch/Star-22
89WinHaven/Star-19
90LynchRS/Team-21
91WinHaven/ClBest-8
91WinHaven/ProC-488

Ryan, Kevin
85Anchora-26
91Bluefld/ProC-4128
91Bluefld/ClBest-17

Ryan, Mike
65T-573R
66T-419
67T-223
67T/Test/RSox-14
68T-306
69MLB/St-177
69OPC-28
69T-28
70MLB/St-93
70T-591
71MLB/St-186
71OPC-533
71T-533
72MB-302
72OPC-324
72T-324
73OPC-467
73T-467
74OPC-564
74T-564
84Phill/TastyK-13CO
85Phill/TastyK-6CO
85Phill/TastyK-8CO
86Phill/TastyK-5CO
87Phill/TastyK-x
88Phill/TastyK-29CO
89Phill/TastyK-29
89Phill/TastyK-30CO
90Phill/TastyK-34CO

Ryan, Nolan
68OPC-177R
68T-177R

69T-533
70MLB/St-81
70OPC-197NLCS
70T-197NLCS
70T-712
70Trans/M-24
71MLB/St-162
71OPC-513
71T-513
72T-595
73K-16
73OPC-220
73OPC-67LL
73T-220
73T-67LL
73T/Comics-17
73T/Lids-45
73T/PinUps-17
74K-8
74OPC-20
74OPC-207LL
74T-20
74T-207LL
74T/DE-41
74T/Puzzles-9
74T/St-147
75Ho-58
75Ho/Twink-58
75K-26
75OPC-312LL
75OPC-500
75OPC-5RB
75OPC-7M
75T-312LL
75T-500
75T-5RB
75T-7M
75T/M-312LL
75T/M-500
75T/M-5RB
75T/M-7M
76Crane-52
76Ho-79
76Laugh/Jub-1
76MSA/Disc
76OPC-330
76SSPC-187
76T-330
77BurgChef-123
77Ho-81
77OPC-264RB
77OPC-65
77OPC-6LL
77Pep-24
77T-234RB
77T-650
77T-6LL
77T/CS-40
78Ho-83
78K-51
78OPC-105
78OPC-241RB
78OPC-6LL
78T-206LL
78T-400
78T-6RB
78Wiffle/Discs-65
79Ho-101
79OPC-51
79T-115
79T-417LL
79T-6LL
79T/Comics-4
80BK/PHR-9
80K-20
80OPC-303
80T-206LL
80T-580
80T/S-20
81Coke
81D-260
81F-57
81F/St-108
81K-6
81OPC-240
81PermaGr/CC-26
81T-240
81T/HT
81T/St-173
81T/St-30
82D-13DK
82D-419
82F-229
82F/St-242M
82F/St-42
82K-11
82OPC-90
82T-167LL
82T-5RB
82T-66TL
82T-90
82T/St-13
82T/St-41
83D-118
83D/AAS-23
83F-463
83K-31
83OPC-360
83OPC-361SV
83T-360
83T-361SV
83T/Gloss40-28
83T/St-235
84D-60
84D/AAS-14
84D/Champs-39
84F-239
84F/St-82
85FunFoodPin-109
84Mother/Ast-1
84Nes/792-470
84Nes/792-4HL
84Nes/792-66TL
84Nes/792-707LL
84OPC-66
84Ralston-14
84Seven-13W
84T-4HL
84T-66TL
84T-470
84T-707LL
84T/Cereal-14
84T/Gloss40-15
84T/St-66
84T/Super-28
85D-60
85D/AAS-20
85D/HL-22
85F-359
85F/LimEd-30
85F/St-115
85Leaf-216
85Mother/Ast-2
85OPC-63
85Seven-1C
85Seven-3S
85T-760
85T-7RB
85T/St-58
85T/Super-23
85Woolwth-32
86D-258
86D/AAS-21
86Drake-33
86F-310
86F/HOF-5
86F/Mini-65
86F/Slug-30
86F/St-102
86Jiffy-13
86Leaf-132
86Mother/Ast-23
86OPC-100
86Pol/Ast-2
86Quaker-12
86Sf-141M
86Sf-143M
86Sf-182M
86Sf-43
86Sf/Dec-63M
86T-100
86T/Gloss60-45
86T/Mini-43
86T/St-24
86T/St-9
86T/Super-47
86TrueVal-26
87Classic-82
87D-138
87D/HL-53
87Drake-32
87F-67
87F/BB-38
87F/St-103
87KMart-20
87Kraft-48
87Leaf-257
87MnM's-22
87Mother/Ast-8
87OPC-155
87Pol/Ast-16
87Ralston-1
87RedFoley/St-121
87Sf-125
87T-757
87T/Coins-40
87T/St-27
88Classic/Red-179
88D-61
88D/Best-232
88F-455
88F/BB/AS-34
88F/Mini-79
88F/St-88
88KMart-23
88Leaf-77
88Mother/Ast-8
88Nestle-43
88OPC-250
88OPC/WaxBox-N
88Panini/St-288
88Panini/St-435
88Pol/Ast-20
88S-575
88Sf-39
88T-250
88T-661TBC
88T-6RB
88T/Big-29
88T/Coins-50
88T/Mini-50
88T/Revco-8
88T/St-7
88T/UK-62
88T/WaxBox-N
88Woolwth-6
89B-225
89Cadaco-46
89Classic/Up/2-164
89D-154
89D/Best-55
89D/Tr-19
89F-368
89F/Up-67
89KingB/Discs-10
89Mother/R-2
89OPC-366
89Panini/St-226
89Panini/St-83
89RedFoley/St-100
89S-300
89S/HotStar-64
89S/Mast-5
89S/Tr-2
89Sf-115
89Smok/Angels-7
89Smok/R-29
89T-530
89T/LJN-114
89T/Mini-15
89T/St-20
89T/Tr-106T
89T/WaxBox-K
89UD-145
89UD-669TC
89UD/Ext-774
90B-486
90B/Ins-8
90BBWit-55
90Classic-1
90Classic/III-84
90Classic/III-91M
90Classic/Up-26
90CollAB-14
90D-166
90D-659
90D-665K
90D/BestAL-49
90D/Learning-24
90D/Preview-7
90F-313
90F-636M
90F/AwardWin-29
90F/LL-31
90F/Up-131
90HOF/St-77
90HotPlay/St-35
90KayBee-28
90KingB/Discs-22
90KMart/SS-25
90Leaf/I-21
90Leaf/I-264CL
90Leaf/II-265K
90Mother/Rang-2
90Mother/Ryan-Set
90MSA/Soda-16
90OPC-1
90OPC-2
90OPC-3
90OPC-4
90OPC-5
90Panini/St-160
90Panini/St-185
90Panini/St-387
90Post-11
90PublInt/St-421
90RedFoley/St-81
90S-250
90S-696HL
90S/100St-44
90S/ComRyan-xx
90Sf-8
90Starline/LJS-13
90Starline/LJS-26
90T-1
90T-2SA
90T-3SA
90T-4SA
90T-5SA
90T/Big-171
90T/Coins-25
90T/DH-53
90T/Gloss60-2
90T/Mini-39
90T/St-242
90T/St-3HL
90T/TVAS-9
90T/WaxBox-O
90Tetley/Discs-20
90UD-34HL
90UD-544
90UD/Ext-734
90WonderBrd-16
90Woolwth/HL-20
91B-280
91BBBest/RecBr-14
91Classic/200-196
91Classic/I-86
91Classic/II-T80
91Classic/II-T97
91Classic/III-79Number 7
91Classic/III-98
91CollAB-3
91D-89
91D-BC15
91D-BC3
91D/Elite-L1(Legend)
91D/Preview-7
91F-302
91F/Ultra-355
91F/Ultra-395EP
91F/Ultra-400CL
91F/WaxBox-3
91JDeanSig-24
91Leaf/GRook-BC25
91Leaf/II-423
91Leaf/Prev-25
91Leaf/Stud-128
91MajorLg/Pins-35
91Mother/Rang-2
91Mother/Ryan-Set
91OPC-1
91OPC-6RB
91OPC/Premier-102
91Pac/Ryan7NH-Set
91Pac/RyanSIns-Set
91Pac/RyanTE-Set
91Panini/FrSt-259
91Panini/FrSt-354
91Panini/St-205
91Panini/St-3
91Panini/Top15-77
91Petro/SU-25
91Post-17
91Post/Can-27
91RedFoley/St-79
91S-4
91S-417HL
91S-686KM
91S-701NH
91S/100SS-25
91S/Cooper-B7
91S/RyanL&T-Set
91Seven/3DCoin-11T
91Seven/3DCoin-12SC
91Seven/3DCoin-14A
91Seven/3DCoin-14F
91Seven/3DCoin-14NW
91Seven/3DCoin-8NC
91SilverSt-2
91Sunflower-20
91T-1
91T-6RB
91T/CJMini/I-1
91T/StClub/I-200
91T/SU-29
91T/WaxBox-N
91UD-345
91UD/Ext-SP2M
91UD/Ryan-Set
91WIZMets-338
91Woolwth/HL-19
92Classic/I-78
92Classic/I-xx
92D/I-154HL
92D/II-555M
92D/II-707
92D/Preview-11
92F-320
92F-682RS
92F-710PV
92S/100SS-50
92S/I-2
92S/I-425NH
92T-1
92T-4RB
92T/GPromo-1
92UD-655
92UD-92HL

Ryan, Ray
T206

Ryan, Reid
90Classic/III-91M

Ryan, Sean
90Batavia/ProC-3076
91Reading/LineD-517
91Reading/ProC-1377
91Single/ClBest-117

Ryan, Wilfred
(Rosy)
90Target-702
E121/120
E121/80
V100
W501-75
W575

Ryba, Dominic
(Mike)
54Hunter
54T-237

Rychel, Kevin
90Augusta/ProC-2461
91Salem/ClBest-19
91Salem/ProC-949

Ryder, Brian
81Colum-14
82Indianap-11
83Indianap-11

Ryder, Scott
90Idaho/ProC-3245
91Pulaski/ClBest-26
91Pulaski/ProC-4003

Ryerson, Gary
No Cards.

Rymer, Carlos
80Ander-16

Saa, Humberto
90Hunting/ProC-3293
91Geneva/ClBest-17
91Geneva/ProC-4227

Saatzer, Michael
82Redwd-10
83Nashua-7
86QuadC-30CO

Saavedra, Ed
81Watlo-27
82Chatt-4
83BuffB-20
84BuffB-22

Saavedra, Justo
80Batavia-23

Saberhagen, Bret
84F/X-U103
84T/Tr-104T
85D-222
85D/HL-26
85F-212
85F/St-124
85OPC-23

85T-23
86D-100
86D-11DK
86D/DKsuper-11
86Drake-29
86F-19
86F/LimEd-38
86F/LL-37
86F/Mini-3
86F/Slug-31
86F/St-103
86KayBee-27
86Kitty/Disc-3
86Leaf-11DK
86NatPhoto-31
86OPC-249
86OPC/WaxBox-O
86Quaker-19
86Sf-10
86Sf-176M
86Sf-185M
86Sf-186M
86T-487
86T-720AS
86T/3D-25
86T/Gloss60-27
86T/Mini-20
86T/St-17WS
86T/St-260
86T/Super-3
86T/WaxBox-O
87Classic-88
87Classic/Up-116
87D-132
87D/HL-6
87F-379
87F/AwardWin-34
87F/LimWaxBox-C5
87F/Slug-36
87Leaf-261
87OPC-140
87Sf-145
87T-140
88Classic/Red-172
88D-96
88D/AS-8
88D/Best-231
88D/PopUp-8
88F-268
88F-626M
88F/LL-33
88F/Mini-26
88F/St-32
88F/TL-32
88Jiffy-15
88Leaf-68
88Nestle-11
88OPC-5
88Panini/St-102
88Panini/St-229
88RedFoley/St-77
88S-89
88S/WaxBox-9
88S/YS/II-17
88Sf-15
88Smok/Royals-16
88T-540
88T/Big-94
88T/Coins-25
88T/Gloss22-10
88T/Mini-14
88T/St-163
88T/St-254
88T/St/Backs-60
88T/UK-63
89B-111
89Classic-62
89D-144
89D/Best-95
89F-291
89OPC-157
89Panini/St-352
89S-251
89Sf-109
89T-750
89T/Big-6
89T/LJN-39
89T/St-263
89Tastee/Discs-11
89UD-37
90B-364
90B/Ins-9
90BBWit-21
90Bz-4
90Classic-139
90Classic/Up-NNO
90CollAB-30
90D-89
90D/BestAL-21
90F-116
90F/AwardWin-30
90F/BB-31
90F/BBMVP-32
90F/LL-32
90Holsum/Discs-5
90HotPlay/St-36
90KMart/SS-26
90Leaf/I-72
90OPC-350
90OPC-393ASen
90Panini/St-81
90PublInt/St-354
90S-195
90Sf-94
90Starline/LJS-19
90Starline/LJS-36
90T-350
90T-393AS
90T/Big-21
90T/Coins-2
90T/DH-54
90T/Gloss60-13
90T/HeadsUp-7
90T/Mini-17
90T/St-266
90T/TVAS-15
90Tetley/Discs-17
90UD-326
90USPlayC/AS-3C
90Windwlk/Discs-4
90Woolwth/HL-3
91B-291
91BBBest/Aces-14
91Classic/200-36
91Classic/III-80
91D-88
91F-567
91F/Ultra-154
91Leaf/I-118
91Leaf/Stud-69
91OPC-280
91Panini/FrSt-283
91Panini/St-225
91Pol/Royal-18
91RedFoley/St-80
91S-6
91S/100SS-59
91T-280
91T/CJMini/II-14
91T/StClub/I-38
91UD-33TC
91UD-435
92D/I-128
92D/II-434HL
92F-167
92S/100SS-11
92S/I-6
92S/II-786HL
92T-75
92UD-233

Sabino, Miguel
87Sumter-3
88Greenvl/Best-7
89Greenvl/ProC-1170
89Greenvl/Star-21
89Greenvl/Best-27
90Canton/Best-15
90Canton/ProC-1305
90Canton/Star-16
91Canton/LineD-94
91Canton/ProC-992

Sable, Luke
88Gaston/ProC-1002
89CharlR/Star-21
90CharlR/Star-25
91Tulsa/LineD-595
91Tulsa/ProC-2782

Sabo, Chris
87Nashvl-18
88D/Best-278
88D/Rook-30
88F/Slug-35
88F/Up-U87
88Kahn/Reds-17
88S/Tr-100T
88T/Tr-98T
89B-309
89Bz-18
89Classic-53
89D-317
89D-4DK
89D/AS-59
89D/Best-222
89D/DKsuper-4DK
89F-170
89F-637M
89F/BBMVP's-33
89F/Excit-35
89F/Superstar-35
89F/WaxBox-C21
89Kahn/Reds-17
89KingB/Discs-7
89KMart/DT-3
89OPC-156
89Panini/St-476
89Panini/St-64
89S-104
89S/HotRook-76
89S/YS/I-10
89Sf-13
89T-490
89T/Big-251
89T/Coins-3
89T/Gloss60-40
89T/JumboR-17
89T/LJN-68
89T/Mini-13
89T/St-142
89T/St-325
89T/UK-65
89ToysRUs-24
89UD-180
89UD-663ROY
89Woolwth-6
90B-53
90CedarDG/Best-4
90Classic/Up-43
90D-242
90D/BestNL-64
90F-433
90Kahn/Reds-25
90KingB/Discs-10
90Leaf/I-146
90MLBPA/Pins-19
90OPC-737
90Panini/St-248
90PublInt/St-39
90S-70
90Starline/LJS-20
90Starline/LJS-25
90T-737
90T/Big-121
90T/St-140
90Tetley/Discs-3
90UD-181
90USPlayC/AS-5H
91B-674
91Classic/200-108
91Classic/I-26
91D-153
91D-412MVP
91D-440AS
91F-80
91F/Ultra-103
91F/UltraG-9
91F/WS-5
91Kahn/Reds-17
91Leaf/I-65
91Leaf/Stud-170
91MooTown-21
91OPC-45
91Panini/FrSt-129
91Panini/FrSt-160
91Panini/St-127
91Pep/Reds-19
91Post-13
91Post/Can-10
91RedFoley/St-125
91RedFoley/St-81
91S-462
91S-795WS
91S/100SS-28
91T-45
91T/CJMini/II-29
91T/StClub/I-165
91UD-135
91UD-77TC
91UD/FinalEd-94F
91USPlayC/AS-12C
91Woolwth/HL-29
92D/I-50
92D/II-424AS
92F-420
92F/TmLIns-3
92S/I-70
92T-485
92UD-123

Sabo, Scott
85Madis-1
85Madis/Pol-21
86Madis-19
86Madis/Pol-17
87Wmsprt-20

Sabol, Tony
46Remar-13
47Remar-15
47Signal
47Smith-13

Saccomanno, Joseph
89BurlB/ProC-1600
89BurlB/Star-19

Sacka, Frank
89Chatt/II/Team-26

Sadecki, Ray
60T-327
61T-32
62T-383
62T/St-190
63T-486
64T-147
65OPC-10LL
65OPC-230
65T-10LL
65T-230
66OPC-26
66T-26
67T-409
68Coke
68Dexter-69
68T-494
69MB-244
69OPC-125
69T-125
70T-679
71MLB/St-163
71OPC-406
71T-406
72MB-303
72T-563
72T-564IA
73OPC-283
73T-283
74OPC-216
74T-216
75OPC-349
75T-349
75T/M-349
77T-26
91WIZMets-339

Sadek, Mike
74OPC-577
74T-577
75Phoenix-3
76OPC-234
76T-234
77T-129
78T-8
79Pol/Giants-3
79T-256
80OPC-240DP
80Pol/Giants-3
80T-462
81D-498
81T-384

Sadler, Alan
85Beloit-21
86Stockton-24
87ElPaso-24
88Stockton/Cal-181
88Stockton/ProC-726
89Denver/CMC-9
89Denver/ProC-44
90Denver/CMC-19
90Denver/ProC-626

Sadler, Sean
90Niagara/Pucko-14
91Fayette/ClBest-15
91Fayette/ProC-1173

Sadowski, Ed
59T-139
60L-113
60T-403
61T-163
62T-569
63T-527
64T-61M

Sadowski, Robert
64T-271
65OPC-156
65T-156
66T-523
78TCMA-167

Sadowski, Robert F.
62Kahn/Atl
62T-595R
63T-568

Sadowski, Ted
61Clover-24
61T-254
61T/St-174

Sadowsky, Clinton
91Bristol/ClBest-17
91Bristol/ProC-3604

Saetre, Damon
90Penin/Star-19
91Penin/ClBest-16
91Penin/ProC-392

Saferight, Harry
75Shrev/TCMA-18
76Shrev
78Colum
79Portl-21
80Richm-16
80T-683R
81Richm-24
82Toledo-10

Saffell, Tom
51B-130
52Mother-36
59DF

Sagawa, Kiyoshi
89Visalia/Cal-103
89Visalia/ProC-1434

Sage, Henry
N172

Sager, A.J.
88Spokane/ProC-1933
89CharRain/ProC-971
90Wichita/Rock-18
91Wichita/LineD-617
91Wichita/ProC-2597

Saier, Vic
14CJ-104
15CJ-104
BF2-66
D328-148
D329-152
D350/2-152
E135-148
M101/4-152
M101/5-152
T207
T222

Sain, Joe
83Wisco/LF-5

Sain, Johnny
47HomogBond-42
47TipTop
48B-12
49B-47
49Eureka-21
51B-314
51FB
51T/BB-9
52BR
52T-49
53B/BW-25
53T-119
54T-205
55Rodeo
55T-193
73OPC-356CO
73T-356CO
74OPC-221CO
74T-221CO
78Richm
79Richm-3CO
80Richm-9CO
81Richm-1CO
82Richm-28CO
83Richm-25CO
84Richm-26CO
85Pol/Atl-33CO
86Pol/Atl-33CO
89Swell-121
91T/Arc53-119
D305
Exh47

R302-122
Sain, Tom
78OrlTw
79Toledo-15
Saitta, Pat
87Dunedin-29
Sajonia, Brian
88James/ProC-1907
Sakata, Lenn
76Spoka
77Spoka
79Vanco-22
80T-668R
81D-499
81F-194
81T-287
82D-644
82F-178
82T-136
83D-205
83F-72
83T-319
84D-620
84F-19
84Nes/792-578
84T-578
85F-189
85T-81
86T-446
86Tacom-20
88SoOreg/ProC-1717
88T-716
89Modesto/Cal-288
91Crown/Orio-399
91Edmon/LineD-175CO
91Edmon/ProC-1533CO
91Pac/SenLg-91
Sakowski, Vince
83TriCit-19
Sala, David J.
87Spring/Best-16
89Savan/ProC-367
Salaiz, David
89ColMud/Best-5
89ColMud/ProC-138
Salamon, John
91Martins/ClBest-18
91Martins/ProC-3453
Salas, Mark
82ArkTr-11
82Nashvl-20
83ArkTr-12
84Louisvl-27
85D-547
85F/Up-U94
85T/Tr-101T
86D-316
86F-402
86F/St-104
86KayBee-28
86Leaf-185
86OPC-43
86Sf-177M
86T-537
86T/St-278
86T/St-315
87F-551
87F/Up-U106
87OPC-87
87T-87
87T/Tr-107T
88Coke/WS-26
88S-232
88S/Tr-52T
88T/Tr-99T
89ColoSp/CMC-20
89ColoSp/ProC-240
89F-511
89S-542
89T-384
89UD-460
90CokeK/Tiger-21
91CokeK/Tiger-27
91D-65
91F-350
91F/Ultra-127
91OPC-498
91T-498
91T/StClub/II-456
91UD-205
92D/II-512
92F-144
92S/I-394
Salava, Randy
82Reading-18
83Reading-19
84Cram/PCL-203
85Cram/PCL-37
85Phill/TastyK-45
Salazar, Argenis
(Angel)
84D-33RR
84Stuart-31
85D-523
85OPC-154
85T-154
86F/Up-U100
86T/Tr-96T
87D-624
87F-380
87T-533
87T/St-259
88Berg/Cubs-18
88D-502
88D/Cubs/Bk-NEW
88F-269
88OPC-29
88Panini/St-109
88S-330
88T-29
89S-527
89T-642
89UD-222
Salazar, Carlos
90SoOreg/Best-19
90SoOreg/ProC-3436
91Modesto/ProC-3099
Salazar, Jeff
83Peoria/LF-17
Salazar, Julian
91Beloit/ClBest-16
91Beloit/ProC-2112
Salazar, Lazerio
86Negro/Frit-93
Salazar, Luis
77Salem
78Salem
80Port-9
81F-501
81T-309
81T/St-228
82D-472
82F-581
82OPC-133
82T-366TL
82T-662
82T/St-101
83D-548
83F-371
83OPC-156
83T-533
84D-356
84F-311
84Mother/Padres-24
84Nes/792-68
84OPC-68
84Smok/Padres-20
84T-68
84T/St-159
85Coke/WS-5
85D-568
85F-43
85F/Up-U95
85T-789
85T/Tr-102T
86D-302
86F-215
86T-103
87T-454
87T/Tr-108T
88F-595
88F/Up-U30
88OPC-276
88Pep/T-12
88S-284
88S/Tr-13T
88StCath/ProC-2006
88T-276
88T/Tr-100T
89Classic-72
89Coke/Padre-15
89D-352
89F-144
89OPC-122
89Panini/St-342
89S-316
89T-553
89T/St-276
89T/Tr-107T
89UD-136
90B-40
90Bristol/ProC-3164
90Bristol/Star-22
90Cub/Mara-17
90D-513
90F/Up-U9
90Leaf/II-388
90OPC-378
90S-92
90T-378
90T/Big-182
90T/TVCub-25
90UD-6
91B-428
91Cub/Mara-10
91D-372
91F-430
91F/Ultra-67
91Leaf/I-185
91OPC-614
91Panini/FrSt-45
91S-207
91T-614
91T/StClub/I-94
91UD-311
92D/I-152
92S/II-508
92T-67
92UD-638
Salazar, Terry
81Buffa-21
Salcedo, Edwin
90Tampa/DIMD-19
Salcedo, Jose
91Kissim/ProC-4182
Salcedo, Luis
87Madis-24
Salcedo, Ron
84CharlO-4
85CharlO-11
87RochR-4
87RochR/TCMA-19
88RochR/Team-19
88RochR/CMC-16
88RochR/Gov-24
88RochR/ProC-200
89ScrWB/CMC-16
89ScrWB/ProC-707
90HagersDG/Best-24
Salee
N172
Salery, Johnny
82Wisco-9
83Wisco/LF-13
Salinas, Manual V.
87BirmB/Best-23
88Jacks/GS-18
88TexLgAS/GS-14
89Jacks/GS-13
89Tidew/ProC-1951
Salisbury, Jim
86Sumter-24
87Durham-24
Salkeld, Bill
49B-88
49Eureka-22
50B-237
Salkeld, Roger
89Belling/Legoe-13
90A&AASingle/ProC-135
90AS/Cal-21
90B-465
90Foil/Best-14
90OPC-44FDP
90SanBern/Best-1
90SanBern/Cal-87
90SanBern/ProC-2632
90S-674DC
90T-44FDP
91B-262
91Classic/II-T59
91Jaxvl/LineD-344
91Jaxvl/ProC-151
91Leaf/GRook-BC19
91Single/ClBest-106
91UD-63TP
92D/I-7RR
92T-676R
92UD-15SR
Sallee, Andy
91Martins/ClBest-7
91Martins/ProC-3464
Sallee, H. Slim
11Helmar-176
14CJ-123
15CJ-123
88Conlon/4-24
88Pac/8Men-82
BF2-94
D327
D328-149
D329-153
D350/2-153
E121/80
E122
E135-149
E254
E270/2
E300
M101/4-153
M101/5-153
M116
T204
T222
T3-37
V100
W514-86
W575
Salles, John
89Peoria/Ko-8P
90CLAS/CL-47
90WinSalem/Team-3
91CharlK/LineD-141
91CharlK/ProC-1687
Salmon, Chico
64T-499R
65OPC-105
65T-105
66T-594
67OPC-43
67T-43
68T-318
69MB-245
69MLB/St-99
69OPC-62
69T-62
69T/St-230
70MLB/St-156
70OPC-301
70T-301
71MLB/St-312
71OPC-249
71T-249
72MB-304
72T-646
91Crown/Orio-400
Salmon, Timothy
88CapeCod/Sum-176
89BendB/Legoe-23
90PalmSp/Cal-215
90PalmSp/ProC-2593
91B-203
91Classic/III-81
91London/LineD-443
91MidldA/ProC-447
91Single/ClBest-329
Saltzgaber, Brian
90Niagara/Pucko-9
91Fayette/ClBest-16
91Fayette/ProC-1174
91SALAS/ProC-SAL21
Salva, Elias
80Wausau-8
Salvior, Troy
90Hamil/Best-10
90Hamil/Star-22
91Single/ClBest-310
91StPete/ClBest-10
91StPete/ProC-2274
Salyer, Ron
75SanAn
Samaniego, Art
79Elmira-5
Sambito, Joe
74Cedar
77T-227
78BK/Ast-10
78T-498
79T-158
80T-571
81Coke
81D-21
81F-65
81OPC-334
81T-385
81T/St-172
82D-65
82F-230
82F/St-47
82T-34
83D-244
83F-464
83OPC-296
83T-662
85D-572
85F-360
85F/Up-U96
85T-264
85T/Tr-103T
86F/Up-U101
86Mother/Ast-19
86T/Tr-97T
87D-421
87F-43
87OPC-262
87T-451
88F-364
88S-314
88T-784
88Tucson/JP-20
89Pac/SenLg-18
89T/SenLg-95
89TM/SenLg-93
91Pac/SenLg-157
91WIZMets-340
Sambo, Ramon
87Vermont-7
88Cedar/ProC-1149
89ElPaso/GS-28
89TexLAS/GS-15
90Vanco/CMC-15
90Vanco/ProC-503
91London/LineD-444
91MidldA/ProC-448
Samboy, Alvaro
91Spokane/ClBest-25
91Spokane/ProC-3949
Samcoff, Ed
48Smith-19
49Remar
Samford, Ron
59T-242
60T-409
79TCMA-102
Sammons, Lee
91Madison/ClBest-28
91Tacoma/ProC-2319
Samonds, Shereen
89Orlan/Best-28
Sampen, Bill
86Watertn-21
87Salem-21
89Harris/ProC-290
89Harris/Star-17
90B-104
90D/Rook-12
90F/Up-U31
90S/Tr-79T
90Swell/Great-118
90T/Tr-108T
90UD/Ext-724
91D-351
91F-247
91Leaf/II-318
91Leaf/Stud-199
91OPC-649
91Panini/FrSt-149
91S-68
91S/100RisSt-64
91Swell/Great-79
91T-649
91T/90Debut-138
91T/StClub/I-249
91ToysRUs-26
91UD-661
92D/II-571
92F-492
92S/I-166
92T-566
Sample, Billy
78Cr/PCL-72
79T-713R
80T-458
81D-268
81F-637

81OPC-283
81T-283
82D-69
82F-330
82OPC-112
82T-112
83D-242
83F-577
83Rang-5
83T-641
84D-403
84F-426
84Nes/792-12
84OPC-12
84Rang-5
84T-12
84T/St-352
85D-464
85F-566
85F/Up-U97
85T-337
85T/St-351
86D-539
86F-118
86F/Up-U102
86Pol/Atl-5
86T-533
86T/Tr-98T
87D-143
87F-527
87T-104

Sample, Deron
89Kingspt/Star-20
90SALAS/Star-41
91StLucie/ClBest-17
91StLucie/ProC-709

Sample, Frank
91Hunting/ClBest-22
91Hunting/ProC-3334

Samples, Todd
90James/Pucko-11
91SALAS/ProC-SAL47
91Sumter/ClBest-24
91Sumter/ProC-2349

Samplinski, Rich
88CapeCod/Sum-104

Sampson, Mark
86Cram/PCL-166

Sampson, Michael
89VeroB/Star-24
90Yakima/Team-3
91VeroB/ClBest-11
91VeroB/ProC-772

Sams, Andre
78Green

Samson, Frederic
(Fred)
87PortChar-14
89Tulsa/GS-23
89Tulsa/Team-22
90CharlR/Star-26
90FSLAS/Star-42
91Tulsa/LineD-596
91Tulsa/ProC-2783

Samson, William
52Park-51
53Exh/Can-54

Samuel, Amado
62T-597R
64T-129
91WIZMets-341

Samuel, Juan
83Portl-2
83Reading-17
84F-47
85FunFoodPin-68
84Phill/TastyK-32
84T/Tr-105T
85CIGNA-1
85D-183
85D-23DK
85D/AAS-56
85D/DKsuper-23
85Drake-27
85F-264
85F-634IA
85F/St-44
85F/St-59
85Leaf-23DK
85OPC-265
85Phill/TastyK-11M
85Phill/TastyK-32
85Seven-15E
85T-265
85T-8RB
85T/Gloss40-31
85T/St-114
85T/St-369YS
85T/Super-28
86BK/AP-10
86CIGNA-1
86D-326
86D/HL-37
86F-449
86F/LimEd-39
86F/LL-38
86F/Mini-93
86F/St-105
86KayBee-29
86Keller-4
86Leaf-196
86OPC-237
86Phill/TastyK-8
86Sf-94
86T-475
86T/Mini-54
86T/St-121
87Champion-3
87D-165
87D/OD-156
87F-185
87F-642M
87F/BB-39
87F/LL-38
87F/Mini-94
87F/St-104
87Leaf-132
87OPC-255
87Phill/TastyK-8
87Sf-123
87T-255
87T/Mini-29
87T/St-125
88Bz-18
88D-288
88D/AS-55
88D/Best-215
88Drake-20
88F-314
88F/AS-10
88F/BB/AS-35
88F/Mini-101
88F/St-110
88F/TL-33
88KayBee-26
88Leaf-146
88Nestle-16
88OPC-19
88Panini/St-359
88Phill/TastyK-22
88S-32
88Sf-96
88Sf/Gamewin-12
88T-398AS
88T-705
88T/Big-67
88T/Coins-51
88T/Gloss60-43
88T/Mini-66
88T/Revco-7
88T/St-120
88T/St/Backs-5
88T/UK-64
89T/Ames-25
89B-405
89Cadaco-47
89Classic-146
89D-76
89D/Best-238
89F-581
89F/Up-102
89Kahn/Mets-7
89OPC-372
89Panini/St-152
89Phill/TastyK-31
89RedFoley/St-101
89S-255
89S/HotStar-26
89S/Tr-21
89Sf-17
89T-575
89T/Big-321
89T/Coins-23
89T/Gloss60-13
89T/Hills-25
89T/LJN-51
89T/Mini-29
89T/St-117
89T/St/Backs-37
89T/Tr-108T
89T/UK-66
89UD-336
90B-91
90Classic/III-45
90D-53
90D/BestNL-29
90F-215
90F/Up-U25
90Leaf/I-226
90Mother/Dodg-7
90OPC-85
90Pol/Dodg-10
90PublInt/St-249
90S-198
90S/Tr-33T
90T-85
90T/Ames-25
90T/Big-283
90T/Mini-68
90T/Tr-109T
90UD-583
90UD/Ext-795
91B-596
91Classic/III-82
91D-62
91F-218
91F/Ultra-168
91Leaf/I-10
91Leaf/Stud-188
91Mother/Dodg-7
91OPC-645
91Panini/FrSt-56
91Pol/Dodg-10
91S-446
91T-645
91T/StClub/II-495
91T/WaxBox-O
91UD-117
91USPlayC/AS-8C
91WIZMets-342
92D/I-105
92F-469
92S/I-73
92T-315
92UD-195

Samuel, Mike
81BurlB-19
82Beloit-19
84ElPaso-9
85Beloit-1

Samuels, Geoff
91BendB/ClBest-10
91BendB/ProC-3695

Samuels, Roger
86ColumAst-23
88F/Up-U131
88Phoenix/CMC-8
88Phoenix/ProC-70
90T/TVMets-57
90Tidew/CMC-19
90Tidew/ProC-543

Sanborn, Kyle
88CapeCod/Sum-112

Sanchez, Adrian
90Hunting/ProC-3281
91Hunting/ClBest-23
91Hunting/ProC-3335

Sanchez, Al
82OkCty-7

Sanchez, Alejandro
83Portl-22
84Cram/PCL-8
85D-43RR
85F-648R
85F/Up-U98
86D-415
86F-236
86T-563
87Tacom-20

Sanchez, Alex
88BBAmer-13
88Knoxvl/Best-1
88OPC-194DP
88SLAS-26
88Tacoma/CMC-17
88Tacoma/ProC-637
89AAA/CMC-25
89B-245
89D-47RR
89F/Up-U71
89Syrac/CMC-10
89Syrac/ProC-813
89Syrac/Team-20
89T/Tr-109T
90D-45RR
90F-92
90OPC-563
90Syrac/CMC-1
90Syrac/ProC-570
90Syrac/Team-20
90T-563
90T/89Debut-107
90Tor/BlueJ-23
90ToysRUs-23
90UD/Ext-757
91Syrac/LineD-515
91Syrac/ProC-2479

Sanchez, Carlos
88Pocatel/ProC-2077

Sanchez, Celerino
73OPC-103
73Syrac/Team-25
73T-103
74OPC-623
74Syrac/Team-24
74T-623

Sanchez, Daniel
90Greens/Best-19
90Greens/ProC-2671
90Greens/Star-21
91PrWill/ClBest-19
91PrWill/ProC-1436

Sanchez, Francisco
87Gaston-28

Sanchez, Frank
78Wausau

Sanchez, Geraldo
86Hagers-17
87Hagers-28

Sanchez, Israel
83CharR-22
85FtMyr-15
87Omaha-18
88F/Up-U34
88Omaha/CMC-11
88Omaha/ProC-1496
89D-474
89T-452
89UD-326
90UD-384
91RochR/LineD-465
91RochR/ProC-1901

Sanchez, Juan
87Clearw-22

Sanchez, Leo
84PrWill-28
85Nashua-22

Sanchez, Luis
73Cedar
74Cedar

Sanchez, Luis M.
82T-653
83D-519
83F-100
83T-623
84D-597
84F-527
84Nes/792-258
84OPC-258
84Smok/Cal-24
84T-258
84T/St-233
85D-352
85F-310
85OPC-42
85Smok/Cal-16
85T-42
86T-124

Sanchez, Orlando
80OkCty
81Louisvl-24
82D-636
82F-126
82Louisvl-26
82T-604
83Louisvl/Riley-24
85Maine-23
91Crown/Orio-401

Sanchez, Osvaldo
87Spokane-1
88Charl/ProC-1200
89Watlo/ProC-1786
89Watlo/Star-25
90Foil/Best-281
90Waterlo/Best-16
90Waterlo/ProC-2391
91HighD/ClBest-28
91HighD/ProC-2411

Sanchez, Pedro
75BurlB
86AubAs-22
87Ashvl-27
88Osceola/Star-23
89ColMud/Best-6
89ColMud/ProC-127
89ColMud/Star-21
90Tucson/CMC-22
90Tucson/ProC-207

Sanchez, Perry
90Gate/ProC-3360
91WPalmB/ClBest-17
91WPalmB/ProC-1233

Sanchez, Raul
57T-393
60T-311
61BeeHive-19

Sanchez, Rey
89OkCty/CMC-18
89OkCty/ProC-1511
91AAAGame/ProC-AAA20
91Iowa/LineD-216
91Iowa/ProC-1067
92D/II-412RR
92T/91Debut-154
92UD-562

Sanchez, Sammye
88LitFalls/Pucko-12

Sanchez, Stan
87SanBern-6
89SanBern/Best-26
89SanBern/Cal-91CO

Sanchez, Zoilo
86Lynch-20
88Jacks/GS-2
89Jacks/GS-15
90T/TVMets-58
90Tidew/CMC-26
90Tidew/ProC-558

Sand, John Henry
(Heinie)
21Exh-150
25Exh-47
26Exh-47
28Exh-23
33G-85
92Conlon/Sport-615
V354-27

Sandberg, Chuck
81Bristol-11

Sandberg, Ryne
80Reading
81OkCty/TCMA-17
82RedLob
83D-277
83F-507
83OPC-83
83T-83
83T/St-328
83Thorn-23
84D-311
84D/AAS-43
84F-504
85FunFoodPin-13
84Nes/792-596
84OPC-64
84SevenUp-23
84T-596
84T/St-45
85D-1DK
85D-67
85D/AAS-24
85D/DKsuper-1
85D/WaxBox-PC2
85Drake-28
85F-630IA
85F-65
85F/LimEd-31
85F/St-11
85F/St-45
85GenMills-8
85Leaf-1DK
85OPC-296
85Seven-11G
85SevenUp-23
85T-460
85T-713AS

85T/3D-7
85T/Gloss22-3
85T/Gloss40-21
85T/St-175FOIL
85T/St-34
85T/Super-1
85ThomMc/Discs-41
86Cub/Unocal-15
86D-67
86D/AAS-32
86Dorman-14
86Drake-19
86F-378
86F/LimEd-40
86F/LL-39
86F/Mini-80
86F/Slug-32
86F/St-106
86Gator-23
86Jay's-15
86Jiffy-12
86Leaf-62
86Meadow/Blank-13
86Meadow/Milk-10
86Meadow/Stat-12
86OPC-19
86Quaker-13
86Sf-127M
86Sf-20
86Sf-51M
86T-690
86T/Gloss60-34
86T/Mini-39
86T/St-55
86T/Super-48
86TrueVal-14
87Berg/Cubs-23
87BK-18
87Classic-35
87D-77
87D/AAS-13
87D/OD-75
87D/PopUp-13
87Drake-21
87F-572
87F-639M
87F/AwardWin-35
87F/LL-39
87F/Mini-95
87F/St-105
87F/WaxBox-C14
87Ho/St-8
87Jiffy-1
87KayBee-28
87Kraft-8
87Leaf-234
87MnM's-4
87OPC-143
87Ralston-15
87RedFoley/St-16
87Sf-116M
87Sf-197M
87Sf-8
87Seven-C14
87Seven-ME11
87T-680
87T/Board-30
87T/Coins-41
87T/Gloss22-3
87T/St-156
87T/St-61
88Berg/Cubs-23
88Bz-19
88ChefBoy-11
88Classic/Red-169
88D-242
88D/AS-35
88D/Best-116
88D/Cubs/Bk-242
88D/PopUp-13
88F-431
88F-628M
88F/BB/MVP-29
88F/Excit-32
88F/Mini-70
88F/SS-C5
88F/St-80
88F/WaxBox-C10
88Leaf-207
88OPC-10
88Panini/St-234M
88Panini/St-260
88S-26
88S/WaxBox-12
88Sf-12
88T-10
88T/Big-16
88T/Coins-52
88T/Gloss22-14
88T/Gloss60-14
88T/St-147
88T/St-57
88T/St/Backs-6
88T/UK-65
89T/Ames-26
89B-290
89Cadaco-48
89D-105
89D/AS-35
89D/Best-26
89D/PopUp-35
89F-437
89F/Heroes-35
89KayBee-26
89KingB/Discs-5
89KMart/DT-24
89Mara/Cubs-23
89OPC-360
89Panini/St-233AS
89Panini/St-56
89S-35
89S/HotStar-54
89S/Mast-23
89Sf-201
89T-360
89T-387AS
89T/Big-212
89T/DH-14
89T/Gloss22-14
89T/Gloss60-34
89T/HeadsUp-9
89T/LJN-110
89T/St-155
89T/St-55
89T/St/Backs-38
89T/UK-67
89UD-120
89UD-675TC
90B-30
90Classic-27
90Classic/III-86
90CollAB-29
90Cub/Mara-18
90D-105
90D-692AS
90D/BestNL-26
90D/Bon/MVP-BC10
90D/Learning-11DK
90F-40
90F-625MV
90F-639M
90F/ASIns-9
90F/AwardWin-31
90F/BB-32
90F/BBMVP-33
90F/LL-33
90HotPlay/St-37
90KMart/SS-2
90Leaf/I-98
90Leaf/II-528CL
90MLBPA/Pins-47
90MSA/Soda-19
90OPC-210
90OPC-398AS
90Panini/St-212
90Panini/St-231
90Post-9
90PublInt/St-201
90PublInt/St-270
90S-561HL
90S-691DT
90S-90
90S/100St-32
90S/McDon-8
90Sf-54
90Sunflower-20
90T-210
90T-398AS
90T/Big-75
90T/Coins-56
90T/DH-55
90T/Gloss22-3
90T/Gloss60-1
90T/HeadsUp-9
90T/Mini-51
90T/St-12HL
90T/St-152AS
90T/St-46
90T/TVAS-51
90T/TVCub-26
90T/WaxBox-P
90Tetley/Discs-12
90UD-324
90USPlayC/AS-4H
90WonderBrd-20
90Woolwth/HL-21
91B-377SLUG
91B-416
91BBBest/HitM-17
91BBBest/RecBr-15
91Bz-9
91Classic/200-107
91Classic/I-29
91Classic/I-NO
91Classic/II-T67
91Colla/Sandberg-Set
91CollAB-15
91Cub/Mara-23
91D-14DK
91D-404MVP
91D-433AS
91D-504
91D-BC7
91D/Elite-S1
91D/Preview-9
91D/SuperDK-14
91F-431
91F-709M
91F-713
91F/ASIns-1
91F/ProVF-3F
91F/Ultra-66
91F/UltraG-10
91JDeanSig-6
91KingB/Discs-19
91Leaf/I-207
91Leaf/Prev-2
91Leaf/Stud-158
91LineD/Sandberg-Set
91MajorLg/Pins-68
91MooTown-5
91OPC-398AS
91OPC-740
91OPC-7RB
91OPC/Premier-103
91Panini/FrSt-159
91Panini/FrSt-44
91Panini/St-40
91Panini/Top15-101
91Panini/Top15-27
91Panini/Top15-34
91Panini/Top15-49
91Panini/Top15-9
91Pep/SS-3
91Petro/SU-4
91Post-16
91RedFoley/St-126
91RedFoley/St-82
91S-3
91S-665AS
91S-815MANYR
91S-862FRAN
91S/100SS-60
91Seven/3DCoin-11MW
91Seven/3DCoin-12T
91Seven/3DCoin-8NW
91T-398AS
91T-740
91T-7RB
91T/CJMini/I-6
91T/StClub/I-230
91T/SU-30
91UD-132
91UD/Ext-725M
91UD/FinalEd-79F
91UD/FinalEd-93F
91UD/SilSlug-SS8
91USPlayC/AS-12S
91Woolwth/HL-20
92Classic/I-79
92D/II-429AS
92D/II-576
92F-389
92F/ASIns-14
92S/100SS-85
92S/I-200
92S/I-442DT
92S/II-774AS
92S/Prev-5
92T-110
92T-387AS
92UD-145

Sander, Mike
88Hagers/Star-18
89EastLDD/ProC-DD40
89Hagers/Best-25
89Hagers/ProC-275
89Hagers/Star-15
90Hagers/Best-21
90Hagers/ProC-1413
90Hagers/Star-22
90HagersDG/Best-25

Sander, Rick
77LodiD

Sanderlin, Rick
77Phoenix
78Cr/PCL-12
79Phoenix

Sanders, Adam
90Utica/Pucko-6

Sanders, Al
88Elmira-10
89Elmira/Pucko-19
89WinHaven/Star-20
90WinHaven/Star-24
91NewBrit/LineD-471
91NewBrit/ProC-352

Sanders, Alexander
N172

Sanders, Barry
91Arena-4

Sanders, Deion
89Albany/Best-1
89Albany/ProC-338
89Albany/Star-23
89Classic/Up/2-200
89D/Rook-6
89F/Up-U53
89S/NWest-22
89T/Tr-110T
90AlbanyDG/Best-1
90Classic-21
90D-427
90F-454
90HotRook/St-38
90Leaf/II-359
90OPC-61
90S-586
90S/100Ris-40
90S/NWest-22
90S/YS/II-27
90Sf-221
90T-61
90T/89Debut-108
90T/TVYank-33
90UD-13
91B-588
91Leaf/II-436
91S/100RisSt-6
91S/RookTr-34T
91T/StClub/II-442
91UD-352
91UD/Ext-743
92Classic/I-80
92D/II-564
92F-368
92S/II-571
92T-645
92UD-247

Sanders, Earl
87Dunedin-24
88Dunedin/Star-15
89Dunedin/Star-14
90Knoxvl/Best-23
90Knoxvl/ProC-1245
90Knoxvl/Star-17
91Greenvl/ClBest-5
91Greenvl/LineD-218
91Greenvl/ProC-2999

Sanders, Ken
66T-356R
69Sunoco/Pin-16
71MLB/St-451
71OPC-116
71T-116
72OPC-391
72T-391
73OPC-246
73T-246
74OPC-638
74T-638
75OPC-366
75T-366
75T/M-366
76OPC-291
76SSPC-550
76T-291
77Spoka
77T-171
91WIZMets-343

Sanders, Lance
89Utica/Pucko-20

Sanders, Matt
91Bluefld/ProC-4129
91Bluefld/ClBest-16

Sanders, Paul
91Eugene/ClBest-8
91Eugene/ProC-3729

Sanders, Ray
47TipTop

Sanders, Reginald
(Reggie)
88Billings/ProC-1822
89Greens/ProC-415
89SALAS/GS-23
90A&AASingle/ProC-128
90Cedar/Best-11
90Cedar/ProC-2334
91B-537
91Chatt/LineD-167
91Chatt/ProC-1973
91Classic/200-70
91Leaf/GRook-BC10
91Single/ClBest-41
91UD-71TP
91UD/FinalEd-11F
91UD/FinalEd-1FCL
92Classic/I-81
92D/II-415RR
92F-421
92S/II-829
92T-283
92T/91Debut-155
92UD-27SR

Sanders, Reginald Jerome
(Reggie)
74OPC-600R
74T-600R
75OPC-617R
75T-617R
75T/M-617R

Sanders, Satch
81Miami-9

Sanders, Scott
91Single/ClBest-338
91Waterlo/ClBest-8
91Waterlo/ProC-1255

Sanders, Stan
82Oneonta-7

Sanders, Tracy
90A&AASingle/ProC-188
90Burllnd/ProC-3023
91CLAS/ProC-CAR19
91Kinston/ClBest-27
91Kinston/ProC-339
91Single/ClBest-202

Sanderski, John
86WinHaven-20
87Greens-24

Sanderson, Scott
79T-720R
80OPC-301
80T-578
81D-450
81F-166
81OPC-235
81OPC/Post-12
81T-235
82D-288
82F-206
82F/St-40
82Hygrade
82OPC-7
82OPC/Post-22
82T-7
82T/St-63
82Zeller-17
83D-446
83F-295
83OPC-54
83Stuart-17
83T-717
84D-341
84F-285
84F/X-U104
84Nes/792-164
84OPC-164
84SevenUp-24

84T-164
84T/Tr-106T
85D-266
85F-66
85Leaf-194
85OPC-373
85SevenUp-21
85T-616
85T/St-40
86Cub/Unocal-16
86D-442
86F-379
86Gator-21
86T-406
87Berg/Cubs-21
87D-447
87F-573
87T-534
87T/St-60
88AlaskaAS70/Team-21
88Berg/Cubs-21
88D-646
88D/Cubs/Bk-646
88F-432
88S-544
88T-311
89D-629
89F/Up-78
89Mara/Cubs-21
89T-212
89UD-342
90B-447
90D-647
90F-41
90F/Up-118
90Leaf/I-194
90Mother/A's-11
90OPC-67
90Publint/St-202
90S-488
90S/Tr-61T
90T-67
90T/Tr-110T
90UD-39
90UD/Ext-739
91B-177
91D-533
91F-23
91F/UltraUp-U43
91Leaf/I-169
91Leaf/Stud-99
91OPC-728
91OPC/Premier-104
91S-118
91S/RookTr-78T
91T-728
91T/Tr-104T
91UD-582
91UD/Ext-750
91USPlayC/AS-3D
92D/DK-DK10
92D/I-227
92F-243
92S/100SS-59
92S/I-211
92T-480
92UD-415

Sanderson, Shaun
89SLCity-17C
90Erie/Star-23

Sandling, Bob
80Elmira-14

Sandlock, Mike
53T-247
54T-104
90Target-703
91T/Arc53-247

Sandoval, Dennis
77Wausau

Sandoval, Guillermo
89Beloit/II/Star-24
90Stockton/Best-22
90Stockton/Cal-183
90Stockton/ProC-2183
91Stockton/ClBest-10

Sandoval, Jesus
86AppFx-20

Sandoval, Mike
87Watertn-31
90Harris/Star-25TR

Sandry, Bill
83AppFx/LF-28

Sands, Charlie
72T-538
74OPC-381
74T-381
75OPC-548
75T-548
75T/M-548
75Tucson-24
76Tucson-39

Sandt, Tommy
75Tucson-1
77T-616
78Syrac
79Portl-6
80Port-8
81Portl-21
82Buffa-18
83LynnP-23
84Cram/PCL-137
85Cram/PCL-233
86Hawaii-6MG
89VFJuice-31CO
90Homer/Pirate-26CO

Sandy, Tim
90Kgsport/Best-17
90Kgsport/Star-22
91Pittsfld/ClBest-8
91Pittsfld/ProC-3436

Sanford, Ed
82ArkTr-8

Sanford, John F.
47TipTop
49B-236
50B-156
51B-145
52Mother
53Mother

Sanford, John S.
(Jack)
57T-387
58Hires-39
58T-264
59T-275
60L-54
60T-165
61P-154
61T-258
61T-383M
61T/St-84
62J-141
62P-141
62P/Can-141
62T-538
63J-110
63P-110
63T-325
63T-7LL
63T/SO
64T-414
65OPC-228
65T-228
66OPC-23
66T-23
67T-549
79TCMA-125

Sanford, Meredith Jr.
(Mo)
89Greens/ProC-423
89SALAS/GS-31
90A&AASingle/ProC-120
90Cedar/Best-23
90Cedar/ProC-2321
91Chatt/LineD-168
91Chatt/ProC-1960
91F/Up-U86
91Single/ClBest-47
92Classic/I-82
92D/II-417RR
92S/II-769
92T-674
92T/91Debut-156
92UD-45

Sanguillen, Manny
68KDKA-35
68T-251
69T-509
70MLB/St-106
70OPC-188
70T-188
71K-13
71MD
71MLB/St-213
71OPC-480
71OPC-62LL
71T-480
71T-62LL
71T/tatt-5
72K-19
72MB-305
72OPC-225WS
72OPC-228WS
72OPC-60
72T-225WS
72T-228WS
72T-60
73K-42
73OPC-250
73T-250
73T/Lids-46
74K-15
74OPC-28
74T-28
74T/DE-22
74T/St-87
75Ho-21
75Ho/Twink-21
75OPC-515
75T-515
75T/M-515
76Crane-53
76Ho-72
76K-42
76MSA/Disc
76OPC-191LL
76OPC-220
76SSPC-571
76T-191LL
76T-220
77BurgChef-111
77OPC-231
77Pep-4
77T-61
78T-658
78Wiffle/Discs-66
79T-447
80T-148
81D-14
81F-376
81T-226
89Swell-29
90Pac/Legend-75
90Swell/Great-126
91Swell/Great-80

Sanjurjo, Jose
91Bristol/ClBest-11
91Bristol/ProC-3620

Sankey, Ben
R314/Can
V355-83

Sanner, Dale
75Tucson-4
76Tucson-14

Sano, Motokuni
88Miami/Star-23

SantaCruz, Nick
88Batavia/ProC-1678
89Spartan/ProC-1043
89Spartan/Star-21
90Spartan/Best-18
90Spartan/ProC-2501
90Spartan/Star-18

Santaella, Alexis
90Tampa/DIMD-20

SantaMaria, Silverio
90Elmira/Pucko-21
91WinHaven/ClBest-9
91WinHaven/ProC-489

Santana, Andres
87Pocatel/Bon-23
88Clinton/ProC-705
88MidwLAS/GS-2
89SanJose/Best-1
89SanJose/Cal-226
89SanJose/ProC-450
89SanJose/Star-23
89Star/Wax-87
90B-230
90Shrev/ProC-1449
90Shrev/Star-22
91AAAGame/ProC-AAA34
91F/Ultra-328
91Phoenix/LineD-393
91Phoenix/ProC-76
91S-762RP
91T/90Debut-139
91UD-87
92S/100RisSt-32

Santana, Ernesto
87Macon-1
88Watertn/Pucko-10
89StCath/ProC-2087
90Utica/Pucko-22

Santana, Jose
89AubAs/ProC-2165
90Ashvl/ProC-2763
90Boise/ProC-3318

Santana, Miguel
88FSLAS/Star-20
90Jaxvl/Best-12
90Jaxvl/ProC-1387

Santana, Rafael
82Louisvl-27
84Tidew-16
85D-610
85F-90
85T-67
86D-319
86F-93
86OPC-102
86T-587
86T/St-102
87D-569
87D/OD-126
87F-21
87Leaf-167
87T-378
88D-633
88D/Best-273
88D/Y/Bk-NEW
88F-149
88F/Up-U50
88Panini/St-344
88S-316
88S/Tr-54T
88T-233
88T/Big-246
88T/Tr-101T
89B-174
89D-309
89F-268
89Panini/St-407
89S-296
89S/NWest-11
89T-792
89T/Big-192
89T/DHTest-21
89T/St-313
89UD-216
90OPC-651
90Publnt/St-546
90T-651
91WIZMets-344

Santana, Raul
91Sumter/ClBest-15
91Sumter/ProC-2338

Santana, Rodolfo
80Elmira-42

Santana, Ruben
90Penin/Star-20
91SanBern/ClBest-20
91SanBern/ProC-1997

Santana, Simon
77Charl

Santangelo, F.P.
88CapeCod/Sum-156
89James/ProC-2132
90WPalmB/Star-19
91Harris/LineD-268
91Harris/ProC-638

Santarelli, Cal
85Water-9
86Water-21

Santiago, Angelo
90Gate/ProC-3354

Santiago, Benito
83Miami-20
85Beaum-21
86F-644R
86LasVegas-14
87Bohem-9
87Classic/Up-132
87D-31RR
87D/HL-45
87D/HL-55
87D/OD-148
87D/Rook-44
87F-429
87Leaf-31
87Sf-118M
87Sf/Rook-19
87Sf/Rook-9
87T/Tr-109T
88Bz-20
88Classic/Blue-219
88Classic/Red-160
88Coke/Padres-9
88D-114
88D-3DK
88D/Best-301
88D/DKsuper-3DK
88F-596
88F/AwardWin-34
88F/BB/MVP-30
88F/Excit-33
88F/Hottest-33
88F/LL-34
88F/Mini-115
88F/RecSet-34
88F/SS-32
88F/St-125
88KMart-24
88Leaf-3DK
88Leaf-58
88MSA/Disc-15
88Nestle-12
88OPC-86
88Panini/St-402
88Panini/St-433
88RedFoley/St-78
88S-25
88S-654HL
88S/YS/I-2
88Sf-22
88Sf-222M
88Sf/Gamewin-10
88Smok/Padres-25
88T-404AS
88T-693
88T-699M
88T-7RB
88T/Big-12
88T/Coins-35
88T/Gloss60-30
88T/JumboR-18
88T/St-112
88T/St-2
88T/UK-66
88ToysRUs-26
88Woolwth-14
89B-453
89Bimbo/Discs-3
89Cadaco-49
89Classic-73
89Coke/Padre-16
89D-205
89F-316
89OPC-256
89Padre/Mag-11
89Panini/St-199
89RedFoley/St-102
89S-4
89S/HotStar-47
89Sf-22
89T-256
89T/Big-134
89T/Coins-24
89T/Gloss60-15
89T/LJN-100
89T/St-101
89T/St/Backs-57
89T/UK-68
89Tetley/Discs-9
89UD-165
90B-218
90Classic/Up-44
90Coke/Padre-16
90D-465
90D-708AS
90D/BestNL-121
90D/Learning-4
90F-167
90F/AwardWin-32
90HOF/St-92
90Leaf/I-207
90MLBPA/Pins-58
90OPC-35
90Padre/MagUno-2
90Padre/MagUno-21
90Panini/St-213
90Panini/St-358
90Publnt/St-271
90Publnt/St-58
90RedFoley/St-82
90S-454

90S/100St-63
90S/McDon-15
90Sf-115
90T-35
90T/Big-125
90T/DH-56
90T/Gloss22-9
90T/St-110
90T/St-153AS
90UD-12TC
90UD-325
90USPlayC/AS-10H
91B-383SLUG
91B-656
91Classic/200-175
91Classic/II-T43
91D-449
91DennyGS-18
91F-542
91F/ASIns-9
91F/Ultra-311
91KingB/Discs-20
91Leaf/II-432
91Leaf/Stud-249
91OPC-760
91OPC/Premier-105
91Panini/FrSt-157
91Panini/FrSt-90
91Panini/St-93
91Panini/Top15-99
91Post/Can-13
91RedFoley/St-83
91S-416RIF
91S-663AS
91S-810
91S-870FRAN
91S-893DT
91S/100SS-61
91Seven/3DCoin-13SC
91T-760
91T/CJMini/I-33
91T/StClub/I-105
91UD-467
91UD/FinalEd-91F
91UD/SilSlug-SS17
91USPlayC/AS-11S
92D/I-40
92D/II-430AS
92F-620
92S/100SS-36
92S/I-245
92T-185
92UD-253

Santiago, Cedric
90Elmira/Pucko-22

Santiago, Delvy
89Princet/Star-19
90Augusta/ProC-2462
91Collnd/ClBest-16
91Collnd/ProC-1483

Santiago, Gus
91Sumter/ClBest-20
91Sumter/ProC-2345

Santiago, Jorge
91Burllnd/ProC-3310

Santiago, Jose G.
56T-59

Santiago, Jose R.
65T-557
66T-203
67T-473
67T/Test/RSox-15
68OPC-123
68T-123
69MB-246
69MLB/St-16
69OPC-21
69T-21
69T/St-137
70T-708

Santiago, Mike
85Durham-11
86Jacks/TCMA-9
88Jacks/GS-9

Santiago, Norm
86FtLaud-19
87Jaxvl-3
88WPalmB/Star-22

Santiago, Rafael
90CharRain/Best-20
90CharRain/ProC-2031

Santiago, Sandi
90Tampa/DIMD-21

91Oneonta/ProC-4153

Santo, Ron
61Bz-3
61P-196
61T-35
61T/St-9
62Bz
62J-184
62P-184
62P/Can-184
62Salada-136
62Shirriff-136
62T-170
62T/St-109
63Exh
63F-32
63J-170
63P-170
63T-252
64T-375
64T/Coins-146AS
64T/Coins-68
64T/S-58
64T/St-33
64T/SU
64Wheat/St-40
65Bz-28
65OPC-110
65OPC-6LL
65T-110
65T-6LL
65T/E-28
65T/trans-67
66Bz-39
66T-290
66T/RO-102
67Bz-39
67OPC-70
67OPC/PI-26
67T-70
67T/PI-26
67T/Test/SU-22
68Bz-15
68Bz-6
68Kahn
68OPC-5LL
68T-235
68T-366AS
68T-5LL
68T/G-19
68T/Post-21
69Citgo-13
69Kahn
69Kelly/Pin-16
69MB-247
69MLB/St-125
69MLBPA/Pin-56
69NTF
69OPC-4LL
69OPC/DE-19
69Sunoco/Pin-8
69T-420AS
69T-4LL
69T-570
69T/DE-19
69T/decal
69T/S-38
69T/St-19
69Trans-42
70Dunkin-5
70K-42
70MB-25
70MLB/St-22
70OPC-454AS
70OPC-63LL
70T-454AS
70T-63LL
70T-670
70T/PI-5
70T/S-21
70Trans-2
71MD
71MLB/St-46
71OPC-220
71T-220
71T/Coins-95
71T/S
71T/tatt-13
72MB-306
72T-555
72T-556A
73K-54
73OPC-115
73T-115

74K-7
74OPC-270
74OPC-334AS
74T-270
74T-334M
74T/St-19
74T/Tr-270T
75OPC-35
75T-35
75T/M-35
78TCMA-22
83MLBPA/Pin-32
88Pac/Leg-97
89Swell-36
90BBWit-14
90Pac/Legend-48
90Swell/Great-64
91LineD-5
91Swell/Great-81
Exh47
WG10-46
WG9-45

SantoDomingo, Rafael
78Indianap-17
80Indianap-22

Santop, Louis
74Laugh/Black-16
90Negro/Star-33

Santora, Steve
85Everett/II/Cram-16
85Everett/Cram-15

Santorini, Al
69T-592R
70OPC-212
70T-212
71MLB/St-237
71OPC-467
71T-467
72T-723
73OPC-24
73T-24

Santos, Don
86Watlo-24
87Watlo-20

Santos, Ed
77LodiD

Santos, Eddie
83Kinston/Team-22

Santos, Faustoe
85Madis-2
85Madis/Pol-22

Santos, Gerald
(Jerry)
91Johnson/ClBest-21
91Johnson/ProC-3977

Santos, Luis
85FtMyr-28

Santovenia, Nelson
83Memphis-8
86Jaxvl/TCMA-8
87Jaxvl-5
87SLAS-5
88F/Up-U103
88Indianap/CMC-18
88Indianap/ProC-500
88S/Tr-96T
88T/Tr-102T
89B-361
89D-366
89D/Best-146
89F-393
89OPC-228
89Panini/St-112
89S-346
89S/HotRook-71
89T-228
89T/Big-98
89T/JumboR-18
89T/St-78
89ToysRUs-25
89UD-380
90D-224
90F-360
90Leaf/II-502
90OPC-614
90Panini/St-289
90Publint/St-187
90S-451
90Sf-162
90T-614
90UD-432
91F-248
91OPC-744

91S-777
91T-744
91T/StClub/II-416
92T-732

Sapienza, Rich
87Tampa-29
88Cedar/ProC-1148

Sarazen, Gene
33SK-22

Sarbaugh, Mike
90AS/Cal-46
91Kinston/ClBest-20
91Kinston/ProC-332

Sarcia, Joe
91Geneva/ClBest-18
91Geneva/ProC-4228

Sardinha, Ed
86Elmira-19

Sarmiento, Manny
76Indianap-16
77Indianap-25
77T-475R
78T-377
79Indianap-21
79OPC-69
79T-149
80Spokane-12
80T-21
81Pawtu-10
81T-649
82Portl-8
83D-502
83F-321
83T-566
84D-200
84F-263
84Nes/792-209
84T-209
85Cram/PCL-248

Sarmiento, Wally
80Toledo-12
81Toledo-8

Sarni, Bill
54T-194
55B-30
55Hunter
55RM-NL9
56T-247
57T-86
79TCMA-106

Sarrett, Daniel
80Water-17

Sartain, Dave
91Elizab/ProC-4299

Sasaki, Shigehi
90Salinas/Cal-118
90Salinas/ProC-2719

Sass, James
90Stockton/Best-10
90Stockton/Cal-195
90Stockton/ProC-2195
91Beloit/ClBest-9
91Beloit/ProC-2118

Sasser, Don
75Cedar
76Cedar

Sasser, Mackey
86Shrev-22
87Phoenix-20
88D-28RR
88D/Mets/Bk-NEW
88D/Rook-51
88F/Up-U106
88Kahn/Mets-2
88Leaf-28RR
88S-642RP
88S/Tr-30T
88T/Tr-103T
89Classic-26
89D-454
89F-48
89Kahn/Mets-2
89S-303
89S/HotRook-82
89S/YS/I-38
89T-457
89T/JumboR-19
89ToysRUs-26
89UD-561
90Classic-78
90D-471
90F-216
90Kahn/Mets-2

90Leaf/II-435
90OPC-656
90Publnt/St-144
90S-510
90T-656
90T/TVMets-22
90UD-185
91Classic/200-37
91D-136
91F-160
91F/Ultra-226
91Kahn/Mets-2
91Leaf/II-361
91OPC-382
91Panini/FrSt-78
91S-307
91S/100SS-75
91T-382
91T/StClub/I-172
91UD-103
91WIZMets-345
92D/I-256
92F-515
92S/II-472
92T-533

Sassone, Mike
87StPete-4
88ArkTr/GS-18

Satnat, Dave
86Salem-24

Satoh, Hiroyuki
90Gate/ProC-3340

Satre, Jason
89Greens/ProC-414
90CharWh/Best-9
90CharWh/ProC-2241
90Foil/Best-42
91Cedar/ClBest-12
91Cedar/ProC-2719

Satriano, Tom
63T-548
64T-521
65OPC-124
65T-124
66T-361
67T-343
68T-238
69MB-248
69OPC-78
69T-78
69T/St-150
70MLB/St-164
70T-581
71MLB/St-330
71OPC-557
71T-557
72MB-307

Satterfield, Cory
88Hamil/ProC-1731
89Spring/Best-18
90StPete/Star-21

Sattler, Bill
82Wichita-16
84Indianap-19

Satzinger, Jeff
86Macon-22
87Kenosha-17
88OrlanTw/Best-13
89Orlan/Best-24
89Orlan/ProC-1330
90OkCty/CMC-8
90OkCty/ProC-433

Saucier, Kevin
79OkCty
80BK/P-22
80T-682R
81F-24
81T-53
81T/Tr-827
82D-485
82F-275
82F/St-158
82OPC-238
82T-238
83T-373

Sauer, Ed
47Signal
49Eureka-196

Sauer, Henry
(Hank)
48B-45
48L-20
49B-5

50B-25
51B-22
51T/BB-49
52Dix
52NTea
52StarCal/L-80E
52T-35
53B/Col-48
53Dix
53Exh/Can-7
53NB
53RM-NL16
53T-111
54RH
54T-4
54Wilson
55T-45
55T/DH-103
56T-41
56T/Hocus-A3
56T/Pin-6
57T-197
58Hires-49
58PacBell-7
58SFCallB-20
58T-378
59T-404
61T-481MV
74Laugh/ASG-52
75OPC-190MV
75T-190MV
75T/M-190MV
88Pac/Leg-23
91T/Arc53-111
Exh47
R302/2-113

Saul, Jim
62Kahn
80ElPaso-7MG
81Holyo-2
82Portl-23
82Portl-24
83Nashvl-18CO
84Nashvl-19CO
85Albany-25
86Albany/TCMA-16
89BurlB/ProC-1615
90BurlB/Best-28MG
90BurlB/ProC-2365MG
90BurlB/Star-27MG

Saulter, Kevin
91Pulaski/ClBest-29
91Pulaski/ProC-4004

Saunders, Dennis
71OPC-423R
71T-423R

Saunders, Doug
89Clmbia/Best-20
89Clmbia/GS-23
91StLucie/ClBest-5
91StLucie/ProC-721

Saunders, Mark
79Elmira-28

Saunier, Randy
82Clinton-12

Sauveur, Rich
84PrWill-23
85Nashua-23
86Nashua-25
87Harris-24
88Jaxvl/Best-3
88Jaxvl/ProC-986
89Indianap/ProC-1228
90Miami/I/Star-23
91Tidew/LineD-567
91Tidew/ProC-2508

Savage, Jack
86Bakers-24
87SanAn-22
87TexLgAS-34
88F-650R
88Tidew/CANDL-27
88Tidew/CMC-1
88Tidew/ProC-1583
89D-618
89Tidew/CMC-5
89Tidew/ProC-1971
90T/Tr-111T
90Target-1060
91OPC-357
91Portl/LineD-417
91Portl/ProC-1564
91T-357

Savage, Jim
90Batavia/ProC-3077
91BendB/ClBest-13
91BendB/ProC-3703
91Spartan/ClBest-18
91Spartan/ProC-903

Savage, John Robert
49B-204

Savage, John
88Reno/Cal-275

Savage, Ted
62T-104
63IDL-19
63T-508
64T-62
66Pep/Tul
67T-552
68OPC-119
68T-119
69Sunoco/Pin-17
69T-471
70McDon-1
70T-602
71MLB/St-434
71OPC-76
71T-76
71T/Coins-44
71T/S-3
71T/tatt-7
72MB-308
90Target-704

Savarino, William
(Bill)
86Cram/PCL-51
87Modesto-2
88Modesto/Cal-75
89AS/Cal-44
89Huntsvl/Best-4
89Modesto/Chong-21

Saverine, Bob
63T-158R
64T-221
65T-427
66T-312
67OPC-27
67T-27
68OPC-149
68T-149
78TCMA-14
91Crown/Orio-402

Saverino, Mike
82Danvl-23
83Peoria/LF-27

Savinon, Odails
89Johnson/Star-19
91Spring/ClBest-24
91Spring/ProC-757

Sawatski, Carl
53T-202
54T-198
55T-122
55T/DH-93
58T-234
59T-56
60L-120
60T-545
61T-198
62J-162
62P-162
62P/Can-162
62Salada-119
62Shirriff-119
62T-106
63T-267
64T-24
89TexLAS/GS-40PRES
91T/Arc53-202
Exh47

Sawkiw, Warren
88CapeCod/Sum-3
90Niagara/Pucko-10
91Lakeland/ClBest-27
91Lakeland/ProC-276

Sawyer, Eddie
49Eureka-145MG
50B-225MG
51B-184MG
60T-226MG

Sawyer, Rick
76SSPC-426
77Padre/SchCd-26
77T-268

Sax, Dave
79Clinton
82Albuq-13
83Pol/Dodg-23
84Cram/PCL-152
84D-519
85Pawtu-15
86T-307
87D-647
87Pawtu/TCMA-25
88BuffB/CMC-22
88BuffB/ProC-1483
89Colum/CMC-26
89Colum/ProC-756
90ColClip/CMC-19
90ColClip/ProC-680
90T/TVYank-59
90Target-705
91ColClip/LineD-117
91ColClip/ProC-600
91Pac/SenLg-34

Sax, Steve
79Clinton
82D-624
82F-21
82Pol/Dodg-52
82T-681R
82T/Tr-103T
83D-336
83F-220
83OPC-245
83PermaGr/AS-15
83Pol/Dodg-3
83Seven-2
83T-245
83T/St-329
84D-104
84F-112
84F-633M
84F/St-90
85FunFoodPin-45
84MiltBrad-22
84Nes/792-610
84OPC-144
84Pol/Dodg-3
84Seven-22W
84Smok/Dodg-3
84T-610
84T/Gloss22-14
84T/St-78
85Coke/Dodg-29
85D-418
85F-384
85F/LimEd-32
85Leaf-90
85OPC-369
85T-470
85T/St-77
86Coke/Dodg-27
86D-540
86D/HL-50
86F-143
86OPC-175
86Pol/Dodg-3
86Sf-60M
86Sf-95
86Sf/Rook-48M
86T-175
86T/St-72
87Classic-20
87D-26DK
87D-278
87D/AAS-28
87D/DKsuper-26
87D/OD-85
87Drake-25
87F-453
87F/AS-4
87F/GameWin-39
87F/Hottest-34
87F/Mini-96
87F/RecSet-34
87F/St-106
87Kraft-38
87Leaf-203
87Leaf-26DK
87MnM's-21
87Mother/Dodg-3
87OPC-254
87Pol/Dodg-2
87Sf-12
87Seven-W10
87Smok/Dodg-32
87Smok/NL-1
87T-596AS
87T-769
87T/Coins-42
87T/Mini-15
87T/St-70
88D-176
88D/Best-204
88F-523
88F/Mini-85
88F/St-93
88Leaf-185
88Mother/Dodg-3
88OPC-305
88Panini/St-311
88Pol/Dodg-3
88S-35
88Smok/Dodg-25
88T-305
88T/Big-46
88T/St-74
89B-178
89Cadaco-50
89Classic/Up/2-179
89D-84
89D/Best-20
89D/Tr-23
89F-70
89F/Up-52
89F/WS-9
89OPC-40
89Panini/St-106
89RedFoley/St-103
89S-69
89S/HotStar-33
89S/NWest-2
89S/Tr-20
89Sf-58
89Smok/Dodg-99
89T-40
89T/Big-111
89T/DHTest-19
89T/LJN-71
89T/Mini-19
89T/St-57
89T/St/Backs-39
89T/Tr-111T
89T/UK-69
89UD-53
89UD/Ext-748
90B-442
90Classic-149
90D-2DK
90D-78
90D/BestAL-24
90D/Bon/MVP-BC22
90D/SuperDK-2DK
90F-455
90F/BB-33
90F/LL-34
90Holsum/Discs-16
90HotPlay/St-38
90Leaf/I-96
90Leaf/Prev-1
90MLBPA/Pins-62
90OPC-560
90Panini/St-129
90Publlnt/St-547
90RedFoley/St-83
90S-125
90S/100St-2
90S/McDon-22
90S/NWest-3
90Sf-12
90T-560
90T/Big-141
90T/Coins-26
90T/DH-57
90T/Gloss60-8
90T/Mini-25
90T/St-310
90T/TVAS-18
90T/TVYank-26
90Target-706
90Tetley/Discs-19
90UD-172
90UD-18TC
90USPlayC/AS-4S
90Windwlk/Discs-7
91B-170
91Classic/200-106
91Classic/II-T17
91D-163
91D-48AS
91F-679
91F/Ultra-242
91Leaf/I-220
91Leaf/Stud-100
91OPC-290
91Panini/FrSt-168
91Panini/FrSt-325
91Panini/St-271
91Panini/Top15-46
91RedFoley/St-127
91RedFoley/St-84
91S-32
91S/100SS-72
91T-290
91T/CJMini/II-30
91T/StClub/I-204
91UD-462
92F-244
92S/II-475
92T-430
92UD-358

Sayler, Barry
83StPete-24

Sayles, Bill
90Target-707

Sayles, Steve
83Miami-24

Scaglione, Tony
88Watlo/ProC-690
89Kinston/Star-22

Scala, Jerry
V362-28

Scales, George
78Laugh/Black-26

Scanlan, William
(Doc)
10Domino-105A
10Domino-105B
11Helmar-151
12Sweet/Pin-76
M116
S74-55
T202
T205
T207

Scanlan, Bob
86Clearw-22
87Phill/TastyK-39B
87Reading-20
88Maine/CMC-9
88Maine/ProC-294
89Reading/Best-8
89Reading/ProC-652
89Reading/Star-21
90ScranWB/CMC-7
90ScranWB/ProC-599
91Cub/Mara-30
91Iowa/LineD-223
91Iowa/ProC-1061
91Leaf/II-520
91S/RookTr-102T
91T/Tr-105T
91UD/FinalEd-48F
92D/II-454
92S/100RisSt-59
92S/I-285
92T-274
92T/91Debut-157

Scanlin, Michael
87Gaston-19
88Tulsa-1

Scanlon, James P.
(Pat)
76SSPC-332
78T-611

Scanlon, Ken
80Ander-23
81Durham-4
82Durham-7
83Durham-12

Scanlon, Steve
88Visalia/Cal-161
88Visalia/ProC-94

Scannell, Larry
87Elmira/Black-5
87Elmira/Red-5
88Elmira-24
89WinHaven/Star-21

Scantlebury, Pat
61BeeHive-20
86Negro/Frit-35

Scarbery, Randy
77SanJose-18
80T-291

Scarborough, Carey

75BurlB
Scarborough, Ray
49B-140
49Royal-14
50B-108
50Drake-29
51B-39
51T/RB-42
52B-140
52Royal
52T-43
52TipTop
53T-213
79TCMA-208
91T/Arc53-213
Scarce, Mac
73OPC-6
73T-6
74OPC-149
74T-149
75OPC-527
75T-527
75T/M-527
76Indianap-22
77Indianap-15
91WIZMets-346
Scarpace, Ken
81Cedar-17
82Water-19
Scarpetta, Dan
83Beloit/LF-25
87Denver-15
88ElPaso/Best-3
88TexLgAS/GS-6
89SanAn/Best-18
Scarsella, Les
46Remar
47Remar-2
47Signal
47Smith-3
48Signal
48Smith-6
49B/PCL-25
49Remar
R314/Can
W711/1
Scarsone, Stephen
86Cram/PCL-135
87CharWh-5
88Clearw/Star-22
89EastLDD/ProC-DD25
89Reading/Best-4
89Reading/ProC-665
89Reading/Star-22
90Clearw/Star-20
91AAAGame/ProC-AAA41
91Reading/LineD-518
91ScranWB/ProC-2548
Schaal, Paul
65T-517R
66T-376
67OPC-58
67T-58
68T-474
69MB-249
69MLB/St-62
69T-352
69T/St-188
70MLB/St-228
70OPC-338
70T-338
71MLB/St-429
71OPC-487
71T-487
72MB-309
72OPC-177
72OPC-178IA
72T-177
72T-178IA
73OPC-416
73T-416
74OPC-514
74T-514
Schacht, Al
39PB-113
40PB-116
87Conlon/2-9
92Conlon/Sport-559
R312/M
R314
V355-29
Schaefer, Bob
82Tidew-22
84Tidew-10
85IntLgAS-1
85Tidew-27
86GlenF-20
87Memphis-10
87Memphis/Best-1
91Pol/Royal-26CO
Schaefer, Chris
88CapeCod/Sum-31
89Eugene/Best-1
90AppFox/Box-23
90AppFox/ProC-2093
Schaefer, Doug
79Phoenix
80Phoenix-3
81Phoenix-7
Schaefer, Herman
(Germany)
09Buster/Pin-13
10Domino-106
11Helmar-76
12Sweet/Pin-63
14Piedmont/St-51
81Detroit-102
D303
D350/2-154
E101
E102
E105
E106
E90/1
E92
M101/5-154
M116
S74-40
T204
T205
T206
T207
T213/blue
T215/blue
T215/brown
T216
Schaefer, Jeff
84RochR-10
85CharlO-12
85Utica-14
86MidldA-21
87SanAn-1
88Vanco/CMC-21
88Vanco/ProC-753
89Coke/WS-25
89Vanco/CMC-24
90Calgary/ProC-660
90T/89Debut-109
91CounHrth-2
91F/Up-U56
91OPC-681
91T-681
92D/II-525
92S/II-629
Schaefer, Jim
79Tulsa-13
80Ashvl-6
Schaefer, Steve
79Elmira-15
Schafer, Bill
90Sumter/Best-18
90Sumter/ProC-2430
Schafer, Dennis
81Clinton-13
Schaffer, Jim
89Hagers/ProC-282
Schaffer, Jimmie
61Union
62T-579
63T-81
64T-359
65T-313
68T-463
78TCMA-152
78TCMA-169
78TCMA-184
91WIZMets-347
Schaffernoth, Joe
61T-58
63T-463
Schaive, John Jr.
82Buffa-6
83LynnP-18
Schaive, John Sr.
61T-259
62T-529
63T-356
Schalk, Ray
14CJ-61
15CJ-61
21Exh-151
25Exh-78
26Exh-78
27Exh-40
50Callahan
60F-56
61F-136
76Motor-6
80Pac/Leg-85
80SSPC/HOF
87Conlon/2-55
88Pac/8Men-100
88Pac/8Men-43
88Pac/8Men-45M
88Pac/8Men-50
88Pac/8Men-51
88Pac/8Men-52
89Kodak/WSox-3M
91Conlon/Sport-48
BF2-17
D327
D328-150
D329-154
D350/2-155
E120
E121/120
E121/80
E122
E126-8
E135-150
E210-23
E254
M101/4-154
M101/5-155
V117-3
V355-124
W501-43
W502-23
W514-60
W515-51
W516-4
W572
W573
W575
Schall, Gene
91Batavia/ClBest-2
91Batavia/ProC-3493
91FrRow/DP-6
Schallock, Art
91Crown/Orio-403
Schammel, Bill
83MidldC-1
Schang, Walter H.
(Wally)
14CJ-58
15CJ-58
16FleischBrd-81
21Exh-152
25Exh-101
28Exh-59
29Exh/4-29
31Exh/4-24
91Conlon/Sport-249
92Conlon/Sport-448
BF2-39
D327
D328-151
D329-155
D350/2-156
E120
E121/80
E122
E135-151
E220
M101/4-155
M101/5-156
T222
V100
V61-20
W501-27
W514-99
W515-17
W572
W573
W575
Schanz, Charley
52Mother-41
53Mother-40
Schanz, Scott
91Penin/ClBest-10
91Penin/ProC-376
Schardt, Wilbur
(Bill)
90Target-708
T207
Scharein, George
47Signal
Scharff, Tony
91SoOreg/ClBest-19
91SoOreg/ProC-3842
Schatter, Jim
89Hagers/Best-10
Schattinger, Jeff
81Omaha-12
82Edmon-25
Schatz, Dan
87Visalia-25
Schatzeder, Dan
78T-709R
79OPC-56
79T-124
80OPC-140
80T-267
81D-248
81F-482
81OPC-112
81T-417
82D-385
82F-281
82OPC-106
82T-691
82T/Tr-104T
83F-296
83OPC-189
83Stuart-22
83T-189
84D-132
84F-286
84Nes/792-57
84OPC-57
84Stuart-7
84T-57
85D-543
85F-409
85Leaf-59
85OPC-293
85T-501
86F-259
86OPC-324
86Provigo-12
86T-324
87D-482
87F-186
87OPC-168
87Phill/TastyK-35
87T-789
88F-21
88Gator-31
88T-218
89F/Up-90
89Lennox/Ast-9
89Tucson/CMC-10
89Tucson/ProC-198
89Tucson/JP-21
90B-69
90D-594
90F-236
90Lennox-21
90Mother/Ast-18
90S-418
91D-497
91WIZMets-348
Schauer, A.J.
(Rube)
16FleischBrd-82
Scheckla, Roddy
88AubAs/ProC-1960
89Ashvl/ProC-946
Scheer, Ron
83Wisco/LF-2
84Visalia-21
86Penin-23
87Penin-17
Scheetz, Rick
82Wisco-11
Scheffing, Bob
48L-160
49B-83
49Eureka-71
50B-168
54T-76
60Lake
60SpicSpan-20CO
60T-464C
61T-223MG
62T-416MG
62T-72M
63T-134MG
Scheffler, Jim
90Pittsfld/Pucko-21
91Pittsfld/ClBest-17
91Pittsfld/ProC-3421
Schefsky, Steve
84Beaum-13
85Beaum-11
Scheib, Carl
49B-25
50B-213
51B-83
52B-46
52T-116
53B/Col-150
53T-57
54B-67
54T-118
91T/Arc53-57
Scheibeck, Frank
N172
Scheid, Rich
87FtLaud-18
88Pittsfld/ProC-1372
89Iowa/CMC-9
89Iowa/ProC-1713
90BirmB/Best-22
90BirmB/ProC-1110
91Vanco/LineD-645
91Vanco/ProC-1594
Scheinblum, Richie
65T-577R
68OPC-16R
68T-16R
69T-479
70OPC-161
70T-161
71OPC-326
71T-326
72OPC-468
72T-468
73OPC-78
73T-78
74OPC-323
74T-323
74T/St-148
Schell, Clyde
(Danny)
55T-79
55T/DH-81
Scheller, Rod
77LodiD
78LodiD
Schellhasse, Albert
N172
Schemer, Mike
47Sunbeam
Schenck, Bruce
91Pocatel/ProC-3781
Schenkle, William
N172
Schenz, Henry
52Mother-30
Scherer, Doug
85Cram/PCL-141
88Knoxvl/Best-11
Scherger, George
73OPC-296CO
73T-296CO
74OPC-326CO
74T-326C
81Water-22MG
82Indianap-2
86TexGold-CO
Scherger, Joe
82Amari-4
Scherman, Fred
71MLB/St-406
71OPC-316
71T-316
72OPC-6
72T-6
73OPC-660
73T-660
74OPC-186
74T-186
74T/Tr-186T
75OPC-252

84Seven-4E
84Seven-4W
84T-132LL
84T-388AS
84T-700
84T-703LL
84T/Cereal-22
84T/Gloss22-15
84T/Gloss40-39
84T/St-101
84T/St-117
84T/St-188FOIL
84T/Super-6
85CIGNA-4
85CircK-19
85D-61
85D/AAS-17
85Drake-29
85F-265
85F-627IA
85F-630IA
85F/LimEd-33
85F/St-17
85F/St-34
85F/St-74SA
85F/St-75
85F/St-76
85F/St-77
85F/St-78
85F/St-79
85GenMills-9
85Leaf-205
85OPC-67
85Phill/TastyK-11M
85Phill/TastyK-33
85Seven-16E
85Seven-1W
85Seven-4C
85Sportflic/Proto-2
85Sportflic/Test-1
85T-500
85T-714AS
85T/3D-1
85T/Gloss22-4
85T/Gloss40-23
85T/St-111
85T/St-193
85T/St-94
85T/Super-12
85ThomMc/Discs-42
86BK/AP-5
86CIGNA-10
86D-61
86D/HL-36
86D/HL-4
86Dorman-8
86Drake-26
86F-450
86F/LimEd-41
86F/Mini-94
86F/Slug-33
86F/St-107
86Jiffy-17
86Keller-5
86Leaf-51
86Meadow/Blank-14
86Meadow/Milk-11
86Meadow/Stat-16
86OPC-200
86Phill/TastyK-20
86Quaker-14
86Sf-139M
86Sf-148M
86Sf-182M
86Sf-44
86Sf-62M
86Sf-68M
86Sf/Dec-55
86T-200
86T/3D-24
86T/Gloss60-17
86T/Mini-55
86T/St-114
86T/Super-49
86TrueVal-28
86Woolwth-30
87BK-17
87Champion-4
87Classic-62
87Classic/Up-101
87D-139
87D/AAS-17
87D/HL-2
87D/OD-160
87D/PopUp-17
87Drake-23
87F-187
87F/AS-6
87F/AwardWin-36
87F/GameWin-40
87F/Hottest-35
87F/BB-40
87F/LL-40
87F/Lim-37
87F/Mini-97
87F/RecSet-35
87F/Slug-37
87F/St-107
87F/WaxBox-C15
87Ho/St-13
87Jiffy-16
87KayBee-29
87KMart-31
87Kraft-30
87Leaf-122
87MnM's-3
87MSA/Discs-11
87OPC-396
87Phill/TastyK-20
87Ralston-14
87RedFoley/St-46
87Sf-115M
87Sf-156M
87Sf-30
87Sportflic/DealP-1
87T-430
87T-597AS
87T/Board-1
87T/Coins-43
87T/Gloss22-4
87T/Gloss60-28
87T/HL-8
87T/Mini-30
87T/St-116
87T/St-160
87Woolwth-8
88ChefBoy-14
88Classic/Red-167
88D-330
88D-BC4
88D/AS-39
88D/Best-271
88D/PopUp-17
88Drake-8
88F-315
88F-636M
88F/AwardWin-35
88F/BB/AS-36
88F/BB/MVP-31
88F/Excit-34
88F/Hottest-34
88F/LL-35
88F/Mini-102
88F/RecSet-35
88F/Slug-36
88F/SS-33
88F/St-111
88F/TL-34
88F/WaxBox-C11
88FanSam-19
88KayBee-27
88KingB/Disc-1
88KMart-25
88Leaf-124
88MSA/Disc-16
88Nestle-6
88OPC-321
88OPC/WaxBox-O
88Panini/St-234M
88Panini/St-360
88Panini/St-429
88Phill/TastyK-23
88RedFoley/St-79
88S-16
88S-657HL
88S/WaxBox-13
88Sf-180M
88Sf-35
88Sf/Gamewin-21
88T-600
88T/Big-88
88T/Coins-53
88T/Gloss22-15
88T/Gloss60-3
88T/Mini-67
88T/RiteAid-8
88T/St-125
88T/St-149
88T/St-9
88T/St/Backs-8
88T/UK-67
88T/WaxBox-O
88Woolwth-7
89T/Ames-27
89B-402
89Cadaco-51
89Classic-48
89Classic/Up/2-153
89T/Crunch-16
89D-193
89F-582
89F/Superstar-36
89F/Up-U131
89KayBee-27
89OPC-100
89Panini/St-153
89Panini/St-3
89Phill/TastyK-32
89MSA/SS-4
89RedFoley/St-104
89S-149
89S/HotStar-76
89Sf-21
89T-100
89T-489TL
89T/Big-220
89T/HeadsUp-24
89T/LJN-122
89T/St-120
89T/UK-70
89T/WaxBox-L
89UD-406
89UD-684TC
90BBWit-39
90D-643
90HOF/St-94
90MSA/AGFA-21
90OPC-662TBC'80
90Phill/TastyK-32
90Phill/TastyK-36BC
90PublInt/St-250
90T-662TBC
90UD-20Special
91BBBest/RecBr-16
91Single/ClBest-1

Schmidt, Robert B.
(Bob)
58SFCallB-21
58T-468
59T-109
60T-501
61P-151
61T-31
62Salada-179
62Shirriff-179
62T-262
63T-94
65T-582
79TCMA-246
84Mother/Giants-14

Schmidt, Walter
92Conlon/Sport-571
E120
V61-113
W572
W573
WG7-46

Schmidt, Willard
53Hunter
53T-168
56T-323
57T-206
58T-214
59T-171
62Kahn/Atl
79TCMA-153
91T/Arc53-168

Schmittou, Larry
89Nashvl/Team-28PRES

Schmitz, Dan
79WHave-5
81Colum-5
82Colum-16
82Colum/Pol-6
82Nashvl-21
83Tidew-17
84Toledo-7
85Visalia-25
86Visalia-18MG

Schmitz, John
47TipTop
48L-48
49B-52
49Eureka-70
50B-24
51B-69
51T/BB-41
52B-224
52NTea
52T-136
53Briggs
54T-33
55B-105
55T-159
56T-298
56T/Hocus-A16
56T/Hocus-B18
90Target-709
91Crown/Orio-407
Exh47

Schmutz, Charlie
90Target-1064

Schneck, Dave
76Indianap-15
91WIZMets-351

Schneider, Dan
63T-299R
64T-351
65T-366
67T-543
68OPC-57
68T-57
69T-656

Schneider, Jeff
80RochR-10
82Spokane-7
82T-21R
83Syrac-11
90F/Up-120
91Crown/Orio-408

Schneider, Paul
83Wausau/LF-19
86Chatt-22
86SLAS-20
87Calgary-8
88Calgary/CMC-2
88Calgary/ProC-793
88SanBern/Best-2

Schneider, Pete
16FleischBrd-83

Schnoor, Chuck
82Lynch-14

Schnurbusch, Chris
88Fayette/ProC-1097
89Cedar/Best-16
89Cedar/ProC-934
89Cedar/Star-17

Schober, Dave
84Madis/Pol-3
85Madis-25TR
85Madis/Pol-23
86Madis-20
86Madis/Pol-25
87Madis-2TR
89Huntsvl/Best-19

Schock, William
(Will)
88Huntsvl/BK-17
88Madis-21
88MidwLAS/GS-54
89Huntsvl/Best-2
90Foil/Best-197
90Huntsvl/Best-9
91Tacoma/LineD-544
91Tacoma/ProC-2304

Schockman, Mark
85Newar-16

Schoen, Jerry
91BendB/ClBest-14
91BendB/ProC-3704

Schoendienst, Albert
(Red)
48B-38
49B-111
49Eureka-197
50B-71
51B-10
51FB
51T/BB-6
52B-30
52BR
52Dix
52RM-NL19
52StarCal/L-81A
52T-91
52TipTop
53B/Col-101
53Dix
53Hunter
53NB
53RM-NL12
53T-78
54B-110
54DanDee
54Dix
54Hunter
54RH
54RM-NL10
55B-29
55Hunter
55RFG-3
55RM-NL18
56T-165
56YellBase/Pin-28
57SpicSpan/4x5-15
57T-154
58T-190
59T-480
60Lake
60MacGregor-22
60NuCard-25
60SpicSpan-21
60T-335
61NuCard-425
61P-111
61T-505
62Salada-151
62Shirriff-151
62T-575
65T-556MG
66OPC-76MG
66T-76MG
67T-512MG
68T-294MG
69T-462MG
70OPC-346MG
70T-346MG
71OPC-239MG
71T-239
72OPC-67MG
72T-67MG
73OPC-497MG
73T-497MG
74Laugh/ASG-50
74OPC-236MG
74T-236MG
75OPC-246MG
75T-246MG
75T/M-246MG
76SSPC-300MG
76T-581MG
79TCMA-94
81D-431MG
88Pac/Leg-2
90T/Tr-113TMG
91T/Arc53-78
Exh47
R423-97

Schoendienst, Kevin
81QuadC-10

Schoenhaus, Ted
76Cedar

Schoenvogel, Chad
91FrRow/DP-3

Schofield, John
86Kinston-23
87PortChar-2

Schofield, John R.
(Ducky)
54Hunter
54T-191
55Hunter
55T-143
58T-106
59T-68
60T-104
61Kahn
61T-453
62T-484
63IDL-20
63Sugar-E
63T-34
64T-284
65OPC-218
65T-218
66OPC-156M
66T-156M
66T-474
67T-381

68T-588
69OPC-18
69T-18
70OPC-251
70T-251
71MLB/St-282
71OPC-396
71T-396
72MB-310
78TCMA-199
85T-138FS

Schofield, Richard C.
(Dick)
82Danvl-27
84D-35RR
84F/X-U105
84Smok/Cal-25
84T/Tr-107T
85D-329
85F-311
85Smok/Cal-13
85T-138FS
85T-629
86D-133
86F-167
86OPC-311
86Smok/Cal-13
86T-311
87D-283
87D/OD-4
87F-92
87OPC-54
87Seven-W9
87Smok/Cal-15
87T-502
87T/St-176
88D-233
88D/Best-195
88F-504
88Leaf-178
88OPC-43
88Panini/St-45
88RedFoley/St-80
88S-274
88Smok/Angels-16
88T-43
88T/Big-204
88T/St-177
89B-46
89D-108
89D/Best-251
89F-488
89OPC-286
89Panini/St-294
89S-16
89T-477
89T/Big-53
89T/St-174
89UD-201
90B-291
90D-288
90D/BestAL-131
90F-144
90Leaf/II-419
90OPC-189
90Publint/St-379
90S-44
90Smok/Angel-15
90T-189
90T/Big-211
90Target-710
90UD-669
91B-191
91D-262
91F-325
91F/Ultra-52
91Leaf/I-59
91OPC-736
91Panini/FrSt-183
91S-776
91Smok/Angel-14
91T-736
91T/StClub/I-59
91UD-169
92D/I-44
92F-69
92S/II-552
92T-230
92UD-269

Scholzen, Jeff
91Pocatel/ProC-3791

Schooler, Michael
86Wausau-21
87Chatt/Best-8
88Calgary/CMC-9
88Calgary/ProC-795
88S/Tr-91T
88T/Tr-105T
89Chatt/II/Team-27
89D-637
89D/Best-275
89F-559
89Mother/Sea-25
89S-528
89S/HotRook-73
89S/YS/II-34
89T-199
89ToysRUs-27
89UD-28
90B-470
90Classic-79
90D-330
90D/BestAL-82
90F-525
90Leaf/I-258
90Mother/Mar-21
90OPC-681
90Panini/St-151
90RedFoley/St-84
90S-149
90Sf-187
90T-681
90T/Big-235
90T/Mini-35
90T/St-228
90UD-214
91B-241
91CounHrth-25
91D-302
91F-461
91Leaf/I-230
91OPC-365
91Panini/FrSt-236
91Panini/St-184
91RedFoley/St-85
91S-489
91Seven/3DCoin-15NW
91T-365
91T/StClub/II-508
91UD-638
92D/II-444
92F-292
92S/II-654
92T-28
92UD-405

Schoonmaker, Jerry
56T-216
57T-334

Schoonover, Gary
88Idaho/ProC-1836
89BurlB/ProC-1602
89BurlB/Star-20

Schoppee, Dave
81Bristol-9
83Pawtu-10

Schorr, Bill
88Butte-8

Schorr, Bradley
91Kingspt/ClBest-22
91Kingspt/ProC-3812

Schott, Arthur Eugene
R312
W711/1

Schourek, Pete
88LitFalls/Pucko-22
89Clmbia/Best-14
89Clmbia/GS-24
90T/TVMets-59
91B-482
91F/Up-U104
91Kahn/Mets-48
91Leaf/GRook-BC15
91OPC/Premier-106
91S/RookTr-87T
91T/Tr-106T
91UD/Ext-766
92D/II-535
92F-516
92S/100RisSt-20
92S/I-332
92T-287
92T/91Debut-158
92UD-673

Schramm, Carl
91Geneva/ClBest-27
91Geneva/ProC-4213

Schrammel, Jamie
80GlenF/C-29bb

Schreckengost, Ossie
E107
E91
T206
WG2-42

Schreiber, Bruce
89Princet/Star-20
90CLAS/CL-23
90Salem/Star-20
91CaroMud/LineD-116
91CaroMud/ProC-1094
91Single/ClBest-225

Schreiber, Marty
84Durham-27
85Durham-12
86Osceola-22

Schreiber, Paul
54T-217

Schreiber, Ted
91WIZMets-352

Schreiner, John
91BBCity/ClBest-21
91BBCity/ProC-1407

Schrenk, Steve
89SoBend/GS-15
90Foil/Best-104
90SoBend/Best-16

Schriver, William
N172

Schroder, Bob
65T-589R

Schroeck, Bob
82ElPaso-16
83ElPaso-24
84ElPaso-3

Schroeder, Alfred W.
(Bill)
81ElPaso-13
82Vanco-3
84D-515
84Nes/792-738
84Pol/Brew-21
84T-738
85D-124
85F-594
85Gard-18
85Pol/Brew-21
85T-176
86D-211
86F-501
86Pol/Brew-21
86T-662
87D-486
87D/OD-49
87F-357
87Pol/Brew-21
87T-302
88D-419
88F-173
88Pol/Brew-21
88S-311
88T-12
89B-44
89D-644
89T-563
89UD-627
90D-567
90ElPasoATG/Team-18
90OPC-244
90S-362
90T-244
90UD-149
91OPC-452
91T-452

Schroeder, Jay
83Kinston/Team-23

Schroeder, Todd
91Welland/ClBest-3
91Welland/ProC-3582

Schroll, Al
55B-319
59T-546
60L-95
60T-357
62T-102

Schrom, Ken
77QuadC
80SLCity-7
81F-425
81OPC-238R
81Syrac-21
81T-577R
82Syrac-7
83Toledo-9
84D-72
84F-572
84Nes/792-11TL
84Nes/792-322
84OPC-322
84T-322
84T/St-308
85D-486
85F-288
85OPC-161
85T-161
86D-635
86F-403
86F/Up-U104
86OhHenry-18
86OPC-71
86T-71
86T/Tr-100T
87D-403
87D/AAS-53
87F-258
87F/Mini-98
87Gator-18
87OPC-171
87Sf-107
87T-635
87T/St-204
88D-501
88F-614
88OPC-256
88S-574
88T-256
90ElPasoATG/Team-36

Schu, Rick
84Cram/PCL-209
85Cram/PCL-34
85D-448
85F/Up-U100
85Phill/TastyK-43
85T/Tr-104T
86D-570
86F-451
86OPC-16
86Phill/TastyK-15
86T-16
86T/St-122
87D-509
87F-188
87Phill/TastyK-15
87T-209
88D-432
88F-316
88French-25
88S-448
88T-731
88T/Big-122
89D-406
89F-619
89Mara/Tigers-35
89OPC-352
89RedFoley/St-105
89RochR/CMC-23
89RochR/ProC-1642
89S-452
89T-352
89T/Big-164
89T/Tr-112T
89UD-490
90D-599
90OPC-498
90T-498
91Crown/Orio-409
91F-326
91ScranWB/LineD-495
91ScranWB/ProC-2547

Schubert, Brian
90Niagara/Pucko-24

Schuble, Henry
33G-4
35G-1H
35G-3F
35G-5F
35G-6F
R337-411
V353-4

Schuckert, Wayne
81AppFx-12
82AppFx-17
83GlenF-19

Schueler, Ron
73OPC-169
73T-169
74JP
74OPC-544
74T-544
74T/Tr-544T
75OPC-292
75T-292
75T/M-292
76OPC-586
76T-586
77T-337
78T-409
79T-686

Schueler, Russ
87BurlEx-14

Schugel, Jeff
84Visalia-14
85Visalia-6

Schuler, Dave
77Watlo
78Cr/PCL-103
79SLCity-17
80SLCity-6
81SLCity-11
82Omaha-8
83Omaha-9
85Richm-8
86Omaha-19
86Omaha/TCMA-19
87Denver-11
88Vermont/ProC-941
90FtLaud/Star-24CO
91PrWill/ClBest-25CO
91PrWill/ProC-1443CO

Schullstrom, Erik
88Alaska/Team-16
89Smok/FresnoSt-20

Schulmerich, Wes
34Exh/4-6
34G-54
88Conlon/NatAS-17

Schult, Art
53T-167
58T-58
60L-123
60T-93
79TCMA-253
91T/Arc53-167

Schulte, Frank
10Domino-108
11Helmar-104
12Sweet/Pin-90
14CJ-101
15CJ-101
91Conlon/Sport-304
BF2-67
D328-152
D329-156
D350/2-158
E135-152
E254
E270/1
E90/3
E91
M101/4-156
M101/5-158
M116
S74-68
T202
T204
T205
T206
T207
T213/blue
T215/blue
T215/brown
T222
T3-117
W514-10
WG4-25

Schulte, Fred
28Exh-60
29Exh/4-30
31Exh/4-29
33G-112
33G-190
35BU-50
35Exh/4-16
91Conlon/Sport-286
R316

Schulte, Joe
86Ashvl-26
87Osceola-14

Schulte, John

90Welland/Pucko-9
Schulte, John C.
33G-186
40PB-12
44Yank/St-23
Schulte, Mark
84ArkTr-13
86ArkTr-22
87FtMyr-12
Schulte, Rich
91AubAS/ClBest-10
91AubAS/ProC-4287
Schulte, Todd
83BurlR-10
83BurlR/LF-2
Schultz, Bob D.
52T-401
53T-144
54B-59
91T/Arc53-144
Schultz, Bobby
91BurlInd/ProC-3317
Schultz, Charles
(Buddy)
78T-301
79T-532
80T-601
82ArkTr-9
Schultz, George
(Barney)
62T-89
62T/St-110
63T-452
65OPC-28
65T-28
66Pep/Tul
73OPC-497CO
73T-497C
74OPC-236CO
74T-236C
78TCMA-15
Schultz, Greg
83Albuq-18
84Cram/PCL-157
85Cram/PCL-196
Schultz, Howie
90Target-711
Schultz, Joseph C. Jr.
(Dode)
47TipTop
62Kahn/Atl
69T-254MG
73OPC-323CO
73T-323CO
89Pac/Leg-162
Schultz, Joseph C. Sr.
(Germany)
90Target-1065
E120
V61-114
W572
W573
Schultz, Scott
87Lakeland-5
Schultz, Ted
76AppFx
Schulz, Harry
75Clinton
Schulz, Jeff
83Butte-28
86Omaha-20
86Omaha/TCMA-6
87Omaha-23
88Omaha/CMC-15
88Omaha/ProC-1508
89Omaha/CMC-22
89Omaha/ProC-1736
90Omaha/CMC-18
90Omaha/ProC-79
90T/89Debut-110
91BuffB/LineD-45
91BuffB/ProC-554
91D-687
91F-568
91S-336RP
91S/100RisSt-25
91UD-607
Schulze, Don
81QuadC-29
83Iowa-9
84Iowa-22
84Wheat/Ind-37
85D-639
85F-454
85T-93
86OhHenry-37
86T-542
87BuffB-22
87F-259
87T-297
87Tidew-25
87Tidew/TCMA-26
88T-131
88Toledo/CMC-3
88Toledo/ProC-604
89Colum/CMC-6
89Colum/Pol-19
89Colum/ProC-753
89Tidew/Candl-11
91WIZMets-353
Schumacher, Hal
33G-129
33G-240
35BU-110
35BU-52
35G-1K
35G-3B
35G-4B
35G-5B
36Wheat
38ONG/Pin-26
39PB-73
40PB-85
48Swell-7
61F-137
88Conlon/NatAS-18
V355-23
Schumacher, Roy
81AppFx-11
Schumate, Jack
79Wisco-22
Schunk, Jerry
87Dunedin-25
88Dunedin/Star-16
89Knoxvl/Best-23
89Knoxvl/ProC-1142
89Knoxvl/Star-19
90Knoxvl/Best-25
90Knoxvl/ProC-1250
90Knoxvl/Star-18
91B-20
91S/ToroBJ-34
91Syrac/LineD-516
91Syrac/ProC-2488
Schupp, Ferdie
16FleischBrd-84
90Target-712
D328-153
E121/120
E121/80
E122
E135-153
W575
Schurr, Wayne
64T-548R
65OPC-149
65T-149
Schuster, Bill
47Signal
Schuster, Mark
79Holyo-7
80Holyo-3
81Vanco-5
82ElPaso-8
84Cram/PCL-7
85Cram/PCL-185
Schwab, Ken
80Clinton-8
Schwabe, Mike
88GlenF/ProC-927
89F/Up-32
89London/ProC-1375
90T/89Debut-111
90Toledo/CMC-9
90Toledo/ProC-148
91F-351
Schwall, Don
62Bz
62J-64
62P-64
62P/Can-64
62Salada-210
62Shirriff-210
62T-35
62T/bucks
62T/St-19
63Sugar-C
63T-344
64T-558
65T-362
66OPC-144
66T-144
67T-267
78TCMA-118
Schwaner, Tom
62Pep/Tul
Schwarber, Mike
80Batavia-10
81Watlo-15
82Chatt-10
Schwarber, Tom
91Bristol/ClBest-23
91Bristol/ProC-3605
Schwartz, Dave
91Elizab/ProC-4300
Schwartz, Randy
67OPC-33R
67T-33R
Schwarz, Jeff
88WinSalem/Star-19
89Hagers/Best-24
89Hagers/ProC-263
89Hagers/Star-16
91ElPaso/LineD-195
91ElPaso/ProC-2748
Schwarz, Tom
86Visalia-19
87Orlan-18
88Reading/ProC-863
Schweighoffer, Mike
85VeroB-18
87SanAn-13
88SanAn/Best-10
Schweitzer, Al
M116
Schwerman, Brian
77Charl
78Charl
Sciortino, Michael
90Pittsfld/Pucko-15
91Pittsfld/ClBest-9
91Pittsfld/ProC-3433
Scioscia, Mike
77Clinton
79Albuq-10
80Albuq-26
81F-131
81Pol/Dodg-14
81T-302R
82D-598
82F-22
82OPC-173
82Pol/Dodg-14
82T-642
83D-75
83F-221
83Pol/Dodg-14
83T-352
84F-113
84Nes/792-64
84Pol/Dodg-14
84T-64
85Coke/Dodg-30
85D-459
85F-385
85Leaf-118
85T-549
85T/St-79
86Coke/Dodg-28
86D-93
86F-144
86Leaf-87
86OPC-111
86Pol/Dodg-14
86Sf-167
86T-468
86T/St-68
87D-130
87D/OD-82
87F-454
87Leaf-123
87Mother/Dodg-10
87OPC-144
87Pol/Dodg-6
87Sf-151M
87Sf-67
87Seven-W12
87T-144
87T/St-73
88D-106
88D/Best-260
88F-524
88Leaf-97
88Mother/Dodg-10
88OPC-225
88Panini/St-307
88Pol/Dodg-14
88S-53
88Sf-110
88T-225
88T/Big-72
88T/St-67
89B-342
89D-77
89D/Best-66
89F-71
89F/AS-9
89F/WS-4
89Mother/Dodg-3
89OPC-7
89Panini/St-104
89Pol/Dodg-9
89S-121
89Sf-138
89Smok/Dodg-31
89T-669TL
89T-755
89T/Big-281
89T/St-58
89UD-116
90B-89
90D-316
90D/BestNL-5
90D/GSlam-7
90F-407
90Leaf/I-49
90Mother/Dodg-4
90OPC-605
90Panini/St-276
90Pol/Dodg-14
90PublInt/St-17
90S-398
90S/100St-48
90Sf-163
90T-605
90T/Big-67
90T/DH-58
90T/Gloss60-34
90T/St-64
90Target-713
90UD-298
90USPlayC/AS-2H
91B-613
91D-112
91D-436AS
91F-219
91F/Ultra-169
91Leaf/I-24
91Leaf/Stud-189
91Mother/Dodg-4
91OPC-305
91OPC-404AS
91Panini/FrSt-54
91Panini/St-57
91Pol/Dodg-14
91RedFoley/St-128
91S-520
91T-305
91T-404AS
91T/StClub/I-19
91UD-139
92D/II-480
92F-470
92S/I-226
92S/II-782AS
92T-13
92UD-152
Sconiers, Daryl
80ElPaso-14
81SLCity-20
82T-653R
83D-141
83T/Tr-99
84D-451
84F-528
84F/St-112
84Nes/792-27
84Smok/Cal-26
84T-27
85D-620
85F-312
85OPC-256
85T-604
86F-168
86SanJose-18
86T-193
87SanJose-28
88Vanco/CMC-22
88Vanco/ProC-766
91London/LineD-445
91MidldA/ProC-443
Scoras, John
78Memphis/Team-9
Score, Herb
55Gol/Ind-26
55Salem
56Carling-7
56T-140
57Sohio/Ind-12
57T-50
58T-352
58T-495AS
59Kahn
59T-88
60Kahn
60T-360
60T/tatt-48
61T-185
61T-337M
61Union
62T-116
79TCMA-134
86Indianap-24
89Pac/Leg-126
89Swell-114
90Pac/Legend-49
90Swell/Great-32
91Swell/Great-82
Exh47
Scott, Charles
86Watlo-25
88ColoSp/CMC-9
88ColoSp/ProC-1529
89ColoSp/CMC-8
90Portl/CMC-7
90Portl/ProC-178
91Portl/LineD-419
91Portl/ProC-1565
Scott, Craig
89Kingspt/Star-21
Scott, Dale
88TM/Umpire-58
89TM/Umpire-56
90TM/Umpire-54
Scott, Darryl
88CapeCod/Sum-34
90Boise/ProC-3313
91QuadC/ClBest-10
91QuadC/ProC-2627
Scott, Dick
82Colum-15
85Albany-19
87Colum-17
88Albany/ProC-1350
89Tacoma/CMC-20
89Tacoma/ProC-1554
90T/89Debut-112
90Tacoma/CMC-24CO
90Tacoma/ProC-103
90Target-714
Scott, Donald M.
(Donnie)
80Ashvl-21
81Tulsa-13
82Tulsa-11
83OKCty-23
84OKCty-19
84Rang-43
85Cram/PCL-81
85D-544
85F-568
85T-496
85T/Tr-105T
86F-474
86RochR-19
86T-568
87ElPaso-3
88ElPaso/Best-2
89Denver/CMC-6
89Denver/ProC-52
90Nashvl/CMC-12
90Nashvl/ProC-237
91Nashvl/LineD-271
91Nashvl/ProC-2160
Scott, Floyd John
(Pete)

33G-70
92Conlon/Sport-578
V354-33
Scott, Gary
89Geneva/ProC-1877
90CLAS/CL-49
90WinSalem/Team-1
91B-535
91Classic/II-T88
91F/UltraUp-U72
91F/Up-U80
91Iowa/ProC-1068
91Leaf/GRook-BC4
91Leaf/Stud-159
91OPC/Premier-107
91S/ASFan-3
91S/RookTr-90T
91T/StClub/II-596
91T/Tr-107T
91UD-58TP
92S/100RisSt-81
92T/91Debut-159
Scott, George
66T-558R
67OPC-75
67T-75
67T/Test/RSox-16
68Bz-7
68Coke
68Dexter-70
68T-233
68T/G-22
69MLB/St-17
69T-574
69T/St-138
70MLB/St-165
70OPC-385
70T-385
71MD
71MLB/St-331
71OPC-9
71T-9
71T/Coins-98
72MB-311
72T-585
73OPC-263
73T-263
73T/Comics-18
73T/Lids-47
73T/PinUps-18
74OPC-27
74T-27
74T/DE-30
74T/St-199
75Ho-26
75Ho/Twink-26
75OPC-360
75T-360
75T/M-360
76A&P/Milw
76Ho-54
76Ho/Twink-54
76K-21
76OPC-15
76OPC-194LL
76OPC-196LL
76SSPC-237
76T-15
76T-194LL
76T-196LL
77Ho-148
77OPC-210
77T-255
78Ho-24
78OPC-12
78PapaG/Disc-15
78T-125
79OPC-340
79T-645
80T-414
PM10/Sm-175
Scott, James
11Helmar-15
14CJ-26
15CJ-26
92Conlon/Sport-341
BF2-18
D329-158
D350/2-159
M101/4-158
M101/5-159
M116
T205
T206
W501-30
WG4-26
Scott, Jeff
77Ashvl
Scott, Jim
86Vermont-17
Scott, Joe
86Negro/Frit-58
Scott, John H.
75OPC-616R
75T-616R
75T/M-616R
76SSPC-131
77OPC-94
77T-473R
78T-547
Scott, John William
91Conlon/Sport-97
W515-25
Scott, Kelly
83Nashvl-19
84Colum-19
84Colum/Pol-22
85Colum-9
85Colum/Pol-19
Scott, Kevin
89AubAs/ProC-2183
90Ashvl/ProC-2752
91Osceola/ClBest-28
91Osceola/ProC-689
91Single/ClBest-37
Scott, L. Everett
21Exh-153
21Exh-154
91Conlon/Sport-149
D327
D328-154
D329-157
D350/2-160
E120
E121/120
E121/80
E122
E135-154
E220
M101/4-157
M101/5-160
V100
W512-7
W514-90
W515-46
W575
Scott, Mark
59HRDerby-17ANN
Scott, Mark
80Charl-2
Scott, Martin
(Marty)
79Tucson-10
81Tulsa-4
82BurlR-25MG
83Tulsa-25
90TulsaDG/Best-34
Scott, Michael Warren
(Mike)
78Tidew
79Tidew-15
80T-681R
80Tidew-23
81D-37
81T-109
82D-128
82F-535
82T-246TL
82T-432
83F-554
83T-679
83T/Tr-100T
84D-136
84F-240
84Mother/Ast-14
84Nes/792-559
84T-559
85D-258
85F-361
85Mother/Ast-18
85OPC-17
85T-17
86D-476
86D/HL-46
86F-311
86F/Mini-66
86F/St-108
86Greenvl/Team-16
86Leaf-235
86Pol/Ast-3
86Sf-195
86T-268
86T/St-27
87Classic-81
87Classic/Up-123
87D-163
87D-18DK
87D/AAS-32
87D/AS/Wax-PC13
87D/DKsuper-18
87D/OD-15
87Drake-33
87F-630M
87F-68
87F/AwardWin-37
87F/Lim-38
87F/Mini-99
87F/RecSet-36
87F/Slug-38
87F/St-108
87Ho/St-10
87Jiffy-18
87KayBee-30
87Kraft-4
87Leaf-18DK
87Leaf-258
87MnM's-18
87Mother/Ast-2
87OPC-330
87Pol/Ast-11
87Sf-119M
87Sf-120M
87Sf-19
87Smok/NL-5
87T-330
87T/Coins-44
87T/HL-18
87T/Mini-11
87T/St-15LCS
87T/St-35
87Woolwth-18
88ChefBoy-19
88Classic/Blue-221
88D-112
88D-BC12
88D/AS-40
88D/Best-206
88D/PopUp-18
88F-456
88F-632M
88F/AwardWin-36
88F/BB/AS-37
88F/BB/MVP-32
88F/Excit-35
88F/Hottest-35
88F/LL-36
88F/Mini-80
88F/RecSet-36
88F/Slug-37
88F/SS-34
88F/St-89
88F/TL-35
88KingB/Disc-13
88KMart-26
88Leaf-54
88Mother/Ast-2
88OPC-227
88Panini/St-233
88Panini/St-289
88Pol/Ast-21
88RedFoley/St-81
88S-335
88S/WaxBox-18
88Sf-66
88T-760
88T/Big-140
88T/Coins-54
88T/Gloss22-21
88T/Gloss60-5
88T/Mini-51
88T/RiteAid-4
88T/St-154FOIL
88T/St-30
88T/St/Backs-26
88T/UK-68
89B-322
89Classic-23
89D-69
89D/Best-94
89D/MVP-BC2
89F-367
89F/BBMVP's-34
89F/LL-34
89F/Superstar-37
89Lennox/Ast-4
89Mother/Ast-2
89OPC-180
89Panini/St-84
89RedFoley/St-106
89S-550
89S/HotStar-60
89S/Mast-4
89Sf-120
89T-180
89T/Big-51
89T/LJN-34
89T/Mini-14
89T/St-15
89UD-295
90B-71
90BBWit-12
90Classic-29
90D-207
90D/BestNL-16
90D/Learning-50
90F-237
90F-636M
90F/ASIns-10
90F/AwardWin-33
90F/LL-35
90HotPlay/St-39
90KingB/Discs-1
90KMart/SS-9
90Leaf/I-4
90Lennox-22
90MLBPA/Pins-43
90Mother/Ast-4
90OPC-405AS
90OPC-460
90Panini/St-262
90Post-20
90PublInt/St-102
90RedFoley/St-85
90S-40
90S-692 DT
90S/100St-97
90Sf-55
90Sunflower-22
90T-405AS
90T-460
90T/Big-249
90T/DH-59
90T/Gloss60-14
90T/Mini-56
90T/St-19
90T/TVAS-42
90UD-125
90UD-88TC
91B-546
91BBBest/Aces-15
91Classic/200-38
91D-483
91F-515
91F/Ultra-140
91Leaf/Stud-180
91Mother/Ast-4
91OPC-240
91Panini/FrSt-14
91Panini/St-16
91Petro/SU-8
91RedFoley/St-86
91S-46
91Seven/3DCoin-9T
91T-240
91T/StClub/I-209
91UD-531
91WIZMets-354
Scott, Michael Wm.
87Greenvl/Best-28
Scott, Philip
90Pittsfld/Pucko-1
91Greens/ProC-3068
Scott, Ralph
(Mickey)
70T-669R
72T-724R
73OPC-553
73T-553
76OPC-276
76T-276
77T-401
78Colum
91Crown/Orio-410
Scott, Rennie
90LynchRS/Team-22
91LynchRS/ClBest-8
91LynchRS/ProC-1198
Scott, Rodney
76SSPC-172
78T-191
79T-86
80OPC-360
80T-712
81D-209
81F-155
81OPC-227
81OPC/Post-2
81T-204M
81T-539
81T/St-185
82D-240
82F-207
82F/St-38
82OPC-259
82OPC/Post-14
82T-259
89Pac/SenLg-177
89T/SenLg-29
89TM/SenLg-94
90EliteSenLg-29
91Pac/SenLg-69
Scott, Shawn
90StCath/ProC-3480
91Dunedin/ClBest-23
91Dunedin/ProC-221
Scott, Steve
87SLCity/Taco-26
Scott, Tary
85Greens-3
86FSLAS-43
86WinHaven-21
87NewBrit-22
Scott, Tim
83Cedar-8
83Cedar/LF-3
87Hawaii-14
87SanAn-4
88Bakers/Cal-258
89SanAn/Best-24
90Albuq/CMC-9
90Albuq/ProC-344
90Albuq/Trib-26
91LasVegas/ProC-235
91LasVegas/LineD-293
92T/91Debut-160
Scott, Tony
76SSPC-339
78T-352
79T-143
80OPC-17
80T-33
81Coke
81D-191
81F-531
81T-165
81T/St-223
81T/Tr-828
82D-522
82F-231
82F/St-46
82T-698
83D-293
83F-465
83T-507
84D-527
84F-241
84Mother/Ast-20
84Nes/792-292
84T-292
85OPC-367
85T-733
89T/SenLg-91
90EliteSenLg-104
91Batavia/ProC-3502CO
91Pac/SenLg-121
Scott, Tyrone
90AubAs/Best-19
90AubAs/ProC-3402
91BurlAs/ClBest-8
91BurlAs/ProC-2799
Scranton, Jim
84Omaha-27
85Omaha-17
86Omaha-21
86Omaha/TCMA-7
Scripture, Billy
78Charl
Scrivener, Wayne

(Chuck)
77T-173
78T-94
Scruggs, Ron
86AppFx-21
87Penin-25
Scruggs, Tony
88CharlR/Star-22
89Tulsa/GS-24
89Tulsa/Team-23
90A&AASingle/ProC-98
90Foil/Best-19
90Gaston/Best-1
90Gaston/ProC-2535
90Gaston/Star-22
90SALAS/Star-22
91B-289
91OkCty/LineD-304
92T/91Debut-161
Scudder, Bill
83VeroB-10
85Cram/PCL-166
Scudder, Scott
87Cedar-7
88Cedar/ProC-1157
88MidwLAS/GS-14
89F/Up-U87
89Nashvl/CMC-8
89Nashvl/ProC-1293
89Nashvl/Team-22
89S/Tr-99
90B-46
90CedarDG/Best-15
90D-435
90F-434
90HotRook/St-39
90Leaf/II-413
90Nashvl/CMC-10
90Nashvl/ProC-232
90OPC-553
90S-518
90S/100Ris-65
90T-553
90T/89Debut-113
90UD-164
91D-265
91F-81
91Kahn/Reds-47
91Leaf/I-183
91OPC-713
91S-642
91T-713
91UD-615
92D/I-306
92F-422
92S/I-209
92T-48
92UD-485
Scull, Angel
53Briggs
54T-204
Scully, Vin
71Ticket/Dodg-20ANN
Scurry, Rod
76Shrev
78Colum
79Portl-22
81F-380
81T-194
82D-185
82F-497
82T-207
83D-376
83F-322
83T-537
84D-235
84F-264
84Nes/792-69
84T-69
85D-142
85F-476
85T-641
86T-449
87D-374
87F-113
87OPC-393
87T-665
88Calgary/CMC-10
88Calgary/ProC-779
89S-516
89UD-208
Seabaugh
E254
Seal, Mike
89Myrtle/ProC-1461
Seals, Joey
89GreatF-15
Sealy, Randy
75Shrev/TCMA-19
76Shrev
80WHave-23
Seaman, Kim
77Wausau
81Hawaii-22
82Hawaii-22
82Wichita-17
Seanez, Rudy
87Watlo-18
88Watlo/ProC-692
89Kinston/Star-23
90A&AASingle/ProC-10
90Canton/Best-24
90Canton/ProC-1293
90F-640R
90Foil/Best-164
90Leaf/II-417
90T/89Debut-114
91ColoSp/LineD-89
91ColoSp/ProC-2181
91D-218
91F-376
91UD-358
92D/II-552
92F-122
92S/II-696
Searage, Ray
77StPete
79ArkTr-20
81Tidew-24
82Charl-10
82T-478
84Cram/PCL-30
85F-595
85Pol/Brew-41
86D-536
86F-502
86T-642
86Vanco-23
87Coke/WS-21
87F-506
87T-149
88Albuq/CMC-4
88Albuq/ProC-262
88D-429
88F-409
88T-788
89F/Up-94
89Mother/Dodg-22
89Pol/Dodg-30
90D-649
90F-408
90Mother/Dodg-22
90OPC-84
90Pol/Dodg-59
90T-84
90Target-1066
91F-220
91ScranWB/LineD-496
91ScranWB/ProC-2538
91WIZMets-355
Search, Michael
90Boise/ProC-3316
90PalmSp/Cal-223
90PalmSp/ProC-2576
Searcy, Steve
86GlenF-21
87Toledo-2
87Toledo/TCMA-16
88Toledo/CMC-4
88Toledo/ProC-609
89B-95
89Classic-78
89D-29RR
89F-145
89S-627RP
89S/HotRook-47
89S/YS/II-27
89T-167FS
89UD/Ext-764
90AAAGame/ProC-AAA20
90F-615
90HotRook/St-40
90OPC-487
90S/100Ris-97
90T-487
90Toledo/CMC-10
90Toledo/ProC-149
90UD-575
91CokeK/Tiger-49
91D-549
91Leaf/I-187
91OPC-369
91S-649
91S/100RisSt-76
91T-369
91T/StClub/II-352
91UD-338
92F-545
92S/II-698
92T-599
Sears, Allen
83Durham-23
Sears, Jimmy
91Boise/ClBest-20
91Boise/ProC-3891
Sears, Ken
44Yank/St-24
Sears, Mike
86FSLAS-44TR
86WinHaven-22TR
87WinHaven-19
Seaton, Tom
14CJ-100
15CJ-100
D329-159
D350/2-161
M101/4-159
M101/5-161
Seats, Dean
81Cedar-13
Seats, Tom
49B/PCL-35
90Target-715
Seaver, Tom
67T-581R
68OPC-45
68T-45
69MB-250
69MLB/St-170
69NTF
69T-480
69T/decal
69T/S-52
69T/St-68
69Trans-48
70K-7
70MB-26
70MLB/St-82
70OPC-195NLCS
70OPC-300
70OPC-69LL
70T-195NLCS
70T-300
70T-69LL
70T/S-5
70T/SO
70Trans-4
70Trans/M-21
71Bz/Test-35
71K-2
71MD
71MLB/St-164
71MLB/St-574
71OPC-160
71OPC-68LL
71OPC-72LL
71T-160
71T-68LL
71T-72LL
71T/Coins-127
71T/S-53
71T/tatt-14
71T/tatt-14a
72K-1
72MB-312
72OPC-347KP
72OPC-445
72OPC-446IA
72OPC-91LL
72OPC-93LL
72OPC-95LL
72T-347KP
72T-445
72T-446IA
72T-91LL
72T-93LL
72T-95LL
72T/Post-13
73K-46
73OPC-350
73T-350
73T/Comics-19
73T/Lids-48
73T/PinUps-19
74K-52
74Laugh/ASG-68
74OPC-206LL
74OPC-207LL
74OPC-80
74T-206LL
74T-207LL
74T-80
74T/DE-9
74T/Puzzles-10
74T/St-70
75Ho-75
75OPC-370
75T-370
75T/M-370
76Crane-55
76Ho-35
76Ho/Twink-35
76K-32
76MSA/Disc
76OPC-199LL
76OPC-201LL
76OPC-203LL
76OPC-5RB
76OPC-600
76SSPC-551
76T-199LL
76T-201LL
76T-203LL
76T-5RB
76T-600
77BurgChef-142
77Ho-7
77OPC-205
77OPC-6LL
77Pep-67
77T-150
77T-6LL
77T/CS-42
78Ho-149
78K-27
78OPC-120
78T-450
78Tastee/Discs-10
78Wiffle/Discs-68
79Ho-65
79K-29
79OPC-44DP
79T-100
79T/Comics-22
80BK/PHR-10
80K-49
80OPC-260
80T-500
80T/S-15
81Coke
81D-422
81D-425
81F-200
81F/St-49
81K-38
81MSA/Disc-29
81OPC-220
81PermaGr/CC-11
81T-220
81T/HT
81T/Nat/Super-14
81T/So-107
81T/St-165
82Coke/Red
82D-148
82D-16DK
82D-628M
82F-645M
82F-82
82F/St-11
82K-8
82OPC-30
82OPC-31IA
82OPC-346AS
82PermaGr/CC-2
82Sqt-21
82T-165LL
82T-30
82T-31IA
82T-346AS
82T-756TL
82T/St-36
82T/St-9
83D-122
83F-601
83OPC-354SV
83OPC-52
83T-580
83T-581SV
83T/St-233
83T/Tr-101T
84D-116
84D/AAS-53
84D/Champs-40
84F-595
84F/X-U106
85FunFoodPin-15
84Nes/792-246TL
84Nes/792-706LL
84Nes/792-707LL
84Nes/792-708LL
84Nes/792-740
84OPC-261
84Ralston-8
84Seven-8E
84T-246TL
84T-706LL
84T-707LL
84T-708LL
84T-740
84T/Cereal-8
84T/St-106
84T/Tr-108T
84TrueVal/WS-27
85Coke/WS-41
85D-424
85D/HL-1
85D/HL-30
85Drake-41
85F-526
85F/LimEd-34
85F/St-68SA
85F/St-69
85F/St-70
85F/St-71
85F/St-72
85F/St-73
85Leaf-101
85OPC-1
85Seven-12G
85Sportflic/Test-45
85T-670
85T/3D-30
85T/St-235
85T/Super-31
85ThomMc/Discs-19
86Coke/WS-41
86D-609
86F-216
86F-630M
86F/HOF-3
86F/LL-40
86F/Mini-46
86F/Slug-34
86F/St-109
86Jay's-16
86Leaf-234
86OPC-390
86Quaker-32
86Sf-130M
86Sf-134M
86Sf-142M
86Sf-182M
86Sf-25
86Sf-56M
86Sf-67M
86Sf-70M
86Sf/Dec-52
86Sf/Rook-47M
86T-390
86T-402TBC
86T/Gloss60-22
86T/St-10
86T/St-287
86T/Super-50
86T/Tr-101T
86TrueVal-12
87D-375
87F-45
87KMart-21
87Leaf-263
87OPC-49
87Sf-28
87T-425
87T/St-246
88AlaskaAS60/Team-3
89T/LJN-57

90BBWit-46
90HOF/St-76
90MSA/AGFA-14
90Pac/Legend-60
90Smok/SoCal-11
90Swell/Great-1
91Swell/Great-107
91WIZMets-356

Seay, Dick
78Laugh/Black-14

Seay, Mark
87SanJose-16

Sebra, Bob
83TriCit-1
85OKCty-19
86Indianap-23
87D-468
87F-331
87Leaf-213
87OPC-314
87T-479
88AAA/ProC-17
88D-458
88F-195
88Indianap/CMC-3
88Indianap/ProC-511
88OPC-93
88S-337
88T-93
89ScrWB/CMC-4
89ScrWB/ProC-718
90Brewer/MillB-22
90Nashvl/CMC-11
90Nashvl/ProC-233
90TulsaDG/Best-8

Sebring, James
90Target-716
T204

Secory, Frank
55B-286ump

Secrest, Charlie
59T-140

Secrist, Don
69T-654R

Seda, Israel
91Penin/ClBest-22
91Penin/ProC-387

Sedar, Ed
83AppFx/LF-18
86Penin-24
87DayBe-19
91Pocatel/ProC-3802CO

See, Larry
82VeroB-20
84Cram/PCL-162
86Albuq-22
87Albuq/Pol-21
89Toledo/CMC-14
89Toledo/ProC-784
90Target-717

Seeburger, John
88Oneonta/ProC-2050
89FtLaud/Star-25

Seeds, Robert Ira
32Orbit/un-52
33Exh/4-10
39PB-32
40PB-91
R305
R314/Can
V355-27

Seefried, Tate
90Tampa/DIMD-22
91Oneonta/ProC-4163

Seeger, Mark
81AppFx-24

Seegers, Pat
78Newar
79BurlB-3

Seelbach, Chuck
73OPC-51
73T-51
74OPC-292
74T-292

Seerey, James Pat
48L-73

Seery, John Emmett
N172
N284
WG1-35

Sefly, Joel
90Visalia/Cal-82TR
91Visalia/ClBest-27TR

Segelke, Herman
82Iowa-23
83Phoenix/BHN-13
84Cram/PCL-10

Segrist, Kal
58Union
91Crown/Orio-411

Segui, Daniel
89Pittsfld/Star-25
90Visalia/Cal-77
90Visalia/ProC-2164

Segui, David
88Hagers/Star-19
89Freder/Star-21
90AAAGame/ProC-AAA54
90B-251A
90B-251B
90F/Up-U69
90HagersDG/Best-26
90S/Tr-95T
90UD/Ext-773
91B-102
91Classic/I-15
91Crown/Orio-412
91D-730
91F-492
91F/Ultra-25
91Leaf/Stud-10
91MajorLg/Pins-30
91OPC-724
91RochR/LineD-466
91RochR/ProC-1910
91S-362RP
91S/100RisSt-61
91S/Rook40-31
91Seven/3DCoin-15A
91T-724
91T/90Debut-140
91T/StClub/I-50
91UD-342
92D/I-321
92F-27
92S/100RisSt-33
92S/II-554
92T-447
92UD-316

Segui, Diego
61Union
63T-157
64T-508
64T/Coins-24
65OPC-197
65T-197
65T/E-24
65T/trans-68
66T-309
68T-517
69T-511
70OPC-2
70T-2
71MLB/St-526
71OPC-215
71OPC-67LL
71T-215
71T-67LL
72T-735
73OPC-383
73T-383
74OPC-151
74T-151
74T/Tr-151T
75OPC-232
75T-232
75T/M-232
76SSPC-423
77T-653
87Pocatel/Bon-30CO
88Pocatel/ProC-2100
89Everett/Star-31
90Everett/ProC-3146CO
90Pac/Legend-104

Segura, Jose
85Kingst-10
86Knoxvl-19
87Syrac-9
87Syrac/TCMA-7
88Coke/WS-27
88F/Up-U20
89Vanco/CMC-6
89Vanco/ProC-591
90Vanco/CMC-12
90Vanco/ProC-490
91Phoenix/LineD-394
91Phoenix/ProC-66
92S/I-278

Sehorn, Jason
90Hunting/ProC-3302

Seibert, Gib
85Cram/PCL-27
87Maine-15
87Maine/TCMA-16

Seibert, Kurt
80Toledo-20
81Toledo-14

Seibert, Mal
90Fayette/ProC-2406

Seibert, Rick
89Penin/Star-22

Seibold, Henry
33DH-38
R316

Seidel, Dick
83Greens-12

Seidensticker, Andy
88Visalia/Cal-172
88Visalia/ProC-106

Seidholz, Don
78Knoxvl
79Knoxvl/TCMA-9

Seifert, Keith
87Watlo-21
88Watlo/ProC-678
90Tampa/DIMD-23
91Greens/ProC-3059

Seilheimer, Rick
80GlenF/B-7
80GlenF/C-8
81GlenF-9
82Edmon-21

Seirra, Ernie
89SanJose/Best-30

Seitz, Charles
T206

Seitz, David
86Sumter-25

Seitzer, Brad
91Bluefld/ProC-4137
91Bluefld/ClBest-8

Seitzer, Kevin
83Butte-20
85FtMyr-9
86Omaha-22
86Omaha/TCMA-3
87Classic/Up-139
87D/HL-26
87D/HL-47
87D/OD-207
87D/Rook-15
87F-652R
87F/Slug-39
87F/Up-U108
87Sf-158R
87Sf/Rook-20
87T/Tr-111T
88Classic/Blue-218
88Classic/Red-159
88D-280
88D-BC17
88D/AS-27
88D/Best-175
88F-270
88F/AwardWin-37
88F/BB/AS-38
88F/BB/MVP-33
88F/Excit-36
88F/Hottest-36
88F/LL-37
88F/Mini-27
88F/RecSet-37
88F/Slug-38
88F/SS-35
88F/St-33
88F/TL-36
88F/WaxBox-C12
88KMart-27
88Leaf-105
88MSA/Disc-8
88OPC-275
88Panini/St-108
88Panini/St-436
88S-6
88S/YS/I-10
88Sf-17
88Sf/Gamewin-13
88Smok/Royals-21
88T-275
88T/Big-115
88T/Gloss60-9
88T/JumboR-9
88T/Mini-15
88T/Revco-22
88T/RiteAid-19
88T/St-261
88T/St-306
88T/UK-69
88ToysRUs-27
89B-123
89Cadaco-52
89Classic-65
89D-10DK
89D-238
89D/Best-207
89D/DKsuper-10DK
89F-292
89F/Excit-36
89F/Heroes-36
89F/WaxBox-C22
89Holsum/Discs-9
89Nissen-9
89OPC-58
89Panini/St-357
89RedFoley/St-107
89S-55
89S/HotStar-17
89Sf-55
89T-670
89T/Big-313
89T/LJN-151
89T/St-264
89Tastee/Discs-2
89UD-510
90B-380
90D-85
90D/BestAL-91
90F-117
90Leaf/I-230
90MLBPA/Pins-102
90OPC-435
90Panini/St-86
90PublInt/St-355
90RedFoley/St-86
90S-199
90S/100St-88
90Sf-46
90T-435
90T/Big-76
90T/Mini-18
90T/St-267
90UD-363
91B-305
91Classic/200-40
91D-73
91F-569
91F/Ultra-155
91KingB/Discs-2
91Leaf/I-133
91Leaf/StudPrev-5
91OPC-695
91Panini/FrSt-278
91Panini/St-227
91Pol/Royal-19
91S-279
91S/100SS-97
91T-695
91T/StClub/I-88
91UD-433
92D/II-577
92F-168
92S/I-310
92T-577
92UD-327

Seja, Aaron
91Fayette/ProC-1184
91Niagara/ClBest-7
91Niagara/ProC-3648

Selbach, Albert
(Kip)
E107

Selby
E254

Sele, Aaron
91Classic/DP-19
91FrRow/DP-2
92S/II-809Draft
92T-504DP

Selig, Kevin
76AppFx

Selkirk, George
34DS-88
37OPC-108
38ONG/Pin-27
39PB-25
40PB-8
92Conlon/Sport-388
V300
V355-11

Sellas, Marcelino
88CapeCod/Sum-91

Sellers, Jeff
86D/Rook-29
86Pawtu-21
87D-544
87F-46
87Leaf-158
87T-12
88D-585
88D/RedSox/Bk-585
88F-366
88S-541
88T-653
89B-299
89D-517
89Nashvl/ProC-1270
89S-491
89T-544

Sellers, Rick
89NiagFls/Pucko-21
90Fayette/ProC-2412
91Lakeland/ClBest-16

Sellheimer, Rick
85BuffB-5

Sellick, John
88SALAS/GS-25
88Savan/ProC-347
89Spring/Best-14
90StPete/Star-22
91ArkTr/LineD-44
91ArkTr/ProC-1296

Sellner, Scott
88Billings/ProC-1807
89Cedar/Best-17
89Cedar/ProC-925
89Cedar/Star-18
91Chatt/LineD-169
91Chatt/ProC-1968

Sells, Dave
74OPC-37
74T-37
90Target-718

Sells, George
88CapeCod/Sum-117
90Hamil/Best-9
90Hamil/Star-23
91StPete/ProC-2275

Selma, Dick
66OPC-67R
66T-67R
67T-386
68T-556
69MLB/St-195
69OPC-197
69T-197
69T/decal
69T/S-62
69T/St-98
70MLB/St-23
70OPC-24
70T-24
71K-21
71MLB/St-187
71OPC-705
71T-705
72T-726
73OPC-632
73T-632
91WIZMets-357

Seltzer, Randy
76AppFx
77AppFx

Semall, Paul
79Colum-3
80Wichita-15
83OKCty-16
84Cram/PCL-125
85Cram/PCL-232

Sember, Mike
79Syrac-10

Sembera, Carroll
66T-539R
67OPC-136
67T-136
68T-207
69T-351

Sementelli, Chris
89Spartan/ProC-1049
Semerano, Bob
77Charl
Seminara, Frank
88Oneonta/ProC-2071
89Oneonta/ProC-2121
89PrWill/Star-18
90CLAS/CL-14
90PrWill/Team-23
91Single/ClBest-382
91Wichita/LineD-618
91Wichita/ProC-2598
92D/I-10RR
Seminick, Andy
49B-30
49Eureka-146
49Lummis
49Royal-7
50B-121
51B-51
51BR-C7
51T/RB-45
52Dix
52Royal
52T-297
53B/BW-7
53Dix
53T-153
54B-172
55B-93
56T-296
91T/Arc53-153
Exh47
PM10/Sm-176
Semprini, John
82Jacks-9
84Chatt-12
Semproch, Roman
58T-474
59T-197
60T-286
61T-174
61T/St-206
Sempsrott, Ed
76Watlo
77DaytB
Sena, Sean
90Yakima/Team-22
Seninger, Glenn
87SLCity/Taco-14PR
Senn, Terry
75Tidew/Team-18
Senne, Michael
87StPete-9
88ArkTr/GS-25
89Shrev/ProC-1840
Senne, Tim
86Visalia-20
87Visalia-14
Senteney, Steve
82Syrac-8
83D-52
83Tidew-10
Sentlinger, Rick
77QuadC
Seoane, Manuel
(Manny)
76OkCty/Team-22
80Wichita-21
81Evansvl-7
Seoane, Mitch
84Greens-25
86PalmSp/Smok-24
87MidldA-20
89QuadC/Best-25
89QuadC/GS-2
91QuadC/ClBest-27MG
91QuadC/ProC-2645MG
Sepanek, Rob
86FtLaud-20
87PrWill-10
88Albany/ProC-1332
89Albany/Best-9
89Albany/ProC-330
89Albany/Star-17
90AlbanyDG/Best-29
90ColClip/CMC-21
90ColClip/ProC-684
Sepela, Thom
86Elmira-21
87Elmira/Black-20
87Elmira/Red-20
Seppala, L.
33SK-48
Septimo, Felix
90MedHat/Best-11
91StCath/ProC-3409
Sepulveda, Jorge
86VeroB-22
Serad, William
N172
Serafini, Rudy
83QuadC-14
Serbin, Scott
90Saraso/Star-30BB
Serena, Bill
50B-230
51B-246
52T-325
53B/Col-122
54B-93
55B-233
Serna, Paul
81LynnS-18
82D-567
83Chatt-2
83T-492
84Chatt-13
85Cram/PCL-79
86Wausau-23
Serna, Ramon
87ElPaso-25
88ElPaso/Best-7
Serra, Armando
88StCath/ProC-2037
Serrano, Andy
79Elmira-17
Serrano, Marty
77DaytB
Serritella, John
83Butte-10
83CharR-23
Serum, Gary
79T-627
80T-61
80Toledo-5
82OrlTw/B-23
Servais, Scott
88T/Tr-106TOLY
89Osceola/Star-20
89Star/Wax-17
89T/Big-291
90Tucson/CMC-21
90Tucson/ProC-206
91Tucson/LineD-618
91Tucson/ProC-2216
91UD/FinalEd-68F
92D/II-763
92F-444
92S/II-816
92T-437
92T/91Debut-162
92UD-561
Servello, Dan
91Eugene/ClBest-12
91Eugene/ProC-3740
Service, Scott
88Reading/ProC-868
89F-653R
89Reading/Best-6
89Reading/ProC-657
89Reading/Star-23
90B-143
90ScranWB/CMC-8
90ScranWB/ProC-600
90UD-35
91Indianap/LineD-193
91Indianap/ProC-461
Servoss, Bob
76Wmsprt
Sevcik, John
65T-597
Severeid, Henry
21Exh-155
25Exh-116
28Exh/PCL-24
D327
D328-155
E120
E121/80
E122
E135-155
T207
V100
V61-25
W572
W573
W575
Severinsen, Al
70OPC-477R
70T-477R
71MLB/St-238
71OPC-747R
71T-747R
72OPC-274
72T-274
72T/Cloth-28
91Crown/Orio-413
Severns, Bill
77Holyo
79Vanco-21
80Vanco-8
Severson, Rich
71MLB/St-430
71OPC-103
71T-103
Sewell, Joe
91AubAS/ClBest-9
91AubAS/ProC-4273
Sewell, Joseph
(Joe)
21Exh-156
25Exh-85
26Exh-84
28Exh-43
28Yueng-10
29Exh/4-21
32Orbit/num-116
33G-165
61F-76
72Laugh/GF-40
80SSPC/HOF
89HOF/St-22
89Pac/Leg-125
90HOF/St-33
90Pac/Legend-67
91Conlon/Sport-275
91Conlon/Sport-40
E120
E121/120
R316
V100
V117-12
V353-89
V61-12
W501-16
W502-10
W507-46
WG7-47
Sewell, Luke
29Exh/4-22
31Exh/4-22
33Exh/4-11
33G-114
33G-163
35BU-155
35G-1F
35G-2F
35G-6F
35G-7F
38Exh/4-10
39PB-5
40PB-48
49Eureka-94
51B-322MG
52B-94MG
61F-138
91Conlon/Sport-193
E220
R312/M
R314
R316
V353-91
V355-62
W753
Sewell, T. Rip
47TipTop
49B-234
49Eureka-172
89Pac/Leg-202
Exh47
Sexauer, Elmer
90Target-1067
Sexton, Jimmy
75Shrev/TCMA-20
76Shrev
77SanJose-22
79T-232
80T-11
80Tucson-2
81Tacom-15
82Tacom-38
83D-449
83F-533
83T-709
Sexton, Wayne
(Twink)
79Jacks-4
Seybold, Ralph
E107
E254
E91
Seyfried, Gordon
64T-499R
Seymour, Bob
82VeroB-25
Seymour, Harold
90LitSun-16
Seymour, James B.
(Cy)
C46-38
E104
E254
E91
M116
T201
T206
WG3-42
Seymour, Paul
81Batavia-29
Seymour, Steve
91Kingspt/ClBest-20
91Kingspt/ProC-3813
Seymour, Winston
89Salem/Star-20
89Welland/Pucko-21
90Augusta/ProC-2475
Sferrazza, Vince
86Fres/Smk-3tr
87Shrev-23
88Shrev/ProC-1284
89Spring/Best-26
Sferrazza, Matt
86Jaxvl/TCMA-13
87GlenF-13
Shaab, Doug
85Osceola/Team-12
Shabazz, Basil
91Johnson/ClBest-15
91Johnson/ProC-3990
Shabosky, Brian
88CapeCod-7
88CapeCod/Sum-186
Shackle, Richard
89Johnson/Star-20
90SALAS/Star-42
90Savan/ProC-2068
91FSLAS/ProC-FSL35
91StPete/ClBest-12
91StPete/ProC-2276
Shaddy, Chris
83Knoxvl-14
86Knoxvl-20
87Knoxvl-2
88Syrac/CMC-22
88Syrac/ProC-833
89Richm/Bob-24
89Richm/CMC-22
89Richm/Ko-10
89Richm/ProC-824
Shade, Mike
(Mick)
83Spring/LF-11
85Louisvl-24
87Jaxvl-14
88Jaxvl/Best-2
88Jaxvl/ProC-985
Shade, Steve
86Erie-26
Shafer
11Helmar-136
Shafer, Frank T.
N172
Shafer, George
N172
Shaffer, Duane
78Knoxvl
79AppFx-21
80GlenF/C-24C
80GlenF/C-25C
Shambaugh, Mike
88Boise/ProC-1611
Shamblin, Bill
87Kinston-1
88Reno/Cal-272
Shamburg, Ken
90Freder/Team-17
91Hagers/LineD-246
91Hagers/ProC-2465
Shamsky, Art
65T-398R
66OPC-119
66T-119
67Kahn
67OPC-96
67T-96
68Kahn
68T-292
69MB-251
69T-221
69T/St-69
70OPC-137
70T-137
70Trans/M-23
71MLB/St-165
71OPC-445
71T-445
71T/Coins-43
72MB-313
72OPC-353
72T-353
72T/Cloth-29
78TCMA-278
91WIZMets-358
Shanahan, Chris
91Pittsfld/ClBest-16
91Pittsfld/ProC-3422
Shanahan, Paul
(Greg)
74Albuq/Team-18
74OPC-599R
74T-599R
90Target-719
Shanks, Howard S.
(Hank)
21Exh-157
D328-156
D329-160
D350/2-162
E120
E135-156
M101/4-160
M101/5-162
V100
Shanks, Willie
85Kingst-11
86Ventura-24
Shannon, Dan
89Hamil/Star-23
90Spartan/Best-21
90Spartan/ProC-2504
90Spartan/Star-19
Shannon, Daniel
N172
Shannon, Maurice J.
E220
Shannon, Mike
61Union
62Kahn/Atl
64T-262R
65OPC-43
65T-43
66T-293
67T-605
68T-445
69MB-252
69MLB/St-215
69OPC-110
69T-110
69T/St-120
70MLB/St-143
70T-614
71MLB/St-283
71OPC-735
71T-735
72MB-314
78TCMA-275
90LitSun-24
Shannon, Robert
86Jamestn-22
Shannon, Scott
91StCath/ClBest-24TR

Shannon, Thomas L.
88Rockford-32GM
89Rockford-32GM
Shannon, Wally
60L-93
Shannon, William P.
T206
Shantz, Bobby
50B-234
51B-227
52Dix-53
52RM-AL20
52StarCal/L-76C
52T-219
53B/Col-11
53NB
53RM-AL20
53T-225
54B-19
54T-21
55B-139M
55B-140
55Rodeo
56Rodeo
56T-261
57T-272
58T-289M
58T-419
59T-222
60T-315
61P-15
61T-379
61T-473MV
61T/St-198
62Salada-188
62Shirriff-188
62T-177
62T/bucks
62T/St-128
63T-533
64PhilBull-21
64T-278
75OPC-190MV
75T-190MV
75T/M-190MV
79TCMA-171
88Pac/Leg-61
89Smok/Ast-7
89Swell-131
90Pac/Legend-105
91Swell/Great-83
91T/Arc53-225
PM10/Sm-177
PM10/Sm-178
Rawl
Shantz, Wilmer
55B-139M
55B-175
55Rodeo
56Rodeo
Sharitt, Kelly
89Oneonta/ProC-2108
90Greens/Star-26TR
90SALAS/Star-25TR
Sharko, Gary
89Clinton/ProC-887
90SanJose/Best-19
90SanJose/Cal-46
90SanJose/ProC-2005
90SanJose/Star-20
91AS/Cal-35
91SanJose/ClBest-21
91SanJose/ProC-10
Sharon, Dick
74OPC-48
74T-48
75OPC-293
75T-293
75T/M-293
Sharp, Bill
74OPC-519
74T-519
75OPC-373
75T-373
75T/M-373
76A&P/Milw
76OPC-244
76SSPC-246
76T-244
77Spoka
Sharp, Gary
82BurlR-9
Sharp, Mike
91Yakima/ClBest-26
91Yakima/ProC-4247
Sharpe, Bayard
C46-31
M116
T205
T206
Sharperson, Mike
83Kinston/Team-24
85Syrac-19
86Syrac-22
87D-565
87D/OD-31
87Tor/Fire-27
88Albuq/CMC-16
88Albuq/ProC-253
88F-525
88Pol/Dodg-27M
89Albuq/CMC-14
89Albuq/ProC-59
89B-348
89F-72
89Pol/Dodg-17
89S-602
90D-603
90Leaf/II-490
90Mother/Dodg-20
90OPC-117
90Pol/Dodg-27
90T-117
90Target-720
91B-602
91D-168
91F-221
91F/Ultra-170
91Mother/Dodg-20
91OPC-53
91Pol/Dodg-27
91S-546
91T-53
91T/StClub/II-541
91UD-598
92D/II-526
92S/II-592
92T-627
Sharpnack, Bob
86Modesto-22
87Madis-25
88Huntsvl/BK-18
89Huntsvl/Best-11
Sharrott, George
90Target-1068
Sharsig, William J.
N172
Sharts, Scott
91Watertn/ClBest-22
91Watertn/ProC-3377
Sharts, Stephen
85Bend/Cram-22
87Clearw-16
88Reading/ProC-865
89Reading/Best-5
89Reading/ProC-651
90ScranWB/CMC-9
90ScranWB/ProC-601
Shaughnessy, Francis
(Shag)
R314/Can
T206
V355-78
Shaute, Joe
90Target-721
Shave, Jon
91Gaston/ClBest-22
91Gaston/ProC-2699
91Single/ClBest-380
Shaver, Jeff
86Madis-21
86Madis/Pol-18
88Tacoma/CMC-8
88Tacoma/ProC-619
89Tacoma/CMC-11
89Tacoma/ProC-1559
Shaw, Al
T206
Shaw, Bob
58T-206
59T-159
60L-83
60T-380
61P-23
61T-352
61T/St-127
62T-109
62T/St-56
63J-154
63P-154
63Salada-7
63T-255
63T-5LL
64T-328
65T-428
65T/E-57
66T-260
67Kahn
67T-470
73OPC-646CO
73T-646C
91WIZMets-359
Shaw, Cedrick
88Butte-9
89CharlR/Star-22
90Tulsa/ProC-1154
91Tulsa/LineD-597
91Tulsa/ProC-2773
Shaw, Curtis
90A&AASingle/ProC-164
90SoOreg/Best-17
90SoOreg/ProC-3427
91Madison/ProC-2132
Shaw, Don
67T-587R
68T-521
69OPC-183
69T-183
70OPC-476
70T-476
71OPC-654
71T-654
72OPC-479
72T-479
88SanDiegoSt-16
91WIZMets-360
Shaw, Jeff
87Watlo-16
88Wmsprt/ProC-1309
89Canton/Best-3
89Canton/ProC-1298
89Canton/Star-19
90B-329
90ColoSp/ProC-33
90D/Rook-53
91ColoSp/LineD-95
91ColoSp/ProC-2182
91S-746RP
91T/90Debut-141
92D/II-595
92S/II-624
92UD-660
Shaw, John W.
N172
Shaw, Kerry
88SLCity-17
89Salinas/Cal-144
89Salinas/ProC-1803
90SanJose/Best-2
90SanJose/Cal-29
90SanJose/ProC-2020
90SanJose/Star-21
Shaw, Kevin
88AppFx/ProC-140
89BBCity/Star-8
89Star/Wax-63
90BBCity/Star-22
91BBCity/ClBest-11
91BBCity/ProC-1398
91FSLAS/ProC-FSL3
Shaw, Malcolm
91Madison/ClBest-14
Shaw, Rick
82Amari-22
Shaw, Robert
C46-83
Shaw, Royal N.
T206
Shaw, Samuel E.
N172
Shaw, Scott
86FtLaud-21
87FtLaud-7
88Albany/ProC-1345
89Albany/Best-4
89Albany/ProC-317
89Albany/Star-18
Shaw, Theo
81CharR-8
84Omaha-17
85FtMyr-20
86Omaha-23
86Omaha/TCMA-20
87Memphis-15
87Memphis/Best-12
88Wmsprt/ProC-1318
89ColoSp/ProC-259
90Calgary/CMC-20
Shawkey, J. Bob
15CJ-164
25Exh-102
26Exh-103
61F-139
88Conlon/5-26
91Conlon/Sport-156
D327
D328-157
D329-161
D350/2-163
E120
E121/120
E121/80
E126-37
E135-157
E210-59
E220
M101/4-161
M101/5-163
R315-A32
R315-B32
V61-39
W501-31
W514-29
W515-9
W572
W573
W575
Shay, Dan
E91
Shea, Bill
90BBWit-27
Shea, Ed
87Watertn-4
Shea, Frank
(Spec)
48B-26
49B-49
50B-155
52B-230
52T-248
53B/Col-141
53Briggs
53T-164
54B-104
55B-207
91T/Arc53-164
PM10/Sm-179
R346-13
Shea, John
87Myrtle-18
88Knoxvl/Best-3
89Knoxvl/Best-24
89Knoxvl/ProC-1140
89Knoxvl/Star-20
90Syrac/CMC-8
90Syrac/ProC-571
90Syrac/Team-21
91Syrac/LineD-517
91Syrac/ProC-2480
Shea, Kevin
87VeroB-29
Shea, Kurt
88Bristol/ProC-1887
89Fayette/ProC-1582
Shea, Mervyn D.J.
29Exh/4-24
90Target-722
92Conlon/Sport-412
Shea, Patrick
(Red)
E121/120
E121/80
W501-63
W575
WG7-48
Shea, Steven F.
69T-499R
Sheaffer, Danny
85Pawtu-12
86Pawtu-22
87Pawtu/TCMA-8
89ColoSp/CMC-21
89ColoSp/ProC-241
90BuffB/CMC-15
90BuffB/ProC-377
90BuffB/Team-24
91Portl/LineD-418
91Portl/ProC-1568
Shean, David
11Helmar-105
E101
E102
E286
E90/1
E92
M116
S74-46
T202
T205
Shean, Larry
W514-116
Shearer, Ray
58T-283
Sheary, Kevin
88Rockford-33
89Rockford-33
Sheckard, James
10Domino-109
11Helmar-106
12Sweet/Pin-91
90Target-723
D328-158
E107
E135-158
E254
E90/1
E90/3
E91
S74-69
T202
T204
T205
T206
T215/brown
WG3-43
Sheehan, Jack
90Target-724
Sheehan, John
87Ashvl-28
88Osceola/Star-24
89Osceola/Star-21
90ColMud/Best-18
90ColMud/ProC-1346
90ColMud/Star-21
Sheehan, Terry
78OrlTw
79Toledo-10
80OrlTw-16
Sheehan, Tommy
90Target-1069
Sheehy, Mark
84Cram/PCL-246C
87Bakers-16C
88SanAn/Best-25
Sheely, Earl Homer
21Exh-158
25Exh-79
26Exh-79
28Exh/PCL-25
28Yueng-37
29Exh/4-13
31Exh/4-2
33Exh/4-1
46Sunbeam
47Centen-26
92Conlon/Sport-515
E120
E121/120
E210-37
V100
V61-34
W501-46
W502-37
W572
W573
W575
Sheen, Charlie
88Pac/8Men-10
Sheets, Larry
84RochR-1
85D-36RR
85F/Up-U101
85T/Tr-106T
86D-350
86F-286

86Sf-177M
86T-147
86T/Gloss60-50
86T/St-308
87D-248
87F-479
87F/Hottest-36
87French-18
87Smok/AL-10
87T-552
87T/St-229
88Classic/Red-188
88D-273
88D/Best-286
88Drake-23
88F-572
88F/AwardWin-38
88F/BB/MVP-34
88F/Excit-37
88F/Hottest-37
88F/LL-38
88F/Mini-3
88F/St-4
88French-18
88OPC-327
88Panini/St-16
88S-219
88Sf-161
88T-327
88T/Big-26
88T/St-230
88T/UK-70
89B-16
89D-333
89F-620
89French-19
89OPC-98
89Panini/St-264
89S-81
89T-381TL
89T-98
89T/Big-113
89T/St-239
89UD-254
90CokeK/Tiger-22
90D-495
90F-189
90F/Up-100
90HagersDG/Best-27
90Leaf/II-350
90OPC-708
90PublInt/St-586
90S-111
90S/Tr-65T
90T-708
90UD-287
91Crown/Orio-414
91F-352
91OPC-281
91S-176
91T-281
91UD-340

Sheffield, Gary
87Stockton-1
88BBAmer-22
88ElPaso/Best-1
88TexLgAS/GS-26
89B-142
89Brewer/YB-1
89Bz-19
89Classic-101
89D-31RR
89D/Best-113
89D/Rook-1
89F-196
89Panini/St-364
89Pol/Brew-1
89S-625RP
89S/HotRook-10
89S/YS/I-25
89Sf-223R
89Sf-41
89T-343FS
89T/Big-55
89T/HeadsUp-13
89T/JumboR-20
89ToysRUs-28
89UD-13SR
90B-391
90Brewer/MillB-23
90Bz-16
90Classic-14
90D-501
90D/BestAL-121
90ElPasoATG/Team-27
90F-336
90HotRook/St-41
90Leaf/I-157
90OPC-718
90Pol/Brew-11
90PublInt/St-504
90PublInt/St-604
90S-97
90S/100Ris-20
90S/McDon-12
90Sf-52
90T-718
90T/Big-163
90T/Coins-27
90T/Gloss60-10
90T/HeadsUp-13
90T/JumboR-25
90T/St-202
90T/St-326FS
90ToysRUs-24
90UD-157
91B-52
91Brewer/MillB-23
91Classic/200-103
91Classic/II-T13
91D-751
91F-596
91F/Ultra-180
91JDeanSig-7
91Leaf/I-173
91Leaf/Stud-76
91OPC-68
91Panini/FrSt-206
91Panini/St-170
91Pol/Brew-20
91Post-15
91S-473
91S/100SS-30
91T-68
91T/StClub/I-95
91UD-266
92D/I-192
92F-188
92S/II-589
92T-695
92UD-234
92UD-84M

Sheffield, Travis
86DayBe-25

Sheffler, Jim
89Kingspt/Star-22

Shehan, Brian
88CapeCod/Sum-38

Sheid, Rich
90Foil/Best-175

Shelby, John
82RochR-17
83T/Tr-102T
84D-291
84F-20
84F/St-114
84Nes/792-86
84T-86
85D-472
85F-190
85OPC-264
85RochR-13
85T-508
85T/St-204
86D-643
86F-287
86F/Mini-60
86T-309
87D-354
87D/OD-139
87F-480
87F/Up-U109
87T-208
87T/Tr-112T
88D-352
88D/Best-290
88F-526
88Mother/Dodg-14
88OPC-307
88Panini/St-316
88Pol/Dodg-31
88S-286
88T-428
88T/Big-218
89B-349
89D-314
89F-73
89Mother/Dodg-14
89OPC-175
89Panini/St-109
89Pol/Dodg-20
89S-103
89T-175
89T/St-63
89UD-75
90Mother/Dodg-25
90Pol/Dodg-31
90PublInt/St-18
90Target-725
91CokeK/Tiger-25
91Crown/Orio-415
91D-563
91F-353
91OPC-746
91S-609
91T-746
91UD-201

Sheldon, Bob
75OPC-623R
75T-623R
75T/M-623R
76OPC-626
76SSPC-256
76T-626
77Spoka

Sheldon, Dave
86AppFx-22

Sheldon, Roland
61T-541
62T-185
63T-507
65OPC-254
65T-254
66OPC-18
66T-18
69T-413

Sheldon, Scott
91SoOreg/ClBest-13
91SoOreg/ProC-3857

Shell, Scott
91Elizab/ProC-4308

Shellenback, Frank
28Exh/PCL-26
88MinorLg/Leg-7

Shellenback, Jim
67T-592R
69T-567R
70OPC-389
70T-389
71MLB/St-549
71OPC-351
71T-351
74OPC-657
74T-657
84Toledo-21
85Toledo-27
87Orlan-7
88Portl/CMC-25CO
88Portl/ProC-644CO
89Portl/CMC-25CO
89Portl/ProC-226CO
90Portl/CMC-21CO
90Portl/ProC-194G
91OrlanSR/LineD-496CO
91OrlanSR/ProC-1867CO

Shelton, Andrew
E270/1

Shelton, Ben
88Augusta/ProC-370
89Augusta/ProC-511
90Salem/Star-21
91Salem/ClBest-8
91Salem/ProC-962

Shelton, Harry
86Geneva-24
87Peoria-19
88CharWh/Best-21
89Peoria/Ko-26
90Miami/I/Star-24
90Miami/II/Star-23

Shelton, Mike
86Reading-24
87Reading-9
88AAA/ProC-25
88Maine/CMC-7
88Maine/ProC-282

Shelton, Ron
90LitSun-17

Shepard, Jack
55T-73
55T/DH-23
79TCMA-112

Shepard, Kelvin
87Jamestn-12
89Rockford/Team-21

Shepard, Ken
88Geneva/ProC-1656

Shepard, Larry
68KDKA-7MG
68T-584
69T-384
73OPC-296CO
73T-296C
74OPC-326CO
74T-326C
79Pol/Giants-8CO

Shepherd, Keith
87Watertn-15
88Augusta/ProC-375
89BBCity/Star-23
90Reno/Cal-276
90SoBend/ClBest-20
90Watertn/Star-19
91SoBend/ProC-2856

Shepherd, Mike
90Pulaski/Best-10
90Pulaski/ProC-3105

Shepherd, Ron
82Knoxvl-20
83Syrac-24
84Syrac-5
85F/Up-U102
86Syrac-23
87Indianap-12
87OPC-117
87T-643
88Indianap/CMC-16
88Indianap/ProC-524
89Louisvl-34
89Louisvl/CMC-22
89Louisvl/ProC-1261

Sheppard, Don
89LittleSun-22
90SoBend/ClBest-11
91SoBend/ProC-2871

Sheppard, Phillip
84Visalia-8

Shepperd, Richard
90Boise/ProC-3329
91Salinas/ClBest-13
91Salinas/ProC-2259

Shepston, Mike
79QuadC-24

Sherdel, Bill
25Exh-63
26Exh-63
91Conlon/Sport-194
92Conlon/Sport-619
E120
E126-12
V61-100
W517-6
W572

Sheridan, Bobby
87Spokane-13
89River/Cal-19
89River/ProC-1418
89Spokane/SP-22

Sheridan, Neil
52Park-16

Sheridan, Pat
81Omaha-24
82Omaha-22
83Omaha-21
84D-588
84F-357
84Nes/792-121
84T-121
84T/St-286
85D-339
85F-213
85T-359
85T/St-272
86D-155
86F-20
86Kitty/Disc-11
86OPC-240
86T-743
87Cain's-18
87Coke/Tigers-6
87F-162
87T-234
88D-522
88F-69
88Panini/St-97
88Pep/T-15
88S-171
88T-514
89B-107
89D-417
89F-146
89Mara/Tigers-15
89Pol/Tigers-15
89S-204
89S/Tr-71T
89T-288
89T/Big-150
89UD-652
90D-367
90F-71
90OPC-422
90PublInt/St-482
90S-509
90T-422
90UD-460
91ColClip/ProC-610

Sheriff, Dave
79WHave-29M
81LynnS-9
82Idaho-33
83Idaho-34

Sherlock, Glenn
85Osceola/Team-15
86Osceola-23
87Colum-7
87Colum/Pol-22
87Colum/TCMA-25
88Colum/ProC-304
89Albany/Best-7
89Albany/ProC-339
90Albany/ProC-1183CO
90Albany/Star-26CO
90Tampa/DIMD-28MG
91FtLaud/ClBest-3MG
91FtLaud/ProC-2443MG

Sherlock, Vince
90Target-726

Sherman, Darrell
89Spokane/SP-26
90A&AASingle/ProC-147
90AS/Cal-10
90Foil/Best-286
90Riversi/Best-17
90Riversi/Cal-3
90Riversi/ProC-2620
91Single/ClBest-153
91Wichita/LineD-619
91Wichita/ProC-2613

Sherman, Jack
47Signal

Sherman, Jim
83ColumAst-5
86Tucson-21

Sherman, Steve
76Cedar
77Cedar

Shermet, Dave
88AubAs/ProC-1958
89Ashvl/ProC-948

Shermeyer, Keith
77Wausau
78Wausau

Sherow, Dennis
80Memphis-18
81WHave-19
82Tacom-18
82WHave-25
83Tacom-27

Sherrill, Dennis
79Colum-19
80Colum-23

Sherrill, Tim
88Savan/ProC-334
89StPete/Star-24
90Louisvl/CMC-22
90Louisvl/ProC-403
90T/TVCard-63
91Louisvl/LineD-247
91OPC-769
91T-769
91T/90Debut-142
92S/100RisSt-90
92S/I-404

Sherry, Larry
60Bz-17
60Morrell
60T-105

61BB-51
61NuCard-431
61P-161
61T-412
61T-521M
61T/St-34
62BB-51
62J-111
62P-111
62P/Can-111
62T-435
63T-565
64T-474
65T-408
66T-289
67T-571
68T-468
90HOF/St-59
90Target-727

Sherry, Norm
59DF
60T-529
61BB-34
61T-521M
62BB-34
62T-238
63T-316
77T-34MG
84Smok/SDP-21C
85Spokane/Cram-21
90Mother/Giant-21M
90Target-728
91Mother/Giant-27CO
91WIZMets-361

Shetrone, Barry
60T-348
63T-276
91Crown/Orio-416

Shevlin, Jim
90Salinas/Cal-138
90Salinas/ProC-2727

Shibata, Keith
88AppFx/ProC-153
88Eugene/Best-29

Shidawara, Cliff
86Phoenix-23TR
87Phoenix-19TR
88Phoenix/ProC-66TR

Shields, Doug
88CapeCod/Sum-40
91BBCity/ClBest-27
91BBCity/ProC-1413

Shields, Mike
79Savan-9

Shields, Steve
81Bristol-17
83Pawtu-11
84Richm-17
85Richm-9
86F-527
86Richm-20
87T/Tr-113T
88Colum/CMC-6
88Colum/Pol-10
88Colum/ProC-314
88D/Y/Bk-NEW
88S-396
88S/Tr-47T
88T-632
89F-269
89Portl/CMC-4
89Portl/ProC-218
89S-578
89T-484
90Publint/St-338

Shields, Tom
86Watertn-23
88Harris/ProC-836
89EastLDD/ProC-DD26
89Harris/ProC-298
89Harris/Star-18
89Star/Wax-20
90BuffB/CMC-21
90BuffB/ProC-384
90BuffB/Team-25
91RochR/LineD-467
91RochR/ProC-1911

Shifflett, Steve
90AppFox/Box-24
90AppFox/ProC-2094
91London/LineD-417
91Memphis/ProC-653

Shiflett, Chris
88Gaston/ProC-1001
89Butte/SP-14
90Tulsa/ProC-1155
91Tulsa/LineD-598
91Tulsa/ProC-2774

Shiflett, Mark
83Nashvl-20
84Nashvl-20
87Memphis-6
87Memphis/Best-13
90Albany/Star-27CO
90Oneonta/ProC-3391CO
91Greens/ProC-3077CO
91SALAS/ProC-SAL30CO

Shiflett, Matt
87Jamestn-25
89Rockford/Team-22
91Durham/ClBest-1
91Durham/ProC-1543

Shikles, Larry
86Greens-22
87WinHaven-4
88NewBrit/ProC-899
89NewBrit/ProC-613
89NewBrit/Star-18
90Pawtu/CMC-4
90Pawtu/ProC-461
90T/TVRSox-59
91Pawtu/LineD-368
91Pawtu/ProC-39

Shillinglaw, Dave
86Madis-22C
86Madis/Pol-26

Shimp, Tommy Joe
80Memphis-19
83Memphis-10
84Tulsa-37
85OKCty-13
86OKCty-20

Shinall, Zakary
88Bakers/Cal-259
89VeroB/Star-25
91B-612
91SanAn/LineD-540
91SanAn/ProC-2972
91Single/ClBest-384

Shindle, William
90Target-729
N172
N300/SC

Shines, Razor
83Memphis-21
84Indianap-17
85D-401
85Leaf-164
86OPC-132
86T-132
87Indianap-8
88Indianap/CMC-12
88Indianap/ProC-514
89Indianap/CMC-12
89Indianap/ProC-1219
91Indianap/LineD-194
91Indianap/ProC-471
91Pac/SenLg-128

Shingledecker, Gary
89Erie/Star-24
90Wausau/Best-19
90Wausau/ProC-2132

Shinholster, Vince
87SanBern-12

Shinners, Ralph
E120
V100
W573

Shiozaki, Kenny
88Butte-11

Shipanoff, Dave
83Knoxvl-7
84Syrac-25
85Cram/PCL-28
86D-34RR
86F-452
86Leaf-29RR
86Phill/TastyK-33
86Portl-20
87Edmon-5

Shipke, William
T204
T206

Shipley, Craig
85Cram/PCL-155
86Albuq-23
87Albuq/Pol-22
88Jacks/GS-12
89Tidew/CMC-22
89Tidew/ProC-1961
90T/TVMets-60
90Target-730
91LasVegas/ProC-245
91WIZMets-362
92D/II-667
92F-621
92S/II-856
92T-308

Shipley, Joe
59T-141
60T-239
62Pep/Tul

Shippy, Greg
75Clinton

Shirahata, Hiro
83SanJose-10

Shireman, Jeff
89Spring/Best-12
90StPete/Star-23
91ArkTr/LineD-45
91ArkTr/ProC-1297

Shires, Charles A.
(Art)
30CEA/Pin-20
92Conlon/Sport-608
R315-C5
R316
W517-43

Shirley, Al
91Classic/DP-14
91FrRow/DP-43
92S/II-802DC
92T-306DP

Shirley, Bart
66T-591R
67T-287R
69T-289
90Target-731
91WIZMets-363

Shirley, Bob
77Padre/SchCd-27
78Padre/FamFun-28
78T-266
79T-594
80OPC-248
80T-476
81D-242
81F-495
81OPC-49
81T-49
81T/Tr-829
82D-120
82F-127
82OPC-33
82T-749
82T/Tr-105T
83F-602
83T-112
83T/Tr-103T
84D-214
84F-141
84Nes/792-684
84T-684
85D-370
85F-145
85T-328
86D-458
86F-119
86T-213
87D-463
87F-114
87T-524
88Syrac/CMC-7
88Syrac/ProC-827
89Pac/SenLg-207
89StCath/ProC-2095
89T/SenLg-6
89TM/SenLg-95
90Syrac/CMC-7CO
90Syrac/ProC-589CO
90Syrac/Team-22CO

Shirley, Mike
91Burllnd/ProC-3318

Shirley, Steve
77LodiD
78LodiD
81Albuq/TCMA-3
82Albuq-8
85Cram/PCL-235
86Albuq-24
87Omaha-14
88Indianap/CMC-4
88Indianap/ProC-505
90Target-732

Shive, Chuck
89Martins/Star-28

Shoch, George
90Target-1071
N172
WG1-70

Shocker, Urban
21Exh-159
25Exh-103
26Exh-104
28Exh-52
91Conlon/Sport-114
E120
E121/120
E126-36
E220
V100
V61-40
W501-2
W515-48
W573
W575

Shockey, Scott
88CapeCod/Sum-63
89Medford/Best-2
90Madison/ProC-2278
91Huntsvl/ClBest-21
91Huntsvl/LineD-293
91HuntsvlProC-1805
91Single/ClBest-237

Shockley, John Costen
(Costen)
65OPC-107R
65T-107R
88Chatt/Team-27

Shoebridge, Terry
77BurlB
78BurlB
80Holyo-9
81ElPaso-5

Shoemaker, John
78LodiD
81VeroB-26
82VeroB-29
83VeroB-26
85VeroB-27
86VeroB-23CO
87VeroB-30
88FSLAS/Star-1MG
89SanAn/Best-25
91SanAn/LineD-549MG
91SanAn/ProC-2991MG

Shoeneck, Lewis
N172
WG1-36

Shoffner, Milburn
39PB-87
40PB-149
W711/1
W711/2

Shofner, Frank S.
48Sommer-9
49Sommer-15

Sholl, Derek
88Eugene/Best-25

Sholton, Craig
91Welland/ClBest-15

Shombert, Otto
N172
N284

Shopay, Tom
70OPC-363
70T-363
72OPC-418
72T-418
76SSPC-401
78Colum
89Pac/SenLg-71
91Crown/Orio-417

Shore, Eddie
33SK-19

Shore, Ernest
(Ernie)
16FleischBrd-85
73F/Wild-31
87Conlon/2-56
90HOF/St-15
91Conlon/Sport-141
92Conlon/Sport-351
D327
D328-159
D329-162
D350/2-164
E135-159
M101/4-162
M101/5-164

Shore, Jeff
89CharlR/Star-23

Shore, Ray
63FrBauer-24

Shore, Roy
52Park-18

Shores, Brad
86BurlEx-19tr
89AppFx/ProC-869
91AppFx/ClBest-21TR

Shores, William
W517-7

Short, Ben
91Oneonta/ProC-4154

Short, Bill
60T-142
61T-252
62T-221
67T-577
68T-536
69T-259
91Crown/Orio-418
91WIZMets-364

Short, Chris
64PhilBull-22
67T-395
68OPC-139
68OPC-7LL
68T-139
68T-7LL
69MB-253
69MLB/St-178
69T-395
69T/decal
69T/S-54
69T/St-78
70K-41
70MLB/St-94
70OPC-270
70T-270
71K-75
71MLB/St-188
71OPC-511
71T-511
72MB-315
72T-665
PM10/L-35

Shorten, Charles
(Chick)
91Conlon/Sport-136
D328-160
E120
E135-160

Shotkoski, David
88Huntsvl/BK-19
88Modesto-31
88Modesto/Cal-57
89Huntsvl/Best-15
91London/LineD-446
91MidldA/ProC-434

Shotton, Burt
14CJ-86
15CJ-86
49Eureka-49
90Target-733
91Conlon/Sport-152
D327
D328-161
D329-163
D350/2-165
E135-161
M101/4-163
M101/5-165
Rawl
W514-78

Shotton, Craig
91Welland/ProC-3590

Shoun, Clyde
50Remar
92Conlon/Sport-379
R423-99
W754

Shoup, Eric
88Bristol/ProC-1876

Shouppe, Jamey

83DayBe-12
Shourds, Jeff
77Cedar
Shouse, Brian
90Welland/Pucko-28
91Augusta/ClBest-11
Show, Eric
81Hawaii
82T/Tr-106T
83D-439
83F-372
83OPC-68
83T-68
83T/St-330
84D-406
84F-312
84Mother/Padres-4
84Nes/792-532
84OPC-238
84Smok/Padres-22
84T-532
84T/St-162
85D-202
85D/AAS-59
85F-44
85Leaf-137
85Mother/Padres-9
85OPC-118
85T-118
85T/St-156
86D-234
86F-334
86Leaf-111
86OPC-209
86T-762
87Bohem-30
87D-164
87D/OD-149
87F-430
87F/Hottest-37
87OPC-354
87T-730
87T/St-112
88Coke/Padres-30
88D-387
88F-597
88Panini/St-400
88S-338
88Smok/Padres-26
88T-303
89B-446
89Coke/Padre-17
89D-482
89F-317
89OPC-147
89Padre/Mag-7
89Panini/St-196
89S-254
89T-427
89T/Big-35
89UD-171
90B-209
90Coke/Padre-18
90D-559
90F-169
90Leaf/I-115
90OPC-239
90Padre/MagUno-5
90Publint/St-59
90S-493
90T-239
90T/Big-71
90T/St-111
90UD-587
91B-223
91F-544
91Leaf/II-354
91Leaf/Stud-108
91Mother/A's-23
91OPC-613
91S-563
91S/RookTr-64T
91SFExam/A's-11
91T-613
91T/StClub/I-138
91UD-293
91UD/Ext-798
92S/II-662
92T-132
Showalter, J.R.
90Boise/ProC-3326
91PalmSp/ProC-2026
Showalter, William N.
(Buck)
79WHave-7
81Colum-20
82Nashvl-22
83Nashvl-21
88FSLAS/Star-27
89Albany/Best-8
89Albany/ProC-326
89Albany/Star-22
92T-201MG
Shreve, Ben
88Geneva/ProC-1652
88Wythe/ProC-1992
Shreve, Leven
N172
Shuba, George
52T-326
53B/Col-145
53T-34
54B-202
54NYJour
55B-66
55Gol/Dodg-27
79TCMA-277
89Rini/Dodg-17
90Target-734
91T/Arc53-34
Shubert, Rich
74Gaston
76SanAn/Team-20
77Holyo
Shuey, Paul
91T/Tr-108T
Shuffield, Jack
83CharR-12
Shull, Mike
87PalmSp-10
90PalmSp/Cal-222
Shulleeta, Mike
82QuadC-11
Shulock, John
88TM/Umpire-39
89TM/Umpire-37
90TM/Umpire-35
Shultis, Chris
86Cram/PCL-22
88Boise/ProC-1613
Shumake, Brooks
86Vermont-18
Shumpert, Terry
88AppFx/ProC-142
89Omaha/CMC-18
89Omaha/ProC-1721
90Classic/III-65
90D/BestAL-134
90D/Rook-55
90F/Up-104
90Leaf/II-409
90S/Tr-110T
90T/Tr-114T
90UD/Ext-733
91B-314
91D-297
91F-570
91F/Ultra-156
91Leaf/I-104
91MajorLg/Pins-22
91OPC-322
91OPC/Premier-108
91Pol/Royal-20
91S-349RP
91S/100RisSt-3
91S/ASFan-9
91S/Rook40-27
91Seven/3DCoin-15F
91T-322
91T/90Debut-143
91T/StClub/I-111
91UD-521
92Classic/I-83
92D/II-562
92F-169
92S/100RisSt-44
92S/I-248
92T-483
92UD-348
Shupe, Wilford
WG7-49
Shwan, Dan
91SLCity/ProC-3229CO
Siberz, Bo
90Oneonta/ProC-3381
91Greens/ProC-3060
Siblerud, Daniel
86Columbia-23
Siddall, Joe
88James/ProC-1908
89Rockford/Team-23
90WPalmB/Star-20
91Harris/LineD-269
91Harris/ProC-633
Siebern, Norm
58T-54
59T-308
60T-11
61P-82
61T-119M
61T-267
61T/Dice-16
61T/St-165
62Bz
62Exh
62J-92
62P-92
62P/Can-92
62Salada-85
62Shirriff-85
62T-127M
62T-275
62T/bucks
62T/St-57
63Bz-4
63Exh
63F-17
63J-85
63P-85
63Salada-51
63T-2LL
63T-430
63T/SO
64T-145
64T/Coins-49
64T/St-14
64T/SU
64T/tatt
64Wheat/St-41
65T-455
66OPC-14
66T-14
67T-299
68T-537
91Crown/Orio-419
Exh47
Siebert, Dick
40PB-192
41DP-128
90Target-735
Siebert, Mac
89Bristol/Star-26
Siebert, Paul
75Iowa/TCMA-17
75OPC-614R
75T-614R
75T/M-614R
89Pac/SenLg-212
91WIZMets-365
Siebert, Rick
86Durham-25
87Durham-18
88Sumter/ProC-402
89Penin/Star-22
Siebert, Sonny
64T-552R
65OPC-96
65T-96
66Kahn
66T-197
66T-222LL
66T-226LL
67Kahn
67OPC-95
67T-463M
67T-95
68OPC-8LL
68T-295
68T-8LL
69MLB/St-43
69T-455
69T/St-167
70MLB/St-166
70T-597
71MLB/St-332
71OPC-710
71T-710
71T/Coins-122
72K-36
72OPC-290
72T-290
73K-14
73OPC-14
73T-14
74OPC-548
74T-548
75OPC-328
75T-328
75T/M-328
76SSPC-484
85Cram/PCL-121
87LasVegas-6
88LasVegas/CMC-25
88LasVegas/ProC-248
91Waterlo/ClBest-26CO
91Waterlo/ProC-1274CO
Siebert, Steve
91Utica/ClBest-15
91Utica/ProC-3251
Siebler, Dwight
64T-516R
65T-326
66T-546
67OPC-164
67T-164
78TCMA-126
Siegel, Bob
86Wausau-24
Siegle, John H.
E101
E105
E216
E90/1
E92
Sieradzki, Al
89Bluefld/Star-21
Sierra, Ruben
85Tulsa-12
86D/Rook-52
86F/Up-U105
86OKCty-21
86Rang-3
86Sf/Rook-16
87Classic/Up-149
87D-346
87D/OD-172
87F-138
87F/Mini-100
87Leaf-225
87Mother/Rang-13
87Smok/R-17
87T-261
87T-6RB
87T/GlossRk-15
87T/St-10
87ToysRUs-24
88Classic/Red-180
88D-223
88D-BC26
88D/Best-200
88F-479
88F/Excit-38
88F/Hottest-38
88F/LL-39
88F/Mini-58
88F/SS-36
88F/St-69
88KayBee-28
88Leaf-206
88Mother/R-10
88OPC-319
88Panini/St-209
88S-113
88S/YS/I-36
88Sf-113
88Smok/R-9
88T-771
88T/Coins-26
88T/Gloss60-4
88T/RiteAid-25
88T/St-234
88T/UK-71
89B-235
89Bimbo/Discs-6
89Classic/Up/2-162
89D-48
89D/Best-111
89D/MVP-BC26
89F-532
89F/BBAS-37
89F/BBMVP's-35
89F/Excit-37
89F/Heroes-37
89Mother/R-7
89OPC-53
89Panini/St-457
89RedFoley/St-108
89S-43
89S/Mast-31
89Sf-189
89Smok/R-30
89T-53
89T/Big-82
89T/Coins-51
89T/Hills-26
89T/St-242
89T/UK-71
89Tulsa/Team-27
89UD-416
89UD-686TC
90B-490
90Classic-59
90Classic-7
90Classic/III-77
90CollAB-7
90D-174
90D-3DK
90D-673AS
90D/BestAL-143
90D/SuperDK-3DK
90F-314
90F/ASIns-11
90F/AwardWin-34
90F/BB-34
90F/BBMVP-34
90F/LL-36
90F/WaxBox-C25
90HotPlay/St-40
90Leaf/I-257
90Mother/Rang-3
90OPC-185
90OPC-390AS
90Panini/St-162
90Panini/St-203
90Publint/St-422
90Publint/St-605
90S-420
90S/100St-85
90Sf-188
90Starline/LJS-33
90Starline/LJS-8
90T-185
90T-390AS
90T/Ames-32
90T/Big-175
90T/Coins-28
90T/DH-60
90T/Gloss22-19
90T/Gloss60-26
90T/HillsHM-20
90T/Mini-40
90T/St-161AS
90T/St-244
90T/TVAS-7
90TulsaDG/Best-35
90UD-355
91B-283
91Classic/200-41
91Classic/III-83
91D-567
91DennyGS-21
91F-303
91F/ProV-3
91F/Ultra-356
91KingB/Discs-9
91Leaf/I-97
91Leaf/Stud-129
91MooTown-16
91Mother/Rang-3
91OPC-535
91OPC/Premier-109
91Panini/FrSt-257
91Panini/St-202
91RedFoley/St-87
91S-495
91S-859FRAN
91S/100SS-12
91Seven/3DCoin-13T
91T-535
91T/CJMini/II-18
91T/StClub/I-123
91UD-455
91USPlayC/AS-9H
92D/I-298
92F-321
92S/100SS-87
92S/I-437AS
92S/II-490

92T-403AS
92T-700
92UD-176

Sierra, Ulises
(Candy)
85Beaum-9
86Beaum-21
87Wichita-20
88Nashvl/Team-21
89F-171
89T-711
90Riversi/Best-23
90Riversi/ProC-2609

Siever, Edward
E107

Sievers, Jason
90Everett/Best-15
90Everett/ProC-3131

Sievers, Roy
50B-16
51B-67
51FB
51T/RB-9
52T-64
53T-67
54T-245
55T-16
55T/DH-79
56T-75
56T/Pin-59OF
57T-89
58T-250
59Armour-15
59Bz
59T-340
59T-465HL
59T-566AS
59T-74M
60NuCard-23
60T-25
61NuCard-423
61P-26
61T-470
61T/St-128
62/Can-46
62J-46
62P-46
62Salada-66
62Shirriff-66
62T-220
62T/bucks
62T/St-169
62T/St-58
63J-177
63P-177
63T-283
64T-43
65T-574
78TCMA-242
79TCMA-206
88Pac/Leg-26
89Swell-47
91T/Arc53-67
Exh47
PM10/L-36

Sigler, Allen
85Cedar-25
86Cedar/TCMA-22

Siglin, W.
(Paddy)
WG7-50

Sigman, Lee
78BurlB
83ElPaso-25

Sikes, Bob
82Jacks-24
83Tidew-27
84Tidew-17

Silch, Edward
N172

Silcox, Rusty
91HighD/ClBest-10
91HighD/ProC-2393

Siler, Mike
87Bakers-26

Silkwood, Joe
83Spring/LF-12
84ArkTr-20

Silton
C46-24

Silva, Freddie
82Spring-6
83StPete-12

Silva, Mark
83Nashvl-22
85Colum-24
85Colum/Pol-20
86Colum-22
86Colum/Pol-20

Silva, Ryan
86Cram/PCL-149

Silvas, Brian
81Batavia-7

Silver, Chad
90Princet/DIMD-18

Silver, Keith
84Everett/Cram-10A
86Shrev-23

Silver, Larry
78StPete

Silver, Roy
86StPete-28
87ArkTr-12
87TexLgAS-2
88Louisvl-44
88Louisvl/CMC-22
88Louisvl/ProC-431
89ArkTr/GS-22
89TexLAS/GS-38
90Louisvl/CMC-16
90Louisvl/ProC-418
90T/TVCard-64
91Savan/ClBest-2CO
91Savan/ProC-1669CO

Silvera, Al
56T-137

Silvera, Charlie
52B-197
52T-168
53T-242
54T-96
55T-188
57T-255
73OPC-323CO
73T-323C
74OPC-379CO
74T-379C
79TCMA-266
91T/Arc53-242

Silverio, Francisco
86Tampa-19
87Cedar-23

Silverio, Luis
76Watlo
77Jaxvl
82Omaha-23
88FSLAS/Star-30CO

Silverio, Nelson
86Madis-23
86Madis/Pol-19
88Charl/ProC-1220

Silverio, Tom
72OPC-213R
72T-213R

Silverio, Victor
91QuadC/ClBest-11
91QuadC/ProC-2628

Silverman, Aaron
52Park-2
V362-19

Silverman, Don
85Iowa-27

Silverstein, Allan
88Myrtle/ProC-1187
89Dunedin/Star-15
90Dunedin/Star-16

Silvestri, David
88T/Tr-107TOLY
89Osceola/Star-22
89Star/Wax-18
89T/Big-141
90PrWill/Team-24
91Albany/ProC-1016

Silvestri, Ken
49Eureka-147
51B-256
52B-200
60T-466CO
73OPC-237CO
73T-237CO
74OPC-634CO
74T-634CO
78Knoxvl
87Portl-23
89Watertn/Star-26
90Watertn/Star-25CO

Sima, Al
52T-93
53T-241
54T-216
88Chatt/Team-28
91T/Arc53-241

Simcox, Larry
82DayBe-23
83ColumAst-7

Simmermacher, Bret
86Cram/PCL-114

Simmons, Al
83Miami-16

Simmons, Aloysius
(Al)
21Exh-160
28Exh-56
31Exh/4-27
32Orbit/num-39
32Orbit/un-53
33CJ/Pin-20
33DH-39
33DL-2
33Exh/4-14
33G-35
34DS-2
34Exh/4-10
34Exh/4-14
35BU-34
35Exh/4-10
35G-1J
35G-3A
35G-5A
35G-6A
35Wheat
38ONG/Pin-28
50Callahn
60Exh/HOF-21
60F-32
61F-77
61GP-20
63Bz-22
69Bz/Sm
80Pac/Leg-119
80Laugh/FFeat-3
80SSPC/HOF
86Sf/Dec-5
88Conlon/4-25
88Conlon/AmAS-22
91Conlon/Sport-311
91Conlon/Sport-49
91T/Arc53-326M
92Conlon/Sport-423
92Conlon/Sport-554
PR1-26
R300
R303/A
R303/B
R305
R306
R308-154
R310
R313
R314
R315-A33
R315-B33
R316
R328-17
R332-1
R337-415
R423-102
V353-35
V355-77
W517-40

Simmons, Brad
77DaytB

Simmons, Curt
49B-14
49Eureka-148
49Lummis
50B-68
51B-111
51BR-D9
52B-184
52StarCal/L-77C
52T-203
53B/Col-64
54B-79
54RM-NL12
55Armour-18
55B-64
55RFG-6
55RM-NL24
56T-290
57T-158
58Hires-28
58T-404
59T-382
60T-451
61T-11
61T/St-93
62J-167
62P-167
62P/Can-167
62T-285
62T-56LL
63T-22
64T-385
65T-373
66T-489
67OPC-39
67T-39
79TCMA-54
91T/Arc53-318
Exh47
PM10/Sm-180

Simmons, Enoch
89Medford/Best-26
90Madison/Best-10
90Madison/ProC-2281
91Modesto/ClBest-23
91Modesto/ProC-3105
91Single/ClBest-256

Simmons, George
C46-75
T205

Simmons, Greg
85Beloit-17
86Beloit-21

Simmons, John
52Park-62
53Exh/Can-35
V362-5

Simmons, Nelson
83BirmB-16
84Evansvl-9
85F/Up-U103
86Cain's-16
86D-272
86F-238
86RochR-21
86T-121
87RochR-18
88Calgary/CMC-19
88Calgary/ProC-802
90Huntsvl/Best-22
91Crown/Orio-420
91Tacoma/LineD-545
91Tacoma/ProC-2320

Simmons, Randy
88Pulaski/ProC-1768
89SALAS/GS-44
89Sumter/ProC-1110
90BurlB/Best-24
90BurlB/ProC-2364
90BurlB/Star-24
90Foil/Best-81
91Durham/ProC-1561

Simmons, Scott
91Hamil/ProC-4038

Simmons, Ted
71OPC-117
71T-117
72OPC-154
72T-154
73OPC-85
73T-85
74K-21
74OPC-260
74T-260
74T/DE-10
74T/St-116
75Ho-95
75OPC-75
75T-75
75T/M-75
76Crane-56
76Ho-113
76K-57
76MSA/Disc
76OPC-191LL
76OPC-290
76SSPC-274
76T-191LL
76T-290
77BurgChef-16
77Ho-61
77OPC-196
77T-470
77T/CS-43
78Ho-65
78OPC-150
78T-380
78Wiffle/Discs-69
79Ho-44
79K-2
79OPC-267
79T-510
79T/Comics-30
80K-44
80OPC-47
80T-85
81D-308
81F-528
81F/St-120
81OPC-352
81PermaGr/CC-17
81T-705
81T/Nat/Super-15
81T/So-63
81T/St-94
81T/Tr-830
82D-106
82F-152
82F/St-137
82OPC-150
82Pol/Brew-23
82T-150
82T/St-201
83D-332
83F-45
83Gard-16
83OPC-284
83OPC-33SV
83PermaGr/AS-5
83Pol/Brew-23
83T-450
83T-451SV
83T/St-85
84D-473
84D/AAS-58
84F-213
85FunFoodPin-124
84Gard-17
84MiltBrad-24
84Nes/792-404AS
84Nes/792-630
84Nes/792-713LL
84Nes/792-726TL
84OPC-122
84OPC-94AS
84Pol/Brew-23
84Ralston-3
84Seven-21C
84T-404AS
84T-630
84T-713LL
84T-726TL
84T/Cereal-3
84T/Gloss22-9
84T/Gloss40-18
84T/St-193
84T/St-293
84T/St/Box-2
85D-414
85F-596
85Gard-19
85Leaf-104
85OPC-318
85Pol/Brew-23
85T-318
85T/St-294
86D-292
86F-503
86F/Up-U106
86Leaf-167
86Pol/Atl-23
86Sf-196
86Sf/Dec-62M
86T-237
86T/St-199
86T/Tr-102T
87D-537
87F-528
87Smok/Atl-13
87T-516
88D-560
88F-549
88Leaf-222

88S-285
88T-791
89F-599
89S-611
89UD-570

Simmons, Todd
86Beaum-22
87LasVegas-11
88F-650R
88LasVegas/CMC-6
88LasVegas/ProC-240
89Denver/CMC-10
89Denver/ProC-30
89F-318

Simms, Michael
87Ashvl-17
88FSLAS/Star-21
88Osceola/Star-25
89ColMud/Best-7
89ColMud/ProC-141
89ColMud/Star-22
89Star/Wax-3
90Tucson/CMC-20
90Tucson/ProC-208
91B-551
91Classic/II-T90
91F-516
91OPC-32
91S-766
91T-32
91T/90Debut-144
91T/StClub/I-281
91Tucson/LineD-619
91Tucson/ProC-2221
91UD-664
92D/II-747
92F-445
92S/II-632
92T-463
92UD-584

Simon, Michael
11Helmar-165
14CJ-25
15CJ-25
D322
M116
T201
T207

Simon, Richard
(Richie)
86AubAs-23
87AubAs-25
88Ashvl/ProC-1069
89Osceola/Star-23
90ColMud/Best-13
90ColMud/ProC-1347
90ColMud/Star-22
91Jacks/LineD-573
91Jacks/ProC-927

Simon, Rick
74Gaston

Simon, Willie
76Wausau

Simond, Rob
80LynnS-6
81LynnS-10

Simonds, Dan
88Fresno/Cal-6
88Fresno/ProC-1230
89EastLDD/ProC-DD29
89Freder/Star-22
89Hagers/Best-23
90Hagers/Best-2
90Hagers/ProC-1417
91Iowa/LineD-217
91Iowa/ProC-1064

Simons, Doug
89AS/Cal-17
89Visalia/Cal-95
89Visalia/ProC-1435
90OrlanSR/Best-21
90OrlanSR/ProC-1082
90OrlanSR/Star-19
91B-463
91Classic/II-T86
91D/Rook-26
91Kahn/Mets-43
91OPC/Premier-110
91S/RookTr-91T
91T/Tr-109T
91UD/FinalEd-63F
92D/II-688
92S/100RisSt-91
92S/II-479
92T-82
92T/91Debut-163

Simons, Mitchel
91James/ClBest-12
91James/ProC-3555

Simons, Neil
82DayBe-15

Simonson, Bob
85Beloit-6
86Beloit-22
88Beloit/GS-9

Simpson, Danny
83TriCit-22

Simpson, Dick
63T-407R
64T-127R
65T-374R
66T-311R
67OPC-6
67T-6
68T-459
69MB-254
69T-608

Simpson, Greg
86Cedar/TCMA-9
87Vermont-6
88Cedar/ProC-1137

Simpson, Harry
(Suitcase)
52B-223
52NumNum-17
52T-193
53B/Col-86
53T-150
55Rodeo
56Rodeo
56T-239
57T-225
58T-299
59T-333
60L-81
60T-180
61Union
79TCMA-79
86Negro/Frit-92
91T/Arc53-150

Simpson, Joe
78Cr/PCL-63
79T-719R
80T-637
81D-168
81F-616
81Pol/Mar-15
81T-116
82D-55
82F-518
82T-382
83F-485
83T-567
83T/Tr-104
84Cram/PCL-115
84D-496
84F-358
84Nes/792-219
84T-219
90Target-736

Simpson, Shelton
90Welland/Pucko-29

Simpson, Wayne
70T-683R
71K-1
71MD
71MLB/St-69
71OPC-339
71OPC-68LL
71T-339
71T-68LL
71T/Coins-53
72T-762
73OPC-428
73T-428
76SSPC-599

Simpson, William
77Ashvl
78Ashvl

Sims, Daniel Jr.
89Idaho/ProC-2018
90Sumter/Best-20
90Sumter/ProC-2448

Sims, Duane
(Duke)
66OPC-169
66T-169
67OPC-3
67T-3
68T-508
69MB-255
69T-414
69T/St-168
70MLB/St-203
70OPC-275
70T-275
71MLB/St-114
71OPC-172
71T-172
71T/Coins-66
71Ticket/Dodg-15
72MB-316
72OPC-63
72T-63
73OPC-304
73T-304
74OPC-398
74T-398
86AppFx-23MG
89Swell-128
90Target-737

Sims, Greg
89Augusta/ProC-517
89SALAS/GS-5
90Salem/Star-22
91Visalia/ProC-1756

Sims, Gregory E.
66T-596R

Sims, Joe Beely
86Jamestn-23
87Jamestn-8

Sims, Kinney
88Reno/Cal-278

Sims, Mark
87Spartan-6
88Clearw/Star-21
89Clearw/Star-20
90EastLAS/ProC-EL22
90Foil/Best-182
90Reading/Best-10
90Reading/ProC-1220
90Reading/Star-22
91Reading/LineD-519
91Reading/ProC-1370

Sims, Mike
83Tampa-29TR
86Vermont-19TR

Simunic, Doug
80Memphis-22
83Charl-7
84BuffB-6
84Maine-5
89AubAs/ProC-2184
89Pac/SenLg-35
89T/SenLg-84
90EliteSenLg-105
91Kissim/ProC-4205CO
91Pac/SenLg-55

Sinatro, Greg
77SanJose-8

Sinatro, Matt
81Richm-20
82D-149
82Richm-12
83D-622
83Richm-11
87Tacom-9
88Tacoma/CMC-18
88Tacoma/ProC-616
89Tucson/CMC-11
89Tucson/ProC-201
90Calgary/CMC-13
90Calgary/ProC-654
90T/Tr-115T
91OPC-709
91T-709

Sinclair, Ken
84Savan-25

Sinclair, Steve
91MedHat/ProC-4100

Siner, Hosea John
E254

Singer, Bill
66T-288R
67OPC-12R
67T-12R
68T-249
69MLB/St-152
69OPC-12LL
69T-12LL
69T-575
69T/St-49
70K-17
70MLB/St-57
70OPC-490
70OPC-71LL
70T-490
70T-71LL
70T/CB
71MLB/St-115
71OPC-145
71T-145
71Ticket/Dodg-16
72MB-317
72OPC-25
72T-25
73OPC-570
73T-570
74K-12
74OPC-210
74T-210
74T/St-149
75Ho-82
75Ho/Twink-82
75OPC-40
75T-40
75T/M-40
76OPC-411
76SSPC-188
76T-411
76T/Tr-411T
77Ho-139
77OPC-85
77T-346
77T/CS-44
87Smok/Dodg-33
88Smok/Dodg-6M
89Smok/Dodg-75
90Target-738

Singer, Tom
90StCath/ProC-3457
91Myrtle/ClBest-10
91Myrtle/ProC-2944

Singletary, Chico
87Savan-15

Singleton, Bert Elmer
49B-147
49Sommer-25
57T-378
59T-548
63MilSau-6

Singleton, Ken
71OPC-16
71T-16
72OPC-425
72OPC-426IA
72T-425
72T-426IA
73OPC-232
73T-232
74K-48
74OPC-25
74T-25
74T/St-60
74Weston-29
75K-40
75OPC-125
75T-125
75T/M-125
76Ho-76
76K-12
76OPC-175
76SSPC-400
76T-175
77BurgChef-41
77Ho-107
77OPC-19
77T-445
78Ho-75
78K-55
78OPC-80
78T-65
79Ho-135
79OPC-324
79T-615
80K-30
80OPC-178
80T-340
80T/S-11
81D-115
81Drake-12
81F-188
81F/St-103
81K-39
81OPC-281
81PermaGr/AS-17
81T-570
81T/So-17
81T/St-33
82D-105
82D-24DK
82Drake-30
82F-179
82F/St-150
82K-58
82OPC-290
82OPC-2AS
82T-290
82T-552AS
82T/St-136
82T/St-144
83D-257
83Drake-26
83F-73
83OPC-85
83T-85
83T/St-28
84D-610
84F-21
84F/St-46
84F/St-55
84Nes/792-165
84OPC-165
84T-165
84T/St-206
84T/St/Box-8
85F-191
85OPC-326
85T-755
85T/St-201
89Swell-26
91Crown/Orio-421
91WIZMets-366

Singley, Joe
87Penin-6
89Utica/Pucko-21
90SoBend/Best-9

Sington, Fred
39PB-68
90Target-739

Sinnett, Lou
85Anchora-40

Sipe, Pat
87WPalmB-8
88Jaxvl/Best-20
88Jaxvl/ProC-981
89Jaxvl/Best-8
89Jaxvl/ProC-165

Sipple, John
89CharlR/Star-24

Siracusa, John
75OkCty

Sirak, Kenny
91Spartan/ClBest-19
91Spartan/ProC-904

Siriano, Rick
82Durham-8
83Durham-13

Sisisky, Terry
79Richm-9M

Sisk, Doug
82Jacks-10
83T/Tr-105T
84D-615
84F-596
84Jacks/Smok-11
84Nes/792-599
84OPC-21
84T-599
85D-441
85F-91
85Leaf-187
85OPC-315
85T-315
85T/Mets/Fan-7
85T/St-103
86F-94
86T-144
86Tidew-26
87F-22
87T-404
88D-642
88F-150
88F/Up-U3
88S-227
88T-763

89F-621
89S-264
89T-13
89UD-261
91Crown/Orio-422
91WIZMets-367

Sisk, Tommie
63T-169R
64T-224
65T-558
66EH-25
66T-441
67OPC-84
67T-84
67T/Test/PP-21
68KDKA-25
68T-429
69MLB/St-196
69OPC-152
69T-152
70MLB/St-118
70OPC-374
70T-374

Sisler, Dave
57T-56
58Hires-40
58T-59
59T-346M
59T-384
60L-64
60T-186
61P-44
61T-239
61T/St-155
62T-171
63T-284

Sisler, Dick
47TipTop
48L-143
49B-205
49Eureka-149
49Royal-19
50B-119
50Drake-10
51B-52
51BR-C8
51T/BB-8
52B-127
52Royal
52T-113
52TipTop
53B/BW-10
53Exh/Can-62
53Hunters
60HenryH-8
63FrBauer-25
64T-162M
65OPC-158MG
65T-158MG
79TCMA-152
89Johnson/Star-24CO
Exh47

Sisler, George Jr.
80Colum-27GM
81Colum-27GM
82Colum-26GM
82Colum/Pol-xx
84Colum-24GM
84Colum/Pol-23GM
85Colum-29GM
85Colum/Pol-21GM
87Colum/Pol-23GM
88Colum/Pol-25GM
89Colum/Pol-25GM

Sisler, George Sr.
21Exh-161
25Exh-117
26Exh-118
27Exh-59
28Yueng-54
29Exh/4-1
40PB-179
48Exh/HOF
50Callahan
60F-13
61F-78
61F-89M
61GP-13
72K/ATG-5
72Laugh/GF-5
73F/Wild-12
79T-411LL
80Pac/Leg-108
80Laugh/3/4/5-24
80Laugh/FFeat-9
80SSPC/HOF
85Woolwth-33
87Conlon/2-58
88Conlon/4-26
90HOF/St-23
91Conlon/Sport-66
92Conlon/Sport-595
BF2-43
D327
D328-162
D329-164
D350/2-166
E120
E121/120
E121/80
E122
E126-49
E135-162
E210-54
E220
M101/4-164
M101/5-166
R423-103
V100
V61-32
W501-4
W502-54
W514-101
W515-11
W572
W573
W575
WG7-51

Sismondo, Ron
83Wausau/LF-24

Sisney, Lorenzo
88Wausau/GS-5

Sisti, Sibby
41DP-42
47TipTop
49B-201
49Eureka-23
50B-164
51B-170
52B-100
52T-293
53JC-13
53T-124
54JC-13
58Union
91T/Arc53-124

Siuda, Matt
85Anchora-33
88Madis-22

Sivik, Mike
77AppFx
79AppFx-13

Siwa, Joe
90Kenosha/Best-14
90Kenosha/ProC-2298
90Kenosha/Star-23
91OrlanSR/LineD-493
91OrlanSR/ProC-1853

Siwy, Jim
81AppFx-10
82Edmon-3
85Maine-12
86LasVegas-15
87LasVegas-25

Sizemore, Ted
69T-552R
70MLB/St-58
70OPC-174
70T-174
71MLB/St-284
71OPC-571
71T-571
71T/Coins-65
72OPC-514
72T-514
73OPC-128
73T-128
74OPC-209
74T-209
74T/St-117
75Ho-75
75OPC-404
75T-404
75T/M-404
76Ho-70
76OPC-522
76SSPC-284
76T-522
77T-366
78OPC-118
78T-136
79OPC-148
79T-297
80OPC-46
80T-81
85SpokAT/Cram-18
90Target-740

Skaalen, Jim
87PortChar-24
88Tulsa-10MG
89OkCty/CMC-23
89OkCty/ProC-1508
90TulsaDG/Best-29MG

Skaff, Francis
(Frank)
52Park-91
54Esskay
90Target-741

Skaggs, David
78T-593
79T-367
80T-211
81T-48
91Crown/Orio-423
91Pac/SenLg-100

Skaggs, Steve
80Cedar-14

Skalski, Joe
87Wmsprt-27
88ColoSp/CMC-10
88ColoSp/ProC-1533
89ColoSp/CMC-9
89UD/Ext-716
90B-323
90ColoSp/CMC-3
90ColoSp/ProC-34
90S-618
90T/89Debut-115

Skeels, Andy
87Spokane-7
88River/Cal-226
88River/ProC-1425
89AS/Cal-20
89River/Best-15
89River/Cal-12
89River/ProC-1414
90Albany/Best-13
90Albany/ProC-1038
90Albany/Star-16
91Albany/ProC-1012

Skeen, Archie
63MilSau-7
64T-428R

Skeete, Rafael
87Hagers-22
88CharlK/Pep-15
89Hagers/Best-22
89Hagers/ProC-278
89Hagers/Star-17

Skelton, John
87Kenosha-28
88Kenosha/ProC-1400

Skiba, Daniel
77Watlo

Skidmore, Robert
(Roe)
71OPC-121R
71T-121R

Skiff, William (Bill)
43Centen-21
44Centen-20MG
45Centen-22MG
WG7-52

Skinner, Bob
55T-88
55T/DH-56
56T-297
57T-209
58Hires-30
58Kahn
58T-94
59Armour-16
59Kahn
59T-320
59T-543M
60Kahn
60T-113
61Kahn
61T-204
61T/St-69
62J-174
62P-174
62P/Can-174
62Salada-143
62Shirriff-143
62T-115
63FrBauer-26
63J-141
63P-141
63Sugar-B
63T-18M
63T-215
64T-377
65T-591
66T-471
69T-369
73OPC-12CO
73T-12CO
74OPC-489CO
74T-489CO
77Padre/SchCd-28CO
79TCMA-248
85T-139FS
86Pol/Atl-4C
89Tucson/CMC-25
89Tucson/ProC-203
90Swell/Great-129
90Tucson/CMC-25MG
90Tucson/ProC-219MG
91AAAGame/ProC-AAA53MG
91Tucson/LineD-624MG
91Tucson/ProC-2228MG

Skinner, Joel
84D-27RR
85BuffB-6
85Coke/WS-22
85D-574
85F-646R
85T-139FS
85T-488
86Coke/WS-22
86D-330
86T-239
87D-545
87D/OD-240
87F-115
87T-626
88D-474
88D/Best-300
88D/Y/Bk-474
88S-532
88T-109
89D-427
89D/Best-224
89D/Tr-22
89F-270
89OPC-127
89S-447
89S/Tr-76T
89T-536
89UD-328
90D-73
90F-501
90Leaf/II-286
90OPC-54
90PublInt/St-567
90T-54
90UD-369
91D-120
91F-377
91Leaf/I-211
91OPC-783
91S-809
91T-783
91T/StClub/II-561
91UD-121
92D/I-99
92F-123
92S/I-227
92T-378
92UD-199

Skinner, John
82AppFx-14

Skinner, Matt
85Newar-23

Skinner, Mike
86RochR-22
87RochR-5
87RochR/TCMA-9

Skizas, Lou
57T-83
58T-319
59T-328
60Union-15

Sklar, Joel
86LitFalls-25

Skodny, Joe
86Cram/PCL-48
87AppFx-11
88BBCity/Star-21

Skoglund, Brad
83Wisco/LF-23

Skok, Craig
79T-363
80Richm-20

Skorochocki, John
77Newar
78BurlB
81ElPaso-4
82Vanco-6

Skowron, Bill
54T-239
55B-160
55T-22
55T/DH-21
56T-61
56T/Pin-30
57T-135
58T-240
58T-477AS
59T-554AS
59T-90
60MacGregor-23
60T-370
60T-553AS
61P-3
61T-371
61T-42LL
61T-568AS
62J-1
62P-1
62P/Can-1
62Salada-59
62Shirriff-59
62T-110
62T/St-91
63J-12
63P-12
63T-180
64T-445
64T/S-60
65OPC-70
65T-70
65T/E-5
65T/trans-69
66Bz-33
66T-199M
66T-590
66T/RO-4
67T-357
78TCMA-230
79TCMA-210
83Kaline-18M
83MLBPA/Pin-17
88Pac/Leg-82
90Target-742
Exh47
PM10/L-37
WG9-46

Skripko, Joseph
85Greens-8

Skripko, Scott
86WinHaven-23
87NewBrit-10
89Lynch/Star-25

Skryd, Chris
89SLCity-19

Skube, Bob
81ElPaso-15
82Vanco-1
83Pol/Brew-26
85Cram/PCL-214

Skurla, John
86Fresno/Smok-23
88Shrev/ProC-1297
88TexLgAS/GS-15
89Phoenix/CMC-23
89Phoenix/ProC-1496
90Edmon/CMC-12
90Edmon/ProC-530

Skurski, Andy
47Signal

Slack, Bill
86Greenvl/Team-17CO
87Durham-15
89Greenvl/ProC-1168

89Greenvl/Best-18
90Greenvl/ProC-1144CO
90Greenvl/Star-24CO
91Greenvl/ClBest-26CO
91Greenvl/LineD-225CO
91Greenvl/ProC-3020CO
Slade, Gordon
28Exh/PCL-27
90Target-743
Slagle, James J.
E91
T206
Slagle, Lee
91James/ClBest-28TR
91James/ProC-3561TR
Slagle, Roger
77WHave
78Cr/PCL-4
80Colum-2
82Nashvl-23
91Pac/SenLg-17
Slater, Bob
76QuadC
79SLCity-21
79T-703R
Slater, Vernon
91AppFx/ClBest-7
91Eugene/ClBest-10
91Eugene/ProC-3741
Slaton, Jim
72T-744
73OPC-628
73T-628
74OPC-371
74T-371
74T/St-200
75OPC-281
75T-281
75T/M-281
76A&P/Milw
76OPC-163
76SSPC-226
76T-163
77BurgChef-83
77Ho-105
77OPC-29
77T-604
78BK/T-7
78Ho-14
78OPC-146
78T-474
79T-541
80OPC-10
80T-24
81D-447
81F-518
81T-357
82D-80
82F-153
82Pol/Brew-41
82T-221
83D-330
83F-46
83Gard-17
83OPC-114
83Pol/Brew-41
83T-114
84D-481
84F-214
84F/X-107
84Nes/792-772
84OPC-104
84Smok/Cal-27
84T-772
84T/St-302
84T/Tr-109
85D-545
85F-313
85Smok/Cal-17
85T-657
86D-402
86F-169
86Smok/Cal-17
86T-579
87F-163
87T-432
89Pac/SenLg-110
89TM/SenLg-96
91SoOreg/ProC-3867CO
Slattery, Chris
88CapeCod/Sum-161
Slattery, Kevin
75Clinton
Slattery, Mike
N172
N338/2
Slaught, Don
82Omaha-12
83D-196
83F-123
84D-419
84F-359
84Nes/792-196
84T-196
85D-496
85F-214
85F/Up-U104
85OPC-159
85Rang-4
85T-542
85T/St-279
85T/Tr-107T
86D-281
86F-572
86Leaf-155
86OPC-24
86Rang-4
86T-761
86T/St-243
87D-136
87D/OD-176
87F-139
87Mother/Rang-12
87OPC-308
87Sf-154M
87Sf-32
87Smok/R-9
87T-308
87T/St-241
88AlaskaAS70/Team-13
88D/Best-188
88D/Y/Bk-NEW
88F/Up-U51
88S-268
88S/Tr-19T
88T-462
88T/Tr-108T
89B-172
89D-190
89D/Best-105
89F-271
89OPC-238
89Panini/St-403
89S-561
89S/NWest-12
89Sf-218
89T-611
89T/Big-138
89UD-178
90B-182
90D-277
90F-456
90F/Up-U51
90Homer/Pirate-27
90Leaf/II-354
90MLBPA/Pins-65
90OPC-26
90PublInt/St-548
90S-79
90S/Tr-13T
90T-26
90T/St-318
90T/Tr-116T
90UD-152
91B-532
91D-213
91F-49
91F/Ultra-286
91Leaf/I-29
91Leaf/Stud-228
91OPC-221
91S-610
91T-221
91T/StClub/II-358
91UD-181
92D/II-653
92F-566
92S/I-280
92T-524
92UD-540
Slaughter, Enos
41DP-40
47HomogBond-43
47TipTop
48B-17
48L-127
49B-65
49Eureka-198
50B-35
50Drake-36
51B-58
51T/BB-30
52B-232
52Dix
52NTea
52RM-NL20
52StarCal/L-81D
52T-65
52TipTop
53B/Col-81
53Dix
53Hunter
53NB
53RM-NL13
53T-41
54B-62
54Dix
54Hunter
54RH
54RM-NL19
54Wilson
55B-60
55Rodeo
56Rodeo
56T-109
57T-215
58T-142
59T-155
74Laugh/ASG-53
79TCMA-240
80Pac/Leg-32
85West/2-27
86Sf/Dec-18
88Pac/Leg-84
89Pac/Leg-137
89Swell-65
90Pac/Legend-50
90Swell/Great-54
91Conlon/Sport-56
91Swell/Great-84
91T/Arc53-41
92Conlon/Sport-642
D305
Exh47
PM10/L-38
PM10/Sm-181
R346-34
R423-96
W754
Slaughter, Garland
89Welland/Pucko-22
Slaughter, Sterling
64T-469R
65T-314
Slavic, Joseph
86Lakeland-21
88Lakeland/Star-23
Slavin, Dave
88Pocatel/ProC-2094
89Clinton/ProC-909
Slavin, Tim
83Wausau/LF-8
Slayback, Bill
73OPC-537
73T-537
Slaymaker, Joe
75BurlB
Sleater, Lou
52T-306
53T-224
55Rodeo
58T-46
91Crown/Orio-424
91T/Arc53-224
Slettvet, Doug
75QuadC
76QuadC
77QuadC
Slezak, Robert
82VeroB-11
83VeroB-12
Slider, Rachel
(Rac)
61Union
85IntLgAS-45
85Pawtu-14
90T/TVRSox-6CO
Slifko, Paul
86NewBrit-22
87WinHaven-20
Sline, Fred
C46-9
Slininger, Dennis
91Johnson/ClBest-20
91Johnson/ProC-3978
Sliwinski, Kevin
86Knoxvl-21
87Knoxvl-10
88Huntsvl/BK-20
88Tacoma/CMC-20
88Tacoma/ProC-626
Sloat, Dwain
(Lefty)
90Target-744
Slocum, Ron
70T-573R
71MLB/St-239
71OPC-274
71T-274
Slocumb, Heathcliff
86LitFalls-26
87WinSalem-7
88WinSalem/Star-16
89Peoria/Ko-9
91B-421
91Classic/III-84
91Cub/Mara-51
91D/Rook-25
91F/UltraUp-U73
91F/Up-U81
91Leaf/II-370
91S/RookTr-84T
91UD/Ext-767
92D/I-334
92F-390
92S/100RisSt-28
92S/I-213
92T-576
92T/91Debut-164
92UD-569
Slominski, Rich
86Wausau-22
Slomkowski, Rich
89Watlo/ProC-1798
89Watlo/Star-19
90Freder/Team-8
Sloniger, Chris
88SLCity-5
89Miami/II/Star-17
Slosson, Bill
91Sumter/ClBest-29TR
Slotnick, Joe
86BurlEx-20
Slowik, Tad
86Peoria-21
87WinSalem-11
Slusarski, Joe
88T/Tr-109TOLY
89Modesto/Cal-266
89Modesto/Chong-15
89T/Big-213
90Foil/Best-203
90Huntsvl/Best-10
91B-233
91Classic/III-85
91S/RookTr-105T
91Tacoma/ProC-2305
91UD/Ext-777
92D/II-626
92F-266
92S/100RisSt-18
92S/I-309
92T-651
92T/91Debut-165
92UD-663
Smajstra, Craig
83AppFx/LF-10
86Water-22
87BuffB-10
88Tucson/CMC-23
88Tucson/ProC-168
88Tucson/JP-21
89Tucson/CMC-12
89Tucson/ProC-200
89Tucson/JP-22
90AAAGame/ProC-AAA40
90Tucson/CMC-9
90Tucson/ProC-209
91Iowa/LineD-205
91Iowa/ProC-1069
Smaldone, Ed
89Geneva/ProC-1861
Small, Aaron
90Myrtle/ProC-2777
91Dunedin/ClBest-10
91Dunedin/ProC-206
91Single/ClBest-361
Small, Chris
88AubAs/ProC-1949
Small, Hank
78Richm
Small, Jeff
86Peoria-22
87WinSalem-24
90AAAGame/ProC-AAA35
90Iowa/CMC-20
90Iowa/ProC-325
90T/TVCub-59
91Iowa/LineD-218
91Iowa/ProC-1070
Small, Jim
56T-207
57T-33
61Union
D301
Small, Mark
89AubAs/ProC-2188
90Ashvl/ProC-2748
91Osceola/ClBest-11
91Osceola/ProC-684
Small, Nataniel
(Lefty)
76Laugh/Clown-7
Small, Robert
89James/ProC-2133
Smalley, Dave
84Greens-13
Smalley, Roy Jr.
75Spoka
76OPC-657
76OPC-70FS
76SSPC-267
76T-657
76T-70FS
77Ho-66
77T-66
78Ho-118
78T-471
79Ho-60
79OPC-110
79T-219
80K-13
80OPC-296
80T-570
80T/S-40
81D-487
81F-551
81F/St-55
81MSA/Disc-30
81OPC-115
81T-115
81T/So-43
81T/St-100
82D-22DK
82D-573
82F-560
82F/St-228
82OPC-197
82T-767
82T/St-207
82T/Tr-107T
83D-209
83F-397
83OPC-38
83RoyRog/Disc-11
83T-460
83T/St-96
84D-225
84F-142
84Nes/792-305
84OPC-305
84T-305
85D-622
85F-527
85F/Up-U105
85OPC-26
85Seven/Minn-6
85T-140FS
85T-26
85T/St-237
85T/Tr-108T
86D-486
86F-404
86Leaf-237
86OPC-156
86T-613

87D-443
87F-552
87OPC-47
87T-744
87T/St-282
88D-566
88F-22
88Leaf-233
88S-606
88T-239
90Smok/SoCal-12
PM10/Sm-182

Smalley, Roy Sr.
48L-77
49Eureka-72
50B-115
51B-44
51FB
51T/BB-17
52B-64
52T-173
53B/BW-56
54B-109
54T-231
55B-252
55JC-30
57T-397
60DF-3
76OPC-70FS
76T-70FS
85T-140FS
91T/Arc53-297

Smalls, Roberto
88Wythe/ProC-1986
89CharWh/Best-15
89CharWh/ProC-1761
90Geneva/ProC-3052
90Geneva/Star-22

Smay, Kevin
81Clinton-9

Smelko, Mark
82Redwd-11
83Redwd-23

Smelser, Don
80ElPaso-15

Smiley, John
85PrWill-22
86PrWill-24
87D/Rook-39
87F/Up-U110
87Sf/Rook-21
87Sf/Rook-7
87T/Tr-114T
88D-449
88D/Best-257
88F-340
88RedFoley/St-82
88S-287
88T-423
88ToysRUs-28
89B-413
89Classic/Up/2-191
89D-329
89D/Best-157
89F-221
89OPC-322
89Panini/St-167
89S-409
89S/YS/I-37
89T-322
89T/Big-85
89T/St-124
89UD-516
89VFJuice-57
90Classic-126
90D-17DK
90D-54
90D/BestNL-21
90D/SuperDK-17DK
90F-480
90Homer/Pirate-30
90Leaf/II-328
90OPC-568
90Panini/St-323
90PublInt/St-165
90S-334
90S/100St-65
90Sf-191
90T-568
90T/Big-79
90T/St-132
90UD-387
91B-509
91Classic/III-86
91D-664
91F-50
91F/UltraUp-U102
91Leaf/I-123
91Leaf/Stud-229
91OPC-143
91S-465
91T-143
91T/StClub/II-471
91UD-669
91USPlayC/AS-3C
92D/I-331
92F-567
92S/100SS-3
92S/II-659
92T-232
92UD-467

Smiley, Reuben
88Pocatel/ProC-2087
89Clinton/ProC-894
90AS/Cal-45
90Foil/Best-310
90SanJose/Best-3
90SanJose/Cal-30
90SanJose/ProC-2024
90SanJose/Star-22
90SanJose/Star-26M
91Shrev/LineD-321
91Shrev/ProC-1836

Smith
10Domino-110
12Sweet/Pin-77
S74-56

Smith, Adam
88Pocatel/ProC-2092

Smith, Al
46Sunbeam
47Signal
47Sunbeam

Smith, Alex
87Durham-14
88Richm-30
88Richm/CMC-13
88Richm/ProC-25
89Richm/Bob-25
89Richm/Ko-14
89Richm/ProC-841

Smith, Alexander B.
(Broadway Aleck)
90Target-1072

Smith, Alfred J.
(Al)
92Conlon/Sport-580

Smith, Alphonse E.
54T-248
55B-20
55Gol/Ind-27
55Salem
55T-197
56Carling-8
56T-105
56T/Pin-11OF
57Sohio/Ind-13
57T-145
58T-177
59T-22
60T-428
61P-24
61T-170
61T-42LL
61T/St-129
62J-48
62P-48
62P/Can-48
62Salada-29
62Shirriff-29
62T-410
63J-38
63P-38
63T-16
64T-317
91Crown/Orio-425

Smith, Anthony
90Target-1075
T204
T205

Smith, Ben
90Kgsport/Star-30BB

Smith, Bernie
83Redwd-29

Smith, Bill
61BeeHive-21

Smith, Bill
83AppFx/LF-1GM

Smith, Billy
85Everett/II/Cram-17

Smith, Billy Edward
76SSPC-199
78T-666
79T-237
80OkCty
80T-367
82F-400
82T-593
91Crown/Orio-426

Smith, Billy Lavern
78DaytB
80Tucson-11
81Tucson-24
82T-441R
82Tucson-18
84Tor/Fire-27CO
85Tor/Fire-26CO
86Tor/Fire-28CO
87Tor/Fire-28CO
88Tor/Fire-42CO

Smith, Bob E.
33G-185
35BU-47
91Conlon/Sport-217
R316

Smith, Bob G.
58T-226
59T-83

Smith, Bob W.
58T-445

Smith, Bob
61BeeHive-22

Smith, Bobby Gene
57T-384
58T-402
59T-162
60T-194
61T-316
62J-196
62P-196
62P/Can-196
62Salada-176A
62Salada-176B
62Shirriff-176
62T-531
91WIZMets-368

Smith, Bobby Glen
78BurlB
79Holyo-6
80Vanco-5
81Vanco-19

Smith, Brad
88Clearw/Star-23

Smith, Brick
84Chatt-5
86Chatt-23
86SLAS-17
87Calgary-12
87Sf/Rook-5
88Calgary/ProC-803
89Chatt/II/Team-28
89Tucson/CMC-17
89Tucson/ProC-193
89Tucson/JP-23

Smith, Bryan
86Bakers-25
87VeroB-24
90AubAs/Best-12
90AubAs/ProC-3406
91BurlAs/ClBest-22
91BurlAs/ProC-2816
91Single/ClBest-313

Smith, Bryn
78Denver
80Memphis-20
82Hygrade
82OPC-118R
82T-118R
83D-88
83F-297
83OPC-234
83Stuart-29
83T-447
84D-453
84F-287
84Nes/792-656
84OPC-77
84Stuart-21
84T-656
85D-209
85F-410
85Leaf-171
85OPC-88
85T-88
85T/St-90
86D-299
86F-260
86F/Mini-55
86F/Slug-35
86F/St-110
86Leaf-174
86OPC-299
86Provigo-19
86Sf-120
86T-299
86T/St-79
86T/Super-51
87D-159
87F-332
87Leaf-60
87OPC-281
87T-505
87T/St-83
88D-335
88D/Best-202
88F-196
88Leaf-129
88OPC-161
88Panini/St-320
88S-356
88T-161
88T/Big-250
89B-353
89D-216
89D/Best-124
89F-394
89OPC-131
89Panini/St-116
89S-428
89T-464
89T/Big-47
89UD-78
90B-184
90D-106
90D-25DK
90D/BestNL-10
90D/SuperDK-25DK
90F-361
90Leaf/II-393
90OPC-352
90PublInt/St-188
90S-419
90S/Tr-55T
90Smok/Card-20
90T-352
90T/St-78
90T/Tr-117T
90T/TVCard-18
90UD-579
90UD/Ext-794
91B-407
91D-113
91F-644
91F/Ultra-294
91Leaf/I-226
91OPC-743
91Pol/Card-36
91S-444
91T-743
91T/StClub/I-17
91UD-307
92D/I-323
92F-590
92S/II-529
92T-31
92UD-591

Smith, Bubba
91Belling/ProC-3675

Smith, C. Bernard
71OPC-204R
71T-204R

Smith, Calvin
91Hunting/ClBest-24
91Hunting/ProC-3344

Smith, Carl R.
(Reggie)
67T-314R
67T/Test/RSox-12
68OPC-61
68T-61
69MB-256
69MLB/St-18
69T-660
69T/St-139
70K-46
70MLB/St-167
70OPC-215
70OPC-62LL
70T-215
70T-62LL
70T/PI-20
71K-52
71MD
71MLB/St-333
71OPC-305
71T-305
71T/Coins-78
71T/S-1
71T/tatt-8
72K-35
72MB-318
72OPC-88LL
72T-565
72T-566IA
72T-88LL
73OPC-40
73T-40
74OPC-285
74T-285
74T/St-118
75Ho-59
75K-3
75OPC-490
75T-490
75T/M-490
76Crane-57
76Ho-30
76Ho/Twink-30
76MSA/Disc
76OPC-215
76SSPC-278
76T-215
77BurgChef-152
77OPC-223
77T-345
78Ho-30
78K-34
78OPC-57
78T-168
78Wiffle/Discs-70
79Ho-72
79OPC-243
79T-465
79T/Comics-25
80OPC-350
80Pol/Dodg-8
80T-695
81D-59
81F-111
81F/St-87
81K-36
81OPC-75
81Pol/Dodg-8
81T-75
81T/HT
81T/So-57
81T/St-178
82D-488
82F-23
82OPC-228IA
82OPC-5
82T-545
82T-546IA
82T/Tr-110T
83D-611
83F-272
83OPC-282
83OPC-283SV
83T-282
83T-283SV
83T/St-12
83T/St-302
87Smok/Dodg-34
88Smok/Dodg-21M
89Smok/Dodg-88
90Target-750

Smith, Carlos
T206

Smith, Chad
89Sumter/ProC-1108
90Durham/Team-23
90Miami/I/Star-25

Smith, Charles
91Belling/ClBest-12

Smith, Charles M.
M116
N172
N284

N300/SC
WG1-62
Smith, Charles W.
60DF-12
62Salada-135A
62Salada-135B
62Shirriff-135
62T-283
63T-424
64T-519
65OPC-22
65T-22
66T-358
67T-257
68T-596
69T-538
78TCMA-289
90Target-745
91WIZMets-369
Smith, Chris W.
80Memphis-21
82Wichita-18
83Phoenix/BHN-22
84D-46RR
Smith, Dan
75Cedar
78Tidew
79Jacks-17
Smith, Dan
90Classic/DP-16
91B-275
91OkCty/LineD-322
91OkCty/ProC-179
91Rockford/ClBest-21
91S-384FDP
Smith, Dan
86Bakers-26
87Orlan-3
Smith, Dana
86Hagers-18
88CharlK/Pep-21
89Hagers/Best-21
89Hagers/ProC-286
89Hagers/Star-18
Smith, Dandy
91Rockford/ProC-2056
Smith, Danny
85Cedar-12
86Vermont-20
Smith, Daryl
80Ashvl-19
83Tulsa-7
86Water-23
87Wmsprt-12
88BirmB/Best-19
90Memphis/Star-24
91Omaha/LineD-345
91Omaha/ProC-1035
91T/90Debut-145
Smith, Dave
76BurlB
77Holyo
78Holyo
Smith, David A.
80Spokane-2
81LynnS-11
82Holyo-9
Smith, David Lee
(D.L.)
87RochR-14
87RochR/TCMA-14
88RochR/CMC-17
89ElPaso/GS-24
89TexLAS/GS-16
90Denver/CMC-10
90Denver/ProC-635
91Denver/LineD-126
91Denver/ProC-132
Smith, David S.
(Dave)
77Cocoa
79Charl-11
81D-23
81F-71
81OPC-287
81T-534
82D-191
82F-232
82OPC-297
82T-761
83D-370
83F-466
83OPC-247
83T-247
84D-548
84F-242
84Mother/Ast-13
84Nes/792-361
84T-361
85D-548
85F-362
85Mother/Ast-21
85T-123
86D-328
86F-312
86F/St-111
86OPC-222
86Pol/Ast-11
86T-408
86T/St-31
87Classic-66
87D-308
87D/AAS-30
87F-6
87F/Hottest-38
87F/St-109
87Leaf-224
87Mother/Ast-20
87OPC-50
87Pol/Ast-17
87Sf-94
87T-50
87T/Mini-12
88AlaskaAS70/Team-24
88D-410
88D/Best-262
88F-457
88F/Hottest-39
88F/Mini-81
88F/St-90
88F/TL-37
88Mother/Ast-20
88OPC-73
88Panini/St-290
88Pol/Ast-22
88RochR/Team-21
88RochR/ProC-195
88SanDiegoSt-17
88S-365
88Sf-208
88T-520
88T/St-26
89B-317
89Classic-22
89D-272
89D/Best-232
89F-369
89F/BBAS-38
89Lennox/Ast-19
89Mother/Ast-19
89OPC-305
89Panini/St-87
89S-245
89T-305
89T/St-13
89UD-302
90B-62
90Classic-94
90D-88
90D/BestNL-40
90F-238
90Leaf/I-122
90Lennox-23
90Mother/Ast-17
90OPC-746
90Panini/St-257
90PublInt/St-103
90RedFoley/St-87
90S-45
90S/100St-19
90Sf-140
90T-746
90T/Big-145
90T/St-16
90T/St-190
90T/TVAS-49
90UD-448
90USPlayC/AS-8D
91B-425
91Classic/III-87
91Cub/Mara-42
91D-212
91F-517
91F/Up-U82
91Leaf/II-456
91Leaf/Stud-160
91OPC-215
91OPC/Premier-111
91Panini/St-12
91S-314
91S/RookTr-9T
91T-215
91T/StClub/II-345
91T/Tr-110T
91UD-513
91UD/Ext-704
92D/I-53
92F-391
92S/I-98
92T-601
92UD-549
Smith, David Wayne
(D.W.)
82Holyo-10
83Nashua-8
83Wausau/LF-27
84Cram/PCL-103
84Newar-11
85Cram/PCL-16
86Edmon-26
Smith, Demond
91Kingspt/ClBest-2
91Kingspt/ProC-3828
Smith, Don
84Cram/PCL-155
85Cram/PCL-171
Smith, Donald
(Snuffy)
47Smith-16
Smith, Dwight
86Peoria-23
87Pittsfld-26
88AAA/ProC-19
88Iowa/CMC-21
88Iowa/ProC-530
89B-297
89D/Best-205
89D/Rook-32
89F/Up-79
89Iowa/CMC-22
89Iowa/ProC-1708
89Mara/Cubs-18
89S-642RP
89S/HotRook-64
89T/Tr-113T
89UD/Ext-780
90B-32
90Classic-30
90Cub/Mara-19
90D-393
90D/BestNL-63
90F-42
90F/BBMVP-35
90F/SoarSt-12
90HotRook/St-42
90Leaf/I-255
90OPC-311
90Panini/St-235
90PublInt/St-204
90S-240
90S/100Ris-4
90S/YS/I-2
90Sf-152
90T-311
90T/89Debut-116
90T/Big-151
90T/Coins-57
90T/HeadsUp-23
90T/JumboR-26
90T/St-52
90T/TVCub-33
90ToysRUs-25
90UD-376
91Cub/Mara-18
91D-559
91F-432
91F/Ultra-68
91OPC-463
91Panini/FrSt-47
91S-301
91T-463
91T/StClub/I-181
91UD-452
92D/II-561
92F-392
92S/II-612
92T-168
Smith, Earl L.
28Yueng-48
E120
V100
W573
Smith, Earl S.
21Exh-162
21Exh-163
25Exh-54
26Exh-54
27Exh-27
28Exh-26
91Conlon/Sport-74
E120
E121/120
E121/80
E220
V100
W501-71
W502-48
W572
W573
W575
Smith, Ed
89SoBend/GS-28
90Saraso/Star-22
91Saraso/ClBest-19
91Saraso/ProC-1121
Smith, Edward Mayo
55T-130MG
56T-60MG
56T/Hocus-A9
56T/Pin-21MG
67T-321MG
68T-544MG
69OPC-40MG
69T-40MG
70OPC-313MG
70T-313MG
81Detroit-35MG
Smith, Elmer E.
N172
Smith, Elmer John
21Exh-164
D328-163
E120
E121/120
E135-163
W501-109
W572
W575
Smith, F.C.
N172
Smith, Forest
(Woody)
75SanAn
77Watlo
78Watlo
81Chatt-24
Smith, Frank
90Kissim/DIMD-25
Smith, Frank T.
52B-186
52T-179
53T-116
54B-188
54T-71
55Hunter
55T-204
91T/Arc53-116
Smith, Frank
(Nig)
14CJ-90
15CJ-90
D303
E101
E102
E105
E254
E270/1
E90/3
E92
M116
T206
T207
T213/blue
T215/blue
T215/brown
T3-118
Smith, Freddie
81Miami-3
Smith, Garry J.
77WHave
79Colum-5
80Colum-5
81Colum-21
82Colum-14
82Colum/Pol-13
Smith, Garry
82Nashvl-24
Smith, Gary
78Cr/PCL-29
Smith, Gene
81BurlB-5
Smith, George A.
90Target-747
V100
Smith, George C.
65T-483
66T-542
67T-444
67T/Test/RSox-18
Smith, George H.
E254
T206
Smith, George J.
(Germany)
90Target-748
N172
Smith, Greg
81VeroB-18
85Beaum-6
86Erie-27
86LasVegas-16
87Erie-11
87OKCty-19
88Spokane/ProC-1932
89CharRain/ProC-979
90Riversi/Best-18
90Riversi/Cal-2
90Riversi/ProC-2621
Smith, Gregory A.
(Greg)
87Peoria-14
88CLAS/Star-35
88WinSalem/Star-17
89CharlK-11
89SLAS-11
90B-31
90F-643
90Iowa/CMC-13
90Iowa/ProC-326
90S-614
90T/89Debut-117
90T/TVCub-27
90UD/Ext-738
91Albuq/LineD-20
91Albuq/ProC-1151
91B-594
91D-574
91F-433
91OPC-560
91T-560
91T/StClub/II-554
Smith, Hal R.
56T-283
57T-111
58T-273
59T-497
60L-58
60L-94M
60T-84
61P-180
61T-549
Smith, Hal W.
55Esskay
55T-8
55T/DH-70
56T-62
56T/Hocus-A15
56T/Pin-3C
57T-41
58T-257
59T-227
60L-119
60L-94M
60T-48
61P-139
61T-242
61T/St-70
61T/St-94
62J-181
62Kahn
62P-181
62P/Can-181
62Salada-190
62Shirriff-190
62T-492
62T/bucks
62T/St-129

63T-153
64T-233
78TCMA-127
89Smok/Ast-12
91Crown/Orio-427
Smith, Harry Thomas
E107
M116
Smith, Henry J.
(Hap)
90Target-1073
T206
Smith, Hilton
78Laugh/Black-34
86Negro/Frit-27
Smith, Jack H.
63T-496R
64T-378R
90Target-749
Smith, Jack
82WHave-9
83ColumAst-20
86Tampa-20
87Tampa-14
88Greens/ProC-1569
89Wmsprt/ProC-643
89Wmsprt/Star-20
91Jaxvl/LineD-345
91Jaxvl/ProC-160
Smith, Jack
21Exh-165
92Conlon/Sport-507
E126-51
V61-75
WG7-53
Smith, Jackie
79Knoxvl/TCMA-17
Smith, James C.
(Red)
16FleischBrd-86
90Target-1074
D327
D328-164
D329-165
D350/2-167
E135-164
E220
M101/4-165
M101/5-167
T222
Smith, Jed
81Louisvl-30
82Louisvl-28
83Louisvl/Riley-30
84Louisvl-10
85Louisvl-10
86Louisvl-29
Smith, Jeff
75Dubuq
76Dubuq
81Redwd-6
82Redwd-12
86Beloit-23
91Eugene/ClBest-20
91Eugene/ProC-3727
Smith, Jim
88Eugene/Best-8
91London/LineD-418
91Memphis/ProC-654
Smith, Jimmy
77Charl
79RochR-13
80RochR-17
80Tidew-20
81Portl-22
83D-402
83F-323
83T-122
Smith, Joel
88SoOreg/ProC-1697
89Rockford/Team-24
90WPalmB/Star-22
Smith, John Francis
N172
Smith, John W.
E102
V100
W572
W573
Smith, John
(Duke)
82Madis-5
Smith, John
78Cedar
Smith, John
89Utica/Pucko-22
90Utica/Pucko-23
Smith, JoJo
91Yakima/ClBest-27
91Yakima/ProC-4248
Smith, Jon
62Pep/Tul
63Pep/Tul
Smith, Keith L.
74Gaston
77Tucson
78Cr/PCL-76
78T-710R
81D-539
81F-534
Smith, Kelly
82Phoenix
Smith, Kelvin
83Clinton/LF-20
Smith, Ken
79Savan-24
80Richm-18
81Richm-4
82BK/Lids-23
82Richm-23
83F-148
83Pol/Atl-11
84Richm-3
85Richm-16
86RochR-23
88Savan/ProC-332
89StPete/Star-25
Smith, Kevin
91Kissim/ProC-4183
Smith, Lance
90Ashvl/ClBest-20
91Ashvl/ProC-572
Smith, Larry
83Idaho-11
85Huntsvl/BK-30
87SanBern-2
Smith, Lawrence
(Larry)
89Miami/I/Star-18
89Welland/Pucko-31
Smith, Lee
80Wichita-12
82D-252
82F-603
82RedLob
82T-452
83D-403
83F-508
83T-699
83Thorn-46
84D-289
84F-505
84F/St-67
85FunFoodPin-108
84Nes/792-176
84OPC-176
84SevenUp-46
84T-176
84T/St-44
85D-311
85F-67
85F/St-105
85Leaf-128
85OPC-43
85SevenUp-46
85T-511
85T/St-41
86Cub/Unocal-17
86D-144
86D/AS/WaxBox-PC8
86F-380
86F/LimEd-42
86F/LL-41
86Gator-46
86Jay's-17
86Leaf-64
86OPC-355
86Sf-45
86Sf-55M
86T-355
86T-636M
86T/St-56
86T/Super-52
87Berg/Cubs-46
87D-292
87F-574
87F/Excit-39
87F/Lim-39
87F/Mini-101
87F/St-110
87Leaf-80
87OPC-23
87RedFoley/St-42
87Sf-104
87Sf-77M
87Seven-C16
87Seven-ME15
87T-23
87T/Mini-3
87T/St-56
88D-292
88D/AS-60
88D/Best-252
88D/RedSox/Bk-NEW
88F-433
88F/Mini-9
88F/Up-U8
88OPC-240
88Panini/St-256
88S-31
88S/Tr-20T
88Sf-179
88T-240
88T/Gloss60-56
88T/Mini-44
88T/St-64
88T/St/Backs-33
88T/Tr-110T
89B-19
89D-66
89D/Best-84
89F-99
89OPC-149
89Panini/St-272
89RedFoley/St-109
89S-150
89S/HotStar-18
89Sf-148
89T-760
89T/St-251
89UD-521
90B-263
90Classic-137
90D-110
90D/BestNL-120
90F-287
90F/Up-U53
90Leaf/II-524
90OPC-495
90Panini/St-14
90Pep/RSox-20
90Publint/St-464
90S-37
90S/Tr-48T
90Smok/Card-21
90T-495
90T/St-262
90T/Tr-118T
90T/TVRSox-17
90UD-393
91B-387
91D-169
91D-403MVP
91F-645
91F/Ultra-295
91Leaf/I-44
91Leaf/Stud-237
91OPC-660
91Panini/FrSt-39
91Panini/St-38
91Panini/Top15-83
91Pol/Card-47
91S-81
91T-660
91T/StClub/I-42
91UD-348
91USPlayC/AS-10C
92D/I-112
92F-591
92F-697LL
92F/ASIns-8
92S/100SS-28
92S/II-630
92S/II-781AS
92T-565
92UD-376
Smith, Leslie
90Miami/II/Star-30PER
Smith, Lonnie
76OkCty/Team-23
79OkCty
79T-722R
80BK/P-14
81Coke
81D-295
81F-15
81OPC-317
81T-317
82D-606
82F-259
82F-641M
82F/St-60
82OPC-127
82T-127
82T/Tr-108T
83D-91
83D/AAS-34
83F-21
83F-636M
83K-30
83OPC-273
83PermaGr/CC-15
83T-465
83T-561TL
83T/St-283
84D-231
84D-625M
84D/Champs-23
84F-335
84F/St-7
84Nes/792-186TL
84Nes/792-580
84OPC-113
84Seven-14C
84T-186TL
84T-580
84T/St-140
84T/St/Box-5
85D-231
85F-239
85F/St-61
85F/Up-U106
85Leaf-225
85OPC-255
85T-255
85T/St-139
85T/Tr-109T
86D-399
86F-21
86F/Mini-4
86F/St-112
86Kitty/Disc-1
86Leaf-188
86NatPhoto-21
86OPC-7
86Sf-186M
86T-617
86T/Mini-21
86T/St-264
87D-225
87F-381
87F/Lim-40
87F/St-111
87T-69
87T/St-262
88D-527
88Panini/St-111
88Richm-5
88Richm/CMC-14
88Richm/ProC-1
88S-263
88T-777
89B-278
89D/Best-114
89F/Up-74
89T/Big-242
89T/LJN-84
89T/Tr-114T
89UD/Ext-731
90B-12
90Classic-52
90D-222
90D/BestNL-86
90F-593
90F/AwardWin-35
90F/LL-37
90KMart/CBatL-19
90Leaf/I-217
90OPC-152
90Panini/St-227
90Publint/St-121
90RedFoley/St-88
90S-399
90S/100St-82
90Sf-65
90T-152
90T/Big-7
90T/Coins-58
90T/DH-61
90T/Mini-46
90T/St-24
90UD-215
91B-567
91D-364
91F-702
91F/Ultra-11
91Leaf/I-13
91OPC-306
91Panini/FrSt-24
91Panini/St-22
91S-543
91T-306A
91T-306B
91T/StClub/I-97
91UD-305
92D/II-517
92F-369
92S/I-13
92T-467
92UD-301
Smith, Mandy
81Wisco-19
Smith, Mark
83BirmB-7
83RochR-8
Smith, Mark
88CapeCod/Sum-146
90Hamil/Best-7
90Hamil/Star-24
91Classic/DP-6
91StPete/ClBest-13
92UD-66TP
Smith, Marvin David
(David)
88Kenosha/ProC-1391
89Belling/Legoe-29
89Visalia/Cal-117
89Visalia/ProC-1448
90SanBern/Best-20
90SanBern/Cal-99
90SanBern/ProC-2647
Smith, Michael A.
(Texas Mike)
86Cedar/TCMA-10
87Vermont-12
88Chatt/Best-21
89RochR/CMC-8
89RochR/CMC-9
89RochR/ProC-1634
89RochR/ProC-1637
90RochR/CMC-8
90RochR/ProC-702
90T/89Debut-118
91Crown/Orio-428
Smith, Michael A.
(Mississippi)
87Indianap-23
88Indianap/CMC-7
88Indianap/ProC-509
90OPC-249
90OPC-552
90T-249
90T-552
90Tampa/DIMD-24
Smith, Mike
76AppFx
82Richm-26
Smith, Mike
80GlenF/B-28bb
80GlenF/C-29bb
Smith, Milt
61Union
Smith, Myrl
79Tucson-2
Smith, Nate
91Crown/Orio-429
Smith, Nick
N172
Smith, Ottis
91Pittsfld/ClBest-15
91Pittsfld/ProC-3423
Smith, Ozzie
78Padre/FamFun-29
79Ho-102
79OPC-52
79T-116
80OPC-205

80T-393
81D-1
81F-488
81OPC-254
81T-207RB
81T-254
81T/SO-68
81T/St-230
82D-21DK
82D-94
82F-582
82F/St-101
82K-6
82OPC-95
82T-95
82T/St-104
82T/Tr-109T
83D-120
83F-22
83F-636M
83K-21
83OPC-14
83PermaGr/AS-17
83PermaGr/CC-16
83T-540
83T/St-168
83T/St-180
83T/St-186
83T/St-288
84D-59
84D-625M
84F-336
85FunFoodPin-71
84MiltBrad-25
84Nes/792-130
84Nes/792-389AS
84Nestle/DT-15
84OPC-130
84OPC-389AS
84Ralston-2
84Seven-19C
84T-130
84T-389
84T/Cereal-2
84T/Gloss22-16
84T/Gloss40-17
84T/St-144
84T/St-187
85D-59
85D/AAS-28
85F-240
85F-631IA
85F/LimEd-35
85GenMills-10
85Leaf-60
85OPC-191
85Seven-16C
85T-605
85T-715AS
85T/Gloss22-5
85T/St-137
85T/St-181
85T/Super-47
86D-59
86D/AAS-8
86D/PopUp-8
86F-46
86F/LL-42
86F/Mini-10
86F/St-113
86KAS/Disc-7
86Leaf-47
86OPC-297
86Quaker-15
86Sf-121
86Schnucks-21
86T-704AS
86T-730
86T/Gloss22-16
86T/Gloss60-46
86T/St-11NLCS
86T/St-153
86T/St-46
86T/Super-53
86TrueVal-9
87BK-14
87Classic-32
87D-5DK
87D-60
87D/AAS-15
87D/DKsuper-5
87D/OD-65
87D/PopUp-15
87F-308
87F/AwardWin-38
87F/BB-41
87F/Mini-102
87F/St-112
87Ho/St-15
87Jiffy-7
87Kraft-16
87Leaf-108
87Leaf-5DK
87MnM's-24
87OPC-107
87Ralston-13
87RedFoley/St-112
87Sf-142
87Sf-79M
87Smok/Cards-17
87Smok/NL-9
87T-598AS
87T-749
87T/Coins-45
87T/Gloss22-5
87T/Gloss60-23
87T/St-162
87T/St-46
88ActPacT-6
88ChefBoy-5
88Classic/Blue-210
88D-263
88D-BC22
88D/AS-37
88D/AS-63
88D/Best-243
88D/PopUp-15
88F-47
88F-628M
88F/AwardWin-39
88F/BB/AS-39
88F/BB/MVP-35
88F/Hottest-40
88F/Mini-109
88F/RecSet-38
88F/St-120
88F/TL-38
88F/WS-4
88FanSam-11
88KingB/Disc-4
88KMart-28
88Leaf-115
88Nestle-5
88OPC-39
88Panini/St-235M
88Panini/St-393
88S-12
88S/WaxBox-14
88Sf-68
88Smok/Card-18
88T-400AS
88T-460
88T/Big-228
88T/Coins-55
88T/Gloss22-16
88T/Gloss60-47
88T/Mini-72
88T/St-153
88T/St-53
88T/St/Backs-12
88T/UK-72
89B-436
89Cadaco-53
89Classic-58
89D-63
89D/AS-37
89D/AS-62
89D/Best-44
89D/MVP-BC14
89D/PopUp-37
89F-463
89F/Excit-38
89F/LL-35
89Holsum/Discs-3
89KayBee-28
89OPC-230
89Panini/St-186
89Panini/St-235AS
89MSA/SS-1
89RedFoley/St-110
89S-80
89S/HotStar-88
89S/Mast-27
89Sf-105
89T-230
89T-389AS
89T/Big-110
89T/Coins-25
89T/DH-16
89T/Gloss22-16
89T/Gloss60-42
89T/HeadsUp-17
89T/LJN-14
89T/Mini-36
89T/St-161
89T/St-44
89T/St/Backs-45
89T/UK-72
89UD-265
89UD-674TC
90B-195
90BBWit-41
90Classic-18
90CollAB-5
90D-201
90D-710AS
90D/BestNL-83
90D/Learning-9
90F-260
90F/AwardWin-36
90F/BB-35
90F/BBMVP-36
90HotPlay/St-41
90KayBee-29
90KingB/Discs-4
90KMart/SS-4
90Leaf/I-142
90Leaf/II-364CL
90Leaf/Prev-12
90MLBPA/Pins-30
90MSA/Soda-10
90OPC-400AS
90OPC-590
90Panini/St-206 M
90Panini/St-338
90Post-6
90PublInt/St-228
90PublInt/St-272
90RedFoley/St-89
90S-285
90S/100St-6
90S/McDon-24
90Sf-16
90Smok/Card-22
90T-400AS
90T-590
90T/Big-203
90T/DH-62
90T/Gloss22-5
90T/Gloss60-16
90T/St-145AS
90T/St-42
90T/TVAS-52
90T/TVCard-29
90UD-225
90USPlayC/AS-6H
90WonderBrd-5
91B-398
91BBBest/RecBr-17
91Classic/200-39
91D-240
91D-437AS
91F-646
91F/Ultra-296
91JDeanSig-20
91Leaf/I-80
91Leaf/Stud-238
91MajorLg/Pins-49
91MooTown-8
91OPC-130
91OPC/Premier-112
91Panini/FrSt-161
91Panini/FrSt-34
91Panini/St-39
91Panini/Top15-103
91Pep/SS-12
91Petro/SU-18
91Pol/Card-1
91Post/Can-8
91RedFoley/St-129
91S-825
91S/100SS-18
91Seven/3DCoin-12MW
91Sunflower-1
91T-130
91T/CJMini/II-27
91T/StClub/I-154
91T/SU-31
91UD-162
91UD/FinalEd-95F
91USPlayC/AS-13S
92D/II-423AS
92D/II-432
92F-592
92S/100SS-47
92S/II-590
92T-396AS
92T-760
92UD-177

Smith, P. Keith
83Nashvl-23
84Nashvl-21
85Colum-19
85Colum/Pol-22
86Colum-23
86Colum/Pol-22
87Denver-25
88Denver/CMC-14
88Denver/ProC-1261
89Vanco/CMC-13
89Vanco/ProC-578
90Vanco/CMC-19
90Vanco/ProC-496

Smith, Paul
54DanDee
54T-11
57T-345
58T-269
63MilSau-8

Smith, Peter J.
86Greenvl/Team-18
87Greenvl/Best-24
88D-571
88D/Best-197
88D/Rook-10
88F-647R
88F/Up-U73
88S/Tr-84T
88T/Tr-111T
89B-269
89D-263
89F-600
89OPC-388
89Panini/St-36
89S-207
89S/HotRook-74
89S/YS/I-19
89T-537
89T/St-31
89ToysRUs-29
89UD-412
90D-499
90F-594
90Leaf/I-144
90OPC-771
90PublInt/St-122
90S-225
90T-771
90T/Big-161
90UD-613
91F-703
91OPC-383
91S-205
91T-383
91T/StClub/II-519
91UD-622
92F-370
92S/II-464
92T-226

Smith, Peter L.
63MilSau-9
64T-428R

Smith, Phil
82DayBe-24

Smith, Randy
76QuadC
90Idaho/ProC-3263CO
91Idaho/ProC-4346CO

Smith, Ray
77Visalia
78OrlTw
79Toledo-22
80Toledo-16
82Toledo-11
84F-573
84Nes/792-46
84T-46
84Toledo-4
85Cram/PCL-114
86Tacom-21
89Elizab/Star-29CO
90Elizab/Star-24CO
91Elizab/ProC-4315MG

Smith, Red
90LitSun-8

Smith, Richard
90Wausau/Best-7
90Wausau/ProC-2120
90Wausau/Star-22

Smith, Richard Arthur
(Dick)
64T-398R
65T-579
90Target-746
91WIZMets-370

Smith, Richard H.
53Mother-3
55B-288

Smith, Rick
88Bakers/Cal-267

Smith, Rick
91AS/Cal-27VP

Smith, Rob
88Stockton/Cal-192
88Stockton/ProC-741
89Stockton/Best-23
89Stockton/Cal-168
89Stockton/ProC-394
89Stockton/Star-18

Smith, Robbie
86Orlan-17
87Orlan-2

Smith, Robbie
90Beloit/Star-19
91Collnd/ClBest-28
91Collnd/ProC-1495

Smith, Robert
21Exh-166
28Exh-3
29Exh/4-2

Smith, Ron
75BurlB
76BurlB
76Watlo
80Penin/B-20
80Penin/C-26

Smith, Ronnie
47Signal

Smith, Roosevelt
91Erie/ClBest-24
91Erie/ProC-4070

Smith, Roy
80Penin/B-12
80Penin/C-4
82Reading-8
83Charl-5
84Maine-3
84Wheat/Ind-33
85D-611
85F-455
85Maine-10
85Polar/Ind-33
85T-381
86D-468
86T-9
87Portl-8
88AAA/ProC-33
88Portl/CMC-6
88Portl/ProC-645
90D-273
90F-386
90Leaf/II-400
90OPC-672
90Panini/St-107
90S-568
90T-672
90UD-284
91D-470
91F-624
91OPC-503
91RochR/ProC-1902
91S-151
91T-503
91UD-490
92F-28
92S/I-256

Smith, Samuel
N172

Smith, Shad
91Greens/ProC-3061

Smith, Sherrod
(Sherry)
21Exh-167
21Exh-168
25Exh-86
26Exh-85
28Yueng-31
90Target-751

92Conlon/Sport-609
E120
E126-22
E210-31
E220
W502-31

Smith, Steve
79Hawaii-14
80Hawaii-18
81Hawaii-3
82Hawaii-3
84Shrev/FB-18
86Beaum-23MG
86Fresno/Smok-17
87TexLgAS-13
87Wichita-9
88LasVegas/CMC-24
88LasVegas/ProC-244
89AAA/ProC-50
89LasVegas/CMC-24
89LasVegas/ProC-25
90OkCty/CMC-21MG
90OkCty/ProC-448MG
90WichSt-31
91Penin/ProC-394MG

Smith, Syd
E270/1
T206
T213/brown

Smith, Terry
86Lakeland-22TR
87Lakeland-11TR
90Lakeland/Star-28TR
90Princet/DIMD-19

Smith, Tim
84Newar-14

Smith, Tim
90Elmira/Pucko-23
91CLAS/ProC-CAR27
91LynchRS/ClBest-9
91LynchRS/ProC-1199
91SoOreg/ClBest-3
91SoOreg/ProC-3843

Smith, Todd
86Miami-23
87Salem-26
89Medford/Best-30
90Modesto/Cal-151
90Modesto/ProC-2212
91Modesto/ClBest-14
91Modesto/ProC-3088

Smith, Tom
81QuadC-18
83Peoria/LF-10

Smith, Tom
89Salem/Star-21
91AppFx/ClBest-25
91AppFx/ProC-1730

Smith, Tommy A.
74OPC-606R
74T-606R
75OPC-619R
75T-619R
75T/M-619R
76SSPC-530
77OPC-92
77T-14

Smith, Tommy
75Lafay
75OkCty
78Cr/PCL-31
80RochR-19

Smith, Tony
C46-32

Smith, Tracy
88Geneva/ProC-1647
89Peoria/Ko-20
90WinSalem/Team-21

Smith, Vinnie
52Mother-59

Smith, Wallace H.
T207

Smith, William G.
63T-241

Smith, Willie
65OPC-85
65T-85
66T-438
67T-397
68T-568
69MB-257
69OPC-198
69T-198
70OPC-318
70T-318
71OPC-457
71T-457
72MB-319

Smith, Willie
88Augusta/ProC-377
90Albany/Best-7
90B-425
90Batavia/ProC-3070
90ColClip/CMC-7
90ColClip/ProC-676
90T/TVYank-60
91Albany/ProC-1008
91B-160
91Single/ClBest-332
91SLCity/ProC-3214

Smith, Woody
88Wythe/ProC-1990
89Peoria/Ko-22
90Peoria/Team-13

Smith, Zane
83Durham-24
85F-651R
85Pol/Atl-34
86D-565
86F-528
86Leaf-222
86OPC-167
86Pol/Atl-34
86T-167
87D-167
87F-529
87OPC-226
87RedFoley/St-73
87Smok/Atl-1
87T-544
88D-167
88D/Best-170
88F-550
88F/Mini-66
88F/St-78
88F/TL-39
88OPC-297
88Panini/St-240
88S-410
88Sf-134
88T-297
88T/Big-193
88T/Mini-42
88T/St-40
88T/UK-73
89B-262
89D-499
89F-601
89F/Up-99
89OPC-339
89RedFoley/St-111
89S-492
89S/Tr-56T
89T-688
89T/St-27
89UD-71
90D-460
90F-362
90Leaf/I-238
90OPC-48
90PublInt/St-123
90S-477
90T-48
90UD-607
91B-524
91Classic/200-82
91D-532
91F-51
91Leaf/II-495
91OPC-441
91Panini/Top15-66
91S-845
91T-441
91T/StClub/I-260
91UD/Ext-759
92D/I-360
92F-568
92S/II-493
92T-345
92UD-486

Smithberg, Roger
89LasVegas/ProC-17
90B-203
90LasVegas/CMC-1
90LasVegas/ProC-124
91HighD/ClBest-11
91HighD/ProC-2394
91Wichita/ProC-2599

Smithson, Mike
81Pawtu-11
83Rang-48
83T/Tr-106T
84D-221
84F-428
84F/X-U108
84Nes/792-89
84T-89
84T/Tr-110T
85D-316
85F-289
85OPC-359
85Seven/Minn-11
85T-483
85T/St-301
86D-147
86F-405
86Leaf-73
86OPC-101
86T-695
86T/Mini-24
86T/St-282
87D-245
87F-553
87OPC-225
87T-225
87T/St-275
88D/RedSox/Bk-NEW
88F-23
88F/Up-U9
88OPC-389
88S/Tr-59T
88T-554
89D-628
89F-100
89S-403
89T-377
89T/Big-222
89UD-38
90D-464
90F-288
90OPC-188
90PublInt/St-465
90S-512
90T-188
90UD-610

Smolen, Bruce
91Batavia/ClBest-11
91Batavia/ProC-3494

Smoll, Clyde
87Elmira/Black-1
87Elmira/Red-1
88Elmira-30GM
89Elmira/Pucko-25

Smoltz, John
86Lakeland-23
87GlenF-24
88F/Up-U74
88Richm-26
88Richm/CMC-3
88Richm/ProC-23
89B-266
89Classic/Up/2-174
89D-642
89D/Best-85
89F-602
89S-616
89T-382
89T/Big-260
89UD-17
90B-10
90Classic-13
90D-121
90D-8DK
90D/BestNL-50
90D/Bon/MVP-BC12
90D/SuperDK-8DK
90F-595
90F/BB-36
90HotPlay/St-42
90Leaf/I-59
90OPC-535
90Panini/St-228
90PublInt/St-124
90RedFoley/St-90
90S-370
90S/100St-35
90S/YS/I-36
90Sf-61
90Starline/LJS-14
90Starline/LJS-34
90T-535
90T/Big-306
90T/Mini-47
90T/St-30
90UD-535
90UD-84TC
91B-580
91Classic/200-180
91Classic/II-T27
91D-75
91F-704
91F/Ultra-12
91Leaf/I-27
91Leaf/Stud-149
91OPC-157
91Panini/FrSt-26
91Panini/St-26
91S-208
91T-157
91T/StClub/II-365
91UD-264
92D/II-442
92F-371
92S/I-287
92T-245
92UD-322

Smoot, Allen
82Clinton-18

Smyth, Harry
90Target-752
R314/Can
V355-79

Snaith, Andy
82AlexD-26

Snead, Jay
89Augusta/ProC-519

Snead, Sam
51Wheat
52Wheat

Snead, Scott
91Billings/ProC-3764

Snedeker, Sean
88GreatF-20
89AS/Cal-21
89Bakers/Cal-181
91VeroB/ClBest-12
91VeroB/ProC-773

Snediker, Jim
86WinHaven-24

Snell, Dave
86Wausau-25
88Vermont/ProC-956

Snell, Nate
85F/Up-U107
85T/Tr-110T
86D-367
86F-288
86Leaf-166
86T-521
87D-396
87F-481
87T-86
88F-70
91Crown/Orio-430

Snider, Duke
49B-226
49Eureka-50
50B-77
50Drake-5
51B-32
51T/RB-38
52B-116
52BR
52NTea
52RM-NL21
52StarCal/L-79E
52T-37
52TipTop
53B/Col-117
53Briggs
53RM-NL14
53SM
54B-170
54DanDee
54NYJour
54RH
54RM-NL16
54SM
54T-32
55Armour-19
55Gol/Dodg-28
55RM-NL19
55SM
55T-210
56T-150
56T/Pin-52
56YellBase/Pin-29
57T-170
57T-400M
58BB
58Hires-61
58T-314M
58T-436M
58T-88
59Bz
59HRDerby-18
59Morrell
59T-20
59T-468HL
60BB-2
60L-37
60Morrell
60NuCard-55
60T-493
61BB-4
61P-167
61T-443
61T/St-35
62BB-4
62J-114
62P-114
62P/Can-114
62Salada-215
62Shirriff-215
62T-500
62T/St-140
63J-118
63P-118
63T-550
63T-68M
64T-155
64Wheat/St-42
76SSPC-351
79TCMA-43
79TCMA-72
80Pac/Leg-19
80SSPC/HOF
82CJ-8
83D/HOF-14
83MLBPA/Pin-33
84D-648PUZ
84West/1-24
85CircK-20
86Sf/Dec-32
87Leaf/SpecOlym-H6
87Nestle/DT-33
88Pac/Leg-55
89B/I-10
89Rini/Dodg-4
89Smok/Dodg-27
89T/LJN-117
90Target-753
91T/Arc53-327
91WIZMets-371
Exh47
PM10/L-39
PM10/Sm-183
PM10/Sm-184
PM10/Sm-185
R423-95
WG9-47

Snider, Kelly
77LodiD
79Albuq-14
80Albuq-4
81Toledo-15
82Toledo-16

Snider, Van
83CharR-13
84Memphis-9
87Omaha-4
88Nashvl/CMC-22
88Nashvl/ProC-473
88Nashvl/Team-22
89D-586
89F-172
89Nashvl/CMC-23
89Nashvl/ProC-1281
89Nashvl/Team-23
89S-640
89S/HotRook-41
89Sf-177
89UD-23
90ColClip/CMC-16
90ColClip/ProC-692
90T/TVYank-61
91ColClip/LineD-118
91ColClip/ProC-611

Snitker, Brian
78Green
79Savan-5
83Durham-28
84Durham-28
86Sumter-26MG
87Durham-6
91Macon/ClBest-18CO
91Macon/ProC-883CO
Snoddy, Ralph
33SK-25
Snodgrass, Fred
11Helmar-137
16FleischBrd-87
60NuCard-54
61NuCard-454
88Conlon/3-26
91Conlon/Sport-168
D328-165
D329-166
D350/2-168
E135-165
E254
E270
M101/4-166
M101/5-168
M116
S74-95
T202
T205
T206
T207
W555
Snover, Colonel L.
E120
Snover, Don
89Pulaski/ProC-1896
Snow, J.T. Jr.
88CapeCod/Sum-125
89Oneonta/ProC-2112
90CLAS/CL-17
90PrWill/Team-25
91Albany/ProC-1017
91Single/ClBest-279
Snuder, Kendall
87Kenosha-4
Snyder, Ben
82DayBe-8
83ColumAst-19
Snyder, Brett
90Beloit/Best-11
90Beloit/Star-20
90Foil/Best-145
Snyder, Brian
80SanJose/JITB-16
81Wausau-7
82SLCity-17
83SLCity-4
84Cram/PCL-178
84Shrev/FB-19
85Cram/PCL-92
86LasVegas-17
86T-174
87LasVegas-15
88Tacoma/CMC-9
88Tacoma/ProC-629
89Tacoma/CMC-4
89Tacoma/ProC-1545
90Richm/Bob-4
90Richm/CMC-25
90Richm/ProC-260
90Richm/Team-28
Snyder, Charles N.
N172
Snyder, Chris
88CapeCod/Sum-9
90Princet/DIMD-20
Snyder, Cory
85T-403OLY
85Water-23
86D-29RR
86D/Rook-15
86F-653R
86Maine-20
86Sf/Rook-18
87Classic/Up-110
87D-526
87D/OD-106
87F-260
87F/Excit-40
87F/Hottest-39
87F/Mini-103
87F/Slug-M5
87F/St-113
87Gator-28
87Kraft-17
87Leaf-157
87OPC-192
87Sf-24
87T-192
87T/Coins-24
87T/Gloss60-9
87T/GlossRk-16
87T/St-213
87ToysRUs-25
88Classic/Red-184
88D-350
88D/Best-224
88F-615
88F-622M
88F/SS-37
88F/St-21
88Gator-28
88KingB/Disc-10
88Leaf-125
88OPC-169
88Panini/St-80
88RedFoley/St-83
88S-92
88S/YS/I-40
88Sf-29
88T-620
88T/Big-43
88T/Coins-27
88T/Gloss60-23
88T/St-208
88T/St/Backs-53
88T/UK-74
89B-89
89Classic-19
89D-191
89D-8DK
89D/Best-168
89D/DKsuper-8DK
89F-412
89F/Superstar-38
89OPC-80
89Panini/St-329
89S-52
89S/HotStar-6
89Sf-196
89T-80
89T/Big-175
89T/LJN-2
89T/St-210
89T/UK-73
89UD-170
89UD-679TC
90B-336
90D-272
90D/BestAL-47
90F-502
90KingB/Discs-12
90Leaf/I-187
90OPC-770
90Panini/St-56
90PublInt/St-568
90RedFoley/St-91
90S-10
90S/100St-28
90Sf-3
90T-770
90T/Big-221
90T/St-211
90UD-126
91B-357
91Classic/200-188
91Classic/II-T8
91D-288
91F-378
91F/Ultra-83
91Kodak/WSox-28
91Leaf/II-506
91OPC-323
91OPC/Premier-113
91Panini/FrSt-221
91RedFoley/St-88
91S-19
91S-695RF
91S/100SS-74
91S/RookTr-61T
91T-323
91T/StClub/II-488
91T/Tr-111T
91UD-123
91UD/Ext-724
92S/II-598
92UD-504
Snyder, Doug
86Osceola-24
87Osceola-9
88Visalia/Cal-158
88Visalia/ProC-100
89Orlan/Best-25
89Orlan/ProC-1327
Snyder, Frank
(Pancho)
21Exh-169
25Exh-38
26Exh-35
40PB-159
91Conlon/Sport-232
E120
E121/120
E121/80
E220
V61-94
W501-66
W515-44
W575
Snyder, Gene W.
59T-522
90Target-1076
Snyder, Gerald
52B-246
54B-216
55B-74
57T-22
Snyder, Jim
76Indianap-1MG
80OkCty
81OkCty/TCMA-23
88T/Tr-112MG
89T-44MG
Snyder, Randy
89Stockton/Best-17
89Stockton/Cal-170
89Stockton/ProC-382
89Stockton/Star-16
90Beloit/Best-13
90Beloit/Star-21
90Foil/Best-215
91Stockton/ClBest-14
91Stockton/ProC-3035
Snyder, Russ
60L-102
60T-81
61T-143
62Salada-206
62Shirriff-206
62T-64
63J-63
63P-63
63T-543
64T-126
65OPC-204
65T-204
66T-562
67T-405
68T-504
69MB-258
69OPC-201
69T-201
70McDon-6
70OPC-347
70T-347
71MLB/St-452
71OPC-653
71T-653
72MB-320
78TCMA-136
91Crown/Orio-431
Soar, Hank
55B-279ump
Soares, Todd
88Jaxvl/ProC-978
91Kissim/ProC-4196
Sobbe, William
81VeroB-19
Sobczyk, Bob
88Beloit/GS-11
89Boise/ProC-1993
Sodders, Mike
82Toledo-18
83Orlan-9
88Geneva/ProC-1642
89Peoria/Ko-10
91CharlK/LineD-142
91CharlK/ProC-1688
Sodders, Randy
89Wythe/Star-24
Soden, Frank
79Richm-9M
Soderholm, Eric
73OPC-577
73T-577
74OPC-503
74T-503
75OPC-54
75T-54
75T/M-54
76K-28
76OPC-214
76SSPC-223
76T-214
77T-273
78Ho-20
78K-32
78OPC-21
78T-602
79Ho-103
79OPC-93
79T-186
80T-441
81D-106
81F-92
81T-383
90Swell/Great-98
91LineD-6
91Swell/Great-85
Soff, Ray
81QuadC-23
83MidldC-22
84MidldC-9
86ArkTr-23
86Louisvl-26
87D-631
87F-309
87Louisvl-27
87OPC-96
87Smok/Cards-1
87T-671
88Portl/CMC-7
88Portl/ProC-662
89Portl/CMC-5
89Portl/ProC-216
90T/TVMets-61
90Tidew/CMC-10
90Tidew/ProC-544
91Tidew/LineD-568
91Tidew/ProC-2509
Sofield, Rick
77Visalia
79T-709R
80T-669R
81D-592
81F-563
81OPC-278
81T-278
82T-42
82Toledo-21
Softy, Mark
79WHave-16
80Wausau-9
Sohn, Young Chul
91Kissim/ProC-4184
Sohns, Thomas
80Water-16
Sojo, Luis
87Myrtle-29
88Myrtle/ProC-1189
88SALAS/GS-18
89Syrac/CMC-22
89Syrac/ProC-809
89Syrac/Team-21
90AAAGame/ProC-AAA3
90B-517
90F/Up-129
90Leaf/II-291
90OPC-594
90Syrac/CMC-18
90Syrac/ProC-580
90Syrac/Team-23
90T-594
91B-197
91D-579
91F-184
91F/UltraUp-U12
91Leaf/II-367
91OPC-26
91OPC/Premier-114
91S-342RP
91S/100RisSt-43
91S/RookTr-49T
91Smok/Angel-15
91T-26
91T/90Debut-146
91T/StClub/II-507
91T/Tr-112T
91UD-297
91UD/Ext-714
92D/I-302
92F-70
92S/I-127
92T-206
92UD-149
Solaita, Tony
75OPC-389
75T-389
75T/M-389
76A&P/KC
76OPC-121
76SSPC-143
76T-121
77T-482
78T-557
79T-18
80OPC-212
80T-407
Solano, Julio
83Tucson-11
84Cram/PCL-63
85F-363
85Mother/Ast-12
85T-353
86Pol/Ast-16
87Pol/Ast-18
88Mother/Sea-24
89Mother/Sea-26
Solano, Ramon
87Fayette-6
Solarte, Jose
88James/ProC-1912
Solimine, Joe
90Utica/Pucko-7
91SoBend/ProC-2861
Solis, Marcelino
59T-214
Solo, Julio
89Pac/SenLg-50
Solomon, Eddie
(Buddy)
74Albuq/Team-19
75OPC-624R
75T-624R
75T/M-624R
78T-598
79OPC-74
79T-156
80T-346
81D-16
81F-384
81T-298
82D-437
82F-498
82T-696TL
82T-73
90Target-754
Solseth, David
89Eugene/Best-12
90AppFox/Box-25
90AppFox/ProC-2099
91BBCity/ClBest-16
91BBCity/ProC-1402
Soltero, Saul
87Spokane-4
88Charl/ProC-1215
89AubAs/ProC-23
89River/Best-16
89River/Cal-31
89River/ProC-1406
89Wichita/Rock/Up-9
Solters, Julius
(Moose)
34DS-85
34G-30
38G-255
38G-279
39PB-78
40PB-126
41DP-71
91Conlon/Sport-285
R313
R314
V354-77
Soma, Katsuya

83SanJose-18
Somers, P.T.
N172
Sommer, David
89James/ProC-2144
90WPalmB/Star-21
91Wmsprt/LineD-642
91Wmsprt/ProC-291
Sommer, Joseph J.
N172
Sommers, Dennis
(Denny)
75Lafay
82BK/Indians-10
82BK/Indians-11
82BK/Indians-12CO
82Wheat/Ind
83Wheat/Ind-25
85Polar/Ind-xx
88Smok/Padres-27
90Padre/MagUno-22CO
Sommers, Joseph A.
N172
Sommers, Scott
86Elmira-22
88Lynch/Star-23
89NewBrit/ProC-623
89NewBrit/Star-19
Sonberg, Erik
85Cram/PCL-159
89Hagers/Best-18
89Hagers/ProC-267
Sondrini, Joe
91Augusta/ClBest-26
91Augusta/ProC-815
Songini, Michael
(Mike)
88Billings/ProC-1829
89Greens/ProC-421
90Erie/Star-24
Sonneberger, Steve
88Hagers/Star-20
Sontag, Alan
86Orlan-18
87Orlan-23
91PalmSp/ProC-2013
Soos, Charles
87Kinston-4
88Kinston/Star-20
Soper, Mike
83BurlR-11
86Colum-24
86Colum/Pol-23
90AS/Cal-52
90Reno/Cal-277
91CLAS/ProC-CAR20
91Kinston/ClBest-12
91Kinston/ProC-324
Sorce, Sam
83BurlR-22
83BurlR/LF-3
85Orlan-11
86Orlan-19
Sorensen, Lary
77Spoka
78T-569
79T-303
80OPC-84
80T-154
81Coke
81D-325
81F-519
81T-379
81T/Tr-831
82D-246
82F-128
82OPC-136
82T-689
82T/Tr-111T
82Wheat/Ind
83D-363
83F-418
83OPC-48
83T-48
83Wheat/Ind-26
84D-635
84F-549
84F/X-U109
84Mother/A's-14
84Nes/792-286
84Nes/792-546TL
84OPC-286
84T-286
84T-546TL
84T/St-259
84T/Tr-111T
85D-131
85F-434
85F/Up-U108
85SevenUp-42
86F-381
86T-744
87F/Up-U111
88Chatt/Best-20
90Swell/Great-63
Sorey, Ron
78Dunedin
Soriano, Hilario
77Clinton
Soriano, Tony
47Remar-24
Soroko, Mark
77Tucson
Sorrel, Mike
81Cedar-14
82CharR-3
Sorrell, Billy
66T-254R
67T-341R
71OPC-17
71T-17
Sorrell, Vic
33G-15
92Conlon/Sport-577
V355-21
Sorrento, Paul
87PalmSp-11
88PalmSp/Cal-110
88PalmSp/ProC-1450
89BBAmerAA/BProC-AA19
89Orlan/Best-1
89Orlan/ProC-1343
89SLAS-13
90B-421
90D-626
90Portl/CMC-25
90Portl/ProC-189
90S-647
90T/89Debut-119
90T/Tr-119T
90UD/Ext-784
91D-745
91OPC-654
91Portl/LineD-420
91Portl/ProC-1574
91S-796
91S/100RisSt-44
91T-654
91T/StClub/II-408
91UD-680
92D/II-752
92F-218
92T-546
Sosa, Elias
74OPC-54
74T-54
74T/St-109
75OPC-398
75T-398
75T/M-398
76OPC-364
76SSPC-558
76T-364
77T-558
78T-694
79T-78
80OPC-153
80T-293
81D-599
81F-151
81OPC-181
81T-181
82D-446
82F-208
82OPC-116
82T-414
82T/Tr-112T
83D-259
83F-342
83T-753
83T/Tr-107T
84F-313
84Nes/792-503
84T-503
87SanJose-18
89Pac/SenLg-8
89Sumter/ProC-1093
89T/SenLg-45
89TM/SenLg-97
90EliteSenLg-14
90Target-755
91Pac/SenLg-137
Sosa, Jose
73Cedar
74Cedar
76OPC-591R
76T-591R
78Charl
90Princet/DIMD-21
Sosa, Miguel
80Ander-24
81Durham-1
82Durham-9
85IntLgAS-3
85Richm-17
86Albany/TCMA-4
86Colum-25
Sosa, Sammy
87Gaston-29
88CharlR/Star-23
89BBAmerAA/BProC-AA29
89D/Best-324
89Tulsa/GS-25
89Tulsa/Team-24
90B-312
90Classic-140
90Coke/WSox-23
90D-489
90D/BestAL-104
90F-548
90HotRook/St-43
90Leaf/I-220
90OPC-692
90S-558
90S/100Ris-35
90S/YS/II-25
90Sf-81
90T-692
90T/89Debut-120
90T/Big-286
90TulsaDG/Best-31
90UD-17
91B-350
91Classic/200-60
91D-147
91F-136
91F/Ultra-82
91Kodak/WSox-25
91Leaf/II-321
91Leaf/Stud-38
91MajorLg/Pins-16
91OPC-414
91Panini/FrSt-316
91S-256
91T-414
91T/StClub/I-6
91UD-265
92D/II-740
92F-98
92S/I-258
92T-94
92UD-438
Sossamon, L. Timothy
(Tim)
86Cram/PCL-148
87CharWh-23
88Reading/ProC-870
90Jaxvl/ProC-1375
Soth, Paul
77AppFx
79AppFx-1
Sothern, Denny
90Target-1077
Sothoron, Allen
21Exh-170
92Conlon/Sport-523
E120
E126-11
R312/M
W573
Soto, Ed
86DayBe-26
87Gaston-14
Soto, Emison
91Elmira/ClBest-15
91Elmira/ProC-3286
Soto, Jose
86Geneva-25
Soto, Mario
77Indianap-21
78Indianap-9
78T-427
79Indianap-28
80T-622
81Coke
81D-63
81F-214
81T-354
81T/HT
82Coke/Reds
82D-103
82F-83
82F/St-19
82T-63
83D-248
83F-603
83OPC-215
83PermaGr/AS-18
83T-215
83T-351TL
83T/St-234
84Borden-36
84D-428
84F-483
84F/St-79
85FunFoodPin-61
84Nes/792-160
84Nes/792-756TL
84OPC-160
84Seven-13C
84T-160
84T-756TL
84T/Gloss22-21
84T/St-51
85D-184
85D-19DK
85D/AAS-3
85D/DKsuper-19
85F-552
85F/LimEd-36
85F/St-116
85F/St-86
85GenMills-11
85Indianap-31
85Leaf-19DK
85OPC-131
85Seven-13G
85T-495
85T/Gloss40-37
85T/St-46
85T/Super-21
86D-184
86F-192
86F/Mini-41
86F/Slug-36
86F/St-114
86Leaf-119
86OPC-28
86Sf-168
86T-725
86T/Mini-42
86T/St-136
86TexGold-36
87D-82
87F-214
87Leaf-140
87OPC-11
87T-517
88T-666
88T/Big-120
89S-588
Soto, Max
86GlenF-22
Soto, Miguel
84Savan-24
Soto, Ozzie
85Cedar-13
86Tampa-21
Soto, Rafael
90Hunting/ProC-3294
91Peoria/ClBest-27
91Peoria/ProC-1351
Soto, Tom
78Newar
79Holyo-10
81Vanco-23
Sottile, Shaun
89Pulaski/ProC-1898
90Sumter/Best-21
90Sumter/ProC-2431
91Durham/ClBest-22
Souchock, Steve
52B-235
52T-234
53B/Col-91
53Glen
54B-103
Southland, Kip
87Everett-8
Southworth, Bill
25Exh-39
27Exh-32
47TipTop
49Eureka-24
51B-207MG
80Pac/Leg-17
91Conlon/Sport-89
92Conlon/Sport-627
E120
E121/120
E126-10
W501-89
W502-118
W514-16
W572
W754
Souza, Brian
91Beloit/ClBest-7
91Beloit/ProC-2102
Souza, Mark
76Watlo
79Ogden/TCMA-17
80Ogden-10
81Tacom-22
Sovern, Jeff
76Indianap-8
78Indianap-25
Sowards, Van
83Clinton/LF-21
84Shrev/FB-20
Sowders, John
N172
Sowders, William J.
E223
N172
N403/Bos
N526
Spaan, Tony
90Elizab/Star-21
Spade, Robert
E254
M116
T206
Spagnola, Glen
83Cedar-5
83Cedar/LF-16
86Vermont-21
87Vermont-18
88ColAst/Best-4
89Calgary/CMC-10
89Calgary/ProC-527
89EastLDD/ProC-DD33
89Wmsprt/Star-21
Spagnuolo, Joe
87VeroB-3
Spahn, Warren E.
47TipTop
48B-18
48L-32
49B-33
49Eureka-25
49Royal-5
50B-19
50Drake-14
51B-134
51BR-B2
51T/RB-30
52B-156
52Dix
52NTea
52RM-NL22
52Royal
52T-33
52TipTop
53B/Col-99
53Dix
53Exh/Can-32
53JC-10
53NB
53RM-NL19
53SpicSpan/3x5-22
53SpicSpan/7x10-12
53T-147
54JC-21
54RH

54RM-NL11
54SpicSpan/PostC-17
54T-20
55Armour-20
55Gol/Braves-27
55JC-21
55RM-NL10
55SpicSpan/DC-16
55T-31
55T/DH-127
56T-10
56T/Hocus-A10
56T/Hocus-B12
56T/Pin-19
57SpicSpan/4x5-15
57T-90
58T-270
58T-494AS
59T-40
59T-571AS
60Bz-19
60Lake
60NuCard-63
60SpicSpan-22
60T-230M
60T-445
60T/tatt-49
61Bz-29
61NuCard-402
61NuCard-463
61P-101
61T-200
61T-47LL
61T-589AS
61T/St-47
62Bz
62Exh
62T-100
62T-312IA
62T-399AS
62T-56LL
62T-58LL
62T/bucks
62T/St-150
63Bz-5
63Exh
63F-45
63Salada-8
63T-320
63T/SO
64Bz-5
64T-3LL
64T-400
64T/Coins-160AS
64T/Coins-88
64T/S-31
64T/St-57
64T/SU
64T/tatt
64Wheat/St-43
65OPC-205
65T-205
73OPC-449CO
73T-449CO
79TCMA-3
80Pac/Leg-57
80Laugh/3/4/5-15
80SSPC/HOF
81Redwd-22
82CJ-3
82F/St-108M
83MLBPA/Pin-34
84West/1-19
86Sf/Dec-27
87Nestle/DT-32
88Pac/Leg-109
89D-588PUZ
89HOF/St-84
90CollAB-24
90HOF/St-68
90Pac/Legend-51
90Swell/Great-12
91K/3D-12
91Swell/Great-86
91T/Arc53-147
91WIZMets-372
Exh47
PM10/L-40
R346-20

Spain, Dan
78OrlTw

Spalding, Al G.
50Callahan
75F/Pion-4
80SSPC/HOF

Spalt, Paul
88Watertn/Pucko-24

Span, Brian
89CharRain/ProC-975
89Spokane/SP-15

Spangler, Al
60L-38
60Lake
60SpicSpan-23
60T-143
61P-114
61T-73
62J-157
62P-157
62P/Can-157
62Salada-196
62Shirriff-196
62T-556
62T/St-130
63F-39
63J-185
63P-185
63Pep
63T-77
64T-406
65OPC-164
65T-164
65T/E-53
65T/trans-70
66OPC-173
66T-173
68T-451
69MB-259
69T8-268
70T-714
72MB-321
74OPC-354CO
74T-354CO
78TCMA-166
78TCMA-171
89Smok/Ast-23

Spann, Tookie
88Bristol/ProC-1891
89Lakeland/Star-19
90Lakeland/Star-23

Spanswick, Bill
63MilSau-10
64T-287R
65T-356
78TCMA-147

Sparks, Donald
89PrWill/Star-19
90Albany/Best-18
90Albany/ProC-1042
90Albany/Star-17
90EastLAS/ProC-EL2
90Foil/Best-237
91ColClip/LineD-119
91ColClip/ProC-605

Sparks, Greg
86CharRain-23
88Huntsvl/BK-21
89AS/Cal-48
89Salinas/ProC-1819
90Albany/Best-19
90Albany/ProC-1043
90Albany/Star-18
90EastLAS/ProC-EL14
90Foil/Best-252
91CaroMud/LineD-117
91CaroMud/ProC-1095

Sparks, Joe
75Iowa/TCMA-18
81Omaha-1
82Omaha-25
83Omaha-24
86Indianap-3MG
87Indianap-4
88AAA/ProC-50
88Indianap/CMC-24
88Indianap/ProC-496
90T/TVYank-5CO
91Toledo/LineD-599MG
91Toledo/ProC-1946MG

Sparks, Steve
88Beloit/GS-24
89Stockton/Best-8
89Stockton/Cal-152
89Stockton/ProC-390
89Stockton/Star-11
91ElPaso/LineD-196
91ElPaso/ProC-2749
91Stockton/ProC-3031

Sparks, Tully
E107
E254
M116

Sparling, Don
85FtMyr-5
87Memphis-19
87Memphis/Best-14

Sparma, Joe
64T-512R
65T-587
66T-267
67OPC-13
67T-13
68T-505
69T-488
70MLB/St-69
70OPC-243
70T-243
88Domino-21

Sparrow, Chris
89Idaho/ProC-2024
90Utica/Pucko-8

Speake, Bob
56T-66
57T-339
58T-437
59T-526

Speaker, Tris
10Domino-111
11Helmar-4
12Sweet/Pin-6
12Sweet/Pin-6A
14CJ-65
14Piedmont/St-52
15CJ-65
16FleischBrd-88
21Exh-171
25Exh-87
26Exh-86
27Exh-64
28Yung-28
33G-89
40PB-170
48Exh/HOF
50Callahan
51T/CM
60Exh/HOF-22
60F-10
61F-79
61GP-309
63Bz-24
69Bz/Sm
72F/FFeat-32
72K/ATG-11
80SSPC/HOF
85Woolwth-34
86Conlon/1-30
87Nestle/DT-6
88Conlon/3-27
89HOF/St-41
90BBWit-72
90Swell/Great-45
91Conlon/Sport-44
91Swell/Great-140
92Conlon/Sport-422
92Conlon/Sport-591
D303
D327
D328-166
E106
E120
E121/120
E121/80
E122
E126-27
E135-166
E210-28
E220
E224
E254
E270/1
E300
E90/1
E91
E94
L1-131
M116
PM1-12
R312/M
R423-104
S74-3
S81-106
T201
T202
T205
T206
T207
T213/blue
T215/blue
T215/brown
T216
T3-36
V100
V354-29
W501-19
W502-28
W512-4
W514-102
W515-28
W516-5
W572
W573
W575
WG4-27
WG5-35
WG6-33

Speakes, Joey
88Pocatel/ProC-2097

Speakman, Tim
85Elmira-21

Speakman, Willie
91Belling/ClBest-14
91Belling/ProC-3669

Spear, Mike
88Butte-20

Spearman, Vernon
91Yakima/ClBest-1
91Yakima/ProC-4261

Spearnock, Mike
86Cram/PCL-99
87PalmSp-1

Speck, R. Cliff
80OkCty
82RochR-6
83RochR-9
86Richm-21
87Richm/Crown-39
87D-571
87Richm/TCMA-25
87T-269
88Colum/CMC-22
88Colum/Pol-11
88Colum/ProC-311

Speckenbach, Paul
64T-548R

Specyalski, Brian
88CapeCod/Sum-89
89BendB/Legoe-19
90Boise/ProC-3322

Speece, Byron
43Centen-22
44Centen-21
45Centen-23

Speed, Horace
75Phoenix-22
76Phoenix
76SSPC-112
77Phoenix
79T-438
80Richm-14

Speek, Frank
90Johnson/Star-24
91Savan/ClBest-11
91Savan/ProC-1652

Speer, V. Floyd
46Remar-18
47Remar-14
47Signal
48Signal
48Smith-18

Spehr, Tim
90Omaha/CMC-21
90Omaha/ProC-69
91AAAGame/ProC-AAA28
91B-298
91Omaha/LineD-346
91Omaha/ProC-1038
92Classic/I-84
92D/II-689
92F-674
92S/I-416
92T-342
92T/91Debut-166

Speier, Chris
72K-28
72OPC-165
72OPC-166IA
72T-165
72T-166IA
73OPC-273
73OPC-345KP
73T-273
73T-345KP
73T/Lids-49
74K-40
74OPC-129
74OPC-335AS
74T-129
74T-335AS
74T/DE-29
74T/St-110
75Ho-73
75Ho/Twink-73
75OPC-505
75T-505
75T/M-505
76Ho-82
76OPC-630
76SSPC-105
76T-630
77BurgChef-108
77OPC-53
77Pep-41
77T-515
78OPC-232
78T-221
79OPC-221
79T-426
80OPC-168
80T-319
81D-329
81F-153
81OPC-97
81OPC/Post-3
81T-97
81T/St-189
82D-366
82F-209
82F/St-32
82Hygrade
82OPC-198
82T-198
82T/St-58
82Zeller-8
83D-266
83F-298
83OPC-121
83Stuart-27
83T-768
83T/St-258
84D-523
84F-288
84Mother/Giants-22
84Nes/792-678
84OPC-328
84Stuart-27
84T-678
84T/St-95
85F/Up-U109
85SevenUp-28
85T-577
85T/Tr-111T
86F-382
86Gator-28
86OPC-212
86T-212
87D-392
87F-575
87F/Up-U112
87Mother/SFG-18
87T-424
87T/Tr-115T
88D-239
88F-96
88Mother/Giants-18
88S-493
88T-329
89D-532
89F-343
89Mother/Giants-18
89S-297
89T-94
89UD-206
90F-72
90OPC-753
90PublInt/St-82
90T-753

Spence, J. Bob
71OPC-186

71T-186
Spence, Samuel
77Watlo
78Watlo
Spence, Stan
49B-102
Exh47
Spencer, Edward
(Tubby)
C46-81
E220
E254
E96
T204
T206
W514-36
Spencer, Daryl
54B-185
56T-277
57T-49
58Hires-51
58SFCallB-22
58T-68
59T-443
60L-129
60MacGregor-24
60T-368
61P-173
61T-357
61T-451M
61T/St-95
62BB-20
62J-103
62P-103
62P/Can-103
62Salada-178A
62Salada-178B
62Shirriff-178
62T-197
62T/St-141
63FrBauer-27
63J-124
63P-124
63T-502
79TCMA-226
90Target-756
Spencer, George
52BR
52T-346
53T-115
55Gol/Giants-25
63MilSau-11
91T/Arc53-115
Spencer, Glenn Edward
33G-84
V354-37
Spencer, Jim
70OPC-255
70T-255
71MLB/St-358
71OPC-78
71T-78
71T/Coins-4
72MB-322
72OPC-419
72T-419
73OPC-319
73T-319
74OPC-580
74T-580
74T/St-239
75OPC-387
75T-387
75T/M-387
76OPC-83
76SSPC-268
76T-83
76T/Tr-83T
77BurgChef-79
77OPC-46
77T-648
78BK/Y-16
78OPC-122
78T-182
79BK/Y-17
79OPC-315
79T-599
80OPC-147
80T-278
81OPC-209
81T-435
81T/Tr-832
82D-265
82F-107
82F/St-127
82OPC-88
82T-729
82T/St-223
Spencer, John
88Elmira-25
89Elmira/Pucko-20
Spencer, Kyle
88Butte-10
89Gaston/ProC-1002
89Gaston/Star-22
90CharlR/Star-27
91CharlR/ClBest-11
91CharlR/ProC-1315
Spencer, Robert
90NewBrit/Best-27
Spencer, Roy
31Exh/4-31
33Exh/4-16
90Target-757
91Conlon/Sport-320
Spencer, Shane
90Tampa/DIMD-25
Spencer, Stan
91B-441
91Harris/LineD-270
91Harris/ProC-628
91Single/ClBest-84
Spencer, Tom
76Indianap-6
78Knoxvl
79Knoxvl/TCMA-25
80Tucson-15
81Tucson-13
86Pittsfld-22MG
88Gator-2CO
89Cedar/Best-25
89Cedar/ProC-917
89Cedar/Star-24
89Pac/SenLg-101
89T/SenLg-24
90Cedar/Best-13
90SanJose/Best-29MG
90SanJose/Cal-53MG
90SanJose/ProC-2026MG
90SanJose/Star-27MG
91CharWh/ClBest-24TR
91Kahn/Mets-51CO
Sperring, Rob
76OPC-323
76SSPC-320
76T-323
77T-514
78Charl
79Charl-16
Sperry, Chris
89Salem/Team-28
Spicer, Len
79Newar-22
Spicer, Robert
52Mother-61
Spiers, Bill
88Stockton/Cal-197
88Stockton/ProC-738
89D/Rook-5
89F/Up-40
89Pol/Brew-6
89S/Tr-82
89T/Tr-115T
89UD/Ext-745
90B-402
90Brewer/MillB-24
90Classic-134
90D-382
90ElPasoATG/Team-26
90F-337
90Leaf/I-203
90OPC-538
90Panini/St-376
90S-449
90S/100Ris-55
90S/YS/I-14
90Sf-206
90T-538
90T/89Debut-121
90T/Big-88
90T/JumboR-27
90ToysRUs-26
90UD-237
91Brewer/MillB-24
91D-310
91F-597
91F/Ultra-181
91Leaf/I-111
91OPC-284
91Panini/FrSt-207
91Panini/St-162
91Pol/Brew-21
91S-84
91T-284
91T/StClub/II-360
91UD-268
92D/I-364
92F-189
92S/I-218
92T-742
92UD-214
Spiers, Mike
90Salinas/Cal-145CO
Spiezio, Ed
65T-431R
66Pep/Tul
67OPC-128
67T-128
68T-349
69MLB/St-197
69T-249
70MLB/St-119
70T-718
71MLB/St-240
71OPC-6
71T-6
72MB-323
72OPC-504
72T-504
Spikes, Charlie
73OPC-614R
73T-614R
74OPC-58
74T-58
74T/DE-33
74T/St-169
75OPC-135
75T-135
75T/M-135
76OPC-408
76SSPC-531
76T-408
77T-168
78T-459
80T-294
81F-259
Spillner, Dan
75OPC-222
75T-222
75T/M-222
76OPC-557
76SSPC-119
76T-557
77Padre/SchCd-29
77T-182
78Padre/FamFun-30
78T-488
79T-359
80T-38
81F-392
81T-276
82D-411
82F-378
82OPC-1
82T-664
82Wheat/Ind
83D-137
83F-419
83OPC-278
83T-725
83T/St-59
83Wheat/Ind-27
84D-582
84F-550
84Nes/792-91
84OPC-91
84T-91
85Coke/WS-37
85F-528
85T-169
86D-122
86F-217
86T-423
91Everett/ProC-3935CO
Spilman, Harry
78Indianap-5
79Indianap-5
79T-717R
80T-677
81D-304
81F-209
81T-94
81T/Tr-833
82F-233
82T-509
82Tucson-11
83D-65
83F-467
83T-193
84D-258
84Mother/Ast-12
84Nes/792-612
84T-612
85Mother/Ast-19
85T-482
86T-352
87F-284
87Mother/SFG-16
87T-64
88D-607
88F-97
88Mother/Giants-16
88S-618
88T-217
89Tucson/CMC-18
89Tucson/ProC-199
89Tucson/JP-24
90Tucson/CMC-14
90Tucson/ProC-210
Spinks, Scipio
70OPC-492R
70T-492R
71MLB/St-92
71OPC-747R
71T-747R
72OPC-202
72T-202
73OPC-417
73T-417
74OPC-576
74T-576
75Iowa/TCMA-19
Spino, Tom
79QuadC-23
Spinosa, John
87WPalmB-28
Spires, Tony
90Everett/Best-19
90Everett/ProC-3135
91SanJose/ClBest-8
91SanJose/ProC-21
91Single/ClBest-113
Spitale, Ben
87BurlEx-12
Spivey, Jim
90Johnson/Star-25
91Savan/ClBest-13
91Savan/ProC-1655
Split, Lickety
90WinSalem/Team-26
Splitt, Steve
77BurlB
78Holyo
79Holyo-19
Splittorff, Paul
71OPC-247R
71T-247R
72OPC-315
72T-315
73OPC-48
73T-48
74OPC-225
74T-225
74T/DE-56
74T/St-190
75OPC-340
75T-340
75T/M-340
76A&P/KC
76OPC-43
76SSPC-163
76T-43
77BurgChef-64
77OPC-41
77T-534
78Ho-11
78T-638
79K-10
79OPC-90
79T-183
80OPC-214
80T-409
81D-342
81F-30
81F/St-95
81T-218
82D-464
82F-423
82OPC-126
82T-759
83D-286
83F-124
83T-316
84D-521
84F-360
84Nes/792-52
84T-52
84T/St-281
Spohrer, Al
31Exh/4-1
33G-161
35G-8L
35G-9L
92Conlon/Sport-602
R310
V353-94
Spoljaric, Paul
91StCath/ClBest-20
91StCath/ProC-3395
Spoolstra, Scott
88Clmbia/GS-20
Spooner, Karl
55Gol/Dodg-29
55T-90
55T/DH-19
56T-83
56T/Hocus-B20
56T/Pin-53P
79TCMA-238
90Target-758
Sposito, Gus
85SpokAT/Cram-19
Spradlin, Jerry
88Billings/ProC-1821
89Greens/ProC-413
90Cedar/ProC-2322
90CharWh/Best-10
91Chatt/LineD-170
91Chatt/ProC-1961
Sprague, Charles
N172
Sprague, Ed
69T-638
72OPC-121
72T-121
75OPC-76
75T-76
75T/M-76
76SSPC-230
Sprague, Ed Jr.
88T/Tr-113T
89B-252
89Dunedin/Star-16
89T/Big-40
90B-511
90Syrac/CMC-19
90Syrac/ProC-581
90Syrac/Team-24
91B-26
91Classic/I-90
91Classic/III-88
91D/Rook-14
91F/UltraUp-U63
91F/Up-U66
91Leaf/II-485
91S/ASFan-7
91S/RookTr-101T
91S/ToroBJ-26
91Syrac/LineD-518
91Syrac/ProC-2484
91T/StClub/II-387
91UD/FinalEd-47F
92D/I-187
92F-340
92S/100RisSt-52
92S/II-504
92T-516
92T/91Debut-167
92UD-242
Spratke, Ken
87Chatt/Best-12
88Memphis/Best-23
89Omaha/CMC-9
89Omaha/ProC-1719
Spratt, Greg
91SALAS/ProC-SAL31TR

Spratt, Henry
(Jack)
T207
Sprick, Scott
91Erie/ClBest-9
91Erie/ProC-4078
91Freder/ClBest-19
91Freder/ProC-2373
Spriggs, George
67T-472R
68T-314R
69T-662R
71MLB/St-431
71OPC-411
71T-411
Spring, Jack
62T-257
63T-572
64T-71
85SpokAT/Cram-20
Springer, Billy
(Steve)
84Jacks-22
85IntLgAS-13
85Tidew-16
85Tidew-17
86Tidew-27
87Tidew-11
87Tidew/TCMA-18
88Tidew/CANDL-12
88Tidew/CMC-21
88Tidew/ProC-1598
89Vanco/CMC-12
89Vanco/ProC-592
Springer, Dennis
88Bakers/Cal-260
89SanAn/Best-20
89TexLAS/GS-18
90Albuq/CMC-12
90Albuq/Trib-27
91SanAn/LineD-541
91SanAn/ProC-2973
Springer, Gary
83SanJose-6
Springer, Russell
87Anchora-27
88CapeCod/Sum-35
90LSUGreat-15
91FSLAS/ProC-FSL18
91FtLaud/ClBest-14
91FtLaud/ProC-2427
Springer, Steve
90ColoSp/CMC-18
90ColoSp/ProC-46
91Calgary/LineD-72
91Calgary/ProC-524
91T/90Debut-147
Sprinz, Joseph C.
48Sommer-28
49Sommer-22
Sproat, Ed
N172
Sproesser, Mark
81Redwd-18
82Redwd-13
Sproviero, Nick
91James/ClBest-19
91James/ProC-3544
Sprowl, Robert
(Bobby)
80Tucson-6
81T-82R
82T-441R
82Tucson-19
83ColumAst-21
Spurgeon, Fred
26Exh-87
Spurgeon, Scott
88AubAs/ProC-1948
89Ashvl/ProC-958
Spurlock, Robert
90Visalia/Cal-85BB
Squires, Mike
79T-704R
80T-466
81D-398
81F-349
81T-292
82D-39
82F-357
82F/St-188
82T-398
83D-495
83F-250
83T-669
83TrueVal/WSox-25
84D-404
84F-71
84Nes/792-72
84T-72
84TrueVal/WS-29
85D-501
85F-529
85OPC-278
85T-543
89Tor/Fire-25CO
90Tor/BlueJ-25CO
91Tor/Fire-6CO
St.Clair, Dan
83Omaha-8
84Omaha-18
St.Claire, Ebba
52B-172
52T-393
53B/BW-34
53JC-16
53SpicSpan/3x5-21
53T-91
54B-128
91T/Arc53-91
St.Claire, Randy
85D-575
85Indianap-19
86D-463
86F-261
86Indianap-15
86Leaf-229
86OPC-89
86T-89
87F/Up-U113
87OPC-366
87T-467
88D-426
88F-197
88OPC-279
88S-397
88T-279
89Portl/CMC-11
89Portl/ProC-213
89T-666
89UD-29
90OPC-503
90T-503
90Tucson/CMC-5
90Tucson/ProC-203
91Richm/LineD-443
91Richm/ProC-2568
92S/II-708
St.Claire, Steve
85Utica-23
86Jamestn-24
87BurlEx-11
St.John, Anthony
89SLCity-16
St.John, Rich
89Watertn/Star-28
90Reno/Cal-289TR
St.Laurent, Jim
85BurlR-15
86DayBe-27
87TexLgAS-17
88OkCty/CMC-23
88OkCty/ProC-39
89OkCty/CMC-17
89OkCty/ProC-1524
90TulsaDG/Best-7
St.Peter, William
(Bill)
88Geneva/ProC-1650
89CharWh/Best-6
89CharWh/ProC-1753
90Peoria/Team-12
91CharlK/LineD-143
91CharlK/ProC-1698
Stablein, George
80Hawaii-15
81Hawaii-15
81T-356R
82Hawaii-15
Stacey, Al
89Geneva/ProC-1874
90Erie/Star-25
Stack, William Edward
(Eddie)
90Target-759
T207
Stackhouse, Brian
86Macon-23tr
Stading, Greg
86PrWill-25
87Salem-6
Stadler, Jeff
78Cedar
Staehle, Marv
65OPC-41R
65T-41R
66OPC-164R
66T-164R
69T-394R
71LaPizza-11
71MLB/St-140
71OPC-663
71T-663
Stafford, Bill
61T-213
61T/St-199
62J-13
62P-13
62P/Can-13
62T-55LL
62T-570
63J-22
63Kahn
63P-22
63T-155
63T-331M
64T-299
65OPC-281
65T-281
WG10-21
WG9-22
Stafford, Gil
75BurlB
Stagg, Bob
47Centen-27
Staggs, Steve
78OPC-94
78T-521
Stahl, Charles
(Chick)
E107
Stahl, Garland
(Jake)
E224
E254
E270/1
E90/1
E91
L1-130
M116
S74-4
S81-105
T202
T204
T205
T206
T215/blue
T215/brown
T3-38
WG2-43
WG5-36
Stahl, Larry
66OPC-107R
66T-107R
69MB-260
69MLB/St-198
69T-271
69T/St-99
70MLB/St-120
70OPC-494
70T-494
71OPC-711
71T-711
72MB-324
72T-782
73OPC-533
73T-533
74OPC-507
74T-507
91WIZMets-373
Stahoviak, Scott
91Classic/DP-23
91FrRow/DP-25
92T-66DP
Staiger, Roy
75Tidew/Team-19
76OPC-592R
76SSPC-560
76T-592R
77T-281
78Cr/PCL-113
79Colum-2
80Colum-9
89Tidew/Candl-10
91WIZMets-374
Stainback, G. Tucker
34DS-52
44Yank/St-25
47Signal
90Target-760
Stairs, Matt
89James/ProC-2141
89WPalmB/Star-22
90WPalmB/Star-23
91Harris/LineD-271
91Harris/ProC-639
Stajduhar, Marty
90Mother/Rang-28TR
Staley, Gerald
(Gerry)
46Sunbeam
51B-121
51T/BB-7
52B-50
52NTea
52StarCal/L-81G
52T-79
53B/Col-17
53Hunter
53RM-NL24
53T-56
54B-14
54Hunter
55B-155
57T-227
58T-412
59T-426
60T-510
60T-57M
61P-29
61T-90
61T/St-130
79TCMA-40
89Kodak/WSox-5M
91T/Arc53-56
R423-98
Staley, Henry E.
N172
Stallard, Tracy
61T-81
62T-567
63T-419
64T-176
65OldLond-18
65T-491
66OPC-7
66T-7
91WIZMets-375
Stallcup, T. Virgil
49B-81
49Eureka-95
50B-116
51B-108
52B-6
52NTea
52T-69
53T-180
91T/Arc53-180
Staller, George
73OPC-136CO
73T-136CO
74OPC-306CO
74T-306CO
Stallings, George T.
15CJ-162
16FleischBrd-89
90HOF/St-21
90Target-761
D329-167
D350/2-169
M101/4-167
M101/5-169
M116
WG5-37
WG6-34
Stalp, Joe
83Cedar-10
83Cedar/LF-4
Stampel, Eric
86Lynch-21
Stamps, Jerry
75Cedar
Stanage, Oscar
11Helmar-37
12Sweet/Pin-31
14Piedmont/St-53
BF2-29
D303
D328-167
D329-168
D350/2-170
E106
E135-167
E90/1
M101/4-168
M101/5-170
M116
T202
T205
T206
T207
T216
W514-115
Stancel, Mark
86Cram/PCL-54
88Modesto-14
88Modesto/Cal-65
90Huntsvl/Best-11
Standaert, Jerry
90Target-762
Standart, Rich
75Shrev/TCMA-21
76Shrev
Standiford, Mark
87Anchora-28
89Salinas/Cal-139
89Salinas/ProC-1801
Standley, Don
75Water
Stanek, Al
64T-99
65T-302
66T-437
Stanfield, Kevin
77Visalia
79T-709R
79Toledo-5
Stanfield, Mike
88Clinton/ProC-713
Stanford, Don
89PrWill/Star-20
90A&AASingle/ProC-21
90Albany/Best-8
90Albany/ProC-1036
90Albany/Star-19
90Foil/Best-92
91Albany/ProC-1009
Stanford, Larry
89Oneonta/ProC-2106
90FSLAS/Star-43
90FtLaud/Star-19
91Albany/ProC-1010
Stange, Albert Lee
61Clover-25
62T-321
63T-246
64T-555
65T-448
66T-371
67OPC-99
67T-99
67T/Test/RSox-19
68T-593
69MB-261
69OPC-148
69T-148
70OPC-447
70T-447
71OPC-311
71T-311
72MB-325
73OPC-131CO
73T-131CO
74OPC-403CO
74T-403CO
89Pawtu/Dunkin-38CO
89Pawtu/ProC-692CO
90Pawtu/ProC-479CO
91WinHaven/ClBest-16CO
Stange, Kurt
87SLCity/Taco-1
88MidwLAS/GS-58
88Wausau/GS-10
89SanBern/Best-13
Stange, Tim

88Elmira-9
90LynchRS/Team-23
Stangel, Chris
84Everett/Cram-18
Stanhope, Chester D.
(Chuck)
86Hagers-19
87CharlO/WBTV-31
88RochR/Gov-25
89Hagers/Best-17
89Hagers/ProC-269
89RochR/CMC-2
90HagersDG/Best-28
Stanhouse, Don
73OPC-352
73T-352
75OPC-493
75T-493
75T/M-493
77K-32
77OPC-63
77T-274
78OPC-162
78T-629
79T-119
80Pol/Dodg-29
80T-517
81D-557
81F-121
81OPC-24
81Pol/Dodg-26
81T-24
90Target-763
91Crown/Orio-432
Stanicek, Pete
86Hagers-20
87CharlO/WBTV-1
88D-541
88D/Best-294
88D/Rook-15
88F-573
88French-17
88RochR/Team-22
88RochR/CMC-18
88RochR/ProC-205
88S-628
88T/Tr-114T
89B-14
89D-169
89F-622
89Hagers/Star-20
89OPC-317
89Panini/St-265
89S-236
89T-497
89T/Coins-52
89T/St-232
89ToysRUs-30
89UD-592
90HagersDG/Best-29
90RochR/ProC-717
91Crown/Orio-433
Stanicek, Steve
84Shrev/FB-21
86ElPaso-19
87Denver-27
88Denver/CMC-22
88Denver/ProC-1266
88F-174
89ScrWB/CMC-12
89ScrWB/ProC-717
90RochR/CMC-15
90ScranWB/CMC-16
90ScranWB/ProC-608
Staniland, Steve
77ArkTr
Stanka, Joe
58Union
Stankiewicz, Andy
87FtLaud-10
88Albany/ProC-1330
88EastLAS/ProC-5
89Albany/Best-15
89Albany/ProC-333
89Albany/Star-19
90AlbanyDG/Best-17
90ColClip/CMC-10
90ColClip/ProC-685
90T/TVYank-62
91ColClip/LineD-120
91ColClip/ProC-606
92T-179R
Stanky, Eddie
49B-104
49Eureka-26
50B-29
50Drake-22
51B-13
51T/CAS
51T/RB-48
52B-160
52BR
52RM-NL23
52T-76
53B/Col-49
53Exh/Can-9
53Hunter
54Hunter
54T-38MG
55B-238MG
55Hunter
55T-191MG
66T-448MG
67OPC-81MG
67T-81MG
68T-564MG
79TCMA-108
89Smok/Dodg-53
90Target-764
91T/Arc53-300
Exh47
R346-31
R423-105
Stanley, Bob
78PapaG/Disc-12
78T-186
79OPC-314
79T-597
80OPC-35
80T-63
81Coke
81D-456
81F-234
81OPC-296
81T-421
81T/HT
82Coke/Bos
82D-134
82F-307
82F/St-169
82OPC-289
82T-289
83D-386
83F-195
83OPC-242
83T-381TL
83T-682
84D-644
84F-409
84F/St-74
85FunFoodPin-81
84Nes/792-320
84OPC-320
84T-320
84T/St-220
85D-91
85Drake-42
85F-169
85OPC-204
85T-555
85T/St-215
86D-91
86F-359
86OPC-158
86Sf-169
86T-785
86T/St-253
87D-216
87D/OD-180
87F-47
87OPC-175
87RedFoley/St-18
87T-175
87T/St-245
88D-92
88D/RedSox/Bk-92
88F-367
88OPC-369
88Panini/St-23
88S-300
88T-573
89B-25
89D-421
89D/Best-233
89F-101
89S-383
89T-37
89T/St-258
89UD-411
90F-289
90PublInt/St-466
90UD-654
Stanley, Carl
90Geneva/Star-23
Stanley, Fred
72OPC-59
72T-59
74OPC-423
74Syrac/Team-25
74T-423
75OPC-503
75T-503
75T/M-503
76OPC-429
76SSPC-442
76T-429
77BK/Y-16
77T-123
78BK/Y-17
78T-664
79BK/Y-16
79T-16
80T-387
81D-585
81F-100
81T-281
81T/Tr-834
82D-449
82F-108
82Granny-15
82T-787
83D-197
83F-534
83T-513
89TM/SenLg-98
91Brewer/MillB-32
91Pac/SenLg-133
91Pac/SenLg-6
91Pol/Brew-x
Stanley, Kevin
83Butte-21
Stanley, Mickey
66T-198
67T-607
68OPC-129
68T-129
69MB-262
69MLB/St-54
69OPC-13
69T-13
69T/St-179
70MLB/St-214
70OPC-383
70T-383
71MLB/St-407
71OPC-524
71T-524
72MB-326
72OPC-385
72T-385
73OPC-88
73T-88
74OPC-530
74T-530
74T/St-180
75OPC-141
75T-141
75T/M-141
76OPC-483
76SSPC-372
76T-483
77T-533
78BK/T-21
78T-232
79OPC-368
79T-692
81Detroit-25
88Domino-22
89Swell-104
Stanley, Mike
86Tulsa-25
87D-592
87D/Rook-28
87F-647R
87OKCty-8
87Sf/Rook-45
87Smok/R-23
87T/Tr-116T
88D-259
88D/Best-223
88F-480
88Mother/R-11
88OPC-219
88Panini/St-199
88S-47
88Smok/R-11
88T-219
88T/St-238
88ToysRUs-29
89D-166
89F-533
89Mother/R-22
89OPC-123
89S-241
89Smok/R-31
89T-587
89T/St-244
89UD-579
90D-579
90Mother/Rang-20
90OPC-92
90T-92
90TulsaDG/Best-6
91Mother/Rang-20
91OPC-409
91S-92
91T-409
91T/StClub/II-526
92D/II-582
92S/II-549
Stanley, Tim
87Anchora-29
88James/ProC-1919
Stansberry
E254
Stantiago, Ramon
90Gaston/Best-29MG
Stanton, Leroy
(Lee)
72OPC-141R
72T-141R
73OPC-18
73T-18
74OPC-594
74T-594
75K-12
75OPC-342
75T-342
75T/M-342
76Ho-39
76Ho/Twink-39
76OPC-152
76SSPC-204
76T-152
77T-226
78Ho-60
78OPC-123
78T-447
79OPC-275
79T-533
87Myrtle-9
88Myrtle/ProC-1180
89Myrtle/ProC-1451
90Myrtle/ProC-2794CO
91Myrtle/ClBest-29CO
91Myrtle/ProC-2963CO
91WIZMets-376
Stanton, Michael Thomas
(Mike)
73Cedar
75Iowa/TCMA-20
78Syrac
81F-400
82D-285
82F-379
82T-473
82T/Tr-113T
83D-433
83F-486
83T-159
84F-619
84Mother/Mar-20
84Nes/792-694
84T-694
85D-562
85F-501
85Mother/Mar-16
85T-256
85T/St-343
Stanton, William Michael
(Mike)
89Greenvl/ProC-1166
89Greenvl/Star-22
89Greenvl/Best-14
90B-4
90Classic/Up-45
90D-508
90D/Rook-7
90F-596
90F/SoarSt-2
90OPC-694
90S-609RP
90S/100Ris-29
90S/YS/II-7
90T-694
90T/89Debut-122
90UD-61
91D-716
91F-705
91Leaf/II-491
91OPC-514
91S-468
91T-514
91T/StClub/II-413
91UD/Ext-749
92D/II-780
92F-372
92S/II-498
92T-788
92UD-653
Staples, Ken
81Wisco-1
82Wisco-3
Stapleton, David E.
(Dave)
86ElPaso-20
88D-521
88D/Rook-4
88Pol/Brew-43
89S-581
89UD-304
Stapleton, David L.
(Dave)
81Coke
81D-544
81F-236
81OPC-81
81T-81
81T/St-215
82D-208
82F-308
82F/St-76
82OPC-93
82T-589
82T/St-85
83D-200
83F-196
83OPC-239
83T-239
83T/St-35
84D-273
84F-410
84Nes/792-653
84OPC-249
84T-653
84T/St-221
85T-322
86T-151
87T-507
Stargell, Tim
89Wausau/GS-26
90Foil/Best-297
90SanBern/Best-24
90SanBern/Cal-108
90SanBern/ProC-2641
91Jaxvl/LineD-346
91Jaxvl/ProC-163
91Single/ClBest-109
Stargell, Willie
63IDL-21
63T-553R
64T-342
65Kahn
65T-377
66EH-8
66Kahn
66OPC-99M
66T-255
66T-99M
66T/RO-44
67Kahn
67OPC-140
67T-140
67T-266M
67T/Test/PP-22
67T/Test/PP-31
68KDKA-8
68OPC-86
68T-86

69MB-263
69MLB/St-188
69T-545
69T/St-89
70K-29
70MLB/St-107
70OPC-470
70T-470
70T/S-19
70T/SO
71K-68
71MLB/St-214
71OPC-230
71T-230
71T/Coins-123
71T/S-43
71T/tatt-8
72K-53
72MB-327
72OPC-343KP
72OPC-447
72OPC-448IA
72OPC-87LL
72OPC-89LL
72T-343KP
72T-447IA
72T-448IA
72T-87LL
72T-89LL
72T/Post-15
73K-25
73OPC-370
73T-370
73T/Comics-20
73T/Lids-50
73T/PinUps-20
74K-37
74Laugh/ASG-65
74OPC-100
74OPC-202LL
74OPC-203LL
74T-100
74T-202LL
74T-203LL
74T/DE-31
74T/Puzzles-11
74T/St-88
75Ho-135
75OPC-100
75T-100
75T/M-100
76Crane-58
76Ho-49
76Ho/Twink-49
76K-22
76MSA/Disc
76OPC-270
76SSPC-573
76T-270
77BurgChef-186
77Ho-27
77OPC-25
77Pep-64
77T-460
77T/CS-45
78Ho-11
78T-510
78Tastee/Discs-11
78Wiffle/Discs-71
79Ho-104
79OPC-22
79T-55
80K-25
80OPC-319
80T-610
80T/S-1
81D-12
81D-132
81F-363
81F/St-15
81K-11
81MSA/Disc-31
81OPC-127
81PermaGr/CC-14
81T-380
82D-639
82F-499
82F/St-106M
82KMart-37
82OPC-188IA
82OPC-372
82PermaGr/CC-5
82T-715
82T-716IA
83D-610
83D-8DK
83F-324
83F-634M
84West/1-6
85CircK-16
86Pol/Atl-8CO
87KMart-22
89HOF/St-27
89Kahn/Coop-10
89T/Gloss22-22
89T/LJN-61
90BBWit-4
91D-702PUZ

Stark, Clinton
61Union
62Pep/Tul
66Pep/Tul

Stark, George
83Kaline-12M

Stark, Jeff
87Spartan-4
88Spartan/ProC-1024

Stark, Matt
86Knoxvl-22
87Tor/Fire-29
90A&AASingle/ProC-47
90BirmB/Best-4
90BirmB/ProC-1113M
90Foil/Best-99M
91Classic/I-30
91D-747
91S-751RP
91Vanco/LineD-646M
91Vanco/ProC-1597M

Stark, Monroe
(Dolly)
39PB-106
40PB-117
90Target-765
T206

Starkovich, Paul
75SanAn

Starks, Bob
76QuadC

Starr, Charles
T201
T206
T213/brown

Starr, Dick
50B-191
51B-137

Starrette, Herm
64T-239
65T-539
74OPC-634CO
74T-634CO
78TCMA-194
86Pol/Brew-38C
88French-31CO
91Crown/Orio-434

Staton, David
88CapeCod/Sum-167
89Spokane/SP-1
90A&AASingle/ProC-148
90AS/Cal-1
90Foil/Best-6
90Riversi/Best-1
90Riversi/Cal-1
90Riversi/ProC-2617
91B-645
91Classic/200-182
91Classic/II-T44
91LasVegas/LineD-294
91LasVegas/ProC-246
91UD-66TP
92T-126R

Statz, Arnold
(Jigger)
21Exh-172
37Wheat
88MinorLg/Leg-9
90Target-766
E120
E126-33
V100
V117-16

Staub, Rusty
63Pep
63T-544R
64T-109
64T/Coins-96
64T/St-88
65T-321
66OPC-106
66T-106
66T-273M
67OPC-73
67T-73
67T/Test/SU-17
68Bz-14
68Coke
68Dexter-71
68T-300
68T/3D
68T/G-28
68T/Post-22
69Citgo-15
69Expos/Pins-7
69Fud's-11
69MB-264
69MLB/St-161
69NTF
69OPC/DE-20
69T-230
69T/DE-22
69T/decal
69T/S-48
69T/St-38
69Trans-39
70Expos/Pins-13
70MLB/St-70
70T-585
70T/CB
70T/S-41
71Bz
71Bz/Test-40
71LaPizza-12
71MD
71MLB/St-141
71MLB/St-575
71OPC-289
71OPC-560
71T-560
71T/Coins-111
71T/GM-35
71T/S-9
71T/tatt-7
72MB-328
74OPC-475WS
74OPC-629
74T-475WS
74T-629
75Ho-129
75OPC-90
75T-90
75T/M-90
76Crane-59
76MSA/Disc
76OPC-120
76SSPC-537
76T-120
76T/Tr-120T
77BurgChef-96
77Ho-82
77OPC-88
77Pep-29
77T-420
77T/CS-46
78BK/T-22
78OPC-188
78T-370
78Wiffle/Discs-72
79Ho-56
79OPC-228
79T-440
79T/Comics-7
80OPC-347
80T-660
81Coke
81F-629
81T-80
81T/HT
81T/Tr-835
82D-56
82F-536
82F/St-82
82OPC-270
82T-270
83D-350
83F-555
83OPC-1
83OPC-51SV
83T-740
83T-741SV
83T/St-14
84D-554
84D-6DK
84D/Champs-28
84F-597
84F/St-40
85FunFoodPin-84
84Nes/792-430
84Nes/792-702LL
84Nes/792-704LL
84OPC-224
84T-430
84T-702LL
84T-704LL
84T/Mets/Fan-6
84T/St-287A
85F-92
85F/St-50
85OPC-190
85T-190
86F-95
86Mother/Ast-6
86Sf-138M
86T-570
90Pac/Legend-52
90Swell/Great-91
91Swell/Great-87
91WIZMets-377

Stauffacher, Stuart
86BurlEx-21

Staydohar, Dave
90Boise/ProC-3328

Stearnes, Turkey
90Negro/Star-15

Stearns, Bill
83OKCty-1
86Tulsa-6MG

Stearns, Dan
N172

Stearns, Don
87SanBern-4

Stearns, John
75IntAS/TCMA-7
76OPC-633
76SSPC-546
76T-633
77BurgChef-140
77T-119
78T-334
79Ho-124
79OPC-280
79T-205RB
79T-545
80K-37
80OPC-41
80T-76
81D-35
81F-317
81OPC-255
81T-428
81T/So-96
81T/St-194
82D-434
82F-537
82F/St-89
82OPC-232
82T-743
83D-380
83D/AAS-25
83F-556
83OPC-212
83T-212
83T/St-264
84F-598
90Knoxvl/Best-9MG
90Knoxvl/ProC-1259MG
90Knoxvl/Star-24MG
91Knoxvl/LineD-374MG
91Knoxvl/ProC-1784MG
91WIZMets-378

Stearns, Norman
78Laugh/Black-4

Stearns, Randy
87SanBern-5

Steck, Dave
76QuadC

Stedman, Tom
75Lafay

Steed, Rick
90StCath/ProC-3473
91Myrtle/ClBest-11
91Myrtle/ProC-2945
91SALAS/ProC-SAL40

Steel, Ed
86Negro/Frit-48

Steele, Don
75Lafay

Steele, Tim
75Water

Steele, Walt
80BurlB-20

Steele, William
(Bill)
11Helmar-177
90Target-1078
T207

Steelman, Farmer
90Target-1080

Steels, James
82Amari-11
83Beaum-20
84Beaum-3
85Cram/PCL-125
86LasVegas-18
87Bohem-21
87D/Rook-50
88D-360
88F/Up-U64
88Mother/R-21
88OkCty/CMC-24
88OkCty/ProC-38
88T-117
90Indianap/CMC-15
90Indianap/ProC-306

Steen, Mike
76SanAn/Team-21

Steen, Scott
86Clearw-23

Steenstra, Kennie
90WichSt-32
91T/Tr-113T

Steevens, Morris
65T-521R
78TCMA-175

Stefan, Todd
91SLCity/ProC-3221

Stefani, Mario
89Bristol/Star-27
90Fayette/ProC-2407

Stefanski, Jim
82Durham-10

Stefaro, John
84D-622
85CharlO-5
87D-541
87F-652R
87T-563
88ColoSp/CMC-11
88ColoSp/ProC-1522
90HagersDG/Best-30
91Crown/Orio-435

Steffen, David
80Evansvl-4
81T-626R

Steffens, Mark
90Princet/DIMD-22
91Spartan/ClBest-27
91Spartan/ProC-912

Steger, Chip
77Tucson

Steger, Kevin
80SanJose/JITB-17
81Wausau-1
83Chatt-22

Stegman, Dave
79T-706R
82Colum-13
82Colum/Pol-23
84Nes/792-664
84T-664
84TrueVal/WS-28
85Syrac-31
85T-194
86Colum/Pol-24

Steigerwald, John
75Lafay

Stein, Bill
76OPC-131
76SSPC-146
76T-131
77Ho-136
77OPC-20
77T-334
78Ho-39
78OPC-147
78T-476
79Ho-18

79OPC-372
79T-698
80OPC-121
80T-226
81D-543
81F-605
81T-532
81T/Tr-836
82D-37
82F-331
82F/St-179
82T-402
82T/St-118
83D-594
83F-579
83Rang-1
83T-64
84F-429
84Nes/792-758
84Rang-1
84T-758
85D-621
85Rang-1
85T-171
86D-403
86T-371
88LitFalls/Pucko-26
89Clmbia/Best-22
89Clmbia/GS-1
89TM/SenLg-99
90SALAS/Star-46MG
91BendB/ClBest-28MG
91BendB/ProC-3710MG

Stein, John
86AppFx-24
87Bakers-9

Stein, Jose
91Boise/ClBest-11

Stein, W. Randy
79T-394
79Vanco-16
80Spokane-13
80T-613
81Spokane-24
82Iowa-24
83Iowa-10

Steinbach, Terry
84Madis/Pol-10
85Huntsvl/BK-16
86SLAS-10
87D-34RR
87D/Rook-26
87F-405
87Leaf-34RR
87Sf-118M
87Sf/Rook-22
87Sf/Rook-1
87T/Tr-117T
88Classic/Red-186
88D-158
88D/A's/Bk-158
88D/Best-78
88F-294
88Mother/A's-4
88OPC-44
88Panini/St-166
88S-82
88S/YS/I-16
88Sf-174
88T-551
88T/Big-39
88T/Coins-28
88T/JumboR-15
88ToysRUs-30
89B-193
89Cadaco-54
89Classic-69
89D-268
89D/AS-31
89D/AS-9
89D/Best-323
89D/PopUp-9
89F-22
89F-634M
89KMart/DT-19
89Mother/A's-3
89OPC-304
89Panini/St-236AS
89Panini/St-419
89S-365
89Sf-119
89T-725
89T/Big-80
89T/Gloss22-9
89T/St-152
89T/St-165
89UD-256
90B-456
90Classic/Up-46
90D-268
90D-637AS
90D/BestAL-137
90F-20
90F/BB-38
90F/WS-3
90F/WS-7
90Leaf/I-252
90MLBPA/Pins-115
90Mother/A's-3
90OPC-145
90Panini/St-143
90Panini/St-205
90PublInt/St-315
90S-162
90S-693DT
90S/100St-55
90Sf-33
90T-145
90T/Big-118
90T/Gloss22-20
90T/St-163AS
90T/St-186
90UD-246
90Woolwth/HL-28
91B-216
91D-329
91F-24
91F/Ultra-253
91Leaf/I-87
91Mother/A's-3
91OPC-625
91Panini/FrSt-191
91S-780
91Seven/3DCoin-11NC
91SFExam/A's-12
91T-625
91T/StClub/II-518
91UD-153
92D/I-104
92F-267
92S/I-440AS
92S/II-633
92T-234
92UD-473

Steinbach, Tom
85Beloit-9

Steinberg, David
83Wisco/LF-8

Steiner, Brian
88Gaston/ProC-1018
89Butte/SP-18
90Gaston/Best-15
90Gaston/ProC-2522
90Gaston/Star-23
91CharlR/ClBest-12
91CharlR/ProC-1316

Steinert, Paul
84Butte-22

Steinfeldt, Harry
12Sweet/Pin-92
90BBWit-57
E107
E254
E90/3
E91
E97
M116
S74-47
S74-70
T202
T204
T205
T206
T207
T215/blue
T215/brown
W555

Steinkamp, Mike
89SLCity-13RHP

Steinmetz, Earl
90Foil/Best-136
90Sumter/Best-22
90Sumter/ProC-2432
91Durham/ClBest-9
91Durham/ProC-1544

Steinmetz, Kevin
83Tampa-21

Steirer, Ricky
80ElPaso-4
81SLCity-12
82Spokane-8
84Cram/PCL-102

Stela, Jose
91Boise/ProC-3883
91QuadC/ClBest-13
91QuadC/ProC-2631

Stellern, Mike
82AubAs-4
85Osceola/Team-25

Stello, Dick
88TM/Umpire-60

Stelmaszek, Rich
70T-599R
73OPC-601R
73T-601R
74OPC-611
74T-611
75OPC-338
75T-338
75T/M-338
77Tucson
78Wisco
79Wisco-23

Stember, Jeff
78Cedar
81Phoenix-5
82Phoenix

Stemberger, Brian
82Knoxvl-9

Stemler, Andy
91Watertn/ClBest-11
91Watertn/ProC-3366

Stemmyer, William
N172

Stengel
N172

Stengel, Charles Dillon
(Casey)
16FleischBrd-90
21Exh-173
40PB-142
46Remar-10
47Remar-8
47Signal
47Smith-1
48Signal
48Smith-20
50B-217MG
51B-181MG
52B-217MG
52RM-AL1
53B/BW-39MG
53RM-AL1
58T-475AS
59T-383M
59T-552AS
60T-227MG
61NuCard-461
62T-29MG
63T-233MG
63T-43M
64T-324MG
64T-393M
65OPC-187MG
65T-187MG
72Laugh/GF-20
76Laugh/Clown-40
80Pac/Leg-47
80Laugh/FFeat-20
80SSPC/HOF
83D/HOF-37
85West/2-35
86Conlon/1-33
88Conlon/HardC-5
89Pac/Leg-218
89Smok/Dodg-28
89Swell-130
90BBWit-85
90HOF/St-60
90Swell/Great-40
90Target-767
91Conlon/Sport-37
91LineD-46
91Swell/Great-136
91T/Arc53-325MG
92Conlon/Sport-558
D327
D328-168
D329-169
D350/2-171
E135-168
E220
M101/4-169
M101/5-171
R312
R423-93
W514-113
W515-24
W575

Stenholm, Richard A.
77WHave
81Colum-1

Stenhouse, Dave
60HenryH-26
62T-592R
63F-30
63J-97
63P-97
63Salada-37
63T-263
63T/SO
64T-498
65T-304
78TCMA-141
84Syrac-26
85T-141FS
86Syrac-24
87Syrac-13
87Syrac/TCMA-11

Stenhouse, Michael
82Wichita-19
84D-29RR
84Indianap-30
84Stuart-26
85D-376
85F-411
85F/Up-U110
85OPC-282
85T-141FS
85T-658
85T/Tr-112T
86F-406
86OPC-17
86Pawtu-23
86T-17
87Toledo-19
87Toledo/TCMA-5

Stennett, Matt
86AubAs-24

Stennett, Rennie
72OPC-219
72T-219
73OPC-348
73T-348
74OPC-426
74T-426
74T/St-89
75Ho-131
75OPC-336
75T-336
75T/M-336
76Crane-60
76Ho-9
76Ho/Twink-9
76MSA/Disc
76OPC-425
76OPC-6RB
76SSPC-575
76T-425
76T-6M
77BurgChef-182
77Ho-101
77OPC-129
77T-35
78Ho-33
78OPC-25
78T-165
79OPC-365
79T-687
80Pol/Giants-6
80T-501
81D-72
81F-438
81OPC-257
81T-257
82D-563
82F-401
82OPC-84
82T-84
89Pac/SenLg-79
89T/SenLg-127
89TM/SenLg-100
90EliteSenLg-89
90HOF/St-82

Stenta, Jeff
91Erie/ClBest-10
91Erie/ProC-4079

Stento, Bernie
87Elmira/Black-28
87Elmira/Red-28

Stenz, Dan
90Boise/ProC-3314

Stepanov, Roman
89EastLDD/ProC-DD16

Steph, Rodney
91Princet/ClBest-9
91Princet/ProC-3514

Stephan, Todd
89Penin/Star-23
90CLAS/CL-3
90Freder/Team-24
91Hagers/LineD-247
91Hagers/ProC-2458

Stephans, Russell
81CharR-13
83Omaha-12
84Omaha-26
85D-42RR
86Omaha-24
86Omaha/TCMA-10

Stephen, Louis
(Buzz)
70OPC-533
70T-533

Stephens, B.F.
N172

Stephens, Bill
91Kissim/ProC-4197

Stephens, Bryan
46Remar-19
V362-11

Stephens, Carl Ray
87TexLgAS-31
88Louisvl-45
88Louisvl/CMC-19
88Louisvl/ProC-422
89ArkTr/GS-23
91Louisvl/LineD-248

Stephens, Darryl
82Redwd-14
83Nashua-15

Stephens, Gene
53T-248
56T-313
57T-217
58Hires-72
58T-227
59T-261
60T-363
61T-102
61T/St-105
62J-95
62P-95
62P/Can-95
62Salada-56
62Shirriff-56
62T-38
62T/St-59
64T-308
65T-498
90HOF/St-48
91Crown/Orio-436
91T/Arc53-248

Stephens, James W.
M116
T201
T204
T206

Stephens, Mark
91Beloit/ClBest-8
91Beloit/ProC-2103
91SLCity/ProC-3211

Stephens, Ray
89ArkTr/GS-23
89TexLAS/GS-21
90Louisvl/CMC-13
90Louisvl/ProC-405
90T/TVCard-65
91AAAGame/ProC-AAA22
91Louisvl/ProC-2918
91S-743RP
91T/90Debut-148
92D/II-764

Stephens, Reggie
91Spokane/ClBest-9
91Spokane/ProC-3963
91Waterlo/ClBest-23

91Waterlo/ProC-1270
Stephens, Ron
88Utica/Pucko-24
89Saraso/Star-22
89Star/Wax-60
90BirmB/Best-23
90BirmB/ProC-1393
90Foil/Best-50
91Vanco/LineD-647
91Vanco/ProC-1595
Stephens, Seth
91Fayette/ClBest-5
Stephens, Vern
47HomogBond-44
47TipTop
48L-161
49B-71
50B-2
50Drake-34
51B-92
51T/RB-4
52B-9
52RM-AL21
52StarCal/L-71D
52T-84
52TipTop
53T-270
54T-54
54Wilson
55B-109
56YellBase/Pin-30
91Crown/Orio-437
91T/Arc53-270
D305
Exh47
R423-94
Stephenson, Chester
(Earl)
72OPC-61R
72T-61R
75IntAS/TCMA-4
78RochR
79Tidew-25
86Hagers-21C
89Pac/SenLg-159
91Crown/Orio-438
Stephenson, Ed
76Baton
Stephenson, Gene
90WichSt-44
Stephenson, J. Riggs
21Exh-174
30CEA/Pin-9
31Exh/4-5
32Orbit/num-3
32Orbit/un-54
33DL-15
33Exh/4-3
33G-204
61F-140
80Pac/Leg-95
88Conlon/4-27
88Conlon/NatAS-19
91Conlon/Sport-218
92Conlon/Sport-441
R305
R308-170
R315-A34
R315-B34
R316
V100
V117-26
Stephenson, Jerry
65OPC-74R
65T-74R
66T-396
67T/Test/RSox-20
68T-519
69OPC-172
69T-172
71OPC-488
71T-488
90Target-768
Stephenson, John
64T-536R
66OPC-17
66T-17
67T-522
68OPC-83
68T-83
71OPC-421
71T-421
91Kodak/WSox-xCO
91WIZMets-379
Stephenson, Joseph
85Greens-11
Stephenson, Phil
83Albany-15
84Cram/PCL-88
85Cram/PCL-132
86Pittsfld-23
87Iowa-18
88Iowa/CMC-17
88Iowa/ProC-540
89D/Rook-36
90AlbanyDG/Best-14
90OPC-584
90S-642RP
90T-584
90T/89Debut-123
90WichSt-35
91F-545
91OPC-726
91S-138
91T-726
91T/StClub/II-420
Sterling, J.C.
N172
Sterling, Randy
75Tidew/Team-20
91WIZMets-380
Stetson, Mike
91AS/Cal-52
Stevanus, Mike
86Macon-24
87Salem-22
88Salem/Star-19
88Watertn/Pucko-11
89Augusta/ProC-502
Steve, Harry
83SanJose-26GM
86SanJose-19GM
89SanJose/Cal-237GM
Stevens, Charles
52Mother-39
53Mother-17
Stevens, Dale
90Hunting/ProC-3282
91Geneva/ProC-4214
91Pocatel/ProC-3782
Stevens, Edward Lee
(Ed)
47TipTop
48L-43
49B-93
49Eureka-173
52Park-25
90Target-769
Exh47
Stevens, J.H.
33SK-47
Stevens, John
89Johnson/Star-21
Stevens, John
55B-258ump
Stevens, Lee
86Cram/PCL-96
87PalmSp-12
88MidldA/GS-18
89AAA/CMC-44
89Edmon/CMC-21
89Edmon/ProC-554
89F/Up-U16
90AAAGame/ProC-AAA42
90B-300
90D-449
90Edmon/CMC-13
90Edmon/ProC-527
90F-145
91AAAGame/ProC-AAA15
91Classic/I-25
91D-754
91Edmon/LineD-170
91Edmon/ProC-1530
91F-327
91F/Ultra-53
91MajorLg/Pins-24
91OPC-648
91S-67
91S/100RisSt-82
91T-648
91T/90Debut-149
91T/StClub/I-293
91UD-573
92Classic/I-85
92D/II-460
92F-71
92S/I-372
92T-702
92UD-634
Stevens, Matt
89Batavia/ProC-1924
90Spartan/Best-8
90Spartan/ProC-2489
90Spartan/Star-20
91Clearw/ClBest-8
91Clearw/ProC-1619
Stevens, Mike
85PrWill-24
86PrWill-26
87Salem-2
Stevens, Paul
77DaytB
80WHave-7
Stevens, R.C.
58T-470
59T-282
61T-526
Stevens, Ray
87ArkTr-22
Stevens, Scott
89Utica/Pucko-23
90SoBend/Best-22
91Saraso/ClBest-10
91Saraso/ProC-1113
Stevens, Tony
80Elmira-22
Stevenson, Bill
85Spokane/Cram-22
86CharRain-24
88Wichita-29
Stevenson, John
78Newar
82Amari-3
84Shrev/FB-22
Stevenson, Stevie
V355-128
Stevenson, Tenoa
82Idaho-12
Steverson, Todd
89Alaska/Team-9
Steward, Charles
(Chuck)
88Fayette/ProC-1092
89Lakeland/Star-20
Steward, Hector
86NewBrit-23
Stewart, Brady
91AppFx/ClBest-20
91AppFx/ProC-1726
Stewart, Carl
88Billings/ProC-1826
90Billings/ProC-3221
91CharWh/ClBest-10
91CharWh/ProC-2887
Stewart, Dave
77Clinton
79Albuq-5
80Albuq-1
81Pol/Dodg-48
82D-410
82F-24
82Pol/Dodg-48
82T-213
83D-588
83F-222
83Pol/Dodg-48
83T-532
84D-343
84F-430
84Nes/792-352
84OPC-352
84Rang-31
84T-352
84T/St-360
85D-343
85F-569
85Rang-48
85T-723
86D-619
86F-453
86Phill/TastyK-48
86T-689
87D-648
87F-406
87Smok/A's-11
87T-14
87T/St-167
88Classic/Red-196
88D-472
88D/A's/Bk-472
88D/Best-99
88F-295
88F/BB/MVP-36
88F/Mini-48
88F/Slug-39
88F/St-57
88F/WaxBox-C14
88Leaf-217
88Mother/A's-3
88OPC-353
88Panini/St-164
88S-458
88Sf-162
88T-476
88T/Gloss60-33
88T/Mini-32
88T/Revco-29
88T/St-168
88T/UK-75
89B-188
89Cadaco-55
89D-214
89D/Best-99
89F-23
89F/Excit-39
89F/LL-36
89Mother/A's-6
89OPC-145
89Panini/St-415
89RedFoley/St-112
89S-32
89S-582M
89S/Mast-14
89Sf-23
89T-145
89T/Big-101
89T/Coins-53
89T/Gloss60-45
89T/Hills-27
89T/Mini-71
89T/St-163
89T/St/Backs-27
89T/UK-74
89UD-185
90B-449
90Classic/Up-47
90CollAB-18
90D-150
90D-6DK
90D-703AS
90D/BestAL-25
90D/Bon/MVP-BC3
90D/Learning-35
90D/Preview-5
90D/SuperDK-6DK
90F-21
90F/AwardWin-37
90F/BB-39
90F/BBMVP-38
90F/WaxBox-C26
90F/WS-8
90Holsum/Discs-14
90Leaf/I-81
90MLBPA/Pins-74
90Mother/A's-5
90OPC-270
90Panini/St-141
90Panini/St-198 M
90Publint/St-295
90Publint/St-316
90S-410
90S/100St-13
90S/McDon-23
90Sf-194
90Sunflower-16
90T-270
90T/Big-64
90T/Coins-29
90T/DH-63
90T/Gloss22-21
90T/Gloss60-4
90T/Mini-32
90T/St-164AS
90T/St-185
90T/TVAS-16
90Target-770
90UD-272
90Woolwth/HL-25
90Woolwth/HL-33
91B-225
91BBBest/Aces-16
91Classic/200-102
91Classic/II-T89
91CollAB-32
91D-102
91D-BC4
91F-25
91F/ProVF-4F
91F/Ultra-254
91F/WaxBox-4
91F/WS-6
91Leaf/II-417
91Leaf/Stud-107
91Mother/A's-5
91OPC-580
91OPC/Premier-115
91Panini/FrSt-199
91Panini/FrSt-355
91Panini/St-144
91Panini/St-4
91Panini/Top15-62
91Panini/Top15-71
91Panini/Top15-93
91RedFoley/St-90
91S-150
91S-702NH
91S-883DT
91S/100SS-24
91Seven/3DCoin-12NC
91SFExam/A's-13
91T-580
91T/CJMini/II-10
91T/StClub/I-1
91T/SU-32
91UD-127
91UD-28TC
91Woolwth/HL-24
92D/I-225
92F-268
92S/100SS-60
92S/II-580
92T-410
92UD-547
Stewart, Duncan
87Nashvl-25M
Stewart, Ed
83Clinton/LF-23
Stewart, Edward P.
(Bud)
48L-104
49B-173
50B-143
51B-159
52B-185
52Hawth/Pin-9
52T-279
Stewart, Glen
(Gabby)
46Remar
47Signal
Stewart, Hector
87Pawtu-11
87Pawtu/TCMA-10
89WinHaven/Star-22
Stewart, James F.
64T-408R
65T-298
66OPC-63
66T-63
67OPC-124
67T-124
70T-636
71MLB/St-70
71OPC-644
71T-644
72MB-329
72T-747
73OPC-351
73T-351
Stewart, Jeff
87Wichita-17
Stewart, Joe
77Visalia
Stewart, John
87Cedar-21
87Durham-13
89SLCity-30
91Salinas/ClBest-19
91Salinas/ProC-2245
Stewart, John F.
(Stuffy)
90Target-771
Stewart, Sammy
79T-206RB
79T-701R

80T-119
81D-474
81F-181
81OPC-262
81T-262
82D-457
82F-180
82OPC-279
82T-426TL
82T-679
83D-203
83F-74
83OPC-347
83T-347
84D-514
84F-22
84Nes/792-59
84T-59
84T/St-25WS
85D-148
85F-192
85Leaf-98
85OPC-213
85T-469
86D-270
86F-289
86F/Up-U107
86OPC-172
86T-597
86T/St-235
86T/Tr-103T
87D-658
87F-48
87T-204
88D-596
88F-616
88T-701
89Pac/SenLg-135
89Pac/SenLg-27
89TM/SenLg-101
90EliteSenLg-48
91Crown/Orio-439

Stewart, Tito
88NewBrit/ProC-905
89NewBrit/Star-5
90Pawtu/CMC-1
90Pawtu/ProC-462
90T/TVRSox-60
91Indianap/LineD-195
91Indianap/ProC-462

Stewart, Vernon
(Bunky)
55T-136
55T/DH-76

Stewart, Walter C.
(Lefty)
31Exh/4-30
33G-121
33G-146
35G-8I
35G-9I
91Conlon/Sport-243
R308-179
V353-75

Stiboro, Tom
80Batavia-13

Stickels, Bob
71MLB/St-527

Stieb, Dave
80OPC-42
80T-77
81D-582
81F-414
81OPC-5
81OPC/Post-22
81T-467
81T/St-142
82D-52
82F-622
82F/St-232
82OPC-380
82OPC-53TL
82OPC/Post-6
82T-380
82T-606TL
82T/St-250
83D-507
83D-9DK
83D/AAS-48
83F-441
83K-36
83OPC-130
83OPC-202TL
83PermaGr/AS-6
83T-130
83T-202
83T/Gloss40-25
83T/St-127
84D-71
84D/AAS-19
84F-167
84F/St-85
85FunFoodPin-75
84MiltBrad-26
84Nes/792-590
84Nes/792-606TL
84OPC-134
84OPC-289TL
84Seven-13E
84T-590
84T-606TL
84T/Gloss22-10
84T/Gloss40-24
84T/St-368
84Tor/Fire-28
85D-193
85D/HL-12
85F-117
85F/LimEd-37
85F/St-110
85F/St-91
85GenMills-23
85Leaf-251CG
85Leaf-54
85OPC-240
85OPC/Post-22
85Seven-14S
85T-240
85T/3D-20
85T/Gloss22-21
85T/Gloss40-40
85T/St-191
85T/St-356
85T/Super-22
85Tor/Fire-27
86Ault-37
86D-146
86D/AAS-55
86Drake-34
86F-642M
86F-70
86F/LL-43
86F/Mini-16
86F/Slug-37
86F/St-115
86Leaf-68
86OPC-353
86Sf-96
86T-650
86T/3D-27
86T/Gloss60-43
86T/Mini-36
86T/St-186
86T/Super-54
86Tor/Fire-29
86TrueVal-19
87D-195
87F-238
87Leaf-72
87OPC-90
87RedFoley/St-81
87T-90
87Tor/Fire-30
88D-148
88D/Best-284
88F-123
88Ho/Disc-17
88Leaf-80
88OPC-153
88Panini/St-215
88S-76
88T-775
88T/Big-172
88T/St-191
88Tor/Fire-37
89B-239
89Classic-49
89D-349
89D/AS-28
89D/Best-143
89F-244
89F/BBAS-40
89OPC-4
89Panini/St-463
89S-197
89Sf-35
89T-460
89T/Big-128
89T/St-194
89Tor/Fire-37
89UD-383
90B-505
90Classic-97
90D-87
90D/BestAL-127
90F-93
90Leaf/I-79
90OPC-320
90Panini/St-173
90PublInt/St-526
90S-201
90S/100St-89
90Sf-26
90Sunflower-7
90T-320
90T/Big-112
90T/Mini-44
90Tor/BlueJ-37
90UD-605
90USPlayC/AS-10C
91B-22
91BBBest/Aces-17
91Classic/I-89
91D-1DK
91D-551
91D-BC21
91D/SuperDK-1DK
91F-185
91F/Ultra-368
91F/WaxBox-9
91Leaf/I-96
91Leaf/Prev-26
91Leaf/Stud-137
91MajorLg/Pins-26
91OPC-460
91OPC/Premier-116
91Panini/FrSt-344
91Panini/FrSt-360
91Panini/St-160
91Panini/St-9
91Panini/Top15-64
91Pep/SS-4
91Post/Can-16
91RedFoley/St-89
91S-30
91S-707NH
91S/100SS-93
91S/ToroBJ-5
91T-460
91T/CJMini/II-32
91T/StClub/I-62
91Tor/Fire-37
91UD-106
92D/II-724
92F-341
92S/100SS-37
92S/II-656
92T-535
92UD-136
92UD-99CL

Stiegele, Rob
89Bluefld/Star-22
90Freder/Team-23

Stieglitz, Al
60T-144

Stigman, Dick
59T-142
60L-85
60T-507
61Clover-26
61T-77
62T-37M
62T-532
63T-89
64T-245
64T-6LL
65T-548
66T-512
78TCMA-162

Stigman, Lee
80Holyo-25
81Vanco-20

Stiles, Will
84LitFalls-1
86Columbia-24
87Lynch-16

Stillman, Royle
76OPC-594R
76SSPC-393
76T-594R
78T-272
79Ogden/TCMA-14
79Spokane-2
80Ogden-18
91Crown/Orio-440

Stillman, Sam
80WHave-18

Stillwell, Kurt
84Cedar-17
86F/Up-U108
86T/Tr-104T
86TexGold-11
87Classic/Up-142
87D-123
87F-215
87Kahn-11
87T-623
87T/GlossRk-17
87ToysRUs-26
88D-265
88D/Best-207
88F-248
88F/Up-U35
88Panini/St-276
88S-221
88S/Tr-4T
88Smok/Royals-23
88T-339
88T/Big-136
88T/Tr-115T
89B-120
89Classic-14
89D-322
89D/AS-29
89D/Best-63
89F-293
89OPC-217
89S-162
89S/YS/II-42
89T-596
89T/Big-161
89T/St-266
89Tastee/Discs-8
89UD-616
90B-376
90CedarDG/Best-6
90Classic/III-29
90D-120
90D/BestAL-106
90F-118
90Leaf/I-256
90MLBPA/Pins-106
90OPC-222
90Panini/St-79
90PublInt/St-356
90S-96
90T-222
90T/Big-293
90T/St-269
90UD-361
91B-307
91D-24DK
91D-520
91D/SuperDK-24DK
91F-571
91F/Ultra-157
91Leaf/I-2
91Leaf/Stud-70
91OPC-478
91Panini/FrSt-279
91Pol/Royal-21
91RedFoley/St-91
91S-295
91T-478
91T/StClub/I-189
91UD-587
92D/II-440
92F-170
92S/I-236
92T-128
92UD-329

Stillwell, Rod
90AppFox/Box-26
90AppFox/ProC-2104

Stimac, Craig
79Hawaii-4
80Hawaii-6
81T-356R
82Charl-13

Stinnett, Kelly
90Watertn/Star-20
91Collnd/ClBest-21
91Collnd/ProC-1488

Stinson, Gorrell R.
(Bob)
70OPC-131R
70T-131R
71MLB/St-285
71OPC-594R
71T-594R
72T-679R
74OPC-653
74T-653
75OPC-471
75T-471
75T/M-471
76OPC-466
76SSPC-166
76T-466
77T-138
78T-396
79Ho-79
79OPC-126
79T-252
80OPC-305
85SpokAT/Cram-21
90Target-772

Stipetich, Mark
75QuadC

Stirnweiss, George
(Snuffy)
39Exh
44Yank/St-26
47TipTop
48B-35
48L-95
49B-165
50B-249
51B-21
52T-217
Exh47

Stitz, John
88Watlo/ProC-669

Stitzel, Glenn
75IntAS/TCMA-19

Stivers, Pat
88Idaho/ProC-1849

Stobbs, Chuck
52T-62
53Briggs
53T-89
54T-185
55T-41
55T/DH-44
56T-68
56T/Pin-60P
57T-101
58T-239
59T-26
60T-432
61Clover-27
61P-94
61Peters-4
61T-431
61T/St-185
62Salada-90A
62Salada-90B
62Shirriff-90
79TCMA-101
81Chatt-19CO
82Chatt-24CO
91T/Arc53-89

Stock, Kevin
83BurlR-23
83BurlR/LF-22

Stock, Milt
21Exh-175
25Exh-14
52T-381CO
90Target-773
D327
D328-169
D329-170
D350/2-172
E120
E121/120
E121/80
E122
E135-169
E220
M101/4-170
M101/5-172
V100
V61-56
W501-77
W572
W575

Stock, Sterling
89StCath/ProC-2089

Stock, Wes
60T-481
61T-26
62T-442
63T-438
64T-382
65OPC-117
65T-117
67OPC-74
67T-74
70McDon-2CO
73OPC-179CO
73T-179CO
77T-597CO
78TCMA-139
78TCMA-154
91Crown/Orio-441
Stockam, Doug
88Durham/Star-19
89Greenvl/ProC-1165
89Greenvl/Star-23
89Greenvl/Best-16
90Greenvl/Best-15
90Greenvl/ProC-1127
90Greenvl/Star-18
Stocker, Bob
86Madis-24
86Madis/Pol-20
88Madis-23
89Huntsvl/Best-8
Stocker, Kevin
91FrRow/DP-10
Stocksdale, Otis
N300/SC
Stockstill, Dave
79Wausau-5
81Tulsa-5
82Tulsa-15
83OKCty-17
84OKCty-8
85OKCty-23
Stoddard, Bob
80Spokane-1
81Spokane-18
82SLCity-18
83T-195
84D-619
84F-620
84Mother/Mar-22
84Nes/792-439
84T-439
85Cram/PCL-90
85F-502
86LasVegas-19
87F-431
87Omaha-12
88Tacoma/CMC-10
88Tacoma/ProC-628
89Denver/CMC-11
89Denver/ProC-31
Stoddard, Tim
78RochR
80T-314
81D-475
81F-176
81OPC-91DP
81T-91
82D-131
82F-181
82T-457
83D-581
83F-75
83OPC-217
83T-217
84D-245
84F-23
84F/X-110
84Nes/792-106
84SevenUp-49
84T-106
84T/Tr-112
85D-144
85F-68
85F/Up-U111
85Mother/Padres-19
85OPC-393
85T-693
85T/Tr-113T
86D-406
86F-335
86T-558
87D-497
87F-116
87OPC-321
87T-788
88D-497
88D/Y/Bk-497
88F-222
88S-257
88T-359
89Pac/SenLg-182
89T/SenLg-37
89TM/SenLg-102
90EliteSenLg-30
91Crown/Orio-442
Stoeckel, Jim
87SanAn-3C
Stoerck, Scott
88Wausau/GS-23
89Wausau/GS-14
Stohr, Bill
90Princet/DIMD-23
Stoker, Mike
87Ashvl-14
88Durham/Star-20
89Durham/Team-20
89Durham/Star-20
Stokes, Gus
81Clinton-15
82Clinton-27
83Clinton/LF-1GM
Stokes, Randall
90Bristol/Star-23
91Fayette/ClBest-28
91Fayette/ProC-1169
Stokke, Doug
80Tucson-24
Stoll, Pete
83Spring/LF-1TR
84ArkTr-23
85Spring-23
Stoll, Rich
85Indianap-4
86Indianap-4
Stoltenberg, Scott
79Wisco-12
Stone, Bill
77Visalia
Stone, Brian
87Beloit-9
88Stockton/Cal-178
88Stockton/ProC-739
91ArkTr/LineD-46
Stone, Dave
88Watertn/Pucko-25
Stone, Dean
54T-114
55T-60
55T/DH-17
56T-87
57T-381
59T-286
62T-574
63T-271
79TCMA-65
91Crown/Orio-443
Stone, Eric
89Lakeland/Star-21
90B-348
90Toledo/CMC-11
90Toledo/ProC-150
91London/LineD-397
91London/ProC-1878
Stone, Fred
WG2-44
Stone, George H.
69T-627
70OPC-122
70T-122
71MLB/St-22
71OPC-507
71T-507
72MB-330
72T-601
73OPC-647
73T-647
74OPC-397
74T-397
75OPC-239
75T-239
75T/M-239
76OPC-567
76SSPC-557
76T-567
91WIZMets-381
Stone, George R.
12Sweet/Pin-55
E254
E90/1
E92
M116
S74-36
T205
T206
T3-119
Stone, George
86AppFx-25
Stone, H. Ron
66T-568R
68T-409R
69T-576R
70OPC-218
70T-218
71MLB/St-189
71OPC-366
71T-366
72T-528
Stone, Jeff
83Reading-20
84Cram/PCL-197
84F/X-U111
84Phill/TastyK-43
85CIGNA-8
85D-624
85F-266
85F/St-119
85Phill/TastyK-12
85Phill/TastyK-39
85T-476
85T/St-116
86D-259
86F-454
86KayBee-30
86Phill/TastyK-14
86Portl-21
86T-686
87D-309
87F-189
87Maine-11
87Maine/TCMA-19
87Phill/TastyK-14
87T-532
88D-482
88F-317
88OPC-154
88RochR/Gov-26
88T-154
88T/Big-146
89Mother/R-26
89OkCty/ProC-1510
89UD-486
90Pawtu/CMC-22
90Pawtu/ProC-475
90T/TVRSox-61
91Crown/Orio-444
91Pawtu/LineD-369
91Pawtu/ProC-52
Stone, John Thomas
(John)
33Exh/4-12
34G-80
35G-8H
35G-9H
37Exh/4-16
38Exh/4-16
81Detroit-41
91Conlon/Sport-289
R314
V354-89
Stone, Michael
77StPete
78Clinton
78LodiD
Stone, Shawn
84PrWill-21
Stone, Steve
82Amari-17
Stone, Steven M.
(Steve)
72OPC-327
72T-327
72T/Cloth-30
73OPC-167
73T-167
74OPC-486
74T-486
74T/Tr-486T
75OPC-388
75T-388
75T/M-388
76OPC-378
76SSPC-302
76T-378
77T-17
78OPC-46
78T-153
79OPC-115
79T-227
80T-688
81D-476
81F-170
81F/St-104
81K-58
81OPC-101
81T-520
81T-5LL
81T/So-49
81T/St-1
81T/St-249
81T/St-40
82D-357
82F-182
82F/St-144
82T-419
90Pac/Legend-63
90Swell/Great-27
91Crown/Orio-445
Stone, Toni
76Laugh/Clown-27
Stonecipher, Eric
91Everett/ClBest-23
91Everett/ProC-3911
Stoneman, Bill
68OPC-179
68T-179
69Expos/Pins-8
69OPC-67
69T-67
70MLB/St-71
70OPC-398
70T-398
71MLB/St-142
71OPC-266
71T-266
72MB-331
72OPC-95LL
72T-610
72T-95LL
73K-23
73OPC-254
73T-254
74OPC-352
74T-352
74Weston-26
Stoner, Lil
92Conlon/Sport-605
Stonikas, Bill
88AppFx/ProC-147
89BBCity/Star-24
Storey, Harvey
49B/PCL-15
Storke, Alan
E91
Story, Jonathan
91Utica/ClBest-14
91Utica/ProC-3256
Stottlemyre, Jeff
80SanJose/JITB-18
81LynnS-27
81Wausau-2
82LynnS-7
83Chatt-16
Stottlemyre, Mel Jr.
86Osceola-25
87ColAst/ProC-6
88Memphis/Best-1
89B-110
89B-261FS
90Leaf/II-310
90Omaha/CMC-7
90Omaha/ProC-66
90OPC-263
90T-263
91D-257
91OPC-58
91S-361RP
91S/100RisSt-23
91T-58
91T/90Debut-150
Stottlemyre, Mel
65OPC-133WS
65T-133WS
65T-550
66Bz-5
66T-224LL
66T-350
66T/RO-58
67Bz-5
67T-225
68OPC-120
68T-120
68T/3D
69Citgo-5
69MB-265
69MLB/St-79
69MLBPA/Pin-27
69NTF
69OPC-9LL
69OPC/DE-21
69T-470
69T-9LL
69T/DE-13
69T/decal
69T/S-25
69T/St-208
69Trans-28
70K-5
70MB-27
70MLB/St-250
70OPC-100
70OPC-70LL
70T-100
70T-70LL
70T/S-27
70T/SO
70Trans-13
71K-40
71MD
71MLB/St-500
71OPC-615
71T-615
71T/Coins-94
71T/S-10
71T/tatt-12
72K-50
72MB-332
72OPC-325
72OPC-492KP
72T-325
72T-492KP
73OPC-520
73Syrac/Team-26
73T-520
74OPC-44
74Syrac/Team-26
74T-44
74T/St-218
75OPC-183
75T-183
75T/M-183
88Kahn/Mets-30CO
88Pac/Leg-22
89B-261FS
89Kahn/Mets-30CO
90BBWit-15A
90BBWit-15B
90Kahn/Mets-30CO
90T/TVMets-6CO
91Kahn/Mets-30CO
WG10-22
Stottlemyre, Todd
86Ventura-25
87Syrac-11
87Syrac/TCMA-8
88D-658
88D/Rook-37
88F/Up-U68
88S/Tr-90T
88T/Tr-116T
88Tor/Fire-16
89B-242
89D-620
89F-245
89OPC-237
89Panini/St-460
89S-453
89S/HotRook-81
89S/YS/II-20
89T-722
89T/Big-298
89Tor/Fire-30
89UD-362
90D-669
90F-94
90Leaf/II-475
90OPC-591

90Panini/St-172
90PubInt/St-527
90S-554
90T-591
90T/Big-240
90Tor/BlueJ-30
90UD-692
91B-10
91Classic/III-89
91D-155
91F-186
91Leaf/I-227
91OPC-348
91Panini/FrSt-349
91S-39
91S/ToroBJ-6
91T-348
91T/StClub/II-564
91Tor/Fire-30
91UD-257
92D/I-263
92F-342
92S/I-74
92T-607
92UD-371

Stotz, Carl
90BBWit-87M

Stouffer, Blair
76SanAn/Team-22

Stout, Jeff
89Augusta/ProC-501

Stout, Tim
82Cedar-22

Stoval, Jerry
80Clinton-5

Stovall, DaRond
91Johnson/ClBest-12
91Johnson/ProC-3991

Stovall, George T.
10Domino-112
11Helmar-65
12Sweet/Pin-19A
12Sweet/Pin-19B
14CJ-11
15CJ-11
D303
E106
E254
E90/1
M116
T201
T202
T205
T206
T207
T213/blue
T216
WG5-38

Stovey, Harry
90Target-774
N172
N693

Stowe
N690

Stowe, Harold
62T-291

Stowell, Brad
91SoOreg/ProC-3844

Stowell, Steve
88Kenosha/ProC-1384
89Visalia/Cal-97
89Visalia/ProC-1444
90Foil/Best-304
90OrlanSR/Best-22
90OrlanSR/ProC-1083
90OrlanSR/Star-20
91OrlanSR/LineD-494
91OrlanSR/ProC-1848

Strahler, Mike
71MLB/St-116
71OPC-188R
71T-188R
72OPC-198R
72T-198R
73OPC-279
73T-279
74Albuq/Team-20
90Target-775

Strain, Joe
78Cr/PCL-7
79Phoenix
79T-726R
80OPC-280
80Pol/Giants-20
80T-538
81D-73
81F-458
81T-361
81T/Tr-837
82Iowa-9
82T-436
83OKCty-21
85Everett/II/Cram-18
86Cram/PCL-180
87Everett-12
89Everett/Star-30

Straker, Les
80Cedar-17
81Water-8
83Water-8
84Albany-19
85Orlan-20
86Toledo-21
87D/Rook-21
87Sf/Rook-46
87T/Tr-118T
88D-73
88F-24
88S-108
88T-264
89Portl/CMC-10
89Portl/ProC-219
89S-244
89T-101
89T/Big-90
89UD-83

Strampe, Bob
73OPC-604R
73T-604R

Strang, Sammy Nicklin
89Chatt/II/Team-21MG
90Target-776
E107
T206

Strange, Alan
W753

Strange, Don
89Pulaski/ProC-1895
90A&AASingle/ProC-94
90Foil/Best-305
90SALAS/Star-43
90Sumter/Best-24
90Sumter/ProC-2433
91Durham/ProC-1545

Strange, Doug
86FSLAS-45
86Lakeland-24
87GlenF-10
88Toledo/CMC-14
88Toledo/ProC-587
89Toledo/CMC-13
89Toledo/ProC-782
90D-535
90OPC-641
90S/100Ris-63
90T-641
90T/89Debut-124
90T/TVCub-60
90Tucson/CMC-16
90Tucson/ProC-211
91Iowa/LineD-219
91Iowa/ProC-1071

Strange, Keith
90SoBend/ClBest-5
90Utica/Pucko-9
91SoBend/ProC-2865

Strange, Kurt
88Wausau/GS-10
89SanBern/Cal-69

Stranski, Scott
80SanJose/JITB-19
81Spokane-3
82LynnS-8
85BuffB-24
86Hagers-22
87Memphis-14
87Memphis/Best-10
90HagersDG/Best-31

Strathairn, David
88Pac/8Men-14

Stratton, C. Scott
N172

Stratton, Drew
88Modesto-29
88Modesto/Cal-69

Stratton, Monty
80Pac/Leg-103

Strauss, Joseph
N172
N284

Strauss, Julio
90WinSalem/Team-23
91CharlK/LineD-144
91CharlK/ProC-1689

Strawberry, Darryl
82Jacks-21
83T/Tr-108T
83Tidew-28
84D-68
84Drake-29
84F-599
84F/St-104
85FunFoodPin-8
84Jacks/Smok-12
84Nes/792-182
84OPC-182
84Seven-17E
84T-182
84T/Gloss40-29
84T/Mets/Fan-7
84T/St-385YS
84T/Super-12
85D-312
85Drake-30
85F-631M
85F-93
85F/LimEd-38
85F/St-36
85Leaf-159
85OPC-126
85Pol/MetYank-M6
85Seven-13S
85T-278FDP
85T-570
85T/3D-9
85T/Gloss22-8
85T/Mets/Fan-8
85T/St-100
85T/St-179
85T/Super-30
86D-197
86D/AAS-5
86D/HL-24
86D/PopUp-5
86Drake-16
86F-632M
86F-96
86F/Mini-21
86F/Slug-38
86F/St-116
86KayBee-31
86Leaf-131
86OPC-80
86Quaker-16
86Sf-60M
86Sf-97
86Sf/Rook-48M
86T-80
86T/3D-26
86T/Gloss22-19
86T/Gloss60-11
86T/Mets/Fan-8
86T/St-150
86T/St-95
86T/Super-55
87BK-19
87Classic-3
87Classic/Up-122
87D-118
87D-4DK
87D/AAS-12
87D/DKsuper-4
87D/HL-42
87D/HL-49
87D/OD-128
87D/PopUp-12
87Drake-1
87F-23
87F-629M
87F-638M
87F/Excit-41
87F/LL-41
87F/Slug-40
87F/St-114
87F/WS-11M
87Jiffy-17
87KayBee-31
87KMart-32
87Kraft-26
87Leaf-4DK
87Leaf-68
87MSA/Discs-1
87OPC-379
87RedFoley/St-58
87Sf-20
87Seven-E13
87T-460
87T-601AS
87T/Board-33
87T/Coins-46
87T/Gloss22-8
87T/Gloss60-32
87T/HL-29
87T/Mets/Fan-7
87T/Mini-26
87T/St-103
87T/St-159
87Woolwth-29
88Bz-21
88Classic/Blue-209
88D-439
88D-BC20
88D/AS-34
88D/Best-182
88D/Mets/Bk-439
88D/PopUp-12
88Drake-3
88F-151
88F-637M
88F/AwardWin-40
88F/BB/AS-40
88F/BB/MVP-37
88F/Excit-39
88F/Head-4
88F/Hottest-41
88F/LL-40
88F/Mini-97
88F/RecSet-39
88F/Slug-40
88F/SS-38
88F/St-106
88F/TL-40
88FanSam-17
88Kahn/Mets-18
88KayBee-29
88KingB/Disc-8
88KMart-29
88Leaf-220
88MSA/Disc-17
88Nestle-18
88OPC-178
88OPC/WaxBox-L
88Panini/St-236M
88Panini/St-347
88S-360
88S/WaxBox-17
88S/YS/II-20
88Sf-155
88Sf/Gamewin-15
88T-710
88T/Big-253
88T/Coins-56
88T/Gloss22-19
88T/Gloss60-22
88T/Mets/Fan-18
88T/Mini-63
88T/RiteAid-7
88T/St-151
88T/St-96
88T/St/Backs-21
88T/UK-76
88T/WaxBox-L
89T/Ames-28
89B-387
89Bz-20
89Cadaco-56
89Classic-108
89Classic-150
89Classic-8
89T/Crunch-7
89D-147
89D/AS-34
89D/Best-40
89D/MVP-BC6
89D/PopUp-34
89F-49
89F-632M
89F/AS-10
89F/BBAS-39
89F/BBMVP's-36
89F/Excit-40
89F/Heroes-38
89F/LL-37
89F/Superstar-39
89F/WaxBox-C25
89Holsum/Discs-10
89Kahn/Mets-18
89KayBee-29
89KingB/Discs-15
89KMart/DT-28
89Nissen-10
89OPC-300
89Panini/St-140
89Panini/St-223
89Panini/St-231AS
89MSA/SS-3
89RedFoley/St-113
89S-10
89S/HotStar-50
89S/Mast-42
89Sf-205
89T-291TL
89T-300
89T-390AS
89T/Big-139
89T/Coins-26
89T/DH-18
89T/DHTest-1
89T/Gloss22-19
89T/Gloss60-8
89T/HeadsUp-6
89T/Hills-28
89T/LJN-10
89T/Mets/Fan-18
89T/Mini-28
89T/St-157
89T/St-98
89T/St/Backs-53
89T/UK-75
89Tetley/Discs-5
89UD-260
89UD-681TC
90B-141
90Classic-33
90CollAB-20
90D-235
90D/BestNL-80
90F-217
90F/AwardWin-38
90F/BB-37
90F/BBMVP-37
90F/LgStand-3
90F/LL-38
90HotPlay/St-43
90Kahn/Mets-18
90Leaf/I-250
90Mets/Fan-18
90MLBPA/Pins-13
90OPC-600
90Panini/St-302
90Post-10
90PubInt/St-145
90PubInt/St-273
90RedFoley/St-92
90S-200
90S/100St-15
90Sf-146
90Starline/LJS-21
90Starline/LJS-37
90T-600
90T/Ames-23
90T/Big-186
90T/DH-64
90T/Gloss60-7
90T/HillsHM-4
90T/St-91
90T/TVAS-56
90T/TVMets-33
90UD-182
90USPlayC/AS-13H
90WonderBrd-10
91B-382SLUG
91B-609
91Classic/200-177
91Classic/I-68
91Classic/I-99
91Classic/II-T73
91Colla/Strawb-Set
91D-408MVP
91D-696
91D/GSlam-13
91F-161
91F/ProV-12
91F/Ultra-171
91F/Up-U96
91JDeanSig-5
91Leaf/II-377
91Leaf/II-444CL

91Leaf/Stud-190
91Mother/Dodg-2
91OPC-200
91OPC-402AS
91OPC/Premier-117
91Panini/FrSt-164
91Panini/FrSt-85
91Panini/St-88
91Panini/Top15-10
91Pol/Dodg-44
91Post-7
91S-640
91S-691MB
91S-864FRAN
91S/100SS-62
91S/RookTr-16T
91Seven/3DCoin-14NE
91Seven/3DCoin-14SC
91T-200
91T-402AS
91T/StClub/II-301
91T/SU-33
91T/Tr-114T
91UD-245
91UD/SilSlug-SS9
91WIZMets-382
92Classic/I-86
92D/II-559
92F-471
92F/TmLIns-16
92S/100SS-55
92S/I-9
92T-550
92UD-174

Strawn, Fla
79Tucson-13
79Tulsa-5
80Charl-14

Strebeck, Rick
91Modesto/ClBest-15

Street, Charles
(Gabby)
10Domino-113A
10Domino-113B
11Helmar-46
12Sweet/Pin-64
12Sweet/Pin-64A
40PB-169
73F/Wild-16
88Conlon/5-27
92Conlon/Sport-652
E254
E91
M116
S74-41
T201
T202
T204
T205
T206
T207
T213/blue
T213/brown
T215/brown
T3-120

Street, Mickey
85Water-7

Streeter, Sam
88Negro/Duques-13

Strelitz, Len
79ArkTr-2

Stricek, Jim
86Modesto-23TR
90WinHaven/Star-28TR
91WinHaven/ClBest-27TR

Stricker, John
N172

Strickland, Bob
86Geneva-26
87CharWh-18
89WinSalem/Star-15

Strickland, Chad
91AppFx/ClBest-14
91AppFx/ProC-1720

Strickland, Dedrick
90Oneonta/ProC-3372

Strickland, George
52B-207
52T-197
54B-36
54DanDee
55B-192
55Gol/Ind-28
55Salem
56Carling-9
57Sohio/Ind-14
57T-263
58T-102
59Kahn
59T-207
60L-30
60T-63
63Sugar-16

Strickland, Jim
72T-778R
73OPC-122
73T-122
75OkCty
76SSPC-512

Strickland, Rick
88CapeCod/Sum-49
89Oneonta/ProC-2116
91FtLaud/ClBest-28
91FtLaud/ProC-2442

Stricklett, Elmer
90Target-777

Strijek, Randy
88CLAS/Star-17
88Hagers/Star-21
89Hagers/Best-20
89Hagers/ProC-265
89Hagers/Star-19
90Shrev/ProC-1452
90Shrev/Star-23

Striker, Jake
60T-169

Strincevich, Nick
47TipTop
V362-17

Stringer, Lou
47Signal
49B-183
50B-187
52Mother-38

Stringfellow, Thornton
(Bean)
86Greenvl/Team-19
87Richm/Crown-31
87Richm/TCMA-7
88Richm-19
88Richm/CMC-4
88Richm/ProC-13

Stripp, Joe
34DS-89
34G-46
35G-1G
35G-3E
35G-4E
35G-5E
90Target-778
R300
V354-91

Strobel, Craig
86Hagers-23TR
87Hagers-8TR
90Spartan/Best-30TR
90Spartan/Star-28TR

Strode, Lester
(Jim)
82FtMyr-19
84Memphis-14
85Omaha-7
86Omaha-25
86Omaha/TCMA-18
88Louisvl-46
89Wythe/Star-29CO
90Peoria/Team-32CO
91Peoria/ClBest-23CO
91Peoria/ProC-1360CO

Strohmayer, John
71OPC-232
71T-232
72T-631
73OPC-457
73T-457
91WIZMets-383

Strom, Brent
73OPC-612R
73T-612R
74OPC-359
74T-359
75OPC-643
75T-643
75T/M-643
76OPC-84
76T-84
77Padre/SchCd-30
77T-348
78T-509
80Tucson-20
81Albuq/TCMA-12
82Albuq-27
83Albuq-13
87Albuq/Pol-3CO
88AlaskaAS60/Team-11
88Albuq/ProC-251
89Albuq/ProC-60
90Tucson/ProC-220CO
91Tucson/LineD-622
91Tucson/ProC-2230CO
91WIZMets-384

Stromer, Rick
83Peoria/LF-11
85Huntsvl/BK-43

Strong, Garret
75Cedar

Strong, Joe
86Modesto-24
88CalLgAS-20
88Reno/Cal-274
89AS/Cal-41
89Reno/Cal-245

Strong, Kevin
91Elizab/ProC-4314

Strong, Steve
89Lakeland/Star-22

Stroud, Derrick
88Geneva/ProC-1649
89Peoria/Ko-11
90WinSalem/Team-9

Stroud, Ed
67T-598R
68OPC-31
68T-31
69MB-266
69MLB/St-108
69T-272
70MLB/St-286
70OPC-506
70T-506
71MLB/St-550
71OPC-217
71T-217
72MB-333

Stroud, Ralph
16FleischBrd-91
C46-58
M116
T201

Stroughter, Steve
78Cr/PCL-45
80Spokane-23
81Toledo-22
82T/Tr-114T

Strube, Bob
86Kenosha-22
87Visalia-5
88Visalia/Cal-162
88Visalia/ProC-101
89Visalia/Cal-99
89Visalia/ProC-1429

Strucher, Mark
82DayBe-25
83ColumAst-6
86Richm-22
87Richm/Crown-5
87Richm/TCMA-15

Struck, J.O.
N172

Struek, Randy
87Hagers-9

Strum, John
41DP-114

Strunk, Amos
14CJ-33
15CJ-33
16FleischBrd-92
D327
D328-170
D329-171
D350/2-173
E104
E120
E121/120
E121/80
E135-170
E270/1
M101/4-171
M101/5-173
M116
T207
T208
T222
W501-44
W573
W575

Stryffeler, Dan
82Spring-9
83Spring/LF-21
84ArkTr-3
86Louisvl-27

Stryker, Dutch
90Target-1081

Stuart, Marlin
52B-147
52T-208
53B/Col-120
54Esskay
91Crown/Orio-446

Stuart, Richard L.
(Dick)
59HRDerby-19
59Kahn
59T-357
60Armour-18
60Bz-6
60Kahn
60T-402
61Kahn
61NuCard-409
61P-127
61T-126
61T/St-71
62Bz
62J-169
62Kahn
62P-169
62P/Can-169
62Salada-120
62Shirriff-120
62Sugar-D
62T-160
62T/bucks
62T/St-180
63J-137
63P-137
63T-18M
63T-285
64T-10LL
64T-12LL
64T-410
64T/Coins-12
64T/Coins-122AS
64T/S-42
64T/St-51
64T/SU
64T/tatt
65OPC-280
65OPC-5LL
65T-280
65T-5LL
65T/trans-29
66T-480
66T/RO-75
90Target-779
91WIZMets-385
PM10/Sm-186

Stubberfield, Chris
86Cram/PCL-18

Stubbs, Franklin
83Albuq-1
84Cram/PCL-151
85Cram/PCL-175
85D-348
85F-386
85T-506
86D-592
86Pol/Dodg-22
86T/Tr-105T
87D-299
87D/OD-83
87F-455
87Mother/Dodg-13
87OPC-292
87Pol/Dodg-10
87Seven-W14
87T-29
87T/St-72
88D-218
88D/Best-331
88F-527
88Leaf-182
88Mother/Dodg-11
88OPC-198
88Panini/St-308
88Pol/Dodg-22
88RedFoley/St-84
88S-147
88T-198
88T/Big-112
88T/St-66
89D-321
89D/GrandSlam-9
89F-74
89Mother/Dodg-11
89Pol/Dodg-13
89S-599
89T-697
89T/Big-32
89UD-91
90D-615
90D/BestNL-143
90Leaf/II-425
90Lennox-24
90Mother/Ast-14
90OPC-56
90Pol/Dodg-22
90PublInt/St-19
90S-478
90S/Tr-40T
90T-56
90T/Tr-120TUER
90Target-780
90UD-550
91B-37
91Brewer/MillB-25
91D-99
91F-518
91F/Up-U34
91Leaf/II-277
91Leaf/Stud-77
91OPC-732
91Panini/FrSt-13
91Pol/Brew-22
91S-308
91S/RookTr-59T
91T-732
91T/StClub/II-461
91T/Tr-115T
91UD-168
91UD/Ext-718
92D/II-618
92S/I-292
92T-329
92UD-396

Stubing, Lawrence
(Moose)
76QuadC
80SLCity-18
81SLCity-25
82Spokane-24
84Cram/PCL-97
89T-444MG

Stuckeman, Al
75Lafay

Studeman, Dennis
87FtMyr-13
89AppFx/ProC-851

Stull, Walt
86Bakers-27
87SanBern-18

Stuper, John
82Louisvl-29
83D-621
83F-23
83T-363
84D-412
84F-337
84Nes/792-186TL
84Nes/792-49
84T-186TL
84T-49
85F/Up-U112
86F-193
86T-497
91Savan/ClBest-28CO
91Savan/ProC-1669CO

Stupur, Dan
89Salem/Team-29

Sturdivant, Dave
89PalmSp/Cal-33
89PalmSp/ProC-486
90PalmSp/Cal-211
90PalmSp/ProC-2582

Sturdivant, Tom
57T-34

58T-127
59T-471
60T-487
61T-293
62T-179
63IDL-22
63T-281
64T-402
91WIZMets-386

Sturgeon, Bob
47TipTop

Sturtze, Tanyon
91Madison/ClBest-2
91Madison/ProC-2133
91MidwLAS/ProC-MWL44

Stutzriem, Jerry
79Wausau-2

Su'a, Murphy
81BurlB-13

Suarez, Ken
66T-588R
68T-218
69OPC-19
69T-19
70OPC-209
70T-209
71MLB/St-383
71OPC-597
71T-597
72MB-334
72OPC-483
72T-483
74OPC-39
74T-39

Suarez, Luis
81Wisco-9

Suarez, Nelson
81Wisco-23

Such, Dick
70T-599R
71OPC-283
71T-283

Sudakis, Bill
69T-552R
70OPC-341
70T-341
71MLB/St-117
71OPC-253
71T-253
71Ticket/Dodg-17
72T-722
73OPC-586
73T-586
74OPC-63
74T-63
74T/St-240
74T/Tr-63T
75OPC-291
75T-291
75T/M-291
90Target-781
91WIZMets-387

Sudbury, Craig
90SoOreg/Best-9
90SoOreg/ProC-3430
91Madison/ClBest-3
91Modesto/ClBest-3
91Modesto/ProC-3089

Suder, Pete
50B-140
51B-154
52B-179
52T-256
53B/BW-8
54B-99
55B-6
R346-15

Sudhoff, John
E107

Sudhoff, William
WG2-45

Sudo, Bob
85Utica-5
86BurlEx-22
87Jaxvl-19
88Spring/Best-11

Suehr, Scott
83Peoria/LF-21
85MidldA-21

Sueme, Hal
43Centen-23
44Centen-22
45Centen-24
47Centen-28
47Signal

Suero, Williams
(William)
88Myrtle/ProC-1186
88SALAS/GS-17
89Dunedin/Star-17
90A&AASingle/ProC-61
90Foil/Best-44
90Knoxvl/Best-5
90Knoxvl/ProC-1249
90Knoxvl/Star-19
91B-8
91Syrac/LineD-519
91Syrac/ProC-2489

Suetsugu, Toshimitsu
87Miami-25

Sugden, Joseph
E107

Suggs, George
10Domino-114
11Helmar-119
12Sweet/Pin-105
14CJ-113
15CJ-113
M116
T202
T205

Suhr, Gus
31Exh/4-13
33CJ/Pin-21
33Exh/4-7
33G-206
34DS-56
35BU-187
35BU-41
35G-8K
35G-9K
37Exh/4-7
38Exh/4-7
39PB-83
40PB-94
R310
R314

Suigiura, Mamoru
87Miami-27

Sukeforth, Clyde
52B-227
52T-364
90Target-782

Sukla, Ed
66T-417R
75Phoenix-6

Sularz, Guy
78Cr/PCL-89
79Phoenix
80Phoenix-21
81Phoenix-15
83D-605
83F-273
83Phoenix/BHN-14
83T-379
84Cram/PCL-22
91Pac/SenLg-129

Sullivan, Brian
89Reno/Cal-246
90Johnson/Star-26
90Rockford/ProC-2690
91Niagara/ClBest-9
91Niagara/ProC-3649

Sullivan, Carl
87DayBe-2
88FSLAS/Star-49
88Tampa/Star-23
89Saraso/Star-23
90Saraso/Star-23
91Saraso/ClBest-25
91Saraso/ProC-1126
91Single/ClBest-303

Sullivan, Dan
86WinHaven-25
87WinHaven-9

Sullivan, Daniel C.
Scrapps

Sullivan, Dave
87Elmira/Black-3
87Elmira/Red-3

Sullivan, Frank
55B-15
55T-106
55T/DH-22
56T-71
56T/Pin-25P
57T-21
58Hires-58
58T-18
59T-323
60T-280
61P-55
61T-281
62T-352
63T-389
79TCMA-57

Sullivan, Glenn
88WinSalem/Star-18
89CharlK-10
90Iowa/CMC-15
90Iowa/ProC-327
91Iowa/LineD-220
91Iowa/ProC-1072

Sullivan, Grant
91Oneonta/ProC-4155

Sullivan, Haywood
57T-336
58T-197
59T-416
60T-474
61P-56
61T-212
62J-99
62P-99
62P/Can-99
62T-184
62T/St-60
63J-92
63P-92
63T-359

Sullivan, Jack
(Twin)
T3/Box-56

Sullivan, Joe
41G-22
R312
R314

Sullivan, John L.
V100

Sullivan, John P.
65T-593R
66T-597
67T-568
76Watlo-MG
84Tor/Fire-29CO
85Tor/Fire-28CO
86Tor/Fire-30CO
87Tor/Fire-31CO
88Tor/Fire-8CO
89Tor/Fire-8
90Tor/BlueJ-8CO
91Tor/Fire-8CO
91WIZMets-388

Sullivan, Marc
84Pawtu-20
86D-614
86T-529
87D-643
87D/OD-187
87OPC-66
87T-66
88S-271
88T-354

Sullivan, Martin J.
E223
N172
N284
N690/2

Sullivan, Michael J.
N172

Sullivan, Mike
81Water-9

Sullivan, Mike
89Batavia/ProC-1929
90Spartan/Best-9
90Spartan/ProC-2490
90Spartan/Star-21
91Clearw/ClBest-9
91Clearw/ProC-1620

Sullivan, Russell
53Glen

Sullivan, Sport
88Pac/8Men-27

Sullivan, William J.
11Helmar-16
61F-141
90Target-783
D329-172
D350/2-174
E107
E254
E270/1
E270/2
E300
E97
M101/4-172
M101/5-174
M116
T206
T207
T3-121
WG1-16

Sultea, Chris
91SLCity/ProC-3210

Summa, Howard Homer
25Exh-88
26Exh-88
29Exh/4-28
91Conlon/Sport-205
V117-6

Summers, Jeff
83SanJose-22
84CharlO-25
85CharlO-16

Summers, John
(Champ)
76OPC-299
76T-299
78Indianap-12
78T-622
79T-516
80OPC-100
80T-176
81D-130
81F-466
81OPC-27
81T-27
81T/So-24
81T/St-76
82D-81
82F-282
82F/St-154
82T-369
82T/Tr-115T
83F-274
83T-428
84F/X-U112
84Mother/Padres-25
84Nes/792-768
84T-768
84T/Tr-113T
85T-208
86Indianap-32
87Colum-6
89Colum/Pol-24CO
89Pac/SenLg-96
89TM/SenLg-103
90T/TVYank-6CO

Summers, Oron Edgar
(Ed)
09Buster/Pin-14
81Detroit-66
E104
E254
E270/1
E90/1
M116
S74-18
T201
T202
T205
T206
T213/blue
T215/blue
T215/brown

Summers, Scott
87Greens-9

Summers, Tom
86Tampa-22

Summers, William
55B-317ump

Sunday, Billy
E223
N172
N284
N403
WG1-63

Sundberg, Jim
75Ho-100
75OPC-567
75T-567
75T/M-567
76Ho-68
76OPC-226
76SSPC-260
76T-226
77BurgChef-23
77Ho-110
77OPC-185
77T-351
78BK/R-2
78Ho-79
78T-492
79Ho-97
79K-60
79OPC-53
79T-120
80OPC-276DP
80T-530
81D-385
81F-619
81OPC-95
81T-95
81T/HT
81T/St-133
82D-268
82F-332
82F/St-181
82OPC-335
82T-335
82T/St-240
83D-609
83D-7DK
83D/AAS-26
83F-580
83K-38
83OPC-158
83Rang-10
83T-665
83T/St-126
84D-178
84F-431
84F/X-U113
84Gard-18
84Nes/792-779
84OPC-251
84Pol/Brew-8
84T-779
84T/St-355
84T/Tr-114T
85D-89
85F-597
85F/Up-U113
85Leaf-78
85OPC-102
85T-446
85T/St-286
85T/Tr-114T
86D-277
86F-22
86Kitty/Disc-18
86Leaf-149
86NatPhoto-8
86OPC-245
86Sf-186M
86T-245
86T/St-15ALCS
86T/St-259
87Berg/Cubs-11
87D-280
87F-382
87F/Up-U114
87OPC-190
87T-190
87T/St-256
87T/Tr-119T
88D-488
88D/Cubs/Bk-488
88F-434
88S-244
88T-516
88T/Big-100
89B-227
89Mother/R-24
89Smok/R-32
89T-78
89T/Big-103
89UD-331
90Publnt/St-423

Sundberg, Richard
82Redwd-15

Sunderlage, Jeff
82Lynch-9
83Lynch-18

Sundgren, Scott
86BurlEx-23

Sundin, Gordie
91Crown/Orio-447
Sundra, Steve
40PB-122
Sunkel, Mark
88Alaska/Team-17
Sunkel, Tom
39PB-146
40PB-110
90Target-784
Sunker, Steve
78Clinton
Sunnen, Gene
88Watertn/Pucko-34
Surane, John
90Idaho/ProC-3250
Surhoff, B.J.
86Vanco-24
87Classic/Up-135
87D-28RR
87D/Rook-17
87F/Up-U115
87Leaf-28RR
87Pol/Brew-5
87Sf/Rook-23
87Sf/Rook-6
87T-216
88Classic/Blue-202
88D-172
88D/Best-277
88F-175
88Leaf-164
88OPC-174
88Panini/St-120
88Pol/Brew-5
88RedFoley/St-85
88S-22
88S/YS/I-8
88Sf-57
88T-491
88T/Big-22
88T/Gloss60-49
88T/JumboR-10
88T/St-202
88T/St/Backs-57
88ToysRUs-31
89B-137
89Brewer/YB-5
89Classic-25
89D-221
89D/Best-221
89F-197
89Gard-5
89OPC-33
89Panini/St-368
89Pol/Brew-5
89S-154
89Sf-208
89T-33
89T/St-200
89UD-343
90B-393
90Brewer/MillB-25
90D-173
90D/BestAL-78
90F-338
90Leaf/II-290
90MLBPA/Pins-84
90OPC-696
90Panini/St-93
90PublInt/St-505
90S-74
90T-696
90T/Big-198
90T/St-203
90UD-159
91B-44
91Brewer/MillB-26
91D-460
91F-598
91F/Ultra-182
91Leaf/I-42
91Leaf/Stud-78
91OPC-592
91Panini/FrSt-203
91Panini/St-169
91Pol/Brew-23
91S-477
91T-592
91T/StClub/I-206
91UD-254
92D/I-70
92F-190
92S/I-78
92T-718
92UD-120
Surhoff, Rich
85Cram/PCL-49
85Phill/TastyK-46
86D-42RR
86OKCty-22
88Iowa/CMC-10
88Iowa/ProC-529
Suris, Jorge
85Spokane/Cram-23
Surkont, Max
52B-12
52T-302
53B/Col-156
53JC-11
53SpicSpan/3x5-23
54B-75
54DanDee
55B-83
56T-209
57T-310
Surner, Ben
82Holyo-26
83Nashua-24
Susce, George
55B-320
55Rodeo
56T-93
57T-229
58T-189
59T-511
Susce, Steve
83AlexD-21
Sutcliffe, Rick
78Cr/PCL-51
80Pol/Dodg-43
80T-544
81D-418
81F-125
81OPC-191
81Pol/Dodg-43
81T-191
82F-25
82OPC-141
82T-609
82T/Tr-116T
82Wheat/Ind
83D-72
83F-420
83T-141
83T-497
83T-707
83T/St-20
83T/St-61
83Wheat/Ind-28
84D-338
84F-551
84F/St-87
84F/X-114
85FunFoodPin-32
84Nes/792-245
84OPC-245
84SevenUp-40
84T-245
84T/St-254
84T/Tr-115
85D-433
85Drake-43
85F-69
85F/LimEd-39
85F/St-89
85Leaf-139
85OPC-72
85Seven-14G
85SevenUp-40
85T-72
85T-720AS
85T/3D-29
85T/Gloss40-9
85T/St-35
85T/St-97
85T/Super-3
85ThomMc/Discs-43
86Cub/Unocal-18
86D-189
86Dorman-17
86F-383
86F/Mini-81
86F/Slug-39
86Gator-40
86Jay's-18
86Leaf-122
86Meadow/Stat-19
86OPC-330
86Sf-134M
86Sf-149M
86Sf-46
86Sf-56M
86Sf-70M
86Sf-72M
86T-330
86T/St-61
86TrueVal-18
87Berg/Cubs-40
87D-68
87D/OD-69
87F-576
87F/Slug-41
87OPC-142
87T-142
88Berg/Cubs-40
88Classic/Blue-224
88D-68
88D/AS-43
88D/Best-138
88D/Cubs/Bk-68
88Drake-31
88F-435
88F/AwardWin-41
88F/BB/AS-41
88F/BB/MVP-38
88F/Excit-40
88F/Hottest-42
88F/LL-41
88F/Mini-71
88F/RecSet-40
88F/SS-39
88F/St-81
88F/TL-41
88KMart-30
88Leaf-91
88OPC-372
88Panini/St-257
88RedFoley/St-86
88S-50
88Sf-27
88T-740
88T/Big-128
88T/Coins-57
88T/Mini-45
88T/Revco-9
88T/St-61
88T/St/Backs-27
88T/UK-77
89B-281
89D-223
89D/Best-138
89F-439
89Mara/Cubs-40
89OPC-394
89Panini/St-51
89S-407
89Sf-217
89T-520
89T/LJN-136
89T/St-52
89UD-303
90B-21
90Cub/Mara-20
90D-157
90F-43
90Leaf/I-6
90MLBPA/Pins-53
90OPC-640
90Panini/St-233
90PublInt/St-205
90S-450
90Sf-181
90T-640
90T/Big-38
90T/St-55
90T/TVCub-15
90Target-785
90UD-109
91B-430
91Cub/Mara-40
91D-462
91F-434
91OPC-415
91S-785
91T-415
91UD-473
92D/II-642
92F-393
92S/II-665
92UD-529
Sutcliffe, Terry
81VeroB-20
Suter, Bill
80OkCty
81OkCty/TCMA-18
Sutey, John
91Bristol/ClBest-10
91Bristol/ProC-3621
Sutherland, Darrell
66OPC-191
66T-191
68T-551
69T/St-59
91WIZMets-389
Sutherland, Gary
67T-587R
68OPC-98
68T-98
69Fud's-12
69T-326
70T-632
71LaPizza-13
71MLB/St-143
71OPC-434
71T-434
72MB-335
72OPC-211
72T-211
73OPC-572
73T-572
74OPC-428
74T-428
74T/Tr-428T
75Ho-146
75OPC-522
75T-522
75T/M-522
76OPC-113
76SSPC-364
76T-113
77Padre/SchCd-31
77T-307
Sutherland, Harry
WG7-54
Sutherland, Leo
77AppFx
79Knoxvl/TCMA-7
81D-42
81T-112R
82Edmon-11
82T-599
Sutko, Glenn
88Billings/ProC-1806
89Greens/ProC-420
90Cedar/Best-2
91B-668
91Chatt/LineD-171
91Chatt/ProC-1963
91MajorLg/Pins-72
91S-767RP
91Single/ClBest-216
91T/90Debut-151
92F-423
92S/100RisSt-98
Sutryk, Tom
87Penin-15
Sutter, Bruce
77T-144
78Ho-5
78K-48
78OPC-196
78T-325
79Ho-130
79K-1
79OPC-238
79T-457
80BK/PHR-11
80K-10
80OPC-4
80T-17
80T/S-32
81Coke
81D-560
81F-294
81F/St-80
81K-56
81OPC-9
81PermaGr/CC-24
81T-590
81T-7LL
81T/St-221
81T/St-32
81T/Tr-838
82D-372
82F-129
82F-631M
82F/St-28
82K-17
82OPC-260
82OPC-347AS
82Sqt-22
82T-168LL
82T-260
82T-347AS
82T/St-10
82T/St-130
82T/St-15
82T/St-94
83D-40
83D/AAS-41
83F-24
83K-37
83OPC-150
83OPC-151SV
83OPC-266AS
83PermaGr/CC-17
83T-150
83T-151SV
83T-407AS
83T-708LL
83T/Gloss40-40
83T/St-166
83T/St-187
83T/St-209
83T/St-284
84D-13DK
84D-534
84F-338
84F/St-70
85FunFoodPin-14
84Nes/792-709LL
84Nes/792-730
84OPC-243
84Ralston-24
84Seven-7C
84T-709LL
84T-730
84T/Cereal-24
84T/St-145
85D-109
85Drake-44
85F-241
85F/St-104
85F/Up-U114
85Ho/Braves-21
85Leaf-163
85OPC-370
85Pol/Atl-40
85Seven-4S
85Seven-5C
85Seven-5G
85Sportflic/Proto-3
85T-370
85T-722AS
85T-9RB
85T/3D-23
85T/Gloss40-22
85T/St-135
85T/St-172
85T/Super-9
85T/Tr-115T
85ThomMc/Discs-44
86D-321
86F-529
86F/Mini-106
86F/St-117
86Leaf-192
86Meadow/Stat-17
86OPC-133
86Pol/Atl-40
86Sf-47
86Sf-65M
86T-620
86T/St-37
86TrueVal-15
87F-530
87OPC-344
87RedFoley/St-125
87T-435
88T-155
89D-458
89F-603
89OPC-11
89Panini/St-39
89RedFoley/St-114
89S-425

89T-11
89T/Big-64
89T/LJN-91
89T/St-25
89T/WaxBox-M
89UD-414
90MSA/AGFA-19
90PublInt/St-125

Suttles, Mule
74Laugh/Black-30
86Negro/Frit-115
90Negro/Star-21

Sutton, Don
66T-288R
67T-445
68OPC-103
68T-103
69MB-267
69MLB/St-153
69OPC-216
69T-216
69T/St-50
70K-8
70MLB/St-59
70T-622
71K-31
71MLB/St-118
71OPC-361
71T-361
71T/Coins-145
71Ticket/Dodg-18
72MB-336
72T-530
73K-5
73OPC-10
73T-10
73T/Comics-21
73T/Lids-51
73T/PinUps-21
74OPC-220
74T-220
74T/DE-12
74T/St-50
75Ho-7
75Ho/Twink-7
75OPC-220
75T-220
75T/M-220
76Crane-61
76K-13
76MSA/Disc
76OPC-530
76SSPC-73
76T-530
77BurgChef-147
77Ho-70
77OPC-24
77Pep-62
77T-620
77T/CS-47
78Ho-70
78K-57
78OPC-96
78T-310
79Ho-92
79OPC-80
79T-170
80OPC-228
80Pol/Dodg-20
80T-440
81Coke
81D-58
81F-112
81F/St-59
81Sqt-16
81T-605
81T-7LL
81T/HT
81T/St-27
81T/Tr-839
82D-443
82F-234
82F/St-43
82K-21
82OPC-305
82OPC-306IA
82T-305
82T-306IA
83D-531
83F-47
83Gard-18
83OPC-145
83OPC-146SV
83Pol/Brew-21
83T-145
83T-146SV
84D-414
84D/Champs-41
84F-215
85FunFoodPin-86
84Gard-19
84Nes/792-35
84Nes/792-715LL
84Nes/792-716LL
84OPC-35
84Pol/Brew-20
84T-35
84T-715LL
84T-716LL
84T/St-300
85D-107
85D-16DK
85D/DKsuper-16
85F-598
85F/Up-U115
85Leaf-16DK
85Mother/A's-3
85OPC-172
85T-10RB
85T-729
85T/St-290
85T/St-7
85T/St-8
85T/Tr-116T
86D-611
86D/HL-16
86F-170
86F/LimEd-43
86F/Mini-35
86Leaf-236
86OPC-335
86Sf-130M
86Sf-175
86Smok/Cal-4
86T-335
87D-181
87F-626M
87F-93
87F/RecSet-37
87F/St-115
87Leaf-153
87OPC-259
87OPC/WaxBox-G
87Ralston-6
87Sf-156M
87Sf-99
87Seven-W11
87Smok/Cal-2
87Smok/Dodg-35
87T-673
87T/WaxBox-G
87T/HL-6
87T/St-183
87Woolwth-6
88D-407
88F-505
88Mother/Dodg-9
88Panini/St-37
88Pol/Dodg-20
88S-105
88Sf-213
88Smok/Dodg-30
88T-575
89S-400
89Smok/Dodg-78
89T/WaxBox-N
90Target-786

Sutton, Doug
89Bluefld/Star-23

Sutton, Ezra
E223
N172
N284
WG1-8

Sutton, Jim
82AppFx-4

Sutton, Johnny
74Gaston
79T-676
80Ogden-13

Sutton, Mark
83BurlR-24
83BurlR/LF-21

Sutton, Rico
80Utica-33
83Kinston/Team-25

Suzuki, Ken
88SanJose/Cal-129
88SanJose/ProC-121

Suzuki, Yasu
89Salinas/Cal-135
89Salinas/ProC-1814

Sveum, Dale
84ElPaso-24
85Cram/PCL-209
86D/Rook-37
86F/Up-U109
86Sf/Rook-4
86T/Tr-106T
86Vanco-25
87D-542
87D/OD-55
87F-358
87Leaf-156
87Pol/Brew-7
87T-327
87T/GlossRk-18
87T/St-309
87ToysRUs-27
88D-232
88D/Best-305
88F-176
88OPC-81
88Panini/St-126
88Pol/Brew-7
88S-120
88T-592
88T/Big-44
88T/St-199
89B-139
89Brewer/YB-7
89D-146
89F-198
89Gard-6
89OPC-12
89Panini/St-374
89Pol/Brew-7
89S-256
89S/YS/II-24
89T-12
89T/Big-126
89T/St-206
89UD-421
90Brewer/MillB-26
90ElPasoATG/Team-8
90OPC-739
90Pol/Brew-7
90PublInt/St-506
90T-739
90UD-499
91Brewer/MillB-27
91Pol/Brew-24
91S-814
92D/II-452
92F-191
92S/I-181
92T-478
92UD-498

Swacina, Harry
E270/1

Swaggerty, Bill
82RochR-7
83RochR-10
84RochR-17
85D-392
85F-193
85RochR-22
85T-147
86D-594
88Omaha/CMC-9
88Omaha/ProC-1498
91Crown/Orio-448

Swaggerty, Glenn
81QuadC-25

Swail, Steve
89Pulaski/ProC-1914
90BurlB/Best-9
90BurlB/ProC-2353
90BurlB/Star-25
91Durham/ClBest-11
91Durham/ProC-1549

Swain, Rob
86Watlo-26
87Kinston-18
88CLAS/Star-36
88Kinston/Star-21
89Canton/Best-26
89Canton/ProC-1303
89Canton/Star-20
90Canton/Best-11
90Canton/ProC-1301

Swain, Steve
82AubAs-16

Swain, Thayer
88Butte-21
90CharlR/Star-28

Swan, Craig
74OPC-602R
74T-602R
75Tidew/Team-21
76OPC-494
76SSPC-558
76T-494
77T-94
78T-621
79Ho-41
79OPC-170
79T-334
79T-7LL
79T/Comics-27
80OPC-1
80T-8
80T/S-41
81Coke
81D-155
81F-319
81OPC-189
81T-189
82D-589
82F-548
82T-592
83D-254
83F-557
83OPC-292
83T-292
83T-621TL
83T/St-262
84D-441
84F-600
84F/X-U115
84Nes/792-763
84T-763
84T/Tr-116T
89Tidew/Candl-9
91WIZMets-391

Swan, Russ
86Cram/PCL-8
88SanJose/Cal-138
88SanJose/ProC-118
89Shrev/ProC-1831
90B-224
90Phoenix/CMC-5
90T/89Debut-125
90T/Tr-121T
91CounHrth-22
91D-621
91F/Up-U57
91OPC-739
91T-739
91T/StClub/II-577
92D/I-382
92F-293
92S/I-281
92T-588
92UD-618

Swank, Ken
82CharR-18

Swank, Randy
91Everett/ClBest-4
91Everett/ProC-3924

Swann, Pedro
91Idaho/ProC-4341

Swanson, Art
56T-204

Swanson, Chad
88Kenosha/ProC-1386
89Kenosha/ProC-1078
90Visalia/Cal-57
90Visalia/ProC-2152

Swanson, Eric
82DayBe-16

Swanson, Evar
33G-195
34Exh/4-10
88Conlon/AmAS-23
92Conlon/Sport-393
R308-174

Swanson, Perry
82CharR-8

Swanson, Stan
72OPC-331
72T-331
72T/Cloth-31

Swartwood, Cyrus
N172

Swartz, Nick
84Omaha-7
85Omaha-3
86Omaha-26C
87Omaha-5
88Omaha/ProC-1500

Swartzbaugh, David
88CapeCod/Sum-66
89Geneva/ProC-1866
90Peoria/Team-28
91Peoria/ProC-1342
91WinSalem/ProC-2829

Swartzel, Parke
N172

Swartzlander, Keith
86Macon-25

Sweatt, George
86Negro/Frit-117

Sweeney, Bill
31Exh/4-18

Sweeney, D.B.
88Pac/8Men-13

Sweeney, Dennis
91Elizab/ProC-4301

Sweeney, Ed
11Helmar-47
11Helmar-81
14CJ-112
15CJ-112
E106
E270/1
E286
E90/1
M116
T201
T202
T205
T206
T213/blue
T216
T222
WG5-39
WG6-35

Sweeney, Jim
89Geneva/ProC-1873
90PeoriaUp/Team-U6

Sweeney, Mark
88CapeCod/Sum-59
91Boise/ClBest-15
91Boise/ProC-3898

Sweeney, Michael
89Idaho/ProC-2023
90Idaho/ProC-3258

Sweeney, Peter
N172

Sweeney, Robert
90Kissim/DIMD-26
91Kissim/ProC-4185

Sweeney, Roger
91Yakima/ProC-4262

Sweeney, William John
D303
E224
E90/1
M116
T204
T206
T207
T213/blue
T213/brown
T215/brown

Sweeney, William
(Bill)
53Mother-23

Sweet, Richard
78Padre/FamFun-31
78T-702R
79Hawaii-3
79OPC-341
79T-646
80Hawaii-20
81Tidew-1
83D-352
83F-487
83Nalley-6
83T-437
84D-196
84F-621
84Nes/792-211
84T-211

88Wausau/GS-1
89Osceola/Star-27
90ColMud/ProC-1361MG
90ColMud/Star-25MG
91Jacks/LineD-574MG
91Jacks/ProC-940MG
91WIZMets-392

Sweetland, Lester L.
29Exh/4-12

Swenson, Mark
82Clinton-31

Swenson, Mickey
82Clinton-30

Swepson, Dobie
86Clinton-23
88Pocatel/ProC-2095

Swepson, Lyle
84Everett/Cram-2

Swetonic, Steve
R310

Swiacki, Bill
79Albuq-4
80Albuq-5
81Albuq/TCMA-6
82Tacom-9

Swift, Bill
85T-404OLY
86D-562
86F-475
86Mother/Mar-16
86T-399
86T/Mini-46
87D-517
87F-597
87T-67
88F/Up-U61
88Mother/Sea-25
88T/Tr-117T
89F-560
89Mother/Sea-17
89OPC-198
89RedFoley/St-115
89S-219
89T-712
89T/St-228
89UD-623
90D-566
90F-526
90Mother/Mar-11
90OPC-574
90PublInt/St-442
90T-574
90Target-787
90UD-313
91CounHrth-12
91D-564
91F-462
91F/UltraUp-U53
91Leaf/II-380
91OPC-276
91S-123
91T-276
91T/StClub/II-372
91UD-498
92D/I-260
92F-294
92S/II-541
92T-144
92UD-620

Swift, Robert V.
(Bob)
47TipTop
49B-148
50B-149
51B-214
52B-131
52T-181
54T-65
60T-470C
81Detroit-42
W753

Swift, Weldon
78BurlB
79Holyo-23
80Holyo-11
81ElPaso-19

Swift, William V.
34G-57
39PB-129
R312
R313
R314

Swim, Greg
91Salinas/ClBest-29
91Salinas/ProC-2253

Swindell, Greg
86Sf/Rook-30
87D-32RR
87F-644M
87F/Up-U116
87Gator-21
87Leaf-32RR
87T-319
88D-227
88D/Best-280
88F-617
88F/Slug-41
88Gator-21
88Leaf-158
88OPC-22
88Panini/St-70
88S-154
88S/YS/II-39
88T-22
88T/Big-156
88T/St-210
89B-76
89Classic-61
89Classic/Up/2-195
89D-232
89D/Best-112
89F-413
89F/LL-38
89OPC-315
89Panini/St-320
89RedFoley/St-116
89S-282
89Sf-4
89T-315
89T/Big-68
89T/Coins-54
89T/Mini-52
89T/St-213
89T/UK-76
89UD-250
90B-325
90Classic/Up-48
90D-310
90D/BestAL-6
90D/Bon/MVP-BC24
90F-503
90F/AwardWin-39
90F/BBMVP-39
90HotPlay/St-44
90Leaf/I-206
90OPC-595
90Panini/St-59
90PublInt/St-569
90PublInt/St-606
90RedFoley/St-93
90S-230
90S/100St-11
90T-595
90T/Big-288
90T/DH-65
90T/St-214
90T/TVAS-32
90UD-574
90WonderBrd-15
91B-58
91Classic/200-101
91Classic/II-T0
91D-546
91F-379
91F/Ultra-117
91Leaf/I-6
91Leaf/Stud-49
91OPC-445
91S-110
91T-445
91T/StClub/II-428
91UD-236
92D/DK-DK23
92D/II-483
92F-124
92S/I-371
92T-735
92UD-336
92UD-95

Swindle, Allen
83Tampa-22

Swingle, Paul
89BendB/Legoe-10
90Boise/ProC-3312
91PalmSp/ProC-2014

Swingle, Russ
52Park-94

Swinton, Jermaine
90Ashvl/ClBest-23
91Ashvl/ProC-581
91Single/ClBest-77

Swisher, Steve
75OPC-63
75T-63
75T/M-63
76OPC-173
76SSPC-319
76T-173
77OPC-23
77T-419
78T-252
79T-304
80T-163
81T-541
81T/Tr-840
82T-764
83D-633
83Richm-12
83T-612
86Watio-27MG
87Wmsprt-18
88ColoSp/CMC-24
88ColoSp/ProC-1546
89Jacks/GS-20
90T/TVMets-62MG
90Tidew/CMC-27MG
90Tidew/ProC-560MG
91AAAGame/ProC-AAA50MG
91Tidew/LineD-574MG
91Tidew/ProC-2526MG

Swob, Tim
87Tampa-9

Swoboda, Ron
65T-533R
66OPC-35
66T-35
66T/RO-23
67OPC-186M
67T-186M
67T-264
67T/Test/SU-5
68Bz-13
68OPC-114
68T-114
68T/3D
68T/Post-17
69Citgo-18
69MB-268
69MLB/St-171
69MLBPA/Pin-57
69T-585
69T/St-70
69Trans-44
70MLB/St-83
70OPC-431
70T-431
70Trans/M-25
71MLB/St-166
71OPC-665
71T-665
72MB-337
72OPC-8
72T-8
73OPC-314
73T-314
91WIZMets-390

Swoope, Bill
77Clinton
78Clinton
79LodiD-13

Swope, Mark
91Single/ClBest-74
91Visalia/ClBest-10
91Visalia/ProC-1741

Sykes, Bob
77T-491R
79T-569
80T-223
81F-533
81T-348
82Colum-12
82Colum/Pol-38
82D-640
82F-130
82Nashvl-25
82T-108

Sylvester, John
77Cedar

Sylvia, Dave
75BurlB

Sylvia, Ronald
81Redwd-7
82Redwd-16
83Nashua-9

Syverson, Dain
85Water-25
86Water-24
87Wmsprt-1

Szczepanski, Joe
91Geneva/ClBest-20
91Geneva/ProC-4215

Szekely, Joe
83CharR-3
85VeroB-6
87SanAn-17
87TexLgAS-35
89Albuq/CMC-19
89Albuq/ProC-77
90Syrac/CMC-11
90Syrac/ProC-574
90Syrac/Team-25
91Richm/LineD-444
91Richm/ProC-2572

Szotkiewicz, Ken
71OPC-749
71T-749

Szymarek, Paul
81Shrev-12
82Phoenix

Szymczak, Dave
83Nashvl-24
84BuffB-13

Szynal, Jon
89Spartan/ProC-1031
89Spartan/Star-22

Tabacheck, Marty
V362-23

Tabaka, Jeff
86Jamestn-25
87WPalmB-5
88WPalmB/Star-23
89Reading/Best-7
89Reading/ProC-663
91Reading/LineD-520
91Reading/ProC-1371

Tabb, Jerry
78T-224

Tabeling, Bob
86Visalia-21

Tabler, Pat
77FtLaud
81Colum-16
82D-529
82Iowa-10
83D-552
83F-509
84D-536
84F-552
84Nes/792-329
84T-329
84T/St-252
84Wheat/Ind-10
85D-460
85F-456
85Leaf-76
85OPC-158
85Polar/Ind-10
85T-158
85T/St-250
86D-129
86F-594
86Leaf-52
86OhHenry-10
86OPC-66
86T-674
86T/St-212
87D-254
87D/OD-107
87F-261
87F/Slug-42
87Gator-10
87Leaf-182
87OPC-77
87Sf-66
87T-575
87T/Mini-52
87T/St-205
88D-219
88D/AS-17
88F-618
88F-633M
88F/Hottest-43
88F/Mini-20
88F/St-22
88F/Up-U36
88Gator-10
88OPC-230
88Panini/St-81
88RedFoley/St-87
88S-23
88S/Tr-22T
88Sf-205
88T-230
88T/Big-173
88T/St-204
88T/Tr-118T
89B-125
89D-326
89F-294
89KMart/Lead-19
89OPC-56
89Panini/St-359
89S-391
89Sf-172
89T-56
89T/Big-67
89T/St-6
89Tastee/Discs-3
89UD-233
89Woolwth-18
90D-444
90F-119
90OPC-727
90PublInt/St-357
90S-242
90Sf-218
90T-727
90T/Big-89
90UD-142
91B-28
91F/Up-U67
91Leaf/II-443
91OPC-433
91OPC/Premier-118
91S-811
91S/RookTr-22T
91S/ToroBJ-19
91T-433
91Tor/Fire-15
91WIZMets-393
92S/I-312
92T-333
92UD-203

Tabor, Greg
82BurlR-10
84Tulsa-19
85OKCty-28
86OKCty-23
87OKCty-21
88F-644R
88Iowa/CMC-18
88Iowa/ProC-548

Tabor, Jim
39PB-14
40PB-36
41DP-58
49B/PCL-33
92Conlon/Sport-542
R303/A

Tabor, Scott
83BirmB-15
86Omaha-27
86Omaha/TCMA-17

Tackett, Jack
(Jeff)
85Newar-5
87CharlO/WBTV-?
88CharlK/Pep-8
89RochR/CMC-17
89RochR/ProC-1645
90RochR/CMC-9
90RochR/ProC-706
91B-106
91RochR/LineD-469
91RochR/ProC-1906
92T/91Debut-168

Tafoya, Dennis
88Ashvl/ProC-1070
88AubAs/ProC-1951
89Osceola/Star-24
90ColMud/Best-24
90ColMud/ProC-1348
90ColMud/Star-23
91CaroMud/LineD-118
91CaroMud/ProC-1086

Tafoya, Rod

89Boise/ProC-1987
90Erie/Star-26
Taft, Dennie
83Clinton/LF-24
Taft, William Howard
90BBWit-107
Taft, Tim
88Clearw/Star-24
Tagi, Anthony
88Fresno/Cal-20
88Fresno/ProC-1234
Tagle, Hank
91Utica/ClBest-26
91Utica/ProC-3239
Tagliaferri, Gino
90Fayette/ProC-2417
90Niagara/Pucko-11
Taguchi, Dragon
89Salinas/Cal-132
89Salinas/ProC-1809
Tahan, Kevin
90Savan/ProC-2078
91Spring/ClBest-25
91Spring/ProC-752
Taitt, D.
29Exh/4-18
Takach, Dave
87Spring/Best-14
88Salem/Star-20
Takacs, John
77Ashvl
Talamantez, Greg
85Newar-4
86Hagers-24
87CharlO/WBTV-35
88FSLAS/Star-22
89Jacks/GS-1
91Wmsprt/LineD-643
91Wmsprt/ProC-292
Talbert, Louis
90AppFox/Box-27
90AppFox/ProC-2095
91London/LineD-419
91Memphis/ProC-655
Talbot, Bob D.
52Mother-16
54T-229
55B-137
Talbot, Fred
65OPC-58
65T-58
66T-403
66T/RO-104
67T-517
68T-577
69T-332
70OPC-287
70T-287
72MB-338
Talbott, Shawn
86Ashvl-27
87Ashvl-18
Talford, Calvin
89Martins/Star-29
Tallent, Ron
91Boise/ClBest-16
91Boise/ProC-3892
Talton, Marion
(Tim)
67T-603R
Tamarez, Carlos
90Madison/ProC-2279
90SoOreg/ProC-3437
Tamargo, John
79Pol/Giants-30
79T-726R
80OPC-351R
80T-680
81D-210
81F-152
81OPC-35DP
81T-519
82Miami-22
87Lynch-22
91StLucie/ClBest-26MG
91StLucie/ProC-727MG
Tamulis, Vito
39PB-139
40PB-145
41G-17
90Target-788
R309/2
R314
V355-101
Tanabe, Collin
82Beloit-13
Tanabe, Nori
86SanJose-20
Tanana, Frank
74OPC-605R
74T-605R
75OPC-16
75T-16
75T/M-16
76Ho-101
76K-30
76OPC-204LL
76OPC-490
76SSPC-189
76T-204LL
76T-490
77BurgChef-122
77Ho-63
77K-45
77OPC-105
77T-200
78Ho-101
78K-54
78OPC-65
78OPC-7LL
78PapaG/Disc-33
78T-207LL
78T-600
78Tastee/Discs-23
78Wiffle/Discs-73
79Ho-47
79OPC-274
79T-530
80OPC-57
80T-105
81Coke
81D-171
81F-276
81OPC-369
81T-369
81T/HT
81T/St-56
81T/Tr-841
82D-326
82F-309
82OPC-4
82T-792
82T/Tr-117T
83D-447
83F-581
83Rang-28
83T-272
84D-98
84F-432
85FunFoodPin-133
84Nes/792-479
84OPC-276
84Rang-28
84T-479
85D-220
85D-9DK
85D/DKsuper-9
85F-570
85Leaf-9DK
85OPC-55
85T-55
85T/St-348
86Cain's-17
86D-491
86F-239
86Leaf-241
86OPC-124
86T-592
87Cain's-20
87Coke/Tigers-5
87D-152
87F-164
87F/Hottest-40
87OPC-231
87Seven-DT10
87T-726
88D-461
88D/Best-259
88F-71
88F/Slug-42
88OPC-177
88Panini/St-86
88Pep/T-26
88Pol/T-11
88S-490
88Sf-133
88T-177
88T/St-264
89B-92
89D-90
89D/Best-91
89F-147
89Mara/Tigers-26
89OPC-299
89Panini/St-336
89Pol/Tigers-26
89RedFoley/St-117
89S-112
89Sf-103
89Smok/Angels-9
89T-603
89T-609TL
89T/LJN-140
89T/St-275
89UD-391
90B-343
90Classic-108
90CokeK/Tiger-23
90D-180
90D/BestAL-48
90F-616
90KayBee-30
90Leaf/I-87
90OPC-343
90Panini/St-72
90PublInt/St-483
90S-57
90T-343
90T/Big-119
90T/St-277
90UD-516
91CokeK/Tiger-26
91D-508
91F-354
91F/Ultra-128
91Leaf/II-497
91Leaf/Stud-57
91OPC-236A
91OPC-236B
91S-328
91T-236A
91T-236B
91T/StClub/I-158
91UD-369
92D/I-111
92F-145
92S/I-271
92T-458
92UD-605
Tanderys, Jeff
91Hamil/ClBest-12
91Hamil/ProC-4039
Tanks, Talmage
76BurlB
Tannahill, Kevin
89Helena/SP-23
91CharlR/ClBest-14
91CharlR/ProC-1318
Tannehill, Jesse
T206
Tannehill, Lee Ford
11Helmar-17
E254
E90/1
M116
S74-9
T202
T205
T206
T207
Tanner, Bruce
85BuffB-25
85F/Up-U116
86BuffB-21
86F-218
87Tacom-8
88Huntsvl/BK-22
89Tacoma/ProC-1540
91CharRain/ClBest-25CO
91CharRain/ProC-112CO
91SALAS/ProC-SAL6CO
Tanner, Chuck
55JC-18
55T-161
56T-69
57T-392
58T-91
59T-234
60L-115
60T-279
61BeeHive-23
71OPC-661MG
71T-661MG
72OPC-98MG
72T-98MG
73OPC-356MG
73T-356MG
74OPC-221MG
74T-221MG
75OPC-276MG
75T-276MG
75T/M-276MG
76SSPC-151MG
76T-656MG
77T-354MG
78T-494MG
79T-244MG
79TCMA-63
81D-257MG
81F-367MG
81T-683R
82D-150
83D-124
83T-696
84Nes/792-291MG
84T-291MG
85T-268MG
86Pol/Atl-7MG
86T-351MG
86T/Tr-107T
87Smok/Atl-26MG
87T-593MG
88T-134MG
Tanner, Ed
(Eddie)
81Batavia-16
82Watlo/B-19
82Watlo/C-22
83Spring/LF-8
84ArkTr-1
86ArkTr-24
87Nashvl-19
88Nashvl/Team-23
89Nashvl/CMC-19
89Nashvl/ProC-1287
89Nashvl/Team-24
90Nashvl/CMC-21
90Nashvl/ProC-243
90SpringDG/Best-6
Tanner, Mark
74Gaston
Tanner, Roy
76Watlo
77DaytB
82CharR-24
83CharR-24
Tanzi, Bobby
80Wausau-12
Tanzi, Michael
82AppFx-25
83GlenF-20
Tapais, Luis
86Kenosha-23
Tapani, Kevin
86Cram/PCL-64
87Modesto-12
88Jacks/GS-23
89Tidew/CMC-10
89Tidew/ProC-1972
90B-407
90Classic/III-16
90D-473
90D/BestAL-93
90D/Rook-35
90F/Up-110
90Leaf/II-269
90OPC-227
90S/Tr-82T
90S/YS/II-31
90T-227
90T/89Debut-126
90T/Big-225
90UD-87
91B-322
91Classic/200-42
91D-116
91F-625
91F/Ultra-196
91Leaf/I-128
91MajorLg/Pins-13
91OPC-633
91Panini/FrSt-307
91Panini/St-249
91S-60
91S/100RisSt-52
91T-633
91T/StClub/I-161
91UD-434
91WIZMets-394
92Classic/I-87
92D/I-236
92F-219
92S/II-507
92T-313
92UD-624
Tapia, Dagoberto
90Martins/ProC-3208
Tapia, Jose
87QuadC-7
87VeroB-2
88PalmSp/Cal-93
88PalmSp/ProC-1446
Tappe, Elvin
53Mother-48
55B-51
55T-129
55T/DH-94
58T-184
60T-457C
Tarangelo, Joseph
84Visalia-23
Tarasco, Tony
89Pulaski/ProC-1904
90Foil/Best-100
90Sumter/Best-23
90Sumter/ProC-2449
91Durham/ClBest-21
91Durham/ProC-1675
Tarchione, Travis
88CapeCod/Sum-23
89SLCity-60F
Tarin, Fernando
77QuadC
Tarjick, Dave
90Pittsfld/Pucko-29PER
Tarnow, Greg
81QuadC-3
83AppFx/LF-21
Tarrh, Jamey
90WichSt-33
Tarrolly, Dave
83Beloit/LF-17GM
Tartabull, Danny
82Water-14
83Chatt-6
84Cram/PCL-170
85Cram/PCL-94
85D-27RR
85F-647R
86D-38
86D/Rook-45
86F-476
86F/Mini-99
86Mother/Mar-22
86Sf-178R
86Sf/Rook-22
86T/Tr-108T
87Classic/Up-145
87D-147
87D/OD-200
87F-598
87F/Up-U117
87Leaf-250
87OPC-332
87RedFoley/St-97
87Sf-23
87T-476
87T/Coins-25
87T/Gloss60-19
87T/GlossRk-19
87T/St-223
87T/St-306
87T/Tr-120T
87ToysRUs-28
88Classic/Blue-235
88D-177
88D-5DK
88D/Best-287
88D/DKsuper-5DK
88F-271
88F/AwardWin-42
88F/Excit-41
88F/Mini-28
88F/SS-40
88F/St-34

88KayBee-30
88Leaf-190
88Leaf-5DK
88OPC-211
88Panini/St-112
88S-106
88S/YS/II-5
88Sf-19
88Smok/Royals-4
88T-724
88T/Big-230
88T/Coins-29
88T/Mini-16
88T/Revco-26
88T/St-257
88T/UK-78
89B-128
89Chatt/II/Team-29
89D-61
89D/Best-39
89D/GrandSlam-10
89F-295
89F/BBMVP's-37
89OPC-275
89Panini/St-360
89RedFoley/St-118
89S-105
89S/HotStar-19
89Sf-46
89T-275
89T/Big-107
89T/Coins-55
89T/St-267
89Tastee/Discs-4
89UD-329
90B-375
90D-322
90D/BestAL-128
90F-120
90Leaf/I-99
90OPC-540
90Panini/St-90
90Publint/St-358
90S-244
90S/100St-72
90Sf-129
90T-540
90T/Ames-33
90T/Big-56
90T/HillsHM-9
90T/St-274
90UD-656
91B-294
91Classic/200-43
91D-463
91DennyGS-16
91F-572
91F/Ultra-158
91Leaf/I-147
91OPC-90
91Panini/FrSt-282
91Pol/Royal-22
91S-515
91T-90
91T/StClub/I-272
91UD-523
91UD/FinalEd-89F
91USPlayC/AS-JK
92Classic/I-88
92D/I-26AS
92D/II-676
92F-171
92F/ASIns-12
92F/TmLIns-18
92S/100SS-90
92S/I-145
92T-145
92UD-237
92UD-88TC

Tartabull, Jose Jr.
86Cram/PCL-108
87Wausau-8
88RedFoley/St-88
88SanBern/Best-13
88SanBern/Cal-36
89SanBern/Best-18
89SanBern/Cal-79

Tartabull, Jose
62T-451
63T-449
64T-276
66OPC-143
66T-143
67OPC-56
67T-56
67T/Test/RSox-21
68T-555
69MB-269
69T-287
70OPC-481
70T-481
72MB-339

Tarumi, Kanenori
88Miami/Star-11

Tarutis, Pete
91James/ClBest-26
91James/ProC-3545

Tarver, LaSchelle
82Lynch-2
84Tidew-21
85IntLgAS-6
85Tidew-13
86Pawtu-24
87Pawtu-10
87Pawtu/TCMA-19

Tasby, Willie
59T-143
60L-100
60T-322
61P-51
61T-458
61T/St-117
62J-70
62P-70
62P/Can-70
62Salada-21
62Shirriff-21
62T-462
91Crown/Orio-449

Tata, Terry
88TM/Umpire-16
89TM/Umpire-14
89TM/Umpire-60M
90TM/Umpire-14

Tatar, Kevin
90Billings/ProC-3222
91CharWh/ClBest-11
91CharWh/ProC-2888
91Single/ClBest-294

Tatarian, Dean
89Utica/Pucko-24
90Utica/Pucko-10
91Saraso/ClBest-20
91Saraso/ProC-1122

Tate, Bennie
91Conlon/Sport-220
R314/Can
V355-80

Tate, Chuck
86Cram/PCL-16

Tate, Edward
N172

Tate, Henry
31Exh/4-20

Tate, Lee W.
59T-544

Tate, Michael
88Boise/ProC-1606

Tate, Randy L.
76OPC-549
76SSPC-555
76T-549
78Colum
91WIZMets-395

Tate, Stuart
(Stu)
84Everett/Cram-12
86Shrev-24
87Shrev-20
88Shrev/ProC-1295
89AAA/ProC-52
89Phoenix/CMC-9
89Phoenix/ProC-1491
90F-643R
90T/89Debut-127
91Phoenix/LineD-395
91Phoenix/ProC-67

Tatis, Bernie
83Kinston/Team-26
86Knoxvl-23
87Knoxvl-16
87SLAS-4
88BuffB/CMC-14
88BuffB/ProC-1475
90OkCty/CMC-20
90OkCty/ProC-447
91Canton/LineD-95
91Canton/ProC-993
91ColoSp/ProC-2194

Tatis, Fausto
90Bakers/Cal-231
90Yakima/Team-33

Tatis, Rafael
73Cedar
74Cedar
75Dubuq

Tatsuno, Derek
82ElPaso-22
87Hawaii-5

Tatterson, Gary
91Watertn/ClBest-12
91Watertn/ProC-3367

Tatum, Jarvis
70T-642R
71MLB/St-334
71OPC-159
71T-159

Tatum, Jim
85Spokane/Cram-24
86CharRain-25
87CharRain-19
88Wichita-18
90Canton/Best-12
90Canton/ProC-1302
91ElPaso/LineD-197
91ElPaso/ProC-2757

Tatum, Ken
70MLB/St-180
70T-658
71MLB/St-335
71OPC-601
71T-601
72MB-340
72T-772
73OPC-463
73T-463

Tatum, Reece
(Goose)
76Laugh/Clown-16
86Negro/Frit-107

Tatum, Tommy
90Target-1082

Tatum, Willie
88Elmira-19
89WinHaven/Star-23
90LynchRS/Team-8
91LynchRS/ClBest-18
91LynchRS/ProC-1208

Taubensee, Edward
(Eddie)
88Greens/ProC-1558
88SALAS/GS-6
89Cedar/Best-12
89Cedar/ProC-937
89Cedar/Star-19
90Cedar/Best-3
90Cedar/ProC-2325
90CedarDG/Best-11
90Foil/Best-184
91ColoSp/LineD-76
91ColoSp/ProC-2187
92D/I-18RR
92S/100RisSt-29
92S/II-871
92T-427
92T/91Debut-169

Tauken, Daniel
87Penin-5

Taussig, Don
62Salada-186
62Shirriff-186
62T-44
89Smok/Ast-22

Tavarez, Alfonso
85Utica-15
86BurlEx-24

Tavarez, Davis
83Clinton/LF-12
84Everett/Cram-21

Tavarez, Hector
90MedHat/Best-27
91MedHat/ProC-4109

Tavarez, Jesus
90Penin/Star-21
91AS/Cal-11
91SanBern/ClBest-24
91SanBern/ProC-2001

Tavener, Jack
28Exh-46
29Exh/4-21
92Conlon/Sport-572

Taveras, Alejandro
75Iowa/TCMA-21

Taveras, Alex
74Cedar
77T-474R
79Albuq-15
81Albuq/TCMA-18
82Albuq-18
83Albuq-10
84Cram/PCL-153
85BuffB-12
89Beloit/I/Star-26M
89Beloit/II/Star-25MG

Taveras, Frank
74OPC-607R
74T-607R
75OPC-277
75OPC-460NLCS
75T-277
75T-460NLCS
75T/M-277
75T/M-460NLCS
76OPC-36
76SSPC-583
76T-36
77BurgChef-184
77T-538
78OPC-4LL
78T-204LL
78T-685
79OPC-79
79T-165
80BK/PHR-32
80OPC-237
80T-456
81Coke
81D-154
81F-320
81OPC-343
81T-343
81T/HT
81T/St-196
82D-98
82F-539
82Hygrade
82OPC-351
82T-782
82T/Tr-118T
91WIZMets-396

Taveras, Marcos
88StCath/ProC-2028
89Dunedin/Star-18
90Dunedin/Star-17

Taveras, Ramon
89Salem/Team-30
90FSLAS/Star-17
90VeroB/Star-25
91SanAn/LineD-542

Taylor, Aaron
89Wythe/Star-25
90Hunting/ProC-3283
91Peoria/ClBest-9
91Peoria/ProC-1343

Taylor, Andrew
86LitFalls-27
88Spring/Best-8
89Savan/ProC-368

Taylor, Antonio S.
(Tony)
58T-411
59T-62
60L-44
60T-294
61P-118
61T-411
61T/St-59
62J-193
62P-193
62P/Can-193
62Salada-156
62Shirriff-156
62T-77
62T/bucks
62T/St-170
63J-178
63P-178
63T-366
64PhilBull-23
64T-585
64T/Coins-113
64T/Coins-144AS
64T/St-9
65T-296
66T-585
67OPC-126
67T-126
68T-327
69MB-270
69MLB/St-179
69OPC-108
69T-108
70MB-28
70MLB/St-95
70OPC-324
70T-324
71K-67
71MLB/St-190
71OPC-246
71T-246
72MB-341
72OPC-511
72T-511
73OPC-29
73T-29
75OPC-574
75T-574
75T/M-574
76OPC-624
76SSPC-474
76T-624
78TCMA-133
88Phill/TastyK-29CO
89Phill/TastyK-33CO
90Shrev/ProC-1459CO
90Shrev/Star-27CO
91Shrev/LineD-325CO
91Shrev/ProC-1840CO

Taylor, Ben
78Laugh/Black-12
90Negro/Star-10

Taylor, Bob
76Baton

Taylor, Bobbie
85Anchora-45

Taylor, Brien
91Classic/DP-1
92T-6DP

Taylor, Bruce
77Evansvl/TCMA-23
78T-701R

Taylor, Carl
68T-559R
69T-357
70OPC-76
70T-76
71MLB/St-286
71MLB/St-432
71OPC-353
71T-353
71T/Coins-55
73OPC-99
73T-99
74OPC-627
74T-627
89Pac/SenLg-160

Taylor, Charley
85Osceola/Team-2
86ColumAst-24C
87Ashvl-11C
88Ashvl/ProC-1067
89Ashvl/ProC-944
90ColMud/Best-21CO
90ColMud/ProC-1362CO
90ColMud/Star-25CO

Taylor, Chuck
63Pep/Tul
70OPC-119
70T-119
71OPC-606
71T-606
72OPC-407
72T-407
73OPC-176
73T-176
74OPC-412
74T-412
75OPC-58
75T-58
75T/M-58
76SSPC-346
91Jacks/LineD-575CO
91Jacks/ProC-942CO
91WIZMets-397

Taylor, Dan
35BU-108

35Exh/4-2
90Target-789
R314
V355-72

Taylor, Dave
87Beloit-25
88Stockton/Cal-195
88Stockton/ProC-729
90Miami/II/Star-24

Taylor, David Michael
(Mike)
88Gaston/ProC-998
89CharlR/Star-25
90Tulsa/ProC-1156

Taylor, Dorn
83AlexD-30
84PrWill-6
85Nashua-24
86Nashua-26
87F/Up-U118
87Vanco-24
88BuffB/CMC-9
88BuffB/Polar-5
88BuffB/ProC-1468
89AAA/ProC-9
89VFJuice-52
90AAAGame/ProC-AAA22
90BuffB/CMC-10
90BuffB/ProC-373
90BuffB/Team-26
91Crown/Orio-451

Taylor, Dwight
82Watlo-23
83BuffB-21
84Maine-18
85Maine-28
86Omaha/TCMA-11
87Omaha-8
89ColoSp/CMC-19
89ColoSp/ProC-234
90ColoSp/ProC-51

Taylor, Eddie
45Centen-25
47Centen-29

Taylor, Edward
26Exh-7

Taylor, Gary
91Hamil/ClBest-14
91Hamil/ProC-4055

Taylor, Gene
91Billings/ProC-3769

Taylor, Harry
90Target-790

Taylor, Jack
26Exh-8
27Exh-4
28Exh-4
90HOF/St-13
WG3-44

Taylor, James
(Zack)
33G-152
51B-315MG
90Target-791
91Conlon/Sport-210
V353-79
W753

Taylor, Jeff
83Memphis-14
86Orlan-20
88Oneonta/ProC-2070
89Oneonta/ProC-2101

Taylor, John W.
E107
E254
E270/1

Taylor, John
81Clinton-17
82AlexD-1
82AppFx-8
83AlexD-12

Taylor, Joseph C.
(Bill)
54T-74
55Gol/Giants-26
55T-53
55T/DH-7
58T-389

Taylor, Joseph F.
54JC
55JC

Taylor, Kerry
89Elizab/Star-25
91Kenosha/ClBest-16
91Kenosha/ProC-2074

Taylor, Luther H.
(Dummy)
C46-41
E91
T206
WG3-45

Taylor, Mark
91Savan/ClBest-15
91Savan/ProC-1656

Taylor, Michael David
(Mike)
88StCath/ProC-2032
89Myrtle/ProC-1462
90Dunedin/Star-18
91Knoxvl/LineD-366
91Knoxvl/ProC-1776

Taylor, Michael Larry
(Mike)
90StCath/ProC-3474
91MedHat/ProC-4101

Taylor, Michael Patrick
91Burllnd/ProC-3305

Taylor, Mike
81Watlo-28
82Watlo-24
87Hawaii-12

Taylor, Phil
86Miami-24

Taylor, Randy
77SanJose-21

Taylor, Rob
90Clinton/Best-27
90Clinton/ProC-2544
90Foil/Best-129
91SanJose/ClBest-22
91SanJose/ProC-11

Taylor, Robert D.
(Hawk)
58T-164
61T-446
62T-406
63T-481
64T-381
65T-329
68OPC-52
68T-52
69T-239
91WIZMets-399

Taylor, Ron
62T-591R
63T-208R
64T-183
65T-568
66OPC-174
66T-174
67T-606
68T-421
69OPC-72
69T-72
69T/St-79
70OPC-419
70T-419
71MLB/St-167
71OPC-687
71T-687
72OPC-234
72T-234
91WIZMets-398

Taylor, Sam
88CapeCod/Sum-121
89Batavia/ProC-1937
91Clearw/ClBest-24
91Clearw/ProC-1635
91Single/ClBest-349

Taylor, Sammy
58T-281
59T-193
60L-131
60T-162
61P-198
61T-253
61T/St-10
62J-189
62P-189
62P/Can-189
62Salada-164
62Shirriff-164
62T-274
63T-273
91WIZMets-400

Taylor, Scott
88CharWh/Best-4
88Elmira-4
88Geneva/ProC-1651
89CharWh/Best-5
89CharWh/ProC-1757
89SALAS/GS-13
89Wausau/GS-11
90Elizab/Star-22
90Foil/Best-246
90LynchRS/Team-24
90SanBern/Best-15
90SanBern/Cal-93
90SanBern/ProC-2633
90WinSalem/Team-22
91B-121
91CharlK/LineD-145
91CharlK/ProC-1692
91CLAS/ProC-CAR3
91Durham/ProC-1546
91Greenvl/LineD-219
91Kenosha/ClBest-17
91Kenosha/ProC-2075
91NewBrit/LineD-472
91NewBrit/ProC-353
91Single/ClBest-83

Taylor, Steve
78Cr/PCL-39
79Colum-20

Taylor, Terry
83Wausau/LF-9
86Chatt-24
87Calgary-17
88Calgary/ProC-781
88CapeCod/Sum-137
89BendB/Legoe-24
89F-651R
89T-597
90Calgary/CMC-5
90Calgary/ProC-651
90PalmSp/Cal-208
90PalmSp/ProC-2587
91London/LineD-420
91London/LineD-447
91Memphis/ProC-656
91MidldA/ProC-444
91Single/ClBest-328

Taylor, Thomas
(Tommy)
89Bluefld/Star-24
90Wausau/Best-9
90Wausau/ProC-2122
90Wausau/Star-23
91Kane/ClBest-10
91Single/ClBest-242

Taylor, Todd
91T/Tr-116T

Taylor, Wade
88FtLaud/Star-21
89PrWill/Star-21
90A&AASingle/ProC-20
90Albany/Best-9
90Albany/ProC-1176
90Albany/Star-20
90EastLAS/ProC-EL12
90Foil/Best-154
90T/TVYank-63
91B-165
91Classic/II-T87
91ColClip/LineD-121
91ColClip/ProC-598
91D/Rook-34
91F/Up-U48
91Leaf/GRook-BC16
91OPC/Premier-119
91S/RookTr-100T
91T/Tr-117T
92D/II-527
92F-245
92S/100RisSt-45
92S/II-631
92T-562
92T/91Debut-170

Taylor, William
(Bill)
75QuadC
76QuadC

Taylor, William Charleston
(Will or Ooiee)
87CharRain-6
88River/Cal-227
88River/ProC-1419
89River/Best-17
89River/Cal-13
89River/ProC-1402
91LasVegas/LineD-295
91LasVegas/ProC-250

Taylor, William H.
N690

Taylor, William Howell
(Bill)
80Ashvl-18
82Wausau-26
83Tulsa-5
84Tulsa-32
85Tulsa-34
86Cram/PCL-179
87OKCty-25
88OkCty/ProC-28
89LasVegas/CMC-10
89LasVegas/ProC-3
89Madis/Star-20
90Madison/Best-24
90Modesto/Cal-154
90Modesto/ProC-2213
90Wichita/Rock-19
91Greenvl/ClBest-6
91Greenvl/ProC-3000

Taylor, William M.
(Joe)
58T-451
60HenryH-22
60Union-13
61Union
91Crown/Orio-450

Tayor, Fiona
85Anchora-38BG

Teague, Scott
89Wythe/Star-26

Teahan, Jim
83Beloit/LF-19

Teasley, Ronald
86Negro/Frit-55

Tebbetts, George
(Birdie)
47HomogBond-45
47TipTop
50Drake-30
51B-257
52B-124
52NumNum-3
52T-282
55B-232
58T-386M
62T-588MG
63Sugar-18
63T-48MG
64T-462MG
65T-301MG
66T-552MG
81Detroit-92
D305
Exh47

Tebbetts, Steve
76QuadC
77QuadC

Tebeau, Oliver
(Patsy)
N172

Techman, Marc
90AubAs/Best-22ASST
91AubAS/ClBest-28GM

Tedder, Scott
89Saraso/Star-24
89Star/Wax-61
90FSLAS/Star-44
90Saraso/Star-24
91Saraso/ClBest-26
91Saraso/ProC-1127

Teegarden, Travis
89Billings/ProC-2040

Teel, Garett
88CapeCod/Sum-171
90Bakers/Cal-252

Tegtmeier, Doug
91Penin/ClBest-11
91Penin/ProC-377

Teich, Mike
91Welland/ClBest-27
91Welland/ProC-3573

Teising, John
78Watlo

Teixeira, Joe
89Bluefld/Star-25
90Wausau/Best-11
90Wausau/ProC-2124

Teixeira, Vince
86Cram/PCL-74
87Madis-5
88Modesto/Cal-80
89Visalia/Cal-113
89Visalia/ProC-1423

Tejada, Alejandro
89James/ProC-2153

Tejada, Domingo
90Martins/ProC-3206

Tejada, Eugenio
88Utica/Pucko-10
89SoBend/GS-25

Tejada, Francisco
88Martins/Star-30
90Princet/DIMD-24

Tejada, Joaquin
86Elmira-23
87Elmira/Black-25
87Elmira/Red-25

Tejada, Leo
90SoBend/Best-6
91Saraso/ClBest-21
91Saraso/ProC-1123

Tejada, Wilfredo
86Jaxvl/TCMA-18
87D-529
87Indianap-25
88Indianap/CMC-19
88Indianap/ProC-523
89B-468
89OPC-391
89Phoenix/CMC-12
89Phoenix/ProC-1489
89T-747
91Huntsvl/LineD-294

Tejeda, Felix
86VeroB-24
87SanAn-15

Tejero, Fausto
90Boise/ProC-3334
91QuadC/ClBest-14
91QuadC/ProC-2632

Tekulve, Kent
76OPC-112
76SSPC-561
76T-112
77T-374
78T-84
79T-223
80OPC-297
80T-573
81Coke
81D-254
81F-362
81F/St-21
81OPC-94
81T-695
82D-311
82F-500
82F/St-73
82OPC-281
82T-485
83D-297
83F-326
83OPC-17
83OPC-18SV
83T-17
83T-18SV
84D-410
84F-265
85FunFoodPin-12
84Nes/792-754
84OPC-74
84T-754
84T/St-132
85D-479
85F-477
85F/Up-U117
85Leaf-119
85OPC-125
85T-125
85T/St-129
85T/Tr-117T
86CIGNA-4
86D-111
86F-455
86OPC-326
86Phill/TastyK-27
86T-326
87D-453
87F-190
87F/Excit-42

87F/Mini-104
87F/St-116
87OPC-86
87Phill/TastyK-27
87T-684
87T/St-118
88D-535
88D/Best-327
88F-318
88OPC-P
88Panini/St-354
88Phill/TastyK-24
88S-425
88T-543
88T/Revco-10
88T/WaxBox-P
89F-583
89Kahn/Reds-43
89S-287
89T/Tr-116T
89T/WaxBox-O
89UD-207
90PublInt/St-40

Telford, Anthony
88Hagers/Star-22
89Freder/Star-23
90Freder/Team-11
90Hagers/Star-23
91Classic/I-16
91Crown/Orio-452
91D-501
91F-493
91OPC-653
91RochR/LineD-470
91RochR/ProC-1903
91S-354RP
91T-653
91T/90Debut-152
91T/StClub/II-330
91UD-304
92D/II-623
92F-29
92S/II-853

Telgheder, Dave
89Pittsfld/Star-22
91Single/ClBest-342
91Wmsprt/LineD-644
91Wmsprt/ProC-293

Tellechea, John
90LSUPol-9

Tellers, David
90Welland/Pucko-30
91CLAS/ProC-CAR37
91Salem/ClBest-20
91Salem/ProC-950

Tellez, Alonzo
87SanAn-5

Tellgren, Scott
83Toledo-25
85Maine-32

Tellmann, Tom
79Hawaii-23
80Hawaii-14
81T-356R
82Hawaii-19
83Pol/Brew-42
83T/Tr-109T
84D-149
84F-216
84Gard-20
84Nes/792-476
84Pol/Brew-42
84T-476
84T/St-297
85Cram/PCL-150
85D-246
85F-599
85Gard-20
85T-112
85T/Tr-118T
86T-693

Temperly, Kevin
89Clinton/ProC-881

Temple, Johnny
55B-31
55Kahn
56Kahn
56T-212
57Kahn
57Sohio/Reds-18
57T-9
58Kahn
58T-205
58T-478AS
59Kahn
59T-335
60Kahn
60MacGregor-25
60T-500
60T/tatt-50
61Kahn
61T-155
61T/St-143
62J-38
62P-38
62P/Can-38
62Salada-52A
62Salada-52B
62Shirriff-52
62T-34
63J-189
63P-189
63Pep
63T-576
91Crown/Orio-453
Rawl

Templeton, Chuck
79TCMA-282
90Target-793

Templeton, Garry
76Tulsa
77Ho-78
77OPC-84
77T-161
78Ho-43
78K-31
78OPC-51
78T-32
79Ho-127
79OPC-181
79T-350
80OPC-308
80T-5HL
80T-587
80T/S-37
81Coke
81D-187
81F-529
81F/St-125
81K-27
81MSA/Disc-32
81OPC-144
81PermaGr/CC-10
81Sqt-12
81T-485
81T/So-82
81T/St-217
81T/St-255
82D-545
82F-131
82F/St-27
82OPC-288
82T-288
82T/St-96
82T/Tr-119T
83D-145
83F-373
83K-17
83OPC-336
83T-505
83T/St-291
84D-185
84F-314
84Mother/Padres-8
84Nes/792-615
84OPC-173
84Smok/Padres-24
84T-615
84T/St-151
85D-356
85F-45
85Mother/Padres-7
85OPC-124
85T-735
85T/St-151
86D-202
86D/AAS-30
86F-336
86F/Mini-71
86F/St-118
86Leaf-133
86OPC-90
86Sf-170
86T-90
86T/St-110
87Bohem-1
87D-141
87D/OD-150
87F-432
87Leaf-63
87OPC-325
87T-325
87T/St-110
88Coke/Padres-1
88D-649
88F-598
88OPC-264
88Panini/St-409
88RedFoley/St-89
88S-189
88Smok/Padres-28
88T-640
88T/St-113
89B-455
89Coke/Padre-18
89D-483
89D/Best-154
89F-319
89Padre/Mag-19
89Panini/St-202
89S-176
89T-121
89T/Big-328
89UD-297
90B-215
90Coke/Padre-19
90D-246
90D/BestNL-133
90F-170
90Leaf/I-102
90OPC-481
90Padre/MagUno-14
90Panini/St-354
90PublInt/St-60
90S-336
90T-481
90T/Big-177
90UD-288
91D-252
91F-546
91F/Ultra-312
91OPC-253
91Panini/FrSt-94
91S-117
91S/RookTr-38T
91T-253
91T/StClub/I-72
91T/Tr-118T
91UD-295
92S/II-588
92T-772
92UD-411

Tena, Paulino
90Watertn/Star-21
91Kinston/ClBest-21
91Kinston/ProC-333

Tenace, Gene
70OPC-21R
70T-21R
71MLB/St-528
71OPC-338
71T-338
72OPC-189
72T-189
73OPC-203WS
73OPC-206WS
73OPC-524
73T-203WS
73T-206WS
73T-524
74OPC-79
74T-79
74T/St-230
75Ho-64
75Ho/Twink-64
75OPC-535
75T-535
75T/M-535
76Ho-122
76OPC-165
76SSPC-493
76T-165
77BurgChef-131
77Ho-141
77OPC-82
77Padre/SchCd-32
77Pep-39
77T-303
78Ho-125
78OPC-35
78Padre/FamFun-32
78T-240
78Tastee/Discs-20
78Wiffle/Discs-74
79Ho-19
79OPC-226
79T-435
80OPC-355
80T-704
81D-241
81F-489
81OPC-29
81T-29
81T/Tr-842
82D-152
82F-132
82F/St-26
82OPC-166
82T-631
83D-442
83F-25
83OPC-252
83T-515
83T/Tr-110T
84D-264
84F-266
84Nes/792-729
84T-729
87Mother/A's-14
90Tor/BlueJ-15CO
91Tor/Fire-18CO

Tenacen, Francisco
86Tampa-23
87Vermont-4
88WinSalem/Star-20
89WinSalem/Star-16

Tenenini, Bob
80Memphis-23
83Memphis-17

Tener, John
N172

Tenhunfeld, Joe
88Batavia/ProC-1679
90Clearw/Star-21

Tennant, Mike
77LodiD
79Albuq-2

Tenney, Fred
D304
E103
E107
E90/1
E91
E98
M116
T204
T206
T3-122
WG3-46

Tenney, Mickey
81QuadC-8

Tepedino, Frank
70T-689
71OPC-342
71T-342
73Syrac/Team-27
74OPC-526
74T-526
75OPC-9
75T-9
75T/M-9

Tepper, Marc
89Miami/I/Star-19
89Watertn/Star-21
90Kinston/Team-11
91Kinston/ClBest-22
91Kinston/ProC-334

Terilli, Joey
91Geneva/ClBest-21
91Geneva/ProC-4232

Terlecky, Greg
76SSPC-299
77T-487R

Terpko, Jeff
77T-137

Terrazas, Marc
82Holyo-24
83Redwd-31

Terrell, James
91Belling/ClBest-6
91Belling/ProC-3681

Terrell, Jerry
74OPC-481
74T-481
75OPC-654
75T-654
75T/M-654
76OPC-159
76SSPC-222
76T-159
77T-513
78T-525
79T-273
80T-98
87FtMyr-29MG
91Pac/SenLg-8

Terrell, Walt
81Tulsa-12
82Tidew-24
83Tidew-12
84D-640
84F-601
84Nes/792-549
84T-549
84T/St-110
85D-597
85F-94
85F/Up-U118
85OPC-287
85T-287
85T/St-109
85T/Tr-119T
86Cain's-18
86D-247
86F-240
86Leaf-123
86OPC-301
86T-461
86T/Mini-16
87Cain's-16
87Coke/Tigers-3
87D-275
87F-165
87Leaf-180
87OPC-72
87T-72
88D-91
88D/Best-293
88F-72
88F/Mini-24
88F/St-28
88OPC-284
88Panini/St-87
88Pep/T-35
88Pol/T-12
88RedFoley/St-90
88S-538
88T-668
89B-445
89Coke/Padre-19
89D-296
89D/Best-245
89D/Tr-28
89F-149
89S-314
89S/Tr-75
89T-127
89T/Tr-117T
89UD-475
89UD/Ext-703
90B-165
90D-309
90F-457
90Homer/Pirate-28
90OPC-611
90PublInt/St-61
90S-463
90T-611
90TulsaDG/Best-11
90UD-661
91CokeK/Tiger-35
91D-717
91OPC-328
91S-801
91T-328
91T/StClub/II-315
91UD-320
91WIZMets-401
92D/II-565
92F-146
92S/I-355
92T-722
92UD-520

Terrill, James
87Everett-19
88Clinton/ProC-702
89SanJose/Best-4
89SanJose/Cal-218

89SanJose/ProC-449
89SanJose/Star-24
91SanAn/LineD-543
91SanAn/ProC-2974

Terrio, Tim
89AS/Cal-26TR
89Bak/Cal-208tr

Terris, Adam
89Rockford/Team-25
90WPalmB/Star-24

Terry, Adonis
90Target-1084

Terry, Brent
88SLCity-6CO

Terry, Brett
88Utica/Pucko-3

Terry, Ralph
57T-391
58T-169
59T-358
60T-96
61T-389
62J-10
62P-10
62P/Can-10
62Salada-77
62Shirriff-77
62T-48
63Bz-20
63F-26
63J-20
63Kahn
63P-20
63Salada-38
63T-10LL
63T-315
63T-8LL
64T-458
65Kahn
65T-406
66OPC-109
66T-109
66T/RO-69
67OPC-59
67T-59
78TCMA-168
88Pac/Leg-64
89Swell-31
91WIZMets-402
WG9-23

Terry, Scott
81Cedar-18
82Cedar-23
83Tampa-23
87Nashvl-20
87T-453
88D-647
88F/Up-U121
88Louisvl-47
88Smok/Card-8
88T/Tr-119T
89D-397
89F-464
89S-397
89Smok/Cards-20
89T-686
89T/Big-31
90CedarDG/Best-7
90D-418
90F-261
90Leaf/I-234
90OPC-82
90Publlnt/St-229
90S-235
90Smok/Card-23
90T-82
90T/TVCard-19
90UD-260
91F-647
91OPC-539
91Pol/Card-37
91S-247
91T-539
91T/StClub/II-469
92D/II-655
92F-593
92S/I-219
92T-117
92UD-688

Terry, William H.
(Bill)
25Exh-40
26Exh-40
28Yueng-46
29Exh/4-9
31Exh/4-10
33CJ/Pin-22
33DL-4
33G-125
33G-20
34DS-14
34Exh/4-5
34G-21
35BU-6
35Exh/4-5
35G-1K
35G-3B
35G-4B
35G-5B
36Exh/4-5
38ONG/Pin-29
50Callahan
60F-52
61F-142
61GP-5
80Pac/Leg-9
80Laugh/3/4/5-7
80SSPC/HOF
86Conlon/1-31
88Conlon/3-28
88Conlon/NatAS-20
89HOF/St-2
91Conlon/Sport-64
92Conlon/Sport-588
E210-46
R300
R306
R311/Gloss
R315-A35
R315-B35
R316
R328-4
R337-405
V353-20
V354-53
V355-7
W502-46
W513-67
W517

Terry, William H.
N172

Terry, Zeb
D327
D328-171
E121/120
E121/80
E135-171
W501-58
W575

Terwilliger, Wayne
50B-114
51B-175
51T/RB-14
52T-7
53Briggs
53T-159
54T-73
55T-34
55T/DH-132
56T-73
59T-496
60L-134
60T-26
77Ashvl
80Tulsa-24
90Target-794
91T/Arc53-159

Terzarial, Anthony
88Billings/ProC-1811
90Cedar/Best-10
90Cedar/ProC-2333

Tesmer, Jim
89Pittsfld/Star-28

Tesreau, Charles
(Jeff)
14CJ-45
15CJ-45
16FleischBrd-96
88Conlon/3-29
92Conlon/Sport-340
BF2-80
D328-172
D329-173
D350/2-175
E135-172
M101/4-173
M101/5-175

Teston, Phil
80Penin/C-1

Teter, Craig
90SoBend/Best-11
90Utica/Pucko-11

Tettleton, Mickey
84Albany-22
85F/Up-U119
85Mother/A's-11
85T/Tr-120T
86D-345
86F-432
86Mother/A's-11
86T-457
87D-349
87D/OD-23
87F-407
87T-649
88D-103
88French-14
88RochR/Team-23
88RochR/CMC-21
88RochR/ProC-202
88S-269
88S/Tr-31T
88T-143
88T/Tr-120T
89D-401
89D/Best-86
89F-623
89French-14
89Panini/St-259
89S-358
89T-521
89T/Big-198
89T/St-231
89UD-553
90AlbanyDG/Best-31
90B-254
90Classic-39
90D-169
90D-5DK
90D/BestAL-15
90D/SuperDK-5DK
90F-190
90F/ASIns-12
90HotPlay/St-45
90KMart/SS-24
90Leaf/I-65
90MLBPA/Pins-111
90OPC-275
90Panini/St-8
90Publlnt/St-587
90RedFoley/St-94
90S-322
90S/100St-9
90Sf-171
90T-275
90T/Coins-30
90T/Gloss60-57
90T/St-237
90T/TVAS-24
90UD-297
90UD-60TC
91B-140
91Classic/II-T62
91CokeK/Tiger-20
91Crown/Orio-454
91D-597
91F-494
91F/UltraUp-U24
91F/Up-U24
91Leaf/II-322
91Leaf/Stud-58
91OPC-385
91Panini/FrSt-239
91S-270
91S/RookTr-25T
91T-385
91T/StClub/II-412
91T/Tr-119T
91UD-296
91UD/Ext-729
92D/I-85
92F-147
92F/ASIns-9
92S/I-134
92T-29
92UD-251

Teufel, Tim
82Orlan/B-12
82OrlTw/A-9
83Toledo-16
84D-37RR
84F-574
84T/Tr-117
85D-192
85F-290
85Leaf-97
85OPC-239
85Seven/Minn-10
85T-239
85T/St-303
86D-242
86F-407
86F/Up-U110
86OPC-91
86T-667
86T/St-280
86T/Tr-109T
87D-581
87D/OD-131
87F-24
87T-158
88D-648
88D/Mets/Bk-648
88F-152
88Kahn/Mets-11
88S-128
88T-508
89B-382
89D-507
89F-50
89Kahn/Mets-11
89S-58
89T-9
89T/DHTest-11
89UD-277
90D-618
90F-218
90Kahn/Mets-11
90Leaf/II-383
90OPC-764
90Publlnt/St-146
90S-501
90T-764
90T/TVMets-29
90UD-492
91D-370
91F-162
91F/UltraUp-U114
91F/Up-U127
91Kahn/Mets-11
91Leaf/II-314
91OPC-302
91S-427
91S/RookTr-67T
91T-302
91T/StClub/I-43
91T/Tr-120T
91UD-370
91WIZMets-403
92D/I-171
92F-622
92S/I-234
92T-413
92UD-349

Teutsch, Mark
79AppFx-15
80GlenF/B-13
80GlenF/C-3

Tevlin, Creighton J.
79Vanco-23
81Syrac-19
82Syrac-22

Tewell, Terry
90Martins/ProC-3202
91Clearw/ClBest-14
91Clearw/ProC-1625

Tewksbury, Bob
84Nashvl-22
85Albany-11
86D/Rook-8
86F/Up-U111
86T/Tr-110T
87Colum/TCMA-9
87D-422
87F-117
87T-254
88Iowa/CMC-5
88Iowa/ProC-534
88T-593
89Louisvl-35
89Louisvl/CMC-11
89Louisvl/ProC-1250
90AlbanyDG/Best-13
90D-714
90Leaf/II-406
90T/Tr-122T
90T/TVCard-20
91B-394
91D-183
91F-648
91Leaf/II-460
91OPC-88
91Panini/St-36
91Pol/Card-39
91S-499
91T-88
91T/StClub/II-417
91UD-630
92D/I-201
92F-594
92S/I-282
92T-623
92UD-512

Texidor, Esteban
78Holyo

Texidor, Jose
91CharlR/ClBest-25
91CharlR/ProC-1329

Thacker, Moe
59T-474
61T-12
62T-546

Thayer, Ernest
90BBWit-98

Thayer, Greg
79Toledo-16

Thayer, Scott
78Green

Thebo, Antonio
T206

Thees, Michael
91SoOreg/ClBest-26
91SoOreg/ProC-3845

Theilman, Harry
WG3-47

Theisen, Mike
86StPete-29

Theiss, Duane
78Richm
79Richm-16
80Ander-3

Thelen, Jeffrey John
90Foil/Best-149
90Kenosha/Best-26
90Kenosha/ProC-2295
90Kenosha/Star-24
91Kenosha/ClBest-18
91Kenosha/ProC-2076

Theobald, Ron
72OPC-77
72T-77

Theodore, George
74OPC-99
74T-8
75Tidew/Team-22
89Tidew/Candl-8
91WIZMets-404

Therrien, Dominic
91Idaho/ProC-4342
91Pulaski/ProC-4021

Therrien, Ed
88CapeCod/Sum-4

Thevenow, Tom J.
31Exh/4-13
33Exh/4-7
33G-36
34Exh/4-7
35G-2B
35G-4B
35G-7B
91Conlon/Sport-69
V353-36

Thibault, Ryan
91Waterlo/ClBest-9
91Waterlo/ProC-1256

Thibert, John
90Tampa/DIMD-26

Thibodeau, John
69OPC-189R
69T-189R

Thibodeaux, Keith
82Buffa-8
83LynnP-8

Thielen, D.J.
91Everett/ClBest-1
91Everett/ProC-3925

Thielker, Dave

85CharlO-6
Thielman, John
T206
Thienpont, Gregg
84Butte-23
Thies, Dave
61Union
Thies, Vernon
(Jake)
55T-12
55T/DH-40
Thiessen, Tim
86WPalmB-26
Thigpen, Arthur
90Niagara/Pucko-25
Thigpen, Bobby
87Coke/WS-22
87D-370
87F-507
87Seven-C13
87T-61
88Coke/WS-28
88D-247
88D/Best-235
88F-410
88F/St-17
88F/TL-42
88S-307
88T-613
88ToysRUs-32
89B-55
89Coke/WS-26
89D-266
89D/Best-25
89F-512
89F/BBMVP's-38
89F/Heroes-39
89F/LL-39
89Kodak/WSox-5M
89OPC-368
89Panini/St-303
89S-399
89S/HotStar-68
89S/YS/I-29
89Sf-207
89T-762
89T/St-305
89UD-647
90B-306
90BirmDG/Best-30
90Classic/III-81
90Coke/WSox-24
90D-266
90D/BestAL-32
90F-549
90F/BB-40
90F/BBMVP-40
90F/LL-39
90Leaf/I-175
90OPC-255
90Panini/St-50
90PublInt/St-401
90RedFoley/St-95
90S-335
90S-694DT
90S/100St-87
90Sf-27
90T-255
90T/Big-295
90T/Mini-12
90T/St-297
90UD-269
90USPlayC/AS-9C
91B-342
91Classic/200-140
91Classic/I-31
91D-399MVP
91D-8DK
91D-90
91D-BC20
91D/SuperDK-8DK
91F-137
91F-712M
91F/Ultra-396EP
91F/Ultra-84
91Kodak/WSox-37
91Leaf/II-336
91Leaf/Stud-39
91MajorLg/Pins-15
91OPC-396AS
91OPC-420
91OPC-8RB
91OPC/Premier-120
91Panini/FrSt-320
91Panini/St-252
91Panini/Top15-85
91Post/Can-25
91RedFoley/St-92
91S-280
91S-401AS
91S-418HL
91S/100SS-95
91Seven/3DCoin-13MW
91Sunflower-22
91T-396AS
91T-420
91T-8RB
91T/CJMini/I-32
91T/StClub/I-256
91UD-261
91UD-93HL
91Woolwth/HL-21
92D/II-708
92F-99
92S/100SS-54
92S/II-570
92T-505
92UD-285
Thigpen, Len
89Penin/Star-24
Thoden, John
88CapeCod/Sum-106
89James/ProC-2157
90Rockford/ProC-2686
91WPalmB/ClBest-12
91WPalmB/ProC-1228
Thoenen, Dick
68T-348R
Thoma, Ray
84Albany-26
85Huntsvl/BK-19
87Pittsfld-1
88Pittsfld/ProC-1358
Thomas, Alphonse
(Tommy)
26Exh-76
27Exh-38
29Exh/4-20
33G-169
91Conlon/Sport-106
92Conlon/Sport-579
R316
Thomas, Andres
83Ander-23
84Durham-14
86D/Rook-10
86F/Up-U112
86Pol/Atl-14
86Sf/Rook-14
86T/Tr-111T
87Classic-7
87D-266
87D/OD-43
87F-531
87F/BB-42
87F/Mini-105
87F/St-117
87Smok/Atl-20
87T-296
87T/GlossRk-20
87T/St-305
87T/St-39
87ToysRUs-29
88D-627
88F-551
88OPC-13
88S-299
88T-13
88T/Big-68
88T/St-41
89B-272
89Cadaco-57
89Classic-21
89D-576
89D/Best-197
89F-604
89OPC-358
89Panini/St-43
89S-406
89S/YS/II-35
89T-171TL
89T-523
89T/St-26
89UD-144
90D-263
90F-597
90Leaf/I-33
90OPC-358
90Panini/St-229
90PublInt/St-126
90S-99
90T-358
90T/St-33
90UD-212
91D-491
91F-706
91OPC-111
91S-613
91T-111
91UD-384
Thomas, Bill
83ArkTr-7
Thomas, C.L.
88Billings/ProC-1823
Thomas, Carey
91Single/ClBest-281
Thomas, Carl
87Kenosha-18
Thomas, Carlos
91Yakima/ClBest-28
91Yakima/ProC-4249
Thomas, Chester David
16FleischBrd-93
D327
D328-173
E121/80
E122
E135-173
T213/blue
T213/brown
W575
Thomas, Chris
83VeroB-11
Thomas, Claude
T207
Thomas, Clinton
91SALAS/ProC-SAL45
89Martins/Star-30
91Spartan/ClBest-20
91Spartan/ProC-905
Thomas, Corey
86Negro/Frit-33
Thomas, Danny
77T-488R
Thomas, Dave
81Holyo-5M
Thomas, Delvin
90Penin/Star-22
91SanBern/ClBest-21
91SanBern/ProC-1998
Thomas, Dennis
82Reading-9
83Reading-9
Thomas, Deron
82Spring-21
83StPete-19
84ArkTr-4
Thomas, Derrel
72OPC-457R
72T-457R
73OPC-57
73T-57
74OPC-518
74T-518
75OPC-378
75T-378
75T/M-378
76OPC-493
76SSPC-106
76T-493
77T-266
78Padre/FamFun-33
78T-194
79OPC-359
79T-679
80OPC-9
80Pol/Dodg-30
80T-23
81D-419
81F-123
81OPC-211
81Pol/Dodg-30
81T-211
82D-537
82F-26
82Pol/Dodg-30
82T-348
83F-223
83Pol/Dodg-30
83T-748
84D-397
84F-114
84F/X-116
84Nes/792-583
84Stuart-28
84T-583
84T/Tr-118
85F-314
85OPC-317
85T-448
85T/Tr-121T
86T-158
89Pac/SenLg-64
89T/SenLg-55
89TM/SenLg-104
90EliteSenLg-90
90Target-795
91Pac/SenLg-87
Thomas, Don
74Gaston
Thomas, Don G.
76SanAn/Team-23
Thomas, Eric
75AppFx
Thomas, Fay
90Target-796
Thomas, Frank J.
54B-155
54DanDee
55Armour-21
55B-58
55RM-NL20
56T-153
57Kahn
57T-140
58Hires-27
58Kahn
58T-409
59Armour-17
59Kahn
59T-17M
59T-490
60Kahn
60T-95
61P-193
61T-382
62J-151
62P-151
62P/Can-151
62Salada-104
62Shirriff-104
62T-7
63J-196
63P-196
63Salada-59
63T-495
64PhilBull-24
64T-345
64T/Coins-73
65OPC-123
65T-123
79TCMA-24
89Pac/Leg-153
90Swell/Great-113
91WIZMets-405
Exh47
Thomas, Frank
(Frankie)
80Holyo-5
81Vanco-6
82Vanco-2
83ElPaso-22
84Cram/PCL-33
Thomas, Frank
88CapeCod-14
88CapeCod/Sum-126
90A&AASingle/ProC-46
90B-320
90BirmB/Best-1
90BirmB/ProC-1116
90Classic/III-93
90Coke/WSox-25
90F/Up-U87
90Foil/Best-1
90Foil/Best-318BC
90Leaf/II-300
90OPC-414
90S-663DC
90S/Tr-86T
90T-414
91Arena-3
91B-366
91BleachFT-1
91BleachFT-2
91BleachFT-3
91Bz-7
91Classic/200-181
91Classic/I-32
91Classic/II-T28
91D-477
91F-138
91F/Ultra-85
91JDeanSig-9
91Kodak/WSox-35
91Kodak/WSox-x
91Leaf/II-281
91Leaf/Stud-40
91MajorLg/Pins-17
91OPC-79
91OPC/Premier-121
91RedFoley/St-111
91S-840
91S-874FRAN
91S/100RisSt-78
91S/HotRook-4
91Seven/3DCoin-14MW
91T-79
91T/90Debut-153
91T/Arc53-283
91T/CJMini/II-20
91T/StClub/I-57
91ToysRUs-27
91UD-246
92Classic/I-89
92D/DK-DK8
92D/Elite-E18
92D/II-592
92F-100
92F-701M
92F-712PV
92F/ASIns-11
92F/RookSIns-1
92S/100SS-51
92S/II-505
92S/II-893DT
92T-555
92UD-166
92UD-87TC
Thomas, George
61T-544
62T-525
62T/St-69
63J-34
63P-34
63T-98
64T-461
65OPC-83
65T-83
66T-277
67OPC-184
67T-184
67T/Test/RSox-22
69T-521
71OPC-678
71T-678
78TCMA-153
Thomas, Gorman
74OPC-288
74Sacra
74T-288
75OPC-532
75T-532
75T/M-532
76OPC-139
76SSPC-243
76T-139
77Spoka
77T-439
79OPC-196
79T-376
80K-11
80OPC-327
80T-202TL
80T-623
80T/S-30
81D-326
81F-507
81F/St-77
81OPC-135
81PermaGr/CC-29
81T-135
81T/St-12
81T/St-96
82D-132
82D-26DK
82F-154

82F/St-134
82OPC-324
82Pol/Brew-20
82T-765
82T/St-204
83D-510
83Drake-27
83F-48
83Gard-19
83K-47
83OPC-10
83PermaGr/CC-32
83Pol/Brew-20
83T-10
83T-702LL
83T/St-17M
83T/St-84
83T/Tr-111T
84D-574
84D/Champs-5
84F-553
84F/X-U117
85FunFoodPin-56
84Mother/Mar-7
84Nes/792-515
84OPC-146
84T-515
84T/St-253
84T/Tr-119T
85F-503
85Mother/Mar-9
85OPC-202
85T-202
86D-440
86F-477
86F/AS-11
86F/St-119
86Leaf-213
86Mother/Mar-9
86OPC-347
86T-750
86T/Gloss60-48
86T/Mini-31
86T/St-216
86T/Super-56
86Woolwth-31
87F-359
87T-495

Thomas, Ira
10Domino-115
11Helmar-59
12Sweet/Pin-50A
12Sweet/Pin-50B
14CJ-34
14Piedmont/St-54
15CJ-34
E103
E104
E300
E90/1
E91
E96
M116
T201
T202
T204
T205
T206
T207
T208
T3-123
W514-97

Thomas, J. Leroy
(Lee)
61T-464
62Bz
62T-154
62T/bucks
62T/St-70
63Bz-32
63Exh
63J-30
63P-30
63T-441
63T/SO
64T-255
64T/St-99
64T/SU
64T/tatt
65OPC-111
65T-111
66T-408
67T-458
68T-438
78TCMA-231
Exh47

Thomas, Jim
83DayBe-23
84Beaum-15
86Tucson-22
87ColAst/ProC-5
88MidldA/GS-23
89Edmon/CMC-22
89Edmon/ProC-550

Thomas, Jim
76SanAn/Team-24

Thomas, John
90Hamil/Best-24
90Hamil/Star-25
91StPete/ClBest-5

Thomas, Keith
53B/BW-62
53T-129
91T/Arc53-129

Thomas, Keith
88Greens/ProC-1554
89Modesto/Chong-32
90Madison/Best-11
90Modesto/Cal-161
90Modesto/ProC-2226
91Madison/ProC-2144

Thomas, Kelvin
90Penin/Star-23
91Erie/ClBest-11
91Erie/ProC-4081
91Penin/ClBest-3
91Penin/ProC-393

Thomas, Larry Jr.
91Utica/ClBest-20
91Utica/ProC-3240

Thomas, Luther
(Bud)
39PB-158
40PB-42

Thomas, Mark
87Watertn-20
89Augusta/ProC-507
89Welland/Pucko-23
91StLucie/ClBest-1
91StLucie/ProC-726

Thomas, Mike
90Pittsfld/Pucko-18
91Bluefld/ProC-4141
91Bluefld/ClBest-5

Thomas, Mitch
86Salem-25
87PortChar-6
88Tulsa-4
90Tulsa/ProC-1157

Thomas, Orlando
87Erie-18
89Savan/ProC-349
90Spring/Best-15
91Spring/ClBest-26
91Spring/ProC-745

Thomas, Randy
79ArkTr-18

Thomas, Ray
90Target-1085

Thomas, Ricky
82Idaho-28

Thomas, Rob
88Bristol/ProC-1888
89Fayette/ProC-1571

Thomas, Rodney
91Princet/ClBest-16
91Princet/ProC-3529

Thomas, Ron
88Pulaski/ProC-1769
89Pulaski/ProC-1889
90Sumter/Best-6
90Sumter/ProC-2434

Thomas, Roy Allen
E107
WG3-48

Thomas, Roy J.
78Charl
78T-711R
79T-563
80T-397
81Tacom-20
82SLCity-19
84F-622
84Mother/Mar-25
84Nes/792-181
84T-181
84T/St-348
85Cram/PCL-82
86F-478
86Mother/Mar-26
86T-626
87Calgary-13
89Pac/SenLg-124
89T/SenLg-121
90EliteSenLg-118
91Pac/SenLg-130

Thomas, Royal Jr.
88Clearw/Star-25
88Spartan/Star-20
88Spartan/Star-4
89Clearw/Star-21
89Clearw/Star-26
90Foil/Best-248
90Riversi/Best-25
90Riversi/Cal-21
90Riversi/ProC-2608
91HighD/ClBest-12
91HighD/ProC-2395

Thomas, Skeets
91StPete/ProC-2291

Thomas, Stan
76OPC-148
76T-148
77T-353
78Cr/PCL-53

Thomas, Steve
90Pittsfld/Pucko-14

Thomas, Terrence
88StPete/Star-24

Thomas, Tim
90Burllnd/ProC-3017
91Watertn/ClBest-28
91Watertn/ProC-3383

Thomas, Todd
86Shrev-25
87Shrev-11

Thomas, Tom
75Shrev/TCMA-22

Thomas, Tom
86Visalia-22
87VeroB-14

Thomas, Tony
77Wausau

Thomas, Troy Gene
87BirmB/Best-25
88Vanco/CMC-18
88Vanco/ProC-775

Thomas, Valmy
58SFCallB-23
58T-86
59T-235
60T-167
61T-319
79TCMA-276
91Crown/Orio-455

Thomas, Vern
80RochR-3

Thomas, Willie
81VeroB-21

Thomason, Mel
76SSPC-600

Thomasson, Gary
74OPC-18
74T-18
75OPC-529
75T-529
75T/M-529
76OPC-261
76SSPC-107
76T-261
77BurgChef-102
77T-496
78T-648
79OPC-202
79T-387
80OPC-70
80Pol/Dodg-9
80T-127
81D-534
81F-138
81T-512
86Kenosha-24
90Target-797

Thomasson, Hal
76Watlo
77DaytB

Thome, Jim
90A&AASingle/ProC-187
90Burllnd/ProC-3018
91B-68
91Canton/LineD-96
91Canton/ProC-989
91Single/ClBest-195
91UD/FinalEd-17F
92Classic/I-90
92D/II-406RR
92F-125
92S/II-859
92T-768
92T/91Debut-171
92UD-1CL
92UD-5SR

Thompson, Al
77Ashvl

Thompson, Averett
46Sunbeam

Thompson, Bob
87Lakeland-19

Thompson, Bobby L.
74Gaston
75Cedar
76SanAn/Team-25
78BK/R-22
79T-336

Thompson, Brian
91AubAS/ClBest-21
91AubAS/ProC-4288

Thompson, Charles
(Tim)
52Park-62
53Exh/Can-40
54T-209
57T-142
58T-57
90CharRain/Best-21
90CharRain/ProC-2035
90Target-800
91CharRain/ClBest-10
91CharRain/ProC-95
V362-18

Thompson, Danny
71MLB/St-474
71OPC-127
71T-127
72OPC-368
72T-368
73OPC-443
73T-443
74K-35
74OPC-168
74T-168
75OPC-249
75T-249
75T/M-249
76OPC-111
76SSPC-225
76T-111

Thompson, Don
90Target-798

Thompson, Eugene
(Junior)
47TipTop
W711/1
W711/2

Thompson, Fay
75Dubuq
76Dubuq
78Dunedin

Thompson, Fletcher
90AubAs/Best-18
90AubAs/ProC-3410
91BurlAs/ClBest-18
91BurlAs/ProC-2812
91MidwLAS/ProC-MWL17

Thompson, Forrest D.
49Remar
58Remar

Thompson, Hank
50B-174
51B-89
51T/RB-32
52B-249
52BR
52T-3
53T-20
54B-217
54NYJour
54T-64
55B-94
55Gol/Giants-27
55RFG-19
55RM-NL11
56T-199
57T-109
79TCMA-150
86Negro/Frit-98
91T/Arc53-20
PM10/Sm-187
R423-107

Thompson, Jason
77BurgChef-99
77Ho-64
77OPC-64
77T-291
78BK/T-12
78Ho-77
78OPC-212
78T-660
79Ho-96
79K-7
79OPC-33
79T-80
80K-17
80OPC-83
80T-150
80T/S-42
81D-293
81F-278
81OPC-373
81T-505
81T/Tr-843
82D-502
82F-501
82T-295
83D-95
83D/AAS-8
83Drake-28
83F-325
83OPC-209
83T-730
83T/St-276
84D-64
84F-267
84Nes/792-355
84OPC-355
84T-355
84T/St-128
85D-322
85F-478
85Leaf-89
85OPC-22
85T-490
85T/St-125
85T/Super-56
86D-322
86F-622
86F/Up-U113
86OPC-153
86Provigo-15
86T-635
86T/St-129

Thompson, John
(Jocko)
49B-161
50B-120
51B-294

Thompson, Justin
91Bristol/ClBest-25
91Bristol/ProC-3606
91Classic/DP-28
91FrRow/DP-31

Thompson, Kelly
87Anchora-39

Thompson, Kirk
89Eugene/Best-10

Thompson, L. Fresco
29Exh/4-11
31Exh/4-3
33G-13
90Target-799
92Conlon/Sport-493
R314
R314/Can
R316
V353-13

Thompson, Marvin W.
78Cr/PCL-87
79Colum-12
80Colum-24
81Syrac-20

Thompson, Michael
88WinHaven/Star-23
89Belling/Legoe-36BB
89Elmira/Pucko-28
89WinHaven/Star-24

Thompson, Michael Wayne
(Mike)
73OPC-564
73T-564
76Indianap-18
76OPC-536
76SSPC-6
76T-536
Thompson, Milt
84Richm-25
85Richm-21
86D-507
86F-530
86F/Up-U114
86Phill/TastyK-24
86T-517
86T/Tr-112T
87D-330
87D/OD-154
87F-191
87Phill/TastyK-24
87T-409
88D-236
88D/Best-296
88F-319
88F/St-112
88OPC-298
88Panini/St-363
88Phill/TastyK-25
88S-115
88Sf-173
88T-298
88T/Big-2
89B-441
89D-313
89D/Best-212
89D/Tr-43
89F-584
89F/Up-121
89OPC-128
89Panini/St-157
89RedFoley/St-119
89S-92
89S/Tr-45
89Sf-169
89Smok/Cards-21
89T-128
89T/Tr-118T
89UD-317
90B-196
90D-82
90F-262
90Leaf/II-308M
90OPC-688
90Panini/St-345
90Publint/St-230
90S-49
90Smok/Card-24
90T-688
90T/Big-126
90T/St-37
90T/TVCard-36
90UD-278
91B-386
91D-225
91F-649
91F/Ultra-297
91Leaf/I-176
91Leaf/Stud-239
91OPC-63
91Panini/FrSt-36
91Pol/Card-25
91S-54
91T-63
91T/StClub/I-66
91UD-309A
91UD-309B
92D/II-513
92F-595
92S/I-114
92T-323
92UD-397
Thompson, Richard
(Rich)
81Watlo-16
82Chatt-5
83Ander-32
83BuffB-7
84BuffB-12
85F/Up-U120
85Maine-11
85Polar/Ind-41
85T/Tr-122T
86F-595
86OPC-242
86T-242
86T/St-215
86Vanco-26
88Memphis/Best-2
89Indianap/CMC-10
89Indianap/ProC-1237
90Indianap/CMC-9
90Indianap/ProC-304
90OPC-474
90T-474
Thompson, Rick
82AubAs-19
Thompson, Rob
89Utica/Pucko-25
Thompson, Robby
86D/Rook-39
86F/Up-U115
86Mother/Giants-16
86Sf/Rook-25
86T/Tr-113T
87D-145
87D/OD-101
87F-285
87F/AwardWin-39
87F/Mini-106
87Leaf-64
87Mother/SFG-10
87MSA/Discs-12
87Sf-46
87T-658
87T/Gloss60-40
87T/GlossRk-21
87T/St-307
87T/St-91
87ToysRUs-30
88D-268
88D/Best-274
88F-98
88Leaf-120
88Mother/Giants-10
88OPC-208
88Panini/St-423
88S-146
88S/YS/I-28
88Sf-24
88T-472
88T/Big-83
88T/St-93
89B-473
89D-98
89D/Best-79
89F-344
89Mother/Giants-10
89OPC-15
89Panini/St-215
89RedFoley/St-120
89S-172
89S/HotStar-84
89Sf-78
89T-15
89T/Big-163
89T/St-87
89UD-172
90B-233
90D-140
90D/BestNL-73
90F-73
90Leaf/I-199
90MLBPA/Pins-26
90Mother/Giant-10
90OPC-325
90Panini/St-371
90Publint/St-83
90S-397
90S/100St-21
90Sf-60
90T-325
90T/Big-169
90T/Coins-59
90T/Mini-88
90T/St-83
90UD-169
91B-623
91Classic/200-44
91D-363
91F-273
91F/Ultra-329
91Leaf/I-107
91Mother/Giant-10
91OPC-705
91Panini/FrSt-68
91Panini/St-77
91PG&E-2
91S-26
91SFExam/Giant-14
91T-705
91T/StClub/I-77
91UD-178
92D/I-52
92F-648
92S/I-247
92T-475
92UD-286
Thompson, Ryan
88StCath/ProC-2035
89StCath/ProC-2072
90Dunedin/Star-19
91Knoxvl/LineD-367
91Knoxvl/ProC-1783
Thompson, Sam
80SSPC/HOF
E223
N172
N284
Scrapps
WG1-25
Thompson, Scot
79T-716R
80OPC-298
80T-574
81Coke
81D-519
81F-296
81T-295
82Iowa-11
82RedLob
83D-378
83T-481
84D-167
85F-621
85Mother/Giants-15
85T-646
86F-262
86Fresno/Smok-21
86OPC-93
86T-93
Thompson, Sean
88Pocatel/ProC-2079
90Salinas/Cal-137
90Salinas/ProC-2734
Thompson, Squeezer
88Spokane/ProC-1927
90CharRain/ProC-2030
Thompson, Tim
61BeeHive-24
Thompson, Tim
82Knoxvl-12
83Syrac-20
84Syrac-30
Thompson, Timothy
84Visalia-11
Thompson, Tom
86BuffB-22
87SanBern-23
Thompson, Tommy
47Signal
47Sunbeam
Thompson, Tommy
79ArkTr-7
81Durham-5
82Durham-11
82FtMyr-3
87Hawaii-9
Thompson, Tommy
86Jaxvl/TCMA-19C
87Jaxvl-25
88BirmB/Best-10
88Jaxvl/Best-24
88Jaxvl/ProC-971
88SLAS-39
89BirmB/Best-27
89BirmB/ProC-104
89Tulsa/GS-1MG
89Tulsa/Team-25MG
90SoBend/CIBest-27MG
90Tulsa/ProC-1172MG
90Utica/Pucko-25
91OkCty/LineD-324MG
91OkCty/ProC-193MG
91Pac/SenLg-86
91SoBend/ProC-2MG
Thompson, Tony
86LitFalls-28
Thompson, William
90CharRain/Best-22
Thompson, Willie
78Knoxvl
79Knoxvl/TCMA-26
Thomsen, Chris
91SoOreg/CIBest-7
91SoOreg/ProC-3858
Thomson, Bobby
47HomogBond-46
48B-47
49B-18
49Eureka-124
49Royal-10
50B-28
50Drake-9
51B-126
52B-2
52BR
52Coke
52RM-NL24
52Royal
52StarCal/L-78A
52T-313
53RM-NL25
53SpicSpan/3x5-24
53SpicSpan/7x10-13
54B-201
54JC-34
54SpicSpan/PostC-18
55B-102
55Gol/Braves-28
55JC-34
55RFG-23
55SpicSpan/DC-17
56T-257
57SpicSpan/4x5-16
57T-262
58Hires-46
58SFCallB-24
58T-430
59T-429
60NuCard-10
60T-153
61NuCard-480
76Laugh/Jub-29
79TCMA-202
80Pac/Leg-115
88Pac/Leg-45
89Swell-133
89T/LJN-45
90HOF/St-46
90Pac/Legend-106
90Swell/Great-21
91B-410M
91Crown/Orio-456
91Swell/Great-88
91T/Arc53-330
D305
Exh47
PM10/Sm-188
R346-41
Thomson, Rob
88Lakeland/Star-24
89EastLDD/ProC-DD45CO
89London/ProC-1379CO
90FtLaud/Star-25CO
91PrWill/CIBest-26CO
91PrWill/ProC-1444CO
Thon, Dickie
76QuadC
78Cr/PCL-112
80T-663R
81D-290
81F-277
81T-209
81T/Tr-844
82F-235
82T-404
83D-191
83F-468
83T-558
84D-304
84D/AAS-44
84F-243
84F-634IA
84F/St-1
84Mother/Ast-7
84Nes/792-692
84OPC-344
84Seven-23W
84T-692
84T/St-64
85F-364
85Mother/Ast-9
85OPC-44
85T-44
85T/St-63
86D-572
86F-313
86Mother/Ast-26
86OPC-166
86Pol/Ast-17
86T-166
86T/St-33
87D-261
87F-70
87Leaf-196
87Mother/Ast-25
87Pol/Ast-14
87T-386
88S/Tr-29T
88Smok/Padres-29
88T/Tr-121T
89B-400
89D-441
89F-320
89OPC-181
89Phill/TastyK-34
89S-234
89S/Tr-55
89T-726
89T/Tr-119T
89UD-258
89UD/Ext-704
90B-155
90D-549
90D/BestNL-81
90F-573
90Leaf/I-105
90MLBPA/Pins-4
90OPC-269
90Panini/St-318
90Phill/TastyK-28
90Publint/St-251
90S-142
90T-269
90T/Big-115
90T/St-115
90UD-439
91B-499
91D-91
91F-412
91F/Ultra-272
91Leaf/I-60
91OPC-439
91Panini/FrSt-106
91Panini/St-106
91Phill/Medford-34
91S-103
91T-439
91T/StClub/I-184
91UD-449
92D/II-510
92F-546
92S/I-24
92T-557
92UD-150
Thon, Frankie
78Cedar
80Clinton-17
Thoney, John
E107
M116
T201
Thor, Audie
80Memphis-30
Thoren, Rick
77AppFx
Thormahlen, H.F.
90Target-801
V100
Thormodsgard, Paul
78OPC-73
78T-162
79T-249
79Toledo-2
80OkCty
Thorn, John
90LitSun-23
Thornton, Al
86Elmira-24
87Elmira/Black-13
87Elmira/Red-13
88Elmira-20
Thornton, Andre
74OPC-604R
74T-604R
75OPC-39

75T-39
75T/M-39
76Crane-62
76MSA/Disc
76OPC-26
76T-26
78OPC-114
78T-148
79Ho-93
79OPC-140
79T-280
79T/Comics-6
80K-28
80OPC-278
80T-534
80T/S-43
81D-198
81OPC-128
81T-388
81T/St-70
82D-324
82F-380
82F/St-201
82OPC-161
82T-746
82T/St-174
82Wheat/Ind
83D-211
83F-421
83F-635M
83K-26
83OPC-344
83T-640
83T/Gloss40-3
83T/St-55
83Wheat/Ind-29
84D-25DK
84D-94
84D/AAS-15
84F-554
85FunFoodPin-125
84Nes/792-115
84OPC-115
84T-115
84T/St-255
84Wheat/Ind-29
85D-468
85F-457
85F/St-32
85F/St-47
85Leaf-102
85OPC-272
85Polar/Ind-29
85T-475
85T/St-244
86D-251
86F-596
86F/St-120
86Leaf-129
86OhHenry-29
86OPC-59
86Sf-171
86T-336M
86T-59
86T/St-208
87D-279
87D/OD-108
87F-262
87Gator-29
87OPC-327
87T-780
88RedFoley/St-91
88S-231
89Swell-117
90Swell/Great-47

Thornton, Eric
89Kingspt/Star-23
90Pittsfld/Pucko-3

Thornton, Lou
85F/Up-U121
85Tor/Fire-29
86F-71
86OPC-18
86Syrac-25
86T-488
87Syrac-3
87Syrac/TCMA-21
89BuffB/CMC-22
89BuffB/ProC-1669
89Tidew/ProC-1954
90Kahn/Mets-1
90T/TVMets-34
90Tidew/CMC-11
90Tidew/ProC-559
91WIZMets-406

Thornton, Woodie A.
T206
T213/brown

Thorp, Bradley S.
81VeroB-22

Thorpe, Benjamin R.
(Bob)
52T-367
53SpicSpan/3x5-25

Thorpe, James F.
(Jim)
33SK-6
73F/Wild-3
87Conlon/2-59
88Conlon/4-28
92Conlon/Sport-403
D350/2-176
M101/5-176

Thorpe, Michael
86Cram/PCL-111
87Wausau-19

Thorpe, Paul
86Hagers-25
87Hagers-23
88CharlK/Pep-17
89Hagers/Best-19
89Hagers/ProC-285
89Hagers/Star-21
90EastLAS/ProC-EL10
90Hagers/Best-26
90Hagers/ProC-1414
90Hagers/Star-24

Thorson, Brian
(Doc)
79Holyo-16
80BurlB-9
81Vanco-7
82Vanco-24
84Albany-9
85Huntsvl/BK-TR
88Madis-24
90Huntsvl/Best-26
91Huntsvl/ClBest-10

Thorton, John
86ElPaso-21

Thoutsis, Paul
87WinHaven-27

Thrams, Jeff
89Boise/ProC-1988

Threadgill, Chris
89PalmSp/Cal-42
89PalmSp/ProC-472

Threadgill, George
85BurlR-8
86DayBe-28
86FSLAS-46
88Tulsa-2
89Tulsa/GS-26

Threatt, Tony
83Tampa-24

Thrift, Jim
87Salem-18
89Penin/Star-26MG
90Kgsport/Best-25MG
90Kgsport/Star-26MG
91Pittsfld/ClBest-25MG
91Pittsfld/ProC-3438MG

Throneberry, M. Faye
52T-376
53T-49
55T-163
57T-356
59T-534
60L-136
60T-9
61T-282
91T/Arc53-49

Throneberry, Marv
58T-175
59T-326
60T-436
61P-85
61T-57
61T/St-166
63J-194
63P-194
63T-78
79TCMA-173
88Pac/Leg-48
90Pac/Legend-62
90Swell/Great-77
91Crown/Orio-457
91Swell/Great-89
91WIZMets-407

Throop, George
76OPC-591R
76T-591R

Thrower, Keith
85Cram/PCL-128
86Tacom-22

Thurberg, Tom
77Wausau
81Louisvl-25
82ArkTr-10
83Louisvl/Riley-25

Thurman, Gary
85FtMyr-18
86SLAS-4
87Omaha-6
88D-44
88D/Rook-33
88F-272
88F/Mini-29
88Leaf-44RR
88Omaha/CMC-14
88Omaha/ProC-1521
88S-631
88S/YS/II-25
88Sf-223
88Smok/Royals-6
88T-89
89D-498
89F-296
89Panini/St-348
89S/HotRook-24
89T-323
89UD-347
90D-416
90F-121
90Omaha/CMC-19
90OPC-276
90PublInt/St-359
90T-276
91B-316
91F-573
91F/UltraUp-U29
91Pol/Royal-23
91T/StClub/II-306
92D/I-346
92F-172
92S/II-512
92T-494
92UD-629

Thurman, Robert
52Mother-49
56Kahn
57Kahn
57T-279
58T-34
59T-341
86Negro/Frit-60

Thurmond, Mark
81Hawaii-21
82Hawaii-21
84D-505
84F-315
84Mother/Padres-26
84Nes/792-481
84Smok/Padres-25
84T-481
85D-284
85F-46
85Leaf-149
85Mother/Padres-21
85OPC-236
85T-236
86D-261
86F-337
86T-37
87Cain's-17
87D-543
87F-166
87T-361
88D-599
88F-73
88S-382
88T-552
89French-21
89T-152
89UD-571
90D-612
90F-191
90OPC-758
90PublInt/St-588
90S-350
90T-758
91Crown/Orio-458
91F-274
91Phoenix/LineD-389

Thurston, Hollis
(Sloppy)
25Exh-80
26Exh-80
28Exh/PCL-28
90Target-802

Thurston, Jerry
91CharRain/ClBest-13
91CharRain/ProC-98
91Single/ClBest-102
91Spokane/ClBest-21
91Spokane/ProC-3952

Tiant, Luis
65Kahn
65OPC-145
65T-145
65T/trans-30
66T-285
67T-377
68Kahn
68T-532
69Kahn
69MB-271
69MLB/St-44
69MLBPA/Pin-28
69OPC-11LL
69OPC-7LL
69OPC-9LL
69OPC/DE-22
69T-11LL
69T-560
69T-7LL
69T-9LL
69T/DE-7
69T/decal
69T/S-13
69T/St-169
69Trans-3
70K-56
70MLB/St-239
70OPC-231
70T-231
71MLB/St-475
71OPC-95
71T-95
72MB-342
73OPC-270
73OPC-65LL
73T-270
73T-65LL
74OPC-167
74T-167
74T/DE-27
74T/St-138
75Ho-102
75K-49
75OPC-430
75T-430
75T/M-430
76Crane-63
76Ho-23
76Ho/Twink-23
76MSA/Disc
76OPC-130
76SSPC-424
76T-130
77BurgChef-34
77Ho-10
77OPC-87
77T-258
77T/CS-48
78OPC-124
78PapaG/Disc-23
78T-345
78Wiffle/Discs-75
79BK/Y-8
79OPC-299
79T-575
80OPC-19
80T-35
81D-231
81F-82
81Portl-23
81T-627
82OPC-160
82T-160
83D-542
83OPC-179SV
83T-178
83T-179SV
89Pac/SenLg-77
89TM/SenLg-105
89TM/SenLg-118M
90EliteSenLg-119
91LineD-11
91Swell/Great-90

Tibbs, Jay
82Lynch-19
83Lynch-16
84Tidew-15
85D-262
85F-553
85T-573
86D-262
86F-194
86F/Up-U116
86Provigo-8
86T-176
86T/Tr-114T
87D-282
87F-333
87Leaf-207
87OPC-9
87T-9
88French-53
88OPC-282
88RochR/Team-24
88RochR/CMC-10
88RochR/ProC-201
88S-608
88T-464
89F-624
89RochR/ProC-1633
89S-262
89T-271
89UD-655
90F-192
90OPC-677
90PublInt/St-589
90S-480
90T-677
91Crown/Orio-459

Tiburcio, Freddy
82Durham-12
83Durham-14
86Greenvl/Team-20
87Toledo-11
87Toledo/TCMA-6

Tidrow, Dick
72OPC-506R
72T-506R
73OPC-339
73T-339
74OPC-231
74T-231
74T/St-170
75OPC-241
75T-241
75T/M-241
76OPC-248
76SSPC-428
76T-248
77BK/Y-9
77OPC-235
77T-461
78BK/Y-6
78T-179
79OPC-37
79T-89
80T-594
81Coke
81D-551
81F-299
81T-352
82D-477
82F-604
82F/St-99
82OPC-249
82RedLob
82T-699
82T/St-27
83F-510
83T-787
83T/St-225
83T/Tr-112T
83TrueVal/WSox-41
84F-72
84Nes/792-153
84T-153
91WIZMets-408

Tidwell, Mike
91Geneva/ClBest-22
91Geneva/ProC-4216

Tiefenauer, Bob
55Hunter

59T-501
62T-227
62T/St-131
64T-522
65OPC-23
65T-23
68T-269
80Penin/B-10C
80Penin/C-27C
83Reading-24
85Cram/PCL-47
86Portl-22C
87Spartan-22C
88Batavia/ProC-1662

Tiernan, Mike
N172
N566-176
WG1-44

Tierney, James A.
(Cotton)
21Exh-176
21Exh-177
90Target-803
E120
V100
W572
W573
WG7-55

Tierney, Tom
91Idaho/ProC-4343

Tijerina, Tony
91Pittsfld/ClBest-1
91Pittsfld/ProC-3426

Tilden, Bill
33SK-16

Tillman, Darren
91Hunting/ClBest-25
91Hunting/ProC-3350

Tillman, J. Bob
61Union
62T-368
63T-384
64T-112
65OPC-222
65T-222
66OPC-178
66T-178
67OPC-36
67T-36
67T/Test/RSox-23
68OPC-174
68T-174
69MB-272
69T-374
70T-668
71MLB/St-453
71OPC-244
71T-244
72MB-343
78TCMA-172

Tillman, Ken
81Redwd-20

Tillman, Rusty
82Tidew-11
83Tidew-19
84Tidew-9
85Cram/PCL-102
86Tacom-23
88Phoenix/CMC-21
88Phoenix/ProC-59
89Phoenix/CMC-15
89Phoenix/ProC-1479
91WIZMets-409

Tillman, Tommy
(Tony)
89Burllnd/Star-23
90Burllnd/ProC-3008

Tillotson, Thad
67T-553R

Tilma, Tommy
90WichSt-34

Tilmon, Pat
89Durham/Team-21
89Durham/Star-21
90Durham/Team-14

Timberlake, Don
83Peoria/LF-13
85MidldA-12
86MidldA-22

Timberlake, Gary
No Cards.

Timko, Andy
81Miami-13
90HagersDG/Best-32

Timlin, Mike
88Myrtle/ProC-1184
89Dunedin/Star-19
90Dunedin/Star-20
90FSLAS/Star-45
91B-15
91Classic/III-90
91D/Rook-27
91F/Up-U68
91Leaf/II-525
91OPC/Premier-122
91S/RookTr-85T
91S/ToroBJ-7
91T/Tr-121T
91UD/Ext-785
92D/I-301
92F-343
92F/RookSlns-12
92S/100RisSt-58
92S/I-214
92T-108
92T/91Debut-172
92UD-409

Timmerman, Tom
70T-554
71MLB/St-408
71OPC-296
71T-296
72OPC-239
72T-239
73OPC-413
73T-413
74OPC-327
74T-327

Timmons, Ozzie
91Geneva/ClBest-23
91Geneva/ProC-4233

Tincup, Frank
44Centen-23

Tingle, Darrel
87Oneonta-3
88PrWill/Star-22

Tingley, Ron
81Hawaii-1
82Hawaii-1
85Cram/PCL-97
86Richm-23
87BuffB-11
88ColoSp/CMC-12
88ColoSp/ProC-1532
89ColoSp/CMC-11
89ColoSp/ProC-257
89F-414
89Panini/St-316
89S/HotRook-56
89T-721
89T/Big-37
90Edmon/CMC-23
90Edmon/ProC-520
91Edmon/LineD-171
91Edmon/ProC-1519
92D/I-287
92S/II-757

Tinker, Harold
88Negro/Duques-19

Tinker, Joe
10Domino-116
11Helmar-107
12Sweet/Pin-93
12Sweet/Pin-93A
14CJ-3
14Piedmont/St-55
15CJ-3
48Exh/HOF
50Callahan
60Exh/HOF-23
60F-40
61F-143
63Bz/ATG-1
69Bz/Sm
80Pac/Leg-42
80SSPC/HOF
BF2-68
D303
D329-174
D350/2-177
E101
E102
E105
E106
E254
E270/1
E300
E90/1
E90/3
E91
E92
E93
E96
E98
L1-122
M101/4-174
M101/5-177
M116
PM1-13
S74-71
S81-97
T202
T204
T205
T206
T207
T213/blue
T215/blue
T215/brown
T216
T3-35
W555
WG5-40
WG6-36

Tinkey, Jim
86SanJose-21

Tinkey, Robert
87Kenosha-13
88Kenosha/ProC-1379

Tinkle, David
86Cram/PCL-27
87FtMyr-5

Tinning, Lyle
32Orbit/num-17
32Orbit/un-55
34G-71
R305

Tinsley, Lee
88SoOreg/ProC-1706
89Madis/Star-21
90Madison/Best-12
90Madison/ProC-2282
91Huntsvl/ClBest-23
91Huntsvl/LineD-295
91HuntsvlProC-1810
91Single/ClBest-207
92T-656M

Tipton, Gordon
88CapeCod/Sum-136

Tipton, Jeff
82Madis-13

Tipton, Joe
49B-103
50B-159
51B-82
52T-134
53B/BW-13
53Briggs
54B-180

Tirado, Aristarco
86Albany/TCMA-25
86FtLaud-22
87PrWill-18
88Albany/ProC-1348
89Albany/Best-18
89Albany/ProC-331
89Albany/Star-20

Tischinski, Tom
70OPC-379
70T-379
71MLB/St-476
71OPC-724
71T-724
74Albuq/Team-21

Tisdale, Freddie
79ArkTr-11
80ArkTr-18
81ArkTr-5

Tisdale, Tom
90Gaston/Best-28TR
91Gaston/ClBest-28TR

Titcomb, Ledell
N172
N338/2

Titus, John
10Domino-117
11Helmar-152
12Sweet/Pin-132A
12Sweet/Pin-132B
E254
M116
S74-105
T201
T202
T205
T206

Tjader, Jimmy
80Ashvl-11

Toale, John
85Elmira-22
86Cram/PCL-7
86Greens-23
87Clinton-2
87WinHaven-16
89London/ProC-1365
90EastLAS/ProC-EL3
90London/ProC-1283
91Albany/ProC-1013

Tobias, Grayling
80Memphis-24

Tobik, Dave
79T-706R
80T-269
81T-102
82D-511
82T-391
83D-385
83F-343
83OPC-186
83Rang-41
83T-691
83T/Tr-113T
84F-433
84Nes/792-341
84T-341
85Cram/PCL-87

Tobin, Dan
91Billings/ProC-3752

Tobin, James A.
39PB-9
41G-30
90HOF/St-41
92Conlon/Sport-372

Tobin, John T.
(Jack)
21Exh-178
25Exh-118
48Sommer-16
49Sommer-27
53Mother-45
88Conlon/5-28
E120
E126-44
E126-50
V100
V61-2
W573

Todd, Alfred
41G-28
90Target-804
91Conlon/Sport-239

Todd, Chuck
86Watlo-28

Todd, Jackson
78T-481
79Syrac-13
80Syrac-4
81D-31
81OPC-142
81T-142
82D-178
82F-623
82OPC-327
82Syrac-9
82T-565
86ElPaso-22CO
87Denver-21CO
88Denver/ProC-1250
89Denver/CMC-24CO
89Denver/ProC-51CO
90Denver/CMC-26CO
90Denver/ProC-642CO
91Gaston/ProC-2706CO
91WIZMets-410

Todd, Jim
75OPC-519
75T-519
75T/M-519
76OPC-221
76SSPC-478
76T-221
77T-31
78T-333
79OPC-46
79T-103
80T-629

Todd, Kyle
86PrWill-27
87Harris-13
88ColAst/Best-9

Todd, Theron
88CLAS/Star-37
88Durham/Star-21
89Durham/Team-22
89Durham/Star-22
89Star/Wax-73
90Durham/Team-15

Todt, Phil
25Exh-70
26Exh-71
27Exh-35
28Exh-36
29Exh/4-18
33G-86
92Conlon/Sport-419
R316
V354-39

Toerner, Sean
81Clinton-20

Toft, Marv
61Union

Tolan, Bob
65OPC-116R
65T-116R
66OPC-179R
66Pep/Tul
66T-179R
67T-474
68OPC-84
68T-84
69MB-273
69T-448
69T/St-30
70MLB/St-36
70OPC-409
70T-409
71MD
71MLB/St-71
71OPC-190
71OPC-200NLCS
71T-190
71T-200NLCS
71T/Coins-81
71T/tatt-12
72MB-344
72OPC-3
72T-3
73K-32
73OPC-335
73T-335
74Greyhound-6M
74McDon
74OPC-535
74T-535
75Ho-1
75Ho/Twink-1
75OPC-402
75T-402
75T/M-402
76Ho-42
76Ho/Twink-42
76OPC-56
76T-56
77T-188
80T-708
84Beaum-21
85Beaum-25
89Erie/Star-27
89Pac/SenLg-1
89T/SenLg-59
89TM/SenLg-106
90EliteSenLg-2
91Pac/SenLg-152

Tolar, Kevin
90SoBend/ClBest-1
90Utica/Pucko-24
91MidwLAS/ProC-MWL12
91Single/ClBest-114
91SoBend/ProC-2857

Tolbert, Mark
90Savan/ProC-2069

Tolentino, Jose
85Cram/PCL-127
86SLAS-6
87Tacom-17

88OkCty/CMC-14
88OkCty/ProC-41
89Tucson/CMC-13
89Tucson/ProC-183
89Tucson/JP-25
90Tucson/CMC-13
90Tucson/ProC-212
91Tucson/LineD-620
91Tucson/ProC-2222
92D/II-589
92T-541
92T/91Debut-173

Toler, Greg
85Cedar-15
86Cedar/TCMA-11

Toliver, Fred
82Cedar-7
83Indianap-19
84Wichita/Rock-20
86CIGNA-15
86D-612
86F-647R
86F/Up-U117
86Phill/TastyK-43
86Portl-23
87Maine-5
87Maine/TCMA-7
87Phill/TastyK-43
87T-63
88Portl/CMC-8
88Portl/ProC-664
88T-203
89B-147
89D-510
89F-126
89S-479
89T-623
89UD-64
90OPC-423
90T-423

Tolleson, Wayne
79Tulsa-1
80Tulsa-16
83D-573
83Rang-3
83T/Tr-114T
84D-464
84F-434
84Nes/792-557
84Rang-3
84T-557
84T/St-358
85D-378
85F-571
85Rang-3
85T-247
86Coke/WS-1
86D-134
86F-573
86F/Up-U118
86Leaf-59
86T-641
86T/Tr-115T
87D-524
87D/OD-245
87F-118
87OPC-224
87T-224
88D-154
88F-223
88OPC-133
88Panini/St-157
88S-117
88T-411
89D-659
89S/NWest-9
89T-716
90PublInt/St-549
90S-386
90S/NWest-26
90T/Tr-123T
90T/TVYank-27
90TulsaDG/Best-3
90UD-320

Tollison, Dave
88CapeCod/Sum-141
90StCath/ProC-3471
91Dunedin/ClBest-19
91Dunedin/ProC-217

Tolliver, Jerome
91Pittsfld/ClBest-7
91Pittsfld/ProC-3437

Tolman, Tim
81Tucson-20
82Tucson-8
84Cram/PCL-57
85Mother/Ast-23
86Nashvl-24
86T-272
87Toledo-12
87Toledo/TCMA-23
88Tidew/CANDL-13
88Tidew/CMC-23
88Tidew/ProC-1584
89Syrac/CMC-14
89Syrac/ProC-815
89Syrac/Team-22
90Tucson/ProC-221CO
91BurlAs/ClBest-27MG
91BurlAs/ProC-2817MG

Toman, Tom
75AppFx
76AppFx
78Knoxvl

Tomanek, Dick
58T-123
59T-369

Tomaselli, Chuck
84Nashvl-23

Tomberlin, Andy
86Sumter-27
89Durham/Team-23
89Durham/Star-23
89Star/Wax-74
90Foil/Best-265
90Greenvl/Best-19
90Greenvl/ProC-1142
90Greenvl/Star-19
90Richm/Bob-20
91Richm/LineD-445

Tomberlin, Rob
86Sumter-28

Tomlin, Dave
75OPC-578
75T-578
75T/M-578
76OPC-398
76SSPC-627
76T-398
77Padre/SchCd-33
77T-241
78T-86
79T-674
80T-126
81Syrac-22
82Indianap-25
84Cram/PCL-126
85Cram/PCL-241
86Indianap-31
87Indianap-7

Tomlin, Randy Leon
88Watertn/Pucko-12
89Salem/Star-22
90A&AASingle/ProC-14
90Harris/ProC-1192
90Harris/Star-17
91B-518
91Classic/I-83
91D-725
91F-52
91F/UltraUp-U103
91Leaf/I-203
91OPC-167
91S-782
91T-167A
91T-167B
91T/90Debut-154
91T/StClub/I-178
91ToysRUs-28
91UD/FinalEd-76F
92D/I-367
92F-569
92S/I-86
92T-571
92UD-537

Tomlin, Rick
90Elizab/Star-25
91Elizab/ProC-4317CO

Tommy, Phillip
N172

Tomori, Denny
88Butte-12

Tompkins, Ron
66OPC-107R
66T-107R
68T-247R

Toms, Tommy
76Phoenix
77Phoenix

Tomsick, Troy
85Durham-13

Tomski, Jeffery
77Watlo
81Chatt-22

Tomso, Matt
91Savan/ClBest-12
91Savan/ProC-1653

Tonascia, Bruce
78Green

Toney, Anthony
(Andy)
88Fayette/ProC-1082
88SALAS/GS-15
89Lakeland/Star-23

Toney, Chris
88Martins/Star-31

Toney, Fred
11Helmar-108
16FleischBrd-94
61F-80
69Bz-1
72F/FFeat-14M
72Laugh/GF-39M
90HOF/St-17M
92Conlon/Sport-347
D327
D328-174
D329-175
D350/2-178
E120
E121/120
E121/80
E135-174
M101/4-175
M101/5-178
W501-69
W575

Tonkin, Wyatt
(Tonk)
78Green

Tonnucci, Norm
86Knoxvl-24
87Knoxvl-25
88Syrac/CMC-6
88Syrac/ProC-809

Tooch, Chuck
91Welland/ProC-3583

Toole, Matt
90Waterlo/Best-24
90Waterlo/ProC-2387

Tooley, Albert
90Target-805
T207

Toolson, Earl
49Remar

Toporcer, George
(Specs)
21Exh-179
25Exh-64
26Exh-64
88Conlon/3-30
91Conlon/Sport-176
92Conlon/Sport-644
E120
E121/120
E126-9
V61-82
W501-79
W573
W575

Torborg, Doug
85Anchora-27
87Watertn-28
88Salem/Star-21
89Miami/II/Star-18

Torborg, Jeff
64T-337R
65T-527
66T-257
67T-398
68T-492
69MB-274
69T-353
70OPC-54
70T-54
71MLB/St-119
71OPC-314
71T-314
72MB-345
72OPC-404
72T-404
73OPC-154
73T-154
78T-351
79T-96
89Coke/WS-3
89T/Tr-120MG
90Coke/WSox-26MG
90OPC-21MG
90T-21MG
90Target-806
91Kodak/WSox-10MG
91OPC-609MG
91T-609MG
92T-759MG

Torchia, Todd
87Spokane-21
88Charl/ProC-1209

Torchia, Tony
81Bristol-8
83Pawtu-25
84Pawtu-3A
84Pawtu-3B
86NewBrit-24MG
87CharRain-17
88River/Cal-229
88River/ProC-1413
89LasVegas/ProC-27
90LasVegas/CMC-24CO
90LasVegas/ProC-139CO
91LasVegas/ProC-255CO
91LasVegas/LineD-300CO

Torgeson, Earl
49B-17
50B-163
50Drake-3
51B-99
51T/BB-34
52B-72
52NTea
52RM-NL25
52T-97
52TipTop
54B-63
55B-210
56T-147
57T-357
58T-138
59T-351
60L-122
60T-299
61T-152
Exh47

Tornay, Nine
53Mother-11

Torre, Frank
56T-172
57T-37
58T-117
59T-65
60Lake
60SpicSpan-24
60T-478
62T-303
63T-161
90Pac/Legend-53
90Swell/Great-74
91Swell/Great-91

Torre, Joe
62J-152
62P-152
62P/Can-152
62Salada-152
62Shirriff-152
62T-218
62T-351M
62T/St-151
63J-156
63P-156
63T-347
64T-70
64T/Coins-118
64T/Coins-155AS
64T/S-26
64T/St-59
64T/SU
64T/tatt
64Wheat/St-44
65Bz-16
65Kahn
65OldLond-19
65OPC-200
65T-200
65T/E-12
65T/trans-31
66Bz-36
66Kahn
66OPC-130
66T-130
66T/RO-120
67Bz-36
67Kahn
67OPC/PI-27
67T-350
67T/PI-27
68Bz-10
68Coke
68Dexter-73
68Kahn
68OPC-30
68T-30
68T/G-31
69Citgo-11
69Kahn
69Kelly/Pin-17
69MB-275
69MLB/St-216
69MLBPA/Pin-58
69T-460
69T/S-36
69T/St-10
69Trans-49
70MLB/St-144
70OPC-190
70T-190
70Trans-3
71K-62
71MLB/St-287
71OPC-370
71OPC-62LL
71T-370
71T-62LL
71T/Coins-11
71T/S-61
71T/tatt-10
72K-10
72MB-346
72OPC-341KP
72OPC-500
72OPC-85LL
72OPC-87LL
72T-341KP
72T-500
72T-85LL
72T-87LL
72T/Post-16
73K-31
73OPC-450
73T-450
73T/Comics-22
73T/Lids-52
73T/PinUps-22
74OPC-15
74T-15
74T/St-119
75Ho-70
75OPC-209MV
75OPC-565
75T-209MV
75T-565
75T/M-209MV
75T/M-565
76Crane-64
76MSA/Disc
76OPC-585
76SSPC-541
76T-585
77T-425
78T-109MG
78TCMA-137
79T-82MG
80T-259MG
81D-506MG
81F-325MG
81T-681MG
82KMart-20
82Pol/Atl-9MG
83D-628MG
83Pol/Atl-9
83T-126MG
84Nes/792-502MG
84Pol/Atl-9MG
84T-502MG
85T-438MG
86Sf/Dec-49M
90MSA/AGFA-4
90Pac/Legend-107
90Swell/Great-130

91Leaf/StudPrev-17MG
91LineD-2
91OPC-351MG
91Pol/Card-9MG
91Swell/Great-92
91T-351MG
91WIZMets-411
92T-549MG

Torrealba, Pablo
76OPC-589R
76T-589R
77T-499
78T-78
79T-242
90Richm25Ann/Team-22

Torres, Al
89Miami/II/Star-19

Torres, Alfredo
77Charl
78Salem
80Buffa-13
81Portl-24
82Buffa-7

Torres, Angel
78Indianap-18
80Indianap-27

Torres, Felix
62T-595R
63J-27
63P-27
63T-482

Torres, Freddy
89Fayette/ProC-1588
89NiagFls/Pucko-22
90Fayette/ProC-2418

Torres, Hector
69T-526
70OPC-272
70T-272
71MLB/St-47
71OPC-558
71T-558
72T-666
76OPC-241
76SSPC-128
76T-241
78Syrac
80Utica-11
82Knoxvl-22
87Syrac-20
87Syrac/TCMA-25
88Syrac/CMC-23
88Syrac/ProC-822
89Syrac/ProC-801
89Syrac/Team-25CO
91Tor/Fire-56

Torres, Jessie
90Augusta/ProC-2468
91Augusta/ClBest-14
91Augusta/ProC-808

Torres, Jose
83Butte-11
89Princet/Star-21

Torres, Leo
89Fayette/ProC-1569
90Fayette/ProC-2408
91Lakeland/ClBest-12
91Lakeland/ProC-267

Torres, Martin
85Tigres-13

Torres, Miguel
88Oneonta/ProC-2054

Torres, Paul
89Wythe/Star-27
90Geneva/ProC-3048
90Geneva/Star-7
90Peoria/Team-14
91Peoria/ClBest-13
91Single/ClBest-174
91WinSalem/ClBest-26
91WinSalem/ProC-2843

Torres, Phil
87VeroB-31
88SanAn/Best-17
89ColMud/Best-27

Torres, Ramon
89Burllnd/Star-24
90Burllnd/ProC-3024
91Collnd/ProC-1502

Torres, Ray
79Knoxvl/TCMA-23
80GlenF/B-8
80GlenF/C-27
81AppFx-25
81GlenF-21

Torres, Rick
88Albany/ProC-1338
89Albany/Best-11
89Albany/ProC-335
89Albany/Star-21
90Albany/Best-10
90Albany/Star-21
90ColClip/CMC-18
90ColClip/ProC-677
90T/TVYank-64

Torres, Ricky
84Greens-17
87PrWill-4

Torres, Rosendo
(Rusty)
72OPC-124R
72T-124R
73OPC-571
73T-571
74OPC-499
74T-499
77T-224
78Cr/PCL-118
80T-36
81Portl-25

Torres, Rudy
83Ander-17

Torres, Salomon
91Clinton/ClBest-8
91Clinton/ProC-834
91MidwLAS/ProC-MWL6
91Single/ClBest-324

Torres, Tony
80Holyo-24
81ElPaso-18

Torrez, Mike
68OPC-162R
68T-162R
69OPC-136R
69T-136R
70OPC-312
70T-312
71MLB/St-288
71OPC-531
71T-531
73OPC-77
73T-77
74OPC-568
74T-568
75OPC-254
75T-254
75T/M-254
76Ho-139
76OPC-25
76SSPC-381
76T-25
77BK/Y-7
77BurgChef-110
77Ho-13
77OPC-144
77T-365
78Ho-127
78PapaG/Disc-21
78T-645
79Ho-22
79OPC-92
79T-185
80OPC-236
80T-455
81D-216
81F-233
81OPC-216
81T-525
82Coke/Bos
82D-235
82F-310
82F/St-160
82T-225
82T-786TL
82T/St-151
83D-512
83F-197
83OPC-312
83T-743
83T/Tr-115
84D-556
84F-602
84Nes/792-78
84OPC-78
84T-78
84T/St-113
89Pac/Leg-168
91Crown/Orio-460
91WIZMets-412

Torrez, Peter
80RochR-21
84CharlO-9

Torricelli, Tim
87Stockton-22
88Beloit/GS-14
89ElPaso/GS-19
90Denver/CMC-8
90Denver/ProC-629

Torrienti, Christobel
74Laugh/Black-18
90Negro/Star-19

Tortorice, Mark
86Modesto-25

Torve, Kelvin
83Phoenix/BHN-12
84Shrev/FB-23
85CharlO-7
86RochR-24
87RochR-21
87RochR/TCMA-15
88Portl/CMC-15
88Portl/ProC-641
89AAA/CMC-32
89Panini/St-380
89Portl/CMC-16
89Portl/ProC-220
89UD-177
90AAAGame/ProC-AAA5
90F/Up-U40
90T/TVMets-63
90Tidew/CMC-22
90Tidew/ProC-554
91F-163
91S-754RP
91Tidew/LineD-569
91Tidew/ProC-2520
91WIZMets-413

Torve, Kenton Craig
87BirmB/Best-20

Tosca, Carlos
83Greens-27
84Greens-1
91BBCity/ClBest-28MG

Tost, Lou
49Remar
50Remar

Toth, Dave
91Idaho/ProC-4334

Toth, Paul
62Kahn/Atl
63T-489
64T-309

Touch, Chuck
91Welland/ClBest-11

Touma, Tim
87WPalmB-2

Toups, Tony
77Watlo

Toussaint, Daris
88Pocatel/ProC-2088

Toutsis, Paul
86Greens-24

Touzzo, John
85LitFalls-10

Tovar, Cesar
65OPC-201R
65T-201R
66T-563R
67T-317
68Coke
68Dexter-72
68T-420
69MB-276
69MLB/St-71
69T-530
69T/St-199
69Trans-9
70MLB/St-240
70OPC-25
70T-25
71K-18
71MD
71MLB/St-477
71OPC-165
71T-165
71T/Coins-52
72MB-347
72OPC-275
72T-275
73OPC-405
73T-405
74OPC-538
74T-538
74T/Tr-538T
75OPC-178
75T-178
75T/M-178
76OPC-246
76T-246
77T-408
78TCMA-174

Tovar, Raul
82Miami-18
83BirmB-1
86MidldA-23

Towers, Kevin
84Beaum-10
86CharRain-26
88LasVegas/CMC-8
88LasVegas/ProC-242
89Spokane/SP-23

Towey, Steve
88Myrtle/ProC-1185
89Modesto/Chong-16

Town, Randall
80Water-6
81Water-10

Townley, Jason
88Dunedin/Star-17
88StCath/ProC-2027
90Dunedin/Star-21
90FSLAS/Star-46
91Knoxvl/LineD-368
91Knoxvl/ProC-1772

Townsend, George
N172
N690

Townsend, Howard
85Everett/Cram-16A
85Everett/Cram-16B
86Clinton-24
87Wausau-5
88SanBern/Cal-45
89Visalia/Cal-100
89Visalia/ProC-1421

Townsend, James
88QuadC/GS-17
89PalmSp/Cal-48
89PalmSp/ProC-463

Townsend, John
E107

Townsend, Ken
77Clinton
78LodiD

Townsend, Lee
88SanBern/Best-3

Townsend, Mike
91Martins/ClBest-30TR

Toy, Tracy
86Watertn-24
87Macon-2
88Augusta/ProC-379

Toyotoshi, Chikada
89Salinas/Cal-131

Traber, Jim
85D-45RR
85RochR-9
86RochR-25
86Sf/Rook-32
87D-477
87F-482
87RochR-26
87RochR/TCMA-20
87T-484
87T/St-232
87ToysRUs-31
88French-28
88RochR/Team-25
88T-544
89B-13
89F-625
89French-28
89OPC-124
89S-590
89T-124
89T/St-233
89UD-294
90D-569
90F-193
90HagersDG/Best-33
90Publint/St-590
90UD-268
91Crown/Orio-461

Tracewski, Dick
64T-154
65OPC-279
65T-279
66T-378
67T-559
68T-488
69MB-277
69OPC-126
69T-126
73OPC-323CO
73T-323CO
88Domino-23
88Pep/T-CO
89Mara/Tigers-CO
90CokeK/Tiger-28CO
90Target-807
91CokeK/Tiger-xCO

Trachsel, Steve
91Geneva/ProC-4217

Tracy, James
(Jim)
80Wichita-2
81D-520
81F-308
82F-605
82F/St-97
82T-403
82Tucson-9
87Myrtle-16
87Peoria-27MG
88Dunedin/Star-18
88Peoria/Ko-29
89Chatt/Best-7
89Chatt/GS-1
89Harris/ProC-309
89Harris/Star-19
90A&AASingle/ProC-13
90EastLAS/ProC-EL27
90Harris/ProC-1193
90Harris/Star-18
91BuffB/LineD-46
91BuffB/ProC-542
91Chatt/LineD-174MG
91Chatt/ProC-1974MG
91Pac/SenLg-70

Tracy, Rich
88Batavia/ProC-1685

Tracy, Rick
87SanJose-20

Traen, Tom
86Jaxvl/TCMA-5
87WPalmB-20

Traffley, William
N172

Trafton, Todd
87DayBe-1
88BirmB/Best-9
89BirmB/Best-19
89BirmB/ProC-97
89SLAS-10
90Vanco/CMC-20
90Vanco/ProC-497
91Chatt/LineD-172
91Chatt/ProC-1969

Tragresser, Walter
16FleischBrd-95

Tramble, Otis
82QuadC-20

Trammell, Alan
78BK/T-15
78T-707R
79OPC-184
79T-358
80OPC-123
80T-232
81Coke
81D-5
81Detroit-68
81F-461
81F/St-89
81K-51
81OPC-133DP
81T-709
81T/So-38
81T/St-75
82D-5DK
82D-76
82F-283
82F/St-155
82OPC-381

82Sqt-4
82T-475
82T/St-181
83D-207
83F-344
83OPC-95
83T-95
83T/St-66
84D-293
84Drake-30
84F-91
84F/St-14
85FunFoodPin-40
84Nes/792-510
84OPC-88
84T-510
84T/St-266
84T/St/Box-9
85Cain's-18
85D-171
85D/AAS-44
85Drake-31
85F-23
85F/LimEd-40
85Leaf-158
85OPC-181
85Seven-15G
85Seven-8D
85T-690
85T/Gloss40-16
85T/St-18WS
85T/St-20
85T/St-258
85T/Super-25
85ThomMc/Discs-20
85Wendy-20
86Cain's-19
86D-171
86D/AAS-45
86F-241
86F-633M
86F/Mini-50
86F/St-121
86Leaf-101
86OPC-130
86Sf-147M
86Sf-172
86T-130
86T/St-267
87Cain's-7
87Coke/Tigers-4
87D-127
87D/HL-51
87D/OD-216
87F-167
87F/Hottest-41
87F/Mini-107
87F/RecSet-38
87F/St-118
87Leaf-126
87OPC-209
87RedFoley/St-62
87Sf-188
87Seven-DT11
87T-687
87T/Mini-56
87T/St-270
88Classic/Blue-231
88D-230
88D-4DK
88D-BC11
88D/AS-22
88D/Best-281
88D/DKsuper-4DK
88Drake-13
88F-635M
88F-74
88F/AS-9
88F/AwardWin-43
88F/BB/AS-42
88F/BB/MVP-39
88F/Excit-42
88F/Hottest-44
88F/LL-42
88F/Mini-25
88F/RecSet-41
88F/SS-41
88F/St-29
88F/TL-43
88FanSam-6
88Jiffy-16
88KayBee-31
88Leaf-167
88Leaf-4DK
88Nestle-35
88OPC-320
88Panini/St-444
88Panini/St-94
88Pep/T-2
88Pol/T-13
88S-37
88S-651M
88Sf-25
88T-320
88T-389AS
88T/Big-8
88T/Coins-30
88T/Gloss60-37
88T/Mini-12
88T/RiteAid-18
88T/St-273
88T/St/Backs-45
88T/UK-79
89T/Ames-29
89B-105
89Cadaco-58
89Classic-128
89T/Crunch-12
89D-180
89D/Best-13
89D/MVP-BC17
89F-148
89F/AS-11
89F/BBAS-41
89F/BBMVP's-39
89F/Excit-41
89F/Heroes-40
89F/LL-40
89F/Superstar-40
89F/WaxBox-C26
89KayBee-30
89KingB/Discs-9
89KMart/Lead-22
89Mara/Tigers-3
89Master/Discs-4
89OPC-49
89Panini/St-343
89Pol/Tigers-3
89MSA/SS-10
89RedFoley/St-121
89S-110
89S/HotStar-7
89Sf-215
89T-400AS
89T-609TL
89T-770
89T/Big-123
89T/Coins-56
89T/DH-4
89T/Gloss60-25
89T/Hills-29
89T/LJN-6
89T/St-281
89T/St/Backs-12
89T/UK-77
89UD-290
89UD-690TC
90B-353
90Classic-106
90CokeK/Tiger-24
90D-90
90D/BestAL-7
90D/Bon/MVP-BC26
90D/Learning-20
90F-617
90F/BB-41
90F/BBMVP-41
90HotPlay/St-46
90Leaf/I-218
90MLBPA/Pins-88
90OPC-440
90Panini/St-70
90Post-28
90PublInt/St-296
90PublInt/St-484
90RedFoley/St-96
90S-9
90S/100St-41
90Sf-154
90Starline/LJS-10
90Starline/LJS-24
90Sunflower-15
90T-440
90T/Big-190
90T/Coins-31
90T/DH-66
90T/St-281
90UD-554
90USPlayC/AS-10S
90WonderBrd-13
91B-154
91B-370SLUG
91Classic/200-97
91Classic/II-T96
91CokeK/Tiger-3
91D-118
91F-355
91F/Ultra-129
91Leaf/II-351
91Leaf/Stud-59
91MajorLg/Pins-33
91OPC-275
91OPC-389AS
91OPC/Premier-123
91Panini/FrSt-291
91Panini/St-238
91Panini/Top15-8
91RedFoley/St-93
91S-40
91S-852FRAN
91S/100SS-63
91Seven/3DCoin-15MW
91T-275
91T-389AS
91T/CJMini/II-26
91T/StClub/I-63
91UD-223
91UD/SilSlug-SS2
92D/I-164
92F-148
92S/II-515
92T-120
92UD-273

Trammell, Marcus
88Utica/Pucko-11

Tramuta, Marc
91Yakima/ClBest-3
91Yakima/ProC-4256

Trapp, Mike
87FtMyr-4

Trautwein, Dave
89Jacks/GS-8
89TexLAS/GS-27
90T/TVMets-64
90Tidew/CMC-12
90Tidew/ProC-545
91Tidew/LineD-570
91Tidew/ProC-2510

Trautwein, John
86Jaxvl/TCMA-7
87Jaxvl-21
87SLAS-14
88D/RedSox/Bk-NEW
88D/Rook-24
88F/Up-U10
89Pawtu/CMC-9
89Pawtu/Dunkin-40
89Pawtu/ProC-685
90Pawtu/CMC-2
90Pawtu/ProC-463
90T/TVRSox-62

Travels, Darren
85Utica-6
86Jamestn-26

Travers, Bill
75OPC-488
75T-488
75T/M-488
76A&P/Milw
76OPC-573
76SSPC-244
76T-573
77BurgChef-90
77Ho-87
77K-9
77OPC-174
77T-125
77T/CS-49
78T-355
79OPC-106
79T-213
80T-109
81D-508
81F-525
81T-704
81T/Tr-845
82T-628
89Pac/SenLg-118
89T/SenLg-21
89TM/SenLg-107

Travers, Steve
82Idaho-13

Travis, Cecil
37OPC-126
37Wheat
38Wheat
39Exh
39PB-114
40PB-16
41DP-75
41PB-48
R303/A
R313
R314
V300

Traxler, Brian
89SanAn/Best-11
90Albuq/Trib-28
90D/Rook-38
91SanAn/LineD-544
91SanAn/ProC-2984
91T/90Debut-155

Traylor, Keith
84LitFalls-9

Traynor, Harold
(Pie)
25Exh-55
26Exh-55
27Exh-28
28Yueng-14
29Exh/4-13
31Exh/4-13
33DL-12
33G-22
34DS-27
34DS-99
34Exh/4-7
35BU-100
35BU-14
35Exh/4-7
35G-2B
35G-4B
35G-7B
36Exh/4-7
50Callahan
60F-77
61F-144
61F-89M
61GP-15
72K/ATG-8
76OPC-343AS
76T-343AS
80Pac/Leg-36
80SSPC/HOF
86Conlon/1-38
86Sf/Dec-11
87Nestle/DT-3
88Conlon/NatAS-21
91Conlon/Sport-268
91Conlon/Sport-36
91Swell/Great-148
92Conlon/Sport-434
E120
E210-14
R311/Gloss
R312/M
R313
R315-A36
R315-B36
R316
R332-23
R337
V117-2
V353-22
W502-14
W513-82
W517-2
W572
WG8-46

Treadway, Andre
82Durham-21
86Richm-24

Treadway, Doug
88WinHaven/Star-24

Treadway, George
90Target-1086

Treadway, Jeff
86Vermont-22
87Nashvl-21
88D-29RR
88D/Rook-17
88F-249
88F/Mini-76
88Kahn/Reds-15
88Leaf-29RR
88S-646RP
88S/YS/II-26
88Sf-225R
88T/Big-214
88T/Tr-122T
89Classic-54
89D-351
89D/Best-141
89F-173
89F/Up-75
89OPC-61
89Panini/St-73
89S-86
89S/HotRook-84
89S/Tr-18
89Sf-107
89T-685
89T/St-139
89T/Tr-121T
89ToysRUs-31
89UD-393
90Classic/III-25
90D-50
90D/BestNL-123
90F-598
90Leaf/II-455
90OPC-486
90Panini/St-218
90S-95
90Sf-219
90T-486
90T/St-29
90UD-141
91B-586
91D-117
91F-707
91F/Ultra-13
91Leaf/I-246
91Leaf/Stud-150
91OPC-139
91Panini/FrSt-20
91Panini/St-28
91S-219
91S/100SS-31
91T-139
91T/StClub/II-497
91UD-499
92D/I-324
92F-373
92S/I-142
92T-99
92UD-389

Treadway, Steven
88CapeCod/Sum-181

Treadwell, Jody
91SanAn/LineD-545
91SanAn/ProC-2975

Treanor, Dean
88Fresno/Cal-26
88Fresno/ProC-1236
90Reno/Cal-288CO

Trebelhorn, Tom
80Port-18
81Portl-2
85Cram/PCL-215
86Pol/Brew-42C
87Pol/Brew-42MG
87T/Tr-121T
88Pol/Brew-42MG
88T-224MG
89Brewer/YB-42MG
89Pol/Brew-42
89T-344MG
90Brewer/MillB-27MG
90OPC-759MG
90Pol/Brew-42MG
90T-759MG
91Brewer/MillB-28MG
91OPC-459MG
91Pol/Brew-25MG
91T-459MG

Trechuck, Frank
V362-6

Tredway, Ed
90Madison/Best-2
90Madison/ProC-2273

Tredway, George
N172

Treece, Jack
44Centen-24

Trella, Steve
75Clinton

Tremark, Nick
90Target-808
Tremblay, Gary
86Pawtu-25
87Pawtu-20
87Pawtu/TCMA-12
88Pawtu/CMC-22
88Pawtu/ProC-450
89Pawtu/CMC-14
89Pawtu/Dunkin-32
89Pawtu/ProC-702
90Pawtu/CMC-13
90Pawtu/ProC-466
90T/TVRSox-63
Tremblay, Wayne
79Elmira-25
85Greens-12
Trembley, Dave
86Kinston-24MG
87Harris-2
88EastLAS/ProC-45
88Harris/ProC-846
89EastLDD/ProC-DD46MG
89Harris/ProC-292MG
91CharRain/ClBest-24MG
91CharRain/ProC-110MG
Tremel, William
55T-52
55T/DH-102
56T-96
56T/Pin-7
Tremper, Overton
90Target-1087
Trent, Ted
78Laugh/Black-1
86Negro/Frit-116
Tresamer, Michael
86Cram/PCL-49
87AppFx-9
88BBCity/Star-22
89Memphis/Best-22
89Memphis/ProC-1197
89Memphis/Star-21
89Star/Wax-45
90Omaha/ProC-65
Tresch, Dave
85Lynch-3
86Lynch-22TR
Tresh, Michael
(Mike)
41DP-69
47TipTop
49B-166
50NumNum
Tresh, Mickey
87PrWill-12
88PrWill/Star-23
89Penin/Star-25
90Lakeland/Star-24
Tresh, Tom
62T-31
63J-23
63P-23
63Salada-54
63T-173
63T-470
64T-395
64T/Coins-10
64Wheat/St-45
65T-440
66Bz-40
66T-205
66T/RO-59
67Bz-40
67T-289
68OPC-69
68T-69
69MB-278
69MLB/St-80
69OPC-212
69T-212
69T/St-209
70MLB/St-215
70T-698
72MB-348
88Pac/Leg-25
89Swell-52
90Swell/Great-17
91Swell/Great-66
WG10-23
WG9-24
Treuel, Ralph
80Evansvl-15
91Toledo/LineD-600CO
91Toledo/ProC-1947CO
Trevino, Alex
77Wausau
78Tidew
80T-537
81Coke
81F-318
81T-23
81T/HT
82Coke/Reds
82D-350
82F-540
82T-368
82T/Tr-120T
83D-374
83F-604
83T-632
83T/St-232
84D-286
84F-484
84F/X-U118
84Nes/792-242
84Pol/Atl-25
84T-242
84T/Tr-120T
85D-565
85F-341
85F/Up-U122
85OPC-279
85T-747
85T/St-30
85T/Tr-123T
86Coke/Dodg-29
86F-550
86F/Up-U119
86OPC-169
86Pol/Dodg-29
86T-444
86T/Tr-116T
87D-546
87F-456
87Mother/Dodg-23
87Pol/Dodg-15
87T-173
88D-376
88Pol/Dodg-29
88S-182
88T-512
88Tucson/CMC-16
88Tucson/JP-22
89B-326
89Lennox/Ast-6
89Mother/Ast-17
89OPC-64
89S-574
89T-64
89UD-262
90D-443
90F-239
90Leaf/II-432
90Lennox-25
90Mother/Ast-21
90OPC-342
90PublInt/St-104
90T-342
90Target-809
90UD-205
91WIZMets-414
Trevino, Tony
88Batavia/ProC-1665
88Spartan/ProC-1040
89Clearw/Star-22
90Clearw/Star-22
90FSLAS/Star-18
91Reading/LineD-521
91Reading/ProC-1378
Triandos, Gus
55Esskay
55T-64
55T/DH-82
56T-80
56T/Pin-4
57Swift-2
57T-156
58T-429
59Armour-18
59Bz
59HRDerby-20
59T-330
59T-568AS
60Armour-19
60Bz-11
60T-60
60T/tatt-51
61Bz-25
61P-69
61T-140
61T/St-106
62J-33
62P-33
62P/Can-33
62Salada-93
62Shirriff-93
62T-420
62T/bucks
62T/St-9
63T-475
64PhilBull-25
64T-83
65OPC-248
65T-248
79TCMA-75
91Crown/Orio-462
Exh47
PM10/Sm-189
Trice, Robert Lee
54T-148
55Rodeo
55T-132
55T/DH-124
86Negro/Frit-43
PM10/Sm-190
Trice, Walter
(Wally)
88AubAs/ProC-1950
89Osceola/Star-25
90ColMud/Best-15
90ColMud/ProC-1349
90ColMud/Star-24
90Foil/Best-205
91BurlAs/ClBest-9
91BurlAs/ProC-2800
91MidwLAS/ProC-MWL18
91Single/ClBest-326
Trillo, Manny
74OPC-597R
74T-597R
75OPC-617R
75T-617R
75T/M-617R
76OPC-206
76SSPC-316
76T-206
77BurgChef-191
77OPC-158
77Pep-59
77T-395
78Ho-69
78OPC-217
78T-123
78Wiffle/Discs-76
79BK/P-14
79OPC-337
79T-639
80BK/P-5
80OPC-50
80T-90
81Coke
81D-22
81F-3
81F/St-96
81OPC-368
81T-470
81T/HT
82D-245
82F-260
82F/St-59
82OPC-220
82PermaGr/AS-18
82T-220
82T/St-122
82T/St-76
83D-294
83F-174
83F-631M
83OPC-174AS
83OPC-73
83PermaGr/AS-8
83T-398AS
83T-535
83T-5M
83T/St-141
83T/St-142
83T/St-268
83T/Tr-116
83Wheat/Ind-30
84D-575
84F-289
84F-627IA
84F/X-119
85FunFoodPin-57
84Nes/792-180
84OPC-180
84T-180
84T/Gloss22-3
84T/St-93
84T/Tr-121T
85D-431
85D/AAS-31
85F-622
85Mother/Giants-5
85OPC-310
85T-310
86Cub/Unocal-19
86D-201
86F-551
86F/Up-U120
86Gator-19
86OPC-142
86T-655
86T/St-88
86T/Tr-117T
87Berg/Cubs-19
87D-570
87F-577
87OPC-32
87T-732
88Berg/Cubs-19
88D-516
88D/Cubs/Bk-516
88F-436
88S-524
88T-287
89B-308
89D-608
89F-440
89S-446
89T-66
89T/Big-295
89UD-127
90PublInt/St-41
Trinkle, Ken
47TipTop
49B-193
49Eureka-150
Triplett, Antonio
82BurlR-11
83BurlR-25
83BurlR/LF-6
86Tulsa-2
87SanBern-21
88Fresno/Cal-1
88Fresno/ProC-1243
Triplett, Coaker
V362-16
W754
Tripodi, Max
89SLCity-20
Tripp, Dave
90SoOreg/Best-23
90SoOreg/ProC-3446
Tritonenkov, Timur
89EastLDD/ProC-DD19
Trlicek, Rick
88Batavia/ProC-1670
90Dunedin/Star-22
91Knoxvl/LineD-369
91Knoxvl/ProC-1765
Troedson, Rich
74OPC-77
74T-77
Trombley, Mike
88CapeCod/Sum-75
90Visalia/Cal-58
90Visalia/ProC-2153
91OrlanSR/LineD-495
91OrlanSR/ProC-1849
Troncoso, Nolberton
90Yakima/Team-25
Tronerud, Rick
80WHave-24
81WHave-15
84Albany-8
89Huntsvl/Best-18
Trosky, Hal
34DS-70
34G-76
35Exh/4-11
35G-1L
35G-2E
35G-6E
35G-7E
36Exh/4-11
37Exh/4-11
37OPC-113
37Wheat
38Exh/4-11
38ONG/Pin-30
40PB-50
41DP-80
41DP-87
41PB-16
41Wheat
61F-145
92Conlon/Sport-385
R303/A
R314
V300
Trott, Sam
N172
Trotter, Bill
39PB-148
40PB-54
W753
Troup, James
89SLCity-27OF
Trouppe, Quincy
78Laugh/Black-33
91Negro/Lewis-16
Trout, Jeff
85Orlan-12
86Orlan-21
Trout, Paul
(Dizzy)
39Exh
39PB-153
40PB-44
47TipTop
48L-10
49B-208
50B-134
51T/BB-23
52NTea
52T-39
53T-169
81Detroit-113
85T-142FS
91Crown/Orio-463
91T/Arc53-169
Trout, Steve
77AppFx
78Knoxvl
80T-83
81D-44
81F-345
81OPC-364
81T-552
82D-243
82F-358
82OPC-299
82T-299
82T/St-169
83D-417
83F-251
83T-461
83T/Tr-117
83Thorn-34
84D-533
84F-506
84Nes/792-151
84OPC-151
84SevenUp-34
84T-151
85D-198
85F-70
85Leaf-243
85OPC-139
85SevenUp-34
85T-142FS
85T-668
85T/St-43
86Cub/Unocal-20
86D-117
86F-384
86Gator-34
86OPC-384
86T-384
86T/St-57
87Berg/Cubs-34
87D-201
87F-578
87OPC-147
87T-750

88D-524
88Mother/Sea-8
88S-342
88T-584
88T/Big-107
89Mother/Sea-24
89S-522
89T-54
90PublInt/St-443

Trowbridge, Bob
57SpicSpan/4x5-16
58T-252
59T-239
60T-66

Trower, Don
48Sommer-10

Trucchio, Frank
83Madis/LF-30C

Trucks, Phil
76Clinton
79Knoxvl/TCMA-2

Trucks, Virgil
47TipTop
48L-5
49B-219
49Royal-21
50B-96
51B-104
52Dix
52T-262
53B/BW-17
53Dix
53T-96
54B-198
55Armour-22
55B-26
56T-117
57T-187
58T-277
59T-417
63IDL-23CO
79TCMA-85
81Detroit-111
89Pac/Leg-120
89Swell-73
91T/Arc53-96
Exh47
R423-106

Trudeau, Kevin
86Watlo-29
87Portl-15
88OrlanTw/Best-14
89MidldA/GS-28

Trudo, Glenn
86Watertn-25TR
87Macon-21
88Augusta/ProC-384

Truesdale, Fred
C46-53

Trujillo, Jose
89Hamil/Star-24
90StPete/Star-24
91StPete/ClBest-23
91StPete/ProC-2286

Trujillo, Louie
83Cedar-11
83Cedar/LF-12

Trujillo, Mike
83AppFx/LF-2
86F-360
86Pawtu-26
86T-687
87D-613
87Mother/Sea-25
87T-402
88T-307
88Toledo/CMC-7
88Toledo/ProC-593
89AAA/ProC-25
89Toledo/CMC-3
89Toledo/ProC-776

Truschke, Mike
88CapeCod/Sum-24

Trusky, Ken
89Welland/Pucko-24
90Augusta/ProC-2479
90SALAS/Star-44
91Salem/ClBest-13
91Salem/ProC-967

Tsamis, George
88CapeCod/Sum-80
90A&AASingle/ProC-143
90AS/Cal-16
90Visalia/Cal-65
90Visalia/ProC-2154
91Portl/LineD-421
91Portl/ProC-1566

Tschida, Tim
88TM/Umpire-59
89TM/Umpire-57
90TM/Umpire-55

Tsitouris, John
60L-63
60T-497
63FrBauer-28
63T-244
64Kahn
64T-275
65Kahn
65OPC-221
65T-221
66OPC-12
66T-12
68T-523

Tsitouris, Marc
90James/Pucko-5
91Sumter/ClBest-21
91Sumter/ProC-2346

Tsotsos, Pete
88CapeCod/Sum-26

Tsoukalas, John
91MedHat/ProC-4110

Tubbs, Gregory Alan
86Greenvl/Team-21
87Greenvl/Best-26
88Richm-15
88Richm/CMC-15
88Richm/ProC-5
89AAA/CMC-23
89Greenvl/ProC-1152
89Richm/Bob-26
89Richm/ProC-823
91BuffB/LineD-47
91BuffB/ProC-555

Tuck, Gary
82Tucson-25
83Tucson-24
84Cram/PCL-248
86Osceola-26CO
87AubAs-12
88Ashvl/ProC-1068
89Colum/Pol-24CO

Tucker, Bill
89Belling/Legoe-34OWN

Tucker, Bob
86VeroB-25

Tucker, Eddie
90Foil/Best-274
90SanJose/Best-13
90SanJose/ProC-2014

Tucker, Mike
81Shrev-8
82Phoenix

Tucker, Scooter
89Clinton/ProC-897
90AS/Cal-37
90SanJose/Cal-37
90SanJose/Star-23
91Shrev/LineD-322
91Shrev/ProC-1825
91Single/ClBest-315

Tucker, Stephen
(Tuck)
90Greens/Best-12
90Greens/ProC-2664
90Greens/Star-22
91PrWill/ClBest-12
91PrWill/ProC-1428

Tucker, Terry
62Pep/Tul-bb
63Pep/Tul-bb

Tucker, Thomas
90Target-810
N172
N300/unif

Tucker, Thurman
47TipTop
50NumNum
51B-222

Tucker, Vance
89CharRain/ProC-972

Tucker, William
78Green

Tuckerman, William
N172

Tudor, John
81D-457
81T-14
82Coke/Bos
82D-260
82F-311
82T-558
83D-563
83F-198
83T-318
84D-416
84F-411
84F/X-U120
84Nes/792-601
84OPC-171
84T-601
84T/St-225
84T/Tr-122T
85D-235
85D/HL-20
85F-479
85F/Up-U123
85OPC-214
85T-214
85T/Tr-124T
86D-260
86Drake-30
86F-47
86F/AS-12
86F/Mini-11
86F/Slug-40
86F/St-122
86KAS/Disc-17
86Leaf-134
86OPC-227
86Sf-122
86Sf-184M
86Sf-185M
86Schnucks-22
86T-474
86T-710
86T/3D-28
86T/Gloss60-53
86T/Mini-64
86T/St-20WS
86T/St-52
86T/Super-57
87Classic-77
87D-170
87D/OD-63
87Drake-30
87F-310
87F/GameWin-41
87F/Mini-108
87F/RecSet-39
87F/St-119
87Kraft-22
87OPC-110
87RedFoley/St-34
87Sf-173
87Smok/Cards-3
87T-110
87T/St-53
88D-553
88D/Best-212
88Drake-33
88F-48
88F/Mini-110
88F/St-121
88F/WS-3
88Leaf-212
88OPC-356
88S-275
88Sf-198
88Smok/Card-9
88T-792
88T/RiteAid-29
88T/St-13
88T/St-21
88Woolwth-23
89Classic-63
89D-195
89F-75
89Mother/Dodg-9
89OPC-35
89Panini/St-100
89Pol/Dodg-19
89RedFoley/St-122
89S-560
89Sf-86
89T-35
89T/LJN-118
89T/Mini-20
89T/St-64
89UD-66
90B-188
90Classic/III-T2
90F/Up-U54
90Leaf/I-176
90PublInt/St-20
90Smok/Card-25
90T/Big-253
90T/Tr-124T
90T/TVCard-21
90Target-811
90UD-396
91F-650
91RedFoley/St-94
91S-53
91S/100SS-47
91UD-329

Tudor, Mark
81Clinton-29
82Clinton-26

Tufts, Bob
80Phoenix-2
81Phoenix-3
82Omaha-9
82T-171R

Tuholald, Tom
89Welland/Pucko-25

Tukes, Stan
89CharRain/ProC-977

Tulacz, Mike
77AppFx

Tuller, Brian
83QuadC-15

Tullier, Mike
86WinSalem-25
87WinSalem-19
88Pittsfld/ProC-1365
89Iowa/CMC-23
89Iowa/ProC-1701
91Bluefld/ProC-4143CO
91Bluefld/ClBest-24CO

Tullish, Bill
76Cedar

Tumbas, Dave
83AlexD-15
84PrWill-27
85Nashua-25

Tumpane, Bob
82Durham-13
83Durham-15
84Durham-12
85IntLgAS-2
86Greenvl/Team-22
87Richm/Crown-9
87Richm/TCMA-16

Tunison, Rich
89Eugene/Best-16
90A&AASingle/ProC-125
90AppFox/Box-28
90AppFox/ProC-2105
91London/LineD-421
91Memphis/ProC-664
91Single/ClBest-200

Tunnell, Lee
82Portl-9
83T/Tr-118T
84D-592
84F-268
84F/St-107
84Nes/792-384
84T-384
85D-288
85F-480
85F-638IA
85T-21
86F-623
86Hawaii-21
86T-161
87F/Up-U119
88F-49
88Louisvl-48
88S-587
89Portl/CMC-6
89Portl/ProC-217
90Tucson/CMC-7
90Tucson/ProC-204
91Tucson/LineD-621
91Tucson/ProC-2213

Tunney, Gene
33SK-18

Tuozzo, John
86Columbia-25

Turang, Brian
88CapeCod-20
88CapeCod/Sum-22
89Belling/Legoe-20
90A&AASingle/ProC-149
90SanBern/Best-18
90SanBern/Cal-106
90SanBern/ProC-2642
91Jaxvl/LineD-347
91Jaxvl/ProC-161

Turco, Frank
91BendB/ClBest-15
91BendB/ProC-3705

Turco, Steve F.
81ArkTr-2
83StPete-25
85Spring-18
91Hamil/ClBest-30CO
91Hamil/ProC-4057CO

Turek, Joseph
88Greens/ProC-1559
88SALAS/GS-8
89Cedar/Best-7
89Cedar/ProC-920
89Cedar/Star-20
90Cedar/Best-18
91Chatt/ProC-1962

Turgeon, David
87Oneonta-12
88FtLaud/Star-22
89PrWill/Star-22
90FtLaud/Star-20

Turgeon, Mike
80Wichita-11
82Phoenix

Turgeon, Steve
83StPete-26
85Spring-19
86Erie-28CO

Turley, Robert
54Esskay
54T-85
55Armour-23
55T-38
55T/DH-64
56T-40
56T/Pin-31P
57T-264
58T-255
58T-493AS
59Armour-19
59Bz
59T-237M
59T-493
59T-570AS
59T-60
60L-103
60NuCard-30
60T-270
61NuCard-430
61P-5
61T-40
61T/St-200
62T-589
63T-322
79TCMA-136
88Pac/Leg-52
91Crown/Orio-464

Turnbull, Keith
83Erie-8

Turner
N172

Turner, Brian
90Greens/Best-26
90Greens/ProC-2678
90Greens/Star-23
90Oneonta/ProC-3374
91Greens/ProC-3069

Turner, Chris
91Boise/ClBest-17
91Boise/ProC-3884

Turner, Col. R.
33SK-27

Turner, Jim
44Yank/St-27
52T-373C
62T-263M
63FrBauer-29
73OPC-116CO
73T-116C
W711/2

Turner, John
(Jerry)
75OPC-619R

75T-619R
75T/M-619R
76OPC-598R
76T-598R
77Padre/SchCd-34
77T-447
78Padre/FamFun-34
78T-364
79T-564
80T-133
81D-244
81F-504
81T-285
81T/St-229
82D-609
82T-736
82Wheat/Ind
83F-345
83T-41

Turner, John
86Peoria-24

Turner, Lloyd
78Watlo
79Wausau-10

Turner, Rick
82Danvl-7
83Redwd-24

Turner, Roy
WG2-46

Turner, Ryan
91BendB/ClBest-16
91BendB/ProC-3709

Turner, Shane
86FSLAS-47
86FtLaud-23
87Colum-13
87Colum/Pol-24
87Colum/TCMA-18
88Maine/CMC-13
88Maine/ProC-288
88Phill/TastyK-27
89F-653M
89Reading/Best-12
89Reading/ProC-655
89Reading/Star-24
89S/HotRook-67
90RochR/CMC-24
90RochR/ProC-711
91RochR/LineD-471
91RochR/ProC-1912

Turner, Terry
10Domino-118
11Helmar-26
12Sweet/Pin-20
14Piedmont/St-56
D328-175
D329-176
D350/2-179
E135-175
E254
E270/1
E94
M101/4-176
M101/5-179
M116
S74-11
T201
T202
T205
T206
T207

Turner, Trent
88CapeCod/Sum-179

Turner, William
(Matt)
87Sumter-2
89Durham/Team-24
89Durham/Star-24
90Greenvl/Best-12
90Greenvl/ProC-1128
90Greenvl/Star-20
91Richm/LineD-446
91Richm/ProC-2569

Turnes, Jose
78DaytB

Turpin, Hal
43Centen-24
44Centen-25
45Centen-26

Turrentine, Richard
90Tampa/DIMD-27
91Greens/ProC-3070

Turri, Shawn
91Niagara/ClBest-22
91Niagara/ProC-3632

Turtletaub, Greg
88LitFalls/Pucko-13

Turvey, Joe
90Hamil/Best-15
90Savan/ProC-2071
91Hamil/ClBest-20
91Hamil/ProC-4042

Tuss, Jeff
91Single/ClBest-364
91WPalmB/ClBest-13
91WPalmB/ProC-1229

Tutt, John
84CharlO-24
85Beaum-22
86LasVegas-20

Tuttle, Bill
55B-35
56T-203
57Swift-14
57T-72
58T-23
59T-459
60L-32
60T-367
61Bz-36
61Clover-28
61P-84
61T-536
61T/St-167
62J-88
62P-88
62P/Can-88
62Salada-87A
62Salada-87B
62Shirriff-87
62T-298
62T/St-80
63T-127
79TCMA-103

Tuttle, David
91T/Tr-122T

Twardoski, Michael
88CLAS/Star-38
88Kinston/Star-22
89Canton/Best-12
89Canton/ProC-1299
89Canton/Star-21
89EastLDD/ProC-DD35
90Foil/Best-155
90NewBrit/Best-9
90NewBrit/Star-18
91Pawtu/LineD-357

Twardy, Glenn
89Belling/Legoe-14

Twellman, Tom
74Cedar
75Dubuq
76Dubuq

Twitchell, Lawrence
E223
N172
WG1-26

Twitchell, Wayne
71OPC-692R
71T-692R
72OPC-14R
72T-14R
73OPC-227
73T-227
74K-26
74OPC-419
74T-419
74T/St-79
75OPC-326
75T-326
75T/M-326
76OPC-543
76T-543
77T-444
78OPC-189
78T-269
79OPC-18
79T-43
91WIZMets-415

Twitty, Jeff
81F-49
82Richm-8

Twitty, Sean
91Belling/ClBest-7
91Belling/ProC-3682

Twombly, Babe
28Exh/PCL-29

Tyler, Brad
91Kane/ClBest-20
91Kane/ProC-2667
91MidwLAS/ProC-MWL35

Tyler, Dave
81Bristol-19

Tyler, George
(Lefty)
15CJ-146
BF2-56
D327
D328-176
D329-177
E121/80
E122
E135-176
M101/4-177
T207
T222
W575

Tyler, Mike
76Dubuq
78Charl
79Charl-7
80Port-1

Tyner, Matt
90HagersDG/Best-34

Tyng, James
N172

Tyrone, Jim
74OPC-598R
74T-598R
76SSPC-604
77SanJose-7
78T-487

Tyson, Albert T.
(Ty)
90Target-1088

Tyson, Mike
74OPC-655
74T-655
74T/St-120
75OPC-231
75T-231
75T/M-231
76Crane-65
76MSA/Disc
76OPC-86
76SSPC-283
76T-86
77BurgChef-18
77Pep-38
77T-599
78T-111
79OPC-162
79T-324
80OPC-252
80T-486
81Coke
81F-315
81T-294
81T/HT
81T/St-155
82D-435
82F-606
82F/St-100
82T-62

Tyson, Terry
77Watlo

Ubina, Alex
90Bristol/ProC-3157
90Bristol/Star-24
91Bristol/ClBest-9
91Bristol/ProC-3609

Ubri, Fermin
84Jacks-24

Uchiyama, Kenichi
90Salinas/Cal-122
90Salinas/ProC-2713

Uecker, Bob
62T-594R
63T-126
64T-543
65T-519
66OPC-91
66T-91
67T-326

Ueda, Joe
88Fresno/ProC-1238

Ueda, Sadahito
83SanJose-16

Ugueto, Jesus
91Johnson/ClBest-10
91Johnson/ProC-3987

Uhal, Bob
88LitFalls/Pucko-8

Uhey, Jackie
76Clinton
82ElPaso-18
85Everett/II/Cram-19CO

Uhlaender, Ted
66T-264R
67T-431
68Coke
68Dexter-74
68OPC-28
68T-28
69MB-279
69MLB/St-72
69OPC-194
69T-194
69T/St-200
70MLB/St-204
70T-673
71MLB/St-384
71OPC-347
71T-347
72MB-349
72T-614
78TCMA-161
90Greens/Best-28CO
90Greens/ProC-2682CO
90Greens/Star-26CO
91FtLaud/ClBest-8CO
91FtLaud/ProC-2445CO

Uhle, George E.
28Exh-44
28Yueng-11
29Exh/4-24
31Exh/4-23
33Exh/4-12
33G-100
40PB-239
61F-146
91Conlon/Sport-224
E120
E210-11
R306
V354-22
V61-16
W502-11
W572
W573
WG7-56

Uhrhan, Kevin
91LynchRS/ClBest-10
91LynchRS/ProC-1200

Ujdur, Gerry
80Evansvl-10
81Evansvl-8
81T-626R
82Evansvl-10
83D-600
83F-346
83T-174

Ullger, Scott
80OrlTw-21
82OrlTw/A-10
82Toledo-22
84D-438
84Nes/792-551
84T-551
84Toledo-12
85IntLgAS-27
85Toledo-18
86Toledo-22
87RochR-7
87RochR/TCMA-21
88Visalia/Cal-170
88Visalia/ProC-99
89AS/Cal-25CO
89Visalia/Cal-118MG
89Visalia/ProC-1433
90AS/Cal-25MG
90Visalia/Cal-79MG
90Visalia/ProC-2170MG
91OrlanSR/LineD-499MG
91OrlanSR/ProC-1865MG

Ulrich, George
89AS/Cal-55UMP

Ulrich, Jeff
80Penin/B-22
80Penin/C-16
81OkCty/TCMA-26
82OkCty-17

Umbach, Arnie
66T-518R

Umbarger, Jim
76OPC-7
76SSPC-257
76T-7
77T-378
79T-518
79Tucson-24

Umbricht, Jim
60T-145
63T-99
64T-389
89Smok/Ast-9

Umdenstock, Bob
79AppFx-19
82CharR-11

Umont, Frank
55B-305ump

Umphlett, Tom
53Briggs
54B-88
55B-45
61Union

Underwood, Bobby
88Watertn/Pucko-13
89Augusta/ProC-500
90Augusta/ProC-2463
91Salem/ClBest-15

Underwood, Pat
80OPC-358
80T-709
81D-368
81Evansvl-9
81F-469
81T-373
82T-133
83D-29
83Evansvl-10
83F-347
83Kaline-70M
83T-588

Underwood, Tom
75OPC-615R
75T-615R
75T/M-615R
76OPC-407
76SSPC-461
76T-407
77T-217
78T-531
79OPC-26
79T-64
80OPC-172
80T-324
81D-108
81F-97
81OPC-114
81T-114
81T/Tr-846
82D-323
82F-109
82T-757
83D-391
83F-535
83Granny-31
83T-466
84D-253
84F-460
84F/X-U121
84Nes/792-642
84OPC-293
84T-642
84T/St-335
84T/Tr-123T
85F-194
85T-289
89Pac/SenLg-169
89TM/SenLg-108
91Crown/Orio-465

Unglaub, Robert
90Niagara/Pucko-26
91Fayette/ClBest-27
91Fayette/ProC-1170
E254
E270/1
E90/1
E91
M116
T204
T206

Ungs, Mike
79Wisco-2

80OrlTw-15
81Wisco-10
Unitas, John
60P
Unrein, Todd
91Kane/ClBest-11
91Kane/ProC-2658
Unser, Al
47Signal
Unser, Del
69MB-280
69T-338
70MLB/St-287
70OPC-336
70T-336
71MLB/St-551
71OPC-33
71T-33
72MB-350
72T-687
73OPC-247
73T-247
74JP
74OPC-69
74T-69
74T/St-80
75OPC-138
75T-138
75T/M-138
76OPC-268
76SSPC-535
76T-268
77BurgChef-155
77OPC-27
77T-471
78OPC-216
78T-348
79OPC-330
79T-628
80BK/P-13
80OPC-12
80T-27
81D-164
81F-26
81OPC-56
81T-566
81T/HT
82D-273
82F-261
82T-713
85Phill/TastyK-7CO
85Phill/TastyK-8CO
86Phill/TastyK-25CO
87Phill/TastyK-x
88Phill/TastyK-29CO
91WIZMets-416
Upham, John
67T-608R
Upp, George
(Jerry)
E90/1
Upshaw, Cecil
67OPC-179R
67T-179R
68T-286
69T-568
70OPC-295
70T-295
71MLB/St-23
71OPC-223
71T-223
72OPC-74
72T-74
73OPC-359
73T-359
74OPC-579
74T-579
74T/Tr-579T
75OPC-92
75T-92
75T/M-92
76SSPC-138
Upshaw, Lee
88Durham/Star-22
89BurlB/ProC-1598
89BurlB/Star-21
90Foil/Best-25
90Greenvl/Best-1
91Greenvl/ClBest-7
91Greenvl/LineD-220
91Greenvl/ProC-3001
Upshaw, Willie
76FtLaud
79OPC-175
79Syrac-4
79T-341
80Syrac-21
82D-652
82F-624
82OPC-196
82T-196
83D-558
83F-442
83OPC-338
83T-556
83T/St-128
84D-315
84F-168
85FunFoodPin-94
84Nes/792-453
84OPC-317
84T-453
84T/St-363
84Tor/Fire-30
85D-10DK
85D-71
85D/AAS-52
85D/DKsuper-10
85F-118
85F-635IA
85F/LimEd-41
85Leaf-10DK
85OPC-75
85OPC/Post-14
85Seven-15S
85T-75
85T/St-358
85Tor/Fire-30
86Ault-26
86D-195
86F-72
86Leaf-128
86OPC-223
86Sf-98
86T-745
86T/St-188
86Tor/Fire-31
87D-367
87D/OD-30
87F-239
87Leaf-231
87OPC-245
87RedFoley/St-107
87T-245
87T/St-186
87Tor/Fire-32
88D-271
88F-124
88F/Up-U25
88Gator-20
88Leaf-131
88OPC-241
88Panini/St-217
88S-279
88S/Tr-42T
88Sf-214
88T-505
88T/St-185
88T/Tr-123T
89D-492
89F-415
89OPC-106
89Panini/St-324
89S-188
89T-106
89UD-157
Upshur, Takashi
80Wausau-11
Upton, Jack
82Iowa-12
Upton, Thomas
52T-71
Urban, Jack E.
58T-367
59T-18
Urban, Luke
92Conlon/Sport-405
Urbanek, Jason
91Martins/ClBest-6
91Martins/ProC-3465
Urbani, Tom
90Johnson/Star-27
91Spring/ClBest-27
91Spring/ProC-742
Urbanski, Bill
33DL-9
33G-212
34DS-37
34Exh/4-1
35BU-59
36Exh/4-1
37Exh/4-1
92Conlon/Sport-408
R313
R314
V355-71
Urbide, Miliciades
88Wythe/ProC-1975
89CharWh/Best-3
89CharWh/ProC-1744
Urbon, Joe
89Batavia/ProC-1933
90Spartan/Best-22
90Spartan/ProC-2505
90Spartan/Star-22
91Clearw/ClBest-25
91Clearw/ProC-1636
Urcioli, John
91Miami/ClBest-24
91Miami/ProC-418
Uremovich, Mike
75Clinton
Uribe, George
84Butte-24
Uribe, Jorge
86Wausau-26
88Vermont/ProC-953
89SanBern/Best-12
89SanBern/Cal-78
Uribe, Jose
81Louisvl-13
84Louisvl-13
85F/Up-U124
85Mother/Giants-13
85T/Tr-125T
86D-236
86F-552
86Mother/Giants-13
86OPC-12
86T-12
86T/St-87
87D-436
87D/OD-99
87F-286
87Mother/SFG-13
87OPC-94
87T-633
88D-559
88D/Best-303
88F-99
88Leaf-218
88Mother/Giants-13
88Nestle-13
88OPC-302
88Panini/St-425
88S-165
88T-302
88T/Big-95
88T/St-91
89B-471
89D-131
89D/Best-106
89F-345
89Mother/Giants-13
89OPC-8
89Panini/St-217
89S-56
89Sf-61
89T-753
89T/Big-258
89T/St-82
89UD-181
90D-335
90D/BestNL-122
90F-74
90Leaf/I-225
90Mother/Giant-17
90OPC-472
90Panini/St-372
90PublInt/St-84
90S-455
90Sf-79
90T-472
90T/Big-213
90UD-188
91B-627
91D-375
91F-275
91F/Ultra-330
91Leaf/II-433
91Mother/Giant-17
91OPC-158
91Panini/FrSt-70
91PG&E-12
91S-628
91SFExam/Giant-15
91T-158
91T/StClub/I-267
91UD-207
92D/II-453
92F-649
92S/II-546
92T-538
92UD-270
Uribe, Juan
88Beloit/GS-8
90Stockton/Best-18
90Stockton/Cal-170
90Stockton/ProC-2179
Uribe, Relito
89Dunedin/Star-20
Urman, Mike
88Pulaski/ProC-1764
89Sumter/ProC-1109
Urrea, John
78T-587
79T-429
81D-190
81T-152
Urso, Salvy
91Penin/ClBest-12
91Penin/ProC-378
Usher, Bob
51B-286
52T-157
57Sohio/Ind-15
58T-124
Utecht, Tim
83Beloit/LF-20
Vaccaro, Sal
86Jamestn-27
87BurlEx-6
87SanJose-4
Vail, Michael
75Tidew/Team-23
76Ho-55
76Ho/Twink-55
76OPC-655
76SSPC-534
76T-655
77T-246
78T-69
79T-663
80OPC-180
80T-343
81D-554
81F-311
81T-471
81T/Tr-848
82Coke/Reds
82F-84
82T-194
83D-597
83F-605
83Mother/Giants-19
83T-554
83T/Tr-119T
84F-290
84F/X-U122
84Nes/792-766
84OPC-143
84T-766
84T/Tr-124T
89Tidew/Candl-6
90Target-812
91WIZMets-417
Vaji, Mark
81QuadC-24
Valasquez, Guillermo
(Gil)
89River/Cal-3
91Wichita/ProC-2607
Valasquez, Ray
89Salinas/Cal-123
Valazquez, Fred
71Richm/Team-17
Valdes, Ramon
88GreatF-25
Valdes, Rene
57T-337
61Union
90Target-813
Valdespino, Sandy
65OPC-201R
65T-201R
66OPC-56
66T-56
68T-304
69MB-281
70McDon
77WHave
85RochR-25
Valdez, Amilcar
88Bakers/Cal-241
Valdez, Angel
82Miami-17
Valdez, Efrain
88Tulsa-5
89Canton/Best-6
89Canton/ProC-1311
89Canton/Star-22
90ColoSp/CMC-4
90ColoSp/ProC-35
91B-60
91ColoSp/LineD-96
91ColoSp/ProC-2183
91OPC-692
91S-723RP
91T-692A
91T-692B
91T/90Debut-156
91T/StClub/II-483
Valdez, Francisco
(Frank)
88Kenosha/ProC-1393
89Gaston/ProC-1020
89Gaston/Star-23
89SALAS/GS-40
89Visalia/Cal-108
89Visalia/ProC-1440
90OrlanSR/Best-14
90OrlanSR/ProC-1094
90OrlanSR/Star-21
91OrlanSR/LineD-479
91OrlanSR/ProC-1864
Valdez, Ismael
91Kissim/ProC-4186
Valdez, Jose
90Kissim/DIMD-27
Valdez, Jose
83Peoria/LF-12
Valdez, Julio
81Pawtu-17
82D-560
82T-381R
83F-199
83T-628
85Iowa-7
86Iowa-25
87Iowa-17
88Pittsfld/ProC-1357
88Wythe/ProC-1988
89Wythe/Star-29INS
Valdez, Miguel
80Elmira-43
Valdez, Pedro
91Hunting/ClBest-27
91Hunting/ProC-3351
Valdez, Rafael
86CharRain-27
87CharRain-15
88Charl/ProC-1201
89River/Best-18
89River/Cal-4
89River/ProC-1398
89Wichita/Rock/HL-6M
89Wichita/Rock/Up-10
90B-210
90F/Up-U58
90LasVegas/CMC-20
90LasVegas/ProC-125
90S/Tr-93T
90UD/Ext-775
91B-663
91LasVegas/ProC-236
91S-360RP
91S/100RisSt-31
91T/90Debut-157
91UD-253
Valdez, Ramon
89Princet/Star-22
Valdez, Sergio
85Utica-7
87Indianap-21
88Indianap/CMC-8

88Indianap/ProC-501
89Indianap/CMC-2
89Indianap/ProC-1215
90D-405
90Leaf/II-496
90OPC-199
90T-199
91ColoSp/LineD-97
91ColoSp/ProC-2184
91D-344
91F-380
91OPC-98
91T-98

Valdez, Sylverio
80Utica-8
83Ander-18

Valdivielso, Jose
56T-237
57T-246
60T-527
61Clover-29
61Peters-25
61T-557
62T-339

Valencia, Gil
89Martins/Star-31
90Batavia/ProC-3083
90Spartan/Best-23
90Spartan/ProC-2506
90Spartan/Star-23

Valencia, Jose
88Sumter/ProC-399

Valente, John
88CapeCod/Sum-2

Valentin, Eddy
89AubAs/ProC-2160

Valentin, John
88CapeCod-11
88CapeCod/Sum-138
89WinHaven/Star-25
90Foil/Best-283
90NewBrit/Best-21
90NewBrit/Star-19
91NewBrit/LineD-473
91NewBrit/ProC-361

Valentin, Jose
87Spokane-23
88Charl/ProC-1198
89AS/Cal-7
89River/Best-19
89River/Cal-8
89River/ProC-1415
89Wichita/Rock/Up-18
90Wichita/Rock-20
91Single/ClBest-33
91Wichita/LineD-620
91Wichita/ProC-2606

Valentine, Bill
80ArkTr-23

Valentine, Bobby
71OPC-188R
71T-188R
72OPC-11
72T-11
73OPC-502
73T-502
74OPC-101
74T-101
74T/DE-11
74T/St-150
75OPC-215
75T-215
75T/M-215
76OPC-366
76T-366
77Padre/SchCd-35
77T-629
78T-712
79OPC-222
79T-428
85Rang-2MG
85SpokAT/Cram-22
85T/Tr-126T
86Rang-2MG
86T-261MG
87Mother/Rang-1
87Smok/R-19MG
87T-118MG
88Mother/R-1MG
88Smok/R-8MG
88T-594MG
89Mother/R-1MG
89Smok/R-33MG
89T-314MG
90Mother/Rang-1MG
90OPC-729MG
90T-729MG
90Target-814
91Mother/Rang-1MG
91OPC-489MG
91T-489MG
91WIZMets-418
92T-789MG

Valentine, Ellis
76OPC-590R
76SSPC-342
76T-590R
77BurgChef-158
77OPC-234
77T-52
78K-19
78OPC-45
78T-185
79Ho-50
79OPC-277
79T-535
80K-21
80OPC-206
80T-395
81F-148
81OPC-244
81OPC/Post-7
81T-445
81T/So-80
81T/St-186
81T/Tr-849
82D-605
82F-541
82F/St-83
82OPC-15
82T-15
82T/St-69
83F-558
83T-653
83T/Tr-120T
84F-529
84Nes/792-236
84OPC-236
84Smok/Cal-29
84T-236
91WIZMets-419

Valentine, Fred
64T-483
66T-351
67OPC-64
67T-64
68T-248
69MB-282
91Crown/Orio-466

Valentine, Harold
(Corky)
55T-44
55T/DH-46
79TCMA-61

Valentinetti, Vito
57T-74
58T-463
59T-44

Valentini, Vincent
80Wichita-19

Valenzuela, Fernando
81F-140
81PermaGr/AS-9
81Pol/Dodg-34
81T-302R
81T/Tr-850
82D-462
82F-27
82F-635M
82F-636M
82F/St-1
82F/St-108M
82F/St-111M
82K-9
82OPC-334
82OPC-345AS
82PermaGr/CC-12
82Pol/Dodg-34
82Sqt-20
82T-166LL
82T-345AS
82T-510
82T-6RB
82T/St-11
82T/St-119
82T/St-50
83D-1DK
83D-284
83D/AAS-53
83F-224
83K-7
83OPC-40
83PermaGr/CC-18
83Pol/Dodg-34
83Seven-8
83T-40
83T-681TL
83T/Gloss40-10
83T/St-250
83T/St/Box-1
84D-52
84D/AAS-13
84F-115
84F/St-81
85FunFoodPin-7
84MiltBrad-27
84Nes/792-220
84OPC-220
84Pol/Dodg-34
84Ralston-10
84Seven-9W
84T-220
84T/Cereal-10
84T/St-16LCS
84T/St-79
84T/Super-30
85Coke/Dodg-31
85D-52
85D/AAS-37
85D/HL-28
85D/HL-6
85F-387
85F/LimEd-42
85F/St-114
85GenMills-12
85Leaf-184
85OPC-357
85Seven-16W
85T-440
85T/3D-21
85T/St-71
85T/Super-52
85ThomMc/Discs-45
86BK/AP-3
86Coke/Dodg-30
86D-215
86D/AAS-27
86D/HL-25
86Drake-36
86F-145
86F-641M
86F/Mini-31
86F/Slug-41
86F/St-123
86Jiffy-14
86Leaf-91
86Meadow/Blank-15
86Meadow/Milk-12
86Meadow/Stat-2
86OPC-178
86OPC/WaxBox-P
86Pol/Dodg-34
86Quaker-17
86Sf-12
86Sf-132M
86Sf-143M
86Sf-56M
86Sf-72M
86Sf/Dec-66
86Sf/Rook-47M
86T-207RB
86T-401TBC
86T-630
86T/3D-30
86T/Gloss60-3
86T/Mini-47
86T/St-64
86T/Super-58
86T/WaxBox-P
86TrueVal-6
87BK-20
87Classic-91
87D-94
87D/AAS-54
87Drake-29
87F-457
87F-631M
87F/AS-10
87F/AwardWin-40
87F/GameWin-42
87F/BB-43
87F/Mini-109
87F/Slug-43
87F/St-120
87Ho/St-11
87Jiffy-15
87KayBee-32
87KMart-33
87Kraft-32
87Leaf-148
87MnM's-19
87Mother/Dodg-4
87OPC-273
87Pol/Dodg-17
87Ralston-11
87RedFoley/St-57
87Sf-119M
87Sf-120M
87Sf-150
87Seven-W16
87Smok/Dodg-36
87Sportflic/DealP-2
87T-410
87T-604AS
87T/Coins-47
87T/Gloss22-11
87T/Gloss60-53
87T/Mini-16
87T/St-75
88ChefBoy-24
88D-53
88D/Best-316
88F-528
88F/BB/MVP-40
88F/Excit-43
88F/Mini-86
88F/St-94
88KingB/Disc-19
88KMart-31
88Leaf-61
88Mother/Dodg-4
88MSA/Disc-20
88OPC-52
88Panini/St-304
88Pol/Dodg-34
88S-600
88Sf-40
88Smok/Dodg-24
88T-489
88T-780
88T/Big-18
88T/Coins-58
88T/Mini-54
88T/Revco-14
88T/St-70
88T/St/Backs-30
88T/UK-80
89B-337
89D-250
89F-76
89KMart/DT-32
89Mother/Dodg-4
89OPC-150
89Panini/St-103
89Pol/Dodg-22
89RedFoley/St-123
89S-437
89Sf-124
89Smok/Dodg-97
89T-150
89T/LJN-78
89T/St-60
89T/UK-78
89UD-656
90D-625
90D/BestNL-90
90D/Learning-39
90F-409
90F-622MVP
90Leaf/I-68
90MLBPA/Pins-7
90Mother/Dodg-2
90OPC-340
90Panini/St-269
90Pol/Dodg-34
90PublInt/St-21
90S-54
90T-340
90T/St-59
90Target-815
90UD-445
91BBBest/RecBr-18
91Classic/200-73
91D-127
91D-BC11
91F-222
91F/WaxBox-5
91OPC-80NH
91Panini/FrSt-356
91Panini/St-5
91Panini/St-59
91S-449
91S-703
91Seven/3DCoin-15SC
91T-80A
91T-80B
91T/StClub/I-90
91UD-175

Valenzuela, Guillermo
83Kinston/Team-27

Valera, Julio
87Columbia-26
88Clmbia/GS-11
89BBAmerAA/BProC-AA28
89Jacks/GS-29
89StLucie/Star-23
89TexLAS/GS-26
90B-123
90T/TVMets-65
90Tidew/CMC-13
90Tidew/ProC-546
91D-39RR
91F-164
91OPC-504
91S-353RP
91T-504
91T/90Debut-158
91Tidew/LineD-571
91Tidew/ProC-2511
91UD-534
91WIZMets-420
92F-517
92S/100RisSt-17

Valera, Wilson
83Watlo/LF-10
85Water-2
86Lynch-23
87Lynch-26

Valette, Ramon
91Elizab/ProC-4309

Valez, Jose
89PalmSp/Cal-46

Valez, Noel
91Cedar/ClBest-24

Valiente, Nestor
84Butte-25

Valla, Mike
88Watertn/Pucko-26

Vallaran, Miguel
77LodiD

Valle, Dave
80SanJose/JITB-20
81LynnS-14
82SLCity-20
83Chatt-26
84Cram/PCL-176
85F/Up-U125
85Mother/Mar-17
86Calgary-24
87D-610
87D/OD-120
87Mother/Sea-9
87T/Tr-122T
88D-393
88F-389
88Mother/Sea-9
88OPC-83
88Panini/St-184
88S-126
88T-583
88T/Big-210
88T/St-220
89B-208
89Chatt/II/Team-30
89D-614
89D/Best-248
89F-561
89Mother/Sea-9
89RedFoley/St-124
89S-27
89T-459
89T-498
89T/Big-56
89UD-320
90B-473
90D-129
90D/BestAL-55
90F-527

90Leaf/I-166
90MLBPA/Pins-120
90Mother/Mar-5
90OPC-76
90Panini/St-156
90PublInt/St-444
90RedFoley/St-97
90S-109
90T-76
90T/Big-266
90UD-451
91B-251
91CounHrth-6
91D-366
91F-463
91F/Ultra-344
91Leaf/II-511
91Leaf/Stud-120
91OPC-178
91Panini/FrSt-227
91RedFoley/St-95
91S-262
91T-178
91T/StClub/I-32
91UD-595
92D/II-462
92F-295
92S/I-343
92T-294
92UD-182

Valle, Hector
65T-561R
66T-314

Valle, John A.
77Evansvl/TCMA-24
78Indianap-14
79Indianap-25
80RochR-14
81RochR-17
82RochR-18
83RochR-18
84RochR-6

Valle, Tony
89Idaho/ProC-2026
90BurlB/Best-8
90BurlB/ProC-2350
90BurlB/Star-26

Valley, Chick
77Salem
78Salem
81ElPaso-16
82Vanco-18

Valo, Elmer
48L-29
49B-66
50B-49
51T/RB-28
52B-206
52T-34
53T-122
54T-145
55Rodeo
55T-145
55T/DH-85
56Rodeo
56T-3
57T-54
58T-323
60L-107
60T-237
61Peters-12
61T-186
63Sugar-17
79TCMA-148
89Pac/Leg-187
90Target-816
91T/Arc53-122

Valrie, Kerry
90SoBend/CIBest-25
90Utica/Pucko-12
91Single/CIBest-243
91SoBend/ProC-2872

Valverde, Miguel
88Augusta/ProC-361
89Salem/Star-23

Van Atta, Russ
33G-215
92Conlon/Sport-611
R312/M
R314

Van Bever, Mark
78Clinton

Van Blaricom, Mark
83Butte-22
85FtMyr-10
86FtMyr-25
87Memphis-12
87Memphis/Best-6
88Memphis/Best-3

Van Brunt, Jim
87Anchora-37bb

Van Brunt, Lefty
85Anchora-28CO
87Anchora-30CO

Van Burkleo, Ty
82Beloit-6
86PalmSp-29
86PalmSp/Smok-20
87MidldA-7

Van Cuyk, Chris
52T-53
53Mother-41
90Target-819

Van DeBrake, Kevin
91Yakima/CIBest-13
91Yakima/ProC-4257

Van DeCasteele, Mike
78Tidew
79Tidew-19

Van Der Beck, Jim
75Water

Van Duzer, Donna L.
88Fresno/ProC-1249TR
91CharlR/CIBest-26TR

Van Dyke, Rod
91Boise/CIBest-7
91Boise/ProC-3879

Van Dyke, William
N172

Van Gilder, Elam
92Conlon/Sport-569
E120
E126-47

Van Gorder, Dave
80Indianap-8
81Indianap-6
82Indianap-12
83D-188
83Indianap-27
83T-322
84Wichita/Rock-10
85D-384
86D-550
86F-195
86T-143
87RochR-2
87RochR/TCMA-11
91Crown/Orio-467

Van Haltren, George
E107
E223
N172
N403
N566-180
N690/2
WG1-17

Van Heyningen, Pat
85Newar-20

Van Horn, Dave
83Ander-24

Van Houten, Jim
85Spring-4
87ColAst/ProC-11

Van Kemper, John
85Everett/II/Cram-20

Van Landingham, William
91Everett/CIBest-24
91Everett/ProC-3913

Van Ornum, John
80Pol/Giants-42

Van Poppel, Todd
90A&AASingle/ProC-160
90Classic/DP-14
90Madison/Best-1
90SoOreg/Best-1
90SoOreg/ProC-3422
91B-218
91Classic/200-151
91Classic/I-75
91Classic/I-77
91Classic/I-NO
91Classic/II-T77
91D/Rook-7
91Huntsvl/CIBest-24
91Huntsvl/LineD-296
91HuntsvlProC-1795
91Leaf/GRook-BC9
91Leaf/Stud-109
91S-389FDP
91Seven/3DCoin-13NC
91Seven/3DCoin-14T
91Single/CIBest-386
91UD-53TP
91UD/FinalEd-12F
92Classic/I-91
92D/I-9RR
92D/Preview-12
92F-269
92F/RookSIns-2
92S/II-865
92T-142
92T/91Debut-175
92UD-22SR

Van Robays, Maurice
47Remar-18
47Signal
47Smith-7
48Signal
48Smith-9
49B/PCL-32
49Remar

Van Ryn, Ben
91Single/CIBest-31
91Sumter/CIBest-11
91Sumter/ProC-2334

Van Rynback, Casper
90Kgsport/Best-19
90Kgsport/Star-23
91Pittsfld/CIBest-14
91Pittsfld/ProC-3424

Van Schaack, Tom
90Watertn/Star-27GM

Van Scoyoc, Aaron
89Oneonta/ProC-2115
90Greens/Best-20
90Greens/ProC-2672
90Greens/Star-24
91FtLaud/ProC-2437

Van Scoyoc, Jim
91Niagara/CIBest-6CO
91Niagara/ProC-3652CO

Van Slyke, Andy
81Louisvl-18
82ArkTr-19
83Louisvl/Riley-18
84D-83
84F-339
84Nes/792-206
84T-206
84T/St-150
85D-327
85F-242
85OPC-341
85T-551
85T/St-138
86D-412
86F-48
86KAS/Disc-19
86KayBee-32
86OPC-33
86Schnucks-23
86T-683
86T/St-51
87D-417
87D/OD-161
87F-311
87F/Up-U121
87OPC-33
87T-33
87T/St-51
87T/Tr-124T
88D-18DK
88D-291
88D-BC8
88D/Best-157
88D/DKsuper-18DK
88F-341
88F/LL-43
88F/Mini-105
88F/St-116
88F/TL-44
88Leaf-102
88Leaf-18DK
88OPC-142
88Panini/St-380
88RedFoley/St-92
88S-416
88Sf-109
88T-142
88T/Big-184
88T/St-126
88T/UK-81
89T/Ames-30
89B-424
89Cadaco-59
89Classic-111
89D-54
89D/AS-61
89D/Best-45
89D/MVP-BC10
89F-222
89F/BBAS-42
89F/BBMVP's-40
89F/Heroes-41
89F/LL-41
89F/WaxBox-C27
89KingB/Discs-19
89OPC-350
89Panini/St-173
89S-174
89S/HotStar-92
89S/Mast-38
89Sf-166
89T-350
89T-392AS
89T/Big-255
89T/Coins-27
89T/DH-19
89T/Gloss60-4
89T/Hills-30
89T/LJN-150
89T/Mini-32
89T/St-132
89T/St/Backs-54
89T/UK-79
89Tetley/Discs-17
89UD-537
89UD-685TC
89VFJuice-18
90B-171
90Classic/III-30
90D-244
90D/BestNL-119
90D/Learning-3
90F-481
90F/AwardWin-40
90F/LL-40
90Homer/Pirate-29
90HotPlay/St-47
90Leaf/I-117
90MLBPA/Pins-36
90OPC-775
90Panini/St-324
90PublInt/St-166
90RedFoley/St-98
90S-440
90S/100St-78
90Sf-101
90T-775
90T/Big-217
90T/Mini-72
90T/St-124
90UD-536
91B-529
91Classic/200-45
91D-552
91F-53
91F/Ultra-287
91Leaf/II-310
91Leaf/Stud-230
91OPC-425
91Panini/FrSt-121
91Panini/St-118
91Panini/Top15-106
91RedFoley/St-96
91S-475
91S-698RF
91S/100SS-22
91T-425
91T/StClub/I-118
91UD-256
92Classic/I-92
92D/I-383
92F-570
92S/II-655
92T-545
92UD-132

Van Stone, Paul
85Everett/II/Cram-21
86Clinton-25

Van Tiger, Tom
91Watertn/CIBest-29
91Watertn/ProC-3384

Van Vuren, Bob
86FtMyr-26

Van Winkle, Dave
89Utica/Pucko-1
90SoBend/Best-4
91AS/Cal-5
91PalmSp/ProC-2015

Vanacore, Derek
85FtMyr-29

Vance, Clarence A.
(Dazzy)
25Exh-15
28Exh-8
29Exh/4-3
31Exh/4-3
33CJ/Pin-23
33Exh/4-2
33G-2
35G-2C
35G-4C
35G-7C
50Callahan
60F-51
61F-81
61GP-26
63Bz/ATG-28
72F/FFeat-4
72Laugh/GF-21
80SSPC/HOF
89HOF/St-73
89Smok/Dodg-29
90Target-817
92Conlon/Sport-377
R310
R315-A37
R315-B37
R316
R332-45
R423-109
V353-2
W517-36
W572

Vance, Gene
(Sandy)
71OPC-34
71T-34
85SpokAT/Cram-23
90Target-818

Vancho, Robert
(Bob)
89Helena/SP-18
90Beloit/Best-23
90Beloit/Star-22
91Stockton/CIBest-4
91Stockton/ProC-3032

VandeBerg, Ed
81Spokane-15
82T/Tr-122T
83D-100
83F-488
83OPC-183
83T-183
83T/St-317
84D-604
84F-623
84Mother/Mar-8
84Nes/792-63
84OPC-63
84T-63
85D-511
85F-504
85Mother/Mar-5
85OPC-207
85T-566
85T/St-336
86Coke/Dodg-31
86D-637
86F-479
86F/Up-U121
86OPC-357
86Pol/Dodg-31
86T-357
86T/Tr-118T
87D-376
87F-458
87F/Up-U120
87Gator-36
87OPC-34
87T-717
87T/Tr-123T
88AlaskaAS70/Team-22
88F-619

88OkCty/CMC-8
88OkCty/ProC-52
88T-421
89F-534
89Iowa/CMC-4
89Iowa/ProC-1710
89T-242
90Calgary/CMC-8
90Target-820
91Calgary/LineD-73
91Calgary/ProC-517

Vandenberg, Hy
40PB-209

Vanderbush, Walt
83Beaum-5
84Cram/PCL-229
85Cram/PCL-111

VanderMeer, John
39Exh
41DP-6
41PB-56
43MP-23
47HomogBond-47
48L-53
48Swell-10
49B-128
49Eureka-96
50B-79
51B-223
60NuCard-5
61F-147
72Laugh/GF-7
74Laugh/ASG-38
76Laugh/Jub-12
80Pac/Leg-110
88Pac/Leg-30
89Swell-11
90BBWit-80
90HOF/St-36
90Swell/Great-99
91Swell/Great-61
92Conlon/Sport-367
92Conlon/Sport-368
D305
Exh47
R346-46
W711/1
W711/2

Vanderwal, John
87Jamestn-14
88FSLAS/Star-23
88WPalmB/Star-24
89Jaxvl/Best-25
89Jaxvl/ProC-161
90Foil/Best-90
90Jaxvl/Best-13
90Jaxvl/ProC-1388
91AAAGame/ProC-AAA17
91Indianap/LineD-197
91Indianap/ProC-476
92D/II-414RR
92T-343
92T/91Debut-174

VanderWeele, Doug
91Everett/ClBest-2
91Everett/ProC-3912

Vanderwel, Bill
86Cram/PCL-84
87PalmSp-13
88PalmSp/Cal-94
88PalmSp/ProC-1457
89QuadC/Best-15
89QuadC/GS-16
90SoBend/Best-23

Vann, Brandy
86Cram/PCL-80
87QuadC-12
88QuadC/GS-29
89PalmSp/Cal-53
89PalmSp/ProC-471
90PalmSp/Cal-218
90PalmSp/ProC-2577
91ElPaso/LineD-198
91Stockton/ProC-3033

Vannaman, Tim
88SoOreg/ProC-1693
89Madis/Star-22
90Modesto/Cal-159
90Modesto/ProC-2227

Vanni, Edo
47Centen-30

Vantrease, Bob
83Idaho-12

Vanzytveld, Jeffrey
90FSLAS/Star-19
90VeroB/Star-26
91VeroB/ClBest-26

Vargas, Eddie
78Charl
80Buffa-15
81Buffa-23
82Portl-17

Vargas, Gonzalo
89StCath/ProC-2083

Vargas, Hector
87Oneonta-5
87PrWill-21
88Oneonta/ProC-2049
89PrWill/Star-23
90FtLaud/Star-21
91Albany/ProC-1018

Vargas, Hedi
85Cram/PCL-236
88Chatt/Best-8
88Nashvl/Team-24
89Chatt/II/Team-31
89MidldA/GS-29

Vargas, Jose
86Osceola-27
86Salem-26
87Osceola-15
87PortChar-17
88ColAst/Best-8
88Tulsa-7
89Osceola/Star-26
91Wmsprt/LineD-645
91Wmsprt/ProC-294

Vargas, Julio
89Martins/Star-32
90Princet/DIMD-25
91Batavia/ClBest-5
91Batavia/ProC-3487

Vargas, Leonel
(Leo)
82Richm-20
83Richm-21
84Richm-12

Vargas, Miguel
87Reading-5

Vargas, Ramon
83Ander-19

Vargas, Roberto
53SpicSpan/3x5-26

Varnell, Dan
90Everett/Best-2
90Everett/ProC-3144

Varner, Buck
88Chatt/Team-29

Varney, Pete
76OPC-413
76SSPC-154
76T-413

Varni, Patrick
88CapeCod/Sum-182
90Miami/II/Star-25

Varoz, Brett
85Anchora-29

Varoz, Eric
86Beaum-24

Varsho, Gary
84MidldC-23
86Pittsfld-24
87Iowa-23
88Berg/Cubs-24
88F/Up-U81
88Iowa/CMC-22
88Iowa/ProC-535
89F-441
89S-604
89T-613
89UD-321
90Iowa/CMC-21
90Iowa/ProC-332
90PublInt/St-206
90T/TVCub-61
91B-510
91D-671
91F-435
91F/UltraUp-U104
91F/Up-U114
91Leaf/II-500
91S/RookTr-72T
92D/II-644
92F-571
92S/II-481
92T-122
92UD-217

Varverde, Miguel
86Watertn-26

Vasquez, Aguedo
88BBCity/Star-23
88FSLAS/Star-50
89Memphis/Best-5
89Memphis/ProC-1186
89Memphis/Star-22
91Wmsprt/LineD-646
91Wmsprt/ProC-295

Vasquez, Angelo
85BurlR-13

Vasquez, Chris
90Billings/ProC-3235
91CharWh/ClBest-26
91CharWh/ProC-2901

Vasquez, Dennis
81GlenF-7

Vasquez, Francisco
79Elmira-18

Vasquez, George
73Cedar

Vasquez, Jesse
80BurlB-12
85Newar-22
86Hagers-26

Vasquez, Julian
89Clmbia/GS-25
91Single/ClBest-359
91StLucie/ClBest-16
91StLucie/ProC-710

Vasquez, Luis
85Elmira-23
86FSLAS-48
86WinHaven-26
87NewBrit-5
88EastLAS/ProC-24
88NewBrit/ProC-889
89Nashvl/CMC-10
89Nashvl/ProC-1285
89Nashvl/Team-25
91Nashvl/LineD-272
91Nashvl/ProC-2156

Vasquez, Rafael
77Salem
80T-672R
80Tacom-9
81Buffa-11

Vasquez, Tony
89Cedar/Best-27

Vatcher, James
88SALAS/GS-26
88Spartan/ProC-1045
88Spartan/Star-21
88Spartan/Star-5
89Clearw/Star-23
89Star/Wax-14
90ScranWB/CMC-17
90ScranWB/ProC-613
91D-753
91F-708
91LasVegas/ProC-251
91LasVegas/LineD-296
91OPC-196
91Padre/MagRal-11
91S-341RP
91T-196
91T/90Debut-159
91UD-604
92D/II-563

Vaughan, Charles
67OPC-179R
67T-179R

Vaughan, J. Floyd
(Arky)
33G-229
34G-22
35BU-21
35Exh/4-7
36Exh/4-7
36Wheat
37Exh/4-7
37Wheat
38Exh/4-7
39Exh
39PB-55
39Wheat
40PB-107
41DP-34
41PB-10
49Sommer-18
60F-11
61F-148
74Laugh/ASG-41
80Pac/Leg-122
88Conlon/NatAS-22
89HOF/St-21
89Pac/Leg-200
89Smok/Dodg-30
90Target-821
91Conlon/Sport-38
R311/Leath
R312/M
R313
R314
V354-70
V355-6
WG8-47

Vaughan, Rick
88StCath/ProC-2033
89Myrtle/ProC-1629

Vaughn, Billy
76Laugh/Clown-10
76Laugh/Clown-38

Vaughn, Derek
91Spokane/ClBest-8
91Spokane/ProC-3964

Vaughn, DeWayne
82Lynch-7
84Jacks-1
86Tidew-28
87Tidew-2
87Tidew/TCMA-8
88D/Rook-25
88Mother/R-24

Vaughn, Fred
47Signal

Vaughn, Greg
87Beloit-2
88BBAmer-24
88ElPaso/Best-20
88TexLgAS/GS-35
89AAA/CMC-8
89AAA/ProC-42
89Denver/CMC-23
89Denver/ProC-36
89F/Up-41
90B-396
90Brewer/MillB-28
90Classic-60
90D-37
90D/BestAL-107
90D/Rook-16
90ElPasoATG/Team-25
90F-339
90HotRook/St-44
90Leaf/I-111
90Leaf/Prev-9
90OPC-57
90Pol/Brew-23
90S-585
90S/100Ris-30
90S/DTRook-B8
90S/YS/I-13
90Sf-135
90T-57
90T/89Debut-128
90ToysRUs-27
90UD-25
91B-33
91Brewer/MillB-29
91Classic/200-46
91Classic/III-91
91D-478
91F-599
91F/Ultra-183
91Leaf/Stud-79
91OPC-347
91Pol/Brew-26
91S-528
91S/100RisSt-65
91T-347
91T/StClub/I-135
91ToysRUs-29
91UD-526
92D/I-224
92F-192
92S/II-639
92T-572
92UD-232
92UD-97

Vaughn, Harry
N172

Vaughn, James
(Hippo)
11Helmar-48
14Piedmont/St-57
15CJ-176
61F-82
69Bz-1
72F/FFeat-14M
72Laugh/GF-39M
90HOF/St-17
92Conlon/Sport-348
BF2-69
D327
D328-177
D329-178
D350/2-180
E121/120
E121/80
E122
E135-177
E220
E300
E98
M101/4-178
M101/5-180
T202
T205
T207
V100
W514-111
W555
W575

Vaughn, Maurice
(Mo)
88CapeCod-16
88CapeCod/Sum-93
90B-275
90Pawtu/ProC-471
90S-675DC
90T/TVRSox-64
91AAAGame/ProC-AAA32
91B-112
91Classic/200-152
91Classic/I-24
91D-430RR
91D/Rook-36
91F/Ultra-387MLP
91F/Up-U7
91Leaf/GRook-BC7
91Leaf/Stud-20
91MajorLg/Pins-10
91OPC/Premier-124
91Pawtu/LineD-370
91Pawtu/ProC-49
91S-750RP
91S/Rook40-6
91T/StClub/II-543
91T/Tr-123T
91UD-5SR
92D/II-514
92F-49
92F-705M
92S/100RisSt-100
92S/II-556
92T-59
92T/91Debut-176
92UD-445

Vaughn, Mike
76Clinton
77Watlo

Vaughn, Randy
88Eugene/Best-10
89AppFx/ProC-850
90BBCity/Star-23

Vaughn, Ron
89Utica/Pucko-28MG

Vaughn, Tim
87Macon-9

Vavra, Joe
85Cram/PCL-153
86Albuq-25
89GreatF-9
91Yakima/ClBest-29MG
91Yakima/ProC-4264MG

Vavrock, Rob
82Madis-24

Vavruska, Paul
76Clinton

Vazquez, Armando
91Negro/Lewis-14

Vazquez, Ed
89Kingspt/Star-24
90Pittsfld/Pucko-22

Vazquez, Jose
89Oneonta/ProC-2126

Vazquez, Marcos
88Sumter/ProC-403
89Sumter/ProC-1115
90Durham/Team-10
91DurhamUp/ProC-4
91Macon/ClBest-11
91Macon/ProC-864
Vazquez, Pedro
90AppFox/Box-29
90AppFox/ProC-2106
91BBCity/ClBest-22
91BBCity/ProC-1408
Veach
N172/PCL
Veach, Robert
15CJ-174
21Exh-180
25Exh-71
81Detroit-118
91Conlon/Sport-159
92Conlon/Sport-486
BF2-30
D327
D328-178
D329-179
D350/2-181
E120
E121/120
E121/80
E122
E135-178
E220
M101/4-179
M101/5-181
V100
V61-33
W501-5
W514-88
W572
W573
W575
Veach, William
N172
Veal, Orville
(Coot)
59T-52
61T-432
62J-68
62P-68
62P/Can-68
62Salada-84
62Shirriff-84
62T-573
Veale, Bob
62T-593R
63IDL-24
63T-87
64Kahn
64T-501
65Bz-13
65Kahn
65OPC-12LL
65OPC-195
65T-12LL
65T-195
65T/trans-32SP
66EH-39
66Kahn
66T-238LL
66T-425
66T/RO-46
67Kahn
67T-238LL
67T-335
67T/Test/PP-23
68Bz-3
68Kahn
68KDKA-39
68OPC-70
68T-70
69Kahn
69MB-283
69MLB/St-189
69OPC-8LL
69T-520
69T-8LL
69T/St-90
70MLB/St-108
70OPC-236
70T-236
71MLB/St-215
71OPC-368
71T-368
72MB-351
72T-729
73OPC-518
73T-518
78Green
78TCMA-114
Veeck, Michael
90Miami/I/Star-29GM
Vega, Jesus
77BurlB
78OrlTw
79Toledo-20
80Toledo-11
81Toledo-16
83D-650
83F-624
83T-308
83Toledo-17
Vegely, Bruce
89QuadC/Best-19
91PalmSp/ProC-2016
Veilleux, Brian
89Modesto/Cal-268
89Modesto/Chong-17
90Huntsvl/Best-12
Veintidos, Juan
75OPC-621R
75T-621R
75T/M-621R
Veit, Steve
90Ashvl/ClBest-17
90AubAs/Best-3
90AubAs/ProC-3400
91Ashvl/ProC-578
Velarde, Randy
86AppFx-26
87Albany-7
88Colum/CMC-17
88Colum/Pol-22
88Colum/ProC-324
88F-646R
89AAA/CMC-19
89AAA/ProC-19
89Colum/CMC-13
89Colum/Pol-20
89Colum/ProC-741
89S/HotRook-18
89T-584
89T/Big-239
89UD-189
90AlbanyDG/Best-19
90B-434
90D-630
90OPC-23
90S-524
90S/NWest-27
90T-23
90T/Big-68
90T/TVYank-28
91OPC-379
91S-134
91T-379
91T/StClub/II-438
92D/II-679
92F-246
92S/I-337
92T-212
92UD-399
Velasquez, Al
82Reading-12
Velasquez, Guillermo
88Charl/ProC-1203
88SALAS/GS-12
89River/Best-20
89River/ProC-1394
90Wichita/Rock-21
91Wichita/LineD-621
Velasquez, Ray
85Visalia-16
86Visalia-23
87Clinton-26
88SanJose/Cal-139
88SanJose/ProC-116
89Salinas/ProC-1807
90Salinas/Cal-125
Velazquel, Ildefonso
85Tigres-9
Velazquez, Carlos
No Cards.
Velazquez, Freddy
No Cards.
Velazquez, Juan
83QuadC-17
Velez, Jose
87Gaston-25
88Gaston/ProC-1011
89PalmSp/ProC-484
91Single/ClBest-208
91Spring/ClBest-28
91Spring/ProC-758
Velez, Noel
90CharWh/Best-18
90CharWh/ProC-2248
90Foil/Best-54
91Cedar/ProC-2734
91Erie/ClBest-12
91Erie/ProC-4082
Velez, Otto
73Syrac/Team-28
74OPC-606R
74Syrac/Team-27
74T-606R
74T/St-219
76SSPC-455
77OPC-13
77T-299
78OPC-67
78T-59
79OPC-241
79T-462
80OPC-354
80T-703
81D-391
81F-410
81OPC-351
81OPC/Post-23
81T-351
81T/So-44
81T/St-138
82D-304
82F-625
82F/St-233
82OPC-155
82OPC/Post-11
82T-155
82T/St-249
83Charl-18
Vella, Greg
88Myrtle/ProC-1183
88SALAS/GS-19
89Dunedin/Star-21
Velleggia, Frank
84Newar-15
Venable, Max
77Clinton
78LodiD
79Pol/Giants-49
80Phoenix-12
81F-443
81Phoenix-6
81T-484
83F-275
83Mother/Giants-16
83T-634
84D-323
84F-385
84Indianap-28
84Nes/792-58
84T-58
85Indianap-9
86D-650
86F-196
86T-428
86TexGold-9
87F-216
87Nashvl-22
87T-226
89Edmon/CMC-23
89Edmon/ProC-556
90Leaf/II-459
91D-510
92S/II-477
Venezia, Mike
81Redwd-8
Venger, Tad
81CharR-24
Venner, Gary
83TriCit-27
Ventress, Leroy
86Cram/PCL-145
88Batavia/ProC-1666
89SALAS/GS-41
89Spartan/ProC-1044
89Spartan/Star-23
90Clearw/Star-23
91Clearw/ClBest-26
91Clearw/ProC-1637
Ventura, Candido
77Charl
Ventura, Jose
86Beloit-24
89SoBend/GS-16
90Saraso/Star-25
91BirmB/LineD-73
91Single/ClBest-271
Ventura, Reynaldo
89BurlInd/Star-25
Ventura, Robin
88T/Tr-124TOLY
89B-65
89BBAmerAA/BProC-AA21
89BirmB/Best-1
89BirmB/ProC-106
89Classic/Up/2-177
89F/Up-23
89SLAS-2
89T-764
89T/Big-65
90B-311
90BirmDG/Best-1
90Classic-5
90Coke/WSox-27
90Coke/WSox-28
90D-28
90D/BestAL-60
90D/Rook-15
90F-550
90F/SoarSt-4
90HotRook/St-45
90Leaf/I-167
90Leaf/Prev-8
90OPC-121
90S-595
90S/100Ris-96
90S/DTRook-B6
90S/YS/II-8
90Sf-222
90T-121
90T/89Debut-129
90ToysRUs-28
90UD-21SR
91B-358
91Bz-15
91Classic/200-52
91D-315
91F-139
91F/Ultra-86
91Kodak/WSox-23
91Kodak/WSox-x
91Leaf/II-271
91OPC-461
91Panini/FrSt-314
91Panini/St-260
91RedFoley/St-97
91S-320
91S/100RisSt-48
91T-461
91T/StClub/I-274
91ToysRUs-30
91UD-263
91UD-677
92D/I-145
92D/Preview-6
92F-101
92F/ASIns-19
92S/100SS-33
92S/I-122
92S/Prev-3
92T-255
92UD-263
Venture, Jose
91BirmB/ProC-1455
Venturini, Peter Paul
(Pete)
86Penin-25
87BirmB/Best-22
88BirmB/Best-11
Venturino, Phil
86MidldA-24
86PalmSp/Smok-18
87MidldA-29
88Edmon/CMC-8
88Edmon/ProC-566
Venuto, Nicholas
88SoOreg/ProC-1695
89Medford/Best-14
Veras, Camilo
86Madis-25
86Madis/Pol-21
87Madis-15
88Huntsvl/BK-23
Veras, Quilvio
91Kingspt/ClBest-10
91Kingspt/ProC-3824
Verban, Emil
48B-28
49B-38
49Eureka-73
Exh47
Verbanic, Joe
67T-442R
68OPC-29
68T-29
69T-541
70OPC-416
70T-416
Verble, Gene
88Chatt/Team-30
Verdi, Frank
78Tidew
79Tidew-4
80Tidew-24
81Colum-17
82Colum-25
82Colum/Pol-26
83SanJose-1MG
84RochR-9
85RochR-24
Verdi, Mike
86SanJose-22CO
87SanJose-19
89Elmira/Pucko-22
90Elmira/Pucko-25MG
91WinHaven/ClBest-5MG
91WinHaven/ProC-505MG
Verducci, John
85Everett/Cram-17
86Shrev-26
87Phoenix-18
Verdugo, Luis
89Miami/II/Star-20
Verdugo, Mando
88SLCity-25
89Miami/I/Star-20
90Kinston/Team-21
Veres, David
86Cram/PCL-53
87Modesto-3
88CalLgAS-10
88Huntsvl/BK-24
88Modesto-32
88Modesto/Cal-56
89Huntsvl/Best-5
90Tacoma/CMC-2
90Tacoma/ProC-90
91Albuq/LineD-21
91Albuq/ProC-1141
Veres, Randy
86Beloit-25
87Beloit-1
88Stockton/Cal-179
88Stockton/ProC-730
89ElPaso/GS-17
89F/Up-42
90B-390
90Brewer/MillB-29
90T/89Debut-130
90T/Tr-125T
91Classic/I-56
91D-755
91OPC-694
91Richm/ProC-2570
91S/100RisSt-12
91T-694
Vergez, Johnny
33G-233
34DS-21
35BU-176
R337-401
V355-5
Verhoeff, Will
77WHave
Verhoeven, John
77T-91
78T-329
79Toledo-12
81D-564
81T-603
82F-547
82T-281
Verkuilen, Mike
85Orlan-13

Verna, Chris
89SanBern/Cal-92TR
90Wmsprt/Best-24
90Wmsprt/Star-27TR
Vernon, Mickey
49B-94
50B-132
51B-65
51T/BB-13
52B-87
52NTea
52T-106
52TipTop
53B/Col-159
53Briggs
53Exh/Can-59
53RM-AL21
54B-152
54RM-AL13
55Armour-24
55B-46
55RM-AL12
56T-228
57T-92
58T-233
59Armour-20
59T-115
60T-467C
61T-134MG
62T-152MG
63T-402MG
76SSPC-621
79Colum-29
79TCMA-87
80Pac/Leg-78
86Sf/Dec-38M
89Swell-54
91T/Arc53-287
Exh47
Versalles, Zoilo
61Clover-30
61Peters-1
61T-21
61T/St-186
62J-86
62P-86
62P/Can-86
62Salada-51A
62Salada-51B
62Shirriff-51
62T-499
62T/St-81
63J-3
63P-3
63T-349
64T-15
64Wheat/St-46
65MacGregor-10
65OPC-157
65T-157
65T/E-33
66T-400
67T-270
68T-315
69MB-284
69MLB/St-45
69OPC-38
69T-38
69T/St-100
70MLB/St-288
70OPC-365
70T-365
72MB-352
75OPC-203M
75T-203MV
75T/M-203MV
82KMart-7
88Pac/Leg-107
90Target-822
Verstandig, Mark
88Spokane/ProC-1943
89CharRain/ProC-990
90Waterlo/Best-25
90Waterlo/ProC-2382
91HighD/ClBest-17
91HighD/ProC-2400
Veryzer, Thomas
75OPC-623R
75T-623R
75T/M-623R
76Ho-109
76OPC-432
76SSPC-367
76T-432
77OPC-188
77T-145
78OPC-14
78T-633
79T-537
80OPC-145
80T-276
81D-199
81F-390
81T-39
82D-450
82F-381
82OPC-387
82T-387
82T/Tr-123T
83F-559
83T-496
83T/Tr-121
83Thorn-29
84Nes/792-117
84T-117
85T-405
91WIZMets-421
Veselic, Bob
80Toledo-19
81Toledo-9
82Toledo-6
83Tucson-9
Vesely, Orece
89QuadC/GS-12
Vesling, Donald
88FSLAS/Star-51
88Lakeland/Star-25
89London/ProC-1374
90Toledo/CMC-1
90Toledo/ProC-151
91Toledo/LineD-598
91Toledo/ProC-1933
Vespe, Will
88CapeCod/Sum-149
89Watertn/Star-22
90Kinston/Team-15
Vessey, Tom
81Tucson-6
Vetsch, Dave
85Visalia-13
86Orlan-22
87Orlan-27
Vezendy, Gerry
65T-509R
Viarengo, Matt
91Idaho/ProC-4328
91Pulaski/ClBest-28
91Pulaski/ProC-4005
Viau, Leon
N172
Vice, Darryl
88CapeCod/Sum-152
89Modesto/Chong-26
90Madison/ProC-2280
91Huntsvl/ClBest-25
91Huntsvl/LineD-297
91HuntsvlProC-1806
Vicente, Alberto
90Martins/ProC-3419
Vick, Ernie
92Conlon/Sport-402
Vickers, Mike
78Ashvl
80Tulsa-25
Vickers, Rube
90Target-1089
C46-37
Vickery, Lou
62Kahn/Atl
63Pep/Tul
Vico, George
48L-47
49B-122
50B-150
53Mother-25
Vidal, Jose
67T-499R
68T-432R
69T-322
Vidmar, Donald
89PalmSp/Cal-50
89PalmSp/ProC-482
90PalmSp/Cal-225
90PalmSp/ProC-2578
91PalmSp/ProC-2017
Viebahn
E270/1
Viebrock, Alan
76Watlo
Viera, John
90PrWill/Team-26
91PrWill/ClBest-23
91PrWill/ProC-1441
Vierra, Jose
90A&AASingle/ProC-190
90Hunting/ProC-3295
91MidwLAS/ProC-MWL9
91Peoria/ClBest-14
91Peoria/ProC-1352
Vierra, Joseph
88Greens/ProC-1574
89Cedar/Best-8
89Cedar/ProC-915
89Cedar/Star-21
90Nashvl/CMC-3
90Nashvl/ProC-234
91Nashvl/LineD-273
91Nashvl/ProC-2157
Viggiano, Matt
88Batavia/ProC-1683
Vike, Jim
86AubAs-27
Vila, Jesus
86VeroB-26
Vilella, Lazaro
84Butte-26
Vilet, Tom
91Batavia/ClBest-15
91Batavia/ProC-3499
Villa, Jose
88StCath/ProC-2008
Villa, Mike
86Fresno/Smok-9
87Tampa-30
88Clinton/ProC-719
Villaescusa, Juan
81VeroB-23
Villalobos, Gary
91LynchRS/ClBest-19
91LynchRS/ProC-1209
Villaman, Rafael
82Nashvl-26
Villanueva, Gilbert
87CharWh-3
88Stockton/Cal-188
88Stockton/ProC-728
Villanueva, Hector
86WinSalem-26
87Pittsfld-3
88EastLAS/ProC-28
88Pittsfld/ProC-1355
89Iowa/CMC-13
89Iowa/ProC-1696
90Cub/Mara-21
90F/Up-U10
90Iowa/CMC-18
90Iowa/ProC-322
90Leaf/II-401
90S/Tr-98T
90T/Tr-126T
90T/TVCub-62
90UD/Ext-741
91Cub/Mara-19
91D-296
91F-436
91F/Ultra-69
91Leaf/I-75
91OPC-362
91S-71
91S/100RisSt-51
91T-362
91T/90Debut-160
91T/StClub/I-213
91UD-171
92D/II-725
92F-394
92S/II-677
92T-181
92UD-102
Villanueva, Juan
86Lynch-24
87Lynch-2
88FSLAS/Star-24
89Jacks/GS-12
90Wichita/Rock-22
Villareal, Juan
90Princet/DIMD-26
Villegas, Mike
84ElPaso-8
Villegas, Ramon
85Tigres-6
Vilorio, Frank
79Toledo-19
83Nashua-16
Viltz, Corey
87Jamestn-15
88WPalmB/Star-25
89WPalmB/Star-23
Viltz, Eski
80Cedar-7
81Water-17
82Water-15
90CedarDG/Best-26
Vincent, Mike
86Cedar/TCMA-12
87Cedar-19
Vines, Ellsworth
33SK-46
Vineyard, Dave
65OPC-169
65T-169
91Crown/Orio-468
Vinson, Chuck
68T-328R
Vinton, William
N172
Viola, Frank
82OrlTw/B-24
82Toledo-7
83D-382
83F-625
83T-586
84D-364
84F-575
84Nes/792-28
84OPC-28
84T-28
84T/St-312
85D-17DK
85D-436
85D/DKsuper-17
85F-291
85F/St-84
85Leaf-17DK
85OPC-266
85Seven/Minn-2
85T-266
85T-710AS
85T/Gloss40-7
85T/St-300
86D-194
86F-408
86F/St-124
86KayBee-33
86Leaf-126
86OPC-269
86Sf-99
86T-742
86T/Mini-25
86T/St-284
87D-196
87D/HL-24
87F-554
87Leaf-74
87OPC-310
87RedFoley/St-127
87T-310
87T/St-277
88ChefBoy-15
88Classic/Red-183
88D-149
88D/Best-214
88Drake-29
88F-25
88F/BB/MVP-41
88F/Mini-38
88F/RecSet-42
88F/SlugWaxBox-C5
88F/St-47
88F/WS-12
88Leaf-94
88Master/Disc-2
88OPC-259
88Panini/St-134
88S-475
88Sf-196
88Smok/Minn-1
88T-625
88T/Big-201
88T/Mini-25
88T/RiteAid-33
88T/St-25
88T/St-282
88T/UK-82
88Woolwth-19
88Woolwth-33WSMVP
89B-150
89Bz-21
89Cadaco-60
89Classic-144
89T/Crunch-4
89D-237
89D-23DK
89D/AS-8
89D/Best-74
89D/DKsuper-23DK
89D/PopUp-8
89F-127
89F/AS-12
89F/BBAS-43
89F/BBMVP's-41
89F/Excit-42
89F/Heroes-42
89F/LL-42
89F/Superstar-41
89F/WaxBox-C28
89Holsum/Discs-17
89KayBee-31
89KingB/Discs-14
89Master/Discs-1
89Nissen-17
89OPC-120
89Panini/St-237AS
89Panini/St-248
89Panini/St-383
89Panini/St-475
89RedFoley/St-125
89S-290
89S/HotStar-5
89S/Tr-67
89Sf-10
89T-120
89T-406AS
89T/Big-140
89T/Coins-30
89T/DH-10
89T/Gloss22-10
89T/Gloss60-18
89T/HeadsUp-7
89T/Hills-31
89T/LJN-158
89T/Mini-64
89T/St-153
89T/St-292
89T/St/Backs-30
89T/UK-80
89UD-397
89UD-658CY
89UD-691TC
89Woolwth-3
90B-122
90Classic-91
90Classic/III-37
90Classic/III-NO
90D-353
90D/BestNL-68
90F-219
90Kahn/Mets-29
90Leaf/I-93
90Mets/Fan-29
90OPC-470
90PublInt/St-297
90PublInt/St-339
90S-500
90Sf-122
90Starline/LJS-18
90Starline/LJS-7
90T-470
90T/Big-162
90T/DH-67
90T/St-95
90T/TVMets-18
90Tetley/Discs-16
90UD-626
90USPlayC/AS-1D
91B-477
91BBBest/Aces-18
91Classic/200-1
91Classic/III-92
91D-529
91F-165
91F/Ultra-227
91Kahn/Mets-29
91Leaf/I-180
91Leaf/Stud-210

91OPC-406AS
91OPC-60
91Panini/FrSt-87
91Panini/St-84
91Panini/Top15-59
91Panini/Top15-68
91Panini/Top15-76
91RedFoley/St-98
91S-460
91S-687KM
91S-882DT
91S/100SS-70
91Seven/3DCoin-15NE
91T-406AS
91T-60
91T/CJMini/I-4
91T/StClub/I-292
91T/SU-34
91UD-122
91USPlayC/AS-7C
91WIZMets-422
92D/II-498
92F-518
92S/100SS-62
92S/I-220
92T-510
92UD-277

Viola, Lance
79Newar-23

Violat, Juan
T206

Viox, James
D329-180
D350/2-182
M101/4-180
M101/5-182

Virdon, Bill
55B-296
55Hunter
56T-170
57T-110
58Hires-45
58T-198
59T-190
59T-543M
60L-40
60T-496
61P-135
61T-70
61T/St-72
62J-175
62Kahn
62P-175
62P/Can-175
62Salada-168
62Shirriff-168
62T-415
62T/St-181
63IDL-25
63J-142
63Kahn
63P-142
63T-55
64Kahn
64T-268M
64T-495
65Kahn
65OPC-69
65T-69
72T-661MG
73OPC-517MG
73T-517MG
74Syrac/Team-28
75OPC-611MG
75T-611MG
75T/M-611MG
76T-147MG
77T-327MG
78BK/Ast-1MG
78T-279MG
79T-381MG
79TCMA-100
81D-384MG
81F-61MG
81T-678MG
82D-144MG
83OPC-6MG
83Stuart-1MG
83T-516MG
84Nes/792-111MG
84OPC-111MG
84Stuart-2MG
84T-111MG
88Pac/Leg-49
89Swell-119
91Swell/Great-93

Virgil, Ossie Jr.
77Spartan
81OkCty/TCMA-19
82T-231R
83D-606
83F-175
83T-383
84D-326
84F-49
84Nes/792-484
84Phill/TastyK-26
84T-484
85CIGNA-3
85D-82
85F-267
85Leaf-250
85OPC-103
85Phill/TastyK-10M
85Phill/TastyK-26
85T-143FS
85T-611
85T/St-110
85ThomMc/Discs-46
86D-137
86D/AAS-26
86F-456
86F/Up-U122
86OPC-95
86Pol/Atl-9
86T-95
86T/St-115
86T/Tr-119T
87D-67
87D/OD-45
87F-532
87OPC-183
87Smok/Atl-12
87T-571
88D-143
88D/AS-50
88D/Best-85
88F-552
88Jiffy-17
88Leaf-64
88OPC-291
88Panini/St-241
88RedFoley/St-93
88S-129
88Sf-217
88T-755
88T/Big-148
88T/St-36
88T/St/Backs-24
89D-145
89F-605
89OPC-179
89RedFoley/St-126
89S-111
89Sf-94
89T-179
89T/St-28
89UD-104
90EliteSenLg-15
90Syrac/CMC-22
90Syrac/ProC-575
90Syrac/Team-26
90Tor/BlueJ-26
91Crown/Orio-469
91Pac/SenLg-150
91Pac/SenLg-159

Virgil, Ossie Sr.
57T-365
58T-107
59T-203
61T-67
62T-327
65T-571
67OPC-132
67T-132
81Detroit-135
84Smok/SDP-26C
85T-143FS
89Pac/SenLg-22
91Pac/SenLg-138MG
91Pac/SenLg-159

Virgilio, George
90Pulaski/Best-19
90Pulaski/ProC-3089
91Pulaski/CIBest-10
91Pulaski/ProC-4016

Viskas, Steve
79QuadC-25

Visner, Joseph
N172

Vitale, Tony
86Fresno/Smok-28

Vitato, Richard
82CharR-14
83CharR-9

Vitiello, Joe
91Classic/DP-5
91Eugene/CIBest-15
91Eugene/ProC-3742
92UD-73TP

Vitko, Joe
90SALAS/Star-45
91StLucie/CIBest-15
91StLucie/ProC-711

Vito, Frank
91Pac/SenLg-158

Vitt, Oscar
(Ossie)
40PB-47
92Conlon/Sport-495
D327
D328-179
D329-181
D350/2-183
E121/120
E121/80
E135-179
M101/4-181
M101/5-183
T222
W501-9
W575

Vivas, Domingo
91Billings/ProC-3753

Vizcaino, Jose
88Bakers/Cal-240
88CalLgAS-47
89Albuq/CMC-23
89Albuq/ProC-82
90Albuq/CMC-20
90Albuq/ProC-355
90Albuq/Trib-29
90B-98
90Classic/Up-49
90F-410
90S-613
90T/89Debut-131
90Target-1090
90UD-44
91B-427
91Cub/Mara-16
91D-724
91F-223
91Leaf/II-323
91S-787
91S/100RisSt-88
91UD-580
92D/I-212
92S/I-169
92T-561

Vizcaino, Junior
87Watertn-14
88CLAS/Star-18
88Salem/Star-22
89Harris/ProC-293
89Harris/Star-20
90Harris/ProC-1202
90Harris/Star-19

Vizquel, Omar
86Wausau-27
88BBAmer-4
88EastLAS/ProC-37
88Vermont/ProC-946
89Calgary/CMC-23
89Calgary/ProC-537
89D/Best-163
89D/Rook-53
89F/Up-62
89Mother/Sea-15
89S/Tr-105
89T/Tr-122T
89UD/Ext-787
90B-474
90D-483
90F-528
90Leaf/I-88
90Mother/Mar-12
90OPC-698
90PublInt/St-445
90S-264
90S/100Ris-37
90S/YS/I-28
90T-698
90T/89Debut-132
90T/Big-140
90T/Gloss60-59
90T/JumboR-28
90UD-233
91B-245
91CounHrth-9
91D-231
91F-464
91F/Ultra-345
91Leaf/I-91
91OPC-298
91Panini/FrSt-231
91S-299
91T-298
91T/StClub/I-195
91UD-593
92D/II-641
92F-296
92S/I-162
92T-101
92UD-401

Vizzini, Dan
90SoOreg/Best-21
90SoOreg/ProC-3447
91SoOreg/CIBest-20
91SoOreg/ProC-3846

Vlasis, Chris
91Johnson/CIBest-13
91Johnson/ProC-3992

Vlcek, Jim
86Salem-27

Vodvarka, Rob
83Butte-12

Voeltz, Bill
87FtLaud-16
87Oneonta-19
87PrWill-16
88FtLaud/Star-23

Vogel, George
84Savan-20

Voigt, Jack
88Hagers/Star-23
89Freder/Star-24
90EastLAS/ProC-EL8
90Foil/Best-103
90Hagers/Best-15
90Hagers/ProC-1430
90Hagers/Star-25
91Hagers/LineD-248
91Hagers/ProC-2470

Voigt, Paul
83Albuq-7

Voiselle, Bill
47TipTop
49Eureka-27
Exh47

Voit, David
89Beloit/I/Star-23
89Helena/SP-12
90Erie/Star-30

Vollmer, Clyde
50B-53
51B-91
52B-57
52T-255
53B/Col-152
53Briggs
53T-32
54B-136
55B-13
91T/Arc53-32

Vollmer, Gus
90Clinton/Best-11
90Clinton/ProC-2562

Vollmer, Robby
83Wausau/LF-16

Voltaggio, Vic
88TM/Umpire-32
89TM/Umpire-30
90TM/Umpire-29

Von Der Ahe, Christian
90BBWit-77
N172
N284
N370

Von Hoff, Bruce
68T-529

Von Ohlen, Dave
79Jacks-15
80Tidew-1
81Louisvl-8
81Tidew-18
82Tidew-23
83Louisvl/Riley-8
84D-205
84F-340
84Louisvl-9
84Nes/792-489
84T-489
85D-412
85F-243
85F/Up-U126
85Polar/Ind-38
85T-177
85T/Tr-127T
86F-597
86Miami-25
86T-632
87F-408
87T-287
87Tacom-7
88Miami/Star-24

Vondran, Steve
89Billings/ProC-2057
89Smok/FresnoSt-21
91Cedar/CIBest-20
91Cedar/ProC-2723
91Single/CIBest-346

Vontz, Doug
87BurlEx-29

Vorbeck, Eric
91Yakima/CIBest-2
91Yakima/ProC-4263

Voorhees, Mark
77Spoka

Vosberg, Ed
84Beaum-6
85Beaum-5
86LasVegas-21
87LasVegas-24
88LasVegas/CMC-7
88LasVegas/ProC-222
89Tucson/CMC-6
89Tucson/ProC-192
89Tucson/JP-26
90Phoenix/CMC-6
90Phoenix/ProC-11
91Edmon/LineD-172
91Edmon/ProC-1516
91S-757RP
91S/100RisSt-80

Vosik, Bill
91Watertn/CIBest-23
91Watertn/ProC-3378

Vosmik, Joe
32Orbit/num-35
32Orbit/un-56
33DH-40
33DL-20
34DS-8
34G-77
35BU-68
35G-8I
35G-9I
36Exh/4-11
36G
36Wheat
38Exh/4-9
38G-247
38G-271
39PB-107
40PB-144
41DP-144
90Target-823
91Conlon/Sport-221
R305
R310
R313
R314
R326-2A
R326-2B
R342-2
V355-76
WG8-48

Voss, Bill
66T-529R
68OPC-142R
68T-142R
69T-621
70OPC-326
70T-326
71MLB/St-454
71OPC-671

71T-671
72T-776
Vossler, Dan
74OPC-602R
74T-602R
Vranjes, Sam
91SanBern/ClBest-28
91SanBern/ProC-1991
Vuchinch, Steve
90Mother/A's-28M
Vuckovich, Pete
77OPC-130
77T-517
78OPC-157
78T-241
79T-407
80OPC-31
80T-57
81D-189
81F-547
81OPC-193
81T-193
81T/Tr-851
82D-458
82F-156
82F/St-14
82OPC-132
82Pol/Brew-50
82T-165LL
82T-643
82T-703TL
82T/St-10LL
82T/St-202
83D-80
83F-49
83Gard-20
83K-19
83OPC-375
83OPC-394AS
83Pol/Brew-50
83T-321TL
83T-375
83T-394AS
83T/St-86
84F-217
84Gard-21
84Nes/792-505
84OPC-313
84Pol/Brew-50
84T-505
85Gard-21
85Pol/Brew-50
85T-254
86D-473
86F-504
86OPC-152
86T-737
90Swell/Great-83
Vukovich, George
81F-21
81OkCty/TCMA-20
81T-598
82F-262
82T-389
83D-315
83F-176
83T-16
83T/Tr-122T
83Wheat/Ind-31
84D-468
84F-555
84Nes/792-638
84T-638
84Wheat/Ind-24
85D-276
85F-458
85Leaf-120
85Polar/Ind-24
85T-212
85T/St-249
86D-346
86F-598
86OPC-337
86T-483
86T/St-214
91Pac/SenLg-45
Vukovich, John
73OPC-451
73T-451
74OPC-349
74T-349
75OPC-602
75T-602
75T/M-602
76SSPC-43
79Ho-87
79OkCty
80BK/P-8
81F-22
83Thorn-26C
88Phill/TastyK-29CO
88Phill/TastyK-38CO
89Phill/TastyK-35CO
90Phill/TastyK-34CO
91Phill/Medford-35CO
Vuksan, Jeff
79AppFx-8
81Durham-12
Vuz, John
87Pocatel/Bon-14
88Clinton/ProC-693
90SanJose/Best-22
90SanJose/Cal-52
90SanJose/ProC-2001
90SanJose/Star-24
Waag, Billy
81Buffa-14
Wabeke, Doug
81Shrev-18
Wacha, Chuck
87Greens-7
Wachs, Thomas
85LitFalls-11
86Columbia-26
87Lynch-3
Wachter, Ed
33SK-5
Wacker, Wade
89Elizab/Star-27
Wada, Hiromi
(Hank)
83SanJose-2C
86SanJose-23C
Waddell, George E.
(Rube)
48Exh/HOF
50Callahan
60F-61
61F-149
80Laugh/FFeat-11
80SSPC/HOF
86Conlon/1-35
88Conlon/5-29
88Conlon/HardC-6
E107
E254
E270/1
E91
E93
M116
T206
W555
WG2-47
Waddell, Tom
84F/X-U123
84T/Tr-125T
84Wheat/Ind-54
85D-582
85F-459
85Polar/Ind-54
85T-453
86D-94
86F-599
86OhHenry-54
86OPC-86
86T-86
86T/St-209
87Gator-54
87T-657
Wade, Ben
52T-389
53T-4
54T-126
59DF
61Union
90Target-824
91T/Arc53-4
Wade, Darrin
88Dunedin/Star-19
88StCath/ProC-2036
Wade, Gale
55T-196
Wade, Jake
V362-3
Wade, Scott
86NewBrit-25
87Pawtu-21
87Pawtu/TCMA-20
88Pawtu/CMC-23
88Pawtu/ProC-458
89Pawtu/CMC-15
89Pawtu/Dunkin-33
89Pawtu/ProC-695
90Pawtu/CMC-23
90Pawtu/ProC-476
90T/TVRSox-65
91ScranWB/LineD-497
91ScranWB/ProC-2554
Wadley, Tony
82Miami-7
83Idaho-13
Waggoner, Aubrey
86AppFx-27
87Penin-8
89BirmB/Best-8
89BirmB/ProC-114
90BirmB/Best-13
90BirmB/ProC-1120
91BirmB/LineD-72
91BirmB/ProC-1468
Waggoner, Jimmy
89Medford/Best-25
90Madison/Best-9
90Modesto/Cal-166
90Modesto/ProC-2223
91Modesto/ClBest-26
91Modesto/ProC-3100
91Single/ClBest-89
Wagner, Adam
90FtLaud/Star-27TR
91PrWill/ClBest-27TR
Wagner, Albert
(Butts)
90Target-1092
Wagner, Charles
(Heinie)
10Domino-119
11Helmar-5
12Sweet/Pin-7
14CJ-31
15CJ-31
E91
M116
T202
T204
T205
T206
T207
T213/blue
T215/blue
T215/brown
T216
Wagner, Charlie
80Elmira-38
87Elmira/Black-33
Wagner, Dan
87Penin-29
88BirmB/Best-13
89BirmB/Best-5
89BirmB/ProC-90
Wagner, Gary
66OPC-151
66T-151
67T-529
68T-448
69T-276
69T/St-158
70T-627
71OPC-473
71T-473
Wagner, Gerald
86Durham-26
87Sumter-28
Wagner, Harold
47TipTop
Wagner, Hector
88Eugene/Best-6
89AppFx/ProC-849
90A&AASingle/ProC-34
90Foil/Best-194
90Memphis/Best-18
90Memphis/ProC-1008
90Memphis/Star-25
91B-299
91Omaha/LineD-347
91Omaha/ProC-1036
91S-730RP
91T/90Debut-161
Wagner, Jeff
83Ander-33
84Durham-7
85Durham-31
Wagner, John
(Honus)
14CJ-68
15CJ-68
16FleischBrd-97
40PB-168
47TipTop
48Exh/HOF
48L-70
50Callahan
51T/CM
60Exh/HOF-24
60F-62
61F-150
61GP-32
63Bz/ATG-10
69Bz/Sm
72F/FFeat-21
72K/ATG-9
76Motor-1
76OPC-344AS
76T-344AS
80Pac/Leg-18
80Laugh/FFeat-1
80SSPC/HOF
83D/HOF-5
85West/2-42
86Conlon/1-55
87Nestle/DT-4
89HOF/St-14
89Pac/Leg-211
89Swell-4
90BBWit-84
90Swell/Great-50
91Conlon/Sport-8
91Swell/Great-126
92S/II-880
BF2-92
D303
D304
D322
D328-180
D329-182
D350/2-184
E101
E102
E103
E105
E106
E107
E135-180
E224
E254
E270/1
E286
E90/1
E90/2
E91
E92
E93
E94
E95
E98
M101/4-182
M101/5-184
M116
R311/Leath
R312/M
R313
T206
W555
WG3-49
WG4-28
WG5-41
WG6-37
Wagner, Leon
59T-257
60T-383
61T-547
61T/Dice-17
62P-77
62P/Can-77
62Salada-57A
62Salada-57B
62Shirriff-57
62T-491
62T/bucks
62T/St-71
63Exh
63F-21
63J-28
63P-28
63Salada-55
63T-335
63T-4LL
64Kahn
64T-41M
64T-530
64T/Coins-130AS
64T/Coins-6
64T/S-54
64Wheat/St-47
65Kahn
65OldLond-36
65T-367
65T/E-31
65T/trans-33
66Bz-8
66OPC-65
66T-65
67Bz-8
67Kahn
67OPC-109M
67OPC/PI-24
67T-109M
67T-360
67T/PI-24
68Kahn
68T-495
69OPC-187
69T-187
78TCMA-125
78TCMA-165
Exh47
Wagner, Mark
75Clinton
77T-490R
78T-598
80OPC-13
80T-29
81D-126
81F-478
81T-358
81T/Tr-852
82D-163
82F-333
82T-443
83D-268
83F-582
83T-144
84Cram/PCL-89
85T-581
89Pac/SenLg-170
91Pac/SenLg-112
91Toledo/LineD-600CO
91Toledo/ProC-1948CO
Wagner, Paul
89Welland/Pucko-26
90Augusta/ProC-2464
91CLAS/ProC-CAR38
91Salem/ClBest-21
91Salem/ProC-951
Wagner, Steve
78OrlTw
Wagner, William G.
(Bull)
90Target-1091
Wahl, Tim
88Beloit/GS-17
89Beloit/I/Star-24
Waid, Patrick
88SLCity-1
89SLCity-10F
Wainhouse, David
89B-358
89WPalmB/Star-24
90WPalmB/Star-25
91Harris/LineD-272
91Harris/ProC-629
92T/91Debut-177
Waitkus, Ed
47TipTop
49B-142
49Eureka-151
49Lummis
50B-30
50Drake-12
51B-28
51BR-C9
51T/BB-51
52B-92
52T-158
52TipTop
54Esskay
55B-4

55Esskay
79TCMA-77
91Crown/Orio-470
Exh47
PM10/Sm-191
Waits, M. Rick
75OkCty
76OPC-433
76SSPC-513
76T-433
77BurgChef-61
77Ho-88
77Pep-16
77T-306
78OPC-191
78T-37
79Ho-35
79OPC-253
79T-484
80OPC-94
80T-168
81D-201
81F-396
81OPC-258
81T-697
82D-33
82F-382
82OPC-142
82T-573
82Wheat/Ind
83D-263
83F-422
83T-779
83T/Tr-123T
83Wheat/Ind-32
84Nes/792-218
84T-218
85Cram/PCL-219
85D-368
85F-600
85T-59
86F-505
86T-614
86Vanco-27
89Pac/SenLg-91
89T/SenLg-60
89TM/SenLg-109
91Pac/SenLg-15
Wakamatsu, Don
86Tampa-24
87Cedar-16
88Chatt/Best-12
89BirmB/Best-16
89BirmB/ProC-107
90Vanco/CMC-22
90Vanco/ProC-491
91Vanco/LineD-648
91Vanco/ProC-1598
92S/II-814
92T/91Debut-178
Wakana, Josh
83Tidew-25
Wakefield, Bill
62Pep/Tul
63Pep/Tul
64T-576R
65OPC-167
65T-167
66T-443
91WIZMets-423
Exh47
Wakefield, Dick
47TipTop
48L-50
49B-91
50Remar
79TCMA-91
Wakefield, Tim
88Watertn/Pucko-27
89Welland/Pucko-27
90Salem/Star-23
91CaroMud/LineD-119
91CaroMud/ProC-1087
Walbeck, Matt
88CharWh/Best-1
89Peoria/Ko-15
90Hunting/ProC-3285
90PeoriaUp/Team-U4
91CLAS/ProC-CAR45
91WinSalem/ClBest-15
91WinSalem/ProC-2832
Walberg, Bill
82Jacks-25
Walberg, George
(Rube)
32Orbit/un-57
33G-145
33G-183
91Conlon/Sport-91
R305
R313
V353-76
W517-41
Walbring, Larry
76Clinton
Walden, Alan
90Burllnd/ProC-3009
91Collnd/ClBest-17
91Collnd/ProC-1484
Walden, Ron
90Classic/DP-9
90Classic/III-82
91B-615
91OPC-596DP
91S-679FDP
91T-596
Walden, Travis
88Clearw/Star-26
Waldenberger, Dave
89Idaho/ProC-2019
Waldron, Joe
91CharRain/ClBest-11
91CharRain/ProC-96
Walewander, James
86GlenF-23
87Toledo-5
87Toledo/TCMA-7
88Pep/T-32
88S-571
88T-106
89D-415
89F-150
89S-311
89T-467
89Toledo/CMC-15
89Toledo/ProC-770
89UD-454
90ColClip/CMC-12
90ColClip/ProC-686
90T/TVYank-65
91ColClip/LineD-122
91ColClip/ProC-607
Walgast, Ad
T3/Box-53
Walk, Bob
81D-393
81F-14
81T-494
81T/Tr-853
82BK/Lids-24
82Pol/Atl-43
82T-296
83D-401
83F-149
83Richm-10
83T-104
84Cram/PCL-141
85Cram/PCL-243
86D-430
86T/Tr-120T
87D-203
87F-623
87T-628
88D-514
88D/Best-269
88F-342
88S-162
88T-349
89B-409
89D-172
89D/AS-58
89D/Best-145
89F-223
89OPC-151
89OPC-66
89S-224
89Sf-34
89T-504
89T/St-123
89UD-438
89VFJuice-17
90B-163
90D-370
90D/BestNL-94
90F-482
90Homer/Pirate-31
90Leaf/I-64
90OPC-754
90Publint/St-167
90S-21
90T-754
90T/Big-23
90T/St-125
90UD-596
91B-526
91D-157
91F-54
91Leaf/II-450
91OPC-29
91S-599
91T-29
91T/StClub/I-14
91UD-689
92D/I-88
92F-572
92S/I-54
92T-486
92UD-619
Walker, Albert
(Rube)
49Eureka-74
52T-319
53T-134
54T-153
55Gol/Dodg-30
55T-108
55T/DH-15
56T-333
57T-147
58Hires-74
58T-203
73OPC-257CO
73T-257CO
74OPC-179CO
74T-179CO
79TCMA-278
80BurlB-13
82Pol/Atl-54CO
83Pol/Atl-54CO
84Pol/Atl-54CO
90Target-826
91T/Arc53-134
Walker, Andy
79QuadC-20
Walker, Anthony
(Tony)
81Water-11
81Water-21
82Water-20
83DayBe-27
86F/Up-U123
86Pol/Ast-20
87F-71
87T-24
Walker, Bernie
87Cedar-25
88Chatt/Best-23
89Chatt/Best-20
89Chatt/GS-22
89SLAS-7
91Chatt/LineD-173
91Nashvl/ProC-2171
Walker, Billy
91Miami/ClBest-4
Walker, Cameron
(Cam)
84ElPaso-22
86ElPaso-23
87ElPaso-18
87Wichita-25
Walker, Chico
81Pawtu-22
83Pawtu-24
84Pawtu-16
85lowa-11
86lowa-26
87Berg/Cubs-29
87D-539
87OPC-58
87T-695
88Edmon/ProC-561
89Syrac/CMC-23
89Syrac/ProC-792
89Syrac/Team-23
91Classic/III-93
91Cub/Mara-24
91F/UltraUp-U74
91Leaf/II-501
92D/II-439
92F-395
92S/II-578
92T-439
92UD-617
Walker, Chris
88Batavia/ProC-1677
89Clearw/Star-24
Walker, Clarence
(Tilly)
21Exh-181
91Conlon/Sport-137
D328-181
D329-183
D350/2-185
E120
E135-181
E254
M101/4-183
M101/5-185
V100
V61-6
W501-99
W515-7
W572
W575
Walker, Clifton
(Cliff)
85Bend/Cram-23
87Spartan-16
Walker, Curtis
21Exh-182
92Conlon/Sport-417
E126-58
Walker, Darcy
86WinSalem-27
Walker, Dennis
89Utica/Pucko-26
90SoBend/Best-12
90SoBend/ClBest-6
91SoBend/ProC-2866
Walker, Doak
52Wheat
Walker, Duane
80Indianap-26
81Indianap-21
82Indianap-6
83D-624
83F-606
83T-243
84D-325
84F-485
84F/St-41
84Nes/792-659
84T-659
85D-608
85F-554
85Leaf-52
85T-441
85T/St-52
86D-500
86F-574
86T-22
86Tucson-23
87Louisvl-28
88Bristol/ProC-1878
88Louisvl-49
88Louisvl/CMC-17
88Louisvl/ProC-425
89Miami/I/Star-24
Walker, Ewart
(Dixie)
T207
Walker, Fred
(Dixie)
34DS-12
34G-39
35G-8E
35G-9E
39Exh
41DP-21
49Eureka-174
53T-190
55Hunter
61F-151
89Smok/Dodg-49
90Target-825
91T/Arc53-190
92Conlon/Sport-506
PM10/Sm-192
R346-45
V354-86
Walker, Frederick
15CJ-173
E254
E270/1
Walker, Gerald
(Gee)
33DH-41
34G-26
35BU-118
35G-8F
35G-9F
37OPC-110
38Wheat-4
41DP-135
41Wheat-10
81Detroit-109
91Conlon/Sport-87
R309/2
R313
R314
V300
V354-81
V355-48
Walker, Glenn
81Wausau-24
82LynnS-16
83SLCity-20
84Cram/PCL-187
86MidldA-25
Walker, Greg
80AppFx
81GlenF-16
83T/Tr-124T
84D-609
84F-73
84Nes/792-518
84T-518
84TrueVal/WS-30
85Coke/WS-29
85D-366
85F-530
85OPC-244
85T-623
85T/St-236
85ThomMc/Discs-21
86Coke/WS-29
86D-135
86F-219
86Jay's-19
86OPC-123
86Sf-174
86T-123
86T/St-293
87Coke/WS-17
87D-25DK
87D-59
87D/DKsuper-25
87D/OD-233
87F-508
87F/LL-42
87F/Mini-110
87Leaf-25DK
87OPC-302
87Seven-C15
87T-397
87T/St-291
88Coke/WS-29
88D-162
88D/Best-193
88F-411
88Leaf-86
88OPC-286
88Panini/St-56
88S-93
88Sf-103
88T-764
88T/Big-105
88T/St-292
88T/UK-83
89Coke/WS-27
89D-135
89Kodak/WSox-1M
89Panini/St-307
89S-37
89Sf-19
89T-21TL
89T-408
89T/Big-4
89UD-231
90F-551
90OPC-33
90Panini/St-45
90Publnt/St-402
90RochR/CMC-18
90RochR/ProC-712
90S-354

90T-33
90UD-350
91Crown/Orio-471

Walker, Harry
48L-137
49B-130
49Eureka-75
50B-180
60T-468C
65T-438MG
66EH-3
66T-318MG
67T-448MG
67T/Test/PP-24MG
69T-633MG
70OPC-32MG
70T-32MG
71OPC-312MG
71T-312MG
72OPC-249MG
72T-249MG
79TCMA-261
89Pac/Leg-190
89Swell-34
90Swell/Great-33
91Swell/Great-94
Exh47
R346-39

Walker, Hugh
89AppFx/ProC-856
89B-127
90BBCity/Star-24
91B-313
91London/LineD-422
91Memphis/ProC-667
91Single/ClBest-58

Walker, J. Luke
66T-498R
67OPC-123R
67T-123R
68T-559R
69OPC-36
69T-36
70OPC-322
70T-322
71MLB/St-216
71OPC-534
71OPC-68LL
71T-534
71T-68LL
71T/S-21
72MB-353
72OPC-471
72T-471
73OPC-187
73T-187
74OPC-612
74T-612
74T/Tr-612T
75OPC-474
75T-474
75T/M-474

Walker, James
87Chatt/Best-5
88Calgary/CMC-7
88Calgary/ProC-791

Walker, Jerry
89Belling/Legoe-35OWN

Walker, Jerry
58T-113
59T-144
60T-399M
60T-540
60T/tatt-52
60T/tatt-96
61T-85
62T-357
62T/bucks
62T/St-61
63Sugar-5
63T-413
64T-77
91Crown/Orio-472

Walker, John
78LodiD
79LodiD-12
80Toledo-9
81Toledo-17

Walker, Johnny
90Pulaski/ProC-3112

Walker, Keith
82Knoxvl-7
83Syrac-12

Walker, Kurt
87Visalia-8
88MidldA/GS-2

Walker, Larry
85Utica-16
86BurlEx-25
87Jaxvl-1
87SLAS-8
89AAA/CMC-7
89Indianap/CMC-23
89Indianap/ProC-1239
90B-117
90Classic/Up-16
90D-578
90D/BestNL-91
90F-363
90F/SoarSt-3
90Greens/Best-15
90Greens/ProC-2667
90Greens/Star-25
90Leaf/II-325
90OPC-757
90S-631
90S/YS/II-9
90T-757
90T/89Debut-133
90T/Big-296
90UD-466
90UD/Ext-702M
91B-442
91Bz-19
91D-359
91F-250
91F/UltraUp-U93
91FtLaud/ClBest-18
91FtLaud/ProC-2431
91Leaf/I-241
91MajorLg/Pins-80
91OPC-339
91Panini/FrSt-145
91Panini/St-65
91S-241
91S/100RisSt-21
91T-339
91T/StClub/I-93
91ToysRUs-31
91UD-536
92D/I-259
92F-493
92S/I-199
92T-531
92UD-249

Walker, Lonnie
88LitFalls/Pucko-14
89Clmbia/Best-27
89Clmbia/GS-26

Walker, Matt
86Clinton-26
86Cram/PCL-186
87Everett-1

Walker, Mike
86Watertn-27
87Harris-23
87Watlo-14
88Harris/ProC-850
88Wmsprt/ProC-1310
89B-77
89ColoSp/ProC-239
90Calgary/CMC-3
90Calgary/ProC-652
90ColoSp/CMC-1
90ColoSp/ProC-36
91D-61
91F-381
91OPC-593
91T-593A
91T-593B
91UD-694

Walker, Moses F.
86Negro/Frit-28

Walker, Pete
91StLucie/ClBest-14
91StLucie/ProC-712

Walker, Peter
90Pittsfld/Pucko-16

Walker, R. Tom
73OPC-41
73T-41
74OPC-193
74T-193
75OPC-627
75T-627
75T/M-627
76OPC-186
76T-186
77T-652
78Colum

Walker, Ray
88Martins/Star-32

Walker, Rich
88Batavia/ProC-1681
90Batavia/ProC-3084TR

Walker, Rod
89LittleSun-6

Walker, Steve
87SanBern-1
88BBCity/Star-24
89Memphis/Best-23
89Memphis/ProC-1196
89Memphis/Star-23
89Star/Wax-46
91Hunting/ClBest-28
91Hunting/ProC-3352

Walker, The
90Everett/Best-7

Walker, Tom
91Hunting/ClBest-29
91Hunting/ProC-3345

Walker, William C.
29Exh/4-7
31Exh/4-7
E120
W575

Walker, William H.
33G-94
35BU-116
R313
V353-57

Walkup, James
39PB-150

Wall, Dave
81AppFx-27

Wall, Donnie
89AubAs/ProC-2182
90Ashvl/ProC-2749
91BurlAs/ClBest-10
91BurlAs/ProC-2801
91MidwLAS/ProC-MWL19

Wall, Jason
90LSUPol-11

Wall, Murray
53T-217
58T-410
59T-42
91T/Arc53-217

Wall, Stan
74Albuq/Team-22
76OPC-584
76T-584
77T-88
90Target-827

Wallace, Alex
85Anchora-30

Wallace, Brooks
81Tulsa-24

Wallace, Curtis
76Baton

Wallace, Dave
76OkCty/Team-24
81VeroB-25
82VeroB-28
84Cram/PCL-245
86Albuq-26CO
90Ashvl/ClBest-24
91Ashvl/ProC-582

Wallace, Don
67T-367R

Wallace, Greg
86Miami-26

Wallace, Jim
49Remar

Wallace, Mike
74OPC-608R
74T-608R
75OPC-401
75T-401
75T/M-401
76SSPC-290
77T-539

Wallace, Roderick
(Bobby)
10Domino-120
11Helmar-66
12Sweet/Pin-56A
12Sweet/Pin-56B
14Piedmont/St-58
50Callahan
80SSPC/HOF
90BBWit-65
E107
E270/1
E90/1
E92
M116
S74-37
T201
T202
T204
T205
T206
T207
WG2-48

Wallace, Tim
83StPete-15
84ArkTr-5
86ArkTr-25
86Louisvl-28
86Peoria-25
87WinSalem-15
88WinSalem/Star-21
89Boise/ProC-1994
90PalmSp/Cal-216
90PalmSp/ProC-2588
91Wichita/LineD-622
91Wichita/ProC-2608

Wallach, Tim
82D-140
82F-210
82Hygrade
82OPC-191
82T-191
83D-392
83F-299
83OPC-229
83Stuart-12
83T-552
83T/St-257
84D-421
84F-291
84Nes/792-232
84OPC-232
84Stuart-14
84T-232
84T/St-94
85D-87
85F-412
85Leaf-199
85OPC-3
85OPC/Post-6
85T-473
85T/St-87
86D-219
86D/AAS-25
86F-263
86F/Mini-56
86Leaf-97
86OPC-217
86Provigo-11
86Sf-123
86T-685
86T-703
86T/St-82
87D-179
87D/OD-88
87F-334
87Ho/St-5
87Leaf-61
87OPC-55
87RedFoley/St-117
87Sf-115M
87Sf-72
87T-55
87T/St-80
88AlaskaAS70/Team-17
88D-222
88D/AS-59
88D/Best-258
88F-198
88F/AwardWin-44
88F/BB/AS-43
88F/BB/MVP-42
88F/Mini-91
88F/St-98
88F/WaxBox-C15
88Ho/Disc-7
88Jiffy-18
88KayBee-32
88Leaf-193
88Leaf-255CG
88Nestle-23
88OPC-94
88Panini/St-327
88RedFoley/St-94
88S-70
88Sf-151
88T-399
88T-560
88T/Big-7
88T/Coins-59
88T/Gloss60-18
88T/Mini-58
88T/Revco-6
88T/St-85
88T/St/Backs-9
88T/UK-84
89B-362
89D-156
89D/Best-34
89F-395
89KMart/DT-25
89OPC-78
89Panini/St-122
89RedFoley/St-127
89S-220
89Sf-114
89T-720
89T/Big-215
89T/LJN-139
89T/St-70
89UD-102
90B-114
90D-220
90D/BestNL-55
90D/Learning-28
90F-364
90F/AwardWin-41
90F/LL-41
90Leaf/I-80
90OPC-370
90Panini/St-286
90PublInt/St-189
90RedFoley/St-99
90S-192
90Sf-182
90T-370
90T/Big-70
90T/Coins-60
90T/DH-68
90T/Mini-64
90T/St-74
90UD-273
90USPlayC/AS-5D
91B-437
91Classic/200-2
91D-406MVP
91D-514
91DennyGS-12
91F-251
91F/Ultra-210
91Leaf/II-388
91Leaf/Prev-6
91Leaf/Stud-200
91OPC-220
91OPC/Premier-125
91Panini/FrSt-141
91Panini/St-64
91Panini/Top15-102
91Petro/SU-10
91Post/Can-2
91RedFoley/St-99
91S-210
91S-865FRAN
91S/100SS-58
91Sunflower-23
91T-220
91T/CJMini/II-21
91T/StClub/II-463
91UD-235
91UD-96
92D/I-34
92F-494
92S/100SS-70
92S/II-595
92T-385
92UD-228

Wallaesa, John
47TipTop

Wallenhaupt, Ron
85Water-16

Waller, Casey Lee
88CapeCod/Sum-113
90Reading/Best-19

90Reading/ProC-1229
90Reading/Star-23
91Reading/LineD-522
91Reading/ProC-1379

Waller, Elliott
(Ty)
78StPete
79ArkTr-9
82F-607
82Iowa-13
82T-51R
84Cram/PCL-60
85Cram/PCL-64
86Tucson-24
87Tucson-6
88River/Cal-233
88River/ProC-1414
88Spokane/ProC-1923
89River/Cal-30CO
90Riversi/Cal-27CO

Waller, Kevin
80Cedar-25
82Madis-22

Waller, Reggie
89AubAs/ProC-2168

Walles, Todd
91Belling/ClBest-8
91Belling/ProC-3676

Wallgren, Chris
90Elizab/Star-23

Wallin, Craig
89SoBend/GS-1

Wallin, Leslie
(Les)
88WinHaven/Star-25
89Lynch/Star-20
90LynchRS/Team-9
91WinHaven/ClBest-21
91WinHaven/ProC-500

Walling, Denny
77SanJose-17
77T-473R
79T-553
80OPC-161
80T-306
81D-144
81F-66
81T-439
82D-496
82F-236
82T-147
83D-419
83F-469
83T-692
84D-641
84F-244
84Mother/Ast-19
84Nes/792-36
84T-36
84T/St-73
85D-527
85F-365
85Mother/Ast-5
85T-382
86D-136
86F-314
86Pol/Ast-7
86T-504
87D-554
87F-72
87Leaf-159
87Mother/Ast-13
87OPC-222
87Pol/Ast-12
87S/Test-145
87T-222
87T/St-33
88D-384
88D/Best-309
88F-458
88Leaf-224
88Mother/Ast-13
88OPC-131
88Panini/St-296
88Pol/Ast-23
88S-145
88T-719
88T/St-31
89Chatt/II/Team-32
89D-279
89F-465
89S-49
89Smok/Cards-22
89T-196
89UD-327
90D-677
90F-263
90OPC-462
90Smok/Card-26
90T-462
90T/TVCard-30
91F-651
91Mother/Rang-18

Walling, Kendall
86Cram/PCL-192
87QuadC-25

Wallis, Joe
76OPC-598R
76T-598R
77BurgChef-190
77T-279
78T-614
79T-406
80T-562

Walls, R. Lee
53Mother-56
55B-82
57Kahn
57T-52
58T-66
59T-105
60Kahn
60L-111
60T-506
61P-119
61T-78
61T/St-60
62BB-56
62T-129
62T/St-160
63J-113
63P-113
63T-11
64T-411
90Target-828

Wallwork, Dave
86Penin-26TR
87Penin-18
88BirmB/Best-6
89BirmB/Best-25
89BirmB/ProC-96
90BirmB/Best-27

Walraven, Randy
78DaytB

Walsh, Dave
84Syrac-21
86Knoxvl-25
87Knoxvl-19
89Albuq/CMC-10
89Albuq/ProC-70
90AAAGame/ProC-AAA33
90Albuq/CMC-11
90Albuq/ProC-345
90Albuq/Trib-30
91Albuq/LineD-22
91OPC-367
91S-351RP
91T-367
91T/90Debut-162

Walsh, Dennis
91Niagara/ClBest-21
91Niagara/ProC-3633

Walsh, Ed
10Domino-121
11Helmar-18
12Sweet/Pin-14
14CJ-36
14Piedmont/St-59
15CJ-36
48Exh/HOF
49Leaf/Prem-8
50Callahan
60F-49
61F-83
63Bz/ATG-7
69Bz/Sm
72F/FFeat-23
80Laugh/FFeat-34
80SSPC/HOF
85Woolwth-35
88Utica/Pucko-25
89HOF/St-77
91Conlon/Sport-273
92Conlon/Sport-337
BF2-19
D329-184
D350/2-187
E224
E270/1
E286
E300
E90/1
E90/3
E98
M101/4-184
M101/5-187
M116
S81-107
T201
T202
T205
T206
WG4-29
WG5-42
WG6-38

Walsh, James C.
15CJ-144
C46-20
D327
D328-182
E135-182

Walsh, Jay
83LynnP-28

Walsh, Jim
81QuadC-11
82QuadC-25
83MidldC-4

Walsh, Joseph
N172

Walter, Craig
85FtMyr-4

Walter, Gene
83Miami-5
84Beaum-9
85Cram/PCL-112
86D/Rook-47
86F-644R
86F/Up-U124
86T/Tr-121T
87D-511
87F-433
87T-248
87Tidew-27
87Tidew/TCMA-21
88D/Mets/Bk-NEW
88F-153
88Kahn/Mets-31
89T-758
89UD-604
91WIZMets-424

Walterhouse, Dick
77Salem

Walters, Alfred
D328-183
E120
E135-183

Walters, Chip
89Nashvl/Team-26COM

Walters, Dan
86Ashvl-28
87Osceola-8
88ColAst/Best-12
89Wichita/Rock-11C
90Wichita/Rock-23
91LasVegas/ProC-240
91LasVegas/LineD-297

Walters, Darryel
85Beloit-13
86Stockton-25
87ElPaso-21
88Denver/CMC-23
88Denver/ProC-1255
89Denver/CMC-16
89Denver/ProC-54
89ElPaso/GS-29
90Denver/CMC-6
90Denver/ProC-640

Walters, David
86Elmira-25
87Greens-26
88Lynch/Star-24
89EastLDD/ProC-DD24
89NewBrit/ProC-614
89NewBrit/Star-20
90NewBrit/Best-25
90NewBrit/Star-20
91Pawtu/LineD-371
91Pawtu/ProC-40

Walters, Ken
60T-511
61P-122
61T-394
62T-328
63FrBauer-30
63T-534

Walters, Mike
80ElPaso-22
81SLCity-13
82Spokane-9
82Toledo-8
83Toledo-10
84Nes/792-673
84T-673
85T-187
85Toledo-11

Walters, Vic
79AppFx-24

Walters, William H.
(Bucky)
37Exh/4-6
38Exh/4-6
39Exh
39PB-22
40PB-73
41DP-8
41DP-96
41PB-3
41Wheat
49Eureka-97
54JC-31CO
55Gol/Braves-29
55JC-31CO
89Pac/Leg-164
92Conlon/Sport-537
Exh47
R314
V355-61
W711/1
W711/2

Walthour, B. Jr.
33SK-31

Walthour, B. Sr.
33SK-7

Walton, Bruce
86Modesto-26
87Modesto-14
88Huntsvl/BK-25
89Tacoma/CMC-8
89Tacoma/ProC-1546
90Tacoma/CMC-6
90Tacoma/ProC-91
91S/RookTr-88T
91Tacoma/LineD-546
91Tacoma/ProC-2306
92T/91Debut-179

Walton, Carlo
91Kissim/ProC-4191

Walton, Danny
69Sunoco/Pin-18
70McDon-73
70OPC-134
70T-134
71K-22
71MLB/St-455
71OPC-281
71T-281
71T/Coins-88
73OPC-516
73T-516
78T-263
79Spokane-4
90Target-829

Walton, Jerome
87Peoria-20
87Peoria/PW-5
88BBAmer-5
88EastLAS/ProC-29
88Peoria/Ko-30
88Pittsfld/ProC-1374
89B-295
89Classic/Up/2-156
89D/Best-172
89D/Rook-26
89F/Up-80
89Mara/Cubs-20
89S/Mast-2
89S/Tr-85
89S/YS/II-36
89T/Tr-123T
89UD/Ext-765
90B-35
90B/Ins-10
90Bz-19
90Classic-34
90CollAB-15
90Cub/Mara-22
90D-285
90D/BestNL-124
90D/Preview-10
90F-44
90F/AwardWin-42
90F/BBMVP-42
90F/LL-42
90F/SoarSt-8
90F/WaxBox-C27
90Holsum/Discs-19
90HotRook/St-46
90KingB/Discs-15
90KMart/SS-7
90Leaf/I-124
90MLBPA/Pins-50
90OPC-464
90Panini/St-230
90PublInt/St-207
90RedFoley/St-100
90S-229
90S/100Ris-2
90Sf-67
90T-464
90T/89Debut-134
90T/Big-267
90T/Coins-35
90T/DH-69
90T/Gloss60-39
90T/HeadsUp-24
90T/JumboR-29
90T/St-327FS
90T/St-50
90T/TVCub-34
90ToysRUs-29
90UD-345
90WonderBrd-8
90Woolwth/HL-6ROY
91B-413
91Classic/200-95
91Classic/II-T29
91Cub/Mara-20
91D-72
91F-437
91F/Ultra-70
91Leaf/I-39
91OPC-135
91Panini/FrSt-48
91Panini/St-44
91S-13
91T-135
91T/StClub/I-162
91UD-332
92D/II-528
92F-396
92S/II-457
92T-543
92UD-463

Walton, Jim
73OPC-646CO
73T-646CO
74T-99CO

Walton, Reggie
75Lafay
79Spokane-9
80Spokane-21
81F-609
81Spokane-14
82Portl-22
82T-711

Walton, Rob
88CharlK/Pep-6

Wambsganss, Bill
25Exh-72
26Exh-112
27Exh-55
72Laugh/GF-49
76Motor-4
88Conlon/4-29
90HOF/St-24
91Conlon/Sport-200
D327
D328-184
D329-185
E120
E121/120
E121/80
E122
E135-184
E220
M101/4-185

V117-29
V61-31
W501-22
W575
Wandler, Mike
87Pocatel/Bon-20
Waner, Lloyd L.
28Yueng-59
29Exh/4-14
31Exh/4-14
33Exh/4-7
33G-164
34DS-16
34Exh/4-7
35BU-157
35BU-17
35G-1E
35G-3C
35G-4C
35G-5C
39PB-89
40PB-105
41DP-119
60F-78
61F-84
72F/FFeat-35
80Pac/Leg-24
80SSPC/HOF
83D/HOF-22M
85Woolwth-36
86Conlon/1-58
89HOF/St-42
89Pac/Leg-128
89Smok/Dodg-32
90Target-830
91Conlon/Sport-265
91Conlon/Sport-6
92Conlon/Sport-429
92Conlon/Sport-562
PR1-27
R300
R306
R310
R312/M
R314
R316
R328-13
R332-16M
R332-2
R423-110
V353-90
W502-59
W513-73
WG8-49
Waner, Paul P.
28Exh-27
28Yueng-45
29Exh/4-14
31Exh/4-14
32Orbit/un-58
33CJ/Pin-24
33Exh/4-7
33G-25
34DS-83
34Exh/4-7
34G-11
35Exh/4-7
35G-1E
35G-3C
35G-4C
35G-5C
36Exh/4-7
36G
37Exh/4-7
38Exh/4-7
38Wheat
39PB-112
40PB-104
41DP-16
50Callahan
60F-76
61F-85
72F/FFeat-24
80Pac/Leg-21
80SSPC/HOF
83D/HOF-22M
86Conlon/1-8
86Sf/Dec-15M
88Conlon/NatAS-23
89HOF/St-45
89Pac/Leg-127
90Target-831
91Conlon/Sport-167
91Conlon/Sport-315
91Conlon/Sport-5
92Conlon/Sport-563
R300
R305
R306
R308-201
R310
R312/M
R314
R315-A38
R315-B38
R316
R326-10A
R326-10B
R328-2
R332-16M
R337-421
R342-10
R423-111
V353-25
V354-67
V355-2
W502-45
W513-70
W517-34
WG8-50
Wanish, John
88Bakers/Cal-261
89StCath/ProC-2086
90Myrtle/ProC-2778
91Dunedin/ClBest-11
91Dunedin/ProC-207
Wanke, Chuck
91Everett/ClBest-25
91Everett/ProC-3914
Wanz, Doug
81Vanco-3
Wapnick, Steve
88Myrtle/ProC-1166
89Dunedin/Star-22
90B-346
90Syrac/CMC-27
90Syrac/ProC-572
90Syrac/Team-27
91Syrac/LineD-520
91Syrac/ProC-2481
91T/90Debut-163
92D/II-743
92S/II-863
Ward, Aaron
21Exh-183
25Exh-104
E120
E121/120
E121/80
E126-7
E220
V100
W501-25
W515-20
W572
Ward, Anthony
88StCath/ProC-2034
89Myrtle/ProC-1630
90Dunedin/Star-23
90FSLAS/Star-47
91Knoxvl/LineD-370
91Knoxvl/ProC-1766
Ward, Chris
75OPC-587
75T-587
75T/M-587
Ward, Chuck
90Target-832
Ward, Colby
85Anchora-31
86Cram/PCL-89
87PalmSp-14
88MidldA/GS-11
89Edmon/CMC-10
89Edmon/ProC-568
90ColoSp/CMC-2
90ColoSp/ProC-37
91D-330
91F-382
91OPC-31
91T-31
91T/90Debut-164
Ward, Colin
83BirmB-19
84Cram/PCL-21
85Cram/PCL-198
86F-645R
86Shrev-27
87Phoenix-9
Ward, Dan
88PalmSp/Cal-95
88PalmSp/ProC-1442
Ward, David
87SLCity/Taco-12
Ward, Duane
83Durham-25
86F/Up-U125
86Pol/Atl-48
87D-45RR
87Leaf-45RR
87OPC-153
87T-153
87Tor/Fire-33
88D-567
88F-125
88OPC-128
88T-696
88Tor/Fire-31
89D-543
89D/Best-216
89F-246
89OPC-392
89S-359
89S/YS/II-13
89T-502
89Tor/Fire-31
89UD-551
90D-307
90F-95
90Leaf/II-501
90OPC-28
90PublInt/St-528
90S-439
90Sf-107
90T-28
90Tor/BlueJ-31
90UD-653
91D-92
91F-187
91F/Ultra-369
91Leaf/I-154
91OPC-181
91S-561
91S/ToroBJ-8
91T-181
91T/StClub/II-363
91Tor/Fire-31
91UD-581
92D/I-308
92F-344
92S/I-48
92T-365
92UD-450
Ward, Gary
77Tacoma
79Toledo-1
80T-669R
81D-594
81T-328R
82D-571
82F-562
82F/St-229
82T-612
83D-429
83D/AAS-18
83F-627
83T-517
83T/St-92
84D-192
84F-576
84F/X-U124
85FunFood/Pin-95
84Nes/792-67
84OPC-67
84Rang-32
84T-67
84T/St-303
84T/Tr-126T
85D-342
85F-572
85Leaf-70
85OPC-84
85Rang-32
85T-414
85T/St-353
86D-20DK
86D-98
86D/AAS-51
86D/DKsuper-20
86F-575
86F/Mini-113
86F/St-125
86Leaf-20DK
86OPC-105
86Rang-32
86Sf-197
86T-105
86T/St-239
87D-427
87D/OD-242
87F-140
87F/Lim-41
87F/RecSet-40
87F/Up-U122
87Leaf-177
87OPC-218
87Sf-91
87T-762
87T/St-235
87T/Tr-125T
88D-251
88D/Y/Bk-251
88F-224
88OPC-235
88Panini/St-160
88RedFoley/St-95
88S-157
88Sf-125
88T-235
88T/Big-195
88T/St-303
89F-273
89F/Up-33
89Mara/Tigers-32
89OPC-302
89S-435
89T-302
89T/Big-206
89T/Tr-124T
89UD-98
90CokeK/Tiger-25
90D-621
90F-618
90Leaf/I-113
90OPC-679
90Panini/St-68
90S-513
90T-679
91D-728
91F-356
91OPC-556
91Panini/FrSt-294
91S-637
91T-556
91UD-412
Ward, Greg
87Savan-8
88Reno/Cal-286
Ward, John Mont.
(Montgomery)
80SSPC/HOF
89Smok/Dodg-33
90Target-833
E223
N172
N28
N284
N300/unif
N338/2
N566-586
N566-587
WG1-45
Ward, John F.
(Jay)
61Union
64T-116R
65T-421R
85Cedar-27
86Vermont-23MG
88CLAS/Star-1
89Wmsprt/Star-24
Ward, Joseph
C46-6
T201
Ward, Kevin
86Phill/TastyK-x
86Reading-25
87Maine/TCMA-22
87Reading-12
88Maine/CMC-22
88Maine/ProC-278
89Huntsvl/Best-22
90Tacoma/CMC-25
90Tacoma/ProC-109
91AAAGame/ProC-AAA21
91LasVegas/ProC-252
91LasVegas/LineD-298
92F-623
92S/100RisSt-42
92S/II-862
92T/91Debut-180
Ward, Max
87FtLaud-12
88Colum/ProC-326
Ward, Pete
63T-324R
64T-85
64T/Coins-21
64T/S-33
64T/St-8
64T/SU
64T/tatt
65Bz-8
65OldLond-37
65OPC-215
65T-215
65T/E-64
65T/trans-71
66OPC-25
66T-25
66T/RO-2
67OPC-143M
67T-143M
67T-436
68OPC-33
68T-33
69Kelly/Pin-18
69MB-285
69MLB/St-35
69MLBPA/Pin-29
69OPC-155
69T-155
69T/decal
69T/S-11
69T/St-159
69Trans-20
70MLB/St-251
70T-659
71MLB/St-501
71OPC-667
71T-667
72MB-354
78TCMA-120
81Portl-1
91Crown/Orio-473
Exh47
WG10-47
WG9-48
Ward, Preston
50B-231
53T-173
54B-139
54T-72
55B-27
55T-95
55T/DH-97
56T-328
57T-226
58T-450
59T-176
79TCMA-111
90Target-834
91T/Arc53-173
Ward, Ricky
90Everett/Best-20
90Everett/ProC-3136
91Clinton/ClBest-24
91Clinton/ProC-844
Ward, Rube
90Target-1093
Ward, Turner
88Colum/CMC-19
88Colum/Pol-17
90ColoSp/CMC-20
90ColoSp/ProC-52
91B-76
91D-429RR
91F-383
91F/Ultra-118
91Leaf/II-449
91Leaf/Stud-138
91OPC-555
91S-732RP
91S/Rook40-4
91T-555
91T/90Debut-165
91T/StClub/II-593
91UD/Ext-762

Warden, Jon
69T-632
88Domino-24
Wardle, Curt
83Visalia/LF-18
85F/Up-U127
86F-600
86Maine-21
86T-303
Wardlow, Jeff
88Butte-17
Wardlow, Joe
89Gaston/ProC-998
89Gaston/Star-24
89Star/Wax-39
90Foil/Best-208
90Gaston/Best-10
90Gaston/ProC-2531
90Gaston/Star-24
91PrWill/ClBest-20
91PrWill/ProC-1437
Wardlow, Mike
77Cedar
Wardwell, Shea
90Elmira/Pucko-8
91Single/ClBest-295
91WinHaven/ClBest-25
91WinHaven/ProC-504
Ware, Derek
87Dunedin-28
Ware, Jeff
91Classic/DP-31
91T/Tr-124T
92T-414
Wares, Clyde E.
(Buzzy)
86Conlon/1-14M
W754
Warfel, Brian
87Elmira/Black-9
87Elmira/Red-9
88Elmira-26
88WinHaven/Star-26
Warhop, John
10Domino-122
11Helmar-49
12Sweet/Pin-38
T206
T207
T213/blue
T215/blue
T215/brown
Waring, Jim
91AubAS/ClBest-22
91AubAS/ProC-4274
Warneke, Lon
32Orbit/num-4
32Orbit/un-59
33CJ/Pin-25
33DL-16
33G-203
34Exh/4-3
35BU-186
35Exh/4-3
36Exh/4-3
36Wheat
37Exh/4-8
38Exh/4-8
38Wheat
39Exh
39PB-41
40PB-114
55B-299ump
88Conlon/NatAS-24
91Conlon/Sport-231
92Conlon/Sport-371
92Conlon/Sport-640
R300
R303/A
R305
R308-194
R312/M
R314
V355-100
W754
WG8-51
Warner, E.H.
N172
Warner, Fred
80Penin/B-5
80Penin/C-8
Warner, Harry
77T-113C
80Syrac-19MG
83Visalia/LF-13
Warner, Jack D.
65T-354R
Warner, Jim
47Signal
47Sunbeam
Warner, John J.
(Jackie)
65T-517R
66T-553R
Warner, John Joseph
26Exh-96
E107
Warner, John R.
(Jack)
33G-178
90Target-835
92Conlon/Sport-410
Warner, Ron
91Hamil/ClBest-21
91Hamil/ProC-4048
Warrecker, William
89BendB/Legoe-11
90PalmSp/Cal-224
90PalmSp/ProC-2579
Warren, Alan
88Oneonta/ProC-2066
Warren, Brian
90Bristol/ProC-3167
91Fayette/ClBest-29
91Fayette/ProC-1171
Warren, Charlie
77Wausau
Warren, Glen
89Everett/Star-29
Warren, Joe
89BendB/Legoe-12
Warren, Marty
86AppFx-28
Warren, Mel
91Kissim/ProC-4204
Warren, Mike
84D-631
84F-461
84F-639IA
84Mother/A's-20
84Nes/792-338
84Nes/792-5HL
84T-338
84T-5HL
84T/St-288B
85D-278
85F-435
85Mother/A's-19
85T-197
86Omaha-28
89Reno/Cal-248
Warren, Randy
88Utica/Pucko-12
89SoBend/GS-17
Warren, Raymond
82BurlR-12
Warren, Ron
86Elmira-26
Warren, Tommy
90Target-836
Warren, Travis
87Clearw-27
Warstler, Harold
(Rabbit)
39PB-120
40PB-59
41G-21
91Conlon/Sport-240
R314
Warthen, Dan
76OPC-374
76SSPC-347
76T-374
77OPC-99
77T-391
79Portl-17
80Port-26
81Buffa-12
82AlexD-20
87Chatt/Best-2
88Calgary/CMC-25
88Calgary/ProC-789
89Calgary/CMC-25
89Calgary/ProC-523
90Calgary/CMC-24CO
90Calgary/ProC-665CO
Warwick, Carl
62J-161
62P-161
62P/Can-161
62Salada-160
62Shirriff-160
62T-202
63J-190
63P-190
63Pep
63T-333
64T-179
65T-357
66T-247
90Target-837
91Crown/Orio-474
WG9-49
Warwick, Clinton
86Geneva-11
Wasdell, James
41DP-19
90Target-838
Wasem, Jim
84Everett/Cram-24
86CharRain-28A
86CharRain-28B
88Charl/ProC-1195
Washburn, Greg
70OPC-74R
70T-74R
Washburn, Ray
62T-19
63J-168
63P-168
63T-206
64T-332
65T-467
66T-399
67OPC-92
67T-92
68T-388
69T-415
70OPC-22
70T-22
Washington, Claudell
75Greyhound-3
75OPC-647
75T-647
75T/M-647
76K-2
76OPC-189
76OPC-198LL
76SSPC-489
76T-189
76T-198LL
77BurgChef-115
77Ho-86
77OPC-178
77T-405
77T/CS-50
78BK/R-19
78T-67
79OPC-298
79T-574
80K-34
80OPC-171
80T-322
81F-329
81Pol/Atl-18
81T-151
81T/Tr-854
82BK/Lids-25
82D-58
82F-449
82F/St-66
82OPC-32
82Pol/Atl-15
82T-126TL
82T-758
82T/St-22
83D-249
83F-150
83OPC-235
83Pol/Atl-15
83T-235
83T/St-216
84D-310
84F-192
84Nes/792-410
84OPC-42
84Pol/Atl-15
84T-294
84T-410
84T/St-32
85D-11
85D-310
85D/DKsuper-11
85F-342
85Ho/Braves-22
85Leaf-11DK
85OPC-166
85Pol/Atl-15
85T-540
85T/St-25
86D-287
86F-531
86F/Mini-107
86Leaf-164
86OPC-303
86Pol/Atl-15
86T-675
86T/St-39
86T/Tr-122T
87F-119
87Mother/A's-15
87T-15
88D-340
88D/Best-217
88D/Y/Bk-340
88F-225
88OPC-335
88S-579
88T-335
88T/Big-178
88T/St-301
89B-52
89D-72
89D/Best-227
89D/Tr-46
89F-272
89F/Up-17
89OPC-185
89S-211
89S/Tr-10T
89Sf-75
89T-185
89T/DHTest-17
89T/Tr-125T
89T/UK-81
89UD-310
89UD/Ext-794
90B-297
90D-52
90F-146
90OPC-705
90Panini/St-30
90PublInt/St-380
90S-298
90S/NWest-8
90S/Tr-45T
90Smok/Angel-17
90T-705
90T/Big-12
90UD-395
91WIZMets-425
Washington, Glenn
86QuadC-31
87PalmSp-15
88PalmSp/Cal-111
88PalmSp/ProC-1455
Washington, Herb
75OPC-407
75T-407
75T/M-407
Washington, Keith
80Penin/B-9
80Penin/C-18
82Reading-19
83Reading-21
Washington, Kraig
89CharWh/Best-4
89CharWh/ProC-1752
90Peoria/Team-7
Washington, Kyle
90Pittsfld/Pucko-2
91Collnd/ClBest-4
91Collnd/ProC-1503
91SALAS/ProC-SAL19
Washington, LaRue
77Tucson
78Cr/PCL-18
80T-233
Washington, Lozando
76Cedar
Washington, Mal
75QuadC
76Clinton
Washington, Randy
81Batavia-24
82Watlo/B-26
82Watlo/C-25
83Watlo/LF-1
84BuffB-20
85Water-3
86Maine-22
87BuffB-12
88ColoSp/CMC-22
88ColoSp/ProC-1525
Washington, Ron
78Cr/PCL-16
79Tidew-9
80Toledo-6
81Toledo-18
82T/Tr-124T
83D-431
83F-626
83OPC-27
83T-458
84D-391
84F-577
84Nes/792-623
84OPC-268
84T-623
85D-391
85F-292
85T-329
86D-560
86F-409
86T-513
86Toledo-23
87RochR-19
87RochR/TCMA-16
87T-169
88Gator-15
88T/Tr-125T
89D-468
89F-416
89Pac/SenLg-178
89T/SenLg-44
89TM/SenLg-110
89Tucson/CMC-19
89Tucson/ProC-190
89Tucson/JP-27
89UD-519
90EliteSenLg-31
90OkCty/CMC-15
90OkCty/ProC-442
90Target-839
91Crown/Orio-475
91Pac/SenLg-47
91Pac/SenLg-48
91Tidew/LineD-575CO
91Tidew/ProC-2528CO
Washington, Tyrone
91Gaston/ClBest-10
91Gaston/ProC-2687
Washington, U.L.
78T-707R
79T-157
80T-508
81Coke
81D-460
81F-34
81OPC-26
81Pol/Royals-8
81T-26
82D-160
82F-424
82F/St-203
82OPC-329
82T-329
83D-490
83F-125
83OPC-67
83Pol/Royals-7
83T-687
84D-543
84F-361
84Nes/792-294
84OPC-294
84T/St-282
85D-521
85F-215
85F/Up-U128
85OPC/Post-4
85T-431
85T/Tr-128T
86D-498
86F-264

86OPC-113
86T-113
87Vanco-25
89Pac/SenLg-205
89T/SenLg-120
89TM/SenLg-111
89Welland/Pucko-30
90EliteSenLg-62
91Pac/SenLg-102

Washko, Patrick
77Watlo

Wasiak, Stan
74Albuq/Team-23MG
77LodiD
78LodiD
79LodiD-14MG
81VeroB-27MG
83VeroB-28MG
85VeroB-26MG
86VeroB-27MG

Wasilewski, Kevin
86AubAs-25
87Ashvl-12

Wasilewski, Tom
86Ventura-26
87Shrev-21

Wasinger, Mark
84Beaum-17
85Beaum-19
86LasVegas-22
87LasVegas-27
88F-100
88Mother/Giants-23
88Phoenix/CMC-17
88Phoenix/ProC-54
88RedFoley/St-96
88S-283
89Colum/CMC-22
89Colum/Pol-21
89Colum/ProC-738
90ColClip/CMC-22
90ColClip/ProC-687
91Edmon/LineD-173
91Edmon/ProC-1525

Waslewski, Gary
69T-438
70T-607
71MLB/St-502
71OPC-277
71T-277
72OPC-108
72T-108

Wasley, Mel
40Hughes-18
47Sunbeam

Wassenaar, Rob
88QuadC/GS-25
89Visalia/Cal-98
89Visalia/ProC-1425
90OrlanSR/Best-18
90OrlanSR/ProC-1084
90OrlanSR/Star-22
91OrlanSR/LineD-497
91OrlanSR/ProC-1850

Watanabe, Curt
80BurlB-26

Watanabe, Masahito
87Miami-12

Waterfield, Bob
52Wheat

Wathan, John
77T-218
78T-343
79T-99
80T-547
81Coke
81D-221
81F-46
81OPC-157
81T-157
82D-86
82F-425
82OPC-383
82T-429
82T/St-192
83D-86
83F-126
83OPC-289
83Pol/Royals-8
83T-6M
83T-746
83T/St-195
83T/St-196
83T/St-78
84D-466
84F-362
84Nes/792-602
84OPC-72
84T-602
84T/St-284
85D-466
85F-216
85T-308
86D-496
86F-23
86Kitty/Disc-12
86T-128
87Omaha-3
88Smok/Royals-1MG
88T-534
89T-374MG
90OPC-789MG
90T-789MG
91OPC-291
91Pol/Royal-24
91T-291

Watkins, Bob C.
70OPC-227R
70T-227R
71MLB/St-93

Watkins, Bud
58Union

Watkins, Darren
87AppFx-12
90BBCity/Star-25
91DurhamUp/ProC-8
91London/LineD-423
91Memphis/ProC-668

Watkins, Dave
70OPC-168
70T-168

Watkins, George
34G-53
35Exh/4-6
90Target-840
91Conlon/Sport-222

Watkins, Jim
81Bristol-22

Watkins, Keith
88Modesto/Cal-71

Watkins, Tim
87Beloit-21
88Denver/CMC-6
88Denver/ProC-1265
89Denver/CMC-2
89Denver/ProC-41
89ElPaso/GS-15
90Denver/CMC-3
90Denver/ProC-627
91CharlK/LineD-146
91CharlK/ProC-1690

Watkins, Troy
86FtMyr-27

Watkins, William H.
N172

Watlington, Julius
52Park-83

Watson, Allen
91Classic/DP-17
91FrRow/DP-44
91Hamil/ClBest-7
91Hamil/ProC-4040
92S/II-799
92T-654

Watson, Bob
69T-562
70OPC-407
70T-407
71MLB/St-94
71OPC-222
71T-222
72OPC-355
72T-355
72T/Cloth-32
73OPC-110
73T-110
74K-11
74OPC-370
74T-370
74T/DE-69
74T/St-39
75Ho-53
75K-6
75OPC-227
75T-227
75T/M-227
76Crane-66
76Ho-5
76Ho/Twink-5
76K-27
76MSA/Disc
76OPC-20
76SSPC-60
76T-20
77BurgChef-6
77Ho-39
77T-540
77T/CS-51
78BK/Ast-12
78Ho-28
78OPC-107
78T-330
78Tastee/Discs-18
78Wiffle/Discs-77
79OPC-60
79T-130
80OPC-250
80T-480
81D-225
81Drake-28
81F-93
81OPC-208
81T-690
81T/HT
82BK/Lids-26
82D-108
82F-54
82OPC-275
82Pol/Atl-8
82T-275
82T/Tr-125T
83D-551
83F-151
83Pol/Atl-8
83T-572
84F-193
84Nes/792-739
84Pol/Atl-8
84T-739
85OPC-51
85T-51
86Mother/Ast-13

Watson, D.J.
87AppFx-5

Watson, Dave
89Princet/Star-23
91Salem/ClBest-22
91Salem/ProC-952

Watson, Dejon
86FtMyr-28
88BBCity/Star-25

Watson, Frankie
88Eugene/Best-28

Watson, John Reeves
E120
W573

Watson, Matt
89Alaska/Team-5
90StCath/ProC-3460

Watson, Milton
W514-77

Watson, Phil
77Ashvl

Watson, Preston
89BurlB/ProC-1604
89BurlB/Star-22
90Greenvl/ProC-1129
90Greenvl/Star-21
91Greenvl/ClBest-8
91Greenvl/LineD-221
91Greenvl/ProC-3002

Watson, Ron
91Boise/ClBest-22
91Boise/ProC-3880

Watson, Shaun
91Kingspt/ClBest-18
91Kingspt/ProC-3814

Watson, Steve
76Cedar
83Tampa-25

Watson, Todd
90CharWh/Best-19
90CharWh/ProC-2249
90Foil/Best-94

Watt, Eddie
66T-442R
67T-271
68OPC-186
68T-186
69T-652
70OPC-497
70T-497
71OPC-122
71T-122
72MB-355
72OPC-128
72T-128
73JP
73OPC-362
73T-362
74OPC-534
74T-534
74T/Tr-534T
75OPC-374
75T-374
75T/M-374
86Tucson-25CO
87Tucson-22
88Tucson/CMC-25
88Tucson/ProC-184
88Tucson/JP-23
89Tucson/ProC-204
90BurlB/Best-12CO
90BurlB/ProC-2367CO
90BurlB/Star-29CO
91Crown/Orio-476

Watters, Mike
86Albuq-27
87Calgary-2
88Calgary/CMC-23
88Calgary/ProC-798

Watts, Andy
86Negro/Frit-17

Watts, Bob
87Dunedin-3
88Dunedin/Star-20
89Beloit/I/Star-25

Watts, Brandon
91Kissim/ProC-4187

Watts, Brian
77Spartan

Watts, Burgess
91Yakima/ClBest-14
91Yakima/ProC-4258

Watts, Harry
63Pep/Tul

Watts, Len
86Reading-26
87Maine-3
87Maine/TCMA-20
87Phill/TastyK-49

Waugh, James
53T-178
91T/Arc53-178

Wauner
E254

Way, Ron
89Welland/Pucko-28
90Augusta/ProC-2465
91Salem/ClBest-23
91Salem/ProC-953

Wayne, Gary
86WPalmB-27
87Jaxvl-22
88Indianap/ProC-508
89D/Rook-27
89S/Tr-91
90D-318
90F-387
90OPC-348
90PublInt/St-340
90S-527
90S/100Ris-15
90S/YS/II-26
90T-348
90T/89Debut-135
90UD-372
91AAAGame/ProC-AAA37
91D-757
91F-626
91OPC-207
91S-283
91T-207
91T/StClub/II-491

Waznik, Allan J.
87Idaho-13
88Sumter/ProC-407
89BurlB/ProC-1612
89BurlB/Star-23

Wearing, Melvin Jr.
89Erie/Star-25
90Foil/Best-293
90Wausau/Best-23
90Wausau/ProC-2137
90Wausau/Star-24
91CLAS/ProC-CAR9
91Freder/ClBest-20
91Freder/ProC-2374
91Single/ClBest-383

Weatherford, Brant
86Tampa-25

Weatherford, Joel
83Beloit/LF-29

Weatherly, Roy
(Stormy)
39PB-152
40PB-49
41PB-17
44Yank/St-28

Weathers, David
88StCath/ProC-2023
89Myrtle/ProC-1475
90Dunedin/Star-24
90EliteSenLg-91
91Knoxvl/LineD-371
91Knoxvl/ProC-1767
91S/ToroBJ-35
91Swell/Great-95
92D/II-418RR
92T/91Debut-181

Weathers, Steven M.
75Tucson-2
76Tucson-2
77SanJose-12

Weathersby, Earl
(Tex)
28Exh/PCL-30

Weaver, D. Floyd
65T-546R
66T-231
71OPC-227
71T-227
78TCMA-176

Weaver, Earl
69T-516MG
70OPC-148MG
70T-148MG
71OPC-477MG
71T-477MG
72OPC-323MG
72T-323MG
73JP
73OPC-136MG
73T-136MG
74OPC-306MG
74T-306MG
75OPC-117MG
75T-117MG
75T/M-117MG
76T-73MG
77T-546MG
78T-211MG
79T-689MG
80T-404MG
81D-356MG
81F-178MG
81T-661MG
82D-27MG
83T-426MG
85T/Tr-129T
86T-321MG
87T-568MG
89Pac/Leg-179
89Pac/SenLg-219M
89Pac/SenLg-56MG
89Swell-98
89T/SenLg-76MG
89TM/SenLg-112MG
89TM/SenLg-120MG
90Pac/Legend-108MG
91LineD-12MG

Weaver, George
(Buck)
73F/Wild-11
87Conlon/2-28
88Pac/8Men-107
88Pac/8Men-12
88Pac/8Men-33
88Pac/8Men-34
88Pac/8Men-40
88Pac/8Men-48M
88Pac/8Men-63
88Pac/8Men-7
88Pac/8Men-71
BF2-20

D328-185
D329-186
D350/2-188
E135-185
M101/4-186
M101/5-188
T207
W514-91

Weaver, James B.
(Jim)
68T-328R
69OPC-134
69T-134

Weaver, James D.
(Jim)
92Conlon/Sport-390
R312/M
W711/1

Weaver, James
83Orlan-3
84Toledo-13
86Maine-23
87Calgary-3
88Tucson/CMC-21
88Tucson/ProC-172
88Tucson/JP-24
89Vanco/CMC-14
89Vanco/ProC-583
90Calgary/CMC-17
90Calgary/ProC-663

Weaver, Monte
33G-111
35G-1C
35G-2C
35G-6C
35G-7C

Weaver, Roger
80Evansvl-1
81Evansvl-10
81T-626R
82Richm-9

Weaver, Trent
89Medford/Best-16
91Modesto/ClBest-2

Weaver, William B.
N172

Webb, Ben
87Watertn-1
88Salem/Star-23
89Harris/ProC-311
89Harris/Star-21
90Harris/ProC-1194
90Harris/Star-20
91CaroMud/LineD-120
91CaroMud/ProC-1088

Webb, Chuck
88Wausau/GS-19

Webb, Cleon Earl
D322

Webb, Dennis
81QuadC-9

Webb, Earl W.
(Billy)
31Exh/4-18
33Exh/4-9
35BU-98M
85Woolwth-37
87Conlon/2-25
91Conlon/Sport-261

Webb, Hank
73OPC-610R
73T-610R
75IntAS/TCMA-24
75OPC-615R
75T-615R
75T/M-615R
76OPC-442
76SSPC-553
76T-442
78Cr/PCL-77
90Target-841
91WIZMets-426

Webb, James
(Skeeter)
No Cards.

Webb, Marvin
75Water

Webb, Normal
(Tweed)
86Negro/Frit-39

Webb, Sam
49Eureka-125

Webb, Spyder
89Belling/Legoe-33TR
91Belling/ClBest-27TR

Webber, Les
90Target-842

Webber, Steve
89Bristol/Star-30

Weber, Ben
91StCath/ClBest-19
91StCath/ProC-3396

Weber, Brent
91Idaho/ProC-4329

Weber, Charles
(Bill)
N172

Weber, Pete
87BuffB-29
90ClintUp/Team-U8
91Shrev/LineD-323
91Shrev/ProC-1837

Weber, Ron
89Johnson/Star-22
90Spring/Best-24
91StPete/ClBest-14
91StPete/ProC-2277

Weber, Steve
90Bristol/Star-29TR

Weber, Todd
88Ashvl/ProC-1078

Weber, Weston
86Cram/PCL-65
87Madis-11
88Modesto-15
89Huntsvl/Best-13
89Modesto/Chong-18
90Tacoma/CMC-5
90Tacoma/ProC-92
91HuntsvlProC-1796

Webster, Casey
86Watlo-30
87Kinston-13
88EastLAS/ProC-43
88Wmsprt/ProC-1317
89Canton/Best-5
89Canton/ProC-1318
89Canton/Star-23
90Canton/Star-17
90ColoSp/CMC-21
90ColoSp/ProC-47

Webster, Lenny
86Kenosha-25
87Kenosha-20
88Kenosha/ProC-1392
88MidwLAS/GS-31
89Visalia/Cal-110
89Visalia/ProC-1442
90A&AASingle/ProC-55
90Foil/Best-45
90OrlanSR/Best-13
90OrlanSR/ProC-1088
90OrlanSR/Star-23
90S-638RP
90T/89Debut-136
90UD/Ext-728
91F/Up-U41
91Portl/LineD-422
91Portl/ProC-1569
92F-220
92S/II-663
92T-585

Webster, Mike
89Eugene/Best-2
90BBCity/Star-26

Webster, Mitch
78Clinton
80Syrac-12
82Syrac-23
83Syrac-25
84Tor/Fire-31
85Tor/Fire-31
86D-523
86F-265
86Leaf-253
86OPC-218
86Provigo-5
86T-629
87D-335
87D/OD-86
87F-335
87F/AwardWin-41
87F/Mini-111
87OPC-263
87Sf-177
87T-442
87T/St-82
88Berg/Cubs-28
88D-257
88D/Best-292
88F-199
88F/St-99
88Ho/Disc-1
88Leaf-198
88OPC-138
88Panini/St-331
88RedFoley/St-97
88S-345
88Sf-105
88T-138
88T/Big-150
89B-296
89D-459
89D/Best-261
89F-442
89Mara/Cubs-33
89OPC-36
89Panini/St-61
89S-71
89Sf-67
89T-36
89UD-65
90D-137
90F-45
90Leaf/II-312
90OPC-502
90Publint/St-208
90S-85
90S/Tr-4T
90T-502
90T/Big-298
90T/Tr-127T
90UD-153
90UD/Ext-730
91B-66
91D-283
91F-384
91F/Ultra-119
91OPC-762
91Panini/St-175
91S-594
91S/RookTr-68T
91T-762
91T/StClub/II-448
91UD-120
92D/II-714
92S/II-643
92T-233

Webster, Ramon
67T-603R
68OPC-164
68T-164
69T-618
72MB-356
75Tucson-6

Webster, Ray G.
59T-531
60T-452

Webster, Rich
82Lynch-21

Webster, Rudy
86Cram/PCL-127
87Wausau-25
88Wausau/GS-17

Wechsberg, Von
90Burllnd/ProC-3010
91Pocatel/ProC-3783

Weck, Steve
85Iowa-31

Wedell, James R.
33SK-26

Wedge, Eric
88CapeCod/Sum-51
89Elmira/Pucko-32
90EastLAS/ProC-EL41
90Foil/Best-2
90Foil/Best-319
90NewBrit/Best-1
90NewBrit/Star-21
90T/TVRSox-66
91Pawtu/LineD-372
91Pawtu/ProC-42
92T/91Debut-182

Wedvick, Jeff
86Jamestn-28
87BurlEx-16

Weeber, Mike
75Dubuq

Weekly, Johnny
62T-204
64T-256
89Smok/Ast-26

Weeks, Ben
91Idaho/ProC-4330

Weeks, Thomas
87Oneonta-13
88FtLaud/Star-24
89PrWill/Star-24
90PrWill/Team-27

Weems, Danny
86Sumter-29
87CharWh-13
88CLAS/Star-39
88Durham/Star-23
89Greenvl/ProC-1157
89Greenvl/Star-24
89Greenvl/Best-13
90Greenvl/Best-16
90Greenvl/ProC-1130
90Greenvl/Star-22

Weese, Dean
88Hamil/ProC-1744
89Savan/ProC-348
90StPete/Star-25
91ArkTr/ProC-1286

Weese, Gary
75SanAn
76Wmsprt

Wegener, Mike
69Fud's-13
69T-284R
70OPC-193
70T-193
71OPC-608
71T-608
75Tidew/Team-24
76Phoenix
77Phoenix

Wegman, Bill
82Beloit-4
85Cram/PCL-216
86D-490
86Pol/Brew-46
86T/Tr-123T
87D-109
87F-360
87Pol/Brew-46
87T-179
88D-151
88D/Best-320
88F-177
88OPC-84
88Panini/St-119
88Pol/Brew-46
88S-296
88T-538
88T/Big-244
88T/St-200
89B-135
89Brewer/YB-46
89D-293
89F-199
89Gard-9
89OPC-354
89Pol/Brew-46
89S-335
89S/YS/II-9
89T-768
89UD-445
90Brewer/MillB-30
90OPC-333
90Pol/Brew-46
90Publint/St-507
90S-188
90T-333
90UD-629
91Brewer/MillB-30
91F/UltraUp-U33
91F/Up-U35
91OPC-617
91Pol/Brew-27
91S-483
91T-617
91T/StClub/II-398
91UD-292
92D/I-378
92F-193
92S/I-374
92T-22
92UD-612

Wegmann, Tom
90Kgsport/Best-20
90Kgsport/Star-24
91StLucie/ClBest-13

Wehmeier, Herm
48B-46
49B-51
49Eureka-98
50B-27
51B-144
51FB
51T/BB-47
52B-150
52T-80
53B/Col-23
53T-110
54T-162
55T-29
55T/DH-131
56T-78
56T/Pin-22P
57T-81
58T-248
59T-421
79TCMA-126
91T/Arc53-110
Exh47

Wehner, John
88Watertn/Pucko-28
89Salem/Star-24
90EastLAS/ProC-EL26
90Harris/ProC-1203
90Harris/Star-21
91CaroMud/LineD-121
91CaroMud/ProC-1096
91F/Up-U115
92Classic/I-93
92D/II-731
92F-573
92S/100RisSt-82
92S/II-752
92T-282
92T/91Debut-183
92UD-469

Wehrmeister, Dave
77Padre/SchCd-36
77T-472R
78Padre/FamFun-35
80Colum-25
81Colum-23
82Colum-11
82Colum/Pol-28
82T-694
83Colum-6
84Cram/PCL-195
84Phill/TastyK-44
85BuffB-26
86BuffB-23
86F-220

Weibel, Randy
83Clinton/LF-27

Weidie, Stuart
86Elmira-27
87WinHaven-12
88Lynch/Star-25
89Lynch/Star-21
90NewBrit/Best-13
90NewBrit/Star-22

Weidman, George
N172

Weiermiller, Mike
82Wisco-4

Weigel, Ralph
48L-86

Weighaus, Thomas
82Wichita-20

Weik, Dick
54T-224

Weiland, Robert
34G-67
35G-8C
35G-9C

Weilman, Carl
16FleischBrd-98

Weimer, Jacob
T206
WG3-50

Weimerskirch, Mike
88CapeCod/Sum-96
91MidwLAS/ProC-MWL49
91Rockford/ClBest-26
91Rockford/ProC-2061
91Single/ClBest-311

Weinbaum, Pete
91Belling/ClBest-20

91Belling/ProC-3663
Weinberg, Barry
76Shrev
90Mother/A's-28TR
Weinberg, Mike
91Fayette/ClBest-26
91Fayette/ProC-1185
Weinberger, Gary
86Jaxvl/TCMA-17
87Jaxvl-10
Weinbrecht, Mark
80Elmira-13
Weinheimer, Wayne
88Wythe/ProC-1977
89CharWh/Best-1
89CharWh/ProC-1751
Weinke, Chris
91StCath/ClBest-6
91StCath/ProC-3405
Weinstein, Bobby
55Gol/Giants-28bb
Weintraub, Phil
37Exh/4-4
92Conlon/Sport-610
V355-135
Weir, Jim
82Clinton-29
83Clinton/LF-5
Weis, A.J.
25Exh-24
Weis, Al
63T-537R
64T-168
65T-516
66OPC-66
66T-66
67T-556
68T-313
69MB-286
69T-269
70MLB/St-84
70OPC-498
70T-498
70Trans/M-21
71MLB/St-168
71OPC-751
71T-751
72MB-357
91WIZMets-427
Weisman
E254
Weisman, Skip
83Ander-3
89Clmbia/GS-4
Weiss, Bill
89AS/Cal-27
90AS/Cal-31STAT
Weiss, Gary
80Albuq-13
81Albuq/TCMA-19
81F-130
90Target-843
Weiss, Jeff
87Durham-3
Weiss, Scott
91Geneva/ClBest-25
91Geneva/ProC-4218
Weiss, Walt
86Madis-26
86Madis/Pol-22
88D/A's/Bk-NEW
88D/Rook-18
88F-652R
88F/Mini-49
88F/Up-U56
88Modesto-34
88Mother/A's-11
88S/Tr-102T
88T/Big-263
88T/Tr-126T
89B-196
89Bz-22
89Classic-68
89D-446
89D/Best-155
89D/GrandSlam-3
89F-24
89F/BBMVP's-42
89F/Superstar-42
89F/WS-10
89KMart/DT-4
89Mother/A's-8
89Mother/ROY's-3
89Mother/ROY's-4M
89OPC-316
89Panini/St-412
89Panini/St-478
89S-165
89S/HotRook-95
89S/YS/I-20
89Sf-116
89T-316
89T-639TL
89T/Big-305
89T/Coins-31
89T/Gloss60-50
89T/JumboR-21
89T/St-168
89T/St-326
89T/UK-82
89Tacoma/ProC-1538
89ToysRUs-32
89UD-374
89UD-660ROY
89Woolwth-5
90B-461
90Classic-46
90D-67
90D/BestAL-95
90F-22
90F/WS-6
90Leaf/I-239
90Mother/A's-10
90OPC-165
90Panini/St-135
90Publint/St-317
90S-110
90Sf-74
90T-165
90UD-542
90Woolwth/HL-26
91B-228
91D-214
91F-26
91F/Ultra-255
91Leaf/I-50
91Mother/A's-10
91OPC-455
91Panini/FrSt-195
91Panini/St-147
91S-171
91SFExam/A's-14
91T-455
91T/StClub/I-49
91UD-192
92D/I-71
92F-270
92S/I-51
92T-691
92UD-151
Weissman, Craig
81QuadC-26
82QuadC-13
86GlenF-24
87ArkTr-17
89ArkTr/GS-24
Weissmuller, John
33SK-21
Weitzel, Brad
90Erie/Star-31CO
Welaj, Johnny
V362-8
Welaj, Lou
V362-40
Welborn, Frank
86Jamestn-29
Welborn, Sam
77Spartan
80LynnS-21
81Spokane-4
82SLCity-21
83Tucson-10
Welborn, Todd
85LitFalls-12
86LitFalls-29
87Columbia-29
88Jacks/GS-16
89Jacks/GS-7
Welborn, Tony
87BurlEx-4
88WPalmB/Star-26
Welch
L1-132
Welch, Bryce
89Everett/Star-32
Welch, Curt
90HOF/St-5
N172
N172/BC
N284/StL
N338/2
N370
N403
Scrapps
Welch, Dan
89Martins/Star-33
90Spartan/Best-24
90Spartan/ProC-2507
90Spartan/Star-24
Welch, Doug
89Geneva/ProC-1864
90WinSalem/Team-7
91CharlK/LineD-147
91CharlK/ProC-1703
Welch, Frank
25Exh-112
E120
Welch, John V.
33G-93
V353-56
Welch, Ken
90Watertn/Star-22
Welch, Michael
(Mickey)
80SSPC/HOF
E223
N172
N338/2
N403
N690/2
Welch, Robert
(Bob)
78Cr/PCL-26
79T-318
80Pol/Dodg-35
80T-146
81D-178
81F-120
81OPC-357
81Pol/Dodg-35
81T-624
81T/HT
82D-75
82F-28
82Pol/Dodg-35
82T-82
83D-410
83F-225
83OPC-288
83Pol/Dodg-35
83T-454
84D-153
84F-116
84Nes/792-306TL
84Nes/792-722
84OPC-227
84Pol/Dodg-35
84T-306TL
84T-722
85Coke/Dodg-32
85D-372
85F-388
85OPC-291
85T-291
86Coke/Dodg-32
86D-459
86F-146
86Leaf-223
86Pol/Dodg-35
86Sf-198
86T-549
86T/Mini-48
87D-475
87F-459
87F/LL-43
87F/St-121
87Mother/Dodg-9
87OPC-328
87Pol/Dodg-18
87Smok/Dodg-37
87T-328
88D-24DK
88D-253
88D/A's/Bk-NEW
88D/Best-134
88D/DKsuper-24DK
88F-529
88F/Mini-50
88F/Up-U57
88Leaf-24DK
88Mother/A's-9
88OPC-118
88Panini/St-305
88RedFoley/St-98
88S-510
88S/Tr-15T
88Sf-167
88T-118
88T/Mini-55
88T/Revco-15
88T/St-73
88T/Tr-127T
89B-186
89Classic-91
89D-332
89D/Best-267
89F-25
89Mother/A's-9
89Panini/St-416
89S-308
89S/HotStar-89
89Sf-91
89Smok/Dodg-92
89T-605
89T/LJN-131
89T/St-166
89UD-191
90D-332
90D/BestAL-67
90F-23
90MLBPA/Pins-76
90Mother/A's-16
90OPC-475
90Panini/St-131
90Publint/St-318
90S-159
90Sf-35
90T-475
90T/Big-106
90T/St-180
90Target-844
90UD-251
90USPlayC/AS-1C
90Windwlk/Discs-3
91B-215
91Bz-3
91Classic/200-199
91Classic/I-76
91CollAB-5
91D-20DK
91D-54AS
91D-645
91D-727CY
91D/Preview-5
91D/SuperDK-20DK
91F-27
91F/Ultra-256
91Leaf/I-64
91Leaf/Stud-110
91Mother/A's-9
91OPC-394AS
91OPC-50
91Panini/FrSt-174
91Panini/St-151
91Panini/Top15-61
91RedFoley/St-130
91S-311
91S-568
91S-877CY
91S/100SS-49
91Seven/3DCoin-14NC
91SFExam/A's-15
91T-394AS
91T-50
91T/CJMini/II-28
91T/StClub/I-79
91UD-425
91Woolwth/HL-4
92D/I-190
92F-271
92S/I-300
92T-285
92UD-452
Welchel, Don
81RochR-18
82RochR-8
84RochR-14
85RochR-23
86OKCty-24
88Omaha/ProC-1511
91Crown/Orio-477
Weldin, David
89Helena/SP-21
Weldon, Paul
91Pocatel/ProC-3792
Weleno, Doug
83MidldC-8
Welish, Scott
89CharRain/ProC-988
89Spokane/SP-16
Welke, Tim
88TM/Umpire-55
89TM/Umpire-53
90TM/Umpire-51
Wellman, Bob
52Park-95
52T-41
79Jacks-6MG
Wellman, Brad
84D-265
84F-386
84Nes/792-109
84T-109
85F-623
85Mother/Giants-26
85T-409
86D-431
86F-553
86Mother/Giants-22
86OPC-41
86T-41
87Albuq/Pol-23
88Smok/Royals-24
89D-380
89S-504
90Target-845
Wellman, Phillip
86Durham-27
87Harris-7
88Pulaski/ProC-1748CO
89Pulaski/ProC-1901
90BurlB/ProC-2368CO
90BurlB/Star-30CO
91Durham/ClBest-26CO
91Durham/ProC-1679CO
Wells
C46-56
Wells, Bob
90Spartan/Best-10
90Spartan/ProC-2491
90Spartan/Star-25
91Clearw/ProC-1621
Wells, David
83Kinston/Team-28
86Ventura-27
87Syrac/TCMA-9
88D-640
88D/Best-311
88D/Rook-26
88F/Up-U69
88T/Tr-128T
88Tor/Fire-36
89D-307
89D/Best-328
89F-247
89OPC-259
89T-567
89T/JumboR-22
89Tor/Fire-36
90D-425
90F-96
90OPC-229
90S-491
90S/YS/I-31
90T-229
90Tor/BlueJ-36
90UD-30
91D-473
91F-188
91F/Ultra-370
91Leaf/I-140
91OPC-619
91Panini/FrSt-350
91Panini/St-153
91S-474
91S/ToroBJ-9
91T-619
91T/StClub/I-133
91Tor/Fire-36
91UD-583
92D/II-620
92F-345
92S/I-49
92T-54
92UD-116
Wells, Ed

34G-73
92Conlon/Sport-389
Wells, Frank
N172
Wells, Greg
(Boomer)
78Dunedin
79Syrac-1
80Syrac-14
81Syrac-16
82OPC-203R
82T-203R
82Toledo-17
Wells, Jacob
N172
Wells, Leo
47Sunbeam
Wells, Terry
86Ashvl-29
87Osceola-1
88ColAst/Best-3
89ColMud/ProC-144
89ColMud/Star-23
90Albuq/CMC-13
90Albuq/ProC-346
90Albuq/Trib-31
91OkCty/LineD-323
91OkCty/ProC-180
91S-359RP
91T/90Debut-166
Wells, Tim
91Gaston/ClBest-11
91Gaston/ProC-2688
Wells, Willie
74Laugh/Black-13
86Negro/Frit-71
88Conlon/NegAS-11
90Negro/Star-11
Welmaker, Roy
52Mother-37
53Mother-52
Welsh, Chris
79Colum-24
80Colum-3
82D-44
82F-584
82T-376
83D-94
83F-374
83OPC-118
83T-118
83T/Tr-125T
84D-498
84F-292
84Indianap-4
85Rang-41
86D-464
86F-576
86T-52
86TexGold-45
87F-217
87T-592
91Pac/SenLg-142
Welsh, Jimmy D.
29Exh/4-10
92Conlon/Sport-494
R316
Wendell, Steven
(Turk)
88Pulaski/ProC-1755
89BurlB/ProC-1616
89BurlB/Star-24
90Foil/Best-122
90Greenvl/Best-8
90Greenvl/ProC-1131
90Greenvl/Star-23
91Greenvl/ClBest-9
91Greenvl/LineD-222
91Greenvl/ProC-3003
92T-676R
Wendelstedt, Harry
88TM/Umpire-6
89TM/Umpire-4
90TM/Umpire-4
Wendlandt, Terry
84Omaha-30
85Omaha-5
Wendler, Doc
55Gol/Dodg-31
Wendt, Glenn
78Watlo
Wengert, Bill
88GreatF-17
89Bakers/Cal-188
90VeroB/Star-27
91VeroB/ClBest-13
91VeroB/ProC-774
Wenrick, Bill
88Boise/ProC-1623
88SLCity-26
Wenrick, John
88LitFalls/Pucko-23
89Clmbia/Best-17
89Clmbia/GS-27
90WPalmB/Star-26
Wensloff, Charles
44Yank/St-29
47TipTop
Wenson, Paul
87Lakeland-25
88GlenF/ProC-921
89Toledo/CMC-8
89Toledo/ProC-780
Wentz, Keith
86Cram/PCL-75
Wentz, Lenny
91CharWh/ClBest-20
91CharWh/ProC-2897
Wenz, Fred
69T-628R
71OPC-92
71T-92
Wera, Julie
91Conlon/Sport-100
Werber, Billy
34DS-61
34G-75
35Exh/4-9
35G-8G
35G-9G
36G
37Exh/4-14
38Exh/4-14
38G-259
38G-283
41DP-10
88Conlon/5-30
R313
R314
W711/1
W711/2
Werd, Norm
75SanAn
Werhas, John
64T-456R
65T-453R
67T-514
90Target-846
Werland, Henry
(Hank)
90Pulaski/Best-11
90Pulaski/ProC-3108
91DurhamUp/ProC-2
91Macon/ClBest-12
91Macon/ProC-865
91Single/ClBest-42
Werle, William
48Sommer-18
49Eureka-175
50B-87
51B-64
51FB
51T/RB-33
52B-248
52T-73
53T-170
54T-144
61Union
91T/Arc53-170
PM10/Sm-193
Werley, George
91Crown/Orio-478
Werley, Jamie
82Colum-10
82Colum/Pol-15
Werner, Dave
89Erie/Star-29
Werner, Don
76Indianap-17
77Indianap-8
78T-702R
79Indianap-22
83D-593
83OKCty-18
83T-504
84Iowa-16
86OKCty-25
87OKCty-5
88OkCty/CMC-21
88OkCty/ProC-37
89James/ProC-2150
91Augusta/ClBest-30MG
91Augusta/ProC-822MG
Wernig, Pat
88Madis-25
88MidwLAS/GS-52
89Huntsvl/Best-23
91Tacoma/LineD-547
91Tacoma/ProC-2307
Werrick, Joe
N172
Wert, Don
62T-299
64T-19
65OPC-271
65T-271
66T-253
67T-511
68OPC-178
68T-178
69MB-287
69T-443
69T/St-180
70OPC-33
70T-33
71MLB/St-552
71OPC-307
71T-307
72MB-358
78TCMA-163
81Detroit-65
88Domino-25
Werth, Dennis
78Cr/PCL-92
79Colum-10
81D-466
81F-102
81Louisvl-22
81T-424R
82F-55
82T-154
82T/Tr-126T
83Louisvl/Riley-22
84Louisvl-30
Wertz, Bill
90Reno/Cal-280
90Watertn/Star-23
91Collnd/ClBest-18
91Collnd/ProC-1485
91Single/ClBest-138
Wertz, Vic
49B-164
50B-9
51B-176
51T/BB-40
52B-39
52BR
52RM-AL22
52StarCal/L-72D
52T-244
53B/Col-2
53T-142
54B-21
54Esskay
55B-40
55Gol/Ind-29
55RM-AL13
55Salem
56T-300
57Sohio/Ind-16
57Swift-6
57T-78
58T-170
59T-500
60T-111
61P-49
61T-173M
61T-340
61T/St-118
62Salada-60
62Shirriff-60
62T-481
63T-348
78TCMA-227
79TCMA-45
81Detroit-123
91Crown/Orio-479
91T/Arc53-142
Exh47
Wesley, Tom
81Cedar-15
Wesolowski, Al
78Newar
Wessel, Troy
89James/ProC-2139
90James/Pucko-26
Wessinger, Jim
79Savan-26
80Richm-21
West, Bobby
89Princet/Star-24
West, Dave
84LitFalls-24
86Lynch-25
87TexLgAS-29
88AAA/ProC-41
88Tidew/CANDL-28
88Tidew/CMC-2
88Tidew/ProC-1592
89Classic-134
89D-41RR
89F-51
89Kahn/Mets-46
89S-650
89S/YS/I-32
89Sf-45
89T-787
89Tidew/CMC-7
89Tidew/ProC-1973
89ToysRUs-33
89UD-7SR
90B-413
90Classic-68
90D-387
90F-388
90HotRook/St-47
90Leaf/II-387
90OPC-357
90S-573
90T-357
90T/Big-325
90T/JumboR-30
90ToysRUs-30
90UD-15
91D-264
91F-627
91OPC-578
91S-158
91T-578
91T/StClub/I-34
91UD-377
91WIZMets-428
92D/II-638
92S/II-669
92T-442
92UD-548
West, Jim
91Waterlo/ClBest-13
91Waterlo/ProC-1260
West, Joe
88TM/Umpire-36
89TM/Umpire-34
90TM/Umpire-33
West, Matt
83Durham-26
85Richm-10
86Richm-25
87Richm/Crown-45
87Richm/TCMA-8
88Calgary/CMC-8
88Calgary/ProC-788
89Pulaski/ProC-1902
90Sumter/ProC-2451CO
90Target-847
91Macon/ClBest-29CO
91Macon/ProC-884CO
West, Milton
N172
West, Reggie
84Cram/PCL-116
85Cram/PCL-8
West, Samuel
33G-166
35G-1F
35G-3D
35G-5D
35G-6D
36Exh/4-15
37Exh/4-15
37OPC-129
38Exh/4-15
39PB-31
40PB-22
74Laugh/ASG-40
91Conlon/Sport-241
R310
R313
V300
West, Tom
86DayBe-29
86FSLAS-49
West, W. Max
39PB-149
40PB-57
41DP-43
41PB-2
52Mother-10
53Mother-19
Westbrook, Mike
84LitFalls-3
86Lynch-26
88CLAS/Star-40
88Kinston/Star-23
89Reno/Cal-251
Westbrooks, Elanis
88Clinton/ProC-716
89SanJose/Best-13
89SanJose/Cal-225
89SanJose/ProC-435
89SanJose/Star-25
90SanJose/Best-14
90SanJose/Cal-32
90SanJose/ProC-2021
90SanJose/Star-25
Westermann, Scott
88Greens/ProC-1565
Westfall, Fred
76Wausau
Westlake, James
T206
Westlake, Wally
46Remar-8
49B-45
49Eureka-176
50B-69
51T/RB-27
52BR
52NTea
52StarCal/L-81B
52T-38
53T-192
54DanDee
54T-92
55Gol/Ind-30
55Salem
55T-102
55T/DH-13
56T-81
91Crown/Orio-480
91T/Arc53-192
Exh47
Westmoreland, Claude
78Cr/PCL-21
79Albuq-21
80Albuq-11
Weston, Mickey
85Lynch-6
86Jacks/TCMA-10
88Jacks/GS-22
89RochR/CMC-6
89RochR/ProC-1638
90OPC-377
90RochR/CMC-3
90S-616
90T-377
90T/89Debut-137
90UD-683
91Crown/Orio-481
91Syrac/LineD-521
91Syrac/ProC-2482
Weston, Tim
88Oneonta/ProC-2065
89Albany/Best-29
89Albany/ProC-323
90Albany/Best-17
90Albany/Star-28TR
Westrope, Jack
(Jockey)
33SK-39
Westrum, Wes
49Eureka-126
51B-161
51FB
51T/RB-37
52B-74

52BR
52Coke
52RM-NL26
52T-75
52TipTop
53RM-NL20
54B-25
54NYJour
54T-180
55B-141
55Gol/Giants-29
56T-156
57T-323
60T-469C
66T-341MG
67T-593MG
75OPC-216MG
75T-216MG
75T/M-216MG
76SSPC-113MG
79TCMA-46
91T/Arc53-323
Exh47
R423-115

Wetherby, Jeff
86Sumter-30
87Greenvl/Best-21
88Richm-22
88Richm/CMC-16
88Richm/ProC-9
89Richm/CMC-16
89Richm/Ko-22
89Richm/ProC-840
90ColoSp/CMC-22
90ColoSp/ProC-53
90OPC-142
90S-540
90S/100Ris-44
90T-142
90T/89Debut-138
90UD-611
91RochR/LineD-472
91RochR/ProC-1917

Wetteland, John
86Bakers-28
87VeroB-1
88BBAmer-28
88SanAn/Best-21
88TexLgAS/GS-7
89Albuq/CMC-11
89Albuq/ProC-63
89S/Tr-90
90B-82
90Classic-110
90D-671
90F-411
90HotRook/St-48
90Mother/Dodg-19
90OPC-631
90Pol/Dodg-57
90S-388
90S/100Ris-25
90S/YS/I-40
90T-631
90T/89Debut-139
90T/JumboR-31
90Target-1094
90ToysRUs-31
90UD-377
91Albuq/LineD-23
91Albuq/ProC-1142
91D-614
91S-267
91UD-668
92Classic/I-94
92D/II-627

Wetzel, Tom
84Everett/Cram-29

Wever, Stefan
82Nashvl-27
83Colum-10

Wex, Gary
83Albany-8

Weyer, Lee
88TM/Umpire-2
89TM/Umpire-62

Weyhing, August
90Target-848
N172

Weyhing, John
N172

Whalen, Mike
84Newar-12

Whalen, Shawn
90Waterlo/Best-17
90Waterlo/ProC-2392
91Single/ClBest-337
91Waterlo/ClBest-24
91Waterlo/ProC-1271

Whaley, Scott Lee
84Madis/Pol-5
85Huntsvl/BK-23
85Madis-3
85Madis/Pol-24

Whaling, Albert
15CJ-163

Whalley, Jarrell
77Spartan

Whatley, Fred
90ClintUp/Team-U9

Wheat, Danny
76SanAn/Team-26
83OKCty-24TR
85Rang-TR
86Rang-TR
90Mother/Rang-28TR

Wheat, Leroy
54T-244

Wheat, Zachary D.
10Domino-123
11Helmar-89
12Sweet/Pin-78
12Sweet/Pin-78A
14CJ-52
14Piedmont/St-60
15CJ-52
16FleischBrd-99
21Exh-184
25Exh-16
26Exh-16
27Exh-56
60F-12
61F-1M
61F-86
80SSPC/HOF
89Smok/Dodg-34
90BBWit-82
90Target-849
90Target-850
91Conlon/Sport-164
D327
D328-187
D329-188
D350/2-186
E120
E121/120
E121/80
E122
E135-187
E220
E270/1
M101/4-188
M101/5-186
S74-57
T201
T202
T205
T206
T207
T213/blue
T215/brown
V100
V61-117
W501-97
W514-110
W515-56
W572
W573
W575
WG5-43
WG6-39

Wheatcroft, Robert
(Bob)
89Bluefld/Star-28
90Wausau/Best-10
90Wausau/ProC-2123
90Wausau/Star-25

Wheeler
C46-51

Wheeler, Bradley
88ElPaso/Best-18

Wheeler, Chris
88Phill/TastyK-39ANN
90Phill/TastyK-35BC

Wheeler, Dave
90Billings/ProC-3226

Wheeler, Ed
90Target-851

Wheeler, Ed
75AppFx

Wheeler, Kenneth Jr.
90Ashvl/ProC-2750
91BurlAs/ClBest-11
91BurlAs/ProC-2802
91MidwLAS/ProC-MWL20

Wheeler, Ralph
(Rocket)
78Dunedin
85Kingst-25
86Syrac-26CO
87Myrtle-19
90Syrac/CMC-28CO
90Syrac/ProC-590CO
90Syrac/Team-28
91Syrac/LineD-525CO
91Syrac/ProC-2498CO

Wheeler, Rodney
86Clearw-24

Wheeler, Tim
82AlexD-18
82Buffa-9
83LynnP-9
84Cram/PCL-140

Wheeler, Winston
90Martins/ProC-3185

Wheelock, Gary
77T-493R
78SanJose-8
78T-596
79Spokane-17
80Spokane-17
87OKCty-2
89Belling/Legoe-32CO
91Belling/ClBest-27CO
91Belling/ProC-3684CO

Wheelock, Warren
N172

Wherry, Cliff
83Tucson-18
84OKCty-4

Whipple, Jack
45Centen-27

Whisenant, Matt
90Princet/DIMD-27
91Batavia/ClBest-17
91Batavia/ProC-3483

Whisenant, Pete
57T-373
58T-466
59T-14
60T-424
61Peters-11
61T-201
61T/St-187
83Albany-20

Whisenton, Larry
78Richm
79Richm-4
79T-715R
80Richm-4
81Richm-6
82BK/Lids-27
82Pol/Atl-28
83D-501
83F-152
83Richm-22
83T-544
84Richm-5

Whisler, Randy
90Gaston/Best-27CO
90Gaston/ProC-2537CO
90Gaston/Star-29CO
91Gaston/ProC-2707CO

Whisman, Rhett
82Wisco-27

Whisonant, John
91Batavia/ClBest-23
91Batavia/ProC-3484

Whistler, Randy
80Ander-19

Whitacre
N172

Whitaker, Darrell
85BurlR-24
86Salem-28
87Gaston-26
88OkCty/CMC-11
88OkCty/ProC-43
88Tulsa-6
89OkCty/CMC-10
89OkCty/ProC-1516

Whitaker, Jeff
91BurlInd/ProC-3311

Whitaker, Lou
78BK/T-13
78T-704R
79Ho-117
79OPC-55
79T-123
80OPC-187
80T-358
81Coke
81D-365
81Detroit-59
81F-463
81OPC-234
81T-234
82D-454
82F-284
82F/St-156
82OPC-39
82T-39
82T/St-187
83D-333
83F-348
83OPC-66
83T-509
83T/St-65
84D-227
84D/AAS-4
84F-92
84F/St-13
84F/St-30
85FunFood/Pin-78
84MiltBrad-28
84Nes/792-398AS
84Nes/792-666TL
84Nes/792-695
84Nestle/DT-2
84OPC-181AS
84OPC-211
84Seven-16C
84T-398AS
84T-666TL
84T-695
84T/Gloss40-30
84T/St-196
84T/St-267
84T/St/Box-1
85Cain's-19
85D-293
85D-5DK
85D/AAS-42
85D/DKsuper-5
85F-24
85GenMills-24
85Leaf-5DK
85OPC-108
85Seven-16S
85Seven-1D
85T-480
85T/Gloss22-14
85T/St-183
85T/St-261
85Wendy-21
86Cain's-20
86D-49
86D/AAS-11
86D/PopUp-11
86F-242
86F/LimEd-44
86F/Mini-51
86F/St-126
86Leaf-33
86OPC-20
86Sf-48
86Sf-74M
86Sf/Dec-73M
86Sf/Rook-48M
86T-20
86T/Gloss22-3
86T/St-156
86T/St-272
86TrueVal-25
87Cain's-8
87Coke/Tigers-16
87D-107
87D/AAS-3
87D/OD-218
87D/PopUp-3
87F-168
87F/Mini-112
87F/RecSet-41
87F/St-122
87Ho/St-23
87Jiffy-11
87Leaf-78
87OPC-106
87RedFoley/St-88
87Sf-112M
87Sf-137
87Seven-DT12
87T-661
87T/Gloss22-14
87T/Gloss60-7
87T/St-153
87T/St-267
88D-173
88D/Best-315
88F-75
88Leaf-169
88OPC-179
88Panini/St-443IA
88Panini/St-92
88Pep/T-1
88Pol/T-14
88S-56
88Sf-30
88T-770
88T/Big-99
88T/Mini-13
88T/St-270
88T/St/Backs-38
89B-103
89ClassicUp/2-188
89D-298
89D/Best-35
89F-151
89Mara/Tigers-1
89OPC-320
89Panini/St-341
89Pol/Tigers-1
89S-230
89Sf-18
89T-320
89T/Big-22
89T/Coins-57
89T/LJN-156
89T/St-282
89T/St/Backs-6
89T/UK-83
89UD-451
90B-356
90CokeK/Tiger-26
90D-16DK
90D-298
90D/BestAL-119
90D/SuperDK-16DK
90F-619
90HotPlay/St-48
90KingB/Discs-24
90Leaf/I-34
90MLBPA/Pins-89
90OPC-280
90Panini/St-71
90PublInt/St-485
90RedFoley/St-101
90S-75
90S/100St-71
90Sf-103
90T-280
90T/Big-130
90T/Coins-32
90T/DH-70
90T/St-275
90UD-327
90UD-41TC
91B-150
91Classic/200-3
91CokeK/Tiger-1
91D-174
91F-357
91F/Ultra-130
91Leaf/I-120
91Leaf/Stud-60
91OPC-145
91Panini/FrSt-289
91Panini/St-233
91S-297
91T-145
91T/StClub/I-101
91UD-367
92D/I-285
92F-149
92S/I-255
92T-570

92UD-516
Whitaker, Stephen E.
(Steve)
67T-277
68T-383
69MLB/St-63
69OPC-71
69T-71
69T/St-189
70OPC-496
70T-496
89Pac/SenLg-67
Whitaker, Steve
91Classic/DP-29
91FrRow/DP-40
92T-369
Whitaker, William
N172
Whitby, William
67T-486R
White, Al
80Penin/B-16
80Penin/C-22
White, Andre
91BurlInd/ProC-3319
White, Bill
82Danvl-6
83VeroB-21
White, Bill D.
59T-359
60T-355
60T/tatt-53
61P-176
61T-232
61T-451M
61T/Dice-18
61T/St-96
62Bz
62J-158
62P-158
62P/Can-158
62Salada-115
62Shirriff-115
62T-14
62T/bucks
62T/St-191
63Bz-28
63F-63
63J-158
63P-158
63T-1LL
63T-290
63T/SO
64T-11LL
64T-240
64T/Coins-141AS
64T/Coins-78
64T/St-10
64T/SU
64Wheat/St-48
65OPC-190
65T-190
65T/E-43
65T/trans-72
66Bz-23
66T-397
66T/RO
67Bz-23
67T-290
68Bz-4
68OPC-190
68T-190
69MB-288
69T-588
72MB-359
78TCMA-12
90Pac/Legend-56
90Swell/Great-9
91LineD-27
91Swell/Great-96
White, Billy
89Geneva/ProC-1884
90CLAS/CL-50
90WinSalem/Team-2
91CharlK/LineD-148
91CharlK/ProC-1699
91Single/ClBest-363
White, Chaney
78Laugh/Black-9
White, Charles
52Park-22
54JC-24
55Gol/Braves-30
55JC-24
55T-103
55T/DH-18
White, Charlie
89Spring/Best-17
91ArkTr/LineD-47
91ArkTr/ProC-1301
White, Chris
91AubAS/ClBest-5
91AubAS/ProC-4275
White, Clinton
89Wythe/Star-28
90Geneva/ProC-3042
90Geneva/Star-24
White, Craig
89GreatF-29
90Yakima/Team-24
White, Darrin
89Helena/SP-25
90Beloit/Best-14
90Beloit/Star-23
91Beloit/ClBest-12
91Beloit/ProC-2106
White, Dave
79AppFx-5
86SLAS-19
87Hawaii-4
White, Derrick
91James/ClBest-3
91James/ProC-3556
White, Devon
82Danvl-21
83Peoria/LF-22
85MidldA-8
86Edmon-27
87ClassicUp-140
87D-38RR
87D/OD-5
87D/Rook-8
87F-646R
87F/Up-U123
87Leaf-38RR
87Sf/Rook-24
87Seven-W13
87Sf/Rook-10
87Smok/Cal-23
87T-139
88Classic/Red-178
88D-283
88D-8DK
88D/Best-227
88D/DKsuper-8DK
88F-506
88F/Excit-44
88F/Mini-12
88Leaf-127
88Leaf-8DK
88OPC-192
88Panini/St-49
88RedFoley/St-99
88S-212
88S/YS/I-12
88Sf-99
88Smok/Angels-13
88T-192
88T/Big-145
88T/Coins-31
88T/Gloss60-29
88T/JumboR-5
88T/St-183
88T/St-313
88ToysRUs-33
89T/Ames-31
89B-54
89D-213
89D/Best-27
89F-489
89OPC-344
89Panini/St-297
89S-323
89Sf-16
89T-602
89T/Big-122
89T/St-179
89UD-110
90B-292
90Classic-63
90D-226
90F-147
90F/BB-42
90F/LL-43
90HotPlay/St-49
90Leaf/I-76
90OPC-65
90Panini/St-29
90PublInt/St-381
90RedFoley/St-102
90S-312
90S/100St-68
90Sf-210
90Smok/Angel-18
90T-65
90T/Big-299
90T/Mini-10
90T/St-168
90UD-129
90UD-5TC
91B-30
91Classic/III-94
91D-150
91F-328
91F/UltraUp-U64
91F/Up-U69
91Leaf/II-394
91Leaf/Stud-139
91OPC-704
91OPC/Premier-126
91Panini/FrSt-185
91S-466
91S/RookTr-48T
91S/ToroBJ-23
91T-704
91T/StClub/II-444
91T/Tr-125T
91Tor/Fire-25
91UD-517
91UD/Ext-783
92Classic/I-95
92D/I-180
92F-346
92S/I-198
92T-260
92UD-352
White, Ernie
W754
White, Foley
T206
White, Frank
74OPC-604R
74T-604R
75OPC-569
75T-569
75T/M-569
76OPC-369
76SSPC-174
76T-369
77T-117
78T-248
79OPC-227
79T-439
80OPC-24
80T-45
81Coke
81D-340
81F-44
81F/St-97
81K-34
81OPC-330
81Pol/Royals-9
81T-330
81T/So-47
81T/St-83
82D-286
82F-426
82F/St-209
82OPC-156
82OPC-183IA
82T-645
82T-646IA
82T/St-193
83D-464
83F-127
83OPC-171
83Pol/Royals-9
83T-525
83T/St-169
83T/St-71
84D-222
84F-363
85FunFood/Pin-44
84Nes/792-155
84OPC-155
84T-155
84T/St-277
85D-175
85F-217
85Leaf-148
85T-743
85T/St-274
86D-130
86F-24
86F/St-127
86Kitty/Disc-13
86Leaf-54
86NatPhoto-20
86OPC-215
86Sf-186M
86T-215
86T/St-23WS
86T/St-263
87D-255
87D/AAS-41
87D/OD-204
87F-383
87F/AwardWin-42
87F/Mini-113
87F/St-123
87Leaf-188
87OPC-101
87Sf-168
87T-692
87T/St-260
88D-225
88D/Best-319
88F-273
88F/St-35
88Nestle-29
88OPC-326
88Panini/St-105
88RedFoley/St-100
88S-79
88Sf-149
88Smok/Royals-25
88T-595
88T/Big-75
88T/St-255
88T/St/Backs-39
89B-122
89D-85
89D/Best-175
89F-297
89OPC-25
89Panini/St-356
89S-390
89T-25
89T/Big-200
89T/LJN-76
89T/St-262
89Tastee/Discs-7
89UD-350
90B-371
90D-262
90F-122
90Leaf/I-204
90MLBPA/Pins-108
90OPC-479
90Panini/St-83
90PublInt/St-360
90S-372
90T-479
90T/Big-105
90UD-382
91F-574
91OPC-352
91T-352
91UD-568
White, Fred
88Kenosha/ProC-1382
89Visalia/Cal-102
89Visalia/ProC-1446
90Visalia/Cal-63
90Visalia/ProC-2155
91Single/ClBest-278
91Visalia/ClBest-11
91Visalia/ProC-1742
White, G. Harris
WG2-49
White, Gabe
91Single/ClBest-61
91Sumter/ClBest-12
91Sumter/ProC-2335
White, Gary
87Clearw-17
88Spartan/ProC-1044
White, Guy
(Doc)
10Domino-124
11Helmar-19
12Sweet/Pin-15
80Laugh/FFeat-15
E254
E286
M116
S74-10
S74-115
T202
T205
T206
T207
T215/blue
T215/brown
White, Harold
51B-320
White, Harry
79Newar-13
White, James
(Deacon)
N172
N284
Scrapps
WG1-27
White, Jerry
75IntAS/TCMA-1
75IntAS/TCMA-6
76OPC-594R
76SSPC-340
76T-594R
77OPC-81
77T-557
79T-494
80OPC-369
80T-724
81D-333
81F-161
81OPC-42
81OPC/Post-11
81T-42
82D-621
82F-211
82Hygrade
82OPC-386
82OPC/Post-24
82T-386
83D-602
83F-300
83OPC-214
83Stuart-19
83T-214
89Pac/SenLg-185
89T/SenLg-8
89TM/SenLg-113
90EliteSenLg-32
91Pac/SenLg-3
White, Jimmy
90Ashvl/ClBest-25
91Ashvl/ProC-583
White, John F.
C46-4
E254
T206
White, John
82Amari-13
White, Johnny
91James/ClBest-1
91James/ProC-3560
White, Joyner C.
(Jo-Jo)
34DS-45
35Wheat
39PB-79
40PB-84
47Centen-31
47Signal
49B/PCL-14
60T-460C
81Detroit-27
92Conlon/Sport-612
R312/M
R314
V355-74
White, Joyner M.
(Mike)
64T-492R
65OPC-31
65T-31
78TCMA-155
White, K.G.
89Bakers/Cal-199
White, Larry
81Chatt-21
82Albuq-10
83Albuq-8
83Pol/Dodg-47
84Cram/PCL-158

85Cram/PCL-168
90Target-852
White, Logan
84Butte-27
White, Marvin
89Butte/SP-29
90Gaston/Best-26CO
90Gaston/ProC-2538CO
90Gaston/Star-27CO
91CharlR/ClBest-28CO
91CharlR/ProC-1331CO
White, Mike
86Bakers-29
87Bakers-12
88FSLAS/Star-25
88VeroB/Star-23
89SanAn/Best-1
91SanAn/LineD-546
91SanAn/ProC-2990
White, Mike
81LynnS-19
White, Myron
77LodiD
80Albuq-12
90Target-853
White, Oliver Kirby
D322
T205
White, Randy
83Greens-13
89Idaho/ProC-2034
White, Rich
80Utica-2
White, Rick
91Augusta/ClBest-12
91Augusta/ProC-806
White, Rondell
90Classic/DP-24
90Classic/DP-xxCL
90Classic/III-80
91B-450
91S-390FDP
91Single/ClBest-360
91Sumter/ClBest-25
91Sumter/ProC-2350
91UD/FinalEd-10F
92UD-51CL
92UD-61TP
White, Roy
46Sunbeam
White, Sammy
52T-345
53B/Col-41
53T-139
54B-34
54RH
54RM-AL14
54Wilson
55B-47
56T-168
57T-163
58Hires-53
58T-414
59T-486
60T-203
62T-494
91T/Arc53-139
PM10/Sm-194
White, Roy
66T-234R
68T-546
69MB-289
69MLB/St-81
69OPC-25
69T-25
69T/S-26
69T/St-210
69Trans-26
70MLB/St-252
70OPC-373
70T-373
70T/PI-14
71K-43
71MD
71MLB/St-503
71OPC-395
71T-395
71T/Coins-34
71T/GM-45
71T/S-26
71T/tatt-13
72MB-360
72OPC-340
72T-340
72T/Cloth-33
73OPC-25
73Syrac/Team-29
73T-25
74OPC-135
74Syrac/Team-29
74T-135
74T/St-220
75K-1
75OPC-375
75T-375
75T/M-375
76OPC-225
76SSPC-435
76T-225
77BK/Y-19
77BurgChef-179
77OPC-182
77T-485
78BK/Y-19
78OPC-48
78T-16
79BK/Y-19
79OPC-75
79T-159
79TCMA-25
80OPC-341
80T-648
90Swell/Great-42
91Swell/Great-97
White, Sherman
51BR-B11
White, Sol
78Laugh/Black-22
White, William D.
N172
Whited, Ed
86AubAs-26
87Ashvl-24
88Greenvl/Best-1
88SLAS-16
89Richm/Bob-27
89Richm/CMC-21
89Richm/Ko-36
89Richm/ProC-837
90OPC-111
90Richm/Bob-16
90Richm/CMC-17
90Richm/ProC-268
90Richm/Team-29
90S-644RP
90S/100Ris-78
90T-111
90T/89Debut-140
90UD-447
Whitehead, Burgess
(Whitey)
34DS-51
39PB-23
40PB-92
41DP-90
41PB-28
R314
V355-59
Whitehead, Chris
88Elmira-21
90LynchRS/Team-10
Whitehead, John
92Conlon/Sport-568
R314
Whitehead, Steve
76QuadC
Whitehead, Steve
(Pitcher)
89James/ProC-2140
90Rockford/ProC-2687
91Rockford/ClBest-28
91Rockford/ProC-2048
Whitehill, Earl
28Exh-47
33G-124
35Exh/4-16
35G-8H
35G-9H
36Exh/4-16
81Detroit-31
87Conlon/2-60
88Conlon/AmAS-24
91Conlon/Sport-127
R308-165
R310
R312/M
R314
R316
V355-60
Whitehouse, Len
77Ashvl
78Ashvl
79Tulsa-3
83T/Tr-126T
84D-558
84F-578
84Nes/792-648
84T-648
85D-513
85T-406
85Toledo-12
Whitehurst, Todd
91Burllnd/ProC-3312
Whitehurst, Wally
86Madis-27
86Madis/Pol-23
88Tidew/CANDL-29
88Tidew/CMC-11
88Tidew/ProC-1589
89B-373
89F/Up-U103
89Tidew/CMC-6
89Tidew/ProC-1958
89UD/Ext-737
90Kahn/Mets-47
90OPC-719
90S-599
90T-719
90T/89Debut-141
90T/TVMets-19
90UD-564
91B-470
91D-511
91F-166
91Kahn/Mets-47
91Leaf/II-333
91OPC-557
91S-529
91S/100RisSt-91
91T-557
91T/StClub/II-458
91ToysRUs-32
91UD-221
91WIZMets-429
92D/I-134
92F-519
92S/I-299
92T-419
92UD-414
Whiteman, Charles
W514-119
Whiten, Mark
87Myrtle-24
88Dunedin/Star-21
89Knoxvl/Best-26
89Knoxvl/Star-21
90AAAGame/ProC-AAA2
90F/Up-130
90Leaf/II-396
90Syrac/CMC-24
90Syrac/ProC-587
90Syrac/Team-29
91B-13
91Classic/200-65
91D-607
91D/Rook-32
91F-189
91F/Ultra-371
91F/UltraUp-U21
91F/Up-U21
91Leaf/I-234
91Leaf/Stud-50
91MajorLg/Pins-28
91OPC-588
91OPC/Premier-127
91S-358RP
91S/100RisSt-24
91S/ASFan-6
91T-588
91T/90Debut-167
91T/StClub/II-452
91T/Tr-126T
91Tor/Fire-23
91UD-561
91UD/FinalEd-75F
92D/I-325
92F-126
92S/II-587
92T-671
92UD-524
Whiteside, Matt
91Gaston/ClBest-12
91Gaston/ProC-2689
Whitfield, Fred
62Kahn/Atl
63Sugar-27
63T-211
64Kahn
64T-367
65OPC-283
65T-283
66Kahn
66OPC-88
66T-88
67Kahn
67T-275
68OPC-133
68T-133
69MB-290
69T-518
Whitfield, Ken
85Kingst-22
86Kinston-25
89Kinston/Star-24
90Reno/Cal-262
91Canton/LineD-98
91Canton/ProC-994
Whitfield, Terry
75OPC-622R
75T-622R
75T/M-622R
76OPC-590R
76SSPC-443
76T-590R
78Ho-136
78T-236
79Ho-10
79OPC-309
79Pol/Giants-45
79T-589
80OPC-361
80Pol/Giants-45
80T-713
81D-435
81F-437
81T-167
81T/So-87
81T/St-233
84F/X-U125
84Pol/Dodg-45
85Coke/Dodg-33
85D-540
85F-389
85T-31
86Coke/Dodg-33
86D-337
86F-147
86Pol/Dodg-45
86T-318
90Target-854
Whitford, Larry
86Beloit-26
Whiting, Don
78Holyo
79Holyo-15
82ElPaso-9
83Beloit/LF-14
Whiting, John
75BurlB
Whiting, Mike
86Elmira-28
Whitlock, Mike
88Beloit/GS-22
89StLucie/Star-24
Whitman, Dick
49Eureka-51
51B-221
90Target-855
Whitman, Jim
91Erie/ClBest-13
91Erie/ProC-4083
Whitmer, Dan
79SLCity-19
80SLCity-2
82Knoxvl-11
82Syrac-28
83Knoxvl-9
Whitmer, Joe
83Chatt-4
84Chatt-17
85Cram/PCL-99
86Calgary-26
Whitmore, Darrell
90Burllnd/ProC-3025
91Watertn/ProC-3385
Whitmyer, Steve
86Water-25
Whitney, Arthur C.
(Pinky)
29Exh/4-12
31Exh/4-11
32Orbit/un-60
33DH-42
36Exh/4-1
37Exh/4-6
38Exh/4-6
38Wheat
39PB-98
91Conlon/Sport-288
R305
R313
R316
Whitney, Arthur W.
N172
N284
N338/2
WG1-71
Whitney, G.
N172
Whitney, James
N172
N284
N403
Whitney, Jeff
90Reno/Cal-278
Whitshire, Vernon
R313
Whitson, Anthony
89CharWh/Best-14
Whitson, Ed
78Colum
79T-189
80Pol/Giants-32
80T-561
81D-74
81F-444
81OPC-336
81T-336
81T/St-240
82D-251
82F-402
82T-656
82T/Tr-127T
82Wheat/Ind
83D-389
83F-423
83T-429
83T/Tr-127T
84D-528
84F-316
84Mother/Giants-26
84Mother/Padres-15
84Nes/792-277
84Smok/Padres-27
84T-277
85D-446
85F-47
85F/Up-U129
85OPC-98
85T-762
85T/St-152
85T/Tr-130T
86D-225
86F-120
86OPC-15
86T-15
86T/St-301
87Bohem-31
87D-360
87F-434
87T-155
88Coke/Padres-31
88D-81
88D/Best-322
88F-599
88OPC-330
88Panini/St-401
88RedFoley/St-101
88S-167
88Smok/Padres-30
88T-330
88T/Big-186
88T/St-107
89B-449
89Coke/Padre-20
89D-229

89D/Best-210
89F-321
89OPC-21
89Padre/Mag-22
89S-329
89T-516
89T/Big-81
89UD-453
90B-204
90Coke/Padre-20
90D-205
90D-26DK
90D/BestNL-98
90D/SuperDK-26DK
90F-171
90Leaf/I-246
90OPC-618
90Padre/MagUno-12
90Panini/St-347
90Publint/St-62
90S-373
90S/100St-69
90Sf-212
90T-618
90T/Big-152
90T/Mini-82
90T/St-107
90UD-308
91B-651
91D-186
91F-547
91F/Ultra-313
91Leaf/II-337
91Leaf/Stud-250
91OPC-481
91Padre/MagRal-14
91Panini/FrSt-98
91Panini/St-91
91Panini/Top15-67
91S-789
91T-481
91T/StClub/I-246
91UD-312
92D/I-380
92F-624
92S/II-564
92T-228
92UD-103

Whitson, Tony
88Wythe/ProC-1984
89CharWh/ProC-1763

Whitt, Ernie
78Syrac
78T-708R
79Syrac-3
79T-714R
81D-390
81F-411
81OPC-282
81OPC/Post-20
81T-407
82D-381
82F-626
82OPC-19
82OPC/Post-3
82T-19
82T/St-247
83D-304
83F-443
83OPC-302
83T-302
83T/St-131
84D-437
84F-169
84Nes/792-506
84OPC-106
84T-506
84T/St-373
84Tor/Fire-32
85D-268
85F-119
85Leaf-181
85OPC-128
85T-128
85Tor/Fire-32
86Ault-12
86D-559
86D/AAS-48
86F-73
86Leaf-217
86OPC-136
86T-673
86Tor/Fire-32
87D-148
87D/HL-39
87D/OD-33
87F-240
87Ho/St-2
87Leaf-69
87OPC-221
87T-698
87Tor/Fire-34
88D-394
88F-126
88Ho/Disc-16
88Leaf-250
88OPC-79
88Panini/St-216
88S-168
88T-79
88T/Big-239
88T/St-187
88Tor/Fire-12
89B-248
89D-591
89D/Best-255
89F-248
89OPC-289
89S-98
89T-289
89T/Big-224
89Tor/Fire-12
89UD-118
90B-16
90D-385
90F-97
90Leaf/II-408
90OPC-742
90Publint/St-529
90S-433
90S/Tr-30T
90T-742
90T/St-189
90T/Tr-128T
90UD-148
91Crown/Orio-501
91Leaf/II-391
91OPC-492
91T-492

Whitt, Mike
85Everett/II/Cram-22
85Everett/Cram-18
86Clinton-27

Whitted, George
(Possum)
15CJ-151
16FleischBrd-100
21Exh-185
90Target-856
D327
D328-188
D329-189
D350/2-190
E121/120
E121/80
E135-188
E220
M101/4-189
M101/5-190
V100
W501-81
W514-92
W575

Whittemore, Reggie
81Bristol-5
83Pawtu-19
84Pawtu-15
85Toledo-19

Whitty, Todd
91AS/Cal-51

Whitworth, Ken
91Miami/CIBest-12
91Miami/ProC-408

Wichman, Mike
89Stockton/Best-26M

Wick, David
82Watlo/B-10
82Watlo/C-13

Wickander, Kevin
87Kinston-2
88BBAmer-9
88EastLAS/ProC-44
88Wmsprt/ProC-1315
89B-75
89ColoSp/CMC-5
89ColoSp/ProC-238
90B-327
90D/Rook-36
90OPC-528
90T-528
90T/89Debut-142
91ColoSp/LineD-98
91ColoSp/ProC-2185
91D-649
91F-385
91OPC-246
91S-355RP
91S/100RisSt-37
91T-246
91T/StClub/II-572

Wicker, Bob
WG3-51

Wicker, Floyd
69Fud's-14
69T-524R
71MLB/St-456
71OPC-97
71T-97

Wicker, Kemp
90Target-857

Wickersham, Dave
61T-381
62T-517
63T-492
64Det/Lids-14
64T-181
64T/Coins-105
64T/S-35
65Bz-25
65OldLond-38
65OPC-9LL
65T-375
65T-9LL
65T/trans-34
66OPC-58
66T-58
67OPC-112
67T-112
68KDKA-40
68T-288
69T-647
78TCMA-195

Wickham, Mike
89Stockton/Star-26M

Wickman, Robert
90SoBend/Best-28
91B-353
91Saraso/CIBest-11
91Saraso/ProC-1114
92UD-76TP

Wickware, Frank
78Laugh/Black-19

Widmar, Al
51B-281
52T-133
53Mother-14
74T-99CO
84Tor/Fire-33CO
85Tor/Fire-33CO
86Tor/Fire-33CO
87Tor/Fire-35CO
88Tor/Fire-41CO
89Tor/Fire-41CO

Widner, Steven
77Watlo

Widner, William
N172

Wieand, F. Ted
60T-146

Wieczorek, Chet
40Hughes-19

Wiedenbauer, Tom
77Cocoa
80Tucson-8
81Tucson-26
83DayBe-13
86Osceola-28MG
87ColAst/ProC-16
88ColAst/Best-25
89ColMud/Best-8
89ColMud/ProC-130

Wiegandt, Scott
89Martins/Star-34
90Spartan/Best-11
90Spartan/ProC-2492
90Spartan/Star-26
91Clearw/CIBest-11
91Clearw/ProC-1622

Wieghaus, Tom
80Memphis-25
84Mother/Ast-18

Wielegman, Phil
86Miami-27

Wieligman, Rich
87Lakeland-4
88GlenF/ProC-922
89Toledo/CMC-23
89Toledo/ProC-775

Wielman, Carl
D327
D328-189
D329-190
D350/2-191
E135-189
M101/4-190
M101/5-191

Wiener, Paul
79Jacks-5

Wiens, Randy
78Dunedin

Wiese, Phil
89Elizab/Star-28
90Visalia/Cal-64
90Visalia/ProC-2156
91OrlanSR/LineD-498
91OrlanSR/ProC-1851

Wieser, Dan
82Omaha-18

Wiesler, Bob
56T-327
57T-126
79TCMA-224

Wiesmiller, Bob
77Salem

Wiesner, Doug
81AppFx-29
82AppFx-29

Wietelmann, William
(Whitey)
52Mother-24
73OPC-12CO
73T-12CO
76SSPC-598
77Padre/SchCd-37CO
78Padre/FamFun-36CO

Wieters, Rick
78Green
79Savan-18
80GlenF/B-12
80GlenF/C-13
81GlenF-8

Wiggins, Alan
79Clinton
83D-397
83F-375
83T-251
84D-568
84F-317
84F/St-89
84Mother/Padres-10
84Nes/792-693
84OPC-27
84Smok/Padres-28
84T-693
84T/St-153
84T/St/Box-3
85D-80
85F-48
85F/St-60
85Leaf-68
85OPC-378
85T-378
85T/St-150
86D-607
86F-290
86T-508
87D/OD-138
87F/Up-U124
87French-2
87T/Tr-126T
88S-291
91Crown/Orio-482

Wiggins, Dave
81Phoenix-14

Wiggins, Jimmy
91Princet/CIBest-26
91Princet/ProC-3515

Wiggins, Kevin
86Orlan-23

Wiggs, James
E107

Wiggs, Johnny
89Belling/Legoe-15
90SanBern/Best-21
90SanBern/Cal-94
90SanBern/ProC-2634
91Penin/CIBest-13
91Penin/ProC-379

Wight, Bill
50B-38
51B-164
52B-117
52T-177
53B/Col-100
53Glen
55B-312
55Gol/Ind-31
56T-286
57T-340
58T-237
79TCMA-131
91Crown/Orio-483

Wihtol, Sandy
79Tacom-16
80T-665R
80Tacom-10
81Charl-7
81T-451R
83Charl-6

Wilber, Del
52B-225
52T-383
53B/BW-24
54B-178

Wilbins, Mike
75Cedar

Wilborn, Ted
80OPC-329R
80T-674R
82Phoenix
83Phoenix/BHN-16
86Hagers-27
87Cedar-20

Wilbur, Bob
80Utica-10

Wilburn, Fred
85MidldA-4

Wilburn, Trey
89Billings/ProC-2041
90CharWh/Best-11
90CharWh/ProC-2242
90Gate/ProC-3355
91Billings/ProC-3758

Wilcox, Milt
71OPC-164R
71T-164R
72OPC-399
72T-399
73OPC-134
73T-134
74OPC-565
74T-565
75OPC-14
75T-14
75T/M-14
76SSPC-306
77Evansvl/TCMA-25
78BK/T-11
78OPC-136
78T-151
79T-288
80OPC-204
80T-392
81D-247
81F-465
81T-658
82D-223
82F-285
82F/St-157
82T-784
82T/St-186
83D-155
83F-349
83T-457
84D-471
84F-93
84Nes/792-588
84T-588
85Cain's-20
85D-105
85F-25
85Leaf-227
85OPC-99
85Seven-6D
85T-99
85T/St-10ALCS

85T/St-17WS
85Wendy-22
86F-243
86Mother/Mar-11
86T-192
89Pac/SenLg-13
89T/SenLg-73
89TM/SenLg-114
90EliteSenLg-16
90MedHat/Best-8
91Pac/SenLg-140
Wilcox, Steve
82Clinton-11
Wild, Jerry
63Pep/Tul
Wilder, Bill
84Memphis-11
Wilder, Dave
82Idaho-29
83Madis/LF-5
87Pittsfld-18
Wilder, John
91Pulaski/ClBest-27
91Pulaski/ProC-4006
Wilder, Mike
83Idaho-25
84Madis/Pol-4
Wilder, Troy
78Watlo
Wiles, Randy
78Charl
Wiley, Charles
91Belling/ClBest-24
91Belling/ProC-3664
Wiley, Craig
87LasVegas-21
88Wichita-12
89NiagFls/Pucko-23
Wiley, Jim
90PrWill/Team-28
91FtLaud/ClBest-15
91FtLaud/ProC-2428
91Single/ClBest-167
Wiley, Keith
88CapeCod/Sum-11
Wiley, Mark
79Syrac-5
83RochR-25
84RochR-3
85RochR-29
87French-31CO
88Gator-35CO
Wiley, Michael
91Kane/ClBest-12
91Kane/ProC-2659
Wiley, Skip
90A&AASingle/ProC-108
90AppFox/Box-30
90AppFox/ProC-2096
91BBCity/ClBest-12
91BBCity/ProC-1399
Wilfong, Rob
76Tacoma
79T-633
80T-238
81D-493
81F-569
81T-453
82D-130
82F-563
82F/St-231
82T-379
82T/St-205
82T/Tr-128T
83D-612
83F-101
83T-158
84D-329
84F-530
84Nes/792-79
84Smok/Cal-30
84T-79
85D-402
85F-315
85Smok/Cal-20
85T-524
86OPC-393
86Smok/Cal-20
86T-658
87D-258
87F-94
87T-251
Wilhelm, Hoyt
52T-392
53B/BW-28
53RM-NL21
53T-151
54B-57
54NYJour
54T-36
55B-1
55Gol/Giants-30
55RM-NL12
56T-307
57T-203
58T-324
59T-349
60L-69
60T-115M
60T-395
61P-80
61T-545
61T/St-107
62J-35
62P-35
62P/Can-35
62T-423M
62T-545
62T/St-10
63Salada-39
63T-108
64T-13
65OPC-276
65T-276
66T-510
67T-422
68T-350
69JB
69MB-291
69T-565
69T/DE-11
69T/decal
69T/St-190
70OPC-17
70T-17
71MLB/St-24
71OPC-248
71T-248
71T/GM-2
72MB-361
72T-777
78Cr/PCL-100
78TCMA-100
79TCMA-270
79WHave-27
80Pac/Leg-121
82Nashvl-28CO
83Nashvl-25CO
84Nashvl-24CO
85West/2-26
88Pac/Leg-76
89HOF/St-81
89Kodak/WSox-5M
89Pac/Leg-171
89Smok/Dodg-35
89Swell-45
90Pac/Legend-57
90Target-858
91Crown/Orio-484
91T/Arc53-151
91T/Arc53-312
Wilhelm, Irvin
(Kaiser)
14Piedmont/St-61
90Target-859
E270/1
M116
T205
T206
T213/blue
V100
Wilhelm, James W.
79Hawaii-7
80T-685R
Wilhelmi, Dave
80Clinton-1
81Clinton-4
84Shrev/FB-24
Wilhoit, Joe
D328-189
E135-189
Wilholte, Arnold
78Ashvl
Wilie, Denney
T207
Wilke, Matt
91MedHat/ProC-4111
Wilkerson, Bill
89London/ProC-1360
Wilkerson, Curtis
(Curt)
82BurlR-13
82Tulsa-25
83OKCty-19
84D-99
84F/X-U126
84Rang-19
84T/Tr-127T
85D-99
85F-573
85OPC-342
85Rang-19
85T-594
85T/St-349
86D-256
86F-577
86OPC-279
86Rang-19
86T-434
86T/St-244
87D-223
87F-141
87Mother/Rang-14
87Smok/R-28
87T-228
88D-592
88F-481
88Mother/R-14
88S-127
88Smok/R-21
88T-53
88T/Big-132
89B-292
89D-402
89D/Tr-34
89F-535
89Mara/Cubs-19
89S-518
89T-331
89T/Tr-126T
89UD-465
90Cub/Mara-23
90D-608
90F-46
90OPC-667
90PublInt/St-209
90S-474
90T-667
90T/TVCub-28
90UD-147
91B-511
91F-438
91Leaf/II-317
91OPC-142
91S-603
91T-142
91T/StClub/II-512
92D/II-489
92S/I-382
92T-712
92UD-490
Wilkerson, Marty
84Omaha-12
85Omaha-20
86Omaha-29
86Omaha/TCMA-9
Wilkerson, Ron
82WHave-18
Wilkerson, Wayne
77Ashvl
Wilkerson, Wayne Sr.
91Princet
91Princet/ClBest-21
91Princet/ProC-3530
Wilkes, Greg
80Hawaii-13
Wilkie, Aldon
47Remar-23
48Signal
Wilkins, Dean
88EastLAS/ProC-30
88Pittsfld/ProC-1368
89Iowa/CMC-10
89Iowa/ProC-1690
90B-26
90F-47
90Iowa/CMC-9
90S-630RP
90T/89Debut-143
90T/TVCub-16
91AAAGame/ProC-AAA54
91Tucson/ProC-2214
Wilkins, Eric
80T-511
80Tacom-25
81Charl-6
81T-99
Wilkins, Mark
81QuadC-28
Wilkins, Michael
88Fayette/ProC-1103
89Lakeland/Star-24
90EastLAS/ProC-EL46
90London/ProC-1269
91SanAn/LineD-547
91SanAn/ProC-2976
Wilkins, Rick
88Peoria/Ko-31
89WinSalem/Star-17
90T/TVCub-63
91B-419
91Classic/III-96
91D/Rook-38
91F/UltraUp-U75
91F/Up-U83
91Iowa/LineD-221
91Iowa/ProC-1065
91S/RookTr-103T
91UD/FinalEd-46F
92D/I-249
92F-397
92S/100RisSt-16
92S/II-483
92T-348
92T/91Debut-184
92UD-373
Wilkins, Steve
76Cedar
Wilkinson, Bill
86Calgary-25
87F/Up-U125
87Mother/Sea-26
87T/Tr-127T
88D-568
88F-390
88Mother/Sea-26
88RedFoley/St-102
88T-376
89Calgary/CMC-6
89T-636
90Omaha/ProC-67
Wilkinson, Brian
89Wausau/GS-13
90Rockford/ProC-2692
91WPalmB/ClBest-14
91WPalmB/ProC-1230
Wilkinson, Ray
V100
Wilkinson, Ron
82Madis-16
Wilkinson, Spencer
88Gaston/ProC-1019
89Gaston/ProC-999
89Gaston/Star-25
Wilks, Ted
47TipTop
49B-137
49Eureka-199
51B-193
52B-138
52T-109
53T-101
79TCMA-218
91T/Arc53-101
Will, Bob
59T-388
60T-147
61T-512
61T/St-11
62Salada-218
62Shirriff-218
62T-47
63T-58
Willard, Gerry
82Reading-11
83Charl-8
84D-520
84Wheat/Ind-16
85D-346
85F-460
85OPC-142
85Polar/Ind-16
85T-504
86D-398
86F-601
86F/Up-U126
86OPC-273
86T-273
86Tacom-24
87D-467
87F-409
87T-137
87Tacom-19
89Vanco/CMC-19
89Vanco/ProC-587
90AAAGame/ProC-AAA37
90Vanco/CMC-23
90Vanco/ProC-492
91D-634
91Richm/ProC-2573
92S/I-188
Willard, Jon
91SLCity/ProC-3212
Willeford, Jerry
76Dubuq
Willett, Robert Edgar
09Buster/Pin-15
11Helmar-38
14Piedmont/St-62
E104
E254
E95
M116
S74-19
T202
T205
T206
T213/blue
T213/brown
T215/brown
Willey, Carlton
(Carl)
58T-407
59T-95
60Lake
60SpicSpan-25
60T-107
61T-105
61T/St-48
62J-155
62P-155
62P/Can-155
62T-174
63T-528
64T-84
64T/Coins-75
64T/St-44
64T/tatt
65T-401
91WIZMets-430
Willhite, Nick
64T-14R
65T-284
66OPC-171
66T-171
67T-249
78Newar
90Target-860
91WIZMets-431
Williams
E254
Williams
E254
T201
Williams, Al
73Cedar
Williams, Alberto
(Al)
80Toledo-17
81T-569
82D-429
82F-564
82T-69
83D-508
83F-628
83T-731
84D-316
84F-579
84Nes/792-183
84T-183
85Colum-10
85Colum/Pol-23
85T-614
Williams, Barry
90Utica/Pucko-13
Williams, Bernard
(Bernie)

70OPC-401R
70T-401R
71MLB/St-264
71OPC-728R
71T-728R
72T-761R
73OPC-557
73T-557

Williams, Bernabe
(Bernie)
87FtLaud-21
87Oneonta-4
88CLAS/Star-19
88PrWill/Star-24
89BBAmerAA/BPro-AA5
89Colum/CMC-21
89Colum/Pol-22
89Colum/ProC-736
90A&AASingle/ProC-31
90Albany/Best-1
90Albany/ProC-1179
90Albany/Star-22
90AlbanyDG/Best-33
90B-439
90Classic-10
90D-689
90EastLAS/ProC-EL45
90Foil/Best-26
90OPC-701
90S-619RP
90T-701
90T/TVYank-66
91AAAGame/ProC-AAA8
91B-173
91Classic/II-T61
91Classic/III-97
91ColClip/LineD-123
91ColClip/ProC-612
91F/UltraUp-U44
91F/Up-U49
91Leaf/StudPrev-7
91OPC/Premier-128
91RedFoley/St-112
91UD-11
92D/I-344
92F-247
92S/100RisSt-34
92S/I-401
92T-374
92T/91Debut-185
92UD-556

Williams, Billy
61T-141
61T/St-12
62Salada-207
62Shirriff-207
62T-288
62T/bucks
62T/St-111
63Exh
63J-172
63P-172
63Salada-30
63T-353
64Bz-17
64T-175
64T/Coins-44
64T/S-52
64T/St-73
64T/SU
64T/tatt
65Bz-17
65OldLond-20
65OPC-220
65OPC-4LL
65T-220
65T-4LL
65T/E-40
65T/trans-35
66Bz-48
66T-217LL
66T-580
66T/RO-101
67Bz-48
67T-315
68Bz-14
68Kahn
68OPC-37
68T-37
69Kahn
69Kelly/Pin-19
69MB-292
69MLB/St-126
69MLBPA/Pin-59
69OPC-4LL
69Sunoco/Pin-9
69T-450
69T-4LL
69T/S-39
69T/St-20
69Trans-38
70Dunkin-6
70K-37
70MLB/St-24
70OPC-170
70T-170
70T/S-40
71Bz
71Bz/Test-26
71K-61
71MLB/St-48
71OPC-350
71OPC-64LL
71OPC-66LL
71T-350
71T-64LL
71T-66LL
71T/Coins-75
71T/GM-37
71T/tatt-12
71T/tatt-12a
72K-46
72MB-362
72OPC-439
72OPC-440IA
72T-439
72T-440IA
72T/Post-21
73K-10
73OPC-200
73OPC-61LL
73T-200
73T-61LL
73T/Comics-23
73T/Lids-53
73T/PinUps-23
74K-32
74OPC-110
74OPC-338AS
74T-110
74T-338AS
74T/St-20
75OPC-545
75T-545
75T/M-545
76OPC-525
76SSPC-496
76T-525
83MLBPA/Pin-35
85CircK-18
86Sf/Dec-51M
87D/HL-20
88Pac/Leg-90
88T/Gloss22-22
89HOF/St-29
89Pac/Leg-184
89Swell-120
89T/LJN-41
90Pac/Legend-58
90Swell/Great-13
91CollAB-36
91K/3D-9
91LineD-28
91Swell/Great-98
Exh47

Williams, Billy
88TM/Umpire-3

Williams, Bo
90SanBern/ProC-2648

Williams, Bob
86BurlEx-26
88CharlK/Pep-2
88Hagers/Star-25

Williams, Brent
91Kissim/ProC-4192

Williams, Brian
91Osceola/ClBest-12
91Osceola/ProC-685
91Single/ClBest-14
92Classic/I-96
92D/II-416RR
92T/91Debut-186
92UD-23SR

Williams, Bruce
83Beloit/LF-9

Williams, Cary
90Clearw/Star-24
91Reading/LineD-523
91Reading/ProC-1384

Williams, Charles
72OPC-388
72T-388
75OPC-449
75T-449
75T/M-449
76OPC-332
76SSPC-98
76T-332
77T-73
78T-561
79T-142
91WIZMets-432

Williams, Charlie
88TM/Umpire-41
89TM/Umpire-39
90TM/Umpire-37

Williams, Charlie
90Kgsport/Best-24
90Kgsport/Star-25

Williams, Claude
(Lefty)
88Pac/8Men-108
88Pac/8Men-11
88Pac/8Men-44
88Pac/8Men-45M
88Pac/8Men-49
88Pac/8Men-60
D327
D328-190
E135-190
W514-35
W575

Williams, Clifford
91BendB/ClBest-17
91BendB/ProC-3698

Williams, Dallas
80RochR-2
81RochR-23
82Indianap-26
83Indianap-7
84Evansvl-12
86Indianap-26
87Indianap-22
91Crown/Orio-485

Williams, Dan
83BirmB-3
88BurlInd/ProC-1799
89Watertn/Star-23
90Kinston/Team-22
91Kinston/ClBest-24CO
91Kinston/ProC-342CO

Williams, Dana
86Pawtu-27
87NewBrit-16
87Pawtu-26
88Pawtu/CMC-21
88Pawtu/ProC-460
89Pawtu/CMC-16
89Pawtu/Dunkin-10
89Pawtu/ProC-690
90F-648M
90T/89Debut-144
90T/TVCub-64
90Vanco/CMC-24
90Vanco/ProC-504

Williams, Dave
52B-178
52T-316
53B/Col-1
53T-120
54B-9
54NYJour
55B-138
55Gol/Giants-31
79TCMA-167
91T/Arc53-120

Williams, Dave
85Orlan-24

Williams, David
90Pulaski/Best-12
90Pulaski/ProC-3091
91Macon/ClBest-13
91Macon/ProC-866

Williams, Deb
40Hughes-20

Williams, Dick H.
52T-396
53T-125
54NYJour
57T-59
58T-79
59T-292
60T-188
61P-86
61T-8
61T/St-168
62J-32
62P-32
62P/Can-32
62Salada-48A
62Salada-48B
62Shirriff-48
62T-382
63T-328
64T-153
67OPC-161MG
67T-161MG
67T/Test/RSox-26MG
68OPC-87MG
68T-87MG
69T-349MG
71OPC-714MG
71T-714MG
72OPC-137MG
72T-137MG
73OPC-179MG
73T-179MG
75OPC-236MG
75T-236MG
75T/M-236MG
76SSPC-192MG
76T-304MG
77OPC-108MG
77T-647MG
78OPC-27MG
78T-522MG
79OPC-349MG
79T-606MG
79TCMA-327
81D-453MG
81F-149MG
81T-616MG
81T-680MG
83D-625MG
83T-366MG
84Mother/SDP-1MG
84Nes/792-742MG
84Smok/SDP-29MG
84T-742MG
85F/St-126MG
85Mother/SDP-1MG
85T-66MG
86D/AAS-38
86Mother/Mar-1
86T-681MG
86T/Gloss22-12
86T/Tr-124T
87Mother/A's-12
87Mother/Sea-1
87T-418MG
88Mother/Sea-1MG
88T-104
89Pac/SenLg-166MG
89Pac/SenLg-183MG
89T/SenLg-22
89TM/SenLg-115MG
89TM/SenLg-120MG
90EliteSenLg-33MG
90Target-861
91Crown/Orio-486
91Swell/Great-99
91T/Arc53-125

Williams, Don
(Spin)
84PrWill-20
85Nashua-26
86Nashua-27CO
87Harris-15
88Harris/ProC-839
90EastLAS/ProC-EL28CO
90Harris/ProC-1209CO
90Harris/Star-24CO
91CaroMud/LineD-125CO
91CaroMud/ProC-1102CO

Williams, Don
77Padre/SchCd-38CO
78Padre/FamFun-37CO

Williams, Don
60T-414

Williams, Dwayne
87Tampa-10

Williams, Earl
71OPC-52R
71T-52R
72OPC-380
72T-380
73JP
73OPC-504
73T-504
74OPC-375
74T-375
74T/St-130
75OPC-97
75T-97
75T/M-97
76Ho-108
76OPC-458
76SSPC-13
76T-458
77OPC-252
77T-223
78Ho-16
78T-604
89Bluefld/Star-29
91Crown/Orio-487

Williams, Eddie
85Cedar-20
86OhHenry-24
87BuffB-13
88ColoSp/CMC-17
88ColoSp/ProC-1547
88D-46RR
88F-620
88Leaf-46RR
88T-758
89Coke/WS-28
89D/Tr-29
89S/YS/II-39
89T/Tr-127T
89UD/Ext-790
90AAAGame/ProC-AAA28
90CedarDG/Best-10
90LasVegas/ProC-131
90PublInt/St-403
90UD-289
90WinSalem/Team-25
91Classic/DP-41
91F-548
91Johnson/ClBest-1
91Johnson/ProC-3980
91SanJose/ClBest-12
91S-552

Williams, Edward
87Peoria-18
88Peoria/Ko-32
89Peoria/Ko-18

Williams, Edwin D.
(Dib)
33G-82
35G-1B
35G-2B
35G-6B
35G-7B
V354-36

Williams, Eric
88Geneva/ProC-1635
89CharWh/Best-2
89CharWh/ProC-1756

Williams, Flavio
88Watertn/Pucko-29
89Augusta/ProC-505
89Welland/Pucko-29
90Salem/Star-24

Williams, Frank
84F/X-U127
84T/Tr-128T
85D-323
85F-624
85Mother/Giants-12
85OPC-254
85T-487
85T/St-169
86F-554
86Phoenix-24
86T-341
87F-287
87F/Up-U127
87Kahn-47
87T-96
87T/Tr-128T
88D-512
88F-250
88Kahn/Reds-47
88S-317
88T-773
89B-100
89D-478
89D/Best-259

89F-174
89F/Up-34
89Mara/Tigers-36
89S-485
89T-172
89T/Tr-128T
89UD-449
90D-327
90F-620
90OPC-599
90Publlnt/St-486
90S-341
90T-599
90UD-539
Williams, Fred
(Cy)
21Exh-186
25Exh-48
28Exh-24
28Yueng-52
29Exh/4-12
91Conlon/Sport-154
D327
D328-191
D329-190
D350/2-191
E120
E121/80
E122
E126-42
E135-191
E210-52
M101/4-190
M101/5-191
V100
V61-118
W501-100
W502-52
W517-18
W572
W573
W575
Williams, Fred
86Stockton-26
87Stockton-26
88ElPaso/Best-19
88TexLgAS/GS-25
89Jaxvl/Best-18
89Jaxvl/ProC-172
90WPalmB/Star-27
Williams, Gary
77Jaxvl
Williams, George
63T-324R
64T-388R
Williams, George
91SoOreg/ClBest-5
91SoOreg/ProC-3851
Williams, Gerald
87Oneonta-6
88PrWill/Star-25
89PrWill/Star-25
90FtLaud/Star-22
91Albany/ProC-1022
91B-161
91Classic/III-99
91F/Ultra-388MLP
91Single/ClBest-127
91UD/FinalEd-15F
92D/II-697
92T-656M
Williams, Glenn
77Ashvl
Williams, Greg
88StCath/ProC-2019
Williams, H
86Nashua-28tr
Williams, Harold
80Ander-25
81Durham-8
87Salem-15
88EastLAS/ProC-46
88Harris/ProC-861
89Harris/ProC-302
Williams, Jaime
88OrlanTw/Best-10
89Orlan/Best-2
89Orlan/ProC-1354
Williams, James
76Laugh/Clown-17
76Laugh/Clown-29
76Laugh/Clown-3
76Laugh/Clown-39
Williams, James A.
70OPC-262R
70T-262R
71OPC-262R
71T-262R
Williams, James A.
N172
Williams, James F.
(Jimy)
66T-544R
75Phoenix-19
77SLCity
79SLCity-22
84Tor/Fire-34CO
85Tor/Fire-34CO
86Tor/Fire-34MG
87OPC-279MG
87T-786MG
87Tor/Fire-36MG
88OPC-314MG
88T-314MG
88Tor/Fire-3MG
89OPC-381MG
89T-594MG
89Tor/Fire-3
Williams, James T.
E107
T206
Williams, James
82DayBe-19
83DayBe-16
84Cram/PCL-58
86Osceola-29
87Visalia-1
88CalLgAS-40
88Visalia/Cal-163
Williams, Jamie
90WichSt-36
Williams, Jay
88Stockton/Cal-203TR
88Stockton/ProC-744TR
89Rockford/Team-31TR
90Jaxvl/Best-28TR
Williams, Jeff
81Miami-19
84CharlO-20
86RochR-26
89Reading/Best-23
89Reading/ProC-675
89Reading/Star-25
90WichSt-37
91Freder/ClBest-9
91Freder/ProC-2364
91Single/ClBest-164
Williams, Jerome
88Wythe/ProC-2002
90Peoria/Team-18
91Single/ClBest-75
91WinSalem/ClBest-27
91WinSalem/ProC-2844
Williams, Jimmy
87French-40CO
88AlaskaAS60/Team-2
90Portl/CMC-10
90Portl/ProC-179
91Phoenix/LineD-396
91Phoenix/ProC-68
Williams, Jody
87Watertn-19
Williams, Joe
90Boise/ProC-3323
Williams, John
86BurlEx-27
Williams, Juan
90Pulaski/Best-25
90Pulaski/ProC-3111
91Macon/ClBest-27
91Macon/ProC-880
Williams, Ken
83AppFx/LF-14
86BuffB-24
87D/Rook-11
87F/Up-U128
87Fayette-25
87Hawaii-2
87Sf/Rook-41
88Coke/WS-30
88D-334
88D/Best-249
88F-412
88F/Mini-17
88F/SS-42
88GlenF/ProC-918
88OPC-92
88Panini/St-65
88S-112
88S/YS/I-6
88Sf-69
88T-559
88T/St-287
89D-337
89D/Tr-17
89Mara/Tigers-25
89S-67
89T-34
89T/Tr-129T
89Toledo/CMC-9
89Toledo/ProC-763
89UD-506
89UD/Ext-714
90CokeK/Tiger-27
90London/ProC-1270
90OPC-327
90Publlnt/St-487
90T-327
90UD-249
91F-190
91Miami/ClBest-13
91Miami/ProC-409
91OPC-274
91T-274
91Tor/Fire-13
91UD-89
92Conlon/Sport-442
92S/I-354
Williams, Kenneth Roy
21Exh-187
25Exh-119
26Exh-119
27Exh-58
E120
E126-48
E220
V100
V61-52
W515-26
W572
W573
Williams, Kerman
85Elmira-24
86Elmira-29
Williams, Kevin
82Orlan-1
83Orlan-4
88Modesto/Cal-59
Williams, Landon
90Penin/Star-24
Williams, Leroy
90Kissim/DIMD-28
Williams, Mark
77SanJose-6
Williams, Mark
91S-498
Williams, Marvin
86Negro/Frit-87
Williams, Matt E.
82Knoxvl-8
83Syrac-13
84Syrac-11
85Syrac-12
86OKCty-26
Williams, Matt
86Cram/PCL-3
87D/Rook-45
87F/Up-U129
87Mother/SFG-22
87Phoenix-2
87Pocatel/Bon-12
87Sf/Rook-25
87T/Tr-129T
88Classic/Blue-246
88D-628
88F-101
88Phoenix/CMC-18
88Phoenix/ProC-56
88S-118
88S/YS/I-18
88S/YS/II-31
88T-372
89AAA/CMC-35
89AAA/ProC-51
89D-594
89F-346
89Mother/Giants-12
89Panini/St-218
89Phoenix/CMC-18
89Phoenix/ProC-1485
89S-612
89T-628
89UD-247
90B-238
90Classic-73
90Classic/Up-11
90D-348
90D/BestNL-61
90D/GSlam-1
90F-75
90Leaf/I-94
90Mother/Giant-9
90Mother/MWilliam-Set
90OPC-41
90Panini/St-366
90S-503
90S/McDon-6
90Sf-70
90T-41
90T/Big-96
90T/St-88
90UD-577
90USPlayC/AS-8H
90Woolwth/HL-30
91B-378SLUG
91B-618
91Classic/200-158
91Classic/I-8
91Classic/III-95
91CollAB-30
91D-18DK
91D-685
91D/Elite-E8
91D/GSlam-8
91D/SuperDK-18DK
91F-276
91F/ASIns-3
91F/Ultra-331
91KingB/Discs-16
91Leaf/I-93
91Leaf/Stud-259
91MajorLg/Pins-65
91Mother/Giant-9
91OPC-190
91OPC-399AS
91Panini/FrSt-69
91Panini/St-76
91Panini/Top15-17
91PG&E-11
91RedFoley/St-100
91S-189
91S-667AS
91S-689MB
91S/100SS-77
91Seven/3DCoin-15NC
91SFExam/Giant-16
91Sunflower-24
91T-190
91T-399AS
91T/CJMini/II-9
91T/StClub/I-295
91T/SU-35
91UD-157
91UD-79
91UD/SilSlug-SS13
92D/I-135
92F-650
92S/100SS-95
92S/I-230
92T-445
92UD-154
Williams, Matthew
87Idaho-19
88Idaho/ProC-1842
89Salinas/Cal-140
89Salinas/ProC-1825
Williams, Mel
83Reading-22
Williams, Mike
76Watlo
77LodiD
79Albuq-3
80Phoenix-1
81Phoenix-8
Williams, Mike
87Pocatel/Bon-19
89Pac/SenLg-16
90Batavia/ProC-3067
91Clearw/ClBest-12
91Clearw/ProC-1623
91Single/ClBest-103
Williams, Mitch
86D/Rook-19
86F/Up-U127
86Rang-28
86Sf/Rook-20
86T/Tr-125T
87D-347
87F-142
87Mother/Rang-17
87Smok/R-7
87T-291
87ToysRUs-32
88D-161
88D/Best-279
88F-482
88F/RecSet-43
88Mother/R-17
88OPC-26
88S-339
88Smok/R-19
88T-26
89B-283
89D-225
89D/Best-60
89D/Tr-38
89F-536
89F/Up-81
89Mara/Cubs-28
89OPC-377
89S-301
89S/Tr-32
89S/YS/I-27
89Sf-151
89T-411
89T/St-247
89T/Tr-130T
89UD-95
89UD/Ext-778
90B-25
90Classic-23
90Cub/Mara-24
90D-275
90D/BestNL-75
90F-48
90F-631M
90F/AwardWin-43
90F/BB-43
90F/BBMVP-43
90Leaf/I-156
90MLBPA/Pins-48
90OPC-520
90Panini/St-232
90Publlnt/St-210
90RedFoley/St-103
90S-262
90S-695DT
90S/100St-93
90Sf-196
90T-520
90T/Big-109
90T/DH-71
90T/Gloss60-47
90T/Mini-52
90T/St-48
90T/TVAS-65
90T/TVCub-17
90UD-174
91D-312
91F-439
91F/Ultra-71
91F/UltraUp-U101
91F/Up-U110
91Leaf/II-420
91OPC-335
91RedFoley/St-101
91S-220
91S/RookTr-27T
91T-335
91T/StClub/I-261
91T/Tr-127T
91UD-173
91UD/Ext-769
92D/I-353
92F-547
92S/I-356
92S/II-892DT
92T-633
92UD-410
Williams, Paul Jr.
86Elmira-30
88WinHaven/Star-27
90CLAS/CL-11
90LynchRS/Team-13
91Wmsprt/LineD-647
91Wmsprt/ProC-303
Williams, Quinn

86Cram/PCL-131
Williams, Ray R.
78StPete
79ArkTr-3
80ArkTr-20
Williams, Ray
88Wausau/GS-13
90SanBern/Best-22
90SanBern/Cal-112
Williams, Reggie
83VeroB-25
86Albuq-28
86D/Rook-5
86F/Up-U128
86Pol/Dodg-51
86Sf/Rook-19
87D-341
87F-460
87F/Hottest-42
87F/Mini-114
87F/St-124
87Mother/Dodg-15
87Pol/Dodg-9
87T-232
88ColoSp/CMC-23
88ColoSp/ProC-1524
89BuffB/CMC-23
89BuffB/ProC-1685
89Clinton/ProC-893
90Target-862
Williams, Rick
73Cedar
78Charl
78Memphis/Team-10
79T-437
80Memphis-26
80T-69
80Tucson-4
81Toledo-10
82Toledo-9
Williams, Rob
85Utica-8
87WPalmB-6
Williams, Robert E.
T207
Williams, Roger
87Pittsfld-21
88Iowa/CMC-11
88Iowa/ProC-545
89Iowa/ProC-1691
Williams, Scott
85Newar-1
Williams, Slim
88Visalia/ProC-96
Williams, Smokey Joe
74Laugh/Black-1
86Negro/Frit-86
88Conlon/NegAS-12
88Negro/Duques-8
90Negro/Star-27
Williams, Stan
59T-53
60BB-16
60L-109
60T-278
61BB-40
61P-162
61T-190
61T-45LL
61T/St-36
62BB-40
62J-115
62P-115
62P/Can-115
62T-515
62T-60LL
63J-122
63P-122
63T-42
64T-505
65T-404
68OPC-54
68T-54
69OPC-118
69T-118
69T/St-170
70OPC-353
70T-353
71MLB/St-478
71OPC-638
71T-638
72OPC-9
72T-9
79Colum-6
89Smok/Dodg-68
90Kahn/Reds-27M
90Target-863
91Kahn/Reds-x
WG9-25
Williams, Steve
75Shrev/TCMA-23
86Clearw-25
87Reading-24
89Erie/Star-26
Williams, Ted
39Exh
39PB-92
40PB-27
41DP-57
41DP-81
41PB-14
43MP-24
47HomogBond-48
48L-76
48Swell-16
50B-98
51B-165
51Wheat
52BR
52RM-AL23
52StarCal/L-71B
52StarCal/L-71C
52Wheat
53Exh/Can-30
54B-66A
54T-1
54T-250
54Wilson
55T-2
55T/DH-69
56T-5
56T/Hocus-A5
56T/Hocus-B7
56T/Pin-26
57T-1
58T-1
58T-321M
58T-485AS
59F/Set
60F-72
60NuCard-39
60NuCard-52
61F-152
61NuCard-439
61NuCard-452
69T-539M
69T-650MG
70OPC-211MG
70T-211MG
71OPC-380MG
71T-380MG
72OPC-510MG
72T-510MG
74Laugh/ASG-46
76Laugh/Jub-27
76OPC-347AS
76T-347AS
78TCMA-260
79TCMA-10
80Pac/Leg-61
80Laugh/3/4/5-20
80Laugh/3/4/5-6
80SSPC/HOF
82F/St-237M
83D/HOF-9
83Kaline-68M
83MLBPA/Pin-18
84D/Champs-14
84West/1-20
85CircK-9
85D/HOF-2
85Woolwth-38
86BLChew-8
86Sf/Dec-25
87Leaf/SpecOlym-H5
87Nestle/DT-18
88Pac/Leg-50
89B/I-11
89HOF/St-28
89Nissen-20
89Pac/Leg-154
89Swell-100
90BBWit-50
90HOF/St-40
90Pac/Legend-59
90Swell/Great-125
91Swell/Great-100
91T/Arc53-319
D305
PM10/L-41
PM10/Sm-195
PM10/Sm-196
PM10/Sm-197
PM10/Sm-198
PM10/Sm-199
PM10/Sm-200
R302-101
R303/A
R346-44
R423-113
Williams, Teddy
86Cram/PCL-123
87Idaho-10
87Wausau-12
88CalLgAS-28
88SanBern/Best-4
88SanBern/Cal-38
88Sumter/ProC-419
89BurlB/ProC-1622
89BurlB/Star-25
89EastLDD/ProC-DD36
89Wmsprt/ProC-636
89Wmsprt/Star-22
90CollAB-23
90Foil/Best-138
90Wmsprt/Best-22
90Wmsprt/ProC-1071
90Wmsprt/Star-23
91Jaxvl/LineD-348
91Jaxvl/ProC-164
Williams, Tim
84Greens-14
88CapeCod/Sum-143
89Alaska/Team-14
Williams, Tom
88CapeCod/Sum-118
Williams, Troy
86Cram/PCL-118
87Wausau-6
Williams, Walter E.
(Walt)
66Pep/Tul
67T-598R
68OPC-172
68T-172
69T-309
70MLB/St-191
70OPC-395
70T-395
70T/CB
71OPC-555
71T-555
71T/Coins-36
72MB-363
72OPC-15
72T-15
73OPC-297
73T-297
74OPC-418
74T-418
76OPC-123
76SSPC-436
76T-123
87Sumter-4
88Durham/Star-24
89Pac/SenLg-123
89T/SenLg-126
89TM/SenLg-116
89Tulsa/GS-2CO
89Tulsa/Team-26CO
90EliteSenLg-120
90Tulsa/ProC-1173CO
91CharlR/ClBest-29CO
Williams, William
(Billy)
89Canton/Best-8
89Canton/ProC-1317
Williams, Willie D.
82Danvl-18
Williams, Woody
47Signal
90Target-864
Williams, Woody
89Dunedin/Star-23
90Foil/Best-210
90Knoxvl/Best-18
90Knoxvl/ProC-1239
90Knoxvl/Star-20
91Knoxvl/LineD-372
91Knoxvl/ProC-1768
Williamson, Bret
87Tampa-13
Williamson, Edward
N172
N284
WG1-18
Williamson, Greg
86Watlo-31
Williamson, Kevin
87Modesto-16
Williamson, Mark
83Beaum-8
85Beaum-3
86LasVegas-23
87D/Rook-3
87French-32
88D-418
88F-574
88SanDiegoSt-18
88T-571
89F-626
89French-32
89S-592
89T-546
89T/Big-147
90B-248
90D-406
90F-194
90Leaf/II-461
90OPC-13
90PublInt/St-591
90S-332
90T-13
90T/St-236
90UD-173
91B-85
91Crown/Orio-488
91D-238
91F-495
91Leaf/I-21
91OPC-296
91T-296
91T/StClub/I-20
91UD-510
92D/II-511
92F-30
92S/I-427NH
92S/II-487
92T-628
92UD-609
Williamson, Mike
77Ashvl
Williamson, Ray
87Watlo-22
88Kinston/Star-24
Willis, Alan
82Watlo-11
Willis, C.H.
N172
Willis, Carl
84Evansvl-22
87F-218
87Nashvl-23
87T-101
88Vanco/CMC-4
88Vanco/ProC-762
89Edmon/CMC-3
89Edmon/ProC-567
90ColoSp/CMC-8
90ColoSp/ProC-38
91Portl/LineD-423
91Portl/ProC-1567
92D/II-665
92S/II-482
Willis, James
54T-67
Willis, Jim
87AppFx-30
Willis, Kent
87Tampa-17
88Rockford-34
88Virgini/Star-22
89Rockford-34
Willis, Marty
89Lakeland/Star-25
90Lakeland/Star-25
91London/LineD-398
91London/ProC-1879
91Single/ClBest-6
Willis, Mike
75IntAS/TCMA-18
75IntAS/TCMA-28
76SSPC-382
77OPC-103
77T-493R
78OPC-227
78T-293
79OPC-366
79T-688
80Syrac-7
81F-426
81OPC-324
81T-324
82OkCty-1
87Maine/TCMA-25
Willis, Ron
67T-592R
68OPC-68
68T-68
69T-273
Willis, Scott
87Cedar-3
Willis, Steve
87Anchora-31
90Wausau/Best-2
90Wausau/ProC-2115
90Wausau/Star-26
91Freder/ClBest-10
Willis, Travis
89Geneva/ProC-1867
90Peoria/Team-29
91CLAS/ProC-CAR46
91WinSalem/ClBest-11
91WinSalem/ProC-2830
Willis, Vic
E104
E107
E90/1
E91
E95
M116
T206
WG3-52
Willoughby, Claude
R316
Willoughby, Jim
73OPC-79
73T-79
74OPC-553
74T-553
76OPC-102
76SSPC-419
76T-102
77T-532
78T-373
79T-266
89Pac/SenLg-37
89T/SenLg-70
91Pac/SenLg-88
Willoughby, Mark
86Columbia-27A
86Columbia-27B
89Pittsfld/Star-23
Wills, Adrian Charles
87Greenvl/Best-8
Wills, Bump
77T-494R
78BK/R-12
78Ho-21
78OPC-208
78T-23
79OPC-190
79T-369
80OPC-373
80T-473
81D-25
81F-628
81OPC-173
81T-173
81T/HT
81T/St-134
82D-289
82F-334
82F/St-175
82OPC-272
82RedLob
82T-272
82T/St-244
82T/Tr-129T
83D-351
83F-511
83T-643
88Butte-29
89Butte/SP-24
91Gaston/ClBest-17
91Gaston/ProC-2704MG

Wills, Frank
82Omaha-10
84Omaha-5
85Cram/PCL-85
86F-480
86Maine-24
86T-419
87BuffB-23
87Gator-22
87T-551
88Syrac/CMC-11
88Syrac/ProC-830
89Syrac/CMC-5
89Syrac/ProC-794
89Syrac/Team-24
89Tor/Fire-44
90F-98
90T/Tr-129T
90Tor/BlueJ-44
91D-691
91F-191
91OPC-213
91S-521
91S/ToroBJ-10
91T-213
91Tor/Fire-44
Wills, Maury
60BB-20
61BB-30
61Morrell
61P-164
62BB-30
62J-104
62P-104
62P/Can-104
62Salada-127A
62Salada-127B
62Shirriff-127
63Exh
63F-43
63J-115
63P-115
63Salada-20
67T-570
68Bz-1
68Bz-4
68KDKA-30
68OPC-175
68T-175
69MB-293
69MLB/St-162
69OPC-45
69OPC/DE-23
69T-45
69T/DE-24
69T/decal
69T/S-49
69T/St-60
70MLB/St-60
70T-595
71Bz/Test-34
71MLB/St-120
71OPC-385
71T-385
71T/GM-29
71T/tatt-14
71Ticket/Dodg-19
72MB-364
72OPC-437
72OPC-438IA
72T-437
72T-438IA
74Greyhound-6M
75OPC-200MV
75T-200MV
75T/M-200MV
77T-435M
78TCMA-70
81F-595MG
81Pol/Mar-14MG
81T-672MG
82KMart-2
83MLBPA/Pin-36
85Woolwth-39
87Smok/Dodg-38
87T-315TBC
88Smok/Dodg-7
89Smok/Dodg-69
90HOF/St-66
90MSA/AGFA-12
90Target-865
Exh47
Wills, Ted
60L-56
61T-548
62T-444
65T-488
78TCMA-138
Willsher, Chris
84CharlO-11
Willson, Rob
87Everett-22
Wilmet, Paul
82Lynch-10
85Spring-30
87ArkTr-10
88EastLAS/ProC-18
88Harris/ProC-852
89OkCty/CMC-9
89OkCty/ProC-1509
90Iowa/CMC-10
90Iowa/ProC-319
90SpringDG/Best-16
90T/89Debut-145
Wilmont, Walter
N172
WG1-72
Wilner, Eric
85Anchora-34
Wilson, A. Parke
N566/2
Wilson, Alan
84LitFalls-20
87CharWh-4
Wilson, Archie C.
52B-210
52T-327
Wilson, Arthur Earl
10Domino-126
15CJ-148
16FleischBrd-101
D328-192
D329-191
D350/2-192
E135-192
E254
M101/4-191
M101/5-192
T207
Wilson, Arthur L.
(Artie)
49Remar
50Remar
52Mother-40
Wilson, Barney
75Cedar
76Cedar
Wilson, Brad
89Bristol/Star-28
90Bristol/ProC-3172
90Bristol/Star-25
91Fayette/ClBest-10
91Fayette/ProC-1175
91Lakeland/ProC-270
Wilson, Brandon
90SoBend/ClBest-7
91MidwLAS/ProC-MWL13
91Single/ClBest-157
91SoBend/ProC-2867
Wilson, Bryan
91Peoria/ClBest-15
91WinSalem/ClBest-22
91WinSalem/ProC-2839
Wilson, Bubba
77Watlo
Wilson, Charles
R314/Can
Wilson, Chaun
88Hagers/Star-24
Wilson, Craig
85Spring-12
87Elmira/Black-18
87Elmira/Red-18
87StPete-2
88Louisvl-50
88Louisvl/CMC-15
88Louisvl/ProC-439
88Lynch/Star-26
89ArkTr/GS-25
89Louisvl-36
89Lynch/Star-22
90Louisvl/CMC-15
90Louisvl/ProC-413
90NewBrit/Best-8
90NewBrit/Star-23
90SpringDG/Best-2
90T/89Debut-146
90T/TVCard-66
91D-544
91F-652
91F/Ultra-298
91Leaf/I-95
91LynchRS/ClBest-13
91LynchRS/ProC-1203
91OPC-566
91Pol/Card-12
91S/100RisSt-97
91T-566
91T/StClub/II-566
91T/Tr-128TUSA
91UD-390
92D/II-744
92S/II-557
92T-646
Wilson, Daniel
88CapeCod/Sum-177
90Classic/DP-7
90Foil/Best-232
91B-687
91CharWh/ClBest-14
91CharWh/ProC-2891
91OPC-767FDP
91S-681FDP
91Single/ClBest-353
91T-767FDP
91T/StClub/II-587
91UD/FinalEd-6F
92D/II-399RR
92UD-72TP
Wilson, Dave
81Clinton-21
Wilson, David
89NiagFls/Pucko-24
90Ashvl/ClBest-11
90AubAs/Best-4
90AubAs/ProC-3404
91Ashvl/ProC-569
91Single/ClBest-274
Wilson, Don
68Bz-13
68OPC-77
68T-77
69MLB/St-143
69OPC-202
69T-202
69T/St-39
69Trans-37
70K-62
70MLB/St-47
70OPC-515
70T-515
71MLB/St-95
71OPC-484
71T-484
71T/Coins-41
72K-51
72MB-365
72OPC-20
72OPC-91LL
72T-20
72T-91LL
73OPC-217
73T-217
74OPC-304
74T-304
75OPC-455
75T-455
75T/M-455
86Mother/Ast-10
Wilson, Doyle
87Kinston-20
88Wmsprt/ProC-1324
Wilson, Earl
60T-249
61T-69
63J-83
63P-83
63T-76
64T-503
65OPC-42
65T-42
66T-575
67T-235LL
67T-237
67T-305
68Kahn
68OPC-10LL
68OPC-160
68T-10LL
68T-160
69MB-294
69T-525
70MLB/St-216
70OPC-95
70T-95
71OPC-301
71T-301
72MB-366
78TCMA-148
81Detroit-51
88Domino-26
91Swell/Great-120
Wilson, Eddie
90Target-1095
Wilson, Eric
86Penin-27
Wilson, Gary
76Dubuq
79Charl-18
80Tucson-5
Wilson, Gary D.
88Batavia/ProC-1688
89Spartan/ProC-1036
89Spartan/Star-24
90Foil/Best-158
90Reading/Best-11
90Reading/ProC-1221
90Reading/Star-24
91ScranWB/LineD-498
91ScranWB/ProC-2539
Wilson, George
79TCMA-189
Wilson, Glenn
81BirmB
83D-580
83F-350
83T-332
83T/St-318
84D-618
84F-94
84F/X-U128
84Nes/792-563
84OPC-36
84Phill/TastyK-40
84T-563
84T/St-270
84T/Tr-129T
85CIGNA-9
85D-609
85F-268
85OPC-189
85Phill/TastyK-12M
85Phill/TastyK-40
85T-454
86BK/AP-7
86CIGNA-16
86D-285
86D/AAS-29
86F-457
86F/Mini-95
86F/St-128
86Keller-6
86Leaf-160
86OPC-318
86Phill/TastyK-12
86T-736
86T/Mini-56
86T/St-118
87D-62
87D/OD-158
87F-192
87F/Mini-115
87Leaf-146
87OPC-97
87Phill/TastyK-12
87Sf-166
87T-97
87T/St-117
88D-262
88D/Best-306
88F-320
88Mother/Sea-12
88OPC-359
88Panini/St-364
88RedFoley/St-103
88S-405
88Sf-204
88T-626
88T/Big-260
88T/St-124
88T/Tr-129T
89B-423
89D-447
89D/Best-241
89F-224
89S-106
89Sf-12
89T-293
89T/Big-284
89VFJuice-11
90BirmDG/Best-31
90D-472
90F-240
90Leaf/II-268
90Lennox-26
90Mother/Ast-22
90OPC-112
90PubIInt/St-168
90RedFoley/St-104
90S-346
90T-112
90T/Big-320
90UD-410
91D-156
91F-519
91OPC-476
91Panini/FrSt-11
91Richm/LineD-447
91Richm/ProC-2582
91S-298
91T-476
91UD-515
Wilson, Jack
86Phoenix-25
Wilson, Jeff
83Wisco/LF-4
86Tampa-26
Wilson, Jim A.
52T-276
53B/Col-37
53JC-12
53SpicSpan/3x5-27
53T-208
54B-16
54JC-19
55B-253
55Gol/Braves-31
55JC-19
55SpicSpan/DC-18
56T-171
57T-330
58T-163
79TCMA-130
91T/Arc53-208
Wilson, Jim
81Bristol-6
83BuffB-14
83Pawtu-18
85IntLgAS-25
85Maine-24
86Maine-25
88EastLAS/ProC-38
88SanDiegoSt-19
88Vermont/ProC-944
89AAA/CMC-39
89AAA/ProC-32
89Calgary/CMC-22
89Calgary/ProC-536
91Crown/Orio-489
91Phoenix/LineD-397
91Phoenix/ProC-77
Wilson, Jimmy
28Exh-32
29Exh/4-15
31Exh/4-15
33G-37
34DS-22
34Exh/4-6
34Ward's/Pin-8
35BU-38
35Exh/4-6
35G-1E
35G-3C
35G-5C
35G-6C
36Exh/4-6
36Wheat
40PB-152
61F-88
91Conlon/Sport-223
R310
R332-30
R337-422
V353-37
V355-99
W711/2
Wilson, John F.
35BU-73
39PB-29

40PB-31
41PB-29
Wilson, John Owen
(Chief)
10Domino-125
11Helmar-138
11Helmar-166
12Sweet/Pin-122A
12Sweet/Pin-122B
12Sweet/Pin-144
14CJ-13
14Piedmont/St-63
15CJ-13
85Woolwth-41
90HOF/St-18
91Conlon/Sport-267
D322
D329-192
D350/2-193
E104
E220
E224
E91
M101/4-192
M101/5-193
M116
S74-116
T202
T205
T206
T207
T213/blue
T213/brown
T215/brown
Wilson, Johnny
85Lynch-24
86Jacks/TCMA-22
Wilson, Jud
74Laugh/Black-12
90Negro/Star-34
Wilson, Lewis R.
(Hack)
28Exh-12
28Yueng-25
29Exh/4-5
30CEA/Pin-10
31Exh/4-5
33DH-43
33G-211
35BU-73
60F-48
61F-87
72F/FFeat-9
72Laugh/GF-27
79T-412LL
80Pac/Leg-97
80Laugh/FFeat-4
80SSPC/HOF
85Woolwth-40
86Conlon/1-56
89Smok/Dodg-36
90BBWit-93
90HOF/St-29
90Target-866
91Conlon/Sport-29
92Conlon/Sport-424
92Conlon/Sport-585
E210-25
R306
R315-A39
R315-B39
R316
R332-14
W502-25
W513-74
W517-42
Wilson, Mark
89Hamil/Star-26
Wilson, Matt
89GreatF-32
90VeroB/Star-31TR
91AS/Cal-25
Wilson, Michael
83Toledo-18
87Idaho-1
Wilson, Mike
77Clinton
80Albuq-15
Wilson, Mookie
79Tidew-7
80Tidew-17
81D-575
81T-259R
82D-175
82F-542
82F/St-86
82OPC-143
82T-143
83D-56
83D/AAS-32
83Drake-29
83F-560
83OPC-55
83T-55
83T-621TL
83T/Gloss40-2
83T/St-266
84D-190
84Drake-31
84F-603
84F/St-91
85FunFood/Pin-65
84Jacks/Smok-13
84Nes/792-246TL
84Nes/792-465
84OPC-270
84T-246TL
84T-465
84T/Mets/Fan-8
84T/St-108
85D-482
85F-95
85Leaf-122
85OPC-11
85Pol/MetYank-M4
85T-775
85T/St-102
86D-604
86F-97
86Leaf-232
86OPC-315
86T-126M
86T-315
87D-487
87D/OD-129
87F-25
87F/Hottest-43
87Leaf-176
87OPC-84
87T-625
87T/Mets/Fan-8
88D-652
88D/Best-208
88D/Mets/Bk-652
88F-154
88Kahn/Mets-1
88Leaf-249
88Panini/St-348
88S-474
88T-255
88T/Big-182
89B-386
89D-152
89F-52
89Kahn/Mets-1
89OPC-144
89Panini/St-141
89S-302
89S/Tr-16
89T-545
89T/Big-231
89T/DHTest-13
89UD-199
90B-516
90D-442
90D/BestAL-28
90F-99
90Leaf/I-263
90OPC-182
90Panini/St-174
90PublInt/St-147
90S-448
90Sf-128
90T-182
90T/Big-179
90Tor/BlueJ-3
90UD-481
91D-585
91F-192
91F/Ultra-372
91Leaf/Stud-140
91OPC-727
91Panini/FrSt-341
91S-42
91S/ToroBJ-24
91T-727
91T/StClub/I-99
91Tor/Fire-3
91UD-512
91WIZMets-433
92F-347
92S/II-458
92T-436
92UD-391
Wilson, Nigel
88StCath/ProC-2017
89StCath/ProC-2081
90Myrtle/ProC-2791
91Dunedin/ClBest-24
91Dunedin/ProC-222
91FSLAS/ProC-FSL10
Wilson, Parker
80Elmira-30
Wilson, Phil
82Watlo/B-13
82Watlo/C-7
83Watlo/LF-14
85Visalia-1
86Orlan-24
87Portl-9
88Portl/CMC-23
88Portl/ProC-661
89Jaxvl/ProC-171
Wilson, Randy
84Newar-22
Wilson, Ric
82Wausau-27
84Chatt-22
87Wausau-27
Wilson, Rick
85Everett/II/Cram-23
Wilson, Robert
(Red)
53T-250
54T-58
56T-92
57T-19
58T-213
59T-24
60T-379
61P-66
79TCMA-281
90Target-867
91T/Arc53-250
Wilson, Roger
86Miami-28
87Wmsprt-21
Wilson, Sam W.
V100
Wilson, Scott
89AS/Cal-51TR
89SanJose/Best-17TR
89SanJose/Cal-234
89SanJose/ProC-454
90SanJose/Best-27
90SanJose/Cal-55TR
90SanJose/Star-30TR
91AS/Cal-49
91SanJose/ClBest-30TR
Wilson, Steve
86Tulsa-10
87PortChar-10
88TexLgAS/GS-5
88Tulsa-8
89B-280
89D/Best-250
89D/Rook-10
89F-640R
89F/Up-U82
89Mara/Cubs-44
89T/Tr-131T
89UD/Ext-799
90B-23
90Cub/Mara-25
90D-394
90F-49
90Leaf/II-420
90OPC-741
90S-531
90S/YS/II-28
90T-741
90T/JumboR-32
90T/TVCub-18
90TulsaDG/Best-9
90UD-341
91D-519
91F-440
91Iowa/LineD-222
91Iowa/ProC-1062
91OPC-69
91S-306
91T-69
91UD-493
92D/II-710
92S/II-812
92T-751
Wilson, Tack
81Albuq/TCMA-23A
82Albuq-23
84Toledo-22
85Cram/PCL-195
87Edmon-10
89OkCty/CMC-22
89OkCty/ProC-1534
90Huntsvl/Best-23
91Pac/SenLg-50
Wilson, Terry
89Myrtle/ProC-1474
Wilson, Tex
90Target-1096
Wilson, Tim
89Helena/SP-5
Wilson, Todd
86Cram/PCL-181
90Billings/ProC-3232
91Cedar/ClBest-21
91Cedar/ProC-2730
Wilson, Tom
86Tampa-27
90Pittsfld/Pucko-17
91Oneonta/ProC-4158
Wilson, Trevor
85Everett/II/Cram-24
86Clinton-28
87Clinton-27
88BBAmer-27
88Shrev/ProC-1298
89F-347
89Phoenix/CMC-10
89Phoenix/ProC-1481
89S/HotRook-31
89T-783
89UD/Ext-733
90D-414
90F/Up-U64
90Leaf/II-489
90OPC-408
90Phoenix/CMC-8
90Phoenix/ProC-12
90T-408
90UD-637
91B-630
91D-263
91F-277
91F/UltraUp-U119
91Mother/Giant-22
91OPC-96
91PG&E-9
91S-657
91T-96
91T/StClub/I-212
91UD-653
92D/II-575
92F-651
92S/II-608
92T-204
92UD-337
Wilson, W.H.
(Chauff)
76Laugh/Clown-36
Wilson, Ward
76Clinton
Wilson, Wayne
84Newar-6
85Newar-11
86Hagers-28
87Hagers-16
Wilson, William D.
54T-222
55Rodeo
55T-86
55T/DH-101
Wilson, William H.
67T-402R
69T-576R
70OPC-28
70T-28
71MLB/St-192
71OPC-192
71T-192
72T-587
73OPC-619
73T-619
Wilson, Willie J.
75Watlo
79T-409
80BK/PHR-33
80OPC-87DP
80T-157
81Coke
81D-223
81F-29
81F/St-106
81K-24
81OPC-360
81PermaGr/CC-31
81Pol/Royals-10
81T-208RB
81T-360
81T/So-20
81T/St-16
81T/St-247
81T/St-81
82D-448
82F-427
82F/St-207
82K-62
82OPC-230
82T-230
82T/St-189
83D-112
83D-15DK
83D/AAS-13
83Drake-30
83F-128
83K-23
83OPC-16
83PermaGr/CC-33
83Pol/Royals-10
83T-471LL
83T-701LL
83T-710
83T/Gloss40-23
83T/St-15
83T/St-161
83T/St-73
84D-175
84F-364
84F/St-94
85FunFood/Pin-82
84Nes/792-525
84OPC-5
84T-525
84T/St-280
84T/St/Box-5
85D-297
85F-218
85Leaf-110
85OPC-6
85T-617
85T/St-277
85ThomMc/Discs-22
85Woolwth-42
86D-175
86F-25
86F/Mini-5
86F/St-129
86Kitty/Disc-15
86Leaf-106
86NatPhoto-6
86OPC-25
86Sf-124
86Sf-128M
86Sf-144M
86Sf-180M
86Sf-186M
86T-25
86T/Mini-22
86T/St-258
86T/Super-59
86Woolwth-32
87D-96
87D/OD-208
87F-384
87F/Excit-43
87F/Mini-116
87F/RecSet-42
87F/St-125
87Leaf-97
87OPC-367
87Sf-85
87T-783
87T/Mini-58
87T/St-261
88D-255
88D/Best-263
88F-274

88Leaf-189
88OPC-222
88Panini/St-113
88S-102
88Sf-192
88Smok/Royals-3
88T-452
88T/Big-21
88T/Mini-17
88T/Revco-25
88T/St-263
89B-124
89D-120
89F-298
89KMart/Lead-17
89OPC-168
89Panini/St-361
89S-28
89Sf-186
89T-168
89T/Big-136
89T/Mini-56
89T/St-268
89Tastee/Discs-5
89UD-244
90D-440
90F-123
90KayBee-31
90Leaf/II-336
90MLBPA/Pins-109
90OPC-323
90Pac/Legend-109
90Publint/St-361
90S-104
90T-323
90T/Big-45
90UD-349
91B-230
91F-575
91F/UltraUp-U48
91Leaf/II-299
91Mother/A's-17
91OPC-208
91OPC/Premier-129
91S/RookTr-15T
91T-208
91T/StClub/II-378
91T/Tr-129T
91UD-609
92S/I-328
92T-536
92UD-238

Wilstead, Randon
(Randy)
90James/Pucko-6
91MidwLAS/ProC-MWL50
91Rockford/ClBest-22
91Rockford/ProC-2057

Wiltbank, Ben
78Salem
79Portl-4
79T-723R
81Buffa-5

Wiltse, George R.
(Hooks)
10Domino-127
11Helmar-139
12Sweet/Pin-123
14Piedmont/St-64
92Conlon/Sport-332
D303
E106
E107
E254
E90/1
E93
E95
M116
S74-96
T201
T202
T205
T206
T207
T215/blue
T215/brown
T216
W555

Wiltse, Lew
WG3-53

Wimmer, Chris
90WichSt-38
91T/Tr-130T

Winbush, Mike
86Salem-29

Windes, Cary
89Smok/FresnoSt-22

Windes, Rodney
88AubAs/ProC-1955
89Ashvl/ProC-947
90Osceola/Star-26
91Osceola/ClBest-13
91Osceola/ProC-686

Windhorn, Gordon
62T-254
90Target-868

Wine, Robbie
86Tucson-26
87Tucson-3
88D-508
88F-459
88OkCty/CMC-22
88OkCty/ProC-42
88S-496
88T-119
89Richm/Bob-28
89Richm/CMC-11
89Richm/Ko-29
89Richm/ProC-843
90Canton/Best-17
90Canton/ProC-1295
91Tidew/LineD-572

Wine, Robert
(Bobby)
63T-71
64PhilBull-26
64T-347
65OPC-36
65T-36
66T-284
67T-466
68T-396
69Expos/Pins-9
69T-648
70Expos/Pins-14
70MLB/St-72
70OPC-332
70T-332
71LaPizza-14
71MLB/St-144
71OPC-171
71T-171
72MB-367
72T-657
73OPC-486CO
73T-486CO
74OPC-119CO
74T-119CO
78TCMA-181
85Pol/Atl-7CO
86T-57MG
PM10/L-42

Winegarner, Ralph
R312

Winfield, Dave
74McDon
74OPC-456
74T-456
74T/St-100
75Ho-37
75OPC-61
75T-61
75T/M-61
76Ho-83
76OPC-160
76SSPC-133
76T-160
77BurgChef-130
77Ho-44
77K-28
77OPC-156
77Padre/SchCd-39
77Padre/SchCd-40
77T-390
77T/CS-52
78Ho-63
78K-11
78OPC-78
78Padre/FamFun-38
78T-530
79Ho-125
79OPC-11
79T-30
79T/Comics-31
80BK/PHR-22
80K-32
80OPC-122
80T-230
80T/S-18
81D-364
81Drake-14
81F-484
81F/St-25
81K-21
81PermaGr/AS-18
81PermaGr/CC-21
81Sqt-19
81T-370
81T/HT
81T/St-111
81T/Tr-855
82D-18DK
82D-31
82D-575M
82Drake-31
82F-56
82F-646M
82F/St-110M
82F/St-113
82K-12
82OPC-352
82OPC-76AS
82PermaGr/CC-14
82Sqt-7
82T-553AS
82T-600
82T/St-137
82T/St-213
83D-409
83D/AAS-36
83Drake-31
83F-398
83F-633M
83K-15
83OPC-258
83PermaGr/AS-7
83PermaGr/CC-34
83RoyRog/Disc-12
83T-770
83T/Gloss40-7
83T/St-99
84D-51
84Drake-32
84F-143
84F/St-5
85FunFood/Pin-1
84MiltBrad-29
84Nes/792-402AS
84Nes/792-460
84Nestle/DT-6
84OPC-266AS
84OPC-378
84Ralston-7
84Seven-7E
84T-402AS
84T-460
84T/Cereal-7
84T/Gloss22-8
84T/Gloss40-16
84T/St-190
84T/St-319
84T/Super-27
85D-51
85D-651M
85D/AAS-12
85D/HL-53
85Drake-32
85F-146
85F-629IA
85F/LimEd-43
85F/St-5
85GenMills-25
85Leaf-127
85Leaf-140M
85OPC-180
85Pol/MetYank-Y4
85Seven-3C
85Seven-3G
85Seven-5E
85Seven-5S
85Seven-5W
85Sportflic/Proto-4
85Sportflic/Proto-5
85T-180
85T-705AS
85T/3D-18
85T/Gloss22-17
85T/Gloss40-14
85T/St-186
85T/St-308
85T/Super-60
85ThomMc/Discs-23
86BK/AP-2
86D-248
86D/AAS-15
86D/PopUp-15
86Dorman-19
86Drake-18
86F-121
86F/Mini-26
86F/St-130
86F/St-S4
86Jiffy-7
86Leaf-125
86Meadow/Blank-16
86Meadow/Stat-7
86OPC-70
86Quaker-33
86Sf-49
86Sf/Dec-74M
86T-70
86T-717AS
86T/3D-29
86T/Gloss22-8
86T/Gloss60-42
86T/Mini-29
86T/St-160
86T/St-298
86T/Super-60
86Woolwth-33
87Classic-11
87D-105
87D-20DK
87D/AAS-2
87D/DKsuper-20
87D/OD-243
87D/PopUp-2
87Drake-5
87F-120
87F/Lim-42
87F/Mini-117
87F/St-126
87KayBee-33
87Kraft-33
87Leaf-20DK
87Leaf-70
87MSA/Discs-9
87OPC-36
87OPC/WaxBox-H
87Ralston-4
87RedFoley/St-28
87Sf-153M
87Sf-41
87Seven-E15
87T-770
87T/WaxBox-H
87T/Board-4
87T/Coins-26
87T/Gloss22-17
87T/St-152
87T/St-298
88AlaskaAS70/Team-16
88Classic/Red-170
88D-298
88D/AS-2
88D/Best-244
88D/PopUp-2
88D/Y/Bk-278
88Drake-12
88F-226
88F/BB/AS-44
88F/BB/MVP-43
88F/Mini-44
88F/Slug-43
88F/St-53
88Jiffy-19
88KayBee-33
88Leaf-116
88Nestle-33
88OPC-89
88Panini/St-161
88Panini/St-231M
88S-55
88S/WaxBox-8
88Sf-7
88Sf/Gamewin-7
88T-392AS
88T-510
88T/Big-24
88T/Gloss22-8
88T/Gloss60-46
88T/St-159
88T/St-302
88T/St/Backs-54
88T/UK-85
89T/Ames-32
89B-179
89Cadaco-61
89Classic-32
89D-159
89D/AS-6
89D/GrandSlam-6
89D/MVP-BC11
89D/PopUp-6
89F-274
89F/BBAS-44
89F/BBMVP's-43
89F/Excit-43
89F/Heroes-43
89F/LL-43
89F/Superstar-43
89KayBee-32
89KingB/Discs-16
89OPC-260
89Panini/St-240AS
89Panini/St-409
89RedFoley/St-128
89S-50
89S/HotStar-3
89S/Mast-41
89S/NWest-7
89Sf-24
89T-260
89T-407AS
89T/Big-314
89T/Coins-58
89T/DHTest-15
89T/Gloss22-8
89T/Gloss60-21
89T/Hills-32
89T/LJN-4
89T/Mini-67
89T/St-149
89T/St-315
89T/St/Backs-20
89T/UK-84
89T/WaxBox-P
89Tetley/Discs-13
89UD-349
90B-432
90D-551
90D/BestAL-87
90F-458
90F/Up-U81
90KayBee-32
90Leaf/II-426
90MLBPA/Pins-64
90MSA/Soda-23
90OPC-380
90Publint/St-298
90Publint/St-550
90S-307
90S/Tr-1T
90Sf-87
90T-380
90T/Ames-1
90T/Big-20
90T/HillsHM-17
90T/Tr-130T
90T/TVYank-34
90UD-337
90UD/Ext-745
91B-210
91D-468
91F-329
91F/Ultra-54
91JDeanSig-22
91Leaf/II-499
91Leaf/Stud-30
91OPC-630
91OPC/Premier-130
91Panini/FrSt-184
91Panini/St-132
91Petro/SU-5
91Post/Can-28
91RedFoley/St-102
91S-83
91S/100SS-66
91Smok/Angel-3
91T-630
91T/StClub/I-263
91UD-337
92D/I-133
92F-686RS
92F-72
92S/100SS-9
92S/I-32
92T-5RB
92T-792

86Leaf-112
86Sf-53M
86Smok/Cal-1
87D-58
87D/AAS-51
87D/OD-2
87F-641M
87F-95
87F/AwardWin-43
87F/GameWin-43
87F/BB-44
87F/Mini-118
87F/Slug-44
87F/St-127
87Kraft-47
87Leaf-111
87MnM's-17
87OPC-92
87RedFoley/St-4
87Sf-59
87Seven-W15
87Smok/Cal-3
87T-760
87T/Gloss60-33
87T/Mini-48
87T/St-179
88D-86
88D/AS-20
88D/Best-307
88F-507
88F-626M
88F/Mini-13
88F/SS-43
88F/St-13
88Leaf-49
88OPC-270
88Panini/St-38
88S-81
88Sf-32
88Smok/Angels-4
88T-270
88T/Big-4
88T/St-174
88T/UK-86
89B-42
89D-372
89F-490
89OPC-190
89Panini/St-286
89RedFoley/St-129
89S-298
89Sf-197
89Smok/Angels-19
89T-190
89T/Coins-59
89T/LJN-8
89T/St-176
89T/UK-85
89UD-555
90Classic/III-49
90D-580
90ElPasoATG/Team-33
90F-148
90OPC-650
90PublInt/St-382
90S-226
90S/NWest-14
90S/Tr-50T
90Smok/Angel-16
90T-650
90UD-548
91D-282
91D-BC1M
91F-680
91F/WaxBox-1M
91Leaf/I-74
91OPC-536
91S-430
91S-699
91T-536
91T/StClub/II-466
91UD-429
92T-357

Wittcke, Darren
91Everett/ClBest-26
91Everett/ProC-3915

Witte, Jerome
47TipTop

Witte, Trey
91Belling/ClBest-18
91Belling/ProC-3665

Wittmayer, Kurt
78OrlTw

Wockenfuss, John
76OPC-13
76T-13
78BK/T-3
78T-723
79T-231
80T-338
81Coke
81D-245
81F-472
81T-468
81T/St-79
82D-459
82F-286
82OPC-46
82T-629
83D-76
83F-351
83T-536
83T/St-64
84D-150
84F-95
84F/X-U129
84Nes/792-119
84Phill/TastyK-27
84T-119
84T/St-274
84T/Tr-130T
85D-549
85F-269
85Phill/TastyK-27
85T-39
86FSLAS-50
86Miami-29
88GlenF/ProC-917
89Toledo/CMC-25
89Toledo/ProC-771

Wohler, Barry
85VeroB-19
87SanAn-8
88SanAn/Best-2

Wohlers, Mark
89Pulaski/ProC-1908
89Sumter/ProC-1099
90Sumter/Best-25
90Sumter/ProC-2435
91B-582
91Greenvl/ClBest-10
91Greenvl/LineD-223
91Greenvl/ProC-3004
91Single/ClBest-331
91UD/FinalEd-77F
92Classic/I-18
92Classic/I-97
92D/I-1RR
92D/II-616
92F-374
92F-700M
92F/RookSIns-18
92S/II-759
92S/II-787
92T-703
92T/91Debut-188
92UD-56TP

Wohlford, Jim
73OPC-611R
73T-611R
74OPC-407
74T-407
75OPC-144
75T-144
75T/M-144
76A&P/KC
76OPC-286
76SSPC-179
76T-286
77T-622
78T-376
79T-596
80Pol/Giants-9
80T-448
81D-316
81F-440
81T-11
82F-403
82T-116
83D-524
83F-276
83Stuart-21
83T-688
83T/Tr-128T
84F-293
84Nes/792-253
84OPC-253
84Stuart-24
84T-253
85D-585
85F-413
85Leaf-82
85OPC-4
85T-787
86D-157
86OPC-344
86Provigo-6
86T-344
87F-336
87OPC-169
87T-527

Woide, Steve
88Myrtle/ProC-1172
90Erie/Star-27

Wojciechowski, Steve
91SoOreg/ClBest-29
91SoOreg/ProC-3847

Wojcik, Jim
81Shrev-5

Wojcik, John
63T-253R

Wojey, Pete
90Target-874

Wojna, Ed
83Reading-10
84Cram/PCL-231
85Cram/PCL-120
86D-505
86F-338
86LasVegas-24
86T-211
87D-589
87T-88
88Vanco/CMC-5
88Vanco/ProC-756
89ColoSp/CMC-4
89ColoSp/ProC-236
90Tacoma/CMC-11
90Tacoma/ProC-93

Wolak, Jerry
89Utica/Pucko-27
90Foil/Best-77
90SoBend/Best-13
91Saraso/ClBest-22
91Saraso/ProC-1128

Wolf, Mike
78Knoxvl

Wolf, Rick
77Wausau

Wolf, Steve
89Smok/FresnoSt-23
90Niagara/Pucko-27
91Lakeland/ClBest-13
91Lakeland/ProC-268

Wolf, Walter
(Wally)
63T-208R
70OPC-74R
70T-74R

Wolf, William
N172

Wolfe, Donn
88StCath/ProC-2013

Wolfe, Joel
91SoOreg/ClBest-1
91SoOreg/ProC-3865

Wolfe, Larry
79T-137
80T-549

Wolfe, Scott
75Lafay

Wolfer, Jim
89Greens/ProC-419

Wolff, Jim
90Hunting/ProC-3286
91Hunting/ClBest-26
91Hunting/ProC-3338

Wolfgang, Meldon
D329-194
D350/2-195
M101/4-194
M101/5-195

Wolkoys, Rob
86Cram/PCL-26
87AppFx-21

Wollenburg, Jay
86Macon-26

Wollenhaupt, Ron
82Watlo/B-28
82Watlo/C-4

Wolten, Brad
87Watlo-5

Wolter, Harry
10Domino-128
11Helmar-50
12Sweet/Pin-39
M116
S74-25
T202
T205

Wolters, Mike
83ArkTr-14

Wolverton, Harry
11Helmar-51
T207

Womack, Dooley
66T-469R
67OPC-77
67T-77
68T-431
69T-594

Womack, Tony
91Welland/ClBest-2
91Welland/ProC-3584

Wong, Dave
81CharR-3
82FtMyr-14

Wong, Kaha
89Reno/Cal-257
90Reno/Cal-273

Wong, Kevin
91Pocatel/ProC-3793

Wood, Andre
78Dunedin
82Knoxvl-14
83Knoxvl-13

Wood, Bill
82Tucson-22

Wood, Brian S.
86Cram/PCL-155
88River/Cal-215
88River/ProC-1420
89SALAS/GS-8
89Wichita/Rock-23RHP
90Wichita/Rock-24
91Wichita/LineD-623
91Wichita/ProC-2600

Wood, Dave
76Clinton

Wood, George
N172
N284
N690
WG1-54

Wood, Jake
61T-514
62J-15
62P-15
62Salada-83
62Shirriff-83
62T-427
62T-72
62T/St-50
63T-453
64T-272
65T-547
66T-509
67T-394
78TCMA-186

Wood, Jason
91SoOreg/ClBest-12
91SoOreg/ProC-3859

Wood, Jeff
85CharlO-17
87CharlO/WBTV-tr
88CharlK/Pep-10

Wood, Joe
14CJ-22
15CJ-22
16FleischBrd-103
21Exh-189
87Conlon/2-57
90HOF/St-16
91Conlon/Sport-254
92Conlon/Sport-336
BF2-7
D327
D328-194
D329-195
D350/2-196
E103
E120
E121/80
E122
E135-194
E254
E270/1
E91
M101/4-195
M101/5-196
M116
T202
T207
V100
W575
WG4-30
WG5-44
WG6-41

Wood, John
90Idaho/ProC-3249

Wood, Johnson
81BurlB-12
82Beloit-5
84ElPaso-2

Wood, Ken
50B-190
51B-209
52T-139
53B/Col-109

Wood, Mike
84Butte-5

Wood, Pete
N172

Wood, Robert Lynn
E107

Wood, Stephen
88VeroB/Star-24

Wood, Ted
88T/Tr-130TOLY
89Shrev/ProC-1842
89T/Big-308
90Shrev/ProC-1456
90Shrev/Star-24
91Phoenix/LineD-398
91Phoenix/ProC-82
92D/II-681
92F-678
92S/II-768
92T-358
92T/91Debut-189
92UD-12SR

Wood, Wilbur
64T-267
65T-478
67T-391
68T-585
69MB-295
69MLB/St-36
69OPC-123
69T-123
69T/St-160
70MLB/St-192
70OPC-342
70T-342
71OPC-436
71T-436
72K-4
72MB-369
72OPC-342KP
72OPC-92LL
72OPC-94LL
72T-342BP
72T-553
72T-554A
72T-92LL
72T-94LL
72T/Post-19
73K-9
73OPC-150
73OPC-66LL
73T-150
73T-66LL
73T/Lids-54
74K-34
74OPC-120
74OPC-205LL
74T-120
74T-205LL
74T/DE-13
74T/St-160
75Ho-68
75Ho/Twink-68
75OPC-110
75T-110
75T/M-110
76Crane-67

76Ho-99
76MSA/Disc
76OPC-368
76SSPC-139
76T-368
77T-198
78T-726
79OPC-108
79T-216
89Pac/Leg-124
89Swell-127
91LineD-35
91Swell/Great-121

Woodall, Brad
91Idaho/ProC-4331

Woodall, Charles L.
(Lawrence)
21Exh-190
25Exh-96
28Exh-48
E120
E126-53
V61-21
W573

Woodard, Darrell
82BirmB-3

Woodard, Mike
81WHave-17
82WHave-19
83Tacom-13
85Cram/PCL-181
86D-46
86F-645M
86Phoenix-26
87Phoenix-10
87T-286
88Vanco/CMC-14
88Vanco/ProC-767
89Colum/CMC-12
89Colum/Pol-23
89Colum/ProC-742
89F-513

Woodbrey, Mark
75Cedar
76Cedar

Woodburn, Eugene
T207

Wooden, Mark
86Cram/PCL-129
87Wausau-16
88Vermont/ProC-939
89Wmsprt/ProC-628
89Wmsprt/Star-23
90Wmsprt/Best-23
90Wmsprt/ProC-1059
90Wmsprt/Star-24

Woodeschick, Hal
59T-106
60T-454
61T-397
62T-526
63T-517
64T-370
64T/St-78
64T/SU
64Wheat/St-49
65OPC-179
65T-179
66T-514
67T-324
78TCMA-123
86Mother/Ast-2
89Smok/Ast-10

Woodfin, Olonzo
89BurlInd/Star-26

Woodhouse, Kevin
84Everett/Cram-9

Woodling, Gene
48Sommer-13
51B-219
51BR-D1
52B-177
52BR
52Dix
52T-99
53B/BW-31
53Dix
53RM-AL12
53T-264
54B-209
54Dix
54NYJour
54RM-AL15
54T-101
55Esskay
55Salem
55T-190
56T-163
56YellBase/Pin-31
57Sohio/Ind-17
57T-172
58T-398
59T-170
60T-190
60T/tatt-54
61Bz-30
61P-70
61T-275
61T/St-207
62Bz
62J-71
62P-71
62P/Can-71
62Salada-96
62Shirriff-96
62T-125
62T/bucks
62T/St-101
63T-342
63T-43M
88Pac/Leg-5
89Swell-102
91Crown/Orio-490
91Swell/Great-101
91T/Arc53-264
91WIZMets-435
Exh47
PM10/L-43
PM10/L-44
PM10/Sm-201
R423-112
TCMA79-156

Woodmansee, Mark
83SLCity-12

Woodruff
E270/1

Woodruff, Pat
89Batavia/ProC-1936
90Clearw/Star-25
91Lakeland/ClBest-28
91Lakeland/ProC-281

Woods, Alvis
(Al)
77OPC-256
77T-479R
78OPC-175
78Syrac
78T-121
79OPC-85
79T-178
80OPC-230
80T-444
81D-32
81F-422
81OPC-165
81OPC/Post-17
81T-703
81T/St-141
82D-180
82F-627
82OPC-49
82OPC/Post-5
82T-49
83F-444
83OPC-59
83T-589
84Syrac-14
85Toledo-25
86Toledo-24

Woods, Anthony
86Wausau-28
87Wausau-13
88SanBern/Best-5
89SanBern/Best-17
89SanBern/Cal-83

Woods, Clancy
79AppFx-7

Woods, Eric
88WinSalem/Star-22
89WinSalem/Star-18

Woods, Gary
76Tucson-3
77OPC-22
77T-492R
78OPC-13
78Syrac
78T-599
79Charl-5
80Tucson-22
81F-75
81T-172
82F-237
82RedLob
82T-483
82T/Tr-130T
83D-631
83F-512
83T-356
83Thorn-25
84D-144
84F-507
84Nes/792-231
84SevenUp-25
84T-231
85D-555
85F-71
85Leaf-49
85SevenUp-25
85T-46
86F-385
86LasVegas-25
86T-611

Woods, George
49B/PCL-4

Woods, Jim
60L-104
61T-59

Woods, Kelly
89Princet/Star-25

Woods, Lyle
87Anchora-41ANN

Woods, Parnell
49Remar

Woods, Preston
88CapeCod/Sum-54

Woods, Ron
69T-544R
70OPC-253
70T-253
71MLB/St-504
71OPC-514
71T-514
72OPC-82
72T-82
73OPC-531
73T-531
74OPC-377
74T-377

Woods, Tony
83QuadC-22
84MidldC-24
86Pittsfld-25
87Miami-5
88Tampa/Star-24
88Wausau/GS-22

Woods, Tyrone
89James/ProC-2134
90Rockford/ProC-2709
91WPalmB/ClBest-29
91WPalmB/ProC-1243

Woods, Walter
E254

Woodson, Dick
70OPC-479
70T-479
71MLB/St-479
71OPC-586
71T-586
72T-634
73OPC-98
73T-98
74OPC-143
74T-143

Woodson, George
69T-244R

Woodson, Kerry
89Belling/Legoe-16
90A&AASingle/ProC-136
90AS/Cal-19
90Foil/Best-308
90SanBern/Best-25
90SanBern/Cal-90
90SanBern/ProC-2635
91B-264

Woodson, Tracy
85VeroB-2
87Albuq/Pol-24
87Mother/Dodg-22
88AAA/ProC-3
88Albuq/CMC-17
88Albuq/ProC-256
88D-499
88F/Up-U98
89Albuq/CMC-16
89Albuq/ProC-75
89F-77
89Pol/Dodg-12
89S-586
89T-306
89T/Big-92
89UD-108
90Target-875
90Vanco/CMC-25
90Vanco/ProC-498
91Richm/LineD-448
91Richm/ProC-2579

Woodward, Jim
82Jacks-17

Woodward, Rob
86D/Rook-53
86F-651R
86Pawtu-28
87Classic-69
87D-652
87Pawtu/TCMA-23
87T-632
88Pawtu/CMC-1
88Pawtu/ProC-448
88S-403
89Pawtu/CMC-10
89Pawtu/Dunkin-25
89Pawtu/ProC-699
90RochR/CMC-2
90RochR/ProC-703
91RochR/LineD-473
91RochR/ProC-1904

Woodward, William
(Woody)
64T-378R
65T-487
66OPC-49
66T-49
67Kahn
67T-546
68Coke
68Dexter-75
68T-476
69OPC-142
69T-142
70OPC-296
70T-296
71MLB/St-72
71OPC-496
71T-496
72MB-370

Woodworth, John
80Utica-9
82Knoxvl-23
83Knoxvl-21
85Syrac-10
86Syrac-27TR
90Dunedin/Star-28TR
91Dunedin/ClBest-30

Woolridge, Floyd
55Hunter

Wooten, Daryl
89AubAs/ProC-2189

Wooten, Earl
49B-189

Wooten, Junior
88Chatt/Team-31

Worden, Bill
82Danvl-20
83Redwd-25
84Nashvl-25
86Water-26

Workman, Michael
86Watlo-32
87Kinston-14

Works, Ralph
E286
T207

Worrell, Tim
91MidwLAS/ProC-MWL31
91Waterlo/ClBest-10
91Waterlo/ProC-1257

Worrell, Todd
81Louisvl-26
83Louisvl/Riley-26
84ArkTr-6
85Louisvl-28
86D-43RR
86D/HL-29
86D/HL-54
86D/Rook-21
86F-49
86KAS/Disc-10
86Sf-179R
86Sf/Rook-35
86Schnucks-24
86T/Tr-127T
87Classic-97
87D-307
87F-312
87F/AS-8
87F/AwardWin-44
87F/Hottest-44
87F/LL-44
87F/Lim-43
87F/Mini-119
87F/RecSet-43
87F/St-128
87Leaf-218
87OPC-67
87Sf-33
87Sf-77M
87Smok/Cards-2
87T-465
87T-605AS
87T-7RB
87T/Coins-48
87T/Gloss60-10
87T/GlossRk-22
87T/HL-13
87T/Mini-34
87T/St-11
87T/St-12
87T/St-310
87T/St-55
87ToysRUs-33
87Woolwth-13
88Bz-22
88ChefBoy-8
88Classic/Red-181
88D-386
88D/Best-268
88F-50
88F/LL-44
88F/Mini-111
88F/RecSet-44
88F/Slug-44
88F/St-122
88F/WaxBox-C16
88F/WS-5M
88KMart-32
88Leaf-229
88OPC-135
88Panini/St-386
88S-202
88Sf-61
88Smok/Card-10
88T-715
88T/Big-149
88T/Coins-60
88T/Mini-73
88T/St-54
88Woolwth-24
89B-429
89Cadaco-62
89D-82
89D/AS-60
89D/Best-243
89F-466
89F/BBMVP's-44
89F/Superstar-44
89Louisvl-37
89OPC-291
89Panini/St-179
89S-265
89S/HotStar-94
89Sf-183
89Smok/Cards-23
89T-535
89T/LJN-124
89T/Mini-37
89T/St-39
89UD-512
90B-185
90BBWit-29
90D-319
90F-264
90MLBPA/Pins-29
90OPC-95
90Panini/St-340
90Publnt/St-231
90Publnt/St-274

90S-392
90Sf-165
90T-95
90T/St-43
90T/TVCard-22
90UD-467
91F-653
91Pol/Card-38
91S-807
Wortham, Rich
80OPC-261DP
80T-502
81D-161
81F-347
81T-107
82Reading-10
Worthington, Al
54NYJour
55Gol/Giants-32
57T-39
58Hires-73
58SFCallB-25
58T-427
59T-28
60T-268
62AmTract-66
63FrBauer-31
63T-556
64T-144
65OPC-216
65T-216
66OPC-181
66T-181
67T-399
68T-473
73OPC-49CO
73T-49CO
79TCMA-269
Worthington, Craig
86Hagers-29
87RochR-23
87RochR/TCMA-17
88D/Rook-23
88F/Up-U4
88RochR/Team-26
88RochR/CMC-19
88RochR/Gov-27
88RochR/ProC-217
89D-569
89D/Best-282
89D/Rook-25
89F-627
89French-11
89Panini/St-252
89S-636
89S/HotRook-6
89S/YS/II-21
89Sf-134
89T-181
89UD/Ext-725
90B-253
90Bz-15
90Classic-31
90D-141
90D/BestAL-71
90F-195
90HagersDG/Best-35
90Leaf/I-170
90OPC-521
90Panini/St-11
90PublInt/St-592
90S-234
90S/100Ris-21
90Sf-117
90T-521
90T/Big-146
90T/Gloss60-49
90T/HeadsUp-22
90T/JumboR-33
90T/St-239
90T/St-328FS
90ToysRUs-32
90UD-444
91Crown/Orio-491
91D-293
91F-496
91F/Ultra-26
91Leaf/II-298
91OPC-73
91Panini/FrSt-242
91Panini/St-198
91S-503
91T-73
91T/StClub/II-467
91UD-141
92F-31
92S/II-724
Wortman, William
(Chuck)
D328-195
E135-195
Wortmann, Russ
82Idaho-15
Wotus, Ron
82Buffa-11
84Cram/PCL-128
86Hawaii-22
87Omaha-20
89Phoenix/CMC-19
89Phoenix/ProC-1501
90Clinton/ProC-2567CO
91AS/Cal-47
91SanJose/ClBest-23MG
91SanJose/ProC-27MG
Woyce, Don
86FtMyr-29
Woyt, Boris
V362-29
Wray, James
88GreatF-13
89AS/Cal-16
89Bakers/Cal-189
91SanAn/LineD-550
91SanAn/ProC-2977
Wren, Frank
80Memphis-28
Wrenn, Luke
76Shrev
Wright, Ab
92Conlon/Sport-407
Wright, Bill
87Idaho-17
Wright, Bill
91Negro/Lewis-10
Wright, Brian
89Idaho/ProC-2009
Wright, Clarence
90Target-876
Wright, Clyde
69T-583
70OPC-543
70T-543
71Bz
71Bz/Test-6
71JB
71K-28
71MLB/St-359
71OPC-240
71OPC-67LL
71T-240
71T-67LL
71T/Coins-60
71T/GM-18
71T/S-39
71T/tatt-14
72MB-371
72OPC-55
72T-55
73OPC-373
73T-373
74OPC-525
74T-525
75OPC-408
75T-408
75T/M-408
76OPC-559
76SSPC-258
76T-559
89Smok/Angels-6
Wright, Don
88AppFx/ProC-146
89AppFx/ProC-855
90BBCity/Star-27
Wright, F. Glenn
25Exh-56
26Exh-56
28Exh-28
28Yueng-47
31Exh/4-4
33Exh/4-2
33G-1453
34Exh/4-2
35G-2B
35G-4B
35G-7B
90Target-877
R306
V353-77
W502-47
W512-5
Wright, George
50Callahan
80SSPC/HOF
91Conlon/Sport-208
Wright, George
78Ashvl
80Tulsa-10
81Tulsa-1
83D-116
83F-583
83Rang-26
83T-299
83T/St-124
84D-525
84F-435
84Nes/792-688
84OPC-314
84Rang-26
84T-688
84T/St-353
85D-256
85F-574
85OKCty-16
85OPC-387
85T-443
86D-220
86F-578
86T-169
86T/Tr-128T
89HOF/St-15
89Phoenix/CMC-24
89Phoenix/ProC-1484
Wright, Goldie
83Redwd-26
Wright, Henderson E.
(Ed)
47TipTop
52T-368
Wright, J.P.
89Kenosha/ProC-1072
89Kenosha/Star-24
Wright, James L.
78PapaG/Disc-18
79OPC-180
79T-722R
80OkCty
80T-524
82D-490
82T-362
Wright, James R.
79T-349
80Penin/B-13
80Penin/C-7
81T-526R
82Syrac-10
86Peoria-26CO
87Pittsfld-5
87Toledo/TCMA-12
88Iowa/CMC-25
88Iowa/ProC-542
89Iowa/CMC-24
89Iowa/ProC-1697
90ScranWB/CMC-23CO
90ScranWB/ProC-614CO
91ScranWB/LineD-500CO
91ScranWB/ProC-2557CO
Wright, Ken
71OPC-504
71T-504
72T-638
73OPC-578
73T-578
76QuadC
77QuadC
Wright, Larry
78Clinton
Wright, Mark
80Batavia-30
81Wisco-11
82Wisco-6
Wright, Mel
73OPC-517
73T-517C
83Stuart-25CO
Wright, Mike
79QuadC-1
Wright, Mitch
79Newar-21
Wright, Paul
82Redwd-17
Wright, Richard
(Ricky)
81Albuq/TCMA-7
82Albuq-11
83F-226
83Pol/Dodg-21
85OKCty-9
86Rang-24
86T/Tr-129T
87T-202
87Toledo-6
90Target-878
Wright, Skipper
88Sumter/ProC-404
89BurlB/ProC-1626
90CLAS/CL-27
90Durham/Team-11
Wright, Taft
40PB-186
41G-10
41PB-32
47TipTop
49B-96
Exh47
Wright, Thomas
51B-271
54T-140
55T-141
55T/DH-75
Wright, W. Henry
(Harry)
50Callahan
75F/Pion-2
80SSPC/HOF
N172
N690
Wright, William S.
T206
Wrightstone, Russell
21Exh-191
26Exh-48
27Exh-24
91Conlon/Sport-238
E120
E126-43
V61-61
W573
Wrigley, Charles
R332-9UMP
Wrigley, Zeke
90Target-1097
Wrona, Bill
86Beaum-25
88Wichita-21
89LasVegas/CMC-19
89LasVegas/ProC-18
90Iowa/CMC-16
90Iowa/ProC-328
90T/TVCub-65
Wrona, Dave
88CapeCod/Sum-39
90Beloit/Star-24
91Beloit/ClBest-23
91Beloit/ProC-2113
91Single/ClBest-213
Wrona, Rick
86WinSalem-28
87Pittsfld-17
89D/Rook-38
90D-512
90OPC-187
90S-557
90S/100Ris-73
90T-187
90T/TVCub-21
90UD-582
91S-519
Wrona, Ron
76BurlB
77Holyo
Wulfemeyer, Mark
75QuadC
Wurm, Garry
89Boise/ProC-2005
90Erie/Star-28
Wuthrich, David
88Pocatel/ProC-2074
Wyatt, Chuck
91Billings/ProC-3754
Wyatt, Dave
83Lynch-19
85Lynch-10
86Tidew-29
87Tidew-14
87Tidew/TCMA-9
Wyatt, John T.
63T-376
64T-108
65OldLond-39
65T-590
66T-521
67T-261
67T/Test/RSox-24
68Coke
68Dexter-76
68T-481
78TCMA-159
Wyatt, John W.
(Whit)
39PB-95
40PB-67
41DP-14
41G-18
41G-18
41PB-55
60Lake
60SpicSpan-26CO
60T-464C
89Smok/Dodg-43
90Target-879
PM10/Sm-202
R314
Wyatt, Porter
78Newar
Wyatt, Reggie
84Memphis-6
Wyde, Rich
91Everett/ClBest-17
Wylie, John
91Boise/ClBest-14
91Boise/ProC-3881
Wynegar, Butch
77BurgChef-53
77Ho-84
77K-56
77OPC-176
77Pep-3
77T-175
78Ho-37
78OPC-104
78T-555
79Ho-141
79OPC-214DP
79T-405
80OPC-159
80T-304
81D-529
81F-558
81OPC-61
81T-61
81T/St-102
82D-508
82Drake-32
82F-565
82OPC-222
82T-222
82T/St-208
82T/Tr-131T
83D-325
83F-399
83OPC-379
83T-617
83T/St-101
84D-458
84F-144
84Nes/792-123
84OPC-123
84T-123
84T/St-321
85D-417
85D/AAS-45
85F-147
85Leaf-165
85OPC-28
85T-585
85T/St-316
86D-274
86F-122
86Leaf-147
86OPC-235
86T-235
86T/St-299
87D/OD-6
87OPC-203
87Smok/Cal-10
87T-464

88S-355
88Smok/Angels-23
88T-737
89S-140

Wynn, Early
49B-110
50B-148
50NumNum
51B-78
51FB
51T/RB-8
52B-142
52RM-AL24
52T-277
53B/Col-146
53RM-AL14
53T-61
54B-164
54DanDee
55B-38
55Gol/Ind-32
55RFG-14
55RM-AL14
55Salem
56Carling-10
56T-187
57Sohio/Ind-18
57T-40
58T-100
59T-260
60Armour-20
60Bz-28
60NuCard-71
60T-1
60T/tatt-55
61NuCard-471
61P-22
61T-337M
61T-455
61T-50LL
61T/St-131
62J-55
62P-55
62P/Can-55
62Salada-97A
62Salada-97B
62Shirriff-97
62T-385
62T/bucks
62T/St-30
63J-43
63P-43
76Laugh/Jub-23
79TCMA-20
80Pac/Leg-73
80Laugh/3/4/5-26
80SSPC/HOF
83D/HOF-42
86Sf/Dec-36
88Pac/Leg-95
89Swell-60
91T/Arc53-61

Wynn, Jim
64T-38
64T/Coins-2
65OPC-257
65T-257
66Bz-35
66T-520
66T/RO-11
67Bz-35
67T-390
67T/Test/SU-24
68Bz-11
68Coke
68Dexter-77
68OPC-5LL
68T-260
68T-5LL
68T/G-24
68T/Post-8
69MLB/St-144
69MLBPA/Pin-60
69T-360
69T/DE-11
69T/decal
69T/S-43
69T/St-40
69Trans-41
70K-9
70MLB/St-48
70OPC-60
70T-60
70T/S-35
70T/SO
70Trans-4
71Bz/Test-43
71MLB/St-96
71OPC-565
71T-565
71T/Coins-69
71T/GM-31
72MB-372
72T-770
73OPC-185
73T-185
74OPC-43
74T-43
74T/St-40
74T/Tr-43T
75Ho-25
75Ho/Twink-25
75OPC-570
75T-570
75T/M-570
76Crane-68
76Ho-129
76MSA/Disc
76OPC-395
76SSPC-89
76T-395
77BK/Y-20
77T-165
86Mother/Ast-7
87Smok/Dodg-39
88Smok/Dodg-20
89Smok/Dodg-86
90Target-880

Wynne, Billy
70T-618
71MLB/St-360
71OPC-718
71T-718
91WIZMets-436

Wynne, Jim
91James/ClBest-18
91James/ProC-3546

Wynne, Marvell
82Tidew-16
83Tidew-21
84D-508
84F-269
84Jacks/Smok-14
84Nes/792-173
84T-173
84T/St-135
85D-113
85F-481
85Leaf-233
85OPC-86
85T-615
85T/St-131
86D-113
86F-625
86F/Up-U130
86OPC-293
86T-525
86T/St-128
87Bohem-16
87D-411
87D/OD-144
87F-435
87T-37
88D-237
88OPC-H
88S-209
88Smok/Padres-31
88T-454
88T/WaxBox-H
89D-347
89D/Best-189
89F-322
89Panini/St-205
89S-203
89T-353
89T/St-107
89UD-154
90Cub/Mara-26
90D-255
90Leaf/II-270
90OPC-256
90PublInt/St-63
90S-337
90T-256
90T/TVCub-35
90UD-14
91F-441
91OPC-714
91S-531
91T-714

Wyrostek, John
48B-44
48L-19
49B-37
49Eureka-99
50B-197
51B-107
51T/BB-44
52B-42
52NTea
52T-13
53B/BW-35
53T-79
55B-237
91T/Arc53-79

Wyse, Henry
47TipTop
51B-192

Wyszynski, Dennis
80WHave-2

Xavier, Joe
88Tacoma/CMC-25
88Tacoma/ProC-613
89Denver/CMC-21
89Denver/ProC-53
90Denver/CMC-7
90Denver/ProC-636

Yacopino, Ed
87Macon-20
88Salem/Star-24
89Harris/ProC-291
89Harris/Star-22
90Harris/ProC-1207
90Harris/Star-22
91CaroMud/LineD-122
91CaroMud/ProC-1099

Yaeger, Chuck
86Albany/TCMA-20

Yagi, Richard
88Fresno/Cal-14
88Fresno/ProC-1239

Yahmann, Jim
88Jaxvl/Best-26

Yamaguchi, Yuji
89Salinas/Cal-133
89Salinas/ProC-1813

Yamamoto, Masahiro
88FSLAS/Star-26
88SanJose/Cal-140
88SanJose/ProC-117
88VeroB/Star-25

Yamano, Mickey
86SanJose-24
87SanJose-11

Yamanouchi, Kenichi
90Salinas/Cal-140
90Salinas/ProC-2724

Yampierre, Eddie
81Wausau-12

Yan, Julian
87Myrtle-1
88Dunedin/Star-23
88FSLAS/Star-52
89Dunedin/Star-24
90Foil/Best-148
90Knoxvl/Best-13
90Knoxvl/ProC-1253
90Knoxvl/Star-22
91Knoxvl/LineD-373
91Knoxvl/ProC-1777

Yan, Roberto
82DayBe-9

Yanagida, Shikato
90AS/Cal-44
90Salinas/Cal-139
90Salinas/ProC-2723

Yancey, William
78Laugh/Black-30
86Negro/Frit-88

Yancy, Hugh
77Indianap-22
79Tacom-10

Yandle, John
80Hawaii-12
81Holyo-6

Yandrick, Jerry
77Charl

Yanes, Eddie
86Visalia-24
87Orlan-19
88OrlanTw/Best-4

Yanus, Bud
80Memphis-29
83Memphis-12
86WPalmB-28CO
87WPalmB-11

Yarbrough, Buddy
77DaytB

Yarrison, Rube
90Target-1099

Yaryan, Clarence
E120
V100

Yastrzemski, Carl
60T-148
61T-287
61T/St-119
62J-61
62P-61
62P/Can-61
62Salada-27
62Shirriff-27
62T-425
62T/bucks
62T/St-20
63Bz-16
63F-8
63J-80
63P-80
63T-115
63T/SO
64Bz-16
64T-210
64T-82M
64T-8LL
64T/Coins-134AS
64T/Coins-26
64T/S-48
64T/St-23
64T/SU
64T/tatt
64Wheat/St-50
65OldLond-40
65T-385
65T/E-1
65T/trans-36SP
66Bz-22
66OPC-70
66T-216LL
66T-70
66T/RO-110
67Bz-22
67OPC/PI-5
67T-355
67T/PI-5
67T/Test/RSox-25
67T/Test/RSox-29
67T/Test/SU-21
68Bz-2
68OPC-152WS
68OPC-192CL
68OPC-2LL
68OPC-4LL
68OPC-6LL
68T-152WS
68T-192CL
68T-250
68T-2LL
68T-369AS
68T-4LL
68T-6LL
68T/G-3
68T/Post-16
69Kelly/Pin-20
69MLBPA/Pin-30
69OPC-130
69OPC-1LL
69OPC/DE-24
69T-130
69T-1LL
69T-425AS
69T/DE-4
69T/decal
69T/S-5
69T/St-140
70MLB/St-168
70OPC-10
70OPC-461AS
70T-10
70T-461AS
70T/S-29
70T/SO
71Bz
71Bz/Test-5
71MLB/St-336
71MLB/St-576
71OPC-530
71OPC-61LL
71OPC-65LL
71T-530
71T-61LL
71T-65LL
71T/Coins-58
71T/GM-40
71T/S-49
71T/tatt-2
71T/tatt-2a
72OPC-37
72OPC-38IA
72T-37
72T-38IA
72T/Post-2
73OPC-245
73T-245
73T/Comics-24
73T/Lids-55
73T/PinUps-24
74Laugh/ASG-70
74OPC-280
74T-280
74T/DE-43
74T/Puzzles-12
74T/St-140
75Ho-48
75K-51
75OPC-205MV
75OPC-280
75T-205MV
75T-280
75T/M-205MV
75T/M-280
76Crane-69
76Ho-149
76K-24
76Laugh/Jub-9
76MSA/Disc
76OPC-230
76SSPC-409
76T-230
77BurgChef-36
77Ho-4
77OPC-37
77Pep-23
77T-434TBC
77T-480
77T/CS-53
78OPC-137
78PapaG/Disc-8
78T-40
78Tastee/Discs-16
78Wiffle/Discs-78
79K-45
79OPC-160
79T-320
79T/Comics-3
80K-27
80OPC-365
80T-1M
80T-720
80T/S-22
81Coke
81D-214
81D-94
81Drake-1
81F-221
81F/St-13
81K-48
81OPC-110
81PermaGr/CC-4
81T-110
81T/HT
81T/St-45
82Coke/Bos
82D-74
82F-312
82F-633M
82F/St-162
82F/St-237M
82K-43
82KMart-11
82OPC-358IA
82OPC-72
82PermaGr/CC-13
82T-650
82T-651IA
82T/St-120
82T/St-155
83D-25DK

83D-326
83D/AAS-44
83Drake-32
83F-200
83F-629M
83K-9
83OPC-126SV
83OPC-4
83PermaGr/CC-35
83T-550
83T-551SV
83T/Gloss40-1
83T/St-31
83T/St-6
84D-660
84D-LLB
84D/Champs-10
84F-412
84F-640IA
84F/St-97
84Nes/792-6HL
84T-6HL
84T/Gloss22-11
85CircK-17
86Sf/Dec-47
87KMart-11
87T-314TBC
89Kahn/Coop-11
89T/LJN-129
90BBWit-34
90CollAB-12
90D-588PUZ
90HOF/St-71
90MSA/AGFA-2
90Pac/Legend-61
90Swell/Great-5
90T/Gloss22-22CAPT
91Swell/Great-108
Exh47
PM10/Sm-203
PM10/Sm-204
WG10-48
WG9-50

Yastrzemski, Mike
84Durham-3
85Durham-32
86SLAS-2
87Hawaii-1
88Vanco/CMC-19
88Vanco/ProC-774
90BirmDG/Best-32

Yasuda, Hideyuki
91AS/Cal-40
91Salinas/ClBest-3
91Salinas/ProC-2248

Yates, Al
No Cards.

Yaughn, Kip
91CLAS/ProC-CAR10
91Freder/ClBest-11
91Freder/ProC-2365

Yawkey, Tom
89HOF/St-93

Yde, Emil
92Conlon/Sport-546

Yeager, Eric
85Anchora-32
87Anchora-32

Yeager, Joseph F.
(Joe)
90Target-881
C46-84
E107
E270/1

Yeager, Steve
73OPC-59
73T-59
74OPC-593
74T-593
75OPC-376
75T-376
75T/M-376
76Ho-147
76OPC-515
76SSPC-83
76T-515
77BurgChef-151
77OPC-159
77T-105
78T-285
79OPC-31
79T-75
80OPC-371
80Pol/Dodg-7
80T-726
81D-297
81F-129
81OPC-318
81Pol/Dodg-7
81T-318
81T/HT
82D-201
82F-29
82OPC-219
82Pol/Dodg-7
82T-477
82T/St-259M
83D-201
83F-227
83OPC-261
83Pol/Dodg-7
83T-555
84D-581
84F-117
84Nes/792-661
84OPC-252
84Pol/Dodg-7
84T-661
84T/St-86
85Coke/Dodg-34
85D-519
85F-390
85OPC-148
85T-148
86D-519
86F/Up-U131
86Mother/Mar-5
86OPC-32
86T-32
86T/Tr-130T
87F-599
87OPC-258
87T-258
90Target-882

Yearout, Mike
86Knoxvl-26
87Knoxvl-3

Yeglinski, John
75Lafay
77ArkTr

Yelding, Eric
85Kingst-23
86Ventura-28
87Knoxvl-12
88AAA/ProC-37
88Syrac/CMC-17
88Syrac/ProC-832
89D/Rook-34
89Lennox/Ast-12
89Mother/Ast-21
89S/HotRook-65
90Classic/III-58
90D-123
90D/BestNL-114
90F/Up-U18
90HotRook/St-49
90Leaf/II-301
90Lennox-27
90Mother/Ast-24
90OPC-309
90S-411
90S/100Ris-16
90S/YS/I-15
90T-309
90T/89Debut-148
90T/Big-317
90UD-427
91B-557
91Classic/200-71
91D-277
91F-520
91F/Ultra-141
91Leaf/I-100
91Mother/Ast-7
91OPC-59
91Panini/FrSt-12
91Panini/St-13
91Panini/Top15-42
91RedFoley/St-103
91S-329
91T-59
91T/StClub/I-16
91UD-197
92D/I-148
92S/I-197
92UD-394

Yellen, Larry
64T-226R
65T-292

Yellowhorse, Moses
21Exh-192

Yelovic, John
43Centen-25

Yelton, Rob
91Bristol/ClBest-7
91Bristol/ProC-3610

Yerkes, Stephen
D328-196
D329-196
D350/2-197
E135-196
E224
M101/4-196
M101/5-197
T207

Yesenchak, Ed
76AppFx
77AppFx

Yett, Rich
81Wisco-12
83Orlan-15
84Toledo-5
85F/Up-U131
85Toledo-30
86Maine-26
86OhHenry-42
87F-263
87Gator-42
87T-134
88F-621
88Gator-42
88S-484
88T-531
89B-79
89D-546
89F-417
89S-467
89T-363
89T/Big-290
89UD/Ext-728
90B-412
90D-509
90F-504
90OPC-689
90Portl/CMC-11
90PublInt/St-570
90S-274
90T-689
90UD-595

Yingling, Earl
90Target-1100
D328-197
E135-197

Yobs, Dave
85BuffB-16
86BuffB-26

Yochim, Ray
49Eureka-200

Yockey, Mark
90Everett/Best-12
90Everett/ProC-3128
91Clinton/ClBest-10
91Clinton/ProC-835

Yoder, Kris
76Wmsprt
78Richm
79Savan-13

Yojo, Minoru
89Visalia/Cal-115
89Visalia/ProC-1424

Yokota, George
86SanJose-25

York, Anthony
47Centen-32
47Signal
49B/PCL-22

York, Jim
72OPC-68
72T-68
73OPC-546
73T-546
75OPC-383
75T-383
75T/M-383
76OPC-224
76T-224

York, Mike
86Lakeland-25
87Macon-7
88Salem/Star-25
89Harris/ProC-310
89Harris/Star-23
89Star/Wax-21
90BuffB/CMC-11
90BuffB/ProC-374
90BuffB/Team-27
91BuffB/LineD-48
91BuffB/ProC-543
91F/Ultra-389MLP
91OPC-508
91S-738RP
91T-508
91T/90Debut-168

York, Rudy
38Exh/4-12
38G-260
38G-284
39Exh
40Wheat-6
47TipTop
60T-456C
72F/FFeat-12
72Laugh/GF-3
74Laugh/ASG-42
81Detroit-9
85Woolwth-43
90HOF/St-35
R346-27

Yorro, Jacinto
90StCath/ProC-3481
91StCath/ProC-3410

Yoshida, Takashi
89Visalia/Cal-120CO
89Visalia/ProC-1430

Yoshinaga, Yoshi
89Salinas/Cal-136
89Salinas/ProC-1810

Yost, Eddie
49B-32
50B-162
51B-41
51T/BB-1
52B-31
52NTea
52RM-AL25
52T-123
52TipTop
53B/Col-116
53Briggs
54B-72
54RH
55B-73
56T-128
57Swift-11
57T-177
58T-173
59T-2
60T-245
61Bz-6
61P-45
61T-413
61T/St-175
62J-76
62P-76
62P/Can-76
62T-176
73OPC-257CO
73T-257CO
74OPC-179CO
74T-179CO
79TCMA-88
90Pac/Legend-73
91Swell/Great-122
R423-117

Yost, Edgar
(Ned)
79T-708R
79Vanco-13
80Vanco-3
81T-659R
82Pol/Brew-5
82T-542
83D-458
83F-50
83Gard-21
83Pol/Brew-5
83T-297
84D-271
84F-218
84F/X-U130
84Jacks/Smok-15
84Nes/792-107
84Rang-7
84T-107
84T/Tr-131T
85D-221
85F-575
85T-777
87Greenvl/Best-12
88SALAS/GS-3
88Sumter/ProC-414
89Sumter/ProC-1095
90Sumter/Best-30MG
90Sumter/ProC-2450MG

Youmans, Floyd
84Jacks-15
86D-543
86F-267
86Leaf-210
86OPC-346
86Provigo-24
86T-732
87Classic-98
87D-257
87D/HL-22
87D/OD-89
87F-337
87F/Mini-120
87F/RecSet-44
87Ho/St-6
87Leaf-206
87Leaf-65CG
87OPC-105
87Sf-103
87T-105
87T/Mini-19
87T/St-79
88D-56
88D/Best-314
88F-201
88Ho/Disc-9
88Leaf-66
88OPC-365
88Panini/St-321
88S-327
88S/YS/II-16
88Sf-108
88T-365
88T/St-82
89B-396
89OPC-91
89Phill/TastyK-36
89T-91
89UD-459
89UD/Ext-730
90PublInt/St-252
90Reading/Star-25

Young, Anthony
88LitFalls/Pucko-24
89Clmbia/Best-16
89Clmbia/GS-28
89SALAS/GS-22
91B-466
91Classic/II-T56
91Leaf/GRook-BC23
91Tidew/LineD-573
91Tidew/ProC-2512
91UD/FinalEd-65F
92D/II-409RR
92F-520
92S/II-756
92T-148
92T/91Debut-190
92UD-535

Young, Bob G.
52B-193
52T-147
53T-160
54B-149
54Esskay
54T-8
55Esskay
91Crown/Orio-492
91T/Arc53-160

Young, Bobby
71Richm/Team-18

Young, Brian
90Elmira/Pucko-24
91WinHaven/ClBest-10
91WinHaven/ProC-490

Young, Cliff
86Knoxvl-27
86SLAS-24
87Knoxvl-27
88Syrac/CMC-8
88Syrac/ProC-807
89Edmon/CMC-4
89Edmon/ProC-557

90Edmon/CMC-1
90Edmon/ProC-518
90F/Up-U82
91B-204
91Edmon/ProC-1517
91F-330
91T/90Debut-169
92F-73
92S/II-813

Young, Curt
83Tacom-8
84Cram/PCL-85
85D-522
85F-436
85Mother/A's-22
85T-293
86T-84
86Tacom-25
87D-344
87D/OD-29
87F-410
87F/GameWin-44
87F/St-129
87Smok/A's-12
87T-519
87T/St-165
88D-97
88D/A's/Bk-97
88D/Best-323
88F-296
88F/St-58
88Mother/A's-17
88OPC-103
88Panini/St-165
88RedFoley/St-104
88S-125
88Sf-209
88T-103
89B-184
89D-304
89F-26
89Mother/A's-14
89S-29
89T-641
89T/Big-254
89UD-392
90D-505
90F-24
90Leaf/II-424
90Mother/A's-24
90OPC-328
90PublInt/St-319
90S-533
90T-328
90UD-4
91B-220
91D-723
91F/Ultra-257
91Mother/A's-24
91OPC-473
91S-236
91T-473
92D/II-469
92F-272
92S/II-722
92T-704

Young, Del E.
48Sommer-27
49Sommer-21

Young, Delwyn
83Cedar-17
86Vermont-24
87BurlEx-15
87SanBern-11
88EastLAS/ProC-12
88GlenF/ProC-916
89Toledo/CMC-22
89Toledo/ProC-764
90Canton/Best-14
90Canton/ProC-1306
90Canton/Star-18

Young, Denton T.
(Cy)
10Domino-129
11Helmar-20
12Sweet/Pin-21A
12Sweet/Pin-21B
48Exh/HOF
50Callahan
60F-47
60NuCard-48
61F-153
61GP-33
61NuCard-448
63Bz/ATG-6
69Bz/Sm
72F/FFeat-11
72K/ATG-12
72Laugh/GF-29
73OPC-477LL
73T-477LL
75F/Pion-19
79T-416LL
80Pac/Leg-91
80Laugh/3/4/5-11
80Laugh/FFeat-30
80SSPC/HOF
83D/HOF-27
84D/Champs-31
85Woolwth-44
88Conlon/4-30
89HOF/St-59
89Swell-5
90BBWit-79
90HOF/St-14
90Swell/Great-100
91Homer/Classic-5
91Swell/Great-135
BF2-31
D304
E101
E106
E107
E120
E121/120
E121/80
E122
E254
E270/1
E90/1
E92
E93
E94
E97
E98
M116
S74-12
T202
T205
T206
T215/brown
T216
W501-68
W555
WG2-51
WG5-45
WG6-42

Young, Derrick
89Clmbia/Best-3
89Clmbia/GS-29
91SanBern/ClBest-25
91SanBern/ProC-2002

Young, Dick
90LitSun-9

Young, Dmitri
91Classic/DP-4
91Johnson/ClBest-11
91Johnson/ProC-3993
91UD/FinalEd-7F
92UD-58TP

Young, Don
66OPC-139R
66T-139R
69T-602R
70OPC-117
70T-117
89Watertn/Star-24

Young, Eric O.
90FSLAS/Star-20
90VeroB/Star-29
91SanAn/LineD-548
91SanAn/ProC-2985
91Single/ClBest-11

Young, Erik
89Watertn/Star-25

Young, Ernest
75Cedar
75Lafay
76Cedar

Young, Ernest Wesley
(Ernie)
90SoOreg/Best-15
90SoOreg/ProC-3438
91Madison/ClBest-18
91Madison/ProC-2145

Young, Ernie
87Hagers-27
88Fresno/Cal-5
88Fresno/ProC-1241

Young, Floyd
WG8-52

Young, Ford
60DF-24

Young, Gerald
85Osceola/Team-26
86ColumAst-25
87Sf/Rook-36
87Tucson-11
88D-431
88D/Best-318
88F-460
88Leaf-210
88Mother/Ast-3
88OPC-368
88Pol/Ast-24
88S-442
88S/YS/II-11
88T-368
89B-333
89D-207
89D/Best-288
89F-370
89Lennox/Ast-20
89Mother/Ast-3
89OPC-95
89Panini/St-93
89S-97
89S/HotStar-72
89Sf-125
89T-95
89T/Coins-28
89T/Mini-16
89T/St-23
89T/UK-86
89UD-135
90B-72
90D-325
90F-241
90Leaf/I-214
90Lennox-28
90MLBPA/Pins-40
90Mother/Ast-8
90OPC-196
90Panini/St-263
90PublInt/St-105
90PublInt/St-618
90S-43
90T-196
90T/Big-49
90T/St-22
90UD-196
91D-689
91F-521
91F/Ultra-142
91OPC-626
91S-844
91T-626
91T/StClub/II-494
91Tucson/LineD-623
91Tucson/ProC-2227
92D/II-477
92F-446
92S/I-346
92T-241

Young, Greg
90SoBend/ClBest-21
91SoBend/ProC-2858
91Utica/ClBest-9
91Utica/ProC-3241

Young, Irving
M116
T206
WG3-54

Young, Jason
90ClintUp/Team-10
90Everett/Best-21
90Everett/ProC-3137
91Clinton/ClBest-25
91Clinton/ProC-850

Young, Jim
91Rockford/ClBest-2TR

Young, John
77ArkTr
80Indianap-31tr
81Indianap-32tr
83Spring/LF-15
84ArkTr-22
87Nashvl-24
88Nashvl/CMC-25
88Nashvl/ProC-495
88Nashvl/Team-25TR
88Watertn/Pucko-30
89Nashvl/CMC-9
89Nashvl/ProC-1276
89Nashvl/Team-29TR
90Nashvl/CMC-26TR
90SpringDG/Best-12

Young, Kenny
81Bristol-14

Young, Kevin
90Welland/Pucko-8
91Salem/ClBest-9
91Salem/ProC-963
91Single/ClBest-239

Young, Kip
79T-706R
80Spokane-11
80T-251
81Indianap-8
82Indianap-3

Young, Larry
88TM/Umpire-54
89TM/Umpire-52
90TM/Umpire-50

Young, Lemuel
(Pep)
35BU-102
39PB-102
40PB-106
92Conlon/Sport-387
D327
D328-198
D329-197
E135-198
E220
M101/4-197
R313
W514-107
W516-28

Young, Mark
88Dunedin/Star-24
89Butte/SP-22
89Dunedin/Star-25
89Myrtle/ProC-1452
90Dunedin/Star-25
90Peoria/Team-30
91Knoxvl/LineD-359
91Knoxvl/ProC-1778

Young, Matt
81Clinton-12

Young, Matt J.
81LynnS-12
82SLCity-22
83T/Tr-129T
84D-16DK
84D-362
84F-624
84Mother/Mar-9
84Nes/792-235
84Nes/792-336TL
84OPC-235
84Seven-24W
84T-235
84T-336TL
84T/St-386YS
85D-267
85F-505
85Mother/Mar-14
85OPC-136
85T-485
85T/St-340
86D-267
86F-481
86Mother/Mar-14
86OPC-274
86T-676
86T/St-220
87D-193
87F-600
87F/Up-U131
87Mother/Dodg-12
87OPC-19
87Pol/Dodg-19
87RedFoley/St-123
87T-19
87T/St-218
87T/Tr-131T
88D-423
88D/A's/Bk-NEW
88F-530
88Mother/A's-21
88OPC-367
88Panini/St-306
88S-357
88T-736
88T/St-72
90F/Up-121
90Leaf/II-509
90Mother/Mar-16
90OPC-501
90T-501
90T/Tr-131T
90Target-883
90UD/Ext-787
91B-128
91D-493
91F-465
91Leaf/I-215
91OPC-108
91Pep/RSox-20
91S-126
91S/RookTr-54T
91T-108
91T/StClub/II-426
91UD-591
91UD/Ext-740
92D/II-635
92S/II-668
92UD-505

Young, Mike
82RochR-19
83RochR-22
84D-621
84F/X-U131
84RochR-19
85D-367
85F-195
85T-173
86D-123
86F-291
86F/Mini-61
86Sf-199
86T-548
86T/St-234
87CharRain-10
87D-150
87F-483
87French-43
87T-309
88D-396
88F-575
88OPC-11
88Panini/St-17
88Phill/TastyK-26
88S-393
88S/Tr-51T
88T-11
89ColoSp/ProC-251
89D-632
89River/Best-21
89River/Cal-18
89River/ProC-1399
89S-494
89T-731
89UD-649
90Geneva/ProC-3046
90Geneva/Star-25
90PublInt/St-571
90Wausau/ProC-2143MG
90Wausau/Star-28MG
91Crown/Orio-493
91Geneva/ClBest-26
91Geneva/ProC-4219
91RochR/LineD-475CO
91RochR/ProC-1920CO

Young, Norman
(Babe)
40PB-212
41DP-32
41DP-93
41G-23
41PB-27
49B-240

Young, Pete
89James/ProC-2136
90FSLAS/Star-21
90WPalmB/Star-28
91Harris/LineD-273
91Harris/ProC-630
91Single/ClBest-189

Young, Ralph S.
E220
V100
W575

Young, Ray
87Dunedin-18
88Modesto-16

88Modesto/Cal-58
89Huntsvl/Best-24
90AAAGame/ProC-AAA48
90Tacoma/CMC-1
90Tacoma/ProC-94
91S-761RP
Young, Rick
75QuadC
Young, Scott
83StPete-13
86ArkTr-26
Young, Shane
84LitFalls-10
86Lynch-28
87TexLgAS-14
88MidldA/GS-5
89MidldA/GS-30
Young, Sly
83Albany-16
Youngbauer, Jeff
79RochR-1
91Pac/SenLg-74
Youngblood, Joel
77T-548
78T-428
79OPC-48
79T-109
80OPC-194
80T-372
81Coke
81D-277
81F-331
81OPC-58
81T-58
81T/St-195
82D-613
82F-543
82OPC-189
82T-655
82T/St-65
83D-572
83F-301
83F-641HL
83Mother/Giants-17
83OPC-265
83T-265
83T/St-143
83T/St-144
83T/Tr-130T
84D-480
84F-387
84Nes/792-727
84OPC-303
84T-727
84T/St-173
85D-79
85F-625
85Leaf-152
85Mother/Giants-19
85OPC-97
85T-567
85T/St-168
86D-567
86F-555
86Mother/Giants-26
86OPC-177
86T-177
87F-288
87Mother/SFG-20
87OPC-378
87T-759
88Mother/Giants-20
88S-509
88T-418
89B-315
89Kahn/Reds-12
89S-539
89S/Tr-66T
89T-304
89UD-458
90PublInt/St-42
90S-344
91Freder/ClBest-28CO
91Pac/SenLg-131
91WIZMets-437
Youngblood, Todd
91Belling/ClBest-25
91Belling/ProC-3666
Younger, Stan
82BirmB-1
83BirmB-5
84Evansvl-7
90BirmDG/Best-33
Youngman, Pete
86Greens-25TR
87Greens-4
89NewBrit/ProC-601
89NewBrit/Star-25
Youngs, Ross M.
21Exh-193
61F-154
80SSPC/HOF
91Conlon/Sport-26
V100
V61-106
W573
W575
Yount, Robin
75Ho-80
75Ho/Twink-80
75OPC-223
75T-223
75T/M-223
76A&P/Milw
76Ho-11
76Ho/Twink-11
76OPC-316
76SSPC-238
76T-316
77BurgChef-88
77Ho-34
77OPC-204
77Pepsi-1
77T-635
77T/CS-54
78Ho-138
78OPC-29
78T-173
79Ho-55
79OPC-41
79T-95
80OPC-139
80T-265
81D-323
81F-511
81F/St-38
81K-57
81OPC-4
81T-515
81T/So-10
81T/St-244
81T/St-95
82D-510
82F-155
82F/St-135
82K-28
82OPC-237
82PermaGr/AS-4
82Pol/Brew-19
82T-435
82T/St-203
83D-258
83D/AAS-56
83Drake-33
83F-51
83F-632M
83Gard-22
83K-14
83OPC-350
83OPC-389AS
83PermaGr/AS-9
83PermaGr/CC-36
83Pol/Brew-19
83T-321TL
83T-350
83T-389AS
83T/Gloss40-5
83T/St-145
83T/St-146
83T/St-150
83T/St-167
83T/St-81
84D-1DK
84D-48
84D/AAS-5
84D/Champs-47
84Drake-33
84F-219
85FunFood/Pin-29
84Gard-22
84MiltBrad-30
84Nes/792-10
84OPC-10
84Pol/Brew-19
84Ralston-21
84Seven-2C
84Seven-2E
84Seven-2W
84T-10
84T/Cereal-21
84T/Gloss22-5
84T/Gloss40-36
84T/St-295
84T/St/Box-6
84T/Super-29
85D-48
85D/AAS-21
85Drake-33
85F-601
85F/LimEd-44
85Gard-22
85GenMills-26
85Leaf-44
85OPC-340
85Pol/Brew-19
85Seven-16G
85T-340
85T/St-284
85T/Super-37
86D-48
86Dorman-16
86F-506
86F/LL-44
86F/Mini-103
86F/Slug-44
86F/St-131
86Jay's-20
86Jiffy-5
86Leaf-31
86OPC-144
86Pol/Brew-19
86Sf-42
86Sf-54M
86Sf-63M
86Sf-71M
86Sf/Dec-73M
86T-780
86T/St-197
86TrueVal-11
87Classic-44
87D-126
87D/OD-58
87F-361
87F/Lim-44
87F/St-130
87F/WaxBox-C16
87Ho/St-25
87Kraft-23
87Leaf-67
87OPC-76
87Pol/Brew-19
87RedFoley/St-126
87Sf-16
87T-773
87T/Board-9
87T/St-196
88D-295
88D/Best-183
88F-178
88F/BB/MVP-44
88F/Mini-33
88F/SS-44
88F/St-40
88Jiffy-20
88KMart-33
88Leaf-106
88OPC-165
88Panini/St-129
88Pol/Brew-19
88S-160
88Sf-34
88T-165
88T/Big-66
88T/Coins-32
88T/Mini-21
88T/St-201
88T/UK-87
89T/Ames-33
89B-144
89Brewer/YB-19
89Classic-83
89T/Crunch-21
89D-55
89D-5DK
89D/Best-53
89D/DKsuper-5DK
89F-200
89F/Excit-44
89F/Heroes-44
89F/LL-44
89Gard-2
89KayBee-33
89KingB/Discs-13
89KMart/Lead-21
89OPC-253
89Panini/St-377
89Pol/Brew-19
89RedFoley/St-130
89S-151
89S/HotStar-28
89Sf-199
89T-615
89T/Big-249
89T/Coins-60
89T/Gloss60-38
89T/Hills-33
89T/LJN-58
89T/Mini-59
89T/St-205
89T/St/Backs-21
89T/UK-87
89UD-285
90B-404
90B/Ins-11
90Brewer/MillB-31
90Bz-2
90Classic-147
90CollAB-9
90D-146
90D/BestAL-22
90D/Learning-37
90F-340
90F/AwardWin-44
90F/BB-44
90F/BBMVP-44
90F/LL-44
90F/WaxBox-C28
90Holsum/Discs-7
90HotPlay/St-50
90KayBee-33
90KingB/Discs-18
90KMart/CBatL-15
90Leaf/I-71
90MLBPA/Pins-82
90MSA/Soda-13
90OPC-290
90OPC-389AS
90Panini/St-92
90Pol/Brew-19
90Post-26
90PublInt/St-508
90S-320
90S/100St-92
90S/McDon-25
90Sf-18
90Sunflower-6
90T-290
90T-389AS
90T/Ames-5
90T/Big-59
90T/Coins-1
90T/DH-72
90T/Gloss60-15
90T/Mini-22
90T/St-198
90T/TVAS-23
90UD-567
90UD-91TC
90WonderBrd-11
90Woolwth/HL-1MVP
90Woolwth/HL-22
91B-55
91BBBest/HitM-18
91Brewer/MillB-31
91Classic/200-59
91D-272
91F-601
91F/Ultra-184
91Leaf/I-116
91Leaf/Stud-80
91MajorLg/Pins-43
91MooTown-17
91OPC-575
91OPC/Premier-131
91Panini/FrSt-208
91Panini/St-166
91Panini/Top15-56
91Pol/Brew-28
91Post/Can-21
91RedFoley/St-104
91S-525
91S-854FRAN
91S/100SS-38
91T-575
91T/CJMini/I-23
91T/StClub/II-509
91T/SU-36
91T/WaxBox-P
91UD-344
91Woolwth/HL-22
92Classic/I-98
92D/I-173
92F-194
92F-708PV
92S/100SS-84
92S/II-525
92T-90
92UD-456
Youse, Bob
73Cedar
74Cedar
Yuhas, John Ed
52T-386
53Hunter
53T-70
54Hunter
91T/Arc53-70
Yuhas, Vince
83Omaha-10
84Memphis-15
84Omaha-16
Yurak, Jeff
75Cedar
76Cedar
77Holyo
78Holyo
79Holyo-28
79Vanco-18
Yurcisin, Scott
90James/Pucko-30
Yurtin, Jeff
86Cram/PCL-176
88Wichita-11
89LasVegas/CMC-20
89LasVegas/ProC-20
90LasVegas/CMC-19
90LasVegas/ProC-132
90LSUGreat-10
Yvars, Sal
52T-338
53T-11
54B-78
54Hunter
91T/Arc53-11
Zachary, Albert M.
(Chink)
90Target-1101
Zachary, Chris
64T-23
66T-313
67T-212
70OPC-471
70T-471
73OPC-256
73T-256
Zachary, J. Tom
31Exh/4-1
33G-91
35G-8A
35G-9A
90Target-884
E120
E210-26
R315-A40
R315-B40
R316
V354-47
V61-3
W572
W573
Zacher, Elmer
E286
Zacher, Todd
82Clinton-8
Zachry, Pat
76OPC-599R
76T-599R
77OPC-201
77Pep-57
77T-86
78OPC-172
78T-171
79K-8
79OPC-327
79T-621
80OPC-220
80T-428
81Coke

81D-275
81F-334
81OPC-224
81T/St-197
82D-254
82F-544
82F/St-88
82OPC-64
82T-399
82T/St-71
83D-560
83F-561
83Pol/Dodg-38
83T-522
83T/Tr-131T
84D-215
84F-118
84Nes/792-747
84Pol/Dodg-38
84T-747
85F-391
85Phill/TastyK-23
85Phill/TastyK-9M
85T-57
87VeroB-8
88SanAn/Best-27
89Pac/SenLg-20
90Target-885
91WIZMets-438

Zahn, Geoff
75OPC-294
75T-294
75T/M-294
76OPC-403
76T-403
78T-27
79K-27
79OPC-358
79T-678
80T-113
81D-532
81F-564
81T-363
81T/Tr-856
82D-164
82F-474
82T-229
83D-66
83F-103
83OPC-131
83T-547
83T/St-42
84D-402
84F-532
84Nes/792-276TL
84Nes/792-468
84OPC-153
84Smok/Cal-32
84T-468
85D-301
85D/AAS-33
85F-317
85Leaf-53
85OPC-140
85Smok/Cal-15
85SpokAT/Cram-24
85T-771
85T/St-221
85ThomMc/Discs-24
86T-42
90Target-886

Zaksek, John
88Utica/Pucko-13
89SoBend/GS-20
90Foil/Best-165
90SoBend/Best-14

Zaleski, Richard
82Danvl-15
83Nashua-22
86MidldA-26TR
87Edmon-15

Zaltsman, Stan
86Erie-29
87Savan-22
88StPete/Star-25

Zambrana, Luis
81Redwd-21
82Redwd-18
83Redwd-27

Zambrano, Eduardo
(Eddie)
85Greens-13
86Greens-26
87WinHaven-21
88NewBrit/ProC-895
89NewBrit/ProC-599
89NewBrit/Star-21
90Kinston/Team-25
91CaroMud/LineD-123
91CaroMud/ProC-1100

Zambrano, Jose
91LynchRS/ClBest-24
91LynchRS/ProC-1214
91Single/ClBest-34

Zambrano, Roberto
85Greens-10
86WinHaven-27
87NewBrit-20
88NewBrit/ProC-911
90Canton/ProC-1307
90Canton/Star-19
91ColoSp/LineD-94
91ColoSp/ProC-2199

Zamora, Oscar
75OPC-604
75T-604
75T/M-604
76OPC-227
76SSPC-304
76T-227
78T-91

Zancanaro, Dave
90A&AASingle/ProC-162
90SoOreg/Best-24
90SoOreg/ProC-3423
91Classic/I-77
91Huntsvl/ClBest-20
91Huntsvl/LineD-298
91HuntsvlProC-1797
91Single/ClBest-124
92UD-54TP

Zane, Kelly
88SLCity-8
89Rockford/Team-27

Zanni, Dom
59T-145
62T-214
63FrBauer-32
63T-354
66T-233

Zapata, Gustavo
91Kissim/ProC-4199

Zapp, Jim
86Negro/Frit-46

Zappelli, Mark
87Anchora-33
89QuadC/Best-17
89QuadC/GS-5
91London/LineD-448
91MidldA/ProC-435

Zarilla, Al
47TipTop
48L-36
49B-156
50B-45
51B-35
51T/RB-49
52B-113
52Hawth/Pin-10
52StarCal/L-73A
52T-70
52TipTop
53T-181
79Hawaii-15C
91T/Arc53-181
Exh47
R423-118

Zarranz, Fernando
86Geneva-27
86Peoria-27
87Peoria-29
88MidwLAS/GS-29
88Peoria/Ko-33
90T/TVCub-66

Zaske, Jeff
82AlexD-17
84Cram/PCL-122
85Cram/PCL-249
86Hawaii-23
87OKCty-26
88Tacoma/CMC-6

Zastoupil, Rich
91Billings/ProC-3755

Zauchin, Norm
55T-176
56T-89
57T-372
58T-422
59T-311
79TCMA-252

Zaun, Greg
90Wausau/Best-15
90Wausau/ProC-2128
90Wausau/Star-27
91Kane/ClBest-14
91Kane/ProC-2661
91MidwLAS/ProC-MWL36
91Single/ClBest-209

Zavaras, Clinton
86Wausau-29
88Vermont/ProC-960
89Calgary/CMC-11
90D-662
90OPC-89
90T-89
90T/89Debut-149

Zawaski, Vince
89Star/Wax-25
89StLucie/Star-25

Zayas, Carlos
85Bend/Cram-24
87Clearw-6
88Spartan/ProC-1039
89Clearw/Star-25

Zayas, Felipe
77StPete
78StPete
80ArkTr-19
81ArkTr-1

Zayas, Pedro
89Spartan/ProC-1051
89Spartan/Star-25

Zazueta, Mauricio
90CLAS/CL-16
90PrWill/Team-29

Zdeb, Joe
78T-408
79T-389

Zeber, George
73Syrac/Team-30
78Cr/PCL-64
78T-591

Zeider, Rollie
14CJ-116
14CJ-60
15CJ-116
D328-199
D329-198
E135-199
E90/3
M101/4-198
T207
W514-32

Zeig, Robert
77WHave
79WHave-23
79WHave-29M

Zeihen, Bob
88Oneonta/ProC-2058
89Star/Wax-81
90Albany/Best-24
90Albany/ProC-1047
90Albany/Star-23
91Erie/ClBest-25CO
91Erie/ProC-4087CO

Zeile, Todd E.
86Erie-30
87Spring/Best-26
88ArkTr/GS-7
88TexLgAS/GS-2
89AAA/CMC-1
89AAA/ProC-14
89F/Up-122
89Louisvl-2
89Louisvl-3
89Louisvl-4
89Louisvl-5
89Louisvl/CMC-13
89Louisvl/ProC-1267
89UD/Ext-754
90B-193
90Bz-12
90Classic-90
90D-29
90D/BestNL-71
90D/Preview-3
90D/Rook-31
90F-265
90F/SoarSt-1
90HotRook/St-50
90Leaf/I-221
90OPC-162
90Panini/St-381
90S-600
90S/100Ris-6
90S/DTRook-B3
90S/YS/II-1
90Sf-177
90Smok/Card-27
90SpringDG/Best-1
90T-162
90T/89Debut-150
90T/Big-294
90T/TVCard-24
90ToysRUs-33
90UD-545
91B-404
91Classic/200-173
91Classic/II-T42
91D-71
91F-654
91F/Ultra-299
91Leaf/II-327
91Leaf/Stud-240
91MajorLg/Pins-48
91OPC-616
91Panini/FrSt-33
91Panini/St-34
91Pol/Card-27
91Post-25
91S-240
91S-869FRAN
91S/100RisSt-81
91T-616
91T/StClub/I-255
91ToysRUs-33
91UD-164
92D/I-132
92F-596
92S/I-52
92T-275
92UD-40TC
92UD-533

Zell, Brian
80Elmira-31

Zellner, Joey
86Macon-27
87Visalia-20
88Visalia/Cal-148
88Visalia/ProC-98

Zello, Mark
91Kane/ClBest-30TR

Zepp, Bill
70T-702R
71MLB/St-480
71OPC-271
71T-271

Zeratsky, Rod
86Cedar/TCMA-13
87Tampa-28

Zerb, Troy
88Batavia/ProC-1690

Zerbe, Chad
91Kissim/ProC-4188

Zernial, Gus
47Signal
50B-4
51B-262
51FB
51T/RB-36
52B-82
52BR
52RM-AL26
52StarCal/L-76A
52T-31
53B/Col-13
53Dix
53NB
53RM-AL13
53T-42
54Dix
54RH
54T-2
55RFG-2
55Rodeo
55T-110
55T/DH-123
56Rodeo
56T-45
56T/Hocus-A13
56T/Hocus-B15
56T/Pin-15
56YellBase/Pin-32
57T-253
58T-112
59T-409
79TCMA-263
91T/Arc53-42
Exh47
PM10/Sm-205
R423-119

Zettelmeyer, Mark
90FtLaud/Star-26GM

Zhigalov, Sergey
89EastLDD/ProC-DD8

Zick, Bill
88QuadC/GS-3
89QuadC/Best-4
89QuadC/GS-4

Ziegler, Bill
84Rang-tr
85Rang-tr
86Rang-tr
90Mother/Rang-28TR

Ziegler, Greg
87Idaho-27

Ziem, Steve
84Durham-23
86Greenvl/Team-23
87Richm/Crown-19
87Richm/TCMA-9
88Greenvl/Best-15
88Richm-28
89Durham/Team-25
89Durham/Star-25
89Richm/Bob-29
90Richm/Bob-2

Zientara, Benny
49Eureka-100

Zimbauer, Jason
91Beloit/ClBest-10
91Beloit/ProC-2104

Zimmer, Charles
N172

Zimmer, Don
55B-65
55Gol/Dodg-32
55T-92
55T/DH-98
56T-99
57T-284
58BB
58Hires-41
58T-77
59Morrell
59T-287
60BB-17
60T-47
61T-493
62Bz
62J-183
62P-183
62P/Can-183
62Salada-123A
62Salada-123B
62Shirriff-123
62T-478
62T/St-161
63T-439
64T-134
64T/Coins-1
64T/St-11
65OPC-233
65T-233
73OPC-12MG
73T-12MG
74OPC-403CO
74T-403CO
77T-309MG
78T-63MG
79T-214MG
79TCMA-228
81F-230MG
81T-673MG
82D-195MG
88Berg/Cubs-4MG
88T/Tr-131MG
89Mara/Cubs-4MG
89Swell-23
89T-134MG
90Cub/Mara-27MG
90OPC-549MG
90T-549MG
90T/TVAS-66MG
90T/TVCub-1MG
90Target-887

91OPC-729MG
91T-729MG
91WIZMets-439
Zimmer, Tom
89Pac/SenLg-25
91Pac/SenLg-136
Zimmerman, Brian
88LitFalls/Pucko-25
Zimmerman, Eric
83AlexD-24
Zimmerman, Gerald
59T-146
60HenryH-9
61Clover-31
62J-130
62P-130
62P/Can-130
62T-222
63T-186
64T-369
65T-299
66OPC-73
66T-73
67T-501
68OPC-181
68T-181
69MB-296
73OPC-377CO
73T-377CO
74OPC-531CO
74T-531CO
78TCMA-117
Zimmerman, Henry
(Heinie)
14CJ-21
15CJ-21
92Conlon/Sport-530
BF2-70
D328-200
D329-199
D350/2-199
E101
E102
E105
E106
E135-200
E224
E254
E254
E270/1
E92
M101/4-199
M101/5-199
M116
T206
T222
Zimmerman, Mike
88CapeCod/Sum-44
90Welland/Pucko-31
91B-519
91Salem/ProC-954
Zimmerman, Roy
50Remar
Zinn, Frank
N172
Zinter, Alan
88CapeCod/Sum-29
89Pittsfld/Star-29
90B-135
90FSLAS/Star-22
90S-671DC
90T/TVMets-66
91Single/ClBest-334
91Wmsprt/LineD-648
91Wmsprt/ProC-297
Zinter, Eddie
88Alaska/Team-18
89Spokane/SP-2
90A&AASingle/ProC-74
90CharRain/Best-23
90CharRain/ProC-2039
91AS/Cal-10
91HighD/ClBest-13
91HighD/ProC-2396
Zipay, Ed
(Bud)
46Sunbeam
47Signal
47Sunbeam
Zipeto, Ted
86Clearw-26tr
Zipfel, M. Bud
63T-69
Zisk, John
79Wausau-11
80Wausau-10
Zisk, Richie
72OPC-392R
72T-392R
73OPC-611R
73T-611R
74OPC-317
74T-317
74T/St-90
75Ho-139
75K-25
75OPC-77
75T-77
75T/M-77
76Crane-70
76MSA/Disc
76OPC-12
76SSPC-574
76T-12
77BurgChef-75
77Ho-127
77OPC-152
77Pep-27
77T-483
77T/CS-55
78BK/R-20
78PapaG/Disc-30
78T-110
78Tastee/Discs-14
78Wiffle/Discs-79
79Ho-140
79K-24
79OPC-130
79T-260
80OPC-325
80T-620
81D-28
81F-620
81F/St-105
81OPC-214
81Pol/Mar-13
81T-517
81T/So-16
81T/St-27
81T/Tr-857
82D-11DK
82D-127
82Drake-33
82F-519
82F/St-223
82K-1
82OPC-66
82T-769
82T/St-229
83D-559
83D/AAS-54
83F-489
83Nalley-3
83OPC-368
83T-368
83T/Gloss40-21
83T/St-116
84D-69
84D/AAS-30
84F-625
84Nes/792-83
84OPC-83
84T-83
84T/St-342
90Peoria/Team-35INST
91Cub/Mara-x
Zitzmann, William
(Billy)
28Exh-16
92Conlon/Sport-570
Zmudosky, Tom
84Albany-20
Zoldak, Sam
49B-78
50B-182
50NumNum
51B-114
52T-231
R423-120
Zollars, Mike
91Burllnd/ProC-3313
Zolzer, Rick
90Spartan/Best-29MG
90Spartan/Star-29GM
Zona, Jeff
89Idaho/ProC-2029
Zosky, Eddie
89Smok/FresnoSt-24
90A&AASingle/ProC-60
90B-523
90Foil/Best-23
90Knoxvl/Best-1
90Knoxvl/ProC-1251
90Knoxvl/Star-23
90S-665DC
91AAAGame/ProC-AAA44
91B-17
91Classic/200-172
91Classic/II-T25
91F/Ultra-390MLP
91Leaf/GRook-BC24
91S/ToroBJ-30
91Syrac/LineD-523
91Syrac/ProC-2490
91UD/Ext-734
91UD/FinalEd-14F
92Classic/I-99
92D/I-8RR
92F-348
92T-72
92T/91Debut-191
92UD-544
Zottneck, Roger
86QuadC-32
87PalmSp-16
Zuber, William
44Yank/St-30
47TipTop
Zupcic, Bob
87Elmira/Red-31
88CLAS/Star-20
88Lynch/Star-27
89NewBrit/ProC-600
89NewBrit/Star-22
90Foil/Best-108
90NewBrit/Best-6
90NewBrit/Star-24
91Pawtu/LineD-373
91Pawtu/ProC-53
92D/II-720
92S/II-850
92T-377
92T/91Debut-192
Zupka, Bill
85Elmira-25
86Greens-27
87NewBrit-3
Zupo, Frank
58T-229
91Crown/Orio-494
Zuvella, Paul
82Richm-17
83Richm-17
84Richm-23
85F-651R
85Pol/Atl-18
86F-532
86Richm-26
86T-572
86T/Tr-131T
87T-102
88ColoSp/CMC-18
88ColoSp/ProC-1528
89AAA/CMC-34
89AAA/ProC-33
89ColoSp/CMC-17
89ColoSp/ProC-245
89S-598
89UD-236
90Omaha/CMC-22
90Omaha/ProC-75
90Richm25Ann/Team-23
91Omaha/LineD-348
91Omaha/ProC-1044
Zuverink, George
52T-199
55B-92
56T-276
57T-11
58Hires-66
58T-6
59T-219
91Crown/Orio-495
Zweig, Ivan
91T/Tr-131T
Zwilling, Edward
(Dutch)
D329-200
D350/2-200
M101/4-200
M101/5-200
M116
Zwolensky, Mitch
82Wausau-19
83Tulsa-9
84OKCty-21
85OKCty-2
88Pittsfld/ProC-1356
90AS/Cal-30
90Stockton/Best-28CO
90Stockton/Cal-201
90Stockton/ProC-2201CO
91Stockton/ClBest-25CO
91Stockton/ProC-3048CO

TEAM CARDS

Atlanta Braves
66T-326
66T/RO-115
67T-477
68T-221
69T/St/Alb-1
69T/T/Post-1
70OPC-472
70T-472
71OPC-652
71T-652
71T/tatt-5
72OPC-21
72T-21
73OPC-521
73T-521
74OPC-483
74T-483
74T/St/Alb-1
75OPC-589
75T-589
75T/M-589
76OPC-631
76T-631
77T-442
78T-551
79T-302
80T-192
81T-675
87Sportflic/TmPrev-24
90PublInt/St-628
90RedFoley/St-130
Baltimore Orioles
56T-100
57T-251
58T-408
59T-48
60T-494
61T-159
61T/RO-85
62T-476
63T-377
64T-473
65T-572
66T-348
67T-302
68T-334
70OPC-387
70T-387
71OPC-1
71T-1
71T/tatt-10
72T-731
73OPC-278
73T-278
74OPC-16
74T-16
75OPC-117
75T-117
75T/M-117
76OPC-73
76T-73
77T-546
78T-96
79T-689
80T-404
81T-661
87Sportflic/TmPrev-21
90PublInt/St-648
90RedFoley/St-108
N690
Boston Braves
48Exh/T-1
T200
Boston Red Sox
51T
56T-111
57T-171
58T-312
59T-248
60T-537
60T/tatt-65
61T-373
61T/RO-5
62T-334
63T-202
64T-579
65T-403
66T-259
66T/RO-109
67T-604
69T/St/Alb-3
69T/T/Post-3
70T-563
71OPC-386
71T-386
71T/tatt-2
72OPC-328
72T-328
72T/Cloth-26
73OPC-596
73T-596
74OPC-567
74T-567
74T/St/Alb-3
75OPC-172
75T-172
75T/M-172
76OPC-118
76T-118
77T-309
78T-424
79T-214
80T-689
81T-662
87Sportflic/TmPrev-9
90PublInt/St-642
90RedFoley/St-109
91Panini/Top15-122
91Panini/Top15-125
R309/2
Brooklyn Dodgers
48Exh/T-13
48Exh/T-15
48Exh/T-3
48Exh/T-9
49Exh/Team
51T
52Exh/Team
55Exh/Team
56Exh/Team
56T-166
57T-324
58T-71
T200
California Angels
61T/RO-6
62T-132
63T-39
64T-213
65T-293
66OPC-131
66T-131
66T/RO-79
67T-327
68T-252
69T/St/Alb-4
69T/T/Post-4
70OPC-522
70T-522
71OPC-442
71T-442
71T/tatt
72OPC-71
72T-71
73OPC-243
73T-243
74OPC-114
74T-114
74T/St/Alb-4
75OPC-236
75T-236
75T/M-236
76OPC-304
76T-304
77T-34
78T-214
79T-424
80T-214
81T-663

87Sportflic/TmPrev-11
90PublInt/St-638
90RedFoley/St-120
91Panini/Top15-132

Chicago Cubs

56T-11
57T-183
58T-327
59T-304
60T-513
60T/tatt-56
61T-122
61T/RO-17
62T-552
63T-222
64T-237
65OPC-91
65T-91
66T-204
66T/RO-97
67T-354
69T/St/Alb-5
69T/T/Post-5
70T-593
71OPC-502
71T-502
71T/tatt-6
72OPC-192
72T-192
73OPC-464
73T-464
74OPC-211
74T-211
74T/St/Alb-5
75OPC-638
75T-638
75T/M-638
76OPC-277
76T-277
77T-518
78T-302
79T-551
80T-381
81T-676
87Sportflic/TmPrev-22
90PublInt/St-632
90RedFoley/St-122
91Panini/Top15-120
T200

Chicago White Sox

51T
56T-188
57T-329
58T-256
59T-94
60T-208
60T/tatt-66
61T-7
61T/RO-9
62T-113
63T-288
64T-496
65OPC-234
65T-234
66T-426
66T/RO-1
67T-573
68T-424
69T/St/Alb-6
69T/T/Post-6
70OPC-501
70T-501
71T-289
71T/tatt-8
72OPC-381
72T-381
73OPC-481
73T-481
74OPC-416
74T-416
74T/St/Alb-6
75OPC-276
75T-276
75T/M-276
76OPC-656
76T-656
77T-418
78T-526
79T-404
80T-112
81T-664
87Sportflic/TmPrev-26
90PublInt/St-639
90RedFoley/St-110
91Panini/Top15-136
91UD-617
T200

Cincinnati Reds

51T
56T-90
57T-322
58T-428
59T-111
60T-164
60T/tatt-57
61T-249
61T/RO-15
62T-465
63T-288
64T-403
65T-316
66OPC-59
66T-59
66T/RO-91
67T-407
68T-574
69T/St/Alb-7
69T/T/Post-7
70OPC-544
70T-544
71OPC-357
71T-357
71T/tatt-6
72T-651
73OPC-641
73T-641
74OPC-459
74T-459
74T/St/Alb-7
75OPC-531
75T-531
75T/M-531
76OPC-104
76T-104
77T-287
78T-526
79T-259
80T-606
81T-677
87Sportflic/TmPrev-4
90PublInt/St-624
90RedFoley/St-107
91Panini/Top15-117
91Panini/Top15-128
91Panini/Top15-131
N690
T200
W711/2

Cleveland Indians

48Exh/T-12
48Exh/T-2
48Exh/Team
54Exh/Team
56T-85
57T-275
58T-158
59T-476
60T-174
60T/tatt-67
61T-467
61T/RO-10
62T-537
63T-451
64T-172
65T-481
66T-303
66T/RO-67
67T-544
69T/St/Alb-8
69T/T/Post-8
70T-637
71OPC-584
71T-584
71T/tatt-7
72T-547
73OPC-629
73T-629
74OPC-541
74T-541
74T/St/Alb-8
75OPC-331
75T-331
75T/M-331
76OPC-477
76T-477
77T-18
78T-689
79T-96
80T-451
81T-665
87Sportflic/TmPrev-3
90PublInt/St-647
90RedFoley/St-105
R309/2
T200

Detroit Tigers

56T-213
57T-198
58T-397
59T-329
60T-72
60T/tatt-68
61T-51
61T/RO-1
62T-24
63T-552
64T-67
65OPC-173
65T-173
66T-583
66T/RO-61
67T-378
68T-528
69T/St/Alb-9
69T/T/Post-9
70T-579
71OPC-336
71T-336
71T/tatt-9
72OPC-487
72T-487
73OPC-191
73T-191
74OPC-94
74T-94
74T/St/Alb-9
75OPC-18
75T-18
75T/M-18
76OPC-361
76T-361
77T-621
78T-404
79T-66
80T-626
81Detroit-108
81Detroit-112
81Detroit-13
81Detroit-22
81Detroit-53
81Detroit-61
81Detroit-7
81Detroit-83
81Detroit-95
81Detroit-98
81T-666
87Sportflic/TmPrev-15
88Negro/Duques-2
90PublInt/St-643
90RedFoley/St-112
91Panini/Top15-123
N690
T200

Houston Astros

63T-312
66T/RO-7
69T/St/Alb-10
69T/T/Post-10
70OPC-448
70T-448
71OPC-722
71T-722
71T/tatt-12
72OPC-282
72T-282
73OPC-158
73T-158
74OPC-154
74T-154
74T/St/Alb-10
75OPC-487
75T-487
75T/M-487
76OPC-147
76T-147
77T-327
78T-112
79T-381
80T-82
81T-678
87Sportflic/TmPrev-8
90PublInt/St-627
90RedFoley/St-117

Kansas City Athletics

56T-236
57T-204
58T-174
59T-172
60T-413
61T-297
61T/RO-7
62T-384
63T-397
64T-151
65OPC-151
65T-151
66T-492
66T/RO-103
67T-262
87Sportflic/TmPrev-13
90PublInt/St-637
90RedFoley/St-126

Kansas City Royals

69T/St/Alb-11
69T/T/Post-11
70OPC-422
70T-422
71OPC-742
71T-742
71T/tatt-4
72T-617
73OPC-347
73T-347
74OPC-343
74T-343
74T/St/Alb-11
75OPC-72
75T/M-72
76OPC-236
76T-236
76T-72
77T-371
78T-724
79T-451
80T-86
81T-667

Los Angeles Dodgers

59T-457
60T-18
60T/tatt-58
61T-86
61T/RO-13
62T-43
63T-337
64T-531
65OPC-126
65T-126
66T-238
66T/RO-13
67T-503
68OPC-168
68T-168
69T/St/Alb-12
69T/T/Post-12
70OPC-411
70T-411
71OPC-402
71T-402
71T/tatt-5
72OPC-522
72T-522
73OPC-91
73T-91
74OPC-643
74T-643
74T/St/Alb-12
75OPC-361
75T-361
75T/M-361
76OPC-46
76T-46
77T-504
78T-259
79T-526
80T-302
81T-679
82T/St-255
82T/St-256
87Sportflic/TmPrev-14
90PublInt/St-623
90RedFoley/St-111

Milwaukee Braves

55Gol/Braves-32
56T-95
57T-114
58T-377
59T-419
60T-381
61T-426
61T/RO-18
62T-158
63T-503
64T-132
65T-426

Milwaukee Brewers

71OPC-698
71T-698
71T/tatt-7
72OPC-106
72T-106
73OPC-127
73T-127
74OPC-314
74T-314
74T/St/Alb-13
75OPC-384
75T-384
75T/M-384
76OPC-606
76T-606
77T-51
78T-328
79T-577
80T-659
81T-668
87Pol/Brew-x
87Sportflic/TmPrev-19
90PublInt/St-644
90RedFoley/St-123
91Panini/Top15-126

Minnesota Twins

61T-542
62T-584
61T/RO-3
63T-162
64T-318
65OPC-24
65T-24
66T-526
66T/RO-49
67T-211
68OPC-137
68T-137
69T/St/Alb-13
69T/T/Post-13
70OPC-534
70T-534
71OPC-522
71T-522
71T/tatt-14
72OPC-156
72T-156
73OPC-654
73T-654
74OPC-74
74T-74
74T/St/Alb-14
75OPC-443
75T-443
75T/M-443
76OPC-556
76T-556
77T-228
78T-451
79T-41
80T-328
81T-669
87Sportflic/TmPrev-17
90PublInt/St-636
90RedFoley/St-124

Montreal Expos

69T/St/Alb-14
69T/T/Post-14
70OPC-509
70T-509
71OPC-674
71T-674
71T/tatt-1
72T-582
73OPC-576
73T-576
74OPC-508
74T-508
74T/St/Alb-15
75OPC-101
75T-101
75T/M-101
76OPC-216
76T-216
77T-647

MISCELLANEOUS

75OPC-306—313
75T-306—313
75T/M-306—313
76OPC-191—205
76T-191—205
77OPC-1—8
77T-1—8
78OPC-201—208
78T-201—208
79T-1—8
80T-201—207
81T-1—8
82T-161—168
82T/St-1—16
83T-701—708

Playoff Games

70OPC-196—202
70T-195—202
71OPC-198
71T-195—202
72OPC-221-222
72T-221—222
73T-201—202
74T-470—471
75T-459—460
75T/M-459, 460
76T-276, 277
78T-411, 412
81T-401, 402
82T/St-253, 254
83T/St-147—158

World Series

60T-385—391
61T-306—313
62T-232—237
63T-142—148
64T-136—140
65OPC-132—139
65T-132—139
67OPC-151—155
67T-151—155
68OPC-151—158
68T-151—158
69OPC-162—169
69T-162—169
70OPC-305—310
70T-305—310
71OPC-327—332
71T-327—332
72OPC-223—230
72T-223—230
73OPC-203—210
73T-203—210
74OPC-472—479
74T-472—479
75OPC-461—466
75T-461—466
75T/M-461—466
76OPC-462
76T-462
77T-411—413
78T-413
81Detroit-37
81Detroit-45
81T-403, 404
82T/St-257—260
83Kaline-37
83Kaline-51
83T/St-179—190
88TM/Umpire-62
89T/LJN-1
89T/LJN-13
89T/LJN-21
89T/LJN-25
89T/LJN-29
89T/LJN-5
89TM/Umpire-61
89UD-666
90F/WS-12
90Panini/St-188—197
90S-700
90S-702
90TM/Umpire-62
91F/WS-8
91Panini/FrSt-176
91Woolwth/HL-32

CHECKLISTS

56T-un
57T-un
58T-134
58T-158
58T-174
58T-19
58T-216
58T-246
58T-256
58T-312
58T-327
58T-341
58T-377
58T-397
58T-408
58T-428
58T-44
58T-475
58T-71
59T-111
59T-172
59T-223
59T-248
59T-304
59T-314
59T-329
59T-397
59T-412
59T-419
59T-457
59T-476
59T-48
59T-510
59T-528
59T-69
59T-8
59T-94
60T-151
60T-164
60T-174
60T-18
60T-208
60T-242
60T-302
60T-332
60T-381
60T-413
60T-43
60T-484
60T-494
60T-513
60T-537
60T-72
61F-1
61F-89
61T-17
61T-189
61T-273
61T-361
61T-437
61T-516
61T-98
62T-192
62T-22
62T-277
62T-367
62T-441
62T-516
62T-98
63F-un
63T-102
63T-191
63T-274
63T-362
63T-431
63T-509
63T-79
64T-102
64T-188
64T-274
64T-362
64T-438
64T-517
64T-76
65OPC-104
65OPC-189
65OPC-273
65OPC-79
65T-104
65T-189
65T-273
65T-361
65T-443
65T-508
65T-79
66OPC-101
66OPC-183
66OPC-34
66T-101
66T-183
66T-279
66T-34
66T-363
66T-444
66T-517
67OPC-103
67OPC-191
67OPC-62
67T-103
67T-191
67T-278
67T-361
67T-454
67T-531
67T-62
68OPC-107
68OPC-192
68OPC-67
68T-107
68T-192
68T-278
68T-356
68T-454
68T-518
68T-67
69OPC-107
69OPC-214
69OPC-57
69T-107
69T-214
69T-314
69T-412
69T-504
69T-57
69T-582
70OPC-128
70OPC-244
70OPC-343
70OPC-432
70OPC-542
70OPC-9
70T-128
70T-244
70T-343
70T-432
70T-542
70T-588
70T-9
71OPC-123
71OPC-206
71OPC-369
71OPC-499
71OPC-54
71OPC-619
71T-123
71T-161Coin
71T-206
71T-369
71T-499
71T-54
71T-619
72OPC-103
72OPC-251
72OPC-378
72OPC-4
72OPC-478
72T-103
72T-251
72T-378
72T-4
72T-478
72T-604
72T/Cloth-5
73OPC-264
73OPC-338
73OPC-453
73OPC-54
73OPC-583
73T-264
73T-338
73T-453
73T-54
73T-588
74OPC-126
74OPC-263
74OPC-273
74OPC-414
74OPC-637
74T-126
74T-263
74T-273
74T-414
74T-637
74T/Tr-un
75OPC-126
75OPC-257
75OPC-386
75OPC-517
75OPC-646
75T-126
75T-257
75T-386
75T-517
75T-646
75T/M-126
75T/M-257
75T/M-386
75T/M-517
75T/M-646
76OPC-119
76OPC-262
76OPC-392
76OPC-526
76OPC-643
76SSPC-589—595
76T-119
76T-262
76T-392
76T-526
76T-643
76T/Tr
77OPC-124
77OPC-179
77T-208
77T-32
77T-356
77T-451
77T-562
77T/CS
78OPC-119
78OPC-183
78T-184
78T-289
78T-435
78T-535
78T-652
78T-74
79OPC-121
79OPC-242
79OPC-353
79T-121
79T-241
79T-353
79T-483
79T-602
79T-699
80OPC-128
80OPC-183
80OPC-249
80OPC-300
80OPC-67
80T-121
80T-241
80T-348
80T-484
80T-533
80T-646
81D-un
81F-641—644
81F-646—649
81F-651
81F-652
81F-654
81F-656
81F-658
81F-659
81OPC-241
81OPC-31
81OPC-331
81OPC-338
81T-241
81T-31
81T-338
81T-446
81T-562
81T-638
81T/Tr-858
82D-un
82F-647—660
82OPC-129
82OPC-226
82OPC-394
82T-129
82T-226
82T-394
82T-491
82T-634
82T-789
82T/Tr-132T
83D-un
83D/AAS-60
83D/HOF-44
83F-647—660
83OPC-129
83OPC-249
83OPC-349
83T-129
83T-249
83T-349
83T-526
83T-642
83T-769
84Cram/PCL-194
84Cram/PCL-217
84D-un
84D/AAS-60
84D/Champs-60
84F-647—660
84F/X-U132
84Nes/792-114
84Nes/792-233
84Nes/792-379
84Nes/792-527
84Nes/792-646
84Nes/792-781
84Nestle/DT-23
84OPC-114
84OPC-233
84OPC-379
84Phill/TastyK-1
84T-114
84T-233
84T-379
84T-527
84T-646
84T-781
84T/Cereal-34
84T/Tr-132T
85D-un
85D/AAS-60
85D/DKsuper-27
85D/HL-56
85F-654—660
85F/Up-U132
85Leaf-260—263
85OPC-121
85OPC-261
85OPC-377
85Phill/TastyK-1
85T-121
85T-261
85T-377
85T-527
85T-659
85T-784
85T/Tr-132T
86D-un
86D/AAS-60
86D/DKsuper-28
86D/HL-56
86D/Rook-56
86F-654—660
86F/Up-U132
86Leaf-261—264
86Negro/Frit-119
86OPC-131
86OPC-263
86OPC-396
86T-131
86T-263
86T-394
86T-527
86T-659
86T-791
86T/Mini-66
86T/Tr-132T
87D-100
87D-200
87D-27DK
87D-300
87D-400
87D-500
87D-600
87D/AAS-60
87D/DKsuper-27
87D/HL-56
87D/Rook-56
87F-654—660
87F/Up-U132
87Leaf-155
87Leaf-259
87Leaf-264
87Leaf-27

87OPC-128
87OPC-214
87OPC-264
87T-128
87T-264
87T-392
87T-522
87T-654
87T-792
87T/Mini-77
87T/Tr-132T
88D-100
88D-200
88D-27DK
88D-300
88D-400
88D-500
88D-600
88D/AS-32
88D/AS-64
88D/Best-288
88D/Best-329
88D/Best-336
88D/Rook-56
88F-654—660
88F/St-132
88F/Up-U132
88Leaf-209
88Leaf-261
88Leaf-264
88Leaf-27
88OPC-253
88OPC-373
88OPC-374
88T-121
88T-253
88T-373
88T-528
88T-646
88T-776
88T/Big-126
88T/Big-216
88T/Big-28
88T/Mini-77
88T/Tr-132T
88T/UK-88
88TM/Umpire-64
89B-481
89B-482
89B-483
89B-484
89D-100
89D-200
89D-27
89D-300
89D-400
89D-500
89D-600
89D/AS-32
89D/AS-64
89D/Best-300
89D/Best-329
89D/Best-332
89D/Rook-56
89D/Tr-56
89F-654—660
89F/Up-132
89OPC-118
89OPC-242
89OPC-247
89Pac/SenLg-187
89Pac/SenLg-218
89Swell-135
89T-118
89T-258
89T-378
89T-524
89T-619
89T-782
89T/Big-176
89T/Big-327
89T/Big-59
89T/LJN-164
89T/Mini-43
89T/SenLg-132
89T/St/Backs-67
89T/Tr-132T
89T/UK-88
89TM/SenLg-121
89UD-27
89UD-694—700
89UD/Ext-701
90B-525
90B-526
90B-527
90B-528
90D-100
90D-200
90D-27
90D-300
90D-400
90D-500
90D-600
90D-700
90D/BestAL-144
90D/BestAL-96
90D/BestNL-144
90D/BestNL-96
90D/Learning-55
90D/Rook-56
90F-654—660
90F/Up-132
90Leaf/I-174
90Leaf/I-264
90Leaf/I-84
90Leaf/II-364
90Leaf/II-444
90Leaf/II-528
90LitSun-1
90Mother/Giant-28
90OPC-128
90OPC-262
90OPC-376
90OPC-526
90OPC-646
90OPC-783
90Swell/Great-135
90T-128
90T-262
90T-376
90T-526
90T-646
90T-783
90T/89Debut-151
90T/89Debut-152
90T/Big-110
90T/Big-220
90T/Big-330
90T/Mini-45
90T/Tr-132T
90TM/Umpire-70
90UD-1
90UD-100
90UD-200
90UD-300
90UD-400
90UD-500
90UD-600
90UD-700
90UD/Ext-800
91B-699—704
91Conlon/Sport-328—330
91D-100
91D-200
91D-27
91D-300
91D-386
91D-500
91D-600
91D-700
91D-760
91D-770
91D/Rook-56
91F-714—720
91F/Ultra-397—400
91F/UltraUp-U120
91F/Up-U132
91Leaf/I-174
91Leaf/I-264
91Leaf/I-84
91Leaf/II-364
91Leaf/II-444
91Leaf/II-528
91Leaf/Stud-261—263
91OPC-131
91OPC-263
91OPC-366
91OPC-527
91OPC-656
91OPC-787
91OPC/Premier-132
91Pol/Royal-27
91Swell/Great-150
91T-131
91T-263
91T-366
91T-527
91T-656
91T-787
91T/90Debut-170
91T/90Debut-171
91T/Arc53-335—337
91T/StClub/I-298—300
91T/StClub/II-598—600
91T/Tr-132T
91Tor/Fire-x
91UD-1
91UD-100
91UD-200
91UD-300
91UD-400
91UD-50
91UD-500
91UD-600
91UD-700
91UD/Ext-800
91UD/FinalEd-100F
91UD/FinalEd-1F
91UD/FinalEd-79F
91WIZMets-xx
92Conlon/Sport-658—660
92D/DK-DK27
92D/I-160
92D/I-240
92D/I-320
92D/I-396
92D/I-80
92D/II-476
92D/II-556
92D/II-636
92D/II-716
92D/II-784
92F-714—720
92T-131
92T-264
92T-366
92T-527
92T-658
92T-787
92T/91Debut-193
92T/91Debut-194
92UD-1
92UD-100
92UD-200
92UD-300
92UD-400
92UD-500
92UD-600
92UD-640
92UD-700
92UD-99

Make Sure You're Fully Equipped!

Order Your Subscription To *Beckett Baseball Card Monthly* Today

Just as a player looks for the right equipment to make him feel comfortable in his game, the sports card collector looks for the right equipment to make him feel comfortable in his hobby. In *Beckett Baseball Card Monthly*, a collector can find many of the things he's looking for to better equip himself for total enjoyment of the hobby.

Each monthly issue features a full-color, superstar cover and Hot hobby art suitable for autographs. Plus, the informative features within the magazine, punctuated by colorful action photos, follow the cards and careers of the Hottest hobby stars, so you can be better informed when adding to your collection.

Active Singles

With regular departments like the "Weather Report" and "Hot Players/Hot Cards," you'll get national rankings to keep you up with who's Hot and who's not, plus tips on building collections. Each month, "Readers Write" answers your hobby questions while keeping you in touch with what other collectors are thinking. And "Fun Cards" provides a little comic relief.

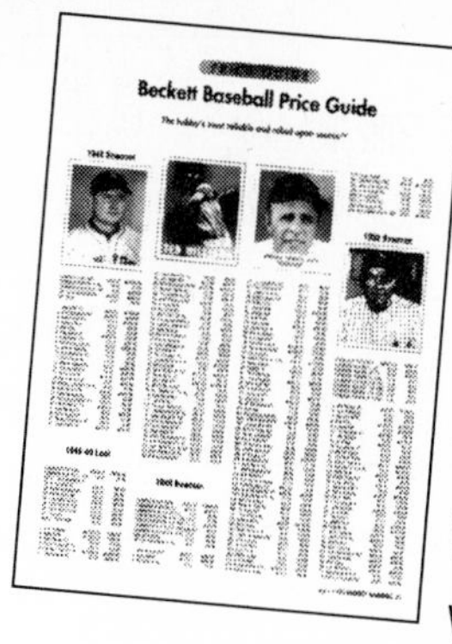

Most important, each month you get the most up-to-date Price Guide in the hobby. You'll find current prices for all the new sets and extensive coverage of older sets. With the monthly Price Guide, you can track the value of your favorite cards and sets, learn about errors and variations, and find out when a player's Rookie Cards were issued.

So make sure you've got the right equipment for maximum enjoyment of your hobby. Subscribe to *Beckett Baseball Card Monthly* today!

And don't forget our other four magazines which make collecting fun. Each gives you the same great hobby coverage and a monthly Price Guide. Try *Beckett Basketball Monthly, Beckett Football Card Monthly, Beckett Hockey Monthly* or *Beckett Focus on Future Stars* today.

Name (Please print) ______________________ Age ____

Address ______________________

City ______________ State ________ Zip ________

Payment enclosed via: ☐ Check or Money Order ☐ VISA/MasterCard (Please do NOT send cash)

Signature ______________________ Exp. ______

Name (Print) ______________________

Credit Card # ☐☐☐☐-☐☐☐☐-☐☐☐☐-☐☐☐☐

BECKETT BASEBALL CARD MONTHLY

Check one please:

		Your Price
☐	**1 year** (a savings of $15.45 for 12 issues)	**$19.95**
☐	**2 years** (a savings of $34.85 for 24 issues)	**$35.95**

All foreign addresses add $12 per year for postage (includes G.S.T.).
All payments payable in U.S. funds. Please allow 6 to 8 weeks for delivery of your first copy.

Mail to: Beckett Publications, Beckett Baseball Card Monthly,
P.O. Box 1915, Marion, OH 43305-1915

DSBA5

PUT TOGETHER A COMPLETE SET

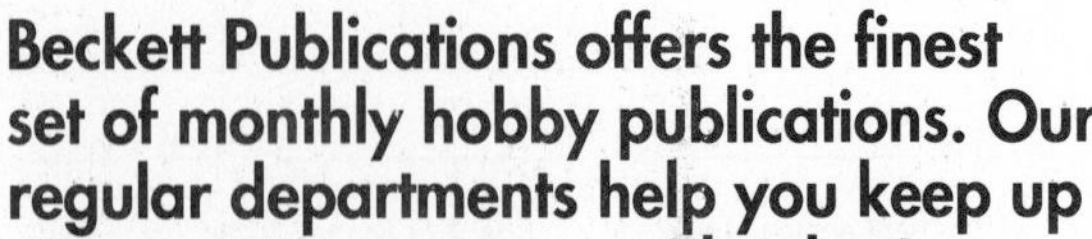

Beckett Publications offers the finest set of monthly hobby publications. Our regular departments help you keep up with what's happening in the hobby today and offer helpful suggestions on how to enhance your collection. Plus, we deliver exciting features on some of the Hottest players going. Add to your collection now.

Subscribe to Beckett today!